THE ROYAL HORTICULTURAL SOCIETY

ENCYCLOPEDIA OF PLANTS & FLOWERS

THE ROYAL HORTICULTURAL SOCIETY

ENCYCLOPEDIA OF PLANTS & FLOWERS

EDITOR-IN-CHIEF

CHRISTOPHER BRICKELL

LONDON, NEW YORK, MUNICH, MELBOURNE, DELHI

FIFTH EDITION

Senior Editor Helen Fewster
Project Editors Emma Callery, Joanna Chisholm, Chauney Dunford, Caroline Reed, Becky Shackleton
Additional Editorial Assistance Monica Byles, May Corfield, Annelise Evans, Diana Vowles, Fiona Wild

RHS Editors Simon Maughan, Rae Spencer-Jones

Senior Art Editors Joanne Doran, Elaine Hewson, Lucy Parissi
Designers Mark Latter, Laura Mingozzi, Vicky Reed, Becky Tennant
Jacket Designer Mark Cavanagh

Database Manager David Roberts
Production Editor Joanna Byrne
Picture Researchers Mel Watson, Janet Johnson
DK Picture Library Jenny Baskaya
Managing Editor Esther Ripley
Managing Art Editor Alison Donovan
Assistant Publisher Liz Wheeler
Art Director Peter Luff, Bryn Walls
Publisher Jonathan Metcalf

FIRST EDITION
Senior Editor Jane Aspden
Editors Liza Bruml, Joanna Chisholm, Roger Smoothy, Jo Weeks
Additional editorial assistance from Jane Birdsell, Lynn Bresler, Jenny Engelmann, Kate Grant, Shona Grimbly, Susanna Longley, Andrew Mikolajski, Diana Miller, Celia Van Oss, Anthony Whitehorn

Senior Art Editor Ina Stradins
Designer Amanda Lunn

First edition published in Great Britain in 1989 by Dorling Kindersley Limited.
Reprinted and updated 1990, 2/1990, 3/1990, 4/1990, 1991, 2/1991

Second edition revised and expanded, published in Great Britain in 1994 by Dorling Kindersley Limited. Reprinted 1995, 1996, 1997

Third edition revised and expanded, published in Great Britain in 1999 by Dorling Kindersley Limited

Fourth revised and updated edition published in Great Britain in 2006 by Dorling Kindersley Limited. Reprinted 2008

Fifth revised and updated edition published in Great Britain in 2010 by Dorling Kindersley Limited. 80 Strand, London WC2R ORL. A Penguin Company

A CIP catalogue record for this book is available from the British Library

ISBN 978-1-4053-5423-3

Colour reproduction by Colourscan, Singapore
Printed and bound by Toppan, China

Discover more at
www.dk.com

PREFACE

What you have in your hands is a very special book. Previous editions of the *RHS Encyclopedia of Plants and Flowers* have sold almost 3 million copies. If you are new to the book it will not take long for you to discover why.

This book is a personal favourite with appeal for gardeners of all levels of experience. It makes selecting plants by size, season, and colour a pleasure – with pictures carefully chosen to reveal the plants' qualities, and rigour in descriptions, names, and cultivation advice. It is easy for a beginner to follow but satisfying for the experienced gardener who will find the breadth of entries in the index invaluable.

At Hergest Croft Gardens in Herefordshire, my family's garden, we use the RHS encyclopedia to help us recognize the wide range of plants growing in the collections and understand their cultivation requirements. The clear illustrations and detailed text help us to identify the species or cultivar and we use the detailed descriptions when choosing a site for a new plant. As an international landscape architect I used it to find plants that would grow in differing climates. It is a book for any aspiring plantsman.

This fifth edition of the encyclopedia has had the most radical overhaul of recent years with every section reviewed, and new cultivars and varieties included. Some chapters have been broadened: for example, water plants include popular bog plants and climbers incorporate wall shrubs. Many tender and exotic trees, shrubs, climbers, and perennials that were scattered through previous editions have been gathered into a dedicated chapter of their own.

As the President of the RHS, with a longstanding involvement with the Society including designing the gardens at Rosemoor, I am delighted to introduce this encyclopedia. I thank the Editor-in-Chief, Chris Brickell, for his meticulous care in this revision: the contributors, and the publishers for their continuing support of this exceptional reference book on garden plants.

Elizabeth Banks

Elizabeth Banks
President, The Royal Horticultural Society, London 2010

CONTRIBUTORS

FIFTH EDITION REVIEWED BY

Zia Allaway — *Bulbs*
Christopher Brickell — *Rock Plants, Climbers*
John R.L. Carter — *Water and Bog Plants*
Philip Clayton — *Perennials*
Philip Harkness — *Roses*
Graham Rice — *Annuals and Biennials, Perennials*
Tony Russell — *Trees, Shrubs*
Julian Shaw — *Tender and Exotics, Plant Dictionary*

FIRST EDITION CONTRIBUTORS

Susyn Andrews — *Hollies*
Larry Barlow with W.B. Wade — *Chrysanthemums*
Kenneth A. Beckett with David Pycraft — *Shrubs, Climbers, Bromeliads, Plant Selector*
John Brookes with Linden Hawthorne — *Introduction*
Eric Catterall with Richard Gilbert — *Begonias*
Allen J. Coombes — *Plant Origins, Trees, Shrubs, Glossary*
Philip Damp with Roger Aylett — *Dahlias*
Kate Donald — *Peonies, Daffodils*
Kath Dryden — *Rock plants*
Raymond Evison — *Clematis*
Diana Grenfell — *Hostas*
Peter Harkness — *Roses*
Linden Hawthorne — *Chapter introductions*
Terry Hewitt — *Cacti and other Succulents*
David Hitchcock — *Carnations and Pinks*
Hazel Key — *Pelargoniums*
Sidney Linnegar — *Irises*
Brian Mathew — *Irises, Bulbs*
Victoria Matthews — *Climbers, Lilies, Tulips*
David McClintock — *Grasses, Bamboos, Rushes and Sedges*
Diana Miller — *Perennials*
with Richard Gilbert — *African violets*
John Paton — *Perennials*
Charles Puddle — *Camellias*
Wilma Rittershausen with Sabina Knees — *Orchids*
Peter Q. Rose with Hazel Key — *Ivies*
Keith Rushforth — *Conifers*
A.D. Schilling — *Rhododendrons and Azaleas*
Arthur Smith — *Gladioli*
Philip Swindells with Peter Barnes — *Ferns*
with Kath Dryden and Jack Wemyss-Cooke — *Primulas*
with Peter Robinson — *Water plants*
John Thirkell — *Delphiniums*
Alan Toogood — *Annuals and Biennials*
Major General Patrick Turpin with David Small — *Heathers*
Michael Upward — *Perennials*
John Wright with Nancy Darnley — *Fuchsias*

CONTENTS

HOW TO USE THIS BOOK

The core of this book is its two main sections – The Plant Catalogue and the Plant Dictionary. Here you will find descriptions and cultivation advice for thousands of plants. Plant Names and Origins explains the system for classifying and naming plants, while the new introduction, Creating a Garden, offers advice on design, planting, and basic pruning.

The Plant Selector

The Plant Selector recommends plants for a variety of sites, soils, and purposes, making it easy to find one to suit your needs. The list is divided into 23 useful categories, including plants for ground-cover in sun or shade, drought-tolerant plants, fragrant plants, and those suitable for hedges and windbreaks. Many are included in the Plant Catalogue and are cross-referenced to a picture and full description.

Photographic reference
Garden themes and uses are illustrated, together with photographs of selected plants.

Top choices
Plants are arranged by group, then listed alphabetically.

The Plant Catalogue

This section combines plant portraits and descriptions in a colourful catalogue of 4,000 plants divided into groups: Trees (including conifers); Shrubs; Roses; Climbers and Wall Shrubs; Perennials (including grasses, bamboos, rushes, sedges, and ferns); Annuals, Biennials, and Bedding Plants; Rock Plants; Bulbs; Water and Bog Plants; and Tender and Exotic Plants. A short introduction to each group is followed by plants arranged by size, season of interest, and colour and includes feature panels on plants with particular appeal.

Catalogue page

If you know a plant but cannot recall its name, have a specimen that you want to identify, or simply wish to choose plants for your garden based on their size or colouring, the Plant Catalogue is the place to start.

Page headings
The headings on each page reflect the way in which each plant group is subdivided – usually by size and main season of interest. (See also Size categories, left.)

Plant portraits
Colour photographs assist in the identification and selection of plants.

Feature panels

Plant types or genera of special interest to the gardener are presented in separate feature panels within the appropriate group.

Key characteristics
The introduction describes the plants and gives guidance on cultivation and planting.

Plant portraits
Close-up photographs of individual flowers or plants allow quick identification or selection.

Plant names
The botanical name is given and the Group or classification where appropriate. Descriptions and cultivation advice appear in the Plant Dictionary.

Size categories

Within most groups in the Plant Catalogue, plants are arranged by size (then subsequently by season of interest). Size categories range from large to small, but are defined differently from group to group. Sizes are based on plant heights. The specific height ranges for large, medium, and small can be found in the introductory section for the relevant plant group.

Colour order

Within each group, plants are arranged by the colour of their main feature. Colours are arranged in the same order: from white through reds, purples and blues to greens, yellows and oranges. Variegated plants are categorized by the colour of their foliage variegation (i.e. white or yellow); succulents are arranged by the colour of their flowers, if produced.

The symbols

☼ Prefers sun
◐ Prefers partial shade
● Tolerates full shade
○ Prefers well-drained soil
◑ Prefers moist soil
● Prefers wet soil
pH Needs acid soil
(!) Toxic plant
♕ Award of Garden Merit
❄ Half hardy: can withstand temperatures down to 0°C (32°F)
❄❄ Frost hardy: can withstand temperatures down to -5°C (23°F)
❄❄❄ Fully hardy: can withstand temperatures down to -15°C (5°F)

***Rhododendron* 'Percy Wiseman'**

Evergreen rhododendron with a domed, compact habit. In late spring produces open funnel-shaped, peach-yellow flowers that fade to white.

Cultivation and hardiness
Symbols show the plant's preferred growing conditions and hardiness. For frost tender plants the minimum temperature required for its cultivation is stated. However, the climatic and soil conditions of your particular site should also be taken into account as they may affect a plant's growth. (See also key, left.)

Toxic plants
This symbol indicates that the plant can be toxic. Details are given in the genus introductions in the Plant Dictionary.

Size and shape
For most plants the approximate height (H) and spread (S) are given at the end of each caption. (The "height" of a trailing plant is the length of its stems, either hanging or spreading.) For Trees, Conifers, and Shrubs a scale drawing shows the size and shape of each plant at maturity.

Award of Garden Merit
This symbol indicates that the plant has received the RHS Award of Garden Merit.

Colour tabs
These indicate a change of colour within the size group for each season.

Tabs
Colour-coded tabs make it easy to find each plant group.

Plant names
The botanical name is given for each plant, and where appropriate, common names are listed in brackets.

Captions
Captions describe the plants in detail and draw attention to any special uses.

Abbreviations

cv(s)	cultivar(s)	illus.	illustrated	subsp.	subspecies
f.	forma	min.	minimum	subspp.	subspecies
H	height (or length of trailing stems)	p(p).	page(s)		(pl.)
		pl.	plural	syn.	synonym(s)
		S	spread	var.	varietas

The Plant Dictionary

The Plant Dictionary contains entries for every genus in the Encyclopedia and includes an additional 4,000 recommended plants to those featured in the Plant Catalogue. It also functions as an index to the Plant Catalogue.

Genus names
The genus name is followed by common names, where appropriate, and family names.

Genus entries
A concise introduction covers the distinctive characteristics and hardiness range of plants in the genus, as well as advice on siting, cultivation, propagation, and, if relevant, pruning, pests and diseases, and toxicity.

Plant names
Botanical names, synonyms and common names are given as appropriate. The genus name is abbreviated; specific epithets (eg. nobile) are abbreviated only if previously given in full.

Plant descriptions
Key characteristics of the plant are described. Hardiness and cultivation needs are included only if specific to the plant. Cultivar entries run on from the species entry, with the binomial omitted.

Illustrated plants
Descriptions for illustrated plants appear in the Plant Catalogue, unless part of a feature panel (see below left).

RHEUM
Rhubarb
POLYGONACEAE

Genus of perennials, grown for their foliage and striking overall appearance. Includes the edible rhubarb and various ornamental plants. Some species are extremely large and require plenty of space. Fully hardy. Prefers sun or semi-shade and deep, rich, well-drained soil. Propagate by division in spring or by seed in autumn. ⓘ Leaves may cause severe discomfort if ingested.

R. nobile. Clump-forming perennial. **H** 15m (5ft), **S** 1m (3ft). Leaves are oblong to oval, leathery, basal, mid-green, 60cm (2ft) long. In late summer produces long stems and conical spikes of large, overlapping, pale cream bracts that hide insignificant flowers.

R. palmatum. Clump-forming perennial. **H** and **S** 2m (6ft). Has 60–75cm (2–2½ft) long, rounded, 5-lobed, mid-green leaves. In early summer has broad panicles of small, creamy-white flowers.

🏆 **'Atrosanguineum'** illus. p.439.

Rhipsalidopsis gaertneri. See *Hatiora gaertneri.*

Rhipsalidopsis rosea. See *Hatiora rosea.*

Cross-references
Synonym cross-references are listed alphabetically.

THE RHS AWARD OF GARDEN MERIT

The Royal Horticultural Society's Award of Garden Merit (AGM) recognizes plants of outstanding excellence for garden decoration or use, whether grown in the open or under glass. Besides being the highest accolade the Society can give to a plant, the AGM is of practical value for ordinary gardeners, helping them in making a choice from the many thousands of plants currently available. The AGM means that plants satisfy the following criteria:

- Excellent for garden use
- Not particularly susceptible to pests and diseases
- Do not require specialist care other than the provision of suitable growing conditions

PLANT NAMES AND ORIGINS

Plants have always been given local names with the result that many of them were called by a different name in different regions and countries. To overcome this problem, a common naming system was devised and developed into the plant naming system that is now used worldwide.

The Binomial System

Greek and Roman scholars laid the foundations of our method of naming plants, but the binomial system used today was largely established in the 18th century by Swedish botanist, Carl Linnaeus (1707–1778). Linnaeus classified each plant with two Latin words, rather than the descriptive phrases used previously. The first word describes the genus (eg. *Ilex*) and the second the epithet (eg. *aquifolium*). Together they provided a name for a particular plant species such as *Ilex aquifolium* (English holly). Other species in the same genus were given different epithets such as *Ilex crenata* and *Ilex serrata*. The system has been developed by scientists so that the entire plant kingdom is divided into a universally recognized "family tree" (see opposite).

The meaning of plant names

Plant names are derived from various sources. Some are commemorative – the *Fuchsia* is a tribute to German physician Leonhart Fuchs – while others indicate a plant's geographic origins, as with *Parrotia persica* (of Persia). A plant may be named after the collector who introduced it, such as *Primula forrestii*, cultivated by George Forrest. Alternatively, the name may describe the plant's characteristics, for example, *quinquefolia* in *Parthenocissus quinquefolia*, which means with foliage made up of five leaflets; it comes from the Latin *quinque* (five) and *folium* (leaf).

A plant name may change either because the plant has been incorrectly identified; or because it has been given an earlier name; or because the name has been found to apply to two different plants; or because new knowledge changes the plant's classification. In this book, synonyms are included so renamed plants can be easily recognised.

Common names

Although many plants have familiar common names, botanical names are used because not all plants possess a common name, or they may share a name with other plants. In addition, a common name may be used in different regions to describe different plants. For example, in Scotland "plane" refers to *Acer pseudoplatanus* (sycamore); in England it refers to the London plane (*Platanus* x *hispanica*), and in America both "plane" and "sycamore" are used for (*Platanus occidentalis*). Common names may also refer to unrelated plants as is the case with sea holly (*Eryngium*), hollyhock (*Alcea*), and summer holly (*Arctostaphylos diversifolia*), none of which is a true holly (*Ilex*). Another problem is that one plant may have several common names: heartsease, love-in-idleness, and Johnny-jump-up all refer to *Viola tricolor*.

Botanical divisions

Divided into a hierachy, plants are classified according to the following groups, which help to identify them:

The family

Plants are grouped in families according to the structure of their flowers, fruits, and other organs. Families may consist of clearly related plants, such as orchids (family Orchidaceae), or embrace diverse plants as in the family Rosaceae: *Alchemilla, Cotoneaster, Crataegus, Malus, Geum, Prunus, Pyracantha, Sorbus* and *Spiraea*.

The genus and its species

A family may contain one genus (for example, *Eucryphia* is the only genus in the family Eucryphiaceae) or many – the daisy family Compositae has over 1,000 genera.

Each genus comprises related plants, such as oaks (genus *Quercus*) or lilies (genus *Lilium*), with several features in common, and a genus may contain one or many species. For example, a member of the genus *Lilium* could be any lily, but *Lilium candidum* denotes just one type.

A species is a group of plants that consistently and naturally reproduce themselves, often by seed or vegetatively, generating plant populations that share similar characteristics.

Subspecies, varieties, and forms

In the wild, even plants of the same species can exhibit slight differences, and these are split into three subdivisions. The subspecies (subsp.) is a distinct variant of the species; the variety (var.) differs slightly in its botanical structure; and the form (f.) has only minor variations, such as the habit or colour of leaf, flower, or fruit.

ABOVE Wild origins
Many plant species that subsequently become garden plants are initially found in the wild. The North Cape Province of South Africa is home to many annuals and succulents, from which breeders have produced new cultivars and hybrids.

Cultivars

Plant breeders are constantly trying to improve a plant's performance, and produce new "cultivars" (a contraction of **culti**vated **var**ieties) that are more vigorous, produce more flowers, or possess other favourable characteristics that differentiate them from the wild form of the species.

Although many cultivars are bred by specialists, others are found in the wild or occur as mutations and are then introduced to cultivation. To reproduce cultivars that exhibit a consistent set of characteristics, many must be propagated vegetatively (cuttings, grafting or division) or grown annually from specially selected seed.

Cultivars have vernacular names, which are printed in Roman type within quotes (eg. *Phygelius aequalis* 'Yellow Trumpet'). When plant breeders raise a new cultivar, it is given a code name that may be different to the name under which the plant is sold. For example, the rose Casino also has the code name 'Macca'; in this book, both names are cited, and styled: *Rosa* CASINO ('Macca').

Hybrids

Sexual crosses between botanically distinct species or genera are known as hybrids and are indicated by a multiplication sign. If the cross is between species in different genera, the result is called an "intergeneric hybrid" and, when two or more genera are crossed, the name given is a condensed form of the the relevant genera; x *Cupressocyparis*, for example, covers hybrids between species of *Chamaecyparis* and *Cupressus*.

If more than three genera are involved, then the hybrids are named after a person and given the ending "-ara". Thus x *Potinara*, a hybrid of *Brassavola*, *Cattleya*, *Laelia* and *Sophronitis*, commemorates M. Potin of the French orchid society. More common are "interspecific hybrids", which are crosses between species in the same genus. These have a collective name preceded by a multiplication sign: *Epimedium* x *rubrum* covers hybrids between *E. alpinum* and *E. grandiflorum*.

When a plant is grafted onto another, a new plant occasionally arises that contains tissues of both parents. These are named in the same way as sexual hybrids, but are denoted by a plus sign: +*Laburnocytisus adamii*, for example, is a graft hybrid between *Laburnum* and *Chamaecytisus*.

Cultivars of hybrids are listed under a botanical name, or if the parentage is complex, by giving the generic name followed solely by the cultivar name (eg. *Rosa* 'Buff Beauty').

Visual Key to Plant Classification

In horticulture, plants are classified according to a hierarchical system and named primarily on the basis of Linnaeus's binomial approach (genus followed by species epithet). As an example, part of the family Roaceae family has been set out below, showing all levels of this system.

FAMILY

A group of several genera that share a set of underlying natural characteristics. Family names usually end in *-aceae*. Family limits are often controversial.

Rosaceae

GENUS (PL. GENERA)

A group of one or more plants that share a range of distinctive characteristics. Several (rarely one) genera are classified into one family. Each genus contains one or more species and its name is printed in italic type with an initial capital letter.

Rosa

Prunus

SPECIES

A group of plants that breeds naturally to produce offspring with similar characteristics; these keep it distinct from other populations in nature. Each species has a two-part name printed in italic type.

Rosa Alba

Prunus lusitanica

SUBSPECIES

A naturally occurring, distinct variant of a species, differing in one or more characteristic. Indicated by 'subsp.' in Roman type and an epithet in italic type.

Prunus lusitanica subsp. *azorica*

VARIETAS* AND *FORMA

A varietas (var.) is a minor species subdivision, differing slightly in botanical structure. A forma (f.) is a minor variant of a species, often differing in flower colour or habit from others in the species.

Rosa gallica var. *officinalis*

Prunus incisa f. *yamadae*

CULTIVAR

Selected or artificially raised, distinct variant of a species, subspecies, *varietas*, *forma*, or hybrid. Indicated by a vernacular name printed in Roman type within single quotation marks.

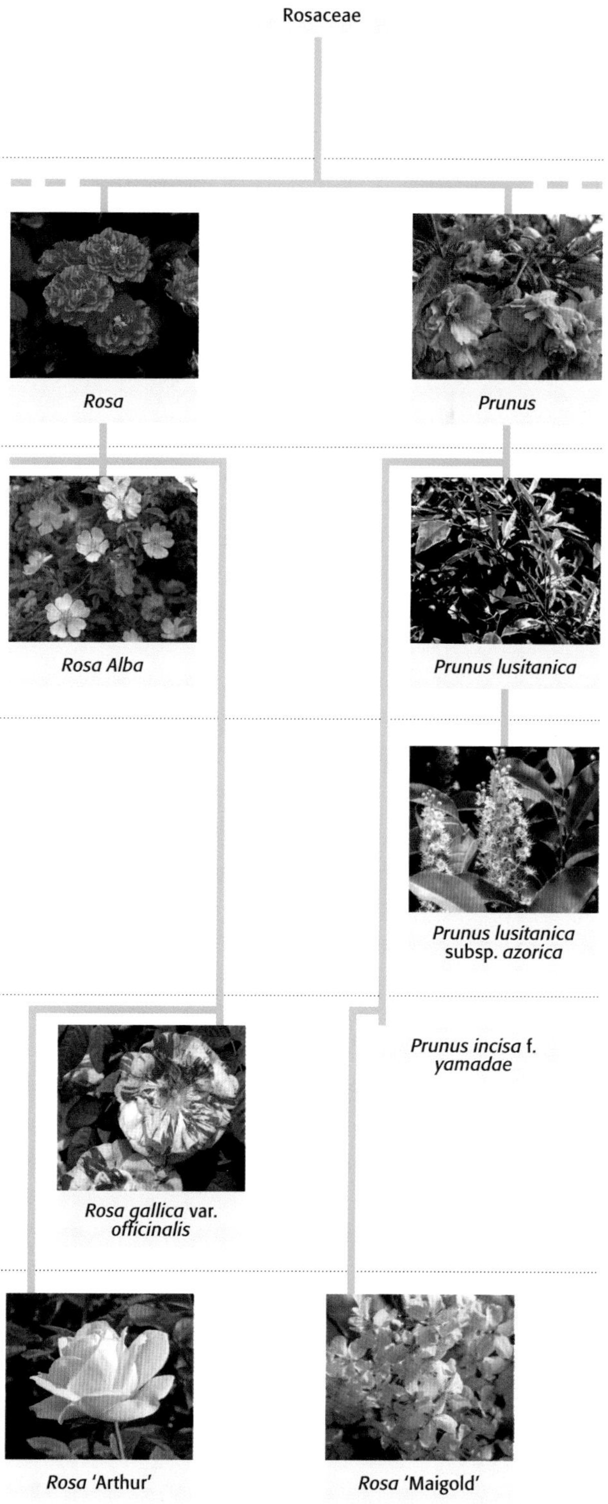

Rosa 'Arthur'

Rosa 'Maigold'

CREATING A GARDEN

A beautiful garden is everyone's dream, and this chapter provides all the information you need to create stunning beds and borders. There is helpful advice on producing colour schemes, including dazzling hot beds, relaxing pastel designs, and elegant white displays, as well as ideas for using plant forms and textures to create arresting images throughout the year. There are also tips to help you select a garden style, whether you prefer the informality of a cottage garden or the ordered symmetry of a formal design. Practical advice on a range of gardening techniques, including preparing the soil, planting methods and pruning basics, completes the picture.

INSPIRATIONAL STYLES

There are many different garden styles, and whether you yearn for neat, symmetrical formality, informal cottage-garden abundance, Japanese minimalism or contemporary urban chic, it is important to select a look that suits both your home and lifestyle if you are to get the best from your outdoor space. Also think about how much time you have to maintain your design, as this will affect your range of choices.

ABOVE Formal by design
The use of symmetry, clear simple geometric shapes, and clipped topiary and hedges are typical of the formal style. The reflective pool and rills bounce light into this primarily green planting scheme.

Formal gardens

A successful formal garden has a balanced design, achieved through symmetry and a clear ground plan. Essential characteristics are straight lines; order and geometry; and clearly delineated garden areas. Organised around a central axis or pathway, formal gardens often focus on a key view through the garden from the house. The geometry is clear, but generous scale and balanced proportions are key considerations.

Geometric shapes feature strongly, but any regular symmetrical shape can be used as long as it sits on at least one axis. Lawns and clipped hedges are important features, the latter defining spaces or views, while dwarf box hedging can be used to edge borders, create decorative parterres or form knot gardens. If space allows, avenues of trees may line paths to accentuate vistas and draw the eye to a distant focal point.

Balustrades, steps, terraces and wide gravel pathways are all key features, with the range of hard-landscaping materials, such as gravel and regular paving stones, kept to a minimum. Decorative elements, such as cobble mosaics or brick designs, are also popular in formal gardens. Other features include classical ornaments, such as Versailles cases, urns and statuary, and topiary, which is often used as a focal point. Water is an important element, and pools with reflective surfaces or jets and fountains appear in many formal designs.

Although the rules of formality are simple and clear, it is still a remarkably flexible style. The overall layout can be completely symmetrical, or you can choose to adopt just a few formal elements in a more contemporary design. For example, one axis can be more dominant than another, or a series of balanced, rectangular beds can be veiled with soft, romantic planting. Another modern interpretation of the formal style is a paved courtyard garden with architectural planting, large-scale containers and a small water feature.

Many formal designs also require very little maintenance, apart from annual hedge clipping and pruning shrubs back.

Informal gardens

Country gardens, cottage gardens, wildlife plots, and prairie-style plantings are all informal designs. Unlike formal schemes, they allow a greater degree of flexibility in the design and planting plans.

Cottage gardens

Cottage gardens are traditionally simple in layout, often with a central path leading to the main door and planting beds filled with flowers, herbs and vegetables on either side. If the garden is large enough, it may also include more naturalistic areas, such as orchards, meadows and informal wildlife ponds.

The edges of flower beds are softened by a rich profusion of planting, with the flowers encouraged to flop over the path and self-seed at random. Typical cottage garden plants include hellebores, lungworts (*Pulmonaria*), grape hyacinths (*Muscari*), aquilegias, and species daffodils and tulips in spring, with hardy geraniums, lilies, lupins, poppies, campanulas, delphiniums, hollyhocks (*Alcea rosea*) and peonies in summer. Plants are often chosen for their range of flower forms, textures and colours. Edible crops, such as herbs, vegetables, and fruit trees and bushes, are mixed with the ornamental plants, adding to the atmosphere of abundance and informality.

Natural stone, brick, cobbles and slate are the best materials for hard landscaping, while simple post-and-rail or picket fences are ideal for boundaries and divisions.

Country gardens

Country gardens also have a relaxed style, with sweeping expanses of lawn and curved, flower-filled mixed beds and borders. Hedges are often used to divide the garden into a series of enclosed spaces with different planting designs and atmospheres in each.

Prairie and wildlife gardens

Prairie planting, championed by many contemporary designers, echoes the tightly woven density of cottage-garden planting by combining broad sweeps of ornamental grasses and sturdy perennials. Grasses such as stipas and calamagrostis are threaded through perennials, such as rudbeckias, echinaceas, heleniums and asters. Prairie schemes suit large open sites in full sun where the bold swathes of planting produce the best effects.

Wildlife gardens are designed to provide habitats for birds, insects and mammals. Domestic gardens can also be wildlife gardens, with naturalistic planting schemes comprising of nectar-rich flowers, and trees for nesting and shelter. An informal pond is usually a feature, to provide homes for amphibians, reptiles, and insects.

Gardeners with more space may opt for a wildflower meadow. These require a sunny site and infertile soil for the rich profusion of native wild flowers and grasses to thrive.

RIGHT **Prairie-style plantings**
Prairie-style gardens combine the soft, feathery effects of grasses with the muted hues of perennials. Planted in informal drifts, this late summer scheme includes eupatorium, echinacea, and sedum.

BELOW **Cottage-garden informality and abundance**
The profuse pink flowers of a climbing rose clambering over an arbour echo the equally abundant planting of cottage-garden perennials in the beds below.

Mediterranean gardens

There are two types of garden associated with the Mediterranean region: formal and informal. The formal gardens feature water and stone, as well as clipped hedges and specimen trees such as pencil cypresses. Decorative parterres are also common, with the plants selected for foliage rather than flower colour. In some gardens in Spain, such as the El Alhambra in Granada, there is a strong Moorish influence, with formal courtyards and water features.

However, the most attainable garden style has an informal structure and relaxed, Mediterranean atmosphere. Gravel is the main hard landscaping material, and is used between areas of planting and to create pathways. Plants native to this region of Europe often have silvery, sage grey-green or blue-tinted foliage, which reflects the strong summer sun. Olive trees, citrus fruits, figs, vines, santolinas and artemisias, as well as herbs like thyme, sage, lavender and rosemary, are popular planting choices.

Another informal approach, often seen in urban areas, is to create a courtyard with walls that have been painted white, warm terracotta, or bold blues or pinks. Mosaic-tiled walls, cobbled floors and terracotta pots planted with bright pelargoniums or white *Convolvulus cneorum* complete the Mediterranean theme. If you live in a cooler climate, a sun-drenched courtyard will also provide some shelter for tender plants. Hot, south-facing gardens call for a shady arbour or pergola festooned with flowering climbers, such as bougainvilleas or jasmine, to create a comfortable area for al fresco dining or relaxation.

ABOVE Cool Mediterranean courtyard
A Mediterranean courtyard, with gleaming white walls and floor that help reflect the heat of the sun, is perfect for growing sun-loving agapanthus.

ABOVE Mediterranean planting
Drought-tolerant plants, including spiky phormiums, rock roses, and artemesias thrive in the gravel of a Mediterranean-style garden on a hot, sunny hillside.

Desert gardens

Dramatic, chic and starkly beautiful, desert gardens have become very fashionable in hot, frost-free locations with low rainfall. Pale-coloured walls, gravel, rocks, boulders and dried driftwood are features, together with tough, drought-tolerant plants like cacti and succulents, such as agaves, aloes and yuccas, which do not need extra irrigation in these hostile environments. In the right place, a desert garden is very eco-friendly, as it focuses on native plants that thrive with little water.

ABOVE Japanese contemplative space
Natural materials, such as carefully positioned rocks and gravel, plants like acers and pines, and ornamental lanterns are typical features of a Japanese garden.

Japanese gardens

The Japanese garden style is designed to reflect the natural landscape using a limited planting palette to produce quiet, contemplative spaces. The key to creating a successful Japanese garden is to consider how the main elements, such as boulders, gravel and plants, relate to one another, and how they are connected both symbolically and spiritually to the natural world.

In many instances, traditional Japanese spiritual beliefs are fundamental to the designs. Both the ancient religion of Shinto, and the Buddhist teachings that were introduced later, celebrate nature, and all natural elements are regarded as sacred and worthy of respect. In Zen gardens, key elements are used to create representations of natural landscapes. For example, raked gravel is used to echo flowing water, with stones symbolizing islands, boats, or animals. The gravel is raked daily, a ritual viewed by Buddhists as an important aid to contemplation, and the gardens often include little or no planting, relying on moss and lichens rather than on large, dramatic plants.

The cultivation of beauty as a spiritual activity is also reflected in Japanese tea gardens in which a *roji* (dewy path) is lit by stone lanterns and leads the visitor on a journey past water basins, stone buddhas and other spiritual symbols to the ceremonial tea house. These gardens are more heavily planted, and include maples (*Acer*), pines, azaleas, and camellias, which are subjected to a tight pruning regime to restrict their size and create miniature forms of larger trees or shrubs. The planting does not simply focus on evergreens and there are splashes of colour in the form of cherry blossom and camellias in the spring, elegant summer irises and the fiery autumn foliage of the maples contributing to the seasonal display.

Contemporary gardens

With many of us living increasingly urban lives, contemporary gardens have had to fulfil a number of different functions, providing a space for planting, relaxation, play, and entertaining. Modern urban gardens can differ in emphasis, and be treated either as purely functional spaces in which hard surfaces prevail along with furniture, lighting effects, and water features to create the ultimate outdoor room, or as green oases in which the planting dominates.

The layout of an urban garden is generally based on simple lines, often with an asymmetrical floor plan, and uses a combination of natural and man-made materials, such as concrete, glass, plastic, Perspex, and steel, to provide textural interest. Furniture often takes the form of integral benches, stylishly coordinated tables and chairs, and recliners, while sculpture provides a focal point, and can be combined with water. Jets or cascades are popular, but tanks of reflective water are becoming increasingly popular.

Contemporary planting designs

As space can be limited in today's urban gardens, the planting often focuses on a more limited choice of species, and those that provide architectural interest. Grasses, bamboos and large-leaved foliage plants, such as the hardy banana (*Musa basjoo*), phormiums and cordylines are popular in contemporary schemes.

Modernist designs employ large block plantings of box (*Buxus*), or small festucas and ophiopogons. These may be used in conjunction with pleached trees planted along the boundaries to provide privacy in overlooked gardens. Dramatic containers made from clay, stone or steel can be used as focal points or lined up in a row to add drama and rhythm to the design. Popular plants for containers include clipped topiary box, bay or Japanese holly (*Ilex crenata*), bamboo, succulents like agaves, or bold grasses.

ABOVE **Contemporary urban chic**
This urban, split-level garden with its smart integral benches shows how contemporary outdoor areas can function on many different levels – both as outdoor rooms and areas for lawns and beautiful plants.

Tropical gardens

Although this style of garden is best suited to tropical and warm-termperate regions, where the native plants are naturally lush, a similar effect can be created in cooler climates with the careful selection of plants.

The design is informal, with man-made structures made from rough-hewn timber and unworked stone, reflecting the traditional crafts of people living in tropical environments. Water plays a large part in designs, mimicking the landscapes that inspired the style, with waterfalls, streams and, occasionally, swimming pools, adding to the lush picture.

A tropical garden is a celebration of foliage shapes, textures and colours. Taller species such as eucalyptus, palms, bamboos and cordylines provide height, with the space below filled with lower-growing shrubs, grasses and flowering perennials, such as birds-of-paradise (*Strelitzia*) and streptocarpus.

This exciting look can be created in temperate areas with exotic architectural plants including tree ferns, bamboos, fatsias, ferns, phormiums and hardy bananas (*Musa basjoo*). For shots of bright detail, use vibrant canna lilies, white arum lilies (*Zantedeschia*), dahlias, crocosmias, agapanthus and lobelias.

BELOW **Tropical abundance**
The striking leaves of elephant ears (*Alocasia*) provide a dramatic focal point in an exotic, jungle-like garden. Bright sparks of colour are provided by the vibrant red cannas which stand out amidst the lush green foliage.

ASSESSING YOUR SITE AND SOIL

It is important to discover as much as possible about the conditions that prevail in your garden before you start planning and planting. Take note of the local environment and climate, as well as the topography and soil conditions, as your plant choices will be determined by these factors. Check the aspect, which influences the sun and shade in a garden, and the soil type, to discover its moisture and nutrient content.

Understanding aspect

Determining how much sun and shade your garden receives is of paramount importance when making plant selections. Some plants prefer full sun, for example, while others need partial or full shade to thrive. You can use a compass to work out which way areas or borders face. Those facing south will be in sun for most of the day, while those that face north will be shady. East-facing areas have morning sun and evening shade, while the opposite applies to those facing west.

Patterns of sun and shade also change throughout the day, and a garden that is in full sun at midday may have areas of shade in the morning and late afternoon. For this reason, it is wise to study your garden on a sunny day and make a note of the way shadows move around the plot. Remember, too, that the seasons can affect the level of sunlight in a garden; for example, an area that is in sun in the summer could be in constant shade during the winter, which may have an effect on evergreens that need a sunny site to thrive.

However much sun your garden receives, there are plenty of plants to choose from that will thrive in those conditions. As well as plants for sun or shade, there are many that are happy with a bit of both.

ABOVE Plants that thrive in sun
Alliums, with their striking globes of rich pinkish-purple flowers, thrive in open, sunny sites, and make great partners for other sun-lovers, like catmints and salvias.

Assessing microclimates

Variations in the conditions in different parts of a garden are described as "microclimates", and may include frost pockets at the bottom of a slope, sheltered hot spots by a warm wall, pockets of wind turbulence, and exposed sites. Rather than limit your plant choice, microclimates actually allow you to grow a wider range of plants, so note the temperature, water levels, and air and wind circulation around your garden.

Types of soil

Knowing your soil type is key to growing healthy plants. It is always preferable to select those that thrive in the soil you have, rather than fighting it by trying to grow plants that are not adapted to your conditions, as they will inevitably suffer.

There are three main types of soil: sand, clay, and silt. They are categorized according to the size of the soil particles, which determines the level of water and plant food they can hold. Most garden soils are a combination of sand and clay, with one type dominating the mix; the ideal soil is "loam", which contains almost equal measures of sand, clay, and silt.

Sandy soils Sandy soil particles are relatively large and water drains freely through the spaces between them. As a result, these soils are free-draining, but because plant nutrients are dissolved in water, they are also quite infertile. Sandy soil is ideal for Mediterranean plants.

Clay soils Clay particles are minute, and trap moisture in between the gaps.

LEFT Growing shade-lovers
Shade-loving plants, such as the hart's tongue fern (*Asplenium scolopendrium*), flourish under the light shade provided by silver birch trees (*Betula pendula*).

The particles are also porous, so these soils are very moisture-retentive and rich in nutrients. However, clay soils can become waterlogged in wet conditions and form impenetrable crusts when dry. They are ideal for "hungry" plants like fruit trees.

Silt soils Pure silt soils are rare, usually occurring on river plains. They have a high nutrient content, but can become compacted and waterlogged like clay.

Loam With equal proportions of sand, clay, and silt, loam offers the best of all worlds, retaining enough water for plant roots to absorb, but allowing excess moisture to drain away and preventing waterlogging. It also holds on to nutrients well, making it the perfect garden soil for most plants.

Improving your soil

Whether you have a dry, sandy soil or a sticky clay one, your plants will grow better if you improve its quality by applying plenty of organic matter, such as well-rotted farmyard manure, garden compost, or spent mushroom compost. Organic matter coats sandy soil particles, helping them to retain more water, while it also opens up the structure of clay soils, allowing water to drain more easily.

Either dig it into the soil when preparing for planting or lay a thick layer as a mulch.

ABOVE **Plants that thrive in dry, sandy soil**
Dry, sandy soils and a sunny site provide the perfect conditions for many euphorbias, Californian poppies, bulbs like eremurus, and succulents, such as agaves.

Worms and micro-organisms will then work it into the soil.

The structure and drainage of heavy clay soils can also be improved by the addition of horticultural grit. Simply dig the grit into the soil over a large area. In extreme circumstances, very heavy, waterlogged soils may require drains.

Understanding pH

The pH of a soil is a measure of its acidity or alkalinity, which also influences the types of plants you can grow successfully. It is measured on a scale from 1 to 14; neutral soil has a pH of 7, a number below this indicates an acid soil, while alkaline soils have a pH above 7. A precise measurement can be obtained by performing a simple soil test (*see right*). Although many plants are tolerant of a wide pH range, there are some that are adapted to particular soil type. Rhododendrons, azaleas and heathers (*Erica*), for example, require an acidic soil, while lilacs (*Syringa vulgaris*) and the pineapple broom (*Cytisus battandieri*) grow best in alkaline soil.

TESTING YOUR SOIL

An easy way to find out what type of soil you have is to dig up a small sample and roll it between your fingers to feel the texture. Soils with a high water content can be rolled into a ball. You can also use a simple kit to test the pH.

Sandy and silty soil
Soils rich in sand feel gritty between your fingers; silty soils feel silky. Both fall apart when rolled into a ball. Sandy soils are easy to dig, and warm up quickly in spring. You may also find that borderline hardy plants survive winters better in these dry soils.

Clay soil
Smooth, sticky and dense, clay soils retain their shape when moulded into a ball, and those with a very high clay content remain intact even when rolled into a horseshoe. They are often described as "heavy" soils because they are difficult to dig.

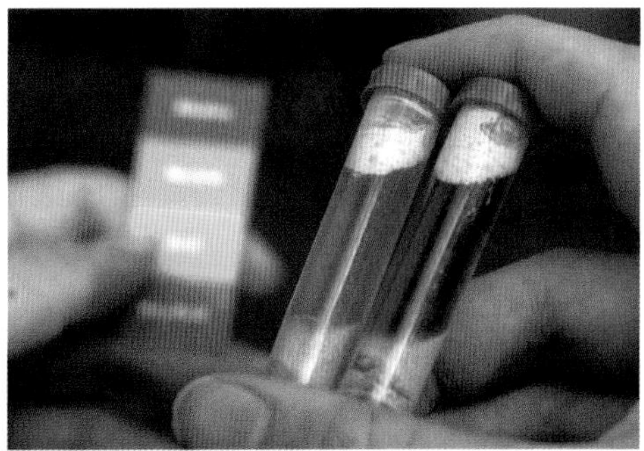

Using a pH testing kit
You can buy pH testing kits from garden centres and DIY stores. Place a small soil sample in the tube and add the solution provided with the kit. Wait until the solution changes colour, and then match it to the chart. Take a few readings from different areas of the garden, as they may have different pH values.

DESIGNING WITH PLANTS

There is a plant for every situation, be it a tree, shrub, perennial, annual or bulb. When designing with plants, you can include examples from all the plant groups to ensure year-round interest, or focus on just one or two groups for a contemporary look. The key to success is to vary shapes, textures, and colours, and consider how each plant will work with others in your border and in the garden as a whole.

Defining plant groups

Different plant groups fulfil different functions in a design, and understanding how each can be used to the best effect will help you to create a balanced, coordinated display. Trees, large shrubs, and some climbers provide the framework for a planting scheme, offering permanent structure, height, and depth, as well as colour and texture. Midrange plants include smaller shrubs, herbaceous perennials, some bulbs and grasses. They help to define the style of your garden, and provide seasonal interest with their flowers and foliage. Focal plants offer eye-catching accents, drawing the eye to a border or vista, while ground-cover plants create a low mat of leaves and blooms at a lower level. Annuals and biennials will put on a show from spring to early autumn in containers, and fill the gaps between more permanent planting groups in borders.

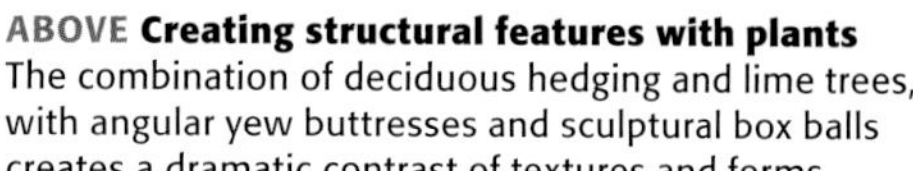

ABOVE Creating structural features with plants
The combination of deciduous hedging and lime trees, with angular yew buttresses and sculptural box balls creates a dramatic contrast of textures and forms.

Structural plants

Permanent structural plants, such as trees, shrubs and hedges, make a vital contribution to the shape and form of the garden, and identifying these key plants, and deciding where to position them, is the first step in producing a coherent design.

Evergreens provide year-round interest, while deciduous trees and shrubs inject dramatic displays of flowers in spring and colourful foliage in autumn. Hedging not only defines boundaries, but also offers shelter and creates privacy. Evergreen hedges make colourful year-round screens and backdrops for other planting groups, while deciduous hedges allow in more light, offer seasonal colour. Either type can be formal or informal in style, with leaf size, colour, and flowers to consider. Leafy shrubs work in a similar way to hedging, providing a green foliage backdrop to smaller midrange plants and ground cover.

You can also use structural plants to frame or block out views, and to lead the eye around the garden. In addition, trees and shrubs can help to create a visual link between the garden and the landscape beyond, extending the display. Repeated plants will also help to make connections between different areas of the garden and different planting areas.

Structural plants come in many different forms and shapes; for example, they may be rounded and neat, such as choisyas and photinias; spiky and textural, like mahonias, hollies, and yuccas; or looser in form, such as laburnums, weeping pears, or garryas. Many plants can be manipulated to create artificial structural effects, such as climbers clambering over arches, arbours and pergolas, or along walls. Others can be clipped into a variety of topiary shapes; box, yew and holly are all good candidates for topiary balls, pyramids, and spirals.

LEFT Creating focal plants
In this beautiful country garden, naturalized tulips in vibrant shades create a carpet of spring colour. The focal plant of this design is the light-reflecting white blossom and architectural shape of a *Malus floribunda*.

Focal plants

These are key specimen plants that can be used to catch the eye in a bed or border, in the centre of a lawn, or at the end of a pathway. Most focal plants are evergreen or have a distinctive shape or foliage form, but they can also include seasonal plants that perform for short times of the year, providing an accent when it is needed most.

Use focal plants to direct the eye to key areas of interest, or as signposts to guide the visitor around the garden. Phormiums, acers, yuccas, cardoons and white-stemmed birches will lead the eye to a particular area or distract attention away from unsightly features, like bins.

Midrange plants

This group of plants are of medium height, and include the vast array of herbaceous perennials, bulbs like tulips, daffodils and alliums, deciduous grasses, and to a lesser extent, small shrubs, including compact hebes and shrubby potentillas.

Some of the most effective midrange plants rely on their leaf shape and texture for interest more than their blooms, although seasonal flower colour is an important feature of many and makes an exciting statement when plants are used *en masse* in a border. When grouped together, those with strong foliage forms, such as acanthus, hostas, ligularias and rodgersias, also create bold plantings, or they can be used to separate plants with looser flowers or foliage forms.

Midrange plants contribute to the structure of the garden, but because many are perennial, dying down in late autumn and appearing again in spring, they are not able to perform the same role as the more permanent woody plants.

Ground-cover plants

Not only are ground-cover plants highly ornamental, providing a tapestry of colour, texture and form, they also create a blanket over the soil, helping to suppress weeds. Ground-cover plants are not restricted to low-growing types, however, and include a range shapes and sizes, the only proviso being that they form a dense canopy.

A dry, sunny site makes an ideal home for drought-tolerant flowering plants, such as dwarf genistas, helianthemums and sedums. Leafy ground-cover plants include thyme and other mat-forming herbs, *Hebe pinguifolia, Santolina chamaecyparissus,* and catmint (*Nepeta*). A cool shady site is perfect for ground-cover plants such as *Cornus canadensis, Geranium macrorrhizum* and epimediums under trees, and bergenias, hellebores and ferns by a wall where the soil is reasonably moist.

Seasonal interest

By combining different plant groups and selecting those with a succession of seasonal highlights, you can easily create a garden with year-round appeal.

In spring, focus on flowering trees, such as cherries, crab apples, magnolias and plums, as well as bulbs like hyacinths, muscari, crocus, daffodils and tulips that provide colour. Summer brings an explosion of flowering perennials, annuals and bulbs, offering a range of colours, heights and flower shapes. The autumn stars are the trees and shrubs, with acers, cotoneasters and cotinus all injecting foliage colour. Team them with late-flowering perennials such as asters. The winter garden also provides seasonal interest, with witch hazels (*Hamamelis*), and sarcococcas offering fragrant flowers, and colour provided by the stems of dogwoods (*Cornus*) and willow (*Salix*), and berries of hawthorns, hollies, and viburnums.

ABOVE **Using midrange plants**
Midrange plants like hostas are ideal feature plants for a mixed shady border. Repeating plants down the length of the border brings cohesion to the design.

ABOVE **Blanketing the ground with plants**
Santolinas, with their button-like, yellow flowers, make excellent ground-cover plants in a gravel planting in full sun, and associate beautifully with spiky eryngiums.

BELOW **Creating winter interest**
The golden yellow flowers of *Mahonia* x *media* 'Lionel Fortescue' make a striking contrast with the flame-red stems of *Cornus alba* 'Sibirica' in a winter border.

USING COLOUR

Colour choice is largely about personal preferences, but there are some useful theories on how to match and blend colours that will help you to create pleasing combinations. Remember, too, that light and shade affect colours and that some visually leap forward, stealing the limelight, while others are more recessive. Colour can also affect mood and tone, so choose carefully to create the desired atmosphere.

Combining colours

Before selecting colours for your beds and borders, it is a good idea to familiarize yourself with some of the principles of colour theory, which will help you combine them more successfully.

Many designers use the colour wheel to make their choices. The wheel is divided into primary, secondary and tertiary colours. The primary colours are red, blue and yellow, and when mixed create the secondary colours, green, orange, and purple. In this way, the primaries blue and red produce secondary purple; red and yellow produce secondary orange; and yellow and blue produce secondary green. Tertiary colours are produced by mixing adjacent primary and secondary colours.

The colour wheel can help you to create harmonious and contrasting schemes. For example, colours directly opposite one another on the wheel, such as yellow and purple or red and green, are considered to be "complementary". When placed next to each other, these contrasting colours create a sense of vibrancy and excitement.

Colours that sit next to each other on the wheel are know as "harmonious" or "analogous colours" and create a sense of order. Examples of harmonious colours are blue, purple and pink, and green, yellow, and pale orange. Harmonious colours can create different moods, depending on whether you choose hot reds and oranges or cool blues and greens.

Triadic colour schemes are created by selecting three colours that are spaced equally apart on the wheel. Green, orange and purple, is one example. The contrasting hues can create eye-catching combinations.

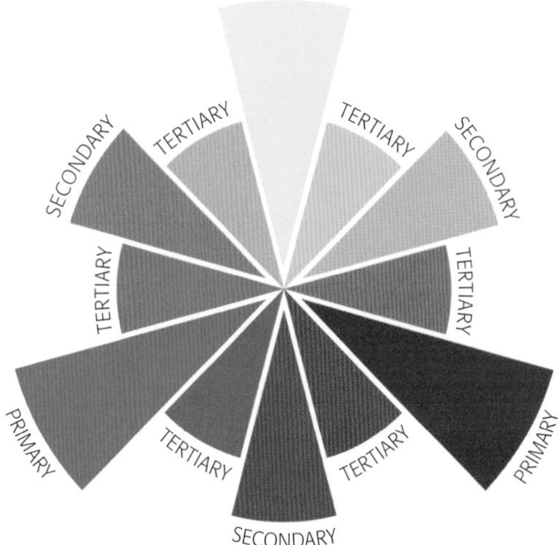

ABOVE The colour wheel
Frequently employed by garden designers, the colour wheel is a simple visual device that shows how to combine colours successfully, whether you want a vibrant scheme or a muted, harmonious grouping.

ABOVE Triadic colours
Green, orange and purple are triadic colours. Using them together creates a sense of exuberance, as shown by the autumn shades of this group of shrubs.

ABOVE Harmonious combination
This border combines adjoining colours: the pale pink *Dictamnus purpureus*, purple-pink *Allium* 'Purple Sensation', and a burgundy-red *Berberis* at the back.

ABOVE Tints and shades
This scheme of pale mauve campanulas, darker purple phlox, and deep pink geraniums, uses tints of mauve together with pink to create a balanced scheme.

LEFT Complementary colours
The contrasting blue-purple veronicas and bright yellow innulas show how hues on opposite sides of the wheel produce an exciting contrast that draws the eye.

Tints and shades

As well as selecting colours from the colour wheel, also consider the effects of tints, shades and tones. As a rule, pure hues or saturated colours are more intense, while colours that have been mixed together are less vibrant. More subtle colours can be created by lightening colours using white to create a tint, or darkening them by adding black to create a shade. When grey is added to a hue it creates a tone.

Tints and shades can be used as transitional colours between stronger hues and help to blend one colour into another. However, too many muted shades can look a bit lifeless, so ensure you inject some stronger colours into your planting schemes to create highlights.

Creating moods and focal points with colour

Colour can convey a mood or message, and has a powerful effect on the atmosphere in a garden. For instance, vivid, hot colours, such as crimson, scarlet, magenta, golden yellow and orange, generate a feeling of excitement, while cool colours like pale blue, pale pink, mauve, muted greys and blue-greens create a tranquil feeling. Use these colours to produce different moods in your garden, perhaps creating a sizzling scheme of hot hues by the house, and cooler

ABOVE **Hot fiery border**
Hot-hued plants in shades of red, orange and yellow are guaranteed to brighten up a garden. This fiery border is perfect for a sunny spot.

BELOW **Cool pastel shades**
The purple flowers of *Salvia* x *sylvestris* 'Mainacht' and the deeper purple leaves of *Persicaria microcephala* 'Red Dragon' contrast with green grasses and green-flowered *Angelica archangelica*. The silvery leaves of Heuchera 'Beauty Colour' are also veined with purple, thus continuing the silver-purple theme.

TEXTURE AND PATTERN

Mixing contrasting plant textures creates a lively effect in a border. Combine glossy and matt, or furry and rough foliage to make an impact. Look, too, at leaf patterns and match a variety of shapes and sizes to add to the interest.

Shiny and glossy
Many hollies (***Ilex***) have glossy leaves that reflect light. Their spiny leaves also add impact to a border, or they can be used as focal plants.

Soft and furry
Plants like lambs ears (***Stachys byzantina***) and sages have a compelling tactile quality. Plant them at the front of a border where they are easy to reach and enjoy.

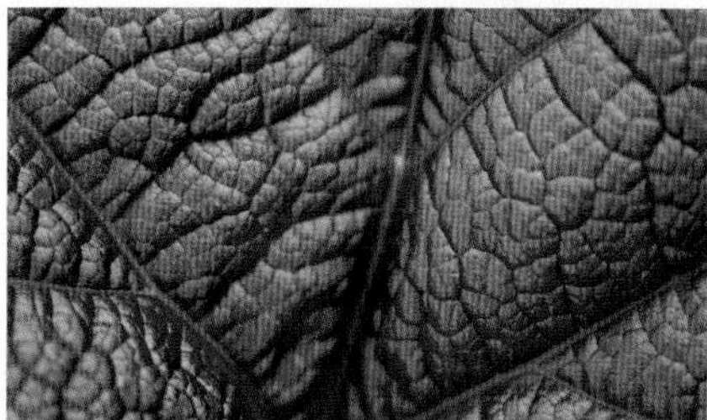

Rough and crinkled
The coarse-textured leaves of this decorative vine (***Vitis coignetiae***), are held on twisted gnarled stems that wrap around its support.

Lace-like tracery
The soft, feathery foliage of an artemisia provides a foil for larger-leaved plants that like the same sunny conditions, such as sedums.

YEAR-ROUND INTEREST

When choosing plants for your garden, try to include a selection of feature trees and shrubs that have more than one season of interest. There is a wide range of trees and shrubs, both deciduous and evergreen, that perform for most of the year.

Cornus alba
A deciduous shrub with white flowers in late spring, as well as striking red shoots in winter. The leaves turn red or orange in autumn.

***Mahonia* x *media* 'Charity'**
Mahonias have shiny evergreen foliage, plus yellow flowers and purple or black fruits. 'Charity' has scented yellow flowers in winter.

Nandina domestica
The leaves of this evergreen shrub have red tints in spring and autumn. Small white summer flowers are followed by bright red berries.

***Prunus* x *subhirtella* 'Autumnalis Rosea'**
This cherry tree has tiny, pale pink flowers that appear in winter. The green leaves are bronze when young, turning golden-yellow in autumn.

tones in a shady woodland area at the far end of the garden. Another option is to use the same bed or border to change in mood as the seasons progress, with bright daffodils and tulips in spring, followed by herbaceous summer planting in blues, purples, pale pinks and whites, and then fiery foliage colour in the autumn.

Single-colour-themed borders, be they white and cream or varying shades of yellow, look highly sophisticated and produce a satisfying cohesion. The restricted plant choices can also make designing a little easier.

You can also use colour to draw attention to a particular feature or planting area. To produce this effect, ensure your plants contrast with the surroundings to increase their visibility. For example, a single, bright orange plant against a recessive background colour, such as green or blue, will create an effective accent. Planting schemes that combine swathes of warm and cool colours also work well, with the cooler colours providing a foil for the hot hues.

You can also exploit the way in which colours can alter perceptions of distance. For instance, bright reds and oranges planted at the end of a garden have a foreshortening effect, making the garden appear shorter, while pale colours can make the garden seem longer.

The effects of light and shade

The way that we perceive colour is influenced by the amount of light it receives. Sunny borders will make colours appear bolder and brighter, while shady areas enhance more subtle colours and white. The colours of plants can therefore change depending on their location, the degree of shade cast on them and on the time of day. For example, pale colours that produce beautiful effects in the early morning or evening may be bleached out by strong midday sunlight. Bear this in mind if you tend to use your garden at a particular time of day. If you work and sit outside mainly in the evenings, choose white and pale flowers that take on a luminous quality in the fading light.

Choose colours that produce the best effects for different areas of the garden. Plant reds, oranges, bright pinks and yellows in sunny spaces, as they will look muddy in the shade. Nature often makes this choice for you, as many hot-hued flowers need a sunny spot to thrive. Woodland plants, on the other hand, tend to produce flowers in whites, pastel shades of yellow, pink and purple, and blues, all of which show up better in shade.

Creating a succession of year-round colour

When selecting plants, try to include a range that flower or are at their peak at different times of the year to sustain the interest. This is particularly important in small gardens, where the planting is on view all year round.

Consider the merits of each plant, including its size, habit, leaf shape, texture and colour, flowers, and fruit. For a prolonged display, focus on foliage, either evergreen for constant colour, or deciduous, which in most cases endures from spring to autumn. This leafy mix provides a backdrop for the succession of flowers that appear. When choosing flowering plants, remember that many have beautiful seedheads, including love-in-a-mist (*Nigella*), poppies, eryngiums, and sedums, that provide two seasons of interest. Also use containers to add an extra dimension to borders and patio displays; one large planter can be used for four different seasonal displays.

Spring

When spring makes a welcome appearance, the garden is soon awash with colour. Some is provided by spring-flowering trees and shrubs, such as amelanchiers, ornamental cherries, apples, plums, and almonds (*Prunus*), magnolias, some viburnums, camellias, and forsythias, as well as a host of tough rock

Spring match
Create a balanced display in your borders with a mixture of tulips, such as 'Bleu Aimable', scented biennial wallflowers (*Erysimum*) and dainty violas providing colour in the foreground.

plants, including aubretias, saxifrages, and violas. Add to these a selection of bulbs and corms, starting with snowdrops (*Galanthus*) in late winter or early spring, and followed by crocuses, grape hyacinths (*Muscari*), daffodils (*Narcissus*), and tulips (*Tulipa*). As the majority of these bold displays of bulbs die down, they are followed by spring-flowering azaleas and rhododendrons which provide a wealth of colours, including magenta, pink, crimson, scarlet, golden yellow, and white. As the new leaves unfurl in late spring, blue ceanothus and the scented flowers of viburnums and lilacs enhance the spring garden further.

Summer

As temperatures rise and light levels increase, the garden is filled with a profusion of perennials, annuals and biennials. Not many trees put on their best performance in summer, but shrubs are a key source of colour. Roses start to bloom early in the season, many continuing well into autumn. Other beautiful summer-flowering shrubs include sweetly scented mock oranges (*Philadelphus*), lavender, hibiscus, and the flowering dogwoods (*Cornus*). Even those that flowered in spring still play their part by providing a leafy backdrop to the flowers that offer the main show at this time of year.

Many climbers are also in full swing in summer. There are a vast number of clematis species and hybrids to choose from, providing colour in the garden from early summer to late in the season, while jasmine, honeysuckle, and the frothy flat heads of climbing hydrangea (*Hydrangea petiolaris*) are other star performers.

Perennials are the real stars of the summer border. There are thousands to choose from, including early summer-flowering aquilegias, and many geraniums and lupins, followed by campanulas, salvias, achilleas, and hemerocallis, with heleniums, rudbeckias, and echinaceas appearing later in the season. Biennials, such as foxgloves, make great partners for shade-loving perennials, while hardy and half hardy annuals produce an explosion of colour in borders and container displays.

Hardy annuals, such as Californian poppies (*Echscholzia californica*), annual mallows (*Malope*), and the shoo-fly plant (*Nicandra*) flower for months on end, offering great value for money, and self seeding to produce a repeat performance the following summer. Together with half-hardy annuals, like cosmos, impatiens, lobelia, and petunias, they provide colour throughout the season, often only ceasing to flower when the frosts arrive in autumn.

Autumn

As summer fades, the foliage of many trees and shrubs flares into the fiery colours of autumn. Some of the best choices for this seasonal display are maples, some cherries, amelanchiers, liquidambars, cotoneasters, sorbus, nyssa, and most forms of smoke bush (*Cotinus*).

Late-flowering perennials, such as Michaelmas daisies (*Aster*) and chrysanthemums, as well as dahlias with their rich variety of flower shapes and colours, brighten up the garden until the arrival of the first frosts. Grasses are also key features of these cooler months. Pampas grasses (*Cortaderia*), fountain grasses (*Pennisetum*), and *Stipa calamagrostis* produce feather- and brush-like seedheads at this time of the year.

Winter

During winter, flower interest is limited, but valuable sources include the scented blooms of winter box (*Sarcococca*) and witch hazels (*Hamamelis*). Bold sculptural shapes and foliage colour provided by evergreens is of most importance now, with conifers, box (*Buxus*), and ivy (*Hedera*), coming into their own.

Deciduous trees and shrubs also play an important role, their intricate skeletons of stems clearly visible at this time of year. Think, too, about bark colour and texture; white-stemmed birches (*Betula*) and the polished coppery-brown stems of *Prunus serrula* are favourite trees, while brightly coloured dogwood (*Cornus*) and willow (*Salix*) stems make exciting focal points. Enhance the winter scene further with berried shrubs, such as hollies (*Ilex*), pyracanthas, and sorbus.

Summer profusion
Perennials often lead the border chorus at this time of year. Crocosomias and veronicastrums provide colour and form, with the pinky-purple domes of stately eupatoriums offering background colour.

Autumn brights
Most perennials are dying down at this time of year but a few leave their best performance till last. Sedums and asters are key features of the autumn border, here offset by buff grasses and red-leaved *Euonymus alata*.

Frosted features
Winter is a quiet time in the garden, but there is still beauty to be found in the form of stark borders filled with frost-encrusted grasses and the enduring seedheads of perennials such as sedums.

BASIC PLANTING TECHNIQUES

Once you have planned your garden, and assessed the aspect and soil, you can begin planting. Giving new plants a good start by improving soil will result in strong, healthy specimens that put on a display year after year. Choose a fine day when the soil is not frozen or waterlogged and, before starting, make sure the soil is free of weeds. Water all plants well in preparation and water them again after planting.

Choosing healthy plants

Before going to the garden centre or nursery, make a list of your chosen plants, and try to stick to it, to avoid making impulsive purchases. If some of the plants are not available, remember to check the eventual size and required growing conditions of any substitutes to ensure that they will fulfil your needs.

Check each plant to ensure you have chosen the healthiest specimen. Look at the leaves and stems for signs of pests and diseases, and reject any plant with wilted foliage. Then turn over the pot and check to see if there is a mass of roots growing through the drainage holes, a sign that the plant is "root bound" and has been growing in the pot for too long. Finally, select plants with lots of leafy stems and plump buds.

Remove the weeds
When weeding, try to remove the root systems completely to prevent the weeds from growing back. Pernicious weeds, such as ground elder and bindweed, may need to be treated with a weedkiller.

Feed the soil
When making a new bed or border, enrich the soil by digging in well-rotted organic matter, such as manure or garden compost, before planting. Apply organic matter as a mulch around plants on existing beds.

Preparing the ground

It is always wise to take a few hours to prepare the soil well before you plant. Clear the site of any large stones and remove all weeds, ensuring that you dig out the whole root system of perennial weeds, like dandelions. Start by hand-weeding the site. You can apply a weedkiller, if necessary, to tackle pernicious weeds such as bindweed, ground elder, Japanese knotweed, horsetail, nettles, and brambles. If weeds are really problematic, consider covering the site with some old carpet or plastic sheeting for a few seasons. This forms a physical barrier against settling weed seeds, and the lack of light and moisture prevents weed growth. When the site has been cleared, enrich the soil with organic matter, such as well-rotted manure or garden compost. On a large plot, dig a series of trenches to the depth of a spade across the area and add manure to the base of each trench. Alternatively, spread an 8cm (3in) layer of organic matter over the border, and dig it into the top 15cm (6in) of soil. Dig in some horticultural grit to heavy clays to improve drainage. Finally, rake the surface.

PLANTING A PERENNIAL OR SHRUB

Shrubs form the backbone of a garden, providing permanent structure, while most perennials die down in winter and emerge again in spring. Plants grown in containers can be planted at any time of year, but avoid times when the ground is frozen or excessively wet or dry. Also, prepare the soil well before you start (see above), to ensure your plants establish quickly and produce healthy growth.

1 Make a planting hole First, water the plants well. Dig out a planting hole for each plant, making sure that it is twice the diameter of the container and a little deeper. Fork the bottom and sides of the hole, and add some controlled-release fertilizer to the excavated soil.

2 Check planting depth Remove the plant from its pot, teasing out the roots if they are congested. Use a cane to check the plant will be at the same depth as it was in its pot. Put the plant in the hole and steadily trickle in water as you backfill with soil, firming as you go.

3 Water and mulch Water the plant. Spread a mulch of organic matter around the plant, avoiding the stems, to conserve moisture and suppress weeds. Water plants in dry spells until fully established. Each spring, rake in a general-purpose fertilizer around the plant.

PLANTING DEPTHS

Most plants need to be planted at the same depth as they were in their pots or, if they are bare-root trees or shrubs, plant them at the depth they were growing at in the field, indicated by a dark soil mark on the stems. Among the exceptions are bearded irises (below); their rhizomes will rot if buried so they should be planted with them exposed. Sun-loving shrubs and perennials, such as verbascums and sedums, also thrive when planted slightly proud of the soil. Moisture-loving plants like hostas prefer to be buried a little deeper than ground level.

Planting in containers

When choosing a container, look at the range of different materials and designs available to find those that suit both your garden style and the types of plants you plan to grow.

In late spring, when all frosts have passed, plant your summer bedding outside in containers, window boxes and hanging baskets. The method for planting containers and window boxes differs slightly from that of hanging baskets (see below) and they require watering daily. If you have less time to spend watering and feeding, opt for pots of drought-tolerant shrubs, such as hebes, lavenders, and phormiums, or rock plants, like sedums and houseleeks (*Sempervivum*).

Trees and large shrubs in containers add height and stature to a design. Those suitable for growing in pots include box (Buxus), many dwarf conifers, *Fatsia japonica*, *Hydrangea serrata* and choisyas. These will need to be watered regularly in dry spells, and in spring, remove the top few centimetres of compost and replace with fresh, together with some all-purpose controlled-release fertilizer.

Choosing pot sizes

When making your container selections, choose pots of different sizes for a traditional grouping, or opt for a series of pots of the same size and line them up for a contemporary look.

The size of your pots will affect the amount of maintenance they require. Tiny pots dry out quickly, and need watering on a daily basis in summer, unless you plant them with drought-tolerant rock plants. Larger pots hold more compost and therefore more moisture and nutrients, reducing the need for such frequent watering and feeding.

Material options

The material a container is made from affects both the price and the maintenance needs of the plants. Clay is a beautiful natural material but because it is porous, it dries out more rapidly than synthetic materials or natural stone. Choose glazed clay or plastic if you want colourful pots.

Terracotta elegance
Natural and the perfect foil for a shrub, such as a hebe, terracotta is porous and dries out quickly. To prevent moisture loss, line with bubble plastic before planting.

Size matters
Choose a pot size that balances your chosen plants. Opt for a tall slim container for a fountain of foliage, or a small wide pot for a rounded shrub or planting group.

PLANTING A SUMMER CONTAINER

You can create exciting displays in containers and window boxes with easy summer flowers. Some grow quickly from seed, or you can buy plug plants via mail order or larger bedding plants from the garden centre. When combining plants, try to balance the shapes, colours and textures. This example includes red dahlias, French marigolds, and yellow bidens.

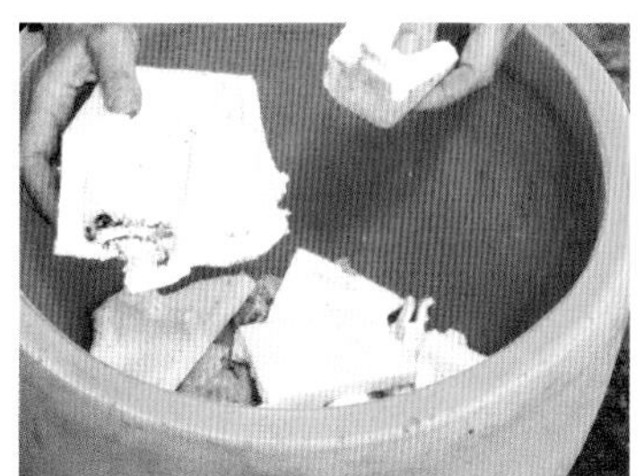

1 Add drainage material

Place a layer of broken clay pot pieces in the base of the pot to help ensure good drainage. For larger pots, you can reduce the amount of potting compost required and the weight of the container by filling the bottom third with pieces of polystyrene.

2 Plant up

Fill the container to about 5cm (2in) from the rim with all-purpose compost. Work in a some slow-release fertilizer granules. Water the plants about 30 minutes before planting. Tip them from their pots or trays and arrange on the compost surface.

Final effects

Plant the tallest plants at the back or in the middle of the container, and fill in around them with shorter or trailing types. Water the container well, and continue to water plants regularly. To exend the flowering period, remove the faded blooms with secateurs at frequent intervals throughout summer.

PLANTING A HANGING BASKET

Globes of flowers and foliage lend an exotic touch to patios and seating areas throughout summer. Plant up a large hanging basket and hang it at about head height where you can see the colours and textures at close quarters. Hanging baskets filled with ivy, small evergreens, violas, and early bulbs also add a splash of colour in autumn and winter.

1 Preparing the basket

Line the basket and add a circle of plastic to the bottom to create a water reservoir. Top with a layer of compost. Cut crosses around the sides of the liner. Protect the leaves of the trailing plants with some plastic and thread them through the crosses, as shown.

2 Planting the top

Cover the roots of the trailing plants with more compost, and then start planting up the top of the basket. Work from the centre out, with the tallest plants (such as verbena) in the middle, with compact bedding and trailing types around the edges.

Finishing touches

Fill in around the plants with compost and work in some slow-release fertilizer granules. Water well and add a layer of gravel over the compost to help retain moisture. Water the basket daily, even if it has rained, and deadhead regularly to extend the flower display throughout the summer.

LOOKING AFTER YOUR GARDEN

To keep your garden in peak condition, you will need to perform regular maintenance tasks throughout the year. Watering is essential for young plants and those in containers, and to win the battle against weeds, you must be vigilant from spring to autumn. It pays to give most plants a feed and a mulch every year – usually in spring. Woody plants may also need to be pruned to keep them in good condition.

Weeding methods

You can limit the growth of weeds by top-dressing the soil with a thick mulch or a membrane, but you will never be completely free of them. The most useful tool for removing annual weeds over a large area is a hoe; as you move it back and forth, the blade slices through the necks of weeds where the stems meet the soil. Choose a dry sunny day for hoeing and leave the weeds on the surface to die – you can then collect them up and compost them.

Although hoeing kills annual weeds, such as chickweed and groundsel, perennial weeds, including brambles, dock, couch grass and ground elder will survive and regrow. Use a weed grubber to remove those with tap roots, such as dandelions, and dig out perennials with fibrous root systems using a spade or trowel. If you have pernicious weeds that you cannot remove by hand, apply a glyphosate weedkiller.

Dealing with dandelions
A grubber is the ideal tool to lever out perennial weeds with deep tap roots, such as dandelions.

Slow-release watering
Seep- or perforated hoses trickle water into the soil above the roots, exactly where it is most needed.

Watering

In summer, watering is the main gardening task. Young plants in beds and borders and container displays are especially vulnerable to drought, and are best watered early in the morning or in the evening when evaporation rates are low. A basic watering can is generally sufficient for small areas or containers, and fits easily under a rainwater butt tap. For seedlings and new plants, fit your can with a rose, so that you do not wash soil away from the roots.

If you have a large new area to water, a garden hose is a more practical option. Attach a spray fitting to give new plantings a gentle shower, and direct the hose on the soil, rather than the leaves or flowers. An even more efficient watering method is to lay perforated hosepipes round your plants; water gradually seeps out at soil level and penetrates deeply with little waste.

Feeding

Once established, most plants growing in reasonably good soil need an annual application of fertilizer in spring. The type of plant food you choose and how often you apply it will be determined by your soil and what you are trying to grow. Plants require a range of essential nutrients. The primary nutrients are nitrogen (N), which plants need for leaf growth; phosphorous (P) for healthy roots; and potassium (K) for good flower and fruit production. The secondary nutrients, calcium, magnesium and sulphur, are required in smaller amounts, while the seven trace elements, such as iron, are needed in very small quantities.

Fertilizers are either organic (derived from plants and animals) or inorganic (chemically manufactured). Most are concentrated for convenience and available

FERTILIZER OPTIONS

Most plants benefit from an application of fertilizer once a year in spring. However, some may need extra nutrients to boost them at key times, such as flowering. Always follow the manufacturer's instructions carefully because too much fertilizer, or using the wrong type for a particular plant, may have a detrimental effect. Your local garden centre or DIY store will stock a selection of organic and inorganic fertilizers.

Growmore
This balanced chemical feed is used to enrich the soil at sowing or planting time. It can also be applied as an annual top dressing in the spring for all types of plant.

Organic matter
Well-rotted manure or garden compost is rich in trace elements and soil-conditioning substances. Dig it into the ground or apply it as a surface mulch.

Blood, fish and bonemeal
This organic, balanced fertilizer can be mixed into the soil when planting, and applied around plants in the spring or early summer.

Soluble food
Fast-acting soluble liquid feeds provide bedding and container plants with the nutrients they need. They can also be used on plants that need a quick boost.

Slow-release granules
These granules are activated by warmth and moisture, and provide a steady supply of nutrients for many weeks in borders and containers.

MULCH OPTIONS

Mulches reduce weed growth and conserve water, which is why they should always be applied when the ground is moist. A gravel mulch helps to keep the leaves and stems of drought-loving plants dry, and prevents them from rotting. As well as being functional, many mulches are also attractive, and produce a decorative surface for borders and containers. Recycled ground glass and dyed shells are colourful options.

Gravel
Gravel laid over landscape fabric creates a weed-suppressant and a decorative foil for alpines and Mediterranean-style plantings. Plant through the fabric by cutting a cross and folding back the flaps. Apply the gravel on top after planting.

Bark chips
Available in different sizes, the smallest being the most attractive, bark breaks down slowly and makes a good weed suppressor. It also helps to conserve soil moisture, but does not supply many nutrients. Top up worn areas annually.

Garden compost
Rotted compost and manure lock moisture into the soil and help to supress weed growth. As the mulch breaks down it also releases plant foods and improves the structure of the soil.

Leafmould
Although low in nutrients, rotted leaves help to improve the soil structure and trap moisture in. They are ideal for woodland and shade-loving plants, many of which would be mulched by leaves in their natural habitats.

as liquids, powders that you dilute in water, or granules. Organic fertilizers include pelleted chicken manure; blood, fish and bonemeal; liquid seaweed fertilizer; and homemade plant feeds, such as the diluted liquor from a wormery or fertilizers made from soaking comfrey leaves. Inorganic fertilizers include sulphate of potash, Growmore and granular rose feeds.

Fertilizers are grouped according to the quantities of N, P, and K they contain. For example, a balanced fertilizer for general use, such as Growmore, contains equal quantities of each primary nutrient, while a fertilizer for lawns has a higher concentration of nitrogen, and those for fruit bushes are rich in potassium.

Apply an all-purpose granular fertilizer to the soil when planting, and spread around plants in spring. Containers, baskets and some bedding annuals may need a regular liquid feed during the growing season, or apply a controlled-release granular fertilizer when planting. Remember to follow the manufacturer's directions carefully.

Mulching

Mulches are materials that are spread on the soil surface, usually around plants. Some mulches serve a practical purpose – feeding the soil, suppressing weeds, retaining moisture or insulating roots in winter – while others are primarily decorative. Decorative mulches include crushed glass or shells, and slate chips.

Mulches are applied at different times of the year, depending on their purpose and the plants' needs. For example, bark chips are spread over the soil surface after planting to suppress weeds, but may take nutrients from the soil as they decompose, so apply a nitrogen-rich fertilizer to compensate for this loss. Organic matter, such as farmyard manure or garden compost, helps to retain soil moisture while also fertilizing the ground. It must be laid over moist soil, either in spring (following autumn and winter rains) or after watering. Apply organic mulches in a thick layer about 10cm (4in) deep, and replenish them annually as worms and soil micro-organisms will break them down throughout the year.

Composting

Disposing of your organic kitchen waste and plant prunings by composting creates an excellent eco-friendly soil improver. There is a wide range of bins available, including standard plastic composters that hold plenty of waste, and more decorative types, such as wooden models that resemble beehives.

To produce good compost, you will need the right mix of ingredients. Too much soft green material, such as grass clippings and vegetable peelings, turns the heap into a slimy mess. On the other hand, if you include too much dry woody material, such as prunings, the heap will rot down too slowly. Aim for an equal measure of green and dry ingredients and add them in layers. A good airflow is also essential to the composting process, so turn over the contents regularly.

MAKING LEAFMOULD

Leafmould is one of the finest soil conditioners, and makes good use of fallen autumn leaves. It is very quick and easy to make, but takes at least a year to rot down, ready for use in the garden.

1 Rake up the leaves
In autumn, rake up the leaves in your garden and place them in large plastic bin bags. If you chop them up first with a garden spade, they will decompose faster.

2 Water, tie and leave
When the bags are half full, sprinkle the leaves with water. Continue to add leaves and water again when full. Tie the bag and make a few holes with a fork to allow in some air. After a year or two, the leafmould will be ready.

Good garden hygiene

By keeping your plants in good health and checking them regularly, you can keep many pests and diseases at bay. Aim to grow your plants in the right conditions because healthy specimens are more able to withstand attacks. Remember, too, that some plants are susceptible to certain diseases so, whenever possible, buy resistant varieties.

A few simple precautions will also pay dividends. Check new plants for signs of pests and diseases to ensure that they do not introduce them to your garden, and keep all tools and equipment clean to guard against the spread of diseases. Tools such as pruners and seed trays are best cleaned with household disinfectant. You can also put up physical barriers, such as cut-off plastic bottles to help protect your plants from pests such as slugs and snails.

If a plant does succumb to a disease, first try to identify the problem to gauge its seriousness, and remove and either burn or bin infected plant material. Minor pest attacks can usually be dealt with by removing the invaders by hand. Also, try to encourage natural predators, such as birds, frogs and toads, ladybirds, hoverflies, spiders and lacewings into your garden, as together they will help to keep many pests under control. Pools, ponds, berried shrubs and trees, and nectar-rich open flowers will help to lure this pest army into your plot. If you have to resort to chemical pesticides and fungicides, use them sparingly and read the manufacturer's instructions carefully.

Pruning guidelines

It is not essential to prune any plant, but thinning and cutting back to varying degrees or selectively removing whole branches can be beneficial.

Pruning can rejuvenate old, congested specimens and help to extend the life of short-lived shrubs. It can also promote the growth of more flowering and fruiting wood, improve the shape of a plant, and reduce the incidence of disease.

Most pruning is performed annually, but if you spot dead, damaged or diseased wood, or a sucker growing from a grafted plant, remove it immediately. A general tip is to prune plants that flower in spring just after they have bloomed, and prune those that flower in summer or autumn in early spring before the buds break. Most evergreens are pruned in late spring.

It is important to use the right tools when pruning, as they will make the task easier. The tool you will require depends on the thickness of the material you need to remove. Use sharp secateurs for stems the width of a pencil or smaller, and a pruning saw or loppers for larger branches. Never prune above head height and call in a professional tree surgeon for large jobs.

MAKING PRUNING CUTS

Trees, shrubs and climbers grow in different ways, and their shoots, buds and stems differ too. Before pruning, identify the type of buds and shoots on the plant and their position. Buds are found at the point where the leaves are about to grow, or where they have previously been attached to the stem. When pruning, cut just above a bud; this stimulates hormones that make the bud develop into a new stem.

Cutting opposite buds
The buds of some plants are opposite each other. Prune above a pair of buds with a flat, straight cut. When the buds grow, they will produce two shoots growing in opposite directions from one another.

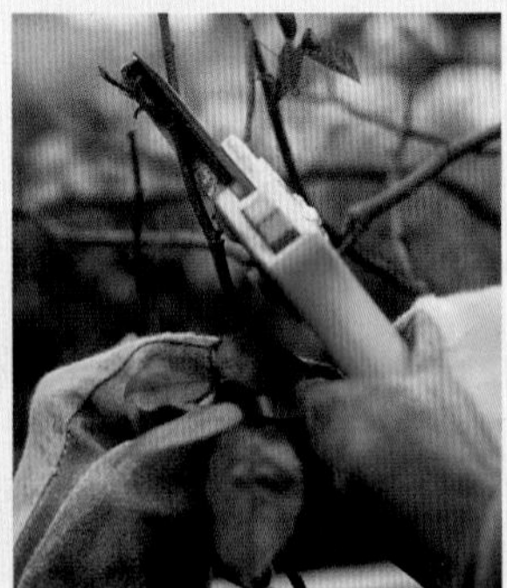

Cutting alternate buds
Where the buds are positioned alternately along the stems, try to prune to one that is facing outwards, away from the centre of the plant. Make a sloping cut above the bud, so that water runs away from it.

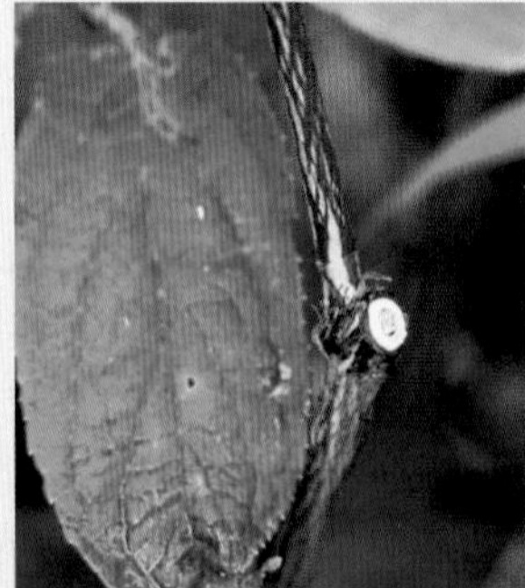

Cutting to new growth
You can recognize new growth because it looks much fresher than old wood. When pruning, cut off old wood just above a new stem, using a sloping cut so that water runs away from the young growth.

WHY PRUNE?

You can achieve many beautiful effects with careful pruning. Some plants are best trimmed lightly to create a natural look, while others can be clipped into elegant topiary. In addition, some pruning techniques encourage more flowering and fruiting stems to form.

Cutting out dead and diseased wood
Whenever you see dead or diseased wood on any woody plant, remove it immediately. If dead wood is left on a plant, disease can enter more easily and move down the stems.

Pruning for shape and form
Some plants need a gentle trim to retain their shape. This *Pittosporum tenuifolium* makes an attractive focal plant. The only pruning it requires is to retain the plant's symmetry by lightly trimming it in late spring.

Crossing and rubbing branches
Branches that rub each other can create open wounds that let in diseases. Remove one of the branches, choosing the weakest one or the stem that has suffered the most damage.

PLANT SELECTOR

The lists in this section suggest plants that are suitable for growing in a range of situations, or that have special uses or characteristics. Although the plants should thrive in the conditions specified, bear in mind that they are not always consistent and much of their success depends on climate, location, aspect and care. The list is subdivided into plant groups for each category, following the arrangement of the Plant Catalogue on pages 56–496. Plants that are featured in the Catalogue are followed by page numbers; refer to the Plant Directory for a whole genus or for a plant not followed by a number.

Plants for sandy soil

Sandy soils are often termed 'light' or 'hungry'. They are usually well-drained, but dry out rapidly and hold low reserves of plant nutrients. Many plants have adapted to such soils by developing deeply penetrating roots. Their leaves are modified to reduce moisture loss: small and reflexed, evergreen and glossy, or covered with fine grey or silver hairs. To improve moisture retention, incorporate some organic matter when planting in autumn; little watering will then be needed and plants are able to establish well before summer.

TREES

Amelanchier lamarckii, p.110
Betula ermanii, p.78
Betula pendula 'Dalecarlica'
Castanea sativa
Celtis australis, p.62
Cercis siliquastrum, p.83
Crataegus laevigata 'Paul's Scarlet', p.84
Genista aetnensis, p.89
Nothofagus obliqua, p.63
Phoenix canariensis
Pinus bungeana, p.78
Pinus sylvestris, p.78
Quercus ilex

CONIFERS

Abies grandis, p.98
x *Cupressocyparis leylandii and cvs*
Juniperus
Larix decidua, p.97
Pinus pinaster, p.97
Pinus radiata, p.98
Pseudotsuga menziesii var. *glauca*, p.96
Thuja occidentalis and cvs

SHRUBS

Acacia dealbata, p.211
Artemisia arborescens 'Faith Raven'
Berberis empetrifolia, p.148
Brachyglottis 'Sunshine'
BUDDLEJAS, p.114
Calluna vulgaris and cvs, p.166
Caragana arborescens 'Lorbergii'
Ceanothus thyrsiflorus and forms
Cistus spp. and cvs, pp.150, 152, 153, 154
Convolvulus cneorum, p.149
Cotoneaster lacteus, p.117
Elaeagnus pungens 'Maculata', p.119
Enkianthus cernuus f. *rubens*, p.123
Erica spp. and cvs, p.166
Gaultheria mucronata 'Mulberry Wine', p.164
Gaultheria mucronata 'Wintertime', p.163
Genista tinctoria, p.148
Halimium 'Susan', p.160
Hippophäe rhamnoides, p.142
Hypericum 'Hidcote', p.160
LAVENDERS, p.158
Olearia nummulariifolia, p.128
Perovskia 'Blue Spire', p.159
Phlomis fruticosa, p.160
Robinia hispida, p.133
Rosa spinosissima
Rosmarinus officinalis, p.157
SALVIAS, p.155
Santolina pinnata subsp. *neapolitana* 'Sulphurea', p.159
Spartium junceum, p.140
Tamarix ramosissima, p.114
Teucrium fruticans 'Azureum'
x *Halimiocistus sahucii*, p.149
Yucca gloriosa, p.132

CLIMBERS AND WALL SHRUBS

CLEMATIS, pp.198–200
Clianthus puniceus, p.193
Eccremocarpus scaber, p.208
Lapageria rosea, p.202
Vitis vinifera 'Purpurea', p.210

PERENNIALS

Acanthus spinosus, p.239
Achillea spp. and cvs, pp.235, 243, 247, 359, 360
Agapanthus 'Northern Star', p.241
Agapanthus 'Phantom'
Agapanthus 'Purple Cloud', p.241
Agapanthus inapertus ssp. pendulus 'Graskop', p.240
Agastache 'Black Adder', p.280
Artemisia ludoviciana 'Valerie Finnis' p.274
Artemisia absinthium 'Lambrook Silver'
Asphodeline
Aster divaricatus, p.249
Aster ericoides f. prostratus 'Snowflurry'
Aster species, selections and hybrids, pp.249, 250, 254, 367
Baptisia australis, p.240
Berkheya purpurea, p.269
Campanula persicifolia
Campanula punctata, C. takesimana, p.241
Campanula species, selections and hybrids, pp.241, 242, 342, 360, 367, 368, 369
CARNATIONS AND PINKS, pp.266–267
Centranthus ruber, p.248
Coreopsis 'Limerock Ruby', p.268
Delphinium grandiflorum 'Blue Butterfly', p.217
Diascia personata, p.223
Eremurus x *isabellinus* 'Cleopatra', p.220
Eryngium pandanifolium
Eryngium x *tripartitum*, p.250
Erysimum 'Bowles Mauve', p.261

BELOW Hot and dry conditions *Acanthus spinosus* and *Phlomis russeliana* make a perfect planting partnership on sandy soil.

PLANT SELECTOR

Francoa sochifolia Rogerson's form
Gaillardia 'Oranges and Lemons', p.277
Gaillardia x *grandiflora* cvs
Libertia ixioides 'Goldfinger', p.277
Limonium latifolium 'Blue Cloud', p.270
Nepeta 'Six Hills Giant', p.240
Nepeta x *faassenii*, p.270
Oenothera fruticosa 'Fyrverkeri', p.275
Origanum vulgare 'Aureum', p.274
ORIENTAL POPPIES, p.238
Phlomis russeliana, p.243
Platycodon grandiflorus, p.269
Potentilla 'Arc-en-ciel', p.268
RED HOT POKER, p.254
Romneya coulteri, p.216
SEDUM, p.279
Solidago 'Goldenmosa', p.251
Stachys officinalis 'Hummelo', p.268
Verbascum spp. and cvs, pp.219, 243, 246, 345

GRASSES AND BAMBOOS

Ampeldesmos mauritanica, p.287
Carex flagellifera, p.289
Chasmanthium latifolium, p.288
Chionochloa rubra, p.285
Cortadera richardii, p.284
Deschampsisa cesoitosa 'Gold Tau', p.289
Elegia capensis, p.285
Eragrostis curvula 'Totnes Burgundy', p.285
Miscanthus sinensis and cvs pp.284, 285, 286
Molinia caerulea subsp. *arundinacea* 'Transparent', p.286
Molinia caerulea subsp. *caerulea* 'Heidebraut', p.285
Panicum virgatum 'Northwind', p.289
Pennisetum spp., pp.286, 311, 312
Stipa spp., pp.286, 287, 288

ANNUALS AND BIENNIALS

Antirrhinum majus and cvs, pp.306, 319, 320
Brachyscome iberidifolia
Cleome hassleriana and cvs, p.304
Coreopsis tinctoria, p.321
Eschscholzia californica, p.326
Glandularia x *hybrida* Series and cvs, pp.303, 307
Limnanthes douglasii, p.321
Limonium sinuatum
Linaria maroccana 'Fairy Lights'
Papaver rhoeas Shirley *Series*, p.310
PELARGONIUMS, p.309
Portulaca grandiflora Series and cvs
Schizanthus 'Dwarf Bouquet', p.304
Senecio cineraria 'Silver Dust', p.315
Tagetes cvs, pp.308, 322, 324, 326
Tanacetum parthenium, p.300
Xanthophthalmum segetum, p.322
Xerochrysum bracteatum Monstrosum Series

ROCK PLANTS

Acaena caesiiglauca, p.374
Achillea x *kellereri*, p.360
Aethionema 'Warley Rose', p.362
Andromeda polifolia 'Compacta', p.333
Arenaria montana, p.360
Armeria juniperifolia, p.352
Cytisus x *beanii*, p.335
Dianthus deltoides
Gaultheria procumbens, p.373
Gypsophila repens
Helianthemum spp. and cvs, pp.336, 337, 338, 340, 344, 345
HOUSELEEKS, p.377
Petrorhagia saxifraga, p.361
Phlox bifida, p.366
Saponaria ocymoides, p.364
Sedum spp. and cvs, pp.315, 345, 371, 374, 375, 377
Tanacetum argenteum, p.346
Vaccinium vitis-idaea subsp. *minus*, p.351

BULBS, CORMS AND TUBERS

Allium aflatunense, p.382
Allium atropurpureum, p.392
Allium cowanii,
Allium 'Gladiator', p.392
Allium 'Globemaster', p.392
Allium 'Mount Everest', p.385
Allium oreophilum, p.418
Allium 'Purple Sensation', p.392
ALSTROEMERIAS, p.387
Anemone blanda 'Violet Star', p.418
Anemone de Caen 'Mr Fokker', p.403
Anemone ranunculoides, p.263
Anomatheca laxa, p.423
Babiana rubrocyanea, p.418
Bellavalia romana, p.399
Brodiaea 'Queen Fabiola'
Calochortus superbus, p.409
Camassia quamash, p.411
Chionodoxa forbesii, p.419
CROCOSMIA, p.410
CROCUS pp.417
Cyclamen coum 'Maurice Dryden', p.428
Cyclamen coum Pewter Group, p.429
DAFFODILS, pp.404–405
DAHLIA, pp.396–398
Fritillaria imperalis 'Lutea', p.382
Fritillaria persica 'Ivory Bells', p.382
Galanthus 'Hill Poe', p.427
Galanthus woronowii, p.428
GLADIOLI, p.384
Gladiolus callianthus murielae
Habenaria radiata, p.408
Hippeastrum 'Black Pearl'
Hyacinthus orientalis 'Blue Jacket', p.403
Hyacinthus orientalis 'White Pearl', p.415
Hymenocallis 'Sulphur Queen', p.412
Incarvillea delavayi, p.265
Ipheion uniflorum 'Froyle Mill', p.419
Iris reticulata and cvs, p.225
Ixia viridiflora, p.406
LILIES, pp.388–391
Muscari spp. and cvs, pp.403, 415, 419, 420, 421
Nerine bowdenii, p.413
Nerine bowdenii 'Nikita'
Ornithogalum, spp. and cvs, pp.382, 399, 408, 414, 415, 416
Polianthes tuberosa 'The Pearl', p.385
Romulea bulbocodium, p.419
Schizostylis 'Mrs Hegarty'
Scilla spp. and cvs, pp.413, 416, 420, 423
Triteleia ixiodes 'Starlight', p.407
Tulbaghia simmleri, p.411
TULIPS, p.400–401
Watsonia meriana, p.385
Zephyranthes spp., pp.413, 424

TENDER AND EXOTIC PLANTS

Trees

Agonis flexuosa, p.450

Shrubs

Boronia megastigma, p.456
Chamelaucium uncinatum, pp.453, 454
Chorizema ilicifolium, p.455
Iochroma australe, p.138
Leucospermum reflexum, p.456

RIGHT A garden on sandy gravel Alliums and lavenders thrive on light, sandy soils and are ideal for gravel gardens in dry areas.

Petrea volubilis, p.463
Plectranthus fructicosus 'James', p.454

Climbers

Bomarea hirsuta
Bomarea multiflora, p.207
Kennedia rubicunda, p.462
Solanum wendlandii, p.463
Streptosolen jamesonii, p.464
Tropaeolum tricolorum, p.461

Perennials

Aphelandra squarrosa 'Louisae', p.476
Billbergia nutans
Cryptanthus zonatus
Gazania rigens var. *uniflora*
Ruellia devosiana, p.465
Sansevieria trifasciata 'Laurentii', p.476
Strelitzia reginae, p.476

Cacti and succulents

AGAVES, p.482
ALOES, p.493
Echeveria montana
Furcraea parmentieri
Rebutia hybrida and cvs, pp.483, 484, 486, 487, 496

Perovskia 'Blue Spire'

Antirrhinum majus Coronette Series

Helianthemum 'Wisley Primrose'

Eccremocarpus scaber

Plants for clay soils

Clay soil is usually wet, glutinous and heavy in winter, and during drier summers it can shrink and crack, damaging plant roots. Whether establishing a new garden on clay or renovating an older one, always choose plants that will grow well in this type of soil. Prepare the planting area thoroughly, digging the soil in the autumn, then leaving it over winter to allow the weathering effects of frost and winter rains to break down large clods. Dig in organic matter, and grit or sharp sand to increase drainage. Plant in early spring, at the beginning of the growing season, to avoid losses over winter.

Caltha palustris 'Plena'

Anemone hupehensis

Kalmia latifolia

Viburnum opulus

LEFT A waterside planting The yellow skunk cabbage *(Lysichiton americanus)* and marsh marigolds *(Caltha palustris)* flourish together in the clay soil beside this stream.

TREES
Alnus glutinosa
Castanospermum australe
Drimys winteri, p.73
FLOWERING DOGWOODS, p.87
Fraxinus spp., pp.60, 66, 71, 74, 79
Juglans nigra, p.63
Magnolia virginiana
Melaleuca viridiflora var. *rubriflora*
Oxydendrum arboreum, p.76
Pinus sylvestris, p.78
Populus spp. and cvs, pp.60, 61, 62, 63, 74
Prunus maackii
Prunus serrula, p.78
Pterocarya fraxinifolia
Quercus palustris, p.66
Quercus robur
Quercus suber, p.78
Salix babylonica var. *pekinensis* 'Tortuosa', p.80
Salix x *sepulcralis* var. *chrysocoma*, p.69
SORBUS, p.91

CONIFERS
Cryptomeria japonica and cvs, p.104
Metasequoia glyptostroboides, p.96
Taxodium distichum, p.99

SHRUBS
Aronia arbutifolia, p.142
Berberis thunbergii 'Rose Glow', p.137
Berberis valdiviana, p.111
Calycanthus floridus
Chaenomeles cathayensis, p.142
Chaenomeles speciosa 'Snow', p.146
Choisya 'Aztec Pearl', p.122
Choisya ternata 'Sundance', p.148
Clethra alnifolia
CORNUS, p.126
Cotoneaster conspicuus, p.142
Cotoneaster frigidus, p.142
Cotoneaster hupehensis
Cotoneaster salicifolius, p.142
Cotoneaster x *watereri* 'John Waterer', p.142
Disanthus cercidifolius, p.141
Elaeagnus umbellata, p.113
Euonymus europaeus 'Red Cascade', p.140
Euonymus spp., pp.117, 142
Fothergilla gardenii, p.163
Fothergilla major, p.117
Genista tenera 'Golden Shower', p.116
Kalmia latifolia, p.136
Ledum groenlandicum, p.145
Photinia serratifolia, p111
Photinia x *fraseri* 'Red Robin', p.111
Ribes sanguineum 'Edward VII', p.146
Ruscus aculeatus, p.167
Salix caprea
Salix exigua, p.112
Salix purpurea
Sambucus racemosa 'Plumosa Aurea', p.139
Spiraea japonica 'Albiflora'
Symphoricarpos albus var. *laevigatus*, p.142
Tetrapanax papyrifer, p.120
Viburnum bitchiuense, p.122
Viburnum lentago
Viburnum opulus and cvs, pp.142, 162
Viburnum tinus 'Eve Price', p.143

CLIMBERS AND WALL SHRUBS
Celastrus scandens
Garrya elliptica 'James Roof', p.211
Humulus lupulus 'Aureus', p.194
Rosa filipes 'Kiftsgate', p.184
Vitis coignetiae, p.209

PERENNIALS
Acanthus mollis 'Hollard's Gold', p.219
Anemone hupehensis
Anemone tomentosa
Bergenia spp. and cvs, pp.255, 256, 280
Chrysosplenium macrophyllum, p.256
Doronicum orientale 'Magnificum', p.263
Eupatorium maculatum Atropurpureum Group 'Reisenschirm', p.221
Filipendula ulmaria 'Aurea', p.274
Geranium 'Orion', p.280
Geranium ROZANNE ='Gerwat', p.271
Geum 'Bell Bank', p.268
Helianthus 'Lemon Queen', p.222
Helonias bullata
Houttuynia cordata 'Chameleon', p.444
Iris laevigata
JAPANESE ANEMONE, p.222
Leucanthemum x *superbum* 'Sonnenschein', p.231
Ligularia 'Britt Marie Crawford', p.445
Ligularia 'The Rocket' AGM, p.219
Lythrum salicaria 'Feuerkerze', p.234
Mimulus guttatus
Omphalodes cappadocia 'Cherry Ingram', p.261
Primula japonica
Rodgersia pinnata 'Fireworks', p.234
Scrophularia auriculata 'Variegata'
Trollius spp. and cvs, pp.358, 436, 445

FERNS
Polystichum setiferum Groups, p.291
Thelypteris palustris, p.291
Woodwardia radicans

GRASSES AND BAMBOOS
Luzula sylvatica 'Hohe Tatra', p.288
Miscanthus sinensis and cvs, pp.284, 285, 286
Phyllostachys spp. and cvs, pp.286, 287, 288, 289

BULBS, CORMS AND TUBERS
Cardiocrinum giganteum, p.385
CANNA, p.394
Zantedeschia 'Cameo', p.395

WATER PLANTS
Aruncus dioicus, p.436
Butomus umbellatus
Caltha palustris, p.444
Darmera peltata, p.438
Gunnera manicata, p.443
Lysichiton americanus, p.444
Matteuccia struthiopteris, p.443
Onoclea sensibilis, p.443
Osmunda regalis, p.443
Pontederia cordata, p.441
Primula florindae, p.445
Ranunculus lingua, p.444
Sagittaria latifolia, p.434
Thalia dealbata

TENDER AND EXOTICS
Perennials
Cyperus papyrus, p.479

Plants for neutral to acid soil

Some plants, notably camellias, rhododendrons, and most heathers, grow naturally in regions such as open woodland, hillsides, or moorland where the soil is neutral to acid, and are intolerant of alkaline soils such as chalk or limestone. These are often termed "lime-haters" or "acid-lovers". Before planting, work in some acidic planting compost or humus. After planting, keep woody plants well mulched. In drier regions, check water needs regularly.

TREES

Acer davidii, p.78
Acer forrestii
Acer griseum, p.78
Acer grosseri, p.78
Acer palmatum and cvs, pp.78, 89, 90, 115, 117, 123, 138, 156
Acer pensylvanicum 'Erythrocladum', p.78
Arbutus menziesii
Arbutus unedo, p.93
Embothrium coccineum, p.86
Eucryphia (most), pp.85, 129
Michelia doltsopa, p.71
Nyssa sinensis, p.77
Nyssa sylvatica, p.66
Oxydendrum arboreum, p.76
Pinus densiflora
Pterostyrax hispida, p.73
Stewartia pseudocamellia, p.78
Stewartia sinensis, p.78
Styrax japonicus, p.72

CONIFERS

Abies spp. and cvs, pp.95, 96, 98, 100, 104, 105
Picea spp. and cvs, pp.98, 99, 100, 101, 103, 105
Pinus densiflora
Pinus pumila
Pseudolarix amabilis, p.102
Pseudotsuga menziesii var. *glauca*, p.96
Sciadopitys verticillata, p.101
Tsuga heterophylla

SHRUBS

Acer palmatum 'Shindeshojo', p.123
Amelanchier lamarckii, p.110
Andromeda polifolia 'Compacta', p.333
Arctostaphylos (some), pp.144, 147
CAMELLIAS, p.120–121
Chamaedaphne calyculata
Cyrilla racemiflora
Enkianthus spp., pp.111, 120, 123
Fothergilla gardenii
Fothergilla major, p.117
Gaultheria spp., pp.145, 154, 163, 164
HEATHERS, p.166, most
Kalmia spp., pp.136, 156
Ledum groenlandicum, p.145
Leiophyllum buxifolium
Leptospermum scoparium 'Snow White', p.135
Leucothöe fontanesiana and cvs, p.167
Lyonia ligustrinum
Menziesia ciliicalyx var. *purpurea*, p.146
Myrica gale, p.162
Philesia magellanica
Pieris spp. and cvs, p.110, 120, 137
RHODODENDRONS, pp.124–125, most
Styrax officinalis, p.112
Telopea speciosissima, p.137
Vaccinium (most), pp.150, 163, 165, 351
WITCH HAZELS, p.118
Zenobia pulverulenta, p.130

CLIMBERS AND WALL SHRUBS

Asteranthera ovata
Berberidopsis corallina, p.202
Crinodendron hookerianum, p.202
Desfontainia spinosa, p.203
Mitraria coccinea, p.193

PERENNIALS

Dianella tasmanica, p.239
Ourisia coccinea, p.269
Smilacina racemosa, p.223
Tolmiea menziesii
Trillium spp., pp.255, 260, 350
Uvularia grandiflora, p.262

FERNS

Adiantum spp., pp.291, 292
Blechnum spp., pp.290, 292
Cryptogramma crispa, p.293

GRASSES AND BAMBOOS

Deschampsisa cespitosa 'Gold Tau', p.289
Molinia caerulea subsp. *arundinacea* 'Transparent', p.286
Molinia caerulea subsp. caerulea 'Heidebraut', p.285

ANNUALS AND BIENNIALS

Calibrachoa cvs, pp.300, 306

ROCK PLANTS

Arctostaphylos spp. and cvs, pp.375, 376
Cassiope spp., pp.322, 349
Cornus canadensis, p.360
Corydalis cashmeriana
Cyananthus spp., pp.359, p.369
Epigaea gaultherioides, p.351
Galax urceolata, p.336
Gaultheria spp., pp.346, 373
Gentiana sino-ornata, p.370
Linnaea borealis, p.363
Lithodora diffusa 'Heavenly Blue', p.343
Mitchella repens
Ourisia spp., p.360, p.362
Phlox adsurgens
Phlox stolonifera
Phyllodoce spp., p.333, 334
Pieris nana
Shortia spp., p.349, p.352

BULBS, CORMS AND TUBERS

Lilium speciosum var. *rubrum*
Lilium superbum, p.390

WATER AND BOG PLANTS

Sarracenia flava, p.445

TENDER AND EXOTIC PLANTS

Shrubs

Boronia megastigma, p.456
Epacris impressa, p.455
Gardenia augusta
Pimelea ferruginea, p.455
Protea spp., p.454

Climbers

Agapetes spp., p.461
Allamanda cathartica

Perennials

Aspidistra spp.
Calanthe striata (syn. C. sieboldii), p.275
Caulokaempferia petelotii
Centropogon cordifolius
Cornukaempferia aurantiflora 'Jungle Gold', p.477
Cypripedium reginae, p.466
Drosera spp., p.473
Nepenthes x *hookeriana*, p.473
Peliosanthes arisanensis, p.472

BELOW A carpet of heather
Heathers (*Erica*) create dramatic sweeps of colour in winter in this heather garden. The majority of heathers thrive in a well-drained, acidic soil in full sun.

Gaultheria mucronata 'Wintertime'

Fothergilla major

Plants for chalk and limestone

Chalk and limestone regions are rich in wildflowers and wildlife, and where there is a reasonable depth of topsoil a wide range of garden plants can be grown. However, often there are only a few centimetres of chalky soil above bedrock and here there is an increased risk of drought in summer. It may be necessary to excavate planting holes and incorporate organic matter to increase plants' chances of survival. On well-drained chalk, plant in autumn or spring; on limestone soils, defer planting until spring. Keep all young woody plants well mulched and watered until established.

TREES

Acer negundo 'Variegatum', p.74
Aesculus x *carnea* 'Briotii', p.60
Arbutus andrachne
Betula albo-sinensis, p.78
Betula ermanii, p.78
Betula nigra, p.78
Betula utilis var. *jacquemontii* cvs, p.78
Catalpa bignonioides, p.73
Cercis siliquastrum, p.83
Crataegus spp. and cvs, pp.80, 84, 90
Eucalyptus pauciflora subsp. *niphophila,* p.78
Fagus sylvatica, p.64
Fraxinus ornus, p.71
Gleditsia triacanthos 'Sunburst', p.72
HOLLIES, p.94
Laurus nobilis p.80
Malus spp. and cvs, pp.71, 83, 90, 110
Morus nigra
Phillyrea latifolia
Prunus avium 'Plena', p.71
Prunus maackii
Prunus serrula, p.78
SORBUS (many), p.91
Tilia tomentosa

CONIFERS

Calocedrus decurrens, p.101
Cedrus libani, p.97
Chamaecyparis lawsoniana and cvs pp.96, 102, 103
Cupressus arizonica var. *glabra*
x *Cupressocyparis* x *leylandii* and cvs
Ginkgo biloba, p.97
Juniperus spp and cvs, pp.100, 103, 105
Picea omorika, p.98
Pinus nigra
Platycladus orientalis and cvs
Taxus baccata and cvs, pp.101, 102, 105
Thuja plicata and cvs

SHRUBS

Abutilon 'Kentish Belle', p.162
Abutilon 'Ashford Red', p.137
Aucuba japonica 'Crotonifolia'
Azara microphylla, p.118
Berberis darwinii, p.111
Berberis valdiviana, p.111
BUDDLEJA, p.114
Ceanothus impressus, p.138
Ceratostigma griffithii
Chaenomeles cathayensis, p.142
Chaenomeles speciosa 'Snow', p.146
Chimonanthus praecox, p.144
Choisya 'Aztec Pearl', p.122
Choisya ternata, p.122
Choisya ternata 'Sundance', p.148
Cistus spp, pp.150, 154
Colletia paradoxa, p.131
Cotinus coggygria 'Golden Spirit', p.116
Cotoneaster conspicuus, p.142
Cotoneaster frigidus, p.142
Cotoneaster hupehensis
Cotoneaster salicifolius, p.142
Cotoneaster x *watereri* 'John Waterer', p.142
Daphne bholua 'Jacqueline Postill', p.143
Deutzia spp. and cvs, pp.132, 149, 152
Edgeworthia chrysantha, p.126
Escallonia 'Donard Beauty', p.154
Euonymus europaeus 'Red Cascade', p.140
Euonymus hamiltonianus, p.142
Euonymus latifolius, p.140
Euonymus oxyphyllus, p.117
Genista tenera 'Golden Shower', p.116
HARDY FUCHSIA, p.154
Hebe carnosula
Hebe 'Great Orme', p.153
Hypericum 'Hidcote', p.160
LAVENDER, p.158
LILACS, p.115
Olearia ilicifolia, p.130
Olearia macrodonta, p.132
Philadelphus spp. and cvs, pp.127, 128, 131, 149
Phlomis fruticosa, p.160
Photinia serratifolia, p.111
Photinia x *fraseri* 'Red Robin', p.111
Potentilla fruticosa and cvs, pp.149, 160, 162
Ribes sanguineum 'Edward VII', p.146
ROSES (most), pp.172–187
Rosmarinus officinalis p.157
Ruscus aculeatus, p.167
Salix exigua, p.112
SALVIA, p.155
Sambucus nigra 'Guincho Purple'
Sambucus racemosa 'Plumosa Aurea', p.139
Spartium junceum, p.140
Spiraea japonica 'Albiflora'
Spiraea nipponica 'Snowmound', p.131
Symphoricarpos albus var. *laevigatus,* p.142
Viburnum bitchiuense, p.122
Viburnum opulus
Viburnum tinus
Viburnum tinus 'Eve Price', p.143
Vitex agnus-castus
Weigela florida 'Variegata', p.152

CLIMBERS AND WALL SHRUBS

Actinidia kolomikta, p.201
Campsis radicans
Carpenteria californica, p.197
Celastrus orbiculatus
CLEMATIS, pp.198–200
Eccremocarpus scaber, p.208
Forsythia suspensa, p.195
Fremontodendron 'California Glory', p.206
Garrya elliptica 'James Roof', p.211
Hedera spp. and cvs, p.211
HONEYSUCKLE, p.207
Jasminum officinale f. *affine,* p.196
Parthenocissus henryana
Passiflora caerulea, p.204
Rosa 'Albéric Barbier', p.184

BELOW **Early summer scent**
A lilac, here combined with deutzia and peonies, grows in the shelter of a wall. Lilacs prefer alkaline chalk soils, as long as they are well-drained.

Philadelphus 'Dame Blanche'

Lathyrus vernus

BELOW **Bright yellow display**
Achillea 'Moonshine' is a perennial that thrives in chalk or limestone soils and will withstand periods of drought. In summer, the flowers attract bees and butterflies.

Rosa 'Albertine', p.185
Solanum crispum 'Glasnevin', p.204
Trachelospermum jasminoides, p.195
Wisteria sinensis

PERENNIALS

Acanthus spinosus, p.239
Anemone tomentosa
Anemone hupehensis
AQUILEGIA. p.226
ASTER, p.249
CAMPANULA, p.241
DELPHINIUM, p.217
Doronicum spp., pp.227, 263
Eryngium spp., p.240, pp.250, 271
Erysimum 'Bowles Mauve', p.261
Eupatorium maculatum Atropurpureum Group 'Reisenscirm', p.221
Geranium ROZANNE = 'Gerwat', p.271
Geranium 'Orion', p.280
Geum 'Bell Bank', p.268
Gypsophila paniculata cvs, p.231
HELENIUM, p.248
Helianthus 'Lemon Queen', p.222
HEUCHERA, p.282
IRISES (most), pp.224–225
JAPANESE ANEMONES, p.222
Leucanthemum x *superbum* 'Sonnenschein', p.231
Nepeta 'Six Hills Giant', p.240
Omphalodes cappadocia 'Cherry Ingram' AGM, p.261
ORIENTAL PAPAVER, p.238
PEONIES, p.229
Potentilla 'Arc-en-ciel', p.268
RUDBECKIA , p.251
SALVIA, p.250
Scabiosa caucasica 'Clive Greaves', p.270
Schizostylis 'Mrs Hegarty'
Sidalcea 'Oberon', p.233
Verbascum spp. and cvs, pp.243, 246
Veronicastrum virginicum 'Fascination', p.220
YARROW, p. 247

FERNS

Asplenium scolopendrium, p.292
Asplenium trichomanes, p.291
Dryopteris filix-mas, p.292
Polypodium vulgare 'Cornubiense'

GRASSES AND BAMBOOS

Ampeldesmos mauritanica, p.287
Stipa tenuissima, p.288

ANNUALS AND BIENNIALS

Ageratum houstonianum and cvs, pp.313, 314
Calendula officinalis and cvs, pp.321, 325, 326
Callistephus chinensis Series and cvs, pp.303, 304, 312
Calomeria amaranthoides
Erysimum cheiri 'Fire King', p.326
Gomphrena globosa, p.303
Lavatera trimestris 'Silver Cup', p.305
Limonium sinuatum
Lobularia maritima
Lunaria annua, p.310
Matthiola 'Giant Excelsior', p.303
Tagetes spp. and cvs, pp.308, 320, 322, 326
Ursinia anthemoides, p.322
Xeranthemum annuum, p.305
Zinnia spp. and cvs, pp.306, 316, 325,

ROCK PLANTS

Aethionema spp. and cvs, pp.338, 362, 364
Androsace lanuginosa, p.363
Aster alpinus, p.367
Campanula (most rock garden species), pp.342, 368, 342
Dianthus (most rock garden species), pp.363, 364, 366
Draba spp., pp.357, 358
Erysimum helveticum, p.358
Gypsophila repens
Helianthemum spp., pp.336, 337, 340, 345
Lathyrus vernus, p.260
Leontopodium alpinum, p.332
Linum arboreum, p.344
Lobularia maritima and cvs, pp.298, 304
Origanum dictamnus
Papaver burseri
Penstemon pinifolius, p.340
Rhodanthemum hosmariense, p.332
Saponaria ocymoides, p.364
Saxifraga, pp.332, 337, 348, 350, 358, 377
Thymus caespititius
Veronica austriaca subsp. *teucrium*, p.343
Veronica prostrata, p.343

BULBS, CORMS AND TUBERS

Allium aflatunense, p.382
Allium atropurpureum, p.392
Allium cowanii, p.409
Allium 'Gladiator', p.392
Allium 'Globemaster', p.392
Allium 'Mount Everest', p.385
Allium oreophilum, p.418
Allium 'Purple Sensation', p.392
Anemone blanda 'Violet Star', p.418
Anemone de Caen 'Mr Fokker', p.403
Anemone ranunculoides, p.263
Anomatheca laxa,p.423
Babiana rubrocyanea,p.418
Bellavalia romana, p.399

Calochortus superbus, p.409
Chionodoxa forbesii, p.419
Colchicum, pp.421, 424, 425
Crinum x *powellii*, p.385
CROCUSES, p.417
Cyclamen coum and cvs, pp.428, 429
Cyclamen hederifolium, p.426
DAFFODILS, pp.404–405
Fritillaria imperalis 'Lutea', p.382
Fritillaria persica 'Ivory Bells', p.382
GLADIOLI, p.384
Gladiolus callianthus murielae
Hermodactylus tuberosus, p.406
Hippeastrum 'Black Pearl'
Hyacinthus orientalis 'Blue Jacket', p.403
Hyacinthus orientalis 'White Pearl', p.415
Hymenocallis 'Sulphur Queen', p.412
Incarvillea delavayi, p.265
Iris reticulata and cvs
Lilium regale, p.388
Muscari spp. and cvs, pp.403, 415, 420, 421
Nerine bowdenii 'Nikita'
Ornithogalum nutans, p.399
Ornithogalum umbellatum, p.416
Pancratium illyricum, p.408
Polianthes tuberosa 'The Pearl', p.385
Scilla spp., pp.413, 416, 420, 423
Triteleia 'Queen Fabiola'
Tulbaghia simmleri, p.411
TULIPS, pp.400–401
Watsonia meriana, p.385
Zephyranthes spp., pp.413, 424

TENDER AND EXOTIC PLANTS

Shrubs

Nerium oleander, p.455

Cacti and succulents

Furcraea parmentieri

BELOW Colourful crevices
Naturally at home in cracks and crevices, these *Saxafraga* form neat mounds of colour. They are ideal for sunny, well-drained rockeries and alpine gardens.

Plants for coastal sites

In coastal regions, salt from sea spray is carried a considerable distance inland on the wind, causing problems for many plants. However, some can tolerate high salt levels, and have hard-surfaced or glossy leaves with low absorbency levels, or foliage covered with fine hairs that prevent salt reaching the surface. Coastal gardens are often exposed, so protect plants with hedges or wattle hurdles. Prepare sandy soil by incorporating organic matter and garden loam, to encourage deep root penetration, and use dense ground-cover plants to stabilize the sand and keep root areas cool.

TREES

Acer pseudoplatanus and cvs, pp.65, 73, 84
Alnus incana, p.61
Arbutus andrachne
Arbutus unedo, p.93
Castanea sativa
Cordyline australis
Crataegus laevigata 'Paul's Scarlet', p.84
Eucalyptus coccifera, p.68
Eucalpytus gunnii, p.68
Fraxinus excelsior
Ilex aquifolium cvs, pp.92, 94
Laurus nobilis, p.80
Luma apiculata, p.78
Melaleuca viridiflora var. *rubriflora*
Melia azedarach, p.71
Populus alba, p.60
Quercus suber, p.78
Salix alba
Schinus molle
SORBUS, p.91

CONIFERS

Cupressus macrocarpa
Juniperus conferta
Pinus contorta var. *latifolia,* p.101
Pinus nigra subsp. *nigra,* p.98
Pinus radiata, p.98
x *Cupressocyparis* x *leylandii*

SHRUBS

Acacia verticillata
Atriplex halimus
Baccharis halimifolia
Berberis darwinii, p.111
Brachyglottis Dunedin Group, p.161
Buddleja globosa, p.116
Bupleurum fruticosum, p.139
Cassinia leptophylla subsp. *fulvida*
Chamaerops humilis, p.165
Choisya ternata, p.122
Cistus ladanifer, p.150
Colutea arborescens, p.139
Corokia x *virgata*
Cotoneaster conspicuus, p.142
Cotoneaster salicifolius, p.142
Cotoneaster frigidus, p.142
Cytisus x *spachianus*
Elaeagnus pungens 'Maculata', p.119
Elaeagnus umbellata, p.113
Erica arborea var. *alpina,* p.166
Erica cinerea 'Eden Valley', p.166
Escallonia 'Donard Beauty', p.154
Escallonia rubra 'Crimson Spire'
Euonymus japonicus
Euphorbia characias subspp.., p.147
Fabiana imbricata
Felicia amelloides 'Santa Anita', p.157
Fuchsia magellanica, p.154
Fuchsia 'Riccartonii', p.154
Genista hispanica, p.160
Genista tenera 'Golden Shower', p.116
Griselinia littoralis
Halimium lasianthum subsp. *formosum,* p.161
Hebe 'White Gem', p.149
Helichrysum italicum
Hippophäe rhamnoides, p.142
Hydrangea macrophylla and cvs, pp.134–135
LAVENDERS, p.158
Lavatera x *clementii* 'Rosea', p.136
Leptospermum scoparium 'Red Damask', p.123
Leycesteria formosa
Lonicera pileata, p.167
Lycium barbarum
Olearia ilicifolia, p.130
Olearia macrodonta, p.132
Ozothamnus ledifolius, p.151
Parahebe perfoliata, p.271
Phillyrea latifolia,
Phlomis fruticosa, p.160
Pittosporum tobira
Pyracantha coccinea 'Lalandei'
Rhamnus alaternus 'Argenteovariegata'
Rosa rugosa, p.176
Rosmarinus officinalis, p.157
Sambucus racemosa and cvs
Spartium junceum, p.140

Spiraea japonica var. albiflora
Tamarix ramosissima, p.114
Ulex europaeus 'Flore Pleno'
Viburnum tinus
Yucca gloriosa, p.132

CLIMBERS AND WALL SHRUBS

Eccremocarpus scaber, p.208
Ercilla volubilis, p.192
Euonymus fortunei 'Coloratus'
Fallopia baldschuanica, p.208
Garrya elliptica 'James Roof', p.211
Hedera canariensis
Muehlenbeckia complexa
Schisandra rubriflora, p.202
Tripterygium regelii
Tropaeolum tuberosum var. lineamaculatum 'Ken Aslet', p.207
Wisteria sinensis

PERENNIALS

Anaphalis margaritacea, p.231
Anchusa azurea 'Loddon Royalist', p.241
Artemisia ludhoviciana 'Valerie Finnis', p.274
Berkheya purpurea, p.269
Centaurea hypoleuca 'John Coutts', p.265
Centranthus ruber, p.248
Crambe maritima, p.264
Dianella caerulea Cassa Blue
Echinacea purpurea, p.221
Erigeron 'Charity'
Eryngium variifolium, p.271
Euphorbia griffithii 'Fireglow', p.246
Francoa sochifolia Rogerson's form
Geranium sanguineum, p.340
Hedychium coccineum 'Tara', p.220
IRISES (some), pp.224–5
Leucanthemum x superbum 'Sonnenschein', p.231
Libertia ixioides 'Goldfinger', p.277
Myosotidium hortensia, p.271
Nepeta 'Six Hills Giant', p.240
Osteospermum jucundum, p.265
Pericallis x hybrida
Phormium tenax
RED HOT POKERS, p.254
Romneya coulteri, p.216
SEDUM, p.279
Stachys byzantina, p.274
Stachys officinalis 'Hummelo', p.268
Verbascum 'Cotswold Beauty', p.246
Veronicastrum virginicum 'Fascination', p.220
YARROW, p.247

BELOW Coastal retreat
Striking agapanthus and architectural phormiums are both ideal plants for exposed, coastal sites with mild winters.

Euphorbia characias characias

Armeria maritima

Felicia amelloides 'Santa Anita'

GRASSES AND BAMBOOS

Ampelodesmos mauritanica, p.287
Calamagrostis brachytricha, p.284
Carex flagellifera, p.289
Chionochloa rubra, p.285
Cortadera richardii, p.284
Cortaderia selloana spp., pp.284, 285
Elegia capensis, p.285
Eragrostis curvula 'Totnes Burgundy', p.285
Miscanthus sinensis cvs, pp.285, 286
Panicum virgatum 'Northwind', p.289
Pennisetum 'Fairy Tails'
Pseudosasa japonica, p.287
Stipa tenuissima, p.288

ANNUALS AND BIENNIALS

Antirrhinum majus and cvs, pp.306, 319, 320
Argyranthemum frutescens, p.298
Bassia scoparia f. trichophylla, p.316
Calendula officinalis and cvs, pp.321, 322, 325, 326
Clarkia amoena 'Sybil Sherwood', p.305
Coreopsis tinctoria, p.321
Cynoglossum amabile 'Firmament', p.315
Dianthus chinensis cvs, pp.305, 307
Dorotheanthus bellidiformis
Duranta erecta
Eschscholzia californica, p.326

Achillea filipendulina 'Parker's Variety'

Eryngium variifolium

Sedum spathulifolium 'Cape Blanco'

Gilia capitata, p.314
Lavatera trimestris cvs, pp.299, 305
Limnanthes douglasii, p.321
Matthiola 'Giant Excelsior', p.303
Portulaca Margarita Series, p.324
Rhodanthe chlorocephala subsp. rosea, p.303
Senecio cineraria 'Silver Dust', p.315
Tagetes

ROCK PLANTS

Achillea clavennae, p.359
Aethionema grandiflorum, p.338
Armeria maritima 'Vindictive', p.365
Aubrieta deltoidea 'Argenteovariegata', p.354
Dianthus deltoides
Draba aizoides
Iberis sempervirens, p.332
Origanum laevigatum, p.340
Oxalis enneaphylla
Parahebe catarractae, p.342
Phlox subulata 'Marjorie', p.365
Pulsatilla vulgaris, p.334
Saxifraga paniculata
Sedum spathulifolium 'Cape Blanco', p.375
Sempervivum arachnoideum, p.377
Silene schafta, p.346
Thlaspi cepaeifolium subsp. rotundifolium, p.352

BULBS, CORMS AND TUBERS

Agapanthus spp. and cvs, pp.240, 241, 242
Crinum spp. and cvs, pp.383, 385
CROCOSMIA, p.410
CROCUSES, p.417
DAFFODILS, pp.404–405
Eucharis amazonica, p.414
Galtonia candicans, p.383
Hyacinthus orientalis and cvs, pp.403, 407, 415
Hymenocallis
Nerine spp. and cvs, pp.413, 414
Scilla spp. and cvs, pp.413, 416, 420, 423
Sprekelia formosissima, p.402
TULIPS, pp.400–401
Veltheimia bracteata, p.414
Zantedeschia aethiopica

TENDER AND EXOTIC PLANTS

Trees

Agonis flexuosa, p.450
Ficus macrophylla
Schefflera actinophylla, p.452
Tabebuia chrysotricha, p.452

Shrubs

Hibiscus rosa-sinensis
Nerium oleander, p.455

Climbers

Bougainvillea glabra, p.462
Pandorea jasminoides, p.459
Pyrostegia venusta, p.464
Solandra maxima, p.464
Ficus pumila

Perennials

Anthurium andraeanum, p.470
Peperomia obtusifolia 'Variegata', p.474
Pilea cadierei, p.465
Tradescantia fluminensis

Cacti and succulents

AGAVE, p.482
Furcraea parmentieri
Lampranthus glaucoides

Trees and shrubs for exposed sites

In cold, inland gardens, particularly those exposed to strong winter winds, only the hardiest plants thrive without the protection of a windbreak. Where providing one is not practical, it is essential to establish a basic framework of trees, shrubs, and conifers that are fully hardy. Carefully positioned within the garden, in groups, they provide sheltered situations where less hardy plants can be grown, while still retaining a degree of openness if desired.

ABOVE Vibrant autumn colour *Cotinus* species and hybrids make a dramatic statement in autumn. They thrive in full sun or partial shade, and tolerate exposed sites.

TREES

Acer platanoides and cvs, pp.60, 67
Acer pseudoplatanus
Betula utilis var. *jacquemontii*
Crataegus laevigata 'Paul's Scarlet', p.84
Crataegus x *lavallei* 'Carrierei'
Fagus sylvatica and cvs, pp.61, 64, 79
Fraxinus excelsior 'Jaspidea', p.60
Fraxinus ornus, p.71
Laburnum x *watereri* 'Vossii', p.84
Populus tremula
SORBUS (many), p.91
Tilia cordata

CONIFERS

Chamaecyparis nootkatensis
Chamaecyparis obtusa and cvs, pp.104, 105
Chamaecyparis pisifera 'Filifera Aurea', p.105
Juniperus communis 'Hibernica'
Juniperus x *pfitzeriana* and cvs, p.105
Picea breweriana, p.99
Pinus nigra subsp. *nigra*, p.98
Pinus sylvestris, p.78
Taxus baccata and cvs, pp.101, 102, 105
Tsuga canadensis, p.102

SHRUBS

Arctostaphylos uva-ursi, p.376
Amorpha canescens
Berberis darwinii, p.111
Berberis 'Rubrostilla', p.162
Berberis x *stenophylla*, p.127
Buddleja davidii 'Royal Red'
Calluna vulgaris and cvs, p.166
Chaenomeles cathayensis, p.142
Cornus alba 'Sibirica', p.143
Corylus maxima 'Purpurea', p.115
Cotinus coggygria 'Golden Spirit', p.116
Cotinus 'Flame', p.117
Cotoneaster 'Gnom'
Cotoneaster lacteus, p.117
Cotoneaster salicifolius, p.142
Cotoneaster simonsii, p.143
Elaeagnus umbellata, p.113
Euonymus europaeus 'Red Cascade', p.140
Euonymus hamiltonianus, p.142
Euonymus hamiltonianus subsp. *sieboldianus*, p.142
Euonymus oxyphyllus, p.117
Ledum groenlandicum, p.145
LILACS, p.115
Lonicera pileata, p.167
Mahonia aquifolium, p.148
Philadelphus 'Beauclerk', p.127
Philadelphus 'Belle Etoile', p.128
Prunus laurocerasus 'Otto Luyken', p.145
Pyracantha x *watereri*, p.128
Ribes sanguineum 'Edward VII', p.146
Rubus thibetanus, p.143
Salix purpurea
Sambucus nigra 'Guincho Purple'
Spiraea japonica 'Albiflora'
Spiraea x *vanhouttei*, p.145
Symphoricarpos x *chenaultii* 'Hancock'
Ulex europaeus 'Flore Pleno'
Viburnum bitchiuense, p.122
Viburnum opulus 'Xanthocarpum'
Viburnum tinus 'Eve Price', p.143

Climbers and shrubs for shady walls

Against cold, north- or east-facing walls, it is essential to choose climbers that grow naturally in shade or semi-shade. These provide reliable and effective foliage cover, and some have attractive flowers. A few climbing roses flower reasonably well in partially shaded situations and, together with climbers and shrubs, add colour to the backs of borders. Shade-tolerant plants prefer moist, woodland-type soils; when planting, dig in organic matter, such as leaf mould.

SHRUBS

Azara microphylla, p.118
CAMELLIAS, pp.120–121
Chaenomeles speciosa 'Moerloosei', p.122
Chaenomeles x *superba* 'Rowallane', p.147
Choisya ternata, p.122
Cotoneaster lacteus, p.117
Cotoneaster salicifolius, p.142
Daphne bholua 'Jacqueline Postill', p.143
Drimys winteri, p.73
Eucryphia x *nymansensis* 'Nymansay', p.73
Fatsia japonica
Jasminum nudiflorum, p.144
Mahonia japonica, p.144
Mahonia x *media* 'Charity', p.118
Muehlenbeckia complexa
Osmanthus decorus
Pyracantha spp. and cvs, pp.118, 128, 141, 144
Ribes laurifolium, p.165
Rosa 'Albéric Barbier', p.184
Rosa 'Madame Alfred Carrière', p.184
Rosa 'Madame Grégoire Staechelin', p.185
Rosa 'Maigold', p.187
Rosa THE PRINCE'S TRUST, p.186
Rosa WHITE STAR, p.184

CLIMBERS AND WALL SHRUBS

Akebia quinata, p.193
Berberidopsis corallina, p.202
Celastrus scandens
Clematis 'Frances Rivis', p.200
Cotoneaster horizontalis, p.208
Crinodendron hookerianum, p.202
Ercilla volubilis, p.192
Euonymus fortunei 'Coloratus',
Euonymus fortunei 'Silver Queen', p.144
x *Fatshedera lizei*, p.211
Forsythia suspensa, p.195
Garrya elliptica 'James Roof', p.211
Hedera colchica 'Dentata Variegata'
Hedera colchica 'Sulphur Heart', p.211
Hedera helix cvs, p.211
HONEYSUCKLE, p.207
Hydrangea petiolaris, p.195
Itea ilicifolia, p.211
Lapageria rosea, p.202
Parthenocissus spp. and cvs, pp.209, 210
Pileostegia viburnoides, p.196
Schisandra rubriflora, p.202
Schizophragma hydrangeoides, p.197
Schizophragma integrifolium, p.197

BELOW Green-themed shade bed Hostas and acers thrive in the shady conditions at the foot of sunless walls, providing attractive foliage patterns.

Drought-tolerant plants

Hot, sunny locations and free-draining, sandy soils demand plants that tolerate dry conditions. Drought-resistant plants will survive the increasing number of long, dry periods which we are experiencing, even in normally wet seasons. All the plants listed here have adapted to thrive in arid conditions, and will need little or no additional irrigation once established, but guard against waterlogged clay soils, in which they will quickly decline and die.

Agapanthus praecox subsp. *orientalis*

Miscanthus sinensis var. *condensatus*

ABOVE Water-wise gardening *Perovskia* and *Echinops* 'Veitch's Blue' can withstand periods of drought, while still providing a spectacular display.

TREES
Arbutus unedo, p.93
Eucalyptus gunnii, p.68
Gleditsia triacanthos
Ilex aquifolium, p.94
Olea europaea
Quercus suber, p.78
Rhus typhina

SHRUBS
Abutilon 'Ashford Red', p.137
Acacia dealbata, p.211
Artemisia abrotanum, p.165
Artemisia arborescens, p.165
Ballota pseudodictamnus, p.347
Ceanothus spp. and cvs, pp.129, 138, 153, 157, 159, 194, 205,
Ceratostigma griffithii
Chaenomeles speciosa 'Snow', p.146
Cistus spp. and cvs, pp.150, 152, 153, 154
Colletia paradoxa, p.131
Convolvulus cneorum, p.149
Cytisus spp. and cvs, pp.116, 148
Elaeagnus umbellata, p.113
Escallonia 'Donard Beauty', p.154
Euonymus hamiltonianus, p.142
Euonymus hamiltonianus subsp. *sieboldianus*, p.142
Euonymus oxyphyllus, p.117
Euphorbia characias subsp. *wulfenii*, p.147
Genista tenera 'Golden Shower', p.116
Hebe spp. and cvs, pp.151, 152, 153, 157, 165
Helichrysum petiolare
Laurus nobilis, p.80
Lonicera nitida
Perovskia 'Blue Spire', p.159
Phlomis fruticosa, p.160
Rosmarinus officinalis, p.157
Santolina spp., p.159
Spartium junceum, p.140
Yucca spp., pp.132, 151

CLIMBERS AND WALL SHRUBS
Eccremocarpus scaber, p.208
Parthenocissus tricuspidata, p.209
Trachelospermum jasminoides, p.195
Vitis coignetiae, p.209

PERENNIALS
Agapanthus 'Northern Star', p.241
Agapanthus 'Phantom'
Agapanthus 'Purple Cloud', p.241
Agapanthus inapertus ssp. *pendulus* 'Graskop', p.240
Anaphalis spp., p.231
Anthemis spp. and cvs, pp.243, 264
Artemisia spp. and cvs, pp.216, 242, 274
Bergenia 'Beethoven', p.256
Bergenia 'Eric Smith'
Berkheya purpurea, p.269
Campanula persicifolia
CARNATIONS AND PINKS, pp.266–267
Echinops bannaticus 'Taplow Blue', p.241
Eremurus x *isabellinus* 'Cleopatra', p.220
Eryngium pandanifolium
Erysimum 'Bowles's Mauve', p.261
Gaillardia 'Oranges and Lemons', p.277
Geranium ROZANNE ='Gerwat', p.271
Geranium 'Orion', p.280
Hedychium coccineum 'Tara', p.220
Lamium maculatum spp., pp.254, 255
Libertia ixioides 'Goldfinger', p.277
Lychnis coronaria, p.268
Nepeta x *faassenii*, p.270
Nepeta 'Six Hills Giant', p.240
ORIENTAL POPPIES, p.238
Osteospermum jucundum, p.265
Persicaria polymorpha, p.234
Phormium spp., p.216
RED HOT POKERS, p.254
SALVIA, p.250
Scabiosa caucasica
SEDUM, p.279
Sisyrinchium striatum, p.274
Stachys byzantina, p.274
Stachys officinalis 'Hummelo', p.268
Verbascum 'Cotswold Beauty', p.246
Verbascum 'Gainsborough', p.243
Verbena bonariensis, p.221
YARROW, p.247

GRASSES AND BAMBOOS
Ampeldesmos mauritanica, p.287
Calamagrostis brachytricha, p.284
Carex flagellifera, p.289
Chionochloa rubra, p.285
Cortadera richardii, p.284
Eragrostis curvula 'Totnes Burgundy', p.285
Festuca glauca
Helictotrichon sempervirens, p.288
Miscanthus sinensis 'Flamingo', p.286
Miscanthus sinensis 'Yakushima Dwarf', p.285
Miscanthus sinensis var. *condensatus*, 'Cosmopolitan', p.285
Panicum virgatum 'Northwind', p.289
Pennisetum 'Fairy Tails'
Pennisetum alopecuroides
Schizostylis 'Mrs Hegarty'
Stipa tenuissima, p.288

ANNUALS AND BIENNIALS
Cleome hassleriana 'Colour Fountain', p.304
Crepis aurea, p.345
Gazania Kiss Series, p.324
Osteospermum ecklonis and cvs, pp.301, 311
PELARGONIUMS, p.309
Rhodanthe chlorocephala subsp. *rosea*, p.303
Zinnia spp. and cvs, pp.298, 306, 307, 316, 325

ROCK PLANTS
Aubrieta spp. and cvs, pp.353, 354, 355
Achillea clavennae, p.359
Armeria maritima 'Vindictive', p.365
Aubrieta deltoidea 'Argenteovariegata', p.354
Dianthus deltoides
Hebe pinguifolia 'Pagei', p.337
Hebe recurva, p.151
Parahebe catarractae, p.342
Sedum spathulifolium 'Cape Blanco', p. 375
HOUSELEEKS, p.377

BULBS
Allium aflatunense, p.382
Allium atropurpureum, p.392
Allium cowanii, p.399
Allium 'Gladiator', p.392
Allium 'Globemaster', p.392
Allium 'Mount Everest', p.385
Allium oreophilum, p.418
Allium 'Purple Sensation', p.392
ALSTROEMERIAS, p.387
Anemone blanda 'Violet Star', p.418
Anemone de Caen 'Mr Fokker', p.403
Anemone ranunculoides, p.263
Anomatheca laxa, p.423
Bellavalia romana, p.399
Brodiaea 'Queen Fabiola'
Calochortus superbus, p.409
Chionodoxa forbesii, p.419
CROCOSMIA, p.410
CROCUSES, p.417
Cyclamen coum 'Maurice Dryden', p.428
Cyclamen coum Pewter Group , p.429
DAHLIAS, pp.396–398
Fritillaria imperalis 'Lutea', p.382
Fritillaria persica 'Ivory Bells', p.382
GLADIOLI, p.384
Gladiolus callianthus murielae
Hippeastrum 'Black Pearl'
Hyacinthus orientalis and cvs, pp.403, 407, 415
Hymenocallis 'Sulphur Queen'
Incarvillea delavayi, p.265
Iris reticulata and cvs
Muscari botryoides 'Album, p.415
Nerine bowdenii 'Nikita'
Ornithogalum nutans, p.399
Ornithogalum umbellatum, p.416
Polianthes tuberosa 'The Pearl', p.385
Scilla bifolia
Scilla siberica 'Alba, p.416
Triteleia ixiodes 'Starlight', p.407
Tulbaghia simmleri, p.411
TULIPS, pp.400–401
Watsonia meriana, p.385

TENDER AND EXOTIC PLANTS
Shrubs
Plectranthus fructicosus 'James', p.454

Cacti and succulents
AGAVE, p.482
ALOE, p.493
Echeveria montana
Furcraea parmentieri
Kalanchoe lactivirens

Plants for hedges and windbreaks

Plants for hedging are often selected for their ornamental qualities, but there are other aspects to consider. Boundary hedges can provide visual privacy, or screen unsightly buildings; they may also be bushy or thorny to keep out animals or intruders. Make sure that plants for screening will grow to the required height, and select conifers or evergreen shrubs for year-round effect. In exposed sites, trees and deciduous shrubs can be used as windbreaks; two or three staggered rows are more effective than a single, close-planted one.

TREES

Arbutus unedo, p.93
Carpinus betulus
Carpinus betulus 'Fastigiata', p.93
Crataegus monogyna
Fagus sylvatica, p.64
HOLLIES, p.94
Laurus nobilis, p.80
Melaleuca viridiflora var. *rubriflora*
Nothofagus dombeyi, p.68
Nothofagus obliqua, p.63
Olea europaea
Populus x *canadensis* 'Robusta', p.62
Prunus lusitanica
Umbellularia californica, p.69

CONIFERS

Abies grandis, p.98
Cedrus deodara, p.96
Cephalotaxus harringtonii
Chamaecyparis lawsoniana
x *Cupressocyparis* 'Castlewellan', p.99
Cupressus macrocarpa
Juniperus communis
Larix decidua, p.97
Picea omorika, p.98
Pinus nigra
Pinus radiata, p.98
Pseudotsuga menziesii var. *glauca*, p.96
Taxus baccata
Thuja plicata
Tsuga canadensis, p.102

SHRUBS

Berberis darwinii, p.111
Berberis thunbergii 'Rose Glow', p.137
Buxus sempervirens 'Suffruticosa', p.167
Choisya ternata, p.122
Cotoneaster salicifolius, p.142
Cotoneaster simonsii, p.143
Elaeagnus umbellata, p.113
Elaeagnus ebbingei
Escallonia 'Langleyensis'
Escallonia 'Donard Beauty', p.154
Euonymus japonicus 'Macrophyllus'
Forsythia x *intermedia* cvs p.127
Griselinia littoralis
Hippophäe rhamnoides, p.142
HYDRANGEAS, p.134
LAVENDERS, p.158
Leptospermum scoparium and cvs, pp.123, 130
Ligustrum ovalifolium, p.119
Lonicera nitida
Pittosporum tenuifolium, p.120
Prunus laurocerasus
Prunus lusitanica
Pyracantha x *watereri*, p.128
Rosa 'Céleste', p.173
Rosa 'Felicia', p.173
Rosa 'Frühlingsmorgen'
Rosa 'Great Maiden's Blush', p.173
Rosa 'Marguerite Hilling', p.173
Rosa 'Nevada', p.173
Rosa 'Penelope', p.172
Rosa gallica 'Versicolor', p.174
Rosa gallica var. *officinalis*
Rosa glauca, p.176
Rosa 'Graham Thomas', p.176
Rosa 'Jacquline du Pre', p.172
Rosa moyesii 'Geranium', p.176
Rosa rugosa, p.176
Rosmarinus officinalis, p.157
Tamarix ramosissima, p.114
Viburnum tinus 'Eve Price', p.143

PERENNIALS

Eupatorium purpureum
Filipendula camtschatica
Phormium tenax

GRASSES AND BAMBOOS

Arundo donax
Chimonobambusa timidissinoda, p.287
Cortaderia selloana 'Sunningdale Silver', p.284
Fargesia nitida
Miscanthus sinensis and cvs, pp.284, 285, 286,
Phyllostachys spp. and cvs, pp.286, 287, 288, 289
Pseudosasa japonica, p.287
Semiarundinaria fastuosa, p.287

TENDER AND EXOTIC PLANTS

Trees

Codiaeum variegatum var. *pictum*, p.459
Metrosideros excelsa, p.450
Syzygium paniculatum, p.450

Shrubs

Dodonaea viscosa 'Purpurea', p.457
Hibiscus rosa-sinensis

Forsythia intermedia

R. gallica Versicolor (Rosa mundi)

Lavandula angustifolia 'Hidcote'

RIGHT **Formal definition**
In this mature garden, yew hedges form green walls, providing shelter as well as excellent structure. Short box hedges give a formal edge to the flower beds.

Architectural plants

Plants that stand out and draw the eye with their strong, distinctive appearance are termed "architectural" plants. They give character and substance to a garden, and help to form the basic framework. Most are trees, conifers, and shrubs, which provide a permanent effect throughout the year, and they usually have a strong shape, such as vertical or conical forms of conifer, or bear striking foliage, such as giant-leaved gunneras and spiky phormiums.

Agave Americana 'Marginata'

Yucca gloriosa (Spanish dagger)

ABOVE Architectural beauty
A tropical effect is created by dramatic *Phoenix canariensis* and the vibrant leaves of *Imperata cylindrica* 'Rubra'.

TREES
Acer griseum, p.78
Betula utilis var *jacquemontti* and cvs, p.78
Cordyline australis 'Atropurpurea', p.451
CORNUS (many), p.126
Eucalyptus spp., pp.67, 68, 79
Kalopanax septemlobus, p.74
Luma apiculata, p.78
MAGNOLIAS, p.70
Paulownia tomentosa, p.72
Phoenix canariensis
Quercus suber, p.78
Trachycarpus fortunei, p.80
Trochodendron aralioides, p.79

CONIFERS
Abies spp., pp.95, 96, 100, 104
Araucaria araucana, p.98
Calocedrus decurrens, p.101
Cedrus spp., pp.95, 96, 97, 104
Juniperus x *pfitzeriana* 'William Pfitzer'
Metasequoia glyptostroboides, p.96
Picea glauca 'Coerulea', p.99
Picea pungens and cvs, pp.99, 105
Pinus bungeana, p.78
Pinus densiflora
Pinus sylvestris, p.78
Pseudolarix amabilis, p.102
Sciadopitys verticillata, p.101
Taxodium distichum, p.99
Tsuga heterophylla

SHRUBS
Aesculus parviflora, p.113
Acer palmatum 'Shindeshojo', p.123
Colletia paradoxa, p.131
FLOWERING DOGWOODS, p.87
Cotoneaster x *watereri* 'John Waterer', p.142
Daphniphyllum macropodum, p.111
Eriobotrya japonica, p.194
Fatsia japonica
Mahonia japonica, p.144
Mahonia x *media* and cvs, p.118
Olearia ilicifolia p.130
Olearia macrodonta p.132
Parkinsonia aculeata
Rhus typhina 'Dissecta', p.117
Yucca spp., pp.132, 151

CLIMBERS
Schizophragma spp., p.197
Vitis coignetiae, p.209
WISTERIA, p.205

PERENNIALS
Acanthus mollis 'Hollard's Gold', p.219
Acanthus spinosus, p.239
Angelica archangelica, p.219
Astelia chathamica, p.242
Begonia grandis subsp. *evansiana*, p.278
Berkheya macrocephala, p.243
Cynara cardunculus, p.216
Echinops bannaticus 'Taplow Blue', p.241
Eremurus x *isabellinus* 'Cleopatra', p.220
Eryngium pandanifolium
Euphorbia characias subsp. *characias*, p.147
Hedychium coccineum 'Tara', p.220
HOSTAS (many), pp.272–273
Kniphofia caulescens, p.254
Kniphofia northiae, p.254
Ligularia 'Britt Marie Crawford', p.445
Ligularia 'The Rocket', p.219
Mathiasella bupleroides 'Green Dream', p.242
Persicaria polymorpha, p.234
Phormium 'Dazzler', p.216
Rodgersia pinnata 'Fireworks'
Rudbeckia maxima, p.251
Verbascum olympicum, p.219

GRASSES AND BAMBOOS
Ampeldesmos mauritanica, p.287
Chimonobambusa timidissinoda, p.287
Chusquea culeou, p.288
Cortadera richardii, p.284
Cortaderia selloana and cvs, pp.284, 285
Elegia capensis, p.285
Miscanthus sinensis and cvs, pp.284, 285, 286
Molinia caerulea subsp. *arundinacea* 'Transparent', p.286
Phyllostachys spp. and cvs, pp.286, 287, 288, 289
Thamnocalamus crassinodus 'Kew Beauty', p.286

FERNS
Asplenium scolopendrium Marginatum Group, p.292
Blechnum tabulare
Dicksonia antarctica, p.290
Polystichum munitum, p.293
Woodwardia radicans

ANNUALS AND BIENNIALS
Alcea rosea
Amaranthus spp. and cvs, pp.307, 308
BEGONIAS, p.317
Calomeria amaranthoides
Onopordum acanthium, p.304
Silybum marianum, p.304

BULBS, CORMS AND TUBERS
Arisaema consanguineum, p.393
Arum creticum, p.407
CANNAS, p.394
Cardiocrinum giganteum, p.385
CROCOSMIA, p.410
Dracunculus vulgaris, p.386
GLADIOLI, p.384
Sauromatum venosum, p.403
Zantedeschia aethiopica

WATER PLANTS
Darmera peltata, p.438
Eichhornia crassipes, p.441
Gunnera manicata, p.443
Ligularia spp., p.445
Lysichiton americanus, p.444
Matteuccia struthiopteris, p.443
Orontium aquaticum, p.444
Pontederia cordata, p.441
Rheum palmatum 'Atrosanguineum', p.439
Sagittaria latifolia, p.434
Thalia dealbata

TENDER AND EXOTIC PLANTS

Trees
Dracaena draco, p.451
Jacaranda mimosifolia, p.451
Washingtonia robusta, p.451

Shrubs
Cycas revoluta, p.457
Protea cynaroides, p.454

Climbers
Epipremnum aureum 'Marble Queen', p.460
Monstera deliciosa, p.463

Perennials
Cyathea australis, p.452
Ensete ventricosum, p.474
GINGERS, p.477
Heliconia psittacorum, p.478
Platycerium bifurcatum, p.479
Puya chilensis, p.471
Strelitzia reginae, p.476

Cacti and succulents
Aeonium tabuliforme, p.491
AGAVES, p.482
ALOES (most), p.493
Carnegiea gigantea, p.492
Cereus spp., p.488
Cyphostemma juttae, p.487
Euphorbia candelabrum
Furcraea parmentieri
Opuntia spp., pp.481, 483, 486, 488, 494, 496

Plants for quick cover

In gardens with steep banks, large spaces that are impractical to turf or cultivate, or areas that have become neglected, or if there is little time for maintenance, plants that have good ground-covering qualities provide a practical solution. Their rapid, dense, leafy or twiggy growth helps to suppress weeds, while creating a decorative blanket of flowers and foliage. Old walls, fences, or screens masking utility areas that also need a quick disguise can be covered with vigorous climbers, such as ivy (*Hedera*). Always select plants that are suitable for the soil conditions.

CONIFERS
Juniperus conferta

SHRUBS
Ceanothus thyrsiflorus var. *repens*, p.159
Cotoneaster conspicuus, p.142
Cotoneaster 'Gnom'
Cotoneaster 'Skogholm'
Gaultheria shallon, p.154
Hypericum calycinum, p.161
Rubus tricolor
Stephanandra incisa 'Crispa'
Symphoricarpos orbiculatus 'Follis Variegatis', p.160

BELOW A tapestry of green shades
The strappy leaves of gardener's garters (*Phalaris arundinacea* var. *picta*) provide excellent ground cover.

CLIMBERS AND WALL SHRUBS
Hedera spp. and cvs, p.211
Hydrangea petiolaris, p.195
Lonicera japonica cvs, p.207
Trachelospermum jasminoides, p.195

PERENNIALS
Alchemilla mollis, p.275
Anemone tomentosa
Anthemis punctata subsp. *cupaniana* p.264
Campanula punctata
Campanula takesimana, p.241
Chelidonium majus 'Flore Pleno', p.227
Chrysosplenium macrophyllum, p.256
Duchesnea indica
Euphorbia amygdaloides var. *robbiae*, p.262
Geranium 'Orion', p.280
Geranium macrorrhizum, p.269
Geranium x *oxonianum* 'Claridge Druce'
Glechoma hederacea 'Variegata', p.277
Lamium maculatum and cvs, pp.254, 255
LUNGWORTS p.261
Nepeta 'Six Hills Giant', p.240
Osteospermum jucundum, p.265
PERSICARIA, p.234
Prunella grandiflora 'Pink Loveliness'
Stachys byzantina, p.274
Symphytum x *uplandicum* 'Variegatum', p.227

GRASSES AND BAMBOOS
Carex flagellifera, p.289
Chimonobambusa timidissinoda, p.287
Luzula sylvatica 'Hohe Tatra', p.288
Phalaris arundinacea var. *picta*

FERNS
Dryopteris dilatata
Polystichum aculeatum
Polystichum setiferum Groups, p.291

ANNUALS AND BIENNIALS
Dichondra argentea Silver Falls
Petunia 'Wave Purple'
Portulaca grandiflora Series and cvs
Sanvitalia procumbens, p.322
Satureja douglasii
Tropaeolum majus Series and cvs, pp.307, 323, 327

ROCK PLANTS
Arabis alpina subsp. *caucasica* and cvs, pp.347, 352
Asarum europaeum, p.375
Aubrieta deltoidea 'Argenteovariegata', p.354
Campanula portenschlagiana, p.368
Cerastium tomentosum, p.350
Helianthemum spp. and cvs, pp.336, 337, 338, 340, 344, 345
Persicaria affinis 'Donald Lowndes', p.365
Persicaria vacciniifolia, p.373
Phlox douglasii and cvs, pp.365, 366
Phuopsis stylosa
Saxifraga stolonifera
Tiarella cordifolia, p.333
Waldsteinia ternata, p.372

TENDER AND EXOTIC PLANTS
Perennials
Heterocentron elegans

Pulmonaria 'Lewis Palmer'

Campanula poscharskyana

Geranium macrorrhizum

Anthemis punctata subsp. *cupaniana*

Hydrangea petiolaris

Persicaria affinis 'Donald Lowndes'

Ground-cover plants for shade

An area that is shaded for some or most of the day may be regarded by some gardeners as a problem space, when in fact it should be viewed as an opportunity to experiment with a different, and often an equally exciting, range of plants. The following ground-cover plants will provide a wealth of colourful flowers and foliage, and may be planted in even deep shade, providing the soil is reasonably fertile. Where the shade is caused by trees and large shrubs, the soil will also be very dry. Keep new plants well watered during their first year until established.

SHRUBS
Cotoneaster conspicuus, p.142
Cotoneaster 'Gnom'
Cotoneaster 'Herbstfeuer'
Daphne laureola subsp. *philippi*, p.147
Epigaea asiatica
Euonymus fortunei 'Kewensis'
Gaultheria shallon, p.154
Hypericum calycinum, p.161
Leucothöe fontanesiana
Lonicera pileata, p.167
Mahonia aquifolium, p.148
Mahonia repens
Paxistima canbyi
Prunus laurocerasus 'Otto Luyken', p.145
Rubus tricolor
Ruscus hypoglossum, p.167
Sarcococca confusa, p.142
Sarcococca humilis, p.164
Vinca spp., pp.164, 165

CLIMBERS AND WALL SHRUBS
Hedera spp. and cvs, p.211

PERENNIALS
Acanthus spinosus, p.239
Ajuga pyramidalis
Ajuga reptans 'Atropurpurea'
Alchemilla mollis, p.275
Anemone apennina
Anemone tomentosa
Arisarum proboscideum
Asarum caudatum
Astrantia maxima, p.278
Brunnera macrophylla
Brunnera macrophylla 'Jack Frost', p.261
Chelidonium majus 'Flore Pleno', p.227
Chrysosplenium macrophyllum, p.256
Convallaria majalis, p.255
Dicentra formosa
Dicentra spectabilis, p.223
Duchesnea indica
Epimedium epsteinii, p.260
Epimedium 'Amber Queen', p.263
Epimedium davidii
Epimedium perralderianum
Euphorbia amygdaloides var. *robbiae*, p.262
Galium odoratum, p.263
Geranium macrorrhizum, p.269
Geranium renardii, p.264
Glechoma hederacea 'Variegata', p.277
HEUCHERA, p.282
HOSTAS (some), pp.272–273
Hypsela reniformis
Lamium maculatum and cvs, pp.254, 255
Liriope muscari, p.280
LUNGWORTS, p.261
Meehania urticifolia
Omphalodes cappadocica
Pachyphragma macrophyllum
Plectranthus oertendahlii
Symphytum grandiflorum
Tellima grandiflora Rubra Group, p.279
Tolmiea menziesii
Vancouveria hexandra

GRASSES AND BAMBOOS
Chasmanthium latifolium, p.288
Luzula sylvatica 'Hohe Tatra', p.288
Phalaris arundinacea var. *picta*

FERNS
Adiantum venustum, p.292
Athyrium spp. and cvs p.290
Blechnum penna-marina, p.290
Blechnum spicant
Polypodium cambricum 'Richard Kayse', p.293
Polypodium vulgare and cvs, p.291
Polystichum setiferum Groups, pp.291

ROCK PLANTS
Asarina procumbens, p.371
Asarum europaeum, p.375
Campanula portenschlagiana, p.368
Campanula poscharskyana, p.367
Cardamine trifolia, p.348
Ceratostigma plumbaginoides, p.346
Cornus canadensis, p.360
Galax urceolata, p.336
Geranium sanguineum, p.340
Homogyne alpina
Maianthemum bifolium, p.348
Mitchella repens
Pachysandra terminalis, p.375
Persicaria affinis 'Donald Lowndes', p.365
Prunella grandiflora, p.368
Saxifraga stolonifera
Saxifraga x *urbium*
Tiarella cordifolia, p.333
Viola riviniana Purpurea Group p.355
Waldsteinia ternata, p.372

TENDER AND EXOTIC PLANTS
Perennials
Elatostema repens
Fittonia albivenis

Astrantia maxima

Geranium sanguineum

Convallaria majalis

Epimedium 'Amber Queen'

RIGHT A covering in shade
Ferns, hostas, and heucheras fill the space and offer interesting textures and contrasts in shady corners.

Ground-cover plants for sun

Many plants grow naturally in dry, sunny conditions. Some have developed foliage characteristics to minimize moisture loss from their leaves; others are densely branched, keeping the soil surface shaded and cool. Most have extensive root systems that penetrate deeply to find moisture. These plants are adapted to well-drained soils; in poorly drained situations, they may not survive prolonged wet conditions. Although adapted to poorer, dry soils, young plants may have been grown in richer composts and well watered, so when planting incorporate organic matter, such as leaf mould or coir, and water in dry periods until well established.

CONIFERS

Juniperus communis 'Prostrata'
Juniperus horizontalis 'Wiltonii'
Juniperus squamata 'Blue Carpet', p.105
Microbiota decussata, p.105
Picea abies 'Inversa'

SHRUBS

Arctostaphylos nevadensis
Arctostaphylos uva-ursi, p.376
Berberis wilsoniae
Brachyglottis Dunedin Hybrids 'Sunshine'
Calluna vulgaris 'White Lawn'
Ceanothus thyrsiflorus var. *repens*, p.159
Cotoneaster cashmiriensis
Cotoneaster 'Skogholm'
Cytisus x *beanii*, p.335
Cytisus scoparius subsp. *maritimus*
Ephedra gerardiana
Erica carnea 'Springwood White', p.166
Euonymus fortunei 'Emerald Gaiety'
Euonymus fortunei 'Kewensis'
Gaultheria myrsinoides
Genista hispanica, p.160
x *Halimiocistus sahucii*, p.149
Hebe carnosula
Hebe pinguifolia 'Pagei', p.337
Hebe 'Youngii'
Hypericum calycinum, p.161
LAVENDERS, p.158
Leiophyllum buxifolium
Leptospermum rupestre, p.151
Potentilla fruticosa 'Abbotswood', p.149
Rosmarinus officinalis 'Prostratus'
Salix repens, p.147
Santolina spp., p.159
Stephanandra incisa 'Crispa'
Symphoricarpos x *chenaultii* 'Hancock',
Ulex europaeus 'Flore Pleno'
Vinca major 'Variegata'

CLIMBERS

Hedera colchica 'Dentata Variegata'
Hedera helix spp. and cvs, p.211
Lathyrus latifolius, p.201

PERENNIALS

Alchemilla mollis, p.275
Anthemis punctata subsp. *cupaniana*, p.264
Artemisia alba 'Canescens'
Aster ericoides f. *prostratus* 'Snowflurry'
Bergenia 'Beethoven', p.256
Bergenia 'Eric Smith'
Campanula takesimana, p.241
Centaurea montana, p.269
Euphorbia polychroma, p.262
Francoa sochifolia Rogerson's form
Geranium ROZANNE 'Gerwat', p.271
Geranium 'Orion', p.280
Geranium sanguineum, p.340
Hypericum
Lysimachia punctata, p.243
Nepeta 'Six Hills Giant', p.240
Nepeta x *faassenii*, p.270
Origanum vulgare 'Aureum', p.274
Osteospermum jucundum, p.265
Persicaria bisorta 'Superba' p.234
Phlomis russeliana, p.243
SEDUM, p.279
Stachys byzantina, p.274
Stachys officinalis 'Hummelo', p.268
Veronica prostrata and cvs, p.343
Waldsteinia ternata, p.372

GRASSES AND BAMBOOS

Chionochloa rubra, p.285

ANNUALS AND BIENNIALS

Calibrachoa CABARET APRICOT
Calibrachoa LIGHT PINK, p.300
Calibrachoa Million Bells Series CHERRY PINK, p.306
Dichondra argentea Silver Falls
Dichondra repens 'Emerald Falls'
Lantana montevidensis, p.310
Tropaeolum spp. and cvs, pp.307, 323, 327

ROCK PLANTS

Acaena microphylla p.374
Antennaria dioica var. *rosea* p.351
Arabis alpina subsp. *caucasica* 'Variegata' p.347
Armeria maritima 'Vindictive' p.365
Aubrieta spp. and cvs, pp.353, 354, 355
Aurinia saxatilis and cvs, p.335
Campanula portenschlagiana p.368
Campanula poscharskyana p.367
Dianthus gratianopolitanus p.363
Dryas octopetala p.361
Helianthemum spp. and cvs, pp.336, 337, 338, 340, 344, 345,
Hypericum olympicum
Iberis sempervirens p.332
Lithodora diffusa 'Heavenly Blue' p.343
Nierembergia repens p.361
Phlox douglasii 'Crackerjack' p.365
Phuopsis stylosa p.338
Thymus 'Bressingham', p.365
Thymus caespititus var. *cilicicus*, p.366
Veronica prostrata 'Kapitan'

BOG PLANTS

Rheum palmatum 'Atrosanguineum', p.439

TENDER AND EXOTIC PLANTS

Climbers
Kennedia rubicunda
Pyrostegia venusta

Perennials
Centropogon cordifolius
Heterocentron elegans

RIGHT Purple and yellow display *Aubrietia deltoides* and *Aurinia saxatilis* provide a bright display of ground-covering colour in sun.

Centaurea montana

Osteospermum jucundum

Tropaeolum majus Alaska Series

Santolina pinnata subsp. *neapolitana* 'Sulphurea'

Plants for dry shade

Dry, shady conditions persist under evergreen trees throughout the year, and although very little moisture penetrates the soil beneath the leaf canopy of deciduous trees, except during prolonged rainfall, a few early-flowering bulbs, such as bluebells (*Hyacinthoides non-scripta*), and woodland plants grow naturally in there, dying down as the trees resume growth in spring. In gardens, dry shade occurs under larger, low-branched trees or where eaves extend over borders. Plant in the autumn so that roots are well established by the following spring, and feed regularly and water during dry periods until the plants are established.

TREES
HOLLIES, p.94

CONIFERS
Taxus baccata 'Adpressa'
Taxus cuspidata, p.104
Tsuga canadensis, p.102

SHRUBS
Berberis thunbergii 'Rose Glow', p.137
Berberis valdiviana, p.111
Buxus sempervirens
Choisya ternata, p.122
Cotoneaster salicifolius, p.142
Daphne laureola and forms
Elaeagnus x *ebbingei*
Euonymus fortunei 'Emerald Gaiety'
Euonymus japonicus
Fatsia japonica
Gaultheria shallon, p.154
Hypericum calycinum, p.161
Hypericum x *inodorum* 'Elstead', p.161
Hypericum x *moserianum*
Lonicera pileata, p.167
Mahonia aquifolium, p.148
Mahonia x media and cvs, p.118
Osmanthus decorus
Osmanthus delavayi, p.110
Pachysandra terminalis, p.375
Prunus laurocerasus 'Otto Luyken', p.145
Prunus laurocerasus 'Zabeliana', p.145
Prunus lusitanica
Rubus tricolor
Ruscus aculeatus, p.167
Ruscus hypoglossum, p.167
Sambucus nigra 'Guincho Purple'
Sarcococca humilis, p.164
Symphoricarpos albus var. *laevigatus*, p.142
Vaccinium angustifolium var. *laevifolium*, p.163
Viburnum rhytidophyllum, p.112
Viburnum tinus
Viburnum tinus 'Eve Price', p.143
Vinca major
Vinca minor, p.165

CLIMBERS AND WALL SHRUBS
Berberidopsis corallina, p.202
Celastrus orbiculatus
Cotoneaster horizontalis, p.208
Hedera canariensis
Hedera helix and cvs, p.211
Lapageria rosea, p.202
Lonicera japonica 'Halliana'
Lonicera periclymenum and cvs, p.207

PERENNIALS
Acanthus mollis 'Hollard's Gold', p.219
Acanthus spinosus, p.239
Ajuga reptans cvs
Alchemilla mollis, p.275
Anemone tomentosa
Aster divaricatus, p.249
Campanula persicifolia
Chelidonium majus 'Flore Pleno', p.227
Corydalis lutea, p.344
Digitalis purpurea
Doronicum x *excelsum* 'Harpur Crewe'
Epimedium spp. and cvs, p.254, 260, 262, 263
Euphorbia amygdaloides var. *robbiae*, p.262
Geranium macrorrhizum, pp.269, 223
Iris foetidissima, p.225
Lamium maculatum
Lunaria rediviva
LUNGWORTS, p.261
Pachysandra terminalis, p.375
Polygonatum x *hybridum*, p.223
Scopolia carniolica, p.260
Symphytum 'Goldsmith'
Symphytum ibericum
Tellima grandiflora
Tolmiea menziesii
Viola riviniana 'Purpurea'

Ferns
Asplenium ceterach, p.293
Asplenium scolopendrium, p.292
Cyrtomium falcatum, p.291
Dryopteris filix-mas, p.293
Polypodium vulgare, p.291
Polystichum aculeatum

GRASSES AND BAMBOOS
Carex flagellifera, p.289
Luzula sylvatica 'Hohe Tatra', p.288

BULBS, CORMS AND TUBERS
Camassia quamash, p.411
Colchicum autumnale, p.426
Cyclamen coum 'Maurice Dryden', p.428
Cyclamen coum Pewter Group, p.429
DAFFODILS, pp.404–405
Galanthus 'Hill Poe', p.427
Galanthus woronowii, p.428
Haemanthus albiflos
Hyacinthoides x *massartiana*, p.403
Hyacinthoides non-scripta, p.403
Incarvillea delavayi, p.265
Scilla siberica 'Alba', p.416

TENDER AND EXOTIC PLANTS
Climbers
Epipremnum aureum 'Marble Queen', p.460
Cissus striata

Perennials
Achimenes
Chirita
Clivia miniata, p.476
Nephrolepsis exaltata
Pteris cretica
Tradescantia zebrina 'Quadricolor'

RIGHT Oceans of blue
English bluebells (*Hyacinthoides non-scripta*) are perfect plants for dry shade, producing a carpet of blue flowers.

Cotoneaster horizontalis

Sarcococca hookeriana var. *digyna*

Geranium phaeum

Plants for moist shade

In areas with high rainfall, the soil in parts of the garden that receive little or no sun may be cool and moist throughout the year. Low-lying gardens with a high water table or drainage problems may also have shady, permanently damp areas. Similar conditions occur along the margins of natural streams, or when an artificial bog is created beside a garden pond. Take advantage of these situations to grow plants such as broad-leaved hostas, ferns, and taller moisture-loving primulas. Plant in spring, enriching lighter soils with well-rotted organic matter. Water during extended dry periods, if necessary.

TREES

Acer spp. and cvs, pp.60, 62, 65, 66, 67, 73, 74, 76, 77, 78, 79, 84, 85, 88, 89, 90, 91, 92, 115, 117, 123, 138, 156
Betula nigra, p.78
Stewartia pseudocamellia, p.78
Stewartia sinensis, p.78

SHRUBS

Anopterus glandulosus, p.110
Cassiope lycopodioides, p.349
Clethra arborea
Crataegus laevigata 'Punicea'
Cyathodes colensoi, p.346
Danäe racemosa
Disanthus cercidifolius, p.141
Gaultheria procumbens, p.373
Kalmia latifolia, p.136
Ledum groenlandicum, p.145
Leucothöe fontanesiana
Lindera benzoin, p.127
Lyonia ligustrina
Myrica gale, p.162
Neillia thibetica, p.133
Paeonia ludlowii, p.229
Paeonia rockii
Paxistima canbyi
Pieris formosa var. *forrestii* 'Wakehurst', p.137
Prunus laurocerasus
RHODODENDRONS, pp.124–125
Ruscus aculeatus, p.167
Salix exigua, p.112
Salix magnifica
Sarcococca spp. and cvs, pp.142, 164
Skimmia japonica, p.164
Spiraea japonica 'Albiflora'
Symphoricarpos albus var. *laevigatus,* p.142
Viburnum opulus and cvs, pp.142, 162
Viburnum 'Pragense', p.131
Viburnum tinus 'Eve Price', p.143

Galanthus elwesii

Passiflora coccinea

LEFT Fresh, cool greens
Ferns and large-leaved hostas, seen here with blue *Corydalis flexuosa*, flourish in cool, moist shade.

CLIMBERS AND WALL SHRUBS

Akebia quinata, p.193
Asteranthera ovata
Garrya elliptica 'James Roof', p.211
Humulus lupulus 'Aureus', p.194
Hydrangea petiolaris, p.195
Lonicera tragophylla, p.207
Pileostegia viburnoides, p.196
Schizophragma integrifolium, p.197

PERENNIALS

Aconitum 'Stainless Steel', p.241
Actaea pachypoda, p.246
Anemone x *hybrida* cvs, pp.220, 222
Anthurium scherzerianum
Asarum europaeum, p.375
Astelia chathamica, p.242
Astrantia major and cvs, pp.238, 278
Begonia grandis subsp. *evansiana,* p.278
Bergenia spp. and cvs, pp.255, 256, 280
Brunnera macrophylla and cvs, p.261
Calanthe striata (syn. *C. sieboldii*), p.275
Cardamine pentaphyllos, p.260
Chrysosplenium macrophyllum, p.256
Cimicifuga racemosa
Convallaria majalis, p.255
Cortusa matthioli, p.341
Cyathodes colensoi, p.346
Deinanthe caerulea
Dianella caerulea CASSA BLUE, p.283
Digitalis x *mertonensis*
Epigaea gaultherioides, p.351
Hacquetia epipactis, p.356
Hedyotis michauxii, p.369
Helleborus x hybridus, p.281
HEUCHERA AND x HEUCHERELLA, p.282
HOSTAS, pp.272–273
Jeffersonia diphylla, p.333
Kirengeshoma palmata, p.251
Lamium maculatum
Lathraea clandestina, p.260
Ligularia 'The Rocket', p.219
Lithophragma parviflorum, p.332
Mitella breweri, p.371
Omphalodes cappadocica and cvs, pp.261, 334
Pachysandra terminalis, p.375
Polygonatum x *hybridum,* p.223
Pratia pedunculata, p.369
PRIMULAS (many), pp.257–259
Prunella grandiflora, p.368
Rodgersia pinnata 'Fireworks', p.234
Tiarella cordifolia, p.333
Trillium grandiflorum, p.255
Uvularia grandiflora, p.262
Vancouveria hexandra

Grasses and bamboos

Chasmanthium latifolium, p.288
Chimonobambusa timidissinoda, p.287
Imperata cylindrica 'Rubra', p.285
Phyllostachys spp. and cvs, pp.286, 287, 288, 289
Thamnocalamus crassinodus 'Kew Beauty', p.286

Ferns

Athyrium 'Ghost', p.290
Athyrium niponicum, p.290
Athyrium niponicum var. *pictum* 'Burgundy Lace', p.290
Blechnum tabulare
Cyathea medullaris
Dicksonia antarctica, p.290
Lygodium japonicum
Osmunda claytoniana
Polypodium cambricum 'Richard Kayse', p.293
Polystichum munitum, p.293
Woodwardia radicans

ANNUALS AND BIENNIALS

BEGONIAS, p.317
Impatiens walleriana and cvs, p.307
Satureja douglasii

BULBS, CORMS AND TUBERS

Arisaema spp., p.393, 406, 408, 412, 422
Arisarum proboscideum
Arum italicum 'Marmoratum', p.421
Camassia leichtlinii, p.383
Cardiocrinum giganteum, p.385
Galanthus elwesii, p.427
Galanthus nivalis and cvs, p.427, 428
Galanthus plicatus subsp. *plicatus*
Leucojum vernum, p.414

WATER AND BOG PLANTS

Aruncus dioicus, p.436
Darmera peltata, p.438
Leucojum aestivum, p.436
Ligularia 'Britt Marie Crawford', p.445
Matteuccia struthiopteris, p.443
Onoclea sensibilis, p.443

TENDER AND EXOTIC PLANTS

Climbers

Dioscorea discolor
Passiflora coccinea, p.462
Thunbergia mysorensis, p.464

Perennials

Alpinia hainanensis, p.477
Alpinia purpurata, p.477
Aspidistra spp. and cvs
Calathea zebrina, p.475
Caulokaempferia petelotii
Cornukaempferia aurantiflora 'Jungle Gold', p.477
Curcuma petiolata, p.477
Curcuma zedoaria, p.477
Cyathea australis, p.452
Dichorisandra reginae, p.473
Hemiorchis patlingii
Lysionotus pauciflorus
Maranta leuconeura 'Erythroneura', p.475
Peliosanthes arisanensis, p.472
Ponerorchis hybrids
Ruellia devosiana, p.465
Selaginella martensii, p.478
Streptocarpus spp. and cvs, pp.465, 469, 473
Xanthosoma sagittifolium, p.474
Zingiber mioga

Shrubs preferring wall protection

Walls can provide favourable growing conditions for shrubs, especially evergreens, that are only moderately frost hardy. Some winter-flowering shrubs also bloom more reliably and freely when given wall protection. The best wall-side situations are warm and sunny, and provide good shelter from cold winds in winter and early spring. The warmth from heat loss through house walls, and the well-drained conditions near the base of walls, also assist the survival of slightly tender shrubs that dislike damp soil.

SHRUBS

Abelia floribunda
Abutilon 'Ashford Red', p.137
Abutilon vitifolium 'Victoria Tennant', p.114
Acacia podalyriifolia
Acacia pravissima, p.92
Acca sellowiana, p.203
Aloysia triphylla, p.132
Artemisia spp. and cvs, p.165, 216, 242, 274
Azara microphylla 'Variegata', p.119
Buddleja asiatica
Cantua buxifolia, p.146
Ceanothus impressus, p.138
Chaenomeles speciosa 'Moerloosei', p.122
Chimonanthus praecox, p.144
Cytisus x *spachianus*
Daphne odora 'Aureomarginata', p.164
Drimys winteri, p.73
Elsholtzia stauntonii
Escallonia 'Iveyi', p.112
Lagerstroemia indica
Leptospermum scoparium 'Red Damask', p.123
Leptospermum scoparium 'Snow White', p.130
Lonicera fragrantissima
Melianthus major, p.145
Myrtus communis, p.122
Olearia x *scilloniensis*
Osteomeles schwerinae, p.129
Robinia hispida, p.133
Rosa 'Mermaid', p.182
Rosmarinus officinalis, p.157
SALVIAS, p.155
Vestia foetida, p.194

CLIMBERS AND WALL SHRUBS

Abutilon megapotanicum, p.203
Azara serrata, p.195
Buddleja crispa, p.204
Callistemon citrinus 'Splendens', p.203
Carpenteria californica, p.197
Coronilla valentina subsp. *glauca*, p.195
Dendromecon rigida, p.206
Fabiana imbricata f. *violacea*, p.204
Fremontodendron 'California Glory', p.206
Garrya elliptica
Itea ilicifolia, p.211
Piptanthus nepalensis, p.206
Solanum crispum 'Glasnevin', p.204

TENDER AND EXOTIC PLANTS

Shrubs

Iochroma australe, p.138
Iochroma cyaneum, p.457
Tibouchina urvilleana, p.457

Leptospermum scoparium 'Red Damask'

Garrya eliptica

Melianthus major

Abutilon megapotamicum

Plants for paving and wall crevices

In mountainous regions, many alpine plants grow in deep cracks and crevices in the rock. Some are clump-forming or trailing in habit; others, such as saxifrages and sempervivums, grow as rosettes extending by means of runners. If laying paving, leave crevices for small plants, but restrict planting to little-used areas where they can survive. When building stone retaining walls, tilt slabs slightly backwards to create deep pockets, and plant them up as the wall is being constructed. Most wall plants thrive in sunny situations, but ramondas and most small ferns prefer moist shade.

ABOVE A wall of bright colour *Geranium* 'Johnson's Blue' and *Helianthemum* 'Cerise Queen' tumble over a dry-stone wall.

PERENNIALS

AQUILEGIAS pp.226
Geum 'Bell Bank', p.268
Ourisia coccinea, p.269

GRASSES AND BAMBOOS

Carex flagellifera, p.289
Imperata cylindrica 'Rubra', p.285
Stipa tenuissima, p.288

FERNS

Asplenium ceterach, p.293
Polypodium cambricum 'Richard Kayse', p.293

ANNUALS AND BIENNIALS (NOT WALLS)

Ageratum houstonianum
Limnanthes douglasii, p.321
Lobelia erinus cvs, pp.311, 314
Lobularia maritima
Malcolmia maritima, p.304
Nemophila maculata, p.299
Nemophila menziesii, p.314
Portulaca grandiflora Series and cvs, p.324

ROCK PLANTS

Acaena microphylla, p.374
Acantholimon glumaceum, p.363
Achillea x *kellereri*, p.360
Aethionema 'Warley Rose', p.362
Androsace sarmentosa
Antennaria dioica
Armeria maritima 'Vindictive', p.365
Artemisia schmidtiana 'Nana', p.374
Aubrieta spp. and cvs, p.353, 354, 355
Aurinia saxatilis and cvs, p.335
Campanula cochleariifolia, p.369
Campanula poscharskyana, p.367
Chamaemelum nobile
Chiastophyllum oppositifolium, p.335
Cyananthus microphyllus, p.369
Cymbalaria muralis
Dianthus deltoides 'Leuchtfunk', p.365
Draba aizoides
Dryas octopetala, p.361
Erigeron karvinskianus, p.363
Erinus alpinus, p.352
Gypsophila repens and cvs, p.362
Haberlea rhodopensis 'Virginalis', p.359
Helianthemum spp. and cvs, pp.336, 338, 337, 340, 344, 345
HOUSELEEKS, p.377
Hypericum olympicum
Lithodora diffusa 'Heavenly Blue', p.343
Mazus reptans, p.351
Mentha requienii
Nierembergia repens, p.361
Parahebe lyallii
Phlox douglasii 'Crackerjack', p.365
Physoplexis comosa (wall), p.366
Ramonda myconi (wall only), p.369
Saxifraga cotyledon
Sedum spathulifolium 'Cape Blanco', p.375
Thymus 'Bressingham', p.365
Thymus caespititus var. *cilicicus*, p.366
Vitaliana primuliflora, p.358

Plants for containers

Containers packed with foliage and flowers can brighten patios, courtyards, and balconies. Large containers are best in sunny, sheltered sites, as they retain more moisture than small ones. Small trees, conifers, or shrubs, together with perennials, give long-term interest with their foliage and forms, and periods of flowering. For colourful displays, plant spring-flowering bulbs, followed by summer bedding, which will flower from late spring to the first frosts.

TREES

Acer negundo
Crataegus laevigata and cvs, p.84
Eucalyptus (when young), pp.67, 68, 78, 79
HOLLIES, p.94
Laurus nobilis, p.80
Malus x *arnoldiana*, p.82
Malus x *magdeburgensis*, p.83
Melia azederach, p.71
Olea europaea

BELOW Springtime tulips
Terracotta containers planted in late autumn with single and double tulip bulbs make a colourful, elegant display the following spring.

CONIFERS

DWARF CONIFERS, p.104–105

SHRUBS

Buxus sempervirens and cvs, pp.144, 167
Choisya ternata, p.122
HARDY FUCHSIAS, p.154
Hebe cupressoides and cvs, pp.165, 347
HYDRANGEAS, p.134–135
LAVENDERS, p.158
Myrtus communis, p.122
Pittosporum tenuifolium 'Tom Thumb', p.164
RHODODENDRONS (most), pp.124–125
ROSES (all patio varieties)
Santolina pinnata subsp. *neapolitana*, p.159
Viburnum tinus and cvs, p.143

CLIMBERS AND WALL SHRUBS

CLEMATIS (small cvs), pp.198–200
Cobaea scandens, p.204
Eccremocarpus scaber, p.208
Hedera helix and cvs, p.211
Ipomoea hederacea, p.204
Ipomoea lobata, p.202
Ipomoea tricolor 'Heavenly Blue', p.205
Jasminum humile and cvs, pp.139, 206
Jasminum polyanthum, p.208
Lathyrus odoratus and cvs, pp.201, 202, 301
HONEYSUCKLE, p.207
Passiflora caerulea, p.204
Tropaeolum speciosum, p.202

PERENNIALS

Agapanthus 'Northern Star', p.241
Agapanthus 'Purple Cloud', p.241
Agapanthus inapertus subsp. *pendulus* 'Graskop', p.240
Astelia chathamica, p.242
Bergenia spp. and cvs, pp.255, 256, 280
DAYLILIES, pp.244–245
Dianella caerulea CASSA BLUE, p.283
Geranium ROZANNE ('Gerwat'), p.271
HEUCHERA and x HEUCHERELLA, p.282
HOSTAS, pp.272–273
LUNGWORTS, p.261
Phormium 'Dazzler', p.216
PRIMULAS, pp.257–259
Rudbeckia fulgida var. *sullivantii* 'Goldsturm', p.251
SALVIA, p.250
Schizostylis 'Mrs Hegarty'
Sedum 'Bertram Anderson' and 'Ruby Glow', p.279
Stachys (some)
Verbena (some)

FERNS

Adiantum (most)
Asplenium scolopendrium Marginatum Group, p.292
Polypodium vulgare 'Cornubiense', p.291
Polystichum setiferum Divisilobum Group, p.291

GRASSES AND BAMBOOS

Carex flagellifera, p.289
Chionochloa rubra, p.285
Elegia capensis, p.285
Eragrostis curvula 'Totnes Burgundy', p.285
Imperata cylindrica 'Rubra', p.285
Miscanthus sinensis 'Yakushima Dwarf', p.285
Pennisetum 'Fairy Tails'
Pennisetum setaceum Rubrum

Ipomoea tricolor 'Heavenly Blue',

Phormium 'Dazzler'

Argyranthemum BUTTERFLY ('Ulyssis')

Pelargonium 'Bulls Eye Salmon'

Viola x *wittrockiana* Joker Series

Tagetes 'Naughty Marietta'

ANNUALS AND BIENNIALS
Ageratum houstonianum and cvs
Antirrhinum spp. and cvs, pp.313, 314
Argyranthemum spp. and cvs, pp.298, 300, 319
Bassia scoparia f. *trichophylla*, p.316
BEGONIAS, p.317
Bidens 'Gold Star', p.319
Brachyscome 'Strawberry Mousse', p.300
Calendula officinalis Series and cvs, pp.321, 322, 325, 326
Calibrachoa Series and cvs pp.300, 306
Callistephus chinensis Series and cvs, pp.303, 304, 312
Catharanthus roseus and cvs, pp.298, 300, 306
Coreopsis 'Rum Punch', p.326
Cosmos atrosanguineus and cvs, pp.238, 306
Cuphea x *purpurea* 'Firecracker', p.306
Diascia LITTLE DANCER (Pendan), p.301
Dichondra argentea 'Silver Falls'
Dichondra repens 'Emerald Falls'
Duranta erecta 'Gold Edge', p.319
Erysimum cheiri 'Treasure Red'
FUCHSIAS, p.302
Helichrysum petiolare, p.165
HOUSELEEKS, p.377
Impatiens spp. and cvs, pp.300, 307, 325
Ipomoea batatus and cvs, pp.311, 318
Lantana camara Lucky Series, p.301
Lobelia erinus cvs
Lobularia maritima 'Snow Crystals'
Lysimachia congestiflora 'Outback Sunset', p.323
Mimulus 'Magic Yellow Blotch', p.320
Nemesia Amelie, p.301
Nemesia strumosa, p.307
Osteospermum ecklonis and cvs, pp.301, p.311
Perilla 'Magilla Vanilla', p.318
x *Petchoa* SuperCal Series, p.303
PELARGONIUMS, p.309
Petunia Series and cvs, pp.308, 311, 312, 316
Plecostachys serpyllifolia
Primula Belarina Series, pp.258, 303
Salpiglossis sinuata Series and cvs
Salvia farinacea 'Strata', p.314
Salvia splendens
Satureja douglasii 'Indian Mint'
Scaevola aemula 'Little Wonder'
Solenostemon scutellarioides Series and cvs, pp.310, 311
Sutera cordata Snowstorm Series GIANT SNOWFLAKE, p.298
Tagetes Series and cvs, pp.308, 322, 324, 326
Tropaeolum majus and cvs, pp.307, 323, 327
Verbena x *hybrida* Series, pp.303, 307
Viola x *wittrockiana* hybrids and cvs, pp.308, 312, 313, 318, 323
Zinnia x marylandica Series, pp.298, 307

ROCK PLANTS
All are suitable, the following being particularly recommended:
Campanula portenschlagiana p.368
Campanula poscharskyana p.367
Dianthus gratianopolitanus p.363
Geranium sanguineum, p.340
Hebe vernicosa p.337
Helianthemum spp. and cvs, pp.336, 337, 338, 340, 344, 345
Hypericum olympicum
Iberis sempervirens p.332
Persicaria affinis 'Donald Lowndes', p.365
Phlox douglasii 'Crackerjack' p.365
Saponaria ocymoides, p.364
Saxifraga stolonifera
Saxifraga x *urbium*
Silene schafta, p.346
Thymus 'Bressingham', p.365
Thymus caespititus var. *cilicicus*, p.366

BULBS, CORMS AND TUBERS
ALSTROEMERIAS, p.387
Anomatheca laxa, p.423
Bellavalia romana, p.399
Calochortus superbus, p.409
CANNAS, p.394
CROCOSMIA, p.410
CROCUSES, p.417
Cyclamen coum and cvs, pp.428, 429
DAFFODILS, pp.404–405
DAHLIAS, pp.396–398
Galanthus 'Hill Poe', p.427
Galanthus woronowii
GLADIOLI, p.428
Gladiolus callianthus murielae
Habenaria radiata, p.408
Hippeastrum 'Black Pearl'
Hyacinthus orientalis 'Blue Jacket', p.403
Hyacinthus orientalis 'White Pearl', p.415
Hymenocallis 'Sulphur Queen', p.412
Incarvillea delavayi, p.265
Iris reticulata and cvs, p.225
LILIES (most), pp.388–391
Muscari botryoides 'Album', p.415
Nerine bowdenii 'Nikita'
Polianthes tuberosa 'The Pearl', p.385
Triteleia ixiodes 'Starlight', p.407
Triteleia 'Queen Fabiola'
Tulbaghia simmleri, p.411
TULIPS, pp.400–401
Watsonia meriana, p.385
Zantedeschia 'Cameo', p.395

WATER AND BOG PLANTS
Acorus calamus 'Argenteostriatus', p.435
Aponogeton distachyos, p.435
Eichhornia crassipes, p.441
Menyanthes trifoliata, p.434
Pontederia cordata, p.441
Thalia dealbata
WATER LILIES (small cvs), p.440
Zantedeschia aethiopica 'Crowborough', p.437

TENDER AND EXOTIC PLANTS
Trees
Cordyline australis 'Atropurpurea', p.451
Ficus spp. pp.450, 452, 458
Jacaranda mimosifolia, p.451
Washingtonia robusta, p.451

Shrubs
Plectranthus fructicosus 'James', p.454

Climbers
Cissus antarctica, p.463
Mandevilla spp., pp.460, 461
Stephanotis floribunda, p.460

Perennials
Browallia speciosa, p.472
Centropogon ferruginensis
Centropogon willdenowianus

Cacti and succulents
AGAVES, p.482
ALOES, *p.493*
Furcraea foetida 'Mediopicta', p.481

Trailing plants for walls or baskets

Many plants grow naturally in crevices, their trailing stems covering large areas of vertical rock. In gardens, they can be used at the top of retaining walls to soften the brickwork. Smaller trailing plants, including tender perennials and annuals, are ideal for hanging baskets. After planting, hang baskets on sturdy brackets on a wall or set them on large, inverted pots on a patio or old tree stump so that the plants form a conical mound of tumbling stems and flowers.

CONIFERS
Juniperus x *pfitzeriana* 'Old Gold', p.105
Juniperus squamata 'Blue Carpet', p.105
Microbiota decussata, p.105

SHRUBS
Arctostaphylos uva-ursi, p.376
Ceanothus thyrsiflorus var. *repens*, p.159
Leptospermum rupestre, p.151
Loiseleuria procumbens, p.364
Nematanthus strigillosus
Salix lindleyana
Salix repens, p.147

CLIMBERS AND WALL SHRUBS
Hedera (most), p.211

PERENNIALS
Campanula isophylla
Chrysosplenium macrophyllum, p.256
Glechoma hederacea 'Variegata', p.277
Tropaeolum polyphyllum, p.276
Verbena 'Sissinghurst', p.268
Verbena peruviana

ANNUALS AND BIENNIALS
Bidens 'Gold Star', p.319
Calceolaria integrifolia
Calibrachoa hybrids and cvs, pp.300, 306
Diascia LITTLE DANCER (Pendan), p.301
Dichondra argentea 'Silver Falls'
Dichondra repens 'Emerald Falls'
Fuchsia procumbens
Helichrysum petiolare, p.165
Ipomoea batatas 'Blackie', p.311
Ipomoea batatas 'Margarita', p.318
Lantana montevidensis, p.310
Lathyrus odoratus 'Cupid Pink', p.301
Limnanthes douglasii, p.321
Lobelia erinus and cvs, p.311, 314, 315
Lotus berthelotii, p.306
Lysimachia congestiflora 'Outback Sunset', p.323
Nemophila maculata, p.299
Nolana paradoxa
Pelargonium peltatum
x *Petchoa* Supercal Series, p.303
Petunia Surfinia Series, p.311, 316
Petunia Tumbelina Series, p.311
Portulaca grandiflora Series and cvs
Sanvitalia procumbens, p.322
Scaevola aemula 'Little Wonder'
Solenostemon scutellarioides 'Inky Fingers', p.311
Sutera cordata GIANT SNOWFLAKE, p.298
Tropaeolum majus Series and cvs, pp.307, 323, 327
Verbena Corsage Series, p.307

ROCK PLANTS
Acaena saccaticupula 'Blue Haze'
Androsace lanuginosa, p.363
Arabis alpina subsp. *caucasica*
Campanula cochleariifolia, p.369
Convolvulus sabatius, p.342
Cymbalaria muralis
Cytisus x *beanii*, p.335
Euphorbia myrsinites, p.357
Genista lydia, p.345
Gypsophila repens
Iberis sempervirens, p.332
Lithodora diffusa cvs, p.343
Oenothera macrocarpa, p.372
Othonna cheirifolia, p.344
Parahebe catarractae, p.342
Parochetus communis, p.370
Persicaria vacciniifolia, p.373
Phlox subulata
Pterocephalus perennis, p.364
Saxifraga stolonifera

TENDER AND EXOTIC PLANTS
Shrubs
Chorizema ilicifolium

Perennials
Achimenes 'Peach Blossom', *p.455*
Aeschynanthus speciosus, *p.478*
Centropogon ferruginensis

Verbena 'Sissinghurst'

Helichrysum petiolare

Petunia Surfinia Lime

Plants with aromatic foliage

The leaves of many plants contain essential aromatic oils, used in medicine or cooking. For gardeners, their value lies in the aromas released naturally or when bruised. Those of culinary value, such as rosemary, are often grown in herb gardens, or plant low-growing thymes next to paths or between paving stones, where they will emit their scent when trodden underfoot. The fragrance from trees is best appreciated as it drifts through the garden on the wind.

TREES

Eucalyptus spp., pp.67, 68, 78, 79
Juglans regia, p.62
Laurus nobilis, p.80
Phellodendron chinense, p.75
Populus balsamifera
Populus trichocarpa
Sassafras albidum, p.64
Umbellularia californica, p.69

BELOW Scented seating
Create a relaxing resting place in the garden with a stylish wooden bench surrounded by aromatic herbs, such as lavender, thyme and marjoram.

CONIFERS

Calocedrus decurrens, p.101
Chamaecyparis spp. and cvs, pp.96, 99, 101, 101, 102, 103, 104, 105
Cupressus spp. and cvs, pp.95, 102, 104
Juniperus spp., pp.100, 103, 105
Pseudotsuga menziesii var. glauca, p.96
Thuja plicata 'Stoneham Gold', p.105

SHRUBS

Aloysia triphylla, p.132
Artemisia abrotanum, p.165
Caryopteris x *clandonensis* 'Arthur Simmonds', p.157
Choisya ternata and cvs, p.122, 148
Cistus laurifolius
Elsholtzia stauntonii
Gaultheria procumbens, p.373
Helichrysum italicum
Hyssopus officinalis, p.157
LAVENDERS, p.158
Lindera benzoin, p.127
Myrtus communis, p.122
Perovskia 'Blue Spire', p.159
Phlomis fruticosa, p.160
Rhododendron rubiginosum
Rosa rubiginosa, p.176
Rosmarinus officinalis, p.157
Salvia officinalis and cvs, p.155
Santolina spp.

PERENNIALS

Achillea filipendulina
Agastache 'Black Adder', p.280
Artemisia spp. and cvs, pp.165, 216, 242, 274, 374
Chamaemelum nobile
Galium odoratum, p.263
Geranium macrorrhizum, p.269
Mentha suaveolens 'Variegata', p.274
Monarda didyma
Myrrhis odorata, p.230
Nepeta 'Six Hills Giant', p.240
Perovskia atriplicifolia
Tanacetum parthenium, p.300

ANNUALS AND BIENNIALS

PELARGONIUMS (scented-leaved forms), p.309
Satureja douglasii

ROCK PLANTS

Mentha requienii
Origanum laevigatum, p.340
Satureja montana,
Thymus spp. and cvs, pp.365, 366, 367

TENDER AND EXOTIC PLANTS

Trees
Agonis flexuosa, p.450

Shrubs
Boronia megastigma
Prostanthera ovalifolia, p.457

Perennials
Kaempferia pulchra, p.477

Phlomis fruticosa

Rosa rubiginosa

Nepeta 'Six Hills Giant'

Plants with fragrant flowers

Fragrance is a compelling feature of many plants. It can be strong, filling the garden with scent, or apparent only when you are close to individual blooms. Some plants release scent continuously, while the perfume of others is more noticeable at night. A sunny, sheltered patio is an ideal situation for fragrant plants, or site them close to paths, and train fragrant climbers over arches and around doorways. Hyacinths provide early spring fragrance indoors.

TREES

Clethra arborea
Crataegus monogyna
Drimys winteri, p.73
Eucryphia lucida, p.85
Fraxinus ornus, p.71
Genista aetnensis, p.89
Laburnum x *watereri* 'Vossii', p.84
MAGNOLIAS, p.70
Malus coronaria 'Charlottae'
Malus hupehensis, p.69
Malus 'Profusion', p.71
Prunus mume 'Beni-chidori', p.123
Prunus padus 'Watereri', p.71
Prunus x *yedoensis*, p.82
Pterostyrax hispida, p.73
Robinia pseudoacacia
Styrax japonicus, p.72
Tilia 'Petiolaris', p.64

SHRUBS

Abelia x *grandiflora*, p.113
Acacia dealbata, p.211
Azara microphylla, p.118
Berberis x *stenophylla*, p.127
Brugmansia arborea
BUDDLEJAS, p.114
Chimonanthus praecox, p.144
Choisya ternata, p.122
Clerodendrum bungei, p.141
Clerodendrum trichotomum, p.142
Clethra delavayi, p.113
Colletia hystrix, p.130
Corylopsis pauciflora, p.126
Cytisus battandieri, p.116
Daphne odora and cvs
Deutzia x *elegantissima* cvs
Edgeworthia chrysantha, p.126
Elaeagnus x *ebbingei* 'Limelight', p.139
Erica lusitanica
Fothergilla major, p.117
WITCH HAZELS, p.118
LAVENDERS, p.158
Ligustrum lucidum
LILACS, p.115
Lupinus arboreus, p.159
MAGNOLIAS, p.70
Osmanthus spp. and cvs, pp.110, 119
Philadelphus spp. and cvs, pp.127, 128, 129, 131, 149
Pittosporum tenuifolium, p.120
ROSES (many), pp.168–187
Sarcococca spp., pp.142, 164
Viburnum spp. and cvs, pp.110, 111, 122, 143, 146

CLIMBERS AND WALL SHRUBS

Clematis montana 'Elizabeth'
Coronilla valentina subsp. *glauca*, p.195
HONEYSUCKLE, p.207
Itea ilicifolia, p.211
Jasminum humile and cvs, pp.139, 206
Jasminum officinale f. *affine*, p.196
Lathyrus odoratus and cvs, pp.201, 202, 203
Mandevilla laxa
ROSES (many)
Trachelospermum spp., p.195, 196
WISTERIA, p.205

PERENNIALS

Anemone sylvestris, p.255
Clematis heracleifolia 'Wyevale'
Convallaria majalis, p.255
Cosmos atrosanguineus, p.*238*
Crambe cordifolia, p.216
CARNATIONS AND PINKS, pp.266–267
Galium odoratum, p.263
Hedychium coccineum 'Tara', p.220
Hemerocallis lilioasphodelus, p.245
Hesperis matronalis, p.230
Impatiens tinctoria, p.216
Iris graminea
Iris unguicularis
Mirabilis jalapa, p.233
Myrrhis odorata, p.230
PEONIES, pp.228–229
Persicaria polymorpha, p.234
Primula elatior, p.259
Primula veris, p.262

ANNUALS AND BIENNIALS

Amberboa moschata
Antirrhinum majus Series, p.303, 319, 320
Argemone mexicana, p.321
Dianthus barbatus and cvs
Erysimum cheiri Series and cvs
Exacum affine
Heliotropium arborescens, p.310
Iberis amara, p.299
Limnanthes douglasii, p.321
Lobularia maritima 'Snow Crystals', p.298
Matthiola incana
Nemesia 'Amelie', p.301
Nicotiana alata, p.231
Nicotiana sylvestris
Petuna 'Priscilla', p.311
Reseda odorata, p.300
Scabiosa atropurpurea
Verbena x *hybrida* Series, pp.303, 307, 312

ROCK PLANTS

Dianthus gratianopolitanus, p.363
Erysimum helveticum, p.358
Papaver croceum
Primula auricula

BULBS, CORMS AND TUBERS

Amaryllis belladonna, p.395
Arisaema candidissimum, p.422
Cardiocrinum giganteum, p.385
Chlidanthus fragrans, p.424
Crinum bulbispermum
Crinum x *powellii*, p.385
Crocus angustifolius
Crocus longiflorus
Cyclamen persicum, p.429
Eucharis amazonica, p.414
Gladiolus murielae, p.383
Habenaria radiata, p.408
Hyacinthus orientalis and cvs, pp.403, 407, 415
Hymenocallis 'Sulphur Queen', p.412
LILIES (several), pp.388–391
Muscari armeniacum, p.420
Narcissus jonquilla and Div.7 hybrids, pp.404–405
Narcissus tazetta and Div.8 hybrids, pp.404, 405, 407
Ornithogalum arabicum, p.408
Polianthes tuberosa 'The Pearl', p.385

WATER PLANTS

Aponogeton distachyos, p.435
Nymphaea 'Blue Beauty', p.440
Nymphaea 'James Brydon', p.440
Nymphaea odorata 'Sulphurea *Grandiflora*'

TENDER AND EXOTIC PLANTS

Trees
Bauhinia variegata
Plumeria rubra

Shrubs
Boronia megastigma
Gardenia augusta 'Veitchii'

Climbers
Hoya carnosa
Stephanotis floribunda

Perennials
Cattleya J.A.Carbone

Lilium regale

Lonicera etrusca 'Michael Rosse's

Wisteria sinensis 'Prolific'

Anemone sylvestris

RIGHT **Classic combination**
Rosa 'Felicia' and *Lavandula angustifolia* provide pretty contrasts and a heady fragrance in a summer border.

Decorative fruit or seedheads

As winter approaches, dull corners or featureless borders can be brightened with the colourful fruits of berberis, cotoneasters, viburnums and other ornamental berried shrubs. On pergolas and trellis, *Celastrus orbiculatus* and *Clematis orientalis* provide late-season interest with trailing skeins of yellow fruits and feathery seeds. Wall-trained pyracanthas will colour drab winter walls with yellow, orange, or scarlet fruits, while hollies (Ilex) also sport berries for winter decoration. The dried seedheads of many plants produce beautiful effects for indoor and outdoor displays.

TREES

Arbutus unedo, p.93
Cornus kousa, p.85
Cotoneaster frigidus, p.142
Crataegus spp., pp.80, 84, 90
HOLLIES (most), p.94
Koelreuteria paniculata, p.89
MAGNOLIAS, p.70
Malus spp. (most), pp.82–110
Photinia davidiana, p.90
SORBUS, p.91

CONIFERS

Abies spp., p.95, 96, 98, 100, 104, 105
Cedrus spp., pp.95, 96, 97, 104
Picea spp., pp.98–105
Pinus spp., pp.78–105

SHRUBS

Aucuba japonica
Berberis spp. and cvs, pp.111, 123, 127, 137, 141, 148, 160, 162
Callicarpa bodinieri var. *giraldii*, p.141
Cotoneaster spp. and cvs, pp.117, 122, 141, 142, 143, 208
Decaisnea fargesii, p.142
Euonymus europaeus 'Red Cascade', p.140
Euonymus latifolius, p.140
Euonymus myrianthus, p.117
Gaultheria mucronata and cvs, p.163, 164
Hippophäe rhamnoides, p.142
Hypericum x *inodorum* 'Elstead', p.161
Leycesteria formosa
Poncirus trifoliata, p.142
Pyracantha spp. and cvs, pp.118, 128, 141, 144, 209
ROSES (most), pp.168–187
Sambucus racemosa 'Plumosa Aurea', p.139
Sarcococca hookeriana var. *digyna*, p.164
Skimmia japonica, p.164
Symphoricarpos spp. and cvs, p.148, 160
Symplocos paniculata, p.142
Viburnum davidii, p.165
Viburnum opulus and cvs, pp.142, 162
Viburnum tinus and cvs, p.143

CLIMBERS AND WALL SHRUBS

Actinidia deliciosa
Billardiera longiflora, p.210
Cardiospermum halicacabum
Celastrus orbiculatus
Clematis orientalis
Holboellia coriacea, p.194
ROSES (several), pp.168–187
Tropaeolum speciosum, p.202

PERENNIALS

Achillea filipendulina
Aconitum 'Stainless Steel', p.241
Actaea pachypoda, p.246
Agapanthus 'Northern Star', p.241
Agapanthus 'Phantom'
Agapanthus 'Purple Cloud', p.241
Clintonia borealis
Disporum hookeri
Duchesnea indica
Echinacea species and cvs, p.221, 234
Eryngium pandanifolium
Eupatorium maculatum Atropurpureum Group 'Reisenschirm', p.221
Francoa sochifolia Rogerson's form
Iris foetidissima, p.225
Ligularia 'The Rocket', p.219
Ophiopogon spp., pp.280, 283
ORIENTAL POPPIES, p.238
PEONIES, pp.228–229
Persicaria polymorpha, p.234
Physalis alkekengi
Podophyllum hexandrum, p.255
Rudbeckia maxima, p.251
SEDUM, p.279
Smilacina racemosa, p.223
Veronicastrum virginicum 'Fascination', p.220

GRASSES AND BAMBOOS

Ampeldesmos mauritanica, p.287
Briza maxima
Calamagrostis brachytricha, p.284
Chasmanthium latifolium, p.288
Cortaderia spp. and cvs, pp.284, 285
Deschampsisa cespitosa 'Gold Tau', p.289
Eragrostis curvula 'Totnes Burgundy', p.285
Miscanthus sinensis and cvs pp.284, 285, 286
Molinia caerulea subsp. *caerulea* 'Heidebraut', p.285
Molinia caerulea subsp. *arundinacea* 'Transparent', p.286
Panicum virgatum 'Northwind', p.289
Pennisetum spp. and cvs, pp.286, 311, 312
Stipa spp. and cvs, pp.286, 287, 288

ANNUALS AND BIENNIALS

Capsicum annuum 'Holiday Cheer'
Lagurus ovatus, p.284
Lunaria annua, p.310
Martynia annua, p.300
Nicandra physalodes
Nigella damascena and cvs, p.314, 315
Solanum capsicastrum

ROCK PLANTS

Acaena microphylla, p.374
Cornus canadensis, p.360
Dryas octopetala, p.361
Gaultheria (most), pp.346, 373
Maianthemum bifolium, p.348
Nertera granadensis, p.373
Pulsatilla spp., p.332, 334, 349
Vaccinium vitis-idaea subsp. *minus*, p.351

BULBS, CORMS AND TUBERS

Allium aflatunense, p.382
Allium atropurpureum, p.392
Allium cowanii
Allium cristophii, p.411
Allium 'Gladiator', p.392
Allium 'Globemaster', p.392
Allium 'Mount Everest', p.385
Allium oreophilum, p.418
Allium 'Purple Sensation', p.392
Arisaema triphyllum, p.406
Arum italicum 'Marmoratum', p.421
Cardiocrinum giganteum, p.385

WATER PLANTS

Ligularia 'Britt Marie Crawford', p.445
Nuphar lutea, p.444
Thalia dealbata

TENDER AND EXOTIC PLANTS

Trees

Cyphomandra betacea, p.456

Shrubs

x *Citrofortunella microcarpa*, p.458

Iris foetidissima

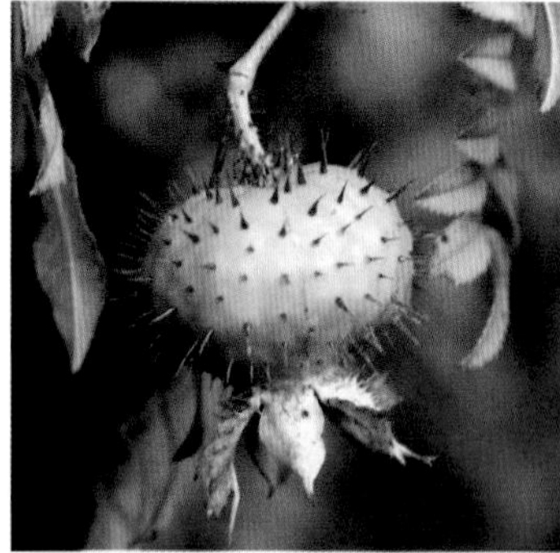

R. roxburghii

Symphoricarpus albus var. *laevigatus*

Ilex aquifolium

BELOW Late-season sculpture The seed heads of *Allium cristophii* complement the brown seed pods of *Nigella damascena*, adding texture to a herbaceous border as winter approaches.

Flowers for cutting

With careful selection, flowers can be cut from the garden at most times of the year, from the Christmas rose (*Helleborus niger*) in midwinter to *Nerine bowdenii* in autumn. In small gardens, integrate plants for cutting into the general scheme, and leave some blooms for display, or plant away from the house so that the cutting is less noticeable. Feed regularly during the growing season, to counteract the weakening effects of cutting the plants.

SHRUBS

CAMELLIA, pp.120–121
Forsythia spp., pp.127, 195
LILACS, p.115
Philadelphus spp. and cvs, pp.127, 128, 129, 131, 149
ROSES (some), pp.168–187
Salix caprea
WITCH HAZELS, p.118

PERENNIALS

Agapanthus 'Northern Star', p.241
Agapanthus 'Purple Cloud', p.241
Agapanthus inapertus subsp. *pendulus* 'Graskop', p.240
Anaphalis spp., p.231
Anchusa azurea
Astrantia major 'Roma', p.278
Astrantia major 'Ruby Wedding', p.238
CARNATIONS and PINKS, pp.266–267
CHRYSANTHEMUMS, pp.252–253
Coreopsis 'Limerock Ruby', p.268
DELPHINIUMS (most), p.217
Francoa sochifolia Rogerson's form,
Gaillardia 'Oranges and Lemons', p.277
Gerbera EVERLAST PINK 'Amberpink'
Helleborus niger, p.281
JAPANESE ANEMONE, p.222
Leucanthemum x *superbum* 'Sonnenschein', p.231
MICHAELMAS DAISIES, p.249
PEONIES, pp.228–229
PHLOX, p.240
Potentilla 'Arc-en-ciel', p.268
RUDBECKIA, p.251

Grasses and bamboos

Calamagrostis brachytricha, p.284
Chasmanthium latifolium, p.288
Cortadera richardii, p.284

ANNUALS AND BIENNIALS

Amaranthus caudatus, p.307
Amberboa moschata
Callistephus chinensis Series, pp.303, 304, 312
Centaurea cyanus and cvs, p.315
Clarkia amoenia 'Sybil Sherwood', p.305
Eustoma grandiflorum, p.299
Gaillardia pulchella 'Lollipops', p.327
Gypsophila elegans, p.299
Lathyrus odoratus and cvs, pp.201, 301
Malope trifida, p.305
Matthiola 'Giant Excelsior', p.303
Moluccella laevis, p.316
Rhodanthe chlorocephala subsp. *rosea*, p.303
Zinnia elegans Series and cvs (tall hybrids), pp.306, 316, 325

BULBS, CORMS AND TUBERS

Allium aflatunense, p.382
Allium atropurpureum, p.392
Allium 'Gladiator', p.392
Allium 'Globemaster', p.392
Allium 'Mount Everest', p.385
Allium 'Purple Sensation', p.392
ALSTROEMERIA, p.387
Brodiaea 'Queen Fabiola'
Camassia quamash, p.411
Cardiocrinum giganteum, p.385
CROCOSMIA, p.410
DAFFODILS (tall species and cvs), pp.404–405
DAHLIAS, pp.396–398
GLADIOLI (most), p.384
Gladiolus murielae, p.383
Hyacinthus orientalis 'Blue Jacket', p.403
Hyacinthus orientalis 'White Pearl', p.415
LILIES (some), pp.388–391
Nerine bowdenii 'Nikita'
Ornithogalum thyrsoides, p.408
Polianthes tuberosa 'The Pearl', p.385
Triteleia ixiodes 'Starlight', p.407
Tulbaghia simmleri (syn. *T. fragrans*), p.411
TULIPS (tall cvs), pp.400–401
Zantedeschia aethiopica and cvs, p.408, 437
Zantedeschia 'Cameo', p.395

TENDER AND EXOTIC PLANTS

Shrubs

Turraea obtusifolia

Perennials

Cymbidium spp.
Phalaenopsis spp.
Strelitzia reginae

RIGHT Late summer beauty
A selection of dahlias in shades of pink planted with vibrant blue agapanthus fill the late summer border and make excellent cut flowers.

Narcissus 'Tahiti'

Allium aflatunense

Clarkia amoena 'Sybil Sherwood'

Tulipa 'Spring Green'

Chrysanthemum 'Chelsea Physic Garden'

Alstroemeria 'Serenade'

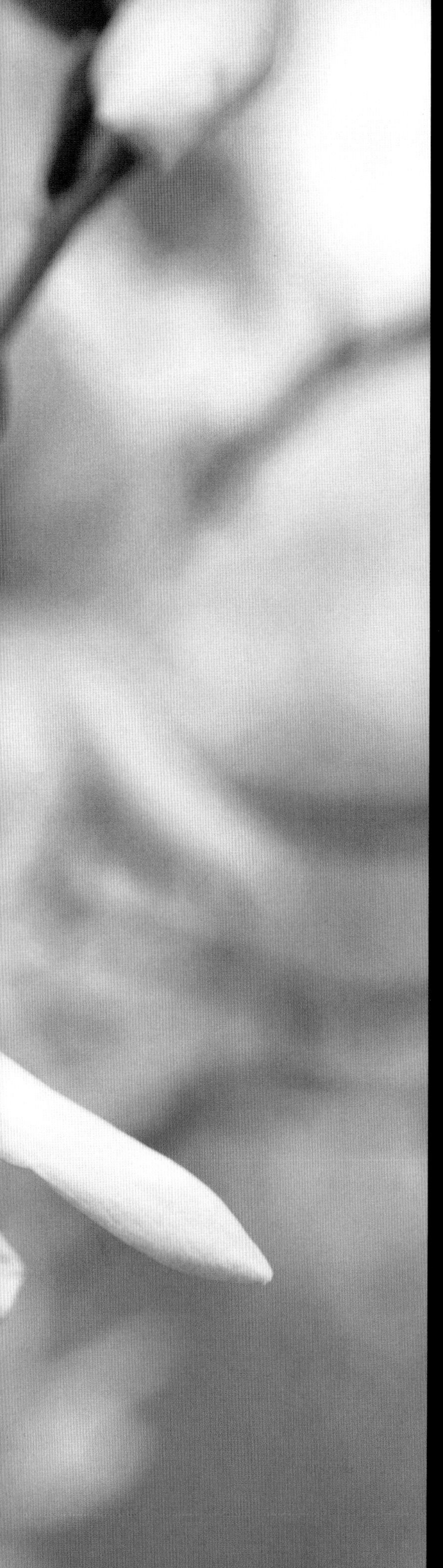

TREES

Trees are the most permanent elements in any planting scheme, making a strong visual impact by virtue of their size alone. There is a wealth of ornamental trees to choose from, with a range to suit your climate and growing conditions, as well as the size and style of your garden. Both deciduous and evergreen trees provide year-round structure and beauty, but they have many other benefits too, providing shade in summer, shelter in winter, and nesting sites and food for birds, insects and other wildlife. Trees can also help to reduce pollution and combat climate change by absorbing carbon dioxide from the atmosphere and replacing it with "clean" oxygen. They can even help to regulate ground water, an important benefit in areas at risk of flooding and soil erosion.

TREES

Dramatic and sculptural, trees are essential plants for gardens large and small. In design terms, they provide height, structure and year-round interest, with flowers, foliage, fruit and attractive bark, while also offering a home and source of food for birds and other wildlife.

SIZE CATEGORIES USED WITHIN THIS GROUP		
Large over 15m (50ft)	**Medium** 10–15m (30–50ft)	**Small** up to 10m (30ft)

What are trees?

Trees are woody plants, with life spans ranging from decades to several centuries. There are deciduous and evergreen trees, and most have a single stem with a crown of branches, although some produce multiple stems, either naturally or as a result of pruning. They range in size from conifers that are less than 1m (3ft) in height, to forest giants that soar up to 90m (300ft) or more. Trees also vary in shape. Some are narrowly conical or columnar, others are rounded or spreading, while some have an elegant, arching, weeping habit. There is also a wide choice of leaf shape and colour.

BELOW Letting in the light
Deciduous trees, such as Acer shirasawanum 'Aureum', can be used to make a wonderful garden centrepiece, underplanted with low plants to extend the interest before and after the main summer season.

Choosing trees

Before buying, match the needs of your chosen tree with the conditions in your garden. A tree is a long-term investment, so consider your site and soil carefully to ensure it will thrive, and that the size, shape and style will suit your design scheme, since trees are difficult to move once established. Also calculate the amount of shade the tree will cast on your or your neighbour's garden when mature, and site large trees away from the house, and where their roots will not undermine walls, pipes, drains or cables.

Designing with trees

Trees have many beautiful features and can be used in various ways to enhance a garden design. For example, several trees can be planted to form enclosures or define spaces; they can be used in pairs to frame a view, or in rows to form an avenue or tunnel. A line of trees also provides excellent wind protection and those that tolerate clipping, such as beech (*Fagus sylvatica*), hornbeam (*Carpinus betulus*) and yew (*Taxus baccata*), make attractive hedges that diffuse wind and noise.

Many trees have eye-catching features that make beautiful focal points – those with colourful stems and bark or large sculptural leaves make good choices. The shape and form of a tree can also help to

REMOVING A TREE BRANCH

The best time to prune most trees is in late winter when the plants are dormant, but wait till mid- to late summer for hornbeam (*Carpinus*), pears (*Pyrus*), plums and cherries (*Prunus*), which are susceptible to disease if cut earlier.

1 Make an undercut first
Shorten the branch first to reduce its weight, and to prevent falling and tearing the bark. Cut half way through the underside of the branch, then saw downwards from the top, further along the branch away from the trunk. Allow the branch to snap off.

2 Cut close to the trunk
Remove the final stump by cutting close to the trunk, but not flush with it. Make a smooth cut, angled away from the tree, just beyond the crease in the bark where the branch meets the trunk.

create a style. For example, the crisp outline of the *Juniperus communis* 'Compressa', suits a formal design, while the shape, flowers and fruit of many crab apples (*Malus* species) lend natural informality.

If you have space for several trees, you can create a small woodland, underplanted with shade-loving perennials. Many small trees, such as *Acer palmatum* and the corkscrew hazel (*Corylus avellana* 'Contorta'), and dwarf conifers are also suitable for growing in containers, and will add height and interest to patios, terraces and roof gardens.

Year-round interest

Broadleaved evergreens, such as hollies (*Ilex*) and bay laurel (*Laurus nobilis*) provide a valuable green backdrop throughout the year, while the needle-like foliage and candle-like cones of conifers offer a useful contrast in shape and texture. Against this permanent display, plant deciduous trees for a seasonally changing palette of leaf colours, flowers and fruit. Japanese cherries (*Prunus*), crab apples (*Malus*) and magnolias have vivid spring flowers, while many trees have large dramatic leaves or colourful foliage that brightens up the summer garden. A few trees, such as *Maackia amurensis* and *Arbutus unedo*, bear flowers in late summer and autumn, but in the case of Japanese maples (*Acer*), the Chinese tupelo (*Nyssa sinensis*), and liquidambars, foliage colour in autumn is the main attraction; they produce luminous colours that set the garden ablaze.

Stem and bark colour is a key feature of winter displays. The bleached white trunks of birches (*Betula*), glossy copper stems of *Prunus serrula*, and shaggy bark of *Acer griseum* provide focal points, while the dainty pink flowers of *Prunus* x *subhirtella* 'Autumnalis' lift winter days.

ABOVE **Spring benefits**
The profusion of large, double pink flowers of *Prunus serrulata* 'Kiku-shidare-sakura', makes a dramatic and colourful focal point in a spring garden.

PLANTING A CONTAINER-GROWN TREE

It is worth taking the time to prepare the site and plant your tree well, as this will increase its chances of survival, and ensure that it thrives. Trees that have been grown in containers can be planted at most times of the year, but the warm, damp soil in autumn provides ideal conditions. Bare-root trees are cheaper and available from autumn to late winter. Plant them as soon as you get them home, unless the soil is frozen.

1 Break up the soil Dig a hole twice the width of the pot and the same depth as the tree's root ball. Do not dig over the bottom of the hole as this may cause the tree to sink once planted. Instead, use a fork to puncture the base and sides.

2 Check planting depth Remove the tree from its pot and put it in the hole. Use a cane to check that the top of the rootball is at the same level or slightly above the soil. Lift out the plant and cut away any roots that are circling the rootball.

3 Firm in Tease out the roots, lower the tree back into the hole, and water it well. Then water again as you backfill the hole to ensure there are no air pockets and the roots are in no danger of drying out. Firm the tree in gently.

4 Stake the tree To prevent the tree from rocking in the wind, which can damage the roots, drive in a wooden tree stake with a mallet at an angle of 45 degrees. Make sure that the stake does not damage the root ball.

5 Fit the tree ties Ensure that the top of the stake faces into the prevailing wind. Fit a tree tie with a spacer one third of the way up the trunk from the base. Knock a nail through the tree tie into the stake to stop it from slipping down.

6 Continue to water in well Water the tree well and apply a moisture-conserving bark mulch over the area around the tree, leaving a space clear around the stem to prevent the bark rotting it. Water the tree during dry spells for two years.

BARE-ROOT TREES

If the ground is frozen when you receive your bare-root trees or you are unable to plant them immediately, find a patch of unfrozen soil or fill a large pot with compost and heel them in. This simply means burying the roots to keep them moist. Plant the trees in the same way as shown here for container-grown plants, but take care to leave no air pockets when filling in around the roots with soil.

SPRING

WHITE

Davidia involucrata (Dove tree, Ghost tree, Pocket handkerchief tree)
Deciduous, conical tree with heart-shaped, vivid green leaves, felted beneath. Large, white bracts appear on mature trees from late spring.

Populus x canescens (Grey poplar)
Vigorous, deciduous, spreading tree with slightly lobed leaves, grey when young, glossy, dark green in summer and yellow in autumn. Usually bears greyish-red catkins in spring.

RED

Acer platanoides 'Crimson King'
Vigorous, deciduous, spreading tree. Leaves are large, lobed and deep reddish-purple, turning orange in autumn. Tiny, red-tinged, deep yellow flowers are carried in mid-spring.

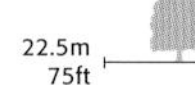

Aesculus x carnea 'Briotii'
Deciduous, round-headed tree. Leaves, consisting of 5 or 7 leaflets, are glossy, dark green. Panicles of red flowers are borne in late spring.

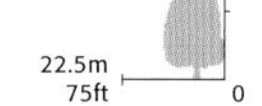

YELLOW

Fraxinus excelsior 'Jaspidea'
Vigorous, deciduous, spreading tree grown for its golden-yellow twigs and black buds, which are most evident in winter. Yellow leaves, with 9–11 oval leaflets, fade to light green and then gold, in autumn.

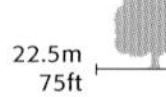

Acer macrophyllum (Oregon maple)
Deciduous, round-headed tree with large, deeply lobed, dark green leaves that turn yellow and orange in autumn. Yellowish-green flowers in spring are followed by pale green fruits.

30m 100ft
22.5m
75ft
0

SUMMER

WHITE

Aesculus chinensis (Chinese horse-chestnut)
Slow-growing, deciduous, spreading tree. Leaves are glossy, dark green with 7 leaflets. Slender spires of white flowers are produced in mid-summer.

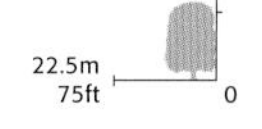

Populus alba (Abele, White poplar)
Deciduous, spreading tree with wavy-margined or lobed leaves, dark green above, white beneath, turning yellow in autumn.

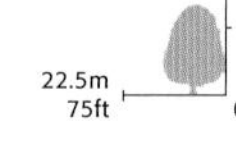

Liriodendron tulipifera (Tulip tree)
Vigorous, deciduous, spreading tree. Deep green leaves, with a cut-off or notched tip and lobed sides, turn yellow in autumn. In mid-summer, has tulip-shaped, orange-marked, greenish-white flowers.

30m 100ft
22.5m
75ft
0

Populus maximowiczii
Fast-growing, deciduous, conical tree. Oval, heart-shaped, bright green leaves have green-veined, white undersides and turn yellow in autumn. Bears long, pendent seed heads surrounded by silky, white hairs in late summer.

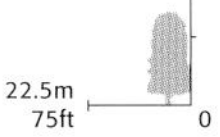

***Castanea sativa* 'Albomarginata'**
Deciduous, spreading tree. Has glossy, white-edged, dark green leaves that turn yellow in autumn. Spikes of creamy-yellow flowers in summer are followed by edible fruits in autumn.

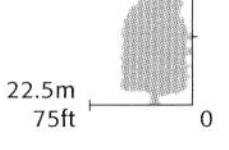

PURPLE

***Fagus sylvatica* 'Rohanii'**
Slow-growing, deciduous tree with oval, deeply cut, deep red-purple leaves, sometimes tinged with green or brown. Leaf margins are deeply cut into triangular teeth, which may bear serrations. Leaf veins and leaf stalk are prominently red.

***Fagus sylvatica* 'Riversii'**
Fast-growing, deciduous, spreading tree with smooth, grey bark and elliptic, wavy-margined, dark purple leaves, which are larger than those of the species. New leaves on young shoots are wine-red and translucent.

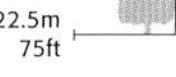

GREEN

***Populus x canadensis* 'Serotina de Selys'**
Fast-growing, deciduous, upright tree. Has broadly oval, grey-green leaves, pale green when young, and red catkins in spring.

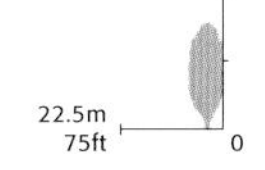

Quercus macranthera
(Caucasian oak)
Deciduous, spreading, stout-branched, handsome tree with large, deeply lobed, dark green leaves.

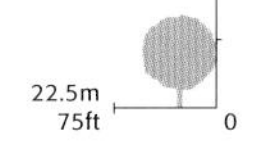

Alnus incana (Grey alder)
Deciduous, conical tree useful for cold, wet areas and poor soils. Yellow-brown catkins are carried in late winter and early spring, followed by oval, dark green leaves.

GREEN

***Populus* x *canadensis* 'Robusta'**
Fast-growing, deciduous, conical tree with upright branches. Broadly oval, bronze, young leaves mature to glossy, dark green. Bears long, red catkins in spring.

30m 100ft
22.5m 75ft 0

Quercus robur* f. *fastigiata
Deciduous, upright, columnar tree of dense habit carrying lobed, dark green leaves.

Quercus muehlenbergii
Deciduous, round-headed tree with sharply toothed, bright green leaves.

30m 100ft
22.5m 75ft 0

Celtis australis (Nettle tree)
Deciduous, spreading tree. Has oval, pointed, sharply toothed, dark green leaves and small, purple-black fruits.

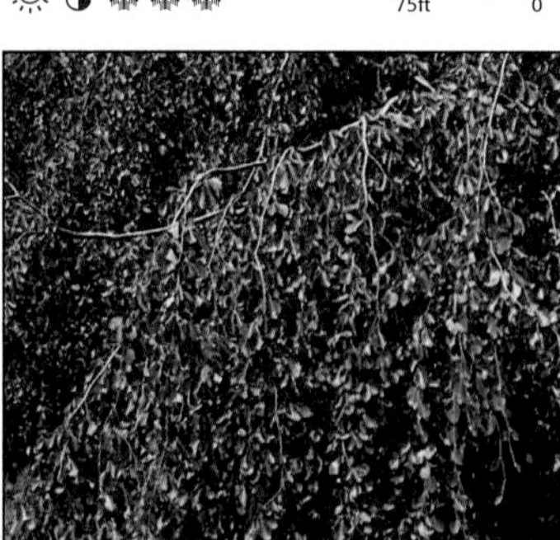

Fagus sylvatica* f. *pendula
(Weeping beech)
Deciduous, weeping tree with oval, wavy-edged, mid-green leaves that in autumn take on rich hues of yellow and orange-brown.

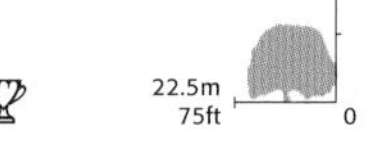

Acer cappadocicum* subsp. *lobelii
(Lobel's maple)
Deciduous tree of narrow, upright habit, well-suited for growing in restricted space. Has wavy-edged, lobed leaves that turn yellow in autumn.

Quercus canariensis (Algerian oak, Mirbeck's oak)
Deciduous or semi-evergreen tree, narrow when young, broadening with age. Large, shallowly lobed, rich green leaves become yellowish-brown in autumn, often persisting into late winter.

30m 100ft
22.5m 75ft 0

Juglans regia (Walnut)
Deciduous tree with a spreading head. Leaves, usually with 5 or 7 leaflets, are aromatic, bronze-purple when young, glossy, mid-green when mature. Produces edible nuts.

Populus nigra 'Italica'
(Lombardy poplar)
Very fast-growing, deciduous, narrowly columnar tree with erect branches, diamond-shaped, bright green leaves and red catkins in mid-spring.

Acer saccharinum (Silver maple)
Fast-growing, deciduous, spreading tree, often with pendent branches. Deeply lobed, sharply toothed, mid-green leaves, with silver undersides, turn yellow in autumn.

Tilia oliveri
Deciduous, spreading, open tree with pointed, heart-shaped leaves, bright green above and silvery-white beneath. Produces small, fragrant, greenish-yellow flowers in summer, followed by winged fruits.

Juglans nigra (Black walnut)
Fast-growing, deciduous, handsome, spreading tree with large, aromatic leaves of many pointed, glossy, dark green leaflets. Produces edible nuts in autumn.

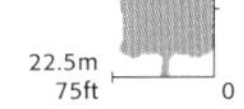

Ailanthus altissima (Tree of heaven)
Fast-growing, deciduous, spreading tree with clusters of small, green flowers in mid-summer, followed by winged, green, then reddish-brown fruits. Large, dark green leaves are divided into paired, oval leaflets.

Quercus petraea 'Columna'
Deciduous, upright, slender tree with large, wavy-edged, leathery, dark green leaves, tinged bronze when young.

Tilia platyphyllos 'Rubra'
(Red-twigged lime)
Deciduous, spreading tree with red winter shoots and rounded, dark green leaves. Bears small, dull yellowish-white flowers in mid-summer.

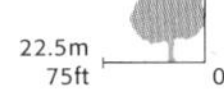

Platanus x hispanica (London plane)
Vigorous, deciduous, spreading tree with ornamental, flaking bark. Has large, sharply lobed, bright green leaves. Spherical fruit clusters hang from shoots in autumn.

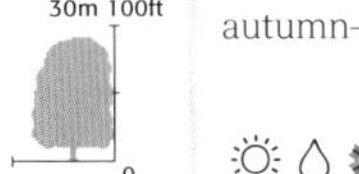

Platanus orientalis (Oriental plane)
Vigorous, deciduous, spreading tree with flaking, grey, brown or cream bark and large, glossy, pale green leaves with 5 deep lobes. Green fruit clusters, later turning brown, persist in autumn–winter.

Nothofagus obliqua (Roblé, Southern beech)
Fast-growing, deciduous, elegant tree with slender, arching branches. Has deep green leaves that turn orange and red in autumn.

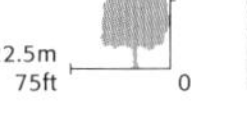

Quercus nigra (Water oak)
Deciduous, spreading tree with glossy, bright green foliage retained until well into winter.

GREEN

Sassafras albidum
Deciduous, upright, later spreading tree. Aromatic, glossy, dark green leaves vary from oval to deeply lobed and turn yellow or red in autumn. Has insignificant, yellowish-green flowers in spring.

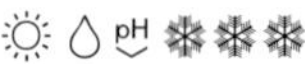
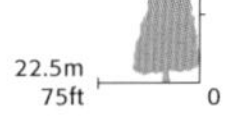

Quercus castaneifolia
Deciduous, spreading tree with sharply toothed leaves, glossy, dark green above, grey beneath.

Fagus sylvatica **(Common beech)**
Deciduous, spreading tree with oval, wavy-edged leaves. These are pale green when young, mid- to dark green when mature, and turn rich yellow and orange-brown in autumn, when nuts are produced.

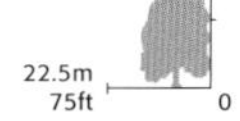

Quercus frainetto **(Hungarian oak)**
Fast-growing, deciduous, spreading tree with a large, domed head and handsome, large, deeply lobed, dark green leaves.

Fagus sylvatica **'Aspleniifolia' (Fern-leaved beech)**
Fast-growing, deciduous, spreading tree. Has narrow, deeply cut, deep green leaves, which give a soft feathery outline to the tree. In autumn, leaves turn golden-brown and persist well into winter.

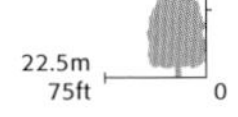

Tilia **'Petiolaris' (Pendent silver lime)**
Deciduous, spreading tree with pendent branches. Pointed, heart-shaped leaves, dark green above, silver beneath, shimmer in the breeze. Has fragrant, creamy-yellow flowers in late summer.

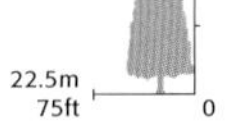

Zelkova carpinifolia **(Caucasian elm)**
Deciduous tree with a short, stout trunk from which many upright branches arise to make an oval, dense crown. Produces oval, sharply toothed, dark green leaves, turning to orange-brown in autumn.

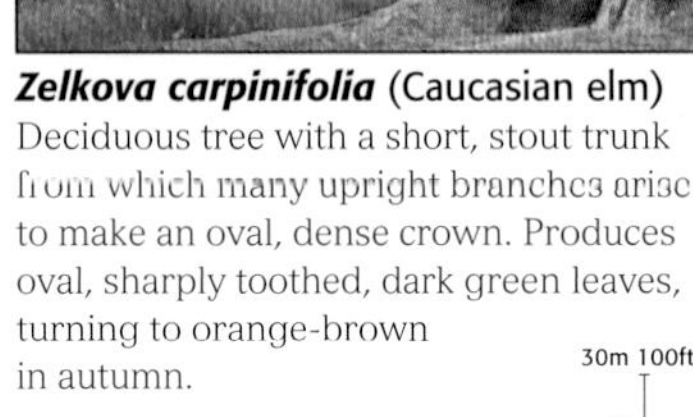

Quercus laurifolia
Deciduous, round-headed tree with narrow, glossy, bright green leaves, bronze-tinged when young, that are retained until late in the year.

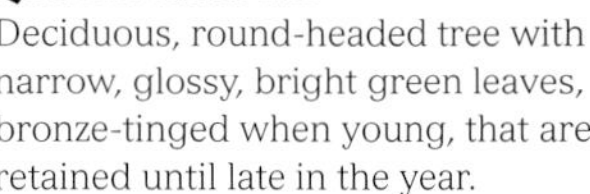

Nothofagus x alpina **(Rauli, Southern beech)**
Fast-growing, deciduous, conical tree. Leaves, with many impressed veins, are dark green, turning orange and red in autumn.

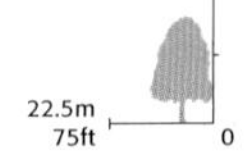

YELLOW

RED

***Liriodendron tulipifera* 'Aureomarginatum'**
Vigorous, deciduous tree. Deep green leaves have yellow margins, cut-off or notched tips and lobed sides. Bears cup-shaped, greenish-white flowers, splashed orange, in summer on mature trees.

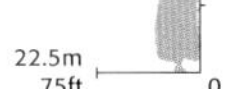

Quercus rubra (Red oak)
Fast-growing, deciduous, spreading tree. Attractively lobed leaves, often large, are deep green becoming reddish- or yellowish-brown in autumn.

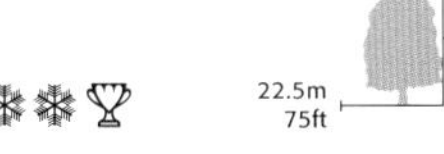

Acer pseudoplatanus* f. *erythrocarpum
Vigorous, deciduous, spreading tree with lobed, deep green leaves. Wings of young autumn fruits are bright red.

Quercus ellipsoidalis
Deciduous, spreading tree with deeply lobed, glossy, dark green leaves that turn dark purplish-red, then red in autumn.

Pterocarya x rehderiana
Very fast-growing, deciduous, spreading tree. Has glossy, bright green leaves consisting of narrow, paired leaflets that turn yellow in autumn and long catkins of winged fruits in late summer and autumn.

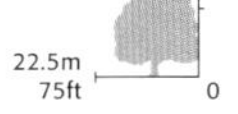

Liquidambar styraciflua (Sweet gum)
Deciduous, conical to spreading tree. Shoots develop corky ridges. Lobed, glossy, dark green leaves turn brilliant orange, red and purple in autumn.

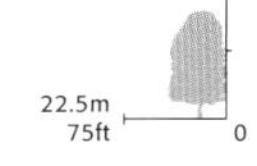

Quercus coccinea (Scarlet oak)
Deciduous, round-headed tree. Glossy, dark green leaves have deeply cut lobes ending in slender teeth. In autumn, they turn bright red, usually persisting for several weeks on the tree.

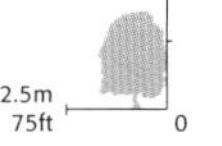

RED

Acer rubrum (Red maple)
Deciduous, round-headed tree. Dark green leaves turn bright red in autumn, producing best colour on acid or neutral soil. In spring, bare branches are covered with tiny, red flowers.

Prunus serotina (Black cherry, Wild rum cherry)
Deciduous, spreading tree. Spikes of fragrant, white flowers appear in early summer followed by red fruits that turn black in autumn. Glossy, dark green leaves become yellow in autumn.

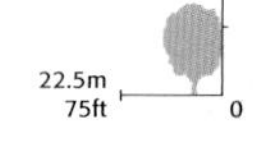

***Acer rubrum* 'Scanlon'**
Deciduous, upright tree. Has lobed, dark green foliage that in autumn becomes bright red, particularly on acid or neutral soil. Clusters of small, red flowers decorate bare branches in spring.

***Fraxinus angustifolia* 'Raywood'** (Claret ash)
Vigorous, deciduous, spreading tree. Leaves have 5–7 narrowly oval, glossy, dark green leaflets that mature to bright reddish-purple in autumn.

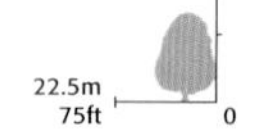

Cercidiphyllum japonicum (Katsura)
Fast-growing, deciduous, spreading tree. Leaves, bronze when young, turn rich green, then yellow to purple in autumn, especially on acid soil. Fallen leaves smell of burnt toffee.

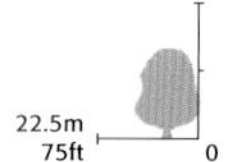

Nyssa sylvatica (Black gum, Tupelo)
Deciduous, broadly conical tree with oval, glossy, dark to mid-green leaves that turn brilliant yellow, orange and red in autumn.

Quercus alba (American white oak)
Deciduous, spreading tree. Deeply lobed, glossy, dark green leaves turn reddish-purple in autumn.

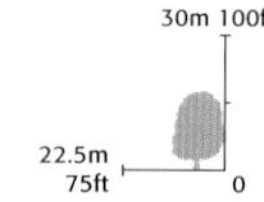

***Acer rubrum* 'Schlesingeri'**
Deciduous, round-headed tree. In early autumn, dark green leaves turn deep red. Tiny, red flowers appear on bare wood in spring.

Quercus palustris (Pin oak)
Fast-growing, deciduous, spreading tree with slender branches, pendulous at the tips. Deeply lobed, glossy, bright green leaves turn scarlet or red-brown in autumn.

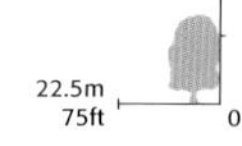

YELLOW

***Acer platanoides* 'Palmatifidum'**
Vigorous, deciduous, spreading tree. Deeply divided, pale green leaves with slender lobes turn yellow or reddish-orange in autumn. Tiny, yellow flowers appear in mid-spring.

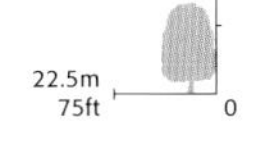

Quercus phellos (Willow oak)
Deciduous, spreading tree of elegant habit. Narrow, willow-like, pale green leaves turn yellow then brown in autumn.

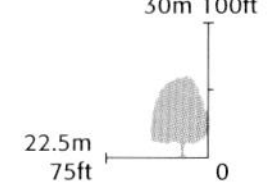

Zelkova serrata
Deciduous, spreading tree with sharply toothed, finely pointed, dark green leaves that turn yellow or orange in autumn.

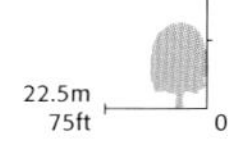

Juglans ailantifolia* var. *cordiformis
Deciduous, spreading tree with large, aromatic leaves consisting of many glossy, bright green leaflets. Long, yellow-green, male catkins are borne in early summer. In autumn has edible nuts.

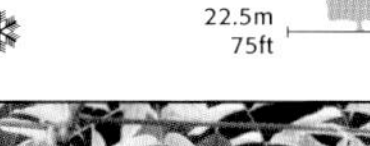

Gymnocladus dioica (Kentucky coffee tree)
Slow-growing, deciduous, spreading tree with small, star-shaped, white flowers borne in early summer. Large leaves, with pairs of oval leaflets, are pink when young, green in summer, then yellow in autumn.

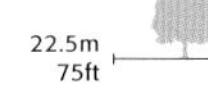

Prunus avium (Gean, Wild cherry)
Deciduous, spreading tree with red-banded bark. Has sprays of white flowers in spring, deep red fruits and dark green leaves that turn red and yellow in autumn.

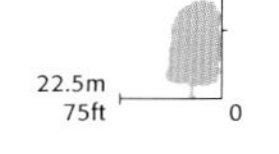

***Sophora japonica* 'Violacea'**
Fast-growing, deciduous, round-headed tree. Large sprays of pea-like, white flowers, tinged with lilac-pink, appear in late summer and early autumn.

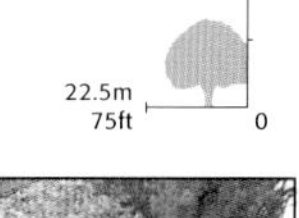

Carya ovata (Shag-bark hickory)
Deciduous tree with flaking, grey bark. Has dark green leaves, usually consisting of 5 slender leaflets, that turn golden-yellow in autumn.

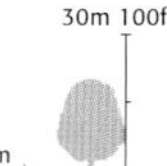

WHITE

Betula papyrifera (Canoe birch, Paper birch)
Vigorous, deciduous, open-branched, round-headed tree with peeling, shiny, white bark, yellowish catkins in spring and oval, coarsely serrated leaves that turn clear yellow in autumn.

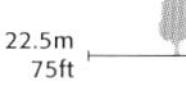

Eucalyptus dalrympleana (Mountain gum)
Vigorous, evergreen tree. Creamy-white, young bark becomes pinkish-grey, then peels. Leaves are long, narrow and pendent. Clusters of white flowers appear in late summer and autumn.

WHITE

***Betula pendula* 'Tristis'**
(Weeping birch)
Deciduous, slender, elegant tree with a strongly weeping habit and white bark. Oval, bright green leaves, with toothed margins, provide excellent golden colour in autumn.

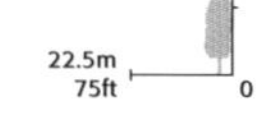

Eucalyptus coccifera (Tasmanian snow gum)
Evergreen tree with peeling, blue-grey and white bark and aromatic, pointed, grey-green leaves. Bears clusters of white flowers, with numerous stamens, in summer.

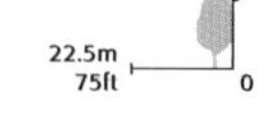

GREEN

Eucalyptus gunnii (Cider gum)
Evergreen, conical tree with peeling, cream, pinkish and brown bark. Leaves are silver-blue when young, blue-green when mature. Clusters of white flowers, with numerous stamens, appear in mid-summer.

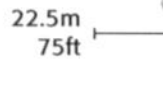

Eucalyptus johnstonii
Fast-growing, evergreen tree with peeling, red to blue-green bark. Leaves are round and apple-green when young and spear-shaped, dark green and glossy when mature. Clusters of white flowers are followed by small, urn-shaped, seed capsules.

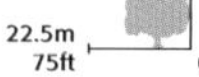

Quercus* x *turneri
Semi-evergreen, rounded, dense tree. Lobed, leathery, dark green leaves fall just before new foliage appears in spring.

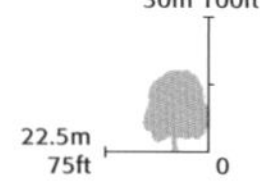

Nothofagus dombeyi
Evergreen, loosely conical tree of elegant habit with shoots that droop at the tips. Leaves are sharply toothed, glossy and dark green.

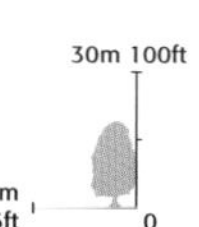

***Quercus* x *hispanica* 'Lucombeana'**
(Lucombe oak)
Semi-evergreen, spreading tree with toothed leaves, glossy, dark green above, grey beneath.

Nothofagus betuloides
Evergreen, columnar tree with dense growth of oval, glossy, dark green leaves on bronze-red shoots.

Nothofagus menziesii (Silver beech)
Evergreen, conical tree with silvery-white bark when young. Produces tiny, rounded, sharply toothed, glossy, dark green leaves.

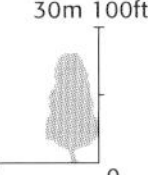

GREEN/YELLOW

Umbellularia californica
(Californian laurel)
Evergreen, spreading tree with aromatic, leathery, glossy, dark green leaves and creamy-yellow flowers in late spring. Pungent leaves may cause nausea and headache when crushed.

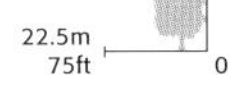

Salix alba* var. *vitellina
(Golden willow)
Deciduous, spreading tree, usually cut back hard to promote growth of strong, young shoots that are bright orange-yellow in winter. Lance-shaped, mid-green leaves appear in spring.

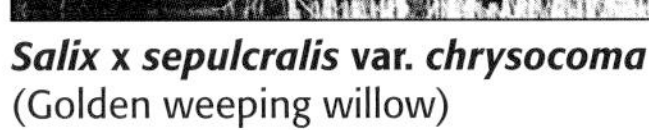

Salix x sepulcralis* var. *chrysocoma
(Golden weeping willow)
Deciduous tree with slender, yellow shoots falling to the ground as a curtain. Yellow-green, young leaves mature to mid-green.

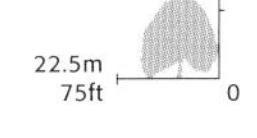

WHITE

Malus baccata* var. *mandschurica
Vigorous, deciduous, spreading tree with dark green leaves and a profusion of white flowers in clusters in mid-spring, followed by long-lasting, small, red or yellow crab apples.

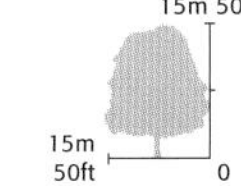

Malus hupehensis (Hupeh crab)
Vigorous, deciduous, spreading tree. Has deep green leaves, large, fragrant, white flowers, pink in bud, from mid- to late spring, followed by small, red-tinged, yellow crab apples in late summer and autumn.

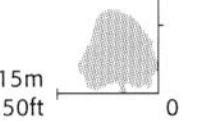

Salix daphnoides (Violet willow)
Fast-growing, deciduous, spreading tree. Has lance-shaped, glossy, dark green leaves, silver, male catkins in spring and purple shoots with bluish-white bloom in winter.

MAGNOLIAS

A mature magnolia in full bloom makes a spectacular sight in spring. Most magnolias are elegant in habit and though slow-growing, eventually form imposing trees and shrubs. The flowers are generally saucer-, star- or goblet-shaped and often have a subtle fragrance. Colours range from pure white, white flushed or stained with pink or purple, to pink and rich red-purple. The genus includes some evergreen, summer-flowering species. These, and cultivars that are not fully hardy, are best planted against a sunny wall. Some magnolias prefer acid or neutral soil, but most tolerate any soil provided it is humus-rich. Plenty of organic matter should be dug into the soil before planting. Avoid planting in exposed sites, as the the flowers can be damaged by frosts.

M. 'Vulcan'

M. *sprengeri* var. *diva*

M. BLACK TULIP ('Jurmag1')

M. *grandiflora* 'Exmouth' 🏆

M. 'Galaxy' 🏆

M. *stellata* 'Rosea'

M. 'Ann' 🏆

M. x *loebneri* 'Leonard Messel' 🏆

M. x *soulangeana* 'Rustica Rubra' 🏆

M. 'Elizabeth' 🏆

M. 'Pinkie' 🏆

M. *stellata* 'Waterlily' 🏆

M. *campbellii* subsp. *mollicomata*

M. 'Butterflies'

M. *wilsonii* 🏆

M. *liliiflora* 'Nigra' 🏆

M. x *brooklynensis* 'Yellow Bird'

WHITE

***Prunus avium* 'Plena'**
Deciduous, spreading tree with reddish-brown bark and masses of double, pure white flowers in spring. Dark green foliage turns red in autumn.

15m 50ft

Halesia monticola
(Silver bell, Snowdrop tree)
Fast-growing, deciduous, conical or spreading tree. Masses of pendent, bell-shaped, white flowers appear in late spring before leaves, followed by 4-winged fruits in autumn.

15m 50ft

PINK

***Malus* 'Profusion'**
Deciduous, spreading tree. Dark green foliage is purple when young. Cup-shaped, deep purplish-pink flowers are freely borne in late spring, followed by small, red-purple crab apples in late summer and autumn.

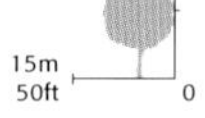

15m 50ft

***Prunus padus* 'Watereri'**
Deciduous, spreading tree with elliptic, matt, dark green leaves. Bears long, stiff racemes of cup-shaped, almond-scented, white flowers, to 20cm (8in) long, in late spring, followed by small, pea-shaped, black fruits, bitter to the taste.

15m 50ft

Michelia doltsopa
Evergreen, rounded tree with oval, glossy, dark green leaves, paler beneath. Strongly scented, magnolia-like flowers, with white to pale yellow petals, appear in winter–spring.

15m 50ft

Melia azedarach
(Bead tree, Persian lilac)
Deciduous, spreading tree. Has dark green leaves with many leaflets and fragrant, star-shaped, pinkish-lilac flowers in spring, followed by pale orange-yellow fruits in autumn.

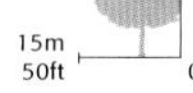

15m 50ft

Fraxinus ornus **(Manna ash)**
Deciduous, round-headed tree. Has deep green leaves with 5–9 leaflets. Panicles of scented, creamy-white flowers appear in late spring and early summer.

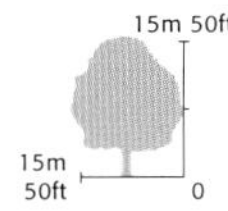

15m 50ft

Prunus mahaleb
Deciduous, round-headed, bushy tree that bears a profusion of fragrant, cup-shaped, white flowers from mid- to late spring. Rounded, glossy, dark green leaves turn yellow in autumn.

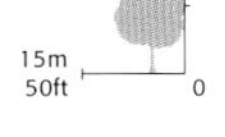

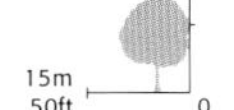

15m 50ft

***Pyrus calleryana* 'Chanticleer'**
Deciduous, conical tree with glossy leaves that turn purplish in autumn. Sprays of small, white flowers appear in spring. Resists fireblight.

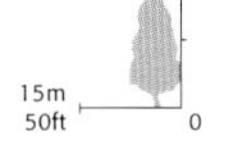

15m 50ft

Prunus jamasakura **(Hill cherry)**
Deciduous, spreading tree bearing cup-shaped, white or pink flowers from mid- to late spring. Oval leaves, bronze when young, mature to deep green.

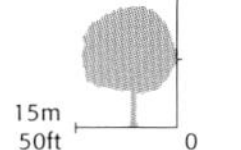

15m 50ft

PINK

***Prunus* 'Kanzan'**
Deciduous, vase-shaped tree. Large, double, pink to purple flowers are borne profusely from mid- to late spring amid bronze, young leaves that mature to dark green.

15m 50ft
15m 50ft 0

***Magnolia* 'Heaven Scent'**
Vigorous, deciduous tree or shrub with fragrant, vase-shaped flowers, each with usually 9 petals that are pink outside, white within, borne from mid-spring to early summer. Leaves are broadly elliptic and glossy green.

15m 50ft
15m 50ft 0

***Aesculus x neglecta* 'Erythroblastos'**
Deciduous, spreading tree. Leaves with 5 leaflets emerge bright pink, turn yellow, then dark green, and finally orange and yellow in autumn. May bear panicles of flowers in summer.

15m 50ft
15m 50ft 0

***Paulownia tomentosa* (Foxglove tree, Princess tree)**
Deciduous, spreading tree. Has large, lobed, mid-green leaves and terminal sprays of fragrant, foxglove-like, pinkish-lilac flowers in spring.

15m 50ft
15m 50ft 0

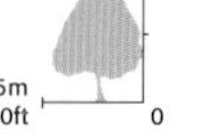

***Prunus padus* 'Colorata'**
Deciduous, spreading tree, conical when young. Produces pendent racemes of fragrant, cup-shaped, pink flowers in late spring, followed by small, black fruits. Oval, purple young leaves mature to dark green and turn red or yellow in autumn.

15m 50ft
15m 50ft 0

YELLOW

***Quercus rubra* 'Aurea'**
Slow-growing, deciduous, spreading tree. Large, lobed leaves are clear yellow when young, becoming green by mid-summer. Produces best colour in an open but sheltered position.

15m 50ft
15m 50ft 0

***Gleditsia triacanthos* 'Sunburst'**
Deciduous, spreading tree with fern-like, glossy foliage that is golden-yellow when young, deep green in summer.

15m 50ft
15m 50ft 0

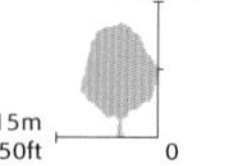

WHITE

Styrax japonicus
Deciduous, spreading tree bearing in early summer a profusion of pendent, fragrant, bell-shaped, white flowers amid glossy, dark green foliage.

15m 50ft
15m 50ft 0

***Ostrya virginiana* (American hop hornbeam, Ironwood)**
Deciduous, conical tree with dark brown bark and deep green leaves, yellow in autumn. Has yellowish catkins in spring, followed by greenish-white fruit clusters.

15m 50ft
15m 50ft 0

Catalpa speciosa
Deciduous, spreading tree. Heads of large, white flowers marked with yellow and purple are borne in mid-summer among glossy, mid-green leaves.

15m 50ft
15m 50ft 0

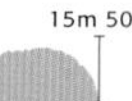

Eucryphia cordifolia (Ulmo)
Evergreen, columnar tree bearing oblong, wavy-edged, dull green leaves, with grey down beneath. Large, saucer-shaped, white flowers are produced in late summer and autumn.

Pterostyrax hispida (Epaulette tree)
Deciduous, spreading tree or shrub with aromatic, grey bark and oblong to oval, mid-green leaves, 20cm (8in) long. Large, drooping panicles of small, bell-shaped, white flowers are borne from early to mid-summer.

***Acer pseudoplatanus* 'Simon Louis Frères'**
Deciduous, spreading tree. Young leaves are marked with creamy-white and pink; older foliage is pale green with white markings.

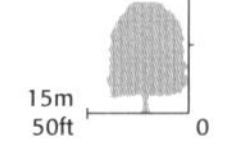

***Aesculus indica* 'Sydney Pearce'**
Deciduous, spreading tree with glossy, dark green leaves, bronze when young and orange or yellow in autumn. Pinkish-white flowers, marked red and yellow, appear from early to mid-summer.

Catalpa bignonioides
(Indian bean tree)
Deciduous, spreading tree. Large, light green leaves are purplish when young. White flowers marked with yellow and purple appear in summer, followed by long, cylindrical, pendent pods.

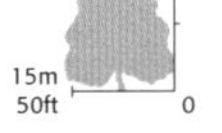

Drimys winteri (Winter's bark)
Evergreen, conical, sometimes shrubby tree with long, glossy, pale or dark green leaves, usually bluish-white beneath. Bears clusters of fragrant, star-shaped, white flowers in early summer.

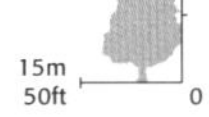

Toona sinensis
Deciduous, spreading tree with shaggy bark when old. Dark green leaves with many leaflets turn yellow in autumn. Bears fragrant, white flowers in mid-summer. Shoots are onion-scented.

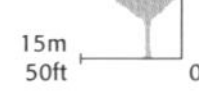

Catalpa fargesii* f. *duclouxii
Deciduous, broadly columnar tree grown for its bell-shaped, foxglove-like, delicate pink flowers, from early to mid-summer, followed by long, pendulous seed pods. Has large, heart-shaped, bright green leaves ending in a long point.

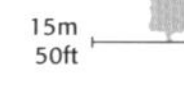

***Quercus cerris* 'Argenteovariegata'**
Deciduous, spreading tree. Strongly toothed or lobed, glossy, dark green leaves are edged with creamy-white.

***Eucryphia x nymansensis* 'Nymansay'**
Evergreen, columnar tree. Some of the leathery, glossy, dark green leaves are simple, others consist of 3 (rarely 5) leaflets. Clusters of large, white flowers open in late summer or early autumn.

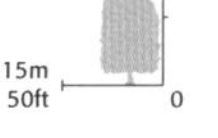

Sorbus pseudohupehensis
Deciduous, spreading tree with leaves of 4–8 pairs of blue-green leaflets turning orange-red in late autumn. White flowers in spring are followed by long-lasting, pink fruits.

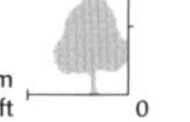

GREEN

Broussonetia papyrifera (Paper mulberry)
Deciduous, round-headed tree. Dull green leaves are large, broadly oval, toothed and sometimes lobed. In early summer, small globes of purple flowers appear on female plants.

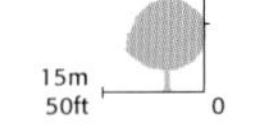

Hovenia dulcis (Raisin-tree)
Deciduous, spreading tree with large, glossy, dark green leaves. In summer it may bear small, greenish-yellow flowers, the stalks of which become red, fleshy and edible.

Fraxinus velutina (Arizona ash)
Deciduous, spreading tree. Leaves vary but usually consist of 3 or 5 narrow, velvety, grey-green leaflets.

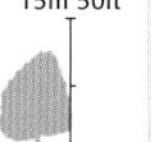

Meliosma veitchiorum
Deciduous, spreading tree with stout, grey shoots and large, dark green, red-stalked leaves with 9 or 11 leaflets. Small, fragrant, white flowers in late spring are followed by violet fruits in autumn.

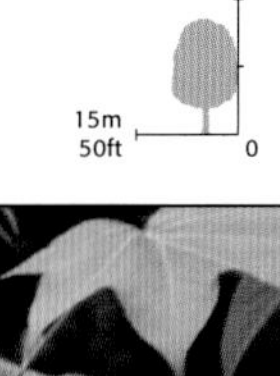

Quercus garryana (Oregon oak)
Slow-growing, deciduous, spreading tree with deeply lobed, glossy, bright green leaves.

***Populus tremula* 'Pendula'** (Weeping aspen)
Vigorous, deciduous, weeping tree. Leaves, reddish when young, grey-green in summer and yellow in autumn, tremble in the wind. Has purplish catkins in late winter and spring.

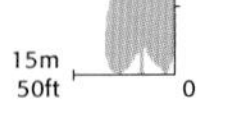

***Acer negundo* 'Variegatum'**
Fast-growing, deciduous, spreading tree. Has pinkish- then white-margined, bright green leaves with 3 or 5 leaflets. Inconspicuous, greenish-yellow flowers appear in late spring.

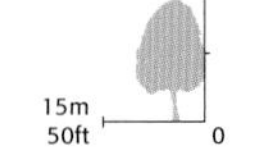

Kalopanax septemlobus
Deciduous, spreading tree with spiny stems, large, 5–7-lobed, glossy, dark green leaves and umbels of small, white flowers, then black fruits in autumn.

***Tilia cordata* 'Rancho'**
Deciduous, conical, dense tree, spreading when young. Has small, oval, glossy, dark green leaves, and clusters of small, fragrant, cup-shaped, yellowish flowers are borne in mid-summer.

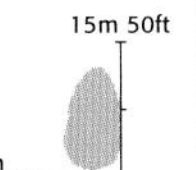

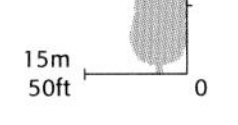

Phellodendron chinense
Deciduous, spreading tree. Aromatic leaves, with 7–13 oblong leaflets, are dark green, turning yellow in autumn. Pendent racemes of greenish flowers in early summer are followed on female trees by berry-like, black fruits.

Idesia polycarpa
Deciduous, spreading tree with large, heart-shaped, glossy, dark green leaves on long stalks. Small, fragrant, yellow-green flowers in mid-summer are followed in autumn, on female plants, by red fruits hanging in clusters.

Quercus marilandica **(Black Jack oak)**
Deciduous, spreading tree. Large leaves, 3-lobed at the apex, are glossy, dark green above, paler beneath, and turn yellow, red or brown in autumn.

Gleditsia japonica
Deciduous, conical tree with a trunk armed with spines. Shoots are purplish when young. Fern-like leaves consist of many small, mid-green leaflets.

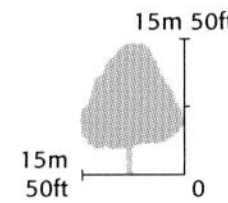

Quercus macrocarpa **(Bur oak)**
Slow-growing, deciduous, spreading tree. Large, oblong-oval, lobed, glossy, dark green leaves turn yellow or brown in autumn.

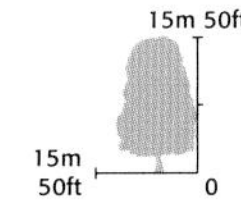

***Alnus glutinosa* 'Imperialis'**
Slow-growing, deciduous, conical tree with rounded, deeply cut, lobed leaves, bright yellow until mid-summer, later becoming pale green. Produces yellow-brown catkins in early spring. Is useful grown in a boggy area.

TREES

Emmenopterys henryi
Deciduous, spreading tree. Large, pointed, dark green leaves are bronze-purple when young. Clusters of white flowers (some bearing a large, white bract) are rarely produced except in hot summers.

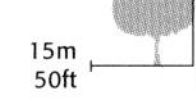

Quercus ithaburensis* subsp. *macrolepis
Deciduous or semi-evergreen, spreading tree. Has grey-green leaves with angular lobes.

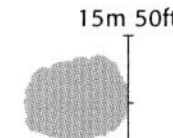
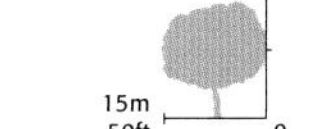

SUMMER

YELLOW

***Catalpa bignonioides* 'Aurea'**
Deciduous, spreading tree with broadly oval, bright yellow leaves, bronze when young. Bell-shaped, white flowers, marked with yellow and purple, borne in summer, are followed by long, pendent, cylindrical pods, often persisting after leaf fall.

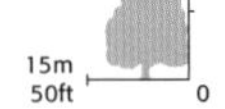

***Ulmus minor* 'Dicksonii'** (Cornish golden elm, Dickson's golden elm)
Slow-growing, deciduous, conical tree of dense habit. Carries small, broadly oval, bright golden-yellow leaves.

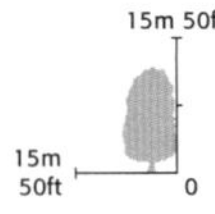

***Robinia pseudoacacia* 'Frisia'**
Deciduous, spreading tree with luxuriant leaves divided into oval leaflets, golden-yellow when young, greenish-yellow in summer and orange-yellow in autumn.

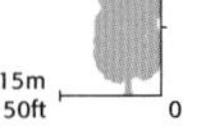

AUTUMN

RED

Acer rufinerve (Snake-bark maple)
Deciduous tree with arching branches striped green and white. In autumn, lobed, dark green leaves turn brilliant red and orange.

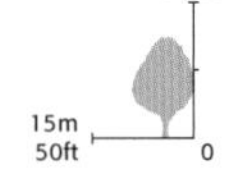

Oxydendrum arboreum (Sorrel tree)
Deciduous, spreading tree with glossy, dark green foliage that turns bright red in autumn. Sprays of white flowers appear in late summer and autumn.

***Acer rubrum* 'Columnare'**
Deciduous, slender, upright tree with lobed, dark green foliage becoming a fiery column of red and yellow in autumn.

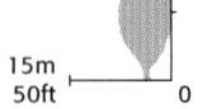

***Acer davidii* 'Madeline Spitta'**
Deciduous tree with upright branches that are striped green and white. Glossy, dark green foliage turns orange in autumn after the appearance of winged, green fruits that ripen reddish-brown.

Stewartia monadelpha
Deciduous, spreading tree with peeling bark and glossy, dark green leaves that turn orange and red in autumn. Small, violet-anthered, white flowers appear in mid-summer, followed by small fruits.

Aesculus flava (Sweet buckeye, Yellow buckeye)
Deciduous, spreading tree. Glossy, dark green leaves, with 5 or 7 oval leaflets, redden in autumn. Has yellow flowers in late spring and early summer followed by round fruits (chestnuts).

Acer henryi
Deciduous, spreading tree. Dark green leaves with 3 oval, toothed leaflets turn bright orange and red in autumn.

Prunus sargentii (Sargent cherry)
Deciduous, spreading tree. Oval, dark green leaves are red when young, turning brilliant orange-red in early autumn. Clusters of blush-pink flowers appear in mid-spring.

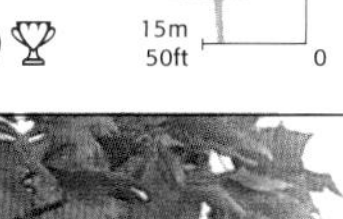

Acer capillipes (Snake-bark maple)
Deciduous, spreading tree. Has lobed, bright green leaves that turn brilliant red and orange in autumn. Older branches are striped green and white.

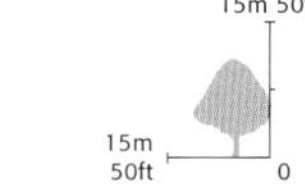
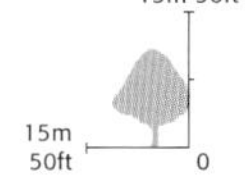

Malus tschonoskii
Deciduous, conical tree with broadly oval, glossy, mid-green leaves that turn brilliant shades of orange, red and purple in autumn. Single, pink-tinged, white flowers, in late spring, are followed by red-flushed, yellowish-green crab apples.

***Acer japonicum* 'Vitifolium'**
Vigorous, deciduous, bushy tree or large shrub with large, rounded, lobed, mid-green leaves that turn a vivid red, orange and purple in autumn.

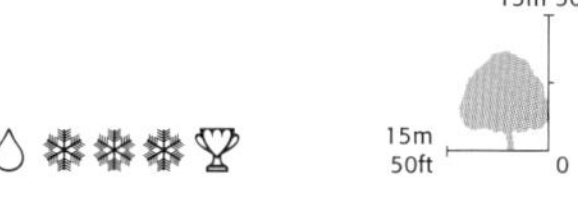

Nyssa sinensis
Deciduous, spreading tree. Has long, narrow, pointed leaves that are purplish when young, dark green when mature and brilliant scarlet in autumn.

***Acer saccharum* 'Temple's Upright'**
Deciduous, columnar tree. In autumn, large, lobed leaves turn brilliant orange and red.

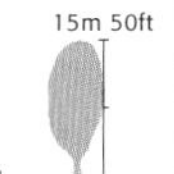

Quercus* x *heterophylla
(Bartram's oak)
Deciduous, spreading tree with toothed, glossy, bright green leaves that turn orange-red and yellow in autumn.

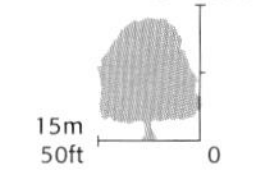

Parrotia persica (Persian ironwood)
Deciduous, spreading, short-trunked tree with flaking, grey and fawn bark. Rich green leaves turn yellow, orange and red-purple in autumn. Small, red flowers are borne on bare wood in early spring.

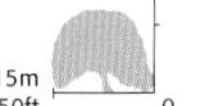

ORNAMENTAL BARK

Of the many ornamental features offered by trees, including flowers, fruit, and foliage, it is probably bark that makes the greatest impact in a garden. This is partly because bark is not transient, and offers interest every day of the year and throughout the mature life of the tree. Chosen carefully, trees with ornamental bark can lighten up the darkest corner and provide superb contrast to other plants. While maple (*Acer*), birch (*Betula*), and cherry (*Prunus*) are obvious choices, there are many other species with stunning, textured or coloured bark, such as the patterned stems of eucalyptus and *Stewartia*. Some trees display their colourful bark from an early age, others may take a few years to develop – but the end result is well worth waiting for.

Stewartia pseudocamellia 🏆

Pinus bungeana

***Acer palmatum* 'Sango-kaku'** 🏆

***Betula utilis* var. *jacquemontii* 'Grayswood Ghost'** 🏆

Eucalyptus pauciflora* subsp. *niphophila 🏆

Pinus sylvestris 🏆

Luma apiculata 🏆

Acer grosseri

Acer griseum 🏆

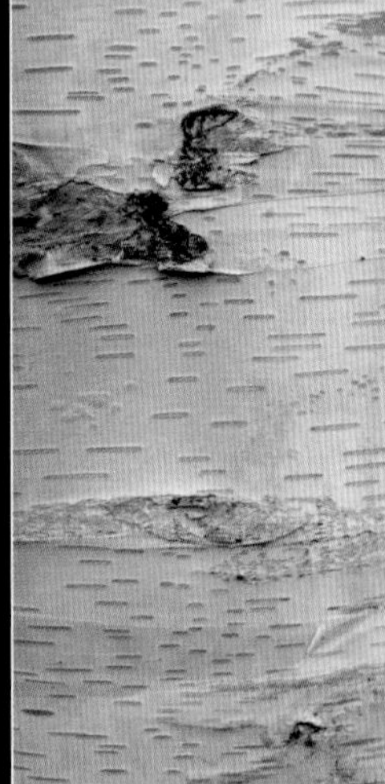

***Betula utilis* var. *jacquemontii* 'Jermyns'** 🏆

Acer davidii

Betula albosinensis 🏆

Prunus serrula 🏆

Betula ermanii

Quercus suber

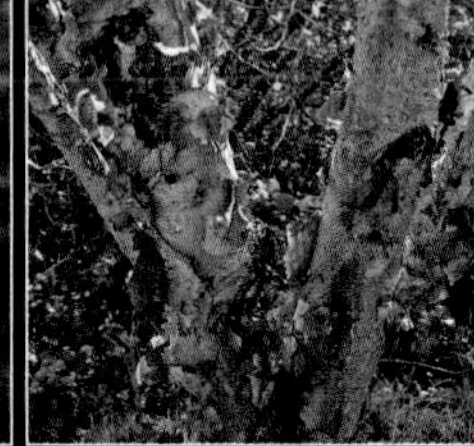

Betula nigra

***Acer pensylvanicum* 'Erythrocladum'**

AUTUMN

YELLOW

Betula lenta (Cherry birch)
Deciduous, broadly spreading tree that gives off a sweet fragrance when leaves, shoots or bark are crushed. Has dark red bark with purple flakes. Oval, mid-green leaves, to 12cm (5in) long, fleetingly turn vibrant gold in autumn.

Cladrastis kentukea (Yellow wood)
Deciduous, round-headed tree. Leaves of 7 or 9 rounded-oval leaflets are dark green, turning yellow in autumn. Clusters of fragrant, pea-like, yellow-marked, white flowers appear in early summer.

Fagus sylvatica 'Dawyck'
Deciduous, narrowly columnar tree with upward-sweeping branches and oval, lime-green leaves, which darken as the season progresses, before turning a rich copper colour in autumn. The tree's form tends to 'broaden out' in maturity.

Fraxinus excelsior 'Pendula'
Deciduous tree with slender, weeping branches, forming a spreading, umbrella-like canopy. Has dull green leaves with 9–11 oval, shallowly toothed leaflets. Most trees are grafted onto *F. excelsior* at 3–5m (10–16ft) above the ground.

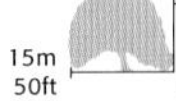

Acer pensylvanicum (Snake-bark maple)
Deciduous, upright tree. Shoots are boldly striped green and white. Large, lobed, mid-green leaves turn bright yellow in autumn.

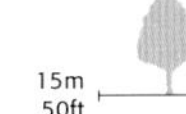

ALL YEAR

GREEN

Arbutus x andrachnoides
Evergreen, bushy, spreading tree with peeling, reddish-brown bark and glossy, dark green foliage. Clusters of small, white flowers in autumn to spring are followed by small, strawberry-like, orange or red fruits.

Eucalyptus pauciflora (White Sally)
Evergreen, spreading tree with peeling, white, young bark and red, young shoots. In summer, white flower clusters appear amid glossy, bright grey-green foliage.

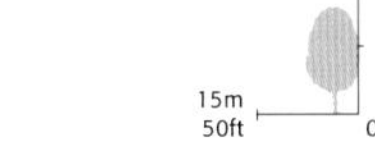

Trochodendron aralioides
Evergreen, broadly conical tree with glossy, dark green foliage. In late spring and early summer bears clusters of unusual, petal-less, wheel-like, green flowers.

GREEN

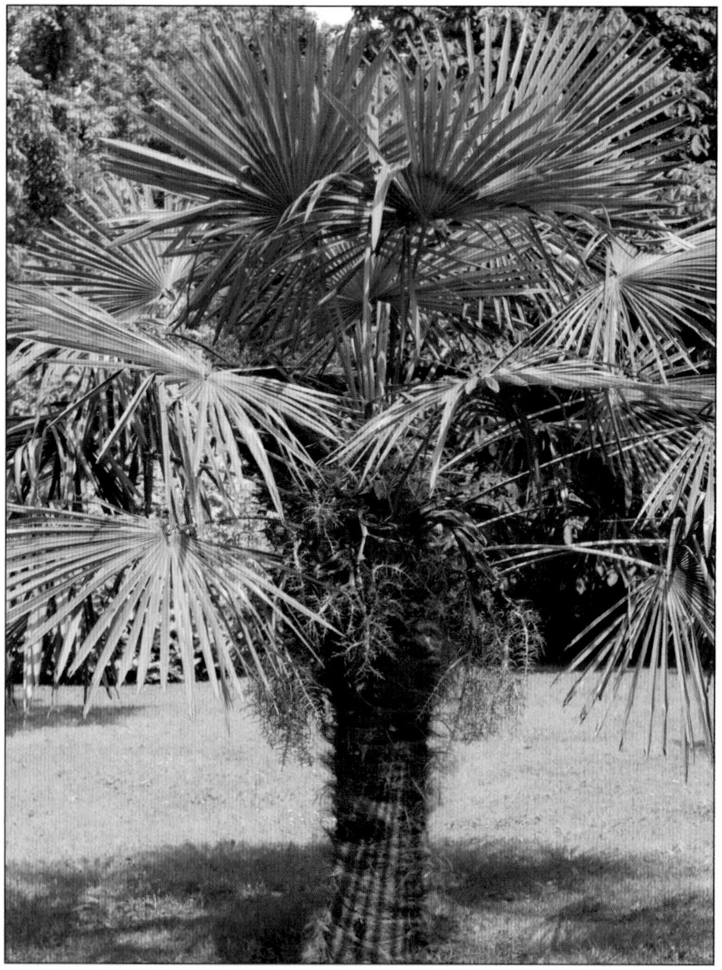

Trachycarpus fortunei
(Chusan palm, Windmill palm)
Evergreen palm with unbranched stem and a head of large, deeply divided, fan-like, mid-green leaves. Sprays of fragrant, creamy-yellow flowers appear in early summer.

Quercus agrifolia
(Californian live oak)
Evergreen, spreading tree bearing rigid, spiny-toothed, glossy, dark green leaves.

WHITE

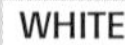

Crataegus flava (Yellow haw)
Deciduous, spreading tree. Has small, dark green leaves and white flowers in late spring and early summer, followed by greenish-yellow fruits.

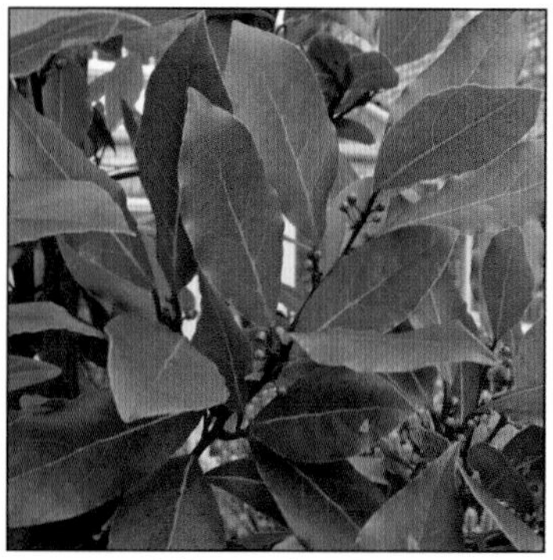

Laurus nobilis (Bay laurel, Sweet bay)
Evergreen, broadly conical tree with narrowly oval, leathery, very aromatic, glossy, dark green leaves. Has small, star-shaped, pale yellow flowers in spring, followed by spherical to egg-shaped, green then black fruits.

Crataegus orientalis
Deciduous, spreading tree with deeply lobed, hairy, dark green leaves. A profusion of white flowers in late spring or early summer is followed by red fruits tinged with yellow.

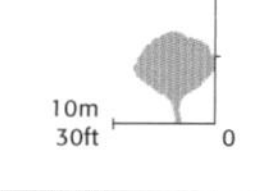

Quercus myrsinifolia
Evergreen, rounded tree with narrow, pointed, glossy, dark green leaves, reddish-purple when young.

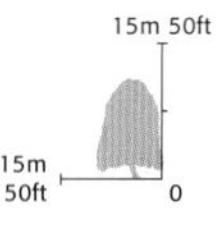

Jubaea chilensis
(Chilean wine palm, Coquito)
Slow growing, evergreen palm with a massive trunk and large, silvery-green leaves. Has small, maroon and yellow flowers in spring and woody, yellow fruits in autumn.

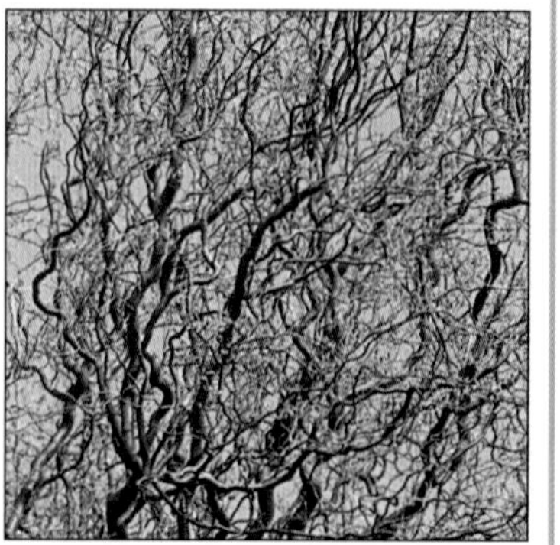

Salix babylonica var. _pekinensis_ 'Tortuosa' (Dragon's-claw willow)
Fast growing, deciduous, spreading tree with curiously twisted shoots and contorted, narrow, tapering, bright green leaves.

Mespilus germanica (Medlar)
Deciduous, spreading tree or shrub. Has dark green leaves that turn orange-brown in autumn, white flowers in spring–summer and brown fruits in autumn, edible when half rotten.

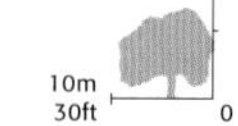

***Prunus* 'Shogetsu'**
Deciduous, round-topped tree. In late spring, pink buds open to large, double, white flowers that hang in clusters from long stalks. Mid-green leaves turn orange and red in autumn.

10m 30ft
10m 30ft 0

***Malus* 'Snowcloud'**
Deciduous, compact tree of upright habit, with oval, bronze leaves that turn dark green. In spring, pink flower buds open to produce masses of semi-double to double, long-lasting, white flowers, followed in late summer by yellow fruits.

10m 30ft
10m 30ft 0

Aesculus californica
(California buckeye)
Deciduous, spreading, sometimes shrubby tree. Dense heads of fragrant, sometimes pink-tinged, white flowers appear in spring and early summer. Small, dark green leaves have 5–7 leaflets.

10m 30ft
10m 30ft 0

Prunus incisa (Fuji cherry)
Deciduous, spreading tree. White or pale pink flowers appear in early spring. Sharply toothed, dark green leaves are reddish when young, orange-red in autumn.

10m 30ft
10m 30ft 0

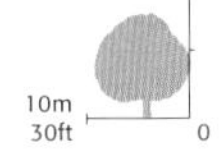

Amelanchier laevis
Deciduous, spreading tree or large shrub. Oval, bronze, young leaves turn dark green in summer, red and orange in autumn. Sprays of white flowers in spring are followed by rounded, fleshy, red fruits.

10m 30ft
10m 30ft 0

WHITE

***Prunus* 'Taihaku'** (Great white cherry)
Vigorous, deciduous, spreading tree. Very large, single, pure white flowers are borne in mid-spring among bronze-red, young leaves that mature to dark green.

***Prunus* 'Ukon'**
Vigorous, deciduous, spreading tree. Semi-double, pale greenish-white flowers open from pink buds in mid-spring amid pale bronze, young foliage that later turns dark green.

***Prunus* 'Shirotae'**
Deciduous, spreading tree with slightly arching branches. Large, fragrant, single or semi-double, pure white flowers appear in mid-spring. Foliage turns orange-red in autumn.

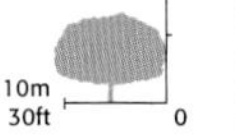

PINK

Prunus x yedoensis (Yoshino cherry)
Deciduous, round-headed tree with spreading, arching branches and dark green foliage. Sprays of pink buds open to white or pale pink flowers in early spring.

***Prunus* 'Spire'**
Deciduous, vase-shaped tree, conical when young. Soft pink flowers appear profusely from early to mid-spring. Dark green leaves, bronze when young, turn brilliant orange-red in autumn.

***Prunus* 'Hokusai'**
Deciduous, spreading tree. Oval, bronze, young leaves mature to dark green, then turn orange and red in autumn. Semi-double, pale pink flowers are borne in mid-spring.

***Prunus* 'Pandora'**
Deciduous tree, upright when young, later spreading. Massed, pale pink flowers appear in early spring. Leaves are bronze when young, dark green in summer and often orange and red in autumn.

Malus x arnoldiana
Deciduous, low, spreading tree with arching branches. In mid- to late spring red buds open to fragrant, pink flowers that fade to white. Bears small, red-flushed, yellow crab apples in autumn. Leaves are oval.

***Prunus* 'Yae-murasaki'**
Deciduous, spreading tree with bright green leaves, bronze when young, orange-red in autumn. Semi-double, deep pink flowers are produced in mid-spring.

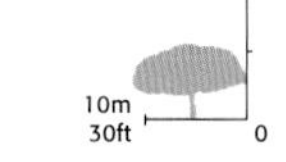

***Prunus pendula* 'Stellata'**
Deciduous, spreading tree. Pink flowers with narrow, pointed petals, red in bud, open from early to mid-spring. Dark green leaves turn yellow in autumn.

***Prunus* 'Accolade'**
Deciduous, spreading tree with clusters of deep pink buds opening to semi-double, pale pink flowers in early spring. Toothed, mid-green leaves turn orange-red in autumn.

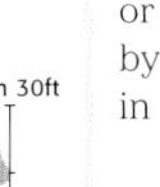

***Cercis siliquastrum* (Judas tree)**
Deciduous, spreading, bushy tree. Clusters of pea-like, bright pink flowers appear in mid-spring, before or with heart-shaped leaves, followed by long, purplish-red pods in late summer.

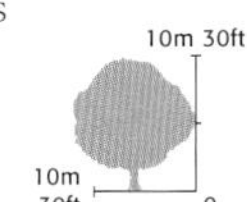

***Prunus* 'Kiku-shidare-zakura'**
Deciduous, weeping tree. Has double, bright pink flowers that cover pendent branches from mid- to late spring.

***Prunus* 'Shirofugen'**
Deciduous, spreading tree with bronze-red leaves turning orange-red in autumn. Pale pink buds open to fragrant, double, white blooms that turn pink before they fade in late spring.

***Prunus* x *subhirtella* 'Pendula Rubra'**
Deciduous, weeping tree that bears deep pink flowers in spring before oval, dark green leaves appear; these turn yellow in autumn.

***Prunus* 'Pink Perfection'**
Deciduous, upright tree that bears double, pale pink flowers in late spring. Oval leaves are bronze when young, dark green in summer.

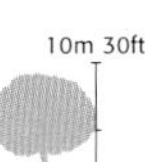

Malus* x *magdeburgensis
Deciduous, spreading tree with dark green foliage. Dense clusters of large, semi-double, deep pink flowers appear in late spring, occasionally followed by small, yellow crab apples in autumn.

***Prunus persica* 'Prince Charming'**
Deciduous, upright, bushy-headed tree with narrow, bright green leaves. Double, deep rose-pink flowers are produced in mid-spring.

PINK

Malus floribunda
Deciduous, spreading, dense-headed tree with pale pink flowers, red in bud, appearing from mid- to late spring, followed by tiny, pea-shaped, yellow crab apples in autumn.

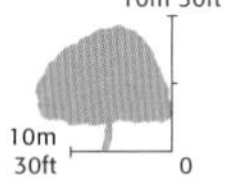

***Prunus* 'Pink Shell'**
Deciduous, spreading tree with oval, bronze-coloured leaves that turn bright green in early summer, then orange in autumn. In mid-spring, a profusion of fragrant, 5-petalled, single, long-stalked, shell-pink flowers cover the branches.

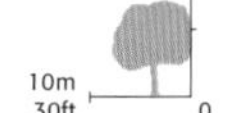

***Acer pseudoplatanus* 'Brilliantissimum'**
Slow-growing, deciduous, spreading tree. Lobed leaves are salmon-pink when young, then turn yellow and finally dark green in summer.

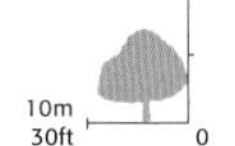

RED

***Crataegus laevigata* 'Paul's Scarlet'**
Deciduous, spreading tree. Has toothed, glossy, dark green leaves and a profusion of double, red flowers in late spring and early summer.

***Acacia baileyana* 'Purpurea'**
Evergreen, spreading tree with divided, fern-like, 2-pinnate, bronze-purple, young leaves that turn silver-grey later in spring. Racemes of sulphur-yellow flowers are produced from late winter to early spring. Is best grown against a wall.

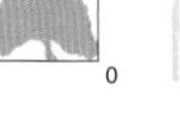

***Malus* 'Royalty'**
Deciduous, spreading tree with glossy, purple foliage. Crimson-purple flowers appear from mid- to late spring, followed by dark red crab apples in autumn.

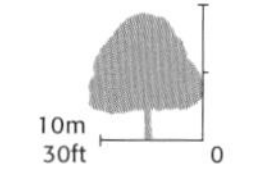

***Malus* 'Lemoinei'**
Deciduous, spreading tree. Oval leaves are deep reddish-purple when young, later becoming tinged with bronze. Wine-red flowers in late spring are followed by dark reddish-purple crab apples in autumn.

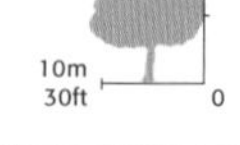

***Cercis canadensis* 'Forest Pansy'**
Deciduous, spreading tree or shrub. In mid-spring has flowers that are magenta in bud, opening to pale pink, before heart-shaped, reddish-purple leaves appear.

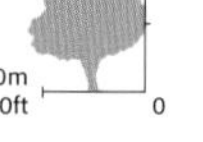

YELLOW

***Laburnum* x *watereri* 'Vossii'**
(Voss's laburnum)
Deciduous, spreading tree. Leaves, consisting of 3 leaflets, are glossy, deep green. Pendent chains of large, yellow flowers are borne in late spring and early summer.

Sophora tetraptera
Semi-evergreen, spreading tree or large shrub with dark green leaves composed of many tiny leaflets. Clusters of golden-yellow flowers appear in late spring.

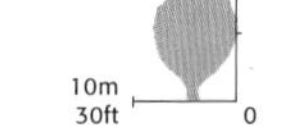

WHITE

Eucryphia lucida
Evergreen, upright, bushy tree with narrow, glossy, dark green leaves and fragrant, white flowers in early or mid-summer.

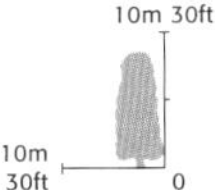
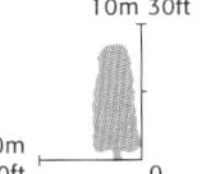
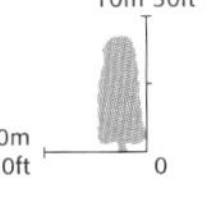

Eucryphia glutinosa
Deciduous, upright or spreading tree. Glossy, dark green leaves, consisting of 3–5 leaflets, turn orange-red in autumn. Large, fragrant, white flowers appear from mid- to late summer.

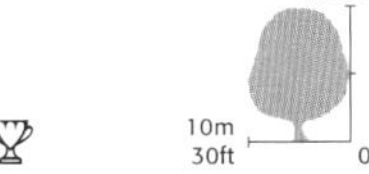

Hoheria lyallii
Deciduous, spreading tree with deeply toothed, grey-green leaves. Clusters of white flowers are borne in mid-summer.

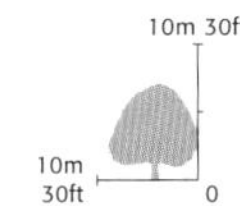

Acer crataegifolium 'Veitchii'
Deciduous, bushy tree with branches streaked with green and white. Small, pointed, dark green leaves, blotched with white and paler green, turn deep pink and reddish-purple in autumn.

Maackia amurensis
Deciduous, spreading tree with deep green leaves consisting of 7–11 leaflets. Dense, upright spikes of white flowers appear from mid- to late summer.

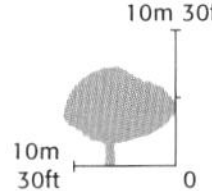

Hoheria angustifolia
Evergreen, columnar tree with narrow, dark green leaves. Shallowly cup-shaped, white flowers are borne from mid- to late summer.

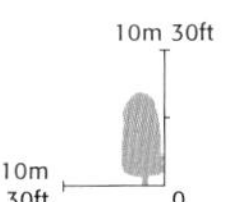

Cornus kousa
Deciduous, vase-shaped tree or shrub with oval, glossy, dark green leaves that turn bright red-purple in autumn. Large, white bracts, surrounding insignificant flowers, in early summer, are followed by strawberry-like fruits.

PINK

***Lagerstroemia indica* 'Seminale'**
Deciduous, compact, rounded tree bearing trusses of mid-pink flowers, with strongly waved petals, from mid-summer to early autumn. Narrowly oval to oblong, dark green leaves are bronze when young.

10m 30ft
10m 30ft 0

***Robinia* x *slavinii* 'Hilleri'**
Deciduous, round-headed tree. Pinnate, pea-green leaves, with 9 or 11 oval-shaped leaflets, turn yellow in autumn. In early summer, pea-like, lilac-pink flowers are borne in loose racemes. Branches are prone to wind damage.

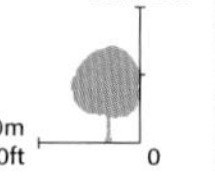

***Albizia julibrissin* (Silk tree)**
Deciduous, spreading tree. Large leaves are light to mid-green and divided into many leaflets. Clusters of brush-like, clear pink flowers appear in late summer or autumn.

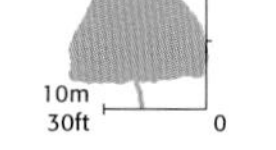

RED

***Aesculus pavia* 'Atrosanguinea'**
Deciduous, round-headed, sometimes shrubby tree. In summer, panicles of deep red flowers appear among glossy, dark green leaves, which have 5 narrow leaflets.

10m 30ft
10m 30ft 0

Embothrium coccineum
(Chilean firebush)
Evergreen or semi-evergreen, upright, suckering tree with lance-shaped, glossy, deep green leaves. Clusters of brilliant orange-red flowers are borne in late spring and early summer.

10m 30ft
10m 30ft 0

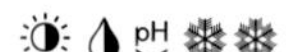

Malus yunnanensis* var. *veitchii
Deciduous, upright tree with lobed, heart-shaped leaves, covered with grey down beneath. Bears white, sometimes pink-tinged, flowers in late spring and a mass of small, red-flushed, brown crab apples in late summer and autumn.

***Prunus cerasifera* 'Nigra'**
Deciduous, round-headed tree with deep purple leaves, red when young. Pink flowers are borne in profusion from early to mid-spring.

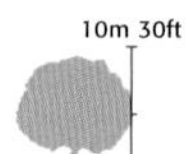

TREES

FLOWERING DOGWOODS

A genus of around 50 species of hardy plants, *Cornus* is perhaps best known for its shrubby dogwoods, such as *Cornus alba* 'Sibirica', which produce brightly coloured winter stems. However, the flowering trees within this genus have much to offer as they are highly ornamental, ideal for small gardens, and easy to grow – many accommodating of a wide range of soil types. The majority flower in late spring or early summer. Their 'flowers' consist of a rounded hub of tiny blooms, surrounded by showy petal-like bracts, up to 7.5cm (3in) across on some cultivars, which range in colour from pure white, cream, and yellow, to pink and red. In good summers, attractive, edible, strawberry-like fruits develop after flowering. Several species, such as *Cornus kousa*, also produce striking autumn leaf colour.

C. kousa **'National'**

C. kousa **'Miss Satomi'** 🏆

C. florida **'Cherokee Princess'**

C. alternifolia

C. nuttallii **'Monarch'**

C. florida **'Rainbow'**

C. florida **'Cherokee Chief'** 🏆

C. controversa

C. alternifolia **'Argentea'** 🏆①

C. 'Porlock' 🏆①

C. mas

C. kousa **var. *chinensis* 'China Girl'**

C. capitata

C. 'Eddie's White Wonder' 🏆①

C. kousa **var. *chinensis*** 🏆

C. mas **'Aureoelegantissima'**

GREEN

Pseudopanax ferox
Evergreen, upright tree with long, narrow, rigid, sharply toothed leaves that are dark bronze-green overlaid white or grey.

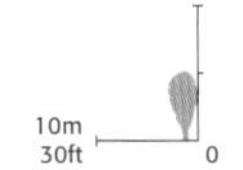

Ehretia dicksonii
Deciduous, spreading tree with stout, ridged branches and large, dark green leaves. Large, flattish heads of small, fragrant, white flowers are borne in mid-summer.

***Cydonia oblonga* 'Vranja'**
(Common quince)
Deciduous, spreading tree. Pale green leaves, grey-felted beneath, mature to dark green and set off large, white or pale pink flowers in late spring and, later, very fragrant, golden-yellow fruits.

Juglans microcarpa
(Little walnut, Texan walnut)
Deciduous, bushy-headed tree with large, aromatic leaves of many narrow, pointed leaflets that turn yellow in autumn.

***Betula pendula* 'Youngii'**
(Young's weeping birch)
Deciduous, weeping tree forming a mushroom-shaped dome of thread-like branchlets. Has triangular, serrated leaves and smooth, white bark that is fissured black at maturity.

***Pyrus salicifolia* 'Pendula'**
Deciduous, weeping, mound-shaped tree with white flowers in mid-spring and narrow, grey leaves.

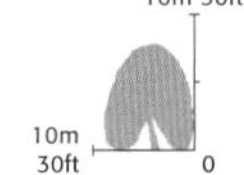

***Ulmus glabra* 'Camperdownii'**
Deciduous, strongly weeping tree with sinuous branches. Leaves are very large, rough and dull green.

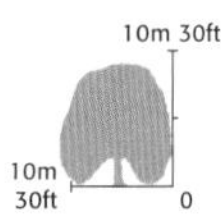

Acer carpinifolium (Hornbeam maple)
Deciduous tree of elegant habit, often with several main stems. Prominent-veined, hornbeam-like leaves turn golden-brown in autumn.

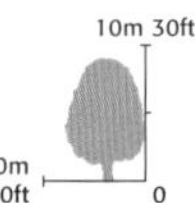

***Morus alba* 'Laciniata'**
(White mulberry)
Deciduous, spreading tree. Has rounded, deeply lobed, glossy leaves that turn yellow in autumn and bears edible, pink, red or purple fruits in summer.

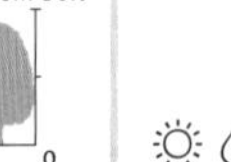

YELLOW

Paraserianthes lophantha
Fast-growing, deciduous, spreading tree. Has fern-like, dark green leaves comprising many leaflets. Creamy-yellow flower spikes appear in spring–summer.

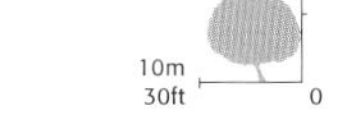

Laburnum alpinum
(Scotch laburnum)
Deciduous, spreading tree. Leaves consist of 3 leaflets and are glossy, dark green. Long, slender chains of bright yellow flowers appear in late spring or early summer.

Koelreuteria paniculata
(Golden-rain tree, Pride of India)
Deciduous, spreading tree with mid-green leaves, turning yellow in autumn. Bears sprays of yellow flowers in summer, followed by inflated, bronze-pink fruits.

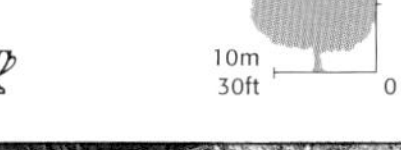

***Acer shirasawanum* 'Aureum'**
Deciduous, bushy tree or large shrub. Has rounded, many-lobed, pale yellow leaves.

Genista aetnensis
(Mount Etna broom)
Almost leafless, rounded tree with many slender, bright green branches and a profusion of fragrant, pea-like, golden-yellow flowers in mid-summer.

RED

***Cornus florida* 'Welchii'**
Deciduous, spreading tree. Bears white bracts, surrounding tiny flowers, in spring. Dark green leaves, edged with white and pink, turn red and purple in autumn.

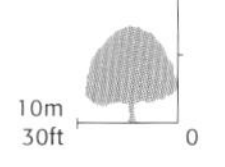

***Acer palmatum* 'Atropurpureum'**
Deciduous, bushy-headed shrub or small tree with lobed, reddish-purple foliage that turns brilliant red in autumn. Small, reddish-purple flowers are borne in mid-spring.

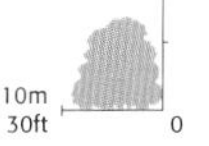

***Malus* 'Veitch's Scarlet'**
Deciduous, spreading tree with dark green foliage. Carries white flowers in late spring and crimson-flushed, scarlet crab apples in autumn.

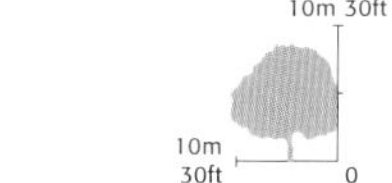

RED

Photinia davidiana
Evergreen, spreading tree or large shrub with narrow, glossy, dark green leaves, older ones turning red in autumn. Sprays of white flowers in early summer are followed by clusters of bright red fruits in autumn.

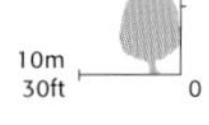

Malus prunifolia
Deciduous, spreading tree. Has dark green leaves and fragrant, white flowers in mid-spring. In autumn bears long-lasting, small, red or occasionally yellowish crab apples.

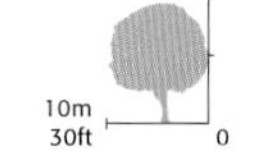

***Malus* 'Cowichan'**
Deciduous, spreading tree. Has dark green foliage, reddish-purple when young. Pink flowers appear in mid-spring, followed by reddish-purple crab apples.

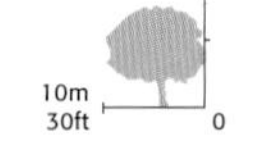

***Acer palmatum* 'Osakazuki'**
Deciduous, bushy-headed shrub or tree with large, 7-lobed, mid-green leaves that turn brilliant scarlet in autumn. Clusters of small, reddish-purple flowers are borne in mid-spring.

***Malus* 'Marshall Oyama'**
Deciduous, upright tree with dark green leaves. Pink-flushed, white flowers borne in late spring are followed by a profusion of large, rounded, crimson and yellow crab apples in autumn.

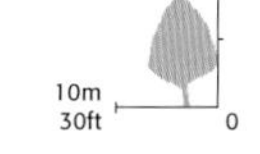

***Acer japonicum* 'Aconitifolium'**
Deciduous, bushy tree or large shrub. Deeply divided, mid-green leaves turn red in autumn. Reddish-purple flowers appear in mid-spring.

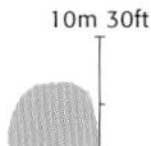

Acer tataricum* subsp. *ginnala
(Amur maple)
Deciduous, spreading tree or large shrub. Clusters of fragrant, creamy-white flowers are borne in early summer amid dainty, bright green leaves that turn red in autumn.

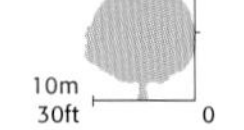

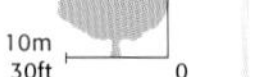

Rhus trichocarpa
Deciduous, spreading tree. Large, ash-like leaves with 13–17 leaflets are pinkish when young, dark green in summer and purple-red to orange in autumn. Bears pendent, bristly, yellow fruits.

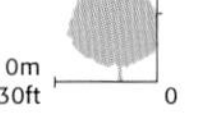

Crataegus pedicellata
Deciduous, spreading tree with sharply toothed, lobed, dark green leaves that turn orange and red in autumn. White flowers with red anthers in late spring are followed by bright red fruits in autumn.

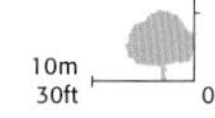

Acer triflorum
Slow-growing, deciduous, spreading tree with peeling, grey-brown bark. Leaves, composed of 3 leaflets, are dark green, turning brilliant orange-red in autumn. Clusters of tiny, yellow-green flowers appear in late spring.

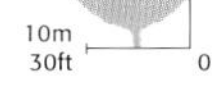

***Malus* 'Professor Sprenger'**
Deciduous, rounded, dense tree. Dark green leaves turn yellow in late autumn. White flowers, pink in bud, open from mid- to late spring and are followed by orange-red crab apples in autumn.

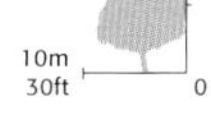

***Malus* 'John Downie'**
Deciduous tree, narrow and upright when young, conical when mature. White flowers, borne amid bright green foliage in late spring, are followed by large, edible, red-flushed, orange crab apples in autumn.

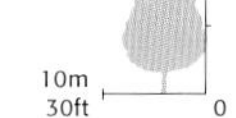

SORBUS

Comprising more than 100 hardy species, *Sorbus* includes a wide range of ornamental trees ideal for small to medium-sized gardens. They provide a year-round display of colour and interest, with fragrant corymbs of cream flowers, attractive, divided foliage, vibrant autumn colour, and decorative berry-like fruits that last well into winter on some species. Most members of this genus fall into one of two categories: the Aucuparia group, which has pinnate leaves like rowan (*Sorbus aucuparia*) and the Aria group that has rounded or oval leaves, such as whitebeam (*Sorbus aria*). Virtually all species are easy to grow, and thrive in full sun or dappled shade, and in well-drained fertile acid or alkaline soil , although species within the Aucuparia group are not long-lived on shallow chalk soils.

S. scalaris

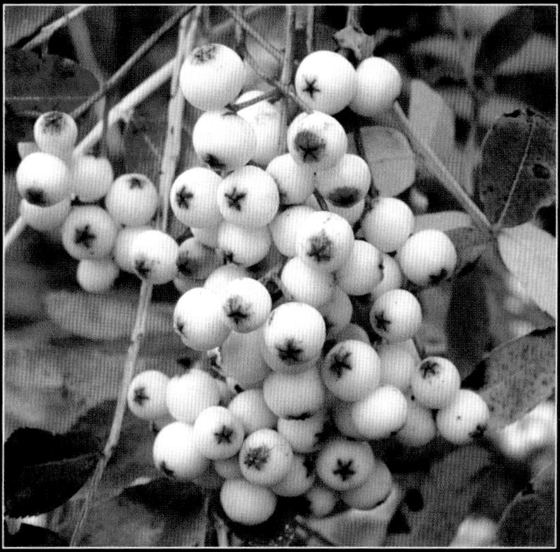

S. forrestii

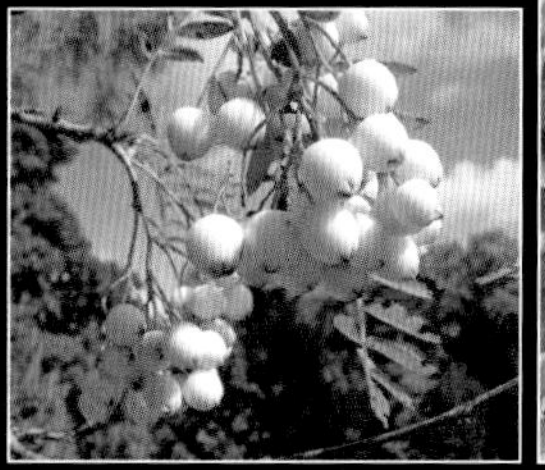

S. cashmiriana ♀ⓘ

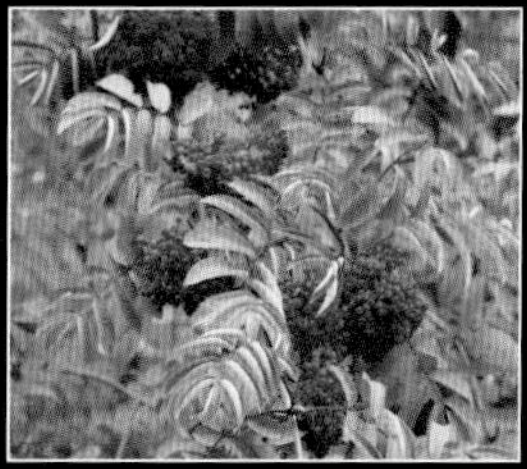

S. aucuparia ⓘ

S. x kewensis

S. commixta ⓘ

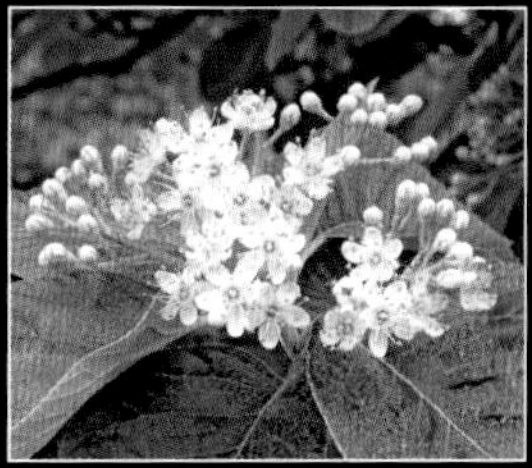

***S. thibetica* 'John Mitchell'** ♀ⓘ

S. vilmorinii ♀ⓘ

S. sargentiana ♀

S. intermedia

***S. aria* 'Lutescens'** ♀ⓘ

S. megalocarpa

S. esserteauana

YELLOW

Malus 'Golden Hornet'
Deciduous, spreading tree with dark green foliage and open cup-shaped, white flowers in late spring. In autumn, branches are weighed down by a profusion of golden-yellow crab apples.

Picrasma quassioides (Quassia)
Deciduous, spreading tree with glossy, bright green leaves, composed of 9–13 leaflets, that turn brilliant yellow, orange and red in autumn.

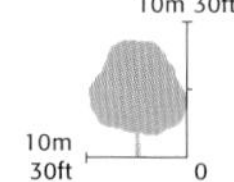

Acer laxiflorum
Deciduous, spreading tree with arching branches streaked with white and green. In late summer has pale red, winged fruits. Pointed, red-stalked, dark green leaves turn orange in autumn.

YELLOW

Acacia pravissima (Ovens wattle)
Evergreen, spreading, arching tree or shrub. Has triangular, spine-tipped, silver-grey phyllodes (flat, leaf-like stalks) and small heads of bright yellow flowers in late winter or early spring.

Acacia baileyana
Evergreen, spreading tree with divided, fern-like, 2-pinnate, silvery-grey or blue-grey leaves. From late winter to early spring produces masses of spherical, golden-yellow flower heads in dense, axillary racemes. Is best grown against a wall.

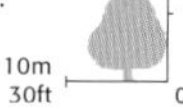

Ilex aquifolium 'Amber'
Evergreen, much-branched, conical, female tree with abundant, amber-yellow berries. Mid-green stems bear elliptic, usually entire, bright green leaves.

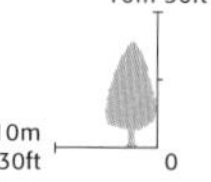

Carpinus betulus **'Fastigiata'**
Deciduous, erect tree, with a very distinctive flame-like outline that becomes more open with age. Oval, prominently veined, dark green leaves turn yellow and orange in autumn.

10m 30ft

10m 30ft 0

Lithocarpus henryi
Slow-growing, evergreen, broadly conical tree with glossy, pale green leaves that are long, narrow and pointed.

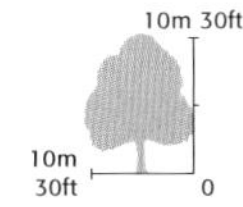

10m 30ft 0

Pittosporum eugenioides **'Variegatum'**
Evergreen, columnar tree. Wavy-edged, glossy, dark green leaves have white margins. Honey-scented, pale yellow flowers are borne in spring.

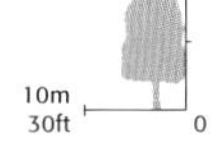

10m 30ft 0

Aralia elata **'Variegata'**
Deciduous tree or shrub with sparse, stout, prickly stems. Large, dark green leaves, with cream margins, are divided into numerous oval, paired leaflets. Billowing heads of tiny, white flowers, forming large panicles, are borne in late summer.

10m 30ft

10m 30ft 0

Arbutus unedo (Strawberry tree)
Evergreen, spreading tree or shrub with rough, brown bark and glossy, deep green leaves. Pendent, urn-shaped, white flowers appear in autumn–winter as previous season's strawberry-like, red fruits ripen.

10m 30ft

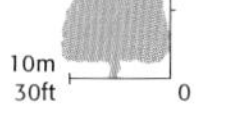

10m 30ft 0

HOLLIES

The common holly, *Ilex aquifolium*, is one of the best-known evergreen trees, but many other Ilex cultivars make attractive garden plants. In size they range from tall, specimen trees to small shrubs. Leaves may be smooth-edged or spiny and vary in colour, several having gold, yellow, cream, white or grey variegation. Small, often white, male and female flowers, borne on separate plants during summer, are followed by red, yellow or black berries. In almost all cases hollies are unisexual, that is the berries are borne on female plants, so to obtain fruits it is usually necessary to grow plants of both sexes. When choosing, don't rely on variety names to sex plants, *I. aquifolium* 'Silver Queen' is male. Hollies respond well to pruning and many may be clipped to form hedges.

***I. x altaclerensis* 'Camelliifolia Variegata'** ①

I. pernyi ①

***I. x koehneana* 'Chestnut Leaf'** 🏆

***I. crenata* 'Convexa'** 🏆①

***I. aquifolium* 'Argentea Marginata'** 🏆①

***I. aquifolium* 'Silver Queen'** 🏆①

***I. aquifolium* 'Madame Briot'** 🏆①

***I. aquifolium* 'Silver Milkmaid'** ①

***I. x altaclerensis* 'Belgica Aurea'** 🏆①

***I. aquifolium* 'Ferox Argentea'** 🏆

***I. x altaclerensis* 'Balearica'** ①

***I. x meserveae* BLUE PRINCESS ('Conapri')** ①

***I. aquifolium* 'Pyramidalis Aureomarginata'** ①

***I. x altaclerensis* 'Golden King'** 🏆

***I. aquifolium* 'Golden Milkboy'** ①

***I. aquifolium* 'Bacciflava'**

I. aquifolium 🏆①

I. verticillata ①

***I. x altaclerensis* 'Camelliifolia'** 🏆①

BLUE

Cedrus atlantica* f. *glauca
(Blue Atlas cedar)
Conical conifer with silvery-blue foliage that is very bright, especially in spring. Erect, cylindrical cones are produced in autumn. Is widely planted as a specimen tree.

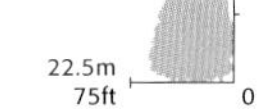

Cupressus cashmeriana
(Kashmir cypress)
Handsome, broadly conical conifer, spreading with age, with aromatic foliage borne in pendent, flat, glaucous blue sprays. Bears small, globose, dark brown, mature cones.

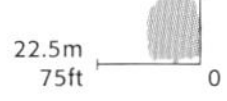

Pinus ayacahuite
(Mexican white pine)
Spreading conifer with weeping leaves made up of lax, blue-green needles, to 16cm (6in) long, in bundles of 5. Pendent cones are often covered with sticky, white resin and may grow 25cm (10in) long.

***Abies concolor* 'Argentea'**
Conical conifer with silvery foliage that contrasts well with dark grey bark. Oblong to ovoid, pale blue or green cones are 8–12cm (3–5in) long.

Pinus* x *holfordiana (Holford pine)
Broadly conical, open conifer with large cones, brown when ripe. Pendent, glaucous blue-green leaves are held in clusters of 5.

SILVER

Abies procera (Noble fir)
Narrowly conical conifer with smooth, silvery-grey bark and grey-green or bright blue-grey leaves. Produces stoutly cylindrical, green cones, 15–25cm (6–10in) long, that ripen to brown.

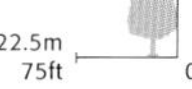

x *Cuprocyparis* 'Haggerston Grey'
Vigorous, upright, columnar conifer, tapering at the apex. Has smooth bark, becoming stringy with age, flat sprays of pointed, grey-green leaves, and dark brown female cones. A popular screening plant.

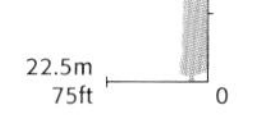

Pinus peuce (Macedonian pine)
Upright conifer, forming a slender pyramid. Has dense, grey-green foliage and cylindrical, green cones with white resin that ripen brown in autumn. Is an attractive tree that grows consistently well in all sites.

30m 100ft

22.5m 75ft 0

GREEN

***Chamaecyparis lawsoniana* 'Intertexta'**
Elegant, weeping conifer with aromatic, grey-green foliage carried in lax, pendulous sprays. Old trees become columnar with some splayed branches.

Wollemia nobilis **(Wollemi pine)**
Erect, bushy, conifer with narrowly oblong, pointed, needle-like, dark green leaves, and "bubbly", brown bark when mature. In winter, shoot tips are covered in a protective, white resin. Catkin-like female cones are borne on shoot tips.

Pinus strobus
(Eastern white pine, Weymouth pine)
Conifer with an open, sparse, whorled crown. Has grey-green foliage and cylindrical cones. Smooth, grey bark becomes fissured with age. Does not tolerate pollution.

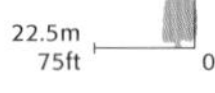

Metasequoia glyptostroboides
(Dawn redwood)
Fast-growing, deciduous, upright conifer with fibrous, reddish bark. Soft, blue-green leaves turn yellow, pink and red in autumn. Cones are globose to ovoid, 2cm (¾in) long.

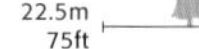

Pseudotsuga menziesii* var. *glauca
(Blue Douglas fir)
Fast-growing, conical conifer with thick, grooved, corky, grey-brown bark, aromatic, glaucous blue-green leaves, and sharply pointed buds. Cones have projecting, 3-pronged bracts.

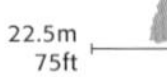

Pinus coulteri
(Big-cone pine, Coulter pine)
Fast-growing conifer with large, broadly ovoid, prickly cones, each 1–2kg (2–4½lb). Grey-green leaves in crowded clusters are sparsely set on branches. Grows in all soils, even heavy clays.

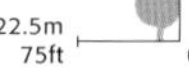

Cedrus deodara **(Deodar cedar)**
Fast-growing conifer, densely conical with weeping tips when young, broader when mature. Has spirally arranged, needle-like, grey-green leaves and barrel-shaped, glaucous cones, 8–12cm (3–5in) long, ripening to brown.

Abies veitchii **(Veitch fir)**
Upright conifer with dark green leaves, silvery beneath, and cylindrical, violet-blue cones.

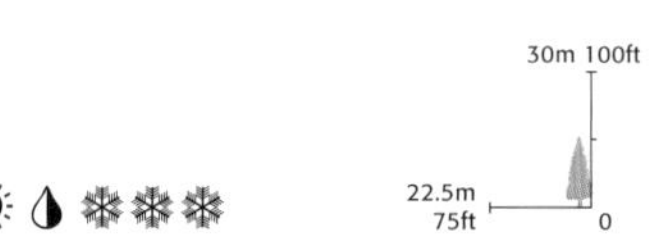

Pinus ponderosa
(Western yellow pine)
Conical or upright conifer, grown for its distinctive, deeply fissured bark, with smooth, brown plates, and bold greyish-green foliage. Bears ovoid, purplish-brown cones.

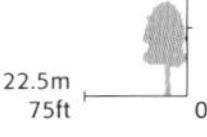

Pinus muricata (Bishop pine)
Fast-growing, often flat-topped conifer. Leaves are blue- or grey-green and held in pairs. Ovoid cones, 7–9cm (3–3½in) long, rarely open. Does particularly well in a poor, sandy soil.

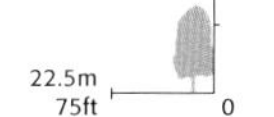

Pinus jeffreyi (Black pine, Jeffrey pine)
Upright, narrow-crowned conifer with stout, grey-green leaves, 12–26cm (5–10in) long. Bark is black with fine, deep fissures and shoots have an attractive, greyish bloom.

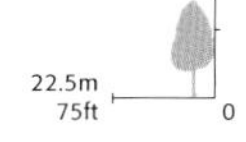

Larix decidua (European larch)
Fast-growing, deciduous conifer with a conical crown when young, broadening on maturity, and spaced branches. Shoots are yellow-brown in winter. Has light green leaves and small, erect, conical cones.

Ginkgo biloba (Maidenhair tree)
Long-lived, deciduous conifer, upright when young, spreading with age. Has fan-shaped, 12cm (5in) long, bright green leaves. Bears fruits with edible kernels in late summer and autumn, if male and female plants are grown together.

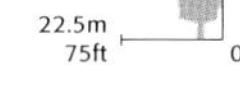

Cedrus libani (Cedar of Lebanon)
Spreading conifer, usually with several arching stems. Branches carry flat layers of dark grey-green foliage and oblong to ovoid, greyish-pink cones, 8–15cm (3–6in) long.

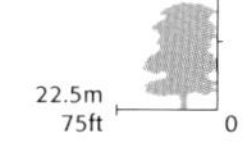

Pinus patula (Mexican weeping pine)
Rounded to broadly spreading conifer with scaling, ochre-coloured bark. Weeping shoots bear narrow, bright green leaves, to 30cm (12in) long, in clusters of 3–5. Long-conical, chestnut-brown cones have a prickle on each scale.

30m 100ft
22.5m
75ft
0

Sequoia sempervirens (Redwood)
Very vigorous, columnar to conical conifer with horizontal branches. Has soft, fibrous, red-brown bark and needle-like, flattened, pale green leaves, spirally arranged. Produces rounded to cylindrical cones, initially green, ripening to dark brown.

30m 100ft
22.5m
75ft
0

Pinus wallichiana
(Bhutan pine, Himalayan pine)
Conical conifer with long, drooping, blue-green leaves in 5s. Has smooth bark, grey-green on young trees, later fissured and dark, and cylindrical cones.

30m 100ft
22.5m
75ft
0

Pinus pinaster
(Cluster pine, Maritime pine)
Vigorous, domed conifer with a long, branchless trunk. Has grey-green leaves and whorls of rich brown cones. Purple-brown bark is deeply fissured. Is well-suited to a dry, sandy soil.

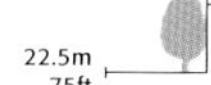

Picea abies
(Common spruce, Norway spruce)
Fast-growing, pyramidal conifer with dark green leaves. Narrow, pendulous, glossy, brown cones are 10–20cm (4–8in) long. Much used as a Christmas tree but less useful as an ornamental.

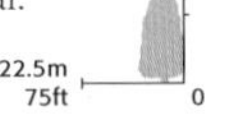

Pinus nigra* subsp. *nigra
(Austrian pine)
Broadly crowned conifer, with well-spaced branches, often with several stems. Paired, dark green leaves are densely tufted. Tolerates an exposed site.

Araucaria araucana
(Chile pine, Monkey puzzle)
Open, spreading conifer with grey bark, wrinkled like elephant hide. Has flattened and sharp, glossy, dark green leaves and 15cm (6in) long cones. Makes a fine specimen tree.

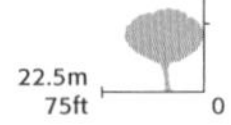

Pinus radiata (Monterey pine)
Very fast growing conifer, conical when young, domed when mature. Black bark contrasts well with soft, bright green leaves. Makes an excellent windbreak.

Picea omorika (Serbian spruce)
Narrow, conical conifer, resembling a church spire, with dark green leaves that are white below. Branches are pendulous and arch out at tips. Violet-purple cones age to glossy brown. Grows steadily in all soils.

Abies grandis (Giant fir, Grand fir)
Very vigorous, narrow, conical conifer, with a neat habit. Mid-green leaves have an orange aroma when crushed. Cones, 7–8cm (3in) long, ripen red-brown. Makes a useful specimen tree.

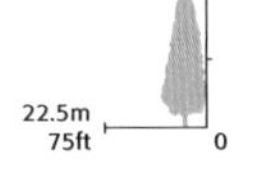
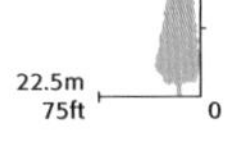

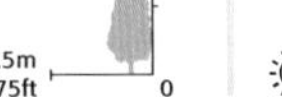

Sequoiadendron giganteum
(Giant redwood, Wellingtonia)
Very fast growing, conical conifer. Has thick, fibrous, red-brown bark and sharp, bluish-green leaves. Is one of the world's largest trees when mature.

Pinus heldreichii (Bosnian pine)
Dense, conical conifer with scaly, ash-grey bark and dark green leaves held in pairs. Ovoid cones, 5–10cm (2–4in) long, are cobalt-blue in early summer, ripening to brown.

GREEN/YELLOW

x *Cuprocyparis* 'Castlewellan'
Upright, vigorous conifer, slightly slower growing than the species, grown for its bronze-yellow foliage.

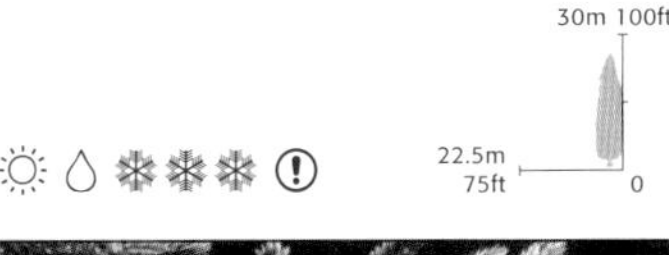

***Picea orientalis* 'Skylands'**
Dense, upright, graceful conifer with short, glossy leaves that retain their creamy-gold colour throughout the year. Narrowly oblong cones are dark purple, males turning brick-red in spring.

30m 100ft
22.5m 75ft
0

Taxodium distichum (Swamp cypress)
Deciduous, broadly conical conifer with small, globose to ovoid cones. Yew-like, fresh green leaves turn rich brown in late autumn. Grows in a very wet site, producing special breathing roots.

30m 100ft
22.5m 75ft
0

BLUE

Picea engelmannii
(Engelmann spruce, Mountain spruce)
Broadly conical conifer. Leaves encircle shoots and are prickly or soft, lush, glaucous or bluish-green. Bears small, cylindrical cones. Is good for a very poor site.

***Picea glauca* 'Coerulea'**
Dense, upright, conical conifer with needle-like, blue-green to silver leaves and ovoid, light brown cones.

Picea breweriana (Brewer's spruce)
Upright conifer with level branches and completely pendulous branchlets, to 2m (6ft) long. Leaves are stout and blue-green. Bears oblong, purplish cones, 6–8cm (2½–3in) long.

***Picea pungens* 'Koster'**
Upright conifer with whorled branches. Has scaly, grey bark and attractive, needle-like, silvery-blue leaves, which fade to green with age. Tends to suffer from aphid attack.

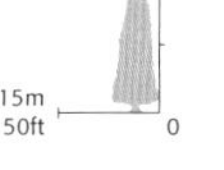

***Chamaecyparis lawsoniana* 'Pembury Blue'**
Magnificent, conical conifer with aromatic, bright blue-grey foliage held in pendulous sprays.

***Tsuga mertensiana* 'Glauca'**
Slow-growing, dwarf or medium-sized, columnar-conical conifer with red-brown shoots bearing spirally arranged, needle-like, flattened, glaucous, silver-grey leaves. Cones are yellow-green to purple, ripening to dark brown.

15m 50ft
15m 50ft
0

Pinus parviflora
(Japanese white pine)
Slow-growing, conical or spreading conifer with fine, bluish foliage and purplish-brown bark. Leaves are held in groups of 5. Bears ovoid cones, 5–10cm (2–4in) long.

15m 50ft
15m 50ft
0

GREEN

Abies forrestii (Forrest fir)
Conical conifer with an open, whorled habit and smooth, silvery-grey bark. Shoots are red-brown, with spherical, white buds. Has dark green leaves, silvery-white beneath, and ovoid-cylindrical, violet-blue cones.

Pinus rigida (Northern pitch pine)
Conical conifer, often with sucker shoots from trunk. Twisted, dark green leaves are borne in 3s. Ovoid to globose, red-brown cones, 3–8cm (1¼–3in) long, persist, open, on the tree.

***Juniperus chinensis* 'Keteleeri'**
Dense, regular, slender, columnar conifer with scale-like, aromatic, greyish-green leaves and peeling, brown bark. Makes a reliable, free-fruiting form for formal use.

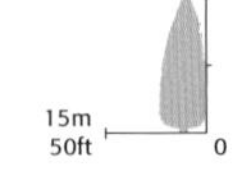

Picea likiangensis (Lijiang spruce)
Upright conifer with bluish-white leaves are well-spaced. Cones, 8–15cm (3–6in) long, are cylindrical, females bright red when young, ripening to purple; male cones are pink.

Podocarpus salignus
Upright conifer. Leaves are willow-like, 5–11cm (2–4in) long, and glossy above. Attractive, fibrous, red-brown bark peels in strips.

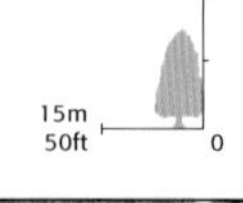

Austrocedrus chilensis
(Chilean incense cedar)
Conical conifer with flattened, feathery sprays of 4-ranked, small, dark green leaves, white beneath.

Fitzroya cupressoides
(Patagonian cypress)
Vase-shaped to sprawling conifer with red-brown bark that peels in long strips. White-lined, dark green leaves are held in open, pendulous, wiry sprays.

Pinus thunbergii
(Japanese black pine)
Rounded conifer, conical when young, with dark green leaves and grey-brown cones, 4–6cm (1½–2½in) long. Buds are covered with a silky cobweb of white hairs. Tolerates sea spray well.

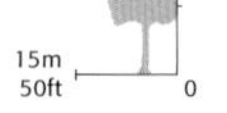

Juniperus recurva* var. *coxii
(Coffin juniper)
Slow-growing, conical conifer with smooth bark flakes in thin sheets. Weeping sprays of long, needle-like, aromatic, incurved leaves are bright green. Globose or ovoid, fleshy berries are black.

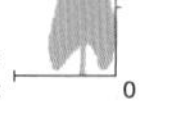

Cunninghamia lanceolata
(Chinese fir)
Upright conifer, mop-headed on a dry site, with distinctive, thick and deeply furrowed, red-brown bark. Glossy, green leaves are sharply pointed and lance-shaped.

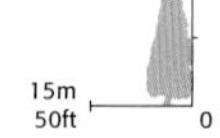

Phyllocladus trichomanoides
Slow-growing conifer, conical when young, developing a more rounded top with age. Leaf-like, deep green, modified shoots, 10–15cm (4–6in) long, have 5–10 lobed segments.

Sciadopitys verticillata
(Japanese umbrella pine)
Conical conifer with reddish-brown bark. Deep green leaves, yellowish beneath, are whorled at the ends of shoots, like umbrella spokes. Ovoid cones ripen over 2 years.

Picea morrisonicola (Taiwan spruce)
Upright, conical conifer, becoming columnar with age. Needle-like, deep green leaves are pressed down on slender, pale brown shoots. Cones are cylindrical and 5–7cm (2–3in) long.

Calocedrus decurrens (Incense cedar)
Upright conifer with short, horizontal branches and flaky, grey bark, brown beneath. Has flat sprays of aromatic, dark green leaves. Resists honey fungus.

Pinus cembra (Arolla pine)
Dense, conical conifer with dark green or bluish-green leaves grouped in 5s. Ovoid, bluish or purplish cones, 6–8cm (2½– 3in) long, ripen brown.

***Taxus baccata* 'Fastigiata'** (Irish yew)
Slow-growing conifer with a broadly conical, later domed crown. Erect branches bear needle-like, flattened, dark green leaves that stand out all around shoots. Female plants bear cup-shaped, fleshy, bright red fruits.

15m 50ft
15m
15ft
0

Pinus contorta* var. *latifolia
(Lodgepole pine)
Conical conifer with bright green leaves, 6–9cm (2½–4in) long. Small, oval cones remain closed on the tree. Is suitable for a wet or coastal site.

Torreya californica
(California nutmeg)
Upright conifer with very prickly, glossy, dark green leaves, yellowish-green beneath, similar to those of yew. Fruits are olive-like.

Chamaecyparis thyoides
(White cypress)
Upright conifer with aromatic, green or blue-grey leaves in rather erratic, fan-shaped sprays on very fine shoots. Cones are small, round and glaucous blue-grey.

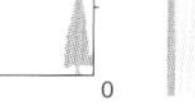

GREEN

Pinus banksiana (Jack pine)
Slender, conical, scrubby-looking conifer with fresh green leaves in twisted, divergent pairs. Curved cones, 3–6cm (1¼–2½in) long, point forward along shoots.

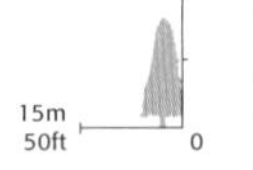

Tsuga canadensis
(Canada hemlock, Eastern hemlock)
Broadly conical conifer, often with several stems. Grey shoots have 2-ranked, dark green leaves, often inverted to show silver lines beneath. Cones are ovoid and light brown.

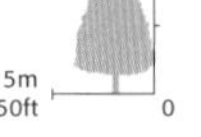
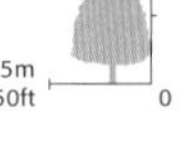

***Cupressus sempervirens* 'Stricta'**
(Italian cypress)
Narrow, columnar conifer with upward sweeping branches. Has fissured bark and scale-like, deep green leaves. Bears globular, prickly, woody, brown cones, to 3cm (1¼in) across.

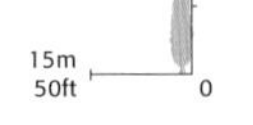

***Chamaecyparis lawsoniana* 'Green Pillar'**
Conical conifer with upright branches. Aromatic foliage is bright green and becomes tinged with gold in spring. Is suitable for hedging as requires little clipping.

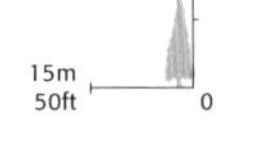

YELLOW

Pinus contorta
(Beach pine, Shore pine)
Dense, conical or domed conifer. Has paired, bright green leaves and conical to ovoid cones, 3–8cm (1¼–3in) long. Is well-suited to a windy, barren site and tolerates waterlogged ground.

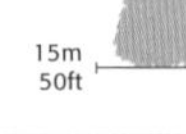

Pinus halepensis (Aleppo pine)
Conical, open-crowned conifer with an open growth of bright green leaves, 6–11cm (2½–4½in) long, and ovoid, glossy, brown cones. Young trees retain glaucous, juvenile needles for several years.

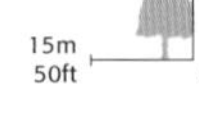

***Chamaecyparis lawsoniana* 'Lanei Aurea'**
Upright conifer that forms a neat column of aromatic, golden-yellow tipped foliage.

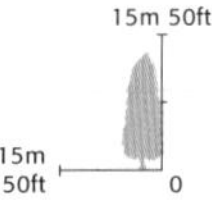

Pseudolarix amabilis (Golden larch)
Deciduous, open-crowned conifer, slow-growing when young. Has clusters of linear, fresh green leaves, 2.5–6cm (1–2½in) long, which gradually turn bright orange-gold in autumn.

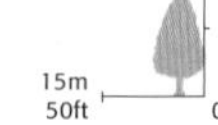

***Taxus baccata* 'Lutea'**
(Yellow-berried yew)
Slow-growing conifer grown for its fleshy, bright golden-yellow fruits. These look particularly striking against the needle-like, dark green leaves and are often borne in great profusion in autumn.

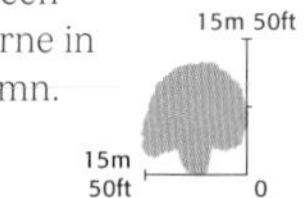

GREEN

Pinus aristata **(Bristle-cone pine)**
Slow-growing, bushy conifer. Leaves are in bundles of 5, very dense and blue-white to grey-green, flecked with white resin. Ovoid cones, 4–10cm (1½–4in) long, have bristly prickles. Is the oldest-known living plant, over 4,000 years old.

Chamaecyparis lawsoniana **'Columnaris'**
Narrow, upright conifer that forms a neat column of aromatic, blue-grey foliage. Will tolerate poor soil and some clipping. Is an effective, small, specimen tree.

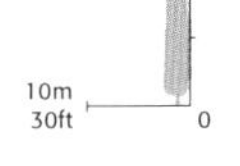

Picea mariana **'Doumetii'**
Densely branched, globose or broadly conical conifer with short, needle-like, silvered, dark green leaves and pendulous, ovoid, purplish cones.

Juniperus recurva **(Drooping juniper, Himalayan weeping juniper)**
Slow-growing, conical conifer with aromatic, incurved, grey- or blue-green leaves and fleshy, black berries. Smooth bark flakes in thin sheets.

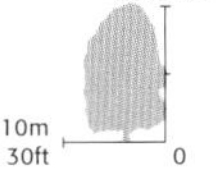

Juniperus chinensis **'Robusta Green'**
Slow-growing, narrow, columnar conifer, making only 7–8cm (3in) a year, with aromatic, blue-green foliage and small, grey-green juniper berries.

Juniperus chinensis **'Obelisk'**
Slender, irregularly columnar conifer. Has ascending branches and long, prickly, needle-like, aromatic, dark green leaves. Tolerates a wide range of soils and conditions but is particularly suited to a hot, dry site.

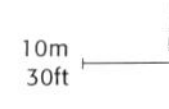

Pinus cembroides
(Mexican stone pine, Pinyon)
Slow-growing, bushy conifer, rarely more than 6–7m (20–22ft) high. Scaly bark is a striking silver-grey or greyish-brown. Leaves, in clusters of 2 or 3, are sparse and dark green to grey-green.

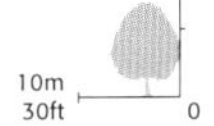

GREEN

Abies koreana (Korean fir)
Broadly conical conifer. Produces cylindrical, violet-blue cones when less than 1m (3ft) tall. Leaves are dark green above, silver beneath.

Cryptomeria japonica 'Pyramidata'
Narrowly columnar or obelisk-shaped conifer. Foliage is blue-green when young, maturing to dark green.

YELLOW

Cedrus deodara 'Aurea'
Slow-growing, upright conifer with pendent branch tips and golden-yellow leaves when young in spring–summer. Foliage matures to yellowish-green. Makes a dramatic, small-garden evergreen.

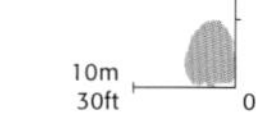

Cryptomeria japonica 'Cristata'
Conical conifer with twisted, curved shoots and soft, fibrous bark. Foliage is bright green, ageing brown.

Taxus cuspidata (Japanese yew)
Evergreen, spreading conifer. Leaves are dark green above, yellowish-green beneath, sometimes becoming tinged red-brown in cold weather. Tolerates very dry and shady conditions.

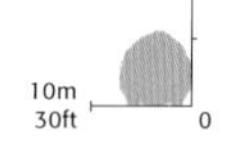

Pinus sylvestris 'Aurea'
Upright conifer that develops a rounded crown with age. Bark is flaking and red-brown on upper trunk, fissured and purple-grey at base. Golden leaves in winter–spring, otherwise blue-green. Conical, green cones ripen to pale grey- or red-brown.

Chamaecyparis obtusa 'Crippsii'
Attractive, small-garden, conical conifer, grown for its flattened sprays of aromatic, bright golden foliage. Bark is stringy and red-brown. Cones are round, 1cm (½in) across, and brown.

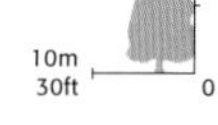

Thujopsis dolabrata 'Variegata'
Slow-growing, broadly conical, bushy conifer. Stout, hatchet-shaped leaves have irregular, creamy patches above and are silvery beneath.

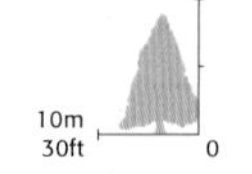

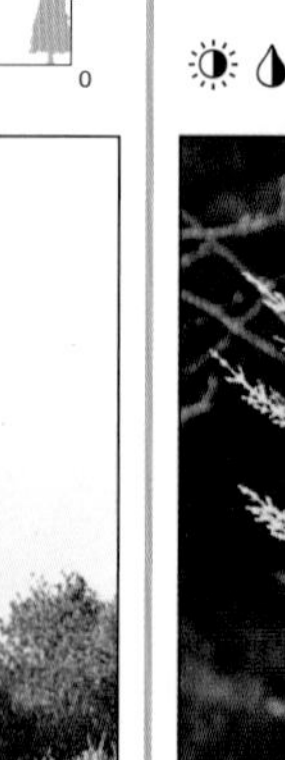

Pinus pinea
(Stone pine, Umbrella pine)
Conifer with a rounded crown on a short trunk. Leaves are dark green, but blue-green, juvenile foliage is retained on young trees. Broadly ovoid cones ripen shiny brown; seeds are edible.

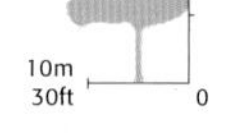

Cupressus macrocarpa 'Goldcrest'
Fast-growing, conical conifer with aromatic, golden-yellow foliage held in plume-like sprays that are useful in flower arrangements. Dislikes clipping.

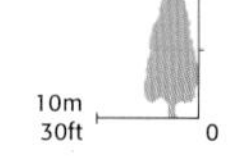

DWARF CONIFERS

Dwarf conifers are valuable plants, especially for the small garden, requiring little attention and providing year-round interest. They can be planted as features in their own right, for their varied shapes, habits and often striking colours, or, in the rock garden, to provide scale or act as a foil for other plants such as bulbs. Several species and cultivars are spreading and good for ground cover. Most conifers are suited to a wide range of growing conditions, although *Cedrus* and *Juniperus* do not tolerate shade, and *Juniperus* and *Pinus* are best for dry, sandy soils. Some species may be clipped to form a low hedge but new growth seldom occurs from wood more than 3 or 4 years old. Dwarf conifers also make excellent container plants.

***Thuja plicata* 'Stoneham Gold'** 🏆

***Pinus heldreichii* 'Smidtii'** 🏆

***Picea pungens* 'Globosa'** 🏆

***Abies cephalonica* 'Meyer's Dwarf'**

Podocarpus nivalis

***Picea abies* 'Ohlendorffii'**

***Juniperus squamata* 'Holger'** 🏆

***Juniperus squamata* 'Blue Carpet'** 🏆

***Taxus baccata* 'Dovastonii Aurea'** 🏆(!)

***Juniperus scopulorum* 'Skyrocket'**

Microbiota decussata 🏆

***Platycladus orientalis* 'Aurea Nana'** 🏆(!)

***Pinus mugo* 'Mops'** 🏆

***J. x pfitzeriana* 'Old Gold'** 🏆

***Abies concolor* 'Compacta'** 🏆

***Chamaecyparis obtusa* 'Nana Gracilis'** 🏆

***Chamaecyparis pisifera* 'Filifera Aurea'** 🏆

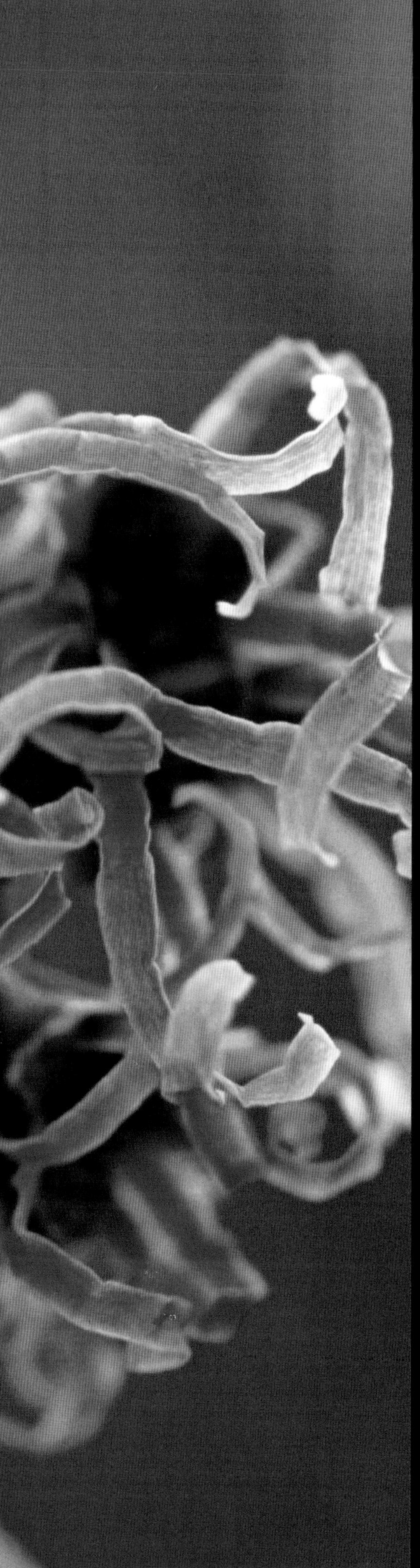

SHRUBS

Shrubs are key to any planting design, and provide colour and interest throughout the seasons with their wide variety of foliage, flowers, fruits and stems. Create a year-round display with a selection of beautiful spring- and summer-flowering shrubs, such as weigelas, buddlejas, and philadelphus, together with those that sport brightly coloured autumn fruits, such as pyracanthas and cotoneasters. You can then include witch hazels and some species of honeysuckle to brighten bleak winter months with their fragrant flowers. Whatever the size or style of your garden, the permanent woody structure of shrubs will form the framework, so make your selection and plant them before the perennials. Some shrubs are also ideal plants for hedges, enclosures, and screens.

SHRUBS

Star performers, shrubs form the backbone of many garden designs. They can be used together in shrub borders or with other plant groups in mixed displays. Providing colour and interest with their foliage, flowers and fruits, many also offer scented blooms and colourful stems.

SIZE CATEGORIES USED WITHIN THIS GROUP		
Large	**Medium**	**Small**
over 3m (10ft)	1.5–3m (5–10ft)	up to 1.5m (5ft)

ABOVE Spring colour
The flowering stems of *Exochorda* x *macrantha* 'The Bride' arch gracefully above forget-me-nots (*Myosotis sylvatica*), daisies (*Bellis perennis*) and *Tulipa* 'Couleur Cardinal'.

What are shrubs?

Shrubs are woody-stemmed, deciduous or evergreen plants that branch out at or near ground level. Some can grow to more than 6m (20ft) in height, although most attain less than half this size. Leaves come in many forms, from large and glossy to grey and needle-like. There is sometimes an overlap between shrubs and trees because larger shrubs, such as flowering dogwoods (*Cornus* species), can be grown on a single stem. Sub-shrubs are another anomaly, with woody stems at the base, but softer top growth that may die back over winter in colder regions like a perennial. Examples include ceratostigmas and fuchsias.

Choosing shrubs

When selecting shrubs, focus on those whose needs match your garden conditions. In general, shrubs with large dark green leaves require shade, plants with grey foliage, such as lavender, require sun, and shrubs with colourful leaves need full sun or partial shade. Also consider the shrub's size and site it where it has space to mature, unless you are planning a topiary display.

Designing with shrubs

When creating a shrub display, try to combine plants with different shapes, habits, flower seasons, and foliage forms and patterns to create a visually balanced scheme and year-round interest. Knit them together in a shrub bed, or use them to provide a backdrop to more transient displays of bulbs, perennials, and annuals in a mixed border.

The shape and habit of shrubs provides a design with structure and form. Contrast low, spreading, prostrate or mat-forming shrubs, such as *Juniperus procumbens* and *Cotoneaster horizontalis*, with more upright forms, such as *Rosmarinus officinalis* 'Miss Jessopp's Upright', and the rounded shapes of bushy shrubs like hebes, skimmias, or box topiary. Mix in shrubs with tiered branch structures, such as *Viburnum plicatum* 'Mariesii', which provide strong horizontal lines in a scheme. Graceful, arching shrubs, such as *Kolkwitzia amabilis*, *Buddleja alternifolia* and *Genista tenera* 'Golden Shower' add an elegant note.

A wide range of shrubs are suitable for creating hedges, enclosures or screens.

RENOVATING A SHRUB

When evergreens such as mahonias have outgrown their allotted space, many can be cut back hard from midwinter to early spring after flowering. The plant may not flower for two years after such drastic pruning, but its overall appearance will be much improved. Other shrubs that respond well to this form of renovation include buddlejas, forsythias, kerrias, and smoke bushes (*Cotinus*). Some, such as rosemary and lavender, do not.

New growth after pruning.

1 Remove tall stems
Remove all dead and diseased wood, taking it back to healthy growth. Then prune back tall stems, removing them a little at a time so that they do not tear at the base. At this stage, cut the stems to about 60cm (2ft) high, keeping in mind the plant's balanced shape as you prune.

2 Make final pruning cuts
Prune out any remaining crossing stems. Once you have cut back the tall growths, check where you can make your final pruning cuts. Cut out the old growths completely to leave five or six strong young stems.

3 Cut back remaining stems
Cut back the young healthy stems that are left, so that they are 30–40cm (12–16in) above the ground. The final cuts should be at an angle so rainwater can run off. Later in the year, a mass of young shoots will appear along these stems (*see left*).

ABOVE: Contrasting foliage
The golden leaves of *Choisya ternata* Sundance ('Lich') provide a glowing contrast with the adjacent rich pink-red *Berberis thunbergii* 'Rose Glow' and dark purple *Cotinus coggygria* 'Royal Purple'.

As well as the evergreen staples like box (*Buxus*), privet (*Ligustrum*) and shrubby honeysuckle (*Lonicera nitida*), which are commonly used, consider colourful deciduous shrubs, like the prickly *Berberis thunbergii* and its cultivars, or the evergreen *Photinia* x *fraseri* 'Red Robin' which produces fiery young foliage in spring and after clipping.

Certain shrubs are also ideal for topiary, their small leaves lending themselves to detailed shaping. Suitable shrubs include box and shrubby honeysuckle.

Shrubs such as fuchsias, hebes, fatsias and choisyas are ideal for containers. Pots also limit the size of larger shrubs.

Year-round interest

There is a shrub in flower almost every month of the year. Interest begins in spring with a range of colourful varieties, including flowering currants (*Ribes*), ceanothus, and rhodododendrons. The display continues with an abundance of summer-flowering shrubs like fuchsias, hydrangeas, buddlejas and spiraeas, followed in autumn by a range of colourful berries offered by plants such as pyracanthas, cotoneasters and *Skimmia japonica*. Many shrubs retain their fruits into winter, providing birds and wildlife with a much-needed supply of food.

As temperatures fall, the fragrant flowers of witch hazel (*Hamamelis*), mahonias, and winter box (*Sarcococca*) open, bringing new interest to the garden. Combine these with the vivid stems of coppiced dogwoods (*Cornus* species) and variegated evergreens for a dramatic winter scheme.

Spring pastels
Ceanothus flowers appear in late spring, decorating the garden with various shades of blue and white. These short-lived evergreens enjoy a warm, sunny site.

Feast of berries
The bright red berries of a female *Skimmia japonica*, produced where plants of both sexes are grown together, persist well into winter.

KEEPING SHRUBS IN SHAPE

Many young plants and shrubs, such as daphnes, produce long, leggy growths in spring or early summer after flowering. They do not require major pruning but a light trim will produce a more compact, bushy shrub that will be covered in flowers the following year.

1 Assess your plant
In early summer, after daphnes have flowered, young leggy shoots sprout from the main stems. Before cutting them back, take a look at the shrub to see where to cut to produce a well-shaped plant.

2 Shorten leggy growths
Using a pair of secateurs, shorten the leggy growths by 15–20cm (6–8in). It is important that you always prune immediately above a leaf bud with an angled, slanting cut, as shown above.

3 Work around the plant
Circle the plant, shortening each of the whippy stems, and checking that you are maintaining a good shape. The cut stems will then produce bushier growth and more flowers the following year.

WHITE

Osmanthus delavayi
Evergreen, rounded, bushy shrub with arching branches. Has small, glossy, dark green leaves and a profusion of very fragrant, tubular, white flowers from mid- to late spring.

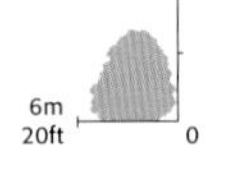

Anopterus glandulosus
Evergreen, bushy shrub or, occasionally, small tree. Has narrow, glossy, dark green leaves, amid which clusters of cup-shaped, white or pink flowers appear from mid- to late spring.

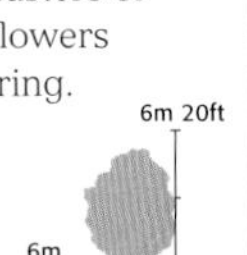

***Viburnum plicatum* f. *tomentosum* 'Mariesii'**
Deciduous, spreading shrub with tiered branches clothed in dark green leaves, which turn reddish-purple in autumn. Large, rounded heads of flowers with white bracts appear in late spring and early summer.

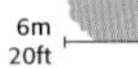

Osmanthus x burkwoodii
Evergreen, rounded, dense shrub. Glossy foliage is dark green and sets off a profusion of small, very fragrant, white flowers from mid- to late spring.

Pieris japonica
Evergreen, rounded, bushy, dense shrub with glossy, dark green foliage that is bronze when young. Produces drooping racemes of white flowers during spring.

Dipelta yunnanensis
Deciduous, arching shrub with peeling bark and glossy leaves. In late spring produces tubular, creamy-white flowers, marked orange inside.

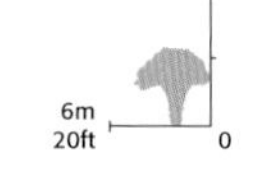

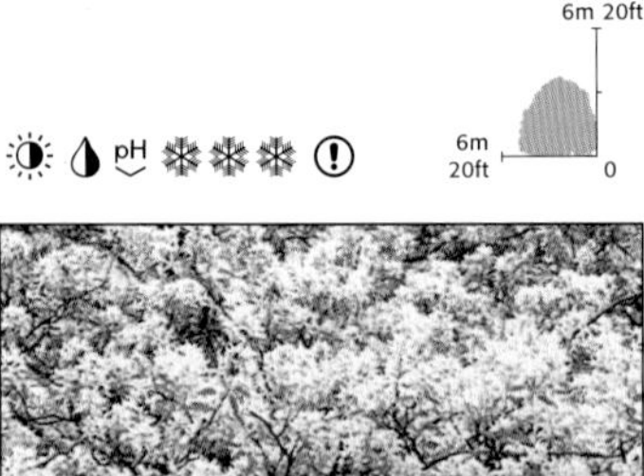

Amelanchier lamarckii
Deciduous, spreading shrub. Young leaves unfold bronze as abundant sprays of star-shaped, white flowers open from mid- to late spring. Foliage matures to dark green, then turns brilliant red and orange in autumn.

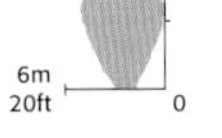

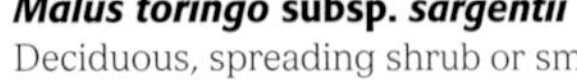

Malus toringo* subsp. *sargentii
Deciduous, spreading shrub or small tree. A profusion of white flowers in late spring is followed by long-lasting, deep red fruits. Oval, dark green leaves are sometimes lobed.

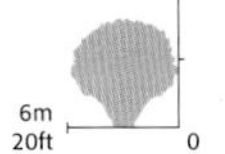

Staphylea pinnata (Bladder nut)
Deciduous, upright shrub that in late spring carries clusters of white flowers, tinted pink with age, followed by bladder-like, green fruits. Foliage is divided and bright green.

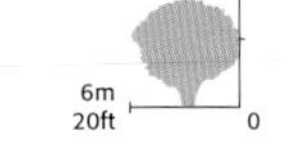

Enkianthus campanulatus
Deciduous, bushy, spreading shrub with red shoots and tufts of dull green leaves that turn bright red in autumn. Small, bell-shaped, red-veined, creamy-yellow flowers appear in late spring.

Viburnum* x *carlcephalum
Deciduous, rounded, bushy shrub. In late spring large, rounded heads of pink buds open to fragrant, white flowers. These are borne amid dark green foliage that often turns red in autumn.

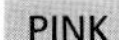

PINK

Dipelta floribunda
Vigorous, deciduous, upright, tree-like shrub with peeling, pale brown bark. Fragrant, pale pink flowers, marked yellow inside, open in late spring and early summer. Has pointed, mid-green leaves.

***Staphylea holocarpa* 'Rosea'**
Deciduous, upright shrub or spreading, small tree. From mid- to late spring bears pink flowers, followed by bladder-like, pale green fruits. Bronze, young leaves mature to blue-green.

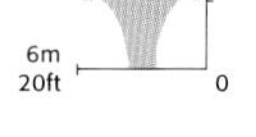

RED

Photinia serratifolia
Evergreen, upright shrub or bushy tree. Oblong, often sharply toothed leaves are red when young, maturing to glossy, dark green. Small, 5-petalled flowers from mid- to late spring are sometimes followed by spherical, red fruits.

***Photinia* x *fraseri* 'Red Robin'**
Evergreen, upright, dense shrub. Oblong, glossy, dark green leaves are brilliant red when young. Bears 5-petalled flowers in late spring. Has good resistance to damage by late frosts.

Daphniphyllum macropodum
Evergreen, bushy, dense shrub with stout shoots and dark green leaves. Small flowers, green on female plants, purplish on male plants, appear in late spring.

YELLOW

Berberis valdiviana
Evergreen shrub with oval to ovate, leathery leaves with 3-pronged spines. Pendulous racemes, to 4cm (1½in) long, of cup-shaped, fragrant, saffron-yellow flowers, in late spring, are followed by egg-shaped, bloomed, purple fruits.

Corylopsis glabrescens
Deciduous, open shrub. Oval leaves, with bristle-like teeth along margins, are dark green above, blue-green beneath. Drooping spikes of fragrant, bell-shaped, pale yellow flowers appear in mid-spring on bare branches.

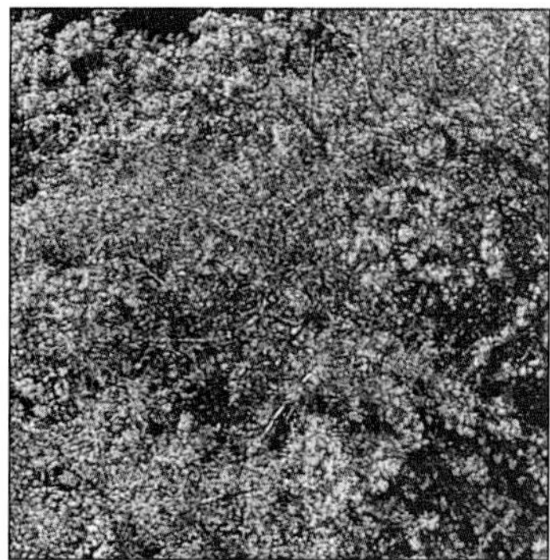

Berberis darwinii (Darwin's barberry)
Vigorous, evergreen, arching shrub. Has small, glossy, dark green leaves and a profusion of rounded, deep orange-yellow flowers from mid- to late spring, followed by bluish berries.

WHITE

Salix exigua (Coyote Willow)
Deciduous, upright shrub with slender, green-grey branches and linear, finely toothed, silky, silvery-white leaves, which move in the breeze. Small, pale lemon catkins are produced in spring, at the same time as the leaves emerge from bud.

Olearia virgata
Evergreen, arching, graceful shrub with very narrow, dark grey-green leaves. Produces an abundance of small, star-shaped, white flower heads in early summer, arranged in small clusters along stems.

Viburnum rhytidophyllum
Vigorous, evergreen, open shrub with long, narrow, deep green leaves. Dense heads of small, creamy-white flowers in late spring and early summer are succeeded by red fruits that mature to black.

Styrax officinalis
Deciduous, loose to dense shrub or small tree. Fragrant, bell-shaped, white flowers appear in early summer among oval, dark green leaves with greyish-white undersides.

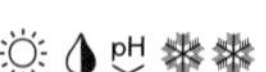

Xanthoceras sorbifolium
Deciduous, upright shrub or small tree with bright green leaves divided into many slender leaflets. In late spring and early summer produces spikes of white flowers with red patches inside at the base of the petals.

Ligustrum sinense
Deciduous or semi-evergreen, bushy, upright shrub with oval, pale green leaves. Large panicles of fragrant, tubular, white flowers are borne in mid-summer, followed by small, purplish-black fruits.

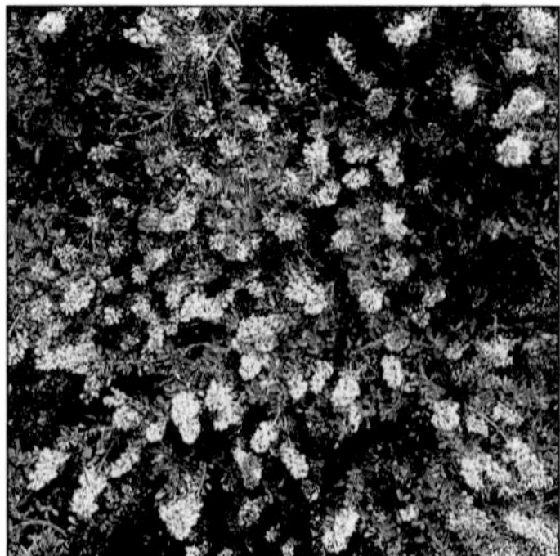

Escallonia leucantha
Evergreen, upright shrub. Narrow, oval, glossy, dark green leaves set off large racemes of small, shallowly cup-shaped, white flowers in mid-summer.

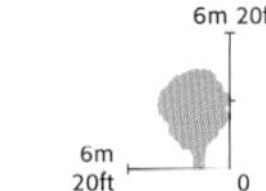

***Escallonia* 'Iveyi'**
Evergreen, upright shrub. Glossy, dark green foliage sets off large racemes of fragrant, tubular, pure white flowers, with short lobes, borne from mid- to late summer.

Chionanthus virginicus (Fringe tree)
Deciduous, bushy shrub or small tree. Has large, glossy, dark green leaves that turn yellow in autumn. Drooping sprays of fragrant, white flowers appear in early summer.

Elaeagnus umbellata
Vigorous, deciduous, bushy shrub with oblong, wavy-edged, bright green leaves, which are silvery when young. Has fragrant, bell-shaped, creamy-yellow flowers in late spring and early summer, followed by egg-shaped, red fruits.

***Syringa vulgaris* 'Madame Florent Stepman'**
Deciduous, upright then spreading shrub with large panicles of fragrant, tubular, single, white flowers borne profusely in late spring. Has heart-shaped, dark green leaves.

Abelia x grandiflora
Vigorous, semi-evergreen, arching shrub. Has glossy, dark green foliage and an abundance of fragrant, pink-tinged, white flowers from mid-summer to mid-autumn.

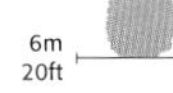

Crinodendron patagua
Vigorous, evergreen, upright shrub with slightly hairy, reddish young shoots and oval to ovate, coarsely toothed, leathery, dark green leaves. Bell-shaped, frilly-edged, white flowers in late summer are followed by angular, red seed pods.

Abutilon vitifolium* var. *album
Fast-growing, deciduous, upright shrub. Large, bowl-shaped, white blooms, pink-tinged when young, are freely borne in late spring and early summer amid deeply lobed, sharply toothed, grey-green leaves.

Aesculus parviflora (Bottlebrush buckeye)
Deciduous, open shrub. Leaves are bronze when young, dark green in summer and yellow in autumn. Panicles of red-centred, white flowers appear from mid- to late summer.

Abelia triflora
Vigorous, deciduous, upright shrub with pointed, deep green leaves. Small, extremely fragrant, white flowers, tinged pale pink, appear in mid-summer.

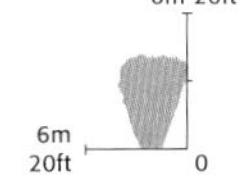

Holodiscus discolor
Fast-growing, deciduous, arching shrub. Has lobed, toothed, dark green leaves and large, pendent sprays of small, creamy-white flowers in mid-summer.

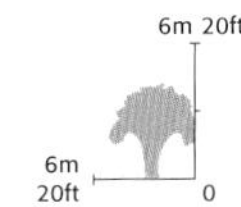

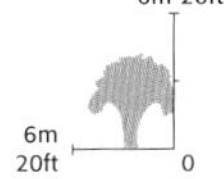

Clethra delavayi
Deciduous, open shrub with lance-shaped, toothed, rich green leaves. Dense, spreading clusters of pink buds opening to scented, white flowers appear in mid-summer.

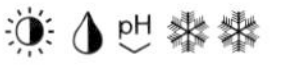

BUDDLEJAS

Buddleja is genus of approximately 100 species of highly ornamental evergreen and deciduous shrubs and small trees, originating predominantly from Asia, Africa and the Americas. Buddlejas are often included in wildlife gardens as they encourage increased insect activity, which has earned one species the common name, butterfly bush, although they all also attract bees and hover flies. They produce small, highly-scented, tubular flowers borne in either plume or globular-shaped clusters. Easy to grow, they thrive in almost any soil, and perform best in a warm, sunny position. They are particularly suited for growing against a south-facing wall.

B. davidii **'White Profusion'** 🏆

B.* x *weyeriana **'Moonlight'**

B. colvilei **'Kewensis'**

B. davidii **'Pink Delight'**

B. salviifolia

B. alternifolia 🏆

B. davidii **'Black Knight'** 🏆

B. davidii **'Dartmoor'** 🏆

B. **'Lochinch'** 🏆

B.* x *weyeriana **'Sungold'** 🏆

Abutilon vitifolium **'Veronica Tennant'**

Fast-growing, generally deciduous, but sometimes semi-evergreen, upright shrub or small tree. Has rounded, toothed, grey-green leaves. In spring and early summer, large, saucer-shaped, purple-blue flowers are borne in profusion.

6m 20ft / 6m 20ft / 0

Kolkwitzia amabilis **'Pink Cloud'**

Deciduous, arching shrub that bears a mass of bell-shaped, pink flowers amid small, oval, mid-green leaves in late spring and early summer.

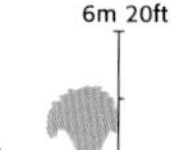

6m 20ft / 6m 20ft / 0

Tamarix ramosissima

Deciduous, arching, graceful shrub or small tree with tiny, narrow, blue-green leaves. In late summer and early autumn bears large, upright plumes of small, pink flowers.

6m 20ft / 6m 20ft / 0

PURPLE

***Cotinus coggygria* 'Notcutt's Variety'**
Deciduous, bushy shrub with deep reddish-purple foliage. Long-lasting, purplish-pink plumes of massed, small flowers are produced in late summer.

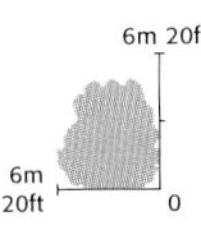

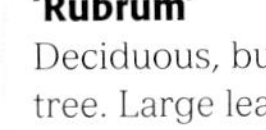

***Acer palmatum* var. *heptalobum* 'Rubrum'**
Deciduous, bushy-headed shrub or small tree. Large leaves are red when young, bronze in summer and brilliant red, orange or yellow in autumn. Has small, reddish-purple flowers in mid-spring.

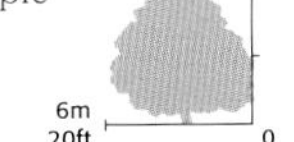

***Corylus maxima* 'Purpurea'**
Vigorous, deciduous, open shrub or small tree with deep purple leaves and purplish catkins, with yellow anthers, that hang from bare branches in late winter. Edible nuts mature in autumn.

***Prunus spinosa* 'Purpurea'**
Deciduous, dense, spiny shrub or small tree. Bright red, young leaves become deep reddish-purple. Bears saucer-shaped, pale pink flowers from early to mid-spring, followed by blue-bloomed, black fruits.

LILACS

The heady scent of the lilac (*Syringa*) epitomizes early summer. Apart from the classic lilacs and mauves, colours include white, pink, cream, and rich red-purple; double forms are also available. Most lilacs grown in gardens are vigorous shrubs derived from *S. vulgaris*. They may eventually become tree-like and are best planted at the back of a shrub border. Spent flower heads should be removed, with care taken not to damage the new shoots. Otherwise little pruning is required, though older plants may be rejuvenated by hard pruning in winter.

***S. pubescens* subsp. *patula* 'Miss Kim'** 🏆

***S. pubescens* subsp. *microphylla* 'Superba'** 🏆

S. x persica 🏆

***S. vulgaris* 'Katherine Havemeyer'** 🏆

***S. vulgaris* 'Andenken an Ludwig Späth'** 🏆

***S. vulgaris* 'Madame Lemoine'** 🏆

***S. meyeri* 'Palibin'** 🏆

***S. x persica* 'Alba'** 🏆

S. komarowii* subsp. *reflexa

***S. vulgaris* 'Firmament'** 🏆

YELLOW

***Genista tenera* 'Golden Shower'**
Vigorous, deciduous, arching shrub with narrowly oblong, grey-green leaves. Racemes of fragrant, pea-like, golden-yellow flowers are produced in early to mid-summer.

6m 20ft / 6m 20ft / 0

Elaeagnus angustifolia **(Oleaster)**
Deciduous, bushy shrub or spreading, small tree. Has narrow, silvery-grey leaves and small, fragrant, creamy-yellow flowers, with spreading lobes, in early summer, followed by small, oval, yellow fruits.

6m 20ft / 6m 20ft / 0

Genista cinerea
Deciduous, arching shrub that produces an abundance of fragrant, pea-like, yellow blooms from early to mid-summer. Has silky, young shoots and narrow, grey-green leaves.

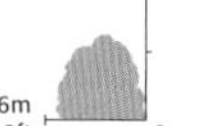

***Cotinus coggygria* GOLDEN SPIRIT ('Ancot') (Golden smoke bush)**
Deciduous, bushy shrub grown for its rounded, golden-yellow leaves, which turn orange in autumn. In summer, tiny, fluffy, plume-like, grey flower clusters, on fine stalks, are borne above the leaves.

6m 20ft / 6m 20ft / 0

Cytisus battandieri
(Moroccan broom, Pineapple broom)
Semi-evergreen, open shrub. Leaves have 3 silver-grey leaflets. Pineapple-scented, yellow flowers appear in summer.

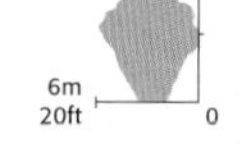

Buddleja globosa
Deciduous or semi-evergreen, open shrub with dark green foliage. Dense, rounded clusters of orange-yellow flowers are carried in early summer.

6m 20ft / 6m 20ft / 0

Caesalpinia gilliesii
Deciduous, open shrub or small tree. Has finely divided, dark green leaves and bears short racemes of yellow flowers with long, red stamens from mid- to late summer.

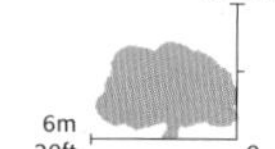

Paliurus spina-christi
(Christ's thorn, Jerusalem thorn)
Deciduous, bushy shrub with slender, thorny shoots. Has oval, glossy, bright green leaves, tiny, yellow flowers in summer and curious, woody, winged fruits in autumn.

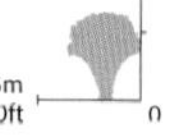

RED

***Cotoneaster* 'Cornubia'**
Vigorous, semi-evergreen, arching shrub. Clusters of white flowers, produced in early summer amid dark green foliage, are followed by large, pendent clusters of decorative, bright red fruits.

6m 20ft / 6m 20ft / 0

Acer palmatum var. heptalobum
Deciduous, bushy-headed shrub or small tree with large, lobed, mid-green leaves that turn brilliant red, orange or yellow in autumn. Bears small, reddish-purple flowers in mid-spring.

6m 20ft / 6m 20ft / 0

Euonymus myrianthus
Evergreen, bushy shrub with pointed, leathery, mid-green leaves. Dense clusters of small, greenish-yellow flowers in summer are followed by yellow fruits that open to show orange-red seeds.

6m 20ft / 6m 20ft / 0

***Rhus typhina* 'Dissecta'**
Deciduous, spreading, open shrub or small tree with velvety shoots. Fern-like, dark green leaves turn brilliant orange-red in autumn, when deep red fruit clusters are also borne.

6m 20ft / 6m 20ft / 0

***Cotinus* 'Flame'**
Deciduous, bushy, tree-like shrub with dark green leaves that turn brilliant orange-red in autumn. From late summer, showy, plume-like, purplish-pink flower heads appear above the foliage.

6m 20ft / 6m 20ft / 0

Euonymus oxyphyllus
Deciduous, upright shrub or tree with oval, dull green leaves turning to purplish-red in autumn. Produces tiny, greenish-white flowers in late spring, then globose, 4- or 5-lobed, deep red fruits with orange-scarlet seeds.

6m 20ft / 6m 20ft / 0

Fothergilla major
Deciduous, upright shrub with glossy, dark green leaves, slightly bluish-white beneath, that turn red, orange and yellow in autumn. Tufts of fragrant, white flowers appear in late spring.

6m 20ft / 6m 20ft / 0

Cotoneaster lacteus
Evergreen, arching shrub suitable for hedging. Oval, dark green leaves set off shallowly cup-shaped, white flowers from early to mid-summer. Long-lasting, red fruits are carried in large clusters in autumn–winter.

6m 20ft / 6m 20ft / 0

SHRUBS

WITCH HAZELS

Species of *Hamamelis* put on a beautiful show of fragrant flowers during the darkest, coldest months, securing their place in any winter planting scheme. The spider-like blooms, ranging in colour from deep red to sulphur yellow, appear on bare branches from late autumn to early spring, the narrow, crepe-paper-like petals withstanding several degrees of frost and snow without damage. Witch hazels prefer a moist but well-drained, fertile, acid to neutral soil in full sun or partial shade. A spring dressing of ericaceous compost or well-rotted leaf mould benefits young plants.

***H. x intermedia* 'Barmstedt Gold'** 🏆

***H. x intermedia* 'Arnold Promise'** 🏆

***H. x intermedia* 'Pallida'** 🏆

***H. x intermedia* 'Jelena'** 🏆

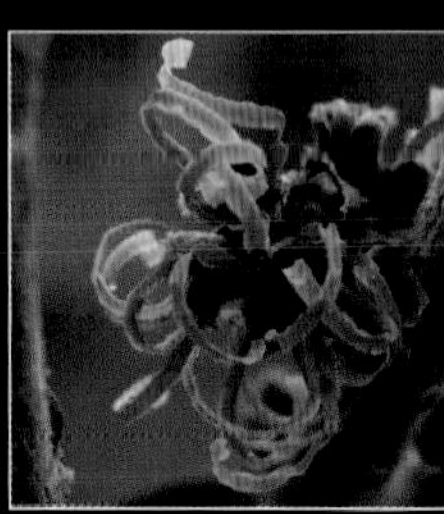

***H. x intermedia* 'Primavera'**

***H. x intermedia* 'Aphrodite'** 🏆

***H. x intermedia* 'Robert'**

***Pyracantha atalantioides* 'Aurea'**
Vigorous, evergreen, upright, spiny shrub, arching with age. Has narrowly oval, glossy, dark green leaves and white flowers in early summer, followed by large clusters of small, yellow berries in early autumn.

6m 20ft / 6m 20ft / 0

***Corylus avellana* 'Contorta'**
(Corkscrew hazel)
Deciduous, bushy shrub with curiously twisted shoots and broad, sharply toothed, mid-green leaves. In late winter, bare branches are covered with pendent, pale yellow catkins.

6m 20ft / 6m 20ft / 0

***Mahonia x media* 'Charity'**
Evergreen, upright, dense shrub with large leaves composed of many spiny, dark green leaflets. Slender, upright, later spreading spikes of fragrant, yellow flowers are borne from early autumn to early spring.

6m 20ft / 6m 20ft / 0

***Hamamelis japonica* 'Sulphurea'**
Deciduous, upright, open shrub. In mid-winter, fragrant, spidery, pale yellow flowers with 4 narrow, crimped petals are borne on leafless branches. Broadly oval, dark green leaves turn yellow in autumn.

6m 20ft / 6m 20ft / 0

***Mahonia x media* 'Buckland'**
Evergreen, upright, dense shrub. Has large leaves with many spiny, dark green leaflets. Clustered, upright then spreading, long, branched spikes of fragrant, yellow flowers appear from late autumn to early spring.

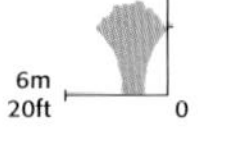

Azara microphylla
Elegant, evergreen shrub or small tree. Has tiny, glossy, dark green leaves and small clusters of vanilla-scented, deep yellow flowers in late winter and early spring.

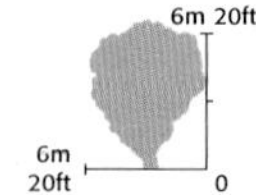

***Azara microphylla* 'Variegata'**
Slow-growing, evergreen, compact shrub. Small, rounded, glossy, dark green leaves have creamy-gold margins. In early spring bears clusters of tiny, chocolate-scented, yellow-green flowers on the underside of the branches.

***Elaeagnus pungens* 'Maculata'**
Evergreen, bushy, slightly spiny shrub. Glossy, dark green leaves are marked with a central, deep yellow patch. Very fragrant, urn-shaped, creamy-white flowers open from mid- to late autumn.

***Osmanthus heterophyllus* 'Aureomarginatus'**
Evergreen, upright shrub. Sharply toothed, holly-like, glossy, bright green leaves have yellow margins. Small, fragrant, white flowers are produced in autumn.

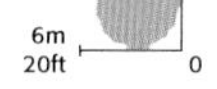

WHITE

Prunus lusitanica* subsp. *variegata
Slow-growing, evergreen, bushy shrub with reddish-purple shoots. Has oval, glossy, dark green, white-edged leaves. Fragrant, shallowly cup-shaped, creamy-white flowers in summer are followed by purple fruits.

***Griselinia littoralis* 'Variegata'**
Evergreen, upright shrub of dense, bushy habit. Leathery leaves are grey-green, marked with bright green and creamy-white. Bears inconspicuous, yellow-green flowers in late spring.

***Pittosporum* 'Garnettii'**
Evergreen, columnar or conical shrub of dense, bushy habit. Rounded, grey-green leaves, irregularly edged creamy-white, become tinged with deep pink in cold areas. May bear small, greenish-purple flowers in spring–summer.

GREEN

***Ligustrum ovalifolium* (Privet)**
Vigorous, evergreen or semi-evergreen, upright, dense shrub with glossy, mid-green leaves. Bears racemes of small, rather unpleasantly scented, tubular, white flowers in mid-summer, followed by black fruits.

Pittosporum dallii
Evergreen, rounded, dense tree or shrub. Has purplish stems and sharply toothed, deep green leaves. Clusters of small, fragrant, shallowly cup-shaped, white flowers are produced in summer.

Prunus lusitanica* subsp. *azorica
Evergreen, bushy shrub with reddish-purple shoots and bright green leaves, red when young. Bears spikes of small, fragrant, white flowers in summer, followed by purple fruits.

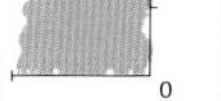

LARGE

ALL YEAR

GREEN

Tetrapanax papyrifer **(Rice-paper plant)**

Evergreen, upright, suckering shrub. Long-stalked, circular leaves are deeply lobed. Has bold sprays of small, creamy-white flowers in summer and black berries in autumn–winter.

6m 20ft

6m 20ft 0

Pittosporum tenuifolium

Evergreen, columnar, later rounded shrub or small tree with purple shoots and wavy-edged, oval, glossy, mid-green leaves. Bears honey-scented, purple flowers in late spring.

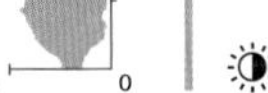

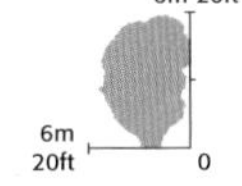

MEDIUM

SPRING

WHITE

Pieris floribunda (Fetterbush, Mountain fetterbush)

Evergreen, bushy, dense, leafy shrub with oval, glossy, dark green leaves. Greenish-white flower buds appear in winter, opening to urn-shaped, white blooms from early to mid-spring.

3m 10ft

3m 10ft 0

Enkianthus perulatus

Deciduous, bushy, dense shrub. Dark green leaves turn bright red in autumn. A profusion of small, pendent, urn-shaped, white flowers is borne in mid-spring.

3m 10ft

3m 10ft 0

***Pieris japonica* 'Scarlett O'Hara'**

Evergreen, rounded, bushy, dense shrub. Young foliage and shoots are bronze-red, leaves becoming glossy, dark green. Produces sprays of white flowers in spring.

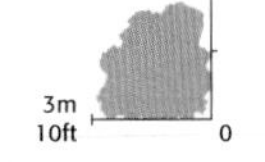

CAMELLIAS

These evergreen shrubs and small trees have long been valued for their luxuriant, rich green foliage and masses of showy flowers, in shades of white, pink, red and yellow, borne mainly in winter and spring. Once thought suitable only for glasshouses, many camellias are frost hardy outdoors if grown in sheltered positions, although blooms may suffer frost and rain damage. Ideal for shady gardens, they grow well against walls. Camellias require lime-free soil but also make good container plants. The main flower forms are illustrated below.

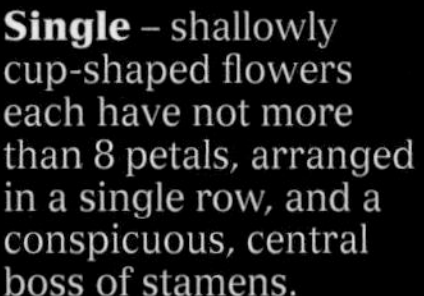

Single – shallowly cup-shaped flowers each have not more than 8 petals, arranged in a single row, and a conspicuous, central boss of stamens.

Semi-double – cup-shaped flowers each have 2 or more rows of 9–21 regular or irregular petals, and conspicuous stamens.

Anemone – rounded flowers each have one or more rows of large, outer petals lying flat or undulating; the domed centre has a mass of intermingled petaloids and stamens.

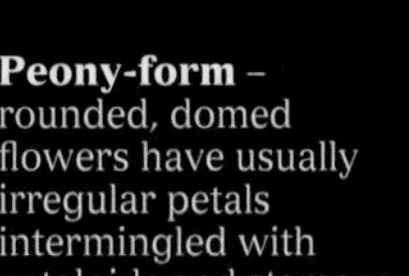

Peony-form – rounded, domed flowers have usually irregular petals intermingled with petaloids and stamens.

Rose-form – cup-shaped flowers each have several rows of overlapping petals and open to reveal stamens in the centre.

Formal double – rounded flowers have rows of regular, neatly overlapping petals that obscure stamens. **Irregular double forms** are similar but often have more loosely arranged, sometimes irregular, petals.

C. **'Cornish Snow'** [single]

C. japonica **'Alba Plena'** [formal double]

C. japonica **'Hagoromo'** [semi-double]

C. japonica **'Janet Waterhouse'** [semi-double]

C. japonica **'Nobilissima'** [peony

SHRUBS

C. japonica 'Lavinia Maggi' 🏆
[formal double]

C. x *williamsii* 'Donation' 🏆
[semi-double]

C. 'Freedom Bell' 🏆
[semi-double]

C. x *williamsii* 'Debbie' 🏆
[peony]

C. 'Spring Festival' 🏆 [double]

C. japonica 'Margaret Davis'
[irregular double]

C. 'Inspiration' 🏆 [semi-double]

C. japonica 'Adolphe Audusson' 🏆
[semi-double]

C. x *williamsii* 'J.C. Williams' 🏆
[single]

C. reticulata 'Captain Rawes'
[semi-double]

C. x *williamsii* 'Water Lily' 🏆
[formal double]

C. 'Leonard Messel' 🏆
[semi-double]

C. japonica 'Bob's Tinsie' 🏆
[anemone]

C. x *williamsii* 'Jury's Yellow' 🏆
[anemone]

C. japonica 'Tricolor' 🏆 [semi-double]

C. 'Black Lace' 🏆 [formal double]

C. japonica 'Brushfield's Yellow' 🏆 [anemone]

WHITE

Choisya 'Aztec Pearl'
Evergreen, compact shrub with aromatic, glossy, dark green leaves composed of 3–5 linear leaflets. Clusters of scented, white flowers, pink flushed in bud, are produced in profusion in spring and then quite often again in early autumn.

Choisya ternata (Mexican orange blossom)
Evergreen, rounded, dense shrub with aromatic, glossy, bright green leaves composed of 3 leaflets. Clusters of fragrant, white blooms open in late spring and often again in autumn.

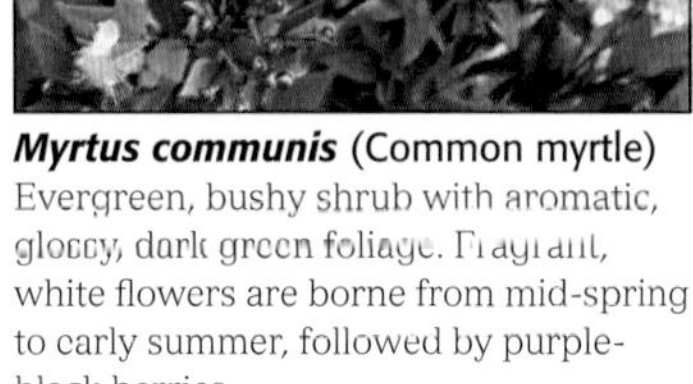

Myrtus communis (Common myrtle)
Evergreen, bushy shrub with aromatic, glossy, dark green foliage. Fragrant, white flowers are borne from mid-spring to early summer, followed by purple-black berries.

PINK

Chaenomeles speciosa 'Moerloosei'
Vigorous, deciduous, bushy shrub. Has glossy, dark green leaves and pink-flushed, white flowers in early spring, followed by greenish-yellow fruits.

Viburnum bitchiuense
Deciduous, bushy shrub with oval, dark green leaves. Rounded heads of fragrant, tubular, pale pink flowers, borne from mid- to late spring, are followed by egg-shaped, flattened, black fruits.

Cotoneaster divaricatus
Deciduous, bushy, spreading shrub. Leaves are glossy, dark green, turning red in autumn. Shallowly cup-shaped, pink-flushed, white flowers in late spring and early summer are followed by deep red fruits.

Rhododendron 'Percy Wiseman'
Evergreen rhododendron with a domed, compact habit. In late spring produces open funnel-shaped, peach-yellow flowers that fade to white.

Camellia x _williamsii_ 'E.G. Waterhouse'
Evergreen, upright shrub with lance-shaped, pale green leaves. Formal double, pink flowers are freely produced in spring.

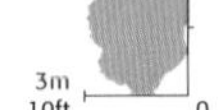

***Ribes sanguineum* 'Pulborough Scarlet'** (Flowering currant)
Deciduous, upright shrub that in spring bears pendent, tubular, deep red flowers amid aromatic, dark green leaves, with 3–5 lobes, sometimes followed by black fruits with a white bloom.

3m 10ft / 3m 10ft

***Prunus mume* 'Beni-chidori'**
Deciduous, spreading shrub with fragrant, single, carmine flowers in early spring before pointed, dark green leaves appear.

3m 10ft / 3m 10ft

Telopea truncata (Tasmanian waratah)
Evergreen, upright shrub, bushy with age. Has deep green leaves and dense, rounded heads of small, tubular, crimson flowers in late spring and summer.

3m 10ft / 3m 10ft

***Acer palmatum* 'Shindeshojo'**
Slow-growing, deciduous, rather twiggy shrub grown for its pink-red leaf colouring in spring. Palmate, deeply lobed leaves then turn bluish-green. Much used for bonsai. Hard frosts can scorch new growth.

3m 10ft / 2m 6ft

***Acer palmatum* 'Corallinum'**
Very slow-growing, deciduous, bushy-headed shrub or small tree. Lobed, bright reddish-pink, young foliage becomes mid-green, then brilliant red, orange or yellow in autumn. Reddish-purple flowers appear in mid-spring.

3m 10ft / 3m 10ft

Enkianthus cernuus* f. *rubens
Deciduous, bushy shrub with dense clusters of dull green leaves that turn deep reddish-purple in autumn. Small, bell-shaped, deep red flowers appear in late spring.

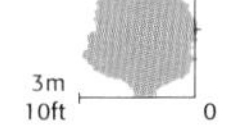

3m 10ft / 3m 10ft

***Leptospermum scoparium* 'Red Damask'**
Evergreen, upright, bushy shrub. Narrow, aromatic, dark green leaves set off sprays of double, dark red flowers in late spring and summer.

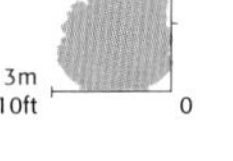

3m 10ft / 3m 10ft

Berberis thunbergii* f. *atropurpurea
Deciduous, arching, dense shrub. Reddish-purple foliage turns bright red in autumn. Globose to cup-shaped, red-tinged, pale yellow flowers in mid-spring are followed by red fruits.

3m 10ft / 3m 10ft

RHODODENDRONS

Rhododendrons and azaleas both belong to the huge genus *Rhododendron*, one of the largest in the plant kingdom. Azalea is the common name used for all the deciduous species and hybrids, and many of the dwarf, small-leaved evergreens. In stature the genus ranges from small alpine shrubs only a few inches high to tall, spreading trees, in the wild reaching 24m (80ft). Rhododendrons require well-drained, acid soil rich in organic matter. Most prefer cool, woodland conditions although many dwarf forms thrive in more open sites. Many grow well in containers, in which it is often easier to provide suitable growing conditions. Once established, they require little attention apart from an annual mulch and occasional feeding, and provide a colourful display for years.

R. pachysanthum 🏆

R. 'Gomer Waterer' 🏆 [rhododendron]

R. decorum 🏆 [rhododendron]

R. 'Polar Bear' 🏆(!) [rhododendron]

R. rex* subsp. *fictolacteum 🏆(!) [rhododendron]

R. yakushimanum (!) [rhododendron]

R. orbiculare 🏆(!) [rhododendron]

R. 'Loderi King George' 🏆(!) [rhododendron]

R. quinquefolium

R. calophytum 🏆(!) [rhododendron]

R. 'Fragrantissimum' 🏆(!) [rhododendron]

R. sinogrande 🏆(!) [rhododendron]

R. falconeri 🏆(!) [rhododendron]

R. williamsianum 🏆(!) [rhododendron]

R. 'Golden Torch' 🏆

R. fulvum 🏆 [rhododendron]

R. 'Purple Splendour' 🏆 [rhododendron]

R. 'Fastuosum Flore Pleno' 🏆 [rhododendron]

R. augustinii ⓘ [rhododendron]

R. 'Blaauw's Pink' 🏆

R. 'Mother's Day' 🏆

R. 'Goldkrone' 🏆ⓘ [rhododendron]

R. 'Pink Pearl' ⓘ [rhododendron]

R. 'Seta' ⓘ [rhododendron]

R. 'Grace Seabrook'

R. 'Hotei' 🏆 [rhododendron]

R. 'Patty Bee' 🏆

R. 'Daviesii' 🏆

R. praecox

R. niveum 🏆

R. 'Curlew' 🏆ⓘ [rhododendron]

R. luteum 🏆ⓘ [azalea]

R. cinnabarinum ⓘ [rhododendron]

R. arboreum ⓘ [rhododendron]

R. 'Blue Danube' 🏆

R. 'Gibraltar' 🏆

CORNUS

Shrubby members of the *Cornus* genus are justifiably popular among gardeners and landscape designers, admired for their highly ornamental brightly coloured winter stems, ranging from lime green and yellow, to orange and crimson, as well as their spring flowers, and, in some cultivars, variegated foliage. Extremely hardy, dogwoods tolerate extreme cold and exposure. They also grow well on most soils, and require little maintenance – simply cut back the stems to just above the ground every two years in late winter. This promotes young growth, which has the most vibrant colour.

C. alba 'Elegantissima'

C. alba 'Spaethii'

C. sericea 'Kelseyi'

C. alba 'Aurea'

C. sericea 'Flaviramea'

C. alba 'Kesselringii'

C. sanguinea 'Winter Beauty'

C. sericea 'White Gold'

C. sanguinea 'Midwinter Fire'

YELLOW

Corylopsis pauciflora

Deciduous, bushy, dense shrub. Oval, bright green leaves, bronze when young, have bristle-like teeth. Bears fragrant, tubular to bell-shaped, pale yellow flowers from early to mid-spring.

3m 10ft

3m 10ft 0

***Rhododendron* 'Yellow Hammer'**

Evergreen, erect, bushy rhododendron. Bears abundant clusters of tubular, bright yellow flowers in spring; frequently flowers again in autumn.

3m 10ft

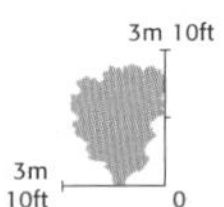

3m 10ft 0

Edgeworthia chrysantha

Deciduous, rounded, open shrub with oval, dark green leaves. Very supple shoots produce terminal, rounded heads of fragrant, tubular, yellow flowers in late winter and early spring.

3m 10ft

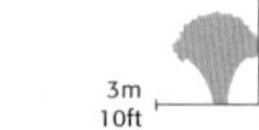

3m 10ft 0

Berberis gagnepainii var. _lanceifolia_
Evergreen, bushy, dense shrub. Massed, globose to cup-shaped, yellow flowers appear among long, narrow, pointed, dark green leaves in late spring. Forms blue-bloomed, black berries.

Forsythia x _intermedia_ 'Spectabilis'
Vigorous, deciduous, spreading shrub with stout growth. A profusion of large, deep yellow flowers is borne from early to mid-spring before sharply toothed, dark green leaves appear.

Lindera benzoin (Benjamin, Spice bush)
Deciduous, bushy shrub with aromatic, bright green leaves that turn yellow in autumn. Tiny, greenish-yellow flowers in mid-spring are followed by red berries on female plants.

Forsythia x _intermedia_ 'Beatrix Farrand'
Vigorous, deciduous, bushy, arching shrub with stout shoots. A profusion of large, deep yellow flowers appears from early to mid-spring before oval, coarsely toothed, mid-green leaves emerge.

Kerria japonica 'Pleniflora'
Vigorous, deciduous, graceful shrub. Double, golden-yellow flowers are borne along green shoots from mid- to late-spring. Leaves are narrowly oval, sharply toothed and bright green.

Berberis x _stenophylla_
Evergreen, arching shrub with slender shoots and narrow, spine-tipped, deep green leaves, blue-grey beneath. Massed, golden-yellow flowers appear from mid- to late spring followed by small, blue-black fruits.

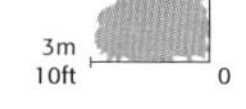

ORANGE

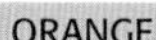

Berberis linearifolia 'Orange King'
Evergreen, upright, stiff-branched shrub with narrow, rigid, dark green leaves. Bears large, globose to cup-shaped, deep orange flowers in late spring.

3m 10ft
3m
10ft
0

Berberis x _lologensis_ 'Stapehill'
Vigorous, evergreen, arching shrub. Glossy, dark green foliage sets off profuse racemes of globose to cup-shaped, orange flowers from mid- to late spring.

Euphorbia mellifera (Honey spurge)
Evergreen, rounded shrub grown mainly for its long, narrowly oblong, rich green leaves with cream midribs. Small, honey-scented, brown flowers, surrounded by showy bracts, are produced in dome-shaped clusters in late spring.

WHITE

Philadelphus 'Beauclerk'
Deciduous, slightly arching shrub. Large, fragrant flowers, white with a small, central, pale purple blotch, are produced from early to mid-summer. Leaves are dark green.

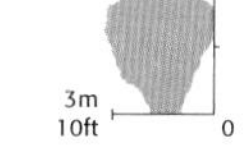

Deutzia scabra
Deciduous, upright shrub with narrowly oval, dark green leaves that, from early to mid-summer, set off dense, upright clusters of 5-petalled, white blooms.

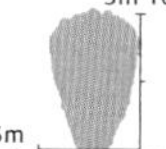
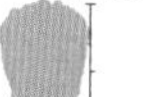

WHITE

***Philadelphus* 'Belle Etoile'**
Deciduous, arching shrub. Very fragrant, white flowers, each with a pale purple mark at the base, are borne profusely among mid-green foliage in late spring and early summer.

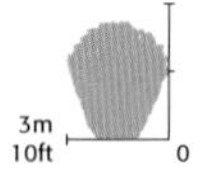

Pyracantha* x *watereri
Evergreen, upright, dense, spiny shrub with glossy, dark green foliage. Shallowly cup-shaped, white flowers in early summer are succeeded by bright red berries in autumn.

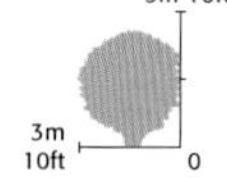

Aronia melanocarpa
(Black chokeberry)
Deciduous, bushy shrub. White flowers appear in late spring and early summer, followed by black fruits. Has glossy, dark green leaves that turn red in autumn.

Spiraea canescens
Deciduous shrub with upright shoots arching at the top. Small heads of white flowers are borne in profusion amid narrowly oval, grey-green leaves from early to mid-summer.

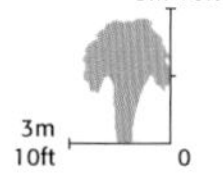

Olearia nummulariifolia
Evergreen, rounded shrub with stiff, upright shoots densely covered with small, very thick, mid- to dark green leaves. Small, fragrant, white flowers appear in mid-summer.

***Rubus* 'Benenden'**
Deciduous, arching, thornless shrub with peeling bark. Large, rose-like, pure white flowers are borne among lobed, deep green leaves in late spring and early summer.

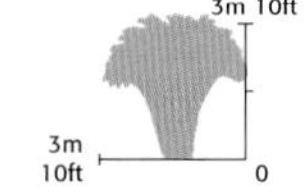

Fallugia paradoxa (Apache plume)
Deciduous, bushy shrub that bears white flowers in mid-summer, followed by silky, pink- and red-tinged, green fruits. Dark green leaves are finely cut and feathery.

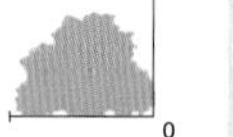

Sorbaria sorbifolia
Deciduous, upright shrub that forms thickets by suckering. Mid-green leaves consist of many sharply toothed leaflets. Large panicles of small, white flowers appear in summer.

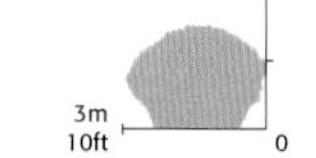

***Philadelphus* 'Boule d'Argent'**
Deciduous, bushy, arching shrub with dark green foliage that sets off clusters of slightly fragrant, semi-double to double, pure white flowers from early to mid-summer.

Eucryphia milliganii

Evergreen, upright, narrow shrub. Has tiny, dark green leaves, bluish-white beneath, and small, white flowers, borne in mid-summer.

***Philadelphus* 'Lemoinei'**
(Mock orange)

Deciduous, upright, slightly arching shrub that produces profuse racemes of small, extremely fragrant, white flowers from early to mid-summer.

Osteomeles schweriniae

Evergreen, arching shrub with long, slender shoots. Leaves, consisting of many small leaflets, are dark green. Clusters of small, white flowers in early summer are followed by red, later blue-black, fruits.

Prinsepia uniflora

Deciduous, arching, spiny shrub. From late spring to summer bears small, fragrant, white flowers amid narrow, glossy, dark green leaves followed by cherry-like, deep red fruits. Grows best in hot sun.

Styrax wilsonii

Deciduous, bushy shrub with slender shoots that produce an abundance of yellow-centred, white flowers in early summer. Leaves are small and deep green.

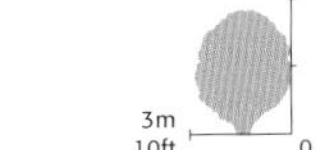

Clethra barbinervis

Deciduous, upright shrub with peeling bark. Has oval, toothed, dark green leaves that turn red and yellow in autumn. Racemes of fragrant, white flowers are borne in late summer and early autumn.

Ceanothus incanus

Evergreen, bushy shrub. Has spreading, spiny shoots, broad, grey-green leaves and large racemes of white flowers in late spring and early summer.

***Philadelphus* 'Dame Blanche'**

Deciduous, bushy, compact shrub with dark, peeling bark. Dark green foliage sets off slightly fragrant, semi-double to loosely double, pure white flowers borne in profusion from early to mid-summer.

WHITE

Escallonia virgata
Deciduous, spreading, graceful shrub with arching shoots and small, glossy, dark green leaves. Bears racemes of small, open cup-shaped, white flowers from early to mid-summer.

***Viburnum dilatatum* 'Catskill'**
Deciduous, low, spreading shrub with sharply toothed, dark green leaves that turn yellow, orange and red in autumn. Flat heads of creamy-white flowers in late spring and early summer are followed by bright red fruits.

Olearia ilicifolia (Mountain holly)
Evergreen, bushy, dense shrub with narrowly oblong, rigid, sharply toothed, musk-scented, grey-green leaves. Fragrant, white flower heads are borne in clusters in summer.

Colletia hystrix
Almost leafless, arching, stoutly branched shrub armed with rigid, grey-green spines. Pink flower buds open in late summer to fragrant, tubular, white blooms that last into autumn.

***Leptospermum scoparium* 'Snow White'** (New Zealand tea-tree)
Evergreen, bushy shrub with small, oval, sharply pointed, green leaves, fragrant when bruised. Produces masses of small, 5-petalled, white flowers from the leaf axils in late spring.

Olearia x haastii (Daisy bush)
Evergreen, bushy, dense shrub, good for hedging. Has small, oval, glossy, dark green leaves and is covered with heads of fragrant, daisy-like, white flowers from mid- to late summer.

Zenobia pulverulenta
Deciduous or semi-evergreen, slightly arching shrub, often with bluish white bloomed shoots. Glossy leaves have a bluish-white reverse when young. Bears fragrant, bell-shaped, white flowers from early to mid-summer.

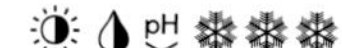

Colletia paradoxa
Deciduous, arching shrub with stiff branches and stout, flattened, blue-green spines. Fragrant, tubular, white flowers are borne in late summer and early autumn.

3m 10ft 3m 10ft 0

***Spiraea nipponica* 'Snowmound'**
Deciduous, spreading shrub with stout, arching, reddish branches. Small, narrow, dark green leaves set off profuse, dense clusters of small, white flowers in early summer.

3m 10ft 3m 10ft 0

***Philadelphus coronarius* 'Variegatus'**
Deciduous, bushy shrub with racemes of very fragrant, creamy-white flowers in late spring and early summer and mid-green leaves broadly edged with white.

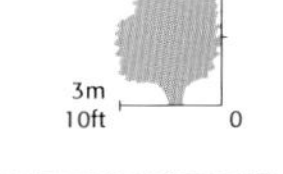

3m 10ft 3m 10ft 0

Lonicera xylosteum (Fly honeysuckle)
Deciduous, upright, bushy, dense shrub. Creamy-white flowers are produced amid grey-green leaves in late spring and early summer, and are followed by red berries.

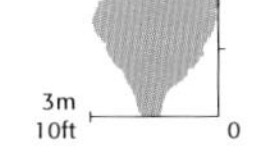

3m 10ft 3m 10ft 0

***Viburnum* 'Pragense'**
Evergreen, rounded, bushy shrub that has dark green foliage and domed heads of white flowers opening from pink buds in late spring and early summer.

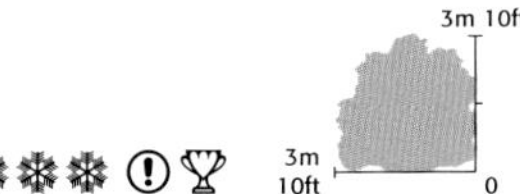

3m 10ft 3m 10ft 0

Leptospermum polygalifolium
Evergreen, arching, graceful shrub with small, glossy, bright green leaves. Bears an abundance of small, pink-tinged, white flowers in mid-summer.

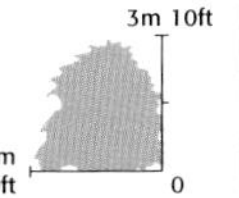

3m 10ft 3m 10ft 0

Philadelphus delavayi* f. *melanocalyx
Deciduous, upright shrub, grown for its extremely fragrant flowers, with pure white petals and deep purple sepals, opening from early to mid-summer. Leaves are dark green.

3m 10ft 3m 10ft 0

***Escallonia* 'Donard Seedling'**
Vigorous, evergreen, arching shrub with small, glossy, dark green leaves. Masses of pink flower buds open to white blooms, flushed with pale pink, from early to mid-summer.

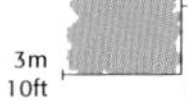

3m 10ft 3m 10ft 0

WHITE

***Hibiscus syriacus* 'Red Heart'**
Deciduous, upright shrub that bears large, white flowers, with conspicuousred centres, from late summer to mid-autumn. Oval leaves are lobed and deep green.

***Deutzia* x *magnifica* 'Staphyleoides'**
Vigorous, deciduous, upright shrub. Large, 5-petalled, pure white blooms, borne in dense clusters in early summer, have recurved petals. Leaves are bright green.

Yucca gloriosa **(Spanish dagger)**
Evergreen shrub with a stout stem crowned with a tuft of long, pointed, deep green leaves, blue-green when young. Bears very long panicles of bell-shaped, white flowers in summer-autumn.

Stephanandra tanakae
Deciduous, arching shrub with orange-brown shoots and sharply toothed, mid-green leaves that turn orange and yellow in autumn. Small, yellow-green buds open to white flowers from early to mid-summer.

Olearia macrodonta
Vigorous, evergreen, upright shrub, often tree-like. Has holly-shaped, sharply toothed, grey-green leaves, silvery-white beneath. Large heads of fragrant, white flowers are produced in early summer.

Aloysia triphylla **(Lemon verbena)**
Deciduous, bushy shrub. Leaves are pale green and lemon-scented. Racemes of tiny, lilac-tinged, white flowers appear in early summer.

***Exochorda* x *macrantha* 'The Bride'**
Deciduous, arching, dense shrub that forms a mound of pendent branches. Large, white flowers are produced in abundance amid dark green foliage in late spring and early summer.

***Escallonia* 'Apple Blossom'**
Evergreen, bushy, dense shrub. From early to mid-summer apple-blossom-pink flowers are borne in profusion amid glossy, dark green leaves.

Lonicera tatarica
Deciduous, bushy shrub. Tubular to trumpet-shaped, 5-lobed, white, pink or red flowers cover dark green foliage in late spring and early summer and are succeeded by red berries.

***Deutzia longifolia* 'Veitchii'**
Deciduous, arching shrub with narrow, pointed leaves and large clusters of 5-petalled, deep pink flowers from early to mid-summer.

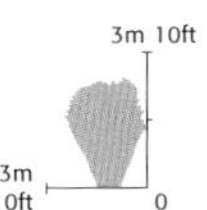

Lavatera assurgentiflora
Semi-evergreen shrub with twisted, grey stems. Clusters of hollyhock-like, darkly veined, deep cerise blooms open in midsummer. Palmate, mid-green leaves are white-haired beneath

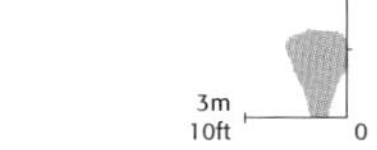

***Robinia hispida* (Rose acacia)**
Deciduous shrub of loose habit with brittle, bristly stems that carry dark green leaves composed of 7–13 leaflets. Pendent racemes of deep rose-pink blooms open in late spring and early summer.

Melaleuca nesophila
(Western tea-myrtle)
Evergreen, bushy shrub or small tree with oval, grey-green leaves. Flowers, consisting of a brush of lavender to rose-pink stamens, are borne in rounded, terminal heads during summer.

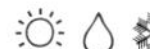

Indigofera heterantha
Deciduous, slightly arching shrub. Has greyish-green leaves consisting of many small leaflets and spikes of small, purplish-pink flowers from early summer to early autumn.

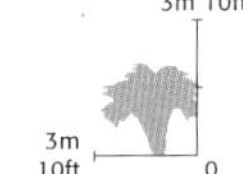

Neillia thibetica
Deciduous, arching shrub. Slender spikes of rose-pink flowers are borne profusely in late spring and early summer. Leaves are sharply toothed.

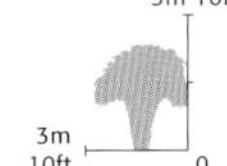

***Hydrangea aspera* Villosa Group**
Deciduous, upright shrub with peeling bark. From late summer to mid-autumn, produces heads of small, blue or purple, central flowers and larger, white, sometimes flushed purplish-pink, outer ones.

HYDRANGEAS

Valued for their late summer flowers, hydrangeas are versatile shrubs that thrive in a variety of situations. Larger-growing species, some of which may become tree-like with age, are suited to light woodland, while the range of cultivars, mostly of *H. macrophylla*, make excellent border plants. Some may also be grown in containers. Colours range from white through pink, red and purple to blue. The truest blue is obtained only on acid soil. Lacecap hydrangeas have a central corymb of small, fertile flowers surrounded by showy, coloured bracts; mopheads (or hortensias) have domed heads of sterile bracts only. *H. paniculata* cultivars bear larger though fewer cone-shaped flower heads if pruned hard in spring.

H. serrata **'Diadem'** 🏆

H. paniculata **PINKY-WINKY ('Dvppinky')** 🏆

H. heteromalla **'Snowcap'**

H. arborescens **'Annabelle'** 🏆⚠

H. macrophylla **'Générale Vicomtesse de Vibraye'** 🏆⚠

H. macrophylla **'Altona'** 🏆⚠

H. quercifolia **'Snowflake'**

H. paniculata **'Big Ben'** 🏆

H. serrata **'Kiyosumi'**

H. macrophylla **'Madame Emile Mouillère'** 🏆

H. paniculata **'Silver Dollar'** 🏆

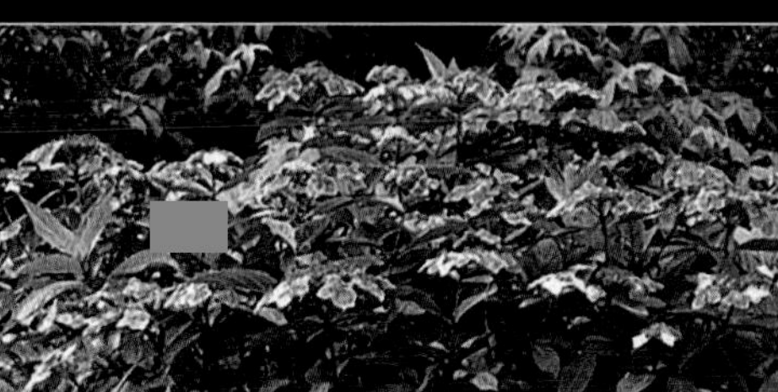

H. macrophylla **'Hamburg'** ⚠

H. paniculata **'Phantom'** 🏆

H. macrophylla **'Lilacina'** 🏆⚠

H. macrophylla 'Ami Pasquier' 🏆

H. macrophylla 'Ayesha'

H. macrophylla 'Europa' 🏆

H. macrophylla 'Möwe' 🏆

H. paniculata 'Dharuma'

H. serrata 'Bluebird' 🏆(!)

H. aspera 'Mauvette'

H. macrophylla 'Libelle'

H. macrophylla 'Blue Bonnet' (!)

H. serrata 'Grayswood' 🏆

H. paniculata PINK DIAMOND ('Interhydia') 🏆(!)

H. aspera subsp. *sargentiana* 🏆

H. paniculata 'Limelight' 🏆

PINK

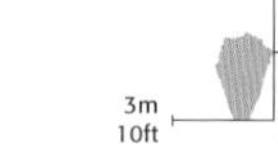

***Lavatera* x *clementii* 'Rosea'**
Semi-evergreen, erect shrub that produces abundant clusters of hollyhock-like, deep pink flowers throughout summer. Has lobed, sage-green leaves.

3m 10ft

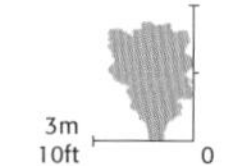

***Hibiscus syriacus* 'Woodbridge'**
Deciduous, upright shrub. From late summer to mid-autumn large, reddish-pink flowers, with deeper-coloured centres, appear amid lobed, dark green leaves.

3m 10ft

Kalmia latifolia (Calico bush)
Evergreen, bushy, dense shrub. In early summer large clusters of pink flowers open from distinctively crimped buds amid glossy, rich green foliage.

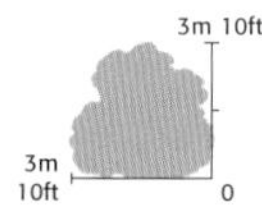

3m 10ft

RED

Paeonia delavayi (Tree peony)
Deciduous, upright, open, suckering shrub. Leaves are divided into pointed-oval leaflets, often with reddish stalks. Produces bowl-shaped, red, orange, yellow or white flowers, 5–6cm (2–2½in) across, with leafy bracts beneath, in late spring.

3m 10ft

Lonicera ledebourii
Deciduous, bushy shrub. Red-tinged, orange-yellow flowers are borne amid dark green foliage in late spring and early summer, and are followed by black fruits. As these ripen, deep red bracts enlarge around them.

3m 10ft

Erythrina* x *bidwillii
Deciduous, upright shrub with pale to mid-green leaves divided into 3 leaflets, up to 10cm (4in) long. Bright red flowers are carried in racemes in late summer or autumn.

3m 10ft

***Pieris formosa* var. *forrestii* 'Wakehurst'**

Evergreen, bushy, dense shrub. Young leaves are brilliant red in early summer, becoming pink, creamy-yellow and finally dark green. Bears urn-shaped, white flowers in spring–summer.

Calycanthus occidentalis
(California allspice)

Deciduous, bushy shrub. Leaves are large, aromatic and dark green. Fragrant, purplish-red flowers with many strap-shaped petals appear during summer.

Erythrina crista-galli
(Cockspur coral-tree)

Deciduous, mainly upright shrub or small tree. Leaves have 3 oval leaflets. Has leafy racemes of crimson flowers in summer-autumn. Dies back to ground level in winter in cold areas.

Telopea speciosissima (Waratah)

Evergreen, erect, fairly bushy shrub with coarsely serrated leaves. Has tubular, red flowers in dense, globose heads, surrounded by bright red bracts, in spring–summer.

Melaleuca elliptica
(Granite bottlebrush)

Evergreen, rounded shrub with long, leathery, usually greyish-green leaves. Flowers, consisting of a brush of red stamens, are borne in dense, terminal spikes in spring–summer.

***Camellia japonica* 'Mathotiana'**

Evergreen, spreading shrub with lance-shaped to oval, slightly twisted, dark green leaves. Very large, formal double, velvety, dark crimson flowers become purplish with age and in warm climates often have rose-form centres.

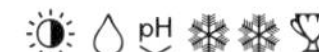

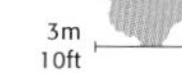

***Berberis thunbergii* 'Rose Glow'**

Vigorous, deciduous, dense shrub with spines. Broadly oval leaves are rich red-purple mottled with pink and cream, when young, maturing to burgundy-red in autumn. Has small, red tinged, yellow flowers in spring.

***Abutilon* 'Ashford Red'**

Strong-growing, evergreen, erect to spreading shrub with maple- to heart-shaped, serrated, pale to mid-green leaves. Pendent, bell-shaped, crimson flowers are borne from spring to autumn.

Callistemon rigidus (Stiff bottlebrush)

Evergreen, bushy, slightly arching shrub with long, narrow, sharply pointed, dark green leaves and dense spikes of deep red flowers in late spring and early summer.

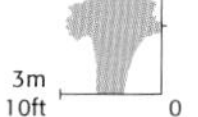

PURPLE

***Acer palmatum* 'Bloodgood'**
Deciduous, bushy-headed shrub or small tree with deep reddish-purple leaves that turn brilliant red in autumn. Small, reddish-purple flowers in mid-spring are often followed by decorative, winged, red fruits.

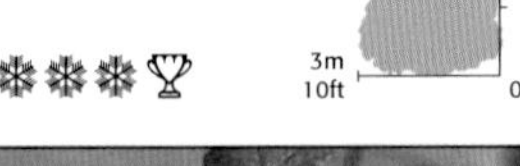

***Abutilon x suntense* 'Violetta'**
Fast-growing, deciduous, upright, arching shrub that carries an abundance of large, bowl-shaped, deep violet flowers in late spring and early summer. Vine-like leaves are sharply toothed and dark green.

Prostanthera rotundifolia
(Round-leaved mint-bush)
Evergreen, bushy, rounded shrub with tiny, sweetly aromatic, deep green leaves and short, leafy racemes of bell-shaped, lavender to purple-blue flowers in late spring or summer.

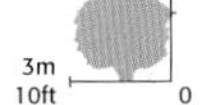

BLUE

Ceanothus impressus
Evergreen, bushy shrub. Spreading growth is covered with small, crinkled, dark green leaves. Deep blue flowers appear in small clusters from mid-spring to early summer.

***Hibiscus syriacus* 'Oiseau Bleu'**
Deciduous, upright shrub that carries large, red-centred, lilac-blue flowers from late summer to mid-autumn. Has lobed, deep green leaves.

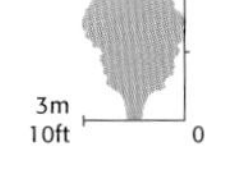

Iochroma australe
Deciduous, erect to spreading shrub with ovate, dark green leaves and bell-shaped, white to blue-purple flowers, 2cm (¾in) long, borne from short spurs in early summer, followed by spherical, yellow-orange fruits, 1.5cm (⅝in) across.

Sophora davidii
Deciduous, bushy shrub with arching shoots. Produces short racemes of small, pea-like, purple and white flowers in late spring and early summer. Grey-green leaves have many leaflets.

***Ceanothus* 'Autumnal Blue'**
Fast-growing, evergreen, bushy shrub. Has glossy, bright green foliage and large panicles of pale to mid-blue flowers from late spring to autumn.

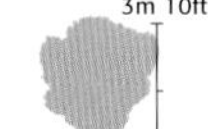

GREEN

Eleutherococcus sieboldianus
Deciduous, bushy, elegant shrub. Has glossy, bright green leaves, divided into 5 leaflets, and is armed with spines. Clusters of small, greenish flowers appear in early summer.

***Ptelea trifoliata* 'Aurea'**
Deciduous, bushy, dense shrub or low tree. Leaves, consisting of 3 leaflets, are bright yellow when young, maturing to pale green. Bears racemes of greenish flowers in summer, followed by winged, green fruits.

Callistemon pallidus
Evergreen, arching shrub. Grey-green foliage is pink-tinged when young and in early summer is covered with dense spikes of creamy-yellow flowers that resemble bottlebrushes.

3m 10ft
3m 10ft 0

Bupleurum fruticosum (Shrubby hare's ear)
Evergreen, bushy shrub with slender shoots. From mid-summer to early autumn rounded heads of small, yellow flowers are borne amid glossy, dark bluish-green foliage.

3m 10ft
3m 10ft 0

Jasminum humile (Yellow jasmine)
Evergreen, bushy shrub that bears bright yellow flowers on long, slender, green shoots from early spring to late autumn. Leaves, with 5 or 7 leaflets, are bright green.

3m 10ft

3m 10ft 0

***Sambucus racemosa* 'Plumosa Aurea'**
Slow-growing, deciduous, bushy shrub with leaves made up of 5 oval leaflets, each deeply cut. Leaves are bronze when young maturing to golden-yellow in early summer. Star-shaped, yellow flowers in spring are followed by scarlet fruits.

3m 10ft
3m 10ft 0

***Elaeagnus x ebbingei* 'Limelight'**
Evergreen, bushy, dense shrub with glossy, dark green leaves, silver beneath, centrally marked yellow and pale green. Bears small, fragrant, white flowers in autumn.

3m 10ft
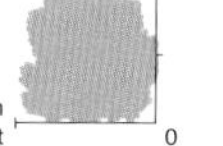
3m 10ft 0

Colutea arborescens (Bladder senna)
Fast-growing, deciduous, open shrub. Has pale green leaves with many leaflets, pea-like, yellow flowers throughout summer, and bladder-like seed pods in late summer and autumn.

3m 10ft

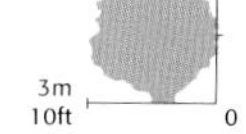
3m 10ft 0

YELLOW

Colutea x _media_
Vigorous, deciduous, open shrub. Grey-green leaves have many leaflets. Racemes of yellow flowers, tinged with copper-orange, appear in summer, followed by bladder-like, papery, red-tinged seed pods.

3m 10ft

Ligustrum 'Vicaryi'
Semi-evergreen, bushy, dense shrub with broad, oval, golden-yellow leaves. Dense racemes of small, white flowers appear in mid-summer.

3m 10ft

Spartium junceum (Spanish broom)
Deciduous, almost leafless, upright shrub that arches with age. Fragrant, pea-like, golden-yellow flowers appear from early summer to early autumn on dark green shoots.

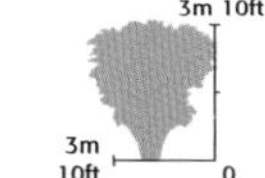

3m 10ft

RED

Euonymus hamiltonianus subsp. _sieboldianus_ 'Red Elf'
Deciduous, upright shrub with mid- to dark green foliage. Decorative, deep pink fruits, borne in profusion after tiny, green flowers in early summer, open in autumn to reveal red seeds.

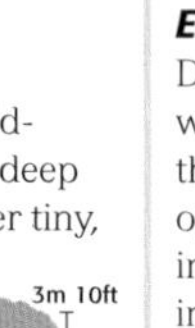

3m 10ft

Euonymus europaeus 'Red Cascade'
Deciduous, bushy shrub or small tree with narrowly oval, mid-green leaves that redden in autumn as red fruits open to show orange seeds. Has inconspicuous, greenish flowers in early summer.

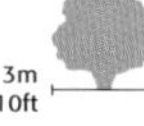

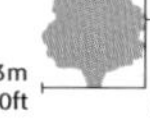

3m 10ft

Rhus glabra (Smooth sumach)
Deciduous, bushy shrub with bluish-white-bloomed, reddish-purple stems. Deep blue-green leaves turn red in autumn. Bears panicles of greenish-red flower heads in summer followed by red fruits on female plants.

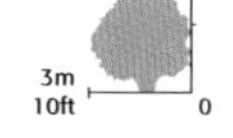

Euonymus latifolius
Deciduous, open shrub. Mid-green foliage turns brilliant red in late autumn. At the same time large, deep red fruits with prominent wings open to reveal orange seeds.

3m 10ft

Euonymus alatus (Winged spindle)
Deciduous, bushy, dense shrub with shoots that develop corky wings. Dark green leaves turn brilliant red in autumn. Inconspicuous, greenish flowers in summer are followed by small, purple-red fruits.

RED/PURPLE

Disanthus cercidifolius
Deciduous, rounded shrub with broadly oval to almost circular, bluish-green leaves that turn yellow, orange, red or purple in autumn. Has small, dark red flowers in autumn as the leaves fall, or later.

3m 10ft / 3m 10ft / 0

Clerodendrum bungei
Evergreen or deciduous, upright, suckering shrub or sub-shrub with heart-shaped, coarsely serrated leaves. Has domed clusters of small, fragrant, red-purple to deep pink flowers in late summer and early autumn.

3m 10ft / 3m 10ft / 0

Callicarpa bodinieri* var. *giraldii
(Beauty berry)
Deciduous, bushy shrub. Leaves are pale green, often bronze-tinged when young. Tiny, lilac flowers in mid-summer are followed by small, violet berries.

3m 10ft / 3m 10ft / 0

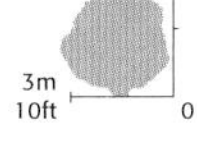

ORANGE

***Pyracantha* 'Golden Charmer'**
Evergreen, bushy, arching, spiny shrub with glossy, bright green leaves. Flattish clusters of white flowers in early summer are succeeded by large, bright orange berries in early autumn.

3m 10ft / 3m 10ft / 0

Leonotis leonurus (Lion's ear)
Semi-evergreen, sparingly branched, erect shrub. Has lance-shaped leaves and whorls of tubular, bright orange flowers in late autumn and early winter.

3m 10ft / 3m 10ft / 0

Zanthoxylum simulans
Deciduous, bushy shrub or small tree with stout spines. Aromatic, glossy, bright green leaves consist of 5 leaflets. Tiny, yellowish-green flowers in late spring and early summer are followed by orange-red fruits.

3m 10ft / 3m 10ft / 0

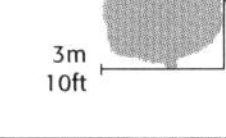

***Berberis* x *carminea* 'Barbarossa'**
Semi-evergreen, arching shrub. Has narrowly oval, dark green leaves and racemes of rounded, yellow flowers in late spring and early summer, followed by globose, orange-scarlet fruits.

3m 10ft / 3m 10ft / 0

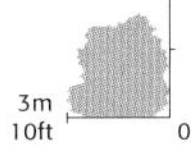

Colquhounia coccinea
Evergreen or semi-evergreen, open shrub. Has aromatic, sage-green leaves and whorls of scarlet or orange flowers in late summer and autumn.

3m 10ft / 3m 10ft / 0

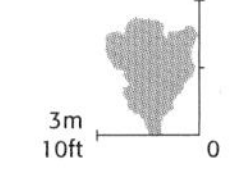

Cotoneaster sternianus
Evergreen or semi-evergreen, arching shrub. Leaves are grey-green, white beneath. Pink-tinged, white flowers in early summer are followed by orange-red fruits.

3m 10ft / 3m 10ft / 0

SHRUBS FOR BERRIES

Most plants produce seed in one form or another, but fruits and berries offer the best decorative value. Shrubs, in particular, offer a huge variety of berries in a range of colours, shapes and sizes. Most appear from summer to late autumn, with many enduring well into winter, brightening up the garden when colour is in short supply, and providing an excellent source of nutrition for birds and wildlife. The most popular berried shrubs are cotoneaster, viburnum, and the snowberry (*Symphoricarpos*), with more unusual fruit produced by *Clerodendrum trichotomum* and *Decaisnea fargesii*, among others. Many of these plants are easy to grow, and will thrive in most soils, if given an annual application of all-purpose granular fertilizer in spring.

***Cornus alba* 'Sibirica Variegata'**

Chaenomeles cathayensis

Poncirus trifoliata

Symphoricarpos albus* var. *laevigatus (!)

Euonymus hamiltonianus* subsp. *sieboldianus (!)

Cotoneaster frigidus

Cotoneaster conspicuus

Cotoneaster salicifolius

***Cotoneaster x watereri* 'John Waterer'** 🏆

Daphne mezereum (!)

Hippophae rhamnoides 🏆

***Viburnum plicatum* 'Pink Beauty'** 🏆(!)

C. sanguinea

Aronia arbutifolia

Viburnum betulifolium (!)

Euonymus hamiltonianus (!)

Clerodendrum trichotomum

Decaisnea fargesii

Symplocos paniculata

Sarcococca confusa 🏆

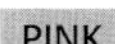

WHITE

Viburnum tinus 'Eve Price'
Evergreen, bushy, very compact shrub with oval, dark green leaves. In winter–spring, deep pink buds open into flattened heads of small, star-shaped, white flowers, which are followed by ovoid, blue fruits.

Viburnum farreri
Deciduous, upright shrub. In late autumn and during mild periods in winter and early spring bears fragrant, white or pale pink flowers. Dark green foliage is bronze when young.

Rubus biflorus
Deciduous, upright shrub with chalky-white, young shoots in winter. Leaves, consisting of 5–7 oval leaflets, are dark green above, white beneath. White flowers in late spring and early summer are followed by edible, yellow fruits.

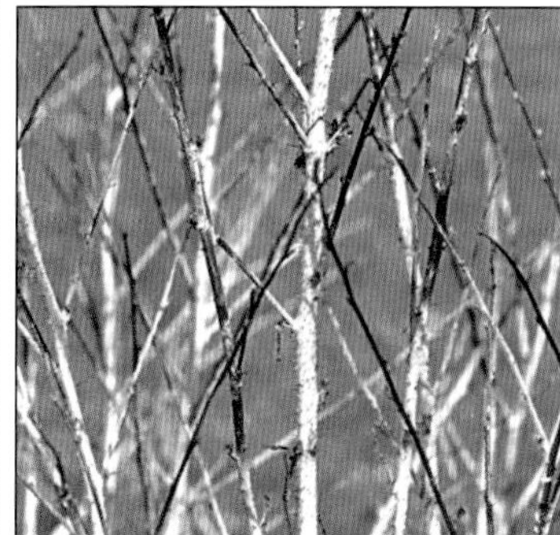

Rubus thibetanus
Deciduous, arching shrub with white-bloomed, brownish-purple, young shoots in winter and fern-like, glossy, dark green foliage, white beneath. Small, pink flowers from mid- to late summer are followed by black fruits.

Viburnum foetens
Deciduous, bushy shrub that has aromatic, dark green leaves. Dense clusters of pink buds open to very fragrant, white flowers from mid-winter to early spring.

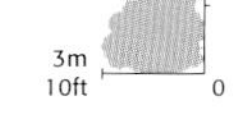

PINK

Viburnum x bodnantense 'Dawn'
Deciduous, upright shrub with oval, bronze, young leaves that mature to dark green. Racemes of deep pink buds open to fragrant, pink flowers during mild periods from late autumn to early spring.

Daphne bholua 'Jacqueline Postill'
Slow-growing, evergreen, upright, compact shrub with oval, leathery, deep green leaves. Masses of highly fragrant flowers, deep pink in bud opening to white, are borne in terminal clusters in late winter and early spring.

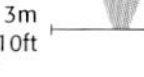

RED

Cornus alba 'Sibirica'
Deciduous, upright shrub with scarlet, young shoots in winter. Has dark green foliage and heads of creamy-white flowers in late spring and early summer, succeeded by rounded, white fruits.

Cotoneaster simonsii
Deciduous or semi-evergreen, upright shrub, suitable for hedging. Has oval, glossy, dark green leaves, shallowly cup-shaped, white flowers in early summer and long-lasting, orange-red fruits in autumn.

Nandina domestica 'Fire Power'
Evergreen or semi-evergreen, elegant, bamboo-like, dwarf shrub. Leaves have dark green leaflets, purplish-red when young and in autumn–winter. Bears small, white flowers in summer followed in warm areas by orange-red fruits.

YELLOW

Mahonia japonica
Evergreen, upright shrub with deep green leaves consisting of many spiny leaflets. Long, spreading sprays of fragrant, yellow flowers appear from late autumn to spring, succeeded by purple-blue fruits.

3m 10ft / 3m 10ft

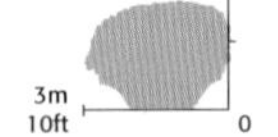

Chimonanthus praecox (Wintersweet)
Deciduous, bushy shrub with oval, rough, glossy, dark green leaves. Bears very fragrant, many-petalled, cup-shaped, yellow flowers, with purple centres, on bare branches in mild periods during winter.

2.5m 8ft / 3m 10ft

WHITE

***Euonymus japonicus* 'Latifolius Albomarginatus'**
Evergreen, upright, bushy and dense shrub with oval, dark green leaves broadly edged with white. Produces clusters of insignificant, greenish-white flowers in late spring.

3m 10ft / 3m 10ft

GREEN

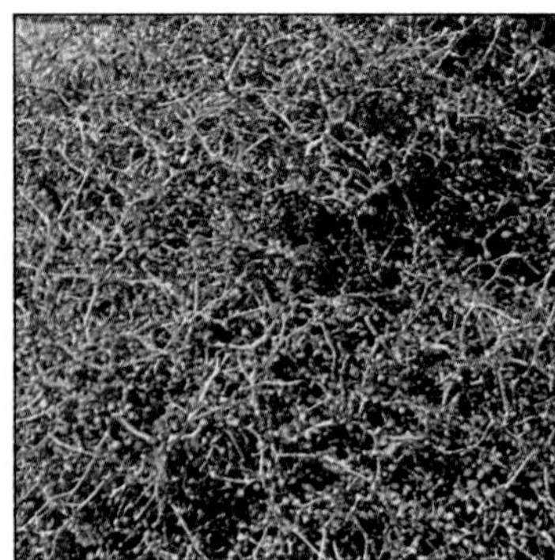

Corokia cotoneaster
(Wire-netting bush)
Evergreen, bushy, open shrub with interlacing shoots. Has small, spoon-shaped, dark green leaves, fragrant, yellow flowers in late spring and red fruits in autumn.

3m 10ft / 3m 10ft

Jasminum nudiflorum
(Winter jasmine)
Deciduous, arching shrub with oval, dark green leaves. Bright yellow flowers appear on slender, leafless, green shoots in winter and early spring.

3m 10ft / 3m 10ft

***Euonymus fortunei* 'Silver Queen'**
Evergreen, bushy, sometimes scandent shrub with a dense growth of dark green leaves, broadly edged with white. Produces insignificant, greenish-white flowers in spring.

3m 10ft / 3m 10ft

Arctostaphylos patula
Evergreen, rounded shrub with reddish-brown bark and bright grey-green foliage. Urn-shaped, white or pale pink flowers appear from mid- to late spring, followed by brown fruits.

3m 10ft / 3m 10ft

Stachyurus praecox
Deciduous, spreading, open shrub with purplish-red shoots. Drooping spikes of pale greenish-yellow flowers open in late winter and early spring, before pointed, deep green leaves appear.

3m 10ft / 3m 10ft

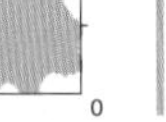

***Pyracantha* 'Golden Dome'**
Evergreen, rounded, very dense, spiny shrub. Dark green foliage sets off white flowers borne in early summer. These are followed by orange-yellow berries in early autumn.

3m 10ft / 3m 10ft

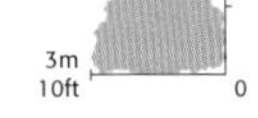

***Fatsia japonica* 'Variegata'**
Evergreen, rounded, bushy and dense shrub with palmate, glossy, dark green leaves, variegated marginally with creamy-white, and large sprays of small, white flowers in autumn.

3m 10ft / 3m 10ft

***Buxus sempervirens* 'Handsworthensis'** (Common box)
Vigorous, evergreen, bushy, upright shrub or small tree. Has broad, very dark green leaves. A dense habit makes it ideal for hedging or screening.

3m 10ft / 3m 10ft

WHITE

Buxus balearica (Balearic box)
Evergreen, tree-like shrub suitable for hedging in mild areas. Has broadly oval, bright green leaves.

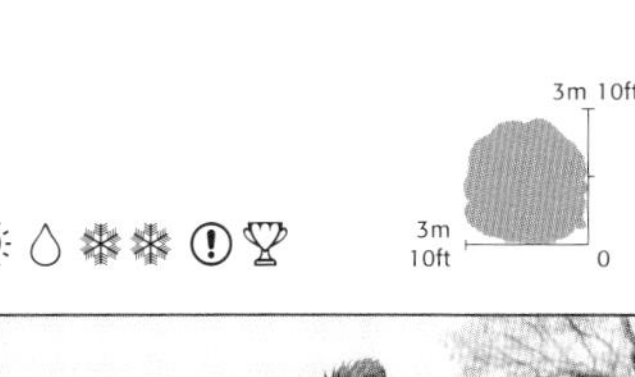

Melianthus major (Honeybush)
Evergreen, sprawling, shrub bearing blue-grey leaves, 25–45cm (10–18in) long, divided into 7–13 oval, toothed leaflets. Tubular, brownish-red flowers are produced in terminal spikes, 30cm (12in) long, in spring and summer.

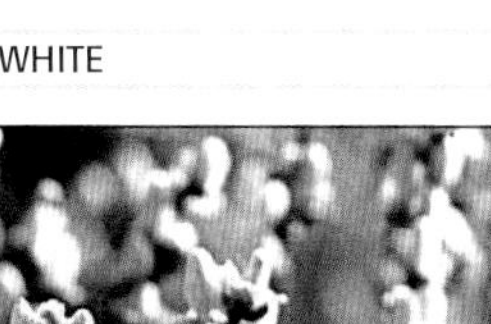

***Salix hastata* 'Wehrhahnii'**
Deciduous, upright-branched shrub with deep purple stems that contrast with silver-grey catkins borne in early spring before foliage appears. Stems later turn yellow. Has oval, bright green leaves.

1.5m 5ft
1.5m 5ft
0

***Prunus glandulosa* 'Alba Plena'**
Deciduous, open shrub, with narrowly oval, mid-green leaves, bearing racemes of double, white flowers in late spring.

Ledum groenlandicum (Labrador tea)
Evergreen, bushy shrub. Foliage is dark green and aromatic. Rounded heads of small, white flowers are carried from mid-spring to early summer.

1.5m 5ft
1.5m 5ft
0

Spiraea* x *vanhouttei (Bridal wreath)
Deciduous, compact shrub with slender, arching shoots. In late spring and early summer abundant, small, dense clusters of white flowers appear amid diamond-shaped, dark green leaves.

Deutzia gracilis
Deciduous, upright or spreading shrub. Massed, 5-petalled, pure white flowers are borne in upright clusters amid bright green foliage in late spring and early summer.

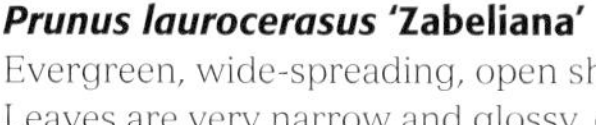

***Prunus laurocerasus* 'Zabeliana'**
Evergreen, wide-spreading, open shrub. Leaves are very narrow and glossy, dark green. Spikes of white flowers in late spring are followed by cherry-like, red, then black, fruits.

***Prunus laurocerasus* 'Otto Luyken'**
Evergreen, very dense shrub. Has upright, narrow, glossy, dark green leaves, spikes of white flowers in late spring, followed by cherry-like, red, then black, fruits.

***Gaultheria* x *wisleyensis* 'Wisley Pearl'**
Evergreen, bushy, dense shrub with oval, deeply veined, dark green leaves. Bears small, white flowers in late spring and early summer, then purplish-red fruits.

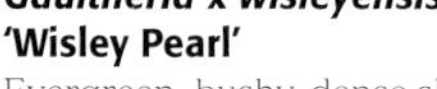

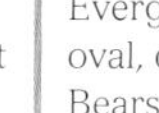

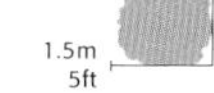

WHITE

Viburnum* x *juddii
Deciduous, rounded, bushy shrub with dark green foliage. Rounded heads of very fragrant, pink-tinged, white flowers open from pink buds from mid- to late spring.

Viburnum carlesii
Deciduous, bushy, dense shrub with dark green leaves that redden in autumn. Rounded heads of very fragrant, white and pink flowers, pink in bud, appear from mid- to late spring, followed by decorative, black fruits.

***Chaenomeles speciosa* 'Snow'**
Slow-growing, deciduous shrub forming a dense framework of interlacing, spiny branches. Has oval, toothed, dark green leaves. Saucer-shaped, pure white flowers, 4cm (1½in) across, in spring are followed by spherical, edible, yellow fruits.

PINK

Deutzia* x *rosea
Deciduous, bushy, dense shrub. In late spring and early summer produces massed, broad clusters of 5-petalled, pale pink flowers. Leaves are oval and dark green.

1.5m 5ft
1.5m 5ft
0

Menziesia ciliicalyx* var. *purpurea
Deciduous, bushy shrub with bright green foliage and racemes of nodding, purplish-pink blooms in late spring and early summer.

1.5m 5ft
1.5m 5ft
0

***Daphne* x *burkwoodii* 'Somerset'**
Semi-evergreen, upright shrub that bears dense clusters of very fragrant, white and pink flowers in late spring, and sometimes again in autumn. Leaves are lance-shaped and pale to mid-green.

Daphne retusa
Evergreen, densely branched, rounded shrub clothed with leathery, glossy leaves notched at the tips. In late spring and early summer, deep purple buds open to very fragrant, pink-flushed, white flowers borne in terminal clusters.

1.5m 5ft
1.5m 5ft
0

Prunus tenella
Deciduous, bushy shrub with upright shoots and narrowly oval, glossy leaves. Shallowly cup-shaped, bright pink flowers appear from mid- to late spring.

1.5m 5ft
1.5m 5ft
0

Prunus* x *cistena
Slow-growing, deciduous, upright shrub with deep reddish-purple leaves, red when young. Small, pinkish-white flowers from mid- to late spring may be followed by purple fruits.

RED

Cantua buxifolia
Evergreen, arching, bushy shrub. Has grey-green foliage and drooping clusters of bright red and magenta flowers from mid- to late spring.

1.5m 5ft
1.5m 5ft
0

***Ribes sanguineum* 'Edward VII'**
Deciduous, upright, compact shrub with rounded, 3–5-lobed, aromatic, dark green leaves. Small, tubular, reddish-pink flowers are borne, from mid- to late spring, and are sometimes followed by spherical, black fruits with a white bloom.

***Chaenomeles* x *superba* 'Rowallane'** (Flowering quince)
Deciduous, low, spreading shrub. Has glossy, dark green foliage and bears a profusion of large, red flowers during spring.

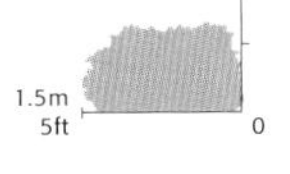

***Chaenomeles* x *superba* 'Nicoline'** (Flowering quince)
Deciduous, bushy, dense shrub. Has glossy, dark green leaves and a profusion of large, scarlet flowers in spring, followed by yellow fruits.

***Arctostaphylos* 'Emerald Carpet'**
Evergreen shrub that, with a low, dense growth of oval, bright green leaves and purple-red stems, makes excellent ground cover. Bears small, urn-shaped, white flowers in spring.

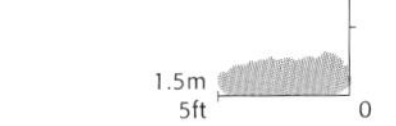

GREEN

Euphorbia characias* subsp. *characias
Evergreen, upright shrub with clusters of narrow, grey-green leaves. During spring and early summer, bears dense spikes of pale yellowish-green flowers with deep purple centres.

Daphne laureola* subsp. *philippi
Evergreen, dwarf shrub with oval, dark green leaves. Slightly fragrant, tubular, pale green flowers with short, spreading lobes appear in late winter and early spring, followed by black fruits.

YELLOW

Salix lanata (Woolly willow)
Deciduous, bushy, dense shrub with stout, woolly, grey shoots and broad, silver-grey leaves. Large, yellowish-green catkins appear in late spring with foliage.

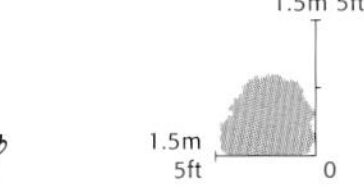

Salix repens (Creeping willow)
Deciduous, prostrate or semi-upright and bushy shrub. Silky, grey catkins become yellow from mid- to late spring, before small, narrowly oval leaves, which are grey-green above, silvery beneath, appear.

Euphorbia characias* subsp. *wulfenii
Evergreen, upright shrub. Stems are biennial, producing clustered, grey-green leaves one year and spikes of yellow-green blooms the following spring.

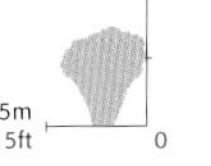

YELLOW

Cytisus x _praecox_ 'Warminster' (Warminster broom)
Deciduous, densely branched shrub. From mid- to late spring, pea-like, creamy-yellow flowers appear in profusion amid tiny, silky, grey-green leaves with 3 leaflets.

1.5m 5ft / 1.5m 5ft / 0

Cytisus x _praecox_ 'Allgold' (Broom)
Deciduous, densely branched shrub with silky, grey-green leaves, divided into 3 leaflets, and a profusion of pea-like, yellow flowers from mid- to late spring.

1.5m 5ft / 1.5m 5ft / 0

Berberis empetrifolia
Evergreen, arching, prickly shrub with narrow, grey-green leaves, globose, golden-yellow flowers in late spring and black fruits in autumn.

1.5m 5ft / 1.5m 5ft / 0

Genista tinctoria (Dyers' greenweed)
Deciduous, spreading, dwarf shrub that bears dense spires of pea-like, golden-yellow flowers in spring and summer. Leaves are narrow and dark green.

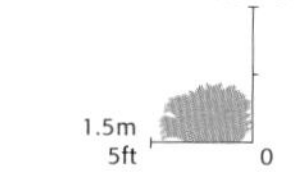

1.5m 5ft / 1.5m 5ft / 0

Mahonia aquifolium (Oregon grape)
Evergreen, open shrub. Leaves, with glossy, bright green leaflets, often turn red or purple in winter. Bunches of small, yellow flowers in spring are followed by blue-black berries.

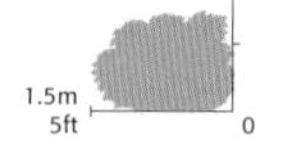

1.5m 5ft / 1.5m 5ft / 0

Caragana arborescens 'Nana'
Deciduous, bushy, dwarf shrub with mid-green leaves consisting of many oval leaflets. Pea-like, yellow flowers are borne in late spring.

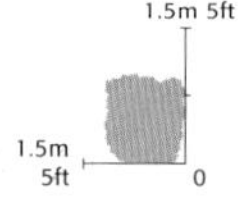

1.5m 5ft / 1.5m 5ft / 0

Ulex europaeus (Gorse)
Leafless or almost leafless, bushy shrub with year-round, dark green shoots and spines that make it appear evergreen. Bears massed, fragrant, pea-like, yellow flowers in spring.

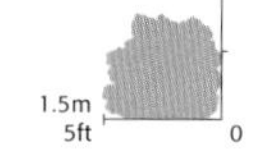

1.5m 5ft / 1.5m 5ft / 0

Choisya ternata SUNDANCE ('Lich')
Evergreen, rounded, dense shrub with aromatic, glossy, bright yellow leaves divided into 3 oblong leaflets. Fragrant, star-shaped, white flowers are produced in clusters in late spring and often again in autumn.

1.5m 5ft / 1.5m 5ft / 0

WHITE

Deutzia monbeigii
Deciduous, arching, elegant shrub. Clusters of small, 5-petalled, white flowers appear in profusion among small, dark green leaves from early- to mid-summer.

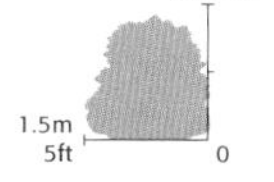

***Hebe* 'White Gem'**
Evergreen, rounded shrub that produces a dense mound of small, glossy leaves covered in early summer with tight racemes of small, white flowers.

Olearia phlogopappa* var. *subrepanda
Evergreen, upright, compact shrub. Heads of daisy-like, white flowers are borne profusely from mid-spring to early summer amid narrow, toothed, grey-green leaves.

Rhodotypos scandens
Deciduous, upright or slightly arching shrub. In late spring and early summer, amid sharply toothed leaves, bears shallowly cupped, white flowers, followed by small, pea-shaped, black fruits.

***Philadelphus* 'Manteau d'Hermine'**
Deciduous, bushy, compact shrub. Clusters of fragrant, double, creamy-white flowers appear amid small, pale to mid-green leaves from early to mid-summer.

***Potentilla fruticosa* 'Abbotswood'**
Deciduous, bushy shrub. Large, pure white flowers are borne amid dark blue-green leaves, divided into 5 narrowly oval leaflets, throughout summer–autumn.

Convolvulus cneorum
Evergreen, rounded, bushy, dense shrub. Pink-tinged buds opening to white flowers with yellow centres are borne from late spring to late summer among narrow, silky, silvery-green leaves.

Halimium umbellatum
Evergreen, upright shrub. Narrow, glossy, dark green leaves are white beneath. White flowers, centrally blotched with yellow, are produced in early summer from reddish buds.

***Potentilla fruticosa* 'Farrer's White'**
Deciduous, bushy shrub with divided, grey-green leaves. Bears an abundance of white flowers during summer to autumn.

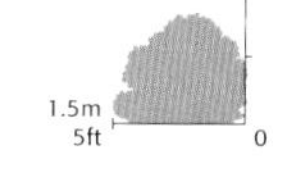

x *Halimiocistus sahucii*
Evergreen, bushy, dense shrub with narrow, dark green leaves that set off an abundance of pure white flowers in late spring and early summer.

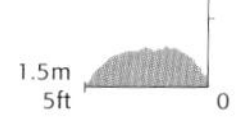

SHRUBS

WHITE

Cistus salviifolius
Evergreen, bushy, dense shrub with slightly wrinkled, grey-green foliage. White flowers, with central, yellow blotches, appear in profusion during early summer.

1.5m 5ft
1.5m 5ft

Cistus* x *hybridus (Rock rose)
Evergreen, bushy, dense shrub. Has wrinkled, wavy-edged, dark green leaves and massed white flowers, with central, yellow blotches, carried in late spring and early summer.

1.5m 5ft
1.5m 5ft

Cistus* x *cyprius
Evergreen, bushy shrub with sticky shoots and narrow, glossy, dark green leaves. In early summer bears large, white flowers, with a red blotch at each petal base, that appear in succession for some weeks but last only a day.

1.5m 5ft
1.5m 5ft

Cassinia leptophylla* subsp. *vauvilliersii
Evergreen, upright shrub. Whitish shoots are covered with tiny, dark green leaves and heads of small, white flowers from mid- to late summer.

1.5m 5ft
1.5m 5ft

***Cistus* x *aguilarii* 'Maculatus'**
Evergreen, bushy shrub with narrow, wavy-edged, slightly sticky, rich green leaves. Large, white flowers, with a central, deep red and yellow pattern, appear from early to mid-summer.

1.5m 5ft
1.5m 5ft

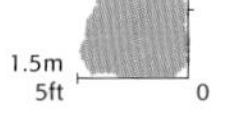

Cistus ladanifer
Evergreen, open, upright shrub. Leaves are narrow, dark green and sticky. Bears large, white flowers, with red markings around the central tuft of stamens, in profusion in early summer.

1.5m 5ft
1.5m 5ft

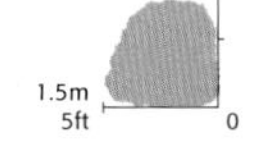

Rhaphiolepis umbellata
Evergreen, bushy shrub with rounded, leathery, dark green leaves and clusters of fragrant, white flowers during early summer.

1.5m 5ft
1.5m 5ft

Vaccinium corymbosum
(Highbush blueberry)
Deciduous, upright, slightly arching shrub. Small, white or pinkish flowers in late spring and early summer are followed by sweet, edible, blue-black berries. Foliage turns red in autumn.

1.5m 5ft
1.5m 5ft

SHRUBS

Yucca whipplei
Evergreen, virtually stemless shrub that forms a dense tuft of slender, pointed, blue-green leaves. Very long panicles of fragrant, greenish-white flowers are produced in late spring and early summer.

Viburnum acerifolium
Deciduous, upright-branched shrub with bright green leaves that turn orange, red and purple in autumn. Decorative, red fruits, which turn purple-black, follow heads of creamy-white flowers in early summer.

Yucca flaccida 'Ivory'
Evergreen, very short-stemmed shrub that produces tufts of narrow, dark green leaves and long panicles of bell-shaped, white flowers from mid- to late summer.

Ozothamnus ledifolius
Evergreen, dense shrub. Yellow shoots are covered with small, aromatic leaves, glossy, dark green above, yellow beneath. Small, white flower heads are borne in early summer.

Lomatia silaifolia
Evergreen, bushy shrub. Spikes of creamy-white flowers, each with 4 narrow, twisted petals, are borne amid deeply divided, dark green leaves from mid- to late summer.

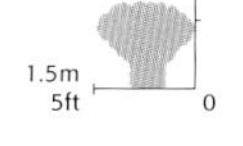

Hebe albicans
Evergreen shrub that forms a dense mound of blue-grey foliage covered with small, tight clusters of white flowers from early to mid-summer.

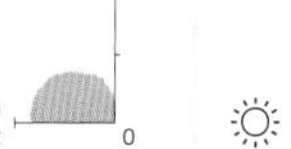

Hebe recurva
Evergreen, open, spreading shrub. Leaves are narrow, curved and blue-grey. Small spikes of white flowers appear from mid- to late summer.

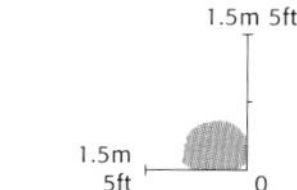

Leptospermum rupestre
Evergreen, semi-prostrate, widely arching shrub with reddish shoots and small, dark green leaves that turn bronze-purple in winter. Small, open cup-shaped, white flowers, red-flushed in bud, appear in early summer.

SHRUBS

WHITE

Weigela florida 'Variegata'
Deciduous, bushy, dense shrub. Carries a profusion of funnel-shaped, pink flowers in late spring and early summer, and has mid-green leaves broadly edged with creamy-white.

1.5m 5ft
1.5m 5ft
0

Coprosma x _kirkii_ 'Variegata'
Evergreen, densely branched shrub, prostrate when young, later semi-erect. White-margined leaves are borne singly or in small clusters. Tiny, translucent, white fruits appear in autumn on female plants if both sexes are grown.

1.5m 5ft
1.5m 5ft
0

PINK

Deutzia 'Mont Rose'
Deciduous, bushy shrub that produces clusters of pink or pinkish-purple flowers, in early summer, with yellow anthers and occasionally white markings. Leaves are sharply toothed and dark green.

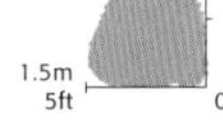

Fuchsia 'Lady Thumb'
Deciduous, upright, dwarf shrub bearing small, semi-double flowers with reddish-pink tubes and sepals, and pink-veined, white petals. May be trained as a miniature standard.

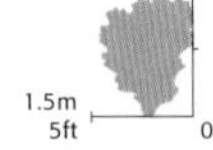

Hebe hulkeana 'Lilac Hint'
Evergreen, upright, open-branched shrub with toothed, glossy, pale green leaves. A profusion of small, pale lilac flowers appears in large racemes in late spring and early summer.

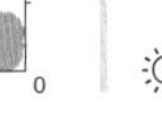

Indigofera dielsiana
Deciduous, upright, open shrub. Dark green leaves consist of 7–11 oval leaflets. Slender, erect spikes of pale pink flowers are borne from early summer to early autumn.

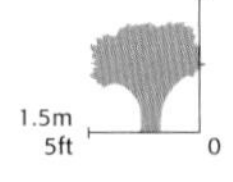

Cistus x _skanbergii_
Evergreen, bushy shrub. A profusion of pale pink flowers appears amid narrow, grey-green leaves from early to mid-summer.

Phlomis italica
Evergreen, upright shrub. In mid-summer, whorls of lilac-pink flowers are borne at the ends of shoots amid narrow, woolly, grey-green leaves.

***Deutzia* x *elegantissima* 'Rosealind'**
Deciduous, rounded, bushy, dense shrub that produces clusters of 5-petalled, deep pink flowers from late spring to early summer.

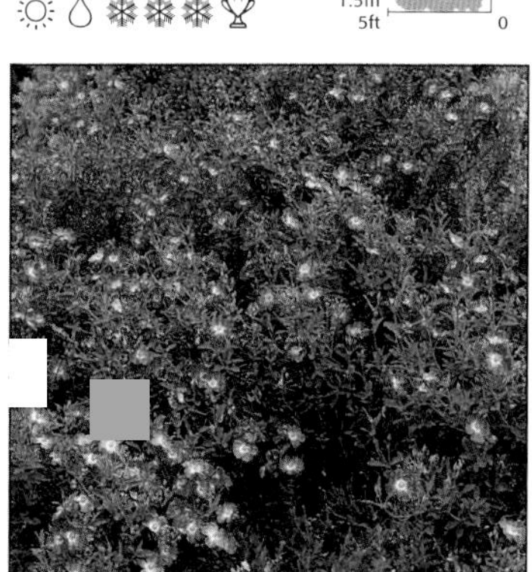

***Cistus* x *argenteus* 'Peggy Sammons'**
Evergreen, bushy shrub with oval, grey-green leaves. Saucer-shaped, pale purplish-pink flowers are produced freely during early summer.

***Weigela florida* 'Foliis Purpureis'**
Deciduous, low, bushy shrub that bears funnel-shaped flowers, deep pink outside, pale pink to white inside, in late spring and early summer. Leaves are dull purple or purplish-green.

Penstemon isophyllus
Slightly untidy, deciduous shrub or sub-shrub that, from mid- to late summer, carries long sprays of large, white- and red-throated, deep pink flowers above spear-shaped, glossy, mid-green leaves.

***Hebe* 'Great Orme'**
Evergreen, rounded, open shrub. Has deep purplish shoots and glossy, dark green foliage. Slender spikes of deep pink flowers that fade to white are produced from mid-summer to mid-autumn.

***Spiraea japonica* 'Little Princess'**
Slow-growing, deciduous, mound-forming shrub that produces copious small heads of rose-pink blooms from mid- to late summer. Small, dark green leaves are bronze when young

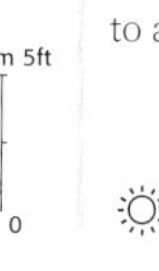

***Ceanothus* 'Perle Rose'**
Deciduous, bushy shrub that from mid-summer to early autumn bears dense racemes of bright carmine-pink flowers amid broad, oval, mid-green leaves.

***Abelia* 'Edward Goucher'**
Deciduous or semi-evergreen, arching shrub. Oval, bright green leaves are bronze when young. Bears a profusion of lilac-pink flowers from mid-summer to autumn.

HARDY FUCHSIAS

With their vivid blooms and long flowering season, hardy fuchsias are outstanding garden shrubs. They flower throughout the summer months, producing an abundance of vibrant, pendant, single to double flowers, with flared or elegantly recurved sepals. These range in colour from deep red and purple, to soft pink and pure white, and are often bicoloured. Unlike tender varieties (see p.302), hardy fuchsias, and can be grown outside all year in full sun or partial shade. They require moist, well-drained soil, and can be grown in large containers.

F. **'Madame Cornélissen'** 🏆

F. magellanica

F. **'Riccartonii'** 🏆

F. **'Rufus'** 🏆

F. magellanica **var. *gracilis*** 🏆

F. **'Mrs Popple'** 🏆

F. **'Corallina'** 🏆

F. magellanica **'Thompsonii'** 🏆 *F.* **'Howlett's Hardy'** 🏆

F. **'Tom Thumb'** 🏆

PINK

Abelia schumannii

Deciduous, arching shrub. Pointed, mid-green leaves are bronze when young. Yellow-blotched, rose-purple and white flowers appear from mid-summer to mid-autumn.

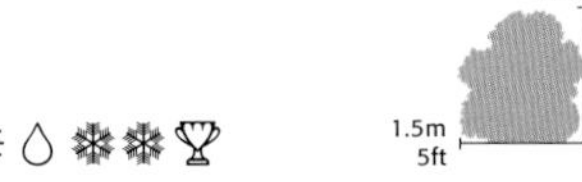

Spiraea japonica **'Anthony Waterer'**

Deciduous, upright, compact shrub. Red, young foliage matures to dark green. Heads of crimson-pink blooms appear from mid- to late summer.

Cistus creticus (Rock rose)

Evergreen, bushy shrub. Pink or purplish-pink flowers, each with a central, yellow blotch, appear amid grey-green leaves from early to mid-summer.

Escallonia **'Donard Beauty'**

Evergreen, arching shrub with slender shoots. Deep pink flowers are produced from early to mid-summer among small, oval, dark green leaves.

Desmodium elegans

Deciduous, upright sub-shrub. Mid-green leaves consist of 3 large leaflets. Large racemes of pale lilac to deep pink flowers appear from late summer to mid-autumn.

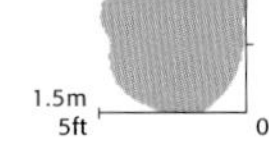

Gaultheria shallon (Shallon)

Evergreen, bushy shrub. Red shoots carry broad, pointed, dark green leaves. Racemes of urn-shaped, pink flowers in late spring and early summer are followed by purple fruit.

SALVIAS

Salvia is a vast genus of 900 species of mainly tender sub-shrubs or herbaceous perennials from North, Central, and South America and Africa. Most species have aromatic leaves and the foliage of common sage, *Salvia officinalis*, has been cultivated for centuries for culinary and medicinal use. The flowers of shrubby salvias, which are primarily white, pink or red, are hooded and borne in whorls along the stems in summer and early autumn. Most species are quite tender and need winter protection in frost-prone areas, although common sage and its cultivars are fully hardy. *S. microphylla* will also withstand a few degrees of frost, but the others featured here are conservatory plants. Grow garden salvias in free-draining soil and full sun.

***S.* x *jamensis* 'Sierra San Antonio'**

***S.* x *jamensis* 'La Luna'**

***S. officinalis* 'Tricolor'**

***S. microphylla* 'Pink Blush'**

***S. microphylla* 'Newby Hall'**

***S. officinalis* 'Berggarten'**

S. officinalis

***S.* x *jamensis* 'Hot Lips'**

***S. microphylla* 'Kew Red'**

***S. microphylla* 'La Foux'**

***S. greggii* 'Icing Sugar'**

***S. officinalis* 'Purpurascens'**

***S.* x *jamensis* 'Maraschino'**

***S.* x *jamensis* 'Red Velvet'**

***S. microphylla* 'Cerro Potosi'**

***S. officinalis* 'Icterina'**

RED

Kalmia angustifolia* f. *rubra
Evergreen, bushy, mound-forming shrub with oval, dark green leaves and clusters of small, deep red flowers in early summer.

***Escallonia rubra* 'Woodside'**
Evergreen, bushy, dense shrub. Has small, glossy, dark green leaves and short racemes of small tubular, crimson flowers in summer–autumn.

***Potentilla fruticosa* 'Red Ace'**
Deciduous, spreading, bushy, dense shrub. Bright vermilion flowers, pale yellow on the backs of petals, are produced among mid-green leaves from late spring to mid-autumn but fade quickly in full sun.

***Spiraea japonica* 'Goldflame'**
Deciduous, upright, slightly arching shrub with orange-red, young leaves turning to bright yellow and finally pale green. Bears heads of deep rose-pink flowers from mid- to late summer.

Salvia fulgens
Evergreen, upright sub-shrub. Oval leaves are white and woolly beneath, hairy above. Racemes of tubular, 2-lipped, scarlet flowers appear in late summer.

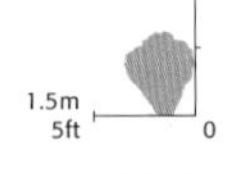

Phygelius aequalis
Evergreen or semi-evergreen, upright sub-shrub. Clusters of tubular, pale red flowers with yellow throats appear from mid-summer to early autumn. Leaves are oval and dark green.

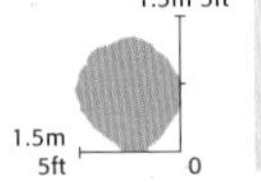

Salvia microphylla* var. *microphylla
Evergreen, well-branched, upright shrub with pale to mid-green leaves. Has tubular, bright red flowers from purple-tinted, green calyces in late summer and autumn.

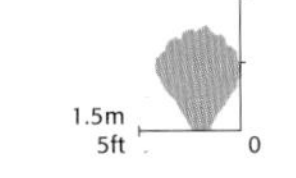

***Acer palmatum* 'Dissectum Atropurpureum'**
Deciduous shrub that forms a mound of deeply divided, bronze-red or purple foliage, which turns brilliant red, orange or yellow in autumn. Has small, reddish-purple flowers in mid-spring.

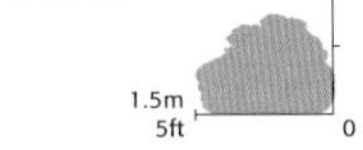

PURPLE

Hebe 'E.A. Bowles'
Evergreen, rounded, bushy shrub with narrow, glossy, pale green leaves and slender spikes of lilac flowers produced from mid-summer to late autumn.

Hebe 'Autumn Glory'
Evergreen shrub that forms a mound of purplish-red shoots and rounded, deep green leaves, over which dense racemes of deep purple-blue flowers appear from mid-summer to early winter.

Hebe 'Purple Queen'
Evergreen, bushy, compact shrub with glossy, deep green leaves that are purple-tinged when young. Dense racemes of deep purple flowers appear from early summer to mid-autumn.

Lavandula stoechas (French lavender)
Evergreen, bushy, dense shrub. Heads of tiny, fragrant, deep purple flowers, topped by rose-purple bracts, appear in late spring and summer. Mature leaves are silver-grey and aromatic.

Hebe 'Bowles's Variety'
Evergreen, rounded shrub with ovate-oblong, slightly glossy, mid-green leaves. In summer, bears mauve-blue flowers in compact, tapered, terminal racemes.

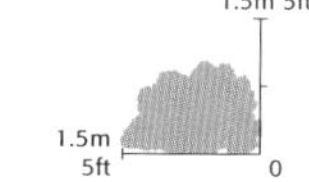

BLUE

Caryopteris x _clandonensis_ 'Arthur Simmonds'
Deciduous, bushy sub-shrub. Masses of blue to purplish-blue flowers appear amid narrowly oval, irregularly toothed, grey-green leaves from late summer to autumn.

Hyssopus officinalis (Hyssop)
Semi-evergreen or deciduous, bushy shrub with aromatic, narrowly oval, deep green leaves. Small, blue flowers appear from mid-summer to early autumn. Sometimes used as a culinary herb.

Felicia amelloides 'Santa Anita'
Evergreen, bushy, spreading shrub. Blue flower heads, with bright yellow centres, are borne on long stalks from late spring to autumn among round to oval, bright green leaves.

Ceanothus 'Gloire de Versailles'
Vigorous, deciduous, bushy shrub. Has broad, oval, mid-green leaves and large racemes of pale blue flowers from mid-summer to early autumn.

Rosmarinus officinalis (Rosemary)
Evergreen, bushy, dense shrub with aromatic, narrow leaves. Small, purplish-blue to blue flowers appear from mid-spring to early summer and sometimes in autumn. Used as a culinary herb.

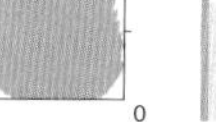

LAVENDERS

Lavendula is a popular genus of about 25 species of aromatic shrubs and herbs that originate predominantly from the Mediterranean region and North-east Africa, and thrive in hot, dry, sunny sites. Most have linear silver-grey foliage and produce erect spikes of fragrant flowers in shades of white, pink, blue, or purple, depending on the type. They are versatile plants, and can be used to edge borders, paths, and hard landscaping, or against a backdrop of stonework, as a dwarf hedge or informal divide, or in association with roses for a typical 'English style' effect. They are also excellent plants for coastal areas, coping well with salt-laden maritime breezes, and thrive in well-drained soil; they will suffer if planted in shade or wet soils.

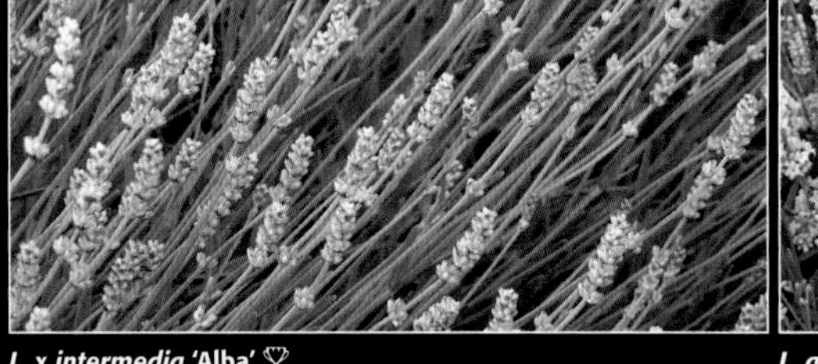

***L.* x *intermedia* 'Alba'** 🏆

L. angustifolia **LITTLE LOTTIE ('Clarmo')** 🏆

***L. angustifolia* 'Miss Katherine'** 🏆

***L.* 'Willow Vale'** 🏆

***L. stoechas* 'Snowman'**

***L. angustifolia* 'Wendy Carlile'** 🏆

***L. pedunculata* subsp. *pedunculata* 'James Compton'**

***L.* 'Fathead'**

***L.* 'Regal Splendour'**

***L. stoechas* f. *rosea* 'Kew Red'**

***L.* 'Helmsdale'**

***L. angustifolia* 'Little Lady'**

***L. angustifolia* 'Loddon Blue'** 🏆

***L. angustifolia* 'Imperial Gem'** 🏆

***L.* x *chaytorae* 'Sawyers'** 🏆

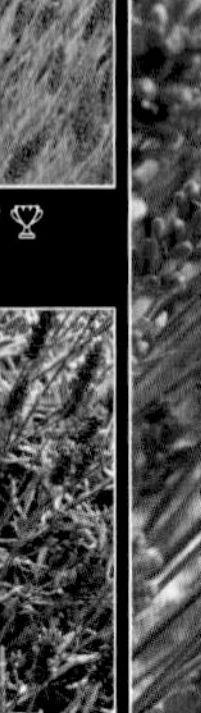

L. lanata 🏆

***L. angustifolia* 'Hidcote'** 🏆

BLUE

Ceanothus thyrsiflorus* var. *repens
(Creeping blue blossom)
Evergreen, shrub that forms a mound of broad, glossy, dark green leaves. Racemes of blue flowers are produced late spring to esarly summer.

***Perovskia* 'Blue Spire'**
Deciduous, upright sub-shrub with grey-white stems. Profuse spikes of violet-blue flowers appear from late summer to mid-autumn above aromatic, deeply cut, grey-green leaves.

1.5m 5ft
1.5m
5ft
0

Ceratostigma willmottianum
Deciduous, open shrub. Has leaves that turn red in late autumn and bright, rich blue flowers from late summer until well into autumn.

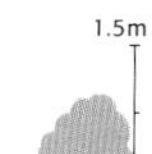

YELLOW

***Physocarpus opulifolius* 'Dart's Gold'**
Deciduous, compact shrub with peeling bark and oval, lobed, golden-yellow leaves. Produces clusters of shallowly cup-shaped, white or pale pink flowers in late spring.

1.5m 5ft
1.5m
5ft
0

***Ruta graveolens* 'Jackman's Blue'**
(Common rue)
Evergreen, bushy, compact sub-shrub. Has aromatic, finely divided, blue foliage. In summer, it produces clusters of small, mustard-yellow flowers.

1.5m 5ft
1.5m
5ft
0

Weigela middendorffiana
Deciduous, bushy, arching shrub. From mid-spring to early summer funnel-shaped, sulphur-yellow flowers, spotted with orange inside, are borne amid bright green foliage.

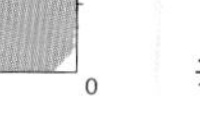

***Potentilla fruticosa* 'Vilmoriniana'**
Deciduous, upright shrub that bears pale yellow or creamy-white flowers from late spring to mid-autumn. Leaves are silver-grey and divided into leaflets.

1.5m 5ft
1.5m
5ft
0

***Santolina pinnata* subsp. *neapolitana* 'Sulphurea'**
Evergreen, rounded, bushy shrub with aromatic, deeply cut, feathery, grey-green foliage. Produces heads of pale primrose-yellow flowers in mid-summer.

Lupinus arboreus (Tree lupin)
Fast-growing, semi-evergreen, sprawling shrub that in early summer usually bears short spikes of fragrant, yellow flowers above hairy, pale green leaves composed of 6–9 leaflets.

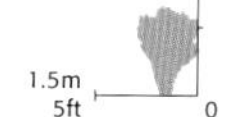

YELLOW

***Symphoricarpos orbiculatus* 'Foliis Variegatis'**
Deciduous, bushy, dense shrub with bright green leaves edged with yellow. Occasionally bears white or pink flowers in summer–autumn.

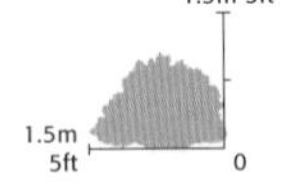

***Phygelius aequalis* 'Yellow Trumpet'**
Evergreen or semi-evergreen, upright sub-shrub. Bears clusters of pendent, tubular, pale creamy-yellow flowers from mid-summer to early autumn.

***Potentilla fruticosa* 'Elizabeth'**
Deciduous, bushy, dense shrub with small, deeply divided leaves and large, bright yellow flowers that appear from late spring to mid-autumn.

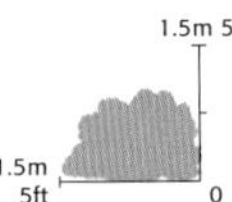

***Potentilla fruticosa* 'Friedrichsenii'**
Vigorous, deciduous, upright shrub. From late spring to mid-autumn pale yellow flowers are produced amid grey-green leaves.

***Hypericum* 'Hidcote'**
Evergreen or semi-evergreen, bushy, dense shrub. Bears an abundance of large, golden-yellow flowers from mid-summer to early autumn amid narrowly oval, dark green leaves.

***Halimium* 'Susan'**
Evergreen, spreading shrub with narrow, oval, grey-green leaves. Numerous single or semi-double, bright yellow flowers with central, deep purple-red markings are borne in small clusters along branches in summer.

***Phlomis fruticosa* (Jerusalem sage)**
Evergreen, spreading shrub with upright shoots. Whorls of deep golden-yellow flowers are produced amid sage-like, grey-green foliage from early to mid-summer.

***Berberis thunbergii* 'Aurea'**
Deciduous, bushy, spiny shrub with small, golden-yellow leaves. Racemes of small, red-tinged, pale yellow flowers in mid-spring are followed by red berries in autumn.

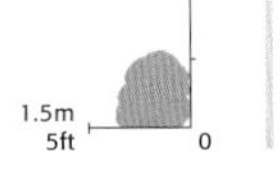

Cytisus nigricans
Deciduous, upright shrub with dark green leaves composed of 3 leaflets. Has a long-lasting display of tall, slender spires of yellow flowers during summer.

***Genista hispanica* (Spanish gorse)**
Deciduous, bushy, very spiny shrub with few leaves. Bears dense clusters of golden-yellow flowers profusely in late spring and early summer.

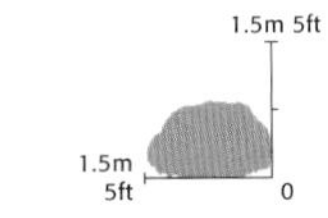

Hypericum x _inodorum_ 'Elstead'
Deciduous or semi-evergreen, upright shrub. Abundant, small, yellow flowers borne from mid-summer to early autumn are followed by ornamental, orange-red fruits. Dark green leaves are aromatic when crushed.

Grindelia chiloensis
Mainly evergreen, bushy shrub with sticky stems. Sticky, lance-shaped, serrated leaves are up to 12cm (5in) long. Has large, daisy-like, yellow flower heads in summer.

Brachyglottis monroi
Evergreen, bushy, dense shrub that makes an excellent windbreak in mild, coastal areas. Has small, wavy-edged, dark green leaves with white undersides. Bears heads of bright yellow flowers in mid-summer.

Brachyglottis Dunedin Group
Evergreen, bushy shrub that forms a mound of silvery-grey, young leaves, later turning dark green. Bears bright yellow flower heads on felted shoots from early to mid-summer.

Hypericum kouytchense
Deciduous or semi-evergreen, arching shrub. Golden-yellow flowers with conspicuous stamens are borne among foliage from mid-summer to early autumn and followed by decorative, bronze-red fruit capsules.

Coriaria terminalis var. _xanthocarpa_
Deciduous, arching sub-shrub. Leaves have oval leaflets and turn red in autumn. Greenish flowers in late spring are followed by decorative, succulent, yellow fruits in late summer and autumn.

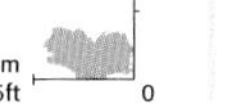

Hypericum calycinum (Aaron's beard, Rose of Sharon)
Evergreen or semi-evergreen dwarf shrub that makes good ground cover. Has large, bright yellow flowers from mid-summer to mid-autumn and dark green leaves.

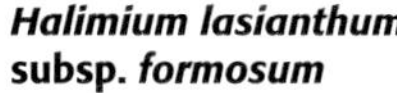

Halimium lasianthum subsp. _formosum_
Evergreen, spreading, bushy shrub. Has grey-green foliage and golden-yellow flowers, with central, deep red blotches, borne in late spring and early summer.

ORANGE

Cytisus scoparius* f. *andreanus
(Common broom)
Deciduous, arching shrub with narrow, dark green leaves that are divided into 3 leaflets. Bears a profusion of bright yellow-and-red flowers along elegant, green branchlets in late spring and early summer.

1.5m 5ft / 1.5m 5ft / 0

***Potentilla fruticosa* 'Daydawn'**
Deciduous, bushy, rather arching shrub. Creamy-yellow flowers, flushed with orange-pink, appear among divided, mid-green leaves from early summer to mid-autumn.

1.5m 5ft / 1.5m 5ft / 0

Mimulus aurantiacus
Evergreen, domed to rounded shrub with sticky, lance-shaped, glossy, rich green leaves. Has tubular, orange, yellow or red-purple flowers from late spring to autumn.

1.5m 5ft / 1.5m 5ft / 0

***Potentilla fruticosa* 'Sunset'**
Deciduous shrub, bushy at first, later arching. Deep orange flowers, fading in hot sun, appear from early summer to mid-autumn. Mid-green leaves are divided into narrowly oval leaflets.

1.5m 5ft / 1.5m 5ft / 0

Cuphea cyanea
Evergreen, rounded sub-shrub with narrowly oval, sticky-haired leaves. Tubular flowers, orange-red, yellow and violet-blue, are carried in summer.

1.5m 5ft / 1.5m 5ft / 0

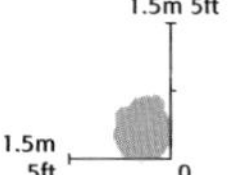

***Abutilon* 'Kentish Belle'**
Semi-evergreen, arching shrub with purple shoots and deeply lobed, purple-veined, dark green leaves. Bears large, pendent, bell-shaped, orange-yellow and red flowers in summer–autumn.

1.5m 5ft / 1.5m 5ft / 0

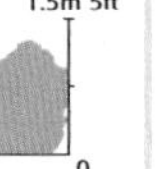

Myrica gale (Bog myrtle)
Deciduous, suckering shrub of dense habit. Produces narrowly oblong to rounded, highly aromatic, dark green leaves, with crinkled margins. Both male and female flowers, borne in mid- and late spring, are erect, golden brown catkins.

1.5m 5ft / 1.5m 5ft / 0

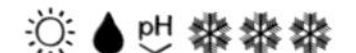

RED

***Berberis* 'Rubrostilla'**
Deciduous, arching shrub. Globose to cup-shaped, pale yellow flowers, appearing in early summer, are followed by a profusion of large, coral-red fruits. Grey-green leaves turn brilliant red in late autumn.

1.5m 5ft / 1.5m 5ft / 0

***Viburnum opulus* 'Compactum'**
Deciduous, dense shrub. Has deep green leaves, red in autumn, and profuse white flowers in spring and early summer, followed by bunches of bright red berries.

1.5m 5ft / 1.5m 5ft / 0

Vaccinium angustifolium var. _laevifolium_ (Low-bush blueberry)
Deciduous, bushy shrub with bright green leaves that redden in autumn. Edible, blue fruits follow white, sometimes pinkish, spring flowers.

***Vaccinium corymbosum* 'Pioneer'**
Deciduous, upright, slightly arching shrub. Dark green leaves turn bright red in autumn. Small, white or pinkish flowers in late spring are followed by sweet, edible, blue-black berries.

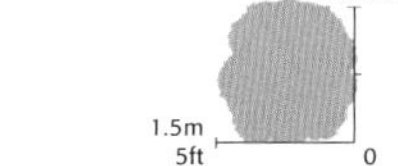

Vaccinium parvifolium
Deciduous, upright shrub. Has small, dark green leaves that become bright red in autumn. Edible, bright red fruits are produced after small, pinkish-white flowers borne in late spring and early summer.

Fothergilla gardenii
Deciduous, bushy, dense shrub. Produces dense clusters of tiny, fragrant, white flowers from mid- to late spring, usually before broadly oval, dark blue-green leaves emerge. Leaves turn to brilliant red in autumn.

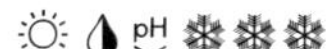

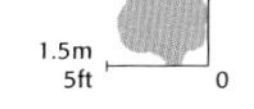

***Skimmia japonica* 'Fructo Albo'**
Evergreen, bushy, dense, dwarf shrub. Has aromatic, dark green leaves and dense clusters of small, white flowers from mid- to late spring, succeeded by white berries.

***Gaultheria mucronata* 'Wintertime'**
Evergreen, bushy, dense shrub. Has prickly, glossy, dark green leaves and white flowers in late spring and early summer, followed by large, long-lasting, white berries.

Lonicera* x *purpusii
Semi-evergreen, bushy, dense shrub with oval, dark green leaves. Small clusters of fragrant, short-tubed, white flowers, with spreading petal lobes and yellow anthers, appear in winter and early spring.

WHITE

Sarcococca humilis **(Christmas box)**
Evergreen, low, clump-forming shrub. Tiny, fragrant, white flowers with pink anthers appear amid glossy, dark green foliage in late winter and are followed by spherical, black fruits.

Sarcococca hookeriana* var. *digyna
Evergreen, clump-forming, suckering, dense shrub with narrow, bright green leaves. Tiny, fragrant, white flowers, with pink anthers, open in winter and are followed by spherical, black fruits.

***Vinca major* 'Variegata'**
(Greater periwinkle)
Evergreen, prostrate, arching, spreading sub-shrub. Has bright green leaves broadly edged with creamy-white and large, bright blue flowers borne from late spring to early autumn.

PINK

***Daphne odora* 'Aureomarginata'**
Evergreen, bushy shrub with glossy, dark green leaves narrowly edged with yellow. Clusters of very fragrant, deep purplish-pink and white flowers appear from mid-winter to early spring.

Gaultheria mucronata
'Mulberry Wine'
Evergreen, bushy, dense shrub with large, globose, magenta berries that mature to deep purple. These follow white flowers borne in spring–summer. Leaves are glossy, dark green.

RED

***Skimmia japonica* 'Rubella'**
Evergreen, upright, dense shrub with aromatic, red-rimmed, bright green foliage. Deep red flower buds in autumn and winter open to dense clusters of small, white flowers in spring.

Correa pulchella
Evergreen, fairly bushy, slender-stemmed shrub with oval leaves. Small, pendent, tubular, rose-red flowers appear from summer to winter, and sometimes at other seasons.

Skimmia japonica* subsp. *reevesiana
'Robert Fortune'
Evergreen, bushy, rather weak-growing shrub with aromatic leaves. Small, white flowers in spring are followed by crimson berries.

Skimmia japonica
Evergreen, bushy, dense shrub. Has aromatic, mid- to dark green leaves and dense clusters of small, white flowers from mid- to late spring, followed on female plants by bright red fruits if plants of both sexes are grown.

Pittosporum tenuifolium
'Tom Thumb'
Evergreen, rounded, dense shrub with pale green, young leaves that contrast with deep reddish-brown, older foliage. Bears cup-shaped, purplish flowers in summer.

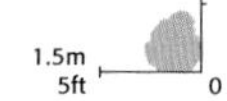

SHRUBS

GREY

GREEN

Helichrysum petiolare 'Variegatum'
Evergreen shrub forming mounds of silver-green shoots and grey-felted leaves, variegated cream. Has creamy-yellow flower heads in summer. Often grown as an annual for ground cover and edging.

1.5m 5ft / 1.5m 5ft / 0

Ribes laurifolium
Evergreen, spreading shrub. Has leathery, deep green leaves and pendent racemes of greenish-yellow flowers in late winter and early spring. Produces edible, black berries on female plants if plants of both sexes are grown.

1.5m 5ft / 1.5m 5ft / 0

Vinca minor (Lesser periwinkle)
Evergreen, prostrate, spreading sub-shrub that forms extensive mats of small, glossy, dark green leaves. Bears small, purple, blue or white flowers, mainly from mid-spring to early summer.

1.5m 5ft / 1.5m 5ft / 0

Artemisia abrotanum
(Lad's love, Old man, Southernwood)
Deciduous or semi-evergreen, moderately bushy shrub. Aromatic, grey-green leaves have many very slender lobes. Has clusters of small, yellowish flower heads in late summer.

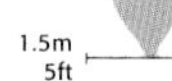

1.5m 5ft / 1.5m 5ft / 0

Viburnum davidii
Evergreen shrub that forms a dome of dark green foliage, over which heads of small, white flowers appear in late spring. If plants of both sexes are grown, female plants bear decorative, metallic-blue fruits.

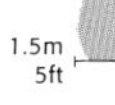

1.5m 5ft / 1.5m 5ft / 0

Chamaerops humilis
(Dwarf fan palm, European fan palm)
Slow-growing, evergreen palm, suckering with age. Fan-shaped leaves, 60–90cm (2–3ft) across, have green to grey-green lobes. Has tiny, yellow flowers in summer.

1.5m 5ft / 1.5m 5ft / 0

Hebe cupressoides
Evergreen, upright, dense shrub with cypress-like, grey-green foliage. On mature plants tiny, pale lilac flowers are borne from early to mid-summer.

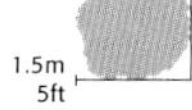

1.5m 5ft / 1.5m 5ft / 0

Artemisia arborescens (Wormwood)
Evergreen, upright shrub, grown for its finely cut, silvery-white foliage. Heads of small, bright yellow flowers are borne in summer and early autumn.

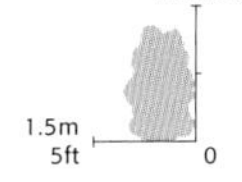

1.5m 5ft / 1.5m 5ft / 0

Ballota acetabulosa
Evergreen sub-shrub that forms a mound of rounded, grey-green leaves, felted beneath. Whorls of small, pink flowers open from mid- to late summer.

1.5m 5ft / 1.5m 5ft / 0

Vaccinium glaucoalbum
Evergreen shrub with deep green leaves that, when young, are pale green above, bluish-white beneath. Pink-tinged, white flowers in late spring and early summer are followed by white-bloomed, blue-black fruits.

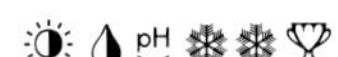

1.5m 5ft / 1.5m 5ft / 0

Eurya emarginata
Slow-growing, evergreen, densely branched, rounded shrub with small, leathery, deep green leaves. Small, greenish-white flowers in late spring or summer are followed by tiny, purple-black berries.

1.5m 5ft / 1.5m 5ft / 0

HEATHERS

As a group, heathers (or heaths) are remarkable in that species and cultivars are available to provide interest at all times of the year. Several are grown for their golden foliage, which often turns a deep burnt orange in winter, while others flower for a long period during summer, autumn or winter. Flowers are in a variety of hues, and are occasionally bicoloured. In habit heathers vary from tree-heaths of up to 6m (20ft) to dwarf, prostrate forms, many of which are excellent for providing ground cover. There are three genera: *Calluna*, *Daboecia* and *Erica*. All *Calluna* and *Daboecia* cultivars and most *Erica* species must be grown in acid soil but otherwise heathers require little attention. Main seasons of interest are given for each plant.

E. arborea* var. *alpina 🏆 [win–spr]

***E.* x *darleyensis* 'White Perfection'** 🏆 [win–spr]

***E. ciliaris* 'David McClintock'** [sum]

***E. carnea* 'Springwood White'** 🏆 [win–spr]

***E. carnea* 'Challenger'** 🏆 [win–spr]

***E.* x *darleyensis* 'Furzey'** 🏆 [win–spr]

***D. cantabrica* 'Bicolor'** 🏆 [spr–aut]

***E. erigena* f. *alba* 'Brian Proudley'** [win–spr]

***E. vagans* 'Birch Glow'** 🏆 [sum]

***E. cinerea* 'C.D. Eason'** 🏆 [sum]

***E. vagans* 'Mrs D. F. Maxwell'** 🏆 [sum]

***E.* x *darleyensis* 'Arthur Johnson'** 🏆 [win–spr]

***E. carnea* 'Golden Starlet'** 🏆 [all year]

***C. vulgaris* 'Wickwar Flame'** 🏆 [all year]

***E. vagans* 'St Keverne'** [sum]

***E. cinerea* 'Eden Valley'** 🏆 [sum]

***C. vulgaris* 'Beoley Gold'** 🏆 [all year]

***E. carnea* 'Ann Sparkes'** 🏆 [win–spr]

***E. erigena* 'Irish Dusk'** 🏆 [win–spr]

***C. vulgaris* 'Dark Star'** 🏆 [sum–aut]

***E. ciliaris* 'Corfe Castle'** [sum]

***C. vulgaris* 'Annemarie'** 🏆 [sum–aut]

***C. vulgaris* 'Peter Sparkes'** 🏆 [sum-aut]

***C. vulgaris* 'Tib'** 🏆 [sum]

GREEN

***Buxus microphylla* 'Green Pillow'**
Evergreen, compact, dwarf shrub, forming a dense, rounded mass of small, oval, dark green leaves. Bears insignificant flowers in late spring or early summer.

***Buxus sempervirens* 'Suffruticosa'**
Evergreen, dwarf shrub that forms a tight, dense mass of oval, bright green leaves. Bears insignificant flowers in late spring or early summer. Trimmed to about 15cm (6in) it is ideal for edging.

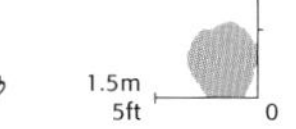

Ruscus hypoglossum
Evergreen, clump-forming shrub with arching shoots. Pointed, glossy, bright green 'leaves' are actually flattened shoots that bear tiny, yellow flowers in spring, followed by large, bright red berries.

Lonicera pileata
Evergreen, low, spreading, dense shrub with narrow, dark green leaves and tiny, short-tubed, creamy-white flowers in late spring, followed by violet-purple berries. Makes good ground cover.

***Ruscus aculeatus* (Butcher's broom)**
Evergreen, erect, thicket-forming shrub with spine-tipped, glossy, dark green 'leaves'. Tiny, star-shaped, green flowers in spring are followed by large, spherical, bright red fruits.

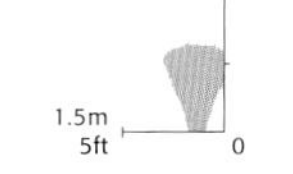

YELLOW

***Leucothöe fontanesiana* 'Rainbow'**
Evergreen, arching shrub with sharply toothed, leathery, dark green leaves that age from pink- to cream-variegated. Racemes of white flowers open below shoots in spring.

***Lonicera nitida* 'Baggesen's Gold'**
Evergreen, bushy shrub with long, arching shoots covered with tiny, bright yellow leaves. Insignificant, yellowish-green flowers in mid-spring are occasionally followed by mauve fruits.

***Euonymus fortunei* 'Emerald 'n' Gold'**
Evergreen, bushy shrub with bright green leaves, margined with bright yellow and tinged with pink in winter.

ROSES

These most romantic of flowers are unsurpassed in beauty and fragrance, and many people consider them indispensable features of the garden. With some 150 species and thousands of cultivars, both ancient and modern, there is a rose to suit almost any situation. They come from a wide range of habitats throughout the northern hemisphere and, with a few exceptions, most roses in cultivation are very hardy. They are also extremely versatile, and can be grown among bulbs, perennials and other shrubs in a mixed border or in a more traditional formal rose garden. Climbing and rambling roses can be trained over arches, arbours and pergolas, creating a blanket of scented blooms and beautiful foliage, or if you have a small garden, you can plant a patio rose or two in a container.

ROSES

Prized for their beauty and fragrance, roses are considered the most romantic of flowers. They are indispensable in informal mixed planting schemes, and add an elegant note to formal parterres. With thousands of colours and forms to choose from, there is a rose for every garden.

Growing roses

With some 150 species and thousands of cultivars, both ancient and modern, there are members of the genus *Rosa* to suit an enormous number of garden situations. They come from a wide range of habitats throughout the northern hemisphere and, with few exceptions, most roses are very hardy. Many modern roses combine the best qualities of old roses, such as flower shape and scent, with disease resistance and extended flowering seasons.

When grown in a suitable site and soil, they will repay you with a profusion of blooms. All roses prefer an open, sunny site in fertile, humus-rich, moist but well-drained soil. However, avoid planting them in an area where roses have been grown before because the soil may be affected by "rose sickness", caused by a build-up of harmful soil organisms, and plants may fail to thrive. Roses also require a good supply of nutrients to perform well, and benefit from an annual application of all-purpose granular fertilizer in the spring.

Year-round interest

Although some roses, notably the climbers and species, bloom for a relatively short period, many hybrids are repeat-flowering, providing a colourful display throughout the summer. 'Frühlingsmorgen' offers the first flush of flowers in early summer, followed by the main flourish from midsummer to the first frosts. To help maintain this display, deadhead your roses regularly, as this redirects the plant's energy from seed formation to flower production. However, if you want attractive fruits (hips) in the autumn, leave the blooms to fade. The best roses for hips include the Rugosa's tomato-like fruit, flask-shaped, vibrant scarlet fruits of *R. moyesii* and the rounded, black hips of *R. pimpinellifolia*.

Ornamental features

Roses embrace almost every colour of the spectrum, apart from true blue, and some have a strong fragrance, such as the heady, sweet scent of the Damasks or musk and spicy fragrances of many modern roses. A few also have ornamental thorns, notably *R. sericea* subsp. *omeiensis* f. *pteracantha*, with its large triangular thorns that glow blood-red when they are backlit.

Foliage can also provide interest. The soft grey-purple leaves of *R. glauca* and blue-green of the Alba roses provide attractive foils for crimson and purple flowers, while foliage textures, ranging from glossy to matt, and delicate fern-like to robustly wrinkled, as in *R.* rugosa, create beautiful contrasts.

Designing with roses

Roses have a diversity of habits each of which can be used to create exciting designs. These include mound-forming ground-cover roses, densely thorny Gallicas, and the arching Chinas and Damasks. A traditional rose garden laid out in a formal style with geometrically ordered beds is particularly suited to the upright growth of many bush roses.

ABOVE Container roses
Some roses have been bred specifically for containers, such as the patio rose Regensburg. Partner them with trailing annuals, such as *Sutera cordata* (syn. *Bacopa*).

LEFT Formal dressing
Here, a sturdy arch clothed with clematis and a vigorous, free-flowering rambler lends height to the scheme and forms a perfect frame to draw the eye to the sculpture used as a focal point.

RIGHT Summer bedfellows
Alliums, bearded irises, campanulas, and verbascums provide perfect companions to a profusion of scented roses in a pink and blue themed summer border. Regular deadheading will prolong the show.

In contemporary schemes, shrub roses are often grown among bulbs, perennials and other shrubs in a mixed border, but when designing these displays, make sure that neighbouring plants do not compete directly for moisture and nutrients. Choose companions that are shallow-rooted, such as the many herbaceous geraniums and pinks (*Dianthus* cultivars), or space plants at a sufficient distance to allow for mulching and feeding around the rose's root zone.

Climbing and rambling roses can be trained on a wall as a colourful backdrop, or on trellis to form a screen. In addition, they provide a cloak of flowers and foliage when grown on arches and over pergolas, and make focal points on free-standing features like tripods and pyramids. Large rampant ramblers, such as *R.* 'Bobbie James' and *R.* 'Seagull', which both can achieve 10m (30ft) or more, will quickly scramble through a tree, offering a profusion of blooms just after most tree blossom has faded.

Many climbing roses are available as weeping standards too. Tall cultivars of dense, thorny shrub roses, such as the Rugosa roses, also make decorative structural features. Use them to create large impenetrable boundary hedges that give privacy and security, or to divide up a garden into compartments. Vigorous ground-cover roses are ideal for clothing sunny and inaccessible banks, since most require little regular pruning.

Not all roses will thrive in containers but smaller patio roses such as *R.* Anna Ford and R. Regensberg are a good choice, while dwarf trailing or spreading cultivars are suitable for hanging baskets.

PRUNING BUSH AND SHRUB ROSES

Modern hybrid tea and floribunda roses, which are commonly grown in gardens, need a hard prune in late winter or early spring to encourage the production of new flowering shoots. Shrub roses require a more gentle pruning regime. Roses also benefit from a light prune in autumn to prevent long stems swaying in the wind and rocking the plant, which may result in root damage. Pruning in a methodical way has other horticultural advantages, helping to control attacks from fungal diseases such as blackspot, to which roses are particularly susceptible, by removing infected wood. Before pruning, use a household disinfectant to clean your secateurs, and apply it again before tackling each new plant to prevent the spread of disease. Also ensure your secateurs are sharp, as clean cuts heal more quickly.

Pruning floribunda roses
Also known as cluster-flowered roses, floribundas produce flushes of blooms through summer and early autumn. In early spring, remove dead, diseased and crossing stems. Prune the other stems to outward-facing buds 20–30cm (8–12in) from the ground using sloping cuts. Aim to leave a framework of 8 to 10 strong, healthy stems.

Pruning hybrid tea roses
These are large-flowered roses, and include some varieties that repeat bloom, although they produce just one flower per stem. In late winter or early spring, cut the oldest stems to the ground, and shorten the remainder to 15cm (6in) from the base. Leave three to five strong young stems after pruning and angle cuts to allow water to drain off the buds.

Pruning shrub and species roses
These usually flower once on wood made in previous years, so prune lightly in early spring. Remove dead, damaged or diseased wood, and thin out congested growth to improve air flow. Also cut some of the oldest stems to the ground. Cut main stems back by a quarter and slightly reduce side shoots by a few centimetres.

ROSE CATEGORIES

Grown for the extraordinary beauty of their flowers, roses have been in cultivation for some hundreds of years. They have been widely hybridized, producing a vast number of shrubs suitable for growing as specimen plants, in the border, as hedges and as climbers for training on walls, pergolas and pillars. Roses are classified into three main groups:

SPECIES

Species, or wild, roses and **species hybrids**, which share most of the characteristics of the parent species, bear flowers generally in one flush in summer and hips in autumn.

Old Garden roses

Alba – large, freely branching roses with clusters of flowers in mid-summer and abundant, greyish-green foliage.
Bourbon – open, remontant shrub roses that may be trained to climb. Flowers are borne, often 3 to a cluster, in summer–autumn.
China – remontant shrubs with flowers borne singly or in clusters in summer–autumn; provide shelter.
Damask – open shrubs bearing loose clusters of usually very fragrant flowers mainly in summer.
Gallica – fairly dense shrubs producing richly coloured flowers, often 3 to a cluster, in the summer months.
Hybrid Perpetual – vigorous, remontant shrubs with flowers borne singly or in 3s in summer–autumn.
Moss – often lax shrubs with a furry, moss-like growth on stems and calyx, and flowers in summer.
Noisette – remontant climbing roses that bear large clusters of flowers, with a slight spicy fragrance, in summer–autumn; provide shelter.
Portland – upright, rather dense, remontant shrubs bearing loose clusters of flowers in summer–autumn.
Provence (Centifolia) – lax, thorny shrubs bearing scented flowers in summer.
Sempervirens – semi-evergreen climbing roses that bear numerous flowers in late summer.
Tea – remontant shrubs and climbers with elegant, pointed buds that open to loose flowers with a spicy fragrance; provide shelter.

Modern Garden roses

Shrub – a diverse group, illustrated here with the Old Garden roses because of their similar characteristics. Most are remontant and are larger than bush roses, with flowers borne singly or in sprays in summer and/or autumn.
Large-flowered bush (Hybrid Tea) – remontant shrubs with large flowers borne in summer–autumn.
Cluster-flowered bush (Floribunda) – remontant shrubs with usually large sprays of flowers in summer–autumn.
Dwarf clustered-flowered bush (Patio) – neat, remontant shrubs with sprays of flowers borne in summer–autumn.
Miniature bush – very small, remontant shrubs with sprays of tiny flowers in summer–autumn.
Polyantha – tough, compact, remontant shrubs with many small flowers in summer–autumn.
Ground cover – trailing and spreading roses, some flowering in summer only, others remontant, flowering in summer–autumn.
Climbing – vigorous climbing roses, diverse in growth and flower, some flowering in summer only, others remontant, flowering in summer–autumn.
Rambler – vigorous climbing roses with flexible stems that bear clusters of flowers mostly in summer.

FLOWER SHAPES

With the mass hybridization that has occurred in recent years, roses have been developed to produce plants with a wide variety of characteristics, in particular different forms of flower, often with a strong fragrance. These flower types, illustrated below, give a general indication of the shape of the flower at its perfect state (which in some cases may be before it has opened fully). Growing conditions may affect the form of the flower. Flowers may be single (4–7 petals), semi-double (8–14 petals), double (15–30 petals) or fully double (over 30 petals).

Flat – open, usually single or semi-double flowers have petals that are almost flat.

Cupped – open, single to fully double flowers have petals curving outwards gently from the centre.

Pointed – elegant, 'Hybrid Tea' shape; semi-double to fully double flowers have high, tight centres.

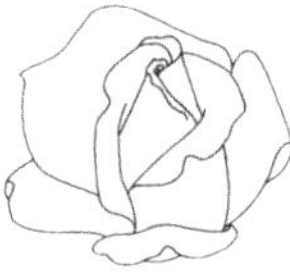

Urn-shaped – classic, curved, flat-topped, semi-double to fully double flowers are of 'Hybrid Tea' type.

Rounded – usually double or fully double flowers have even-sized, overlapping petals that form a bowl-shaped or rounded outline.

Rosette – usually double or fully double flowers are rather flat with many confused, slightly overlapping petals of uneven size.

Quartered-rosette – rather flat, usually double or fully double flowers have confused petals of uneven size arranged in a quartered pattern.

Pompon – small, rounded, double or fully double flowers, usually borne in clusters, have masses of small petals.

WHITE

***R.* 'Penelope'**
Dense, bushy shrub rose with good disease resistance and plentiful, dark green foliage. Bears clusters of many scented, cupped, double, pink-cream flowers, 8cm (3in) across, in a single flush in summer. **H** and **S** 1m (3ft), more if lightly pruned.

***R.* 'Madame Hardy'**
Vigorous, upright Damask rose with good disease resistance. Plentiful, leathery, matt leaves. Richly fragrant, quartered-rosette, fully double flowers, 10cm (4in) across, white with green eyes, are borne in a single flush in summer. **H** 1.5m (5ft), **S** 1.2m (4ft).

***R.* JACQUELINE DU PRE ('Harwanna')**
Compact, bushy shrub rose with good disease resistance and repeat-flowering in summer–autumn. Bears semi-double, red-stamened, white flowers, 10cm (4in) across, often with a pink blush and a strong musk perfume. Has glossy, dark green leaves. **H** 1.2m (4ft), **S** 1m (3ft).

***R.* 'Dupontii'** (Snowbush rose)
Upright, bushy shrub rose with very good disease resistance and abundant, greyish foliage. Clusters of fragrant, flat, single, white flowers, tinged with blush-pink, 6cm (2½in) across, are borne in a single flush in summer. **H** and **S** 2.2m (7ft).

***R.* 'Nevada'**
Dense, arching shrub rose with very good disease resistance and abundant, light green leaves. Scented, flat, semi-double, creamy-white flowers, 10cm (4in) across, are borne in a single flush in summer. **H** and **S** 2.2m (7ft).

***R.* 'Sally Holmes'**
Bushy shrub rose with good disease resistance and prolific, glossy, deep green leaves. Substantial clusters of slightly scented, single, white flowers, 15cm (6in) across, with pink-peach buds, are borne in summer and again in autumn. **H** 1.5m (5ft), **S** 1.2m (4ft).

PINK

***R.* 'Fantin-Latour'**
Vigorous, shrubby Provence rose with good disease resistance. Flowers appear in a single flush in summer and are fragrant, cupped to flat, fully double, blush-pink, with neat, green button eyes, and 10cm (4in) across. Has broad, dark green leaves. **H** 1.5m (5ft), **S** 1.2m (4ft).

***R.* 'Céleste'**
Vigorous, spreading, bushy Alba rose with good disease resistance. Fragrant, cupped, double, light pink flowers, 8cm (3in) across, appear in a single flush in summer. Makes a good hedge. **H** 1.5m (5ft), **S** 1.2m (4ft).

***R.* 'Great Maiden's Blush'**
Vigorous, upright Alba rose with good disease resistance. Very fragrant, rosette, fully double, pinkish-white flowers, 8cm (3in) across, appear in a single flush in summer. **H** 2m (6ft), **S** 1.3m (4½ft).

***R.* 'Marguerite Hilling'**
Dense, arching shrub rose with good disease resistance. Many scented, flat, semi-double, rose-pink flowers, 10cm (4in) across, are borne in a single flush in summer. Has light green foliage. **H** and **S** 2.2m (7ft).

***R.* 'Felicia'**
Vigorous shrub rose with good disease resistance and abundant, healthy, greyish-green foliage. Scented, cupped, double flowers, 8cm (3in) across, are light pink, tinged with apricot, and are borne in a single flush in summer. **H** 1.5m (5ft), **S** 2.2m (7ft).

***R.* 'Reine Victoria'**
Lax Bourbon rose with good disease resistance, slender stems and light green leaves. Sweetly scented, rosette, double flowers, 8cm (3in) across, in shades of pink, are borne in a single flush in summer. Grows well on a pillar. **H** 2m (6ft), **S** 1.2m (4ft).

PINK

***R.* ALISSAR PRINCESS OF PHONECIA ('Harsidon')**
Compact, upright, sturdy shrub rose with good disease resistance. Red leaves mature green. Slightly scented, flat, semi-double, dark-eyed, pink flowers, 10cm (4in) across, open summer and autumn. **H** 1.2m (4ft), **S** 90cm (3ft).

***R.* x *odorata* 'Mutabilis'**
Open species rose with coppery young foliage and good disease resistance. Bears shallowly cup-shaped, single, buff-yellow flowers, 6cm (2½in) across, in a single flush in summer, that age to coppery-pink or -crimson. **H** and **S** 1m (3ft), to 2m (6ft) against a wall.

***R.* 'Mrs John Laing'**
Bushy Hybrid Perpetual rose with good disease resistance and plentiful, light green foliage. Produces many richly fragrant, rounded, fully double, pink flowers, 12cm (5in) across, in a single flush in summer. **H** 1m (3ft), **S** 80cm (2½ft).

***R.* x *odorata* 'Pallida'**
(Old blush china, Parson's pink china)
Bushy China rose with good disease resistance that may be trained as a climber on a sheltered wall. Cupped, double, pink flowers, 6cm (2½in) across, open in a single flush in summer. **H** 1m (3ft), **S** 80cm (2½ft) or more.

***R.* 'Complicata'**
Very vigorous Gallica rose with good disease resistance and thorny, arching growth. Useful as a large hedge. Slightly fragrant, cupped, single flowers, 11cm (4½in) across, are pink with pale centres and appear in a single flush in summer. **H** 2.2m (7ft), **S** 2.5m (8ft).

***R.* CONSTANCE SPRY ('Austance')**
Shrub rose of arching habit and good disease resistance that will climb if supported. Cupped, fully double, pink flowers, 12cm (5in) across, with a spicy scent, are borne in a single flush in summer. Leaves are large and plentiful. **H** 2m (6ft), **S** 1.5m (5ft).

***R.* *gallica* 'Versicolor'** (Rosa mundi)
Neat, bushy Gallica rose with good disease resistance. In a single flush in summer produces striking, slightly scented, flat, semi-double flowers, 5cm (2in) across, very pale blush-pink with crimson stripes. **H** 75cm (2½ft), **S** 1m (3ft).

***R.* STRAWBERRY HILL ('Ausrimini')**
Bushy shrub rose with very good disease resistance. Has plentiful, glossy, mid-green leaves. Rosette, fully double, rich-pink flowers, 7cm (3in) across, with a strong myrrh scent, summer and autumn. The flowers fade with age. **H** 1.5m (5ft), **S** 1.2m (4ft).

***R.* 'Madame Isaac Pereire'**
Vigorous, arching Bourbon rose with good disease resistance. Fragrant, cupped to quartered-rosette, fully double flowers, 15cm (6in) across, are deep purple-pink and are produced in a single flush in summer. **H** 2.2m (7ft), **S** 2m (6ft).

***R.* GERTRUDE JEKYLL ('Ausbord')**
Upright shrub rose with good disease resistance and broad, matt, mid-green, well-spaced leaves. Plump, rounded buds open into rosette, fully double, deep pink flowers, 12cm (5in) across, with a rich sweet-myrrh scent, summer and autumn. **H** 2m (6ft), **S** 1.2m (4ft).

***R.* 'Roseraie de l'Haÿ'**
Vigorous, dense shrub rose with very good disease resistance. Bears many strongly scented, cupped to flat, double, reddish-purple flowers, 11cm (4½in) across, in summer and again in autumn. Light green leaves are abundant.
H 2.2m (7ft), **S** 2m (6ft).

RED

***R.* BENJAMIN BRITTEN ('Ausencart')**
Willowy shrub rose with very good disease resistance, an open habit and large, matt-green leaves. Fully double, cupped, red flowers, 12cm (5in) across, with hints of scarlet and a strong fruity scent, open summer and autumn.
H 2m (6ft), **S** 1.5m (5ft).

***R.* CARDINAL HUME ('Harregale')**
Bushy, spreading shrub rose with good disease resistance. Cupped, fully double, reddish-purple flowers, 7.5cm (3in) across, are borne in dense clusters in summer and again in autumn, and have a musky scent. **H** and **S** 1m (3ft).

***R.* 'Henri Martin'**
Vigorous, upright Moss rose with good disease resistance. Rosette, double, purplish-crimson flowers, 9cm (3½in) across, appear in a single flush in summer and have a light scent and some furry, green 'mossing' of the calyces underneath. **H** 1.5m (5ft), **S** 1m (3ft).

PURPLE

***R.* 'Cardinal de Richelieu'**
Vigorous, compact Gallica rose with good disease resistance and plentiful, dark green foliage. Bears fragrant, rounded, fully double, deep burgundy-purple flowers, 8cm (3in) across, in a single flush in summer.
H 1.2m (4ft), **S** 1m (3ft).

***R.* RHAPSODY IN BLUE ('Frantasia')**
Upright shrub rose with good disease resistance and large, light green leaves. Cupped, semi-double, purple flowers, 12cm (5in) across, with white eyes, yellow stamens and a pungent, spicy perfume, summer and autumn. **H** 1.8m (6ft), **S** 1.2m (4ft).

***R.* 'William Lobb'**
Moss rose with good disease resistance and strong, arching, prickly stems. Will climb if supported. In a single flush in summer bears rosette, double, deep purplish-crimson flowers, 9cm (3½in) across, that fade to lilac-grey.
H and **S** 2m (6ft).

HIPS AND THORNS

Roses have many beautiful features that provide interest for many months of the year. Although most are grown for their spectacular flowers, many also produce decorative hips that provide glowing autumn and winter colour, offer birds a valuable source of food, and create a stunning picture in frost and snow. Fertilized flowers produce the hips, so avoid dead-heading the blooms as this will also remove the fruit. Thorns offer another attractive feature on some species. For example, the winger thorn rose (*R. sericea* subsp. *omeiensis* f. *pteracantha*) has translucent thorns, while the fine prickly thorns of moss roses look furry, adding to their attraction. Prune these roses hard to ensure a supply of young, thorny wood.

R. roxburghii

R. multibracteata

R. sericea* subsp. *omeiensis* f. *pteracantha

R. rubiginosa

R. glauca 🏆

R. rugosa

***R. moyesii* 'Geranium'**

YELLOW

***R.* THE PILGRIM ('Auswalker')**
Bushy shrub rose with very good disease resistance. Produces rosette, fully double, creamy-white flowers, 10cm (4in) across, with rich yellow centres and a strong, sweet perfume, in summer and again in autumn. Has glossy, dark green leaves. **H** 1.2m (4ft), **S** 1m (3ft).

***R.* TEASING GEORGIA ('Ausbaker')**
Upright, lax, shrub rose with good disease resistance. Produces dark green leaves with a deep sheen. Slightly scented, rosette, fully double, pale yellow flowers, 12cm (5in) across, with deeper centres, open summer and autumn. **H** 1.8m (6ft), **S** 1.2m (4ft).

***R.* GRAHAM THOMAS ('Ausmas')**
Vigorous, arching shrub rose with good disease resistance. Lax in habit, with glossy, bright green leaves. In summer, and again in autumn, bears cupped, fully double, yellow flowers, 11cm (4½in) across, with some scent. **H** 1.2m (4ft), **S** 1.5m (5ft).

ORANGE

***R.* 'Buff Beauty'**
Dense, rounded Hybrid musk rose with good disease resistance. Masses of cupped, double, apricot-yellow to buff-yellow flowers, 7cm (3in) across, with a light musk scent, open in a single summer flush. Has glossy, mid-green leaves. **H** and **S** 1.2m (4ft).

***R.* EVELYN ('Aussaucer')**
Slightly lax, arching shrub rose with good disease resistance and large, mid-green leaves. Bears strongly scented, rosette, fully double flowers, 12cm (5in) across, peach with hints of pastel pink and lemon, in summer and autumn. **H** 1.5m (5ft), **S** 1.2m (4ft).

***R.* SUMMER SONG ('Austango')**
Upright shrub rose with very good disease resistance and large, matt, mid-green leaves. Produces quartered-rosette, fully double, burnt-orange flowers, 10cm (4in) across, scented with traces of banana, summer and autumn. **H** 1.5m (5ft), **S** 1.2m (4ft).

WHITE

***R.* KENT ('Poulcov')**
Dense ground-cover rose with very good disease resistance and glossy, mid-green leaves. Produces large clusters of flat, semi-double, pure white flowers, 5cm (2in) across. Repeat-flowering, summer–autumn. **H** 80cm (32in), **S** 90cm (36in).

***R.* ISN'T SHE LOVELY ('Diciluvit')**
Upright Hybrid Tea rose with good disease resistance and semi-glossy, green leaves. Pointed, fully double, pale white-pink flowers, 10cm (4in) across, with creamy-peach centres and a fruity scent, are borne in summer and autumn. **H** 1m (3ft), **S** 60cm (2ft).

***R.* CHAMPAGNE MOMENTS ('Korvanaber')**
Vigorous Floribunda rose with very good disease resistance, repeat-flowering summer–autumn. Produces clustered slightly scented, double flowers, 7cm (3in) across, cream to golden-amber. **H** 1m (3ft), **S** 80cm (32in).

***R.* ICEBERG ('Korbin')**
Floribunda bush rose with moderate disease resistance, repeat-flowering summer–autumn. Produces many sprays of cupped, fully double, white flowers, 7cm (3in) across. Has abundant, glossy leaves. **H** 75cm (30in), **S** 65cm (26in) or more.

***R.* MARGARET MERRIL ('Harkuly')**
Upright, Floribunda bush rose with moderate disease resistance. Very fragrant, double, blush-white or white flowers, are well-formed, urn-shaped, 10cm (4in) across, and are borne singly or in clusters in summer and again in autumn. **H** 1m (3ft), **S** 60cm (2ft).

***R.* SILVER ANNIVERSARY ('Poulari')**
Vigorous Hybrid Tea rose with good disease resistance and slightly scented, pointed, double, almost pure white flowers, 12cm (5in) across, produced in summer and again in autumn. Leaves are mid-green and semi-glossy. **H** 1.2m (4ft), **S** 80cm (32in).

PINK

***R.* MAID OF HONOUR ('Jacwhink')**
Bushy patio rose with very good disease resistance. Produces dense, small, glossy, leaves and abundant, flat, single flowers, 3cm (1¼in) across, with pink and white petals, and bright yellow stamens. Repeat-flowering, summer–autumn. **H** and **S** 80cm (32in).

***R.* 'The Fairy'**
Dense, cushion-forming, dwarf cluster-flowered bush rose with good disease resistance and abundant, small, glossy leaves. Rosette, double, pink flowers, 2.5cm (1in) across, are borne freely in a single flush in summer. **H** and **S** 60cm (24in).

***R.* PAUL SHIRVILLE ('Harqueterwife')**
Spreading, Hybrid Tea bush rose with moderate disease resistance. Bears fragrant, pointed, fully double, rosy salmon-pink flowers, 9cm (3½in) across, in summer and again in autumn. Leaves are glossy, reddish and abundant. **H** and **S** 75cm (30in).

***R.* 'Queen Elizabeth'**
Upright, Floribunda bush rose with moderate disease resistance. Bears long-stemmed, fully double, pink flowers, 10cm (4in) across, singly or in clusters, summer and autumn. Leaves are large and leathery. **H** 1.5m (5ft), **S** 75cm (2½ft) more if not pruned hard.

***R.* MANY HAPPY RETURNS ('Harwanted')**
Spreading Floribunda rose with good disease resistance and semi-glossy, light green leaves. In summer and autumn it bears big clusters of slightly fragrant, cupped, semi-double, light pink flowers, 7cm (3in) across. **H** and **S** 80cm (32in).

***R.* APHRODITE ('Tanetidor')**
Sturdy Floribunda rose with good disease resistance and large, glossy, dark green leaves. Slightly scented, rounded, fully double, pale pink flowers, 10cm (4in) across, with dense, darker centres, open summer and autumn. **H** 1m (3ft), **S** 80cm (32in).

***R.* CHANDOS BEAUTY ('Harmisty')**
Extremely vigorous Hybrid Tea rose with good disease resistance. Produces a strong, classic Tea-rose scent, from pointed, fully double, light pink flowers, 12cm (5in) across. Has tough, glossy, green leaves. Repeats summer–autumn. **H** 1.5m (5ft), **S** 1m (3ft).

***R.* SUSAN DANIEL ('Harlibra')**
Vigorous Floribunda rose with very good disease resistance, repeat flowering summer–autumn. Has glossy, dark green leaves. Bears cupped, double, apricot flowers, to 10cm (4in) across, with creamy-white flashes. Scent is spicy but mild. **H** 1m (3ft), **S** 80cm (32in).

***R.* SAVOY HOTEL ('Harvintage')**
Spreading Hybrid Tea rose with good disease resistance and matt, mid-green leaves. Long-lasting, pointed, fully double, pink flowers, 12cm (5in) across, often with green on the outer petals, open summer and autumn. **H** 1.2m (4ft), **S** 1m (3ft).

***R.* CHRIS BEARDSHAW ('Wekmeredoc')**
Sturdy Hybrid Tea rose with good disease resistance. Pointed, double, pale pink flowers, to 12cm (5in) across, with a strong, sweet scent, are produced summer and autumn. **H** 1.2m (4ft), **S** 80cm (32in).

***R.* GORDON'S COLLEGE ('Cocjabby')**
Vigorous Floribunda rose with good disease resistance and matt, dark green leaves. Strongly scented, urn-shaped, deep salmon-pink flowers, 10cm (4in) across, are borne in small clusters in summer and again in autumn. **H** 1.2m (4ft), **S** 80cm (32in).

***R.* BELMONTE ('Harpearl')**
Vigorous Floribunda rose with very good resistance and large, semi-glossy, mid-green leaves. Pointed, double, pearl-pink flowers, darker in the centre, 10cm (4in) across, with a strong, fruity perfume, open summer and autumn. **H** 1.1m (3½ft), **S** 80cm (32in).

***R.* WARM WISHES ('Fryxotic')**
Bushy Hybrid Tea rose with very good disease resistance and matt, mid-green leaves. Pointed, fully double, coral-pink flowers, 10cm (4in) across, in summer and again in autumn, mature to rose-pink. Floral scent is slight spice and myrrh. **H** 1m (3ft), **S** 80cm (32in).

***R.* FLOWER CARPET ('Noatraum')**
Spreading ground-cover rose with good disease resistance. Forms a dense prostrate mound of small, glossy, green leaves. Cupped, semi-double, fuchsia-pink flowers, 5cm (2in) across, are borne in summer and again in autumn. **H** 45cm (18in), **S** 1.2m (4ft).

***R.* JOIE DE VIVRE ('Korfloci 01')**
Compact, well-branched, bushy Floribunda rose with very good disease resistance and dense, mid-green leaves. Scented, quartered-rosette, double, pink to light apricot flowers, 10cm (4in) across, open summer and autumn. **H** 90cm (36in), **S** 60cm (24in).

***R.* SWEET DREAM ('Fryminicot')**
Bushy Patio rose with good disease resistance. Produces slightly scented, rounded, double flowers, 5cm (2in) across, apricot-peach, summer and autumn. Has small, mid-green leaves. Ideal in a pot or planter. **H** 45cm (18in), **S** 30cm (12in).

***R.* NOSTALGIA ('Taneiglat')**
Bushy Hybrid Tea rose with good disease resistance and large, dark green leaves. Pointed, fully double, creamy-white flowers, 12cm (5in) across, with pink-edged outer petals, open summer and autumn. The flowers age to red. **H** 1.2m (4ft), **S** 80cm (32in).

***R.* CRAZY FOR YOU ('Wekroalt')**
Sturdy, branching Floribunda rose with good disease resistance and emerald leaves. Summer and autumn, produces cupped, semi-double, cream flowers, 10cm (4in) across, splashed with cherry flecks, and with a fruity perfume. **H** 1.5m (5ft), **S** 1.1m (3½ft).

PINK

***R.* SIMPLY SALLY ('Harpaint')**
Rounded patio rose with very good disease resistance. Has numerous, small, matt, mid-green leaves. Slightly scented, flat, single flowers, 5cm (2in) across, open to pink with yellow centres. Repeat-flowering summer–autumn. **H** 80cm (32in), **S** 60cm (24in).

***R.* PINK PERFECTION ('Korpauvio')**
Vigorous, bushy Hybrid Tea rose with very good disease resistance and glossy, mid-green leaves. Bears slightly scented, rounded, double, sugar-pink flowers, to 7cm (3in) across, with white veining and lighter reverses, in summer and again in autumn. **H** 1m (3ft), **S** 80cm (32in).

RED

***R.* DOUBLE DELIGHT ('Andeli')**
Hybrid Tea bush rose of upright, uneven growth with good disease resistance. Fragrant, rounded, fully double flowers, 12cm (5in) across, are creamy-white, edged with red, and are borne in summer and again in autumn. **H** 1m (3ft), **S** 60cm (2ft).

***R.* ANNA FORD ('Harpiccolo')**
Dwarf cluster-flowered bush rose with good disease resistance. Has urn-shaped (opening flat), double, orange-red flowers, 4cm (1½in) across, borne in summer and again in autumn, and many small, dark green leaves. **H** 45cm (18in), **S** 38cm (15in).

***R.* ROYAL WILLIAM ('Korzaun')**
Vigorous, Hybrid Tea bush rose with good disease resistance and large, dark green leaves. Slightly scented, pointed, fully double, deep crimson flowers, 12cm (5in) across, are carried on long stems in summer and again in autumn. **H** 1m (3ft), **S** 75cm (2½ft).

***R.* ALEXANDER ('Harlex')**
Vigorous, upright, Hybrid Tea bush rose with good disease resistance and abundant, dark green foliage. Slightly scented, pointed, double, bright red flowers, 12cm (5in) across, are borne on long stems in summer and again in autumn. **H** 1.5m (5ft), **S** 75cm (2½ft).

***R.* THE TIMES ROSE ('Korpeahn')**
Spreading, Floribunda bush rose with good disease resistance. Slightly scented, cupped, double, deep crimson flowers, 8cm (3in) across, are borne in wide clusters in summer and again in autumn. Foliage is dark green and plentiful. **H** 60cm (24in), **S** 75cm (30in).

***R.* CARRIS ('Harmanna')**
Compact Hybrid Tea rose with very good disease resistance. Has a mass of glossy, mid-green leaves. Produces urn-shaped, bright scarlet flowers, to 12cm (5in) across, with a spicy myrrh scent. Repeat-flowering summer–autumn. **H** 1m (3ft), **S** 80cm (32in).

***R.* GEORGE BEST ('Dichimanher')**
Bushy patio rose with very good disease resistance and small, matt, mid-green leaves. Slightly scented, urn-shaped, semi-double, deep red flowers, 5cm (2in) across, are borne in clusters in summer and autumn. **H** and **S** 45cm (18in).

***R.* RED FINESSE ('Korvillade')**
Compact Floribunda rose with very good disease resistance and repeat-flowering in summer–autumn. Produces abundant, glossy, dark green leaves and clusters of up to 15 cupped, double, red flowers, 7cm (3in) across. **H** 90cm (36in), **S** 60cm (24in).

***R.* REMEMBRANCE ('Harxampton')**
Well-branched Floribunda rose with good disease resistance and glossy leaves. Long-lasting, rounded, double, scarlet flowers, 7cm (3in) across, have darker outer petals, fading with age. Repeat-flowers summer–autumn. **H** 80cm (32in), **S** 60cm (24in).

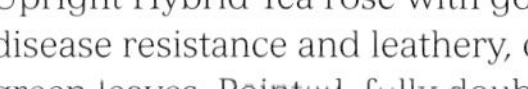

***R.* LOVING MEMORY ('Korgund')**
Upright Hybrid Tea rose with good disease resistance and leathery, dark green leaves. Pointed, fully double, crimson flowers, 12cm (5in) across, are borne in summer and autumn. Perfume is light but sweet. **H** 1.2m (4ft), **S** 80cm (32in).

***R.* ALEC'S RED ('Cored')**
Vigorous, Hybrid Tea bush rose with moderate disease resistance. Bears strongly fragrant, deep cherry-red flowers that are pointed and fully double, 15cm (6in) across, in summer and again in autumn. **H** 1m (36in), **S** 60cm (24in).

***R.* LANCASHIRE ('Korstesgli')**
Ground-cover rose with good disease resistance and small, matt, dark green leaves. Cupped, semi-double, cherry-red flowers, 5cm (2in) across, fading to cerise, are produced in clusters of at least 7 in summer and again in autumn. **H** 60cm (24in), **S** 90cm (36in).

PURPLE

***R.* GUY SAVOY ('Delstrimen')**
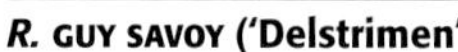
Upright Floribunda rose with good disease resistance and glossy, dark green leaves. Produces cupped, semi-double white-striped, purple flowers, 7cm (3in) across, in large clusters. Repeat-flowering summer–autumn. **H** 1.5m (5ft), **S** 1m (3ft).

***R.* BURGUNDY ICE ('Prose')**
Open Floribunda rose with good disease resistance, repeat-flowering in summer–autumn. Has matt, light green leaves. Clusters of up to 7 cupped, double, mauve flowers, 7cm (3in) across, have pale mauve margins. **H** 1.2m (4ft), **S** 1m (3ft).

YELLOW

***R.* 'Arthur Bell'**
Upright Floribunda rose with good disease resistance and large, glossy, mid-green leaves. Strongly scented, cupped, double, butter-yellow flowers, 7cm (3in) across, fading to creamy-white, are borne in summer and again in autumn. **H** 1m (3ft), **S** 60cm (2ft).

***R.* PEACE ('Madame A. Meilland')**
Vigorous, shrubby, large-flowered bush rose with moderate disease resistance. Scented, pointed to rounded, fully double flowers, 15cm (6in) across, are borne freely in clusters in summer and again in autumn. Has abundant, large, glossy foliage. **H** 1.2m (4ft), **S** 1m (3ft).

***R.* EASY GOING ('Harglow')**
Bushy Floribunda rose with good disease resistance and repeat-flowering in summer–autumn. Has rich glossy, pale green leaves. Pointed buds open into cupped, double, deep amber flowers, 10cm (4in) across, with a moderately fruity scent. **H** 80cm (32in), **S** 60cm (24in).

***R.* GOLDEN MEMORIES ('Korholesea')**
Bushy Floribunda rose with very good disease resistance and glossy, dark green leaves. In summer and autumn, clusters of urn-shaped, fully double flowers, 7.5cm (3in) across, open wide to show stamens, deep yellow centres and paler yellow margins. **H** 1m (3ft), **S** 80cm (32in).

***R.* ABSOLUTELY FABULOUS ('Wekvossutono')**
Vigorous Floribunda rose with very good disease resistance and repeat-flowering in summer–autumn. Bears urn-shaped, yellow flowers, 10cm (4in) across, and glossy, green leaves. Scent has liquorice overtones. **H** 1m (3ft), **S** 60cm (2ft).

***R.* GOLDEN BEAUTY ('Korberbeni')**
Bushy Floribunda rose with very good disease resistance and glossy, mid-green leaves. In summer and autumn produces clusters of 3–5 slightly scented, rounded, fully double, golden-yellow flowers, 8cm (3in) across, deepening to amber-gold in centres. **H** 1m (3ft), **S** 75cm (30in).

***R.* FREEDOM ('Dicjem')**
Neat, large-flowered bush rose with good disease resistance, many shoots, and abundant, glossy foliage. Bears many lightly scented, rounded, double, bright yellow flowers, 9cm (3½in) across, in summer–autumn. **H** 75cm (30in), **S** 60cm (24in).

***R.* MOUNTBATTEN ('Harmantelle')**
Shrubby, cluster-flowered bush rose with good disease resistance. Bears scented, rounded, fully double, yellow flowers, 10cm (4in) across, singly or in clusters, in summer and again in autumn. **H** 1.2m (4ft), **S** 75cm (2½ft).

***R.* GUY'S GOLD ('Harmatch')**
Well-branched, bushy Hybrid Tea rose with very good disease resistance and repeat-flowering in summer–autumn. Has glossy, mid-green leaves and masses of slightly scented, pointed, double, bright yellow flowers, 12cm (5in) across. **H** 80cm (32in), **S** 60cm (24in).

R. RACHEL ('Tangust')
Bushy Hybrid Tea rose with good disease resistance and large, mid-green leaves. Sweetly scented, rounded, fully double, orange-apricot flowers, 10cm (4in) across, in summer and again in autumn, turn lighter with pink tones as they age. **H** 1m (3ft), **S** 60cm (24in).

R. 'Southampton'
Upright, cluster-flowered bush rose with very good disease resistance and glossy foliage. Bears fragrant, pointed, double, apricot flowers, 8cm (3in) across, singly or in clusters in summer and again in autumn. **H** 1m (3ft), **S** 60cm (24in).

R. SWEET MAGIC ('Dicmagic')
Branching, dwarf cluster-flowered bush rose with good disease resistance and repeat-flowering in summer–autumn. Bears sprays of lightly fragrant, urn-shaped, double, pink-flushed, golden-orange flowers, 4cm (1½in) across. **H** 38cm (15in), **S** 30cm (12in).

R. REMEMBER ME ('Cocdestin')
Vigorous, dense, large-flowered bush rose with good disease resistance. Pointed, fully double, copper-orange flowers, 9cm (3½in) across, are borne freely in summer and again in autumn. Leaves are abundant and glossy. **H** 1m (3ft), **S** 75cm (2½ft).

R. EASY DOES IT ('Harpagent')
Compact Floribunda rose with very good disease resistance and repeat-flowering in summer–autumn. Has matt, mid-green leaves. Produces spicy-scented, tangerine flowers, 10cm (4in) across, fading to pink. Many petals have wavy edges. **H** 1m (3ft), **S** 60cm (24in).

R. SIMPLY THE BEST ('Macamster')
Bushy Hybrid Tea rose with good disease resistance and dark green leaves. In summer and again in autumn produces abundant, scented, urn-shaped, double, light orange flowers, 10cm (4in) across. Colouring lightens as it ages. **H** 1.2m (4ft), **S** 80cm (32in).

R. FELLOWSHIP ('Harwelcome')
Bushy Floribunda rose with good disease resistance and repeat-flowering in summer–autumn. Has large, glossy, green leaves. Spicy-scented, cupped, double flowers, 10cm (4in) across, have orange outer petals, lightening inwards to tangerine. **H** 75cm (30in), **S** 60cm (24in).

R. 'Just Joey'
Branching, open, large-flowered bush rose with good disease resistance and repeat-flowering in summer–autumn. Bears rounded, fully double flowers, 12cm (5in) across, with waved copper-pink petals and some scent. Has leathery, green leaves. **H** 75cm (30in), **S** 60cm (2ft).

R. SUPER TROOPER ('Fryleyeca')
Bushy Floribunda rose with very good disease resistance and lush, dark green leaves. Scented, pointed, double, bright orange flowers, flashed yellow beneath, open in small clusters, 10cm (4in) across, in summer and autumn. **H** 1m (3ft), **S** 80cm (32in).

WHITE

***R.* 'Albéric Barbier'**
Vigorous, semi-evergreen rambler rose with very good disease resistance. Clusters of slightly fragrant, rosette, fully double, creamy-white flowers, 8cm (3in) across, appear in a single flush in summer. Leaves are small and bright green. **H** to 5m (15ft), **S** 3m (10ft).

***R.* 'Paul's Lemon Pillar'**
Stiff, upright climbing rose with good disease resistance and large, dark green leaves. Scented, pointed to rounded, fully double, lemon-white flowers, 15cm (6in) across, appear in a single flush in summer. Prefers a sunny, sheltered wall. **H** 5m (15ft), **S** 3m (10ft).

***R. filipes* 'Kiftsgate'**
Rampant climbing rose with very good disease resistance and abundant, glossy, light green foliage. Clusters of cupped to flat, single, creamy-white flowers, 2.5cm (1in) across, appear in a single flush in summer. Use to grow up a tree or in a wild garden. **H** and **S** 10m (30ft) or more.

***R.* 'Félicité Perpétue'**
Sempervirens climbing rose with long, slender stems. Clusters of rosette, fully double, blush-pink to white flowers, 4cm (1½in) across, appear in mid-summer. Small leaves are semi-evergreen. Prune spent wood only. **H** 5m (15ft), **S** 4m (12ft).

***R.* 'Madame Alfred Carrière'**
Noisette climbing rose with good disease resistance and slender, smooth stems. Very fragrant, rounded, double flowers are creamy-white, tinged pink, 4cm (1½in) across, and are borne in a single flush in summer. **H** to 5.5m (18ft), **S** 3m (10ft).

***R.* 'Gloire de Dijon'**
Stiffly branched Noisette or climbing Tea rose with good disease resistance. Fragrant, quartered-rosette, fully double, creamy-buff flowers, 10cm (4in) across, are borne in a single flush in summer. **H** 4m (12ft), **S** 2.5m (8ft).

***R.* WHITE STAR ('Harquill')**
Climber with very good disease resistance and repeat-flowering in summer–autumn. Glossy, dark green leaves are lighter when young. Slightly scented, flat, semi-double, pure white flowers, 10cm (4in) across, have bright yellow stamens. **H** 2.5m (8ft), **S** 1.8m (6ft).

***R.* 'Rambling Rector'**
Rampant rambler rose with very good disease resistance. Clusters of scented, cupped to flat, semi-double, creamy-white flowers, 4cm (1½in) across, with golden stamens, appear in a single flush in summer, followed by red hips. Has greyish-green foliage. **H** and **S** 6m (20ft).

R. 'New Dawn'
Vigorous, very hardy climbing rose with good disease resistance. Fragrant, cupped, double, pale pearl-pink flowers, 8cm (3in) across, are borne in clusters in summer and again in autumn. Tolerates a north-facing wall. **H** and **S** 5m (15ft).

R. 'Zéphirine Drouhin' (Thornless rose)
Lax, arching Bourbon rose that will climb if supported. Bears fragrant, cupped, double, deep pink flowers, 8cm (3in) across, in a single flush in summer. Is prone to mildew. May be grown as a hedge. **H** to 2.5m (8ft), **S** to 2m (6ft).

R. HIGH HOPES ('Haryup')
Vigorous, upright and arching, long-stemmed climbing rose with good disease resistance. Scented, urn-shaped to rounded, double, light pink flowers, 8cm (3in) across, are freely borne in summer–autumn. Has purplish-green foliage. **H** 4m (12ft), **S** 2.2m (7ft).

R. 'Veilchenblau'
Vigorous rambler rose with good disease resistance. Rosette, double, violet flowers, streaked white, 2.5cm (1in) across, have a fruity scent and appear in clusters in a single flush in summer. **H** 4m (12ft), **S** 2.2m (7ft).

R. 'Albertine'
Vigorous rambler rose with good disease resistance and arching, thorny, reddish stems. Abundant clusters of scented, cup-shaped, fully double, salmon-pink flowers, 8cm (3in) across, are borne in a single flush in summer. Prone to mildew in a dry site. **H** to 5m (15ft), **S** 3m (10ft).

R. 'Aloha'
Strong-growing, bushy climbing rose with good disease resistance. Fragrant, cupped, fully double, rose- and salmon-pink flowers, 9cm (3½in) across, appear in summer and again in autumn. Leaves are leathery and dark green. May be grown as a shrub. **H** and **S** 2.5m (8ft).

R. 'Madame Grégoire Staechelin'
Vigorous, arching climbing rose with good disease resistance. Bears large clusters of rounded to cupped, fully double flowers, 13cm (5in) across, with ruffled, clear pink petals, shaded carmine, in a single flush in summer. **H** to 6m (20ft), **S** to 4m (12ft).

R. 'Compassion'
Upright, free-branching climbing rose with good disease resistance. Fragrant, rounded, double, pink-tinted, salmon-apricot flowers, 10cm (4in) across, are borne in summer and again in autumn. Has glossy, dark leaves on reddish stems. **H** 3m (10ft), **S** 2.5m (8ft).

R. 'Chaplin's Pink Companion'
Vigorous climbing rose with very good disease resistance and glossy, dark green foliage. Slightly scented, rounded, double, light pink flowers, 5cm (2in) across, are borne freely in large clusters in a single flush during summer. **H** and **S** 3m (10ft).

PINK

R. 'Cécile Brünner'
Vigorous climber with good disease resistance and light green leaves. Masses of sweetly-scented, pointed, double, blush-pink flowers, 4cm (1½in) across, fading to pearl, are borne in a single flush in summer. **H** 3.5m (11½ft), **S** 2.5m (8ft).

R. DANCING QUEEN ('Fryfestoon')
Climber with good disease resistance and large, mid-green leaves. Small clusters of slightly scented, rounded, double, rose-pink flowers, 10cm (4in) across, with a basal white flash on each outer petal, are produced in summer and autumn. **H** 2.4m (8ft), **S** 1.8m (6ft).

R. PENNY LANE ('Hardwell')
Climber with very good disease resistance and glossy, mid-green leaves. Wide clusters of quartered-rosette, fully double flowers, 12cm (5in) across, in light pink with champagne, scented with myrrh and musk, are borne in summer and autumn. **H** 2.5m (8ft), **S** 1.8m (6ft).

RED

R. 'Sympathie'
Vigorous, free-branching climbing rose with moderate disease resistance. Slightly scented, cupped, fully double, bright red flowers, 8cm (3in) across, are borne in summer and autumn, usually in clusters. Has plentiful, glossy, dark green foliage. **H** 3m (10ft), **S** 2.5m (8ft).

R. DUBLIN BAY ('Macdub')
Dense, shrubby climbing rose with good disease resistance that may be pruned to grow as a shrub. Bears clusters of cupped, double, bright crimson flowers, 10cm (4in) across, in summer and again in autumn. Foliage is glossy, dark green and plentiful. **H** and **S** 2.2m (7ft).

R. THE PRINCE'S TRUST ('Harholding')
Climber with good disease resistance and glossy, light to mid-green leaves. Produces dense clusters of slightly scented, cupped, double, bright red flowers, 10cm (4in) across, in summer and autumn. **H** 3m (10ft), **S** 1.8m (6ft).

R. 'Dortmund'
Upright climbing rose with very good disease resistance that may be pruned to make a shrub. Flat, single, red flowers, 10cm (4in) across, with white eyes and a slight scent, are borne freely in clusters in summer and autumn. Has dark green foliage. **H** 3m (10ft), **S** 1.8m (6ft).

R. 'Guinée'
Vigorous, stiffly branched climbing rose with moderate disease resistance. Fragrant, cupped, fully double, blackish-red to maroon flowers, 11cm (4½in) across, are borne in a single flush in summer. Leaves large and leathery. **H** 5m (15ft), **S** 2.2m (7ft).

YELLOW

***R.* GARDENERS GLORY ('Chewability')**
Climber with very good disease resistance and light green leaves. Clusters of cupped, double, yellow flowers, 5cm (2in) across, fading to light yellow, are borne in summer and again in autumn. **H** 2.2m (7ft), **S** 1.5m (5ft).

***R.* 'Emily Gray'**
Semi-evergreen rambler rose with good disease resistance. Trusses of slightly fragrant, cupped, fully double, butter-yellow flowers, 5cm (2in) across, appear in a single flush in summer. Has long, lax stems and dark green leaves. Is prone to mildew. **H** 5m (15ft), **S** 3m (10ft).

***R.* 'Mermaid'**
Slow-growing climbing rose with good disease resistance and repeat-flowering in summer–autumn. Produces flat, single, primrose-yellow flowers, 12cm (5in) across. Has stiff, reddish stems, large, hooked thorns and glossy, dark green leaves. **H** and **S** to 6m (20ft).

***R.* LAURA FORD ('Chewarvel')**
Upright, stiffly branching climbing rose with good disease resistance. Sprays of scented, urn-shaped to flat, yellow flowers, 4.5cm (1¾in) across, appear in summer and again in autumn. Has small, dark, glossy leaves. Good for pillars. **H** 2.2m (7ft), **S** 1.2m (4ft).

***R.* 'Maigold'**
Vigorous climbing rose with very good disease resistance and prickly, arching stems. Fragrant, cupped, semi-double, bronze-yellow flowers, 10cm (4in) across, are borne freely in a single flush in summer. May be pruned to grow as shrub. **H** and **S** 2.5m (8ft).

ORANGE

***R.* BRIDGE OF SIGHS ('Harglow')**
Climber with good disease resistance, repeat-flowering in summer–autumn. Has highly glossy, dark green leaves. Dense clusters of flat, semi-double, deep golden-amber flowers, 10cm (4in) across, have yellow stamens and a sweet spicy perfume. **H** 2.5m (8ft), **S** 1.8m (6ft).

***R.* ALIBABA ('Chewalibaba')**
Climber with very good disease resistance, repeat-flowering summer–autumn. Produces mid-green leaves and sweet-scented, cupped, double flowers, 8cm (3in) across, with ruffled petal edges, in shades of peach-salmon and red. **H** 2.2m (7ft), **S** 1.2m (4ft).

***R.* SUMMER WINE ('Korizont')**
Climber with good disease resistance and large, dark green leaves. Small clusters of flat, semi-double, salmon-pink flowers, to 10cm (4in) across, fading to pink, are produced in summer and again in autumn. **H** 3m (10ft), **S** 1.8m (6ft).

CLIMBERS AND WALL SHRUBS

Versatile and decorative, climbers offer great scope for imaginative garden design, their scrambling stems veiling other plants and structures with flowers and foliage. A few, such as ivy, will also trail across the ground, helping to suppress weeds. Climbers are often used as a backdrop to other plantings, or grown over arbours and gazebos to provide shade. You can also create focal points by weaving them through trees, pyramids and up pillars, or train them over trellis to form boundary screens or dividers between different areas of the garden. The rigid stems of wall shrubs add another dimension to vertical schemes, covering walls and fences with foliage, blooms and berries.

CLIMBERS AND WALL SHRUBS

One of the most versatile of plant groups, climbers bring height to the garden, adding interest to walls and fences, and clothing structures such as arches and pergolas with flowers and foliage. A number of shrubs can also be trained against walls and fences to create textures, patterns, and backdrops to beds and borders.

What are climbers and wall shrubs?

Most climbers are woody, evergreen or deciduous plants, while a few are herbaceous perennials, or summer-flowering annuals. Climbers can be self-clinging or twining (with or without tendrils), or scandent – scrambling species that do not cling. It is important to identify the climbing method of your plant, since this dictates the method of support it needs. Self-clingers such as Virginia creeper (*Parthenocissus quinquefolia*) climb up their supports using adhesive pads, while ivies (*Hedera*) and the Swiss cheese plant (*Monstera deliciosa*) use aerial roots to attach themselves to vertical surfaces. Self-clinging climbers may initially need to be guided to their support with canes (see box below) but will then become self supporting. By contrast, twiners coil around the slim stems of a host plant or they will need wires, mesh, or trellis to cling to if they are wall-trained. Clematis, passion flowers (*Passiflora*), hop (*Humulus lupulus*) sweet peas (*Lathyrus*) and morning glory (*Ipomoea*) fall into this group.

Scrambling plants like winter jasmine (*Jasminum nudiflorum*) attach themselves loosely by threading their flexible stems through host plants or over a framework of their old stems made in previous seasons. On smooth surfaces, such as walls and fences, their stems must be tied into wires or trellis attached to the support, as they have no other means of clinging.

Wall shrubs such as chaenomeles, pyracanthas, and ceanothus are not natural climbers, but can be trained to decorate walls or fences. Some are best grown in this way as they require the additional shelter and support a wall provides.

Ornamental features

Climbing plants have a range of attractive foliage forms, from the lobed leaves of *Tropaeolum speciosum* and palmate foliage of x *Fatshedera lizei*, to the heart-shaped leaves of *Actinidia deliciosa*. Leaf surfaces also offer textural contrasts, from the downy *Vitis vinifera* to glossy ivies (*Hedera*).

ABOVE Wisteria-clad wall
Climbers, such as *Wisteria sinensis*, need a sturdy trellis or wall for support to display their heavy flowers to perfection. When grown around a window the subtle scent of its flowers can be appreciated indoors and out.

PLANTING A CLIMBER

Before planting, attach eye screws and horizontal wires, or a trellis, to the wall or fence. The lowest wire should be about 50cm (20in) above soil level, and the others 30–45cm (12–18in) apart. Work plenty of organic matter into the soil.

1 Dig a planting hole
Water the climber before planting. Dig a hole twice the diameter and deeper than the rootball, 45cm (18in) from the fence. Dig a slightly deeper hole for clematis, since they need to be planted 10cm (4in) deeper than the top of their rootball.

2 Plant the climber
Arrange a fan of canes in the hole. Place the climber in the hole and slant towards the canes. Backfill with some soil enriched with rotted organic matter. Untie the stems from their original support and spread them out ready to attach to the canes.

3 Tie in the stems
Using soft garden twine, tie the stems to the canes using a figure of eight. Train the lower stems on to the lower wires and any tall stems at the centre of the plant to cover the high wires.

4 Firm in the soil
Firm in the climber and create a shallow saucer shape around the base of the plant so that moisture runs into the area above the roots. Water, and apply a bark mulch, keeping it clear of the plant stems.

Colours range from golden-hued *Humulus lupulus* 'Aureus' to the deep green of many jasmines, as well as the purple tints of plants such as *Vitis vinifera* 'Purpurea'. Others have bright, variegated foliage, such as *Actinidia kolomikta*, with its green leaves tipped with splashes of cream and pink. Some, most notably species of vitis and parthenocissus, produce their finest displays in autumn when both fire up with burning shades of red.

Climbers such as passion flowers (*Passiflora*) and clematis bear beautiful flowers, while some, especially wisteria, honeysuckles (*Lonicera*) and jasmines, are deliciously fragrant. The flower colours span the spectrum from the creamy whites of *Schizophragma integrifolium* and *Hydrangea petiolaris* to the magentas of bougainvillea, blues and purples of a whole range of clematis, and chocolate-maroon of *Rhodochiton atrosanguineus*. With many climbers their season is further prolonged by silky seed heads, as in clematis, or striking berries, notably the oblong, purple fruits of *Billardiera longiflora* and the orange-yellow fruits of *Celastrus orbiculatus*.

Annual climbers such as sweet peas (*Lathyrus odoratus*) climb rapidly to the top of wigwams made from garden canes, producing a succession of scented flowers from mid- to late summer that are ideal for cutting. Morning glory (*Ipomoea tricolor* 'Heavenly blue'), with its sky-blue trumpets and black-eyed Susan (*Thumbergia alata*), also offer a quick-fix solution, covering bare trellis, or adding height to containers on patios.

Wall shrubs are also valued for their attractive foliage and blooms. Ceanothus, for example, has both evergreen and deciduous forms, with flowers in varying shades of blue, white and pink. The flowering quince (*Chaenomeles*) produces a profusion of cupped white, pink, orange, or scarlet-red flowers early in the year, followed by yellow fruits in the autumn. Thorny pyracanthas make excellent security hedges, deterring intruders, and sport glossy evergreen foliage with an abundance of yellow, orange, or red berries in the autumn.

Designing with climbers and wall shrubs

Growing climbers as a backdrop for other plants is one way of adding height to a border but they can also be grown on free-standing supports to form screens or divisions between different parts of the garden. Grown through trees or on pillars and pyramids, they also create focal points.

Where a garden lacks shade, climbers allowed to ramble over pergolas and arbours offer a cool place to sit. You can also use climbers and wall shrubs to soften the lines of hard landscaping, while vigorous climbers will help to camouflage unsightly structures. Left unsupported, some climbers trail on the ground and, when pegged at the nodes, will root to form a carpet of ground cover. When growing climbers through other plants, make sure that you synchronise their flowering times for a dual effect, and match their pruning needs.

As well as growing shrubs such as pyracanthas and chaenomeles against walls, you can train them into fans and espaliers for a formal effect.

ABOVE *Clematis* **'Bill MacKenzie'**
This small-bloomed, late-flowering Group 3 clematis provides a natural, rambling backdrop of nodding yellow flowers and fluffy seedheads.

PRUNING CLEMATIS

Some clematis flower well if pruned lightly or not at all, while others bloom more effectively when cut back hard. They are divided into three groups, each with different pruning requirements. Group 1 clematis (including *C. montana*, and *C. armandii*) are vigorous plants that flower in late spring on the previous year's growth. Group 2 clematis, such as *C.* 'Corona', and *C.* 'Henryi', flower in early summer on the previous year's growth. Group 3 clematis include small-flowered viticella and texensis types, *C.* 'Gravetye Beauty', for example, and some large-flowered types including *C.* 'Perle d'Azur'. They bloom from mid-summer to autumn on new growth formed earlier in the year.

Pruning Group 1 clematis
Plants in this group need little or no pruning once established, except to remove dead and damaged stems, or to keep them in check. After flowering, give them a light trim if necessary. Prune the leggy new season's growth, cutting above a pair of healthy buds, but do not cut them back hard.

Pruning Group 2 clematis
Prune this group in early spring when the buds are in growth and are clearly visible. Work from the top of the clematis, pruning each stem back to the first pair of healthy buds or shoots. Remove dead, diseased or damaged wood; it will be brown and dry. The pruned stems will produce new growth and then flowers in early summer.

Pruning Group 3 clematis
Left unpruned, these clematis form flowers at the top of the plant, leaving bare, straggly stems at the bottom. In late winter before the buds break, remove the tangle of shoots from their support and cut back all the stems hard to within 30cm (12in) of the ground. This encourages strong new shoots and flowers to form along their length.

WHITE

Decumaria sinensis
Evergreen, woody-stemmed, root climber with oval, often toothed leaves, 2.5–8cm (1–3in) long. Conical clusters of small, honey-scented, cream flowers are produced in late spring and early summer. **H** to 2m (6ft) or more.

Clianthus puniceus* f. *albus
Evergreen or semi-evergreen, woody-stemmed, scrambling climber, grown for its drooping clusters of claw-like, creamy-white flowers that open in spring and early summer. Mid-green leaves consist of many small leaflets. **H** 4m (12ft).

Holboellia latifolia [white form]
Variable, evergeen, twining climber with glossy, mid-green leaves divided into 3–9 ovate or oblong leaflets. Bears racemes of 3–7 sweetly scented, creamy-white, male flowers and greenish, female flowers in early summer, and sausage-shaped, purple fruit. **H** to 5m (16ft).

Stauntonia hexaphylla
Evergreen, woody-stemmed, twining climber. Leaves have 3–7 oval leaflets, 5–13cm (2–5in) long. In spring bears racemes of fragrant, cup-shaped, violet-tinged white flowers, followed by egg-shaped, edible, purple fruits, if plants of both sexes are grown. **H** to 10m (30ft).

Acradenia frankliniae
Evergreen, upright, stiffly branched shrub with aromatic, dark green leaves divided into 3 narrowly lance-shaped leaflets. From late spring to early summer bears small clusters of star-shaped, white flowers. **H** 3m (10ft), **S** 1.5m (5ft).

PINK

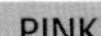

***Prostanthera rotundifolia* 'Rosea'**
Evergreen, bushy, rounded shrub with tiny, sweetly aromatic, deep green leaves and short, leafy racemes of bell-shaped, purple-anthered, pale pink flowers in late spring or summer. **H** 2–4m (6–13ft), **S** 1–3m (3–10ft).

Ercilla volubilis
Evergreen, root climber with oval to heart-shaped, mid-green leaves, 2.5–5cm (1–2in) long. Spikes of petal-less flowers, each consisting of 5 greenish or purple sepals and 6–8 white stamens, are borne in spring. **H** to 10m (30ft) or more.

***Campsis radicans* 'Indian Summer'**
Deciduous, woody-stemmed, root climber with leaves divided into 7–11 oval, toothed leaflets. Small clusters of trumpet-shaped, yellow-throated, orange-red flowers, 6–8cm (2½–3in) long, are produced in late summer and early autumn. **H** 12m (40ft).

Mitraria coccinea
Evergreen, woody-stemmed, scrambling climber with oval, toothed leaves. Small, tubular, orange-red flowers are borne singly in leaf axils during late spring to summer. **H** to 2m (6ft).

Ribes speciosum
Deciduous, bushy, spiny shrub bearing slender, drooping, tubular, red flowers, with long, red stamens, in mid–late spring. Fruits are spherical and red. Has red, young shoots and oval, 3–5-lobed, glossy, bright green leaves. **H** and **S** 2m (6ft).

Akebia quinata (Chocolate vine)
Woody-stemmed, twining climber, semi-evergreen in mild winters or warm areas, with leaves of 5 leaflets. Vanilla-scented, brownish-purple flowers appear in late spring, followed by sausage-shaped, purplish fruits. **H** 10m (30ft) or more.

***Chaenomeles* x *superba* 'Crimson and Gold'** (Flowering quince)
Deciduous, dense shrub with thorns and oval, glossy, green leaves. Bears masses of 5-petalled, deep red flowers, with conspicuous, golden-yellow anthers, in spring, followed by round, yellow fruits. **H** 1m (3ft), **S** 2m (6ft).

Clianthus puniceus (Parrot's bill)
Evergreen or semi-evergreen, woody-stemmed, scrambling climber with leaves composed of many leaflets. In spring and early summer bears drooping clusters of unusual, claw-like, brilliant red flowers. **H** 4m (12ft).

Jasminum beesianum
Evergreen, woody-stemmed, scrambling climber, deciduous in cool areas. Has lance-shaped leaves. Fragrant, tubular, usually 6-lobed, pinkish-red flowers, 1–3 together, borne in early summer, are followed by shiny, black berries. **H** to 5m (15ft).

PURPLE

Akebia* x *pentaphylla
Mainly deciduous, woody-stemmed, twining climber. Mid-green leaves, bronze-tinted when young, have 3 or 5 oval leaflets. Pendent racemes of small, 3-petalled, purple flowers (female at base, male at apex) are borne in spring. **H** to 10m (30ft).

Hardenbergia comptoniana
Evergreen, woody-stemmed, twining climber with leaves of 3 or 5 lance-shaped leaflets. Has racemes of pea-like, deep purple-blue flowers in spring. **H** to 2.5m (8ft).

Holboellia latifolia [purple form]
Variable, evergeen, twining climber with glossy, mid-green leaves divided into 3–9 ovate leaflets. Has racemes of 3–7 sweetly scented, plum-purple, male flowers and greenish-white female flowers in early summer, followed by sausage-shaped, purple fruit. **H** to 5m (16ft) or more.

BLUE

***Ceanothus arboreus* 'Trewithen Blue'**
Vigorous, evergreen, bushy, spreading shrub with broadly oval to rounded, dark green leaves. In spring and early summer bears large, pyramidal clusters of rich blue flowers. **H** 6m (20ft), **S** 8m (25ft).

Sollya heterophylla
Evergreen, woody-based, twining climber with narrowly lance-shaped to oval leaves, 2–6cm (¾-2½in) long. Nodding clusters of 4–9 broadly bell-shaped, sky-blue flowers are carried from spring to autumn. **H** to 3m (10ft).

YELLOW

Eriobotrya japonica (Loquat)
Evergreen, bushy shrub or spreading tree with stout shoots bearing large, oblong, prominently veined, glossy, dark green leaves. Fragrant, 5-petalled, white flowers borne in clusters in early autumn are followed by pear-shaped, orange-yellow fruits. **H** and **S** 8m (25ft).

***Humulus lupulus* 'Aureus'**
Herbaceous, twining climber with rough, hairy stems and toothed, yellowish leaves divided into 3 or 5 lobes. Greenish, female flower spikes are borne in pendent clusters in autumn. **H** to 6m (20ft).

Vestia foetida
Evergreen, upright shrub with pendent, tubular, pale yellow flowers from mid-spring to mid-summer. Oblong, glossy, dark green leaves have an unpleasant scent. **H** 2m (6ft), **S** 1.5m (5ft).

Azara serrata

Evergreen, upright shrub with glossy, bright green foliage and rounded bunches of fragrant, yellow flowers in late spring or early summer. **H** 4m (12ft), **S** 3m (10ft).

Coronilla valentina* subsp. *glauca
Evergreen, bushy, dense shrub. Has blue-grey leaves with 5 or 7 leaflets. Fragrant, pea-like, yellow flowers are borne from mid-spring to early summer. **H** 1.5m (5ft), **S** 1.5m (5ft).

Forsythia suspensa
Deciduous, arching, graceful shrub with slender shoots. Nodding, narrow, trumpet-shaped, bright yellow flowers open from early to mid-spring, before mid-green leaves appear. **H** 3m (10ft), **S** 3m (10ft).

Gelsemium sempervirens
Moderately vigorous, evergreen, twining climber with pointed, lustrous leaves. Clusters of fragrant, funnel-shaped, pale to deep yellow flowers are borne from late spring to late summer. **H** to 6m (20ft).

Jasminum mesnyi (Primrose jasmine)
Evergreen or semi-evergreen, woody-stemmed, scrambling climber. Leaves are divided into 3 leaflets; semi-double, pale yellow flowers appear in spring. **H** to 3m (10ft).

WHITE

Trachelospermum jasminoides
(Confederate jasmine, Star jasmine)
Evergreen, woody-stemmed, twining climber with oval leaves up to 15cm (6in) long. Has very fragrant, white flowers in summer, then pairs of pods, up to 15cm (6in) long. **H** to 9m (28ft).

Araujia sericifera (Cruel plant)
Evergreen, woody-stemmed, twining climber with leaves that are white-downy beneath. Has scented, white flowers, often striped pale maroon inside, from late summer to autumn. **H** to 7m (23ft).

***Ampelopsis brevipedunculata* var. *maximowiczii* 'Elegans'**
Vigorous, deciduous, woody-stemmed, twining, tendril climber with hairy young stems. Has variable, densely white-mottled, pink-tinged leaves. Tiny flowers are produced in summer, followed by blue berries. **H** 5m (16ft).

***Solanum laxum* 'Album'** (Potato vine)
Semi-evergreen, woody-stemmed, scrambling climber. Oval to lance-shaped leaves are sometimes lobed or divided into leaflets. Has star-shaped, white flowers, 2–2.5cm (¾–1in) across, in summer–autumn. **H** to 6m (20ft).

Hydrangea petiolaris
(Climbing hydrangea)
Deciduous, woody-stemmed, root climber. Has toothed leaves and lacy heads of small, white flowers in summer, only sparingly borne on young plants. **H** to 15m (50ft).

WHITE

Pileostegia viburnoides
Slow-growing, evergreen, woody-stemmed, root climber. Tiny, white or cream flowers, with many prominent stamens, are borne in heads from late summer to autumn. **H** to 6m (20ft).

***Wisteria floribunda* 'Alba'**
Deciduous, woody-stemmed, twining climber with leaves of 11–19 oval leaflets. Scented, pea-like, white flowers are carried in drooping racemes, up to 60cm (2ft) long, in early summer. **H** to 9m (28ft).

Hydrangea seemannii
Evergreen, woody-stemmed climber with elliptic to lance-shaped, leathery, mid-green leaves. In summer produces domed flower heads consisting of small, clustered, greenish-white, fertile flowers surrounded by larger, white, sterile flowers. **H** 15m (50ft).

Jasminum officinale* f. *affine
(Common jasmine)
Semi-evergreen or deciduous, woody-stemmed, twining climber with leaves comprising 7 or 9 leaflets. Clusters of fragrant, 4- or 5-lobed flowers, white inside and pink outside, are borne in summer–autumn. **H** to 12m (40ft).

Hydrangea serratifolia
Vigorous, evergreen, woody-stemmed climber with elliptic, sharply toothed, dark green leaves. In summer produces rounded clusters of small, white, fertile flowers opening from large, rounded buds. **H** 15–20m (50–70ft).

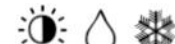

Trachelospermum asiaticum
Evergreen, woody-stemmed, twining climber with oval, glossy, dark green leaves, 2.5cm (1in) long. Scented, tubular, cream flowers that age to yellow, are produced in summer. Pairs of long, slender pods, 12–22cm (5–9in) long, contain silky seeds. **H** to 6m (20ft).

Dregea sinensis
Evergreen, woody-stemmed, twining climber. Oval, green leaves, 3–10cm (1¼–4in) long, are greyish beneath. In summer produces clusters of 10–25 small, fragrant, star-shaped flowers, red-marked white or cream, followed by pairs of slender seed pods. **H** to 3m (10ft).

Anredera cordifolia
Fast-growing, evergreen, tuberous, twining climber with oval to lance-shaped, fleshy leaves. Tiny, fragrant, white flowers are borne in clusters from upper leaf axils in summer. **H** to 6m (20ft).

Drimys lanceolata (Mountain pepper)
Evergreen, upright, dense shrub or tree with deep red shoots and oblong, dark green leaves. Produces clusters of star-shaped, white flowers in spring. **H** 4m (12ft), **S** 2.5m (8ft).

Schizophragma integrifolium
Deciduous, woody-stemmed, root climber with oval or heart-shaped leaves. In summer, white flowers are borne in flat heads up to 30cm (12in) across, marginal sterile flowers each having a large, white bract. **H** to 12m (40ft).

Prostanthera cuneata
Evergreen, bushy, erect to spreading shrub with small, aromatic, shiny, dark green leaves. In late spring and early summer produces dense racemes of shortly tubular, 2-lipped, white flowers, with purple and yellow markings in the throat. **H** and **S** 90cm (3ft).

Schizophragma hydrangeoides
Deciduous, woody-stemmed, climber with broadly oval leaves. Small white flowers, in flat heads, are produced on pendent side-branches in summer; these are surrounded by marginal, sterile flowers, each with an oval, pale yellow sepal. **H** to 12m (40ft).

Carpenteria californica
Evergreen, bushy shrub. Glossy, dark green foliage sets off fragrant, yellow-centred, white flowers borne during summer. **H** 2m (6ft) or more, **S** 2m (6ft).

CLEMATIS

Among the climbers, clematis are unsurpassed in their long period of flowering (with species flowering in almost every month of the year), the variety of flower shapes and colours, and their tolerance of almost any aspect and climate. Some spring-flowering species and cultivars are vigorous and excellent for rapidly covering buildings, old trees and pergolas. Other, less rampant cultivars display often large, exquisite blooms from early summer to autumn in almost every colour. Flower colours may vary according to your climatic conditions; generally speaking, the warmer the climate, the darker the flowers are likely to be.

Clematis look attractive when trained on walls or trellises and when grown in association with other climbers, trees or shrubs, treating them as hosts. Less vigorous cultivars may also be left unsupported to scramble at ground level, where their flowers will be clearly visible.

The various types of clematis (see the Plant Dictionary) may be divided into 3 groups, each of which has different pruning requirements. Incorrect pruning may result in cutting out the stems that will produce flowers in the current season, so the following guidelines should be followed closely.

Group 1

Early-flowering species, Alpina, Macropetala and Montana types

Flower stems are produced direct from the previous season's ripened stems. Prune after flowering to allow new growth to be produced and ripened for the next season. Remove dead or damaged stems and cut back other shoots that have outgrown their allotted space.

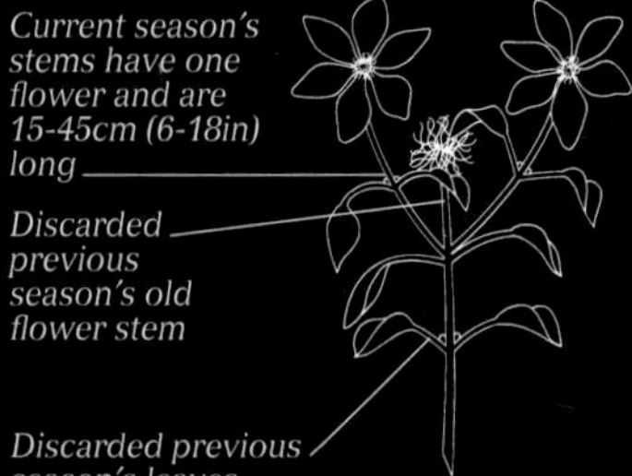

Group 2

Early, large-flowered cultivars

Flowers are produced on short, current season's stems, so prune before new growth starts, in early spring. Remove dead or damaged stems and cut back all others to where strong, leaf-axil buds are visible. (These buds will produce the first crop of flowers.)

Group 3

Late, large-flowered cultivars, Late-flowering species, Small-flowered cultivars and Herbaceous types

Flowers are produced on the current season's growth only, so prune before new growth commences, in early spring. Remove all of the previous season's stems down to a pair of strong, leaf-axil buds, 15-30cm (6-12in) above the soil.

C. x *cartmanii* 'Joe' [1, early]

C. 'Andromeda' [2, early-large-fl.]

C. ARCTIC QUEEN ('Evitwo') 🏆 [2, early large-fl.]

C. *fasciculiflora* [1, early small-fl.]

C. 'White Columbine' 🏆 [1, early small-fl.]

C. *armandii* [1, early small-fl.]

C. 'Guernsey Cream' [2, early large-fl.]

C. x *cartmanii* 'Avalanche' 🏆 [1, early]

C. 'Bella' [2, early large-fl.]

C. 'Early Sensation' [3, late]

C. *montana* [1, Montana]

C. CHANTILLY ('Evipo021') [2, early large-fl.]

C. *florida* PISTACHIO ('Evirida') [3, late large-fl.]

C. *montana* var. *rubens* [1, Montana]

C. 'Alionushka' 🏆 [3, early small-fl.]

C. 'Fireworks' [2, early large-fl.]

C. *cirrhosa* [1, early small-fl.]

C. 'Jacqueline du Pré' 🏆 [1, early small-fl.]

C. *montana* var. *rubens* 'Tetrarose' 🏆 [1, Montana]

C. 'Lincoln Star' [2, early large-fl.]

C. VIENNETTA ('Evipo006') [3, large-fl.]

C. 'Sunrise' [1, early]

C. 'Jan Lindmark' [1, early small-fl.]

C. 'Henryi' 🏆 [2, early large-fl.]

C. BLUE MOON ('Evirin') [3, late large-fl.]

C. 'Corona' [2, early large-fl.]

C. 'Charissima' [2, late large-fl.]

C. 'Nelly Moser' 🏆 [2, early large-fl.]

C. *florida* var. *sieboldiana* [3, small-fl.]

C. 'Huldine' 🏆 [3, late large-fl.]

C. 'Barbara Jackman' [2, early large-fl.]

C. 'Barbara Dibley' [2, early lge-fl.]

C. 'Kakio' [2, early large-fl.]

C. **'Gravetye Beauty'** [3, small-fl.]

C. **'Etoile Violette'** ♡ [3, late]

C. **'Abundance'** ♡ [3, late-fl.]

C. **'Madame Julia Correvon'** ♡ [3, late-fl.]

C. **'Purpurea Plena Elegans'** ♡ [3, late-fl.]

C. **'Rosy O' Grady'** ♡ [1, early and late]

C. **'Jackmanii'** ♡ [3, late large-fl.]

C. **AVANT-GARDE ('Evipo033')** [3, mid-season small-fl.]

C. **ROSEMOOR ('Evipo002')** [2, early large-fl.]

C. **BOURBON ('Evipo018')** [2, early large-fl.]

C. **VINO ('Poulvo')** [2, early large-fl.]

C. **'Polish Spirit'** ♡ [3, late large-fl.]

C. **'Frankie'** ♡ [1, early small-fl.]

C. **'Kardynal Wyszynski'** [2, early large-fl.]

C. **ANNA LOUISE ('Evithree')** ♡ [2, early large-fl.]

C. cirrhosa **var.** ***purpurascens*** **'Freckles'** ♡ [1, early small-fl.]

C. **'Black Prince'** [3, late]

C. **'Perle d'Azur'** [3, late large-fl.]

C. **'Frances Rivis'** ♡ [1, early small-fl.]

C. **'Silver Moon'** [2, early large-fl.]

C. ***flammula*** [3, late]

C. **'Westerplatte'** [2, early large-fl.]

C. **'Ernest Markham'** [3, late lge fl.]

C. **'Columella'** [1, early]

C. **'Betty Corning'** ♡ [3, early]

C. ***rehderiana*** ♡ [3, late fl.]

PINK

***Lathyrus odoratus* 'Mrs Bernard Jones'**
Vigorous, annual, tendril climber with mid-green leaves. Produces large, strongly scented, wavy-edged, sugar-pink flowers, suffused white at the margins, from summer to early autumn. **H** 2m (6ft).

***Lathyrus odoratus* 'Charles Unwin'**
Vigorous, annual, tendril climber with oval, mid-green leaves. Produces large, scented, wavy-margined, soft salmon-pink flowers with cream keels, paling to salmon-tinted cream at the margins in summer and early autumn. **H** 2m (6ft).

Actinidia kolomikta
Deciduous, woody-stemmed, twining climber with 8–16cm (3–6in) long leaves, the upper sections often creamy-white and pink. Has small, cup-shaped, white flowers in summer, male and female on separate plants. **H** 4m (12ft).

Lathyrus latifolius
(Everlasting pea, Perennial pea)
Herbaceous, tendril climber with winged stems. Leaves have broad stipules and a pair of leaflets. Has small racemes of pink-purple flowers in summer and early autumn. **H** 2m (6ft) or more.

Jasminum* x *stephanense
Vigorous, deciduous, twining climber with simple or pinnate, matt green leaves. Produces loose clusters of fragrant, 5-lobed, pale pink flowers, from early to mid-summer, sometimes producing a second flush later in the season. **H** 5–7m (16–22ft).

***Lathyrus odoratus* 'Lady Diana'**
Moderately fast-growing, slender, annual, tendril climber with oval, mid-green leaves. Fragrant, pale violet-blue flowers are borne from summer to early autumn. **H** 2m (6ft).

***Grevillea* 'Canberra Gem'**
Vigorous, evergreen shrub with silky stems and linear, pointed, green leaves, to 3cm (11/4in) long. Late winter to mid-summer, and occasionally through the year, produces short racemes of small, tubular, white-tipped, pink-red flowers. **H** and **S** 2–4m (6–13ft).

Bomarea edulis
Deciduous, twining climber with lance-shaped, mid-green leaves. From early summer to autumn bears umbel-like clusters of narrowly bell-shaped flowers, to 3.5cm (1½in) long, pink–light red, with yellow-flecked throats. **H** 2–3m (6–10ft).

RED

Lapageria rosea **(Chilean bellflower, Copihue)**
Evergreen, woody-stemmed, twining climber with oblong to oval, leathery leaves. Has pendent, fleshy, pink to red flowers, 7–9cm (2¾–3½in) long, with paler flecks, from summer to late autumn. **H** to 5m (15ft).

***Lathyrus odoratus* 'Barry Dare'**
Vigorous, annual, tendril climber with ovate, mid-green leaves and large, sweetly-scented, bright orange-red, pea-flowers from summer to autumn. **H** 2m (6ft).

Cestrum elegans
Vigorous, evergreen, arching shrub. Nodding shoots carry downy, deep green foliage. Dense racemes of tubular, purplish-red flowers in late spring and summer are followed by deep red fruits. **H** and **S** 3m (10ft).

Schisandra rubriflora
Deciduous, woody-stemmed, twining climber with leathery, toothed leaves, paler beneath. Has small, crimson flowers in spring or early summer and drooping, red fruits in late summer. **H** to 6m (20ft).

Ipomoea lobata
Deciduous or semi-evergreen, twining climber with 3-lobed leaves, usually grown as an annual. One-sided racemes of small, tubular, dark red flowers fade to orange, then creamy-yellow, in summer. **H** to 5m (15ft).

Berberidopsis corallina **(Coral plant)**
Evergreen, woody-stemmed, twining climber with oval to heart-shaped, leathery leaves edged with small spines. Bears pendent clusters of globular, deep red flowers in summer to early autumn. **H** 4.5m (14ft).

Ipomoea quamoclit **(Cypress vine)**
Annual, twining climber with oval, bright green leaves cut into many thread-like segments. Slender, tubular, orange or scarlet flowers are carried in summer–autumn. **H** 2–4m (6–12ft).

Tropaeolum speciosum **(Flame creeper, Flame nasturtium)**
Herbaceous, twining climber with a creeping rhizome and lobed, blue-green leaves. Bears scarlet flowers in summer, followed by bright blue fruits surrounded by deep red calyces. Roots should be in shade. **H** to 3m (10ft).

Crinodendron hookerianum **(Lantern tree)**
Evergreen, stiffly-branched shrub. In late spring and early summer, lantern-like, red flowers hang from shoots clothed with narrow, dark green leaves. **H** 6m (20ft), **S** 5m (15ft).

Desfontainia spinosa
Evergreen, bushy, dense shrub with spiny, holly-like, glossy, dark green leaves. Long, tubular, drooping, red flowers, tipped with yellow, are borne from mid-summer to late autumn.
H and **S** 2m (6ft).

***Callistemon citrinus* 'Splendens'** (Crimson bottlebrush)
Evergreen, arching shrub with broad, lemon-scented, grey-green leaves that are bronze-red when young. In early summer bright red flowers are borne in bottlebrush-like spikes. **H** 2–8m (6–25ft), **S** 1.5–6m (5–20ft).

Acca sellowiana (Pineapple guava)
Evergreen, bushy shrub or tree. Dark green leaves have white undersides. In mid-summer bears large, dark red flowers with white-edged petals, followed by edible, red-tinged, green fruits. **H** 2m (6ft), **S** 2.5m (8ft).

Grevillea rosmarinifolia
Evergreen, rounded, well-branched shrub. Dark green leaves are needle-shaped with reflexed margins, silky-haired beneath. Has short, dense clusters of tubular, red, occasionally pink or white flowers in summer.
H 0.6–3m (2–10ft), **S** 1–5m (3–15ft).

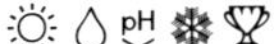

Campsis grandiflora
Deciduous, woody-stemmed, root climber. Leaves have 7 or 9 oval, toothed leaflets. Drooping clusters of trumpet-shaped, orange or red flowers, 5–8cm (2–3in) long, are produced in late summer and autumn, abundantly in warm areas. **H** 7–10m (22–30ft).

Callistemon subulatus
Evergreen, arching shrub with narrowly oblong, bright green leaves. Dense spikes of crimson flowers are produced in summer. **H** 1.5m (5ft), **S** 2m (6ft).

***Cestrum* 'Newellii'**
Evergreen, arching shrub bearing clusters of tubular, crimson flowers in late spring and summer. Leaves are large, broadly lance-shaped and dark green. **H** and **S** 3m (10ft).

Abutilon megapotamicum
Evergreen shrub with long, slender branches normally trained against a wall. Pendent, bell-shaped, yellow-and-red flowers are produced from late spring to autumn. Leaves are oval, with heart-shaped bases, and dark green.
H and **S** 2m (6ft).

Rhodochiton atrosanguineus
Evergreen, leaf-stalk climber, usually grown as an annual, with toothed leaves. Has tubular, blackish-purple flowers, with bell-shaped, red-purple calyces, from late spring to late autumn.
H to 3m (10ft). Min. 5°C (41°F).

Lablab purpureus (Australian pea, Hyacinth bean, Lablab)
Deciduous, woody-stemmed, twining climber, often grown as an annual. Purple, pinkish or white flowers in summer are followed by long pods with edible seeds. **H** 10m (30ft).
Min. 5°C (41°F).

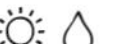

PURPLE

Ipomoea hederacea
Annual, twining climber with heart-shaped or 3-lobed, mid- to bright green leaves. Has funnel-shaped, red, purple, pink or blue flowers in summer to early autumn. **H** 3–4m (10–12ft).

Akebia trifoliata
Deciduous, woody-stemmed, twining climber. Mid-green leaves, bronze-tinted when young, have 3 oval leaflets. Drooping racemes of purple flowers in spring are followed by sausage-shaped, purplish fruits. **H** to 10m (30ft) or more.

Buddleja crispa
Deciduous, upright, bushy shrub that, from mid- to late summer, bears racemes of small, fragrant, lilac flowers with white eyes. Has woolly, white shoots and oval, greyish-green leaves. **H** and **S** 3m (10ft).

Cobaea scandens
(Cup-and-saucer vine)
Evergreen or deciduous, woody-stemmed, tendril climber, grown as an annual. From late summer to first frosts has flowers that open yellow-green and age to purple. **H** 4–5m (12–15ft). Min. 4°C (39°F).

Passiflora caerulea
(Common passion flower)
Fast-growing, evergreen or semi-evergreen, woody-stemmed, tendril climber. Has white flowers, sometimes pink-flushed, with blue- or purple-banded crowns, in summer-autumn. **H** 10m (30ft).

Fabiana imbricata* f. *violacea
Evergreen, upright shrub with shoots that are densely covered with tiny, heath-like, deep green leaves. Tubular, lilac flowers are borne profusely in early summer. **H** and **S** 2.5m (8ft).

Aristolochia macrophylla
(Dutchman's pipe)
Vigorous, deciduous climber with heart-shaped, dark green leaves, to 30cm (12in) long. In summer produces malodorous, trumpet-shaped, cream-coloured flowers, strongly mottled yellow, purple and brown. **H** 10m (30ft).

Aconitum hemsleyanum
Wiry, scandent, fibrous perennial with hooded, lilac flowers produced in drooping clusters in late summer. Leaves are divided and mid-green. Is best grown where it can scramble through a shrub or be supported. **H** 2–2.5m (6–8ft), **S** 1–1.2m (3–4ft).

***Solanum crispum* 'Glasnevin'**
(Chilean potato tree)
Vigorous, evergreen or semi-evergreen, woody-stemmed, scrambling climber with oval leaves. Has clusters of lilac to purple flowers, 2.5cm (1in) across, in summer. **H** to 6m (20ft).

Codonopsis convolvulacea
Herbaceous, twining climber with 5cm (1–2in) long, oval or lance-shaped leaves. Widely bell- to saucer-shaped, bluish-violet flowers, 5cm (1–2in) across, are borne in summer. **H** to 2m (6ft).

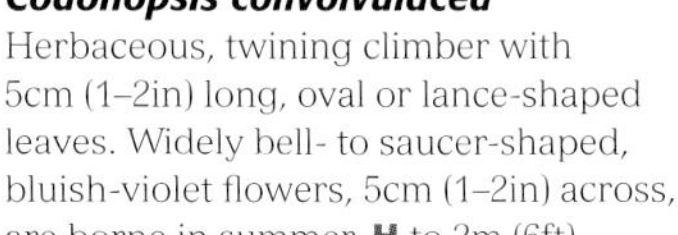

***Ipomoea tricolor* 'Heavenly Blue'** (Morning glory)
Fast-growing, annual, twining climber with heart-shaped leaves and large, funnel-shaped, sky-blue flowers borne from summer to early autumn. **H** to 3m (10ft).

Plumbago auriculata (Cape leadwort)
Fast-growing, evergreen, woody-stemmed, scrambling climber. Trusses of sky-blue flowers are carried from summer to early winter. **H** 3–6m (10–20ft).

***Ceanothus* 'Puget Blue'**
Vigorous, evergreen, spreading shrub with arching branches clothed with small, oval, wrinkled, dark green leaves. In mid-spring produces abundant clusters of small, deep blue flowers. Is best grown trained as a wall shrub. **H** and **S** 3–4m (10–13ft).

***Ceanothus* 'Burkwoodii'**
Evergreen, bushy, dense shrub producing dense panicles of bright blue flowers from mid-summer to mid-autumn. Has oval, glossy, dark green leaves, downy and grey beneath. **H** 1.5m (5ft), **S** 2m (6ft).

WISTERIA

Wisterias are large, vigorous, deciduous climbers, which flower late-spring to early summer, producing pendent racemes 45cm (18in) long or more, of scented, pea-like flowers. These open in shades of white, through pale lilac-blue, to dark purple, and are sweetly scented. Often seen growing over the front of buildings, wisterias need strong support as they become heavy with age, and their roots may damage building foundations. They prefer fertile, moist, well-drained soil in full sun or partial shade. Unless the soil is very poor, don't feed them as this encourages excess growth. Choosing wisteria can be confusing because many varieties are commonly mislabelled.

***W. brachybotrys* 'Shiro-kapitan'** ⓘ

***W. floribunda* 'Hon-Beni'** ⓘ

***W. brachybotrys* 'White Silk'** ⓘ

***W. floribunda* 'Domino'** ⓘ

***W. floribunda* 'Lawrence'** ⓘ

***W. floribunda* 'Yae-kokuryu'** ⓘ

***W. sinensis* 'Prolific'** ⓘ

YELLOW

Thladiantha dubia
Fast-growing, herbaceous or deciduous, tendril climber. Oval to heart-shaped, mid-green leaves, 10cm (4in) long, are hairy beneath; bell-shaped, yellow flowers are carried in summer.
H 3m (10ft).

Grevillea juniperina* f. *sulphurea
Evergreen, rounded, bushy shrub with almost needle-like leaves, recurved and dark green above, silky-haired beneath. Has clusters of small, spidery, pale yellow flowers in spring–summer.
H 1.5–2m (5–6ft), **S** 2–3m (6–10ft).

***Hypericum* 'Rowallane'**
Semi-evergreen, arching shrub with oval, rich green leaves. Bears large, bowl-shaped, deep golden-yellow flowers from mid-summer to mid- or late autumn. Is cut to ground level in severe winters. **H** to 1.8m (6ft), **S** to 1m (3ft).

Dendromecon rigida
Vigorous, evergreen, upright shrub, best grown against a wall. Large, fragrant, golden-yellow flowers appear amid grey-green foliage from spring to autumn. **H** and **S** 3m (10ft).

***Fremontodendron* 'California Glory'**
Very vigorous, evergreen or semi-evergreen, upright shrub. Has rounded, lobed, dark green leaves and large, bright yellow flowers from late spring to mid-autumn. **H** 6m (20ft), **S** 4m (12ft).

Lonicera* x *americana (Honeysuckle)
Very free-flowering, deciduous, woody-stemmed, twining climber. Leaves are oval, upper ones united and saucer-like. Has clusters of strongly fragrant, yellow flowers, flushed with red-purple, in summer. **H** to 7m (23ft).

Piptanthus nepalensis
Deciduous or semi-evergreen, open shrub with leaves consisting of 3 large, dark blue-green leaflets. Racemes of pea-like, bright yellow flowers appear in spring–summer. **H** 2.5m (8ft), **S** 2m (6ft).

***Jasminum humile* 'Revolutum'**
Evergreen, bushy shrub with glossy, bright green leaves divided into 3–7 oval leaflets. Bears large, fragrant, tubular, upright, bright yellow flowers, with 5 spreading lobes, on long, slender, green shoots from early spring to late autumn.
H 2.5m (8ft), **S** 3m (10ft).

Campsis radicans* f. *flava
Deciduous, woody-stemmed, root climber with leaves divided into 7–11 oval, toothed leaflets, downy beneath. Small clusters of trumpet-shaped, yellow flowers, 6–8cm (2½–3in) long, are produced in late summer and early autumn. **H** 12m (40ft).

Thunbergia alata **(Black-eyed Susan)**
Moderately fast-growing, annual, twining climber. Has toothed, oval to heart-shaped leaves and rounded, rather flat, small flowers, orange-yellow with very dark brown centres, from early summer to early autumn. **H** 3m (10ft).

***Tropaeolum tuberosum* var. *lineamaculatum* 'Ken Aslet'**
Herbaceous climber with yellowish, red-streaked tubers and blue-green leaves. From mid-summer to autumn has flowers with red sepals and orange petals. In cool areas, lift and store tubers in winter. **H** to 2.5m (8ft).

Bomarea multiflora
Herbaceous, twining climber with rounded clusters of 5–40 tubular to funnel-shaped, orange-red flowers, spotted crimson within, in summer. **H** 3–4m (10–12ft).

HONEYSUCKLE

Fragrant, colourful, and easy to grow, honeysuckles (*Lonicera*) can illuminate a border, wall, or fence with their distinctive blooms. They are mainly cultivated for their flowers, which are tubular or funnel- to bell-shaped, and come in a range of colours, from the bright golden-yellow of *L. etrusca* 'Superba', to the deep pink of *L. periclymenum* 'Red Gables'. The genus includes deciduous, semi-evergreen or evergreen shrubs and twining climbers, which have a sweet fragrance that intensifies at night. Honeysuckles need fertile, well-drained soil, in sun or semi-shade. Prune back young growth soon after flowering. Most produce berries, which should not be eaten.

***L. etrusca* 'Superba'** 🏆

L. etrusca 'Michael Rosse'

***L. japonica* 'Aureoreticulata'**

L. henryi

L. sempervirens 🏆(!)

***L. periclymenum* 'Serotina'** 🏆 ***L. periclymenum* 'Red Gables'**

ORANGE

Eccremocarpus scaber
(Chilean glory flower, Glory vine)
Evergreen, sub-shrubby, tendril climber, often grown as an annual. In summer has racemes of small, orange-red flowers, followed by inflated fruit pods containing many winged seeds. **H** 2–3m (6–10ft).

Mutisia decurrens
Evergreen, tendril climber with narrowly oblong leaves, 7–13cm (2¾–5in) long. Flower heads, 10–13cm (4–5in) across with red or orange ray flowers, are produced in summer. Proves difficult to establish, but is worthwhile. **H** to 3m (10ft).

***Campsis radicans* 'Flamenco'**
Deciduous, woody-stemmed, root climber with leaves divided into 7–11 oval, toothed leaflets, downy beneath. Small clusters of trumpet-shaped, orange-red flowers, 6–8cm (2½–3in) long, are produced in late summer and early autumn. **H** 12m (40ft).

WHITE

Fallopia baldschuanica
(Mile-a-minute plant, Russian vine)
Vigorous, deciduous, woody-stemmed, twining climber with drooping panicles of pink or white flowers in summer–autumn. **H** 12m (40ft) or more.

Jasminum polyanthum
Evergreen, woody-stemmed, twining climber. Dark green leaves have 5 or 7 leaflets. Large clusters of fragrant, 5-lobed, white flowers, sometimes reddish on the outside, are carried from late summer to winter. **H** 3m (10ft) or more.

RED

Campsis* x *tagliabuana
'Madame Galen'
Deciduous, woody-stemmed, root climber with leaves of 7 or more narrowly oval, toothed leaflets. Trumpet-shaped, orange-red flowers are borne in pendent clusters from late summer to autumn. **H** to 10m (30ft).

***Vitis* 'Brant'**
Deciduous, woody-stemmed, tendril climber with lobed, toothed, green leaves, 10–22cm (4–9in) long. In autumn leaves mature to brown-red, except for the veins. Produces tiny flowers in summer, followed by green or purple fruits. **H** to 7m (22ft) or more.

***Cotoneaster horizontalis* (Wall-spray)**
Deciduous, stiff-branched, spreading shrub. Glossy, dark green leaves redden in late autumn. Bears pinkish-white flowers from late spring to early summer, followed by red fruits. **H** 1m (3ft), **S** 1.5m (5ft).

***Pyracantha coccinea* 'Mohave'**
Evergreen, dense, bushy shrub with oval, dark green leaves. Dense clusters of small, 5-petalled, white flowers in early summer are followed by spherical, bright red fruits. **H** and **S** 4m (12ft).

Parthenocissus tricuspidata
(Boston ivy, Japanese ivy)
Vigorous, deciduous, woody-stemmed, tendril climber. Has spectacular, crimson, autumn leaf colour and dull blue berries. Will cover large expanses of wall. **H** to 20m (70ft).

***Celastrus orbiculatus* 'Diana'**
Vigorous, deciduous, twining climber with small, rounded, toothed leaves. Clusters of 2–4 small, green flowers are borne in summer. Tiny, long-lasting, green fruit turns black in autumn and finally splits, showing yellow insides and red seeds. **H** to 14m (46ft).

Vitis coignetiae (Crimson glory vine)
Vigorous, deciduous, woody-stemmed, tendril climber. Large leaves, brown-haired beneath, are brightly coloured in autumn. Has tiny, pale green flowers in summer, followed by purplish-bloomed, black berries. **H** to 15m (50ft).

Cayratia thomsonii
Deciduous, woody-stemmed, tendril climber. Has glossy, green leaves with 5 leaflets that turn red-purple in autumn, and black berries. Provide some shade for best autumn colour. **H** to 10m (30ft).

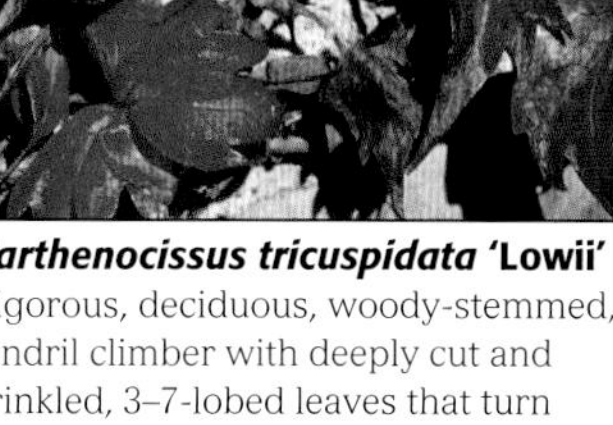

***Parthenocissus tricuspidata* 'Lowii'**
Vigorous, deciduous, woody-stemmed, tendril climber with deeply cut and crinkled, 3–7-lobed leaves that turn crimson in autumn. Has insignificant flowers, followed by dull blue berries. **H** to 20m (70ft).

PURPLE

Billardiera longiflora
Evergreen, woody-stemmed, twining climber with narrow leaves. Small, bell-shaped, sometimes purple-tinged, green-yellow flowers are produced singly in leaf axils in summer, followed by purple-blue fruits in autumn. **H** to 2m (6ft).

Ampelopsis megalophylla
Vigorous, deciduous climber with glaucous shoots and large, pinnate to 2-pinnate, dark green leaves, glaucous beneath. Axillary clusters of small, green flowers, in summer, are followed by small, top-shaped, purple fruits that later turn black. **H** 10m (30ft).

Ampelopsis brevipedunculata* var. *maximowiczii
Vigorous, deciduous, woody-stemmed twining, tendril climber with dark green leaves that vary in size and shape. Bears inconspicuous, greenish flowers in summer, followed by pinkish-purple, later bright blue berries. **H** to 5m (15ft).

***Vitis vinifera* 'Purpurea'**
Deciduous, woody-stemmed, tendril climber with toothed, 3- or 5-lobed, purplish leaves, white-haired when young. Has tiny, pale green flowers in summer and tiny, green or purple berries. **H** to 7m (23ft).

***Parthenocissus tricuspidata* 'Veitchii'**
Vigorous, deciduous, woody-stemmed, tendril climber. Has spectacular, red-purple, autumn leaf colour and dull blue berries. Greenish flowers are insignificant. **H** to 20m (70ft).

GREEN

***Hedera helix* 'Glacier'**
Vigorous, evergreen, self-clinging climber or trailing perennial bearing 5-lobed, silvery-grey-green leaves.
H 3m (10ft).

x *Fatshedera lizei* (Tree ivy)
Evergreen, loose-branched shrub that forms a mound of deeply lobed, glossy, deep green leaves. May also be trained as a climber. Sprays of small, white flowers appear in autumn.
H 1.2–2m (4–6ft), **S** 3m (10ft).

***Garrya elliptica* 'James Roof'**
Evergreen, bushy, dense shrub with oval, wavy-edged, leathery, dark green leaves. Very long, grey-green catkins, with yellow anthers, are borne from mid- or late winter to early spring.
H and **S** 4m (12ft).

***Hedera colchica* 'Sulphur Heart'**
Evergreen, self-clinging climber or trailing perennial with large, oval, unlobed leaves variegated yellow and light green. Is suitable for growing against a wall. **H** 5m (15ft).

YELLOW

Acacia dealbata
(Mimosa, Silver wattle)
Fast-growing, evergreen, spreading tree. Has feathery, blue-green leaves with many leaflets. Racemes of globular, fragrant, bright yellow flower heads are borne in winter–spring.
H 15m (50ft), **S** 15m (50ft).

***Hedera helix* 'Oro di Bogliasco'**
Vigorous, evergreen, self-clinging climber or trailing perennial bearing 5-lobed, dark green leaves with bright yellow centres. Is slow to establish, then grows rapidly; is not suitable for ground cover. **H** 6m (20ft).

Itea ilicifolia
Evergreen, bushy shrub with arching shoots and oval, sharply toothed, glossy, dark green leaves. Long, catkin-like racemes of small, greenish flowers appear in late summer and early autumn.
H 3–5m (10–15ft), **S** 3m (10ft).

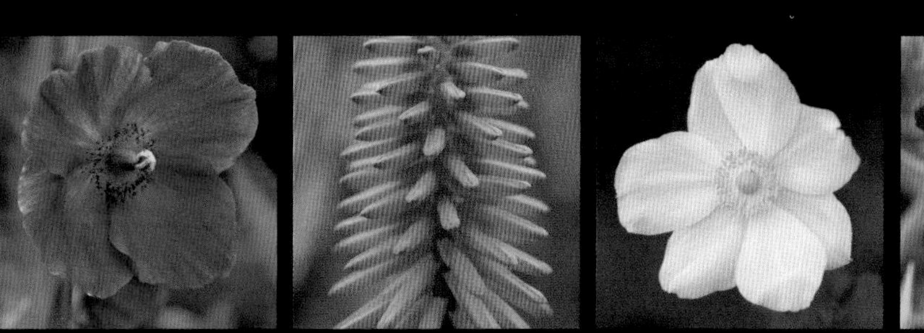

PERENNIALS

One of the largest plant groups, perennials offer seasonal colour, fragrance, form and texture, with a wealth of plants to suit every size and style of garden. They are traditionally grown in herbaceous borders, using a wall or hedge as the backdrop for the main summer display, but since most gardens are not large enough for long borders solely devoted to perennials, they are usually grown in mixed borders, together with shrubs, annuals, biennials and bulbs that extend the seasons of interest. Although some perennials are evergreen, most die back each autumn and emerge again in spring. While this can leave borders bare in winter, the seedheads and dried stems of some perennials, including rudbeckias, echinops, and sedums, provide a beautiful display when others have disappeared.

PERENNIALS

One of the largest and most versatile plant groups, perennials offer a seasonally changing diversity of colour, fragrance, form, and texture. The choice of perennials is vast, and there is a huge choice to suit any garden style, from traditional to modern.

SIZE CATEGORIES USED WITHIN THIS GROUP		
Large over 1.2m (4ft)	**Medium** 60cm–1.2m (2–4ft)	**Small** up to 60cm (2ft)

What are perennials?

Perennials are non-woody plants that live for two or more years and, when mature, produce flowers annually. The term often includes grasses and ferns. Although some perennials are evergreen, most are herbaceous and will die back each autumn, emerging again in spring.

Choosing perennials

When making your selections, first ensure that the plants suit the climate, aspect, soil type, and light levels in your garden. Plants struggling in unsuitable conditions will not fulfil their intended purpose if they fail to flower or grow to fill their allotted space. The best results are usually achieved by grouping plants with similar cultivation needs; you may also find inspiration for garden planting schemes by looking at natural landscapes for symbiotic planting groups. For example, a deciduous woodland may feature a range of shade-loving ferns that marry well together.

When perennials are massed together in borders, consider their eventual height and spread to ensure vigorous types do not overshadow or swamp more delicate plants.

Designing with perennials

Long herbaceous borders, often 3m (10ft) or more in depth, flanked by turf and backed by a wall or hedge, were traditionally planted with perennials that create a spectacular display in summer. Today, most people do not have space for such a scheme, and perennials are now more commonly used in smaller beds and borders with other plants, such as shrubs, bulbs, and annuals. However, the design ideas employed in these large borders can used in more modest schemes, with tall plants sited at the back, midrange types in the middle, and compact perennials planted at the front, ensuring that all can be seen clearly and no plants are obscured by taller neighbours. Plants are grouped in swathes of three or more of the same species, which lends borders a visual unity and rhythm.

Groups of tall verbascums, eupatoriums, and delphiniums create a backdrop for the border plants in front, while low, ground-covering perennials such as *Cerastium tomentosum* and *Stachys byzantina* are ideal at the front. Superb effects can then be created by using large specimens as a focal points, especially those that have an architectural form, such as cardoons (*Cynara cardunculus*) and bears breeches (*Acanthus*), or a tall grass such as a miscanthus, or *Stipa gigantea*.

Introduce variety of shape and texture by combining the rounded forms of sedums and geraniums, with the upright spires of *Kniphofia* or salvias, for instance, or finely-cut *Corydalis flexuosa* leaves with the

ABOVE Frosted seedheads
Most perennials die down in winter leaving borders bare, but a few, such as *Echinacea purpurea* 'Kims Knee High' form decorative seedheads that remain for many months in winter.

LEFT Contrasting colours and forms
This design focuses on matching the blues and yellows of delphiniums, echinops, salvias, *Thalictrum flavum* subsp. *glaucum*, nepetas, verbascums and foxgloves. Contrasting flower forms intensify the effect.

ABOVE Contrasting foliage
In damp, dappled shade, elegant contrasts of foliage form and texture create an atmosphere of lush abundance. A selection of bergenias, hostas, ferns and ligularias are included in this lush scheme.

bolder outlines of hostas in shady areas. Or use the stems of bleeding heart (*Dicentra spectabilis*) and *Polygonatum* x *hybridum* to gracefully arch over shorter plants, such as heucheras and *Alchemilla mollis*.

When making your selections, consider the foliage shape, form, and texture as well as flower colours. The boldly pleated foliage of veratrums and delicate, pinnate leaves of *Polemonium caeruleum* are worthy of consideration, while furry verbascums are seductively tactile.

The disadvantage of planting herbaceous perennials is that the garden looks bare in winter, unless you plant sturdy types with long-lasting seedheads, such as sedum, rudbeckias, and many grasses. These can be left to stand and provide interest until new shoots appear in spring. Prairie-style schemes use these types of plants for year-round interest; rather than planting in long borders, perennials and grasses are used in large bold groups, with tall see-through plants in front of shorter ones. Just a few plant species are used, and repeated to mirror nature. The effects of prairie schemes are best seen in larger gardens.

STAKING BORDER PERENNIALS

Many tall perennials, such as delphiniums and achilleas, become top heavy and require some form of support. If you provide plant supports early in the season, the plants will grow through and disguise them. Plants staked at a later date, especially once they have already flopped, always tend to look trussed up.

Using canes
Bamboo canes are ideal for supporting tall flowers such as delphiniums. Use soft twine to tie the stems to the supports.

Using twiggy sticks
Plants with mound-like growth will grow through and be supported by twiggy sticks placed around stems in spring.

Using metal spirals
Metal spirals provide good support for perennials such as this *Pimpinella* and also make decorative features.

DIVIDING PERENNIALS

This easy method of propagation can be used to propagate most herbaceous perennials as well as to rejuvenate large, tired clumps that are no longer flowering well. You can also divide newly bought perennials, providing they are large enough and have clearly divisible stems, to make the most of your purchases. Most perennials can be divided in autumn or early spring just as the shoots appear.

1 Dig up the plant
In early spring, select a clump of plants and water them well. Cut back any old top growth to the ground. Using a fork, lift the clump of plants, taking great care to keep the whole rootball intact.

2 Divide with forks
Cut solid crowns into portions with a spade or old bread knife. If you cannot prise other pieces apart by hand, use two forks held back-to-back to split the clump into smaller sections.

3 Replant the divisions
Discard the dead central portions of overgrown clumps. Replant healthy, hand-sized pieces with strong buds in soil improved with well-rotted organic matter, such as manure. Water in well.

WHITE

Sanguisorba tenuifolia 'Alba'
Clump-forming, upright perennial with branched, slender stems and pinnate, toothed leaves. Pendent, bottlebrush-like spikes of fluffy, white flowers are borne in late summer. **H** 1.8m (6ft), **S** 90cm (3ft).

Crambe cordifolia
Robust perennial with clouds of small, fragrant, white flowers borne in branching sprays in summer above mounds of large, crinkled and lobed, dark green leaves. **H** to 2m (6ft), **S** 1.2m (4ft).

Artemisia lactiflora (White mugwort)
Vigorous, erect perennial. Many sprays of creamy-white buds open to off-white flowers in summer. Dark green leaves are jagged-toothed. Needs staking and is best as a foil to stronger colours. **H** 1.2–1.5m (4–5ft), **S** 50cm (20in).

Romneya coulteri (Tree poppy)
Vigorous, bushy, shrubby perennial, grown for its large, fragrant, white flowers, with prominent centres of golden stamens, that appear in late summer. Has deeply divided, grey leaves. **H** and **S** 2m (6ft).

Epilobium angustifolium f. _album_ (White rosebay)
Vigorous, upright perennial bearing sprays of pure white flowers along wand-like stems in late summer. Leaves are small and lance-shaped. May spread. **H** 1.2–1.5m (4–5ft), **S** 50cm (20in) or more.

Impatiens tinctoria
Vigorous, upright, tuberous perennial with fleshy, branched stems and oval, toothed, dark green leaves. In late summer produces large, night-scented, white-and-purple flowers. Needs shelter and fertile soil. **H** 1.5m (5ft), **S** 90cm (3ft).

PINK

Eremurus robustus
Upright perennial with strap-like leaves that die back during summer as huge racemes of cup-shaped, pink blooms appear. Cover crowns in winter with compost or bracken. Needs staking. **H** 2.2m (7ft), **S** 1m (3ft).

Macleaya microcarpa 'Kelway's Coral Plume'
Clump-forming perennial that in summer produces branching spikes of rich pink-buff flowers. Large, rounded, lobed leaves are grey-green above, grey-white beneath. **H** 2–2.5m (6–8ft), **S** 1–1.2m (3–4ft).

PURPLE

Cynara cardunculus (Cardoon)
Stately perennial with large clumps of arching, pointed, divided, silver-grey leaves, above which rise large, thistle-like, blue-purple flower heads borne singly on stout, grey stems in summer. Flower heads dry well. **H** 2m (6ft), **S** 1m (3ft).

Veratrum nigrum (Black false hellebore)
Erect, stately perennial that from late summer onwards bears long spikes of chocolate-purple flowers at the ends of stout, upright stems. Stems are clothed with ribbed, oval to narrowly oval leaves. **H** 2m (6ft), **S** 60cm (2ft).

Phormium 'Dazzler'
Evergreen, upright perennial with tufts of bold, stiff, pointed leaves in tones of yellow, salmon-pink, orange-red and bronze. Bluish-purple stems carry panicles of reddish flowers in summer. **H** 2–2.5m (6–8ft) in flower, **S** 1m (3ft).

DELPHINIUMS

Delphiniums make a bold statement in summer gardens, with their elegant, showy spires of single or double flowers. Their classic colour is blue, but hybrids are now available in a broad range of colours, from white and pastel shades of pink and lilac, to rich mauves, violet-purples, and new red selections. Grow tall delphiniums in a mixed border or island bed, and dwarf types in a rock garden. Plants thrive in full sun and well-drained soil, and apart from dwarf species and cultivars, all require staking securely to support their heavy flower spikes. In growth, water all plants freely, applying a balanced liquid fertilizer every 2–3 weeks. Dead-head by cutting spent flower spikes back to small, flowering sideshoots. Protect plants from slugs and snails.

D. **'Gillian Dallas'** 🏆ⓘ

D. **'Can-Can'** 🏆ⓘ

D. **'Olive Poppleton'** 🏆ⓘ

D. **'Sandpiper'** 🏆ⓘ

D. **'Langdon's Royal Flush'** 🏆ⓘ

D. **'Min'** 🏆ⓘ

D. **'Cliveden Beauty'** ⓘ

D. **'Elizabeth Cook'** 🏆ⓘ

D. **'Bruce'** 🏆ⓘ

D. **'Spindrift'** 🏆ⓘ

D. grandiflorum **'Blue Butterfly'** ⓘ

D. **'Red Caroline'** ⓘ

D. **'Lucia Sahin'** 🏆ⓘ

D. **'Michael Ayres'** 🏆ⓘ

D. **'Alice Artindale'** ⓘ

D. **'Loch Leven'** 🏆ⓘ

PURPLE

Thalictrum 'Elin'
Clump-forming perennial with fern-like, blue-green leaves. Erect, sturdy, purplish-green stems bear billowing panicles of tiny, fluffy, creamy-yellow and purple flowers in summer.
H 2.5m (8ft), **S** 90cm (3ft) or more.

Galega x _hartlandii_ 'Lady Wilson'
Vigorous, upright perennial with spikes of small, pea-like, blue and pinkish-white flowers in summer above bold leaves divided into oval leaflets. Needs staking.
H to 1.5m (5ft), **S** 1m (3ft).

BLUE

Meconopsis grandis (Blue poppy)
Erect perennial with oblong, slightly toothed, hairy, mid-green leaves produced in rosettes at the base. Stout stems bear slightly nodding, cup-shaped, deep blue flowers in early summer. Divide every 2–3 years.
H 1–1.5m (3–5ft), **S** 30cm (1ft).

HIMALAYAN POPPIES

With delicate flowers in a wide range of colours, including beautiful shades of sky blue, *Meconopsis* (Himalayan poppies) are striking garden plants. Some also have attractive rosettes of foliage that develop slowly before the first flowers appear. Many are suited to moist, woodland conditions in light or partial shade, and acidic, well-drained soil; others are best treated as alpines in raised beds or troughs. All prefer cooler conditions. Most of the big blue poppy cultivars are sterile and very long-lived. Other Meconopsis are monocarpic perennials, living for a few years before flowering, setting seed, and then dying.

***M.* x *cookei* 'Old Rose'**

***M.* Infertile Blue Group 'Slieve Donard'**

***M.* Infertile Blue Group 'Crewdson Hybrid'**

GREEN

Angelica archangelica **(Angelica)**
Upright perennial, usually grown as a biennial, with deeply divided, bright green leaves and white or green flowers in late summer. Stems have culinary usage and when crystallized may be used for confectionery decoration.
H 2m (6ft), **S** 1m (3ft).

Musa basjoo **(Japanese banana)**
Evergreen, palm-like, suckering perennial with arching leaves to 1m (3ft) long. Has drooping, pale yellow flowers with brownish bracts in summer followed by green fruits.
H 3–5m (10–15ft), **S** 2–2.5m (6–8ft).

YELLOW

Acanthus mollis **'Hollard's Gold'**
Semi-evergreen perennial with large, oval, deeply cut, glossy leaves. New leaves are golden-yellow, fading to green. Spires of white and mauve flowers are borne in summer.
H 1.5m (5ft), **S** 60cm (2ft) or more.

Verbascum olympicum
Semi-evergreen, rosette-forming biennial or short-lived perennial. Branching stems, arising from felt-like, grey foliage at the plant base, bear sprays of 5-lobed, bright golden flowers from mid-summer onwards.
H 2m (6ft), **S** 1m (3ft).

Inula magnifica
Robust, clump-forming, upright perennial with a mass of lance-shaped to elliptic, rough leaves. Leafy stems bear terminal heads of large, daisy-like, yellow flower heads in late summer. Needs staking. **H** 1.8m (6ft), **S** 1m (3ft).

Ferula communis **(Giant fennel)**
Upright perennial. Large, cow-parsley-like umbels of yellow flowers are borne from late spring to summer on the tops of stems that arise from a mound of finely cut, mid-green foliage.
H 2–2.3m (6–7ft), **S** 1–1.2m (3–4ft).

Delphinium **'Sungleam'**
Elatum Group herbaceous perennial with spikes, 40–75cm (16–30in) long, of semi-double, white flowers, 5–7cm (2–3in) across, overlaid with pale yellow and with yellow eyes, produced in mid-summer. **H** 1.7–2m (5½–6ft), **S** 60–90cm (24–36in).

Ligularia **'The Rocket'**
Clump-forming perennial with triangular, deeply toothed leaves on tall stems. In summer produces dark-stemmed racemes of daisy-like, bright yellow flower heads.
H 1.8m (6ft), **S** 1m (3ft).

SUMMER

ORANGE

***Heliopsis helianthoides* var. *scabra* 'Light of Loddon'**
Upright perennial bearing dahlia-like, double, bright orange flower heads on strong stems in late summer. Dark green leaves are coarse and serrated. **H** 1.2–1.5m (4–5ft), **S** 60cm (2ft).

***Hedychium* x *moorei* 'Tara'**
Erect, rhizomatous perennial with stout, leafy stems bearing lance-shaped, grey-green leaves. Cylindrical racemes of tubular, spidery, scented, orange flowers, with prominent stamens, are borne in late summer. **H** 1.5m (5ft), **S** 60cm (2ft) or more.

***Eremurus* x *isabellinus* 'Cleopatra'**
Clump-forming perennial with narrowly strap-shaped, soft green leaves. In summer produces stout, dense spikes of star-shaped, coppery-orange flowers. **H** 1.5m (5ft), **S** 50cm (20in).

AUTUMN

WHITE

Cimicifuga simplex
Upright perennial with arching spikes of tiny, slightly fragrant, star-shaped, white flowers in autumn. Leaves are glossy and divided. Needs staking. **H** 1.2–1.5m (4–5ft), **S** 60cm (2ft).

Leucanthemella serotina
Erect perennial with lance-shaped, toothed, dark green leaves. Leafy stems produce sprays of large, green-centred, white flower heads in late autumn. **H** 1.5m (5ft), **S** 90cm (3ft).

***Anemone* x *hybrida* 'Honorine Jobert'**
Vigorous branching perennial. Slightly cupped, white flowers with contrasting yellow stamens are carried on wiry stems in late summer and early autumn above deeply divided, dark green leaves. **H** 1.5m (5ft), **S** 60cm (2ft).

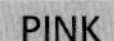

PINK

***Thalictrum delavayi* 'Hewitt's Double'**
Clump-forming perennial with fern-like, mid-green leaves. Bears large billowing panicles of tiny, double, lavender flowers from late summer to autumn. **H** 1.5m (5ft), **S** 60cm (2ft) or more.

***Veronicastrum virginicum* 'Fascination'**
Upright perennial with stout stems bearing erect racemes of tiny, star-shaped, mauve flowers, which are darker at the tips, in mid- and late summer. Has lance-shaped, whorled, dark green leaves. **H** 1.5cm (5ft), **S** 40cm (16in).

PURPLE

***Salvia involucrata* 'Bethellii'**
Sub-shrubby perennial that produces long racemes of large, cerise-crimson blooms, with pink bracts, in late summer and autumn. Leaves are oval to heart-shaped. **H** 1.2–1.5m (4–5ft), **S** 1m (3ft).

***Eupatorium maculatum* 'Riesenschirm'**
Upright, deciduous perennial with rounded, fluffy, purple-pink flower heads in late summer, which are attractive to insects. Oval to lance-shaped, reddish-green leaves are arranged in whorls up purple stems. Is superb for the back of a deep border. **H** 2.5m (8ft), **S** 1.5m (5ft).

Verbena bonariensis
Perennial with a basal clump of dark green leaves. Upright, wiry stems carry tufts of tiny, purplish-blue flowers in summer–autumn. **H** 1.5m (5ft), **S** 60cm (2ft).

ECHINACEA

Admired for their cone- and daisy-like flowers, *Echinacea* cultivars have expanded their repertoire; while once they were restricted to purple, pink, and white, a range of green, orange, yellow, and red flowers are now available, as well as double-flowered forms. They create bold and beautiful late summer and early autumn displays, and the faded flower heads also offer structural interest into winter. Grow plants in well-drained, humus-rich soil in full sun, although they will tolerate some shade. Protect young plants from slug and snail damage.

E. angustifolia

***E.* 'Harvest Moon'**

E. paradoxa

***E. purpurea* 'Coconut Lime'**

***E. purpurea* 'Fragrant Angel'**

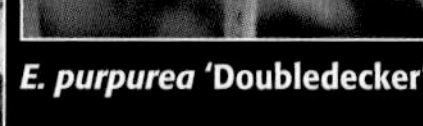

***E. purpurea* 'Doubledecker'**

***E. purpurea* 'Razzmatazz'**

***E. purpurea* 'Magnus'** 🏆

***E. purpurea* 'Sundown'**

JAPANESE ANEMONES

These useful plants fill the late summer and early autumn garden with single or double flowers held on slender stems above handsome, divided, ground-covering foliage. The blooms are available in white and shades of pink and purple and are ideal for the middle to back of mixed borders, and in woodland gardens, injecting interest when many other flowers have faded. Border anemones are easy to grow, and thrive in a wide range of soil conditions and in sun or light shade. Once the plants are established, they develop into large clumps, which can be lifted and divided in autumn or spring.

***A.* x *hybrida* 'Robustissima'**

***A. hupehensis* var. *japonica* 'Bressingham Glow'** (!)

***A. hupehensis* var. *japonica* 'Pamina'** 🏆

***A.* x *hybrida* 'Konigin Charlotte'** 🏆

***A.* x *hybrida* 'September Charm'** 🏆(!)

***A. hupehensis* 'Praecox'**

***A.* x *hybrida* 'Whirlwind'**

***A. hupehensis* 'Bowles's Pink'** 🏆

YELLOW

***Helianthus* 'Lemon Queen'**

Vigorous, upright, rhizomatous perennial with stout, branched stems bearing oval, rough, dark green leaves. Bears masses of large, daisy-like, pale yellow flower heads in summer–autumn. **H** 1.5m (5ft), **S** 60cm (2ft) or more.

***Rudbeckia laciniata* 'Goldquelle'**

Erect perennial. In late summer and autumn, daisy-like, double, bright yellow flower heads with green centres are borne singly on stout stems. Has deeply divided, mid-green foliage. **H** 1.5–2m (5–6ft), **S** 60–75cm (2–2½ft).

☼ 💧 ❄❄❄ 🏆

***Helianthus* x *multiflorus* 'Loddon Gold'**

Upright perennial bearing showy, large, vivid deep yellow flower heads with rounded, double centres in late summer and early autumn. Needs staking and may spread quickly. **H** 1.5m (5ft), **S** 60cm (2ft).

☼ 💧 ❄❄❄ (!) 🏆

Helianthus salicifolius
(Willow-leaved sunflower)

Upright, clump-forming perennial grown for its whorls of lance-shaped, dark green leaves. Clusters of daisy-like, yellow flowers are borne on branching stems in autumn. Is best at the back of a border. **H** 2m (6ft), **S** 60cm (2ft) or more.

WHITE

Smilacina racemosa (False spikenard)
Arching perennial. Has oval, light green leaves terminating in feathery sprays of white flowers that appear from spring to mid-summer and are followed by fleshy, reddish fruits. **H** 75–90cm (30–36in), **S** 45cm (18in).

Ranunculus aconitifolius
Vigorous, clump-forming perennial with deeply divided, dark green leaves. Single, white flowers, about 3cm (1in) across, are borne in spring and early summer. **H** and **S** 1m (3ft).

Polygonatum* x *hybridum (Solomon's seal)
Arching, leafy perennial with fleshy rhizomes. In late spring, clusters of small, pendent, tubular, greenish-white flowers are produced in axils of neat, oval leaves. **H** 1.2m (4ft), **S** 1m (3ft).

Dicentra spectabilis* f. *alba
Leafy perennial forming a hummock of fern-like, deeply cut, light green foliage with arching sprays of pendent, heart-shaped, pure white flowers in late spring and summer. **H** 60–75cm (24–30in), **S** 60cm (24in).

PINK

Dicentra spectabilis (Bleeding heart, Dutchman's trousers)
Leafy perennial forming a hummock of fern-like, mid-green foliage, above which rise arching stems of pendent, heart-shaped, pinkish-red and white flowers in late spring and summer. **H** 75cm (30in), **S** 50cm (20in).

Diascia personata
Semi-evergreen, semi-erect perennial with masses of lobed, dusky-pink flowers held in spires from late spring to the first frosts. Small, narrowly ovate, mid-green leaves are borne on rather lax, brittle stems, which require support. **H** 1.2m (4ft), **S** 90cm (3ft).

PURPLE

***Aquilegia vulgaris* var. *stellata* 'Black Barlow'**
Clump-forming, perennial with mid-green leaves divided into lobed leaflets. In later spring and early summer bears dark purple, bell-shaped flowers, and spreading petals in shades of blue or pink. **H** 90cm (36in), **S** 45cm (18in).

Geranium phaeum (Mourning widow)
Clump-forming perennial with lobed, soft green leaves and maroon-purple flowers, with reflexed petals, borne on rather lax stems in late spring. **H** 75cm (30in), **S** 45cm (18in).

IRISES

Few other perennials show such diversity of flower colour as irises; and you will find one for almost every position in the garden. They have a long flowering season, the earliest appearing in the first months of the year, the latest in early autumn. Their flowers often have "beards" (short hairs) or crests that add to their appeal, while a few are grown for their foliage or seed heads. The genus is classified into many divisions. Of these, the easiest to grow are the bearded, crested, and Xiphium irises. Siberian and Japanese types are ideal for bog gardens or by water, but they will tolerate drier sites. Juno, Oncocyclus, and Regelia irises are more difficult to grow, though their beautiful flowers are worth the effort. For more information, see the Plant Dictionary.

I. 'Ringo' (!) [bearded]

I. *ensata* 'Rose Queen' ♀(!) [bearded]

I. *japonica* ♀(!) [Evansia]

I. 'Bold Print' (!) [bearded]

I. 'Autumn Circus' (!) [bearded]

I. x *robusta* 'Gerald Darby' [beardless] ♀(!)

I. *confusa* ♀(!) [crested]

I. 'Green Spot' ♀(!)

I. *hoogiana* ♀(!) [Regelia]

I. *ensata* 'Moonlight Waves' (!) [beardless]

I. 'Mountain Lake' (!) [Siberian]

I. *cristata* ♀(!) [Evansia]

I. 'Dreaming Yellow' ♀(!) [Siberian]

I. 'Champagne Elegance' (!) [bearded]

I. *sanguinea* 'Snow Queen' (!) [beardless]

I. *germanica* 'Florentina' (!) [bearded]

I. *unguicularis* subsp. *cretensis* (!) [beardless]

I. 'Oriental Eyes' (!) [beardless]

I. *magnifica* ♀(!) [Juno]

I. *bucharica* ♀(!) [Juno]

I. 'Frost and Flame' (!) [bearded]

I. *orientalis* ♀(!) [beardless]

I. 'English Cottage' (!) [bearded]

I. 'Deep Black' (!)

I. 'Tropic Night' (!) [Siberian]

I. 'Joyce' (!) [Reticulata]

I. 'Eyebright' 🏆(!) [bearded]

I. variegata 🏆(!) [bearded]

I. winogradowii 🏆(!) [Reticulata]

I. 'Bumblebee Deelite' 🏆(!) [bearded]

I. pseudacorus 🏆(!) [beardless]

I. versicolor 'Kermesina' (!) [beardless]

I. 'Ola Kala' (!) [bearded]

I. 'Perry's Blue' (!) [beardless]

I. 'Berlin Tiger' 🏆(!)

I. sibirica 'Papillon' (!)

I. sibirica 'Soft Blue' 🏆(!) [Siberian]

I. 'Katharine Hodgkin' 🏆(!) [Reticulata]

I. reticulata 'Cantab' (!) [Reticulata]

I. 'Kent Pride' (!) [bearded]

I. 'Holden Clough' [beardless] 🏆(!)

I. sibirica 'Shirley Pope' [Siberian] 🏆(!)

I. chrysographes 🏆(!) [Siberian]

I. 'Blue Rhythm' (!) [bearded]

I. foetidissima [beardless] 🏆(!)

I. 'Carnaby' (!) [bearded]

AQUILEGIAS

Commonly known as columbines, *Aquilegia* are ideal cottage garden plants, well suited to growing in borders, rock gardens, and as fillers between summer-flowering shrubs. Most are graceful, elegant plants with divided basal foliage topped in late spring and summer by a succession of delicate, bell-shaped, usually spurred flowers, although some have rounded double blooms. They vary in colour from light and dark blue, purple, almost black, dark red, and pink, to orange, yellow, and white; many are bicoloured. *Aquilegia* thrive in moist but well-drained soil, and full sun or dappled shade. They are normally raised from seed, which is freely produced, and once established, they tend to self-seed, although most do not come true to type.

***A. vulgaris* var. *stellata* 'Ruby Port'**

A. flabellata* var. *pumila

A. 'Dove' (Songbird Series)

A. 'Hensol Harebell'

***A. vulgaris* 'William Guiness'**

***A. vulgaris* 'Nivea'**

A. 'Bluebird' (Songbird Series)

A. 'Dragonfly'

A. coerulea

A. 'Bunting' (Songbird Series)

A. viridiflora

***A. vulgaris* var. *stellata* 'Nora Barlow'**

A. triternata

A. chrysantha

A. longissima

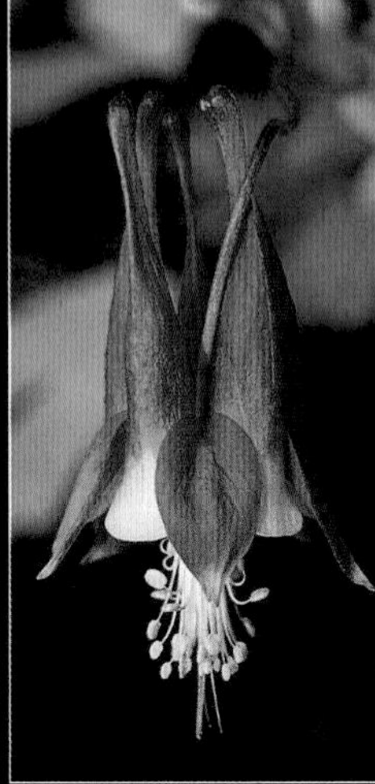

A. canadensis

BLUE

***Symphytum* x *uplandicum* 'Variegatum'**
Perennial with large, hairy, grey-green leaves that have broad, cream margins. In late spring and early summer, pink or blue buds open to tubular, blue or purplish-blue flowers. **H** 1m (3ft), **S** 60cm (2ft).

Symphytum caucasicum
Clump-forming perennial carrying clusters of pendent, azure-blue flowers in spring above rough, hairy, mid-green foliage. Is best suited to a wild garden. **H** and **S** 60–90cm (24–36in).

YELLOW

***Iris* 'Butter and Sugar'**
Rhizomatous, beardless Siberian iris with large, yellow and white flowers produced from late spring to early summer. **H** 1m (3ft), **S** indefinite.

Paeonia mlokosewitschii
Clump-forming perennial with soft bluish-green leaves, sometimes edged reddish-purple. Produces large, single, lemon-yellow flowers in late spring and early summer. **H** and **S** 75cm (30in).

***Chelidonium majus* 'Flore Pleno'**
Upright perennial with divided, bright green leaves and many cup-shaped, double, yellow flowers borne on branching sprays in late spring and early summer. Seeds freely and is best in a wild garden. **H** 60–90cm (24–30in), **S** 30cm (12in).

***Doronicum columnae* 'Miss Mason'**
Clump-forming, rhizomatous perennial with heart-shaped leaves. Slender stems bear daisy-like, bright yellow flower heads, 8cm (3in) across, held well above the foliage, in mid- and late spring. **H** and **S** 60cm (24in).

Asphodeline lutea (Yellow asphodel)
Neat, clump-forming perennial that bears dense spikes of star-shaped, yellow flowers amid narrow, grey-green leaves in late spring. **H** 1–1.2m (3–4ft), **S** 60cm–1m (2–3ft).

Aciphylla aurea (Golden Spaniard)
Evergreen, rosette-forming perennial with long, bayonet-like, yellow-green leaves. Bears spikes of golden flowers up to 2m (6ft) tall from late spring to early summer. **H** and **S** in leaf 60–75cm (24–30in).

Euphorbia rigida
Mound-forming, evergreen perennial with semi-upright stems with whorls of lance-shaped, blue-green leaves. Terminal umbels of bright yellow-green flowers are borne in spring. **H** 60cm (24in), **S** 60cm (24in) or more.

PEONIES

Peonies (*Paeonia* species and cultivars) are valued for their showy blooms, filling borders with whites, pinks, yellows, and reds in late spring and early- to mid-summer. Flowers include single, double, or anemone forms (with broad, outer petals and a mass of petaloids in the centre); some are scented. They may need support when in full bloom and make good cut flowers. The foliage is striking, too, often tinged bronze when young and rich red in autumn. As well as many attractive species and a wide range of herbaceous hybrids, there are several tree peonies (cultivars of *P. suffruticosa*), and intersectional hybrids, which are crosses between the latter two. Peonies prefer sun but will tolerate light shade and need a rich well-drained soil. These long-lived plants resent transplanting so are best left undisturbed.

***P.* 'Kelway's Fairy Queen'** [semi-double]

***P.* 'Sarah Bernhardt'** 🏆(!) [double]

***P. suffruticosa* 'Hana-kisoi'** (!) [tree peony]

***P. suffruticosa* 'Hakuo-jisi'** [tree peony]

***P.* 'White Wings'** (!) [single]

***P.* 'Whitleyi Major'** 🏆(!) [single]

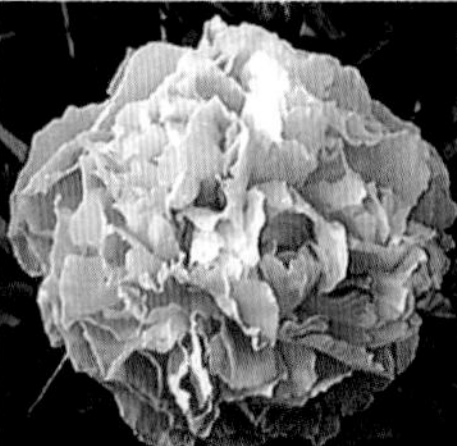

***P.* 'Shirley Temple'** (!) [double]

***P.* 'Bowl of Beauty'** 🏆(!) [anemone]

P. cambessedesii 🏆(!) [single]

***P.* 'Cheddar Gold'** 🏆 [semi-double]

***P.* 'Festiva Maxima'** 🏆 [double]

***P.* 'Lady Alexandra Duff'** 🏆 [semi-double]

***P.* 'Pillow Talk'** [double]

***P. suffruticosa* 'Yachiyo-tsubaki'** [tree peony]

P. obovata* var. *alba 🏆(!) [single]

P. japonica [single]

***P.* 'Jan van Leeuwen'** [single]

P. emodi (!) [single]

***P.* 'Coral Charm'** [semi-double]

P. suffruticosa **'Rimpo'** [tree peony]

P. 'Kelway's Gorgeous' ⓘ [single]

P. 'Magic Orb' ⓘ [double]

P. suffruticosa **'Cardinal Vaughan'** ⓘ [semi-double]

P. 'Bartzella' [double]

P. 'Paul M. Wild' [double]

P. 'America' ⓘ [single]

P. 'Laura Dessert' ♀ⓘ [double]

P. 'Claire de Lune' [single]

P. 'Félix Crousse' ♀ [double]

P. 'Knighthood' ⓘ [double]

P. veitchii ⓘ [single]

P. 'Garden Treasure' [tree peony]

P. x ***lemoinei*** **'L'Espérance'** ⓘ [tree peony]

P. x ***lemoinei*** **'High Noon'** [tree peony]

P. officinalis **'Rubra Plena'** ♀ⓘ [double]

P. peregrina **'Otto Froebel'** ♀ⓘ [single]

P. 'Buckeye Belle' [semi-double]

P. 'Thunderbolt' [single]

P. ludlowii ♀ⓘ [single]

WHITE

***Ranunculus aconitifolius* 'Flore Pleno'**
Clump-forming perennial with deeply divided, dark green leaves. Double, pure white flowers are borne on strong, branched stems in spring–summer. **H** 60–75cm (24–30in), **S** 50cm (20in).

Asphodelus albus (White asphodel)
Upright perennial with clusters of star-shaped, white flowers borne in late spring and early summer. Has narrow, basal tufts of mid-green leaves. **H** 1m (3ft), **S** 45cm (1½ft).

Libertia grandiflora (New Zealand satin flower)
Loosely clump-forming, rhizomatous perennial. In early summer produces spikes of white flowers above grass-like, dark green leaves that turn brown at the tips. Has decorative seed pods in autumn. **H** 75cm (30in), **S** 60cm (24in).

***Leucanthemum* x *superbum* 'Aglaia'**
Robust perennial with large, daisy-like, semi-double, yellow-centred, pure white flower heads, on stout, upright stems, borne singly in early summer. Has spoon-shaped, toothed, glossy, dark green leaves. **H** 70cm (28in), **S** 50cm (20in).

***Phlox paniculata* 'Mount Fuji'**
Upright perennial with star-shaped, white flowers borne in conical heads in late summer. Has oval, mid-green leaves. **H** 1.2m (4ft), **S** 60cm (2ft).

Dictamnus albus* var. *albus
(Burning bush)
Upright perennial bearing, in early summer, spikes of fragrant, star-shaped, white flowers with long stamens. Light green leaves are divided into oval leaflets. Dislikes disturbance. **H** 1m (3ft), **S** 60cm (2ft).

Selinum wallichianum
Upright, architectural perennial with dainty, long-lasting, lacy umbels of star-shaped, white flowers, borne on leafy, branched stems, in mid- and late summer. Has very finely divided, fern-like, bright green leaves. **H** 1.2m (4ft), **S** 40cm (16in).

Hesperis matronalis (Dame's violet, Sweet rocket)
Upright perennial with long spikes of many 4-petalled, white or violet flowers borne in summer. Flowers have a strong fragrance in the evening. Leaves are smooth and narrowly oval. **H** 75cm (30in), **S** 60cm (24in).

Myrrhis odorata (Sweet Cicely)
Graceful perennial that resembles cow parsley. Has aromatic, fern-like, mid-green foliage and fragrant, bright creamy-white flowers in early summer. **H** 60–90cm (24–36in), **S** 60cm (24in).

***Aruncus dioicus* 'Kneiffii'**
Hummock-forming perennial that has deeply cut, feathery leaves with lance-shaped leaflets on elegant stems and bears branching plumes of tiny, star-shaped, creamy-white flowers in mid-summer. **H** 90cm (3ft), **S** 50cm (20in).

Nicotiana alata
Rosette-forming perennial, often grown as an annual, that in late summer bears clusters of tubular, creamy-white flowers, pale brownish-violet externally, which are fragrant at night. Has oval, mid-green leaves. **H** 75cm (30in), **S** 30cm (12in).

***Leucanthemum x superbum* 'Sonnenschein'**
Erect perennial with large, daisy-like, single, creamy-yellow flower heads, each with a darker yellow centre, borne from mid- to late summer. Has spoon-shaped, toothed, dark green leaves. May need staking. **H** 90cm (36in), **S** 50cm (20in).

Morina longifolia
Evergreen perennial that produces rosettes of large, spiny, thistle-like, rich green leaves. Whorls of hooded, tubular, white flowers, flushed pink within, are borne well above foliage in mid-summer. **H** 60–75cm (2–2½ft), **S** 30cm (1ft).

Ageratina altissima **(Hardy age, Mist flower, White snakeroot)**
Erect perennial with nettle-like, grey-green leaves. In late summer bears dense, flat, white flower heads. **H** 1.2m (4ft), **S** 45cm (1½ft).

***Anaphalis triplinervis* 'Sommerschnee'**
Variable, clump-forming perennial with obovate to elliptic, white-woolly leaves, prominently 3-veined. In mid- to late summer produces clusters of yellow-centred flower heads with bright silvery-white bracts. **H** 50cm (20in), **S** 45–60cm (18–24in).

Gillenia trifoliata
Upright perennial with many wiry, branching stems carrying clusters of dainty, white flowers with reddish-brown calyces in summer. Leaves are dark green and lance-shaped. Needs staking. Thrives in most situations. **H** 1–1.2m (3–4ft), **S** 60cm (2ft).

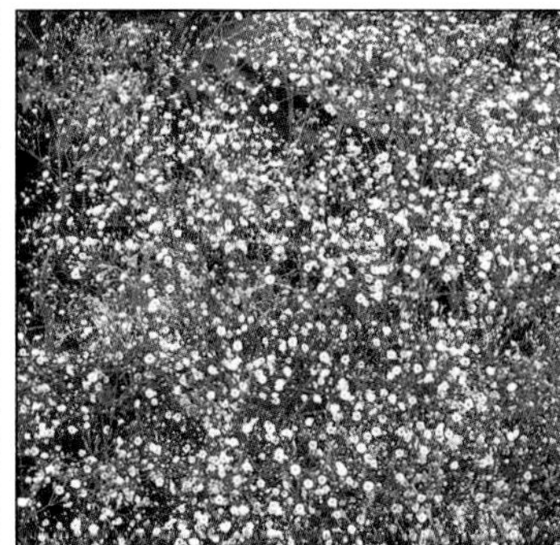

***Gypsophila paniculata* 'Bristol Fairy'**
Perennial with small, dark green leaves and wiry, branching stems bearing panicles of tiny, double, white flowers in summer. **H** 60–75cm (2–2½ft), **S** 1m (3ft).

Anaphalis margaritacea **(Pearl everlasting)**
Bushy perennial that has lance-shaped, grey-green or silvery-grey leaves with white margins and many heads of small, white flowers on erect stems in late summer. Flower heads dry well. **H** 60–75cm (24–30in), **S** 60cm (24in).

Valeriana officinalis **(Cat's valerian, Common valerian)**
Clump-forming, fleshy perennial that bears spikes of white to deep pink flowers in summer. Leaves are deeply toothed and mid-green. Has the disadvantage of attracting cats. **H** 1–1.2m (3–4ft), **S** 1m (3ft).

Gaura lindheimeri
Bushy perennial with racemes of star-shaped, 4-petalled, butterfly-like, pink-tinged or white flowers, borne on wand-like stems, in summer. Leaves are lance-shaped and mid-green. Grows well with grasses and other dainty perennials. **H** 90cm (36in), **S** 60cm (24in).

ASTILBES

These elegant, colourful, tough perennials are useful plants for moist sites. Their feathery plumes open mainly in summer and are composed of hundreds, sometimes thousands, of tiny flowers that create diverse forms, from dense and upright to open and arching. Colours range from white through shades of pink, to deep reds and purples. The blooms are set against neatly lobed or divided foliage, which, in some cultivars, has attractive metallic, bronze, or red tints. All prefer moist soil – they tolerate clay well – in sun or partial shade, and they make compact clumps in bog or waterside gardens. Watch out for signs of plant collapse as astilbe are susceptible to vine weevil attack.

***A.* 'Sprite'** 🏆

***A.* 'Deutschland'**

***A.* 'Straussenfeder'** 🏆

***A.* x *crispa* 'Perkeo'** 🏆

***A.* 'Europa'**

***A.* 'Feuer'**

***A.* 'Montgomery'**

***A.* 'Irrlicht'**

***A.* 'Granat'**

***A.* 'Amethyst'**

PINK

***Linaria purpurea* 'Canon J. Went'**
Upright perennial bearing spikes of snapdragon-like, pink blooms with orange-tinged throats from mid- to late summer. Has narrow, grey-green leaves. **H** 60cm–1m (2–3ft), **S** 60cm (2ft).

***Tanacetum coccineum* 'Eileen May Robinson'**
Upright perennial with slightly aromatic, feathery leaves. Daisy-like, pink flowers with yellow centres are produced on strong stems in summer. **H** 75cm (30in), **S** 45cm (18in).

Malva moschata
Bushy, branching perennial producing successive spikes of saucer-shaped, rose-pink flowers during early summer. Narrow, lobed, divided leaves are slightly scented. **H** 60cm–1m (2–3ft), **S** 60cm (2ft).

***Lupinus* 'The Chatelaine'**
Clump-forming perennial carrying spikes of pink-and-white flowers above divided, mid-green foliage in early summer. **H** 1.2m (4ft), **S** 45cm (1½ft).

Centaurea pulcherrima
Upright perennial with deeply cut, silvery leaves. Rose-pink flower heads, with thistle-like centres paler than surrounding star-shaped ray petals, are borne singly on slender stems in summer. **H** 75cm (2½ft), **S** 60cm (2ft).

Mirabilis jalapa **(Four o'clock flower, Marvel of Peru)**
Bushy, tuberous perennial. Fragrant, trumpet-shaped, crimson, pink, white or yellow flowers, opening in evening, cover mid-green foliage in summer. **H** 60cm–1.2m (2–4ft), **S** 60–75cm (2–2½ft).

Physostegia virginiana **'Variegata'**
Erect perennial. In late summer produces spikes of tubular, purplish-pink blooms that can be placed into position. Toothed, mid-green leaves are white-variegated. **H** 1–1.2m (3–4ft), **S** 60cm (2ft).

Penstemon **'Evelyn'**
Semi-evergreen, bushy perennial with racemes of small, tubular, pink flowers produced from mid-summer to mid-autumn. Broadly lance-shaped leaves are mid-green. **H** and **S** 45cm (18in).

Geranium psilostemon
Clump-forming perennial that has broad, deeply cut leaves with good autumn colour and many cup-shaped, single, black-centred, magenta flowers in mid-summer. **H** and **S** 1.2m (4ft).

Thalictrum aquilegiifolium **'Thundercloud'**
Clump-forming perennial with a mass of fern-like, silvery-green leaves. Bunched heads of fluffy, dark lilac flowers, on sturdy stems, are borne in summer. **H** 1m (3ft), **S** 30cm (1ft).

Monarda **'Croftway Pink'**
Clump-forming perennial carrying whorls of hooded, soft pink blooms throughout summer above neat mounds of aromatic foliage. **H** 1m (3ft), **S** 45cm (1½ft).

Sidalcea **'Oberon'**
Upright perennial with rounded, deeply cut leaves divided into narrowly oblong segments. In summer, produces racemes of shallowly cup-shaped, clear pink flowers. **H** 60cm (24in), **S** 45cm (18in).

PINK

***Astilbe* 'Venus'**
Leafy perennial bearing feathery, tapering plumes of tiny, pale pink flowers in summer. Foliage is broad and divided into leaflets; flowers remain on the plant, dried and brown, well into winter. Prefers humus-rich soil. **H** and **S** to 1m (3ft).

***Lythrum salicaria* 'Feuerkerze'**
Clump-forming perennial for a waterside or bog garden. Bears spikes of intense rose-red blooms from mid-to late summer. Small, lance-shaped leaves are borne on flower stems. **H** 1m (3ft), **S** 45cm (1½ft).

***Echinacea purpurea* 'Robert Bloom'**
Upright perennial. Has lance-shaped, dark green leaves and large, daisy-like, deep crimson-pink flower heads, with conical, brown centres, borne singly on strong stems in summer. Needs humus-rich soil. **H** 1.2m (4ft), **S** 50cm (20in).

Rehmannia elata
Straggling perennial bearing foxglove-like, yellow-throated, rose-purple flowers in leaf axils of notched, stem-clasping, soft leaves from early to mid-summer. **H** 1m (3ft), **S** 45cm (1½ft). Min. 1°C (34°F).

PERSICARIA

In recent years *Persicaria* have increased in popularity, as gardeners realise that the value of these plants in a range of different situations. Most flower profusely for many weeks in summer, while those with handsome foliage and are prized for the beauty of their leaves rather than their flowers. Taller selections are usually self supporting while lower growing types form weed-suppressing ground cover. Grow *Persicaria* in moist soil in sun or partial shade; *P. bistorta* tolerates drier soil. A word of warning: some, such as *P.* 'Red Dragon', can be invasive and need to be kept under control.

***P. campanulata* 'Rosenrot'**

***P.* 'Red Dragon'**

P. campanulata ⓘ

***P. affinis* 'Superba'** 🏆

***P. virginiana* 'Lance Corporal'**

P. polymorpha

***P. bistorta* 'Superba'** 🏆ⓘ

***P. amplexicaulis* 'Firetail'** 🏆ⓘ

***P. virginiana* 'Painter's Palette'** ⓘ

Knautia macedonica
Upright perennial with deeply divided leaves and many rather lax, branching stems bearing double, almost globular, bright crimson flower heads in summer. Needs staking. **H** 75cm (30in), **S** 60cm (24in).

Hedysarum coronarium
(French honeysuckle)
Spreading, shrubby perennial or biennial. Spikes of pea-like, bright red flowers are produced in summer above divided, mid-green leaves. **H** and **S** 1m (3ft).

***Achillea* 'Fanal'**
Herbaceous perennial with slightly greyish-green, fern-like leaves that forms spreading, drought-resistant clumps. In early summer bears flat-topped, bold crimson flower heads that atttract bees and butterflies. **H** 75cm (30in), **S** 60cm (24in).

***Phlox paniculata* 'Prince of Orange'**
Upright perennial with tubular, 5-lobed, orange-red flowers borne in conical heads in late summer. Has oval, mid-green leaves. **H** 1.2m (4ft), **S** 60cm (2ft).

***Hemerocallis* 'Red Precious'**
Evergreen, clump-forming perennial bearing small, intensely red flowers, with a slim, greenish-yellow stripe on each petal and a golden throat, in late summer. **H** and **S** 50cm (20in).

Lychnis chalcedonica
(Jerusalem cross, Maltese cross)
Neat, clump-forming perennial that bears flat heads of small, vermilion flowers at the tips of stout stems in early summer. Foliage is mid-green. **H** 1–1.2m (3–4ft), **S** 30–45cm (1–1½ft).

***Monarda* 'Cambridge Scarlet'**
Clump-forming perennial that throughout summer bears whorls of hooded, rich red flowers above neat mounds of aromatic, hairy foliage. **H** 1m (3ft), **S** 45cm (1½ft).

***Papaver orientale* 'Beauty of Livermere'**
Hairy-leaved perennial with deep, fleshy roots. Large, solitary, cup-shaped, crimson-scarlet flowers, with a black mark at the base of each petal, are borne from late spring to mid-summer. **H** 1–1.2m (3–4ft), **S** 1m (3ft).

PENSTEMONS

Valued for their racemes of foxglove-like flowers, Penstemons are elegant and reliable border perennials. Numerous cultivars are available, in colours that include white, pale and dark pink, warm cherry-red, clear blue, and shades of purple. Many flowers have contrasting white throats or are streaked with other colours. Penstemons flower prolifically in summer and the display can be prolonged, provided the plants are regularly dead-headed. Some taller cultivars may need staking. All types thrive in well-drained soil, preferably in full sun. Some are not fully hardy, and where winters are severe, plants should be overwintered in a cold frame. Plants are more likely to survive frost if grown in a sheltered spot and mulched in autumn. Penstemons are simple to propagate, and can easily be raised as cuttings.

***P.* 'Stromboli'**

***P.* 'Hidcote Pink ' ♡**

***P.* 'Stapleford Gem' ♡**

***P. fruticosus* var. *scouleri* f. *albus* ♡**

***P.* 'White Bedder' ♡**

***P.* 'Apple Blossom' ♡**

***P.* 'Alice Hindley' ♡**

***P.* 'Beech Park' ♡**

***P.* 'Mother of Pearl'**

***P.* 'The Juggler'**

***P. digitalis* 'Husker Red'**

***P.* 'Margery Fish ' ♡**

***P.* 'Flamingo'**

***P.* 'Osprey' ♡**

P. kunthii

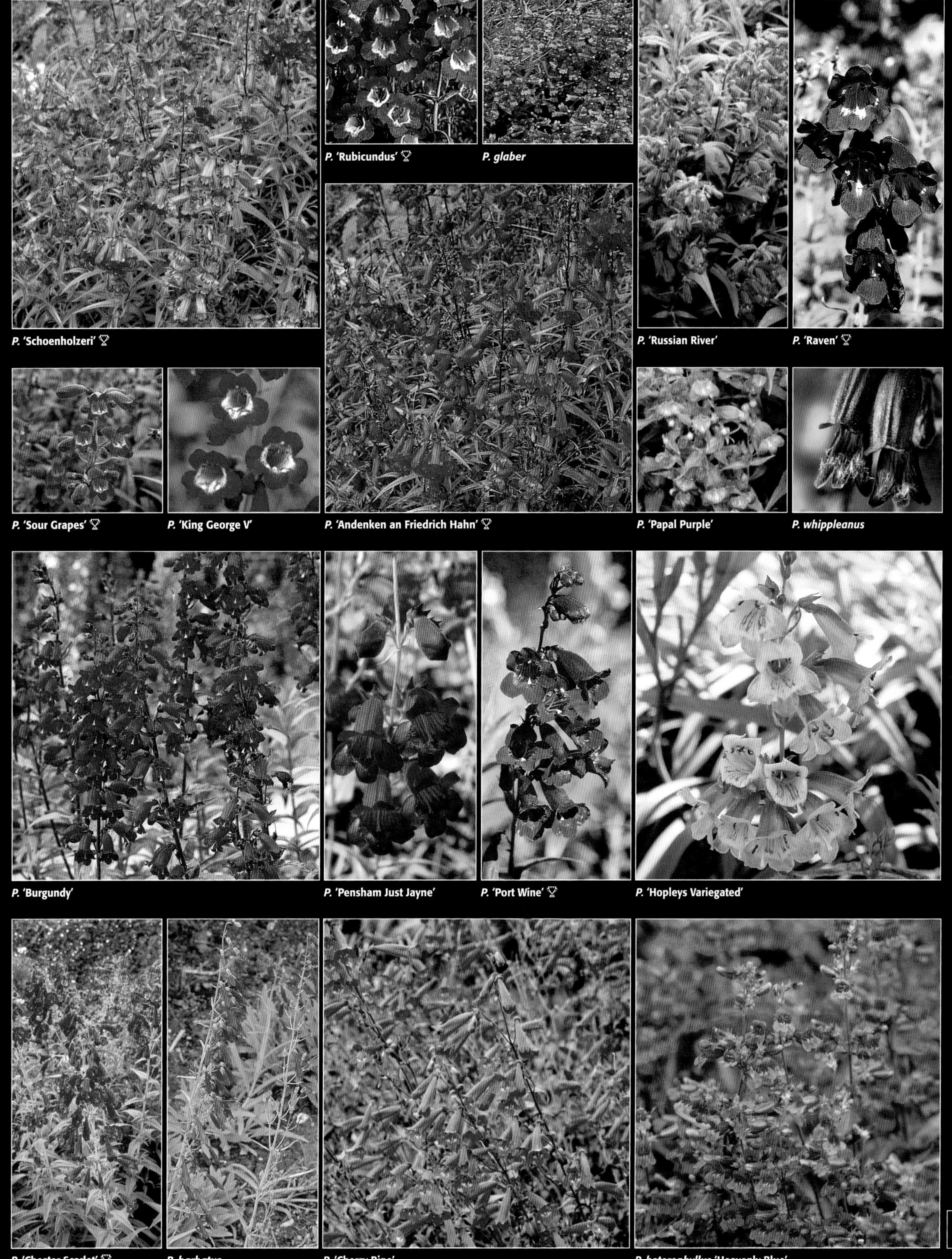
P. 'Schoenholzeri' 🏆

P. 'Rubicundus' 🏆

P. *glaber*

P. 'Russian River'

P. 'Raven' 🏆

P. 'Sour Grapes' 🏆

P. 'King George V'

P. 'Andenken an Friedrich Hahn' 🏆

P. 'Papal Purple'

P. *whippleanus*

P. 'Burgundy'

P. 'Pensham Just Jayne'

P. 'Port Wine' 🏆

P. 'Hopleys Variegated'

P. 'Chester Scarlet' 🏆

P. *barbatus*

P. 'Cherry Ripe'

P. *heterophyllus* 'Heavenly Blue'

RED

***Astrantia major* 'Ruby Wedding'**
Clump-forming perennial producing ruby-red flower heads on tall, slender stems throughout summer above a mass of divided, purple-flushed, mid-green leaves. **H** and **S** 60cm (24in).

Cosmos atrosanguineus
(Chocolate cosmos)
Upright, tuberous perennial with chocolate-scented, maroon-crimson flower heads in late summer. In warm sites tubers may overwinter if protected. **H** 60cm (24in) or more, **S** 45cm (18in).

Filipendula purpurea
Upright perennial with deeply divided leaves. Produces large, terminal heads of masses of tiny, rich reddish-purple flowers in summer. Makes a good waterside plant. **H** 1.2m (4ft), **S** 60cm (2ft).

PURPLE

Geranium palmatum
Evergreen perennial with large, palmate, bright, rather glossy, light green leaves held on sturdy stalks, growing from a central, rather woody stem. In early summer has tall, branched stems of 5-petalled, magenta flowers. **H** 1m (3ft), **S** 60cm (2ft).

ORIENTAL POPPIES

The large-flowered selections of *Papaver orientale* are stars of the early summer garden, their huge yet delicate blooms, some with fringed petals, appearing in profusion above mounds of hairy foliage. Numerous selections are available, with flowers in pastel shades of white, pink, and plum-purple, or red and orange for dramatic hot-hued borders. Large round seed heads keep the display going for a few more weeks after the flowers have faded. Poppies thrive in fertile soil in full sun, but plants die down in mid-summer; ensure other later performers fill the gaps.

***P. orientale* 'Karine'** ♀

***P.* 'Medallion'** (Super Poppy Series)

***P. orientale* 'Turkish Delight'**

Acanthus spinosus
Stately perennial that has very large, arching, deeply cut and spiny-pointed, glossy, dark green leaves. Spires of funnel-shaped, soft mauve and white flowers are borne freely in summer. **H** 1.2m (4ft), **S** 60cm (2ft) or more.

Dianella tasmanica
Upright perennial with nodding, star-shaped, bright blue or purple-blue flowers carried in branching sprays in summer, followed by deep blue berries in autumn. Has untidy, evergreen, strap-shaped leaves. **H** 1.2m (4ft), **S** 50cm (20in).

***Geranium sylvaticum* 'Mayflower'**
Upright perennial with a basal clump of deeply lobed leaves, above which rise branching stems of cup-shaped, violet-blue flowers in early summer. **H** 1m (3ft), **S** 60cm (2ft).

***Geranium pratense* 'Mrs Kendall Clark'**
Clump-forming perennial with hairy stems and deeply divided leaves. In early to mid-summer, bears erect, saucer-shaped, pearl-grey or violet-blue flowers with white or pale pink veins. **H** 60–90cm (24–36in), **S** 60cm (24in).

Thalictrum aquilegiifolium
Clump-forming perennial with a mass of finely divided, grey-green leaves, resembling those of maidenhair fern. Bunched heads of fluffy, lilac-purple flowers are borne on strong stems in summer. **H** 1–1.2m (3–4ft), **S** 45cm (1½ft).

***Veronica spicata* 'Romiley Purple'**
Clump-forming perennial that in summer freely produces large spikes of purple flowers above whorled, mid-green leaves. **H** 1–1.2m (3–4ft), **S** 30–60cm (1–2ft).

Linaria triornithophora
(Three birds toadflax)
Upright perennial that from early to late summer produces spikes of snapdragon-like, purple and yellow flowers above narrow, grey-green leaves. **H** 1m (3ft), **S** 60cm (2ft).

Monarda fistulosa
Clump-forming perennial that produces small heads of lilac-purple flowers from mid- to late summer. **H** 1.2m (4ft), **S** 45cm (1½ft).

***Aconitum x cammarum* 'Bicolor'**
Compact, tuberous perennial with violet-blue and white flowers borne in summer along upright stems. Has deeply cut, divided, glossy, dark green leaves and poisonous roots. **H** 1.2m (4ft), **S** 50cm (20in).

Galega orientalis
Vigorous, upright but compact perennial that in summer bears spikes of pea-like, blue-tinged, violet flowers above delicate leaves divided into oval leaflets. Needs staking. Spreads freely. **H** 1.2m (4ft), **S** 60cm (2ft).

PHLOX

Border phlox (cultivars of *P. maculata* and *P. paniculata*) are an elegant mainstay of the mid- to late summer border. Their dome-shaped or conical panicles of flowers, often delicately scented, are produced in white, pink, red, and purple, many with contrasting eyes. Some cultivars also have strikingly variegated foliage. Phlox thrive in sun or partial shade in fertile, well-drained soil; taller types may need staking. For larger flowers, reduce the number of stems in spring by pinching out the weakest shoots. To prolong flowering, dead-head regularly to encourage side shoots to bloom.

***P. paniculata* 'Fujiyama'**

***P. paniculata* 'Eva Cullum'**

***P. paniculata* 'Mia Ruys'**

***P. paniculata* 'Brigadier'** 🏆

***P. paniculata* 'Windsor'** 🏆

***P. paniculata* 'Norah Leigh'**

***P. paniculata* 'Amethyst'**

***P. paniculata* 'Hampton Court'**

PURPLE

Baptisia australis (False indigo)
Upright perennial bearing spikes of pea-like, violet-blue flowers in summer. Bright green leaves are divided into oval leaflets. Dark grey seed pods may be used for winter decoration. **H** 75cm (30in), **S** 60cm (24in).

☼ 💧 ❄❄❄ 🏆

***Erigeron* 'Dunkelste Aller'**
Clump-forming perennial with a mass of daisy-like, deep purple flower heads, with yellow centres, in summer. Has narrowly oval, greyish-green leaves. **H** 80cm (32in), **S** 60cm (24in) or more.

☼ 💧 ❄❄❄ 🏆

BLUE

Eryngium alpinum
Upright perennial with basal rosettes of heart-shaped, deeply toothed, glossy foliage. In summer stout stems bear heads of conical, purplish-blue flower heads, surrounded by blue bracts and soft spines. **H** 75cm–1m (2½–3ft), **S** 60cm (2ft).

☼ 💧 ❄❄❄ 🏆

***Agapanthus inapertus* subsp. *pendulus* 'Graskop'**
Clump-forming perennial with compact, rounded clusters of pendent, dark violet-blue flowers, in summer. Has narrowly strap-shaped, rich green leaves. **H** 90cm (36in), **S** 50cm (20in).

☼ 💧 ❄❄

***Nepeta* 'Six Hills Giant'**
Vigorous, clump-forming perennial with narrowly oval, toothed, hairy, aromatic, grey-green leaves. In summer bears loose spikes of tubular, 2-lipped, lavender-blue flowers. **H** 90cm (3ft), **S** 1.2m (4ft).

***Anchusa azurea* 'Loddon Royalist'**
Upright perennial that bears flat, single, deep blue flowers on branching spikes in early summer. Most of the lance-shaped, coarse, hairy leaves are at the base of plant. Needs staking. **H** 1.2m (4ft), **S** 60cm (2ft).

Eryngium* x *oliverianum
Upright perennial that produces large, rounded heads of thistle-like, blue to lavender-blue flowers in late summer. Has heart-shaped, jagged-edged, basal, mid-green leaves. **H** 60cm–1m (2–3ft), **S** 45–60cm (1½–2ft).

***Agapanthus* 'Purple Cloud'**
Compact, clump-forming perennial with large, rounded clusters of violet-blue flowers in summer followed by long-lasting seed heads. Has broadly strap-shaped, slightly silver-grey leaves. **H** 1.2m (4ft), **S** 60cm (2ft) or more.

***Echinops bannaticus* 'Taplow Blue'**
Upright perennial with narrowly oval, divided, prickly, greyish-green leaves. Erect stems produce thistle-like, rounded heads of steely-blue flowers from mid- to late summer. Is suitable even for poor soils. Is attractive to insects. **H** 1.2m (4ft), **S** 90cm (3ft).

***Agapanthus* 'Northern Star'**
Clump-forming perennial bearing large, rounded clusters of inky-blue flowers, with reflexed petals, in summer, followed by long-lasting seed heads. Has narrowly strap-shaped, mid-green leaves stained purple at the bases. **H** 1.2m (4ft), **S** 60cm (2ft) or more.

***Aconitum* 'Stainless Steel'**
Erect, tuberous perennial with dense spikes of hooded, silvery-blue flowers in mid- to late summer, held above deeply divided, dark green leaves. **H** 1m (3ft), **S** 60cm (2ft).

CAMPANULA

Archetypal cottage garden plants, tall campanulas are valued for their spires of pastel bell-shaped flowers, which appear from early- to mid-summer. They make good candidates for herbaceous borders, naturalistic planting schemes – perhaps at the edge of a woodland garden – or with shrubs such as roses. Developments using *C. punctata* have produced some superb, compact plants with dramatic drooping flowers suitable for the front of the border. *C. lactiflora* and tall types may need some support. Most are easily grown in sun or light shade in reasonably fertile, moist but well-drained soil.

C. alliariifolia

***C. punctata* 'Cherry Bells'**

***C. trachelium* 'Bernice'**

***C. lactiflora* 'Loddon Anna'** ♕

***C. glomerata* 'Superba'** ♕

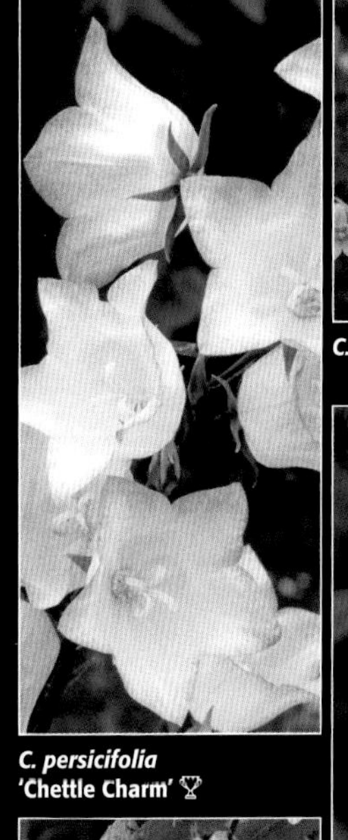

***C. persicifolia* 'Chettle Charm'** ♕

C. takesimana

***C. lactiflora* 'Prichard's Variety'** ♕

BLUE

Agapanthus praecox* subsp. *orientalis
Perennial with large, dense umbels of sky-blue flowers borne on strong stems in late summer over clumps of broad, almost evergreen, dark green leaves. Makes a good plant for pots. **H** 1m (3ft), **S** 60cm (2ft).

Cichorium intybus (Chicory)
Clump-forming perennial with basal rosettes of light green leaves and daisy-like, bright blue flower heads borne along upper parts of willowy stems in summer. Flowers are at their best before noon. **H** 1.2m (4ft), **S** 45cm (1½ft).

***Campanula persicifolia* 'Telham Beauty'**
Perennial with basal rosettes of narrow, bright green leaves. In summer, large, nodding, cup-shaped, light blue flowers are borne on slender spikes. **H** 1m (3ft), **S** 30cm (1ft).

SILVER

***Artemisia* 'Powis Castle'**
Semi-evergreen, upright sub-shrub with woody stems, usually grown as a perennial, with fern-like, silvery-grey leaves, making an excellent foil for other plants. If old growth is retained, insignificant, yellow flowers are borne in summer. **H** and **S** 1m (3ft).

Astelia chathamica
Evergreen, clump-forming perennial with sword-shaped, erect, bright silvery-grey leaves. Panicles of insignificant, frothy, yellow flowers are borne in summer. **H** and **S** 1.2m (4ft).

GREEN

Aciphylla squarrosa (Bayonet plant)
Evergreen, clump-forming perennial with tufts of pointed, divided leaves. In summer bears spiky, yellow flowers in compound umbels with male and female flowers often mixed. **H** and **S** 1–1.2m (3–4ft).

***Mathiasella bupleuroides* 'Green Dream'**
Upright, deciduous perennial with divided, silvery-blue leaves. In early summer has umbels of bell-shaped, pendent, jade-green flowers, which turn pinkish as they age. Needs good winter drainage. **H** 1m (3ft), **S** 60cm (24in).

Euphorbia sikkimensis
Spreading, upright perennial bearing yellow cyathia cupped by pale to greenish-yellow involucres in mid- to late summer. Young shoots are bright pink and the leaves deep green. **H** 1.2m (4ft), **S** 45cm (18in).

***Verbascum* 'Gainsborough'**
Semi-evergreen, rosette-forming, short-lived perennial bearing branched racemes of 5-lobed, pale sulphur-yellow flowers throughout summer above oval, mid-green leaves borne on flower stems. **H** 60cm–1.2m (2–4ft), **S** 30–60cm (1–2ft).

Inula hookeri
Clump-forming perennial with lance-shaped to elliptic, hairy leaves and a mass of slightly scented, daisy-like, greenish-yellow flower heads borne in summer. **H** 75cm (30in), **S** 45cm (18in).

Aconitum lycoctonum* subsp. *vulparia
(Wolf's bane)
Upright, fibrous perennial that has hooded, straw-yellow flowers during summer. Leaves are dark green and deeply divided. Requires staking. **H** 1–1.2m (3–4ft), **S** 30–60cm (1–2ft).

Thermopsis rhombifolia
Upright perennial bearing spikes of bright yellow flowers above divided, mid-green leaves in summer. **H** 60cm–1m (2–3ft), **S** 60cm (2ft).

Gentiana lutea (Great yellow gentian)
Erect, unbranched perennial with oval, stalkless leaves to 30cm (1ft) long. In summer has dense whorls of tubular, yellow flowers in axils of greenish bracts. **H** 1–1.2m (3–4ft), **S** 60cm (2ft).

Phlomis russeliana
Evergreen perennial, forming excellent ground cover, with large, rough, heart-shaped leaves. Stout flower stems bear whorls of hooded, butter-yellow flowers in summer. **H** 1m (3ft), **S** 60cm (2ft) or more.

Lysimachia punctata
(Garden loosestrife)
Clump-forming perennial that in summer produces spikes of bright yellow flowers above mid-green leaves. **H** 60–75cm (24–30in), **S** 60cm (24in).

***Anthemis tinctoria* 'E.C. Buxton'**
Clump-forming perennial with a mass of daisy-like, lemon-yellow flower heads borne singly in summer on slim stems. Cut back hard after flowering to promote a good rosette of crinkled leaves for winter. **H** and **S** 1m (3ft).

Berkheya macrocephala
Upright perennial bearing large, daisy-like, yellow flower heads on branched, spiny-leaved stems throughout summer. Prefers rich soil and a warm, sheltered position. **H** and **S** 1m (3ft).

***Achillea filipendulina* 'Gold Plate'**
Upright perennial with stout, leafy stems carrying broad, flat, terminal heads of yellow flowers in summer, above filigree foliage. Flowers retain colour if dried. Divide plants regularly. **H** 1.2m (4ft), **S** 60cm (2ft).

DAYLILIES

Although they belong to the lily family (*Liliaceae*), daylilies (*Hemerocallis*) are not true lilies; their common name comes from their lily-like flowers that last just one day, but appear in succession for many weeks in summer. Daylilies range in size from compact plants that grow 30–38cm (12–15in) tall, to large plants that may reach 1.5m (5ft). They form clumps of arching, strappy foliage, and flower colours range from creamy-white, yellow, orange, red, pink, and purple, to almost black; some also have bands of contrasting colours on the petals. The flower forms are classified as single, double, or spider, and some are fragrant. They thrive in most soils, except waterlogged, in sun or shade, but flower best when in sun for at least part of the day.

***H.* 'Pardon Me'**

***H.* 'Neyron Rose'** 🏆

***H.* 'Joan Senior'**

***H.* 'Stoke Poges'** 🏆

***H.* 'Always Afternoon'**

***H.* 'Siloam Baby Talk'**

***H.* 'Luxury Lace'**

***H.* 'Pink Damask'** 🏆

***H.* 'Summer Wine'**

***H.* 'Canadian Border Patrol'**

***H.* 'Cherry Cheeks'**

***H.* 'Night Beacon'**

***H.* 'Prairie Blue Eyes'**

H. 'Green Flutter' 🏆

H. 'Whichford' 🏆

H. 'Bonanza'

H. 'Lemon Bells' 🏆

H. 'Little Wine Cup'

H. lilioasphodelus 🏆

H. dumortieri

H. fulva

H. 'Missenden' 🏆

H. citrina

H. 'Cream Drop'

H. 'Little Grapette'

H. 'Golden Chimes' 🏆

H. 'Cartwheels' 🏆

H. fulva 'Flore Pleno'

H. 'Mauna Loa'

H. 'Frans Hals'

H. 'Chicago Sunrise'

H. 'Stafford'

H. 'Burning Daylight' 🏆

H. 'Black Magic'

H. 'Cathy's Sunset'

ORANGE

***Euphorbia griffithii* 'Fireglow'**
Bushy perennial that bears orange-red flowers in terminal umbels in early summer. Leaves are lance-shaped, mid-green and have pale red midribs. **H** to 1m (3ft), **S** 50cm (20in).

Sphaeralcea ambigua
Branching, shrubby perennial. Broadly funnel-shaped, orange-coral blooms are produced singly in leaf axils from summer until the onset of cold weather. Leaves are soft, hairy and mid-green. **H** and **S** 75–90cm (30–36in).

Asclepias tuberosa **(Butterfly weed)**
Erect, tuberous perennial with long, lance-shaped leaves. Small, 5-horned, bright orange-red flowers are borne in summer and followed by narrow, pointed pods, to 15cm (6in) long. **H** to 75cm (30in), **S** 45cm (18in).

***Verbascum* 'Cotswold Beauty'**
Rosette-forming perennial with sometimes-branched spires of 5-petalled, pale coppery-apricot flowers, each with a soft purple centre, in summer. Has oval, grey-green leaves. May be short-lived in rich soil. **H** 1.2m (4ft), **S** 40cm (16in).

AUTUMN

WHITE

Actaea pachypoda
(Doll's eyes, White baneberry)
Compact, clump-forming perennial with spikes of small, fluffy, white flowers in summer and clusters of white berries, borne on stiff, fleshy scarlet stalks, in autumn. **H** 1m (3ft), **S** 50cm (20in).

Leucanthemum* x *superbum
'Wirral Pride'
Robust, clump-forming perennial with glossy, dark green, slightly toothed leaves. Bears numerous, solitary, white double flower heads with yellowish anemone centres from early summer to autumn. **H** to 1m (3ft), **S** 60cm (24in).

PINK

***Chrysanthemum* 'Clara Curtis'**
Bushy perennial producing many clusters of flat, daisy-like, clear pink flower heads throughout summer and autumn. Divide plants every other spring. **H** 75cm (30in), **S** 45cm (18in).

Tricyrtis formosana
Upright, rhizomatous perennial. In early autumn bears spurred flowers, heavily spotted with purplish-pink and with yellow-tinged throats. Glossy, dark green leaves clasp stems. **H** 60cm–1m (2–3ft), **S** 45cm (18in).

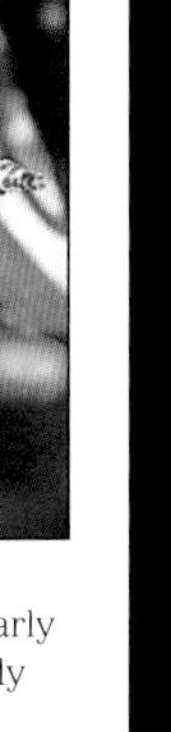

***Anemone hupehensis* 'Hadspen Abundance'**
Erect, branching perennial that bears pink flowers with rounded, dark reddish-pink outer tepals from summer to autumn. Leaves are dark green and deeply divided, with toothed leaflets. **H** 60cm–1.2m (2–4ft), **S** 45cm (18in).

YARROW

Stalwarts of the summer garden, Yarrow (*Achillea*) are easy-to-grow perennials for sunny sites and well-drained soils. Taller types are best planted toward the back of herbaceous borders, while shorter forms associate well with grasses in naturalistic planting schemes. Both selections also look at home in mixed beds and gravel gardens. Most have flattened flower heads, creating a horizontal plane that contrasts well with vertical flower spikes. Available in a range of colours, including white, yellow, pink, peach, and red, the flowers change colour as they age, creating a two-tone effect. Many make good cut flowers; some can also be dried.

***A. millefolium* 'Red Velvet'**

***A. ptarmica* 'The Pearl'**

A. 'Heidi'

A. 'Belle Epoque'

***A. millefolium* 'Kelwayi'**

***A. filipendulina* 'Parker's Variety'**

A. 'Christine's Pink'

A. 'Terracotta'

A. 'Lachsschönheit'

HELENIUM

Of all late-summer, daisy-flowered perennials, *Helenium* are among the most colourful. They have become increasingly popular with the rise of naturalistic plantings, to which they are well suited, although they also add a dramatic note to herbaceous borders. The stout stems bear shuttlecock-shaped flowers in fiery tones of red, orange, and yellow that last for many weeks. Plants seldom need staking and form slowly spreading clumps if grown in sun and fertile soil. To lengthen the flowering season, select a variety of forms, and cut back some in early summer to promote later flowering.

***H.* 'Indianersommer'**

***H.* 'Potter's Wheel'**

***H.* 'Bruno'** ⓘ

***H.* 'Double Trouble'**

***H.* 'Red Army'**

***H.* 'Butterpat'** 🏆

***H.* 'Feuersiegel'** 🏆

***H.* 'Rubinzwerg'** 🏆

***H.* 'Waltraut'** 🏆

Centranthus ruber **(Red valerian)**
Perennial forming spreading colonies of fleshy leaves. Branching heads of small, star-shaped, deep reddish-pink or white flowers are borne above foliage from late spring to autumn. Thrives in poor, exposed sites. **H** 60–90cm (24–36in), **S** 45–60cm (18–24in) or more.

Lobelia cardinalis **'Queen Victoria'**
Clump-forming perennial. From late summer to mid-autumn spikes of blazing red flowers on branching stems arise from basal, deep red-purple foliage. **H** 1m (3ft), **S** 30cm (12in).

MICHAELMAS DAISIES

Invaluable border plants, Michaelmas daisies (*Aster* species and cultivars; mostly *A. novae-angliae* and *A. novi-belgii*) flower later than many other perennials and continue the display until late autumn. The smaller-flowered species and selections associate well with grasses and naturalistic planting schemes, while the larger flowers are excellent for cutting. The daisy-like, single or double flowers range in colour from white, pink, and red, to purple and blue. Michaelmas daisies thrive in sun or partial shade and well-drained soil, and tall cultivars may need staking. For large flowers pinch out weaker shoots in spring; to produce bushier plants with a greater number of smaller flowers, pinch out the top 2.5–5cm (1–2in) of all shoots in late spring.

***A.* 'Coombe Fishacre'** 🏆 ***A.* 'Photograph'** 🏆 ***A. novi-belgii* 'Chequers'**

A. divaricatus

***A. novi-belgii* 'Apple Blossom'**

***A.* x *frikartii* 'Wunder von Stäfa'** 🏆

***A. novae-angliae* 'Violetta'**

***A. novi-belgii* 'Marie Ballard'**

***A. novae-angliae* 'Harrington's Pink'** 🏆

***A. novae-angliae* 'Rosa Sieger'** 🏆

***A.* 'Little Carlow'** 🏆

***A. ericoides* 'Golden Spray'** 🏆

***A. cordifolius* 'Silver Spray'**

***A.* 'Sunhelene'**

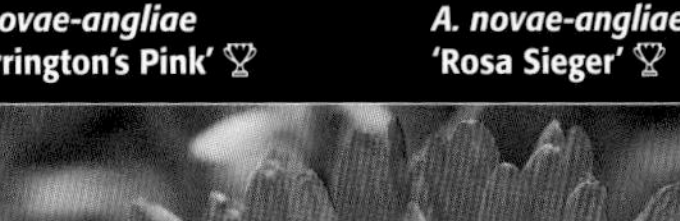

***A. novi-belgii* 'Carnival '**

***A. ericoides* 'White Heather'**

***A. novi-belgii* 'Freda Ballard'** ***A. novi-belgii* 'Orlando'**

***A. novi-belgii* 'Professor Anton Kippenberg'**

BLUE

Strobilanthes atropurpureus
Upright, branching perennial with oval, toothed leaves. Spikes of numerous, violet-blue to purple flowers appear in summer–autumn. **H** to 1.2m (4ft), **S** to 60cm (2ft).

PURPLE

***Aster amellus* 'King George'**
Bushy perennial with oval, rough leaves. In autumn produces many large, terminal, daisy-like, deep blue-violet flower heads with yellow centres. **H** and **S** 50cm (20in).

Gentiana asclepiadea
(Willow gentian)
Arching perennial with narrow, oval leaves to 8cm (3in) long. In late summer to autumn has arching sprays of trumpet-shaped, deep blue flowers, spotted and striped inside. **H** to 90cm (36in), **S** to 60cm (24in).

Eryngium x tripartitum
Perennial with wiry stems above a basal rosette of coarsely toothed, grey-green leaves. Conical, metallic-blue flower heads on blue stems are borne in summer–autumn and may be dried for winter decoration. **H** 1–1.2m (3–4ft), **S** 50cm (20in).

SALVIAS

Hardy perennial salvias are useful plants, many flowering profusely in late summer and lasting well into autumn. The genus is quite diverse, with plants in a range of sizes and flower colours, including white, true blue, purple, pink, and red. A few, such as *S. argentea*, are also grown for their foliage, which in many species is aromatic. Salvias thrive in hot, sunny sites and free-draining soil, and grow quickly, many developing into shrub-like plants within a season. To ensure they survive cold winters, in autumn spread a thick mulch over the plants to protect the roots.

***S. pratensis* 'Pink Delight'**

***S. x sylvestris* 'Blauhügel'**

***S. x sylvestris* 'Mainacht'**

***S. nemorosa* 'Caradonna'**

***S. pratensis* 'Indigo'**

***S. nemorosa* 'Lubecca'**

***S. guaranitica* 'Black and Blue'**

***S. pratensis* 'Swan Lake'**

S. uliginosa

S. argentea

***S. nemorosa* 'Amethyst'**

***S. nemorosa* 'Ostfriesland'**

***S. verticillata* 'Purple Rain'**

S. patens

S. glutinosa

Kniphofia 'Percy's Pride'
Upright perennial with large, terminal spikes of creamy flowers, tinged green and yellow, borne on erect stems in autumn. Protect crowns with winter mulch. **H** 1m (3ft), **S** 50cm (20in).

Kirengeshoma palmata
Upright perennial with rounded, lobed, bright green leaves, above which strong stems bearing clusters of narrowly funnel-shaped, creamy yellow flowers appear in late summer to autumn. **H** 1m (3ft), **S** 60cm (2ft).

Euphorbia schillingii
Robust, clump-forming perennial that produces long-lasting, yellow cyathia and rounded, greenish-yellow bracts from mid-summer to mid-autumn. Stems are erect and leaves are dark green with pale green or white veins. **H** 1m (3ft), **S** 30cm (1ft).

***Solidago* 'Goldenmosa'**
Clump-forming perennial. Sprays of tufted, mimosa-like, yellow flower heads are carried in late summer and autumn above lance-shaped, toothed, hairy, yellowish-green leaves. **H** 1m (3ft), **S** 60cm (2ft).

RUDBECKIA

The golden daisy flowers of *Rudbeckia* illuminate late summer and early autumn borders, perennial schemes, and gravel gardens. Most are just over knee-height, but some forms of *R. hirta* are small and compact, ideal for the front of beds or containers, while others, like *R.* 'Herbstonne' tower above the rest, reaching up to 2.5m (8ft) in height. *R. maxima* also has attractive glaucous blue foliage. All types produce large flowers on stout stems that seldom need staking, and the blooms also attract beneficial insects. *Rudbeckia* thrive in an open, sunny situation, and moist but free-draining soil.

***R. occidentalis* 'Green Wizard'**

R. maxima

R. triloba

R. fulgida* var. *speciosa

***R. fulgida* var. *sullivantii* 'Goldsturm'**

***R. laciniata* 'Herbstsonne'**

R. fulgida* var. *deamii

CHRYSANTHEMUMS

Florist's chrysanthemums, as well as those that are grown as hardy garden plants, are grouped according to their differing flower forms, approximate flowering season (early, mid- or late autumn) and habit. The best groups for garden decoration are the sprays, pompons and semi-pompons, the hardy Korean and early, reflexed chrysanthemums. The dwarf Charm-types, forming dense, domed masses of flowers, are most attractive displayed in pots for both indoor and outdoor use in autumn. Most of the various flower forms are described below, with further details provided in the Plant Dictionary under Chrysanthemum.

Incurved – fully double, dense, spherical flowers have incurved petals arising from the base of the flower and closing tightly over the crown.

Fully reflexed – fully double flowers have curved, pointed petals reflexing outwards and downwards from the crown, back to touch the stem.

Reflexed – fully double flowers are similar to those of fully reflexed forms except that the petals are less strongly reflexed and form an umbrella-like or spiky outline.

Intermediate – fully double, roughly spherical flowers have loosely incurving petals, which may close at the crown or may reflex for the bottom half of each flower.

Anemone-centred – single flowers each have a central, dome-shaped disc, up to half the diameter of the bloom, and up to 5 rows of flat, or occasionally spoon-type, ray petals at right angles to the stem.

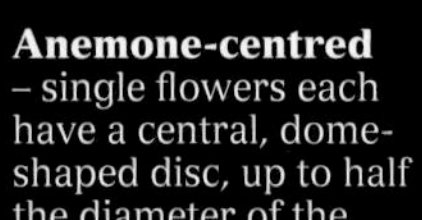

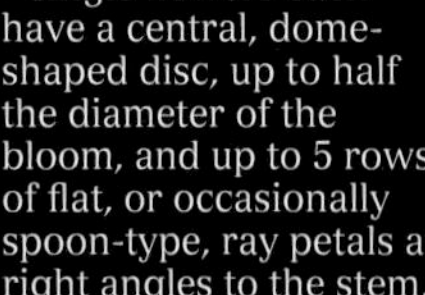

Single – flowers each have about 5 rows of flat petals, borne at right angles to the stem, that may incurve or reflex at the tips; the prominent, central disc is golden throughout or has a small, green centre.

Pompon – fully double, dense, spherical, or occasionally hemispherical, flowers, have tubular petals with flat, rounded tips, growing outwards from the crown.

Spoon-type – flowers are similar to those of single forms except that the ray petals are tubular and open out at their tips to form a spoon shape.

Spider-form – double flower heads with long, thin ray-florets; the outer ray-florets are more or less pendent, the inner ones curling upwards.

Quill-shaped – double flower heads with tubular ray-florets that open out at their tips to form spoon shapes.

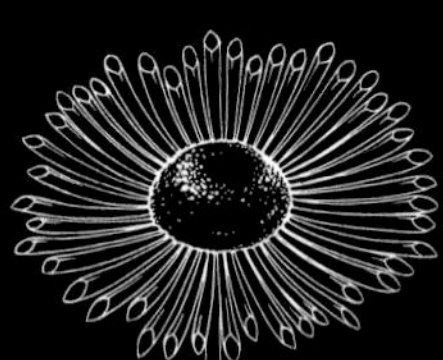

C. 'Innocence' ⓘ [single]

C. 'Pennine Oriel' 🏆ⓘ [spray, anemone]

C. 'Nell Gwynn' ⓘ [Korean Group]

C. 'Purleigh White' ⓘ [semi-pompon]

C. 'Emperor of China' ⓘ [double]

C. 'Enbee Wedding' 🏆ⓘ [spray, single]

C. 'Chesapeake' ⓘ [spray, quill]

C. 'Spartan Seagull' ⓘ [Korean Group]

C. 'Aunt Millicent' ⓘ [Korean Group]

C. 'Anastasia' ⓘ [semi-pompon]

C. 'Tapestry Rose' ⓘ [Korean Group]

C. 'Ruby Mound' 🏆ⓘ [Korean Group]

C. 'Mary Stoker' ⓘ [single]

C. 'Nantyderry Sunshine' 🏆ⓘ [semi-pompon]

C. 'Carmine Blush' ⓘ [single]

C. 'Rumpelstilzchen' ⓘ [Korean Group]

C. 'Golden Chalice' ⓘ [Charm]

C. 'Yellow John Hughes' 🏆ⓘ [incurved]

C. 'Grandchild' ⓘ [double]

C. 'Perry's Peach' ⓘ [Korean Group]

C. 'Chelsea Physic Garden' ⓘ [double]

C. 'Bronze Elegance' ⓘ [semi-pompon]

C. 'Sea Urchin' 🏆ⓘ [Korean Group]

C. 'Mrs Jessie Cooper' ⓘ [single]

C. 'George Griffiths' 🏆ⓘ [reflexed]

C. 'Doctor Tom Parr' ⓘ [semi-pompon]

C. 'Cottage Apricot' ⓘ [Korean Group]

C. 'Apollo' ⓘ [Korean Group]

C. 'Duchess of Edinburgh' ⓘ [Korean Group]

C. 'Paul Boissier' ⓘ [semi-double]

RED HOT POKERS

Red hot pokers *(Kniphofia)* are dramatic hardy perennials, their upright forms providing focal points in borders, gravel gardens, and perennial schemes. Spires of tubular flowers in a range of fiery colours, or more muted shades of green, ivory, and pale yellow, rise from clumps of slender, often evergreen, foliage. Selections flower from mid-summer to late autumn, and they enjoy an open site in full sun, with shelter from cold winds, and fertile, well-drained soil that does not dry out. Give them space to spread, as too much competition may limit their success. Protect plants over winter with a deep mulch.

K. 'Royal Standard'

K. 'Green Jade' **K. 'Wrexham Buttercup'** **K. 'Atlanta'**

K. *caulescens*

K. 'Toffee Nosed' **K. *thomsonii* var. *snowdenii***

K. 'Bees' Sunset' **K. 'Prince Igor'** **K. *rooperi***

MEDIUM

AUTUMN

ORANGE

***Helenium* 'Moerheim Beauty'**
Upright perennial with strong, branching stems bearing sprays of daisy-like, rich reddish-orange flower heads in early autumn above dark green foliage. Needs regular division in spring or autumn. **H** 1m (3ft), **S** 60cm (2ft).

Aster linosyris (Goldilocks)
Upright, unbranched perennial with numerous small, dense, single, golden-yellow flower heads in late summer and autumn. Leaves are narrowly lance-shaped. **H** 60cm (24in), **S** 30cm (12in).

SMALL

SPRING

WHITE

***Epimedium* x *youngianum* 'Niveum'**
Compact, ground-cover perennial with heart-shaped, serrated, bronze-tinted leaflets that turn green in late spring, when small, cup-shaped, snow-white flowers are borne. **H** 15–30cm (6–12in), **S** 30cm (12in).

***Lamium maculatum* 'White Nancy'**
Semi-evergreen, mat-forming perennial with white-variegated, mid-green foliage and spikes of hooded, white flowers in late spring and summer. **H** 15cm (6in), **S** 1m (3ft).

***Pulmonaria* 'Sissinghurst White'**
Semi-evergreen, clump-forming perennial that bears funnel-shaped, white flowers in spring above long, elliptic, mid-green, paler spotted leaves. **H** 30cm (12in), **S** 45–60cm (18–24in).

Anemone narcissiflora
Leafy perennial that in late spring and early summer produces cup-shaped, single, white flowers with a blue or purplish-pink stain on reverse of petals. Leaves are dark green and deeply divided. **H** to 60cm (24in), **S** 50cm (20in).

Trillium grandiflorum (Wake-robin)
Clump-forming perennial. Large, pure white flowers that turn pink with age are borne singly in spring just above large, 3-parted, green leaves. **H** 38cm (15in), **S** 30cm (12in).

***Lamium maculatum* 'Album'**
Semi-evergreen, mat-forming perennial that has dark green leaves with central, white stripes. Bears clusters of hooded, white flowers in spring–summer. **H** 20cm (8in), **S** 1m (3ft).

***Bergenia* 'Silberlicht'**
Evergreen, clump-forming perennial that has flat, oval, mid-green leaves with toothed margins. Clusters of white flowers, sometimes suffused with pink, are borne on erect stems in spring. **H** 30cm (12in), **S** 50cm (20in).

Convallaria majalis (Lily-of-the-valley)
Low-growing, rhizomatous perennial with narrowly oval, mid- to dark green leaves and sprays of small, very fragrant, pendulous, bell-shaped, white flowers. Likes humus-rich soil. **H** 15cm (6in), **S** indefinite.

Sinopodophyllum hexandrum
(Himalayan May apple)
Perennial with pairs of 3-lobed, brown-mottled leaves followed by white or pink flowers in spring and fleshy, red fruits in summer. **H** 30–45cm (12–18in), **S** 30cm (12in).

Pachyphragma macrophyllum
Creeping, mat-forming perennial with rosettes of rounded, long-stalked, glossy, bright green leaves, each to 10cm (4in) long. Bears many racemes of tiny, white flowers in spring. **H** to 30cm (12in), **S** indefinite.

Trillium ovatum
Clump-forming perennial with white flowers, later turning pink, that are carried singly in spring just above red-stalked, 3-parted, green foliage. **H** 25–38cm (10–15in), **S** 20cm (8in).

Trillium chloropetalum
Clump-forming perennial with reddish-green stems carrying 3-parted, grey-marbled, dark green leaves. Flowers vary from purplish-pink to white and appear above foliage in spring. **H** and **S** 30–45cm (12–18in).

Anemone sylvestris
(Snowdrop windflower)
Carpeting perennial that may be invasive. Fragrant, semi-pendent, white flowers with yellow centres are borne in spring and early summer. Has divided, mid-green leaves. **H** and **S** 30cm (12in).

***Helleborus* x *ericsmithii* 'Bob's Best'**
Evergreen, clump-forming perennial with toothed, green leaves flushed in pewter and divided into 3–5 leaflets. From mid-winter to late spring bears saucer-shaped, pink-tinted, white flowers. **H** 38cm (15in), **S** 45cm (18in).

WHITE

Chrysosplenium macrophyllum
Evergreen, ground-cover perennial with large, rounded, fleshy, mid green leaves covered in silvery hairs. Lacy heads of flattish, pink-tinted, creamy flowers are borne in early spring. Spreads freely by runners. **H** 20cm (8in), **S** 90cm (36in).

Helleborus* x *ericsmithii
IVORY PRINCE ('Walivor')
Evergreen, clump-forming perennial with silver-veined, bluish-green leaves divided into 3–5 leaflets. From mid-winter to spring bears pink-tinted cream flowers, often striped in green and with darker petal backs. **H** 38cm (15in), **S** 45cm (18in).

Bergenia ciliata
Evergreen, clump-forming perennial with attractive, large, rounded, hairy leaves. In spring bears clusters of white flowers that age to pink. Leaves are often damaged by frost, although fresh ones will appear in spring. **H** 30cm (12in), **S** 50cm (20in).

PINK

***Cypripedium* Ulla Silkens gx**
Deciduous, terrestrial orchid with 1–3 pouched, pastel white and pink flowers, 5–7cm (2–3in) long, borne in spring. Has broadly lance-shaped leaves, to 30cm (12in) long. **H** 30cm (12in), **S** 60cm (24in).

***Dicentra* 'Spring Morning'**
Neat, leafy perennial with small, heart-shaped, pink flowers hanging in arching sprays in late spring and summer. Attractive, fern-like foliage is grey-green and finely cut. **H** and **S** 30cm (12in).

***Bergenia* 'Beethoven'**
Evergreen, ground-covering perennial with masses of pink-tinged, white flowers, borne in branched panicles, in spring. Has spoon-shaped, leathery, mid-green leaves. Protect from spring frosts. **H** 40cm (16in), **S** 60cm (24in) or more.

Geranium macrorrhizum
'Ingwersen's Variety'
Compact, carpeting perennial, useful as weed-suppressing ground cover. Small, soft rose-pink flowers appear in late spring and early summer. Aromatic leaves turn bronze- and scarlet-tinted in autumn. **H** 30cm (12in), **S** 60cm (24in).

Heloniopsis orientalis
Clump-forming perennial with basal rosettes of narrowly lance-shaped leaves, above which rise nodding, rose-pink flowers in spring. **H** and **S** 30cm (12in).

Helleborus thibetanus
Clump-forming perennial with palmate, mid-green leaves deeply divided into 7–9 toothed lobes. Bears deeply cup-shaped flowers, 4–6.5cm (1½–2¾in) across, in late winter–early spring that vary from white to white with pink veins, which darken with age. **H** and **S** to 30cm (12in).

PRIMULAS

There are primulas to suit most garden situations, ranging from boggy areas and pond margins, to woodlands, rock gardens, and containers. Of the various botanical groups, Candelabra, Auricula, and Primrose-Polyanthus primulas are the most widely grown. Auriculas are compact evergreen plants with leathery leaves and flowers with beautiful markings; they grow well in moist but well-drained soil. Candelabras prefer damp soil, and are taller and deciduous, with flowers arranged in rings up sturdy stems. The Primrose-Polyanthus group include a diverse range of small winter to spring-flowering plants, often sold as bedding or for containers, that thrive in moist soil. Most prefer some shade. For full cultivation details see the Plant Dictionary.

***P.* 'Guinevere'** 🏆

P. vialii 🏆

***P.* 'Lady Greer'** 🏆

P. denticulata* var. *alba

P. allionii 🏆

P. frondosa 🏆

***P. japonica* 'Miller's Crimson'** 🏆

***P.* 'Dawn Ansell'**

***P.* Husky Mixed** [white]

***P.* 'Woodland Walk'**

***P.* Crescendo Series** [pink and rose shades] 🏆

***P. vulgaris* 'Alba Plena'**

***P. japonica* 'Postford White'** 🏆

***P. sieboldii* 'Geisha Girl'**

***P.* 'Charisma Red'**

P. sieboldii ♡

P. vulgaris subsp. *sibthorpii* ♡

P. 'Elizabeth Killelay'

P. 'Mark' [Auricula]

P. pulverulenta ♡

P. 'Inverewe' ♡

P. Barnhaven Blues Group ♡

P. Charisma Series [blue] ♡

P. Crescendo Series

P. Crescendo Series 'Crescendo Bright Red' ♡

P. polyneura

P. beesiana

P. Belarina Series 'Belarina Cobalt Blue'

P. 'Don Keefe'

P. 'Matthew Yates' [Auricula]

P. 'Miss Indigo'

P. 'Fransisca'

P. sikkimensis 🏆

P. chungensis

P. palinuri

P. 'Margaret Martin' [Auricula]

P. 'Blairside Yellow' [Auricula]

P. forrestii

P. bulleyana 🏆

P. aureata

P. elatior 🏆

P. verticillata

P. kewensis 🏆

P. veris 'Katy McSparron'

P. Gold-laced Group

P. alpicola 🏆

P. vulgaris 🏆

P. 'Trouble' [Auricula]

RED

Epimedium* x *rubrum
Carpeting perennial with dense, heart-shaped, divided leaves that are dark brownish-red in spring, when clusters of cup-shaped, crimson flowers with yellow spurs appear. **H** 30cm (12in), **S** 20cm (8in).

Trillium erectum
(Birthroot, Squawroot)
Clump-forming perennial with 3-lobed, mid-green leaves and bright maroon-purple flowers in spring. **H** 30–45cm (12–18in), **S** 30cm (12in).

Trillium sessile
(Toadshade, Wake-robin)
Clump-forming perennial that in spring bears red-brown flowers, nestling in a collar of 3-lobed leaves, marked white, pale green or bronze. **H** 30–38cm (12–15in), **S** 30–45cm (12–18in).

PURPLE

Glaucidium palmatum
Leafy perennial that has large, lobed leaves and, in spring, large, delicate, cup-shaped, lavender flowers. A woodland plant, it requires humus-rich soil and a sheltered position. **H** and **S** 50cm (20in).

Cardamine pentaphyllos
Upright perennial spreading by fleshy, horizontal rootstocks. Produces clusters of large, white or pale purple flowers in spring. **H** 30–60cm (12–24in), **S** 45–60cm (18–24in).

Scopolia carniolica
Clump-forming perennial that carries spikes of nodding, purplish-brown flowers, yellow inside, in early spring. **H** and **S** 60cm (24in).

Helleborus purpurascens
Neat, clump-forming perennial with small, nodding, cup-shaped, deep purple or green flowers, splashed with deep purple on outside, in early spring. Dark green leaves are palmate and deeply divided into narrowly lance-shaped, toothed segments. **H** and **S** 30cm (1ft).

Epimedium epsteinii
Rather compact, semi-evergreen, rhizomatous perennial with glossy green leaves divided into narrowly oval, toothed leaflets. Has clusters of pendent, long-spurred, white-and-purple flowers in spring. Good for ground cover. **H** 30cm (12in), **S** 40cm (16cm).

Lathyrus vernus
Clump-forming perennial bearing in spring small, pea-like, bright purple and blue flowers veined with red, several on each slender stem. Leaves are soft and fern-like. Proves difficult to transplant successfully. **H** and **S** 30cm (12in).

Lathraea clandestina **(Toothwort)**
Spreading perennial that grows as a parasite on willow or poplar roots. Fleshy, underground stems have colourless scales instead of leaves. Bears bunches of hooded, purple flowers from late winter to early spring. **H** 10cm (4in), **S** indefinite.

Lamium orvala
Clump-forming perennial that forms a mound of mid-green leaves, sometimes with central white stripes. Clusters of pink or purple-pink flowers open in late spring to early summer. **H** and **S** 30cm (12in).

***Erysimum* 'Bowles's Mauve'**
Shrubby, short-lived perennial with many clusters of purple flowers, each with 4 spreading petals, from early spring to early summer. Has narrowly lance-shaped, dark green leaves. Is best in poor soil. **H** 60cm (24in), **S** 40cm (16in).

BLUE

Mertensia virginica
Elegant perennial with rich blue flowers, hanging in clusters in spring. Leaves are soft blue-green. Dies down in summer. Crowns are prone to slug damage. **H** 30–60cm (12–24in), **S** 30–45cm (12–18in).

***Omphalodes cappadocica* 'Cherry Ingram'**
Clump-forming, rhizomatous perennial with oval, deeply veined, pointed, mid-green leaves. In spring bears loose racemes of 5-petalled, dark blue flowers. **H** 30cm (12in), **S** 60cm (24in).

***Brunnera macrophylla* 'Jack Frost'**
Ground-cover perennial with heart-shaped, silvery-grey leaves. Delicate sprays of small, star-shaped, forget-me-not-like, blue flowers are produced in spring. Is ideal in the front of a border. **H** 60cm (24in), **S** 60cm (24in) or more.

LUNGWORTS

Invaluable shade-loving perennials, lungworts, *Pulmonaria*, produce clusters of bell-shaped spring flowers and hairy, ground-covering foliage. Selections are available in a range of colours, from white through to pink, blue and purple; *P. rubra* has red blooms. Some cultivars have also been selected for the beauty of their foliage, which may be spotted or streaked with white or silver or variegated. Easy to grow, *Pulmonaria* thrive in cool areas in soil that does not dry out. During summer, trim off the old foliage and fresh leaves, often more prominently marked, soon appear.

***P. rubra* 'David Ward'**

P. rubra

***P.* 'Lewis Palmer'**

***P.* 'Excalibur'**

***P.* OPAL ('Ocupol')**

***P.* 'Margery Fish'**

***P.* 'Mary Mottram'**

***P.* 'Mawson's Blue'**

GREEN

***Helleborus argutifolius* 'Pacific Frost'**
Clump-forming perennial with pink shoot tips and evergreen, divided, spiny, dark green leaves densely speckled in cream. Produces large clusters of cup-shaped, pale green flowers in winter–spring.
H 60cm (24in), **S** 45cm (18in).

Euphorbia cyparissias
Rounded, leafy perennial with a mass of slender, grey-green leaves and umbels of small, bright lime-green flowers in late spring. May be invasive. **H** and **S** 30cm (12in).

Euphorbia amygdaloides* var. *robbiae
Evergreen, spreading perennial with rosettes of dark green leaves, useful as ground cover even in poor, dry soil and semi-shade. Bears open, rounded heads of lime-green flowers in spring.
H 45–60cm (18–24in), **S** 60cm (24in).

Helleborus* x *sternii
Evergreen, clump-forming perennial with divided leaves and cup-shaped, often pink-tinged, pale green flowers borne in terminal clusters in winter and early spring. **H** and **S** 45cm (18in).

***Helleborus argutifolius* 'Silver Lace'**
Clump-forming perennial with evergreen, divided, spiny, bluish-green leaves and flared, cup-shaped, pale green flowers borne in large clusters in winter–spring. **H** 60cm (24in), **S** 45cm (18in).

YELLOW

Anemone* x *lipsiensis
Prostrate, carpeting perennial that in spring has many single, pale yellow flowers with bright yellow stamens. Leaves are deeply cut with long leaflets.
H 15cm (6in), **S** 30cm (12in).

***Epimedium* x *versicolor* 'Neosulphureum'**
Carpeting perennial with dense, heart-shaped, divided leaves, tinted reddish-purple in spring when it bears cup-shaped, pale yellow flowers in small, pendent clusters on wiry stems.
H and **S** 30cm (12in).

Uvularia grandiflora
(Bellwort, Merry-bells)
Clump-forming perennial. Clusters of long, bell-shaped, yellow flowers hang gracefully from slender stems in spring.
H 45–60cm (18–24in), **S** 30cm (12in).

***Valeriana phu* 'Aurea'**
Perennial with rosettes of lemon- to butter-yellow young foliage that turns mid-green by summer, when heads of insignificant, white flowers appear.
H 38cm (15in), **S** 30–38cm (12–15in).

Adonis vernalis
Clump-forming perennial that in early spring produces buttercup-like, greenish-yellow blooms singly at the tips of stems. Mid-green leaves are delicately dissected. **H** and **S** 23–30cm (9–12in).

Euphorbia polychroma
Rounded, bushy perennial with mid-green leaves and heads of bright yellow flowers carried for several weeks in spring. **H** and **S** 50cm (20in).

Primula veris **(Cowslip)**
Very variable, rosette-forming, evergreen or semi-evergreen perennial with tight clusters of fragrant, tubular, yellow flowers produced on stout stems in spring. Leaves are oval to lance-shaped, toothed and mid-green. **H** and **S** 25cm (10in).

Doronicum orientale **'Magnificum'**
Clump-forming perennial with heart-shaped, lush, soft green leaves. Short stems bear daisy-like, bright yellow flower heads in spring. Plants may die down by late summer. **H** 45cm (18in), **S** 40cm (16in).

Anemone ranunculoides
Spreading perennial for damp woodland, bearing buttercup-like, single, deep yellow flowers in spring. Divided leaves have short stalks. **H** and **S** 20cm (8in).

ORANGE

Epimedium* x *warleyense
Carpeting perennial with heart-shaped, divided, light green leaves, tinged purple-red, and cup-shaped, rich orange flowers borne in clusters on wiry stems in spring. **H** and **S** 30cm (12in).

Meconopsis cambrica **(Welsh poppy)**
Spreading perennial that in late spring carries lemon-yellow or rich orange blooms. Double forms are available. Has deeply divided, fern-like foliage. **H** 30–45cm (12–18in), **S** 30cm (12in).

Epimedium **'Amber Queen'**
Evergreen, clump-forming perennial with clusters of spidery, pendent, long-spurred, orange flowers, held on wiry stems, in spring. Dark green leaves are mottled when young and divided into rounded heart-shaped, toothed leaflets. **H** 30cm (12in), **S** 40cm (16in).

WHITE

Anthericum liliago **(St Bernard's lily)**
Upright perennial that in early summer bears tall racemes of trumpet-shaped, white flowers above clumps of long, narrow, grey-green leaves. **H** 45–60cm (18–24in), **S** 30cm (12in).

Tradescantia **Andersoniana Group 'Osprey'**
Clump-forming perennial with narrow, lance-shaped leaves, 15–30cm (6–12in) long. Has clusters of white flowers with purple-blue stamens, surrounded by 2 leaf-like bracts, in summer. **H** to 60cm (24in), **S** 45cm (18in).

***Leucanthemum* x *superbum* 'Esther Read'**
Robust perennial with large, daisy-like, double, white flower heads borne singly on strong stems in summer. **H** and **S** 45cm (18in).

Galium odoratum **(Woodruff)**
Carpeting perennial that bears whorls of star-shaped, white flowers above neat, whorled leaves in summer. All parts of plant are aromatic. **H** 15cm (6in), **S** 30cm (12in) or more.

Geranium clarkei **'Kashmir White'**
Carpeting, rhizomatous perennial with divided leaves and loose clusters of cup-shaped flowers, white with pale lilac-pink veins, borne for a long period in summer. **H** and **S** 45–60cm (18–24in).

WHITE

Deinanthe bifida
Slow-growing, clump-forming perennial with nodding, cup-shaped, white flowers. Has oval, bristly, soft green leaves on short stems. **H** 40cm (16in), **S** 30cm (12in).

Diplarrhena moraea
Clump-forming perennial with fans of long, strap-shaped leaves and clusters of iris-like, white flowers, with centres of yellow and purple, borne on wiry stems in early summer. **H** 45cm (18in), **S** 23cm (9in).

Anthemis punctata* subsp. *cupaniana
Evergreen, carpeting perennial with dense, finely cut, silvery foliage that turns green in winter. Small, daisy-like, white flower heads with yellow centres are borne singly on short stems in early summer. **H** and **S** 30cm (12in).

Geranium renardii
Compact, clump-forming perennial with lobed, circular, sage-green leaves and purple-veined, white flowers, borne in early summer. **H** and **S** 30cm (12in).

Crambe maritima **(Sea kale)**
Robust perennial with a mound of wide, curved, lobed, silvery-green leaves. Bears large heads of small, fragrant, white flowers, opening into branching sprays in summer. **H** and **S** 60cm (24in).

Melittis melissophyllum
(Bastard balm)
Erect perennial that in early summer bears white flowers with purple lower lips in axils of rough, oval, mid-green leaves. **H** and **S** 30cm (12in).

PINK

Mimulus naiandinus
Spreading perennial, with hairy leaves, that in summer bears snapdragon-like, rose-pink flowers tipped with creamy-yellow and spotted deep pink. **H** 23cm (9in), **S** 25cm (10in).

***Erigeron* 'Charity'**
Clump-forming perennial with a mass of daisy-like, light pink flower heads with greenish-yellow centres borne for a long period in summer. May need some support. **H** and **S** to 60cm (24in).

x *Heucherella tiarelloides*
Evergreen, ground-cover perennial that has dense clusters of leaves and feathery sprays of tiny, bell-shaped, pink flowers in early summer. **H** and **S** 45cm (18in).

***Geranium* x *oxonianum* 'Wargrave Pink'**
Semi-evergreen, carpeting perennial with dense, dainty, lobed, basal leaves acting as weed-suppressing ground cover. Cup-shaped, bright salmon-pink flowers are borne throughout summer. **H** 45cm (18in), **S** 60cm (24in).

Persicaria macrophylla
Compact perennial carrying neat spikes of rich rose-pink blooms above narrow, lance-shaped, leaves in late summer. **H** 45–60cm (18–24in), **S** 30cm (12in).

Lychnis flos-jovis
Clump-forming perennial with round clusters of deep rose-pink flowers, opening in mid-summer, that are set off by grey foliage. **H** and **S** 45cm (18in).

Osteospermum jucundum
Evergreen, neat, clump-forming perennial with mid-green leaves. In late summer, soft pink flower heads, mostly dark-eyed, are borne singly but in great abundance. **H** and **S** 30cm (12in).

***Potentilla nepalensis* 'Miss Willmott'**
Clump-forming perennial with palmate, strawberry-like, bright green leaves. Numerous slender, branching stems carry cherry-red-centred, pink flowers throughout summer. **H** 50cm (20in), **S** 60cm (24in).

***Centaurea hypoleuca* 'John Coutts'**
Upright perennial. Deep rose-red flower heads, with thistle-like centres encircled by star-shaped ray petals, are borne on slender stems in summer. Deeply divided leaves are white-grey beneath. **H** 60cm (24in), **S** 45cm (18in).

Incarvillea delavayi
Clump-forming perennial with deeply divided leaves and erect stems bearing several trumpet-shaped, pinkish-red flowers in early summer. Has attractive seed pods. **H** 45–60cm (18–24in), **S** 30cm (12in).

Erodium manescaui
Mound-forming perennial with divided, ferny, blue-green leaves. Produces loose clusters of single, deep pink, darker blotched flowers throughout summer. **H** 45cm (18in), **S** 60cm (24in).

Incarvillea mairei
Compact, clump-forming perennial that has short stems bearing several trumpet-shaped, purplish-pink flowers in early summer. Leaves are divided into oval leaflets. Protect crowns with winter mulch. **H** and **S** 30cm (12in).

Dactylorhiza foliosa
Deciduous, terrestrial orchid with spikes of bright purple or pink flowers, 1–2cm (1/2–3/4in) long, borne in spring-summer. Has lance-shaped or triangular leaves, 10–20cm (4–8in) long, arranged spirally on stem. **H** 60cm (24in), **S** 15cm (6in).

***Lychnis viscaria* 'Splendens Plena'**
Clump-forming perennial bearing spikes of double, magenta flowers in early summer. Stems and large, oval to lance-shaped, basal leaves are covered in sticky hairs. **H** 30–45cm (12–18in), **S** 23cm (9in) or more.

CARNATIONS AND PINKS

Although perhaps best known for providing excellent, long-lasting cut flowers, carnations and pinks (*Dianthus* cultivars) are highly ornamental border subjects, valued for their usually fragrant, clove-scented, blooms, produced over a long period in summer, and their distinctive, silvery- or grey-green foliage. Shorter-growing cultivars – the old-fashioned and modern pinks – make excellent edging plants. Many of the flowers are attractively marked or have fringed petals. Carnations and pinks need an open, sunny position, preferably in alkaline soil. All except the perpetual-flowering carnations are frost hardy, and most can be easily propagated from cuttings. The myriad of carnation and pinks cultivars are divided into the following groups:

Border carnations – plants are of upright habit and flower prolifically in mid-summer in a single flush; each stem bears 5 or more flowers. Picotee-flowered forms, with petals outlined in a darker, contrasting colour, are available.

Perpetual-flowering carnations – similar in habit to border carnations, they are usually grown for cut flowers and bloom year-round under glass. Plants are normally disbudded, leaving one flower per stem, but spray forms have up to 5 flowers per stem.

Malmaison carnations – these produce intensely fragrant flowers sporadically throughout the year under glass.

Old-fashioned pinks – these have a low, spreading habit and form neat cushions of foliage; masses of fragrant flowers are produced in mid-summer. Good for border edging and cutting.

Modern pinks – usually more vigorous than old-fashioned pinks, they are repeat-flowering and produce 2 or 3 main flushes of flowers in summer. Cut or deadhead to encourage further flowering.

Alpine pinks – in early summer, these plants form cushions of small, scented flowers. Good for edging, in a rockery, raised bed, trough, or alpine house.

***D.* 'Coquette'** 🏆
[perpetual-flowering carnation]

***D.* CANDY FLOSS ('Devon Flavia')** 🏆
[modern pink]

***D.* 'Milky Way'** 🏆
[perpetual-flowering carnation]

***D.* 'White Ladies'**
[old-fashioned pink]

***D.* 'Lady Madonna'** 🏆
[modern pink]

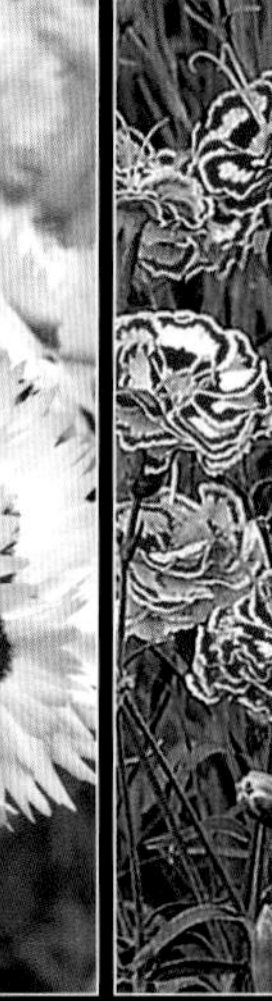

***D.* 'Becky Robinson'** 🏆
[modern pink]

***D.* 'Mrs Sinkins'**
[old-fashioned pink]

***D.* 'Musgrave's Pink'**
[old-fashioned pink]

***D.* 'Gran's Favourite'** 🏆
[old-fashioned pink]

***D.* 'Haytor White'** 🏆
[modern pink]

***D.* 'Doris'** 🏆
[modern pink]

***D.* 'Duchess of Westminster'**
[Malmaison carnation]

***D.* 'Dad's Favourite'**
[old-fashioned pink]

***D.* 'Brilliant Star'** 🏆
[modern pink]

***D.* 'Cranmere Pool'** 🏆 [modern]

***D.* 'Devon Dove'** 🏆 [modern]

***D.* 'Inchmery'** [old-fashioned pink]

***D.* 'Evening Star'** 🏆 [modern pink]

D. 'Rose de Mai'
[old-fashioned pink]

D. STARLIGHT ('Hilstar')
[modern pink]

D. 'Tickled Pink'
[modern pink]

D. 'Neon Star' 🏆
[modern pink]

D. 'Fusilier'
[modern pink]

D. superbus 'Crimsonia'
[old-fashioned pink]

D. 'Monica Wyatt' 🏆
[modern pink]

D. 'Feuerhexe' [alpine pink]

D. 'Valda Wyatt' 🏆
[modern pink]

D. 'Tayside Red'
[Malmaison carnation]

D. 'India Star' 🏆
[modern pink]

D. 'Pixie Star' 🏆
[modern pink]

D. 'Moulin Rouge' 🏆
[modern pink]

D. 'Queen of Sheba'
[old-fashioned pink]

D. 'Prado Mint' 🏆
[perpetual-flowering carnation]

D. 'Lily the Pink'
[modern pink]

D. 'Devon Wizard' 🏆 [modern]

D. 'Pink Jewel' [alpine pink]

D. 'Passion' [modern pink]

D. 'Golden Cross' 🏆 [border carnation]

PINK

Glandularia 'Sissinghurst'
Mat-forming perennial that throughout summer bears heads of brilliant pink flowers above mid-green foliage. Is excellent for edging a path or growing in a tub. **H** 15–20cm (6–8in), **S** 45cm (18in).

Stachys officinalis 'Hummelo'
Mat-forming perennial with oblong, round-toothed, hairy, dark green leaves. Upright, sturdy stems bear whorls of small, tubular, 2-lipped, pink flowers in summer. **H** and **S** 60cm (24in).

Dianthus 'Houndspool Ruby'
Modern pink with compact growth and an abundance of strongly scented, semi-double, ruby-pink flowers, each with a deeper eye. **H** 30–45cm (12–18in), **S** 23–30cm (9–12in).

Geum 'Bell Bank'
Clump-forming perennial with cup-shaped, nodding, semi-double, pink flowers, slender, branching, hairy stems, in early summer. Has pinnate, lobed, mid-green leaves. Is easily grown in any moist soil. **H** 60cm (24in), **S** 30cm (12in).

RED

Dicentra 'Stuart Boothman'
Tufted perennial with oval, finely cut, deep grey-green leaves. In spring–summer, produces arching sprays of heart-shaped, carmine flowers. **H** 30cm (12in), **S** 40cm (16in).

Lychnis coronaria
Clump-forming perennial, often grown as a biennial. From mid-to late summer, brilliant rose-crimson flowers are borne in panicles on branched, grey stems, above grey leaves. **H** 45–60cm (18–24in), **S** 45cm (18in).

Potentilla 'Arc-en-ciel'
Clump-forming perennial with arching stems bearing loose sprays of large, saucer-shaped, double, yellow-centred, red flowers in late spring and summer. Has rounded, 3-lobed, toothed, mid-green basal leaves. **H** and **S** 30cm (12in).

Crusea coccinea
Prostrate, creeping perennial with ovate, ribbed, light green leaves, 3–5cm (1¼–2in) long. Trumpet-shaped, bright red flowers, 2.5–4cm (1–1½in) long, in long-stalked, few-flowered, axillary clusters, are borne in summer–autumn. **H** 15cm (6in), **S** 20–40cm (8–16in).

Rhodiola heterodonta
Clump-forming perennial with heads of yellow or red, sometimes greenish flowers from spring to early summer. Stems bear toothed, blue-green leaves. **H** 45cm (18in), **S** 25cm (10in).

Coreopsis 'Limerock Ruby'
Upright perennial producing masses of daisy-like, ruby-red flower heads, on branched, slender stems, throughout summer. Has small lance-shaped, dark green leaves. **H** 40cm (16in), **S** 45cm (18in).

Ourisia coccinea
Mat-forming, evergreen perennial with rosettes of oval, toothed, strongly veined, bright green leaves. Loose racemes of tubular, nodding, rich red flowers are borne in mid- to late summer. **H** 20cm (8in), **S** 30cm (12in).

Potentilla atrosanguinea
Clump-forming perennial with hairy, palmate, strawberry-like leaves. Loose clusters of dark red flowers are borne throughout summer. **H** 45cm (18in), **S** 60cm (24in).

PURPLE

Polemonium carneum
Clump-forming perennial that carries clusters of cup-shaped, pink or lilac-pink flowers in early summer. Foliage is finely divided. **H** and **S** 45cm (18in).

Verbena rigida
Neat, compact perennial bearing heads of pale violet flowers from mid-summer onwards. Has lance-shaped, rough, mid-green leaves borne on flower stems. **H** 45–60cm (18–24in), **S** 30cm (12in).

Centaurea montana
Spreading perennial with many rather lax stems carrying, in early summer, one or more large, purple, blue, white or pink flower heads with thistle-like centres encircled by star-shaped ray petals. **H** 50cm (20in), **S** 60cm (24in).

Geranium macrorrhizum
Semi-evergreen, carpeting perennial bearing magenta flowers in early summer. Rounded, divided, aromatic leaves make good, weed-proof ground cover and assume bright tints in autumn. **H** 30–38cm (12–15in), **S** 60cm (24in).

Berkheya purpurea
Clump-forming perennial with large, daisy-like, lavender flower heads in summer. Has oblong-lance-shaped, spiny, silvery-grey basal leaves. **H** 60cm (24in), **S** 30cm (12in).

Geranium x magnificum
Clump-forming perennial with hairy, deeply lobed leaves and cup-shaped, prominently veined, violet-blue flowers borne in small clusters in summer. **H** 45cm (18in), **S** 60cm (24in).

Platycodon grandiflorus
(Balloon flower)
Neat, clump-forming perennial with clusters of large, balloon-like buds, opening to bell-shaped, purplish-blue flowers in summer. Stems are clothed with bluish leaves. **H** 45–60cm (18–24in), **S** 30–45cm (12–18in).

Tradescantia Andersoniana Group 'Purple Dome'
Clump-forming perennial with narrow, lance-shaped leaves, 15–30cm (6–12in) long. Has clusters of rich purple flowers, surrounded by 2 leaf-like bracts, in summer. **H** to 60cm (24in), **S** 45cm (18in).

Stokesia laevis
Perennial with overwintering, evergreen rosettes. In summer, cornflower-like, lavender- or purple-blue flower heads are borne freely. Leaves are narrow and mid-green. **H** and **S** 30–45cm (12–18in).

PURPLE

***Stachys macrantha* 'Superba'**
Clump-forming perennial with heart-shaped, soft, wrinkled, green leaves. Produces stout stems with whorls of hooded, purple-violet flowers in summer. **H** 30–45cm (12–18in), **S** 30–60cm (12–24in).

Nepeta x faassenii (Catmint)
Bushy, clump-forming perennial, useful for edging. Forms mounds of small, greyish-green leaves, from which loose spikes of tubular, soft lavender-blue flowers appear in early summer. **H** and **S** 45cm (18in).

Anemonopsis macrophylla
(False anemone)
Clump-forming perennial producing waxy, nodding, purple-blue flowers, borne on slender, branching stems in summer above fern-like leaves.
H 45–60cm (18–24in), **S** 50cm (20in).

BLUE

***Geranium* 'Johnson's Blue'**
Vigorous, clump-forming perennial with many divided leaves and cup-shaped, deep lavender-blue flowers borne throughout summer.
H 30cm (12in), **S** 60cm (24in).

Eryngium bourgatii
Clump-forming perennial that, from mid- to late summer, carries heads of thistle-like, blue-green, then lilac-blue, flowers on branched, wiry stems well above deeply cut, basal, grey-green leaves. **H** 45–60cm (18–24in), **S** 30cm (12in).

Polemonium caeruleum
(Jacob's ladder)
Clump-forming perennial. Clusters of cup-shaped, lavender-blue flowers with orange-yellow stamens open in summer amid finely divided foliage. **H** and **S** 45–60cm (18–24in).

***Catananche caerulea* 'Major'**
Perennial forming clumps of grassy, grey-green leaves, above which rise wiry, branching stems each carrying a daisy-like, lavender-blue flower head in summer. Propagate regularly by root cuttings. **H** 45–60cm (18–24in), **S** 30cm (24in).

Polemonium caeruleum
BRISE D'ANJOU ('Blanjou')
Clump-forming, short-lived perennial with clusters of cup-shaped, lavender-blue flowers in summer. Has finely divided, mid-green leaves with creamy-yellow margins. **H** 60cm (24in), **S** 25–30cm (10–12in).

Amsonia orientalis
Neat, clump-forming perennial. In summer, heads of small, star-shaped, grey-blue flowers open on tops of wiry stems clothed with green, sometimes greyish, leaves. **H** 45–60cm (18–24in), **S** 30–45cm (12–18in).

Eryngium variifolium
Evergreen, rosette-forming perennial with stiff stems that, in late summer, bear heads of thistle-like, grey-blue flowers, each with a collar of white bracts. Jagged-edged leaves are mid-green, marbled with white. **H** 45cm (18in), **S** 25cm (10in).

***Scabiosa caucasica* 'Clive Greaves'**
Clump-forming perennial that throughout summer has violet-blue flower heads with pincushion-like centres. Basal, mid-green leaves are lance-shaped and slightly lobed on the stems. **H** and **S** 45–60cm (18–24in).

***Geranium* ROZANNE ('Gerwat')**
Sprawling, deciduous perennial producing masses of large, shallowly cup-shaped, blue flowers during summer and into autumn. Rounded, deeply divided basal leaves are green with marbled, paler markings. **H** 35cm (14in), **S** 60cm (24in) or more.

Myosotidium hortensia
(Chatham Island forget-me-not)
Evergreen, clump-forming perennial bearing large clusters of forget-me-not-like, blue flowers in summer above a basal mound of large, ribbed, glossy leaves. **H** 45–60cm (18–24in), **S** 60cm (24in).

Veronica gentianoides
Mat-forming perennial with spikes of very pale blue flowers opening in early summer on tops of stems that arise from glossy, basal leaves. **H** and **S** 45cm (18in).

Parahebe perfoliata
(Digger's speedwell)
Evergreen sub-shrub with willowy stems clasped by leathery, glaucous leaves. Elegant, long, branching sprays of blue flowers are borne in summer. **H** 45–60cm (18–24in), **S** 45cm (18in).

Veronica peduncularis
Mat-forming perennial with ovate to lance-shaped, glossy, purple-tinged, mid-green leaves. Bears abundant, saucer-shaped, deep blue flowers, with small, white eyes, over a long period from early spring to summer. **H** to 10cm (4in), **S** 60cm (24in) or more.

Veronica spicata* subsp. *incana
Mat-forming perennial, densely covered with silver hairs, with linear to lance-shaped leaves. In summer, bears spikes of small, star-shaped, clear blue flowers. **H** and **S** 30cm (12in).

HOSTAS

Their luxuriant foliage and attractive habit have made hostas, or plantain lilies, increasingly sought after as garden plants. Native to the East, they add an exotic touch to waterside or damp, shady corners, and large patio containers. Hostas vary in size from plants a few centimetres in height, to tall forms that make clumps up to 1.5m (5ft) across. Their elegant, deciduous leaves appear in mid-spring and are incredibly diverse in shape, texture, and colour, with dramatic variegations and shadings. Many produce decorative flower spikes, which rise gracefully above the foliage in mid-summer and may be scented, according to variety. Although hostas are essentially shade- and moisture-loving plants, preferring rich, well-drained soils, they also tolerate drier soils. Protect the leaves from slug damage.

***H.* 'Cherry Berry'**

***H.* 'Devon Green'**

***H.* 'Antioch'**

***H.* 'Regal Splendor'**

***H.* 'Gold Edger'**

***H.* 'Invincible'**

H. nigrescens

H. sieboldiana

***H.* 'Night Before Christmas'**

***H.* 'Hadspen Blue'**

H. tokudama* f. *flavocircinalis

***H.* 'Ground Master'**

***H.* 'Minuteman'**

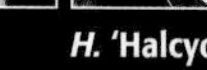

***H.* 'Halcyon'**

***H.* 'June'** ♡

H. lancifolia ♀

H. 'Fire and Ice'

H. 'Golden Prayers'

H. 'Fragrant Bouquet'

H. 'Golden Tiara' ♀

H. 'August Moon'

H. 'Whirlwind'

H. 'Brim Cup'

H. 'Hydon Sunset'

H. 'Blue Wedgwood'

H. 'Allan P. McConnell'

H. 'Dream Weaver'

H. 'Revolution'

H. 'Birchwood Parky's Gold'

H. 'So Sweet'

H. 'Remember Me'

H. 'Sagae' ♀

H. 'Ginko Craig'

H. 'Great Expectations'

H. 'Tattoo'

GREY

***Artemisia ludoviciana* 'Valerie Finnis'**
Semi-evergreen, upright then arching perennial with silvery-grey leaves, the lower ones are broad and lobed while the upper ones are narrow and spear-shaped. Bears spires of insignificant, yellowish flowers in late summer. **H** 60cm (2ft), **S** 90cm (3ft).

Stachys byzantina **(Lamb's tongue)**
Evergreen, mat-forming perennial with woolly, grey foliage that is excellent for a border front or as ground cover. Bears mauve-pink flowers in summer. **H** 30–38cm (12–15in), **S** 60cm (24in).

GREEN

***Mentha suaveolens* 'Variegata'**
(Variegated apple mint)
Spreading perennial with soft, woolly, mid-green leaves, splashed with white and cream, that smell of apples. Seldom produces flowers. **H** 30–45cm (12–18in), **S** 60cm (24in).

***Filipendula ulmaria* 'Aurea'**
Leafy perennial, grown for its divided foliage, which is bright golden-yellow in spring and pale green in summer. Clusters of creamy-white flowers are carried in branching heads in mid-summer. **H** and **S** 30cm (12in).

Hosta tokudama* f. *aureonebulosa
Slow-growing, clump-forming perennial bearing cup-shaped, puckered, blue leaves with irregular, cloudy-yellow centres. Racemes of trumpet-shaped, pale lilac-grey flowers, on scapes 40cm (16in) long, are produced mid-summer. **H** 45cm (18in), **S** 75cm (30in).

YELLOW

Sisyrinchium striatum
Semi-evergreen perennial that forms tufts of long, narrow, grey-green leaves. Bears slender spikes of purple-striped, straw-yellow flowers in summer. Self seeds freely. **H** 45–60cm (18–24in), **S** 30cm (12in).

***Origanum vulgare* 'Aureum'**
Woody-based perennial forming a dense mat of aromatic, golden-yellow, young leaves that turn pale yellow-green in mid-summer. Occasionally bears tiny, mauve flowers in summer. **H** in leaf 8cm (3in), **S** indefinite.

***Stachys byzantina* 'Primrose Heron'**
Evergreen, mat-forming perennial with woolly, yellowish-grey leaves, to 10cm (4in) long. Erect stems bear interrupted spikes of pink-purple flowers from early summer to early autumn. **H** 45cm (18in), **S** 60cm (24in).

Alchemilla mollis (Lady's mantle)
Clump-forming, ground-cover perennial that has rounded, pale green leaves with crinkled edges. Bears small sprays of tiny, bright greenish-yellow flowers, with conspicuous outer calyces, in mid-summer that may be dried. **H** and **S** 50cm (20in).

Calanthe striata
Deciduous, terrestrial orchid with erect spikes of fragrant, yellow or yellow-and-brown flowers, each with a 3-lobed lip, borne in late spring and early summer, before the 2–3 long, broadly oblong, ribbed leaves fully expand. **H** 80cm (32in), **S** 50cm (20in).

Patrinia triloba
Clump-forming perennial with broad, 3- to 5-lobed, bright green leaves that turn yellow in autumn. In summer upright stems bear panicles of small, fragrant, 5-petalled, bright yellow flowers. **H** 50cm (20in), **S** 30cm (12in).

***Oenothera fruticosa* 'Fyrverkeri'**
Clump-forming perennial that from mid- to late summer bears spikes of fragrant, cup-shaped flowers. Has reddish stems and glossy, mid-green foliage. **H** and **S** 30–38cm (12–15in).

Alchemilla conjuncta
Clump-forming perennial that has wavy, star-shaped leaves with pale margins. In mid-summer, bears loose clusters of tiny, greenish-yellow flowers, with conspicuous, outer calyces, which may be dried for winter decoration. **H** and **S** 30cm (12in).

***Ranunculus constantinopolitanus* 'Plenus'**
Clump-forming perennial with divided, toothed leaves sometimes spotted grey and white. Neat, pompon-like, double, yellow flowers appear in early summer. **H** 50cm (20in), **S** 30cm (12in).

***Helichrysum* 'Schwefellicht'**
Clump-forming perennial that bears silver-grey leaves and a mass of ever-lasting, fluffy, sulphur-yellow flowers from mid- to late summer. **H** 40–60cm (16–24in), **S** 30cm (12in).

Solidago x luteus
Clump-forming perennial. From mid-summer onwards, slender stems carry dense heads of bright creamy-yellow flowers above narrow, mid-green leaves. **H** 60cm (24in), **S** 75cm (30in).

YELLOW

***Geum* 'Lady Stratheden'**
Clump-forming perennial with lobed leaves and cup-shaped, double, bright yellow flowers with prominent, green stamens borne on slender, branching stems for a long period in summer. **H** 45–60cm (18–24in), **S** 45cm (18in).

Coreopsis verticillata
Bushy perennial with finely divided, dark green foliage and many tiny, star-shaped, golden flower heads borne throughout summer. Divide in spring. **H** 40–60cm (16–24in), **S** 30cm (12in).

Potentilla megalantha
Clump-forming perennial with large, palmate, hairy, soft green leaves. Large, rich yellow flowers are produced in summer. **H** 20cm (8in), **S** 15cm (6in).

Eriophyllum lanatum
Perennial forming low cushions of divided, silvery leaves. Daisy-like, yellow flower heads are produced freely in summer, usually singly, on grey stems. **H** and **S** 30cm (12in).

***Ranunculus acris* 'Flore Pleno'**
(Double meadow buttercup)
Clump-forming perennial. Wiry stems with lobed and cut leaves act as a foil for rosetted, double, golden-yellow flowers in late spring and early summer. **H** and **S** 45–60cm (18–24in).

Buphthalmum salicifolium
(Yellow ox-eye)
Spreading perennial that carries daisy-like, deep yellow flower heads singly on willowy stems throughout summer. May need staking. Divide regularly; spreads on rich soil. **H** 60cm (24in), **S** 90cm (36in).

Tropaeolum polyphyllum
Prostrate perennial with spurred, short, trumpet-shaped, rich yellow flowers, borne singly in summer above trailing, grey-green leaves and stems. May spread widely once established but is good on a bank. **H** 5–8cm (2–3in), **S** 30cm (12in) or more.

Coreopsis lanceolata
Bushy perennial that in summer freely produces daisy-like, bright yellow flower heads on branching stems. Lance-shaped leaves are borne on flower stems. Propagate by seed or division. **H** 45cm (18in), **S** 30cm (12in).

Hieracium lanatum
Clump-forming perennial that produces mounds of broad, downy, grey leaves, above which dandelion-like, yellow flower heads appear on wiry stems in summer. **H** 30–45cm (12–18in), **S** 30cm (12in).

ORANGE

Inula royleana
Upright, clump-forming perennial with dark green stems and hairy leaves. Bears solitary, orange-yellow flower heads, 10–12cm (4–5in) across, from mid-summer to early autumn. **H** 45–60cm (18–24in), **S** 45cm (18in).

***Libertia ixioides* 'Goldfinger'**
Evergreen, clump-forming rhizomatous perennial grown for its lance-shaped, golden-orange leaves, the colour intensifying in winter. Has short panicles of saucer-shaped, white flowers in summer. **H** and **S** 60cm (24in).

***Calceolaria* 'John Innes'**
Vigorous, evergreen, clump-forming perennial that in spring–summer produces large, pouch-like, reddish-brown-spotted, deep yellow flowers, several to each stem. Has broadly oval, basal, mid-green leaves. **H** 15–20cm (6–8in), **S** 25–30cm (10–12in).

Inula ensifolia
Clump-forming perennial with small, lance-shaped to elliptic leaves, bearing many daisy-like, yellow flower heads, singly on wiry stalks, in late summer. **H** and **S** 30cm (12in).

***Gaillardia* 'Oranges and Lemons'**
Upright, rather open perennial that produces daisy-like, yellow-tipped, peachy-orange flower heads all through summer. Has lance-shaped, toothed, hairy, mid-green leaves. Plants may be short-lived. Is excellent in a border. **H** and **S** 60cm (24in).

WHITE

Tricyrtis hirta* var. *alba
Upright, rhizomatous perennial that bears clusters of large, bell-shaped, spurred, white flowers, occasionally purple-spotted, in upper leaf axils of hairy, stem-clasping, dark green leaves during late summer and early autumn. **H** 45–60cm (18–24in), **S** 45cm (18in).

***Aspidistra elatior* 'Variegata'**
Evergreen, rhizomatous perennial with upright, narrow, glossy, dark green leaves which are longitudinally cream-striped. Occasionally has inconspicuous, cream to purple flowers near soil level. **H** 60cm (24in), **S** 45cm (18in).

***Glechoma hederacea* 'Variegata'**
(Variegated ground ivy)
Evergreen, carpeting perennial that has small, heart-shaped leaves, with white marbling, on trailing stems. Bears insignificant flowers in summer. Spreads rapidly but is useful for a container. **H** 15cm (6in), **S** indefinite.

PINK

Begonia grandis* subsp. *evansiana
Tuberous begonia with oval, toothed, often red- or bronze-tinged, olive-green leaves, up to 15cm (6in) long, and pendant fragrant, single, pink flowers, to 3cm (1¼in) across in late summer and autumn. **H** 60cm (24in), **S** 30cm (12in).

***Astrantia major* 'Roma'**
Clump-forming perennial bearing masses of sterile, pink flower heads, which gradually fade to green, borne on slender stems from summer until the first frosts. **H** and **S** 60cm (24in).

Astrantia maxima
Clump-forming perennial that bears rose-pink flower heads during summer-autumn. **H** 60cm (24in), **S** 30cm (12in).

***Schizostylis coccinea* 'Sunrise'**
Clump-forming, rhizomatous perennial that in early autumn produces spikes of large, shallowly cup-shaped, pink flowers above grassy, mid-green foliage. **H** 60cm (24in), **S** 23–30cm (9–12in).

Begonia taliensis
Erect, tuberous perennial with pointed, oval, light green leaves marbled silver and purple-brown. Produces many small, single, shell-pink flowers in late autumn. **H** 50cm (20in), **S** 35cm (14in).

***Diascia barberae* 'Blackthorn Apricot'**
Mat-forming perennial with narrowly heart-shaped, tapering leaves. From summer to autumn, produces loose racemes of apricot-pink flowers with small, narrow 'windows' and almost straight, downward-pointing spurs. **H** 25cm (10in), **S** to 50cm (20in).

***Sedum spectabile* 'Brilliant'**
(Ice-plant)
Clump-forming perennial that from late summer to autumn produces flat heads of bright rose-pink flowers. These are borne over a mass of fleshy, grey-green leaves and attract butterflies. **H** and **S** 30–45cm (12–18in).

Senecio pulcher
Perennial with leathery, hairy, dark green leaves. In summer–autumn produces handsome, daisy-like, yellow-centred, bright purplish-pink flower heads. **H** 45–60cm (18–24in), **S** 50cm (20in).

RED

Tellima grandiflora **Rubra Group**
Semi-evergreen, clump-forming perennial with a mass of hairy, basal, reddish-purple leaves, underlaid dark green. In late spring, erect stems bear spikes of bell-shaped, pinkish-cream flowers. **H** and **S** 60cm (24in).

Schizostylis coccinea **'Major'**
Rhizomatous perennial with long, narrow, grass-like leaves. Gladiolus-like spikes of cup-shaped, bright crimson flowers appear in autumn. **H** 60cm (24in) or more, **S** 30cm (12in) or more.

Cautleya spicata
Upright perennial that in summer and early autumn bears spikes of light orange or soft yellow flowers in maroon-red bracts. Has handsome, long, mid-green leaves. Needs a sheltered site and rich, deep soil. **H** 60cm (24in), **S** 50cm (20in).

SEDUM

With fleshy, drought-resistant foliage and heads of tiny, star-shaped flowers from summer to autumn, *Sedum* are useful perennials for herbaceous borders and gravel gardens, while their nectar-rich blooms also make them a good choice for wildlife and naturalistic schemes. The flowers of the taller herbaceous plants are mostly in shades of pink and red, although white and yellow blooms are also available. Many have purple-tinged or variegated foliage, which extends their season of interest; the faded flowers and seed heads also provide a colourful display in late autumn and winter. Plants thrive in full sun and free-draining soil, and will bulk up quickly. Divide them regularly to prevent clumps flopping open, and stake taller varieties. Protect young growth from slugs in spring and early summer.

S. telephium **'Purple Emperor'** 🏆

S. erythrostictum **'Mediovariegatum'**

S. 'Ruby Glow' 🏆

S. 'Red Cauli' 🏆

S. spectabile **'Iceberg'**

S. 'Matrona' 🏆

S. telephium **'Gooseberry Fool'**

S. telephium **'Strawberries and Cream'**

S. aizoon **'Aurantiacum'** ①

PURPLE

Tulbaghia violacea
Vigorous, semi-evergreen, clump-forming perennial that in summer–autumn carries umbels of lilac-purple or lilac-pink flowers above a mass of narrow, glaucous, blue-grey leaves.
H 45–60cm (18–24in), **S** 30cm (12in).

Liriope muscari
Evergreen, spreading perennial that in autumn carries spikes of thickly clustered, rounded-bell-shaped, lavender or purple-blue flowers among narrow, glossy, dark green leaves.
H 30cm (12in), **S** 45cm (18in).

***Physostegia virginiana* 'Vivid'**
(Obedient plant)
Erect, compact perennial that in late summer and early autumn bears spikes of tubular, dark lilac-pink flowers that can be placed in postion. Has toothed, mid-green leaves. **H** and **S** 30–60cm (12–24in).

Bergenia purpurascens
Evergreen, clump-forming perennial with oval to spoon-shaped, flat, dark green leaves turning to beetroot-red in late autumn. In spring bears racemes of open cup-shaped rich red flowers.
H 40cm (16in), **S** 60cm (42in) or more.

***Ophiopogon planiscapus* 'Nigrescens'**
Evergreen, spreading, clump-forming perennial, grown for its distinctive, grass-like, black leaves. Racemes of lilac flowers in summer are followed by black fruits. **H** 23cm (9in), **S** 30cm (12in).

***Heuchera* 'Plum Pudding'**
Evergreen, clump-forming perennial with rounded, deeply lobed, silvery-purple leaves. Long sprays of tiny, bell-shaped, pinkish flowers are borne in summer. Rejuvenate regularly to keep it healthy. A good foil for other plants.
H 50cm (20in), **S** 30cm (12in).

***Agastache* 'Black Adder'**
Upright perennial with whorled spires of smoky, purple-blue flowers from early summer to mid-autumn, above oval, pointed, toothed, aromatic, mid-green leaves. Is good for attracting insects.
H 60cm (24in), **S** 45cm (18in).

***Geranium* 'Orion'**
Deciduous, clump-forming perennial producing masses of large, shallowly cup-shaped, violet-blue flowers from early summer until mid-autumn. Has deeply lobed, mid-green basal leaves, each divided to the base into 7 sections.
H and **S** 50cm (20in).

WHITE

***Helleborus niger* 'Potter's Wheel'**
Evergreen, clump-forming perennial with divided, deep green leaves and cup-shaped, nodding, pure white flowers, with overlapping petals and green "eyes", borne in winter or early spring. **H** and **S** 30cm (12in).

***Helleborus niger* 'HGC Josef Lemper'**
Evergreen, clump-forming, upright perennial with divided, rich, dark green leaves. Slightly fragrant, rounded, pure white flowers, with overlapping petals, are borne on sturdy stems from mid-autumn to late winter. **H** to 30cm (12in), **S** 45cm (18in).

Helleborus* x *nigercors
Evergreen, clump-forming perennial with matt green leaves, to 35cm (14in) long with 3–5 broad, evenly toothed segments. From mid-winter–early spring bears branched clusters of 10–20 saucer-shaped, green-tinted, cream or white flowers. **H** 40cm (16in), **S** 50cm (20in).

LENTEN ROSES

Helleborus x hybridus (lenten rose) are the hybrids between *H. orientalis* and other species. They flower winter and spring, and are so varied that they're often sold by description or collection, rather than as named varieties. Their single or double flowers last for a few months and open in a range of whites, yellows, pinks and purples, often spotted or with darker-edges. Most are evergreen, with large, toothed, divided leaves, and prefer moist, neutral to alkaline soil, but need protection from strong, winter winds. They will naturally hybridize and self-seed, and, it's worth allowing your own seedlings to develop.

Harvington hybrids
[single, white]

[single, red]

[double, slate]

Bradfield hybrids
[double, apricot with spots]

[double, plum]

Ashwood Garden hybrids
[double, black]

[single, green]

[double, white]

[double, white with spots]

Harvington hybrids
[double, apricot]

[single, white with spots]

[single, apricot]

Ashwood Garden hybrids [double, pink]

[single, yellow]

[single, yellow with spots]

HEUCHERA AND X HEUCHERELLA

Once regarded as a useful cottage garden ground-covering perennial, grown for its sprays of red flowers and evergreen foliage, the selections of *Heuchera* bred in recent years have transformed this humble plant into a horticultural superstar. The leaves come in many colours, from near black and purple, to pink, peach, and yellow-green, and plants are ideal for containers as well as borders. Selections of x *Heucherella*, a cross between *Heuchera* and *Tiarella*, are smaller and more dainty. Plant all types in moist but well-drained soil and partial shade, but site brighter-leaved cultivars in a sunnier position. Most plants should be split and replanted every few years to prevent the crown from becoming woody and to keep them in good health.

***Heuchera* 'Black Beauty'**

***Heuchera* 'Ginger Ale'**

***Heuchera* 'Midnight Rose'**

***Heuchera* 'Chocolate Ruffles'**

***Heuchera* CRÈME BRÛLÉE ('Tnheu041')**

***Heuchera sanguinea* 'Snow Storm'**

***Heuchera* 'Pewter Moon'**

***Heuchera* 'Purple Petticoats'** 🏆

***Heuchera* 'Southern Comfort'**

***Heuchera* 'Silver Scrolls'**

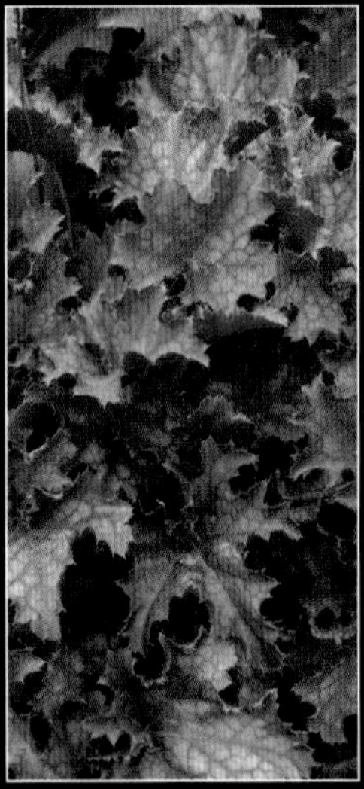

***Heuchera* 'Blackbird'** 🏆

***Heuchera* 'Green Spice'**

***Heuchera* 'Ebony and Ivory'**

***Heuchera* 'Can-can'** 🏆

***Heuchera* 'Beauty Colour'**

x *Heucherella tiarelloides* 'Kimono'

***Heuchera* 'Tiramisu'**

***Heuchera* 'Peach Flambé'**

***Heuchera* 'Peppermint Spice'**

***Heuchera* 'Lime Rickey'**

x *Heucherella tiarelloides* 'Stoplight'

***Heuchera* 'Cinnabar Silver'**

***Heuchera* 'Amber Waves'**

***Heuchera* 'Georgia Peach'**

GREEN

Ophiopogon japonicus
Evergreen, clump or mat-forming perennial with grass-like, glossy, dark green foliage. Spikes of lilac flowers in late summer are followed by blue-black berries. **H** 30cm (12in), **S** indefinite, **S** indefinite

***Helleborus* x *sternii* 'Boughton Beauty'**
Evergreen, clump-forming perennial with purple-pink stems and divided, veined, mid-green leaves. Cup-shaped, pink-purple flowers, with green insides, are borne in terminal clusters in winter–early spring. **H** and **S** 50–60cm (20–24in).

Helleborus foetidus
(Stinking hellebore)
Evergreen, clump-forming perennial with deeply divided, dark green leaves and, in late winter and early spring, panicles of cup-shaped, red-margined, pale green flowers. **H** and **S** 45cm (18in).

***Helleborus foetidus* Wester Flisk Group**
Evergreen, semi-woody perennial with small, cup-shaped, purple-rimmed pale green flowers, borne on floppy, red-green stems in winter and spring. Has red-stalked, dark grey-green leaves divided into slender, slightly toothed leaflets. **H** 60–90cm (24–36in), **S** 45cm (18in).

***Dianella caerulea* CASSA BLUE ('Dbb03')**
Evergreen, tuft-forming perennial with narrowly lance-shaped, upright, dusky-blue leaves arising from a slowly creeping rootstock. Star shaped, blue flowers in panicles in spring are followed by blue berries. **H** 50cm (20in), **S** 20cm (8in).

Helleborus odorus
Semi-evergreen, clump-forming perennial with deeply divided, deep green basal leaves, hairy beneath, with 5 central leaflets. From early winter–early spring bears clusters of 3–5 fragrant, saucer-shaped, bright green to yellow-green flowers. **H** and **S** to 30cm (12in).

Soleirolia soleirolii
(Baby's tears, Mind-your-own-business)
Usually evergreen, invasive, prostrate perennial with small, round, vivid green leaves that form a carpet. May choke other plants if not controlled. **H** 5cm (2in), **S** indefinite.

Helleborus cyclophyllus
Clump-forming perennial with palmate, deeply divided, bright green leaves. In early spring produces shallowly cup-shaped, yellow-green flowers with prominent, yellowish-white stamens. **H** 60cm (24in), **S** 45cm (18in).

WHITE

Pleioblastus variegatus
(Dwarf white-stripe bamboo)
Evergreen, slow-spreading bamboo with narrow, slightly downy, white-striped leaves. Stems are branched near the base. **H** 80cm (30in), **S** indefinite.

Sasa veitchii
Evergreen, slow-spreading bamboo. Leaves, 25cm (10in) long, soon develop white edges. Stems, often purple, produce a single branch at each node. White powder appears beneath nodes. **H** to 1.5m (5ft), **S** indefinite.

Lagurus ovatus (Hare's-tail grass)
Tuft-forming, annual grass that in early summer bears dense, egg-shaped, soft panicles of white flower spikes, with golden stamens, lasting well into autumn. Leaves are long, narrow and flat. Self seeds readily. **H** 45cm (18in), **S** 15cm (6in).

Cortaderia selloana
'Sunningdale Silver'
Evergreen, clump-forming, perennial grass with narrow, sharp-edged, recurved leaves, 1.5m (5ft) long. Bears long-lasting, feathery panicles of creamy-white spikelets in late summer. **H** 2.1m (7ft), **S** 1.2m (4ft).

***Miscanthus sinensis* 'Zebrinus'**
Herbaceous, clump-forming, perennial grass. Leaves, hairy beneath, have transverse, yellowish-white ring markings. May carry awned, hairy, white spikelets in fan-shaped panicles in autumn. **H** 1.2m (4ft), **S** 45cm (1½ft).

Luzula nivea (Snowy woodrush)
Evergreen, slow-spreading, perennial rush with fairly dense clusters of shining, white flower spikes in early summer. Leaves are edged with white hairs. **H** 60cm (24in), **S** 45–60cm (18–24in).

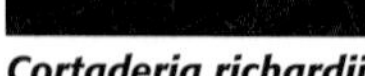

Cortaderia richardii
Evergreen, clump-forming, perennial grass with blade-like, sharply edged, upright, olive-green leaves. In summer has plume-like, 1-sided, parchment-coloured panicles on tall stems. **H** 2.5m (8ft), **S** 1m (3ft).

Calamagrostis brachytricha
Herbaceous, clump-forming, perennial grass with linear, arching, grey-green leaves. In late summer has tall erect stems bearing slender, grey-green inflorescences in narrow panicles, which last into winter, turning straw coloured. **H** 1.4m (4½ft), **S** 50cm (20in).

***Miscanthus sinensis* 'Yakushima Dwarf'**
Compact, herbaceous, clump-forming, perennial grass with fine, arching, silvery-green leaves borne on short, upright stems. In late summer produces plume-like panicles of long-lasting, grey-white spikelets. **H** 1m (3ft), **S** 60cm (24in).

***Cortaderia selloana* 'Silver Comet'**
Evergreen, clump-forming, perennial grass with very narrow, sharp-edged, recurved leaves, 1m (3ft) long, that have silver margins. Carries plume-like panicles of spikelets from late summer. **H** 1.2–1.5m (4–5ft), **S** 1m (3ft).

***Miscanthus sinensis* var. *condensatus* 'Cosmopolitan'**
Herbaceous, clump-forming, perennial grass with white-striped leaves borne on upright, stout stems. Plume-like panicles of silver-white spikelets appear from late summer. Dried stems remain attractive into winter. **H** 2m (6ft), **S** 80cm (32in).

RED

Chionochloa rubra
Evergreen, tussock-forming, perennial grass with linear, arching, tightly inrolled, reddish-green leaves. In summer produces panicles of dainty, bronze-coloured spikelets amid the leaves. Makes a superb potted specimen. **H** and **S** 70cm (28in).

***Eragrostis curvula* 'Totnes Burgundy'**
Herbaceous, densely tufted, perennial grass with narrowly linear, arching, dark green leaves, which turn dark burgundy-red from the tips downwards. Nodding panicles of brownish spikelets are borne in summer. **H** 90cm (36in), **S** 60cm (24in).

***Imperata cylindrica* 'Rubra'**
Herbaceous, clump-forming, perennial grass. Linear, upright, bright green leaves turn red in late summer and autumn, dying down in winter. Narrow, spike-like panicles of silvery-white spikelets are borne occasionally, in late summer. **H** and **S** 50cm (20in) or more.

Elegia capensis
Evergreen, clump-forming perennial with tall, horsetail-like, arching stems bearing whorls of soft, slender, dark green, needle-shaped, leaf-like shoots. Stout, red-green shoots, with papery sheaths at each node, are produced from the base in spring. **H** 1.5m (5ft), **S** 1m (3ft).

***Molinia caerulea* subsp. *caerulea* 'Heidebraut'**
Herbaceous, clump-forming, erect, perennial grass with linear, mid-green leaves that turn golden-yellow in autumn. Has masses of tall, arching stems bearing purplish spikelets in late summer. **H** 1.5m (5ft), **S** 60cm (24in).

RED

***Miscanthus sinensis* 'Flamingo'**
Herbaceous, clump-forming, perennial grass with narrow, arching, mid-green leaves borne on sturdy stems. In late summer has plume-like panicles of feathery, pinkish-red spikelets. These remain in good shape well into winter. **H** 1.5m (5ft), **S** 60cm (24in).

***Miscanthus sinensis* 'Gracillimus'**
Herbaceous, clump-forming, perennial grass with very narrow leaves, hairy beneath, often turning bronze. May bear fan-shaped panicles of awned, hairy, white spikelets in early autumn. **H** 1.2m (4ft), **S** 45cm (11/2ft).

PURPLE

***Melica altissima* 'Atropurpurea'**
Evergreen, tuft-forming, perennial grass with broad leaves, short-haired beneath. Purple spikelets in narrow panicles, 10cm (4in) long, hang from the tops of stems during summer. **H** and **S** 60cm (24in).

***Phyllostachys nigra* (Black bamboo)**
Evergreen, clump-forming bamboo with greenish-brown stems that turn black in second season. Almost unmarked culm sheaths bear bristled auricles and mid-green leaves. Flowers are rarely produced. **H** 6–8m (20–25ft), **S** indefinite.

GREEN

***Molinia caerulea* subsp. *arundinacea* 'Transparent'**
Herbaceous, clump-forming, erect, perennial grass with linear, mid-green leaves that turn straw-yellow in autumn. Tall, supple stems bear open panicles of purplish-green spikelets in summer. **H** 2m (6ft), **S** 60cm (24in).

***Pennisetum villosum* (Feather-top)**
Herbaceous, tuft-forming, perennial grass with long-haired stems. In autumn has panicles of creamy-pink spikelets, fading to pale brown, with long, bearded bristles. **H** to 1m (3ft), **S** 50cm (20in).

Stipa calamagrostis
Herbaceous or semi-evergreen, perennial grass forming tufts of linear, inrolled, bluish-green leaves, turning yellowish in autumn. In summer has feathery, arching panicles of silvery-white spikelets, which age to reddish brown. **H** and **S** 80cm (32in).

***Hordeum jubatum* (Foxtail barley, Squirrel tail grass)**
Tufted, short-lived perennial or annual grass. In summer to early autumn has flat, arching, feathery, plume-like flower spikes with silky awns. **H** 30–60cm (12–24in), **S** 30cm (12in).

***Thamnocalamus crassinodus* 'Kew Beauty'**
Evergreen or semi-evergreen, clump-forming bamboo with small, lance-shaped, greyish-green leaves on arching, blue-grey stems that age gradually to reddish-brown. Needs shelter. **H** 3m (10ft), **S** 1.5m (5ft).

***Juncus effusus* f. *spiralis* (Corkscrew rush)**
Evergreen, tuft-forming, perennial rush with leafless stems that twist and curl and are often prostrate. Fairly dense, greenish-brown flower panicles form in summer. **H** 1m (3ft), **S** 60cm (2ft).

Stipa gigantea (Golden oats)
Evergreen, tuft-forming, perennial grass with narrow leaves, 45cm (18in) or more long. In summer carries elegant, open panicles of silvery spikelets, with long awns and dangling, golden anthers, which persist well into winter. **H** 2.5m (8ft), **S** 1m (3ft).

Phyllostachys nigra f. henonis
Evergreen, clump-forming bamboo with bristled auricles on culm sheaths and a profusion of leaves. **H** 10m (30ft), **S** 2–3m (6–10ft).

Phyllostachys viridiglaucescens
Evergreen, clump-forming bamboo with greenish-brown stems that arch at the base. Has white powder beneath nodes. **H** 6–8m (20–25ft), **S** indefinite.

Phyllostachys bambusoides
(Timber bamboo)
Evergreen, clump-forming bamboo with stout, erect, green stems. Bears leaf sheaths with prominent bristles, and large, broad mid-green leaves. **H** 6–8m (20–25ft), **S** indefinite.

Pseudosasa japonica
(Arrow bamboo, Metake)
Evergreen, clump-forming bamboo that may run. Has long-persistent, roughly pubescent, brown sheaths and broad leaves, 35cm (14in) long. **H** 5m (15ft), **S** indefinite.

Shibataea kumasasa
Evergreen, clump-forming bamboo with stubby, side branches on greenish-brown stems. Leaves are 5–10cm (2–4in) long. **H** 1–1.5m (3–5ft), **S** 30cm (1ft).

Semiarundinaria fastuosa
(Narihira bamboo)
Evergreen, clump-forming bamboo with 15cm (6in) long leaves and short, tufted branches at each node. Culm sheaths open to reveal polished, purplish interiors. **H** 6m (20ft), **S** indefinite.

Ampelodesmos mauritanica
Dense, evergreen, clump-forming, perennial grass with linear, grey-green leaves, to 1m (3ft) long, with dark green undersides. In summer, long-lasting one-sided panicles of purplish-green flowers are borne on upright, lofty stems. **H** 2.5m (8ft), **S** 1m (3ft).

Chimonobambusa timidissinoda
Vigorous, evergreen, rhizomatous bamboo with curiously prominent, green stems, flared at each node. Lance-shaped, dark green leaves have a feathery look. May spread. **H** and **S** 5m (16ft) or more.

GREEN

Chasmanthium latifolium
Herbaceous, clump-forming, perennial grass with broadly lance-shaped, short-stemmed, light green leaves that turn pale beige in winter. In summer has open panicles of oat-like, arching, green spikelets aging to beige. **H** 1m (3ft), **S** 60cm (24in).

Helictotrichon sempervirens **(Blue oat grass)**
Evergreen, tufted, perennial grass with stiff, silvery-blue leaves up to 30cm (12in) or more long. Produces erect panicles of straw-coloured flower spikes in summer. **H** 1m (3ft), **S** 60cm (2ft).

***Yushania anceps* 'Pitt White'**
Very vigorous, evergreen, rhizomatous, clump-forming bamboo with upright, shiny, dark green stems that arch with age. Produces almost weeping branches of narrowly lance-shaped, fresh green leaves, with purple-tinted stalks. **H** 10m (30ft), **S** indefinite.

Chusquea culeou **(Chilean bamboo)**
Slow-growing, evergreen, clump-forming bamboo. Bears long-lasting culm sheaths, shining white when young, at the swollen nodes of stout, solid stems. **H** to 5m (15ft), **S** 2.5m (8ft) or more.

***Luzula sylvatica* 'Hohe Tatra'**
Evergreen, mound-forming, perennial sedge with broadly linear, bright golden-yellow leaves turning yellowish-green in summer. Short stems bear open panicles of brown flowers in summer. **H** 40cm (16in), **S** 30cm (12in).

YELLOW

Phyllostachys aurea **(Golden bamboo)**
Vigorous, evergreen, clump-forming bamboo with upright, grooved, yellow-green stems and cup-shaped swellings beneath each node. Has narrowly lance-shaped, pointed, green leaves. **H** 6m (20ft), **S** 4m (13ft) or more.

***Carex oshimensis* 'Evergold'**
Evergreen, tuft-forming, perennial sedge with narrow, yellow-striped leaves, 20cm (8in) long. Solid, triangular stems may carry insignificant flower spikes in summer. **H** 20cm (8in), **S** 15–20cm (6–8in).

Stipa tenuissima
Deciduous, tuft-forming, perennial grass with narrowly linear, upright, tightly inrolled, bright green leaves. From early summer has plume-like panicles of silvery-green spikelets, turning to pale beige as seeds form. **H** 60cm (24in), **S** 40cm (16in).

***Deschampsia cespitosa* 'Goldtau'**
Evergreen, tuft-forming, perennial grass with cloud-like panicles of tiny, golden-yellow spikelets in summer. Both spikelets and the linear, sharp-edged, dark green leaves turn golden in autumn. **H** 70cm (28in), **S** 50cm (20in).

ORANGE

***Alopecurus pratensis* 'Aureovariegatus'** (Golden foxtail)
Herbaceous, tuft-forming, perennial grass with yellow or yellowish-green-streaked leaves and dense flower spikes in summer. **H** and **S** 23–30cm (9–12in).

***Spartina pectinata* 'Aureomarginata'**
Herbaceous, spreading, rhizomatous grass with long, arching, yellow-striped leaves, which turn orange-brown in late autumn to winter. **H** to 2m (6ft), **S** indefinite.

***Panicum virgatum* 'Northwind'**
Herbaceous, clump-forming, erect, perennial grass with broad, dark bluish-green leaves turning golden-yellow in autumn, when tall, narrow panicles of pinkish-green spikelets are borne and age to silvery-green. **H** 1.5m (5ft), **S** 90cm (36in).

Pleioblastus viridistriatus
Evergreen, slow-spreading bamboo with purple stems and broad, softly downy, bright yellow leaves with green stripes. **H** 1.5m (5ft), **S** indefinite.

Phyllostachys vivax* f. *aureocaulis
Evergreen, clump-forming, slow-growing bamboo with bright lemon-yellow stems. Narrowly lance-shaped, dark evergreen leaves make the perfect foil for the stems. **H** 6m (20ft), **S** 3m (10ft) or more.

***Hakonechloa macra* 'Aureola'**
Slow-growing, herbaceous, shortly rhizomatous grass with purple stems and green-striped, yellow leaves that age to reddish-brown. Open panicles of reddish-brown flower spikes appear in early autumn and last into winter. **H** 40cm (16in), **S** 45–60cm (18–24in).

Stipa lessoniana
(Pheasant's tail grass)
Evergreen/semi-evergreen, tuft-forming, perennial grass with linear, olive-green leaves tinted orange. In summer, bears arching, open panicles of tiny, purplish-green spikelets. Has good winter colour and form. **H** 50cm (20in), **S** 80cm (32in).

Carex flagellifera
Evergreen, tuft-forming, perennial sedge with grass-like, reddish-brown leaves, upright, then arching, to the ground. Triangular stems bear insignificant, brown flower spikes in summer. Is good for winter colour. **H** 80cm (32in), **S** 60cm (24in) or more.

PURPLE

Athyrium niponicum* var. *pictum
'Burgundy Lace'
Deciduous fern with a slow-creeping, reddish-brown rhizome and broadly triangular, divided, spreading fronds of metallic purplish-bronze with silver-grey tips and bright pink-purple veins. **H** 50cm (20in), **S** 40cm (16in).

***Athyrium* 'Ghost'**
Deciduous fern producing lance-shaped, rather upright, silvery-white fronds, with contrasting, purplish-green veins, in spring. Coloration is most pronounced in spring. **H** 60cm (24in), **S** 20cm (8in) or more.

GREEN

Polystichum setiferum
'Pulcherrimum Bevis'
Evergreen or semi-evergreen fern with broadly lance-shaped, daintily cut, sharp-edged fronds that are yellowish-green in spring and mature to a glossy, rich dark green. **H** 60cm (24in), **S** 75cm (30in).

Blechnum penna-marina
Fast-growing, evergreen, carpeting fern. Has narrow, ladder-like, dark green fronds, red-tinged when young. Outer, sterile fronds are spreading; inner, fertile ones erect. **H** 15–30cm (6–12in), **S** 30–45cm (12–18in).

Dicksonia antarctica
(Australian tree fern)
Evergreen, tree-like fern. Stout trunks are covered with brown fibres and crowned by spreading, somewhat arching, broadly lance-shaped, much-divided, palm-like fronds. **H** 10m (30ft) or more, **S** 4m (12ft).

Asplenium trichomanes
(Maiden-hair spleenwort)
Semi-evergreen fern that has long, slender, tapering fronds with glossy, black, later brown, midribs bearing many rounded-oblong, bright green pinnae. Is suitable for limestone soils. **H** 15cm (6in), **S** 15–30cm (6–12in).

***Polystichum setiferum* Divisilobum Group**
Evergreen or semi-evergreen fern. Broadly lance-shaped or oval, soft-textured, much-divided, spreading fronds are clothed with white scales as they unfurl. **H** 60cm (24in), **S** 45cm (18in).

Adiantum pedatum
(Northern maidenhair fern)
Semi-evergreen fern with a stout, creeping rootstock. Dainty, divided, finger-like, mid-green fronds are produced on glossy, dark brown or blackish stems. **H** and **S** to 45cm (18in).

Thelypteris palustris
(Marsh buckler fern, Marsh fern)
Deciduous fern. Has strong, erect, lance-shaped, pale green fronds, with widely separated, deeply cut pinnae, produced from wiry, creeping, blackish rhizomes. Grows well beside a pool or stream. **H** 75cm (30in), **S** 30cm (12in).

***Polystichum setiferum* Plumosodivisilobum Group**
Evergreen fern that produces a "shuttlecock" of lance-shaped, divided fronds with segments narrowed towards the frond tips; lower pinnae often overlap. **H** 1.2m (4ft), **S** 1m (3ft).

Cyrtomium falcatum
(Fishtail fern, Holly fern)
Evergreen fern. Fronds are lance-shaped and have holly-like, glossy, dark green pinnae; young fronds are often covered with whitish or brown scales. **H** 30–60cm (12–24in), **S** 30–45cm (12–18in).

Adiantum aleuticum
Semi-evergreen fern with a short root-stock. Has glossy, dark brown or blackish stems and dainty, divided, finger-like fronds, with blue-green pinnae, that are more crowded than those of *A. pedatum*. Grows well in alkaline soils. **H** and **S** to 45cm (18in).

***Polypodium interjectum* 'Cornubiense'**
Evergreen fern with narrow, lance-shaped, divided, fresh green fronds; segments are further sub-divided to give an overall lacy effect. **H** and **S** 25–30cm (10–12in).

Polypodium vulgare
(Common polypody, Polypody)
Evergreen fern with narrow, lance-shaped, divided, herring-bone-like, mid-green fronds, arising from creeping rhizomes covered with copper-brown scales. Suits a rock garden. **H** and **S** 25–30cm (10–12in).

GREEN

Asplenium scolopendrium
(Hart's-tongue fern)
Evergreen fern with stocky rhizomes and tongue-shaped, leathery, bright green fronds. Is good in alkaline soils. **H** 45–75cm (18–30in), **S** to 45cm (18in).

Asplenium scolopendrium
Marginatum Group
Evergreen fern with stocky, upright rhizomes and lobed, slightly frilled, tongue-shaped fronds that are leathery and bright green. Is good in alkaline soils. **H** and **S** 30cm (12in) or more.

Adiantum venustum
Deciduous fern. Bears delicate, pale green fronds, tinged brown when young, consisting of many small, triangular pinnae, on glossy stems. **H** 23cm (9in), **S** 30cm (12in).

pH

Blechnum chilense
Splendid evergreen fern with broadly lance-shaped, leathery, dark green fronds on upright, scaly brownish stems arise from a creeping rootstock. Eventually forms a large colony. **H** and **S** 1m (3ft).

pH

Polystichum tsussimense
Evergreen fern bearing broadly lance-shaped, rather leathery, dark green fronds with narrowly oblong, spiny toothed, pointed pinnae. Is suitable for a shaded rock garden or alpine house. **H** 25cm (10in), **S** 20cm (8in).

Dryopteris wallichiana
(Wallich's wood fern)
Deciduous, clump-forming or often solitary fern with an erect rhizome and a 'shuttlecock' of lance-shaped, divided, bright yellow-green fronds, ageing to dark green with scaly, brownish-black stems. **H** 90cm (3ft), **S** 30cm (12in).

Dryopteris erythrosora
(Japanese shield fern)
Usually evergreen, clump-forming fern with broadly triangular, arching, shiny, coppery-red flushed, pinkish-green ageing to bronze then bright green.
H 40cm (16in), **S** 30cm (12in).

Asplenium ceterach (Rusty-back fern)
Semi-evergreen fern with lance-shaped, leathery, dark green fronds divided into alternate, bluntly rounded lobes. Backs of young fronds are covered with silvery scales that mature to reddish-brown.
H and **S** 15cm (6in).

Cryptogramma crispa (Parsley fern)
Deciduous fern with broadly oval to triangular, finely divided, bright pale green fronds that resemble parsley. In autumn, fronds turn bright rusty-brown and persist during winter.
H 15–23cm (6–9in), **S** 15–30cm (6–12in).

Dryopteris filix-mas (Male fern)
Deciduous or semi-evergreen fern with 'shuttlecocks' of elegantly arching, upright, broadly lance-shaped, mid-green fronds that arise from crowns of large, upright, brown-scaled rhizomes. **H** 1.2m (4ft), **S** 1m (3ft).

Polystichum munitum
(Giant holly fern)
Evergreen fern with erect, leathery, lance-shaped, dark green fronds that consist of small, spiny-margined pinnae. **H** 1.2m (4ft), **S** 30cm (1ft).

Polypodium cambricum
'Richard Kayse'
Evergreen fern with a slow-creeping rhizome and lance-shaped to triangular-oval, lacy, bright green fronds. New fronds appear in late summer and die back in late spring. Sori are yellow in winter. **H** 30cm (12in), **S** 20cm (8in).

ANNUALS, BIENNIALS AND BEDDING

Invaluable for their rapid growth, instant colour and relatively low cost, annuals and biennials are ideal gap fillers between newly planted trees and shrubs, as well as in perennial displays that might need reviving after the first flush of spring. They are also useful as bedding in formal schemes, such as parterres, and in containers of all types. An important ingredient in cottage gardens and wildflower meadows, they also help to shape informal schemes.

ANNUALS, BIENNIALS, AND BEDDING

Indispensable in pots, containers and borders, many of these colourful plants flower from early summer to early autumn, and some also provide beautiful foliage. Combine them with plants that bloom in winter and spring to brighten up your garden all year round.

ABOVE Shades of pink
Create an elegant basket using shades of pink. Dark cherry pink petunias, pale busy Lizzies, starry isotomas, and raspberry-coloured diascias combine beautifully.

What are annuals and biennials?

Annuals are plants that grow, bloom, set seed and die in a single growing season. Biennials complete their lifecycle in two seasons: most are sown in late spring or summer and make leafy growth in the first year, then flower, set seed and die in the next. Bedding plants usually refer to half-hardy or tender annuals that are traditionally used in summer flower schemes. Some plants in this category are technically perennials or even shrubs, but are referred to as annuals because they are used for just one season. Examples include pelargoniums, nemesias, and brachyscome, which are perennials, and marguerites (*Argyranthemum* species), and fuchsias, which are tender shrubs. Plants in this group are also sometimes described as "summer seasonals" and "spring seasonals".

BELOW Summer harmonies
Combine the shapes and colours of annuals for a balanced display. Begonias, heliotropes, silver-leaved senecio, and zinnias create a vibrant mix.

Growing annuals and biennials

Plants in this category can be grown from seed, bought as young seedlings known as "plug" plants, or purchased as mature specimens ready to plant.

Sowing seed is the most cost-effective option if you have a large space or lots of containers to fill; there are many half hardy or frost-tender types that are very easy to grow in pots or trays on a windowsill or in a greenhouse, including petunias, French marigolds (*Tagetes*), and tobacco plants (*Nicotiana*). The seedlings should be hardened off for a few weeks in spring by placing them outside during the day and bringing them back under cover at night. Then plant them outside in late spring when all danger of frost has passed.

Hardy annuals are easier still, as they can be sown outside in spring where they are to flower. For earlier summer blooms, plants like love-in-a-mist (*Nigella*) and poppies (*Papaver rhoeas*) can be sown in early autumn in free-draining soil. Sow your seeds in straight lines or curves, so that you can distinguish them from weed seedlings when they germinate.

For winter and spring colour, most suitable plants, such as violas, are raised from seed sown in summer. Alternatively buy young plants in the autumn.

Biennials can be grown from seed or bought as plug plants in the summer before they bloom. Find a quiet corner of the garden to sow your seed as they will be there for many months, and may be swamped by other plants if sown directly into a summer bed or border.

Ornamental features

Annuals and biennials are available in a wide range of shapes and sizes, from low hummock-forming cultivars of *Ageratum houstonianum* and trailing petunias to the tall spires of foxgloves (*Digitalis purpurea*) and dramatic Scotch thistles (*Onopordum acanthium*) that shoot up to 1.8m (6ft).

Flowers offer a vast choice of colours and forms, including scented types such as heliotropes (*Heliotropium arborescens*), tobacco plants (*Nicotiana* species), and the chocolate-scented *Cosmos atrosanguineus*. Colours extend from the opalescent whites of *Lavatera trimestris* 'Mont Blanc' to the vibrant scarlets of pelargoniums, bright orange and yellow Californian poppies (*Eschscholzia californica*) and intense magentas and purples of petunias.
For more subtle pastel schemes, opt for plants such as *Anoda cristata*, blue *Silene*

coeli-rosa, baby blue eyes (*Nemophilia menziesii*), and pale green blooms of *Nicotiana langsdorfii*.

To provide a foil for the flowers, consider the wealth of foliage plants available. These include the vast variety of coleus (*Solenostemon*) with their multi-coloured leaves, the bright silver foliage of *Senecio cineraria*, and dark purple-lobed leaves of *Ipomoea batatus* 'Blackie'.

Design options

Annuals and biennials provide an extended season of colour in formal schemes, and are particularly useful for filling beds and gaps in borders. In addition, they can be used to edge flower beds and borders or to create Victorian-style bedding schemes, which are enjoying renewed popularity.

Hardy annuals like poppies, cornflowers (*Centaurea*), and California bluebell (*Phacelia campanularia*) are ideal for naturalistic or wildlife schemes. For mixed schemes, grow them in pots like half-hardy annuals or buy plug plants and set them between more permanent perennials and shrubs (many annual seeds will not germinate in these situations due to competition from neighbouring plants).

Annuals and bedding plants make striking features in seasonal containers, window boxes, and hanging baskets. Use feature plants, such as fuchsias, zinnias, and begonias in the centre, together with trailers like *Helichrysum petiolatum* or trailing petunias to soften the edges of your pots. In autumn and winter displays, combine dwarf conifers, such as *Juniperus communis* 'Compressa', with dainty violas.

Year-round colour

The long flowering season of annuals and biennials provides months of colour. Violas flower in winter but put on their best show in spring, when they are joined by forget-me-nots (*Myosotis*) and wallflowers (*Erysimum cheiri*), which look particularly beautiful when combined with bulbs such as daffodils and tulips. Follow these with any of the summer annuals and biennials, such as foxgloves (*Digitalis*). Busy lizzies (*Impatiens*) are particularly useful for shady sites. Autumn stars include Chinese asters (*Callistephus chinesis*) and in warm climes, the fruits of *Solanum pseudocapsicum* will brighten a winter's day. In cold areas, bring these bushy evergreens indoors.

POTTING UP PLUG PLANTS

If you do not have the space or time to sow seed, look out for seedlings, known as "plugs". Many popular plants, including busy Lizzies, begonias, lobelias, and fuchsias are available in this form, with the largest choice available from mail-order specialists. Pot up small plug plants and grow them on indoors until the frosts have passed.

1 Remove plugs Water the plugs as soon as they arrive. Fill large modular trays or 8cm (3in) pots with good quality potting compost designed for seedlings. Use the blunt end of a pencil or a dibber to gently push them out of their original containers from the bottom.

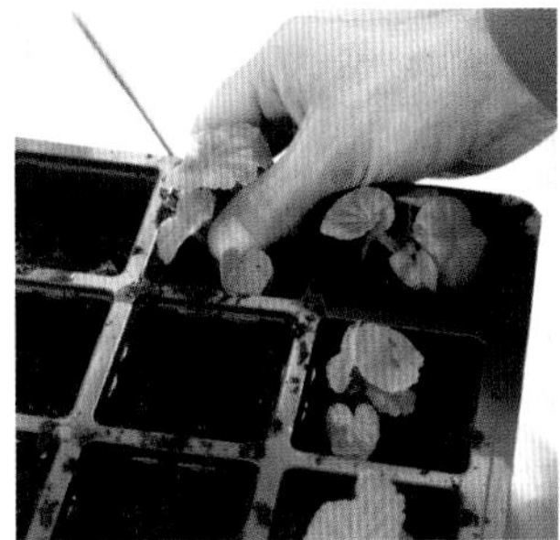

2 Plant up modules Make a hole in the compost with your finger or the pencil and insert a plug into each module or pot. Firm the compost around the plants with your fingers, ensuring there are no air gaps, and taking care not to compact the soil or damage the roots.

3 Water the plants Using a water can fitted with a fine rose, water the plugs well. Keep them in a cool, light, frost-free place, and keep them well watered. Harden the young plants off before planting them outside after the risk of frost has passed.

SOWING SEED IN TRAYS

Growing summer bedding plants from seed can be very cost-effective, especially if you have several containers or beds to fill. Sowing seed in trays indoors is the ideal option for half-hardy or frost-tender plants, allowing you to start them off early in spring so that plants are mature and ready to flower when planted outside. Small seeds, such as petunias, are difficult to space evenly in trays; seedlings will need to be transplanted when they have a few leaves to larger trays, pots, or modules. Seed specialists offer a huge variety of plants via mail order or online.

Pot of seed-sown annuals.

1 Fill seed trays Using good quality seed compost, fill some clean seed trays to within 2cm (1in) of the top. Gently press another seed tray on top to level out and firm the surface. Water the compost with a can fitted with a fine rose and allow to drain.

2 Sow seeds Pour some seeds into your hand and carefully space them out on the compost surface. Sprinkle sieved compost over the seeds, and cover to the depth specified on the seed packet. Also check the seeds' required germination temperature.

3 Cover and keep moist Label the seed tray, and cover with a lid or a clear plastic bag. Place in a light spot. Keep the soil moist, and remove the lid or plastic bag as soon as the seedlings emerge. Harden them off before planting the seedlings outside.

Argyranthemum frutescens
(Marguerite)
Evergreen, woody-based, bushy perennial that bears many daisy-like, white, yellow or pink flower heads throughout summer. Attractive leaves are fresh green. **H** and **S** 70cm (28in).

Catharanthus roseus
(Rose periwinkle)
Evergreen, spreading shrub, becoming untidy with age. Has white to rose-pink flowers in spring to autumn, also in winter in warm areas. **H** and **S** 30–60cm (12–24in). Min. 5–7°C (41–5°F).

Euphorbia hypericifolia
DIAMOND FROST ('Inneuphe')
Bushy perennial, grown as an annual, with slender, repeatedly branched stems bearing elliptical, greyish-green leaves. Small, white florets are produced in cloud-like flower heads in summer–autumn. **H** 18cm (7in), **S** 40cm (16in).

***Sutera cordata* Snowstorm Series**
GIANT SNOWFLAKE ('Danova906')
Spreading or trailing annual with small, rounded, mid-green leaves and 5-lobed, bright white flowers throughout summer. Is excellent in a hanging basket or trailing from a tub. **H** 10–20cm (4–8in), **S** 20–30cm (8–12in).

***Lobularia maritima* 'Snow Crystals'**
Ground-hugging, mound-forming annual with narrow, mid-green leaves and heads of unusually large, fragrant, 4-petalled, white flowers in summer–autumn. Neater than older types. **H** 15–25cm (6–10in), **S** 30–35cm (12–14in).

***Plectranthus forsteri* 'Marginatus'**
Evergreen, bushy perennial. Oval leaves, to 6cm (2½in) long, are greyish-green with scalloped, white margins. Irregularly has tubular, white to pale mauve flowers. **H** 25cm (10in), **S** to 1m (3ft). Min. 10°C (50°F).

***Osteospermum* 'Whirlygig'**
Evergreen, clump-forming, semi-woody perennial of lax habit that produces bluish-white flower heads singly, but in great profusion, during summer. Leaves are grey-green. **H** and **S** 60cm (24in).

***Dahlia* 'Gallery Art Fair'**
Well-branched, small-flowered decorative dahlia, grown as an annual. Produces a prolific display of white flowers, 10cm (4in) across, with greenish-yellow centres, in summer–autumn. Is ideal in a container. **H** 30–35cm (12–14in), **S** 25–30cm (10–12in).

***Zinnia* x *marylandica* Zahara Series 'Zahara Starlight Rose'**
Mound-forming, disease-resistant annual with ovate, mid-green leaves and, in summer–autumn, bears bright, double, daisy-like, red-and-white, bicoloured flower heads. Is drought tolerant. **H** and **S** 30–45cm (12–18in).

Digitalis purpurea f. albiflora
Slow-growing, short-lived perennial, grown as a biennial. Has a rosette of large, pointed-oval leaves and erect stems carrying tubular, white flowers in summer. **H** 1–1.5m (3–5ft), **S** 30–45cm (12–18in).

Dimorphotheca pluvialis (Rain daisy)
Branching annual with oval, hairy, deep green leaves. In summer has small, daisy-like flower heads, the rays purple beneath and white above, with brownish-purple centres. **H** 20–30cm (8–12in), **S** 15cm (6in).

Euphorbia marginata (Snow-in-summer, Snow-on-the-mountain)
Moderately fast-growing, upright, bushy annual. Has pointed-oval, bright green leaves; upper leaves are white-margined. Broad, petal-like, white bracts surround tiny flowers in summer. **H** 60cm (24in), **S** 30cm (12in).

Eustoma grandiflorum
Slow-growing, upright annual with lance-shaped, deep green leaves. Poppy-like, pink, purple, blue or white flowers, 5cm (2in) wide, are carried in summer. **H** 60cm (24in), **S** 30cm (12in). Min. 4–7°C (39–45°F).

Gypsophila elegans
Fast-growing, erect, bushy annual. Has lance-shaped, greyish-green leaves and clouds of tiny, white flowers in branching heads from summer to early autumn. **H** 60cm (24in), **S** 30cm (12in) or more.

Iberis amara
Fast-growing, erect, bushy annual with lance-shaped, mid-green leaves. Has flattish heads of small, scented, 4-petalled, white flowers in summer. **H** 30cm (12in), **S** 15cm (6in).

Lavatera trimestris 'Mont Blanc'
Moderately fast-growing, erect, branching annual with oval, lobed leaves. Shallowly trumpet-shaped, brilliant white flowers appear from summer to early autumn. **H** to 60cm (24in), **S** 45cm (18in).

Nemophila maculata (Five-spot baby)
Fast-growing, spreading annual with lobed leaves. Small, bowl-shaped, white flowers with purple-tipped petals are carried in summer. **H** and **S** 15cm (6in).

Nicotiana x sanderae 'Saratoga Series' [white]
Slow-growing, bushy annual with ovate, mid-green leaves. In summer and early autumn produces a long display of sparkling, white, long-tubed, salverform flowers. **H** and **S** 30cm (12in).

Omphalodes linifolia (Venus's navelwort)
Fairly fast-growing, slender, erect annual with lance-shaped, grey-green leaves. Tiny, slightly scented, rounded, white flowers, rarely tinged blue, are carried in summer. **H** 15–30cm (6–12in), **S** 15cm (6in).

Reseda odorata (Mignonette)
Moderately fast-growing, erect, branching annual with oval leaves. Conical heads of small, very fragrant, somewhat star-shaped, white flowers with orange-brown stamens are carried in summer and early autumn. **H** 30–60cm (12–24in), **S** 30cm (12in).

Tanacetum parthenium (Feverfew)
Moderately fast-growing, short-lived, bushy perennial, grown as an annual. Has aromatic leaves and small, white flower heads in summer and early autumn. **H** and **S** 20–45cm (8–18in).

Hibiscus trionum (Flower-of-the-hour)
Fairly fast-growing, upright annual with oval, serrated leaves. Trumpet-shaped, creamy-white or pale yellow flowers, with purplish-brown centres, are borne from late summer to early autumn. **H** 60cm (24in), **S** 30cm (12in).

Impatiens balsamina (Balsam)
Fairly fast-growing, erect, compact, bushy annual with lance-shaped leaves. Small, cup-shaped, spurred, pink or white flowers are borne in summer and early autumn. **H** to 75cm (30in), **S** 45cm (18in).

Martynia annua (Unicorn plant)
Fairly fast-growing, upright annual with long stalked leaves. Has foxglove like, lobed, creamy-white flowers marked red, pink and yellow in summer, followed by horned, green, then brown, fruits. **H** 60cm (24in), **S** 30cm (12in).

Hypoestes phyllostachya (Freckle face, Polka-dot plant)
Evergreen, bush perennial or sub-shrub. Dark green leaves are covered with irregular, pink spots. Bears small, tubular, lavender flowers intermittently. **H** and **S** 75cm (30in). Min. 10°C (50°F).

Pentas lanceolata (Egyptian star, Star-cluster)
Mainly evergreen, loosely rounded shrub with hairy, bright green leaves. In summer–autumn produces dense clusters of pink, lilac, red or white flowers. **H** 2m (6ft), **S** 1m (3ft). Min. 10–15°C (50–59°F).

Argyranthemum 'Summer Melody'
Evergreen, prolific shrub, grown as an annual, with daisy like, fully double, dark-centred, pale pink flower heads, 3cm (1¼in) across, from early summer and into autumn. Has lobed, glossy, dull green leaves. **H** 28cm (11in), **S** 17cm (7in).

Brachyscome 'Strawberry Mousse'
Twiggy, semi-trailing, short-lived perennial, grown as an annual. Daisy-like flower heads, 3–4cm (1¼–1½in) across, have slightly reflexed, deep pink ray petals and yellow eyes. Good for the edges of a raised bed or window box. **H** 15cm (6in), **S** 35cm (14in).

Calibrachoa Cabaret Series LIGHT PINK ('Balcablitpi')
Mound-forming and trailing, prolific perennial, grown as an annual. In summer–autumn, trumpet-shaped, vivid pink flowers, 4cm (1½in) across, are borne on twiggy stems with linear, dark green leaves. **H** 15cm (6in), **S** 45cm (18in).

Catharanthus roseus Boa Series 'Boa Peach'
Evergreen, semi trailing shrub, grown as an annual. Flattish, rounded, very pale pink flowers, 5cm (2in) across, with a neat ring of reddish-pink around the tiny eye, are borne in summer. **H** 15cm (6in), **S** 45–60cm (18–24in).

Diascia **LITTLE DANCER ('Pendan')**
Mound-forming or semi-trailing perennial, usually grown as an annual. Spikes of tubular, coral-pink flowers are borne in clouds from late spring to autumn. Has heart-shaped, pale green leaves. **H** 30cm (12in), **S** 45cm (18in).

Lathyrus odoratus **Cupid Series 'Cupid Pink'**
Neat, compact, annual with fragrant, pink-and-white, bicoloured flowers in summer. Has pairs of mid-green, 2.5–5cm (1–2in) leaves and no tendrils. Is good at the front of the border, or in a container. **H** 20cm (8in), **S** 30cm (12in).

Nemesia **AMELIE ('Fleurame')**
Mound-forming, twiggy perennial, grown as an annual, with very fragrant, trumpet-shaped, 2-tone pink flowers, 4cm (1½in) across, with yellow lips, in summer. Has lance-shaped, neatly toothed, dark green leaves. Good for a container. **H** 13cm (5in), **S** 15cm (6in).

Lantana camara **Lucky Series LUCKY HONEY BLUSH ('Baluclush')**
Evergreen, mound-forming shrub, grown as an annual. Bears clusters of tubular, 5-lobed, yellow flowers, maturing to pink, with a spicy scent, in late spring–autumn. Has oval, finely wrinkled, deep green leaves. **H** 18cm (7in), **S** 30cm (12in).

Gaura lindheimeri **'Rosyjane'**
Upright, woody-based perennial, usually grown as an annual. Racemes of tubular, white flowers, with bright pink margins, are borne in summer–autumn on twiggy stems with lance-shaped leaves. **H** 75cm (30in), **S** 45cm (18in).

Osteospermum **Sunny Series 'Sunny Marina'**
Evergreen, compact, slightly shrubby perennial, grown as an annual. In summer–autumn, bears blue-eyed flowers with purple rays, shading to white. Has narrow, slightly toothed, dark green leaves. **H** and **S** 20–25cm (8–10in).

Fuchsia **'Leonora'**
Vigorous, deciduous, upright shrub bearing bell-shaped, single, pink flowers with green-tipped sepals. Is good for training as a standard. **H** 1.5m (5ft), **S** 1m (3ft).

FUCHSIAS

Flowering freely all summer and throughout early autumn until the first frosts, fuchsias make excellent container and border plants. The single or double blooms vary from small and dainty to bold and blowsy, their colourful outer sepals held above petals in similar or contrasting hues. A few also boast variegated foliage. Ranging in habit from strongly upright, through broad and bushy, to arching and trailing, there are fuchsias for many garden situations. Upright and bushy types inject summer colour into permanent mixed border schemes or seasonal bedding displays, while larger types make good container specimens, combining well with other summer flowers. Trailing fuchsias are ideal for hanging baskets and window boxes.

F. triphylla **'Firecracker'**

F. Mojo Series 'Beebop'

F. 'Lye's Unique' 🏆

F. 'Celia Smedley' 🏆

F. 'Annabel' 🏆

F. 'Pink Galore'

F. 'Joanna Lumley'

F. 'Jack Shahan' 🏆

F. 'Dollar Prinzessin' 🏆

F. 'Mrs Lovell Swisher' 🏆

F. Windchimes Series WINDCHIMES PINK AND WHITE ('Kiefuwind')

F. Shadowdancer Series PEGGY ('Goetzpeg')

F. 'Nellie Nuttall' 🏆

F. 'Golden Marinka' 🏆

F. California Dreamers Series 'Snowburner'

F. 'Bicentennial'

F. 'Swingtime' 🏆

F. 'Sunray'

F. 'Thalia' 🏆

F. 'Coralle'

F. 'Red Spider'

F. fulgens 🏆

***Primula* Belarina Series**
BELARINA PINK ICE ('Kerbelpice')
Rosette-forming, semi-evergreen, Primrose Group primula. Double white flowers, 3cm (1¾in) across, mature to light pink-purple in late winter and spring. Has oval, deeply veined, dark green leaves. **H** 16cm (6in), **S** 30cm (12in).

***Glandularia* x *hybrida* AZTEC DARK PINK MAGIC ('Balazdapima')**
Trailing or ground-cover perennial, grown as an annual. Stems bear oval, dark green leaves divided into slender leaflets with tubular, lobed, white-eyed, rose pink flowers, 6cm (2½in) across, in summer. **H** 12cm (5in), **S** 40cm (16in).

Gomphrena globosa
(Globe amaranth)
Moderately fast-growing, upright, bushy annual with oval, hairy leaves. Has oval, clover-like flower heads in pink, yellow, orange, purple or white in summer and early autumn. **H** 30cm (12in), **S** 20cm (8in).

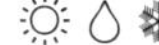

Rhodanthe chlorocephala* subsp. *rosea
Moderately fast-growing, erect annual. Lance-shaped leaves are greyish-green; small, daisy-like, papery, semi-double, pink flower heads appear in summer. Flowers dry well. **H** 30cm (12in), **S** 15cm (6in).

***Antirrhinum* Luminaire Series LUMINAIRE HOT PINK ('Balumhopi')**
Semi-trailing sub-shrub, grown as an annual with vibrant pink, 2-lipped flowers, each with a yellow throat. Has lance-shaped, dark green leaves. Is ideal in a mixed basket or trailing over the edge of a tub. **H** 15cm (6in), **S** 30cm (12in).

x *Petchoa* Supercal Series SUPERCAL NEON ROSE ('Kakegawa S89')
Trailing evergreen perennial, grown as an annual with abundant, flared, trumpet-shaped yellow-eyed, vivid pink flowers borne continuously all summer. Is a Petunia/Calibrachoa hybrid. **H** 25cm (10in), **S** 35cm (14in).

***Matthiola* 'Giant Excelsior'**
Fast-growing, erect, bushy biennial, grown as an annual. Lance-shaped leaves are greyish-green; long spikes of highly scented flowers in shades of pink, red, pale blue or white appear in summer. **H** to 75cm (30in), **S** 30cm (12in).

***Callistephus chinensis* Ostrich Plume Series**
Fast-growing, bushy annual with long, branching stems. From late summer to late autumn, produces spreading, feathery, reflexed, double flowers, mainly in pinks and crimsons. **H** to 60cm (24in), **S** 30cm (12in).

***Papaver somniferum* Paeoniiflorum Group**
Fast-growing, erect annual with lobed, pale greyish-green leaves. Has large, rounded, often cup-shaped, double flowers in a mixture of colours – red, pink, purple or white – in summer. **H** 75cm (30in), **S** 30cm (12in).

Silene coeli-rosa
Moderately fast-growing, erect annual with lance-shaped, greyish-green leaves. Has 5-petalled, pinkish-purple flowers with white centres in summer. **H** 45cm (18in), **S** 15cm (6in).

***Agrostemma githago* 'Milas'**
Fast-growing, slender, upright, thin-stemmed annual. Has lance-shaped leaves and 5-petalled, purplish-pink flowers, 8cm (3in) wide, in summer. **H** 60–90cm (24–36in), **S** 30cm (12in).

***Lobularia maritima* 'Rosie O'Day'**
Fast-growing, compact annual with lance-shaped, mid-green leaves. In summer bears rounded, compact heads of small, sweet-scented flowers, which open white but become red-purple. **H** to 15cm (6in), **S** to 25cm (10in).

***Schizanthus* 'Dwarf Bouquet' [mixed]**
Moderately fast-growing, erect annual with fern-like, mid-green leaves. Bears massed, 2-lipped, open-faced flowers in a range of colours from pink to red, purple, yellow or white in summer and autumn. **H** and **S** 20–25cm (8–10in).

***Malcolmia maritima* (Virginian stock)**
Fast-growing, slim, erect annual with oval, greyish-green leaves. Carries tiny, fragrant, 4-petalled, pink, red or white flowers from spring to autumn. Sow in succession for a long flowering season. **H** 20cm (8in), **S** 5–8cm (2–3in).

Silybum marianum
(Blessed Mary's thistle)
Biennial with a basal rosette of deeply lobed, very spiny, heavily white-marbled, deep green leaves. Has thistle-like, dark purplish-pink flower heads on erect stems in summer and early autumn. **H** 1.2m (4ft), **S** 60cm (2ft).

***Cleome hassleriana* 'Colour Fountain'**
Fast-growing, bushy annual with hairy stems and divided leaves. In summer has heads of narrow-petalled flowers, with long, protruding stamens, in shades of pink, purple or white. **H** 1–1.2m (3–4ft), **S** 45–60cm (1½–2ft).

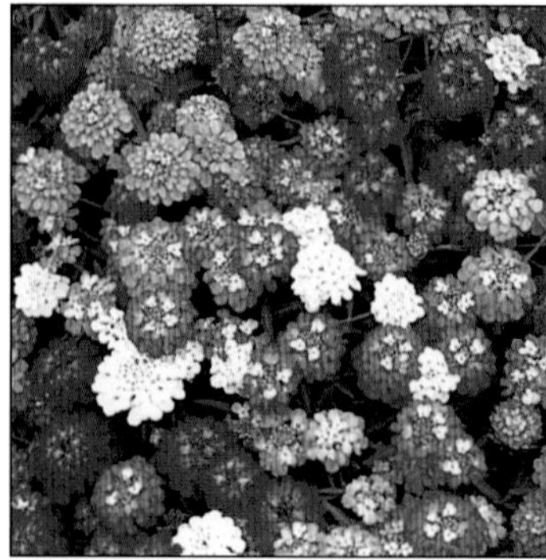

***Iberis umbellata* Fairy Series**
Fast-growing, upright, bushy annual with lance-shaped, mid-green leaves. Heads of small, 4-petalled flowers, in shades of pink, red, purple or white, are carried in summer and early autumn. **H** and **S** 20cm (8in).

Onopordum acanthium
(Cotton thistle, Scotch thistle)
Slow-growing, erect, branching biennial. Large, lobed, spiny leaves are hairy and bright silvery-grey; winged, branching flower stems bear deep purplish-pink flower heads in summer. **H** 1.8m (6ft), **S** 90cm (3ft).

Callistephus chinensis
Milady Super Series [rose]
Moderately fast-growing, erect, bushy annual with oval, toothed leaves. Has large, daisy-like, double, rose-pink flower heads in summer and early autumn. **H** 25–30cm (10–12in), **S** 30–45cm (12–18in).

***Clarkia amoena* 'Sybil Sherwood'**
Erect annual with lance-shaped, sometimes toothed leaves. Single, fluted, salmon-pink flowers, fading to white at the margins, are borne at the tips of long, leafy shoots in summer.
H to 45cm (18in), **S** 30cm (12in).

***Phlox drummondii* 'Chanal'**
Erect to spreading, but compact, bushy, hairy annual with very variable, stem-clasping leaves. In late spring, bears cymes of double, almost rose-like, pink flowers. **H** 10–45cm (4–18in), **S** to 25cm (10in) or more.

***Clarkia* 'Brilliant'**
Fast-growing, erect, bushy annual with oval leaves. Large, rosette-like, double, bright reddish-pink flowers are carried in long spikes in summer and early autumn. **H** to 60cm (24in), **S** 30cm (12in).

***Cosmos bipinnatus* Sensation Series**
Moderately fast-growing, bushy, erect annual. Has feathery, mid-green leaves and daisy-like flower heads, to 10cm (4in) wide, in shades of red, pink or white, from early summer to early autumn.
H 90cm (36in), **S** 60cm (24in).

***Lavatera trimestris* 'Silver Cup'**
Moderately quick-growing, erect, branching annual with oval, lobed leaves. Shallowly trumpet-shaped, rose-pink flowers are carried summer to autumn. **H** 60cm (24in), **S** 45cm (18in).

***Dianthus chinensis* Baby Doll Series**
Neat, bushy annual or biennial, grown as an annual. Light or mid-green leaves are lance-shaped; small, single, zoned flowers in various colours are carried in summer and early autumn. **H** 15cm (6in), **S** 15–30cm (6–12in).

Malope trifida
Moderately quick-growing, erect, branching annual with round, lobed leaves. Flared, trumpet-shaped, reddish-purple flowers, to 8cm (3in) wide and with deep pink veins, are produced in summer and early autumn.
H 90cm (36in), **S** 30cm (12in).

***Xeranthemum annuum* [double]**
Erect annual with lance-shaped, silvery leaves and branching heads of daisy-like, papery, double flower heads in shades of pink, mauve, purple or white, in summer. Suitable for drying. **H** 60cm (24in), **S** 45cm (18in).

Nicotiana x sanderae
Saratoga Series [deep rose]
Slow-growing, bushy annual with ovate mid-green leaves. In summer and early autumn produces a long display of long-tubed, deep-rose flowers.
H and **S** 30cm (12in).

PINK

***Calibrachoa* Million Bells Series CHERRY PINK ('Sunbelrichipi')**
Semi-trailing, prolific perennial, grown as an annual. In summer–autumn, trumpet-shaped, deep cherry-pink flowers, 4cm (1½in) across, are borne on twiggy stems with linear, dark green leaves. **H** 20cm (8in), **S** 55cm (22in).

***Lunaria annua* 'Variegata'**
Fast-growing, erect biennial with pointed-oval, serrated, white-variegated leaves. Heads of small, scented, 4-petalled, deep purplish-pink flowers are borne in spring and early summer followed by rounded, silvery seed pods. **H** 75cm (30in), **S** 30cm (12in).

***Brassica* Northern Lights Series**
Moderately fast-growing, evergreen biennial. Has compact heads of large, tightly packed, bluish green leaves, crinkled at the edges, opening purple, pink or creamy-white in the centre. Is used for autumn and winter colour. **H** and **S** 30–40cm (12–16in).

RED

Lotus berthelotii (Coral gem)
Semi-evergreen, straggling perennial suitable for a hanging basket or large pan in an alpine house. Has hairy, silvery branches and leaves, and clusters of pea-like, scarlet flowers in summer. **H** 30cm (12in), **S** indefinite. Min. 5°C (41°F).

Gerbera jamesonii (Barberton daisy)
Evergreen, upright perennial with daisy-like, variably coloured flower heads, borne intermittently on long stems, and basal rosettes of large, jagged leaves. Flowers are excellent for cutting. **H** 60cm (24in), **S** 45cm (18in).

***Catharanthus roseus* Cobra Series 'Cobra Burgundy'**
Evergreen, well-branched, disease-resistant shrub, grown as an annual, with oval, glossy, dark green leaves. Produces flat, rounded, 5-petalled, deep burgundy-red flowers in summer. **H** 35–40cm (14–16in), **S** 55–65cm (22–26in).

***Zinnia elegans* Dreamland Series** [scarlet]
Moderately fast-growing, sturdy, erect annual with ovate, mid-green leaves. In summer and autumn produces large, daisy-like, semi-double, bright scarlet flower heads. **H** and **S** 30cm (12in).

***Antirrhinum majus* 'Black Prince'**
Erect, bushy perennial, grown as an annual. Lance-shaped, bronze leaves offset spikes of 2-lipped, deep crimson flowers produced in summer–autumn. Dead-head regularly. **H** 45cm (18in), **S** 30cm (12in).

***Cosmos atrosanguineus* CHOCAMOCHA 'Thomocha'**
Bushy, tuberous perennial, grown as an annual, with slightly bowl-shaped, strongly chocolate-scented, deep red flower heads, 4cm (1½in) across, in summer–autumn. Has pinnate, dark green leaves. **H** and **S** 35–38cm (14–15in).

***Cuphea* x *purpurea* 'Firecracker'**
Semi-trailing, sub-shrubby perennial, grown as an annual. Sticky stems bear lance-shaped, dark green leaves and, from late spring to autumn, 2-lipped, bright red flowers. Is good in a mixed container. **H** 23cm (9in), **S** 40cm (16in).

***Dahlia* HAPPY SINGLE ROMEO ('HS Romeo')**
Bushy, single dahlia, grown as an annual, bearing deep purple leaves with oval leaflets. Produces dark-centred, deep red flowers, 10cm (4in) across, in summer and autumn. **H** 55cm (22in), **S** 40cm (16in).

Glandularia* x *hybrida
Corsage Series 'Corsage Red'
Trailing perennial, grown as an annual. Stems have oval, neatly lobed, dark green leaves and, in summer, bear clusters, 7cm (3in) across, of tubular, lobed, double, vibrant red flowers. **H** 35cm (14in), **S** 70cm (28in).

Zinnia* x *marylandica
Profusion Series 'Profusion Cherry'
Mound-forming, well-branched, disease-resistant annual with ovate, mid-green leaves. Has semi-double, rich cherry red flower heads, 5–7.5cm (2–3in) across, in summer–autumn. **H** 30–45cm (12–18in), **S** 40–60cm (16–24in).

***Nemesia strumosa* Carnival Series**
Fairly fast-growing, bushy annual with serrated, pale green leaves. In summer has small, somewhat trumpet-shaped flowers in a range of colours, including yellow, red, orange, purple and white. **H** 20–30cm (8–12in), **S** 15cm (6in).

Impatiens walleriana
MASQUERADE ('Tuckmas')
Mound-forming, well-branched, prolific perennial, grown as an annual. Oval, fresh green leaves have yellow or cream margins. In summer produces flattish, 5-petalled, spurred, single, bright orange-red flowers. **H** and **S** 38–45cm (15–18in).

Tropaeolum majus
'Hermine Grashoff'
Trailing, short-lived perennial, grown as an annual, with large, rounded, slightly wavy-edged, pale green leaves. Produces double, sterile, bright red flowers in summer–autumn. Is best in a large container. **H** 45cm (18in), **S** 60cm (24in).

***Pelargonium* 'Happy Thought'**
Fancy-leaved zonal pelargonium with single, light crimson flowers in clusters borne in summer. Rounded leaves each have a green-yellow butterfly marking in the centre. **H** 40–45cm (16–18in), **S** 20–25cm (8–10in). Min. 2°C (36°F).

***Dianthus chinensis* 'Fire Carpet'**
Slow-growing, bushy annual or biennial, grown as an annual. Lance-shaped leaves are light or mid-green. Small, rounded, single, bright red flowers are carried in summer and early autumn. **H** 20cm (8in), **S** 15–30cm (6–12in).

Amaranthus caudatus
(Love-lies-bleeding, Tassel flower)
Bushy annual with oval, pale green leaves. Pendulous panicles of tassel-like, red flowers, 45cm (18in) long, are carried in summer–autumn. **H** to 1.2m (4ft), **S** 45cm (1½ft).

***Impatiens* Expo Series 'Expo Pink'**
(Busy lizzie)
Fast-growing, evergreen, bushy perennial usually grown as an annual. Has pointed, ovate leaves and from late spring to autumn bears spurred, flat-faced, red, pink or white flowers. **H** 10–15cm (4–6in), **S** 15–30cm (6–12in).

***Linum grandiflorum* 'Rubrum'**
Fairly fast-growing, slim, erect annual. Lance-shaped leaves are grey-green; small, rounded, flattish, deep red flowers are carried in summer. **H** 45cm (18in), **S** 15cm (6in).

***Petunia* 'Mirage Velvet'**
Branching, bushy perennial, grown as an annual, with oval, dark green leaves. Large, flared, trumpet-shaped, rich red flowers, with almost black centres, appear in summer–autumn. **H** 25m (10in), **S** 30cm (12in).

***Viola* x *wittrockiana* Floral Dance Series**
Fairly fast-growing, bushy perennial, grown as an annual or biennial. Has oval, mid-green leaves and rounded, 5-petalled flowers in a wide range of colours in winter. **H** 15–20cm (6–8in), **S** 20cm (8in).

***Salvia splendens* Vista Series [red]**
Slow-growing, bushy perennial grown as an annual, with dark green, ovate, toothed leaves. Produces long-tubed, 2-lipped, bright scarlet flowers in dense, terminal spikes during summer and autumn. **H** and **S** 30cm (12in).

***Tagetes* 'Cinnabar'**
Fast-growing, bushy annual with aromatic, very feathery, deep green leaves. Heads of rounded, daisy-like, single, rich rust-red flowers, yellow-red beneath, are carried in summer and early autumn. **H** and **S** 30cm (12in).

***Amaranthus hypochondriacus* (Prince's feather)**
Bushy annual with upright, sometimes flattened panicles, 15cm (6in) long or more, of dark red flowers in summer–autumn. Leaves are heavily suffused purple. **H** to 1.2m (4ft), **S** 45cm (1½ft).

***Ricinus communis* 'Impala'**
Fast-growing, evergreen, erect shrub, usually grown as an annual. Has deeply lobed, bronze leaves to 30cm (12in) wide, and clusters of small, red flowers in summer, followed by globular, prickly, red seed heads. **H** 1.5m (5ft), **S** 90cm (3ft).

***Cuphea ignea* (Cigar flower)**
Evergreen, spreading, bushy sub-shrub with bright green leaves. From spring to autumn has tubular, dark orange-red flowers, each with a dark band and white ring at the mouth. **H** 30–75cm (12–30in), **S** 30–90cm (12–36in). Min. 2°C (36°F).

***Alonsoa warscewiczii* (Mask flower)**
Perennial, grown as an annual, with slender, branching, red stems carrying oval, toothed, deep green leaves. Spurred, bright scarlet flowers are produced during summer–autumn. **H** 30–60cm (12–24in), **S** 30cm (12in).

PELARGONIUMS

Pelargoniums are perfect for containers and beds, and flower almost continuously in warm climates or under glass. Most fall into one of four main groups. Zonal geraniums have rounded leaves, clearly marked with a darker 'zone', and single to double flowers. Regal types are shrubby with serrated leaves and delicate, trumpet-shaped flowers. Ivy-leaved pelargoniums are trailing plants with lobed leaves and single to double flowers – a good choice for hanging baskets. Scented-leaved types and species have small, star-shaped flowers and are grown principally for their fragrant foliage. Unique types are tall sub-shrubs with regal, brightly coloured flowers; some also have scented leaves. To flower well, all types need sun and well-drained soil.

P. **'Alberta'** ⓘ
[zonal]

P. **Fireworks Series FIREWORKS SCARLET ('Fiwoscarlet')**

P. **'Clorinda'** ⓘ
[scented-leaved]

P. **'Evka'**

P. **Maverick Series 'Maverick Star'**

P. **'Fraiche Beauté'** ⓘ
[zonal]

P. **'Lady Plymouth'** 🏆ⓘ
[scented-leaved]

P. **'Voodoo'** 🏆ⓘ
[unique]

P. **Regalia Series 'Regalia Chocolate'**

P. **Horizon Deva Series 'Horizon Deva Raspberry Ripple'**

P. **Decora Series 'Decora Dark Pink'**

P. **'Lachskönigin'** ⓘ
[ivy-leaved]

P. **'Tip Top Duet'** 🏆ⓘ
[regal]

P. **Bulls Eye Series 'Bulls Eye Salmon'**

P. **'Brookside Primrose'** ⓘ
[zonal]

P. **Antik Series ANTIK SALMON ('Tiksal')**

P. **BLUE WONDER ('Pacbla')**

P. **Horizon Deva Series 'Horizon Deva Orange Ice'**

RED

***Papaver rhoeas* Shirley Group** [single]
Fast-growing, slender, erect annual with lobed, light green leaves. Rounded, often cup-shaped, single flowers, in shades of red, pink, salmon or white, appear in summer. **H** 60cm (24in), **S** 30cm (12in).

Lunaria annua (Honesty)
Fast-growing, erect biennial with pointed-oval, serrated leaves. Heads of scented, 4-petalled, white to deep purple flowers in spring and early summer are followed by rounded, silvery seed pods. **H** 75cm (30in), **S** 30cm (12in).

***Solenostemon scutellarioides* Kong Series 'Kong Scarlet'**
Fast-growing, large-leaved perennial, grown as an annual. Deepest crimson leaves are feathered to green at the margins and have a slender, central, cerise flash. Pinch out flower spikes. **H** and **S** 45–60cm (18–24in).

PURPLE

***Aeonium* 'Zwartkop'**
Bushy, perennial succulent with stems each crowned by a rosette, to 15cm (6in) across, of narrow, purple leaves. Bears golden pyramids of flowers in spring on 2–3-year-old stems, which then die. **H** 60cm (2ft), **S** 1m (3ft). Min. 5°C (41°F).

***Lycianthes rantonnetii* 'Royal Robe'**
Evergreen, loosely rounded shrub with smooth, bright green leaves. In summer has clusters of rich purple-blue flowers that open almost flat. **H** and **S** 1–2m (3–6ft). Min. 7°C (45°F).

Streptocarpus saxorum
(False African violet)
Evergreen, rounded, woody-based perennial with small, oval, hairy leaves in whorls. Lilac flowers with white tubes arise from leaf axils in summer–autumn. **H** and **S** 30cm (12in) or more. Min. 10–15°C (50–59°F).

Lantana montevidensis
Evergreen, trailing or mat-forming shrub with serrated leaves. Has heads of rose-purple flowers, each with a yellow eye, intermittently all year but mainly in summer. **H** 20–100cm (8–39in), **S** 60–120cm (24–48in). Min. 10–13°C (50–55°F).

***Tradescantia pallida* 'Purpurea'**
Evergreen, creeping perennial with dark purple stems and slightly fleshy leaves. Has pink or pink-and-white flowers in summer. **H** 30–40cm (12–16in), **S** 30cm (12in) or more. Min. 15°C (59°F).

Heliotropium arborescens
Evergreen, bushy shrub. Semi-glossy, dark green leaves are finely wrinkled. Purple to lavender flowers are borne in dense, flat clusters from late spring to winter. **H** 45cm (18in), **S** 30–45cm (12–18in). Min. 7°C (45°F).

***Alternanthera dentata* 'Purple Knight'** (Joseph's coat)
Vigorous, evergreen perennial, grown as an annual. Forms a spreading mound of upright, purple stems clad in ovate, slightly glossy, dark purple leaves.
H 60–90cm (2–3ft), **S** 90–120cm (3–4ft). Min. 15–18°C (59–64°F).

***Angelonia angustifolia* AngelMist Series 'AngelMist Lavender Stripe'**
Evergreen, upright perennial, grown as an annual, with lance-shaped, toothed leaves. Slender racemes of 2-lipped flowers, 2cm (¾in) across, purple above and white below, are borne in summer.
H 30cm (12in), **S** 35cm (14in).

***Solenostemon scutellarioides* 'Inky Fingers'**
Fast-growing, semi-trailing, bushy perennial, grown as an annual. Rounded, blackish-red leaves are cut into 5–11 deep lobes and edged in green. Pinch out once or twice when young. **H** 30–60cm (12–24in), **S** 60–100cm (24–39in).

***Solenostemon* 'Chocolate Mint'**
Fast-growing perennial, grown as an annual, with broadly oval, chocolate-brown leaves margined in fresh mint-green. Pinch out any flower spikes.
H 35–50cm (14–20in), **S** 30–35cm (12–14in).

***Dahlia* HAPPY SINGLE WINK ('HS Wink')**
Bushy, single dahlia, grown as an annual, bearing deep purple leaves with oval leaflets. Pale purple flowers, 8cm (3in) across, each have a dark purple ring around the eye. Is good in a mixed border. **H** 70cm (28in), **S** 45cm (18in).

***Ipomoea batatas* 'Blackie'**
Evergreen, tuberous, trailing perennial grown as an annual, with 3-lobed, almost black leaves. In summer may produce trumpet-shaped, purple-throated, lavender flowers, 2.5cm (1in) across. Is good in a mixed container.
H 15–25cm (6–10in), **S** 45–60cm (18–24in).

***Lobelia erinus* Waterfall Series 'Waterfall Light Lavender'**
Mound-forming, semi-trailing perennial, grown as an annual, with narrowly oval to lance-shaped, dark green leaves. Bears 2-lipped, lobed, pale violet flowers, 2cm (¾in) across, with white eyes, in summer.
H 15–20cm (6–8in), **S** 20–30cm (8–12in).

***Petunia* Surfinia Series SURFINIA BLUE VEIN ('Sunsolos')**
Vigorous, trailing perennial, grown as an annual. In summer, almost white flowers, 5cm (2in) across, developing mauve tints, are borne with vivid purple-blue veins and dark throats. Is good in a basket.
H 25cm (10in), **S** 60cm (24in).

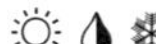

***Pennisetum glaucum* 'Purple Majesty'** (Pearl millet)
Tall, upright perennial, grown as an annual, with long, strap-like, arching purple leaves. Bold, bristly, vertical flower spikes, borne in summer, turn from tan to purple. **H** 60–90cm (24–36in), **S** 40–70cm (16–28in). Min. 2°C (36°F).

***Petunia* Tumbelina Series PRISCILLA ('Kerpril')**
Semi-trailing, well-branched perennial, grown as an annual, with lance-shaped, dark green leaves. Produces fragrant, double, mauve flowers, veined in dark purple, in summer and autumn.
H 30cm (12in), **S** 50cm (20in).

Strobilanthes dyerianus (Purple Shield)
Evergreen, relatively unbranched sub-shrub, grown as an annual, with elliptical, dark green, leaves, 15cm (6in) long, almost fully flushed in silvery purple, leaving only a pattern of dark green veins. **H** and **S** 90cm (36in).

***Osteospermum* Cape Daisy Series NASINGA PURPLE 'Aksullo'**
Evergreen, slightly woody perennial, grown as an annual, with lance-shaped, slightly toothed leaves. In summer bears blue-eyed flowers, 7cm (3in) across, with fuchsia-purple rays, spooned at the tips.
H 30–38cm (12–15in), **S** 20–30cm (8–12in).

***Viola* x *wittrockiana* Imperial Series 'Imperial Frosty Rose'**
Erect, bushy perennial, grown as an annual or biennial, with oval leaves. In summer, bears large, unusual, rose-purple flowers fading to pink and white. **H** 16–23cm (6–9in), **S** 23–30cm (9–12in).

Collinsia grandiflora
Moderately fast-growing, slender-stemmed annual. Upper leaves are lance-shaped; lower are oval. Whorls of pale purple flowers, with purplish-blue lips, are carried in spring–summer. **H** and **S** 15–30cm (6–12in).

***Callistephus chinensis* Milady Super Series** [blue]
Moderately fast-growing, erect, bushy annual with oval, toothed leaves. Has large, daisy-like, double, purplish-blue flower heads in summer and early autumn. **H** 25–30cm (10–12in), **S** 30–45cm (12–18in).

***Pennisetum setaceum* 'Rubrum'**
Clump-forming, herbaceous perennial grass, grown as an annual, with slender, upright, rather rough, dark purple leaves. In summer produces dense, cylindrical panicles of crimson spikelets, with bearded bristles, fading to green. **H** 90cm (36in), **S** 45cm (18in).

***Nierembergia linariifolia* 'Purple Robe'**
Moderately fast-growing, rounded, branching perennial, grown as an annual, with narrow, lance-shaped leaves. Has cup-shaped, dark bluish-purple flowers in summer and early autumn. **H** and **S** 15–20cm (6–8in).

***Viola* Joker Series**
Bushy, spreading perennial, usually grown as an annual or biennial. Large, rounded, 5-petalled, purplish-blue flowers, with black and white 'faces' and yellow eyes, appear in summer. **H** and **S** 15cm (6in).

***Viola* x *wittrockiana* Sorbet Series 'Sorbet Black Delight'**
Neat, prolific perennial, grown as a biennial. Small, 5-petalled, deep black flowers, each with a small, gold eye, are borne in winter and spring over ovate, sparsely toothed, mid-green leaves. **H** and **S** 15–20cm (6–8in).

***Cerinthe major* 'Purpurascens'**
Annual of lax habit with oval to spoon-shaped leaves, to 6cm (2½in) long. Bears terminal sprays of nodding, tubular, pale to mid-yellow flowers, with violet-tinged tips. Bracts around flowers are strongly suffused purple. **H** and **S** 60cm (24in).

***Petunia* Daddy Series 'Sugar Daddy'**
Fairly fast-growing, branching, bushy, perennial, grown as an annual, with oval leaves. In early summer to autumn, has large, purple flowers with dark veins. **H** to 35cm (14in), **S** 30–90cm (12–36in).

***Salvia farinacea* 'Victoria'**
Moderately fast-growing perennial, grown as an annual, with many erect stems. Has oval or lance-shaped leaves and spikes of tubular, violet-blue flowers in summer. **H** 45cm (18in), **S** 30cm (12in).

***Glandularia* x *hybrida* AZTEC SILVER MAGIC ('Balazsilma')**
Trailing or ground-cover, mildew-tolerant perennial, grown as an annual, with small, finely lobed, green leaves. In summer, clusters, 6cm (2½in) across, of pale violet flowers are borne along the stems. **H** 8cm (3in), **S** 50cm (20in).

***Campanula medium* 'Bells of Holland'**

Slow-growing, evergreen, clump-forming, erect biennial with lance-shaped, toothed leaves. In spring and early summer has bell-shaped flowers in blue, lilac, pink or white. **H** to 60cm (24in), **S** 30cm (12in).

Salvia sclarea* var. *turkestanica

Moderately fast-growing, erect biennial, grown as an annual. Has aromatic, oval, hairy leaves and panicles of tubular, white and lavender-purple flowers with prominent, lavender-purple bracts in summer. **H** 75cm (30in), **S** 30cm (12in).

***Myosotis* Sylva Series**

Compact, bushy, early-flowering perennial, grown as a biennial. Has lance-shaped, hairy leaves and, from mid spring to early summer, clustered spikes of small, 5-lobed flowers in blue, pink or white. **H** and **S** 23cm (9in).

***Viola* x *wittrockiana* Ultima Radiance Series** [deep blue]

Spreading perennial, grown as a biennial. Produces large, neatly rounded, 5-petalled, deep blue flowers, with white faces, yellow lips and dark whiskers, in winter and spring. Leaves are oval and mid-green. **H** and **S** 15–20cm (6–8in).

Trachelium caeruleum (Throatwort)

Moderately fast-growing, erect perennial, grown as an annual. Has oval, serrated leaves and clustered heads of small, tubular, lilac-blue or white flowers in summer. **H** 60–90cm (24–36in), **S** 30cm (12in).

***Isotoma* Avant-Garde Series**

Neat, domed, woody-based perennial, grown as an annual. Rounded mounds of slender, lobed leaves are topped by star-shaped, 5-petalled flowers, in blue purple, pink and white, in summer. Is good in a container. **H** 15–30cm (6–12in), **S** 23–38cm (9–15in).

***Ageratum houstonianum* 'Blue Danube'**

Moderately fast-growing, hummock-forming annual with pointed-oval leaves. Has clusters of feathery, brush-like, lavender-blue flower heads in summer–autumn. Makes a useful edging plant. **H** and **S** 15cm (6in).

***Salvia farinacea* 'Strata'**
Upright, slightly tuberous perennial, grown as an annual. White-mealy stems bear spikes of blue flowers, with broad lower lips, 2cm (¾in) long, each in a white calyx, in summer–autumn. Has glossy, narrowly lance-shaped, grey-green leaves. **H** 60cm (24in), **S** 30cm (12in).

Nigella damascena
Persian Jewels Series
Fast-growing, erect annual with feathery leaves. Small, semi-double flowers, in shades of blue, pink or white, appear in summer, followed by inflated seed pods which can be cut and dried. **H** 45cm (18in), **S** 20cm (8in).

Nemophila menziesii
(Baby blue-eyes)
Fast-growing, spreading annual with serrated, greyish-green leaves. Small, bowl-shaped, blue flowers with white centres are carried in summer. **H** 20cm (8in), **S** 15cm (6in).

Phacelia campanularia
(California bluebell)
Moderately fast-growing, branching, bushy annual with oval, serrated, deep green leaves. Bell-shaped, pure blue flowers, 2.5cm (1in) wide, are carried in summer and early autumn. **H** 20cm (8in), **S** 15cm (6in).

Gilia capitata
Erect, branching annual. Has very feathery, mid-green leaves and tiny, dense, rounded heads of soft lavender-blue flowers in summer and early autumn. Is good for cut flowers. **H** 45cm (18in), **S** 20cm (8in).

***Lobelia erinus* Waterfall Series 'Waterfall Blue'**
Mound-forming, semi-trailing perennial, grown as an annual, with narrowly oval to lance-shaped, toothed, green leaves. Racemes of 2-lipped, mid-blue flowers, 2cm (¾in) across, are borne in summer. **H** 15–20cm (6–8in), **S** 20–30cm (8–12in).

***Pericallis* Senetti Series SENETTI BLUE BICOLOR ('Sunseneribuba')**
Mound-forming, bushy perennial, grown as an annual. Daisy-like, white flowers, 7cm (3in) across, with vivid blue tips and magenta eyes, are borne in spring. Has oval, serrated, mid–deep green leaves. **H** 38–45cm (15–18in), **S** 30–38cm (12–15in).

***Lobelia erinus* 'Sapphire'**
Slow-growing, pendulous, spreading annual or occasionally perennial. Oval to lance-shaped leaves are pale green; small, sapphire-blue flowers with white centres are produced continuously in summer and early autumn. **H** 20cm (8in), **S** 15cm (6in).

***Convolvulus tricolor* 'Blue Flash'**
Moderately fast-growing, upright, bushy annual with oval to lance-shaped leaves. Has small, saucer-shaped, intense blue flowers with cream and yellow centres in summer. **H** 20–30cm (8–12in), **S** 20cm (8in).

***Ageratum houstonianum* 'Blue Mink'**
Moderately fast-growing, hummock-forming annual. Has pointed-oval leaves and clusters of feathery, brush-like, pastel blue flower heads in summer–autumn. Is a useful edging plant. **H** and **S** 20–30cm (8–12in).

Cynoglossum amabile **'Firmament'**
Slow-growing, upright, bushy annual or biennial with lance-shaped, hairy, grey-green leaves. Pendulous, tubular, pure sky-blue flowers are carried in summer. **H** 45cm (18in), **S** 30cm (12in).

Commelina coelestis (Day flower)
Fairly fast-growing, upright perennial, usually grown as an annual, with lance-shaped, mid-green leaves. Small, 3-petalled, bright pure blue flowers are freely produced from late summer to mid-autumn. **H** to 45cm (18in), **S** 30cm (12in).

Myosotis sylvatica **'Blue Ball'**
Slow-growing, bushy, compact perennial, often grown as a biennial. Has lance-shaped leaves and, in spring and early summer, spikes of tiny, 5-lobed, deep blue flowers. **H** to 20cm (8in), **S** 15cm (6in).

Senecio cineraria **'Silver Dust'**
Moderately fast-growing, evergreen, bushy sub-shrub, usually grown as an annual, with deeply lobed, silver leaves. Small, daisy-like, yellow flower heads appear in summer but are best removed. **H** and **S** 30cm (12in).

Anchusa capensis **'Blue Angel'**
Bushy biennial, grown as an annual. Has lance-shaped, bristly leaves. Heads of shallowly bowl-shaped, brilliant blue flowers are borne in summer. **H** and **S** 20cm (8in).

Centaurea cyanus [tall, blue] (Cornflower)
Fast-growing, erect, branching annual. Has lance-shaped, grey-green leaves and branching heads of daisy-like, blue flowers in summer and early autumn. **H** to 90cm (36in), **S** 30cm (12in).

Borago officinalis (Borage)
Spreading, clump-forming, annual herb. Has oval, crinkled, rough-haired leaves and sprays of star-shaped, blue flowers in summer and early autumn. Young leaves are sometimes used as a coolant in drinks. Self seeds prolifically. **H** 90cm (36in), **S** 30cm (12in).

Nigella damascena **'Miss Jekyll'**
Fast-growing, slender, erect annual. Feathery leaves are bright green; small, rounded, many-petalled, semi-double, blue flowers are carried in summer, followed by inflated seed pods which can be cut and dried. **H** 45cm (18in), **S** 20cm (8in).

Lobelia erinus **'Crystal Palace'**
Slow-growing, spreading, compact, bushy annual or occasionally perennial. Bronzed leaves are oval to lance-shaped; small, deep blue flowers are produced continuously in summer and early autumn. **H** 10–20cm (4–8in), **S** 10–15cm (4–6in).

Sedum caeruleum
Moderately fast-growing annual with branching flower stems. Oval, light green leaves become red-tinged when clusters of small, star-shaped, light blue flowers with white centres are borne in summer. **H** and **S** 10–15cm (4–6in).

Leucophyta brownii
Evergreen, intricately branched shrub with velvety, grey branches and tiny, scale-like leaves. Clusters of flowers, silver in bud, yellowish when expanded, appear in summer. **H** 40–75cm (16–30in), **S** 40–90cm (16–36in). Min. 7–10ºC (45–50ºF).

Bassia scoparia* f. *trichophylla
(Burning bush, Summer cypress)
Moderately fast-growing, erect, very bushy annual. Narrow, lance-shaped, light green leaves, 5–8cm (2–3in) long, turn red in autumn. Has insignificant flowers. **H** 90cm (36in), **S** 60cm (24in).

Nicotiana langsdorffii
Fairly slow-growing, erect, branching perennial, grown as an annual, with oval to lance-shaped leaves. Slightly pendent, bell-shaped, pale green to yellow-green flowers appear in summer. **H** 1–1.5m (3–5ft), **S** 30cm (1ft).

Moluccella laevis
(Bells of Ireland, Shell flower)
Fairly fast-growing, erect, branching annual. Rounded leaves are pale green; spikes of small, tubular, white flowers, each surrounded by a conspicuous, pale green calyx, appear in summer. **H** 60cm (24in), **S** 20cm (8in).

***Zinnia elegans* 'Envy'**
Moderately fast-growing, sturdy, erect annual. Has oval to lance-shaped, pale or mid-green leaves and large, daisy-like, double, green flower heads in summer and early autumn. **H** 60cm (24in), **S** 30cm (12in).

***Petunia* Surfinia Series**
SURFINIA LIME ('Keiyeul')
Vigorous, trailing perennial grown as an annual, with slightly star-shaped, white flowers, 6cm (2½in) across, shading to lime-yellow in the throats, in summer. Is good in a basket. **H** 25cm (10in), **S** 60cm (24in).

BEGONIAS

The genus *Begonia* is one of the most versatile, providing interest throughout the year. Semperflorens begonias are excellent for summer bedding, while the *Rex-cultorum* group offers distinctive, handsome foliage in a huge variety of decorative shades and unusual textures. Other begonias, such as the *Tuberhybrida* cultivars with their large, showy blooms, are grown mostly for their flowers. Most begonias are not suitable for permanent outdoor cultivation in frost-prone areas as they are not hardy, but they make attractive house plants and displays in summer containers. Begonias may be fibrous-rooted, rhizomatous, or tuberous, the tubers becoming dormant in winter. Grow them in a light position, shaded from direct sun.

B. serratipetala

***B. boliviensis* 'Bonfire'**

***B. x tuberhybrida* Non Stop Series** [White]

***B.* 'Ingramii'**

***B. x tuberhybrida* Mocha Series** [Scarlet]

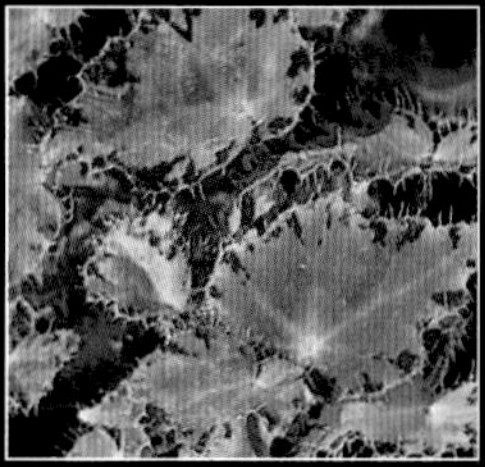

B. bowerae

***B.* 'Orpha C. Fox'**

B. masoniana 🏆

B. albopicta

***B.* 'Merry Christmas'** 🏆

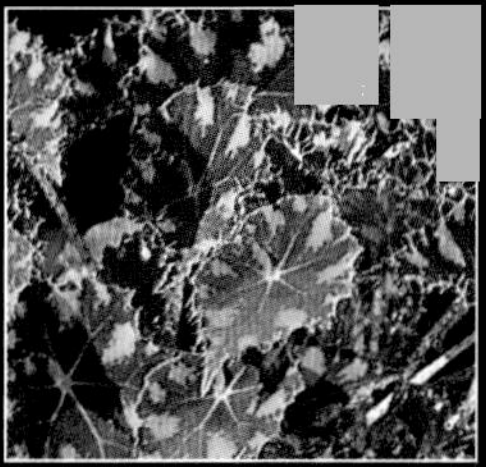

***B.* DRAGON WING RED ('Bepared')**

***B.* 'Tiger Paws'** 🏆

B. dregei 🏆

B. prismatocarpa

B. scharffii

***B.* 'Ikon White Blush'**

***B.* Illumination Series 'Illumination Salmon Pink'** 🏆

***B.* 'Orange Rubra'** 🏆

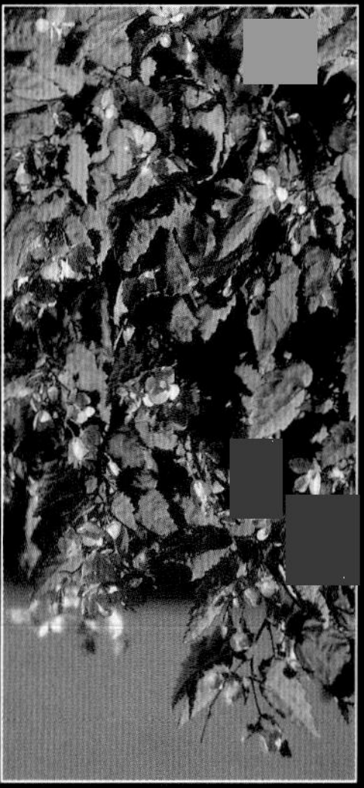

B. sutherlandii 🏆

Ricinus communis **(Castor-oil plant)**
Fast-growing, evergreen, erect shrub, usually grown as an annual. Has large, deeply lobed, mid-green leaves and heads of green and red flowers in summer, followed by globular, prickly seed pods. **H** 1.5m (5ft), **S** 90cm (3ft).

Ipomoea batatas **'Margarita'**
Evergreen, tuberous, trailing perennial grown as an annual, with 3-lobed, bright lime green leaves. In summer, may produce trumpet-shaped, purple-throated, lavender flowers, 2.5cm (1in) across. Is good in a mixed container. **H** 15–30cm (6–12in), **S** 45–60cm (18–24in).

Viola **'Green Goddess'**
Evergreen, clump-forming perennial, often grown as an annual, with small, oval, toothed, dark green leaves. Flattish, 5-petalled flowers, with whiskered, yellow centres surrounded by hazy green zones, are borne from spring to autumn. **H** 15cm (6in), **S** 25cm (10in).

Perilla **'Magilla Vanilla'**
Fast-growing perennial, grown as an annual, with broadly oval, bright green leaves brightly splashed in the centres in rich cream. Spikes of tiny, bell-shaped flowers are occasionally borne in late summer; pinch them out. **H** 60–90cm (24–36in), **S** 45–60cm (18–24in).

Setaria macrostachya **(Italian millet)**
Upright, clump-forming, perennial grass, grown as an annual. Has long, pointed, coarse, mid-green leaves each with a pale central stripe. Erect spikes of bristly, vivid green flower heads are produced in summer. **H** 90cm (3ft), **S** 60cm (2ft).

***Argyranthemum* 'Jamaica Primrose'**
Evergreen, woody-based perennial with fern-like, pale green leaves. Daisy-like, single, soft yellow flower heads are borne in summer. Take stem cuttings in early autumn. **H** and **S** to 1m (3ft).

***Osteospermum* 'Buttermilk'**
Evergreen, upright, semi-woody perennial. Daisy-like, pale yellow flower heads, with dark eyes, are borne singly amid grey-green foliage from mid-summer to autumn. **H** 60cm (24in), **S** 30cm (12in).

***Brugmansia* x *candida* 'Grand Marnier'**
Evergreen, robust shrub with large, oval to elliptic leaves. Pendent, flared, trumpet-shaped, apricot flowers open from an inflated calyx in summer. **H** 3–5m (10–15ft), **S** 1.5–2.5m (5–8ft). Min. 7–10ºC (45–50ºF).

***Iresine herbstii* 'Aureoreticulata'**
Evergreen, bushy perennial with red stems and inconspicuous flowers. Rounded, mid-green leaves, 10cm (4in) long, have yellow or red veins and notched tips. **H** to 60cm (24in), **S** 45cm (18in). Min. 10–15ºC (50–59ºF).

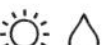

Euryops pectinatus
Evergreen, upright shrub. Deeply cut, grey-green leaves set off large heads of daisy-like, bright yellow flowers, borne in late spring and early summer and often again in winter. **H** and **S** 1m (3ft). Min. 5–7ºC (41–5ºF).

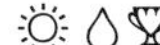

***Argyranthemum* BUTTERFLY ('Ulyssis')**
Evergreen sub-shrub, grown as an annual, with finely divided, dark green leaves. Prolific, daisy-like, single, bright yellow flower heads are produced in summer–autumn. **H** 45–90cm (18–36in), **S** 38–45cm (15–18in).

Duranta erecta
(Pigeon berry, Skyflower)
Fast-growing, usually evergreen, bushy shrub. Has spikes of lilac-blue flowers, mainly in summer, followed by yellow fruits. **H** 3–6m (10–20ft), **S** 2–3m (6–10ft). Min. 10ºC (50ºF).

***Bidens* 'Gold Star'**
Rather spreading, short-lived perennial, grown as an annual. Semi-trailing stems have divided leaves and bear star-shaped, golden-eyed, bright yellow flower heads in summer–autumn. **H** 30cm (12in), **S** 45cm (18in).

***Duranta erecta* 'Gold Edge'**
Evergreen, fast-growing, bushy shrub, grown as an annual, with oval, toothed, glossy, bright green leaves, 5–7.5cm (2–3in) long, irregularly margined in bright yellow. Rarely flowers. **H** and **S** 60cm (24in).

***Antirrhinum majus* Liberty Classic Series 'Liberty Yellow'**
Erect perennial, grown as an annual, branching from the base. Has lance-shaped, dull green leaves and in summer–autumn bears spikes of tubular, 2-lipped, 2-tone yellow flowers. **H** 45–55cm (18–22in), **S** 30–35cm (12–14in).

Glaucium flavum **(Horned poppy)**
Slow-growing, erect biennial with oval, lobed, light greyish-green leaves. Poppy-like, vivid yellow flowers, 8cm (3in) wide, are borne in summer and early autumn. **H** 30–60cm (12–24in), **S** 45cm (18in).

Tagetes **Gold Coins Series**
Fast-growing, erect, bushy annual. Has aromatic, feathery, glossy, deep green leaves and large, daisy-like, double flower heads in shades of yellow and orange in summer and early autumn. **H** 90cm (36in), **S** 30–45cm (12–18in).

Sanvitalia procumbens
(Creeping zinnia)
Moderately fast-growing, prostrate annual with pointed-oval leaves. Daisy-like, yellow flower heads, 2.5cm (1in) wide, with black centres, are borne in summer. **H** 15cm (6in), **S** 30cm (12in).

Nemesia **Sunsatia Series**
SUNSATIA MANGO ('Inupyel')
Evergreen, semi-trailing, woody-based perennial, grown as an annual, with lance-shaped, green leaves. Racemes of 2-lipped, yellow flowers, with golden lips and purple throats, are borne in summer. **H** 23cm (9in), **S** 45cm (18in).

Xerochrysum bracteatum **Sundaze Series SUNDAZE GOLD ('Redbragol')**
Bushy, rounded, short-lived perennial, grown as an annual, with lance-shaped, mid-green leaves. Produces small, papery, daisy-like, yellow flower heads, with orange centres, in summer–autumn. **H** 20–30cm (8–12in), **S** 30cm (12in).

Rudbeckia hirta **'Toto Gold'**
Upright, strong-stemmed biennial or short-lived perennial, often grown as an annual, with ovate to lance-shaped, mid-green leaves. Has large, daisy-like, bright yellow flower heads with very dark brown centres in summer and early autumn. **H** and **S** to 45cm (18in).

Antirrhinum majus
Chimes Series [yellow]
Erect perennial usually grown as an annual, with branching shoots and mid- to dark green, lance-shaped leaves. During summer and autumn produces racemes of bright yellow, 2-lipped flowers. **H** 30cm (12in), **S** 20cm (8in).

Platystemon californicus
(Cream cups)
Moderately fast-growing, upright, compact annual with lance-shaped, greyish-green leaves. Saucer-shaped, cream or pale yellow flowers, about 2.5cm (1in) across, appear in summer. **H** 30cm (12in), **S** 10cm (4in).

Argemone mexicana
(Devil's fig, Prickly poppy)
Spreading perennial, grown as an annual, with leaves divided into white-marked, greyish-green leaflets. In summer has fragrant, poppy-like, yellow or orange flowers, 8cm (3in) wide. **H** to 60cm (24in), **S** 30cm (12in).

***Calendula officinalis* 'Daisy May'**
Fast-growing, bushy annual with aromatic, lance-shaped, mid-green leaves and numerous, semi-double, yellow flower heads from late spring to autumn. **H** and **S** 30–40cm (12–16in).

***Coreopsis grandiflora* 'Sunray'**
Spreading, clump-forming perennial, grown as an annual by sowing under glass in early spring. Has lance-shaped, serrated leaves and daisy-like, double, bright yellow flower heads in summer. **H** 45cm (18in), **S** 30–45cm (12–18in).

Smyrnium perfoliatum
Slow-growing, upright biennial. Upper leaves, rounded and yellow-green, encircle stems which bear heads of yellowish-green flowers in summer. **H** 60cm–1m (2–3ft), **S** 60cm (2ft).

Cladanthus arabicus
Moderately fast-growing, hummock-forming annual with aromatic, feathery, light green leaves. Has fragrant, daisy-like, single, deep yellow flower heads, 5cm (2in) wide, in summer and early autumn. **H** 60cm (24in), **S** 30cm (12in).

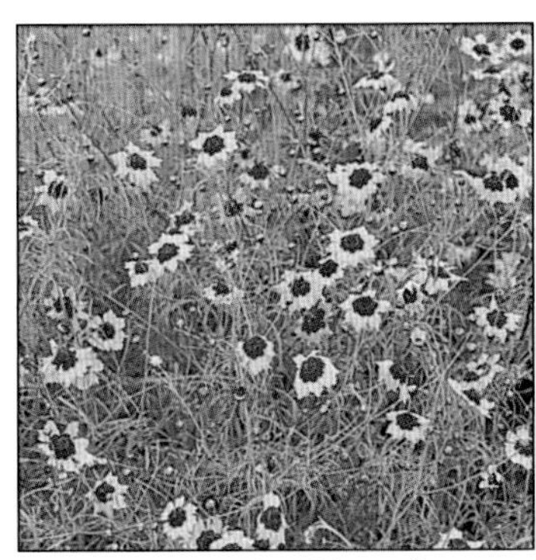

Coreopsis tinctoria (Tick-seed)
Fast-growing, erect, bushy annual with lance-shaped leaves. Large, daisy-like, bright yellow flower heads with red centres are carried in summer and early autumn. **H** 60–90cm (24–36in), **S** 20cm (8in).

Eschscholzia caespitosa
Fast-growing, slender, erect annual with feathery, bluish-green leaves. Cup-shaped, 4-petalled, yellow flowers, 2.5cm (1in) wide, appear in summer and early autumn. **H** and **S** 15cm (6in).

Limnanthes douglasii
(Meadow foam, Poached-egg flower)
Fast-growing, slender, erect annual. Feathery leaves are glossy, light green; slightly fragrant, cup-shaped, white flowers with yellow centres are carried from early to late summer. **H** 15cm (6in), **S** 10cm (4in).

***Mimulus* Magic Series 'Magic Yellow Blotch'**
Erect, well-branched perennial, grown as an annual. Fleshy stems bear small, oval, toothed, mid-green leaves and in summer bear flared, tubular flowers in bright yellow heavily blotched in red. **H** and **S** 15–20cm (6–8in).

***Helianthus annuus* 'Teddy Bear'**
Fast-growing, compact, hairy-stemmed annual with toothed, roughly hairy leaves. Produces daisy-like, double, deep yellow flower heads, to 13cm (5in) across, in summer. **H** 90cm (36in), **S** to 60cm (24in).

Ursinia anthemoides
Moderately fast-growing, bushy annual with feathery, pale green leaves. Small, daisy-like, purple-centred flower heads with orange-yellow rays, purple beneath, appear in summer and early autumn. **H** 30cm (12in), **S** 20cm (8in).

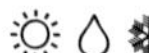

***Helianthus annuus* 'Music Box'**
Fast-growing, free-flowering, many-branched, hairy-stemmed annual. Bears daisy-like flower heads, 10–12cm (4–5in) across, with ray-florets ranging from creamy-yellow to dark red, and black disc-florets, in summer. **H** 70cm (28in), **S** to 60cm (24in).

Xanthophthalmum segetum
Moderately fast-growing, erect annual with lance-shaped, grey-green leaves. Daisy-like, single flower heads, to 8cm (3in) wide, in shades of yellow, are carried in summer and early autumn. **H** 45cm (18in), **S** 30cm (12in).

***Calendula officinalis* Pacific Beauty Series 'Lemon Queen'**
Fast-growing, erect annual with softly hairy, aromatic leaves. Daisy-like, double, lemon-yellow flower heads, with red-brown disc-florets, are borne summer–autumn. **H** to 45cm (18in), **S** 30–45cm (12–18in).

***Tagetes* 'Naughty Marietta'**
Fast-growing, bushy annual with aromatic, deeply cut, deep green leaves. Heads of daisy-like, bicoloured flowers, deep yellow and maroon, are carried in summer and early autumn. **H** and **S** 30cm (12in).

***Begonia* 'Herzog von Sagan'**
Upright Tuberhybrida begonia with few side shoots. Double, yellow flowers, 20cm (8in) across, with rough-edged, red petals, are borne in summer. **H** 30cm (12in), **S** 50cm (20in). Min. 5–7°C (41–45°F).

***Gazania* Daybreak Series 'Daybreak Bright Yellow'**
Spreading perennial, grown as an annual, with narrowly lance-shaped, green leaves. Daisy-like, vivid yellow flowers, 7.5cm (3in) across, with a dark ring round each golden eye, are borne all summer. **H** and **S** 20cm (8in).

***Viola* x *wittrockiana* Angel Series 'Tiger Eye'**
Clump-forming, short-lived perennial, grown as a biennial or annual, with small, oval, toothed, leaves. 5-petalled, burnished-gold flowers, patterned with chestnut-brown whiskers, are borne in spring. **H** and **S** 20cm (8in).

***Lysimachia congestiflora* 'Outback Sunset'**
Mat-forming or trailing perennial. Lance-shaped, red-tinged, leaves, 5cm (2in) long, irregularly splashed in yellow. Has clusters of 5-lobed, trumpet-shaped, yellow flowers in summer. **H** 10cm (4in), **S** 30cm (12in).

Carthamus tinctorius (False saffron)
Moderately fast-growing, upright annual with coarse, spine-edged, linear foliage. Produces tufted, thistle-like flowers, surrounded by stiff green bracts, in summer. Suitable for drying. **H** and **S** 30–60cm (12–24in).

***Tropaeolum majus* Alaska Series**
Fast-growing, bushy annual with rounded, variegated leaves. Spurred, trumpet-shaped flowers, in shades of red or yellow, appear in summer and early autumn. **H** and **S** 30cm (12in).

***Rudbeckia hirta* 'Marmalade'**
Moderately fast-growing, erect, branching perennial, grown as an annual, with lance-shaped leaves. In summer–autumn bears daisy-like, deep golden-orange flower heads, 8cm (3in) wide, with black centres. **H** 45cm (18in), **S** 30cm (12in).

***Erysimum* x *allionii* 'Orange Bedder'**
Slow-growing, short-lived, evergreen, bushy perennial, grown as a biennial. Has lance-shaped, mid-green leaves. Heads of scented, 4-petalled, brilliant orange flowers appear in spring. **H** and **S** 30cm (12in).

***Sanvitalia procumbens* 'Mandarin Orange'**
Moderately fast-growing, prostrate annual. Has pointed-oval, mid-green leaves and daisy-like, orange flower heads, 2.5cm (1in) wide, in summer. **H** 15cm (6in), **S** 30cm (12in).

***Gazania* Kiss Series 'Kiss Orange Flame'**
Spreading perennial, grown as an annual, with long, narrowly lance-shaped, dark green leaves. All summer produces daisy-like, orange flowers, 7.5cm (3in) across, with mahogany-striped petals. **H** and **S** 20cm (8in).

***Portulaca* Sundial Series 'Mango'**
Spreading, slightly succulent perennial, grown as an annual, with lance-shaped, fleshy, red-tinted, dark green leaves. In summer bears bowl-shaped, semi-double, peach flowers, 5cm (2in) across. **H** 20–38cm (8–15in), **S** 25–30cm (10–12in).

***Tagetes* Boy Series** [orange]
Compact annual that bears double, crested flower heads in a range of colours, including shades of golden-yellow, yellow, orange or reddish-brown, with deep orange or yellow crests, in late spring and early summer. **H** to 15cm (6in), **S** to 30cm (12in).

***Tithonia rotundifolia* 'Torch'**
Slow-growing, erect annual with rounded, lobed leaves. Has daisy-like, bright orange or scarlet flower heads, 5–7cm (2–3in) wide, in summer and early autumn. **H** 90cm (36in), **S** 30cm (12in).

***Rudbeckia hirta* 'Goldilocks'**
Moderately fast-growing, erect, branching perennial, grown as an annual. Has lance-shaped leaves and daisy-like, double or semi-double, golden-orange flowers, 8cm (3in) across, in summer–autumn. **H** 60cm (24in), **S** 30cm (12in).

***Abutilon pictum* 'Thompsonii'**
Robust, evergreen, upright shrub with 3–5-lobed, serrated, rich green, heavily yellow-mottled leaves. Yellow-orange flowers with crimson veins are borne from summer to autumn. **H** 5m (15ft), **S** 2–5m (6–15ft). Min. 5–7°C (41–5°F).

Calendula officinalis
Fiesta Gitana Group
Fast-growing, bushy annual with strongly aromatic, lance-shaped, pale green leaves. Daisy-like, double flower heads, ranging from cream to orange in colour, are carried from spring to autumn. **H** and **S** 30cm (12in).

***Zinnia haageana* 'Orange Star'**
Dwarf, bushy annual with daisy-like, broad-petalled, orange flower heads, borne in summer. Is mildew-resistant and good for ground cover. **H** to 25cm (10in), **S** to 30cm (12in).

***Lantana* 'Spreading Sunset'**
Evergreen, rounded to spreading shrub with finely wrinkled, deep green leaves. Has tiny, tubular flowers in a range of colours, carried in dense, rounded heads from spring through to autumn. **H** and **S** 1–2m (3–6ft). Min. 10–13°C (50–55°F).

***Impatiens* Sunpatiens Series**
SUNPATIENS COMPACT ORANGE ('Sakimp011')
Mound-forming, well-branched, prolific perennial, grown as an annual. Has flattish, 5-petalled, spurred, thick-petalled, vivid orange flowers, 6cm (2½in) across, in summer. **H** and **S** 60cm (24in).

***Impatiens* Fusion Series**
FUSION PEACH FROST ('Balfuspeafro')
Evergreen, bushy perennial, grown as an annual, with elliptical, pale green leaves margined in cream. Tubular, 5-petalled, peach-pink flowers, 1.5cm (⅝in) across, with orange centres, are borne in summer. **H** and **S** 25–40cm (10–16in).

***Tagetes* 'Tangerine Gem'**
Fast-growing, bushy annual with aromatic, feathery leaves. Small, single, deep orange flower heads appear in summer and early autumn.
H 20cm (8in), **S** 30cm (12in).

***Coreopsis* 'Rum Punch'**
Bushy, rather spreading, prolific but short-lived perennial, grown as an annual. Slender stems have divided, dark green leaves and in summer–autumn bear daisy-like, coppery-pink flower heads, 3.5cm (1½in) across.
H 45cm (18in), **S** 60cm (24in).

***Calendula officinalis* 'Geisha Girl'**
Fast-growing, bushy annual with strongly aromatic, lance-shaped, pale green leaves. Heads of double, orange flowers with incurved petals are borne from late spring to autumn.
H 60cm (24in), **S** 30–60cm (12–24in).

Eschscholzia californica
Fast-growing, slender, erect annual with feathery, bluish-green leaves. Cup-shaped, 4-petalled, vivid orange-yellow flowers are borne in summer–autumn. **H** 30cm (12in), **S** 15cm (6in).

***Erysimum cheiri* 'Fire King'**
Moderately fast-growing, evergreen, bushy perennial, grown as a biennial. Lance-shaped leaves are mid- to deep green; heads of 4-petalled, reddish-orange flowers are carried in spring.
H 38cm (15in), **S** 30–38cm (12–15in).

Emilia coccinea (Tassel flower)
Moderately fast-growing, upright annual with lance-shaped, greyish-green leaves and double, red or yellow flower heads in summer. **H** 30–60cm (12–24in), **S** 30cm (12in).

Solanum pseudocapsicum **'Red Giant'**
Fairly slow-growing, evergreen, bushy shrub, usually grown as an annual. Has lance-shaped, deep green leaves, small, white flowers in summer and large, round, orange-red fruits in winter. **H** and **S** 30cm (12in). Min. 5°C (41°F).

Tropaeolum **Jewel Series**
Fast-growing, bushy annual with rounded leaves. Spurred, trumpet-shaped flowers, in shades of red, yellow or orange, are held well above leaves from early summer to early autumn. **H** and **S** 30cm (12in).

Dahlia **Dahlietta Series 'Surprise Kelly'**
Compact, bushy, well-branched, tuberous perennial, grown as an annual. In summer has pointed-oval, toothed leaves and flat heads of daisy-like, golden-yellow flowers, very heavy speckled in dark orange. **H** 25–30cm (10–12in), **S** 35–40cm (14–16in).

Eschscholzia californica **Thai Silk Series**
Fast-growing, compact, slender, erect annual with feathery, bluish-green leaves. In summer–autumn, produces single or semi-double, fluted, bronze-tinged flowers in red, pink or orange. **H** 20–25cm (8–10in), **S** 15cm (6in).

Gaillardia pulchella **'Lollipops'**
Moderately fast-growing, upright annual with lance-shaped, hairy, greyish-green leaves. Daisy-like, double, red-and-yellow flower heads, 5cm (2in) wide, are carried in summer. **H** and **S** 30cm (12in).

Dahlia **'Dandy'**
Well-branched, erect, bushy, tuberous perennial, grown as an annual. Has pointed-oval, serrated leaves and heads of daisy-like flowers, with contrasting central collars of quilled petals, in shades of red, yellow or orange in summer. **H** and **S** 60cm (24in).

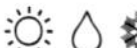

Solanum pseudocapsicum **'Balloon'**
Evergreen, bushy shrub, grown as an annual. Has lance-shaped leaves and, in summer, small, star-shaped, white flowers. Large, cream fruits turn orange in winter. **H** 30cm (12in), **S** 30–45cm (12–18in). Min. 5°C (41°F).

ROCK PLANTS

Rock plants are prized for their natural charm, foliage forms, and, in many cases, masses of colourful flowers in spring and summer. Grow them in areas that mimic the conditions in which they thrive in the wild, which are usually exposed sites with stony, rapidly draining soils. As long as they have sharp drainage and protection from excessive winter moisture, you can grow rock plants in small gardens in a trough or container, or where there is more space, in a rock garden or scree bed. If the soil in your garden is unsuitable, you can also grow these ground-hugging plants in raised beds to create landscapes in miniature. Raised beds also have the advantage of bringing the small plants closer to eye level so that you can admire their tiny, delicate features in more detail.

ROCK PLANTS

The delicate flowers and foliage of many rock plants belies their tough nature, withstanding the burning sun and harsh winds typical of their alpine habitats. They make excellent plants for the garden, and are perfect for rock and scree gardens, wall crevices, troughs, and pots.

SIZE CATEGORIES USED WITHIN THIS GROUP		
Large over 15cm (6in)	**Medium** ———	**Small** up to 15cm (6in)

What are rock plants?

The term rock plants includes bulbs and mat- and cushion-forming perennials – many of which are evergreen – as well as dwarf conifers and both evergreen and deciduous shrubs. Some are true alpines from mountain regions, while others are simply compact plants suitable for rock-garden planting schemes. While some alpines have specialized needs, many species and cultivars, including aubrietas and geraniums, are easy to grow and thrive in any well-drained soil and sunny site.

True alpines are found at high altitudes above the tree-line on mountains, growing on scree slopes, in short turf, or finding protection from the wind by squeezing into rock crevices. Sub-alpine plants live below the tree-line on rocky slopes or in high pastures or meadows. Most alpines are compact in habit and frequently deep-rooting, usually with small leaves that are leathery, fleshy or covered in fine hair. These adaptations help them survive the drying, high-velocity winds, brilliant, burning sun, and extreme temperature fluctuations of their natural habitats.

Most rock plants grow in areas that have stony soils with rapid drainage, which explains why few can cope with wet soil around the roots, which is experienced at lower-altitudes. They also dislike warm, humid summers.

In the wild, high-growing species are insulated from winter cold by a blanket of snow, beneath which they remain dormant at temperatures around 0°C (32°F) until spring. Those environments that mimic conditions in the wild, such as rock gardens, scree and gravel beds, troughs, pots, raised beds, and open frames, are therefore ideal for growing rock plants. You can grow alpines successfully even in areas where the soil is unsuitable by filling raised beds, pots and troughs with free-draining soil and horticultural grit.

Designing with rock plants

One of the major attractions of this group is their diminutive size, which allows you to grow a huge number of different plant types in a relatively confined space. In a rock garden – as in larger-scale plantings – use small shrubs, such as the highly fragrant *Daphne cneorum* and *D. retusa* or the catkin-bearing *Salix bockii* and *S. apoda*, to form the structural framework of your design. Miniature conifers, such as *Juniperus communis* 'Compressa', provide vertical accents and year-round colour, and work well in combination with the contrasting forms of rounded or domed plants, such as the evergreen *Hebe cupressoides* 'Boughton Dome' and *Cassiope lycopodioides*. This structure can then be filled in with mat- and cushion-forming plants, such as sandworts (*Arenaria*) or *Dianthus deltoides*,

ABOVE Mediterranean mountains
Recreate a Mediterranean alpine scene with clay pots and pebbles decorating beds that include a range of sedums, saxifrages, thymes, and arabis, with clipped box balls providing structure.

LEFT Colourful tapestry
Siting a rock garden on a gentle slope assists rapid drainage, while an open sunny site is perfect for alpines. Choose plants with contrasting forms, such as tear-shaped, upright conifers and mats of colourful blooms.

PLANTING A GRAVEL OR SCREE GARDEN

Gravel gardens are ideal for alpines and rock plants. Stones can be worked into a scheme to create a rock garden, or a variety of rock and stone sizes used on a slope to form a natural scree. A gravel or slate chip mulch helps to keep the plant leaves and stems dry, and prevents rotting but lay a weed-suppressing fabric over the garden first. This elimates light and stops weed seeds germinating but still allows moisture through to the plant.

A weed-free gravel garden

1 Lay the fabric
Measure your bed, and buy sufficient weed-suppressing fabric to cover it. Overlap the edges when joining two pieces together. Cut crosses where you plan to plant.

2 Plant up
Fold back the flaps, and dig a hole, putting the excavated soil on a plastic sheet. Insert the plant, water in, and backfill with soil. Firm in and replace the flaps around the plant stems.

3 Add gravel mulch
Trim the fabric around the stems and continue to plant in this way. When the bed is planted, spread a 5–8cm (2–3in) layer of gravel over the fabric and around each plant.

at the feet of slightly taller, feathery-leaved pulsatillas or the airy *Linum narbonense*. As well as shape and form, think too about contrasting textures. Candidates include the almost bead-like foliage of certain sedums, spiky houseleek (*Sempervivum*) rosettes, and the pointy-tipped grey leaves of *Euphorbia myrsinites*, which would make eye-catching partners for the white-haired leaves of edelweiss (*Leontopodium*) or the silky, silver leaves of celmisias.

Most alpines like an open sunny site and will not thrive if shaded by overhanging trees or neighbouring plants. Plant them with space to spread and use a dry mulch, such as gravel, to keep the stems and leaves dry at all times. Mulches also act as a foil for the plants.

If you have limited space, plant a selection of different alpines in small pots filled with gritty compost. Many plants in this group are drought-tolerant and thrive in containers, and when grouped together make colourful displays. Troughs can be given a modern make-over by planting alpines between slate chips (*see box right*), or using a ground glass or shell mulch.

Raised beds offer another design option for those with small gardens. They are also useful for people with reduced mobility, allowing them to access the plants more easily. Use raised beds to create miniature landscapes with plants spreading between rocks and pebbles. Dry stone walls offer ideal sites for many crevice-lovers, such as aubretias and sedums, while cascading alpines, such as *Saxifraga* 'Tumbling Waters', are perfect for the tops of walls.

Year-round interest

Many alpines flower in spring and early summer, just after the snow melts and before the heat of midsummer in their natural habitat. For colour earlier in the year, plant spring bulbs, such as alpine narcissus or crocuses, among evergreen perennials, conifers, and small shrubs. The choice of flower at the peak flowering times is vast, so coordinate your colour schemes for a dramatic performance. Hot colours, such as the bright yellow sedums and wall flowers (*Erysimum*) and scarlet and orange helianthemums, create highlights against more subdued blues and purples. As the summer progresses, select later-flowering rock plants, including phlox, crepis, and diascias, followed by the pink *Silene schafta*, gentians, and berry-bearing gaultherias in the autumn.

PLANTING A SLATE-FILLED TROUGH

Topped with slate chips, this decorative trough mirrors a natural mountain scree, and provides a long season of colour in spring and summer. Plants included in this display are *Draba* species, erigerons, saxifrages, *Silene acaulis* and *Townsendia grandiflora*. However, any small alpines that have different leaf textures and flower colours will work equally well. Move your trough to its final position before you start, as it will be very heavy once planted.

1 Prepare the trough
Cover the drainage holes at the base of the trough with crocks. Add a 5cm (2in) layer of gravel. Fill up the trough with equal parts of soil-based compost and sand, to 5cm (2in) from the top.

2 Add slates and plants
Push the slate chips vertically into the compost, leaving spaces for the alpines. Water the plants, and plant them into the gaps, making sure the roots are covered with the sand and compost mix. Water well.

WHITE

Leontopodium alpinum (Edelweiss)
Short-lived perennial with lance-shaped, woolly leaves. Small, silvery-white flower heads, in spring or early summer, are surrounded by petal-like, felted bracts in a star shape. Dislikes wet. **H** and **S** 15–20cm (6–8in).

Lithophragma parviflorum
Clump-forming, tuberous perennial that has small, open clusters of campion-like, white or pink flowers in spring above a basal cluster of deeply toothed, kidney-shaped leaves. Lies dormant in summer. **H** 15–20cm (6–8in), **S** to 20cm (8in).

Iberis sempervirens
Evergreen, spreading sub-shrub, with narrow, oblong, dark green leaves, bearing dense, rounded heads of white flowers in late spring and early summer. Trim after flowering. **H** 15–30cm (6–12in), **S** 45–60cm (18–24in).

Pulsatilla alpina (Alpine anemone)
Tufted perennial with feathery leaves. Has upright, or nodding, cup-shaped, white, sometimes blue- or pink-flushed flowers singly in spring and early summer, then feathery seed heads. **H** 15–30cm (6–12in), **S** to 10cm (4in).

Saxifraga granulata (Fair maids of France, Meadow saxifrage)
Clump-forming perennial that loses its kidney-shaped, crumpled, glossy leaves in summer. Sticky stems carry loose panicles of rounded, white flowers in late spring. **H** 23–38cm (9–15in), **S** to 15cm (6in) or more.

Rhodanthemum hosmariense
Evergreen, shrubby perennial with finely cut, bright silvery-green leaves that clothe lax, woody stems. From late spring to early autumn, white flower heads are borne singly above foliage. **H** 15cm (6in) or more, **S** 30cm (12in).

Andromeda polifolia 'Alba'
Evergreen, open, twiggy shrub bearing terminal clusters of pitcher-shaped, white flowers in spring and early summer. Glossy, dark green leaves are leathery and lance-shaped. **H** 45cm (18in), **S** 60cm (24in).

Cassiope 'Muirhead'
Evergreen, loose, bushy shrub with scale-like, dark green leaves on upright branches. In spring, these bear tiny, virtually stemless, bell-shaped, white flowers along their length. **H** and **S** 20cm (8in).

Cassiope tetragona
Evergreen, upright shrub with dense, scale-like, dark green leaves concealing branched stems. In spring, leaf axils bear solitary pendent, bell-shaped, white flowers in red calyces. **H** 10–25cm (4–10in), **S** 10–15cm (4–6in).

ROCK PLANTS

Jeffersonia diphylla
Slow-growing, tufted perennial with distinctive, 2-lobed, light to mid-green leaves. Bears solitary cup-shaped, white flowers with prominent, yellow stamens in late spring. Do not disturb roots.
H 15–23cm (6–9in), **S** to 23cm (9in).

***Saxifraga* 'Tumbling Waters'**
Slow-growing, evergreen, mat-forming perennial with a tight rosette of narrow, lime-encrusted leaves. After several years produces arching sprays of white flowers in conical heads; main rosette then dies but small offsets survive.
H to 60cm (24in), **S** to 20cm (8in).

PINK

***Andromeda polifolia* 'Compacta'**
Evergreen, compact, twiggy shrub that bears delicate, terminal clusters of pitcher-shaped, coral-pink flowers, with white undertones, in spring and early summer. Leaves are lance-shaped and glossy, dark green. **H** 15–23cm (6–9in), **S** 30cm (12in).

Daphne cneorum
Evergreen, low-growing shrub with trailing branches clothed in small, oval, leathery, dark green leaves. Fragrant, deep rose pink flowers are borne in terminal clusters in late spring. Prefers humus-rich soil. **H** 23cm (9in), **S** to 2m (6ft).

Daphne blagayana
Evergreen, prostrate shrub with trailing branches each bearing a terminal cluster of oval, leathery leaves and, in early spring, dense clusters of fragrant, tubular, white flowers. Likes humus-rich soil. **H** 30–40cm (12–16in), **S** 60–80cm (24–32in) or more.

Daphne alpina
Compact and upright deciduous shrub with softly hairy, oval, grey-green leaves. In late spring produces terminal clusters of small, white flowers that are sweetly scented. These are followed by spherical, orange-red fruits. **H** and **S** to 60cm (24in).

Dodecatheon hendersonii
Clump-forming perennial with a flat rosette of kidney-shaped leaves, above which deep pink flowers with reflexed petals appear in late spring. Needs a dry, dormant summer period. **H** 30cm (12in), **S** 8cm (3in).

Tiarella cordifolia (Foamflower)
Vigorous, evergreen, spreading perennial. Lobed, pale green leaves sometimes have darker marks; veins turn bronze-red in winter. Bears many spikes of profuse white flowers in late spring and early summer. **H** 15–20cm (6–8in), **S** to 30cm (12in) or more.

Dodecatheon meadia* f. *album
Clump-forming perennial with basal rosettes of oval, pale green leaves. In spring, strong stems bear several white flowers with dark centres and reflexed petals. Lies dormant in summer.
H 20cm (8in), **S** 15cm (6in).

***Phyllodoce* x *intermedia* 'Drummondii'**
Evergreen, bushy, dwarf shrub with narrow, heath-like, glossy leaves. From late spring to early summer bears terminal clusters of pitcher-shaped, rich pink flowers on slender, red stalks.
H and **S** 23cm (9in).

***Dodecatheon pulchellum* 'Red Wings'**
Clump-forming perennial with a basal cluster of oblong, soft, pale green leaves. In late spring and early summer bears small, loose clusters of deep magenta flowers, with reflexed petals, on strong stems. Lies dormant in summer.
H 20cm (8in), **S** 10cm (4in).

PINK

Phyllodoce empetriformis
Evergreen, mat-forming shrub with fine narrow, heath-like leaves and terminal clusters of bell-shaped, purplish-pink flowers in late spring and early summer. **H** 15–23cm (6–9in), **S** 20cm (8in).

Phyllodoce caerulea
Evergreen, dwarf shrub with fine, narrow, heath-like leaves. Bears bell-shaped, purple to purplish-pink flowers, singly or in clusters, in late spring and summer. **H** and **S** to 30cm (12in).

***Daphne x hendersonii* 'Blackthorn Rose'**
Evergreen, domed shrub with glossy, dark green leaves, to 2.5cm (1in) long. In spring produces numerous, rounded deep red-purple buds that open to very fragrant, pink flowers with spreading lobes. **H** 20–30cm (8–12in), **S** 45cm (18in).

PURPLE

Pulsatilla halleri
Tufted perennial, intensely hairy in all parts, that in spring bears nodding, later erect, cup-shaped flowers in shades of purple. Has feathery leaves and seed heads. **H** 15–38cm (6–15in), **S** 15–20cm (6–8in).

Pulsatilla vulgaris (Pasque flower)
Tufted perennial with feathery, light green leaves. In spring bears nodding, cup-shaped flowers, in shades of purple, red, pink or white, with bright yellow centres. Flower stems rapidly elongate as feathery seeds mature. **H** and **S** 15–23cm (6–9in).

Erinacea anthyllis (Hedgehog broom)
Slow growing, evergreen sub-shrub with hard, blue-green spines. Pea-like, soft lavender flowers appear in axils of spines in late spring to early summer. **H** and **S** 15–25cm (6–10in).

BLUE

Aquilegia alpina (Alpine columbine)
Short-lived, upright perennial with spurred, clear blue or violet-blue flowers on slender stems in spring and early summer. Has basal rosettes of rounded, finely divided leaves. Needs rich soil. **H** 45cm (18in), **S** 15cm (6in).

Omphalodes verna
Semi-evergreen, clump-forming perennial that in spring bears long, loose sprays of flat, bright blue flowers with white eyes. Leaves are oval and mid-green. **H** and **S** 20cm (8in) or more.

Omphalodes cappadocica
Spreading perennial with creeping underground stems and many loose sprays of flat, bright blue flowers in spring-summer above tufts of oval, hairy, basal leaves. **H** 15–20cm (6–8in), **S** 25cm (10in) or more.

Betula nana (Arctic birch)
Deciduous, bushy, dwarf shrub with small, toothed leaves that turn bright yellow in autumn. Has tiny, yellowish-brown catkins in spring. **H** 30cm (12in), **S** 45cm (18in).

Chiastophyllum oppositifolium
Evergreen, trailing perennial with large, oblong, serrated, succulent leaves. In late spring and early summer bears many tiny, yellow flowers in arching sprays. **H** 15–20cm (6–8in), **S** 15cm (6in).

Hylomecon japonica
Vigorous, spreading perennial with large, cup-shaped, bright yellow flowers that are borne singly on slender stems in spring. Soft, dark green leaves are divided into 4 unequal lobes. **H** to 30cm (12in), **S** 20cm (8in).

Corydalis cheilanthifolia
Evergreen perennial with fleshy roots. Produces spreading rosettes of fern-like, near-prostrate, sometimes bronze-tinted, mid-green leaves. Has dense spikes of short-spurred, yellow flowers in late spring and early summer. **H** 20–30cm (8–12in), **S** 15–20cm (6–8in).

***Aurinia saxatilis* 'Citrina'**
Evergreen, clump-forming perennial with oval, hairy, grey-green leaves. Bears racemes of many, small, pale lemon-yellow flowers in late spring and early summer. **H** 23cm (9in), **S** 30cm (12in).

Cytisus x beanii
Deciduous, low-growing shrub with arching sprays of pea-like, golden-yellow flowers that appear in late spring and early summer on previous year's wood. Leaves, divided into 3 leaflets, are small, linear and hairy. **H** 15–40cm (6–16in), **S** 30–75cm (12–30in).

***Erysimum* 'Moonlight'**
Mat-forming, evergreen perennial with narrowly oval leaves. In early summer, produces clusters of pale, sulphur-yellow flowers on short, leafy stems. Prefers an open site and gritty soil. **H** 25cm (10in), **S** 45cm (18in).

Salix helvetica
Deciduous, spreading, much-branched, dwarf shrub that has small, oval, glossy leaves, white-haired beneath. In spring bears short-stalked, silky, grey, then yellow catkins. **H** 60cm (24in), **S** 30cm (12in).

Corydalis wilsonii
Evergreen perennial with a fleshy rootstock. Forms rosettes of near-prostrate, divided, bluish-green leaves. Loose racemes of spurred, green-tipped, yellow flowers are produced in spring. **H** and **S** 10–25cm (4–10in).

***Aurinia saxatilis* 'Variegata'**
Evergreen perennial that bears racemes of many small, yellow flowers in spring above a mat of large, oval, soft grey-green leaves with cream margins. **H** 23cm (9in), **S** 30cm (12in).

Aurinia saxatilis (Gold dust)
Evergreen perennial forming low clumps of oval, hairy, grey-green leaves. Has substantial spikes of small, chrome-yellow flowers in spring. **H** 23cm (9in), **S** 30cm (12in).

YELLOW

***Erysimum* 'Bredon'**
Semi-evergreen, rounded, woody perennial clothed in oval, dark green leaves. In late spring bears dense spikes of flat, bright mustard-yellow flowers. **H** 30–45cm (12–18in), **S** 45cm (18in).

***Erysimum* x *kewense* 'Harpur Crewe'**
Evergreen, shrubby perennial with stiff stems and narrow leaves. Fragrant, double, deep yellow flowers open in succession from late spring to mid-summer. Grows best in poor soil and a sheltered site. **H** and **S** 30cm (12in).

***Berberis* x *stenophylla* 'Corallina Compacta'**
Evergreen, neat, dwarf shrub with spiny stems clothed in small, narrowly oval leaves. In late spring bears many tiny, bright orange flowers. Is slow-growing and difficult to propagate. **H** and **S** to 25cm (10in).

WHITE

Parnassia palustris
(Grass of Parnassus)
Perennial with low, basal tufts of heart-shaped, pale to mid-green leaves. Bears saucer-shaped, white flowers, with dark green or purplish-green veins, on erect stems in late spring and early summer. **H** 20cm (8in), **S** 6cm (2½in) or more.

Armeria pseudarmeria
Evergreen, clump-forming perennial with large, spherical heads of white flowers occasionally suffused pink; these are borne in summer on stiff stems above long, narrow, glaucous leaves. **H** and **S** 30cm (12in).

Celmisia walkeri
Evergreen, loose, spreading perennial with long, oval or lance-shaped leaves, glossy, green above and hairy, white beneath. Has large, daisy-like, white flower heads in summer. **H** 23cm (9in), **S** to 2m (6ft).

Helianthemum apenninum
Evergreen, spreading, much-branched shrub that bears saucer-shaped, pure white flowers in mid-summer. Stems and small, linear leaves are covered in white down. **H** and **S** 45cm (18in).

Galax urceolata
Evergreen, clump-forming perennial. Large, round, leathery, mid-green leaves on slender stems turn bronze in autumn-winter. Has dense spikes of small, white flowers in late spring and early summer. **H** 15–20cm (6–8in), **S** to 30cm (12in).

***Helianthemum* 'Wisley White'**
Evergreen, spreading shrub, with oblong, grey-green leaves, bearing saucer-shaped, white flowers for a long period in summer. **H** 23cm (9in), **S** 30cm (12in) or more.

Chamaecytisus purpureus* f. *albus
Deciduous, low-growing shrub with semi-erect stems clothed in leaves, divided into 3 leaflets. A profusion of pea-like, white flowers appear in early summer on previous year's wood. **H** 45cm (18in), **S** 60cm (24in).

***Diascia* ICE CRACKER ('Hecrack')**
Mat-forming perennial with narrowly ovate, mid to dark green leaves. From summer to autumn produces upright racemes of 2-lipped, hooded, shallowly bell-shaped, spurred, white flowers, touched pink at the base. **H** 30cm (12in), **S** 5–20cm (6–8in).

Saxifraga cuneifolia
Evergreen, carpeting perennial with neat rosettes of rounded leaves. In late spring and early summer bears panicles of tiny, white flowers, frequently with yellow, pink or red spots, on slender stems. **H** 15–20cm (6–8in), **S** 30cm (12in) or more.

Saxifraga callosa
Evergreen, tightly rosetted perennial with long, linear, stiff, lime-encrusted leaves and, in early summer, upright, then arching panicles of star-shaped, red-spotted white flowers. Rosettes die after flowering. Suits a rock pocket. **H** 25cm (10in), **S** to 20cm (8in).

***Hebe pinguifolia* 'Pagei'**
Evergreen, semi-prostrate shrub with small, oblong, slightly cupped, intensely glaucous leaves. Bears short spikes of small, white flowers in late spring or early summer. Is excellent for ground or rock cover. **H** 15–30cm (6–12in), **S** 60cm (24in).

Hebe vernicosa
Evergreen, bushy, compact shrub with small, oval, glossy, dark green leaves densely packed on stems. In early and mid-summer, spikes of small, 4-lobed, white flowers are freely produced. **H** 60cm (2ft), **S** 1.2m (4ft).

Corydalis ochroleuca
Evergreen, clump-forming perennial with fleshy, fibrous roots and much divided, basal, grey-green leaves. Bears slender, yellow-tipped, creamy-white flowers in late spring and summer. **H** and **S** 20–30cm (8–12in).

PINK

Aethionema grandiflorum
(Persian stone cress)
Short-lived, evergreen or semi-evergreen, lax shrub. Bears tiny, pale to deep rose-pink flowers in loose sprays in spring–summer. Blue-green leaves are narrow and lance-shaped. **H** 30cm (12in), **S** 23cm (9in).

Rhodothamnus chamaecistus
Evergreen, low-growing, dwarf shrub with narrow, oval leaves, edged with bristles. In late spring and early summer bears cup-shaped, rose- to lilac-pink flowers, with dark stamens, in leaf axils. **H** 15–20cm (6–8in), **S** to 25cm (10in).

Phuopsis stylosa
Low-growing perennial with whorls of pungent, pale green leaves and rounded heads of small, tubular, pink flowers in summer. Is good grown over a bank or large rock. **H** 30cm (12in), **S** 30cm (12in).

***Lewisia* 'George Henley'**
Evergreen, clump-forming perennial with rosettes of narrow, fleshy, dark green leaves. Bears dense sprays of open cup-shaped, deep pink flowers, with magenta veins, from late spring to late summer. **H** 15cm (6in) or more, **S** 10cm (4in).

Onosma alborosea
Semi-evergreen, clump-forming perennial covered in fine hairs, which may irritate skin. Clusters of long, pendent, tubular flowers, borne for a long period in summer, open white and then turn pink. **H** 15–30cm (6–12in), **S** 20cm (8in).

Anthyllis montana
Rounded, bushy or somewhat spreading perennial with loose branches and finely cut foliage. Heads of clover-like, pale pink flowers with red markings are borne in late spring and early summer. **H** and **S** 30cm (12in).

***Helianthemum* 'Rhodanthe Carneum'**
Evergreen, lax shrub with saucer-shaped, soft, pale pink flowers with orange centres borne for a long period in summer. Has oblong, grey-green leaves. **H** and **S** 30cm (12in) or more.

***Saxifraga* 'Southside Seedling'**
Evergreen, mat-forming perennial, with large, pale green rosettes of leaves, dying after flowering. In late spring and early summer bears arching panicles of open cup-shaped, white flowers, strongly red-banded within. **H** and **S** to 30cm (12in).

Oxalis tetraphylla
Tuft-forming, tuberous perennial with brown marked, basal leaves, usually divided into 4 leaflets. Produces loose sprays of widely funnel-shaped, deep pink flowers in late spring and summer. Needs shelter. **H** 15–30cm (6–12in), **S** 10–15cm (4–6in).

***Origanum* 'Kent Beauty'**
Prostrate perennial with trailing stems clothed in aromatic, rounded-oval leaves. In summer bears short spikes of tubular, pale pink flowers with darker bracts. Is suitable for a wall or ledge. **H** 15–20cm (6–8in), **S** 30cm (12in).

Crassula sarcocaulis
Evergreen or, in severe climates, semi-evergreen, bushy sub-shrub with tiny, oval, succulent leaves. Bears terminal clusters of tiny, red buds opening to pale pink flowers in summer. **H** and **S** 30cm (12in).

Diascia rigescens
Trailing perennial with semi-erect stems covered in heart-shaped, mid-green leaves. Spurred, flat-faced, salmon-pink flowers are borne along stem length in summer and early autumn. **H** 23cm (9in), **S** to 30cm (12in).

Geranium orientalitibeticum
Perennial spreading by tuberous, underground runners. Has cup-shaped, pink flowers, with white centres, in summer. Leaves are deeply cut and marbled in shades of green. Invasive. **H** in flower 15–25cm (6–10in), **S** indefinite.

***Astilbe* x *crispa* 'Perkeo'**
Erect, compact perennial bearing small plumes of tiny, salmon-pink flowers from mid- to late summer on fine stems. Has stiff, deeply cut, crinkled leaves. **H** 15–20cm (6–8in), **S** 10cm (4in).

***Diascia barberae* 'Fisher's Flora'**
Prostrate perennial with stems clothed in heart-shaped, pale green leaves. Bears terminal clusters of spurred, flat-faced, bright pink flowers in summer and early autumn. **H** 15–20cm (6–8in), **S** 20cm (8in).

Ononis fruticosa (Shrubby restharrow)
Deciduous shrub that in summer bears pendent clusters of large, pea-like, purplish-pink blooms with darker streaks. Leaves are divided into 3 serrated leaflets, which are hairy when young. **H** and **S** 30–60cm (12–24in).

Dianthus carthusianorum
Evergreen perennial carrying rounded, upward-facing, cherry-red or deep pink flowers on slender stems in summer above small tufts of grass-like leaves. **H** 20cm (8in), **S** 7cm (3in).

PINK

***Lewisia* Cotyledon Hybrids**
Evergreen, clump-forming perennials with rosettes of large, thick, toothed leaves. In early summer bear clusters of flowers, in various shades of pink to purple, on erect stems. Is good for a rock crevice or an alpine house. **H** to 30cm (12in), **S** 15cm (6in) or more.

Penstemon newberryi* f. *humilior
Evergreen, mat-forming shrub with arching branches clothed in small, leathery, dark green leaves. Bears short sprays of tubular, lipped, cherry-red to deep pink flowers in early summer. **H** 15–20cm (6–8in), **S** 30cm (12in).

Geranium sanguineum
(Bloody cranesbill)
Hummock-forming, spreading perennial with many cup-shaped, deep magenta-pink flowers borne in summer above round, deeply divided, dark green leaves. Makes good ground cover. **H** to 25cm (10in), **S** 30cm (12in) or more.

Origanum laevigatum
Deciduous, mat-forming sub-shrub with small, aromatic, dark green leaves, branching, red stems and a profusion of tiny, tubular, cerise-pink flowers, surrounded by red-purple bracts, in summer. **H** 23–30cm (9–12in), **S** 20cm (8in) or more.

Erigeron alpinus **(Alpine fleabane)**
Clump-forming perennial of variable size that bears daisy-like, lilac-pink flower heads on erect stems in summer. Leaves are long, oval and hairy. Suits a sunny border, bank or large rock garden. **H** 25cm (10in), **S** 20cm (8in).

RED

Delphinium nudicaule
Short-lived, upright perennial with erect stems bearing deeply divided, basal leaves and, in summer, spikes of hooded, red or occasionally yellow flowers, with contrasting stamens. **H** 20cm (8in), **S** 5–10cm (2–4in).

Penstemon pinifolius
Evergreen, bushy shrub with branched stems clothed in fine, dark green leaves. In summer, very narrow, tubular, orange-red flowers are borne in loose, terminal spikes. **H** 10–20cm (4–8in), **S** 15cm (6in).

***Zauschneria californica* 'Dublin'**
Clump-forming, woody-based perennial with lance-shaped, grey-green leaves. From late summer to early autumn bears terminal clusters of tubular, deep orange-scarlet flowers. **H** 30cm (12in), **S** 45cm (18in).

Punica granatum* var. *nana
(Dwarf pomegranate)
Slow-growing, deciduous, rounded shrub that, in summer, bears funnel-shaped, red flowers with somewhat crumpled petals, followed by small, rounded, orange-red fruits. **H** and **S** 30–90cm (12–36in).

***Helianthemum* 'Fire Dragon'**
Evergreen, spreading shrub with saucer-shaped, orange-scarlet flowers in late spring and summer. Leaves are linear and grey-green. **H** 23–30cm (9–12in), **S** 45cm (18in).

Cortusa matthioli
Clump-forming perennial with a basal rosette of rounded, dull green leaves and, in late spring and early summer, one-sided racemes of small, pendent, bell-shaped, reddish- or pinkish-purple flowers. **H** 15–20cm (6–8in), **S** 10cm (4in).

Erodium cheilanthifolium
Compact, mound-forming perennial with pink flowers, veined and marked with purple-red, borne on stiff stems in late spring and summer. Greyish-green leaves are crinkled and deeply cut. **H** 15–20cm (6–8in), **S** 20cm (8in) or more.

Scabiosa lucida
Clump-forming perennial with tufts of oval leaves and rounded heads of pale lilac to deep mauve flowers, borne on erect stems in summer. **H** 20cm (8in), **S** 15cm (6in).

Semiaquilegia ecalcarata
Short-lived, upright perennial with narrow, lobed leaves. In summer each slender stem bears several pendent, open bell-shaped, dusky-pink to purple flowers, with no spurs. **H** 20cm (8in), **S** 7cm (3in).

Calceolaria arachnoidea
Evergreen, clump-forming perennial with a basal rosette of wrinkled leaves, covered in white down. Upright stems carry spikes of many pouch-shaped, dull purple flowers in summer. Is best treated as a biennial. **H** 25cm (10in), **S** 12cm (5in).

Penstemon serrulatus
Semi-evergreen sub-shrub, deciduous in severe climates, that has small, elliptic, dark green leaves and tubular, blue to purple flowers borne in loose spikes in summer. Soil should not be too dry. **H** 60cm (24in), **S** 30cm (12in).

Wulfenia amherstiana
Evergreen perennial with rosettes of narrowly spoon-shaped, toothed leaves. Erect stems bear loose clusters of small, tubular, purple or pinkish-purple flowers in summer. **H** 15–30cm (6–12in), **S** to 30cm (12in).

***Phlox divaricata* subsp. *laphamii* 'Chattahoochee'**
Short-lived, clump-forming perennial that has saucer-shaped, red-eyed, bright lavender flowers throughout summer-autumn. Narrow, pointed leaves are dark reddish-purple when young. **H** 15–20cm (6–8in), **S** 30cm (12in).

Phlox divaricata* subsp. *laphamii
Semi-evergreen, creeping perennial with oval leaves and upright stems bearing loose clusters of saucer-shaped, pale to deep violet-blue flowers in summer. **H** 30cm (12in), **S** 20cm (8in).

PURPLE

Parahebe catarractae
Evergreen sub-shrub with oval, toothed, mid-green leaves and, in summer, loose sprays of small, open funnel-shaped, white flowers, heavily zoned and veined pinkish-purple. **H** and **S** 30cm (12in).

***Sisyrinchium* 'E.K. Balls'**
Clump-forming, variable perennial with fans of narrowly sword-shaped, upright, mid-green leaves. In summer produces a succession of many star-shaped, bluish-mauve flowers. **H** 20cm (8in), **S** 15cm (6in).

Campanula wanneri
Clump-forming perennial with branching stems and hairy, oval leaves. In summer bears pendent, bell-shaped, blue to violet-blue flowers in loose, terminal spikes. **H** 15–23cm (6–9in), **S** 25cm (10in).

BLUE

Campanula barbata
(Bearded bellflower)
Evergreen perennial with a basal rosette of oval, hairy, grey-green leaves. In summer bears one-sided racemes of bell-shaped, white to lavender-blue flowers. Is short lived but sets seed freely. **H** 20cm (8in), **S** 12cm (5in).

Linum perenne
Upright perennial with slender stems, clothed in grass-like leaves, that bear terminal clusters of open funnel-shaped, clear blue flowers in succession throughout summer. **H** 30cm (12in), **S** to 15cm (6in).

Convolvulus sabatius
Trailing perennial with slender stems clothed in small, oval leaves and open trumpet-shaped, vibrant blue-purple flowers in summer and early autumn. Shelter in a rock crevice in a cold site. **H** 15–20cm (6–8in), **S** 30cm (12in).

Phyteuma scheuchzeri
Tufted perennial with narrow, dark green leaves and terminal heads of spiky, blue flowers that are borne in summer. Seeds freely; dislikes winter wet. **H** 15–20cm (6–8in), **S** 10cm (4in).

Lithodora oleifolia
Evergreen shrub with oval, pointed, silky, mid green leaves. Curving stems carry loose sprays of several small, funnel-shaped, light blue flowers in early summer. **H** 15–20cm (6–8in), **S** to 1m (3ft).

Moltkia suffruticosa
Deciduous, upright sub-shrub. In summer bears clusters of funnel-shaped, bright blue flowers, pink in bud, on hairy stems. Leaves are long, pointed and hairy. **H** 15–40cm (6–16in), **S** 30cm (12in).

Veronica prostrata
(Prostrate speedwell)
Dense, mat-forming perennial that has upright spikes of small, saucer-shaped, brilliant blue flowers in early summer. Foliage is narrow, oval and toothed. **H** to 30cm (12in), **S** indefinite.

***Lithodora diffusa* 'Heavenly Blue'**
Evergreen, prostrate shrub with trailing stems bearing pointed, oblong, hairy leaves and, in summer, many open funnel-shaped, deep blue flowers in leaf axils. Trim stems hard after flowering. **H** 15–30cm (6–12in), **S** to 45cm (18in).

***Veronica prostrata* 'Trehane'**
Dense, mat-forming perennial bearing upright spikes of small, saucer-shaped, deep violet-blue flowers in early summer above narrow, toothed, yellow or yellowish-green leaves. **H** in flower 15–20cm (6–8in), **S** indefinite.

***Veronica austriaca* subsp. *teucrium* 'Kapitan'**
Dense, mat-forming perennial bearing erect spikes of small, saucer-shaped, bright deep blue flowers in early summer. Foliage is narrow, oval and toothed. **H** to 30cm (12in), **S** indefinite.

Veronica austriaca* subsp. *teucrium
Spreading perennial with narrow spikes of small, flat, outward-facing, bright blue flowers in summer. Leaves are small, divided, hairy and greyish-green. **H** and **S** 25–60cm (10–24in).

Erodium chrysanthum
Mound-forming perennial, grown for its dense, silvery stems and finely cut, fern-like leaves. Has small sprays of cup-shaped, sulphur- or creamy-yellow flowers in late spring and summer. **H** and **S** 23cm (9in).

***Hypericum olympicum* f. *uniflorum* 'Citrinum'**
Deciduous, dense, rounded sub-shrub with tufts of upright stems, clothed in small, oval, grey-green leaves. Bears terminal clusters of lemon-yellow flowers throughout summer. **H** and **S** 15–30cm (6–12in).

***Verbascum* 'Letitia'**
Evergreen, stiff-branched shrub with toothed, grey leaves. Bears outward-facing, 5-lobed, bright yellow flowers with orange centres continuously from late spring to mid-autumn. Hates winter wet; is good in an alpine house. **H** and **S** to 25cm (10in).

Linum arboreum
Evergreen, compact shrub with blue-green leaves. In summer has a succession of funnel-shaped, bright yellow flowers opening in sunny weather and borne in terminal clusters. **H** to 30cm (12in), **S** 30cm (12in).

Corydalis lutea
Evergreen, clump-forming perennial with fleshy, fibrous roots, semi-erect, basal, grey-green leaves. Bears racemes of slender, yellow flowers, with short spurs, in late spring and summer. **H** and **S** 20–30cm (8–12in).

Euryops acraeus
Evergreen, dome-shaped shrub with stems clothed in toothed, silvery-blue leaves. Bears solitary daisy-like, bright yellow flower heads in late spring and early summer. **H** and **S** 30cm (12in).

Chrysogonum virginianum
Mat-forming perennial with daisy-like, yellow flower heads borne on short stems in summer-autumn and oval, toothed, mid-green leaves. Although plant spreads by underground runners, it is not invasive. **H** 15–20cm (6–8in), **S** 10–15cm (4–6in) or more.

Helianthemum 'Wisley Primrose'
Fast-growing, evergreen, compact shrub with saucer-shaped, soft pale yellow flowers in summer. Has oblong, grey-green leaves. **H** 23cm (9in), **S** 30cm (12in) or more.

Othonna cheirifolia
Evergreen shrub with narrow, somewhat fleshy, grey leaves. In early summer bears daisy-like, yellow flower heads singly on upright stems. Needs a warm, sheltered site. **H** 20–30cm (8–12in), **S** 30cm (12in) or more.

Eriogonum umbellatum
Evergreen, prostrate to upright perennial with mats of green leaves, white and woolly beneath. In summer carries heads of tiny, yellow flowers that later turn copper. Dwarf forms are available. **H** 8–30cm (3–12in), **S** 15–30cm (6–12in).

Verbascum dumulosum
Evergreen, mat-forming, shrubby perennial with hairy, grey or grey-green leaves. In late spring and early summer bears a succession of 5-lobed, bright yellow flowers in short racemes. Dislikes winter wet. **H** 15cm (6in) or more, **S** 23–30cm (9–12in) or more.

Ranunculus gramineus
Erect, slender perennial with grass-like, blue-green leaves. Bears several cup-shaped, bright yellow flowers in late spring and early summer. Prefers rich soil. Seedlings will vary in height and flower size. **H** 40–50cm (16–20in), **S** 8–10cm (3–4in).

Sedum rupestre
(Reflexed stonecrop)
Evergreen perennial with loose mats of rooting stems bearing narrow, fleshy leaves. Carries flat, terminal heads of tiny, bright yellow flowers in summer. Makes good ground cover. **H** 15–20cm (6–8in), **S** indefinite.

Genista lydia
Deciduous, domed shrub with slender, arching branches and blue-green leaves. Massed terminal clusters of pea-like, bright yellow flowers appear in late spring and early summer. Will trail over a large rock or wall. **H** 45–60cm (18–24in), **S** 60cm (24in) or more.

Ononis natrix
(Large yellow restharrow)
Deciduous, compact, erect shrub with pea-like, red-streaked, yellow flowers in pendent clusters in summer. Hairy leaves are divided into 3 leaflets. **H** and **S** 30cm (12in) or more.

ORANGE

***Diascia* 'Salmon Supreme'**
Mat-forming perennial with heart-shaped leaves. Dense spikes of pretty, pale-apricot flowers with very small, deeply concave "windows" are produced over a long period, from summer through to autumn. **H** 15cm (6in), **S** to 50cm (20in).

***Helianthemum* 'Ben More'**
Evergreen, spreading, twiggy shrub that bears a succession of saucer-shaped, reddish-orange flowers in loose, terminal clusters in late spring and summer. Has small, glossy, dark green leaves. **H** 23–30cm (9–12in), **S** 30cm (12in).

Crepis aurea
Clump-forming perennial with a basal cluster of oblong, light green leaves. In summer produces dandelion-like, orange flower heads, singly, on stems covered with black and white hairs. **H** 10–30cm (4–12in), **S** 15cm (6in).

AUTUMN

PINK

Sorbus reducta
Deciduous shrub forming a low thicket of upright branches. Small, grey-green leaves, divided into leaflets, turn bronze-red in late autumn. In early summer bears loose clusters of flat, white flowers, followed by pink berries. **H** and **S** to 30cm (12in) or more.

Silene schafta
Spreading perennial with tufts of narrow, oval leaves. Bears sprays of 5-petalled, rose-magenta flowers from late summer to late autumn. **H** 25cm (10in), **S** 30cm (12in).

BLUE

Ceratostigma plumbaginoides
Bushy perennial that bears small, terminal clusters of single, brilliant blue flowers on reddish, branched stems in late summer and autumn. Oval leaves turn rich red in autumn. **H** 45cm (18in), **S** 20cm (8in).

Gentiana septemfida
Evergreen perennial with many upright, then arching stems clothed with oval leaves. Bears heads of trumpet-shaped, mid-blue flowers in summer–autumn. Likes humus-rich soil but tolerates reasonably drained, heavy clay. **H** 15–20cm (6–8in), **S** 30cm (12in).

WINTER

WHITE

Gaultheria cuneata
Evergreen, compact shrub with stiff stems clothed in leathery, oval mid-green leaves. In summer bears nodding, urn-shaped, white flowers, in leaf axils, followed by white berries in autumn. **H** and **S** 30cm (12in).

Ranunculus calandrinioides
Clump-forming perennial that loses its long, oval, blue-green leaves in summer; in a reasonable winter will bear a succession of cup-shaped, pink-flushed, white flowers for many weeks. Needs very sharp drainage. **H** and **S** to 20cm (8in).

Leucopogon colensoi
Evergreen, low-growing shrub with stiff stems clothed in tiny, grey-green leaves. Bears clusters of small, tubular, white flowers in spring at the ends of new growth. Red or white berries in late summer are rare in cultivation. **H** and **S** 30cm (12in).

SILVER

Tanacetum argenteum
Mat-forming perennial, usually evergreen, grown for its finely cut, bright silver leaves. Has a profusion of small, daisy-like, white flower heads in summer. **H** in flower 15–23cm (6–9in), **S** 20cm (8in).

Celmisia semicordata
Evergreen perennial with sword-like, silver leaves in large clumps and, in summer, daisy-like, white flower heads borne singly on hairy stems. **H** and **S** 30cm (12in).

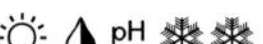

Tanacetum densum* subsp. *amani
Clump-forming perennial retaining fern-like, hairy, grey leaves in winter in mild climates. Bears daisy-like, yellow flower heads with woolly bracts in summer. Dislikes winter wet. **H** and **S** 20cm (8in).

Ozothamnus coralloides
Evergreen, upright shrub with grey stems clothed in neat, dark green leaves, marked silver. Occasionally bears fluffy, yellow flower heads. Suits a cold frame or an alpine house. Hates winter wet. **H** 15–23cm (6–9in), **S** 15cm (6in).

Salix* x *boydii
Very slow-growing, deciduous, upright shrub forming a gnarled, branched bush. Has oval, rough-textured leaves; catkins are rarely produced. Will tolerate light shade. **H** to 15–23cm (6–9in), **S** to 30cm (12in).

GREEN

***Hebe cupressoides* 'Boughton Dome'**
Slow-growing, evergreen, dome-shaped shrub with scale-like, stem-clasping, dark grey-green leaves. Has terminal clusters of small, 4-lobed, blue-tinged, white flowers in summer. **H** 30cm (12in), **S** to 60cm (24in).

Ozothamnus selago
Evergreen, upright shrub with stiff stems covered in scale-like leaves. Intermittently bears fluffy, creamy-white flower heads. Makes a good foil for spring bulbs. **H** and **S** 15–23cm (6–9in).

Ballota pseudodictamnus
Evergreen, mound-forming sub-shrub with rounded, grey-green leaves and stems covered with woolly, white hairs. In summer bears whorls of small, pink flowers with conspicuous, enlarged, pale green calyces. **H** 60cm (2ft), **S** 90cm (3ft).

WHITE

Androsace vandellii
Evergreen, dense, cushion-forming perennial with narrow, grey leaves and a profusion of stemless, white flowers in spring. Needs careful cultivation with a deep collar of grit under the cushion. **H** 2.5cm (1in), **S** to 10cm (4in).

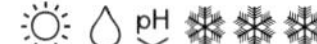

***Arabis alpina* subsp. *caucasica* 'Variegata'**
Evergreen, mat-forming perennial with rosettes of oval, cream-splashed, mid-green leaves. Bears bunches of single, sometimes pink-flushed, white flowers from early spring to summer. **H** and **S** 15cm (6in).

Arenaria balearica
Prostrate perennial that is evergreen in all but the most severe winters. Will form a green film over a wet, porous rock face. Minute, white flowers stud mats of foliage in late spring and early summer. **H** less than 1cm (½in), **S** indefinite.

WHITE

Saxifraga scardica
Slow-growing, evergreen perennial with hard cushions composed of blue-green rosettes of leaves. In spring bears small clusters of upward-facing, cup-shaped, white flowers. Does best in an alpine house or sheltered scree. **H** 2.5cm (1in), **S** 8cm (3in).

Saxifraga burseriana
Slow-growing, evergreen perennial with hard cushions of spiky, grey-green leaves. In spring open cup-shaped, white flowers are borne on short stems. **H** 2.5–5cm (1–2in), **S** to 10cm (4in).

Sanguinaria canadensis (Bloodroot)
Rhizomatous perennial with fleshy, underground stems that exude red sap when cut. In spring bears white flowers, sometimes pink-flushed or slate-blue on reverses, as blue-grey leaves unfurl. **H** 10–15cm (4–6in), **S** 30cm (12in).

Weldenia candida
Perennial with rosettes of strap-shaped, wavy-margined leaves, growing from tuberous roots. Bears a succession of upright, cup-shaped, pure white flowers in late spring and early summer. **H** and **S** 8–15cm (3–6in).

Maianthemum bifolium
Spreading, rhizomatous perennial with pairs of large, oval, glossy, dark green leaves arising direct from rhizomes. Stems produce a raceme of 4-petalled, white flowers in early summer, followed by small, spherical, red fruits. May be invasive. **H** 10cm (4in), **S** indefinite.

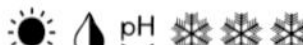

Dicentra cucullaria
(Dutchman's breeches)
Compact perennial with fern-like foliage and arching stems each bearing a few small, yellow-tipped, white flowers, like tiny, inflated trousers, in spring. Lies dormant in summer. **H** 15cm (6in), **S** to 30cm (12in).

Cardamine trifolia
Ground-cover perennial with creeping stems clothed in rounded, toothed, 3-parted leaves. In late spring and early summer bears loose heads of open cup-shaped, white flowers on bare stems. **H** 10–15cm (4–6in), **S** 30cm (12in).

Arenaria tetraquetra
Evergreen perennial that forms a grey-green cushion of small leaves. Stemless, star-shaped, white flowers appear in late spring. Is well-suited for a trough or an alpine house. **H** 2.5cm (1in), **S** 15cm (6in) or more.

Pulsatilla vernalis
Tufted perennial with rosettes of feathery leaves. Densely hairy, brown flower buds appear in late winter and open in early spring to somewhat nodding, open cup-shaped, pearl-white flowers. Buds dislike winter wet. **H** 5–10cm (2–4in), **S** 10cm (4in).

Corydalis popovii
Tuberous perennial with leaves divided into 3–6 bluish-green leaflets. In spring bears loose racemes of deep red-purple and white flowers, each with a long spur. Keep dry when dormant. **H** and **S** 10–15cm (4–6in).

Scoliopus bigelowii
Compact perennial with basal, veined leaves, sometimes marked brown. In early spring bears flowers with purple inner petals and greenish-white outer petals with deep purple lines. **H** 8–10cm (3–4in), **S** 10–15cm (4–6in).

Ranunculus alpestris
(Alpine buttercup)
Short-lived, evergreen, clump-forming perennial that bears cup-shaped, white flowers on erect stems from late spring to mid-summer. Glossy, dark green leaves are rounded and serrated. **H** 2.5–12cm (1–5in), **S** 10cm (4in).

Ranunculus ficaria* var. *albus
Mat-forming perennial bearing in early spring cup-shaped, single, creamy-white flowers with glossy petals. Leaves are heart-shaped and dark green. Can spread rapidly; is good for a wild garden. **H** 5cm (2in), **S** 20cm (8in).

Cassiope mertensiana
Evergreen, dwarf shrub with scale-like, dark green leaves tightly pressed to stems. In early spring carries bell-shaped, creamy-white flowers, with green or red calyces, in leaf axils. **H** 15cm (6in), **S** 20cm (8in).

Gypsophila cerastioides
Prostrate perennial with a profusion of small, saucer-shaped, purple-veined, white flowers borne in late spring and early summer above mats of rounded, velvety, mid-green foliage. **H** 2cm (¾in), **S** to 10cm (4in) or more.

Androsace villosa
Evergreen, mat-forming perennial with very hairy rosettes of tiny leaves. Bears umbels of small, white flowers, with yellow centres that turn red, in spring. **H** 2.5cm (1in), **S** 20cm (8in).

Cassiope lycopodioides
Evergreen, prostrate, mat-forming shrub with slender stems densely set with minute, scale-like, dark green leaves. In spring, short, reddish stems carry tiny, bell-shaped, white flowers, in red calyces, singly in leaf axils. **H** 8cm (3in), **S** 30cm (12in).

Leptinella atrata* subsp. *luteola
Evergreen, mat-forming perennial that in late spring and early summer bears blackish-red flower heads with creamy-yellow stamens. Leaves are small, finely cut and dark green. Needs adequate moisture; best in an alpine house. **H** 2.5cm (1in), **S** to 25cm (10in).

Shortia galacifolia (Oconee bells)
Evergreen, clump-forming, dwarf perennial with round, toothed, leathery, glossy leaves. In late spring bears cup- to trumpet-shaped, often pink-flushed, white flowers with deeply serrated petals. **H** to 15cm (6in), **S** 15–23cm (6–9in).

WHITE

Cerastium tomentosum
(Snow-in-summer)
Very vigorous, ground-cover perennial, only suitable for a hot, dry bank, with prostrate stems covered by tiny, grey leaves. In late spring and summer bears star-shaped, white flowers above foliage. **H** 8cm (3in), **S** indefinite.

Androsace pyrenaica
Evergreen perennial with small rosettes of tiny, hairy leaves, tightly packed to form hard cushions. Minute, stemless, single, white flowers appear in spring. **H** 4cm (1½in), **S** to 10cm (4in).

Anemone trullifolia
Creeping, fibrous rooted perennial with wedge-shaped, semi-erect, mid-green basal leaves, each with 3 deeply toothed lobes. Rounded flowers of 5 petals, varying from rich blue to near white, are borne in early summer and late summer. **H** and **S** 20cm (8in).

PINK

Anemonella thalictroides
Perennial with delicate, fern-like leaves growing from a cluster of small tubers. From spring to early summer bears small, cup-shaped, white or pink flowers, singly on finely branched stems. Needs humus-rich soil. **H** 10cm (4in), **S** 4cm (1½in) or more.

Trillium rivale
Perennial with oval leaves, divided into 3 leaflets. In spring bears open cup-shaped, white or pale pink flowers with dark-spotted, heart-shaped petals, singly on upright, later arching stems. **H** to 15cm (6in), **S** 10cm (4in).

Daphne jasminea
Evergreen, compact shrub. Bears small, white flowers, pink-flushed externally, in late spring and early summer and again in autumn. Brittle stems are clothed in grey-green leaves. Suits an alpine house or a dry wall. **H** 8–10cm (3–4in), **S** to 30cm (12in).

***Saxifraga* x *irvingii* 'Jenkinsiae'**
Slow-growing perennial with very tight, grey-green cushions of foliage. Carries a profusion of open cup-shaped, lilac-pink flowers on slender stems in early spring. **H** 8–10cm (3–4in), **S** to 15cm (6in).

Paraquilegia anemonoides
Tufted perennial with fern-like, blue-green leaves. In spring, pale lavender-blue buds open to pendent, cup-shaped, almost white flowers borne singly on arching stems. May be difficult to establish. **H** and **S** 10–15cm (4–6in).

Androsace carnea
Evergreen, cushion-forming perennial that has small rosettes of pointed leaves with hairy margins. In spring, 2 or more stems rise above each rosette, bearing tiny, single, pink flowers. Suits a trough. **H** and **S** 5cm (2in).

Arenaria purpurascens
Evergreen, mat-forming perennial with sharp-pointed, glossy leaves, above which rise many small clusters of star-shaped, pale to deep purplish-pink flowers in early spring. **H** 1cm (½in), **S** to 15cm (6in).

Antennaria rosea
Semi-evergreen perennial forming a spreading mat of tiny, oval, woolly leaves. Bears fluffy, rose-pink flower heads in small, terminal clusters in late spring and early summer. Is good as ground cover with small bulbs. **H** 2.5cm (1in), **S** to 40cm (16in).

Daphne arbuscula
Evergreen, prostrate shrub. In late spring bears many very fragrant, tubular, deep pink flowers in terminal clusters. Narrow, leathery, dark green leaves are crowded at the ends of the branches. Likes humus-rich soil. **H** 10–15cm (4–6in), **S** 50cm (20in).

***Daphne petraea* 'Grandiflora'**
Slow-growing, evergreen, compact shrub that bears terminal clusters of fragrant, rich pink flowers in late spring and tiny, glossy leaves. Suits an alpine house, a sheltered, humus-rich rock garden or a trough. **H** to 15cm (6in), **S** to 25cm (10in).

Vaccinium vitis-idaea* subsp. *minus
Evergreen, mat-forming sub-shrub with tiny, oval, leathery leaves. In late spring produces small, erect racemes of many tiny, bell-shaped, deep pink or deep pink-and-white flowers. **H** 5–8cm (2–3in), **S** 10–15cm (4–6in).

Epigaea gaultherioides
Evergreen, prostrate sub-shrub with cup-shaped, shell-pink flowers borne in terminal clusters in spring. Hairy stems carry heart-shaped, dark green leaves. Is difficult to grow and propagate. **H** to 10cm (4in), **S** to 25cm (10in) or more.

Lewisia tweedyi
Evergreen, rosetted perennial with large, fleshy leaves and stout, branched stems that bear open cup-shaped, many-petalled, white to pink flowers in spring. Best grown in an alpine house. **H** 15cm (6in), **S** 12–15cm (5–6in).

Claytonia megarhiza* var. *nivalis
Evergreen perennial with a rosette of spoon-shaped, succulent leaves. Bears small heads of tiny, deep pink flowers in spring. Grows best in a deep pot of gritty compost in an alpine house. **H** 1cm (½in), **S** 8cm (3in).

Mazus reptans
Prostrate perennial that has tubular, purple or purplish-pink flowers, with protruding, white lips, spotted red and yellow, borne singly on short stems in spring. Narrow, toothed leaves are in pairs along stem. **H** to 5cm (2in), **S** 30cm (12in) or more.

PINK

Silene acaulis **(Moss campion)**
Evergreen, cushion-forming perennial with minute, bright green leaves studded with tiny, stemless, 5-petalled, pink flowers in spring. May be difficult to bring into flower; prefers a cool climate. **H** to 2.5cm (1in), **S** 15cm (6in).

Oxalis adenophylla
Mat-forming, fibrous-rooted, tuberous perennial with grey-green leaves divided into narrow, wavy lobes. In spring bears rounded, purplish-pink flowers, each 2.5–4cm (1–1½in) across, with darker purple eyes. **H** to 5cm (2in), **S** 8–10cm (3–4in).

Thlaspi cepaeifolium* subsp. *rotundifolium
Clump-forming perennial with dense tufts of round leaves and small, open cup-shaped, pale to deep purplish- or lilac-pink flowers in spring. Needs cool conditions. May be short-lived. **H** 5–8cm (2–3in), **S** 10cm (4in).

Armeria juniperifolia
Evergreen, cushion-forming perennial composed of loose rosettes of sharp-pointed, mid- to grey-green leaves. Pale pink flowers are borne in spherical umbels in late spring and early summer. **H** 5–8cm (2–3in), **S** 15cm (6in).

Erinus alpinus
Semi-evergreen, short-lived perennial with rosettes of soft, mid-green leaves covered, in late spring and summer, with small, purple, pink or white flowers. Self seeds freely. **H** and **S** 5–8cm (2–3in).

Oxalis acetosella* var. *subpurpurascens
Creeping, rhizomatous perennial forming mats of 3-lobed leaves. Cup-shaped, soft pink flowers, each 1cm (½in) across, with 5 darker-veined petals, are produced in spring. **H** 5cm (2in), **S** indefinite.

***Arabis alpina* subsp. *caucasica* 'Douler Angevine'**
Evergreen, mat forming perennial bearing loose rosettes of obovate, toothed, mid-green leaves with irregular, creamy-yellow margins. In spring produces fragrant, 4-petalled, bright pink flowers. **H** 15cm (6in), **S** 50cm (20in).

Shortia soldanelloides
Evergreen, mat-forming perennial with rounded, toothed leaves and small, pendent, bell-shaped and fringed, deep pink flowers in late spring. **H** 5–10cm (2–4in), **S** 10–15cm (4–6in).

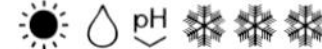

***Anagallis tenella* 'Studland'**
Short-lived perennial that forms prostrate mats of tiny, bright green leaves studded in spring with honey-scented, star-shaped, bright pink flowers. **H** 1cm (½in), **S** 15cm (6in) or more.

Saxifraga oppositifolia
(Purple mountain saxifrage)
Evergreen, prostrate perennial with clusters of tiny, white-flecked leaves. Has open cup-shaped, dark purple, purplish-pink or, rarely, white flowers in early spring. Likes an open position. **H** 2.5–5cm (1–2in), **S** 15cm (6in).

Androsace carnea* subsp. *laggeri
Evergreen, cushion-forming perennial composed of small, tight rosettes of pointed leaves. Cup-shaped, deep pink flowers are borne in small clusters above cushions in spring. **H** and **S** 5cm (2in).

Polygonatum hookeri
Slow-growing, dense, rhizomatous perennial that bears loose spikes of several small, bell-shaped, lilac-pink flowers in late spring and early summer. Leaves are tiny and lance-shaped. Suits a peat bed. **H** to 5cm (2in), **S** to 30cm (12in).

***Aubrieta* 'Joy'**
Vigorous, evergreen, trailing perennial that forms mounds of soft green leaves. In spring bears double, pale mauve-pink flowers on short stems. **H** 10cm (4in), **S** 20cm (8in).

Arabis blepharophylla
'Frühlingszauber'
Short-lived, evergreen, mat-forming perennial bearing loose rosettes of dark green leaves with grey margins. Compact racemes of fragrant, 4-petalled, dark purple-pink flowers are produced in spring. **H** 12cm (5in), **S** 20cm (8in).

***Corydalis solida* 'George Baker'**
Tuberous perennial with fern-like, divided leaves and dense racemes of spurred, rich deep rose-red flowers in spring. **H** and **S** 10–15cm (4–6in).

Saxifraga federici-augusti
subsp. *grisebachii* 'Wisley Variety'
Evergreen perennial with rosettes of lime-encrusted leaves. Crosier-shaped stems with pale pink to bright red hairs, bear dense racemes of dark red flowers in spring. **H** 10cm (4in), **S** 15cm (6in).

Saxifraga sempervivum
Evergreen, hummock-forming perennial with tight rosettes of tufted, silvery-green leaves. Crosier-shaped flower stems, covered in silvery hairs and emerging from rosettes, bear racemes of dark red flowers in early spring. **H** and **S** 10–15cm (4–6in).

PURPLE

***Aubrieta deltoidea* 'Argenteovariegata'**
Evergreen, compact perennial, grown for its trailing, green leaves which are heavily splashed with creamy-white. Produces pinkish-lavender flowers in spring. **H** 5cm (2in), **S** 15cm (6in).

Saxifraga stribrnyi
Evergreen, mound-forming perennial with small, lime-encrusted rosettes of leaves. Crosier-shaped stems, covered in pinkish-buff hairs, bear racemes of deep maroon-red flowers above leaves in late spring and early summer. **H** 8cm (3in), **S** 10–12cm (4–5in).

***Aubrieta* 'J.S. Baker'**
Evergreen perennial with single, reddish-purple flowers with a white eye borne in spring above mounds of small, soft green leaves. **H** 10cm (4in), **S** 20cm (8in).

Soldanella alpina (Alpine snowbell)
Evergreen, clump-forming perennial with tufts of leaves and short, bell-shaped, fringed, pinkish-lavender or purplish-pink flowers in early spring. Is difficult to flower well. **H** to 8cm (3in), **S** 8–10cm (3–4in).

Polygala chamaebuxus* var. *grandiflora
Evergreen, woody-based perennial with terminal clusters of pea-like, reddish-purple and yellow flowers in late spring and early summer. Leaves are small, oval, leathery and dark green. **H** to 15cm (6in), **S** to 30cm (12in).

Soldanella villosa
Evergreen, clump-forming perennial with round, leathery, hairy-stalked leaves and nodding, bell-shaped, fringed, purplish-lavender flowers borne on erect stems in early spring. Dislikes winter wet. **H** 10cm (4in), **S** 10–15cm (4–6in).

***Aubrieta* 'Greencourt Purple'**
Evergreen, mat-forming perennial with rosetted, mid-green leaves. Produces masses of double, bright purple flowers in spring. Is very good on a dry wall. **H** 10–15cm (4–6in), **S** 30cm (12in) or more.

Corydalis diphylla
Tuberous perennial with semi-erect, basal leaves, divided into narrow leaflets, and loose racemes of purple-lipped flowers with white spurs in spring. Protect tubers from excess moisture in summer. **H** 10–15cm (4–6in), **S** 8–10cm (3–4in).

Viola calcarata
Clump-forming perennial, with oval leaves, that bears flat, outward-facing, single, white, lavender or purple flowers for a long period from late spring to summer. Prefers rich soil. **H** 10–15cm (4–6in), **S** to 20cm (8in).

Viola tricolor **(Heartsease, Wild pansy)**
Short-lived perennial or annual with neat, flat-faced flowers in combinations of white, yellow and shades of purple from spring through to autumn. Self seeds profusely. **H** 5–15cm (2–6in), **S** 5–15cm (2–6in) or more.

Hepatica nobilis **var. *japonica***
Slow-growing perennial with leathery, lobed leaves, semi-evergreen in all but very cold or arid climates. Bears slightly cupped, lilac-mauve, pink or white flowers in spring. **H** to 8cm (3in), **S** to 12cm (5in).

Jeffersonia dubia
Tufted perennial with 2-lobed, blue-green leaves, sometimes flushed pink when unfolding. Bears cup-shaped, pale lilac to purplish blue flowers singly in spring. **H** 10–15cm (4–6in), **S** to 23cm (9in).

Synthyris missurica **var. *stellata***
Evergreen, mounded, rhizomatous perennial that bears dense spikes of small, violet-blue flowers in spring above rounded, deeply toothed leaves. Tolerates sun if soil remains moist. **H** 10–15cm (4–6in), **S** 15cm (6in).

Aubrieta **'Purple Charm'**
Evergreen, mat-forming perennial with rosetted, mid-green leaves. In spring, roduces masses of single, lavender-purple flowers, with yellow eyes. Is very good on a dry wall. **H** 10–15cm (4–6in), **S** 30cm (12in) or more.

Jancaea heldreichii
Perennial with rosettes of thick, hairy, silver-green leaves, above which rise slender stems bearing clusters of tiny, lavender-blue flowers in late spring. Is rare and difficult to grow and is best in an alpine house. **H** and **S** to 8cm (3in).

Viola pedata **(Bird's-foot violet)**
Clump-forming perennial with finely divided foliage and yellow-centred, pale violet, rarely white flowers borne singly on slender stems in late spring and early summer. Needs sharp drainage; grow in an alpine house. **H** 5cm (3in), **S** 8cm (3in).

Viola riviniana **Purpurea Group**
Clump-forming perennial with tiny, flat-faced, purple flowers in spring-summer. Leaves are kidney-shaped and dark purple-green. Is invasive but suits a bank, woodland or wild garden. **H** 2.5–5cm (1–2in), **S** indefinite.

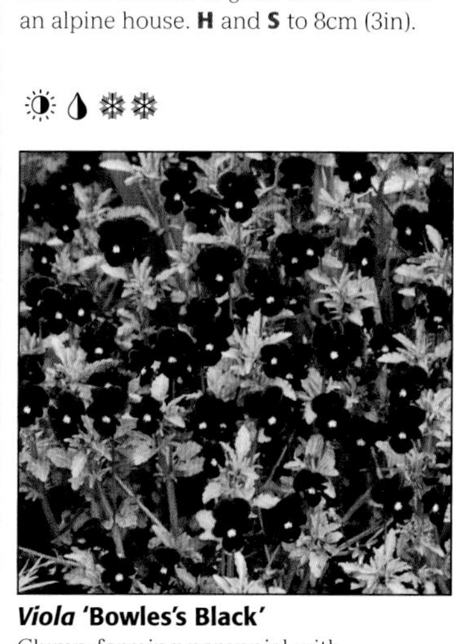

Viola **'Bowles's Black'**
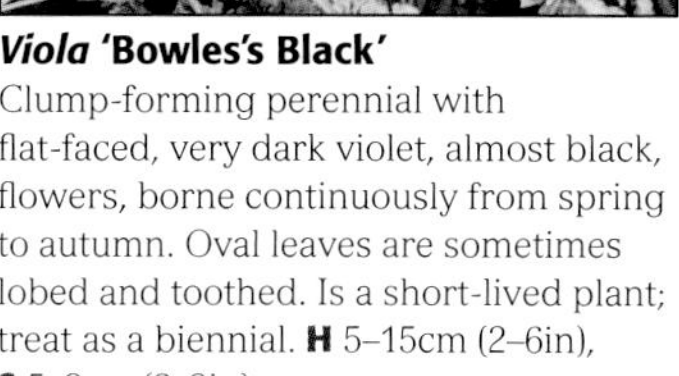
Clump-forming perennial with flat-faced, very dark violet, almost black, flowers, borne continuously from spring to autumn. Oval leaves are sometimes lobed and toothed. Is a short-lived plant; treat as a biennial. **H** 5–15cm (2–6in), **S** 5–8cm (2–3in).

BLUE

Myosotis alpestris
(Alpine forget-me-not)
Short-lived, clump-forming perennial producing dense clusters of tiny, bright blue flowers with creamy-yellow eyes in late spring and early summer, just above tufts of hairy leaves. Prefers gritty soil. **H** and **S** 10–15cm (4–6in).

Anchusa cespitosa
Evergreen, mound-forming perennial with rosettes of lance-shaped, dark green leaves. In spring, stemless, white-centred, blue flowers appear in centres of rosettes. Old plants do not flower well; take early summer cuttings. **H** 2.5–5cm (1–2in), **S** to 23cm (9in).

Viola cornuta 'Minor'
Rhizomatous perennial with oval, toothed leaves and flat-faced, rather angular, spurred, lavender-blue, occasionally white flowers in spring and much of summer. **H** 7–10cm (3–4in), **S** to 15cm (6in).

Gentiana verna (Spring gentian)
Evergreen perennial, often short-lived, with small rosettes of oval, dark green leaves. In early spring, tubular, bright blue flowers with white throats are held upright on short stems. **H** and **S** to 5cm (2in).

Mertensia maritima
Prostrate perennial with oval, fleshy, bright silver-blue or silver grey leaves. Stout stems carry clusters of pendent, funnel-shaped, sky-blue flowers in spring. Is prone to slug damage. Needs very sharp drainage. **H** 10–15cm (4–6in), **S** 12cm (5in).

GREY

Leucogenes grandiceps
Evergreen, dense, woody-based perennial with neat rosettes of downy, silver leaves. Yellow flower heads, within woolly, white bracts, are borne singly in spring or early summer. **H** and **S** 10–15cm (4–6in).

Salix apoda
Slow-growing, deciduous, prostrate shrub. In early spring, male forms bear fat, silky, silver catkins with orange to pale yellow stamens and bracts. Oval, leathery leaves are hairy when young, becoming dark green later. **H** to 15cm (6in), **S** 30–60cm (12–24in).

YELLOW

Mandragora officinarum
Rosetted, fleshy-rooted perennial with coarse, wavy-edged leaves. Bears funnel-shaped, yellowish- or purplish-white flowers in spring, followed by large, tomato-like, shiny yellow fruits. **H** 5cm (2in), **S** 30cm (12in).

Hacquetia epipactis
Clump-forming perennial spreading by short rhizomes. In late winter and early spring bears yellow or yellow-green flower heads, encircled by apple-green bracts, before rounded, 3-parted leaves appear. **H** 6cm (2½in), **S** 15–23cm (6–9in).

Saxifraga x _boydii_
'Hindhead Seedling'
Evergreen perennial that forms a hard dome of small, tufted, spiny, blue-green leaves. In spring bears upward-facing, open, cup-shaped, pale yellow flowers, 2 or 3 to each short stem. **H** 2.5cm (1in), **S** 8cm (3in).

Euphorbia myrsinites
Evergreen, prostrate perennial with terminal clusters of bright yellow-green flowers in spring. Woody stems are clothed in small, pointed, fleshy, grey leaves. Is good on a wall or ledge. **H** 5–8cm (2–3in), **S** to 20cm (8in) or more.

Salix reticulata **(Net-veined willow)**
Deciduous, spreading, mat-forming shrub. Carries plump, reddish-brown, then yellow catkins on male plants in spring and rounded, slightly crinkled leaves. Likes cool, peaty soil. **H** 5–8cm (2–3in), **S** 20cm (8in) or more.

Saxifraga* x *apiculata
'Gregor Mendel'
Evergreen perennial with a tight cushion of bright green foliage. Bears clusters of open, cup-shaped, pale yellow flowers in early spring. **H** 10–15cm (4–6in), **S** 15cm (6in) or more.

Saxifraga* x *elizabethae
Evergreen, cushion-forming perennial, composed of densely packed, tiny rosettes of spiny leaves. In spring, tight upward-facing, bright yellow flowers are carried on tops of red-based stems. **H** 2.5cm (1in), **S** 10–15cm (4–6in).

Draba rigida
Evergreen perennial with tight hummocks of minute, dark green leaves. Tiny clusters of bright yellow flowers on fine stems cover hummocks in spring. Suits a rough, scree garden or alpine house. Dislikes winter wet. **H** 4cm (1½in), **S** 6cm (2½in).

Ranunculus ficaria **Flore Pleno Group**
Mat-forming perennial with heart-shaped, dark green leaves and, in early spring, double, bright yellow flowers with glossy petals. May spread rapidly. Is good for a wild garden. **H** 2.5–5cm (1–2in), **S** 20cm (8in).

Draba longisiliqua
Semi-evergreen, cushion-forming perennial composed of firm rosettes of tiny, silver leaves. Bears sprays of small, yellow flowers on long stalks in spring. Needs plenty of water in growth; is best grown in an alpine house. **H** 5–8cm (2–3in), **S** 15cm (6in).

YELLOW

Vitaliana primuliflora
Evergreen, prostrate perennial with a mat of rosetted, mid-green leaves that are covered in spring with many small clusters of stemless, tubular, bright yellow flowers. **H** 2.5cm (1in), **S** 20cm (8in).

Morisia monanthos
Prostrate perennial with flat rosettes of divided, leathery, dark green leaves. Bears stemless, flat, bright yellow flowers in late spring and early summer. Needs very sharp drainage. **H** 2.5cm (1in), **S** to 8cm (3in).

Dionysia tapetodes
Evergreen, prostrate perennial producing a tight mat of tiny, grey-green leaves. Bears small, upward-facing, yellow flowers in early spring. **H** 1cm (½in), **S** to 15cm (6in).

Trollius pumilus
Tufted perennial with leaves divided into 5 segments, each further lobed. Carries solitary cup-shaped, bright yellow flowers in late spring and early summer. **H** 15cm (6in), **S** 15cm (6in) or more.

Erysimum helveticum
Semi-evergreen, clump-forming perennial with closely-packed tufts of long, narrow leaves and many fragrant, bright yellow flowers borne in flat heads in late spring and early summer. **H** 10cm (4in), **S** 15cm (6in).

Saxifraga sancta
Evergreen, mat-forming perennial with tufts of bright green leaves. Bears short racemes of upward-facing, open cup-shaped, bright yellow flowers in spring. **H** 5cm (2in), **S** 15cm (6in).

Draba mollissima
Semi-evergreen, cushion-forming perennial with clusters of tiny, yellow flowers on slender stems in spring. Minute leaves form a soft green dome, which should be packed beneath with small stones. Grow in an alpine house. **H** 4cm (1½in), **S** 15cm (6in) or more.

Dionysia aretioides
Evergreen perennial forming cushions of soft, hairy, greyish green leaves that are covered in early spring by scented, stemless, round, bright yellow flowers. **H** 5–10cm (2–4in), **S** 15–30cm (6–12in).

WHITE

***Viola* 'Jackanapes'**
Clump-forming perennial with oval, toothed leaves. Produces flat-faced flowers with reddish-brown, upper petals and yellow, lower ones in late spring and summer. **H** 8–12cm (3–5in), **S** to 20cm (8in) or more.

Viola aetolica
Clump-forming perennial bearing flat-faced, yellow flowers singly on upright stems in late spring and early summer. Leaves are oval and mid-green. **H** 5–8cm (2–3in), **S** 15cm (6in).

Ranunculus ficaria* var. *aurantiacus
Mat-forming perennial bearing in early spring cup-shaped, single, orange flowers with glossy petals. Leaves are heart-shaped and mid-green. May spread rapidly. Is good for a wild garden. **H** 5cm (2in), **S** 20cm (8in).

Silene alpestris
Perennial with branching stems and narrow leaves. Bears small, rounded, fringed, white, occasionally pink-flushed flowers in late spring and early summer. Self seeds freely. **H** 10–15cm (4–6in), **S** 20cm (8in).

***Phlox stolonifera* 'Ariane'**
Evergreen, low-growing perennial with flowering sideshoots that bear heads of open, saucer-shaped, white blooms in early summer. Has oval, pale green leaves. Cut back flowered shoots by half after flowering. **H** to 15cm (6in), **S** 30cm (12in).

Achillea clavennae
Semi-evergreen, carpeting perennial that bears loose clusters of white flower heads with gold centres from summer to mid-autumn. Leaves are narrowly oval, many-lobed and covered with fine, white hairs. Dislikes winter wet. **H** 15cm (6in), **S** 23cm (9in) or more.

***Haberlea rhodopensis* 'Virginalis'**
Evergreen perennial with small, arching sprays of funnel-shaped, pure white flowers borne in late spring and early summer above neat rosettes of oval, toothed, dark green leaves. **H** and **S** in flower 10–15cm (4–6in).

Potentilla alba
Vigorous mat-forming perennial bearing loose sprays of flat, single, white flowers in summer. Leaves are divided into oval leaflets and are silvery beneath. **H** 5–8cm (2–3in), **S** 8cm (3in).

Cyananthus lobatus* f. *albus
Prostrate perennial with branched stems clothed in small, wedge-shaped, dull green leaves. Bears funnel-shaped, single, white flowers with spreading lobes in late summer. **H** 8cm (3in), **S** 30cm (12in).

WHITE

***Campanula carpatica* 'Bressingham White'**
Clump-forming perennial bearing open cup-shaped, white flowers, singly on unbranched stems, in summer. Has abundant, rounded, bright green leaves. **H** 10–15cm (4–6in), **S** 15cm (6in).

Arenaria montana
Prostrate perennial that forms loose mats of small, narrowly oval leaves and bears large, round, white flowers in summer. Suits a wall or rock crevice. Must have adequate moisture. **H** 5cm (2in), **S** 12cm (5in).

Cornus canadensis
(Creeping dogwood)
Ground-cover perennial with whorls of oval leaves. In late spring and early summer bears green, sometimes purple-tinged flowers, within white bracts, followed by red berries. **H** 10–15cm (4–6in), **S** 30cm (12in) or more.

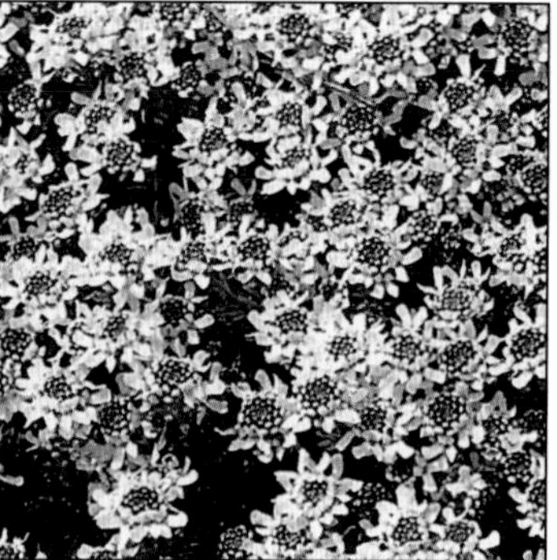

Iberis saxatilis
Evergreen, dwarf sub-shrub that in late spring and early summer produces large heads of numerous small, white flowers, which become tinged violet with age. Glossy, dark leaves are linear and cylindrical. Trim after flowering. **H** 8–12cm (3–5in), **S** 30cm (12in).

Celmisia ramulosa
Evergreen, shrubby perennial with small, hairy, grey-green leaves. Daisy-like, white flower heads are borne singly on short stems in late spring and early summer. **H** and **S** 10cm (4in).

Ourisia caespitosa
Evergreen, prostrate perennial with creeping rootstocks and stems bearing tiny, oval leaves and many outward-facing, open cup-shaped, white flowers in late spring and early summer. **H** 2.5cm (1in), **S** 10cm (4in).

Anacyclus pyrethrum* var. *depressus
Short-lived, prostrate perennial that has white flower heads, with red reverses to ray petals, in summer. Flowers close in dull light. Stems are clothed in fine leaves. Dislikes wet. **H** 2.5–5cm (1–2in) or more, **S** 10cm (4in).

Lewisia rediviva [white form]
(Bitter root)
Tufted, rosetted perennial with clusters of fine, narrow leaves that are summer-deciduous. Bears large, white flowers that open in bright weather in late spring and early summer. **H** 1–4cm (½–1½in), **S** to 5cm (2in).

Epilobium glabellum of gardens
Mat- or clump-forming, semi-evergreen perennial with elliptic to ovate, finely toothed, deep green leaves. Cup-shaped, creamy-white to pink flowers are borne on branching stems in summer. **H** and **S** 20cm (8in).

Achillea x kellereri
Semi-evergreen perennial that bears daisy-like, white flower heads in loose clusters in summer. Leaves are feathery and grey-green. Is good for a wall or bank. Dislikes winter wet and must have perfect drainage. **H** 15cm (6in), **S** 23cm (9in) or more.

Nierembergia repens
Mat-forming perennial with upright, open bell-shaped, yellow-centred, white flowers, occasionally flushed pink with age, borne for a long period in summer. Leaves are small, oval and light green. Is useful for cracks in paving. **H** 5cm (2in), **S** 20cm (8in) or more.

Petrocosmea kerrii
Evergreen perennial with compact rosettes of oval, pointed, hairy, rich green leaves. In summer bears clusters of short, outward-facing, tubular, open-mouthed white flowers. Suits an alpine house. **H** to 8cm (3in), **S** 12–15cm (5–6in). Min. 2–5°C (36–41°F).

Penstemon hirsutus* var. *pygmaeus
Short-lived, evergreen, compact sub-shrub that bears tubular, lipped, hairy, purple- or blue-flushed, white flowers in summer. Has tightly packed, dark green leaves and is suitable for a trough. **H** and **S** 8cm (3in).

Dryas octopetala
Evergreen, prostrate perennial forming mats of oval, lobed, leathery, dark green leaves on stout stems. In late spring and early summer, cup-shaped, creamy-white flowers are borne just above foliage, followed by attractive, feathery seeds. **H** 6cm (2½in), **S** indefinite.

Carlina acaulis (Alpine thistle)
Clump-forming perennial that in summer-autumn bears large, stemless, thistle-like, single, off-white or pale brown flower heads, with papery bracts, on rosettes of long, spiny-margined, deeply-cut leaves. **H** 8–10cm (3–4in), **S** 15–23cm (6–9in).

Alstroemeria hookeri
Tuberous perennial with narrow leaves and loose heads of widely flared, orange-suffused, pink flowers in summer; upper petals are spotted and blotched red and yellow. **H** 10–15cm (4–6in), **S** 45–60cm (18–24in).

Petrorhagia saxifraga (Tunic flower)
Mat-forming perennial with tufts of grass-like leaves. In summer bears a profusion of small, pale pink flowers, veined deeper pink, on slender stems. Grows best on poor soil and self-seeds easily. **H** 10cm (4in), **S** 15cm (6in).

PINK

***Gypsophila repens* 'Dorothy Teacher'**
Semi-evergreen, prostrate perennial. Sprays of small, rounded, white flowers, which age to deep pink, cover mats of narrow, bluish-green leaves in summer. trim stems after flowering. **H** 2.5–5cm (1–2in), **S** 30cm (12in) or more.

Convolvulus althaeoides
Vigorous perennial with long, trailing stems clothed in heart-shaped, cut, mid-green leaves, overlaid silver. Bears large, open trumpet-shaped pink flowers in summer. May be invasive in a mild climate. **H** 5cm (2in), **S** indefinite.

Geranium sanguineum* var. *striatum
Hummock-forming, spreading perennial that has cup-shaped, pink flowers, with darker veins, borne singly in summer above round, deeply divided, dark green leaves. **H** 10–15cm (4–6in), **S** 30cm (12in) or more.

***Rhodohypoxis* 'Margaret Rose'**
Perennial with a tuber-like rootstock and an erect, basal tuft of narrowly lance-shaped, hairy leaves. Bears a succession of upright, flattish, pale pink flowers on slender stems in spring and early summer. **H** 5–10cm (2–4in), **S** 2.5–5cm (1–2in).

Ourisia microphylla
Semi-evergreen, mat-forming perennial, with neat, scale-like, pale green leaves, bearing a profusion of small, pink flowers in late spring and early summer. Is difficult to grow in an arid climate. **H** 5–10cm (2–4in), **S** 15cm (6in).

Asperula suberosa
Clump-forming perennial with a mound of loose stems bearing tiny, hairy, grey leaves and, in early summer, many tubular, pale pink flowers. Dislikes winter wet but needs moist soil in summer. Is best in an alpine house. **H** 8cm (3in), **S** to 30cm (12in).

Erodium corsicum
Compact, clump-forming perennial that has soft, grey-green leaves with wavy margins. Bears flat-faced, pink flowers, with darker veins, on stiff, slender stems in late spring and summer. Is best in an alpine house as dislikes winter wet. **H** 8cm (3in), **S** 15cm (6in).

Saponaria* x *olivana
Compact perennial with a firm cushion of narrow leaves. Flowering stems, produced around edges of the cushion, bear flat, single, pale pink flowers in summer. Needs very sharp drainage. **H** 8cm (3in), **S** 10cm (4in).

***Aethionema* 'Warley Rose'**
Short-lived, evergreen or semi-evergreen, compact sub-shrub with tiny, linear, bluish-green leaves. Bears racemes of small, pink flowers on short stems in profusion in spring-summer. **H** and **S** 15cm (6in).

***Phlox adsurgens* 'Wagon Wheel'**
Evergreen, prostrate perennial forming wide mats of woody stems, clothed in oval leaves. Bears heads of wheel-shaped, pink flowers with narrow petals in summer. Needs humus-rich soil. **H** 10cm (4in), **S** 30cm (12in).

Androsace lanuginosa
Evergreen, trailing perennial with loose stems, covered in silky hairs, carrying deep green leaves and, in summer, clusters of small, flat, lilac-pink or pale pink flowers with dark pink or yellow eyes. **H** 4cm (1½in), **S** to 18cm (7in).

Linnaea borealis (Twin flower)
Evergreen, mat-forming, sub-shrubby perennial with rooting stems bearing small, oval leaves, above which in summer rise thread-like stems bearing pairs of small, fragrant, tubular, pale pink and white flowers. **H** 2cm (¾in), **S** 30cm (12in) or more.

Acantholimon glumaceum
Evergreen, cushion-forming perennial with hard, spiny, dark green leaves and short spikes of small, star-shaped, pink flowers in summer. **H** 10cm (4in), **S** 20cm (8in).

***Dianthus* 'Little Jock'**
Evergreen, compact, clump-forming perennial with spiky, silvery-green foliage. In summer produces strongly fragrant, rounded, semi-double, pink flowers, with darker eyes, above foliage. **H** and **S** 10cm (4in).

Geranium dalmaticum
Prostrate, spreading perennial with outward-facing, almost flat, shell-pink flowers borne in summer above divided, dark green leaves. Will grow taller in partial shade and is evergreen in all but severest winters. **H** 8–10cm (3–4in) or more, **S** 12–20cm (5–8in).

Erigeron karvinskianus
Spreading perennial with lax stems bearing narrow, lance-shaped, hairy leaves and, in summer-autumn, daisy-like flower heads that open white, turn pink and fade to purple. **H** 10–15cm (4–6in), **S** indefinite.

Dianthus pavonius
Evergreen, prostrate perennial with comparatively large, rounded, pale to deep pink flowers, buff on reverses, borne on short stems in summer above low mats of spiky leaves. **H** 5cm (2in), **S** 8cm (3in).

Dianthus gratianopolitanus
(Cheddar pink)
Evergreen perennial with loose mats of narrow, grey-green leaves. In summer, produces very fragrant, flat, pale pink flowers on slender stems. **H** to 15cm (6in), **S** to 30cm (12in).

PINK

Loiseleuria procumbens
(Alpine azalea, Trailing azalea)
Evergreen, prostrate shrub with small, oval leaves, hairy and beige beneath. Has terminal clusters of open funnel-shaped, rose-pink to white flowers in early summer. **H** to 8cm (3in), **S** 10–15cm (4–6in).

Saponaria ocymoides (Tumbling Ted)
Perennial with compact or loose, sprawling mats of hairy, oval leaves, above which a profusion of tiny, flat, pale pink to crimson flowers is carried in summer. Is excellent on a dry bank. **H** 2.5–8cm (1–3in), **S** 40cm (16in).

Oxalis depressa
Tuberous perennial with 3-lobed leaves and short-stemmed, widely funnel-shaped, bright rose-pink flowers, 2cm (¾in) across, in summer. Needs a sheltered site or cool greenhouse. **H** 5cm (2in), **S** 8–10cm (3–4in).

***Dianthus* 'Pike's Pink'**
Evergreen, compact, cushion-forming perennial, with spiky, grey-green foliage, that bears fragrant, rounded, double, pink flowers in summer. **H** and **S** 10cm (4in).

Pterocephalus perennis
Semi-evergreen, mat-forming perennial with crinkled, hairy leaves. Bears tight, rounded heads of tubular, pinkish-lavender flowers, singly on short stems in summer, followed by feathery seed heads. **H** 5cm (2in), **S** 10cm (4in).

Dianthus myrtinervius
Evergreen, spreading perennial with numerous small, rounded, pink flowers that appear in summer above tiny, grass-like leaves. **H** 5cm (2in), **S** 20cm (8in).

Aethionema armenum
Short-lived, evergreen or semi-evergreen, dense sub-shrub with narrow, blue-green leaves. Carries loose sprays of tiny, pale to deep pink flowers in summer. **H** and **S** 15cm (6in).

Saponaria caespitosa
Mat-forming perennial with small, lance-shaped leaves. Tiny, flat, single, pink to purple flowers are borne in small heads in summer. Needs very sharp drainage. **H** 8cm (3in), **S** 10cm (4in).

Dianthus alpinus (Alpine pink)
Evergreen, compact perennial that bears comparatively large, rounded, rose-pink to crimson flowers, singly in summer, above mats of narrow, dark green foliage. Likes humus-rich soil. **H** 5cm (2in), **S** 8cm (3in).

***Dianthus* 'Annabelle'**
Evergreen, compact, clump-forming perennial with spiky, grey-green foliage. In summer bears fragrant, rounded, semi-double, cerise-pink flowers, singly on slender stems. **H** and **S** 10cm (4in).

***Phlox* 'Camla'**
Evergreen mound-forming perennial with wiry, arching stems and fine leaves. Has a profusion of open saucer-shaped, rich pink flowers in early summer. Trim after flowering. Needs humus-rich soil. **H** 12cm (5in), **S** 30cm (12in).

***Phlox subulata* 'Marjorie'**
Evergreen, mound-forming perennial with fine leaves and a profusion of flat, star-shaped, bright rose-pink flowers in early summer. Trim after flowering. **H** 10cm (4in), **S** 20cm (8in).

***Dianthus* 'La Bourboule'**
Evergreen perennial with small clumps of tufted, spiky foliage. Bears a profusion of strongly fragrant, small, single, pink flowers in summer. **H** 5cm (2in), **S** 8cm (3in).

***Persicaria affinis* 'Donald Lowndes'**
Evergreen, mat-forming perennial that has stout, branching, spreading stems clothed with pointed leaves. In summer bears dense spikes of small, red flowers, which become paler with age. **H** 8–15cm (3–6in), **S** to 15cm (6in).

***Phlox douglasii* 'Crackerjack'**
Evergreen, compact, mound-forming perennial. Has a profusion of saucer-shaped, bright crimson or magenta flowers in early summer. Leaves are lance-shaped and mid-green. Cut back after flowering. **H** to 8cm (3in), **S** 20cm (8in).

***Armeria maritima* 'Vindictive'**
Evergreen, clump-forming perennial with grass-like, dark blue-green leaves, above which rise stiff stems bearing spherical heads of small, deep rose-pink flowers for a long period in summer. **H** 10cm (4in), **S** 15cm (6in).

Lewisia rediviva [pink form]
(Bitter root)
Tufted, rosetted perennial. Clusters of narrow leaves are summer-deciduous. Large, many-petalled, pink flowers open on bright days in late spring and early summer. Suits an alpine house. **H** 1–4cm (½–1½in), **S** to 5cm (2in).

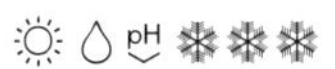

***Rhodohypoxis* 'Albrighton'**
Perennial with tuber-like rootstock and an erect, basal tuft of narrowly lance-shaped, hairy leaves. Bears a succession of erect, deep pink flowers singly on slender stems in spring and early summer. **H** 5–10cm (2–4in), **S** 2.5–5cm (1–2in).

***Dianthus deltoides* 'Leuchtfunk'**
Evergreen, mat-forming perennial. Many small, flat, upward-facing, brilliant cerise flowers are borne singly above tiny, oblong, pointed leaves. **H** 10–15cm (4–6in), **S** 20cm (8in).

***Thymus* 'Bressingham'**
Evergreen, mat-forming, aromatic sub-shrub with creeping stems and elliptic, white-hairy, mid-green leaves. Bears numerous, small, 2-lipped, purple-pink flowers, splashed dark crimson, in summer. **H** 3cm (1¼in), **S** 12cm (5in).

PINK

Phlox bifida (Sand phlox)
Evergreen, mound-forming perennial with lance-shaped leaves. Bears a profusion of small heads of star-shaped, lilac or white flowers with deeply cleft petals in summer. Cut back stems by half after flowering. **H** 10–15cm (4–6in), **S** 15cm (6in).

***Geranium cinereum* 'Ballerina'**
Spreading, rosetted perennial that bears cup-shaped, purplish-pink flowers, with deep purple veins, on lax stems in late spring and summer. Basal leaves are round, deeply divided and soft. **H** 10cm (4in), **S** 30cm (12in).

Dianthus microlepis
Evergreen perennial with tiny tufts of minute, fine, grass-like leaves, above which rise numerous small, rounded, pink flowers in early summer. Is best suited to a trough. **H** 5cm (2in), **S** 20cm (8in).

PURPLE

Thymus caespititius
Compact, cushion-forming, aromatic sub-shrub with upright stems covered in small, prominently veined, dark-green leaves. In early summer, bears lilac or mauve flowers in dense rounded heads. **H** 15cm (6in), **S** 20cm (8in).

Androsace villosa* var. *jacquemontii
Evergreen, mat-forming perennial with small rosettes of hairy, grey-green leaves. Bears tiny, pinkish-purple flowers on red stems in late spring and early summer. Suits an alpine house. **H** 1–4cm (½–1½in), **S** 20cm (8in).

Teucrium polium
Deciduous, dome-shaped sub-shrub that has much-branched, woolly, white or yellowish stems and leaves with scalloped margins. Bears yellowish-white or pinkish-purple flowers in flat heads in summer. Requires very sharp drainage. **H** and **S** 15cm (6in).

Geranium subcaulescens
Spreading perennial with round, deeply divided, soft leaves. In summer bears brilliant purple-magenta flowers, with striking, black eyes and stamens, on lax stems. **H** 10cm (4in), **S** 30cm (12in).

***Phlox douglasii* 'Boothman's Variety'**
Evergreen, mound-forming perennial with lance-shaped leaves and masses of pale lavender-blue flowers, with violet-blue markings around eyes, in early summer. Cut back after flowering. **H** to 5cm (2in), **S** 20cm (8in).

Physoplexis comosa
Tufted perennial with deeply cut leaves and round heads of bottle-shaped, violet-blue, rarely white, flowers in summer. Suits crevices but dislikes winter wet. **H** 8cm (3in), **S** 10cm (4in).

Aster alpinus
Clump-forming, spreading perennial with lance-shaped, dark green leaves. Bears daisy-like, purplish-blue or pink-purple flower heads, with yellow centres, from mid- to late summer. **H** 15cm (6in), **S** 30–45cm (12–18in).

***Thymus* 'Peter Davis'**
Evergreen, aromatic, mound-forming sub-shrub with fine, twiggy stems and narrow leaves fringed with white hairs. Bears dense heads of small, pinkish-purple flowers with purple bracts in summer. **H** 10–12cm (4–5in), **S** 15cm (6in).

***Phlox* 'Emerald Cushion'**
Evergreen perennial with emerald-green mounds of fine leaves, studded in late spring and early summer with large, saucer-shaped, bright violet-blue flowers. Trim after flowering. **H** 8cm (3in), **S** 15cm (6in).

***Viola* 'Nellie Britton'**
Clump-forming perennial with small, oval, toothed leaves and flat-faced, lavender-pink flowers borne from late spring to late summer. Soil should not be too dry. **H** 8–15cm (3–6in), **S** to 20cm (8in).

Campanula poscharskyana
Rampant, spreading perennial with bell-shaped, violet flowers borne on leafy stems in summer. Leaves are round with serrated edges. Vigorous runners make it suitable for a bank or a wild garden. **H** 10–15cm (4–6in), **S** indefinite.

Globularia meridionalis
Evergreen, dome-shaped sub-shrub. In summer, globular, fluffy, lavender to lavender-purple flower heads are borne singly just above glossy leaves. **H** to 10cm (4in), **S** to 20cm (8in).

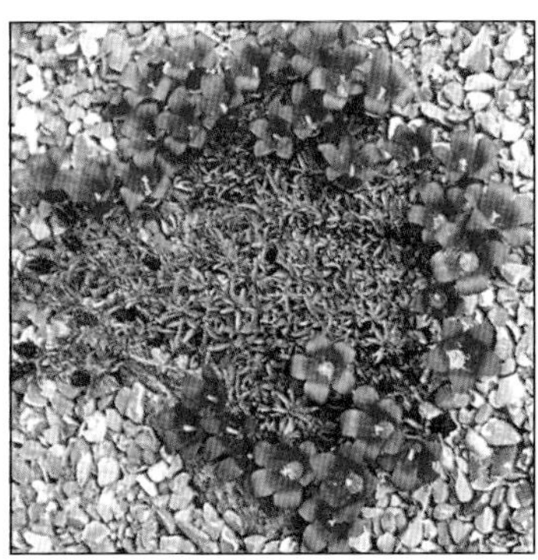

Edraianthus serpyllifolius
Evergreen, prostrate perennial with tight mats of tiny leaves and small, bell-shaped, deep violet flowers, borne on short stems in early summer. Is uncommon and seldom sets seed in gardens. **H** 1cm (½in), **S** to 5cm (2in).

***Campanula carpatica* 'Jewel'**
Low-growing, compact and clump-forming perennial with mid-green, toothed leaves on branching stems. Bright, purple-blue, upturned, bell-shaped flowers are produced over several months in summer. **H** and **S** 10–15cm (4–6in).

PURPLE

***Viola* 'Huntercombe Purple'**
Perennial forming wide clumps of neat, oval, toothed leaves. Has a profusion of flat-faced, rich violet flowers from spring to late summer. Divide clumps every 3 years. **H** 10–15cm (4–6in), **S** 15–30cm (6–12in) or more.

Campanula portenschlagiana
Vigorous, evergreen, prostrate perennial with dense mats of small, ivy-shaped leaves and large clusters of erect, open bell-shaped, violet flowers in summer. **H** 15cm (6in), **S** indefinite.

***Campanula* 'G.F. Wilson'**
Neat, mound-forming perennial with large, upturned, bell-shaped, violet flowers in summer. Has rounded, pale yellow-green leaves. **H** 8–10cm (3–4in), **S** 12–15cm (5–6in).

Pinguicula grandiflora
Clump-forming perennial with a basal rosette of sticky, oval, pale green leaves. In summer produces spurred, open funnel-shaped, violet-blue to purple flowers singly on upright, slender stems. **H** 12–15cm (5–6in), **S** 5cm (2in).

Aquilegia jonesii
Compact perennial that bears short-spurred, violet-blue flowers in summer, a few to each slender stem. Has small rosettes of finely divided, blue-grey or grey-green leaves. Is uncommon, suitable for an alpine house only. **H** 2.5cm (1in), **S** to 5cm (2in).

Prunella grandiflora
(Large self-heal)
Semi-evergreen, spreading, mat-forming perennial with basal rosettes of leaves. In mid-summer bears short spikes of funnel-shaped, purple flowers in whorls. **H** 10–15cm (4–6in), **S** 30cm (12in).

***Campanula* 'Birch Hybrid'**
Vigorous, evergreen perennial with tough, arching, prostrate stems and ivy-shaped, bright green leaves. Bears many open bell-shaped, deep violet flowers in summer. **H** 10cm (4in), **S** 30cm (12in) or more.

Edraianthus pumilio
Short-lived perennial with low tufts of fine, grass-like leaves. In early summer, upturned, bell-shaped, pale to deep lavender flowers, on very short stems, appear amid foliage. **H** 2.5cm (1in), **S** 8cm (3in).

Cyananthus microphyllus
Mat-forming perennial with very fine, red stems clothed in tiny leaves. Bears funnel-shaped, violet-blue flowers at the end of each stem in late summer. Likes humus-rich soil. **H** 2cm (¾in), **S** 20cm (8in).

Townsendia grandiflora
Short-lived, evergreen perennial with basal rosettes of small, spoon-shaped leaves. Upright stems carry solitary daisy-like, violet or violet-blue flower heads in late spring and early summer. **H** to 15cm (6in), **S** 10cm (4in).

***Polygala calcarea* 'Lillet'**
Evergreen, prostrate, very compact perennial with rosettes of small, narrowly oval leaves and loose heads of bright blue flowers in spring and early summer. Likes humus-rich soil. Suits a trough. **H** 2.5cm (1in), **S** 8–10cm (3–4in).

Hedyotis michauxii
(Creeping bluets)
Vigorous perennial with rooting stems. Produces mats of mid-green foliage studded with star-shaped, violet-blue flowers in late spring and early summer. **H** 8cm (3in), **S** 30cm (12in).

Ramonda myconi
Evergreen, rosette-forming perennial with hairy, crinkled leaves and, in late spring and early summer, flat, blue-mauve, pink or white flowers, borne on branched stems. **H** 8cm (3in), **S** to 10cm (4in).

Sisyrinchium idahoense
Semi-evergreen, upright, clump-forming perennial that for a long period in summer and early autumn has many flowering stems carrying tiny tufts of iris-like, blue to violet-blue flowers. Foliage is grass-like. Self seeds readily. **H** to 12cm (5in), **S** 10cm (4in).

Globularia cordifolia
Evergreen, mat-forming, dwarf shrub with creeping, woody stems clothed in tiny, oval leaves. Bears stemless, round, fluffy, blue to pale lavender-blue flower heads in summer. **H** 2.5–5cm (1–2in), **S** to 20cm (8in).

Campanula cochleariifolia
(Fairy thimbles)
Spreading perennial. Runners produce mats of rosetted, tiny, round leaves. Bears small clusters of white, lavender or pale blue flowers in summer on many thin stems above foliage. **H** 8cm (3in), **S** indefinite.

Pratia pedunculata
Vigorous, evergreen, creeping perennial with small leaves and a profusion of star-shaped, pale to mid-blue or occasionally purplish-blue flowers borne in summer. Makes good ground cover in a moist site. **H** 1cm (½in), **S** indefinite.

Trachelium asperuloides
Mat-forming perennial with thread-like stems clothed in minute, mid-green leaves, above which rise many tiny, upright, tubular, pale blue flowers in summer. Do not remove old stems in winter. **H** 8cm (3in), **S** to 15cm (6in).

GENTIANS

Although there are gentians large enough to hold their own in the herbaceous border, most are low-growing, deciduous or evergreen perennials, best suited to rock gardens, where they can form spreading mats. Flowering between spring and autumn, they are renowned for their vivid blue trumpet-shaped flowers, which are produced in pale shades, such as *G.* 'Strathmore', to intensely dark, such as *G. acaulis,* although there are also white and yellow-flowered forms. All are fully hardy and require a cool position, sheltered from hot summer sun. Most need light, rich, moist but well-drained neutral soil; autumn-flowering species and cultivars, such as *G. sino-ornata* require acidic conditions to thrive. Protect from slugs and snails, particularly in spring.

G. saxosa

***G.* 'Ettrick'**

***G.* 'Strathmore'** 🏆

***G.* 'Soutra'**

***G.* 'Eugen's Allerbester'**

***G.* 'Blue Silk'**

***G.* 'Shot Silk'**

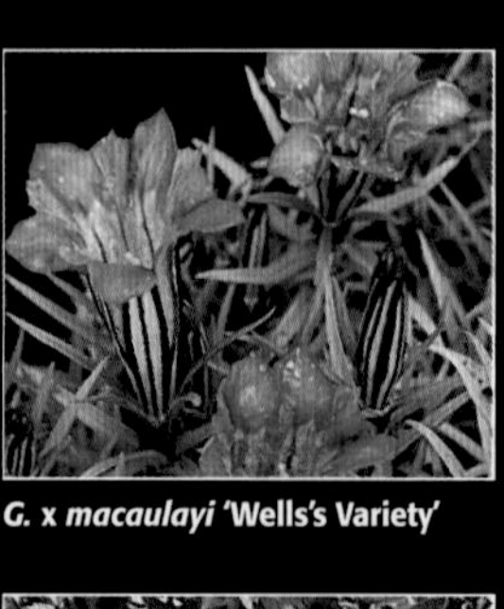

***G.* x *macaulayi* 'Wells's Variety'**

***G.* 'Inverleith'** 🏆

G. sino-ornata 🏆

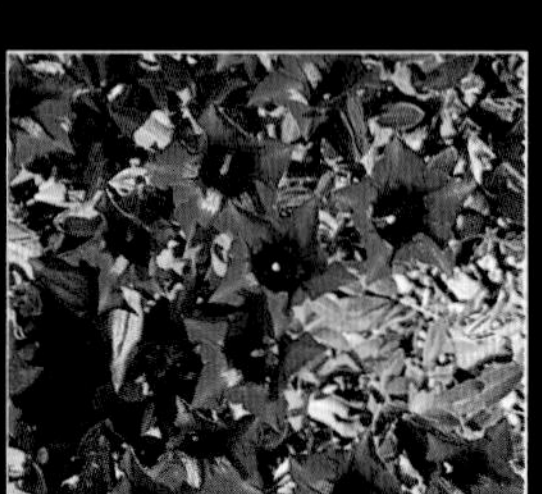

G. acaulis 🏆

Eritrichium nanum

Clump-forming perennial with tufts of hairy, grey-green leaves. Bears small, stemless, flat, pale blue flowers in late spring and early summer. Requires sharp drainage. Is only suitable for an alpine house. **H** 2cm (¾in), **S** 2.5cm (1in).

Parochetus communis
(Shamrock pea)

Evergreen, prostrate perennial with clover-like leaves and pea-like, brilliant blue flowers that are borne almost continuously. Grows best in an alpine house. **H** 2.5–5cm (1–2in), **S** indefinite.

Polygala calcarea

Evergreen, prostrate, occasionally upright, perennial. Has small, narrowly oval leaves and pale to dark blue flowers in late spring and early summer. Likes humus-rich soil. Suits a trough. May be difficult to establish. **H** 2.5cm (1in), **S** to 15cm (6in).

Mitella breweri
Neat, clump-forming, rhizomatous perennial with slender, hairy stems bearing small, pendent, tubular, greenish-white flowers, with flared mouths, in summer. Has lobed, kidney-shaped, basal green leaves. **H** and **S** 15cm (6in).

Gunnera magellanica
Mat-forming perennial, grown for its rounded, toothed leaves, often bronze-tinged when young, on short, creeping stems. Small, green, unisexual flowers, with reddish-bracts, are borne on male and female plants. Likes peaty soil. **H** 2.5cm (1in), **S** to 30cm (12in).

Polygala chamaebuxus
Evergreen, woody-based perennial with tiny, hard, dark green leaves. In late spring and early summer bears many racemes of small, pea-like, white-and-yellow flowers, sometimes marked brown. Needs humus-rich soil. **H** 5cm (2in), **S** 20cm (8in).

Asarina procumbens
Semi-evergreen perennial with trailing stems bearing soft, hairy leaves and tubular, pale cream flowers, with yellow palates, throughout summer. Dislikes winter wet. Self seeds freely. **H** 1–2.5cm (½–1in), **S** 23–30cm (9–12in).

***Sedum acre* 'Aureum'**
Evergreen, mat-forming perennial with spreading shoots, yellow-tipped in spring and early summer, clothed in tiny, fleshy, yellow leaves. Has flat heads of tiny, yellow flowers in summer. Is invasive but easy to control. **H** 2.5–5cm (1–2in), **S** to 23cm (9in).

Sedum acre
(Biting stonecrop, Common stonecrop)
Evergreen, mat-forming perennial with dense, spreading shoots and tiny, fleshy, pale green leaves. Bears flat, terminal heads of tiny, yellow summer flowers. Is invasive but easily controlled. **H** 2.5–5cm (1–2in), **S** indefinite.

Calceolaria tenella
Vigorous, evergreen, prostrate perennial with creeping, reddish stems and oval, mid-green leaves, above which rise small spikes of pouch-shaped, red-spotted, yellow flowers in summer. **H** 10cm (4in), **S** indefinite.

Oxalis perdicaria
Clump-forming perennial with woolly-coated tubers. Mid-green leaves have up to 5 rounded lobes. Produces racemes of widely funnel-shaped, bright yellow flowers, 1–2cm (½–¾in) across, in late summer and autumn. **H** 5cm (2in), **S** 8–10cm (3–4in).

YELLOW

Waldsteinia ternata
Semi-evergreen perennial with loose, spreading mats of toothed, 3-parted leaves. Bears saucer-shaped, yellow flowers in late spring and early summer. Is good on a bank. **H** 10cm (4in), **S** 20–30cm (8–12in).

***Lysimachia nummularia* 'Aurea'**
(Golden creeping Jenny)
Prostrate perennial. Creeping, rooting stems bear pairs of round, soft yellow leaves, which later turn greenish-yellow or green in dense shade. Has bright yellow flowers in leaf axils in summer. **H** 2.5–5cm (1–2in), **S** indefinite.

Scutellaria orientalis
Rhizomatous perennial with hairy, grey, rooting stems. Has terminal spikes of tubular, yellow flowers, with brownish-purple lips, in summer. Leaves are toothed and oval. May be invasive in a small space. **H** 5–10cm (2–4in), **S** to 23cm (9in).

***Linum flavum* 'Compactum'**
Shrubby perennial with narrow leaves and terminal clusters of many upward-facing, open funnel-shaped, single, bright yellow flowers in summer. Provide a sunny, sheltered position and protection from winter wet. **H** and **S** 15cm (6in).

Potentilla eriocarpa
Clump-forming perennial with tufts of oval, dark green leaves divided into leaflets. Flat, single, pale yellow flowers are borne throughout summer just above leaves. **H** 5–8cm (2–3in), **S** 10–15cm (4–6in).

Cytisus ardoinoi
Deciduous, hummock-forming, dwarf shrub with arching stems. In late spring and early summer, pea-like, bright yellow flowers are produced in pairs in leaf axils. Leaves are divided into 3 leaflets. **H** 10cm (4in), **S** 15cm (6in).

Potentilla aurea
Rounded perennial, with a woody base, that in late summer bears loose sprays of flat, single, yellow flowers with slightly darker eyes. Leaves are divided into oval, slightly silvered leaflets. **H** 10cm (4in), **S** 20cm (8in).

Oenothera macrocarpa
Spreading perennial with stout stems and oval leaves. Throughout summer bears a succession of wide, bell-shaped, yellow flowers, sometimes spotted red, that open at sundown. **H** to 10cm (4in), **S** to 40cm (16in) or more.

***Calceolaria* 'Walter Shrimpton'**
Evergreen, mound-forming perennial with glossy, dark green leaves. In early summer bears short spikes of many pouch-shaped, bronze-yellow flowers, spotted rich brown, with white bands across centres. **H** 10cm (4in), **S** 23cm (9in).

Papaver fauriei
Short-lived, clump-forming perennial with basal rosettes of finely cut, hairy, soft grey leaves. Bears pendent, open cup-shaped, pale yellow flowers in summer. Dislikes winter wet. **H** and **S** 5–10cm (2–4in).

Hypericum empetrifolium subsp. _tortuosum_
Evergreen, prostrate shrub with angled branches and bright green leaves that have curled margins. Bears flat heads of small, bright yellow flowers in summer. Needs winter protection. **H** 2cm (¾in), **S** 30cm (12in).

Hippocrepis comosa
(Horseshoe vetch)
Vigorous perennial with prostrate, rooting stems bearing open spikes of pea-like, yellow flowers in summer and leaves divided into leaflets. Self seeds freely and may spread rapidly. **H** 5–8cm (2–3in), **S** indefinite.

Persicaria vacciniifolia
Evergreen, perennial with woody, red stems. Leaves are tinged red in autumn. Bears deep pink or rose-red flowers in late summer and autumn. **H** 10–15cm (4–6in), **S** to 30cm (12in).

Genista sagittalis
Deciduous, semi-prostrate shrub with winged stems bearing a few oval, dark green leaves. Pea-like, yellow flowers appear in dense, terminal clusters in early summer, followed by hairy seed pods. **H** 8cm (3in), **S** 30cm (12in) or more.

Nertera granadensis (Bead plant)
Prostrate perennial with dense mats of tiny, bright green leaves. In early summer bears minute, greenish-white flowers, then many shiny, orange or red berries. Needs ample moisture in summer. **H** to 1cm (½in), **S** 10cm (4in).

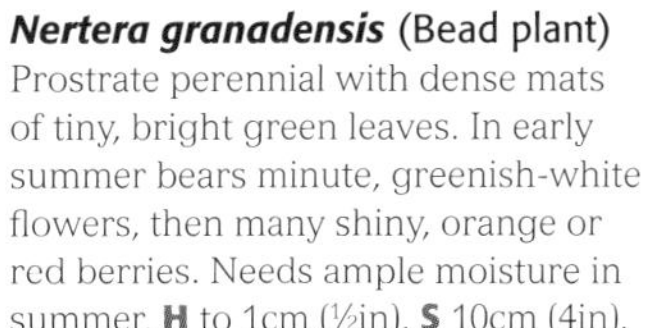

Gaultheria procumbens
Vigorous, evergreen sub-shrub with prostrate stems carrying clusters of oval, leathery leaves that turn red in winter. In summer, solitary bell-shaped, pink-flushed, white flowers appear in leaf axils, followed by scarlet berries. **H** 5–15cm (2–6in), **S** indefinite.

RED

Sedum lydium
Evergreen, mat-forming perennial with reddish stems and narrow, fleshy, often red-flushed leaves. Bears flat-topped, terminal clusters of tiny, white flowers in summer. **H** 5cm (2in), **S** to 15cm (6in).

Acaena microphylla
Compact, mat-forming perennial, usually evergreen, with leaves divided into tiny leaflets, bronze-tinged when young. Heads of small flowers with spiny, dull red bracts are borne in summer and develop into decorative burs. **H** 5cm (2in), **S** 15cm (6in).

Jovibarba hirta
Evergreen, mat-forming perennial with rosettes of hairy, mid-green leaves, often suffused red, and terminal clusters of star-shaped, pale yellow flowers in summer. Dislikes winter wet. **H** 8–15cm (3–6in), **S** 10cm (4in).

Sedum obtusatum
Evergreen, prostrate perennial with small, fat, succulent leaves that turn bronze-red in summer. Loose, flat sprays of tiny, bright yellow flowers are borne in summer. Dislikes summer wet. **H** 5cm (2in), **S** 10–15cm (4–6in).

Sedum spathulifolium
Evergreen, mat-forming perennial with rosettes of fleshy, green or silver leaves, usually strongly suffused bronze-red, and small clusters of tiny, yellow flowers borne just above foliage in summer. Tolerates shade. **H** 5cm (2in), **S** indefinite.

GREY

***Artemisia schmidtiana* 'Nana'**
Prostrate perennial with fern-like, silver foliage. Has insignificant sprays of daisy-like, yellow flowers in summer. Is suitable for a wall or bank. **H** 8cm (3in), **S** 20cm (8in).

Raoulia hookeri* var. *albosericea
Evergreen, prostrate perennial with tiny rosettes of silver leaves. Flower heads appear briefly in summer as fragrant, yellow fluff. Is best in poor, gritty humus in an alpine house. Dislikes winter wet. **H** to 1cm (½in), **S** 25cm (10in).

Acaena caesiiglauca
Vigorous, ground-cover perennial, usually evergreen. Has hairy, glaucous blue leaves divided into leaflets. Heads of small flowers with spiny, brownish-green bracts, borne in summer, develop into brownish-red burs. **H** 5cm (2in), **S** 75cm (30in) or more.

Paronychia kapela subsp. _serpyllifolia_
Evergreen, very compact, mat-forming perennial with minute, silver leaves. Inconspicuous flowers, borne in summer, are surrounded by papery, silver bracts. Is good for covering tufa. **H** to 1cm (½in), **S** 20cm (8in).

Asarum europaeum **(Asarabacca)**
Vigorous, evergreen, prostrate, rhizomatous perennial with large, kidney-shaped, leathery, glossy leaves that hide tiny, brown flowers appearing in spring. **H** 15cm (6in), **S** indefinite.

Arabis procurrens **'Variegata'**
Evergreen, mat-forming perennial with small, oval, green leaves, splashed with cream. Bears small, white flowers in spring and early summer. May revert to type, with plain green leaves. **H** 2cm (¾in), **S** 30cm (12in).

Trifolium repens **'Purpurascens'**
Vigorous, semi-evergreen, ground-cover perennial, grown for its divided, bronze-green foliage, variably edged bright green. Produces heads of small, pea-like, white blooms in summer. Suits a wild bank. **H** in flower 8–12cm (3–5in), **S** 20–30cm (8–12in) or more.

Arctostaphylos uva-ursi **'Point Reyes'**
Evergreen, prostrate shrub with long shoots and glossy leaves. In late spring and early summer bears terminal clusters of urn-shaped, pale pink to white flowers, followed by red berries. **H** 10cm (4in), **S** 50cm (20in).

Sedum spathulifolium **'Cape Blanco'**
Evergreen perennial with rosettes of fleshy leaves, frequently suffused purple. Tiny, yellow flowers appear above foliage in summer. Tolerates shade. **H** 5cm (2in), **S** indefinite.

Pachysandra terminalis
Evergreen, creeping perennial that has smooth leaves clustered at the ends of short stems. Bears spikes of tiny, white flowers, sometimes flushed purple, in early summer. Makes excellent ground cover in a moist or dry site. **H** 10cm (4in), **S** 20cm (8in).

Sempervivum ciliosum
Evergreen, mat-forming perennial with rosettes of hairy, grey-green leaves and, in summer, heads of small, star-shaped, yellow flowers. Dislikes winter wet; is best grown in an alpine house. **H** 8–10cm (3–4in), **S** 10cm (4in).

GREEN

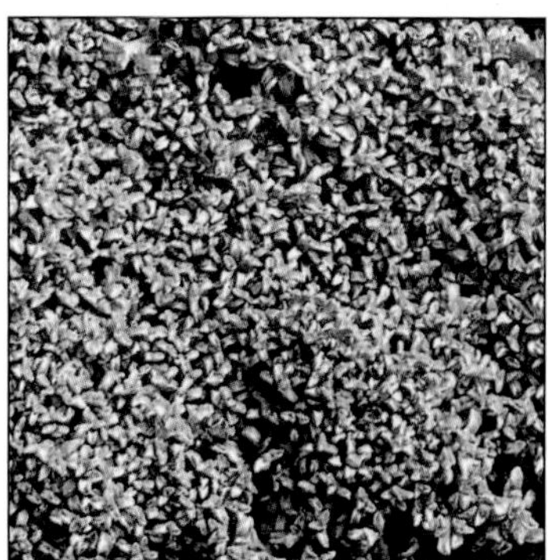

Raoulia australis
Evergreen, carpeting perennial forming a hard mat of grey-green leaves. Bears tiny, fluffy, sulphur-yellow flower heads in summer. **H** to 1cm (½in), **S** 25cm (10in).

Azorella trifurcata
Evergreen perennial forming tight, hard cushions of tiny, leathery, oval leaves in rosettes. Bears many small, stalkless umbels of yellow flowers in summer. **H** to 10cm (4in), **S** 15cm (6in).

Raoulia haastii
Evergreen perennial forming low, irregular hummocks of minute leaves that are apple-green in spring, dark green in autumn and chocolate-brown in winter. Occasionally has small, fluffy, yellow flower heads in summer. **H** to 1cm (½in), **S** 25cm (10in).

Sagina boydii
Evergreen perennial with hard cushions of minute, stiff, bottle-green leaves in small rosettes. Bears insignificant flowers in summer. Is difficult and slow-growing. **H** 1cm (½in), **S** to 20cm (8in).

Arctostaphylos uva-ursi
Evergreen, low-growing shrub with arching, intertwining stems clothed in small, oval, bright green leaves. Bears urn-shaped, pinkish-white flowers in summer followed by scarlet berries. **H** 10cm (4in), **S** 50cm (20in).

Plantago nivalis
Evergreen perennial with neat rosettes of thick, silver-haired, green leaves. Bears spikes of insignificant, dull grey flowers in summer. Dislikes winter wet. **H** in leaf 2.5cm (1in), **S** 5cm (2in).

Bolax gummifer
Very slow-growing, evergreen perennial with neat rosettes of small, blue-green leaves forming extremely hard cushions. Insignificant, yellow flowers are rarely produced. Grows well on tufa. **H** 2.5cm (1in), **S** 10cm (4in).

***Sedum kamtschaticum* 'Variegatum'**
Semi-evergreen, prostrate perennial with fleshy, cream-edged leaves. Has fleshy stems and leaf buds in winter and loose, terminal clusters of orange-flushed, yellow flowers in early autumn.
H 5–8cm (2–3in), **S** 20cm (8in).

***Saxifraga exarata* subsp. *moschata* 'Cloth of Gold'**
Evergreen hummock-forming perennial with small, soft rosettes of bright golden foliage; produces best colour in shade. Has star-shaped, white flowers on slender stems in summer.
H 10–15cm (4–6in), **S** 15cm (6in).

HOUSELEEKS

The main attraction of houseleeks is their colourful rosettes of leaves. These range from bright yellow, through various shades of green, grey, pink, purple, red and orange, to almost black. The leaves may be dull or glossy, or covered with soft down or longer hairs. Leaf shape can also vary from short and succulent to long and tapering. The rosettes are most striking in the spring and summer but, even in the winter, many varieties remain attractively coloured. It is the endless range of different leaf shapes, shades and textures that make this group so interesting to enthusiasts. They do not like damp or shaded conditions, but thrive in well-drained soil in full sun. Houseleeks are ideal for pots or sink gardens on a south-facing patio, or can planted out in rockeries or in the crevices of stone walls.

S. calcareum

S. **'Rosie'**

S. calcareum **'Extra'** 🏆

S. **'Blood Tip'**

S. tectorum 🏆

S. arachnoideum 🏆

S. giuseppii 🏆

S. montanum

S. **'Gulle Dame'**

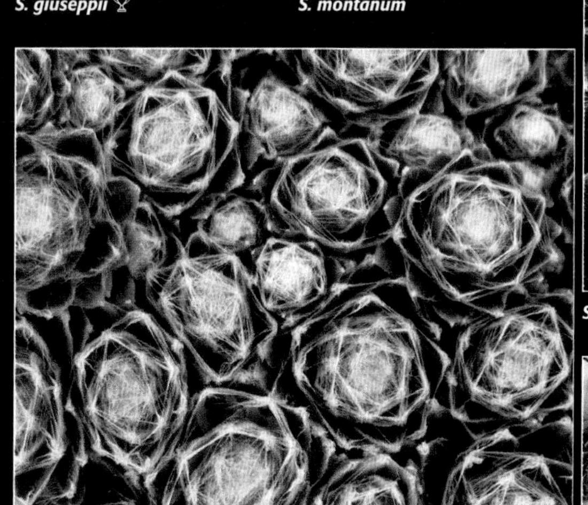

S. **'Kappa'**

S. **'Gallivarda'** 🏆

BULBS

Bulbous plants are found throughout the world in habitats as diverse as woodland and scrub, meadows, river banks, the edges of streams, and rocky hills and mountains. There are ones to suit every garden site and design, from the tiny *Iris danfordiae* for a rock garden, to daffodils and tulips in beds and borders, and the carpeting erythroniums or statuesque *Cardiocrinum giganteum* for a woodland garden. Most have a distinct flowering season, yet with careful planning it is possible to extend or enhance this period of interest. Although most bloom in spring or early summer, producing splashes of colour before many shrubs and perennials reach their peak, plant snowdrops for late winter colour, and colchicums, cyclamen and some crocuses to brighten an autumn day.

BULBS

Embracing a wide range of decorative plants, bulbs provide exciting effects throughout the year, with large drifts of snowdrops in late winter, daffodils and tulips in spring, the exquisite perfume of lilies and vibrant dahlia colours in summer, and spidery flowers of nerines in autumn.

SIZE CATEGORIES USED WITHIN THIS GROUP		
Large	**Medium**	**Small**
over 75cm (30in)	23–75cm (9–30in)	up to 23cm (9in)

BULB DEFINITIONS

Bulbs are divided into smaller plant categories, including true bulbs, corms and tubers. All of these swollen, underground, food-storage organs help the bulb to survive periods of drought.

Bulb
A true bulb is a storage organ made up of stems and fleshy leaves inside. Examples include daffodils, tulips, and eucomis (above).

Corm
Swollen stems that have adapted to store food are known as corms. They appear solid throughout, and include crocuses (above).

Tuber
Tuberous plants have swollen underground roots or stems. Examples include cyclamen, dahlias (above) and begonias.

What are bulbs?

The term bulb can be used to describe all swollen, underground, food-storage organs, and includes true bulbs as well as corms, rhizomes and tubers. True bulbs have fleshy scales – modified leaves or leaf bases – that overlap and are often enclosed in a papery tunic, as in narcissi, or they may be naked and loosely arranged like lily bulbs.

Corms are compressed and enlarged stem bases, usually enclosed in a fibrous or papery tunic, as in the crocus. Each corm lasts one year, and is replaced by a new one after flowering. Tubers, such as cyclamen, are solid, underground sections of modified stem or root and seldom possess scales or tunics. Rhizomes are modified stems that creep at or just below soil level, and may be thin and wiry or swollen and fleshy.

A few bulbs are evergreen, but most grow and bloom during a short season, and then die back to below ground level. Their leaves produce the food store for the following year, which is why the foliage must not be cut down after flowering but allowed to wither naturally.

When below ground, bulbs are described as dormant but they are, in fact, ripening and developing the following year's flowers, and must be planted in a suitable site to thrive. Bulbs that originate from dry, hot climates, such as nerines and watsonias, need warm, dry conditions when dormant to aid ripening and flower formation, while those from woodland or other damp, shaded habitats, such as bluebells (*Hyacinthoides*) and snowdrops (*Galanthus*) require a cool, slightly moist spot.

Designing with bulbs

There are bulbs to suit all garden designs and planting styles. They range in size from the tiny *Iris danfordiae* and autumn daffodil (*Sternbergia lutea*), both suitable for a scree or rock garden, to carpeting erythroniums for the dappled shade of a woodland garden, midrange alliums and tulips for a hot, sunny border, and tall, slender regal lilies that produce highly scented flowers on stems up to 1.8m (6ft) in height. The

BELOW Carpets of spring colour
A selection of daffodils has been naturalized in the grass beneath silver birches and spring-flowering trees, creating a sea of nodding yellow flowers.

flower forms also lend themselves to certain garden styles. Tulips with sculptural cupped flowers planted *en masse*, and the sharp flower shapes of many dahlias are ideal for formal schemes, while the looser flower forms of nectaroscordums and turks-cap lilies, and arching spikes of crocosmias create an informal look. Turf spangled with crocuses or snake's-head fritillaries (*Fritillaria meleagris*) mimics their wild habitat and provides early colour in naturalistic schemes.

Bulbs add seasonal colour and interest to mixed borders with annuals, shrubs and perennials. Daffodils (*Narcissus*), crown imperials (*Fritillaria imperialis*), alliums, and dahlias, all blend well with other types of planting. Unscented lilies make good partners for scented roses, while exotic looking cannas and alstroemerias add spice to a tropical design. If you can't squeeze bulbs into your border, many are perfectly at home in containers and baskets.

LAYERING BULBS IN CONTAINERS

Pots brimming with spring bulbs lift the spirits after a long winter, but you need to plan ahead to create the most spectacular displays. In autumn, look out for bulbs at garden centres or in mail-order catalogues, and check flowering times for a synchronized display of tulips, daffodils and grape hyacinths (*Muscari*).

A multi-coloured display.

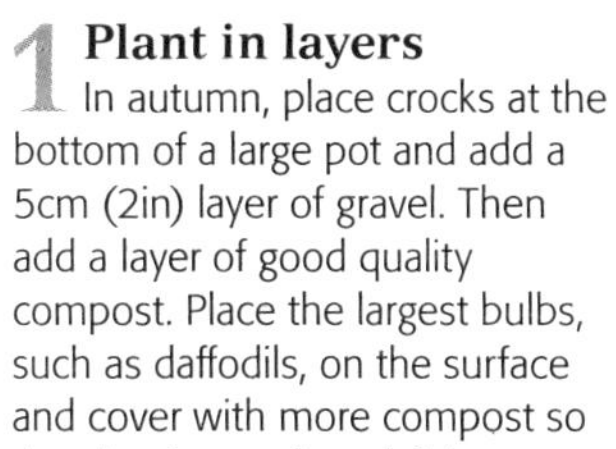

1 Plant in layers In autumn, place crocks at the bottom of a large pot and add a 5cm (2in) layer of gravel. Then add a layer of good quality compost. Place the largest bulbs, such as daffodils, on the surface and cover with more compost so that the tips are just visible.

2 Cover the bulbs Now place the next layer of bulbs, such as tulips, between the daffodil bulbs, and cover with more potting compost. Finally add small bulbs, like grape hyacinths, on this top layer, and cover with compost. Press down lightly with your hands, and leave the pot in a sheltered sunny spot.

Year-round interest

Choose carefully, and you can have a bulb in flower for most of the year. The first to appear in late winter are the snowdrops (*Galanthus*) and winter aconites (*Eranthis*), while early narcissus, muscari, crocuses, scillas, chionodoxas, dwarf iris and *Anemone blanda* mark the onset of spring.

In mid-spring, fill your garden with vibrant yellow daffodils and bright tulips, or opt for the same plants in pastel shades – the choice is vast for both genera. Summer-flowering bulbs, such as *Galtonia candicans*, most alliums, the Peruvian daffodil (*Hymenocallis naricissiflora*) and ornithogalums offer colourful highlights.

These are followed in late summer by gladioli, crinums, dahlias, and crocosmias, which may continue to bloom into the autumn until the frosts arrive. When the summer spectacle is over, select autumn-flowering nerines, crocuses, colchicums and cyclamen, and to end the year display, use *Cyclamen hederifolium*, whose marbled foliage often persists into winter.

For scented bulbs, choose hyacinths, bluebells, and scented daffodils for spring, and lilies and crinums for summer displays.

NATURALIZING BULBS

You can create spectacular effects by naturalizing bulbs in a lawn or under trees. Choose robust plants, such as snowdrops, daffodils and crocuses, which are able to compete with trees roots and grass. To achieve a natural random effect, toss the bulbs in the air and plant them individually where they fall. For each bulb, dig out a small plug of soil and turf, two to three times the depth of the bulb. After flowering, when the leaves have died, mow the grass.

BULB PLANTING PLANNER

Type of bulb	Planting Time	Planting depth	Preferred Conditions
Agapanthus	spring	10cm (4in)	Full sun in moist, but well drained soil
Allium	autumn	5–15cm (2–6in)	Full sun in moist, but well drained soil
Colchicum	late summer	10cm (4in)	Full sun in well-drained soil
Crocus (spring)	autumn	8cm (3in)	Full sun in well-drained soil
Crocus (autumn)	late summer	8cm (3in)	Full sun in well-drained soil
Cyclamen	autumn	10cm (4in)	Partial shade in well-drained soil
Galanthus	early autumn	2.5–5cm (1–2in)	Full sun or partial shade in moist soil that does not dry out in summer
Hyacinthus	autumn	10cm (4in)	Full sun or partial shade in moist, well-drained soil
Lilium	autumn	10–15cm (4–6in)	Full sun or partial shade; most prefer acid to neutral well-drained soil.
Muscari	autumn	5cm (2in)	Full sun in well-drained soil
Narcissus	autumn	10–15cm (4–6in)	Sun or partial shade in any reasonable, well-drained garden soil
Tulipa	late autumn	8–15cm (3–6in)	Full sun in well-drained soil

WHITE

Ornithogalum magnum
Late spring-flowering bulb with linear, grey-green basal leaves. Produces upright, pyramid-shaped racemes of small, star-shaped, white flowers, with a green stripe on the reverse. **H** 60–80cm (24–32in), **S** 10cm (4in).

Fritillaria verticillata
Spring-flowering bulb with slender leaves in whorls up the stem, which bears a loose spike of 1–15 bell-shaped, white flowers, 2–4cm (¾–1½in) long and chequered green or brown. **H** to 1m (3ft), **S** 8–10cm (3–4in).

***Fritillaria persica* 'Ivory Bells'**
Robust, late spring-flowering bulb with lance-shaped, grey-green leaves on sturdy, upright stems. Produces a terminal raceme of 10–30 pendent, bell-shaped, creamy-white to green-white flowers. **H** 75–100cm (30–39in), **S** 10cm (4in).

PURPLE

Fritillaria persica
Spring-flowering bulb with narrow, lance-shaped, grey-green leaves along stem. Produces a spike of 10–20 or more narrow, bell-shaped, black- or brownish-purple flowers, 1.5–2cm (⅝–¾in) long. **H** 1.5m (5ft), **S** 10cm (4in).

Allium aflatunense
Late spring-flowering bulb with strap-shaped, mid-green, basal leaves. Dense, spherical, terminal umbels of small, star-shaped, lilac-purple flowers are borne on sturdy stems. Seed heads may be dried for decorative use. **H** 80cm (32in), **S** 10–15cm (4–6in).

YELLOW

***Fritillaria imperialis* 'Lutea'**
Spring-flowering bulb with whorls of lance-shaped, shiny, light green leaves and a head of up to 8 pendent, bell-shaped, bright yellow flowers, to 6cm (2in) long, crowned by a tuft of small, leaf-like bracts. **H** 1m (3ft), **S** 25cm (10in).

Fritillaria raddeana
Robust, spring-flowering bulb with lance-shaped leaves in whorls on lower half of stem. Has a head of up to 20 widely conical, pale or greenish-yellow flowers, 3–4cm (1¼–1½in) long, topped by a 'crown' of small leaves. **H** to 1m (3ft), **S** 15–23cm (6–9in).

ORANGE

Fritillaria imperialis (Crown imperial)
Spring-flowering bulb with glossy, pale green leaves carried in whorls on leafy stems. Has up to 5 widely bell-shaped, orange flowers crowned by small, leaf-like bracts. **H** to 1.5cm (5ft), **S** 23–30cm (9–12in).

Fritillaria recurva (Scarlet fritillary)
Spring-flowering bulb with whorls of narrow, lance-shaped, grey-green leaves. Bears a spike of up to 10 narrow, yellow-chequered, orange–red flowers. **H** to 1m (30in), **S** 8–10cm (3–4in).

WHITE

***Crinum x powellii* 'Album'**
Late summer- or autumn-flowering bulb, with a long neck, producing a group of semi-erect, strap-shaped leaves. Leafless flower stems carry heads of fragrant, widely funnel-shaped, white flowers. **H** to 1m (3ft), **S** 60cm (2ft).

Camassia leichtlinii
Tuft-forming bulb with long, narrow, erect, basal leaves. Each leafless stem bears a dense spike of 6-petalled, star-shaped, bluish-violet or white flowers, 4–8cm (1½–3in) across, in summer. **H** 1–1.5m (3–5ft), **S** 20–30cm (8–12in).

Crinum moorei
Summer-flowering bulb with a long neck, up to 1m (3ft) tall, and strap-shaped, semi-erect, grey-green leaves. Leafless flower stems bear heads of long-tubed, funnel-shaped, white to deep pink flowers. **H** 50–70cm (20–28in), **S** 60cm (24in).

Gladiolus murielae
Mid-summer-flowering corm with a loose spike of up to 10 sweetly scented, hooded, funnel-shaped, maroon-eyed, pure white flowers. Has linear, pleated leaves. Is good for cutting. **H** 80cm (32in), **S** 5cm (2in).

Galtonia candicans
(Summer hyacinth)
Late summer- or autumn-flowering bulb with wide strap-shaped, fleshy, semi-erect, basal, grey-green leaves. Leafless stem has a spike of up to 30 pendent, short-tubed, white flowers. **H** 1–1.2m (3–4ft), **S** 18–23cm (7–9in).

GLADIOLI

Comprising about 180 species, with over 10,000 hybrids and cultivars for garden cultivation, exhibiting, and cutting, gladioli are prized for their showy spikes of usually open, funnel-shaped flowers. *Gladiolus* hybrids are divided into the Grandiflorus Group, with long, densely packed flower spikes, categorized as miniature, small, medium-sized, large, or giant, according to the width of the lowest flowers, and the Primulinus and Nanus Groups, which have loose spikes of small flowers. Plant gladioli in borders or pots for late spring to early autumn displays, and store corms in a frost-free place over winter. In cold areas, grow them by a sheltered, sunny wall; winter-flowering South African gladioli require a cool greenhouse. For more information see the Plant Dictionary.

***G.* 'Purple Flora'** [Grandiflorus Group]

***G.* 'Her Majesty'** [Grandiflorus Group]

***G.* 'Blue Frost'** [Grandiflorus Group]

***G.* 'White Prosperity'** [Grandiflorus Group]

***G.* 'Columbine'** [small]

***G.* 'Velvet Eyes'** [Grandiflorus Group]

***G.* 'Impressive'** [Nanus Group]

***G.* 'Nova Lux'** [Grandiflorus Group]

***G.* 'Morning Gold'** [Grandiflorus Group]

***G.* 'Green Woodpecker'** [medium]

***G.* 'Drama'** [large]

***G.* 'Sancerre'** [Grandiflorus Group]

***G.* x *colvillii* 'The Bride'** 🏆 [Nanus Group]

***G.* 'White Ice'** [medium]

***G.* 'Wine and Roses'** [Grandiflorus Group]

***G.* 'Nymph'** [Nanus Group]

***G.* 'Oscar'** [Grandiflorus Group]

***G.* 'Stella'** [Grandiflorus Group]

***G.* 'Peter Pears'** [large]

WHITE

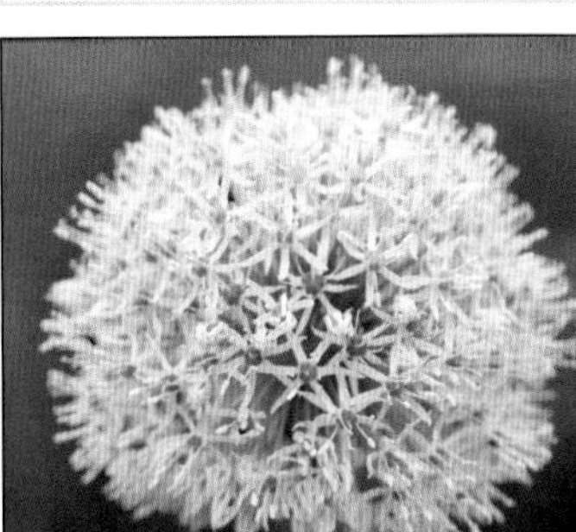

***Allium* 'Mount Everest'**
Late spring to early summer-flowering bulb with sturdy stems bearing spherical umbels, 12–15cm (5–6in) in diameter, of tiny star-shaped, white flowers, with green stamens. The basal strap-shaped, semi-erect, leaves are greyish-green. **H** 1.1m (3½ft), **S** 15cm (6in).

Cardiocrinum giganteum (Giant lily)
Stout, leafy-stemmed bulb. In summer has long spikes of fragrant, slightly pendent, cream flowers, 15cm (6in) long, with purple-red streaks inside, then brown seed pods. **H** to 3m (10ft), **S** 75cm–1.1m (2½–3½ft).

Nectaroscordum siculum* subsp. *bulgaricum
Late spring- to early summer-flowering bulb with pendent, bell-shaped, white flowers, flushed purple-red and green. In seed, stalks bend upwards, holding dry seed pods erect. **H** to 1.2m (4ft), **S** 30–45cm (1–1½ft).

***Polianthes tuberosa* 'The Pearl'**
Late summer-flowering, rhizomatous perennial. Sweetly scented, flared, funnel-shaped, double, white flowers are borne in pairs above long, lance-shaped, upright, basal leaves. Keep tuber dry when dormant. **H** 1m (3ft), **S** 15cm (6in).

Nomocharis pardanthina
Summer-flowering bulb with stems bearing whorls of lance-shaped leaves and up to 15 outward-facing, white or pale pink flowers, each with purple blotches and a dark purple eye. **H** to 1m (3ft), **S** 12–15cm (5–6in).

PINK

Crinum* x *powellii
Late summer- or autumn-flowering bulb with a long neck producing a group of strap-shaped, semi-erect leaves. Leafless flower stems bear heads of fragrant, widely funnel-shaped, pink flowers. **H** to 1m (3ft), **S** 60cm (2ft).

Watsonia meriana
Clump-forming, summer-flowering corm with sword-shaped, erect leaves at base, with smaller, sheath-like leaves on the stem. Produces a loose spike of trumpet-shaped flowers, 5–6cm (2–2½in) long, in bright pink to vivid orange or red. **H** 1.2m (4ft), **S** 15cm (6in).

PINK

Dierama pulcherrimum
Upright, summer-flowering corm with long, narrow, strap-like, evergreen leaves, above which rise elegant, arching, wiry stems bearing funnel-shaped, deep pink flowers. Prefers deep, rich soil. **H** 1.5m (5ft), **S** 30cm (1ft).

Notholirion campanulatum
Early summer-flowering bulb with long, narrow leaves in a basal tuft. Leafy stem bears a spike of 10–40 pendent, funnel-shaped flowers, each 4–5cm (1½–2in) long, with green-tipped, deep rose-purple petals. **H** to 1m (3ft), **S** 8–10cm (3–4in).

Watsonia borbonica
Very robust, summer-flowering corm with narrowly sword-shaped leaves both at base and on stem. Produces a loose, branched spike of rich pink flowers, with 6 spreading, pointed, rose-red lobes. **H** 1–1.5m (3–5ft), **S** 45–60cm (1½–2ft).

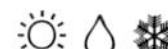

RED

Watsonia pillansii
Summer-flowering corm with long, sword-shaped, erect leaves, some basal and some on stem. Stem carries a dense, branched spike of tubular, orange-red flowers, each 6–8cm (2½–3in) long, with 6 short lobes. **H** to 1m (3ft), **S** 30–45cm (1–1½ft).

Scadoxus multiflorus* subsp. *katherinae (Blood flower)
Very robust, clump-forming bulb with lance-shaped, wavy-edged leaves. Bears an umbel of up to 200 red flowers in summer. **H** to 1.2m (4ft), **S** 30–45cm (1–1½ft). Min. 10°C (50°F).

Dracunculus vulgaris (Dragon's arum)
Spring- and summer-flowering tuber with deeply divided leaves at apex of thick, blotched stem. A blackish-maroon spadix protrudes from a deep maroon spathe, 35cm (14in) long. **H** to 1m (3ft), **S** 45–60cm (1½–2ft).

***Gloriosa superba* 'Rothschildiana'** (Glory lily)
Deciduous, summer-flowering, tuberous, tendril climber. Upper leaf axils each bear a large flower that has 6 reflexed, red petals with scalloped, yellow edges. **H** to 2m (6ft), **S** 30–45cm (1–1½ft). Min. 8°C (46°F).

***Dahlia* 'Hillcrest Royal'**
Medium-flowered cactus dahlia producing rich purple flowers, with incurving petals, held on strong stems in summer–autumn. **H** 1.1m (3½ft), **S** 60cm (2ft).

ALSTROEMERIAS

Commonly known as the Peruvian Lily, Lily of the Incas, or Parrot Lily, these South American tuberous perennials are prized for their delicate funnel-shaped blooms in yellow, orange, pink, red, white, or purple, with decorative markings in contrasting colours. They also have an exceptionally long flowering season, from mid-summer to the first frosts, and make excellent cut flowers. Most suppliers offer plants, rather than tubers, which are best planted in spring after the late frosts in a sunny site and free-draining soil, giving the roots time to establish before winter. Although reasonably hardy, young plants are vulnerable to cold, wet conditions – protect them in winter with a thick mulch of well-rotted compost or manure.

A. PRINCESS JULIETA **('Zaprijul')** ①   ***A.*** PRINCESS ARIANE **('Zapriari')** ①

A. **'Elvira'** ①

A. **'Polka'** ①

A. **'Friendship'** ♕①

A. **'Apollo'** ♕①

A. **'Tara'** ①

A. **'Blushing Bride'** ①

A. **'Serenade'** ①

A. aurea **'Orange King'** ①

A. **'Moulin Rouge'** ①

A. **'Red Beauty'** ①

A. INCA ICE **'Koice'** ①

A. psittacina ①

A. INCA TROPIC **'Kotrop'** ①

LILIES

Lilies (*Lilium* species and cultivars) make elegant additions to summer borders and containers. Their flamboyant flowers range from nodding, upright, and trumpet-shaped forms, to turkscaps with recurved petals. The blooms are often spotted with a darker or contrasting colour, or have conspicuous stamens. Many lilies have a powerful, sweet fragrance, most notably the Oriental and Longiflorum hybrids, although a few species are unpleasantly scented. The hybrids thrive in sun and well-drained soil, and are available in a dazzling array of colours, from white, pink, and red, to shades of yellow and orange. Lily species prefer partially-shaded sites; some also require acid soil. Leave plants undisturbed once established, as the bulbs are easily damaged. For more information see the Plant Dictionary.

***L.* 'Casa Blanca'** 🏆

L. martagon* var. *album 🏆

***L.* TRIUMPHATOR ('Zanlophator')**

***L.* 'White Heaven'**

***L.* 'Sterling Star'**

***L.* 'Mona Lisa'**

***L.* 'Olivia'**

***L.* 'Nymph'**

***L.* 'Black Magic'**

***L.* 'Lady Alice'**

***L.* 'Arena'**

L. longiflorum 🏆

L. auratum* var. *platyphyllum

L. regale 🏆

***L.* 'Altari'**

L. 'Tom Pouce'

L. 'Rosita'

L. 'Elodie'

L. 'Sumatra'

L. 'Miss Lucy'

L. 'Côte d'Azur'

L. 'Star Fighter'

L. rubellum

L. mackliniae

L. cernuum

L. 'Sweet Lord'

L. 'Tiger Woods'

L. 'Black Out'

L. martagon 🏆

L. lankongense

L. 'Journey's End'

L. 'Netty's Pride'

L. 'Conca d'Or'

L. canadense

L. pyrenaicum

L. 'Bright Star'

L. leichtlinii

L. 'Rosemary North'

L. superbum

L. 'Connecticut King'

L. rosthornii

L. medeoloides

L. pardalinum subsp. *wigginsii*

L. regale 'Royal Gold'

L. monadelphum

L. 'Limelight'

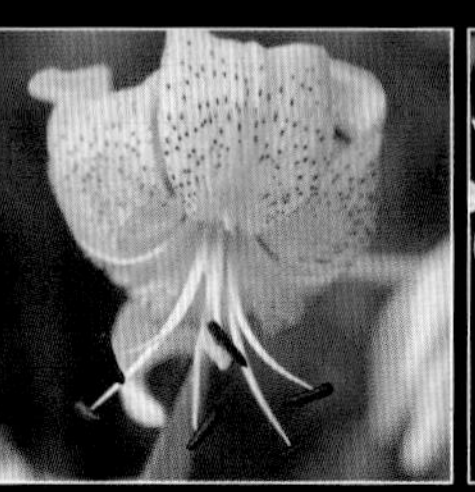

L. Citronella Group

L. 'Roma'

L. 'Boogie Woogie'

L. 'Apollo' 🏆

L. African Queen Group 🏆

L. hansonii

L. pyrenaicum f. *rubrum*

L. 'Crimson Pixie'

L. bulbiferum var. *croceum*

L. henryi 🏆

L. 'Orange Pixie'

L. 'Grand Cru' 🏆

L. 'Red Carpet'

L. tsingtauense

L. 'Lady Bowes Lyon'

L. 'Enchantment'

L. lancifolium var. *splendens* 🏆

L. chalcedonicum

L. 'Orange Electric'

L. pomponium

L. 'Karen North'

L. pardalinum 🏆

L. 'Gran Paradiso'

PURPLE

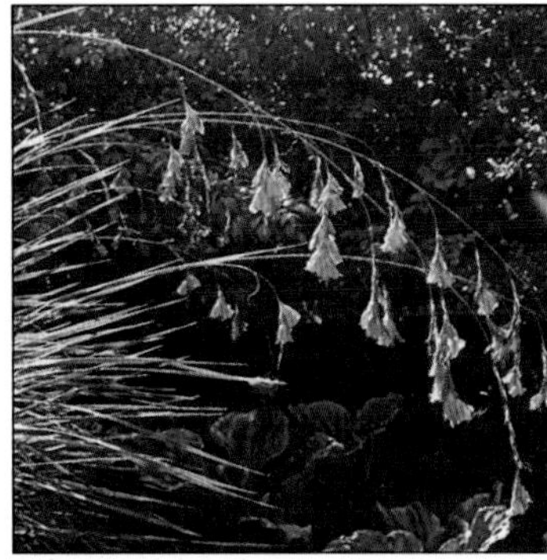

Dierama pendulum
(Angel's fishing rod)
Clump-forming, late summer-flowering corm with arching, basal leaves. Bears pendulous, loose racemes of bell-shaped, pinkish-purple flowers, 2.5cm (1in) long. **H** to 1.5m (5ft), **S** 15–20cm (6–8in).

Allium giganteum
Robust, summer-flowering bulb with long, wide, semi-erect, basal leaves. Produces a stout stem with a dense, spherical umbel, 12cm (5in) across, of 50 or more star-shaped, purple flowers. **H** to 2m (6ft), **S** 30–35cm (12–14in).

***Allium* 'Globemaster'**
Summer-flowering bulb with dense spherical umbels, 15–20cm (6–8in) across, of small, star-shaped, deep violet flowers. Has strap-shaped, semi-erect, glossy, grey-green, basal leaves. **H** 80cm (32in), **S** 20cm (8in).

Allium atropurpureum
Summer-flowering bulb with compact, domed umbels, 8cm (3in) wide, of small, star-shaped, deep red-purple flowers borne from early to mid-summer. Basal leaves are strap-shaped, semi-erect and grey-green. **H** 80cm (32in), **S** 10cm (4in).

***Allium* 'Purple Sensation'**
Early summer-flowering bulb with long, strap-shaped, semi-erect, grey-green, basal leaves. Produces spherical umbels of 50 or more star-shaped, rich purple flowers on sturdy stems in early summer. Is good for cut flowers. **H** 80cm (32in), **S** 7cm (3in).

***Allium* 'Gladiator'**
Summer-flowering bulb with long, strap-shaped, semi-erect, grey-green, basal leaves. Produces large, densely packed, spherical umbels of star-shaped, lilac-purple flowers on sturdy stems in summer. **H** 1.2m (4ft), **S** 20cm (8in).

Dichelostemma congestum
Early summer-flowering bulb with semi-erect, basal leaves dying away when a dense head of funnel-shaped, purple flowers, each 1.5–2cm (⅝–¾in) long, appears. **H** to 1m (3ft), **S** 8–10cm (3–4in).

Aristea capitata
Robust, evergreen, clump-forming rhizome with sword-shaped, erect leaves, to 2.5cm (1in) across, and dense spikes of purple-blue flowers on short stalks in summer. **H** to 1m (3ft), **S** 45–60cm (1½–2ft).

Neomarica caerulea
Summer-flowering rhizome with sword-shaped, semi-erect leaves in basal fans. Stems each bear a leaf-like bract and a succession of iris-like, blue flowers, with white, yellow and brown central marks. **H** to 1m (3ft), **S** 1–1.5m (3–5ft). Min. 10°C (50°F).

Arisaema consanguineum
Summer-flowering tuber with robust, spotted stems and erect, umbrella-like leaves with narrow leaflets. Produces purplish-white- or white-striped, green spathes, 15–20cm (6–8in) long, and bright red berries. **H** to 1m (3ft), **S** 30–45cm (1–1½ft)).

Galtonia viridiflora
Clump-forming, summer-flowering bulb with widely strap-shaped, fleshy, semi-erect, basal, grey-green leaves. Leafless stem bears a spike of up to 30 pendent, short-tubed, funnel-shaped, pale green flowers. **H** 1–1.2m (3–4ft), **S** 18–23cm (7–9in).

***Lilium* Golden Splendor Group**
Vigorous, variable Division 6a lilies. In mid-summer, strong, sturdy stems produce umbels of large, scented, shallowly trumpet-shaped, almost bowl-shaped flowers in shades of yellow with dark burgundy-red bands outside. **H** 1.2–2m (4–6ft), **S** 30cm (12in).

Moraea huttonii
Summer-flowering corm with long, narrow, semi-erect, basal leaves. Tough stem bears a succession of iris-like, yellow flowers, 5–7cm (2–3in) across, with brown marks near the centre. **H** 75cm–1m (2½–3ft), **S** 15–25cm (6–10in).

Zantedeschia elliottiana
(Golden arum lily)
Summer-flowering tuber with heart-shaped, semi-erect, basal leaves with transparent marks. Bears a 15cm (6in) long, yellow spathe surrounding a yellow spadix. **H** 60cm–1m (2–3ft), **S** 45–60cm (1½–2ft). Min. 10°C (50°F).

CANNAS

Grown as much for their dramatic foliage as for their flamboyant flowers, cannas are ideal for lush tropical planting schemes, as an accent plant in a border, or as a bold addition to container displays. Large paddle- or broadly lance-shaped leaves are produced in a range of colours, from green to dark maroon, and many are striped or variegated, while the vibrant red, orange, or yellow flowers bloom for many months from summer to early autumn. Plant these tender South American rhizomatic perennials after the frosts in spring in fertile soil and full sun – they require heat to flower well. In autumn, cut down the stems and leaves when frost blackens the foliage, and store the rhizomes in a frost-free place over winter.

C. 'Striata' 🏆

C. 'Stuttgart'

C. 'Lucifer'

C. 'Ambassadour'

C. x *ehemanii* 🏆

C. 'Brillant'

C. 'Picasso' 🏆

C. 'Wyoming' 🏆

C. 'Richard Wallace'

C. 'Louis Cottin'

C. 'Königin Charlotte'

C. 'Durban'

ORANGE

Canna iridiflora
Very robust, spring- or summer-flowering, rhizomatous perennial with broad, oblong leaves and spikes of pendent, long-tubed, reddish-pink or orange flowers, each 10–15cm (4–6in) long, with reflexed petals. **H** 3m (10ft), **S** 45–60cm (1½–2ft).

Littonia modesta
Deciduous, summer-flowering, tuberous, scandent climber with slender stems and lance-shaped leaves with tendrils at apex. Leaf axils bear bell-shaped, pendent, orange flowers, 4–5cm (1½–2in) across. **H** 1–2m (3–6ft), **S** 10–15cm (4–6in). Min. 16°C (61°F).

***Zantedeschia* 'Cameo'**
Summer-flowering, tuberous perennial with arrow-shaped, erect, white-spotted, mid-green leaves. Produces long-lasting, peach to salmon-orange spathes each with a dark maroon eye. **H** 70cm (28in), **S** 20cm (8in).

WHITE

***Amaryllis belladonna* 'Hathor'**
Autumn-flowering bulb with a stout, purple stem bearing fragrant, pure white flowers, 10cm (4in) long, with yellow throats. Strap-shaped, semi-erect, basal leaves appear in late winter or spring. **H** 50–80cm (20–32in), **S** 30–45cm (12–18in).

Gladiolus papilio
Clump-forming, summer- or autumn-flowering corm with stolons. Bears up to 10 yellow or white flowers, suffused violet, with hooded, upper petals and darker yellow patches on lower petals. **H** to 1m (3ft), **S** 15cm (6in).

Dietes bicolor
Evergreen, tuft-forming, summer-flowering rhizome with tough, long and narrow, erect, basal leaves. Branching stems each bear a succession of flattish, iris-like, pale to mid-yellow flowers; each large petal has a brown patch. **H** to 1m (3ft), **S** 30–60cm (1–2ft).

PINK

x *Amarcrinum memoria-corsii*
Evergreen, clump-forming bulb with wide, semi-erect, basal leaves. Stout stems carry fragrant, rose-pink flowers in loose heads in late summer and autumn. **H** and **S** to 1m (3ft).

x *Amarygia parkeri*
Early autumn-flowering bulb. Stout stem carries a large head of funnel-shaped, deep rose flowers with yellow and white throats. Produces strap-shaped, semi-erect, basal leaves after flowering. **H** to 1m (3ft), **S** 60cm–1m (2–3ft).

Amaryllis belladonna
(Belladonna lily)
Autumn-flowering bulb with a stout, purple stem bearing fragrant, funnel-shaped, pink flowers, 10cm (4in) long. Forms strap-shaped, semi-erect, basal leaves after flowering. **H** 50–80cm (20–32in), **S** 30–45cm (12–18in).

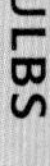

DAHLIAS

The wide spectrum of dahlia hybrids offers a bold display of colour and form from summer to the first frosts in autumn. Flower colours range from deep red, crimson, purple, mauve, and vibrant pink, to white, apricot, orange, bronze, and bright scarlet, while the blooms range from tiny 5cm (2in) pompons to huge exhibition blooms more than 25cm (10in) across.

Dahlias flower prolifically – in the right conditions a single plant may produce up to 100 blooms. They make beautiful border plants, compact types are ideal for containers, and all are good for cutting. In addition, no special skills are required to grow them, but protect the tubers from frost. The flower types below indicate the recognized groups.

Single – flowers usually have 8–10 broad petals surrounding an open, central disc.

Anemone – fully double flowers each with one or more rings of flattened ray petals surrounding a dense group of shorter, tubular petals, usually longer than petals of single dahlias.

Collerette – single flowers with 8–10 broad, outer petals, and an inner 'collar' of smaller petals surrounding an open, central disc.

Water-lily – fully double flowers with large, generally sparse ray petals, which are flat or with slightly incurved or recurved margins, giving the flower a flat appearance.

Decorative – fully double flowers with no visible central disc, and broad, flat petals, sometimes twisted, that incurve slightly at their margins.

Ball – spherical, fully double flowers, sometimes slightly flattened on top, with densely packed, almost tubular, petals.

Pompon – a miniature form of ball flowers, but more spherical in shape, with fully double flowers no more than 5cm (2in) in diameter.

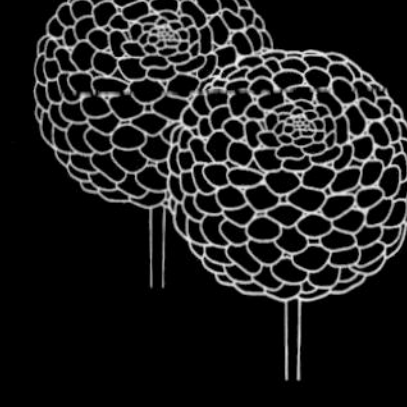

Cactus – fully double flowers have narrow, pointed petals that can be straight or curl inwards and have recurved edges for more than two-thirds of their length.

Semi-cactus – fully double flowers similar to cactus types, but with broader-based petals, the edges of which are generally recurved towards their tips.

Miscellaneous – flowers that fall into a wide range of unclassified types, including orchid-like (shown right), single, and double forms.

***D.* 'Eveline'**
[decorative]

***D.* 'Trelyn Kiwi'** 🏆
[semi-cactus]

***D.* 'White Moonlight'**
[semi-cactus]

***D.* 'Café au Lait'**
[decorative]

***D.* 'Small World'** 🏆
[pompon]

***D.* 'B. J. Beauty'** [decorative]

***D.* 'White Alva's'** 🏆 [cactus]

***D.* 'White Klankstad'** [cactus]

***D.* 'White Ballet'** 🏆 [collerette]

***D.* 'Jura'** [semi-cactus]

***D.* 'Brian's Dream'**
[decorative]

***D.* 'Roxy'**
[single]

D. coccinea
[single]

***D.* 'Carolina Moon'**
[decorative]

***D.* 'Lilac Marston'** 🏆
[decorative]

***D.* 'Sorbet'**
[semi-cactus]

***D.* 'Tiptoe'**
[decorative]

***D.* 'Hillcrest Jessica'**
[decorative]

***D.* 'Gerrie Hoek'**
[water-lily]

***D.* 'Franz Kafka'**
[pompon]

***D.* 'New Dimension'**
[cactus]

***D.* 'Karma Choc'**
[decorative]

***D.* 'Bishop of Auckland'**
[single]

***D.* 'Ruskin Charlotte'**
[semi-cactus]

***D.* 'Ryecroft Gem'**
[decorative]

***D.* 'Berwick Wood'**
[decorative]

***D.* 'Natal'**
[pompon]

***D.* 'Sascha'** 🏆
[water-lily]

***D.* 'Mermaid of Zennor'**
[single]

***D.* 'Gallery Art Nouveau'** [decorative]

***D.* 'Wootton Cupid'** 🏆 [ball]

***D.* 'Cornel'** [ball]

***D.* 'Arabian Night'** [decorative]

***D.* 'Preston Park'** 🏆 [single]

***D.* 'Bishop of Llandaff'** 🏆 [miscellaneous]

***D.* 'Comet'** [anemone]

***D.* 'Chimborazo'** [collerette]

***D.* 'Akita'** [miscellaneous]

***D.* 'Hamari Gold'** 🏆 [decorative]

***D.* 'Zorro'** 🏆 [decorative]

***D.* 'Black Narcissus'** [semi-cactus]

***D.* 'Alva's Supreme'** 🏆 [decorative]

***D.* 'Kenora Superb'** [semi-cactus]

***D.* 'Biddenham Sunset'** [decorative]

***D.* 'Charlie Dimmock'** 🏆 [water-lily]

***D.* 'Hamari Katrina'** [semi-cactus]

***D.* 'Trengrove Millennium'** [decorative]

***D.* 'Hexton Copper'** [ball]

***D.* 'Hamari Accord'** 🏆 [semi-cactus]

***D.* 'Moonglow'** [cactus]

***D.* 'Bishop of York'** [single]

***D.* 'Ellen Huston'** 🏆 [miscellaneous]

***D.* 'Oosterbeck Remembered'** [semi-cactus]

***D.* 'Onslow Renown'** [semi-cactus]

***D.* 'Yellow Hammer'** 🏆 [single]

***D.* 'Wootton Impact'** 🏆 [semi-cactus]

***D.* HAPPY SINGLE FIRST LOVE** [single]

***D.* 'So Dainty'** 🏆 [semi-cactus]

Ornithogalum nutans
Late spring-flowering bulb with 1-sided racemes of semi-pendent, funnel-shaped, silvery-white flowers, with a broad pale green stripe down the centre of each petal. Strap-shaped, semi-erect, mid-green leaves each have a central, silver stripe. **H** 25cm (10in), **S** 5cm (2in).

Erythronium californicum 'White Beauty'
Vigorous, clump-forming tuber with basal, mottled leaves. In spring has a loose spike of 1–10 reflexed, white flowers, each with a brown ring near the centre. Spreads rapidly. **H** 20–30cm (8–12in), **S** 10–12cm (4–5in).

Pamianthe peruviana
Evergreen, spring-flowering bulb with a stem-like neck and semi-erect leaves with drooping tips. Stem has a head of 2–4 fragrant, white flowers, each with a bell-shaped cup and 6 spreading petals. **H** 50cm (20in), **S** 45–60cm (18–24in). Min. 12°C (54°F).

Allium neapolitanum
Spring-flowering bulb with narrow, semi-erect leaves on the lower quarter of flower stems. Stems each develop an umbel, 5–10cm (2–4in) across, of up to 40 white flowers. **H** 20–50cm (8–20in), **S** 10–12cm (4–5in).

Calochortus venustus
Late spring-flowering bulb with 1 or 2 narrow, erect leaves near the base of the branched stem. Bears 1–4 white, yellow, purple or red flowers, with a dark red, yellow-margined blotch on each large petal. **H** 20–60cm (8–24in), **S** 5–10cm (2–4in).

Bellevalia romana
Late spring-flowering bulb with loose conical racemes of bell-shaped, lightly fragrant, white flowers, 8mm (3/8in) long, ageing to purplish-brown. Strap-shaped, basal leaves are erect and mid-green. **H** 30cm (12in), **S** 8cm (3in).

Erythronium oregonum
Clump-forming, spring-flowering tuber with 2 semi-erect, mottled, basal leaves. Has up to 3 pendent, white flowers, with yellow eyes and often brown rings near centre; petals reflex as flowers open. Increases rapidly by offsets. **H** to 35cm (14in), **S** 12cm (5in).

TULIPS

Tulips are excellent in the rock garden, in formal bedding, as elegant cut flowers and for containers. Their bold flowers are generally simple in outline and held upright, often with bright, strong colours. Many of the species deserve to be more widely grown alongside the large variety of hybrids currently available. *Tulipa* is classified in 15 divisions, which are described below.

Div.1 Single early – cup-shaped, single flowers, often opening wide in sun, are borne from early to mid-spring.

Div.2 Double early – long-lasting, double flowers open wide in early and mid-spring.

Div.3 Triumph – sturdy stems bear rather conical, single flowers, becoming more rounded, in mid- and late spring.

Div.4 Darwin hybrids – large, single flowers are borne on strong stems from mid- to late spring.

Div.5 Single late – single flowers, usually with pointed petals, are borne in late spring and very early summer.

Div.6 Lily-flowered – strong stems bear narrow-waisted, single flowers, with long, pointed, often reflexed petals, in late spring.

Div.7 Fringed – flowers are similar to those in Div.6, but have fringed petals.

Div.8 Viridiflora – variable, single flowers, with partly greenish petals, are borne in late spring.

Div.9 Rembrandt – flowers are similar to those in Div.6, but have striped or feathered patterns caused by virus, and appear in late spring.

Div.10 Parrot – has large, variable, single flowers, with frilled or fringed and usually twisted petals, in late spring.

Div.11 Double late (peony-flowered) – usually bowl-shaped, double flowers appear in late spring.

Div.12 Kaufmanniana hybrids – single flowers are usually bicoloured, open flat in sun and appear in early spring; leaves often mottled or striped.

Div.13 Fosteriana hybrids – large, single flowers open wide in the sun from early to mid-spring. Leaves are often mottled or striped.

Div.14 Greigii hybrids – large, single flowers appear in mid- and late spring. Mottled or striped leaves are often wavy-edged.

Div.15 Miscellaneous – a diverse category of other species and their cultivars and hybrids. Flowers appear in spring and early summer.

T. 'White Dream' ① [Div. 3]

T. 'White Triumphator' 🏆① [Div. 6]

T. 'Purissima' 🏆① [D

T. 'Spring Green' 🏆① [Div. 8]

T. turkestanica 🏆① [Div. 15]

T. saxatilis ① [Div. 15]

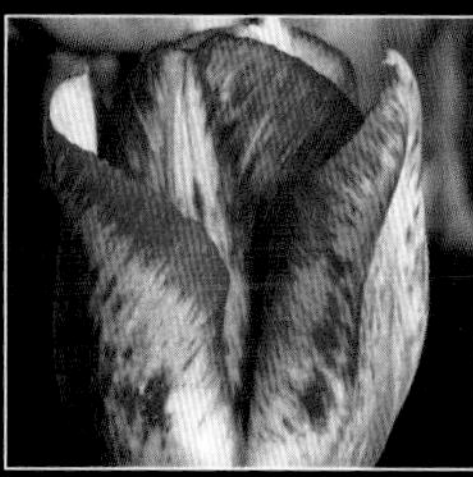

T. 'Shirley' ①

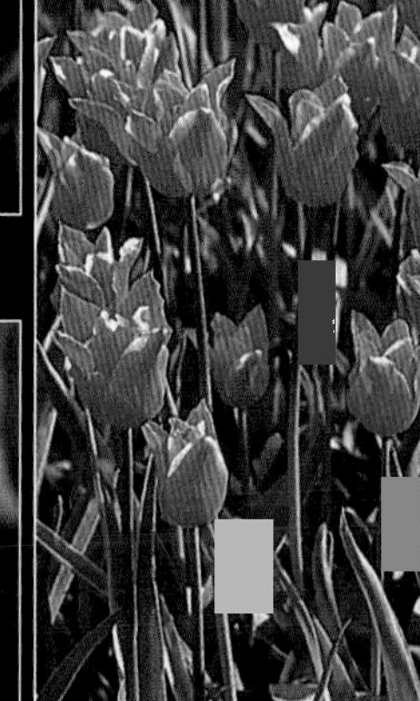

T. 'China Pink' 🏆① [Div. 6]

T. 'Albert Heijn' ①

T. 'Dreamland' 🏆① [Div. 5]

T. 'Ballade' 🏆① [Div. 6]

T. 'Carnaval de Nice' 🏆① [Div. 11]

T. 'Bird of Paradise' ① [Div. 10]

T. 'Estella Rijnveld' ① [Div. 10]

T. 'Groenland' ① [Div. 8]

T. 'Esperanto' 🏆①

T. 'Bellona' ⚠ [Div. 1]

T. kaufmanniana ⚠ [Div. 15]

T. clusiana var. *chrysantha* 🏆⚠ [Div. 15]

T. 'Red Riding Hood' 🏆⚠ [Div. 14]

T. 'Maja' ⚠ [Div. 7]

T. 'Apeldoorn's Elite' 🏆⚠ [Div. 4]

T. 'Candela' 🏆⚠ [Div. 13]

T. orphanidea ⚠ [Div. 15]

T. sprengeri 🏆⚠ [Div. 15]

T. 'Negrita' ⚠

T. 'Prinses Irene' 🏆⚠ [Div. 1]

T. 'Madame Lefèber' ⚠ [Div. 13]

T. 'Uncle Tom' ⚠ [Div. 11]

T. 'Queen of Night' ⚠ [Div. 5]

T. 'Golden Apeldoorn' ⚠ [Div. 4]

T. 'Glück' 🏆⚠ [Div. 12]

T. praestans 'Unicum' ⚠ [Div. 15]

T. 'Blue Parrot' ⚠ [Div. 10]

T. 'Dreaming Maid' ⚠ [Div. 3]

T. sylvestris ⚠ [Div. 15]

T. 'Menton' 🏆⚠ [Div. 5]

T. 'Artist' 🏆⚠ [Div. 8]

T. acuminata ⚠ [Div. 15]

T. 'Abu Hassan' ⚠

T. 'Black Hero' ⚠

T. 'Ballerina' 🏆⚠

PINK

Erythronium hendersonii
Spring-flowering tuber with 2 semi-erect, basal, brown- and green-mottled leaves. Flower stem carries up to 10 lavender or lavender-pink flowers, with reflexed petals and deep purple, central eyes. **H** 20–30cm (8–12in), **S** 10–12cm (4–5in).

Allium unifolium
Late spring-flowering bulb with one semi-erect, basal, grey-green leaf. Each flower stem carries a domed umbel, 5cm (2in) across, of up to 30 purplish-pink flowers. **H** to 30cm (12in), **S** 8–10cm (3–4in).

RED

Anemone pavonina
Leafy tuber with cup-shaped, single, dark-centred, scarlet, purple or blue flowers rising above divided, frilly leaves in early spring. **H** 40cm (16in), **S** 20cm (8in).

Sprekelia formosissima
(Aztec lily, Jacobean lily)

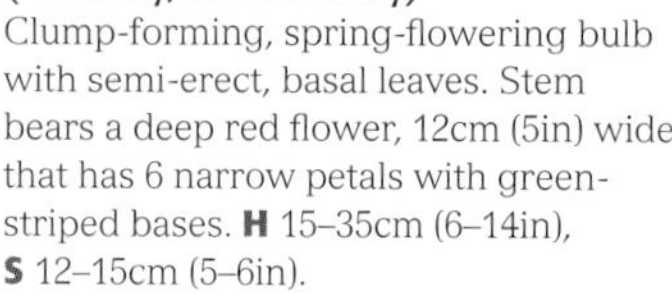

Clump-forming, spring-flowering bulb with semi-erect, basal leaves. Stem bears a deep red flower, 12cm (5in) wide, that has 6 narrow petals with green-striped bases. **H** 15–35cm (6–14in), **S** 12–15cm (5–6in).

Fritillaria meleagris
(Snake's-head fritillary)
Spring-flowering bulb with slender stems producing scattered, narrow, grey-green leaves. Has solitary bell-shaped, prominently chequered flowers, in shades of pinkish-purple or white. **H** to 30cm (12in), **S** 5–8cm (2–3in).

Fritillaria camschatcensis
(Black sarana)
Spring-flowering bulb. Stout stems carry lance-shaped, glossy leaves, mostly in whorls. Bears up to 8 deep blackish-purple or brown flowers. Needs humus-rich soil. **H** 15–60cm (6–24in), **S** 8–10cm (3–4in).

Sauromatum venosum
(Monarch-of-the-East, Voodoo lily)
Early spring-flowering tuber. Bears a large, acrid, purple-spotted spathe, then a lobed leaf on a long, spotted stalk. **H** 30–45cm (12–18in), **S** 30–35cm (12–14in). Min. 5–7°C (41–45°F).

Fritillaria pyrenaica
Spring-flowering bulb with scattered, lance-shaped leaves, often rather narrow. Develops 1, or rarely 2, broadly bell-shaped flowers with flared-tipped, chequered, deep brownish- or blackish-purple petals. **H** 15–30cm (6–12in), **S** 5–8cm (2–3in).

***Anemone coronaria* De Caen Group 'Mister Fokker'**
Spring-flowering perennial with a knobbly tuber. Bears shallowly cup-shaped, single, violet-blue flowers, with black stamens, above rounded, divided, finely lobed, semi-erect, basal leaves. **H** 25cm (10in), **S** 8cm (3in).

Muscari latifolium
Spring-flowering bulb with one strap-shaped, semi-erect, basal, grey-green leaf. Has a dense spike of tiny, bell-shaped, blackish-violet to -blue flowers with constricted mouths; upper ones are paler and smaller. **H** to 25cm (10in), **S** 5–8cm (2–3in).

Hyacinthoides x massartiana
(Spanish bluebell)
Spring-flowering bulb with strap-shaped, glossy leaves and pendent, bell-shaped, blue, white or pink flowers. **H** to 30cm (12in), **S** 10–15cm (4–6in).

***Hyacinthus orientalis* 'Blue Jacket'**
Mid-spring-flowering bulb with a dense, cylindrical spike of highly fragrant, bell-shaped, waxy, navy-blue flowers with purple veining. Has lance-shaped, channelled, erect, bright green, basal leaves. **H** 25cm (10in), **S** 8cm (3in).

Hyacinthoides non-scripta
(English bluebell)
Tuft-forming, spring-flowering bulb with strap-shaped leaves. An erect stem, arching at the apex, bears fragrant, blue, pink or white flowers. **H** 20–40cm (8–16in), **S** 8–10cm (3–4in).

Ixiolirion tataricum
Spring- to early summer-flowering bulb with long, narrow, semi-erect leaves on the lower part of stem. Has a loose cluster of blue flowers with a darker, central line along each petal. **H** to 40cm (16in), **S** 8–10cm (3–4in).

DAFFODILS

Narcissus species and hybrids grace the garden from early to late spring with diverse flowers, ranging from the tiny Cyclamineus types, with their swept-back petals, to the stately trumpet daffodils. Some are also scented, including the Poeticus, Jonquilla, and many of the small-flowered forms. Daffodils can be naturalized to form a carpet in grass or a wild garden, or used to brighten up beds and borders, but dwarf forms are best in rock or gravel gardens, or planted in pots and troughs.

The genus is classified in 13 divisions. Their flower forms are illustrated below, with the exception of Div.12, miscellaneous, and Div.13, which comprise mostly wild species. Both have varying flowers, including hoop-petticoat forms, and are produced between autumn and early summer.

Div. 1 Trumpet – usually solitary flowers, each with a trumpet that is as long as, or longer, than the petals. Early to late spring-flowering.

Div. 2 Large-cupped – solitary flowers, each with a cup at least one-third the length of, but shorter than, the petals. Spring-flowering.

Div. 3 Small-cupped – flowers are often borne singly, each with a cup not more than one-third the length of the petals. Spring- or early summer-flowering.

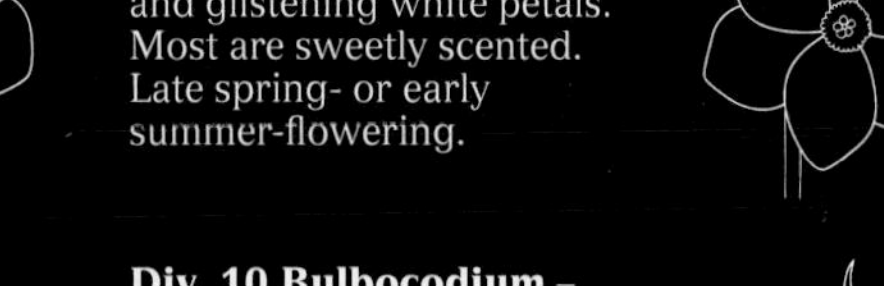

Div. 4 Double – most have solitary large, fully or semi-double flowers with the cup and petals, or just the cup, replaced by petaloid structures. Some have smaller flowers in clusters of 4 or more. Spring- or early summer-flowering.

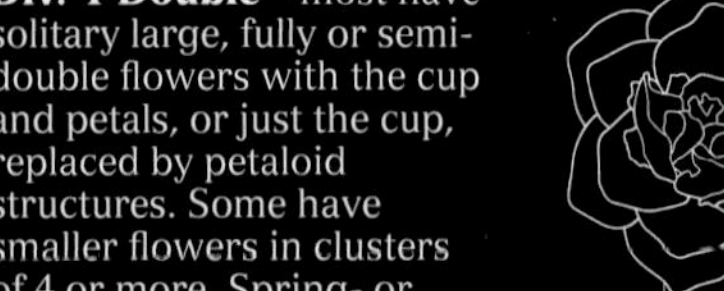

Div. 5 Triandrus – 2–6 nodding flowers per stem, each with a short, sometimes straight-sided cup and narrow, reflexed petals. Spring-flowering.

Div. 6 Cyclamineus – usually 1 or 2 flowers per stem with cups that are sometimes flanged and often longer than those of Div. 5. Petals are narrow, pointed and reflexed. Early to mid-spring flowering.

Div. 7 Jonquilla and Apodanthus – sweetly scented flowers, usually 1–5 per stem. Cups are short, sometimes flanged; petals are often flat, fairly broad and rounded. Mid- to late spring-flowering.

Div. 8 Tazetta – clusters of 12 or more small, fragrant flowers per stem, or 3 or 4 large ones. Cups are small and often straight-sided; petals are broad and mostly pointed. Late autumn- to mid-spring-flowering.

Div. 9 Poeticus – 1–2 flowers per stem, each with a small, coloured cup and glistening white petals. Most are sweetly scented. Late spring- or early summer-flowering.

Div. 10 Bulbocodium – flowers usually borne singly on very short stems, with insignificant petals and large, widely flaring cups. Winter- to spring-flowering.

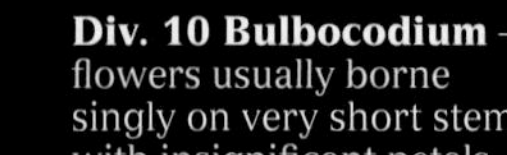

Div. 11 Split-cupped – usually solitary flowers with cups split along more than half their length. Spring-flowering.

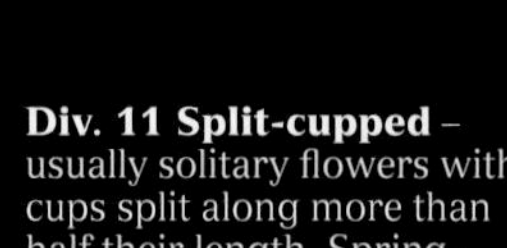

(a) Collar – wide cup segments lie back on the petals.

(b) Papillon – narrower cup segments have tips arranged at the margin of the petals.

N. 'Dove Wings' ♕ⓘ [Div. 6]

N. 'Ice Follies' ♕ⓘ [Div. 2]

N. 'Actaea' ♕ⓘ [Div. 9]

N. 'Canaliculatus' ⓘ [Div. 8]

N. 'Mount Hood' ♕ⓘ [Div. 1]

N. 'Cheerfulness' ♕ⓘ [Div. 4]

N. 'Empress of Ireland' ♕ⓘ [Div. 1]

N. 'Thalia' ⓘ [Div. 5]

N. 'Bridal Crown' ♕ⓘ [Div. 4]

N. 'Broadway Star' ⓘ [Div. 11b]

N. 'Fragrant Breeze' ⓘ [Div. 2]

N. 'Sir Winston Churchill' 🏆(!) [Div. 8]

N. 'Jack Snipe' 🏆(!) [Div. 6]

N. bulbocodium 🏆(!) [Div. 13]

N. 'Home Fires' (!) [Div. 2]

N. 'Aircastle' (!) [Div. 3]

N. 'Stratosphere' 🏆(!) [D

N. 'Avalanche' 🏆(!) [Div. 8]

N. 'Charity May' 🏆(!) [Div. 6]

N. 'Pencrebar' (!) [Div. 4]

N. 'Pipit' 🏆(!) [Div. 7]

N. 'Bartley' (!) [Div. 6]

N. 'Panache' (!) [D

N. 'February Silver' (!) [Div. 6]

N. 'Liberty Bells' (!) [Div. 5]

N. 'Suzy' 🏆(!) [Div. 7]

N. 'Hawera' 🏆(!) [Div. 5]

N. 'Jenny' 🏆(!) [D

N. 'Cassata' (!) [Div. 11a]

N. 'Binkie' (!) [Div. 2]

N. 'Tahiti' 🏆(!) [Div. 4]

N. 'Passionale' 🏆(!) [Div. 2]

N. 'Irene Copeland' (!) [Div. 4]

N. 'Spellbinder' 🏆(!) [Div. 1]

N. 'Golden Ducat' (!) [Div. 4]

N. 'Ambergate' (!) [Div. 2]

N. 'Altruist' (!) [Div. 3]

GREEN

Fritillaria acmopetala
Spring-flowering bulb with slender stems that bear narrowly lance-shaped, scattered leaves, and 1 or 2 broadly bell-shaped, green flowers, with brown-stained petals flaring outwards at the tips. **H** 15–40cm (6–16in), **S** 5–8cm (2–3in).

Fritillaria pontica
Spring-flowering bulb with stems carrying lance-shaped, grey-green leaves, the topmost in a whorl of 3. Has solitary broadly bell shaped, green flowers, 3–4.5cm (1¼–1¾in) long, often suffused brown. **H** 15–45cm (6–18in), **S** 5–8cm (2–3in).

Fritillaria cirrhosa
Spring-flowering bulb with slender stems and narrow, whorled leaves; upper leaves have tendril-like tips. Produces up to 4 widely bell-shaped flowers, purple or yellowish-green with dark purple chequered patterns. **H** to 60cm (24in), **S** 5–8cm (2–3in).

Hermodactylus tuberosus
(Widow iris)
Spring-flowering perennial with finger-like tubers. Long, narrow, grey-green leaves are square in cross-section. Has a fragrant, yellowish-green flower with large, blackish-brown-tipped petals. **H** 20–40cm (8–16in), **S** 5–8cm (2–3in).

Arisaema triphyllum
(Jack-in-the-pulpit)
Summer-flowering tuber with 3-lobed, erect leaves. Produces green or purple spathes, hooded at tips, followed by bright red berries. **H** 40–50cm (16–20in), **S** 30–45cm (12–18in).

Ixia viridiflora
Spring- to early summer-flowering corm with very narrow, erect leaves mostly at stem base. Carries a spike of flattish, jade-green flowers, 2.5–5cm (1–2in) across, with purple-black eyes. **H** 30–60cm (12–24in), **S** 2.5–5cm (1–2in).

YELLOW

Calochortus luteus
(Yellow mariposa)
Late spring-flowering bulb with long, narrow, erect leaves near the base of the loosely branched stem. Each branch produces a 3-petalled, yellow flower with central, brown blotches. **H** 20–45cm (8–18in), **S** 5–10cm (2–3in).

***Erythronium* 'Pagoda'**
Robust, spring-flowering tuber with 2 semi-erect, basal, faintly mottled, glossy leaves. Flower stem produces up to 10 pendent, pale yellow flowers with reflexed petals. **H** 25–35cm (10–14in), **S** 15–20cm (6–8in).

Fritillaria pallidiflora
Robust, spring-flowering bulb with broadly lance-shaped, grey-green leaves, scattered or in pairs on stem. Has 1–5 widely bell-shaped, yellow to greenish-yellow flowers, usually faintly chequered brownish-red within. **H** 15–70cm (6–28in), **S** 8–10cm (3–4in).

ORANGE

***Tulipa* 'Giuseppe Verdi'**
Mid-spring-flowering bulb (Div.12) with purple-marked leaves. Yellow-margined, carmine-red flowers are golden-yellow with small, red marks inside. **H** 20cm (8in), **S** to 20cm (8in).

***Narcissus* 'Silver Chimes'**
Sturdy, mid- to late spring-flowering bulb (Div.8) with dark green leaves. Bears up to 10 fragrant flowers, each with broad, milk-white petals and a straight, shallow, creamy-primrose cup. Thrives in a warm site. **H** 32cm (13in), **S** to 20cm (8in).

***Triteleia ixioides* 'Starlight'**
Free-flowering, late spring-flowering corm with grass-like, semi-erect, basal leaves. Open umbels, to 12cm (5in) across, of star-shaped, creamy-yellow flowers have a central, green stripe on each petal. Is good for cut flowers. **H** 40cm (16in), **S** 8cm (3in).

***Hyacinthus orientalis* 'City of Haarlem'**
Late spring-flowering bulb with lance-shaped, channelled, erect, bright green, basal leaves. Has a dense, cylindrical spike of fragrant, bell-shaped, primrose-yellow flowers. **H** 25cm (10in), **S** 8cm (3in).

Arum creticum
Spring-flowering tuber that bears white or yellow spathes, each bottle-shaped at the base, slightly reflexed at the apex and with a protruding, yellow spadix. Has arrow-shaped, semi-erect, deep green leaves in autumn. **H** 30–50cm (12–20in), **S** 20–30cm (8–12in).

Ferraria crispa
Spring-flowering corm with leafy stem bearing a succession of upward-facing, brown or yellowish-brown flowers, 4–5cm (1½–2in) across, with 6 wavy-edged, spreading petals that are conspicuously lined and blotched. **H** 20–40cm (8–16in), **S** 8–10cm (3–4in).

Stenomesson miniatum
Late spring-flowering bulb with strap-shaped, semi-erect, basal leaves. Bears a head of red or orange flowers, 2–4cm (¾–1½in) long, with yellow anthers. **H** 20–30cm (8–12in), **S** 10–15cm (4–6in). Min. 5°C (41°F).

Stenomesson variegatum
Clump-forming bulb. Bears reddish-yellow, pink or white flowers, with 6 green lobes at the apex, in winter or spring. **H** 30–60cm (12–24in), **S** 30cm (12in). Min. 10°C (50°F).

WHITE

Triteleia hyacinthina
Late spring- to early summer-flowering corm with long, narrow, semi-erect or spreading, basal leaves. Heads of white, sometimes purple-tinged flowers are borne on wiry stems. **H** 30–45cm (12–20in), **S** 8–10cm (3–4in).

Ornithogalum narbonense
Clump-forming, late spring- to summer-flowering bulb with long, narrow, semi-erect, basal, grey-green leaves. Leafless stem produces a spike of star-shaped, white flowers, 2cm (¾in) wide. **H** 30–40cm (12–16in), **S** 10–15cm (4–6in).

Pancratium illyricum
Bulb with strap-shaped, semi-erect, basal, greyish-green leaves. Leafless stem has 5–12 fragrant, 6-petalled, white flowers, 8cm (3in) across in summer. **H** 45cm (18in), **S** 25–30cm (10–12in).

***Zantedeschia aethiopica* 'Green Goddess'**
Robust, summer-flowering tuber with arrow-shaped, semi-erect, basal, green leaves. Bears several green spathes, each with a large, central, green-splashed, white area. **H** 45cm–1m (18–39in), **S** 45–60cm (18–24in).

Ismene narcissiflora
(Peruvian daffodil)
Spring- or summer-flowering bulb with semi-erect, basal leaves, dying down in winter. Bears a loose head of 2–5 fragrant, white flowers. **H** to 60cm (24in), **S** 30–45cm (12–18in).

Arisaema sikokianum
Early summer-flowering tuber with erect leaves divided into 3–5 leaflets. Produces deep brownish-purple and white spathes, 15cm (6in) long, with club-like, white spadices protruding from the mouths. **H** 30–50cm (12–20in), **S** 30–45cm (12–18in).

Ornithogalum thyrsoides
(Chincherinchee)
Summer-flowering bulb with strap-shaped, semi-erect, basal leaves. Bears a dense, conical spike of cup-shaped, white flowers, 2–3cm (¾–1¼in) across. **H** 30–45cm (12–18in), **S** 10–15cm (4–6in).

Habenaria radiata
Evergreen–deciduous, terrestrial orchid with fleshy tubers and linear, grey-green, basal leaves. In mid-summer, each slender flower stem bears 2 or 3 white flowers that resemble egret birds in flight. **H** 30cm (12in), **S** 10cm (4in).

Ornithogalum arabicum
Early summer-flowering bulb with strap-shaped, semi-erect leaves in a basal cluster. Has a flattish head of up to 15 scented, white or creamy-white flowers, 4–5cm (1½–2in) across, with black centres. **H** 30–45cm (12–18in), **S** 10–15cm (4–6in).

Allium neapolitanum Cowanii Group
Late spring-flowering bulb with large umbels of up to 30 star-shaped, white flowers in late spring or early summer, after the lance-shaped, semi-erect, mid-green, basal leaves have withered. Is good for cut flowers. **H** 40cm (16in), **S** 5cm (2in).

Eucomis pallidiflora
(Giant pineapple lily)
Summer-flowering bulb with sword-shaped, crinkly edged, semi-erect, basal leaves. Bears a dense spike of star-shaped, greenish-white flowers, topped with a cluster of leaf-like bracts. **H** to 75cm (30in), **S** 30–60cm (12–24in).

Calochortus superbus
Bulb with linear, grey-green, basal leaves. In early summer, branched stems bear 1–3 upward-facing, cup-shaped, white, creamy-yellow or lavender-blue flowers, with purplish-brown markings at the base of each petal. **H** 40cm (16in), **S** 8cm (3in).

PINK

Eucomis comosa
Clump-forming bulb with strap-shaped, wavy-margined leaves, spotted purple beneath. Purple-spotted stem bears a spike of white or greenish-white, sometimes pink-tinted flowers, with purple ovaries. **H** to 70cm (28in), **S** 30–60cm (12–24in).

Tritonia disticha subsp. _rubrolucens_
Late summer-flowering corm with narrowly sword-shaped, erect leaves in a flattish, basal fan. Has pink flowers in a loose, one-sided spike. **H** 30–50cm (12–20in), **S** 8–10cm (3–4in).

Allium schubertii
Early summer-flowering bulb with widely strap-shaped, semi-erect, basal leaves. Bears large umbels of 40 or more star-shaped, pink or purple flowers on very unequal stalks, then brown seed capsules. **H** 30–60cm (12–24in), **S** 15–20cm (6–8in).

Allium senescens subsp. _montanum_
Vigorous, clump-forming, summer-flowering bulb with strap-shaped, often twisted, grey-green leaves. Has dense umbels, 2cm (¾in) across, of up to 30 long-lasting, cup-shaped, pink flowers. **H** 45cm (18in), **S** 60cm (24in).

Allium cernuum
Clump-forming, summer-flowering bulb with narrow, semi-erect, basal leaves. Each stem produces up to 30 cup-shaped, pink or white flowers in a loose, nodding umbel, 2–4cm (¾–1½in) across. **H** 30–70cm (12–28in), **S** 8–12cm (3–5in).

CROCOSMIA

Cormous perennials with flowers in vibrant shades of yellow, orange, and red, and sword-shaped, pleated foliage, crocosmias are real crowd-pleasers. The flowers are held on elegant arching stems and bloom for many weeks between mid-summer and autumn. Most are easy to grow, spreading quickly when the conditions are right for them. Plants, rather than corms, are the best choice for beginners, and should be planted in spring in moist but well-drained fertile soil in sun or partial shade. Although many are hardy, borderline types benefit from a warm site near a protective wall.

C. 'Lucifer' 🏆 C. 'Honey Angels'

C. 'Solfatare' 🏆

C. 'George Davison'

C. *masoniorum* 🏆

C. 'Severn Sunrise' 🏆

C. 'Star of the East' 🏆

C. 'Jackanapes'

RED

Rhodophiala advena
Clump-forming, spring- to summer-flowering bulb with basal, grey-green leaves. Leafless stem carries a head of 2–8 narrowly funnel-shaped, red flowers, 5cm (2in) long. **H** to 40cm (16in), **S** 15–20cm (6–8in).

Ranunculus asiaticus
(Persian buttercup)
Early summer-flowering perennial with claw-like tubers and long-stalked leaves both at base and on stem. Has single or double flowers in red, white, pink, yellow or orange. **H** 45–55cm (18–22in), **S** 10cm (4in).

Lycoris radiata (Red spider lily)
Late summer-flowering bulb with a head of 5 or 6 bright rose-red flowers with narrow, wavy-margined, reflexed petals and conspicuous anthers. Has strap-shaped, semi-erect, basal leaves after flowering time. **H** 30–40cm (12–16in), **S** 10–15cm (4–6in).

Phaedranassa carmioli
Spring- and summer-flowering bulb with upright, elliptic or lance-shaped, basal leaves. Bears a head of 6–10 pendent, pinkish-red flowers, with green bases and yellow-edged, green lobes at each apex. **H** 50–70cm (20–28in), **S** 30–45cm (12–18in).

Gladiolus communis* subsp. *byzantinus
Early summer-flowering corm with a dense spike of up to 20 deep purplish-red or purplish-pink flowers, 4–6cm (1½–2½in) long. Produces a fan of sword-shaped, erect, basal leaves. **H** to 70cm (28in), **S** 10–15cn (4–6in).

PURPLE

Tulbaghia simmleri
Semi-evergreen, bulbous perennial with clusters of narrow, grass-like, mid-green leaves. Produces terminal umbels of fragrant, tubular, light to deep purple flowers in early to mid-summer.
H 60cm (24in), **S** 25cm (10in).

Allium cristophii
Summer-flowering bulb with semi-erect, hairy, grey leaves that droop at tips. Has a large, spherical umbel of 50 or more star-shaped, purplish-violet flowers, which dry well. **H** 15–40cm (6–16in), **S** 15–20cm (6–8in).

Roscoea auriculata
Early autumn-flowering tuber with linear to broadly lance-shaped, semi-erect, dark green leaves. Orchid-like, rich purple flowers are borne from upper leaf axils from late summer to autumn. **H** 45cm (18in), **S** 15cm (6in).

BLUE

Camassia quamash
(Common camassia, Quamash)
Clump-forming bulb with racemes of shallowly cup-shaped, rich to pale blue or white flowers in late spring and early summer. Has long, linear, erect, basal leaves. **H** 30cm (12in), **S** 5cm (2in).

***Triteleia laxa* 'Koningin Fabiola'**
Mid-summer-flowering corm with linear, semi-erect, basal leaves. These often die back before a loose umbel of funnel-shaped, deep violet-blue flowers, on long, slender stalks, is produced. Is good for cut flowers. **H** 30cm (12in), **S** 5cm (2in).

Allium caeruleum
Clump-forming, summer-flowering bulb with narrow, erect leaves on the lower third of slender flower stems, which bear 30–50 star-shaped, blue flowers in a dense, spherical umbel, 3–4cm (1¼–1½in) across. **H** 20–80cm (8–32in), **S** 10–15cm (4–6in).

Triteleia laxa
Early summer-flowering corm with narrow, semi-erect, basal leaves. Stem carries a large, loose umbel of funnel-shaped, deep to pale purple-blue flowers, 2–5cm (¾–2in) long, mostly held upright. **H** 10–50cm (4–20in), **S** 8–10cm (3–4in).

GREEN

Eucomis bicolor
Summer-flowering bulb with wavy-edged, semi-erect, basal leaves. Stem, often spotted purple, bears a spike of green or greenish-white flowers, with 6 purple-edged petals, topped by a cluster of leaf-like bracts. **H** 30–50cm (12–20in), **S** 30–60cm (12–24in).

Arisaema jacquemontii
Summer-flowering tuber with 1 or 2 erect leaves, divided into wavy-edged leaflets. Produces slender, white-lined, green spathes that are hooded at tips and drawn out into long points. **H** 30–50cm (12–20in), **S** 30–38cm (12–15in).

Arisaema griffithii
Summer-flowering tuber with large, erect leaves above a green or purple spathe, 20–25cm (8–10in) long, strongly netted with paler veins and expanded like a cobra's hood. Protect in winter or lift for frost-free storage. **H** to 60cm (24in), **S** 45–60cm (18–24in).

YELLOW

Ranunculus asiaticus* var. *flavus
(Persian buttercup)
Early summer-flowering perennial with claw-like tubers and long-stalked, palmate leaves at base and on stem. Has single or double flowers in yellow, white, pink, red or orange. **H** 45–55cm (18–22in), **S** 8–10cm (3–4in).

Cypella herbertii
Summer-flowering bulb with a fan of narrow, sword-shaped, erect, basal leaves. Branched flower stem carries a succession of short-lived, iris-like, orange-yellow flowers, each spotted purple in the centre. **H** 30–50cm (12–20in), **S** 8–10cm (3–4in).

Calochortus barbatus
Summer-flowering bulb with narrow, erect leaves near the base of the loosely branched stem. Each branch bears a pendent, yellow or greenish-yellow flower that is hairy inside. **H** 30–60cm (12–24in), **S** 5–10cm (2–4in).

Allium flavum
Clump-forming, summer-flowering bulb. Leaves are linear and semi-erect on lower half of slender flower stem. Produces a loose umbel of up to 60 small, bell-shaped, yellow flowers on thin, arching stalks. **H** 10–35cm (4–14in), **S** 5–8cm (2–3in).

Cyrtanthus mackenii* var. *cooperi
Clump-forming, summer-flowering bulb with long, narrow, semi-erect, basal leaves. Leafless stems each carry a head of up to 10 fragrant, tubular, cream or yellow flowers, 5cm (2in) long and slightly curved. **H** 30–40cm (12–16in), **S** 8–10cm (3–4in).

***Ismene* x *spofforthiae* 'Sulphur Queen'**
Summer-flowering bulb with strap-shaped, dark green, basal leaves. Bears terminal umbels of up to 6 large, fragrant, sulphur-yellow flowers, each with a frilly-edged, light yellow cup with green stripes and 6 spreading petals. **H** 60cm (24in), **S** 30cm (12in). Min. 15°C (59°F).

***Crocosmia* 'Golden Fleece'**
Clump-forming, late summer-flowering corm with sword-shaped, erect, basal, grey-green leaves. Flowers are funnel-shaped and clear golden-yellow. **H** 60–75cm (24–30in), **S** 15–20cm (6–8in).

ORANGE

Polianthes geminiflora
Summer-flowering tuber with narrowly strap-shaped, semi-erect leaves in a basal tuft. Stems each carry long spikes of downward-curving, tubular, red or orange flowers in pairs. **H** 20–40cm (8–16in), **S** 10–15cm (4–6in).

***Alstroemeria* Ligtu Hybrids**
Summer-flowering tuber with narrow, twisted leaves and heads of widely flared flowers in shades of pink, yellow or orange, often spotted or streaked with contrasting colours. **H** 45–60cm (1½–2ft), **S** 60cm–1m (2–3ft).

Sandersonia aurantiaca
(Chinese-lantern lily)
Deciduous, summer-flowering, tuberous climber with a slender stem bearing scattered, lance-shaped leaves, some tendril-tipped. Orange flowers are produced in axils of upper leaves. **H** 60cm (24in), **S** 25–30cm (10–12in).

Tigridia pavonia
(Peacock flower, Tiger flower)
Summer-flowering bulb with sword-shaped, pleated, erect leaves near stem base. A succession of short-lived flowers vary from white to orange, red or yellow, often with contrasting spots. **H** to 45cm (18in), **S** 12–15cm (4–6in).

PINK

Zephyranthes carinata
Late summer- to early autumn-flowering bulb with narrowly strap-shaped, semi-erect, basal leaves. Each stem bears a funnel-shaped, pink flower, held almost erect. **H** 20–30cm (8–12in), **S** 8–10cm (3–4in).

Nerine bowdenii
Autumn-flowering bulb with a stout stem and strap-shaped, semi-erect, basal leaves. Carries a head of 5–10 glistening, pink flowers with petals that widen slightly towards wavy-margined, recurved tips. **H** 45–60cm (18–24in), **S** 12–15cm (5–6in).

Scilla scilloides
Late summer- and autumn-flowering bulb with 2–4 narrowly strap-shaped, semi-erect, basal leaves. Stem bears a slender, dense spike of up to 30 flattish, pink flowers, 0.5–1cm (¼–½in) across. **H** to 30cm (12in), **S** 5cm (2in).

Nerine bowdenii* f. *alba
Autumn-flowering bulb with a stout stem and strap-shaped, semi-erect, basal leaves. Produces a head of 5–10 white, often pink-flushed flowers; petals widen slightly towards wavy-margined, recurved tips. **H** 45–60cm (18–24in), **S** 12–15cm (5–6in).

***Nerine* 'Orion'**
Autumn-flowering bulb with strap-shaped, semi-erect, basal leaves. Stout, leafless stem bears a head of pale pink flowers with very wavy-margined petals that have recurved tips. **H** 30–50cm (12–20in), **S** 20–25cm (8–10in).

Nerine undulata
Autumn-flowering bulb with narrowly strap-shaped, semi-erect, basal leaves. Flower stem carries a head of pink flowers with very narrow petals crinkled for their whole length. **H** 30–45cm (12–18in), **S** 10–12cm (4–5in).

MEDIUM

AUTUMN

ORANGE

Dahlia 'Harvest Inflammation'
Single dahlia bearing orange flowers, 5cm (2in) across, suffused orange-red, each with a central, orange-yellow disc, in summer–autumn. **H** 55cm (22in), **S** 40cm (16in).

Nerine sarniensis (Guernsey lily)
Autumn-flowering bulb with strap-shaped, semi-erect, basal leaves. Leafless stem carries a spherical head of up to 20 deep orange-pink flowers, 6–8cm (2½–3in) across, with wavy-margined petals. **H** 45–60cm (18–24in), **S** 12–15cm (5–6in).

WINTER

WHITE

Eucharis amazonica
Evergreen, clump-forming bulb with strap-shaped, semi-erect, basal leaves. Bears a head of up to 6 fragrant, slightly pendent, white flowers at almost any season. **H** 40–60cm (16–24in), **S** 60cm–1m (2–3ft). Min. 15°C (59°F).

Hippeastrum 'Apple Blossom'
Winter- to spring-flowering bulb with strap-shaped, semi-erect, basal leaves produced as, or just after, flowers form. Stout stem has a head of 2–6 white flowers, becoming pink at petal tips. **H** 30–50cm (12–20in), **S** 30cm (12in). Min. 13°C (55°F).

Hippeastrum 'Striped'
Winter- to spring-flowering bulb with strap-shaped, semi-erect, basal leaves produced with or just after flowers. Stout stem has a head of 2–6 widely funnel-shaped flowers, striped white and red. **H** 50cm (20in), **S** 30cm (12in). Min. 13°C (55°F).

RED

Hippeastrum 'Red Lion'
Tuft-forming, winter- and spring-flowering bulb with a stout stem bearing a head of 2–6 dark red flowers with yellow anthers. Strap-shaped leaves appear with or just after flowers. **H** 30–50cm (12–20in), **S** 30cm (12in). Min. 13°C (55°F).

Hippeastrum aulicum
Winter- and spring-flowering bulb with a basal cluster of strap-shaped, semi-erect leaves. Stout stem bears two red flowers with green-striped petals and green throats. **H** 30–50cm (12–20in), **S** 30cm (12in). Min. 13–15°C (55–59°F).

Veltheimia bracteata
Clump-forming, winter-flowering bulb with semi-erect, strap-shaped, basal, glossy leaves and dense spikes of pendent, tubular, pink, red or yellowish-red flowers. **H** 30–45cm (12–18in), **S** 25–38cm (10–15in). Min. 10°C (50°F).

SMALL

SPRING

WHITE

Anemone blanda 'White Splendour'
Knobbly tuber with semi-erect leaves that have 3 deeply toothed lobes. Bears upright, flattish, white flowers, 4–5cm (1½–2in) across, with 9–14 narrow petals, in early spring. **H** 5–10cm (2–4in), **S** 10–15cm (4–6in).

Leucojum vernum (Spring snowflake)
Spring-flowering bulb with strap-shaped, semi-erect, basal leaves. Leafless stem carries 1 or 2 pendent, bell-shaped flowers, 1.5–2cm (⅝–¾in) long, with 6 green-tipped, white petals. **H** 10–15cm (4–6in), **S** 8–10cm (3–4in).

Ornithogalum balansae
Spring-flowering bulb with 2 almost prostrate, inversely lance-shaped, mid-green basal leaves. Has a broad head of 2–5 flowers, glistening white inside, bright green outside, that open wide. **H** 5–15cm (2–6in), **S** 5–8cm (2–3in).

Sternbergia candida
Spring-flowering bulb. Strap-shaped, semi-erect, basal, greyish-green leaves appear together with a fragrant, funnel-shaped, white flower, 4–5cm (1½–2in) long, borne on a leafless stem. **H** 10–20cm (4–8in), **S** 8–10cm (3–4in).

***Puschkinia scilloides* var. *libanotica* 'Alba'**
Spring-flowering bulb with usually 2 strap-shaped, semi-erect, basal leaves. Produces a dense spike of star-shaped, white flowers, 1.5–2cm (⅝–¾in) across. **H** 15cm (6in), **S** 2.5–5cm (1–2in).

***Muscari botryoides* 'Album'**
Late spring-flowering bulb with 3–4 narrow, semi-erect, basal leaves that widen slightly at the tips. Produces dense, conical-shaped racemes of tiny, fragrant, white flowers. **H** 15cm (6in), **S** 5cm (2in).

Erythronium californicum
Clump-forming, spring-flowering tuber. Has 2 semi-erect, basal, mottled leaves. Up to 3 white or creamy-white flowers, sometimes reddish-brown externally, have reflexed petals, yellow eyes and often brown rings near centres. **H** 15–35cm (6–14in), **S** 10–12cm (4–5in).

Ornithogalum montanum
Clump-forming, spring-flowering bulb with strap-shaped, semi-erect, basal, grey-green leaves. Leafless stem produces a head of star-shaped, white flowers, 3–4cm (1¼–1½in) across, striped green outside. **H** and **S** 10–15cm (4–6in).

***Iris* 'Natascha'**
Bulbous iris with solitary, slightly fragrant, very pale blue, almost white flowers, with a yellow spot on each petal, borne in early spring. Has linear, mid-green leaves. **H** 15cm (6in), **S** 2cm (¾in).

Ornithogalum lanceolatum
Spring-flowering, dwarf bulb with a rosette of prostrate, lance-shaped, basal leaves. Carries a head of flattish, star-shaped, white flowers, 3–4cm (1¼–1½in) across, broadly striped green outside. **H** 5–10cm (2–4in), **S** 10–15cm (4–6in).

***Hyacinthus orientalis* 'White Pearl'**
Mid-spring-flowering bulb with linear to lance-shaped, channelled, erect, bright green, basal leaves. Produces a dense, cylindrical raceme of sweetly scented, tubular to bell-shaped, pure white flowers. **H** 25cm (10in), **S** 8cm (3in).

WHITE

Ornithogalum umbellatum
Late spring-flowering bulb with linear, semi-erect, mid-green leaves with a whitish-green midrib. These fade as stems each bearing 6–20 star-shaped, white flowers, with green reverses, are produced in late spring and early summer. **H** 20cm (8in), **S** 10cm (4in).

***Scilla siberica* 'Alba'**
Early to mid-spring-flowering bulb with 2–4 broadly linear, erect, basal leaves, widening towards the tips. Racemes of small, pendent, bowl-shaped, white flowers are produced at the same time as the leaves. **H** 15cm (6in), **S** 5cm (2in).

PINK

Allium akaka
Spring-flowering bulb with 1–3 broad, prostrate and basal, grey-green leaves and an almost stemless, spherical umbel, 5–7cm (2–3in) across of 30–40 star-shaped, white to pinkish-white flowers with red centres. **H** 15–20cm (6–8in), **S** 12–15cm (5–6in).

Anemone tschaernjaewii
Spring-flowering tuber with 3-palmate, oval, mid-green leaves, the leaflets shallowly lobed. Has 5-petalled, saucer-shaped, purple-centred, white or pink flowers, 2–4.5cm (¾–1¾in) across. Needs warm, dry, summer dormancy. **H** 5–10cm (2–4in), **S** 5–8cm (2–3in).

***Chionodoxa* 'Pink Giant'**
Early spring-flowering bulb with 2 narrow, semi-erect, basal leaves. Leafless stem produces a spike of 5–10 flattish, white-eyed, pink flowers, 2–2.5cm (¾–1in) across. **H** 10–25cm (4–10in), **S** 2.5–5cm (1–2in).

Allium acuminatum
Spring-flowering bulb with 2–4 long, narrow, semi-erect, basal leaves. Stem bears an umbel, 5cm (2in) across, of up to 30 small, purplish-pink flowers. **H** 10–30cm (4–12in), **S** 5–8cm (2–3in).

Allium karataviense
Late spring-flowering bulb with narrowly elliptic to elliptic, prostrate, basal, greyish-purple leaves. Stem bears 50 or more star-shaped, pale purplish-pink flowers in a spherical umbel, 15cm (6in) or more across. **H** to 20cm (8in), **S** 25–30cm (10–12in).

CROCUSES

Crocus species and cultivars are versatile dwarf bulbous plants. Most flower in late winter or early spring; a few bloom in autumn. Colours range from white, cream, and yellow to pinkish-lilac and purple, and many are attractively striped or feathered with other colours. The goblet-shaped flowers open wide in full sun, in some cases revealing contrasting centres or conspicuous stamens. Most crocuses are also fragrant. Plant in rock or gravel gardens with other early flowering dwarf bulbs or perennials, in drifts in grass, or beneath deciduous trees and shrubs, where they will rapidly spread. If naturalized in grass, delay mowing until the leaves have died down. Feed with an all-purpose granular fertilizer once the flowers have faded.

C. sieberi **'Hubert Edelsten'** 🏆

C. vernus **'Remembrance'**

C. goulimyi 🏆 [Autumn]

C. **'Eyecatcher'**

C. vernus **'Pickwick'**

C. **'E.P. Bowles'**

C. **'Dorothy'**

C. **'Snow Bunting'** 🏆

C. **'Blue Bird'**

C. etruscus **'Zwanenburg'**

C. **'Zwanenberg Bronze'** 🏆

C. hadriaticus 🏆 [Autumn]

C. sieberi **subsp.** ***sublimis*** **f.** ***tricolor*** 🏆

C. tommasinianus **'Ruby Giant'**

C. speciosus **'Conqueror'** [Autumn]

C. vernus **'Queen of the Blues'**

C. kotschyanus 🏆 [Autumn]

C. speciosus 🏆 [Autumn]

C. **'Cream Beauty'** 🏆

PINK

Allium oreophilum
Spring- and summer-flowering, dwarf bulb with 2 narrow, semi-erect, basal leaves. Has loose, domed umbels of up to 10 widely bell-shaped, deep rose-pink flowers, 1.5–2cm (⅝–¾in) across. **H** 5–10cm (2–4in), **S** 8–10cm (3–4in).

Cyclamen libanoticum
Spring-flowering tuber with ivy-shaped, dull green leaves with lighter patterns and purplish-green undersides. Has musty-scented, clear pink flowers, each with deep carmine marks at the mouth. Grows best in an alpine house. **H** to 10cm (4in), **S** 10–15cm (4–6in).

Bulbocodium vernum
Spring-flowering corm with stemless, widely funnel-shaped, reddish-purple flowers. Narrow, semi-erect, basal leaves appear with flowers but do not elongate until later. Dies down in summer. **H** 3–4cm (1¼–1½in), **S** 3–5cm (11/4–2in).

Erythronium dens-canis (Dog's-tooth violet)
Spring-flowering tuber with 2 basal, mottled leaves. Stem has a pendent, pink, purple or white flower, with bands of brown, purple and yellow near the centre and reflexed petals. **H** 15–25cm (6–10in), **S** 8–10cm (3–4in).

Anemone blanda var. _rosea_ 'Radar'
Knobbly tuber with semi-erect, deep green leaves with 3 deeply toothed lobes. In early spring, stems each bear an upright, flattish, white-centred, deep reddish-carmine flower with 9–14 narrow petals. **H** 5–10cm (2–4in), **S** 10–15cm (4–6in).

RED

Anemone x _fulgens_
Spring- or early summer-flowering tuber with deeply divided, semi-erect, basal leaves. Stout stems each carry an upright, bright red flower, 5–7cm (2–3in) across, with 10–15 petals. **H** 10–30cm (4–12in), **S** 8–10cm (3–4in).

Sparaxis tricolor
Spring-flowering corm with erect, lance-shaped leaves in a basal fan. Stem produces a loose spike of up to 5 flattish, orange, red, purple, pink or white flowers, 5–6cm (2–2½in) across, with black or red centres. **H** 10–30cm (4–12in), **S** 8–12cm (3–5in).

PURPLE

Iris 'Pixie'
Bulbous iris with solitary, slightly fragrant, rich deep purple-blue flowers, with yellow midribs and white stripes, borne in late winter and early spring. Has linear, mid-green leaves. **H** 15cm (6in), **S** 2cm (¾in).

Babiana rubrocyanea (Winecups)
Spring-flowering corm with lance-shaped, erect, folded leaves in a basal fan. Carries short spikes of 5–10 flowers, each with 6 petals, purple-blue at the top and red at the base. **H** 15–20cm (6–8in), **S** 5–8cm (2–3in). Min. 10°C (50°F).

Anemone blanda 'Violet Star'
Knobbly tuber with rounded, semi-erect, dark green, basal leaves with divided, irregularly lobed leaves. In spring, stems each bear a saucer-shaped, white-centred, amethyst-violet flower that resembles a daisy. **H** and **S** 15cm (6in).

BLUE

***Ipheion uniflorum* 'Froyle Mill'**
Spring-flowering bulb with narrow, semi-erect, basal, pale green leaves that smell of onions if crushed. Each leafless stem carries a star-shaped, violet-blue flower, 3–4cm (1¼–1½in) across. **H** 10–15cm (4–6in), **S** 5–8cm (2–3in).

Bellevalia hyacinthoides
Spring-flowering bulb with prostrate, narrow leaves in a basal cluster. Bears a dense spike of up to 20 bell-shaped, pale lavender-blue, almost white flowers with darker, central veins. **H** 5–15cm (2–6in), **S** 5cm (2in).

Chionodoxa forbesii
Early spring-flowering bulb with 2 semi-erect, narrow, basal leaves. Bears a spike of 5–10 outward-facing, rich blue-lilac flowers with white eyes. **H** 10–25cm (4–10in), **S** 2.5–5cm (1–2in).

***Anemone blanda* 'Atrocaerulea'**
Knobbly tuber with semi-erect, dark green leaves that have 3 deeply toothed lobes. In early spring, stems bear an upright, flattish, bright blue flower, 4–5cm (1½–2in) across, with 9–14 narrow petals. **H** 5–10cm (2–4in), **S** 10–15cm (4–6in).

Romulea bulbocodium
Spring-flowering corm with long, semi-erect, thread-like leaves in a basal tuft. Slender flower stems each carry 1–6 upward-facing flowers, usually pale lilac-purple with yellow or white centres. **H** 5–10cm (2–4in), **S** 2.5–5cm (1–2in).

x *Chionoscilla allenii*
Early spring-flowering bulb with 2 narrow, semi-erect, basal, dark green leaves and flattish, star-shaped, deep blue flowers, 1–2cm (½–¾in) across, in a loose spike. **H** 10–15cm (4–6in), **S** 2.5–5cm (1–2in).

Moraea sisyrinchium
Spring-flowering corm with 1 or 2 semi-erect, narrow, basal leaves. Wiry stems each carry a succession of lavender- to violet-blue flowers, 3–4cm (1¼–1½in) across, with white or orange patches on the 3 larger petals. **H** 10–20cm (4–8in), **S** 8–10cm (3–4in).

***Muscari comosum* 'Plumosum'**
(Feather grape hyacinth)
Spring-flowering bulb with up to 5 strap-shaped, semi-erect, basal, grey-green leaves. Sterile flowers are replaced by a fluffy mass of purple threads. **H** to 25cm (10in), **S** 10–12cm (4–5in).

Brimeura amethystina
Late spring-flowering bulb with very narrow, semi-erect, basal leaves. Each leafless stem bears a spike of up to 15 pendent, tubular, blue flowers. **H** 10–25cm (4–10in), **S** 2.5–5cm (1–2in).

BLUE

Chionodoxa luciliae
Early spring-flowering bulb with 2 somewhat curved, semi-erect, basal leaves. Leafless stem bears 1–3 upward-facing, blue flowers with white eyes. **H** 5–10cm (2–4in), **S** 2.5–5cm (1–2in).

Scilla mischtschenkoana
Early spring-flowering bulb with 2 or 3 strap-shaped, semi-erect, basal, mid-green leaves. Stems elongate as cup-shaped or flattish, pale blue flowers, with darker blue veins, open. **H** 5–10cm (2–4in), **S** 5cm (2in).

***Scilla siberica* 'Atrocoerulea'**
Early spring-flowering bulb with 2–4 strap-shaped, semi-erect, basal, glossy leaves, widening towards tips. Bell-shaped, deep rich blue flowers, 1–1.5cm (½–⅝in) long, are borne in a short spike. **H** 10–15cm (4–6in), **S** 5cm (2in).

Muscari neglectum
Spring-flowering bulb. Bears 4–6 often prostrate leaves from autumn to early summer. Has small, ovoid, deep blue or blackish-blue flowers with white-rimmed mouths. Increases rapidly. **H** 10–20cm (4–8in), **S** 8–10cm (3–4in).

Tecophilaea cyanocrocus* var. *leichtlinii
Spring-flowering corm with 1 or 2 narrowly lance-shaped, semi-erect, basal leaves and solitary upward-facing, widely funnel-shaped, pale blue flowers with large, white centres. **H** 8–10cm (3–4in), **S** 5–8cm (2–3in).

Muscari aucheri
Spring-flowering bulb with 2 strap-shaped, greyish-green leaves. Bears small, almost spherical, bright blue flowers with white-rimmed mouths; upper flowers are often paler. **H** 5–15cm (2–6in), **S** 5–8cm (2–3in).

Muscari armeniacum
Spring-flowering bulb with 3–6 long, narrow, semi-erect, basal leaves. Carries a dense spike of small, fragrant, bell-shaped, deep blue flowers with constricted mouths that have a rim of small, paler blue or white "teeth". **H** 15–20cm (6–8in), **S** 8–10cm (3–4in).

Tecophilaea cyanocrocus
(Chilean blue crocus)
Spring-flowering corm with 1 or 2 lance-shaped, semi-erect, basal leaves. Carries upward-facing, funnel-shaped, deep gentian-blue flowers, 4–5cm (1½–2in) across, with white throats. **H** 8–10cm (3–4in), **S** 5–8cm (2–3in).

Puschkinia scilloides* var. *libanotica
(Striped squill)
Spring-flowering bulb with usually 2 strap-shaped, semi-erect, basal leaves. Carries a dense spike of star-shaped, pale blue flowers with a darker blue stripe down each petal centre.
H 15cm (6in), **S** 2.5–5cm (1–2in).

Hyacinthella leucophaea
Spring-flowering bulb with 2 narrowly strap-shaped, semi-erect, basal leaves and a thin, wiry, leafless flower stem. Carries a short spike of tiny, bell-shaped, very pale blue, almost white flowers.
H 10cm (4in), **S** 2.5–5cm (1–2in).

***Crocus* 'Blue Pearl'**
Early spring-flowering corm bearing narrow, semi-erect, basal leaves, with white lines along the centres. Fragrant, long-tubed, funnel-shaped, soft lavender-blue flowers, bluish-white within, have golden-yellow throats.
H 7cm (3in), **S** 5cm (2in).

Ledebouria socialis
Evergreen, spring-flowering bulb with lance-shaped, semi-erect, basal, dark-spotted, grey or green leaves. Produces a short spike of bell-shaped, purplish-green flowers.
H 5–10cm (2–4in), **S** 8–10cm (3–4in).

***Arum italicum* 'Marmoratum'**
Late spring-flowering tuber. Produces semi-erect leaves, with cream or white veins, in autumn, followed by pale green or creamy-white spathes, then red berries in autumn. Is good for flower arrangements. **H** 15–25cm (6–10in), **S** 20–30cm (8–12in).

Colchicum luteum
Spring-flowering corm with wineglass-shaped, yellow flowers – the only known yellow Colchicum. Semi-erect, basal leaves are short at flowering time but later expand. **H** 5–10cm (2–4in), **S** 5–8cm (2–3in).

Erythronium americanum
Spring-flowering tuber with 2 semi-erect, basal leaves, mottled green and brown, and a pendent, yellow flower, often bronze outside, with petals reflexing in sunlight. Forms clumps by stolons. **H** 5–25cm (2–10in), **S** 5–8cm (2–3in).

Muscari macrocarpum
Spring-flowering bulb with 3–5 semi-erect, basal, greyish-green leaves. Carries a dense spike of fragrant, brown-rimmed, bright yellow flowers. Upper flowers may initially be brownish-purple. **H** 10–20cm (4–8in), **S** 10–15cm (4–6in).

ORANGE

Dipcadi serotinum
Spring-flowering bulb with 2–5 very narrow, semi-erect, basal leaves. Leafless stem has a loose spike of nodding, tubular, brown or dull orange flowers, 1–1.5cm (½–⅝in) long. **H** 10–30cm (4–12in), **S** 5–8cm (2–3in).

Fritillaria pudica (Yellow fritillary)
Spring-flowering bulb with stems bearing scattered, narrowly lance-shaped, grey-green leaves. Has 1 or 2 deep yellow, sometimes red-tinged flowers, 1–2.5cm (½–1in) long. **H** 5–20cm (2–8in), **S** 5cm (2in).

WHITE

Arisaema candidissimum
Early summer-flowering tuber with large, cowl-like, pink-striped, white spathes, enclosing tiny, fragrant flowers on spadices, followed by broad, 3-palmate, semi-erect leaves, 30cm (12in) long. **H** 10–15cm (4–6in), **S** 30–45cm (12–18in).

Albuca humilis
Summer-flowering, dwarf bulb with very narrow, basal, dark green leaves. Carries a loose head of 1–3 cup-shaped, white flowers, 1cm (½in) long, striped green, later reddish, outside. **H** 5–10cm (2–4in), **S** 5–8cm (2–3in).

PINK

Allium schoenoprasum (Chives)
Clump-forming, summer-flowering bulb with narrow, hollow, erect, dark green leaves at base. Stems each carry up to 20 tiny, bell-shaped, pale purple or pink flowers in a dense umbel up to 5cm (2in) across. **H** 12–25cm (5–10in), **S** 5–10cm (2–4in).

Allium narcissiflorum
Clump-forming, summer-flowering bulb with very narrow, erect, grey-green leaves on the lower part of the flower stem. Has an umbel of up to 15 bell-shaped, pinkish-purple flowers. **H** 15–30cm (6–12in), **S** 8–10cm (3–4in).

Cyclamen purpurascens
Summer- and autumn-flowering tuber with rounded, silver-patterned leaves. Bears very fragrant, lilac-pink to reddish-purple flowers. **H** to 10cm (4in), **S** 10–15cm (4–6in).

Cyrtanthus brachyscyphus
Clump-forming, summer-flowering bulb with strap-shaped, semi-erect, basal, bright green leaves. Leafless stem bears a head of 6–12 tubular, orange- or brilliant red flowers with 6 lobes. **H** 20–30cm (8–12in), **S** 10–15cm (4–6in).

Anomatheca laxa
Early summer-flowering corm with a loose spike of up to 6 small, long-tubed, funnel-shaped, red or orange-red flowers, with darker red marks on the lower petals, borne among narrowly sword-shaped, erect, mid-green leaves. **H** 20cm (8in), **S** 5cm (2in).

Haemanthus coccineus (Blood lily)
Summer-flowering bulb with 2 elliptic leaves, hairy beneath, that lie flat on the ground. Spotted stem, forming before leaves, bears a cluster of tiny, red flowers with prominent stamens, within fleshy, red or pink bracts. **H** to 30cm (12in), **S** 20–30cm (8–12in). Min. 10°C (50°F).

Roscoea humeana
Summer-flowering tuber. Erect, broadly lance-shaped, rich green leaves form a stem-like sheath at base. Has up to 10 long-tubed, purple flowers, each with a hooded, upper petal, a wide, pendent lip and 2 narrower petals. **H** 15–25cm (6–10in), **S** 15–20cm (6–8in).

Allium cyathophorum* var. *farreri
Clump-forming, summer-flowering bulb with tufts of narrow, erect, basal leaves. Each stem bears a small, loose umbel, 1.5–4cm (⅝–1½in) wide, of up to 30 bell-shaped, dark reddish-purple flowers with sharply pointed petals. **H** 15–30cm (6–12in), **S** 10–15cm (4–6in).

Scilla peruviana
Early summer-flowering bulb with a basal cluster of up to 10 lance-shaped, semi-erect leaves. Stem bears a broadly conical head of up to 50 flattish, violet-blue flowers, 1.5–3cm (⅝–1¼in) across. **H** 10–25cm (4–10in), **S** 15–20cm (6–8in).

YELLOW

Allium moly
Clump-forming, summer-flowering bulb with 1–3 broad, semi-erect, basal, grey-green leaves. Stems each bear up to 40 star-shaped, yellow flowers in a fairly dense umbel, 4–8cm (1½–3in) across. **H** 10–35cm (4–14in), **S** 10–12cm (4–5in).

Chlidanthus fragrans
Summer-flowering bulb with narrow, semi-erect leaves in a basal tuft. Leafless stem carries a head of 3–5 fragrant, funnel-shaped, yellow flowers, 4–7cm (1½–2¾in) long. **H** 10–30cm (4–12in), **S** 8–10cm (3–4in).

Roscoea cautleyoides
Summer-flowering tuber. Erect, lance-shaped leaves form a stem-like sheath at base. Has up to 5 long-tubed, yellow flowers, each with a hooded, upper petal, a broad, 2-lobed, lower lip and 2 narrower petals. **H** 15–25cm (6–10in), **S** 10–15cm (4–6in).

WHITE

***Colchicum speciosum* 'Album'**
Vigorous, autumn-flowering corm with large, semi-erect, basal leaves in late winter or spring. Cup-shaped, white flowers successfully withstand bad weather. **H** and **S** 15–20cm (6–8in).

Acis autumnalis **(Autumn snowflake)**
Autumn-flowering bulb with thread-like, erect, basal leaves appearing with, or just after, flowers. Slender stems each produce a head of 1–4 bell-shaped, white flowers, tinged pink at bases. **H** 10–15cm (4–6in), **S** 2.5–5cm (1–2in).

Cyclamen hederifolium* f. *albiflorum
Autumn-flowering tuber. Pure white flowers, with reflexed petals, appear before or with leaves, which vary but are often ivy-shaped with silvery-green patterns. **H** to 10cm (4in), **S** 10–15cm (4–6in).

Zephyranthes candida
Autumn-flowering bulb with narrow, erect, basal leaves forming rush-like tufts. Each leafless stem carries crocus-like, white flowers, to 6cm (2½in) across. **H** 15–25cm (6–10in), **S** 5–8cm (2–3in).

Cyclamen africanum
Autumn-flowering tuber with ivy-shaped, deep green leaves with lighter patterns. Bears pendent, white or pink flowers, with reflexed petals and darker stains around mouths, as or just before leaves appear. **H** to 10cm (4in), **S** 10–15cm (4–6in).

Colchicum bivonae
Autumn-flowering corm with large, funnel-shaped, pinkish-purple flowers, strongly chequered darker purple and with purple anthers. Produces 8–10 erect leaves in spring. **H** 10–15cm (4–6in), **S** 15–20cm (6–8in).

Colchicum cilicicum
Autumn-flowering corm with large, cup-shaped, pale pink to deep rose-purple flowers, sometimes slightly chequered. Very broad, semi-erect, basal leaves, ribbed lengthways, appear soon after flowers have faded. **H** and **S** 15–20cm (6–8in).

***Colchicum* 'Waterlily'**
Autumn-flowering corm with rather broad, semi-erect, basal leaves in winter or spring. Tightly double flowers have 20–40 pinkish-lilac petals. **H** 10–15cm (4–6in), **S** 15–20cm (6–8in).

Colchicum agrippinum
Early autumn-flowering corm. Narrow, slightly waved, semi-erect, basal leaves develop in spring. Bears erect, funnel-shaped, bright purplish-pink flowers with a darker chequered pattern and pointed petals. **H** 10–15cm (4–6in), **S** 8–10cm (3–4in).

Cyclamen graecum
Autumn-flowering tuber with heart-shaped, toothed, velvety, dark green leaves, patterned silver or light green. Flowers are pink or white, with purple stains around mouths. Grows best in an alpine house. **H** to 10cm (4in), **S** 10–15cm (4–6in).

Cyclamen mirabile
Autumn-flowering tuber with pale pink flowers with toothed petals and dark purple-stained mouths. Heart-shaped, patterned leaves, purplish-green beneath, are minutely toothed on margins. **H** to 10cm (4in), **S** 5–8cm (2–3in).

PINK

Cyclamen hederifolium
Autumn-flowering tuber. Pale to deep pink flowers, stained darker at mouths, appear before or with foliage. Leaves vary but are often ivy-shaped with silvery-green patterns. **H** to 10cm (4in), **S** 10–15cm (4–6in).

Cyclamen rohlfsianum
Autumn-flowering tuber with coarsely toothed leaves, zoned with light and dark green patterns, and pale pink-lilac flowers, stained darker at mouths. **H** to 10cm (4in), **S** 10–15cm (4–6in).

Colchicum x byzantinum
Robust, autumn-flowering corm with up to 20 large, funnel-shaped, pale purplish-pink flowers, 10–15cm (4–6in) long. In spring produces very broad, semi-erect, basal leaves, ribbed lengthways. **H** and **S** 15–20cm (6–8in).

Habranthus robustus
Late summer- to early autumn-flowering bulb with narrowly strap-shaped, semi-erect, basal leaves. Leafless flower stems each bear a funnel-shaped, pink flower inclined at an angle. **H** 20–30cm (8–12in), **S** 8–10cm (3–4in).

Colchicum autumnale
(Autumn crocus, Meadow saffron)
Autumn-flowering corm with up to 8 long-tubed, wineglass-shaped, purple, pink or white flowers, followed by 3–5 large, strap-shaped, semi-erect, basal, glossy leaves in spring. **H** and **S** 10–15cm (4–6in).

Cyclamen cilicium
Autumn-flowering tuber with broadly heart-shaped leaves that have light and dark green zones. Has white or pink flowers, each with a dark purple stain at the mouth, just before or with leaves. **H** to 10cm (4in), **S** 5–10cm (2–4in).

Galanthus 'Atkinsii'
Vigorous, late winter- and early spring-flowering bulb with strap-shaped, semi-erect, basal, greyish-green leaves. Each stem carries a slender, white flower with a green mark at the apex of each inner petal. **H** 10–25cm (4–10in), **S** 5–9cm (2–3½in).

Galanthus nivalis 'Flore Pleno'
(Double common snowdrop)
Late winter- and early spring-flowering bulb with semi erect, basal, grey-green leaves. Bears rosetted, many-petalled, double, white flowers, some inner petals having a green mark at the apex. **H** 10–15cm (4–6in), **S** 5–8cm (2–3in).

Galanthus elwesii
Late winter- and early spring-flowering bulb with semi-erect, basal, grey-green leaves that widen gradually towards tips. Each inner petal of the white flowers bears green marks at the apex and base, which may merge. **H** 10–30cm (4–12in), **S** 5–8cm (2–3in).

Galanthus 'Hill Poë'
Early spring-flowering bulb with strap-shaped, semi-erect, grey-green leaves. Produces rosetted, double, white flowers, to 3cm (1¼in) long, with 4 larger outer petals and shorter, tightly packed, green-tipped inner petals. **H** 10–18cm (4–7in), **S** 5–8cm (2–3in).

Galanthus nivalis 'Pusey Green Tip'
Late winter- and early spring-flowering bulb with narrowly strap-shaped, semi-erect, basal, grey-green leaves. Each stem bears a white flower with many mostly green-tipped petals. **H** 10–15cm (4–6in), **S** 5–8cm (2–3in).

Crocus sieberi 'Albus'
Spring-flowering corm bearing narrow, semi-erect, basal leaves, with white lines along the centres. Scented, white flowers have large, deep yellow areas in throats and purple staining outside. **H** 3–4.5cm (1¼in–1¾in), **S** 5cm (2in).

Galanthus gracilis
Late winter- and early spring-flowering bulb with slightly twisted, strap-shaped, semi-erect, basal, grey-green leaves. Bears white flowers with 3 inner petals, each marked with a green blotch at the apex and base. **H** 10–15cm (4–6in), **S** 5–8cm (2–3in).

Galanthus ikariae
Late winter- and early spring-flowering bulb with strap-shaped, semi-erect, basal, glossy, bright green leaves. Produces one white flower, 1.5–2.5cm (⅝–1in) long, marked with a green patch at the apex of each inner petal. **H** 10–25cm (4–10in), **S** 5–8cm (2–3in).

Galanthus plicatus subsp. _byzantinus_
Late winter- and early spring-flowering bulb. Semi-erect, basal, deep green leaves have a grey bloom and reflexed margins. White flowers have green marks at bases and tips of inner petals. **H** 10–20cm (4–8in), **S** 5–8cm (2–3in).

WHITE

***Galanthus nivalis* 'Sandersii'**
Late winter- and early spring-flowering bulb with narrowly strap-shaped, semi-erect, basal, grey-green leaves. Flowers, 1.5–2cm (⅝–¾in) long, are white with yellow patches at the apex of each inner petal. **H** 10cm (4in), **S** 2.5–5cm (1–2in).

Galanthus woronowii
Late winter- to early spring-flowering bulb with inversely lance-shaped, semi-erect, basal, glossy to matt, dark to mid-green leaves. Produces white flowers, 2–2.5cm (¾–1in) long, with a green mark at the apex of each inner petal. **H** 10–15cm (4–6in), **S** 5–8cm (2–3in).

Galanthus rizehensis
Late winter- and early spring-flowering bulb with very narrow, strap-shaped, semi-erect, basal, dark green leaves. Produces white flowers, 1.5–2cm (⅝–¾in) long, with a green patch at the apex of each inner petal. **H** 10–20cm (4–8in), **S** 5cm (2in).

Cyclamen coum* f. *albissimum
Winter-flowering tuber with rounded, deep green leaves, sometimes silver-patterned. Carries white flowers, each with a maroon mark at the mouth. **H** to 10cm (4in), **S** 5–10cm (2–4in).

***Galanthus nivalis* 'Scharlockii'**
Vigorous, late winter- and early spring-flowering bulb with semi-erect, basal, grey-green leaves. Has white flowers, with green marks at the apex of inner petals, overtopped by 2 narrow spathes that resemble a donkey's ears. **H** 10–15cm (4–6in), **S** 5–8cm (2–3in).

***Cyclamen coum* Pewter Group 'Maurice Dryden'**
Winter- to early spring-flowering tuber with rounded, silver leaves edged dark green. Produces a succession of white flowers, occasionally pink flushed, with dark purple-pink mouths. **H** and **S** 10–12cm (4–5in).

PINK

***Cyclamen coum* Pewter Group**
Winter- to early spring-flowering tuber with rounded, dark green-margined, silvery-green leaves, each with a variably-sized, dark green centre. Produces a succession of flowers in shades of pink with dark purple-pink mouths. **H** and **S** 10–12in (4–5in).

Cyclamen coum
Winter-flowering tuber with rounded leaves, plain deep green or silver-patterned. Produces bright carmine flowers with dark stains at mouths. **H** to 10cm (4in), **S** 5–10cm (2–4in).

Cyclamen persicum
Winter- or spring-flowering tuber with heart-shaped leaves, marked light and dark green, and silver. Bears fragrant, slender, white or pink flowers, 3–4cm (1¼–1½in) long, with carmine mouths. **H** 10–20cm (4–8in), **S** 10–15cm (4–6in). Min. 5–7°C (41–45°F).

YELLOW

Eranthis hyemalis (Winter aconite)
Clump-forming tuber. Bears stalkless, cup-shaped, yellow flowers, 2–2.5cm (¾–1in) across, from late winter to early spring. A cut, leaf-like bract forms a ruff beneath each bloom. **H** 5–10cm (2–4in), **S** 8–10cm (3–4in).

***Lachenalia aloides* 'Nelsonii'**
Winter- to spring-flowering bulb with 2 strap-shaped, purple-spotted, semi-erect, basal leaves. Has a spike of 10–20 pendent, tubular, green-tinged, bright yellow flowers, 3cm (1¼in) long. **H** 15–25cm (6–10in), **S** 5–8cm (2–3in).

Lachenalia aloides* var. *quadricolor
Winter- to spring-flowering bulb with 2 strap-shaped, semi-erect, basal leaves. Has a spike of 10–20 purplish-red buds opening to greenish-yellow or -orange flowers. **H** 15–25cm (6–10in), **S** 5–8cm (2–3in).

WATER AND BOG PLANTS

The sound and reflective qualities of water have long been used to animate garden designs, and whether tiny or large, formal or informal, every garden has space for a water feature. A pond, pool or container also greatly extends the range of plants that you can grow. They are classified according to the depth of water required for them to thrive, and include deep water aquatics, marginal plants, and moisture-lovers or bog plants. Together, they offer a succession of interest, providing a diversity of foliage, form and flower colour. Informal ponds with sloping sides and richly planted banks, will also encourage a wide range of wildlife, including frogs, toads and birds.

WATER AND BOG PLANTS

Still or moving water reflects light and adds a dynamic quality to garden designs. It also greatly extends the range of plants that you can grow, with aquatic and moisture-loving types injecting colour, texture, and form into water features. They also provide an excellent wildlife habitat.

What are water plants?

The broad definition of water plants includes all plants that grow rooted, submerged or floating in water. They are further subdivided into deep-water aquatics, surface- or free-floating plants, marginals, and bog or moisture-loving plants, depending on the depth of water they require.

Water plants are grown for their beauty and ornamental value, but when a wide range of plants are grown together they also create a healthy ecosystem that maintains the quality of the water in a feature or pond. A balanced range of plants will regulate the levels of light, oxygen, and nutrients, helping to keep the water clear.

Submerged plants like hornwort (*Ceratophyllum demersum*) are known as "oxygenators". These purify the water by using up nutrients and excluding light, which prevents algal growth. Surface-floaters, such as water hyacinths (*Eichhornia crassipes*), also absorb dissolved nutrients. Deep-water plants, including water lilies (*Nymphaea*), root at the bottom of ponds, while their flowers and leaves shade the surface, again helping to prevent the growth of algae. The roots of marginal plants are submerged, but their top growth is visible above the water, providing shelter for fish, amphibians, and other wildlife.

ABOVE Patio feature
Tiny but perfectly formed, this patio water feature, fringed by ferns, supports flowering irises and arum lilies. Flow from a pump helps to oxygenate the water.

Ornamental planting

To maximize your pond or pool's planting potential, create areas at varying depths to accommodate different types. Begin planting at the centre of your pond, using deep-water plants, such as Cape pondweed (*Aponogeton distachyos*) with its white flowers that pop up at the surface, and the floating water soldier (*Stratiotes aloides*) which has spiky leaves; both require a depth of about 60–90cm (24–36in). (See box below for details on plant depths.) Most water lilies need to root at depths of 30–100cm (12in–3ft), depending on the species or cultivar. Dwarf water lilies, such as *Nymphaea tetragona* or slender water irises (*Iris laevigata)* are good choices for a

PLANTING DEPTHS

A pond with a range of planting depths allows you to grow a wide range of plants. Place plants at their appropriate depths, measured from the top of the soil in their containers to the water surface. Support young deep water aquatics on bricks and lower them to their final depth as they grow. Fill the pool a few days before planting to allow the water to reach the air temperature and become populated with beneficial micro-organisms.

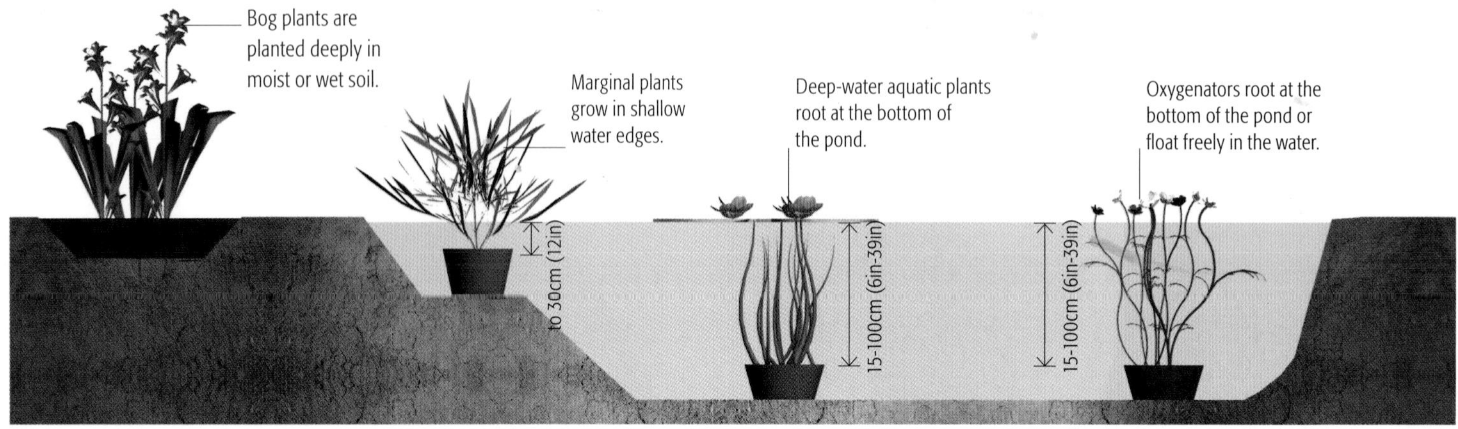

small pond or water feature. Marginal plants thrive in shallow water. Many are planted just below the surface, while water irises prefer a depth of about 15cm (6in) and pickerel weeds (*Pontederia*) like their roots submerged to a depth of 30cm (12in).

Marginals help to disguise liners at the edges of ponds, create reflections, and provide wildlife cover. They have a range of habits, from the bog bean (*Menyanthes trifoliata*) with its clusters of white flowers in spring, to the flowering rush (*Butomus umbellatus*) with its umbels of small pink flowers, and the large, arum-like blooms of skunk cabbages (*Lysichiton*). Larger areas can be enhanced by bold clumps of bullrushes (*Typha latifolia*), while architectural plants such as *Pontederia cordata* provide focal points with their leaves and flower spikes.

The damp areas around the edges of a pond provide ideal conditions for bog natives and moisture-lovers. In very wet bogs, marginals will survive, but in drier conditions, opt for moisture-lovers. Bog gardens must have either drainage or water flowing through them to provide oxygen for the plant roots.

ABOVE Marginal planting
The curving edges of an informal pool offer ideal conditions for marginals such as *Pontederia cordata* and *Sagittaria latifolia*. Marginals disguise plastic liners and provide shelter for wildlife.

Designing with water plants

Every garden has space for a water feature and its associated plants but try to match your plants to the size and design of your pond. Informal pools are designed with sloping sides and boggy banks to attract amphibians, birds, and small mammals that prey on garden pests. In winter, water that is more than 60cm (24in) deep will help creatures to survive a long freeze. The great advantage of an informal pool is that it offers versatility: its sinuous margins are longer than straight-sided ponds of a similar size, and the sloping banks provide a range of planting depths, increasing your choice of plants.

In small gardens, avoid vigorously spreading plants, such as the flag iris (*Iris pseudacorus*) or *Glyceria maxima*. For architectural plants for bogs, try *Filipendula camtschatica* and *Miscanthus sacchariflorus*. Astilbes, trollius, primulas, and ferns provide colour around the edges.

Seasonal care

In autumn, cut away dead foliage, trim over-large plants, and remove weeds. It is also a good idea to place a net over ponds close to deciduous trees, as the fallen leaves can foul the water. Aim to reach a balance, so that rotting vegetation releases enough nutrition for next year's growth, but not so much as to encourage algae.

Water plants are best divided and repotted in spring as they start into growth. Keep planting baskets weeded, removing annual weed seedlings as they appear, as well as surplus water-plant seedlings. This task can be eased by dead-heading the plants after flowering. Small ponds and water features will also need topping up in summer, using rainwater if possible.

PLANTING UP A POND

Submerged plants are planted in baskets rather than pots, using aquatic compost. Garden soil is unsuitable because it often contains nutrients that encourage the growth of algae. When choosing plants look for healthy specimens that are free of algae and pond weeds. All submerged plants, such as water lilies and oxygenators, can be planted in the same way. Lift them from the pond for dividing and repotting every two or three years.

Established water lily pond

1 Use a pond basket Choose a pond basket with small holes to prevent soil leaking out into the water. Place a layer of aquatic compost in the bottom.

2 Position the plant Remove the plant from its pot and put it in the centre of the basket at the same level. Fill around the plant with more compost, firming as you go.

3 Mulch with gravel Clean any algae or duckweed from the plant's leaves and stems. Wash some pea gravel and apply a thin layer to stabilize the soil's surface.

Menyanthes trifoliata **(Bog bean)**
Deciduous, perennial, marginal water plant with 3-parted, green leaves on floating, spreading stems. To control, cut off extremities and replant. The fringed, white flowers open from cerise buds in early spring. **H** 23cm (9in), **S** indefinite.

Lysichiton camtschatcensis
Vigorous, deciduous, perennial, marginal water or bog plant. Pure white spathes, surrounding spikes of small, insignificant flowers, are borne in spring, before large, oblong to oval, bright green leaves emerge. **H** 75cm (30in), **S** 60cm (24in).

Hydrocharis morsus-ranae **(Frogbit)**
Deciduous, perennial, floating water plant with rosettes of kidney-shaped, olive-green leaves and small, white flowers during summer. Dormant buds can be eaten by fish in winter, so move a few plantlets to a protected place. **S** 10–100cm (4–39in).

Calla palustris **(Bog arum)**
Deciduous or semi-evergreen, perennial, spreading, marginal water plant with heart-shaped, glossy, mid- to dark green leaves. In spring produces large, white spathes usually followed by red or orange fruits. **H** 25cm (10in), **S** 30cm (12in).

Sagittaria latifolia
(American arrowhead, Duck potato)
Deciduous, perennial, marginal water plant with curved, soft green leaves and sprays of white flowers in summer. It can be invasive, so confine it in a basket. **H** 1.5m (5ft), **S** 60cm (2ft).

Alisma plantago-aquatica
(Water plantain)
Deciduous, perennial, marginal water plant with upright, oval, bright green leaves held well above water. Bears loose, conical panicles of small, pinkish to white flowers in summer. May be invasive. **H** 75cm (30in), **S** 45cm (18in).

Saururus cernuus (Lizard's tail)
Deciduous, perennial, marginal water or bog plant. Has clumps of heart-shaped, mid-green leaves and racemes of creamy flowers in summer. It can become invasive. In small ponds and water features keep this confined in a basket. **H** 23cm (9in), **S** 30cm (12in).

Astilboides tabularis
Deciduous, clump-forming perennial, bog plant with rounded, mid-green leaves, 1m (3ft) across. In mid-summer produces plume-like panicles of numerous, tiny, white flowers. **H** 1.2m (4ft), **S** 1.5m (5ft).

***Acorus calamus* 'Argenteostriatus'**
Semi-evergreen, perennial, marginal water plant. Sword-like, tangerine-scented, mid-green leaves have cream variegation and are flushed rose-pink in spring. Increase by division in April. **H** 75cm (30in), **S** 60cm (24in).

Aponogeton distachyos
(Cape pondweed, Water hawthorn)
Deciduous, perennial, deep-water plant with floating, oblong, mid- to dark green leaves, often splashed with purple. Very fragrant, 'forked', white flowers are borne throughout summer, often into winter. **S** 1.2m (4ft).

Caltha leptosepala
Deciduous, perennial, marginal water plant with heart-shaped, dark green leaves and buttercup-like, white flowers produced in late spring and early summer. Increase by division in April. **H** and **S** 30cm (12in).

Hottonia palustris (Water violet)
Deciduous, perennial, submerged water plant. Dense whorls of much-divided, light green leaves form a spreading mass of foliage. Lilac or whitish flowers appear above water surface in summer. Helps to suppress algae. Increase by division. **S** indefinite.

***Acorus gramineus* 'Variegatus'**
Semi-evergreen, perennial, marginal or submerged water plant. Narrow, stiff, grass-like leaves are dark green with cream variegation. Other cultivars with different coloured foliage are available. Useful for patio ponds. **H** 25cm (10in), **S** 15cm (6in).

Stratiotes aloides (Water soldier)
Semi-evergreen, perennial, submerged, free-floating water plant. Spiny, olive-green leaves are arranged in rosettes. Produces cup-shaped, white, sometimes pink-tinged flowers in summer. Increases by producing small water buds. **S** 30cm (12in).

Aruncus dioicus (Goat's beard)
Hummock-forming perennial carrying large leaves with lance-shaped leaflets on tall stems and above them, in mid-summer, branching plumes of tiny, creamy-white flowers. **H** 2m (6ft), **S** 1.2m (4ft).

***Glyceria maxima* 'Variegata'**
Herbaceous, spreading, perennial grass with cream-striped leaves, often tinged pink at the base. Bears open panicles of greenish spikelets in summer. **H** 80cm (30in), **S** indefinite.

Leucojum aestivum
(Summer snowflake)
Spring-flowering bulb with long, strap-shaped, semi-erect, basal leaves. Bears heads of pendent, long-stalked, bell-shaped, green-tipped, white flowers on leafless stems. **H** 50cm–1m (1½–3ft), **S** 10–12cm (4–5in).

Rodgersia podophylla
Clump-forming, rhizomatous perennial with large, many-veined leaves that are bronze when young and later become mid-green, then copper-tinted. Panicles of creamy-white flowers are borne well above foliage in summer. **H** 1.2m (4ft), **S** 1m (3ft).

***Schoenoplectus lacustris* subsp. *tabernaemontani* 'Zebrinus'**
Evergreen, spreading, perennial sedge with leafless stems, striped horizontally with white, and brown spikelets in summer. Withstands brackish water. **H** 1.5m (5ft), **S** indefinite.

Arundo donax* var. *versicolor
Herbaceous, rhizomatous, perennial grass with strong stems bearing broad, creamy-white-striped leaves. May bear dense, erect panicles of whitish-yellow spikelets in late summer. **H** 2.5–3m (8–10ft), **S** 60cm (2ft).

Filipendula ulmaria (Meadowsweet)
Deciduous, perennial, bog plant with plume-like spikes of creamy-white flowers in mid-summer. Leafy stems bear divided, mid-green leaves. Self-seeds quite vigorously. **H** 1m (3ft), **S** 60cm (24in).

***Trollius x cultorum* 'Alabaster'**
Clump-forming perennial producing rounded, yellowish-white flowers in spring. These emerge from a basal mass of rounded, deeply divided, mid-green leaves. **H** 60cm (24in), **S** 45cm (18in).

***Zantedeschia aethiopica* 'Crowborough'**
Early to mid-summer-flowering tuber with arrow-shaped, semi-erect, basal, deep green leaves. Produces a succession of arum-like, white spathes, each with a yellow spadix. **H** 45cm–1m (1½–3ft), **S** 35–45cm (1–1½ft).

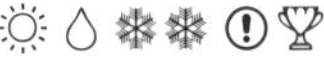

Sanguisorba canadensis
(Canadian burnet)
Clump-forming perennial. In late summer bears slightly pendent spikes of bottlebrush-like, white flowers on stems that arise from toothed, divided, mid-green leaves. **H** 1.2–2m (4–6ft), **S** 60cm (2ft).

***Iris laevigata* 'Rowden Starlight'**
Deciduous, perennial, marginal water plant with single, white flowers in late spring and early summer. Leaves are linear, smooth and mid-green. **H** 75cm (30in), **S** 45cm (18in)

Rhynchospora colorata
Slow-growing, deciduous, spreading, perennial, marginal water plant or bog plant with pointed, green-tipped, white bracts surrounding an inconspicuous flower head in late summer. Has linear, slightly hairy, mid-green leaves. **H** 45cm (18in), **S** indefinite.

Rodgersia sambucifolia
Deciduous, clump-forming, perennial, bog plant with emerald-green leaves, sometimes bronze-tinged, divided into large, lobed leaflets. Bears broad spires of creamy-white flowers in summer. **H** 1.5m (5ft), **S** 1m (3ft).

Rodgersia aesculifolia
Clump-forming, rhizomatous perennial that is excellent for a bog garden or pool side. In mid-summer, plumes of fragrant, pinkish-white flowers rise from crinkled, bronze foliage like that of a horse-chestnut tree. **H** and **S** 1m (3ft).

Lysimachia clethroides
Vigorous, clump-forming, spreading perennial carrying spikes of small, white flowers above mid-green foliage in late summer. **H** 1m (3ft), **S** 60cm–1m (2–3ft).

Anemone rivularis
Perennial with stiff, free-branching stems bearing delicate, cup-shaped, white flowers in summer above deeply divided, dark green leaves. **H** 60cm (24in), **S** 30cm (12in).

Nelumbo nucifera **(Sacred lotus)**
Vigorous, deciduous, perennial, marginal water plant. Sturdy stems carry very large, plate-like, blue-green leaves and, in summer, large, vivid rose-pink flowers, maturing to flesh-pink. Grow under glass. **H** 1–1.5m (3–5ft) above water, **S** 1.2m (4ft). Min. 7°C (45°F).

Darmera peltata **(Umbrella plant)**
Spreading perennial with large, rounded leaves. Has clusters of white or pale pink flowers in spring on white-haired stems before foliage appears. **H** 1–1.2m (3–4ft), **S** 60cm (2ft).

Cardamine raphanifolia
Deciduous, almost evergreen, perennial, bog plant with panicles of dark lilac flowers in late spring. Mid-green leaves are divided into oval to rounded leaflets. Self-seeds readily. **H** 50cm (20in), **S** 20cm (8in).

Iris versicolor **'Rowden Cadenza'**
Deciduous, perennial, marginal water plant or bog plant with single, white flowers heavily veined cerise, borne in late spring and early summer. Has linear, erect to slightly arching, mid-green leaves. **H** 75cm (30in), **S** 45cm (18in).

Butomus umbellatus **(Flowering rush)**
Deciduous, perennial, rush-like, marginal water plant with narrow, twisted, mid-green leaves and umbels of pink to rose-red flowers in summer. **H** 1m (3ft), **S** 45cm (1½ft).

Chelone obliqua **(Turtle-head)**
Upright perennial that bears terminal spikes of hooded, lilac-pink flowers in late summer and autumn. Leaves are dark green and lance-shaped. **H** 1m (3ft), **S** 50cm (20in).

Cardamine pratensis **(Lady's smock)**
Deciduous, clump-forming, perennial, marginal water plant or bog plant with dense panicles of single or double, lilac or white flowers in spring. Has rosettes of glossy, dark green leaves divided into rounded leaflets. **H** 45cm (18in), **S** 15cm (6in).

Filipendula rubra
Vigorous, upright perennial with large, jagged leaves and feathery plumes of tiny, soft pink flowers on tall, branching stems in mid-summer. Will rapidly colonize a boggy site. **H** 2–2.5m (6–8ft), **S** 1.2m (4ft).

Liatris spicata
Clump-forming perennial. In late summer bears spikes of crowded, rose-purple flower heads on stiff stems that arise from basal tufts of grassy, mid-green foliage. **H** 60cm (24in), **S** 30cm (12in).

***Rheum palmatum* 'Atrosanguineum'**
Clump-forming perennial with very large, lobed, deeply cut leaves that are deep red-purple when young. Bears large, fluffy panicles of crimson flowers in early summer. **H** and **S** 2m (6ft).

Lobelia cardinalis **(Cardinal flower)**
Deciduous, perennial, bog plant with narrowly lance-shaped, fresh green leaves. Produces spires of 2-lipped, brilliant scarlet flowers in summer. **H** 75cm (30in), **S** 23in (9in).

***Astilbe* 'Fanal'**
Leafy perennial with strong stems. In summer bears neat, tapering, feathery panicles of tiny, crimson red flowers that turn brown and keep their shape in winter. Broad leaves are divided into leaflets. Prefers humus-rich soil. **H** 60cm (24in), **S** to 90cm (36in).

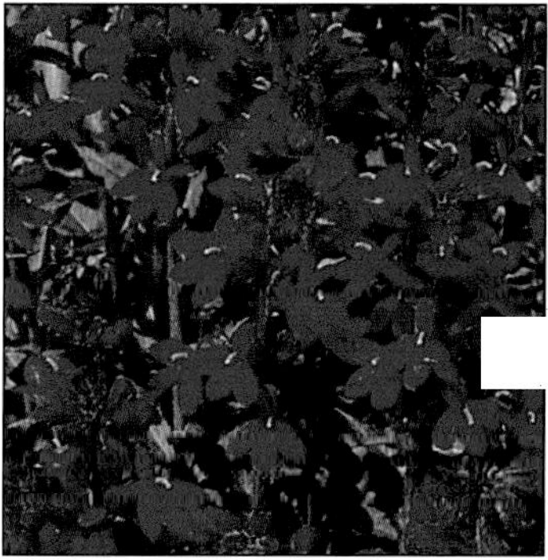

***Lobelia* 'Cherry Ripe'**
Clump-forming perennial bearing spikes of cerise-scarlet flowers from mid- to late summer. Leaves, usually fresh green, are often tinged red-bronze. **H** 1m (3ft), **S** 23cm (9in).

Geum coccineum
Clump-forming perennial with irregularly lobed leaves, above which rise slender, branching, hairy stems bearing single, orange flowers with prominent, yellow stamens in summer. **H** and **S** 30cm (12in).

Iris fulva
Rhizomatous, beardless iris. In late spring or summer produces a slender, slightly branched stem with 4–6 (occasionally more) copper- or orange-red flowers, 5–7cm (2–3in) across, with 2 flowers per leaf axil. **H** 45–80cm (18–32in), **S** indefinite.

Sarracenia purpurea **(Common pitcher plant, Huntsman's cup)**
Evergreen, erect to semi-prostrate, rosette-forming perennial. Inflated, green pitchers are tinged purple-red. In spring, 5-petalled, purple flowers are borne above. **H** 30cm (12in), **S** 30–40cm (12–16in). Min. 5°C (41°F).

WATER LILIES

These beautiful plants are often the focal point in a pond, or water feature, be it naturalistic or formal. The leaves and flowers float on the surface, helping to control algae and providing cover for fish and wildlife. There are nearly 400 species and selections on offer, with flower colours in shades of white, yellow, pink, and red. Blue water lilies are not hardy in frost-prone climates. Lilies range in size, and include miniature types that spread up to 60cm (24in) in diameter and need a water depth of just 20cm (8in); medium lilies, ranging from 1–1.5m (3–5ft); and large types that extend 1.5–4m (5–12ft) or more – these require a water depth of 60cm (24in) or more. All water lilies thrive in full sun and must be grown in still water. For more details, see the Plant Dictionary.

***N.* 'Froebelii'**
[medium]

***N.* Laydekeri Group 'Fulgens'**
[medium]

***N.* 'Blue Beauty'**
[tropical]

***N.* 'James Brydon'** ♀
[medium]

N. odorata* var. *minor
[medium]

***N.* 'American Star'**
[large]

***N.* 'Rose Arey'**
[medium]

***N.* 'Black Princess'**
[medium]

***N.* 'Helvola'** [miniature]

***N.* Marliacea Group 'Chromatella'** ♀ [large]

***N.* 'Gonnère'** ♀
[large]

***N. tetragona* 'Alba'**
[miniature]

***N.* 'Attraction'**
[large]

***N.* 'Firecrest'**
[medium]

***N.* 'Lucidia'**
[medium]

***N.* 'Lemon Chiffon'**
[medium]

***N.* Marliacea Group 'Albida'** [large]

***N.* 'Escarboucle'** ♀ [large]

***N.* 'Sunrise'** [medium]

Mimulus ringens
Deciduous, perennial, marginal water plant or bog plant with snapdragon-like, mauve-blue flowers borne in the leaf axils on tall stems from early to mid-summer. Has lance-shaped to narrowly oblong, toothed, mid-green leaves. **H** 60cm (24in), **S** 15cm (6in).

Eichhornia crassipes (Water hyacinth)
Fully- or semi-evergreen, perennial water plant with glossy leaves and air-filled stalks. Bears spikes of blue-lilac flowers in summer in warmer climates but may be invasive. Ideal for indoor pools. **S** 23cm (9in). Min. 1°C (34°F).

Iris ensata (Japanese flag)
Rhizomatous, beardless Japanese iris. Branched stem produces 3–15 purple or red-purple flowers, 8–15cm (3–6in) across, with a yellow blaze on each fall, from early to mid-summer. Many garden forms, including doubles and bicolours. **H** 60–90cm (2–3ft), **S** indefinite.

Iris setosa (Bristle-pointed iris)
Rhizomatous, beardless iris, very variable in stature. Bears 2–13 deep blue or purple-blue flowers, 5–8cm (2–3in) across, from each spathe in late spring and early summer. Falls have paler blue or white marks; each standard is reduced to a bristle.

Iris sibirica (Siberian flag)
Rhizomatous, beardless Siberian iris. From late spring to early summer, a branched stem bears 2 or 3 dark-veined, blue or blue-purple flowers, 5–10cm (2–4in) across, from each spathe. **H** 50–120cm (20–48in), **S** indefinite.

Pontederia cordata (Pickerel weed)
Deciduous, perennial, marginal water plant. In late summer, dense spikes of blue flowers emerge between lance-shaped, glossy, dark green leaves. **H** 75cm (30in), **S** 45cm (18in).

Lobelia siphilitica
(Blue cardinal flower)
Clump-forming perennial with narrowly oval, green leaves. Racemes of 2-lipped, blue flowers are produced in late summer and autumn. **H** 1m (3ft), **S** 23cm (9in).

***Myosotis scorpioides* 'Mermaid'**
(Water forget-me-not)
Deciduous, perennial, marginal water plant for mud or very shallow water. Narrow, mid-green leaves form sprawling mounds. Bears small, blue, forget-me-not flowers during summer. **H** 15cm (6in), **S** 30cm (12in).

BLUE

Iris versicolor **(Blue flag, Wild iris)**
Robust, rhizomatous, beardless iris. Branched stem produces 3–5 or more purple-blue, reddish-purple, lavender or slate-purple flowers, 5–10cm (2–4in) across, from early to mid-summer. Falls usually have a central white area veined purple. **H** 20–80cm (8–32in).

Veronica beccabunga **(Brooklime)**
Usually evergreen, marginal water plant with creeping, hollow, fleshy stems and rounded, mid-green leaves. Bears blue flowers with white centres from late spring to late summer. Grow in wet soil or water to 12cm (5in) deep. Invasive. **H** 10cm (4in), **S** indefinite.

Iris laevigata **'Weymouth Midnight'**
Deciduous, perennial, marginal water plant with double, deep blue flowers in late spring and early summer. Has linear, smooth, mid-green leaves. **H** 75cm (30in), **S** 45cm (18in).

GREEN

Typha latifolia **(Bulrush)**
Deciduous, perennial, marginal water plant with large clumps of mid-green foliage. Produces spikes of beige flowers in late summer, followed by decorative, dark brown seed heads. Invasive. Smaller species available. **H** to 2.5m (8ft), **S** 60cm (2ft).

Potamogeton crispus
(Curled pondweed)
Deciduous, perennial, submerged water plant that produces spreading colonies of seaweed-like, bronze-or mid-green foliage. Insignificant, flowers are borne in summer. Prefers cool water. Helps to keep the water clear. **S** indefinite.

Pistia stratiotes **(Water lettuce)**
Deciduous, perennial, floating water plant for a pool or aquarium, evergreen in tropical conditions. Hairy, soft green foliage is lettuce-like in arrangement. Does not survive outdoors in cooler climates. Replace annually. **H** and **S** 10cm (4in). Min. 10–15°C (50–59°F).

Trapa natans **(Water chestnut)**
Annual, floating water plant with diamond-shaped, mid-green leaves, often marked purple, arranged in rosettes. Bears white flowers in summer. In cooler climates it will not survive the winter. Replace annually. **S** 23cm (9in).

Sparganium erectum
(Branched bur reed)
Vigorous, deciduous or semi-evergreen, perennial, marginal water plant with narrow, mid-green leaves. Bears small, greenish-brown burs in summer. In small to medium ponds, control in a basket. **H** 1m (3ft), **S** 60cm (2ft).

Typha minima
Deciduous, perennial, marginal water plant with grass-like leaves. Spikes of rust-brown flowers in late summer are succeeded by decorative, black, cylindrical seed heads. Confine in a basket to keep under control.
H 45–60cm (18–24in), **S** 30cm (12in).

Gunnera manicata
Architectural perennial with rounded, prickly-edged leaves, to 1.5m (5ft) across. Has conical, light green flower spikes in early summer, followed by orange-brown seed pods. Needs mulch cover for crowns in winter and a sheltered site. **H** 2m (6ft), **S** 2.2m (7ft).

Matteuccia struthiopteris
(Ostrich-feather fern, Ostrich fern)
Deciduous, rhizomatous fern. Lance-shaped, erect, divided fronds are arranged like a shuttlecock; outermost, fresh green, sterile fronds surround denser, dark brown, fertile fronds.
H 1m (3ft), **S** 45cm (1½ft).

Myriophyllum verticillatum
(Whorled water milfoil)
Deciduous, perennial, spreading, submerged water plant, overwintering by club-shaped winter buds. Slender stems are covered with whorls of finely divided, olive-green leaves. An excellent water conditioner. **S** indefinite.

Peltandra virginica
Deciduous, perennial, marginal water plant with arrow-shaped, glossy, dark green leaves, 25cm (10in) long. Produces an inconspicuous, green spathe with a paler green spadix in late summer.
H and **S** 60cm (24in).

Onoclea sensibilis (Sensitive fern)
Deciduous, creeping fern with handsome, arching, almost triangular, divided, fresh pale green fronds, often suffused pinkish-brown in spring. In autumn, fronds turn an attractive yellowish-brown. **H** and **S** 45cm (18in).

Osmunda regalis (Royal fern)
Deciduous fern with elegant, broadly oval to oblong, divided, bright green fronds, pinkish when young. Mature plants bear tassel-like, rust-brown fertile flower spikes at ends of taller fronds.
H 2m (6ft), **S** 1m (3ft).

***Houttuynia cordata* 'Chameleon'**
Vigorous, deciduous, perennial, ground-cover, marginal water plant. Aromatic, leathery leaves are splashed yellow and red. Has small sprays of white flowers in summer. Needs some sun to enhance variegation. Potentially invasive. **H** 10cm (4in), **S** indefinite.

Lysichiton americanus
(Yellow skunk cabbage)
Vigorous, deciduous, perennial, marginal water or bog plant. In spring, before large, fresh green leaves appear, produces bright yellow spathes. Avoid planting near streams, it spreads rapidly. **H** 1m (3ft), **S** 75cm (2.5ft).

***Caltha palustris* 'Plena'**
Deciduous, perennial, marginal water plant with rounded, dark green leaves. Bears clusters of double, bright golden-yellow flowers in spring. Increase by division in March. **H** and **S** 25cm (10in).

Ranunculus lingua
Deciduous, perennial, marginal water plant with stout stems and lance-shaped, glaucous leaves. Clusters of yellow flowers are borne in late spring. Increase by division in March. Spreads rapidly. Confine to a basket in smaller ponds. **H** 90cm (3ft), **S** 45cm (1½ft).

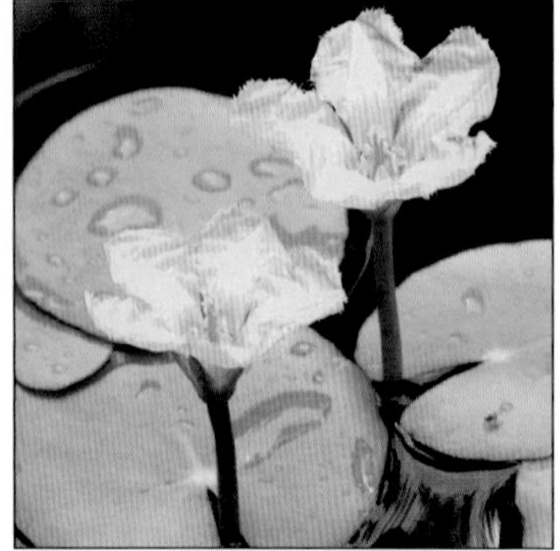

Nymphoides peltata (Water fringe)
Deciduous, perennial, deep-water plant with floating, small, round, mid-green leaves, often spotted and splashed with brown. Produces small, fringed, yellow flowers throughout summer. In smaller ponds, keep it under control in a basket. **S** 60cm (24in).

Caltha palustris
(Marsh marigold)
Deciduous, perennial, marginal water plant that has rounded, dark green leaves and bears clusters of cup-shaped, bright golden yellow flowers in spring. There are several varieties available. **H** 60cm (24in), **S** 45cm (18in).

Orontium aquaticum (Golden club)
Deciduous, perennial, deep-water plant or, less suitably, marginal water plant. In spring, pencil-like, gold-and-white flower spikes emerge from floating, oblong, blue-grey or blue-green leaves. Needs a large basket. Increase by division or seed. **S** 60cm (24in).

Nuphar lutea (Yellow water lily)
Vigorous, deciduous, perennial, deep-water plant for a large pool. Mid-green leaves are leathery. Small, sickly-smelling, bottle-shaped, yellow flowers open in summer, followed by decorative seed heads. Increase by division in early spring. **S** 1.5m (5ft).

Primula prolifera
Rosette-forming, evergreen, Candelabra primula with bell-shaped, yellow flowers borne in summer. Leaves are oval, toothed and pale green.
H and **S** 60cm (24in).

Mimulus x hybridus (Monkey flower)
Deciduous, perennial, marginal water plant or bog plant bearing snapdragon-like, yellow flowers, with red spots in the throat, from mid-spring to summer. Bears toothed, mid- to dark green leaves. Self-seeds freely. **H** 45cm (18in), **S** 30cm (12in).

Iris pseudacorus* var. *bastardii
Deciduous, perennial, marginal water plant or bog plant with single, pale lemon-yellow flowers in late spring and early summer. Leaves are broadly linear, ridged and mid-green. **H** 1m (3ft), **S** 60cm (24in).

***Ligularia* 'Britt Marie Crawford'**
Clump-forming perennial with heart-shaped, dark purple leaves and stems. In mid-summer has sturdy racemes of large, daisy-like, orange flower heads. **H** 1.5m (5ft), **S** 1m (3ft).

Ligularia przewalskii
Loosely clump-forming perennial with stems clothed in deeply cut, round, dark green leaves. Narrow spires of small, daisy-like, yellow flower heads appear mid- to late summer. **H** 1.2–2m (4–6ft), **S** 1m (3ft).

Primula florindae (Giant cowslip)
Bold, rosette-forming perennial with broadly lance-shaped, toothed, mid-green leaves. In summer produces large heads of pendent, bell-shaped, scented, sulphur-yellow flowers.
H 1.2m (4ft), **S** 1m (3ft).

***Carex elata* 'Aurea'**
(Bowles' golden sedge)
Evergreen, tuft-forming, perennial sedge with golden-yellow leaves. Solid, triangular stems bear dark brown flower spikes in summer. **H** to 40cm (16in), **S** 15cm (6in).

Sarracenia flava
(Yellow pitcher plant)
Erect perennial with red-marked, yellow-green pitchers (modified leaves) that have hooded tops. From late spring to early summer bears nodding, yellow or greenish-yellow flowers.
H and **S** 45cm (18in). Min. 5°C (41°F).

Trollius europaeus (Globeflower)
Clump-forming perennial that in spring bears rounded, lemon- to mid-yellow flowers above deeply divided, mid-green leaves.
H 60cm (24in), **S** 45cm (18in).

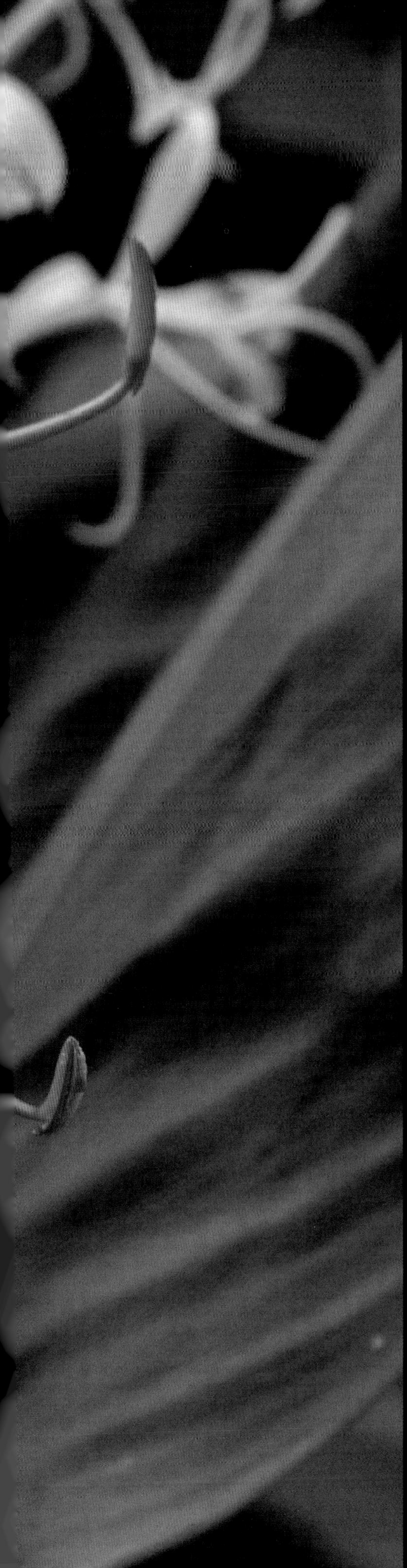

TENDER AND EXOTIC PLANTS

Tropical and subtropical regions are home to a huge range of plants, each thriving in varying growing conditions. If you live in these areas, you can grow tender plants outside and create dramatic planting schemes with architectural forms and exotic flowers. In temperate regions, either grow these exotic plants under glass or indoors as house plants. There is a wealth of form, colour and texture on offer, from plants with handsome foliage to those with beautiful blooms, including bougainvilleas and peace lilies. Unlike those grown outside, indoor plants are not subject to seasonal extremes, and many need relatively little attention, apart from watering, feeding and potting on annually.

TENDER AND EXOTIC PLANTS

Gardeners have long been fascinated by tender and exotic plants that bring colour and interest from all corners of the world. In warmer regions many of these can be grown in the garden, but in cooler areas they're best treated as house plants, at least for part of the year.

What are tender and exotic plants?

This group of plants originate from many parts of the world, including tropical and subtropical areas, where they require temperatures no lower than 1–18°C (34–64°F), even in winter. Their specific cultural demands vary between plants and can be complex. In addition to warmth, many also require high light levels, long growing seasons, and often either very arid or humid growing conditions. A small few, including cacti and succulents, can tolerate frost if kept dry, but most cannot.

Where the climate allows, tender and exotic plants can be grown in the garden; where it doesn't, they must be grown indoors. The most tender plants require permanent protection and are commonly grown as house plants, including flamingo flower, *Anthurium andraeanum*, peace lily, *Spathiphyllum wallisii*, and Madagascar jasmine, *Stephanotis floribunda*. Other plants are more robust and can spend the summer in sheltered positions in the garden, being brought back in before the first frosts. These include *Banksia coccinea*, the Australian heath, *Epracris impressa*, and king protea, *Protea cynaroides*.

Designing with tender plants

The range of tender and exotic plants is vast, and includes many with bold flowers, attractive foliage, or an architectural habit. With such a diverse variety to grow, they are ideal for many different situations and planting styles. In areas where they can be grown outdoors all year they can form the mainstay of beds and borders, even entire gardens, from jungle schemes to desert-style borders. In cooler areas, where they can only spend the warm summer months outside, they can still play a prominent role. Pot-grown plants like *Agave americana*, *Ensete ventricosum*, and even the bird of paradise, *Strelitzia reginae*, for example, will all give a dramatic, but temporary display in the garden, or on the patio or roof terrace.

Indoors, tender and exotic plants can be put to many uses, from statement plants in grand reception rooms, and year-round greenery in conservatory planters, to lone windowsill pot plants for seasonal colour.

BELOW Dramatic foliage
The Japanese sago palm (*Cycas revoluta*) is one of many tender shrubs that can be enjoyed indoors during winter, but can be stood outside for summer. It is grown for its sculptural foliage and habit.

ABOVE Exotic flowers for indoors
Frangipani (*Plumeria rubra*) is famed for its rich scent and must be grown permanently in a large heated conservatory, where it can become very large. It needs a minimum winter temperature of 10°C (50°F).

ABOVE Conservatory climber
Bougainvillea is a vigorous shrubby climber in warmer climates. It needs a minimum temperature of 7°C (45°F), and must be treated as a large conservatory plant in cooler areas.

LEFT In a natural setting
In their native hot, dry climates, cacti and other succulents can achieve spectacular dimensions. Even in cooler temperate gardens they can still make a bold impression but must be brought in for the winter, and repositioned outside again each summer.

When choosing and positioning tender plants indoors, consider the conditions they require. Light levels may be poor, even near windows, and air-conditioning and central heating can create a dry atmosphere, which many plants dislike. Another consideration is how large the plants will become; many exotic plants commonly grown as house plants, such as Swiss-cheese plant, *Monstera deliciosa*, and *Bougainvillea*, occupy considerable space over time, although they can be pruned and trained.

Caring for tender plants

Tender and exotic plants, like any other garden plant, all have their preferred growing conditions, so consider your site, soil and aspect carefully when planting outdoors. This is even more important when growing them indoors as the plants are reliant on you for their care. The best approach is to try and mirror their natural conditions as closely as possible, providing the same degree of heat, light, shade, humidity and ventilation. It is also very important to observe their natural growing seasons by feeding and watering them more frequently when they're in growth, less so, if at all, when they are dormant.

Heated conservatories and greenhouses provide the best indoor habitat for most tender plants, although many also thrive in houses. The care they require depends on the plant but as a guide, position sun-loving plants nearer the windows, shade-lovers further away, and maintain high humidity levels by standing your plants on trays of moist gravel and misting them regularly. Some plants, such as moth orchids, *Phalaenopsis*, require good light but not direct sunlight. This can be achieved by positioning them on a north-facing window, or on a shelf close to a bright window. Also watch out for pests, which can flourish in the favourable conditions you provide.

Finding areas that provide optimal growing conditions for house plants indoors can difficult, so it is worth making best use of them where they occur. A good approach is to plant 'community planters' and grow plants that enjoy similar conditions together in a single container. This is ideal for sun-loving cacti, as well as epiphytic orchids and bromeliads that need high humidity, and insectivorous plants which prefer very moist soil.

MAKING AN ORCHID PLANTER

Orchids, such as *Colmanara* Masai gx 'Red', all require particular conditions to perform at their best. Where you have a suitable spot indoors, take full advantage of it and position two or more plants in the same container, at least while they're in flower. This will serve as a temporary community-planter, which will benefit the plants, and also create a more attractive display than growing them as individual specimens.

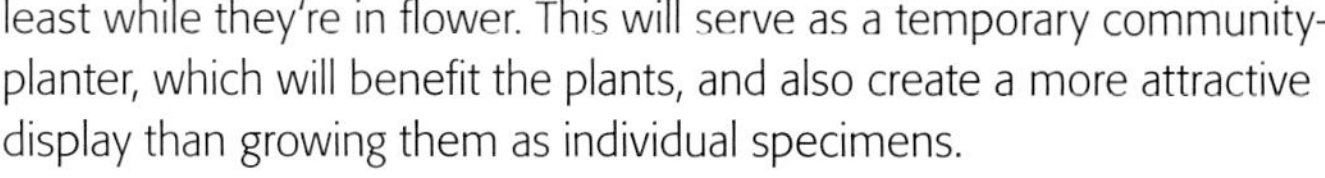

The completed planter

1 Make a base
Fill the base of a large, plastic-lined container with clay pebbles to hold the orchids in place, and to provide drainage and humidity. In a permanent community planter you should use a suitable compost mix.

2 Position the plants
Place the orchids into the container, making sure the top of their pots sit just below the rim. Ensure the plants are upright and facing the right direction, before adding more pebbles to hold the plants in place.

3 Dress the top
Add a layer of moss or decorative material around the orchids to disguise their pots below. This will also help maintain humidity, although if you use natural moss, it will need to be sprayed regularly to keep it healthy.

WHITE

Syzygium paniculatum
(Australian brush cherry)
Evergreen tree with glossy leaves, coppery when young. Has creamy-white flowers, with reddish sepals, and fragrant, rose-purple fruits. **H** 10m (30ft) or more, **S** 3–10m (10–30ft). Min. 10°C (50°F).

***Ficus elastica* 'Doescheri'**
(Rubber plant)
Strong-growing, evergreen, upright then spreading tree with oblong to oval, leathery, lustrous, deep green leaves, patterned with grey-green, yellow and white. **H** 30–60m (100–200ft), **S** 20–60m (70–200ft). Min. 10°C (50°F).

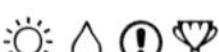

Agonis flexuosa
(Peppermint tree, Willow myrtle)
Evergreen, weeping tree. Aromatic, lance-shaped, leathery leaves are bronze-red when young. In spring–summer, mature trees bear masses of small, white flowers. **H** 6–12m (20–40ft), **S** 5–10m (15–30ft). Min. 10ºC (50ºF).

***Ficus benjamina* 'Variegata'**
Evergreen, dense, round-headed, weeping tree, often with aerial roots. Has slender, pointed, lustrous leaves that are rich green with white variegation. **H** 30m (100ft) or more, **S** 15m (50ft) or more. Min. 15–18°C (59–64°F).

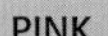

PINK

Dombeya x cayeuxii **(Pink snowball)**
Evergreen, bushy tree with rounded, toothed, hairy leaves to 20cm (8in) long. Pink flowers appear in pendent, ball-like clusters in winter or spring. **H** 3–5m (10–15ft), **S** 2–3m (6–10ft). Min. 10–13ºC (50–55ºF).

Chorisia speciosa **(Floss silk tree)**
Fast-growing, deciduous tree, the trunk and branches studded with thick, conical thorns. Pink to burgundy flowers appear as indented, light green leaves fall. **H** 15m (50ft), **S** 1.5m (5ft). Min. 15°C (59°F).

Bauhinia variegata
Deciduous, rounded tree with broadly oval, deeply notched leaves. Fragrant, magenta to lavender flowers, to 10cm (4in) across, appear in winter–spring, sometimes later. **H** 8–12m (25–40ft), **S** 3–8m (10–25ft). Min. 15–18ºC (59–64ºF).

RED

Metrosideros excelsa **(New Zealand Christmas tree, Pohutukawa)**
Evergreen, wide-spreading tree. Oval, grey-green leaves are white felted beneath. Bears showy tufts of crimson stamens in winter. **H** to 20m (70ft), **S** 10–20m (30–70ft). Min. 5°C (41°F).

Brachychiton acerifolius
(Illawarra flame tree)
Deciduous tree with clusters of bright scarlet flowers in late winter, spring or summer before 3–7-lobed, lustrous leaves develop. **H** 15–35m (50–120ft), **S** 8–12m (25–40ft). Min. 7–10°C (45–50°F).

Grevillea banksii
Evergreen, loosely branched tree or tall shrub. Has leaves divided into 5–11 slender leaflets, silky-downy beneath. Spider-like, red flowers appear in dense heads intermittently throughout the year. **H** 1–10m (3–30ft), **S** 2–5m (6–15ft). Min. 10ºC (50ºF).

PURPLE

***Cordyline australis* 'Atropurpurea'**
Slow-growing, evergreen tree with purple to purplish-green leaves. Has terminal sprays of white flowers in summer and small, globular, white fruits in autumn. **H** 3–10m (10–30ft), **S** 1–4m (3–12ft). Min. 5°C (41°F).

Jacaranda mimosifolia
Fast-growing, deciduous, rounded tree with fern-like leaves of many tiny, bright green leaflets. Has trusses of vivid blue to blue-purple flowers in spring and early summer. **H** 15m (50ft), **S** 7–10m (22–30ft). Min. 7°C (45°F).

SILVER

***Leucadendron argenteum* (Silver tree)**
Evergreen, conical to columnar tree, spreading with age. Leaves are covered with long, silky, white hairs. Has insignificant flowers set in silvery bracts in autumn–winter. **H** 6–10m (20–30ft), **S** 2–4m (6–12ft). Min. 7°C (45°F).

***Dracaena draco* (Dragon tree)**
Slow-growing, evergreen tree with a wide-branched head. Has stiff, lance-shaped, grey- or blue-green leaves. Mature trees bear clusters of orange fruits from mid- to late summer. **H** 3–10m (10–30ft) or more, **S** 2–8m (6–25ft) or more. Min. 13°C (55°F).

GREEN

***Firmiana simplex* (Chinese parasol tree)**
Robust, deciduous tree with large, lobed leaves, small, showy, lemon-yellow flowers and papery, leaf-like fruits. **H** 15m (50ft), **S** 10m (30ft). Min. 2°C (36°F).

***Meryta sinclairii* (Puka, Pukanui)**
Evergreen, round-headed tree with large, glossy, deep green leaves. Greenish flowers appear sporadically in spring to autumn, followed by berry-like, black fruits. **H** 10m (39ft), **S** 5m (15ft). Min. 5°C (41°F).

***Livistona chinensis* (Chinese fan palm, Chinese fountain palm)**
Slow-growing, evergreen palm with a stout trunk. Has fan-shaped, glossy leaves, 1–3m (3–10ft) across. Mature trees bear loose clusters of berry-like, black fruits in autumn. **H** 12m (40ft), **S** 5m (15ft). Min. 7°C (45°F).

***Beaucarnea recurvata* (Elephant's foot, Pony-tail)**
Slow-growing, evergreen tree or shrub with a sparsely branched stem. Recurving leaves, 1m (3ft) long, persist after turning brown. **H** 4–8m (12–25ft), **S** 2–4m (6–12ft). Min. 7°C (45°F).

Corynocarpus laevigatus
Evergreen, upright tree, spreading with age. Has leathery leaves and clusters of small, greenish flowers in spring–summer. Plum-like, orange fruits appear in winter. **H** 10–15m (30–50ft), **S** 2–5m (6–15ft). Min. 7–10°C (45–50°F).

***Washingtonia robusta* (Thread palm)**
Fast-growing, evergreen palm with large, fan-shaped leaves and, in summer, tiny, creamy-white flowers in large, long-stalked sprays. Black berries appear in winter–spring. **H** 25m (80ft), **S** 2.5–5m (8–15ft). Min. 10°C (50°F).

GREEN

***Dracaena marginata* 'Tricolor'**
Slow-growing, evergreen, upright tree or shrub with narrow, strap-shaped, cream-striped, rich green leaves, prominently edged with red. **H** 2–5m (6–15ft), **S** 1–3m (3–10ft). Min. 13°C (55°F).

Cyathea australis
(Australian tree fern)
Evergreen, upright tree fern with a robust, almost black trunk. Finely divided leaves, 2–4m (6–12ft) long, are light green, bluish beneath. **H** 1–3m (3–10ft), **S** 3–5m (10–15ft). Min. 13°C (55°F).

Ficus benghalensis **(Banyan)**
Evergreen, wide-spreading tree with trunk-like prop roots. Has oval, leathery leaves, rich green with pale veins, to 20cm (8in) long, and small, fig-like, brown fruits. **H** 20–30m (70–100ft), **S** 200m (700ft). Min. 15–18°C (59–64°F).

Archontophoenix alexandrae
(Alexandra palm, Northern bungalow palm)
Evergreen palm with feather-shaped, arching leaves. Mature trees bear sprays of small, white or cream flowers. **H** 25m (80ft), **S** 5–7m (15–22ft). Min. 15°C (59°F).

Schefflera actinophylla
(Queensland umbrella tree)
Evergreen, upright tree with large, spreading leaves of 5–16 leaflets. Has large sprays of small, dull red flowers in summer or autumn. **H** 12m (40ft), **S** 6m (20ft). Min. 16°C (61°F).

Dypsis lutescens
(Golden-feather palm, Yellow palm)
Evergreen, suckering palm, forming clumps of robust, cane-like stems. Has long, arching leaves of slender, yellowish-green leaflets. **H** 9m (28ft), **S** 6m (20ft). Min. 16°C (61°F).

YELLOW

Tecoma stans
(Yellow bells, Yellow elder)
Evergreen, rounded, upright tree or large shrub. Leaves have 5–13 leaflets. Has funnel-shaped, yellow flowers from spring to autumn. **H** 5–9m (15–28ft), **S** 3–5m (10–15ft). Min. 13°C (55°F).

Tabebui chrysotricha
(Golden trumpet tree)
Deciduous, round-headed tree with dark green leaves, divided into 3–5 oval leaflets, and rich yellow flowers, 7cm (3in) long, borne in late winter or early spring. **H** 25m (80ft), **S** 18m (60ft). Min. 16–18°C (61–4°F).

ORANGE

Plumeria rubra (Frangipani)
Deciduous, spreading tree or large shrub, sparingly branched. Has fragrant flowers, in shades of yellow, orange, pink, red and white, in summer–autumn. **H** 7m (22ft), **S** 5m (15ft). Min. 13°C (55°F).

Spathodea campanulata (African tulip tree, Flame-of-the-forest)
Evergreen, showy tree. Leaves have 9–19 deep green leaflets. Clusters of tulip-shaped, scarlet or orange-red flowers appear intermittently. **H** 18–25m (60–80ft), **S** 10–18m (30–60ft). Min. 16–18°C (61–64°F).

WHITE

Chamelaucium uncinatum [white] (Geraldton waxflower)
Evergreen, wiry-stemmed, bushy shrub. Each needle-like leaf has a tiny, hooked tip. Flowers ranging from deep rose-purple to pink, lavender or white appear in late winter or spring. **H** 2–5m (6–15ft), **S** 2–4m (6–12ft). Min. 5°C (41°F).

Azorina vidalii
Evergreen sub-shrub with erect stems. Has coarsely serrated, glossy, dark green leaves and racemes of bell-shaped, white or pink flowers in spring and summer. **H** and **S** 40–60cm (16–24in). Min. 5°C (41°F).

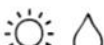

Westringia fruticosa (Australian rosemary)
Evergreen, rounded, compact shrub. Crowded leaves, in whorls of 4, are white-felted beneath. White to palest blue flowers open in spring–summer. **H** and **S** 1–1.5m (3–5ft). Min. 5–7°C (41–45°F).

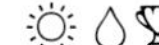

Eriogonum arborescens
Evergreen, sparingly branched shrub. Small leaves have recurved edges and woolly, white undersides. Leafy umbels of small, white or pink flowers appear from spring to autumn. **H** and **S** 60cm–150cm (2–5ft). Min. 5°C (41°F).

Sparrmannia africana (African hemp)
Evergreen, erect shrub or small tree. Has large, shallowly lobed leaves and clusters of white flowers, with yellow and red-purple stamens, in late spring and summer. **H** 3–6m (10–20ft), **S** 2–4m (6–12ft). Min. 7°C (45°F).

Acokanthera oblongifolia (Wintersweet)
Evergreen, rounded shrub. Has fragrant, white or pinkish flowers in late winter and spring and poisonous, black fruits in autumn. **H** 3–6m (10–20ft), **S** 1.5–4m (5–12ft). Min. 10°C (50°F).

***Carissa macrocarpa* 'Tuttlei'**
Evergreen, compact and spreading shrub with thorny stems and leathery leaves. Has fragrant flowers in spring–summer and edible, plum-like, red fruits in autumn. **H** 2–3m (6–10ft) or more, **S** 3m (10ft) or more. Min. 13°C (55°F).

Dracaena sanderiana (Ribbon plant)
Evergreen, upright shrub with seldom branching, cane-like stems. Lance-shaped leaves, 15–25cm (6–10in) long, are pale to grey-green, with bold, creamy-white edges. **H** 1.5m (5ft), **S** 40–80cm (16–32in). Min. 13°C (55°F).

Calliandra eriophylla (Fairy duster)
Evergreen, stiff, dense shrub. Leaves have numerous tiny leaflets. From late spring to autumn has pompons of tiny, pink-anthered, white florets, followed by brown seed pods. **H** 1m (3ft), **S** 80cm (32in). Min. 13°C (55°F).

WHITE

***Pandanus tectorius* 'Veitchii'** (Veitch's screw pine)
Evergreen, upright, arching shrub with rosettes of long, light green leaves that have spiny, white to cream margins.
H 3–6m (10–20ft), **S** 2–4m (6–12ft).
Min. 13–16°C (55–61°F).

***Gardenia jasminoides* 'Veitchii'**
Fairly slow-growing, evergreen, leafy shrub with oval, glossy leaves up to 10cm (4in) long and fragrant, double, white flowers from summer to winter.
H 2–12m (6–40ft), **S** 1–3m (3–10ft).
Min. 15°C (59°F).

***Dracaena fragrans* Deremensis Group 'Warneckei'**
Slow-growing, evergreen shrub. Erect to arching, lance-shaped leaves are banded grey-green and cream.
H 5–15m (15–50ft), **S** 1–3m (3–10ft).
Min. 15–18°C (59–64°F).

PINK

Myoporum parvifolium
Evergreen, spreading to prostrate shrub with semi-succulent leaves. In summer has clusters of small, honey-scented flowers, white or pink with purple spots, and tiny, purple fruits in autumn.
H 60cm (24in), **S** 60–90cm (24–36in).
Min. 2–5°C (36–41°F).

***Plectranthus fructicosus* 'James'**
Evergreen, erect, shrub. Purple stems bear broadly ovate, coarsely toothed, fleshy, purple-veined, mid-green leaves. Bears terminal panicles of tubular pink flowers, with darker spots, to 30cm (12in) long, in late summer. **H** and **S** 1.5m (5ft).
Min. 5°C (41°F).

***Chamelaucium uncinatum* [pink]** (Geraldton waxflower)
Evergreen, wiry-stemmed, bushy shrub. Each needle-like leaf has a tiny, hooked tip. Flowers ranging from deep rose-purple to pink, lavender or white appear in late winter or spring. **H** 2–5m (6–15ft), **S** 2–4m (6–12ft). Min. 5°C (41°F).

Protea cynaroides (King protea)
Evergreen, bushy, rounded shrub. Water lily-shaped flower heads, 13–20cm (5–8in) wide, with silky-haired, petal-like, pink to red bracts, appear in spring–summer. Leaves are oval and mid- to dark green. **H** and **S** 1–2m (3–6ft).
Min. 5–7°C (41–45°F).

Protea neriifolia
Evergreen, bushy, upright shrub with narrow leaves. Flower heads, about 13cm (5in) long, are red, pink or white, the bracts tipped with tufts of black hair, and appear in spring-summer.
H and **S** 3m (10ft). Min. 5–7°C (41–45°F).

***Calliandra haematocephala* [pink form]**
Evergreen, spreading shrub. Leaves have 16–24 narrowly oval leaflets. Flower heads consist of many pink-stamened florets from late autumn to spring. **H** 3–6m (10–20ft), **S** 2–4m (6–12ft).
Min. 7°C (45°F).

Pimelea ferruginea
Evergreen, dense, rounded shrub with tiny, recurved, deep green leaves. Small, tubular, rich pink flowers appear in dense heads in spring or early summer.
H 1–2m (3–6ft), **S** 1–1.5m (3–5ft).
Min. 7°C (45°F).

Chorizema ilicifolium (Holly flame pea)
Evergreen, sprawling or upright shrub, with spiny-toothed, leathery leaves. Has spikes of bicoloured, orange and pinkish-red flowers in spring–summer.
H and **S** 1–3m (3–10ft). Min. 7°C (45°F).

Nerium oleander (Oleander)
Evergreen, upright, bushy shrub with leathery, deep green leaves. Clusters of salver-form, pink, white, red, apricot or yellow flowers appear from spring to autumn, often on dark red stalks. **H** 2–6m (6–20ft), **S** 1–3m (3–10ft). Min. 10°C (50°F).

***Hibiscus rosa-sinensis* 'The President'**
Evergreen, bushy shrub with toothed, oval, glossy, dark green leaves. In summer bears large, magenta-centred, bright pink flowers with prominent, yellow anthers. **H** 2.5–5m (8–15ft), **S** 1.5–3m (5–10ft). Min. 15°C (59°F).

Euphorbia pulcherrima (Poinsettia)
Evergreen, sparingly branched shrub. Has small, greenish-red flowers surrounded by bright red, pink, yellow or white bracts from late autumn to spring. **H** 2–4m (6–12ft), **S** 1–2.5m (3–8ft). Min. 15°C (59°F).

Epacris impressa (Australian heath)
Evergreen, usually erect, fairly open, heath-like shrub with short, red-tipped leaves. Tubular, pink or red flowers appear in late winter and spring. **H** 30–120cm (12–48in), **S** 30–90cm (12–36in). Min. 5°C (41°F).

Justicia carnea (King's crown)
Evergreen, sparingly branched shrub with velvety-haired leaves. Produces spikes of pink to rose-purple flowers in summer–autumn. **H** 2m (6ft), **S** 1m (3ft). Min. 10–15°C (50–59°F).

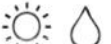

Justicia brandegeeana (Shrimp plant)
Evergreen, rounded shrub intermittently, but mainly in summer, producing white flowers surrounded by shrimp-pink bracts. **H** 1m (3ft), **S** 60–90cm (24–36in). Min. 10–15°C (50–59°F).

Medinilla magnifica
Evergreen, upright shrub, with sparingly produced, 4-angled, robust stems and boldly veined leaves. Pink to coral-red flowers hang in long trusses beneath large, pink bracts in spring–summer. **H** 1–2m (3–6ft), **S** 60cm–150cm (2–5ft). Min. 16–18°C (61–64°F).

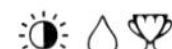

Greyia sutherlandii
Deciduous or semi-evergreen, rounded shrub. Coarsely serrated, leathery leaves turn red in autumn. Spikes of small, bright red flowers appear in spring with new foliage. **H** 2–5m (6–15ft), **S** 1.5–3m (5–10ft). Min. 7–10°C (45–50°F).

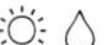

RED

Nymania capensis
Evergreen, more or less rounded, rigidly branched shrub or small tree. In spring has flowers with upright, pink to rose-purple petals. Bears papery, inflated, red fruits in autumn. **H** 2–3m (6–10ft) or more, **S** 1–2m (3–6ft). Min. 7–10°C (45–50°F).

Euphorbia milii (Crown of thorns)
Fairly slow-growing, mainly evergreen, spiny, semi-succulent shrub. Clusters of tiny, yellowish flowers, enclosed by 2 bright red bracts, open intermittently during the year. **H** 1m (3ft) or more, **S** 45cm (18in). Min. 8°C (46°F).

Solanum betaceum (Tree tomato)
Evergreen, sparingly branched shrub or small tree, upright when young, with large, heart-shaped, rich green leaves. Has edible, tomato-like, red fruits from summer to winter. **H** 2–3m (6–10ft), **S** 1–2m (3–6ft). Min. 10°C (50°F).

Sutherlandia frutescens
Evergreen, upright shrub. Has leaves of 13–21 grey-haired, deep green leaflets; bright red flowers in late spring and summer are followed by pale green, later red-flushed, inflated seed pods. **H** 0.6–2m (2–6ft), **S** 1–1.5m (3–5ft). Min. 10°C (50°F).

Bouvardia ternifolia
(Scarlet trompetilla)
Mainly evergreen, bushy, upright shrub with leaves in whorls of 3. Has tubular, bright scarlet flowers from summer to early winter. **H** 60–90cm (24–36in), **S** 30–60cm (12–24in). Min. 7–10°C (45–50°F).

Leucospermum reflexum
Evergreen, erect shrub with ascending branchlets. Has small, blue-grey or grey-green leaves. Slender, tubular, crimson flowers with long styles are carried in tight, rounded heads in spring–summer. **H** 3m (10ft), **S** 2–4m (6–12ft). Min. 10°C (50°F).

Ixora coccinea
Evergreen, rounded shrub with glossy, dark green leaves to 10cm (4in) long. Small, tubular, red, pink, orange or yellow flowers appear in dense heads in summer. **H** 2.5m (8ft), **S** 1.5–2m (5–6ft). Min. 13–16°C (55–61°F).

Boronia megastigma
Evergreen, well branched, wiry-stemmed shrub. Small leaves have 3–5 narrow leaflets. Fragrant, bowl-shaped, brownish-purple and yellow flowers hang from leaf axils in late winter and spring. **H** 1–3m (3–10ft), **S** 1–2m (3–6ft). Min. 7–10°C (45–50°F).

Banksia coccinea
Evergreen, dense shrub with toothed, dark green leaves, grey-green beneath. Flower heads comprising clusters of bright red flowers with prominent styles and stigmas are borne in late winter and spring. **H** 4–8m (12–25ft), **S** 1.5–4m (5–12ft). Min. 10°C (50°F).

Ardisia crenata
(Coralberry, Spiceberry)
Evergreen, upright, open shrub. Has fragrant, star-shaped, white flowers in early summer, followed by long-lasting, bright red fruits. **H** to 2m (6ft), **S** 60cm (24in). Min. 10°C (50°F).

Acalypha wilkesiana
(Copperleaf, Jacob's coat)
Evergreen, bushy shrub. Oval, serrated leaves are 10cm (4in) or more long, rich copper-green, variably splashed with shades of red. **H** 2m (6ft), **S** 1–2m (3–6ft). Min. 16°C (61°F).

Prostanthera ovalifolia
Evergreen, bushy, rounded shrub with tiny, sweetly aromatic, oval, thick-textured leaves. Cup-shaped, 2-lipped, purple flowers appear in short, leafy racemes in spring–summer. **H** 2.5–4m (8–12ft), **S** 1.5–2.5m (5–8ft). Min. 5°C (41°F).

***Dodonaea viscosa* 'Purpurea'**
Evergreen, bushy shrub or tree. Firm-textured leaves are flushed copper-purple. Has clusters of small, reddish or purplish seed capsules in late summer or autumn. Makes a good hedge in a windy site. **H** 1–5m (3–15ft), **S** 1–3m (3–10ft). Min. 5°C (41°F).

Tibouchina urvilleana (Glory bush)
Evergreen, slender-branched shrub. Velvet-haired leaves are prominently veined. Has satiny, blue-purple flowers in clusters from summer to early winter. **H** 3–6m (10–20ft), **S** 2–3m (6–10ft). Min. 7°C (45°F).

Polygala x dalmaisiana
Evergreen, erect shrub with small, greyish-green leaves. White-veined, rich purple flowers appear from late spring to autumn. **H** and **S** 1–2.5m (3–8ft). Min. 7°C (45°F).

Iochroma cyaneum
Evergreen, semi-upright, slender-branched shrub. Tubular, deep purple-blue flowers, with flared mouths, appear in dense clusters from late autumn to early summer. **H** 3m (10ft), **S** 1.5–2m (5–6ft). Min. 7–10°C (45–50°F).

***Brunfelsia pauciflora* 'Macrantha'**
Evergreen, spreading shrub with leathery leaves. Blue-purple flowers, ageing to white in about 3 days, appear from winter to summer. **H** 1–3m (3–10ft), **S** 0.6–1.5m (2–5ft). Min. 10–13°C (50–55°F).

Sabal minor (Dwarf palmetto)
Evergreen, suckering fan palm with stems mainly underground. Has leaves of 20–30 green or grey-green lobes. Erect sprays of small, white flowers are followed by shiny, black fruits. **H** 1–2m (3–6ft), **S** 3m (10ft). Min. 5°C (41°F).

Portulacaria afra (Elephant bush)
Semi-evergreen, upright shrub with horizontal branches and tiny, fleshy, bright green leaves. Clusters of pale pink flowers appear in late spring and summer. **H** 2–3m (6–10ft), **S** 1.5m (5ft). Min. 7–10°C (45–50°F).

Encephalartos ferox
Slow-growing, evergreen, palm-like plant, almost trunkless for many years. Feather-shaped leaves, 60–180cm (2–6ft) long, have many serrated and spine-tipped, leathery, greyish leaflets. **H** 1m (3ft), **S** 2–3m (6–10ft). Min. 10–13°C (50–55°F).

Schefflera elegantissima
(False aralia)
Evergreen, upright, open shrub. Large leaves have 7–10 coarsely toothed, lustrous, grey-green, sometimes bronze-tinted, leaflets. **H** 8–15m (25–50ft), **S** 2–3m (6–10ft). Min. 13°C (55°F).

Cycas revoluta (Japanese sago palm)
Slow-growing, evergreen, palm-like plant that may produce several trunks. Leaves have spine-tipped leaflets with rolled margins. Bears tight clusters of reddish fruits in autumn. **H** and **S** 1–2m (3–6ft). Min. 13°C (55°F).

Mimosa pudica
(Humble plant, Sensitive plant)
Short-lived, evergreen shrub with prickly stems; needs support. Fern-like leaves fold when touched. Has minute, pale mauve-pink flowers in summer–autumn. **H** 30–75cm (12–30in), **S** 40–90cm (16–36in). Min. 13–16°C (55–61°F).

GREEN

Rhapis excelsa **(Bamboo palm, Slender lady palm)**
Evergreen fan palm, eventually forming clumps. Leaves are 20–30cm (8–12in) long, composed of 20 or more narrow, glossy, deep green lobes in fan formation. **H** and **S** 1.5–5m (5–15ft). Min. 15°C (59°F).

Philodendron bipinnatifidum
Evergreen, unbranched shrub. Glossy leaves, to 60cm (2ft) or more long, are divided into many finger-like lobes. Occasionally produces greenish-white spathes. **H** and **S** 5m (15ft). Min. 15–18°C (59–64°F).

Ficus deltoidea **(Mistletoe fig)**
Slow-growing, evergreen, bushy shrub with bright green leaves, red-brown-tinted beneath. Bears small, greenish-white fruits that mature to dull yellow. **H** 5–7m (15–22ft), **S** 1–3m (3–10ft). Min. 15–18°C (59–64°F).

Polyscias filicifolia **(Fern-leaf aralia)**
Evergreen, erect, sparingly branched shrub. Leaves are 30cm (12in) long and are divided into many small, serrated, bright green leaflets. **H** 2–2.5m (6–8ft), **S** 1m (3ft). Min. 15–18°C (59–64°F).

***Polyscias guilfoylei* 'Victoriae'** **(Lace aralia)**
Slow-growing, evergreen, rounded shrub or small tree with leaves that are divided into several oval to rounded, serrated, white-margined, deep green leaflets. **H** 1.5m (5ft), **S** 80cm (32in). Min. 15–18°C (59–64°F).

Chamaedorea elegans **(Dwarf mountain palm, Parlour palm)**
Evergreen, slender palm, suckering with age. Feather-shaped leaves of many glossy leaflets are 60–100cm (2–3ft) long. **H** 2–3m (6–10ft), **S** 1–2m (3–6ft). Min. 18°C (64°F).

YELLOW

x *Citrofortunella microcarpa* **(Calamondin)**
Evergreen, bushy shrub with leathery, leaves. Intermittently has tiny, fragrant flowers followed by orange-yellow fruits. **H** 3–6m (10–20ft), **S** 2–3m (6–10ft). Min. 5–10°C (41–50°F).

Hibbertia cuneiformis
Evergreen, upright, bushy shrub with small, oval leaves, serrated at tips. Has small clusters of bright yellow flowers, with spreading petals, in spring–summer. **H** 1–2m (3–6ft), **S** 1–1.5m (3–5ft). Min. 5–7°C (41–45°F).

Acacia pulchella **(Western prickly Moses)**
Semi-evergreen or deciduous shrub of diffuse habit, with spiny twigs and rich green foliage. Tiny, deep yellow flowers appear in dense, globular heads in spring. **H** 0.6–1.5m (2–5ft), **S** 1–2m (3–6ft). Min. 5–7°C (41–45°F).

Senna corymbosa

Vigorous, evergreen or semi-evergreen shrub. Leaves have 4–6 oval, bright green leaflets; sprays of bowl-shaped, rich yellow flowers appear in late summer. **H** 2–4m (6–12ft), **S** 1.5m–3m (5–10ft). Min. 7°C (45°F).

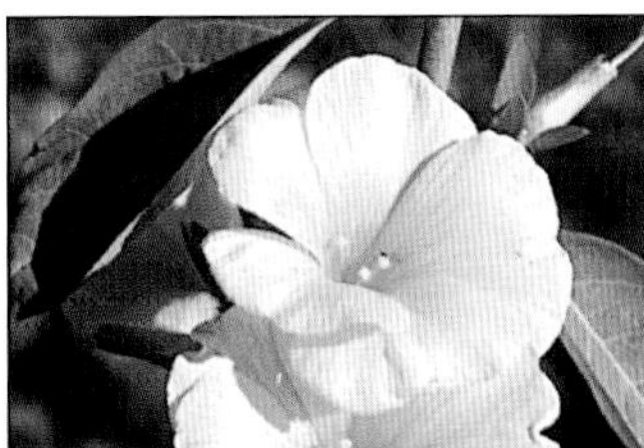

Reinwardtia indica (Yellow flax)

Evergreen, upright sub-shrub, branching from the base. Has greyish-green leaves and small clusters of yellow flowers mainly in summer but also during the year. **H** and **S** 60–90cm (24–36in). Min. 10°C (50°F).

Senna didymobotrya
(Golden wonder)

Evergreen, rounded, sometimes spreading shrub with leaves of several leaflets. Spikes of rich yellow flowers open from glossy, blackish-brown buds throughout the year. **H** 2.5m (8ft), **S** 1.5–3m (5–10ft). Min. 13°C (55°F).

Pachystachys lutea (Lollipop plant)

Evergreen, loose, more or less rounded shrub, often grown annually from cuttings. Has tubular, white flowers in tight, golden-bracted spikes in spring–summer. **H** 1m (3ft), **S** 45–75cm (18–30in). Min. 13°C (55°F).

Crotalaria agatiflora
(Canary-bird bush)

Evergreen, loose, somewhat spreading shrub with grey-green leaves. Racemes of greenish-yellow flowers appear in summer and also intermittently during the year. **H** 2–3m (6–10ft), **S** 1–2m (3–6ft). Min. 15°C (59°F).

ORANGE

Codiaeum variegatum* var. *pictum
(Croton)

Evergreen, erect, sparingly branched shrub. Leathery, glossy leaves vary greatly in size and shape, and are variegated with red, pink, orange or yellow. **H** 1–2m (3–6ft), **S** 0.6–1.5m (2–5ft). Min. 10–13°C (50–55°F).

Nematanthus gregarius

Evergreen, prostrate or slightly ascending shrub with fleshy, glossy leaves. Inflated, orange and yellow flowers appear mainly from spring to autumn. **H** 80cm (32in), **S** 90cm (36in) or more. Min. 13–15°C (55–59°F).

Isoplexis canariensis

Evergreen, rounded, sparingly branched shrub. Bears foxglove-like, yellow to red- or brownish-orange flowers in dense, upright spikes, to 30cm (12in) tall, in summer. **H** 1.5m (5ft), **S** 1m (3ft). Min. 7°C (45°F).

WHITE

Pandorea jasminoides (Bower vine)

Evergreen, woody-stemmed, twining climber with leaves of 5–9 leaflets. Has clusters of funnel-shaped, white flowers, with pink-flushed throats, from late winter to summer. **H** 5m (15ft). Min. 5°C (41°F).

Dioscorea dodecaneura
(Ornamental yam)

Evergreen, woody-stemmed, twining climber. Heart-shaped, olive-green leaves are 12–15cm (5–6in) long, marbled silver, paler green and brown, and are red beneath. **H** to 2m (6ft). Min. 5°C (41°F).

Beaumontia grandiflora
(Herald's trumpet)

Vigorous, evergreen, woody-stemmed, twining climber with rich green leaves that are hairy beneath. Has large, fragrant, white flowers from late spring to summer. **H** 8m (25ft). Min. 7–10°C (45–50°F).

WHITE

***Bougainvillea glabra* 'Snow White'**
Vigorous, evergreen or semi-evergreen, woody-stemmed, scrambling climber with oval leaves. In summer has clusters of white floral bracts with green veins. **H** to 5m (15ft). Min. 7–10°C (45–50°F).

***Epipremnum aureum* 'Marble Queen'**
Fairly fast-growing, evergreen, woody-stemmed, root climber. Leaves are marbled with white. Is less robust than the species. **H** 3–10m (10–30ft). Min. 15–18°C (59–64°F).

Clerodendrum thomsoniae
Vigorous, evergreen, woody-stemmed, scandent shrub with oval, rich green leaves. Flowers with crimson petals and bell-shaped, pure white calyces appear in clusters in summer. **H** 3m (10ft) or more. Min. 16°C (61°F).

Hoya lanceolata* subsp. *bella
Evergreen, woody-stemmed, trailing shrub with narrowly oval, pointed leaves. In summer bears tiny, star-shaped, white flowers, with red centres, in pendulous, flattened clusters. **H** 45cm (18in). Min. 10–12°C (50–54°F).

Stephanotis floribunda
(Madagascar jasmine)
Moderately vigorous, evergreen, woody-stemmed, twining climber with leathery, glossy leaves. Scented, waxy, white flowers appear in small clusters from spring to autumn. **H** 5m (15ft) or more. Min. 13–16°C (55–61°F).

Syngonium podophyllum
'Trileaf Wonder'
Evergreen, woody-stemmed, root climber with tufted stems and arrow-head-shaped leaves when young. Mature leaves have 3 glossy leaflets with pale green or silvery-grey veins. **H** 2m (6ft) or more. Min. 18°C (64°F).

PINK

Lophospermum erubescens
Evergreen, soft-stemmed, scandent, perennial climber, sometimes woody-stemmed, often grown as an annual. Stems and leaves are downy. Rose-pink flowers, 7cm (2¾in) long, are borne in summer–autumn. **H** to 3m (10ft) or more. Min. 5°C (41°F).

Hoya carnosa (Wax plant)
Moderately vigorous, evergreen, woody-stemmed, twining, root climber. Scented, star-shaped flowers, white, fading to pink, with deep pink centres, are borne in dense trusses in summer–autumn. **H** to 5m (15ft) or more. Min. 5–7°C (41–45°F).

Mandevilla splendens
Evergreen, woody-stemmed, twining climber. Has lustrous leaves and trumpet-shaped, rose-pink flowers, with yellow centres, appearing in late spring or early summer. **H** 3m (10ft). Min. 7–10°C (45–50°F).

TENDER AND EXOTIC PLANTS

***Mandevilla* x *amabilis* 'Alice du Pont'**
Vigorous, evergreen, woody-stemmed, twining climber with oval leaves. Has large clusters of trumpet-shaped, pink flowers in summer. **H** 3m (10ft) or more. Min. 7–10°C (45–50°F).

Distictis buccinatoria
(Mexican blood flower)
Vigorous, evergreen, woody-stemmed, tendril climber. Has trumpet-shaped, rose-crimson flowers, orange-yellow within, from early spring to summer. **H** to 5m (15ft) or more. Min. 5°C (41°F).

Clytostoma callistegioides
Fast-growing, evergreen, woody-stemmed, tendril climber. Each leaf has 2 oval leaflets and a tendril. Small, nodding clusters of purple-veined, lavender flowers, fading to pale pink, borne spring–summer. **H** to 5m (15ft). Min. 10–13°C (50–55°F).

Agapetes variegata* var. *macrantha
Evergreen or semi-evergreen, loose, scandent shrub that may be trained against supports. Has lance-shaped leaves and narrowly urn-shaped, white or pinkish-white flowers, patterned in red, in winter. **H** 1–2m (3–6ft). Min. 15–18°C (59–64°F).

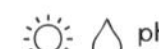

Tropaeolum tricolorum
Herbaceous climber with delicate stems, small tubers and 5–7-lobed leaves. Small, orange or yellow flowers with black-tipped, reddish- orange calyces are borne from early spring to early summer. **H** to 1m (3ft). Min. 5°C (41°F).

Agapetes serpens
Evergreen, arching to pendulous, scandent shrub, best grown with support as a perennial climber. Has small, lance-shaped, lustrous leaves and pendent flowers, rose-red with darker veins, in spring. **H** 2–3m (6–10ft). Min. 5°C (41°F).

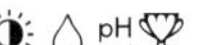

RED

Kennedia rubicunda
(Dusky coral pea)
Fast-growing, evergreen, woody-stemmed, twining climber with leaves divided into 3 leaflets. Coral-red flowers are borne in small trusses in spring–summer. **H** to 3m (10ft). Min. 5–7°C (41–45°F).

Quisqualis indica (Rangoon creeper)
Fairly fast-growing, deciduous or semi-evergreen, scandent shrub, often grown as an annual. From late spring to late summer has fragrant flowers, varying from orange to red, sometimes pink. **H** 3–5m (10–15ft). Min. 10°C (50°F).

Passiflora coccinea
(Red passion flower)
Vigorous, evergreen, woody-stemmed, tendril climber with rounded, oblong leaves. Has bright deep scarlet flowers, with red, pink and white crowns, from spring to autumn. **H** 3–4m (10–12ft). Min. 15°C (59°F).

PURPLE

Hoya macgillivrayi
Strong-growing, twining climber with thick stems and lustrous, dark green leaves. From spring to summer, bears large, cup-shaped, red-purple, purple or brownish-red flowers, with dark red, occasionally white-centred coronas. **H** 5–8m (15–25ft). Min. 7°C (45°F).

Ipomoea indica (Blue dawn flower)
Vigorous, perennial climber with evergreen, mid-green leaves. From late spring to autumn bears abundant, funnel-shaped, rich purple-blue to blue flowers, often maturing to purplish-red. **H** 6m (20ft) or more. Min. 7°C (45°F).

***Hardenbergia violacea* 'Happy Wanderer'**
Evergreen, woody-stemmed, twining climber. In spring, bears pendent panicles of deep mauve-purple flowers, with yellow marks on upper petals. **H** to 3m (10ft). Min. 7°C (45°F).

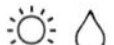

***Bougainvillea glabra* 'Sanderiana'**
Vigorous, mainly evergreen, woody-stemmed, scrambling climber. Rounded-oval, dark green leaves are edged with creamy-white. Has many bright purple floral bracts in summer. **H** to 5m (15ft). Min. 7–10°C (45–50°F).

Bougainvillea glabra
Vigorous, evergreen or semi-evergreen, woody-stemmed, scrambling climber with rounded-oval leaves. Clusters of floral bracts, in shades of cyclamen-purple, appear in summer. **H** to 5m (15ft). Min. 7–10°C (45–50°F).

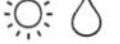

Passiflora quadrangularis
(Giant granadilla)
Strong-growing, evergreen, woody-stemmed climber with angled, winged stems. White, pink, red or pale violet flowers, the crowns banded white and deep purple, appear mainly in summer. **H** 5–8m (15–25ft). Min. 10°C (50°F).

Aristolochia littoralis (Calico flower)
Fast-growing, evergreen, woody-stemmed, twining climber with heart-to kidney-shaped leaves. Heart-shaped, 12cm (5in) wide flowers, maroon with white marbling, are carried in summer. **H** to 7m (22ft). Min. 13°C (55°F).

Gynura aurantiaca (Velvet plant)
Evergreen, woody-based, soft-stemmed, semi-scrambling climber or lax shrub with purple-haired stems and leaves. Clusters of daisy-like, orange-yellow flower heads are borne in winter. **H** 2–3m (6–10ft), less as a shrub. Min. 16°C (61°F).

Solanum seaforthianum
(Italian jasmine, St Vincent lilac)
Evergreen, scrambling climber with nodding clusters of star-shaped, blue, purple, pink, or white flowers, with yellow stamens, from spring to autumn, followed by scarlet fruits. **H** 2–3m (6–10ft). Min. 7°C (45°F).

Solanum wendlandii
Robust, mainly evergreen, prickly-stemmed, scrambling climber with oblong, variably lobed leaves. Lavender flowers appear in late summer and autumn. **H** 3–6m (10–20ft). Min. 10°C (50°F).

Petrea volubilis
Strong-growing, evergreen, woody-stemmed, twining climber with elliptic, rough-textured leaves and deep violet and lilac-blue flowers carried in simple or branched spikes from late winter to late summer. **H** 6m (20ft) or more. Min. 13–15°C (55–59°F).

Cissus antarctica (Kangaroo vine)
Moderately vigorous, evergreen, woody-stemmed, tendril climber. Oval, pointed, coarsely serrated leaves are lustrous, rich green. **H** to 5m (15ft). Min. 7°C (45°F).

Asparagus scandens
Evergreen, scrambling climber with lax stems and short, curved, leaf-like shoots in whorls of 3. Tiny, nodding, white flowers appear in clusters of 2–3 in summer, followed by red fruits. **H** 1m (3ft) or more. Min. 10°C (50°F).

Tetrastigma voinierianum
(Chestnut vine)
Strong-growing, evergreen, woody-stemmed, tendril climber. Young stems and leaves are rust-coloured and hairy; mature leaves turn lustrous, deep green above. **H** 10m (30ft) or more. Min. 15–18°C (59–64°F).

Monstera deliciosa
(Swiss-cheese plant)
Robust, evergreen, woody-stemmed, root climber with large-lobed, holed leaves, 40–90cm (16–36in) long. Mature plants bear cream spathes, followed by scented, edible fruits. **H** to 6m (20ft). Min. 15–18°C (59–64°F).

Syngonium podophyllum
Evergreen, woody-stemmed, root climber with tufted stems and arrowhead-shaped leaves when young. Mature plants have leaves of 7–9 glossy leaflets up to 30cm (12in) long. **H** 2m (6ft). Min. 16–18°C (61–64°F).

Philodendron scandens (Heart leaf)
Fairly fast-growing, evergreen, woody-based, root climber. Rich green leaves are 10–15cm (4–6in) long when young, to 30cm (12in) long on mature plants. **H** 4m (12ft) or more. Min. 15–18°C (59–64°F).

YELLOW

***Tecoma capensis* 'Aurea'**
Erect, scrambling, evergreen shrub or climber with lustrous, mid- to dark green leaves. Racemes, to 15cm (6in) long, of slender, tubular, yellow flowers, to 5cm (2in) long, are borne mainly in summer. **H** 4m (12ft), **S** 2m (6ft). Min. 5°C (41°F).

Solandra maxima
(Copa de oro, Golden-chalice vine)
Strong-growing, evergreen, woody-stemmed, scrambling climber with glossy leaves. In spring–summer bears fragrant, pale yellow, later golden flowers. **H** 7–10m (23–30ft) or more. Min. 13–16°C (55–61°F).

Thunbergia mysorensis
Evergreen, woody-stemmed, twining climber. Has narrow leaves and pendent spikes of flowers with yellow tubes and recurved, reddish-brown lobes from spring to autumn. **H** 6m (20ft). Min. 15°C (59°F).

Allamanda cathartica* 'Hendersonii'
Fast-growing, evergreen, woody-stemmed, scrambling climber. Has lance-shaped leaves in whorls and trumpet-shaped, rich bright yellow flowers in summer–autumn. **H** to 5m (15ft). Min. 13–15°C (55–59°F).

***Senecio macroglossus* 'Variegatus'**
Evergreen, woody-stemmed, twining climber with triangular, fleshy leaves, bordered in white to cream, and, mainly in winter, daisy-like, cream flower heads. **H** 3m (10ft). Min. 7°C (45°F).

Stigmaphyllon ciliatum
Fast growing, evergreen, woody-stemmed, twining climber with heart-shaped, pale green leaves fringed with hairs. Bright yellow flowers with ruffled petals appear in spring–summer. **H** 5m (15ft) or more. Min. 15–18°C (59–64°F).

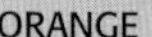

ORANGE

Canarina canariensis
(Canary Island bellflower)
Herbaceous, tuberous, scrambling climber with triangular, serrated leaves. Has waxy, orange flowers with red veins from late autumn to spring. **H** 2–3m (6–10ft). Min. 7°C (45°F).

Streptosolen jamesonii
(Marmalade bush)
Evergreen or semi-evergreen, loosely scrambling shrub. Has oval, finely corrugated leaves and, mainly in spring–summer, many bright orange flowers. **H** 2–3m (6–10ft). Min. 7°C (45°F).

***Pyrostegia venusta* (Flame flower, Flame vine, Golden shower)**
Fast-growing, evergreen, woody-stemmed, tendril climber with clusters of tubular, golden-orange flowers from autumn to spring. **H** 10m (30ft) or more. Min. 13–15°C (55–59°F).

WHITE

***Streptocarpus* 'Crystal Ice'**
Herbaceous, stemless, basal-rosetted perennial with long, narrowly strap-shaped, wrinkled, lightly hairy, green leaves. Produces clusters of 7–13 funnel-shaped, white flowers, with blue veins, in winter. **H** 40cm (16in), **S** 30cm (12in). Min. 5°C (41°F).

Coelogyne cristata
Evergreen, epiphytic orchid for a cool greenhouse. In winter produces crisp, white flowers, 5cm (2in) across, and marked orange on each lip. Narrowly oval leaves are 8–10cm (3–4in) long. Needs good light in summer. **H** 30cm (12in), **S** 60cm (24in). Min. 10°C (50°F).

***Chlorophytum comosum* 'Vittatum'**
Evergreen, tufted, rosette-forming perennial. Long, narrow, lance-shaped, creamy-white leaves have green stripes and margins. Irregularly has small, star-shaped, white flowers on thin stems. **H** and **S** 30cm (12in). Min. 5°C (41°F).

Pilea cadierei (Aluminium plant)
Evergreen, bushy perennial with broadly oval leaves, each with a sharply pointed tip and raised, silvery patches that appear quilted. Has insignificant, greenish flowers. **H** and **S** 30cm (12in). Min. 10°C (50°F).

Peperomia caperata (Emerald ripple)
Evergreen, bushy perennial with pinkish leaf stalks. Has oval, fleshy, wrinkled, dark green leaves, to 5cm (2in) long, with sunken veins; spikes of white flowers appear irregularly. **H** and **S** to 15cm (6in). Min. 10°C (50°F).

***Ctenanthe oppenheimiana* 'Tricolor'**
Robust, evergreen, bushy perennial. Has leathery, lance-shaped leaves, over 30cm (12in) long, splashed with large, cream blotches, and, intermittently, spikes of 3-petalled, white flowers. **H** and **S** 1m (3ft). Min. 15°C (59°F).

***Dieffenbachia seguine* 'Exotica'**
Evergreen, tufted perennial, sometimes woody at the base. Broadly lance-shaped leaves, to 45cm (18in) long, are blotched with creamy-white. **H** and **S** 1m (3ft) or more. Min. 15°C (59°F).

Anthurium crystallinum
(Crystal anthurium)
Evergreen, erect, tufted perennial. Long, velvety, dark green leaves are distinctively pale green- to white-veined. Has long-lasting, red-tinged, green spathes. **H** to 75cm (30in), **S** to 60cm (24in). Min. 15°C (59°F).

Ruellia devosiana
Evergreen, bushy sub-shrub with spreading, purplish branches. Leaves are broadly lance-shaped, dark green with paler veins above and purple below. Has mauve-tinged, white flowers in spring–summer. **H** and **S** to 45cm (18in) or more. Min. 15°C (59°F).

Episcia dianthiflora (Lace flower)
Evergreen perennial with creeping prostrate stems. Has thick, velvety leaves with brownish midribs and, intermittently, pure white flowers with fringed petals. **H** 15cm (6in), **S** 30cm (12in). Min. 15°C (59°F).

ORCHIDS

Elegant and exotic, orchids are prized for their unusual flowers. There are two main groups. Terrestrials [t] grow in a wide range of habitats in the wild; many are at least frost hardy. Epiphytes [e], the more showy of the two and mostly native to the tropics, cling to tree branches or rocks, obtaining nourishment through their leaves and aerial roots. An aura of mystique surrounds these plants, but their cultivation is not always difficult and some thrive happily indoors as house plants. They need special composts and in cool climates must be grown under glass. An orchid hybrid is called a grex [gx] from the Latin for a flock. A grex name applies to all the individual seedlings from any given cross, the individual plants of which may also be given cultivar names. Several cultivars may also be given a Group name within a grex. See also the Plant Dictionary.

Calanthe vestita [t]

***Paphiopedilum* Freckles gx** ⓘ [t]

Rhynchostele rossii [e]

***Cymbidium* Portelet Bay** ⓘ [e]

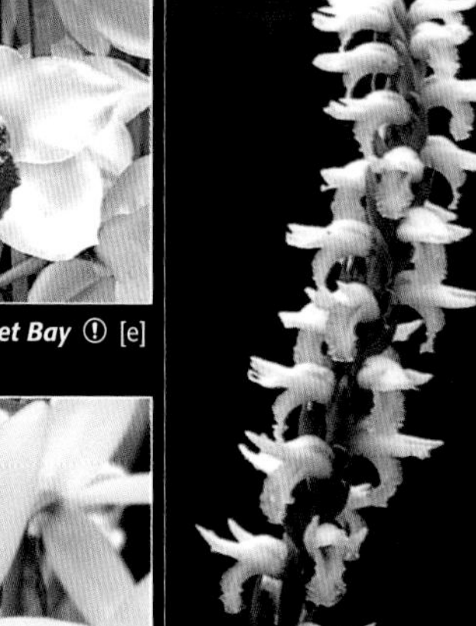

Masdevallia tovarensis [e]

Oncidium alexandrae [e]

Cypripedium reginae [t]

Spiranthes cernua [t]

Brassavola nodosa [e]

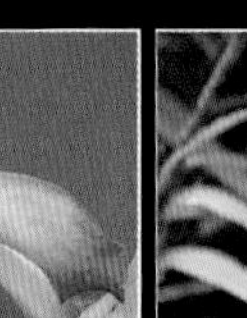

***Miltoniopsis* Robert Strauss gx 'Ardingly'** [e]

Dendrobium infundibulum [e]

Coelogyne nitida [e]

Coelogyne flaccida [e]

Ophrys tenthredinifera [t]

Laelia anceps [e]

x *Rhyncholaeliocattleya* Mount Adams gx [e]

Pleione bulbocodioides [t]

Dendrobium nobile [e]

***Vanda* Rothschildiana gx** [e]

Anacamptis morio [t]

Oncidium sotoanum [e]

***Phalaenopsis* Lady Pink Lips gx** [e]

Bletilla striata [t]

Guarianthe bowringiana [e]

Masdevallia coccinea [e]

***Zygopetalum* Perrenoudii gx** [e]

Oncidium Hambühren Stern gx 'Cheam' [e]

Cymbidium Strathkanaid gx ⓘ [e]

Phaius tankervilleae [t]

Miltoniopsis Anjou gx 'St Patrick' [e]

Ada aurantiaca [e]

Cymbidium Caithness Ice gx 'Trinity' ⓘ [e]

x *Oncidopsis* Cambria gx 'Lensing's Favorite' [e]

x *Cattlianthe* Rojo gx 'Mont Millais' [e]

Oncidium Tigersun gx 'Orbec' [e]

Masdevallia wagneriana [e]

Oncidium Artur Elle gx 'Colombien' [e]

Paphiopedilum bellatulum ⓘ [t]

Oncidium Memoria Commander Wiggs gx 'Kay' [e]

Phalaenopsis Lundy gx [e]

Paphiopedilum Buckhurst gx 'Mont Millais' ⓘ [t]

Paphiopedilum Lyric gx 'Glendora' ⓘ [t]

Paphiopedilum Maudiae gx ⓘ [t]

Paphiopedilum fairrieanum ⓘ [t]

Paphiopedilum armeniacum [t]

Rossioglossum grande [e]

Oncidium Eric Young gx [e]

Paphiopedilum rothschildianum [t]

Gomesa flexuosa [e]

Brasiliorchis porphyrostele [e]

Oncidium Julie Barbara Good gx [e]

Lycaste cruenta [e]

x *Cattlianthe* Hazel Boyd gx 'Apricot Glow' [e]

Cymbidium elegans ⓘ [e]

Oncidium tigrinum [e]

Ophrys lutea [t]

Phragmipedium besseae [t]

Psychopsis papilio [e]

WHITE

***Spathiphyllum* 'Mauna Loa'**
Robust, evergreen, rhizomatous perennial. Has long, lance-shaped, glossy leaves. Irregularly throughout the year bears fleshy, white spadices of fragrant flowers enclosed in large, oval, pure white spathes. **H** and **S** 45–60cm (18–24in). Min. 15°C (59°F).

***Fittonia albivenis* Argyroneura Group (Silver net-leaf)**
Evergreen, creeping perennial with small, oval, white-veined, green leaves. Remove any flowers. **H** to 15cm (6in), **S** indefinite. Min. 15°C (59°F).

***Aglaonema commutatum* 'Treubii'**
Evergreen, erect, tufted perennial. Lance-shaped leaves, to 30cm (12in) long, are marked with pale green or silver. Occasionally has greenish-white spathes. **H** and **S** to 45cm (18in). Min. 15°C (59°F).

***Tradescantia fluminensis* 'Albovittata'**
Strong-growing, evergreen perennial with trailing, rooting stems. Blue-green leaves have broad, white stripes. Bears small, white flowers. **H** 30cm (12in), **S** indefinite. Min. 15°C (59°F).

***Spathiphyllum wallisii* (Peace lily)**
Evergreen, tufted, rhizomatous perennial. Has clusters of long, lance-shaped leaves. Fleshy, white spadices of fragrant flowers in white spathes are irregularly produced. **H** and **S** 30cm (12in) or more. Min. 15°C (59°F).

Angraecum sesquipedale
Evergreen, epiphytic orchid. Waxy, white flowers, 8cm (3in) across, each with a 30cm (12in) long spur, are borne, usually 2 per stem, in winter. Has narrow, semi-rigid, horizontal leaves, 15cm (6in) long. **H** and **S** 30cm (12in) or more. Min. 13°C (55°F).

***Achimenes* 'Little Beauty'**
Bushy perennial with oval, toothed leaves. Large, funnel-shaped, deep pink flowers with yellow eyes are carried in summer. **H** 25cm (10in), **S** 30cm (12in). Min. 10°C (50°F).

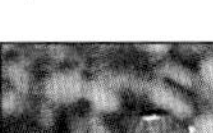

***Streptocarpus* 'Nicola'**
Evergreen, stemless perennial with a rosette of strap-shaped, wrinkled leaves. Funnel-shaped, rose-pink flowers are produced intermittently in small clusters. **H** 25cm (10in), **S** 50cm (20in). Min. 10–15°C (50–59°F).

***Saintpaulia* 'Colorado'**
Evergreen, rosette-forming perennial with broadly ovate to oval, dark green leaves. Produces star-shaped, frilled, single, magenta flowers all year. **H** 15–20cm (6–8in). Min. 15°C (59°F).

Tradescantia sillamontana
Evergreen, erect perennial. Oval, stem-clasping leaves are densely covered with white, woolly hairs. Has clusters of small, bright purplish-pink flowers in summer. **H** and **S** to 30cm (12in). Min. 10–15°C (50–59°F).

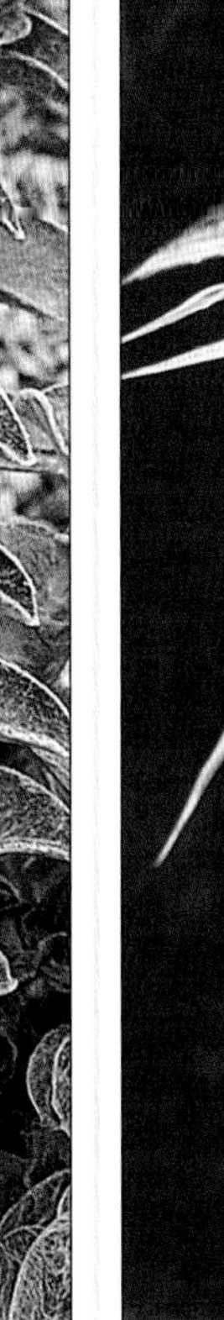

***Oplismenus africanus* 'Variegatus'**
Evergreen, creeping, perennial grass with wiry, rooting stems. White-striped leaves, with wavy margins, are often tinged pink. Bears inconspicuous flowers intermittently. **H** 20cm (8in) or more, **S** indefinite. Min. 12°C (54°F).

Kohleria digitaliflora
Erect, bushy, rhizomatous perennial with white-haired stems. Has scalloped, hairy leaves and clusters of tubular, hairy, pink-and-white flowers, with purple-spotted, green lobes, summer to autumn. **H** 60cm (24in) or more, **S** 45cm (18in). Min. 15°C (59°F).

Tradescantia zebrina
(Silver inch plant)
Evergreen, trailing or mat-forming perennial. Blue-green leaves, purple-tinged beneath, have 2 broad, silver bands. Has pink or violet-blue flowers intermittently all year. **H** 15cm (6in), **S** indefinite. Min. 15°C (59°F).

PINK

Musa ornata (Flowering banana)
Evergreen, palm-like, suckering perennial with oblong, waxy, bluish-green leaves to 2m (6ft) long. In summer has erect, yellow-orange flowers with pinkish bracts and greenish-yellow fruits. **H** to 3m (10ft), **S** 2.2m (7ft). Min. 18°C (64°F).

Caladium bicolor 'Pink Beauty'
Tufted, tuberous perennial. Has long-stalked, triangular, pink-mottled, green leaves, to 45cm (18in) long, with darker pink veins. White spathes appear in summer. **H** and **S** 90cm (36in). Min. 19°C (66°F).

RED

Anigozanthos manglesii (Red-and-green kangaroo paw)
Vigorous, bushy perennial that bears racemes of large, tubular, woolly, red-and-green flowers in spring and early summer. Has long, narrow, grey-green leaves. May suffer from ink disease. **H** 1m (3ft), **S** 45cm (1½ft).

Doryanthes palmeri
Evergreen perennial with a rosette of arching, ribbed leaves, to 2m (6ft) long. Intermittently bears panicles of small, red-bracted, orange-red flowers, white within. Flowers are often replaced by bulbils. **H** 2–2.5m (6–8ft), **S** 2.5m (8ft). Min. 10°C (50°F).

Bromelia balansae (Heart of flame)
Evergreen, clump-forming, basal-rosetted perennial bearing strap-shaped, arching, grey-green leaves with hooked spines. Club-shaped panicles of tubular, red or purple flowers, with long, bright red bracts, are borne in spring–summer. **H** 1m (3ft), **S** 1.5m (5ft). Min. 15°C (59°F).

Columnea x banksii
Evergreen, trailing perennial with oval, fleshy leaves, glossy above, purplish-red below. Tubular, hooded, brilliant red flowers, to 8cm (3in) long, appear from spring to winter. Makes a useful plant for a hanging basket. **H** 1m (3ft), **S** indefinite. Min. 15°C (59°F).

Russelia equisetiformis (Coral plant)
Evergreen, branching, bushy sub-shrub with rush-like stems and tiny leaves. Showy, pendent clusters of tubular, scarlet flowers appear in summer–autumn. **H** to 1m (3ft) or more, **S** 60cm (2ft). Min. 15°C (59°F).

Kohleria eriantha
Robust, bushy, rhizomatous perennial with reddish-haired stems. Oval leaves, to 13cm (5in) long, are edged with red hairs. Has tubular, red flowers, with yellow-spotted lobes, in nodding clusters in summer. **H** and **S** 1m (3ft) or more. Min. 15°C (59°F).

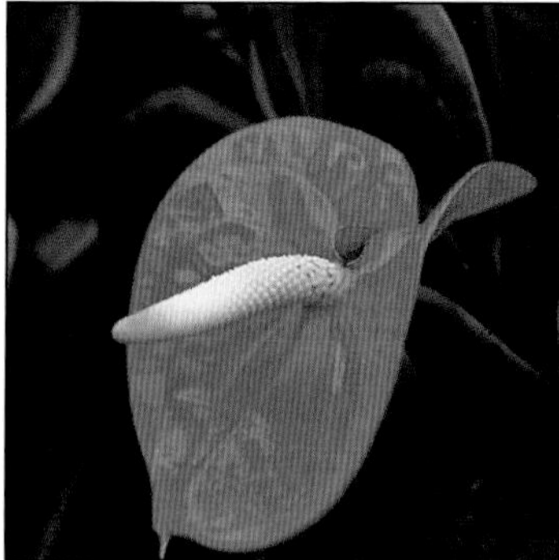

Anthurium andraeanum (Flamingo flower)
Evergreen, erect perennial. Long-stalked, oval leaves, with a heart-shaped base, are 20cm (8in) long. Has long-lasting, bright red spathes with yellow spadices. **H** 60–75cm (24–30in), **S** 50cm (20in). Min. 15°C (59°F).

Sinningia 'Switzerland'
Short-stemmed, tuberous perennial with rosettes of oval, velvety leaves, to 20cm (8in) long. In summer has large, fleshy, trumpet-shaped, bright scarlet flowers with ruffled, white borders. **H** to 30cm (12in), **S** 45cm (18in). Min. 15°C (59°F).

Columnea crassifolia
Evergreen, shrubby perennial with fleshy, lance-shaped leaves. Erect, tubular, hairy, scarlet flowers, about 8cm (3in) long, each with a yellow throat, are carried from spring to autumn. **H** and **S** to 45cm (18in). Min. 15°C (59°F).

Smithiantha 'Orange King'
Strong-growing, erect, rhizomatous perennial. Large, scalloped, velvety leaves are emerald-green with dark red-marked veins. In summer–autumn has tubular, orange-red flowers, red-spotted within and with yellow lips. **H** and **S** to 60cm (24in). Min. 15°C (59°F).

Episcia cupreata (Flame violet)
Evergreen, creeping perennial. Has small, downy, wrinkled leaves, usually silver-veined or -banded, and, intermittently, scarlet flowers marked yellow within. **H** 10cm (4in), **S** indefinite. Min. 15°C (59°F).

Nautilocalyx lynchii
Robust, evergreen, erect, bushy perennial. Broadly lance-shaped, slightly wrinkled leaves are glossy, greenish-red above, reddish beneath. In summer has tubular, red-haired, pale yellow flowers with red calyces. **H** and **S** to 60cm (24in). Min. 15°C (59°F).

BROMELIADS

Bromeliads, or plants that belong to the family *Bromeliaceae*, are distinguished by their bold, usually rosetted foliage and showy flowers in shades of white, red or purple, borne in dense, cylindrical or conical inflorescences in summer. The flowers are followed by ovoid yellow fruits containing large brown seeds. Many bromeliads are epiphytes, or air plants (absorbing their food through moisture in the atmosphere), and will grow outdoors only in tropical regions. In cooler climates, bromeliads make attractive house plants or will thrive in a warm greenhouse. Follow watering instructions with care.

Tillandsia argentea ♀

Ananas bracteatus var. *tricolor* ♀

Aechmea fasciata ♀

Cryptanthus bivittatus 'Pink Starlight' ♀

Aechmea recurvata

Neoregelia concentrica

Vriesea splendens ♀

Tillandsia stricta

Tillandsia lindenii ♀

Puya chilensis

AFRICAN VIOLETS

African violet is the common name for the genus *Saintpaulia*, although it is often applied to the numerous cultivars derived from *S. ionantha*. These low-growing, rosetted, evergreen perennials have a wide range of attractive flower colours, varying from white, pink, blue, and violet, to bi- or multi-coloured. Their petal edges can be ruffled, rounded, frilled, or fringed, and leaves are somewhat succulent, usually hairy, and, in some cases, variegated. They may be grown as summer bedding in warm, humid climates but also make attractive indoor pot plants, flowering freely throughout the year if kept in a suitable draught-free, light, humid position.

S. 'Garden News'

S. 'Powder Keg'

S. 'Starry Trail'

S. 'Pip Squeek'

S. 'Porcelain'

S. 'Ice Maiden'

S. 'Falling Raindrops'

S. 'Zoja'

S. 'Bright Eyes'

PURPLE

Peliosanthes arisanensis

Evergreen perennial with slow-spreading rhizomes. Stems have oblong, pleated, thin-textured, light green leaves, 20–30cm (8–12in) long, and in spring bear spikes of up to 20, 6-petalled, nodding, purple-centred, yellow flowers. **H** 30cm (12in), **S** 40cm (16in).

Tetranema roseum **(Mexican violet)**

Short-stemmed perennial with crowded, stalkless leaves, bluish-green beneath. Intermittently, has nodding, purple flowers with paler throats. **H** to 20cm (8in), **S** 30cm (12in). Min. 13°C (55°F).

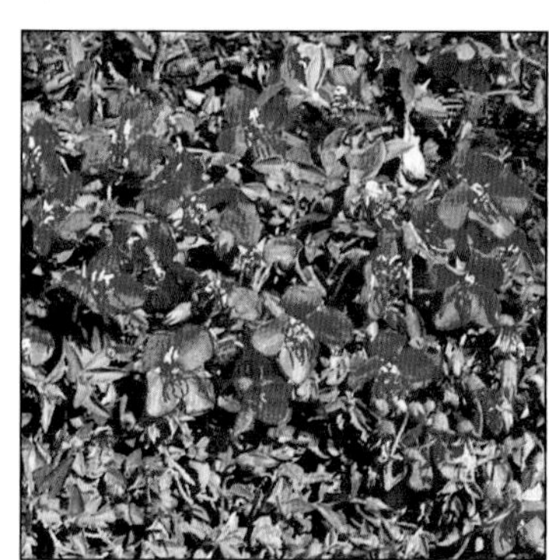

Heterocentron elegans

Evergreen, mat-forming perennial with dense, creeping, mid-green foliage. Massed, bright deep purple flowers open summer–autumn and, under glass, in winter. **H** 5cm (2in), **S** indefinite. Min. 5°C (41°F).

Calathea sanderiana

Evergreen, clump-forming perennial. Broadly oval, leathery, glossy leaves, to 60cm (2ft) long, are dark green with pink to white lines above, and purple beneath. Intermittently has short spikes of white to mauve flowers. **H** 1.2–1.5m (4–5ft), **S** 1m (3ft). Min. 15°C (59°F).

Browallia speciosa **(Bush violet)**

Bushy perennial, usually grown as an annual, propagated by seed each year. Has oval leaves to 10cm (4in) long and showy, violet-blue flowers with white eyes, the season depending when sown. **H** 60–75cm (24–30in), **S** 45cm (18in). Min. 10–15°C (50–59°F).

Alocasia cuprea

Evergreen, tufted perennial. Oval leaves 30cm (12in) long, with a metallic sheen and darker, impressed veins above, purple below; leaf stalks arise from the lower surface. Purplish spathes appear intermittently. **H** and **S** to 1m (3ft). Min. 15°C (59°F).

Chirita lavandulacea
Evergreen, erect perennial with downy, pale green leaves to 20cm (8in) long. In leaf axils has clusters of lavender-blue flowers with white tubes. May be sown in succession to flower from spring to autumn. **H** and **S** 60cm (24in). Min. 15°C (59°F).

Hemigraphis repanda
Evergreen, prostrate perennial with spreading, rooting stems. Lance-shaped, toothed, purple-tinged leaves, 5cm (2in) long, are darker purple below. Has tiny, tubular, white flowers intermittently. **H** to 15cm (6in). Min. 15°C (59°F).

Elatostema repens
(Watermelon begonia)
Evergreen, creeping perennial with rooting stems. Broadly oval, olive-green leaves have purplish-brown edges and paler green centres. Flowers are insignificant. **H** 10cm (4in), **S** indefinite. Min. 15°C (59°F).

Nepenthes x hookeriana
Evergreen, epiphytic, insectivorous perennial with oval, leathery leaves to 30cm (12in) long and pendent, pale green pitchers, with reddish-purple markings and a spurred lid, to 13cm (5in) long. **H** 60–75cm (24–30in). Min. 18°C (64°F).

Dichorisandra reginae
Evergreen, erect, clump-forming perennial. Glossy, often silver-banded and flecked leaves are purple-red beneath. Has small spikes of densely set, purple-blue flowers in summer–autumn. **H** 60–75cm (24–30in), **S** to 30cm (12in). Min. 20°C (68°F).

BLUE

***Streptocarpus* 'Amanda'**
Evergreen, stemless perennial with a few, long, strap-shaped, wrinkled, finely hairy, mid-green leaves. Funnel-shaped, rich blue flowers, with darker veining and white throat, are produced in tight clusters in spring. **H** 30cm (12in), **S** 20cm (8in). Min. 5°C (41°F).

Pycnostachys dawei
Strong-growing, bushy perennial with toothed, oblong leaves, 12–30cm (5–12in) long, that are reddish below. Has compact spikes of tubular, 2-lipped, bright blue flowers in winter–spring. **H** 1.2–1.5m (4–5ft), **S** 30–90cm (1–3ft). Min. 15°C (59°F).

GREEN

Dionaea muscipula (Venus flytrap)
Evergreen, insectivorous perennial with rosettes of 6 or more spreading, hinged leaves, pink-flushed inside, edged with stiff bristles. Has clusters of tiny, white flowers in summer. **H** 10cm (4in), **S** 30cm (12in). Min. 5°C (41°F).

Drosera spatulata
Evergreen, insectivorous perennial with rosettes of spoon-shaped leaves that have sensitive, red, glandular hairs. Has many small, pink or white flowers on leafless stems in summer. **H** and **S** 8cm (3in). Min. 5–10°C (41–50°F).

Drosera capensis (Cape sundew)
Evergreen, insectivorous perennial. Rosettes of narrow leaves have sensitive, red, glandular hairs. Many small, purple flowers are borne on leafless stems in summer. **H** and **S** to 15cm (6in). Min. 5–10°C (41–50°F).

GREEN

Ensete ventricosum
Evergreen, palm-like perennial with small, banana-like fruits. Has 6m (20ft) long leaves with reddish midribs and, intermittently, reddish-green flowers with dark red bracts. **H** 6m (20ft), **S** 3m (10ft) or more. Min. 10°C (50°F).

Peperomia marmorata (Silver heart)
Evergreen, bushy perennial with insignificant flowers. Has oval, long-pointed, fleshy, dull green leaves, marked with greyish-white and quilted above, reddish below. **H** and **S** to 20cm (8in). Min. 10°C (50°F).

Pilea nummulariifolia
(Creeping Charlie)
Evergreen, mat-forming perennial with creeping, rooting, reddish stems. Rounded, pale green leaves, 2cm (¾in) wide, have a ridged surface. Flowers are insignificant. **H** to 5cm (2in), **S** 30cm (12in). Min. 10°C (50°F).

Peperomia glabella (Wax privet)
Evergreen perennial with wide-spreading, red stems. Has broadly oval, fleshy, glossy, bright green leaves, to 5cm (2in) long, and insignificant flowers. **H** to 15cm (6in), **S** 30cm (12in). Min. 10°C (50°F).

Xanthosoma sagittifolium
Spreading, tufted perennial with thick stems. Broadly arrow-shaped leaves, 60cm (2ft) or more long, on long leaf stalks, are green with a greyish bloom. Has green spathes intermittently during the year. **H** to 2m (6ft) in flower, **S** 2m (6ft) or more. Min. 15°C (59°F).

Asparagus densiflorus
Evergreen, trailing perennial with clusters of narrow, bright green, leaf-like stems. In summer has pink-tinged, white flowers, followed by red fruits. Suits a hanging basket. **H** to 1m (3ft), **S** 50cm (20in). Min. 10°C (50°F).

***Asparagus densiflorus* 'Myersii'**
(Foxtail fern)
Evergreen, erect perennial with spikes of tight, feathery clusters of leaf-like stems and pinkish-white flowers in summer, then red fruits. **H** to 1m (3ft), **S** 50cm (20in). Min. 10°C (50°F).

***Peperomia obtusifolia* 'Variegata'**
Evergreen, bushy perennial with spade-shaped, fleshy leaves, to 20cm (8in) long, that have irregular, yellowish-green to creamy-white margins and usually greyish centres. Flowers are insignificant. **H** and **S** to 15cm (6in). Min. 10°C (50°F).

Dieffenbachia seguine
'Rudolph Roehrs'
Evergreen, tufted perennial, sometimes woody at the base. Leaves, to 45cm (18in) long, are yellowish-green or white with green midribs and margins. **H** and **S** 1m (3ft). Min. 15°C (59°F).

***Columnea microphylla* 'Variegata'**
Evergreen, trailing perennial. Has rounded leaves narrowly bordered with cream and tubular, hooded, scarlet flowers, with yellow throats, in winter–spring. **H** 1m (3ft) or more, **S** indefinite. Min. 15°C (59°F).

***Calathea zebrina* (Zebra plant)**
Robust, evergreen, clump-forming perennial with long-stalked, velvety, dark green leaves, to 60cm (2ft) long (less if pot-grown), with paler veins, margins and midribs. Has short spikes of white to pale purple flowers. **H** and **S** to 90cm (3ft). Min. 15°C (59°F).

Aglaonema pictum
Evergreen, erect, tufted perennial. Oval leaves, to 15cm (6in) long, are irregularly marked with greyish-white or grey-green. Has creamy-white spathes in summer. **H** and **S** to 60cm (24in). Min. 15°C (59°F).

***Aglaonema* 'Silver King'**
Evergreen, erect, tufted perennial. Broadly lance-shaped, mid-green leaves, to 30cm (12in) long, are marked with dark and light green. Has greenish-white spathes in summer. **H** and **S** to 45cm (18in). Min. 15°C (59°F).

***Maranta leuconeura* 'Erythroneura' (Herringbone plant)**
Evergreen perennial. Oblong leaves have veins marked red, with paler yellowish-green midribs, and are upright at night, flat by day. **H** and **S** to 30cm (12in). Min. 15°C (59°F).

***Sansevieria trifasciata* 'Hahnii'**
Evergreen, stemless perennial with a rosette of about 5 stiff, erect, broadly lance-shaped and pointed leaves, banded horizontally with pale green or white. Occasionally has small, pale green flowers. **H** 15–30cm (6–12in), **S** 10cm (4in). Min. 15°C (59°F).

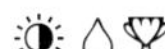

***Calathea makoyana* (Peacock plant)**
Evergreen, clump-forming perennial. Horizontal leaves, 30cm (12in) long, are dark and light green above, reddish-purple below. Has short spikes of white flowers intermittently. **H** to 60cm (2ft), **S** to 1.2m (4ft). Min. 15°C (59°F).

***Maranta leuconeura* 'Kerchoveana' (Rabbit tracks)**
Evergreen perennial that intermittently bears white to mauve flowers. Oblong leaves with dark brown blotches become greener with age and are upright at night, flat by day. **H** and **S** to 30cm (12in). Min. 15°C (59°F).

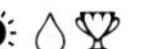

YELLOW

Arctotheca calendula
(Cape dandelion)
Carpeting perennial. Leaves are woolly below, rough-haired above. Heads of daisy-like, bright yellow flowers, with darker yellow centres, appear from late spring to autumn. **H** 30cm (12in), **S** indefinite. Min. 5°C (41°F).

***Sansevieria trifasciata* 'Laurentii'**
Evergreen, stemless perennial with a rosette of about 5 stiff, erect, lance-shaped and pointed leaves with yellow margins. Occasionally has pale green flowers. Propagate by division to avoid reversion. **H** 45cm–1.2m (1½–4ft), **S** 10cm (4in). Min. 10–15°C (50–59°F).

Hedychium gardnerianum
Upright, rhizomatous perennial. In late summer and early autumn has many spikes of short-lived, fragrant, lemon-yellow and red flowers. Lance-shaped leaves are greyish-green, most markedly when young. **H** 1.5–2m (5–6ft), **S** 75cm (2½ft). Min. 5°C (41°F).

***Aphelandra squarrosa* 'Louisae'**
Evergreen, erect perennial. Long, oval, glossy, slightly wrinkled, dark green leaves have white veins and midribs. Bears dense spikes of golden-yellow flowers from axils of yellow bracts in late summer to autumn. **H** to 1m (3ft), **S** 60cm (2ft). Min. 13°C (55°F).

***Sansevieria trifasciata* 'Golden Hahnii'**
Evergreen, stemless perennial with a rosette of about 5 stiff, erect, broadly lance-shaped leaves with wide, yellow borders. Sometimes bears small, pale green flowers. **H** 15–30cm (6–12in), **S** 10cm (4in). Min. 15°C (59°F).

Impatiens repens
Evergreen, creeping perennial with rooting stems. Has small, oval to rounded leaves and, in summer, yellow flowers, each with a large, hairy spur. **H** to 5cm (2in), **S** indefinite. Min. 10°C (50°F).

***Peristrophe hyssopifolia* 'Aureovariegata'**
Evergreen, bushy perennial. Small leaves are broadly lance-shaped with long, pointed tips and central, creamy-yellow blotches. Has tubular, rose-pink flowers in winter. **H** to 60cm (2ft) or more, **S** 1.2m (4ft). Min. 15°C (59°F).

Anigozanthos flavidus
(Yellow kangaroo paw)
Bushy perennial with racemes of large, woolly, tubular, yellowish-green flowers, with reddish anthers, borne in spring–summer. Narrow leaves, to 60cm (2ft) long, are mid-green. **H** 1.2m (4ft), **S** 45cm (1½ft).

ORANGE

Strelitzia reginae
(Bird-of-paradise flower)
Evergreen, clump-forming perennial with long-stalked, bluish-green leaves. Has beak-like, orange-and-blue flowers in boat-shaped, red-edged bracts mainly in spring. **H** over 1m (3ft), **S** 75cm (2½ft). Min. 5–10°C (41–50°F).

Clivia miniata
Evergreen, tuft-forming rhizome with strap-shaped, semi-erect, basal, dark green leaves, 40–60cm (16–24in) long. Stems each produce a head of 10–20 orange or red flowers in spring or summer. **H** 40cm (16in), **S** 30–60cm (12–24in). Min. 10°C (50°F).

GINGERS

Gingers have been cultivated in Europe for over 100 years and bring colourful, intricate flowers, tropical foliage and, quite literally, spice to the garden. Evergreen types need to be over-wintered under glass or gradually dried off in autumn to induce artificial dormancy, whereas many deciduous types such as *Roscoea* and *Cautleya* will die off naturally and, being frost hardy, can remain in the ground with a protective mulch. Most gingers do not tolerate wet winter conditions and benefit from some shade. A brighter location encourages flowering, whereas shade encourages better foliage, so site accordingly. They should not be allowed to dry out while in growth, and are heavy feeders, so give them frequent applications of liquid feed.

Alpinia zerumbet

Hedychium thyrsiforme

Hedychium stenopetalum

Hedychium yunnanense

Alpinia hainanensis

Costus speciosus

Curcuma petiolata

Roscoea scillifolia

Alpinia purpurata

Curcuma zedoaria

Hedychium maximum

Cornukaempferia aurantiiflora 'Jungle Gold'

Hedychium densiflorum

Globba winitii

ORANGE

Heliconia psittacorum (Parrot's flower, Parrot's plantain)
Tufted perennial with long-stalked, lance-shaped leaves. In summer, mature plants carry green-tipped, orange flowers with narrow, glossy, orange-red bracts. **H** to 2m (6ft), **S** 1m (3ft). Min. 18°C (64°F).

Aeschynanthus speciosus
Evergreen, trailing perennial with waxy, narrowly oval leaves usually carried in whorls. Erect, tubular, bright orange-red flowers are borne in large clusters in summer. **H** and **S** 30–60cm (12–24in). Min. 18°C (64°F).

GREEN

Cyperus involucratus
Evergreen, tuft-forming, perennial sedge with leaf-like bracts forming a whorl beneath the clustered flower spikes in summer. **H** to 1m (3ft), **S** 30cm (1ft). Min. 4–7°C (39–45°F).

Cyperus papyrus (Paper reed, Papyrus)
Evergreen, clump-forming, perennial sedge with stout, triangular, leafless stems, carrying in summer huge umbels of spikelets with up to 100 rays. Grows in water. **H** to 3–5m (10–15ft), **S** 1m (3ft). Min. 7–10°C (45–50°F).

Microlepia speluncae
Large, terrestrial fern with a spreading rhizome and triangular, divided, softly hairy fronds, consisting of triangular to lance-shaped pinnae. **H** to 1.2m (4ft), **S** to 2m (6ft). Min. 5–10°C (41–50°F).

Selaginella martensii
Evergreen, moss-like perennial with dense, much-branched, frond-like sprays of glossy, rich green foliage. **H** and **S** 23cm (9in). Min. 5°C (41°F).

***Pteris cretica* 'Wimsettii'**
Evergreen or semi-evergreen fern with broadly ovate fronds divided into narrow pinnae, each with an incised margin and crested tip. **H** 45cm (18in), **S** 30cm (12in). Min. 5°C (41°F).

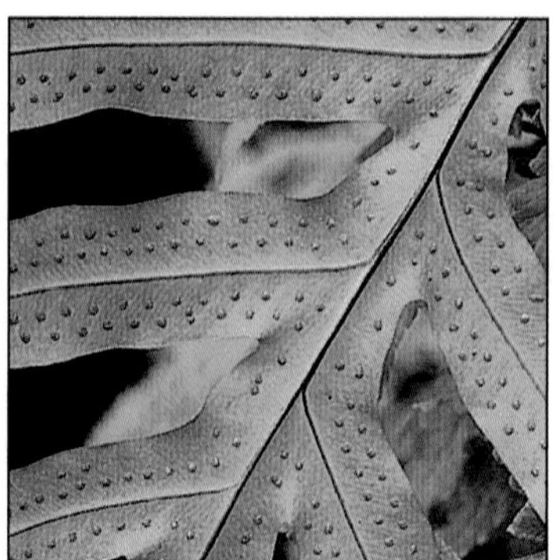

Phlebodium aureum
Evergreen fern with creeping, golden-scaled rhizomes. Has arching, deeply lobed, mid-green or glaucous fronds with attractive, orange-yellow sporangia on reverses. **H** 90cm–1.5m (3–5ft), **S** 60cm (2ft). Min. 5°C (41°F).

Nephrolepis exaltata (Sword fern)
Evergreen fern. Has erect, sometimes spreading, lance-shaped, divided, pale green fronds borne on wiry stems. **H** and **S** 90cm (36in) or more. Min. 5°C (41°F).

Selaginella kraussiana
Evergreen, trailing, more or less prostrate, moss-like perennial with bright green foliage. **H** 1cm (½in), **S** indefinite. Min. 5°C (41°F).

WHITE

Asplenium nidus (Bird's-nest fern)
Evergreen fern. Produces broadly lance-shaped, glossy, bright green fronds in a shuttlecock-like arrangement. **H** 60cm–1.2m (2–4ft), **S** 30–60cm (1–2ft). Min. 5°C (41°F).

***Phlebodium aureum* 'Mandaianum'**
Evergreen fern with creeping rhizomes. Has arching, deeply lobed, glaucous fronds with attractive, orange-yellow sporangia on reverses; pinnae are deeply cut and wavy. **H** 1–1.5m (3–5ft), **S** 60cm (2ft). Min. 5°C (41°F).

Platycerium bifurcatum
(Common stag's-horn fern)
Evergreen, epiphytic fern with broad, plate-like sterile fronds and long, arching or pendent, forked, grey-green fertile fronds bearing velvety, brownish spore patches beneath. **H** and **S** 1m (3ft). Min. 5°C (41°F).

Selenicereus grandiflorus
(Queen-of-the-night)
Climbing, perennial cactus. Has 7-ribbed, 1–2cm (½–¾in) wide, green stems with yellow spines. White flowers, 18–30cm (7–12in) across, open at night in summer. **H** 3m (10ft), **S** indefinite. Min. 5°C (41°F).

Pereskia aculeata (Barbados gooseberry, Lemon vine)
Fast-growing, deciduous, climbing cactus with broad, glossy leaves. Orange-centred, creamy-white flowers appear in autumn, only on plants over 1m (3ft) high. **H** to 10m (30ft), **S** 5m (15ft). Min. 5°C (41°F).

Cephalocereus senilis
(Old-man cactus)
Very slow-growing, columnar, perennial cactus with a green stem covered in long, white hairs, masking short, white spines. Is unlikely to flower in cultivation. **H** 15m (50ft), **S** 15cm (6in). Min. 5°C (41°F).

Cleistocactus strausii (Silver torch)
Fast-growing, columnar, perennial cactus with 8cm (3in) wide stems and short, dense, white spines. Tubular, red flowers appear in spring on plants over 60cm (2ft) high. **H** 30cm (10ft), **S** 1–2m (3–6ft). Min. 5°C (41°F).

Mammillaria hahniana
(Old-woman cactus)
Spherical to columnar, perennial cactus with a green stem bearing long, woolly, white hairs. Carries cerise flowers in spring and spherical, red fruits in autumn. **H** 40cm (16in), **S** 15cm (6in). Min. 5°C (41°F).

WHITE

Coryphantha cornifera
Spherical to columnar, perennial cactus with angular tubercles, each bearing a curved, dark, central spine and shorter, radial spines. Has funnel-shaped, yellow flowers in summer. **H** 15cm (6in), **S** 10cm (4in). Min. 5°C (41°F).

Crassula socialis
Spreading, perennial succulent with short, dense rosettes of fleshy, triangular, green leaves, to 1cm (½in) across. Produces clusters of star-shaped, white flowers on 3cm (1¼in) tall stems in spring. **H** 5cm (2in), **S** indefinite. Min. 5°C (41°F).

Escobaria vivipara
Spherical, perennial cactus with a green stem densely covered with grey spines. Bears funnel-shaped, pink flowers, 3.5cm (1½in) across, in summer. Is much more difficult to grow than many other species in this genus. **H** and **S** 5cm (2in). Min. 5°C (41°F).

Gasteria bicolor* var. *liliputana
Perennial succulent that forms rosettes of dark green leaves blotched with white. Flower stems, to 15cm (6in) long, bear spikes of bell-shaped, orange-green flowers in spring. **H** 7cm (3in), **S** 10cm (4in). Min. 5°C (41°F).

Haworthia attenuata
Clump-forming, perennial succulent with a basal rosette of triangular, 3cm (1¼in) long, dark green leaves, that have pronounced white dots. Has tubular, white flowers, with spreading petals, from spring to autumn. **H** 7cm (3in), **S** 25cm (10in). Min. 5°C (41°F).

Gasteria carinata* var. *verrucosa
Clump-forming, perennial succulent with stiff, dark green leaves, with raised, white dots and incurved edges. Has spikes of bell-shaped, orange-green flowers in spring. **H** 10cm (4in), **S** 30cm (12in). Min. 5°C (41°F).

Mammillaria geminispina
Clump-forming, perennial cactus. Has a spherical, green stem densely covered with short, white, radial spines and very long, white, central spines. Has red flowers, 1–2cm (½–¾in) across, in spring. **H** 25cm (10in), **S** 50cm (20in). Min. 5°C (41°F).

Mammillaria bocasana
(Powder-puff cactus)
Clump-forming, perennial cactus. Long, white hairs cover a hemispherical stem. Has cream or rose-pink flowers in summer and red seed pods the following spring–summer. **H** 10cm (4in), **S** 30cm (12in). Min. 5°C (41°F).

TENDER AND EXOTIC PLANTS

Opuntia polyacantha
Bushy, perennial cactus with a green stem of 15cm (6in) long, flattened segments. Areoles bear 6–15 flattened, 20cm (8in) long, hair-like spines. Has masses of saucer-shaped, red or yellow flowers in summer. **H** 50cm (20in), **S** 2m (6ft). Min. 5°C (41°F).

Crassula ovata (Friendship tree, Jade tree, Money tree)
Perennial succulent with a swollen stem crowned by glossy, green leaves, at times red-edged. Bears 5-petalled, white flowers in autumn–winter. **H** 4m (12ft), **S** 2m (6ft). Min. 5°C (41°F).

Strombocactus disciformis
Very slow-growing, hemispherical, perennial cactus with a grey-green to brown stem set with a spiral of blunt tubercles. Woolly crown has bristle-like spines, which soon fall off, and cream flowers in summer. **H** 3cm (1¼in), **S** 10cm (4in). Min. 5°C (41°F).

Senecio rowleyanus (String-of-beads)
Pendent, perennial succulent. Very slender, green stems bear cylindrical, green leaves. Has heads of fragrant, tubular, white flowers from spring to autumn. Suits a hanging pot. **H** 1m (3ft), **S** indefinite. Min. 5°C (41°F).

Lithops karasmontana
Egg-shaped, perennial succulent, divided into 2 unequal-sized, grey leaves, that have pink, upper surfaces with sunken, darker pink marks. Bears a white flower in late summer or early autumn. **H** to 4cm (1½in), **S** 5cm (2in). Min. 5°C (41°F).

Echinopsis oxygona
Spherical to columnar, perennial cactus with a 13–15-ribbed, green stem and long spines. Has 10cm (4in) wide, tubular, white to lavender flowers, to 20cm (8in) long, in spring–summer. **H** and **S** 30cm (12in). Min. 5°C (41°F).

Trichodiadema mirabile
Bushy to prostrate, perennial succulent with cylindrical, dark green leaves tipped with dark brown bristles and covered in papillae. Stem tip bears white flowers, 4cm (1½in) across, from spring to autumn. **H** 15cm (6in), **S** 30cm (12in). Min. 5°C (41°F).

Agave americana 'Striata'
Basal-rosetted, perennial succulent. Has sharply pointed, sword-shaped, blue-green leaves with yellow edges. Stem carries white flowers, each 9cm (3½in) long, in spring–summer. Offsets freely. **H** and **S** 2m (6ft).

Gibbaeum velutinum
Clump-forming, perennial succulent with paired, finger-like, velvety, bluish grey-green leaves, to 6cm (2½in) long. Produces daisy-like, pink, lilac or white flowers, 5cm (2in) across, in spring. **H** 8cm (3in), **S** 30cm (12in). Min. 5°C (41°F).

Gymnocalycium gibbosum
Spherical to columnar, perennial cactus that has a dark green stem with 12–19 rounded ribs, pale yellow spines, darkening with age, and white flowers, to 7cm (3in) long, in summer. **H** 30cm (12in), **S** 20cm (8in). Min. 5°C (41°F).

Furcraea foetida 'Mediopicta'
Basal-rosetted, perennial succulent with broad, sword-shaped, green leaves, striped with creamy-white, to 2.5m (8ft) long. Has bell-shaped, green flowers, with white interiors, in summer. **H** 3m (10ft), **S** 5m (15ft). Min. 6°C (43°F).

AGAVES

Tough plants originating from the Americas, agaves are able to withstand drought, heat, and full sun. Some species are frost hardy too. Agaves arrest attention with bold rosettes of thick sculptured leaves, often of great architectural value. The rosette slowly increases in size over several years before producing a flower spike, sometimes of tree-like proportions, so site carefully. Some species die after flowering, but may produce seed, bulbils amongst the flowers, and offsets around the base of the old rosette. Care should be taken when planting due to sharp thorns at the end of the leaves.

A. parrasana

A. potatorum 🏆

A. macroacantha

A. polianthiflora

A. parviflora 🏆

***A. americana* 'Marginata'** 🏆

A. victoriae-reginae 🏆

A. filifera 🏆

WHITE

***Kalanchoe blossfeldiana* 'Calandiva'**

Bushy, perennial succulent with oval to oblong, toothed, glossy, dark green leaves. Clusters of tubular, double, red, orange, pink, purple or white flowers, 0.5cm (¼in) across, of any combination of these colours, appear year-round. **H** and **S** 30cm (12in). Min. 10°C (50°F).

Echinocereus leucanthus

Clump-forming, tuberous cactus with spined, 6- or 7-ribbed, prostrate stems. In spring bears often terminal, dark-throated, white flowers, softly streaked purple, with green stigmas. **H** 20cm (8in), **S** 30cm (12in). Min. 8°C (46°F).

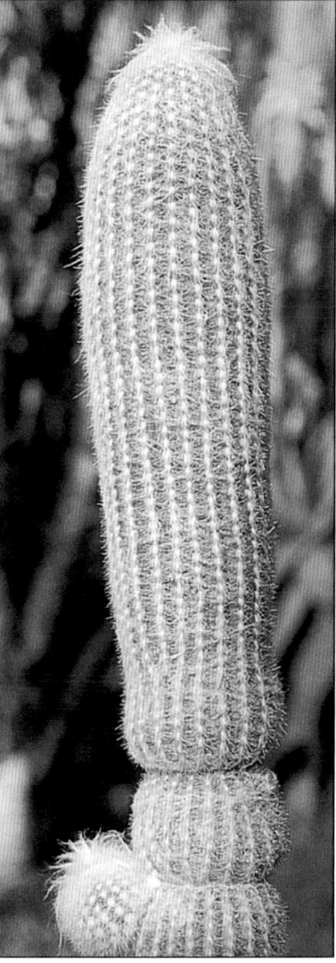

Espostoa lanata

(Cotton ball, Peruvian old-man cactus)

Very slow-growing, columnar, perennial cactus with a branching, woolly, green stem. Foul-smelling, white flowers appear in summer, only on plants over 1m (3ft) high. **H** to 4m (12ft), **S** 2m (6ft). Min. 10°C (50°F).

Epiphyllum laui

Bushy, perennial cactus, usually with strap-shaped, red-tinged, glossy stems, which may also be spiny, cylindrical or 4-angled. Has fragrant, white flowers, with brown sepals, in spring–summer. **H** 30cm (12in), **S** 50cm (20in). Min. 10°C (50°F).

***Kalanchoe fedtschenkoi* 'Variegata'**

Bushy, perennial succulent. Blue-green and cream leaves also colour red. Bears a new plantlet in each leaf notch. Has brownish-pink flowers in late winter. **H** and **S** to 1m (3ft). Min. 10°C (50°F).

Mammillaria plumosa
Clump-forming, perennial cactus. Has a spherical, green stem that is completely covered with feathery, white spines. Carries cream flowers in mid-winter. Is difficult to grow. Add calcium to soil. **H** 12cm (5in), **S** 40cm (16in). Min. 10°C (50°F).

Neolloydia conoidea
Clump-forming, perennial cactus. Has a columnar, blue-green stem densely covered with white, radial spines and longer, black, central spines. Bears funnel-shaped, purple-violet flowers in summer. **H** 10cm (4in), **S** 15cm (6in). Min. 10°C (50°F).

Pachycereus pringlei
Slow-growing, columnar, perennial cactus with a branched, bluish-green stem that has 10–15 ribs. Large areoles each have 15–25 black-tipped, white spines. Is unlikely to flower in cultivation. **H** 11m (35ft), **S** 3m (10ft). Min. 10°C (50°F).

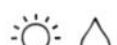

Opuntia microdasys* var. *albispina
Bushy, perennial cactus with green, flattened, oval segments. Spineless areoles, with slender, barbed, white hairs, are set in diagonal rows. Funnel-shaped, yellow flowers appear in summer. **H** 60cm (24in), **S** 30cm (12in). Min. 10°C (50°F).

***Euphorbia tithymaloides* 'Variegata'**
(Redbird flower)
Bushy, perennial succulent with stems angled at each node. Leaves have white or pink marks. Stem tips carry small, greenish flowers in red to yellowish-green bracts in summer. **H** to 3m (10ft), **S** 30cm (12in). Min. 10°C (50°F).

Rhipsalis cereuscula (Coral cactus)
Pendent, perennial cactus with 4- or 5-angled or cylindrical, green stems and branches, to 3cm (1¼in) long in whorls. Bell-shaped, white flowers on stem tips in winter–spring. **H** 60cm (24in), **S** 50cm (20in). Min. 10°C (50°F).

Pilosocereus leucocephalus
Columnar, perennial cactus with a 10–12-ribbed stem and white-haired crown. Bears tubular, pink flowers, with cream anthers, at night in summer, on plants over 1.5m (5ft) tall. **H** to 6m (20ft), **S** 1m (3ft). Min. 11°C (52°F).

Aporocactus flagelliformis
(Rat's-tail cactus)
Pendent, perennial cactus with pencil-thick, green stems bearing short, golden spines. Has double, cerise flowers along stems in spring. Is good for a hanging basket. **H** 1m (3ft), **S** indefinite.

***Rebutia* 'Carnival'**
Clump-forming, spherical, perennial cactus with low, tuberculate ribs bearing areoles of white hairs and thin spines. In spring produces masses of funnel-shape flowers around the base; in white, pink, salmon, orange or orange-red. **H** 5cm (2in), **S** 15cm (6in). Min. 5°C (41°F).

PINK

Rebutia 'Jenny'
Clump-forming, perennial cactus with low, tuberculate ribs bearing areoles with short, white spines. In spring produces funnel-shaped flowers, the outer sepals dark pink shading to off-white towards the centre. **H** 5cm (2in), **S** 15cm (6in). Min. 5°C (41°F).

Echinocereus pentalophus
Clump-forming, perennial cactus with spined, green stems, 3–4cm (1¼–1½in) wide, that have 4–8 ribs, later rounded. Has trumpet-shaped, bright pink flowers, paler at the base, to 12cm (5in) across, in spring. **H** 60cm (2ft), **S** 1m (3ft). Min. 5°C (41°F).

Echeveria elegans
Clump-forming, perennial succulent with a basal rosette of broad, fleshy, pale silvery-blue leaves, edged with red, and yellow-tipped, pink flowers in summer. Keep dry in winter. Makes a good bedding plant. **H** 5cm (2in), **S** 50cm (20in). Min. 5°C (41°F).

Stenocactus obvallatus
Spherical, perennial cactus with wavy-margined ribs. White areoles each bear 5–12 greyish-brown spines. In spring, has pale yellow to pale pink flowers, with a purplish-red stripe on each petal. **H** and **S** 8cm (3in). Min. 7°C (45°F).

Hesperaloe parviflora
Basal-rosetted, perennial succulent, often with peeling, white fibres at leaf edges. Flower stems each bear a raceme of bell-shaped, pink to red flowers in summer–autumn. **H** 1m (3ft) or more, **S** 2m (6ft). Min. 3°C (37°F).

Mammillaria sempervivi
Slow-growing, spherical, perennial cactus. Has a dark green stem with short, white spines. Has white wool between short, angular tubercles on plants over 4cm (1½in) high. Bears cerise flowers in spring. **H** and **S** 7cm (3in). Min. 5°C (41°F).

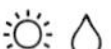

Aptenia cordifolia
Fast-growing, prostrate, perennial succulent with oval, glossy, green leaves and, in summer, daisy-like, bright pink flowers. Is ideal for ground cover. **H** 5cm (2in), **S** indefinite. Min. 7°C (45°F).

Thelocactus bicolor
Spherical to columnar, perennial cactus with an 8–13-ribbed stem. Areoles each have 4 usually flattened, yellow, central spines, or bicoloured yellow and red, and numerous shorter, radial spines. Flowers are purple-pink. **H** and **S** 20cm (8in). Min. 7°C (45°F).

Conophytum concordans
Clump-forming, perennial succulent with 2 fleshy, grey-green leaves that are broad, erect and united for most of their length but have distinctly divided, upper lobes. Pale pink flowers appear in late summer. **H** 2.5cm (1in), **S** 1cm (½in). Min. 5°C (41°F).

Lampranthus spectabilis
Spreading, perennial succulent with erect stems and narrow, cylindrical, grey-green leaves. In summer produces daisy-like flowers, cerise with yellow centres or golden-yellow throughout. **H** 30cm (12in), **S** indefinite. Min. 5°C (41°F).

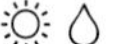

Echinocereus reichenbachii var. baileyi
Columnar, perennial cactus with a slightly branched stem bearing 12–23 ribs and yellowish-white, 3cm (1¼in) long spines. Produces pink flowers with darker bases in spring. **H** 30cm (12in), **S** 20cm (8in). Min. 7°C (45°F).

Crassula multicava
Bushy, perennial succulent with oval, grey-green leaves, 8cm (3in) across. Carries numerous clusters of small, star-shaped, pink flowers on elongated stems in spring, followed by small plantlets. **H** 15cm (6in), **S** 1m (3ft). Min. 7°C (45°F).

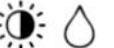

Crassula schmidtii
Carpeting, perennial succulent with dense rosettes of linear, dark green leaves, pitted and marked, each 3–4cm (1¼–1½in) long. Bears masses of star-shaped, bright pink-red flowers in clusters in winter. **H** 10cm (4in), **S** 30cm (12in). Min. 7°C (45°F).

Oscularia deltoides
Spreading, perennial succulent. Has chunky, triangular, blue-green leaves, to 1cm (½in) long, with small-toothed, often reddened leaf margins. Fragrant, pink flowers, 1–2cm (½–¾in) wide, appear in early summer. **H** 15cm (6in), **S** 1m (3ft). Min. 7°C (45°F).

Eriosyce napina
Flattened spherical, perennial cactus with very short, grey spines pressed flat against a greenish-brown stem. Produces white, pink, carmine or brown flowers, 5cm (2in) across, from the crown in summer. **H** 2cm (¾in), **S** 3.5cm (1½in). Min. 8°C (46°F).

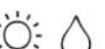

***Disocactus* 'Gloria'**
Erect, then pendent, perennial cactus. Strap-shaped, flattened, green stems have toothed edges. Produces pinkish-red flowers, 10cm (4in) across, in spring. **H** 30cm (1ft), **S** 1m (3ft). Min. 10°C (50°F).

Frithia pulchra
Basal-rosetted, perennial succulent with erect, rough, grey leaves, cylindrical with flattened tips. Produces masses of stemless, daisy-like, bright pink flowers, with paler centres, in summer. **H** 3cm (1¼in), **S** 6cm (2½in). Min. 10°C (50°F).

***Disocactus* 'M.A. Jeans'**
Erect, then pendent, perennial cactus. Strap-shaped, flattened, green stems have shallowly toothed edges. In spring has deep pink flowers, 8cm (3in) across, with white anthers. **H** 30cm (12in), **S** 50cm (20in). Min. 10°C (50°F).

***Kalanchoe* 'Wendy'**
Semi-erect, perennial succulent with narrowly oval, glossy, green leaves, 7cm (3in) long. In late winter bears bell-shaped, pinkish-red flowers, 2cm (¾in) long, with yellow tips. Is ideal for a hanging basket. **H** and **S** 30cm (12in). Min. 10°C (50°F).

Hatiora rosea
Bushy, perennial cactus with slender, 3- or 4-angled, bristly, green stem segments, usually tinged purple, to 5cm (2in) long. Has masses of bell-shaped, pink flowers, to 4cm (1½in) across, in spring. **H** and **S** 10cm (4in). Min. 10°C (50°F).

Graptopetalum bellum
Basal-rosetted, perennial succulent with triangular to oval, grey leaves, 5cm (2in) long. Has clusters of deep pink to red flowers, 2cm (¾in) across, in spring–summer. **H** 3cm (1¼in), **S** 15cm (6in). Min. 10°C (50°F).

***Disocactus phyllanthoides* 'Deutsche Kaiserin'**
Pendent, epiphytic, perennial cactus with flattened, toothed, glossy, green stems, each 5cm (2in) across. Stem margins each bear pink flowers, to 10cm (4in) across, in spring. **H** 60cm (2ft), **S** 1m (3ft). Min. 10°C (50°F).

Pereskia grandifolia (Rose cactus)
Deciduous, bushy, perennial cactus with black spines. Single rose-like, pink flowers form in summer–autumn only on plants over 30cm (1ft) high. **H** 5m (15ft), **S** 3m (10ft). Min. 10°C (50°F).

PINK

Mammillaria zeilmanniana
(Rose pincushion)
Clump-forming, perennial cactus with a spherical, green stem that has hooked spines and bears a ring of deep pink to purple flowers in spring. **H** 15cm (6in), **S** 30cm (12in). Min. 10ºC (50ºF).

Oroya peruviana
Spherical, perennial cactus with a much-ribbed stem covered in yellow spines, 1.5cm (⅝in) long, with darker bases. Pink flowers, with yellow bases, open in spring–summer. **H** 25cm (10in), **S** 20cm (8in). Min. 10ºC (50ºF).

***Senecio articulatus* 'Variegatus'**
Deciduous, spreading, perennial succulent with grey-marked stems. Has cream- and pink-marked, blue-green leaves in summer and yellow flower heads from autumn to spring. **H** 60cm (24in), **S** indefinite. Min. 10ºC (50ºF).

Parodia mueller-melchersii
Columnar, perennial cactus. Areoles each have about 15 radial spines and 2 upward- or downward-pointing, central spines. Has cream-centred, pink flowers in summer. **H** 10cm (4in), **S** 5cm (2in). Min. 10ºC (50ºF).

***Schlumbergera* 'Gold Charm'**
Erect, then pendent, perennial cactus. Has flattened, oblong, green stem segments with toothed margins. Yellow flowers in early autumn turn pinkish-orange in winter. **H** 15cm (6in), **S** 30cm (12in). Min. 10ºC (50ºF).

Adenium obesum
Tree-like, perennial succulent with a fleshy, tapering, green trunk and stems crowned by oval, glossy, green leaves, dull green beneath. Carries funnel-shaped, pink to pinkish-red flowers, white inside, in summer. **H** 2m (6ft), **S** 50cm (20in). Min. 15ºC (59ºF).

RED

Echinopsis chamaecereus
(Peanut cactus)
Clump-forming, perennial cactus with spined stems, initially erect, then prostrate. Has funnel-shaped, orange-red flowers in late spring. **H** 10cm (4in), **S** indefinite. Min. 3ºC (37ºF).

Opuntia verschaffeltii
Clump-forming, perennial cactus with cylindrical, usually spineless stems, to 25cm (10in) long. Stem tips each bear short-lived, cylindrical leaves from spring to autumn. Has orange-red flowers in spring. **H** 15cm (6in), **S** 1–2m (3–6ft). Min. 5ºC (41ºF).

Rebutia deminuta
Clump-forming, perennial cactus with a spherical, spined, green stem, to 4cm (1½in) across, becoming columnar with age. Bears masses of slender-tubed, orange-red flowers at base in late spring. **H** 10cm (4in), **S** 20cm (8in). Min. 5ºC (41ºF).

Rebutia minuscula
Clump-forming, perennial cactus with a tuberculate, dark green stem. Bears prominent, white areoles with very short, white spines. Trumpet-shaped, bright red flowers, to 5cm (2in) across, appear at stem base in spring. **H** 5cm (2in), **S** 20cm (8in). Min. 5ºC (41ºF).

Ferocactus hamatacanthus
Slow-growing, spherical to columnar, perennial cactus with a 13-ribbed stem that bears hooked, red spines, to 12cm (5in) long. Has yellow blooms in summer, then spherical, red fruits. **H** and **S** 60cm (24in). Min. 5ºC (41ºF).

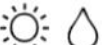

Echeveria secunda
Clump-forming, perennial succulent with short stems each crowned by a rosette of broad, fleshy, light green to grey leaves, reddened near the tips. Bears cup-shaped, red-and-yellow flowers in spring–summer. **H** 4cm (1½in), **S** 30cm (12in). Min. 5°C (41°F).

Parodia haselbergii* subsp. *haselbergii (Scarlet ball cactus)
Slow-growing, perennial cactus with a stem covered in white spines. Slightly sunken crown bears red flowers, with yellow stigmas, in spring. **H** 10cm (4in), **S** 25cm (10in). Min. 10°C (50°F).

Parodia nivosa
Ovoid, perennial cactus that has a much-ribbed, green stem with stiff, white spines, each 1–2cm (½–¾in) long. Has a white, woolly crown and bright red flowers, to 5cm (2in) across, in summer. **H** to 15cm (6in), **S** 10cm (4in). Min. 10°C (50°F).

Cyphostemma juttae
Perennial succulent. Swollen stem has peeling bark and deciduous, scandent branches with broad leaves. Bears inconspicuous, yellow-green flowers in summer. Green fruits turn yellow or red. **H** and **S** 2m (6ft). Min. 10°C (50°F).

Stenocactus coptonogonus
Spherical, perennial cactus. White areoles each have 3–5 flat, upward-curving, pale brownish-red spines. Bears purple to white flowers, with pink-purple or violet-purple stripes, in spring. **H** 10cm (4in), **S** 16cm (6in). Min. 7°C (45°F).

Parodia microsperma
Clump-forming, perennial cactus. Has a much-ribbed, green stem densely covered with brown, radial spines and red, central spines, some of which are hooked. Bears blood-red, occasionally yellow flowers in spring. **H** 8cm (3in), **S** 30cm (12in). Min. 10°C (50°F).

***Kalanchoe* 'Tessa'**
Prostrate to pendent, perennial succulent with narrowly oval, green leaves, 3cm (1¼in) long. Bears tubular, orange-red flowers, 2cm (¾in) long, in late winter. **H** 30cm (12in), **S** 60cm (24in). Min. 10°C (50°F).

Schlumbergera truncata
(Crab cactus, Lobster cactus)
Erect, then pendent, perennial cactus. Oblong stem segments have toothed margins. Bears purple-red flowers in early autumn and winter. **H** 15cm (6in), **S** 30cm (12in). Min. 10°C (50°F).

Kalanchoe blossfeldiana
Bushy, perennial succulent with oval to oblong, toothed, glossy, green leaves. Produces clusters of yellow, orange, pink, red or purple flowers, year-round. Makes an excellent house plant. **H** and **S** 30cm (12in). Min. 10°C (50°F).

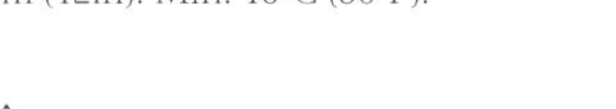

***Gymnocalycium mihanovichii* 'Red Head'**
Perennial cactus with a red stem, 8 angular ribs and curved spines. Must be grafted on to any fast-growing stock as it contains no chlorophyll. Has pink flowers in spring–summer. **H** and **S** as per graft stock. Min. 10°C (50°F).

Rebutia steinbachii* subsp. *tiraquensis
Variable, perennial cactus with a green stem. Elongated areoles bear spines of gold or bicoloured red and white. Has dark pink- or orange-red flowers in spring. **H** 15cm (6in), **S** 10cm (4in). Min. 10°C (50°F).

Hatiora gaertneri (Easter cactus)
Bushy, perennial cactus with flat, oblong, glossy, green stem segments, each to 5cm (2in) long, often tinged red at the edges. Segment ends each bear orange-red flowers in spring. **H** 15cm (6in), **S** 20cm (13in). Min. 13°C (55°F).

PURPLE

***Schlumbergera* 'Bristol Beauty'**
Erect, then pendent, perennial cactus with flattened, green stem segments with toothed margins. Bears reddish-purple flowers, with silvery-white tubes, in early autumn and winter. **H** 15cm (6in), **S** 30cm (12in). Min. 10°C (50°F).

Orbea variegata (Star flower)
Clump-forming, branching, perennial succulent with 4-angled, indented stems. Flowers, variable in colour and blotched yellow, purple- or red-brown, appear in summer-autumn. **H** to 10cm (4in), **S** indefinite. Min. 11°C (52°F).

Argyroderma delaetii
Prostrate, egg-shaped, perennial succulent with 2 very fleshy, silvery-green leaves between which daisy-like, pink-purple flowers, 5cm (2in) across, appear in late summer. **H** 3cm (1½in), **S** 5cm (2in). Min. 5°C (41°F).

Huernia macrocarpa
Clump-forming, perennial succulent with finger-shaped, 4- or 5-sided, green stems. Produces short-lived, deciduous leaves and, in autumn, bell-shaped, white-haired, dark purple flowers with recurved petal tips. **H** and **S** 10cm (4in). Min. 8°C (46°F).

Stapelia grandiflora
Clump-forming, perennial succulent with 4-angled, hairy, toothed, green stems. In summer-autumn carries star-shaped, purple-brown flowers, to 10cm (4in) across, ridged with white or purple hairs. **H** to 20cm (8in), **S** indefinite. Min. 11°C (52°F).

BLUE

Crassula deceptor
Slow-growing, clump-forming, perennial succulent with branching stems surrounded by fleshy, grey leaves set in 4 rows. Each leaf has minute lines around raised dots. Bears insignificant flowers in spring. **H** and **S** 10cm (4in). Min. 5°C (41°F).

Browningia hertlingiana
Slow-growing, columnar, perennial cactus with a silvery-blue stem, golden spines and tufted areoles. Nocturnal, white flowers appear in summer, only on plants over 1m (3ft) high. **H** 8m (25ft), **S** 4m (12ft). Min. 7°C (45°F).

Opuntia robusta
Bushy, perennial cactus. Silvery-blue stem has flattened, oval segments with either no spines or 8–12 white ones, to 5cm (2in) long, per areole. Saucer-shaped, yellow flowers, 7cm (3in) across, appear in spring-summer. **H** and **S** 5m (15ft). Min. 5°C (41°F).

Cereus hildmannianus
Columnar, perennial cactus. Has a branching, silvery-blue stem and golden spines on 4–8 indented ribs. Bears cup-shaped, white flowers, 10cm (4in) across, at night in summer, and pear-shaped, red fruits. **H** 5m (15ft), **S** 4m (12ft). Min. 7°C (45°F).

Aloinopsis schooneesii
Dwarf, mounded, perennial succulent with tuberous roots and fleshy, almost spherical, blue-green leaves arranged tightly in tufts. Produces flattish, yellow flowers in winter-spring. **H** 3cm (1½in), **S** to 7cm (3in). Min. 7°C (45°F).

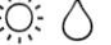

Cereus hankeanus
Columnar, perennial cactus with a branching, blue-green stem bearing dark spines on 4–7 prominent ribs. Has 25cm (10in) long, cup-shaped, white flowers at night in summer, followed by red fruits. **H** 7m (22ft), **S** 3m (10ft). Min. 7°C (45°F).

Copiapoa cinerea
Very slow-growing, clump-forming, perennial cactus. Blue-green stem bears up to 25 ribs and black spines. Has a woolly, white-grey crown and, on plants over 10cm (4in) across, yellow flowers in spring-summer. **H** 50cm (20in), **S** 2m (6ft). Min. 10°C (50°F).

Aeonium haworthii **(Pinwheel)**
Bushy, perennial succulent. Freely branching stems bear rosettes, 12cm (5in) across, of blue-green leaves, often with red margins. Has a terminal spike of star-shaped, pink-tinged, pale yellow flowers in spring. **H** 60cm (2ft), **S** 1m (3ft). Min. 5°C (41°F).

Agave attenuata
Perennial succulent with a thick stem crowned by a rosette of sword-shaped, spineless, pale green leaves. Arching flower stem, to 1.5m (5ft) long, is densely covered with yellow flowers in spring-summer. **H** 1m (3ft), **S** 2m (6ft). Min. 5°C (41°F).

Crassula perfoliata* var. *falcata
(Aeroplane propeller)
Bushy, perennial succulent that branches freely. Long leaves each twist like a propeller. Has large clusters of fragrant, red flowers in late summer. **H** and **S** 1m (3ft). Min. 7°C (45°F).

Echinopsis lageniformis
Columnar, perennial cactus with 4–8-ribbed stems branching at base. Areoles each produce up to 6 spines. Scented, funnel-shaped, white flowers open at night in summer. **H** to 5m (15ft), **S** 1m (3ft). Min. 10°C (50°F).

Agave parryi
Basal-rosetted, perennial succulent with stiff, broad, grey-green leaves, each to 30cm (12in) long with a solitary dark spine at its pointed tip. Flower stem, to 4m (12ft) long, bears creamy-yellow flowers in summer. **H** 50cm (20in), **S** 1m (3ft). Min. 5°C (41°F).

Myrtillocactus geometrizans
(Blue candle)
Columnar, perennial cactus with a branched, 5- or 6-ribbed, blue-green stem. Bears short, black spines, on plants over 30cm (1ft) tall, and white flowers at night in summer. **H** to 4m (12ft), **S** 2m (6ft). Min. 12°C (54°F).

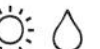

Graptopetalum paraguayense
(Mother-of-pearl plant)
Clump-forming, perennial succulent with a basal rosette, 15cm (6in) across, of grey-green leaves, often tinged pink. Bears star-shaped, yellow-and-red flowers in summer. **H** 10cm (4in), **S** 1m (3ft). Min. 5°C (41°F).

Lithops marmorata
Egg-shaped, perennial succulent, divided into 2 unequal-sized, swollen, pale grey leaves with dark grey marks on convex, upper surfaces. Bears a white flower in late summer or early autumn. **H** 2–3cm (¾–1¼in), **S** 5cm (2in). Min. 5°C (41°F).

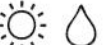

GREY

Leuchtenbergia principis
Basal-rosetted, perennial cactus with narrow, angular, dull grey-green tubercles, each 10cm (4in) long and crowned by papery spines to 10cm (4in) long. Crown bears yellow flowers, to 7cm (3in) across, in summer. **H** and **S** 30cm (12in). Min. 6°C (43°F).

Crassula arborescens (Silver jade plant)
Perennial succulent with a thick, robust stem crowned by branches bearing rounded, silvery-blue leaves, often with red edges. Has 5-petalled, pink flowers in autumn–winter. **H** 4m (12ft), **S** 2m (6ft). Min. 7°C (45°F).

Ceropegia linearis (Heart vine, Rosary vine, String-of-hearts)
Semi-evergreen, trailing, succulent sub-shrub with tuberous roots. Leaves redden in sun. Has hairy, pinkish-green flowers from spring to autumn. **H** 1m (3ft), **S** indefinite. Min. 7°C (45°F).

Dudleya pulverulenta
Basal-rosetted, perennial succulent with strap-shaped, pointed, silvery-grey leaves. Bears masses of star-shaped, red flowers in spring–summer. **H** 60cm (24in), **S** 30cm (12in). Min. 7°C (45°F).

x _Pachyveria glauca_
Clump-forming, perennial succulent with a dense, basal rosette of fleshy, incurved, oval, silvery-blue leaves, to 6cm (2½in) long, with darker marks. Bears star-shaped, yellow flowers, each with a red tip, in spring. **H** and **S** 30cm (12in). Min. 7°C (45°F).

Eriosyce villosa
Clump-forming, perennial cactus with a branched, green to dark grey-green stem. Has dense, sometimes curved, grey spines, 3cm (1¼in) long. Produces tubular, pink or white flowers in spring or autumn. **H** 15cm (6in), **S** 10cm (4in). Min. 8°C (46°F).

Pachyphytum oviferum (Moonstones, Sugared-almond plum)
Clump-forming, perennial succulent with a basal rosette of oval, pinkish-blue leaves. Stem bears 10–15 bell-shaped flowers, with powder-blue calyces and orange-red petals, in spring. **H** 10cm (4in), **S** 30cm (12in). Min. 10°C (50°F).

Kalanchoe tomentosa (Panda plant, Pussy ears)
Bushy, perennial succulent with thick, oval, grey leaves, covered with velvety bristles and often edged with brown at tips. Has yellowish-purple flowers in winter. **H** 50cm (20in), **S** 30cm (12in). Min. 10°C (50°F).

GREEN

Beschorneria yuccoides
Clump-forming, perennial succulent with a basal rosette of up to 20 rough, greyish-green leaves, to 1m (3ft) long and 5cm (2in) across. Produces pendent, tubular, bright red flowers in summer in spikes over 2m (6ft) tall. **H** 1m (3ft), **S** 3m (10ft).

Maihuenia poeppigii
Slow-growing, clump-forming, perennial cactus. Has a cylindrical, branched, spiny, green-brown stem. Most branches produce a spike of cylindrical, green leaves at the tip, with a funnel-shaped, yellow flower in summer. **H** 6cm (2½in), **S** 30cm (12in).

Frailea pygmaea
Columnar, perennial cactus with a much-ribbed, dark green stem bearing white to light brown spines. Buds, which rarely open to flattish, yellow flowers in summer, become tufts of spherical, spiny seed pods. **H** to 5cm (2in), **S** 2cm (¾in). Min. 5°C (41°F).

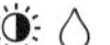

Aeonium tabuliforme
Prostrate, almost stemless, short-lived, perennial succulent with a basal rosette, to 30cm (12in) across, like a flat, bright green plate. Has star-shaped, yellow flowers in spring, then dies. Propagate from seed. **H** 5cm (2in), **S** 30cm (12in). Min. 5°C (41°F).

Mammillaria microhelia
Columnar, perennial cactus with a 5cm (⅝in) wide, green stem bearing cream or brown spines, discolouring with age. Has 5cm (⅝in) wide, yellow or pink flowers in spring. Offsets slowly with age. **H** 20cm (8in), **S** 40cm (16in). Min. 5°C (41°F).

Argyroderma pearsonii
Prostrate, egg-shaped, perennial succulent. A united pair of very fleshy, silvery-grey leaves has a deep fissure in which a red flower, 3cm (1¼in) across, appears in summer. **H** 3cm (1¼in), **S** 5cm (2in). Min. 5°C (41°F).

Lithops lesliei* var. *albinica
Egg-shaped, perennial succulent, divided into 2 unequal-sized leaves; convex, pale green, upper surfaces have dark green and yellow marks. Bears a white flower in late summer or early autumn. **H** 2–3cm (¾–1¼in), **S** 5cm (2in). Min. 5°C (41°F).

Schwantesia ruedebuschii
Mat-forming, perennial succulent with cylindrical, bluish-green leaves, 3–5cm (1–2in) long, with expanded tips. Leaf edges each produce 3–7 minute, blue teeth with brown tips. Has yellow flowers in summer. **H** 5cm (2in), **S** 20cm (8in). Min. 5°C (41°F).

Echinopsis marsoneri
Columnar, perennial cactus with a 20–25-ribbed, bluish- to dark green stem that has yellow, radial spines with longer, darker, central ones. In summer produces yellow flowers, 7cm (3in) across, with red throats. **H** 30cm (12in), **S** 15cm (6in). Min. 5°C (41°F).

Echinopsis pentlandii
Clump-forming or solitary, variable, perennial cactus with a 10–20-ribbed stem and 6–20 spined aeroles. Has white, pink, purple or orange flowers, with paler throats, in summer. **H** 8cm (3in), **S** 10cm (4in). Min. 5°C (41°F).

Argyroderma fissum
Clump-forming, perennial succulent with finger-shaped, fleshy leaves, 5–10cm (2–4in) long and often reddish at the tip. Has light red flowers between leaves in summer. **H** 15cm (6in), **S** 10cm (4in). Min. 5°C (41°F).

Lithops dorotheae
Egg-shaped, perennial succulent, divided into 2 unequal-sized leaves, pale pink-yellow to green with darker areas and red marks on upper surfaces. Produces a daisy-like, yellow flower in summer or autumn. **H** 2–3cm (¾–1¼in), **S** 5cm (2in). Min. 5°C (41°F).

Pachyphytum compactum
Clump-forming, perennial succulent with a basal rosette of green leaves, each narrowing to a blunt point, with angular, paler edges. Stems each bear 3–10 flowers with green to pink calyces and orange petals in spring. **H** 15cm (6in), **S** indefinite. Min. 5°C (41°F).

Echinopsis backebergii
Clump-forming, almost spherical, perennial cactus with a 10–15-ribbed, spined, dark green stem. Has funnel-shaped, pink, red or purple flowers, with paler throats, in summer. **H** 10cm (4in), **S** 15cm (6in). Min. 5°C (41°F).

Haworthia arachnoidea
Slow-growing, clump-forming, perennial succulent with a basal rosette of triangular leaves. Bears soft, white teeth along leaf margins. Has white flowers from spring to autumn. **H** 5cm (2in), **S** 10cm (4in). Min. 6°C (43°F).

GREEN

Carnegiea gigantea **(Saguaro)**
Very slow-growing, perennial cactus with a thick, 12–24-ribbed, spiny, green stem. Tends to branch and bears short, funnel-shaped, fleshy, white flowers at stem tips in summer, only when over 4m (12ft) high. **H** to 12m (40ft), **S** 3m (10ft). Min. 7°C (45°F).

Kalanchoe daigremontiana
(Mexican hat plant)
Erect, perennial succulent with a stem bearing fleshy, boat-shaped, toothed leaves. Produces a plantlet in each leaf notch. Umbels of pink flowers appear at stem tops in winter. **H** to 1m (3ft), **S** 30cm (1ft). Min. 7°C (45°F).

Adromischus maculatus
Clump-forming, perennial succulent with rounded, glossy, green leaves with purple marks. Leaf tips are often wavy. Carries tubular, purplish-white flowers, on a 30cm (12in) tall stem, in summer. **H** 6cm (2½in), **S** 10–15cm (4–6in). Min. 7°C (45°F).

Echinopsis spachiana **(Torch cactus)**
Clump-forming, perennial cactus with glossy, green stems bearing 10–15 ribs and pale golden spines. Fragrant, funnel-shaped, white flowers open at night in summer. **H** and **S** 2m (6ft). Min. 8°C (46°F).

Echinopsis candicans
Clump-forming, branching, perennial cactus with up to 11 ribs. Areoles each have 10–15 radial spines and 4 central ones. Fragrant, funnel-shaped, white flowers open at night in summer. **H** 1m (3ft), **S** indefinite. Min. 8°C (46°F).

Echinocereus schmollii
(Lamb's-tail cactus)
Erect to prostrate, tuberous cactus with 8–10-ribbed, purplish-green stems and mostly white spines. Has pinkish-purple flowers in spring-summer. **H** and **S** 30cm (12in). Min. 8°C (46°F).

Aloe vera
Clump-forming, perennial succulent with basal rosettes of tapering, thick leaves, mottled green, later grey-green. Flower stems carry bell-shaped, yellow flowers in summer. Propagate by offsets as plant is sterile. **H** 60cm (24in), **S** indefinite. Min. 10°C (50°F).

Haworthia truncata
Clump-forming, perennial succulent with a basal fan of broad, erect, rough, blue-grey leaves with pale grey lines and flat ends. Produces small, tubular, white flowers, with spreading petals, from spring to autumn. **H** 2cm (¾in), **S** 10cm (4in). Min. 10°C (50°F).

Dioscorea elephantipes
(Elephant's foot)
Very slow-growing, deciduous, perennial succulent with a domed, woody trunk, annual, climbing stems and yellow flowers in autumn. **H** 50cm (20in), **S** 1m (3ft). Min. 10°C (50°F).

Lophophora williamsii
(Dumpling cactus, Mescal button)
Very slow-growing, clump-forming, perennial cactus with an 8-ribbed, blue-green stem. Masses of pink flowers appear in summer on plants over 3cm (1¼in) high. **H** 5cm (2in), **S** 8cm (3in). Min. 10°C (50°F).

Pachycereus schottii
Columnar, perennial cactus, branching with age. Olive- to dark green stem, covered with small, white spines, bears 4–15 ribs. Funnel-shaped, pink flowers are produced at night in summer. **H** 7m (22ft), **S** 2m (6ft). Min. 10°C (50°F).

Rhipsalis floccosa
Pendent, perennial cactus with cylindrical, green stems, to 1cm (½in) across, branching less than many other Rhipsalis species. Has masses of very pale pink flowers in early summer, then pinkish-white fruits. **H** 1m (3ft), **S** 50cm (20in). Min. 10°C (50°F).

Oreocereus celsianus
(Old man of the Andes)
Slow-growing, perennial cactus. Has heavy and wispy spines. Mature plants bear pink flowers in summer. **H** 1m (3ft), **S** 30cm (1ft). Min. 10°C (50°F).

Epithelantha micromeris
Slow-growing, spherical, perennial cactus with a green stem completely obscured by close-set areoles bearing tiny, white spines. Bears funnel-shaped, pale pinkish-red flowers, 0.5cm (¼in) across, on a woolly crown in summer. **H** and **S** 4cm (1½in). Min. 10°C (50°F).

Duvalia corderoyi
Clump-forming, perennial succulent. Has a prostrate, leafless stem with 6 often purple, indistinct ribs. Bears star-shaped, dull green flowers, 1cm (½in) across and covered in purple hairs, in summer–autumn. **H** 5cm (2in), **S** 60cm (24in). Min. 10°C (50°F).

Euphorbia obesa (Gingham golf ball)
Spherical, perennial succulent. Spineless, dark green stem, often chequered light green, has 8 low ribs. Crown bears rounded heads of cupped, yellow flowers in summer. **H** 12cm (5in), **S** 15cm (6in). Min. 10°C (50°F).

ALOES

Aloes are abundant in Mediterranean and African gardens. There is a huge range of species and hybrids providing a kaleidoscope of growth forms, flowers, and leaf variegation. Unlike agaves, aloes do not die after flowering, but gradually produce a trunk, becoming shrubs or small trees. Aloes typically produce their leaves singly, and the centre of the rosette is usually hollow, reminiscent of a bromeliad. A few species, such as *A. aristata* are frost hardy, and can be grown in rock gardens or at the base of a south facing wall.

A. arborescens 'Variegata'

A. striata

A. variegata

A. ferox

A. aristata

A. ciliaris

A. hemmingii

GREEN

Pachypodium lamerei
Tree-like, perennial succulent with a spiny, pale green stem crowned by linear leaves. Has fragrant, trumpet-shaped, creamy-white flowers in summer, on plants over 1.5m (5ft) tall. Stems branch after flowering. **H** 6m (20ft), **S** 2m (6ft). Min.11°C (52°F).

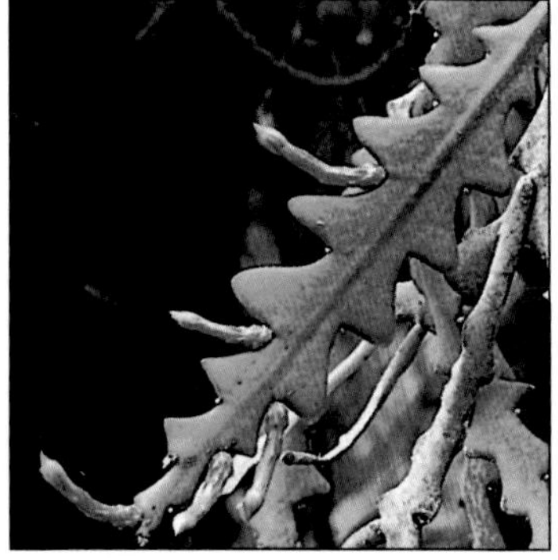

Epiphyllum anguliger
(Fishbone cactus)
Erect, then pendent, perennial cactus. Has strap-shaped, flattened, green stems with heavily indented margins. Produces tubular, 10cm (4in) wide, white flowers in summer. **H** 1m (3ft), **S** 40cm (16in). Min. 11°C (52°F).

Pachycereus marginatus
(Organ-pipe cactus)
Columnar, perennial cactus with a 5- or 6-ribbed, branching, stem. Areoles bear minute spines. Produces funnel-shaped, white flowers in summer. **H** 7m (22ft), **S** 3m (10ft). Min. 11°C (52°F).

Neobuxbaumia euphorbioides
Columnar, perennial cactus. Has grey-green to dark green stems, 10cm (4in) across, with 8–10 ribs and 1 or 2 black spines per areole. Funnel-shaped, wine-red flowers appear in summer. **H** 3m (10ft), **S** 1m (3ft). Min. 15°C (59°F).

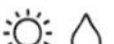

Caralluma joannis
Clump-forming, perennial succulent with blue-grey stems and rudimentary leaves on stem angles. Bears clusters of star-shaped, purple flowers, with short, fine hairs on petal tips, in late summer near stem tips. **H** 20cm (8in), **S** 1m (3ft). Min. 11°C (52°F).

Melocactus intortus (Melon cactus)
Flattened spherical, perennial cactus. Has an 18–20-ribbed stem with yellow-brown spines. Crown matures to a white column with brown spines. Bears pink flowers in summer. **H** 20cm (8in), **S** 25cm (10in). Min. 15°C (59°F).

YELLOW

Opuntia humifusa
Prostrate, perennial cactus. Each areole bears up to 3 spines, 3cm (1¼in) long. Has flat, rounded to oval, purple-tinged, dark green stem segments, 7–18cm (3–7in) long. Bears 8cm (3in) wide, yellow flowers spring–summer. Keep dry in winter. **H** 15cm (6in), **S** 1m (3ft).

Astrophytum myriostigma
(Bishop's cap)
Slow-growing, spherical to slightly elongated, perennial cactus. A fleshy stem has 4–6 ribs and is flecked with tiny tufts of white spines. Bears yellow flowers in summer. **H** 30cm (12in), **S** 20cm (8in). Min. 5°C (41°F).

Conophytum bilobum
Slow-growing, clump-forming, perennial succulent with 2-lobed, fleshy, green leaves, 4cm (1½in) long, 2cm (¾in) wide. Has flared, yellow flowers, 3cm (1¼in) across, in autumn. **H** 4cm (1½in), **S** 15cm (6in). Min. 4°C (39°F).

Ferocactus cylindraceus
Slow-growing, columnar, perennial cactus, spherical when young. Green, 10–20-ribbed stem has large, hooked, red or yellow spines. Funnel-shaped, yellow flowers form in summer on plants 25cm (10in) across. **H** 3m (10ft), **S** 80cm (32in). Min. 5°C (41°F).

Mammillaria elongata (Lace cactus)
Clump-forming, perennial cactus. Has columnar, green stems, 3cm (1¼in) across, densely covered with yellow, golden or brown spines. Bears cream flowers in summer. **H** 15cm (6in), **S** 30cm (12in). Min. 5°C (41°F).

Rhombophyllum rhomboideum
Clump-forming, perennial succulent. Linear, glossy, grey-green leaves have expanded middles and white margins. Stems, 2–5cm (¾–2in) long, bear 3–7 yellow flowers, to 4cm (1½in) across, in summer. **H** 5cm (2in), **S** 15cm (6in). Min. 5°C (41°F).

Astrophytum ornatum
Spherical, perennial cactus with a very fleshy, 8-ribbed stem. Crown of each rib bears 5–11cm (2–4½in) long spines on each raised areole. Has yellow flowers, 8cm (3in) across, in summer. **H** 15cm (6in), **S** 12cm (5in). Min. 5°C (41°F).

Lithops pseudotruncatella* subsp. *dendritica
Egg-shaped, perennial succulent, divided into 2 unequal-sized, grey leaves with dark green and red marks on upper surfaces. Has a bright yellow flower in summer or autumn. **H** 2–3cm (¾–1¼in), **S** 4cm (1½in). Min. 5°C (41°F).

Pleiospilos bolusii (Living rock)
Clump-forming, perennial succulent with 1 or 2 pairs of grey leaves, often wider than long, and narrowing at incurved tips. Has golden flowers in early autumn. **H** 10cm (4in), **S** 20cm (8in). Min. 5°C (41°F).

Echinopsis aurea
Columnar, perennial cactus. Has narrow, much-ribbed, green stems covered with pale, radial spines often surrounded by 1–3 very stout, central spines, to 2.5cm (1in) long. Produces funnel-shaped, yellow flowers in summer. **H** and **S** 10cm (4in). Min. 5°C (41°F).

Glottiphyllum nelii
Clump-forming, perennial succulent with semi-cylindrical, fleshy, green leaves, to 5cm (1½in) long. Carries daisy-like, golden flowers, 5cm (1½in) across, in spring–summer. **H** 5cm (2in), **S** 30cm (12in). Min. 5°C (41°F).

Pleiospilos compactus
Clump-forming, perennial succulent with 1 or 2 pairs of thick, grey leaves, to 8cm (3in) long. Bears coconut-scented, yellow flowers in early autumn. **H** 10cm (4in), **S** 30cm (12in). Min. 5°C (41°F).

Lithops schwantesii
Egg-shaped, perennial succulent, divided into 2 unequal-sized leaves with blue or red marks on upper surface. Produces a yellow flower late summer or autumn. **H** 2–3cm (¾–1¼in), **S** 3cm (1¼in). Min. 5°C (41°F).

***Aichryson* x *aizoides* var. *domesticum* 'Variegatum'**
Prostrate, perennial succulent with stems crowned by rosettes of hairy, cream-marked, green leaves, often pure cream. Has star-shaped, yellow flowers in spring. **H** 15cm (6in), **S** 40cm (16in). Min. 5°C (41°F).

Fenestraria rhopalophylla* subsp. *aurantiaca (Baby's toes)
Clump-forming, perennial succulent with a basal rosette of glossy leaves. Has yellow flowers in late summer to autumn. **H** 5cm (2in), **S** 30cm (12in). Min. 6°C (43°F).

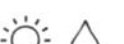

Faucaria tigrina (Tiger-jaws)
Clump-forming, stemless, perennial succulent. Fleshy, green leaves, 5cm (2in) long, have 9-10 teeth along each margin. Has yellow flowers, 5cm (2in) across, in autumn. **H** 10cm (4in), **S** 50cm (20in). Min. 6°C (43°F).

Thelocactus setispinus
Slow-growing, perennial cactus with a 13-ribbed stem and yellow or white spines. Fragrant, yellow flowers with red throats appear in summer on mature plants over 5cm (2in) across. **H** and **S** 30cm (12in). Min. 7°C (45°F).

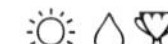

Sclerocactus scheeri
Spherical to columnar, perennial cactus. Stem bears spines and, in spring, funnel-shaped, straw-coloured flowers. Lowest and longest spines are darker and hooked. **H** 10cm (4in), **S** 6cm (2½in). Min. 7–10°C (45–50°F).

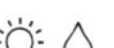

YELLOW

Titanopsis calcarea
Clump-forming, perennial succulent with a basal rosette of very fleshy, triangular, blue-grey leaves covered in wart-like, grey-white and beige tubercles. Has yellow flowers from autumn to spring. **H** 3cm (1¼in), **S** 10cm (4in). Min. 8°C (46°F).

Rebutia arenacea
Spherical, perennial cactus. Has a brown-green stem with white spines on spirally arranged tubercles. Has golden-yellow blooms, to 3cm (1¼in) across, in spring. **H** 5cm (2in), **S** 6cm (2½in). Min. 10°C (50°F).

Parodia chrysacanthion
Spherical, perennial cactus with a much-ribbed, green stem densely covered with bristle-like, golden spines, each 1–2cm (½–¾in) long. Crown bears yellow flowers in spring and, often, pale yellow wool. **H** and **S** 30cm (1ft). Min. 10°C (50°F).

***Discocactus* 'Jennifer Ann'**
Erect, then pendent, perennial cactus. Has strap-shaped, flattened, green stems with toothed margins. Bears yellow flowers, 15cm (6in) across, in spring. **H** 30cm (12in), **S** 50cm (20in). Min. 10°C (50°F).

Opuntia tunicata
Mounded, perennial cactus. Cylindrical, green stem segments are covered with 5cm (2in) long, golden spines, enclosed in a silver papery sheath. Bears shallowly saucer-shaped, yellow flowers in spring-summer. **H** 60cm (2ft), **S** 1m (3ft). Min. 10°C (50°F).

Stapelia gigantea
Clump-forming, perennial succulent. In summer-autumn bears star-shaped, red-marked, yellow-brown flowers, 30cm (12in) across, with white-haired, recurved edges. **H** to 20cm (8in), **S** indefinite. Min. 11°C (52°F).

ORANGE

Echinocereus triglochidiatus* var. *paucispinus
Clump-forming, perennial cactus with a 10cm (4in) wide, dark green stem that has 6 or 7 ribs, and 4–6 spines, 3–4cm (1¼–1½in) long, per areole. Has orange-red flowers in spring. **H** 20cm (8in), **S** 50cm (20in). Min. 5°C (41°F).

Conophytum frutescens
Slow-growing, spherical, perennial succulent forming clumps of 2-lobed, very fleshy, grey-green leaves, often with a red spot on edge of fissure between the lobes. Carries copper-orange flowers in autumn. **H** 3cm (1¼in), **S** indefinite. Min. 4°C (39°F).

Rebutia fiebrigii
Clump-forming, perennial cactus. Has a dark green stem densely covered with soft, white spines, to 0.5cm (¾–1¼in) long. Bears bright orange flowers, 0.5cm (¾–1¼in) across, in late spring. **H** 10cm (4in), **S** 15cm (6in). Min. 5°C (41°F).

Lampranthus aurantiacus
Erect, then prostrate, sparse-branching perennial succulent with short, cylindrical, tapering, grey-green leaves. Masses of daisy-like, bright orange flowers, 5cm (2in) wide, open in summer sun. **H** 50cm (20in), **S** 70cm (28in). Min. 5°C (41°F).

Malephora crocea
Erect or spreading, perennial succulent with semi-cylindrical, blue-green leaves on short shoots. Carries solitary daisy-like, orange-yellow flowers, reddened on outsides, in spring–summer. **H** 20cm (8in), **S** 1m (3ft). Min. 5°C (41°F).

Kalanchoe delagoensis
Erect, perennial succulent with long, almost cylindrical, grey-green leaves with reddish-brown mottling and flattened, notched tips that form plantlets. Bears an umbel of orange-yellow flowers in late winter. **H** to 1m (3ft), **S** 30cm (1ft). Min. 8°C (46°F).

PLANT DICTIONARY

A complete listing of more than 8,000 plants, suitable for growing in temperate gardens worldwide. Includes full descriptions of the characteristics and cultivation of over 4,000 plants not already described in the Plant Catalogue.

A

ABELIA

CAPRIFOLIACEAE

Genus of deciduous, semi-evergreen or evergreen shrubs, grown for their foliage and freely borne flowers. Fully to half hardy, but in cold areas does best against a south- or west-facing wall. Requires a sheltered, sunny position and fertile, well-drained soil. Remove dead wood in late spring and prune out older branches after flowering to restrict growth, if required. Propagate by softwood cuttings in summer.

A. 'Edward Goucher' illus. p.153.

🏆 **A. *floribunda*.** Evergreen, arching shrub. **H** 3m (10ft), **S** 4m (12ft). Half hardy. Has oval, glossy, dark green leaves and, in early summer, drooping, tubular, bright red flowers.

🏆 **A. x *grandiflora*** illus. p.113. **'Francis Mason'** is a vigorous, semi-evergreen, arching shrub. **H** 2m (6ft), **S** 3m (10ft). Frost hardy. Has coppery-yellow young shoots and oval, yellowish-green leaves, darker in centres. Bears a profusion of fragrant, bell-shaped, white flowers, tinged with pink, from mid-summer to mid-autumn.

🏆 **A. *schumannii*** illus. p.154.

A. *triflora* illus. p.113.

ABELIOPHYLLUM

OLEACEAE

Genus of one species of deciduous shrub, grown for its winter flowers. Fully hardy, but in cold areas grow against a south- or west-facing wall. Requires plenty of sun and fertile, well-drained soil. Thin out excess older shoots after flowering each year to encourage vigorous young growth. Propagate by softwood cuttings in summer.

A. *distichum*. Deciduous, open shrub. **H** and **S** 1.2m (4ft). In late winter produces fragrant, star-shaped, white flowers, tinged with pink, on bare stems; flowers may be damaged by hard frosts. Leaves are oval and dark green.

ABIES

Silver fir

PINACEAE

Genus of tall conifers with whorled branches. Spirally arranged leaves are needle-like, flattened, usually soft and often have silvery bands beneath. Bears erect cones that ripen in their first autumn to release seeds and scales. See also CONIFERS.

A. *alba*. Fast-growing, conical conifer. **H** 15–25m (50–80ft), **S** 5–8m (15–25ft). Fully hardy. Has silvery-grey bark and dull green leaves, silvery beneath. Cylindrical cones, 10–15cm (4–6in) long, ripen to red-brown.

A. *amabilis* (Pacific fir). Conical conifer. **H** 15m (50ft), **S** 4–5m (12–15ft). Fully hardy. Dense, notched, square-tipped, glossy, dark green leaves, banded with white beneath, are borne on hairy, grey shoots. Oblong, violet-blue cones are 9–15cm (3½–6in) long. **'Spreading Star'**, **H** 50cm (20in), **S** 4–5m (12–15ft), is a procumbent form suitable for ground cover.

A. *balsamea* (Balsam fir). 🏆 **f. *hudsonia***, syn. Hudsonia Group, is a dense, dwarf conifer of flattened to globose habit. **H** and **S** 60cm–1m (2–3ft). Fully hardy. Has smooth, grey bark and grey-green leaves that are semi-spirally arranged. **Hudsonia Group** see *A.b.* f. *hudsonia*. **'Nana'** is another dwarf form that makes a dense, globose mound with leaves that are spirally arranged.

A. *cephalonica* (Greek fir). Upright conifer with a conical crown; old trees have massive, spreading, erect branches. **H** 20–30m (70–100ft), **S** 5–10m (15–30ft). Fully hardy. Sharp, stiff, glossy, deep green leaves are whitish-green beneath. Cylindrical, tapered cones, 10–15cm (4–6in) long, are brown when ripe. **'Meyer's Dwarf'** (illus. p.105), **H** 50cm (20in), **S** 1.5m (5ft), has short leaves and forms a spreading, flat-topped mound.

🏆 **A. *concolor*** (White fir). Upright conifer. **H** 15–30m (50–100ft), **S** 5–8m (15–25ft). Fully hardy. Has widely spreading, blue-green or grey leaves and cylindrical, green or pale blue cones, 8–12cm (3–5in) long. **'Argentea'** illus. p.95. 🏆 **'Compacta'** (syn. *A.c.* 'Glauca Compacta'; illus. p.105), **H** to 2m (6ft), **S** 2–3m (6–10ft), is a cultivar with steel-blue foliage.

A. *delavayi* (Delavay's fir). Upright conifer producing tiered, spreading branches. **H** 10–15m (30–50ft), **S** 4–6m (12–20ft). Fully hardy. Has maroon shoots and curved, bright deep green leaves, spirally arranged, with vivid silver bands beneath and rolled margins. Cones are narrowly cylindrical, 6–15cm (2½–6in) long, and violet-blue.

A. *forrestii* (Forrest fir) illus. p.100.

A. *grandis* (Giant fir, Grand fir) illus. p.98.

A. *homolepis* (Nikko fir). Conifer that is conical when young, later columnar. **H** 15m (50ft), **S** 6m (20ft). Fully hardy. Pink-grey bark peels in fine flakes. Has pale green leaves, silver beneath, and cylindrical, violet-blue cones, 8–12cm (3–5in) long. Tolerates urban conditions.

A. *koreana* (Korean fir) illus. p.104.

A. *lasiocarpa* (Subalpine fir). Narrowly conical conifer. **H** 10–15m (30–50ft), **S** 3–4m (10–12ft). Fully hardy. Has grey or blue-green leaves and cylindrical, violet-blue cones, 6–10cm (2½–4in) long. 🏆 **var. *arizonica* 'Compacta'**, **H** 4–5m (12–15ft), **S** 1.5–2m (5–6ft), is a slow-growing, ovoid to conical tree with corky bark and blue foliage. **'Roger Watson'**, **H** and **S** 75cm (2½ft), is dwarf and conical, with silvery-grey leaves.

🏆 **A. *nordmanniana*** (Caucasian fir). Columnar, dense conifer. **H** 15–25m (50–80ft), **S** 5m (15ft). Fully hardy. Luxuriant foliage is rich green. Cylindrical cones, 10–15cm (4–6in) long, are green-brown, ripening to brown. 🏆 **'Golden Spreader'**, **H** and **S** 1m (3ft), is a dwarf form with a spreading habit and bright golden-yellow leaves.

🏆 **A. *procera*** (Noble fir) illus. p.95

A. *veitchii* (Veitch fir) illus. p.96.

ABUTILON

MALVACEAE

Genus of evergreen, semi-evergreen or deciduous shrubs, perennials and annuals, grown for their flowers and foliage. Frost hardy to frost tender, min. 5–7°C (41–5°F). Needs full sun or partial shade and fertile, well-drained soil. Water containerized specimens freely when in full growth, less at other times. In the growing season, young plants may need tip pruning to promote bushy growth. Mature specimens may have previous season's stems cut back har **S** d annually in early spring. Tie lax-growing species to a support if necessary. Propagate by seed in spring or by softwood, greenwood or semi-ripe cuttings in summer. Whitefly and red spider mite may be troublesome.

A. 'Ashford Red' illus. p.137.

A. 'Golden Fleece'. Strong-growing, evergreen, rounded shrub. **H** and **S** 2–3m (6–10ft). Half hardy. Has maple- to heart-shaped, serrated, rich green leaves. Pendent, bell-shaped, yellow flowers are carried from spring to autumn.

🏆 **A. 'Kentish Belle'** illus. p.162.

🏆 **A. *megapotamicum*** illus. p.203.

A. *pictum*, syn. *A. striatum* of gardens.**'Thompsonii'** illus. p.325.

A. *striatum* of gardens. See *A. pictum*.

A. x *suntense*. Fast-growing, deciduous, upright, arching shrub. **H** 5m (15ft), **S** 3m (10ft). Frost hardy. Has oval, lobed, toothed, dark green leaves. Produces an abundance of large, bowl-shaped, pale to deep purple, occasionally white, flowers from late spring to early summer. **'Violetta'** illus. p.138.

A. *vitifolium*. Fast-growing, deciduous, upright shrub. **H** 4m (12ft), **S** 2.5m (8ft). Frost hardy. Masses of large, bowl-shaped, purplish-blue flowers are produced in late spring and early summer. Has oval, lobed, sharply toothed, grey-green leaves. **var. *album*** illus. p.113. **'Veronica Tennant'** illus. p.114.

ACACIA

Mimosa

LEGUMINOSAE/MIMOSACEAE

Genus of evergreen, semi-evergreen or deciduous trees and shrubs, grown for their tiny flowers, composed of massed stamens, and for their foliage. Many species have phyllodes instead of true leaves. Frost hardy to frost tender, min. 5–7°C (41–5°F). Requires full sun and well-drained soil. Propagate by seed in spring. Red spider mite and mealy bug may be problematic.

🏆 **A. *baileyana*** illus. p.92. 🏆 **'Purpurea'** illus. p.84.

🏆 **A. *dealbata*** (Mimosa, Silver wattle) illus. p.211.

A. *juniperina*. See *A. ulicifolia*.

A. *longifolia* (Sydney golden wattle). Evergreen, spreading tree. **H** and **S** 6m (20ft). Frost hardy. Has narrowly oblong, dark green phyllodes. Bears cylindrical clusters of golden-yellow flowers in early spring.

A. *podalyriifolia* (Mount Morgan wattle, Queensland silver wattle). Evergreen, arching shrub. **H** 3–5m (10–15ft), **S** 3–4m (10–12ft). Half hardy. Has blue-green phyllodes and produces racemes of bright yellow flowers in spring.

🏆 **A. *pravissima*** (Ovens wattle) illus. p.92.

A. *pulchella* (Western prickly Moses) illus. p.458.

A. *ulicifolia*, syn. *A. juniperina*. Evergreen, bushy shrub. **H** 1m (3ft), **S** 1.5m (5ft). Frost hardy. Has very narrow, cylindrical, spine-like, rich green phyllodes and, in mid-spring, globular clusters of pale yellow flowers.

A. *verticillata* (Prickly Moses). Evergreen, spreading tree or bushy shrub. **H** and **S** 9m (28ft). Half hardy. Has needle-like, dark green phyllodes and, in spring, dense, bottle brush-like spikes of bright yellow flowers.

ACAENA

ROSACEAE

Genus of mainly summer-flowering sub-shrubs and perennials, evergreen in all but the severest winters, grown for their leaves and coloured burs and as ground cover. Has tight, rounded heads of small flowers. Is good for a rock garden. Some species may be invasive. Fully to frost hardy. Needs sun or partial shade and well-drained soil. Propagate by division in early spring or by seed in autumn.

A. anserinifolia of gardens. See *A. novae-zelandiae*.

A. buchananii. Vigorous, evergreen, prostrate perennial. **H** 2cm (¾in), **S** 75cm (30in) or more. Fully hardy. Bears glaucous leaves composed of 11–17 oval, toothed leaflets. Globose, green flower heads are borne in summer and develop into spiny, yellow-green burs.

A. caerulea. See *A. caesiiglauca*.

A. caesiiglauca, syn. *A. caerulea*, illus. p.374.

♀ ***A. microphylla*** illus. p.374.

A. novae-zelandiae, syn. *A. anserinifolia* of gardens. Vigorous, evergreen, prostrate sub-shrub. **H** 10cm (4in), **S** 75cm (30in) or more. Fully hardy. Has brown-green leaves, divided into 9–13 oval, toothed leaflets. In summer, red-spined, brownish burs develop from spherical heads of greenish-brown flowers.

A. 'Pewter'. See *A. saccaticupula* 'Blue Haze'.

***A. saccaticupula* 'Blue Haze'**, syn. *A.* 'Pewter'. Vigorous, evergreen, prostrate perennial. **H** 10cm (4in), **S** 75cm (30in) or more. Fully hardy. Leaves are divided into 9–15 oval, toothed, steel-blue leaflets. Produces spherical, brownish-red flower heads that develop in autumn to dark red burs with pinkish-red spines.

A

ACALYPHA

EUPHORBIACEAE

Genus of evergreen shrubs and perennials, grown for their flowers and foliage. Frost tender, min. 10–13°C (50–55°F), but best at min. 16°C (61°F). Needs partial shade and humus-rich, well-drained soil. Water containerized plants freely when in full growth, much less at other times and in low temperatures. Stem tips of young plants may be removed in growing season to promote branching. Propagate by softwood, greenwood or semi-ripe cuttings in summer. Red spider mite, whitefly and mealy bug may be troublesome.

♀ ***A. hispida*** (Red-hot cat's tail). Evergreen, upright, soft-stemmed shrub. **H** 2m (6ft) or more, **S** 1–2m (3–6ft). Has oval, toothed, lustrous, deep green leaves. Tiny, crimson flowers hang in long, dense, catkin-like spikes, intermittently year-round. May be grown as a short-lived cordon.

A. wilkesiana (Copperleaf, Jacob's coat) illus. p.456.

ACANTHOLIMON

PLUMBAGINACEAE

Genus of evergreen perennials, grown for their flowers and tight cushions of spiny leaves. Is suitable for rock gardens and walls. Fully hardy. Prefers sun and well-drained soil. Dislikes damp winters. Seed is rarely set in cultivation. Propagate by softwood cuttings in late spring.

A. glumaceum illus. p.363.

A. venustum. Evergreen, cushion-forming perennial. **H** and **S** 10cm (4in). Small spikes of star-shaped, pink flowers, on 3cm (1¼in) stems, are produced from late spring to early summer amid rosetted, spear-shaped, spiny, blue-green leaves that are edged with silver. Needs a very hot, well-drained site. Makes an excellent alpine house plant.

Acanthopanax. See *Eleutherococcus* except for ***A. ricinifolius*** for which see *Kalopanax septemlobus*.

ACANTHUS

Bear's breeches

ACANTHACEAE

Genus of perennials, some of which are semi-evergreen, grown for their large, deeply cut leaves and their spikes of flowers. Fully hardy. Prefers full sun, warm conditions and well-drained soil, but will tolerate shade. Protect crowns in first winter after planting. Long, thong-like roots make plants difficult to eradicate if wrongly placed. Propagate by seed or division in early autumn or spring, or by root cuttings in winter.

A. balcanicus. See *A. hungaricus*.

A. dioscoridis. Upright, architectural perennial. **H** to 1m (3ft), **S** 45cm (18in). Has oval, deeply cut, rigid, basal leaves and hairy stems. Dense spikes of small, funnel-shaped, purple-and-white flowers are produced in summer.

A. hungaricus, syn. *A. balcanicus, A. longifolius*. Upright perennial. **H** 60cm–1m (2–3ft), **S** 1m (3ft). Has long, deeply cut, basal, dark green leaves. Spikes of white or pink-flushed flowers, set in spiny, red-purple bracts, are carried in summer.

A. longifolius. See *A. hungaricus*.

A. mollis. Semi-evergreen, stately, upright perennial. **H** 1.2m (4ft), **S** 45cm (18in). Has long, oval, deeply cut, bright green leaves and, in summer, produces many spikes of funnel-shaped, mauve-and-white flowers. **'Hollard's Gold'** illus. p.219.

♀ ***A. spinosus*** illus. p.239.

ACCA

SYN. FEIJOA

MYRTACEAE

Genus of evergreen, opposite-leaved shrubs, grown for their shallowly cup-shaped flowers. Frost hardy. Needs a sheltered, sunny site and light, well-drained soil. Propagate by seed sown as soon as ripe or by semi-ripe cuttings in summer.

A. sellowiana (Pinapple guava) illus. p.203.

ACER

Maple

ACERACEAE/SAPINDACEAE

Genus of deciduous or evergreen trees and shrubs, grown for their foliage, which often colours brilliantly in autumn and, in some cases, for their ornamental bark or stems. Small, but often attractive flowers are followed by 2-winged fruits. Fully to frost hardy. Requires sun or semi-shade and fertile, moist but well-drained soil. Many acers produce their best autumn colour on neutral to acid soil. Propagate species by seed as soon as ripe or in autumn; cultivars by various grafting methods in late winter or early spring, or by budding in summer. Leaf-eating caterpillars or aphids sometimes infest plants, and maple tar spot may affect *A. platanoides* and *A. pseudoplatanus*.

A. buergerianum (Trident maple). Deciduous, spreading tree. **H** 10m (30ft) or more, **S** 8m (25ft). Fully hardy. Has 3-lobed, glossy, dark green leaves, usually providing an attractive, long-lasting display of red, orange and purple in autumn.

♀ ***A. capillipes*** (Snake-bark maple) illus. p.77.

A. cappadocicum (Cappadocian maple). Deciduous, spreading tree. **H** 20m (70ft), **S** 15m (50ft). Fully hardy. Has 5-lobed, bright green leaves that turn yellow in autumn. ♀ **'Aureum'** has bright yellow young leaves that turn light green in summer and assume yellow autumn tints. **subsp. *lobelii*** (syn. *A. lobelii*, Lobel's maple) illus. p.62

A. carpinifolium (Hornbeam maple) illus. p.88.

A. circinatum (Vine maple). Deciduous, spreading, bushy tree or shrub. **H** 5m (15ft) or more, **S** 6m (20ft). Fully hardy. Rounded, 7–9-lobed, mid-green leaves turn brilliant orange and red in autumn. Bears clusters of small, purple-and-white flowers in spring.

A. cissifolium. Deciduous, spreading tree. **H** 8m (25ft), **S** 12m (40ft). Fully hardy. Leaves consist of 3 oval, toothed leaflets, bronze-tinged when young, dark green in summer, turning red and yellow in autumn. Does best in semi-shade and on neutral to acid soil. **subsp. *henryi*** see *A. henryi*.

A. crataegifolium (Hawthorn maple). Deciduous, arching tree. **H** and **S** 10m (30ft). Fully hardy. Branches are streaked green and white. Small, oval, mid-green leaves turn orange in autumn. **'Veitchii'** illus. p.85.

A. davidii (Père David's maple, Snake-bark maple; illus. p.78). Deciduous tree with upright branches. Fully hardy. **H** and **S** 15m (50ft). Branches are striped green and white. Oval, glossy, dark green leaves often turn yellow or orange in autumn. **subsp. *grosseri*** see *A. grosseri*. **'Madeline Spitta'** illus. p.76.

A. ginnala. See *A. tataricum* subsp. *ginnala*.

A. giraldii. Deciduous, spreading tree. **H** and **S** 10m (30ft). Frost hardy. Shoots have a blue-grey bloom. Large, sycamore-like, shallowly lobed leaves, with long, pink stalks, are dark green above, blue-white beneath.

A. grandidentatum. See *A. saccharum* subsp. *grandidentatum*.

♀ ***A. griseum*** (Paper-bark maple; illus. p.78). Deciduous, spreading tree. **H** and **S** 10m (30ft). Fully hardy. Has striking, peeling, orange-brown bark. Dark green leaves have 3 leaflets and turn red and orange in autumn.

A. grosseri, syn. *A. davidii* subsp. *grosseri* (Snake-bark maple; illus. p.78). Deciduous, upright and spreading tree. **H** and **S** 10m (30ft). Fully hardy. Has white-striped trunk and branches. Broadly oval, deeply lobed, bright green leaves turn red in autumn.

A. henryi, syn. *A. cissifolium* subsp. *henryi*, illus. p.76.

A. japonicum (Full-moon maple, Japanese maple). Deciduous, bushy tree or shrub. **H** and **S** 10m (30ft). Fully hardy. Rounded, lobed leaves are mid-green, turning red in autumn. Clusters of small, reddish-purple flowers open in mid-spring. Shelter from strong winds. ♀ **'Aconitifolium'** illus. p.90. **'Aureum'** see *A. shirasawanum* 'Aureum'. ♀ **'Vitifolium'** illus. p.77.

A. laxiflorum, syn. *A. pectinatum* subsp. *laxiflorum*, illus. p.92.

A. lobelii. See *A. cappadocicum* subsp. *lobelii*.

A. macrophyllum (Oregon maple) illus. p.60.

A. maximowiczianum, syn. *A. nikoense* (Nikko maple). Slow-growing, deciduous, round-headed tree. **H** and **S** 12m (40ft). Fully hardy. Leaves have 3 oval, bluish-green leaflets that turn brilliant red and yellow in autumn.

A. monspessulanum (Montpelier maple). Deciduous, usually compact, round-headed tree or shrub. **H** and **S** 12m (40ft). Fully hardy. Small, 3-lobed, glossy, dark green leaves remain on tree until late autumn.

A. negundo (Ash-leaved maple, Box elder). Fast-growing, deciduous, spreading tree. **H** 15m (50ft), **S** 8m (25ft). Fully hardy. Bright green leaves have 3–5 oval leaflets. Clusters of inconspicuous, greenish-yellow flowers are borne in late spring. **'Variegatum'** illus. p.74. **var. *violaceum*** has purplish branchlets covered in a glaucous bloom and prominent clusters of tassel-like, purplish-pink flowers.

A. nikoense. See *A. maximowiczianum*.

A. opalus (Italian maple). Deciduous, round-headed tree. **H** and **S** 15m (50ft). Fully hardy. Clusters of small, yellow flowers emerge from early to mid-spring, before foliage. Leaves are broad, 5-lobed and dark green, turning yellow in autumn.

A. palmatum (Japanese maple). Deciduous, bushy-headed shrub or tree. **H** and **S** 6m (20ft) or more. Fully hardy. Palmate, deeply lobed, mid-green leaves turn brilliant orange, red or yellow in autumn. Clusters of small, reddish-purple flowers are borne in mid-spring. **'Atropurpureum'** illus. p.89. ♀ **'Bloodgood'** illus. p.138. **'Butterfly'** has grey-green leaves edged with cream and pink. ♀ **'Chitose-yama'** has mid-green foliage that gradually turns brilliant red from late summer to autumn. **'Corallinum'** illus. p.123. **var. *coreanum*** has mid-green leaves turning brilliant red in autumn. **'Dissectum Atropurpureum'** (syn. *A.p.* 'Ornatum'), illus. p.156. **var. *heptalobum*** illus. p.117. **var. *heptalobum* 'Lutescens'** has large leaves that become clear yellow in autumn. Winged fruits follow flowers. **var. *heptalobum* 'Rubrum'** illus. p.115. **'Ornatum'** see *A.p.* 'Dissectum Atropurpureum. ♀ **'Osakazuki'** illus.

p.90. 🏆 **'Sango-kaku'** (syn. *A.p.* 'Senkaki', Coral-bark maple) illus. p.78. **'Shindeshojo'** illus. p.123.
***A. pectinatum* subsp. *laxiflorum*.** See *A. laxiflorum*.
🏆 ***A. pensylvanicum*** (Snake-bark maple) illus. p.79. **'Erythrocladum'** (illus. p.70) is a deciduous, upright tree. **H** 10m (30ft), **S** 6m (20ft). Fully hardy. Has brilliant candy-pink, young shoots in winter and large, boldly lobed, mid-green leaves that turn bright yellow in autumn.
🏆 ***A. platanoides*** (Norway maple). Vigorous, deciduous, spreading tree. **H** 25m (80ft), **S** 15m (50ft). Fully hardy. Has large, broad, sharply lobed, bright green leaves that turn yellow or orange in autumn and clusters of yellow flowers borne in mid-spring before the leaves appear. **'Columnare'**, **H** 12m (40ft), **S** 8m (25ft), is dense and columnar. 🏆 **'Crimson King'** illus. p.60. **'Drummondii'** has leaves broadly edged with creamy-white. **'Emerald Queen'** is upright when young. **'Globosum'**, **H** 8m (25ft), **S** 10m (30ft), has a dense, round crown. **'Lorbergii'** see *A.p.* 'Palmatifidum'. **'Palmatifidum'** (syn. *A.p.* 'Lorbergii') illus. p.67. **'Royal Red'** has deep reddish-purple leaves. Those of 🏆 **'Schwedleri'** are bright red when young, maturing to purplish-green in summer and turn orange-red in autumn. **'Summershade'** has dark green leaves.
A. pseudoplatanus (Sycamore). Fast-growing, deciduous, spreading tree. **H** 30m (100ft), **S** 15m (50ft). Fully hardy. Has broadly 5-lobed, dark green leaves. Makes a fine specimen tree and is good for an exposed position. 🏆 **'Brilliantissimum'** illus. p.84. **f. *erythrocarpum*** illus. p.65. **'Simon-Louis Frères'** illus. p.73.
A. rubrum (Red maple) illus. p.66. **'Columnare'** illus. p.76. **'Franksred'** see *A.p.* Red Sunset. 🏆 **'October Glory'** is a deciduous, spreading tree. **H** 20m (70ft), **S** 12m (40ft). Fully hardy. Has 3- or 5-lobed, glossy, dark green leaves that become intense red in autumn, particularly on neutral to acid soil. In spring, bare branches are covered with clusters of tiny, red flowers. **Red Sunset ('Franksred')** has dense growth that also turns brilliant red in autumn. **'Scanlon'** and **'Schlesingeri'** illus. p.66.
🏆 ***A. rufinerve*** (Snake-bark maple) illus. p.76. **'Hatsuyuki'** (syn. *A.r.* f. *albolimbatum)* is a deciduous, arching tree. **H** 10m (30ft), **S** 8m (25ft). Fully hardy. Branches are striped green and white. Has 3-lobed, mid-green leaves, mottled and edged with white, that turn orange and red in autumn.
A. saccharinum (Silver maple) illus. p.63. **f. *laciniatum* 'Wieri'** is a fast-growing, deciduous, spreading tree with pendent, lower branches. **H** 25m (80ft), **S** 15m (50ft). Fully hardy. Deeply lobed, mid-green leaves, with silver undersides, turn yellow in autumn.
A. saccharum (Sugar maple). **subsp. *grandidentatum*** (syn. *A. grandidentatum*) is a deciduous, spreading tree. **H** and **S** 10m (30ft) or more. Fully hardy. Broad 3-or 5-lobed, bright green leaves turn bright orange-red in early autumn. **'Green Mountain'**, **H** 20m (70ft), **S** 12m (40ft), is upright. Large, 5-lobed leaves turn brilliant scarlet in autumn.
'Temple's Upright' illus. p.77.
🏆 ***A. shirasawanum* 'Aureum'**, syn. *A. japonicum* 'Aureum', illus. p.89.
A. tataricum* subsp. *ginnala, (syn. *A. ginnala*, Amur maple) illus. p.90.
🏆 ***A. triflorum*** illus. p.91.
A. velutinum*.** Deciduous, spreading tree. **H** 20m (70ft), **S** 15m (50ft). Fully hardy. Produces large, sycamore-like, lobed, dark green leaves, with undersides covered with pale brown down. **var. *vanvolxemii (Van Volxem's maple) has even larger leaves, slightly glaucous and smooth beneath.

ACHILLEA

ASTERACEAE/COMPOSITAE

Genus of mainly upright perennials, some of which are semi-evergreen, suitable for borders and rock gardens. Has fern-like foliage and large, usually plate-like, flower heads mainly in summer. Flower heads may be dried for winter decoration. Fully hardy. Tolerates most soils but does best in a sunny, well-drained site. Tall species and cultivars need staking. Propagate by division in early spring or autumn or by softwood cuttings in early summer.
(!) Contact with foliage may aggravate skin allergies.
A. aegyptica of gardens. See *A.* 'Taygetea'.
***A. argentea*.** See *Tanacetum argenteum*.
A. argentea of gardens. See *A. clavennae*.
***A.* 'The Beacon'**. See. *A.* 'Fanal'.
🏆 ***A.* 'Belle Epoque'** (illus. p.247). Semi-evergreen, upright perennial. **H** 1m (3ft), **S** 40cm (16in). Has feathery, dark green, basal leaves and bears flat heads of rose-red flowers, maturing to lemon-yellow, in summer.
🏆 ***A.* 'Christine's Pink'** (illus. p.247). Semi-evergreen, upright perennial. **H** 90cm (3ft), **S** 40cm (16in). Has feathery, dark green, basal leaves. In summer produces flat heads of pale pink flowers, which fade as they age.
A. clavennae, syn. *A. argentea* of gardens, illus. p.359.
***A. clypeolata*.** Semi-evergreen, upright perennial. **H** 45cm (18in), **S** 30cm (12in). Has divided, hairy, silver leaves and dense, flat heads of small, yellow flowers in summer. Divide plants regularly in spring.
🏆 ***A.* 'Coronation Gold'**. Upright perennial. **H** 1m (3ft), **S** 60cm (2ft). Has feathery, silvery leaves. Produces large, flat heads of small, golden flower heads in summer that dry well for winter decoration. Divide and replant every third year.
***A.* 'Fanal'**, syn. *A.* 'The Beacon', illus. p.235.
***A. filipendulina*.** Upright perennial. **H** 1–1.2m (3–4ft), **S** 60cm (2ft). Has deeply divided, pale green, basal leaves. In summer, erect flowering stems bear dense, domed heads of tiny, daisy-like, bright yellow flowers. Is good for cut flowers and drying them. 🏆 **'Gold Plate'** illus. p.243. 🏆 **'Parker's Variety'** (illus. p.247), **H** to 1.4m (4½ft), has rather rounded flower heads.
🏆 ***A.* 'Heidi'** (illus. p.247). Semi-evergreen, upright perennial. **H** 60cm (24in) or more, **S** 40cm (16in). Has feathery, dark green, basal leaves. Bears flat heads of pink flowers, maturing to near white, in summer.
A. x kellereri illus. p.360.
🏆 ***A.* 'Lachsschönheit'** (illus. p.247). Semi-evergreen, upright perennial. **H** 1m (3ft) or more, **S** 40cm (16in). Has feathery, dark green, basal leaves. Bears flat heads of pinkish-orange flowers, maturing to pinkish-cream, in summer.
🏆 ***A. x lewisii* 'King Edward'**. Semi-evergreen, rounded, compact, woody-based perennial. **H** 10cm (4in), **S** 23cm (9in) or more. Has feathery, soft, grey-green leaves. Bears compact heads of minute, buff-yellow flower heads in summer. Is suitable for a rock garden, wall or bank.
🏆 ***A.* 'Lucky Break'**. Semi-evergreen, upright perennial. **H** 80cm (32in) or more, **S** 50cm (20in). Has feathery, silvery green, basal leaves. Bears flat heads of pale yellow flowers, maturing to creamy-white, in summer.
A. millefolium (Yarrow). Variable, spreading, sometimes invasive perennial. **H** to 1.2m (4ft), **S** 60cm (2ft) or more. Has long, narrow, divided, dark green, basal leaves. From late spring to late summer, erect flowering stems bear flattened heads of tiny, daisy-like, white or sometimes pink flowers. Thrives on poor soil. **'Fire King'** has dark green leaves and rich red flowers in summer. 🏆 **'Kelwayi'** (illus. p.247), **H** 60cm (2ft), produces heads of rich red flower heads. **'Red Velvet'** (illus. p.247), **H** 60cm (24in), bears rich rose-red flowers. **'Tickled Pink'**, **H** 80–100cm (32–39in), is variable and produces flower heads from rich red-pink to softer, pastel shades.
🏆 ***A.* 'Moonshine'**. Upright perennial. **H** 60cm (24in), **S** 50cm (20in). Has flat heads of bright yellow flowers throughout summer above a mass of small, feathery, grey-green leaves. Divide plants regularly in spring.
***A.* 'Paprika'**. Semi-evergreen, Upright perennial. **H** 80cm (32in) or more, **S** 40cm (16in). Has feathery, silvery-green, basal leaves. Bears flat heads of rich rusty-red flowers in summer.
***A.* 'Pretty Belinda'**. Semi-evergreen, upright perennial. **H** 50cm (20in), **S** 40cm (16in) or more. Has feathery, dark green, basal leaves. In summer bears a succession of rounded, deep pink flower heads, fading gradually to a softer colour, creating a 2-tone effect.
🏆 ***A. ptarmica* 'The Pearl'** (illus. p.247). Upright perennial. **H** and **S** 75cm (30in). Has large heads of small, pompon-like, white flowers in summer and tapering, glossy, dark green leaves. May spread rapidly.
***A.* 'Schwellenburg'**. Spreading perennial. **H** 45cm (18in), **S** 60cm (24in). Has branched stems and grey-green leaves. Silvery buds are followed by lemon-yellow flower heads from early summer to early autumn.
🏆 ***A.* 'Summerwine'**. Semi-evergreen, upright perennial. **H** 80cm (32in) or more, **S** 40cm (16in) or more. Has feathery, dark-green, basal leaves. In summer bears flat heads of deep red flowers maturing to soft purplish-brown.
***A.* 'Taygetea'**, syn. *A. aegyptica* of gardens. Upright perennial. **H** 60cm (24in), **S** 50cm (20in). Has lemon-yellow flowers above clumps of feathery, grey leaves. Divide and replant every third year.
***A.* 'Terracotta'** (illus. p.247). Semi-evergreen, upright perennial. **H** 1m (3ft), **S** 60cm (2ft). Has feathery, grey-green, basal leaves. Bears flat heads of burnt-orange flowers, maturing to cream, in summer.

ACHIMENES

Hot-water plant

GESNERIACEAE

Genus of erect or trailing perennials with small rhizomes and showy flowers. Frost tender, min. 10°C (50°F). Prefers bright light, but not direct sunlight, and well-drained soil. Use tepid water for watering pot-grown plants. Allow plants to dry out after flowering and store rhizomes in a frost-free place over winter. Propagate by division of rhizomes or by seed, if available, in spring or by stem cuttings in summer.
***A. antirrhina*.** Erect perennial. **H** and **S** 35cm (14in) or more. Has oval, toothed leaves, to 5cm (2in) or more long and of unequal size in each opposite pair. In summer bears funnel-shaped, red-orange flowers, to 4cm (1½in) long, with yellow throats.
***A.* 'Brilliant'**. Erect, compact perennial. **H** and **S** 30cm (12in). Has oval, toothed leaves and, in summer, large, funnel-shaped, scarlet flowers.
***A. coccinea*.** See *A. erecta*.
A. erecta, syn. *A. coccinea, A. pulchella*. Erect, bushy, branching perennial. **H** and **S** 45cm (18in). Has narrowly oval, toothed leaves, often arranged in whorls of 3. Tubular, scarlet flowers with yellow eyes are produced in summer.
***A. grandiflora*.** Erect perennial. **H** and **S** to 60cm (24in). Oval, toothed leaves are often reddish below. In summer has tubular, dark pink to purple flowers with white eyes.
***A.* 'Little Beauty'** illus. p.469.
🏆 ***A.* 'Paul Arnold'**. Erect, compact, free-flowering perennial. **H** and **S** 30cm (12in). Has oval, toothed leaves. Bears large, funnel-shaped, purple flowers in summer.
***A.* 'Peach Blossom'**. Trailing perennial. **H** and **S** to 25cm (10in). Has oval, toothed leaves, and large, funnel-shaped, peach-coloured flowers in summer.
***A. pulchella*.** See *A. erecta*.

***Achnatherum calamagrostis*.** See *Stipa calamagrostis*.
***Acidanthera bicolor* var. *murieliae*.** See *Gladiolus murielae*.
***Acidanthera murieliae*.** See *Gladiolus murielae*.

ACIPHYLLA

UMBELLIFERAE/APIACEAE

Genus of evergreen perennials, grown mainly for the architectural value of their spiky foliage but also for their flowers, which are produced more freely on male plants. Frost hardy. Requires sun and well-drained soil. Protect neck of plant from winter wet with a deep layer of stone chippings. Propagate by seed when fresh, in late summer, or in early spring.
A. aurea (Golden Spaniard) illus. p.227.
A. scott-thomsonii (Giant Spaniard). Evergreen, rosette-forming perennial.

H to 4.5m (14ft), S 60cm–1m (2–3ft). Much-dissected, spiny foliage is bronze when young, maturing to silver-grey. Prickly spikes of tiny, creamy-yellow flowers are rarely produced. Prefers a moist but well-drained site.
A. squarrosa (Bayonet plant) illus. p.242.

ACIS

AMARYLLIDACEAE

Genus of bulbs, grown for their pendent, bell-shaped, white or pink flowers in autumn or spring. Fully to frost hardy. Some species prefer a moist, partially shaded site, others do best in sun and well-drained soil. Propagate by division in spring or early autumn or by seed in autumn.
♀***A. autumnalis***, syn. *Leucojum autumnale* (Autumn snowflake) illus. p.424.
A. rosea, syn. *Leucojum roseum*. Early autumn-flowering bulb. H to 10cm (4in), S 2.5–5cm (1–2in). Frost hardy. Slender stems bear usually solitary, pale pink flowers, 1cm (½in) long. Thread-like, erect, basal leaves appear with, or just after, flowers. Prefers sun and well-drained soil.

Acnistus australis. See *Iochroma australe.*

ACOKANTHERA

APOCYNACEAE

Genus of evergreen shrubs and trees, grown for their flowers and overall appearance. Frost tender, min. 10°C (50°F). Requires full light and good drainage. Water containerized plants moderately, less when not in full growth. Propagate by seed in spring or autumn or by semi-ripe cuttings in summer. ⓘThe sap and small, plum-like fruits that follow the flowers are highly toxic if ingested.
A. oblongifolia, syn. *A. spectabilis, Carissa spectabilis* (Wintersweet) illus. p.453.
A. spectabilis. See *A. oblongifolia.*

ACONITUM

Aconite, Monkshood, Wolf's bane

RANUNCULACEAE

Genus of perennials with poisonous, tuberous or fibrous roots and upright, sometimes scandent, stems, bearing curious, hooded flowers in summer. Leaves are mostly rounded in outline. Is good when grown in rock gardens and borders. Fully hardy. Prefers a position in sun, but tolerates some shade and this may enhance flower colour. Requires fertile, well-drained soil. Propagate by division in autumn, every 2–3 years, or by seed in autumn. ⓘContact with the foliage may irritate skin; all parts are highly toxic if ingested.
A. anthora. Compact, tuberous perennial. H 60cm (24in), S 50cm (20in). Has erect, leafy stems that bear several hooded, yellow flowers in summer. Leaves are divided and dark green.
A. x bicolor. See *A. x cammarum* 'Bicolor'.
♀***A. 'Bressingham Spire'.*** Compact, upright, tuberous perennial. H 1m (3ft), S 50cm (20in). Very erect spikes of hooded, violet-blue flowers are produced in summer. Bears deeply divided leaves that are glossy and dark green.
♀***A. x cammarum* 'Bicolor'**, syn. *A. x bicolor*, illus. p.239.
♀***A. carmichaelii* 'Arends'**, syn. *A.c.* 'Arendsii'. Erect, tuberous perennial. H 1.5m (5ft), S 30cm (1ft). Has divided, rich green leaves and, in autumn, spikes of hooded, rich deep blue flowers. Upright stems may need staking, particularly if planted in a shady site.
A. hemsleyanum, syn. *A. volubile* of gardens, illus. p.204.
***A.* 'Ivorine'.** Upright, tuberous perennial. H 1.5m (5ft), S 50cm (20in). Bears hooded, creamy-white flowers in erect spikes in early summer. Strong stems bear deeply divided, glossy, green leaves.
A. lycoctonum* subsp. *vulparia, syn. *A. orientale* of gardens, *A. vulparia* (Wolf's bane) illus. p.243.
A. napellus (Helmet flower, Monkshood). Upright, tuberous perennial. H 1.5m (5ft), S 30cm (1ft). Bears tall, slender spires of hooded, light indigo-blue flowers in late summer and deeply cut, mid-green leaves. **subsp. *vulgare* 'Albidum'** (syn. *A.n.* 'Albiflorus') has white flowers.
***A.* 'Newry Blue'.** Upright, tuberous perennial. H 1.2m (4ft), S 50cm (20in). Produces hooded, dark blue flowers on erect stems in summer and has deeply divided, glossy, dark green leaves.
A. orientale of gardens. See *A. lycoctonum* subsp. *vulparia*.
♀***A.* 'Spark's Variety'.** Upright, tuberous perennial. H 1.2m (4ft), S 50cm (20in). Bears violet-blue flowers on branching stems in summer and has deeply divided, glossy, dark green leaves.
***A.* 'Stainless Steel'** illus. p.241.
A. volubile of gardens. See *A. hemsleyanum.*
A. vulparia. See *A. lycoctonum* subsp. *vulparia.*

ACORUS

ARACEAE

Genus of semi-evergreen, perennial, marginal and submerged water plants, grown for their frequently aromatic foliage. Fully to frost hardy. Needs an open, sunny position. *A. calamus* requires up to 25cm (10in) depth of water. Tidy up fading foliage in autumn and lift and divide plants every 3 or 4 years, in spring, as clumps become congested.
***A. calamus* 'Argenteostriatus'** illus. p.435.
***A. gramineus* var. *pusillus*.** Semi-evergreen, perennial, marginal water plant or submerged aquarium plant. Frost hardy. H and S 10cm (4in). Has narrow, grass-like, stiff leaves. Rarely, insignificant, greenish flower spikes are produced in summer. **'Variegatus'** illus. p.435.

ACRADENIA

RUTACEAE

Genus of evergreen shrubs, grown for their foliage and flowers. Half hardy. Requires a sheltered position in sun or semi-shade and fertile, well-drained soil. Does best planted against a south- or west-facing wall. Propagate by semi-ripe cuttings in summer.
A. frankliniae, illus. p.192.

Acroclinium. See *Rhodanthe.*
A. roseum. See *Rhodanthe chlorocephala* subsp. *rosea*

ACTAEA

Baneberry

RANUNCULACEAE

Genus of clump-forming perennials, grown for their colourful, poisonous berries. Fully hardy. Likes woodland conditions – moist, peaty soil and shade. Propagate by division in spring or by seed in autumn. ⓘThe berries are highly toxic if ingested.
A. alba. See *A. pachypoda.*
A. alba of gardens. See *A. rubra* f. *neglecta.*
A. erythrocarpa of gardens. See *A. rubra.*
♀***A. pachypoda***, syn. *A. alba*, (Doll's eyes, White baneberry) illus. p.246.
A. racemosa. See *Cimicifuga racemosa.*
♀***A. rubra***, syn. *A. erythrocarpa* of gardens (Red baneberry). Clump-forming perennial. H 50cm (20in), S 30cm (12in). Small, fluffy, white flowers are followed in autumn by clusters of poisonous, rounded, scarlet berries, borne above oval, divided, bright green leaves. **f. *neglecta*** (syn. *A. alba* of gardens) has white berries.
A. simplex. See *Cimicifuga simplex.*

ACTINIDIA

ACTINIDIACEAE

Genus of mainly deciduous, woody-stemmed, twining climbers. Fully hardy to frost tender, min. 10°C (50°F). Grows in partial shade but needs sun for fruit to form and ripen. Grow in any well-drained soil that does not dry out. Prune in winter if necessary. Propagate by seed in spring or autumn, by semi-ripe cuttings in mid-summer or by layering in winter.
A. arguta. Deciduous, woody-stemmed, twining climber. H 7–10m (22–30ft). Fully hardy. Has ovate to oblong-ovate, bristle-toothed, dark green leaves, to 12cm (5in) long. In early summer produces clusters of fragrant, cup-shaped, white, unisexual flowers which in male plants have purple anthers. Oblong, smooth-skinned, edible, yellow-green fruits, to 2.5cm (1in) long, are produced on female plants. **'Issai'** is self-fertile.
A. chinensis of gardens. See *A. deliciosa.*
A. deliciosa, syn. *A. chinensis* of gardens (Chinese gooseberry, Kiwi fruit). Vigorous, mainly deciduous, woody-stemmed, twining climber. H 9–10m (28–30ft). Frost hardy. Heart-shaped leaves are 13–20cm (5–8in) long. In summer bears clusters of cup-shaped, white flowers that later turn yellowish, followed by edible, hairy, brown fruits. To obtain fruits, both male and female plants must usually be grown.
♀***A. kolomikta*** illus. p.201.
A. pilosula. Vigorous, deciduous, woody-stemmed, twining climber. H 5–7m (16–22ft). Fully hardy. Has lance-shaped, pointed, bristle-margined, dark green leaves with silvery-white markings at the leaf tips that often also cover half the leaf surface. Clusters of cup-shaped, pink, unisexual flowers are borne singly or in small clusters in the leaf axils in spring. Egg-shaped, edible, yellow-green fruits may be produced on female plants.
A. polygama (Silver vine). Mainly deciduous, woody-stemmed, twining climber. H 4–6m (12–20ft). Frost hardy. Heart-shaped leaves, 7–13cm (3–5in) long, are bronze when young and sometimes have creamy upper sections. In summer has scented, cup-shaped, white flowers, usually arranged in groups of 3 male, female or bisexual, followed by edible but not very palatable, egg-shaped, bright yellow fruits.

ADA

ORCHIDACEAE

See also ORCHIDS.
A. aurantiaca (illus. p.467). Evergreen, epiphytic orchid for a cool greenhouse. H 23cm (9in). Bears sprays of tubular, orange flowers, 2.5cm (1in) long, in early spring. Has narrowly oval leaves, 10cm (4in) long. Needs shade in summer.

ADANSONIA

Baobab

BOMBACACEAE

Genus of deciduous or semi-evergreen, mainly spring-flowering trees, grown for their characteristically swollen trunks, their foliage and for shade. Has flowers only on large, mature specimens. Frost tender, min. 13–16°C (55–61°F). Requires full light and sharply drained soil. Allow soil of containerized specimens almost to dry out between waterings. Propagate by seed sown in spring. Pot specimens under glass are susceptible to red spider mite.
A. digitata. Slow-growing, semi-evergreen, rounded tree. H and S 15m (50ft) or more. Has palmate leaves of 5–7 lustrous, green leaflets. Produces fragrant, pendent, long-stalked, white flowers, with 5 reflexed petals, in spring, followed by edible, sausage-shaped, brown fruits.

ADENIUM

Desert rose

APOCYNACEAE

Genus of perennial succulents with fleshy, swollen trunks. Frost tender, min. 15°C (59°F). Needs sun or partial shade and well-drained soil; plants are very prone to rotting. Propagate by seed sown in spring or summer. ⓘThe milky sap that exudes from broken stems may irritate skin and cause severe discomfort if ingested.
♀***A. obesum*** illus. p.486.

ADENOCARPUS

LEGUMINOSAE/PAPILIONACEAE

Genus of deciduous or semi-evergreen shrubs, grown for their profuse, broom-like, yellow flowers, which are produced in spring or early summer. Frost to half hardy. Requires a site in full sun and well-drained soil. Does best grown against a south-or west-facing wall. Propagate by seed sown in autumn.
A. viscosus. Semi-evergreen, arching shrub. H and S 1m (3ft). Frost hardy. Grey-green leaves with 3 narrowly lance-shaped leaflets densely cover shoots. Produces dense, terminal racemes of orange-yellow flowers in late spring.

ADENOPHORA

Gland bellflower

CAMPANULACEAE

Genus of summer-flowering, fleshy-rooted perennials. Fully hardy. Requires a site in [illegible] over-dry soil. May sometimes become invasive but resents disturbance. Propagate by basal cuttings taken in early spring or by seed sown in autumn.

A. potaninii. Rosette-forming perennial. **H** 45cm (18in) or more, **S** 60cm (24in). Arching sprays of bell-shaped, pale bluish-lavender flowers are produced in late summer. Has oval to lance-shaped, basal, mid-green leaves.

Adhatoda duvernoia. See *Justicia adhatoda.*

ADIANTUM

ADIANTACEAE/PTERIDACEAE

Genus of deciduous, semi-evergreen or evergreen ferns. Fully hardy to frost tender, min. 7–13°C (45–55°F). Prefers semi-shade and moist, neutral to acid soil (*A. aleuticum* prefers alkaline soil). Remove fading fronds regularly. Propagate by spores in summer.

🏆 ***A. aleuticum***, syn. *A. pedatum* var. *aleuticum*, illus. p.291.

A. capillus-veneris (Maidenhair fern). Semi-evergreen or evergreen fern. **H** and **S** 30cm (12in). Half hardy. Has dainty, triangular to oval, segmented, arching, light green fronds borne on black stems.

A. cuneatum. See *A. raddianum.*

🏆 ***A. pedatum*** (Northern maidenhair fern) illus. p.291. **var. *aleuticum*.** See *A. aleuticum*.

🏆 ***A. raddianum***, syn. *A. cuneatum* (Delta maidenhair). Semi-evergreen or evergreen fern. **H** and **S** 30cm (12in). Frost tender, min. 7°C (45°F). Triangular, divided, pale green segments are borne on finely dissected fronds that have purplish-black stems. 🏆 **'Fritz Lüthi'** has bright green fronds. **'Grandiceps'** (Tassel maidenhair) has elegant, tasselled fronds.

A. tenerum. Semi-evergreen or evergreen fern. **H** 30cm–1m (1–3ft), **S** 60cm–1m (2–3ft). Frost tender, min. 13°C (55°F). Broadly lance-shaped, much-divided, spreading, mid-green fronds consist of rounded or diamond-shaped pinnae.

🏆 ***A. venustum*** illus. p.292.

ADLUMIA

PAPAVERACEAE/FUMARIACEAE

Genus of one species of herbaceous, biennial, leaf-stalk climber, grown for its leaves and flowers. Frost hardy. Grow in semi-shade in any soil. Propagate by seed in spring.

A. cirrhosa. See *A. fungosa.*

A. fungosa, syn. *A. cirrhosa* (Allegheny vine, Climbing fumitory). Herbaceous, biennial, leaf-stalk climber. **H** 3–4m (10–12ft). Delicate leaves have numerous leaflets. Tiny, tubular, spurred, white or purplish flowers are borne in drooping panicles in summer.

ADONIS

RANUNCULACEAE

Genus of spring-flowering perennials, grown for their foliage and flowers. Fully hardy. Some thrive in semi-shade, others [illegible] Propagate by seed when fresh, in late summer, or by division after flowering.

A. amurensis Clump-forming perennial. **H** 30cm (12in), **S** 23–30cm (9–12in). Mid-green leaves are finely cut. Bears cup-shaped, golden flowers singly at the tips of stems in late winter and early spring.

A. brevistyla. Clump-forming perennial. **H** and **S** 15–23cm (6–9in). Mid-green leaves are finely cut. Has cup-shaped, white flowers, tinged blue outside and borne singly at the tips of stems in early spring.

A. vernalis illus. p.262.

ADROMISCHUS

CRASSULACEAE

Genus of perennial succulents and evergreen sub-shrubs with rounded, thin or fat leaves. Frost tender, min. 7°C (45°F). Needs partial shade and very well-drained soil. Propagate by leaf or stem cuttings in spring or summer.

A. cooperi, syn. *Cotyledon cooperi, Echeveria cooperi.* Freely branching perennial succulent. **H** 10cm (4in), **S** to 15cm (6in). Has greyish-brown stems and inversely lance-shaped, glossy, grey-green leaves, to 5cm (2in) long, often purple-marked above. In summer, produces tubular, green-and-red flowers, with white-margined, pink or purple lobes, on a stem 25cm (10in) or more long.

A. maculatus illus. p.492.

AECHMEA

BROMELIACEAE

Genus of evergreen, rosette-forming, epiphytic perennials, cultivated for their foliage, flowers and fruits. Frost tender, min. 10–15°C (50–59°F). May be grown in full light or a semi-shaded site. Provide a rooting medium of equal parts humus-rich soil and either sphagnum moss or bark or plastic chips used for orchid culture. Using soft water, water moderately in summer, sparingly at all other times, and keep cup-like, rosette centres filled with water from spring through to autumn. Propagate by offsets in late spring.

A. distichantha. Evergreen, basal-rosetted, epiphytic perennial. **H** and **S** to 1m (3ft). Forms dense rosettes of narrowly oblong, round-tipped, arching leaves that are dull green above, grey and scaly beneath. Has panicles of small, tubular, purple or blue flowers among white-felted, pink bracts, usually in summer.

🏆 ***A. fasciata***, syn. *Billbergia rhodocyanea* (Silver vase plant, Urn plant; illus. p.471). Evergreen, tubular-rosetted, epiphytic perennial. **H** 40–60cm (16–24in), **S** 30–50cm (12–20in). Has loose rosettes of broadly oblong, round-tipped, incurved, arching leaves with dense, grey scales and silver cross-banding. Bears dense, pyramidal panicles of tubular, blue-purple flowers among pink bracts, just above foliage, from spring to autumn.

🏆 ***A.* Foster's Favorite Group** (Lacquered wine-cup). Evergreen, basal-rosetted, epiphytic perennial. **H** and **S** 30–60cm (12–24in). Has loose rosettes of strap-shaped, arching, lustrous, wine-red leaves. Drooping spikes of small, tubular, [illegible] summer, followed later by pear-shaped, red fruits.

A. fulgens (Coral berry). Evergreen, basal-rosetted, epiphytic perennial. **H** and **S** 40–75cm (16–30in). Forms loose rosettes of broadly oblong, arching, glossy, mid-green leaves with grey scales beneath and rounded or pointed tips. In summer produces, above foliage, erect panicles of small, tubular, violet-purple flowers that turn red with age. These are succeeded by small, rounded to ovoid, red fruits on red stalks.

🏆 ***A. nudicaulis.*** Evergreen, basal-rosetted, epiphytic perennial. **H** and **S** 40–75cm (16–30in). Produces loose rosettes of a few broadly strap-shaped, arching, olive-green leaves with spiny edges and usually banded with grey scales beneath. Spikes of small, tubular, yellow flowers open above large, red bracts in summer.

A. recurvata (illus. p.471). Evergreen, basal-rosetted, epiphytic perennial. **H** and **S** 15–20cm (6–8in). Narrowly triangular, tapered, spiny-edged, arching, red-flushed, mid-green leaves are produced in dense rosettes. In summer bears a short, dense spike of tubular, red-and-white flowers, with red bracts, just above leaves.

AEGOPODIUM

Bishop's weed, Gout weed, Ground elder

UMBELLIFERAE/APIACEAE

Genus of invasive, rhizomatous perennials, most of which are weeds although *A. podagraria* 'Variegatum' provides excellent ground cover. Fully hardy. Tolerates sun or shade and any well-drained soil. Propagate by division of rhizomes in spring or autumn.

***A. podagraria* 'Variegatum'.** Vigorous, spreading perennial. **H** 10cm (4in), **S** indefinite. Fully hardy. Has lobed, creamy-white-variegated leaves. Insignificant, white flowers, borne in summer, are best removed.

AEONIUM

CRASSULACEAE

Genus of perennial succulents, some of which are short-lived, and evergreen, succulent shrubs, grown for their rosettes of bright green or blue-green, occasionally purple, leaves. Frost tender, min. 5°C (41°F). Prefers partial shade and very well-drained soil. Most species grow from autumn to spring and are semi-dormant in mid-summer. Propagate by seed in summer or, for branching species, by stem cuttings in spring or summer.

🏆 ***A. arboreum.*** Bushy, perennial succulent. **H** to 60cm (2ft), **S** 1m (3ft). Branched stems are each crowned by a rosette, up to 15cm (6in) across, of broadly lance-shaped, glossy, bright green leaves. In spring produces cones of small, star-shaped, golden flowers on 2–3-year-old stems, which then die back. **'Schwarzkopf'** see *A.* 'Zwartkop'.

🏆 ***A. haworthii*** (Pinwheel) illus. p.489.

🏆 ***A. tabuliforme*** illus. p.491.

🏆 ***A.* 'Zwartkop'**, syn. *A. arboreum* 'Schwarzkopf', illus. p.310.

AESCHYNANTHUS

GESNERIACEAE

Genus of evergreen, climbing, trailing or creeping perennials, useful for growing in hanging baskets. Frost tender, min. 15–18°C (59–64°F). Needs a fairly humid atmosphere and a position out of direct sun. Water sparingly in low temperatures. Propagate by tip cuttings in spring or summer.

***A.* 'Black Pagoda'.** Semi-trailing perennial. **H** 60cm (24in), **S** to 45cm (18in). Has elliptic leaves, to 10cm (4in) long, pale green with dark brown marbling above, and purple beneath. Bears terminal clusters of deep burnt-orange flowers, with green calyces, from summer to winter.

A. longicaulis, syn. *A. marmoratus, A. zebrinus.* Evergreen, trailing perennial. **H** and **S** to 60cm (24in). Oval, waxy leaves are dark green, veined yellowish-green above, purplish below. Produces tubular, greenish flowers, with dark brown markings, borne in terminal clusters in summer.

🏆 ***A. pulcher*** (Lipstick plant, Royal red bugler). Evergreen, climbing or trailing perennial. **H** and **S** indefinite. Produces thick, oval leaves and small, tubular, hooded, bright red flowers, with yellow throats, borne in terminal clusters from summer to winter.

🏆 ***A. speciosus***, syn. *A. splendens*, illus. p.478.

A. splendens. See *A. speciosus.*

A. zebrinus. See *A. marmoratus.*

AESCULUS

Buckeye, Horse-chestnut

HIPPOCASTANACEAE/SAPINDACEAE

Genus of deciduous trees and shrubs, grown for their bold, divided leaves and conspicuous, upright panicles or clusters of flowers, followed by fruits (horse-chestnuts) sometimes with spiny outer casings. Fully to frost hardy. Requires sun or semi-shade and fertile, well-drained soil. Propagate species by sowing seed in autumn, cultivars by budding in late summer or by grafting in late winter. Leaf spot may affect young foliage, and coral spot fungus may attack damaged wood.

① All parts of these plants may cause mild stomach upset if ingested.

A. californica (California buckeye) illus. p.81.

A. x carnea (Red horse-chestnut). 🏆 **'Briotii'** illus. p.60.

A. chinensis (Chinese horse chestnut) illus. p.60.

🏆 ***A. flava***, syn. *A. octandra* (Sweet buckeye, Yellow buckeye) illus. p.76.

A. glabra (Ohio buckeye). Deciduous, round-headed, sometimes shrubby tree. **H** and **S** 10m (30ft). Fully hardy. Leaves, usually composed of 5 narrowly oval leaflets, are dark green. Bears 4-petalled, greenish-yellow flowers in upright clusters in late spring and early summer.

A

♀ ***A. hippocastanum***. Vigorous, deciduous, spreading tree. **H** 18m (60ft), **S** 15m (50ft). Fully hardy. Has large leaves with 5 or 7 leaflets and spires of white flowers, flushed pink and yellow in centres in spring. Spiny fruits contain glossy, brown nuts in autumn. ♀ **'Baumannii'**, **H** 30m (100ft), has dark green leaves turning to yellow in autumn and double, yellow- or red-marked, white flowers.
A. indica (Indian horse-chestnut). Deciduous, spreading, elegant tree. **H** 20m (70ft), **S** 12m (40ft). Frost hardy. Glossy, dark green leaves with usually 7 narrowly oval leaflets are bronze when young, orange or yellow in autumn. Upright panicles of 4-petalled, pink-tinged, white flowers, marked with red or yellow, appear in mid-summer. ♀ **'Sydney Pearce'** illus. p.73.
A. x neglecta (Sunrise horse-chestnut). ♀ **'Erythroblastos'** illus. p.72.
A. octandra. See *A. flava.*
♀ ***A. parviflora*** (Bottlebrush buckeye) illus. p.113.
♀ ***A. pavia*** (Red buckeye). Deciduous, round-headed, sometimes shrubby tree. **H** 5m (15ft), **S** 3m (10ft). Fully hardy. Glossy, dark green leaves consist of 5 narrowly oval leaflets. Has panicles of 4-petalled, red flowers in early summer. **'Atrosanguinea'** illus. p.86.
A. turbinata (Japanese horse-chestnut). Deciduous, spreading, stout-branched tree. **H** 20m (70ft), **S** 12m (40ft). Fully hardy. Large, dark green leaves consist of 5 or 7 narrowly oval leaflets. Panicles of creamy-white flowers appear in late spring and early summer.

AETHIONEMA

BRASSICACEAE/CRUCIFERAE

Genus of short-lived, evergreen or semi-evergreen shrubs, sub-shrubs and perennials, grown for their prolific flowers. Fully hardy. Needs sun and well-drained soil. Propagate by softwood cuttings in spring or by seed in autumn. Most species self-seed readily.
A. armenum illus. p.364.
♀ ***A. grandiflorum***, syn. *A. pulchellum,* (Persian stone cress) illus. p.338.
A. iberideum. Evergreen or semi-evergreen, rounded, compact shrub. **H** and **S** 15cm (6in). Bears small, lance-shaped, grey-green leaves and, in summer, 2cm (¾in) stems each bear a raceme of small, saucer-shaped, white flowers.
A. pulchellum. See *A. grandiflorum.*
♀ ***A.* 'Warley Rose'** illus. p.362.
***A.* 'Warley Ruber'.** Evergreen or semi-evergreen, rounded, compact sub-shrub. **H** and **S** 15cm (6in). Has tiny, linear, bluish-green leaves. Racemes of small, deep rose-pink flowers are produced on 2–3cm (¾–1¼in) stems in spring–summer.

AGAPANTHUS

LILIACEAE/ALLIACEAE

Genus of clump-forming perennials, some of which are evergreen, with erect stems that carry large umbels of bell- to tubular-bell-shaped or trumpet-shaped flowers, usually blue and often fading to purple with age. Leaves are strap-shaped. Narrow-leaved forms are frost hardy, broad-leaved ones half hardy. Grow in full sun and in moist, well-drained soil. Protect crowns in winter with ash or mulch. Plants increase slowly but may be propagated by division in spring; may also be raised from seed in autumn or spring. Named cultivars will not come true from seed.
♀ ***A. africanus*** (African lily). Evergreen, clump-forming perennial. **H** 1m (3ft), **S** 50cm (20in). Half hardy. In late summer has rounded umbels of deep blue flowers on upright stems, above broad, dark green leaves.
***A.* 'Alice Gloucester'.** Clump-forming perennial. **H** 1m (3ft), **S** 50cm (20in). Frost hardy. Produces large, dense, rounded umbels of white flowers in summer, above narrow, mid-green leaves.
***A.* 'Ben Hope'.** Clump-forming perennial. **H** 1–1.2m (3–4ft), **S** 50cm (20in). Frost hardy. Erect stems support dense, rounded umbels of deep blue flowers in late summer and early autumn, borne over narrow, greyish-green leaves.
***A.* 'Blue Giant'.** Clump-forming perennial. **H** 1.2m (4ft), **S** 60cm (24in). Frost hardy. Has rounded heads of open, bell-shaped rich blue flowers in mid- to late summer.
A. campanulatus. Clump-forming perennial. **H** 60cm–1.2m (2–4ft), **S** 50cm (20in). Frost hardy. Rounded umbels of blue flowers are borne on strong stems in summer, above narrow, greyish-green leaves.
***A.* 'Cherry Holley'.** Clump-forming perennial. **H** 1m (3ft), **S** 50cm (20in). Frost hardy. Rounded umbels of dark blue flowers, carried in summer above narrow leaves, do not fade to purple with age.
***A.* 'Dorothy Palmer'.** Clump-forming perennial. **H** 1m (3ft), **S** 50cm (20in). Frost hardy. Rounded umbels of rich blue flowers, fading to reddish-mauve, are borne on erect stems above narrow, greyish-green leaves in late summer.
A. inapertus. Clump-forming perennial. **H** 1.5m (5ft), **S** 60cm (2ft). Frost hardy. Pendent, narrowly tubular, blue flowers are borne on very erect stems, above narrow, bluish-green leaves, in late summer and autumn. **subsp. *pendulus* 'Graskop'** illus. p.240.
***A.* 'Lilliput'.** Compact, clump-forming perennial. **H** 80cm (32in), **S** 50cm (20in). Frost hardy. Has small, rounded umbels of dark blue flowers that are produced in summer. Leaves are narrow and mid-green.
♀ ***A.* 'Loch Hope'.** Clump-forming perennial. **H** 1–1.2m (3–4ft), **S** 50cm (20in). Frost hardy. Bears large, rounded umbels of deep blue flowers in late summer and early autumn, above narrow, greyish-green leaves.
***A.* 'Northern Star'** illus. p.241.
A. orientalis. See *A. praecox* subsp. *orientalis.*
***A.* 'Phantom'.** Evergreen, clump-forming perennial. **H** 1.2m (4ft), **S** 60cm (2ft) or more. Frost hardy. Large, rounded clusters of white flowers, flushed pale blue at the edges, are borne on stout stems in mid- to late summer. Has broadly strap-shaped, bright green leaves
A. praecox* subsp. *orientalis, syn. *A. orientalis,* illus. p.242.
***A.* 'Purple Cloud'** illus. p.241.

AGAPETES

SYN. PENTAPTERYGIUM

ERICACEAE

Genus of evergreen or deciduous, scandent shrubs and semi-scrambling climbers, grown for their flowers. Frost tender, min. 5–18°C (41–64°F). Provide full light or partial shade and a humus-rich, well-drained but not dry, neutral to acid soil. Water potted specimens freely when in full growth, but moderately at other times. Overlong stems may be cut back to promote branching, but they are best tied to supports. Propagate by seed sown in spring or by semi-ripe cuttings taken in late summer.
A. incurvata, syn. *A. rugosa* var. *rugosa* of gardens. An evergreen, loose shrub with arching or spreading stems. **H** and **S** to 3m (10ft). Min. 5°C (41°F). Leaves are lance-shaped, wrinkled and bright green. In spring, clusters of pendent, urn-shaped, white flowers, patterned with purple-red, are borne from leaf axils.
♀ ***A.* 'Ludgvan Cross'.** Evergreen, scandent shrub with arching or pendulous stems. **H** and **S** 2–3m (6–10ft). Min. 5°C (41°F). Lance-shaped leaves are dark green. Urn-shaped, red flowers with darker patterns are produced in spring.
A. macrantha. See *A. variegata* var. *macrantha.*
A. rugosa. See *A. incurvata.*
♀ ***A. serpens*** illus. p.461.
A. variegata* var. *macrantha, syn. *A. macrantha,* illus. p.461.

AGASTACHE

Mexican giant hyssop

LABIATAE/LAMIACEAE

Genus of summer-flowering perennials with aromatic leaves. Half hardy. Requires full sun and fertile, well-drained soil. Plants are short-lived and should be propagated each year by softwood or semi-ripe cuttings taken in late summer.
***A.* 'Black Adder'** illus. p.280.
A. mexicana, syn. *Brittonastrum mexicanum, Cedronella mexicana.* Upright perennial with aromatic leaves. **H** to 1m (3ft), **S** to 30cm (1ft). In summer bears whorls of small, tubular flowers in shades of pink to crimson. Leaves are oval, pointed, toothed and mid-green.

Agathaea. See *Felicia.*

AGATHOSMA

RUTACEAE

Genus of evergreen shrubs, grown for their flowers and overall appearance. Frost tender, min. 5–7°C (41–5°F). Needs full light and well-drained, acid soil. Water containerized specimens moderately, less when not in full growth. Propagate by semi-ripe cuttings in late summer.
A. pulchella, syn. *Barosma pulchella.* Evergreen, rounded, wiry, aromatic shrub. **H** and **S** to 1m (3ft). Has a dense mass of small, oval, leathery leaves. Small, 5-petalled, purple flowers are freely produced in terminal clusters in spring–summer.

AGAVE

AGAVACEAE

Genus of rosetted, perennial succulents with sword-shaped, sharp-toothed leaves. Small species, to 30cm (1ft) high, flower only after 5–10 years; tall species, to 5m (15ft) high, may take 20–40 years to flower. The majority of species that have hard, blue-grey leaves are half hardy; grey-green- or green-leaved species are usually frost tender, requiring min. 5°C (41°F). Requires full sun and well-drained soil. Propagate by seed or offsets in spring or summer.
♀ ***A. americana*** (Century plant). Basal-rosetted, perennial succulent. **H** 1–2m (3–6ft), **S** 2–3m (6–10ft) or more. Half hardy. Has sharply pointed, toothed leaves, to 1.5–2m (5–6ft) long. Branched flower stem, to 8m (25ft) long, bears dense, tapering spikes of bell-shaped, white to pale creamy-yellow flowers, each 9cm (3½in) long, in spring–summer. Offsets freely. ♀ **'Marginata'** (illus. p.482). **H** and **S** 2m (6ft), has yellow margins and a central green zone to each leaf. ♀ **'Mediopicta'**, **H** and **S** 2m (6ft), has central, yellow stripes along leaves. **'Striata'** illus. p.481.
A. attenuata illus. p.489.
A. duplicata. See *Polianthes geminiflora.*
♀ ***A. filifera*** (Thread agave; illus. p.482). Basal-rosetted, perennial succulent. **H** 1m (3ft), **S** 2m (6ft). Half hardy. Has narrow, green leaves, each spined at the tip. White leaf margins gradually break away, leaving long, white fibres. Produces yellow-green flowers on a 2.5m (8ft) tall stem in summer. Offsets freely.
A. flexispina. Basal-rosetted, perennial succulent. **H** 35cm (14in), **S** 75cm (30in). Frost tender, min. 5°C (41°F). Sword-shaped, glaucous to yellowish-green leaves have wavy margins and flexible, brown spines. Flower stem, to 3.5m (11½ft) long, bears a rather open panicle of cylindrical, red-tinged, greenish-yellow flowers, 2cm (¾in) long, in summer.
A. macroacantha (illus. p.482). Basal-rosetted, perennial succulent. **H** 30–40cm (12–16in), **S** 25–40cm (10–16in). Frost hardy. Has narrowly sword-shaped, toothed, bluish-grey leaves with dark brown spines. Flower stem, to 2m (6ft) long, bears slender panicles of tubular, purple-tinged, green flowers, 5cm (2in) long, and sometimes bulbils, in summer.
A. maculosa, syn. *Manfreda maculosa.* Basal-rosetted, perennial succulent. **H** 20–60cm (24–72in), **S** 30–90cm (12–36in). Frost tender, min. 5°C (41°F). Lance-shaped, grooved, dark green leaves, with small, distantly spaced teeth, sometimes have dark green- or brown-spotted patterns. Flower stem, to 1.8m (6ft) long, bears narrow spikes of bell-shaped, white to yellowish-white flowers, 1.5cm (⅝in) long, in summer.
A. parrasana (illus. p.482). Basal-rosetted, compact, perennial succulent. **H** 30–40cm (12–16in), **S** 30–45cm (12–18in). Frost hardy. Ovate, closely packed and overlapping, thick, rigid, light grey leaves have toothed margins with short, greyish-brown spines. Flower stem, 3–4m (10–13ft) long, produces ellipsoidal panicles of bell-shaped, pale yellow flowers, 5cm (2in) long, flushed red or purple, in summer.

A. parryi illus. p.489.
🏆 **A. parviflora** (illus. p.482). Basal-rosetted, perennial succulent. **H** 1.5m (5ft), **S** 50cm (20in). Frost tender, min. 5°C (41°F). Has narrow, white-marked, dark green leaves with white fibres peeling from edges. Produces white flowers in [illegible]
A. pollanthes. See Polianthes tuberosa.
A. polianthiflora (illus. p.482). Basal-rosetted, perennial succulent. **H** 10–20cm (4–8in), **S** 10–30cm (4–12in). Frost tender, min. 5°C (41°F). Lance-shaped, white-marked, mid-green leaves have wispy, white filaments on the margins; minute teeth are borne only towards leaf bases. Red flower stem, 1–2m (3–6ft) long, bears narrow spikes of tubular, pink and red flowers, 4cm (1½in) long, in summer.
🏆 **A. potatorum** (illus. p.482). Basal-rosetted, compact, perennial succulent. **H** 30cm (12in), **S** 30–45cm (12–18in). Frost tender, min. 5°C (41°F). Broadly sword-shaped, glaucous-white to green leaves have wavy to notched margins and sharp, sinuous, chestnut-brown spines. Red to purple flower stem, 3–4m (10–13ft) long, produces egg-shaped panicles of bell-shaped, red-tinged, light green to yellowish flowers, 5–8cm (2–3in) long, in summer.
A. schottii. Basal-rosetted, perennial succulent. **H** 20–40cm (8–16in), **S** 30–45cm (12–18in). Frost tender, min. 5°C (41°F). Narrowly linear, yellowish green to green leaves have margins bearing brittle threads. Often crooked flower stem, to 2m (6ft) long, produces slender spike of tubular, yellow flowers, 3–4cm (1¼–1½in) long, in summer.
A. utahensis. Basal-rosetted, perennial succulent. **H** 23cm (9in) or more, **S** 2m (6ft). Half hardy. Has rigid, blue-grey leaves, each with spines up margins and a long, dark spine at tip. Flower stem, to 1.5m (5ft) long, carries yellow flowers in summer.
🏆 **A. victoria-regina** illus. p.482. **'Compacta'** is a very slow-growing, basal-rosetted, perennial succulent. **H** 30cm (12in), **S** 45cm (18in). Frost hardy. Has tight fitting, tapered, deep green leaves, each with a small, terminal spine and smooth, spineless, white margins. Flower stem, to 5m (16ft) long, bears a narrow, dense spike of funnel-shaped, purple- or red-tinged, cream flowers, 2–3cm (¾–1¼) long, in summer.
A. zebra. Basal-rosetted, perennial succulent. **H** 1m (4ft), **S** 45–60cm (1½–3ft). Frost tender, min. 5°C (41°F). Lance-shaped, thick, rigid, rough, wavy-margined, patterned, light grey leaves have curved, grey spines. Flower stem, 6–8m (20–25ft) long, produces narrow, panicle of bell-shaped, yellow flowers, 4.5cm (1¾in) long, in summer.

AGERATINA
COMPOSITAE/ASTERACEAE

Genus of perennials, sub-shrubs and shrubs, many of which are evergreen, grown mainly for their flowers, some also for their architectural foliage. Fully hardy to frost tender, min. 5–13°C (41–55°F). Requires full light or partial shade. Will grow in any conditions, although most species prefer moist but well-drained soil. Water containerized plants freely when in full growth, moderately at other times. Prune shrubs lightly after flowering or in spring. Propagate by seed in spring; shrubs and sub-shrubs may also be propagated by softwood or greenwood cuttings in summer, perennials by division in early spring or autumn. Red spider mite and whitefly may be troublesome.
A. altissima, syn. *Eupatorium ageratoides, E. rugosum, E. urticifolium* (Hardy age, Mist flower, White snakeroot). Erect perennial. **H** 1.2m (4ft), **S** 45cm (1½ft). Fully hardy. Has nettle-like, grey-green leaves. In late summer bears dense, flat, white flower heads.
🏆 **A. ligustrina**, syn. *Eupatorium ligustrinum, E. micranthum, E. weinmannianum*. Evergreen, rounded shrub. **H** and **S** 2–4m (6–12ft). Half hardy. Has elliptic to lance-shaped, bright green leaves and, in autumn, fragrant, groundsel-like, white or pink flowers are produced in flattened clusters, 10–20cm (4–8in) wide.

AGERATUM
Floss flower
COMPOSITAE/ASTERACEAE

Genus of annuals and biennials. Half hardy. Grow in sun and in fertile, well-drained soil, which should not be allowed to dry out otherwise growth and flowering will be poor. Dead-head regularly to ensure continuous flowering. Propagate by seed sown outdoors in late spring.
A. houstonianum. Moderately fast-growing, hummock-forming annual. Tall cultivars, **H** and **S** 30cm (12in); medium, **H** and **S** 20cm (8in); dwarf, **H** and **S** 15cm (6in). All have oval, mid-green leaves and clusters of feathery, brush-like flower heads throughout summer and into autumn. Is useful for bedding. 🏆 **'Blue Danube'** (dwarf) illus. p.313. **'Blue Mink'** (tall) illus. p.314. **Hawaii Series** includes uniform, compact plants, with deep to pale blue or white flower heads. 🏆 **'Pacific'** (medium) is neat, with tight clusters of deep violet-blue flower heads. **'Swing Pink'** (dwarf) has attractive, pink flower heads.

AGLAONEMA
Chinese evergreen
ARACEAE

Genus of evergreen, erect, tufted perennials, grown mainly for their foliage. Frost tender, most species requiring min. 15°C (59°F). Tolerates shade, although the variegated forms need more light, and prefers moist but well-drained soil. Water moderately when in full growth, less in winter. Propagate by division or stem cuttings in summer. Mealy bug may be a problem.
A. commutatum. Evergreen, erect, tufted perennial. **H** and **S** to 45cm (18in) or more. Broadly lance-shaped leaves are 30cm (12in) long and dark green with irregular, greyish-white patches along lateral veins. Has greenish-white spathes produced in summer. **'Malay Beauty'** (syn. *A.c.* 'Pewter') bears very dark green leaves mottled greenish-white and cream. **'Pewter'** see *A.c.* 'Malay Beauty'. **'Treubii'** illus. p.468.
A. pictum illus. p.475.
A. 'Silver King' illus. p.475.

AGONIS
Willow myrtle
MYRTACEAE

Genus of evergreen, mainly spring-flowering shrubs and trees, grown for their foliage, flowers and graceful appearance. Frost tender, min. 10°C (50°F). Needs full light and well-drained but moisture-retentive soil. Water containerized specimens moderately, scarcely at all in winter. Pruning is tolerated when necessary. Propagate by seed in spring or by semi-ripe cuttings in summer.
A. flexuosa (Peppermint tree, Willow myrtle) illus. p.450.

AGROSTEMMA
Corn cockle
CARYOPHYLLACEAE

Genus of summer-flowering annuals. Fully hardy. Grow in sun; flowers best in very well-drained soil that is not very fertile. Support with sticks and dead-head to prolong flowering. Propagate by seed sown *in situ* in spring or early autumn.
⚠ Seeds may cause severe discomfort if ingested.
A. coeli-rosa. See *Silene coeli-rosa*.
A. githago. Fast-growing, erect annual with thin stems. **H** 60cm–1m (2–3ft), **S** 30cm (1ft). Has lance-shaped, mid-green leaves and, in summer, produces 5-petalled, open trumpet-shaped, pink flowers, 8cm (3in) wide. Seeds are tiny, rounded, dark brown and poisonous. **'Milas'** illus. p.304.

AICHRYSON
CRASSULACEAE

Genus of annual and perennial succulents, often shrub-like, grown for their fleshy, spoon-shaped to rounded, hairy leaves. Most species are short-lived, dying after flowering. Frost tender, min. 5°C (41°F). Requires a position in full sun or partial shade and very well-drained soil. Propagate by seed or stem cuttings in spring or summer.
🏆 **A. x aizoides var. domesticum 'Variegatum'**, syn. *A. x domesticum* 'Variegatum', illus. p.495.

AILANTHUS
SIMAROUBACEAE

Genus of deciduous trees, grown for their foliage and 3–5-winged fruits; they can be particularly useful as they are extremely tolerant of urban pollution. Fully hardy. Needs sun or semi-shade and deep, fertile, well-drained soil. To grow as shrubs, cut back hard in spring, after which vigorous shoots bearing very large leaves are produced. Propagate by seed sown in autumn or by suckers or root cuttings taken in winter. Male flowers are unpleasantly scented; the pollen may cause an allergic reaction.
🏆 **A. altissima**, syn. *A. glandulosa* (Tree of heaven) illus. p.63.
A. glandulosa. See *A. altissima*.

AJUGA
LABIATAE/LAMIACEAE

Genus of annuals and perennials, some of which are semi-evergreen or evergreen and excellent as ground cover. Fully hardy. Tolerates sun or shade and any soil, but grows more vigorously in moist conditions. Propagate by division in spring.
A. pyramidalis (Pyramidal bugle). Semi-evergreen perennial. **H** 15cm (6in), **S** 45cm (18in). Forms a creeping carpet of oblong to spoon-shaped, deep green leaves, above which appear spikes of whorled, 2-lipped, blue flowers in spring. **'Metallica Crispa'** has crisp, curled leaves, with a metallic-bronze lustre, and dark blue flowers.
A. reptans 'Atropurpurea'. Evergreen, ground-cover perennial, spreading freely by runners. **H** 15cm (6in), **S** 90cm (36in). Has small rosettes of ovate to oblong-spoon-shaped, toothed or slightly lobed, glossy, deep bronze-purple leaves. Short spikes of 2-lipped, blue flowers are borne in spring. **'Jungle Beauty'**, **H** 38cm (15in), **S** 60cm (24in), is semi-evergreen and has large, dark green leaves, sometimes suffused purple. **'Multicolor'** (syn. *A.r.* 'Rainbow'), **H** 12cm (5in), **S** 45cm (18in), has dark green leaves, marked with cream and pink. **'Rainbow'** see *A.r.* 'Multicolor'.

AKEBIA
LARDIZABALACEAE

Genus of deciduous or semi-evergreen, woody-stemmed, twining climbers, grown for their leaves and flowers. Individual plants seldom produce fruits; cross-pollination between 2 individuals is required for fruit formation. Frost hardy. Prefers a position in full sun and any good, well-drained soil. Tolerates an east- or north-facing position. Dislikes disturbance. May be propagated in a number of ways: by seed sown in autumn or spring; by semi-ripe cutings taken in summer; or by layering in winter.
A. lobata. See *A. trifoliata*.
A. x pentaphylla illus. p.194.
A. quinata (Chocolate vine) illus. p.193.
A. trifoliata, syn. *A. lobata*, illus. p.204.

ALANGIUM
ALANGIACEAE

Genus of deciduous or evergreen trees and shrubs, grown for their foliage and flowers. Frost hardy. Needs full sun and any fertile, well-drained soil. Propagate by sowing seed in spring or by taking softwood cuttings in summer.
A. platanifolium. Deciduous, upright, tree-like shrub. **H** 3m (10ft), **S** 2m (6ft). Produces maple-like, 3-lobed, mid-green leaves. Fragrant, tubular, white flowers are borne from early to mid-summer.

ALBIZIA
LEGUMINOSAE/MIMOSACEAE

Genus of deciduous or semi-evergreen trees, grown for their feathery foliage and unusual flower heads, composed of numerous stamens and resembling bottlebrushes. Half hardy, so it is best

grown against a south- or west-facing wall; in cold areas, do not risk planting out until late spring. Requires full sun and well-drained soil. *A. julibrissin* may be grown as a summer bedding plant for its foliage. Propagate by seed in autumn.
A. distachya. See *Paraserianthes lophantha.*
A. julibrissin (Silk tree) illus. p.86.
A. lophantha. See *Paraserianthes lophantha.*

ALBUCA

HYACINTHACEAE/LILIACEAE

Genus of spring- or summer-flowering bulbs. Half hardy to frost tender, min. 10°C (50°F). Needs an open, sunny position and well-drained soil. Dies down in spring or late summer after flowering. Propagate by seed in spring or by offsets when dormant.
A. canadensis, syn. *A. major, A. minor.* Spring-flowering bulb. **H** 15cm (6in), **S** 8–10cm (3–4in). Half hardy. Has 3–6 narrowly lance-shaped, erect, basal leaves. Produces a loose spike of tubular, yellow flowers, 1.5–2cm (⅝–¾in) long, with a green stripe on each petal.
A. humilis illus. p.422.
A. major. See *A. canadensis.*
A. minor. See *A. canadensis.*

ALCEA

Hollyhock

MALVACEAE

Genus of biennials and short-lived perennials, grown for their tall spikes of flowers. Fully hardy. Needs full sun and well-drained soil. Propagate by seed in late summer or spring. Rust may be a problem.
A. rosea, syn. *Althaea rosea.* Erect biennial. **H** 1.5–2m (5–6ft), **S** to 60cm (2ft). Has rounded, lobed, rough-textured leaves. Spikes of single flowers, in a range of colours including pink, yellow and cream, are borne in summer and early autumn. **Chater's Double Group**, **H** 1.8–2.4m (6–8ft), bears double flowers in several different colours in summer and early autumn. **'Majorette'**, **H** 60cm (24in), **S** to 30cm (12in), produces double flowers, in several different colours, in summer and early autumn. **'Summer Carnival'** (annual or biennial), **H** 1.8–2.4m (6–8ft), **S** to 60cm (2ft), has double flowers in mixed colours.

ALCHEMILLA

Lady's mantle

ROSACEAE

Genus of perennials that produce sprays of tiny, greenish-yellow flowers, with conspicuous outer calyces, in summer. Some are good for ground cover. Fully hardy. Grow in sun or partial shade, in all but boggy soils. Propagate by seed or division in spring or autumn.
A. alpina (Alpine lady's mantle). Mound-forming perennial. **H** 15cm (6in), **S** 60cm (24in) or more. Rounded, lobed, pale green leaves are covered in silky hairs. Bears upright spikes of tiny, greenish-yellow flowers, with conspicuous, green, outer calyces, in summer. Is suitable for ground cover and a dry bank.
A. conjuncta illus. p.275.
🏆***A. mollis*** (Lady's mantle) illus. p.275.

x ALICEARA

ORCHIDACEAE

See also ORCHIDS.
x *A.* Dark Warrior. Evergreen, epiphytic orchid for a cool greenhouse. **H** 25cm (10in). Produces sprays of wispy, mauve-brown, cream-yellow or green flowers, 4cm (1½in) across; flowering season varies. Leaves, 10cm (4in) long, are narrowly oval. Grow in semi-shade in summer.
x *A. Eurostar* gx, syn. x *Beallara* Eurostar. Evergreen, epiphytic orchid for a cool greenhouse. **H** 60cm (24in), **S** 40cm (16in). Frost tender, min. 10°C (50°F). In spring bears star-shaped, maroon sepals and petals, each with white or cream tips and a large, spade-shaped, weakly 3-lobed lip, which is white in lower half and pink, maroon or speckled in upper half. Large, elliptic, compressed pseudobulb produces 1–3 strap-shaped leaves. Needs shade in summer.

ALISMA

ALISMATACEAE

Genus of deciduous, perennial, marginal water plants, grown for their foliage and flowers. Fully to frost hardy. Requires an open, sunny position in mud or up to 25cm (10in) depth of water. Tidy up fading foliage in autumn and remove dying flower spikes before ripening seeds are dispersed. May be propagated by division in spring or by seed in late summer. ⚠Contact with sap may irritate skin; all parts may cause mild stomach upset if ingested.
A. natans. See *Luronium natans.*
A. plantago-aquatica (Water plantain) illus. p.434.
A. ranunculoides. See *Baldellia ranunculoides.*

ALLAMANDA

SYN. ALLEMANDA

APOCYNACEAE

Genus of evergreen, woody-stemmed, scrambling climbers, grown for their trumpet-shaped flowers. Frost tender, min. 13–15°C (55–59°F). Prefers partial shade in summer and humus-rich, well-drained, neutral to acid soil. Water regularly, less when not in full growth. Stems must be tied to supports. Prune previous season's growth back to 1 or 2 nodes in spring. Propagate by softwood cuttings in spring or summer. Whitefly and red spider mite may be troublesome. ⚠Contact with sap may irritate skin; all parts may cause mild stomach upset if ingested.
A. cathartica (Golden trumpet).
🏆**'Hendersonii'** illus. p.464.

ALLIUM

Onion

LILIACEAE/ALLIACEAE

Genus of perennials, some of which are edible, with bulbs, rhizomes or fibrous rootstocks. Nearly all have narrow, basal leaves smelling of onions when crushed, and most have small flowers packed together in a dense, spherical or shuttlecock-shaped umbel. Dried umbels of tall border species are good for winter decoration. Fully to frost hardy. Requires an open, sunny situation and well-drained soil; is best left undisturbed to form clumps. Plant in autumn. Propagate by seed in autumn or by division of clumps – spring-flowering varieties in late summer and summer-flowering ones in spring. ⚠Contact with the bulbs may irritate skin or aggravate skin allergies.
A. acuminatum, syn. *A. murrayanum*, illus. p.416.
A. aflatunense illus. p.382.
A. aflatunense of gardens. See *A. hollandicum.*
A. akaka illus. p.416.
A. albopilosum. See *A. cristophii.*
A. atropurpureum illus. p.392.
A. azureum. See *A. caeruleum.*
A. beesianum. Clump-forming, late summer-flowering bulb. **H** 20–30cm (8–12in), **S** 5–10cm (2–4in). Fully hardy. Has linear, grey-green leaves and, in late summer, pendent heads of bell-shaped, blue flowers.
🏆***A. caeruleum***, syn. *A. azureum*, illus. p.411.
A. campanulatum. Clump-forming, summer-flowering bulb. **H** 10–30cm (4–12in), **S** 5–10cm (2–4in). Frost hardy. Linear, semi-erect, basal leaves die away before flowering time. Bears a domed umbel, 2.5–7cm (1–3in) wide, of up to 30 small, star-shaped, pale pink or white flowers.
🏆***A. carinatum* subsp. *pulchellum***, syn. *A. pulchellum.* Clump-forming, summer-flowering bulb. **H** 30–60cm (12–24in), **S** 8–10cm (3–4in). Fully hardy. Linear, semi-erect leaves sheathe lower two-thirds of stem. Has an umbel of pendent, cup-shaped, purple flowers.
A. cernuum illus. p.409.
A. christophii. See *A. cristophii.*
A. cowanii. See *A. neapolitanum.*
🏆***A. cristophii***, syn. *A. albopilosum*, illus. p.411.
🏆***A. cyaneum.*** Tuft-forming, summer-flowering bulb. **H** 10–30cm (4–12in), **S** 5–8cm (2–3in). Fully hardy. Leaves are thread-like and erect. Stems each bear a small, dense umbel of 5 or more pendent, cup-shaped, blue or violet-blue flowers, 0.5cm (¼in) long.
A. cyathophorum* var. *farreri illus. p.423.
🏆***A. flavum*** illus. p.412.
🏆***A. giganteum*** illus. p.392.
🏆***A.* 'Gladiator'** illus. p.392.
🏆***A.* 'Globemaster'** illus. p.392.
🏆***A. hollandicum***, syn. *A. aflatunense* of gardens. Tuft-forming, summer-flowering bulb. **H** 1m (3ft), **S** 10cm (4in). Frost hardy. Has mid-green, basal leaves dying away by flowering time. Carries numerous star-shaped, purplish-pink flowers in a dense, spherical umbel, 10cm (4in) across.
A. kansuense. See *A. sikkimense.*
🏆***A. karataviense*** illus. p.416.
A. macranthum. Tuft-forming, summer-flowering bulb. **H** 20–30cm (8–12in), **S** 10–12cm (4–5in). Fully hardy. Has linear leaves on lower part of flower stem, which bears a loose umbel of up to 20 bell-shaped, deep purple flowers, each 1cm (½in) long, on slender stalks.
A. mairei. Clump-forming, late summer- to autumn-flowering bulb. **H** 10–20cm (4–8in), **S** 10–12cm (4–5in). Fully hardy. Leaves are erect, thread-like and basal. Wiry stems, each carry a small, shuttlecock-shaped umbel of up to 20 upright, bell-shaped, pink flowers, each 1cm (½in) long.
A. moly illus. p.424.
***A.* 'Mount Everest'** illus. p.385.
A. murrayanum. See *A. acuminatum.*
A. murrayanum of gardens. See *A. unifolium.*
A. narcissiflorum, syn. *A. pedemontanum* of gardens, illus. p.422.
A. neapolitanum, syn. *A. cowanii*, illus. p.399. **Cowanii Group** illus. p.409.
A. oreophilum, syn. *A. ostrowskianum*, illus. p.418.
A. ostrowskianum. See *A. oreophilum.*
A. pedemontanum of gardens. See *A. narcissiflorum.*
A. pulchellum. See *A. carinatum* subsp. *pulchellum.*
🏆***A.* 'Purple Sensation'** illus. p.392.
A. rosenbachianum. Tuft-forming, summer-flowering bulb. **H** 1m (3ft), **S** 10cm (4in). Frost hardy. Has ridged stems and grey-green strap-like, basal leaves. Carries 50 or more star-shaped, deep purple flowers in a spherical umbel, 10cm (4in) across.
A. schoenoprasum (Chives) illus. p.422.
A. schubertii illus. p.409.
A. senescens* var. *calcareum*.** See *A.s.* subsp. *montanum.* **subsp. *montanum (syn. *A.s.* var. *calcareum*) illus. p.409.
A. sikkimense, syn. *A. kansuense.* Tuft-forming, summer-flowering bulb. **H** 10–25cm (4–10in), **S** 5–10cm (2–4in). Fully hardy. Leaves are linear, erect and basal. Up to 15 bell-shaped, blue flowers, 0.5–1cm (¼–½in) long, are borne in a small, pendent umbel.
A. sphaerocephalon. Clump-forming, summer-flowering bulb. **H** to 60cm (24in), **S** 8–10cm (3–4in). Fully hardy. Has linear, semi-erect leaves on basal third of slender, wiry stems and a very dense umbel, 2–4cm (¾–1½in) across, of up to 40 small, bell-shaped, pinkish-purple flowers.
A. stipitatum Summer-flowering bulb. **H** to 1–1.5m (3–4ft), **S** 15–20cm (6–8in). Frost hardy. Stout stems with strap-like, semi-erect, basal leaves carry 50 or more star-shaped, purplish-pink flowers in a spherical umbel, 8–12cm (3–5in) across.
🏆***A. unifolium***, syn. *A. murrayanum* of gardens illus. p.402.

ALNUS

Alder

BETULACEAE

Genus of deciduous trees and shrubs, grown mainly for their ability to thrive in wet situations. Flowers are borne in catkins in late winter or early spring, the males conspicuous and attractive, the females forming persistent, woody, cone-like fruits. Fully hardy. Most do best in sun and any moist or even waterlogged soil, but *A. cordata* will also grow well on poor, dry soils. Propagate species by seed sown in autumn, cultivars by budding in late summer or by hardwood cuttings taken in early winter.

♀ ***A. cordata*** (Italian alder). Fast-growing, deciduous, conical tree. **H** 18m (60ft), **S** 9m (30ft). Yellow, male catkins appear in late winter and early spring, followed by heart-shaped, glossy, deep green leaves. Has persistent, round, woody fruits in autumn.
A. glutinosa (Black alder, Common alder). **'Aurea'** is a slow-growing, deciduous, conical tree. **H** to 25m (80ft), **S** 10m (30ft). Has rounded leaves, bright yellow until mid-summer, later becoming pale green. Produces yellow-brown catkins in early spring. Is useful grown in a boggy area. ♀ **'Imperialis'** illus. p.75.
A. incana (Grey alder) illus. p.61. **'Aurea'** is a deciduous, conical tree. **H** 20m (70ft), **S** 8m (25ft). Has reddish-yellow or orange shoots in winter and broadly oval, yellow leaves. Reddish-yellow or orange catkins are borne in late winter and early spring. Is useful for cold, wet areas and poor soils. **'Ramulis Coccineis'** has red winter shoots and buds, and orange catkins.

ALOCASIA

ARACEAE

Genus of evergreen perennials with underground rhizomes, grown for their attractive foliage. Produces tiny flowers on a spadix enclosed in a leaf-like spathe. Frost tender, min. 15°C (59°F). Needs high humidity, partial shade and well-drained soil. Propagate by seed, stem cuttings or division of rhizomes in spring. ⓘ Contact with sap may irritate skin; all parts may cause mild stomach upset if ingested.
A. cuprea illus. p.472.
A. longiloba, syn. *A. lowii* var. *picta, A.l.* var. *veitchii, A. veitchii.* Evergreen, tufted perennial. **H** 1m (3ft) or more, **S** 75cm (30in). Narrow leaves, triangular with arrow-shaped bases, are 45cm (18in) long and green with greyish midribs, veins and margins, purple below. Greenish spathes.
A. lowii* var. *picta. See *A. longiloba.* **var. *veitchii.*** See *A. longiloba.*
A. macrorrhiza (Giant elephant's ear, Taro). Evergreen, tufted perennial with a thick, trunk-like stem. **H** to 3m (10ft) or more, **S** 2m (6ft). Broad, arrow-shaped, glossy, green leaves, to 1m (3ft) long, are carried on stalks 1m (3ft) long. Has yellowish-green spathes to 20cm (8in) high.
A. veitchii. See *A. longiloba.*

ALOE

LILIACEAE/ASPHODELACEAE

Genus of evergreen, rosetted trees, shrubs, perennials and scandent climbers with succulent foliage and tubular to bell-shaped flowers. Frost tender, min. 7–10°C (45–50°F). Tree aloes and shrubs with a spread over 30cm (1ft) prefer full sun; most smaller species prefer partial shade. Needs very well-drained soil. Propagate by seed, stem cuttings or offsets in spring or summer.
A. arborescens. Evergreen, bushy, succulent-leaved shrub. **H** and **S** 2m (6ft). Stems are crowned by rosettes of widely spreading, long, slender, curved, dull blue-green leaves with toothed margins. Long flower stems produce masses of tubular to bell-shaped, red flowers 4cm (1½in) long in late winter and spring. ♀ **'Variegata'** (illus. p.493) has numerous spikes of red flowers in late winter and spring.
♀ ***A. aristata*** (Lace aloe, Torch plant; illus. p.493). Clump-forming, perennial succulent. **H** 10cm (4in), **S** 30cm (12in). Has a basal rosette of pointed, dull green leaves with white spots and soft-toothed edges. Has orange flowers in spring. Offsets freely.
A. barbadensis. See *A. vera.*
♀ ***A. brevifolia.*** Basal-rosetted, perennial succulent, producing many offsets. **H** 15cm (6in), **S** 30cm (12in). Has broadly sword-shaped, fleshy, blue-green leaves with a few teeth along edges. In spring, flower stems, 50cm (20in) long, carry narrowly bell-shaped, bright red flowers 3–4cm (1¼–1½in) long.
A. broomii. Basal-rosetted, perennial succulent. **H** 10cm (4in), **S** 30cm (12in). Frost tender, min. 1°C (34°F). Ovate to lance-shaped, mid-green leaves have minutely-toothed, red-brown margins and sharp, terminal spines. In summer unbranched flower stems, to 1m (3ft) long, bear dense spikes of tubular, pale lemon flowers, 2cm (3/4in) long.
A. ciliaris (illus. p.493). Climbing, perennial succulent. **H** 5m (15ft), **S** 30cm (1ft). Has a slender stem crowned by a rosette of narrow, green leaves and white teeth where leaf base joins stem. Bears bell-shaped, scarlet flowers, with yellow and green mouths, in spring.
A. concinna. See *A. squarrosa.*
♀ ***A. descoingsii.*** Clump-forming, basal-rosetted, perennial succulent. **H** 10cm (in), **S** 15cm (6in). Frost tender, min. 5°C (41°F). Triangular, dull green leaves have white-toothed margins and many raised, white spots. In summer, unbranched flower stems, 15cm (6in) long, produce urn-shaped, red-orange flowers, 7mm (1/4in) long.
A. erinacea. See *A. melanacantha* var. *erinacea.*
A. ferox (illus. p.493). Evergreen, succulent tree. **H** to 3m (10ft), **S** 1.5–2m (5–6ft). Has a woody stem crowned by a dense rosette of sword-shaped, blue-green leaves that have spined margins. Carries an erect spike of bell-shaped, orange-scarlet flowers in spring.
♀ ***A. haworthioides.*** Stemless, perennial succulent suckering to form clumps. **H** 20cm (8in), **S** 10cm (4in). Frost tender, min. 5°C (41°F). Has dense rosettes of lance-shaped, dark green leaves, with many raised, white bristles and margins with small, white teeth set close together. Unbranched flower stems, 15–30cm (8–12in) long, bear bell-shaped, white to pale pink flowers, 8cm (3in) long, in summer.
A. hemmingii (illus. p.493). Basal-rosetted, perennial succulent. **H** 15cm (6in), **S** 25cm (10in). Frost tender, min. 5°C (41°F). Ovate to lance-shaped, olive-green leaves, 10cm (4in) long, with dull, white streaks, have short, sharp teeth at the margins. Produces unbranched flower stems, 30cm (12in) long, with tubular, minutely spotted, flamingo-pink to pale rose flowers, 2.5cm (1in) long, in summer.
A. humilis. Rosetted, perennial succulent. **H** 10cm (4in), **S** 30cm (12in). Has a dense, basal rosette of narrowly sword-shaped, spine-edged, fleshy, blue-green leaves, often erect, with incurving tips. Produces flower stems 30cm (12in) long, each bearing a spike of narrowly bell-shaped, orange flowers in spring 3.5–4.5cm (1½–1¾in) long. Offsets freely.
A. [illegible]. Solitary or sometimes clump-forming, perennial succulent. **H** 50cm (20in), **S** to 100cm (39in). Frost tender, min. 5°C (41°F). Has dense rosettes of lance-shaped, smooth, glossy, dark green leaves with many small, pale green spots and margins bearing firm, reddish-brown teeth. In summer, produces branched flower spikes, to 1.2m (4ft) long, of tubular, strawberry-red to pink flowers, 2.5cm (1in) long.
A. melanacantha* var. *erinacea, syn. *A. erinacea.* Slow-growing, clump-forming, perennial succulent. **H** 15cm (6in), **S** 30cm (12in). Frost tender, min. 1°C (34°F) if kept dry in winter. Compact rosettes of triangular to lance-shaped, dull-green leaves have sharp, black spines at the margins and a black spine at each tip. Unbranched flower stems, to 1m (3ft) long, produce dense, cylindrical clusters of bell-shaped, scarlet flowers, 3cm (1¼in) long, fading to yellow, in summer.
A. microstigma. Basal-rosetted, perennial succulent. **H** 30cm (12in), **S** 25–60cm (10–24in). Frost tender, min. 1°C (34°F). Lance-shaped to triangular, red-tinged, mid-green leaves, often white spotted, especially beneath, have reddish-brown margins with small, reddish-brown teeth. Unbranched flower stems, 60cm (24in) long, bears conical racemes of bell-shaped, orange flowers, 25cm (10in) long, fading to greenish-yellow, in summer.
A. plicatilis. Perennial succulent with leaves in opposite pairs up the stem. **H** and **S** to 60cm (24in). Frost tender, min. 1°C (34°F). Has strap-shaped, smooth, dull to glaucous green leaves with margins almost without teeth. In summer, unbranched flower stems, to 50cm (20in) long, produce cylindrical spikes of bell-shaped, scarlet flowers, 5cm (2in) long.
A. punctata. See *A. variegata.*
♀ ***A. rauhii.*** Basal-rosetted, perennial succulent eventually forming dense clumps. **H** to 10cm (4in), **S** 20cm (8in). Frost tender, min. 5°C (41°F). Unbranched flower stems, to 25cm (10in) long, of tubular, scarlet flowers, 2.5cm (1in) long, pale red to greenish towards mouths, are borne throughout the year. Lance-shaped, greyish or bright green leaves have many elongated, white spots and small, white teeth at the margins. In some forms, the leaves have raised dots or are almost white with green dots.
♀ ***A. somaliensis.*** Basal-rosetted, perennial succulent. **H** 30cm (12in), **S** 25cm (10in). Frost tender, min. 5°C (41°F). Lance-shaped, glossy olive-green leaves, 20–40cm long, with dull, white streaks, have short, sharp teeth at the margins. Branched flower stems, 30–60cm (12–24in) long, with tubular, minutely spotted, flamingo-pink to pale rose flowers, 2.5cm (1in) long, are borne in summer.
A. squarrosa, syn. *A. concinna.* Prostrate, perennial succulent. **H** 30cm (12in), **S** 20cm (8in). Frost tender, min. 5°C (41°F). Has lance-shaped, strongly recurved, toothed, white-speckled, mid-green leaves borne along short stems. Unbranched, pendulous flower stems, 10–25cm (4–10in) long, of tubular, red flowers, 2.5cm (1in) long, are produced in summer.
A. striata (illus. p.493). Basal-rosetted, perennial succulent. **H** and **S** 1m (3ft). Has broad, blue-green leaves, with white margins and marks, that become suffused red in full sun. Produces reddish-orange flowers in spring. Makes a good house plant.
♀ ***A. variegata***, syn. *A. punctata* (Partridge-breasted aloe; illus. p.493). Humped, perennial succulent. **H** 30cm (12in), **S** 10cm (4in). Has triangular, white-marked, dark green leaves with pronounced keels beneath. Bears a spike of pinkish-red flowers in spring. Makes a good house plant.
♀ ***A. vera***, syn. *A. barbadensis,* illus. p.492.
A. zebrina. Basal-rosetted, perennial succulent. **H** 20cm (8in), **S** 40cm (16in). Frost tender, min. 4°C (39°F). Lance-shaped, dull green leaves, with white chevrons, have sharp, brown teeth at the margins. Branched flower stems, 1m (3ft) long, of tubular, coral-red to dull red flowers, 3cm (1¼in) long, are produced in summer

ALOINOPSIS

AIZOACEAE

Genus of dwarf, tuberous, perennial succulents with daisy-like flowers from late summer to early spring. Frost tender, min. 7°C (45°F). Requires a sunny site and very well-drained soil. Is very susceptible to overwatering. Propagate by seed in summer.
A. schooneesii illus. p.488.

ALONSOA

SCROPHULARIACEAE

Genus of perennials, grown as annuals. May be used for cut flowers. Half hardy. Grow in sun and in rich, well-drained soil. Flowering may be poor outdoors in a wet summer. Young plants should have growing shoots pinched out to encourage bushy growth. Propagate by seed sown outdoors in late spring. Aphids may be troublesome, particularly under glass.
A. warscewiczii (Mask flower) illus. p.308.

ALOPECURUS

GRAMINEAE/POACEAE

See also GRASSES, BAMBOOS, RUSHES and SEDGES.
***A. pratensis* 'Aureovariegatus'**, syn. *A.p.* 'Aureomarginatus', (Golden foxtail) illus. p.289.

ALOYSIA

VERBENACEAE

Genus of deciduous or evergreen, summer-flowering shrubs, grown for their aromatic foliage and sprays of tiny flowers. Frost to half hardy; in cold areas plant against a south- or west-facing wall or raise afresh each year. Needs full sun and well-drained soil. Cut out any dead wood in early

A

summer. Propagate by softwood cuttings in summer.
♀ ***A. triphylla***, syn. *Lippia citriodora*, (Lemon vebena) illus. p.132.

ALPINIA

ZINGIBERACEAE

Genus of mainly evergreen perennials with fleshy rhizomes, grown for their flowers. Frost tender, min. 18°C (64°F). Needs well-drained soil with plenty of humus, partial shade and a moist atmosphere. Not easy to grow successfully in containers. Propagate by division in late spring or early summer. Red spider mite may be a problem.
A. calcarata (Indian ginger). Evergreen, upright, clump-forming perennial. **H** and **S** to 1m (3ft). Has stalkless, aromatic, lance-shaped leaves, to 30cm (1ft) long. At any time of year may bear horizontal spikes of whitish flowers, with 2.5cm (1in) long, yellow lips marked reddish-purple.
A. hainanensis (illus. p.477). Evergreen, clump-forming perennial. **H** and **S** 90–120cm (36–48in). Min. 18°C (64°F). Has short stalked, lance-shaped, slightly hairy, mid-green leaves, to 40cm (16in) long. In spring-summer, honey-scented, white flowers, with red-lined lips 4.5cm (1¾in) long, are borne on old stems.
A. nutans of gardens. See *A. zerumbet*.
A. purpurata (Cone ginger; illus. p.477). Vigorous, evergreen, upright perennial. **H** to 3m (10ft), **S** 1m (3ft). Min. 18°C (64°F). In summer produces cone-like spires, 35cm (14in) long, of many small, white flowers, to 2.5cm (1in) long, in the axils of persistent, red or pink bracts. Has stalked, oblong, hairless, mid-green leaves, to 90cm (36in) long. Is good for cut flowers.
A. speciosa. See *A. zerumbet*.
A. zerumbet, syn. *A. nutans* of gardens, *A. speciosa* (Shell flower, Shell ginger; illus. p.477). Evergreen, clump-forming perennial. **H** 3m (10ft), **S** 1m (3ft). Has racemes of white flowers, with yellow lips and pink- or red-marked throats, mainly in summer.

Alsobia dianthiflora. See *Episcia dianthiflora*.
Alsophila. See *Cyathea*.

ALSTROEMERIA

ALSTROEMERIACEAE

Genus of mostly summer- to autumn-flowering, tuberous perennials with showy, funnel-shaped, multicoloured flowers. Flowers are good for cutting as they last well. Produces erect stems with alternate or scattered, linear to lance-shaped, mid- to grey-green leaves, usually 7–12cm (3–5in) long, held on twisted leaf stalks. Frost hardy, but in very cold winters protect by covering dormant tubers with dry bracken or loose peat. Needs sun and well-drained soil. Propagate by seed or division in early spring. ⓘ Contact with foliage may aggravate skin allergies.
♀ ***A. 'Apollo'*** (illus. p.387). Mid-summer to autumn-flowering, tuberous perennial. **H** 1m (3ft), **S** 75cm (2½ft). Bears large, open, white flowers with brown markings and yellow throats.
A. aurantiaca. See *A. aurea*.
A. aurea, syn. *A. aurantiaca*. Summer-flowering, tuberous perennial. **H** to 1m (3ft), **S** 60cm–1m (2–3ft). Produces orange flowers, tipped with green and streaked dark red. **'Orange King'** (illus. p.387) has bright orange flowers, with brown-speckled throats, from mid-summer to autumn.
A. 'Blushing Bride' (illus. p.387). Mid-summer to autumn-flowering, tuberous perennial. **H** and **S** 60cm (2ft). Produces cream flowers with brown-speckled, pink and pale yellow throats.
A. 'Charm'. Mid-summer-flowering, tuberous perennial. **H** 75cm (2½ft), **S** 60cm (2ft). Produces pale peach flowers with brown speckles and primrose-yellow throats.
A. 'Elvira' (illus. p.387). Mid-summer to autumn-flowering, tuberous perennial. **H** 75cm (2½ft), **S** 60cm (2ft). Produces cream flowers with bold, pink flecks on outer edges of petals and at the throats.
♀ ***A. 'Friendship'*** (illus. p.387). Mid-summer to autumn-flowering, tuberous perennial. **H** 1m (3ft), **S** 75cm (2½ft). Produces pale lime-yellow flowers with brown-red speckled, yellow throats.
A. hookeri illus. p.361.
A.* INCA ICE *('Koice') illus. p.387. Late spring to autumn-flowering, tuberous perennial. **H** and **S** to 1m (3ft). Produces cream and pale yellow flowers with pink throats and purple-brown speckling on the upper and lower petals.
A.* INCA TROPIC *('Kotrop') illus. p.387. Mid-summer to autumn-flowering, tuberous perennial. **H** and **S** 45cm (18in). Produces orange flowers with yellow throats flecked with brown markings. Young leaves are brown tinged.
A. 'Koice'. See *A.* INCA ICE.
A. 'Kotrop'. See *A.* INCA TROPIC.
A. Ligtu Hybrids illus. p.413.
A. 'Little Miss Tara'. Mid-summer to autumn-flowering, tuberous perennial. **H** and **S** 15cm (6in). Produces relatively large reddish-pink flowers with brown markings and yellow throats.
***A.* MARGARET *('Stacova')*.** Mid- to late summer-flowering tuberous perennial. **H** 1m (3ft), **S** 60cm–1m (2–3ft). Produces widely flared, funnel-shaped, deep red flowers.
A. 'Moulin Rouge' (illus. p.387). Mid-summer to autumn-flowering, tuberous perennial. **H** and **S** 45cm (18in). Produces soft red flowers with dark brown-speckled, yellow throats.
A. 'Parigo Charm'. Summer-flowering, tuberous perennial. **H** 1m (3ft), **S** 60cm (24in). Produces salmon-pink flowers with primrose-yellow inner tepals, marked carmine-red.
A. pelegrina. Summer-flowering, tuberous perennial. **H** 30–60cm (1–2ft), **S** 60cm–1m (2–3ft). Each leafy stem has 1–3 white flowers, stained pinkish-mauve and spotted yellow and brownish-purple.
A. 'Polka' (illus. p.387). Mid-summer to autumn-flowering, tuberous perennial. **H** 75cm (2½ft), **S** 60cm (2ft). Produces bright magenta-blushed, pale pink flowers with dark brown-speckled, yellow throats.
A.* PRINCESS ARIANE *('Zapriari') illus. p.387. Mid-summer to autumn-flowering, tuberous perennial. **H** 20cm (8in), **S** 15cm (6in). Produces yellow-flowers with purple-marked petal tips and dark brown speckled throats.
A.* PRINCESS JULIETA *('Zaprijul') illus. p.387. Mid-summer to autumn-flowering, tuberous perennial. **H** and **S** 30cm (12in). Produces pale purple flowers with darker purple markings and white throats.
***A.* PRINCESS PAOLA *('Stapripal')*.** Mid-summer to autumn-flowering, tuberous perennial. **H** 25cm (10in), **S** 20cm (8in). Produces pale pink flowers with dark pink markings and dark brown-speckled, yellow throats.
A. psittacina, syn. *A. pulchella* (illus. p.387). Summer-flowering, tuberous perennial. **H** 1m (3ft), **S** 45cm (1½ft). Mauve-spotted stems bear open umbels of red-marked, green flowers.
A. 'Red Beauty' (illus. p.387). Mid-summer to autumn-flowering, tuberous perennial. **H** 1m (3ft), **S** 75cm (2½ft). Produces bright scarlet flowers with dark brownish-black-speckled, yellow throats.
A. 'Serenade' (illus. p.387). Mid-summer to autumn-flowering, tuberous perennial. **H** 75cm (2½ft), **S** 60cm (2ft). Produces pale pink flowers with deep magenta markings and black-speckled, yellow throats.
A. 'Stacova'. See *A.* MARGARET.
A. 'Tara' (illus. p.387). Late spring to autumn-flowering, tuberous perennial. **H** 10–30cm (4–12in), **S** 30cm (12in). Produces dark brownish-black-speckled, red flowers with yellow throats.
A. 'Walter Fleming'. Summer-flowering, tuberous perennial. **H** to 1m (3ft), **S** 60cm–1m (2–3ft). Each leafy stem produces narrowly lance-shaped, twisted leaves and widely funnel-shaped, deep yellow flowers, 5–6cm (2–2½in) across, flushed purple with reddish-purple spots.
A. 'Zapriari'. See *A.* PRINCESS ARIANE.
A. 'Zaprijul'. See *A.* PRINCESS JULIETA.
A. 'Stapripal'. See *A.* PRINCESS PAOLA.

ALTERNANTHERA

AMARANTHACEAE

Genus of bushy perennials, grown for their attractive, coloured foliage. Is useful for carpeting or bedding. Frost tender, min. 15–18°C (59–64°F). Needs sun or partial shade and moist but well-drained soil. Propagate by tip cuttings or division in spring.
A. amoena. See *A. ficoidea* var. *amoena*.
***A. dentata* 'Purple Knight'** (Joseph's coat) illus. p.311.
A. ficoidea (Parrot leaf). **var. *amoena*** (syn. *A. amoena*) is a mat-forming perennial. **H** 5cm (2in), **S** indefinite. Has narrowly oval, green leaves, marked red, yellow and orange, with wavy margins. **'Versicolor'** (syn. *A. versicolor*) is an erect form, **H** and **S** to 30cm (12in), with rounded to spoon-shaped leaves shaded brown, red and yellow.
A. versicolor. See *A. ficoidea* 'Versicolor'.

Althaea rosea. See *Alcea rosea*.
Alum root. See *Heuchera*.

ALYSSOIDES

CRUCIFERAE/BRASSICACEAE

Genus of one species of short-lived, evergreen sub-shrub, grown for its flowers and swollen fruits. It is particularly suitable for dry banks and rock gardens. Frost hardy. Needs sun and well-drained soil. Propagate by seed sown in autumn.
A. utriculata. Evergreen, rounded sub-shrub. **H** and **S** 30cm (12in). Has oval, glossy, dark green leaves. Loose sprays of small, bright yellow flowers, which are produced in spring, are followed later by balloon-like, buff seed pods.

ALYSSUM

CRUCIFERAE/BRASSICACEAE

Genus of perennials, some of which are evergreen, and annuals, grown for their flowers. Fully hardy. Requires a sunny site and well-drained soil. Cut back lightly after flowering. Propagate either by softwood cuttings taken in late spring or by seed sown in autumn.
A. maritimum. See *Lobularia maritima*.
A. montanum. Evergreen, prostrate perennial. **H** and **S** 15cm (6in). Leaves are small, oval, hairy and grey. Flower stems, 15cm (6in) long, each bear an open, spherical raceme carrying small, highly fragrant, soft yellow flowers in summer. Is a good plant for a rock garden.
A. saxatile. See *Aurinia saxatilis*.
A. spinosum, syn. *Ptilotrichum spinosum*. Semi-evergreen, rounded, compact shrub. **H** 20cm (8in) or more, **S** 30cm (12in). Intricate branches bear spines and narrowly oval to linear, silver leaves. Spherical heads of tiny, 4-petalled, white to purple-pink flowers appear in early summer.
A. wulfenianum. Prostrate perennial. **H** 2cm (¾in), **S** 20cm (8in). Loose heads of small, bright yellow flowers appear in summer above small, oval, grey leaves.

AMARANTHUS

AMARANTHACEAE

Genus of annuals, grown for their dense panicles of tiny flowers or their colourful foliage. Half hardy. Grow in a sunny position in rich or fertile, well-drained soil. Propagate from seed sown outdoors in late spring. Aphids may be a problem.
A. caudatus (Love-lies-bleeding, Tassel flower) illus. p.307.
A. hypochondriacus (Prince's feather) illus. p.308.
***A. tricolor* 'Joseph's Coat'.** Bushy annual. **H** to 1m (3ft), **S** 45cm (1½ft) or more. Has oval, scarlet, green and yellow leaves, to 20cm (8in) long, and produces small panicles of tiny, red flowers in summer. Leaves of **'Molten Fire'** are crimson, bronze and purple.

x AMARCRINUM

AMARYLLIDACEAE

Hybrid genus (*Amaryllis* x *Crinum*) of one robust, evergreen bulb, grown for its large, funnel-shaped flowers. Frost hardy. Needs a sunny position and well-drained soil. Plant with neck just covered by soil. Propagate by division in spring.
x *A. memoria-corsii*, syn. x *Crinodonna corsii*. Evergreen, clump-forming bulb. **H** and **S** to 1m (3ft). Has wide, semi-erect, basal leaves. Stout stems bear fragrant, rose-pink flowers in loose heads in late summer and autumn.

A

x AMARYGIA

AMARYLLIDACEAE

Hybrid genus (*Amaryllis* x *Brunsvigia*) of stout, autumn-flowering bulbs, which are cultivated for their large, showy flowers. Frost hardy. Needs full sun and, preferably, the shelter of a wall. Plant bulbs just beneath the surface of well-drained soil. Propagate by division in spring.
x *A. parkeri*, syn. x *Brunsdonna parkeri*. Early autumn-flowering bulb. **H** to 1m (3ft), **S** 60–100cm (2–3ft). Stout stem bears a large head of funnel-shaped, deep rose flowers with yellow and white throats. Produces strap-shaped, semi-erect, basal leaves after flowering.

AMARYLLIS

AMARYLLIDACEAE

Genus of autumn-flowering bulbs, grown for their funnel-shaped flowers. Frost hardy, but in cool areas should be grown against a south-facing wall for protection. Requires well-drained soil and a sheltered, sunny situation. Plant bulbs in at least 8cm (3in) of soil. Propagate by division in late spring as leaves die down, or in late summer, before growth recommences.
♀***A. belladonna*** (Belladonna lily) and **'Hathor'** illus. p.395.

AMBERBOA

Sweet sultan

COMPOSITAE/ASTERACEAE

Genus of erect annuals or biennials, grown for their cornflower-like flower heads, which are borne from spring to autumn. Fully hardy. Needs full sun and moderately fertile, well-drained soil. Dead-head to prolong flowering. Propagate by seed in spring or autumn.
A. moschata, syn. *Centaurea moschata* (Sweet sultan). Fast-growing, upright, slender-stemmed annual. **H** 45cm (18in), **S** 20cm (8in). Has lance-shaped, greyish-green leaves and large, fragrant flower heads, in a range of colours, in summer and early autumn.

AMELANCHIER

Juneberry, Serviceberry, Shadbush

ROSACEAE

Genus of deciduous, spring-flowering trees and shrubs, grown primarily for their profuse flowers and their foliage, which is frequently brightly coloured in autumn. Fully hardy. Requires sun or semi-shade and well-drained but not too dry, preferably neutral to acid soil. Propagate in autumn by seed, in late autumn to early spring by layering or, in the case of suckering species, by division. Fireblight may sometimes be troublesome.
A. alnifolia. Deciduous, upright, suckering shrub. **H** 4m (12ft) or more, **S** 3m (10ft) or more. Leaves are oval to rounded and dark green. Erect spikes of star-shaped, creamy-white flowers are borne in late spring, followed by small, edible, juicy, rounded, purple-black fruits.
A. arborea. Deciduous, spreading, sometimes shrubby, tree. **H** 10m (30ft), **S** 12m (40ft). Clusters of star-shaped, white flowers appear in mid-spring as oval, white-haired, young leaves unfold. Foliage matures to dark green, turning to red or yellow in autumn. Rounded fruits are small, dry and reddish-purple.
A. asiatica. Deciduous, spreading tree or shrub of elegant habit. **H** 8m (25ft), **S** 10m (30ft). Leaves are oval and dark green, usually woolly when young and turning yellow or red in autumn. Star-shaped, white flowers are borne profusely in late spring, followed by edible, juicy, rounded, blackcurrant-like fruits.
A. canadensis. Deciduous, upright, dense shrub. **H** 6m (20ft), **S** 3m (10ft). Star-shaped, white flowers are borne from mid- to late spring amid unfolding, oval, white-haired leaves that mature to dark green and turn orange-red in autumn. Fruits are edible, rounded, blackish-purple, sweet and juicy.
A. laevis illus. p.81.
♀***A. lamarckii*** illus. p.110.

Amomyrtus luma. See *Luma apiculata*.
***Amomyrtus luma* 'Glanleam Gold'.** See *Luma apiculata* 'Glanleam Gold'.

AMORPHA

LEGUMINOSAE/PAPILIONACEAE

Genus of deciduous shrubs and sub-shrubs, grown for their flowers and foliage. Is a useful plant for cold, dry, exposed positions. Fully hardy. Requires full sun and well-drained soil. May be propagated by softwood cuttings taken in summer or by seed sown in autumn.
A. canescens (Lead plant). Deciduous, open sub-shrub. **H** 1m (3ft), **S** 1.5m (5ft). Dense spikes of tiny, pea-like, purple flowers, with orange anthers, are produced in late summer and early autumn, amid oval, grey-haired leaves divided into 21–41 narrowly oval leaflets.

AMORPHOPHALLUS

ARACEAE

Genus of tuberous perennials, cultivated for their huge and dramatic, but foul-smelling, spathes, which surround tiny flowers on stout spadices. Frost tender, min. 10°C (50°F). Requires partial shade and humus-rich soil kept continuously moist during the growing season. Keep tubers dry in winter. Propagate by seed sown in spring or by offsets in spring or summer.
A. konjac, syn. *A. rivieri*. Summer-flowering, tuberous perennial. **H** to 40cm (16in), **S** 60cm–1m (2–3ft). Produces a flattish, wavy-edged, dark reddish-brown spathe, to 40cm (16in) long, from which protrudes an erect, dark brown spadix. Brownish-green-mottled, pale green stem, 1m (3ft) long, bears one large, deeply lobed leaf after flowering.
A. rivieri. See *A. konjac*.

AMPELODESMOS

POACEAE/GRAMINEAE

See also GRASSES, BAMBOOS, RUSHES AND SEDGES.
A. mauritanica illus. p.287.

AMPELOPSIS

VITACEAE

Genus of deciduous, woody-stemmed, tendril climbers, some of which are twining, grown for their leaves. Frost hardy. Grow in a sheltered position in sun or partial shade in any soil. Needs plenty of room as grows quickly and can cover a large area. Propagate by greenwood or semi-ripe cuttings in mid-summer.
A. aconitifolia, syn. *Vitis aconitifolia*. Fast-growing, deciduous, woody-stemmed, twining, tendril climber. **H** to 12m (40ft). Rounded leaves have 3 or 5 toothed, lobed, dark green leaflets. Inconspicuous, greenish flowers, in late summer, are followed by orange berries.
A. brevipedunculata* var. *maximowiczii, syn. *A. glandulosa* var. *brevipedunculata*, *A. heterophylla*, *Vitis heterophylla*, illus. p.210. **'Elegans'** (syn. *A. brevipedunculata* 'Tricolor', *A.b.* 'Variegata') illus. p.195.
***A. glandulosa* var. *brevipedunculata*.** See *A. brevipedunculata* var. *maximowiczii*.
A. heterophylla. See *A. brevipedunculata* var. *maximowiczii*.
A. megalophylla illus. p.210.
A. sempervirens. See *Cissus striata*.
A. veitchii. See *Parthenocissus tricuspidata* 'Veitchii'.

AMSONIA

Blue star

APOCYNACEAE

Genus of slow-growing, clump-forming, summer-flowering perennials. Fully hardy. Grow in full sun and in well-drained soil. Is best left undisturbed for some years. May be propagated by division in spring, by softwood cuttings in summer or by seed in autumn. ⓘContact with the milky sap may irritate skin.
A. orientalis, syn. *Rhazya orientalis*, illus. p.271.
A. tabernaemontana Clump-forming perennial. **H** 45–60cm (18–24in), **S** 30cm (12in). Leaves are small and narrow. Willowy stems bear drooping clusters of small, tubular, pale blue flowers in summer.

ANACAMPTIS

ORCHIDACEAE

See also ORCHIDS.
A. morio, syn. *Orchis morio* (Gandergoose, Green-veined orchid; illus. p.466). Deciduous, terrestrial orchid. **H** 40cm (16in). Half hardy. Reddish-purple, mauve or rarely white flowers, 1cm (½in) long, with green veins on the cupped sepals, open along stems in spring. Has a basal cluster of lance-shaped or broadly oblong, pale to mid-green leaves, 10–16cm (4–6in) long. Requires sun or semi-shade.

Anacharis densa. See *Egeria densa*.

ANACYCLUS

COMPOSITAE/ASTERACEAE

Genus of summer-flowering, prostrate perennials with stems radiating from a central rootstock. Frost hardy. Needs full sun and well-drained soil. Propagate by softwood cuttings in spring or by seed in autumn.
A. depressus. See *A. pyrethrum* var. *depressus*.
A. pyrethrum* var. *depressus, syn. *A. depressus*, illus. p.[illegible]

ANAGALLIS

PRIMULACEAE

Genus of annuals and creeping perennials, grown for their flowers. Fully to frost hardy. Plant in an open, sunny site in fertile, moist soil. Propagate by seed or division in spring. Raise *A. tenella* by soft-tip cuttings in spring or early summer.
A. tenella (Bog pimpernel). **'Studland'** illus. p.353.

ANANAS

BROMELIACEAE

Genus of evergreen, rosette-forming perennials, grown for their foliage and edible fruits (pineapples). Frost tender, min. 13–15°C (55–9°F). Prefers full light, but tolerates some shade. Needs fertile, well-drained soil. Water moderately during growing season, sparingly at other times. Propagate by suckers or cuttings of 'leafy' fruit tops in spring or summer.
A. bracteatus (Red pineapple, Wild pineapple). ♀**var. *tricolor*** (syn. *A.b.* 'Striatus', *A.b.* 'Tricolor', illus. p.471) is an evergreen, basal-rosetted perennial. **H** and **S** 1m (3ft). Forms dense rosettes of strap-shaped, spiny-edged, arching, deep green leaves, longitudinally yellow-striped and often with marginal, red spines. Dense spikes of small, tubular, lavender-violet flowers, with prominent, reddish-pink bracts, appear usually in summer. These are followed by brownish-orange-red fruits that are 15cm (6in) or more long.
***A. comosus* 'Variegatus'.** Evergreen, basal-rosetted perennial. **H** and **S** 60cm (24in) or more. Produces very narrowly strap-shaped, channelled, rigid, grey-green leaves that are suffused pink, have cream margins, are grey-scaled beneath and sometimes have spiny edges. Produces tubular, purple-blue flowers with inconspicuous, green bracts; fruits are the edible pineapples grown commercially, but are much smaller on pot-grown plants.

ANAPHALIS

Pearl everlasting

ASTERACEAE/COMPOSITAE

Genus of perennials with heads of small, papery flowers, used dried for winter decoration. Fully hardy. Prefers sun but will grow in semi-shade. Soil should be well-drained but not too dry. Propagate by seed in autumn or by division in winter or spring.
A. margaritacea (Pearl everlasting) illus. p.231.
A. nepalensis* var. *monocephala, syn. *A. nubigena*. Dwarf, leafy perennial. **H** 20–30cm (8–12in), **S** 15cm (6in). Woolly, silvery stems bear lance-shaped leaves. Bears dense, terminal clusters of white flower heads in late summer.
A. nubigena. See *A. nepalensis* var. *monocephala*.

A

♀ ***A. triplinervis.*** Variable, clump-forming perennial. **H** 80–90cm (32–36in), **S** 45–60cm (18–24in). Has obovate to elliptic, white-woolly leaves, prominently 3-veined. In mid- to late summer produces clusters of white-bracted, yellow-centred flower heads. ♀ **'Sommerschnee'** (syn. *A.t.* Summer Snow) illus. p.231.

ANAPHALIOIDES

Pearl everlasting

ASTERACEAE/COMPOSITAE

Genus of summer flowering perennials and drawf shrubs grown for silver foliage and "everlasting" flower heads. Hardy to -10°C (14°F). Requires full sun and very well drained soil. Propagate by heel or semi-ripe cuttings in summer.

A. bellidioides, syn. *Helichrysum bellidioides*. Evergreen, prostrate shrub. **H** 5cm (2in), **S** 23cm (9in). Fully hardy. Has small, rounded, fleshy, dark green leaves and, in early summer, terminal clusters of daisy-like, white flower heads.

ANCHUSA

BORAGINACEAE

Genus of annuals, biennials and perennials, some of which are evergreen, usually with blue flowers. Fully to frost hardy. Needs sun and well-drained soil; resents too much winter wet. Tall perennial species may need to be staked and allowed room to spread. Propagate perennials by root cuttings in winter, annuals and biennials by seed in autumn or spring.

A. azurea, syn. *A. italica*.**'Little John'** is a clump-forming perennial. **H** 50cm (20in), **S** 60cm (24in). Fully hardy. Mainly basal leaves are narrowly oval and hairy. Bears branching racemes of large, open cup-shaped, dark blue flowers in early summer. ♀ **'Loddon Royalist'** illus. p.241. **'Opal'**, **H** 1.2m (4ft), has paler blue flowers.

A. caespitosa. See *A. cespitosa*.

***A. capensis* 'Blue Angel'** illus. p.315. **'Blue Bird'** is a bushy biennial, grown as an annual. **H** to 45cm (18in), **S** 20cm (8in). Frost hardy. Has lance-shaped, bristly, mid-green leaves and, in summer, heads of shallowly bowl-shaped, sky-blue flowers.

A. cespitosa, syn. *A. caespitosa*, illus. p.356.

A. italica. See *A. azurea*.

Ancistrocactus megarhizus. See *Sclerocactus scheeri*.

Ancistrocactus scheeri. See *Sclerocactus scheeri*.

Ancistrocactus uncinatus. See *Sclerocactus uncinatus*.

ANDROMEDA

ERICACEAE

Genus of evergreen shrubs with an open, twiggy habit. Fully hardy. Needs full light and humus-rich, moist, acid soil. Propagate by semi-ripe cuttings taken in late summer or by seed sown in spring.

A. polifolia. Evergreen, open, twiggy shrub. **H** 30–45cm (12–18in), **S** 60cm (24in). Has narrow, leathery, glossy, mid-green leaves. Bears terminal clusters of pitcher-shaped, pink flowers in spring and early summer. **'Alba'** illus. p.332. ♀ **'Compacta'** illus. p.333.

ANDROSACE

PRIMULACEAE

Genus of annuals and evergreen perennials, usually compact cushion-forming and often with soft, hairy leaves. Many species are suitable for cold greenhouses and troughs with winter cover. Fully to frost hardy. Needs sun and very well-drained soil; some species prefer acid soil. Resents wet foliage in winter. Propagate by tip cuttings in summer or by seed in autumn. Is prone to botrytis and attack by aphids.

A. carnea illus. p.350. ♀ **subsp. *laggeri*** illus. p.353.

A. chamaejasme. Evergreen, basal-rosetted, variable perennial with easily rooted stolons. **H** 3–6cm (1¼–2½in), **S** to 15cm (6in). Fully hardy. Has open, hairy rosettes of oval leaves. In spring bears clusters of 2–8 flattish, white flowers, each with a yellow eye that sometimes turns red with age.

A. cylindrica. Evergreen, basal-rosetted perennial. **H** 1–2cm (½–¾in), **S** 10cm (4in). Fully hardy. Leaves are linear and glossy. Flower stems each carry up to 10 small, flattish, white flowers, each with a yellow-green eye, in early spring. Is suitable for a cold greenhouse.

A. hedraeantha. Evergreen, tight cushion-forming perennial. **H** 1–2cm (½–¾in), **S** to 10cm (4in). Fully hardy. Bears loose rosettes of narrowly oval, glossy leaves. Umbels of 5–10 flattish, yellow-throated, pink flowers are produced in spring. Is best in a cold greenhouse.

A. hirtella. Evergreen, tight cushion-forming perennial. **H** 1cm (½in), **S** to 10cm (4in). Fully hardy. Produces rosettes of small, thick, linear to oblong, hairy leaves. Almond-scented, flattish, white flowers are borne in spring on very short stems, 1 or 2 per rosette.

A. imbricata. See *A. vandellii*.

♀ ***A. lanuginosa*** illus. p.363.

A. pyrenaica illus. p.350.

A. sarmentosa. Evergreen, mat-forming perennial, spreading by runners. **H** 4–10cm (1½–4in), **S** 30cm (12in). Fully hardy. Has open rosettes of small, narrowly elliptic, hairy leaves. Large clusters of flattish, yellow-eyed, bright pink flowers open in spring. Is a good rock plant in all but extremely wet areas.

♀ ***A. sempervivoides.*** Evergreen, mat-forming, rosetted perennial with stolons. **H** 1–7cm (½–3in), **S** 30cm (12in). Fully hardy. Has leathery, oblong or spoon-shaped leaves. In spring produces small heads of 4–10 flattish, pink flowers, with yellow, then red, eyes. Is a good rock plant.

A. vandellii, syn. *A. imbricata*, illus. p.347.

A. villosa illus. p.349. **var. *jacquemontii*** illus. p.366.

Anemanthele lessoniana. See *Stipa lessoniana*.

ANEMONE

Windflower

RANUNCULACEAE

Genus of spring-, summer- and autumn-flowering perennials, sometimes tuberous or rhizomatous, with mainly rounded, shallowly cup-shaped flowers. Leaves are rounded to oval, often divided into 3–15 leaflets. Fully to frost hardy. Most thrive in full light or semi-shade in humus-rich, well-drained soil. Propagate by division in spring, by seed sown in late summer, when fresh, or by root cuttings in winter. ⚠Contact with the sap may irritate skin.

♀ ***A. apennina*** (Apennine anemone). Spreading, spring-flowering, rhizomatous perennial. **H** and **S** 15–20cm (6–8in). Fully hardy. Fern-like leaves have 3 deeply toothed lobes. Each stem carries a large, upright, flattish, blue, white or pink flower, with 10–20 narrow petals.

♀ ***A. blanda.*** Spreading, early spring-flowering perennial with a knobbly tuber. **H** 5–10cm (2–4in), **S** 10–15cm (4–6in). Fully hardy. Leaves are broadly oval and semi-erect, with 3 deeply toothed lobes. Each stem bears an upright, flattish, blue, white or pink flower, 4–5cm (1½–2in) across, with 9–14 narrow petals. **'Atrocaerulea'** illus. p.419. **'Ingramii'** bears purple-backed, deep blue flowers. ♀ **var. *rosea* 'Radar'**, syn. *A.b.* 'Radar', illus. p.418. **'Violet Star'** illus. p.418. ♀ **'White Splendour'** illus. p.414.

A. coronaria. Spring-flowering perennial with a misshapen tuber. **H** 5–25cm (2–10in), **S** 10–15cm (4–6in). Frost hardy. Produces parsley-like, divided, semi-erect leaves. Each stiff stem carries a large, 5–8-petalled, shallowly cup-shaped flower in shades of red, pink, blue or purple. Garden groups include **De Caen Group** and **Saint Bridgid Group**, which have larger flowers varying in colour from white through red to blue. **'Mister Fokker'** illus. p.403.

A. x fulgens illus. p.418.

A. hepatica. See *Hepatica nobilis*.

A. hupehensis. Erect perennial with a creeping, woody-based rootstock. **H** 100cm (36in), **S** 100cm (36in) or more. Fully hardy. Large, rounded, dark green leaves have 3 toothed lobes. In late summer, flower stems bear smaller leaves and 5-petalled, slightly cupped, pale pink or white flowers, 5–6cm (2–2½in) across, with yellow stamens. ♀ **'Bowles's Pink'** (illus. p.222) bears rich purple-pink flowers. ♀ **'Hadspen Abundance'** illus. p.247. **var. *japonica* 'Bressingham Glow'** (syn. *A.* x *hybrida* 'Bressingham Glow'; illus. p.222), **H** 1.2–1.5m (4–5ft), **S** 60cm (2ft), has semi-double, rose-purple flowers on wiry stems. ♀ **var. *japonica* 'Pamina'** (illus. p.222), **H** 80cm (32in), bears masses of rather small, semi-double, reddish-purple flowers. ♀ **var. *japonica* 'Prinz Heinrich'** (syn. *A.* x *hybrida* 'Prince Henry') has single, deep pink flowers on slender stems. **'Praecox'** (illus. p.222), **H** 80cm (32in), bears single, pink flowers in mid-summer. **'September Charm'** see *A.* x *hybrida* 'September Charm'.

A. x hybrida, syn. *A. japonica* of gardens (Japanese anemone). Group of vigorous, branching, perennials. **H** 1.5m (5ft), **S** 60cm (2ft). Fully hardy. Bears shallowly cup-shaped, single, semi-double or double flowers in late summer and early autumn. Leaves are deeply divided and dark green. **'Bressingham Glow'** see *A. hupehensis* var. *japonica* 'Bressingham Glow'. ♀ **'Elegans'** (syn. *A.* x *h.* 'Max Vogel') has semi-double, pinkish-mauve flowers on wiry stems. ♀ **'Honorine Jobert'** (single) illus. p.220. ♀ **'Königin Charlotte'** (illus. p.222), **H** 1.2m (4ft), has large, semi-double, bright pink flowers. **'Lady Gilmour'**, **H** 1m (3ft), produces crested leaves and pink flowers with often uneven, twisted petals. **'Max Vogel'** see *A.* x *h.* 'Elegans'. **'Montrosa'**, **H** 1.2m (4ft), has large, double, soft reddish-pink flowers with rather twisted petals. **'Prince Henry'** see *A. hupehensis* var. *japonica* 'Prinz Heinrich'. **'Richard Ahrens'**, **H** 1.2m (4ft), bears large, single, soft pink flowers in mid-summer. **'Robustissima'** (illus. p.222), **H** 1.2m (4ft), has single, dark pink flowers borne on reddish stems. ♀ **'September Charm'** (syn. *A. hupehensis* 'September Charm'; illus. p.222), H 75cm (30in), **S** 50cm (20in), has single, clear pink flowers on wiry stems. **'Whirlwind'** (syn. *A.* x *h.* Wirbelwind; illus. p.222), **H** 80–100cm (32–39in), bears irregularly formed double, white flowers, with some petals green flushed. **Wirbelwind** see *A.* x *h.* 'Whirlwind'.

A. x intermedia. See *A.* x *lipsiensis*.

A. japonica of gardens. See *A.* x *hybrida*.

A. x lipsiensis, syn. *A.* x *intermedia*, *A.* x *seemannii*, illus. p.262.

A. narcissiflora illus. p.255.

♀ ***A. nemorosa*** (Wood anemone). Vigorous, carpeting, rhizomatous perennial. **H** 15cm (6in), **S** 30cm (12in). Fully hardy. Produces masses of star-shaped, single, white flowers, with prominent, yellow stamens, in spring and early summer, above deeply cut, mid-green leaves. Likes woodland conditions. ♀ **'Allenii'** produces many large, cup-shaped, single, rich lavender-blue flowers in spring. ♀ **'Robinsoniana'** has lavender-blue flowers, pale creamy-grey beneath, on maroon stems. ♀ **'Vestal'** has anemone-centred, double, white flowers. **'Wilks' Giant'** (syn. *A.n.* 'Wilk's Giant') has larger, single, white flowers.

A. pavonina illus. p.402.

♀ ***A. ranunculoides*** illus. p.263. **'Pleniflora'** (syn. *A.r.* 'Flore Pleno') is a spreading, rhizomatous perennial. **H** and **S** 20cm (8in). Fully hardy. Bears buttercup-like, double, yellow flowers in spring. Leaves are divided. Likes damp, woodland conditions.

A. rivularis illus. p.437.

A. x seemannii. See *A.* x *lipsiensis*.

A. sylvestris (Snowdrop windflower) illus. p.255. **'Macrantha'** is a clump-forming perennial that can be invasive. **H** and **S** 30cm (12in). Fully hardy. Large, fragrant, semi-pendent, shallowly cup-shaped, white flowers are produced in spring and early summer. Leaves are divided and mid-green.

A. tomentosa, syn. *A. vitifolia* of gardens. Vigorous, clump-forming perennial with a creeping rootstock. **H** 1.2m (4ft), **S** 1.5m (5ft) or more. Fully hardy. Large, 3–7 lobed mid-green leaves with toothed margins have white-hairy undersides. In summer, flower stems bear 5-petalled, slightly cupped, pale pink flowers, 5–6cm (2–2½in) across, with yellow stamens.

A. trullifolia illus. p.350.

A. tschaernjaewii illus. p.416.

A. vitifolia. Branching, clump-forming perennial. **H** 1.2m (4ft), **S** 50cm (20in). Fully

hardy. In summer bears open cup-shaped, occasionally pink-flushed, white flowers with yellow stamens. Vine-like leaves are woolly beneath.
A. vitifolia of gardens. See *A. tomentosa.*

ANEMONELLA

RANUNCULACEAE

Genus of one species of tuberous perennial, grown for its flowers. Fully hardy. Needs shade and humus-rich, moist soil. Propagate by seed when fresh or by division every 3–5 years in autumn.
A. thalictroides illus. p.350. **'Oscar Schoaf'** (syn. *A.t.* 'Schoaf's Double') is a slow-growing, tuberous perennial. **H** 10cm (4in), **S** 4cm (1½in) or more. Has delicate, fern-like leaves. From spring to early summer bears small, cup-shaped, double, strawberry-pink flowers, singly on finely branched, slender stems.

ANEMONOPSIS

False anemone

RANUNCULACEAE

Genus of one species of perennial, related to Anemone. Fully hardy. Likes a sheltered, semi-shaded position and humus-rich, moist but well-drained soil. Propagate by division in spring or by seed sown in late summer, when fresh.
A. macrophylla (False anemone) illus. p.270.

ANEMOPAEGMA

BIGNONIACEAE

Genus of evergreen, tendril climbers, grown for their flowers. Frost tender, min. 13–15°C (55–9°F). Needs partial shade in summer and humus-rich, well-drained soil. Water regularly and freely when in full growth, less at other times. Provide support and in summer thin out stems at intervals; shorten all growths by half in spring. Propagate by softwood or semi-ripe cuttings in spring or summer.
A. chamberlaynei. Fast-growing, evergreen, tendril climber. **H** to 6m (20ft). Leaves have 2 pointed, oval leaflets and a 3-hooked tendril. Foxglove-like, primrose-yellow flowers are carried in pairs from upper leaf axils in summer.

ANGELICA

UMBELLIFERAE/APIACEAE

Genus of summer-flowering, often short-lived perennials, some of which have culinary and medicinal uses. Fully hardy. Grows in sun or shade and in any well-drained soil. Remove seed heads when produced, otherwise plants may die. Propagate by seed when ripe.
A. archangelica (Angelica) illus. p.219.

ANGELONIA

SCROPHULARIACEAE

Genus of evergreen sub-shrubs and soft-stemmed perennials, grown for summer display in containers and borders. Half hardy to frost tender, min. 10°C (50°F). Grow in moist but well-drained, fertile soil in sun. Propagate by seed or softwood cuttings or spring.
A. angustifolia **AngelMist Series 'AngelMist Lavender Stripe'** illus. p.311

ANGRAECUM

ORCHIDACEAE

See also ORCHIDS.
A. sesquipedale, illus. p.460.

ANGULOA

ORCHIDACEAE

See also ORCHIDS.
A. clowesii (Cradle orchid). Deciduous, epiphytic orchid for a cool greenhouse. **H** 60cm (24in). Fragrant, erect, cup-shaped, lemon-yellow flowers, 10cm (4in) long, each with a loosely hinged, yellow lip, are produced singly in early summer. Broadly oval, ribbed leaves are 45cm (18in) long. Grow in semi-shade in summer.

ANIGOZANTHOS

Kangaroo paw

HAEMODORACEAE

Genus of perennials, with thick rootstocks and fans of sword-shaped leaves, grown for their curious flowers. Half hardy. Needs an open, sunny position and does best in well-drained, peaty or leafy, acid soil. Propagate by division in spring or by seed when fresh, in late summer.
A. flavidus illus. p.476.
♀***A. manglesii*** illus. p.470.
A. rufus. Tufted perennial. **H** 1m (3ft), **S** 60cm (2ft). Panicles of 2-lipped, rich burgundy flowers, covered with purple hairs, appear in spring. Has long, sword-shaped, stiff, mid-green leaves.

ANISODONTEA

MALVACEAE

Genus of evergreen shrubs and perennials, grown for their flowers. Frost tender, min. 3–5°C (37–41°F). Needs full light and well-drained soil. Water containerized plants freely when in full growth, very little at other times. In growing season, young plants may need tip pruning to promote a bushy habit. Propagate by seed in spring or by greenwood or semi-ripe cuttings in late summer.
A. capensis, syn. *Malvastrum capensis.* Evergreen, erect, bushy shrub. **H** to 1m (3ft), **S** 60cm (2ft) or more. Each oval leaf has 3–5 deep lobes. Bowl-shaped, 5-petalled, rose-magenta flowers, with darker veins, appear from spring to autumn.

ANNONA

Cherimoya, Custard apple, Sweet sop

ANNONACEAE

Genus of deciduous or evergreen shrubs and trees, grown for their edible fruits and ornamental appearance. Frost tender, min. 15°C (59°F), preferably higher. Needs full light or partial shade and fertile, moisture-retentive but well-drained soil. Water specimens in containers moderately when in full growth, sparingly in winter. Propagate by seed in spring or by semi-ripe cuttings in late summer. Red spider mite may be a nuisance.
A. reticulata (Bullock's heart, Custard apple). Mainly deciduous, rounded tree. **H** 6m (20ft) or more, **S** 3–5m (10–15ft). Has oblong to lance-shaped, 13–25cm (5–10in) long leaves. Cup-shaped, olive-green flowers, often flushed purple, appear in summer, followed by edible, heart-shaped, red-flushed, greenish-brown fruits, each 13cm (5in) long.

Anoiganthus breviflorus. See *Cyrtanthus breviflorus.*
Anoiganthus luteus. See *Cyrtanthus breviflorus.*

ANOMATHECA

IRIDACEAE

Genus of upright, summer-flowering corms, grown for their trumpet- to funnel-shaped, red flowers, followed by egg-shaped seed pods that split to reveal red seeds. Frost hardy. Plant 5cm (2in) deep in an open, sunny situation and in well-drained soil. In cold areas, lift corms and store dry for winter. Propagate by seed in spring.
A. cruenta. See *A. laxa.*
♀***A. laxa,*** syn. *A. cruenta, Freesia laxa, Lapeirousia cruenta, L. laxa,* illus. p.423.

ANOPTERUS

ESCALLONIACEAE

Genus of evergreen shrubs or small trees, grown for their foliage and flowers. Half hardy. Needs shade or semi-shade and moist but well-drained, lime-free soil. Propagate by semi-ripe cuttings in summer.
A. glandulosus illus. p.110.

ANREDERA

Madeira vine, Mignonette vine

BASELLACEAE

Genus of evergreen, tuberous, twining climbers, grown for their luxuriant foliage and small, scented flowers. Frost tender, min. 7°C (45°F). If grown in cool areas will die down in winter. Requires a position in full light and well-drained soil. Water moderately in growing season, but sparingly at other times. Provide support. Cut back the previous season's growth by half or to just above ground level in spring. Propagate by tubers, produced at stem bases, in spring or by softwood cuttings in summer.
A. cordifolia, syn. *Boussingaultia baselloides* of gardens, illus. p.197.

ANTENNARIA

Cat's ears

COMPOSITAE/ASTERACEAE

Genus of evergreen or semi-evergreen perennials, grown for their almost stemless flower heads and mats of often woolly leaves. Makes good ground cover. Fully hardy. Needs sun and well-drained soil. Propagate by seed or division in spring.
A. dioica. Semi-evergreen, mat-forming, dense perennial. **H** 2.5cm (1in), **S** 25cm (10in). Leaves are tiny, oval, usually woolly and greenish-white. Short stems carry fluffy, white or pale pink flower heads in late spring and early summer. Is good when grown in a rock garden. Compact **'Nyewoods'** has very deep rose-pink flowers. **var. *rosea*** see *A. rosea.*
♀***A. rosea***, syn. *A. dioica* var. *rosea,* illus. p.[illegible]

ANTHEMIS

Dog's fennel

COMPOSITAE/ASTERACEAE

Genus of carpeting and clump-forming perennials, some of which are evergreen, grown for their daisy-like flower heads and fern-like foliage. Fully to frost hardy. Prefers a position in sun and well-drained soil. May need staking for support. Cut to ground level after flowering to produce good leaf rosettes in winter. Propagate by division in spring or, for some species, by basal cuttings in late summer, autumn or spring.
A. nobilis. See *Chamaemelum nobile.*
♀***A. punctata* subsp. *cupaniana*** illus. p.264.
A. sancti-johannis. Evergreen, spreading, bushy perennial. **H** and **S** 60cm (24in). Frost hardy. In summer bears many daisy-like, bright orange flower heads among fern-like, shaggy, mid-green leaves.
A. tinctoria. Evergreen, clump-forming perennial. **H** and **S** 1m (3ft). Fully hardy. Produces a mass of daisy-like, yellow flower heads in mid-summer, borne singly above a basal clump of fern-like, crinkled, mid-green leaves. Propagate by basal cuttings in spring or late summer.
'E.C. Buxton' illus. p.243.

ANTHERICUM

Spider plant

LILIACEAE/ANTHERICACEAE

Genus of upright perennials with saucer- or trumpet-shaped flowers rising in spike-like racemes from clumps of leaves. Fully hardy. Likes a sunny site and fertile, well-drained soil that does not dry out in summer. Propagate by division in spring or by seed in autumn.
A. graminifolium. See *A. ramosum.*
A. liliago (St Bernard's lily) illus. p.263.
A. ramosum, syn. *A. graminifolium.* Upright perennial. **H** 1m (3ft), **S** 30cm (1ft). Erect racemes of small, saucer-shaped, white flowers are borne in summer above a clump of grass-like, greyish-green leaves.

Antholyza paniculata. See *Crocosmia paniculata.*

ANTHURIUM

ARACEAE

Genus of evergreen, erect, climbing or trailing perennials, some grown for their foliage and others for their bright flower spathes. Frost tender, min. 15°C (59°F). Prefers bright light in winter and indirect sun in summer; needs a fairly moist atmosphere and moist, but not waterlogged, peaty soil. Propagate by division in spring. ⓘ All parts may cause mild stomach disorder if digested; contact with sap may irritate skin.

♀ **A. andraeanum** (Flamingo flower) illus. p.470.
♀ **A. crystallinum** (Crystal anthurium) illus. p.465.
♀ **A. scherzerianum** (Flamingo flower). Evergreen, erect, tufted perennial. **H** and **S** 30–60cm (12–24in). Has oblong, leathery, dark green leaves, to 20cm (8in) long. Produces large, long-lasting, bright red spathes and fleshy, orange to yellow spadices. **'Rothschildianum'**, **H** and **S** 30cm (12in), bears white-spotted, red spathes and yellow spadices.
A. veitchii (Queen anthurium). Evergreen, erect, short-stemmed perennial. **H** 1m (3ft) or more, **S** to 1m (3ft). Glossy, corrugated leaves, to 1m (3ft) long, are oval, with heart-shaped bases on 60cm–1m (2–3ft) long leaf stalks. Intermittently bears a long-lasting, leathery, green to white spathe that surrounds a cream spadix.

ANTHYLLIS

LEGUMINOSAE/PAPILIONACEAE

Genus of rounded, bushy perennials, grown for their flowers and finely divided leaves. Frost hardy. Needs sun and well-drained soil. Propagate by softwood cuttings in summer or by seed in autumn.
A. hermanniae. Rounded, bushy perennial. **H** and **S** to 60cm (24in). Spiny, tangled stems bear simple or 3-parted, bright green leaves. Has small, pea-like, yellow flowers in summer. Is good for a rock garden.
A. montana illus. p.338. ♀ **'Rubra'** is a rounded or spreading, woody-based perennial. **H** and **S** 30cm (12in). Divided leaves consist of 17–41 narrowly oval leaflets. Heads of clover-like, bright pink flowers are borne in late spring and early summer. Is good for a rock garden.

ANTIGONON

Coral vine

POLYGONACEAE

Genus of evergreen, woody-stemmed, tendril climbers, grown for their foliage and profuse clusters of small flowers. Frost tender, min. 15°C (59°F). Grow in full light and any fertile, well-drained soil. Water freely in growing season, sparingly at other times. Needs tropical conditions to flower well. Provide support. Thin out congested growth in early spring. Propagate by seed in spring or by softwood cuttings in summer.
A. leptopus. Fast-growing, evergreen, woody-stemmed, tendril climber. **H** 6m (20ft). Has crinkly, pale green leaves. Dense trusses of bright pink, sometimes red or white, flowers grow mainly in summer, but all year in tropical conditions.

ANTIRRHINUM

Snapdragon

SCROPHULARIACEAE

Genus of perennials and semi-evergreen sub-shrubs, usually grown as annuals, flowering from spring to autumn. Fully to half hardy. Needs sun and rich, well-drained soil. Dead-head to prolong flowering season. Propagate by seed sown outdoors in late spring or by stem cuttings in early autumn or spring. Rust disease may be a problem with *A. majus*, but rust-resistant cultivars are available.
A. asarina. See *Asarina procumbens*.
A. 'Balumhopi'. See A. Luminaire Series LUMINAIRE HOT PINK.
A. Luminaire Series LUMINAIRE HOT PINK ('Balumhopi') illus. p.303.
A. majus. Erect perennial that branches from the base. Cultivars are grown as annuals and are grouped according to size and flower type: tall, **H** 60cm–1m (2–3ft), **S** 30–45cm (12–18in); intermediate, **H** and **S** 45cm (18in); dwarf, **H** 20–30cm (8–12in), **S** 30cm (12in); regular tubular-shaped (hyacinth-like) flowers; penstemon, trumpet-shaped flowers; double; and irregular tubular-shaped flowers. Half hardy. All have lance-shaped leaves and, from spring to autumn, carry spikes of usually 2-lipped, sometimes double, flowers in a variety of colours, including white, pink, red, purple, yellow and orange. **Bells Series** (dwarf, regular) is early-flowering, with long-lasting flowers in purple, purple and white, red, rose-pink, pink, bronze, yellow, or white. ♀ **Bells Series 'Pink Bells'** has pink flowers. **'Black Prince'** illus. p.306. **Chimes Series** (dwarf, regular) is very compact, producing flowers in a wide colour range including several bicolours. **Chimes Series** (Yellow), illus. p.320. ♀ **Coronette Series** (tall, regular) is compact with tubular, 2-lipped flowers in a wide range of colours. **'Floral Showers'** (dwarf, regular) is early-flowering, bearing flowers in up to 10 colours, including some bicolours; tolerates wet weather. ♀ **Kim Series** (intermediate, regular) has flowers in scarlet, deep rose, deep orange, primrose-yellow and white as well as orange bicolour. **Liberty Classic Series 'Liberty Yellow'** illus. p.319. **Madame Butterfly Series** (tall, peloric) is available in a mixture of colours. **Rocket Series** (tall, regular) is vigorous, with flowers in a broad colour range; they are excellent for cut flowers. ♀ **Sonnet Series** (intermediate, regular) is bushy and has flowers in a variety of colours. **'Trumpet Serenade'** (dwarf, penstemon) has bicoloured flowers in a mixture of pastel shades.

APHELANDRA

ACANTHACEAE

Genus of evergreen shrubs and perennials with showy flowers. Frost tender, min. 13°C (55°F). Grows best in bright light but out of direct sun in summer. Use soft water and keep soil moist but not waterlogged. Benefits from feeding when flower spikes are forming. Propagate by seed or tip cuttings from young stems in spring.
A. squarrosa (Zebra plant).**'Dania'** is an evergreen, compact perennial. **H** 1m (3ft), **S** slightly less. Oval, glossy, dark green leaves, with white veins and mid-ribs, are nearly 30cm (1ft) long. Has dense, 4-sided spikes, to 15cm (6in) long, of 2-lipped, bright yellow flowers in axils of yellow bracts in autumn. ♀ **'Louisae'** illus. p.476.

APHYLLANTHES

LILIACEAE/APHYLLANTHACEAE

Genus of one species of summer-flowering perennial. Frost hardy, but shelter from cold wind. Grow in a sunny, warm, sheltered corner, preferably in an alpine house, and in well-drained, sandy, peaty soil. Resents disturbance. Propagate by seed in autumn or spring.
A. monspeliensis. Tuft-forming perennial. **H** 15–20cm (6–8in), **S** 5cm (2in). Star-shaped, pale to deep blue flowers are borne singly or in small groups at tops of wiry, glaucous green stems from early to mid-summer. Leaves are reduced to red-brown sheaths surrounding stems.

APONOGETON

APONOGETONACEAE

Genus of deciduous, perennial, deep-water plants, grown for their floating foliage and often heavily scented flowers. Frost hardy to frost tender, min. 16°C (61°F). Requires an open, sunny position. Tidy fading foliage in autumn. Propagate by division in spring or by seed while still fresh.
A. distachyos (Cape pondweed, Water hawthorn) illus. p.435.

APOROCACTUS

CACTACEAE

Genus of perennial cacti, grown for their pendent, slender, fleshy stems and bright flowers. Is suitable for hanging baskets. Half hardy to frost tender, min. 5°C (41°F). Needs partial shade and very well-drained soil. Occasional light watering in winter will stop stems dying back from the tips. Propagate by stem cuttings in spring or summer.
A. flagelliformis, syn. *Disocactus flagelliformis,* (Rat's tail cactus) illus. p.483.

APTENIA

AIZOACEAE

Genus of fast-growing, perennial succulents, with trailing, freely branching stems, that make good ground cover. Frost tender, min. 7°C (45°F). Requires full sun and very well-drained soil. Keep dry in winter. Propagate by seed or stem cuttings in spring or summer.
♀ **A. cordifolia**, syn. *Mesembryanthemum cordifolium*, illus. p.484. **'Variegata'** is a fast-growing, prostrate, perennial succulent. **H** 5cm (2in), **S** indefinite. Has oval, glossy, bright green leaves, with creamy-white margins, and small, daisy-like, bright pink flowers in summer.

AQUILEGIA

Columbine

RANUNCULACEAE

Genus of graceful, clump-forming, short-lived perennials, grown for their mainly bell-shaped, spurred flowers in spring and summer. Is suitable for rock gardens. Fully to frost hardy. Prefers an open, sunny site and well-drained soil. Propagate species by seed in autumn or spring. Selected forms only occasionally come true from seed (e.g. *A. vulgaris* 'Nora Barlow') as they cross freely; they should be widely segregated. Is prone to aphid attack. ⓘ Contact with sap may irritate skin.

A. akitensi. See *A. flabellata* var. *pumila*.
A. alpina (Alpine columbine) illus. p.334.
A. atrata (Black columbine). Clump-forming, hardy perennial **H** 60–70 cm (24–28in), **S** 30cm (12in). Bell-shaped, fluted, deep purple-violet flowers with spreading sepals and short 1cm-long, strongly hooked spurs appear in early summer above mid-green, glaucous-backed leaves divided into 9 segments.
♀ **A. bertolonii,** syn. *A. reuteri*. Clump-forming, compact, hardy perennial. **H** 10–30cm (4–12in), **S** 8–20cm (3–8in). Bell-shaped, blue-violet flowers with spreading sepals and short, 1cm-long curved spurs appear in late spring and early summer above dark green leaves divided into 9 segments.
A. Biedermeier Group. Short-stemmed, compact, hardy perennials. **H** 30–35cm (12–14in), **S** 20–30cm (8–12in). More or less upward-facing, open bell shaped flowers in colours varying from purple-blue to lilac, red, pink or white appear from late spring to mid-summer above the bluish-green divided foliage.
♀ **A. 'Bluebird' (Songbird Series)** illus. p.226. Clump-forming. Compact, hardy perennial **H** 60–70cm (24–28in), **S** 35–40 cm (14–16in). Open bell-shaped, very large, fluted flowers with white petals, soft, pale violet-blue sepals and long, slightly curved spurs appear in late spring and early summer above fern-like, divided, mid-green leaves.
♀ **A. 'Bunting' (Songbird Series)** illus. p.226. Clump-forming, compact, hardy perennial. **H** 60cm (24in), **S** 30–35cm (12–14in). Open bell-shaped, fluted flowers with white, blue-flushed petals, violet-blue sepals and long spurs are produced in late spring and early summer above fern-like, divided, mid-green leaves.
♀ **A. canadensis** (Canadian columbine; illus. p.226). Clump-forming, leafy perennial. **H** 60cm (24in), **S** 30cm (12in). Fully hardy. In early summer bears semi-pendent, bell-shaped flowers, with yellow sepals and red spurs, several per slender stem, above fern-like, dark green foliage.
A. 'Cardinal' (Songbird Series). Clump-forming, compact, hardy perennial. **H** 50cm (20in), **S** 30–35cm (12–14in). Open bell-shaped, fluted flowers with white petals, deep red-pink at the base, dark red sepals and long, curved spurs are produced in late spring and early summer above fern-like, divided, mid-green leaves.
A. chrysantha (illus. p.226). Vigorous, clump-forming perennial. **H** 1.2m (4ft), **S** 60cm (2ft). Fully hardy. Bears semi-pendent, bell-shaped, from pale to bright yellow flowers, with long spurs, several per stem, in early summer. Has fern-like, divided, mid-green leaves. **'Yellow Queen'** has golden-yellow flowers.
♀ **A. coerulea** (Rocky mountain columbine) illus. p.226. Upright, hardy perennial. **H** 60–80cm (24–32in), **S** 30–40cm (12–16in). More or less upward-facing flowers, with open-spreading white sepals, pale to deep sky-blue petals and long spurs

A

are borne from late spring to mid-summer above mid-green, divided leaves.

🏆**A. 'Dove' (Songbird Series)** illus. p.226. Clump-forming, compact, hardy perennial. **H** 75cm (30in), **S** 35–40cm (14–16in). Open bell-shaped, fluted, large flowers with white petals, sepals and long spurs are produced in late spring and early summer above fern-like, divided, light green leaves.

A. 'Dragonfly' (illus. p.226). Upright, hardy perennial. **H** 60cm (24in), **S** 30cm (12in). Bell-shaped, upright to semi-horizontally-placed, fluted, large flowers with yellow, basally red-flushed petals and purplish-red sepals and spurs are produced from late spring to mid-summer above fern-like, mid-green, divided leaves.

🏆***A. flabellata***. Clump-forming perennial. **H** 25cm (10in), **S** 10cm (4in). Fully hardy. Bell-shaped, soft blue flowers, each with fluted petals and a short spur, are produced in summer. Rounded, finely divided leaves form an open, basal rosette. Needs semi-shade and moist soil. **var. *alba* 'White Jewel'** has white flowers. The flowers of **Jewel Series** vary from blue to pink or white. **'Ministar'** has slightly nodding blooms with contrasting purple-blue, spreading sepals and white, blue-based petals. **'Nana Alba'** see *A.f.* var. *pumila* f. *alba*. 🏆**var. *pumila*** (syn. *A. akitensis*; illus. p.226) grows to 10cm (4in) and has deep blue and white petals. 🏆**var. *pumila* f. *alba*** (syn. *A.f.* 'Nana Alba'), **H** 10cm (4in), is compact and has white flowers.

🏆**A. 'Florida' (State Series).** Clump-forming, upright, hardy perennial. **H** 60cm (24in), **S** 30cm (12in). Open, bell-shaped, fluted flowers with mid-yellow petals, creamy-yellow, spreading sepals and long spurs are produced during late spring and early summer above fern like, divided, light green leaves.

A. fragrans. Upright, hardy perennial. **H** 15–40cm (6–16in), **S** 15–20cm (6–8in). Nodding, bell-shaped, fragrant flowers with creamy-white petals and bluish- or pinkish-white sepals and spurs to 2cm (¾in.) long are borne in midsummer above finely divided bluish-green leaves.

A. 'Goldfinch' (Songbird Series). Clump-forming, compact, hardy perennial. **H** 60–70cm (24–28in), **S** 35cm (14in). Open bell-shaped, fluted flowers with bright yellow petals, sepals and long spurs appear in late spring and early summer above fern-like, divided, mid-green leaves.

🏆**A. 'Hensol Harebell'** (illus. p.226). Clump-forming, compact perennial. **H** 60cm (2ft), **S** 30cm (1ft). Fully hardy. Has fern-like, divided, pale green leaves. In late spring, tall, slender stems bear pendent, bell-shaped, short-spurred, soft blue flowers.

A. jonesii illus. p.368.

A. karelinii. Clump-forming, hardy perennial. **H** 20–80cm (8–32in), **S** 12–30cm (5–12in) . Nodding, bell-shaped flowers with violet to wine-purple petals, spreading sepals and short, hooked spurs are produced above the light green, slightly glaucous leaves in early summer.

🏆***A. longissima*** (illus. p.226). Clump-forming, leafy perennial. **H** 60cm (24in), **S** 50cm (20in). Fully hardy. Bell-shaped, pale yellow flowers, with very long, bright yellow spurs, are borne, several per stem, in early summer, above fern-like, divided, mid-green leaves.

A. 'Mrs Scott Elliott'. See *A.* Mrs Scott Elliott Hybrids.

A. Mrs Scott Elliott Hybrids, syn. *A.* 'Mrs Scott Elliott'. Clump-forming, leafy perennial. **H** 1m (3ft), **S** 50cm (20in). Fully hardy. Bell-shaped flowers of various colours, often bicoloured, have long spurs and appear in early summer on branching, wiry stems. Has fern-like, divided, bluish-green leaves.

A. 'Nuthatch' (Songbird Series). Clump-forming, compact, hardy perennial. **H** 60–70cm (24–28in), **S** 30cm (12in). Open, bell-shaped, fluted flowers with white, pink-based petals, deep pink sepals and long spurs appear in late spring and early summer above fern-like divided, mid-green leaves.

A. 'Robin' (Songbird Series). Clump-forming, compact, hardy perennial. **H** 60cm (24in), **S** 30cm (12in). Open bell-shaped, fluted flowers with white petals, pink-flushed at the base, dusky pink, spreading sepals and long spurs are produced in late spring and early summer above fern-like, divided, pale mid-green leaves.

A. rockii. Upright, hardy perennial. **H** 50–80cm (20–32in), **S** 30–35cm (12–14in). Nodding to semi-erect, narrowly bell-shaped, deep purple flowers with spreading sepals and curved spurs, to 2cm (¾in) long, are borne above the mid-green, divided leaves, which are glaucous beneath, in late spring and early summer.

A. scopulorum. Clump-forming perennial. **H** 6cm (2½in), **S** 9cm (3½in). Frost hardy. In summer produces bell-shaped, fluted, pale blue, or rarely pink, flowers, each with a cream centre and very long spurs. Leaves are divided into 9 oval, glaucous leaflets.

A. 'Sunburst Ruby'. Clump-forming, hardy perennial. **H** 60cm (24in), **S** 30cm (12in). Semi-double to double, deep ruby-red, semi-upright flowers are borne above golden, fern-like, divided leaves in late spring and early summer.

A. triternata (illus. p.226). Upright, hardy perennial. **H** 20–60cm (8–24in), **S** 20–30cm (8–12in). Narrowly bell-shaped, nodding flowers with short, yellow, sometimes red-flushed petals, red sepals and 2.5cm (1in) long spurs are produced in early summer above the 3-parted, mid-green leaves.

A. viridiflora (illus. p.226). Upright, short-lived, hardy perennial. **H** 20–50cm (8–20in), **S** 10–20cm (4–8in). In late spring and early summer produces fragrant, nodding, bell-shaped flowers with purple, chocolate-brown or sometimes yellow-green petals with contrasting green sepals and 2cm (¾in) long spurs above the 3-parted, mid-green leaves.

A. vulgaris (Granny's bonnets). Clump-forming, leafy perennial. **H** 1m (3ft), **S** 50cm (20in). Fully hardy. Many funnel-shaped, short-spurred flowers, in shades of pink, crimson, purple and white, are borne, several per long stem, in early summer. Leaves are grey-green, rounded and divided into leaflets. **var. *alba*** produces white flowers. **'Magpie'** see 'William Guiness'. **'Munstead White'** see 'Nivea'. 🏆**'Nivea'** (syn. 'Munstead White'; illus. p.226) has grey-green leaves and glistening white flowers. **var. *stellata* 'Black Barlow'** (illus. p.223) bears spurless, deep purple-black, double flowers. 🏆**var. *stellata* 'Nora Barlow'** (illus. p.226) produces double red flowers, pale green at the tips. **var. *stellata* 'Ruby Port'** (illus. p.226) has spurless, deep ruby-red double flowers. **'William Guiness'** (syn. *A.v.* 'Magpie'; illus. p.226) has nodding, deep blue-purple flowers with the tips of the petals white.

A. 'Winky Red-White' (Winky Series). Clump-forming, compact, hardy perennial. **H** 35–50cm (14–20in), **S** 30cm (12in). Double or semi-double flowers with a mix of red and white petals are produced in late spring and early summer above fern-like leaves that are divided and coloured pale mid-green.

ARABIS

CRUCIFERAE/BRASSICACEAE

Genus of robust, evergreen perennials. Makes excellent ground cover in a rock garden. Fully to frost hardy. Needs sun and well-drained soil. Propagate by softwood cuttings in summer or by seed in autumn.

A. albida. See *A. alpina* subsp. *caucasica*.

A. alpina* subsp. *caucasica, syn. *A. albida*, *A. caucasica*. Evergreen, mat-forming perennial. **H** 15cm (6in), **S** 50cm (20in). Fully hardy. Bears loose rosettes of obovate, toothed, mid-green leaves and, in late spring and summer, fragrant, 4-petalled, white, occasionally pink, flowers. Is excellent on a dry bank. Trim back after flowering. **'Douler Angevine'** illus. p.352. 🏆**'Flore Pleno'** (syn. *A. caucasica* 'Plena') has double, white flowers. **'Variegata'** (syn. *A. caucasica* 'Variegata') illus. p.347.

***A. x arendsii* 'Rosabella'**, syn. *A. caucasica* 'Rosabella'. Evergreen, mat-forming perennial. **H** 15cm (6in), **S** 30cm (12in). Fully hardy. Has large rosettes of small, oval, soft green leaves and a profusion of single, deep pink flowers in spring and early summer.

A. blepharophylla. Short-lived, evergreen, mat-forming perennial. **H** 12cm (5in), **S** 20cm (8in). Fully hardy, but dislikes winter wet. Has oval, toothed, dark green leaves, with hairy, grey margins, borne in loose rosettes. Fragrant, 4-petalled, bright pink to white flowers are produced in spring. 🏆**'Frühlingszauber'** (syn. *A.b.* Spring Charm) illus. p.353.

A. caucasica. See *A. alpina* subsp. *caucasica*.**'Plena'** see *A. alpina* subsp. *caucasica* 'Flore Pleno'. **'Rosabella'** see *A. x arendsii* 'Rosabella'. **'Variegata'** see *A. alpina* subsp. *caucasica* 'Variegata'.

***A. ferdinandi-coburgi* 'Variegata'.** See *A. procurrens* 'Variegata'.

🏆***A. procurrens* 'Variegata'**, syn. *A. ferdinandi-coburgi* 'Variegata', illus. p.375.

ARALIA

ARALIACEAE

Genus of deciduous trees, shrubs and perennials, grown for their bold leaves and small, but profusely borne flowers. Fully hardy. Requires sun or semi-shade, some shelter and fertile, well-drained soil. Propagate those listed below by seed in autumn or by suckers or root cuttings in late winter.

🏆***A. elata*** (Japanese angelica tree). Deciduous tree or suckering shrub with sparse, stout, prickly stems. **H** and **S** 10m (30ft). Has large, dark green leaves with numerous oval, paired leaflets. Billowing heads of tiny, white flowers, forming a large panicle, 30–60cm (12–24in) long, are borne in late summer and autumn. **'Albomarginata'** see *A.e.* 'Variegata'. **'Aureovariegata'** has leaflets broadly edged with yellow. Leaflets of 🏆**'Variegata'** (syn. *A.e.* 'Albomarginata') illus. p.93.

A. elegantissima. See *Schefflera elegantissima*.

A. japonica. See *Fatsia japonica*.

A. sieboldii. See *Fatsia japonica*.

ARAUCARIA

ARAUCARIACEAE

See also CONIFERS.

A. araucana (Chile pine, Monkey puzzle) illus. p.98.

A. excelsa of gardens. See *A. heterophylla*.

🏆***A. heterophylla***, syn. *A. excelsa* of gardens (Norfolk Island pine). Upright conifer. **H** 30m (100ft), **S** 5–8m (15–25ft). Half hardy. Has spirally set, needle-like, incurved, fresh green leaves. Cones are seldom produced in cultivation. Is often grown as a shade-tolerant house plant.

ARAUJIA

ASCLEPIADACEAE/APOCYNACEAE

Genus of evergreen, twining climbers with woody stems that exude milky juice when cut. Half hardy. Needs sun and fertile, well-drained soil. Propagate by seed in spring or by stem cuttings in late summer or early autumn.

A. sericifera (Cruel plant) illus. p.195.

ARBUTUS

ERICACEAE

Genus of evergreen trees and shrubs, grown for their leaves, clusters of small, urn-shaped flowers, ornamental bark and strawberry-like fruits, which are edible but insipid. Frost hardy, but must be protected from strong, cold winds when young. Prefers a position in full sun and needs fertile, well-drained soil; *A. menziesii* requires acid soil. May be propagated by semi-ripe cuttings in late summer or by seed sown in autumn.

A. andrachne (Grecian strawberry tree). Evergreen, spreading tree or shrub. **H** and **S** 6m (20ft). Has oval, glossy, dark green leaves and peeling, reddish-brown bark. Panicles of urn-shaped, white flowers in late spring, are followed by orange-red fruits. Prefers a sheltered position.

🏆***A. x andrachnoides*** illus. p.79.

🏆***A. menziesii*** (Madroña, Madroñe). Evergreen, spreading tree. **H** and **S** 15m (50ft). Has smooth, peeling, reddish bark and oval, dark green leaves. Large, upright, terminal panicles of urn-shaped, white flowers in early summer are followed by orange or red fruits.

🏆***A. unedo*** (Strawberry tree) illus. p.93.

ARCHONTOPHOENIX
King palm

PALMAE/ARECACEAE

Genus of evergreen palms, grown for their majestic appearance. Frost tender, min. 15°C (59°F). Needs full light or partial shade and humus-rich, well-drained soil. Water container specimens moderately, less when temperatures are low. Propagate by seed in spring at not less than 24°C (75°F). Red spider mite may be troublesome.

A. alexandrae (Alexandra palm, Northern bungalow palm) illus. p.452.

♀***A. cunninghamiana*** (Illawarra palm, Piccabeen palm). Evergreen palm. **H** 15–20m (50–70ft), **S** 2–5m (6–15ft). Has long, arching, feather-shaped leaves. Mature trees produce large clusters of small, lavender or lilac flowers in summer, followed by large, egg-shaped, red fruits.

Arcterica nana. See *Pieris nana.*

ARCTOSTAPHYLOS
Manzanita

ERICACEAE

Genus of evergreen trees and shrubs, grown for their foliage, flowers and fruits. Some species are also grown for their bark, others for ground cover. Fully hardy to frost tender, min. 7°C (45°F). Provide shelter from strong winds. Does best in full sun and well-drained, acid soil. Propagate by semi-ripe cuttings in summer or by seed in autumn.

A. alpina, syn. Arctous alpinus. Deciduous, creeping shrub. **H** 5cm (2in), **S** to 12cm (5in). Produces drooping, terminal clusters of tiny, urn-shaped, pink-flushed, white flowers in late spring. These are followed by rounded, purple-black berries. Leaves are oval, toothed, glossy and bright green.

A. diversifolia, syn. *Comarostaphylis diversifolia* (Summer holly). Evergreen, upright shrub or tree. **H** 5m (15ft), **S** 3m (10ft). Half hardy. Leaves are oblong, glossy and dark green. Terminal racemes of fragrant, urn-shaped, white flowers appear from early to mid-spring, followed by spherical, red fruits.

***A.* 'Emerald Carpet'** illus. p.147.

***A. hookeri* 'Monterey Carpet'**, syn. *A. uva-ursi* subsp. *hookeri* 'Monterey Carpet'. Evergreen, open shrub. **H** 10–15cm (4–6in), **S** 40cm (16in) or more. Half hardy. Has hairy branchlets bearing glossy, pale green leaves and, in early summer, urn-shaped, white flowers, sometimes flushed pink, that are followed by globose, red fruits.

A. manzanita. Evergreen, upright shrub. **H** and **S** 2m (6ft) or more. Frost hardy. Has peeling, reddish-brown bark and oval, leathery, grey-green leaves. From early to mid-spring produces small, urn-shaped, deep pink flowers.

A. nevadensis (Pine-mat manzanita). Evergreen, prostrate shrub. **H** 10cm (4in), **S** 1m (3ft). Frost hardy. Has small, oval leaves. In summer, pendent, urn-shaped, white flowers are borne in clusters in leaf axils, followed by globose, brownish-red fruits. Is useful as ground cover.

A. nummularia. Evergreen, erect to prostrate shrub. **H** 30cm (1ft) or more, **S** 1m (3ft). Frost hardy. Leaves are small, rounded, leathery and toothed. Pendent, urn-shaped, white flowers are borne in clusters from leaf axils in summer, followed by globose, green fruits. Makes good ground cover.

A. patula illus. p.144.

A. stanfordiana (Stanford manzanita). Evergreen, erect shrub. **H** and **S** 1.5m (5ft). Half hardy. Bark is smooth and reddish-brown. Has narrowly oval, glossy, bright green leaves. Bears drooping clusters of urn-shaped, pink flowers from early to mid-spring.

A. uva-ursi illus. p.376. **subsp. *hookeri* 'Monterey Carpet'** see *A. hookeri* 'Monterey Carpet'.**'Point Reyes'** illus. p.375. **'Vancouver Jade'** is an evergreen, trailing, sometimes arching shrub. **H** 10cm (4in), **S** 50cm (20in). Fully hardy. Has small, oval, bright green leaves and bears urn-shaped, white flowers in summer.

ARCTOTHECA

COMPOSITAE/ASTERACEAE

Genus of creeping perennials. Frost tender, min. 5°C (41°F). Requires a position in bright light and fertile, well-drained soil; dislikes humid conditions. Propagate by seed or division in spring.

A. calendula, syn. *Cryptostemma calendulaceum*, (Cape dandelion) illus. p.476.

ARCTOTIS
SYN. x VENIDIOARCTOTIS

COMPOSITAE/ASTERACEAE

Genus of annuals and perennials, grown for their flower heads and foliage. Half hardy to frost tender, min. 1–5°C (34–41°F). Requires full sun and leafy loam with sharp sand added. Propagate by seed in autumn or spring or by stem cuttings year-round.

***A.* Harlequin Hybrids**, syn. *A.* x *hybrida*. Fairly slow-growing, upright, branching perennial, usually grown as an annual. **H** and **S** 45cm (18in). Half hardy. Lance-shaped, lobed leaves are greyish-green above, white below. In summer has large, daisy-like flower heads in many shades, including yellow, orange, bronze, purple, pink, cream and red. **'Bacchus'** has purple flower heads; **'China Rose'** deep pink; **'Sunshine'** yellow; **'Tangerine'** orange-yellow; and **'Torch'** bronze.

A.* x *hybrida. See *A.* Harlequin Hybrids.

A. stoechadifolia. See *A. venusta*.

A. venusta, syn. *A. stoechadifolia* (African daisy). Compact perennial, often grown as an annual. **H** 50cm (20in) or more, **S** 40cm (16in). Half hardy. Daisy-like, creamy-white flower heads with blue centres are borne singly throughout summer and into autumn. Chrysanthemum-like leaves are dark green above, grey beneath.

Arctous alpinus. See *Arctostaphylos alpina*.

ARDISIA

MYRSINACEAE

Genus of evergreen shrubs and trees, grown for their fruits and foliage. Half hardy to frost tender, min. 10°C (50°F). Needs partial shade and humus-rich, well-drained but not dry soil. Water potted plants freely when in full growth, moderately at other times. Cut back old plants in early spring if required. Propagate by seed in spring or by semi-ripe cuttings in summer.

A. crenata, syn. *A. crenulata*, (Coralberry, Spiceberry) illus. p.456.

A. crenulata. See *A. crenata*.

Areca lutescens of gardens. See *Dypsis lutescens*.

Arecastrum romanozoffianum. See *Syagrus romanozoffiana*.

Aregelia carolinae. See *Neoregelia carolinae*.

ARENARIA
Sandwort

CARYOPHYLLACEAE

Genus of spring- and summer-flowering annuals and perennials, some of which are evergreen. Fully to frost hardy. Most need sun and well-drained, sandy soil. Propagate by division or softwood cuttings in early summer or by seed in autumn or spring.

A. balearica illus. p.347.

♀***A. montana*** illus. p.360.

A. purpurascens illus. p.351.

A. tetraquetra illus. p.348.

ARGEMONE

PAPAVERACEAE

Genus of robust perennials, most of which are best treated as annuals. Fully to half hardy. Grow in sun and in very well-drained soil without supports. Dead-head to prolong the flowering season. Propagate by seed sown outdoors in late spring.

A. mexicana (Devil's fig, Prickly poppy) illus. p.321.

ARGYRANTHEMUM

COMPOSITAE/ASTERACEAE

Genus of evergreen sub-shrubs, grown for their daisy-like flowers. Frost to half hardy. Needs full sun and moderately fertile, well-drained soil. Propagate by semi-ripe cuttings in summer or root greenwood cuttings in spring.

♀***A.* BUTTERFLY ('Ulyssis')** illus. p.319.

A. frutescens, syn. *Chrysanthemum frutescens* (Marguerite), illus. p.298.

♀***A.* 'Jamaica Primrose'**, syn. *Chrysanthemum frutescens* 'Jamaica Primrose', illus. p.319.

***A.* 'Mary Wootton'**, syn. *Chrysanthemum frutescens* 'Mary Wootton'. Evergreen, woody-based, bushy perennial. **H** and **S** to 1m (3ft). Half hardy. Has fern-like, divided, pale green foliage bearing daisy-like, pink flower heads throughout summer.

***A.* 'Summer Melody'** illus. p.300.

***A.* 'Ulyssis'.** See *A.* BUTTERFLY.

ARGYREIA

CONVOLVULACEAE

Genus of evergreen, twining climbers, closely allied to *Ipomoea* and grown for their showy flowers. Frost tender, min. 13°C (55°F). Needs full light and fertile, well-drained soil. Water freely when in full growth, sparingly at other times. Support is needed. Thin out previous season's growth in spring. Propagate by seed in spring or by softwood or greenwood cuttings in summer. Red spider mite and whitefly may be troublesome.

A. nervosa, syn. *A. speciosa* (Woolly morning glory). Evergreen, twining climber. **H** 8–10m (25–30ft). Oval, silver-backed leaves are 18–27cm (7–11in) long. Clusters of funnel-shaped, lavender-blue flowers with darker bases and white downy in bud, appear in summer–autumn.

A. speciosa. See *A. nervosa*.

Argyrocytisus battandieri. See *Cytisus battandieri*.

ARGYRODERMA

AIZOACEAE

Genus of perennial succulents, grown for their very fleshy, grey-green leaves united in a prostrate, egg shape. In summer, daisy-like flowers appear in central split between leaves. Frost tender, min. 5°C (41°F). Needs full sun and extremely well-drained soil. Propagate by seed in summer.

A. aureum. See *A. delaetii*.

A. blandum. See *A. delaetii*.

A. brevipes. See *A. fissum*.

A. delaetii, syn. *A. aureum, A. blandum*, illus. p.488.

A. fissum, syn. *A. brevipes*, illus. p.491.

A. pearsonii, syn. *A. schlechteri*, illus. p.491.

A. schlechteri. See *A. pearsonii*.

ARIOCARPUS
Living rock

CACTACEAE

Genus of very slow-growing, perennial cacti with large, swollen roots. Has flattened, spherical, green stems with angular tubercles and tufts of wool. Frost tender, min. 5°C (41°F). Prefers full sun and extremely well-drained, lime-rich soil. Is very prone to rotting. Propagate by seed in spring or summer.

A. fissuratus. Very slow-growing, flattened spherical, perennial cactus. **H** 10cm (4in), **S** 15cm (6in). Grey stem is covered with rough, triangular tubercles each producing a tuft of wool. Has 4cm ($1^1/_2$in) wide, pink-red flowers in autumn.

ARISAEMA

ARACEAE

Genus of tuberous perennials, grown for their large, curious, hooded spathes, each enclosing a pencil-shaped spadix. Forms spikes of fleshy, red fruits in autumn, before dying down. Fully to half hardy. Needs sun or partial shade and moist but well-drained humus-rich soil. Plant tubers 15cm (6in) deep in spring. Propagate by seed in autumn or spring or by offsets in spring.

A. atrorubens. See *A. triphyllum*.

♀***A. candidissimum*** illus. p.422.

A. consanguineum illus. p.393.

A. griffithii illus. p.412.

A. jacquemontii illus. p.412.

A. ringens. Early spring-flowering, tuberous perennial. **H** 25–30cm (10–12in), **S** 30–45cm (12–18in). Half hardy. Bears 2 erect leaves, each with

A

3 long-pointed lobes, and a widely hooded, green spathe, enclosing the spadix, that has paler green stripes and is edged with dark brown-purple.
A. sikokianum illus. p.408.
A. tortuosum. Summer-flowering, tuberous perennial. **H** 30cm–1m (1–3ft), **S** 30–45cm (1–1½ft). Half hardy. Each dark green-mottled, pale green stem bears 2–3 erect leaves, divided into several oval leaflets. A hooded, green or purple spathe, with a protruding, S-shaped spadix, overtops leaves. Produces spikes of attractive, fleshy, red fruits in autumn.
A. triphyllum, syn. *A. atrorubens*, (Jack-in-the-pulpit), illus. p.406.

ARISARUM

ARACEAE

Genus of tuberous perennials, grown mainly for their curious, hooded spathes enclosing spadices with minute flowers. Frost hardy. Needs partial shade and humus-rich, well-drained soil. Propagate in autumn by dividing established clumps of tubers, which produce offsets freely.
A. proboscideum (Mouse plant). Clump-forming, spring-flowering, tuberous perennial. **H** to 10cm (4in), **S** 20–30cm (8–12in). Leaves are arrow-shaped and prostrate. Produces a spadix of minute flowers concealed in a hooded, dark brown spathe that is drawn out into a tail up to 15cm (6in) long, creating a mouse-like effect.

ARISTEA

IRIDACEAE

Genus of evergreen, clump-forming, rhizomatous perennials, grown for their spikes of blue flowers in spring or summer. Half hardy. Prefers a sunny position and well-drained soil. Established plants cannot be moved satisfactorily. Propagate by seed in autumn or spring.
A. capitata, syn. *A. major, A. thyrsiflora*, illus. p.393.
A. ecklonii. Evergreen, clump-forming, rhizomatous perennial. **H** 30–60cm (12–24in), **S** 20–40cm (8–16in). Has long, sword-shaped, tough leaves, overtopped in summer by loosely branched spikes of saucer-shaped, blue flowers, produced in long succession.
A. major. See *A. capitata*.
A. thyrsiflora. See *A. capitata*.

ARISTOLOCHIA

Birthwort

ARISTOLOCHIACEAE

Genus of evergreen or deciduous, woody-stemmed, twining and scrambling climbers, grown for their foliage and flowers. Frost hardy to frost tender, min. 10–13°C (50–55°F). Requires partial shade in summer and well-drained soil. Water regularly, less when not in full growth. Provide support. Cut back previous season's growth to 2 or 3 nodes in spring. Propagate by seed in spring or by semi-ripe cuttings in summer. Red spider mite and whitefly may be a nuisance.
A. durior. See *A. macrophylla*.
A. elegans. See *A. littoralis*.
A. gigas. See *A. grandiflora*.
A. grandiflora, syn. *A. gigas* (Pelican flower, Swan flower). Fast-growing, evergreen, woody-stemmed, twining climber. **H** 7m (22ft) or more. Frost tender. Leaves are broadly oval, 15–25cm (6–10in) long. In summer bears large, unpleasant-smelling, tubular, purple-veined, white flowers, each with a long tail and expanding at the mouth into a heart-shaped lip.
A. griffithii, syn. *Isotrema griffithii*. Moderately vigorous, evergreen, woody-stemmed, twining climber. **H** 5–6m (15–20ft). Half hardy; deciduous in cold winters. Has heart-shaped leaves and tubular, dark red flowers, each with an expanded, spreading lip, in summer.
🏆 ***A. littoralis***, syn. *A. elegans*, (Calico flower) illus. p.462.
A. macrophylla, syn. *A. durior, A. sipho*, (Dutchman's pipe) illus. p.204.
A. sipho. See *A. macrophylla*.

ARISTOTELIA

ELAEOCARPACEAE

Genus of evergreen shrubs and deciduous trees, grown for their foliage. Needs separate male and female plants in order to obtain fruits. Frost hardy, but in most areas protect by growing against other shrubs or a south- or west-facing wall. Needs sun or semi-shade and fertile, well-drained soil. Propagate by semi-ripe cuttings in summer.
A. chilensis, syn. *A. macqui*. Evergreen, spreading shrub. **H** 3m (10ft), **S** 5m (15ft). Leaves are oval, glossy and deep green. Tiny, star-shaped, green flowers are borne in summer, followed by small, spherical, black fruits.
A. macqui. See *A. chilensis*.

ARMERIA

PLUMBAGINACEAE

Genus of evergreen perennials and, occasionally, sub-shrubs, grown for their tuft-like clumps or rosettes of leaves and their flower heads. Fully to frost hardy. Needs sun and well-drained soil. Propagate by semi-ripe cuttings in summer or by seed in autumn.
A. 'Bees Ruby', syn. *A. pseudarmeria* 'Bees Ruby'. Evergreen, clump-forming, dwarf sub-shrub. **H** and **S** 30cm (12in). Fully hardy. Round heads of many small, ruby-red flowers are produced in summer on stiff stems above narrow, grass-like, dark green leaves.
A. caespitosa. See *A. juniperifolia*.
🏆 ***A. juniperifolia***, syn. *A. caespitosa*, illus. p.352. 🏆 **'Bevans Variety'** is an evergreen, densely cushioned sub-shrub. **H** 5–8cm (2–3in), **S** 15cm (6in). Fully hardy. Has narrow, pointed, mid- to grey-green leaves in loose rosettes. Round heads of small, deep pink flowers are borne in late spring and early summer.
A. latifolia. See *A. pseudarmeria*.
A. maritima (Sea pink, Thrift). Evergreen, clump-forming perennial or dwarf sub-shrub. **H** 10cm (4in), **S** 15cm (6in). Fully hardy. Leaves are narrow, grass-like and dark green. Stiff stems carry round heads of many small, white to pink flowers in summer. Makes a good edging plant. 🏆 **'Vindictive'** illus. p.365.
A. pseudarmeria, syn. *A. latifolia*, illus. p.336. **'Bees Ruby'** see *A.* 'Bees Ruby'.

ARNEBIA

BORAGINACEAE

Genus of perennials with hairy leaves, suitable for rock gardens and banks. Fully hardy. Needs sun and gritty, well-drained soil. Propagate by seed in autumn, by root cuttings in winter or by division in spring.
A. echioides. See *A. pulchra*.
A. pulchra, syn. *A. echioides, Echioides longiflorum, Macrotomia echioides* (Prophet flower). Clump-forming perennial. **H** 23–30cm (9–12in), **S** 25cm (10in). Leaves are lance-shaped to narrowly oval, hairy and light green. In summer produces loose racemes of tubular, bright yellow flowers, each with 5 spreading lobes and fading dark spots at petal bases.

ARNICA

COMPOSITAE/ASTERACEAE

Genus of rhizomatous perennials, grown for their large, daisy-like flower heads. Is suitable for large rock gardens. Fully hardy. Prefers sun and humus-rich, well-drained soil. Propagate by division or seed in spring. ⓘ All parts may cause severe discomfort if ingested, and contact with sap may aggravate skin allergies.
A. montana. Tufted, rhizomatous perennial. **H** 30cm (12in), **S** 15cm (6in). Bears narrowly oval to oval, hairy, grey-green leaves and, in summer, solitary daisy-like, golden flower heads, 5cm (2in) wide. Prefers acid soil.

ARONIA

Chokeberry

ROSACEAE

Genus of deciduous shrubs, cultivated for their flowers, fruits and colourful autumn foliage. Fully hardy. Needs sun (for autumn colour at its best) or semi-shade and fertile, well-drained soil. May be propagated in several ways: by softwood or semi-ripe cuttings taken in summer; by seed sown in autumn; or by division from early autumn to spring.
A. arbutifolia (Red chokeberry; illus. p.142). Deciduous shrub, upright when young, later arching. **H** 3m (10ft), **S** 1.5m (5ft). Clusters of small, white flowers, with red anthers, in late spring, are followed by red berries. Dark green leaves turn red in autumn.
A. melanocarpa (Black chokeberry) illus. p.128.
A. x prunifolia. Deciduous, upright shrub. **H** 3m (10ft), **S** 2.5m (8ft). Oval, glossy, dark green leaves redden in autumn. Produces star-shaped, white flowers in late spring and early summer, followed by spherical, purplish-black fruits.

ARRHENATHERUM

GRAMINEAE/POACEAE

See also GRASSES, BAMBOOS, RUSHES and SEDGES.
A. elatius (False oat grass). **subsp. *bulbosum* 'Variegatum'** is a loosely tuft-forming, herbaceous, perennial grass. **H** 50cm (20in), **S** 20cm (8in). Fully hardy. Has a basal stem swelling, hairless, grey-green leaves, with white margins, and open panicles of brownish spikelets in summer.

ARTEMISIA

Wormwood

COMPOSITAE/ASTERACEAE

Genus of perennials and spreading, dwarf sub-shrubs and shrubs, some of which are evergreen or semi-evergreen, grown mainly for their fern-like, silvery foliage that is sometimes aromatic. Fully to half hardy. Prefers an open, sunny, well-drained site; dwarf types benefit from a winter protection of sharp grit or gravel. Trim lightly in spring. Propagate by division in spring or autumn or by softwood or semi-ripe cuttings in summer.
🏆 ***A. abrotanum*** (Lad's love, Old man, Sourthernwood) illus. p.165.
🏆 ***A. absinthium* 'Lambrook Silver'.** Evergreen, bushy perennial, woody at base. **H** 80cm (32in), **S** 50cm (20in). Frost hardy. Has a mass of finely divided, aromatic, silvery-grey leaves. Produces tiny, insignificant, grey flower heads, borne in long panicles, in summer. Needs protection in an exposed site.
🏆 ***A. alba* 'Canescens'**, syn. *A. canescens, A. splendens*. Semi-evergreen, bushy perennial. **H** 50cm (20in), **S** 30cm (12in). Fully hardy. Has delicate, finely cut, curling, silvery-grey leaves. In summer, insignificant, yellow flower heads are borne on erect, silver stems. Makes good ground cover.
A. arborescens (Wormwood) illus. p.165. **'Brass Band'** see *A.* 'Powis Castle'. **'Faith Raven'** is an evergreen, upright shrub. **H** 1.2m (4ft), **S** 1m (3ft). Differs from the species only in that it is frost hardy. Has finely cut, aromatic, silvery-white foliage and, in summer and early autumn, rounded heads of small, bright yellow flowers.
A. assoana. See *A. caucasica*.
A. canescens. See *A. alba* 'Canescens'.
🏆 ***A. caucasica***, syn. *A. assoana, A. lanata, A. pedemontana*. Evergreen or semi-evergreen, prostrate perennial. **H** and **S** 30cm (12in). Fully hardy. Fern-like foliage is densely covered with silvery-white hairs. Small clusters of small, rounded, yellow flower heads are borne in summer. Suits a rock garden or wall.
🏆 ***A. frigida.*** Semi-evergreen, mat-forming perennial with a woody base. **H** 30cm (12in) in flower, **S** 30cm (12in) or more. Fully hardy. Bears small, fern-like, aromatic, silky, grey-white leaves, divided into many linear lobes. In summer produces narrow panicles of small, rounded, yellow flower heads.
🏆 ***A. lactiflora*** (White mugwort) illus. p.216.
A. lanata. See *A. caucasica*.
A. ludoviciana. Semi-evergreen, rhizomatous, clump-forming perennial. **H** 1.2m (4ft), **S** 60cm (2ft). Fully hardy. Has aromatic, lance-shaped, woolly, silvery-grey leaves with jagged margins. Bears slender plumes of tiny, greyish-white flower heads in summer. 🏆 **'Silver Queen'**, **H** 75cm (30in), has densely white-woolly panicles of brownish-yellow flower

A

heads from mid-summer to autumn. ♀ **'Valerie Finnis'** illus. p.274.
A. pedemontana. See *A. caucasica.*
A. pontica (Roman wormwood). Vigorous, upright perennial. **H** 60cm (24in), **S** 20cm (8in). Fully hardy. Has aromatic, feathery, silver-green foliage and tall spikes of small, greyish flower heads in summer. May spread.
♀ ***A.* 'Powis Castle'**, syn. *A. arborescens* 'Brass Band', illus. p.242.
♀ ***A. schmidtiana.*** Semi-evergreen, hummock-forming perennial with creeping stems. **H** 8–30cm (3–12in), **S** 60cm (24in). Frost hardy. Has fern-like, very finely and deeply cut, silver leaves and, in summer, produces short racemes of small, rounded, pale yellow flower heads. Is good for a large rock garden, wall or bank. Needs sandy, peaty soil. ♀ **'Nana'** illus. p.374.
A. splendens. See *A. alba* 'Canescens'.
A. stelleriana. Evergreen, rounded, rhizomatous perennial with a woody base. **H** 30–60cm (1–2ft), **S** 60cm–1m (2–3ft). Fully hardy. White-haired, silver leaves are deeply lobed or toothed. Bears slender sprays of small, yellow flower heads in summer. Needs light soil. **'Boughton Silver'** (syn. *A.s.* 'Mori', *A.s.* 'Silver Brocade'), **S** 1m (3ft), is vigorous and arching in habit. **'Mori'** see *A.s.* 'Boughton Silver'. **'Silver Brocade'** see *A.s.* 'Boughton Silver'.

ARTHROPODIUM

LILIACEAE/ANTHERICACEAE

Genus of tufted perennials, grown for their flowers. Half hardy. Prefers a position against a sunny, sheltered wall in fertile soil. Propagate by division in spring or by seed in spring or autumn.
A. cirratum, syn. *A. cirrhatum* (Rienga lily, Rock lily). Branching perennial. **H** 1m (3ft), **S** 30cm (1ft). Bears sprays of nodding, shallowly cup-shaped, white flowers on wiry stems in early summer. Has a basal tuft of narrowly sword-shaped leaves and fleshy roots.
A. cirrhatum. See *A. cirratum.*

ARUM

Cuckoo pint, Lords and ladies

ARACEAE

Genus of tuberous perennials, grown for their leaves and spathes, each enclosing a pencil-shaped spadix of tiny flowers. Fully to half hardy. Requires sun or partial shade and moist but well-drained soil. Propagate by seed in autumn or by division in early autumn.
A. creticum illus. p.407.
A. dioscoridis. Spring-flowering, tuberous perennial. **H** 20–35cm (8–14in), **S** 30–45cm (12–18in). Frost hardy. Has a sail-like, green or purple spathe, blotched dark purple, surrounding a blackish-purple spadix. Arrow-shaped, semi-erect leaves appear in autumn. Needs a sheltered, sunny site.
A. dracunculus. See *Dracunculus vulgaris.*
♀ ***A. italicum* 'Marmoratum'**, syn. *A.i.* 'Pictum', illus. p.421.
A. pictum. Autumn-flowering, tuberous perennial. **H** 15–25cm (6–10in), **S** 15–20cm (6–8in). Half hardy. Arrow-shaped, semi-erect, glossy leaves, with cream veins, appear at same time as cowl-like, deep purple-brown spathe and dark purple spadix.

ARUNCUS

ROSACEAE

Genus of perennials, grown for their hummocks of broad, fern-like leaves and their plumes of white flowers in summer. Fully hardy. Thrives in full light and any well-drained soil. Propagate by seed in autumn or by division in spring or autumn.
♀ ***A. dioicus***, syn. *A. sylvester, Spiraea aruncus,* (Goat's beard), illus. p.436. **'Kneiffii'** illus. p.231.
A. sylvester. See *A. dioicus.*

Arundinaria anceps. See *Yushania anceps.*
Arundinaria auricoma. See *Pleioblastus viridistriatus.*
Arundinaria falconeri. See *Himalayacalamus falconeri.*
Arundinaria fastuosa. See *Semiarundinaria fastuosa.*
Arundinaria fortunei. See *Pleioblastus variegatus.*
Arundinaria japonica. See *Pseudosasa japonica.*
Arundinaria jaunsarensis. See *Yushania anceps.*
Arundinaria murieliae. See *Fargesia murieliae.*
Arundinaria nitida. See *Fargesia nitida.*

ARUNDO

GRAMINEAE/POACEAE

See also GRASSES, BAMBOOS, RUSHES and SEDGES.
A. donax (Giant reed). Herbaceous, rhizomatous, perennial grass. **H** to 6m (20ft), **S** 1m (3ft). Half hardy. Has thick stems that bear broad, floppy, blue-green leaves. Produces dense, erect panicles of whitish-yellow spikelets in summer. Can be grown in moist soil. **var. *versicolor*** (syn. *A.d.* 'Variegata') illus. p.436. **'Variegata'** see *A.d.* var. *versicolor.*

ASARINA

SCROPHULARIACEAE

Genus of evergreen climbers and perennials, often with scandent stems, grown for their flowers. Is herbaceous in cold climates. Frost hardy to frost tender, min. 5°C (41°F). Grow in a position with full light and in any well-drained soil. Propagate by seed in spring.
A. barclayana. See *Maurandya barclayana.*
A. erubescens. See *Lophospermum erubescens.*
A. procumbens, syn. *Antirrhinum asarina,* illus. p.371.

ASARUM

SYN. HEXASTYLIS

Wild ginger

ARISTOLOCHIACEAE

Genus of rhizomatous perennials, some of which are evergreen, with pitcher-shaped flowers carried under kidney- or heart-shaped leaves. Makes good ground cover, although leaves may become damaged in severe weather. Fully hardy. Prefers shade and humus-rich, moist but well-drained soil. Propagate by division in spring. Self seeds readily.
A. caudatum. Evergreen, prostrate, rhizomatous perennial. **H** 8cm (3in), **S** 25cm (10in) or more. Heart-shaped, leathery, glossy, dark green leaves, 5–10cm (2–4in) across, conceal small, pitcher-shaped, reddish-brown or brownish-purple flowers, with tail-like lobes, in early summer.
♀ ***A. europaeum*** (Asarabacca) illus. p.375.
A. hartwegii. Evergreen, prostrate, rhizomatous perennial. **H** 8cm (3in), **S** 25cm (10in) or more. Pitcher-shaped, very dark brown, almost black, flowers, with tail-like lobes, appear in early summer beneath heart-shaped, silver-marked, mid-green leaves, 5–10cm (2–4in) wide.
A. shuttleworthii. Evergreen, prostrate, rhizomatous perennial. **H** 8cm (3in), **S** 25cm (10in) or more. Has broadly heart-shaped, usually silver-marked, mid-green leaves, 8cm (3in) across. Bears pitcher-shaped, dark brown flowers, mottled violet inside, in early summer.

ASCLEPIAS

Silk weed

ASCLEPIADACEAE/APOCYNACEAE

Genus of tuberous perennials or sub-shrubs, some of which are evergreen, grown for their flowers. Stems exude milky, white latex when cut. Fully hardy to frost tender, min. 5–10°C (41–50°F). Fully to half hardy species prefer a position in sun and a humus-rich, well-drained soil. Propagate by division or seed in spring. Frost tender species require sun and a moist atmosphere; cut back during periods of growth. Water very sparingly in low temperatures. Propagate by tip cuttings or seed in spring. ⚠ Contact with the milky sap may irritate skin.
A. curassavica (Blood flower). Evergreen, bushy, tuberous sub-shrub. **H** and **S** 1m (3ft). Frost tender. Has narrowly oval leaves to 15cm (6in) long. Umbels of small, but showy, 5-horned, orange-red flowers with yellow centres appear in summer-autumn and are followed by narrowly ovoid, pointed fruits, 8cm (3in) long, with silky seeds.
A. hallii. Upright, tuberous perennial. **H** to 1m (3ft), **S** 60cm (2ft). Fully hardy. Has oblong leaves, to 13cm (5in) long. Umbels of small, 5-horned, dark pink flowers are carried in summer; tightly packed silky seeds are enclosed in narrowly ovoid fruits, to 15cm (6in) long.
A. physocarpa. See *Gomphocarpus physocarpus.*
A. syriaca. Upright, tuberous perennial. **H** and **S** 1m (3ft) or more. Fully hardy. Bears oval leaves to 20cm (8in) long. Produces umbels of small, 5-horned, purplish-pink flowers carried on drooping flower stalks in summer, followed by narrowly ovoid fruits, to 15cm (6in) long and filled with silky seeds.
A. tuberosa (Butterfly weed) illus. p.246.

ASIMINA

ANNONACEAE

Genus of deciduous or evergreen shrubs and trees, grown for their foliage and flowers. Fully hardy. Prefers full sun and fertile, deep, moist but well-drained soil. Propagate by seed in autumn or by layering or root cuttings in winter.
A. triloba (Pawpaw). Deciduous, open shrub. **H** and **S** 4m (12ft). Large, oval, mid-green leaves emerge in late spring or early summer, just after, or at the same time as, 6-petalled, purplish-brown flowers. Later it produces small, globular, brownish, edible fruits.

ASPARAGUS

LILIACEAE/ASPARAGACEAE

Genus of perennials and scrambling climbers and shrubs, some of which are evergreen, grown for their foliage. Fully hardy to frost tender, min. 10°C (50°F). Grow in partial shade or bright light, but not direct sun, in any fertile, well-drained soil. Propagate by seed or division in spring.
A. densiflorus illus. p.474. ♀ **'Myersii'** (syn. *A. meyeri, A.* 'Myers', Foxtail fern) illus. p.474.
A. meyeri. See *A. densiflorus* 'Myersii'.
***A.* 'Myers'.** See *A. densiflorus* 'Myersii'.
A. scandens illus. p.463.

ASPERULA

RUBIACEAE

Genus of annuals and perennials; some species make good alpine house plants. Fully to frost hardy. Most species need sun and well-drained soil with moisture at roots. Dislikes winter wet on crown. Propagate by softwood cuttings or seed in early summer.
A. athoa of gardens. See *A. suberosa.*
A. odorata. See *Galium odoratum.*
A. suberosa, syn. *A. athoa* of gardens, illus. p.362.

ASPHODELINE

LILIACEAE/ASPHODELACEAE

Genus of perennials with thick, fleshy roots. Frost to half hardy. Requires sun and not over-rich soil. Propagate by division in early spring, taking care not to damage roots, or by seed in autumn or spring.
A. liburnica. Neat, clump-forming perennial. **H** 25–60cm (10–24in), **S** 30cm (12in). Frost hardy. In spring produces racemes of shallowly cup-shaped, yellow flowers on slender stems above linear, grey-green leaves.
A. lutea (Yellow asphodel) illus. p.227.

ASPHODELUS

LILIACEAE/ASPHODELACEAE

Genus of spring- or summer-flowering annuals and perennials. Frost to half hardy. Requires sun; most prefer fertile, well-drained soil. *A. albus* prefers light, well-drained soil. Propagate by division in spring or by seed in autumn.
A. acaulis. Prostrate perennial. **H** 5cm

A

(2in), **S** 23cm (9in). Half hardy. In spring or early summer, stemless, funnel-shaped, flesh-pink flowers appear in the centre of each cluster of grass-like, mid-green leaves. Is suitable for an alpine house.

A. aestivus, syn. *A. microcarpus* (Asphodel). Upright perennial. **H** 1m (3ft), **S** 30cm (1ft). Frost hardy. Dense panicles of star-shaped, white flowers are borne in late spring. Has basal rosettes of upright, then spreading, grass-like, channelled, leathery, mid- green leaves.
A. albus (White asphodel) illus. p.230.
A. microcarpus. See *A. aestivus.*

ASPIDISTRA

LILIACEAE/CONVALLARIACEAE

Genus of evergreen, rhizomatous perennials that spread slowly, grown mainly for their glossy foliage. Frost tender, min. 5–10°C (41–50°F). Very tolerant, but is best grown in a cool, shady position away from direct sunlight and in well-drained soil. Water frequently when in full growth, less at other times. Propagate by division of rhizomes in spring.
A. attenuata. Evergreen, rhizomatous perennial. **H** 100cm (36in), **S** 50cm (20in) or more. Frost tender, min. 1°C (34°F). Has long-stalked, pointed, elliptic, yellow-spotted, glossy, deep green leaves, 45–50cm (18–20in) long. Small, urn-shaped red and yellow flowers are produced at ground level in spring or autumn.
A. daibuensis. Evergreen, rhizomatous perennial. **H** 100cm (36in), **S** 50cm (20in) or more. Frost tender, min. 1°C (34°F). Produces lance-shaped, yellow-spotted, glossy, deep green leaves, 40–60cm (16–24in) long. Cup-shaped, yellow flowers are borne near ground level, in summer-autumn.
🏆 ***A. elatior*** (Cast-iron plant). Evergreen, rhizomatous perennial. **H** 60cm (24in), **S** 45cm (18in). Has upright, narrow, pointed-oval leaves, to 60cm (24in) long; inconspicuous, cream to purple flowers are occasionally produced on short stalks near soil level. **'Asahi'** has variegated leaves each with a narrow, inverted wedge-shaped, white zone extending down the leaf from the apex.
🏆 **'Variegata'** illus. p.277.
***A. zongbayi* 'Uan Fat Lady'.** Evergreen, rhizomatous perennial. **H** 50cm (20in), **S** 30cm (12in) or more. Frost tender, min. 1°C (34°F). Slender leaf stalks bear broadly oval, wavy-margined, bright green leaves, 20cm (8in) long, speckled with greenish-yellow and with a central, broad, pale stripe. Cup-shaped, purple flowers are produced near ground level from late summer to autumn.

ASPLENIUM

ASPLENIACEAE

Genus of evergreen or semi-evergreen ferns. Fully hardy to frost tender, min. 5°C (41°F). Plants described prefer partial shade, but *A. trichomanes* tolerates full sun. Grow in any moist soil, although containerized plants should be cultivated in a compost that includes chopped sphagnum moss or coarse peat. Regularly remove any fronds that are fading. Propagate by spores or bulbils, if produced, in late summer.
A. bulbiferum (Hen-and-chicken fern, Mother spleenwort). Semi-evergreen or evergreen fern. **H** 15–30cm (6–12in), **S** 30cm (12in). Frost tender. Lance-shaped, finely divided, dark green fronds produce bulbils from which young plants develop.
A. ceterach, syn. *Ceterach officinarum* (Rusty-back fern) illus. p.293.
🏆 ***A. nidus*** (Bird's-nest fern) illus. p.479.
🏆 ***A. scolopendrium***, syn. *Phyllitis scolopendrium*, *Scolopendrium vulgare*, (Hart's-tongue fern) illus. p.292.
Marginatum Group (syn. *Phyllitis scolopendrium* 'Marginatum') illus. p.292.
🏆 ***A. trichomanes*** (Maiden-hair spleenwort) illus. p.291.

ASTELIA

ASTELIACEAE

Genus of clump-forming perennials, grown mainly for their foliage. Frost to half hardy. Prefers full sun or semi- shade and fertile soil that does not dry out readily. Propagate by division in spring.
🏆 ***A. chathamica*** illus. p.242.
A. nervosa. Clump-forming perennial. **H** 60cm (2ft), **S** 1.5m (5ft). Frost hardy. Has long, sword-shaped, arching, silvery-grey leaves, above which, in summer, rise graceful, branching panicles of small, star-shaped, pale brown flowers.

ASTER

Michaelmas daisy

COMPOSITAE/ASTERACEAE

Genus of perennials and deciduous or evergreen sub-shrubs with daisy-like flower heads borne in summer-autumn. Fully to half hardy. Prefers sun or partial shade and fertile, well-drained soil, with adequate moisture all summer. Tall asters require staking. Propagate by softwood cuttings in spring or by division in spring or autumn. Spray modern forms of *A. novi-belgii* against mildew and insect attack. Other species may suffer too. See also feature panel, p.249.
A. acris. See *A. sedifolius.*
A. albescens, syn. *Microglossa albescens.* Deciduous, upright, slender- stemmed sub-shrub. **H** 1m (3ft), **S** 1.5m (5ft). Frost hardy. Has narrowly lance- shaped, grey-green leaves and flattish sprays of lavender-blue flower heads, with yellow centres, in mid-summer.
🏆 ***A. alpinus*** illus. p.367. **'Dark Beauty'** see *A.a.* 'Dunkle Schöne'. **'Dunkle Schöne'** (syn. *A.a.* 'Dark Beauty') is a clump-forming perennial. **H** 25cm (10in), **S** 45cm (18in). Fully hardy. Leaves are lance-shaped and dark green. Deep purple flower heads are borne from mid- to late summer. Is suitable for a rock garden.
🏆 ***A. amellus* 'King George'** illus. p.250. **'Mauve Beauty'** is a bushy perennial. **H** and **S** 50cm (20in). Fully hardy. In autumn, bears clusters of large, terminal, daisy-like, violet flower heads with yellow centres. Leaves are lance-shaped, coarse and mid-green.
'Nocturne', **H** 75cm (30in), has deep lilac flower heads with yellow centres.
'Rudolph Goethe' with large, violet-blue flower heads, **'Sonia'** with pink flower heads and 🏆 **'Veilchenkönigin'** (syn. *A.a.* 'Violet Queen') with deep violet flower heads are other good cultivars. **'Violet Queen'** see *A.a.* 'Veilchenkönigin'.
A. capensis. See *Felicia amelloides.*
🏆 ***A.* 'Coombe Fishacre'** (illus. p.249). Clump-forming, upright perennial. **H** to 90cm (36in), **S** 35cm (14in). Fully hardy. Has lance-shaped, mid-green leaves. In late summer, erect stems bear masses of daisy-like, pinkish-mauve flower heads with yellow centres that age to red.
***A. cordifolius* 'Silver Spray'** (illus. p.249). Bushy perennial. **H** 1.2m (4ft), **S** 1m (3ft). Fully hardy. Dense, arching stems carry sprays of small, pink-tinged, white flower heads in autumn. Mid-green leaves are lance-shaped. Needs staking.
A. diffusus. See *A. lateriflorus.*
A. divaricatus (illus. p.249). Spreading, upright perennial. **H** 40cm (16in), **S** 30cm (12in). Fully hardy. Has pointed, oval, toothed, glossy, dark green leaves. In late summer, purplish-black, wiry, branching, arching stems bear daisy-like, white flower heads. Is best in shade, where it makes good ground cover.
A. ericoides. Clump-forming, bushy perennial. **H** 1m (3ft), **S** 30cm (1ft). Fully hardy. From late summer to late autumn produces daisy-like, yellow-centred, white flower heads, sometimes shaded pink or blue, in lax panicles. Has small, lance-shaped, mid-green leaves and slender, freely branched stems. 🏆 **'Blue Star'**, **H** 80cm (32in), has soft mauve-blue ray florets. 🏆 **'Golden Spray'** (illus. p.249) produces pink-tinged, white flower heads, with golden-yellow centres. 🏆 **'Pink Cloud'**, **H** 80cm (32in), is vigorous, with arching sprays of pale pink flower heads. **f. *prostratus*,** **H** to 20cm (8in), **S** 60cm (24in), makes good ground cover and has tiny, needle-like leaves and white or pale mauve flower heads. 🏆 **f. *prostratus* 'Snow Flurry'** has pure white flowers; is good in gravel or in a rock garden. **'White Heather'** (illus. p.249) produces long-lasting, neat, white flower heads in late autumn and wire stems that may need support.
🏆 ***A.* x *frikartii* 'Mönch'.** Bushy perennial. **H** 75cm (30in), **S** 45cm (18in). Fully hardy. Bears daisy-like, single, soft lavender-blue flower heads with yellowish-green centres continuously from mid-summer to late autumn. Leaves are oval and rough. May need staking. 🏆 **'Wunder von Stäfa'** (illus. p.249) is similar but has lavender flowers.
🏆 ***A.* 'Kylie'.** Clump-forming, upright perennial. **H** 100cm (36in), **S** 45cm (18in). Fully hardy. Has lance-shaped, mildew-resistant, deep-green leaves. In late summer, upright then arching sprays of small, daisy-like, clear pastel-pink flower heads are borne in profusion.
A. laevis. Variable, clump-forming perennial. **H** 120cm (48in), **S** 50cm (20in). Fully hardy. Has long, lance-shaped, mildew-resistant, mid-green leaves. In late summer, upright purplish stems bear abundant sprays of daisy-like, pale purple flowers. **'Bluebird'** has violet-blue flowers.
A. lateriflorus, syn. *A. diffusus.* Branching perennial. **H** 60cm (24in), **S** 50cm (20in). Fully hardy. Bears sprays of tiny, mauve flower heads, with pinkish-brown centres, in autumn. Lance-shaped leaves are small and dark green. 🏆 **var. *horizontalis*** has flower heads that are sometimes tinged pink, with darker pink centres. **'Lady in Black'**, **H** 1.2m (4ft), has bronze-purple leaves and yellow-centred, white flower heads and retains its leaf colouring well during the growing season.**'Prince'**, **H** 50cm (20in), has bronze-purple leaves, which fade to dark green, and small, pink-centred, white flower heads.
A. linosyris (Goldilocks) illus. p.254.
🏆 ***A.* 'Little Carlow'** (illus. p.249). Clump-forming, upright perennial. **H** 120cm (48in), **S** 45cm (18in). Fully hardy. Has lance-shaped, mildew-resistant, deep-green leaves. In autumn, upright sprays bear masses of daisy-like, bright mauve-blue flower heads.
***A. novae-angliae* 'Andenken an Alma Pötschke'.** Vigorous, upright perennial. **H** 75cm (30in), **S** to 60cm (24in). Fully hardy. In autumn produces clusters of single, pink flower heads on stiff stems. Has lance-shaped, rough leaves. May need staking. **'Autumn Snow'** see *A.n-a.* 'Herbstschnee'. **'Barr's Pink'** bears semi-double, bright rose-pink flower heads in summer-autumn.
🏆 **'Harrington's Pink'** (illus. p.249), **H** 1.2–1.5m (4–5ft), has single, clear pink flower heads with yellow centres. Those of **'Herbstschnee'** (syn. *A.n-a.* 'Autumn Snow'), **H** 75cm–1.1m (2½–3½ft), are white with yellow centres. 🏆 **'Rosa Sieger'**(illus. p.249), **H** 1.2m (4ft), has pink flower heads. **'Violetta'** (illus. p.249), **H** 1.5m (5ft), produces yellow-centred, bright violet-purple flower heads.
***A. novi-belgii* 'Apple Blossom'** (illus. p.249). Vigorous, spreading perennial. **H** 90cm (36in), **S** 60–75cm (24–30in). Fully hardy. Panicles of single, pale soft pink flowers are borne in autumn amid lance-shaped, mid-green leaves. **'Carnival'** (illus. p.249), **H** 75cm (30in), **S** to 45cm (18in), bears double, cerise-red flower heads with yellow centres. Leaves are dark green. Is prone to mildew. **'Chequers'** (illus. p.249), **H** 90cm (36in), **S** 60–75cm (24–30in), has single, purple flowers. **'Climax'**, **H** 1.5m (5ft), **S** 60cm (2ft), bears single, light blue flowers. Is mildew-resistant. The flower heads of **'Fellowship'**, **H** 1.2m (4ft), **S** 50cm (20in), are large, double and clear, deep pink; those of **'Freda Ballard'** (illus. p.249) are semi-double and rich rose-red. **'Kristina'**, **H** 30cm (12in), **S** 45cm (18in), has large, semi-double, white flower heads with yellow centres. **'Lassie'**, **H** 1.2m (4ft), **S** 75cm (30in), produces large, single, clear pink flowers. **'Little Pink Beauty'**, **H** 45cm (18in), **S** 50cm (20in), is a good dwarf semi-double, pink cultivar. **'Marie Ballard'** (illus. p.249), **H** to 1m (3ft), **S** to 45cm (18in), has double, mid-blue flowers. Is prone to mildew. **'Orlando'** (illus. p.249), **H** 1m (3ft), **S** to 45cm (18in), has large, single, bright pink flower heads with golden centres. Leaves are dark green. Mildew may be a problem. **'Patricia Ballard'**, **H** 1.2m (4ft), **S** 75cm (30in), produces semi-double, pink flowers. Large, single flowers of **'Peace'** are mauve; **'Professor Anton Kippenberg'**

(illus. p.249) **H** 30cm (12in), **S** to 45cm (18in), are clear blue with yellow centres; and those of **'Raspberry Ripple'**, **H** 75cm (30in), **S** 60cm (24in), are smaller and reddish-violet. **'Royal Ruby'**, **H** and **S** to 45cm (18in), bears semi-double, rich red flower heads with yellow centres. Is prone to mildew. **'Royal Velvet'**, **H** 1.2m (4ft), **S** 75cm (30in), has single deep violet flowers. **'Sandford White Swan'**, **H** 90cm (36in), **S** 60cm (24in), bears white flower heads.

♀ ***A.* 'Photograph'** (illus. p.249). Clump-forming, upright, compact perennial. **H** 1m (3ft), **S** 30cm (1ft). Fully hardy. Has heart-shaped, mid-green leaves. In autumn, upright then arching, branched sprays bear masses of daisy-like, glowing violet-blue flower heads.

♀ ***A. pilosus* var. *demotus***, syn. *A. tradescantii* of gardens. Erect perennial. **H** 1.2m (4ft), **S** 50cm (20in). Fully hardy. Has lance-shaped, mid- green leaves. In autumn, clusters of small, white flower heads appear on wiry, leafy stems and provide a good foil to bright, autumn leaf colours.

♀ ***A.* 'Ringdove'.** Clump-forming, upright, compact perennial. **H** 1m (3ft), **S** 30cm (1ft). Fully hardy. Has narrowly lance-shaped, mid-green leaves. In autumn, upright then arching, branched sprays bear masses of small, daisy-like, yellow-centred, soft lilac flower heads.

A. sedifolius, syn. *A. acris.* Bushy perennial. **H** 1m (3ft), **S** 60cm (2ft). Fully hardy. Produces clusters of almost star-shaped, lavender-blue flower heads, with yellow centres, in autumn. Has small, narrowly oval, bright green leaves. **'Nanus'**, **H** and **S** 50cm (20in), makes a compact dome of blooms.

***A.* 'Sunhelene'** (illus. p.249). Clump-forming, upright, compact perennial. **H** 100cm (36in), **S** 40cm (16in). Fully hardy. Has lance-shaped , mildew-resistant, mid-green leaves. In late summer and autumn, upright, branched sprays bear masses of daisy-like, double, blue-mauve flower heads

A. thomsonii. Upright perennial. **H** 1m (3ft), **S** 50cm (20in). Fully hardy. Produces long-petalled, pale lilac flower heads, freely in autumn. Leaves are slightly heart-shaped. **'Nanus'** is more compact, **H** 45cm (18in), **S** 23cm (9in).

A. tongolensis. Mat-forming perennial. **H** 50cm (20in), **S** 30cm (12in). Fully hardy. Large, lavender-blue flower heads, with orange centres, are borne singly in early summer. Has lance-shaped, hairy, dark green leaves.

A. tradescantii of gardens. See *A. pilosus* var. *demotus*.

♀ ***A. turbinellus.*** Clump-forming perennial. **H** 1.5m (5ft), **S** 1m (3ft). Fully hardy. Has lance-shaped, dark green leaves. In late summer and autumn, upright, wiry purplish-green stems bear panicles of daisy-like, yellow-centred, pale violet flowers.

ASTERANTHERA

GESNERIACEAE

Genus of one species of evergreen, root climber. May be grown up mossy tree-trunks, trained against walls or used as ground cover. Frost hardy. Needs a dampish, semi-shaded position and neutral to slightly acid soil. Propagate by tip cuttings in summer or by stem cuttings in late summer or early autumn.

A. ovata. Evergreen, root climber with stems covered in white hairs. **H** to 4m (12ft). Has small, oblong, toothed leaves. Tubular, reddish-pink flowers, 5–6cm (2–2½in) long, often with yellow-striped, lower lips, appear singly or in pairs in leaf axils in summer.

ASTILBE

SAXIFRAGACEAE

Genus of summer-flowering perennials, grown for their panicles of flowers that remain handsome even when dried brown in winter. Is suitable for borders and rock gardens. Fully hardy. Needs partial shade for most species, and a rich, moist soil. Leave undisturbed if possible, and give a spring mulch of well-rotted compost. Propagate species by seed sown in autumn, others by division in spring or autumn.

***A.* 'Amethyst'** (x *arendsii* hybrid; illus. p.232). Clump-forming perennial. **H** and **S** 1m (3ft). Tiny, star-shaped, vivid purple flowers are borne in long, rather open, slightly arching panicles in mid-summer above sharply divided, matt, dark green leaves. Is good towards the back of a border.

***A.* 'Beauty of Ernst'** (x *arendsii* hybrid). Clump-forming perennial. **H** 25–30cm (10–12in), **S** 45cm (18in). Compact, oval, sharply divided, vivid green leaves become increasingly tinted wine-red and purple, then develop fiery autumn colours. Tiny, star-shaped, pale pink flowers, maturing to apricot, are borne in open sprays in early summer.

♀ ***A.* 'Brautschleier'**, syn. *A.* Bridal Veil (x *arendsii* hybrid). Clump-forming perennial. **H** and **S** 75cm (30in). Conical plumes of tiny, star-shaped, white flowers open in mid-summer from bright green buds then fade to cream. Oval, sharply divided leaves are glossy and bright green. Is less vigorous than many taller cultivars.

***A.* 'Bressingham Beauty'.** Leafy, clump-forming perennial. **H** and **S** to 1m (3ft). In summer bears feathery, tapering panicles of small, star-shaped, rich pink flowers on strong stems. Broad leaves are divided into oblong to oval, toothed leaflets.

***A.* Bridal Veil.** See *A.* 'Brautschleier'.

♀ ***A.* 'Bronce Elegans'** (*simplicifolia* hybrid). Compact, clump-forming perennial. **H** 30cm (12in), **S** 25cm (10in). Pyramidal, slightly drooping panicles of tiny, star-shaped, purplish-pink flowers are borne in late summer on reddish stems. Oval, sharply divided, dark green leaves slowly turn to reddish-purple.

***A.* 'Bumalda'** (x *arendsii* hybrid) Clump-forming perennial. **H** and **S** 75cm (30in). Tiny, star-shaped, bright white flowers are borne in open panicles in mid-summer. Has more or less oval, jaggedly toothed, red-tinted, bronze leaves.

♀ ***A. chinensis* var. *pumila.*** Clump-forming perennial. **H** 30cm (12in), **S** 20cm (8in). Lower two-thirds of flower stem bears deeply dissected, coarse, toothed, hairy, dark green leaves. Dense, fluffy spikes of tiny, star-shaped, deep raspberry-red flowers appear in summer. Is good for a shaded, moist rock garden.

♀ **var. *taquetii* 'Superba'**, **H** and **S** 1.3m (4½ft), is vigorous and has narrow, upright spikes of vivid magenta-purple flowers. **'Vision in Red'**, **H** 70cm (28in), **S** 65cm (26in), has a vigorous, upright habit, very dark, slightly metallic green leaves and strong, dark purple stems and leaf stalks bearing purple flowers.

♀ ***A.* x *crispa* 'Perkeo'**, syn. *A.* 'Perkeo', illus. p. 339.

***A.* 'Deutschland'** (*japonica* hybrid; illus. p.232). Early-flowering, slow-spreading, clump-forming, robust perennial. **H** 50cm (20in), **S** 30cm (12in). Has oval, sharply divided, bright green leaves. Slightly arching panicles of tiny, star-shaped, white flowers are produced in late spring.

***A.* 'Dusseldorf'** (*japonica* hybrid). Tightly clump-forming perennial. **H** 60cm (24in), **S** 45cm (18in). Produces neat, regular panicles of tiny, star-shaped, salmon-pink flowers in mid summer above oval, sharply divided, slightly bronze- or deep-red tinted, dark green leaves.

***A.* 'Eliblo'.** See *A.* Elizabeth Bloom.

***A.* Elizabeth Bloom ('Eliblo')** (x *arendsii* hybrid). Vigorous, clump-forming perennial. **H** 80cm (32in), **S** 60cm (24in). Oval, densely packed panicles of tiny, star-shaped, pale purplish pink flowers are borne in mid-summer. Has oval, sharply divided, glossy, very dark green leaves.

***A.* 'Europa'** (*japonica* hybrid; illus. p.232). Early-flowering, clump-forming perennial. **H** 60cm (24in), **S** 45cm (18in). In early summer produces tiny, star-shaped, unusually broad-petalled, pale purplish-pink flowers in dense panicles. Has oval, sharply divided, glossy, mid-green leaves.

♀ ***A.* 'Fanal'** illus. p.439.

***A.* 'Feuer'**, syn. *A.* Fire (x *arendsii* hybrid; illus. p.232). Clump-forming perennial. **H** and **S** 1m (3ft). Conical plumes of tiny, star-shaped, rich purplish-red flowers are borne in early summer above oval, sharply divided, glossy, bright green leaves.

***A.* Fire.** See *A.* 'Feuer'.

♀ ***A. glaberrima* var. *saxatilis.*** Mound-forming perennial. **H** 10cm (4in), **S** 15cm (6in). In summer produces tiny, star-shaped, white-tipped, mauve flowers in short spikes. Oval, sharply divided, glossy, deeply toothed, dark green leaves are tinted red underneath. Thrives in consistently moist soil.

***A.* 'Gnom'**, syn. *A. simplicifolia* 'Gnom'. Arching, clump-forming, slender-stemmed perennial. **H** 15cm (6in), **S** 10cm (4in). Has oval, deeply lobed or cut, crimped, reddish-green leaves in a basal rosette. Produces dense racemes of tiny, star-shaped, pink flowers in summer. Is good for a shaded, moist rock garden or peat bed. Self seeds in damp places but will not come true.

***A.* 'Granat'** (illus. p.232). Clump-forming, leafy perennial. **H** 60cm (2ft), **S** to 1m (3ft). Produces pyramidal trusses of tiny, star-shaped, deep red flowers in summer above broad, bronze-flushed, rich green leaves, which are divided into oblong to oval, toothed leaflets.

***A.* 'Irrlicht'** (illus. p.232). Leafy perennial. **H** 45–60cm (1½–2ft), **S** to 1m (3ft). Bears tapering, feathery plumes of tiny, white flowers in summer. Foliage is dark green and flowers remain on the plant, dried and brown, well into winter.

***A.* 'Koln'** (*japonica* hybrid). Clump-forming perennial. **H** 60cm (24in), **S** 45cm (18in). Panicles of tiny, star-shaped, deep pink flowers are borne in mid-summer. Oval, sharply divided, dark green leaves are tinted bronze or deep red.

***A.* 'Montgomery'** (illus. p.232). Leafy perennial. **H** 75cm (2½ft), **S** to 1m (3ft). Bears tapering, feathery plumes of tiny, deep salmon-red flowers in summer. Foliage is broad and divided into leaflets; flowers, brown when dried, remain on the plant well into winter.

***A.* 'Ostrich Plume'.** See *A.* 'Straussenfeder'.

***A.* 'Perkeo'.** See *A.* x *crispa* 'Perkeo'.

***A* 'Professor van der Wielen'** (*thunbergii* hybrid). Clump-forming perennial. **H** 1.2m (4ft), **S** 1m (3ft). Arching sprays of tiny, star-shaped, pure white flowers are borne in early summer above oval, sharply divided, fresh green leaves.

♀ ***A.* 'Rheinland'** (*japonica* hybrid). Clump-forming perennial. **H** 50cm (20in), **S** 45cm (18in). Compact, conical, upright panicles of tiny, star-shaped, deep pink flowers are produced in early and mid-summer above conspicuously divided, mid-green leaves.

***A. simplicifolia* 'Gnom'.** See *A.* 'Gnom'.

♀ ***A.* 'Sprite'** (illus. p.232). Clump-forming, dwarf, leafy perennial. **H** 50cm (20in), **S** to 1m (3ft). Has feathery, tapering panicles of tiny, star-shaped, shell-pink flowers in summer, borne above broad leaves divided into narrowly oval, toothed leaflets.

♀ ***A.* 'Straussenfeder'**, syn *A.* 'Ostrich Plume' (illus. p.232). Leafy perennial. **H** and **S** to 1m (3ft). Has divided leaves. Arching, feathery, tapering plumes of tiny, coral-pink flowers in summer; dry, brown flowers remain on plant well into winter.

***A.* 'Venus'** illus. p.234.

***A.* 'Willie Buchanan'** (*simplicifolia* hybrid). Clump-forming perennial. **H** 20–30cm (8–12in), **S** 20cm (8in). Produces neat clumps of divided, red- or bronze-tinted, green leaves. Loose, conical sprays of tiny, star-shaped, pale pink flowers, with white petals, are borne in mid- and late summer.

ASTILBOIDES

SAXIFRAGACEAE

A genus of a single species of hardy perennial grown for interesting foliage with turns reddish in autumn, requiring a semi-shady, moist, but well drained position. Propagate by division or seed sown in autumn.

A. tabularis, syn. *Rodgersia tabularis*, illus. p.435.

ASTRANTIA

Masterwort

UMBELLIFERAE/APIACEAE

Genus of perennials, widely used in flower arrangements. Fully hardy. Requires sun or semi-shade and well-drained soil. Propagate by division in spring or by seed when fresh, in late summer.

A. major Clump-forming perennial. **H** 60cm (24in), **S** 45cm (18in). Produces greenish-white, sometimes pink-tinged flower heads throughout summer–autumn above a dense mass of divided, mid-green leaves. **subsp. *carinthiaca*** see *A.m.* subsp. involucrata.**'Hadspen Blood'** has dark red bracts and flowers. **subsp. *involucrata*** (syn. *A.m.* subsp. *carinthiaca*) has pink-tinged flower heads with long bracts through summer. **'Roma'** illus. p.278. **'Ruby Wedding'** illus. p.238.
♀***A. maxima*** illus. p.278.

ASTROPHYTUM

CACTACEAE

Genus of slow-growing, perennial cacti, grown for their freely produced, flattish, yellow flowers, some with red centres. Frost tender, min. 5°C (41°F). Prefers sun and very well-drained, lime-rich soil. Allow to dry completely in winter. Is prone to rot if wet. Propagate by seed sown in spring or summer.
A. asterias, syn. *Echinocactus asterias* (Sea urchin, Silver dollar cactus). Slow-growing, slightly domed, perennial cactus. **H** 8–10cm (3–4in), **S** 10cm (4in). Spineless stem has about 8 low ribs bearing small, tufted areoles. Produces bright yellow flowers, to 6cm (2½in) across, in summer.
♀***A. myriostigma***, syn. *Echinocactus myriostigma* (Bishop's cap, Bishop's mitre) illus. p.494.
A. ornatum, syn. *Echinocactus ornatus*, illus. p.495.

Asystasia bella. See *Mackaya bella.*

ATHEROSPERMA

ATHEROSPERMATACEAE/ MONIMIACEAE

Genus of evergreen trees, grown for their foliage and flowers in summer. Frost tender, min. 3–5°C (37–41°F). Needs full light or partial shade and well-drained soil. Water containerized specimens moderately, less in winter. Pruning is tolerated if necessary. Propagation is by seed sown in spring or by semi-ripe cuttings taken in summer.
A. moschatum (Australian sassafras, Tasmanian sassafras). Evergreen, spreading tree, conical when young. **H** 15–25m (50–80ft), **S** 5–10m (15–30ft). Has lance-shaped, nutmeg-scented, glossy leaves, slightly toothed and covered with white down beneath. Produces small, saucer-shaped, creamy-white flowers in summer.

ATHROTAXIS

TAXODIACEAE

Genus of conifers with awl-shaped leaves that clasp stems. See also CONIFERS.
A. selaginoides (King William pine). Irregularly conical conifer. **H** 15m (50ft) or more, **S** 5m (15ft). Half hardy. Has tiny, thick-textured, loosely overlapping, dark green leaves and insignificant, globular cones.

ATHYRIUM

ATHYRIACEAE/WOODSIACEAE

Genus of deciduous or, occasionally, semi-evergreen ferns. Fully hardy to frost tender, min. 5°C (41°F). Needs shade and humus-rich, moist soil. Remove fading fronds regularly. Propagate by spores in late summer or by division in autumn or winter.
♀***A. filix-femina*** (Lady fern). Deciduous fern. **H** 60cm–1.2m (2–4ft), **S** 30cm–1m (1–3ft). Fully hardy. Dainty, lance-shaped, much-divided, arching fronds are pale green. Has very variable frond dissection.
***A.* 'Ghost'** illus. p.290.
A. goeringianum. See *A. niponicum.*
A. niponicum, syn. *A. goeringianum, A. nipponicum.* **var. *pictum* 'Burgundy Lace'** illus. p.290.
A. nipponicum. See *A. niponicum.*
♀***A. otophorum.*** Semi-evergreen fern. **H** and **S** to 75cm (30in). Fully hardy (borderline). Has arching, broadly ovate, mid-green or purple- tinged, divided fronds, 45–75cm (18–30in) long. Stalk and midrib are a contrasting deep wine-purple.

ATRIPLEX

CHENOPODIACEAE

Genus of annuals, perennials and evergreen or semi-evergreen shrubs, grown for their foliage. Grows well by the coast. Fully to half hardy. Needs full sun and well-drained soil. Propagate by softwood cuttings taken in summer or by seed sown in autumn.
A. halimus (Tree purslane). Semi-evergreen, bushy shrub. **H** 2m (6ft), **S** 3m (10ft). Frost hardy. Oval leaves are silvery-grey. Produces flowers very rarely.
A. hortensis* var. *rubra (Red mountain spinach, Red orach). Fast-growing, erect annual. **H** 1.2m (4ft), **S** 30cm (1ft). Half hardy. Triangular, deep red leaves, to 15cm (6in) long, are edible. Bears insignificant flowers in summer.

AUBRIETA

CRUCIFERAE/BRASSICACEAE

Genus of evergreen, trailing and mound-forming perennials. Is useful on dry banks, walls and in rock gardens. Fully hardy. Thrives in a sunny position and in any well-drained soil. To maintain a compact shape, cut back hard after flowering. Propagate by greenwood cuttings in summer or by semi-ripe cuttings in late summer or autumn.
***A.* 'Carnival'.** See *A.* 'Hartswood Purple'.
***A.* 'Cobalt Violet'.** Evergreen, mound-forming perennial. **H** 10cm (4in), **S** 20cm (8in). Has small, soft green leaves. Single, blue-violet flowers are borne in short, terminal spikes in spring.
***A. deltoidea* 'Argenteovariegata'** illus. p.354.
♀***A.* 'Doctor Mules'.** Vigorous, evergreen, mound-forming perennial. **H** 5–8cm (2–3in), **S** 30cm (12in). Has rounded, toothed, soft green leaves and, in spring, large, single, rich purple flowers on short spikes.
♀***A.* 'Greencourt Purple'** illus. p.354.
***A.* 'Gurgedyke'.** Evergreen, mound-forming perennial. **H** 10cm (4in), **S** 20cm (8in). Bears rounded, toothed, soft green leaves. Produces 4-petalled, deep purple flowers in spring.
***A.* 'Hartswood Purple'**, syn. *A.* 'Carnival'. Vigorous, evergreen, mound-forming perennial. **H** 10cm (4in), **S** 30cm (12in). Has small, soft green leaves and many short spikes of large, single, violet-purple flowers borne in spring.
***A.* 'Joy'** illus. p.353.
***A.* 'J.S. Baker'** illus. p.354.
***A.* 'Purple Charm'** illus. p.355.

AUCUBA

CORNACEAE/AUCUBACEAE

Genus of evergreen shrubs, grown for their foliage and fruits. To obtain fruits, grow both male and female plants. Makes good house plants when kept in a cool, shaded position. Fully to frost hardy. Tolerates full sun through to dense shade. Grow in any but water- logged soil. To restrict growth, cut old shoots back hard in spring. Propagate by semi-ripe cuttings taken in summer.
A. japonica. Evergreen, dense, bushy shrub. **H** 2.5m (8ft), **S** 2.5m (8ft). Frost hardy. Has stout, green shoots and glossy, dark green leaves. Small, purplish flowers in mid-spring are followed on female plants by rounded to egg-shaped, bright red berries. ♀**'Crotonifolia'**, **H** 2m (6ft), **S** 2m (6ft), has leaves heavily mottled yellow. **'Gold Dust'** has gold-speckled, dark green leaves. Bright green leaves of **'Picturata'** (male) each have a central, golden blotch. Some plants of 'Crotonifolia' and 'Picturata' are known to be female and have produced fruits.

AURINIA

BRASSICACEAE/CRUCIFERAE

Genus of evergreen perennials, grown for their grey-green foliage and showy flower sprays. Is suitable for rock gardens, walls and banks. Fully hardy. Needs sun and well-drained soil. Propagate by softwood or greenwood cuttings in early summer or by seed in autumn.
♀***A. saxatilis***, syn. *Alyssum saxatile*, (Gold dust) illus. p.335. ♀**'Citrina'** illus. p.335. **'Dudley Nevill'** is an evergreen, clump-forming perennial. **H** 23cm (9in), **S** 30cm (12in). Has oval, hairy, grey-green leaves and, in late spring and early summer, produces racemes of many small, 4-petalled, buff-yellow flowers.
'Variegata' illus. p.335.

AUSTROCEDRUS

CUPRESSACEAE

Genus of conifers with flattish sprays of scale-like leaves. See also CONIFERS.
A. chilensis, syn. *Libocedrus chilensis*, (Chilean incense cedar) illus. p.100.

Austrocylindropuntia cylindrica. See *Opuntia cylindrica*
Austrocylindropuntia verschaffeltii. See *Opuntia verschaffeltii*
Avena candida. See *Helictotrichon sempervirens.*
Avena sempervirens. See *Helictotrichon sempervirens.*

AZARA

FLACOURTIACEAE

Genus of evergreen shrubs and trees, grown for their foliage and also for their yellow flowers that are composed of a mass of stamens. Frost to half hardy; in cold climates, plants are best grown situated against a south- or west-facing wall for added protection. Grows in sun or shade, and in fertile, well-drained soil. Propagate by semi- ripe cuttings in summer.
A. lanceolata. Evergreen, bushy shrub or spreading tree. **H** and **S** 6m (20ft). Frost hardy. Has narrowly oval, sharply toothed, bright green leaves. Has small, rounded clusters of pale yellow flowers in late spring or early summer.
♀***A. microphylla*** illus. p.118.
'Variegata' illus. p.119.
♀***A. serrata*** illus. p.195.

AZOLLA

AZOLLACEAE

Genus of deciduous, perennial, floating water ferns, grown for their decorative foliage and also to control algal growth by reducing light in water beneath. Frost to half hardy. Grows in sun or shade. If not kept in check, may be invasive; reduce spread by removing portions with a net. Propagate by redistributing clusters of plantlets when they appear.
A. caroliniana. See *A. filiculoides.*
A. filiculoides, syn. *A. caroliniana*, (Fairy moss, water fern). Deciduous, perennial, floating water fern. **S** indefinite. Half hardy. Divided fronds vary from red to purple in full sun and from pale green to blue-green in shade.

AZORELLA

UMBELLIFERAE/APIACEAE

Genus of evergreen, tufted or spreading perennials, grown for their flowers and neat, rosetted foliage. Is useful as an alpine house plant. Fully hardy. Thrives in full light and well-drained soil. Propagate by division in spring.
A. nivalis. See *A. trifurcata.*
A. trifurcata, syn. *A. nivalis*, illus. p.376.

AZORINA

CAMPANULACEAE

Genus of one species of erect evergreen shrub with bell-shaped flowers. Frost tender, min. 5°C (41°F). Needs full light and fertile, moist but well-drained soil. Propagate by seed in spring or take softwood or semi-ripe cuttings in summer.
A. vidalii, syn. *Campanula vidalii*, illus. p.453.

Azureocereus hertlingianus. See *Browningia hertlingiana.*

B

BABIANA

IRIDACEAE

Genus of spring- and early summer-flowering corms, valued for their brightly coloured flowers, which are somewhat like freesias. Frost tender, min. 10°C (50°F). Requires a position in sun and well-drained soil. Propagate in autumn by seed or natural division of corms.
B. disticha. See *B. fragrans*.
B. fragrans, syn. *B. disticha, B. plicata*. Spring-flowering corm. **H** 10–20cm (4–8in), **S** 5–8cm (2–3in). Has a fan of lance-shaped, erect, basal leaves and short spikes of funnel-shaped, violet-blue flowers, 4–5cm (1½–2in) long, with yellow-patched petals.
B. plicata. See *B. fragrans*.
B. rubrocyanea (Winecups) illus. p.418.
♀ ***B. stricta.*** Spring-flowering corm. **H** 10–20cm (4–8in), **S** 5–8cm (2–3in). Produces a fan of narrowly lance-shaped, erect, basal leaves and short spikes of up to 10 funnel-shaped, purple, blue, cream or pale yellow flowers, 2.5–4cm (1–1½in) long and sometimes red-centred.

BACCHARIS

COMPOSITAE/ASTERACEAE

Genus of evergreen or deciduous, mainly autumn-flowering shrubs, grown for their foliage and fruits. Is useful for exposed, coastal gardens and dry soil. Fully hardy. Requires a position in full sun and well-drained soil. Propagate by softwood cuttings in summer.
B. halimifolia (Bush groundsel). Vigorous, deciduous, bushy shrub. **H** and **S** 4m (12ft). Has grey-green, sharply toothed, oval leaves. Large clusters of tiny, white flower heads in mid-autumn are followed by fluffy, white heads of tiny fruits.

Bahia lanata. See *Eriophyllum lanatum*.

BALDELLIA

ALISMATACEAE

Genus of deciduous or evergreen, perennial, bog plants and submerged water plants, grown for their foliage. Frost hardy. Prefers a position in sun, but tolerates shade. Remove fading foliage and excess growth as required. Propagate by division in spring or summer.
B. ranunculoides, syn. *Alisma ranunculoides, Echinodorus ranunculoides*. Deciduous, perennial, bog plant or submerged water plant. **H** 23cm (9in), **S** 15cm (6in). Has lance-shaped, mid-green leaves and, in summer, umbels of small, 3-parted, pink or white flowers with basal, yellow marks.

BALLOTA

LABIATEA/LAMIACEAE

Genus of perennials and evergreen or deciduous sub-shrubs, grown for their foliage and flowers. Frost hardy. Requires very well-drained soil and full sun. Cut back in spring before growth starts. Propagate by semi-ripe cuttings in summer.
♀ ***B. acetabulosa*** illus. p.165.
♀ ***B. pseudodictamnus*** illus. p.347.

BAMBUSA

GRAMINEAE/POACEAE

See also GRASSES, BAMBOOS, RUSHES and SEDGES.
B. glaucescens. See *B. multiplex*.
B. multiplex, syn. *B. glaucescens* (Hedge bamboo). Evergreen, clump-forming bamboo. **H** to 15m (50ft), **S** indefinite. Has narrow leaves, 10–15cm (4–6in) long. Is useful for a hedge or windbreak.

BANKSIA

PROTEACEAE

Genus of evergreen shrubs and trees, grown for their flowers and foliage. Frost tender, min. 7–10°C (45–50°F). Requires full light and sharply drained, sandy soil that contains little phosphates or nitrates. Water containerized plants moderately when in full growth, sparingly at other times. Freely ventilate plants grown under glass. Propagate by seed in spring.
B. baxteri. Evergreen, spreading, open shrub. **H** and **S** 2–3m (6–10ft). Leathery, mid-green leaves are strap-shaped, cut from the midrib into triangular, sharply pointed lobes. Produces dense, spherical heads of small, tubular, yellow flowers in summer.
B. coccinea illus. p.456.
B. ericifolia (Heath banksia). Evergreen, irregularly rounded, wiry, freely branching shrub. **H** and **S** to 3m (10ft). Has small, needle-like leaves and dense, upright, bottlebrush-like spikes, each 10–15cm (4–6in) long, of small, tubular, bronze-red or yellow flowers in late winter and spring.
B. serrata. Evergreen, bushy, upright shrub or tree. **H** 3–10m (10–30ft), **S** 1.5–3m (5–10ft). Oblong to lance-shaped, saw-toothed, leathery leaves are mid- to deep green. Small, tubular, reddish-budded, cream flowers appear in dense, upright, bottlebrush-like spikes, each 10–15cm (4–6in) long, from spring to late summer.

BAPTISIA

LEGUMINOSAE/PAPILIONACEAE

Genus of summer-flowering perennials, grown for their flowers. Fully hardy. Requires full sun and deep, well-drained, preferably neutral to acid soil. Is best not disturbed once planted. Propagate by division in early spring or by seed in autumn.
♀ ***B. australis*** (False indigo) illus. p.240.

Barbacenia elegans. See *Vellozia elegans*.

BARBAREA

CRUCIFERAE/BRASSICACEAE

Genus of summer-flowering perennials, biennials and annuals. Most species are weeds or winter salad plants, but the variegated form of *B. vulgaris* is grown for decorative purposes. Fully hardy. Grows in a sunny or shady position and in any well-drained but not very dry soil. Propagate by seed or division in spring.
B. vulgaris (Winter cress, Yellow rocket). **'Variegata'** is a rosette-forming perennial. **H** 25–45cm (10–18in), **S** to 23cm (9in). Has long, toothed, glossy leaves, blotched with cream. Produces heads of small, silvery-yellow flowers in early summer.

BARLERIA

ACANTHACEAE

Genus of evergreen shrubs and perennials, grown for their flowers. Frost tender, min. 7–18°C (45–64°F). Needs full light or partial shade and fertile soil. Water potted plants well when in full growth, moderately at other times. In the growing season, prune tips of young plants to encourage branching. For a more compact habit, shorten long stems after flowering. May be propagated by seed in spring or by greenwood or semi-ripe cuttings in summer.
B. cristata (Philippine violet). Evergreen, semi-erect shrub. **H** and **S** 60cm–1.2m (2–4ft). Min. 15–18°C (59–64°F). Has elliptic, coarsely haired leaves. Tubular, light violet flowers, sometimes pale pink or white, are produced from upper leaf axils in summer.
B. obtusa. Evergreen, erect, spreading shrub. **H** and **S** to 1m (3ft). Min. 7–10°C (45–50°F). Leaves are elliptic. Tubular, mauve flowers appear from upper leaf axils in winter–spring.

Barosma pulchella. See *Agathosma pulchella*.
Bartonia aurea. See *Mentzelia lindleyi*.

BARTLETTINA

COMPOSITAE/ASTERACEAE

Genus of perennials, sub-shrubs and shrubs, many of which are evergreen, grown mainly for their flowers, some also for their architectural foliage. Fully hardy to frost tender, min. 5–13°C (41–55°F). Requires full light or partial shade. Will grow in any conditions, although most species prefer moist but well-drained soil. Water containerized plants freely when in full growth, moderately at other times. Prune shrubs lightly after flowering or in spring. Propagate by seed in spring; shrubs and sub-shrubs may also be propagated by softwood or greenwood cuttings in summer, perennials by division in early spring or autumn. Red spider mite and whitefly may be troublesome.
B. sordida, syn. *Eupatorium ianthinum, E. sordidum*. Evergreen, rounded, robust-stemmed shrub. **H** and **S** 1–2m (3–6ft). Frost tender, min. 10–13°C (50–55°F). Oval, serrated, deep green leaves are red haired. Produces fragrant, pompon-like, violet-purple flower heads in flattened clusters, 10cm (4in) wide, mainly in winter.

BASSIA

SYN. KOCHIA

CHENOPODIACEAE

Genus of annuals and perennials, grown for their habit, the feathery effect of their leaves and their autumn tints. Half hardy. Does best in sun and in fertile, well-drained soil. May require support in very windy areas. Propagate by seed sown under glass in early to mid-spring, or outdoors in late spring.
B. scoparia f. trichophylla illus. p.316.

BAUERA

CUNONIACEAE

Genus of evergreen shrubs, grown mainly for their flowers. Frost tender, min. 3–5°C (37–41°F). Needs full sun and humus-rich, well-drained, neutral to acid soil. Water potted plants moderately, less when not in full growth. Remove straggly stems after flowering. May be propagated by seed sown in spring or by semi-ripe cuttings taken in late summer.
B. rubioides. Evergreen, bushy, wiry-stemmed shrub, usually of spreading habit. **H** and **S** 30–60cm (1–2ft). Leaves each have 3 oval to lance-shaped, glossy leaflets. Bowl-shaped, pink or white flowers appear in early spring and summer.

BAUHINIA

LEGUMINOSAE/PAPILIONACEAE

Genus of evergreen, semi-evergreen or deciduous trees, shrubs and scandent climbers, grown for their flowers. Frost tender, min. 5–18°C (41–64°F). Requires full light and fertile, well-drained soil. Water containerized specimens freely when in full growth, less in winter. Thin out congested growth after flowering. Propagate by seed in spring.
B. galpinii, syn. *B. punctata*. Semi-evergreen or evergreen, spreading shrub, occasionally semi-climbing. **H** 3m (10ft), **S** 2m (8ft). Frost tender, min. 5°C (41°F). Has 2-lobed leaves and, in summer, fragrant, bright brick-red flowers.
B. punctata. See *B. galpinii*.
B. variegata illus. p.450. **'Candida'** is a deciduous tree, rounded when young, spreading with age. **H** 2m (8ft), **S** 3m (10ft). Frost tender, min. 15–18°C (59–64°F). Has broadly oval, deeply notched leaves and fragrant, pure white flowers, 10cm (4in) across, in winter–spring or sometimes later.

BEAUCARNEA

AGAVACEAE/DRACAENACEAE

Genus of evergreen shrubs and trees, grown mainly for their intriguing, overall appearance. Frost tender, min. 7°C (45°F). Needs full light and sharply drained, fertile soil; drought conditions are tolerated. Water potted specimens moderately; allow compost almost to dry out between waterings. Propagate by seed or suckers in spring or by stem-tip cuttings in summer.
♀ ***B. recurvata***, syn. *Nolina recurvata, N. tuberculata*, illus. p.451.

BEAUMONTIA

APOCYNACEAE

Genus of evergreen, woody-stemmed, twining climbers, grown for their large, fragrant flowers and handsome leaves. Frost tender, min. 7–10°C (45–50°F). Requires fertile, well-drained soil and full light. Water freely in growing season, sparingly otherwise. Provide support.

Thin out previous season's growth after flowering. Propagate by semi-ripe cuttings in late summer.
B. grandiflora illus. p.459.

BEGONIA

BEGONIACEAE

Genus of evergreen or deciduous shrubs and small, tree-like plants, perennials and annuals, grown for their colourful flowers and/or ornamental leaves. Prefers slightly acidic soil. Is susceptible to powdery mildew and botrytis from late spring to early autumn. Commonly cultivated begonias are divided into the following groupings, each with varying cultivation requirements. See also feature panel p.317.

Cane-stemmed begonias
Evergreen, woody perennials, many known as 'Angelwings', with usually erect, cane-like stems bearing regularly spaced, swollen nodes and flowers in large, pendulous panicles. Encourage branching by pinching out growing tips. New growth develops from base of plant. Frost tender, min. 10°C (50°F). Grow under glass in good light but not direct sun (poor light reduces quantity of flowers) and in free-draining, loam-based compost. Stake tall plants. Propagate in spring by seed or tip cuttings.

Rex-cultorum begonias
Mostly evergreen, rhizomatous perennials of variable habit derived from crosses of *B. rex* and related species. They are grown for their brilliantly coloured, oval to lance-shaped leaves, 8–30cm (3–12in) long, that are sometimes spirally twisted. Frost tender, min. 13–15°C (55–9°F), but preferably 21–4°C (70–75°F), with 40–75% relative humidity. Grow under glass in cool climates, in partial shade and in well-drained soil; water only sparingly. Do not allow water to remain on the leaves, otherwise they become susceptible to botrytis. Propagate in spring by seed, leaf cuttings or division of rhizomes.

Rhizomatous begonias
Variable, mostly evergreen, rhizomatous perennials, grown for their foliage and small, single flowers. Smooth, crested or puckered, green or brown leaves, 8–30cm (3–12in) long, often marked silver, are sometimes spirally twisted. Creeping cultivars are more freely branched than erect ones and are useful for hanging baskets. Frost tender, min. 13–15°C (55–9°F), but preferably 19°C (66°F), with 40–75% relative humidity. Grow under glass in cool climates, in partial shade and in well-drained soil; water only sparingly. Do not allow water to remain on the leaves, otherwise they become susceptible to botrytis. Propagate in spring by seed, leaf cuttings or division of rhizomes.

Semperflorens begonias
Evergreen, bushy perennials, derived from *B. cucullata* var. *hookeri*, *B. schmidtiana* and other species, often grown as half-hardy bedding annuals. Stems are soft, succulent and branch freely, bearing generally rounded, green, bronze or variegated leaves, 5cm (2in) long. Flowers are single or double. Pinch out growing tips to produce bushy plants. Frost tender, min. 10–15°C (50–59°F). Needs sun or partial shade and well-drained soil. Propagate in spring by seed or stem cuttings.

Shrub-like begonias
Evergreen, multi-stemmed, bushy perennials, usually freely branched with flexible, erect or pendent stems, often hairy. Leaves may be hairy or glabrous and up to 15cm (6in) across, 10–30cm (4–12in) long. Single flowers are pink, cream or white. Frost tender, min. 7°C (45°F) with 55% relative humidity. Grow under glass in good light and moist but well-drained soil. Propagate in spring by seed or stem cuttings.

Tuberous begonias (including the Tuberhybrida, Multiflora and Pendula begonias)
Mostly upright, bushy, tuberous, winter-dormant perennials grown for their foliage and flowers. Tuberhybrida begonias, **H** and **S** 75cm (30in), vary from pendent to erect, with sparsely branched, succulent stems and oval, pointed, glossy, bright to dark green leaves, 20cm (8in) long. Most are summer flowering and mainly double-flowered. Multiflora cultivars, **H** and **S** 30cm (12in), are more bushy and have 8cm (3in) long leaves and single, semi-double or double, flowers, each 4–5cm (1½–2in) across, in summer; tolerates full sun. Pendula cultivars, **H** to 1m (3ft), have long, thin, trailing stems; leaves are 6–8cm (2½–3in) long. Masses of single or double flowers are borne in summer. Frost tender, min. 5–7°C (41–5°F). Outdoors, grow in dappled shade and moist conditions; under glass, plant in cool shade with 65–70% relative humidity. Tubers are dormant in winter. Start into growth in spring for mid-summer to early autumn flowering. Remove all flower buds until stems show at least 3 pairs of leaves; with large-flowered types allow only central male bud to flower, so remove flanking buds. Plants may require staking. Propagate in spring by seed, stem or basal cuttings or division of tubers.

Winter-flowering begonias
Evergreen, low-growing, very compact perennials, with succulent, thin stems, that are often included in the tuberous group. Two main groups are recognized: the single-flowered, usually pink or white, Lorraine, Cheimantha or Christmas begonias; and the single, semi-double or double, Elatior and Rieger begonias that occur in a wide range of colours. Leaves are green or bronze, 5cm (2in) long. Flowers are borne mainly from late autumn to mid-spring. Frost tender, min. 18°C (64°F) with 40% relative humidity. Indirect sun and moist soil are preferred. Cut back old stems to 10cm (4in) after flowering. Propagate in spring by seed or stem cuttings.

B. albopicta (illus. p.317). Fast-growing, evergreen, cane-stemmed begonia. **H** to 1m (3ft), **S** 30cm (1ft). Freely branched, green stems turn brown-green when mature. Narrowly oval to lance-chaped, wavy-edged, green leaves are silver-spotted. Has clusters of single, green-white flowers in summer-autumn.
B. angularis, syn. *B. compta*, *B. stipulacea* of gardens, *B zebrina*. Evergreen, cane-stemmed begonia. **H** 60cm–1.2m (2–4ft), **S** 30cm (1ft). Bears well-branched, angular stems and oval, wavy-edged, 20cm (8in) long, grey-green leaves, with silver-grey veins, pale green beneath. Single, white flowers are produced in winter-spring.
***B.* 'Apricot Cascade'**. Pendent Tuberhybrida begonia. **H** and **S** 60cm (2ft). Has emerald-green leaves and, from early summer to mid-autumn, double, orange-apricot flowers. Other cascades are **'Bridal Cascade'** (pink-edged, white petals), **'Crimson Cascade'**, **'Gold Cascade'** and **'Orange Cascade'.**
***B.* 'Beatrice Haddrell'.** Evergreen, creeping, rhizomatous begonia. **H** 20–30cm (8–12in), **S** 25–30cm (10–12in). Oval leaves are deeply cleft, 8–15cm (3–6in) long, and dark green with paler veins. Produces single, pink flowers, above foliage, in winter and early spring.
***B.* 'Bethlehem Star'.** Evergreen, creeping, rhizomatous begonia. **H** 20–30cm (8–12in), **S** 25–30cm (10–12in). Oval, slightly indented, almost black leaves, less than 8cm (3in) long, each have a central, creamy-green star. Bears masses of single, pale pink flowers, with darker pink spots, from late winter to early spring.
***B.* 'Billie Langdon'.** Upright Tuberhybrida begonia. **H** 60cm (2ft), **S** 45cm (18in). In summer has masses of heavily veined, double, white flowers, each 18cm (7in) across, with a perfect rose-bud centre.
***B.* 'Bokit'.** Evergreen, erect, rhizomatous begonia. **H** 20–30cm (8–12in), **S** 25–35cm (10–14in). Has oval, spirally twisted, yellow-green leaves with brown tiger stripes. Bears masses of single, white flowers, flecked with pink, in winter.
***B. boliviensis* 'Bonfire'** (illus. p.317). Semi-trailing begonia. **H** 75cm (30in), **S** 100cm (36in). Succulent stems bear lance-shaped, slightly hairy leaves, 12cm (5in) long, with narrow, toothed, red edges. Produces abundant, pendulous, single, orange-red flowers from late spring to autumn.
B. bowerae (Eyelash begonia; illus. p.317). Evergreen, creeping, rhizomatous begonia. **H** 25–30cm (10–12in), **S** 20–25cm (8–10in). Has oval, bright green leaves, 2.5cm (1in) long, with chocolate marks and bristles around edges. Bears single, pink-tinted, white flowers freely in winter.
***B.* 'Bridal Cascade'.** See *B.* 'Apricot Cascade'.
***B.* 'Can-can',** see *B.* 'Herzog von Sagan'.
***B.* 'City of Ballarat'.** Vigorous, upright Tuberhybrida begonia. **H** 60cm (2ft), **S** 45cm (18in). Leaves are rich dark green. Carries double, glowing orange flowers, each 18cm (7in) across, with broad petals and a formal centre, in summer.
B. coccinea (Angelwing begonia). Evergreen, cane-stemmed begonia. **H** 1.2m (4ft), **S** 30cm (1ft). Produces narrowly oval, glossy, green leaves, buff-coloured beneath, and, in spring, many single, pink or coral-red flowers.
♀ ***B.* 'Cocktail Series'.** Semperflorens begonia. **H** and **S** 20–30cm (8–12in). Produces rounded, wavy, green-bronze leaves and pink, red or white flowers from summer until autumn frosts.
***B.* 'Corallina de Lucerna'.** See *B.* 'Lucerna'.
***B.* 'Crimson Cascade'.** See *B.* 'Apricot Cascade'.
***B.* 'Curly Merry Christmas'.** Rex-cultorum begonia. **H** 25cm (10in), **S** 30cm (12in). Is a sport of *B.* 'Merry Christmas' with spirally twisted leaves.
B. dichroa. Evergreen, cane-stemmed begonia. **H** 35cm (14in), **S** 25cm (10in). Oval leaves are mid-green, 12cm (5in) long; occasionally new leaves bear silver spots. Produces small, single, orange flowers, each with a white ovary, in summer.
***B.* Dragon Wing Red ('Bepared')** (Dragon Wing Series) illus. p.317. Vigorous, Semperflorens begonia. **H** and **S** 45cm (18in). Semi-trailing, succulent stems bear oval, slightly waxy, mid-green leaves, 5–7.5cm (2–3in). Produces clusters of single, scarlet flowers from late summer to autumn.
♀ ***B. dregei*** (Mapleleaf begonia; illus. p.317). Semi-tuberous begonia. **H** 75cm (30in), **S** 35cm (14in). Has small, maple-like, lobed, purple-veined, bronze leaves, red beneath and at times silver-speckled when young. Has profuse, pendent, single, white flowers in summer. Needs winter rest.
***B.* 'Duartei'.** Rex-cultorum begonia. **H** and **S** 45–60cm (18–24in). Has spirally twisted, red-haired, very dark green leaves, over 15cm (6in) long, with silver-grey streaks and almost black edges. Is difficult to grow to maturity.
B.* x *erythrophylla. See *B.* 'Erythrophylla'.
***B.* 'Erythrophylla'**, syn. *B.* x *erythrophylla*, *B.* 'Feastii'. Evergreen, creeping, rhizomatous begonia. **H** 20cm (8in), **S** 23–30cm (9–12in). Thick, mid-green leaves, 8–15cm (3–6in) long, are almost rounded, with leaf stalks attached to centre of red undersides; slightly wavy margins have white hairs. Produces single, light pink flowers well above foliage, in early spring.
***B.* 'Feastii'.** See *B.* 'Erythrophylla'.
***B.* 'Flamboyant'.** Upright Tuberhybrida begonia. **H** 17cm (7in), **S** 15cm (6in). Leaves are slender and bright green. Has single, scarlet flowers in profusion in summer.
B. foliosa. Evergreen, shrub-like begonia. **H** 30–50cm (12–20in), **S** 30–35cm (12–14in). Bears erect, then arching stems and oval, toothed, dark green leaves, 1cm (½in) long. Has very small, single, white flowers in spring and autumn. Is susceptible to whitefly. ♀ **var. *miniata,*** syn. *B. fuchsiioides* (Fuchsia begonia). Evergreen, shrub-like begonia. **H** to 1.2m (4ft), **S** 30cm (1ft). Oval, toothed leaves are numerous and dark green, 4cm (1½in) long. Pendent, single, bright red flowers are borne in winter.
B. fuchsioides. See *B. foliosa* var. *miniata*.
***B.* 'Gloire de Lorraine'** (Christmas begonia, Lorraine begonia). Evergreen, winter-flowering, Cheimantha begonia. **H** 30cm (12in), **S** 30–35cm (12–14in). Is well-branched with rounded, bright green leaves and single, white to pale pink flowers. Male flowers are sterile, female, highly infertile.
***B.* 'Gold Cascade'.** See *B.* 'Apricot Cascade'.
B. gracilis* var. *martiana, syn. *B. martiana*. Tuberous begonia. **H** 60–75cm (24–30in), **S** 40cm (16in). Has small, oval to lance-shaped, lobed, pale green or brown-

B

green leaves with tapering tips and large, fragrant, single, pink flowers, 2.5cm (1in) across, in summer.
♀ ***B. grandis* subsp. *evansiana*** illus. p.278.
B. haageana. See *B. scharffii*.
♀ ***B.* 'Helen Lewis'.** Rex-cultorum begonia. **H** and **S** 45–60cm (18–24in). Has an erect rhizome and silky, deep royal purple leaves, 15–20cm (6–8in) long, with silver bands. Slightly hairy, single, cream flowers are produced in early summer.
***B.* 'Herzog von Sagan',** syn. *B.* 'Can-can', illus. p.322.
***B.* 'Ikon white Blush'** (illus. p.317). Semperflorens begonia. **H** and **S** to 15cm (6in). Has broadly oval, pointed, slightly bronzed, mid-green leaves. Produces clusters of single, pink and white flowers in summer–autumn.
***B.* Illumination Series.** Double and semi-double Pendula begonia. **H** 60cm (24in), **S** 30cm (12in). Has oval, toothed, brightly veined, mid- to dark green leaves. Bears prolific, double flowers, 7.5cm (3in) across, in red, pink, orange and yellow shades and white including bicolours. ♀ **'Illumination Salmon Pink'** (illus. p.317) is pale salmon-pink.
B. imperialis. Rhizomatous begonia. **H** 13cm (5in), **S** 23cm (9in). Ovate, toothed, light green leaves, 10cm (4in) long, have puckered edges and silver-green splashes on the main veins. Has sprays of sparse white flowers, to 1.5cm (½in) wide, in winter.
***B.* 'Ingramii'** (illus. p.317). Evergreen, shrub-like begonia. **H** 70cm (28in), **S** 45cm (18in). Produces elliptic, toothed, bright green leaves, 8cm (3in) long, and, intermittently from spring to autumn, masses of single, pink flowers on spreading branches.
***B.* 'Iron Cross'.** See *B. masoniana*.
***B.* 'Krefeld'.** Evergreen, winter-flowering, Rieger begonia. **H** 25cm (10in), **S** 30cm (12in). Is semi-tuberous with succulent stems, oval, mid-green leaves and masses of single, vivid orange or bright crimson flowers. Is very susceptible to botrytis and mildew at base of stems, so water by pot immersion.
***B.* 'Lucerna'**, syn. *B.* 'Corallina de Lucerna'. Vigorous, evergreen, cane-stemmed begonia. **H** 2–2.2m (6–7ft), **S** 45–60cm (1½–2ft). Has oval, silver-spotted, bronze-green leaves, 25–35cm (10–14in) long, with tapered tips and, year-round, large panicles of single, deep pink flowers; male flowers remain almost closed.
***B.* 'Mac's Gold'.** Evergreen, creeping, rhizomatous begonia. **H** and **S** 20–25cm (8–10in). Star-shaped, lobed, yellow leaves, 8–15cm (3–6in) long, have chocolate-brown marks. Has single, pink flowers intermittently in spring-summer but in moderate quantity.
***B.* 'Madame Richard Galle'.** Upright Tuberhybrida begonia. **H** 25cm (10in), **S** 20cm (8in). Has masses of small, double, soft apricot flowers in summer.
B. manicata. Evergreen, erect, rhizomatous begonia. **H** 60cm (24in), **S** 30–40cm (12–16in). Bears large, oval, brown-mottled, green leaves and, below each leaf base, a collar of stiff, red hairs around leaf stalk. Produces single, pale pink flowers in very early spring. Propagate by plantlets during growing season. **'Crispa'** (syn. *B.m.* 'Cristata') has deeper pink flowers and light green leaves with crested margins. **'Cristata'** see *B.m.* 'Crispa'.
B. martiana. See *B. gracilis* var. *martiana*.
♀ ***B. masoniana***, syn. *B.* 'Iron Cross' (Iron cross begonia; illus. p.317). Evergreen, creeping, rhizomatous begonia. **H** 45–60cm (18–24in), **S** 30–45cm (12–18in). Bears oval, toothed, rough, bright green leaves, 15cm (6in) long, with tapering tips and cross-shaped, black or dark brown centres. Has single, pink-flushed, white flowers during summer.
B. mazae. Evergreen, trailing, rhizomatous begonia. **H** to 23cm (9in), **S** indefinite. Bears rounded, red-veined, bronze-green leaves and in early spring fragrant, single, red-spotted, pink flowers. Is good for a hanging basket.
♀ ***B.* 'Merry Christmas'** (syn. *B.* 'Ruhrtal'; illus. p.317). Rex-cultorum begonia. **H** and **S** 25–30cm (10–12in). Has satiny, red leaves, 15–20cm (6–8in) long, each with an outer, broad band of emerald-green and a deep velvet-red centre, sometimes edged with grey.
♀ ***B. metallica*** (Metal-leaf begonia). Evergreen, shrub-like begonia. **H** 50cm–1.2m (20in–4ft), **S** 45cm (18in). Bears white-haired stems and oval, toothed, silver-haired, bronze-green leaves, 18cm (7in) long, with dark green veins, red beneath. Has single, pink flowers, with red bristles, in summer-autumn.
***B.* 'Oliver Twist'.** Evergreen, creeping, rhizomatous begonia. **H** 45–60cm (18–24in), **S** 25–45cm (10–18in). Oval leaves are pale to mid-green, to 30cm (12in) long, with heavily crested edges. Has single, pink flowers in early spring.
B. olsoniae. Evergreen, compact, shrub-like begonia. **H** 23–30cm (9–12in), **S** 30cm (12in). Rounded, satiny, bronze-green leaves have cream veins. Bears single, very pale pink flowers, year-round, on arching, 30cm (12in) long stems.
***B.* 'Orange Cascade'.** See *B.* 'Apricot Cascade'.
♀ ***B.* 'Orange Rubra'** (illus. p.317). Slow-growing, evergreen, cane-stemmed begonia. **H** 50cm (20in), **S** 45cm (18in). Oval leaves are light green. Produces abundant clusters of single, orange flowers all year.
***B.* 'Organdy'.** Weather-resistant Semperflorens begonia. **H** and **S** 15cm (6in). Has rounded, waxy, green-bronze leaves and pink, red or white flowers throughout summer until autumn frosts.
***B.* 'Orpha C. Fox'** (illus. p.317). Evergreen, cane-stemmed begonia. **H** 1m (3ft), **S** 30cm (1ft). Oval, silver-spotted, olive-green leaves, 15cm (6in) long, are maroon beneath. Produces large clusters of single, bright pink flowers year-round.
B. paulensis. Evergreen, creeping, rhizomatous begonia. **H** and **S** 25–30cm (10–12in). Erect stems produce rounded, mid-green leaves, 15cm (6in) long, with 'seersucker' surfaces criss-crossed with a spider's web of veins. Produces single, cream-white flowers, with wine-coloured hairs, in late spring.
***B.* 'Président Carnot'.** Vigorous, evergreen, cane-stemmed begonia. **H** to 2.2m (7ft), **S** 45cm (1½ft). Erect stems bear 28cm (11in) long, 'angelwing', green leaves, with lighter spots. Produces large panicles of single, pink flowers, each 4cm (1½in) across, year-round.
♀ ***B.* 'Princess of Hanover'.** Rex-cultorum begonia. **H** and **S** 25–30cm (10–12in). Has spirally twisted, deep green leaves, 20cm (8in) long, with bands of silver edged with ruby-red; entire leaf surfaces are covered with fine, pink hairs.
B. prismatocarpa (illus. p.317). Evergreen, creeping, rhizomatous begonia. **H** 15–20cm (6–8in), **S** 20–25cm (8–10in). Leaves are oval, lobed, light green and less than 8cm (3in) long. Produces single, bright yellow flowers year-round. Needs 60–65% relative humidity.
B. pustulata. Evergreen, creeping, rhizomatous begonia. **H** 15–20cm (6–8in), **S** 20–25cm (8–10in). Bears oval, fine-haired, dark green leaves, with small blisters or pustules, and single, rose-pink flowers in summer. Prefers min. 22–4°C (72–5°F) and 70–75% relative humidity. **'Argentea'** (syn. *B.* 'Silver') has silver-splashed leaves and creamy-white flowers.
***B.* 'Red Ascot'.** Semperflorens begonia. **H** and **S** 15cm (6in). Has rounded, emerald-green leaves and masses of crimson-red flowers in summer.
B. rex. Rhizomatous begonia, the parent of the Rex-cultorum begonias. **H** 25cm (10in), **S** 30cm (12in). Has 20–25cm (8–10in) long, heart-shaped, deep green leaves, with a metallic sheen, zoned silvery-white above. Produces pink flowers in winter.
***B.* 'Roy Hartley'.** Upright Tuberhybrida begonia. **H** 60cm (2ft), **S** 45cm (18in). In summer, bears double, salmon-coloured flowers, with soft pink tinge. Colour depth depends on light intensity. Has few side shoots.
***B.* 'Ruhrtal'.** See *B.* 'Merry Christmas'.
B. scharffii, syn. *B. haageana* (illus. p.317). Evergreen, shrub-like begonia. **H** 60cm–1.2m (2–4ft), **S** 60cm (2ft). Stems are often covered with white hairs. Has oval, fine-haired, dark metallic-green leaves, 28cm (11in) long, with tapered tips and reddish-green undersides. Produces single, pinkish-white flowers, each with a pink beard, from autumn to summer.
***B.* 'Scherzo'.** Evergreen, creeping, rhizomatous begonia. **H** 25–30cm (10–12in), **S** 30–35cm (12–14in). Oval leaves are small, highly serrated and yellow with black marks. Bears single, white flowers in early spring.
B. serratipetala (illus. p.317). Evergreen, trailing, shrub-like begonia. **H** and **S** 45cm (18in). Obliquely oval leaves are highly serrated and bronze-green, with raised, deep pink spots. Produces mostly female, single, deep pink flowers intermittently throughout the year. Prefers 60% relative humidity, but with fairly dry roots.
***B.* 'Silver'.** See *B. pustulata* 'Argentea'.
***B.* 'Silver Helen Teupel'.** Rex-cultorum begonia. **H** and **S** 30–35cm (12–14in). Has long, deeply cut, silver leaves, each with a glowing pink centre, giving a feathered effect.
B. stipulacea of gardens. See *B. angularis*.
***B.* 'Sugar Candy'.** Tuberhybrida begonia. **H** 60cm (24in), **S** 45cm (18in). Leaves are mid-green. Produces double, clear pink flowers in summer.
♀ ***B. sutherlandii*** (illus. p.317). Trailing, tuberous begonia. **H** 1m (3ft), **S** indefinite. Slender stems carry small, lance-shaped, lobed, bright green leaves, with red veins, and, in summer, loose clusters of single, orange flowers in profusion. In late autumn, leaves and stems collapse prior to winter dormancy. Makes an excellent hanging-basket plant. Is particularly susceptible to mildew.
B. taliensis illus. p.278.
♀ ***B.* 'Thurstonii'.** Evergreen, shrub-like begonia. **H** to 1.2m (4ft), **S** 45cm (1½ft). Has rounded to oval, smooth, glossy, bronze-green leaves, with dark red veins, and, in summer, bears single, pink flowers.
♀ ***B.* 'Tiger Paws'** (illus. p.317). Evergreen, creeping, rhizomatous begonia. **H** 15cm (6in), **S** 25–30cm (10–12in). Small, rounded, striking bright green leaves, with yellow and brown splashes, have bristly, white hairs on the margins. Many clusters of small, white flowers are carried well above the foliage in spring.
***B.* x *tuberhybrida* Mocha Series.** Bushy, dark-leaved, Tuberhybrida begonia. **H** and **S** 30cm (12in). Has green-veined, chocolate-brown leaves and, held tightly above the foliage, double flowers, 7.5–10cm (3–4in) across, in about 6 varied, individual colours. **'Mocha Scarlet'** (illus. p.317) is deep red with very dark leaves.
***B.* x *tuberhybrida* Non Stop Series.** Bushy Tuberhybrida begonia. **H** and **S** 30cm (12in). Has double flowers, 7.5–10cm (3–4in) across, in about 12 varied individual colours and mixtures held close to heart-shaped, mid-green leaves. **'Non Stop White'** (illus. p.317) has creamy-centred, white flowers opening from pink buds.
B. versicolor. Evergreen, creeping, rhizomatous begonia. **H** 15cm (6in), **S** 15–30cm (6–12in). Produces broadly oval or oblong, velvety leaves, 8cm (3in) long, in shades of mahogany, apple-green and maroon, and, in spring-summer, single, salmon-pink flowers. Provide min. 16–19°C (61–6°F) with 65–70% relative humidity.
B.* x *weltoniensis. See *B.* 'Weltoniensis'.
***B.* 'Weltoniensis'**, syn. *B.* x *weltoniensis*. (Mapleleaf begonia). Semi-tuberous begonia with a shrub-like habit. **H** 30–50cm (12–20in), **S** 30cm (12in). Has small, oval, long-pointed, toothed, dark green leaves. Heads of 5–8 single, pink or white flowers appear from leaf axils in summer.
B. xanthina. Evergreen, bushy, creeping, rhizomatous begonia. **H** 25–30cm (10–12in), **S** 30–35cm (12–14in). Bears oval, dark green leaves, 15–23cm (6–9in) long, with yellow veins, purple and hairy beneath. Pendent, single, orange-yellow flowers are borne in summer. Provide min. 21–4°C (70–75°F) with 75% relative humidity.
B. zebrina. See *B. angularis*.

BELAMCANDA

IRIDACEAE

Genus of summer-flowering bulbs, grown for their iris-like flowers. Frost hardy, but needs protection in cold winters. Requires sun and well-drained, humus-rich soil. Propagate by seed in spring.
B. chinensis, syn. *Iris domestica*. Summer-flowering bulb. **H** 45cm–1m (1½–3ft), **S** 15–25cm (6–10in). Carries a fan of sword-shaped, semi-erect leaves. A loosely branched stem bears a succession of flattish, orange-red flowers, 4–5cm (1½–2in) across, with darker blotches. Seeds are shiny and black.

B

BELLEVALIA

LILIACEAE/HYACINTHACEAE

Genus of spring-flowering bulbs, similar to *Muscari*, but with longer, more tubular flowers. Some species have ornamental [illegible] but most are uninteresting horticulturally. Frost hardy. Needs an open, sunny position and well-drained soil that dries out in summer. Propagate by seed, preferably in autumn.

B. hyacinthoides, syn. *Strangweja spicata*, illus. p.419.

B. paradoxa of gardens. See *B. pycnantha*.

B. pycnantha, syn. *B. paradoxa* of gardens, *Muscari paradoxum* of gardens, *M. pycnantha*. Spring-flowering bulb. **H** to 40cm (16in), **S** 5–8cm (2–3in). Has strap-shaped, semi-erect, basal, greyish-green leaves. Tubular, deep dusky-blue flowers, 0.5cm (¼in) long and with yellow tips, are produced in a dense, conical spike.

B. romana illus. p.399.

BELLIS

Daisy

COMPOSITAE/ASTERACEAE

Genus of perennials, some grown as biennials for spring bedding. Fully hardy. Grow in sun or semi-shade and in fertile, very well-drained soil. Dead-head regularly. Propagate by seed in early summer or by division after flowering.

B. perennis (Common daisy). Stoloniferous, carpeting perennial. Cultivars are grown as biennials. **H** and **S** 15–20cm (6–8in). All have inversely lance-shaped to spoon-shaped, mid-green leaves and semi-double to fully double flower heads in spring. Large-flowered (flower heads to 8cm/3in wide) and miniature-flowered (flower heads to 2½cm/1in wide) cultivars are available. **Habanera Series** cultivars bear long-petalled, pink, white or red flower heads, to 6cm (2.5in) across, in early summer. **Pomponette Series** cultivars bear double, pink, white or red flower heads, to 4cm (1½in) across, with quilled petals. **Roggli Series** cultivars flower early and prolifically, with semi-double, red, rose-pink, salmon-pink or white flower heads, to 3cm (1¼in) across. ♀ **Tasso Series** cultivars have double, pink, white or red flower heads, to 6cm (2½in) across, with quilled petals.

Beloperone guttata. See *Justicia brandegeeana*.

BERBERIDOPSIS

FLACOURTIACEAE/ BERBERIDOPSIACEAE

Genus of one species of evergreen, woody-stemmed, twining climber. Frost hardy. Dislikes strong winds and strong sun and is best grown in a north or west aspect. Soil, preferably lime-free, should be moist but well-drained. Cut out dead growth in spring; train to required shape. Propagate by seed in spring or by stem cuttings or layering in late summer or autumn.

B. corallina (Coral plant) illus. p.202.

BERBERIS

Barberry

BERBERIDACEAE

Genus of deciduous, semi-evergreen or evergreen, spiny shrubs, grown mainly for their rounded to cup-shaped flowers, with usually yellow sepals and petals, and for their fruits. The evergreens are also cultivated for their leaves, the deciduous shrubs for their colourful autumn foliage. Fully to frost hardy. Requires sun or semi-shade and any but waterlogged soil. Propagate species by seed in autumn, deciduous hybrids and cultivars by softwood or semi-ripe cuttings in summer, evergreen hybrids and cultivars by semi-ripe cuttings in summer. ⓘ All parts may cause mild stomach upset if ingested; contact with the spines may irritate skin.

B. aggregata. Deciduous, bushy shrub. **H** and **S** 1.5m (5ft). Fully hardy. Oblong to oval, mid-green leaves redden in autumn. Dense clusters of pale yellow flowers appear in late spring or early summer and are followed by egg-shaped, white-bloomed, red fruits.

B. buxifolia. Semi-evergreen or deciduous, arching shrub. **H** 2.5m (8ft), **S** 3m (10ft). Fully hardy. Has oblong to oval, spine-tipped, leathery, dark green leaves. Deep orange-yellow flowers appear from early to mid-spring and are followed by spherical, black fruits with a white bloom.

B. calliantha. Evergreen, bushy shrub. **H** and **S** 1–1.5m (3–5ft). Fully hardy. Has oblong, sharply spiny, glossy, green leaves, white beneath, and large, pale yellow flowers in late spring, followed by egg-shaped, black fruits with a white bloom.

B. candidula. Evergreen, bushy, compact shrub. **H** and **S** 1m (3ft). Fully hardy. Leaves are narrowly oblong, glossy, dark green, white beneath. Has bright yellow flowers in late spring, then egg-shaped, blue-purple fruits.

***B.* x *carminea* 'Barbarossa'** illus. p.141. **'Pirate King'** is a deciduous, arching shrub. **H** 2m (6ft), **S** 3m (10ft). Fully hardy. Produces oblong, dark green leaves. In late spring and early summer produces clusters of yellow flowers, followed by spherical, pale red fruits.

***B.* 'Chenault'.** See *B.* 'Chenaultii'.

***B.* 'Chenaultii'**, syn. *B.* 'Chenault'. Evergreen, bushy shrub. **H** 1.5m (5ft), **S** 2m (6ft). Fully hardy. Narrowly oblong, wavy-edged, glossy, dark green leaves set off golden-yellow flowers in late spring and early summer. Bears egg-shaped, blue-black fruits.

B. coxii. Evergreen, bushy, dense shrub. **H** 2m (6ft), **S** 3m (10ft). Fully hardy. Produces narrowly oval, glossy, dark green leaves with white undersides and, in late spring, yellow flowers. Egg-shaped, blue-black fruits have a grey-blue bloom.

♀ ***B. darwinii*** illus. p.111.

B. empetrifolia illus. p.148.

B. gagnepainii* var. *lanceifolia illus. p.127.

B. jamesiana. Vigorous, deciduous, arching shrub. **H** and **S** 4m (12ft). Fully hardy. Yellow flowers in late spring are followed by pendent racemes of spherical, red berries. Oval, dark green leaves redden in autumn.

♀ ***B. julianae.*** Dense, bushy, evergreen shrub. **H** 2.5m (8ft), **S** 3m (10ft). Fully hardy. Has glossy, dark green leaves, yellow flowers in late spring–early summer, and egg-shaped, blue-black fruits in autumn.

***B. linearifolia* 'Orange King'** illus. p.127.

***B.* x *lologensis*.** Vigorous, evergreen, arching shrub. **H** 3m (10ft), **S** 5m (15ft). Fully hardy. Has broadly oblong, glossy, dark green leaves. Profuse clusters of orange flowers are borne from mid- to late spring. **'Stapehill'** illus. p.127.

***B.* x *ottawensis* 'Purpurea'.** See *B.* x *o.* f. *purpurea* 'Superba'. ♀ **f. *purpurea* 'Superba'** (syn. *B.* x *o.* 'Purpurea') is a deciduous, arching shrub. **H** and **S** 2.5m (8ft). Fully hardy. Produces rounded to oval, deep reddish-purple leaves. Bears small, red-tinged, yellow flowers in late spring, then egg-shaped, red fruits in autumn.

***B.* 'Park Jewel'.** See *B.* 'Parkjuweel'.

***B.* 'Parkjuweel'**, syn. *B.* 'Park Jewel'. Semi-evergreen, bushy, rounded shrub. **H** and **S** 1m (3ft). Fully hardy. Leaves are oval, glossy and bright green; some turn red in autumn. Flowers are of little value.

B. polyantha of gardens. See *B. prattii*.

B. prattii, syn. *B. polyantha* of gardens. Deciduous, bushy shrub. **H** and **S** 3m (10ft). Fully hardy. Produces oblong, glossy, dark green leaves. Large clusters of small, yellow flowers in late summer are followed by a profusion of long-lasting, egg-shaped, coral-pink fruits.

***B.* x *rubrostilla*.** See *B.* 'Rubrostilla'.

***B.* 'Rubrostilla'**, syn. *B.* x *rubrostilla*, illus. p.162.

B. sargentiana. Evergreen, bushy shrub. **H** and **S** 2m (6ft). Fully hardy. Leaves are oblong, glossy, bright green. Yellow flowers are produced in late spring and early summer and are succeeded by egg-shaped, blue-black fruits.

♀ ***B.* x *stenophylla*** illus. p.127.

♀ **'Corallina Compacta'** illus. p.336.

♀ ***B. thunbergii*.** Deciduous, arching, dense shrub. **H** 2m (6ft), **S** 3m (10ft). Fully hardy. Broadly oval, pale to mid-green leaves turn brilliant orange-red in autumn. Small, red-tinged, pale yellow flowers appear in mid-spring, followed by egg-shaped, bright red fruits. **f. *atropurpurea*** illus. p.123. ♀ **'Atropurpurea Nana'** (syn. *B.t.* 'Crimson Pygmy'), **H** and **S** 60cm (24in), bears reddish-purple foliage. **'Aurea'** illus. p.160. **'Crimson Pygmy'** see *B.t.* 'Atropurpurea Nana'. Upright branches of **'Erecta'** spread with age. ♀ **'Golden Ring'** has purple leaves narrowly margined with golden-yellow, turning red in autumn, and produces red fruit. ♀ **'Rose Glow'** illus. p.137.

B. valdiviana illus. p.111.

♀ ***B. verruculosa*.** Slow-growing, evergreen, bushy shrub. **H** and **S** 1.5m (5ft). Fully hardy. Glossy, dark green leaves have blue-white undersides. Clusters of small, cup-shaped, bright yellow flowers in late spring and early summer are followed by blue-black fruits.

***B. wilsoniae*.** Deciduous or semi-evergreen, bushy shrub. **H** 1m (3ft), **S** 1.5m (5ft). Fully hardy. Narrowly oblong, grey-green leaves turn bright orange-red in autumn. In late spring and early summer produces yellow flowers, then showy, spherical, coral-red fruits.

BERCHEMIA

RHAMNACEAE

Genus of deciduous, twining climbers, grown for their leaves and fruit. Is useful for covering walls, fences and tree stumps. Fully hardy. Grow in sun or shade, in any well-drained soil. Propagate by seed in autumn or spring, by semi-ripe cuttings in summer or by layering or root cuttings in winter.

***B. racemosa* 'Variegata'.** Deciduous, twining climber. **H** 5m (15ft) or more. Produces heart-shaped, green leaves, 3–8cm (1¼–3in) long and paler beneath, that are variegated creamy-white. Small, bell-shaped, greenish-white flowers in summer are followed by rounded, green fruits that turn red, then black.

BERGENIA

SYN. MEGASEA

SAXIFRAGACEAE

Genus of evergreen perennials with thick, usually large, rounded to oval or spoon-shaped, leathery leaves, with indented veins, that make ideal ground cover. Fully to frost hardy. Tolerates sun or shade and any well-drained soil, but leaf colour is best on poor soil and in full sun. Propagate by division in spring after flowering.

***B.* 'Abendglut'**, syn. *B.* 'Evening Glow'. Evergreen, clump-forming perennial. **H** 23cm (9in), **S** 30cm (12in). Fully hardy. Bears rosettes of oval, crinkled, short-stemmed, maroon leaves, from which arise racemes of open cup-shaped, semi-double, deep magenta flowers in spring.

♀ ***B.* 'Ballawley'.** Evergreen, clump-forming perennial. **H** and **S** 60cm (24in). Fully hardy. Large, rounded to oval, flat, deep green leaves turn red in winter. Racemes of cup-shaped, bright crimson flowers are borne on red stems in spring. Shelter from cold winds.

***B.* 'Beethoven'** illus. p.256.

***B. beesiana*.** See *B. purpurascens*.

B. ciliata illus. p.256.

***B. cordifolia*.** Evergreen, clump-forming perennial. **H** 45cm (18in), **S** 60cm (24in). Fully hardy. Leaves are rounded, puckered and crinkle-edged. Produces racemes of open cup-shaped, light pink flowers in spring. ♀ **'Purpurea'** **H** and **S** 50cm (20in). Has large, rounded, purple-tinged, deep green leaves. Clusters of bell-shaped, rose-pink flowers are carried on red stems from late winter to early spring.

***B. crassifolia*.** Evergreen, clump-forming perennial. **H** 30cm (12in), **S** 45cm (18in). Fully hardy. Has oval- or spoon-shaped, fleshy, flat leaves that turn mahogany in winter. Bears spikes of open cup-shaped, lavender-pink flowers in spring.

***B.* 'Eric Smith'.** Evergreen, groundcover perennial. **H** 40cm (16in), **S** 60cm (24in) or more. Fully hardy. Has large, rounded, rather upright, leathery, mid-green leaves, which in winter are reddish tinted. Rich pink flowers are borne on stout stalks in spring.

***B.* 'Evening Glow'.** See *B.* 'Abendglut'.

♀ ***B.* 'Morgenröte'**, syn. *B.* 'Morning Red'. Evergreen, clump-forming perennial. **H** 45cm (18in), **S** 30cm (12in). Fully hardy. Leaves are rounded, crinkled and deep green. Spikes of open cup-shaped, deep

carmine flowers in spring are often followed by a second crop in summer.
***B.* 'Morning Red'.** See *B.* 'Morgenröte'.
♀ ***B. purpurascens***, syn. *B. beesiana* illus, illus p.280.
♀ ***B.* x *schmidtii*.** Evergreen, clump-forming perennial. **H** 30cm (12in), **S** 60cm (24in). Fully hardy. Oval, flat leaves have toothed margins. Sprays of open cup-shaped, soft pink flowers are borne in early spring on short stems.
♀ ***B.* 'Silberlicht'**, syn. *B.* 'Silver Light', illus. p.255.
***B.* 'Silver Light'.** See *B.* 'Silberlicht'.
***B. stracheyi*.** Evergreen, clump-forming perennial. **H** 23cm (9in), **S** 30cm (12in). Fully hardy. Small, rounded, flat leaves form neat rosettes, among which nestle heads of open cup-shaped, white or pink flowers in spring.
***B.* 'Sunningdale'.** Evergreen, clump-forming perennial. **H** 60cm (24in), **S** 30cm (12in). Fully hardy. Rounded, slightly crinkled, deep green leaves are mahogany beneath. Bears racemes of open cup-shaped, lilac-carmine flowers on red stalks in spring.

BERKHEYA

COMPOSITAE/ASTERACEAE

Genus of summer-flowering perennials. Frost to half hardy, but, except in mild areas, grow most species against a south- or west-facing wall. Needs full sun and fertile, well-drained soil. Sow seed in autumn or divide in spring.
B. macrocephala illus. p.243.
B. purpurea illus. p.269.

BERTOLONIA

MELASTOMATACEAE

Genus of evergreen perennials, grown for their foliage. Frost tender, min. 15°C (59°F) but preferably warmer. Requires a fairly shaded position and high humidity, although soil should not be waterlogged. Propagate by tip or leaf cuttings in spring or summer.
***B. marmorata*.** Evergreen, rosette-forming perennial. **H** 15cm (6in) or more in flower, **S** 45cm (18in). Broadly oval, slightly fleshy leaves have heart-shaped bases, silvery midribs and puckered surfaces, and are reddish-purple below, velvety green above. Intermittently produces spikes of saucer-shaped, pinkish-purple flowers.

BERZELIA

BRUNIACEAE

Genus of evergreen, heather-like, summer-flowering shrubs, grown for their flowers. Frost tender, min. 7°C (45°F). Requires full sun and well-drained, neutral to acid soil. Water containerized plants moderately, less when not in full growth. Plants may be cut back lightly after flowering. Propagate by seed in spring or by semi-ripe cuttings in late summer.
***B. lanuginosa*.** Evergreen, erect shrub with soft-haired, young shoots. **H** and **S** to 1m (3ft). Has small, heather-like leaves. Compact, spherical heads of tiny, creamy-white flowers are carried in dense, terminal clusters in summer.

BESCHORNERIA

AGAVACEAE

Genus of perennial succulents with narrowly lance-shaped leaves forming erect, almost stemless, basal rosettes. Half hardy. Needs full sun and very well-drained soil. Propagate by seed or division in spring or summer.
♀ ***B. yuccoides*** illus. p.490.

BESSERA

LILIACEAE/ALLIACEAE

Genus of summer-flowering bulbs, grown for their striking, brightly coloured flowers. Half hardy. Needs an open, sunny situation and well-drained soil. Propagate by seed in spring.
B. elegans (Coral drops). Summer-flowering bulb. **H** to 60cm (24in), **S** 8–10cm (3–4in). Has long, narrow, erect, basal leaves. Each leafless stem bears pendent, bell-shaped, bright red flowers on long, slender stalks.

***Betonica officinalis*.** See *Stachys officinalis*.

BETULA

Birch

BETULACEAE

Genus of deciduous trees and shrubs, grown for their bark and autumn colour. Fully hardy. Needs sun and moist but well-drained soil; some species prefer acid soil. Transplant young trees in autumn. Propagate by grafting in late winter or by softwood cuttings in early summer.
♀ ***B. albosinensis*** (White Chinese birch; illus. p.78). Deciduous, open-branched, elegant tree. **H** 25m (80ft), **S** 10m (30ft). Has serrated, oval to lance-shaped, pale green leaves. Peeling bark is honey-coloured or reddish-maroon with a grey bloom.
B. alleghaniensis, syn. *B. lutea* (Yellow birch). Deciduous, upright, open tree, often multi-stemmed. **H** 12m (40ft) or more, **S** 3m (10ft). Smooth, glossy, golden-brown bark peels in thin shreds. Oval, mid- to pale green leaves rapidly turn gold in autumn. Bears yellow-green catkins in spring.
B. ermanii (illus. p.78). Deciduous, open-branched, elegant tree. **H** 20m (70ft), **S** 12m (40ft). Oval, glossy, green leaves give excellent autumn colour. Has peeling, pinkish-white bark, distinctively marked with large lenticels.
***B. jacquemontii*.** See *B. utilis* var. *jacquemontii*.
***B.* 'Jermyns'.** See *B. utilis* var. *jacquemontii* 'Jermyns'.
B. lenta (Cherry Birch) illus. p.79.
***B. lutea*.** See *B. alleghaniensis*.
B. maximowicziana (Monarch birch). Fast-growing, deciduous, broad-headed tree. **H** 18m (60ft), **S** 3m (10ft). Has orange-brown or pink bark, and racemes of yellowish catkins in spring. Large, oval, mid-green leaves turn bright butter-yellow in autumn.
B. nana (Arctic birch) illus. p.335.
B. nigra (River birch; illus. p.78). Deciduous, conical then spreading tree with peeling, pink-orange bark, which becomes fissured with age. **H** 15m (50ft), **S** 10m (30ft). Diamond-shaped, glossy, mid-green leaves turn golden-orange in autumn. Bears yellow, male catkins in spring. Can be coppiced to encourage multiple, brightly coloured stems. Grows well in damp soil.
B. papyrifera (Canoe birch) illus. p.67.
♀ ***B. pendula*** (Silver birch). Deciduous, broadly columnar or conical, graceful tree. **H** 25m (80ft) or more, **S** 10m (30ft). Has slender, drooping shoots and silver-white bark that becomes black and rugged at base of trunk with age. Yellow-brown catkins appear in spring. Oval, bright green leaves turn yellow in autumn. **'Dalecarlica'** has a more upright habit, with pendent, shorter shoots at the end of the branches, and has much more deeply cut leaves. ♀ **'Laciniata'** develops a narrow crown. ♀ **'Tristis'** (Weeping birch) illus. p.68. **'Youngii'** illus. p.88.
***B. platyphylla* var. *szechuanica*.** See *B. szechuanica*.
B. szechuanica, syn. *B. platyphylla* var. *szechuanica* (Szechuan birch). Vigorous, deciduous, open tree with stiff branches. **H** 14m (46ft), **S** 2.5m (8ft). Bark is strikingly chalky-white when mature. Has triangular to oval, serrated, leathery, deep green leaves that turn brilliant gold in autumn. Produces yellow-green catkins in spring.
B. utilis (Himalayan birch). Deciduous, upright, open tree. **H** 18m (60ft), **S** 10m (30ft). Paper-thin, peeling bark varies from creamy-white to dark copper-brown. Yellow-brown catkins are borne in spring. Oval, mid-green leaves, hairy beneath when young, turn golden-yellow in autumn. **var. *jacquemontii*** (syn *B. jacquemontii*) has bright white bark and oval, serrated, mid-green leaves that turn clear yellow in autumn. ♀ **var. *jacquemontii* 'Grayswood Ghost'** (illus. p.78) has bright, white bark, slightly pendent branchlets and dark green leaves. **'Jermyns'** (syn. *B.* 'Jermyns', illus. p.78), **H** 15m (50ft), **S** 10m (30ft), produces bright white bark and very long, elegant, yellow, male catkins.

BIARUM

ARACEAE

Genus of mainly autumn-flowering, tuberous perennials with tiny flowers carried on a pencil-shaped spadix, enclosed within a tubular spathe. Upper part of spathe is hooded or flattened out and showy. Frost hardy, but during cold, wet winters protect in a cold frame or greenhouse. Needs a sunny position and well-drained soil. Dry out tubers when dormant in summer. Propagate in autumn by seed or offsets.
***B. eximium*.** Early autumn-flowering, tuberous perennial. **H** and **S** 8–10cm (3–4in). Lance-shaped, semi-erect, basal leaves follow stemless, tubular, velvety, blackish-maroon spathe, up to 15cm (6in) long and often lying flat on ground. Upper part is flattened out. Spadix is upright and black.
B. tenuifolium Late summer- or autumn-flowering tuberous perennial. **H** to 20cm (8in), **S** 8–10cm (3). Produces clusters of acrid, narrow, erect, basal leaves after which stemless, upright and often twisted, blackish-purple spathes appear.

BIDENS

ASTERACEAE/COMPOSITAE

A large genus of about 200 species, annuals and perennials, a few perennials usually treated as annuals are grown as creeping hanging basket and container plants for their large yellow flowers and finely dissected leaves. Propagate by seed sown in spring and perennials by division.
***B. atrosanguinea*.** See *Cosmos atrosanguineus*.
***B.* 'Gold Star'** illus. p.319.

BIGNONIA

BIGNONIACEAE

Genus of one species of evergreen, tendril climber. Frost hardy; in cool areas may lose its leaves in winter. Requires a position in sun and in fertile soil to flower well. If necessary, prune in spring. Propagate by stem cuttings in summer or autumn or by layering in winter.
***B. capensis*.** See *Tecoma capensis*.
B. capreolata, syn. *Doxantha capreolata* (Cross vine, Trumpet flower). Evergreen, tendril climber. **H** 10m (30ft) or more. Each leaf has 2 narrowly oblong leaflets and a branched tendril. In summer, funnel-shaped, reddish-orange flowers appear in clusters in leaf axils. Pea-pod-shaped fruits, to 15cm (6in) long, are produced in autumn.
***B. grandiflora*.** See *Campsis grandiflora*.
***B. jasminoides*.** See *Pandorea jasminoides*.
***B. pandorana*.** See *Pandorea pandorana*.
***B. radicans*.** See *Campsis radicans*.
***B. stans*.** See *Tecoma stans*.

***Bilderdykia*.** See *Fallopia*.

BILLARDIERA

PITTOSPORACEAE

Genus of evergreen, woody-stemmed, twining climbers, grown mainly for their fruits. Half hardy. Grow in any well-drained soil, in a sheltered position and partial shade. Propagate by seed in spring or stem cuttings in summer or autumn.
♀ ***B. longiflora*** illus. p.210.

BILLBERGIA

BROMELIACEAE

Genus of evergreen, rosette-forming perennials, grown for their flowers and foliage. Frost tender, min. 5–7°C (41–5°F). Requires semi-shade and well-drained soil, ideally adding sphagnum moss or plastic chips used for orchid culture. Water moderately when in full growth, sparingly at other times. Propagate by division or offsets after flowering or in late spring.
B. nutans (Queen's tears). Evergreen, clump-forming, tubular-rosetted perennial. **H** and **S** to 40cm (16in). Strap-shaped leaves are usually dark green. In spring, pendent clusters of tubular, purple-blue-edged, lime-green flowers emerge from pink bracts.
***B. rhodocyanea*.** See *Aechmea fasciata*.
♀ ***B.* x *windii*** (Angel's tears). Evergreen, clump-forming, tubular-rosetted perennial. **H** and **S** to 40cm (16in). Is similar to

B. nutans, but produces broader, spreading, grey-green leaves and larger bracts. Flowers intermittently from spring to autumn.

Biota orientalis. See *Platycladus orientalis.*

BLECHNUM

BLECHNACEAE

Genus of evergreen or semi-evergreen ferns. Fully hardy to frost tender, min. 5°C (41°F). Most species prefer semi-shade. Requires moist, neutral to acid soil. Remove fading fronds regularly. Propagate *B. penna-marina* by division in spring, other species by spores in late summer.
B. alpinum. See *B. penna-marina.*
♀ ***B. chilense***, syn. *B. tabulare*, illus. p.292.
♀ ***B. penna-marina***, syn. *B. alpinum*, illus. p.290.
♀ ***B. spicant*** (Hard fern). Evergreen fern. **H** 30–75cm (12–30in), **S** 30–45cm (12–18in). Fully hardy. Bears narrowly lance-shaped, indented, leathery, spreading, dark green fronds. Prefers shade and peaty or leafy

BLETILLA

ORCHIDACEAE

See also ORCHIDS.
B. hyacinthina. See *B. striata.*
B. striata, syn. *B. hyacinthina* (illus. p.466). Deciduous, terrestrial orchid. **H** to 60cm (24in). Half hardy. In late spring or early summer produces magenta or white flowers, 3cm (1¼in) long, and broadly lance-shaped leaves, 50cm (20in) long. Needs shade in summer.

BLOOMERIA

LILIACEAE/ALLIACEAE

Genus of onion-like, spring-flowering bulbs, with spherical flower heads on leafless stems, which die down in summer. Frost hardy. Requires a sheltered, sunny situation and well-drained soil. Propagate by seed in autumn or by division in late summer or autumn.
B. crocea. Late spring-flowering bulb. **H** to 30cm (12in), **S** to 10cm (4in). Long, narrow, semi-erect, basal leaves die at flowering time. Each leafless stem carries a loose, spherical head, 10–15cm (4–6in) across, of star-shaped, dark-striped, yellow flowers.

Bocconia cordata. See *Macleaya cordata.*

BOENNINGHAUSENIA

RUTACEAE

Genus of one species of deciduous sub-shrub, usually with soft, herbaceous stems, grown for its foliage and flowers. Frost hardy, although cut to ground level in winter. Needs full sun and fertile, well-drained but not too dry soil. Propagate by softwood cuttings in summer or by seed in autumn.
B. albiflora. Deciduous, bushy sub-shrub. **H** and **S** 1m (3ft). Has pungent, mid-green leaves, divided into oval leaflets. Bears loose panicles of small, cup-shaped, white flowers from mid-summer to early autumn.

BOLAX

UMBELLIFERAE/APIACEAE

Genus of evergreen, hummock- and cushion-forming perennials, often included in *Azorella*. Is grown for its symmetrical rosettes of small, thick, tough leaves. Flowers only rarely in cultivation. Is suitable for gritty screes, troughs and alpine houses. Fully hardy. Needs sun and humus-rich, well-drained soil. Propagate by rooting rosettes in summer.
B. gummifera illus. p.376.

BOMAREA

ALSTROEMERIACEAE

Genus of herbaceous or evergreen, tuberous-rooted, scrambling and twining climbers, grown for tubular or bell-shaped flowers. Frost hardy to frost tender, min. 5°C. Grow in well-drained soil in full light. Water regularly in growth, sparingly when dormant. Provide support. Some species grow well out of doors planted beneath shrubs through which they can climb; mulch to protect tubers before winter. Cut out old flowering stems at ground level when leaves yellow. Propagate by seed or division in early spring.
B. andimarcana, syn. *B. pubigera* of gardens. Deciduous, scrambling climber with straight, slender stems. **H** 2–3m (6–10ft). Frost tender, min. 5°C (45°F). Has lance-shaped leaves, white and hairy beneath. Bears nodding, tubular, green-tipped, pale yellow flowers, suffused pink, from early summer to autumn.
B. caldasii. See *B. multiflora.*
B. edulis illus. p.201.
B. hirsuta. Herbaceous, twining climber. **H** 1–2m (3–6ft). Frost tender, min. 1°C (34°F). Has narrowly ovate, mid-green leaves, softly hairy beneath. Bears tight clusters of pendent, bell-shaped, reddish-orange flowers, with yellow-orange interiors, from mid-summer to autumn.
B. kalbreyeri of gardens. See *B. multiflora.*
B. multiflora, syn. *B. caldasii*, *B. kalbreyeri* of gardens, illus. p.207.
B. pubigera of gardens. See *B. andimarcana.*
B. salsilla. Herbaceous, twining climber. **H** 1–1.5m (3–5ft). Half hardy. Ovate leaves are greyish-green. Produces open clusters of pendent, bell-shaped, green-tipped, cerise flowers in summer.

BORAGO

Borage

BORAGINACEAE

Genus of annuals and perennials, grown for culinary use as well as for their flowers. Fully hardy. Requires sun and fertile, well-drained soil. For culinary use gather only young leaves. Propagate by seed sown outdoors in spring. Some species will self seed prolifically and may become invasive.
B. officinalis (Borage) illus. p.315.

BORONIA

RUTACEAE

Genus of evergreen shrubs, grown primarily for their flowers. Frost tender, min. 7–10°C (45–50°F). Requires full light and sandy, neutral to acid soil. Water potted specimens moderately, less when they are not in full growth. For a compact habit, shorten long stems after flowering. Propagate by seed in spring or by semi-ripe cuttings in late summer. Red spider mite may be a problem.
B. megastigma illus. p.4[illegible].

BOUGAINVILLEA

NYCTAGINACEAE

Genus of deciduous or evergreen, woody-stemmed, scrambling climbers, grown for their showy floral bracts. Frost tender, min. 7–10°C (45–50°F). Grow in fertile, well-drained soil and in full light. Water moderately in the growing season; keep containerized plants almost dry when dormant. Tie to a support. Cut back previous season's lateral growths in spring, leaving 2–3cm (¾–1¼in) long spurs. Propagate by semi-ripe cuttings in summer or by hardwood cuttings when dormant. Whitefly and mealy bug may attack.
B. x buttiana. Vigorous, evergreen, woody-stemmed, scrambling climber. **H** 8–12m (25–40ft). Has ovate, mid-green leaves, to 8cm (3in) long, lighter below. Bears large clusters of strongly waved, golden-yellow, purple or red floral bracts from summer to autumn. **'California Gold'** see *B.* x *b.* 'Enid Lancaster'. **'Crimson Lake'** see *B.* x *b.* 'Mrs Butt'. Floral bracts of **'Enid Lancaster'** (syn. *B.* x *b.* 'California Gold', *B.* x *b.* 'Golden Glow') are orange-yellow. **'Golden Glow'** see *B.* x *b.* 'Enid Lancaster'. ♀ **'Miss Manila'** (syn. *B.* 'Miss Manila') has pink floral bracts. Those of ♀ **'Mrs Butt'** (syn. *B.* x *b.* 'Crimson Lake') are crimson-magenta; those of **'Scarlet Queen'** are scarlet.
***B.* 'Dania'.** Vigorous, mainly evergreen, woody-stemmed, scrambling climber. **H** to 5m (15ft). Has rounded-oval, mid-green leaves and bears clusters of deep pink floral bracts in summer..
♀ ***B. glabra*** illus. p.462. **'Sanderiana'** illus. p.462. **'Snow White'** illus. p.460.
***B.* 'Miss Manila'.** See *R.* x *buttiana* 'Miss Manila'.
B. spectabilis. Strong-growing, mainly evergreen, woody-stemmed, scrambling climber; stems usually have a few spines. **H** to 7m (22ft). Has elliptic to oval leaves and, in summer, large trusses of red-purple floral bracts.
***B.* 'Tango'.** See *B.* 'Miss Manila'.

Boussingaultia baselloides of gardens. See *Anredera cordifolia.*

BOUTELOUA

GRAMINEAE/POACEAE

See also GRASSES, BAMBOOS, RUSHES and SEDGES.
B. gracilis, syn. *B. oligostachya* (Blue grama, Mosquito grass). Semi-evergreen, tuft-forming, narrow-leaved, perennial grass. **H** 50cm (20in), **S** 20cm (8in). Fully hardy. In summer bears comb-like flower spikes, 4cm (1½in) long, held at right-angles to stems.
B. oligostachya. See *B. gracilis.*

BOUVARDIA

RUBIACEAE

Genus of deciduous, semi-evergreen or evergreen shrubs and perennials, grown for their flowers. Frost tender, min. 7–10°C (45–50°F), , but 13–15°C (55–9°F) for winter-flowering species. Prefers full light and fertile, well-drained soil. Water freely when in full growth, and moderately at other times. Cut back stems by half to three-quarters after flowering. Propagate by softwood cuttings in spring or by greenwood or semi-ripe cuttings in summer. Whitefly and mealy bug may be troublesome.
B. humboldtii. See *B. longiflora.*
B. longiflora, syn. *B. humboldtii.* Semi-evergreen, spreading shrub. **H** and **S** 1m (3ft) or more. Min. 13–15°C (55–9°F), until flowering ceases, then 7°C (45°F). Has lance-shaped leaves, and terminal clusters of fragrant, white flowers, with slender tubes and 4 petal lobes, from summer to early winter.
B. ternifolia, syn. *B. triphylla*, illus. p.456.
B. triphylla. See *B. ternifolia.*

BOWIEA

LILIACEAE/HYACINTHACEAE

Genus of summer-flowering, bulbous succulents with scrambling, branched, green stems that produce no proper leaves. Frost tender, min. 10°C (50°F). Needs sun and well-drained soil; plant with half of bulb above soil level. Support with sticks or canes. Propagate by seed, sown under glass in winter or spring. May produce offsets.
B. volubilis. Bulbous summer-flowering succulent. **H** 1–2m (3–6ft), **S** 45–60cm (1½–2ft). Has climbing, much-branched, slender stems and no proper leaves. Produces small, star-shaped, green flowers at tips of stems. Provide support.

BOYKINIA

SAXIFRAGACEAE

Genus of mound-forming perennials. Fully hardy. Most species require shade and humus-rich, moist but well-drained, acid soil. Propagate by division in spring or by seed in autumn.
B. aconitifolia. Mound-forming perennial. **H** 1m (3ft), **S** 15cm (6in). Has rounded to kidney-shaped, lobed leaves. In summer, flower stems carry very small, bell-shaped, white flowers.
B. jamesii, syn. *Telesonix jamesii.* Mound-forming, rhizomatous perennial. **H** and **S** 15cm (6in). Each woody stem bears a rosette of kidney-shaped leaves with lacerated edges. In early summer bears open bell-shaped, frilled, pink flowers with green centres.

Brachychilum horsfieldii. See *Hedychium horsfieldii.*

BRACHYCHITON

STERCULIACEAE

Genus of evergreen or deciduous, mainly spring-and summer-flowering trees, grown for their flowers and overall appearance. Frost tender, min. 7–10°C

(45–50°F). Needs full light and humus-rich, well-drained, preferably acid soil. Water containerized plants moderately, much less in winter. Prune if needed. Propagate by seed in spring. Red spider mite may be a nuisance.
B. acerifolius (Illawarra flame tree), syn. *Sterculia acerifolia*, illus. p.450.
B. populneus, syn. *Sterculia diversifolia* (Kurrajong). Evergreen, conical tree, pyramidal when young. **H** and **S** 15–20m (50–70ft). Pointed or 3–5 lobed, glossy, deep green leaves are chartreuse when young. In spring-summer has panicles of saucer-shaped, cream or greenish-white flowers with red, purple or yellow throats.

BRACHYGLOTTIS

COMPOSITAE/ASTERACEAE

Genus of evergreen shrubs and trees, grown for their bold foliage and daisy-like flower heads. Fully hardy to frost tender, min. 3°C (37°F). Needs full light or partial shade and well-drained soil. Water containerized plants freely in summer, moderately at other times. Take semi-ripe cuttings in late summer.
B. compacta, syn. *Senecio compactus*. Evergreen, bushy, dense shrub. **H** 1m (3ft), **S** 2m (6ft). Frost hardy. Bears small, oval, white-edged, dark green leaves, white below, and daisy-like, bright yellow flowers in clustered heads from mid- to late summer. Felt-like, white hairs cover the shoots.
♀ ***B. Dunedin Group***, syn. *Senecio* Dunedin Hybrids, *S. greyi* of gardens, *S. laxifolius* of gardens, illus. p.161.
B. laxifolia, syn. *Senecio laxifolius*. Evergreen, bushy, spreading shrub. **H** 1m (3ft), **S** 2m (6ft). Frost hardy. Oval, grey-white leaves become dark green. Has large clusters of daisy-like, golden-yellow flower heads in summer.
♀ ***B. monroi***, syn. *Senecio monroi*, illus. p.161.
B. repanda (Pukapuka, Rangiora). Evergreen, bushy shrub or tree. **H** 3m (10ft), **S** 3m (10ft) or more. Upright when young, with robust, downy, white stems and veined leaves that are white beneath. Produces fragrant, white flower heads in summer.
B. rotundifolia, syn. *Senecio reinholdii*, *S. rotundifolius*. Evergreen, rounded, dense shrub. **H** and **S** 1m (3ft). Frost hardy. Has rounded, leathery, glossy leaves, dark green above, white-felted below, and tiny, yellow flower heads from early to mid-summer. Withstands salt winds in mild coastal areas.

BRACHYSCOME

COMPOSITAE/ASTERACEAE

Genus of annuals and perennials, grown for their daisy-like flower heads and very variable, often finely divided foliage. Fully hardy. Requires sun, a sheltered position and rich, well-drained soil. Pinch out growing shoots of young plants to encourage a bushy habit. Propagate by seed sown under glass in spring or outdoors in late spring.
B. iberidifolia (Swan River daisy). Moderately fast-growing, thin-stemmed, bushy annual. **H** and **S** to 45cm (18in). Has deeply cut leaves and small, fragrant, daisy-like flowers, usually blue but also pink, mauve, purple or white, in summer and early autumn.
B. 'Strawberry Mousse' illus. p.300.

Bracteantha. See *Xerochrysum*.
Brasiliopuntia brasiliensis. See *Opuntia brasiliensis*.

BRASILIORCHIS

ORCHIDACEAE

See also ORCHIDS.
B. picta, syn. *Maxillaria picta*. Evergreen, epiphytic orchid for a cool greenhouse. **H** 23cm (9in). Fragrant, deep yellow to white flowers, 2.5cm (1in) across, marked purple to dark reddish-brown outside, are produced singly beneath foliage in winter. Has narrowly oval leaves, 15–23cm (6–9in) long. Requires semi-shade in summer.
B. porphyrostele, syn. *Maxillaria porphyrostele* (illus. p.467). Evergreen, epiphytic orchid for a cool greenhouse. **H** 8cm (3in). White- and red-lipped, yellow flowers, 1cm (½in) across, are borne singly in summer-autumn. Narrowly oval leaves are 8cm (3in) long. Grow in good light during summer.

Brassaia. See *Schefflera*.

BRASSAVOLA

ORCHIDACEAE

See also ORCHIDS.
B. nodosa (Lady-of-the-night; illus. p.466). Evergreen, epiphytic orchid for an intermediate greenhouse. **H** 23cm (9in). Narrow-petalled, pale green flowers, 5cm (2in) across and each with a white lip, are produced, 1–3 to a stem, in spring; they are fragrant at night. Leaves, 8–10cm (3–4in) long, are thick and cylindrical. Is best grown on a bark slab. Provide good light in summer.

BRASSICA

CRUCIFERAE/BRASSICACEAE

Genus of annuals and evergreen biennials and perennials. Most are edible vegetables, eg. cabbages and kales, but forms of *B. oleracea* are grown for ornamental foliage. Fully hardy. Grow in sun and fertile, well-drained soil. Lime-rich soil is preferable, though not essential. Propagate by seed sown outdoors in spring or under glass in early spring. Is susceptible to club root.
B. oleracea forms (Ornamental cabbage). Moderately fast-growing, evergreen, rounded biennial, grown as an annual. **H** and **S** 30–45cm (12–18in). Has heads of large, often crinkled leaves, in combinations of red/green, white/pink, pink/green. Do not allow to flower.
B. Northern Lights Series illus. p.306.

x *Brassocattleya* x *B.* Mount Adams. See x *Rhyncholaeliocattleya* Mount Adams.
x *Brassolaeliocattleya* Hetherington Horace 'Coronation'. See x *Rhyncholaeliocattleya* Hetherington Horace 'Coronation'.
x *Brassolaeliocattleya* St Helier. See x *Rhyncholaeliocattleya* St Helier.
Bravoa geminiflora. See *Polianthes geminiflora*.

BREYNIA

EUPHORBIACEAE/PHYLLANTHACEAE

Genus of evergreen shrubs and trees, grown for their foliage. Frost tender, min. 13°C (55°F). Requires full light or partial shade and fertile, well-drained soil. Water containerized plants freely when in full growth, moderately at other times. Large bushes should be cut back hard after flowering. Propagate by greenwood or semi-ripe cuttings in summer. Whitefly, red spider mite and mealy bug may be troublesome.
B. disticha, syn. *B. nivosa*, *Phyllanthus nivosus* (Snow bush). Evergreen, well-branched shrub with slender stems. **H** 1m (3ft) or more, **S** 60–100cm (24–39in). Leaves are green with white marbling. Tiny, greenish flowers, borne intermittently, have no petals. **'Roseopicta' H** and **S** to 1m (3ft). Has broadly oval, green leaves variably bordered and splashed with white and flushed pink. Insignificant, petalless flowers are borne in spring-summer.
B. nivosa. See *B. disticha*.

Bridgesia. See *Ercilla*.

BRIGGSIA

GESNERIACEAE

Genus of evergreen perennials, grown for their rosettes of hairy leaves. Frost tender, min. 2–5°C (36–41°F). Needs shade and peaty soil with plenty of moisture in summer and good air circulation in winter. Protect against damp in winter. Propagate by seed in spring.
B. muscicola. Evergreen, basal-rosetted perennial. **H** 8–10cm (3–4in), **S** 23cm (9in). Leaves are oval, silver-haired and pale green. Arching flower stems bear loose clusters of tubular, pale yellow flowers, with protruding tips, in early summer. Is best grown in an alpine house.

BRIMEURA

LILIACEAE/HYACINTHACEAE

Genus of spring-flowering bulbs, similar to miniature bluebells, cultivated for their attractive flowers. Is suitable for rock gardens and shrub borders. Frost hardy. Requires partial shade and prefers humus-rich, well-drained soil. Propagate by sowing seed in autumn or by division in late summer.
♀ ***B. amethystina***, syn. *Hyacinthus amethystinus*, illus. p.419.

Brittonastrum mexicanum. See *Agastache mexicana*.

BRIZA

Quaking grass

GRAMINEAE/POACEAE

See also GRASSES, BAMBOOS, RUSHES and SEDGES.
B. maxima (Greater quaking grass). Robust, tuft-forming, annual grass. **H** to 50cm (20in), **S** 8–10cm (3–4in). Fully hardy. Mid-green leaves are mainly basal. Produces loose panicles of up to 10 pendent, purplish-green spikelets, in early summer, that dry particularly well for winter decoration. Self seeds readily.
B. media (Common quaking grass). Evergreen, tuft-forming, rhizomatous, perennial grass. **H** 30–60cm (12–24in), **S** 8–10cm (3–4in). Fully hardy. Mid-green leaves are mainly basal. In summer produces open panicles of up to 30 pendent, purplish-brown spikelets that dry well for winter decoration.

BRODIAEA

LILIACEAE/ALLIACEAE

Genus of mainly spring-flowering bulbs with colourful flowers produced in loose heads on leafless stems. Frost hardy. Needs a sheltered, sunny situation and light, well-drained soil. Dies down in summer. Propagate in autumn by seed or in late summer and autumn by freely produced offsets.
B. capitata. See *Dichelostemma pulchellum*.
B. congesta. See *Dichelostemma congestum*.
B. coronaria, syn. *B. grandiflora*. Late spring- to early summer-flowering bulb. **H** 10–25cm (4–10in), **S** 8–10cm (3–4in). Long, narrow, semi-erect, basal leaves die down by flowering time. Leafless stems each carry a loose head of erect, funnel-shaped, violet-blue flowers on long, slender stalks.
B. grandiflora. See *B. coronaria*.
B. hyacinthina. See *Triteleia hyacinthina*.
B. ida-maia. See *Dichelostemma ida-maia*.
B. ixioides. See *Triteleia ixioides*.
B. lactea. See *Triteleia hyacinthina*.
B. laxa. See *Triteleia laxa*. **'Queen Fabiola'** see *Triteleia laxa* 'Koningin Fabiola'.
B. lutea. See *Triteleia ixioides*.
B. peduncularis. See *Triteleia peduncularis*.
B. pulchella. See *Dichelostemma pulchellum*.

BROMELIA

BROMELIACEAE

Genus of evergreen, rosette-forming perennials, grown for their overall appearance. Frost tender, min. 5–7°C (41–45°F). Needs full light and well-drained soil. Water moderately in summer, sparingly at other times. Propagate by suckers in spring.
B. balansae (Heart of flame) illus. p.470.

BROMUS

GRAMINEAE/POACEAE

See also GRASSES, BAMBOOS, RUSHES and SEDGES.
B. ramosus (Hairy brome grass). Evergreen, tuft-forming, perennial grass. **H** to 2m (6ft), **S** 30cm (1ft). Fully hardy. Mid-green leaves are lax and hairy. Produces long, arching panicles of nodding, grey-green spikelets in summer. Prefers shade.

BROUSSONETIA

MORACEAE

Genus of deciduous trees and shrubs, grown for their foliage and unusual flowers. Male and female flowers are produced on different plants. Frost hardy. Requires a position in full sun and well-

drained soil. Propagate by softwood cuttings in summer or by seed in autumn.
B. papyrifera (Paper mulberry) illus. p.74.

BROWALLIA

SOLANACEAE

Genus of shrubby perennials, usually grown as annuals, with showy, open trumpet-shaped flowers. Frost tender, min. 4–15°C (39–59°F). Grows best in sun or partial shade and in fertile, well drained soil that should not dry out completely. Feed when flowering if container-grown and pinch out young shoots to encourage bushiness. Propagate by seed in spring; for winter flowers, sow in late summer.
B. americana, syn. *B. elata*. Moderately fast-growing, bushy perennial, usually grown as an annual. **H** 30cm (12in), **S** 15cm (6in). Min. 4°C (39°F). Produces oval, mid-green leaves and, in summer, trumpet-shaped, blue flowers, 4cm (1½in) wide.
B. elata. See *B. americana*.
B. speciosa (Bush violet) illus. p.472.

BROWNINGIA

SYN. AZUREOCEREUS

CACTACEAE

Genus of slow-growing, eventually tree-like, perennial cacti. Spiny, silvery-or green-blue stems, with up to 20 or more ribs, are crowned by stiff, erect, green-blue branches. Frost tender, min. 7°C (45°F). Requires a position in full sun and very well-drained soil. Propagate by seed in spring or summer.
B. hertlingiana, syn. *Azureocereus hertlingianus*, illus. p.488.

Bruckenthalia spiculifolia. See *Erica spiculifolia*.

BRUGMANSIA

Angels' trumpets

SOLANACEAE

Genus of evergreen or semi-evergreen shrubs, trees and annuals, grown for their flowers borne mainly in summer–autumn. Frost hardy to frost tender, min. 7–10°C (45–50°F). Prefers full light and fertile, well-drained soil. Water containerized specimens freely in full growth, moderately at other times. May be pruned hard in early spring. Propagate by seed sown in spring or by greenwood or semi-ripe cuttings in early summer or later. Whitefly and red spider mite may be troublesome.
⚠ All parts are highly toxic if ingested.
B. arborea, syn. *B. versicolor* of gardens. Evergreen or semi-evergreen, rounded, robust shrub. **H** and **S** to 3m (10ft). Frost tender. Bears narrowly oval leaves, each 20cm (8in) or more long. Produces strongly fragrant, pendent, trumpet-shaped, white flowers, each 16–20cm (6–8in) long with a spathe-like calyx, in summer and autumn.
B. aurea. Evergreen, rounded shrub or tree. **H** and **S** 6–11m (20–35ft). Frost tender. Has oval leaves, 15cm (6in) long. In summer–autumn, produces pendent, trumpet-shaped, white or yellow flowers, 15–25cm (6–10in) long.
B. x candida Semi-evergreen, rounded shrub or small tree. **H** 3–5m (10–15ft), **S** 1.5–2.5m (5–8ft). Frost tender, min. 10°C (50°F). Has downy, oval leaves and strongly scented, pendulous, white flowers, sometimes cream or pinkish, in summer–autumn. ♀ **'Grand Marnier'** (syn. *B.* 'Grand Marnier') illus. p.319.
B. 'Grand Marnier'. See *B.* x *candida* 'Grand Marnier'.
B. rosei of gardens. See *B. sanguinea*.
B. sanguinea, syn. *B. rosei* of gardens. Semi-evergreen, erect to rounded shrub or small tree. **H** 3–5m (10–15ft), **S** 2–3m (6–10ft). Frost tender, min. 10°C (50°F). Has lobed, young leaves and large, trumpet-shaped, yellow and orange-red flowers from late summer to winter.
B. versicolor of gardens. See *B. arborea*.

BRUNFELSIA

SOLANACEAE

Genus of evergreen shrubs, grown for their flowers. Frost tender, min. 10–13°C (50–55°F), , but 15–18°C (59–64°F) for good winter flowering. Needs semi-shade and humus-rich, well-drained soil. Water containerized plants moderately, much less in low temperatures. Remove stem tips to promote branching in growing season. Propagate by semi-ripe cuttings in summer. Mealy bug and whitefly may be a problem.
B. calycina. See *B. pauciflora*.
B. eximia. See *B. pauciflora*.
♀ **B. pauciflora**, syn. *B. calycina*, *B. eximia* (Yesterday-today-and-tomorrow). Evergreen, spreading shrub. **H** and **S** 60cm (2ft) or more. Bears oblong to lance-shaped, leathery, glossy leaves. Blue-purple flowers, each with a tubular base and 5 overlapping, wavy-edged petals, are carried from winter to summer. **'Macrantha'** illus. p.457.

BRUNNERA

BORAGINACEAE

Genus of spring-flowering perennials. Fully hardy. Prefers light shade and moist soil. Propagate by division in spring or autumn or by seed in autumn.
♀ **B. macrophylla** (Siberian bugloss). Clump-forming perennial. **H** 45cm (18in), **S** 60cm (24in). Delicate sprays of small, star-shaped, forget-me-not-like, bright blue flowers in early spring are followed by heart-shaped, rough, long-stalked leaves. Makes good ground cover. **'Dawson's White'** has delicate sprays of small, bright blue flowers in spring. Shelter from wind to prevent leaf damage. **'Jack Frost'** illus. p.261.

x *Brunsdonna parkeri*. See x *Amarygia parkeri*.

BRUNSVIGIA

AMARYLLIDACEAE

Genus of autumn-flowering bulbs with heads of showy flowers. Half hardy. Requires sun and well-drained soil. Water in autumn to encourage bulbs into growth and continue watering until summer, when the leaves will die away and dormant bulbs should be kept fairly dry and warm. Propagate by seed sown in autumn or by offsets in late summer.
B. josephinae (Josephine's lily). Autumn-flowering bulb. **H** to 45cm (18in), **S** 45–60cm (18–24in). Bears a stout, leafless stem with a spherical head of 20–30 funnel-shaped, red flowers, 7–9cm (3–3½in) long, with recurved petal tips. Semi-erect, oblong leaves appear after flowering.

Bryophyllum. See *Kalanchoe*.

BUDDLEJA

BUDDLEJACEAE

Genus of deciduous, semi-evergreen or evergreen shrubs and trees, grown for their clusters of small, often fragrant flowers. Fully to half hardy. Requires full sun and fertile, well-drained soil. *B. crispa*, *B. davidii*, *B. fallowiana*, *B.* 'Lochinch' and *B.* x *weyeriana* should be cut back hard in spring. Prune *B. alternifolia* by removing shoots that have flowered. Other species may be cut back lightly after flowering. Propagate by semi-ripe cuttings in summer.
B. agathosma. Deciduous, upright shrub. **H** and **S** 3m (10ft). Fully hardy. Large, triangular-shaped, felt-like, silvery-green leaves have wavy margins. Fragrant, tubular, lilac flowers, with orange centres, are borne in late spring.
♀ **B. alternifolia** (illus. p.114). Deciduous, arching shrub that can be trained as a weeping tree. **H** and **S** 4m (12ft). Has slender, pendent shoots and narrow, grey-green leaves. Neat clusters of fragrant, lilac-purple flowers appear in early summer.
♀ **B. asiatica.** Evergreen, arching shrub. **H** and **S** 3m (10ft). Half hardy. Long plumes of very fragrant, tubular, white flowers appear amid long, narrow, dark green leaves in late winter and early spring. Grow against a south- or west-facing wall.
B. colvilei Deciduous, arching shrub, often tree-like with age. **H** and **S** 6m (20ft). Frost hardy. Has dark green foliage among which large, white-centred, deep pink to purplish-red flowers are borne in drooping racemes during early summer. **'Kewensis'** (illus. p.114), **H** and **S** 5m (15ft), has lance-shaped, dark green leaves. Large, tubular, white-throated, deep red flowers hang in drooping clusters in early summer.
B. crispa illus. p.204.
B. davidii (Butterfly bush). Variable, fast-growing, deciduous shrub. **H** 3–5m (10–16ft), **S** to 5m (16ft). Fully hardy. Long, arching branches bear lance-shaped, pointed, mid- to grey-green leaves, to 25cm (10in) long. Bears dense, semi-pendent panicles, to 20cm (8in) or more, of small, very fragrant, tubular, lilac to purple or white flowers from mid-summer to autumn. Is tolerant of dry conditions. ♀ **'Black Knight'** (illus. p.114) has dark green leaves with white-felted undersides and dark violet-purple flowers. ♀ **'Dartmoor'** (illus. p.114) has deeply cut leaf margins and produces large, branched panicles of deep rich lilac-purple flowers. ♀ **'Empire Blue'** has rich violet-blue flowers. **'Harlequin'** has red-purple flowers. **'Peace'** bears long plumes of white flowers. ♀ **'Pink Delight'** (illus. p.114) has panicles, 30cm (12in) long, of orange-eyed, bright pink flowers. **'Pink Pearl'** produces pale lilac-pink flowers. ♀ **'Royal Red'** has rich purple-red flowers. ♀ **'White Profusion'** (illus. p.114) bears masses of snow-white flowers, each with a yellow eye.
B. fallowiana. Deciduous, arching shrub. **H** 2m (6ft), **S** 3m (10ft). Frost hardy. Shoots and lance-shaped leaves, when young, are covered with white hairs; foliage then becomes dark grey-green. Has fragrant, tubular, lavender-purple flowers in late summer and early autumn. Is often damaged in very severe winters; grow against a wall in cold areas. ♀ **var. alba** has white flowers.
♀ **B. globosa** illus. p.116.
♀ **B. 'Lochinch'** (illus. p.114). Deciduous, arching shrub. **H** and **S** 3m (10ft). Frost hardy. Long plumes of fragrant, tubular, lilac-blue flowers are borne above lance-shaped, grey-green leaves in late summer and autumn.
♀ **B. madagascariensis**, syn. *Nicodemia madagascariensis*. Evergreen, arching shrub. **H** and **S** 4m (12ft) or more. Half hardy. Has narrowly lance-shaped, dark green leaves, white beneath, and, in late winter and spring, long clusters of tubular, orange-yellow flowers. Grow against a south- or west-facing wall.
B. salviifolia (South African sage wood; illus. p.114). Semi-evergreen, arching shrub. **H** 4m (13ft), **S** 3m (10ft). Half hardy. Has sage-like, lance-shaped, wrinkled, blue-green leaves, covered in fine hairs. Fragrant, tubular, white to pale lilac flowers are produced in early summer.
B. x weyeriana. Deciduous, arching shrub. **H** and **S** 4m (12ft). Fully hardy. Bears lance-shaped, dark green leaves, and loose, rounded clusters of tubular, orange-yellow flowers, often tinged purple, from mid-summer to autumn. **'Moonlight'** (illus. p.114) bears pale cream flowers with deep orange-yellow throats. ♀ **'Sungold'** (illus. p.114) has dense clusters of dark orange-yellow flowers.

BULBOCODIUM

LILIACEAE/COLCHICACEAE

Genus of spring-flowering corms, related to *Colchicum* and with funnel-shaped flowers. Is particularly suitable for rock gardens and cool greenhouses. Fully hardy. Requires an open, sunny site and well-drained soil. Propagate by seed sown in autumn or by division in late summer and early autumn.
B. vernum illus. p.418.

BULBOPHYLLUM

ORCHIDACEAE

See also ORCHIDS.
B. careyanum illus. p.000. Evergreen, epiphytic orchid for an intermediate greenhouse. **H** 8cm (3in). Oval leaves are 8–10cm (3–4in) long. In spring produces tight sprays of many slightly fragrant, brown flowers, 0.5cm (¼in) across. Grows best in a hanging basket. Needs semi-shade in summer.

BUPHTHALMUM

COMPOSITAE/ASTERACEAE

Genus of summer-flowering perennials. Fully hardy. Requires full sun; grows well in any but rich soil. Propagate by seed in spring or autumn or by division in autumn. Needs frequent division to curb invasiveness.

B. salicifolium (Yellow ox-eye) illus. p.276.
B. speciosum. See *Telekia speciosa.*

BUPLEURUM

UMBELLIFERAE/APIACEAE

Genus of perennials and evergreen shrubs, grown for their foliage and flowers. Grows well in coastal gardens. Frost hardy. Needs full sun and well-drained soil. Propagate by semi-ripe cuttings in summer.
B. fruticosum (Shrubby hare's ear) illus. p.139.

BUTIA

Yatay palm

ARECACEAE/PALMAE

Genus of evergreen palms, grown for their overall appearance. Frost hardy to frost tender, min. 5°C (41°F). Grow in fertile, well-drained soil and in full light or partial shade. Water regularly, less in winter. Propagate by seed in spring at min. 24°C (75°F). Red spider mite may be a problem.
B. capitata, syn. *Cocos capitata* (Jelly palm). Slow-growing, evergreen palm. **H** 4–6m (12–20ft), **S** 3–5m (10–15ft). Feather-shaped leaves, 2m (6ft) or more long and composed of many leathery leaflets are strongly arching to recurved.

BUTOMUS

BUTOMACEAE

Genus of one species of deciduous, perennial, rush-like, marginal water plant, grown for its fragrant, cup-shaped flowers. Fully hardy. Requires an open, sunny situation in up to 25cm (10in) depth of water. Propagate by division in spring or by seed in spring or late summer.
♀ ***B. umbellatus*** (Flowering rush) illus. p.438.

BUXUS

Box

BUXACEAE

Genus of evergreen shrubs and trees, grown for their foliage and habit. Is excellent for edging, hedging and topiary work. Flowers are insignificant. Fully to frost hardy. Requires sun or semi-shade and any but waterlogged soil. Trim hedges in summer. Promote new growth by cutting back stems to 30cm (12in) or less in late spring. Propagate by semi-ripe cuttings in summer. ⓘ Contact with box sap may irritate skin.
♀ ***B. balearica*** (Balearica box) illus. p.145.
B. microphylla (Small-leaved box). Evergreen, bushy shrub. **H** 1m (3ft), **S** 1.5m (5ft). Fully hardy. Forms a dense, rounded mass of small, oblong, dark green leaves. **'Green Pillow'** illus. p.167.
♀ ***B. sempervirens*** (Common box). Evergreen, bushy shrub or tree. **H** and **S** 5m (15ft). Fully hardy. Produces leaves that are oblong, glossy and dark green. Is useful for hedging and screening. **'Handsworthensis'** (Common box) illus. p.144. ♀ **'Suffruticosa'** illus. p.167.
B. wallichiana (Himalayan box). Slow-growing, evergreen, bushy shrub with open habit. **H** and **S** 2m (6ft). Frost hardy. Produces long, narrow, glossy, bright green leaves.

C

CABOMBA

CABOMBACEAE

Genus of deciduous or semi-evergreen, perennial, submerged water plants with finely divided foliage. Is suitable for aquariums. Frost tender, min. 5°C (41°F). Prefers partial shade. Propagate by stem cuttings in spring or summer.
C. caroliniana (Fanwort, Fish grass, Washington grass). Deciduous or semi-evergreen, perennial, submerged water plant. **S** indefinite. Forms dense, spreading hummocks of fan-shaped, coarsely cut, bright green leaves. Is used as an oxygenating plant.

CAESALPINIA

LEGUMINOSAE/CAESALPINIACEAE

Genus of deciduous or evergreen shrubs, trees and scrambling climbers, grown for their foliage and flowers. Frost hardy to frost tender, min. 5–10°C (41–50°F). Needs full sun and fertile, well-drained soil. Propagate by softwood cuttings in summer or by seed in autumn or spring.
C. gilliesii, syn. *Poinciana gilliesii*, illus. p.116.
C. pulcherrima, syn. *Poinciana pulcherrima* (Barbados pride). Evergreen shrub or tree of erect to spreading habit. **H** and **S** 3–6m (10–20ft). Frost tender, min. 5°C (41°F). Has fern-like leaves composed of many small, mid-green leaflets. In summer bears cup-shaped, yellow flowers, 3cm (1¼in) wide, with very long, red anthers, in short, dense, erect racemes.

CALADIUM

ARACEAE

Genus of perennials with tubers from which arise long-stalked, ornamental leaves. Frost tender, min. 18–19°C (64–6°F). Requires partial shade and moist, humus-rich soil. After leaves have died down, store tubers in a frost-free, dark place. Propagate by separating small tubers when planting in spring. ⓘ Contact with all parts may irritate skin, and may cause mild stomach upset if ingested.
C. bicolor (Angels' wings). **'Candidum'** is a tufted perennial. **H** and **S** to 90cm (36in). Triangular, green-veined, white leaves, to 45cm (18in) long, have arrow-shaped bases and long leaf stalks. Intermittently bears white spathes; small flowers clustered on spadix sometimes produce whitish berries. **'John Peed'** has purple stems and waxy, green leaves with metallic orange-red centres and scarlet veins. **'Pink Beauty'** illus. p.470. **'Pink Cloud'** has large, dark green leaves with mottled pink centres, and pink to white areas along the veins.

CALAMAGROSTIS

GRAMINAE/POACEAE

See also GRASSES, BAMBOOS, RUSHES and SEDGES.
Calamagrostis brachytricha, illus. p.284.

Calandrinia megarhiza of gardens. See *Claytonia megarhiza*.

CALANTHE

ORCHIDACEAE

See also ORCHIDS.
C. sieboldii. See *C. striata*.
C. striata, syn. *C. sieboldii*, illus. p.275.
C. vestita (illus. p.466). Deciduous, terrestrial orchid. **H** 60cm (24in). Frost tender, min. 18°C (64°F). In winter bears sprays of many white flowers, 4cm (1½in) across, each with a large, red-marked lip. Has broadly oval, ribbed, soft leaves, 30cm (12in) long. In summer requires semi-shade and regular feeding.

CALATHEA

MARANTACEAE

Genus of evergreen perennials with brightly coloured and patterned leaves. Frost tender, min. 15°C (59°F). Prefers a shaded, humid position, without fluctuations of temperature, in humus-rich, well-drained soil. Water with soft water, sparingly in low temperatures, but do not allow to dry out completely. Propagate by division in spring.
C. lindeniana. Evergreen, clump-forming perennial. **H** 1m (3ft), **S** 60cm (2ft). Lance-shaped, long-stalked, more or less upright leaves, over 30cm (1ft) long, are dark green, with paler green, feathered midribs above and marked with reddish-purple below. Intermittently bears short, erect spikes of 3-petalled, pale yellow flowers.
***C. majestica* 'Roseolineata'**, syn. *C. ornata* 'Roseolineata'. Evergreen, clump-forming, stemless perennial. **H** to 2m (6ft), **S** to 1.5m (5ft). Narrowly oval, leathery leaves, to 60cm (2ft) long, are dark green, with close-set, fine, pink stripes along the lateral veins and reddish-purple below. Intermittently bears short, erect spikes of 3-petalled, white to mauve flowers. **'Sanderiana'** see *C. sanderiana*.
♀ ***C. makoyana*** illus. p.475.
C. oppenheimiana. See *Ctenanthe oppenheimiana*.
***C. ornata* 'Roseolineata'.** See *C. majestica* **'Roseolineata'**.
C. sanderiana, syn. *C. majestica* 'Sanderiana', illus. p.472.
♀ ***C. zebrina*** (Zebra plant) illus. p.475.

CALCEOLARIA

SCROPHULARIACEAE

Genus of annuals, biennials and evergreen perennials, sub-shrubs and scandent climbers, some of which are grown as annuals. Fully hardy to frost tender, min. 5–7°C (41–5°F). Most prefer sun but some like a shady, cool site and moist but well-drained soil, incorporating sharp sand and compost, and dislike wet conditions in winter. Propagate by softwood cuttings in late spring or summer or by seed in autumn.
C. acutifolia. See *C. polyrrhiza*.
***C.* Anytime Series.** Compact, bushy annuals or biennials. **H** 20cm (8in), **S** 15cm (6in). Half hardy. Has oval, slightly hairy, mid-green leaves and, in spring-summer, heads of 5cm (2in) long, rounded, pouched flowers in red and yellow shades, including bicolours.
C. arachnoidea illus. p.341.
***C.* 'Bright Bikinis'.** Compact, bushy annual or biennial. **H** and **S** 20cm (8in). Frost tender, min. 5°C (41°F). Has oval, slightly hairy, mid-green leaves, and heads of small, rounded, pouched flowers in shades of yellow, orange or red in summer.
C. darwinii. See *C. uniflora* var. *darwinii*.
C. fothergillii. Evergreen, clump-forming, short-lived perennial. **H** and **S** 12cm (5in). Frost hardy. Has a rosette of rounded, light green leaves with hairy edges and, in summer, solitary pouch-shaped, sulphur-yellow flowers with crimson spots. Is good for a sheltered rock ledge or trough or in an alpine house. Needs gritty, peaty soil. Is prone to aphid attack.
♀ ***C. integrifolia.*** Evergreen, upright sub-shrub, sometimes grown as an annual. **H** to 1.2m (4ft), **S** 60cm (2ft). Half hardy. In summer bears crowded clusters of pouch-shaped, yellow to red-brown flowers above oblong to elliptic, mid-green leaves, sometimes rust-coloured beneath.
♀ **'Sunshine'** is compact and bushy with oval, mid-green leaves and heads of small, rounded, pouched, bright golden-yellow flowers in late spring and summer. **H** and **S** 20cm (8in).
***C.* 'John Innes'** illus. p.277.
***C.* 'Monarch'.** Group of bushy annuals or biennials. **H** and **S** 30cm (12in). Half hardy. Has oval, lightly hairy, mid-green leaves and, in spring-summer, bears heads of large, rounded, pouched flowers, 5cm (2in) long, in a wide range of colours.
C. pavonii. Robust, evergreen, scandent climber. **H** 2m (6ft) or more. Frost tender, min. 7°C (45°F). Has oval, serrated, soft-haired leaves with winged stalks. Pouched, yellow flowers with brown marks appear in large trusses from late summer–winter.
C. polyrrhiza, syn. *C. acutifolia*. Evergreen, prostrate perennial. **H** 2.5cm (1in), **S** 15cm (6in). Frost hardy. Has rounded, hairy, mid-green leaves along flower stem, which bears pouch-shaped, purple-spotted, yellow flowers in summer. Is good for a shady rock garden. May also be propagated by division in autumn or spring.
C. tenella illus. p.371.
C. uniflora* var. *darwinii, syn. *C. darwinii*. Evergreen, clump-forming, short-lived perennial. **H** 8cm (3in), **S** 10cm (4in). Fully hardy. Bears rounded, wrinkled, glossy, dark green leaves. In late spring, flower stems carry pendent, pouch-shaped, yellow flowers with dark brown spots on lower lips and central, white bands. Is difficult to grow. Needs a sheltered, sunny site in moist, gritty, peaty soil. Is prone to attack by aphids.
***C.* 'Walter Shrimpton'** illus. p.372.

CALENDULA

Marigold

COMPOSITAE/ASTERACEAE

Genus of annuals and evergreen shrubs. Annuals are fully hardy; shrubs are frost tender, min. 4°C (39°F). Grow in sun or partial shade and in any well-drained soil. Dead-head regularly to prolong flowering. Propagate annuals by seed sown outdoors in spring or autumn, shrubs by stem

B

cuttings in summer. Annuals may self-seed. Cucumber mosaic virus and powdery mildew may cause problems.
C. officinalis (Pot marigold). Fast-growing, bushy annual. Tall cultivars, **H** and **S** 60cm (24in); dwarf forms, **H** and **S** 30cm (12in). All have lance-shaped, strongly aromatic, pale green leaves. Daisy-like, single or double flower heads in a wide range of yellow and orange shades are produced from spring to autumn. **'Daisy May'** illus. p.321. **Fiesta Gitana Group,** syn. *C.o.* 'Fiesta Gitana', illus. p.325. **'Geisha Girl'** (tall) illus. p.326. **Pacific Beauty Series 'Lemon Queen'** illus. p.322.

CALIBRACHOA

SOLANACEAE

A genus of about 25 half hardy shrubby perennials, once included in Petunia, grown for showy flowers. Most hybrids will withstand light frost. Propagation is mainly by semi-ripe cuttings, seed may be sown in spring when available. They make good hanging basket and container plants.
***C.* 'Balcabrose'.** See *C.* Cabaret Series Cabaret Rose.
***C.* Cabaret Series Cabaret Apricot ('Balcabapt').** Mound-forming and trailing, prolific, perennial, grown as an annual. **H** 13cm (5in), **S** 45cm (18in). Has twiggy stems with narrowly ovate, dark green leaves. Trumpet-shaped flowers, 3–4cm (1¼–1½in) across, flecked in apricot, cream and yellow, are borne in summer-autumn. **Cabaret Light Pink ('Balcablitpi')** illus. p.300.
***C.* Million Bells Series Million Bells Cherry Pink ('Sunbelrichipi')** illus. p.306.
***C.* 'Sunbelrichipi'.** See *C.* Million Bells Series Million Bells Cherry Pink.

CALLA

ARACEAE

Genus of one species of deciduous or semi-evergreen, perennial, spreading, marginal water plant, grown for its foliage and showy spathes that surround insignificant flower clusters. Fully hardy. Requires a sunny position, in mud or in water to 25cm (10in) deep. Propagate by division in spring or by seed in late summer. ⚠ Contact with the foliage may aggravate skin allergies.
C. palustris (Bog arum) illus. p.434.

CALLIANDRA

LEGUMINOSAE/MIMOSACEAE

Genus of evergreen trees, shrubs and scandent semi-climbers, grown for their flowers and overall appearance. Frost tender, min. 7–18°C (45–64°F). Requires full light or partial shade and well-drained soil. Water containerized plants freely when in full growth, much less when temperatures are low. To restrict growth, cut back stems by one-half to two-thirds after flowering. Propagate by seed sown indoors in spring. Whitefly and mealy bug may be troublesome.
C. eriophylla (Fairy duster) illus. p.453.
C. haematocephala [pink] illus. p.454. [white]. Evergreen, spreading shrub. **H** 3–6m (10–20ft), **S** 2–4m (6–12ft). Frost tender, min. 7°C (45°F). Leaves have 16–24 leaflets. Flower heads comprising many white-stamened florets appear from late autumn to spring.

CALLIANTHEMUM

RANUNCULACEAE

Genus of perennials, grown for their daisy-like flowers and thick, dissected leaves. Is excellent for rock gardens and alpine houses. Fully hardy. Needs sun and moist but well-drained soil. Propagate by seed when fresh.
C. coriandrifolium, syn. *C. rutifolium.* Prostrate perennial with upright flower stems. **H** 8cm (3in), **S** 20cm (8in). Leaves, forming open rosettes, are long-stalked, very dissected and blue-green. In spring has short-stemmed, many-petalled, white flowers with yellow centres. Is susceptible to slugs.
C. rutifolium. See *C. coriandrifolium.*

CALLICARPA

VERBENACEAE/LAMIACEAE

Genus of deciduous, summer-flowering shrubs, grown for their small but striking, clustered fruits. Fully hardy. Does best in full sun and fertile, well-drained soil. Propagate by softwood cuttings in summer.
C. bodinieri. Deciduous, bushy shrub. **H** 3m (10ft), **S** 2.5m (8ft). Has oval, dark green leaves. Tiny, star-shaped, lilac flowers in mid-summer are followed by dense clusters of spherical, violet fruits. **var. *giraldii*** (Beauty berry) illus. p.141.

CALLISIA

COMMELINACEAE

Genus of evergreen, prostrate perennials, grown for their ornamental foliage and trailing habit. Frost tender, min. 10–15°C (50–59°F). Grow in full light, but out of direct sunlight, in fertile, well-drained soil. Propagate by tip cuttings in spring, either annually or when plants become straggly.
C. navicularis, syn. *Tradescantia navicularis.* Evergreen, low-growing perennial with creeping, rooting shoots, 50cm (20in) or more long. **H** 5–8cm (2–3in), **S** indefinite. Has 2 rows of oval, keeled leaves, 2.5cm (1in) long, sheathing the stem, and stalkless clusters of small, 3-petalled, pinkish-purple flowers in leaf axils in summer–autumn.
C. repens Evergreen, creeping perennial with rooting stems. **H** 10cm (4in), **S** indefinite. Has densely packed leaves, sometimes white-banded and often purplish beneath. Rarely, has inconspicuous, white flowers in winter.

CALLISTEMON

Bottlebrush

MYRTACEAE

Genus of evergreen shrubs, usually with narrow, pointed leaves, grown for their clustered flowers, which, with their profusion of long stamens, resemble bottlebrushes. Fully hardy to frost tender, min. 5°C (41°F); in cool areas, grow half hardy and tender species against a south-or west-facing wall or in a cool greenhouse. Requires full sun and fertile, well-drained soil. Propagate by semi-ripe cuttings in summer or by seed in autumn or spring.
🏆 ***C. citrinus* 'Splendens'** illus. p.203.
C. pallidus illus. p.139.
C. paludosus. See *C. sieberi.*
C. pityoides. Evergreen, compact, upright shrub. **H** 1.5m (5ft), **S** 1m (3ft). Fully hardy. Is densely covered with sharply pointed, dark green leaves, and has short spikes of yellow flowers in mid- and late summer.
C. rigidus (Stiff bottlebrush) illus. p.137.
C. sieberi, syn. *C. paludosus.* Evergreen, bushy, dense shrub. **H** 1.5m (5ft), **S** 1m (3ft). Frost hardy. Has short, narrowly lance-shaped, rigid, mid-green leaves and, from mid- to late summer, small clusters of pale yellow flowers.
C. speciosus (Albany bottlebrush). Evergreen, bushy shrub. **H** and **S** 3m (10ft). Half hardy. Produces long, narrow, grey-green leaves. Cylindrical clusters of bright red flowers appear in late spring and early summer.
C. subulatus, illus. p.203.
C. viminalis. Evergreen, arching shrub. **H** and **S** 5m (15ft). Half hardy. Narrowly oblong, bronze, young leaves mature to dark green. Bears clusters of bright red flowers in summer.

CALLISTEPHUS

China aster

COMPOSITAE/ASTERACEAE

Genus of one species of annual. Half hardy. Requires sun, a sheltered position and fertile, well-drained soil. Tall cultivars need support; all should be dead-headed. Propagate by seed sown under glass in spring; seed may also be sown outdoors in mid-spring. Wilt disease, virus diseases, foot rot, root rot and aphids may be a problem.
C. chinensis. Moderately fast-growing, erect, bushy annual. Tall cultivars, **H** 60cm (24in), **S** 45cm (18in); intermediate, **H** 45cm (18in), **S** 30cm (12in); dwarf, **H** 25–30cm (10–12in), **S** 30–45cm (12–18in); very dwarf, **H** 20cm (8in), **S** 30cm (12in). All have oval, toothed, mid-green leaves and flower in summer and early autumn. Different forms are available in a wide colour range, including pink, red, blue and white. **Duchesse Series** (tall) has incurved, chrysanthemum-like flower heads.
🏆 **Milady Super Series** (dwarf) has incurved, fully double flower heads available either in mixed or single colours (blue, illus. p.312; rose, illus. p.304). **Ostrich Plume Series** (tall) illus. p.303. **Pompon Series** (tall) has small, double flower heads. **Princess Series** (tall) has double flower heads with quilled petals.

CALLUNA

ERICACEAE

See also HEATHERS.
C. vulgaris (Ling, Scotch heather). Evergreen, bushy shrub. **H** to 60cm (24in), **S** 45cm (18in). Fully hardy. Slightly fleshy, linear leaves, in opposite and overlapping pairs, may range in colour from bright green to many shades of grey, yellow, orange and red. Spikes of bell- to urn-shaped, single or double flowers are produced from mid-summer to late autumn. Unlike *Erica*, most of the flower colour derives from the sepals. The following cultivars are **H** 45cm (18in), have mid-green leaves and bear single flowers in late summer and early autumn, unless otherwise stated. **'Alba Plena'**, **H** 30–45cm (12–18in), bears double, white flowers. 🏆 **'Alexandra'**, **H** 30cm (12in), **S** 40cm (16in), has an upright habit, dark green foliage, and deep crimson buds until early winter. 🏆 **'Alicia'**, **H** 30cm (12in), **S** 40cm (16in), has white buds until early winter, and a neat, compact habit.
🏆 **'Allegro'**, **H** 60cm (24in), is compact in habit and produces purple-red flowers. **'Alportii'**, **H** 60–90cm (24–36in), has purple-red flowers. 🏆 **'Anette'**, **H** 35cm (14in), **S** 40cm (16in), has clear pink buds until early winter. 🏆 **'Annemarie'** (illus. p.166), **H** 50cm (20in), **S** 60cm (24in), has outstanding, double, rose-pink flowers, ideal for cutting. 🏆 **'Anthony Davis'** has grey leaves and white flowers. 🏆 **'Beoley Gold'** (illus. p.166), **S** 50cm (20in), has golden foliage and white flowers. **'Beoley Silver'**, **H** 40cm (16in), has silver foliage and white flowers. **'Blazeaway'**, **H** 35cm (14in), **S** 60cm (24in), has gold foliage in summer that turns orange, then fiery red in winter. **'Bonfire Brilliance'**, **H** 30cm (12in), has bright, flame-coloured foliage and mauve-pink flowers. **'Boskoop'**, **H** 30cm (12in), is compact with golden foliage that turns deep orange in winter and lilac-pink flowers. 🏆 **'County Wicklow'**, **H** 30cm (12in), **S** 35cm (14in), is compact with double, shell-pink flowers.
🏆 **'Dark Beauty'**, **H** 20cm (8in), **S** 35cm (14in), is neat and compact, and bears bright, semi-double, crimson flowers.
🏆 **'Darkness'**, **H** 40cm (16in), **S** 35cm (14in), is compact with crimson flowers.
🏆 **'Dark Star'**, illus, p.166. **H** 20cm (8in), **S** 35cm (14in), has short racemes of semi-double, deep crimson flowers. 🏆 **'Elsie Purnell'** is a spreading cultivar with greyish-green leaves and double, pale pink flowers. **'Finale'** bears dark pink flowers from late autumn to early winter.
🏆 **'Firefly'**, 50cm (20in), with deep mauve flowers, has foliage that is terracotta in summer, brick-red in winter. **'Foxii Nana'**, **H** 15cm (6in), forms low mounds of bright green foliage and produces a few mauve-pink flowers. **'Fred J. Chapple'** has bright pink- and coral-tipped foliage in spring; mauve-pink flowers are borne on long stems. 🏆 **'Gold Haze'** has bright golden foliage and white flowers. **'Golden Feather'** has bright yellow foliage, turning orange in winter, and mauve-pink flowers. **'Hammondii Aureifolia'**, **H** 30cm (12in), **S** 40cm (16in), has white flowers. Foliage is light green, tipped yellow in spring and early summer. **'H. E. Beale'**, **H** 50cm (20in), is one of the best double-flowered heathers, with pale pink flowers on long stems.🏆 **'J.H. Hamilton'**, **H** 20cm (8in), **S** 40cm (16in), is compact with double, salmon-pink flowers. 🏆 **'Joy Vanstone'** has golden foliage, turning to orange and bronze, and mauve-pink flowers. 🏆 **'Kerstin'**, **H** 30cm (12in), produces mauve flowers and has downy, deep lilac-grey foliage in winter, tipped pale yellow and red in spring.
🏆 **'Kinlochruel'**, **H** 30cm (12in), **S** 35cm (14in), bears an abundance of large, double, white flowers. **'Loch Turret'**,

H 30cm (12in), has emerald-green foliage and produces white flowers in early summer. ♀ **'Mair's Variety'**, an old cultivar, has white flowers on long spikes. **'Marleen'** is unusual in that its long-lasting, dark mauve flower buds, borne from early to late autumn, do not open fully. ♀ **'Mullion'** **H** 25cm (10in), **S** 50cm (20in), is a spreading cultivar with rich mauve-pink flowers. **'Multicolor'**, **H** 20cm (8in), is compact with foliage in shades of yellow, orange, red and green year-round; flowers are mauve-pink. ♀ **'My Dream'** (syn. *C.v.* 'Snowball'), **H** 50cm (20in), produces double, white flowers that are borne on long, tapering stems. ♀ **'Peter Sparkes'** (illus. p.166), **H** 50cm (20in), **S** 55cm (22in), bears double, deep pink flowers. ♀ **'Robert Chapman'** is a spreading cultivar and grown mainly for its foliage, which is golden-yellow in summer, turning orange and brilliant red in winter; flowers are mauve-pink. **'Ruth Sparkes'**, **H** 25cm (10in), has golden foliage and white flowers. **'Silver Knight'**, **H** 30cm (12in), is of upright habit with grey leaves and mauve-pink flowers. ♀ **'Silver Queen'**, **H** 40cm (16in), **S** 55cm (22in), is a spreading cultivar with dark mauve-pink flowers. ♀ **'Sir John Charrington'** has bright-coloured foliage, varying from golden-yellow in summer to orange and red in winter, and dark mauve-pink flowers. ♀ **'Sister Anne'**, **H** 15cm (6in), has grey leaves and pale mauve-pink flowers. **'Snowball'** see *C.v.* 'My Dream'. ♀ **'Spring Cream'** has bright green leaves, which have cream tips in spring, and white flowers. **'Spring Torch'**, **H** 40cm (16in), **S** 60cm (24in), has mauve flowers with cream, orange and red tips in spring. ♀ **'Sunset'**, **H** 25cm (10in), has brightly coloured foliage, changing from golden-yellow in spring to orange in summer and fiery red in winter; flowers are mauve-pink. ♀ **'Tib'** (illus. p.166), **H** 30cm (12in), **S** 40cm (16in), is the earliest-flowering double cultivar, producing small, double, deep pink flowers in early summer. ♀ **'White Lawn'**, **H** 10cm (4in), is a creeping cultivar with bright green foliage and white flowers on long stems; is suitable for a rock garden. ♀ **'Wickwar Flame'** (illus. p.166) is primarily a foliage plant with leaves in shades of yellow, orange and flame that are particularly effective in winter; flowers are mauve-pink.

CALOCEDRUS

CUPRESSACEAE

See also CONIFERS.
♀ ***C. decurrens*** (Incense cedar), syn. *Libocedrus decurrens*, illus. p.101.

Calocephalus brownii. See *Leucophyta brownii.*

CALOCHONE

RUBIACEAE

Genus of evergreen, scrambling climbers, grown for their flowers. Frost tender, min. 18°C (64°F). Needs full light and humus-rich, well-drained soil. Water regularly, less in cold weather. Needs tying to a support. Thin out stems after flowering. Propagate by semi-ripe cuttings in summer.

C. redingii. Moderately vigorous, evergreen, scrambling climber. **H** 3–5m (10–15ft). Has oval, pointed, hairy leaves, 7–12cm (3–5in) long. Trusses of primrose-shaped, red to orange-pink flowers appear in winter.

CALOCHORTUS

Cat's ears, Fairy lantern, Mariposa tulip

LILIACEAE

Genus of bulbs, grown for their spring and summer flowers. Frost hardy. Needs a sheltered, sunny site and well-drained soil. In cold, damp climates, cover or lift spring-flowering species when dormant, or grow in cold frames or cold houses. After flowering, remove bulbils for propagation. Propagate by seed or bulbils: spring-flowering species in autumn, summer-flowering species in spring.

C. albus. (Fairy lantern, Globe lily). Spring-flowering bulb. **H** 20–50cm (8–20in), **S** 5–10cm (2–4in). Has long, narrow, erect, grey-green leaves near the base of the loosely branched stem. Each branch carries a pendent, globose, white or pink flower.

C. barbatus, syn. *Cyclobothra lutea*, illus. p.412.

C. luteus (Yellow mariposa) illus. p.406.

C. monophyllus. Summer-flowering bulb. **H** 8–20cm (3–8in), **S** 5cm (2in). Has an erect, branched stem with 1–3 slender leaves and one long, narrow basal leaf. Bears cup-shaped, deep yellow flowers, often with a reddish mark on the claws. Petals are fringed and densely bearded.

C. splendens. Late spring-flowering bulb. **H** 20–60cm (8–24in), **S** 5–10cm (2–4in). Bears 1 or 2 linear, erect leaves near base of branched stem and 1–4 upward-facing, saucer-shaped, pale purple flowers, 5–7cm (2–3in) across, with a darker blotch at the base of each of the 3 large petals.

C. superbus illus. p.409.

C. venustus illus. p.399.

C. vestae. Late spring-flowering bulb. **H** 20–60cm (8–24in), **S** 5–10cm(2–4in). Is similar to *C. splendens*, but flowers are white or purple, with a rust-brown mark near the base of each of the 3 large petals.

C. weedii. Summer-flowering bulb. **H** 30–60cm (12–24in), **S** 5–10cm (2–4in). Has a linear, erect leaf near base of stem. Carries usually 2 upright, saucer-shaped flowers, 4–5cm (1½–2in) across, that are orange-yellow with brown lines and flecks and hairy inside.

CALODENDRUM

RUTACEAE

Genus of evergreen trees, grown for their flowers that are produced mainly in spring-summer. Frost tender, min. 7–10°C (45–50°F). Needs full light and fertile, well-drained but moisture-retentive soil. Water containerized specimens freely when in full growth, less at other times. Tolerates some pruning. Propagate by seed in spring or by semi-ripe cuttings in summer.

C. capense (Cape chestnut). Fairly fast growing, evergreen, rounded tree. **H** and **S** to 15m (50ft) or more. Has oval leaves patterned with translucent dots. Terminal panicles of 5-petalled, light pink to deep mauve flowers appear from spring to early summer.

CALOMERIA

SYN. HUMEA

COMPOSITAE/ASTERACEAE

Genus of perennials and evergreen shrubs. Only *C. amaranthoides* is cultivated, usually as a biennial. Frost tender, min. 4°C (39°F). Needs sun and fertile, well-drained soil. Propagate by seed sown under glass in mid-summer.

C. amaranthoides, syn. *C. elegans* (Incense plant). Erect, branching biennial. **H** to 1.8m (6ft), **S** 90cm (3ft). Has lance-shaped leaves and heads of tiny, pink, brownish-red or crimson flowers with a strong fragrance of incense in summer-autumn.

C. elegans. See *C. amaranthoides.*

Calonyction aculeatum. See *Ipomoea alba.*

CALOSCORDUM

LILIACEAE/ALLIACEAE

Genus of one species of summer-flowering bulb, related and similar to *Allium*. Is suitable for a rock garden. Frost hardy. Needs an open, sunny situation and well-drained soil. Lies dormant in winter. Propagate in early spring by seed or division before growth starts.

C. neriniflorum, syn. *Nothoscordum neriniflorum.* Clump-forming bulb. **H** 10–25cm (4–10in), **S** 8–10cm (3–4in). Thread-like, semi-erect, basal leaves die down at flowering time. Each leafless stem produces a loose head of 10–20 small, funnel-shaped, pinkish-red flowers in late summer.

CALOTHAMNUS

MYRTACEAE

Genus of evergreen, summer-flowering shrubs, grown for their flowers and overall appearance. Thrives in a dryish, airy environment. Frost tender, min. 5°C (41°F). Requires full sun and well-drained, sandy soil. Water containerized plants moderately when in full growth, less at other times. Propagate by seed or semi-ripe cuttings in summer.

C. quadrifidus (Common net bush). Erect to spreading, evergreen shrub. **H** 2–4m (6–12ft), **S** 2–5m (6–15ft). Has linear, greyish to dark green or grey leaves. Irregular, axillary, one-sided spikes of rich red, feathery flowers, 2.5cm (1in) long, are produced from late spring to autumn, often forming clusters, 20cm (8in) or more across, around the stems.

CALTHA

RANUNCULACEAE

Genus of deciduous, perennial, marginal water plants, bog plants and rock garden plants, grown for their attractive flowers. Fully hardy. Most prefer an open, sunny position. Smaller growing species are suitable for rock gardens, troughs and alpine houses and require moist but well-drained soil; larger species are best in marginal conditions. Propagate species by seed in autumn or by division in autumn or early spring, selected forms by division in autumn or early spring.

C. leptosepala illus. p.435.

♀ ***C. palustris*** (Kingcup, Marsh marigold) illus. p.444. **var. *alba*** (syn. *C.p.* 'Alba') is a compact, deciduous, perennial, marginal water plant. **H** 22cm (9in), **S** 30cm (12in). Has rounded, glossy, dark green leaves, and bears solitary, white flowers with yellow stamens in early spring, often before the foliage develops. ♀ **'Plena'**, syn. *C.p.* 'Flore Pleno', illus. p.444.

CALYCANTHUS

CALYCANTHACEAE

Genus of deciduous, summer-flowering shrubs, grown for their purplish- or brownish-red flowers with strap-shaped petals. Fully hardy. Requires sun or light shade and fertile, deep, moist but well-drained soil. Propagate by softwood cuttings in summer or by seed in autumn.

C. floridus (Carolina allspice). Deciduous, bushy shrub. **H** and **S** 2m (6ft). Has oval, aromatic, dark green leaves and, from early to mid-summer, fragrant, brown-red flowers with masses of spreading petals.

C. occidentalis (California allspice) illus. p.137.

CALYPSO

ORCHIDACEAE

See also ORCHIDS.

C. bulbosa. Deciduous, terrestrial orchid. **H** 5–20cm (2–8in). Fully hardy. Corm-like stem produces a single, oval, pleated leaf, 3–10cm (1¼–4in) long. Purplish-pink flowers, 1.5–2cm (⅝–¾in) long, with hairy, purple-blotched, white or pale pink lips, are produced singly in late spring or early summer. Requires a damp, semi-shaded position with a mulch of leaf mould.

CAMASSIA

LILIACEAE/HYACINTHACEAE

Genus of summer-flowering bulbs, suitable for borders and pond margins. Frost hardy. Requires sun or partial shade and deep, moist soil. Plant bulbs in autumn, 10cm (4in) deep. Lies dormant in autumn–winter. Propagate by seed in autumn or by division in late summer. If seed is not required, cut off stems after flowering.

C. esculenta. See *C. quamash.*

♀ ***C. leichtlinii*** illus. p.383. **'Semiplena'** is a tuft-forming, summer-flowering bulb. **H** 1–1.5m (3–5ft), **S** 20–30cm (8–12in). Has long, narrow, erect, basal leaves. Each leafless stem carries a dense spike of narrow-petalled, double, creamy-white flowers, 4–8cm (1½–3in) across.

C. quamash, syn. *C. esculenta* (Common camassia, Quamash), illus. p.411.

CAMELLIA

THEACEAE

Genus of evergreen shrubs and trees, grown for their flowers and foliage. Flowers are classified according to the following types: single, semi-double, anemone-form, peony-form, rose-form, formal double and irregular double. See feature panel pp.120–121 for illustrations and descriptions. Grows well against walls and in containers. Fully hardy to frost tender, min. 7–10°C (45–50°F). Most forms prefer a sheltered position and semi-

shade. Well-drained, neutral to acid soil is essential. Prune to shape after flowering. Propagate by semi-ripe or hardwood cuttings from mid-summer to early winter or by grafting in late winter or early spring. Aphids, thrips and scale insects may cause problems under glass.
C. 'Anticipation'. See *C.* x *williamsii* 'Anticipation'.
🏆 **C. 'Black Lace'** (illus. p.121). Slow-growing, dense, upright shrub. **H** 1.5–2.5m (5–8ft), **S** 1–2.5m (3–8ft). Fully hardy. Has ovate, dark green leaves, 8cm (3in) long, and large, formal double, deep velvet-red flowers from early to late spring.
C. chrysantha. See *C. nitidissima.*
🏆 **C. 'Cornish Snow'** (illus. p.120). Fast-growing, evergreen, upright, bushy shrub. **H** 3m (10ft), **S** 1.5m (5ft). Frost hardy. Has lance-shaped leaves, bronze when young, maturing to dark green. In early spring, bears a profusion of small, cup-shaped, single, white flowers.
C. cuspidata. Evergreen, upright shrub becoming bushy with age. **H** 3m (10ft), **S** 1.5m (5ft). Frost hardy. Has small, lance-shaped leaves, bronze when young, maturing to purplish-green. Small, cup-shaped, single, pure white flowers are freely produced from leaf axils in early spring.
🏆 **C. 'Dr Clifford Parks'.** Evergreen, spreading shrub. **H** 4m (12ft), **S** 2.5m (8ft). Frost hardy. In mid-spring has large, flame-red flowers, often semi-double, peony- and anemone-form on the same plant. Leaves are large, oval and dark green.
🏆 **C. 'Francie L.'.** Vigorous shrub with long, fan-shaped branches. **H** 5m (15ft), **S** 6m (20ft). Fully hardy (if trained on a wall). Leaves are lance-shaped and dark green, 6–10cm (2½–4in) long. Has large, semi-double, salmon-red to deep rose-red flowers from late winter to late spring.
🏆 **C. 'Freedom Bell'** (illus. p.121). Evergreen, dense, rounded shrub. **H** and **S** 2.2m (7ft). Fully hardy. Has masses of semi-double, bright red flowers, from late winter to early spring, and ovate, glossy, rich green leaves.
C. granthamiana. Evergreen, open shrub. **H** to 3m (10ft), **S** 2m (6ft). Half hardy. Oval, leathery leaves are crinkly and glossy, deep green. In late autumn bears large, saucer-shaped, single, white flowers, to 18cm (7in) across, with up to 8 broad petals.
C. hiemalis. Evergreen, upright, bushy shrub. **H** 2–3m (6–10ft), **S** 1.5m (5ft). Frost hardy. Has small, lance-shaped leaves and fragrant, single, cup-shaped, semi- or irregular double, white, pink or red flowers borne in late autumn and winter. Is good for hedging.
C. hongkongensis. Evergreen, bushy shrub or tree. **H** to 3m (10ft), **S** 2m (6ft). Half hardy. Lance-shaped leaves, 10cm (4in) long, are dark red when young, maturing to dark green. Bears cup-shaped, single, deep crimson flowers, velvety beneath, in late spring.
C. 'Innovation'. Evergreen, open, spreading shrub. **H** 5m (15ft), **S** 3m (10ft). Frost hardy. Has large, oval, leathery leaves and, in spring, produces large, peony-form, lavender-shaded, claret-red flowers with twisted petals.
🏆 **C. 'Inspiration'** (illus. p.121). Evergreen, upright shrub. **H** 4m (12ft), **S** 2m (6ft). Frost hardy. Leaves are oval and leathery. Saucer-shaped, semi-double, phlox-pink flowers are freely produced in spring.
C. japonica (Common camellia). Evergreen shrub that is very variable in habit, foliage and floral form. **H** 10m (30ft), **S** 8m (25ft). Frost hardy. Numerous cultivars are available; they are spring-flowering unless otherwise stated.
🏆 **'Adolphe Audusson'** (illus. p.121) is a very reliable, old cultivar that is suitable for all areas and will withstand lower temperatures than most other variants. Produces large, saucer-shaped, semi-double, dark red flowers with prominent, yellow stamens. Leaves are broadly lance-shaped and dark green. 🏆 **'Alba Plena'** (illus. p.120) has an erect habit with elliptic, mid-green leaves and large, formal double, white flowers. **'Alba Simplex'** is bushy in habit with broadly lance-shaped, mid-to yellow-green leaves and cup-shaped, single, white flowers in early spring.
🏆 **'Alexander Hunter',** an upright, compact shrub, has flattish, single, deep crimson flowers, with some petaloids, and lance-shaped, dark green leaves.
'Althaeiflora' has a vigorous, bushy habit, large, peony-form, dark red flowers and broadly oval, very dark green leaves.
'Apollo' (syn. *C.j.* 'Paul's Apollo') is a vigorous, branching shrub that produces semi-double, red flowers sometimes blotched with white. Leaves are glossy, dark green. 🏆 **'Berenice Boddy'** is a vigorous shrub that bears semi-double, light pink flowers amid lance-shaped, dark green leaves. **'Betty Sheffield Supreme'** is upright in habit with lance-shaped, mid-green leaves. Irregular double flowers have white petals bordered with shades of rose-pink. 🏆 **'Bob's Tinsie'** (illus. p.121) has a dense, upright habit, and bears miniature, anemone-form, brilliant red flowers from early to late spring. 🏆 **'Brushfield's Yellow'** (illus. p.121) has an erect, compact habit, elliptic, dark green leaves and anemone-form, cream flowers, each with a pale yellow centre.
🏆 **'Coquettii'** (syn. *C.j.* 'Glen 40') is a slow-growing, erect shrub. In early and mid-spring, bears profuse, medium to large, deep red flowers, sometimes formal double, sometimes peony-form.
'Donckelaeri' see *C.j.* 'Masayoshi'.
🏆 **'Elegans'** has a spreading habit and anemone-form, deep rose-pink flowers with central petaloids often variegated white. Leaves are broadly lance-shaped and dark green. **'Glen 40'** see *C.j.* 'Coquettii'. 🏆 **'Gloire de Nantes'** is an upright shrub, becoming bushy with age, that bears flattish to cup-shaped, semi-double, bright rose-pink flowers over a long period. Has oval to lance-shaped, glossy, dark green leaves. 🏆 **'Guilio Nuccio'** is an upright, free-flowering cultivar that spreads with age. Produces large, cup-shaped, semi-double, rose-red flowers with wavy petals and often a confused centre of petaloids and golden stamens. Dark green leaves are lance-shaped and occasionally have 'fish-tail' tips. 🏆 **'Hagoromo'** (syn. *C.j.* 'Magnoliiflora; illus. p.120) has a bushy habit and flattish to cup-shaped, semi-double, blush-pink flowers. Twisted, light green leaves point downwards. **'Janet Waterhouse'** (illus. p.120) is strong-growing and has semi-double, white flowers with golden anthers borne amid dark green foliage. **'Julia Drayton'** has an upright habit and large, crimson flowers varying from formal double to peony-form. Dark green leaves are oval to lance-shaped and slightly twisted.
'Jupiter' is an upright shrub that bears lance-shaped, dark green leaves and large, saucer-shaped, single, pinkish-red flowers with golden stamens.
'Kumasaka' (syn. *C.j.* 'Lady Marion') has an upright habit with narrowly lance-shaped, mid-green leaves. Produces formal double, or occasionally peony-form, deep rose-pink flowers. **'Lady Marion'** see *C.j.* 'Kumasaka'. **'Lady Vansittart'** is upright, with unusual, holly-like, twisted, mid-green foliage. Saucer-shaped, semi-double, white flowers are flushed rose-pink; flower colour is variable and often self-coloured mutations appear. 🏆 **'Lavinia Maggi'** (illus. p.121) has an upright habit and formal double, white flowers striped with pink and carmine. Sometimes sports red flowers. **'Magnoliiflora'** see *C.j.* 'Hagoromo'. **'Margaret Davis'** (illus. p.121) is a spreading cultivar, with oval to lance-shaped, dark green leaves. Has irregular double blooms with ruffled, creamy-white petals, often lined with pink. Edges of each petal are bright rose-red. 🏆 **'Masayoshi'** (syn. *C.j.* 'Donckelaeri') is slow-growing, bushy and pendulous with saucer-shaped, semi-double, red flowers, often white-marbled. Has lance-shaped, dark green leaves.
'Mathotiana', illus. p.137. **'Mrs D.W. Davis'** is a dense, spreading cultivar that bears very large, pendulous, cup-shaped, semi-double, delicate pink flowers that are backed by oval to lance-shaped, dark green leaves. **'Nobilissima'** (illus. p.120) has a semi-erect habit, elliptic, dark green leaves and peony-form, lemon-tinted, white flowers in late winter and early spring. **'Paul's Apollo'** see *C.j.* 'Apollo'.
🏆 **'R.L. Wheeler'** has robust, upright growth; large, broadly oval, leathery, very dark green leaves and very large, flattish, anemone-form to semi-double, rose-pink flowers, with distinctive rings of golden stamens, often including some petaloids. 🏆 **'Rubescens Major'** is an upright cultivar, becoming bushy with age, with oval to lance-shaped, dark green leaves. Bears formal double, crimson-veined, rose-red flowers.
'Sieboldii' see *C.j.* 'Tricolor'.
'Tomorrow Park Hill', one of the best of many mutations of 'Tomorrow', is of vigorous, upright habit. Has lance-shaped, mid-green leaves and bears irregular double flowers with deep pink, outer petals gradually fading to soft pink centres that are often variegated with white. **'Tomorrow's Dawn'** is similar to 'Tomorrow Park Hill', but produces pale pink flowers, each with a white border and frequently red-streaked.
🏆 **'Tricolor'** (syn. *C.j.* 'Sieboldii; illus. p.121) has bright green, crinkled, holly-like leaves, and bears medium, single or semi-double, red flowers, striped pink and white, in early spring.
🏆 **C. 'Leonard Messel'** (illus. p.121). Evergreen, open shrub. **H** 4m (12ft), **S** 2.5m (8ft). Frost hardy. Has large, oval, leathery, dark green leaves. In spring bears a profusion of large, flattish to cup-shaped, semi-double, rose-pink flowers.
C. x maliflora. Evergreen, upright, bushy shrub. **H** 2m (6ft), **S** 1m (3ft). Frost hardy. Has small, broadly oval, thin-textured, light green leaves and, in spring, produces flattish to cup-shaped, semi-double, pale pink- or white-centred flowers with rose-pink margins.
C. nitidissima, syn. *C. chrysantha*. Fast-growing, evergreen, open shrub or tree. **H** 6m (20ft) or more, **S** 3m (10ft). Half hardy. Has large, oval, leathery, veined leaves. Small, stalked, cup-shaped, single, clear yellow flowers are produced from leaf axils in spring.
C. oleifera. Evergreen, bushy shrub. **H** 2m (6ft), **S** 1.5m (5ft). Frost hardy. Leaves are oval and dull green. Has cup-shaped, single, sometimes pinkish, white flowers in early spring.
C. reticulata. Evergreen, open, tree-like shrub. **H** 10m (30ft) or more, **S** 5m (15ft). Half hardy. Has large, oval, leathery leaves; large, saucer-shaped, single, rose-pink and salmon-red flowers are borne in spring. Needs shelter. **'Arch of Triumph'** bears very large, loose peony-form, orange-tinted, crimson-pink flowers. **'Butterfly Wings'** see *C.r.* 'Houye Diechi'. **'Captain Rawes'** (illus. p.121) has a profusion of large, semi-double, carmine-rose blooms.
'Houye Diechi' (syn. *C.r.* 'Butterfly Wings') produces very large, flattish to cup-shaped, semi-double, rose-pink flowers with wavy, central petals.
'Mandalay Queen' has large, semi-double, deep rose-pink flowers. **'Robert Fortune'** see *C.r.* 'Songzilin'. **'Songzilin'** (syn. *C.r.* 'Robert Fortune') is upright and has large, formal double, deep red flowers.
C. rosiflora. Evergreen, spreading shrub. **H** and **S** 1m (3ft). Frost hardy. Leaves are oval and dark green. In spring bears small, saucer-shaped, single, rose-pink flowers.
C. saluenensis. Fast-growing, evergreen, bushy shrub. **H** to 4m (12ft), **S** to 2.5m (8ft). Half hardy. Has lance-shaped, stiff, dull green leaves. Cup-shaped, single, white to rose-red flowers are freely produced in early spring. Some forms may withstand lower temperatures.
C. sasanqua. Fast-growing, evergreen, dense, upright shrub. **H** 3m (10ft), **S** 1.5m (5ft). Frost hardy. Has lance-shaped, glossy, bright green leaves. In autumn, bears a profusion of fragrant, flattish to cup-shaped, single, rarely semi-double, white flowers; they may occasionally be pink or red. Does best in a hot, sunny site.
🏆 **'Hugh Evans'** is vigorous and has an upright habit, so can be trained against a wall, and bears single, pale pink flowers in winter. 🏆 **'Jean May'** produces large, peony-form to double, pale pink flowers, from winter to early spring.
'Narumigata' has large, cup-shaped, single, white flowers, sometimes pink-flushed. **'Shishigashira'** has small, semi-double to rose-form, double, pinkish-red flowers.
C. 'Satan's Robe'. Vigorous, erect shrub. **H** 3–5m (10–15ft), **S** 2–3m (6–10ft). Frost hardy. Leaves are broadly elliptic, glossy and dark green, 12–16cm (5–6in) long. From early to late spring, produces large,

C

semi-double, bright carmine-red flowers, with yellow stamens.
***C.* 'Shiro-wabisuke'.** Slow-growing, compact shrub. **H** 2.5m (8ft), **S** 1.5m (5ft). Fully hardy. Has narrow, mid-green leaves. From mid-winter to early spring produces small, single, bell-shaped, white flowers.
***C.* 'Spring Festival'** (illus. p.121). Evergreen, upright shrub. **H** 2–4m (6–13ft), **S** 0.6–2m (2–6ft). Fully hardy. Has elliptic, dark green leaves. Miniature, formal double, pink flowers, maturing to pale pink, are produced in mid-spring.
C. tsaii. Evergreen, bushy shrub. **H** 4m (12ft), **S** 3m (10ft). Half hardy. Small, lance-shaped, light green leaves turn bronze with age. Small, cup-shaped, single, white flowers are freely produced in spring.
C.* x *vernalis. Fast-growing, evergreen, upright shrub. **H** to 3m (10ft), **S** 1.5m (5ft). Frost hardy. Has lance-shaped, bright green leaves and, in late winter, fragrant, flattish to cup-shaped, single, white, pink or red flowers. Some forms produce irregular double flowers.
***C.* 'William Hertrich'.** Strong-growing, evergreen, open shrub. **H** 5m (15ft), **S** 3m (10ft). Half hardy. Is free-flowering with large, flattish to cup-shaped, semi-double blooms of a bright cherry-red in spring. Petal formation is very irregular, and petals often form a confused centre with only a few golden stamens. Leaves are large, oval and deep green.
***C.* x *williamsii* 🏆 'Anticipation'.** Robust, evergreen, upright shrub. **H** 3m (10ft), **S** 1.5m (5ft). Frost hardy. Has lance-shaped, dark green leaves. Large, peony-form, deep rose-pink blooms are freely produced in spring. **'Bow Bells'**, **H** 4m (12ft), **S** 2.5m (8ft), has a spreading habit, is fully hardy, has small, mid-green leaves and, in early spring, masses of cup-shaped, single, rose-pink flowers with deeper pink centres and veins. 🏆 **'Brigadoon'** is a bushy shrub, bearing semi-double, rose-pink flowers with broad, down-curving petals. 🏆**'Debbie'** (illus. p.121) bears large, peony-form, rose-pink flowers. 🏆 **'Donation'** (illus. p.121) is a compact, upright plant that is very floriferous, with large, cup-shaped, semi-double, pink flowers. **'Dream Boat'** has a spreading habit, and bears medium, formal double, pale purplish-pink flowers, with incurved petals, in mid-spring. **'E. G. Waterhouse'** (illus. p.122) is an upright, free-flowering cultivar bearing formal double, pink flowers among pale green foliage. **'Elizabeth de Rothschild'** is vigorous and upright; cup-shaped, semi-double, rose-pink flowers appear among glossy foliage. 🏆**'Elsie Jury'** has glossy, deep green leaves and large, full peony-form, clear pink flowers. **'Francis Hanger'** has an upright habit and carries single, white flowers with gold stamens. 🏆 **'George Blandford'** is spreading and bears semi-double, bright crimson-pink flowers in early spring. **'Golden Spangles'** is a cup-shaped, single, deep pink cultivar with unusual, variegated foliage, yellowish in centres of leaves with dark green margins. 🏆 **'J.C. Williams'** (illus. p.121) is of pendulous habit when mature and bears cup-shaped, single, pink flowers from early winter to late spring. 🏆 **'Joan Trehane'** has strong, upright growth and large, rose-form, double, rose-pink flowers. 🏆 **'Jury's Yellow'** (illus. p.121) is narrow and erect, bearing medium, anemone-form, white flowers, with centres of yellow petaloids. **'Ruby Wedding'** produces anemone to peony-form, vivid red flowers, which are sometimes specked white in the centre. 🏆 **'Saint Ewe'** has glossy, light green foliage and funnel-shaped, single, deep pink flowers. 🏆 **'Water Lily'** (illus. p.121) is an upright, compact cultivar with dark green leaves that bears formal double, mid-pink flowers with incurving petals in mid- to late spring. 🏆 **'Wilber Foss'** is rounded with dark green foliage and large, broad, peony-form, brilliant pink-red flowers.

CAMPANULA

Bellflower

CAMPANULACEAE

Genus of spring- and summer-flowering annuals, biennials and perennials, some of which are evergreen. Fully to half hardy. Grows in sun or shade, but delicate flower colours are preserved best in shade. Most forms prefer moist but well-drained soil. Propagate by softwood or basal cuttings in summer or by seed or division in autumn or spring. Is prone to slug attack, and rust may be a problem in autumn.
C. alliariifolia (illus. p.241). Mound-forming perennial. **H** 60cm (24in), **S** 50cm (20in). Fully hardy. Has heart-shaped leaves, above which rise nodding, bell-shaped, creamy-white flowers borne along arching, wiry stems throughout summer.
C. armena, syn. *Symphyandra armena.* Upright or spreading perennial. **H** 30–60cm (1–2ft), **S** 30cm (1ft). Produces panicles of upright, bell-shaped, blue or white flowers in summer. Leaves are oval, irregularly toothed, hairy and mid-green.
C. barbata illus. p.342.
🏆 ***C. betulifolia.*** Prostrate, slender-stemmed perennial. **H** 2cm (¾in), **S** 30cm (12in). Fully hardy. In summer, long, branching flower stems each carry a cluster of open bell-shaped, single, white to pink flowers, deep pink outside. Leaves are wedge-shaped.
🏆 ***C.* 'Birch Hybrid'** illus. p.368.
C.* x *burghaltii. See *C.* 'Burghaltii'.
🏆 ***C.* 'Burghaltii'**, syn. *C.* x *burghaltii.* Mound-forming perennial. **H** 60cm (24in), **S** 30cm (12in). Fully hardy. Leaves are oval, soft and leathery. Produces long, pendent, funnel-shaped, pale lavender flowers on erect, wiry stems in summer. May need staking.
🏆 ***C. carpatica.*** Clump-forming perennial. **H** 8–10cm (3–4in), **S** to 30cm (12in). Fully hardy. Leafy, branching stems bear rounded to oval, toothed leaves and, in summer, broadly bell-shaped, blue or white flowers. **'Bressingham White'** illus. p.360. **'Jewel'**, illus. p.367.. Flowers of **'Turbinata'** (syn. *C.c.* var. *turbinata*) are pale lavender.
🏆 ***C. cochleariifolia*** (Fairy thimbles), syn. *C. pusilla*, illus. p.369.
🏆 ***C. garganica.*** Spreading perennial. **H** 5cm (2in), **S** 30cm (12in). Fully hardy. Has small, ivy-shaped leaves along stems. Bears clusters of star-shaped, single, pale lavender flowers from leaf axils in summer. Makes an excellent wall or bank plant.
🏆 **'W.H. Paine'** has bright lavender-blue flowers, each with a white eye.
🏆 ***C.* 'G.F. Wilson'** illus. p.368.
🏆 ***C. glomerata* 'Superba'** (illus. p.241). Vigorous, clump-forming perennial. **H** 75cm (2½ft), **S** 1m (3ft) or more. Fully hardy. Has dense, rounded heads of large, bell-shaped, purple flowers borne in summer. Bears oval leaves in basal rosettes and on flower stems. Must be divided and replanted regularly.
C.* x *haylodgensis. See *C.* x *haylodgensis* 'Plena'. **'Plena'** (syn. *C.* x *haylodgensis*) is a spreading perennial. **H** 5cm (2in), **S** 20cm (8in). Fully hardy. Has small, heart-shaped leaves and, in summer, pompon-like, double, deep lavender-blue flowers. Is suitable for a rock garden or wall.
🏆 ***C. isophylla.*** Evergreen, dwarf, trailing perennial. **H** 10cm (4in), **S** 30cm (12in). Half hardy. In summer, star-shaped, blue or white flowers are borne above small, heart-shaped, toothed leaves. Is ideal for a hanging basket. **Kristal Hybrids 'Stella Blue'** is compact and free-flowering, producing large, upright, saucer-shaped, pale blue flowers are produced in mid-summer.. **H** 15–20cm (6–8in), **S** to 30cm (12in).
🏆 ***C.* 'Joe Elliott'.** Mound-forming perennial. **H** 8cm (3in), **S** 12cm (5in). Fully hardy. In summer, large, funnel-shaped, mid-lavender-blue flowers almost obscure small, heart-shaped, downy, grey-green leaves. Is good for an alpine house, trough or rock garden. Needs well-drained, alkaline soil. Protect from winter wet. Is prone to slug attack.
🏆***C.* 'Kent Belle'.** Sturdy, spreading but clump-forming perennial. **H** 70cm (28in), **S** 45cm 18in or more. Fully hardy. Has rounded, toothed, glossy, mid-green leaves. In summer produces large, pendent, bell-shaped, violet-blue flowers.
C. lactiflora. Upright, branching perennial. **H** 1.2m (4ft), **S** 60cm (2ft). Fully hardy. In summer, slender stems bear racemes of large, nodding, bell-shaped, blue, occasionally pink or white flowers. Leaves are narrowly oval. Needs staking on a windy site. 🏆 **'Loddon Anna'** (illus. p.241) has soft dusty-pink flowers. 🏆 **'Prichard's Variety'** (illus. p.241) has violet-blue flowers from early summer to late autumn.
***C. latifolia* 'Amethyst'.** Clump-forming, spreading perennial. **H** 90–100cm (36–39in), **S** 60cm (24in). Fully hardy. Strong stems are clothed with large, open bell-shaped, pastel amethyst-blue flowers in summer. Oval, toothed leaves are rough-textured. **'Brantwood'** has violet-purple flowers.
C. latiloba. Rosette-forming perennial. **H** 1m (3ft), **S** 45cm (1½ft). Fully hardy. Leaves are oval. Widely cup-shaped flowers, in shades of blue, occasionally white, are borne in summer. 🏆 **'Hidcote Amethyst'** has large, vivid violet-blue flowers with purple highlights. 🏆 **'Percy Piper'** has lavender flowers.
C. medium (Canterbury bell). Slow-growing, evergreen, erect, clump-forming biennial. Tall cultivars, **H** 1m (3ft), **S** 30cm (1ft); dwarf, **H** 60cm (2ft), **S** 30cm (1ft). Fully hardy. All have lance-shaped, toothed, fresh green leaves. Bell-shaped, single or double flowers, white or in shades of blue and pink, are produced in spring and early summer. **'Bells of Holland'** illus. p.313.
C. morettiana. Tuft-forming perennial. **H** 2.5cm (1in), **S** 7cm (3in). Frost hardy. Leaves are ivy-shaped with fine hairs. Arching flower stems each carry a solitary, erect, bell-shaped, violet-blue flower in late spring and early summer. Needs gritty, alkaline soil and a dry but not arid winter climate. Red spider mite may be troublesome.
C. pendula, syn. *Symphyandra pendula.* Arching perennial. **H** 30–60cm (1–2ft), **S** 30cm (1ft). Produces panicles of pendent, bell-shaped, cream flowers in summer. Has oval, hairy, pale green leaves. Becomes woody at base with age.
C. persicifolia. Rosette-forming, spreading perennial. **H** 1m (3ft), **S** 30cm (1ft). Fully hardy. In summer, nodding, bell-shaped, papery, white or blue flowers are borne above narrowly lance-shaped, bright green leaves. 🏆**'Chettle Charm'** (illus. p.241), **H** 60cm (2ft), bears large, white flowers with violet-blue margins. 🏆 **'Fleur de Neige'** has double, white flowers. **'Pride of Exmouth'** bears double, powder-blue flowers. **'Telham Beauty'** illus. p.242.
🏆 ***C. portenschlagiana*** illus. p.368.
C. poscharskyana illus. p.367.
C. pulla. Often short-lived perennial that spreads by underground runners. **H** 2.5cm (1in), **S** 10cm (4in). Fully hardy. Tiny, rounded leaves form 1cm (½in) wide rosettes, each bearing a flower stem with a solitary, pendent, bell-shaped, deep violet flower from late spring to early summer. Is good for a scree or rock garden. Needs gritty, alkaline soil that is not too dry. Slugs may prove troublesome.
C. punctata. Vigorous, clump-forming but spreading perennial. **H** 40cm (16in), **S** 60cm (24in) or more. Fully hardy. Has heart-shaped, light green, basal leaves. In summer, tall flowering stems bear sprays of pendent, tubular, dusky-pink flushed, creamy-white flowers. **'Alina's Double'**, **H** 30cm (12in), has large, hose-in-hose, double, rich pink flowers. **'Cherry Bells'** (illus. p.241), **H** 50cm (20in), bears cream-tipped, rose-pink flowers. **'Wine 'n' Rubies'**, **H** 30cm (12in), has dark green leaves and bears large, rich purple-red flowers, with heavily speckled interiors, in mid-summer.
***C.* 'Purple Sensation'.** Clump-forming perennial. **H** 40cm (16in), **S** 30cm (12in) or more. Fully hardy. Has oval, dark green leaves. Pendent, tubular, deep violet-black flowers are produced in summer.
C. pusilla. See *C. cochleariifolia.*
C. pyramidalis (Chimney bellflower). Erect, branching biennial. **H** 2m (6ft), **S** 60cm (2ft). Half hardy. Produces long racemes of star-shaped, blue or white flowers in summer. Leaves are heart-shaped. Needs staking.
🏆 ***C. raineri.*** Perennial that spreads by underground runners. **H** 4cm (1½in), **S** 8cm (3in). Frost hardy. Leaves are oval, toothed and grey-green. Flower stems each carry a large, upturned, bell-shaped, pale lavender flower in summer. Is suitable for an alpine house or trough that is protected from winter wet. Requires semi-shade.
C. takesimana (illus. p.241). Vigorous, spreading perennial. **H** 75cm (30in), **S** 100cm (39in). Fully hardy. Forms rosettes of heart-shaped, glossy, mid-green leaves. In summer and autumn, flowering stems bear pendent, tubular to bell-shaped,

ivory-white flowers with red speckled interiors. Is best in sun.
C. trachelium (Nettle-leaved bellflower). Upright perennial. **H** 60cm–1m (2–3ft), **S** 30cm (1ft). Fully hardy. Has rough, serrated, oval, pointed, basal leaves. Wide, bell-shaped, blue or purple-blue flowers are spaced along erect stems in summer. **'Bernice'** (illus. p.211) has double purple-violet flowers.
C. vidalii. See *Azorina vidalii.*
C. wanneri, syn. *Symphyandra wanneri,* illus. p.342.
C. zoysii. Tuft-forming perennial. **H** 5cm (2in), **S** 10cm (4in). Frost hardy. Has tiny, rounded, glossy green leaves. In summer, flower stems each bear a bottle-shaped, lavender flower held horizontally. Needs gritty, alkaline soil. Is difficult to grow and encourage to flower, dislikes winter wet and is prone to slug attack.

CAMPSIS

BIGNONIACEAE

Genus of deciduous, woody-stemmed, root climbers, grown for their flowers. Frost hardy; in cooler areas needs protection of a sunny wall. Grow in sun in fertile, well-drained soil, and water regularly in summer. Prune in spring. Propagate by semi-ripe cuttings in summer or by layering in winter.
C. chinensis. See *C. grandiflora.*
C. grandiflora, syn. *Bignonia grandiflora, Campsis chinensis, Tecoma grandiflora* (Chinese trumpet creeper), illus. p.203.
C. radicans, syn. *Bignonia radicans, Tecoma radicans* (Trumpet creeper, Trumpet honeysuckle, Trumpet vine). Deciduous, woody-stemmed, root climber. **H** to 12m (40ft). Leaves of 7–11 oval, toothed leaflets are downy beneath. Small clusters of trumpet-shaped, orange, scarlet or yellow flowers, 6–8cm (2½–3in) long, open in late summer and early autumn. **'Flamenco'** illus. p.208. 🏆 **f. *flava*** (syn. *C. r.* 'Yellow Trumpet') illus. p.206. **'Indian Summer'** illus. p.193. **'Yellow Trumpet'** see *C. r.* f. *flava.*
🏆 ***C. x tagliabuana* 'Madame Galen'** illus. p.208.

CANARINA

CAMPANULACEAE

Genus of herbaceous, tuberous, scrambling climbers, grown for their flowers. Frost tender, min. 7°C (45°F). Grow in full light and in any fertile, well-drained soil. Water moderately from early autumn to late spring, then keep dry. Needs tying to a support. Remove dead stems when dormant. Propagate by basal cuttings or seed sown in spring or autumn.
C. campanula. See *C. canariensis.*
🏆 ***C. canariensis*** (Canary Island bellflower), syn. *C. campanula,* illus. p.464.

Candollea cuneiformis. See *Hibbertia cuneiformis.*

CANNA

CANNACEAE

Genus of robust, showy, rhizomatous perennials, grown for their striking flowers and ornamental foliage. Is generally used for summer-bedding displays and container growing. Half hardy to frost tender, min. 5–15°C (41–59°F). Requires a warm, sunny position and humus-rich, moist soil. If grown under glass or for summer bedding, encourage into growth in spring at 16°C (61°F) and store rhizomes in slightly damp soil or peat in winter. Propagate in spring by division or in winter by seed sown at 20°C (68°F) or more.
***C.* 'Ambassadour'** (illus. p.394). Rhizomatous perennial. **H** to 2m (6ft), **S** 60–90cm (24–36in). Half hardy. Has broadly lance-shaped, slightly glaucous, mid-green leaves. From mid-summer to autumn produces large, creamy-white flowers flushed orange-yellow within at the bases.
***C.* 'Assault'.** See *C.* 'Assaut'.
***C.* 'Assaut'**, syn. *C.* 'Assault'. Summer-flowering, rhizomatous perennial. **H** to 1.2m (4ft), **S** 45–60cm (1½–2ft). Half hardy. Has stout, leafy stems bearing wide, purple-green leaves with a spike of scarlet flowers surrounded by purple bracts.
***C.* 'Bengal Tiger'.** See *C.* 'Striata'.
***C.* 'Black Knight'.** Rhizomatous perennial. **H** 1.8m (6ft), **S** 45–60cm (1½–2ft). Half hardy. Stout stems bear broadly lance-shaped, bronze-green leaves. From mid-summer to early autumn has large racemes of gladiolus-like, very dark red flowers, 7cm (3in) across, with wavy petals.
***C.* 'Brilliant'** (illus. p.394). Mid-summer to early-autumn-flowering, rhizomatous perennial. **H** 1m (3ft), **S** 50cm (20in). Half hardy. Produces iris-like, bright red flowers and broadly lance-shaped, mid-green leaves.
***C.* 'Durban'** (illus. p.394). Mid-summer to early-autumn-flowering, rhizomatous perennial. **H** 1.6m (5½ft), **S** 50cm (20in). Half hardy. Produces gladiolus-like, dark orange-red flowers above broadly elliptical, pink-veined, purple leaves fading to orange.
🏆 ***C. x ehemanii***, syn. *C. iridiflora* 'Ehemanii' (illus. p.394). Mid-summer to early-autumn-flowering, rhizomatous perennial. **H** 2m (6ft), **S** 60cm (2ft). Half hardy. Broadly elliptical, dark bluish-green leaves have red margins. Produces trumpet-shaped, bright pinkish-red flowers.
***C.* 'Ermine'.** Clump-forming, mid-summer to early-autumn-flowering, rhizomatous perennial. **H** 100cm (36in), **S** 50cm (20in). Half hardy. Has broadly lance-shaped, mid-green leaves. Very large, gladiolus-like, creamy-white flowers are pale yellow flushed toward the centres.
***C.* 'Gnom'.** Mid-summer to early-autumn-flowering, rhizomatous perennial. **H** 60cm (24in), **S** 45cm (18in). Half hardy. Produces gladiolus-like, salmon-pink flowers, with overlapping petals, and broadly elliptical, mid-green leaves.
C. iridiflora illus. p.395. **'Ehemanii'** see *C. x ehemanii.*
***C.* 'King Midas'.** See *C.* 'Richard Wallace'.
***C.* 'Königin Charlotte'** syn *C.* 'Queen Charlotte' (illus. p.394). Mid-summer to early-autumn-flowering, rhizomatous perennial. **H** 1–1.2m (3–4ft), **S** 50cm (20in). Half hardy. Has broadly lance-shaped, mid-green leaves. From mid-summer to early autumn produces velvety, blood-red flowers, the petals with canary-yellow margins.
***C.* 'Louis Cottin'** (illus. p.394). Mid-summer to early-autumn-flowering, rhizomatous perennial. **H** 1.2m (4ft), **S** 50cm (1½ft). Half hardy. Produces trumpet-shaped, apricot flowers and broadly lance-shaped, dark blackish-green leaves.
***C.* 'Lucifer'** (illus. p.394). Compact, mid-summer to early-autumn-flowering, rhizomatous perennial. **H** 60cm (24in), **S** 50cm (20in). Half hardy. Produces relatively small, iris-like, red and yellow flowers and elliptic, mid-green leaves.
🏆 ***C.* 'Musifolia'.** Mid-summer to early-autumn-flowering, rhizomatous perennial. **H** 3m (10ft), **S** 1.5m (5ft). Half hardy. Bears small, iris-like, orange flowers. Very long, oval, mid-green leaves have dark margins and red-tinted midribs.
🏆 ***C.* 'Picasso'** (illus. p.394). Mid-summer to early-autumn-flowering, rhizomatous perennial. **H** 1.2m (4ft), **S** 50cm (20in). Half hardy. Produces gladiolus-like, yellow flowers with orange and red spots. Has large, broadly ovate, mid-green leaves.
***C.* 'Pretoria'.** See *C.* 'Striata'.
***C.* 'Queen Charlotte'.** See *C.* 'Königin Charlotte'.
***C.* 'Richard Wallace'**, syn. *C.* 'King Midas' (illus. p.394). Mid-summer to early-autumn-flowering, rhizomatous perennial. **H** 1.5m (5ft), **S** 50cm (½ft). Half hardy. Produces gladiolus-like, bright yellow flowers, with spotted throats and frilly-edged petals, and elliptical, apple-green leaves.
🏆 ***C.* 'Striata'**, syn. *C.* 'Bengal Tiger', *C.* 'Pretoria' (illus. p.394). Mid-summer to early-autumn-flowering, rhizomatous perennial. **H** 1.5m (5ft), **S** 50cm (½ft). Half hardy. Gladiolus-like, bright orange flowers are produced above ovate, light green to yellow-green leaves, with bright yellow veins.
***C.* 'Stuttgart'** (illus. p.394). Mid-summer to early-autumn-flowering, rhizomatous perennial. **H** 2.1m (7ft), **S** 60cm (2ft). Half hardy. Produces small, iris-like, pale apricot flowers, fading to pink. Broadly lance-shaped, white-and-green leaves require some shade to prevent burning.
🏆 ***C.* 'Whithelm Pride'.** Mid-summer to early-autumn-flowering, rhizomatous perennial. **H** 1m (3ft), **S** 50cm (½ft). Half hardy. Produces large, gladiolus-like, pink flowers and ovate, bronze leaves.
🏆 ***C.* 'Wyoming'** (illus. p.394). Mid-summer to early-autumn-flowering, rhizomatous perennial. **H** 1.8m (6ft), **S** 50cm (20in). Half hardy. Produces gladiolus-like, soft orange flowers and large, ovate, purple-bronze leaves, with darker purple

CANTUA

POLEMONIACEAE

Genus of evergreen shrubs, grown for their showy flowers in spring. Only one species is in general cultivation. Half hardy; is best grown against a south- or west-facing wall. Requires full sun and fertile, well-drained soil. Propagate by semi-ripe cuttings in summer.
🏆 ***C. buxifolia***, syn. *C. dependens*, illus. p.146.
C. dependens. See *C. buxifolia.*

CAPSICUM

SOLANACEAE

Genus of evergreen shrubs, sub-shrubs and short-lived perennials, usually grown as annuals. Some species produce edible fruits (eg. sweet peppers), others small, ornamental ones. Frost tender, min. 4°C (39°F). Grow in sun and in fertile, well-drained soil. Spray flowers with water to encourage fruit to set. Propagate by seed sown under glass in spring. Red spider mite may cause problems.
C. annuum (Ornamental pepper). **'Holiday Cheer'** is a moderately fast-growing, evergreen, bushy perennial, grown as an annual. **H** and **S** 20–30cm (8–12in). Has oval, mid-green leaves. Bears small, star-shaped, white flowers in summer and, in autumn–winter, spherical, green fruits maturing to red.

CARAGANA

LEGUMINOSAE/PAPILIONACEAE

Genus of deciduous shrubs, grown for their foliage and flowers. Fully hardy. Requires full sun and fertile but not over-rich, well-drained soil. Propagate species by softwood cuttings in summer or by seed in autumn, cultivars by softwood or semi-ripe cuttings or budding in summer or by grafting during winter.
C. arborescens. Fast-growing, deciduous, upright shrub. **H** 6m (20ft), **S** 4m (12ft). Has spine-tipped, dark green leaves, each composed of 8–12 oblong leaflets. Produces clusters of pea-like, yellow flowers in late spring. Arching **'Lorbergii'**, **H** 3m (10ft), **S** 2.5m (8ft), has very narrow leaflets and smaller flowers and is often grown as a tree by top-grafting. **'Nana'** illus. p.148. **'Walker'**, **H** 30cm (1ft), **S** 2–3m (6–10ft), is prostrate but is usually top-grafted to form a weeping tree, **H** 2m (6ft), **S** 75cm (2½ft).
***C. frutex* 'Globosa'.** Slow-growing, deciduous, upright shrub. **H** and **S** 30cm (1ft). Mid-green leaves each have 4 oblong leaflets. Pea-like, bright yellow flowers are borne only rarely in late spring.

CARALLUMA

ASCLEPIADACEAE/APOCYNACEAE

Genus of perennial succulents with 4–6-ribbed, finger-like, blue-grey or blue-green to purple stems. Frost tender, min. 11°C (52°F). Needs sun and extremely well-drained soil. Water sparingly, only in the growing season. May be difficult to grow. Propagate by seed or stem cuttings in summer.
C. europaea, syn. *Stapelia europaea.* Clump-forming, perennial succulent. **H** 20cm (8in), **S** 1m (3ft). Rough, 4-angled, erect to procumbent, grey stems often arch over and root. Has clusters of small, star-shaped, yellow and brownish-purple flowers near stem crown from mid- to late summer, then twin-horned, grey seed pods. Flowers smell faintly of rotten meat. Is one of the easier species to grow.
C. joannis illus. p.494.

CARDAMINE
Bitter cress
CRUCIFERAE/BRASSICACEAE

Genus of spring-flowering annuals and perennials. Some are weeds, but others are suitable for informal and woodland gardens. Fully hardy. Requires sun or semi-shade and moist soil. Propagate by seed or division in autumn.
C. enneaphyllos, syn. *Dentaria enneaphyllos*. Lax perennial spreading by fleshy, horizontal rootstocks. **H** 30–60cm (12–24in), **S** 45–60cm (18–24in). In spring, nodding, pale yellow or white flowers open at the ends of shoots arising from deeply divided leaves.
C. latifolia. See *C. raphanifolia*.
🏆 ***C. pentaphyllos***, syn. *Dentaria pentaphyllos*, illus. p.260.
C. pratensis (Cuckoo flower, Lady's smock) illus p.438. **'Flore Pleno'** is a neat, clump-forming perennial. **H** 45cm (18in), **S** 30cm (12in). Bears dense sheaves of double, lilac flowers in spring. Mid-green leaves are divided into rounded leaflets. May also be propagated by leaf-tip cuttings in mid-summer. Prefers a moist or wet site.
C. raphanifolia, syn. *C. latifolia*, illus. p.438.
C. trifolia illus. p.348.

CARDIOCRINUM
LILIACEAE

Genus of summer-flowering, lily-like bulbs, grown for their spectacular flowers. Frost hardy. Needs partial shade and deep, humus-rich, moist soil. Plant bulbs just below soil surface, in autumn. Water well in summer and mulch with humus. Provide a deep mulch in winter. After flowering, main bulb dies, but produces offsets. To produce flowers in up to 5 years, propagate by offsets in autumn; may also be propagated by seed in autumn or winter and will then flower in 7 years.
C. giganteum (Giant lily) illus. p.385. **var. *yunnanense*** is a stout, leafy-stemmed bulb. **H** 1.5–2m (5–6ft), **S** 75cm–1m (2½–3ft). Has bold, heart-shaped, bronze-green leaves. Fragrant, pendent, trumpet-shaped, cream flowers, 15cm (6in) long, with purple-red streaks inside, are borne in long spikes in summer and are followed by decorative seed heads.

CARDIOSPERMUM
SAPINDACEAE

Genus of herbaceous or deciduous, shrubby climbers, grown mainly for their attractive fruits. Is useful for covering bushes or trellises. Frost tender, min. 5°C (41°F). Grow in full light and any soil. Propagate by seed in spring.
C. halicacabum (Balloon vine, Heart pea, Heart seed, Winter cherry). Deciduous, shrubby, scandent, perennial climber, usually grown as an annual or biennial. **H** to 3m (10ft). Has toothed leaves of 2 oblong leaflets. Inconspicuous, whitish flowers are produced in summer, followed by downy, spherical, inflated, 3-angled, straw-coloured fruits containing black seeds, each with a heart-shaped, white spot.

CAREX
CYPERACEAE

See also GRASSES, BAMBOOS, RUSHES and SEDGES.
🏆 ***C. buchananii*** (Leatherleaf sedge). Evergreen, tuft-forming, perennial sedge. **H** to 60cm (24in), **S** 20cm (8in). Fully hardy. Very narrow, copper-coloured leaves turn red towards base. Solid, triangular stems bear insignificant, brown spikelets in summer.
C. elata, syn. *C. stricta* (Tufted sedge). Evergreen, tuft-forming, perennial sedge. **H** to 1m (3ft), **S** 15cm (6in). Fully hardy. Leaves are somewhat glaucous. Solid, triangular stems bear blackish-brown spikelets in summer. 🏆 **'Aurea'** illus. p.445.
C. flagellifera, illus. p.289.
C. grayi (Mace sedge). Evergreen, tuft-forming, perennial sedge. **H** to 60cm (24in), **S** 20cm (8in). Fully hardy. Has bright green leaves. Large, female spikelets, borne in summer, mature to pointed, knobbly, greenish-brown fruits.
🏆 ***C. hachijoensis* 'Evergold'.** See *C. oshimensis* 'Evergold'.
C. morrowii of gardens. See *C. oshimensis*.
C. oshimensis, syn. *C. morrowii* of gardens. Evergreen, tuft-forming, perennial sedge. **H** 20–50cm (8–20in), **S** 20–25cm (8–10in). Fully hardy. Has narrow, mid-green leaves. Solid, triangular stems bear insignificant spikelets in summer. 🏆 **'Evergold'**, syn. *C. hachijoensis* 'Evergold', illus. p.288.
C. pendula (Pendulous sedge). Evergreen, tuft-forming, graceful, perennial. **H** 1m (3ft), **S** 30cm (1ft). Fully hardy. Has narrow, green leaves, 45cm (18in) long. Solid, triangular stems freely produce pendent, greenish-brown flower spikes in summer.
C. riparia (Greater pond sedge). **'Variegata'** is a vigorous, evergreen, perennial sedge. **H** 60cm–1m (2–3ft), **S** indefinite. Fully hardy. Has broad, white-striped, mid-green leaves and solid, triangular stems that bear narrow, bristle-tipped, dark brown spikelets in summer.
C. stricta. See *C. elata*.

CARISSA
APOCYNACEAE

Genus of evergreen, spring- to summer-flowering shrubs, grown for their flowers and overall appearance. Frost tender, min. 10–13°C (50–55°F). Needs partial shade and well-drained soil. Water containerized specimens moderately, less when temperatures are low. Propagate by seed when ripe or in spring or by semi-ripe cuttings in summer. ⓘ Seeds are poisonous.
C. grandiflora. See *C. macrocarpa*.
C. macrocarpa, syn. *C. grandiflora* (Natal plum). **'Tuttlei'** illus. p.453.
C. spectabilis. See *Acokanthera oblongifolia*.

CARLINA
Thistle
COMPOSITAE/ASTERACEAE

Genus of annuals, biennials and perennials, grown for their ornamental flower heads. Fully hardy. Requires a sunny position and well-drained soil. Propagate by seed: annuals in spring, perennials in autumn.
C. acaulis (Alpine thistle) illus. p.361.

CARMICHAELIA
LEGUMINOSAE/PAPILIONACEAE

Genus of deciduous, usually leafless shrubs, grown for their profusion of tiny flowers in summer. Flattened, green shoots assume function of leaves. Frost to half hardy. Needs full sun and well-drained soil. Cut out dead wood in spring. Propagate by semi-ripe cuttings in summer or by seed in autumn or spring.
C. arborea. Deciduous, upright shrub. **H** 2m (6ft), **S** 1.5m (5ft). Frost hardy. Small clusters of pea-like, pale lilac flowers appear from early to mid-summer. May need staking when mature.
C. carmichaeliae, syn. *Notospartium carmichaeliae* (Pink broom). Leafless, arching shrub. **H** 2m (6ft), **S** 1.5m (5ft). Short, dense spikes of pea-like, purple-blotched, pink flowers are produced in mid-summer on slender, drooping, green shoots.
C. enysii. Deciduous, mound-forming, dense shrub. **H** and **S** 30cm (1ft). Frost hardy. Shoots are rigid. Pea-like, violet flowers are borne in mid-summer. Is best grown in a rock garden.
C. stevensonii, syn. *Chordospartium stevensonii*. Deciduous, almost leafless, arching shrub. **H** 3m (10ft), **S** 2m (6ft). Produces small, pea-like, purplish-pink flowers in cylindrical racemes in mid-summer.

CARNEGIEA
CACTACEAE

Genus of one species of very slow-growing, perennial cactus with thick, 12–24-ribbed, spiny stems. Is unlikely to flower or branch at less than 4m (12ft) high. Frost tender, min. 7°C (45°F). Requires full sun and very well-drained soil. Propagate by seed in spring or summer.
C. gigantea (Saguaro) illus. p.492.

CARPENTERIA
HYDRANGEACEAE

Genus of one species of evergreen, summer-flowering shrub, cultivated for its flowers and foliage. Frost hardy. Grows well against a south- or west-facing wall. Prefers full sun and fairly moist but well-drained soil. Propagate by greenwood cuttings in summer or by seed in autumn.
🏆 ***C. californica*** illus. p.197.

CARPINUS
Hornbeam
CORYLACEAE/BETULACEAE

Genus of deciduous trees, grown for their foliage, autumn colour and clusters of small, winged nuts. Fully hardy. Needs sun or semi-shade and fertile, well-drained soil. Propagate species by seed in autumn, cultivars by budding in late summer.
🏆 ***C. betulus*** (Common hornbeam). Deciduous, round-headed tree. **H** 25m (80ft), **S** 20m (70ft). Has a fluted trunk and oval, prominently veined, dark green leaves that turn yellow and orange in autumn. Bears green catkins from late spring to autumn, when clusters of winged nuts appear. 🏆 **'Fastigiata'** (syn. *C.b.* 'Pyramidalis'), illus. p.93. **'Pyramidalis'** see *C.b.* 'Fastigiata'.
C. caroliniana (American hornbeam). Deciduous, spreading tree with branches that droop at tips. **H** and **S** 10m (30ft). Has a fluted, grey trunk, green catkins in spring and oval, bright green leaves that turn orange and red in autumn, when clusters of winged nuts appear.
C. tschonoskii. Deciduous, rounded tree of elegant habit, with branches drooping at tips. **H** and **S** 12m (40ft). Has oval, sharply toothed, glossy, dark green leaves. Green catkins are carried in spring and clusters of small, winged nuts appear in autumn.
🏆 ***C. turczaninowii.*** Deciduous, spreading tree of graceful habit. **H** 12m (40ft), **S** 10m (30ft). Green catkins are borne in spring. Produces clusters of small, winged nuts in autumn, when small, oval, glossy, deep green leaves turn orange.

CARPOBROTUS
AIZOACEAE

Genus of mat-forming, perennial succulents with triangular, fleshy, dark green leaves and daisy-like flowers. Is excellent for binding sandy soils. Half hardy to frost tender, min. 5°C (41°F). Needs full sun and well-drained soil. Propagate by seed or stem cuttings in spring or summer.
C. edulis (Hottentot fig, Kaffir fig). Carpeting, perennial succulent. **H** 15cm (6in), **S** indefinite. Frost tender. Prostrate, rooting branches bear leaves 1.5cm (⅝in) thick and 12cm (5in) long. Yellow, purple or pink flowers, 12cm (5in) across, open in spring–summer from about noon in sun. Bears edible, fig-like, brownish fruits in late summer and autumn.

CARRIEREA
FLACOURTIACEAE

Genus of deciduous trees. Only *C. calycina*, grown for its flowers, is in general cultivation. Frost hardy. Requires full sun and fertile, well-drained soil. Propagate by softwood cuttings in summer.
C. calycina. Deciduous, spreading tree. **H** 8m (25ft), **S** 10m (30ft). Oval, glossy, mid-green leaves set off upright clusters of cup-shaped, creamy-white or greenish-white flowers borne in early summer.

CARTHAMUS
ASTERACEAE

A genus of 14 species of hardy annuals grown for flowers, foliage and medicinal properties. Propagate by seed sown in spring.
C. tinctorius illus. p.323.

CARYA
Hickory
JUGLANDACEAE

Genus of deciduous trees, grown for their stately habit, divided leaves, autumn colour and, in some cases, edible nuts. Has insignificant flowers in spring. Fully hardy. Requires sun or semi-shade and deep,

C

fertile soil. Plant young seedlings in a permanent position during their first year since older plants resent transplanting. Propagate by seed in autumn.
C. cordiformis (Bitternut, Bitternut hickory). Vigorous, deciduous, spreading tree. **H** 25m (80ft), **S** 15m (50ft). Bark is smooth at first, later fissured. Bright yellow winter leaf buds develop into large, dark green leaves, with usually 7 oval to oblong leaflets; these turn yellow in autumn. Nuts are pear-shaped or rounded, 2–4cm (¾–1½in) long, each with a bitter kernel.
C. glabra (Pignut, Pignut hickory). Deciduous, spreading tree. **H** 25m (80ft), **S** 20m (70ft). Dark green leaves, with usually 5 narrowly oval leaflets, turn bright yellow and orange in autumn. Pear-shaped or rounded nuts, 2–4cm (¾–1½in) long, each have a bitter kernel.
C. ovata (Shag-bark hickory) illus. p.67.

CARYOPTERIS

VERBENACEAE/LAMIACEAE

Genus of deciduous sub-shrubs, grown for their foliage and small, but freely produced, blue flowers. Frost hardy. Prefers full sun and light, well-drained soil. Cut back hard in spring. Propagate species by greenwood or semi-ripe cuttings in summer or by seed in autumn; propagate cultivars by cuttings only, in summer.
C. x clandonensis ♀ **'Arthur Simmonds'** illus. p.157. **'Heavenly Blue'** is a deciduous, bushy sub-shrub. **H** and **S** 1m (3ft). Forms an upright, compact mass of lance-shaped, grey-green leaves. Dense clusters of tubular, blue to purplish-blue flowers, with prominent stamens, are borne from late summer to autumn.
C. incana, syn. *C. mastacanthus*. Deciduous, bushy sub-shrub. **H** and **S** 1.2m (4ft). Bears tubular, violet-blue flowers, with prominent stamens, amid lance-shaped, grey-green leaves from late summer to early autumn.
C. mastacanthus. See *C. incana*.

CASSIA

LEGUMINOSAE/CAESALPINIACEAE

Genus of annuals, perennials and evergreen or deciduous trees and shrubs, grown for their flowers mainly produced from winter to summer. Fully hardy to frost tender, min. 7–18°C (45–64°F). Needs full light and fertile, well-drained soil. Water containerized specimens freely when in full growth, moderately to sparingly in winter. Pruning is tolerated, severe if need be, but trees are best left to grow naturally. Propagate by seed in spring.
C. artemisioides. See *Senna artemisioides*.
C. corymbosa. See *Senna corymbosa*. **var. *plurijuga*** of gardens. See *Senna* x *floribunda*.
C. didymobotrya. See *Senna didymobotrya*.
C. fistula (Golden shower, Indian laburnum, Pudding pipe-tree). Fast-growing, almost deciduous, ovoid tree. **H** 8–10m (25–30ft), **S** 4–6m (12–20ft). Frost tender, min. 16°C (61°F). Has 30–45cm (12–18in) long leaves, each with 4–8 pairs of oval leaflets, coppery when young. In spring produces racemes of small, fragrant, 5-petalled, cup-shaped, bright yellow flowers. Cylindrical, dark brown pods, to 60cm (24in) long, yield cassia pulp.
C. x floribunda. See *Senna* x *floribunda*.
C. siamea. See *Senna siamea*.

CASSINIA

COMPOSITAE/ASTERACEAE

Genus of evergreen shrubs, grown for their foliage and flowers. Frost hardy, but avoid cold, exposed positions. Needs full sun and fertile, well-drained soil. Propagate by softwood cuttings in summer.
C. fulvida. See *C. leptophylla* subsp. *fulvida*.
C. leptophylla* subsp. *fulvida, syn. *C. fulvida*. Evergreen, bushy shrub. **H** and **S** 2m (6ft). Has yellow shoots, small, oblong, dark green leaves and, in mid-summer, clustered heads of minute, white flowers. **subsp. *vauvilliersii*** (syn. *C. vauvilliersii*) illus. p.150.
C. vauvilliersii. See *C. leptophylla* subsp. *vauvilliersii*.

CASSIOPE

ERICACEAE

Genus of evergreen, spring-flowering shrubs, suitable for peat beds and walls and for rock gardens. Fully hardy. Needs a sheltered, shaded or semi-shaded site and moist, peaty, acid soil. Propagate by semi-ripe or greenwood cuttings in summer or by seed in autumn or spring.
♀ ***C.* 'Edinburgh'.** Evergreen, dwarf shrub. **H** and **S** 20cm (8in). Has tiny, dark green leaves tightly pressed to upright stems. In spring, many small, bell-shaped, white flowers are borne singly in leaf axils.
C. fastigiata. Evergreen, upright, loose shrub. **H** 30cm (12in), **S** 15–20cm (6–8in). In spring, bell-shaped, creamy-white flowers, resting in green or red calyces, are borne on short stalks in leaf axils. Leaves are tiny and scale-like. Needs semi-shade.
♀ ***C. lycopodioides*** illus. p.349.
C. mertensiana illus. p.349.
♀ ***C.* 'Muirhead'** illus. p.332.
C. selaginoides. Evergreen, spreading shrub. **H** 25cm (10in), **S** 15cm (6in). Stem is hidden by dense, scale-like, mid-green leaves. Bears solitary, relatively large, pendent, bell-shaped, white flowers in spring. Needs a shaded site.
C. tetragona illus. p.332.
C. wardii. Evergreen, upright to spreading, loose shrub. **H** 15cm (6in), **S** 20cm (8in). Semi-upright stems are densely clothed with scale-like, dark green leaves that give them a squared appearance. Bell-shaped, white flowers, set close to stems, open in spring. Needs shade in all but cool areas. May also be propagated by division of runners in spring.

CASTANEA

Chestnut

FAGACEAE

Genus of deciduous, summer-flowering trees and shrubs, grown for their foliage, stately habit, flowers and edible fruits (chestnuts). Fully hardy. Requires sun or semi-shade; does particularly well in hot, dry areas. Needs fertile, well-drained soil; grows poorly on shallow, chalky soil. Propagate species by seed in autumn, cultivars by budding in summer or by grafting in late winter.
C. dentata (American chestnut). Deciduous, spreading tree with rough bark. **H** 30m (100ft), **S** 15m (50ft). Oblong, toothed, dull green leaves turn orange-yellow in autumn. Has catkins of greenish-white flowers in summer, then typical spiny 'chestnut' fruits.
♀ ***C. sativa*** (Spanish chestnut, Sweet chestnut). Deciduous, spreading tree. **H** 30m (100ft), **S** 15m (50ft). Bark becomes spirally ridged with age. Oblong, glossy, dark green leaves turn yellow in autumn. Produces spikes of small, creamy-yellow flowers in summer, followed by edible fruits in rounded, spiny husks.
♀ **'Albomarginata'** illus. p.61.

CASTANOPSIS

FAGACEAE

Genus of evergreen shrubs and trees, grown for their habit and foliage. Flowers are insignificant. Frost hardy. Needs a sheltered position in sun or semi-shade and fertile, well-drained but not too dry, acid soil. Propagate by seed when ripe, in autumn.
C. cuspidata. Evergreen, bushy, spreading shrub or tree with drooping shoots. **H** and **S** 8m (25ft) or more. Bears long, oval, slender-tipped, leathery leaves, glossy, dark green above, bronze beneath.

CASTANOSPERMUM

Black bean tree, Moreton Bay chestnut

LEGUMINOSAE/PAPILIONACEAE

Genus of one species of evergreen tree, grown for its overall ornamental appearance and for shade. Frost tender, min. 10–15°C (50–59°F). Requires full light and fertile, moisture-retentive but well-drained soil. Water containerized specimens freely when in full growth, moderately at other times. Propagate by seed in spring.
C. australe. Strong-growing, evergreen, rounded tree. **H** 15m (50ft) or more, **S** 8m (25ft) or more. Has 45cm (18in) long leaves of 8–17 oval leaflets. Racemes of large, pea-like, yellow flowers, that age to orange and red, are produced in autumn, but only on mature trees, and are succeeded by cylindrical, reddish-brown pods, each 25cm (10in) long, containing large, chestnut-like seeds.

CATALPA

BIGNONIACEAE

Genus of deciduous, summer-flowering trees and shrubs, extremely resistant to urban pollution, grown for their foliage and bell- or trumpet-shaped flowers with frilly lobes. Trees are best grown as isolated specimens. Fully hardy. Prefers full sun and does best in hot summers. Needs deep, fertile, well-drained but not too dry soil. Propagate species by seed in autumn, cultivars by softwood cuttings in summer or by budding in late summer.
♀ ***C. bignonioides*** (Indian bean tree) illus. p.73. ♀ **'Aurea'** illus. p.76.
♀ ***C. x erubescens* 'Purpurea'.** Deciduous, spreading tree. **H** and **S** 15m (50ft). Broadly oval or 3-lobed, very dark purple, young leaves age to dark green. Fragrant, bell-shaped, white flowers, marked with yellow and purple, appear from mid- to late summer.
C. fargesii* f. *duclouxii illus. p.73.
C. ovata. Deciduous, spreading tree. **H** and **S** 10m (30ft). Bears 3-lobed, purplish leaves when young, maturing to pale green. Has large clusters of bell-shaped, white flowers, spotted with red and yellow, from mid- to late summer.
C. speciosa illus. p.72.

CATANANCHE

Blue cupidone

COMPOSITAE/ASTERACEAE

Genus of perennials with daisy-like flower heads that may be successfully dried for winter flower arrangements. Fully hardy. Needs sun and light, well-drained soil. Propagate by seed in spring or by root cuttings in winter.
♀ ***C. caerulea* 'Major'** illus. p.270.

CATHARANTHUS

APOCYNACEAE

Genus of evergreen shrubs, grown for their flowers. *C. roseus* is often grown annually from seed or cuttings and used as a summer bedding plant in cool climates. Frost tender, min. 5–7°C (41–5°F). Needs full light and well-drained soil. Water potted specimens moderately, less when temperatures are low. Prune long or straggly stems in early spring to promote a more bushy habit. Propagate by seed in spring or by greenwood or semi-ripe cuttings in summer.
♀ ***C. roseus*** (Rose periwinkle), syn. *Vinca rosea*, illus. p.298. **Boa Series 'Boa Peach'** illus. p.300. **Cobra Series 'Cobra Burgundy'** illus. p.306.

CATTLEYA

ORCHIDACEAE

See also ORCHIDS.
C. bowringiana. See *Guarianthe bowringiana*.
***C.* J.A. Carbone gx.** Evergreen, epiphytic orchid for an intermediate greenhouse. **H** 45cm (18in). Large heads of fragrant, pinkish-mauve flowers, 10cm (4in) across and each with a yellow-marked, deep pink lip, open in early summer. Has oval, stiff leaves, 10–15cm (4–6in) long. Avoid spraying from overhead.
C. cinnabarina, syn. *Laelia cinnabarina*. Evergreen, epiphytic orchid for an intermediate greenhouse. **H** 15cm (6in). Produces sprays of slender, orange flowers, 5cm (2in) or more across, usually in winter. Has narrowly oval, rigid leaves, 8–10cm (3–4in) long. Needs good light in summer.
x *C.* Trizac gx 'Purple Emperor', syn. x *Sophrolaeliocattleya* Trizac gx 'Purple Emperor'. Evergreen, epiphytic orchid for an intermediate greenhouse. **H** 10cm (4in). In spring, has crimson-lipped, pinkish-purple flowers, 6cm (2½in) across, in small heads. Has oval, rigid leaves, 10cm (4in) long. Provide good light in summer.

x CATTLIANTHE

ORCHIDACEAE

See also ORCHIDS.

x C. Hazel Boyd gx 'Apricot Glow', syn. x *Sophrolaeliocattleya* Hazel Boyd 'Apricot Glow' (illus. p.467). Evergreen, epiphytic orchid for an intermediate greenhouse. **H** 10cm (4in). In spring and early summer produces small heads of apricot-orange flowers, 9cm (3½in) across, with crimson marks on lips. Has oval, rigid leaves, 10cm (4in) long. Grow in good light in summer.

x C. Rojo gx 'Mont Millais', syn. x *Laeliocattleya* Rojo gx 'Mont Millais' (illus. p.467). Evergreen, epiphytic orchid for an intermediate greenhouse. **H** 30cm (12in). In winter-spring bears arching heads of slender, reddish-orange flowers, 2cm (¾in) across. Oval leaves are up to 15cm (6in) long. Provide good light in summer.

CAULOKAEMPFERIA

ZINGIBERACEAE

Genus of herbaceous, rhizomatous perennials, grown for small but numerous, bright flowers, which are produced from late spring until autumn, from the same stem as the leaves. Probably frost hardy when dormant, but is best grown in a shade house or protected in winter. Requires moist, humus-rich soil in a shady, sheltered position. Propagate by division or seed in early spring.

C. petelotii. Herbaceous, rhizomatous perennial. **H** and **S** 20cm (8in). Has 6–8 narrowly lance-shaped, mid-green leaves. Clusters of broad-lipped, bright canary yellow flowers, surrounded by long, narrow, green bracts, are borne from spring into autumn.

CAUTLEYA

ZINGIBERACEAE

Genus of summer-and autumn-flowering perennials. Frost hardy. Grow in a sunny, wind-free position and in deep, rich, moist but well-drained soil. Propagate by seed or division in spring.

C. spicata illus. p.279.

CAYRATIA

VITACEAE

Genus of deciduous, woody-stemmed, tendril climbers, grown for their leaves and autumn colour. Tendril tips have sucker-like pads that cling to supports. Insignificant greenish flowers appear in summer. Half-hardy. Grow in shade or semi-shade and well-drained soil. Propagate by softwood or greenwood cuttings in summer or by hardwood cuttings in early spring. ⓘThe berries may cause mild stomach upset if ingested.

C. thomsonii, syn. *Parthenocissus thomsonii*, illus. p.209.

CEANOTHUS

RHAMNACEAE

Genus of evergreen or deciduous shrubs and small trees, grown for their small but densely clustered, mainly blue flowers. Frost to half hardy; in cold areas plant against a south-or west-facing wall. Needs a sheltered site in full sun and light, well-drained soil. Cut dead wood from evergreens in spring and trim their side-shoots after flowering. Cut back shoots of deciduous species to basal framework in early spring. Propagate by semi-ripe cuttings in summer.

♀ ***C. arboreus* 'Trewithen Blue'** illus. p.194.

♀ ***C.* 'Autumnal Blue'** illus. p.138.

♀ ***C.* 'Blue Mound'.** Evergreen, bushy, dense shrub. **H** 1.5m (5ft), **S** 2m (6ft). Frost hardy. Forms a mound of oblong, glossy, dark green leaves, covered, in late spring, with rounded clusters of deep blue flowers.

♀ ***C.* 'Burkwoodii'** illus. p.205.

***C.* 'Burtonensis'.** Evergreen, bushy, spreading shrub. **H** 2m (6ft) or more, **S** 4m (12ft). Frost hardy. Has small, rounded, almost spherical, crinkled leaves that are lustrous and dark green. Small, deep blue flowers appear in clusters, 2cm (¾in) wide, from mid-spring to early summer.

♀ ***C.* 'Cascade'.** Vigorous, evergreen, arching shrub. **H** and **S** 4m (12ft). Frost hardy. Leaves are narrowly oblong, glossy and dark green. Large panicles of powder-blue flowers open in late spring and early summer.

***C.* 'Delight'.** Fast-growing, evergreen, bushy shrub. **H** 3m (10ft), **S** 5m (15ft). Frost hardy. Bears oblong, glossy, deep green leaves. Long clusters of rich blue flowers appear in late spring.

♀ ***C.* x *delileanus* 'Gloire de Versailles'.** See *C.* 'Gloire de Versailles'.

C. dentatus. Evergreen, bushy, dense shrub. **H** 1.5m (5ft), **S** 2m (6ft). Frost hardy. Produces small, oblong, glossy, dark green leaves and is covered, in late spring, with rounded clusters of bright blue flowers.

C. dentatus of gardens. See *C.* x *lobbianus*.

♀ ***C.* 'Gloire de Versailles'**, syn. *C.* x *delileanus* 'Gloire de Versailles', illus. p.157.

C. gloriosus. Evergreen, prostrate shrub. **H** 30cm (1ft), **S** 2m (6ft). Frost hardy. Leaves are oval and dark green. Rounded clusters of deep blue or purplish-blue flowers appear from mid- to late spring. May suffer from chlorosis on chalky soils.

C. impressus illus. p.138. **'Puget Blue'** see *C.* 'Puget Blue'.

C. incanus illus. p.129.

♀ ***C.* 'Italian Skies'.** Evergreen, bushy, spreading shrub. **H** 1.5m (5ft), **S** 3m (10ft). Frost hardy. Has small, oval, glossy, dark green leaves. Produces dense, conical clusters of bright blue flowers during late spring.

C.* x *lobbianus, syn. *C. dentatus* of gardens. Evergreen, bushy, dense shrub. **H** and **S** 2m (6ft). Frost hardy. Rounded clusters of bright, deep blue flowers are borne in late spring and early summer amid oval, dark green leaves.

***C.* 'Marie Simon'.** Deciduous, bushy shrub. **H** and **S** 1.5m (5ft). Frost hardy. Has broadly oval, mid-green leaves. Conical clusters of soft pink flowers are carried in profusion from mid-summer to early autumn.

C. papillosus. Evergreen, arching shrub. **H** 3m (10ft), **S** 5m (15ft). Frost hardy. Leaves are narrowly oblong, glossy, dark green and sticky. Produces dense racemes of blue or purplish-blue flowers during late spring.

***C.* 'Perle Rose'** illus. p.153.

♀ ***C.* 'Puget Blue',** syn. *C. impressus* 'Puget Blue', illus. p.205.

C. rigidus. See *C. rigidus* var. *rigidus*.

***C. rigidus* var. *ridigus*,** syn. *C. rigidus* (Monterey ceanothus). Evergreen, bushy shrub of dense, spreading habit. **H** 1.2m (4ft), **S** 2.5m (8ft). Frost hardy. Bears oblong to rounded, glossy, dark green leaves and, from mid-spring to early summer, produces rounded clusters of deep purplish-blue flowers.

♀ ***C.* 'Southmead'.** Evergreen, bushy, dense shrub. **H** and **S** 1.5m (5ft). Frost hardy. Has small, oblong, glossy, dark green leaves. Deep blue flowers are produced in rounded clusters in late spring and early summer.

C. thyrsiflorus. Evergreen, bushy shrub or spreading tree. **H** and **S** 6m (20ft). Frost hardy. Has broadly oval, glossy, mid-green leaves and, in late spring and early summer, rounded clusters of pale blue flowers. ♀ **var. *repens*** illus. p.159.

***C.* x *veitchianus*.** Vigorous, evergreen, bushy shrub. **H** and **S** 3m (10ft). Frost hardy. Dense, oblong clusters of deep blue flowers are borne in late spring and early summer amid oblong, glossy, dark green leaves.

Cedrela sinensis. See *Toona sinensis*.

Cedronella mexicana. See *Agastache mexicana*.

CEDRUS

Cedar

PINACEAE

See also CONIFERS.

C. atlantica, syn. *C. libani* subsp. *atlantica* (Atlas cedar). Conifer that is conical when young, broadening with age. **H** 15–25m (50–80ft), **S** 5–10m (15–30ft). Fully hardy. Leaves are spirally arranged, needle-like, dull green or bright blue-grey. Has ovoid cones, males pale brown, females pale green, ripening to brown. **f. *fastigiata*** (syn. *C.a.* Fastigiata Group), **S** 4–5m (12–15ft), has a narrower, more upright habit. ♀ **f. *glauca*** (Blue Atlas cedar), syn. *C.a.* Glauca Group, illus. p.95.

♀ ***C. deodara*** (Deodar cedar) illus. p.96. ♀ **'Aurea'** illus. p.104.

♀ ***C. libani*** (Cedar of Lebanon), illus. p.97. **subsp. *atlantica*** see *C. atlantica*. **'Comte de Dijon'**, **H** 1–2m (3–6ft), **S** 60cm–1.2m (2–4ft), is a dwarf form that grows only 5cm (2in) a year. **'Sargentii',** **H** and **S** 1–1.5m (3–5ft), has horizontal, then weeping branches and makes a bush that is rounded in shape.

CEIBA

BOMBACACEAE

Genus of evergreen, semi-evergreen or deciduous trees, grown for their overall appearance and for shade. Frost tender, min. 15°C (59°F). Requires full light or light shade and fertile, moisture-retentive but well-drained soil. Water potted specimens freely while in full growth, less at other times. Pruning is tolerated if necessary. Propagate by seed in spring or by semi-ripe cuttings in summer.

C. pentandra (Kapok, Silk cotton tree). Fast-growing, semi-evergreen tree with a spine-covered trunk. **H** and **S** 25m (80ft) or more. Hand-shaped leaves have 5–9 elliptic leaflets, red when young, becoming mid-green. Bears clusters of 5-petalled, white, yellow or pink flowers in summer, followed by woody, brownish seed pods containing silky kapok fibre.

C. speciosa. See *Chorisia speciosa*.

CELASTRUS

CELASTRACEAE

Genus of deciduous shrubs and twining climbers, grown for their attractive fruits. Most species bear male and female flowers on separate plants, so both sexes must be grown to obtain fruits; hermaphrodite forms of *C. orbiculatus* are available. Fully to frost hardy. Grow in any soil and in full or partial shade. Likes regular feeding. Prune in spring to cut out old wood and maintain shape. Propagate by seed in autumn or spring or by semi-ripe cuttings in summer.

C. articulatus. See *C. orbiculatus*.

C. orbiculatus, syn. *C. articulatus* (Oriental bittersweet, Staff vine). Vigorous, deciduous, twining climber. **H** to 14m (46ft). Frost hardy. Has small, rounded, toothed leaves. Clusters of 2–4 small, green flowers are produced in summer; tiny, long-lasting, spherical fruits begin green, turn black in autumn, and finally split and show yellow insides and red seeds. **'Diana'**, illus. p.209.

C. scandens (American bittersweet, Staff tree). Deciduous, twining climber. **H** to 10m (30ft). Frost hardy. Oval leaves are 5–10cm (2–4in) long. Tiny, greenish flowers are borne in small clusters in leaf axils in summer. Long-lasting, spherical fruits are produced in bunches, 5–8cm (2–3in) long; each fruit splits to show an orange interior and scarlet seeds.

CELMISIA

COMPOSITAE/ASTERACEAE

Genus of evergreen, late spring- and summer-flowering perennials, grown for their foliage and daisy-like flower heads. Is suitable for rock gardens and peat beds, but may be difficult to grow in hot, dry climates. Frost hardy. Needs a sheltered, sunny site and humus-rich, moist but well-drained, sandy, acid soil. Propagate by division in early summer or by seed when fresh.

C. bellidioides. Evergreen, mat-forming perennial. **H** 2cm (¾in), **S** to 15cm (6in). Has rounded, leathery, dark green leaves. Bears almost stemless, 1cm (½in) wide, daisy-like, white flowers in early summer.

C. coriacea of gardens . See *C. semicordata*.

C. ramulosa illus. p.360.

C. semicordata, syn. *C. coriacea* of gardens, illus. p.346.

C. traversii. Slow-growing, evergreen, clump-forming perennial. **H** 15cm (6in), **S** 20cm (8in). Sword-shaped, dark green leaves have reddish-brown margins and cream undersides. In summer, carries 6–7cm (2½–3in) wide, daisy-like, white flower heads. Is difficult to establish.

C. walkeri, syn. *C. webbiana*, illus. p.336.

C. webbiana. See *C. walkeri*.

CELOSIA

AMARANTHACEAE

Genus of erect perennials, grown as annuals. Half hardy. Grows best in a sunny, sheltered position and in fertile, well-drained soil. Propagate by seed sown under glass in spring.

C. argentea. Moderately fast-growing, erect, bushy perennial, grown as an annual. **H** 30–60cm (12–24in), **S** to 45cm (18in). Has oval to lance-shaped, pale to mid-green leaves and, in summer, silvery-white, pyramid-shaped, feathery flower heads, to 10cm (4in) long. Cultivars are available in red, orange, yellow and cream. Dwarf cultivars, **H** 30cm (12in), include **'Fairy Fountains'**, which has flower heads, to 15cm (6in) tall, in a wide range of colours in summer-autumn, and **Olympia Series**, which has crested, coral-like heads of tightly clustered flowers, 8–12cm (3–5in) across, in colours such as golden yellow, scarlet, light red, deep cerise and purple.

CELTIS

Hackberry, Nettle tree

ULMACEAE

Genus of deciduous trees, with inconspicuous flowers in spring, grown for their foliage and small fruits. Fully hardy. Needs full sun (doing best in hot summers) and fertile, well-drained soil. Propagate by seed in autumn.

C. australis illus. p.62.

C. occidentalis (Common hackberry). Deciduous, spreading tree. **H** and **S** 20m (70ft). Oval, sharply toothed, glossy, bright green leaves turn yellow in autumn, when they are accompanied by globose, yellowish-red, then red-purple fruits.

C. sinensis. Deciduous, rounded tree. **H** and **S** 10m (30ft). Has oval, glossy, dark green leaves, with fine teeth, and small, globose, orange fruits.

CENTAUREA

Knapweed

COMPOSITAE/ASTERACEAE

Genus of annuals and perennials, grown for their flower heads that each have a thistle-like centre surrounded by a ring of slender ray petals. Fully hardy. Requires sun; grows in any well-drained soil, even poor soil. Propagate by seed or division in autumn or spring.

C. cyanus (Bluebottle, Cornflower). Fast-growing, upright, branching annual. **H** 30cm–1m (1–3ft), **S** 30cm (1ft). Has lance-shaped, grey-green leaves and, in summer and early autumn, branching stems with usually double, daisy-like flower heads in shades of blue, pink, red, purple or white. Flowers are excellent for cutting. Tall (blue, illus. p.315) and dwarf cultivars are available. **Baby Series** (dwarf), **H** to 30cm (1ft), has blue, white or pink flower heads.

C. dealbata. Erect perennial. **H** 1m (3ft), **S** 60cm (2ft). Lilac-purple flower heads are borne freely in summer, one or more to each stem. Has narrowly oval, finely cut, light green leaves. **'Steenbergii'**, **H** 60cm (2ft), has carmine-lilac flowers.

***C. hypoleuca* 'John Coutts'** illus. p.265.

C. macrocephala. Robust, clump-forming perennial. **H** 1m (3ft), **S** 60cm (2ft). In summer, stout stems bear large, yellow flower heads, within papery, silvery-brown bracts. Mid-green leaves are narrowly oval and deeply cut.

C. montana illus. p.269.

C. moschata. See *Amberboa moschata*.

C. pulcherrima illus. p.232.

CENTRADENIA

MELASTOMATACEAE

Genus of evergreen perennials and shrubs, grown for their flowers and foliage. Frost tender, min. 13°C (55°F). Needs light shade and fertile, well-drained soil. Water containerized plants freely when in full growth, moderately at other times. Tip prune young plants to promote a bushy habit; old plants become straggly unless trimmed each spring. Propagate from early spring to early summer by seed or by softwood or greenwood cuttings. If grown as pot plants, propagate annually.

C. floribunda. Evergreen, loosely rounded, soft-stemmed shrub. **H** and **S** to 60cm (24in). Lance-shaped leaves are prominently veined, glossy, green above, bluish-green beneath. Large, terminal clusters of 4-petalled, pink or white flowers develop from pink buds in late winter and spring.

CENTRANTHUS

VALERIANACEAE

Genus of late spring- to autumn-flowering perennials. Fully hardy. Requires sun. Thrives in an exposed position and in poor, alkaline soil. Propagate by seed in autumn or spring.

C. ruber (Red valerian) illus. p.248.

CENTROPOGON

CAMPANULACEAE

Genus of herbaceous or sub-shrubby, upright, scrambling or climbing, deciduous or evergreen perennials, grown for their tubular, bright pink to red, orange or yellow flowers borne singly on stalks from between the uppermost leaves, which are sometimes patterned or variegated. Half hardy to frost tender, min. 5°C (41°F). Needs humus-rich, moist but well-drained soil in sun or partial shade. Propagate by seed in spring.

C. ayavacensis, syn. *C. willdenowianus*. Deciduous, trailing perennial. **H** and **S** 1m (3ft). Frost tender. Flexuous, purple stems have rounded to broadly elliptic, mid-green leaves, to 5cm (2in) long. Bears tubular, cerise flowers, 5–6cm (2–2½in) long, with reflexed petals, from early spring to summer. Needs a sunny position. Protect roots from frost.

C. cordifolius. Herbaceous, weakly climbing or trailing perennial. **H** 0.5m (½ft), **S** 1–2m (3–6ft). Frost tender. Red stems have heart-shaped, toothed, grey-green leaves, to 7.5cm (3in) long, and bear flared, tubular, cerise flowers, 4cm (1½in) long, from late spring to summer. Requires a sunny position. Protect roots from frost.

C. ferrugineus. Herbaceous, trailing perennial. **H** 0.5–2m (½–6ft), **S** 1–2m (3–6ft). Frost tender. Long, wiry, pendent stems bear narrowly ovate, silver-marked, mid-green leaves, 6–13cm (2½–5in) long, with narrowly toothed margins. Flared, tubular, bright pink flowers, 4–5cm (1½–2in) long, from summer into autumn, are followed by spherical fruits. Is best in a container.

C. willdenowianus. See *C. ayavacensis*.

CEPHALARIA

DIPSACACEAE

Genus of coarse, summer-flowering perennials, best suited to large borders and wild gardens. Fully hardy. Prefers sun and well-drained soil. Propagate by division in spring or by seed in autumn.

C. gigantea, syn. *C. tatarica* (Giant scabious, Yellow scabious). Robust, branching perennial. **H** 2m (6ft), **S** 1.2m (4ft). In early summer, wiry stems bear pincushion-like heads of primrose-yellow flowers above lance-shaped, deeply cut, dark green leaves.

C. tatarica. See *C. gigantea*.

CEPHALOCEREUS

CACTACEAE

Genus of slow-growing, columnar, perennial cacti with 20–30-ribbed, green stems. Frost tender, min. 5°C (41°F). Prefers full sun and extremely well-drained, lime-rich soil. Is prone to rot if overwatered. Propagate by seed in spring or summer.

C. senilis (Old-man cactus) illus. p.479.

CEPHALOPHYLLUM

AIZOACEAE

Genus of clump-forming, bushy, perennial succulents with semi-cylindrical to cylindrical, green leaves. Flowers are borne after 1 or 2 years. Frost tender, min. 5°C (41°F). Needs sun and well-drained soil. Propagate by seed in spring or summer.

C. alstonii (Red spike). Prostrate, perennial succulent. **H** 10cm (4in), **S** 1m (3ft). Has cylindrical, grey-green leaves, to 7cm (3in) long. Carries daisy-like, dark red flowers, 8cm (3in) across, in summer.

C. pillansii. Clump-forming, perennial succulent. **H** 8cm (3in), **S** 60cm (24in). Leaves are cylindrical, 6cm (2½in) long, dark green and covered in darker dots. Short flower stems produce daisy-like, red-centred, yellow flowers, 6cm (2½in) across, from spring to autumn.

CEPHALOTAXUS

CEPHALOTAXACEAE

See also CONIFERS.

C. harringtonii (Cow's-tail pine, Plum yew). Bushy, spreading conifer. **H** 5m (15ft), **S** 3m (10ft). Frost hardy. Needle-like, flattened leaves are glossy, dark green, greyish beneath, radiating around erect shoots. Bears ovoid, fleshy, green fruits that ripen to brown.

CERASTIUM

CAROPHYLLACEAE

Genus of annuals and perennials with star-shaped flowers. Some species are useful as ground cover. Fully hardy. Needs sun and well-drained soil. Propagate by division in spring.

C. alpinum (Alpine mouse-ear). Prostrate perennial. **H** 8cm (3in), **S** 40cm (16in). Tiny, oval, grey leaves cover stems. Flower stems carry solitary, 1cm (½in) wide, star-shaped, white flowers throughout summer.

C. tomentosum illus. p.350.

CERATOPHYLLUM

CERATOPHYLLACEAE

Genus of deciduous, perennial, submerged water plants, grown for their foliage. Is suitable for pools and cold-water aquariums. Fully to half hardy. Prefers an open, sunny position, but tolerates shade better than most submerged plants. Propagation occurs naturally when scaly young shoots or winter buds separate from main plants. Take stem cuttings in growing season.

C. demersum (Hornwort). Deciduous, perennial, spreading, submerged water plant that occasionally floats. **S** indefinite. Fully hardy. Has small, dark green leaves with 3 linear lobes. Is best suited to a cool-water pool.

CERATOPTERIS

PARKERIACEAE

Genus of deciduous or semi-evergreen, perennial, floating water ferns, grown for their attractive foliage. Is suitable for aquariums. Frost tender, min. 10°C (50°F). Prefers a sunny position. Remove fading fronds regularly. Propagate in summer by division or by buds that develop on the leaves.

C. thalictroides (Water fern). Semi-evergreen, perennial, spreading, floating water fern that sometimes roots and becomes submerged. **S** indefinite. Lance- or heart-shaped, soft green fronds are wavy-edged.

CERATOSTIGMA

PLUMBAGINACEAE

Genus of deciduous, semi-evergreen or evergreen shrubs and perennials, grown for their blue flowers and autumn colour. Fully hardy to frost tender, min. 10°C (50°F). Requires a sunny position, with well-drained soil. Cut out old, dead wood from shrubs in spring. Propagate shrubs by softwood cuttings in summer, perennials by division in spring.

C. griffithii. Evergreen or semi-evergreen, bushy, dense shrub. **H** 1m (3ft), **S** 1.5m (5ft). Half hardy. Spoon-shaped, bristly, purple-edged, dull green leaves redden in autumn. Clusters of tubular, bright blue flowers, with spreading petal lobes, appear in late summer and autumn.

🏆 ***C. plumbaginoides*** illus. p.346.

🏆 ***C. willmottianum*** illus. p.159.

CERCIDIPHYLLUM

CERCIDIPHYLLACEAE

Genus of deciduous trees, grown for their foliage and often spectacular autumn colour. Fully hardy. Late frosts may damage young foliage, but do not usually cause lasting harm. Requires sun or semi-shade and fertile, moist but well-drained soil. Propagate by seed in autumn.

🏆 ***C. japonicum*** (Katsura) illus. p.66.

CERCIS

Judas tree, Redbud

LEGUMINOSAE/PAPILIONACEAE

Genus of deciduous shrubs and trees with sometimes shrubby growth, cultivated for their foliage and small, pea-like flowers, borne profusely in spring. Fully hardy. Requires a position in full sun with deep, fertile, well-drained soil. Plant out as young specimens. Resents transplanting. Propagate species by seed sown in autumn, cultivars by budding in summer.

C. canadensis (Eastern redbud). Deciduous, spreading tree or shrub. **H** and **S** 10m (30ft). Heart-shaped, dark green leaves turn yellow in autumn. Pea-like flowers are magenta in bud, opening to pale pink in mid-spring before leaves emerge. ♀ **'Forest Pansy'** illus. p.84.

♀ ***C. siliquastrum*** illus. p.83.

CEREUS

CACTACEAE

Genus of columnar, perennial cacti with spiny stems, most having 4–10 pronounced ribs. Cup-shaped flowers usually open at night. Frost tender, min. 7°C (45°F). Needs full sun and very well-drained soil. Propagate in spring by seed or, for branching species, by stem cuttings.

C. forbesii. See *C. hankeanus.*

C. hankeanus, syn. *C. forbesii*, illus. p.488.

C. hildmannianus, syn. *C. peruvianus* of gardens, illus. p.488. **'Monstrosus'** is a columnar, perennial cactus. **H** 5m (15ft), **S** 4m (12ft). Swollen, occasionally fan-shaped, silvery-blue stems bear golden spines on 4–8 (or more) uneven ribs. Is unlikely to flower in cultivation.

C. peruvianus of gardens. See *C. hildmannianus.*

C. spachianus. See *Echinopsis spachiana.*

CERINTHE

BORAGINACEAE

Genus of annuals, biennials, and perennials with somewhat fleshy stems and leaves. Fully to frost hardy. Requires a site in full sun, with dry to moist, but well-drained soil. Propagate by seed sown in autumn or spring.

***C. major* 'Purpurascens'** illus. p.312.

CEROPEGIA

ASCLEPIADACEAE/APOCYNACEAE

Genus of semi-evergreen, succulent shrubs and sub-shrubs, most with slender, climbing or pendent stems, grown for their unusual flowers. Frost tender, min. 7–11°C (45–52°F). Needs partial shade and very well-drained soil. Propagate by seed or stem cuttings in spring or summer. *C. woodii* is often used as grafting stock for difficult asclepiads.

C. distincta* subsp. *haygarthii. See *C. haygarthii.*

C. haygarthii, syn. *C. distincta* subsp. *haygarthii*. Semi-evergreen, climbing, succulent sub-shrub. **H** 2m (6ft) or more, **S** indefinite. Min. 11°C (52°F). Bears oval or rounded, dark green leaves, 1–2cm (½–¾in) long. In summer, produces masses of small, white or pinkish-white flowers, each with a pitcher-shaped tube, widening towards the top and then united at the tip by purplish-spotted petals that form a short stem ending in 5 'knobs' edged with fine hairs. The whole resembles an insect hovering over a flower.

C. linearis, syn. *C.l.* subsp. *woodii, C. woodii*.. (Heart vine, Rosary vine, String-of-hearts), illus. p.490.

♀ ***C. linearis* subsp. *woodii***, see. *C linearis.*

C. sandersoniae. See *C. sandersonii.*

♀ ***C. sandersonii***, syn. *C. sandersoniae* (Fountain flower, Parachute plant). Semi-evergreen, scrambling, succulent sub-shrub. **H** 2m (6ft), **S** indefinite. Min. 11°C (52°F). Leaves are triangular to oval, fleshy and 2cm (¾in) long. In summer–autumn has tubular, green flowers, 5cm (2in) long, with paler green to white marks; the petals are flared widely at tips to form 'parachutes'.

C. woodii. See *C. linearis* .

CESTRUM

SOLANACEAE

Genus of deciduous or evergreen shrubs and semi-scrambling climbers, grown for their showy flowers. Foliage has an unpleasant scent. Frost hardy to frost tender, min. 7–10°C (45–50°F); in cold areas, grow frost hardy species against a south-or west-facing wall or in a greenhouse. Requires a sheltered, sunny position and fertile, well-drained soil. Water containerized specimens freely when in full growth, moderately at other times. Support is needed for scrambling species. Propagate frost hardy species by softwood cuttings in summer, tender species by seed in spring or by semi-ripe cuttings in summer.

C. aurantiacum. Mainly evergreen semi-scrambler that remains a rounded shrub if cut back annually. **H** and **S** to 2m (6ft). Frost tender, min. 7–10°C (45–50°F); is deciduous at low temperatures. Bears oval, bright green leaves. Tubular, bright orange flowers are carried in large, terminal trusses in summer and may be followed by spherical, white fruits. Prune annually, cutting out old stems to near base after flowering.

C. elegans, syn. *C. purpureum* of gardens, illus. p.202.

♀ ***C.* 'Newellii'** illus. p.203.

♀ ***C. parqui.*** Deciduous, open shrub. **H** and **S** 2m (6ft). Frost hardy. Large clusters of tubular, yellowish-green flowers, fragrant at night, are borne in profusion in summer amid narrowly lance-shaped, mid-green leaves.

C. purpureum of gardens. See *C. elegans.*

Ceterach officinarum. See *Asplenium ceterach.*

CHAENOMELES

Flowering quince, Japonica

ROSACEAE

Genus of deciduous, usually thorny, spring-flowering shrubs, grown for their showy flowers and fragrant fruits, produced in autumn and used for preserves. Fully hardy. Prefers sun and well-drained soil. On wall-trained shrubs cut back side-shoots after flowering to 2 or 3 buds and shorten shoots growing away from wall during growing season. Propagate species by softwood or greenwood cuttings in summer or by seed in autumn, cultivars by cuttings only in summer. Fireblight and, on chalk soils, chlorosis are common problems.

C. cathayensis (illus. p.142). Deciduous, spreading, open shrub with thorns. **H** and **S** 3m (10ft) or more. Produces long, narrow, pointed, mid-green leaves. Small, 5-petalled, pink-flushed, white flowers appear from early to mid-spring, followed by large, egg-shaped, yellow-green fruits.

C. japonica (Japanese quince, Japonica). Deciduous, bushy, spreading shrub with thorns. **H** 1m (3ft), **S** 2m (6ft). Has oval, mid-green leaves and, in spring, a profusion of 5-petalled, red or orange-red flowers, then spherical, yellow fruits.

C. speciosa. Vigorous, deciduous, bushy shrub with thorns. **H** 2.5m (8ft), **S** 5m (15ft). Leaves are oval, glossy and dark green. Clustered, 5-petalled, red flowers are borne from early to mid-spring, and are followed by spherical, greenish-yellow fruits. ♀ **'Moerloosei'** illus. p.122. Flowers of **'Nivalis'** are pure white. **'Simonii'**, **H** 1m (3ft), **S** 2m (6ft), bears masses of semi-double, deep red flowers. **'Snow'**, illus. p.146.

♀ ***C. x superba* 'Etna'.** Deciduous, bushy, dense shrub with thorns. **H** 1.5m (5ft), **S** 3m (10ft). Has oval, glossy, dark green leaves. Bears masses of 5-petalled, scarlet flowers, with conspicuous, golden-yellow anthers, in spring, followed by round, yellow fruits. ♀ **'Crimson and Gold'** illus. p.193. ♀ **'Knap Hill Scarlet'**, **H** 1.5m (5ft), **S** 3m (10ft), produces large, brilliant red flowers. ♀ **'Nicoline'** illus. p.147. ♀ **'Rowallane'** illus. p.147.

CHAMAEBATIARIA

ROSACEAE

Genus of one species of deciduous shrub, grown for its foliage and summer flowers. Frost hardy. Needs a sheltered, sunny position and well-drained soil. Propagate by semi-ripe cuttings in summer.

C. millefolium. Deciduous, upright, open shrub. **H** and **S** 1m (3ft). Has finely divided, aromatic, grey-green leaves. Shallowly cup-shaped, white flowers, with yellow stamens, are borne in terminal, branching panicles from mid- to late summer.

Chamaecereus silvestrii. See *Echinopsis chamaecereus.*

CHAMAECYPARIS

False Cypress

CUPRESSACEAE

ⓘ Contact with the foliage may aggravate skin allergies. See also CONIFERS.

C. lawsoniana (Lawson cypress). Upright, columnar conifer with branches drooping at tips. **H** 15–25m (50–80ft), **S** 3–4m (10–12ft). Fully hardy. Bears flattened sprays of scale-like, aromatic, dark green leaves and globular cones, the males brick-red, the females insignificant and green. **'Columnaris'** illus. p.103. ♀ **'Ellwoodii'**, **H** 3m (10ft), **S** 1.5m (5ft), is erect with incurved, blue-grey leaves. ♀ **'Fletcheri'**, **H** 5–12m (15–40ft), **S** 2–3m (6–10ft), has grey leaves that are incurved. **'Gnome'**, **H** and **S** 50cm (20in), is a dwarf, bun-shaped form with blue foliage. **'Green Pillar'** illus. p.102. ♀ **'Intertexta'** illus. p.96. ♀ **'Kilmacurragh'**, **H** 10–15m (30–50ft), **S** 1m (3ft), has very bright green foliage. ♀ **'Lanei Aurea'** illus. p.102. **'Minima'**, **H** and **S** 1m (3ft), is dwarf and globular, and has light green foliage. ♀ **'Pembury Blue'** illus. p.99. **'Tamariscifolia'** (syn. *C.l.* Tamariscifolia Group), **H** 3m (10ft), **S** 4m (12ft), is a dwarf, spreading form. **'Triomf van Boskoop'**, **H** 20m (70ft), is broadly columnar, with grey-blue foliage. ♀ **'Wisselii'**, **H** 15m (50ft), **S** 2–3m (6–10ft), is fast-growing, with erect branches and blue-green leaves.

C. nootkatensis (Nootka cypress). Almost geometrically conical conifer. **H** 15m (50ft), **S** 6m (20ft). Fully hardy. Bears long, pendent sprays of scale-like, aromatic, grey-green leaves and globular, hooked, dark blue and green cones that ripen to brown. **'Pendula'** has a gaunt crown of arching, weeping foliage.

C. obtusa (Hinoki cypress). Conical conifer. **H** 15–20m (50–70ft), **S** 5m (15ft). Fully hardy. Has stringy, red-brown bark and scale-like, aromatic, dark green leaves with bright silver lines at sides and incurving tips. Small, rounded cones ripen to yellow-brown. **'Coralliformis'**, **H** to 50cm (20in), **S** 1m (3ft), is dwarf, with thread-like shoots. ♀ **'Crippsii'** illus. p.104. **'Intermedia'**, **H** to 30cm (12in), **S** 40cm (16in), is a globular, open, dwarf shrub with downward-spreading, light green foliage. **'Kosteri'**, **H** 1–2m (3–6ft), **S** 2–3m (6–10ft), forms a sprawling bush with twisted, lustrous foliage. Extremely slow-growing. ♀ **'Nana'**, eventual **H** 1m (3ft), **S** 1.5–2m (5–6ft), makes a flat-topped bush. ♀ **'Nana Aurea'**, **H** and **S** 2m (6ft), is a form with golden-yellow leaves. ♀ **'Nana Gracilis'** (illus. p.105), **H** 2m (6ft), **S** 1.5–2m (5–6ft), is a form with glossy foliage. **'Nana Pyramidalis'** (illus. p.105), **H** and **S** to 60cm (2ft), is a slow-growing, dense, conical, dwarf cultivar with horizontal, cup-shaped leaves. **'Tetragona Aurea'**, **H** 10m (30ft), **S** 2–3m (6–10ft), produces golden- or bronze-yellow leaves.

C. pisifera (Sawara cypress). Conical conifer with horizontal branches. **H** 15m (50ft), **S** 5m (15ft). Fully hardy. Has ridged, peeling, red-brown bark, scale-like, aromatic, fresh green leaves, white at sides and beneath, and angular, yellow-brown cones. ♀ **'Boulevard'** has silver-blue foliage. **'Filifera'** has whip-like, hanging shoots and dark green foliage. ♀ **'Filifera Aurea'** (illus. p.105), **H** 12m (40ft), **S** 3–5m (10–15ft), also has whip-like shoots, but with golden-yellow leaves. **'Filifera Nana'**, **H** 60cm (2ft), **S** 1m (3ft), is a dwarf form with whip-like branches. **'Nana'**, **H** and **S** 50cm (20in), is also dwarf, with dark bluish-green foliage. **'Plumosa'** is broadly conical to columnar, with yellowish-grey-green leaves. **'Plumosa Rogersii'**, **H** 2m (6ft), **S** 1m (3ft), has yellow foliage. Slow-growing **'Squarrosa'**, **H** to 20m (70ft), has a broad crown and soft, blue-grey foliage.

C. thyoides illus. p.101. **'Andelyensis'** is a slow-growing, conical, dwarf conifer. **H** 3m (10ft), **S** 1m (3ft). Fully hardy. Has wedge-shaped tufts of scale-like, aromatic, blue-green leaves. Globular cones are glaucous blue-grey.

CHAMAECYTISUS

LEGUMINOSAE/PAPILIONACEAE

Genus of evergreen and deciduous trees, shrubs and sub-shrubs, grown for pea-like flowers. Fully to half hardy. Best in full sun and moderately fertile, well-drained soil. Propagate by seed in autumn or spring, or by semi-ripe cuttings in summer.

C. albus, syn *Cytisus albus, Cytisus leucanthus*. Deciduous, spreading shrub. **H** 30cm (1ft), **S** 1m (3ft). Fully hardy. Has oval leaves, each with 3 tiny leaflets and, from early to mid-summer, creamy-white flowers borne in dense clusters.

C. demissus, syn. *C. hirsutus* var. *demissus, Cytisus demissus*. Slow-growing, deciduous, prostrate shrub. **H** 8cm (3in), **S** 20–30cm (8–12in). Fully hardy. Densely hairy stems bear tiny, bright green leaves with 3-palmate, obovate leaflets. Produces axillary clusters of 2–4 bright yellow flowers, each with a brown keel, in early summer. Is good for a rock garden or trough.

***C. hirsutus* var. *demissus*.** See *C. demissus*.

C. purpureus, syn. *Cytisus purpureus* (Purple broom). Deciduous, arching shrub. **H** 45cm (18in), **S** 60cm (24in). Fully hardy. Semi-erect stems are clothed with leaves of 3-palmate, obovate leaflets. Clusters of 2–3 pale lilac to purple flowers open in early summer on previous year's wood. Suits a bank or sunny border. **f. *albus*** illus. p.337.

C. supinus, syn. *Cytisus supinus*. Deciduous, bushy, rounded shrub. **H** and **S** 1m (3ft). Fully hardy. Dense, terminal heads of large, yellow flowers are borne from mid-summer to autumn amid grey-green leaves with 3-palmate, oblong-elliptic leaflets.

CHAMAEDAPHNE

ERICACEAE

Genus of one species of evergreen shrub, grown for its white flowers. Fully hardy. Needs sun or semi-shade and moist, peaty, acid soil. Propagate by semi-ripe cuttings in summer.

C. calyculata (Leatherleaf). Evergreen, arching, open shrub. **H** 75cm (2½ft), **S** 1m (3ft). Leaves are small, oblong, leathery and dark green. Leafy racemes of small, urn-shaped flowers appear on slender branches in mid- to late spring.

CHAMAEDOREA

ARECACEAE/PALMAE

Genus of evergreen palms, grown for their overall appearance. Frost tender, min. 18°C (64°F). Needs shade or semi-shade and humus-rich, well-drained soil. Water containerized plants moderately, less when temperatures are low. Propagate by seed in spring at not less than 25°C (77°F). Red spider mite may be troublesome.

🏆 ***C. elegans***, syn. *Neanthe bella*, illus. p.458.

CHAMAEMELUM

COMPOSITAE/ASTERACEAE

Genus of evergreen perennials, suitable as ground cover or for a lawn. Flowers may be used to make tea. Fully hardy. Needs sun and well-drained soil. Propagate by division in spring or by seed in autumn.

C. nobile, syn. *Anthemis nobilis* (Chamomile). Evergreen, mat-forming, invasive perennial. **H** 10cm (4in), **S** 45cm (18in). Has finely divided, aromatic leaves and daisy-like heads of white flowers, with yellow centres, borne in late spring or summer. **'Treneague'** is a non-flowering, less invasive cultivar that, requiring less mowing, is better for a lawn.

***Chamaenerion*.** See *Epilobium*.
***Chamerion*.** See *Epilobium*.
***Chamaepericlymenum canadense*.** See *Cornus canadensis*.

CHAMAEROPS

ARECACEAE/PALMAE

Genus of evergreen palms, cultivated for their overall appearance. Half hardy to frost tender, min. 7°C (45°F). Needs full light and fertile, well-drained soil. Water containerized plants moderately, less when not in full growth. Propagate by seed in spring at not less than 22°C (72°F) or by suckers in late spring. Red spider mite may be a nuisance.

🏆 ***C. humilis*** illus. p.165.

***Chamaespartium sagittale*.** See *Genista sagittalis*.
***Chamaespartium sagittale* subsp. *delphinense*.** See *Genista delphinensis*.

CHAMELAUCIUM

MYRTACEAE

Genus of evergreen shrubs, grown for their flowers and overall appearance. Frost tender, min. 5°C (41°F), but best at 7–10°C (45–50°F). Requires full sun and well-drained, sandy, neutral to acid soil. Water containerized specimens moderately, sparingly when not in full growth. To maintain a more compact habit, cut back flowered stems by half when the last bloom falls. Propagate by seed in spring or by semi-ripe cuttings in summer.

C. uncinatum [pink] illus. p.454, [white] illus. p.453.

CHASMANTHE

IRIDACEAE

Genus of corms, grown for their showy flowers. Frost to half hardy. Needs a site in full sun or partial shade and well-drained soil, with plenty of water in late winter and early spring. Reduce watering in summer–autumn. Propagate by division in autumn.

***C. aethiopica*.** Spring- and early summer-flowering corm. **H** to 80cm (32in), **S** 12–18cm (5–7in). Frost hardy. Has narrowly sword-shaped, erect, basal leaves in a flat fan. Produces a spike of scarlet flowers, all facing one way, with yellow tubes, 5–6cm (2–2½in) long, and hooded, upper lips.

***C. floribunda*.** Summer-flowering corm. **H** to 80cm (32in), **S** 12–18cm (5–7in). Half hardy. Is similar to *C. aethiopica*, but the leaves are much wider, and the longer, orange or scarlet flowers do not all face the same way.

CHASMANTHIUM

GRAMINEAE/POACEAE

See also GRASSES, BAMBOOS, RUSHES and SEDGES.

C. latifolium illus. p.288.

CHEILANTHES

ADIANTACEAE

Genus of evergreen ferns. Half hardy. Needs full light and humus-rich, well-drained soil. Do not overwater containerized plants or splash water on fronds. Remove fading foliage regularly. Propagate by spores in summer.

C. lanosa of gardens. See *C. tomentosa*.

C. tomentosa, syn. *C. lanosa* of gardens. Evergreen fern. **H** and **S** 15–23cm (6–9in). Leaves are triangular or lance-shaped and have much divided, soft green fronds on hairy, black stems.

***Cheiranthus*.** See *Erysimum*.

CHEIRIDOPSIS

AIZOACEAE

Genus of clump-forming, perennial succulents with pairs of semi-cylindrical leaves. Frost tender, min. 5°C (41°F). Needs sun and well-drained soil. Water in autumn to encourage flowers. Propagate by seed or stem cuttings in spring or summer.

***C. candidissima*.** See *C. denticulata*.

🏆 ***C. denticulata***, syn. *C. candidissima*. Clump-forming, perennial succulent. **H** 10cm (4in), **S** 20cm (8in). Has semi-cylindrical, slender, fleshy, blue-grey leaves, each 10cm (4in) long with a flat top, joined in pairs for almost half their length. Bears daisy-like, shiny, white flowers, to 6cm (2½in) across, in spring.

***C. purpurata*.** See *C. purpurea*.

C. purpurea, syn. *C. purpurata*. Carpeting, perennial succulent. **H** 10cm (4in), **S** 30cm (12in). Has semi-cylindrical, thick, short, glaucous green leaves, each with a flat top. In early spring produces daisy-like, purple-pink flowers, 4cm (1½in) across.

CHELIDONIUM

Celandine, Greater Celandine

PAPAVERACEAE

Genus of one species of perennial that rapidly forms ground cover. Fully hardy. Grows in sun or shade and in any but very wet soil. Propagate by seed or division in autumn. ⓘ Contact with the sap may cause skin blisters.

***C. majus* 'Flore Pleno'** illus. p.227.

CHELONE

Turtle-head

SCROPHULARIACEAE

Genus of summer- and autumn-flowering perennials. Fully hardy. Needs semi-shade and moist soil. Propagate by soft-tip cuttings in summer or by division or seed in autumn or spring.

***C. barbata*.** See *Penstemon barbatus*.

C. obliqua (Turtle-head) illus. p.438.

CHIASTOPHYLLUM

CRASSULACEAE

Genus of one species of evergreen perennial, grown for its succulent leaves and attractive sprays of small, yellow flowers. Thrives in rock crevices. Fully hardy. Needs shade and well-drained soil that is not too dry. Propagate by side shoot cuttings in early summer or by seed in autumn.

🏆 ***C. oppositifolium***, syn. *Cotyledon simplicifolia*, illus. p.335.

CHIMONANTHUS

CALYCANTHACEAE

Genus of deciduous or evergreen, winter-flowering shrubs, grown for their flowers. Frost hardy, but in cold areas reduce susceptibility of flowers to frost by training plants against a south- or west-facing wall. Needs full sun and fertile, well-drained soil. Propagate species by seed when ripe, in late spring and early summer, cultivars by softwood cuttings in summer.

***C. fragrans*.** See *C. praecox*.

C. praecox, syn. *C. fragrans*, illus. p.144. 🏆 **'Luteus'** (syn. *C.p.* var. *concolor, C.p.* 'Concolor', *C.p.* var. *luteus*) has pure yellow flowers.

CHIMONOBAMBUSA

GRAMINEAE/POACEAE

See also GRASSES, BAMBOOS, RUSHES and SEDGES.

C. timidissinoda illus. p.287.

CHIONANTHUS

OLEACEAE

Genus of deciduous shrubs, grown for their profuse, white flowers. Flowers more freely in areas with hot summers. Fully hardy. Prefers full sun and fertile, well-drained but not too dry soil. Propagate by seed in autumn.

C. retusus (Chinese fringe tree). Deciduous, often tree-like, arching shrub. **H** and **S** 3m (10ft). From early to mid-summer, star-shaped, pure white flowers appear in large clusters amid oval, bright green leaves.

C. virginicus (Fringe tree) illus. p.112.

CHIONOCHLOA

GRAMINEAE/POACEAE

See also GRASSES, BAMBOOS, RUSHES and SEDGES.

C. conspicua (Hunangemoho grass). Evergreen, tussock-forming, perennial grass. **H** 1.2–1.5m (4–5ft), **S** 1m (3ft). Fully hardy. Very long, mid-green leaves are tinged reddish-brown. Has stout, arching stems with long, loose, open panicles of cream spikelets in summer.

C. rubra illus. p.285.

CHIONODOXA

Glory-of-the-snow

LILIACEAE/HYACINTHACEAE

Genus of spring-flowering bulbs, related to *Scilla*. Is suitable for rock gardens and for naturalizing under shrubs, in sun or partial shade. Fully hardy. Requires well-

drained soil, top dressed with leaf mould or mature garden compost in autumn. Propagate by seed in autumn or by division in late summer or autumn.
C. forbesii, syn. *C. luciliae* of gardens, *C. siehei*, *C. tmolusii*, illus. p.419.
C. gigantea. See *C. luciliae*.
♀ ***C. luciliae***, syn. *C. gigantea*, illus. p.420.
C. luciliae of gardens. See *C. forbesii*.
C. 'Pink Giant' illus. p.416.
♀ ***C. sardensis.*** Early spring-flowering bulb. **H** 10–20cm (4–8in), **S** 2.5–5cm (1–2in). Has 2 narrowly lance-shaped, semi-erect, basal leaves. Leafless stem has 4–15 flattish, slightly pendent or outward-facing, deep rich blue flowers, 1.5–2cm (⅝–¾in) across and with, or without an indistinct, white eye.
♀ ***C. siehei.*** See *C. forbesii*.
C. tmolusii. See *C. forbesii*.

x CHIONOSCILLA

LILIACEAE/HYACINTHACEAE

Hybrid genus (*Chionodoxa* x *Scilla*) of spring-flowering bulbs, suitable for rock gardens. Fully hardy. Needs full sun or partial shade and humus-rich, well-drained soil. Propagate by division in late summer or autumn.
x *C. allenii*, illus. p.419.

CHIRITA

GESNERIACEAE

Genus of evergreen perennials or sub-shrubs, grown for their flowers. Frost tender, min. 15°C (59°F). Requires well-drained soil, a fairly humid atmosphere and a light position out of direct sunlight. Propagate by tip cuttings in summer or, if available, seed in late winter or spring.
♀ ***C. lavandulacea*** illus. p.473.
♀ ***C. sinensis.*** Evergreen, stemless, rosetted perennial. **H** to 15cm (6in), **S** 25cm (10in) or more. Has oval, almost fleshy leaves, the corrugated, hairy surfaces usually patterned with silver marks. In spring–summer, clusters of tubular, lavender flowers are held above leaves.

CHLIDANTHUS

AMARYLLIDACEAE

Genus of one species of summer-flowering bulb, grown for its showy, funnel-shaped flowers. Half hardy.Needs a sunny site and well-drained soil. Plant in the open in spring and after flowering, if necessary, lift and dry off for winter. Propagate by offsets in spring.
C. fragrans illus. p.424.

CHLOROGALUM

LILIACEAE/HYACINTHACEAE

Genus of summer-flowering bulbs, grown more for botanical interest than for floral display. Frost hardy, but in cold areas plant in a sheltered site.Requires sun and well-drained soil.Propagate by seed in autumn or spring.
C. pomeridianum. Summer-flowering bulb. **H** to 2.5m (8ft), **S** 15–20cm (6–8in). Semi-erect, basal leaves are long, narrow and grey-green, with wavy margins. Carries a large, loosely branched head of small, saucer-shaped, white flowers, with a central, green or purple stripe on each petal, that open after midday.

CHLOROPHYTUM

LILIACEAE/ANTHERICACEAE

Genus of evergreen, stemless perennials with short rhizomes, grown for their foliage. Frost tender, min. 5°C (41°F). Grow in a light position, away from direct sun, in fertile, well-drained soil. Water freely in growing season but sparingly at other times if pot-grown. Propagate by seed, division or plantlets (produced on flower stems of some species) at any time except winter.
C. capense. Evergreen, tufted perennial. **H** 30cm (12in), **S** indefinite. Forms rosettes of lance- or strap-shaped, bright green leaves, to 60cm (24in) long. Tiny, white flowers in racemes, to 60cm (24in) long, are borne in summer. Does not produce plantlets.
C. capense of gardens. See *C. comosum*.
C. comosum, syn. *C. capense* of gardens. (Spider plant). Evergreen, tufted perennial. **H** 30cm (12in), **S** indefinite. Very narrow leaves, to 45cm (18in) long, spread from a rosette. Racemes of many small, star-shaped, white flowers are carried on thin stems, 60cm (24in) or more long, at any time. Small rosettes of leaves may appear on flower stems, forming plantlets.
♀ **'Vittatum'** illus. p.465.

CHOISYA

RUTACEAE

Genus of evergreen shrubs, grown for their foliage and flowers. Frost to half hardy; in most areas needs some shelter. Requires full sun and fertile, well-drained soil. Propagate by semi-ripe cuttings in late summer.
C. 'Aztec Pearl' illus. p.122.
♀ ***C. ternata*** (Mexican orange blossom) illus. p.122. ♀ **SUNDANCE ('Lich')** illus p.148.

Chordospartium. See *Carmichaelia*.

CHORISIA

BOMBACACEAE

Genus of deciduous trees, usually with spine-covered trunks, grown mainly for their flowers in autumn and winter and their overall appearance. Frost tender, min. 15°C (59°F). Needs full light and well-drained soil. Water containerized specimens freely when in full growth, very little when leafless. Pruning is tolerated if necessary. Propagate by seed in spring. Red spider mite may be troublesome.
C. speciosa (Floss silk tree) , syn. Ceiba speciosa, illus. p.450.

CHORIZEMA

LEGUMINOSAE/PAPILIONACEAE

Genus of evergreen sub-shrubs, shrubs and scandent climbers, grown mainly for their flowers. Frost tender, min. 7°C (45°F). Requires full light and humus-rich, well-drained, sandy soil, preferably neutral to acid. Water potted plants moderately, less when not in full growth. Tie climbers to supports, or grow in hanging baskets. Propagate by seed in spring or by semi-ripe cuttings in summer.
C. ilicifolium (Holly flame pea) illus. p.454.

Chrysalidocarpus lutescens. See *Dypsis lutescens*.

CHRYSANTHEMUM

COMPOSITAE/ASTERACEAE

Genus of annuals, perennials, some of which are evergreen, and evergreen sub-shrubs, grown for their flowers. Each flower head is referred to horticulturally as a flower, even though it does in fact comprise a large number of individual flowers or florets; this horticultural usage has been followed in the descriptions below. Leaves are usually deeply lobed or cut, often feathery, oval to lance-shaped. Florists' chrysanthemums (nowadays considered to belong to the genus *Dendranthema*) comprise the vast majority of chrysanthemums now cultivated and are perennials grown for garden decoration, cutting and exhibition. Annuals are fully to half hardy. Florists' chrysanthemums are fully hardy to frost tender, min. 10°C (50°F); those that are half hardy or frost tender should be lifted and stored in a frost-free place over winter. Other perennial chrysanthemums are fully to half hardy. Provide a sunny site and reasonably fertile, well-drained soil. If grown for exhibition will require regular feeding. Pinch out growing tips to encourage lateral growths on which flowers will be borne, and stake tall plants with canes. Propagate annuals by seed sown in position in spring; thin out, but do not transplant. Propagate hardy perennials by division in autumn, after flowering, or in early spring. Florists' chrysanthemums should be propagated from basal softwood cuttings in spring. Spray regularly to control aphids, capsids, froghoppers, earwigs, mildew and white rust.

Florists' chrysanthemums
Florists' chrysanthemums are grouped according to their widely varying flower forms, approximate flowering season (early, mid- or late autumn) and habit. They are divided into disbudded and non-disbudded types. For descriptions and illustrations of flower forms, see feature panel pp.252–3.

Disbudded types – single, anemone-centred, incurved, intermediate and reflexed – are so called because all buds, except the one that is to flower, are removed from each stem. To produce exhibition flowers, incurved, intermediate and reflexed chrysanthemums may be restricted to only 2 blooms per plant by removing all except the 2 most vigorous lateral growths. In gardens, allow 4 or 5 blooms per plant to develop. Single and anemone-centred flowers should be reduced to 4–8 blooms per plant for exhibition, according to their vigour, and 10 or more for garden decoration or cutting.

Non-disbudded types – charm, pompon and spray chrysanthemums – have several flowers per stem.
Charm chrysanthemums are dwarf plants that produce hundreds of star-shaped, single flowers, 2.5cm (1in) across, densely covering each plant to form a hemispherical to almost spherical head. For exhibition, finish growing in at least 30cm (12in) pots. Plants for indoor decoration are grown in smaller pots and have correspondingly smaller, though equally dense, heads of blooms.
Pompon chrysanthemums are also dwarf. Each plant has 50 or more dense, spherical or occasionally hemispherical, fully double flowers that have tubular petals (for illustrations see p.252). They are excellent for growing in borders.
Semi-pompon chrysanthemums, sometimes called Japanese pompon, have similar flowers to those of the pompon but as they mature the yellow centres are revealed.
Spray chrysanthemums have a variety of flower forms: single, anemone-centred, intermediate, reflexed, pompon, spoon-shaped (in which each straight, tubular floret opens out like a spoon at its tip), quill-shaped and spider-form. Each plant should be allowed to develop 4 or 5 stems with at least 5 flowers per stem. Grow late-flowering sprays on up to 3 stems per plant. With controlled day length, to regulate flowering dates for exhibition purposes, late sprays should be allowed to develop at least 12 flowers per stem; without day length control, 6 or 7 flowers per stem.
Korean Group chrysanthemums have a variety of flower forms: anemone-centred, pompon, reflexed, single, intermediate, spider, quill and spoon. All are derived from plants originally developed in Connecticut in the 1930s and the prime quality, which they all have in common, is their dependable hardiness: they can be left in the ground all winter without protection. They are ideal for general garden use, in fact they require little special treatment other than good winter drainage; their hardiness can be compromised if grown in poorly drained soil. Some are usefully late in coming into flower, some need support while others are short and bushy. The taller types make good cut flowers.

Those most suitable for garden decoration are sprays, pompons and early reflexed chrysanthemums. All are suitable for cutting, except for charms. Late-flowering chrysanthemums are only suitable for growing under glass as flowers need protection from poor weather; they should be grown in pots and placed in a greenhouse in early autumn, when the flower buds have developed. Intermediate cultivars are also less suitable for garden decoration as florets may collect and retain rain and thus become damaged. Those cultivars suitable for exhibition are noted below. Measurements of flowers given are the greatest normally achieved and may vary considerably depending on growing conditions.

C. 'Alison Kirk'. Incurved florists' chrysanthemum. **H** 1.2m (4ft), **S** 30–60cm (1–2ft). Half hardy. Produces white flowers, to 12–15cm (5–6in) across, in early autumn. Is more suitable for exhibition than for garden use.

C

C. alpinum. See *Leucanthemopsis alpina.*
🏆 ***C.* 'Amber Yvonne Arnaud'.** Reflexed florists' chrysanthemum. **H** 1.2m (4ft), **S** 60–75cm (2–2½ft). Half hardy. Is a sport of *C.* 'Yvonne Arnaud' with fully reflexed, amber flowers in early autumn.
***C.* 'Anastasia'** (illus. p.253). Semi-pompon chrysanthemum. **H** 60cm (24in), **S** 50cm (20in). Fully hardy. Has flat-topped, dark purplish-pink flowers, 3cm (1¼in) across, with yellow centres, in mid-autumn.
***C.* 'Apollo'** (illus. p.253). Korean Group chrysanthemum. **H** 90cm (36in), **S** 75cm (30in). Fully hardy. Single, bronze-red flowers, 5cm (2in) across, with petals of uneven length, open from dark red buds in late autumn.
***C.* 'Aunt Millicent'** (illus. p.252). Korean Group chrysanthemum. **H** 75cm (30in), **S** 60cm (24in). Fully hardy. Produces abundant, single, silvery-pink flowers, 4cm (1½in) across, each with a pale zone around the yellow centre, in mid-autumn. Has rather large leaves.
***C.* 'Autumn Days'.** Intermediate florists' chrysanthemum. **H** 1.1–1.2m (3½–4ft), **S** to 75cm (2½ft). Half hardy. Bears loosely incurving, bronze flowers, 12cm (5in) across, in early autumn.
🏆 ***C.* 'Beacon'.** Intermediate florists' chrysanthemum. **H** 1.2m (4ft), **S** 60cm (2ft). Frost tender. Bears red, sometimes bronze, flowers, to 18cm (7in) wide, in late autumn. Is good for exhibition.
***C.* 'Bill Wade'.** Intermediate florists' chrysanthemum. **H** 1.35m (4½ft), **S** 60cm (2ft). Half hardy. Loosely incurving, white flowers, 18–20cm (7–8in) across, are borne in early autumn. Is more suitable for exhibition than for garden use.
🏆 ***C.* 'Brietner'.** Reflexed florists' chrysanthemum. **H** 1.1–1.2m (3½–4ft), **S** 75cm (2½ft). Half hardy.Fully reflexed, pink flowers, to 12cm (5in) wide, appear in early autumn.
***C.* 'Bronze Elegance'** (illus. p.253). Semi-pompon chrysanthemum. **H** 60cm (24in), **S** 50cm (20in). Fully hardy. Light bronze flowers, 2.5cm (1in) across, with yellow centres, are borne on small-leaved plants in mid-autumn.
🏆 ***C.* 'Bronze Fairie'.** Pompon florists' chrysanthemum. **H** 30–60cm (1–2ft), **S** 60cm (2ft). Fully hardy. Has bronze flowers, 4cm (1½in) across, in early autumn.
***C.* 'Bronze Hedgerow'.** Single florists' chrysanthemum. **H** 1.5m (5ft), **S** 75cm–1m (2½–3ft). Frost tender. Produces bronze flowers, 12cm (5in) across, in late autumn.
***C.* 'Bronze Yvonne Arnaud'.** Reflexed florists' chrysanthemum. **H** 1.2m (4ft), **S** 60–75cm (2–2½ft). Half hardy. Is a sport of *C.* 'Yvonne Arnaud' with fully reflexed, bronze flowers in early autumn.
***C.* 'Buff Margaret'.** Spray florists' chrysanthemum. **H** 1.2m (4ft), **S** to 75cm (2½ft). Fully hardy. Has reflexed, pale bronze flowers, to 9cm (3½in) wide, in early autumn.
C. carinatum. See *Ismelia carinata.*
***C.* 'Carmine Blush'** (illus. p.253). Rubellum Group chrysanthemum. **H** 60cm (24in), **S** 45cm (18in). Fully hardy. Produces single, clear rose-pink flowers, 4cm (1½in) across, each with a greenish yellow centre, from mid-autumn to early winter.
***C.* 'Chelsea Physic Garden'** (illus. p.253). Rubellum Group chrysanthemum. **H** 115cm (45in), **S** 90cm (36in). Fully hardy. In late autumn bears double, bronze flowers, 6cm (2½in) across, with yellow-petalled undersides.
***C.* 'Chesapeake'** (illus. p.252). Spider-form florists' chrysanthemum. **H** 1.2m (48in), **S** 50cm (20in). Half hardy. Quill-shaped, white flowers, to 20cm (8in) across, are borne in autumn when disbudded.
***C.* 'Chessington'.** Intermediate florists' chrysanthemum. **H** 2–2.2m (6–7ft), **S** 75cm (2½ft). Half hardy. Produces fairly tightly incurving, white flowers, 18–20cm (7–8in) across, in early autumn. Is more suitable for exhibition than for garden use.
***C.* 'Christina'.** Intermediate florists' chrysanthemum. **H** 1.35–1.5m (4½–5ft), **S** 60–75cm (2–2½ft). Half hardy. Bears loosely incurving, white flowers, to 14cm (5½in) wide, in early autumn. Is suitable for exhibition.
***C.* 'Claire Louise'.** Reflexed florists' chrysanthemum. **H** 1.2–1.35m (4–4½ft), **S** 75cm (2½ft). Half hardy. Produces fully reflexed, bronze flowers, to 15cm (6in) across, in early autumn. Is ideal for exhibition.
***C.* 'Clara Curtis'**, illus. p.247.
C. coccineum. See *Tanacetum coccineum.*
C. coronarium. See *Xanthophthalmum coronarium.*
***C.* 'Cottage Apricot'** (illus. p.253). Korean Group chrysanthemum. **H** 75cm (30in), **S** 60cm (24in). Fully hardy. Single, bright orange flowers, 6cm (2½in) across, each with a narrow yellow ring around the yellow centre, are borne in mid-autumn.
C. densum. See *Tanacetum densum* subsp. *amani.*
***C.* 'Doctor Tom Parr'** (illus. p.253). Semi-pompon chrysanthemum. **H** and **S** 45cm (18in). Fully hardy. Rather flat, rose-madder flowers, 3cm (1¼in), with gold flashes fading to beige, are produced in mid-autumn. Is a darker sport of *C.* 'Anastasia'.
***C.* 'Duchess of Edinburgh'** (illus. p.253). Korean Group chrysanthemum. **H** and **S** 60cm (24in). Fully hardy. In early and mid-autumn bears semi-double, rich coppery-red flowers, 5cm (2in) across, with yellow centres, some with tufts of petals in the centre.
***C.* 'Elsie Prosser'.** Fully reflexed florists' chrysanthemum. **H** 1.3–1.5m (4½–5ft), **S** 30cm (1ft). Frost tender. Bears pink flowers, 25cm (10in) wide, in late autumn. Is good for exhibition.
***C.* 'Emperor of China'** (illus. p.252). Rubellum Group chrysanthemum. **H** 1.2m (4ft), **S** 60cm (2ft). Fully hardy. Double, silvery pink flowers, 5cm (2in) across, with quilled petals, are borne in late autumn above red-tinted leaves.
🏆 ***C.* 'Enbee Wedding'** (illus. p.252). Spray florists' chrysanthemum. **H** 1.2m (4ft), **S** 75cm (2½ft). Fully hardy. Has single, light pink flowers, to 8cm (3in) wide, in early autumn. Is good for exhibition.
***C.* 'Fairweather'.** Incurved florists' chrysanthemum. **H** 1.1m (3½ft), **S** 60cm (2ft). Frost tender. Bears pale purplish-pink flowers, 14cm (5½in) wide, in late autumn. Is good for exhibition.
***C.* 'Fiona Lynn'.** Reflexed florists'chrysanthemum. **H** 1.5m (5ft), **S** 75cm (2½ft). Fully reflexed, pink flowers, to 18–20cm (7–8in) across, appear in early autumn. Is ideal for exhibition.
C. frutescens. See *Argyranthemum frutescens.* **'Jamaica Primrose'** see *A.* 'Jamaica Primrose'. **'Mary Wootton'** see *A.* 'Mary Wootton'.
🏆 ***C.* 'George Griffiths'** (illus. p.253). Reflexed florists' chrysanthemum. **H** 1.2–1.35m (4–4½ft), **S** 75cm (2½ft). Half hardy. Produces fully reflexed, deep red flowers, to 14cm (5½in) wide, in early autumn. Is excellent for exhibition.
***C.* 'Gigantic'.** Tightly incurved or loosely reflexed florists' chrysanthemum, its form depending on the amount of warmth provided. **H** 1.3m (4½ft), **S** 30cm (1ft). Frost tender. Has salmon-pink flowers, 25–27cm (10–11in) wide, in late autumn. Is good for exhibition.
***C.* 'Ginger Nut'.** Intermediate florists' chrysanthemum. **H** 1.2m (4ft), **S** 60–75cm (2–2½ft). Half hardy. Bears tightly incurving, light bronze flowers, to 14cm (5½in) across, occasionally closing at top to form a true incurved flower, in early autumn. Is good for exhibition.
***C.* 'Golden Chalice'** (illus. p.253). Charm florists' chrysanthemum. **H** and **S** 1m (3ft). Frost tender. Bears single, yellow flowers, 2.5cm (1in) wide, in late autumn. Is good for exhibition.
***C.* 'Golden Gigantic'.** Tightly incurved or loosely reflexed florists' chrysanthemum. **H** 1.3m (4½ft), **S** 30cm (1ft). Frost tender. Produces large, gold flowers, 25–27cm (10–11in) wide, in late autumn. Is good for exhibition.
***C.* 'Golden Woolman's Glory'.** Single florists' chrysanthemum. **H** 1.5m (5ft), **S** 1m (3ft). Frost tender. Golden flowers, to 18cm (7in) across, appear in late autumn. Is excellent for exhibition.
***C.* 'Grandchild'** (illus. p.253). Korean Group chrysanthemum. **H** 45cm (18in), **S** 40cm (16in). Fully hardy. Has double, bright mauve flowers, 5cm (2in) across, in early autumn.
***C.* 'Green Satin'.** Intermediate florists' chrysanthemum. **H** 1.2m (4ft), **S** 60cm (2ft). Frost tender. Produces loosely incurving, green flowers, to 12cm (5in) wide, in late autumn.
C. haradjanii. See *Tanacetum haradjanii.*
C. hosmariense. See *Rhodanthemum hosmariense.*
***C.* 'Idris'.** Incurved florists'chrysanthemum. **H** 1.3m (4½ft), **S** 45cm (1½ft). Frost tender. Has salmon-pink flowers, 21–25cm (8–10in) wide, in late autumn.
***C.* 'Innocence'** (illus. p.252). Rubellum Group chrysanthemum. **H** 80cm (32in), **S** 50cm (20in). Fully hardy. Single, palest pink flowers, 6cm (2½in) across, with several layers of petals and a narrow, white ring round the green-centred, yellow centre, are produced in mid- and late autumn over red-tinted leaves.
***C.* 'John Wingfield'.** Reflexed florists' chrysanthemum. **H** 1.5m (5ft), **S** 45–60cm (1½–2ft). Frost tender. Produces white, often pink-flushed, flowers, 12cm (5in) wide, in late autumn. Is good for exhibition.
***C.* 'Keith Luxford'.** Incurved florists' chrysanthemum. **H** 1.5m (5ft), **S** 45cm (1½ft). Frost tender. Bears pink flowers, 21–25cm (8–10in) wide, in late autumn. Is good for exhibition.
***C.* 'Lemon Rynoon'.** Spray florists' chrysanthemum. **H** 1.5m (5ft), **S** 75–100cm (30–39in). Frost tender. Has single, yellow-centred flower heads, 8cm (3in) across, in pale lemon-yellow fading to white, in late autumn.
***C.* 'Lundy'.** Fully reflexed florists' chrysanthemum. **H** 1.5m (5ft), **S** 45cm (1½ft). Frost tender. Bears white flowers 21–25cm (8–10in) wide, often broader than they are deep, in late autumn. Is good for exhibition.
🏆 ***C.* 'Madeleine'.** Spray florists' chrysanthemum. **H** 1.2m (4ft), **S** 75cm (2½ft). Fully hardy. Has reflexed, pink flowers, to 8cm (3in) across, in early autumn. Is good for exhibition.
***C.* 'Majestic'.** Fully reflexed florists' chrysanthemum. **H** 1.3m (4½ft), **S** 45cm (1½ft). Frost tender. Has light bronze flowers, 21–25cm (8–10in) wide, in late autumn. Is good for exhibition.
***C.* 'Maria'.** Pompon florists' chrysanthemum. **H** 45cm (1½ft), **S** 30–60cm (1–2ft). Fully hardy. Bears masses of pink flowers, to 4cm (1½in) across, in early autumn.
***C.* 'Marian Gosling'.** Reflexed florists' chrysanthemum. **H** 1.2–1.35m (4–4½ft), **S** 60cm (2ft). Half hardy. Fully reflexed, pale pink flowers, to 14cm (5½in) wide, are produced in early autumn. Is good for exhibition.
***C.* 'Marion'.** Spray florists' chrysanthemum. **H** 1.2m (4ft), **S** 75cm (2½ft). Fully hardy. Produces reflexed, pale yellow flowers, to 8cm (3in) wide, from late summer.
***C.* 'Mary Stoker'** (illus. p.253). Rubellum Group chrysanthemum. **H** 100cm (39in), **S** 90cm (36in). Fully hardy. Bears slightly ragged-looking, single, creamy-apricot flowers, 5cm (2in) across, each with a domed, yellow centre, in mid-autumn. Tends to run at the roots.
***C.* 'Mason's Bronze'.** Single florists' chrysanthemum. **H** 1.35–1.5m (4½–5ft), **S** to 1m (3ft). Frost tender. Has bronze flowers, to 12cm (5in) wide, in late autumn. Is excellent for exhibition.
C. maximum of gardens. See *Leucanthemum* x *superbum.*
***C.* 'Mei-kyo'.** Semi-pompon chrysanthemum. **H** and **S** 50cm (20in). Fully hardy. In mid- and late autumn produces pale mauve flowers, 2.5cm (1in) across, each with a small, yellow centre and with new petals in the centre a darker shade. Has small leaves.
***C.* 'Mrs Jessie Cooper'** (illus. p.253). Rubellum Group chrysanthemum. **H** 90cm (36in), **S** 60cm (24in). Fully hardy. Single, vivid cerise-pink, flowers, 5cm (2in) across, each with a slender, white ring around the domed, yellow centre, are borne in mid- and late autumn above broad, dark green leaves.
🏆 ***C.* 'Myss Saffron'.** Spray chrysanthemum. **H** 85cm (34in), **S** 75cm (30in). Fully hardy. In late summer and early autumn bears erect sprays of double, Yellow flowers, 6cm (2½in) across, fade to cream.
***C.* 'Nancye Furneaux'.** Reflexed florists' chrysanthemum. **H** 1.5m (5ft), **S** 45cm (1½ft). Frost tender. Has yellow flowers, 21–25cm (8–10in) wide, in late autumn. Is good for exhibition.
🏆 ***C.* 'Nantyderry Sunshine'** (illus.

p.253). (illus. p.253). Semi-pompon chrysanthemum. **H** and **S** 50cm (20in). Fully hardy. Bright yellow flowers, 2.5cm (1in) across, each with a small, yellow centre, are borne in mid- to late autumn. May occasionally revert to the pink of *C.* 'Mei-kyo'.
***C.* 'Nell Gwynn'** (illus. p.252). Korean Group chrysanthemum. **H** 75cm (30in), **S** 60cm (24in). Fully hardy. Single, rose-pink flowers, 6.5cm (2¾in) across, each with a primrose-yellow ring around the yellow centre, are produced in late summer and early autumn above broad, mid-green leaves.
***C.* 'Oracle'.** Intermediate florists' chrysanthemum. **H** 1.2m (4ft), **S** 60–75cm (2–2½ft). Half hardy. Produces loosely incurving, pale bronze flowers, to 12cm (5in) wide, in early autumn. Is useful for exhibition.
C. parthenium. See *Tanacetum parthenium.*
***C.* 'Paul Boissier'** (illus. p.253). Rubellum Group chrysanthemum. **H** 1m (39in), **S** 75cm (30in). Fully hardy. Has semi-double, orange-bronze flowers, 5cm (2in) across, with sharp-pointed petals, in mid- to late autumn.
***C.* 'Peach Brietner'.** Reflexed florists' chrysanthemum. **H** 1.1–1.2m (3½–4ft), **S** 75cm (2½ft). Half hardy. Is a sport of *C.* 'Brietner' with fully reflexed, peach-coloured flowers.
♀ ***C.* 'Pennine Alfie'.** Spray florists' chrysanthemum. **H** 1.2m (4ft), **S** 60–75cm (2–2½ft). Fully hardy. Spoon-shaped, pale bronze flowers, to 6–8cm (2½–3in) wide, appear in early autumn. Is suitable for exhibition.
♀ ***C.* 'Pennine Flute'.** Quill-shaped florists' chrysanthemum. **H** 1.2m (4ft), **S** 60–75cm (2–2½ft). Fully hardy. Is similar to *C.* 'Pennine Alfie', but has pink flowers.
♀ ***C.* 'Pennine Oriel'** (illus. p.252). Spray florists' chrysanthemum. **H** 1.2m (4ft), **S** 60–75cm (2–2½ft). Fully hardy. Anemone-centred, white flowers, to 9cm (3½in) across, appear in early autumn. Is very good for exhibition.
***C.* 'Perry's Peach'** (illus. p.253). Korean Group chrysanthemum. **H** 50cm (20in), **S** 40cm (16in). Fully hardy. Single, peach-pink flowers, 5cm (2in) across, each with a narrow, cream band round the golden-yellow centre, are produced in mid-autumn over red-tinted leaves.
***C.* 'Peterkin'.** Semi-pompon chrysanthemum. **H** and **S** 50cm (20in). Fully hardy. In mid- and late autumn bears golden-yellow flowers, 2.5cm (1in) across, with each petal tipped in rusty-orange, becoming paler with age, and with a small, yellow centre. Has small leaves.
***C.* 'Peter Rowe'.** Incurved florists' chrysanthemum. **H** 1.35m (4½ft), **S** 60–75cm (2–2½ft). Half hardy. Produces yellow flowers, to 14cm (5½in) across, in early autumn. Is ideal for exhibition.
***C.* 'Primrose Fairweather'.** Incurved florists' chrysanthemum. **H** 1–1.1m (3–3½ft), **S** to 75cm (2½ft). Half hardy. Produces pale yellow flowers, to 14–15cm (5½–6in) wide, in late autumn. Is good for exhibition.
***C.* 'Primrose John Hughes'.** Perfectly incurved florists' chrysanthemum. **H** 1.2m (4ft), **S** 60–75cm (2–2½ft). Frost tender. Bears primrose-yellow flowers, 12–14cm (5–5½in) wide, in late autumn. Is good for exhibition.
***C.* 'Primrose West Bromwich'.** Reflexed florists' chrysanthemum. **H** 2.2m (7ft), **S** 45–60cm (1½–2ft). Fully reflexed, pale yellow flowers, to 18cm (7in) or more wide, appear in mid-autumn. Use only for exhibition.
***C.* 'Purleigh White'** (illus. p.252). Semi-pompon chrysanthemum. **H** and **S** 50cm (20in). Fully hardy. In mid- and late autumn bears white flowers, 2.5cm (1in) across, slightly blushed in pink, each with a small, yellow centre. Has small leaves.
♀ ***C.* 'Purple Pennine Wine'.** Spray florists' chrysanthemum. **H** 1.2m (4ft), **S** 60–75cm (2–2½ft). Half hardy. Bears reflexed, purplish-red flowers, to 8cm (3in) wide, in early autumn. Is very good for exhibition.
***C.* 'Ringdove'.** Charm florists' chrysanthemum. **H** and **S** 1m (3ft). Frost tender. Has masses of pink flowers, 2.5cm (1in) across, in late autumn. Is excellent for exhibition.
♀ ***C.* 'Robeam'.** Spray florists' chrysanthemum. **H** 1.5m (5ft), **S** 75–100cm (2½–3ft). Frost tender. Produces reflexed, yellow flowers, to 8cm (3in) wide, in late autumn. Is good for exhibition.
***C.* 'Rose Yvonne Arnaud'.** Reflexed florists' chrysanthemum. **H** 1.2m (4ft), **S** 60–75cm (2–2½ft). Half hardy. Is a sport of *C.* 'Yvonne Arnaud', producing fully reflexed, red flowers in early autumn.
♀ ***C.* 'Roy Coopland'.** Intermediate to loosely incurved florists' chrysanthemum. **H** 1.3m (4½ft), **S** 60cm (2ft). Frost tender. Produces bronze flowers, 15cm (6in) wide, in late autumn. Is good for exhibition.
***C. rubellum* 'Clara Curtis'.** See *C.* 'Clara Curtis'.
♀ ***C.* 'Ruby Mound'** (illus. p.253). Korean Group chrysanthemum. **H** 90cm (36in), **S** 80cm (32in). Fully hardy. Prolific, fully double, rich deep maroon flowers, 6cm (2½in) across, are borne in mid- and late autumn.
***C.* 'Rumpelstilzchen'** (illus. p.253). Korean Group chrysanthemum. **H** 60cm (24in), **S** 50cm (20in). Fully hardy. Single, rich red flowers, 4cm (1½in) across, with several layers of petals and a narrow, yellow ring around the yellow centre, are produced in early autumn. Dislikes wet soil in winter.
***C.* 'Rytorch'.** Spray florists' chrysanthemum. **H** 1.5m (5ft), **S** 75–100cm (30–39in). Frost tender. Produces single, light bronze, yellow- centred flower heads, to 8cm (3in) across, in late autumn.
♀ ***C.* 'Salmon Fairie'.** Pompon florists' chrysanthemum. **H** 30–60cm (1–2ft), **S** 60cm (2ft). Fully hardy. Is similar to *C.* 'Bronze Fairie', but has salmon flowers.
***C.* 'Salmon Margaret'.** Spray florists' chrysanthemum. **H** 1.2m (4ft), **S** to 75cm (2½ft). Is similar to *C.* 'Buff Margaret', but has salmon flowers.
♀ ***C.* 'Sea Urchin'** (illus. p.253). Korean Group chrysanthemum. **H** 60cm (24in), **S** 50cm (20in). Fully hardy. Produces spider-form, fully double, lemon-yellow flowers, 7cm (3in) across, in early and mid-autumn. Dislikes winter wet.
C. segetum. See *Xanthophthalmum segetum.*
***C.* 'Senkyo Emiaki'.** Spider-form florists' chrysanthemum. **H** 30–60cm (1–2ft), **S** to 60cm (2ft). Frost tender. Bears light pink flowers, 15cm (6in) wide, in early autumn. Is good for exhibition.
C. serotinum. See *Leucanthemella serotina.*
***C.* 'Spartan Seagull'** (illus. p.252). Korean Group chrysanthemum. **H** 70cm (28in), **S** 50cm (20in). Fully hardy. Slightly ruffled, single, white flowers, 7cm (3in) across, are borne in early autumn. Has dark green leaves.
C. x superbum. See *Leucanthemum x superbum.*
***C.* 'Talbot Jo'.** Spray florists' chrysanthemum. **H** 1.3m (4½ft), **S** 75cm (30). Fully hardy. Bears single, yellow-centred, pink flower heads, 8cm (3in) across, in early autumn. Is good for exhibition.
***C.* 'Tapestry Rose'** (illus. p.253). Korean Group chrysanthemum. **H** 90cm (36in), **S** 60cm (24in). Fully hardy. Slightly messy, rich rose-pink flowers, 4cm (1½in) across, with green-centred, yellow centres, are produced in mid-autumn.
C. tricolor. See *Ismelia carinata.*
C. uliginosum. See *Leucanthemella serotina.*
***C.* 'Venice'.** Reflexed florists' chrysanthemum. **H** 1.2m (4ft), **S** 60–75cm (2–2½ft). Half hardy. Reflexed, pink flowers, to 15cm (6in) wide, are produced in early autumn. Is good for exhibition.
♀ ***C.* 'Wendy'.** Spray florists' chrysanthemum. **H** 1.2m (4ft), **S** 60–75cm (2–2½ft). Fully hardy. Produces reflexed, pale bronze flowers, to 8cm (3in) wide, in early autumn. Is excellent for exhibition.
C. weyrichii. Mat-forming, rhizomatous perennial. **H** 30cm (12in), **S** 45cm (18in). Fully hardy. In autumn bears single, yellow-centred, pink or white flowers, 5cm (2in) across.
***C.* 'Woking Rose'.** Intermediate florists' chrysanthemum. **H** 1.5m (5ft), **S** 45cm (1½ft). Frost tender. Has rose-pink flowers, to 21cm (8in) wide, in late autumn. Is good for exhibition.
***C.* 'Yellow Brietner'.** Reflexed florists' chrysanthemum. **H** 1.1–1.2m (3½–4ft), **S** 75cm (2½ft). Half hardy. Is a sport of *C.* 'Brietner' with fully reflexed, yellow flowers in early autumn.
♀ ***C.* 'Yellow John Hughes'** (illus. p.253). Incurved florists' chrysanthemum. **H** 1.2m (4ft), **S** 60–75cm (2–2½ft). Frost tender. Yellow flowers, to 12–14cm (5–5½in) wide, appear in late autumn. Is excellent for exhibition.
♀ ***C.* 'Yvonne Arnaud'.** Reflexed florists' chrysanthemum. **H** 1.2m (4ft), **S** 60–75cm (2–2½ft). Half hardy. Fully reflexed, purple flowers, to 12cm (5in) wide, are produced in early autumn.

CHRYSOGONUM

COMPOSITAE/ASTERACEAE

Genus of one species of summer- to autumn-flowering perennial. Suits a rock garden. Fully hardy. Needs partial shade and moist but well-drained, peaty, sandy soil. Propagate by division in spring or by seed when fresh.
C. virginianum illus. p.344.

CHRYSOSPLENIUM

SAXIFRAGACEAE

A genus of about 60 species of creeping hardy perennials grown for foliage and early spring flowers, requiring moist, shady conditions. Propagate by division, seed sown in autumn, and runners or bulbils in some species.
C. macrophyllum illus. p.256.

CHUSQUEA

GRAMINEAE/POACEAE

See also GRASSES, BAMBOOS, RUSHES and SEDGES.
♀ ***C. culeou*** (Chilean bamboo) illus. p.288.

CICERBITA,

SYN. MULGEDIUM

COMPOSITAE/ASTERACEAE

Genus of perennials, grown for their attractive flower heads. Fully hardy. Needs shade and damp but well-drained soil. Propagate by division in spring or by seed in autumn. Some species may be invasive.
C. alpina, syn. *Lactuca alpina* (Mountain sow thistle). Branching, upright perennial. **H** to 2m (6ft), **S** 60cm (2ft). Mid-green leaves are lobed, with a large, terminal lobe. Bears elongated panicles of thistle-like, pale blue flower heads in summer.
C. bourgaei, syn. *Lactuca bourgaei.* Rampant, erect perennial. **H** to 2m (6ft), **S** 60cm (2ft). Leaves are oblong to lance-shaped, toothed and light green. Many-branched panicles of thistle-like, mauve-blue or purplish-blue flower heads appear in summer.

CICHORIUM

Chicory

COMPOSITAE/ASTERACEAE

Genus of annuals, biennials and perennials, grown mainly as ornamental plants (*C. intybus* has edible leaves). Fully hardy. Needs full sun and well-drained soil. Propagate by seed in autumn or spring. ⓘ Contact with all parts of the plants may irritate skin or aggravate skin allergies.
C. intybus (Chicory) illus. p.242.

CIMICIFUGA

Bugbane

RANUNCULACEAE

Genus of perennials, grown for their flowers, which have an unusual, slightly unpleasant smell. Fully hardy. Grow in light shade and moist soil. Needs staking. Propagate by seed when fresh or by division in spring. Sometimes included in the closely related genus *Actaea*, which has fleshy, berry-like, fruits, whereas the pods of *Cimicifuga* are dry and not fleshy.
C. cordifolia, syn. *C. racemosa* var. *cordifolia*, *C. rubifolia*. Clump-forming perennial. **H** 1.5m (5ft), **S** 60cm (2ft). Feathery plumes of star-shaped, creamy-white flowers are produced in mid-summer above broadly oval to lance-shaped, dissected, light green leaves.
♀ ***C. racemosa***, syn. *Actaea racemosa.* Clump-forming perennial. **H** 30–150cm (1–5ft), **S** 60cm (2ft). Spikes of bottlebrush-

like, pure white flowers are borne in mid-summer above broadly oval, divided, fresh green leaves. **var. *cordifolia*** see *C. cordifolia.*
C. rubifolia. See *C. cordifolia.*
C. simplex, syn. *Actaea simplex*, illus. p.220. **'Elstead'** is an upright perennial. **H** 1.2m (4ft), **S** 60cm (2ft). Purple stems bear arching racemes of fragrant, bottlebrush-like, white flowers in autumn. Has broadly oval to lance-shaped, divided, glossy leaves.
'Prichard's Giant', **H** 2.2m (7ft), has large, much-divided leaves and produces white flowers on arching panicles.

Cineraria cruentus of gardens. See *Pericallis* x *hybrida.*
Cineraria* x *hybridus. See *Pericallis* x *hybrida.*

CINNAMOMUM
LAURACEAE

Genus of evergreen trees, grown for their foliage and to provide shade. Frost tender, min. 10°C (50°F). Requires full light or partial shade and fertile, moisture-retentive but well-drained soil. Water containerized specimens freely when in full growth but less at other times. May be pruned if necessary. Propagate by seed in spring or by semi-ripe cuttings in summer.
C. camphora. Moderately fast-growing, evergreen, rounded tree. **H** and **S** 12m (40ft) or more. Oval, lustrous, rich green leaves, tinted blue-grey beneath, reddish or coppery when young, are camphor-scented when bruised. Produces insignificant flowers in spring.

CIONURA
ASCLEPIADACEAE/APOCYNACEAE

Genus of one species of deciduous, twining climber, grown for its flowers. Half hardy. Grow in any soil and in full sun. Prune after flowering. Propagate by seed in spring or by stem cuttings in late summer or early autumn. ⓘ Contact with the latex exuded by cut leaves and stems may irritate skin or cause blisters, and may cause severe discomfort if ingested.
C. erecta, syn. *Marsdenia erecta.* Deciduous, twining climber. **H** 3m (10ft) or more. Heart-shaped, greyish-green leaves are 3–6cm (1¼–2¼in) long. In summer, clusters of fragrant, white flowers, with 5 spreading petals, are borne in leaf axils, followed by 7cm (3in) long fruits, containing many silky seeds, in autumn.

CIRSIUM
COMPOSITAE/ASTERACEAE

Genus of annuals, biennials and perennials. Most species are not cultivated – indeed some are pernicious weeds – but *C. rivulare* has decorative flower heads. Fully hardy. Tolerates sun or shade and any but wet soil. Propagate by division in spring or by seed in autumn.
***C. rivulare* 'Atropurpureum'.** Erect perennial. **H** 1.2m (4ft), **S** 60cm (2ft). Heads of pincushion-like, deep crimson flowers are borne on erect stems in summer. Leaves are narrowly oval to oblong or lance-shaped and deeply cut, with weakly spiny margins.

CISSUS
VITACEAE

Genus of evergreen, woody-stemmed, mainly tendril climbers, grown for their attractive foliage. Bears insignificant, greenish flowers, mainly in summer. Half hardy to frost tender, min. 7–18°C (45–64°F). Provide fertile, well-drained soil, with semi-shade in summer. Water regularly, less in cold weather. Needs tying to supports. Thin out crowded stems in spring. Propagate by semi-ripe cuttings in summer.
♀ ***C. antarctica*** illus. p.463.
C. bainesii. See *Cyphostemma bainesii.*
C. discolor (Rex begonia vine). Moderately vigorous, evergreen, tendril climber with slender, woody stems. **H** to 3m (10ft). Frost tender, min. 18°C (64°F). Oval, pointed leaves, 10–15cm (4–6in) long, are deep green with silver bands above, maroon beneath.
C. hypoglauca. Evergreen, woody-stemmed, scrambling climber. **H** 2–3m (6–10ft). Frost tender, min. 7°C (45°F). Leaves are divided into 4 or 5 oval leaflets that are pale green above and blue-grey beneath.
C. juttae. See *Cyphostemma juttae.*
♀ ***C. rhombifolia***, syn. *Rhoicissus rhombifolia, R. rhomboidea* (Grape ivy). Moderately vigorous, evergreen, woody-stemmed, tendril climber. **H** 3m (10ft) or more. Frost tender, min. 7°C (45°F). Has lustrous leaves divided into 3 coarsely toothed leaflets.
C. striata, syn. *Ampelopsis sempervirens, Parthenocissus striata, Vitis striata* (Ivy of Uruguay, Miniature grape ivy). Fast-growing, evergreen, woody-stemmed, tendril climber. **H** 10m (30ft) or more. Half hardy. Has leaves of 3–5 oval, serrated, lustrous, green leaflets. Mature plants may produce pea-shaped, glossy, black berries in autumn.
C. voinieriana. See *Tetrastigma voinierianum.*

CISTUS
Rock rose
CISTACEAE

Genus of evergreen shrubs, grown for their succession of freely borne, short-lived, showy flowers. Is good in coastal areas, withstanding sea winds well. Frost to half hardy; in cold areas needs shelter. Does best in full sun and light, well-drained soil. Resents being transplanted. Cut out any dead wood in spring, but do not prune hard. Propagate species by softwood or greenwood cuttings in summer or by seed in autumn, hybrids and cultivars by cuttings only in summer.
♀ ***C.* x *aguilarii* 'Maculatus'** illus. p.150.
C. albidus. Evergreen, bushy shrub. **H** and **S** 1m (3ft). Half hardy. Leaves are oblong and white-felted. Saucer-shaped, pale rose-pink flowers, each with a central, yellow blotch, open in early summer.
C. algarvensis. See *Halimium ocymoides.*
♀ ***C.* x *argenteus* 'Peggy Sammons'** illus. p.153.
C.* x *corbariensis. See *C.* x *hybridus.*
C. creticus (Rock rose), syn. *C. incanus* subsp. *creticus*, illus. p.154.
♀ ***C.* x *cyprius*** illus. p.150.
C.* x *dansereaui, syn. *C.* x *lusitanicus* of gardens. Evergreen, bushy, compact shrub. **H** and **S** 1m (3ft). Frost hardy. Leaves are narrowly oblong and dark green. Saucer-shaped, white flowers, each with a central, deep red blotch, appear from early to mid-summer.
C.* x *hybridus (Rock rose), syn. *C.* x *corbariensis*, illus. p.150.
C. incanus* subsp. *creticus. See *C. creticus.*
♀ ***C. ladanifer***, syn. *C. ladaniferus*, illus. p.150.
C. ladaniferus. See *C. ladanifer.*
♀ ***C. laurifolius.*** Evergreen, bushy, dense shrub. **H** and **S** 2m (6ft). Frost hardy. Has oval, aromatic, dark green leaves and, in summer, saucer-shaped, white flowers, each with a central, yellow blotch.
***C.* x *lenis* Graysword Pink',** syn. *C.* 'Silver Pink'. Evergreen, bushy shrub. **H** 60cm (2ft), **S** 1m (3ft). Frost hardy. Oval, dark green leaves set off large, saucer-shaped, clear pink flowers, each with conspicuous, yellow stamens, from early to mid-summer.
C.* x *lusitanicus of gardens. See *C.* x *dansereaui.*
C. monspeliensis Evergreen, bushy shrub. **H** 1m (3ft), **S** 1.5m (5ft). Frost hardy. Has narrow, wrinkled, dark green leaves and small, white flowers freely borne from early to mid-summer.
C. parviflorus. Evergreen, bushy, dense shrub. **H** and **S** 1m (3ft). Frost hardy. Small, saucer-shaped, pale pink flowers appear among oval, grey-green leaves in early summer.
♀ ***C.* x *purpureus.*** Evergreen, bushy, rounded shrub. **H** and **S** 1m (3ft). Frost hardy. Produces saucer-shaped, deep purplish-pink flowers, each blotched with deep red, from early to mid-summer. Leaves are narrowly lance-shaped and grey-green.
C. revolii of gardens. See x *Halimiocistus sahucii.*
C. salviifolius illus. p.150.
***C.* 'Silver Pink'.** See *C.* x *lenis* 'Grayswords Pink'.
♀ ***C.* x *skanbergii*** illus. p.152.

x CITROFORTUNELLA
RUTACEAE

Hybrid genus (*Citrus* x *Fortunella*) of evergreen shrubs and trees, grown for their flowers, fruits and overall appearance. Frost tender, min. 5–10°C (41–50°F). Needs full light and fertile, well-drained but not dry soil. Water containerized specimens freely when in full growth, moderately at other times. Propagate by seed when ripe or by greenwood or semi-ripe cuttings in summer. Whitefly, red spider mite, mealy bug, lime-induced and magnesium-deficiency chlorosis may be troublesome.
♀ **x *C. microcarpa***, syn. x *C. mitis, Citrus mitis*, illus. p.458.
x *C. mitis.* See x *C. microcarpa.*

Citrus mitis. See x *Citrofortunella microcarpa.*

CLADANTHUS
COMPOSITAE/ASTERACEAE

Genus of one species of annual, grown for its fragrant foliage and daisy-like flower heads. Fully hardy. Grow in sun and in reasonably fertile, very well-drained soil. Dead-head to prolong flowering. Propagate by seed sown outdoors in mid-spring.
C. arabicus illus. p.321.

CLADRASTIS
LEGUMINOSAE/PAPILIONACEAE

Genus of deciduous, summer-flowering trees, grown for their pendent, wisteria-like flower clusters and autumn foliage. Fully hardy. Requires full sun and fertile, well-drained soil. Propagate by seed in autumn or by root cuttings in late winter. The wood is brittle: old trees are prone to damage by strong winds.
C. kentukea, syn. *C. lutea*, illus. p.79.
C. lutea. See *C. kentukea.*

CLARKIA
SYN. GODETIA
ONAGRACEAE

Genus of annuals, grown for their flowers, which are good for cutting. Fully hardy. Grow in sun and in reasonably fertile, well-drained soil. Avoid rich soil as this encourages vegetative growth at the expense of flowers. Propagate by seed sown outdoors in spring, or in early autumn in mild areas. Botrytis may be troublesome.
C. amoena. Fast-growing annual with upright, thin stems. **H** to 60cm (24in), **S** 30cm (12in). Has lance-shaped, mid-green leaves. Spikes of 5-petalled, single or double flowers, in shades of lilac to pink, are produced in summer. Tall forms, **H** 60cm (24in), have double flowers in shades of pink or red. **Grace Series**, intermediate, **H** to 50cm (20in), has single, lavender-pink, red, salmon-pink or pink flowers with contrasting centres. **Princess Series**, dwarf, **H** 30cm (12in), has frilled flowers in shades of pink. **Satin Series**, dwarf, **H** to 20cm (8in), has single flowers in various colours, many with white margins or contrasting centres. **'Sybil Sherwood'** illus. p.305.
***C.* 'Brilliant'** illus. p.305.

CLAYTONIA
PORTULACACEAE

Genus of mainly evergreen perennials with succulent leaves; is related to *Lewisia.* Grows best in alpine houses. Fully hardy. Tolerates sun or shade and prefers well-drained soil. Propagate by seed or division in autumn. May be difficult to grow.
C. megarhiza, syn. *Calandrinia megarhiza* of gardens. Evergreen, basal-rosetted perennial with a long tap root. **H** 1cm (½in), **S** 8cm (3in). Leaves are spoon-shaped and fleshy. Bears small heads of tiny, bowl-shaped, white flowers in spring. Prefers sun and gritty soil. Is prone to aphid attack. **var. *nivalis*** illus. p.351.
C. virginica (Spring beauty). Clump-forming perennial with flat, black tubers. **H** 10cm (4in), **S** 20cm (8in) or more. Narrowly spoon-shaped leaves, reddish when young, later turn green and glossy. Branched stems bear cup-shaped, white or pink flowers, striped deep pink, in early spring. Needs shade.

CLEISTOCACTUS
SYN. BORZICACTUS
CACTACEAE

Genus of columnar, perennial cacti with branched, cylindrical, much-ribbed stems with spines. Is one of the faster-growing cacti, some reaching 2m (6ft) in 5 years or less. Tubular flowers contain plenty of nectar and are pollinated by hummingbirds. Frost tender, min. 5°C (41°F). Needs full sun and very well-drained soil. Propagate by seed or stem cuttings in spring or summer.

C. baumannii. Erect, then prostrate, perennial cactus. **H** 1m (3ft) or more, **S** 5m (15ft). Thick stems produce long, uneven, variable-coloured spines. Has S-shaped, tubular, bright orange-red flowers in spring–summer.

C. celsianus. See *Oreocereus celsianus*.

C. smaragdiflorus. Erect, then prostrate, perennial cactus. **H** 1.5m (5ft), **S** 6m (20ft). Is similar to *C. baumannii*, but has straight, tubular flowers with green-tipped petals.

🏆 ***C. strausii*** illus. p.479.

C. trollii. See *Oreocereus trollii*.

CLEMATIS
Old man's beard, Travellers' joy
RANUNCULACEAE

Genus of evergreen or deciduous, mainly twining climbers and herbaceous perennials, cultivated for their mass of flowers, often followed by decorative seed heads, and grown on walls and trellises and together with trees, shrubs and other host plants. Only early-flowering species are evergreen, although some later-flowering species are semi-evergreen. Most species have nodding, bell-shaped flowers, with 4 petals (botanically known as perianth segments), or flattish flowers, each usually with 4–6 generally pointed petals. Large-flowered cultivars also bear flattish flowers, but with 4–10 petals. Flower colour may vary according to climatic conditions: in general, the warmer the climate, the darker the flower colour. Fully to half hardy. May be grown in partial shade or full sun, but prefers rich, well-drained soil with roots shaded. Propagate cultivars in early summer by softwood or semi-ripe cuttings or layering, species from seed sown in autumn. Aphids, mildew and clematis wilt may cause problems.

Clematis may be divided into groups according to their flowering seasons, habit and pruning needs. See also feature panel pp.198–200.

Group 1
Early-flowering species prefers a sheltered, sunny site with well-drained soil. Small, single flowers, either bell-shaped or open-bell-shaped, 2–5cm (¼–2in) long, or saucer-shaped, 4–5cm (1¼–2in) across, are borne on the previous season's ripened shoots in spring or, occasionally, in late winter. Leaves are evergreen and glossy, or deciduous, and usually divided into 3 lance-shaped, 12cm (5in) long leaflets or into 3 fern-like, 5cm (2in) long leaflets. Fully to half hardy.
***C. alpina, C. macropetala* and their cultivars** tolerate cold, exposed positions. Small, bell-shaped to open bell-shaped, single, semi-double, or double flowers, 3–7cm (1¼–3in) across, are borne on the previous season's ripened shoots in spring, occasionally also on the current season's shoots in summer. Deciduous, pale to mid-green leaves are divided into 3–5 lance-shaped to broadly oblong, toothed leaflets, 3cm (1¼in) long. Fully hardy.
***C. montana* and its cultivars** are vigorous, deciduous climbers, suitable for growing over large buildings and trees. Small, flat to saucer-shaped, usually single flowers, 5–7cm (2–3in) across, are borne on the previous season's ripened shoots in late spring. Leaves are mid- to purplish-green and divided into 3 lance-shaped to broadly oval, serrated leaflets, 8cm (3in) long with pointed tips. Fully hardy.

Prune all group 1 clematis after flowering to allow new growth to be produced and ripened for the following season. Remove dead or damaged stems and cut back other shoots that have outgrown their allotted space. This will encourage new growth to bear flowers in the following season.

Group 2
Early- to mid-season, large-flowered cultivars bearing mostly saucer-shaped, single, semi-double, or fully double flowers, 10–20cm (4–8in) across, that are borne on the previous season's ripened shoots, in late spring and early summer, and on new shoots in mid- and late summer. Generally the second flush of flowers on semi-double and double forms produces single flowers. Deciduous, pale to mid-green leaves are usually 10–15cm (4–6in) long and divided into 3 ovate or lance-shaped leaflets, or are simple and ovate, and to 10cm (4in) long. Fully to frost hardy.

Prune before new growth starts, in early spring. Remove any dead or damaged stems and cut back all remaining shoots to where strong buds are visible. These buds provide a framework of second-year shoots which, in turn, produce sideshoots that flower in late spring and early summer. The flowers may then be removed. Young shoots bear more flowers later in the summer.

Group 3
Late, large-flowered cultivars producing outward-facing, usually saucer-shaped, single flowers, 7–15cm (3–6in) across, borne on new shoots in summer or early autumn. Leaves are deciduous and similar to those of early cultivars (group 2), described above. Fully hardy.
Late-flowering species and small-flowered cultivars that bear small, single or double flowers on the current season's shoots in summer–autumn. Flowers vary in shape and may be star-shaped, tubular, bell-shaped, flattish or resembling nodding lanterns; they vary in size from 1cm (½in) to 10cm (4in) across. Have generally deciduous, pale to dark green or grey-green leaves divided into 3 lance-shaped to broadly oval leaflets, each 1cm (½in) long, or hairy and/or toothed leaves divided into 5 or more lance-shaped to broadly oval leaflets, each 1–10cm (½–4in) long. Fully to half hardy.
Herbaceous species and cultivars producing single flowers that are either saucer-shaped, 1–2cm (½–¾in) wide, or bell-shaped or tubular, 1–4cm (½–1½in) long, and are produced on the current season's shoots in summer. Mid- to dark green or grey-green leaves are simple and lance-shaped to elliptic, 2.5–15cm (1–6in) long, or are divided into 3–5 lance-shaped to ovate, serrated leaflets, each 10–15cm (4–6in) long with a pointed tip. Fully to frost hardy.

Prune all group 3 clematis before new growth begins, in early spring. Cut back all the previous season's stems to a pair of strong buds, 15–20cm (6–8in) above soil level.

***C.* 'Abundance'**, syn. *C. viticella* 'Abundance' (illus. p.200). Late-flowering clematis (group 3). **H** 2–3m (6–10ft), **S** 1m (3ft). Fully hardy. Produces flattish, deep purplish-red flowers, 5cm (2in) across, with cream anthers, in summer.

🏆 ***C.* ALABAST ('Poulala').** Vigorous, long flowering, large-flowered clematis (group 2). **H** 3m (10ft), **S** 1m (3ft). Fully hardy. Freely produces creamy-green, rounded, large flowers 12–15cm (5–6in) across, with creamy-yellow anthers, in late spring and again from mid- to late summer.

🏆 ***C.* 'Alionushka'** (illus. p.199). Semi-herbaceous, non-clinging clematis (group 3). **H** 1–1.2m (3–4ft), **S** 1m (3ft). Fully hardy. In mid-summer to early autumn, produces single, rich mauvish-pink flowers, 6–8cm (2½–3in) wide, with a satin sheen when young, with deep ridges on the reverse and crumpled edges; the petal tips recurve and twist as they age.

🏆 ***C. alpina.*** Alpina clematis (group 1). **H** 2–3m (6–10ft), **S** 1.5m (5ft). Fully hardy. Has lantern-shaped, single, blue flowers, 4–7cm (1½–3in) long, in spring and, occasionally, summer. Forms attractive, fluffy, silvery seed heads in summer. Is ideal for a north-facing or very exposed site. **'Columbine'** see *C.* 'Columbine'. **'Constance'**see *C.* 'Constance'. **'Frances Rivis'** see *C.* 'Frances Rivis'. **'Frankie'** see *C.* 'Frankie'.

***C.* 'Andromeda'** (illus. p.198). Early, large-flowered clematis (group 2). **H** 2–3m (6–10ft), **S** 1m (3ft). Fully hardy. Semi-double, white flowers, with bright pink stripes in the centre of each sepal, are produced in spring and again later in the year when they are single.

***C.* ANGELIQUE ('Evipo017')**. Compact, mid- to late season clematis (group 2). **H** 90cm–1.2m (3–4ft), **S** 1m (3ft). Fully hardy. Produces an abundance of lilac-blue, brown-anthered flowers, 10cm (4in) across, from early summer to late autumn.

🏆 ***C.* ANNA LOUISE ('Evithree')** (illus. p.200). Compact, early, large-flowered clematis (group 2). **H** 1–1.2m (3–4ft), **S** 1m (3ft). Fully hardy. Freely produces single flowers with violet petals with a contrasting red-purple central bar, and striking brown anthers, in late spring to early summer, and again in late summer to early autumn.

🏆 ***C.* ARCTIC QUEEN ('Evitwo')** (illus. p.198). Early, large-flowered clematis (group 2). **H** 3m (10ft), **S** 1m (3ft). Fully hardy. From early summer to early autumn, freely produces double, clear creamy-white flowers, 10–18cm (4–7in) across, with yellow anthers.

C. armandii (illus. p.198). Strong-growing, evergreen, early-flowering clematis (group 1). **H** 3–5m (10–15ft), **S** 2–3m (6–10ft). Frost hardy. Bears scented, flattish, single, white flowers, 4cm (1½in) across, in early spring. Needs a sheltered, south- or south-west-facing site.

***C.* 'Ascotiensis'.** Vigorous, late, large-flowered clematis (group 3). **H** 3–4m (10–12ft), **S** 1m (3ft). Frost hardy. Single, bright violet-blue flowers, 9–12cm (3½–5in) across, with pointed petals and brownish-green anthers, are produced in summer.

***C.* AVANT-GARDE ('Evipo033')** (illus. p.200). Vigorous, mid-season clematis (group 3). **H** 3m (10ft), **S** 1m (3ft). Fully hardy. Free-flowering climber, producing deep red flowers to 5cm (2in) across, with central pom-pons of pink, petaloid stamens, in abundance from mid-summer to autumn.

***C.* 'Barbara Dibley'** (illus. p.199). Early, large-flowered clematis (group 2). **H** 2.5m (8ft), **S** 1m (3ft). Fully hardy. In late spring produces single, petunia-red flowers, to 23cm (9in) across, with carmine-red to red-purple stripes along each sepal and red-purple stamens.

***C.* 'Barbara Jackman'** (illus. p.199). Early, large-flowered clematis (group 2). **H** to 3m (10ft), **S** 1m (3ft). Fully hardy. In early summer produces single, bluish-mauve flowers, with crimson stripes and creamy-white stamens, followed in late summer by a further flush. Grow in semi-shade as flowers fade in full sun.

***C.* 'Bees Jubilee'.** Compact, early, large-flowered clematis (group 2). **H** 2.5m (8ft), **S** 1m (3ft). Frost hardy. In early summer, bears a profusion of single, deep pink flowers, 10–12cm (4–5in) across, with brown anthers and a central, rose-madder stripe on each petal. Prefers partial shade.

***C.* 'Bella'** (illus. p.198). Early, large-flowered clematis (group 2). **H** to 3m (10ft), **S** 1m (3ft). Fully hardy. Single, white flowers, with white anthers and purple-red filaments, are produced in spring and again in late summer.

🏆***C.* 'Betty Corning'** (illus. p.200). Late, small-flowered clematis (group 3). **H** to 4m (13ft), **S** 1m (3ft). Fully hardy. Slightly scented, bell-shaped, lilac to pinkish-mauve flowers, 4–6cm (1½– 2½in) across, are borne from early summer to early autumn.

🏆 ***C.* 'Bill MacKenzie'.** Vigorous, late-flowering clematis (group 3). **H** 7m (22ft), **S** 3–4m(10–12ft). Fully hardy. Has dark green leaves. Flowers are yellow and 6–7cm (2½–3in) wide. Is best pruned with shears.

***C.* 'Black Prince'** (illus. p.200). Late, small-flowered clematis (group 3). **H** to 4m (13ft), **S** 1m (3ft). Fully hardy. In mid-summer produces bell-shaped, semi-nodding, very dark blackish-claret-red flowers, to 9cm (3½in) across, with maroon stamens.

***C.* BLUE MOON ('Evirin')** (illus. p.199). Compact, free-flowering, early, large-flowered clematis (group 2). **H** 2.5–3m (8–10ft), **S** 1m (3ft). Fully hardy. Bears single, white flowers, 15–18cm (6–7in) wide, suffused with pale lilac becoming darker at the wavy petal edges, in late spring to early summer. In late summer to early autumn, flowers are slightly smaller and darker.

***C.* BONANZA ('Evipo031').** Vigorous, mid-season clematis (group 3). **H** 3m (10ft),

S 1m (3ft). Fully hardy. Free-flowering climber producing blue-purple blooms to 7cm (3in) across, with pale yellow anthers, from mid-summer to autumn.
C. Bourbon ('Evipo018') (illus. p.200). Compact, mid-season clematis (group 2). **H** 1.2–2m (4–6ft), **S** 1m (3ft). Fully hardy. Produces an abundance of vibrant, red, yellow centred flowers, 8cm (3in) across, from early to mid-summer.
C. 'Broughton Star', syn. *C. montana* 'Broughton Star'. Vigorous Montana clematis (group 1). **H** 4–5m (12–15ft), bears semi-double to fully double, cup-shaped, dusty pink flowers, with slightly darker veins.
C. calycina. See *C. cirrhosa*.
C. 'Carnaby'. Compact, early, large-flowered clematis (group 2). **H** 2.5m (8ft), **S** 1m (3ft). Frost hardy. In early summer has a profusion of single, deep pink flowers, 8–10cm (3–4in) across, with a darker stripe on each petal and red anthers. Prefers partial shade.
C. x cartmanii (*C. marmoraria* x *C. paniculata*). Evergreen, clump-forming, bushy shrub (group 1) with some procumbent stems. **H** 20–25cm (8–10in). **S** 50cm (20in). Frost hardy. Has dissected, leathery, shiny, dark green leaves varying in shape. Leafy panicles of shallowly cup-shaped, pure white flowers, 2–4cm (¾–1½in) across, with white anthers, are freely produced in early spring. ♀**'Avalanche'** (illus. p.198), **H** and **S** 3–5m (10–16ft), is fully to frost hardy, has roughly ovate, deeply toothed leaves and white flowers flushed pale green at the base. **'Joe'** (illus. p.198), **H** to 2m (6ft), has 3-parted, toothed leaves; procumbent stems can be trained upwards.
C. Cassis ('Evipo020'). Vigorous, long-flowering clematis (group 3). **H** 2–3m (6–10ft). Fully hardy. Free-flowering climber with fully double, plum red, rosetted flowers, 8cm (3in) across, borne from early summer to early autumn.
C. Cezanne ('Evipo023'). Compact, long-flowering clematis (group 2). **H** 90cm–1.2m (3–4ft), **S** 1m (3ft). Fully hardy. Free-flowering, producing sky-blue flowers, 10cm (4in) across, with broad overlapping sepals and yellow anthers, blooming from early summer to late autumn.
C. Chantilly ('Evipo021') (illus. p.199). Compact, long-flowering clematis (group 2). **H** 90cm–1.2m (3–4ft), **S** 1m (3ft). Fully hardy. Free-flowering climber producing single, occasionally semi-double, pale pink flowers, to 10cm (4in) across, the sepals with a pronounced, deeper pink central bar, in abundance from early summer to late autumn.
C. 'Charissima' (illus. p.199). Free-flowering, early, large-flowered clematis (group 2). **H** 2.5–3m (8–10ft), **S** 1m (3ft). Fully hardy. In late spring to early summer, produces single flowers, 15–18cm (6–7in) across, with pointed, cerise-pink petals, a deeper pink bar and veins throughout the flower, and dark maroon anthers.
C. Chinook ('Evipo013'). Low growing, scandent, non-clinging clematis (group 3). **H** 1m (3ft), **S** 60cm (2ft). Fully hardy. Produces numerous, nodding, mid-violet-blue flowers, 12cm (5in) across, with twisted sepals, each with a prominent, central boss of yellow stamens, from mid-summer to early autumn.

C. cirrhosa, syn. *C. calycina* (illus. p.199). Evergreen, early-flowering clematis (group 1). **H** 2–3m (6–10ft), **S** 1–2m (3–6ft). Frost hardy. Produces bell-shaped, cream flowers, 3cm (1¼in) across and spotted red inside, in late winter and early spring during frost-free weather. **var. *balearica*** has fragrant, pale cream flowers, speckled reddish brown. ♀ **var. *purpurascens* 'Freckles'** (illus. p.200) has creamy-pink flowers, 5–8cm (2–3in) across, heavily speckled red within.
C. Clair de Lune ('Evirin'). Vigorous, large-flowered clematis (group 2). **H** 2.5–3m (8–10ft), **S** 1–1.5m (3–5ft). Fully hardy. Produces an abundance of large, blue-purple flowers, to 12cm (5in) across, with paler central bands on the sepals and dark anthers, from late spring to early summer and again from late summer to early autumn.
C. 'Columbine' (Atragene Group), syn. *C. alpina* 'Columbine'. Deciduous, early-flowering climber. **H** 2–4m (6–12ft). In early and mid-spring, produces soft lavender-blue, nodding, bell-shaped flowers, 4–5cm (2in) across, with creamy-white or green staminodes, sometimes blooming again in summer.
C. 'Columella' (Atragene Group; illus. p.200). Deciduous, early-flowering climber (group 1). **H** 3m (10ft), **S** 1m (3ft). Fully hardy. From mid- to late spring produces strongly scented, broadly bell-shaped, pendent, purplish-violet to deep rosy-pink flowers, to 6.5cm (2¾in) across, with yellow staminodes.
♀ **C. 'Comtesse de Bouchaud'.** Strong-growing, late, large-flowered clematis (group 3). **H** 2–3m (6–10ft), **S** 1m (3ft). Fully hardy. In summer has masses of single, bright mauve-pink flowers, 8–10cm (3–4in) across, with yellow anthers.
C. Confetti ('Evipo036'). Vigorous, mid-season clematis (group 3). **H** 3m (10ft), **S** 1m (3ft). Fully hardy. Free flowering climber with nodding, pink flowers produced from mid-summer to autumn.
♀ **C. 'Constance'** (Atragene Group), syn. C. alp*ina* 'Constance'. Deciduous, early-flowering climber. **H** 2–4m (6–12ft), **S** 1m (3ft). Semi-double, nodding, rich purple-pink or reddish-pink, bell-like flowers, 2.5–6cm (1–2½in) across, with purple or creamy-white staminodes, are produced from early to mid-spring and occasionally again in summer.
C. 'Corona' (illus. p.199). Moderately vigorous, early, large-flowered clematis (group 2). **H** to 3.5m (11½ft), **S** 1m (3ft). Fully hardy. Bears numerous single, rich velvety-crimson flowers, with red and white stamens, in late spring and early summer, followed in late summer by a further flush of slightly smaller, paler flowers.
C. Crystal Fountain ('Evipo038'). Compact, large-flowered clematis (group 2), **H** 1.5–2m (4–6ft), **S** 1m (3ft). Fully hardy. Produces an abundance of double, deep lilac-blue flowers, to 10cm (4in) across, with a central boss of narrow staminodes, from late spring to early summer and again in early autumn.
♀ **C. 'Daniel Deronda'.** Vigorous, early, large-flowered clematis (group 2). **H** 3m (10ft), **S** 1m (3ft). Frost hardy. Has double and semi-double, deep purple-blue flowers, 10–14cm (4–5½in) across, with cream anthers, then single flowers in late summer.
C. 'Doctor Ruppel'. Early, large-flowered clematis (group 2). **H** 2.5m (8ft), **S** 1m (3ft). Fully hardy. Single flowers, 10–15cm (4–6in) across, with deep rose-pink petals with darker central bands and light chocolate anthers, are freely produced throughout summer.
C. 'Duchess of Albany'. Vigorous, small-flowered clematis (group 3). **H** 2.5m (8ft), **S** 1m (3ft). Frost hardy. In summer and early autumn has masses of small, tulip-like, single, soft pink flowers, 6cm (2½in) long, with brown anthers and a deeper pink stripe inside each petal.
C. 'Duchess of Edinburgh'. Early, large-flowered clematis (group 2). **H** 2–3m (6–10ft), **S** 1m (3ft). Frost hardy. In summer produces double, white flowers, 8–10cm (3–4in) across, with yellow anthers and green, outer petals. May be weak-growing.
♀ ***C. x durandii.*** Semi-herbaceous, late-flowering clematis (group 3). **H** 1–2m (3–6ft), **S** 45cm–1.5m (1½–5ft). Frost hardy. In summer has flattish, single, deep blue flowers, 6–8cm (2½–3in) across, with 4 petals and yellow anthers. Leaves are elliptic.
C. 'Early Sensation' (Forsteri Group; illus. p.198). Evergreen, late flowering clematis (group 1). **H** 2m (6ft), **S** 1m (3ft). Half hardy. Dark green leaves are bronzed when young. From early to mid-spring bears scented, bell- to cup-shaped, white flowers, with yellow anthers often tinged purple.
C. 'Elizabeth', syn. *C. montana* 'Elizabeth'. Vigorous Montana clematis (group 1). **H** 10–12m (30–40ft), has scented, soft pink flowers with widely spaced petals.
C. 'Elsa Spath'. Early, large-flowered clematis (group 2). **H** 2–3m (6–10ft), **S** 1m (3ft). Frost hardy. Bears masses of single, 12cm (5in) wide flowers, with overlapping, rich mauve-blue petals and red anthers, throughout summer.
♀ **C. 'Ernest Markham'** (illus. p.200). Vigorous, late, large-flowered clematis (group 3). **H** 3–4m (10–12ft), **S** 1m (3ft). Fully hardy. In summer bears 10cm (4in) wide, single flowers with blunt-tipped, vivid magenta petals and chocolate anthers. Thrives in full sun.
♀ **C. 'Etoile Violette'**, syn. *C. viticella* 'Etoile Violette' (illus. p.200). Vigorous, late-flowering clematis (group 3). **H** 3–5m (10–15ft), **S** 1.5m (5ft). Fully hardy. Produces masses of flattish, single, violet-purple flowers, 4–6cm (½–2½in) wide, with yellow anthers, in summer.
C. 'Evifour'. See *C.* Royal Velvet.
C. Evijohill. See *C.* 'Josephine'.
C. 'Evione'. See *C.* Sugar Candy.
C. 'Evipo001'. See *C.* Wisley.
C. 'Evipo002'. See *C.* Rosemoor.
C. 'Evipo003'. See *C.* Ice Blue.
C. 'Evipo004'. See *C.* Harlow Carr.
C. 'Evipo005'. See *C.* Peppermint.
C. 'Evipo006. See *C.* Vienetta.
C. 'Evipo007'. See *C.* Victor Hugo.
C. 'Evipo008'. See *C.* Franziska Maria.
C. 'Evipo009'. See *C.* Hyde Hall.
C. 'Evipo012'. See *C.* Parisienne.
C. 'Evipo013'. See *C.* Chinook.
C. 'Evipo014'. See *C.* Gazelle.
C. 'Evipo015'. See *C.* Savannah.
C. 'Evipo017'. See *C.* Avant-garde.
C. 'Evipo018'. See *C.* Bourbon.
C. 'Evipo019'. See *C.* Medley.
C. 'Evipo020'. See *C.* Cassis.
C. 'Evipo021'. See *C.* Chantilly.
C. 'Evipo023'. See *C.* Cezanne.
C. 'Evipo031'. See *C.* Bonanza.
C. 'Evipo032'. See *C.* Galore.
C. 'Evipo033'. See *C.* Angelique.
C. 'Evipo036'. See *C.* Confetti.
C. 'Evipo038'. See *C.* Crystal Fountain.
C. 'Evirida'. See *C.* Florida Pistachio.
C. 'Evirin'. See *C.* Clair de Lune.
C. 'Evirin'. See *C.* Blue Moon.
C. 'Evisix'. See *C.* Petit Faucon.
C. 'Evithree'. See *C.* Anna Louise.
C. 'Evitwo'. See *C.* Arctic Queen.
C. fasciculiflora (illus. p.198). Evergreen, early-flowering species (group 1). **H** and **S** 6m (20ft) or more. Half hardy. Dark green leaves have silver midribs. From late winter to mid-spring produces fragrant, bell-shaped, nodding, creamy-white to yellowish-white, solitary or clustered flowers. Needs a warm, sunny position.
C. 'Fireworks' (illus. p.199). Early, large-flowered clematis (group 2). **H** 4m (13ft), **S** 1m (3ft). Fully hardy. In late spring and early summer produces single, blue-mauve flowers, with wine-red and white stamens and a central, bright cerise-purple stripe on each sepal. Late summer flowers are slightly smaller.
C. flammula (illus. p.200). Vigorous, late-flowering clematis; may be semi-evergreen (group 3). **H** 3–5m (10–15ft), **S** 2m (6ft). Frost hardy. Produces masses of almond-scented, flattish, single, white flowers, 2cm (¾in) across, in summer and early autumn.
C. florida. **'Bicolor'**. See *C.f.* var. *sieboldiana*. **Pistachio ('Evirida')** (illus. p.199). Vigorous, long-flowering clematis (group 3). **H** 3m (10ft), **S** 1m (3ft). Fully hardy. From early summer to late autumn produces an abundance of creamy-white, rounded flowers 6–9cm (2½–3½in) across, each with a central cluster of pinkish-grey anthers and green styles. **'Sieboldii'**, see *C.f.* var. *sieboldiana*. **var. *sieboldiana*** syn. *C.f.* 'Bicolor', *C.f.* 'Sieboldii' (illus. p.199). Weak-growing, small-flowered clematis (group 3). **H** 2–3m (6–10ft), **S** 1m (3ft). Frost hardy. In summer has passion-flower-like, single blooms, each 8cm (3in) wide, with creamy-white petals and a domed boss of petal-like, rich purple stamens. Needs a sheltered aspect.
♀ **C. 'Frances Rivis'** (Atragene Group), syn. C. alpina 'Frances Rivis' (illus. p.200). Deciduous, early-flowering climber. **H** 2–4m (6–12ft), **S** 1m (3ft). In early and mid-spring produces an abundance of deep blue, nodding, bell-shaped flowers, 5–8cm (2–3in) across, with white staminodes.
♀ **C. 'Frankie'** (Atragene Group), syn. C. alpina 'Frankie' (illus. p.200). Deciduous, early-flowering climber. **H** 2.2–4m (7–12ft), **S** 1m (3ft). In early and mid-spring produces nodding, bell-shaped, mid-blue to deep mauve-blue flowers, to 2.5–6cm (1–2½in) across, with creamy-white, blue-tipped staminodes.
C. Franziska Maria ('Evipo008'). Compact, very long-flowering clematis (group 2). Fully hardy. Free-flowering climber producing fully double, deep blue-purple flowers, 10–15cm (4–6in) across, with yellow anthers, from early summer to early autumn.

C

C. GALORE ('Evipo032'). Vigorous, mid-season, small-flowered clematis (group 3). H 3m (10ft), S 1m (3ft). Fully hardy. From mid-summer to autumn has numerous, deep purple flowers to 7cm (3in) across, with contrasting yellow anthers.
C. GAZELLE ('Evipo014'). Low growing, scandent, non-clinging clematis (group 3). H 1m (3ft), S 60cm (2ft). Fully hardy. Produces numerous nodding, slightly scented, white flowers, to 6cm (2½in) across, with twisted sepals and yellow stamens, from mid-summer to early autumn.
C. **'Général Sikorski'.** Early, large-flowered clematis (group 2). H 3m (10ft), S 1m (3ft). Frost hardy. Has numerous 10cm (4in) wide, single flowers, with large, overlapping, blue petals and cream anthers, in summer.
♡ *C.* **'Gipsy Queen'.** Vigorous, late, large-flowered clematis (group 3). H 3m (10ft), S 1m (3ft). Fully hardy. Bears single, 10cm (4in) wide flowers, with velvety, violet-purple petals and red anthers, in summer.
C. **'Gravetye Beauty'** (illus. p.200). Vigorous, small-flowered clematis (group 3). H 2.5m (8ft), S 1m (3ft). Frost hardy. In summer and early autumn has masses of small, tulip-like, single, bright red flowers, 6cm (2½in) long, with brown anthers. Is similar to *C.* 'Duchess of Albany', but flowers are more open.
C. **'Guernsey Cream'** (illus. p.198). Early, large-flowered clematis (group 2). H 2.5m (8ft), S 1m (3ft). Fully hardy. Bears single flowers, 12cm (5in) across, with creamy yellow petals and anthers, in early summer. Flowers are smaller and creamy white in late summer. Fades in full sun.
C. **'Hagley Hybrid'.** Vigorous, late, large-flowered clematis (group 3). H 2.5m (8ft), S 1m (3ft). Fully hardy. Produces 8–10cm (3–4in) wide, single flowers with boat-shaped, rose-mauve petals and red anthers, in summer. Prefers partial shade.
C. **Harlow Carr ('Evipo004').** Scandent, herbaceous clematis (group 3). H 2–3m (6–10ft), S 1m (3ft). Fully hardy. From early to late summer produces semi-pendent, dark violet-blue, open flowers, to 7cm (3in) across, each with 4 twisted petals, dark brown anthers and white filaments.
♡ *C.* **'Henryi'** (illus. p.199). Vigorous, early, large-flowered clematis (group 2). H 3m (10ft), S 1m (3ft). Frost hardy. Has 12cm (5in) wide, single flowers, with white petals and dark chocolate anthers, in summer.
C. ***heracleifolia*** of gardens. See *C. tubulosa*.
C. ***heracleifolia* var. *davidiana*.** See *C. tubulosa*.
C. **'H.F. Young'.** Compact, early, large-flowered clematis (group 2). H 2.5m (8ft), S 1m (3ft). Frost hardy. Bears 10cm (4in) wide, single flowers, with violet-tinged, blue petals and cream anthers, in summer. Is ideal for a container or patio garden.
♡ *C.* **'Huldine'** (illus. p.199). Very vigorous, late, large-flowered clematis (group 3). H 3–4m (10–12ft), S 2m (6ft). Fully hardy. In summer has 6cm (2½in) wide, single, white flowers, mauve beneath and with cream anthers. Is ideal for an archway or pergola.
C. HYDE HALL ('Evipo009'). Vigorous, large-flowered clematis (group 2). H 2–2.5m (6–8ft), S 1m (3ft). Fully hardy. Flowers prolifically from early to mid-summer producing large, creamy-white blooms, 12–18cm (5–7in) across, sometimes tinged pink or green, with chocolate-brown anthers.
C. ICE BLUE ('Evipo003'). Early, large-flowered clematis (group 2). H 2–2.5m (6–8ft), S 1m (3ft). Fully hardy. In late spring and early summer produces an abundance of very large, ice-blue flowers, 15–20cm (6–8in) across, repeat-flowering during late summer and early autumn.
C. ***integrifolia*.** Herbaceous clematis (group 3). H and S 75cm (30in). Fully hardy. Leaves are narrowly lance-shaped. In summer bears bell-shaped, single, deep blue flowers, 3cm (1¼in) long, with cream anthers, followed by attractive, grey-brown seed heads.
♡ *C.* **'Jackmanii'** (illus. p.200). Vigorous, late, large-flowered clematis (group 3). H 3m (10ft), S 1m (3ft). Fully hardy. Bears masses of velvety, single, dark purple flowers, fading to violet, 8–10cm (3–4in) across, with light brown anthers, in mid-summer.
C. **'Jackmanii Superba'.** Vigorous, late, large-flowered clematis (group 3). Is similar to *C.* 'Jackmanii', but has more rounded, darker flowers.
♡ *C.* **'Jacqueline du Pré'** (Atragene Group; illus. p.199). Deciduous, early-flowering climber (group 1). H 2.5–4m (8–13ft), S 1.5m (5ft). Fully hardy. Has bell-shaped, nodding, rosy-mauve flowers, with silvery-pink sepal margins and pink-flushed, white staminodes, in spring.
C. **'Jan Lindmark'** (Atragene Group; illus. p.199). Deciduous, early-flowering clematis (group 1). H to 4m (13ft), S 1m (3ft). Fully hardy. In spring produces bell-shaped, pendent, purple-mauve flowers, with purple, outer stamens and shorter, white, inner staminodes.
♡ *C.* **'John Huxtable'.** Late, large-flowered clematis (group 3). H 2–3m (6–10ft), S 1m (3ft). Fully hardy. Bears masses of 8cm (3in) wide, single, white flowers, with cream anthers, in mid-summer.
♡ *C.* JOSEPHINE' (Evijohill). Early, large-flowered clematis (group 2). H 2.5m (8ft), S 1m (3ft). Fully hardy. From early summer to early autumn, bears double flowers, 12cm (5in) across, with almost bronze, green-tinged petals with a darker central bar; the petals become lilac in mid-summer, with a pink bar. Best colour in sun.
C. **x *jouiniana*.** Sprawling, sub-shrubby, late-flowering clematis (group 3). H 1m (3ft), S 3m (10ft). Frost hardy. Has coarse foliage and, in summer, masses of tubular, single, soft lavender or off-white flowers, 2cm (¾in) wide, with reflexed petal tips. Is non-clinging. **'Praecox'**, see *C.* 'Praecox'.
C. **'Kakio'**, syn. *C.* PINK CHAMPAGNE (illus. p.199). Early, large-flowered clematis (group 2). H 3m (10ft), S 1m (3ft). Fully hardy. In late spring and early summer produces single, vivid purple-red to deep pink flowers, with central, white stripes on each sepal.
C. **'Kardynal Wyszyñski'** (illus. p.200). Early, large-flowered clematis (group 2). H 3m (10ft), S 1m (3ft). Fully hardy. Produces single, bright crimson flowers, with pale violet filaments and dark brown anthers, from early to late summer.
C. **'Kathleen Wheeler'.** Early, large-flowered clematis (group 2). H 2.5–3m (8–10ft), S 1m (3ft). Frost hardy. Has single, plum-mauve flowers, 12–14cm (5–5½in) across with yellow anthers, in early summer.
♡ *C.* **'Lasurstern'.** Vigorous, early, large-flowered clematis (group 2). H 2–3m (6–10ft), S 1m (3ft). Frost hardy. In summer bears single, blue flowers, 10–12cm (4–5in) across, with overlapping, wavy-edged petals and cream anthers.
C. **'Lincoln Star'** (illus. p.199). Early, large-flowered clematis (group 2). H 2–3m (6–10ft), S 1m (3ft). Frost hardy. Has 10–12cm (4–5in) wide, single, raspberry-pink flowers, with red anthers, in early summer. Early flowers are darker than late ones, which have very pale pink petal edges. Prefers partial shade.
C. ***macropetala*.** Macropetala clematis (group 1). H 3m (10ft), S 1.5m (5ft). Fully hardy. During late spring and summer has masses of semi-double, mauve-blue flowers, 5cm (2in) long and lightening in colour towards the centre, then fluffy, silvery seed heads. **'Markham's Pink'** has pink flowers.
C. **'Madame Edouard André'.** Late, large-flowered clematis (group 3). H 2.5m (8ft), S 1m (3ft). Fully hardy. Freely produces single, deep red flowers, 8–10cm (3–4in) across, with silver undersides, pointed petals, and yellow anthers, in mid-summer.
♡ *C.* **'Madame Julia Correvon'**, syn. *C. viticella* 'Madame Julia Correvon' (illus. p.200). Late-flowering clematis (group 3). H 2.5–3.5m (8–11ft), S 1m (3ft). Fully hardy. Has flattish, single, wine-red flowers, 5–7cm (2–3in) wide, with twisted petals, in summer.
C. **'Madame Le Coultre'.** See *C.* 'Marie Boisselot'.
♡ *C.* **'Marie Boisselot'**, syn. *C.* 'Madame Le Coultre'. Vigorous, early, large-flowered clematis (group 2). H 3m (10ft), S 1m (3ft). Frost hardy. Bears single flowers, 12cm (5in) across, with overlapping, white petals and cream anthers, in summer.
♡ *C.* **'Markham's Pink'**,See *C. macropetala* 'Markham's Pink'.
♡ *C.* MEDLEY ('Evipo019'). Low-growing, scandent, non-clinging clematis (group 3). H 1m (3ft), S 60cm (2ft). Fully hardy. From mid-summer to autumn produces light pink, nodding, slightly scented flowers, 4–5cm (1½–2in) across, with twisted sepals that open to reveal a boss of yellow stamens in the centre.
♡ *C.* **'Miss Bateman'.** Compact, early, large-flowered clematis (group 2). H 2.5m (8ft), S 1m (3ft). Frost hardy. Masses of single, white flowers, 8–10cm (3–4in) across, with red anthers, are produced in summer. Is good for a container or patio garden.
C. ***montana*** (illus. p.198). Vigorous, Montana clematis (group 1). H 7–12m (22–40ft), S 2–3m (6–10ft). Fully hardy. In late spring bears masses of single, white flowers, 4–5cm (1½–2in) across, with yellow anthers.**'Broughton Star'**, see *C.* 'Broughton Star'. **'Elizabeth'**, see *C.* 'Elizabeth'. **var. *rubens*** (illus. p.199). ♡ **var. *rubens* 'Tetrarose'** (illus. p.199).
♡ *C.* **'Mrs Cholmondeley'.** Early, large-flowered clematis (group 2). H 2–3m (6–10ft), S 1m (3ft). Frost hardy. In summer has single, light bluish-lavender flowers, 10–12cm (4–5in) across, with widely spaced petals and light chocolate anthers.
♡ *C.* **'Mrs George Jackman'.** Early, large-flowered clematis (group 2). H 2–3m (6–10ft), S 1m (3ft). Frost hardy. Bears 10cm (4in) wide, semi-double flowers, with creamy-white petals and light brown anthers, in early summer.
C. **'Mrs N. Thompson'.** Compact, early, large-flowered clematis (group 2). H 2.5m (8ft), S 1m (3ft). Frost hardy. Produces masses of 8–10cm (3–4in) wide, single, magenta flowers, with a central, slightly darker stripe on each bluish-purple-edged petal and red anthers, in summer. Is good for a container or patio garden.
♡ *C.* **'Nelly Moser'** (illus. p.199). Early, large-flowered clematis (group 2). H 3.5m (11ft), S 1m (3ft). Frost hardy. In early summer has 12–16cm (5–6½in) wide, single, rose-mauve flowers, with reddish-purple anthers and, on each petal, a carmine stripe that fades in strong sun. Prefers a shaded, east-, west- or north-facing situation.
♡ *C.* **'Niobe'.** Early, large-flowered clematis (group 2). H 2–3m (6–10ft), S 1m (3ft). Frost hardy. Throughout summer produces masses of single, rich deep red flowers, 10–14cm (4–5½in) across, with yellow anthers.
C. ***orientalis*.** Late-flowering clematis (group 3). H 3–4m (10–12ft), S 1.5m (5ft). Fully hardy. Leaves are grey- to dark green. In summer lantern-shaped, single, greenish-yellow flowers, 3cm (1¼in) wide, with recurved petal tips, are followed by feathery seed heads.
C. PARISIENNE ('Evipo012'). Compact, medium-flowered clematis (group 2). H 90–120cm (3–4ft), S 60cm (2ft). Fully hardy. Produces an abundance of pale violet flowers, 7–10cm (3–4in) across, with wavy-edged sepals and red anthers, from early summer to late autumn.
C. PEPPERMINT ('Evipo005'). Vigorous, medium-flowered clematis (group 3). H 2–3m (6–10ft), S 1m (3ft). Fully hardy. From early summer to late autumn has numerous creamy-white, rosetted flowers, 7–10cm (3–4in) across, with 6 large, outer sepals, which drop as the tight, inner rosette of smaller sepals expand. The late season's flowers are greenish-white.
C. **'Perle d' Azur'** (illus. p.200). Late, large-flowered clematis (group 3). H 3m (10ft), S 1m (3ft). Fully hardy. Single, azure-blue flowers, 8cm (3in) across, with recurved petal tips and creamy-green anthers, open in summer.
♡ *C.* PETIT FAUCON ('Evisix'). Vigorous, scandent, non-clinging clematis (group 3). H 1–1.5m (3–5ft), S 60cm (2ft). Fully hardy. From summer to early autumn produces broadly bell-shaped, nodding to semi-pendent, deep blue-violet flowers, 5–8cm (2–3in) across, with violet filaments and orange-yellow anthers.
C. PINK CHAMPAGNE, see *C.* 'Kakio'.
♡ *C.* **'Polish Spirit'** (illus. p.200). Strong-growing, late, large-flowered clematis (group 3). H to 4m (13ft), S 1m (3ft). Fully hardy. Single, velvety, deep purple flowers, with dark purple-red and greenish-white stamens, are produced from early summer to early autumn.

C

***C.* 'Poulala'.** See *C.* ALABAST.
***C.* 'Poulvo'.** See *C.* VINO.
🏆 ***C.* 'Praecox',** syn. *C.* x *jouiniana* 'Praecox'. Sprawling, sub-shrubby, late-flowering clematis (group 3). **H** 1m (3ft), **S** 3m (10ft). Frost hardy. Has coarse foliage and, in summer, masses of tubular, single, soft lavender or off white flowers, 2cm (¾in) wide, with reflexed petal tips. Is non-clinging.
🏆 ***C.* 'Purpurea Plena Elegans',** syn. *C. viticella* 'Purpurea Plena Elegans' (illus. p.200). **H** 2–3m (6–10ft), **S** 1m (3ft). Fully hardy. Late-flowering clematis (group 3). Bears abundant, double flowers, with many purplish-mauve sepals, occasionally green outer sepals, and no anthers, from mid-summer to late autumn.
***C.* 'Ramona'.** Early, large-flowered clematis (group 2). **H** 3m (10ft), **S** 1m (3ft). Frost hardy. Has coarse, dark green leaves offset, in summer, by single, pale blue flowers, 10–12cm (4–5in) across, with red anthers. Prefers a south-or south-west-facing position.
***C. recta*.** Clump-forming, herbaceous clematis (group3). **H** 1–2m (3–6ft), **S** 50cm (20in). Fully hardy. Leaves are dark or grey-green. Bears masses of sweetly scented, flattish, single, white flowers, 2cm (¾in) across, in mid-summer.
🏆 ***C. rehderiana*** (illus. p.200). Vigorous, late-flowering clematis (group 3). **H** 6–7m (20–22ft), **S** 2–3m (6–10ft). Frost hardy. Bears loose clusters of fragrant, tubular, single, yellow flowers, 1–2cm (½–¾in) long, in late summer and early autumn. Leaves are coarse-textured.
***C.* 'Rhapsody'.** Compact, early, large-flowered clematis (group 2). **H** 2.5m (8ft), **S** 1m (3ft). Fully hardy. From early summer to early autumn, bears single, sapphire-blue flowers, 10–13cm (4–5in) across, with splayed, creamy-yellow anthers. Colour deepens with age.
🏆 ***C.* 'Richard Pennell'.** Early, large-flowered clematis (group 2). **H** 2–3m (6–10ft), **S** 1m (3ft). Frost hardy. Produces 10–12cm (4–5in) wide, single flowers, with rich purple-blue petals and golden-yellow anthers, in summer.
***C.* 'Rouge Cardinal'.** Early, large-flowered clematis (group 3). **H** 2–3m (6–10ft), **S** 1m (3ft). Frost hardy. In summer has single, velvety, crimson flowers, 8–10cm (3–4in) across, with red anthers.
***C.* ROSEMOOR ('Evipo002')** illus. p.200. Vigorous, large-flowered, long-flowering clematis (group 2). **H** 2–2.5m (6–8ft), **S** 1m (3ft). Fully hardy. From early summer to autumn deep red flowers, 12–15cm (5–6in) across, with contrasting yellow anthers, are produced in abundance.
🏆 ***C.* 'Rosy O'Grady'** (Atragene Group; illus. p.200). Deciduous, early-flowering climber (group 1). **H** 3–4m (10–13ft), **S** 1m (3ft). Fully hardy. Open, bell-shaped, deep pink to mauve-pink flowers, 6–12cm (2½–5in) across, with creamy-white staminodes, are produced from late spring to early summer and again in autumn.
***C.* ROYAL VELVET ('Evifour').** Early, large-flowered clematis (group 2). **H** 2–2.5m (6–8ft), **S** 1m (3ft). Fully hardy. In early and mid-summer, bears single flowers, 10–15cm (4–6in) wide, with bluish, rich velvet-purple petals, with darker central bands, and red anthers.
***C.* SAVANNAH ('Evipo015').** Low-growing, scandent, non-clinging clematis (group 3). **H** 1m (3ft), **S** 60cm (2ft). Fully hardy. From mid-summer to autumn produces dark pink, nodding flowers, to 6cm (2½in) across, with twisted sepals that open to reveal clusters of yellow stamens in the centre.
***C.* 'Silver Moon'** (illus. p.200). Early, large-flowered clematis (group 2). **H** to 4m (13ft), **S** 1m (3ft). Fully hardy. Produces single, silvery-mauve flowers from late spring to early autumn.
***C.* 'Souvenir du Capitaine Thuilleaux'.** Compact, early, large-flowered clematis (group 2). **H** 2.5m (8ft), **S** 1m (3ft). Frost hardy. In early summer bears 8–10cm (3–4in) wide, single flowers, with red anthers and deep pink-striped, cream-pink petals. Is ideal for a container or patio garden.
***C.* 'Star of India'.** Vigorous, late, large-flowered clematis (group 3). **H** 3m (10ft), **S** 1m (3ft). Fully hardy. Bears masses of 8–10cm (3–4in) wide, single, deep purple-blue flowers, with light brown anthers, in mid-summer; each petal has a deep carmine-red stripe.
***C.* SUGAR CANDY ('Evione').** Vigorous, early, large-flowered clematis (group 2). **H** 3m (10ft), **S** 1m (3ft). Fully hardy. Has masses of pinkish-mauve to light purple flowers, 10–18cm (4–6in) across, with darker, central bars on the sepals and yellow anthers.
***C.* 'Sunrise'** (illus. p.199). Vigorous, Montana clematis (group 1). **H** and **S** 8–10m (25–30ft). Fully hardy. Leaves are reddish-purple when young. Slightly scented, semi-double or double, deep pink, single flowers are borne in spring.
***C. tangutica*.** Vigorous, late-flowering clematis (group 3). **H** 5–6m (15–20ft), **S** 2–3m (6–10ft). Fully hardy. Has lantern-shaped, single, yellow flowers, 4cm (1½in) long, throughout summer and early autumn; these are followed by fluffy, silvery seed heads.
🏆 ***C.* 'The President'.** Early, large-flowered clematis (group 2). **H** 2–3m (6–10ft), **S** 1m (3ft). Frost hardy. In early summer bears masses of single, rich purple flowers, silver beneath, 10cm (4in) wide, with red anthers.
***C. tubulosa*,** syn. *C. heracleifolia* of gardens, *C. heracleifolia* var. *davidiana*. Herbaceous clematis (group 3). **H** 1m (3ft), **S** 75cm (2½ft). Fully hardy. In summer, thick stems bear axillary clusters of scented, tubular, single, pale blue flowers, 2–3cm (¾–1¼in) long, with reflexed petal tips. 🏆 **'Wyevale'** has strongly scented, dark blue flowers.
***C.* VICTOR HUGO ('Evipo007').** Vigorous, scandent, non-clinging clematis (group 3). **H** 2.5–3m (8–10ft), **S** 1m (3ft). Fully hardy. Produces an abundance of red-violet flowers, 8cm (3in) across, with dark, violet-tipped stamens, from early summer until autumn.
***C.* VIENNETTA ('Evipo006')** illus. p.199. Vigorous, medium-flowered clematis (group 3). **H** 2–3m (6–10ft), **S** 1m (3ft). Fully hardy. Between early summer and autumn produces unusual, passion-flower-like, rounded blooms with 6 creamy-white, regularly placed sepals, surrounding a ring of purple, modified stamens and a dark centre. In autumn the outer sepals develop a greenish hue.
***C.* 'Ville de Lyon'.** Late, large-flowered clematis (group 3). **H** 2–3m (6–10ft), **S** 1m (3ft). Fully hardy. In mid-summer has single, bright carmine-red flowers, 8–10cm (3–4in) across, with darker petal edges and yellow anthers. Lower foliage tends to become scorched by late summer.
***C.* VINO ('Poulvo')** (illus. p.200). Vigorous, early, large-flowered clematis (group 2). **H** 3m (10ft), **S** 1m (3ft). Fully hardy. Produces numerous, deep petunia-red flowers, 10–18cm (4–7in) across, with contrasting, white to cream filaments and yellow anthers, in late spring and again in late summer and early autumn.
🏆 ***C. viticella*.** Late-flowering clematis (group 3). **H** 2–3m (6–10ft), **S** 1m (3ft). Fully hardy. Produces nodding, open bell-shaped, single, purple-mauve flowers, 3.5cm (1½in) long, in summer. **'Abundance'** see *C.* 'Abundance'. **'Etoile Violette'** see *C.* 'Etoile Violette'. **'Madame Julia Correvon'** see *C.* 'Madame Julia Correvon'. **'Purpurea Plena Elegans'** see *C.* 'Purpurea Plena Elegans'.
***C.* 'Vyvyan Pennell'.** Early, large-flowered clematis (group 2). **H** 2–3m (6–10ft), **S** 1m (3ft). Frost hardy. Has double, lilac flowers, 10–12cm (4–5in) wide, with a central, lavender-blue rosette of petals and golden-yellow anthers, in early summer, then single, blue-mauve flowers.
***C.* 'W.E. Gladstone'.** Vigorous, early, large-flowered clematis (group 2). **H** 3–4m (10–12ft), **S** 1m (3ft). Frost hardy. Produces single, lavender flowers, 15cm (6in) wide, with red anthers, in summer.
***C.* 'Westerplatte'** (illus. p.200). Early, large-flowered clematis (group 2). **H** 2.5m (8ft), **S** 1m (3ft). Fully hardy. From late spring to early summer and again from late summer to early autumn produces single, dark velvet-red flowers, with white filaments and deep red anthers.
🏆 ***C.* 'White Columbine'** (Atragene Group; illus. p.198). Deciduous, early-flowering climber (group 1). **H** and **S** 2–3m (6–10ft). Fully hardy. In spring produces purple-tinted buds that open into bell-shaped, nodding, single, creamy-white flowers, maturing to pure white, with petal-like, greenish-white staminodes.
***C.* 'William Kennett'.** Early, large-flowered clematis (group 2). **H** 2–3m (6–10ft), **S** 1m (3ft). Frost hardy. In summer has masses of single flowers, 10–12cm (4–5in) across, with red anthers and tough, lavender-blue petals, each bearing a central, darker stripe that fades as the flower matures.
***C.* WISLEY ('Evipo001').** Strong growing, mid-season large-flowered clematis (group3). **H** 2.5–3m (8–10ft), **S** 1m (3ft). Fully hardy. From mid-summer to early autumn produces numerous, slightly nodding, violet-blue, yellow-anthered flowers, 10–12cm (4–5in) across.

CLEOME

Spider flower

CAPPARACEAE

Genus of annuals and a few evergreen shrubs, grown for their unusual, spidery flowers. Half hardy to frost tender, min. 4°C (39°F). Grow in sun and in fertile, well-drained soil. Remove dead flowers. Propagate by seed sown outdoors in late spring. Aphids may be a problem.
***C. hassleriana*,** syn. *C. spinosa* of gardens. Fast-growing, bushy annual. **H** to 1.2m (4ft), **S** 45cm (1½ft). Half hardy. Has hairy, spiny stems and mid-green leaves divided into lance-shaped leaflets. Large, rounded heads of narrow-petalled, pink-flushed, white flowers, with long, protruding stamens, are produced in summer. **'Colour Fountain'** illus. p.304. **'Rose Queen'** has rose-pink flowers.
C. spinosa of gardens. See *C. hassleriana*.

CLERODENDRUM

VERBENACEAE/LAMIACEAE

Genus of evergreen or deciduous, small trees, shrubs, sub-shrubs and woody-stemmed, twining climbers, grown for their showy flowers. Fully hardy to frost tender, min. 10–16°C (50–61°F). Needs humus-rich, well-drained soil and full sun, with partial shade in summer. Water freely in growing season, less at other times. Stems require support. Thin out crowded growth in spring. Propagate by seed in spring, by softwood cuttings in late spring or by semi-ripe cuttings in summer. Whitefly, red spider mite and mealy bug may be a problem.
C. bungei illus. p.141.
🏆 ***C. chinense* var. *chinense*,** syn. *C.c.* 'Pleniflorum', *C. fragrans* 'Pleniflorum', *C. philippinum*. Evergreen or deciduous, bushy shrub. **H** and **S** to 2.5m (8ft). Frost tender, min. 10°C (50°F). Leaves are broadly oval, coarsely and shallowly toothed and downy. Fragrant, double, pink or white flowers are borne in domed, terminal clusters in summer.
***C. fallax*.** See *C. speciosissimum*.
***C. fragrans* 'Pleniflorum'.** See *C. chinense* var. *chinense*.
***C. philippinum*.** See *C. chinense* var. *chinense*.
***C. speciosissimum*,** syn. *C. fallax*. Evergreen, erect to spreading, sparingly branched shrub. **H** and **S** to 3m (10ft). Frost tender, min. 15°C (59°F). Bears broadly heart-shaped, wavy-edged leaves, each to 30cm (1ft) across, on long stalks and, from late spring to autumn, tubular, scarlet flowers, with spreading petal lobes, in 30cm (1ft) long, terminal clusters. Makes a good pot plant.
🏆 ***C. splendens*.** Vigorous, evergreen, woody-stemmed, twining climber. **H** 3m (10ft) or more. Frost tender, min. 15°C (59°F). Has oval to elliptic, rich green leaves. Clusters of 5-petalled, tubular, scarlet flowers, 2.5cm (1in) wide, are produced in summer.
🏆 ***C. thomsoniae*** illus. p.460.
C. trichotomum (illus. p.142). Deciduous, upright, bushy-headed, tree-like shrub. **H** and **S** 5–6m (15–20ft). Fully hardy. Clusters of deep pink and greenish-white buds open to fragrant, white flowers above large leaves from late summer to mid-autumn, followed by decorative, blue berries.

CLETHRA

CLETHRACEAE

Genus of deciduous or evergreen shrubs and trees, grown for their fragrant, white flowers. Fully to half hardy. Needs semi-shade and moist, peaty, acid soil.

C

Propagate by softwood cuttings in summer or by seed in autumn.
C. alnifolia (Sweet pepper-bush). Deciduous, bushy shrub. **H** and **S** 2.5m (8ft). Fully hardy. Has oval, toothed, mid-green leaves and, in late summer and early autumn, slender spires of small, bell-shaped flowers.
C. arborea (Lily-of-the-valley tree). Evergreen, bushy, dense shrub or tree. **H** 8m (25ft), **S** 6m (20ft). Half hardy. Bears long, nodding clusters of small, strongly fragrant, bell-shaped flowers among oval, toothed, rich green leaves from late summer to mid-autumn.
🏆 ***C. barbinervis*** illus. p.129.
C. delavayi illus. p.113.

CLEYERA
THEACEAE

Genus of evergreen, summer-flowering shrubs and trees, grown for their foliage and flowers. Frost to half hardy. Requires a sheltered position in sun or semi-shade and moist, acid soil. Propagate by semi-ripe cuttings in summer.
***C. fortunei* 'Variegata'.** See *C.japonica* 'Fortunei'.
C. japonica. Evergreen, bushy shrub. **H** and **S** 3m (10ft). Frost hardy. Small, fragrant, bowl-shaped, creamy-white flowers are borne in summer amid narrowly oblong to oval-oblong, glossy, dark green leaves. Occasionally has small, spherical, red fruits, ripening to black. **'Fortunei'** (syn. *C. fortunei* 'Variegata', *Eurya japonica* 'Variegata' of gardens), **H** and **S** 2m (6ft), is half hardy and produces pink-flushed, young leaves, later green edged with creamy-white.
'Tricolor' see *C. j.* 'Fortunei'.

CLIANTHUS
LEGUMINOSAE/PAPILIONACEAE

Genus of evergreen or semi-evergreen, woody-stemmed, scrambling climbers, grown for their attractive flowers. Half hardy to frost tender, min. 7°C (45°F). Grow outdoors in warm areas in well-drained soil and full sun. In cooler areas needs to be under glass. In spring prune out growing tips to give a bushier habit and cut out any dead wood. Propagate by seed in spring or stem cuttings in late summer.
🏆 ***C. puniceus*** (Parrot's bill) illus. p.193.
🏆 ***f. albus*** illus. p.192.

CLINTONIA
LILIACEAE/CONVALLARIACEAE

Genus of late spring- or summer-flowering, rhizomatous perennials. Fully hardy. Prefers shade and moist but well-drained, peaty, neutral to acid soil. Propagate by division in spring or by seed in autumn.
C. andrewsiana. Clump-forming, rhizomatous perennial. **H** 60cm (24in), **S** 30cm (12in). In early summer produces clusters of small, bell shaped, pinkish purple flowers at tops of stems, above sparse, broadly oval, glossy, rich green leaves. Bears globose, blue fruits in autumn.
C. borealis. Clump-forming, rhizomatous perennial. **H** and **S** 30cm (12in). Is similar to *C. andrewsiana*, but has nodding, yellowish-green flowers and small, globose, blackish fruits.
C. uniflora (Queencup). Spreading, rhizomatous perennial. **H** 15cm (6in), **S** 30cm (12in). Has oval, glossy, green leaves. Slender stems bear solitary star-shaped, white flowers in late spring, then large, globose, blue-black fruits.

CLITORIA
LEGUMINOSAE/PAPILIONACEAE

Genus of perennials and evergreen shrubs and twining climbers, grown for their large, pea-like flowers. Frost tender, min. 15°C (59°F). Grow in full light and in any fertile, well-drained soil. Water moderately, less when not in full growth. Provide support for stems. Thin out crowded stems in spring. Propagate by seed in spring or by softwood cuttings in summer. Whitefly and red spider mite may be a problem.
C. ternatea. Evergreen, twining climber with slender stems. **H** 3–5m (10–15ft). Leaves are divided into 3 or 5 oval leaflets. Clear bright blue flowers, 7–12cm (3–5in) wide, are carried in summer.

CLIVIA
AMARYLLIDACEAE

Genus of robust, evergreen, rhizomatous perennials, cultivated for their funnel-shaped flowers. Suits borders and large containers. Frost tender, min. 10°C (50°F). Needs partial shade and well-drained soil. Water well in summer, less in winter. Propagate by seed in winter or spring or by division in spring or summer after flowering. Mealy bugs may cause problems. ⓘ All parts of *C. miniata* may cause mild stomach upset if ingested, and the sap may irritate skin.
🏆 ***C. miniata*** illus. p.476.
🏆 ***C. nobilis.*** Evergreen, spring- or summer-flowering, rhizomatous perennial. **H** 30–40cm (12–16in), **S** 30–60cm (12–24in). Has strap-shaped, semi-erect, basal leaves, 40–60cm (16–24in) long. Each leafless stem bears a dense, semi-pendent head of over 20 narrowly funnel-shaped, red flowers, with green tips and yellow margins to petals.

CLUSIA
CLUSIACEAE

Genus of evergreen, mainly summer-flowering climbers, shrubs and trees, grown for their foliage and flowers. Frost tender, min. 16–18°C (61–4°F). Needs partial shade and well-drained soil. Water potted specimens moderately, very little when temperatures are low. Pruning is tolerated if necessary. Propagate by layering in spring or by semi-ripe cuttings in summer. Whitefly and red spider mite may be a problem.
C. major. See *C. rosea.*
C. rosea, syn. *C. major* (Autograph tree, Copey, Fat pork tree, Pitch apple). Slow growing, evergreen, rounded tree or shrub. **H** and **S** to 15m (50ft). Bears oval, lustrous, deep green leaves. Cup-shaped, pink flowers, 5cm (2in) wide, are produced in summer, followed by globose, greenish fruits that yield a sticky resin.

CLYTOSTOMA
BIGNONIACEAE

Genus of evergreen, woody-stemmed, tendril climbers, grown for their flowers. Frost tender, min. 10–13°C (50–55°F). Grow in well-drained soil, with partial shade in summer. Water freely in summer, less at other times. Provide support for stems. Thin out congested growth after flowering or in spring. Propagate by semi-ripe cuttings in summer.
C. callistegioides, syn. *Pandorea lindleyana*, illus. p.461.

COBAEA
COBAEACEAE/POLEMONIACEAE

Genus of evergreen or deciduous, woody-stemmed, tendril climbers. Only one species, *C. scandens*, is generally cultivated. Frost tender, min. 4°C (39°F). Grow outdoors in warm areas in full light and in any well-drained soil. In cool regions may be grown under glass or treated as an annual. Propagate by seed in spring.
🏆 ***C. scandens*** illus. p.204. 🏆 ***f. alba*** is an evergreen, woody-stemmed, tendril climber. **H** 4–5m (12–15ft). Has long-stalked, bell-shaped, green, then white flowers from late summer until first frosts. Leaves have 4 or 6 oval leaflets.

Cocos capitata. See *Butia capitata.*

CODIAEUM
EUPHORBIACEAE

Genus of evergreen shrubs, grown for their foliage. Frost tender, min. 10–13°C (50–55°F). Prefers partial shade and fertile, moist but well-drained soil. Remove tips from young plants to promote a branched habit. Propagate by greenwood cuttings from firm stem tips in spring or summer. Mealy bug and soft scale may be a nuisance. ⓘ Contact with the foliage may aggravate skin allergies.
C. variegatum* var. *pictum illus. p.459.

CODONOPSIS
CAMPANULACEAE

Genus of perennials and mostly herbaceous, twining climbers, grown for their bell- or saucer-shaped flowers. Fully to frost hardy. Needs a position in semi-shade, with light, well-drained soil. Train over supports or leave to scramble through other, larger plants. Propagate by seed sown in autumn or spring.
C. clematidea. Herbaceous, twining climber. **H** to 1.5m (5ft). Frost hardy. Has small, oval, mid-green leaves. In summer produces nodding, bell-shaped, white flowers, 2.5cm (1in) long; they are tinged with blue, and marked inside with darker veining and 2 purple rings.
🏆 ***C. convolvulacea*** illus. p.205.
C. ovata. Upright perennial with scarcely twining stems. **H** to 30cm (12in). Frost hardy. Has small, oval leaves and, in summer, small, bell-shaped, pale blue flowers, often with darker veins.

COELOGYNE
ORCHIDACEAE

See also ORCHIDS.
C. cristata illus. p.465.
C. flaccida (illus. p.466). Evergreen, epiphytic orchid for a cool greenhouse. **H** 15cm (6in). During spring bears drooping spikes of fragrant, star-shaped, light buff flowers, 4cm (1½in) across, with yellow and brown marks on each lip. Has narrowly oval, semi-rigid leaves, 8–10cm (3–4in) long. Grow in semi-shade in summer.
C. nitida, syn. *C. ochracea* (illus. p.466). Evergreen, epiphytic orchid for a cool greenhouse. **H** 12cm (5in). In spring produces sprays of very fragrant, white flowers, 2.5cm (1in) across and with a yellow mark on each lip. Narrowly oval, semi-rigid leaves are 8–10cm (3–4in) long. Requires semi-shade in summer.
C. ochracea. See *C. nitida*.
C. speciosa. Vigorous, evergreen, epiphytic orchid for an intermediate greenhouse. **H** 25cm (10in). In summer, produces pendent, light green flowers, 6cm (2½in) across, with brown- and white-marked lips, that open in succession along stems. Has broadly oval leaves, 23–25cm (9–10in) long. Grow in good light in summer.

COIX
GRAMINEAE/POACEAE

See also GRASSES, BAMBOOS, RUSHES and SEDGES.
C. lacryma-jobi (Job's tears). Tuft-forming, annual grass. **H** 45–90cm (18–36in), **S** 10–15cm (4–6in). Half hardy. Has broad leaves and insignificant spikelets followed by hard, bead-like, green fruits turning shiny, greyish-mauve in autumn.

COLCHICUM
LILIACEAE/COLCHICACEAE

Genus of spring- and autumn-flowering corms, grown for their mainly goblet-shaped blooms, up to 20cm (8in) long, most of which emerge before leaves. Each corm bears 2–7 narrowly strap-shaped to broadly elliptic, basal leaves. Fully to frost hardy. Needs an open, sunny situation and well-drained soil. Propagate by seed or division in autumn. ⓘ All parts are highly toxic if ingested and, if in contact with skin, may cause irritation.
🏆 ***C. agrippinum*** illus. p.425.
C. autumnale illus. p.426. **'Alboplenum'** is an autumn-flowering corm. **H** and **S** 10–15cm (4–6in). Fully hardy. In spring has 3–5 large, semi-erect, basal, glossy, green leaves. Produces a bunch of up to 8 long-tubed, rounded, double, white flowers with 15–30 narrow petals.
***C.* 'Beaconsfield'.** Robust, autumn-flowering corm. **H** and **S** 15–20cm (6–8in). Fully hardy. Bears large, goblet-shaped, rich pinkish-purple flowers, faintly chequered and white in centres. Large, semi erect, basal leaves appear in spring.
C. bivonae, syn. *C. bowlesianum, C. sibthorpii*, illus. p.425.
C. bowlesianum. See *C. bivonae*.
🏆 ***C. x byzantinum*** illus. p.426.
C. cilicicum illus. p.425.
***C.* 'Lilac Wonder'.** Vigorous, autumn-

C

flowering corm. **H** and **S** 15–20cm (6–8in). Fully hardy. Has goblet-shaped, deep lilac-pink flowers, 15–20cm (6–8in) long. Broad, semi-erect, basal leaves appear in spring.
C. luteum illus. p.421.
C. sibthorpii. See *C. bivonae.*
🏆 ***C. speciosum.*** Vigorous, autumn-flowering corm. **H** and **S** 15–20cm (6–8in). Fully hardy. Bears goblet-shaped, pale to deep pinkish-purple flowers, 15–20cm (6–8in) long, often with white throats. Large, semi-erect, basal leaves develop in winter or spring. 🏆 **'Album'** illus. p.424.
***C.* 'The Giant'.** Robust, autumn-flowering corm. **H** and **S** 15–20cm (6–8in). Fully hardy. Produces up to 5 funnel-shaped, deep mauve-pink flowers, each 15–20cm (6–8in) long and fading to white in the centre. Broad, semi-erect, basal leaves form in winter or spring.
C. variegatum. Autumn-flowering corm. **H** 10–15cm (4–6in), **S** 8–10cm (3–4in). Frost hardy. Bears widely funnel-shaped, reddish-purple flowers with strong chequered patterns. More or less horizontal, basal leaves with wavy margins appear in spring. Needs a hot, sunny site.
🏆 ***C.* 'Waterlily'** illus. p.425.

COLEONEMA

RUTACEAE

Genus of evergreen, heath-like shrubs, grown for their flowers and overall appearance. Frost tender, min. 3–5°C (37–41°F). Requires a position in full sun and well-drained, neutral to acid soil. Water potted plants moderately when in full growth, sparingly at other times. For a more compact habit, clip after flowering. Propagate by seed sown in spring or by semi-ripe cuttings in late summer.
C. pulchrum. Evergreen, spreading to domed shrub with wiry stems. **H** 60cm–1.2m (2–4ft), **S** 1–1.5m(3–5ft). Has soft, needle-like, bright green leaves. Carries 5-petalled, pale pink to red flowers in spring-summer.

Coleus.* See** *Solenostemon* except for: ***C. thyrsoideus for which see *Plectranthus thyrsoideus.*

COLLETIA

RHAMNACEAE

Genus of deciduous, usually leafless shrubs, grown for their curious, spiny shoots and profuse, small flowers. Shoots assume function of leaves. Frost hardy. Requires a sheltered, sunny site and well-drained soil. Propagate by semi-ripe cuttings in late summer.
C. armata. See *C. hystrix.*
C. cruciata. See *C. paradoxa.*
C. hystrix. syn. *C. armata*, illus. p.130. **'Rosea'** is a deciduous, stoutly branched shrub. **H** 2.5m (8ft), **S** 5m (15ft). Shoots have rigid, grey-green spines. Bears fragrant, tubular, pink flowers in late summer and early autumn.
C. paradoxa. syn. *C. cruciata*, illus. p.131.

COLLINSIA

SCROPHULARIACEAE

Genus of spring- to summer-flowering annuals. Fully hardy. Grow in partial shade and in fertile, well-drained soil. Support with thin sticks. Propagate by seed sown outdoors in spring or early autumn.
C. grandiflora illus. p.312.

COLOCASIA

ARACEAE

Genus of deciduous or evergreen, perennial, marginal water plants, grown for their foliage. Has edible tubers, known as 'taros', for which it is widely cultivated. Is suitable for the edges of frost-free pools; may also be grown in wet soil in pots. Frost tender, min. 1°C (34°F); with min. 25°C (77°F) is evergreen. Grows in sun or light shade and in mud or shallow water. Propagate by division in spring. ⚠ All parts may cause mild stomach upset if ingested without cooking, and contact with the sap may irritate the skin.
C. antiquorum. See *C. esculenta.*
🏆 ***C. esculenta***, syn. *C. antiquorum.* **'Fontanesii'** is a deciduous, perennial, marginal water plant. **H** 1.1m (3½ft), **S** 60cm (2ft). Has large, bold, oval, mid-green leaves with dark green veins and margins and blackish-violet leaf stalks and spathe tubes. **'Illustris'** has brownish-purple leaf stalks and dark green leaf blades with purple spots.

COLQUHOUNIA

LABIATAE/LAMIACEAE

Genus of evergreen or semi-evergreen shrubs, grown for their flowers in late summer and autumn. Frost hardy, but is cut to ground level in cold winters. Needs a sheltered, sunny position and well-drained soil. Propagate by softwood cuttings in summer.
C. coccinea illus. p.141.

COLUMNEA

GESNERIACEAE

Genus of evergreen, creeping or trailing perennials or sub-shrubs, grown for their showy flowers. Trailing species are useful for hanging baskets. Frost tender, min. 15°C (59°F). Needs bright but indirect light, a fairly humid atmosphere and moist soil, except in winter. Propagate by tip cuttings after flowering.
🏆 ***C.* x *banksii*** illus. p.470.
C. crassifolia illus. p.470.
C. gloriosa (Goldfish plant). Evergreen, trailing perennial with more or less unbranched stems. **H** and **S** to 90cm (3ft). Oval leaves have reddish hairs. Has tubular, hooded, scarlet flowers, to 8cm (3in) long, with yellow throats, in winter–spring.
C. microphylla. Evergreen perennial, sparsely branched on each trailing stem. **H** and **S** 1m (3ft) or more. Has small, rounded leaves with brown hairs. Hooded, tubular, scarlet flowers, to 8cm (3in) long, with yellow throats, are produced in winter–spring. **'Variegata'** illus. p.475.

COLUTEA

LEGUMINOSAE/PAPILIONACEAE

Genus of deciduous, summer-flowering shrubs, grown for their foliage, pea-like flowers and bladder-shaped seed pods. Fully hardy. Grow in full sun and any but waterlogged soil. Propagate by softwood cuttings in summer or by seed in autumn. ⚠ Seeds may cause mild stomach upset if ingested.
C. arborescens illus. p.139.
C.* x *media illus. p.140.
C. orientalis. Deciduous, bushy shrub. **H** and **S** 2m (6ft). Has blue-grey leaves consisting of 7 or 9 oval leaflets. Clusters of yellow-marked, coppery-red flowers produced in summer are followed by inflated, green, then pale brown seed pods.

Comarostaphylis diversifolia. See *Arctostaphylos diversifolia.*

COMBRETUM

COMBRETACEAE

Genus of evergreen trees, shrubs and scandent to twining climbers, grown for their small, showy flowers. Frost tender, min. 16°C (61°F). Provide humus-rich, well-drained soil, with partial shade in summer. Water freely in summer, less at other times. Support for stems is necessary. Thin out and spur back congested growth after flowering. Propagate by semi-ripe cuttings in summer. Red spider mite may be a problem.
C. grandiflorum. Moderately vigorous, evergreen, scandent to twining climber. **H** to 6m (20ft). Has oblong to elliptic, pointed leaves, 10–20cm (4–8in) long. Tubular, bright red flowers with long stamens are borne in summer in one-sided spikes, 10–13cm (4–5in) long.
C. indicum. See *Quisqualis indica.*

COMMELINA

COMMELINACEAE

Genus of perennials, usually grown as annuals. Half hardy. Grow in a sunny, sheltered position and in fertile, well-drained soil. Crowns should be lifted before the frosts and overwintered in slightly moist, frost-free conditions. Propagate by seed sown under glass or by division of the crown in spring.
C. coelestis, syn. *C. tuberosa* Coelestis Group, illus. p.315.
***C. tuberosa* Coelestis Group.** See *C. coelestis.*

CONANDRON

GESNERIACEAE

Genus of one species of tuberous perennial, grown for its fleshy leaves and drooping flower clusters. Frost hardy. Grow in alpine houses. Needs shade and humus-rich, well-drained soil. Keep containerized plants moist in summer, dry when dormant in winter. Propagate by division or seed in spring.
C. ramondoides. Hummock-forming, tuberous perennial. **H** 30cm (12in), **S** 20cm (8in). Bears broadly oval, fleshy, wrinkled, mid-green leaves with toothed edges. In mid-summer, each flower stem carries 5–25 tubular flowers, usually lilac, but white, purple or pink forms also occur.

CONIFERS

Group of trees and shrubs distinguished botanically from others by producing seeds exposed or uncovered on the scales of fruits. Most conifers are evergreen, have needle-like leaves and bear woody fruits (cones). All genera in the Cupressaceae family, however, have needle-like juvenile leaves and, excepting many junipers and some other selected forms, scale-like adult leaves.

Conifers described in this book are evergreen unless otherwise stated. Conifers are excellent garden plants. Most provide year-round foliage, which may be green, blue, grey, bronze, gold or silver. They range in height from trees 40m (130ft) or more tall to dwarf shrubs that grow less than 5cm (2in) every 10 years. Tall conifers may be planted as specimen trees or to provide shelter, screening or hedging. Dwarf conifers make good features in their own right as well as in groups; they also associate well with heathers, add variety to rock gardens and provide excellent ground cover. They may also be grown in containers.

Hardiness

Nearly all conifers described in this book are fully hardy. Some, such as *Picea sitchensis, P. omorika* and *Pinus contorta*, thrive in the coldest, most windswept sites. *Araucaria, Cupressus* and *Pinus* are good for coastal conditions. *Athrotaxis, Austrocedrus, Cephalotaxus, Podocarpus* and certain species noted in other genera are frost to half hardy and flourish only in mild localities. Elsewhere they need a very sheltered position or may be grown indoors as dwarf plants.
Frost may damage new growth of several genera, especially *Abies, Larix, Picea* and *Pseudotsuga*, and severe cold, dry spells in winter may temporarily harm mature foliage.

Position and soil

x *Cupressocyparis, Cupressus, Larix* and *Pinus* need full sun. *Cedrus, Juniperus* and *Pseudolarix* do not tolerate shade. All other conifers will thrive in sun or shade, and most *Abies* and all *Cephalotaxus, Podocarpus, Taxus, Thuja, Torreya* and *Tsuga* will grow in deep shade once established. *Wollemia* prefers a sheltered location out of full sun.
Conifers grow well on most soils, but certain genera and species will not do well on soils over chalk or limestone. In this book, such conifers are: *Abies, Pseudolarix, Pseudotsuga* and *Tsuga*; also *Picea*, except *P. likiangesis, P. omorika* and *P. pungens*; and *Pinus*, except *P. aristata, P. armandii, P. cembroides, P. halepensis, P. heldreichii, P. nigra, P. peuce* and *P.wallichiana.*
Certain conifers tolerate extreme conditions. *Abies alba, A. homolepis, A. nordmanniana, Cryptomeria, Cunninghamia, Metasequoia, Pinus coulteri, P. peuce, P. ponderosa, Sciadopitys, Sequoia, Sequoiadendron* and *Taxodium* will grow on heavy clay soils. *Picea omorika, P. sitchensis, Pinus contorta, Sciadopitys verticillata* and *Thuja plicata* are all happy on wet soil, and *Metasequoia* and *Taxodium thrive* in waterlogged conditions. *Cupressus, Juniperus* and *Pinus* grow well on dry, sandy soil.

Pruning

If a conifer produces more than one leader, remove all but one. Bear in mind when trimming hedges that most conifers will not make new growth when cut back into old wood or from branches that have turned brown. This does not, however, apply to *Cephalotaxus, Cryptomeria, Cunninghamia, Sequoia, Taxus,Torreya,* and *Wollemia,* and these conifers may be kept to a reasonable size in the garden by cutting back the main stem, which will later coppice (make new growth).Young specimens of *Araucaria, Ginkgo, Metasequoia* and *Taxodium* will sometimes do the same.

Propagation
Seed is the easiest method of propagation, but forms selected for leaf colour (other than blue in some species) do not come true. Sow in autumn or spring. All genera apart from *Abies, Cedrus, Picea* (except young plants or dwarf forms), *Pinus, Pseudolarix, Pseudotsuga* and *Tsuga* (except young plants or dwarf forms) may be raised fairly easily from cuttings: current growth from autumn to spring for evergreens, softwood cuttings in summer for deciduous conifers. Tall-growing forms of Pinaceae (*Abies, Cedrus, Picea, Pinus, Pseudolarix, Pseudotsuga* and *Tsuga*) are usually propagated by grafting in late summer, winter or early spring. Layering may be possible for some dwarf conifers. It is illegal to propagate *Wollemia nobilis.*

Pests and diseases
Honey fungus attacks many conifers, especially young plants. Most resistant to the disease are *Abies, Calocedrus, Larix, Pseudotsuga* and *Taxus.* Green spruce aphid may be a problem on *Picea,* and conifer spinning mite may defoliate *Abies, Picea* and some *Pinus.*
Conifers are illustrated on pp.95–105, dwarf forms on pp.105. See also *Abies, Araucaria, Athrotaxis, Austrocedrus, Calocedrus, Cedrus, Cephalotaxus, Chamaecyparis, Cryptomeria, Cunninghamia,* x *Cupressocyparis, Cupressus, Fitzroya, Ginkgo, Juniperus, Larix, Metasequoia, Microbiota, Phyllocladus, Picea, Pinus, Podocarpus, Pseudolarix, Pseudotsuga, Saxegothaea, Sciadopitys, Sequoia, Sequoiadendron, Taxodium, Taxus, Thuja, Thujopsis, Torreya, Tsuga,* and *Wollemia.*

CONOPHYTUM

AIZOACEAE

Genus of slow-growing, clump-forming, perennial succulents with spherical or 2-eared leaves that grow for only 2 months each year, after flowering. In early summer, old leaves gradually shrivel to papery sheaths from which new leaves and flowers emerge in late summer. Frost tender, min. 4°C (39°F) if dry. Needs full sun and well-drained soil. Keep dry in winter. Propagate by seed from spring to autumn or by division in late summer.
♀ ***C. bilobum*** illus. p.494.
C. concordans, syn. *Ophthalmophyllum villetii*, illus. p.484.
C. frutescens, syn. *C. notabile*, illus. p.496.
♀ ***C. longum***, syn. *Ophthalmophyllum herri, O. longum.* Clump-forming, perennial succulent. **H** 3cm (1¼in), **S** 1.5cm (⅝in). Has 2 almost united, cylindrical, very fleshy, erect, grey-green to brown leaves. In late summer bears daisy-like, white to pink flowers, 2cm (¾in) across.
C. notabile. See *C. frutescens.*
♀ ***C. truncatum*** Slow-growing, clump-forming, perennial succulent. **H** 1.5cm (⅝in), **S** 15cm (6in). Has pea-shaped, dark spotted, blue-green leaves, each with a sunken fissure at the tip. Produces cream flowers, 1.5cm (⅝in) across, in autumn.

CONSOLIDA

Larkspur

RANUNCULACEAE

Genus of annuals, providing excellent cut flowers. Fully hardy. Needs sun and fertile, well-drained soil. Support stems of tall-growing plants with sticks. Propagate by seed sown outdoors in spring, or in early autumn in mild areas. Protect young plants from slugs and snails. The seeds are poisonous.
C. ajacis, syn. *C. ambigua, Delphinium consolida.* Fast-growing, upright, branching annual. Giant forms, **H** to 1.2m (4ft), **S** 30cm (1ft); dwarf, **H** and **S** 30cm (1ft). All have feathery, mid-green leaves and, throughout summer, spikes of rounded, spurred flowers. **Dwarf Hyacinth Series** has spikes of tubular flowers in shades of pink, mauve, blue or white. **Giant Imperial Series** (Giant larkspur) has spikes of rounded, spurred, double flowers in pink, blue or white.
C. ambigua. See *C. ajacis.*

CONVALLARIA

Lily-of-the-valley

LILIACEAE/CONVALLARIACEAE

Genus of spring-flowering, rhizomatous perennials. Fully hardy. Prefers partial shade and humus-rich, moist soil. Propagate by division after flowering or in autumn. ⓘThe seeds of *C. majalis* may cause mild stomach upset if ingested.
♀ ***C. majalis*** illus. p.255. **'Flore Pleno'** is a low-growing, rhizomatous perennial. **H** 23–30cm (9–12in), **S** indefinite. Sprays of small, very fragrant, pendent, bell-shaped flowers that are double and white open in spring. Narrowly oval leaves are mid-to dark green. **'Fortin's Giant'**, **H** 45cm (18in), has larger flowers and leaves that appear a little earlier.

CONVOLVULUS

CONVOLVULACEAE

Genus of dwarf, bushy and climbing annuals, perennials and evergreen shrubs and sub-shrubs. Fully hardy to frost tender, min 2°C (36°F). Grow in sun and in poor to fertile, well-drained soil. Dead-head to prolong flowering. Propagate by seed sown outdoors in mid-spring for hardy plants or under glass in spring for tender plants, perennials and sub-shrubs by softwood cuttings in late spring or summer.
C. althaeoides illus. p.362.
♀ ***C. cneorum*** illus. p.149.
C. mauritanicus. See *C. sabatius.*
C. minor. See *C. tricolor.*
C. purpureus. See *Ipomoea purpurea.*
♀ ***C. sabatius***, syn. *C. mauritanicus*, illus. p.342.
C. tricolor, syn. *C. minor.* Moderately fast-growing, upright, bushy or climbing annual. **H** 20–30cm (8–12in), **S** 20cm (8in). Fully hardy. Has oval to lance-shaped, mid-green leaves. In summer bears saucer-shaped, blue or white flowers, 2.5cm (1in) wide, with yellowish-white throats. Tall, climbing forms, **H** to 3m (10ft), are half hardy and have flowers to 10cm (4in) wide. **'Blue Flash'** (bushy) illus. p.314. **'Flying Saucers'** (climber) has blue-and-white-striped flowers.

COPIAPOA

CACTACEAE

Genus of slow-growing, perennial cacti with funnel-shaped, yellow flowers. Many species have large tap roots. Frost tender, min. 8–10°C (46–50°F). Needs partial shade and very well-drained soil. Propagate by seed or grafting in spring or summer.
C. cinerea illus. p.489.
C. coquimbana. Clump-forming, spherical, then columnar, perennial cactus. **H** to 30cm (1ft), **S** 1m (3ft). Min. 8°C (46°F). Dark grey-green stem has 10–17 ribs. Areoles each bear 8–10 dark brown radial spines and 1 or 2 stouter central spines. Yellow flowers, 3cm (1¼in) across, appear in summer. Is slow to form clumps.
C. echinoides. Flattened spherical, perennial cactus, ribbed like a sea urchin. **H** 15cm (6in), **S** 10cm (4in). Min. 10°C (50°F). Solitary grey green stem bears dark brown spines, 3cm (1¼in) long, which soon fade to grey. In summer produces pale yellow flowers, 4cm (1½in) across.
C. marginata. Clump-forming, perennial cactus. **H** 60cm (2ft), **S** 30cm (1ft). Min. 10°C (50°F). Grey-green stem bears very close-set areoles with dark-tipped, pale brown spines, to 3cm (1¼in) long. Has yellow flowers, 2–5cm (¾–2in) across, in spring–summer.

COPROSMA

RUBIACEAE

Genus of evergreen shrubs and trees, grown for their foliage and fruits. Separate male and female plants are needed to obtain fruits. Half hardy to frost tender, min. 2–5°C (36–41°F). Prefers full light and well-drained soil. Water containerized specimens freely in summer, moderately at other times. Propagate by seed in spring or by semi-ripe cuttings in late summer.
C. baueri of gardens. See *C. repens.*
C. baueriana. See *C. repens.*
C. x kirkii. Evergreen, prostrate, then semi-erect, densely branched shrub. **H** to 1m (3ft), **S** 1.2–2m (4–6ft). Half hardy. Narrowly oblong to lance-shaped, leathery, glossy leaves are borne singly or in small clusters. In late spring has insignificant flowers, followed on female plants by tiny, egg-shaped, translucent, white fruits with red speckles. **'Variegata'** illus. p.152.
C. repens, syn. *C. baueri* of gardens, *C. baueriana.* Evergreen, spreading, then erect shrub. **H** and **S** to 2m (6ft). Frost tender, min. 2°C (36°F). Has broadly oval, leathery, lustrous, rich green leaves. Carries insignificant flowers in late spring, followed on female plants by egg-shaped, orange-red fruits from late summer to autumn. Leaves of ♀ **'Picturata'** each have a central, cream blotch.

CORDYLINE

AGAVACEAE

Genus of evergreen shrubs and trees, grown primarily for their foliage, although some also have decorative flowers. Half hardy to frost tender, min. 5–16°C (41–61°F). Provide fertile, well-drained soil and full light or partial shade. Water potted plants moderately, less in winter. Propagate by seed or suckers in spring or by stem cuttings in summer. Red spider mite may be a nuisance.
♀ ***C. australis***, syn. *Dracaena australis* (New Zealand cabbage palm). Slow-growing, evergreen, sparsely branched tree. **H** 15m (50ft) or more, **S** 5m (15ft) or more. Half hardy. Each stem is crowned by a rosette of strap-shaped, 30cm–1m (1–3ft) long leaves. Has small, scented, white flowers in large, open panicles in summer and, in autumn, globose, white fruits. **'Atropurpurea'** illus. p.451. Long, sword-shaped leaves of **'Veitchii'** have red bases and midribs.
C. fruticosa, syn. *C. terminalis* (Good-luck plant, Ti tree). Slow-growing, evergreen, upright shrub, sparingly branched and suckering. **H** 2–4m (6–12ft), **S** 1–2m (3–6ft). Frost tender, min. 13°C (55°F). Broadly lance-shaped, glossy, deep green leaves are 30–60cm (1–2ft) long. Produces branched panicles of small, white, purplish or reddish flowers in summer. Foliage of ♀ **'Baptistii'**, is deep green with pink and yellow stripes and spots.
'Imperialis' has red- or pink-marked, deep green leaves.
C. indivisa, syn. *Dracaena indivisa.* Slow-growing, evergreen, erect tree or shrub. **H** 3m (10ft) or more, **S** 2m (6ft). Half hardy. Bears lance-shaped, 60cm–2m (2–6ft) long, green leaves, orange-brown veined above, blue-grey tinted beneath. In summer tiny, star-shaped, white flowers in dense clusters, 60cm (2ft) or more long, are followed by tiny, spherical, blue-purple fruits.
C. terminalis. See *C. fruticosa.*

COREOPSIS

Tickseed

COMPOSITAE/ASTERACEAE

Genus of annuals and perennials, grown for their daisy-like flower heads. Fully to frost hardy. Needs full sun and fertile, well-drained soil. Propagate annuals by seed in spring; *C. lanceolata* by seed or division in spring; *C. auriculata* 'Superba', *C.* 'Goldfink' and *C. grandiflora* 'Badengold' by softwood cuttings or division in spring or summer; and *C. verticillata* by division in spring.
C. auriculata **'Superba'.** Bushy perennial. **H** and **S** 45cm (18in). Fully hardy. Daisy-like, rich yellow flower heads, with central, purple blotches, are borne in summer. Oval to lance-shaped leaves are lobed and light green. Some plants grown as *C. auriculata* are the closely related annual *C. basalis.*
C. **Coloropsis Series 'Jive'.** Bushy, well-branched, prolific perennial grown as an annual. **H** 30–45cm (12–18in), **S** 45–60cm (18–24in). Frost hardy. Has narrowly lance-shaped, dark green leaves. Daisy-like, deep crimson flower heads, 5cm (2in) across,

C

margined in pure white, are borne in summer-autumn.
***C.* 'Goldfink'.** See *C. lanceolata* 'Goldfink'.
***C. grandiflora* 'Badengold'.** Short-lived, erect perennial with lax stems. **H** 75cm (30in), **S** 60cm (24in). Fully hardy. Bears large, daisy-like, rich buttercup-yellow flower heads in summer and broadly lance-shaped, divided, bright green leaves. **'Sunray',** syn. *C.* 'Sunray', illus. p.321.
C. lanceolata illus. p.276. **'Goldfink',** syn. *C.* 'Goldfink'. Short-lived, dwarf, bushy perennial. **H** and **S** 30cm (12in). Fully hardy. Sprays of daisy-like, deep yellow flower heads appear in summer above narrowly oval, deep green leaves.
***C. rosea* 'American Dream'.** Upright perennial. **H** 35cm (14in), **S** 30cm (12in). Fully hardy. Has small, lance-shaped, dark green leaves. Produces masses of daisy-like, yellow-centred, pink flower heads, borne on self-supporting, branched stems, in mid-summer.
***C.* 'Limerock Ruby'**, illus. p.268.
***C.* 'Rum Punch'** illus. p.326.
***C.* 'Sunray'.** See *C. grandiflora* 'Sunray'.
C. tinctoria illus. p.321. **'Golden Crown'** is a fast-growing, upright, bushy annual. **H** 60cm (24in), **S** 20cm (8in). Fully hardy. Has lance-shaped, deep green leaves and, in summer and early autumn, large, daisy-like, deep yellow flower heads with brown centres.
C. verticillata illus. p.276.

CORIARIA

CORIARIACEAE

Genus of deciduous, spring- or summer-flowering shrubs and sub-shrubs, grown for their habit, foliage and fruits. Frost to half hardy. Needs full sun and fertile, well-drained soil. Propagate by softwood cuttings in summer or by seed in autumn. ⚠The leaves and fruits of some species may cause severe stomach upset if ingested; in other species, the fruits are edible, although the seeds are thought to be poisonous.
C. terminalis. Deciduous, arching sub-shrub. **H** 1m (3ft), **S** 2m (6ft). Frost hardy. Broadly lance-shaped, fern-like, mid-green leaves turn red in autumn. Minute, green flowers in late spring are succeeded by small, spherical, black fruits. **var. *xanthocarpa*** illus. p.161.

CORNUKAEMPFERIA

ZINGIBERACEAE

Genus of herbaceous perennials with underground rhizome, grown for its large, colourful leaves and flowers. Frost tender, min. 10°C (50°F). Grow in moist but well-drained soil in partial or full shade. Keep dry when dormant. Propagate by division in spring or by seed in spring.
C. aurantiflora. Herbaceous, rhizomatous perennial. **H** 70cm (28in), **S** 50cm (20in). Has ovate, ribbed, dark green and silver leaves, to 25cm (10in) long, with purple undersides, borne close to the ground. Tubular, orange flowers, 5cm (2in) long, are borne, in summer, from short stalks in the leaf axils. Requires full shade. **'Jungle Gold'** (illus. p.477) has largely silver leaves and deep orange-red buds that open into orange-gold flowers, with red lines.

CORNUS

Dogwood

CORNACEAE

Genus of deciduous shrubs and deciduous or evergreen trees, grown for their flowers, foliage or brightly coloured winter stems. Fully to half hardy. Needs sun or semi-shade and fertile, well-drained soil. Those grown for winter stem colour do best in full sun. *C. florida, C. kousa* and *C. nuttallii* dislike shallow, chalky soil. *C. canadensis* prefers acid soil. Plants grown for their stems should be cut back almost to ground level each year in early spring. Propagate *C. alba* and *C. stolonifera* 'Flaviramea' by softwood cuttings in summer or by hardwood cuttings in autumn or winter; variegated forms of *C. alternifolia* and *C.controversa* by grafting in winter; *C. canadensis* by division in spring or autumn; *C. capitata, C. florida* and *C.kousa* by seed in autumn or by softwood cuttings in summer; *C.nuttallii* by seed in autumn; all others described here by softwood cuttings in summer. ⚠The fruits of some species may cause mild stomach upset if ingested; contact with the leaf hairs may irritate skin.
C. alba (Red-barked dogwood). Vigorous, deciduous, upright, then spreading shrub. **H** and **S** 3m (10ft). Fully hardy. Young shoots are bright red in winter. Has oval, dark green leaves, often red or orange in autumn. Bears flattened heads of star-shaped, creamy-white flowers in late spring and early summer, followed by spherical, sometimes blue-tinted, white fruits. 🏆**'Aurea'** (illus. p.126) has pale greenish-yellow leaves in summer. 🏆 **'Elegantissima'** (illus. p.126) has white-edged, grey-green leaves. **'Gouchaultii'** has pink-flushed leaves broadly edged with yellow. **'Kesselringii'** (illus. p.126) has dark green leaves flushed reddish-purple in autumn. 🏆 **'Sibirica'** illus. p.143. **'Sibirica Variegata'** (illus. p.142) has grey-green leaves with creamy-white margins. 🏆 **'Spaethii'** (illus. p.126) has bright green leaves with yellow edges.
C. alternifolia (illus. p.87). Deciduous, spreading tree or bushy shrub, with tiered branches. **H** and **S** 6m (20ft). Fully hardy. Oval, bright green leaves, which each taper to a point, often turn red in autumn. Clusters of tiny, star-shaped, creamy-white flowers in early summer are followed by small, rounded, blue-black fruits. 🏆 **'Argentea'** (illus. p.87) narrowly oval, white-variegated leaves.
🏆 ***C. canadensis*** (Creeping dogwood), syn. *Chamaepericlymenum canadense*, illus. p.360.
C. capitata. syn. *Dendrobenthamia capitata* (Bentham's corne; illus. p.87). Evergreen or semi-evergreen, spreading tree. **H** and **S** up to 12m (40ft). Frost to half hardy. Pale yellow bracts, surrounding insignificant flowers, appear in early summer, followed by large, strawberry-like, red fruits. Has oval, grey-green leaves. Is good for mild coastal areas.
C. controversa (illus. p.87). Deciduous tree with layered branches. **H** and **S** 15m (50ft). Fully hardy. Leaves are oval, pointed and bright green, turning purple in autumn Clusters of small, star-shaped, white flowers appear in summer. 🏆 **'Variegata'** (Wedding-cake tree), **H** and **S** 8m (25ft), leaves are bright green with broad, creamy-white margins and turn yellow in autumn.
🏆 ***C.* 'Eddie's White Wonder'** (illus. p.87). Deciduous, spreading tree or shrub. **H** 6m (20ft), **S** 5m (15ft). Fully hardy. Large, white bracts, surrounding insignificant flowers, appear in late spring. Oval leaves are mid-green, turning red and purple in autumn.
C. florida (Flowering dogwood). Deciduous, spreading tree. **H** 6m (20ft), **S** 8m (25ft). Fully hardy. In late spring bears white or pinkish-white bracts surrounding tiny, insignificant flowers. Oval, pointed, dark green leaves turn red and purple in autumn. **'Apple Blossom'** has pale pink bracts. 🏆**'Cherokee Chief'** (illus. p.87) bears pink-red bracts, fading to white close to each flower. **'Cherokee Princess'** (illus. p.87) has bronze-coloured leaves that mature to dark green. **'Rainbow'** (illus. p.87) has a compact, erect habit, white bracts and yellow-edged leaves turning purple-red in autumn. **f. *rubra*** bears pink or red bracts. **'Spring Song'** has pink bracts. **'Welchii'** illus. p.89. **'White Cloud'** has large white bracts.
C. kousa, illus. p.85. 🏆**'Miss Satomi'** (illus. p.87) has deep pink bracts and bright green leaves turning orange and red in autumn. **'National'** (illus. p.87) is vigorous, has bright green leaves turning to orange and red in autumn, and bears large, white bracts that mature to pink. **'Rosea'** has rose-pink bracts. 🏆**var. *chinensis*** (illus. p.87) has larger flower heads and more narrowly pointed bracts. **var. chinensis 'China Girl'** (illus. p.87) bears creamy-white bracts and mid-green leaves turning orange-red in autumn.
C. macrophylla. Deciduous, spreading tree. H 12m (40ft), S 8m (25ft). Fully hardy. Glossy, bright green leaves are large, pointed and oval. Clusters of small, creamy-white flowers appear in summer.
C. mas (Cornelian cherry; illus. p.87). Deciduous, spreading, open shrub or tree. **H** and **S** 5m (15ft). Fully hardy. Oval, dark green leaves change to reddish-purple in autumn. Produces small, star- shaped, yellow flowers on bare shoots in late winter and early spring, then edible, oblong, bright red fruits. **'Aureoelegantissima'**, syn. *C.m.* 'Elegantissima', illus. p.87. **H** 2m (6ft), **S** 3m (10ft). has pink-tinged leaves edged with yellow. **'Elegantissima'** see *C.m.* 'Aureoelegantissima'. 🏆 **'Variegata'** Deciduous, bushy, dense shrub or small tree. Small, star-shaped, yellow flowers appear on bare branches in early spring before white-edged, dark green leaves.
🏆 ***C.* 'Norman Hadden'.** Deciduous, spreading tree. **H** and **S** 8m (25ft). Fully hardy. Creamy-white bracts around tiny flowers turn to deep pink in summer. These are often followed by strawberry-like fruits in autumn.
C. nuttallii (Mountain dogwood, Pacific dogwood). Deciduous, conical tree. **H** 12m (40ft), **S** 8m (25ft). Fully hardy. Has oval, dark green leaves and large, white bracts, surrounding tiny flowers, appear in late spring. **'Monarch'** (illus. p.87) is a vigorous, deciduous, spreading tree. **H** to 12m (40ft), **S** 8m (25ft). Fully hardy. Large, rounded, white bracts, surrounding tiny flowers, are produced in mid-spring. Purple-blushed shoots bear ovate, mid-green leaves.
🏆 ***C.* 'Porlock'** (illus. p.87). Deciduous, spreading tree. **H** 10m (30ft), **S** 5m (15ft). Fully hardy. Creamy-white bracts around tiny flowers turn to deep pink in summer. These are often followed by heavy crops of strawberry-like fruits in autumn.
C. sanguinea (Common dogwood; illus. p.142). Deciduous, upright shrub. **H** to 3m (10ft), **S** 1m (3ft). Fully hardy. Reddish-green, sometimes entirely green, winter shoots are a deep red colour when young. Ovate, mid-green leaves turn reddish-purple in autumn. Flattened heads of star-shaped, white flowers, in late spring, are followed by ovoid, blue-black fruits. Grows well in damp soil. **'Midwinter Fire'** (illus. p.126) produces flame-coloured stems – yellow at the bases rising to scarlet-red on younger growth. **'Winter Beauty'** (illus. p.126) has orange-yellow winter stems, tipped with crimson, and yellow-red autumn leaf colour.
C. sericea, syn. *C. stolonifera* (Red osier dogwood). 🏆**'Flaviramea'** (illus. p.126) is a vigorous, deciduous shrub. **H** 2m (6ft), **S** 4m (13ft). Fully hardy. Has olive-green to yellow, young shoots in winter and ovate, mid-green leaves. Flattened heads of small, star-shaped cream flowers, in late spring and early summer, are followed by ovoid, creamy-white fruits. **'Kelseyi'** (illus. p.126), **H** 75cm (2½ft), **S** 1.5m (5ft), is compact and has yellow-green winter stems tipped with orange-red. 🏆 **'White Gold'** (syn. *C.s.* 'White Spot'; illus. p.126) has mid-green leaves margined and mottled with white. **'White Spot'** see *C.s.* 'White Gold'.
C. stolonifera. See *C. sericea.*

COROKIA

ESCALLONIACEAE/ARGOPHYLLACEAE

Genus of evergreen shrubs, grown for their habit, foliage, flowers and fruits. Is good in mild, coastal areas, where it is very wind-tolerant. Frost to half hardy; in cold areas protect from strong winds. Needs full sun and fertile, well-drained soil. Propagate by softwood cuttings in summer.
C. buddlejoides. Evergreen, upright shrub. **H** 3m (10ft), **S** 2m (6ft). Half hardy. Has slender, grey shoots and narrowly oblong, glossy, dark green leaves. Bears panicles of star-shaped, yellow flowers in late spring, followed by spherical, blackish-red fruits.
C. cotoneaster illus. p.144.
C. x virgata. Evergreen, upright, dense shrub. **H** and **S** 3m (10ft). Frost hardy. Leaves are oblong and glossy, dark green above, white beneath. Produces star-shaped, yellow flowers in mid-spring, then egg-shaped, bright orange fruits. Makes a good hedge, especially in coastal areas.

CORONILLA

LEGUMINOSAE/PAPILIONACEAE

Genus of deciduous or evergreen shrubs and perennials, grown for their foliage and flowers. Fully to half hardy; in cold areas grow half hardy species against a south- or west-facing wall. Requires full

sun and light, well-drained soil. Propagate by softwood cuttings in summer.
C. glauca. See *C. valentina* subsp. *glauca*.
♀ ***C. valentina* subsp. *glauca***, syn. *C. glauca*, illus. p.195.

CORREA

RUTACEAE

Genus of evergreen shrubs, grown for their flowers. Half hardy to frost tender, min. 3–5°C (37–41°F). Prefers full light or partial shade and fertile, well-drained, neutral to acid soil. Water potted specimens moderately, less when not in flower. Propagate by seed in spring or by semi-ripe cuttings in late summer.
♀ ***C. backhouseana.*** Evergreen, rounded, well-branched shrub. **H** and **S** 2m (6ft). Half hardy. Leaves are oval to elliptic and dark green, with dense, pale buff down beneath. Tubular, pale yellow-green to white flowers appear in spring and intermittently until autumn.
C.* x *harrisii. See *C.* 'Mannii'.
***C.* 'Harrisii'.** See *C.* 'Mannii'.
♀ ***C.* 'Mannii'**, syn. *C.* x *harrisii*, *C.* 'Harrisii'. Evergreen, bushy, slender-stemmed shrub. **H** and **S** 2m (6ft). Frost tender. Has narrowly oval leaves with short hairs beneath. Tubular, scarlet flowers are carried in summer–autumn, sometimes in other seasons.
♀ ***C. pulchella*** illus. p.164.
♀ ***C. reflexa***, syn. *C. speciosa*. Evergreen, bushy, slender-stemmed shrub. **H** and **S** to 2m (6ft). Frost tender. Oval leaves have thick down beneath. Bears tubular, greenish-yellow to crimson or rose flowers, with greenish-white petal tips, in summer–autumn, sometimes in other seasons.
C. speciosa. See *C. reflexa*.

CORTADERIA

GRAMINEAE/POACEAE

See also GRASSES, BAMBOOS, RUSHES and SEDGES.
C. richardii illus. p.284.
C. selloana (Pampas grass). Evergreen, clump-forming, stately, perennial grass. **H** to 2.5m (8ft), **S** 1.2m (4ft). Frost hardy. Has narrow, very sharp-edged, outward-curving leaves, 1.5m (5ft) long. In late summer, erect, plume-like, silvery panicles, up to 60cm (2ft) long, are borne above mid-green leaves. Male and female flowers are produced on separate plants; females, with long, silky hairs, are more decorative.
♀ **'Aureolineata'** (syn. *C.s.* 'Gold Band'), **H** to 2.2m (7ft), is compact, and has leaves with rich yellow margins ageing to dark golden-yellow. **'Gold Band'** see *C.s.* 'Aureolineata'. **'Silver Comet'**, illus. p.285.
♀ **'Sunningdale Silver'** illus. p.284.

CORTUSA

PRIMULACEAE

Genus of clump-forming, spring- and summer-flowering perennials, related to *Primula*, with one-sided racemes of bell-shaped flowers. Fully hardy. Is not suited to hot, dry climates as needs shade and humus-rich, moist soil. Propagate by seed when fresh or by division in autumn.
C. matthioli illus. p.341.

CORYDALIS

PAPAVERACEAE/FUMARIACEAE

Genus of spring- and summer-flowering annuals and tuberous or fibrous-rooted perennials, some of which are evergreen, grown for their tubular, spurred, 2-lipped flowers or for their fern-like leaves. Fully to frost hardy. Needs full sun or partial shade and well-drained soil; some require humus-rich soil and cool growing conditions. Propagate by seed in autumn or by division when dormant: autumn for spring-flowering species, spring for summer-flowering species.
C. ambigua of gardens. See *C. fumariifolia*.
C. bulbosa of gardens. See *C. cava*.
C. cashmeriana. Tuft-forming, fibrous-rooted perennial. **H** 10–25cm (4–10in), **S** 8–10cm (3–4in). Fully hardy. Has divided, semi-erect, basal leaves and, in summer, dense spikes of 2-lipped, brilliant blue flowers. Needs cool, partially shaded, humus-rich, neutral to acid soil. Is good for a rock garden. Dies down in winter.
C. cava, syn. *C. bulbosa* of gardens. Spring-flowering, tuberous perennial. **H** 10–20cm (4–8in), **S** 8–10cm (3–4in). Fully hardy. Leaves are semi-erect, basal and much divided. Carries dense spikes of tubular, dull purple flowers. Dies down in summer.
C. cheilanthifolia illus. p.335.
C. diphylla illus. p.354.
C. fumariifolia, syn. *C. ambigua* of gardens. Tuberous perennial, flowering from spring to early summer. **H** to 15cm (6in), **S** to 10cm (4in). Fully hardy. Stem bears much-divided leaves and a short spike of 2-lipped, azure blue or purplish-blue flowers, with flattened, triangular spurs. Dies down in summer.
C. halleri. See *C. solida*.
C. lutea, syn. *Pseudofumaria lutea*, illus. p.344.
C. nobilis. Perennial with long, fleshy, fibrous roots. **H** and **S** 20–35cm (8–14in). Fully hardy. Bears much-divided leaves on lower part of flower stems, each of which carries a dense spike of long-spurred, pale yellow flowers, with lips tipped green or brown, in early summer.
C. ochroleuca of gardens, syn *Pseudofumaria alba, Pseudofumaria ochroleuca*, illus. p.337.
C. popovii illus. p.349.
C. solida, syn. *C. halleri*. Tuft-forming, tuberous perennial. **H** 10–20cm (4–8in), **S** 8–12cm (3–5in). Fully hardy. Leaves alternate on flower stems, each of which carries a dense spike of dull purplish-red flowers in spring. Dies down in summer.
♀ **'George Baker'** (syn. *C.s.* 'G.P. Baker') illus. p.353.
C. wilsonii illus. p.335.

CORYLOPSIS

HAMAMELIDACEAE

Genus of deciduous shrubs and trees, grown for their fragrant, yellow flowers, which are produced before hazel-like leaves emerge. Fully hardy, but late frosts may damage flowers. Prefers semi-shade and fertile, moist but well-drained, acid soil. Propagate by softwood cuttings in summer or by seed in autumn.
C. glabrescens illus. p.111.
♀ ***C. pauciflora*** illus. p.126.
♀ ***C. sinensis***, syn. *C. willmottiae*. Vigorous, deciduous, spreading, open shrub. **H** and **S** 4m (12ft). Leaves are bright green above, blue-green beneath. Clusters of bell-shaped, pale yellow flowers open from early to mid-spring. **'Spring Purple'** has deep plum-purple, young leaves.
C. spicata. Deciduous, spreading, open shrub. **H** 2m (6ft), **S** 3m (10ft). Bristle-toothed leaves are dull, pale green above, blue-green beneath. Drooping clusters of bell-shaped, pale yellow flowers are borne in mid-spring.
C. willmottiae. See *C. sinensis*.

CORYLUS

Hazel

CORYLACEAE/BETULACEAE

Genus of deciduous trees and shrubs, grown for their habit, catkins and often edible fruits (nuts). Fully hardy. Prefers sun or semi-shade and fertile, well-drained soil. Cut out suckers as they arise. Propagate species by seed in autumn, cultivars by grafting in late summer or by suckers or layering in late autumn to early spring. Mildew may cause defoliation; other fungi and insects may spoil nuts.
C. avellana (Cobnut). ♀ **'Contorta'** (Corkscrew hazel) illus. p.118.
♀ ***C. colurna*** (Turkish hazel). Deciduous, conical tree. **H** 20m (70ft), **S** 7m (22ft). Has broadly oval, strongly toothed, almost lobed, dark green leaves. Long, yellow catkins are borne in late winter. Clusters of nuts are set in fringed husks.
C. maxima (Filbert). Vigorous, deciduous, bushy, open shrub or tree. **H** 6m (20ft), **S** 5m (15ft). Bears oval, toothed, mid green leaves, long, yellow catkins in late winter and edible, egg-shaped, brown nuts.
♀ **'Purpurea'** illus. p.115.

CORYNOCARPUS

CORYNOCARPACEAE

Genus of evergreen trees, grown for their foliage and overall appearance. Frost tender, min. 7–10°C (45–50°F). Needs full light or partial shade and fertile, moisture-retentive but well-drained soil. Water containerized specimens moderately, less when temperatures are low. Pruning is tolerated if necessary. Propagate by seed when ripe or by semi-ripe cuttings in summer.
C. laevigatus illus. p.451.

CORYPHANTHA

CACTACEAE

Genus of perennial cacti with roughly spherical, spiny, green stems. Stems have elongated areoles in grooves running along upper sides of tubercles; many species only show this groove on very old plants. Funnel-shaped flowers are produced in summer, followed by cylindrical, green seed pods. Frost tender, min. 5°C (41°F). Needs a site in full sun with very well-drained soil. Propagate by seed in spring or summer.
C. cornifera, syn. *C. radians*, illus. p.480.
C. radians. See *C. cornifera*.
C. vivipara. See *Escobaria vivipara*.

COSMOS

COMPOSITAE/ASTERACEAE

Genus of summer- and early autumn-flowering annuals and tuberous perennials. Fully hardy to frost tender, min. 5°C (41°F). Needs sun and does best in moist but well-drained soil. In mild areas, tubers of half hardy *C. atrosanguineus* may be overwintered in ground if protected with a deep mulch. Propagate half-hardy species by basal cuttings in spring, annuals by seed in autumn or spring.
C. atrosanguineus, syn. *Bidens atrosanguinea*, illus. p.238. **CHOCAMOCHA ('Thomocha')** illus. p.306.
C. bipinnatus. Upright, bushy annual. **H** to 1.5m (5ft), **S** 45cm (1½ft). Half hardy. Has feathery, mid-green leaves, and, throughout summer, produces solitary, bowl- or saucer-shaped flower heads in white, pink, or crimson, with yellow centres. **'Candy Stripe'**, **H** to 90cm (3ft), has white flower heads, edged and flecked with crimson. **'Sea Shells'**, **H** to 90cm (3ft), produces carmine-red, pink, or white flower heads with tubular florets. **Sensation Series** illus. p.305.
***C. sulphureus* Ladybird Series.** Group of upright, bushy annuals. **H** 30–40cm (12–16in), **S** 20cm (8in). Frost tender. Has feathery, mid-green leaves, and in summer produces clusters of semi-double, bowl-shaped flower heads in yellow, orange, or scarlet, with black centres.

COSTUS

ZINGIBERACEAE

Genus of mostly clump-forming, rhizomatous perennials, grown for their showy, solitary or paired, tubular flowers with basal bracts. Frost tender, min. 18°C (64°F). Grow in a humid atmosphere, out of direct sunlight, in humus-rich soil. Propagate by division in spring. Pot-grown plants may be attacked by red spider mite.
C. speciosus (Malay ginger; illus. p.477). Clump-forming, rhizomatous perennial. **H** 2m (6ft) or more, **S** 1m (3ft). Has narrowly oval, downy leaves, to 25cm (10in) long. Reddish bracts are spine-tipped, each surrounding one white or pink-flushed flower, to 10cm (4in) wide with a broad, yellow-centred lip; flowers are produced intermittently throughout the year.

COTINUS

ANACARDIACEAE

Genus of deciduous shrubs and trees, grown for their foliage, flower heads and autumn colour. Individual flowers are inconspicuous. Fully hardy. Requires a position in full sun or semi-shade, with fertile but not over-rich soil. Purple-leaved forms need full sun to bring out their best colours. Propagate species by softwood or greenwood cuttings in summer or by seed in autumn, cultivars by cuttings only in summer.
C. americanus. See *C. obovatus*.
♀ ***C. coggygria***, syn. *Rhus cotinus* (Smoke tree, Venetian sumach). Deciduous, bushy shrub. **H** and **S** 5m (15ft). Leaves are

rounded or oval and light green, becoming yellow or red in autumn. From late summer, as insignificant fruits develop, masses of tiny flower stalks form showy, pale fawn, later grey, plume-like clusters. **'Flame'** see *C.* 'Flame'. **GOLDEN SPIRIT ('Ancot')** (Golden Smoke Bush), illus. p.116. **'Notcutt's Variety'** illus. p.115. ♀ **'Royal Purple'** has deep pink plumes and deep purplish-red leaves.
♀ ***C.* 'Flame'**, syn. *C. coggygria* 'Flame', illus. p.117
♀ ***C. obovatus***, syn. *C. americanus, Rhus cotinoides*. Vigorous, deciduous, bushy shrub or tree. **H** 10m (30ft), **S** 8m (25ft). Has large, oval leaves that are bronze-pink when young, maturing to mid-green and turning orange, red and purple in autumn.

COTONEASTER

ROSACEAE

Genus of deciduous, semi-evergreen or evergreen shrubs and trees, grown for their foliage, flowers and fruits. Some species make fine specimen plants; others may be used for hedging or ground cover. Fully to frost hardy. Deciduous species and cultivars prefer full sun, but evergreens do well in either sun or semi-shade. All resent waterlogged soil and are particularly useful for dry sites. Propagate species by cuttings in summer or by seed in autumn, hybrids and cultivars by cuttings only, in summer. Take semi-ripe cuttings for evergreens and semi-evergreens, softwood cuttings for deciduous plants. Fireblight is a common problem. ⓘThe seeds may cause mild stomach upset if ingested.
♀ ***C. adpressus.*** Deciduous, arching shrub. **H** 30cm (1ft), **S** 2m (6ft). Fully hardy. Rounded, wavy-edged, dark green leaves redden in autumn. Produces small, 5-petalled, pink flowers in early summer, then spherical, red fruits.
***C.* 'Autumn Fire'.** See *C.* 'Herbstfeuer'.
C. bullatus* 'Firebird'**, syn. *C.* 'Firebird'. Deciduous, bushy, open shrub. **H** and **S** 3m (10ft). Fully hardy. Large, oval, deeply veined, dark green leaves redden in autumn. Small, 5-petalled, white flowers in early summer are followed by masses of spherical, bright red fruits. **var. *macrophyllus see *C. rehderi*.
♀ ***C. cashmiriensis.*** syn. *C. cochleatus* of gardens, *C. microphyllus* var. *cochleatus* of gardens. Evergreen, prostrate shrub. **H** to 45cm (1½ft), **S** 2m (6ft). Has small, oval, notched, dark green leaves. Small, white flowers are produced in late spring, followed by spherical, red fruits.
C. cochleatus of gardens. See *C. cashmiriensis*.
C. congestus. Evergreen, prostrate shrub. **H** 20cm (8in), **S** 2m (6ft). Fully hardy. Forms dense mounds of oval, dull green leaves. Produces small, 5-petalled, pinkish-white flowers in early summer, followed by spherical, bright red fruits. Is excellent for a rock garden.
C. conspicuus, syn. *C.c.* var. *decorus* (illus. p.142). Evergreen, prostrate, arching shrub. **H** 30cm (1ft), **S** 2–3m (6–10ft). Fully hardy. Leaves are oblong, glossy, very dark green. Small, 5-petalled, white flowers in late spring are succeeded by large, spherical, scarlet or orange-red fruits.
***C.* 'Coral Beauty'.** Evergreen, arching, dense shrub. **H** 1m (3ft), **S** 2m (6ft). Fully hardy. Has small, oval, glossy, dark green leaves and, in early summer, produces small, 5-petalled, white flowers. Fruits are spherical and bright orange-red.
♀ ***C.* 'Cornubia'** illus. p.117.
C. dielsianus. Deciduous, arching shrub. **H** and **S** 2.5m (8ft). Fully hardy. Slender shoots are clothed in oval, dark green leaves. Produces small, 5-petalled, pink flowers in early summer, followed by spherical, glossy, red fruits.
C. divaricatus illus. p.122.
***C.* 'Exburiensis'.** Evergreen or semi-evergreen, arching shrub. **H** and **S** 5m (15ft). Frost hardy. Has narrowly lance-shaped, bright green leaves, small, 5-petalled, white flowers, in early summer, and spherical, yellow fruits, sometimes tinged pink later.
***C.* 'Firebird'.** See *C. bullatus* 'Firebird'.
C. franchetii. Evergreen or semi-evergreen, arching shrub. **H** and **S** 3m (10ft). Fully hardy. Oval, grey-green leaves are white beneath. Bears small, 5-petalled, pink-tinged, white flowers in early summer, then a profusion of oblong, bright orange-red fruits. **var. *sternianus*** see *C. sternianus*.
C. frigidus (Tree cotoneaster; illus. p.142). Vigorous, deciduous tree, upright when young, arching when mature. **H** and **S** 10m (30ft). Fully hardy. Has large, broadly oval, wavy-edged, dull green leaves and broad heads of small, 5-petalled, white flowers borne in early summer, followed by large clusters of long-lasting, small, spherical, bright red fruits.
C. glaucophyllus. Evergreen, arching, open shrub. **H** and **S** 3m (10ft). Fully hardy. Leaves are oval, dark green, bluish-white beneath. Produces small, 5-petalled, white flowers in mid-summer, followed by small, spherical, deep red fruits in autumn. **var. *serotinus*** see *C. serotinus*.
***C.* 'Gnom'**, syn. *C.* 'Gnome', *C. salicifolius* 'Gnom'. Evergreen, prostrate shrub. **H** 20cm (8in), **S** 2m (6ft). Fully hardy. Bears narrowly lance-shaped, dark green leaves, small, 5-petalled, white flowers, in early summer, and clusters of small, spherical, red fruits. Makes good ground cover.
***C.* 'Gnome'.** See *C.* 'Gnom'.
***C.* 'Herbstfeuer'**, syn. *C.* 'Autumn Fire'. Evergreen, prostrate or arching shrub. **H** 30cm (1ft), **S** 2m (6ft). Fully hardy. Has lance-shaped, bright green leaves. Small, 5-petalled, white flowers in early summer are followed by spherical, bright red fruits. May be grown as ground cover or as a weeping standard.
♀ ***C. horizontalis*** illus. p.208.
C. hupehensis. Deciduous, arching shrub. **H** 2m (6ft), **S** 3m (10ft). Fully hardy. Oval, bright green leaves become yellow in autumn. Masses of small, 5-petalled, white flowers in late spring are succeeded by large, spherical, bright red fruits.
***C.* 'Hybridus Pendulus'.** Evergreen, prostrate shrub, almost always grown as a weeping standard. **H** 2m (6ft), **S** 1.5m (5ft). Frost hardy. Has oblong, dark green leaves. Small, 5-petalled, white flowers in early summer are followed by spherical, deep red fruits.
C. integrifolius, syn. *C. microphyllus* of gardens Evergreen, spreading, dense shrub. **H** 1m (3ft), **S** 2m (6ft). Fully hardy. Rigid shoots are clothed in small, oval, dark green leaves. Small, 5-petalled, white flowers in late spring are followed by spherical, red fruits.
♀ ***C. lacteus*** illus. p.117.
C. linearifolius, syn. *C. microphyllus* var. *thymifolius* of gardens. Evergreen, prostrate shrub. **H** 60cm (2ft), **S** 2m (6ft). Fully hardy. Rigid branches bear tiny, narrow, blunt-ended, glossy leaves. Produces small, white flowers in late spring, followed by spherical red fruits.
C. microphyllus of gardens. See *C. integrifolius*. **var. *cochleatus*** of gardens see *C. cashmiriensis*.
var. *thymifolius* of gardens see *C. linearifolius*.
C. prostratus of gardens. See *C. rotundifolius*.
C. rehderi, syn. *C. bullatus* var. *macrophyllus*. Deciduous, bushy, open shrub. **H** 5m (15ft), **S** 3m (10ft). Fully hardy. Very large, oval, deeply veined, dark green leaves change to red in autumn. Clusters of small, 5-petalled, pink flowers appear in late spring and early summer, succeeded by spherical, bright red fruits.
♀ ***C.* 'Rothschildianus'.** Evergreen or semi-evergreen, arching shrub. **H** and **S** 5m (15ft). Frost hardy. Has narrowly oval, bright green leaves, small, 5-petalled, white flowers, in early summer, and large clusters of spherical, golden-yellow fruits.
C. rotundifolius, syn. *C. prostratus* of gardens. Evergreen, arching shrub. **H** 1.5m (5ft), **S** 2.5m (8ft). Fully hardy. Has small, oval, glossy, dark green leaves. Produces small, 5-petalled, white flowers in early summer, followed by spherical, deep red fruits.
C. salicifolius (illus. p.142). Vigorous, evergreen, arching shrub. **H** and **S** 5m (15ft). Fully hardy. Has narrowly lance-shaped, dark green leaves. Small, 5-petalled, white flowers, in early summer, are followed by clusters of small, spherical, red fruits. **'Gnom'** see *C.* 'Gnom'.
C. serotinus, syn. *C. glaucophyllus* var. *serotinus*. Evergreen, arching, open shrub. **H** and **S** 6m (20ft). Fully hardy. Has oval, dark green leaves. Small white flowers are borne from mid- to late summer and the fruits last until spring.
♀ ***C. simonsii*** illus. p.143.
***C.* 'Skogsholmen'.** See *C.* x *suecicus* 'Skogholm'.
***C.* x *suecicus* 'Skogholm'**, syn. *C.* 'Skogsholmen'. Evergreen, arching, wide-spreading shrub. **H** 60cm (2ft), **S** 3m (10ft). Fully hardy. Leaves are small, oval and glossy, dark green. Bears small, 5-petalled, white flowers during early summer, then rather sparse, spherical, red fruits. Makes good ground cover.
♀ ***C. sternianus***, syn. *C. franchetii* var. *sternianus*, illus. p.141.
♀ ***C.* x *watereri* 'John Waterer'** (illus. p.142). Vigorous, evergreen or semi-evergreen, arching shrub. **H** and **S** 5m (15ft). Frost hardy. Has lance-shaped, dark green leaves. Bears small, 5-petalled, white flowers, in early summer, and produces a profusion of spherical, red fruits in large clusters.

COTULA

COMPOSITAE/ASTERACEAE

Genus of perennials and a few marginal water plants, most of which are evergreen, grown for their neat foliage and button-like flower heads. Many species are useful for cracks in paving stones, but may be invasive. Fully to frost hardy. Most need a position in full sun, with well-drained soil that is not too dry. Propagate by division in spring.
C. atrata. See *Leptinella atrata*.
C. coronopifolia (Brass buttons). Short-lived, deciduous, perennial, marginal water plant. **H** 15cm (6in), **S** 30cm (12in). Frost hardy. Has fleshy stems, small, lance-shaped, mid-green leaves and, in summer, button-like, yellow flower heads.

COTYLEDON

CRASSULACEAE

Genus of evergreen, succulent shrubs and sub-shrubs, grown for their diverse foliage that ranges from large, oval, grey leaves to small, cylindrical, mid-green leaves. Frost tender, min. 5–7°C (41–5°F). Likes a sunny or partially shaded site and very well-drained soil. Propagate by seed or stem cuttings in spring or summer.
C. cooperi. See *Adromischus cooperi*.
C. orbiculata. Evergreen, upright, succulent shrub. **H** and **S** 50cm (20in) or more. Min. 7°C (45°F). Swollen stem bears thin, oval, mid-green leaves, densely coated in white wax and sometimes red-edged. Flower stems, to 70cm (28in) long, have pendent, tubular, orange flowers in autumn. **var. *oblonga*** (syn. *C. undulata*) has flat, wavy tips to the leaves with bell-shaped orange flowers.
C. paniculata. See *Tylecodon paniculatus*.
C. reticulata. See *Tylecodon reticulatus*.
C. simplicifolia. See *Chiastophyllum oppositifolium*.
***C. tomentosa* subsp. *ladismithensis*.** Evergreen, freely branching, later prostrate, succulent sub-shrub. **H** and **S** 20cm (8in). Frost hardy to min. 5°C (41°F). Has fleshy, green leaves, swollen and blunt at tips and covered with short, golden-brown hairs. Clusters of tubular, brownish-red flowers appear in autumn..
C. undulata. See *C. orbiculata* var. *oblonga*.
C. wallichii. See *Tylecodon wallichii*.

CRAMBE

BRASSICACEAE/CRUCIFERAE

Genus of annuals and perennials, grown for their bold leaves and large sprays of white flowers in summer. Leaf shoots of *C. maritima* (Sea kale) are eaten as a spring vegetable. Fully hardy. Will grow in any well-drained soil; prefers an open position in full sun but tolerates some shade. Propagate by division in spring or by seed in autumn or spring.
♀ ***C. cordifolia*** illus. p.216.
♀ ***C. maritima*** (Sea kale) illus. p.264.

CRASPEDIA

COMPOSITAE/ASTERACEAE

Genus of basal-rosetted, summer-flowering perennials, some of which are best treated as annuals. Half hardy to frost tender, min. 5°C (41°F). Needs a site in sun and well-drained soil. Propagate by seed sown when very fresh in summer.
C. incana. Basal-rosetted perennial. **H** 20–30cm (8–12in), **S** 10cm (4in). Frost tender. Has narrowly oval, basal leaves, with

dense, woolly, white hairs beneath, and smaller leaves on flower stem. In summer, many domed heads of 3–10 tiny, tubular, yellow flowers are produced in large, terminal clusters.

CRASSULA

CRASSULACEAE

Genus of perennial succulents and evergreen, succulent shrubs and sub-shrubs, ranging from 2cm (¾in) high, very succulent-leaved species to 5m (15ft) shrubby types. Most are easy to grow. Frost hardy to frost tender, min. 5–7°C (41–45°F). Most prefer full sun; others like partial shade. Needs very well-drained soil and a little water in winter. Propagate by seed or stem cuttings in spring or autumn.
C. arborescens illus. p.490.
C. argentea of gardens. See *C. ovata.*
C. coccinea. syn. *Rochea coccinea.* Evergreen, erect, succulent shrub. **H** to 60cm (24in), **S** 30cm (12in) or more. Alternate pairs of fleshy, oval to oblong-oval, hairy-margined, dull green leaves, each united at the base, are arranged at right angles in 4 rows up the woody, green stems. Produces umbels of tubular, bright red flowers in summer or autumn.
C. cooperi. See *C. exilis* subsp. *cooperi.*
C. deceptor, syn. *C. deceptrix,* illus. p.488.
C. deceptrix. See *C. deceptor.*
C. exilis subsp. cooperi, syn. *C. cooperi.* Carpeting, perennial succulent. **H** 2cm (¾in), **S** 30cm (12in). Frost tender, min. 7°C (45°F). Has small, spoon- to lance-shaped, light green leaves, pitted with darker green or blackish-green marks. Produces clusters of minute, 5-petalled, white to pale pink flowers in winter.
C. falcata. See *C. perfoliata* var. *minor.*
C. lactea. Prostrate to semi-erect, perennial succulent. **H** 20cm (8in), **S** 1m (3ft). Frost tender, min. 5°C (41°F). Leaves are triangular-oval, glossy and dark green. In winter produces masses of small, 5-petalled, white flowers in terminal clusters. Likes partial shade
C. lycopodioides. See *C. muscosa.*
C. multicava illus. p.484.
C. muscosa, syn. *C. lycopodioides.* Dense, bushy, woody-based, perennial succulent. **H** 15cm (6in), **S** 30cm (12in). Frost tender, min. 5°C (41°F). Bears small, scale-like, neatly overlapping, mid-green leaves arranged in 4 rows around erect stems. In spring, produces tiny, 5-petalled, greenish-yellow flowers. Likes partial shade.
♀ ***C. ovata,*** syn. *C. argentea* of gardens, *C. portulacea,* illus. p.481.
C. perfoliata var. falcata, syn. *C. falcata* (Aeroplane propellor), illus. p.489.
C. portulacea. See *C. ovata.*
C. sarcocaulis illus. p.339.
C. schmidtii illus. p.485.
C. socialis illus. p.480.

+ CRATAEGOMESPILUS

ROSACEAE

Group of grafted, hybrid, deciduous trees *(Crataegus and Mespilus),* grown for their flowers, foliage and fruits. Fully hardy. Requires sun or semi-shade and fertile, well-drained soil. Propagate by grafting in late summer.
+ *C. dardarii* (Bronvaux medlar). **'Jules d'Asnières'** is a deciduous, spreading tree. **H** and **S** 6m (20ft). Has drooping branches and spiny shoots. Variable, oval or deeply lobed, dark green leaves, grey when young, turn orange and yellow in autumn. Clusters of saucer-shaped, white, sometimes rose-tinted, flowers in late spring or early summer are followed by small, rounded, red-brown fruits.

CRATAEGUS

Hawthorn, Thorn

ROSACEAE

Genus of deciduous, or more rarely semi-evergreen, spiny, often spreading trees and shrubs, grown for their clustered, 5-petalled, occasionally double flowers in spring–summer, ornamental fruits and, in some cases, autumn colour. Fully hardy. Prefers full sun but is suitable for most sites and may be grown in any but very wet soil. Is useful for growing in polluted urban areas, exposed sites and coastal gardens. Propagate species by seed in autumn, cultivars by budding in late summer. Fireblight is sometimes a problem. ⓘ The seeds may cause mild stomach upset if ingested.
C. cordata. See *C. phaenopyrum.*
C. crus-galli (Cockspur thorn). Deciduous, flat-topped tree. **H** 8m (25ft), **S** 10m (30ft). Has shoots armed with long, curved thorns and oval, glossy, dark green leaves that turn bright crimson in autumn. Clusters of white flowers, with pink anthers, in late spring are followed by long-lasting, rounded, bright red fruits.
C. crus-galli of gardens. See *C. persimilis* 'Prunifolia'.
C. ellwangeriana. Deciduous, spreading tree. **H** and **S** 6m (20ft). Broadly oval, dark green leaves are shallowly toothed and lobed. Bears clusters of white flowers, with pink anthers, in late spring, followed by rounded, glossy, crimson fruits.
C. flava (Yellow haw) illus. p.80.
C. laciniata of gardens. See *C. orientalis.*
C. laevigata, syn. *C. oxyacantha* of gardens (Hawthorn, May). ♀ **'Paul's Scarlet'** illus. p.84. **'Punicea'** is a deciduous, spreading tree. **H** and **S** 6m (20ft). In late spring and early summer, oval, lobed, toothed, glossy, dark green leaves set off clusters of crimson flowers, which are followed by rounded, red fruits.
♀ ***C. x lavallei* 'Carrierei'.** Vigorous, deciduous, spreading tree. **H** 7m (22ft), **S** 10m (30ft). Oval, glossy, dark green leaves turn red in late autumn. Has clusters of white flowers in late spring, followed by long-lasting, rounded, orange-red fruits.
C. macrosperma var. acutiloba. Deciduous, spreading tree. **H** 6m (20ft), **S** 8m (25ft). Has broad, sharply toothed, dark green leaves. White flowers with red anthers in late spring are followed by bright red fruits in autumn.
C. mollis. Deciduous, spreading tree. **H** 10m (30ft), **S** 12m (40ft). Large, broadly oval, lobed, dark green leaves have white-haired undersides when young. Bears heads of large, white flowers in late spring, followed by short-lived, rounded, red fruits.
C. monogyna (Common hawthorn). Deciduous, round-headed tree. **H** 10m (30ft), **S** 8m (25ft). Has broadly oval, deeply lobed, glossy, dark green leaves. Clusters of fragrant, white flowers are borne from late spring to early summer, followed by rounded, red fruits. Makes a dense hedge. **'Biflora'** (Glastonbury thorn) has flowers and leaves in mild winters as well as in spring.
C. orientalis, syn. *C. laciniata* of gardens, illus. p.80.
C. oxyacantha of gardens. See *C. laevigata.*
C. pedicellata illus. p.90.
♀ ***C. x persimilis* 'Prunifolia',** syn. *C. crus-galli* of gardens, *C.* x *prunifolia.* Deciduous, spreading, thorny tree. **H** 8m (25ft), **S** 10m (30ft). Oval, glossy, dark green leaves turn red or orange in autumn. Has clusters of white flowers, with pink anthers, in early summer, then rounded, dark red fruits.
C. phaenopyrum, syn. *C. cordata* (Washington thorn). Deciduous, round-headed tree. **H** and **S** 10m (30ft). Broadly oval leaves are sharply lobed, glossy and dark green. Clusters of white flowers, with pink anthers, are produced from early to mid-summer, followed by rounded, glossy, red fruits that last through winter.
C. x prunifolia. See *C. persimilis* 'Prunifolia'.
C. tanacetifolia (Tansy-leaved thorn). Deciduous, upright, usually thornless tree. **H** 10m (30ft), **S** 8m (25ft). Has oval to diamond-shaped, deeply cut, grey-green leaves, clusters of fragrant, white flowers, with red anthers, in mid-summer and small, apple-shaped, yellow fruits.

CREMANTHODIUM

COMPOSITAE/ASTERACEAE

Genus of basal-rosetted perennials, grown for their pendent, half-closed, daisy-like flower heads. Is often very difficult to grow in all but very cool areas with snow cover. Dislikes winter wet. Fully to frost hardy. Needs shade and humus-rich, moist but well-drained soil. Propagate by seed when fresh.
C. reniforme. Basal-rosetted perennial. **H** and **S** 20cm (8in). Fully hardy. Leaves are large and kidney-shaped. Stout stems each carry a large, daisy-like, yellow flower head in summer.

CREPIS

Hawk's beard

COMPOSITAE/ASTERACEAE

Genus of summer-flowering annuals, biennials and perennials, some of which are evergreen, with long tap roots and leaves in flat rosettes. Many species are persistent weeds, but some are grown for their many-petalled, dandelion-like flower heads. Fully hardy. Tolerates sun or shade and prefers well-drained soil. Propagate annuals and biennials by seed in autumn, perennials by root cuttings (not from tap root) in late winter, although most species self-seed freely.
C. aurea illus. p.345.
♀ ***C. incana*** (Pink dandelion). Basal-rosetted perennial. **H** 20cm (8in), **S** 10cm (4in). Bears oblong, divided, hairy, greyish-green leaves. Uneven discs of ragged, pink flower heads are produced on stiff stems in summer. Is good for a sunny rock garden or border.
C. rubra. Fairly fast-growing, rosette-forming annual. **H** 30cm (12in), **S** 15cm (6in). Has lance-shaped, serrated leaves. In summer bears dandelion-like, pink, occasionally red or white flower heads.

CRINODENDRON

ELAEOCARPACEAE

Genus of evergreen shrubs and trees, grown for their flowers and foliage. Frost to half hardy. Requires shade or semi-shade, with plant base in cool shade. Soil should be fertile, moist but well-drained, and acid. Propagate by softwood cuttings in summer or by seed in autumn.
♀ ***C. hookerianum*** (Lantern tree), syn. *Tricuspidaria lanceolata,* illus. p.202.
C. patagua illus. p.113.

x *Crinodonna corsii.* See x *Amarcrinum memoria-corsii.*

CRINUM

AMARYLLIDACEAE

Genus of robust bulbs, grown for their often fragrant, funnel-shaped flowers. Frost hardy to frost tender, min. 16°C (61°F). Needs full sun, shelter and rich, well-drained soil. Propagate by offsets in spring or by seed when fresh or in spring. ⓘ All parts may cause severe discomfort if ingested; contact with the sap may irritate skin.
C. americanum. Tuft-forming, spring- and summer-flowering bulb. **H** 40–75cm (16–30in), **S** 60cm (24in). Half hardy. Has 6–10 strap-shaped, semi-erect, basal leaves. Leafless stem bears a head of up to 6 fragrant, long-tubed, white flowers with narrow petals.
C. asiaticum. Clump-forming bulb. **H** 45–60cm (1½–2ft), **S** 60cm–1m (2–3ft). Has strap-shaped, semi-erect, basal, dark green leaves, 1m (3ft) long. Leafless flower stems produce heads of long-tubed, white flowers, with narrow petals, in spring or summer.
C. bulbispermum. syn. *C. longifolium.* Summer-flowering bulb. **H** to 1m (3ft), **S** 60cm (2ft). Half hardy. Leafless flower stem has a head of fragrant, long-tubed, white or pinkish-red flowers with darker red stripes. Bears long, strap-shaped, semi-erect leaves grouped in a tuft on a short stalk.
C. longifolium. See *C. bulbispermum.*
C. macowanii. Autumn-flowering bulb. **H** and **S** 60cm (2ft) or more. Half hardy. Is similar to *C. bulbispermum,* but leaves are wavy-edged.
C. moorei illus. p.383.
♀ ***C. x powellii.*** illus. p.385. ♀ **'Album'** illus. p.383.

CROCOSMIA

Montbretia

IRIDACEAE

Genus of corms, grown for their brightly coloured flowers produced mainly in summer. Forms dense clumps of sword-shaped, erect leaves. Frost hardy. Requires well-drained soil and an open, sunny site. In very cold areas, plant in a sheltered position or lift and store corms over winter. Propagate by division as growth starts in spring.
C. aurea. Tuft-forming, summer-flowering corm. **H** 50–75cm (20–30in),

S 15–20cm (6–8in). Erect, basal leaves are long, narrow and sword-shaped. Carries a loosely branched spike of tubular, orange or yellow flowers, each 3–5cm (1–2in) long and with 6 spreading petals.
***C.* 'Bressingham Blaze'.** Clump-forming, late summer-flowering corm. **H** 75cm (30in), **S** 15–20cm (6–8in). Has sword-shaped, pleated, basal, erect leaves. Branched stem bears widely funnel-shaped, fiery-red flowers.
***C.* 'Citronella'** of gardens. See *C.* 'Golden Fleece'.
***C.* x *crocosmiiflora*.** Robust, sometimes invasive, variable, late summer-flowering corm. **H** 60cm (24in), **S** 8cm (3in). Has erect, sword-shaped, pale green, basal leaves. Produces thin, slightly arching, sometimes branched spikes of funnel-shaped, orange or yellow flowers in summer. **'George Davison'** See *C.* 'George Davison'. **'Honey Angels'** See *C.* 'Honey Angels'. ♀ **'Solfatare'** See *C.* 'Solfatare'.
***C.* 'Emily McKenzie'.** Compact, late summer-flowering corm. **H** to 60cm (24in), **S** 15–20cm (6–8in). Leaves are erect, basal and sword-shaped. Bears a dense spike of widely funnel-shaped, deep orange flowers, each with a dark mahogany throat.
***C.* 'George Davison'** (illus. p.410). Mid- to late summer-flowering corm. **H** 90–120cm (3–4ft), **S** 15cm (6in). Has sword-shaped, erect, pleated, mid-green basal leaves. Produces branched stems bearing large, trumpet-shaped, pale orange-yellow flowers, tinted deeper orange externally.
***C.* 'Golden Dew'.** Late summer-flowering corm. **H** 75cm (30in), **S** 8cm (3in). Has erect, sword-shaped, mid-green, basal leaves. Produces large funnel-shaped, yellow and gold flowers on wiry, dark reddish stems.
***C.* 'Golden Fleece'**, syn. *C.* 'Citronella' of gardens, illus. p.412.
***C.* 'Harlequin'.** Late summer-flowering corm. **H** 90cm (36in), **S** 8cm (3in). Has erect, sword-shaped, mid-green, basal leaves. Well-branched, upright stems bear funnel-shaped, bright yellow flowers with alternate, red and orange outer petals.
***C.* 'Honey Angels'** (illus. p.410). Summer-flowering corm. **H** 75cm (30in), **S** 15cm (6in). Has sword-shaped, erect, pleated, bronzed-green leaves and trumpet-shaped, pale yellow flowers.
***C.* 'Jackanapes'** (illus. p.410). Clump-forming, late summer-flowering corm. **H** 40–60cm (16–24in), **S** 15–20cm (6–8in). Has sword-shaped, erect, basal leaves. Produces striking bicoloured, yellow and orange-red flowers.
***C.* 'John Boots'.** Mid- to late summer-flowering corm. **H** 45cm (18in), **S** 8cm (3in). Has erect, sword-shaped, mid-green, basal leaves. Bears funnel-shaped, golden-yellow flowers.
♀ ***C.* 'Lucifer'** (illus. p.410) . Robust, clump-forming corm. **H** to 1m (3ft), **S** 20–25cm (8–10in) Has sword-shaped, erect, basal, bright green leaves. Bears funnel-shaped, deep rich red flowers in dense, branching spikes in mid-summer.
♀ ***C. masoniorum*.** syn. *C. masonorum* (illus. p.410). Robust, clump-forming corm. **H** to 1.5m (5ft), **S** 30–45cm (1–1½ft). Has erect, basal, deep green leaves, pleated lengthways. Erect, branched stem has a horizontal, upper part, which carries upright, reddish-orange flowers in summer-autumn. ♀ **'Rowallane Yellow'**, **H** 1m (3ft), **S** 8cm (3in) and has upward-facing, funnel-shaped, warm yellow flowers.
***C. masonorum*.** See *C. masoniorum*.
***C. paniculata*,** syn. *Antholyza paniculata*, *Curtonus paniculatus*. Summer-flowering corm. **H** to 1.5m (5ft), **S** 30–45cm (1–1½ft). Has sword-shaped, erect, basal leaves, pleated lengthways. Carries long-tubed, orange flowers on branched stems, which are strongly zig-zag in shape.
♀ ***C.* 'Severn Sunrise'** (illus. p.410). Late summer-flowering corm. **H** 90cm (36in), **S** 8cm (3in). Has erect, sword-shaped, mid-green, basal leaves. Produces tightly clustered, funnel-shaped flowers in shades of salmon, apricot and yellow.
♀ ***C.* 'Solfatare'** (illus. p.410). Mid- to late summer-flowering corm. **H** 65–70cm (26–28in), **S** 15cm (6in). Bears sword-shaped, erect, pleated, bronzed-green leaves and trumpet-shaped pale to mid-yellow flowers.
♀ ***C.* 'Star of the East'** (illus. p.410). Late summer-flowering corm. **H** 70cm (28in), **S** 8in (3in). Has sword-shaped, erect, basal, mid-green leaves. Bears horizontal-facing, funnel-shaped, clear orange flowers, with a paler orange centre, on branched stems.

CROCUS

IRIDACEAE

Genus of mainly spring- or autumn-flowering corms with funnel-shaped to rounded, long-tubed flowers. Has long, very narrow, semi-erect, basal leaves, each with a white line along centre, usually 1–5 per corm. Some autumn-flowering species have no leaves at flowering time, these appearing in winter or spring. Most species are less than 10cm (4in) tall when in flower and have a spread of 2.5–8cm (1–3in). Is ideal for rock gardens and for forcing in bowls for an early indoor display. Fully to frost hardy. Most require well-drained soil and a sunny situation; *C. banaticus* prefers moist soil and semi-shade. Plant 5–6cm (2–2½in) deep, in late summer or early autumn. Propagate in early autumn by seed or division of corm clumps. See also feature panel p.417.
***C.* 'Advance'.** Late winter- to mid-spring-flowering corm. Fully hardy. Funnel-shaped flowers are buttercup yellow inside and paler yellow outside, suffused violet-bronze.
C. aerius of gardens. See *C. biflorus* subsp. *pulchricolor*.
***C. ancyrensis*.** Spring-flowering corm. Frost hardy. Produces up to 7 fragrant, bright orange-yellow flowers, 5–6cm (2–2½in) long.
♀ ***C. angustifolius*,** syn. *C. susianus* (Cloth-of-gold crocus). Spring-flowering corm. Fully hardy. Fragrant flowers are bright golden-yellow, striped or stained bronze outside.
***C. aureus*.** See *C. flavus*.
***C. balansae*.** See *C. olivieri* subsp. *balansae*.
♀ ***C. banaticus*,** syn. *C. iridiflorus*. Autumn-flowering corm. Fully hardy. Usually has one long-tubed, pale violet flower; outer 3 petals are much larger than inner 3. Very narrow, semi-erect, basal leaves, each with a paler line along the centre, appear in spring.
***C. baytopiorum*.** Spring-flowering corm. Frost hardy. Each corm bears 1 or 2 rounded, clear turquoise-blue, slightly darker-veined flowers.
C. biflorus*.** Early spring-flowering corm. Fully hardy. Has narrow, semi-erect, basal leaves, each with a white line along the centre. Bears fragrant, white or purplish-white flowers, with yellow throats, vertically striped purple outside. **subsp. *alexandri has fragrant, deep violet flowers, with white insides. **subsp. *pulchricolor*** (syn. *C. aerius* of gardens) has rich deep blue flowers with golden-yellow centres.
***C.* 'Blue Bird'** (illus. p.417). Late winter- to mid-spring-flowering corm. Fully hardy. Funnel-shaped flowers are white inside with deep yellow throats and violet margined with white outside.
♀ ***C.* 'Blue Pearl'** illus. p.421.
***C. boryi*.** Autumn-flowering corm. Frost hardy. Flowers are ivory-white, sometimes veined or flushed with mauve outside.
***C. cancellatus*.** Autumn-flowering corm. Frost hardy. Slender flowers are pale blue, slightly striped outside. Leaves form after flowering, in spring.
♀ ***C. cartwrightianus*.** Autumn-flowering corm. Frost hardy. Produces leaves at same time as strongly veined, violet or white flowers, each 4–6cm (1½–2½in) across and with 3 long, bright red stigmas, similar to those of *C. sativus*.
♀ ***C. chrysanthus*.** Spring-flowering corm. Fully hardy. Scented flowers are orange-yellow throughout with deeper orange-red stigmas. ♀ ***C.* 'Cream Beauty'** (illus. p.417). Spring-flowering corm. Fully hardy. Scented rich cream flowers, with deep yellow throats, are stained purplish-brown outside at base. Bears very narrow, semi-erect, basal, dark green leaves, each with a white, central line.
***C. cvijicii*.** Spring-flowering corm. Fully hardy. Usually has one funnel-shaped, yellow flower. Produces very narrow, semi-erect, basal leaves, each with a white line along the centre, which scarcely show at flowering time.
***C. dalmaticus*.** Spring-flowering corm. Fully hardy. Very narrow, semi-erect leaves have central, white lines. Bears 1–3 purple-veined, pale violet flowers, with yellow centres, overlaid with silver or yellow outside.
***C.* 'Dorothy'** (illus. p.417). Spring-flowering corm. Fully hardy. Scented flowers are pale lemon-yellow.
***C.* 'Dutch Yellow'.** See *C.* 'Golden Yellow'.
♀ ***C.* 'E.P. Bowles'**, syn. *C.* 'E.A. Bowles', (illus. p.417). Early spring-flowering corm. Fully hardy. Has scented, funnel-shaped, deep yellow flowers, stained bronze near base on outside. Has narrow, semi-erect leaves, each with a central white line. Increases well by offsets.
♀ ***C. etruscus*.** Spring-flowering corm. Frost hardy. Has very narrow, semi-erect, basal, dark green leaves with central, white lines. Bears long-tubed, funnel-shaped, pale purple-blue flowers, washed silver outside, with violet veining. **'Zwanenburg'** (illus. p.417) has pale purple-blue flowers, washed with biscuit-brown and flecked violet outside.
***C.* 'Eyecatcher'** (illus. p.417). Late winter- to mid-spring-flowering corm. Fully hardy. Funnel-shaped, grey-white, yellow-throated flowers have white-edged, deep purple outer segments.
♀ ***C. flavus*,** syn. *C. aureus*. Spring-flowering corm. Fully hardy. Fragrant flowers are bright yellow or orange-yellow throughout; often several flowers are produced together or in quick succession.
***C. gargaricus*.** Spring-flowering corm. Frost hardy. Bears yellow flowers, 4–5cm (1½–2in) long. Increases by stolons. Tolerates slightly damper conditions than most crocuses.
***C.* 'Golden Yellow'**, syn. *C.* 'Dutch Yellow', *C.* x *luteus* 'Golden Yellow'. Very vigorous, clump-forming, spring-flowering corm. Fully hardy. Bears yellow flowers, 8–10cm (3–4in) long and faintly striped outside at bases. Naturalizes well in grass.
♀ ***C. goulimyi*** (illus. p.417). Autumn-flowering corm. Frost hardy. Usually has one long-tubed, pale lilac to pinkish-lilac flower, with a white throat and 3 inner petals usually paler than the 3 outer ones. Leaves and flowers appear together. Needs a warm site.
♀ ***C. hadriaticus*** (illus. p.417). Autumn-flowering corm. Frost hardy. Leaves appear with the white flowers, which usually have yellow throats and may be lilac-feathered at the base.
♀ ***C. imperati*.** Strikingly bicoloured, spring-flowering corm. Frost hardy. Develops 1 or 2 scented, purple flowers, 6–8cm (2½–3in) long, fawn with purple striping outside and with yellow throats. In **'De Jager'**, flowers are rich violet-purple inside and biscuit-coloured with violet feathering outside.
***C. iridiflorus*.** See *C. banaticus*.
C. korolkowii (Celandine crocus). Spring-flowering corm. Fully hardy. Produces up to 20 narrow leaves. Carries fragrant, yellow flowers that are speckled or stained brown or purple outside. When open in sun, petals have glossy surfaces.
♀ ***C. kotschyanus*,** syn. *C. zonatus* (illus. p.417). Autumn-flowering corm. Fully hardy. Pinkish-lilac or purplish-blue flowers have yellow centres and white anthers. Narrow, semi-erect, basal leaves, with white lines along centres, appear in winter-spring. **var. *leucopharynx*** has pale lilac-blue flowers with white centres and white anthers. Leaves appear in winter–spring.
♀ ***C.* 'Ladykiller'.** Late winter- to mid-spring-flowering corm. Fully hardy. Has funnel-shaped flowers, white or pale lilac within and deep violet-purple with white margins outside.
♀ ***C. laevigatus*.** Very variable corm, flowering intermittently for a month or more in autumn or winter depending on the form. Frost hardy. Fragrant flowers are produced with leaves and are usually lilac-purple with bold stripes on outside; inside each has a yellow eye and cream-white anthers.
♀ ***C. longiflorus*.** Autumn-flowering corm. Frost hardy. Produces fragrant, slender, purple flowers, which are striped darker purple outside, at the same time as leaves. Flowers have yellow centres and anthers and red stigmas.
♀ ***C.* x *luteus* 'Golden Yellow'.** See *C.* 'Golden Yellow'.
♀ ***C. malyi*.** Spring-flowering corm. Fully hardy. Has 1 or 2 funnel-shaped, white

flowers with yellow throats, brown or purple tubes and showy, bright orange stigmas. Leaves are very narrow, semi-erect and basal with central, white lines.
♀ ***C. medius.*** Autumn-flowering corm. Frost hardy. Has 1 or 2 funnel-shaped, uniform rich purple flowers, with yellow anthers and red stigmas cut into many thread-like branches. Linear, basal leaves appear in winter–spring, after flowering.
C. minimus. Late spring-flowering corm. Frost hardy. Has very narrow, semi-erect, basal, dark green leaves that have central, white lines. Bears 1 or 2 flowers, purple inside and stained darker violet or sometimes darker striped on outside.
C. niveus. Autumn-flowering corm. Frost hardy. Produces 1 or 2 white or pale lavender flowers, 10–15cm (4–6in) long, with conspicuous, yellow throats. Leaves appear with flowers or just afterwards. Needs a warm, sunny site.
C. nudiflorus (Autumn crocus) Autumn-flowering corm. Fully hardy. Has linear, basal leaves in winter–spring. Usually bears one slender, long-tubed, rich purple flower, with a frilly, bright orange or yellow stigma. Naturalizes in grass.
C. olivieri. Spring-flowering corm. Frost hardy. Bears rounded, bright orange flowers. Flowers of **subsp. *balansae*** (syn. *C. balansae*) are stained or striped bronze-brown outside.
♀ ***C. pulchellus.*** Autumn-flowering corm. Fully hardy. Bears long-tubed, pale lilac-blue flowers with darker veins, conspicuous, yellow throats and white anthers. Leaves are very narrow, semi-erect and basal, with white lines along centres.
C. salzmannii. See *C. serotinus* subsp. *salzmannii*.
C. sativus, syn. *C.s.* var. *cashmirianus* (Saffron crocus). Autumn-flowering corm. Fully hardy. Leaves appear with saucer-shaped, dark-veined, purple flowers, 5–7cm (2–3in) across, each with 3 long, bright red stigmas that yield saffron.
C. serotinus* subsp. *salzmannii, syn. *C. salzmannii*. Autumn-flowering corm. Frost hardy. Lilac-blue flowers, to 10cm (4in) long, sometimes with yellow throats, appear with leaves.
♀ ***C. sieberi.*** Spring-flowering corm. Fully hardy. Has scented white flowers with yellow throats and purple staining outside, either in horizontal bands or vertical stripes. **'Albus'** (syn. *C.s.* 'Bowles' White'), illus. p.427. **subsp. *atticus*** has pale lilac to violet-blue flowers with frilly, orange stigmas. ♀ **'Bowles' White'** see. *C.s.* 'Albus'. ♀ **'Hubert Edelsten'** (illus p.417) has yellow-throated, pale lilac flowers, the outer segments of which are white, tipped, centrally marked and feathered with rich purple. ♀ **subsp. *sublimis* f. *tricolor*** (illus. p.417) has unusual flowers, divided into 3 distinct bands of lilac, white and golden yellow.
♀ ***C.* 'Snow Bunting'** (illus. p.417). Spring-flowering corm. Fully hardy. Fragrant long-tubed, funnel-shaped, white flowers have mustard yellow centres and orange stigmas. Very narrow, semi-erect, basal leaves are dark green with white, central lines.
♀ ***C. speciosus*** (illus. p.417). Autumn-flowering corm. Fully hardy. Produces lilac-blue to deep purple-blue flowers, usually with a network of darker veins and a much-divided, orange stigma. Leaves appear in winter-spring. **'Conqueror'** (illus. p.417) has large, deep sky-blue flowers. **'Oxonian'** produces dark violet-blue flowers with prominent darker veining externally.
C. susianus. See *C. angustifolius*.
♀ ***C. tommasinianus.*** Spring-flowering corm. **H** to 10cm (4in), **S** 2.5–8cm (1–3in). Fully hardy. Bears slender, long-tubed, funnel-shaped flowers, varying in colour from lilac or purple to violet, sometimes with darker tips to petals and occasionally silver outside. Naturalizes well. **f. *albus*** has white flowers. **'Ruby Giant'** (illus. p.417) bears clusters of large rich reddish-purple flowers.**'Whitewell Purple'** has slender, reddish-purple flowers.
♀ ***C. tournefortii.*** Autumn-flowering corm. Frost hardy. Leaves appear at same time as 1 or 2 pale lilac-blue flowers that open flattish to reveal a much-divided, orange stigma and white anthers. Requires a warm, sunny site.
C. vernus (Dutch crocus, Spring crocus). Spring-flowering corm. **H** to 10cm (4in), **S** 2.5–8cm (1–3in). Fully hardy. Variable in colour from white to purple or violet and often striped and feathered. Stigmas are large, frilly and orange or yellow. Is suitable for naturalizing. **subsp. *albiflorus*** has small, white flowers, sometimes slightly marked or striped purple. **'Jeanne d'Arc'** has white flowers with a deep purple base. **'Pickwick'** (illus. p.417) has pale, greyish-white flowers, with dark violet stripes and purplish bases. **'Prinses Juliana'** has mid-purple flowers with darker veins. **'Purpureus Grandiflorus'** has shiny, violet-purple flowers. **'Queen of the Blues'** (illus. p.417) has rich blue flowers that have higher margins and a darker base. **'Remembrance'** (illus. p.417) has shiny, violet flowers. **'Vanguard'**, a very early cultivar, has bluish-lilac flowers, paler and silvered outside.
♀ ***C.* 'Zephyr'.** Autumn-flowering corm. Fully hardy. Bears very pale silver-blue flowers, veined darker, each with a conspicuous yellow throat and white anthers.
C. zonatus. See *C. kotschyanus*.
♀ ***C.* 'Zwanenburg Bronze'**, syn. *C. Chrysanthus* 'Zwanenberg Bronze', (illus. p.417). Spring-flowering corm. **H** to 10cm (4in), **S** 2.5–8cm (1–3in). Fully hardy. Has bicoloured flowers, rich yellow inside, stained bronze outside.

CROSSANDRA

ACANTHACEAE

Genus of evergreen perennials, sub-shrubs and shrubs, grown mainly for their flowers. Frost tender, min. 15°C (59°F). Needs partial shade or full light and humus-rich, well-drained soil. Water potted plants freely when in full growth, moderately at other times. For a strong branch system, cut back flowered growth by at least half in late winter. Propagate by seed in spring or by greenwood cuttings in late spring or summer. Whitefly may be troublesome.
♀ ***C. infundibuliformis***, syn. *C. undulifolia*. Evergreen, erect to spreading, soft-stemmed shrub or sub-shrub. **H** to 1m (3ft), **S** 60cm (2ft). Has oval to lance-shaped, glossy, deep green leaves and, in summer–autumn or earlier, fan-shaped, salmon-red flowers in conical spikes, each 10cm (4in) long.
C. nilotica. Evergreen, upright to spreading, leafy shrub. **H** 30–60cm (12–24in), **S** to 35cm (14in). Has oval, pointed, rich green leaves. Small tubular, apricot to pale brick-red flowers with spreading petals are carried in short spikes from spring to autumn.
C. undulifolia. See *C. infundibuliformis*.

CROTALARIA

LEGUMINOSAE/PAPILIONACEAE

Genus of evergreen shrubs, perennials and annuals, grown mainly for their flowers. Frost tender, min. 10–15°C (50–59°F). Requires full light and well-drained soil. Water containerized specimens freely when in full growth, less at other times. For a more compact habit, cut back old stems by half after flowering. Propagate by seed in spring or by semi-ripe cuttings in summer. Red spider mite may be troublesome.
C. agatiflora illus. p.459.

CRUSEA

RUBIACEAE

Genus of annuals and perennials grown for their showy flowers. Frost to half hardy. Needs semi- to full shade in moist but well-drained, humus-rich soil. Propagate by seed in spring, by division in spring or summer or by cuttings in summer.
C. coccinea illus. p.268.

CRYPTANTHUS

BROMELIACEAE

Genus of evergreen, rosette forming perennials, grown for their attractive foliage. Frost tender, min. 10–13°C (50–55°F). Needs semi-shade and well-drained soil, preferably mixed with sphagnum moss. Water moderately in the growing season, sparingly at other times. Propagate by offsets or suckers in late spring.
C. acaulis (Green earth star). Evergreen, clump-forming, basal-rosetted perennial. **H** to 10cm (4in), **S** 15–30cm (6–12in). Loose, flat rosettes of lance-shaped to narrowly triangular, wavy, mid-green leaves have serrated edges. A cluster of fragrant, tubular, white flowers appears from each rosette centre, usually in summer. **'Ruber'** has red-flushed foliage.
♀ ***C. bivittatus***. Evergreen, clump-forming, basal-rosetted perennial. **H** to 15cm (6in), **S** 25–38cm (10–15in). Loose, flat rosettes of broadly lance-shaped, wavy, mid- to yellowish-green leaves have finely toothed margins and are striped lengthways with 2 coppery-fawn to buff bands. Small clusters of tubular, white flowers appear from centre of each rosette, usually in summer. ♀ **'Pink Starlight'** (illus. p.471). Vigorous, evergreen, spreading, basal-rosetted perennial. **H** 20cm (8in) or more, **S** 35cm (14in) or more. Strap-shaped, wavy, finely toothed, arching, green leaves are striped yellowish-green, and heavily suffused deep pink. Clusters of tubular, white flowers occasionally appear from each rosette centre in summer.
C. bromelioides (Rainbow star). Evergreen, spreading, basal-rosetted perennial. **H** 20cm (8in) or more, **S** 35cm (14in) or more. Strap-shaped, wavy, finely toothed, arching, mid- to bright green leaves are produced in dense rosettes. Occasionally bears clusters of tubular, white flowers in centre of each rosette, usually in summer. ♀ **'Tricolor'** has carmine-suffused, white-striped foliage.
♀ ***C. zonatus.*** Evergreen, basal-rosetted perennial. **H** 10–15cm (4–6in), **S** 30–40cm (12–16in). Forms loose, flat rosettes of strap-shaped, wavy, finely toothed, sepia-green leaves, cross-banded with grey-buff and with greyish-white scales beneath. A cluster of tubular, white flowers opens in each rosette, usually in summer. **'Zebrinus'** produces silver-banded foliage.

x CRYPTBERGIA

BROMELIACEAE

Hybrid genus (*Cryptanthus* x *Billbergia*) of evergreen, rosette-forming perennials, grown for their foliage. Frost tender, min. 8–10°C (46–50°F). Needs semi-shade and fertile, well-drained soil. Water moderately during growing season, sparingly in winter. Propagate by suckers or offsets in spring.
x *C.* 'Rubra'. Evergreen, clump-forming, basal-rosetted perennial. **H** and **S** 15–30cm (6–12in). Loose rosettes comprise strap-shaped, pointed, bronze-red leaves. Rarely, small, tubular, white flowers are produced in rosette centres in summer.

CRYPTOCORYNE

ARACEAE

Genus of semi-evergreen, perennial, submerged water plants and marsh plants, grown for their foliage. Is suitable for tropical aquariums. Frost tender, min. 10°C (50°F). Needs sun and rich soil. Remove fading foliage, and divide plants periodically. Propagate by division in spring or summer.
***C. beckettii* var. *ciliata*.** See *C. ciliata*.
C. ciliata, syn. *C. beckettii* var. *ciliata*. Semi-evergreen, perennial, submerged water plant. **S** 15cm (6in). Lance-shaped, deep green leaves have paler midribs. Small, hooded, fringed, purplish spathes appear intermittently at base of plant.
C. spiralis. Semi-evergreen, perennial, submerged water plant. **S** 15cm (6in). Small, hooded, purplish spathes are borne intermittently among lance-shaped, purplish-green leaves.

CRYPTOGRAMMA

ADIANTACEAE/CRYPTOGRAMMACEAE

Genus of deciduous or semi-evergreen ferns. Fully to frost hardy. Needs partial shade and moist but well-drained, neutral or acid soil. Remove fading fronds. Propagate by spores in late summer.
C. crispa illus. p.293.

CRYPTOMERIA

TAXODIACEAE

See also CONIFERS.
♀ ***C. japonica*** (Japanese cedar). Fast-growing, columnar to conical, open conifer. **H** 15–20m (50–70ft), **S** 5–8m

(15–25ft). Fully hardy. Has soft, fibrous, red-brown bark, needle-like, incurved, mid- to dark green leaves, spirally arranged, and globular, brown cones.
🏆 **'Bandai-sugi'**, **H** and **S** 2m (6ft), makes an irregularly rounded shrub with foliage that turns bronze in winter. **'Cristata'** illus. p.104.
🏆 **'Elegans Compacta'**, **H** 2–5m (6–15ft), **S** 2m (6ft), is a dwarf form. **'Pyramidata'** illus. p.104.
'Sekkan-sugi', **H** 10m (30ft), **S** 3–4m (10–12ft), has semi-pendulous branches and light golden-cream foliage. **'Spiralis'**, **H** and **S** 2–3m (6–10ft), forms a tree or dense shrub with spirally twisted foliage and is very slow-growing.
🏆 **'Vilmoriniana'**, **H** and **S** 1m (3ft), forms a globular mound of yellow-green foliage that turns bronze in winter.

CRYPTOSTEGIA

ASCLEPIADACEAE/APOCYNACEAE

Genus of evergreen, twining climbers, grown for their flowers. Frost tender, min. 15°C (59°F). Provide fertile, well-drained soil and full light. Water regularly, less when not in full growth. Stems require support. Spur back previous season's old flowering stems in spring. Propagate by seed in spring or by softwood cuttings in summer.
C. grandiflora (Rubber vine). Strong-growing, evergreen, twining climber. **H** 10m (30ft) or more. Has thick-textured, oval, glossy leaves. Funnel-shaped, reddish to lilac-purple flowers appear in summer. ⚠ Stems yield a poisonous latex that may cause severe discomfort if ingested.

Cryptostemma calendulaceum. See *Arctotheca calendula.*

CTENANTHE

MARANTACEAE

Genus of evergreen, bushy perennials, grown for their ornamental foliage.Frost tender, min. 15°C (59°F).Requires a humid atmosphere, even temperature and partial shade. Prefers moist but well-drained soil and soft water; do not allow to dry completely. Propagate by division in spring.
🏆 ***C. lubbersiana.*** Evergreen, clump-forming, bushy perennial. **H** and **S** to 75cm (30in) or more. Long-stalked, lance-shaped, sharply pointed leaves are 25cm (10in) long, green above, irregularly marked and striped with pale yellowish-green, and pale greenish-yellow below. Intermittently bears dense, one-sided spikes of many small, 3-petalled, white flowers.
C. oppenheimiana, syn. *Calathea oppenheimiana*. Robust, evergreen, bushy perennial. **H** and **S** 1m (3ft) or more. Lance-shaped, leathery leaves are over 30cm (1ft) long, red below, dark green above with pale green or white bands along veins on either side of midribs. Dense, one-sided spikes of many small, 3-petalled, white flowers are borne intermittently.
🏆 **'Tricolor'** illus. p.465.

Cudrania tricuspidata. See *Maclura tricuspidata.*

CUNNINGHAMIA

TAXODIACEAE

See also CONIFERS.
C. lanceolata (Chinese fir) illus. p.100.

CUNONIA

CUNONIACEAE

Genus of evergreen, summer-flowering trees, grown for their foliage, flowers and overall appearance. Frost tender, min. 10°C (50°F). Requires full light and well-drained soil. Water potted plants moderately, less in winter. Pruning is tolerated. Propagate by seed in spring or by semi-ripe cuttings in summer.
C. capensis (African red alder). Moderately fast-growing, evergreen, rounded tree. **H** and **S** 10–15m (30–50ft), more in rich soil. Has lustrous, dark green leaves, divided into pairs of lance-shaped, serrated leaflets. Tiny, long-stamened, white flowers appear in dense, bottlebrush-like spikes, each 10–13cm (4–5in) long, in late summer.

CUPHEA

LYTHRACEAE

Genus of annuals, perennials and evergreen shrubs and sub-shrubs, grown for their flowers. Half hardy to frost tender, min. 2–7°C (36–45°F).Prefers full sun and fertile, well-drained soil. Water freely when in full growth, moderately at other times. Remove flowered shoots after flowering to maintain a bushy habit. Propagate by seed in spring or by greenwood cuttings in spring or summer. Red spider mite may be troublesome.
C. cyanea illus. p.162.
🏆 ***C. ignea***, syn. *C. platycentra*, illus. p.308.
C. platycentra. See *C. ignea*.
***C. x purpurea* 'Firecracker'** illus. p.306.

x CUPRESSOCYPARIS

CUPRESSACEAE

⚠ Contact with the foliage may aggravate skin allergies. See also CONIFERS.
x *C. leylandii* 'Castlewellan' illus. p.99.
'Haggerston Grey' illus. p.95.
'Harlequin' is a very fast-growing, columnar conifer with a conical tip. **H** 25–35m (80–120ft), **S** 4–5m (12–15ft). Fully hardy. Grey-green foliage, with patches of clear ivory-white, is held in plume-like sprays. **'Leighton Green'** bears flattened sprays of paired, scale-like, rich green leaves and globular, glossy, dark brown cones. 🏆 **'Robinson's Gold'**, **H** 15–20m (50–70ft), has bright golden leaves.

CUPRESSUS

Cypress

CUPRESSACEAE

See also CONIFERS.
C. arizonica* var. *glabra, syn. *C. glabra* (Arizona cypress, Smooth cypress). Conical conifer. **H** 10–15m (30–50ft), **S** 3–5m (10–15ft). Fully hardy. Has smooth, flaking, reddish-purple bark and upright, spirally arranged sprays of scale-like, aromatic, glaucous blue-grey leaves that are flecked with white resin. Globular cones are chocolate-brown.
🏆 ***C. cashmeriana***, syn. *C. torulosa* 'Cashmeriana', illus. p.95.
C. glabra. See *C. arizonica* var. *glabra*.
C. lusitanica (Cedar of Goa, Mexican cypress). Conical conifer. **H** 20m (70ft), **S** 5–8m (15–25ft). Fully hardy. Has fissured bark and spreading, spirally arranged sprays of scale-like, aromatic, grey-green leaves. Bears small, globular cones that are glaucous blue when young, ripening to glossy brown.
C. macrocarpa (Monterey cypress). Fast-growing, evergreen conifer, columnar when young, often wide-spreading with age. **H** 20m (70ft), **S** 6–25m (20–80ft). Fully hardy. Bark is shallowly fissured. Scale-like, aromatic, bright to dark green leaves are borne in plume-like sprays. Globular cones are glossy and brown.
🏆 **'Goldcrest'** illus. p.104.
***C. sempervirens* 'Stricta'** (Italian cypress), illus. p.102.
***C. torulosa* 'Cashmeriana'.** See *C. cashmeriana.*

CURCUMA

Hidden ginger, Siam tulip

ZINGIBERACEAE

Genus of herbaceous perennials, grown for their patterned leaves and showy bracts atop the flower spikes. The lower bracts form pouches from which the flowers emerge, the upper bracts are without flowers, but larger and brightly coloured or white. Half hardy to frost tender, min. 5°C (41°F). Grow in humus-rich, moist but well-drained soil in partial shade. Keep completely dry in winter. Propagate by division of the rhizome in spring.
C. cordata. See *C. zedoaria*.
C. petiolata (illus p.477). Herbaceous, clump-forming perennial. **H** 120cm (48in), **S** 50cm (20in). Frost tender. Narrowly ovate, strongly ribbed, mid-green leaves are to 60cm (24in) long. In summer produces a spike, to 35cm (14in) long, of lemon-yellow flowers and bright pink upper bracts.
C. zedoaria, syn. *C. cordata* (illus. p.477). Herbaceous, clump-forming perennial. **H** 150cm (60in), **S** 50cm (20in). Frost tender. Has ovate, ribbed, mid-green leaves, to 90cm (36in) long, with dark red stripes on upper sides. In mid- to late spring bears a spike, 5–8cm (2–3in) long, of yellow flowers and pink to purple-red upper bracts.

Curtonus paniculatus. See *Crocosmia paniculata*.

CYANANTHUS

CAMPANULACEAE

Genus of late summer-flowering perennials, suitable for rock gardens, walls and troughs. Fully hardy. Needs partial shade and humus-rich, moist but well-drained soil. Propagate by softwood cuttings in spring or by seed in autumn.
🏆 ***C. lobatus.*** Prostrate perennial. **H** 2cm (¾in), **S** 20cm (8in). Branched stems are clothed in small, wedge-shaped, dull green leaves. In late summer, each stem carries a funnel-shaped, blue flower. **f. *albus*** illus. p.359.
🏆 ***C. microphyllus*** illus. p.369.

CYANOTIS

COMMELINACEAE

Genus of evergreen, creeping perennials, grown for their foliage. Frost tender, min. 10–15°C (50–59°F).Prefers a position in sun or partial shade, with humus-rich, well-drained soil. Propagate by tip cuttings from spring to autumn.
🏆 ***C. kewensis*** (Teddy-bear vine). Evergreen perennial forming rosettes with trailing stems. **H** 5cm (2in), **S** 30cm (12in). Clasping the stem are 2 rows of overlapping, oval leaves, to 5cm (2in) long, dark green above, purple with velvety, brown hairs below. Stalkless clusters of 3 petalled, purplish-pink flowers are produced in axils of leaf-like bracts almost all year round.
🏆 ***C. somaliensis*** (Pussy ears). Evergreen, creeping perennial. **H** 5cm (2in), **S** indefinite. Small, narrow, glossy, dark green leaves with white hairs surround stems. Has purplish-blue flowers in leaf axils in winter-spring.

CYATHEA

SYN. ALSOPHILA, SPHAEROPTERIS

CYATHEACEAE

Genus of evergreen tree ferns, grown for their foliage and overall appearance. Frost tender, min. 10–13°C (50–55°F). Needs a humid atmosphere, sun or partial shade and humus-rich, moisture-retentive but well-drained soil. Water potted plants freely in summer, moderately at other times. Propagate by spores in spring.
C. australis (Australian tree fern), syn. *Alsophila australis* illus. p.452.
C. medullaris (Black tree fern, Mamaku). Evergreen, upright tree fern with a slender, black trunk. **H** 7–16m (22–52ft), **S** 6–12m (20–40ft). Has arching fronds, each to 7m (22ft) long, divided into small, oblong, glossy, dark green leaflets, paler beneath.

Cyathodes. See *Leucopogon*.

CYBISTAX

BIGNONIACEAE

Genus of deciduous trees, grown for their spring flowers and for shade.Frost tender, min. 16–18°C (61–4°F).Needs full light and fertile, moisture-retentive but well-drained soil. Will not bloom when confined to a container.Young plants may be pruned to shape when leafless; otherwise pruning is not required. Propagate by seed or air-layering in spring or by semi-ripe cuttings in summer.
C. donnell-smithii, syn. *Tabebuia donnell-smithii*. Fairly fast-growing, deciduous, rounded tree. **H** and **S** 10m (30ft) or more. Leaves have 5–7 oval, 5–20cm (2–8in) long leaflets. Bell-shaped, 5-lobed, bright yellow flowers appear in spring before the leaves, often in great profusion.

CYCAS

CYCADACEAE

Genus of slow-growing, evergreen, woody-stemmed perennials, grown for their palm-like appearance. Frost tender,

min. 10–13°C (50–55°F). Prefers a position in full light and humus-rich, well-drained soil. Water potted specimens moderately, less when not in full growth. Propagate in spring by seed or suckers taken from mature plants.
♀ ***C. revoluta*** illus. p.457.

CYCLAMEN

PRIMULACEAE

Genus of tuberous perennials, some of which are occasionally evergreen, grown for their pendent flowers, each with 5 reflexed petals and a mouth often stained with a darker colour. Fully hardy to frost tender, min. 5–7°C (41–5°F). Grow in sun or partial shade, and in humus-rich, well-drained soil. If grown in containers, in summer dry off tubers of all except *C. purpurascens* (which is evergreen and flowers in summer); repot in autumn and water to restart growth. Propagate by seed in late summer or autumn. *C. persicum* and its cultivars are susceptible to black root rot. ⓘ All parts may cause severe discomfort if ingested.
C. africanum illus. p.424.
C. alpinum, syn. *C. trochopteranthum*. Spring-flowering, tuberous perennial. **H** 10cm (4in), **S** 5–10cm (2–4in). Fully hardy. Bears rounded or heart-shaped leaves, zoned with silver. Produces musty-scented, pale carmine or white flowers, stained dark carmine at mouths; petals are twisted and propeller-shaped.
C. caucasicum. See *C. coum* subsp. *caucasicum*.
♀ ***C. cilicium*** illus. p.426.
♀ ***C. coum*** illus. p.429. **f. *albissimum*** (syn. *C.c.* 'Album') illus. p.428. **subsp. *caucasicum*** (syn. *C. caucasicum*) is a winter flowering, tuberous perennial. **H** to 10cm (4in), **S** 5–10cm (2–4in). Frost hardy. Has heart-shaped, silver-patterned leaves and produces a succession of bright carmine flowers, each with a dark stain at the mouth. ♀ **Pewter Group** illus. p.429. **Pewter Group 'Maurice Dryden'** illus. p.428.
C. creticum. Spring-flowering, tuberous perennial. **H** to 10cm (4in), **S** 5–10cm (2–4in). Frost hardy. Produces heart-shaped, dark green leaves, sometimes silver-patterned, and fragrant, white flowers.
C. cyprium. Autumn-flowering, tuberous perennial. **H** to 10cm (4in), **S** 5–10cm (2–4in). Frost hardy. Heart-shaped, toothed, dark green leaves, patterned with lighter green, appear with or just after fragrant, white flowers, each with carmine marks around the mouth.
C. europaeum. See *C. purpurascens*.
C. fatrense. See *C. purpurascens*.
C. graecum illus. p.425.
♀ ***C. hederifolium***, syn. *C. neapolitanum*, illus. p.426. **f. *albiflorum*** illus. p.424.
C. libanoticum illus. p.418.
♀ ***C. mirabile*** illus. p.425.
C. neapolitanum. See *C. hederifolium*.
C. persicum illus. p.429. **'Esmeralda'** is a winter-flowering tuberous perennial. **H** 10–20cm (4–8in), **S** 15–20cm (6–8in). Has heart-shaped, silver-patterned leaves and broad-petalled, carmine-red flowers. **Halios Series, H** 30cm (12in), **S** 18cm (7in). Frost tender. Blunt-toothed, heart-shaped, dark green leaves have silver marbling. Produces a succession of white, pink, scarlet, lilac or purple flowers in late summer or autumn. **Kaori Series**, **H** 10–20cm (4–8in), **S** 15–20cm (6–8in). Produces fragrant flowers, 4cm (1½in) long, in a wide range of colours in winter. **'Pearl Wave'**, **H** 10–20cm (4–8in), **S** 10–15cm (4–6in), has leaves marked light and dark green and silver. Produces fragrant, slender, deep pink flowers in winter and spring, with 5–6cm (2–2½in) long, frilly-edged petals. **'Renown'**, **H** 10–20cm (4–8in), **S** 10–15cm (4–6in), has silver-green leaves, each with a central, dark green mark. Carries fragrant, slender, scarlet flowers, 5–6cm (2–2½in) long, in winter and spring. **'Scentsation'**, **H** 15cm (6in), bears strongly scented flowers in pink, carmine-red or crimson from early winter to early spring.
♀ ***C. pseudibericum.*** Spring-flowering, tuberous perennial. **H** to 10cm (4in), **S** 10–15cm (4–6in). Frost hardy. Has heart-shaped, toothed leaves patterned with silvery- and dark green zones. Flowers are deep carmine-purple with darker, basal stains and white-rimmed mouths.
♀ ***C. purpurascens***, syn. *C. europaeum*, *C. fatrense*, illus. p.422.
♀ ***C. repandum.*** Spring-flowering, tuberous perennial. **H** to 10cm (4in), **S** 10–15cm (4–6in). Frost hardy. Has heart-shaped, jagged-toothed, dark green leaves with lighter patterns. Bears fragrant, slender, reddish-purple flowers.
C. rohlfsianum illus. p.426.
C. trochopteranthum. See *C. alpinum*.

Cyclobothra lutea. See *Calochortus barbatus*.

CYDONIA

ROSACEAE

Genus of one species of deciduous, spring-flowering tree, grown for its flowers and fruits, which are used as a flavouring and for preserves. Fully hardy, but grow against a south- or west-facing wall in cold areas. Requires sun and fertile, well-drained soil. Propagate species by seed in autumn, cultivars by softwood cuttings in summer. Mildew, brown rot and fireblight are sometimes a problem.
C. oblonga (Quince). **'Lusitanica'** is a deciduous, spreading tree. **H** and **S** 5m (15ft). Broadly oval, dark green leaves are grey-felted beneath. Has a profusion of large, 5-petalled, pale pink flowers in late spring, followed by fragrant, pear-shaped, deep yellow fruits. ♀ **'Vranja'** illus. p.88.
C. sinensis. See *Pseudocydonia sinensis*.

Cylindropuntia tunicata. See *Opuntia tunicata*.

CYMBALARIA

SCROPHULARIACEAE

Genus of annuals, biennials and short-lived perennials, related to *Linaria*, grown for their tiny flowers on slender stems. Is good for rock gardens, walls and banks, but may be invasive. Fully hardy. Needs shade and moist soil.Propagate by seed in autumn. Self-seeds readily.
C. muralis (Ivy-leaved toadflax, Kenilworth ivy). Spreading perennial. **H** 5cm (2in), **S** 12cm (5in). Bears small, ivy-shaped, pale green leaves and, in summer, masses of tiny, tubular, spurred, sometimes purple-tinted, white flowers.

CYMBIDIUM

ORCHIDACEAE

ⓘ Contact with the foliage may aggravate skin allergies. See also ORCHIDS.
***C.* Caithness Ice gx 'Trinity'** (illus. p.467). Evergreen, epiphytic orchid for a cool greenhouse. **H** 75cm (30in). Sprays of green flowers, 10cm (4in) across, each with a red-marked, white lip, are borne in early spring. Has narrowly oval leaves, to 60cm (24in) long. Needs a position in semi-shade in summer.
***C.* Christmas Angel gx 'Cooksbridge Sunburst'.** Evergreen, epiphytic orchid for a cool greenhouse. **H** 75cm (30in). In winter produces sprays of yellow flowers, 10cm (4in) across and with red-spotted lips. Narrowly oval leaves are up to 60cm (24in) long. Grow in semi-shade in summer.
C. devonianum. Evergreen, epiphytic orchid for a cool greenhouse. **H** 60cm (24in). In early summer bears pendent spikes of 2.5cm (1in) wide, olive-green flowers overlaid with purple and with purple lips. Has broadly oval, semi-rigid leaves, to 30cm (12in) long. Needs semi-shade in summer.
C. elegans, syn. *Cyperorchis elegans* (illus. p.467). Evergreen, epiphytic orchid for a cool greenhouse. **H** 75cm (30in). Dense, pendent sprays of fragrant, tubular, yellow flowers, 4cm (1½in) across, appear in early summer. Has narrowly oval leaves, to 60cm (24in) long. Requires semi-shade in summer.
C. grandiflorum. See *C. hookerianum*.
C. hookerianum, syn. *C. grandiflorum*. Evergreen, epiphytic orchid for a cool greenhouse. **H** 75cm (30in). In winter produces sprays of deep green flowers, 8cm (3in) across, each with a hairy, brown-spotted, creamy-white lip. Narrowly oval leaves are up to 60cm (24in) long. Grow in semi-shade in summer.
♀ ***C.* King's Loch gx 'Cooksbridge'.** Evergreen, epiphytic orchid for a cool greenhouse. **H** 60cm (24in). Sprays of green flowers, 5cm (2in) across and each with a purple-marked, white lip, open in spring. Leaves are narrowly oval and up to 60cm (24in) long. Provide semi-shade in summer.
***C.* Pontac gx 'Mont Millais'.** Evergreen, epiphytic orchid for a cool greenhouse. **H** 75cm (30in). Bears sprays of 8cm (3in) wide, rich deep red flowers, edged and marked with white, in spring. Has narrowly oval leaves, to 60cm (24in) long. Grow in semi-shade in summer.
***C.* Portelet Bay gx** (illus. p.466). Evergreen, epiphytic orchid for a cool greenhouse. **H** 75cm (30in). Red-lipped, white flowers, 10cm (4in) across, are borne in sprays in spring. Has narrowly oval leaves, to 60cm (24in) long. Provide semi-shade in summer.
***C.* Strathbraan gx.** Evergreen, epiphytic orchid for a cool greenhouse. **H** 60cm (24in). In spring produces slightly arching spikes of off-white flowers, 5cm (2in) across, with red marks on each lip. Leaves are narrowly oval, to 60cm (24in) long. Requires semi-shade in summer.
***C.* Strathkanaid gx** (illus. p.467). Evergreen, epiphytic orchid for a cool greenhouse. **H** 60cm (24in). In spring bears arching spikes of deep red flowers, 5cm (2in) across. Lips are white, marked deep red. Narrowly oval leaves are up to 60cm (24in) long. Requires semi-shade in summer.
♀ ***C.* Strathdon gx 'Cooksbridge Noel'.** Evergreen, epiphytic orchid for a cool greenhouse. **H** 1m (3ft). Sprays of rich pink flowers, 5cm (2in) across, with red-spotted, yellow-tinged lips, appear in winter. Has narrowly oval leaves, up to 60cm (24in) long. Needs semi-shade in summer.
C. tracyanum. Evergreen, epiphytic orchid for a cool greenhouse. **H** 75cm (30in). In autumn produces long spikes of fragrant, olive-green flowers, 8cm (3in) across, overlaid with reddish dots and dashes. Has narrowly oval leaves, to 60cm (24in) long. Grow in semi-shade in summer.

CYNARA

COMPOSITAE/ASTERACEAE

Genus of architectural perennials, grown for their large heads of flowers.The plant described is grown both as a vegetable and as a decorative border plant. Frost hardy. Requires sun and fertile, well-drained soil. Propagate by seed or division in spring.
♀ ***C. cardunculus*** (Cardoon) illus. p.216.

CYNOGLOSSUM

Hound's tongue

BORAGINACEAE

Genus of annuals, biennials and perennials, grown for their long flowering period from late spring to early autumn. Fully hardy. Needs sun and fertile but not over-rich soil.Propagate by division in spring or by seed in autumn or spring.
***C. amabile* 'Firmament'** illus. p.315.

CYPELLA

IRIDACEAE

Genus of summer-flowering bulbs, grown for their short-lived, iris-like flowers that have 3 large, spreading outer petals and 3 small, incurved inner ones. Half hardy; may survive outdoors in cool areas if planted near a sunny wall. Needs full sun and well-drained soil. Lift bulbs when dormant; partially dry off in winter. Propagate by seed in spring.
C. herbertii illus. p.412.

Cyperorchis elegans. See *Cymbidium elegans*.

CYPERUS

CYPERACEAE

See also GRASSES, BAMBOOS, RUSHES and SEDGES.
C. albostriatus, syn. *C. diffusus* of gardens, *C. elegans* of gardens. Evergreen, perennial sedge. **H** 60cm (24in), **S** indefinite. Frost tender, min. 7°C (45°F). Stem has prominently veined, mid-green leaves and up to 8 leaf-like, green bracts surrounding a well-branched umbel of brown spikelets, produced in summer.

'Variegatus' has white-striped leaves and bracts.
C. alternifolius of gardens. See *C. involucratus*.
C. diffusus of gardens. See *C. albostriatus*.
C. elegans of gardens. See *C. albostriatus*.
C. flabelliformis. See *C. involucratus*.
🏆 ***C. involucratus***, syn. *C. alternifolius* of gardens, *C. flabelliformis*, illus. p.478.
C. isocladus of gardens. See *C. papyrus* 'Nanus'.
C. longus (Galingale). Deciduous, spreading, perennial sedge. **H** 1.5m (5ft), **S** indefinite. Fully hardy. Bears rough-edged, glossy, dark green leaves and, in summer, attractive umbels of narrow, flattened, milk-chocolate-coloured spikelets that keep their colour well. Tolerates its roots in water.
🏆 ***C. papyrus*** (Paper reed, Papyrus) illus. p.478. 🏆 **'Nanus'** (syn. *C. isocladus* of gardens) is an evergreen, spreading, perennial sedge with a red rhizome; it is a dwarf variant of the species, sometimes considered distinct, and is often grown under misapplied names. **H** 80cm (32in), **S** indefinite. Frost tender, min. 7–10°C (45–50°F). Triangular, leafless stems bear umbels of brown spikelets on 8–10cm (3–4in) stalks in summer.

Cyphomandra betacea. See *Solanum betaceum*.
Cyphomandra crassicaulis. See *Solanum betaceum*.

CYPHOSTEMMA

VITACEAE

Genus of deciduous, perennial succulents with very thick, fleshy, almost woody caudices and branches.Leaf undersides often exude droplets of resin. Frost tender, min. 10°C (50°F).Needs full sun and very well-drained soil. Keep dry in winter. Is difficult to grow. Propagate by seed in spring.
C. bainesii. syn. *Cissus bainesii*. Deciduous, perennial succulent. **H** and **S** 60cm (24in). Has a thick, swollen, bottle-shaped trunk, often unbranched, covered in peeling, papery, yellow bark. Fleshy, silvery-green leaves, with deeply serrated edges, are divided into 3 oval leaflets, silver-haired when young. Bears tiny, cup-shaped, yellow-green flowers in summer, then grape-like, red fruits.
C. juttae, syn. *Cissus juttae*, illus. p.487.

CYPRIPEDIUM

Slipper orchid

ORCHIDACEAE

See also ORCHIDS.
C. acaule (Moccasin flower). Deciduous, terrestrial orchid. **H** to 40cm (16in). Fully hardy. Yellowish-green or purple flowers, 4–6cm (1½–2½in) long, each with a pouched, pink or white lip, are borne singly in spring–summer. Leaves are broadly lance-shaped, pleated and 10–30cm (4–12in) long. Does best in partial shade.
C. calceolus (Lady's slipper orchid, Yellow lady's slipper orchid). Deciduous, terrestrial orchid. **H** 75cm (30in). Fully hardy. In spring–summer bears paired or solitary yellow-pouched, purple flowers, 3–7cm (1¼–3in) long. Broadly lance-shaped leaves, 5–20cm (2–8in) long, are arranged in a spiral up stem. Stems and leaves are slightly hairy. Prefers partial shade. **var. *pubescens*** see *C. pubescens*.
C. macranthon. See *C. macranthos*.
C. macranthos, syn. *C. macranthon*. Deciduous, terrestrial orchid. **H** 50cm (20in). Fully hardy. Pouched, violet or purplish-red flowers, 4–6cm (1½–2½in) long, usually borne singly, open in spring–summer. Stems and oval leaves, 4–7cm (1½–3in) long, are slightly hairy. Prefers partial shade.
C. pubescens, syn. *C. calceolus* var. *pubescens*. Deciduous, terrestrial orchid. **H** 75cm (30in). Fully hardy. Has large, purple-marked, greenish-yellow flowers, 8–10cm (3–4in) long, in spring–summer. Large, broadly lance-shaped leaves, 15–20cm (6–8in) long, are arranged in a spiral up stem. Stems and leaves are hairy. Prefers partial shade.
C. reginae (Showy lady's slipper orchid; illus. p.466). Deciduous, terrestrial orchid. **H** to 1m (3ft). Fully hardy. In spring–summer, white flowers, 2–5cm (¾–2in) long, each with a pouched, white-streaked, pink lip, are borne singly or in groups of 2 or 3. Stem and oval leaves, 10–25cm (4–10in) long, are hairy. Does best in partial shade.
***C.* Ulla Silkens gx** illus. p.256.

CYRILLA

CYRILLACEAE

Genus of one very variable species of deciduous or evergreen shrub, grown for its flowers in late summer and autumn. Fully to half hardy. Prefers full sun and needs peaty, acid soil.Propagate by semi-ripe cuttings in summer.
C. racemiflora (Leatherwood). Deciduous or evergreen, bushy shrub. **H** and **S** 1.2m (4ft). Oblong, glossy, dark green leaves redden in autumn. Slender spires of small, 5-petalled, white flowers are borne in late summer and autumn.

CYRTANTHUS

AMARYLLIDACEAE

Genus of bulbs with brightly coloured flowers, usually in summer. Frost hardy to frost tender, min. 15°C (59°F).Requires full sun and free-draining, light soil. In frost-free areas may flower for much of the year. Plant in spring. Water freely in the growing season. Propagate by seed or offsets in spring.
C. brachyscyphus, syn. *C. parviflorus*, illus. p.423.
C. breviflorus, syn. *Anoiganthus breviflorus, A. luteus*. Clump-forming, summer-flowering bulb. **H** 20–30cm (8–12in), **S** 8–10cm (3–4in). Frost hardy. Has narrowly strap-shaped, semi-erect, basal leaves. Leafless flower stem bears up to 6 funnel-shaped, yellow flowers, 2–3cm (¾–1¼in) long. Prefers a warm, sheltered situation.
🏆 ***C. elatus***, syn. *C. purpureus, Vallota speciosa*. Clump-forming, summer-flowering bulb. **H** 30–50cm (12–20in), **S** 12–15cm (5–6in). Half hardy. Bears widely strap-shaped, semi-erect, basal, bright green leaves. Stout stem produces a head of up to 5 widely funnel-shaped, scarlet flowers, 8–10cm (3–4in) long. Makes an excellent house plant.
C. mackenii. Clump-forming, summer-flowering bulb. **H** 30–40cm (12–16in), **S** 8–10cm (3–4in). Half hardy. Bears strap-shaped, semi-erect, basal leaves. Leafless stems each carry an umbel of up to 10 fragrant, tubular, white flowers, 5cm (2in) long and slightly curved. **var. *cooperi*** illus. p.412.
C. obliquus. Clump-forming, summer-flowering bulb. **H** 20–60cm (8–24in), **S** 12–15cm (5–6in). Half hardy. Bears widely strap-shaped, semi-erect, basal, greyish-green leaves, twisted lengthways. Carries a head of up to 12 pendent, tubular, red-and-yellow flowers, each 7cm (3in) long.
C. parviflorus. See *C. brachyscyphus*.
C. purpureus. See *C. elatus*.
C. sanguineus. Clump-forming, summer-flowering bulb. **H** 30–50cm (12–20in), **S** 12–15cm (5–6in). Half hardy. Has strap-shaped, semi-erect, basal, bright green leaves. Stout stem bears 1 or 2 long-tubed, scarlet flowers, 8–10cm (3–4in) long.

CYRTOMIUM

DRYOPTERIDACEAE

Genus of evergreen ferns. Fully to half hardy. Does best in semi-shade and humus-rich, moist soil. Remove fading fronds. Propagate by division in spring or summer or by spores in summer.
🏆 ***C. falcatum*** (Fishtail fern, Holly fern) illus. p.291.
🏆 ***C. fortunei***, syn. *Phanerophlebia fortunei*. Evergreen fern. **H** 60cm (24in), **S** 40cm (16in). Fully hardy. Has erect, dull, pale green fronds, 30–60cm (12–24in) long, with broadly sickle-shaped pinnae, 2.5–5cm (1–2in) long.

CYSTOPTERIS

WOODSIACEAE

Genus of deciduous ferns, suitable for rock gardens. Fully hardy. Does best in semi-shade and in soil that is never allowed to dry out. Remove fronds as they fade. Propagate by division in spring, by spores in summer or by bulbils when available.
C. bulbifera (Berry bladder fern). Deciduous fern. **H** 15cm (6in), **S** 23cm (9in). Broadly lance-shaped, much-divided, dainty, pale green fronds produce tiny bulbils along their length. Propagate by bulbils as soon as mature.
C. dickieana. Deciduous fern. **H** 15cm (6in), **S** 23cm (9in). Has broadly lance-shaped, divided, delicate, pale green fronds, with oblong, blunt, indented pinnae, that arch downwards.
C. fragilis (Brittle bladder fern). Deciduous fern. **H** 15cm (6in), **S** 23cm (9in). Broadly lance-shaped, pale green fronds are delicate and much divided into oblong, pointed, indented pinnae.

CYTISUS

Broom

LEGUMINOSAE/PAPILIONACEAE

Genus of deciduous or evergreen shrubs, grown for their abundant, pea-like flowers. Fully to half hardy. Prefers full sun and fertile, but not over-rich, well-drained soil. Resents being transplanted. Propagate species by semi-ripe cuttings in summer or by seed in autumn, hybrids and cultivars by semi-ripe cuttings in late summer. ⓘ All parts, especially the seeds, may cause mild stomach upset if ingested.
C. albus. See *Chamaecytisus albus*.
C. ardoinii. See *C. ardoinoi*.
🏆 ***C. ardoinoi.*** syn. *C. ardoinii*, illus. p.372.
🏆 ***C. battandieri*** (Moroccan broom, Pineapple broom), syn. *Argyrocytisus battandieri*, illus. p.116.
🏆 ***C.* x *beanii*** illus. p.335.
C. canariensis of gardens. See *Genista* x *spachiana*.
C. demissus. See *Chamaecytisus demissus*.
***C.* 'Firefly'.** Deciduous, bushy shrub with slender, arching shoots. **H** and **S** 1.5–2m (5–6ft). Fully hardy. Small, mid-green leaves are oblong and have 3 tiny leaflets. Produces masses of yellow flowers, marked with red, from late spring to early summer.
🏆 ***C.* x *kewensis.*** Deciduous, arching shrub. **H** 30cm (1ft), **S** to 2m (6ft). Fully hardy. Has leaves, each composed of 3 tiny leaflets, along downy stems. In late spring bears creamy-white flowers. Is good for a bank or large rock garden.
C. leucanthus. See *Chamaecytisus albus*.
C. nigricans, syn. *Lembotropis nigricans*, illus. p.160.
🏆 ***C.* x *praecox* 'Allgold'** (Broom) illus. p.148. 🏆 **'Warminster'** (Warminster broom), illus. p.148.
C. purpureus. See *Chamaecytisus purpureus*.
C. racemosus of gardens. See *Genista* x *spachiana*.
C. scoparius (Common broom).
🏆 **f. *andreanus*** (Common broom), illus. p.162. **subsp. *maritimus***, syn. *C.s.* var. *prostratus*, is a deciduous, prostrate shrub forming dense mounds of interlocking shoots. **H** 20cm (8in), **S** 1.2–2m (4–6ft). Fully hardy. Small, grey-green leaves usually have 3 oblong leaflets, but may be reduced to a single leaflet. Has masses of golden-yellow flowers in late spring and early summer. **var. *prostratus*** see *C.s.* subsp. *maritimus*.
C.* x *spachianus. See *Genista* x *spachiana*.
C. supinus. See *Chamaecytisus supinus*.
***C.* 'Windlesham Ruby'.** Deciduous, bushy shrub with slender, arching shoots. **H** and **S** 1.5–2m (5–6ft). Fully hardy. Small, mid-green leaves have 3 oblong leaflets. Large, rich red flowers are borne in profusion in late spring and early summer.
🏆 ***C.* 'Zeelandia'.** Deciduous, bushy shrub with slender, arching shoots. **H** and **S** 1.5–2m (5–6ft). Fully hardy. Small, mid-green leaves have 3 oblong leaflets. Has masses of bicoloured, creamy-white and lilac-pink flowers from late spring to early summer.

DABOECIA

ERICACEAE

See also HEATHERS.

D. azorica. Evergreen, compact shrub. **H** to 15cm (6in), **S** to 60cm (24in). Half hardy. Lance-shaped leaves are dark green above, silver-grey beneath. Urn- to bell-shaped flowers are vivid red and open in late spring or early summer.

D. cantabrica (St Dabeoc's heath). Evergreen, straggling shrub. **H** to 45cm (18in), **S** 60cm (24in). Frost hardy; top growth may be damaged by frost and cold winds, but plants respond well to hard pruning and produce new growth from base. Leaves are lance-shaped to oval, dark green above, silver-grey beneath. Bears bell- to urn-shaped, single or double, white, purple or mauve flowers from late spring to mid-autumn. 🏆 **'Bicolor'** (illus. p.166) bears white, purple and striped flowers on the same plant. **'Praegerae'**, **H** 35cm (14in), has glowing deep pink flowers. **'Snowdrift'** has bright green foliage and long racemes of large, white flowers.

D. subsp. scotica, syn. *D. cantabrica* subsp. *scotica*. Evergreen, compact shrub. **H** to 15cm (6in), **S** to 60cm (2ft). Frost hardy. Lance-shaped to oval leaves are dark green above, silver-grey beneath. Bears bell- to urn-shaped, white, purple or mauve flowers from late spring to mid-autumn. 🏆 **'Jack Drake'**, **H** 20cm (8in), has small, dark green leaves and ruby-coloured flowers. 🏆 **'Silverwells'** has small, bright green leaves and large, white flowers. 🏆 **'William Buchanan'**, **H** 45cm (18in), is a vigorous cultivar with dark green leaves and deep purple flowers.

DACTYLIS

GRAMINEAE/POACEAE

See also GRASSES, BAMBOOS, RUSHES and SEDGES.

D. glomerata (Cock's-foot, Orchard grass). **'Variegata'** is an evergreen, tuft-forming, perennial grass. **H** 1m (3ft), **S** 20–25cm (8–10in). Fully hardy. Silver-striped, red-green leaves arise from tufted rootstock. In summer bears panicles of densely clustered, awned, purplish-green spikelets.

DACTYLORHIZA

ORCHIDACEAE

See also ORCHIDS.

🏆 ***D. elata***, syn. *Orchis elata*. Deciduous, terrestrial orchid. **H** 1.1m (3½ft). Frost hardy. Spikes of pink or purple flowers, 1–2cm (½–¾in) long, open in spring–summer. Lance-shaped leaves, 15–25cm (6–10in) long, are spotted with brownish-purple and arranged spirally on stem. Requires shade outdoors; keep pot plants semi-shaded in summer.

🏆 ***D. foliosa***, syn. *D. maderensis*, *Orchis maderensis*, illus. p.265.

D. maderensis. See *D. foliosa*.

DAHLIA

COMPOSITAE/ASTERACEAE

Genus of bushy, summer- and autumn-flowering, tuberous perennials, grown as bedding plants or for their flower heads, which are good for cutting or exhibition. Dwarf forms are used for mass-planting and are also suitable for containers. Half hardy. Needs a sunny position and well-drained soil. All apart from dwarf forms require staking. After flowering, lift tubers and store in a frost-free place; replant once all frost danger has passed. In frost-free areas, plants may be left in ground as normal herbaceous perennials, but they benefit from regular propagation to maintain vigour. Propagate dwarf forms by seed sown under glass in late winter, others in spring by seed, basal shoot cuttings or division of tubers. Dahlias may be subject to attack by aphids, red spider mite and thrips. In recent years, powdery mildew has become a problem in certain areas, and spraying is essential. Dahlias also succumb quickly to virus infection. See also feature panel pp.396–98.

Border dahlias

Prolific and long-flowering, various species of *Dahlia* have been hybridized and, with constant breeding and selection, have developed into many forms and have a wide colour range (although there is no blue). Shoots may be stopped, or pinched out, to promote vigorous growth and a bushy shape. Spread measurements depend on the amount of stopping carried out and the time at which it is done: early stopping encourages a broader shape, stopping later in the growing season results in a taller plant with much less spread, even in the same cultivar. Leaves are generally mid-green and divided into oval leaflets, some with rounded tips and some with toothed margins. Each flower head is referred to horticulturally as a flower, even though it does in fact comprise a large number of individual flowers. This horticultural usage has been followed in the descriptions below. All forms with flower heads to 15cm (6in) across are suitable for cutting; those suitable for exhibition are so noted.

Groups and flower sizes

Dahlias are divided into groups, according to the size and type of their flower heads, although the latter may vary in colour and shape depending on soil and weather conditions. The groups are: (1) single; (2) anemone; (3) collerette; (4) water-lily; (5) decorative; (6) ball; (7) pompon; (8) cactus; (9) semi-cactus; (10) miscellaneous; (11) fimbriated; (12) single orchid; (13) double orchid. For illustrations and descriptions see p.396. Certain groups have been subdivided; flower sizes are as follows:

Groups 4, 5, 8 and 9

A – giant-flowered; usually over 25cm (10in) in diameter. B – large-flowered, usually 20–25cm (8–10in) in diameter. C – medium-flowered; usually 15–20cm (6–8in) in diameter. D – small-flowered; usually 10–15cm (4–6in) in diameter. E – miniature-flowered; usually not exceeding 10cm (4in) in diameter.

Group 6

A – small ball dahlias; usually 10–15cm (4–6in) in diameter. B – miniature ball dahlias; usually 5–10cm (2–4in) in diameter.

Group 7

Pompon dahlias; not exceeding 5cm (2in) in diameter.

***D.* 'Akita'** (illus. p.398). Miscellaneous dahlia. **H** 1.2m (4ft), **S** 60cm (2ft). In summer and autumn produces dark crimson to red flowers, to 13cm (5in) across, with yellow centres. The reverses of the petals are tipped white.

🏆 ***D.* 'Alva's Supreme'** (illus. p.398). Giant-flowered decorative dahlia. **H** 1.2m (4ft), **S** 60cm (2ft). Produces yellow flowers in summer–autumn. Is suitable for exhibition.

***D.* 'Anniversary Ball'**, syn. *D.* 'Brookfield Enid'. Miniature ball dahlia. **H** 1m (3ft), **S** 60cm (2ft). Produces lilac and pink flowers in summer–autumn.

***D.* 'Appetiser'**. Small-flowered semi-cactus dahlia. **H** 1.2m (4ft), **S** 60cm (2ft). Produces yellow-and-pink flowers in summer–autumn.

***D.* 'Arabian Night'** (illus. p.397) Small-flowered decorative dahlia. **H** 1.2m (4ft), **S** 50cm (½ft). Has dark green leaves. Double, dark burgundy-red flowers are borne in summer–autumn.

***D.* 'Aranka'**. Collerette dahlia. **H** 1.2m (4ft), **S** 60cm (2ft). Produces flowers, 7–10cm (3–4in) across, with white-tipped, dark pink outer petals, white inner petals and yellow centres, in summer–autumn.

***D.* 'Autumn Fairy'**. Miniature-flowered, semi-cactus dahlia. **H** 40cm (16in), **S** 30cm (12in). Soft orange flowers, with darker centres, are produced from mid-summer to autumn.

***D.* 'Avoca Cree'**. Small-flowered semi-cactus dahlia. **H** 1.5m (5ft), **S** 60cm (2ft). Produces masses of bright orange flowers in summer–autumn. Is good for cutting.

***D.* 'Avoca Kiowa'**. Small-flowered semi-cactus dahlia. **H** 1.2m (4ft), **S** 60cm (2ft). Produces masses of lavender-tipped, pale yellow flowers in summer–autumn. Is good for cutting.

***D.* 'Barry Williams'**. Medium-flowered decorative dahlia. **H** 1.2m (4ft), **S** 60cm (2ft). Bears pink-and-yellow flowers in summer–autumn.

***D.* 'Berwick Wood'** (illus. p.397). Medium-flowered decorative dahlia. **H** 1.3m (4½ft), **S** 60cm (2ft). In summer and autumn produces dark-centred, purple flowers on strong stems.

***D.* 'Bicentenary'**. Medium-flowered decorative dahlia. **H** 1.2m (4ft), **S** 60cm (2ft). In summer and autumn produces dark orange flowers, fading to pale orange at the tips. Is good for cutting.

***D.* 'Biddenham Sunset'** (illus. p.398). Small-flowered decorative dahlia. **H** 1.1m (3½ft), **S** 60cm (2ft). Orange-red flowers are borne in mid-summer and autumn.

***D.* 'Bishop of Auckland'** (illus. p.397). Single dahlia. **H** 80cm (32in), **S** 45cm (18in). Produces matt blackish-green leaves and single, open-centred, dusky-red flowers from mid-summer to autumn.

🏆 ***D.* 'Bishop of Llandaff'** (illus. p.398). Miscellaneous dahlia. **H** 1m (3ft), **S** 45cm (18in). Has bronze-green leaves and single, open-centred, dark red flowers, 78mm (3in) across, in summer–autumn. It is excellent as a bedding plant.

***D.* 'Bishop of York'** (illus. p.398). Single dahlia. **H** 80cm (32in), **S** 45cm (18in). Produces dark purple leaves and single, open-centred, orange-blushed, golden flowers from mid-summer to autumn.

***D.* 'B. J. Beauty'** (illus. p.396). Medium-flowered decorative dahlia. **H** 1.2m (4ft), **S** 60cm (2ft). Double, white flowers are borne on strong stems in summer–autumn.

***D.* 'Black Narcissus'** (illus. p.398). Medium-flowered semi-cactus dahlia. **H** 1.5m (5ft), **S** 60cm (2ft). Produces intensely dark red blooms in summer–autumn.

***D.* 'Brian's Dream'** (illus. p.397). Miniature-flowered decorative dahlia. **H** 1–1.2m (3–4ft), **S** 60cm (2ft). Produces creamy-white flowers with the tips of the petals suffused purplish-pink, in summer and autumn.

***D.* 'Brookfield Enid'**. See *D.* 'Anniversary Ball'.

***D.* 'Butterball'**. Miniature-flowered decorative dahlia. **H** 60cm (2ft), **S** 30cm (1ft). Produces bright yellow flowers in early summer.

***D.* 'Café au Lait'** (illus. p.396). Giant-flowered decorative dahlia. **H** 90cm (36in), **S** 60cm (24in). Cream flowers that merge into pale peach in the centres are borne from mid-summer to autumn.

***D.* 'Cameo'**. Small-flowered water-lily dahlia. **H** 75cm (30in), **S** 45cm (18in). Cream flowers with a yellow base appear from mid-summer to autumn.

🏆 ***D.* 'Candy Cupid'**. Miniature ball dahlia. **H** 1.1m (3½ft), **S** 60cm (2ft). In summer and autumn bears lavender-pink flowers that are good for exhibition.

***D.* 'Carolina Moon'** (illus. p.397). Small-flowered decorative dahlia. **H** 1.2m (4ft), **S** 60cm (2ft). Lilac-edged, white flowers are produced from mid-summer to autumn.

🏆 ***D.* 'Charlie Dimmock'** (illus. p.398). Small-flowered water-lily dahlia. **H** 1.6m (5½ft), **S** 60cm (2ft). Produces apricot flowers on a pale yellow ground, during summer and autumn.

***D.* 'Chat Noir'**. Medium-flowered semi-cactus dahlia. **H** 1m (3ft), **S** 60cm (2ft). Produces deep reddish-black flowers from mid-summer to autumn.

***D.* 'Cherokee Beauty'**. Giant-flowered decorative dahlia. **H** 1.3m (4½ft), **S** 60–80cm (24–32in). In summer–autumn has pink flowers.

🏆 ***D.* 'Cherwell Skylark'**. Small-flowered semi-cactus dahlia. **H** 1m (3ft), **S** 50–60cm (20–24in). Bears orange-flushed, salmon-pink blooms in summer and autumn.

***D.* 'Chimborazo'** (illus. p.398). Collerette dahlia. **H** 1.1m (3½ft), **S** 60cm (2ft). Leaves are glossy, dark green. Has 102mm (4in) wide flowers, with red, outer petals and yellow, inner petals, in summer–autumn. Flowers are good for exhibition.

🏆 ***D.* 'Clair de Lune'**. Collerette dahlia. **H** 1.1m (3½ft), **S** 60cm (2ft). Has 102mm (4in) wide flowers, with lemon-yellow, outer petals and paler yellow, inner petals, in summer–autumn. Is good for exhibition.

D. coccinea (illus. p.397). Tuberous-rooted herbaceous perennial. **H** 2–3m (6–10ft), **S** 1–2m (3–6ft). From summer to

D

late autumn produces sprays of single, yellow, orange-red, maroon or purple-red flowers, 5–8cm (2–3in) across. Is a parent of many garden dahlias.
***D.* 'Coltness Gem'.** Description dahlia. **H** and **S** 45cm (18in). Has deeply lobed leaves and daisy-like, single flower heads in many colours throughout summer until autumn frosts..
***D.* 'Comet'** (illus. p.398). Anemone dahlia. **H** 1.1m (3½ft), **S** 60cm (2ft). Leaves are glossy, dark green. Dark red flowers, 10–15cm (4–6in) across, are produced in summer–autumn.
***D.* 'Cornel'** (illus. p.397). Small-flowered ball dahlia. **H** 1.2m (4ft), **S** 60cm (2ft). Deep maroon-red flowers are produced from mid-summer to autumn.
***D.* 'Cottesmore'.** Medium-flowered water-lily dahlia. **H** 1.1m (3½ft), **S** 60cm (2ft). Produces purplish-pink flowers, with yellow shading at the petal bases, in summer and autumn.
***D.* 'Currant Cream'.** Small ball dahlia. **H** 1.2m (4ft), **S** 60cm (2ft). In summer and autumn produces dark pink flowers with the pink-and-white petal bases. Is good for cutting.
***D.* Dahlietta Series 'Surprise Kelly'** illus. p.327.
***D.* 'Dancing Queen'.** Small-flowered semi-cactus dahlia. **H** 1.1m (3½ft), **S** 60cm (2ft). In summer and autumn produces pink flowers, with deeper pink centres. Petals are primrose-yellow at the bases.
***D.* 'Dandy'** illus. p.327.
***D.* 'Davenport Sunlight'.** Medium-flowered semi-cactus dahlia. **H** 1.2m (4ft), **S** 60cm (2ft). Has bright yellow flowers in summer and autumn. Is good for exhibition.
***D.* 'Deborah's Kiwi'.** Small-flowered cactus dahlia. **H** 1.1m (3½ft), **S** 60cm (2ft). Produces pink flowers, with white bases to the petals, during summer and autumn.
***D.* 'Demi Schneider'.** Collerette dahlia. **H** 1.5m (5ft), **S** 60cm (2ft). In summer and autumn produces single, red flowers, to 14cm (5½in) across, with yellow centres.
***D.* 'Downham Royal'.** Miniature-flowered ball dahlia. **H** 1.2m (4ft), **S** 60cm (2ft). Produces deep claret-red flowers from mid-summer to autumn.
***D.* 'Dutch Triumph'.** Large-flowered water-lily dahlia. **H** 1.1m (3½ft), **S** 60cm (2ft). Bears yellow-pink flowers in summer–autumn.
***D.* 'East Anglian'.** Small-flowered decorative dahlia. **H** 1m (3ft), **S** 60cm (2ft). Has orange-yellow flowers in summer–autumn.
***D.* 'Easter Sunday'.** Collerette dahlia. **H** 1m (3ft), **S** 60cm (2ft). Leaves are glossy, dark green. Produces 102mm (4in) wide flowers, with white, inner and outer petals and dark yellow centres, in summer–autumn. Is good for exhibition.
🏆 ***D.* 'Ellen Huston'** (illus. p.398) Dwarf bedding dahlia. **H** 40cm (16in), **S** 45cm (18in). Has dark bronzed leaves and produces rich orange flowers from mid-summer to autumn.
***D.* 'Embrace'.** Small-flowered cactus dahlia. **H** 1.1m (3½ft), **S** 60cm (2ft). Pale orange flowers are borne from mid-summer to autumn.
***D.* 'Eveline'** (illus. p.396). Small-flowered decorative dahlia. **H** 1m (3ft), **S** 60cm (2ft). White flowers, with a touch of purple at the centres and petal tips, are produced from mid-summer to autumn.
🏆 ***D.* 'Fascination'.** Dwarf miscellaneous dahlia. **H** 45cm (18in), **S** 30cm (12in). Has single, light purple flowers, 78mm (3in) across, in summer–autumn. Is useful for bedding.
***D.* 'Franz Kafka'** (illus. p.397). Miniature-flowered pompon dahlia. **H** 80cm (32in), **S** 55cm (22in). Produces lilac flowers from mid-summer to autumn.
🏆 ***D.* 'Fusion'.** Small-flowered decorative dahlia. **H** 1m (3ft), **S** 60cm (2ft). In summer and autumn produces white flowers, the outer petals flushed pale pink, the inner petals veined purple-violet. Has bronze-tinged, dark green foliage.
🏆 ***D.* 'Gallery Art Deco'.** Miniature-flowered, decorative dahlia. **H** 30–45cm (12–18in), **S** 20cm (8in). Produces dark green leaves and bears double, red-centred, deep orange flowers, 10cm (4in) across, from mid-summer to autumn.
🏆 ***D.* 'Gallery Art Nouveau'** (illus. p.397). Miniature-flowered, decorative dahlia. **H** 30–45cm (12–18in), **S** 20cm (8in). From mid-summer to autumn produces double, pink and purple flowers, 10cm (4in) across, above dark green foliage.
***D.* 'Gallery Art Fair'** illus. p.298.
***D.* 'Gateshead Festival'.** See *D.* 'Peach Melba'.
***D.* 'Gay Princess'.** Small-flowered decorative dahlia. **H** 1.2m (4ft), **S** 60cm (2ft). Produces lilac-lavender flowers in summer–autumn.
***D.* 'Geerling's Moonlight'.** Medium-flowered semi-cactus dahlia. **H** 1.3m (4½ft), **S** 60cm (2ft). Produces brilliant yellow flowers in summer and autumn.
***D.* 'Gerrie Hoek'** (illus. p.397). Small-flowered water-lily dahlia. **H** 1m (3ft), **S** 60cm (2ft). Abundant, rose-pink flowers are borne on sturdy stems from mid-summer to autumn.
***D.* 'Gilwood Terry G'.** Small-flowered semi-cactus dahlia. **H** 1.3m (4½ft), **S** 1–1.2m (3–4ft). Flowers have bronze-tinted, orange outer petals and yellow inner petals, borne in summer–autumn. Excellent for cutting.
***D.* 'Giraffe'.** Double orchid dahlia. **H** 1m (3ft), **S** 60cm (2ft). In summer and autumn has spotted, yellow-bronze flowers, to 8cm (3in) across. Is good for cutting.
🏆 ***D.* 'Glorie van Heemstede'.** Small-flowered water-lily dahlia. **H** 1.35m (4½ft), **S** 60cm (2ft). Clear yellow flowers are produced on sturdy stems from mid-summer to autumn.
***D.* 'Grenidor Pastelle'.** Medium-flowered semi-cactus dahlia. **H** 1.3m (4½ft), **S** 60cm (2ft). Bears salmon-pink flowers, with cream petal bases, in summer–autumn. Is good for exhibition.
***D.* 'Gwyneth'.** Small-flowered water-lily dahlia. **H** 1.8m (6ft), **S** 60cm (2ft). Bears bronze-tinted, orange flowers in summer–autumn. Is good for cutting.
🏆 ***D.* 'Hamari Accord'** (illus. p.398). Large-flowered semi-cactus dahlia. **H** 1.2m (4ft), **S** 60cm (2ft). Has clear yellow flowers held on strong stems in summer–autumn. Is good for exhibition.
🏆 ***D.* 'Hamari Gold'** (illus. p.398). Giant-flowered decorative dahlia. **H** 1.1m (3½ft), **S** 60cm (2ft). Has golden orange-bronze flowers in summer–autumn. Is suitable for exhibition.
***D.* 'Hamari Katrina'** (illus. p.398). Large-flowered semi-cactus dahlia. **H** 1.2m (4ft), **S** 60cm (2ft). Bears deep butter-yellow flowers in summer–autumn. Is good for exhibition.
***D.* Happy Single First Love ('HS First Love')** illus. p.398. Single dahlia. **H** 60cm (24in), **S** 45cm (18in). Produces dark purple leaves. Peach flowers, with a central red ring, appear from mid-summer to autumn.
***D.* Happy Single Juliet ('HS Juliet').** Single dahlia. **H** 60cm (24in), **S** 45cm (18in). Produces fuchsia-pink flowers, from mid-summer to autumn, and dark purple leaves.
***D.* Happy Single Kiss ('HS Kiss')** Single dahlia. **H** 60cm (24in), **S** 45cm (18in). Flowers with salmon-pink petals that blend into yellow at the centre with a dark brown eye are produced from mid-summer to autumn above dark purple foliage.
***D.* Happy Single Romeo ('HS Romeo')** illus. p.306.
***D.* Happy Single Wink ('HS Wink').** Single dahlia. **H** 60cm (24in), **S** 45cm (18in). Produces lilac-pink flowers, each with a central, red ring around a dark eye, from mid-summer to autumn. Leaves are dark purple.
🏆 ***D.* 'Harvest Inflammation'** illus. p.414.
***D.* 'Hayley Jayne'.** Small-flowered semi-cactus dahlia. **H** 1.1m (3½ft), **S** 60cm (2ft). Produces flowers that are white at base with purple-red tips, in summer and autumn. Is good for exhibition.
***D.* 'Hexton Copper'** (illus. p.398). Small ball dahlia. **H** 1.1m (3½ft), **S** 60cm (2ft). In summer–autumn has orange flowers.
***D.* 'Hillcrest Jessica'** (illus. p.397). Large-flowered decorative dahlia. **H** 1.25m (4ft), **S** 60cm (2ft). Bears red-purple flowers in summer and autumn.
🏆 ***D.* 'Hillcrest Royal'.** **H** 1.1m (3½ft), **S** 60cm (2ft). In summer–autumn has rich purple flowers, with incurving petals, held on strong stems.
***D.* 'Hillcrest Ultra'.** Small-flowered decorative dahlia. **H** 1.2m (4ft), **S** 60cm (2ft). Produces flowers, with pink outer petals and lemon-yellow inner petals, in summer and autumn.
🏆 ***D.* 'Honka'.** Single orchid dahlia. **H** 1–1.2m (3–4ft), **S** 60cm (2ft). Has masses of star-shaped, bright yellow flowers, 5cm (2in) across, with darker yellow discs, in summer and autumn. Is good for cutting.
***D.* 'HS First Love'.** See *D.* Happy Single First Love.
***D.* 'HS Juliet'.** See *D.* Happy Single Juliet.
***D.* 'HS Kiss'.** See *D.* Happy Single Kiss.
***D.* 'HS Romeo'.** See *D.* Happy Single Romeo.
***D.* 'HS Wink'.** See *D.* Happy Single Wink.
🏆 ***D.* 'Jaldec Joker'.** Small-flowered semi-cactus dahlia. **H** 1.1m (3½ft), **S** 60cm (2ft). In summer and autumn has bright orange-red flowers, shading to yellow at the bases. Petals are tipped white.
🏆 ***D.* 'Jean Fairs'.** Miscellaneous dahlia. **H** 1.3m (4½ft), **S** 60cm (2ft). In summer and autumn produces semi-double, orange-yellow flowers, to 10cm (4in) across, the yellow outer petals strongly flushed orange, the inner petals orange-red.
🏆 ***D.* 'Jeanette Carter'.** Miniature-flowered decorative dahlia. **H** 1.1m (3½ft), **S** 60cm (2ft). Bears yellow flowers, sometimes flushed pink in the centres, in summer–autumn.
***D.* 'Jescot Julie'.** Double orchid dahlia. **H** 60cm (24in), **S** 45cm (18in). Has sparse, mid-green foliage and orange-purple flowers, 78mm (3in) across, with purple-backed petals, in summer–autumn.
***D.* 'Jim Branigan'.** Large-flowered semi-cactus dahlia. **H** 1.3m (4½ft), **S** 60cm (2ft). Bright red flowers are held well above the foliage in summer–autumn. Is good for exhibition.
***D.* 'Julie One'.** Double orchid dahlia. **H** 1.2m (4ft), **S** 60cm (2ft). In summer and autumn produces bronze-purple flowers, 8cm (3in) across. Is good for cutting.
***D.* 'Jura'** (illus. p.396). Small-flowered semi-cactus dahlia. **H** 1.2m (4ft), **S** 60cm (2ft). In summer and autumn produces purple-tipped, white flowers.
***D.* 'Kaiser Waltzer'.** See *D.* 'Kaiserwalzer'.
***D.* 'Kaiserwalzer'**, syn. *D.* 'Kaiser Waltzer'. Collerette dahlia. **H** 1.1m (3½ft), **S** 60cm (2ft). Produces flowers, 10cm (4in) across, with large, red outer petals and narrower, yellow inner petals, in summer and autumn. Is good as a border plant.
***D.* 'Karma Amanda'.** Small-flowered decorative dahlia. **H** 85cm (34in), **S** 60cm (24in). From mid-summer to autumn produces white flowers with lilac petal tips and darker lilac colouring extending towards the base.
***D.* 'Karma Choc'** (illus. p.397). Small-flowered decorative dahlia. **H** 1.25m (4ft), **S** 60cm (2ft). Has black-green leaves. Velvety, dark maroon flowers are produced from mid-summer to autumn.
🏆 ***D.* 'Kathryn's Cupid'.** Miniature ball dahlia. **H** 1.2m (4ft), **S** 60cm (2ft). In summer–autumn, produces peach flowers that are good for exhibition.
🏆 ***D.* 'Kenora Sunset'.** Medium-flowered semi-cactus dahlia. **H** 1.2m (4ft), **S** 60cm (2ft). Bears bicoloured, brilliant red and yellow blooms in summer and autumn.
***D.* 'Kenora Superb'** (illus. p.398). Giant-flowered semi-cactus dahlia. **H** 1.2m (4ft), **S** 60cm (2ft). Produces bright orange-and-yellow flowers in summer–autumn.
***D.* 'Klondike'**, syn. *D.* 'Klondyke'. Large-flowered semi-cactus dahlia. **H** 1.2m (4ft), **S** 60cm (2ft). Produces white flowers in summer and autumn.
***D.* 'Klondyke'.** See *D.* 'Klondike'.
🏆 ***D.* 'Lakeland Sunset'.** Small-flowered cactus dahlia. **H** 1.65m (5½ft), **S** 60cm (2ft). Bears yellow-orange flowers, with brighter yellow centres, in late summer and autumn. Good for cutting.
***D.* 'Lavender Athalie'.** Small-flowered cactus dahlia. **H** 1.2m (4ft), **S** 60cm (2ft). Is a sport of *D.* 'Athalie'. Bears soft lilac-lavender flowers in summer–autumn.
🏆 ***D.* 'Lilac Marston'.** Miniature-flowered decorative dahlia. **H** 1.2m (4ft), **S** 60cm (2ft). Bears warm lilac flowers from mid-summer to autumn.
***D.* 'Lilac Time'.** Medium-flowered decorative dahlia. **H** 1.2m (4ft), **S** 60cm (2ft). Produces white-edged, lilac flowers from mid-summer to autumn.
***D.* 'Mabel Ann'.** Giant-flowered decorative dahlia. **H** 1m (3ft), **S** 60cm (2ft). Apricot flowers, with pale yellow centres, are produced from mid-summer to autumn.

***D.* 'Marie Schnugg'.** Single orchid dahlia. **H** 1.1m (3½ft), **S** 60cm (2ft). Bears star-like, red flowers, 5–7cm (2–3in) across, in summer and autumn. Is good as a border plant as well as for cutting.
***D.* 'Mark Hardwick'.** Giant-flowered decorative dahlia. **H** 1.1m (3½ft), **S** 60cm (2ft). Compact plant bearing bright, deep yellow flowers, on strong stems, in summer–autumn. Is good for exhibition.
***D.* 'Mary Richards'.** Small-flowered decorative dahlia. **H** 1.2m (4ft), **S** 60cm (2ft). In summer and autumn produces white flowers strongly suffused lavender-pink.
***D.* 'Mermaid of Zennor'** (illus. p.397). Single dahlia. **H** 75cm (30in), **S** 60cm (2ft). In summer–autumn produces lavender flowers, 2.5cm (1in) across, above delicate foliage. Is good as a border plant.
🏆 ***D.* 'Minley Carol'.** Pompon dahlia. **H** 1m (3ft), **S** 60cm (2ft). Pale orange flowers, with a hint of red at the petal tips, are produced from mid-summer to autumn.
***D.* 'Mi Wong'.** Pompon dahlia. **H** 1.1m (3½ft), **S** 60cm (2ft). Bears white flowers, suffused pink, in summer–autumn. Is good for exhibition.
🏆 ***D.* 'Moonfire'.** Dwarf, single dahlia. **H** 45cm (18in), **S** 30cm (12in). Produces dark foliage before yellow-red flowers, 5–7cm (2–3in) across, appear in summer–autumn. Is very good as a container plant and in a border.
***D.* 'Moonglow'** (illus. p.398). Large-flowered semi-cactus dahlia. **H** 1m (3ft), **S** 60cm (2ft). Pale creamy-yellow flowers are produced from mid-summer to autumn.
***D.* 'Moor Place'.** Pompon dahlia. **H** 1m (3ft), **S** 60cm (2ft). Leaves are glossy, dark green. Has red-purple flowers in summer–autumn. Is a good exhibition cultivar.
***D.* 'Mum's Lipstick'.** Fimbriated cactus dahlia. **H** 1–1.2m (3–4ft), **S** 60cm (2ft). Bears red-tipped, yellow flowers, 7–10cm (3–4in) across, in summer–autumn.
***D.* 'Nargold'.** Medium-flowered semi-cactus dahlia. **H** 90cm (3ft), **S** 60cm (2ft). Produces rich orange flowers with fringed petals from summer to autumn.
***D.* 'Natal'** (illus. p.397). Pompon dahlia. **H** 90cm (3ft), **S** 60cm (2ft). Dark red flowers are produced from mid-summer to autumn.
***D.* 'New Dimension'** (illus. p.397). Small-flowered semi-cactus dahlia. **H** 75cm (30in), **S** 40cm (16in). Produces light rose-pink flowers, with pale yellow centres, from mid-summer to autumn.
***D.* 'Noreen'.** Pompon dahlia. **H** 1m (3ft), **S** 60cm (2ft). In summer–autumn produces dark pinkish-purple flowers Is good for exhibition.
🏆 ***D.* 'NZ's Robert'.** Miniature water-lily dahlia. **H** 50cm (20in), **S** 30cm (12in). Produces red-pink flowers, with greeny-yellow discs, in summer and autumn. Is a good container plant.
***D.* 'Onesta'.** Small-flowered water-lily dahlia. **H** 1.2m (4ft), **S** 60cm (2ft). Produces masses of flowers, with dark pink inner petals fading to pale pink outer petals, in summer–autumn. Is good for cutting.
***D.* 'Onslow Renown'** (illus. p.398). Large-flowered semi-cactus dahlia. **H** 1.2m (4ft), **S** 60cm (2ft). Bears yellowish-orange flowers in summer and autumn.
***D.* 'Oosterbeck Remembered'** (illus. p.398). Small-flowered semi-cactus dahlia. **H** 1.2m (4ft), **S** 60cm (2ft). Bears dark orange flowers, with bright yellow inner petals, in summer–autumn. Is good for cutting.
***D.* 'Orange Berger's Record'.** Medium-flowered semi-cactus dahlia. **H** 1.2m (4ft), **S** 60cm (2ft). Bears yellowish-orange flowers in summer–autumn.
***D.* 'Park Princess'.** Small-flowered cactus dahlia. **H** 60cm (24in), **S** 45cm (18in). Pink flowers are borne in profusion from mid-summer to autumn.
***D.* 'Peach Melba',** syn. *D.* 'Gateshead Festival'. Small-flowered decorative dahlia. **H** 1.2m (4ft), **S** 60cm (2ft). In summer–autumn, bears peach to orange flowers with lemon-yellow petal bases. Is good for exhibition.
🏆 ***D.* 'Pearl of Heemstede'.** Small-flowered water-lily dahlia. **H** 1m (3ft), **S** 45cm (18in). Produces pale silvery-pink flowers on long, thin stems in summer–autumn. Is extremely free-flowering.
***D.* 'Pink Jupiter'.** Giant-flowered semi-cactus dahlia. **H** 1.3m (4½ft), **S** 60cm (2ft). In summer–autumn produces deep pinkish-mauve flowers. Is good for exhibition.
***D.* 'Pink Shirley Alliance'.** Small-flowered cactus dahlia. **H** 1.2m (4ft), **S** 60cm (2ft). Has soft lilac-pink flowers in summer–autumn.
***D.* 'Pink Symbol'.** Medium-flowered semi-cactus dahlia. **H** 1–1.2m (3–4ft), **S** 60cm (2ft). Bears pink flowers in summer–autumn. Is good for exhibition.
***D.* 'Pontiac'.** Small-flowered cactus dahlia. **H** 1m (3ft), **S** 60cm (2ft). Leaves are glossy, dark green. Bears dark pinkish-purple flowers in summer–autumn.
***D.* 'Pooh'.** Collerette dahlia. **H** 1m (3ft), **S** 60cm (2ft). Produces yellow-tipped, scarlet flowers, with central, yellow collars, from mid-summer to autumn.
🏆 ***D.* 'Preston Park'** (illus. p.398). Dwarf single dahlia. **H** 45cm (18in), **S** 30cm (12in). Bedding plant with nearly black foliage. In summer–autumn bears bright scarlet flowers, to 78mm (3in) across, with prominent yellow anthers, on short stems.
***D.* 'Rhonda'.** Pompon dahlia. **H** 1m (3ft), **S** 60cm (2ft). In summer–autumn produces whitish-lilac flowers. Good for exhibition.
***D.* 'Rip City'.** Small-flowered semi-cactus dahlia. **H** 1m (3ft), **S** 60cm (2ft). Produces maroon flowers, with darker maroon-black centres, from mid-summer to autumn.
***D.* 'Roxy'** (illus. p.397). Single dahlia. **H** 45cm (18in), **S** 40cm (16in). Bedding plant with magenta-purple flowers, borne from mid-summer to autumn, and dark green-black leaves.
***D.* 'Ruskin Charlotte'** (illus. p.397). Large-flowered semi-cactus dahlia. **H** 1m (3ft), **S** 60cm (2ft). Lavender-pink flowers, with white bases, are produced from mid-summer to autumn.
***D.* 'Ryecroft Gem'** (illus. p.397). Miniature-flowered decorative dahlia. **H** 90cm (3ft), **S** 60cm (2ft). In summer–autumn produces violet-margined, lavender-pink flowers. Is good for exhibition.
🏆 ***D.* 'Sascha'** (illus. p.397). Small-flowered water-lily dahlia. **H** 1.8m (6ft), **S** 60cm (2ft). Bears bright purple-pink flowers, fading to paler purple-pink towards the margins, in summer–autumn.
***D.* 'Shandy'.** Small-flowered semi-cactus dahlia. **H** 1.1m (3½ft), **S** 60cm (2ft). Produces pale orange-brown flowers in summer–autumn.
***D.* 'Shirley Alliance'.** Small-flowered cactus dahlia. **H** 1.3m (4½ft), **S** 60cm (2ft). In summer–autumn bears soft orange flowers with a gold base to each petal. Is good for exhibition.
***D.* 'Sir Alf Ramsey'.** Giant-flowered decorative dahlia. **H** 1.1m (3½ft), **S** 60cm (2ft). In summer and autumn produces lavender-pink flowers, with white petal bases.
🏆 ***D.* 'Small World'** (illus. p.396). Pompon dahlia. **H** 1m (3ft), **S** 60cm (2ft). Leaves are glossy, dark green. Has white flowers in summer–autumn. Is suitable for exhibition.
***D.* 'Smokey O'.** Medium-flowered semi-cactus dahlia. **H** 1–1.2m (3–4ft), **S** 60cm (2ft). Produces dark pink flowers in summer–autumn.
🏆 ***D.* 'So Dainty'** (illus. p.398). Miniature-flowered semi-cactus dahlia. **H** 1.1m (3½ft), **S** 60cm (2ft). Produces bronze-coloured flowers in summer–autumn that are suitable for exhibition.
***D.* 'Sorbet'** (illus. p.397). Medium-flowered semi-cactus dahlia. **H** 1.2m (4ft), **S** 60cm (2ft). Produces white flowers, with dark purple-red tips, from mid-summer to autumn.
***D.* 'Swanvale'.** Small-flowered decorative dahlia. **H** 1.1m (3½ft), **S** 60cm (2ft). Bears yellow flowers in summer–autumn.
***D.* 'Tiptoe'** (illus. p.397). Miniature-flowered decorative dahlia. **H** 90cm (3ft), **S** 60cm (2ft). Wine-red flowers, with white-tipped petals, are borne from mid-summer to autumn.
🏆 ***D.* 'Trelyn Kiwi'** (illus. p.396). Small-flowered semi-cactus dahlia. **H** 1.2m (4ft), **S** 60cm (2ft). Produces pink-flushed, white flowers, with darker pink central petals, in summer and autumn.
***D.* 'Trengrove Millennium'** (illus. p.398). Medium-flowered decorative dahlia. **H** 1.2m (4ft), **S** 60cm (2ft). Produces yellow flowers in summer–autumn. Is suitable for exhibition.
***D.* 'Tui Ruth'.** Small-flowered semi-cactus dahlia. **H** 1.1m (3½ft), **S** 60cm (2ft). Produces pink-yellow flowers from summer to autumn.
***D.* 'Vicky Crutchfield'.** Small-flowered water-lily dahlia. **H** 1m (3ft), **S** 60cm (2ft). Bears pink flowers in summer–autumn. Is suitable for exhibition.
***D.* 'Vulkan'.** Large-flowered semi-cactus dahlia. **H** 1m (3ft), **S** 60cm (2ft). Scarlet-striped, yellow flowers are borne from mid-summer to autumn.
***D.* 'Wanda's Capella'.** Giant-flowered decorative dahlia. **H** 1.2m (4ft), **S** 60cm (2ft). Has bright yellow flowers in summer–autumn. Is suitable for exhibition.
🏆 ***D.* 'Weston Pirate'.** Miniature-flowered cactus dahlia. **H** 1.3m (4½ft), **S** 50–60cm (20–24in). Produces prolific, semi-double, dark red flowers in summer–autumn. Is good for cutting.
🏆 ***D.* 'Weston Spanish Dancer'.** Miniature-flowered cactus dahlia. **H** 1m (3ft), **S** 60cm (2ft). Bright scarlet flowers, with yellow bases, are produced from mid-summer to autumn. Good for exhibition.
***D.* 'Whale's Rhonda'.** Pompon dahlia. **H** 1m (3ft), **S** 60cm (2ft). Leaves are glossy, very dark green. In summer–autumn has bright purple flowers. Good for exhibition.
🏆 ***D.* 'White Alva's** (illus. p.396). Giant-flowered decorative dahlia. **H** 1.2m (4ft), **S** 60cm (2ft). Produces pure white flowers, held well above the foliage on strong stems, in summer–autumn. Is good for exhibition.
🏆 ***D.* 'White Ballet'** (illus. p.396). Small-flowered water-lily dahlia. **H** 1m (3ft), **S** 60cm (2ft). Produces pure white flowers in summer–autumn.
***D.* 'White Klankstad'** (illus. p.396). Small-flowered cactus dahlia. **H** 1.1–1.2m (3½–4ft), **S** 60cm (2ft). Is a sport of *D.* 'Klankstad Kerkrade' with white flowers in summer–autumn.
***D.* 'White Moonlight'** (illus. p.396). Medium-flowered semi-cactus dahlia. **H** 1.2m (4ft), **S** 60cm (2ft). White flowers are produced on sturdy stems from mid-summer to autumn.
🏆 ***D.* 'Wootton Cupid'** (illus. p.397). Miniature ball dahlia. **H** 1.1–1.2m (3½–4ft), **S** 60cm (2ft). Has pink flowers in summer–autumn. Is good for exhibition.
🏆 ***D.* 'Wootton Impact'** (illus. p.398). Medium-flowered semi-cactus dahlia. **H** 1.2m (4ft), **S** 60cm (2ft). Has flowers in shades of bronze, held well above the foliage on strong stems, in summer–autumn. Is good for exhibition.
🏆 ***D.* 'Yellow Hammer'** (illus. p.398). Dwarf, single dahlia. **H** 45cm (18in), **S** 30cm (12in). Has rich yellow flowers, 78mm (3in) across, in summer–autumn.
***D.* 'Yelno Enchanted'.** See *D.* 'Yelno Enchantment'.
***D.* 'Yelno Enchantment',** syn. *D.* 'Yelno Enchanted'. Small-flowered water lily dahlia. **H** 1.2m (4ft), **S** 60cm (2ft). Bears pale pink flowers in summer–autumn. Is good for cutting.
***D.* 'Yelno Firelight'.** Small-flowered water-lily dahlia. **H** 1.2m (4ft), **S** 60cm (2ft). In summer–autumn has red and yellow flowers, with a neat petal formation, held on strong stems.
🏆 ***D.* 'Zorro'** (illus. p.398). Giant-flowered decorative dahlia. **H** 1.2m (4ft), **S** 60cm (2ft). Bears bright blood-red flowers in summer–autumn. Is good for exhibition.

DAIS

THYMELAEACEAE

Genus of deciduous, summer-flowering shrubs, grown for their flowers and overall appearance. Frost tender, min. 5°C (41°F). Requires full sun and well-drained soil. Water containerized plants well when in full growth, less when leafless. Propagate by seed in spring or by semi-ripe cuttings in summer.
D. cotinifolia. Deciduous, bushy, neat shrub. **H** and **S** 2–3m (6–10ft). Has small, oval to oblong, lustrous leaves. In summer bears scented, star-shaped, rose-lilac flowers in flattened clusters, 8cm (3in) across. Bark yields fibres strong enough to be used as thread.

Daiswa polyphylla. See *Paris polyphylla.*

DANÄE

LILIACEAE/RUSCACEAE

Genus of one species of evergreen shrub, with inconspicuous flowers, grown for its attractive, flattened, leaf-like shoots. Frost hardy. Grows in sun or shade and in moist soil. Propagate by seed in autumn or by division from autumn to spring.

D. racemosa (Alexandrian laurel). Evergreen, arching, dense shrub. **H** and **S** 1m (3ft). Has slender stems, lance-shaped, leaf-like, glossy, green shoots and pointed, glossy, bright green 'leaves'. Occasionally bears spherical, red berries.

DAPHNE

THYMELAEACEAE

Genus of evergreen, semi-evergreen or deciduous shrubs, grown for their usually fragrant, tubular flowers, each with 4 spreading lobes, and, in some species, for their foliage or fruits (seeds are poisonous). Dwarf species and cultivars are good for rock gardens. Fully to frost hardy. Most need full sun (although *D. alpina, D. arbuscula* and *D. blagayana* may be grown in semi-shade and *D. laureola* tolerates deep shade) and fertile, well-drained but not over-dry soil. Resents being transplanted. Propagate species by seed when fresh or by semi-ripe cuttings in summer, cultivars by cuttings only. Is susceptible to viruses that cause leaf mottling. ① All parts, including the seed, are highly toxic if ingested, and contact with the sap may irritate skin.

D. alpina illus. p.333. Deciduous, erect shrub. **H** 50cm (20in), **S** 40cm (16in). Fully hardy. Leaves are oval, downy and grey-green. Carries terminal clusters of fragrant, white flowers in late spring. Is suitable for a rock garden.

♀ ***D. arbuscula*** illus. p.351.

D. bholua Evergreen, occasionally deciduous, upright shrub. **H** 2–4m (6–12ft), **S** 1.5m (5ft). Frost hardy. Has leathery, dark green foliage. Terminal clusters of richly fragrant, purplish-pink and white flowers are borne in winter.

♀ **'Jacqueline Postill'** illus. p.143.

D. blagayana illus. p.333.

***D. x burkwoodii* 'Somerset'** illus. p.146. **'Somerset Variegated'** is a semi-evergreen, upright shrub. **H** 1.5m (5ft), **S** 1m (3ft). Fully hardy. Bears dense clusters of very fragrant, white-throated, pink flowers in late spring, sometimes again in autumn. Narrowly oblong, grey-green leaves are edged with creamy-white or pale yellow.

D. cneorum illus. p.333. ♀ **'Eximia'** is an evergreen, prostrate shrub. **H** 10cm (4in), **S** to 50cm (20in) or more. Fully hardy. Has small, oval, leathery, dark green leaves and, in late spring, terminal clusters of fragrant, white flowers, crimson outside and often pink-flushed within.

D. collina. Evergreen, domed, compact shrub. **H** and **S** 50cm (20in). Frost hardy. Oval, dark green leaves densely cover upright branches. Has terminal clusters of small, fragrant, purple-rose flowers in late spring. Is good for a rock garden or shrubbery.

D. genkwa. Deciduous, upright, open shrub. **H** and **S** 1.5m (5ft). Fully hardy after a hot summer, otherwise frost hardy. Oval, dark green leaves are bronze when young. Large, faintly scented, lilac flowers are borne from mid- to late spring.

D. giraldii. Deciduous, upright shrub. **H** and **S** 60cm (2ft). Fully hardy. Clusters of fragrant, golden-yellow flowers are produced amid oblong, pale blue green leaves in late spring and early summer and are followed by egg-shaped, red fruits.

***D. x hendersonii* 'Blackthorn Rose'** illus. p.334.

D. jasminea illus. p.350.

D. laureola (Spurge laurel). Evergreen, bushy shrub. **H** 1m (3ft), **S** 1.5m (5ft). Fully hardy. Has oblong, dark green leaves. Slightly fragrant, pale green flowers are borne from late winter to early spring, followed by spherical, black fruits.

subsp.*philippi* illus. p.147.

D. mezereum (Mezereon); (illus. p.142). Deciduous, upright shrub. **H** 1.2m (4ft), **S** 1m (3ft). Fully hardy. Very fragrant, purple or pink blooms clothe the bare stems in late winter and early spring, followed by red fruits. Mature leaves are narrowly oval and dull grey-green. **f. *alba*** is a deciduous, upright to spreading shrub. **H** and **S** 1.2m (4ft). Fully hardy. Bears very fragrant, white or creamy-white flowers that clothe bare stems in late winter and early spring. Has spherical, yellow fruits. Leaves are oblong and dull grey-green.

D. odora. Evergreen, bushy shrub. **H** and **S** 1.5m (5ft). Frost hardy. Has oval, glossy, dark green leaves and, from mid-winter to early spring, very fragrant, deep purplish-pink-and-white flowers.

♀ **'Aureomarginata'** illus. p.164.

***D. petraea* 'Grandiflora'** illus. p.351.

D. retusa, see. *D. tangutica* Retusa Group.

♀ ***D. tangutica.*** Evergreen, bushy shrub with stout shoots. **H** and **S** 1m (3ft). Fully hardy. Narrowly oval, leathery leaves are dark green. Bears clusters of fragrant, white-flushed, purple-pink flowers in mid- to late spring. ♀ **Retusa Group** illus. p.146.

DAPHNIPHYLLUM

DAPHNIPHYLLACEAE

Genus of evergreen trees and shrubs, grown for their habit and foliage. Male and female flowers are borne on separate plants. Frost hardy. Needs a sheltered position in sun or semi-shade and deep, fertile, well-drained but not too dry soil. Propagate by semi-ripe cuttings in summer.

D. himalaense* subsp. *macropodum. See *D. macropodum.*

D. macropodum, syn. *D. himalaense* subsp. *macropodum*, illus. p.111.

DARMERA

SYN. PELTIPHYLLUM

Umbrella plant

SAXIFRAGACEAE

Genus of one species of perennial, grown for its unusual foliage. Makes fine marginal water plants. Fully hardy. Grows in sun or shade and requires moist soil. Propagate by division in spring or by seed in autumn or spring.

♀ ***D. peltata*** illus. p.438.

DARWINIA

MYRTACEAE

Genus of evergreen, spring-flowering shrubs, grown for their flowers and overall appearance. Frost tender, min. 7–10°C (45–50°F). Needs full light and moist, neutral to acid soil, not rich in nitrogen. Water moderately when in full growth, sparingly at other times. Propagate by seed in spring or by semi-ripe cuttings in late summer. Is difficult to root and to grow under glass.

D. citriodora. Evergreen, rounded, well-branched shrub. **H** and **S** 60cm–1.2m (2–4ft). Oblong to broadly lance-shaped, blue-green leaves are lemon-scented when bruised. In spring produces pendent, terminal heads of usually 4 small, tubular, yellow or red flowers, each surrounded by 2 red or yellowish bracts.

DASYLIRION

Bear grass

DRACAENACEAE

Genus of evergreen, palm-like perennials, grown for their foliage and flowers. Male and female flowers are produced on separate plants. Frost tender, min. 10°C (50°F). Requires well-drained soil and a sunny position. Water freely when in full growth, sparingly at other times. Propagate by seed in spring.

D. texanum. Evergreen, palm-like perennial with a 75cm (30in) high trunk. **H** over 1m (3ft), **S** 3m (10ft). Has a rosette of narrow, drooping, green leaves, each 60–90cm (2–3ft) long, with yellowish prickles along margins. Stems, 5m (15ft) long, emerge from centre of plant carrying dense, narrow panicles of small, bell-shaped, whitish flowers in summer. Dry, 3-winged fruits appear in autumn.

DAVALLIA

DAVALLIACEAE

Genus of evergreen or semi-evergreen, often epiphytic ferns, suited to growing in pots and baskets. Half hardy to frost tender, min. 5°C (41°F). Needs semi-shade and fibrous, moist, peaty soil. Cut off fading fronds regularly. Propagate by division in spring or summer or by spores in summer.

♀ ***D. canariensis*** (Hare's-foot fern). Semi-evergreen fern. **H** and **S** 30cm (12in). Frost tender. Broadly lance-shaped, mid-green fronds, with triangular pinnae, arise from a scaly, brown rootstock.

♀ ***D. mariesii*** (Squirrel's-foot fern). Evergreen fern. **H** 15cm (6in), **S** 23cm (9in). Half hardy. Broadly triangular, delicately divided, leathery, mid-green fronds arise from a creeping, scaly, brown rootstock.

DAVIDIA

CORNACEAE/DAVIDIACEAE

Genus of one species of deciduous, spring- and summer-flowering tree, grown for its habit and showy, white bracts surrounding insignificant flowers. Fully hardy; needs shelter from strong winds. Requires sun or semi-shade and fertile, well-drained but moist soil. Propagate by semi-ripe cuttings in spring or by seed when ripe in autumn.

♀ ***D. involucrata*** illus. p.60.

DECAISNEA

LARDIZABALACEAE

Genus of deciduous, summer-flowering shrubs, grown for their foliage, flowers and sausage-shaped fruits. Frost hardy. Requires a sheltered, sunny situation and fertile soil that is not too dry. Propagate by seed in autumn.

D. fargesii (illus. p.142). Deciduous, semi-arching, open shrub. **H** and **S** 6m (20ft). Has blue-bloomed shoots and large, deep green leaves of paired leaflets. Racemes of greenish flowers in early summer are followed by pendent, sausage-shaped, bluish fruits.

DECUMARIA

HYDRANGEACEAE

Genus of evergreen or deciduous, woody-stemmed, root climbers. Half hardy. Prefers sun and loamy, well-drained soil that does not dry out. Prune, if necessary, after flowering. Propagate by stem cuttings in late summer or early autumn.

D. barbara. Deciduous climber. **H** to 10m (30ft). Frost hardy. Has ovate to ovate-oblong, glossy, dark green leaves. In summer produces rounded, terminal clusters, 1.5cm (5/8in) across, of small, white flowers each with a central "brush" of white or creamy-white stamens.

D. sinensis illus. p.192.

DEINANTHE

HYDRANGEACEAE

Genus of slow-growing perennials with creeping, underground rootstocks. Is useful for rock gardens and peat beds. Fully hardy. Needs shaded, moist soil. Propagate by division in spring or by seed when fresh.

D. bifida illus. p.264.

D. caerulea. Slow-growing, mound-forming perennial. **H** 20cm (8in), **S** to 15cm (6in). Stems, each carrying a cluster of nodding, bowl-shaped, pale violet-blue flowers, rise above 3–4 oval, toothed leaves in summer.

Delairea odorata. See *Senecio mikanioides.*

DELOSPERMA

AIZOACEAE

Genus of densely branched, trailing, perennial, sometimes shrubby succulents, some with tuberous roots. Frost tender, min. 5°C (41°F). Requires full sun and very well-drained soil. Propagate by seed or stem cuttings in spring or summer.

D. cooperi. Spreading, mat-forming, perennial succulent. **H** 5cm (2in), **S** indefinite. Has cylindrical, fleshy, light green leaves, 5cm (2in) long, and, in mid- to late summer, solitary, daisy-like, magenta flowers.

DELPHINIUM

RANUNCULACEAE

Genus of perennials, biennials, and annuals, grown for their spikes of irregularly cup-shaped, sometimes hooded, spurred flowers. Fully to half hardy. Needs an open, sunny position and fertile or rich, well-drained soil. Tall cultivars need staking and ample feeding and watering in spring and early summer. In spring, remove thin growths from well-established plants, leaving 5–7 strong shoots. If flower spikes are removed after they fade, a second flush may be produced in late summer, provided plants are fed and watered well. Propagate species by seed in autumn or spring; Belladonna Group cultivars by division or basal cuttings of young shoots in spring; Elatum Group cultivars by cuttings only. ⓘ All parts may cause severe discomfort if ingested, and contact with foliage may irritate skin. See also feature panel p.217.

For ease of reference, delphinium cultivars have been grouped as follows:

Belladonna Group. Upright, branched perennials with palmately lobed leaves. **H** 1–1.2m (3–4ft), **S** to 45cm (18in). Fully hardy. Wiry stems bear loose, branched spikes, 30cm (12in) long, of elf cap-shaped, single flowers, 2cm (¾in) or more across, with spurs up to 3cm (1¼in) long, in early and late summer.
Elatum Group. Erect perennials with large, palmate leaves. **H** 1.5–2m (5–6ft), **S** 60–90cm (24–36in). Fully hardy. In summer, produce closely packed spikes, 40cm–1.2m (16in–4ft) long, of regularly spaced, semi-double, rarely fully double flowers, 8–10cm (3–4in) wide, in a range of colours from white to blue and purple, sometimes red-pink, usually with contrasting eyes.
Pacific Hybrids. Similar to Elatum Group cultivars, but grown as annuals or biennials. They produce short-lived, large, semi-double flowers on spikes in early and mid-summer.
University Hybrids. Erect, branched herbaceous perennials with palmately lobed, mid-green leaves. **H** 1–1.2m (3–4ft), **S** to 45cm (18in). Fully hardy. In summer, stems bear loose, branched spikes of large, semi-double or double flowers in a range of colours in shades of red, orange or pink. Plants need careful cultivation to succeed.

***D.* 'Ailsa'.** Elatum Group herbaceous perennial. **H** 1.7m (5½ft). In early to mid-summer produces semi-double, off-white or very pale greyish-white flowers, 6–7.5cm (2½–3in) across, with white eyes, on spikes 70–90cm (28–36in) long.
***D.* 'Alice Artindale'** (illus. p.217). Elatum Group herbaceous perennial. **H** 1.5m (5ft). Produces neat, button-like, fully double, bicolour, rosy-mauve and sky-blue flowers, to 3cm (1¼in) across, on narrow spikes, 50–60cm (20–24in) or more long, in early to mid-summer.
***D.* 'Ann Woodfield'.** Elatum Group herbaceous perennial. **H** 1.5m (5ft). In mid-summer produces semi-double, pale blue flowers, to 10cm (4in) across, suffused pale mauve, on tapering spikes to 1m (3ft) long.
***D.* 'Anne Kenrick'.** Elatum Group herbaceous perennial. **H** 1.5m (5ft). In mid-summer produces semi-double, pale blue flowers to 8cm (3in) across, with a pink suffusion towards the central white eye, borne on tapering spikes to 1m (3ft) long.
♀ ***D.* 'Atlantis'.** Vigorous, Belladonna Group herbaceous perennial. **H** 1.4m (4½ft), **S** 50cm (20in). Produces spikes of mauve-flushed, deep blue flowers, 3cm (1¼in) across, in mid-summer. Has dark green leaves.
***D.* Black Knight Group.** Short-lived, Pacific Hybrids herbaceous perennial. **H** 1.5–1.7m (5–5½ft). Produces semi-double, purple to deep purple, black-eyed flowers, to 8cm (3in) across, on spikes, 60–100cm (2–3ft), in early to mid-summer.
♀ ***D.* 'Blue Dawn'.** Elatum Group herbaceous perennial. **H** 2.4m (8ft). In mid-summer, spikes to 1.25m (4ft) long bear pale blue flowers, to 7cm (3in) wide, with dark brown eyes.
***D.* Blue Fountains Group.** Short-lived, Pacific Hybrids herbaceous perennial. **H** 1.5m (5ft). In early to mid-summer has variable, white-eyed, mid-blue flowers, to 7cm (3in) across, on spikes 70–100cm (2–3ft) long.
***D.* 'Blue Lagoon'.** See *D.* 'Langdon's Blue Lagoon'.
♀ ***D.* 'Blue Nile'.** Elatum Group herbaceous perennial. **H** 1.5–1.8m (5–6ft). In mid-summer has rich blue flowers, 6–7cm (2½–3in), with lightly blue-streaked, white eyes, on spikes to 85cm (34in) long.
♀ ***D.* 'Bruce'** (illus. p.217). Elatum Group herbaceous perennial. **H** 1.7–2.2m (5½–7ft). In mid-summer, spikes to 1.2m (4ft) long bear deep violet-purple flowers, to 8cm (3in), silver-flushed towards centres and with dark brown eyes.
***D. brunonianum*.** Upright herbaceous perennial. **H** and **S** to 20cm (8in). Fully hardy. Hairy stems bear rounded, 3- or 5-lobed leaves. In early summer, flower stems each produce a spike, to 15cm (6in) long, of hooded, single, pale blue to purple flowers, 4cm (1½in) wide, with short, black spurs. Is good for a rock garden.
***D.* 'Butterball'.** Elatum Group herbaceous perennial. **H** 1.5–1.7m (5–5½ft). In mid-summer bears cream-eyed, white flowers, to 8cm (3in), overlaid with very pale greenish-yellow, on spikes to 50cm (20in) long.
♀ ***D.* 'Can-can'** (illus. p.217). Elatum Group herbaceous perennial. **H** 1.9m (6ft). In mid-summer, spikes to 75cm (30in) long bear fully double flowers, to 9cm (3½in) across, the outer sepals margined dark blue, the inner sepals purple-mauve with darker veining.
***D. cardinale*.** Short-lived, upright herbaceous perennial. **H** 1–2m (3–6ft), **S** 60cm (2ft). Half hardy. In summer has single, scarlet flowers, 4cm (1½in) wide, with yellow eyes, on spikes, 30–45cm (12–18in) long, above palmate, finely divided leaves.
***D.* 'Chelsea Star'.** Elatum Group herbaceous perennial. **H** 2m (6ft). Has rich deep violet flowers, 6–8cm (2½–3in) across, with white eyes, on spikes to 1.1m (3½ft) long in mid-summer.
***D. chinense*.** See *D. grandiflorum*.
♀ ***D.* 'Claire'.** Elatum Group herbaceous perennial. **H** 1.4m (4½ft). In mid-summer, semi-double, pale mauve-pink flowers, to 5cm (2in) across, with cream to pale brown eyes, are borne on spikes to 55cm (22in) long.
***D.* 'Clifford Lass'.** Elatum Group herbaceous perennial. **H** 1.3m (4½ft). In mid-summer, spikes 80–100cm (32–36in) long bear semi-double, dusky-pink flowers, to 7.5cm (3in) across, with white-tipped, dark brown eyes.
♀ ***D.* 'Clifford Sky'.** Elatum Group herbaceous perennial. **H** 2m (6ft). In mid-summer bears semi-double, white-eyed, sky-blue flowers, to 7.5cm (3in) across, on spikes to 1m (3ft) long.
***D.* 'Cliveden Beauty'** (illus. p.217). Belladonna Group herbaceous perennial. **H** 1–1.2m (3–4ft). Produces sky-blue flowers, 2–3cm (½–1in) across, on spikes 30cm (12in) long in early to mid-summer.
***D. consolida*.** See *Consolida ajacis*.
♀ ***D.* 'Conspicuous'.** Elatum Group herbaceous perennial. **H** 1.5m (5ft). In mid-summer produces semi-double, pale mauve and blue flowers, 5–6cm (2–2½in) across, with prominent dark eyes, in dense spikes to 60cm (2ft) long.
***D.* 'Crown Jewel'.** Elatum Group herbaceous perennial. **H** 1.5m (5ft). Spikes, to 85cm (34in) long, bear semi-double, pale blue and mauve flowers, to 5cm (2in) across, with deep brown eyes, in summer.
***D.* 'Dora Larkan'.** Elatum Group herbaceous perennial. **H** 2m. (6ft). In mid-summer produces spikes, 60cm (2ft) long, of deep mid-blue flowers, to 6cm (2½in) across, with white eyes.
***D.* 'Dunsden' Green'.** Elatum Group herbaceous perennial. **H** 1.3m (4½ft). Spikes, 60cm (2ft) long, of semi-double, lime-green-suffused, white flowers, to 5cm (2in) across, with small, green eyes, are produced in mid-summer.
♀ ***D.* 'Elizabeth Cook'** (illus. p.217). Elatum Group herbaceous perennial. **H** 1.5–1.7m (5–5½ft), **S** 50cm (1½ft). In mid-summer bears white flowers, 6cm (2½in) across, held in spires that gradually taper towards the tips.
♀ ***D.* 'Emily Hawkins'.** Elatum Group herbaceous perennial. **H** 2–2.2m (6–7ft). Semi-double, purple-mauve flowers, to 6cm (2½in) across, with light yellowish-brown eyes are borne in mid-summer on spikes to 80cm (32in) long.
***D.* 'Fanfare'.** Elatum Group herbaceous perennial. **H** 2–2.2m (6–7ft). In mid-summer bears pale blue to silvery-mauve flowers, 6–7cm (2½–3in) across, with white-and-violet eyes, on 60–75cm (2–2½ft) spikes.
♀ ***D.* 'Fenella'.** Elatum Group herbaceous perennial. **H** 1–1.65m (3–5½ft). Bears purple-flushed, gentian-blue blooms, 5–6cm (2–2½in) across, with black eyes, on spikes to 1m (3ft) long in mid-summer.
♀ ***D.* 'Foxhill Nina'.** Elatum Group herbaceous perennial. **H** 1.2m (4ft). Bears semi-double, white-eyed, pale pink flowers, 5–6cm (2–2½in) across, on spikes, to 60cm (2ft) long, in mid-summer.
***D.* 'Franjo Sahin'.** Elatum Group herbaceous perennial. **H** 2m (6ft). In mid-summer, tapering spikes, to 1.1m (3½ft) long, produce semi-double, purplish–mauve flowers, to 10cm (4in) across, with black eyes.
♀ ***D.* 'Galileo'.** Elatum Group herbaceous perennial. **H** 1.8m (6ft). In early and mid-summer, tapering spikes, to 80cm (32in) long, bear semi-double, violet-blue blooms, 7cm (3in) wide, paling slightly towards the centre, with brownish-black eyes.
***D.* 'Gemini'.** Elatum Group herbaceous perennial. **H** 1.8m (6ft). In mid-summer, spikes to 85cm (34in) long bear semi-double, pale violet flowers, to 7.5cm (3in) across, edged reddish-violet with dark black-brown eyes, white near the centre.
***D.* 'Gemma'.** Elatum Group herbaceous perennial. **H** 2m (6ft). Semi-double, pale lavender flowers, to 7.5cm (3in) across, with white eyes, are borne in mid-summer on spikes to 1m (3ft) long.
***D.* 'Gertrude Sahin'.** Elatum Group herbaceous perennial. **H** 1.7–1.9m (5½–6ft). In mid-summer produces mid- to light blue flowers, 7.5–9.5cm (3–3½in) across, with prominent white eyes, on spikes to 1m (3ft) long.
♀ ***D.* 'Gillian Dallas'** (illus. p.217). Elatum Group herbaceous perennial. **H** 2.1m (6½ft). In mid-summer has spikes, to 90cm (3ft) long, of blue-violet flowers, to 8cm (3in) across, with white eyes and violet flecks.
♀ ***D.* 'Giotto'.** Elatum Group herbaceous perennial. **H** 1.7–2m (5½–6ft). In mid-summer, spikes to 80cm (32in) long bear semi-double flowers, to 7.5cm (3in) wide, with deep purple inner sepals, dark blue outer sepals and light yellow-brown eyes.
***D.* 'Gordon Forsyth'.** Elatum Group herbaceous perennial. **H** 2m (6ft). In mid-summer produces semi-double, amethyst-purple blooms, 6–7cm (2½–3in) across, with violet-flecked, black eyes, on spikes 60–70cm (24–28in) long.
***D. grandiflorum*,** syn. *D. chinense*. **'Blue Butterfly'** (illus. p.217) is a short-lived, erect herbaceous perennial, usually grown as an annual. **H** 45cm (1½ft), **S** 30cm (1ft). Fully hardy. Has palmate, divided leaves. In summer produces loose, branching spikes, to 15cm (6in) long, of single, deep blue flowers, 3.5cm (1½in) wide. Is useful as a bedding plant.
♀ ***D.* 'Holly Cookland Wilkins'.** Elatum Group herbaceous perennial. **H** 1.5m (5ft). Produces tapering spikes. 1m (3ft) long. of semi-double, black-eyed, lavender flowers, to 7.5cm (3in) across, in mid-summer.
***D.* 'Joan Edwards'.** Elatum Group herbaceous perennial. **H** 1.5m (5ft). In mid-summer, tapering spikes, 80–90cm (32–36in) long, bear semi-double, vivid purplish-blue flowers, 5.5–7.5cm (2¼–3in) across, becoming paler and purple striated towards the central, white eye.
♀ ***D.* 'Kennington Classic'.** Elatum Group herbaceous perennial. **H** 1.5m (5ft). Semi-double, rich cream flowers, to 8cm (3in) across, with well-formed, yellow eyes are borne in mid-summer on spikes to 90cm (3ft) long.
♀ ***D.* 'Langdon's Blue Lagoon'**, syn. *D.* 'Blue Lagoon'. Elatum Group herbaceous perennial. **H** 2m (6ft). Tapering spikes, to 90cm long, bear semi-double, pale to mid-blue flowers, to 7cm (3in) across, which are paler towards the centre, with blue-specked, white eyes.
♀ ***D.* 'Langdon's Royal Flush'** (illus. p.217). Elatum Group herbaceous perennial. **H** 2m (6ft). In mid-summer has semi-double, magenta-pink flowers, 5–6cm (2–2½in) across, on spikes to 85cm (34in) long; upper petals are a darker shade than lower ones.
♀ ***D.* 'Loch Leven'** (illus. p.217). Elatum Group herbaceous perennial. **H** to 1.5m (5ft). Bears semi-double, mid-blue flowers, to 7.5cm (3in) across, with white eyes, on 1m (3ft) spikes in early to mid-summer.
♀ ***D.* 'Lord Butler'.** Elatum Group herbaceous perennial. **H** 1.5–1.7m (5–5½ft). Produces semi-double, mid-blue flowers, to 7.5cm (3in) across, lightly flushed with

D

pale lilac and with blue-marked, white eyes, on spikes to 75cm (30in) long.
🏆 **D. 'Lucia Sahin'** (illus. p.217). Elatum Group herbaceous perennial. **H** 2m (6ft). In mid-summer, spikes to 90cm (36in) long bear semi-double, deep purple-pink flowers, to 7.5cm (3in) across, with dark brown eyes.
🏆 **D. 'Michael Ayres'** (illus. p.217). Elatum Group herbaceous perennial. **H** 1.8m (6ft). In early and mid summer, semi-double, deep purple-blue flowers, to 6cm (2½in) across, with black-brown eyes, are borne on spikes to 80cm (32in) long.
D. 'Mighty Atom'. Elatum Group herbaceous perennial. **H** 1.5–2m (5–6ft). In mid-summer has semi-double, mid-violet flowers, to 6cm (2½in) across, with violet-marked, yellowish-brown eyes, on spikes to 75cm (2½ft) long.
🏆 **D. 'Min'** (illus. p.217). Elatum Group herbaceous perennial. **H** 1.6–2m (5½–6ft). In mid-summer, tapering spikes, to 1m (3ft) long, bear semi-double, pale lavender flowers, to 9.5cm (3¾in) across, with deep lavender suffusions and veining, as well as dark brown eyes.
D. 'Nobility'. Elatum Group herbaceous perennial. **H** 1.6m (5½ft). Semi-double, deep purple and dark mauve flowers, to 7.5cm (3in) across, with prominent white eyes, are borne in mid-summer on spikes to 1m (3ft) long.
D. nudicaule illus. p.340.
🏆 **D. 'Olive Poppleton'** (illus. p.217). Elatum Group herbaceous perennial. **H** 2–2.5m (6–8ft). Off-white flowers, 5–6cm (2–2½in) across, sometimes very faintly flushed pink and with fawn eyes, are borne on spikes to 1m (3ft) long in mid-summer.
D. 'Pink Ruffles'. Elatum Group herbaceous perennial. **H** 1.5m (5ft). Fully double, shell-pink flowers, to 7.5cm (3in) across, are borne in mid-summer on spikes to 80cm (32in) long.
D. 'Red Caroline' (illus. p.217). University Hybrids herbaceous perennial. **H** 1m (3ft), **S** 30cm (1ft). Fully hardy. Has large, palmate, soft green, basal leaves. In summer produces spikes of flattish, bright red flowers.
D. x ruysii (Elatum Group delphinium and D. nudicale). University Hybrids herbaceous perennial. **H** 80–100cm (32–39in), **S** 40cm (16in). Has palmate, mid-green, basal leaves. In early summer produces loose branched spikes of cup-shaped flowers in shades of red and pink. **'Pink Sensation'** has slightly mauve-tinged, salmon-pink flowers.
🏆 **D. 'Sandpiper'** (illus. p.217). Elatum Group herbaceous perennial. **H** 1–1.5m (3–4ft). In mid-summer has semi-double, white flowers, to 6cm (2½in) across, with dark creamy-brown eyes, on spikes to 75cm (2½ft) long.
D. 'Shimmer'. Elatum Group herbaceous perennial. **H** 1.8m (6ft). In mid-summer produces semi-double, bright blue flowers, 5–7cm (2–3in) across, with prominent white eyes, on spikes to 80cm (32in) long.
🏆 **D. 'Spindrift'** (illus. p.217). Elatum Group herbaceous perennial. **H** 1.7–2m (5½–6ft). In early and mid-summer produces spikes, to 1m (3ft) long, of semi-double, pinkish-purple flowers, 5–7cm (2–3in) across, overlaid with pale blue and with creamy-white eyes; towards centres, the pinkish-purple becomes paler and the blue darker. Flower colour varies according to different types of soil; on acid soil, flowers are greenish.
D. 'Strawberry Fair'. Elatum Group herbaceous perennial. **H** 1.7m (5½ft). Has semi-double, white-eyed, mulberry-pink flowers, 5–7cm (2–3in) across, on spikes to 78cm (31in) long in mid-summer.
🏆 **D. 'Sungleam'** illus. p.219.
🏆 **D. 'Sunkissed'.** Elatum Group herbaceous perennial. **H** 1.7m (5½ft). In mid-summer, spikes to 80cm (32in) long bear semi-double, cream flowers, to 6.5cm (2¾in) across, with canary-yellow eyes.
D. tatsienense. Short-lived, upright herbaceous perennial. **H** 30cm (12in), **S** 5–10cm (2–4in). Fully hardy. Loose spikes, to 15cm (6in) long, of small-spurred, single, bright blue flowers, 2.5cm (1in) long, are borne in summer. Leaves are rounded to oval and deeply cut. Suits a rock garden. Requires soil that is gritty.
🏆 **D. 'Tiddles'.** Elatum Group herbaceous perennial. **H** 1.8m (6ft). In mid-summer, semi-double to almost double, greyish-violet flowers, 5–6cm (2–2½in) across, with brown eyes, are borne on spikes to 90cm (3ft) long.
D. 'Tiger Eye'. Elatum Group herbaceous perennial. **H** 1.7m (5½ft). In mid-summer, spikes 60–70cm (24–28in) long bear semi-double, light violet flowers, 5–6cm (2–2½in) across, with yellow-edged, brown eyes.

Dendrathema. See *Chrysanthemum*.
Dendrobenthamia capitata. See *Cornus capitata*.

DENDROBIUM

ORCHIDACEAE

See also ORCHIDS.
D. aphyllum, syn. *D. pierardii*. Deciduous, epiphytic orchid for an intermediate greenhouse. **H** to 60cm (24in). In early spring produces pairs of soft pink flowers, 4cm (1½in) across and each with a large, cream lip. Has oval leaves, 5–8cm (2–3in) long. Requires semi-shade in summer. Is best grown hanging from a bark slab.
D. chrysotoxum. Deciduous, epiphytic orchid for an intermediate greenhouse. **H** 60cm (24in). Trusses of cup-shaped, deep yellow flowers, 2cm (¾in) across and with hairy, red-marked lips, are borne in spring. Oval leaves are 5–8cm (2–3in) long. Provide good light in summer.
D. infundibulum (illus. p.466). Evergreen, epiphytic orchid for a cool greenhouse. **H** 30cm (12in). In spring, stems each produce up to 6 pure white flowers, 8cm (3in) wide and each with a yellow-marked lip. Has oval leaves, 5–8cm (2–3in) long. Grow in semi-shade in summer.
D. Momozono gx 'Princess'. Evergreen, epiphytic orchid for an intermediate greenhouse. **H** 60cm (24in), **S** 30cm (12in). In spring, produces pairs of dark pink flowers, 7cm (3in) across, fading to white in the centres, and with white and pink marks on the lips. Oblong leaves are 10cm (4in) long. Requires semi-shade in summer.
D. nobile (illus. p.466). Deciduous, epiphytic orchid (often evergreen in cultivation) for a cool greenhouse. **H** 30cm (12in). Trusses of delicate, rose-pink flowers, 5cm (2in) across and each with a prominent maroon lip, are borne in spring. Oval leaves are 5–8cm (2–3in) long. Requires semi-shade in summer.
D. 'Oriental Paradise'. Evergreen, epiphytic orchid. **H** 60cm (24in). White flowers, 7cm (3in) across, with dark pink notches on the petals and yellow marks on the lips, are borne in pairs in spring. Oblong leaves are 10cm (4in) long. Requires semi-shade in summer.
D. pierardii. See *D. aphyllum*.

DENDROCHILUM

ORCHIDACEAE

See also ORCHIDS.
D. glumaceum (Silver chain). Evergreen, epiphytic orchid for a cool greenhouse. **H** 10cm (4in). Pendent sprays of fragrant, pointed, orange-lipped, creamy-white flowers, 1cm (½in) long, are produced in autumn. Narrowly oval leaves are 15cm (6in) long. Requires semi-shade in summer.

DENDROMECON

PAPAVERACEAE

Genus of evergreen shrubs, grown for their foliage and showy flowers. Frost to half hardy. Plant against a sunny wall in cold areas. Requires full sun and very well-drained soil. Propagate by softwood cuttings in summer, by seed in autumn or spring or by root cuttings in winter.
D. rigida illus. p.206.

Dentaria enneaphyllos. See *Cardamine enneaphyllos*.
Dentaria pentaphyllos. See *Cardamine pentaphyllos*.

DESCHAMPSIA

GRAMINEAE/POACEAE

See also GRASSES, BAMBOOS, RUSHES and SEDGES.
D. cespitosa (Tufted hair grass). Evergreen, tuft-forming, perennial grass. **H** to 1m (3ft), **S** 25–30cm (10–12in). Fully hardy. Has narrow, rough-edged, dark green leaves. In summer produces dainty, open panicles of tiny, pale brown spikelets that last well into winter. Tolerates sun or shade. **'Gold Tau'** illus. p.289.

DESFONTAINIA

DESFONTAINIACEAE/LOGANIACEAE

Genus of evergreen shrubs, grown for their foliage and tubular flowers. Frost to half hardy. Provide shelter in cold areas. Needs some shade, particularly in dry areas, and moist, peaty, preferably acid soil. Propagate by semi-ripe cuttings in summer.
🏆 ***D. spinosa***, illus. p.203.

DESMODIUM

LEGUMINOSAE/PAPILIONACEAE

Genus of perennials and deciduous shrubs and sub-shrubs, grown for their flowers. Fully to frost hardy. Needs full sun and well-drained soil. Propagate by softwood cuttings in late spring or by seed in autumn. May also be divided in spring.
🏆 ***D. elegans***, syn. *D. tiliifolium*, illus. p.154.
D. tiliifolium. See *D. elegans*.

DEUTZIA

HYDRANGEACEAE

Genus of deciduous shrubs, grown for their profuse, 5-petalled flowers. Fully to frost hardy. Needs full sun and fertile, well-drained soil. Plants benefit from regular thinning out of old shoots after flowering. Propagate by softwood cuttings in summer.
***D. x elegantissima* 'Fasciculata'.** Deciduous, upright shrub. **H** 2m (6ft), **S** 1.5m (5ft). Fully hardy. From late spring to early summer produces large clusters of 5-petalled, pale pink flowers. Leaves are oval, toothed and mid-green. 🏆 **'Rosealind'** illus. p.153.
D. gracilis illus. p.145.
🏆 ***D. x hybrida* 'Mont Rose'** illus. p.152.
D. 'Joconde'. Deciduous, upright shrub. **H** and **S** 1.5m (5ft). Fully hardy. Bears 5-petalled, white flowers, striped purple outside, in early summer. Oval, mid-green leaves have long points.
D. longifolia. Deciduous, arching shrub. **H** 2m (6ft), **S** 3m (10ft). Fully hardy. Large clusters of 5-petalled, deep pink flowers are produced from early to mid-summer. Narrowly lance-shaped leaves are grey-green. 🏆 **'Veitchii'** illus. p.133.
D. x magnifica. Vigorous, deciduous, upright shrub. **H** 2.5m (8ft), **S** 2m (6ft). Fully hardy. Produces dense clusters of 5-petalled, pure white flowers in early summer. Leaves are narrowly oval and bright green. **'Staphyleoides'** illus. p.132.
D. monbeigii illus. p.149.
D. pulchra. Vigorous, deciduous, upright shrub. **H** 2.5m (8ft), **S** 2m (6ft). Frost hardy. Has peeling, orange-brown bark and lance-shaped, dark green leaves. Slender, pendulous panicles of 5-petalled, pink-tinged, white flowers appear in late spring and early summer.
D. x rosea illus. p.146.
D. scabra illus. p.127. 'Plena' (syn. *D.s.* 'Flore Pleno') is a deciduous, upright shrub. **H** 3m (10ft), **S** 2m (6ft). Fully hardy. Narrowly oval, dark green leaves set off dense, upright clusters of double, white flowers, purplish-pink outside, from early to mid-summer.
🏆 ***D. setchuenensis* var. *corymbiflora*.** Deciduous, upright shrub with peeling, pale brown bark when mature. **H** 2m (6ft), **S** 1.5m (5ft). Frost hardy. Small, 5-petalled, white flowers are borne in broad clusters in early and mid-summer. Produces lance-shaped, long-pointed, grey-green leaves.

DIANELLA

Flax lily

LILIACEAE/PHORMIACEAE

Genus of evergreen, summer-flowering perennials. Frost to half hardy; is suitable outdoors only in mild areas and elsewhere requires a cold greenhouse or frame. Needs sun and well-drained, neutral to acid soil. Propagate by division or seed in spring.
D. caerulea. Evergreen, tuft-forming perennial. **H** 75cm (30in), **S** 30cm (12in). Half hardy. In summer has panicles of small, star-shaped, blue flowers, above grass-like leaves, followed by blue berries. **Cassa Blue ('Dbb03')** illus. p.307.
D. tasmanica illus. p.239.

DIANTHUS

Carnation, Pink

CARYOPHYLLACEAE

Genus of evergreen or semi-evergreen, mainly summer-flowering perennials, annuals and biennials, grown for their mass of flowers, often scented, some of which are excellent for cutting. Carnations and pinks (see below) are excellent for cut flowers and border decoration, the biennial *D. barbatus* (Sweet William) is suitable for bedding and smaller, tuft-forming species and cultivars are good for rock gardens. Fully to half hardy. Needs an open, sunny position and well-drained, slightly alkaline soil, except for *D. pavonius*, which prefers acid soil. Dead-heading of repeat-flowering types is beneficial. Tall forms of carnations and pinks have a loose habit and need staking. Propagate border carnations by layering in late summer, other named forms by softwood cuttings in early to mid-summer and species by seed at any time. Is susceptible to rust, red spider mite and virus infection through aphids, but many cultivars are available from virus-free stock.

Carnations and pinks have narrowly lance-shaped, silvery- or grey-green leaves, scattered up flower stems, which may coil outwards on carnations. They are divided into the following groups, all with self-coloured and bicoloured cultivars. See also feature panel pp.266–267.

Carnations

Border carnations are annuals or evergreen perennials that flower prolifically once in mid-summer and are good for border decoration and cutting. Each stem bears 5 or more often scented, semi-double or double flowers, to 8cm (3in) across; picotee forms (with petals outlined in a darker colour) are available. **H** 75cm–1.1m (2½–3½ft), **S** to 30cm (1ft). Frost hardy.

Perpetual-flowering carnations are evergreen perennials that flower year-round if grown in a greenhouse, but more prolifically in summer. They are normally grown for cut flowers: flower stems should be disbudded, leaving one terminal bud per stem. Fully double flowers, to 10cm (4in) across, are usually unscented and are often flecked or streaked. **H** 1–1.5m (3–5ft), **S** 30cm (1ft) or more. Half hardy.

Spray forms are not disbudded so have 5 or more flowers per stem, each 5–6cm (2–2½in) across. **H** 60cm–1m (2–3ft), **S** to 30cm (1ft).

Malmaison carnations are evergreen perennials, derived from *D.* 'Souvenir de la Malmaison'. Grown under glass, they bear large, double, scented flowers sporadically during the year. The flowers can reach up to 13cm (5in) across. They are mostly self-coloured, and tend to split their calyces. **H** 50–70cm (20–28in), **S** 40cm (16in). Half hardy.

Pinks

Evergreen, clump-forming perennials, grown for border decoration and cutting, that in summer produce a succession of basal shoots, each bearing 4–6 fragrant, single to fully double flowers, 3.5–6cm (1½–2in) across. **H** 30–45cm (12–18in), **S** 23–30cm (9–12in) or more. Frost hardy.

Old-fashioned pinks have a low, spreading habit and produce masses of flowers in one flowering period in mid-summer. Mule types (a border carnation crossed with a Sweet William) and laced types (in which the central colour extends as a loop around each petal) are available.

Modern pinks, obtained by crossing an old-fashioned pink with a perpetual-flowering carnation, are more vigorous than old-fashioned pinks, and are repeat-flowering with two or three main flushes of flowers in summer.

Alpine pinks are evergreen species and cultivars forming neat mat or cushion plants. They will grow at the edge of a border or in a rock garden, trough or alpine house. In early summer, they bear single, semi-double or double, often scented flowers. Foliage is grey-green. **H** 8–10cm (3–4in), **S** 20cm (8in). Fully hardy.

***D.* 'A.J. MacSelf'.** See *D.* 'Dad's Favourite'.

***D.* 'Albisola'.** Perpetual-flowering carnation. Fully double flowers are clear tangerine-orange.

***D.* 'Aldridge Yellow'.** Border carnation. Semi-double flowers are clear yellow.

***D.* 'Alice'.** Modern pink. Has clove-scented, semi-double, ivory-white flowers, each with a bold, crimson eye.

♀ ***D. alpinus*** (Alpine pink) illus. p.364.

***D.* 'Annabelle'** illus. p.364.

D. armeria (Deptford pink). Evergreen, tuft-forming perennial, sometimes grown as an annual. **H** 30cm (12in), **S** 45cm (18in). Fully hardy. Has narrowly lance-shaped, dark green leaves. In summer, tall stems each carry small, 5-petalled, cerise-pink flowers in small bunches. Is good for a rock garden or bank.

D. barbatus (Sweet William). **Roundabout Series** (dwarf). Slow-growing, upright, bushy biennial. **H** 15cm (6in), **S** 20–30cm (8–12in). Fully hardy. Has lance-shaped leaves. In early summer bears flat heads of single and bicoloured flowers in shades of pink, red and white.

♀ ***D.* 'Becky Robinson'** (illus. p.266). Modern pink. Has strongly clove-scented, double, rose-pink flowers laced and flecked with crimson.

***D.* 'Bombardier'.** Evergreen, tuft-forming perennial. **H** and **S** 10cm (4in). Frost hardy. Has a basal tuft of linear, grey-green leaves and, in summer, small, double, scarlet flowers. Is good for a rock garden.

***D.* 'Bookham Fancy'.** Border carnation. Produces bright yellow flowers, margined and flecked carmine-purple, on short, stiff stems.

***D.* 'Bookham Perfume'.** Perennial border carnation. Has scented, semi-double, crimson flowers.

♀ ***D.* 'Bovey Belle'.** Modern pink. Has clove-scented, fully double, bright purple flowers that are excellent for cutting.

♀ ***D.* 'Brilliant Star'** illus. p.266.

***D.* 'Brympton Red'.** Old-fashioned pink. Flowers are single, bright crimson with deeper shading.

D. caesius. See *D. gratianopolitanus.*

D. carthusianorum illus. p.339.

♀ ***D.* Candy Floss 'Devon Flavia'** illus. p.266.

***D.* 'Charles Musgrave'.** See *D.* 'Musgrave's Pink'.

D. chinensis (Indian pink). Slow-growing, bushy annual. **H** and **S** 15–30cm (6–12in). Fully hardy. Lance-shaped leaves are pale or mid-green. Tubular, single or double flowers, 2.5cm (1in) or more wide and with open, spreading petals, in shades of pink, red or white, are produced in summer and early autumn. **Baby Doll Series** illus. p.305. **'Fire Carpet'** illus. p.307. **Heddewigii Group**, **H** 30cm (12in), has flowers in mixed colours.

***D.* 'Christine Hough'.** Perennial border carnation. Semi-double apricot flowers, overlaid and streaked with rose-pink.

***D.* 'Christopher'.** Modern pink. Produces lightly scented, fully double, bright salmon-red flowers.

***D.* 'Clara'.** Perpetual-flowering carnation. Fully double flowers are yellow with salmon flecks.

***D.* 'Constance Finnis'.** See *D.* 'Fair Folly'.

♀ ***D.* 'Coquette'** (illus. p.266). Perpetual-flowering, spray carnation. Double, slightly purplish-red flowers have toothed, almost white margins.

♀ ***D.* 'Cranmere Pool'** (illus. p.266). Modern pink. Double, pink-tinted, white flowers have crimson centres and a light fragrance.

***D.* 'Cream Sue'.** Perpetual-flowering carnation. Flowers are cream coloured. Is a sport of *D.* 'Apricot Sue'.

***D.* 'Crompton Princess'.** Perpetual-flowering carnation. Flowers are white.

***D.* 'Dad's Favourite'**, syn. *D.* 'A.J. MacSelf' (illus. p.266). Old-fashioned pink. Bears scented, semi-double, white flowers with chocolate-brown lacing.

♀ ***D. deltoides*** (Maiden pink). Evergreen, mat-forming, basal-tufted perennial. **H** 15cm (6in), **S** 30cm (12in). Fully hardy. In summer, small, 5-petalled, white, pink or cerise flowers are borne singly above tiny, lance-shaped leaves. Is good for a rock garden or bank. Trim back after flowering. **'Leuchtfunk'**, syn. *D.d.* 'Flashing Light', illus. p.365.

***D.* 'Denis'.** Modern pink. Strongly clove-scented, fully double, magenta flowers.

***D.* 'Devon Dove'.** See D. Devon Series 'Devon Dove'.

***D.* 'Devon Flavia'.** See *D.* Scent First Series Candy Floss.

***D.* 'Devon PP 11'.** See *D.* Scent First Series Tickled Pink.

***D.* Devon Series.** Modern pink. Prolific, double-flowered, long-flowering, medium to tall plants raised in Devon. ♀ **'Devon Dove'** (illus. p.266) produces well-scented, pure white flowers with lacy tips. ♀ **'Devon Wizard'** (illus. p.266) is vigorous, and bears vibrant, well-scented, cerise-purple flowers with deep red centres.

♀ ***D.* 'Doris'** (illus. p.266). Modern pink. Has compact growth and an abundance of fragrant, semi-double, pale pink flowers, each with a salmon-red ring towards base of flower. Good for cutting.

***D.* 'Duchess of Westminster'** (illus. p.266). Vigorous Malmaison carnation. Bears salmon-pink flowers with stronger calyces than most Malmaison carnations.

***D.* 'Emile Paré'.** Old-fashioned, mule pink. Has clusters of semi-double, salmon-pink flowers and, unusually for a pink, mid-green foliage.

***D.* 'Eva Humphries'.** Perennial border carnation. Has fragrant, semi-double flowers with white petals, each outlined in purple.

♀ ***D.* 'Evening Star'** See *D.* Star Series 'Evening Star.'

***D.* 'Fair Folly'**, syn. *D.* 'Constance Finnis'. Modern pink. Flowers are single and usually dusky-pink to dusky-purple with 2 white splashes on each petal.

***D.* 'Feuerhexe'** (illus. p.267). Alpine pink. Strongly scented, fringed, single, magenta flowers are produced throughout summer. Has silvery-blue leaves.

***D.* 'Forest Treasure'.** Perennial border carnation. Has double, white flowers with reddish-purple splashes on each petal.

***D.* 'Freckles'.** Modern pink. A compact cultivar, it has fully double flowers that are red-speckled and dusky-pink.

***D.* 'Fusilier'** (illus. p.267). Dwarf, modern pink. **H** 15cm (6in). Fragrant, single, rose-red flowers have blood-red eyes.

♀ ***D.* 'Golden Cross'** (illus. p.267). Border carnation. Produces bright yellow flowers on short, stiff stems.

♀ ***D.* 'Gran's Favourite'** (illus. p.266). Old-fashioned pink. Bears fragrant, semi-double, white flowers with deep raspberry lacing.

♀ ***D. gratianopolitanus***, syn. *D. caesius*, illus. p.363.

***D.* 'Green Eyes'.** See *D.* 'Musgrave's Pink'.

D. haematocalyx. Evergreen, tuft-forming perennial. **H** 12cm (5in), **S** 10cm (4in). Fully hardy. Leaves are lance-shaped and usually glaucous. Bears 5-petalled, toothed, beige-backed, deep pink flowers on slender stems in summer. Suits a rock garden or scree.

***D.* 'Happiness'.** Perennial border carnation. Semi-double flowers are yellow, striped scarlet-orange.

***D.* 'Haytor'.** See *D.* 'Haytor White'.

♀ ***D.* 'Haytor White'**, syn. *D.* 'Haytor' (illus. p.266). Modern pink. Fully double, white flowers, borne on strong stems, have a good scent. Is widely grown, especially to provide cut flowers.

***D.* 'Hidcote'.** Evergreen, tufted, compact perennial. **H** and **S** 10cm (4in). Fully hardy. Bears a basal tuft of linear, spiky, grey-green leaves and, in summer, double, red flowers. Suits a rock garden.

***D.* 'Hilstar'.** See *D.* Starlight.

♀ ***D.* 'Houndspool Ruby'**, syn. *D.* 'Ruby', *D.* 'Ruby Doris', illus. p.268.

***D.* 'Ibiza'.** Perpetual-flowering, spray carnation. Fully double flowers are shell-pink.

***D.* 'Iceberg'.** Modern pink. Fragrant flowers are semi-double and pure white. Has a somewhat looser habit than *D.* 'Haytor White'.

***D.* 'Inchmery'** (illus. p.266). Old-fashioned, mule pink. Highly scented, double, pale pink flowers are borne above blue-green leaves. Does well on heavy soil.

♀ ***D.* 'India Star'** See *D.* Star Series 'India Star'.

♀ ***D.* 'Joy'**. Modern pink. Bears semi-double, pink flowers that are strongly scented and good for cutting.

***D.* 'Kobusa'.** See *D.* Pierrot.

***D.* 'La Bourbille'.** See *D.* 'La Bourboule'.

D

♀ **D. 'La Bourboule'**, syn. D. 'La Bourbille', illus. p.365.
D. 'Laced Monarch'. Modern pink. Double flowers are pink, laced with maroon-red.
D. 'Laced Prudence'. See D. 'Prudence'.
D. 'Lady Madonna' (illus. p.266). Modern pink. Double, white flowers have fringed petals, bright ruby centres and a powerful clove fragrance.
D. 'Lavender Clove'. Vigorous border carnation. Bears lavender-grey flowers on long stems.
D. Lily the Pink ('WP05 Idare') (illus. p.267). Modern pink. Fringed, double, vivid lavender-pink flowers have redder centres and a sweet, spicy fragrance. Is unusually vigorous.
D. 'Little Jock' illus. p.363.
D. 'London Brocade'. Modern pink. Has clove-scented, crimson-laced, pink flowers.
D. 'London Delight'. Old-fashioned pink. Fragrant flowers are semi-double and lavender, laced with purple.
D. 'Manon'. Perpetual-flowering carnation. Is one of the best deep pink cultivars with fully double flowers.
D. 'Mars'. Evergreen, tuft-forming perennial. **H** and **S** 10cm (4in). Frost hardy. Has small, double, cherry-red flowers in summer. Bears a basal tuft of linear, grey-green leaves. Is good in a rock garden.
D. 'Master Stuart'. Perennial border carnation. Has striking, semi-double flowers that are white with scarlet stripes.
D. microlepis illus. p.366.
♀ **D. 'Milky Way'** (illus. p.266). Perpetual-flowering, spray carnation. Shallowly toothed, double, white flowers may be slightly cream in the centres.
D. Miss Pinky. See D. 'Valda Wyatt'.
♀ **D. 'Monica Wyatt'** (illus. p.267). Modern pink. Fragrant, fringed, double, deep pink flowers, with crimson centres, are borne over an unusually long season.
D. monspessulanus. Evergreen, mat-forming perennial. **H** 30cm (12in), **S** 10–15cm (4–6in). Fully hardy. In summer, masses of strongly fragrant, 5-petalled, deeply fringed, pale lavender flowers rise on slender stems above short tufts of fine, grass-like leaves. Is good for a rock garden. Needs gritty soil.
♀ **D. 'Moulin Rouge'** (illus. p.267). Modern pink. Has double, pink flowers with burgundy lacing, rich burgundy centres and a strong clove scent.
D. 'Mrs Sinkins' (illus. p.266). Old-fashioned pink. Flowers are heavily scented, fringed, fully double and white.
D. 'Murcia'. Perpetual-flowering carnation. Has fully double, deep golden-yellow flowers.
D. 'Musgrave's Pink', syn. D. 'Charles Musgrave', D. 'Green Eyes' (illus. p.266). Old-fashioned pink. Bears single, white flowers with green eyes.
D. myrtinervius illus. p.364.
D. neglectus. See *D. pavonius*.
♀ **D. 'Neon Star'** See D. Star Series 'Neon Star'.
D. 'Nina'. Perpetual-flowering carnation. Is one of the best crimson cultivars. Fully double flowers have smooth-edged petals.
D. Passion ('WP Passion') See D. Scent First Series 'Passion'.
♀ ***D. pavonius***, syn. *D. neglectus*, illus. p.363.
D. Pierrot ('Kobusa'). Perpetual-flowering carnation. Bears fully double, light rose-lavender flowers with purple-edged petals.
♀ **D. 'Pike's Pink'** illus. p.364.
D. 'Pink Calypso'. See D. 'Truly Yours'.
D. 'Pink Jewel' (illus. p.267). Alpine pink. Has strongly scented, semi-double, pink flowers.
♀ **D. 'Pixie Star'** illus. p.267.
♀ **D. 'Prado Mint'** (illus. p.267). Perpetual-flowering carnation. Double, pale yellowish-green flowers have shallowly toothed margins.
D. 'Prudence', syn. D. 'Laced Prudence'. Old-fashioned pink. Fragrant flowers are semi-double and pinkish-white with purple lacing. Has a spreading habit.
D. 'Queen of Sheba' (illus. p.267). Old-fashioned pink. Has clove-scented, single, white flowers laced and flaked with magenta-purple.
D. 'Raggio di Sole'. Perpetual-flowering carnation. Fully double flowers are bright orange.
D. 'Red Barrow'. Perpetual-flowering, spray carnation. Fully double, bright scarlet flowers are borne in abundance.
D. 'Rose de Mai' (illus. p.267). Old-fashioned, mule pink. Double, mauve-pink flowers have darker centres.
D. 'Ruby'. See D. 'Houndspool Ruby'.
D. 'Ruby Doris'. See D. 'Houndspool Ruby'.
D. 'Sam Barlow'. Old-fashioned pink. Bears very fragrant, frilly, fully double, white flowers with brown centres.
♀ **D. 'Sandra Neal'.** Border carnation. Fully double, golden-apricot flowers are flaked deep rose-pink.
D. Scent First Series. Modern pink. Compact, repeat-flowering, strongly scented plants which tolerate extreme weather conditions. **Candy Floss ('Devon Flavia')** illus. p.266, has highly scented, double, bright sugar-pink flowers, with lacy tips and richer pink centres. **Passion ('WP Passion')** illus. p.267, produces rounded, fragrant, double, bright red flowers over an unusually long season. **Tickled Pink ('Devon PP 11')** (illus. p.267) bears rounded, semi-double, fringed, deep lavender flowers, with a strong spicy scent, over a long season.
D. 'Show Ideal'. Modern pink. Flat-petalled, semi-double flowers are white with red eyes and are strongly scented. Is excellent for exhibition.
D. 'Sops-in-wine'. Old-fashioned pink. Bears fragrant, single, maroon flowers with white markings.
D. Star Series. Prolific Modern pink with single or semi-double flowers over mounded foliage. ♀ **'Brilliant Star'** (illus. p.266) has fragrant, semi-double, glistening white flowers, with rich velvet-red centres. ♀ **'Evening Star'** (illus. p.266) bears single or semi-double, rounded, bright deep pink flowers with gently rippled edges and crimson eyes. ♀ **'India Star'** (illus. p.267) produces single, rich rose-pink flowers with bold, deep red eyes and a fine fragrance. ♀ **'Neon Star'** (illus. p.267) has silvery-green leaves and single, vivid magenta flowers over a very long season. ♀ **'Pixie Star'** (illus. p.267) bears single, rose-lavender flowers with slightly wavy petals and deep pink eyes.
D. Starlight ('Hilstar') illus. p.267. Modern pink. Strongly scented, single, rose-lavender flowers turn to lilac, then mature to almost white.
D. superbus. Evergreen, mat-forming perennial. **H** to 20cm (8in), **S** 15cm (6in). Fully hardy. Has narrowly lance-shaped, pale green leaves. In summer, slender stems bear very fragrant, 5-petalled, deeply fringed, pink flowers with darker centres. Suits a rock garden. **'Crimsonia'** (illus. p.267). Old-fashioned pink. Slender, rather floppy stems bear fragrant, high dissected, single, scarlet flowers.
D. 'Tayside Red' (illus. p.267). Malmaison carnation. Produces brick-red flowers through summer and into autumn. Does best in a cool glasshouse or conservatory.
D. 'Tickled Pink' illus. p.267.
D. 'Tigré'. Perpetual-flowering carnation. Has fully double, yellow flowers with a uniform, pinkish-purple stripe and edging to each petal.
D. 'Tony'. Perpetual-flowering, spray carnation. Fully double flowers are yellow with red stripes.
D. 'Truly Yours', syn. D. 'Pink Calypso'. Perpetual-flowering carnation. Fully double flowers are a good pink.
♀ **D. 'Valda Wyatt'**, syn. D. Miss Pinky (illus. p.267). Modern pink. Very fragrant flowers are fully double and rose-lavender.
D. 'Valencia'. Perpetual-flowering carnation. Has fully double, orange blooms.
♀ **D. 'Whatfield Magenta'.** Alpine pink. Fragrant, single, brilliant magenta flowers have paler throats. Has deep blue leaves.
D. 'White Ladies' (illus. p.266). Old-fashioned pink. Produces very fragrant, fully double, white flowers with greenish centres.
♀ **D. 'Widecombe Fair'.** Modern pink. Semi-double flowers, borne on strong stems, are of unusual colouring – peach-apricot, opening to blush-pink.
D. 'WP05 Idare'. See D. Lily the Pink.
D. 'WP Passion'. See D. Scent First Series Passion.

DIAPENSIA

DIAPENSIACEAE

Genus of evergreen, spreading sub-shrubs, suitable for rock gardens and troughs. Fully hardy. Needs partial shade and peaty, sandy, acid soil. Is very difficult to grow in hot, dry climates at low altitudes. Propagate by seed in spring or by semi-ripe cuttings in summer.
D. lapponica. Evergreen, spreading sub-shrub. **H** and **S** 7cm (3in). Has tufts of small, rounded, leathery leaves. Carries solitary tiny, bowl-shaped, white flowers in early summer.

DIASCIA

SCROPHULARIACEAE

Genus of summer- and autumn-flowering annuals and perennials, some of which are semi-evergreen, grown for their tubular, pink flowers. Is suitable for banks and borders. Frost hardy. Needs sun and humus-rich, well-drained soil that is not too dry. Cut back old stems in spring. Propagate by softwood cuttings in late spring, by semi-ripe cuttings in summer or by seed in autumn.
♀ ***D. barberae* 'Blackthorn Apricot'**, syn. D. 'Blackthorn Apricot', illus. p.278. **'Fischer's Flora'**, syn. *D. cordata* of gardens, illus. p.339. ♀ **'Ruby Field'** is a mat-forming perennial. **H** 8cm (3in), **S** 15cm (6in). Heart-shaped, pale green leaves clothe short, wiry stems. Produces tubular, wide-lipped, salmon-pink flowers throughout summer.
D. 'Blackthorn Apricot'. See *D. barberae* 'Blackthorn Apricot'.
D. cordata of gardens. See *D. barberae* 'Fischer's Flora'.
D. Ice Cracker ('Herack') illus. p.337.
D. Little Dancer ('Pendan') illus. p.301.
♀ ***D. rigescens*** illus. p.339.
D. 'Salmon Supreme' illus. p.345.
♀ ***D. vigilis.*** Prostrate perennial. **H** 30–40cm (12–16in), **S** 60cm (24in). Pale green leaves are small, rounded and toothed. Upright branchlets carry loose spikes of flattish, outward-facing, pale pink flowers in summer.

DICENTRA

PAPAVERACEAE/FUMARIACEAE

Genus of perennials, grown for their elegant sprays of pendent flowers. Fully hardy. Most do best in semi-shade and humus-rich, moist but well-drained soil. Propagate by division when dormant in late winter, species also by seed in autumn. ⓘ Contact with the foliage may aggravate skin allergies.
D. 'Adrian Bloom'. Spreading, tuft-forming perennial. **H** 45cm (18in), **S** 30cm (12in). Has sprays of pendent, heart-shaped, rich carmine-pink flowers above oval, grey-green leaves.
D. cucullaria illus. p.348.
D. eximia of gardens. See *D. formosa*.
D. formosa, syn. *D. eximia* of gardens. Spreading, tufted perennial. **H** 45cm (18in), **S** 30cm (12in). In spring–summer bears slender, arching sprays of pendent, heart-shaped, pink or dull red flowers above oval, finely cut, grey-green leaves.
D. peregrina. Tuft-forming perennial. **H** 8cm (3in), **S** to 5cm (2in). Locket-shaped, pink flowers appear in spring-summer above fern-like, blue-green leaves. Needs gritty soil. Is suitable for an alpine house.
D. spectabilis, syn. *Lamprocapnos spectabilis*, illus. p.223. ***f. alba*** syn. *Lamprocapnos spectabilis* f. *alba*, illus. p.223.
D. 'Spring Morning' illus. p.256.
♀ **D. 'Stuart Boothman'** illus. p.268.

DICHELOSTEMMA

LILIACEAE/ALLIACEAE

Genus of summer-flowering bulbs, grown for their dense flower heads on leafless stems. Is related to *Brodiaea* and is similar to *Allium* in appearance. Frost hardy, but in cold areas grow in a sheltered site. Needs sunny and well-drained soil. Water freely in spring, but dry out after flowering. Propagate by seed in autumn or spring or by offsets in autumn before growth commences.
D. congestum, syn. *Brodiaea congesta*, illus. p.392.
D. ida-maia, syn. *Brodiaea ida-maia*. Early summer-flowering bulb. **H** to 1m (3ft), **S** 8–10cm (3–4in). Long, narrow leaves are semi-erect and basal. Leafless stem carries a dense head of 2–2.5cm (¾–1in)

long flowers, each with a red tube and 6 green petals.
D. pulchellum, syn. *Brodiaea capitata, B. pulchella.* Early summer-flowering bulb. **H** 30–60cm (12–24in), **S** 8–10cm (3–4in). Long, narrow leaves are semi-erect and basal. Leafless stem bears a dense head of narrowly funnel-shaped, pale to deep violet flowers, 1–2cm (½–¾in) long, with violet bracts.

DICHORISANDRA

COMMELINACEAE

Genus of erect, clump-forming, evergreen perennials, grown for their ornamental foliage. Frost tender, min. 15–20°C (59–68°F). Prefers fertile, moist but well-drained soil, humid conditions and partial shade. Propagate by division in spring or by stem cuttings in summer.
D. reginae illus. p.473.

Dichromena colorata. See *Rhynchospora colorata.*

DICKSONIA

DICKSONIACEAE

Genus of evergreen or semi-evergreen, tree-like ferns that resemble palms and that are sometimes used to provide height in fern plantings. Half hardy to frost tender, min. 5°C (41°F). Needs semi-shade and humus-rich, moist soil. Remove faded fronds regularly. Propagate by spores in summer.
♀ ***D. antarctica*** illus. p.290.
♀ ***D. fibrosa.*** Evergreen, tree-like fern (deciduous in cold climates). **H** to 6m (20ft), **S** to 4m (12ft). Half hardy. Stout trunks are crowned by a rosette of spreading, divided, lance-shaped, dark green fronds, to 2m (6ft) long.
♀ ***D. squarrosa.*** Evergreen, tree-like fern (deciduous in cold climates). **H** to 6m (20ft), **S** to 4m (12ft). Half hardy. Slender trunks are crowned by a rosette of spreading, divided, lance-shaped, mid-green fronds, to 2m (6ft) long, with blackish stalks and midribs.

DICTAMNUS

RUTACEAE

Genus of summer-flowering perennials. Fully hardy. Requires full sun and fertile, well-drained soil. Resents disturbance. Propagate by seed sown in late summer when fresh. ⓘThe foliage, roots and seeds of *D. albus* may cause mild stomach upset if ingested, and contact with the foliage may cause photodermatitis.
♀ ***D. albus* var. *albus*** illus. p.230. ♀ **var. *purpureus*** (syn. *D. fraxinella*). Upright perennial. **H** 1m (3ft), **S** 60cm (2ft). Has light green leaves divided into oval leaflets. In early summer bears spikes of fragrant, star-shaped, purplish-pink flowers with long stamens.
D. fraxinella. See *D. albus* var. *purpureus.*

Didiscus coeruleus. See *Trachymene coerulea.*

DIDYMOCHLAENA

DRYOPTERIDACEAE/ASPIDIACEAE

Genus of one species of evergreen fern. Frost tender, min. 10°C (50°F). Has tufts of glossy, mid-green fronds, tinged with rose-pink or red when young. Requires partial shade, high humidity and moist, humus-rich soil. Propagate by spores as soon as ripe, or divide in spring.
D. lunulata. See *D. truncatula.*
D. truncatula, syn. *D. lunulata.* Evergreen fern. **H** and **S** to 1m (3ft). Has erect rhizomes and triangular, divided fronds, 60cm–1.5m (2–5ft) long, with simple diamond-shaped segments.

DIEFFENBACHIA

Dumb cane, Leopard lily

ARACEAE

Genus of evergreen, tufted perennials, grown for their foliage. Frost tender, min. 15°C (59°F). Grow in fertile, well-drained soil and in partial shade. Propagate in spring or summer by stem cuttings or pieces of leafless stem placed horizontally in compost. Scale insect or red spider mite may be troublesome. ⓘAll parts may cause severe discomfort if ingested, and contact with sap may irritate skin.
D. amoena of gardens. See *D. seguine* 'Amoena'.
***D.* 'Exotica'.** See *D. seguine* 'Exotica'.
***D. maculata* 'Exotica'.** See *D. seguine* 'Exotica'. **'Rudolph Roehrs'** see *D. seguine* 'Rudolph Roehrs'.
***D.* 'Memoria'.** See *D. seguine* 'Memoria Corsii'.
D. seguine. Evergreen, tufted perennial. **H** and **S** 1m (3ft) or more. Broadly lance-shaped leaves, to 45cm (18in) long, are glossy and dark green. Insignificant, tiny, greenish-white flowers, clustered on the spadix, are surrounded by a narrow, leaf-like spathe that appears intermittently. **'Amoena'** (syn. *D. amoena* of gardens) is robust. **H** to 2m (6ft), with creamy-white bars along lateral veins on the leaves. ♀ **'Exotica'** (syn. *D.* 'Exotica', *D. maculata* 'Exotica') illus. p.465. **'Memoria Corsii'** (syn. *D.* 'Memoria') has grey-green leaves, marked dark green and spotted white. **'Rudolph Roehrs'** (syn. *D. maculata* 'Rudolph Roehrs', *D.s.* 'Roehrs') illus. p.474.

DIERAMA

Angel's fishing rod, Wandflower

IRIDACEAE

Genus of evergreen, clump-forming, summer-flowering corms with pendent, funnel- or bell-shaped flowers on long, arching, wiry stems. Flourishes near pools. Frost to half hardy. Prefers a warm, sheltered, sunny site and well-drained soil that should be kept moist in summer when in growth. Dies down partially in winter. Propagate by division of corms in spring or by seed in autumn or spring. Resents disturbance, and divisions take a year or more to settle and start flowering again.
***D.* 'Blackbird'.** Evergreen, upright perennial. **H** 1.5m (5ft), **S** 30cm (1ft). Frost hardy. Produces cascades of nodding, funnel-shaped, violet-mauve flowers on wiry, pendulous stems in summer above grass-like leaves.
D. dracomontanum, syn. *D. pumilum.* Vigorous, evergreen, upright perennial. **H** 75cm (30in), **S** 30cm (12in). Frost hardy. In summer freely produces nodding, funnel-shaped flowers, in shades of pink and violet, on wiry stems. Leaves are grass-like.
D. ensifolium. See *D. pendulum.*
D. pendulum, syn. *D. ensifolium*, illus. p.392.
D. pulcherrimum illus. p.386.
D. pumilum. See *D. dracomontanum.*

DIERVILLA

CAPRIFOLIACEAE

Genus of deciduous, summer-flowering shrubs. Is similar to *Weigela.* Frost hardy. Needs partial shade or full sun and moderately fertile, well-drained soil. To keep the shrub neat, remove 2- and 3-year-old stems in winter or after flowering. Propagate by semi-ripe cuttings in late summer or hardwood cuttings in autumn.
D. sessilifolia. Deciduous, spreading shrub. **H** and **S** 1–1.5m (3–5ft). Narrowly oval, pointed, serrated, green leaves are often copper-tinted when young. Has terminal and lateral clusters of tubular, pale yellow flowers in summer. To treat as an herbaceous perennial, cut back to ground level each spring and apply a mulch and a fertilizer.

DIETES

IRIDACEAE

Genus of evergreen, iris-like, rhizomatous perennials, grown for their attractive flowers in spring or summer. Half hardy. Needs sun or partial shade and humus-rich, well-drained soil that does not dry out excessively. Propagate by seed in autumn or spring or by division in spring (although divisions do not become re-established very readily).
D. bicolor illus. p.395.
D. iridioides, syn. *D. vegeta* of gardens. Evergreen, spring- and summer-flowering, rhizomatous perennial. **H** to 60cm (2ft), **S** 30–60cm (1–2ft). Bears sword-shaped, semi-erect, basal leaves in a spreading fan. Branching, wiry stems bear iris-like, white flowers, 6–8cm (2½–3in) across; each of the 3 large petals has a central, yellow mark.
D. vegeta of gardens. See *D. iridioides.*

DIGITALIS

Foxglove

SCROPHULARIACEAE

Genus of biennials and perennials, some are evergreen, grown for their summer flower spikes. Fully to frost hardy. Species mentioned grow in most conditions, even dry, exposed sites, but do best in semi-shade and moist but well-drained soil. Propagate by seed in autumn. ⓘAll parts may cause severe discomfort if ingested. Contact with foliage may irritate skin.
D. ambigua. See *D. grandiflora.*
D. canariensis. See *Isoplexis canariensis.*
D. eriostachya. See *D. lutea.*
♀ ***D. ferruginea.*** Perennial best treated as a biennial. **H** 1–1.2m (3–4ft), **S** 30cm (1ft). Fully hardy. Long, slender spikes bear funnel-shaped, orange-brown and white flowers in mid-summer above basal rosettes of oval, rough leaves.
♀ ***D. grandiflora***, syn. *D. ambigua* (Yellow foxglove). Evergreen, clump-forming perennial. **H** 75cm (30in), **S** 30cm (12in). Fully hardy. Racemes of downward-pointing, tubular, creamy-yellow flowers appear in summer above a rosette of oval to oblong, smooth, strongly veined leaves.
D. lutea, syn. *D. eriostachya.* Upright perennial. **H** 75cm (30in), **S** 30cm (12in). Fully hardy. In summer, delicate spires of downward-pointing, narrowly tubular, creamy-yellow flowers are borne above a rosette of oval, smooth, mid-green leaves.
♀ ***D. x mertonensis.*** Clump-forming perennial. **H** 75cm (30in), **S** 30cm (12in). Fully hardy. Produces spikes of downward-pointing, tubular, rose-mauve to coppery flowers in summer, above a rosette of oval, hairy, soft leaves. Divide after flowering.
D. purpurea. Upright, short-lived perennial, grown as a biennial. **H** 1–1.5m (3–5ft), **S** 60cm (2ft). Fully hardy. Has a rosette of oval, rough, deep green leaves and, in summer, tall spikes of tubular flowers in shades of pink, red, purple or white. ♀ **f. *albiflora*** (syn. *D.p.* f. *alba*) illus. p.299.

DILLENIA

DILLENIACEAE

Genus of evergreen or briefly deciduous, spring-flowering trees, grown for their flowers and foliage and for shade. Frost tender, min. 16°C (61°F). Needs moisture-retentive, fertile soil and full light. Water potted plants freely while in full growth, less in winter. Propagate by seed in spring.
D. indica (Elephant apple). Briefly deciduous, spreading tree. **H** and **S** 8–12m (25–40ft). Has oval, serrated, boldly parallel-veined, glossy leaves, each 30cm (1ft) long. Nodding, cup-shaped, white flowers, each 15–20cm (6–8in) wide, are produced in spring, followed by edible, globular, greenish fruits.

DIMORPHOTHECA

African daisy, Cape marigold

COMPOSITAE/ASTERACEAE

Genus of annuals, perennials and evergreen sub-shrubs. Half hardy. Grow in sun and fertile, very well-drained soil. Dead-head to prolong flowering. Propagate annuals by seed sown under glass in mid-spring, perennials by semi-ripe cuttings in summer. Is susceptible to botrytis in wet summers.
D. annua. See *D. pluvialis.*
D. barberae of gardens. See *Osteospermum jucundum.*
D. pluvialis, syn. *D. annua*, illus. p.299.

DIONAEA

DROSERACEAE

Genus of evergreen, insectivorous, rosette-forming perennials. Frost tender, min. 5°C (41°F). Needs partial shade and a humid atmosphere; grow in a mixture of peat and moss, kept constantly moist. Propagate by seed or division in spring.
D. muscipula illus. p.473.

DIONYSIA

PRIMULACEAE

Genus of evergreen, cushion-forming perennials. Fully hardy. Grow in an alpine house in sun and very gritty, well-drained soil. Position deep collar of grit under cushion and ensure good ventilation at all times. Dislikes winter wet. Propagate by softwood cuttings in summer. Plants are susceptible to botrytis.

♀ ***D. aretioides*** illus. p.358.

D. microphylla. Evergreen perennial. **H** 5cm (2in), **S** 15cm (6in). Rosettes of oval to rounded, often sharply pointed, grey-green leaves, with a mealy, yellow coating beneath, form tight cushions. Small, short-stemmed, 5-petalled, white-eyed, pale to deep violet-yellow flowers, with darker petal bases, appear in early spring.

D. tapetodes illus. p.358.

DIOON

ZAMIACEAE

Genus of evergreen shrubs, grown for their palm-like appearance. Frost tender, min. 13–18°C (55–64°F). Requires full sun and fertile, well- drained soil. Water potted specimens moderately, less when not in full growth. Propagate by seed in spring.

♀ ***D. edule*** (Virgin's palm). Slow-growing, evergreen, palm-like shrub, eventually with a thick, upright trunk. **H** 2–4m (6–12ft), **S** 1.5–3m (5–10ft). Leaves are feather-like, 60cm–1.2m (2–4ft) long, with spine-tipped, blue-green leaflets.

DIOSCOREA

DIOSCOREACEAE

Genus of tuberous perennials, some of which are succulent, and herbaceous or evergreen, twining climbers, grown mainly for their decorative leaves. Insignificant flowers are generally yellow. Frost tender, min. 5–13°C (41–55°F). Prefers full sun or partial shade and fertile, well-drained soil. Propagate by division, or by cutting off sections of tuber in spring or autumn or by seed in spring.

D. discolor. See *D. dodecaneura.*

D. dodecaneura, syn. *D. discolor* (Common yam), illus. p.459.

♀ ***D. elephantipes***, syn. *Testudinaria elephantipes*, illus. p.492.

DIOSMA

RUTACEAE

Genus of evergreen, wiry-stemmed shrubs, grown for their flowers and overall appearance. Frost tender, min. 7°C (45°F). Needs full light and well-drained, neutral to acid soil. Water potted specimens moderately, less when not in full growth. To create a compact habit shorten flowered stems after flowering. Propagate by seed in spring or by semi-ripe cuttings in late summer.

D. ericoides (Breath of heaven). Fast-growing, evergreen, loosely rounded shrub. **H** and **S** 30–60cm (1–2ft). Aromatic, needle-like leaves are crowded on stems. In winter–spring carries a profusion of small, fragrant, 5-petalled, white flowers, sometimes tinted red.

Diosphaera. See *Trachelium.*

DIOSPYROS

EBENACEAE

Genus of deciduous or evergreen trees and shrubs, grown for their foliage and fruits. Fully to frost hardy. Needs full sun and does best in hot summers. Requires fertile, well-drained soil. To obtain fruits, plants of both sexes should be grown. Propagate by seed in autumn.

D. kaki (Chinese persimmon, Kaki, Persimmon). Deciduous, spreading tree. **H** 10m (30ft), **S** 7m (22ft). Frost hardy. Oval, glossy, dark green leaves turn orange, red and purple in autumn. Tiny, yellowish-white flowers in summer are followed on female trees by large, edible, rounded, yellow or orange fruits.

D. lotus (Date plum). Deciduous, spreading tree. **H** 10m (30ft), **S** 6m (20ft). Fully hardy. Has oval, glossy, dark green leaves, tiny, red-tinged, green flowers from mid- to late summer and, on female trees, unpalatable, rounded, purple or yellow fruits.

DIPCADI

LILIACEAE/HYACINTHACEAE

Genus of spring-flowering bulbs, grown mainly for botanical interest. Frost hardy, but will not tolerate cold, wet winters, so is best grown in a cold frame or alpine house. Needs a warm, sunny situation and light, well-drained soil. Is dormant in summer. Propagate by seed in autumn.

D. serotinum illus. p.422.

DIPELTA

CAPRIFOLIACEAE

Genus of deciduous shrubs, with bold, long-pointed leaves, grown for their showy, tubular flowers and peeling bark. After flowering, bracts beneath flowers enlarge and become papery and brown, surrounding the fruits. Fully hardy. Requires sun or semi- shade and fertile, well-drained soil. Benefits from the occasional removal of old shoots after flowering. Propagate by softwood cuttings in summer.

♀ ***D. floribunda*** illus. p.111.

D. yunnanensis illus. p.110.

DIPHYLLEIA

BERBERIDACEAE

Genus of perennials with creeping rootstocks and umbrella-like leaves. Is best suited to woodland gardens. Fully hardy. Needs semi-shade and moist soil. Propagate by division in spring or by seed in autumn.

D. cymosa (Umbrella leaf). Rounded perennial. **H** 60cm (24in), **S** 30cm (12in). Has large, rounded, 2-lobed leaves. In spring bears loose heads of inconspicuous, white flowers followed by indigo-blue berries on red stalks.

Dipidax. See *Onixotis.*

Diplacus glutinosus. See *Mimulus aurantiacus.*

Dipladenia. See *Mandevilla.*

DIPLARRHENA

IRIDACEAE

Genus of one species of summer-flowering perennial. Half hardy. Needs sun and well-drained soil. Propagate by seed or division in spring.

D. moraea illus. p.264.

DIPSACUS

Teasel

DIPSACACEAE

Genus of biennials or short-lived perennials grown for their flower heads, which are good for drying. Fully hardy. Requires sun or partial shade and any fertile soil. Sow seed in autumn or spring.

D. fullonum. Prickly biennial. **H** 1.5–2m (5–6ft), **S** 30–80cm (12–32in). In the first year produces a basal rosette of toothed, dark green leaves covered in spiny pustules. Thistle-like, pinkish-purple or white flower heads, with stiff, prickly bracts, are borne terminally on upright stems with paired leaves in mid- and late summer of the second year.

DIPTERONIA

ACERACEAE/SAPINDACEAE

Genus of deciduous trees, grown for their foliage and fruits. Fully hardy. Needs full sun and fertile, well-drained soil. Propagate by softwood cuttings in summer or by seed in autumn.

D. sinensis. Deciduous, spreading, sometimes shrubby tree. **H** 10m (30ft), **S** 6m (20ft). Large, mid-green leaves have 7–11 oval to lance-shaped leaflets. Inconspicuous, greenish-white flowers in summer are followed by large clusters of winged, red fruits.

DISA

ORCHIDACEAE

See also ORCHIDS.

D. uniflora. Deciduous, terrestrial orchid. **H** 45–60cm (1½–2ft). Frost tender, min. 7–10°C (45–50°F). Has narrowly lance-shaped, glossy, dark green leaves, to 22cm (9in) long. In early summer each stem bears up to 7 hooded, scarlet flowers, 8–10 cm (3–4in) long, that have darker veins and are suffused yellow. Needs partial shade and continually moist soil. Raise from seed or propagate by division of offsets when dormant.

DISANTHUS

HAMAMELIDACEAE

Genus of one species of deciduous, autumn-flowering shrub, grown for its overall appearance and autumn colour. Frost hardy. Needs partial shade and humus-rich, moist but not wet, neutral to acid soil. Propagate by layering in spring or by seed when ripe or in spring.

♀ ***D. cercidifolius*** illus. p.141.

DISCARIA

RHAMNACEAE

Genus of deciduous or almost leafless shrubs and trees, grown for their habit and flowers. Spiny, green shoots assume function of leaves. Frost hardy. Needs a sheltered, sunny site and fertile, well-drained soil. Propagate by softwood cuttings in summer.

D. toumatou (Wild Irishman). Deciduous or almost leafless, bushy shrub. **H** and **S** 2m (6ft). Shoots have sharp, rigid spines. Tiny, star-shaped, greenish-white flowers are borne in dense clusters in late spring

DISOCACTUS

CACTACEAE

Genus of epiphytic, perennial cacti with flattened, strap-shaped stems. Is closely related to *Epiphyllum*, with which it hybridizes. Spines are insignificant. Stems may die back after flowering. Frost tender, min. 10°C (50°F). Needs partial shade and rich, well-drained soil. Propagate by stem cuttings in spring or summer.

D. ackermannii, syn. *Epiphyllum ackermannii, Nopalxochia ackermannii* (Red orchid cactus). Erect, then pendent, epiphytic, perennial cactus. **H** 30cm (1ft), **S** 60cm (2ft). Has fleshy, toothed, green stems, to 7cm (3in) across and 40cm (16in) long; 15cm (6in) wide, funnel-shaped, red flowers in spring–summer along indented edges of stems.

D. flagelliformis. See *Aporcactus flagelliformis.*

D. 'Gloria' illus. p.485.

D. 'Jennifer Ann' illus. p.496.

D. 'M.A. Jeans' illus. p.485.

***D. phyllanthoides* 'Deutsche Kaiserin'** illus. p.485.

DISPORUM

Fairy bells

LILIACEAE/CONVALLARIACEAE

Genus of spring- or early summer-flowering perennials. Is best suited to woodland gardens. Fully hardy. Requires a cool, semi-shaded position and humus-rich soil. Propagate by division in spring or by seed in autumn.

D. hookeri. Clump-forming perennial. **H** 75cm (30in), **S** 30cm (12in). Leaves are narrowly oval and mid-green. Orange-red berries in autumn follow clusters of drooping, open bell-shaped, greenish-white flowers in spring.

***D. sessile* 'Variegatum'.** Rapidly spreading, clump-forming perennial. **H** 45cm (18in), **S** 30cm (12in). Solitary tubular-bell-shaped to bell-shaped, creamy-white flowers are produced in spring. Narrowly oval, pleated leaves are irregularly striped with white.

DISTICTIS

BIGNONIACEAE

Genus of evergreen, woody-stemmed, tendril climbers, grown for their colourful, trumpet-shaped flowers. Frost tender, min. 5–7°C (41–5°F). Well-drained soil is suitable with full light. Water freely in summer, less at other times. Support for stems is necessary. Thin out congested growth in spring. Propagate by softwood cuttings in early summer or by semi-ripe cuttings in late summer.

D. buccinatoria, syn. *Phaedranthus buccinatorius*, illus. p.461.

DISTYLIUM

HAMAMELIDACEAE

Genus of evergreen shrubs and trees, grown for their foliage and flowers. Frost hardy. Prefers a sheltered, partially shaded position and moist, peaty soil. Propagate by semi-ripe cuttings in summer.

D. racemosum. Evergreen, arching shrub. **H** 2m (6ft), **S** 3m (10ft). Leaves are oblong, leathery, glossy and dark green. Bears small flowers, with red calyces and purple anthers, late spring–early summer.

Dizygotheca elegantissima. See *Schefflera elegantissima.*

DOCYNIA

ROSACEAE

Genus of evergreen or semi-evergreen, spring-flowering trees, grown for their flowers and foliage; is related to *Cydonia*. Half hardy. Requires full sun and well-drained soil. Other than shaping while young, pruning is not necessary. Propagate by seed in spring or autumn, by budding in summer or by grafting in winter. Caterpillars may be troublesome.

D. delavayi. Evergreen or semi-evergreen, spreading tree. **H** and **S** 8m (25ft) or more. Oval to lance-shaped leaves are white-felted beneath. In spring has fragrant white flowers, pink in bud; ovoid, downy, yellow fruits follow in autumn.

D

DODECATHEON

Shooting stars

PRIMULACEAE

Genus of spring- and summer-flowering perennials, grown for their flowers, with reflexed petals and prominent stamens. Once fertilized, flowers turn skywards – hence their common name. Is dormant after flowering. Fully to frost hardy. Prefers sun or partial shade and moist but well-drained soil. Propagate by seed in autumn or by division in winter.

♀ ***D. dentatum.*** Clump-forming perennial. **H** 7cm (3in), **S** 25cm (10in). Fully hardy. Leaves are long, oval and toothed. In late spring, bears white flowers with prominent, dark stamens and reflexed petals. Prefers a partially shaded position.

♀ ***D. hendersonii***, illus. p.333.

D. latifolium. See *D. hendersonii.*

♀ ***D. meadia.*** Clump-forming perennial. **H** 20cm (8in), **S** 15cm (6in). Fully hardy. Leaves are oval and pale green. In spring, bears pale pink flowers, with reflexed petals, above foliage. Prefers a partially shaded site. ♀ ***f. album*** illus. p.333.

D. pauciflorum of gardens. See *D. pulchellum.*

♀ ***D. pulchellum***, syn. *D. pauciflorum* of gardens. Clump-forming perennial. **H** 15cm (6in), **S** 10cm (4in). Fully hardy. Is similar to *D. meadia*, but flowers are usually deep cerise.

***D.* 'Red Wings'** illus. p.333.

DODONAEA

SAPINDACEAE

Genus of evergreen trees and shrubs, grown mainly for their foliage and overall appearance. Half hardy to frost tender, min. 3–5°C (37–41°F). Prefers full sun and well-drained soil. Water potted plants freely when in full growth, less at other times. Cut back in late summer and in spring if needed, to maintain a balanced shape. Propagate by seed in spring or by semi-ripe cuttings in late summer.

***D. viscosa* 'Purpurea'** illus. p.457.

Dolichos lablab. See *Lablab purpureus.*

Dolichos purpureus. See *Lablab purpureus.*

DOMBEYA

STERCULIACEAE

Genus of evergreen shrubs and trees, grown for their flowers. Frost tender, min. 5–13°C (41–55°F). Needs full sun or partial shade and fertile, well-drained soil. Water potted plants freely when in full growth, less when temperatures fall. Cut back after flowering. Propagate by seed in spring or by semi-ripe cuttings in summer. Whitefly and red spider mite may be a nuisance.

D. burgessiae, syn. *D. mastersii.* Evergreen shrub. **H** 2–4m (6–12ft), **S** 1.5–3m (5–10ft). Frost tender, min. 5°C (41°F). Has rounded, 3-lobed, downy leaves and dense clusters of fragrant, white flowers, with pink to red veins, in autumn–winter.

D. x cayeuxii illus. p.450.

D. mastersii. See *D. burgessiae.*

Dondia. See *Hacquetia.*

DORONICUM

Leopard's bane

COMPOSITAE/ASTERACEAE

Genus of perennials, grown for their daisy-like flowers, which are good for cutting. Fully hardy. Most prefer full sun or part shade and moist, well-drained soil. Propagate by division in autumn.

D. austriacum. Clump-forming perennial. **H** 45cm (18in), **S** 30cm (12in). Bears daisy-like, pure yellow flower heads on slender stems in spring. Heart-shaped, wavy-edged bright green leaves are hairy.

D. columnae, syn. *D. cordatum.*

♀ ***D.* 'Miss Mason'** illus. p.227.

D. cordatum. See *D. columnae.*

***D. x excelsum* 'Harpur Crewe'**, syn. *D. plantagineum* 'Excelsum'. Elegant, clump-forming perennial. **H** 1m (3ft), **S** 60cm (2ft). Large, daisy-like, buttercup-yellow flower heads are borne, 3 or 4 to a stem, in spring. Leaves are heart-shaped and bright green. Good for a dry, shaded site.

***D.* 'Frühlingspracht'**, syn. *D.* 'Spring Beauty'. Clump-forming perennial. **H** 45cm (18in), **S** 30cm (12in). Produces daisy-like, double, bright yellow flower heads in spring. Bears heart-shaped, bright green leaves.

***D. orientale* 'Magnificum'** illus. p.263.

***D. plantagineum* 'Excelsum'.** See *D. x excelsum* 'Harpur Crewe'.

***D.* 'Spring Beauty'.** See *D.* 'Frühlingspracht'.

DOROTHEANTHUS

AIZOACEAE

Genus of succulent annuals, suitable for hot, dry places such as rock gardens, screes and gaps in paving. Half hardy. Needs sun and grows well in poor, very well-drained soil. Dead-head to prolong flowering. Propagate by seed sown under glass in early spring, or outdoors in mid-spring. Protect from slugs and snails.

♀ ***D. bellidiformis***, syn. *Mesembryanthemum criniflorum* (Ice-plant, Livingstone daisy). **'Magic Carpet'** is a carpeting annual. **H** 15cm (6in), **S** 30cm (12in). Has lance-shaped, pale green leaves. Daisy-like flowers, in bright shades of red, pink, yellow or white, open in sun.

DORYANTHES

LILIACEAE/DORYANTHACEAE

Genus of evergreen, rosette-forming perennials, grown for their flowers. Frost tender, min. 10°C (50°F). Needs a sunny position and humus-rich, well-drained soil. Propagate by mature bulbils, by seed in spring or by suckers after flowering.

D. palmeri illus. p.470.

Dorycnium hirsutum. See *Lotus hirsutus.*

Douglasia vitaliana. See *Vitaliana primuliflora.*

Doxantha. See *Macfadyena* except for:

Doxantha capreolata. See *Bignonia capreolata.*

DRABA

CRUCIFERAE/BRASSICACEAE

Genus of spring-flowering annuals and evergreen or semi-evergreen, cushion- or mat-forming perennials. Some species form soft, green cushions that in winter turn brown except at the tips, appearing dead. Is suitable for alpine houses. Fully to frost hardy. Needs sun and gritty, well-drained soil. Dislikes winter wet. Propagate by softwood cuttings of the rosettes in late spring or by seed in autumn.

D. aizoides (Yellow whitlow grass). Semi-evergreen, mat-forming perennial. **H** 2.5cm (1in), **S** 15cm (6in). Fully hardy. Has lance-shaped, stiff-bristled leaves in rosettes and, in spring, 4-petalled, bright yellow flowers. Suits a scree.

D. bryoides. See *D. rigida* var. *bryoides.*

D. hispanica. Semi-evergreen, cushion-forming perennial. **H** 5cm (2in), **S** 10cm (4in). Frost hardy. Pale green leaves are oval and soft. Clusters of flat, 4-petalled, pale yellow flowers are borne in spring.

♀ ***D. longisiliqua*** illus. p.357.

D. mollissima illus. p.358.

D. polytricha. Semi-evergreen, cushion-forming perennial. **H** 6cm (2½in), **S** 15cm (6in). Fully hardy. Forms rosettes of tiny round leaves. Bears flat, 4-petalled, golden-yellow flowers in spring. Is difficult to grow. Keep stones under cushion at all times. Remove dead rosettes at once.

D. rigida illus. p.357. **var. *bryoides*** (syn. *D. bryoides*) is an evergreen, hummock-forming perennial. **H** 4cm (1½in), **S** 6cm (2½in). Fully hardy. Has tiny, round, dark green leaves. Produces small clusters of almost stemless, 4-petalled, bright yellow flowers that cover hummocks in spring.

DRACAENA

AGAVACEAE/DRACAENACEAE

Genus of evergreen trees and shrubs, grown for their foliage. Frost tender, min. 13–18°C (55–64°F). Needs full sun or partial shade and well-drained soil. Water containerized plants moderately, much less in low temperatures. Rejuvenate leggy plants by cutting back to near soil level in spring. Propagate by seed or air-layering in spring or by tip or stem cuttings in summer. Mealy bug may be a nuisance.

D. australis. See *Cordyline australis.*

D. deremensis. See *D. fragrans* Deremensis Group. **'Souvenir de Schrijver'** see *D. fragrans* Deremensis Group 'Warneckei'. **'Warneckei'** see *D. fragrans* Deremensis Group 'Warneckei'.

♀ ***D. draco*** illus. p.451.

D. fragrans (Corn plant). ***Deremensis Group***, syn. *D. deremensis*, is a slow-growing sparsely branched shrub. **H** 2m (6ft) or more, **S** 1m (3ft) or more. Has lance-shaped, erect to arching, glossy, deep green leaves, to 45cm (18in) long. Mature plants may bear large panicles of small, red-and-white flowers in summer. ♀ ***Deremensis Group* 'Warneckei'** (syn. *D. deremensis* 'Souvenir de Schrijver', *D.d.* 'Warneckei') illus. p.454. **'Massangeana'.** Evergreen, erect, sparsely branched shrub. **H** 3–6m (10–20ft), **S** 1–3m (3–10ft). Has strap-shaped, arching leaves, to 60cm (2ft) long, with longitudinal bands of yellow and pale green. In early summer, fragrant, star-shaped, yellow flowers, rarely produced, are followed by rounded-oblong, orange-red fruits.

D. indivisa. See *Cordyline indivisa.*

♀ ***D. marginata*** (Madagascar dragon tree). Slow-growing, evergreen, erect shrub or tree. **H** 3m (10ft) or more, **S** 1–2m (3–6ft) or more. Leaves are narrowly strap-shaped and rich green with red margins. Flowers are rarely produced. ♀ **'Tricolor'** illus. p.452.

♀ ***D. sanderiana*** illus. p.453.

DRACOCEPHALUM

Dragon's head

LABIATAE/LAMIACEAE

Genus of summer-flowering annuals and perennials, suitable for rock gardens and borders. Fully hardy. Prefers sun and fertile, well-drained soil. Propagate by seed or division in spring or autumn or by basal cuttings of young growth in spring.

D. ruyschiana. Erect perennial. **H** 45–60cm (18–24in), **S** 30cm (12in). Freely bears whorled spikes of 2-lipped, violet-blue flowers from early to mid-summer. Mid-green leaves are linear to lance-shaped.

D. sibiricum. See *Nepeta sibirica.*

DRACUNCULUS

ARACEAE

Genus of tuberous perennials that produce triangular, foul-smelling spathes. Frost hardy, but protect dormant tubers with a cloche or dead bracken in severe winters. Needs sun and well-drained soil that dries out in summer. Propagate by offsets in late summer or by seed in autumn.

D. vulgaris, syn. *Arum dracunculus*, illus. p.386.

DREGEA

ASCLEPIADACEAE/APOCYNACEAE

Genus of evergreen, woody-stemmed, twining climbers, grown for botanical interest. Frost hardy. Grow in sun and

in any well-drained soil. Propagate by seed in spring or by stem cuttings in summer or autumn.
D. corrugata. See *D. sinensis.*
D. sinensis, syn. *D. corrugata, Wattakaka sinensis*, illus. p.197.

Drejerella guttata. See *Justicia brandegeeana.*
Drepanostachyum falconeri. See *Himalayacalamus falconeri.*

DRIMIA

SYN. URGINEA

LILIACEAE/HYACINTHACEAE

Genus of late summer- or early autumn-flowering bulbs, growing on or near soil surface, with spear-shaped flower spikes up to 1.5m (5ft) high. Frost to half hardy. Needs sun and well-drained soil that dries out while bulbs are dormant in summer. Plant in mid- to late summer. Water until leaves die down. Propagate by seed in autumn or by offsets in late summer.
D. maritima, syn. *Urginea maritima.* Late summer- or early autumn-flowering bulb. **H** 1.5m (5ft), **S** 30–45cm (1–1½ft). Half hardy. Bears broadly sword-shaped, erect, basal leaves in autumn after long spikes of small star-shaped, white flowers.

DRIMYS

WINTERACEAE

Genus of evergreen trees and shrubs, grown for their foliage and star-shaped flowers. Frost hardy, but in cold areas grow against a sunny wall. Needs sun or semi-shade and fertile, moist but well-drained soil. Propagate by semi-ripe cuttings in summer or by seed in autumn.
D. aromatica. See *D. lanceolata.*
D. axillaris. See *Pseudowintera axillaris.*
D. colorata. See *Pseudowintera colorata.*
D. lanceolata, syn. *D. aromatica*, illus. p.197.
♀ ***D. winteri***, syn. *Wintera aromatica*, illus. p.73.

DROSANTHEMUM

AIZOACEAE

Genus of erect or prostrate, succulent shrubs with slender stems and summer flowers. Frost tender, min. 5°C (41°F). Needs full sun and very well-drained soil. Propagate by seed or stem cuttings in spring or summer.
D. hispidum. Shrub with arching or spreading branches that root down. **H** 60cm (2ft), **S** 1m (3ft). Has cylindrical, light green leaves, 1.5–2.5cm (⅝–1in) long. In summer, bears masses of shiny, daisy-like, purple flowers, to 3cm (1¼in) across.
D. speciosum. Erect, shrubby succulent. **H** 60cm (2ft), **S** 1m (3ft). Has semi-cylindrical leaves, 1–2cm (½–¾in) long. Masses of daisy-like, green-centred, orange-red flowers, to 5cm (2in) across, appear in summer.

DROSERA

Sundew

DROSERACEAE

Genus of evergreen, insectivorous perennials. Fully hardy to frost tender, min. 5–10°C (41–50°F). Grow in sun, in a mixture of peat and moss that is not allowed to dry out. Propagate by seed or division in spring.
D. capensis illus. p.473.
D. spatulata illus. p.473.

DRYANDRA

PROTEACEAE

Genus of evergreen, spring- to summer-flowering shrubs and trees, grown for their flowers, foliage and overall appearance. Frost tender, min. 7°C (45°F). Needs full light and well-drained, sandy soil that is low in nutrients. Is difficult to grow. Water containerized plants moderately, less in low temperatures. Plants under glass must be freely ventilated. Propagate by seed in spring.
D. formosa. Evergreen, bushy shrub. **H** 2–5m (6–15ft), **S** 1.5–3m (5–10ft). Strap-shaped leaves are divided into triangular, closely set lobes, creating a saw-blade effect. In spring carries small, scented, tubular, orange-yellow flowers in domed, terminal heads.

DRYAS

Mountain avens

ROSACEAE

Genus of evergreen, prostrate, woody-based perennials with oak-like leaves and cup-shaped flowers. Is useful on banks and walls, in rock gardens and as ground cover. Fully hardy. Prefers sun and gritty, well-drained, peaty soil. Propagate by seed or by semi-ripe cuttings in summer.
D. drummondii. Evergreen, prostrate, woody-based perennial. **H** 5cm (2in), **S** indefinite. Stout stems are clothed in small, oval, lobed, leathery, dark green leaves. Bears nodding, cream flowers in early summer that never fully open.
♀ ***D. octopetala*** illus. p.361.
♀ ***D. x suendermannii.*** Evergreen, prostrate, woody-based perennial. **H** 5cm (2in), **S** indefinite. Is similar to *D. drummondii*, but has slightly nodding, pale cream flowers that open horizontally.

DRYOPTERIS

DRYOPTERIDACEAE/ASPIDIACEAE

Genus of deciduous or semi-evergreen ferns, many of which form regular, shuttlecock-like crowns. Fully to half hardy. Requires shade and moist soil. Regularly remove fading fronds. Propagate by spores in summer or by division in autumn or winter.
♀ ***D. affinis***, syn. *D. borreri, D. pseudomas* (Golden male fern). Virtually evergreen fern. **H** and **S** to 1m (3ft). Fully hardy. Has a "shuttlecock" of lance-shaped, divided fronds, 20–80cm (8–32in) tall, from an erect rhizome. Fronds are pale green as they unfurl in spring, in contrast to the scaly, golden brown midribs; they mature to dark green and often remain green through winter. Distinguished from *D. filix-mas* by a dark spot where each pinna joins the midrib.
D. atrata of gardens. See *D. cycadina.*
D. austriaca. See *D. dilatata.*
D. borreri. See *D. affinis.*
D. carthusiana (Narrow buckler fern). Deciduous or semi-evergreen, creeping, rhizomatous fern. **H** 1m (3ft), **S** 45cm (18in). Fully hardy. Produces lance-shaped, much-divided, mid-green fronds with triangular to oval pinnae.
♀ ***D. cycadina***, syn. *D. atrata* of gardens, *D. hirtipes.* Deciduous fern. **H** 60cm (24in), **S** 45cm (18in). Fully hardy. Has an erect rhizome producing a "shuttlecock" of lance-shaped, divided, bright green fronds, 45cm (18in) tall, with green midribs.
♀ ***D. dilatata***, syn. *D. austriaca* (Broad buckler fern). Deciduous or semi-evergreen fern. **H** 1m (3ft), **S** 45cm (18in). Fully hardy. Has much-divided, arching, mid-green fronds, with triangular to oval pinnae, on stout, dark brown stems.
♀ ***D. erythrosora*** (Japanese shield fern) illus. p.293.
♀ ***D. filix-mas*** illus. p.293.
♀ **'Grandiceps Wills'** is a deciduous fern. **H** and **S** 90m (3ft). Fully hardy. Has "shuttlecocks" of broadly lance-shaped, tasselled, elegantly arching, mid-green fronds, arising from crowns of large, upright, brown-scaled rhizomes. The tip of each frond has a heavy crest, and the pinnae are also finely crested.
D. goldieana (Giant wood fern). Deciduous fern. **H** 1m (3ft), **S** 60cm (2ft). Fully hardy. Has broadly oval, light green fronds divided into numerous oblong, indented pinnae.
D. hirtipes. See *D. cycadina.*
D. marginalis. Deciduous fern. **H** 60cm (24in), **S** 30cm (12in). Fully hardy. Fronds are lance-shaped, dark green and divided into numerous oblong, slightly indented pinnae.
D. pseudomas. See *D. affinis.*
D. sieboldii. Semi-evergreen, tufted fern. **H** and **S** 30–60cm (1–2ft). Fully or frost hardy. Produces long-stalked, erect or arching, yellowish-green fronds, 20–50cm (8–20in) long, with up to 6 pairs of narrowly lance-shaped pinnae, 15–30cm (6–12in) long.
♀ ***D. wallichiana*** (Wallich's wood fern) illus. p.293.

DUCHESNEA

ROSACEAE

Genus of perennials, some of which are semi-evergreen, grown as ground cover as well as for their flowers. May be used in hanging baskets. Fully hardy. Grow in well-drained soil and in sun or partial shade. Propagate by division in spring, by rooting plantlets formed at ends of runners in summer or by seed in autumn.
D. indica, syn. *Fragaria indica.* Semi-evergreen, trailing perennial. **H** to 10cm (4in), **S** indefinite. Dark green leaves have 3 toothed leaflets like those of strawberries. Solitary, 5-petalled, bright yellow flowers, to 2.5cm (1in) wide and with leafy, green frills of sepals, appear from spring to early summer. Strawberry-like, tasteless, red fruits appear in late summer.

DUDLEYA

CRASSULACEAE

Genus of basal-rosetted, perennial succulents, closely related to *Echeveria.* Frost tender, min. 7°C (45°F). Requires full sun and very well-drained soil. Water sparingly when plants are semi-dormant in mid-summer. Propagate by seed or division in spring or summer.
D. brittonii. Basal-rosetted, perennial succulent. **H** 20–60cm (8–24in) or more when in flower, **S** 50cm (20in). Has narrowly lance-shaped, tapering, fleshy, silvery-white leaves. Masses of star-shaped, pale yellow flowers are produced in spring-summer.
D. pulverulenta illus. p.490.

DURANTA

VERBENACEAE

Genus of fast-growing, evergreen or partially deciduous trees and shrubs, grown for their flowers and overall appearance. Frost tender, min. 10–13°C (50–55°F). Needs full light and fertile, well-drained soil. Water potted plants freely when in full growth, moderately at other times. Prune as necessary to curb vigour. Propagate by seed in spring or by semi-ripe cuttings in summer. Whitefly may be troublesome.
D. erecta, syn. *D. plumieri, D. repens*, illus. p.319. **'Gold Edge'** illus. p.319.
D. plumieri. See *D. erecta.*
D. repens. See *D. erecta.*

DUVALIA

ASCLEPIADACEAE/APOCYNACEAE

Genus of clump-forming or carpeting, perennial succulents with short, thick, leafless stems; is closely related to *Stapelia.* Star-shaped flowers have thick, fleshy petals recurved at tips. Frost tender, min. 10°C (50°F), but best at 20°C (68°F). Requires partial shade and very well-drained soil. Propagate by seed or stem cuttings in spring or summer.
D. corderoyi illus. p.493.

Duvernoia adhatodoides. See *Justicia adhatoda.*

DYCKIA

BROMELIACEAE

Genus of evergreen, rosette-forming perennials. Frost tender, min. 7–10°C (45–50°F). Requires full light and well-drained soil containing sharp sand or grit. Water moderately in summer, scarcely or not at all in winter, sparingly at other times. Propagate by offsets or division in spring.
D. remotiflora Evergreen, basal-rosetted perennial. **H** and **S** 30–50cm (12–20in). Has dense rosettes of very narrowly triangular, pointed, thick-textured, arching, dull green leaves with hooked spines and grey scales beneath. Woolly spikes of tubular, orange-yellow flowers are produced above the foliage in summer–autumn.

DYPSIS

PALMAE/ARECACEAE

Genus of evergreen palms, grown for their elegant appearance. Frost tender, min. 16°C (61°F). Needs full light or partial shade and fertile, well-drained soil. Water potted specimens moderately, much less when temperatures are low. Propagate by seed in spring at not less than 26°C (79°F). Red spider mite may sometimes be a nuisance.
♀ ***D. lutescens***, *syn. Areca lutescens, Chrysalidocarpus lutescens*, illus. p.452.

E

ECCREMOCARPUS

BIGNONIACEAE

Genus of evergreen, sub-shrubby, tendril climbers grown for their flowers, which appear over a long period. One species only is commonly grown. Half hardy; in cold areas treat as an annual. Grow in full sun and in any well-drained soil. Propagate by seed in early spring.
E. scaber illus. p.208.

ECHEVERIA

CRASSULACEAE

Genus of rosetted, perennial succulents with long-lasting flowers. Leaves take on their brightest colours from autumn to spring. Half hardy to frost tender, min. 5–7°C (41–5°F). Needs sun, good ventilation and very well-drained soil. Propagate by seed, stem or leaf cuttings, division or offsets in spring or summer.
♀***E. agavoides.*** Basal-rosetted, perennial succulent. **H** 15cm (6in), **S** 30cm (12in). Frost tender, min. 5°C (41°F). Has tapering, light green leaves, often red-margined. Carries cup-shaped, red flowers, 1cm (½in) long, in summer.
E. cooperi. See *Adromischus cooperi.*
♀***E. derenbergii.*** Clump-forming, perennial succulent. **H** 4cm (1½in), **S** 30cm (12in). Min. 5°C (41°F). Produces a short-stemmed rosette of rounded, grey-green leaves. Flower stem, 8cm (3in) long, produces cup-shaped, yellow-and-red or orange flowers in spring. Offsets freely. Is often used as a parent in breeding.
♀***E. elegans*** illus. p.484.
E. gibbiflora. Rosetted, perennial succulent. **H** 10–25cm (4–10in), **S** 30cm (12in). Min. 7°C (45°F). Rosettes of spoon-shaped, pointed, grey-green leaves, often tinged red-brown, are stemless or borne on short stems. Cup-shaped, red flowers, yellow within, are borne on stems, 90cm (3ft) long, in autumn–winter. ♀ **var. *metallica*** (syn. *E.g.* 'Metallica') has white- or red-margined, purple-green leaves that mature to green-bronze.
♀***E. harmsii***, syn. *Oliveranthus elegans.* Bushy, perennial succulent. **H** 20cm (8in), **S** 30cm (12in). Min. 7°C (45°F). Erect stems are each crowned by a 6cm (2½in) wide rosette of short, narrowly lance-shaped, pale green leaves, covered in short hairs. In spring bears cup-shaped, orange-tipped, red flowers, yellow within.
E. montana. Rosetted, perennial succulent. **H** 30cm (12in), **S** 10cm (4in). Half hardy. Spoon-shaped, pointed, waxy-bloomed, light green leaves are produced in a small, short-stemmed, clustered rosette. Slender flower stem, 30–40cm (12–16in) long, bears cup-shaped, yellow to orange flowers in summer.
♀***E. pulvinata*** (Plush plant). Bushy, perennial succulent. **H** 30cm (12in), **S** 50cm (20in). Frost tender, min. 5°C (41°F). Has brown-haired stems topped by a rosette of thick, rounded, green leaves that become red-edged in autumn. Leaves have short white hairs. Bears red flowers in spring.
E. secunda illus. p.487.
♀***E. setosa*** (Mexican firecracker). Basal-rosetted, perennial succulent. **H** 4cm (1½in), **S** 30cm (12in). Min. 7°C (45°F). Has long, narrow, mid-green leaves covered in short, thick, white hairs. Bears cup-shaped, red-and-yellow flowers in spring. Is prone to rotting: do not water foliage.

ECHINACEA

Coneflower

COMPOSITAE/ASTERACEAE

Genus of summer-flowering perennials. Fully hardy. Prefers sun and humus-rich, moist but well-drained soil. Propagate by division or root cuttings in spring.
E. angustifolia (illus. p.221). Clump-forming perennial. **H** 80cm (32in), **S** 45cm (18in). Has narrowly lance-shaped, hairy, dark green leaves. In summer, upright stems bear solitary, daisy-like flower heads with narrow, reflexed, pale pinkish-purple ray florets and a central, orange-brown cone. Needs an open position.
***E.* 'CBG Cone 2'.** See *E.* Pixie Meadowbrite.
***E.* 'Green Envy'.** Clump-forming, erect perennial. **H** 100cm (36in), **S** 30cm (12in). Has lance-shaped, dark green leaves. In summer, upright stems bear solitary, daisy-like, lime-green flower heads with a central, greenish-purple cone and rather broad, overlapping ray florets, which are pinkish-purple at the bases.
***E.* 'Green Jewel'.** Clump-forming, erect perennial. **H** 50–60cm (20–24in), **S** 30cm 12in). Has lance-shaped, dark green leaves. In summer, upright stems bear solitary, daisy-like, soft-green flower heads with rather short, overlapping ray florets and a central, bright green cone.
***E.* 'Harvest Moon'** (illus. p.221). Clump-forming, erect perennial. **H** to 60cm (24in), **S** 30cm (12in). Has lance-shaped, dark green leaves. In summer, upright often branched stems bear daisy-like flower heads with rather reflexed, orange-tinged, soft yellow ray florets and a central, greenish-yellow cone.
E. paradoxa (illus. p.221). Clump-forming perennial. **H** 1m (3ft), **S** 30cm (12in) or more. Has narrowly lance-shaped, dark green leaves. In summer, upright stems bear solitary, daisy-like, bright yellow flower heads with drooping, long, slender ray florets and a central, dark brown cone. Needs an open position.
***E.* Pixie Meadowbrite ('CBG Cone 2').** Compact perennial. **H** 50cm (20in), **S** 30cm (12in). Has lance-shaped, dark green leaves. In summer, stout, well-branched stems bear solitary, daisy-like, bright pink flower heads with horizontal ray florets and a central, greenish-pink cone, which matures to crimson.
E. purpurea, syn. *Rudbeckia purpurea.* Erect perennial. **H** 1.2m (4ft) or more, **S** 45cm (1½ft) or more. Has oval, hairy, dark green, basal leaves. From summer to mid-autumn, branching stems bear solitary, daisy-like, pinkish-purple or white flower heads with horizontal or reflexed ray florets and a central, orange-brown cone. Is best in an open position. **'Coconut Lime'** (illus. p.221), **H** to 60cm (2ft), has reflexed, white ray florets and a central cone that develops into a rounded pompom of shorter, green florets forming a shuttlecock-shaped head. **Doppelganger** see *E.p.* 'Doubledecker'. **'Doubledecker'** (syn. *E.p.* Doppelganger; illus. p.221), **H** 1m (3ft), has reflexed, magenta-pink ray florets and a central, dark brown cone, out of which develop more, smaller ray florets. ♀ **Elton Knight ('Elbrook'), H** 60cm (2ft), has a compact, bushy habit and produces numerous flower heads with horizontal, bright pink ray florets and a central, purplish-red cone. **'Fragrant Angel'** (illus. p.221), **H** 1m (3ft), bears fragrant flower heads with overlapping, horizontal, white ray florets, sometimes green tinged, and a central, orange cone. **'Kim's Knee High', H** 60cm (2ft), has a compact habit and produces masses of small, warm pink flower heads with reflexed ray florets and a central, orange cone. **'Kim's Mop Head', H** 50–60cm (20–24in), has a compact habit and produces near-horizontal, white ray florets and a central, greenish-orange cone.
♀**'Magnus'** (illus. p.221), **H** 1m (3ft), produces large, red-pink flower heads with rather broad, overlapping, horizontal ray florets. **'Razzmatazz'** (illus. p.221), **H** 90cm (36in), has soft pink flower heads, the central cone of which develops into a rounded pompom of shorter, reddish-pink ray florets. May need staking. **'Robert Bloom'** illus. p.234. ♀**'Rubinstern', H** 80cm (32in), bears large, reddish-pink flowers with horizontal ray florets and a central, brownish-red cone. ♀**'Ruby Giant', H** 80cm (32in), produces sturdy stems bearing rich pink flower heads with a second row of ray florets; these are held at the horizontal, giving flowers an impression of greater size than selections with drooping ray florets. **'Sundown'** (illus. p.221), **H** 80cm (32in), has a variable form and flower colour, and bears usually overlapping, near-horizontal, warm orange, ray florets and a central, dark orange cone. **'White Lustre', H** 1.2m (4ft), has lance-shaped leaves and produces strong stems bearing white flower heads with a prominent, central orange-brown cone. **'White Swan', H** 70cm (28in), bears rather reflexed, warm white ray florets and a central, orange-brown cone.
***E.* 'Tiki Torch'.** Clump-forming, erect perennial. **H** 70cm (28in), **S** 30cm (12in). Has lance-shaped, dark green leaves. In summer, upright stems bear solitary, daisy-like, bright orange flower heads with a central, reddish-brown cone and rather reflexed ray florets, which are darkest at the bases.
***E.* 'Tomato Soup'.** Clump-forming, erect perennial. **H** 80cm (32in), **S** 30cm (12in). Has lance-shaped, dark green leaves. In summer, upright stems bear daisy-like, fiery orange-red flower heads with ray florets held more or less horizontally and a central, greenish-brown cone.

ECHINOCACTUS

CACTACEAE

Genus of slow-growing, hemispherical, perennial cacti. Frost tender, min. 11°C (52°F); lower temperatures cause yellow patches on *E. grusonii.* Requires full sun and very well-drained soil. Yellow-flowered species are easy to grow. Propagate by seed in spring.
E. asterias. See *Astrophytum asterias.*
E. chilensis. See *Eriosyce chilensis.*
E. eyriesii. See *Echinopsis oxygona.*
E. grusonii (Golden barrel cactus, Mother-in-law's cushion). Slow-growing, hemispherical, perennial cactus. **H** to 60cm (24in) **S** to 80cm (32in). Spined, green stem has 30 ribs. Woolly crown bears a ring of straw-coloured flowers in summer, only on stems over 38cm (15in) wide.
E. ingens. See *E. platyacanthus.*
E. myriostigma. See *Astrophytum myriostigma.*
E. ornatus. See *Astrophytum ornatum.*
E. platyacanthus, syn. *E. ingens.* Slow-growing, hemispherical, perennial cactus. **H** 3m (10ft), **S** 2m (6ft). Grey-blue stem has a woolly crown and up to 50 ribs. Funnel-shaped, yellow flowers, 3cm (1¼in) across, appear in summer only on plants over 40cm (16in) in diameter.
E. scheeri. See *Sclerocactus scheeri.*
E. uncinatus. See *Sclerocactus uncinatus.*

ECHINOCEREUS

CACTACEAE

Genus of spherical to columnar, perennial cacti, freely branching with age, some with tuberous rootstocks. Buds, formed inside spiny stem, burst through skin, producing long-lasting flowers, with reflexed petal tips and prominent, green stigmas, followed by pear-shaped, spiny seed pods. Frost tender, min. 5–8°C (41–46°F); some species tolerate light frost if dry. Needs full sun and very well-drained soil. Propagate by seed or stem cuttings in spring or summer.
E. baileyi. See *E. reichenbachii* var. *baileyi.*
E. cinerascens. Clump-forming, perennial cactus. **H** 30cm (1ft), **S** 1m (3ft). Min. 5°C (41°F). Has 7cm (3in) wide stems, each with 5–12 ribs. Areoles each bear 8–15 yellowish-white spines. Mature plants produce masses of trumpet-shaped, bright pink or purple flowers, 12cm (5in) across and with paler petal bases, in spring.
E. leucanthus, syn. *Wilcoxia albiflora,* illus. p.482.
E. pectinatus. Columnar cactus. **H** 35cm (14in), **S** 20cm (8in). Min. 7°C (45°F). Has sparsely branched, green stems with 12–23 ribs and short, comb-like spines, often variably coloured. In spring bears trumpet-shaped, purple, pink or yellow flowers, 12cm (5in) across, with paler bases.
E. pentalophus, syn. *E. procumbens,* illus. p.484.
E. procumbens. See *E. pentalophus.*
♀***E. reichenbachii.*** Columnar cactus. **H** 35cm (14in), **S** 20cm (8in). Min. 7°C (45°F). Slightly branched, multi-coloured stem with 12–23 ribs has comb-like spines, 1.5cm (⅝in) long. Trumpet-shaped, pink or purple flowers, 12cm (5in) across, with darker petal bases, appear in spring. **var. *baileyi*** (syn. *E. baileyi*) illus. p.484.
E. schmollii, syn. *Wilcoxia schmollii,* illus. p.492.
E. triglochidiatus. Clump-forming, perennial cactus. **H** 30cm (12in), **S** 15cm (6in). Min. 5°C (41°F). Has a short, thick, dark green stem with 3–5 spines, each to 2.5cm (1in) long, per areole. In spring bears funnel-shaped, bright red flowers, 7cm (3in) across, with prominent, red stamens and green stigmas. **var. *paucispinus*** illus. p.496.

Echinodorus ranunculoides. See *Baldellia ranunculoides.*
Echinofossulocatus lamellosus. See *Stenocactus crispatus.*
Echinofossulocactus. See *Stenocactus.*
Echinomastus macdowellii. See *Thelocactus macdowellii.*

ECHINOPS

Globe thistle

COMPOSITAE/ASTERACEAE

Genus of summer-flowering perennials, grown for their globe-like, spiky flower heads. Fully hardy. Does best in full sun and in poor soil. Propagate by division or seed in autumn or by root cuttings in winter. Flower heads dry well.
E. bannaticus. Upright perennial. **H** 1.2–1.5m (4–5ft), **S** 75cm (2½ft). Has narrow, deeply cut leaves and pale to mid-blue heads of spherical flowers, borne on branching stems in late summer. ♀**'Taplow Blue'** illus p. 241.
***E. ritro* 'Veitch's Blue'.** Upright perennial. **H** 1.2m (4ft), **S** 75cm (2½ft). Sharply divided dark green leaves are covered in down beneath. Has round, thistle-like, purplish-blue heads of flowers carried in late summer on silvery stems.
E. sphaerocephalus. Massive, bushy perennial. **H** 2m (6ft), **S** 1m (3ft). Has deeply cut, mid-green leaves, pale grey beneath, and grey stems bearing round, greyish-white flower heads in late summer.

ECHINOPSIS

CACTACEAE

Genus of spherical to columnar, perennial cacti, mostly freely branching; it is sometimes held to include *Trichocereus.* Frost tender, min. 5–10°C (41–50°F). Requires full sun and well-drained soil. Propagate by seed or offsets in spring or summer.
♀***E. aurea***, syn. *Lobivia aurea, L. cylindrica, Pseudolobivia aurea,* illus p.495.
E. backebergii, syn. *E. backerbergii* subsp. *backebergii, Lobivia backebergii,* illus. p.491.
E. bridgesii. See *E. lageniformis.*
E. candicans, syn. *Trichocereus candicans,* illus. p.492.
♀***E. chamaecereus***, syn. *Chamaecereus silvestrii, Lobivia silvestrii,* illus. p.486.
E. cinnabarina, syn. *Lobivia cinnabarina.* Spherical, perennial cactus. **H** and **S** 15cm (6in). Glossy, dark green stem has about 20 warty ribs and mostly curved, dark spines. In summer bears funnel-shaped to flattish, carmine-red flowers, 8cm (3in) across.
E. eyriesii. See *E. oxygona.*
E. lageniformis, syn. *E. bridgesii, Trichocereus bridgesii,* illus. p.489.
E. marsoneri, syn. *Lobivia haageana,* illus. p.491.
E. multiplex. See *E. oxygona.*
E. oxygona, syn. *E. eyriesii, E. multiplex, Echinocactus eyriesii,* illus. p.481. Flattened spherical, perennial cactus. **H** 30cm (12in), **S** 50cm (20in). Has slowly branching, mid-green stems with 11–18 ribs and very short spines. Tubular, white flowers appear in spring–summer.
E. pentlandii, syn. *Lobivia pentlandii,* illus. p.491.
E. rhodotricha. Spherical to columnar, perennial cactus. **H** 60cm (2ft), **S** 20cm (8in). Produces branching, dark green stems, 9cm (3½in) across, with 8–13 ribs. Curved, dark spines, 2cm (¾in) long, later turn pale. Has tubular, white to pink flowers in spring–summer.
E. spachiana, syn. *Cereus spachianus, Trichocereus spachianus,* illus. p.492.

Echioides longiflorum. See *Arnebia pulchra.*

ECHIUM

BORAGINACEAE

Genus of annuals and evergreen shrubs, biennials and perennials, grown for their flowers. Fully hardy to frost tender, min. 3°C (37°F). Needs full sun and fertile, well-drained soil. Water containerized specimens freely in summer, moderately at other times. Propagate by seed in spring or by greenwood or semi-ripe cuttings in summer. Whitefly may sometimes be troublesome. ⓘ All parts may cause mild stomach upset if ingested; contact with the foliage may irritate skin.
E. bourgaeanum. See *E. wildpretii.*
E. vulgare [dwarf] Moderately fast-growing, erect, bushy annual or biennial. **H** 30cm (12in), **S** 20cm (8in). Fully hardy. Has lance-shaped, dark green leaves. Spikes of tubular flowers, in white, pink, blue or purple, appear in summer.
♀***E. wildpretii***, syn. *E. bourgaeanum.* Evergreen, erect, unbranched biennial that dies after fruiting. **H** 2.5m (8ft) or more, **S** 60cm (2ft). Half hardy. Narrowly lance-shaped, silver-haired leaves, 30cm (1ft) long, form a dense rosette. Has compact spires, 1–1.5m (3–5ft) long, of small, funnel-shaped, red flowers in late spring and early summer.

EDGEWORTHIA

THYMELAEACEAE

Genus of deciduous shrubs, grown for their flowers in late winter and early spring. Frost hardy, but flowers are susceptible to frost damage. Is best grown against a south- or west-facing wall in most areas. Requires full sun and well-drained soil. Dislikes being transplanted. Propagate by semi-ripe cuttings in summer or by seed in autumn.
E. chrysantha, syn. *E. papyrifera,* illus. p.126.
E. papyrifera. See *E. chrysantha.*

EDRAIANTHUS

CAMPANULACEAE

Genus of short-lived perennials; some are evergreen. In winter, a small bud is just visible from each rootstock. In spring, prostrate stems radiate to carry leaves and flowers. Is suitable for rock gardens, screes and troughs. Fully hardy. Needs sun and well-drained soil. Propagate by softwood cuttings from side shoots in early summer or by seed in autumn.
E. dalmaticus. Upright, then arching perennial. **H** 10cm (4in), **S** 15cm (6in). Bears narrowly lance-shaped, pale green leaves and, in early summer, terminal clusters of bell-shaped, violet-blue flowers, 2.5cm (1in) across.
♀***E. pumilio*** illus. p.368.
E. serpyllifolius, syn. *Wahlenbergia serpyllifolia,* illus. p.367. **'Major'** is an evergreen, prostrate perennial. **H** 1cm (½in), **S** to 5cm (2in). Has tight mats of tiny, oval, dark green leaves. In early summer, bell-shaped, deep violet flowers, 1.5cm (⅝in) wide, are borne on very short stems. Needs a sheltered site. Seldom sets seed.

Edwardsia microphylla. See *Sophora microphylla.*

EGERIA

HYDROCHARITACEAE

Genus of semi-evergreen or evergreen, perennial, floating or submerged water plants, grown for their foliage. Is similar to *Elodea*, but has more conspicuous flowers, held above water surface. Plants are useful for oxygenating water and provide a suitable depository for fish spawn. Frost tender, min. 1°C (34°F). Needs a sunny position. Thin regularly to keep under control. Propagate by stem cuttings in spring or summer.
E. densa, syn. *Anacharis densa, Elodea densa.* Semi-evergreen perennial, spreading, submerged water plant. **S** indefinite. Forms a mass of whorled, small, lance-shaped, dark green leaves borne on long, wiry stems. Small, 3-parted, white flowers appear in summer.

EHRETIA

BORAGINACEAE

Genus of deciduous, summer-flowering trees, grown for their foliage and star-shaped flowers. Frost hardy, but is susceptible to frost damage when young. Requires sun or semi-shade and fertile, well-drained soil. Propagate by softwood cuttings in summer.
E. dicksonii illus. p.88.

EICHHORNIA

PONTEDERIACEAE

Genus of evergreen or semi-evergreen, perennial, floating and marginal water plants. Frost tender, min. 1°C (34°F). Needs an open, sunny position in warm water. Grows prolifically and requires regular thinning year-round. Propagate by detaching young plants as required.
E. crassipes, syn. *E. speciosa,* illus. p.441.
E. speciosa. See *E. crassipes.*

ELAEAGNUS

ELAEAGNACEAE

Genus of deciduous or evergreen shrubs and trees, grown for their foliage and small, usually fragrant flowers, and ornamental fruits. Evergreens make good shelter belts or hedging, particularly in coastal areas. Fully to frost hardy. Most evergreen species thrive in sun or shade, but silver-leaved and deciduous species prefer full sun. Requires fertile, well-drained soil. Trim hedges in late summer. Propagate by seed in autumn, evergreen forms also by semi-ripe cuttings in summer, deciduous forms by softwood or semi-ripe cuttings in summer.
E. angustifolia illus. p.116.
E. x ebbingei. Evergreen, bushy, dense shrub. **H** and **S** 5m (15ft). Fully hardy. Has oblong to oval, glossy, dark green leaves, silvery beneath. Fragrant, bell-shaped, silvery-white flowers are borne from mid- to late autumn. Leaves of ♀**'Gilt Edge'** have golden-yellow margins. **'Limelight'** illus. p.139.
E. macrophylla. Evergreen, bushy, dense shrub. **H** and **S** 3m (10ft). Frost hardy. Broadly oval leaves are silvery-grey when young, becoming glossy and dark green above, but remaining silvery-grey beneath, when mature. Fragrant, bell-shaped, creamy-yellow flowers, silvery outside, appear from mid- to late autumn, followed by egg-shaped, red fruits.
***E. pungens* 'Maculata'**, syn. *E. pungens* 'Aureovariegata', illus. p.119.
E. umbellata illus. p.113.

ELAEOCARPUS

ELAEOCARPACEAE

Genus of evergreen, spring- and summer-flowering shrubs and trees, grown for their flowers and foliage. Half hardy to frost tender, min. 5°C (41°F). Requires full sun or partial shade and fertile, well-drained but not dry soil. Water containerized plants freely when in growth, less in winter. Current season's growth may be cut back in winter. Propagate by seed in spring or by semi-ripe cuttings in summer. Red spider mite and whitefly may cause problems.
E. cyaneus, syn. *E. reticulatus* (Blueberry ash). Evergreen, rounded shrub or tree. **H** and **S** 3m (10ft), sometimes to 12m (40ft) or more. Frost tender. Bears elliptic to lance-shaped, toothed, lustrous leaves and, in summer, bell-shaped, fringed, white flowers, and globular, blue fruits in autumn.
E. reticulatus. See *E. cyaneus.*

ELATOSTEMA

SYN. PELLIONIA

URTICACEAE

Genus of evergreen, creeping perennials and subshrubs with attractive foliage that makes useful ground cover. Frost tender, min. 15°C (59°F). Requires humid conditions, indirect light and moist soil. Propagate from stem cuttings in spring or summer.
E. pulchra, syn. *E. repens* var. *pulchra.* Evergreen, slightly fleshy perennial with rooting, creeping stems. **H** 8–10cm (3–4in), **S** 60cm (2ft) or more. Broadly oval leaves, 5cm (2in) long, are blackish-green with dark green veins above, purple below. Flowers are insignificant.
♀***E. repens***, syn. *Pellionia daveauana, P. repens* (Watermelon begonia), illus. p.473. **var. *pulchra*** see *E. pulchra.*

ELEGIA

RESTIONACEAE

See also GRASSES, BAMBOOS, RUSHES and SEDGES.
E. capensis illus. p.285.

ELEOCHARIS

CYPERACEAE

See also GRASSES, BAMBOOS, RUSHES and SEDGES.
E. acicularis (Needle spike-rush). Evergreen, rhizomatous, perennial sedge. **H** to 10cm (4in), **S** indefinite. Fully hardy. Basal, mid-green leaves are very narrow. Hairless, unbranched, square stems produce solitary tiny brown spikelets in summer.

ELEUTHEROCOCCUS

SYN. ACANTHOPANAX

ARALIACEAE

Genus of deciduous shrubs and trees, grown for their foliage and fruits. Produces tiny, usually greenish-white flowers. Fully hardy. Prefers full sun and needs well-drained soil. Propagate by seed in spring or by root cuttings in late winter.
E. sieboldianus illus. p.138.

Elliottia paniculata. See *Tripetaleia paniculata.*
Elodea crispa of gardens. See *Lagarosiphon major.*
Elodea densa. See *Egeria densa.*

ELSHOLTZIA

LABIATAE/LAMIACEAE

Genus of perennials and deciduous shrubs and subshrubs, grown for their flowers. Frost hardy. Needs full sun and fertile, well-drained soil. Cut back old shoots hard in early spring. Propagate by softwood cuttings in summer.
E. stauntonii. Deciduous, open sub-shrub. **H** and **S** 1.5m (5in). Sharply toothed, mint-scented, dark green leaves turn red in autumn. Slender spires of pale purple blooms appear in late summer–autumn.

Elymus arenarius. See *Leymus arenarius.*

EMBOTHRIUM

PROTEACEAE

Genus of evergreen or semi-evergreen trees, grown for their flowers. Frost hardy, but shelter from cold winds. Needs semi-shade and moist but well-drained, acid soil. Propagate by suckers in spring or autumn or by seed in autumn.
E. coccineum illus. p.86.

EMILIA

COMPOSITAE/ASTERACEAE

Genus of annuals and perennials with flowers that are good for cutting. Is ideal for hot, dry areas and coastal soils. Half hardy. Requires sun and very well-drained soil. Propagate by seed sown under glass in spring, or outdoors in late spring.
E. coccinea, syn. *E. flammea, E. javanica* of gardens, illus. p.327.
E. flammea. See *E. coccinea.*
E. javanica of gardens. See *E. coccinea.*

EMMENOPTERYS

RUBIACEAE

Genus of deciduous trees, grown for their foliage; flowers only appear in hot summers. Frost hardy, but young growths may be damaged by late frosts. Needs full sun and deep, fertile, well-drained soil. Propagate by softwood cuttings in summer.
E. henryi illus. p.75.

ENCEPHALARTOS

ZAMIACEAE

Genus of evergreen shrubs and trees, grown for their palm-like leaves. Frost tender, min. 10–13°C (50–55°F). Needs full sun and well-drained soil. Water potted plants moderately when in full growth, less at other times. Propagate by seed in spring.
E. ferox illus. p.457.
E. longifolius. Slow-growing, evergreen tree, sometimes branched with age. **H** 3m (10ft) or more, **S** 1.5–2.5m (5–8ft). Has feather-shaped leaves, each 60cm–1.5m (2–5ft) long, divided into narrowly lance-shaped to oval, blue-green leaflets, usually with hook-tipped teeth. Cone-like, brown flower heads appear intermittently.

ENCYCLIA

ORCHIDACEAE

See also ORCHIDS.
E. cochleata. Evergreen, epiphytic orchid for a cool greenhouse. **H** 30cm (12in). Upright spikes of green flowers, 5cm (2in) long, with dark purple lips at the top and ribbon-like sepals and petals, are produced in summer and, on mature plants, intermittently throughout the year. Leaves are narrowly oval and 15cm (6in) long. Requires semi-shade in summer.
E. radiata. Evergreen, epiphytic orchid for a cool greenhouse. **H** 25cm (10in). Bears upright spikes of very fragrant, rounded, creamy-white flowers, 1cm (½in) across, with red-lined white lips, in summer. Narrowly oval leaves are 10–15cm (4–6in) long.

Endymion. See *Hyacinthoides.*

ENKIANTHUS

ERICACEAE

Genus of deciduous or semi-evergreen, spring-flowering shrubs and trees, grown for their mass of small, bell- or urn-shaped flowers and their autumn colour. Fully to frost hardy. Needs sun or semi-shade and moist, peaty, acid soil. Propagate by semi-ripe cuttings in summer or by seed in autumn.
♀ ***E. campanulatus*** illus. p.111.
♀ ***E. cernuus* f. *rubens*** illus. p.123.
♀ ***E. perulatus*** illus. p.120.

ENSETE

MUSACEAE

Genus of evergreen perennials, grown for their foliage, which resembles that of bananas, and fruits. Has false stems made of overlapping leaf sheaths that die after flowering. Frost tender, min. 10°C (50°F). Grow in sun or partial shade and humus-rich soil. Propagate by seed in spring or by division year-round.
♀ ***E. ventricosum***, syn. *Musa arnoldiana, M. ensete*, illus. p.474.

EOMECON

PAPAVERACEAE

Genus of one species of perennial. Is suitable for large rock gardens. Fully hardy. Needs sun and well-drained soil. Propagate by seed or runners in spring.
E. chionantha (Snow poppy). Vigorous, spreading perennial. **H** to 40cm (16in), **S** indefinite. Leaves are large, palmate and grey. Erect stems carry long panicles of small, poppy-like, white summer flowers.

EPACRIS

ERICACEAE/EPACRIDACEAE

Genus of evergreen, heath-like shrubs, grown for their flowers. Frost tender, min. 5°C (41°F). Needs full sun and humus-rich, well-drained, neutral to acid soil. Water potted plants moderately when in full growth, less at other times. Cut back flowered stems after flowering to maintain a neat habit. Propagate by seed in spring or semi-ripe cuttings in late summer.
E. impressa illus. p.155.

EPHEDRA

EPHEDRACEAE

Genus of evergreen shrubs, grown for their habit and green shoots. Makes good ground cover in dry soil. Grow male and female plants together in order to obtain fruits. Fully hardy. Requires full sun and well-drained soil. Propagate by seed in autumn or division in autumn or spring.
E. gerardiana. Evergreen, spreading shrub with slender, erect, rush-like, green shoots. **H** 60cm (2ft), **S** 2m (6ft). Leaves and flowers are inconspicuous. Bears small, spherical, red fruits.

EPIDENDRUM

ORCHIDACEAE

See also ORCHIDS.
E. difforme. Evergreen, epiphytic orchid for an intermediate greenhouse. **H** 23cm (9in). Large heads of semi-translucent, green flowers, 0.5cm (¼in) across, open in autumn. Has oval, rigid leaves, 2.5–5cm (1–2in) long. Requires shade in summer. Avoid spraying, which can cause spotting of leaves. Propagate by division in spring.
E. ibaguense, syn. *E. radicans.* Evergreen, epiphytic orchid for a cool greenhouse. **H** 2m (6ft) or more. Produces a constant succession of feathery-lipped, deep red blooms, 0.5cm (¼in) across. Leaves, 2.5–5cm (1–2in) long, are oval and rigid. Grow in semi-shade in summer. Propagate by tip cuttings in spring.
E. radicans. See *E. ibaguense.*

EPIGAEA

ERICACEAE

Genus of evergreen, prostrate, spring-flowering sub-shrubs. Fully to frost hardy. Needs shade and humus-rich, moist, acid soil. Most are difficult to cultivate. Propagate by seed in spring or by softwood cuttings in early summer.
E. asiatica. Evergreen, creeping sub-shrub. **H** to 10cm (4in), **S** to 20cm (8in). Fully hardy. Stems and heart-shaped, deep green leaves are covered with brown hairs. Bears terminal clusters of 3–6 tiny, slightly fragrant, urn-shaped, white or pink flowers in spring.
E. gaultherioides, syn. *Orphanidesia gaultherioides*, illus. p.351.
E. repens (Mayflower, Trailing arbutus). Evergreen, creeping sub-shrub. **H** 10cm (4in), **S** 30cm (12in). Fully hardy. Hairy stems, bearing heart-shaped, leathery leaves, root at intervals. In spring produces terminal clusters of 4–6 cup-shaped, white flowers, sometimes flushed pink. Is relatively easy to grow.

EPILOBIUM

SYN. CHAMAENERION, CHAMERION
Willow herb

ONAGRACEAE

Genus of annuals, biennials, semi-evergreen and deciduous perennials and sub-shrubs, grown for their deep pink to white flowers in summer. Is useful on dry banks; many species are invasive. Fully to frost hardy. Tolerates sun or shade and prefers moist but well-drained soil. Propagate species by seed in autumn, selected forms by softwood cuttings from side-shoots in spring.
E. angustifolium* f. *album illus. p.216.
E. californicum. See *Zauschneria californica.*
E. canum. See *Zauschneria californica* subsp. *cana.*
E. chlorifolium* var. *kaikourense. Clump-forming, deciduous, woody-based perennial. **H** 30cm (12in), **S** 15cm (6in). Fully hardy. Has persistent, oval, hairy, bronze and dark green leaves. Produces short spikes of funnel-shaped, white to pink flowers in summer.
E. glabellum of gardens illus. p.360.
E. obcordatum. Clump-forming perennial. **H** 15cm (6in), **S** 10cm (4in). Frost hardy. Oval leaves are glossy green. Spikes of open cup-shaped, deep rose-pink flowers are borne in summer. Is good for a rock garden or alpine house. Requires a sheltered position and full sun. In cultivation may not retain character, especially in mild climates.
E. septentrionale. See *Zauschneria septentrionalis.*

EPIMEDIUM

Barrenwort

BERBERIDACEAE

Genus of spring-flowering perennials, some of which are evergreen. Flowers are cup-shaped with long or short spurs. Makes good ground cover. Fully hardy. Does best in partial shade and humus-rich, moist but well-drained soil. Cut back just before new growth appears in spring. Propagate by division in spring or autumn.
E. alpinum. Evergreen, clump-forming perennial. **H** 23cm (9in), **S** to 30cm (12in). Racemes of pendent, short-spurred flowers, with crimson sepals and yellow petals, appear in spring. Has finely toothed,

E

glossy leaves divided into oval, angled, mid-green leaflets, bronze when young.
***E.* 'Amber Queen'** illus. p.263.
***E. davidii*.** Vigorous, evergreen, ground-cover perennial. **H** 30cm (12in), **S** 40cm (16in). Dainty, mid-green leaves are tinged bronze when young and divided into rounded heart-shaped, toothed leaflets. Produces clusters of pendent, long-spurred, butter-yellow flowers in spring.
E. epsteinii illus. p.260.
E. grandiflorum* 'Crimson Beauty'.** Clump-forming perennial. **H** and **S** 30cm (12in). Racemes of pendent, long-spurred, copper-crimson flowers are produced in spring at the same time as heart-shaped, copper-marked, light green leaves, divided into oval leaflets, which mature to mid-green. ♀**'Rose Queen'** has wiry stems bearing clusters of cup-shaped, deep pink flowers with white-tipped spurs in spring. ***f. violaceum has young leaves that are flushed bronze and produces purple-and-white flowers.
♀***E.* x *perralchicum*.** Evergreen, carpeting perennial. **H** 45cm (18in), **S** 30cm (12in). Short spires of pendent, yellow flowers, with short spurs, appear in spring. Leaves, divided into rounded to oval leaflets, are dark green.
***E. perralderianum*.** Semi-evergreen, carpeting perennial. **H** 30cm (12in), **S** 45cm (18in). Clusters of small, pendent, short-spurred, bright yellow flowers are borne in spring. Has large, toothed, glossy, deep green leaves, divided into rounded to oval leaflets.
♀***E. pinnatum* subsp. *colchicum*.** Evergreen, carpeting perennial. **H** and **S** 30cm (12in). In spring, clusters of small, pendent, bright yellow flowers with short spurs appear above dark green leaves, hairy when young, divided into oval leaflets.
***E. pubigerum*.** Evergreen, carpeting perennial. H and S 45cm (18in). Grown for its dense, smooth, heart-shaped, divided foliage and clusters of cup-shaped, creamy-white or pink flowers in spring.
♀***E.* x *rubrum*** illus. p.260.
***E.* x *versicolor*.** Clump-forming perennial. **H** and **S** 30cm (12in). Small, pendent clusters of yellow flowers, with long, red-tinged spurs, appear in spring. Heart-shaped, fresh green leaves are divided into oval leaflets that are tinted reddish-purple. **'Neosulphureum'** illus. p.262.
E.* x *warleyense illus. p.263.
♀***E.* x *youngianum* 'Niveum'** illus. p.254.

EPIPHYLLUM
Orchid cactus, Strap cactus
CACTACEAE

Genus of perennial cacti with strap-shaped, flattened, green stems that have notched edges. Flowers are produced at notches. Frost tender, min. 5–11°C (41–52°F). Grow in sun or partial shade and in rich, well-drained soil. Propagate by stem cuttings in spring or summer.
***E. ackermannii*.** See *Disocactus ackermannii*.
E. anguliger illus. p.494.
***E. crenatum*.** Erect, then pendent, perennial cactus. **H** and **S** 3m (10ft). Min. 11°C (52°F). Has a flattened stem. Bears lightly perfumed, funnel-shaped, broad-petalled, white flowers, 20cm (8in) across, in spring–summer. Is often used as a parent for breeding.
E. laui illus. p.482.
***E. oxypetalum*.** Erect, then pendent, perennial cactus. **H** 3m (10ft), **S** 1m (3ft). Min. 11°C (52°F). Produces freely branching, flattened stems, 12cm (5in) across. In spring–summer bears nocturnal, tubular, white flowers, 25cm (10in) long. Makes a good house plant.

EPIPREMNUM
SYN. POTHOS
ARACEAE

Genus of evergreen, woody-stemmed, root climbers, including *Pothos*, grown for their handsome leaves. Frost tender, min. 15–18°C (59–64°F). Grow in light shade away from direct sun; any well-drained, moisture-retentive soil is suitable. Water regularly, less in cold weather. Stems need good supports. Remove shoot tips to induce branching at any time. Propagate by leaf-bud or stem-tip cuttings in late spring or by layering in summer. ⓘAll parts may cause severe discomfort if ingested, and contact with the sap of *E. aureum* may irritate skin.
***E. aureum* 'Marble Queen'**, syn. *Scindapsus aureus* 'Marble Queen', illus. p.460.
***E. pictum* 'Argyraeum'.** See *Scindapsus pictus* 'Argyraeus'.

EPISCIA
GESNERIACEAE

Genus of evergreen, low-growing and creeping perennials, grown for their ornamental leaves and colourful flowers. Is useful as ground cover or in hanging baskets. Frost tender, min. 15°C (59°F). Requires high humidity, a shaded site and humus-rich, well-drained soil. Keep well watered, but avoid waterlogging. Propagate in summer by stem cuttings, division or removing rooted runners.
E. cupreata (Flame violet) illus. p.471. **'Metallica'** is an evergreen, creeping perennial. **H** 10cm (4in), **S** indefinite. Has oval, downy, wrinkled leaves, tinged pink to copper and with broad, silvery bands along midribs. Funnel-shaped, orange-red flowers, marked yellow within, are borne intermittently. **'Tropical Topaz'** has yellow flowers.
E. dianthiflora, syn. *Alsobia dianthiflora*, illus. p.465.
***E. lilacina*.** Evergreen, low-growing perennial, with runners bearing plantlets. **H** 10cm (4in), **S** indefinite. Has oval, hairy, pale green leaves, to 8cm (3in) long. Funnel-shaped, white flowers, tinged mauve and with yellow eyes, are produced in small clusters from autumn to spring. Leaves of **'Cuprea'** are bronze-tinged.

EPITHELANTHA
CACTACEAE

Genus of very slow-growing, spherical, perennial cacti densely covered with very short spines. Frost tender, min. 10°C (50°F). Needs full sun and well-drained soil; prone to rotting if overwatered. Propagate by grafting, seed or stem cuttings in spring or summer.
E. micromeris illus. p.493.

ERAGROSTIS
GRAMINEAE/POACEAE

See also GRASSES, BAMBOOS, RUSHES and SEDGES.
***E. curvula* 'Totnes Burgundy'** illus. p.285.

ERANTHEMUM
ACANTHACEAE

Genus of perennials and evergreen shrubs, grown for their flowers. Frost tender, min. 15–18°C (59–64°F). Requires full light or partial shade and fertile, well-drained soil. Water containerized plants freely when in full growth, moderately at other times. In spring or after flowering remove at least half of each spent flowering stem to encourage a bushier habit. Propagate by softwood cuttings in late spring. Whitefly may be a nuisance.
***E. atropurpureum*.** See *Pseuderanthemum atropurpureum*.
***E. nervosum*.** See *E. pulchellum*.
♀***E. pulchellum***, syn. *E. nervosum*. Evergreen, erect shrub. **H** 1–1.2m (3–4ft), **S** 60cm (2ft) or more. Produces elliptic to oval, prominently veined, deep green leaves. Blue flowers, each with a 3cm (1¼in) long tube and rounded petal lobes, are produced in winter-spring.

ERANTHIS
RANUNCULACEAE

Genus of clump-forming perennials, with knobbly tubers, grown for their cup-shaped flowers surrounded by leaf-like ruffs of bracts. Fully to frost hardy. Prefers partial shade and humus-rich soil, well-drained but not drying out excessively. Dies down in summer. Propagate by seed in autumn or by division of clumps immediately after flowering while still in leaf. ⓘAll parts may cause mild stomach upset if ingested, and contact with the sap may irritate skin.
♀***E. hyemalis*** illus. p.429.
♀***E.* x *tubergenii* 'Guinea Gold'.** Late winter- or early spring-flowering, tuberous perennial. **H** 8–10cm (3–4in), **S** 4–6cm (1½–2½in). Frost hardy. Stems each bear a stalkless, deep golden-yellow flower, 3–4cm (1¼–1½in) across, surrounded by a bronze-green bract, cut into narrow lobes. Rounded leaves are divided into finger-shaped lobes.

ERCILLA
SYN. BRIDGESIA
PHYTOLACCACEAE

Genus of evergreen, root climbers, grown for their neat, green leaves and green and purple flower spikes. Frost hardy. Grow in sun or partial shade and in any well-drained soil. Prune after flowering, if required. Propagate by stem cuttings in late summer or autumn.
***E. spicata*.** See *E. volubilis*.
E. volubilis, syn. *E. spicata*, illus. p.192.

EREMURUS
Foxtail lily, King's spear
LILIACEAE/ASPHODELACEAE

Genus of perennials, with fleshy, finger-like roots, grown for their stately spires of shallowly cup-shaped flowers in summer. Fully to frost hardy. Requires a sunny, warm position and well-drained soil. Tends to come into growth very early, and young shoots may be frosted. Provide a covering of dry bracken in late winter to protect the crowns when shoots are first developing. Stake tall species and hybrids. Propagate by division in spring or early autumn or by seed in autumn.
***E. himalaicus*.** Upright perennial. **H** 2–2.25m (6–8ft), **S** 1m (3ft). Frost hardy. Has strap-shaped, bright green basal leaves. In early summer tall stems bearing dense racemes of open cup-shaped, pure white blooms with long stamens appear.
***E.* x *isabellinus* 'Cleopatra'** illus. p.220.
♀***E. robustus*** illus. p.216.
***E.* Shelford Hybrids.** Perennials of varying habit and flower colour. **H** 1.5m (5ft), **S** 60cm (2ft). Frost hardy. Long racemes of orange, buff, pink or white flowers are borne freely in mid-summer. Leaves are strap-shaped, in basal rosettes.
***E. spectabilis*.** Erect perennial. **H** 1.2m (4ft), **S** 60cm (2ft). Frost hardy. Bears long racemes of pale yellow flowers, with brick-red anthers, in early summer. Leaves are strap-shaped, in basal rosettes.

ERIA
ORCHIDACEAE

See also ORCHIDS.
E. coronaria, syn. *Trichosma suavis*. Evergreen, epiphytic orchid for a cool greenhouse. **H** 23cm (9in). Sprays of fragrant, rounded, creamy-white flowers, 1cm (½in) across, each with a red- and yellow-marked lip, open in autumn. Has broadly oval, glossy leaves, 10cm (4in) long. Needs semi-shade in summer and moist compost year-round.

ERICA
ERICACEAE

See also HEATHERS.
E. arborea (Tree heath). Evergreen, upright, shrub-like tree heath. **H** 6m (20ft), **S** 1.5m (5ft). Frost hardy, but liable to damage from frost and cold winds. Has needle-like, bright green leaves in whorls of 3 or 4 and bears scented, bell-shaped, white flowers from late winter to late spring. May tolerate slightly alkaline soil. ♀**'Albert's Gold'**, **H** 2m (6ft), retains its golden foliage year-round. ♀**var. *alpina*** (illus. p.166) has vivid green foliage and compact racemes of white flowers. May be pruned hard to keep its shape and to encourage new growth.
♀***E. australis*** (Spanish heath, Spanish tree heath). Evergreen, shrub-like tree heath. **H** to 2.2m (7ft), **S** 1m (3ft). Frost hardy, but stems may be damaged by snow and frost. Has needle-like leaves in whorls of 4 and tubular to bell-shaped, white or purplish-pink flowers in spring. May tolerate slightly alkaline soil. ♀**f. *albiflora* 'Mr Robert'** has white flowers. ♀**'Riverslea'** has bright purple-

pink flowers, mostly in clusters of 4.
♀ ***E. canaliculata*** (Channelled heath). Evergreen, erect shrub. **H** to 3m (10ft), **S** 1m (3ft). Half hardy. Produces whorls of 3 dark green narrow, needle-like leaves. Cup-shaped, pearl-white flowers, sometimes rose-tinted, with dark brown, almost black anthers, are borne in winter (under glass) or early spring (in the open). Requires acid soil.
E. carnea, syn. *E. herbacea* (Alpine heath, Winter heath). Evergreen, spreading shrub. **H** to 30cm (12in), **S** to 45cm (18in) or more. Fully hardy. Produces whorls of needle-like, mid- to dark green leaves and bears tubular to bell-shaped flowers that are in shades of pink and red, occasionally white, from early winter to late spring. Tolerates limestone and some shade. Makes good ground cover. **'Altadena'** has golden foliage and pale pink flowers. ♀ **'Ann Sparkes'** (illus. p.166), **H** 15cm (6in), has golden foliage, turning to bronze in winter, and rose-pink flowers. **'Bell's Extra Special'**, **H** 15cm (6in), **S** 40cm (16in), has a neat habit, with crimson flowers borne on distinctive, whisky-coloured foliage, flecked with tints of orange and gold. **'Cecilia M. Beale'**, **H** 15cm (6in), bears an abundance of white flowers from mid-winter to early spring. ♀ **'Challenger'** (illus. p.166) has magenta flowers, with deep pink sepals, set against dark green leaves. **'December Red'** has a spreading habit and vigorous growth. Deep rose-pink flowers are borne in winter. ♀ **'Foxhollow'**, a vigorous, spreading cultivar, has foliage that is golden-yellow in summer, with orange tips in spring, and a few pale pink flowers. ♀ **'Golden Starlet'** (illus. p.166), **H** 15cm (6in), **S** 40cm (16in), bears white flowers set on lime-green foliage that turns a glowing yellow in summer. ♀ **'Ice Princess'**, **H** 15cm (6in), **S** 35cm (14in), has white flowers held erect on bright green foliage. ♀ **'Isabell'**, **H** 15cm (6in), **S** 35cm (14in), has large, white flowers on bright green foliage, and an erect but spreading habit. **'King George'**, **H** 20cm (8in), has dark green foliage and deep rose-pink flowers from early winter to mid-spring. ♀ **'Loughrigg'**, **H** 15cm (6in), produces dark purplish-red flowers from late winter to spring. **'March Seedling'** has a spreading habit, dark green foliage and rich, rose-purple flowers. ♀ **'Myretoun Ruby'**, **H** 20cm (8in), is vigorous but compact with brilliant deep purple-red flowers in late winter and early spring. ♀ **'Nathalie'**, **H** 15cm (6in), **S** 40cm (16in), the deepest and brightest of the *E. carnea* cultivars, has purple flowers, neat, dark green foliage and a compact, upright habit. ♀ **'Pink Spangles'**, **H** 15cm (6in), is vigorous with flowers that have shell-pink sepals and deeper pink corollas. **'Pirbright Rose'** is very floriferous with bright pink flowers from early winter to early spring. ♀ **'R.B. Cooke'**, **H** 20cm (8in), bears clear pink flowers from early winter to early spring. ♀ **'Rosalie'**, **H** 15cm (6in), **S** 35cm (14in), has bright pink flowers, bronze-green foliage and a low, upright but spreading habit. ♀ **'Springwood White'** (illus. p.166), **H** 15cm (6in), the most vigorous white cultivar, is excellent as ground cover and bears large, white flowers, with brown anthers, from late winter to spring. ♀ **'Vivellii'**, **H** 15cm (6in), has dark bronze-green foliage and deep purple-pink flowers from late winter to spring. ♀ **'Westwood Yellow'** is compact with golden-yellow foliage and deep pink flowers. **'Winter Sun'** see *E.c.* 'Wintersonne'. **'Wintersonne'**, **H** 15cm (6in), **S** 35cm (14in), has magenta flowers and red-brown foliage.
E. ciliaris (Dorset heath). Evergreen, loose shrub. **H** to 30cm (12in), **S** 40cm (16in). Fully hardy, but may be damaged in severe weather. Has needle-like, dark green leaves in whorls of 3. Bears long racemes of bell-shaped, bright pink flowers in tiers of 3 or 4 in summer. Requires acid soil and prefers warm, moist conditions. **'Aurea'** has somewhat straggly growth with golden foliage and clear pink flowers. **'Corfe Castle'** (illus. p.166) produces salmon-pink flowers from summer to early autumn. **'David McClintock'** (illus. p.166) has light grey-green foliage and bears white flowers, with deep pink tips, from summer to early autumn. ♀ **'Mrs C.H. Gill'** has dark grey-green foliage and clear red flowers. **'White Wings'**, a sport of 'Mrs C.H. Gill', has dark grey-green foliage and white flowers.
E. cinerea (Bell heather). Evergreen, compact shrub. **H** 30cm (12in), **S** 45–60cm (18–24in). Fully hardy. Has needle-like, mid- to deep green leaves and bears bell-shaped flowers that are in shades of pink and dark red, occasionally white, from early summer to early autumn. Prefers a warm, dry position. Requires acid soil. **'Atropurpurea'** has deep purple flowers in long racemes. ♀ **'C.D. Eason'** (illus. p.166) has distinctive, dark green foliage and bright red flowers. **'Cevennes'** is upright in habit and bears a profusion of mauve flowers. ♀ **'C.G. Best'** has mid-green foliage and rose-pink flowers. **'Domino'** produces white flowers that contrast with dark brown stems and sepals and almost black stigmas. ♀ **'Eden Valley'** (illus. p.166), **H** 20cm (8in), bears white flowers with lavender-mauve tips. ♀ **'Fiddler's Gold'**, **H** 25cm (10in), has golden-yellow foliage, deepening to red in winter, and lilac-pink flowers. ♀ **'Golden Hue'**, **H** 35cm (14in), has amethyst flowers set on pale yellow foliage, tipped orange in winter. **'Hookstone White'**, **H** 35cm (14in), has bright green foliage and bears long racemes of large, white flowers. ♀ **'Lime Soda'**, **H** 35cm (14in), bears soft lavender flowers in profusion on lime-green foliage. ♀ **'Pentreath'** has rich purple flowers. ♀ **'Pink Ice'**, **H** 20cm (8in), is compact with soft pink flowers. ♀ **'P.S. Patrick'** is a vigorous cultivar with purple flowers and dark green foliage. **'Purple Beauty'** has purple flowers and dark foliage. ♀ **'Stephen Davis'**, **H** 25cm (10in), has brilliant, almost fluorescent, red flowers. ♀ **'Velvet Night'**, **H** 25cm (10in), produces very dark purple, almost black flowers. ♀ **'Windlebrooke'**, **H** 25cm (10in), is vigorous, with golden foliage, turning bright orange-red in winter, and mauve flowers.
E.* x *darleyensis. Evergreen, bushy shrub. **H** 45cm (18in), **S** 1m (3ft) or more. Fully hardy. Has needle-like, mid-green foliage, with cream, pink or red, young growth in late spring. Bell-shaped, white, pink or purple flowers are borne in racemes from early winter to late spring. Tolerates limestone. **'Archie Graham'**, **H** 50cm (20in), is vigorous with mauve-pink flowers. ♀ **'Arthur Johnson'** (illus. p.166), **H** 1m (3ft), has young foliage with cream and pink tips in spring and long racemes of mauve-pink flowers from mid-winter to spring. **'Darley Dale'** bears pale mauve flowers from mid-winter to spring. ♀ **'Furzey'** (illus. p.166) has a compact, vigorous habit and bears deep pink flowers and dark green leaves. **'George Rendall'** carries deep pink flowers from early winter to early spring. ♀ **'Ghost Hills'** has cream-tipped foliage in spring and a profusion of pink flowers from mid-winter to spring. **'Jack H. Brummage'**, **H** 30cm (12in), has golden foliage, with yellow and orange tints, and mauve flowers. ♀ **'J.W. Porter'**, **H** 30cm (12in), has reddish, young shoots in spring and mauve-pink flowers from mid-winter to late spring. ♀ **'Kramer's Rote'** (syn. *E.* x *d.* 'Kramer's Red') has dark bronze-green foliage with deep purple-red flowers from late autumn to late spring. Spring foliage does not have cream or red tips. **'Molten Silver'** see *E.* x *d.* 'Silberschmelze'. **'Silberschmelze'** (syn. *E.* x *d.* 'Molten Silver') is vigorous and produces young shoots with creamy-pink tips in spring and white flowers. **'White Glow'**, **H** 30cm (12in), bears white flowers. ♀ **'White Perfection'** (illus. p.166) has bright green foliage and white flowers.
E. erigena, syn. *E. mediterranea*, *E. hibernica*, Evergreen, upright shrub. **H** to 2.5m (8ft), **S** to 1m (3ft). Frost hardy; top growth may be damaged in severe weather, but plant recovers well from the base. Has needle-like, mid-green leaves and, usually, bell-shaped, mauve-pink flowers from early winter to late spring. Tolerates limestone. Flowers of some cultivars have a pronounced scent of honey. **f. *alba* 'Brian Proudley'** (illus. p.166), **H** 90cm (36in), **S** 40cm (16in), is a vigorous, erect cultivar with bright green leaves and long racemes of white flowers borne from late autumn to mid-spring. **'Brightness'**, **H** 45cm (18in), has bronze-green foliage and mauve-pink flowers in spring. ♀ **'Golden Lady'**, **H** 30cm (12in), has a neat, compact habit with year-round, golden foliage and white flowers in late spring. ♀ **'Irish Dusk'** (illus. p.166), **H** 45cm (18in), has dark green foliage and salmon-pink flowers from mid-winter to early spring. **'Superba'**, **H** 2m (6ft), bears strongly scented, rose-pink flowers during spring. ♀ **'W.T. Rackliff'**, **H** 60cm (2ft), has dark green foliage and produces thick clusters of white flowers from late winter to late spring.
E. gracilis. Evergreen, compact shrub. **H** and **S** to 30cm (12in). Frost tender, min. 5°C (41°F). Has needle-like, mid-green leaves and clusters of small, bell-shaped, cerise flowers from early autumn to early spring. Is usually grown as a pot plant; may be planted outdoors in summer in a sheltered site.
E. herbacea. See *E. carnea*.
E. hibernica. See *E. erigena*.
E.* x *hiemalis. Evergreen, bushy shrub. **H** and **S** 30cm (12in). Half hardy. Has needle-like, mid-green foliage and racemes of tubular to bell-shaped, pink-tinged, white flowers from late autumn to mid-winter.
♀ ***E. lusitanica*** (Portuguese heath). Evergreen, upright, bushy tree heath. **H** to 3m (10ft), **S** 1m (3ft). Frost hardy. Has feathery, bright green leaves and, from late autumn to late spring, bears tubular to bell-shaped flowers that are pink in bud but pure white when fully open. **'George Hunt'** has golden foliage; is frost hardy but needs a sheltered position.
E. mackaiana. See *E. mackayana*.
E. mackayana, syn. *E. mackaiana* (Mackay's heath). Evergreen, spreading shrub. **H** to 25cm (10in), **S** 40cm (16in). Fully hardy. Has needle-like, mid-green leaves and bears umbels of rounded, pink, mauve-pink or white flowers from mid-summer to early autumn. Likes damp, acid soil. **'Dr Ronald Gray'**, **H** 15cm (6in), has dark green foliage and pure white flowers. **'Plena'**, **H** 15cm (6in), has double, deep-pink flowers, shading to white in centres.
E. mediterranea. See *E. erigena*.
E. pageana. Evergreen, bushy shrub. **H** to 60cm (2ft), **S** 30cm (1ft). Half hardy. Has needle-like, mid-green leaves and, from late spring to early summer, bell-shaped, rich yellow flowers.
E. perspicua (Prince of Wales heath). Variable, evergreen shrub. **H** to 2m (6ft), **S** 1m (3ft). Half hardy. Has overlapping, needle-like, grey-green leaves and, mainly from early autumn to winter, tubular flowers in white, pink-and-white, red-and-white, purple-and-white or red. Needs damp soil.
E.* x *praegeri. See *E.* x *stuartii*.
E. scoparia (Besom heath). Evergreen, bushy shrub. **H** to 3m (10ft), **S** 1m (3ft). Frost hardy. Has needle-like, dark green leaves. Clusters of rounded, bell-shaped, greenish-brown flowers appear in late spring and early summer. Requires acid soil. **'Minima'**, **H** 30cm (12in), has bright green foliage.
E. spiculifolia, syn. *Bruckenthalia spiculifolia* (Spike heath). Evergreen, heath-like shrub. **H** and **S** 15cm (6in). Needle-like, glossy, dark green leaves clothe stiff stems. Terminal clusters of tiny, pink flowers appear in summer.
E. stricta. See *E. terminalis*.
E.* x *stuartii, syn. *E.* x *praegeri*. Evergreen, compact shrub. **H** 15cm (6in), **S** 30cm (12in). Fully hardy. Has needle-like, dark green leaves. Numerous umbels of bell-shaped, pink flowers are produced in late spring and summer. Prefers moist, acid soil. ♀ **'Irish Lemon'** produces young foliage with lemon-yellow tips in spring and bright pink flowers. **'Irish Orange'** has orange-tipped young foliage and dark pink flowers.
♀ ***E. terminalis***, syn. *E. stricta* (Corsican heath). Evergreen, shrub-like tree heath with stiff, upright growth. **H** and **S** to 2.5m (8ft). Frost hardy. Has needle-like, mid-green foliage. Bell-shaped, mauve-pink flowers, borne from early summer to early autumn, turn russet as they fade in winter. Tolerates limestone.
E. tetralix (Cross-leaved heath). Evergreen, spreading shrub. **H** to 30cm (12in), **S** 45cm (18in). Fully hardy. Has needle-like, grey-green leaves in whorls of 4. Umbels of bell-shaped, pink flowers appear from summer to early autumn.

Requires acid, preferably moist soil. 🏆 **'Alba Mollis'** has silver-grey foliage and bears white flowers from early summer to late autumn. 🏆 **'Con Underwood'** has dark red flowers. **'Hookstone Pink'** has silver-grey foliage and bears rose-pink flowers from late spring to early autumn. 🏆 **f. *stellata* 'Pink Star'** produces pink flowers held upright in a star-like pattern.
E. umbellata. Evergreen, bushy shrub. **H** and **S** 60cm (2ft). Frost hardy. Has needle-like, mid-green foliage and bell-shaped, mauve flowers, with chocolate-brown anthers, in late spring.
E. vagans (Cornish heath). Vigorous, evergreen, bushy shrub. **H** and **S** 75cm (30in). Fully hardy. Leaves are needle-like and mid-green. Rounded, bell-shaped, pink, mauve or white flowers appear from mid-summer to late autumn. Tolerates some limestone. Responds well to hard pruning. 🏆 **'Birch Glow'** (illus. p.166), **H** 45cm (18in), has bright green foliage and glowing rose-pink flowers. 🏆 **'Lyonesse'**, **H** 45cm (18in), has dark green foliage and long, tapering spikes of white flowers with brown anthers. 🏆 **'Mrs D.F. Maxwell'** (illus. p.166), **H** 45cm (18in), has dark green foliage and glowing deep pink flowers. **'St Keverne'** (illus. p.166), **H** 45cm (18in), is a neat, bushy shrub with rose-pink flowers; may be used for a low hedge. 🏆 **f. *aureifolia* 'Valerie Proudley'**, **H** 45cm (18in), has golden evergreen foliage when grown in full light, and bears sparse white flowers in late summer and autumn.
E.* x *veitchii. Evergreen, bushy, shrub-like tree heath. **H** to 2m (6ft), **S** 1m (3ft). Frost hardy. Has needle-like, mid-green leaves. Scented, tubular to bell-shaped, white flowers are produced in dense clusters from mid-winter to spring. 🏆 **'Exeter'** has a profusion of white flowers, almost obscuring the foliage. 🏆 **'Gold Tips'** is similar to 'Exeter', but young foliage has golden tips in spring. **'Pink Joy'** has pink flower buds that open to clear white.
E. verticillata. Evergreen, erect shrub. **H** to 60cm (2ft), **S** 30cm (1ft). Frost tender, min. 5–7°C (41–5°F). Has an unusual and attractive arrangement of flowers tightly packed in whorls at intervals along an otherwise almost bare stem. The tubular, pale mauve-pink flowers, 1.5cm (½in) long, appear intermittently throughout the year.
E.* x *watsonii. Evergreen, compact shrub. **H** 30cm (12in), **S** 38cm (15in). Fully hardy. Needle-like, mid-green leaves often have bright-coloured tips in spring. Bears rounded, bell-shaped, pink flowers from mid- to late summer. **'Cherry Turpin'** has long racemes of pale pink flowers from mid-summer to mid-autumn. 🏆 **'Dawn'** produces young foliage with orange-yellow tips and bears deep mauve-pink flowers in compact clusters all summer.
E.* x *williamsii. Evergreen, spreading shrub. **H** 30cm (12in), **S** 60cm (24in). Fully hardy. Has needle-like, dark green leaves, with bright yellow tips when young in spring. Bears bell-shaped, mauve or pink flowers in mid-summer. Prefers acid soil. **'Gwavas'** has pale pink flowers on a neat, compact plant from mid-summer to autumn. 🏆 **'P.D. Williams'**, **H** 45cm (18in), has dark mauve-pink flowers; sometimes keeps its golden foliage tips all summer.

ERIGERON
Fleabane

COMPOSITAE/ASTERACEAE

Genus of mainly spring- and summer-flowering annuals, biennials and perennials, grown for their daisy-like flowers. Ideal for rock gardens or borders. Fully to frost hardy. Prefers sun and well-drained soil but should not be allowed to dry out during growing season. Resents winter damp. Propagate by division in spring or early autumn or by seed in autumn, selected forms by softwood cuttings in early summer.
E. alpinus (Alpine fleabane) illus. p.340.
E. aurantiacus. Clump-forming perennial. **H** 15cm (6in), **S** 30cm (12in). Fully hardy. Has long, oval, grey-green leaves and produces daisy-like, brilliant orange flower heads in summer. Propagate by seed or division in spring.
E. aureus. Short-lived, clump-forming perennial. **H** 5–10cm (2–4in), **S** 15cm (6in). Fully hardy. Bears small, spoon-shaped to oval, hairy leaves. Slender stems each bear a relatively large, daisy-like, golden-yellow flower head in summer. Dislikes winter wet with no snow cover. Is excellent for a scree, trough or alpine house; is prone to aphid attack. 🏆 **'Canary Bird'**, **H** to 10cm (4in), is longer lived, and bears bright canary-yellow flower heads.
***E.* 'Charity'** illus. p.264.
***E.* 'Darkest of All'.** See *E.* 'Dunkelste Aller'.
🏆 ***E.* 'Dunkelste Aller'**, syn. *E.* 'Darkest of All', illus. p.240.
🏆 ***E.* 'Foersters Liebling'.** Clump-forming perennial. **H** 80cm (32in), **S** 60cm (24in). Fully hardy. In summer daisy-like, semi-double, pink flower heads, with yellow centres, are borne above narrowly oval, greyish-green leaves.
***E. glaucus* 'Elstead Pink'.** Tufted perennial. **H** 30cm (12in), **S** 15cm (6in). Fully hardy. Daisy-like, dark lilac-pink flower heads appear throughout summer above oval, grey-green leaves.
🏆 ***E. karvinskianus***, syn. *E. mucronatus*, illus. p.363.
E. mucronatus. See *E. karvinskianus.*
***E.* 'Quakeress'.** Clump-forming perennial. **H** 80cm (32in), **S** 60cm (24in). Fully hardy. Produces a mass of daisy-like, delicate lilac-pink flower heads, with yellow centres, in summer. Narrowly oval leaves are greyish-green.
***E.* 'Serenity'.** Clump-forming perennial. **H** and **S** to 60cm (24in). Fully hardy. Daisy-like, violet-mauve flower heads, with yellow centres, are appear early–mid-summer.

ERINACEA

LEGUMINOSAE/PAPILIONACEAE

Genus of one species of slow-growing, evergreen sub-shrub with hard, sharp, blue-green spines and pea-like flowers. In spring produces short-lived, soft leaves. Frost hardy. Needs a sheltered position with full sun and deep, gritty, well-drained soil. Propagate by seed when available or by softwood cuttings in late spring or summer.
🏆 ***E. anthyllis***, syn. *E. pungens*, illus. p.334.
E. pungens. See *E. anthyllis.*

ERINUS
Fairy foxglove

SCROPHULARIACEAE

Genus of short-lived, semi-evergreen perennials, suitable for rock gardens, walls and troughs. Fully hardy. Needs sun and well-drained soil. Propagate species by seed in autumn (but seedlings will vary considerably), selected forms by softwood cuttings in early summer. Self-seeds freely.
🏆 ***E. alpinus*** illus. p.352. **'Dr Hähnle'** (syn. *E.a.* 'Dr Haenele') is a semi-evergreen, basal-rosetted perennial. **H** and **S** 5–8cm (2–3in). Small, flat, 2-lipped, deep pink flowers open in late spring and summer. Leaves are small, oval and mid-green.

ERIOBOTRYA

ROSACEAE

Genus of evergreen, autumn-flowering trees and shrubs, grown for their foliage, flowers and edible fruits. Frost hardy, but in cold areas grow against a south- or west-facing wall. Fruits, which ripen in spring, may be damaged by hard, winter frosts. Requires sunny, fertile, well-drained soil. Propagate by seed in autumn or spring.
🏆 ***E. japonica*** illus. p.194.

ERIOGONUM
Wild buckwheat

POLYGONACEAE

Genus of annuals, biennials and evergreen perennials, sub-shrubs and shrubs, grown for their rosetted, hairy, often silver or white leaves. Fully hardy to frost tender, min. 5°C (41°F). Needs full sun and well-drained, even poor soil. In cool, wet-winter areas protect shrubby species and hairy-leaved perennials. Water potted plants moderately in summer, less in spring and autumn, very little in winter. Remove flower heads after flowering unless seed is required. Propagate by seed in spring or autumn or by semi-ripe cuttings in summer. Divide perennial root clumps in spring.
E. arborescens illus. p.453.
E. crocatum. Evergreen, sub-shrubby perennial. **H** to 20cm (8in), **S** 15cm (6in). Frost hardy. Oval, hairy leaves have woolly, white undersides. Heads of minute, sulphur-yellow flowers are borne in summer. Is a good alpine house plant.
E. giganteum (St Catherine's lace). Evergreen, rounded shrub. **H** and **S** 1–2m (3–6ft). Frost hardy. Has oblong to oval, grey leaves, white-downy beneath. In summer, small, white flowers are carried in branching clusters to 30cm (12in) long.
E. ovalifolium. Evergreen, domed perennial. **H** 30cm (12in), **S** 10cm (4in). Fully hardy. In summer tiny, bright yellow flowers in umbels above branched stems appear. Has tiny, spoon-shaped, hairy, grey leaves.Excellent for an alpine house.
E. umbellatum illus. p.344.

ERIOPHYLLUM

COMPOSITAE/ASTERACEAE

Genus of summer-flowering perennials and evergreen sub-shrubs, with silvery foliage and daisy-like flowers. Suitable for rock gardens. Frost hardy. Needs sun and well-drained soil. Propagate by division in spring or by seed in autumn.
E. lanatum, syn. *Bahia lanata*, illus. p.276.

ERIOSYCE

CACTACEAE

Genus of spherical to columnar, perennial cacti. Produces sgg-shaped, red, brown or green seed pods which are similar to those of *Wigginsia*. Frost tender, min. 8°C (46°F). Requires full sun and very well-drained soil. Propagate by seed in spring or summer.
E. chilensis, syn. *Echinocactus chilensis, Neoporteria chilensis.* Spherical, then columnar, perennial cactus. **H** 30cm (12in), **S** 10cm (4in). Pale green stem has a dense covering of stout, golden spines. Crown bears flattish, pink-orange or white flowers, to 5cm (2in) across, in summer.
E. kunzei, syn. *Neoporteria nidus.* Spherical to columnar, perennial cactus. **H** 10cm (4in), **S** 8cm (3in). Long, soft, grey spines completely encircle a dark greenish-brown stem. During spring or autumn, the crown produces tubular, pink to cerise flowers that are 3–5cm (1¼–2in) long, with paler bases, and open only at the tips.
🏆 ***E. napina***, syn. *Neochilenia mitis* of gardens, *Neoporteria mitis, Neoporteria napina*, illus. p.485.
E. subgibbosa, syn. *Neoporteria subgibbosa, Neoporteria litoralis.* Spherical to columnar, perennial cactus. **H** 30cm (12in), **S** 10cm (4in). Light green to dark grey-green stem bears large, woolly areoles and stout, amber spines. In late summer, crown bears flattish, carmine-pink flowers, 4cm (1½in) across.
E. villosa, syn. *Neoporteria villosa*, illus. p.490.

ERITRICHIUM

BORAGINACEAE

Genus of short-lived perennials with soft, grey-green leaves and forget-me-not-like flowers. Is suitable for rock gardens and alpine houses. Fully hardy. Needs sun and well-drained, peaty, sandy soil with a deep collar of grit; dislikes damp conditions. Is extremely difficult to grow. Propagate by seed when available or by softwood cuttings in summer.
E. elongatum. Tuft-forming perennial. **H** 2cm (¾in), **S** 3cm (1¼in). Leaves are oval, hairy and grey-green. Short flower stems each carry small, rounded, flat, blue flowers in early summer.
E. nanum illus. p.370.

ERODIUM

GERANIACEAE

Genus of mound-forming perennials, suitable for rock gardens. Fully to half hardy. Needs sun and well-drained soil. Propagate by semi-ripe cuttings in summer or by seed when available.
E. chamaedryoides. See *E. reichardii.*
E. cheilanthifolium, syn. *E. petraeum* subsp. *crispum*, illus. p.341.
E. chrysanthum illus. p.343.
E. corsicum illus. p.362.
E. foetidum, syn. *E. petraeum.* Compact, mound-forming perennial. **H** 15–20cm (6–8in), **S** 20cm (8in). Frost hardy. Produces

E

saucer-shaped, single, red-veined, pink flowers in summer. Oval, grey leaves have deeply cut edges.
E. manescaui, syn. *E. manescavii*, illus. p.265.
E. manescavii. See *E. manescaui.*
E. petraeum. See *E. foetidum.* **subsp. *crispum*** see *E. cheilanthifolium.*
E. reichardii, syn. *E. chamaedryoides.* Mound-forming perennial. **H** 2.5cm (1in), **S** 6–8cm (2½–3in). Half hardy. In summer saucer-shaped, single flowers, either white or pink with darker veins, are borne above tiny, oak-like leaves. Is good for a rock garden or trough.
***E.* x *variabile* 'Flore Pleno'.** Variable, cushion-forming or spreading perennial. **H** 10cm (4in), **S** 30cm (12in). Fully hardy. Has oval to narrowly oval, dark to grey-green leaves with scalloped edges and long stalks. From spring to autumn, flower stems each bear 1 or 2 rounded, double, pink flowers with darker veins; outer petals are rounded, inner petals narrower. **'Ken Aslet'** has single, deep pink flowers.

Erpetion reniforme. See *Viola hederacea.*

ERYNGIUM
Sea holly
UMBELLIFERAE/APIACEAE

Genus of biennals and perennials, some evergreen, grown for their flowers and foliage. Fully to half hardy. Needs sun and fertile, well-drained soil. Propagate species by seed in autumn, selected forms by division in spring or root cuttings in winter.
E. agavifolium, syn. *E. bromeliifolium* of gardens. Evergreen, clump-forming perennial. **H** 1.5m (5ft), **S** 60cm (2ft). Half hardy. Forms rosettes of sword-shaped, sharply toothed, rich green leaves. Thistle-like, greenish-white flower heads are produced on branched stems in summer.
♀***E. alpinum*** illus. p.240.
E. amethystinum. Rosette-forming perennial. **H** and **S** 60cm (24in). Fully hardy. Mid-green oval leaves are divided and spiny. In summer, bears branched stems of small, thistle-like, blue flowers surrounded by spiky, darker blue bracts.
E. bourgatii illus. p.270.
E. bromeliifolium of gardens. See *E. agavifolium.*
E. eburneum, syn. *E. paniculatum.* Evergreen perennial. **H** 1.5–2m (5–6ft), **S** 60cm (2ft). Frost hardy. Has spiny, linear, mid-green leaves. Bears heads of thistle-like, green flowers with white stamens on branched arching stems in late summer.
♀***E. giganteum.*** Clump-forming biennial or short-lived perennial that dies after flowering. **H** 1–1.2m (3–4ft), **S** 75cm (2½ft). Fully hardy. Heart-shaped, basal leaves are mid-green. Has large, rounded heads of thistle-like, blue flowers, surrounded by spiny, silvery bracts, in late summer.
♀***E.* x *oliverianum*** illus. p.241.
♀ ***E. pandanifolium.*** Clump-forming, evergreen perennial. **H** 2.5m (8ft), **S** 1.5m (5ft). Frost hardy. Has narrowly sword-shaped, arching, slightly toothed, pale green basal leaves. Bears towering umbels of small, thistle-like, greenish-purple flower heads in summer.
E. paniculatum. See *E. eburneum.*
♀***E.* x *tripartitum*** illus. p.250.
E. variifolium illus. p.271.
***E.* x *zabelii* 'Violetta'.** Upright perennial. **H** 75cm (30in), **S** 60cm (24in). Fully hardy. Has rounded, mid-green divided leaves. Loose heads of thistle-like, deep violet flowers, surrounded by narrow, spiny, silvery-blue bracts, appear in late summer.

ERYSIMUM
Wallflower
CRUCIFERAE/BRASSICACEAE

Genus of annuals, biennials, evergreen or semi-evergreen, short-lived perennials and sub-shrubs, grown for their flowers. Is closely related to *Cheiranthus* and is suitable for borders, banks and rock gardens. Fully to frost hardy. Requires sun and well-drained soil. Propagate by seed in spring or autumn or by softwood cuttings in summer.
♀***E.* x *allionii***, syn. *E.* x *marshallii* (Siberian wallflower). **'Orange Bedder'** illus. p.324.
♀***E.* 'Bowles's Mauve'**, syn. *Cheiranthus* 'Bowles' Mauve', *E.* 'E.A. Bowles', illus. p.261.
♀***E.* 'Bredon'**, syn. *Cheiranthus* 'Bredon', illus. p.336.
E. cheiri, syn. *Cheiranthus cheiri.* Evergreen, bushy perennial, grown as a biennial. **H** 25–80cm (10–32in), **S** 30–40cm (12–16in). Fully hardy. Has lance-shaped, mid- to deep green leaves. Heads of fragrant, 4-petalled flowers in red, yellow, bronze, white and orange, appear in spring. **Bedder Series** is dwarf and has golden-yellow, primrose-yellow, orange or scarlet-red flowers. **Fair Lady Series** produces flowers in pale pink, yellow and creamy white, with some reds. **'Fire King'** illus. p.326. Flowers of **'Ivory White'** are creamy white. **Treasure Series 'Treasure Red'** is frost hardy with red flowers.
***E.* 'E.A. Bowles'.** See *E.* 'Bowles' Mauve'.
E. helveticum, syn. *E. pumilum*, illus. p.358.
♀***E.* x *kewense* 'Harpur Crewe'**, syn. *Cheiranthus cheiri* 'Harpur Crewe', illus. p.336.
E. linifolium. Short-lived, semi-evergreen, open, dome-shaped sub-shrub. **H** to 30cm (12in), **S** 20cm (8in) or more. Frost hardy. Leaves are narrowly lance-shaped and blue-grey. Tight heads of small, 4-petalled, pale violet flowers appear in early summer.
E.* x *marshallii. See *E.* x *allionii.*
♀***E.* 'Moonlight'**, syn. *Cheiranthus* 'Moonlight', illus. p.335.
E. pumilum. See *E. helveticum.*

ERYTHRINA
LEGUMINOSAE/PAPILIONACEAE

Genus of deciduous or semi-evergreen trees, shrubs and perennials, grown for their flowers. Half hardy to frost tender, min. 5°C (41°F). Requires full sun and well-drained soil. Water potted plants moderately, very little in winter or when leafless. Propagate by seed in spring or semi-ripe cuttings in summer. Red spider mite may be a problem.
E. americana. See *E. coralloides.*
E.* x *bidwillii illus. p.136.
E. coralloides, syn. *E. americana* (Flame coral tree, Naked coral tree). Deciduous, untidily rounded shrub or tree with somewhat prickly stems. **H** and **S** 3–6m (10–20ft). Frost tender. Has leaves of 3 triangular leaflets, the largest central one 11cm (4½in) long. Racemes of pea-like, red flowers are borne on leafless stems in early spring and summer.
E. crista-galli illus. p.137.

ERYTHRONIUM
LILIACEAE

Genus of spring-flowering, tuberous perennials, grown for their pendent flowers and, in some cases, mottled leaves. Fully to frost hardy. Requires partial shade and humus-rich, well-drained soil, where tubers will not dry out in summer while dormant. Propagate by seed in autumn. Some species increase by offsets, which can be divided in late summer. Do not allow tubers to dry out before replanting, 15cm (6in) deep.
E. americanum illus. p.421.
♀***E. californicum*** illus. p.415. ♀**'White Beauty'** illus. p.399.
♀***E. dens-canis*** illus. p.418.
E. grandiflorum. Spring-flowering, tuberous perennial. **H** 10–30cm (4–12in), **S** 5–8cm (2–3in). Fully hardy. Has 2 lance-shaped, semi-erect, basal, plain bright green leaves. Stem carries 1–3 pendent, bright yellow flowers with reflexed petals.
E. hendersonii illus. p.402.
E. oregonum illus. p.399.
♀***E.* 'Pagoda'** illus. p.406.
♀***E. revolutum.*** Tuberous perennial. **H** 20–30cm (8–12in), **S** 15cm (6in). Frost hardy. Has lance-shaped, semi-erect, basal, brown-mottled, green leaves and a loose spike of 1–4 pendent, pale to deep pink flowers with reflexed petals in spring.
♀***E. tuolumnense.*** Tuberous perennial. **H** to 30cm (12in), **S** 12–15cm (5–6in). Frost hardy. Has 2 lance-shaped, semi-erect, basal, glossy, plain green leaves. Carries a spike of up to 10 pendent, bright yellow flowers with reflexed petals.

ESCALLONIA
ESCALLONIACEAE

Genus of evergreen, semi-evergreen or deciduous shrubs and trees, grown for their 5-petalled flowers and glossy foliage. Thrives in mild areas, where *Escallonia* is wind-resistant and ideal for hedging in coastal gardens. Frost hardy, but in cold areas protect from strong winds and grow against a south- or west-facing wall. Requires full sun and fertile, well-drained soil. Trim hedges and wall-trained plants after flowering. Propagate by softwood cuttings in summer.
♀***E.* 'Apple Blossom'** illus. p.133.
***E.* 'Donard Beauty'** illus. p.154.
***E.* 'Donard Seedling'** illus. p.131.
***E.* 'Edinensis'.** Vigorous, evergreen, arching shrub. **H** 2m (6ft), **S** 3m (10ft). Bears small, oblong, bright green leaves. Small, pink flowers are produced from early to mid-summer. Is one of the more hardy escallonias.
♀***E.* 'Iveyi'** illus. p.112.
♀***E.* 'Langleyensis'.** Evergreen or semi-evergreen, arching shrub. **H** 2m (6ft), **S** 3m (10ft). Has small, glossy, bright green leaves and an abundance of rose-red flowers from early to mid-summer.
E. leucantha illus. p.112.
♀***E. rubra* 'Crimson Spire'.** Very vigorous, evergreen, upright shrub. **H** and **S** 3m (10ft). Has oval, rich green leaves and, throughout summer, tubular, deep red flowers. **'Woodside'** illus. p.156.
E. virgata illus. p.130.

ESCHSCHOLZIA
California poppy
PAPAVERACEAE

Genus of annuals, grown for their bright, poppy-like flowers. Is suitable for rock gardens and gaps in paving. Fully hardy. Requires sun and poor, very well-drained soil. Dead-head regularly to ensure a long flowering period. Propagate by seed sown outdoors in spring or early autumn.
♀***E. caespitosa*** illus. p.321.
♀***E. californica*** illus. p.326, [mixed] Fast-growing, slender, erect annual. **H** 30cm (12in), **S** 15cm (6in). Feathery leaves are bluish-green; cup-shaped, 4-petalled, single flowers, in shades of red, orange, yellow or cream, are borne in summer–autumn. **Ballerina Series** has flowers in shades of red, orange, yellow or cream.
♀**Thai Silk Series** illus. p.327.

ESCOBARIA
CACTACEAE

Genus of mainly spherical to columnar, perennial cacti. The stems are studded with tubercles (each with a furrow immediately above it) and very spiny, generally white areoles. Frost tender, min. 5°C (41°F). Needs full sun and poor to moderately fertile, well-drained soil. Propagate by seed in spring or by offsets in summer.
E. vivipara, syn. *Coryphantha vivipara*, illus. p.480.

ESPOSTOA
CACTACEAE

Genus of columnar, perennial cacti, each with a 10–30-ribbed stem, eventually becoming bushy or tree-like with age. Most species are densely covered in woolly, white hairs masking short, sharp spines. Bears cup-shaped flowers, as well as extra wool down the side of stems facing the sun, only after about 30 years. Frost tender, min. 10°C (50°F). Needs full sun and very well-drained soil. Propagate by seed in spring or summer.
E. lanata illus. p.482.

EUCALYPTUS
Gum tree
MYRTACEAE

Genus of evergreen trees and shrubs, grown for their bark, flowers and aromatic foliage. Frost hardy to frost tender, min. 1–10°C (34–50°F). Needs full sun, shelter from cold winds, and fertile, well-drained soil. Plant smallest obtainable trees. Water potted plants moderately, less in winter. Attractive, young foliage of some species, may be retained by cutting growth back hard in spring. Propagate by seed in spring or autumn.

E. camaldulensis (Murray red gum, River red gum). Fast-growing, drought-resistant evergreen, rounded tree. **H** 30m (100ft) or more, **S** 20m (70ft) or more. Frost tender, min. 3–5°C (37–41°F). Young bark is grey, brown and cream; leaves are lance-shaped, slender, green or blue-green. Has umbels of small, cream flowers in summer.
E. coccifera illus. p.68.
♀ ***E. dalrympleana*** illus. p.67.
E. ficifolia (Flowering gum). Moderately fast-growing, evergreen, rounded tree. **H** and **S** to 8m (25ft). Frost tender, min. 1–3°C (34–7°F). Has broadly lance-shaped, glossy, deep green leaves and, in spring–summer, large panicles of many-stamened, pale to deep red flowers. Best grown in acid soil.
E. glaucescens (Tingiringi gum). Evergreen, spreading tree. **H** 12m (40ft), **S** 8m (25ft). Frost hardy. Young bark is white. Leaves are silvery-blue and rounded when young; long, narrow and blue-grey when mature. In autumn bears clusters of many-stamened, white flowers.
E. globulus (Blue gum, Tasmanian blue gum). Very fast-growing, evergreen, spreading tree. **H** 30m (100ft), **S** 12m (40ft). Half hardy. Bark peels in ribbons. Large, oval to oblong, silvery-blue leaves are long, narrow and glossy, mid-green when mature. White flowers, consisting of tufts of stamens, appear in summer–autumn, often year-round.
♀ ***E. gunnii*** illus. p.68.
♀ ***E. johnstonii*** illus. p.68.
E. niphophila. See *E. pauciflora* subsp. *niphophila*.
E. pauciflora illus. p.79. ♀ **subsp. *niphophila*** (syn. *E. niphophila*; Snow gum; illus. p.78). Evergreen, spreading tree. **H** to 8m (25ft), **S** 6–15m (20–50ft). Frost hardy. Flaking bark reveals yellow, bronze, or greenish patches. The lance-shaped foliage is blue-green, grey-green when young. Bears whitish-cream flowers in summer.
E. perriniana (Spinning gum). **H** 4–10m (12–30ft), **S** 3–8m (10–25ft). Fast-growing, evergreen, spreading tree with rounded, grey-blue, young leaves joined around stems. Leaves on mature trees are long and pendulous. White flowers appear in late summer.
E. viminalis (Manna gum, Ribbon gum). Vigorous, evergreen, spreading tree. **H** 30m (100ft), **S** 15m (50ft). Frost tender, min. 5°C (41°F). Bark peels on upper trunk. Lance-shaped, dark green leaves become very long, narrow and pale green when mature. Bears clusters of stamened, white flowers in summer.

EUCHARIS

AMARYLLIDACEAE

Genus of evergreen bulbs, grown for their fragrant, white flowers that resemble large, white daffodils, with a cup and 6 spreading petals. Frost tender, min. 15°C (59°F). Prefers at least 50% relative humidity. Needs partial shade and humus-rich soil. Water freely in summer. Propagate by seed when ripe or by offsets in spring.
♀ ***E. amazonica***, syn. *E. grandiflora* of gardens, illus. p.414.
E. grandiflora of gardens. See *E. amazonica*.

EUCOMIS

Pineapple flower

LILIACEAE/HYACINTHACEAE

Genus of summer- and autumn-flowering bulbs, grown for their dense spikes of flowers, which are overtopped by a tuft of small, leaf-like bracts, as in a pineapple. Frost hardy, but in severe winters protect with dead bracken or loose, rough peat. Needs full sun and well-drained soil. Plant in spring and water freely in summer. Propagate by seed or division of clumps in spring.
♀ ***E. autumnalis***, syn. *E. undulata*. Late summer- to autumn-flowering bulb. **H** 20–30cm (8–12in), **S** 60–75cm (24–30in). Has strap-shaped, wavy-edged leaves in a semi-erect, basal tuft. Leafless stem bears small, star-shaped, pale green or white flowers in a dense spike, with cluster of leaf-like bracts at apex.
♀ ***E. bicolor*** illus. p.412.
E. comosa illus. p.409.
♀ ***E. pallidiflora*** illus. p.409.
E. undulata. See *E. autumnalis*.

EUCOMMIA

EUCOMMIACEAE

Genus of one species of deciduous tree, grown for its unusual foliage. Fully hardy. Needs full sun and fertile, well-drained soil. Propagate by softwood cuttings in summer.
E. ulmoides (Gutta-percha tree). Deciduous, spreading tree. **H** 12m (40ft), **S** 8m (25ft). Drooping, oval leaves are pointed and glossy, dark green; when pulled apart, leaf pieces stay joined by rubbery threads. Inconspicuous flowers appear in late spring before leaves.

EUCRYPHIA

EUCRYPHIACEAE/CUNONIACEAE

Genus of evergreen, semi-evergreen or deciduous trees and shrubs, grown for their foliage and often fragrant, white flowers. Frost hardy. Needs a sheltered, semi-shaded position in all but mild, wet areas, where it will withstand more exposure. Does best with roots in a cool, moist, shaded site and crown in sun. Needs fertile, well-drained, lime-free soil, except for *E. cordifolia* and *E.* x *nymansensis*. Propagate by semi-ripe cuttings in late summer.
E. cordifolia illus. p.73.
♀ ***E. glutinosa*** illus. p.85.
E. lucida illus. p.85.
E. milliganii illus. p.129.
♀ ***E.* x *nymansensis* 'Nymansay'** illus. p.73.

Eugenia australis of gardens. See *Syzygium paniculatum*.
Eugenia paniculata. See *Syzygium paniculatum*.
Eugenia ugni. See *Ugni molinae*.
Euodia. See *Tetradium*.

EUONYMUS

CELASTRACEAE

Genus of evergreen or deciduous shrubs and trees, sometimes climbing, grown for their foliage, autumn colour and fruits. Fully to frost hardy. Needs sun or semi-shade and any well-drained soil, although, for evergreen species in full sun, soil should not be very dry. Propagate by semi-ripe cuttings in summer or by seed in autumn. *E. europaeus* and *E. japonicus* may be attacked by caterpillars; *E. japonicus* is susceptible to mildew. ⓘ All parts may cause mild stomach upset if ingested.
♀ ***E. alatus*** illus. p.140. ♀ **'Compactus'** is a deciduous, bushy, dense shrub. **H** 1m (3ft), **S** 3m (10ft). Fully hardy. Shoots have corky wings. Oval, dark green leaves turn brilliant red in autumn. Bears inconspicuous, greenish-white flowers in summer, followed by small, 4-lobed, purple or red fruits.
***E. cornutus* var. *quinquecornutus*.** Deciduous, spreading, open shrub. **H** 2m (6ft), **S** 3m (10ft). Frost hardy. Has narrowly lance-shaped, dark green leaves. Small, purplish-green flowers in summer are followed by showy, 5-horned, pink fruits that open to reveal orange-red seeds.
E. europaeus (Spindle tree). ♀ **'Red Cascade'** illus. p.140.
E. fortunei. Evergreen shrub, grown only as **var. *radicans*** and its cultivars, which are climbing or prostrate. **H** 5m (15ft) if supported, **S** indefinite. Fully hardy. Bears oval, dark green leaves and inconspicuous, greenish-white flowers from early to mid-summer. Makes good ground cover. Foliage of **'Coloratus'** turns reddish-purple in autumn–winter. ♀ **'Emerald Gaiety'**, **H** 1m (3ft), **S** 1.5m (5ft), is bushy, with rounded, white-edged, deep green leaves. ♀ **'Emerald 'n' Gold'** illus. p.167. **'Gold Tip'** see E.f. 'Golden Prince'. Young, rounded leaves of **'Golden Prince'** (syn. *E.f.* 'Gold Tip') are edged bright yellow, ageing to creamy-white. **'Kewensis'**, **H** 10cm (4in) or more, has slender stems and tiny leaves, and forms dense mats of growth. **'Sarcoxie'**, **H** and **S** 1.2m (4ft), is vigorous, upright and bushy, with glossy, dark green leaves. **'Silver Queen'** illus. p.144. **'Sunspot'** bears deep green leaves, each marked in centre with golden-yellow.
E. hamiltonianus (illus. p.142). Deciduous, tree-like shrub or small tree, sometimes semi-evergreen. **H** and **S** 8m (25ft). Fully hardy. Oval, mid-green leaves often turn pink and red in autumn. Tiny, green flowers in late spring and early summer are followed by 4-lobed, rose-pink fruits enclosed in a bright red casing. **subsp. *sieboldianus***, (syn. *E. yedoensis*; illus. p.142), **H** and **S** 6m (20ft) or more, has pink fruits. **subsp. *sieboldianus* 'Red Elf'** illus. p.140.
E. japonicus (Japanese spindle). **'Latifolius Albomarginatus'** (syn. *E.j.* 'Macrophyllus Albus') illus. p.144. **'Macrophyllus'** is an evergreen, upright, dense shrub. **H** 4m (12ft), **S** 2m (6ft). Frost hardy. Has large, oval, glossy, dark green leaves and, in summer, small, star-shaped, green flowers, followed by spherical, pink fruits with orange seeds. Is good for hedging, particularly in coastal areas. **'Macrophyllus Albus'** see *E.j.* 'Latifolius Albomarginatus'. Leaves of ♀ **'Ovatus Aureus'** are broadly edged with golden-yellow.
E. latifolius illus. p.140.
E. myrianthus illus. p.117.
E. oxyphyllus illus. p.117.
♀ ***E. planipes***, syn. *E. sachalinensis* of gardens. Deciduous, upright, shrub. **H** and **S** 3m (10ft). Fully hardy. Bears oval, mid-green leaves that turn to brilliant red in autumn, as large, 4- or 5-lobed, red fruits open to reveal bright orange seeds. Star-shaped, green flowers open in late spring.
E. sachalinensis of gardens. See *E. planipes*.
E. yedoensis. See *E. hamiltonianus* var. *sieboldianus*.

EUPATORIUM

COMPOSITAE/ASTERACEAE

Genus of perennials, sub-shrubs and shrubs, many of which are evergreen, grown mainly for their flowers, some also for their architectural foliage. Fully hardy to frost tender, min. 5–13°C (41–55°F). Requires full light or partial shade. Will grow in any conditions, although most species prefer moist but well-drained soil. Water containerized plants freely when in full growth, moderately at other times. Prune shrubs lightly after flowering or in spring. Propagate by seed in spring; shrubs and sub-shrubs may also be propagated by softwood or greenwood cuttings in summer, perennials by division in early spring or autumn. Red spider mite and whitefly may be troublesome.
E. ageratoides. See *Ageratina altissima*.
E. ianthinum. See *Bartlettina sordida*.
E. ligustrinumm. See *Ageratina ligustrina*.
***E. maculatum* 'Riesenschirm'** illus. p.221
E. micranthum. See *Ageratina ligustrina*.
E. purpureum (Joe Pye weed). Stately, upright perennial. **H** to 2.2m (7ft), **S** to 1m (3ft). Fully hardy. Oval leaves are arranged in whorls along purplish stems. Terminal heads of tubular, pinkish-purple flowers appear in late summer–early autumn.
E. rugosum. See *Ageratina altissima*.
E. sordidum. See *Bartlettina sordida*.
E. urticifolium. See *Ageratina altissima*.
E. weinmannianum. See *Ageratina ligustrina*.

EUPHORBIA

Milkweed, Spurge

EUPHORBIACEAE

Genus of shrubs, succulents and perennials, some of which are semi-evergreen or evergreen, and annuals. Flower heads consist of cup-shaped bracts, in various colours and usually each containing several flowers lacking typical sepals and petals. Fully hardy to frost tender, min. 5–15°C (41–59°F). Does best in sun or partial shade and in moist but well-drained soil. Propagate by basal cuttings in spring or summer, by division in spring or early autumn or by seed in autumn or spring. ⓘ All parts may cause severe discomfort if ingested; contact with their milky sap may irritate skin.
E. amygdaloides (Wood spurge). **'Purpurea'** is a semi-evergreen, erect perennial. **H** and **S** 30cm (1ft). Fully hardy. Stems and narrowly oval leaves are green, heavily suffused purple-red. Has flower heads of cup-shaped, yellow bracts in spring. Is susceptible to mildew. ♀ **var. *robbiae*** (syn. *E. robbiae*) illus. p.262.
E. bicompacta* var. *rubra, syn.

Synadenium compactum var. *rubrum*, *S. grantii* of gardens 'Rubrum'. Evergreen, erect, robust-stemmed shrub. **H** 3–4m (10–12ft), **S** 2m (6ft) or more. Has very small, red flowers in autumn, largely concealed by lance-shaped to oval, glossy, purplish-green leaves, red-purple beneath.
E. biglandulosa. See *E. rigida.*
E. candelabrum. Deciduous, tree-like, perennial succulent. **H** 10m (30ft), **S** 5m (15ft). Frost tender, min. 10°C (50°F). Erect, 3–5-angled, deeply indented, glossy, dark green stems, often marbled white, branch and rebranch candelabra-like. Has short-lived, spear-shaped leaves. Rounded heads of small flowers, with cup-shaped, yellow bracts, are produced in spring.
E. characias* subsp. *characias and ♀ **subsp. *wulfenii*** illus. p.147.
E. cyparissias illus. p.262.
E. epithymoides. See *E. polychroma.*
♀ ***E. fulgens*** (Scarlet plume). Evergreen shrub of erect and arching habit. **H** 1–1.5m (3–5ft), **S** 60cm–1m (2–3ft). Frost tender, min. 5–7°C (41–5°F). Has elliptic to lance-shaped, mid- to deep green leaves, to 10cm (4in) long. From winter to spring, bears leafy, wand-like sprays of small flowers, each cluster surrounded by 5 petal-like, scarlet bracts, 2–3cm (¾–1¼in) across.
E. gorgonis (Gorgon's head). Deciduous, hemispherical, perennial succulent. **H** 8cm (3in), **S** 10cm (4in). Frost tender, min. 10°C (50°F). Has a much-ribbed, green main stem crowned by 3–5 rows of prostrate, 1cm (½in) wide stems that are gradually shed. In spring, crown also bears rounded heads of small, fragrant flowers with cup-shaped, yellow bracts.
***E. griffithii* 'Fireglow'** illus. p.246.
***E. hypericifolia* Diamond Frost ('Inneuphe')** illus. p.298.
***E.* 'Inneuphe'.** See *E. hypericifolia* Diamond Frost.
E. marginata illus. p.299.
♀ ***E. mellifera*** (Honey spurge) illus. p.127.
♀ ***E. milii*** illus. p.456. ♀ **var. *splendens*** (syn. *E. splendens*) is a slow-growing, mainly evergreen, spreading, spiny, semi-succulent shrub. **H** to 2m (6ft), **S** to 1m (3ft). Frost tender, min. 5–7°C (41–5°F). Has oblong to oval leaves and, intermittently year-round but especially in spring, clusters of tiny flowers enclosed in large, petal-like, red bracts.
♀ ***E. myrsinites*** illus. p.357.
E. nicaeensis. Clump-forming perennial with a woody base. **H** 75cm (30in), **S** 45cm (18in). Fully hardy. Has narrowly oval, fleshy, grey-green leaves. Umbels of greenish-yellow flower heads with cup-shaped bracts are borne throughout summer.
♀ ***E. obesa*** (Gingham golf ball), illus. p.493.
♀ ***E. palustris.*** Bushy perennial. **H** and **S** 1m (3ft). Fully hardy. Clusters of yellow-green flower heads with cup-shaped bracts appear in spring above oblong to lance-shaped, yellowish-green leaves.
♀ ***E. polychroma***, syn. *E. epithymoides*, illus. p.262.
E. pulcherrima (Poinsettia), illus. p.455. **'Paul Mikkelson'** is a mainly evergreen, erect, freely branching shrub. **H** and **S** 3–4m (10–12ft). Frost tender, min. 5–7°C (41–5°F). Bears oval to lance-shaped, shallowly lobed leaves. From late autumn to spring, has flattened heads of small, greenish-white flowers with large, leaf-like, bright red bracts.
♀ ***E. rigida***, syn. *E. biglandulosa*, illus. p.227.
E. robbiae. See *E. amygdaloides* var. *robbiae.*
♀ ***E. schillingii*** illus. p.251.
E. seguieriana. Clump-forming, semi-evergreen perennial. **H** and **S** 45cm (18in). Has narrow, lance-shaped, glaucous leaves on slender stems. Bears large, terminal clusters of yellowish-green flowers in late spring.
♀ ***E. sikkimensis*** illus. p.242.
E. splendens. See *E. milii* var. *splendens.*
E. tithymaloides, syn. *Pedilanthus tithymaloides.* Bushy, perennial succulent. **H** 3m (10ft), **S** 30cm (1ft). Min 10°C (50°F). Has thin, erect stems zigzagging at each node. Leaves are mid-green and boat-shaped, with prominent ribs beneath. Red to yellowish-green bracts are produced at each of the stem tips in summer. Prefers partial shade.
♀ **'Variegata'** illus. p.403.

EUPTELEA

EUPTELEACEAE

Genus of deciduous trees, grown for their foliage. Fully to half hardy. Grows best in full sun and fertile, well-drained soil. Propagate by seed in autumn.
E. polyandra. Deciduous, bushy-headed tree. **H** 8m (25ft), **S** 6m (20ft). Fully hardy. Long-stalked, narrowly oval, pointed, sharply toothed leaves are glossy and bright green, turning red and yellow in autumn. Has inconspicuous flowers in spring before leaves emerge.

EURYA

THEACEAE

Genus of evergreen shrubs and trees, grown for their foliage. Insignificant flowers are produced from spring to summer. Half hardy to frost tender, min. 7°C (45°F). Tolerates partial shade or full light and needs fertile, well-drained soil. Water containerized specimens freely when in full growth, less at other times. Propagate by seed when ripe or in spring or by semi-ripe cuttings in late summer.
E. emarginata illus. p.165.
E. japonica. Evergreen, bushy shrub or small tree. **H** and **S** 10m (30ft). Frost hardy. Has elliptic to lance-shaped, bluntly toothed, leathery, dark green leaves. Inconspicuous, green flowers, borne from spring to summer, are followed on female plants by tiny, spherical, purple-black fruits. **'Variegata'** of gardens see *Cleyera japonica* Fortunei'.

EURYALE

NYMPHAEACEAE

Genus of one species of annual, deep-water plant, grown for its floating foliage; is suitable only for a tropical pool. Frost tender, min. 5°C (41°F). Needs full light, constant warmth and heavy feeding. Propagate by seed in spring.
E. ferox. Annual, deep-water plant. **S** 1.5m (5ft). Has floating, rounded, spiny, olive-green leaves with rich purple undersides and bears small, red or violet-purple shuttlecock-like flowers in summer.

EURYOPS

COMPOSITAE/ASTERACEAE

Genus of evergreen shrubs and sub-shrubs, grown for their attractive leaves and showy, daisy-like flower heads. Is suitable for borders and rock gardens. Fully hardy to frost tender, min. 5–7°C (41–45°F). Needs sun and moist but well-drained soil. May not tolerate root disturbance. Propagate by softwood cuttings in summer.
♀ ***E. acraeus***, syn. *E. evansii* of gardens, illus. p.344.
E. evansii of gardens. See *E. acraeus.*
♀ ***E. pectinatus*** illus. p.319.

EUSTOMA

GENTIANACEAE

Genus of annuals and perennials with poppy-like flowers that are good for cutting. Makes a good container-grown plant. Frost tender, min. 4–7°C (39–45°F). Needs sun and well-drained soil. Propagate by seed sown under glass in late winter.
E. grandiflorum, syn. *E. russellianum*, *Lisianthus russellianus*, illus. p.299. **Heidi Series** produces flowers in shades of rose-pink, blue, white and bicolours.
E. russellianum. See *E. grandiflorum.*

Evodia. See *Tetradium.*

EXACUM

GENTIANACEAE

Genus of annuals, biennials and perennials, grown for their profusion of flowers, that are excellent as pot plants. Frost tender, min. 7–10°C (45–50°F). Grow in sun and in well-drained soil. Propagate by seed sown in early spring for flowering the same year or in late summer for the following year.
♀ ***E. affine*** (Persian violet). Evergreen, bushy perennial, usually grown as an annual. **H** and **S** 20–30cm (8–12in). Frost tender, min 7–10°C (45–50°F). Has oval, glossy leaves and masses of tiny, scented, saucer-shaped, purple, rose-pink or white flowers, with yellow stamens, in summer and early autumn.

EXOCHORDA

ROSACEAE

Genus of deciduous shrubs, grown for their abundant, showy, white flowers. Fully hardy. Does best in full sun and fertile, well-drained soil. Improve vigour and flowering by thinning out old shoots after flowering. Propagate by softwood cuttings in summer or by seed in autumn. Chlorosis may be a problem on shallow, chalky soil.
E. giraldii. Deciduous, widely arching shrub. **H** and **S** 3m (10ft). Has pinkish-green, young growths and oblong leaves. Bears upright racemes of large, 5-petalled, white flowers in late spring.
♀ ***E. x macrantha* 'The Bride'** illus. p.132.
E. racemosa. Deciduous, arching shrub. **H** and **S** 4m (12ft). Has upright clusters of 5-petalled, white flowers in late spring. Leaves are oblong and deep blue-green. Prefers acid soil.

F

FABIANA

SOLANACEAE

Genus of evergreen shrubs, grown for their foliage and flowers. Frost hardy, but in cold areas plant in a sheltered position. Requires full sun and fertile, well-drained soil. Propagate by softwood cuttings in summer.
F. imbricata* 'Prostrata'.** Evergreen, mound-forming, very dense shrub. **H** 1m (3ft), **S** 2m (6ft). Shoots are densely covered with tiny, heath-like, deep green leaves. Bears a profusion of tubular, white flowers in early summer. ♀ **f. *violacea, syn. *F.i.* 'Violacea', illus. p.204.

FAGUS

Beech

FAGACEAE

Genus of deciduous trees, grown for their habit, foliage and autumn colour. Insignificant flowers appear in late spring and hairy fruits ripen in autumn to release edible, triangular nuts. Fully hardy. Requires sun or semi-shade; purple-leaved forms prefer full sun, yellow-leaved forms a little shade. Grows well in any but waterlogged soil. *F. sylvatica*, when used as hedging, should be trimmed in summer. Propagate species by seed sown in autumn, and selected forms by budding in late summer. Problems may be caused by bracket fungi, canker-causing fungi, aphids and beech coccus.
F. americana. See *F. grandifolia.*
F. grandifolia, syn. *F. americana* (American beech). Deciduous, spreading tree. **H** and **S** 10m (30ft). Oval, silky, pale green young leaves mature to dark green in summer, then turn golden-brown in autumn.
F. orientalis (Oriental beech). Deciduous, spreading tree. **H** 20m (70ft), **S** 15m (50ft). Has large, oval, wavy-edged, dark green leaves that turn yellow in autumn.
♀ ***F. sylvatica*** (Common beech) illus. p.64. ♀ **'Aspleniifolia'** (Fern-leaved beech) illus. p.64. **f. *atropunicea*,** syn. *F.s.* Atropurpureum Group, *F.s.* f. *purpurea* (Copper beech, Purple beech) is a deciduous, round-headed tree, **H** 25m (80ft), **S** 15m (50ft), with oval, wavy-margined, purple leaves that turn a rich coppery colour in autumn. **'Aurea Pendula'** is a deciduous, slender tree with pendulous branches. **H** 30m (100ft), **S** 25m (80ft). Oval, wavy-edged leaves are bright yellow and become rich yellow and orange-brown in autumn. ♀ **'Dawyck'** illus. p.79. ♀ **'Dawyck Purple'** is similar, but has deep purple foliage. Leaves of **f. *laciniata*** are deeply cut. ♀ **f. *pendula***, (syn. *F. s.* 'Pendula'; Weeping beech) illus. p.62. **f. *purpurea*** see *F. s.* Atropurpureum Group. **'Purpurea Pendula'**, **H** and **S** 3m (10ft), has stiff, weeping branches and blackish-purple foliage. ♀ **'Riversii'** illus. p.61. **'Rohanii'** illus. p.61. **'Zlatia'** produces yellow, young foliage that later becomes mid- to dark green.

FALLOPIA

SYN. BILDERDYKIA, REYNOUTRIA

POLYGONACEAE

Genus of rhizomatous, climbing or scrambling, woody-based perennials that are good for training on pergolas and deciduous trees or for covering unsightly structures. Fully hardy. Grow in full sun or partial shade and moist but well-drained soil. Propagate by seed sown as soon as ripe or in spring or by semi-ripe cuttings in summer or hardwood cuttings in autumn.

F. aubertii, syn. *Polygonum aubertii* (Mile-a-minute plant, Russian vine). Vigorous, deciduous, woody-stemmed, twining climber. **H** to 12m (40ft) or more. Fully hardy. Leaves are broadly heart-shaped. Panicles of small, white or greenish flowers, ageing to pink, are carried in summer-autumn; they are followed by angled, pinkish-white fruits. Is often confused with *F. baldschuanica*.

F. aubertii of gardens. See *Fallopia baldschuanica*.

F. baldschuanica, syn. *F. aubertii* of gardens, *Polygonum baldschuanicum*, (Mile-a-minute plant, Russian vine), illus. p.208.

FALLUGIA

ROSACEAE

Genus of one species of deciduous shrub, grown for its flowers and showy fruit clusters. Frost hardy, but in cold areas needs protection in winter. Requires a hot, sunny position and well-drained soil. Propagate by softwood cuttings taken in summer or by seed sown in autumn.

F. paradoxa (Apache plum) illus. p.128.

FARFUGIUM

COMPOSITAE/ASTERACEAE

Genus of perennials, grown for their foliage and daisy-like flower heads. Frost hardy. Grow in sun or semi-shade and in moist but well-drained soil. Propagate by division in spring or by seed in autumn or spring.

F. japonicum, syn. *Ligularia tussilaginea*. Loosely clump-forming perennial. **H** and **S** 60cm (24in). Frost hardy. Has large, rounded, toothed, basal, mid-green leaves, above which rise woolly, branched stems bearing clusters of daisy-like, pale yellow flower heads in late summer.

♀ **'Aureomaculatum'** (Leopard plant) has variegated, gold-and-white leaves and is half hardy.

FARGESIA

GRAMINEAE/POACEAE

See also GRASSES, BAMBOOS, RUSHES and SEDGES.

♀ ***F. murieliae***, syn. *Arundinaria murieliae, Fargesia spathacea* of gardens, *Sinarundinaria murieliae, Thamnocalamus murieliae, T. spathaceus* of gardens (Muriel bamboo). Evergreen, clump-forming bamboo. **H** 4m (12ft), **S** indefinite. Frost hardy. Has attractive, grey young culms with loose, light brown sheaths and broad, apple-green leaves, each very long, drawn-out at its tip. Flower spikes are unimportant.

F. nitida, syn. *Arundinaria nitida, Sinarundinaria nitida*. Evergreen, clump-forming bamboo. **H** 5m (15ft), **S** indefinite. Frost hardy. Has small, pointed, mid-green leaves on dark purple stalks and several branches at each node. Stems are often purple with close sheaths.

F. spathacea of gardens. See *F. murieliae*.

FASCICULARIA

BROMELIACEAE

Genus of evergreen, rosette-forming perennials, grown for their overall appearance. Half hardy. Prefers full light; any well-drained soil is suitable. Water moderately from spring to autumn, sparingly in winter. Propagate by offsets or division in spring.

F. andina. See *F. bicolor*.

F. bicolor, syn. *F. andina*. Evergreen, rosetted perennial forming congested hummocks. **H** to 45cm (18in), **S** to 60cm (24in). Has dense rosettes of linear, tapered, arching, mid- to deep green leaves. In summer produces a cluster of tubular, pale blue flowers, surrounded by bright red bracts, at the heart of each mature rosette. Is best grown at not less than 2°C (36°F).

x FATSHEDERA

ARALIACEAE

Hybrid genus (*Fatsia japonica* 'Moseri' x *Hedera helix* 'Hibernica') of one evergreen, autumn-flowering shrub, grown for its foliage. Is good trained against a wall or pillar or, if supported by canes, cultivated as a house plant. Frost hardy. Thrives in a sunny or shaded position and in fertile, well-drained soil. Propagate by semi-ripe cuttings in summer.

♀ ***x F. lizei*** illus. p.211. ♀ **'Variegata'** is an evergreen, mound-forming, loose-branched shrub. **H** 1.5m (5ft), or more if trained as a climber, **S** 3m (10ft). Has rounded, deeply lobed, glossy, deep green leaves, narrowly edged with creamy-white. From mid- to late autumn bears sprays of small, white flowers.

FATSIA

ARALIACEAE

Genus of one species of evergreen, autumn-flowering shrub, grown for its foliage, flowers and fruits. Is excellent for conservatories. Frost hardy, but in cold areas shelter from strong winds. Tolerates sun or shade and requires fertile, well-drained soil. May be propagated by semi-ripe cuttings taken in summer or by seed sown in autumn or spring.

♀ ***F. japonica***, syn. *Aralia japonica, A. sieboldii* (Japanese aralia). Evergreen, rounded, dense shrub. **H** and **S** 3m (10ft). Has stout shoots and very large, rounded, deeply lobed, glossy, dark green leaves. Dense clusters of tiny, white flowers are produced in mid-autumn, and these are followed by rounded, black fruits.

♀ **'Variegata'** illus. p.144.

F. papyrifera. See *Tetrapanax papyrifer*.

FAUCARIA

AIZOACEAE

Genus of clump-forming, stemless, perennial succulents with semi-cylindrical or 3-angled, fleshy, bright green leaves and yellow flowers that open in late afternoons in autumn. Buds and dead flowers may appear orange or red. Frost tender, min. 6°C (43°F). Requires full sun and well-drained soil. Keep dry in winter and water sparingly in spring. Propagate by seed or stem cuttings in spring or summer.

F. tigrina (Tiger jaws) illus. p.495.

Feijoa. See *Acca*.

FELICIA

SYN. AGATHAEA

COMPOSITAE/ASTERACEAE

Genus of annuals, evergreen sub-shrubs and (rarely) shrubs, grown for their daisy-like, mainly blue flower heads. Fully hardy to frost tender, min. 5–7°C (41–5°F). Requires a position in full sun and well-drained soil. Water potted plants moderately, less when not in full growth; dislikes wet conditions, particularly in low temperatures. Cut off dead flowering stems and cut back straggly shoots regularly. Propagate by seed in spring or by greenwood cuttings in summer or early autumn.

F. amelloides, syn. *Aster capensis* (Blue marguerite). Bushy sub-shrub, grown as an annual. Bears deep green leaves, to 3cm (1¼in) long, and light to deep blue flowers from summer to autumn. ♀ **'Santa Anita'** illus. p.157.

F. bergeriana (Kingfisher daisy). Fairly fast-growing, mat-forming annual. **H** and **S** 15cm (6in). Fully hardy. Lance-shaped, hairy, grey-green leaves. Small, daisy-like, blue flower heads with yellow centres open only in sunshine in summer and early autumn.

FENESTRARIA

AIZOACEAE

Genus of clump-forming, perennial succulents with basal rosettes of fleshy leaves that have grey 'windows' in their flattened tips. Frost tender, min. 6°C (43°F). Needs sun and very well-drained soil. Keep bone dry in winter. Propagate by seed in spring or summer.

F. aurantiaca. See *F. rhopalophylla* subsp. *aurantiaca*.

F. rhopalophylla. Clump-forming, perennial succulent. **H** 5cm (2in), **S** 20cm (8in). Forms open cushions of erect, club-shaped, glossy, glaucous to mid-green leaves, each with a flattened tip. Bears daisy-like, white flowers on long stems in late summer and autumn. ♀ **subsp. *aurantiaca***, syn. *F. aurantiaca* (Baby's toes) illus. p.495.

FEROCACTUS

Barrel cactus

CACTACEAE

Genus of slow-growing, spherical, perennial cacti, becoming columnar after many years. Frost tender, min. 5°C (41°F). Needs full sun and very well-drained soil. Propagate by seed in spring or summer. Treat blackened areoles with systemic fungicide and ensure plants have good ventilation.

F. acanthodes. See *F. cylindraceus*.

F. chrysacanthus. Slow-growing, spherical, perennial cactus. **H** 1m (3ft), **S** 60cm (2ft). Green stem, with 15–20 ribs, is fairly densely covered with curved, yellow-white spines. In summer bears funnel-shaped, yellow, rarely red, flowers, 5cm (2in) across, only on plants 25cm (10in) or more in diameter.

F. cylindraceus, syn. *F. acanthodes* illus. p.494.

F. hamatacanthus, syn. *Hamatocactus hamatacanthus* illus. p.486.

F. latispinus. Slow-growing, flattened spherical, perennial cactus. **H** 20cm (8in), **S** 40cm (16in). Green stem, with 15–20 ribs, bears broad, hooked, red or yellow spines. Funnel-shaped, pale yellow or red flowers appear in summer on plants over 10cm (4in) wide.

F. setispinus. See *Thelocactus setispinus*.

F. wislizenii. Slow-growing, spherical, perennial cactus. **H** 2m (6ft), **S** 1m (3ft). Green stem, with up to 25 ribs, is covered in flattened, fish-hook, usually reddish-brown spines, to 5cm (2in) long. Funnel-shaped, orange or yellow flowers, 6cm (2½in) across, appear in late summer, on plants over 25cm (10in) wide, which should attain this size 10–15 years after raising from seed.

FERRARIA

IRIDACEAE

Genus of spring-flowering corms, grown for their curious flowers with 3 large, outer petals and 3 small, inner ones, with very wavy edges. Is unpleasant-smelling to attract flies, which pollinate flowers. Half hardy. Requires full sun and well-drained soil. Plant in autumn, water during winter and dry off after flowering. Dies down in summer. Propagate by division in late summer or by seed in autumn.

F. crispa, syn. *F. undulata*, illus. p.407.

F. undulata. See *F. crispa*.

FERULA

Giant fennel

UMBELLIFERAE/APIACEAE

Genus of mainly summer-flowering perennials, grown for their bold, architectural form. Should not be confused with culinary fennel, *Foeniculum*. Frost hardy. Needs sun and well-drained soil. Propagate by seed when fresh, in late summer.

F. communis (Giant fennel) illus. p.219.

FESTUCA

GRAMINEAE/POACEAE

See also GRASSES, BAMBOOS, RUSHES and SEDGES.

F. glauca, syn. *F. ovina* var. *glauca* (Blue fescue). Group of evergreen, tuft-forming, perennial grasses. **H** and **S** 10cm (4in). Fully hardy. Bears narrow leaves in various shades of blue-green to silvery-white. Produces unimportant panicles of spikelets in summer. Is good for bed

edging. Divide every 2–3 years in spring.
***F. ovina* var. *glauca*.** See *F. glauca*.

***Ficaria verna*.** See *Ranunculus ficaria*.

FICUS

MORACEAE

Genus of evergreen or deciduous trees, shrubs and scrambling or root climbers, grown for their foliage and for shade; a few species also for fruit. All bear insignificant clusters of flowers in spring or summer. Frost hardy to frost tender, min. 5–18°C (41–64°F). Prefers full light or partial shade and fertile, well-drained soil. Water potted specimens moderately, very little when temperatures are low. Propagate by seed in spring or by leaf-bud or stem-tip cuttings or air-layering in summer. Red spider mite may be a nuisance. ⓘThe foliage may cause mild stomach upset if ingested; the sap may irritate skin or aggravate allergies.
F. benghalensis (Banyan) illus. p.452.
♀ ***F. benjamina*** (Weeping fig). Evergreen, weeping tree, often with aerial roots. **H** and **S** 18–20m (60–70ft). Frost tender, min. 10°C (50°F). Has slender, oval leaves, 7–13cm (3–5in) long, in lustrous, rich green. **'Variegata'** illus. p.450.
♀ ***F. deltoidea*** (Mistletoe fig) illus. p.458.
F. elastica (India rubber tree, Rubber plant). ♀ **'Decora'** is a strong-growing, evergreen, irregularly ovoid tree. **H** to 30m (100ft), **S** 15–20m (50–70ft). Frost tender, min. 10°C (50°F). Has broadly oval, leathery, lustrous, deep green leaves, pinkish-bronze when young.
♀ **'Doescheri'** (Rubber plant) illus. p.450. Leaves of **'Variegata'** are cream-edged, mottled with grey-green.
♀ ***F. lyrata*** (Fiddle-leaf fig). Evergreen, ovoid, robust-stemmed tree. **H** 15m (50ft) or more, **S** to 10m (30ft). Frost tender, min. 15–18°C (59–64°F). Fiddle-shaped leaves, 30cm (1ft) or more long, are lustrous, deep green.
F. macrophylla (Australian banyan, Moreton Bay fig). Evergreen, wide-spreading, dense tree with a buttressed trunk when mature. **H** 20–30m (70–100ft), **S** 30–40m (100–130ft). Frost tender, min. 15–18°C (59–64°F). Oval leaves, to 20cm (8in) long, are leathery, glossy, deep green.
♀ ***F. pumila***, syn. *F. repens* (Creeping fig). Evergreen, root climber. **H** 8m (25ft), 1.5m (5ft) as a pot-grown plant. Frost tender, min. 5°C (41°F). Bright green leaves are heart-shaped and 2–3cm (¾–1¼in) long when young, 3–8cm (1¼–3in) long, leathery and oval when mature. Unpalatable fruits are 6cm (2½in) long, orange at first, then flushed red-purple. Only reaches adult stage in very warm regions or under glass. Pinch out branch tips to encourage branching. The young leaves of **'Minima'** are shorter and narrower.
F. religiosa (Bo, Peepul, Sacred fig tree). Mainly evergreen, rounded to wide-spreading tree with prop roots from branches. **H** and **S** 20–30m (70–100ft). Frost tender, min. 15–18°C (59–64°F). Leaves, 10–15cm (4–6in) long, are broadly oval to almost triangular with long, thread-like tips, pink-flushed when expanding.
***F. repens*.** See *F. pumila*.
♀ ***F. rubiginosa*** (Port Jackson fig, Rusty-leaved fig). Evergreen, dense-headed tree with a buttressed trunk. **H** and **S** 20–30m (70–100ft) or more. Frost tender, min. 15–18°C (59–64°F). Elliptic, blunt-pointed leaves, to 10cm (4in) long, are glossy, dark green above, usually with rust-coloured down beneath.

FILIPENDULA

Meadowsweet

ROSACEAE

Genus of spring- and summer-flowering perennials. Fully hardy. Most grow in full sun or partial shade, in moist but well-drained, leafy soil; some species, e.g. *F. rubra*, will thrive in boggy sites. *F. vulgaris* needs a drier site, in full sun. Propagate by seed in autumn or by division in autumn or winter.
F. camtschatica, syn. *F. kamtschatica*. Clump-forming perennial. **H** to 1.5m (5ft), **S** 1m (3ft). In mid-summer, produces frothy, flat heads of scented, star-shaped, white or pale pink flowers above large, lance-shaped, divided and cut leaves.
***F. hexapetala*.** See *F. vulgaris*. **'Flore Pleno'** see *F. vulgaris* 'Multiplex'.
***F. kamtschatica*.** See *F. camtschatica*.
F. purpurea illus. p.238.
F. rubra illus. p.438.
F. ulmaria, syn. *Spiraea ulmaria*, illus. p.436. **'Aurea'** illus. p.274.
F. vulgaris, syn. *F. hexapetala* (Dropwort). **'Multiplex'** (syn. *F. hexapetala* 'Flore Pleno') is an upright, rosette-forming perennial with fleshy, swollen roots. **H** 1m (3ft), **S** 45cm (1½ft). In summer, produces flat panicles of rounded, double, white flowers, sometimes flushed pink, above fern-like, finely divided, toothed, hairless, dark green leaves.

FIRMIANA

STERCULIACEAE

Genus of mainly deciduous trees and shrubs, grown for their foliage and to provide shade. Half hardy, but to reach tree proportions needs min. 2–5°C (36–41°F). Requires well-drained but moisture-retentive, fertile soil and full light or partial shade. Water containerized specimens freely when in full growth, less in winter. Pruning is tolerated if necessary. Propagate by seed when ripe or in spring.
***F. platanifolia*.** See *F. simplex*.
F. simplex, syn. *F. platanifolia*, *Sterculia platanifolia*, (Chinese parasol tree), illus. p.451.

FITTONIA

ACANTHACEAE

Genus of evergreen, creeping perennials, grown mainly for their foliage. Is useful as ground cover. Frost tender, min. 15°C (59°F). Needs a fairly humid atmosphere. Grow in shade and well-drained soil; keep well watered but avoid waterlogging, especially in winter. If it becomes too straggly, cut back in spring. Propagate in spring or summer, with extra heat, by division or stem cuttings.
♀ ***F. albivenis* Argyroneura Group**, syn. *F. argyroneura*, *F. verschaffeltii* var. *argyroneura*, (Silver net-leaf), illus. p.468. ♀ **Verschaffeltii Group**, syn. *F. verschaffeltii* (Painted net-leaf) is an evergreen, creeping perennial. **H** to 15cm (6in), **S** indefinite. Small, oval, red-veined, olive-green leaves. Flowers are best removed if they form.
***F. argyroneura*.** See *F. albivenis* Argyroneura Group.
F. verschaffeltii*.** See *F. albivenis* Verschaffeltii Group. **var. *argyroneura see *F. albivenis* Argyroneura Group.

FITZROYA

CUPRESSACEAE

See also CONIFERS.
F. cupressoides, syn. *F. patagonica*, (Patagonian cypress), illus. p.100.
***F. patagonica*.** See *F. cupressoides*.

FOENICULUM

UMBELLIFERAE/APIACEAE

Genus of summer-flowering biennials and perennials, some of which are grown for their umbels of yellow flowers. Is also grown for its leaves, which are both decorative in borders and used for culinary flavouring. Fully to frost hardy. Grow in an open, sunny position and in fertile, well-drained soil. Remove flower heads after fading to prevent self seeding. Propagate by seed in autumn.
F. vulgare (Fennel). **'Purpureum'** is an erect, branching perennial. **H** 2m (6ft), **S** 45cm (1½ft). Fully hardy. Has very finely divided, hair-like, bronze leaves and, in summer, large, flat umbels of small, yellow flowers.

FONTINALIS

Water moss

SPHAGNACEAE/FONTINALACEAE

Genus of evergreen, perennial, submerged water plants, grown for their foliage, which provides dense cover for fish and a good site for the deposit of spawn. Fully hardy. Grows in sun or semi-shade in streams and other running water; tolerates still water if cool, but then does not grow to full size. Propagate by division in spring.
F. antipyretica (Water moss, Willow moss). Evergreen, perennial, submerged water plant. **H** 2.5cm (1in), **S** indefinite. Forms spreading colonies of moss-like, dark olive-green leaves.

FORSYTHIA

OLEACEAE

Genus of deciduous, spring-flowering shrubs, grown for their usually profuse, yellow flowers, which are produced before the leaves emerge. *F.* x *intermedia* 'Beatrix Farrand' and *F.* x *i.* 'Lynwood' make attractive, flowering hedges. Fully hardy. Prefers a position in full sun and in fertile, well-drained soil. Thin out old shoots and trim hedges immediately after flowering. Propagate by softwood cuttings in summer or by hardwood cuttings in autumn or winter.
***F.* 'Flo Jar'.** See *F.* x *intermedia* MINIGOLD
***F.* x *intermedia* 'Arnold Giant'.** Deciduous, bushy shrub. **H** 1.5m (5ft), **S** 2.5m (8ft). Has stout shoots and oblong, sharply toothed, mid-green leaves. Large, 4-lobed, deep yellow flowers are produced sparsely from early to mid-spring. **'Beatrix Farrand'** illus. p.127. **'Karl Sax'**, **H** 2.5m (8ft), is dense-growing, with an abundance of flowers. Some leaves turn red or purple in autumn.
♀ **'Lynwood'**, **H** 3m (10ft), is very free-flowering, vigorous and upright.
MINIGOLD ('Flo Jar'), **H** and **S** 2m (6ft), has oblong, mid-green leaves, and produces masses of small, 4-lobed, yellow flowers from early to mid-spring.
'Spectabilis' illus. p.127.
'Spring Glory', **H** 2m (6ft), **S** 1.5m (5ft), has clusters of large, 4-lobed, pale yellow flowers borne in mid-spring and oblong, toothed, bright green leaves.
***F. ovata*.** Deciduous, bushy shrub. **H** and **S** 1.5m (5ft). Bears broadly oval, toothed, dark green leaves. Produces small, 4-lobed, bright yellow flowers in early spring.
'Tetragold' has larger flowers.
F. suspensa illus. p.195.

FOTHERGILLA

HAMAMELIDACEAE

Genus of deciduous, spring-flowering shrubs, grown for their autumn colour and fragrant flowers, each with a dense, bottlebrush-like cluster of stamens, which open before or as leaves emerge. Fully hardy. Grows in sun or semi-shade, but colours best in full sun. Requires moist, peaty, acid soil. Propagate by softwood cuttings taken in summer.
F. gardenii illus p.163.
♀ ***F. major***, syn. *F. monticola*, illus. p.117.
***F. monticola*.** See *F. major*.

***Fragaria indica*.** See *Duchesnea indica*.

FRAILEA

CACTACEAE

Genus of spherical to columnar, perennial cacti with tuberculate ribs. Bears short spines, mostly bristle-like. In summer produces masses of buds, most of which develop into small, spherical, shiny pods without opening. Frost tender, min. 5°C (41°F). Needs partial shade and very well-drained soil. Is not well-adapted to long periods of drought. Propagate by seed in spring or summer.
***F. pulcherrima*.** See *F. pygmaea*.
F. pygmaea, syn. *F. pulcherrima*, illus. p.490.

FRANCOA

SAXIFRAGACEAE/MELIANTHACEAE

Genus of summer- and early autumn-flowering perennials. Frost hardy. Needs full sun and fertile, well-drained soil. Propagate by seed or division in spring.
F. appendiculata (Bridal wreath). Clump-forming perennial. **H** 60cm (24in), **S** 45cm (18in). Racemes of small, bell-shaped, pale pink flowers, spotted with deep pink at base, appear on graceful, erect stems from summer to early autumn, above oblong to oval, lobed, hairy, crinkled, dark green leaves.
***F. sonchifolia*.** Clump-forming perennial. **H** 75cm (30in), **S** 45cm (18in). Bears racemes of cup-shaped, red-marked, pink

flowers from summer to early autumn. Lobed leaves each have a large, terminal lobe. **Rogerson's form** **H** 60cm (24in), **S** 60cm (24in) or more, has lance-shaped, lobed, dark green leaves and slender, wand-like racemes of star-shaped, rich pink and red flowers in summer. Is good for ground-cover.

FRANKLINIA

THEACEAE

Genus of one species of deciduous tree or shrub, grown for its flowers and autumn colour. Fully hardy, but thrives only during hot summers. Requires a position in full sun and moist but well-drained, neutral to acid soil. Propagate by softwood cuttings in summer, by seed in autumn or by hardwood cuttings in early winter.

F. alatamaha. Deciduous, upright tree or shrub. **H** and **S** 5m (15ft) or more. Large, shallowly cup-shaped, white flowers with yellow stamens open in late summer and early autumn. Oblong, glossy, bright green leaves turn red in autumn.

FRAXINUS

Ash

OLEACEAE

Genus of deciduous trees and shrubs, grown mainly for their foliage of paired leaflets; flowers are usually insignificant. Fully hardy. Requires a position in sun and fertile, well-drained but not too dry soil. Propagate species by seed in autumn, selected forms by budding in summer. ⓘContact with lichens on the bark may aggravate skin allergies.

F. americana (White ash). Fast-growing, deciduous, spreading tree. **H** 25m (80ft), **S** 15m (50ft). Leaves are dark green, with 5–9 oval to lance-shaped leaflets, sometimes turning yellow or purple in autumn.

F. angustifolia* subsp. *oxycarpa, syn. *F. oxycarpa* (Narrow-leaved ash). Deciduous, spreading, elegant tree. **H** 25m (80ft), **S** 12m (40ft). Leaves usually consist of 9–11 slender, lance-shaped, glossy, dark green leaflets that are golden-yellow in autumn.

F. excelsior (Common ash). Vigorous, deciduous, spreading tree. **H** 30m (100ft), **S** 20m (70ft). Dark green leaves, with usually 9–11 oval leaflets, sometimes become yellow in autumn. Black leaf buds are conspicuous in winter. ***f. diversifolia*** has leaves that are simple or with only 3 leaflets. ♀ **'Jaspidea'** illus. p.60.
♀ **'Raywood'** (Claret ash) illus. p.66.
♀ **'Pendula'** illus. p.79.

F. mariesii. See *F. sieboldiana.*
♀ ***F. ornus*** (Manna ash) illus. p.71.

F. oxycarpa. See *F. angustifolia* subsp. *oxycarpa.*

F. pennsylvanica (Green ash, Red ash). Fast-growing, deciduous, spreading tree. **H** and **S** 20m (70ft). Leaves of usually 7 or 9 narrowly oval, dull green leaflets are often velvety beneath, like the shoots, and turn yellow in autumn. **'Patmore'** is disease-resistant, with long-lasting, glossy leaves, but does not bear fruit.

F. sieboldiana, syn. *F. mariesii.* Slow-growing, deciduous, compact-headed tree. **H** 6m (20ft), **S** 5m (15ft). Leaves consist of 3–5 oval, dark green leaflets, each on a purple stalk. Produces clusters of small, fragrant, star-shaped, creamy-white flowers in early summer, followed by narrowly oblong, purple fruits.

F. velutina (Arizona ash) illus. p.74.

FREESIA

IRIDACEAE

Genus of winter- and spring-flowering corms, grown for their usually fragrant, funnel-shaped flowers, which are popular for cutting. Half hardy. Requires full sun and well-drained soil. Plant in autumn and water throughout winter. Support with twigs or small canes. Dry off corms after flowering. Plant specially prepared corms outdoors in spring for flowering in summer. Propagate by offsets in autumn or by seed in spring.

F. alba, syn. *F. refracta* var. *alba.* Late winter- and spring-flowering corm. **H** 20–30cm (8–12in), **S** 4–6cm (1½–2½in). Has narrowly sword-shaped, erect leaves in a basal fan. Leafless stems bear loose spikes of very fragrant, white flowers, sometimes with a yellow blotch on the lowest petal, each 5–8cm (2–3in) long.

F. alba of gardens. See *F. caryophyllacea.*

F. armstrongii. See *F. corymbosa.*

F. caryophyllacea, syn. *F. alba* of gardens, *F. lactea. F. xanthospila.* Late winter- and spring-flowering corm. **H** to 15cm (6in), **S** 4–6cm (1½–2½in). Has narrow, sword-shaped leaves growing at an angle. Short, leafless stems bear spikes of white, narrow, tubular flowers, 3–5cm (1¼–2in) long, with the lower 3 petals usually marked with yellow.

F. corymbosa, syn. *F. armstrongii.* Late winter-and spring-flowering corm. **H** to 30cm (12in), **S** 4–6cm (1½–2½in). Has narrowly sword-shaped, erect, basal leaves. Flower stem bends horizontally near the top and bears a spike of unscented, upright, pink flowers, 3–3.5cm (1¼–1½in) long, with yellow bases.

***F.* 'Golden Melody'.** Winter- and spring-flowering corm. **H** to 30cm (12in), **S** 4–6cm (1½–2½in). Is similar to *F. corymbosa*, but has larger, fragrant flowers, yellow throughout.

F. lactea. See *F. caryophyllacea.*

F. laxa. See *Anomatheca laxa.*

***F.* 'Oberon'.** Winter- and spring-flowering corm. **H** to 40cm (16in), **S** 4–6cm (1½–2½in). Has narrow, erect, basal leaves and yellow flowers, 4–5cm (1½–2in) long, light blood-red inside; the throats are lemon-yellow with small, red veins.

F. refracta* var. *alba. See *F. caryophyllacea.*

***F.* 'Romany'.** Winter- and spring-flowering corm. **H** to 30cm (12in), **S** 4–6in (1½–2½in). Is similar to F.corymbosa, but has fragrant, double, pale mauve flowers.

***F.* 'White Swan'.** Winter- and spring-flowering corm. **H** to 30cm (12in), **S** 4–6cm (1½–2½in). Is similar to *F. corymbosa*, but has very fragrant, white flowers with cream throats.

F. xanthospila. See *F. caryophyllacea.*

Fremontia. See *Fremontodendron.*

FREMONTODENDRON

SYN. FREMONTIA

Flannel flower

STERCULIACEAE

Genus of vigorous, evergreen or semi-evergreen shrubs, grown for their large, very showy flowers. Frost hardy, but in cold areas plant against a south- or west-facing wall. Needs full sun and light, not too rich, well-drained soil. In mild areas may be grown as a spreading shrub, but needs firm staking when young. Resents being transplanted. Propagate by semi-ripe cuttings in summer or by seed in autumn or spring. ⓘContact with the foliage and shoots may irritate the skin.

♀ ***F.* 'California Glory'** illus. p.206.

F. californicum. Vigorous, evergreen or semi-evergreen, upright shrub. **H** 6m (20ft), **S** 4m (12ft), when grown against a wall. Large, saucer-shaped, bright yellow flowers are borne amid dark green leaves, each with 3 rounded lobes, from late spring to mid-autumn.

F. mexicanum. Vigorous, evergreen or semi-evergreen, upright shrub. **H** 6m (20ft), **S** 4m (12ft) when grown against a wall. Dark green leaves have 5 deep, rounded lobes. Bears masses of large, saucer-shaped, deep golden-yellow flowers from late spring to mid-autumn.

***F.* 'Pacific Sunset'.** Upright, evergreen shrub. **H** 5m (15ft), **S** 3–4m (10–12ft). Rounded, strongly lobed leaves are dark green. In summer produces saucer-shaped, bright yellow flowers, to 6cm (2½in) across, with long, slender-pointed lobes.

FRITHIA

AIZOACEAE

Genus of one species of rosette-forming, perennial succulent. Frost tender, min. 10°C (50°F). Needs sun and well-drained soil. Propagate by seed in spring or summer.

♀ ***F. pulchra*** illus. p.485.

FRITILLARIA

LILIACEAE

Genus of spring-flowering bulbs, grown for their pendent, mainly bell-shaped flowers on leafy stems. Fully to frost hardy; protect smaller, 5–15cm (2–6in) high species in cold frames or cold greenhouses. Needs full sun or partial shade and well-drained soil that dries out slightly in summer when bulbs are dormant but that does not become sunbaked. Grow *F. meleagris*, which is good for naturalizing in grass, in moisture-retentive soil. Propagate by offsets in summer or by seed in autumn or winter.

♀ ***F. acmopetala*** illus. p.406.

F. bucharica. Spring-flowering bulb. **H** 10–35cm (4–14in), **S** 5cm (2in). Frost hardy. Stems each bear scattered, lance-shaped, grey-green leaves and a raceme of up to 10 cup-shaped, green-tinged, white flowers, 1.5–2cm (⅝–¾in) long.

F. camschatcensis (Black sarana) illus. p.403.

F. chitralensis. Spring- to early summer-flowering bulb. **H** 50–80cm (20–32in), **S** 10cm (4in). Fully hardy.Has ovate, mid- to light green leaves and open umbels of 4 or 5 conical, pendent, bright yellow flowers. Similar to F. imperialis.

F. cirrhosa illus. p.406.

F. crassifolia. Spring-flowering bulb. **H** 10–20cm (4–8in), **S** 5cm (2in). Frost hardy. Has scattered, lance-shaped, grey leaves. Stems each produce 1–3 bell-shaped, green flowers, 2–2.5cm (¾–1in) long and chequered with brown.

F. delphinensis. See *F. tubiformis.*

F. imperialis (Crown imperial) illus. p.383. **'Lutea'** illus. p.382. **'Rubra Maxima'** is a very robust, spring-flowering bulb. **H** to 1.5m (5ft), **S** 23–30cm (9–12in). Leafy stems each bear lance-shaped, light green leaves in whorls and a head of up to 5 widely bell-shaped, red flowers, 5cm (2in) long, crowned by small, leaf-like bracts.

F. meleagris (Snake's-head fritillary) illus. p.402.

♀ ***F. michailovskyi.*** Spring-flowering bulb. **H** 10–20cm (4–8in), **S** 5cm (2in). Frost hardy. Has lance-shaped, grey leaves scattered on stem. Bears 1–4 bell-shaped, 2–3cm (¾–1¼in) long flowers, coloured purplish-brown with upper third of petals bright yellow.

♀ ***F. pallidiflora*** illus. p.406.

F. persica illus. p.382. ♀ **'Adiyaman'** is a spring-flowering bulb. **H** to 1.5m (5ft), **S** 10cm (4in). Frost hardy. Has narrowly lance-shaped, grey leaves along stem. Produces a spike of 10–20 or more narrowly bell-shaped, deep blackish-purple flowers, 1.5–2cm (⅝–¾in) long. **'Ivory Bells'** illus. p.382.

F. pontica illus. p.406.

F. pudica (Yellow fritillary) illus. p.422.

♀ ***F. pyrenaica*** illus. p.403.

F. raddeana illus. p.382.

F. recurva (Scarlet fritillary) illus. p.383.

F. sewerzowii, syn. *Korolkowia sewerzowii.* Spring-flowering bulb. **H** 15–25cm (6–10in), **S** 8–10cm (3–4in). Frost hardy. Stems bear scattered, broadly lance-shaped leaves. Produces a spike of up to 10 narrowly bell-shaped, green or metallic purplish-blue flowers, 2.5–3.5cm (1–1½in) long, with flared mouths.

F. tubiformis, syn. *F. delphinensis.* Spring-flowering bulb. **H** 15–35cm (6–14in), **S** 5–8cm (2–3in). Frost hardy. Stems carry scattered, narrowly lance-shaped, grey leaves and a solitary, broadly bell-shaped, purplish-pink flower, 3.5–5cm (1½–2in) long, conspicuously chequered and suffused grey outside.

F. verticillata illus. p.382.

FUCHSIA

ONAGRACEAE

Genus of deciduous or evergreen shrubs and trees, grown for their flowers, usually borne from early summer to early autumn. Frost hardy to frost tender, min. 5°C (41°F). If temperature remains above 4°C (39°F), deciduous plants are evergreen, but temperatures above 32°C (90°F) should be avoided. Prolonged low temperatures cause loss of top growth. If top growth dies in winter, cut back to ground level in spring. Needs a sheltered, partially shaded position, except where stated otherwise, and fertile, moist but well-drained soil.

When grown as pot plants in a greenhouse, fuchsias also need high-nitrogen feeds and, when flowering, plenty of potash. Propagate by softwood cuttings in any season.

Tubular flowers are almost always pendulous and often bicoloured, with petals of one hue, and a tube and 4 sepals of another. Leaves are oval and mid-green unless otherwise stated. Spherical to cylindrical, usually blackish-purple fruits are edible, but mostly poor-flavoured. Upright types may be trained as compact bushes or standards or, with more difficulty, as pyramids. Lax or trailing plants are good for hanging baskets, but may be trained on trellises; if they are used for summer bedding they require staking. Heights given in descriptions below are of plants grown in frost-free conditions. See also feature panels, p.154 (hardy fuchsias) and p.302 (tender fuchsias).

♀ ***F.* 'Alice Hoffman'.** Deciduous, compact shrub. **H** and **S** 75cm (2½ft). Frost hardy. Has bronze foliage and small, semi-double flowers with rose-red tubes and sepals and rose-veined, white petals.

♀ ***F.* 'Annabel'** (illus. p.302). Deciduous, upright shrub. **H** 1m (3ft), **S** 75cm (2½ft). Half hardy. Produces large, double, pink-tinged, creamy-white flowers amid pale green leaves. Makes an excellent standard.

***F.* 'Applause'.** Deciduous, lax, upright shrub. **H** 30–40cm (12–18in), **S** 45–60cm (18–24in). Half hardy. Bears very large, double flowers with short, thick, pale carmine tubes, very broad, carmine sepals with a pale central streak, and many, spreading, deep orange-red petals. Produces best colour in shade. Needs staking as a bush, but will trail with weights.

F. arborea. See *F. arborescens.*

F. arborescens, syn. *F. arborea* (Tree fuchsia). Evergreen, upright tree. **H** 8m (25ft), **S** 2.5m (8ft). Frost tender. Foliage is mid- to dark green. Erect heads of tiny, pale mauve to pink flowers, borne year-round, are followed by black fruits with grey-blue bloom. May also be grown as a pot plant.

***F.* 'Auntie Jinks'.** Deciduous, trailing shrub. **H** 15–20cm (6–8in), **S** 20–40cm (8–16in). Half hardy. Bears small, single flowers with pink-red tubes, cerise-margined white sepals, and white-shaded purple petals.

♀ ***F.* 'Autumnale'**, syn. *F.* 'Burning Bush'. Deciduous, lax shrub, grown mainly for its foliage. H2m (6ft), **S** 50cm (20in). Half hardy. Bears variegated red, gold and bronze leaves. Flowers have red tubes and sepals with reddish-purple petals. Is suitable for a hanging basket or for training as a weeping standard.

F. x bacillaris, syn. F. *parviflora* of gardens. Group of deciduous, lax shrubs. **H** and **S** 75cm (2½ft). Frost hardy. Small leaves are mid- to dark green. Bears minute, white, pink or crimson flowers (colour varying according to sun), sometimes followed by glossy, black fruits. Is suitable for a rock garden or hanging basket.

♀ ***F.* 'Ballet Girl'.** Deciduous, upright shrub. **H** 30–45cm (12–18in), **S** 45–75cm (18–30in). Half hardy. Produces large, double flowers with bright cerise tubes and sepals, and white petals with cerise veins at the base.

***F.* 'Bicentennial'** (illus. p.302). Deciduous, lax shrub. **H** 30–45cm (12–18in), **S** 45–60cm (18–24in). Half hardy. Bears medium, double flowers with thin white tubes, orange sepals, and double corollas with magenta centres surrounded by orange petals.

F. boliviana. Fast-growing, deciduous, upright shrub. **H** 3m (10ft), **S** 1m (3ft). Frost tender. Has large, soft, grey-green leaves with reddish midribs. Long-tubed, scarlet flowers, bunched at ends of branches, are followed by pleasantly flavoured, black fruits. Needs a large pot and plenty of space to grow well. Resents being pinched back. Is very susceptible to whitefly.

♀ **var. *alba*** (syn. *F.b.* var. *luxurians* 'Alba', *F. corymbiflora* 'Alba') has flowers with white tubes and sepals and scarlet petals, followed by green fruits.

***F.* 'Bon Accorde'.** Vigorous, deciduous, upright shrub. **H** 1.5m (5ft), **S** 50cm (20in). Half hardy. Small, erect flowers have white tubes and sepals and pale purple petals.

***F.* 'Brookwood Belle'.** Deciduous, lax, bushy shrub with strong, short-jointed stems. **H** and **S** 45–60cm (18–24in). Frost hardy. Medium, double flowers have deep cerise tubes and sepals, and white petals flushed pink and veined deep rose-pink.

♀ ***F.* 'Brutus'.** Vigorous, deciduous, upright shrub. **H** 1.5m (5ft), **S** 1m (3ft). Frost hardy. Single or semi-double flowers have crimson-red tubes and sepals and deep purple petals.

***F.* 'Burning Bush'.** See *F.* 'Autumnale'.

***F.* California Dreamer Series** Deciduous, semi-trailing shrub. **H** and **S** 45cm (18in). Half hardy. Produces very large, blowsy, fully double flowers. Is ideal in a large container. **'Snowburner'** (illus. p.302) has wavy, horizontal, red sepals and ruffled, white petals delicately patterned with red veins.

***F.* 'Cascade'.** Deciduous, trailing shrub. **H** 2m (6ft), **S** indefinite. Half hardy. Bears red-tinged, white tubes and sepals and deep carmine petals. Is excellent grown in a hanging basket.

♀ ***F.* 'Celia Smedley'** (illus. p.302). Vigorous, deciduous, upright shrub. **H** 1.5m (5ft), **S** 1m (3ft). Half hardy. Large, single or semi-double flowers have greenish-white tubes, pale pinkish-white sepals and currant-red petals. Is best when trained as a standard.

♀ ***F.* 'Checkerboard'.** Vigorous, deciduous, upright shrub with strong stems. **H** 75–90cm (30–36in), **S** 45–75cm (18–30in). Half hardy. Produces medium, single flowers with slightly recurved, long red tubes, red sepals turning white and white-based, dark red petals.

***F.* 'Cloverdale Pearl'.** Deciduous, upright shrub. **H** 1m (3ft), **S** 75cm (2½ft). Half hardy. Foliage is mid-green with crimson midribs. Flowers have pinkish-white tubes, pink-veined, white petals and green-tipped, pink sepals. Is readily trained as a standard.

***F.* 'Coquet Bell'.** Vigorous, deciduous, upright shrub. **H** 1.5m (5ft), **S** 1m (3ft). Half hardy. Has a profusion of single or semi-double flowers with pinkish-red tubes and sepals and red-veined, pale mauve petals.

***F.* 'Coralle'**, syn. *F.* 'Koralle' (illus. p.302). Deciduous, upright shrub. **H** and **S** 1m (3ft). Frost tender. Foliage is velvety and deep green. Salmon-orange flowers, with long, narrow tubes and small sepals and petals, are bunched at branch ends. Is useful for summer bedding and as a specimen plant. Prefers sun.

♀ ***F.* 'Corallina'** (illus. p.154). Deciduous, spreading shrub. **H** 40cm (16in), **S** 1.5m (60in). Frost hardy. Has burgundy-red stems and mid-green leaves flushed pink at the bases. Pendent, medium flowers have narrow, spreading, scarlet sepals and broader, shorter, purple petals tinted red at the bases.

***F. corymbiflora* 'Alba'.** See *F. boliviana* var. *alba.*

♀ ***F.* 'Dancing Flame'.** Deciduous, lax shrub. **H** and **S** 45cm (18in). Half hardy. Strong stems bear small, oval, deep green leaves. Double, purple and blue flowers have bright pink sepals.

♀ ***F.* 'Dark Eyes'.** Deciduous, bushy, upright shrub. **H** 45–60cm (18–24in), **S** 60–75cm (24–30in). Half hardy. Bears medium, double flowers that hold their shape for a long period. The tubes and upturned sepals are deep red, and the petals deep violet-blue.

F. denticulata. Deciduous, straggling shrub. **H** 4m (12ft), **S** indefinite. Frost tender. Leaves are glossy, dark green above and reddish-green beneath. Flowers have long, crimson tubes, green-tipped, pale pink sepals and vermilion petals. With good cultivation under glass, flowers appear throughout autumn and winter.

♀ ***F.* 'Display'.** Deciduous, upright shrub. **H** 1m (3ft), **S** 75cm (2½ft). Frost hardy. Bears saucer-shaped flowers in shades of pink.

***F.* 'Dollar Princess'.** See *F.* 'Dollar Prinzessin'.

♀ ***F.* 'Dollar Prinzessin'**, syn. 'Dollar Princess' (illus. p.302). Deciduous, upright shrub. **H** 1m (3ft), **S** 75cm (2½ft). Frost hardy. Small, double flowers have cerise-red tubes and sepals and purple petals.

***F.* 'Estelle Marie'.** Deciduous, upright shrub. **H** 1m (3ft), **S** 50cm (20in). Half hardy. Flowers with white tubes, green-tipped, white sepals and mauve petals are borne above foliage. Is excellent for summer bedding.

♀ ***F.* 'Flash'.** Fast-growing, deciduous, stiffly erect shrub. **H** 2.5m (8ft), **S** 50cm (20in). Frost hardy. Produces small, red flowers amid small leaves.

***F.* 'Flirtation Waltz'.** Vigorous, deciduous, upright shrub. **H** 1m (3ft), S75cm (2½ft). Half hardy. Produces large, double flowers with petals in shades of pink, and white tubes and sepals.

♀ ***F. fulgens*** (illus. p.302). Deciduous, upright shrub with tubers. **H** 2m (6ft), **S** 1m (3ft). Frost tender. Long-tubed, orange flowers hang in short clusters amid large, pale green leaves and are followed by edible but acidic, green fruits. Tubers may be stored dry for winter. May also be propagated by division of tubers in spring. Is highly susceptible to whitefly.

♀ ***F.* 'Garden News'.** Deciduous, upright shrub with strong stems. **H** and **S** 45–60cm (18–24in). Frost hardy (borderline). Medium, double flowers have short, thick, pink tubes, frost-pink sepals and magenta-rose petals becoming rose-pink at the base.

♀ ***F.* 'Genii'.** Deciduous, erect shrub. **H** 1.5m (5ft), **S** 75cm (2½ft). Frost hardy. Has golden-green foliage. Produces small flowers with cerise-red tubes and sepals and reddish-purple petals. Makes a good standard.

***F.* 'Golden Dawn'.** Deciduous, upright shrub. **H** 1.5m (5ft), **S** 75cm (2½ft). Half hardy. Flowers are salmon-pink. Is good for training as a standard.

♀ ***F.* 'Golden Marinka'** (illus. p.302). Deciduous, trailing shrub. **H** 2m (6ft), **S** indefinite. Half hardy. Has red flowers and variegated golden-yellow leaves with red veins. Is excellent for a hanging basket.

***F.* 'Gruss aus dem Bodethal'.** Deciduous, upright shrub. **H** 1m (3ft), **S** 75cm (2½ft). Half hardy. Small, single or semi-double, crimson flowers open almost black, becoming larger and paler with age.

***F.* 'Harry Gray'.** Deciduous, lax shrub. **H** 2m (6ft), **S** indefinite. Half hardy. Bears a profusion of double flowers with pale pink tubes, green-tipped, white sepals and white to pale pink petals. Is excellent in a hanging basket.

***F.* 'Heidi Weiss'**, syn. *F.* 'White Ann' of gardens, *F.* 'White Heidi Ann' of gardens. Deciduous, upright shrub. **H** 1m (3ft), **S** 75cm (2½ft). Half hardy. Has double flowers with red tubes and sepals and cerise-veined, white petals. Is good for training as a standard.

♀ ***F.* 'Howlett's Hardy'** (illus. p.154). Deciduous, mound-forming shrub. **H** 40cm (16in). **S** 60cm (24in). Frost hardy. Dark red-purple stems bear slightly bronzed, mid-green leaves. Throughout summer produces numerous, pendent, medium flowers with spreading to reflexed, scarlet sepals and bright purple petals veined red at the bases.

***F.* 'Hula Girl'.** Deciduous, trailing shrub. **H** 2m (6ft), **S** indefinite. Half hardy. Bears large, double flowers with deep rose-pink tubes and sepals and pink-flushed, white petals. Does best in a large hanging basket or when trained against a trellis.

♀ ***F.* 'Jack Shahan'** (illus. p.302). Vigorous, deciduous, trailing shrub. **H** 2m (6ft), **S** indefinite. Half hardy. Has large, pale to deep pink flowers. Is excellent for a hanging basket or for training into a weeping standard or upright against a trellis.

***F.* 'Joanna Lumley'** (illus. p.302). Deciduous, semi-trailing shrub. **H** and **S** 30–38cm (12–15in). Half hardy. Has large, double flowers with rather upright, blushed white sepals and lilac petals stained pink at the bases.

***F.* 'Joy Patmore'.** Vigorous, deciduous, upright shrub. **H** 1.5m (5ft), **S** 1m (3ft). Half hardy. Flowers have white tubes, green-tipped, white sepals and cerise petals with white bases. Makes a good standard.

***F.* 'Koralle'.** See *F.* 'Coralle'.

♀ ***F.* 'La Campanella'.** Deciduous, trailing shrub. **H** 1.5m (5ft), **S** indefinite. Half hardy. Has small, semi-double flowers with white tubes, pink-flushed, white sepals and cerise-purple petals. Does best in a hanging basket or trained against a trellis.

♀ ***F.* 'Lady Thumb'** illus. p.152.

♀ *F.* **'Lena'.** Deciduous, lax shrub. **H** and **S** 1m (3ft). Frost hardy. Bears double flowers with pale pink sepals and tubes and pink-flushed, purple petals. Makes a good standard.
F. **'Leonora'** illus. p.301.
♀ *F.* **'Love's Reward'.** Deciduous, upright, short-jointed shrub. **H** and **S** 30–45cm (12–18in). Half hardy. Small to medium, single flowers have white to pale pink tubes and sepals and violet-blue petals.
♀ *F.* **'Lye's Unique'** (illus. p.302). Vigorous, deciduous, upright shrub. **H** 1.5m (5ft), **S** 1m (3ft). Half hardy. Has small flowers with long, white tubes and sepals and orange-red petals. Is excellent for training as a large pyramid.
♀ *F.* **'Madame Cornélissen'** (illus. p.154). Deciduous, arching shrub. **H** and **S** to 1m (3ft). Frost hardy. Has long, white tubes and mauve-red sepals.
F. magellanica (Lady's eardrops; illus. p.154). Deciduous, upright shrub. **H** 3m (10ft), **S** 2m (6ft). Frost hardy. Small flowers with red tubes, long, red sepals and purple petals are followed by black fruits. **'Alba'** see *F.m.* var. *molinae*. ♀**var. *gracilis*** (illus. p.154). Compact, mound-forming shrub. **H** 80cm (32in), **S** 1.2m (48in). Frost hardy. Has rich red stems. In summer and early autumn produces pendent, medium flowers with narrow, slightly spreading, scarlet sepals and shorter, deep purple petals. **var. *molinae*** (syn. *F.m.* 'Alba') has very pale pink flowers. **var. *molinae* 'Enstone'** has gold and green, variegated foliage. **var. *molinae* 'Sharpitor'** produces cream and pale green, variegated leaves. ♀**'Thompsonii'** (illus. p.154), **H** 1.5m (5ft), **S** 1m (3ft), has bright red sepals and purple petals, red-tinted at the bases.
♀ *F.* **'Margaret Brown'.** Deciduous, free-flowering, upright shrub. **H** and **S** 60–90cm (2–3ft). Has strong stems and light green foliage, and bears small, single, 2-tone pink flowers in summer.
♀ *F.* **'Marinka'.** Deciduous, trailing shrub. **H** 2m (6ft), **S** indefinite. Half hardy. Red flowers with darker petals that are folded at outer edges are produced amid dark green leaves with crimson midribs. Foliage becomes discoloured in full sun or cold winds. Is excellent in a hanging basket.
♀ *F.* **'Micky Goult'.** Vigorous, deciduous, upright shrub. **H** 1m (3ft), **S** 75cm (2½ft). Half hardy. Small flowers, with white tubes, pink-tinged, white sepals and pale purple petals, are produced amid pale green foliage.
♀ *F.* **'Mieke Meursing'.** Deciduous, upright shrub. **H** 1m (3ft), **S** 75cm (2½ft). Half hardy. Single to semi-double flowers have red tubes and sepals and pale pink petals with cerise veins.
F. **Mojo Series** Deciduous, bushy, well-branched shrub. **H** 25–35cm (10–14in), **S** 30–40cm (12–16in). Half hardy. Produces small, nodding or slightly outward-facing, bicoloured flowers from mid-spring to autumn in a range of colour combinations. **'Beebop'** (illus. p.302) has slightly upturned, pale pink sepals and magenta petals, paler at the bases.
♀ *F.* **'Mrs Lovell Swisher'** (illus. p.302). Deciduous, upright shrub. **H** 45–60cm (18–24in), **S** 30–60cm (12–24in). Half hardy. Produces masses of small, single flowers with flesh-pink tubes, pinkish-white sepals and deep rose-pink petals.
♀ *F.* **'Mrs Popple'** (illus. p.154). Vigorous, deciduous, upright shrub. **H** 1.5m (5ft), **S** 75cm (2½ft). Frost hardy. Has flowers with red tubes, overhanging, red sepals and purple petals. In a sheltered area may be grown as a hedge.
F. **'Mrs Rundle'.** Vigorous, deciduous, lax shrub. **H** and **S** 75cm (2½ft). Frost tender. Produces large flowers with long, pink tubes, green-tipped, pink sepals and vermilion petals. Is good for training as a standard or growing in a large hanging basket.
F. **'Nancy Lou'.** Vigorous, deciduous, upright shrub. **H** and **S** 1m (3ft). Half hardy. Large, double flowers have pink tubes, upright, green-tipped, pink sepals and bright white petals.
♀ *F.* **'Nellie Nuttall'** (illus. p.302). Vigorous, deciduous, upright shrub. **H** 1m (3ft), **S** 75cm (2½ft). Half hardy. Flowers, with rose-red tubes and sepals and white petals, are borne well above foliage. Is especially suitable for summer bedding; is also good as a standard.
F. **'Other Fellow'.** Deciduous, upright shrub. **H** 1.5m (5ft), **S** 75cm (2½ft). Half hardy. Has small flowers with white tubes and sepals and pink petals.
F. **'Pacquesa'.** Vigorous, deciduous, upright shrub. **H** 1m (3ft), **S** 75cm (2½ft). Half hardy. Has flowers with deep red tubes and sepals and red-veined, white petals. Is good for training as a standard.
F. parviflora of gardens. See *F.* x *bacillaris*.
F. **'Peppermint Stick'.** Deciduous, upright shrub. **H** and **S** 1m (3ft). Half hardy. Double, carmine-red flowers have a central, white stripe and royal purple sepals.
♀ *F.* **'Phyllis'.** Deciduous, upright shrub. **H** 2m (6ft), **S** 1m (3ft). Frost hardy. Single to semi-double flowers, with rose-red tubes and sepals and crimson petals, are followed by masses of black fruits. In a sheltered area may be grown as a hedge.
F. **'Pink Fantasia'.** Deciduous, stiff, upright shrub. **H** 30–40cm (12–18in), **S** 45–60cm (18–24in). Half hardy. Bears single, upward-looking flowers, in profusion, with white tubes and sepals blushed dark pink, and dark purple petals, veined pink, with white bases. Is excellent for borders or pots.
F. **'Pink Galore'** (illus. p.302). Deciduous, trailing shrub. **H** 1.5m (5ft), **S** indefinite. Half hardy. Has large, double, pale pink flowers. Grows best in a large hanging basket or when trained against a trellis.
F. procumbens. Deciduous, prostrate shrub. **H** 10cm (4in), **S** indefinite. Half hardy. Produces tiny, erect, petalless, yellow-tubed flowers with purple sepals and bright blue pollen. Has small, dark green leaves and large, red fruits. Suits a rock garden as well as a hanging basket. Encourage flowering by root restriction or growing in poor, sandy soil.
F. **'Red Spider'** (illus. p.302). Deciduous, trailing shrub. **H** 1.5m (5ft), **S** indefinite. Half hardy. Has long, red flowers with long, narrow, spreading sepals and darker petals. Is best in a large hanging basket or when trained against a trellis.
♀ *F.* **'Riccartonii'** (illus. p.154). Deciduous, stiff, upright shrub. **H** 2m (6ft), **S** 1.5m (5ft). Frost hardy, but, with good drainage and wind protection, is sometimes fully hardy. Has small flowers with red tubes, broad, overhanging, red sepals and purple petals. In a sheltered area may be grown as a hedge. Many plants sold under name of F. 'Riccartonii' are lax hybrids of *F. magellanica*.
F. **'Rose Fantasia'.** Deciduous, stiff, upright shrub. **H** 30–40cm (12–18in), **S** 45–60cm (18–24in). Half hardy. Produces single, upward-looking flowers, in profusion, with rose-pink tubes, dark rose-pink sepals with green tips and red-purple petals, veined rose-pink. Is excellent plant for either borders or pots.
♀ *F.* **'Rose of Castile'.** Vigorous, deciduous, upright shrub. **H** 1.5m (5ft), **S** 1m (3ft). Frost hardy. Produces small flowers with white tubes, green-tipped, white sepals and purple-flushed, pink petals. Makes a good standard.
F. **'Rough Silk'.** Vigorous, deciduous, trailing shrub. **H** 2m (6ft), **S** indefinite. Half hardy. Bears large flowers with pink tubes, long, spreading, pink sepals and wine-red petals. Grows best in a large hanging basket or when trained against a trellis.
♀ *F.* **'Royal Velvet'.** Vigorous, deciduous, upright shrub. **H** 1.5m (5ft), **S** 75cm (2½ft). Half hardy. Has large, double flowers with red tubes and sepals and deep purple petals, splashed deep pink. Is an excellent standard.
♀ *F.* **'Rufus'** (illus. p.154). Vigorous, deciduous, upright shrub. **H** 1.5m (5ft), **S** 75cm (2½ft). Half hardy. Has a profusion of small, bright red flowers. Is easily trained as a standard.
F. **Shadowdancer Series** Deciduous, bushy, well-branched shrubs. **H** and **S** 20–30cm (8–12in). Half hardy. Cultivars produce small single flowers and bloom continuously from spring to late summer or autumn. Ideal in a small container or as edging. **Peggy ('Goetzpeg')** (illus. p.302) has pale pink sepals and rich pink petals tinted in vivid orange.
F. **'Shelford'.** Deciduous, upright, short-jointed shrub. **H** 35–50cm (14–20in), **S** 45–60cm (18–24in). Half hardy. Bears masses of medium-sized, single flowers with slightly fluted, baby-pink tubes, long, narrow, baby-pink sepals and white petals with slight pink veining at the base. Suitable for all forms of training.
♀ ***F. splendens.*** Deciduous, upright shrub. **H** 2m (6ft), **S** 1m (3ft). Half hardy. Small flowers, with broad, orange tubes, pinched in their middles, and short, green sepals and petals, are produced in spring amid pale green foliage. Is extremely susceptible to whitefly.
F. **'Strawberry Delight'.** Deciduous, lax shrub. **H** and **S** 1m (3ft). Half hardy. Leaves are yellowish-green and slightly bronzed. Produces large, double flowers with red tubes and sepals and pink-flushed, white petals. Is excellent as a standard or hanging basket plant.
F. **'Sunray'** (illus. p.302). Deciduous, upright shrub. **H** and **S** to 70cm (28in). Frost tender. White-edged, light green leaves are sometimes pink flushed. Red-violet flowers, with deep pink sepals, are borne freely in summer–autumn.
♀ *F.* **'Swingtime'** (illus. p.302). Vigorous, deciduous, lax shrub. **H** and **S** 1m (3ft). Half hardy. Has large, double flowers with red tubes and sepals and red-veined, creamy-white petals. Makes a good standard or hanging basket plant.
F. **'Texas Longhorn'.** Deciduous, lax shrub. **H** and **S** 75cm (2½ft). Half hardy. Produces very large, double flowers with red tubes, long, spreading, red sepals and cerise-veined, white petals. Grow as a standard or in a hanging basket.
♀ *F.* **'Thalia'** (illus. p.302). Deciduous, upright shrub. **H** and **S** 1m (3ft). Frost tender. Foliage is dark maroon and velvety. Long, slender flowers, with long, red tubes, small, red sepals and small, orange-red petals, are bunched at ends of branches. Makes an excellent specimen plant in summer bedding schemes. Prefers a position in full sun.
F. thymifolia. Deciduous, lax shrub. **H** and **S** 1m (3ft). Half hardy. Has pale green foliage and a few minute, greenish-white flowers that age to purplish-pink. Bears black fruits on female plants if pollen-bearing plants of this species or of *F.* x *bacillaris* are also grown.
♀ *F.* **'Tom Thumb'** (illus. p.154). Deciduous, upright shrub. **H** and **S** 50cm (20in). Frost hardy. Bears small flowers with red tubes and sepals and mauve-purple petals. May be trained as a miniature standard.
F. **'Tom West'.** Deciduous, upright, lax shrub. **H** and **S** 30–60cm (12–24in). Half hardy. Has green and cream variegated foliage and small, single flowers with red tubes and sepals, and purple petals.
F. triphylla. Deciduous, upright shrub, sometimes confused with F. 'Thalia'. **H** and **S** 50cm (20in). Frost tender. Spikes of narrow, long-tubed, bright reddish-orange flowers, with small petals and sepals, are borne above dark bronze-green leaves that are purple beneath. Is very difficult to grow. **'Firecracker'** (illus. p.302) has pink-veined, olive-green leaves edged in cream and bears bright orange flowers.
F. **'Waveny Gem'** Deciduous, trailing shrub. **H** and **S** 30–45cm (12–18in). Frost hardy. Produces medium, single white and mauve-pink flowers from early summer.
F. **'White Ann'** of gardens. See *F.* 'Heidi Weiss'.
F. **'White Heidi Ann'** of gardens. See *F.* 'Heidi Weiss'.
♀ *F.* **'Whiteknights Pearl'** Deciduous, upright shrub. **H** and **S** 1m (3ft) or more. Fully hardy. From summer–autumn, freely produces small, single flowers with long, thin, white tubes, pale pink sepals with small green tips, and clear pink corollas with rounded petals.
F. **Windchimes Series** Deciduous, semi-trailing, slightly mound-forming shrubs. **H** and **S** 45cm (18in). Half hardy. Cultivars have a spreading, branching habit and produce single flowers continuously from spring to late summer or early autumn. Suitable for use in a hanging basket, or at the edge of a large container, as well as in garden plantings. **Windchimes Pink and White** ('Kiefuwind') illus. p.302. Has narrow, salmon-pink sepals and white petals.
♀ *F.* **'Winston Churchill'** Deciduous,

bushy, upright, extremely free-flowering shrub. **H** and **S** 45–75cm (18–30in). Half hardy. Produces medium, fully double flowers with green-tipped pink tubes, broad, reflexed sepals, and lavender-blue corollas, maturing purple. Is good for summer bedding,or trained as a standard in containers.

FURCRAEA

AGAVACEAE

Genus of perennial succulents with dense clusters of sword-shaped, fleshy, toothed leaves in terminal or basal rosettes; rosettes die after flowering. Resembles *Agave*, but has short-tubed flowers. Frost hardy to frost tender, min. 6°C (43°F). Requires a position in full sun and in well-drained soil. Protect from winter wet. Propagate by bulbils, borne on lower stems, when developed.

F. bedinghausii. See *F. parmentieri*.

F. foetida, syn. *F. gigantea*. Basal-rosetted, perennial succulent. **H** 3m (10ft), **S** 5m (15ft). Frost tender, min. 6°C (43°F). Has broadly sword-shaped, fleshy, mid-green leaves, to 2.5m (8ft) long, with edges toothed only at the base. Flower stems, to 8m (25ft), produce scented, bell-shaped, green flowers, which are white within, in summer. **'Mediopicta'** (syn. *F.f.* var. *mediopicta, F.f.* 'Variegata') illus. p.481.

F. gigantea. See *F. foetida*.

F. parmentieri, syn. *F. bedinghausii*. Basal-rosetted, perennial succulent. **H** 60cm (24in), **S** 1m (3ft). Frost hardy. Sword-shaped, minutely toothed, glaucous, mid-green leaves. In summer produces a large, pyramidal, erect spike, to 2m (6ft), with drooping branches and clusters of 2–4 creamy flowers, 3–4cm (1¼–1½in), followed by numerous bulbils. Often incorrectly labelled *F. longaeva*.

G

GAGEA

LILIACEAE

Genus of spring-flowering bulbs, grown for their clusters of funnel- or star-shaped, white or yellow flowers. Is suitable for rock gardens. Frost to half hardy. Prefers full light and well-drained soil that does not become too hot and dry. Dies down in summer. Propagate by division in spring or autumn or by seed in autumn.

G. graeca, syn. *Lloydia graeca*. Spring-flowering bulb. **H** 5–10cm (2–4in), **S** 3–5cm (1¼–2in). Half hardy. Thread-like, semi-erect leaves form at ground level and on wiry stems. Bears up to 5 widely funnel-shaped, purple-veined, white flowers, 1–1.5cm (½–¾in) long.

G. peduncularis. Spring-flowering bulb. **H** 5–15cm (2–6in), **S** 2.5–5cm (1–2in). Frost hardy. Has thread-like, semi-erect leaves at base and on stem. Produces a loose head of flat, star-shaped, yellow flowers, each 1.5–3cm (⅝–1¼in) across, with green stripes outside.

GAILLARDIA

Blanket flower

COMPOSITAE/ASTERACEAE

Genus of summer-flowering annuals and perennials that tend to be short-lived. Fully to frost hardy. Requires sun and prefers well-drained soil. May need staking. Propagate species by seed in autumn or spring, selected forms by root cuttings in winter.

G. aristata (Blanket flower). Upright, rather open perennial. **H** 60cm (24in), **S** 50cm (20in). Fully hardy. Has large, terminal, daisy-like, single flower heads, yellow with red centres, over summer, and aromatic, divided leaves.

♀ ***G. x grandiflora* 'Dazzler'.** Upright, rather open perennial. **H** 60cm (24in), **S** 50cm (20in). Fully hardy. Bears large, terminal, daisy-like, yellow-tipped, red flower heads for a long period in summer. Leaves are soft and divided. **'Wirral Flame'** is a clump-forming, short-lived perennial with deep cardinal-red flower heads during summer. Leaves are lance-shaped, lobed and soft green.

***G.* 'Oranges and Lemons'** illus. p.277.

G. pulchella. Moderately fast-growing, upright annual or short-lived perennial. **H** 45cm (18in), **S** 30cm (12in). Fully hardy. Has lance-shaped, hairy, greyish-green leaves and, in summer, daisy-like, double, crimson-zoned, yellow, pink or red flower heads. **'Lollipops'** illus. p.327

GALANTHUS

Snowdrop

AMARYLLIDACEAE

Genus of bulbs, grown for their pendent, white flowers, one on each slender stem between 2 basal leaves. Is easily recognized by its 3 large, outer petals and 3 small, inner ones forming a cup, which is green-marked. Fully to frost hardy. Needs a cool, partially shaded position and humus-rich, moist soil. Do not allow bulbs to dry out excessively. Propagate by division in spring after flowering or during late summer or autumn when bulbs are dormant.

① All parts may cause mild stomach upset if ingested; contact with the bulbs may irritate skin.

♀ ***G.* 'Atkinsii'** illus. p.427.

♀ ***G. elwesii*** illus. p.427.

G. gracilis, syn. G. *graecus* of gardens, illus. p.427.

G. graecus of gardens. See *G. gracilis*.

***G.* 'Hill Poë'** illus. p.427.

G. ikariae illus. p.427.

♀ ***G. nivalis*** (Common snowdrop). Late winter- and early spring-flowering bulb. **H** 10–15cm (4–6in), **S** 5–8cm (2–3in). Fully hardy. Produces narrowly strap-shaped, semi-erect, basal, grey-green leaves. Flowers are 2–2.5cm (¾–1in) long with a green mark at the tip of each inner petal.**'Flore Pleno'** illus. p.427. **'Lutescens'** see *G.n.* 'Sandersii'. **'Pusey Green Tip'** illus. p.427. **'Sandersii'** (syn. *G.n.* 'Lutescens') illus. p.428. **'Scharlockii'** illus. p.428. **'Viridapicicis'** has a very long spathe, sometimes split in 2, and green marks on the outer tepals.

♀ ***G. plicatus* subsp. *plicatus*.** Late winter- and early spring-flowering bulb. **H** 10–20cm (4–8in), **S** 5–8cm (2–3in). Fully hardy. Bears broadly strap-shaped, semi-erect, basal, deep green leaves that have grey bands along the centres and reflexed margins. White flowers, 2–3cm (¾–1¼in) long, have a green patch at the tip of each inner petal.

subsp. *byzantinus* illus. p.427.

G. rizehensis illus. p.428.

♀ ***G. woronowii*** illus. p.428.

GALAX

DIAPENSIACEAE

Genus of one species of evergreen perennial, grown for its foliage and for its flowers, borne in late spring and summer. Is useful for underplanting shrubs. Fully hardy. Requires shade and moist, peaty, acid soil. Propagate by division of rooted runners in spring.

G. aphylla. See *G. urceolata*.

G. urceolata, syn. *G. aphylla*, illus. p.336.

GALEGA

Goat's rue

LEGUMINOSAE/PAPILIONACEAE

Genus of summer-flowering perennials. Fully hardy. Grow in an open, sunny position and in any well-drained soil. Requires staking. Propagate by seed in autumn or by division in winter.

***G.* 'Her Majesty'.** See *G.* 'His Majesty'.

***G.* 'His Majesty'**, syn. *G.* 'Her Majesty'. Vigorous, upright perennial. **H** to 1.5m (5ft), **S** 1m (3ft). In summer, produces spikes of small, pea-like, clear lilac-mauve and white flowers. Bold, oblong to lance-shaped leaves consist of oval leaflets.

♀ ***G. x hartlandii* 'Lady Wilson'** illus. p.218.

G. orientalis illus. p.239.

GALIUM

Bedstraw

RUBIACEAE

Genus of spring- and summer-flowering perennials, many of which are weeds; *G. odoratum* is cultivated as ground cover. Fully hardy. Grows well in partial shade, but tolerates sun and thrives in any well-drained soil. Propagate by division in early spring or autumn.

G. odoratum, syn. *Asperula odorata*, illus. p.263.

GALTONIA

LILIACEAE/HYACINTHACEAE

Genus of summer- and autumn-flowering bulbs, grown for their elegant spikes of pendent, funnel-shaped, white or green flowers. Frost hardy. Needs a sheltered, sunny site and fertile, well-drained soil that does not dry out in summer. Dies down in winter. May be lifted for replanting in spring. Propagate by seed in spring or by offsets in autumn or spring.

♀ ***G. candicans*** illus. p.383.

G. viridiflora illus. p.393.

GARDENIA

RUBIACEAE

Genus of evergreen shrubs and trees, grown for their flowers and foliage. Frost tender, min. 15°C (59°F). Prefers partial shade and humus-rich, well-drained, neutral to acid soil. Water containerized specimens freely when in full growth, moderately at other times. After flowering, shorten strong shoots to maintain a shapely habit. Propagate by greenwood cuttings in spring or by semi-ripe cuttings in summer. Whitefly and mealy bug may cause problems.

G. augusta. See *G. jasminoides*.

G. capensis. See *Rothmannia capensis*.

G. florida. See *G. jasminoides*.

G. grandiflora. See *G. jasminoides*.

♀ ***G. jasminoides***, syn. *G. augusta, G. florida, G. grandiflora* (Cape jasmine, Common gardenia). **'Veitchii'** illus. p.454.

G. rothmannia. See *Rothmannia capensis*.

G. thunbergia. Evergreen, bushy shrub with white stems. **H** and **S** to 2m (6ft) or more. Has elliptic, glossy, deep green leaves. Fragrant, 7–9-petalled, white flowers, 6–10cm (2½–4in) wide, are borne in winter–spring.

GARRYA

GARRYACEAE

Genus of evergreen shrubs and trees, grown for their catkins in winter and spring, which are longer and more attractive on male plants. Frost hardy. Hard frosts may damage catkins. Requires a sheltered, sunny site and tolerates any poor soil. Is suitable for a south- or west-facing wall. Dislikes being transplanted. Propagate by semi-ripe cuttings in summer.

G. elliptica (Silk tassel bush). Bushy, dense shrub. **H** and **S** 4m (12ft). Has leathery, wavy-edged, dark green leaves.

F

Grey-green catkins are borne from mid-winter to early spring. ♀ **'James Roof'** has very long, grey-green catkins with yellow anthers (illus. p.211).

GASTERIA

LILIACEAE/ALOACEAE

Genus of perennial succulents with thick, fleshy leaves, usually arranged in a fan, later becoming a tight rosette. Frost tender, min. 5°C (41°F). Is easy to grow, needing sun or partial shade and very well-drained soil. Propagate by seed, leaf cuttings or division in spring or summer.
G. bicolor* var. *bicolor, syn. *G. caespitosa*. Fan-shaped, perennial succulent. **H** 15cm (6in), **S** 30cm (12in). Produces triangular, thick, dark green leaves, 15cm (6in) long, with horny borders. Upper leaf surfaces have numerous white or pale green dots, usually in diagonal rows. Bears spikes of bell-shaped, orange-green flowers in spring. **var. *liliputana***, syn. *G. liliputana*, illus. p.480.
G. caespitosa. See *G. bicolor* var. *bicolor*.
G. carinata* var. *verrucosa, syn. *G. verrucosa*, illus. p.480.
G. liliputana. See *G. bicolor* var. *liliputana*.
G. verrucosa. See *G. carinata* var. *verrucosa*.

x *Gaulnettya* 'Pink Pixie'. See *Gaultheria* x *wisleyensis* 'Pink Pixie'.
x *Gaulnettya* 'Wisley Pearl'. See *Gaultheria* x *wisleyensis* 'Wisley Pearl'.

GAULTHERIA

ERICACEAE

Genus of evergreen shrubs and sub-shrubs, grown for their foliage, flowers and fruits. Fully to half hardy. Grows best in shade or semi-shade and requires moist, peaty, acid soil. Will tolerate sun provided the soil is permanently moist. Propagate by semi-ripe cuttings in summer or by seed in autumn; for *G. shallon and G. trichophylla*, propagate by division in autumn or spring. ① All parts may cause mild stomach upset if ingested, except the fruits, which are edible.
♀ ***G. cuneata*** illus. p.346.
G. forrestii. Evergreen, rounded shrub. **H** and **S** 1.5m (5ft). Half hardy. Has oblong, glossy, dark green leaves and racemes of small, fragrant, rounded, white flowers, in spring, followed by rounded, blue fruits.
G. miqueliana. Evergreen, compact shrub. **H** and **S** 25cm (10in). Frost hardy. Has oval, leathery leaves clothing stiff stems. In late spring, produces bell-shaped, pink-tinged, white flowers, up to 6 per stem, followed by rounded, white or pink fruits.
G. mucronata, syn. *Pernettya mucronata*. Evergreen, bushy, dense shrub, spreading by underground stems. **H** and **S** 1.2m (4ft). Fully hardy. Oval, prickly, glossy, dark green leaves set off tiny, urn-shaped, white flowers in late spring and early summer. Spherical, fleshy fruit are produced and these vary in colour between cultivars. Sprays of fruit are good for indoor display. Fruits of **'Cherry Ripe'** (female) are large and bright cherry-red. **'Edward Balls'** (male) produces stout, upright, red shoots and sharply spined, bright green leaves. ♀ **'Mulberry Wine'** (female) illus.p.164. ♀ **'Wintertime'** (female) illus.p.163.
G. myrsinoides, syn. *G. prostrata, Pernettya prostrata*. Evergreen, spreading shrub. **H** 15–30cm (6–12in), **S** 30cm (12in) or more. Fully hardy. Bears oval, leathery, dark green leaves. Urn-shaped, white flowers are produced in early summer and are followed by large, rounded, blue-purple fruits. Is suitable for a rock garden or peat bed.
G. nummularioides. Evergreen, compact shrub. **H** 10–15cm (4–6in), **S** 20cm (8in). Frost hardy. Leaves are oval to heart-shaped and leathery. Egg-shaped, pink-flushed, white flowers are produced from the upper leaf axils in late spring or summer. Produces rounded, blue-black fruits, but only rarely.
♀ ***G. procumbens*** illus. p.373.
G. prostrata. See *G. myrsinoides*.
G. pumila, syn. *Pernettya pumila*. Evergreen, mat-forming, creeping shrub. **H** 5cm (2in), **S** 30–60cm (12–24in). Fully hardy. Prostrate branches bear tiny, bell-shaped, white flowers in early summer among tiny, rounded, leathery leaves. Rounded fruits are pink or white. Is good for a rock garden or peat bed.
G. shallon illus. p.154.
G. tasmanica, syn. *Pernettya tasmanica*. Evergreen, mat-forming shrub. **H** 5–8cm (2–3in), **S** 20cm (8in). Frost hardy. Has oval, toothed, leathery leaves with wavy edges. Bell-shaped, white flowers in early summer are followed by rounded, red fruits. Is good for a rock garden or peat bed.
G. trichophylla. Evergreen, compact shrub with creeping, underground stems. **H** 7–15cm (3–6in), **S** 20cm (8in). Frost hardy. Bell-shaped, pink flowers in early summer are followed by egg-shaped, blue fruits produced from leaf axils. Leaves are small and oval.
***G.* x *wisleyensis* 'Pink Pixie'**, syn. x *Gaulnettya* 'Pink Pixie'. Evergreen, dense, bushy shrub. **H** and **S** 1m (3ft). Bears broadly oval, deeply veined, dark green leaves. Small, urn-shaped, pale pink flowers, produced in late spring and early summer, are followed by spherical, purplish-red fruits. **'Wisley Pearl'**, syn. x *aulnettya* 'Wisley Pearl', illus. p.145.

GAURA

ONAGRACEAE

Genus of summer-flowering annuals and perennials that are sometimes short-lived. Fully hardy. Prefers full sun and light, well-drained soil. Propagate by softwood or semi-ripe cuttings in summer or by seed in autumn or spring.
♀ ***G. lindheimeri*** (illus. p.231). Bushy perennial. **H** 90cm (36in), **S** 60cm (24in). In summer produces racemes of star-shaped, pink-suffused, white flowers. Leaves are lance-shaped and mid-green. **'Rosyjane'** illus. p.301.

GAYLUSSACIA

Huckleberry

ERICACEAE

Genus of deciduous occasionally evergreen shrubs, grown for their flowers, fruits and autumn colour. Fully hardy. Needs sun or semi-shade and moist, peaty, acid soil. Propagate by softwood cuttings in summer or by seed in autumn.
G. baccata (Black huckleberry). Deciduous, bushy shrub. **H** and **S** 1m (3ft). Oval, sticky, dark green leaves redden in autumn. Produces clusters of small, urn-shaped, dull red flowers in late spring, then edible, spherical, black fruits.

GAZANIA

COMPOSITAE/ASTERACEAE

Genus of evergreen perennials, often grown as annuals and useful for summer bedding, pots and tubs. Half hardy. Requires sun and sandy soil. Propagate by seed in spring or by heel cuttings in spring or summer.
***G.* Daybreak Series.** Carpeting perennial, grown as an annual. **H** and **S** 20cm (8in). Has lance-shaped leaves and, in summer, large, daisy-like flower heads in a mixture of orange, yellow, pink, bronze and white. Flowers remain open in dull weather. **'Daybreak Bright Yellow'** illus. p.323.
***G.* Kiss Series 'Kiss Orange Flame'** illus. p.324.
G. pinnata. Mat-forming perennial. **H** 15cm (6in), **S** 30cm (12in). Daisy-like, orange-red flower heads, with central, black rings, appear singly in early summer above oval, finely cut, hairy, bluish-grey leaves.
♀ ***G. rigens* var. *uniflora***, syn. *G. uniflora*. Mat-forming perennial, grown as an annual in all except mildest areas. **H** 23cm (9in), **S** 20–30cm (8–12in). Yellow or orange-yellow flower heads, sometimes with central white spots, are borne singly in early summer above rosettes of narrow, silver-backed leaves.
♀ ***G.* Talent Series.** Vigorous perennials. **H** and **S** to 25cm (10in). Have highly ornamental, mid-green leaves, to 15cm (6in) long, grey-felted on both surfaces. In summer, produce solitary, yellow, orange, pink or brown flower heads on short stems just above the leaves.
G. uniflora. See *G. rigens* var. *uniflora*.

GELSEMIUM

LOGANIACEAE

Genus of evergreen, twining climbers, grown for their fragrant, jasmine-like flowers. Half hardy. In cool climates best grown under glass. Provide full light and fertile, well-drained soil. Water regularly, less in cold weather. Stems require support and should be thinned out after flowering or during spring. Propagate by seed sown in spring or by semi-ripe cuttings in summer.
♀ ***G. sempervirens*** illus. p.195.

GENISTA

Broom

LEGUMINOSAE/PAPILIONACEAE

Genus of deciduous, sometimes almost leafless, shrubs and trees, grown for their mass of small, pea-like flowers. Fully to half hardy. Does best in full sun and not over-rich, well-drained soil. Resents being transplanted. Propagate species by softwood or semi-ripe cuttings in summer or by seed in autumn, selected forms by softwood cuttings only in summer.
♀ ***G. aetnensis*** (Mount Etna broom) illus. p.89.
G. cinerea. illus. p.116.
♀ ***G. delphinensis***, syn. *Chamaespartium sagittale* subsp. *delphinense, G. sagittalis* subsp. *delphinensis*. Deciduous, prostrate shrub. **H** 1cm (½in), **S** 20cm (8in). Frost hardy. Has tangled, winged branches, covered with minute, oval, dark green leaves. Masses of golden-yellow flowers are produced along stems in early summer. Suitable for a rock garden or wall.
G. fragrans of gardens. See *Genista* x *spachiana*.
G. hispanica. (Spanish gorse) illus. p.160.
♀ ***G. lydia.*** illus. p.345.
G. monosperma. See *Retama monosperma*.
G. pilosa. Deciduous, domed shrub. **H** and **S** 30cm (12in). Fully hardy. Narrowly oval leaves are silky-haired beneath. Bright yellow flowers on short stalks are borne in leaf axils in summer. Is useful on a bank or as ground cover. Propagate by semi-ripe cuttings in summer.
G. sagittalis, syn. *Chamaespartium sagittale*, illus. p.373. ♀ **subsp. *delphinensis.*** See *G. delphinensis*.
♀ ***G.* x *spachiana*,** syn. *Cytisus canariensis* of gardens, *C. racemosus* of gardens, *Genista fragrans* of gardens. Vigorous, evergreen, arching shrub. **H** and **S** 3m (10ft). Half hardy. Has dark green leaves with 3 oval leaflets. Produces long, slender clusters of fragrant, golden-yellow flowers in winter and early spring. Is often grown as a houseplant.
***G. tenera* 'Golden Shower'** illus. p.116.
G. tinctoria illus. p.148. ♀ **'Royal Gold'** is a deciduous, upright shrub. **H** and **S** 1m (3ft). Fully hardy. Produces long, conical panicles of golden-yellow flowers in spring–summer and leaves that are narrowly lance-shaped and dark green.

GENTIANA

Gentian

GENTIANACEAE

Genus of annuals, biennials and perennials, some of which are semi-evergreen or evergreen, grown for their usually blue flowers. Is excellent for rock gardens and peat beds. Fully hardy. Prefers sun or semi-shade and humus-rich, well-drained, moist, neutral to acid soil. Some species grow naturally on limestone soils. Propagate by division or offshoots in spring or by seed in autumn.

Divide autumn-flowering species and *G. clusii* every 3 years in early spring and replant in fresh soil. See also feature panel p.370.

♀ ***G. acaulis***, syn. *G. excisa*, *G. kochiana* (Stemless gentian; illus. p.370). Evergreen, clump-forming perennial. **H** in leaf 2cm (¾in), **S** to 10cm (4in) or more. Has narrowly oval, glossy leaves and trumpet-shaped, deep blue flowers, with green-spotted throats, on short stems in spring and often in autumn. Tolerates alkaline soils.

G. angustifolia. Evergreen, clump-forming perennial. **H** 10cm (4in), **S** 20cm (8in). Has rosettes of oblong, dull green leaves and, in summer, solitary, tubular, sky-blue flowers on 7cm (3in) stems. Tolerates alkaline soils.

♀ ***G. asclepiadea*** (Willow gentian) illus. p.250.

***G.* 'Blue Silk'** (illus. p.370). Evergreen, procumbent perennial. **H** 5cm (2in), **S** to 12cm (5in) or more. Has basal rosettes of lance-shaped, mid-green leaves. In late summer and autumn produces upright, trumpet-shaped, deep blue flowers, banded white and dark blue on the outer surfaces. Requires acid soil.

G. clusii (Trumpet gentian). Evergreen, clump-forming perennial. **H** 5cm (2in), **S** 15–23cm (6–9in). Has rosettes of oval, glossy, dark green leaves. Trumpet-shaped, azure-blue flowers, with green-spotted, paler throats, are borne on 2.5–10cm (1–4in) stems in early summer. Tolerates alkaline soils.

***G.* 'Ettrick'** (illus. p.370). Evergreen, procumbent, perennial. **H** 5cm (2in), **S** to 12cm (5in) or more. Has basal rosettes of linear-lance-shaped, mid-green leaves. In late summer and autumn produces upright, trumpet-shaped, clear white flowers, flecked with blue spots on the inner surfaces. Requires acid soil.

***G.* 'Eugen's Allerbester'** (illus. p.370). Vigorous, evergreen, procumbent perennial. **H** 5cm (2in), **S** to 20cm (8in) or more. Has basal rosettes of linear, mid-green leaves. In late summer and autumn produces upright, trumpet-shaped, double, deep blue flowers, banded white on the outer surfaces. Requires acid soil.

G. excisa. See *G. acaulis.*

G. gracilipes. Semi-evergreen, tufted perennial with arching stems. **H** 15cm (6in), **S** 20cm (8in). Forms a central rosette of long, strap-shaped, dark green leaves from which lax flower stems bearing tubular, dark purplish-blue flowers, greenish within, are produced in summer. Tolerates some shade.

♀ ***G.* 'Inverleith'** (illus. p.370). Vigorous, evergreen, procumbent perennial. **H** 5cm (2in), **S** to 12cm (5in) or more. Has basal rosettes of linear-lance shaped, mid-green leaves. In late summer produces upright, trumpet-shaped, bright blue flowers, banded green on the outer surfaces. Requires acid soil.

G. kochiana. See *G. acaulis.*

G. lutea illus. p.243.

***G. x macaulayi* 'Wells's Variety'**, syn. *G. 'Wellsii'* (illus. p.370). Evergreen, prostrate perennial. **H** in flower 5cm (2in), **S** 20cm (8in). Has trumpet-shaped, mid-blue flowers in late summer and autumn. Spreading stems are clothed in narrow, mid-green leaves. Requires moist, acid soil.

G. ornata. Semi-evergreen, clump-forming perennial with small, over-wintering rosettes. **H** 5cm (2in), **S** 10cm (4in). Forms a central rosette of grass-like leaves. In autumn, each stem tip carries an upright, bell-shaped, mid-blue flower, with a white throat and deep blue stripes shading to creamy-white outside. Requires acid soil and a moist atmosphere.

G. saxosa (illus. p.370). Evergreen, hummock-forming perennial. **H** 5cm (2in), **S** 15cm (6in). Is clothed in small, spoon-shaped, fleshy, dark green leaves. Produces small, upturned, bell-shaped, white flowers in early summer. Is a short-lived scree plant. Tolerates alkaline soils.

***G.* scabra.** Deciduous, upright perennial. **H** 30cm (12in), **S** 20–30cm (8–12in). Has long, ovate to lance-shaped, deep green stem leaves borne in opposite pairs on herbaceous stems. Narrowly bell-shaped, deep blue flowers are borne in terminal clusters and also in pairs in upper leaf axils in mid-autumn. Requires acid soil.

♀ ***G. septemfida*** illus. p.346.

***G.* 'Shot Silk'** (illus. p.370). Evergreen, procumbent perennial. **H** 5cm (2in), **S** to 12cm (5in) or more. Has basal rosettes of linear-lance-shaped, deep green leaves. In late summer and autumn produces upright, trumpet-shaped, silky, deep purple-blue flowers, banded green and purple on the outer surfaces. Requires acid soil.

♀ ***G. sino-ornata*** (illus. p.370). Evergreen, prostrate, spreading perennial. **H** in flower 5cm (2in), **S** to 30cm (12in). In autumn, bears trumpet-shaped, rich blue flowers singly at the ends of stems. Leaves are narrow. Requires acid soil.

***G.* 'Soutra'** (illus. p.370). Evergreen, procumbent, perennial. **H** 5cm (2in), **S** to 12cm (5in) or more. Has basal rosettes of linear-lance-shaped, mid-green leaves. In late summer and autumn produces upright, trumpet-like, white flowers, suffused pale green on the outer surfaces. Requires acid soil.

♀ ***G.* 'Strathmore'** (illus. p.370). Evergreen, procumbent perennial. **H** 5cm (2in), **S** to 12cm (5in) or more. Has basal rosettes of linear-lance-shaped, pale green leaves. In late summer and autumn produces upright, trumpet-shaped, blue-mauve flowers, with vertical, greenish-white stripes on the outer surfaces. Requires acid soil.

***G.* 'Susan Jane'.** Vigorous, semi-evergreen, spreading perennial with small, overwintering rosettes. **H** 5cm (2in), **S** 30cm (12in). Prostrate stems bear grass-like leaves. Large, trumpet-shaped, white-throated, deep blue flowers, greenish within, appear in autumn. Requires acid soil.

♀ ***G. verna*** illus. p.356.

***G.* 'Wellsii'.** See *G.* x *macaulayi* 'Wells's Variety'.

GERANIUM

Cranesbill

GERANIACEAE

Genus of perennials, some of which are semi-evergreen, grown for their flowers and often as ground cover. Compact species are suitable for rock gardens. Fully to half hardy. Most species prefer sun, but some do better in shade. Will grow in all but waterlogged soils. Propagate by semi-ripe cuttings in summer or by seed or division in autumn or spring. Cultivars should be propagated by division or cuttings only.

G. anemonifolium. See *G. palmatum.*

♀ ***G.* 'Ann Folkard'.** Spreading perennial. **H** 50cm (20in), **S** 1m (36in). Fully hardy. Has rounded, deeply cut, yellowish-green leaves and, in summer–autumn, masses of shallowly cup-shaped, rich magenta flowers with black veins.

G. armenum. See *G. psilostemon.*

G. cinereum. Semi-evergreen, rosetted perennial with spreading flowering stems. **H** 15cm (6in), **S** 30cm (12in). Fully hardy. Has cup-shaped flowers, either white to pale pink, strongly veined with purple, or pure white, on lax stems in late spring and summer. Basal leaves are rounded, deeply divided, soft and grey-green. Is good for a large rock garden. ♀ **'Ballerina'** illus. p.366. **var. *subcaulescens*** see *G. subcaulescens.*

***G. clarkei* 'Kashmir Purple'**, syn. *G. pratense* 'Kashmir Purple'. Carpeting, rhizomatous perennial. **H** and **S** 45–60cm (18–24in). Fully hardy. Bears loose clusters of cup-shaped, deep purple flowers in summer. Rounded leaves are deeply divided and finely veined. ♀ **'Kashmir White'** (syn. *G. pratense* 'Kashmir White') illus. p.263.

♀ ***G. dalmaticum*** illus. p.363.

♀ ***G. endressii.*** Semi-evergreen, compact, carpeting perennial. **H** 45cm (18in), **S** 60cm (24in). Fully hardy. Has small, lobed leaves and cup-shaped, rose-pink flowers borne throughout summer. **'Wargrave Pink'** see *G.* x *oxonianum* 'Wargrave Pink'.

G. farreri. Rosetted perennial with a tap root. **H** 10cm (4in), **S** 10–15cm (4–6in) or more. Fully hardy. Outward-facing, flattish, very pale mauve-pink flowers set off blue-black anthers in early summer. Has kidney-shaped, matt green leaves. Both flower and leaf stems are red.

G. grandiflorum. See *G. himalayense.*

G. himalayense, syn. *G. grandiflorum, G. meeboldii.* Clump-forming perennial. **H** 30cm (12in), **S** 60cm (24in). Fully hardy. Has large, cup-shaped, violet-blue flowers borne on long stalks in summer over dense tufts of neatly cut leaves.

G. ibericum. Clump-forming perennial. **H** and **S** 60cm (24in). Fully hardy. In summer, produces sprays of 5-petalled, saucer-shaped, violet-blue flowers. Has heart-shaped, lobed or cut, hairy leaves.

G. incanum. Semi-evergreen, spreading, mounded perennial. **H** 30–38cm (12–15in), **S** 60cm–90cm (24–36in). Frost hardy. Shallowly cup-shaped flowers are variable, but usually deep pink, and borne singly in summer above aromatic, deeply divided, grey-green leaves with linear segments.

♀ ***G.* 'Johnson's Blue'** illus. p.270.

G. macrorrhizum illus. p.269.

♀ **'Ingwersen's Variety'** illus. p.256.

G. maculatum. Clump-forming perennial. **H** 75cm (30in), **S** 45cm (18in). Fully hardy. In spring, bears heads of flattish, pinkish-lilac flowers above rounded, lobed or scalloped, mid-green leaves that turn fawn and red in autumn.

♀ ***G. maderense.*** Vigorous, semi-evergreen, bushy perennial with a woody base. **H** and **S** 1m (3ft). Half hardy. Produces large sprays of shallowly cup-shaped, deep magenta flowers in summer above palmate, finely cut, dark green leaves.

♀ ***G.* x *magnificum*** illus. p.269.

G. meeboldii. See *G. himalayense.*

G. nodosum. Clump-forming perennial. **H** and **S** 45cm (18in). Fully hardy. Has lobed, glossy leaves and delicate, cup-shaped, lilac or lilac-pink flowers borne in spring and summer. Tolerates deep shade.

G. orientalitibeticum, syn. *G. stapfianum* var. *roseum* of gardens, illus. p.339.

♀ ***G.* 'Orion'** illus. p.280.

***G.* x *oxonianum* 'Claridge Druce'.** Vigorous, semi-evergreen, carpeting perennial. **H** and **S** 60–75cm (24–30in). Fully hardy. Bears clusters of cup-shaped, darker-veined, mauve-pink flowers throughout summer. Has dainty, rounded, lobed leaves. ♀ **'Wargrave Pink'** (syn. *G. endressii* 'Wargrave Pink') illus. p.265. **'Winscombe'**, **H** 60–75cm (24–30in), **S** 45cm (18in), has cup-shaped, deep pink flowers, which fade to pale pink, borne throughout summer.

♀ ***G. palmatum***, syn. *G. anemonifolium.* (illus. p.238). Vigorous, semi-evergreen, bushy perennial with a woody base. **H** 45cm (18in), **S** 60cm (24in). Half hardy. Has palmate, deeply lobed, dark green leaves and, in late summer, large sprays of shallowly cup-shaped, purplish-red flowers.

G. phaeum illus. p.223.

G. pratense (Meadow cranesbill). Clump-forming perennial. **H** 75cm (30in), **S** 60cm (24in). Fully hardy. Bears 5-petalled, saucer-shaped, violet-blue flowers on branching stems in summer. Rounded, lobed to deeply divided, mid-green leaves become bronze in autumn. **'Kashmir Purple'** see *G. clarkei* 'Kashmir Purple'. **'Kashmir White'** see *G. clarkei* 'Kashmir White'. ♀ **'Mrs Kendall Clark'** illus. p.239. ♀ **'Plenum Violaceum'** is more compact than the species with double, deep violet flowers.

G. procurrens. Carpeting perennial. **H** 30cm (12in), **S** 60cm (24in). Fully hardy. Has rounded, lobed, glossy leaves and, in summer, clusters of saucer-shaped, deep rose-purple flowers.

♀ ***G. psilostemon***, syn. *G. armenum*, illus. p.233.

G. pylzowianum. Spreading perennial with underground runners and tiny tubers. **H** 12–25cm (5–10in), **S** 25cm (10in) or more. Fully hardy. Bears semi-circular, deeply cut, dark green leaves and, in late spring and summer, trumpet-shaped, green-centred, deep rose-pink flowers. May be invasive.

♀ ***G. renardii*** illus. p.264.

♀ ***G.* x *riversleaianum* 'Russell Prichard'.** Semi-evergreen, clump forming perennial. **H** 30cm (1ft), **S** 1m (3ft). Frost hardy. Saucer-shaped, clear pink flowers are borne singly or in small clusters from early summer to autumn. Rounded leaves are lobed and grey-green.

♀ ***G.* Rozanne ('Gerwat')** illus. p.271.

G. sanguineum illus. p.340. ♀ ***var. striatum*** illus. p.362.
G. stapfianum* var. *roseum of gardens. See *G. orientalitibeticum*.
♀ ***G. subcaulescens***, syn. *G. cinereum* var. *subcaulescens*, illus. p.366.
♀ ***G. sylvaticum* 'Mayflower'** illus. p.239.
***G. traversii* var. *elegans*.** Semi-evergreen, rosetted perennial with spreading stems. **H** 10cm (4in), **S** 25cm (10in). Frost hardy. Large, upward-facing, saucer-shaped, pale pink flowers, with darker veins, rise above rounded, lobed, grey-green leaves in summer. Is suitable for a sheltered ledge or rock garden. Protect from winter wet. Requires gritty soil.
♀ ***G. wallichianum* 'Buxton's Variety'**, syn. *G.w.* 'Buxton's Blue'. Spreading perennial. **H** 30–45cm (12–18in), **S** 90cm (36in). Fully hardy. Has luxuriant, white-flecked leaves and large, white-centred, blue or blue-purple flowers from mid-summer to autumn. Prefers partial shade.
***G. wlassovianum*.** Clump-forming perennial. **H** and **S** 60cm (24in). Fully hardy. Has velvety stems and rounded, lobed, dark green leaves. Saucer-shaped, deep purple flowers are borne singly or in small clusters in summer.

GERBERA

COMPOSITAE/ASTERACEAE

Genus of perennials, flowering from summer to winter depending on growing conditions. Frost to half hardy. Grow in full sun and in light, sandy soil. Propagate by heel cuttings from side shoots in summer or by seed in autumn or early spring.
G.* 'Amgerbpink'**. See G. ***Everlast Pink.
G. Everlast Pink ('Amgerbpink'). Clump-forming perennial. **H** 35cm (14in), **S** 30cm (12in). Frost hardy. Has oval, irregularly lobed leaves. Large, daisy-like, soft pink flower heads are borne on tall, slender stems in mid- and late summer.
G. jamesonii illus. p.306.

GEUM

Avens

ROSACEAE

Genus of summer-flowering perennials. Fully hardy. Does best in sun and prefers moist but well-drained soil. Propagate by division or by seed in autumn.
***G.* 'Bell Bank'** illus. p.268.
G. x borisii of gardens. See *G. coccineum*.
G. chiloense, syn. *G. coccineum* of gardens. Clump-forming perennial. **H** 40–60cm (16–24in), **S** 60cm (24in). Saucer-shaped, scarlet flowers are produced from early to late summer. Pinnate leaves are deeply lobed and toothed.
G. coccineum, syn. *G.* x *borisii* of gardens, illus. p.439.
G. coccineum of gardens. See *G. chiloense*.
♀ ***G.* 'Fire Opal'.** Clump-forming perennial. **H** 80cm (32in), **S** 45cm (18in). Rounded, double, bronze-scarlet flowers are borne in small clusters in summer above oblong to lance-shaped, lobed, fresh green leaves.
***G.* 'Goldball'.** See *G.* 'Lady Stratheden'.
♀ ***G.* 'Lady Stratheden'**, syn. *G.* 'Goldball', illus. p.276.
***G.* 'Lionel Cox'.** Clump-forming perennial. **H** and **S** 30cm (12in). In early summer, produces small clusters of 5-petalled, cup-shaped, shrimp-red flowers above oblong to lance-shaped, lobed, fresh green leaves.
♀ ***G. montanum*** (Alpine avens). Dense, clump-forming, rhizomatous perennial that spreads slowly. **H** 10cm (4in), **S** 23cm (9in). Shallowly cup-shaped, golden-yellow flowers in early summer are followed by fluffy, buff-coloured seed heads. Leaves are pinnate, each with a large, rounded, terminal lobe. Suitable for a rock garden.
♀ ***G.* 'Mrs J. Bradshaw'**. Clump-forming perennial. **H** 80cm (32in), **S** 45cm (18in). Rounded, double, crimson flowers are borne in small sprays in summer. Fresh green leaves are oblong to lance-shaped and lobed.

GEVUINA

PROTEACEAE

Genus of evergreen trees, grown for their foliage and flowers in summer. Frost hardy. Requires semi-shade and fertile, moist but well-drained soil. Propagate by semi-ripe cuttings during late summer or by seed in autumn.
G. avellana (Chilean hazel). Evergreen, conical tree. **H** and **S** 10m (30ft). Has large, glossy, dark green leaves divided into numerous oval, toothed leaflets. Slender spires of spidery, white flowers in late summer are followed by cherry-like, red, then black fruits.

GIBBAEUM

AIZOACEAE

Genus of clump-forming, perennial succulents with pairs of small, swollen leaves, often of unequal size. Frost tender, min. 5°C (41°F). Needs full sun and very well-drained soil. Water very lightly in early winter. Propagate by seed or stem cuttings in spring or summer.
***G. petrense*.** Carpeting, perennial succulent. **H** 3cm (1½in), **S** 30cm (12in) or more. Each branch carries 1 or 2 pairs of thick, triangular, pale grey-green leaves, 1cm (½in) long. Bears daisy-like, pink-red flowers, 1.5cm (⅝in) across, in spring.
G. velutinum illus. p.481.

GILIA

POLEMONIACEAE

Genus of summer- and autumn-flowering annuals. Fully hardy. Grows best in sun and in fertile, very well-drained soil. Stems may need support, especially on windy sites. Propagate by seed sown outdoors in spring, or in early autumn for early flowering the following year.
***G. achilleifolia*.** Fast-growing, upright, bushy annual. **H** 60cm (24in), **S** 20cm (8in). Finely divided, mid-green leaves are hairy and sticky. Heads of funnel-shaped, blue flowers, 2.5cm (1in) wide, are produced in summer.
G. capitata illus. p.314.

GILLENIA

ROSACEAE

Genus of summer-flowering perennials. Fully hardy. Grow in sun or shade and any well-drained soil. Needs staking. Propagate by seed in autumn or spring.
♀ ***G. trifoliata*** illus. p.231.

GINKGO

GINKGOACEAE

See also CONIFERS.
♀ ***G. biloba*** illus. p.97.

GLADIOLUS

IRIDACEAE

Genus of corms, each producing a spike of funnel-shaped flowers and a fan of erect, sword-shaped leaves on basal part of flower stem. Is suitable for cutting or for planting in mixed borders; most hybrids are also good for exhibition. Frost to half hardy. Needs a sunny and fertile, well-drained site. Plant 10–15cm (4–6in) deep and the same distance apart in spring. Water well in summer and support tall cultivars with canes. Lift half-hardy types in autumn, cut off stems and dry corms in a frost-free but cool place. Pot up spring-flowering species and cultivars in autumn and place in a cool greenhouse; after flowering, dry off corms during summer months and repot in autumn.

Propagate by seed or by removal of young cormlets from parent. Seed sown in early spring in a cool greenhouse will take 2–3 years to flower and may not breed true to type. Cormlets, removed after lifting, should be stored in frost-free conditions and then be planted out 5cm (2in) deep in spring; lift in winter as for mature corms. They will flower in 1–2 years.

While in store, corms may be attacked by various rots. Protect sound, healthy corms by dusting with a fungicide or soaking in a fungicide solution before drying; store in an airy, cool, frost-free place. Gladiolus scab causes blotches on leaves; gladiolus yellows shows as yellowing stripes on leaves, which then die; in both cases destroy affected corms. As a preventative measure, always plant healthy corms in a new site each year. See also feature panel p.384.

Gladiolus hybrids

Most hybrids are derived from *G.* x *hortulanus*. All have stiff leaves, 20–50cm (8–20in) long, ranging from pale willow-green or steely blue-green to almost bottle-green. Half hardy. All are good for flower arranging. They are divided into Grandiflorus, Primulinus, and Nanus Groups.
Grandiflorus Group produces long, densely packed spikes of funnel-shaped flowers, with ruffled, thick-textured petals or plain-edged, thin-textured ones. Giant-flowered hybrids have a bottom flower of over 14cm (5½in) across (flower head is 65–80cm (26–32in) long); large-flowered 11–14cm (4½–5½in) across (flower head 60cm–1m (24–36in) long); medium-flowered 9–11cm (3½–4½in) across (flower head 60–80cm (24–32in) long); small-flowered 6–9cm (2½–3½in) across (flower head 50–70cm (20–28in) long); and miniature-flowered 3.5–6cm (1½–2½in) across (flower head 40–60cm (16–24in) long).
Primulinus Group has fairly loose spikes of plain-edged, funnel-shaped flowers, 6–8cm (2½–3in) across, each with a strongly hooded, upper petal over the stigma and anthers. Flower heads are 30cm (12in) long.
Nanus Group produces 2 or 3 slender spikes, with loosely arranged flowers, 4–5cm (1½–2in) across. Flower heads are 22–35cm (9–14in) long.

***G.* 'Amanda Mahy'.** Nanus Group gladiolus. **H** 80cm (32in), **S** 8–10cm (3–4in). Produces spikes of up to 7 salmon-pink flowers, with lip tepals flecked violet and white, in early summer.
***G.* 'Amsterdam'.** Grandiflorus Group, giant-flowered gladiolus. **H** 1.7m (5½ft), **S** 30cm (1ft). Spikes of up to 27 slightly upward-facing, finely ruffled, white flowers are produced in late summer. Is good for exhibition.
***G.* 'Amy Beth'.** Grandiflorus Group, small-flowered gladiolus. **H** 1.2m (4ft), **S** 20–25cm (8–10in). Produces spikes of up to 22 heavily ruffled, lavender flowers, with thick, waxy, cream-lipped petals, in late summer.
***G.* 'Anna Leorah'.** Grandiflorus Group, large-flowered gladiolus. **H** 1.6m (5½ft), **S** 15cm (6in). In mid-summer bears spikes of up to 25 strongly ruffled, mid-pink flowers with large, white throats. Is good for exhibition.
***G.* 'Atlantis'.** Grandiflorus Group, medium-flowered gladiolus. **H** 1.5m (5ft), **S** 20–25cm (8–10in). Produces spikes of up to 20 lightly ruffled, deep violet-blue flowers with small, white throats, in late summer.
***G.* 'Beau Rivage'.** Grandiflorus Group, large-flowered gladiolus. **H** to 1.2m (4ft), **S** 30cm (1ft). Spikes of up to 15 ruffled, deep coral-pink flowers are produced in summer. Is good for exhibition.
***G.* 'Beauty of Holland'.** Grandiflorus Group, large-flowered gladiolus. **H** 1.7m (⁵⁄₂ft), **S** 15cm (6in). Produces spikes of up to 27 ruffled, pink-margined, white flowers in mid-summer. Is good for exhibition.
***G.* 'Black Jack'.** Grandiflorus Group, medium-flowered gladiolus. **H** 90cm (36in), **S** 8cm (3in). Bears spikes of black-edged, dark maroon flowers in summer.
***G.* 'Black Lash'.** Grandiflorus Group, small-flowered gladiolus. **H** 1.35m (4½ft), **S** 15–20cm (6–8in). Bears spikes of up to 25 lightly ruffled, deep black-rose flowers, with pointed, slightly reflexed petals, from late summer to early autumn.
***G. blandus*.** See *G. carneus*.
***G.* 'Blue Frost'** (illus. p.384). Grandiflorus Group, large-flowered gladiolus. **H** 120cm (48in), **S** 15cm (6in). In mid-summer produces spikes of white flowers with ruffled, lilac edges and darker purple eyes.
***G.* Butterfly Group.** Small-flowered gladiolus. **H** 80cm (32in), **S** 8cm (3in). From mid- to late summer produces spikes of wavy, ruffled, bicoloured flowers with petals that resemble the wings of a

G

butterfly. They are produced in a range of colours, including red, orange, pink and yellow, and have contrasting colours at the throat.
G. byzantinus. See *G. communis* subsp. *byzantinus*.
G. callianthus. See *G. murielae*.
G. cardinalis. Summer-flowering corm. **H** to 1.2m (4ft), **S** 10–15cm (4–6in). Half hardy. Arching stem bears a spike of up to 12 widely funnel-shaped flowers, each 8cm (3in) long and bright red with spear-shaped, white marks on lower 3 petals.
G. carneus, syn. *G. blandus*. Spring-flowering corm. **H** 20–40cm (8–16in), **S** 8–10cm (3–4in). Half hardy. Stem bears a loose spike of 3–12 widely funnel-shaped, white or pink flowers, 4–6cm (1½–2½in) long, marked on lower petals with darker red or yellow blotches.
***G.* 'Charmer'.** Grandiflorus Group, large-flowered gladiolus. **H** 1.7m (5½ft), **S** 15cm (6in). In early and mid-summer, produces spikes of up to 27 strongly ruffled, almost translucent, light pink flowers. Is good for exhibition.
***G.* 'Charming Lady'.** Nanus Group gladiolus. **H** 70cm (28in), **S** 8cm (3in). Produces spikes of pink flowers, with pale lilac throats, from early to mid-summer.
***G.* 'Christabel'.** Spring-flowering corm (a hybrid of G. tristis). **H** to 45cm (18in), **S** 8–10cm (3–4in). Half hardy. Loose spikes of up to 10 fragrant, widely funnel-shaped, primrose-yellow flowers, 6–8cm (2½–3in) across, with purple-brown-veined, upper petals, are produced in spring.
***G.* 'Columbine'** (illus. p.384). Grandiflorus Group, small-flowered gladiolus. **H** 90cm (36in), **S** 8cm (3in). In early summer produces spikes of light carmine-rose flowers with creamy-white throats.
♀ ***G. x colvillii* 'The Bride'** (illus. p.384).
♀ ***G. communis* subsp. *byzantinus***, syn. *G. byzantinus*, illus. p.410.
***G.* 'Côte d' Azur'.** Grandiflorus Group, giant-flowered gladiolus. **H** 1.7m (5½ft), **S** 15cm (6in). Bears spikes of up to 23 ruffled, mid-blue flowers, with pale blue throats, in early summer. Is good for exhibition.
G. dalenii, syn. *G. natalensis*, *G. primulinus*, *G. psittacinus*. Vigorous, summer-flowering corm. **H** to 1.5m (5ft), **S** 10–15cm (4–6in). Half hardy. Produces up to 14 red, yellow-orange, yellow or greenish-yellow flowers, 8–12cm (3–5in) long, each with a hooded, upper petal and often flecked or streaked red.
***G.* 'Dancing Queen'.** Grandiflorus Group, large-flowered gladiolus. **H** 1.5m (5ft), **S** 12–15cm (5–6in). In mid- to late summer, produces spikes of up to 20 white flowers, with feathered, dark red markings at the base of the lower petals.
***G.* 'Deliverance'.** Grandiflorus Group, large-flowered gladiolus. **H**.1.7m (5½ft), **S** 12–15cm (5–6in). In mid- to late summer, produces spikes of 20 or more ruffled, coral-pink flowers, deeper peach-pink at the margins, with yellow-tinted, white throats.
***G.* 'Drama'** (illus. p.384). Grandiflorus Group, large-flowered gladiolus. **H** 1.7m (5½ft), **S** 25–30cm (10–12in). In late summer, produces spikes of up to 26 lightly ruffled, deep watermelon-pink flowers with red-marked, yellow throats. Is superb for exhibition.
***G.* 'Dutch Mountain'.** Grandiflorus Group, large-flowered gladiolus. **H** 1.7m (5½ft), **S** 15cm (6in). In mid-summer, produces spikes of up to 25 slightly ruffled, white flowers with small green marks in the throats. Is good for exhibition.
***G.* 'Esta Bonita'.** Grandiflorus Group, giant-flowered gladiolus. **H** 1.7m (5½ft), **S** 30cm (1ft). Produces spikes of up to 24 apricot-orange flowers, slightly darker towards petal edges, in late summer. Is good for exhibition.
***G.* 'Firestorm'.** Grandiflorus Group, miniature-flowered gladiolus. **H** 1.1m (3½ft), **S** 8–10cm (3–4in). Spikes of up to 22 loosely spaced, ruffled, vivid scarlet flowers, with yellowish-white flecks on the outer tepals, are produced in early summer. Is good for exhibition.
***G.* 'Flevo Bambino'.** Grandiflorus Group, medium-flowered gladiolus. **H** 60cm (2ft), **S** 8cm (3in). From late summer to early autumn produces spikes of pale yellow flowers with purple throats.
***G.* 'Florence C'.** Grandiflorus Group, large-flowered gladiolus. **H** 1.7m (5½ft), **S** 15cm (6in). In late summer produces spikes of up to 26 strongly ruffled, white flowers.
***G.* 'Georgette'.** Grandiflorus Group, small-flowered gladiolus. **H** 1.2m (4ft), **S** 8–10cm (3–4in). Produces spikes of up to 22 slightly ruffled, yellow-suffused, orange flowers, with large lemon-yellow throats, in mid-summer. Is good for exhibition.
***G.* 'Green Isle'.** Grandiflorus Group, medium-flowered gladiolus. **H** 1.35m (4½ft), **S** 20–25cm (8–10in). Spikes carrying up to 22 slightly informal flowers, lime-green throughout with chiselled ruffling, are produced in late summer.
***G.* 'Green Woodpecker'** (illus. p.384). Grandiflorus Group, medium-flowered gladiolus. **H** 1.5m (5ft), **S** 30cm (1ft). Has spikes of up to 25 lime-green flowers, with wine-red throats, in late summer. Is very good for exhibition.
***G.* 'Halley'.** Nanus Group gladiolus. **H** 1m (3ft), **S** 8–10cm (3–4in). In early summer produces spikes carrying up to 7 white-flushed, pale yellow flowers, each with bright red marks in the throats.
***G.* 'Her Majesty'** (illus. p.384). Grandiflorus Group, large-flowered gladiolus. **H** 115cm (46in), **S** 5cm (6in). Produces spikes of sky-blue flowers, with much paler throats, in mid-summer.
***G.* 'Ice Cap'.** Grandiflorus Group, large-flowered gladiolus. **H** 1.7m (5½ft), **S** 25–30cm (10–12in). Produces spikes of up to 27 heavily ruffled, ice-white flowers from late summer to early autumn.
***G.* 'Impressive'** (illus. p.384). Nanus Group gladiolus. **H** 70cm (28in), **S** 8cm (3in). Spikes of pale pink flowers, with hot pink markings, are borne in early summer.
***G.* 'Inca Queen'.** Grandiflorus Group, large-flowered gladiolus. **H** 1.5m (5ft), **S** 20–25cm (8–10in). Bears spikes of up to 25 heavily ruffled, waxy, deep salmon-pink flowers, with lemon-yellow lip petals and throats, in late summer.
G. italicus, syn. *G. segetum*. Early summer-flowering corm. **H** to 1m (3ft), S 10–15cm (4–6in). Frost hardy. Carries a loose spike of up to 20 pinkish-purple flowers, 4–5cm (1½–2in) long, and has a fan of erect, sword-shaped leaves from the basal part of stem.
***G.* 'Little Darling'.** Primulinus Group gladiolus. **H** 1.1m (3½ft), **S** 8–10cm (3–4in). Bears spikes of up to 16 loosely spaced, salmon- to rose-pink flowers, with lemon lip tepals, in mid-summer. Is good for exhibition.
***G.* 'Magistral'.** Grandiflorus Group, large-flowered gladiolus. **H** 1.8m (6ft), **S** 15cm (6in). Produces spikes of up to 24 ruffled, oyster-white flowers, with magenta lines, in mid-summer. Is good for exhibition.
***G.* 'Melodie'.** Grandiflorus Group, small-flowered gladiolus. **H** 1.2m (4ft), **S** 15–20cm (6–8in). Produces spikes of up to 17 salmon-rose flowers, with longitudinal, spear-like, red-orange marks in throats, in late summer.
***G.* 'Mi Mi'.** Grandiflorus Group, small-flowered gladiolus. **H** 1.3m (4½ft), **S** 8–10cm (3–4in). In mid-summer bears spikes of up to 24 strongly ruffled, deep lavender-pink flowers with white throats. Is good for exhibition.
***G.* 'Miss America'.** Grandiflorus Group, medium-flowered gladiolus. **H** 1.5m (5ft), **S** 30cm (1ft). In late summer, produces spikes of up to 24 deep pink flowers that are heavily ruffled. Is excellent for exhibition.
***G.* 'Morning Gold'** (illus. p.384). Grandiflorus Group, large-flowered gladiolus. **H** 100cm (39in), **S** 10cm (4in). Spikes of green-tinted, golden-yellow flowers are produced from mid-summer to early autumn.
♀ ***G. murielae***, syn. *Acidanthera bicolor* var. *murielae*, *A. murieliae*, *G. callianthus*. (illus. p.383). Late summer-flowering corm. **H** to 1m (3ft), **S** 10–15cm (4–6in). Half hardy. Has a loose spike of up to 10 fragrant flowers, each with a curved, 10cm (4in) long tube and 6 white petals, each with a deep purple blotch at the base.
G. natalensis. See *G. dalenii*.
***G.* 'Nova Lux'** (illus. p.384). Grandiflorus Group, giant-flowered gladiolus. **H** 100cm (39in), **S** 15cm (6in). Spikes of clear yellow flowers are borne in mid-summer.
***G.* 'Nymph'** (illus. p.384). Nanus Group gladiolus. **H** 70cm (28in), **S** 8cm (3in). In early summer produces spikes of creamy-white flowers, with teardrop-shaped, pink-edged markings on the lower petals.
***G.* 'Oscar'** (illus. p.384). Grandiflorus Group, large-flowered gladiolus. **H** 100cm (39in), **S** 15cm (6in). Produces spikes of velvety-red flowers in mid-summer.
G. papilio, syn. *G. purpureoauratus*, illus. p.395.
***G.* 'Parade'.** Grandiflorus Group, giant-flowered gladiolus. **H** 1.7m (5½ft), **S** 25–35cm (10–14in). Produces spikes of up to 27 finely ruffled, salmon-pink flowers, with small, cream throats, in early autumn. Is superb for exhibition.
***G.* 'Passos'.** Grandiflorous Group, large-flowered gladiolus. **H** 120cm (48in), **S** 15cm (6in). Spikes of purple-flecked, pale lilac to white flowers, with dark purple throats, are produced in mid-summer.
***G.* 'Peace'.** Grandiflorus Group, giant-flowered gladiolus. **H** 1.7m (5½ft), **S** 15cm (6in). Bears spikes of up to 26 strongly ruffled, cream flowers, with pale lemon throats and pale pink margins, in mid-summer. Is good for exhibition.
***G.* 'Peter Pears'** (illus. p.384). Grandiflorus Group, large-flowered gladiolus. **H** 1.7m (5½ft), **S** 35cm (14in). In late summer, has spikes of up to 26 apricot-salmon flowers with red throat marks. Is excellent for exhibition.
***G.* 'Pink Flare'.** Grandiflorus Group, small-flowered gladiolus. **H** 1.3m (4½ft), **S** 8–10cm (3–4in). Spikes of up to 25 ruffled, mid-pink flowers, each with a small, white throat, are produced in mid-summer. Is good for exhibition.
***G.* 'Pink Lady'.** Grandiflorus Group, large-flowered gladiolus. **H** 1.5m (5ft), **S** 25–30cm (10–12in). Has spikes of up to 25 lightly ruffled, deep rose-pink flowers, with large, white throats, in late summer and early autumn.
G. primulinus. See *G. dalenii*.
G. psittacinus. See *G. dalenii*.
***G.* 'Pulchritude'.** Grandiflorus Group, medium-flowered gladiolus. **H** 1.3m (4½ft), **S** 12cm (5in). Produces spikes of up to 27 ruffled, light lavender-pink flowers, deepening at the tepal margins, and with a magenta-red mark on each lip tepal, in mid-summer. Is good for exhibition.
***G.* 'Purple Flora'** (illus. p.384). Grandiflorus Group, large-flowered gladiolus. **H** 100cm (39in), **S** 15cm (6in). Produces spikes of rich deep purple flowers, with paler lilac markings, in mid-summer.
G. purpureoauratus. See *G. papilio*.
***G.* 'Renegade'.** Grandiflorus Group, large-flowered gladiolus. **H** 1.5m (5ft), **S** 12–15cm (5–6in). In mid- to late summer produces spikes of 15–20 ruffled, deep red flowers.
***G.* 'Rose Supreme'.** Grandiflorus Group, giant-flowered gladiolus. **H** 1.7m (5½ft), **S** 25–30cm (10–12in). Spikes of up to 24 rose-pink flowers, flecked and streaked darker pink towards petal tips, and with cream throats, are produced in late summer.
***G.* 'Royal Dutch'.** Grandiflorus Group, large-flowered gladiolus. **H** 1.7m (5½ft), **S** 25–30cm (10–12in). Produces spikes of up to 27 flowers, each pale lavender blending into a white throat, from late summer to early autumn. Is very good for exhibition.
***G.* Sancerre** (illus. p.384). Grandiflorus Group, large-flowered gladiolus. **H** 120cm (48in), **S** 15cm (6in). Spikes of pure white flowers are borne in mid-summer.
G. segetum. See *G. italicus*.
***G.* 'Stardust'.** Grandiflorus Group, miniature-flowered gladiolus. **H** 1.2m (4ft), **S** 8–10cm (3–4in). Has spikes of up to 21 ruffled, pale yellow flowers, with lighter yellow throats, in mid-summer. Is good for exhibition.
***G.* 'Stella'** (illus. p.384). Grandiflorus Group, medium-flowered gladiolus. **H** 60cm (24in), **S** 8cm (3in). Spikes of yellow flowers, with a star-shaped, dark red mark at the throat, are produced in mid-summer.
***G.* 'Tendresse'.** Grandiflorus Group, medium-flowered gladiolus. **H** 1.5m (5ft), **S** 20–25cm (8–10in). In late summer, has spikes of up to 28 slightly ruffled, dark pink flowers, with small, cream throats marked with longitudinal, faint rose-pink "spears".
***G.* 'Tesoro'.** Grandiflorus Group,

medium-flowered gladiolus. **H** 1.5m (5ft), **S** 20–25 cm (8–10in). Bears spikes of up to 26 silky flowers, slightly ruffled and glistening yellow, in early autumn. Is among the top exhibition gladioli.
♀ ***G.* 'The Bride'.** Nanus Group gladiolus. **H** 80cm (32in), **S** 8–10cm (3–4in). Produces spikes of up to 7 white flowers, with green-marked throats, in early summer.
***G.* 'Trader Horn'** Grandiflorus Group, large-flowered gladiolus. **H** 120cm (48in), **S** 15cm (6in). Tall spikes of scarlet flowers, with a white mark on the throat, are produced in mid-summer.
***G.* 'Vaucluse'.** Grandiflorus Group, giant-flowered gladiolus. **H** 1.9m (6ft), **S** 15cm (6in). In late summer, bears spikes of up to 27 slightly ruffled, vermilion-red flowers with small, creamy-white throats. Is good for exhibition.
***G.* 'Velvet Eyes'** (illus. p.384). Grandiflorus Group, large-flowered gladiolus. **H** 120cm (48in), **S** 15cm (6in). Produces spikes of dark bluish-purple flowers, with reddish-purple throats, in mid-summer.
***G.* 'Victor Borge'.** Grandiflorus Group, large-flowered gladiolus. **H** 1.7m (5½ft), **S** 35cm (14in). Spikes of up to 22 vermilion-orange flowers, with pale cream throat marks, are produced in late summer.
***G.* 'White Ice'** (illus. p.384). Grandiflorus Group, medium-flowered gladiolus. **H** 1.5m (5ft), **S** 12cm (5in). Produces spikes of up to 25 ruffled, white flowers in late summer. Is good for exhibition.
***G.* 'White Prosperity'** (illus. p.384). Grandiflorus Group, large-flowered gladiolus. **H** 120cm (48in), **S** 15cm (6in). Spikes of pure white flowers, with ruffled petals, are borne in mid-summer.
***G.* 'Wine and Roses'** (illus. p.384). Grandiflorus Group, large-flowered gladiolus. **H** 120cm (48in), **S** 15cm (6in). Spikes of soft pink flowers, with burgundy-red throats, are produced in mid-summer.
***G.* 'Zephyr'.** Grandiflorus Group, large-flowered gladiolus. **H** 1.7m (5½ft), **S** 5cm (6in). In mid-summer, has spikes of up to 26 light lavender-pink flowers with small, ivory throats. Is good for exhibition.

Glandulicactus uncinatus. See *Sclerocactus uncinatus.*

GLANDULARIA

VERBENACEAE

Genus of summer- and autumn-flowering evergreen perennials, often treated as annuals. Frost hardy to frost tender, min. 1°C (23°F). Grow in sun and well-drained soil. Propagate by stem cuttings in late summer and autumn or by layering or seed sown in autumn or spring.
***G.* 'Balazdapima'.** See *G.* x *hybrida* Aztec Dark Pink Magic.
***G.* 'Balazsilma'.** See *G.* x *hybrida* Aztec Silver Magic.
***G.* x *hybrida*,** syn. *V.* x *hortensis*, *V.* x *hybrida*. **Aztec Dark Pink Magic** (**'Balazdapima'**) illus. p.303. ♀ **Aztec Silver Magic** (**'Balazsilma'**) illus. p.312. ♀ **Corsage Series 'Corsage Red',** illus. p.307. **Derby Series** are erect, bushy perennials, grown as annuals. **H** 25cm (10in), **S** 30cm (12in). Half hardy. Have oval, serrated, mid- to deep green leaves. Clusters of small, tubular, lobed flowers, in a wide colour range, including red, pink, blue, mauve and white, appear in summer and early autumn. Cultivars of **Novalis Series** are erect and bushy, with flowers in rose-pink, deep blue, pinkish-red and scarlet, as well as single colours of bright scarlet, white or rose-pink. **'Peaches and Cream'** is spreading and branching, and produces pastel orange-pink flowers, maturing to apricot-yellow, and eventually creamy-yellow. Cultivars of **'Quartz Mix'** are compact and bushy with lance-shaped, leaves, and rounded heads of pink, red, maroon or purple flowers with white "eyes". **Romance Series** cultivars are erect and bushy, and have flowers in deep wine-red, intense scarlet, carmine-rose-red and blue-purple, as well as single colours of white, bright scarlet, dark rose or lavender-pink. '
***G.* x *maonettii*,** syn. *Verbena alpina* of gardens, *V. tenera* var. *maonetti*. Spreading perennial with a slightly woody base. **H** 8cm (3in), **S** 15cm (6in). Half hardy. Has oblong to oval leaves, deeply cut into linear, toothed, mid-green segments, and, in summer, terminal clusters of small, tubular, reddish-violet flowers, with white-edged lobes.
***G. peruviana*,** syn. *Verbena chamaedrifolia*, *V. chamaedrioides*. Semi-evergreen, prostrate perennial. **H** to 8cm (3in), **S** 1m (3ft). Frost tender. Heads of small, tubular, brilliant scarlet flowers, with spreading petal lobes, are produced from early summer to early autumn. Oval, toothed leaves are mid-green. Prefers to grow in dry soil that is not too rich.
♀ ***G.* 'Sissinghurst',** syn. *Verbena* 'Sissinghurst', illus. p.268.

GLAUCIDIUM

GLAUCIDIACEAE/RANUNCULACEAE

Genus of one species of spring-flowering perennial. Is excellent in woodland gardens. Fully hardy. Needs a partially shaded, sheltered position and moist, peaty soil. Propagate by seed in autumn.
♀ ***G. palmatum*** illus. p.260.

GLAUCIUM

Horned poppy

PAPAVERACEAE

Genus of annuals, biennials and perennials, grown for their bright, poppy-like flowers. Fully hardy. Grow in sun and in fertile, well-drained soil. Propagate annuals by seed sown outdoors in spring; perennials by seed sown outdoors in spring or autumn; biennials by seed sown under glass in late spring or early summer. ⓘRoots are toxic if ingested.
G. flavum illus. p.320.

GLECHOMA

LABIATAE/LAMIACEAE

Genus of evergreen, summer-flowering perennials. Makes good ground cover, but may be invasive. Fully hardy. Tolerates sun or shade. Prefers moist but well-drained soil. Propagate by division in spring or autumn or by softwood cuttings in spring.
G. hederacea (Ground ivy). **'Variegata'** illus. p.277.

GLEDITSIA

LEGUMINOSAE/CAESALPINIACEAE

Genus of deciduous, usually spiny trees, grown for their foliage. Has inconspicuous flowers, often followed by large seed pods after hot summers. Fully hardy, but young plants may suffer frost damage. Requires plenty of sun and fertile, well-drained soil. Propagate species by seed in autumn, selected forms by budding in late summer.
G. caspica (Caspian locust). Deciduous, spreading tree. **H** 12m (40ft), **S** 10m (30ft). Trunk is armed with long, branched spines. Has fern-like, glossy, mid-green leaves.
G. japonica illus. p.75.
G. triacanthos (Honey locust). Deciduous, spreading tree. **H** 20m (70ft), **S** 15m (50ft). Trunk is very thorny. Fern-like, glossy, dark green leaves turn yellow in autumn. **f. *inermis*** is thornless. **'Shademaster'** is vigorous, with long-lasting leaves. **'Skyline'** is thornless, broadly conical and has golden-yellow foliage in autumn.
♀ **'Sunburst'** illus. p.72.

GLOBBA

ZINGIBERACEAE

Genus of evergreen or herbaceous, clump-forming perennials, grown for their flowers. Frost tender, min. 7–18°C (45–64°F). Needs partial shade, high humidity and humus-rich, well-drained soil. Keep plants dry when dormant in winter. Propagate by division or seed in spring or by mature bulbils that fall off plants. See also feature panel p.477.
***G. platystachya*.** Herbaceous, clump-forming perennial. H and **S** 1m (3ft). Frost tender, min. 7°C (45°F). Has lance-shaped, silver-patterned, mid-green leaves, to 30cm (12in) long. Pendent racemes of small, tubular, golden-yellow flowers are borne at the shoot tips along with bulbils in late summer.
G. winitii (illus. p.477). Evergreen, clump-forming perennial. **H** 1m (3ft), **S** 30cm (1ft). Frost tender, min. 18°C (64°F). Has lance-shaped leaves to 20cm (8in) long. Intermittently has pendent racemes of tubular, yellow flowers with large, reddish-purple, reflexed bracts.

GLOBULARIA

GLOBULARIACEAE

Genus of mainly evergreen, summer-flowering shrubs and sub-shrubs, grown for their dome-shaped hummocks and usually blue or purple flower heads. Fully to frost hardy. Needs full sun and well-drained soil. Propagate by division in spring, by softwood or semi-ripe cuttings in summer or by seed in autumn.
***G. bellidifolia*.** See *G. meridionalis*.
♀ ***G. cordifolia*** illus. p.369. **subsp. *bellidifolia*** see *G. meridionalis*.
***G. meridionalis*,** syn. *G. bellidifolia*, *G. cordifolia* subsp. *bellidifolia*, *G. pygmaea*, illus. p.367.
***G. pygmaea*.** See *G. meridionalis*.

GLORIOSA

LILIACEAE/COLCHICACEAE

Genus of deciduous, summer-flowering, tendril climbers with finger-like tubers. Frost tender, min. 8–10°C (46–50°F). Needs full sun and rich, well-drained soil. Water freely in summer and liquid feed every 2 weeks. Provide support. Dry off tubers in winter and keep cool but frost free. Propagate by seed or division in spring. ⓘHighly toxic if ingested; handling tubers may irritate the skin.
***G. rothschildiana*.** See *G. superba* 'Rothschildiana'.
♀ ***G. superba*** (Glory lily). Deciduous, tendril climber with tubers. **H** to 2m (6ft), **S** 30–45cm (1–1½ft). Min. 8°C (46°F). Slender stems bear scattered, broadly lance-shaped leaves. In summer, upper leaf axils carry large, yellow or red flowers, with 6 sharply reflexed, wavy-edged petals, changing to dark orange or deep red. Stamens are prominent. **'Rothschildiana'** (syn. *G. rothschildiana*) illus. p.386.

GLOTTIPHYLLUM

AIZOACEAE

Genus of clump-forming, perennial succulents with semi-cylindrical leaves often broader at tips. Frost tender, min. 5°C (41°F). Grow in full sun and poor, well-drained soil. Propagate by seed or stem cuttings in spring or summer.
***G. difforme*,** syn. *G. semicylindricum*. Clump-forming, perennial succulent. **H** 8cm (3in), **S** 30cm (12in) or more. Has semi-cylindrical, bright green leaves, 6cm (2½in) long, with a tooth half-way along each margin. Short-stemmed, daisy-like, golden-yellow flowers, 4cm (1½in) across, appear in spring–summer.
G. nelii illus. p.495.
***G. semicylindricum*.** See *G. difforme*.

GLOXINIA

GESNERIACEAE

Genus of late summer- to autumn-flowering, rhizomatous perennials. Frost tender, min. 10°C (50°F). Needs partial shade and humus-rich, well-drained soil. Dies down in late autumn or winter; then keep rhizomes nearly dry. Propagate by division or seed in spring or by stem or leaf cuttings in summer.
***G. perennis*.** Late summer- to autumn-flowering rhizome. **H** to 60cm (24in), **S** 30–35cm (12–14in). Has heart-shaped, toothed, hairy leaves on spotted stems and bell-shaped, lavender-blue flowers, with rounded lobes and purple-blotched throats.
***G. speciosa*.** See *Sinningia speciosa*.

GLYCERIA

GRAMINEAE/POACEAE

See also GRASSES, BAMBOOS, RUSHES and SEDGES.
***G. aquatica* 'Variegata'.** See *G.maxima* 'Variegata'.
***G. maxima* 'Variegata',** syn. *G. aquatica* 'Variegata', illus. p.436.

GLYCYRRHIZA

Liquorice

LEGUMINOSAE/PAPILIONACEAE

Genus of summer-flowering perennials. Fully hardy. Needs sun and deep, rich, well-drained soil. Propagate by division in spring or seed in autumn or spring.
G. glabra. Upright perennial. **H** 1.2m (4ft), **S** 1m (3ft). Has pea-like, purple-blue and white flowers, borne in short spikes on erect stems in late summer, and large leaves divided into oval leaflets. Is grown commercially for production of liquorice.

Godetia. See *Clarkia.*

GOMESA

ORCHIDACEAE

See also ORCHIDS.
G. flexuosum, syn. *Oncidium flexuosum* (Dancing-doll orchid; illus. p.467). Evergreen, epiphytic orchid for a cool or intermediate greenhouse. **H** 23cm (9in). In autumn produces terminal sprays of many small, large-lipped, bright yellow flowers, 0.5cm (¼in) across, with red-brown markings on the sepals and petals. Bears narrowly oval leaves, 10cm (4in) long. Is best grown on a bark slab. Keep in semi-shade in summer. See also feature panel p.467.
G. planifolia. Evergreen, epiphytic orchid for a cool greenhouse. **H** 23cm (9in). Sprays of star-shaped, pea-green flowers, 0.5cm (¼in) across, are produced in autumn. Narrowly oval leaves are 15cm (6in) long. Grow in semi-shade during summer.

GOMPHOCARPUS

ASCLEPIADACEAE/APOCYNACEAE

Genus of evergreen and deciduous sub-shrubs and perennials. Hooded, cup-shaped flowers are followed by seed pods that are usually inflated. Half hardy to frost tender, min. 5°C (41°F). Grows in sun or partial shade and in any well-drained soil. Propagate by seed or softwood cuttings in spring. ⓘ Some species exude a milky sap, which may aggravate skin allergies.
G. physocarpus, syn. *Asclepias physocarpa*. Deciduous, erect, hairy sub-shrub. **H** to 2m (6ft), **S** to 60cm (2ft). Half hardy. Has lance-shaped leaves, 10cm (4in) long, and umbels of 5-horned, creamy-white flowers in summer, followed by large, inflated, globose seed pods with soft bristles.

GOMPHRENA

AMARANTHACEAE

Genus of annuals, biennials and perennials. Only one species, *G. globosa*, is usually cultivated; its flower heads are good for cutting and drying. Half hardy. Grows best in sun and in fertile, well-drained soil. Propagate by seed sown under glass in spring.
G. globosa (Globe amaranth) illus. p.303.

GONGORA

ORCHIDACEAE

See also ORCHIDS.
G. quinquenervis Evergreen, epiphytic orchid for an intermediate greenhouse. **H** 25cm (10in). In summer, fragrant, brown, orange and yellow flowers, 1cm (½in) across, which resemble birds in flight, are produced in long, pendent spikes. Has oval, ribbed leaves, 12–15cm (5–6in) long. Is best grown in a hanging basket. Requires semi-shade in summer.

Gordonia. See *Polyspora.*

GRAPTOPETALUM

CRASSULACEAE

Genus of rosetted, perennial succulents very similar to *Echeveria*, with which it hybridizes. Frost tender, min. 5–10°C (41–50°F). Is easy to grow, needing sun or partial shade and very well-drained soil. Propagate by seed or by stem or leaf cuttings in spring or summer.
G. amethystinum. Clump-forming, prostrate, perennial succulent. **H** 40cm (16in), **S** 90cm (36in). Min. 10°C (50°F). Produces thick, rounded, blue-grey to red leaves, 7cm (3in) long, in terminal rosettes and star-shaped, yellow-and-red flowers, 1–2cm (½–¾in) across, in spring–summer.
♀ ***G. bellum***, syn. *Tacitus bellus,* illus. p.485.
G. paraguayense illus. p.489.

GRAPTOPHYLLUM

ACANTHACEAE

Genus of evergreen shrubs, grown mainly for their foliage. Frost tender, min. 16–18°C (61–4°F). Needs partial shade and fertile, well-drained soil. Water potted plants freely when in full growth, much less when temperatures are low. Young plants need tip pruning after flowering to promote branching; leggy specimens may be cut back hard after flowering or in spring. Propagate by greenwood or semi-ripe cuttings in spring or summer.
G. pictum (Caricature plant). Evergreen, erect, loose shrub. **H** to 2m (6ft), **S** 60cm (2ft) or more. Has oval, pointed, glossy, green leaves with central, yellow blotches. Bears short, terminal spikes of tubular, red to purple flowers in spring and early summer.

GRASSES, BAMBOOS, RUSHES AND SEDGES

Group of evergreen or herbaceous, perennial and annual grasses or grass-like plants belonging to the Gramineae (including Bambusoideae), Juncaceae and Cyperaceae families. They are grown mainly as foliage plants, adding grace and contrast to borders and rock gardens, although several grasses have attractive flower heads in summer that may be dried for winter decoration. Dead foliage may be cut back on herbaceous perennials when dormant. Propagate species by seed in spring or autumn or by division in spring; selected forms by division only. Pests and diseases usually give little trouble. Grasses, bamboos, rushes and sedges are illustrated on pp.284–289.

Grasses (Gramineae)
Family of evergreen, semi-evergreen or herbaceous, sometimes creeping perennials, annuals and marginal water plants, usually with rhizomes or stolons, that form tufts, clumps or carpets. All have basal leaves and rounded flower stems that bear alternate, long, narrow leaves. Flowers are bisexual (males and females in same spikelet) and are arranged in panicles, racemes or spikes. Each flower head comprises spikelets, with one or more florets, that are covered with glumes (scales) from which awns (long, slender bristles) may grow. Fully hardy to frost tender, min. 5–12°C (41–54°F). Unless otherwise stated, grasses will tolerate a range of light conditions and flourish in any well-drained soil. Many genera, such as *Briza*, self-seed readily.
See also *Alopecurus, Anemanthele, Arrhenatherum, Arundo, Bouteloua, Briza, Bromus, Chionochloa, Coix, Cortaderia, Dactylis, Deschampsia, Festuca, Glyceria, Hakonechloa, Helictotrichon, Holcus, Hordeum, Lagurus, Lamarckia, Leymus, Melica, Melinis, Milium, Miscanthus, Molinia, Oplismenus, Panicum, Pennisetum, Phalaris, Sesleria, Setaria, Spartina, Stenotaphrum, Stipa, Zea* and *Zizania.*

Bamboos (Bambusoideae)
Sub-family of Gramineae, comprising evergreen, rhizomatous perennials, sometimes grown as hedging as well as for ornamentation. Most bamboos differ from other perennial grasses in that they have woody stems (culms). These are hollow (except in *Chusquea*), mostly greenish-brown and, due to their silica content, very strong, with a circumference of up to 15cm (6in) in some tropical species. Leaves are lance-shaped with cross veins that give a tessellated appearance, which may be obscured in the more tender species. Flowers are produced at varying intervals but are not decorative. After flowering, stems die down but few plants die completely. Fully to half hardy. Bamboos thrive in a sheltered, not too dry situation in sun or shade, unless otherwise stated.
See also *Bambusa, Chusquea, Fargesia, Himalayacalamus, Phyllostachys, Pleioblastus, Pseudosasa, Sasa, Semiarundinaria, Shibataea* and *Yushania.*

Rushes (Juncaceae)
Family of evergreen, tuft-forming or creeping, mostly rhizomatous annuals and perennials. All have either rounded, leafless stems or stems bearing long, narrow, basal leaves that are flat and hairless except *Luzula* (woodrushes) which has flat leaves, edged with white hairs. Rounded flower heads are generally unimportant. Fully to half hardy. Most rushes prefer sun or partial shade and a moist or wet situation, but *Luzula* prefers drier conditions. See also *Isolepis, Juncus* and *Luzula.*

Sedges (Cyperaceae)
Family of evergreen, rhizomatous perennials that form dense tufts. Stems are triangular and bear long, narrow leaves, sometimes reduced to scales. Spikes or panicles of florets covered with glumes are produced and contain both male and female flowers, although some species of *Carex* have separate male and female flower heads on the same stem. Fully hardy to frost tender, min. 4–7°C (39–45°F). Grow in sun or partial shade. Some sedges grow naturally in water, but many may be grown in any well-drained soil.
See also *Carex, Cyperus, Eleocharis, Schoenoplectus* and *Scirpoides.*

GREVILLEA

PROTEACEAE

Genus of evergreen shrubs and trees, grown for their flowers and foliage. Frost hardy to frost tender, min. 5–10°C. Grow in full sun and well-drained, preferably acid soil. Water potted specimens moderately, very little in winter. Pruning is tolerated if necessary. Propagate by seed in spring or by semi-ripe cuttings in summer. ⓘ All parts may aggravate skin allergies.
G. alpestris. See *G. alpina.*
G. alpina, syn. *G. alpestris*. Evergreen, rounded, wiry-stemmed shrub. **H** and **S** 30–60cm (1–2ft). Half hardy. Has narrowly oblong or oval leaves, dark green above, silky-haired beneath. Bears tubular, red flowers in small clusters in spring–summer.
G. banksii illus. p.450.
♀ ***G. 'Canberra Gem'*** illus. p.201.
G. juniperina* f. *sulphurea, syn. *G. sulphurea*, illus. p.206.
G. 'Poorinda Constance'. Evergreen, bushy, rounded shrub. **H** and **S** to 2m (6ft). Half hardy. Has small, lance-shaped, mid- to deep green leaves with prickly toothed margins. Tubular, bright red flowers in conspicuous clusters are borne from spring to autumn, sometimes longer.
♀ ***G. robusta*** (Silky oak). Fast-growing, evergreen, upright to conical tree. **H** 30m (100ft), **S** to 15m (50ft). Frost tender, min. 5°C (41°F). Fern-like leaves are 15–25cm (6–10in) long. Mature specimens bear upturned bell-shaped, bright yellow or orange flowers in dense, one-sided spikes, 10cm (4in) or more long, in spring–summer.
G. 'Robyn Gordon'. Evergreen, sprawling shrub. **H** 1–1.5m (3–5ft), **S** 50–150cm (20–60in). Frost tender, min. 5–10°C (41–50°F). Has leathery, dark green leaves and arching stems that bear racemes of crimson flowers with protruding, recurved styles from early spring to late summer.
♀ ***G. rosmarinifolia.*** (illus. p.203). Evergreen, rounded, well-branched shrub. **H** and **S** to 2m (6ft). Half hardy. Dark green leaves are needle-shaped with reflexed margins, silky-haired beneath. Has short, dense clusters of tubular, red, occasionally pink or white flowers in summer.
G. sulphurea. See *G. juniperina* f. *sulphurea*.

GREYIA

GREYACEAE/MELIANTHACEAE

Genus of evergreen, semi-evergreen or deciduous, spring-flowering shrubs and trees, grown for their flowers and overall appearance. Frost tender, min. 7–10°C

G

(45–50°F). Needs full light and well-drained soil. Water containerized specimens moderately, less when not in full growth. Remove or shorten flowered stems after flowering. Propagate by seed in spring or by semi-ripe cuttings in summer. Plants grown under glass need plenty of ventilation.
G. sutherlandii illus. p.455.

GRINDELIA

COMPOSITAE/ASTERACEAE

Genus of annuals, biennials, evergreen perennials and sub-shrubs, grown for their flower heads. Frost to half hardy, but in cold areas grow in a warm, sheltered site. Requires sun and well-drained soil. Water potted specimens moderately, less when not in full growth. Remove spent flowering stems either as they die or in following spring. Propagate by seed in spring or by semi-ripe cuttings in late summer.
G. chiloensis, syn. G. *speciosa*, illus. p.161.
G. speciosa. See *G. chiloensis*.

GRISELINIA

CORNACEAE/GRISELINIACEAE

Genus of evergreen shrubs and trees, with inconspicuous flowers, grown for their foliage. Thrives in mild, coastal areas where it is effective as a hedge or windbreak as it is very wind- and salt-resistant. Frost to half hardy; in cold areas provide shelter. Requires sun and fertile, well-drained soil. Restrict growth and trim hedges in early summer. Propagate by semi-ripe cuttings in summer.
♀ ***G. littoralis*** (Broadleaf). Fast-growing, evergreen, upright shrub of dense habit. **H** 6m (20ft), **S** 5m (15ft). Frost hardy. Bears oval, leathery leaves that are bright apple-green. Tiny, inconspicuous, yellow-green flowers are borne in late spring. **'Dixon's Cream'**, **H** 3m (10ft), **S** 2m (6ft), is slower-growing and has central, creamy-white leaf variegation. ♀ **'Variegata'** illus. p.119.
G. lucida. Fast-growing, evergreen, upright shrub. **H** 6m (20ft), **S** 5m (15ft). Half hardy. Is similar to *G. littoralis*, but has larger, glossy, dark green leaves.

GUARIANTHE

ORCHIDACEAE

See also ORCHIDS.
G. bowringiana, syn. *Cattleya bowringiana*, (illus. p.466). Evergreen, epiphytic orchid for a cool greenhouse. **H** 45cm (18in). In autumn bears large heads of rose-purple-lipped, magenta flowers, 8cm (3in) across. Has oval, stiff leaves, 8–10cm (3–4in) long. Grow in semi-shade during summer and do not spray from overhead.

GUNNERA

GUNNERACEAE/HALORAGIDACEAE

Genus of summer-flowering perennials, grown mainly for their foliage. Some are clump-forming with very large leaves; others are mat-forming with smaller leaves. Frost hardy, but shelter from wind in summer and cover with bracken or compost in winter. Some require sun while others do best in partial shade; all need moist soil. Propagate by seed in autumn or spring; small species by division in spring.
G. chilensis. See *G. tinctoria*.
G. magellanica illus. p.371.
♀ ***G. manicata*** illus. p.443.
G. scabra. See *G. tinctoria*.
♀ ***G. tinctoria***, syn. *G. chilensis, G. scabra.* Robust, rounded, clump-forming perennial. **H** and **S** 1.5m (5ft) or more. Has very large, rounded, puckered and lobed leaves, 45–60cm (1½–2ft) across. In early summer, produces dense, conical clusters of tiny, dull reddish-green flowers.

GUZMANIA

BROMELIACEAE

Genus of evergreen, rosette-forming, epiphytic perennials, grown for their overall appearance. Frost tender, min. 10–15°C (50–59°F). Needs semi-shade and a rooting medium of equal parts humus-rich soil and either sphagnum moss, or bark or plastic chips used for orchid culture. Using soft water, water moderately during growing season, sparingly at other times, and keep rosette centres filled with water from spring to autumn. Propagate by offsets in spring or summer.
♀ ***G. lingulata*** Evergreen, basal-rosetted, epiphytic perennial. **H** and **S** 30–45cm (12–18in). Forms loose rosettes of broadly strap-shaped, arching, mid-green leaves. Bears a cluster of tubular, white to yellow flowers, surrounded by a rosette of bright red bracts, usually in summer.
♀ ***var. minor***, **H** and **S** 15cm (6in), has yellow-green leaves and red or yellow bracts.
♀ ***G. monostachia***, syn. *G. monostachya, G. tricolor* (Striped torch) . Evergreen, basal-rosetted, epiphytic perennial. **H** and **S** 30–40cm (12–16in). Has dense rosettes of strap-shaped, erect to arching, pale to yellowish-green leaves. In summer, elongated spikes of tubular, white flowers emerge from axils of oval bracts, the upper ones red, the lower ones green with purple-brown stripes.
G. monostachya. See *G. monostachia*.
♀ ***G. sanguinea.*** Evergreen, basal-rosetted, epiphytic perennial. **H** 20cm (8in), **S** 30–35cm (12–14in). Has dense, slightly flat rosettes of broadly strap-shaped, arching, mid- to deep green leaves. In summer, a compact cluster of tubular, yellow flowers, surrounded by red bracts, appears at the heart of each mature rosette.
G. tricolor. See *G. monostachia*.
G. vittata. Evergreen, basal-rosetted, epiphytic perennial. **H** and **S** 35–60cm (14–24in). Produces fairly loose rosettes of strap-shaped, erect, dark green leaves with pale green cross-bands and recurved tips. Stem bears a compact, egg-shaped head of small, tubular, white flowers in summer.

GYMNOCALYCIUM

CACTACEAE

Genus of perennial cacti with masses of funnel-shaped flowers in spring–summer. Crowns generally bear smooth, scaly buds. Frost tender, min. 5–10°C (41–50°F). Needs full sun or partial shade and very well-drained soil. Propagate by seed or offsets in spring or summer.
♀ ***G. andreae.*** Clump-forming, spherical, perennial cactus. **H** 6cm (2½in), **S** 10cm (4in). Frost tender, min. 10°C (50°F). Has a glossy, dark green stem bearing 8 rounded ribs and up to 8 pale yellow-white spines per areole. Yellow flowers, 5cm (2in) wide, appear in spring and summer.
G. gibbosum illus. p.481.
***G. mihanovichii* 'Red Head'**, syn. *G.m* 'Hibotan', *G.m.* 'Red Cap', illus. p.487.
♀ ***G. quehlianum.*** Flattened spherical, perennial cactus. **H** 5cm (2in), **S** 7cm (3in). Frost tender, min. 5°C (41°F). Grey-blue to brown stem has 11 or so rounded ribs. Areoles each produce 5 curved spines. Has white flowers, 5cm (2in) across, with red throats, in spring–summer. Is easy to flower.
G. schickendantzii. Spherical, perennial cactus. **H** and **S** 10cm (4in). Frost tender, min. 5°C (41°F). Dark green stem has 7–14 deeply indented ribs and long, red-tipped, grey-brown spines. Bears greenish-white to pale pink flowers, 5cm (2in) across, in summer.

GYMNOCARPIUM

DRYOPTERIDACEAE/WOODSIACEAE

Genus of deciduous, rhizomatous, terrestrial ferns with triangular fronds, ideal for ground cover. Fully hardy. Grow in deep shade and preferably neutral to acid, leafy, moist soil. Propagate from spores when ripe, or divide in spring.
♀ ***G. dryopteris*** (Oak fern). Deciduous fern. **H** 20cm (8in), **S** indefinite. Bears distinctive, divided fronds, each with a leaf-blade 10–18cm (4–7in) long and across, on a stem 10cm (4in) long. Pinnae are triangular, with oblong to ovate, toothed and scalloped segments. Pale yellowish green when young, the fronds darken to vivid rich green as they mature.

GYMNOCLADUS

LEGUMINOSAE/CAESALPINIACEAE

Genus of deciduous trees, grown for their foliage. Fully hardy. Needs full sun and deep, fertile, well-drained soil. Propagate by seed in autumn.
G. dioica illus. p.67.

Gynandriris sisyrinchium. See *Moraea sisyrinchium*.

GYNURA

COMPOSITAE/ASTERACEAE

Genus of evergreen perennials, shrubs and semi-scrambling climbers, grown for their ornamental foliage or flower heads. Frost tender, min. 16°C (61°F). Requires a lightly shaded position in summer and any fertile, well-drained soil. Water moderately throughout the year, less in cool conditions; do not overwater. Provide support for stems. Remove stem tips to encourage branching. Propagate by softwood or semi-ripe cuttings in spring or summer.
G. aurantiaca illus. p.462. ♀ **'Purple Passion'** (syn. *G. sarmentosa* of gardens) is an evergreen, erect, woody-based, soft-stemmed shrub or semi-scrambling climber. **H** 60cm (2ft) or more. Stems and lance-shaped, lobed, serrated leaves are covered with velvety, purple hairs. Leaves are purple-green above, deep red-purple beneath. In winter, clusters of daisy-like, orange-yellow flower heads are produced and these become purplish as they mature.
G. sarmentosa of gardens. See *G. aurantiaca* 'Purple Passion'.

GYPSOPHILA

CARYOPHYLLACEAE

Genus of spring- to autumn-flowering annuals and perennials, some of which are semi-evergreen. Fully hardy. Needs sun. Will grow in dry, sandy and stony soils, but does best in deep, well-drained soil. Resents being disturbed. Cut back after flowering for a second flush of flowers. Propagate *G. paniculata* cultivars by grafting in winter; others by softwood cuttings in summer or by seed in autumn or spring.
G. cerastioides illus. p.349.
G. elegans illus. p.299.
♀ ***G. paniculata* 'Bristol Fairy'** illus. p.231. **'Flamingo'** is a spreading, short-lived perennial. **H** 60–75cm (2–2½ft), **S** 1m (3ft). In summer, bears panicles of numerous, small, rounded, double, pale pink flowers on wiry, branching stems. Has small, linear, mid-green leaves.
♀ ***G. repens.*** Semi-evergreen, prostrate perennial with much-branched rhizomes. **H** 2.5–5cm (1–2in) or more, **S** 30cm (12in) or more. In summer, produces sprays of small, rounded, white, lilac or pink flowers on slender stems on which are borne narrowly oval, bluish-green leaves. Is excellent for a rock garden, wall or dry bank. May also be propagated by division in spring. **'Dorothy Teacher'** illus. p.362.

HAAGEOCERUS

CACTACEAE

Genus of perennial cacti with ribbed, densely spiny, columnar, green stems branching from the base. Frost tender, min. 11°C (52°F). Requires full sun and very well-drained soil. Propagate by seed or stem cuttings in spring or summer.
H. ambiguus. See *H. decumbens.*
H. chosicensis. See *H. pseudomelanostele.*
H. decumbens, syn. *H. ambiguus, H.litoralis.* Prostrate, perennial cactus. **H** 30cm (1ft), **S** 1m (3ft). Stems, 6cm (2½in) across, with 20 or so ribs, have dark brown, central spines, 5cm (2in) long, and shorter, dense, golden, radial spines. Tubular, white flowers, 8cm (3in) across, are produced in summer near crowns, only on mature plants.
H. litoralis. See *H. decumbens.*
H. pseudomelanostele, syn. *H. chosicensis.* Upright, perennial cactus. **H** 1.5m (5ft), **S** 1m (3ft). Green stem, 10cm (4in) across, with 19 or so ribs, bears white, golden or red, central spines and shorter, dense, bristle-like, white, radial ones. Has tubular, white, lilac-white or pinkish-red flowers, 7cm (3in) long, near crown in summer.
H. versicolor. Columnar, perennial cactus. **H** to 2m (6ft), **S** 1m (3ft). Dense, radial spines, golden, red or brown, at times form coloured bands around a longer, central spine up the green stem. Long-tubed, white flowers appear near crown of plant in summer.

HABENARIA

ORCHIDACEAE

See also ORCHIDS.
H. radiata illus. p.408.

HABERLEA

GESNERIACEAE

Genus of evergreen, rosetted perennials, grown for their elegant sprays of flowers. Is useful on walls. Fully hardy. Needs partially shaded, moist soil. Resents disturbance to roots. Propagate by seed in spring or by leaf cuttings or offsets in early summer.
H. ferdinandi-coburgii. Evergreen, dense, basal-rosetted perennial. **H** 10–15cm (4–6in), **S** 30cm (12in). Has oblong, toothed, dark green leaves, hairy below, almost glabrous above. Sprays of funnel-shaped, blue-violet flowers, each with a white throat, appear on long stems in late spring and early summer.
♀ ***H. rhodopensis***. Evergreen, dense, basal-rosetted perennial. **H** 10cm (4in), **S** 15cm (6in) or more. Is similar to *H. ferdinandi-coburgii*, but leaves are hairy on both surfaces. **'Virginalis'** illus. p.359.

HABRANTHUS

AMARYLLIDACEAE

Genus of summer- and autumn-flowering bulbs, grown for their funnel-shaped flowers. Frost to half hardy. Needs a sheltered, sunny site and fertile soil, which is well supplied with moisture in growing season. Propagate by seed or offsets in spring.
H. andersonii. See *H. tubispathus.*
H. brachyandrus. Summer-flowering bulb. **H** to 30cm (12in), **S** 5–8cm (2–3in). Half hardy. Long, linear, semi-erect, narrow leaves form a basal cluster. Each flower stem bears a semi-erect, widely funnel-shaped, pinkish-red flower, 7–10cm (3–4in) long.
♀ ***H. robustus***, syn. *Zephyranthes robusta*, illus. p.426.
♀ ***H. tubispathus***, syn. *H. andersonii.* Summer-flowering bulb. **H** to 15cm (6in), **S** 5cm (2in). Frost hardy. Has linear, semi-erect, basal leaves and a succession of flower stems each bearing solitary, 2.5–3.5cm (1–1½in) long, funnel-shaped flowers, yellow inside, copper-red outside.

HACQUETIA

SYN. DONDIA

UMBELLIFERAE/APIACEAE

Genus of one species of clump-forming, rhizomatous perennial that creeps slowly, grown for its yellow or yellow-green flower heads borne on leafless plants in late winter and early spring. Is good in rock gardens. Fully hardy. Prefers a position in shade and in humus-rich, moist soil. Resents disturbance to roots. Propagate by division in spring, by seed when fresh in autumn or by root cuttings in winter.
♀ ***H. epipactis*** illus. p.356.

HAEMANTHUS

AMARYLLIDACEAE

Genus of summer-flowering bulbs with dense heads of small, star-shaped flowers, often brightly coloured. Frost tender, min. 10°C (50°F). Prefers full sun or partial shade and well-drained soil or sandy compost. Liquid feed in the growing season. Leave undisturbed as long as possible before replanting. Propagate by offsets or seed before growth commences in early spring. ⓘ All parts may cause mild stomach upset if ingested; contact with the sap may irritate skin.
♀ ***H. albiflos*** (Paintbrush). Summer-flowering bulb. **H** 5–30cm (2–12in), **S** 20–30cm (8–12in). Has 2–6 almost prostrate, broadly elliptic leaves with hairy edges. Flower stem, appearing between leaves, bears a brush-like head of up to 50 white flowers with very narrow petals and protruding stamens.
♀ ***H. coccineus*** illus. p.423.
H. katherinae. See *Scadoxus multiflorus* subsp. *katherinae.*
H. magnificus. See *Scadoxus puniceus.*
H. multiflorus. See *Scadoxus multiflorus.*
H. natalensis. See *Scadoxus puniceus.*
H. puniceus. See *Scadoxus puniceus.*
H. sanguineus. Summer-flowering bulb. **H** to 30cm (12in), **S** 20–30cm (8–12in). Bears 2 prostrate, elliptic, rough, dark green leaves, hairy beneath. Brownish-purple-spotted, green flower stem, forming before leaves, produces a dense head of small, narrow-petalled, red flowers, surrounded by whorls of narrow, leaf-like, red or pink bracts.

HAKEA

PROTEACEAE

Genus of evergreen shrubs and trees, grown for their often needle-like leaves and their flowers. Is very wind-resistant, except in cold areas. Frost hardy to frost tender, min. 5–7°C (41–5°F). Requires a position in full sun and fertile, well-drained soil. Water containerized specimens moderately in growing season, but only sparingly in winter. Propagate by semi-ripe cuttings in summer or by seed in autumn.
H. drupacea, syn. *H. suaveolens.* Evergreen, rounded shrub. **H** and **S** 2m (6ft) or more. Frost tender. Leaves are divided into cylindrical, needle-like leaflets or occasionally are undivided and lance-shaped. Small, fragrant, tubular, white flowers, carried in short, dense clusters, are produced from summer to winter.
H. lissosperma, syn. *H. sericea* of gardens. Evergreen, upright, densely branched shrub of pine-like appearance. **H** 5m (15ft), **S** 3m (10ft). Frost hardy. Bears long, slender, sharply pointed, grey-green leaves and produces, in late spring and early summer, clusters of small, spidery, white flowers.
H. sericea of gardens. See *H. lissosperma.*
H. suaveolens. See *H. drupacea.*

HAKONECHLOA

GRAMINEAE/POACEAE

See also GRASSES, BAMBOOS, RUSHES and SEDGES.
♀ ***H. macra* 'Aureola'** illus. p.289.

HALESIA

Silver bell, Snowdrop tree

STYRACACEAE

Genus of deciduous, spring-flowering trees and shrubs, grown for their showy, pendent, bell-shaped flowers and their curious, winged fruits. Fully hardy, but needs a sunny, sheltered position. Prefers moist but well-drained, neutral to acid soil. Propagate by softwood cuttings in summer or by seed in autumn.
H. carolina, syn. *H. tetraptera.* Deciduous, spreading tree or shrub. **H** 8m (25ft), **S** 10m (30ft). Oval leaves are mid-green. Masses of bell-shaped, white flowers, hanging from bare shoots, are produced in late spring, and are followed by 4-winged, green fruits.
H. monticola illus. p.71.
H. tetraptera. See *H. carolina.*

x HALIMIOCISTUS

CISTACEAE

Hybrid genus (*Cistus* x *Halimium*) of evergreen shrubs, grown for their flowers. Frost hardy, but in cold areas needs shelter. Requires full sun and well-drained soil. Propagate by semi-ripe cuttings in summer.
♀ **x *H. sahucii***, syn. *Cistus revolii* of gardens, illus. p.149.
♀ **x *H. wintonensis***, syn. *Halimium wintonense.* Evergreen, bushy shrub. **H** 60cm (2ft), **S** 1m (3ft). Saucer-shaped, white flowers, each with deep red bands and a yellow centre, open amid lance-shaped, grey-green leaves in late spring and early summer.

HALIMIUM

CISTACEAE

Genus of evergreen shrubs, grown for their showy flowers. Is good for coastal gardens. Frost hardy, but in cold areas needs shelter. Does best in full sun and light, well-drained soil. Propagate by semi-ripe cuttings in summer.
H. formosum. See *H. lasianthum* subsp. *formosum.*
♀ ***H. lasianthum.*** Evergreen, bushy, spreading shrub. **H** 1m (3ft), **S** 1.5m (5ft). Leaves are oval and grey-green. In late spring and early summer, bears saucer-shaped, golden-yellow flowers, sometimes with small, central, red blotches. **subsp. *formosum*** (syn. *H. formosum*) illus. p.161.
♀ ***H. ocymoides***, syn. *Cistus algarvensis.* Evergreen, bushy shrub. **H** 60cm (2ft), **S** 1m (3ft). Narrowly oval leaves, covered in white hairs when young, mature to dark green. In early summer, has upright clusters of saucer-shaped, golden-yellow flowers, conspicuously blotched with black or purple. **'Susan'.** See *H.* 'Susan'.
♀ ***H.* 'Susan'**, syn. *H. ocymoides* 'Susan', illus. p.160.
H. umbellatum, syn. *Helianthemum umbellatum*, illus. p.149.
H. wintonense. See x *Halimiocistus wintonensis.*

HAMAMELIS

Witch hazel

HAMAMELIDACEAE

Genus of deciduous, autumn- to early spring-flowering shrubs, grown for their autumn colour and fragrant, frost-resistant flowers, each with 4 narrowly strap-shaped petals. Fully hardy. Flourishes in sun or semi-shade and fertile, well-drained, peaty, acid soil, although tolerates good, deep soil over chalk. Propagate species by seed in autumn, selected forms by softwood cuttings in summer, by budding in late summer or by grafting in winter. See also feature panel p.118.
♀ ***H.* x *intermedia* 'Aphrodite'** (illus. p.118). Deciduous, upright shrub. **H** and **S** 4m (12ft) or more. Has oval, bright green leaves. Bears masses of large, fragrant, spidery, golden-orange flowers, along bare branches, in winter. ♀ **'Arnold Promise'** (illus. p.118) has a spreading habit, leaves turning to yellow in autumn and bears yellow flowers in mid- and late winter. ♀ **'Barmstedt Gold'** (illus. p.118) has deep golden-yellow flowers, with red-tinted bases, and leaves that turn to yellow in autumn. ♀ **'Diane'** has deep red flowers from mid- to late winter. Leaves turn yellow and red in autumn. ♀ **'Jelena'** (illus. p.118) has coppery-orange flowers from early to mid-winter and bright orange or red leaves in autumn.
♀ **'Pallida'**, syn. *H. mollis* 'Pallida' (illus. p.118), S 3m (10ft), bears dense clusters of large, sulphur-yellow flowers.
'Primavera' (illus. p.118) has yellow flowers in late winter and early spring.
'Robert' (illus. p.118) has orange-red flowers. ♀ **'Vesna'** produces golden-yellow flowers flushed with red.

H. japonica (Japanese witch hazel). Deciduous, upright, open shrub. **H** and **S** 4m (12ft). Broadly oval, glossy, mid-green leaves turn yellow in autumn. Fragrant, yellow flowers, with crinkled petals, are produced on bare branches from mid- to late winter. **'Sulphurea'** illus. p.118. **'Zuccariniana'** bears paler, lemon-yellow flowers in early spring and leaves turn orange-yellow in autumn.
♡ ***H. mollis*** (Chinese witch hazel). Deciduous, upright, open shrub. **H** and **S** 4m (12ft) or more. Broadly oval, mid-green leaves turn yellow in autumn. Produces extremely fragrant, spidery, yellow flowers, along bare branches, in mid- and late winter. **'Coombe Wood'** has golden-yellow flowers. ♡ **'Jermyn's Gold'** bears large clusters of broad-petalled, bright yellow flowers.
♡ **'Pallida'** see *H.* x *intermedia* 'Pallida'.
♡ ***H. vernalis* 'Sandra'.** Deciduous, upright, open shrub. **H** and **S** 5m (15ft). Bears small, fragrant, spidery, deep yellow blooms in late winter and early spring. Oval leaves are purple when young, mid-green in summer, and purple, red, orange and yellow in autumn.
H. virginiana (Virginian witch hazel). Deciduous, open, upright shrub. **H** and **S** 5m (15ft). Small, fragrant, spidery, yellow flowers with 4 narrow petals open in autumn as leaves fall. Broadly oval leaves turn yellow in autumn.

Hamatocactus hamatacanthus. See *Ferocactus hamatacanthus*.
Hamatocactus setispinus. See *Thelocactus setispinus*.
Hamatocactus uncinatus. See *Sclerocactus uncinatus*.

HARDENBERGIA

LEGUMINOSAE/PAPILIONACEAE

Genus of evergreen, woody-stemmed, twining climbers or sub-shrubs, grown for their curtains of leaves and racemes of pea-like flowers. Half hardy to frost tender, min. 7°C (45°F). Grows best in sun and in well-drained soil that does not dry out. Propagate by stem cuttings in late summer or autumn or by seed (soaked before sowing) in spring.
♡ ***H. comptoniana*** illus. p.194.
H. monophylla. See *H. violacea*.
♡ ***H. violacea***, syn. *H. monophylla* (Australian sarsparilla, Coral pea, Vine lilac). Evergreen, woody-stemmed, twining climber. **H** to 3m (10ft). Frost tender. Narrowly oval leaves are 2.5–12cm (1–5in) long. Violet, occasionally pink or white, flowers, with yellow blotches on upper petals, are borne in spring. Brownish pods, 3–4cm (1¼–1½in) long, are borne in autumn. **'Happy Wanderer'** illus. p.462.

HATIORA

CACTACEAE

Genus of perennial, epiphytic cacti with short, jointed, cylindrical stems, each swollen at one end like a bottle. Frost tender, min. 10–13°C (50–55°F). Requires partial shade and very well-drained soil. Keep damp in summer; water a little in winter. Propagate by stem cuttings in spring or summer.
H. clavata. See *Rhipsalis gaertneri*.
♡ ***H. gaertneri***, syn. *Rhipsalidopsis gaertneri*, (Easter Cactus) illus. p.487.
♡ ***H. rosea***, syn. *Rhipsalidopsis rosea*, illus. p.485.
♡ ***H. salicornioides***, syn. *Rhipsalis salicornioides* (Bottle plant, Drunkard's dream). Bushy, perennial, epiphytic cactus. **H** and **S** 30cm (1ft). Frost tender, min. 11°C (52°F). Has freely branching stems, 3cm (1¼in) long. Has joints with expanded tips and terminal, bell-shaped, golden-yellow flowers in spring.

HAWORTHIA

LILIACEAE/ALOACEAE

Genus of basal-rosetted, clump-forming, perennial succulents with triangular to rounded, green leaves. Roots tend to wither in winter or during long periods of drought. Frost tender, min. 5–10°C (41–50°F). Needs partial shade to stay green and grow quickly; if planted in full sun turns red or orange and grows slowly. Requires very well-drained soil. Keep dry in winter. Propagate by seed or division from spring to autumn.
H. arachnoidea, syn. *H. setata*, illus. p.491.
H. attenuata illus. p.480.
H. x cuspidata. Clump-forming, perennial succulent. **H** 5cm (2in), **S** 25cm (10in). Min. 5°C (41°F). Produces a basal rosette of smooth, rounded, fleshy, light green leaves covered with translucent marks. Tubular to bell-shaped, white flowers appear from spring to autumn on long, slender stems.
H. fasciata. Slow-growing, clump-forming, perennial succulent. **H** 15cm (6in), **S** 30cm (12in). Min. 5°C (41°F). Has raised, white dots, mostly in bands, on undersides of triangular, slightly incurved leaves, to 8cm (3in) long, which are arranged in a basal rosette. Bears tubular to bell-shaped, white flowers, on long, slender stems, from spring to autumn.
H. setata. See *H. arachnoidea*.
♡ ***H. truncata*** illus. p.492.

HEATHERS

ERICACEAE

Heathers (otherwise known as heaths) are evergreen, woody-stemmed shrubs, grown for their flowers and foliage, both of which may provide colour in the garden all year round. There are 3 genera: *Calluna, Daboecia* and *Erica*. *Calluna* has only one species, *C. vulgaris*, but it contains a large number of cultivars that flower mainly from mid-summer to late autumn. *Daboecia* has 2 species, both of which are summer-flowering. The largest genus is *Erica*, which, although broadly divided into 2 groups – winter-and summer-flowering species – has some species also flowering in spring and autumn. They vary in height from tree heaths, which may grow to 6m (20ft), to dwarf, prostrate plants that, if planted 30–45cm (12–18in) apart, soon spread to form a thick mat of ground cover.

Heathers are fully hardy to frost tender, min. 5–7°C (41–5°F). They prefer an open, sunny position and require humus-rich, well-drained soil. *Calluna* and *Daboecia* dislike limestone and must be grown in acid soil; some species of *Erica* tolerate slightly alkaline soil but all are better grown in acid soils. Prune lightly after flowering each year to keep plants bushy and compact. Propagate species by seed in spring or by softwood cuttings, division or layering in summer. Seed cannot be relied on to come true. All cultivars should be vegetatively propagated. Heathers are illustrated on p.166.

HEBE

SCROPHULARIACEAE

Genus of evergreen shrubs, grown for their often dense spikes, panicles or racemes of flowers and their foliage. Grows well in coastal areas. Smaller species and cultivars are suitable for rock gardens. Fully to half hardy. Requires position in full sun and well-drained soil. Growth may be restricted, or leggy plants tidied, by cutting back in spring. Propagate by semi-ripe cuttings in summer.
♡ ***H. albicans*** illus. p.151. **'Cranleigh Gem'** is an evergreen, rounded shrub. **H** 60cm (2ft), **S** 1m (3ft). Frost hardy. Has dense spikes of small, 4-lobed, white flowers, with conspicuous, black anthers, amid narrowly oval, grey-green leaves in early summer.
H. 'Alicia Amherst'. Fast-growing, evergreen, upright shrub. **H** and **S** 1.2m (4ft). Frost hardy. Has large, oblong, glossy, dark green leaves and, in late summer–autumn, large spikes of small, 4-lobed, deep violet-purple flowers.
H. 'Andersonii Variegata'. See *H.* x *andersonii* 'Variegata'.
***H. x andersonii* 'Variegata'**, syn. *H.* 'Andersonii Variegata'. Evergreen, bushy shrub. **H** and **S** 2m (6ft). Half hardy. Leaves are oblong and dark green, each with a grey-green centre and creamy-white margins. Has dense spikes of small, 4-lobed, lilac flowers from mid-summer to autumn.
H. 'Autumn Glory' illus. p.157.
H. 'Bowles's Variety' illus. p.157.
H. brachysiphon. Evergreen, bushy, dense shrub. **H** and **S** 2m (6ft). Fully hardy. Has oblong, dark green leaves. Produces dense spikes of small, 4-lobed, white flowers in mid-summer. **'White Gem'** see *H.* 'White Gem'.
H. buchananii. Evergreen, dome-shaped shrub. **H** and **S** 15cm (6in) or more. Frost hardy. Very dark stems bear oval, bluish-green leaves. In summer, produces clusters of small, 4-lobed, white flowers at stem tips. **'Minor'**, **H** 5–10cm (2–4in), has smaller leaves.
H. canterburiensis, syn. *H.* 'Tom Marshall'. Evergreen, low-growing, spreading shrub. **H** and **S** 30–90cm (1–3ft). Frost hardy. Small, oval, glossy, dark green leaves are densely packed on stems. In early summer, short racemes of small, white flowers are freely produced in leaf axils.
H. 'Carl Teschner'. See *H.* 'Youngii'.
H. carnosula. Evergreen, prostrate shrub. **H** 15–30cm (6–12in), **S** 30cm (12in) or more. Frost hardy. Has small, oblong to oval, slightly convex, fleshy, glaucous leaves. Terminal clusters of many small, white flowers, with 4 pointed lobes, are borne in late spring or early summer.
H. cupressoides illus. p.165. **'Boughton Dome'** illus. p.347.
H. 'E.A. Bowles' illus. p.157.
H. 'Eveline', syn. *H.* 'Gauntlettii'. Evergreen, upright shrub. **H** and **S** 1m (3ft). Frost hardy. Has long spikes of small, 4-lobed, pink flowers, each with a purplish tube, amid rich green, oblong leaves from late summer to late autumn.
H. 'Fairfieldii'. Evergreen, upright shrub. **H** and **S** 60cm (2ft). Frost hardy. Oval, toothed, glossy, bright green leaves are red-margined. Large, open panicles of small, 4-lobed, pale lilac flowers are produced in late spring and early summer.
***H. x franciscana* 'Blue Gem'.** Evergreen, spreading shrub. **H** 60cm (2ft), **S** 1.2m (4ft). Frost hardy. Has oblong, densely arranged, mid-green leaves. Dense spikes of small, 4-lobed, violet-blue flowers are borne from mid-summer until early winter.
H. 'Gauntlettii'. See *H.* 'Eveline'.
♡ ***H. 'Great Orme'*** illus. p.153.
♡ ***H. hulkeana.*** Evergreen, upright, open shrub. **H** and **S** 1m (3ft). Frost hardy. Oval, toothed, glossy, dark green leaves have red margins. Has masses of small, 4-lobed, pale lilac flowers in large, open panicles in late spring and early summer. **'Lilac Hint'** illus. p.152.
H. 'La Séduisante', syn. *H.* 'Ruddigore', *H. speciosa* 'Ruddigore'. Evergreen, upright shrub. **H** and **S** 1m (3ft). Frost hardy. Oval, glossy, deep green leaves are purple beneath. Produces small, 4-lobed, deep purplish-red flowers in large spikes from late summer to late autumn.
♡ ***H. macrantha.*** Evergreen, bushy shrub. **H** 60cm (2ft), **S** 1m (3ft). Frost hardy. Has oval, toothed, fleshy, bright green leaves and produces racemes of large, 4-lobed, pure white flowers in early summer. May become bare at base.
♡ ***H. 'Midsummer Beauty'.*** Evergreen, rounded, open shrub. **H** 2m (6ft), **S** 1.5m (5ft). Frost hardy. Long, narrow, glossy, bright green leaves are reddish-purple beneath. Long spikes of small, 4-lobed, lilac flowers that fade to white are borne from mid-summer to late autumn.
H. ochracea. Evergreen, bushy, dense shrub. **H** and **S** 1m (3ft). Fully hardy. Slender shoots are densely covered with tiny, scale-like, ochre-tinged, olive-green leaves. Clusters of small, 4-lobed, white flowers appear in late spring and early summer.
H. pinguifolia (Disk-leaved hebe).
♡ **'Pagei'** illus. p.337.
H. 'Purple Queen' illus. p.157.
♡ ***H. rakaiensis.*** Evergreen, rounded, compact shrub. **H** 1m (3ft), **S** 1.2m (4ft). Fully hardy. Produces small, dense spikes of 4-lobed, white flowers amid small, oblong, mid-green leaves from early to mid-summer.
H. recurva illus. p.151.
H. 'Ruddigore'. See *H.* 'La Séduisante'.
H. salicifolia. Evergreen, upright shrub. **H** and **S** 2.5m (8ft). Frost hardy. Has long, narrow, pointed, pale green leaves and, in summer, produces slender spikes of small, 4-lobed, white or pale lilac flowers.
***H. speciosa* 'Ruddigore'.** See *H.* 'La Séduisante'.
H. 'Tom Marshall'. See *H. canterburiensis*.

H

♀ ***H. vernicosa*** illus. p.337.
♀ ***H.* 'White Gem'**, syn. *H. brachysiphon* 'White Gem', illus. p.149.
♀ ***H.* 'Youngii'**, syn. *H.* 'Carl Teschner'. Evergreen, prostrate, becoming dome-shaped, shrub. **H** 15cm (6in), **S** 30cm (12in) or more. Frost hardy. Blackish-brown stems are covered in small, oval, glossy, dark green leaves. Bears short racemes of tiny, 4-lobed, white-throated, purple flowers in summer. Is excellent as a border plant.

HEDERA

Ivy

ARALIACEAE

Genus of evergreen, woody-stemmed, trailing perennials and self-clinging climbers with adventitious rootlets, used for covering walls and fences and as ground cover. Takes a year or so to become established, but thereafter growth is rapid. On the ground and while climbing, mostly bears roughly triangular, usually lobed leaves. Given extra height and access to light, leaves become less lobed and, in autumn, umbels of small, yellowish-green flowers are produced, followed by globose, black, occasionally yellow, fruits. Fully to half hardy. Ivies with green leaves are very shade tolerant and do well against a north-facing wall. Those with variegated or yellow leaves prefer more light, are usually less hardy and may sustain frost and wind damage in severe winters. All prefer well-drained, alkaline soil. Prune in spring to control height and spread, and to remove any damaged growth. Propagate in late summer by softwood cuttings or rooted layers. Red spider mite may be a problem when plants are grown against a south-facing wall or in dry conditions. ⓘ All parts of ivy may cause severe discomfort if ingested; contact with the sap may aggravate skin allergies or irritate skin.

H. algeriensis, syn *H. canariensis* of gardens. Fast-growing, evergreen, self-clinging climber. **H** to 6m (20ft), **S** 5m (15ft). Half hardy; may be damaged in severe winters but soon recovers. Has oval to triangular, unlobed, glossy, mid-green leaves and reddish-purple stems. Is suitable for growing against a wall in a sheltered area. ♀ **'Gloire de Marengo'** has silver-variegated leaves. ♀ **'Ravensholst'** is vigorous with large leaves; makes good ground cover.

H. canariensis of gardens, see *H. algeriensis*.

♀ ***H. colchica*** (Persian ivy). Evergreen, self-clinging climber or trailing perennial. **H** 10m (30ft), **S** 5m (15ft). Fully hardy. Has large, oval, unlobed, dark green leaves. Is suitable for growing against a wall. ♀ **'Dentata'** (Elephant's ears) is more vigorous and has large, light green leaves that droop, hence its common name. Is good when grown against a wall or for ground cover. ♀ **'Dentata Variegata'**, **H** 5m (15ft), has variegated, cream-yellow leaves; is useful to brighten a shady corner. **'Paddy's Pride'** see 'Sulphur Heart'. ♀ **'Sulphur Heart'** (syn. *H.c.* 'Paddy's Pride') illus. p.211.

H. cypria, syn. *H. pastuchovii* var. *cypria*. Vigorous, evergreen, self-clinging climber. **H** 3m (10ft, **S** 2m (6ft). Fully hardy. Has shield-shaped, glossy, dark green leaves with prominent, grey-green veins. Should only be grown against a wall.

H. helix (Common English ivy). Vigorous, evergreen, self-clinging climber or trailing perennial. **H** 10m (30ft), **S** 5m (15ft). Fully hardy. Has 5-lobed, dark green leaves. Makes good ground and wall cover, but may be invasive; for a small garden, the more decorative cultivars are preferable. **'Adam'**, **H** 1.2m (4ft), **S** 1m (3ft), is half hardy and has small, light green leaves variegated-yellow; may suffer leaf damage in winter, but will recover. ♀ **'Angularis Aurea'**, **H** 4m (12ft), **S** 2.5m (8ft), has glossy, light green leaves, with bright yellow variegation; is not suitable as ground cover. **'Anna Marie'**, **H** 1.2m (4ft), **S** 1m (3ft), is frost hardy and has light green leaves with cream variegation, mostly at margins; may suffer leaf damage in winter. **'Atropurpurea'** (syn. *H.h.* 'Purpurea'; Purple-leaved ivy), **H** 4m (12ft), **S** 2.5m (8ft), has dark green leaves that turn deep purple in winter. **var. *baltica*** (syn. *H.h.* 'Baltica'), an exceptionally hardy cultivar, has small leaves and makes good ground cover in an exposed area. **'Buttercup'**, **H** 2m (6ft), **S** 2.5m (8ft), is frost hardy and has light green leaves that turn rich butter-yellow in full sun. **'Caenwoodiana'** see *H.h.* 'Pedata'. ♀ **'Congesta'**, **H** 45cm (1½ft), **S** 60cm (2ft), is a non-climbing, erect cultivar with spire-like shoots and small leaves; is suitable for a rock garden. **'Conglomerata'** (Clustered ivy), **H** and **S** 1m (3ft), will clamber over a low wall or grow in a rock garden; has small, curly, unlobed leaves. **'Cristata'** see *H.h.* 'Parsley Crested'. **'Curlylocks'** see *H.h.* 'Manda's Crested'. **'Deltoidea'** see *H. hibernica* 'Deltoidea'. **'Digitata'** see *H. hibernica* 'Digitata'. ♀ **'Erecta'**, **H** 1m (3ft), **S** 1.2m (4ft), is a non-climbing, erect cultivar similar to *H.h.* 'Congesta'. **'Eva'**, **H** 1.2m (4ft), **S** 1m (3ft), is frost hardy and has small, grey-green leaves with cream variegation; may suffer leaf damage in winter. **'Glacier'** illus. p.211. **'Glymii'**, **H** 2.5m (8ft), **S** 2m (6ft), has glossy, dark green leaves that turn deep purple in winter; is not suitable for ground cover. ♀ **'Goldchild'** (syn. *H.h.* 'Gold Harald'), **H** 1m (3ft), is frost hardy and has small, 3- to 5-lobed, grey-green leaves with broad yellow margins. **'Gold Harald'** see *H.h.* 'Goldchild'. **'Goldheart'** see *H.h.* 'Oro di Bogliasco'. **'Gracilis'** see *H. hibernica* 'Gracilis'. **'Green Ripple'**, **H** and **S** 1.2m (4ft), is frost hardy and has mid-green leaves with prominent, light green veins; is good for ground cover or for growing against a low wall. **'Hahn's Self-branching'** see *H.h.* 'Pittsburgh'. **'Heise'**, **H** 30cm (1ft), **S** 60cm (2ft), is frost hardy and has small, grey-green leaves with cream variegation; is suitable as ground cover for a small, sheltered area. **var. *hibernica*** see *H. hibernica*. ♀ **'Ivalace'**, **H** 1m (3ft), **S** 1.2m (4ft), is frost hardy and has curled and crimped, glossy leaves; is good for ground cover and for growing against a low wall. **'Jubiläum Goldherz'** see *H.h.* 'Oro di Bogliasco'. **'Jubilee Goldheart'** see *H.h.* 'Oro di Bogliasco'. **'Königers Auslese'** (syn. *H.h.* 'Sagittifolia' of gardens), **H** 1.2 m (4ft), **S** 1m (3ft), is frost hardy and has finger-like, deeply cut leaves; is not suitable for ground cover. **'Little Diamond'** is frost hardy, slow-growing and has entire, diamond-shaped, grey-green leaves, variegated creamy-white. **'Lobata Major'** see *H. hibernica* 'Lobata Major'. ♀ **'Manda's Crested'** (syn. *H.h.* 'Curlylocks'), **H** and **S** 2m (6ft), is frost hardy and has elegant, wavy-edged, mid-green leaves that turn a coppery shade in winter. **'Merion Beauty'**, **H** 1.2m (4ft), **S** 1m (3ft), is frost hardy with delicately lobed leaves; is not suitable for ground cover. **'Nigra'**, **H** and **S** 1.2m (4ft), has small, very dark green leaves that turn purple-black in winter. **'Oro di Bogliasco'** (syn. *H.h.* 'Goldheart', *H.h.* 'Jubiläum Goldherz', *H.h.* 'Jubilee Goldheart') illus. p.211. ♀ **'Parsley Crested'** (syn. *H.h.* 'Cristata'), **H** 2m (6ft), **S** 1.2m (4ft), is frost hardy and has light green leaves, crested at margins; is not suitable for ground cover. **'Pedata'** (syn. *H.h.* 'Cacnwoodiana'; Bird's-foot ivy), **H** 4m (12ft), **S** 3m (10ft), has grey-green leaves shaped like a bird's foot; is not suitable for ground cover. **'Pittsburgh'** (syn. *H.h.* 'Hahn's Self-branching'), **H** 1m (3ft), **S** 1.2m (4ft), is frost hardy and has mid-green leaves; is suitable for growing against a low wall and for ground cover. **f. *poetarum*** syn. *H.h.* 'Poetica', *H.h.* 'Poetica Arborea' (Italian Ivy, Poet's Ivy), **H** 3m (10ft), is slow-growing with large, 5-lobed, shiny, mid-green leaves. Often grown as a "bush ivy", as it bears distinctive, orange-yellow fruit, even on comparatively young plants. **'Poetica'** see *H.h.* f. *poetarum*. **'Poetica Arborea'** see *H.h.* f. *poetarum*. **'Purpurea'** see *H.h.* 'Atropurpurea'. **'Sagittifolia'** of gardens see *H.h.* 'Königers Auslese'. **'Telecurl'**, **H** and **S** 1m (3ft), is frost hardy and has elegantly twisted, light green leaves. **'Triton'**, **H** 45cm (1½ft), **S** 1m (3ft), is a non-climbing, frost-hardy cultivar that has leaves with deeply incised lobes that resemble whips; makes good ground cover. **'Woeneri'**, **H** 4m (12ft), **S** 3m (10ft), is a vigorous cultivar that has bluntly lobed, grey-green leaves, with lighter coloured veins, that turn purple in winter.

♀ ***H. hibernica***, syn. *H. helix* var. *hibernica* (Irish ivy). Vigorous, evergreen climber. **H** 5m (15ft), **S** 6m (20ft). Fully hardy. Has large, mid-green leaves. Is good for covering a large area, either on the ground or against a wall. ♀ **'Deltoidea'** (syn. *H. helix* 'Deltoidea'; Shield ivy, Sweetheart ivy), **H** 5m (15ft), **S** 3m (10ft), has heart-shaped leaves; is suitable only for growing against a wall. **'Digitata'** (syn. *H. helix* 'Digitata'; Finger-leaved ivy), **H** 6m (20ft), has large leaves; is not suitable for ground cover. **'Gracilis'** (syn. *H. helix* 'Gracilis'), **H** 5m (15ft), has sharply lobed, dark green leaves that turn bronze-purple in winter; is not suitable for ground cover. **'Lobata Major'** (syn. *H. helix* 'Lobata Major'), **H** 5m (15ft), is vigorous with large, 3-lobed leaves. **'Sulphurea'**, **H** and **S** 3m (10ft), has medium-sized leaves with sulphur-yellow variegation; is suitable for growing against a wall or for ground cover, and as a foil for brightly coloured plants.

H. nepalensis (Nepalese ivy). Evergreen, self-clinging climber. **H** 4m (12ft), **S** 2.5m (8ft). Half hardy; young growth may suffer damage from late frosts. Has oval to triangular, toothed, olive-green leaves and is suitable only for growing against a sheltered wall. **'Suzanne'**, **H** 2m (6ft), is less vigorous than the species and has 5-lobed leaves with backward-pointing basal lobes.

H. pastuchovii. Moderately vigorous, evergreen, self-clinging climber. **H** 2.5m (8ft), **S** 2m (6ft). Fully hardy. Has shield-shaped, glossy, dark green leaves and should only be grown against a wall. **var. *cypria*** see *H. cypria*.

H. rhombea (Japanese ivy). Evergreen, self-clinging climber. **H** and **S** 1.2m (4ft). Frost hardy. Has small, fairly thick, diamond-shaped, unlobed, mid-green leaves. Is suitable only for growing against a low wall. **'Variegata'** has leaves with narrow, white margins.

HEDYCHIUM

Garland flower, Ginger lily

ZINGIBERACEAE

Genus of perennials with stout, fleshy rhizomes. Fragrant, showy flowers are short-lived, but borne profusely. Grow in sheltered borders and conservatories. Frost hardy to frost tender, min. 5°C (41°F). Requires a position in sun and in rich, moist soil. Propagate by division in spring; should not be divided when dormant. See also feature panel p.477.

H. coccineum. Upright, rhizomatous perennial. H and **S** to 2m (6ft). Half hardy. Has long-stalked, narrowly lance-shaped, greyish-green leaves. Bears spikes of short-lived, orange to red flowers, each with a 2-lobed lip, in summer. Is very variable, with many named forms, some of which are frost hardy. **'Tara'.** See *H.* x *moorei* 'Tara'.

H. coronarium (White ginger lily). Upright, rhizomatous perennial. **H** 1.5m (5ft), **S** 60cm–1m (2–3ft). Frost tender, min. 5°C (41°F). Produces dense spikes of very fragrant, butterfly-like, white flowers with basal, yellow blotches in mid-summer. Lance-shaped, mid-green leaves are downy beneath.

H. densiflorum (illus. p.477). Clump-forming, rhizomatous perennial. **H** 1.2–2m (4–6ft), **S** 60cm (2ft). Frost hardy. Bears a profusion of short-lived, fragrant, orange or yellow flowers in dense spikes during late summer. Broadly lance-shaped leaves are glossy, mid-green.

H. flavescens. Upright, rhizomatous perennial. H 1–2m (3–6ft), **S** 1m (3ft). Frost tender, min. 5°C (41°F). Lance-shaped, mid-green leaves are softly hairy. Produces spikes of short-lived, very fragrant, pale to lemon-yellow flowers, each with a 2-lobed lip, in late autumn. Is good in a tub.

H. gracile. Arching, rhizomatous perennial. H 120cm (48in), **S** 50cm (20in). Frost tender, min. 5°C (41°F). In summer, thin stems bear short-lived, sometimes fragrant, white flowers, each with a narrow, 2-lobed lip, narrow sepals and red stamens. Has lance-shaped, mid-green leaves. Requires staking. Is good in a raised container or on a bank.

♀ ***H. gardnerianum*** illus. p.476.

H. horsfieldii, syn. *Brachychilum horsfieldii*. Clump-forming, tufted perennial. **H** and **S** to 1m (3ft). Frost tender, min. 5°C (41°F). Has short-stalked, lance-shaped, leathery leaves, to 30cm (1ft) long. Produces showy, tubular, yellow-and-white flowers, to 8cm (3in) across, in summer, followed by orange fruits that open to reveal red seeds.
H. maximum (illus. p.477). Upright, rhizomatous perennial. **H** 2–3m (6–10ft), **S** 1m (3ft). Frost tender, min. 5°C (41°F). Has large, thick-stems, bearing lance-shaped, mid-green leaves. Short-lived, fragrant, pale yellow flowers, with golden centres and 2-lobed lip, are produced in autumn.
♀ ***H. x moorei* 'Tara',** (illus. p.220).
H. stenopetalum (illus. p.477). Upright, rhizomatous perennial. **H** 3–4m (10–13ft), **S** 1m (3ft) or more. Frost tender, min. 5°C (41°F). Has very large, thick-stems bearing lance-shaped, deep green leaves that are hairy beneath. Short-lived, white flowers, each with a 2-lobed lip, are borne in a spike, to 45cm (18in) long, in late summer and autumn. Is prone to wind damage.
H. thyrsiforme (illus. p.477). Upright, rhizomatous perennial. **H** 1–2m (3–6ft), **S** 50cm (20in). Frost tender, min. 5°C (41°F). Broadly lance-shaped leaves are dark green. Small, short-lived, white flowers, each with a 2-lobed lip and very long stamens, are borne in autumn-winter. Flower spike is wider than tall, which distinguishes it from other species.
H. yunnanense (illus. p.477). Upright, rhizomatous perennial. **H** 50–80cm (20–32in), **S** 30cm (12in). Half hardy. Has broadly lance-shaped, mid-green leaves. Short-lived, fragrant, cream and white flowers, each with a 2-lobed lip, are produced in summer.

HEDYOTIS

RUBIACEAE

Genus of mat-forming, summer-flowering perennials. Fully hardy. Thrives in a position in shade and on moist, sandy leaf mould. Propagate by division in spring or by seed in autumn.
H. michauxii, syn. *Houstonia serpyllifolia*, (Creeping bluets), illus. p.369.

HEDYSARUM

LEGUMINOSAE/PAPILIONACEAE

Genus of perennials, biennials and deciduous sub-shrubs. Fully hardy. Prefers a position in sun and in well-drained soil. Roots resent being disturbed. Propagate by seed in autumn or spring.
H. coronarium illus. p.235.

Heeria. See *Heterocentron*.
Heimerliodendron brunonianum. See *Pisonia umbellifera*.

HELENIUM

Sneezeweed

COMPOSITAE/ASTERACEAE

Genus of late summer- and autumn-flowering perennials, grown for their daisy-like flower heads, each with a prominent, central disc. Fully hardy. Needs a site in full sun and any well-drained soil. Propagate by division in spring or autumn. ⓘ All parts may cause severe discomfort if ingested; contact with foliage may aggravate skin allergies. See also feature panel p.248.
H. 'Biedermeier'. Clump-forming, erect, bushy perennial. **H** 120cm (48in), **S** 45cm (18in). Has lance-shaped, mid-green leaves. In late summer, erect stems bear sprays of yellow-tipped, red flower heads with a central, dark brown disc. The ray florets become reflexed with age.
H. 'Blopip'. See *H.* PIPSQUEAK.
H. 'Bressingham Gold'. Erect, bushy perennial with stout stems clothed in lance-shaped, mid-green leaves. **H** 1m (3ft), **S** 60cm (2ft). Sprays of bright yellow flower heads are produced in late summer and autumn.
H. 'Bruno' (p.248). Erect, bushy perennial. **H** 1.2m (4ft), **S** 75cm (2½ft). Sprays of deep bronze-red flower heads are borne in late summer–autumn. Stout stems are clothed in lance-shaped leaves.
♀ **H. 'Butterpat'** (illus. p.248). Compact perennial. **H** 1m (3ft), **S** 60cm (2ft). Has stout stems clothed in lance-shaped leaves. Bears sprays of rich deep yellow flower heads in late summer and autumn.
H. 'Coppelia'. Clump-forming, erect, bushy perennial. **H** to 80cm (32in), **S** 45cm (18in). Has lance-shaped, mid-green leaves. In mid–to late summer bears sprays of deep reddish-orange flower heads, which fade with age, with central, brown discs.
H. 'Double Trouble' (illus. p.248). Clump-forming, erect, bushy perennial. **H** to 80cm (32in), **S** 45cm (18in). Has lance-shaped, mid-green leaves. In mid- to late summer produces sprays of double, bright yellow flower heads with twin layers of ray florets, held horizontally.
H. 'Dunkelpracht'. Clump-forming, erect, bushy perennial. **H** to 1m (3ft), **S** 45cm (18in). Has lance-shaped, mid-green leaves. In late summer bears sprays of dark brown-red flower heads.
♀ **H. 'Feuersiegel'** (illus. p.248). Clump-forming, erect, bushy perennial. **H** to 100cm (36in) or more, **S** 45cm (18in). Has lance-shaped, mid-green leaves. In mid- to late summer produces sprays of rich yellow flower heads with horizontally held ray florets, marked with an irregular, orange-red band, and central, soft brown discs.
H. 'Indianersommer' (illus. p.248). Clump-forming, erect, bushy perennial. **H** to 100cm (36in) or more, **S** 45cm (18in). Has lance-shaped, mid-green leaves. In mid- to late summer bears sprays of dark brownish-red flower heads, ageing to orange and yellow, and central, greenish-brown discs.
♀ **H. 'Moerheim Beauty'** illus. p.254.
H. PIPSQUEAK ('Blopip'). Clump-forming, compact, bushy perennial. **H** to 60cm (2ft), **S** 30cm (1ft). Has lance-shaped, mid-green leaves. In mid- to late summer produces sprays of shuttlecock-shaped, yellow flower heads with short, reflexed ray florets and large, central, rich brown discs.
H. 'Potter's Wheel' (illus. p.248). Clump-forming, erect, bushy perennial. **H** to 80cm (32in), **S** 45cm (18in). Has lance-shaped, mid-green leaves. From mid-summer to autumn bears sprays of dark red flower heads with gold-edged ray florets and central, brown discs.
H. 'Red Army' (illus. p.248). Clump-forming, erect, bushy perennial. **H** to 90cm (36in), **S** 45cm (18in). Has lance-shaped, mid-green leaves. From mid-summer to mid-autumn produces sprays of reddish-orange flower heads, intensifying in colour as they age to dark red, with central, dark brown discs.
H. 'Riverton Gem'. Erect, bushy perennial. **H** 1.4m (4½ft), **S** 1m (3ft). Has sprays of red-and-gold flower heads in late summer–autumn. Stems are clothed in lance-shaped leaves.
♀ **H. 'Rubinzwerg'** (illus. p.248). Clump-forming, erect, bushy perennial. **H** to 100cm (39in), **S** 45cm (18in). Has lance-shaped, mid-green leaves. From mid-summer to autumn bears sprays of rich red flower heads with reflexed ray florets and central, dark brown discs.
♀ **H. 'Sahin's Early Flowerer'.** Clump-forming, erect, bushy perennial. **H** to 90cm (36in), **S** 45cm (18in). Has lance-shaped, mid-green leaves. From mid-summer until the first frosts produces large, bright reddish-orange flower heads with long ray florets, ageing to orange and warm yellow, and central, brown discs.
H. 'The Bishop'. Clump-forming, erect, bushy perennial. **H** to 90cm (36in), **S** 45cm (18in). Has lance-shaped, mid-green leaves. From mid-summer to autumn produces sprays of yellow flower heads with reflexed ray florets and large, central, brown discs.
♀ **H. 'Waltraut'** (illus. p.248). Clump-forming, erect, bushy perennial. **H** to 90cm (36in), **S** 45cm (18in). Has lance-shaped, mid-green leaves. From late summer produces sprays of copper-orange and yellow flower heads that intensify in colour as they age; the central disc is brown.
H. 'Wyndley'. Bushy perennial with branching stems. **H** 80cm (30in), **S** 50cm (20in). Bears sprays of daisy-like, orange-yellow flower heads for a long period in late summer and autumn. Foliage is dark green. Needs regular division in spring or autumn.

HELIANTHEMUM

Rock rose

CISTACEAE

Genus of evergreen, spring- to autumn-flowering shrubs and sub-shrubs, grown for their flowers. Is useful for rock gardens and dry banks. Fully to frost hardy. Needs full sun and well-drained soil. Cut back lightly after flowering. Propagate by semi-ripe cuttings in early summer.
♀ **H. 'Amy Baring'.** Evergreen, spreading shrub. **H** 10–15cm (4–6in), **S** 60cm (24in). Fully hardy. Small, oblong, light grey leaves are hairy beneath. In summer, bears a succession of saucer-shaped, orange-centred, deep yellow flowers in loose, terminal clusters.
H. apenninum illus. p.336.
H. 'Ben Hope'. Evergreen, domed shrub. **H** 23–30cm (9–12in), **S** 45cm (18in). Fully hardy. Bears small, linear, grey-green leaves and saucer-shaped, carmine-red flowers in mid-summer.
H. 'Ben More' illus. p.345.
H. 'Ben Nevis'. Evergreen, hummock-forming, compact shrub. **H** and **S** 15–23cm (6–9in). Fully hardy. Has small, linear, dark green leaves and, in mid-summer, saucer-shaped, orange flowers with bronze centres.
♀ **H. 'Fire Dragon'** illus. p.340.
H. 'Golden Queen'. Evergreen, domed, compact shrub. **H** 23cm (9in), **S** 30cm (12in). Fully hardy. Saucer-shaped, golden-yellow flowers appear amid small, linear, dark green leaves in mid-summer.
H. guttatum. See *Tuberaria guttata*.
♀ **H. 'Jubilee'.** Evergreen, domed, compact shrub. **H** 15–23cm (6–9in), **S** 23–30cm (9–12in). Fully hardy. Has small, linear, dark green leaves. Bears saucer-shaped, double, pale yellow flowers from spring to late summer.
H. oelandicum subsp. alpestre. Evergreen, open, twiggy shrub. **H** 7–12cm (3–5in), **S** 15cm (6in) or more. Fully hardy. Produces terminal clusters of 3–6 saucer-shaped, bright yellow flowers from early to mid-summer. Leaves are tiny, oblong and mid-green. Is suitable for growing in a trough.
H. 'Raspberry Ripple'. Evergreen, spreading shrub. **H** 15–23cm (6–9in), **S** 23–30cm (9–12in). Fully hardy. Saucer-shaped, red-centred, white flowers are borne in mid-summer. Has small, linear, grey-green leaves.
♀ **H. 'Rhodanthe Carneum'**, syn. *H.* 'Wisley Pink', illus. p.338.
H. umbellatum. See *Halimium umbellatum*.
H. 'Wisley Pink'. See *H.* 'Rhodanthe Carneum'.
♀ **H. 'Wisley Primrose'** illus. p.344.
H. 'Wisley White' illus. p.337.

HELIANTHUS

Sunflower

COMPOSITAE/ASTERACEAE

Genus of summer- and autumn-flowering annuals and perennials, grown for their large, daisy-like, usually yellow flower heads. May be invasive. Fully hardy. All need sun and well-drained soil; some prefer moist conditions. Needs staking. Propagate by seed or division in autumn or spring. ⓘ Contact with the foliage may aggravate skin allergies.
H. annuus. Fast-growing, erect annual. **H** 1–3m (3–10ft) or more, **S** 30–45cm (12–18in). Has oval, serrated, mid-green leaves. Daisy-like, brown- or purplish-centred, yellow flower heads, 30cm (12in) or more wide, are produced in summer. Tall, intermediate and dwarf cultivars are available. **'Music Box'** (dwarf) illus. p.322. **'Russian Giant'** (tall), **H** 3m (10ft) or more, produces yellow flower heads with green-brown centres. **'Teddy Bear'** (dwarf) illus. p.322.
***H. debilis* subsp. *cucumerifolius* 'Italian White'.** Erect perennial. **H** 1.2m (4ft), **S** 45–60cm (1½–2ft). In summer, has large, black-centred, creamy-white flower heads. Purple-mottled stems bear coarsely hairy, sharply toothed, glossy, mid-green leaves.
♀ **H. 'Lemon Queen'** illus. p.222.
♀ **H. 'Monarch'.** Erect perennial. **H** 2.2m (7ft), **S** 1m (3ft). Bears terminal, daisy-like, semi-double, golden-yellow flower heads on branching stems in late summer. Has lance-shaped, coarse, mid-green leaves.

Replant each spring to keep in check.
H. x multiflorus. Upright perennial. **H** 1.5m (5ft), **S** 60cm (2ft). Has large, yellow flower heads, with double centres surrounded by larger, rayed segments, in late summer and early autumn. Leaves are lance-shaped, coarse and mid-green.
♀ **'Capenoch Star'**, **H** 1.2m (4ft), has lemon-yellow flower heads. ♀ **'Loddon Gold'** illus. p.222.
H. orgyalis. See *H. salicifolius.*
♀ ***H. salicifolius***, syn. *H. orgyalis,* (Willow-leaved sunflower), illus. p.222.

HELICHRYSUM

COMPOSITAE/ASTERACEAE

Genus of summer- and autumn-flowering perennials, annuals and evergreen sub-shrubs and shrubs. When dried, flower heads are "everlasting". Fully hardy to frost tender, min. 5°C (41°F). Needs sun and well-drained soil. Propagate shrubs and sub-shrubs by heel or semi-ripe cuttings in summer; perennials by division or seed in spring; annuals by seed in spring.
H. angustifolium. See *H. italicum.*
H. bellidioides. See *Anaphalioides bellidioides.*
H. coralloides. See *Ozothamnus coralloides.*
♀ ***H. italicum***, syn. *H. angustifolium* (Curry plant). Evergreen, bushy sub-shrub. **H** 60cm (2ft), **S** 1m (3ft). Frost hardy. Has linear, aromatic, silvery-grey leaves. Broad clusters of small, oblong, bright yellow flower heads are produced on long, upright, white shoots during summer. **subsp. *serotinum*** (syn. *H. serotinum*), **H** and **S** 15cm (6in), is dome-shaped; stems and oval leaves are densely felted with white hairs. Dislikes winter wet and cold climates.
H. ledifolium. See *Ozothamnus ledifolius.*
H. marginatum of gardens. See *H. milfordiae.*
♀ ***H. milfordiae***, syn. *H. marginatum* of gardens. Evergreen, mat-forming, dense sub-shrub. **H** 5cm (2in), **S** 23cm (9in). Frost hardy. On sunny days in early summer, large, conical, red buds open into daisy-like, white flower heads with red-backed petals; they close in dull or wet weather. Has basal rosettes of oval, hairy, silver leaves. Prefers very gritty soil. Dislikes winter wet. Propagate in spring by rooting single rosettes.
♀ ***H. petiolare,*** syn. H. petiolatum of gardens. Evergreen shrub. **H** 50cm (20in), **S** 2m (6ft). Half hardy. Forms mounds of silver-green shoots and oval to heart-shaped, grey-felted leaves. Has daisy-like, creamy-yellow flower heads in summer. Is often grown as an annual for ground cover and edging. ♀ **'Limelight'** has lime-yellow leaves. **'Variegatum'** illus. p.165.
H. petiolatum of gardens. See *H. petiolare.*
H. rosmarinifolium. See *Ozothamnus rosmarinifolius.*
***H.* 'Schwefellicht'**, syn. *H.* 'Sulphur Light', illus. p.275.
H. selago. See *Ozothamnus selago.*
H. serotinum. See *H. italicum* subsp. *serotinum.*
♀ ***H. splendidum.*** Evergreen, bushy, dense shrub. **H** and **S** 1.2m (4ft). Frost hardy. Woolly, white shoots are clothed in small, oblong, silvery-grey leaves. Small, oblong, bright yellow flower heads produced in clusters from mid-summer to autumn or sometimes into winter.
***H.* 'Sulphur Light'.** See *H.* 'Schwefellicht'.

HELICONIA

Lobster claws

HELICONIACEAE/MUSACEAE

Genus of tufted perennials, evergreen in warm climates, grown for their spikes of colourful flowers and for the attractive foliage on younger plants. Frost tender, min. 18°C (64°F). Needs partial shade and humus-rich, well-drained soil. Water generously in growing season, very sparingly when plants die down in winter. Propagate by seed or division of rootstock in spring.
H. metallica. Tufted perennial. **H** to 3m (10ft), **S** 1m (3ft). Oblong, long-stalked leaves, to 60cm (2ft) long, are velvety-green above with paler veins, sometimes purple below. In summer, mature plants bear erect stems with tubular, glossy, greenish-white-tipped, red flowers enclosed in narrow, boat-shaped, green bracts.
H. psittacorum illus. p.478.

HELICTOTRICHON

GRAMINEAE/POACEAE

See also GRASSES, BAMBOOS, RUSHES and SEDGES.
♀ ***H. sempervirens***, syn. *Avena candida, A. sempervirens,* illus. p.288.

HELIOPSIS

COMPOSITAE/ASTERACEAE

Genus of summer-flowering perennials. Fully hardy. Requires sun and any well-drained soil. Propagate by seed or division in autumn or spring.
***H.* 'Ballet Dancer'.** Upright perennial. **H** 1–1.2m (3–4ft), **S** 60cm (2ft). Flowers freely in late summer, bearing double, yellow flower heads with frilled petals. Dark green leaves are coarse and serrated.
H. helianthoides* 'Incomparabilis'**. Upright perennial. **H** to 1.5m (5ft), **S** 60cm (2ft). Bears daisy-like, single, orange flower heads in late summer. Leaves are narrowly oval, coarsely toothed and mid-green. **'Patula'** bears flattish, semi-double, orange-yellow flower heads. **subsp. *scabra (syn. *H. scabra*) has very rough stems and leaves and double, orange-yellow flower heads. ♀ **subsp. *scabra* 'Light of Loddon'** (syn. *H.* 'Light of Loddon') illus. p.220.
***H.* 'Light of Loddon'.** See *H. helianthoides* subsp. *scabra* 'Light of Loddon'.
H. scabra. See *H. helianthoides* subsp. *scabra.*

HELIOTROPIUM

BORAGINACEAE

Genus of annuals, evergreen sub-shrubs and shrubs, grown for their fragrant flowers. Frost hardy to frost tender, min. 5–7°C (41–5°F). Needs full sun and fertile, well-drained soil. Water potted plants freely when in full growth, moderately at other times. In spring, tip prune young plants to promote a bushy habit and cut leggy, older plants back hard. Propagate by seed in spring, by greenwood cuttings in summer or by semi-ripe cuttings in early autumn.
H. arborescens, syn. *H. peruvianum,* illus. p.310.
H. peruvianum. See *H. arborescens.*

Helipterum manglesii. See *Rhodanthe manglesii.*
Helipterum roseum. See *Rhodanthe chlorocephala* subsp. *rosea.*

HELLEBORUS

Christmas rose

RANUNCULACEAE

Genus of perennials, some of which are evergreen, grown for their winter and spring flowers. Most deciduous species retain their old leaves over winter. These should be cut off in early spring as flower buds develop. Is excellent in woodlands. Fully to half hardy. Prefers semi-shade and moisture-retentive, well-drained soil. Propagate by fresh seed or division in autumn or very early spring. Is prone to aphid attack in early summer. ⓘ All parts may cause severe discomfort if ingested, and the sap may irritate skin on contact. See also feature panel p.281.
♀ ***H. argutifolius***, syn. *H. corsicus, H. lividus* subsp. *corsicus.* Evergreen, clump-forming perennial. **H** 60cm (24in), **S** 45cm (18in). Frost hardy. Divided, spiny, dark green leaves. Cup-shaped, pale green flowers are borne in large clusters in winter and spring. **'Pacific Frost'** illus. p.262. **'Silver Lace'** illus. p.262.
H. atrorubens of gardens. See *H. orientalis* subsp. *abchasicus* Early Purple Group.
***H. x ballardiae* 'December Dawn'**. Clump-forming perennial with deep bluish-green leaves. **H** to 35cm (14in), **S** 30cm (12in). Fully hardy. From mid-winter to early spring, bears saucer-shaped, white flowers, 6–8cm (2½–3in) across, flushed pinkish-purple, maturing to a dull metallic purple.
H. corsicus. See *H. argutifolius.*
H. cyclophyllus illus. p.283.
***H. x ericsmithii* 'Bob's Best'** illus. p.255. Ivory Prince **('Walivor')** illus. p.256.
♀ ***H. foetidus*** illus. p.283. **Wester Flisk Group**, illus. p.283.
H. x hybridus (Lenten rose). Evergreen, clump-forming perennial. **H** and **S** 45cm (18in). Fully hardy. Has dense, divided foliage, above which rise nodding, cup-shaped, white, pink or purple flowers, sometimes darker spotted, in winter or early spring. There is a range of single- and double-flowered cultivars available in various colours, including the following: double, plum; double, slate; double, white; double, white with spots; single, apricot; single, green; single, red; single, white with spots; single, yellow; single, yellow with spots (all illus. p.281). Ashwood Garden hybrids (double, black, illus. p.281; double, pink, illus. p.281). Bradfield hybrids (double, apricot with spots, illus. p. 281). Harvington hybrids (double, apricot, illus. p. 281; single, white, illus. p.281).
♀ ***H. lividus.*** Evergreen, clump-forming perennial. **H** and **S** 45cm (18in). Half hardy. Has 3-parted, mid-green leaves, marbled pale green, purplish-green below, with obliquely oval, slightly toothed or entire leaflets. Produces large clusters of cup-shaped, purple-suffused, yellow-green flowers in late winter. **subsp. *corsicus*** see *H. argutifolius.*
♀ ***H. x nigercors*** illus. p.281.
♀ ***H. niger*** (Christmas rose). Evergreen, clump-forming perennial. **H** and **S** 30cm (12in). Fully hardy. Has divided, deep green leaves and cup-shaped, nodding, white flowers, with golden stamens, borne in winter or early spring. **'HGC Josef Lemper'**, illus. p.281. **'Potter's Wheel'** illus. p.281.
H. odorus illus. p.283.
***H. orientalis* subsp. *abchasicus* Early Purple Group,** syn. *H. atrorubens* of gardens. Clump-forming perennial. **H** and **S** 30cm (1ft). Fully hardy. Shallowly cup-shaped, deep purple flowers are borne in late winter. Has palmate, deeply divided, toothed, glossy, dark green leaves.
H. purpurascens illus. p.260.
H. x sternii illus. p.262. **'Boughton Beauty'** illus. p.283.
H. thibetanus, illus. p.256.
H. viridis (Green hellebore). Deciduous, clump-forming perennial. **H** and **S** 30cm (12in). Fully hardy. Has divided, dark green leaves and cup-shaped, green flowers in late winter or early spring.

HELONIAS

LILIACEAE/MELIANTHACEAE

Genus of one species of spring-flowering perennial. Fully hardy. Is excellent when grown in bog gardens. Requires an open, sunny position and moist to wet soil. Propagate by division in spring or by seed in autumn.
H. bullata (Swamp pink). Rosetted, clump-forming perennial. **H** 38–45cm (15–18in), **S** 30cm (12in). Produces rosettes of strap-shaped, fresh green leaves, above which dense racemes of small, fragrant, star-shaped, pinkish-purple flowers are borne in spring.

HELONIOPSIS

LILIACEAE/MELANTHIACEAE

Genus of spring-flowering, rosette-forming perennials. Fully hardy. Grow in semi-shade and in moist soil. Propagate by division in autumn or by seed in autumn or spring.
H. orientalis illus. p.256.

HELWINGIA

HELWINGIACEAE

Genus of deciduous shrubs, bearing flowers and showy fruits directly on leaf surfaces, grown mainly for botanical interest. Requires separate male and female plants in order to produce fruits. Fully hardy. Needs sun or semi-shade and moist soil. Propagate by softwood cuttings in summer.
H. japonica. Deciduous, bushy, open shrub. **H** and **S** 1.5m (5ft). Oval, bright green leaves have bristle-like teeth. In early summer, has tiny, star-shaped, green flowers at centre of each leaf, then spherical, black fruits.

Helxine soleirolii. See *Soleirolia soleirolii.*

HEMEROCALLIS

Daylily

LILIACEAE/HEMEROCALLIDACEAE

Genus of perennials, some of which are semi-evergreen or evergreen. Flowers, borne in succession, each last for only a day. Fully hardy. Does best in full sun and fertile, moist soil. Propagate by division in autumn or spring. Cultivars raised from seed will not come true to type; species may come true if grown in isolation from other daylilies. Slug and snail control is essential in early spring when young foliage appears. See also feature panel pp.244–245.

***H.* 'Always Afternoon'** (illus. p.244). Robust, semi-evergreen, clump-forming perennial. **H** 55cm (22in), **S** to 75cm (2½ft). In summer and again in autumn, produces rounded, slightly ruffled, lavender-mauve flowers, each with a dark purple band above the yellow-green throat.

***H.* 'Arctic Snow'.** Deciduous, clump-forming perennial. **H** 55cm (22in), **S** 50cm (20in). Produces huge, funnel-shaped, ivory-white flowers, with green throats and black anthers, from mid-summer to early autumn.

H. aurantiaca. Robust, semi-evergreen perennial, spreading freely from underground runners. **H** 90cm (3ft), **S** 1m (3ft) or more. Produces numerous funnel-shaped, burnt-orange flowers, with yellowish midribs, over a long period in summer.

♡ ***H.* 'Berlin Red'.** Vigorous, deciduous or semi-evergreen, clump-forming perennial. **H** 70–90cm (28–36in), **S** 60cm (24in). In mid-summer, produces open, rounded, rich velvety-red flowers with a blackish-red bloom at the margins and yellow midribs and throats.

***H.* 'Betty Woods'.** Robust, cream spreading evergreen, clump-forming perennial. **H** 65cm (26in), **S** 60cm (2ft). Large, peony-like, yellow flowers are borne in mid- and late summer.

***H.* 'Black Magic'** (illus. p.245). Deciduous, clump-forming perennial. **H** and **S** 90cm (36in). Has star-shaped, pale-edged, dark reddish-black flowers, with green throats, from mid-summer to early autumn.

***H.* 'Bonanza'** (illus. p.245). Vigorous, deciduous or semi-evergreen, clump-forming perennial. **H** 1m (3ft), **S** 70cm (28in). Produces open, star-like, bright yellow flowers, with strongly red-marked centres, in mid-summer.

***H.* 'Brocaded Gown'.** Semi-evergreen, clump-forming perennial. **H** and **S** to 60cm (2ft). In summer, has rounded, ruffled creamy-yellow flowers.

♡ ***H.* 'Burning Daylight'** (illus. p.245). Robust, deciduous or semi-evergreen, clump-forming perennial. **H** 75cm (2½ft), **S** 60cm (2ft). Produces orange-brown flowers, with paler midribs and red marks around the throat bases, over a long period in summer.

***H.* 'Canadian Border Patrol'** (illus. p.244). Vigorous, semi-evergreen, clump-forming perennial. **H** 65cm (26in), **S** 60cm (24in). Produces masses of funnel-shaped, cream flowers with purple throats from mid-summer to early autumn.

♡ ***H.* 'Cartwheels'** (illus. p.245). Deciduous, clump-forming perennial. **H** 75cm (30in), **S** 60cm (24in). In mid-summer has trumpet-shaped, broad, deep yellow to orange flowers, with small, green throats and widely spreading petals.

***H.* 'Cathy's Sunset'** (illus. p.245). Deciduous, clump-forming perennial. **H** 60cm (24in), **S** 50cm (20in). From mid-summer to early autumn; bears small, funnel-shaped flowers each with 3 yellow-striped, brick-red, inner petals and 3 yellow, outer petals.

***H.* 'Cat's Cradle'.** Semi-evergreen, clump-forming perennial. H 1m (3ft), **S** 75cm (2½ft). In summer, produces large, spider-shaped, bright yellow flowers.

***H.* 'Cherry Cheeks'** (illus. p.244). Vigorous, deciduous or semi-evergreen, clump-forming perennial. **H** 80cm (32in), **S** 50cm (20in). Produces bright cherry-red flowers, with white midribs, over a long period in summer.

***H.* 'Chicago Apache'.** Very vigorous, deciduous, clump-forming perennial. **H** 65cm (26in), **S** 50cm (20in). Funnel-shaped, ruffled, rich scarlet flowers with white midribs, lemon-green throats and black anthers, are borne above prolific leaves in summer. Is very adaptable.

***H.* 'Chicago Sunrise'** (illus. p.245). Vigorous, clump-forming perennial. **H** 70cm (28in), **S** 85cm (34in). Very rounded, slightly ruffled, rich yellow flowers, with faint bronze bands and darker throats, are borne in summer.

***H.* 'Children's Festival'.** Deciduous, clump-forming perennial. **H** 55cm (22in), **S** 50cm (20in). Unusually thick petals form funnel-shaped flowers, with rosy tints and apricot throats, from mid-summer to early autumn.

***H.* 'Christmas Is'.** Vigorous, deciduous, clump-forming perennial. **H** and **S** 60cm (24in). Funnel-shaped flowers, with green throats, open from mid-summer to early autumn.

***H.* 'Chorus Line'.** Extended-blooming, semi-evergreen, clump-forming perennial. **H** 50cm (20in), **S** 60cm (24in). Produces remontant, triangular, slightly fragrant, bright pink flowers, with pink- and yellow-marked petals and dark green throats, from early to mid-summer.

H. citrina (illus. p.245). Vigorous, coarse-growing, clump-forming perennial. **H** and **S** 75cm (2½ft). Many large, very fragrant, trumpet-shaped, rich lemon-yellow flowers open at night in mid-summer; each lasts one day.

♡ ***H.* 'Corky'.** Clump-forming perennial. **H** and **S** 45cm (18in). Bears trumpet-shaped, lemon-yellow flowers, brown on outsides, in late spring and early summer. Flowers, borne prolifically, last only a day.

***H.* 'Cream Drop'** (illus. p.245). Robust, deciduous or semi-evergreen, clump-forming perennial. **H** 60cm (2ft), **S** 45cm (18in). In mid-summer, produces numerous, scented, well-formed, creamy-yellow flowers, with slightly ruffled margins.

***H.* 'Crimson Pirate'.** Vigorous, deciduous, clump-forming perennial. **H** 75cm (2½ft). **S** 50cm (20in). Produces open, star-shaped, bright crimson-red blooms, with paler midribs, in mid- and late summer.

***H.* 'Custard Candy'.** Vigorous, deciduous, clump-forming perennial. **H** 60cm (2ft), **S** 40cm (16in). In early and mid-summer produces an abundance of rounded, creamy-yellow flowers, each with a feathered band around the greenish-yellow eye.

H. dumortieri (illus. p.245). Compact, clump-forming perennial. **H** 45cm (1½ft), **S** 60cm (2ft). In early summer, produces fragrant, trumpet-shaped, brown-backed, golden-yellow flowers. Mid-green leaves are strap-shaped, stiff and coarse.

***H.* 'Ed Murray'.** Vigorous, free-flowering, deciduous or semi-evergreen, clump-forming perennial. **H** 65–70cm (26–28in), **S** 50cm (20in). Has rounded, ruffled, deep maroon-red flowers, with yellowish-green throats, in early and mid-summer.

***H.* 'Eenie Weenie'.** Clump-forming perennial. **H** and **S** 30cm (1ft). Has masses of clear yellow flowers in early summer.

H. flava. See *H. lilioasphodelus.*

***H.* 'Frans Hals'** (illus. p.245). Strong-growing, free-flowering, deciduous, clump-forming perennial. **H** 60cm (2ft), **S** 40cm (16in). In mid- and late summer, bears open, star-like flowers, with yellow outer petals and three cinnamon-red inner petals with yellow midribs.

H. fulva (Fulvous daylily, Tawny daylily; illus. p.245). Vigorous, clump-forming perennial. **H** 1m (3ft), **S** 75cm (2½ft). Trumpet-shaped, tawny-orange flowers appear from mid- to late summer above a mound of strap-shaped, light green leaves. **'Flore Pleno'** (illus. p.245), **H** 75cm (30in), has double flowers with dark red eyes. **'Kwanzo Variegated'** has leaves variably marked with white.

***H.* 'Gentle Shepherd'.** Semi-evergreen, clump-forming perennial. **H** 70cm (28in), **S** 60cm (24in). In early and mid-summer, has ruffled, white flowers, with green throats.

♡ ***H.* 'Golden Chimes'** (illus. p.245). Clump-forming perennial of graceful habit. **H** 75cm (2½ft), **S** 60cm (2ft). Bears small, delicate, trumpet-shaped, golden-yellow flowers, with a brown reverse, lasting only a day, from early to mid-summer.

***H.* 'Golden Prize'.** Vigorous, deciduous, clump-forming perennial. **H** 65–70cm (26–28in), **S** 40–50cm (16–20in). Produces large, rounded, golden-yellow flowers in mid- and late summer.

***H.* 'Grape Velvet'.** Deciduous, clump-forming perennial. **H** 50cm (20in), **S** 60cm (24in). From early to late summer; produces funnel-shaped flowers, each with rather pointed, deep wine-red petals, a central, paler stripe and a yellow-green throat.

♡ ***H.* 'Green Flutter'** (illus. p.245). Semi-evergreen, clump-forming perennial. **H** 50cm (20in), **S** 40cm (16in). Produces masses of star-shaped, ruffled, canary-yellow flowers, with bright green throats, in late summer and early autumn.

***H.* 'Happy Returns'.** Deciduous, clump-forming perennial. **H** 40cm (16in), **S** 60cm (24in). Bears small, fragrant, rounded flowers from early to late summer.

♡ ***H.* 'Helle Berlinerin'.** Evergreen, clump-forming perennial. **H** 75cm (30in), **S** 80cm (32in). Has rounded flowers, with a faint apricot blush and yellow throats, borne on unusually strong stems in mid-summer.

***H.* 'Hyperion'.** Clump-forming perennial. **H** and **S** 90cm (3ft). In mid-summer, has very fragrant, lily-like, pale lemon-yellow flowers.

***H.* 'Joan Senior'** (illus. p.244). Vigorous, semi-evergreen, clump-forming perennial. **H** 63cm (25in), **S** 1m (3ft). Open trumpet-shaped, almost pure white flowers are produced on well-branched stems from mid- to late summer.

***H.* 'Jolyene Nichole'.** Semi-evergreen, clump-forming perennial. **H** and **S** 50cm (20in). Bears rounded, ruffled, rose-pink flowers amid lush, blue-green leaves.

***H.* 'Lady Fingers'.** Semi-evergreen, clump-forming perennial with narrow leaves. **H** 80cm (32in), **S** 75cm (30in). In mid-summer, bears spider-shaped, pale yellow-green flowers with green throats and spoon-shaped petals.

***H.* 'Lark Song'.** Vigorous, deciduous, clump-forming perennial. **H** 80–90cm (32–36in), **S** 60cm (2ft). Has fragrant, open bowl-shaped, bright pale yellow blooms, on blackish stems, in mid- and late summer.

♡ ***H.* 'Lemon Bells'** (illus. p.245). Evergreen, clump-forming perennial. **H** 85cm (24in), **S** 60cm (24in). Produces prolific sprays of small, orange-yellow flowers, with green-tinted throats, in mid-summer.

♡ ***H. lilioasphodelus,*** syn. *H. flava* (illus. p.245). Robust, clump-forming, spreading perennial. **H** and **S** 60cm (2ft) or more. Very fragrant, delicate, lemon- to chrome-yellow flowers, lasting only 1 or 2 days, are borne in late spring and early summer. Strap-shaped leaves are mid-green.

***H.* 'Little Grapette'** (illus. p.245). Free-flowering, deciduous, clump-forming perennial. **H** 45cm (18in), **S** 30cm (12in). Has lightly ruffled, wine-purple flowers, with yellow throats, in mid- and late summer.

***H.* 'Little Wine Cup'** (illus. p.245). Vigorous, deciduous, clump-forming perennial. **H** 45cm (18in), **S** 30cm (12in). Produces masses of lightly ruffled, wine-red flowers, with paler midribs and yellow-green throats, in early and mid-summer.

***H.* 'Luxury Lace'** (illus. p.244). Vigorous, deciduous, clump-forming perennial. **H** 75cm (30in), **S** 40cm (16in). Has fragrant, funnel-shaped, vibrant orange flowers with dark green throats from mid-summer to early autumn.

***H.* 'Mallard'.** Deciduous, clump-forming perennial. **H** and **S** 60cm (24in). Produces funnel-shaped flowers, with a slender, central, pale stripe on each petal, from mid-summer to early autumn.

♡ ***H.* 'Marion Vaughn'.** Clump-forming perennial. **H** 1m (3ft), **S** 60cm (2ft). Produces fragrant, trumpet-shaped, green-throated, pale lemon-yellow flowers, in late summer, each lasting only a day. Each petal has a raised, near-white midrib.

***H.* 'Mauna Loa'** (illus. p.245). Vigorous, free-flowering, evergreen, clump-forming perennial. **H** 55cm (22in), **S** 1m (3ft). Produces rounded, bright tangerine-orange flowers, with chartreuse throats

and contrasting black anthers, in mid- to late summer.
***H.* 'Michele Coe'.** Vigorous, evergreen or semi-evergreen, clump-forming perennial. **H** 70cm (28in), **S** 85cm (34in). In mid-summer, has rounded, pale apricot flowers with light lavender-pink midribs.
***H.* 'Millie Schlumpf'.** Vigorous, free-flowering, evergreen, clump-forming perennial. **H** 50cm (20in), **S** 60cm (24in). Triangular to rounded, pale pink flowers, with deeper pink bands and green throats, are borne in early to mid-summer.
H. minor (Grass-leaved daylily). Compact, clump-forming perennial. **H** 40cm (16in), **S** 45cm (18in). In early summer bears fragrant, trumpet-shaped, lemon-yellow flowers, with tawny-backed, outer petals. Has narrowly strap-shaped, mid-green leaves that die back in early autumn.
♀ ***H.* 'Missenden'** (illus. p.245). Vigorous, deciduous, clump-forming perennial. **H** 1.1m (3½ft), **S** 60–70cm (24–28in). In mid-summer has large, funnel-shaped, rich velvety-red flowers with a velvety, black sheen and yellow midribs.
♀ ***H.* 'Neyron Rose'** (illus. p.244). Vigorous, deciduous, clump-forming perennial. **H** 1m (3ft), **S** 60–70cm (24–28in). In early and mid-summer, has pink-suffused, orange-brown flowers, with white midribs.
***H.* 'Night Beacon'** (illus. p.244). Evergreen, clump-forming perennial. **H** 70cm (28in), **S** 75cm (30in). In early and mid-summer, produces rounded, very dark burgundy-black flowers, with black-purple bands, lemon-green throats and pearl-white midribs.
***H.* 'Pardon Me'** (illus. p.244). Deciduous, clump-forming perennial. **H** 45cm (18in), **S** 60cm (24in). Small, fragrant, funnel-shaped, bright burgundy-red flowers, with greenish-yellow throats, are borne from mid-summer to early autumn.
♀ ***H.* 'Pink Damask'** (illus. p.244). Vigorous, deciduous, free-flowering, clump-forming perennial. **H** 1m (3ft), **S** 60–70cm (24–28in). Produces masses of rich salmon-pink flowers in summer.
***H.* 'Prairie Blue Eyes'** (illus. p.244). Semi-evergreen, clump-forming perennial. **H** 80cm (32in), **S** 90cm (36in). In mid-summer, produces lavender flowers, banded with blue-purple, that have green throats.
***H.* 'Real Wind'.** Vigorous, free-flowering, evergreen, clump-forming perennial with dense foliage. **H** 65cm (26in), **S** 1m (3ft). Produces triangular to round, pale buff to salmon-pink flowers, with bold rose-pink eyes, in mid- to late summer.
♀ ***H.* 'Red Precious'** illus. p.235.
***H.* 'Rose Emily'.** Semi-evergreen, clump-forming perennial. **H** and **S** 45cm (18in). In mid-summer, bears rounded, rose-pink flowers with ruffled margined petals and pale green throats.
***H.* 'Ruffled Apricot'.** Slow-growing, clump-forming perennial. Large, deep apricot flowers, with lavender-pink midribs, are ruffled at margins.
***H.* 'Scarlet Oak'.** Vigorous, semi-evergreen, clump-forming perennial. **H** 1.1m (3½ft), **S** 60–70cm (24–28in). In mid- and late summer, has open rounded, scarlet flowers, with white midribs.
***H.* 'Scarlet Orbit'.** Semi-evergreen, clump-forming perennial. **H** 50cm (20in), **S** 65cm (26in). Scarlet flowers with green throats, open flat in mid-summer.
***H.* 'Siloam Baby Talk'** (illus. p.244). Vigorous, free-flowering, deciduous, clump-forming perennial. **H** 35–40cm (14–16in), **S** 20–25cm (8–10in). Has rounded, ruffled-margined, creamy-pink flowers, with pale purple bands above bright green throats, in mid-summer.
***H.* 'Siloam Ethel Smith'.** Evergreen, clump-forming perennial. **H** 50cm (20in), **S** 45cm (18in). In mid-summer, bears masses of rounded, creamy-beige flowers, with triangular, red, yellow and olive-green eyes.
***H.* 'Siloam Virginia Henson'.** Clump-forming perennial. **H** 45cm (18in), **S** 65cm (26in). In early summer, bears rounded, ruffled, creamy-pink flowers banded with rose-pink and with green throats.
***H.* 'Solano Bulls Eye'.** Vigorous, free-flowering, evergreen, clump-forming perennial. **H** 50cm (20in), **S** 75cm (30in). Produces round, bright yellow flowers, with deep brownish-purple eyes, over a long period from early to late summer.
***H.* 'Stafford'** (illus. p.245). Vigorous, evergreen, clump-forming perennial. **H** 70cm (28in), **S** 1m (3ft). In mid-summer, bears masses of star-shaped, scarlet flowers with yellow midribs and throats.
♀ ***H.* 'Stoke Poges'** (illus. p.244). Deciduous, clump-forming perennial. **H** 70cm (28in), **S** 50cm (20in). In mid-summer has fragrant, funnel-shaped, salmon-pink flowers with reflexed petal tips and a deep pink zone around each golden throat.
***H.* 'Strawberry Candy'.** Robust, deciduous or semi-evergreen, clump-forming perennial. **H** 75cm (30in), **S** 50cm (20in). In early and mid-summer, bears bright apricot-pink flowers, with red picotee margins and ruby-red marks around yellowish throats.
***H.* 'Strutter's Ball'.** Deciduous, clump-forming perennial. **H** and **S** 60cm (24in). Has funnel-shaped, rich deep, blue-purple flowers, each with a silvery zone above small, lemon-yellow throat, from mid-summer to early autumn.
***H.* 'Summer Wine'** (illus. p.244). Strong-growing, deciduous, clump-forming perennial. **H** 60cm (2ft), **S** 45cm (18in). In early and mid-summer, bears open, soft purple flowers, with yellowish-green throats and very pale purple to white midribs. Broad inner petals are slightly ruffled.
***H.* 'Super Purple'.** Clump-forming perennial. **H** 68cm (27in), **S** 65cm (26in). Bears rounded, ruffled, velvety, red-purple flowers, with lime-green throats, in mid-summer.
♀ ***H.* 'Whichford'** (illus. p.245). Deciduous, clump-forming perennial. **H** 70cm (28in), **S** 50cm (20in). Fragrant, slightly star-shaped, green-budded, clear lemon-yellow flowers, with green throats, are borne on stout stems from mid-summer.
***H.* 'White Temptation'.** Semi-evergreen, clump-forming perennial. **H** 75cm (30in), **S** 65cm (26in). Funnel-shaped white flowers, with slightly crinkled edges and green throats, are produced from mid-summer to early autumn.

HEMIGRAPHIS

ACANTHACEAE

Genus of annuals and evergreen perennials, usually grown for their foliage. Frost tender, min. 15°C (59°F). Grows well in bright but not direct sunlight and in moist but well-drained soil. Water frequently during growing season, less in winter. Regularly cut back straggly stems to tidy. Propagate by stem cuttings in spring or summer.
H. repanda illus. p.473.

HEMIORCHIS

ZINGIBERACEAE

Genus of herbaceous, rhizomatous perennials, grown for their orchid-like flowers, which emerge above ground before the leaves. Frost hardy to frost tender, min. 5°C (41°F). Grow in humus-rich, moist but well-drained soil in shade. Is more tolerant of winter wet than most gingers, so water occasionally during dormancy. Propagate by division of the rhizome in early spring.
H. patlingii. Herbaceous, rhizomatous perennial. **H** and **S** 30cm (12in). Frost hardy if dormant. Stem, 10–15cm (4–6in) long, produces up to 20 flowers, opening in succession in spring, each with 3 pale brown outer lobes surrounding a deep red-veined, golden-yellow inner lobe. Has broadly lance-shaped, glossy, mid-green leaves, to 15cm (6in) long.

HEPATICA

RANUNCULACEAE

Genus of very variable perennials, some of which are semi-evergreen. Flowers are produced in early spring before new leaves are properly formed. Fully hardy. Needs partial shade and deep, humus-rich, moist soil. Stout, much-branched rootstock resents disturbance. Propagate by seed when fresh or by division or removing side shoots in spring.
H. angulosa. See *H. transsilvanica*.
***H. x media* 'Ballardii'.** Slow-growing, dome-shaped perennial. **H** 10cm (4in), **S** 30cm (12in). Has rounded, 3-lobed, stalked, soft green leaves and, in early spring, shallowly cup-shaped, many-petalled, intense blue flowers. Fully double, coloured forms are also known. Propagate by division only.
♀ ***H. nobilis***, syn. *Anemone hepatica, H. triloba*. Slow-growing, semi-evergreen, dome-shaped perennial. **H** 8cm (3in), **S** 10–12cm (4–5in). Bears rounded, 3-lobed, fleshy, mid-green leaves. Shallowly cup-shaped, many-petalled flowers – white through pink to carmine, pale to deep blue or purple – are produced in early spring. Fully double, coloured forms are also known. Is excellent in a woodland or rock garden. **var. *japonica*** illus. p.355.
♀ ***H. transsilvanica***, syn. *H. angulosa*. Semi-evergreen, spreading perennial. **H** 8cm (3in), **S** 20cm (8in). Shallowly cup-shaped, many-petalled flowers, varying from blue to white or pink, are produced in early spring amid rounded, 3-lobed, hairy, green leaves. Fully double, coloured forms are also known.
H. triloba. See *H. nobilis*.

Heptapleurum. See *Schefflera*.

HERBERTIA

IRIDACEAE

Genus of spring-flowering bulbs, grown mainly for their iris-like flowers. Half hardy. Requires full sun and well-drained soil. Reduce watering when bulb dies down after flowering. Propagate by seed in autumn.
H. pulchella. Spring-flowering bulb. **H** 10–15cm (4–6in), **S** 3–5cm (1¼–2in). Leaves are narrowly lance-shaped, pleated, erect and basal. Bears a succession of upward-facing, violet-blue flowers, 5–6cm (2–2½in) wide and usually with dark-spotted centres.

HERMANNIA

STERCULIACEAE

Genus of evergreen sub-shrubs and shrubs, grown mainly for their flowers. Frost tender, min. 7°C (45°F). Prefers full light and fertile, well-drained soil. Water containerized plants freely when in full growth, moderately at other times. Tip prune young plants to produce well-branched specimens. Propagate by softwood or greenwood cuttings in late spring or summer.
H. candicans. See *H. incana*.
H. incana, syn. *H. candicans*. Evergreen, bushy sub-shrub. **H** and **S** 60cm (24in) or more. Oval to oblong leaves are covered with white down beneath. Produces small, nodding, bell-shaped, bright yellow flowers, carried in terminal clusters, to 15cm (6in) long, in spring–summer.

HERMODACTYLUS

IRIDACEAE

Genus of one species of spring-flowering tubers, with elongated, finger-like rootstock, grown mainly for its iris-like flowers. Fully hardy. Requires a hot, sunny site, where tubers will ripen well in summer, and well-drained soil. Grows particularly successfully on hot, chalky soils. Propagate by division in late summer.
H. tuberosus, syn. *Iris tuberosa*, illus. p.406.

HESPERALOE

AGAVACEAE

Genus of basal-rosetted, perennial succulents with very narrow, strap-shaped, grooved, dark green leaves, that often have peeling, white fibres at their margins. Is closely related to *Agave* and *Yucca*. Frost tender, min. 3°C (37°F). Grows well in a sunny situation and in very well-drained soil. Propagate by seed or division in spring or summer, or from offsets, freely produced at base.
H. parviflora, syn. *Yucca parviflora*, illus. p.484.

HESPERANTHA

IRIDACEAE

Genus of spring-flowering corms with spikes of small, funnel- or cup-shaped flowers. Half hardy. Needs full sun and

well-drained soil. Plant in autumn, water through winter and dry off corms after flowering. Propagate by seed in autumn or spring.
H. buhrii. See *H. cucullata*.
♀ ***H. coccinea.*** See *Schizostylis coccinea*.
H. cucullata, syn. *H. buhrii*. Spring-flowering corm. **H** 20–30cm (8–12in), **S** 3–5cm (1¼–2in). Has linear, erect leaves on lower part of branched stems, each of which produces a spike of up to 7 cup-shaped, white flowers, flushed pink or purple outside, that open only at evening.

HESPERIS

CRUCIFERAE/BRASSICACEAE

Genus of late spring- or summer-flowering annuals and perennials. Fully hardy. Requires a sunny site and well-drained soil. *H. matronalis* tolerates poor soil. Tends to become woody at base, so raise new stock from seed every few years. Propagate by basal cuttings in spring or by seed in autumn or spring.
H. matronalis illus. p.230.

HESPEROCALLIS

LILIACEAE/HYACINTHACEAE

Genus of spring- to summer-flowering bulbs. Half hardy. Needs a sunny, well-drained site. Is difficult to cultivate in all but warm, dry areas; in cool, damp climates, protect in a cool greenhouse. Requires ample water in spring, followed by a hot, dry period during its summer dormancy. Propagate by seed in autumn.
H. undulata. Spring- to summer-flowering bulb. **H** 20–50cm (8–20in), **S** 10–15cm (4–6in). Has a cluster of long, narrow, wavy-margined leaves, semi-erect or prostrate, at base. Stout stems each bear a spike of upward-facing, funnel-shaped, white flowers, with a central, green stripe along each of the 6 petals.

Hesperoyucca. See *Yucca*.

HETEROCENTRON,

SYN. HEERIA

MELASTOMATACEAE

Genus of evergreen, summer- and autumn-flowering perennials and shrubs. Frost tender, min. 5°C (41°F). Requires sun and well-drained soil. Propagate by softwood or stem-tip cuttings in late winter or early spring.
H. elegans, syn. *Schizocentron elegans*, illus. p.472.

HETEROMELES

ROSACEAE

Genus of one species of evergreen tree or large shrub, grown mainly for its showy clusters of holly-like fruits. Frost hardy. Requires fertile, well-drained soil in full sun, with protection from cold, drying winds in winter. Propagate by seed in autumn or by semi-ripe cuttings in summer.
H. arbutifolia. See *H. salicifolia*.
H. salicifolia, syn. *H. arbutifolia*, *Photinia arbutifolia* (Christmas berry, Toyon). Evergreen, bushy, spreading shrub or tree. **H** 6m (20ft), **S** 8m (25ft). Has oblong, sharply toothed, leathery, glossy, dark green leaves. Broad, flat heads of small, 5-petalled, white flowers, produced in late summer, are succeeded by large clusters of rounded, red fruits.

HEUCHERA

Alum root

SAXIFRAGACEAE

Genus of evergreen, summer-flowering perennials forming large clumps of leaves, that are often tinted bronze or purple. Makes good ground cover. Fully to frost hardy. Prefers semi-shaded position and moisture-retentive but well-drained soil. Propagate species by seed in autumn or by division in autumn or spring, and cultivars by division only, using young, outer portions of crown. See also feature panel p.282.
***H.* 'Amber Waves'** (illus. p.282). Evergreen, clump-forming perennial. **H** 20–30cm (8–12in), **S** to 50cm (20in). Fully hardy. Rounded, lobed, lightly ruffled orange-yellow leaves are pale burgundy underneath. In summer, produces loose sprays of small, pendent, bell-shaped, light-rose flowers.
***H. americana* 'Harry Hay'.** Vigorous, evergreen, clump-forming perennial. **H** 50–100cm (20–39in), **S** 80cm (32in) or more. Fully hardy. Has large, rounded, lobed, purplish-brown leaves. In summer, produces tall spires of pendent, bell-shaped, white flowers.
***H.* 'Beauty Colour'** (illus. p.282). Evergreen, clump-forming perennial. **H** 20–30cm (8–12in), **S** to 50cm (20in). Fully hardy. Rounded, lobed, burgundy-veined leaves are marbled with silver and bordered with green. Leaf colour intensifies in cold periods. In summer, produces loose, arching sprays of small, pendent, bell-shaped, ivory flowers.
***H.* 'Black Beauty'** (illus. p.282). Evergreen, clump-forming, rather compact perennial. **H** 20–25cm (8–10in), **S** to 25cm (10in). Fully hardy. Rounded, lobed, ruffled, glossy, dark purple-black leaves are held rather upright. In summer, produces loose sprays of small, pendent, bell-shaped, white flowers.
♀ ***H.* 'Blackbird'** (illus. p.282). Evergreen, clump-forming perennial. **H** 25–30cm (10–12in), **S** to 30cm (12in). Fully hardy. Has rounded, lobed, rather ruffled, maroon-brown leaves. In summer, produces loose sprays of small, pendent, bell-shaped, rose-pink flowers.
♀ ***H.* 'Can-can'** (illus. p.282). Vigorous, evergreen, clump-forming perennial. **H** and **S** 50cm (20in). Fully hardy. Rounded, lobed, ruffled, dark-veined, silver-grey leaves are rich wine-red beneath; leaves turn pinkish with cooler conditions. In summer, produces loose sprays of small, pendent, bell-shaped, ivory flowers.
***H.* 'Coral Cloud'.** Evergreen, clump-forming perennial. **H** 45–75cm (18–30in), **S** 30–45cm (12–18in). Fully hardy. In early summer, bears long, feathery sprays of small, pendent, bell-shaped, coral-red flowers. Leaves are rounded, lobed, toothed, glistening and dark green.
***H.* 'Chocolate Ruffles'** (illus. p.282). Evergreen, clump-forming perennial. **H** and **S** 30cm (12in). Fully hardy. Rounded, lobed, ruffled, chocolate-brown leaves have burgundy undersides. In summer, produces loose sprays of small, pendent, bell-shaped, white flowers.
***H.* 'Cinnabar Silver'** (illus. p.282). Evergreen, clump-forming perennial. **H** 30cm (12in), **S** 50cm (20in). Fully hardy. Forms a mound of beautiful rounded, lobed, purple-flushed silver leaves; the purple colour intensifies in cool conditions. In summer, produces loose sprays of small, red pendent, bell-shaped flowers.
***H.* 'Citronelle'.** Evergreen, clump-forming perennial. **H** and **S** 50cm (20in). Fully hardy. Has rounded, lobed, lime-green leaves. In summer, produces loose sprays of small, pendent, bell-shaped, white flowers.
***H.* Crème Brûlée ('Tnheu041')** illus. p.282. Evergreen, clump-forming perennial. **H** 40–50cm (16–20in), **S** 40cm (16in). Fully hardy. Rounded, lobed, glowing caramel, bronze and gold leaves fade in intensity as they age. In summer, produces loose sprays of small, pendent, bell-shaped, white flowers.
***H. cylindrica* 'Greenfinch'.** Evergreen, clump-forming perennial. **H** 45–60cm (18–24in), **S** 50cm (20in). Fully hardy. Has rosettes of lobed, heart-shaped leaves and, in summer, spikes of small, bell-shaped, pale green or greenish-white flowers.
***H.* 'E and I'.** See *H.* Ebony and Ivory.
***H.* Ebony and Ivory ('E and I')** illus. p.282. Evergreen, clump-forming, rather compact perennial. **H** and **S** 30cm (12in). Fully hardy. Has rounded, lobed, rather ruffled, ebony-black leaves. In summer, produces numerous loose sprays of small, pendent, bell-shaped, ivory-white flowers.
***H.* 'Firebird'.** Evergreen, compact perennial. **H** 60cm (2ft), **S** 30cm (1ft). Fully hardy. In early summer, bears long, feathery sprays of small, pendent, bell-shaped, crimson-scarlet flowers. Leaves are rounded, lobed, toothed and dark green.
***H.* 'Georgia Peach'** (illus. p.282). Evergreen, clump-forming perennial. **H** 30cm (12in), **S** 50cm (20in). Fully hardy. Large, rounded, lobed, silvery pinkish-peach leaves are most vibrant when young. In summer, produces loose sprays of small, pendent, bell-shaped, white flowers.
***H.* 'Ginger Ale'** (illus. p.282). Evergreen, clump-forming perennial. **H** 30–40cm (12–16in), **S** 30cm (12in). Fully hardy. Has rounded, lobed, silvery-white-marbled, pale orange leaves. In summer, produces loose sprays of small, pendent, bell-shaped, creamy-pink flowers.
***H.* 'Green Spice'** (illus. p.282). Evergreen, clump-forming perennial. **H** 20–30cm (8–12in), **S** 30cm (12in). Fully hardy. Rounded, lobed, silvery-green leaves have dark purple veins and dark grey edges. In summer, produces loose sprays of small, pendent, bell-shaped, greenish-white flowers.
***H.* Key Lime Pie ('Tnheu042').** Evergreen, clump-forming perennial. **H** and **S** 40cm (16in). Fully hardy. Has rounded, lobed, lime-green leaves. In summer, produces loose sprays of small, pendent, bell-shaped, pinkish-white flowers.
***H.* 'Lime Rickey'** (illus. p.282). Strong-growing, evergreen, clump-forming perennial. **H** 40–50cm (16–20in), **S** 50cm (20in). Fully hardy. Rounded, lobed, ruffled, lime-green leaves are brightest in spring. In summer, produces loose sprays of small, pendent, bell-shaped, white flowers.
***H. micrantha* var. *diversifolia* 'Palace Purple'.** See *H.* 'Palace Purple'.
***H.* 'Midnight Rose'** (illus. p.282). Evergreen, clump-forming perennial. **H** and **S** 50cm (20in). Fully hardy. Rounded, lobed, dark purple leaves have pink speckles that get larger as the season progresses and may fade to cream. In summer, produces loose sprays of small, pendent, bell-shaped, cream flowers.
***H.* 'Obsidian'.** Evergreen, clump-forming perennial. **H** and **S** 50cm (20in). Fully hardy. Has rounded, lobed, smooth, glossy, dark purple-black leaves. In summer, produces loose sprays of small, pendent, bell-shaped, ivory flowers on red stems.
***H.* 'Palace Purple'.** Clump-forming perennial. **H** and **S** 45cm (18in). Fully hardy. Has persistent, heart-shaped, deep purple leaves and sprays of small, white flowers in summer. Cut leaves last well in water.
***H.* 'Peach Flambé'** (illus. p.282). Evergreen, clump-forming perennial. **H** and **S** 50cm (20in). Fully hardy. Large, rounded, lobed, smooth, rich peach leaves develop purplish hues in winter. In summer, produces loose sprays of small, pendent, bell-shaped, white flowers.
***H.* 'Pearl Drops'.** Evergreen, clump-forming perennial. **H** 60cm (2ft), **S** 30cm (1ft). Fully hardy. In early summer, bears small, pendent, bell-shaped, white flowers tinged pink. Leaves are rounded, lobed, toothed and dark green.
***H.* 'Peppermint Spice'** (illus. p.282). Evergreen, clump-forming, rather compact perennial. **H** 40cm (16in), **S** 30–40cm (12–16in). Fully hardy. Has rounded, lobed, purple-veined, silver green leaves. In summer produces loose sprays of small, pendent, bell-shaped, soft pink flowers.
***H.* 'Pewter Moon'** (illus. p.282). Evergreen, clump-forming perennial. **H** 40cm (16in), **S** 30–50cm (12–20in). Fully hardy. Rounded, lobed, veined, silvery-green leaves have deep maroon undersides. In summer, produces loose sprays of small, pendent, bell-shaped, soft pink flowers on maroon stems.
***H.* 'Plum Pudding'** illus. p.280.
♀ ***H.* 'Purple Petticoats'** (illus. p.282). Evergreen, clump-forming perennial. **H** 40cm (16in), **S** 30–50cm (12–20in). Fully hardy. Rounded, lobed, ruffled, rich purple leaves are a brighter reddish-purple beneath. In summer, produces loose sprays of small, pendent, bell-shaped, cream flowers.
***H.* 'Red Spangles'.** Evergreen, clump-forming perennial. **H** and **S** 30cm (12in). Fully hardy. Has heart-shaped, purplish-green leaves and spikes of small, bell-shaped, crimson-scarlet flowers in summer.
***H. sanguinea* var. *pulchra* 'Snow Storm'** (illus. p.282). Slow-growing, evergreen, clump-forming perennial. **H** 40cm (16in), **S** 30–40cm (12–16in). Fully hardy. Rather small, rounded, lobed, green

leaves each have a large, creamy-white centre. In summer, produces loose sprays of small, pendent, bell-shaped, coral-pink flowers. May be short-lived.
🏆 ***H.* 'Scintillation'.** Evergreen, clump-forming perennial. **H** 45–75cm (18–30in), **S** 30–45cm (12–18in). Fully hardy. In early summer, produces long, feathery sprays of small, pendent, bell-shaped, deep pink flowers, each rimmed with coral-pink. Bears rounded, lobed, toothed and dark green leaves.
***H.* 'Silver Scrolls'** (illus. p.282). Evergreen, clump-forming perennial. **H** 50cm (20in), **S** 40–50cm (16–20in). Fully hardy. Rounded, lobed, silver and burgundy leaves are at their most vibrant when young. In summer, produces loose sprays of small, pendent, bell-shaped, pinkish-white flowers.
***H.* 'Southern Comfort'** (illus. p.282). Strong-growing, evergreen, clump-forming perennial. **H** 50–60cm (20–24in), **S** 60–70cm (24–28in). Fully hardy. Large, rounded, lobed, rather hairy, brownish-peach leaves age to burnt-copper. In summer, produces loose sprays of small, pendent, bell-shaped, white flowers.
***H.* 'Stormy Seas'.** Evergreen, clump-forming perennial. **H** 40cm (16in), **S** 40–50cm (16–20in). Fully hardy. Rounded, lobed, grey-silver-mottled, glossy, maroon-purple leaves, aging to bronze-green, have vivid purple undersides. In summer, produces loose sprays of small, pendent, bell-shaped, cream flowers.
***H.* 'Tiramisu'** (illus. p.282). Evergreen, clump-forming perennial. **H** 30–40cm (12–16in), **S** 30cm (12in). Fully hardy. Has rounded, lobed, red-flushed, copper-yellow leaves. In summer, produces loose sprays of small, pendent, bell-shaped, pinkish flowers.
***H.* 'Tnheu041'.** See *H.* CRÈME BRÛLÉE.
***H.* 'Tnheu042'.** See *H.* KEY LIME PIE.

H

x HEUCHERELLA

SAXIFRAGACEAE

Hybrid genus (*Heuchera* x *Tiarella*) of evergreen, mainly late spring- and summer-flowering perennials. Fully hardy. Prefers semi-shade and needs fertile, well-drained soil. Propagate by basal cuttings in spring or by division in spring or autumn. See also feature panel p.282.
x *H. alba* 'Bridget Bloom'. Evergreen, clump-forming perennial. **H** 45cm (18in), **S** 30cm (12in). Has dense, bright green leaves and, in early summer, many feathery sprays of tiny, bell-shaped, rose-pink flowers, which continue intermittently until autumn.
🏆 **x *H. tiarelloides*** illus. p.264. **'Alabama Sunrise'** is an evergreen, ground-cover perennial. **H** and **S** 30cm (12in). Rounded, deeply lobed, red-veined, golden-yellow young leaves fade to bright green and develop orange tints in autumn. In early summer produces feathery sprays of small, bell-shaped, pendent, white flowers. **'Dayglow Pink'**, **H** and **S** 30–40cm (12–16in), has dark-veined, rich green leaves and numerous feathery sprays of bright pink flowers. **'Heart of Darkness'**, **H** and **S** 40cm (16in), has green leaves, each with a large dark purple central zone surrounded by silver-grey, and produces white flowers. **'Kimono'** (illus. p.282), **H** and **S** 40cm (16in), is vigorous and has very deeply lobed, purple-veined, silvery-purple and green leaves and loose sprays of cream flowers. **'Stoplight'** (illus. p.282), **H** and **S** 40cm (16in), has red-veined, bright yellow leaves and white flowers.

Hexastylis. See *Asarum.*

HIBBERTIA

SYN. CANDOLLEA

DILLENIACEAE

Genus of evergreen shrubs and twining climbers, grown for their flowers. Frost tender, min. 5–10°C (41–50°F). Grow in well-drained soil, in full light or semi-shade. Water freely in summer, less at other times. Provide stems with support. Thin out congested growth in spring. Propagate by semi-ripe cuttings in summer.
H. cuneiformis illus. p.458.
🏆 ***H. scandens***, syn. *H. volubilis.* Vigorous, evergreen, twining climber. **H** 6m (20ft). Has 4–9cm (1½–3½in) long, oblong to lance-shaped, glossy, deep green leaves. Saucer-shaped, bright yellow flowers, 4cm (1½in) across, are produced mainly in summer.
H. volubilis. See *H. scandens.*

HIBISCUS

MALVACEAE

Genus of evergreen or deciduous shrubs, trees, perennials and annuals, grown for their flowers. Fully hardy to frost tender, min. 5–15°C (41–59°F). Needs full sun and humus-rich, well-drained soil. Water containerized specimens freely when in full growth, moderately at other times. Tip prune young plants to promote bushiness; cut old plants back hard in spring. Propagate by seed in spring; shrubs and trees by greenwood cuttings in late spring or by semi-ripe cuttings in summer; and perennials by division in autumn or spring. Whitefly may cause problems.
H. mutabilis (Confederate rose, Cotton rose). Evergreen, erect to spreading shrub or tree. **H** and **S** 3–5m (10–15ft). Frost tender, min 5°C (41°F). Rounded leaves have 5–7 shallow lobes. In summer–autumn bears funnel-shaped, sometimes double, white or pink flowers, 7–10cm (3–4in) wide, that age from pink to deep red. In light frost dies back to ground level.
H. rosa-sinensis. Evergreen, rounded, leafy shrub. **H** and **S** 1.5–3m (5–10ft) or more. Frost tender, min. 10–13°C (50–55°F). Oval, glossy leaves are coarsely serrated. Produces funnel-shaped, bright crimson flowers, 10cm (4in) wide, mainly in summer but also in spring and autumn. Many colour selections are grown including **'The President'** illus. p.455.
🏆 ***H. schizopetalus.*** Evergreen, upright, spreading, loose shrub. **H** to 3m (10ft), **S** 2m (6ft) or more. Frost tender, min. 10–13°C (50–55°F). Has oval, serrated leaves and, in summer, pendent, long-stalked flowers, 6cm (2½in) wide, with deeply fringed, reflexed, pink or red petals. May be trained as a climber.
***H. syriacus* 'Blue Bird'.** See *H.s.* 'Oiseau Bleu'. 🏆 **'Diana'** is a deciduous, upright shrub. **H** 3m (10ft), **S** 2m (6ft). Fully hardy. Has oval, lobed, deep green leaves and very large, trumpet-shaped, pure white flowers, with wavy-edged petals, from late summer to mid-autumn. 🏆 **'Oiseau Bleu'** (syn. *H.s.* 'Blue Bird') illus. p.138. 🏆 **'Red Heart'** illus. p.132. 🏆 **'Woodbridge'** illus. p.136.
H. trionum illus. p.300.

HIDALGOA

Climbing dahlia

COMPOSITAE/ASTERACEAE

Genus of evergreen, leaf stalk climbers, grown for their single, dahlia-like flower heads. Frost tender, min. 10°C (50°F). Requires full light and humus-rich, well-drained soil. Water freely when in full growth, less at other times. Needs support. In spring, thin out crowded stems or cut back all growth to ground level. Propagate by softwood cuttings in spring. Aphids, red spider mite and whitefly may be troublesome.
H. wercklei. Moderately vigorous, evergreen, leaf stalk climber. **H** 5m (15ft) or more. Oval leaves are divided into 3, 5 or more, coarsely serrated leaflets. In summer, bears dahlia-like, scarlet flower heads, yellowish in bud.

HIERACIUM

Hawkweed

COMPOSITAE/ASTERACEAE

Genus of perennials; most are weeds, but the species described is grown for its foliage. Fully hardy. Needs sun and poor, well-drained soil. Propagate by seed or division in autumn or spring.
H. lanatum illus. p.277.

HIMALAYACALAMUS

GRAMINEAE/POACEAE

See also GRASSES, BAMBOOS, RUSHES and SEDGES.
H. falconeri, syn. *Arundinaria falconeri, Drepanostachyum falconeri, Thamnocalamus falconeri.* Evergreen, clump-forming bamboo. **H** 5–10m (15–30ft), **S** 1m (3ft). Half hardy. Greenish-brown stems have a dark purple ring beneath each node. Has yellowish-green leaves, 10–15cm (4–6in) long, without visible tessellation, and unimportant flower spikes.

HIPPEASTRUM

AMARYLLIDACEAE

Genus of bulbs, grown for their huge, funnel-shaped flowers. Is often incorrectly cultivated as *Amaryllis.* Frost hardy to frost tender, min. 13–15°C (55–9°F). Requires a position in full sun or partial shade and well-drained soil. Plant large-flowered hybrids in autumn, half burying bulb; after the leaves die away, dry off bulb until following autumn. Smaller, summer-flowering species should be kept dry while dormant in winter. Propagate by seed in spring or by offsets in spring (summer-flowering species) or autumn (large-flowered hybrids). ⚠ All parts may cause mild stomach upset if ingested.
H. advenum. See *Rhodophiala advena.*
***H.* 'Apple Blossom'** illus. p.414.
H. aulicum, syn. *H. morelianum*, illus. p.414.
🏆 ***H.* 'Belinda'.** Winter- and spring-flowering bulb with a basal leaf cluster. **H** 30–50cm (12–20in), **S** 30cm (12in). Frost tender, min. 13°C (55°F). Is similar to *H. aulicum*, but flowers are deep velvety-red throughout, stained darker towards centres.
***H.* 'Black Pearl'.** Winter-flowering bulb. **H** 50cm (20in), **S** 30cm (12in). Half hardy. Has a stout stem bearing 4–5 large, funnel-shaped, dark maroon flowers and strap-shaped, semi-erect, basal leaves that develop with or after the flowers.
***H.* 'Bouquet'.** Winter- and spring-flowering bulb with a basal leaf cluster. **H** 30–50cm (12–20in), **S** 30cm (12in). Frost tender, min. 13°C (55°F). Is similar to *H. aulicum*, but has very wide, salmon-pink flowers, with deep red veins and red centres.
H. morelianum. See *H. aulicum.*
🏆 ***H.* 'Orange Sovereign'.** Winter- to spring-flowering bulb. **H** 30–50cm (12–20in), **S** 30cm (12in). Frost tender, min. 13°C (55°F). Has strap-shaped, semi-erect, basal, grey-green leaves produced as, or just after, flowers form. Stout stem bears head of 2–6 rich orange-red flowers.
H. procerum. See *Worsleya procera.*
***H.* 'Red Lion'** illus. p.414.
H. reginae. Summer-flowering bulb. **H** to 50cm (20in), **S** 20–25cm (8–10in). Frost tender, min. 13°C (55°F). Flower stem produces a head of 2–4 scarlet flowers, each 10–15cm (4–6in) across, and with a star-shaped, green mark in the throat. Long, strap-shaped, semi-erect leaves develop at base after flowering has finished.
H. rutilum. See *H. striatum.*
H. striatum, syn. *H. rutilum.* Spring- and summer-flowering bulb. **H** 30cm (12in), **S** 20–25cm (8–10in). Frost tender, min. 15°C (59°F). Has strap-shaped, semi-erect, bright green, basal leaves. Funnel-shaped flowers have pointed, scarlet petals with central, green stripes.
***H.* 'Striped'** illus. p.414.
H. vittatum. Vigorous, spring-flowering bulb. **H** 1m (3ft), **S** 30cm (1ft). Frost tender, min. 13°C (55°F). Leaves are broadly strap-shaped, semi-erect and basal. Stout, leafless stem precedes leaves and terminates in a head of 2–6 red-striped, white flowers, each 12–20cm (5–8in) across.
***H.* 'White Dazzler'.** Winter- and spring-flowering bulb with a basal leaf cluster. **H** 30–50cm (12–20in), **S** 30cm (12in). Frost tender, min. 13°C (55°F). Is similar to *H. aulicum*, but has pure white flowers.

HIPPOCREPIS

Vetch

LEGUMINOSAE/PAPILIONACEAE

Genus of annuals and perennials, grown for their pea-like flowers. Fully hardy. Requires full sun and well-drained soil. Propagate by seed in spring or autumn. Self-seeds readily. May be invasive.
H. comosa (Horseshoe vetch) illus. p.373. **'E.R. Janes'** is a vigorous, prostrate, woody-based perennial. **H** 5–8cm (2–3in),

S 15cm (6in) or more. Rooting stems bear small, loose spikes of pea-like, yellow flowers from late spring to late summer. Leaves are divided, with 3–8 pairs of narrowly oval leaflets.

HIPPOPHAE

ELAEAGNACEAE

Genus of deciduous shrubs and trees, with inconspicuous flowers, grown for their foliage and showy fruits. Separate male and female plants are required in order to obtain fruits. Is suitable for coastal areas, where it is wind-resistant and excellent when grown as hedging. Fully hardy. Needs sun and is especially useful for poor, dry or very sandy soil. Propagate by softwood cuttings in summer or by seed in autumn. See also feature panel p.142.

♀ ***H. rhamnoides*** (Sea buckthorn; illus. p.142). Deciduous, bushy, arching shrub or small tree. **H** and **S** 6m (20ft). Has narrow, silvery leaves. Tiny, yellow flowers borne in mid-spring are followed in autumn by bright orange berries on female plants.

HOHERIA

MALVACEAE

Genus of deciduous, semi-evergreen or evergreen trees and shrubs, grown for their flowers produced mainly in summer. Frost hardy, but in cold areas grow against a south- or west-facing wall. Requires sun or semi-shade and fertile, well-drained soil. Propagate by semi-ripe cuttings in summer or by seed in autumn.

H. angustifolia illus. p.85.

♀ ***H. 'Glory of Amlwch'.*** Semi-evergreen, spreading tree. **H** 7m (22ft), **S** 6m (20ft). Has long, narrowly oval, glossy, bright green leaves and a profusion of large, 5-petalled, white flowers from mid- to late summer.

♀ ***H. lyallii*** illus. p.85.

H. populnea (Lace-bark). Evergreen, spreading tree. **H** 12m (40ft), **S** 10m (30ft). Bears narrowly oval, glossy, dark green leaves and produces dense clusters of 5-petalled, white flowers in late summer and early autumn. Bark on mature trees is pale brown and white and often flaky.

H. sexstylosa (Ribbonwood). Fast-growing, evergreen, upright tree or shrub. **H** 8m (25ft), **S** 6m (20ft). Glossy, pale green leaves are narrowly oval and sharply toothed. Star-shaped, 5-petalled, white flowers are borne in clusters from mid- to late summer.

HOLBOELLIA

LARDIZABALACEAE

Genus of evergreen, twining climbers, grown mainly for their fine foliage. Fully hardy. Both male and female flowers are borne on the same plant. Grow in any well-drained soil, in a position in shade or full light. Propagate by stem cuttings in late summer or autumn.

H. brachyandra. Evergreen climber to 10m (30ft) bearing alternate, trifoliate, ovate to elliptic, mid-green leaves to 12cm (5in) long. In summer produces racemes of 4–8, large, white, fragrant flowers with sepals of female flowers reaching 3–4cm (1½in) long. Hardy to at least -5°C (23°F).

H. coriacea. Evergreen, twining climber. **H** to 5m (16ft). Fully hardy. Has glossy, mid- to dark green leaves divided into 3 ovate to elliptic leaflets. In early summer produces racemes of 5–8 fragrant, bell-shaped flowers with sepals of female flowers reddish-purple; white, male flowers have purple lines at bases. Flowers are sometimes followed by ovoid, light purple fruits.

H. latifolia [purple form] illus. p.194; [white form] illus. p.192.

HOLCUS

GRAMINEAE/POACEAE

See also GRASSES, BAMBOOS, RUSHES and SEDGES.

H. mollis (Creeping soft grass). **'Albovariegatus'** (syn. *H.m.* 'Variegatus'). Evergreen, spreading, variegated, perennial grass. **H** 30–45cm (12–18in), **S** indefinite. Fully hardy. Has white-striped leaves and hairy nodes. In summer produces purplish-white flower spikes.

HOLMSKIOLDIA

VERBENACEAE/LAMIACEAE

Genus of evergreen shrubs or scrambling climbers. Frost tender, min. 16°C (61°F). Any fertile, well-drained soil is suitable in a position in full light. Water freely in growing season, less at other times. Requires tying to supports. Crowded growth should be thinned out in spring or after flowering has finished. Propagate by seed in spring or by softwood or semi-ripe cuttings in summer. Whitefly and red spider mite may be troublesome.

H. sanguinea (Chinese hat plant, Mandarin's hat plant). Evergreen, straggly shrub. **H** to 5m (15ft), **S** 2m (6ft). Leaves are 5–10cm (2–4in) long, oval and serrated. Produces showy, red or orange flowers, with saucer-shaped calyces and central, 5-lobed tubes, in autumn through to winter.

HOLODISCUS

ROSACEAE

Genus of deciduous shrubs, grown for their flowers in summer. Fully hardy. Needs sun or semi-shade and any but very dry soil. Propagate by softwood cuttings in summer.

H. discolor illus. p.113.

HOMERIA

IRIDACEAE

Genus of spring- or summer-flowering corms with widely funnel-shaped, cup-shaped or flattish flowers. Half hardy. Needs a sunny site and well-drained soil. To produce flowers in spring, pot in autumn in a cool greenhouse, water until after flowering, then dry off for summer. To produce flowers in summer, plant in the open in spring. Propagate by seed, division or offsets in autumn. ⓘ *H. collina* is toxic to livestock.

H. ochroleuca. Spring- or summer-flowering corm. **H** to 55cm (22in), **S** 5–8cm (2–3in). Slender, wiry stems each bear 1 or 2 long, narrow, semi-erect leaves on lower part of stem. Bears a succession of upright, cup-shaped to flattish, yellow flowers, each sometimes with a central, orange stain.

HOMOGYNE

COMPOSITAE/ASTERACEAE

Genus of evergreen perennials, useful for ground cover in rock gardens and woodland. Fully hardy. Needs shade and moist soil. Propagate by division in spring or by seed when fresh.

H. alpina (Alpine coltsfoot). Mat-forming, rhizomatous perennial. **H** 8–15cm (3–6in), **S** 15cm (6in) or more. Has kidney-shaped, toothed, glossy leaves and in summer, stems, 8–15cm (3–6in) or more long, each carry a daisy-like, rose-purple flower head.

HOODIA

ASCLEPIADACEAE/APOCYNACEAE

Genus of branching, perennial succulents with firm, erect, green stems, generally branching from the base. Frost tender, min. 10–15°C (50–59°F). Needs full sun and very well-drained soil. Is difficult to cultivate. Water sparingly at all times. Propagate by seed or grafting in spring or summer.

H. bainii. See *H. gordonii.*

H. gordonii, syn. *H. bainii*. Variable, erect, clump-forming, perennial succulent. **H** 80cm (32in), **S** 30cm (12in). Min 10°C (50°F). Green stem is covered with short, spine-tipped tubercles in distorted rows. Often branches into clumps. Produces 5-lobed, flesh-coloured to brownish flowers in late summer.

HORDEUM

GRAMINEAE/POACEAE

See also GRASSES, BAMBOOS, RUSHES and SEDGES.

H. jubatum illus. p.286.

HORMINUM

LABIATAE/LAMIACEAE

Genus of one species of basal-rosetted perennial, suitable for rock gardens. Fully hardy. Requires a position in sun and in well-drained soil. Propagate by division in spring or by seed in autumn.

H. pyrenaicum (Dragon's mouth). Basal-rosetted perennial. **H** and **S** 20cm (8in). In summer, carries whorls of nodding, short-stalked, funnel-shaped, blue-purple or white flowers above oval, leathery, dark green leaves, 8–10cm (3–4in) long.

HOSTA

Plantain lily

LILIACEAE/HOSTACEAE

Genus of perennials, grown mainly for their decorative foliage. Forms large clumps that are excellent for ground cover (heights given are those of foliage). Fully hardy. Most species prefer shade and rich, moist but well-drained, neutral soil. Propagate by division in early spring. Seed-raised plants (except of *H. ventricosa*) very rarely come true to type. Slug and snail control is essential. See also feature panel pp.272–73.

H. albomarginata. See *H. sieboldii* 'Paxton's Original'.

H. 'Allan P. McConnell' (illus. p.273). Clump-forming perennial. **H** 15–20cm (6–8in), **S** 30–45cm (12–18in). Has broadly to narrowly ovate, olive-green leaves with narrow, white margins. In mid-summer produces bell-shaped, purple flowers on scapes 35–40cm (14–16in) long.

H. 'American Halo'. Robust, densely mounded, clump-forming perennial. **H** 55cm (22in), **S** 1.5m (5ft). Has large, broadly ovate, strongly veined, dark blue-green leaves, with heart-shaped bases and wide, irregular, yellow margins becoming ivory-white as they mature. In early and mid-summer produces broadly funnel-shaped, pure white flowers on scapes 60cm (2ft) long.

H. 'Antioch' (illus. p.272). Robust, clump-forming perennial. **H** 50cm (20in), **S** 90cm (36in). Has broadly ovate, matt, dark green leaves irregularly margined grey-green and creamy-yellow, fading to white. In mid-summer bears funnel-shaped, lavender-blue flowers on scapes 90cm (36in) long.

H. 'August Moon' (illus. p.273). Vigorous, clump-forming perennial. **H** 50cm (20in), **S** 75cm (30in). Has rounded to heart-shaped, cupped, puckered, pale green leaves becoming golden-yellow with a faint glaucous bloom. In summer bears bell-shaped, greyish-white flowers on scapes 90cm (36in) long.

H. 'Big Daddy'. Clump-forming perennial. **H** 60cm (2ft), **S** 1m (3ft). Has rounded to heart-shaped, cupped, deeply puckered, glaucous, grey-blue leaves. In early summer bears bell-shaped, greyish-white flowers on scapes 80cm (32in) long.

H. 'Birchwood Parky's Gold', syn. *H.* 'Golden', *H.* 'Golden Nakaiana' (illus. p.273). Vigorous, clump-forming perennial. **H** 35–40cm (14–16in), **S** indefinite. Has heart-shaped, matt, yellow-green leaves becoming rich yellow with age. In mid-summer bears bell-shaped, pale lavender-blue flowers on scapes 70cm (28in) long.

♀ ***H. 'Blue Angel'.*** Slow-growing, clump-forming perennial. **H** 35cm (14in), **S** 60cm (24in). Has ovate to heart-shaped, wavy, glaucous, bluish-grey leaves. In mid-summer bears bell-shaped, greyish- or mauvish-white flowers on scapes 1m (3ft) long.

H. 'Blue Cadet'. Clump-forming perennial. **H** 35–40cm (14–16in), **S** 75cm (30in). Has small, broadly ovate leaves, blue-green above and glaucous beneath, with heart-shaped bases. Produces funnel-shaped, rich lavender flowers in long, dense racemes, 55cm (22in) long, from mid- to late summer.

H. 'Blue Moon'. Slow-growing, compact, clump-forming perennial. **H** 12cm (5in), **S** 30cm (12in). Oval to rounded, greyish-blue leaves taper to a point. In mid-summer, dense clusters of trumpet-shaped, mauve flowers, on scapes 20–25cm (8–10in) long, are borne just above leaves. Is suitable for a rock garden. Prefers partial shade.

H. 'Blue Mouse Ears'. Slow-growing, clump-forming perennial. **H** 15cm (6in), **S** 30cm (12in). Has very small, shallowly cupped, ovate, rich blue-green leaves, which in mature plants are almost round

in shape. Produces clusters of bell-shaped, lavender-striped, rich violet flowers, on scapes 20cm (8in) long, in mid- and late summer.
***H.* 'Blue Wedgwood'** (illus. p.273). Slow-growing, clump-forming perennial. **H** 30cm (1ft), **S** 45cm (1½ft). Has wedge-shaped, deeply quilted, blue leaves and, in summer, produces lavender flowers on scapes 40cm (16in) long.
***H.* 'Brim Cup'** (illus. p.273). Slow-growing, clump-forming perennial. **H** 30cm (12in), **S** 35–40cm (14–16in). Erect, heart-shaped, slightly cupped and puckered, thick, dark green leaves are irregularly margined with cream fading to white. Bears pale lavender-blue flowers, on scapes 45cm (18in) long, in summer.
***H.* 'Buckshaw Blue'.** Slow-growing, clump-forming perennial. **H** 35cm (14in), **S** 60cm (24in). Has ovate to heart-shaped, concave, puckered, glaucous, deep blue-green leaves. In early summer bears bell-shaped, greyish-white flowers on scapes to 45cm (18in) long.
***H.* 'Candy Hearts'.** Vigorous, clump-forming perennial. **H** 35–40cm (14–16in), **S** 55cm (22in). Has heart-shaped, pointed, greenish-grey-blue leaves. In summer bears bell-shaped, pale lavender-blue to off-white flowers on scapes to 50cm (20in) long.
***H.* 'Cherry Berry'** (illus. p.272) Mounded, clump-forming perennial. **H** 30cm (12in), **S** 60cm (24in). Has broadly lance-shaped, creamy-yellow leaves, becoming ivory-white, with broad, irregular, green margins. In mid- to late summer produces funnel-shaped, deep purple flowers on red scapes 45cm (18in) long.
***H. decorata*.** Stoloniferous perennial. **H** 30cm (12in), **S** 45cm (18in). Oval to rounded, dark green leaves have white margins. Dense racemes of trumpet-shaped, deep violet or sometimes white flowers, on scapes to 50cm (20in) long, are borne in mid-summer.
f. *normalis* has plain green leaves.
***H.* 'Devon Green'** (illus. p.272). Clump-forming perennial. **H** 45cm (18in), **S** 40cm (16in). Red-spotted leaf stalks bear lance-shaped, glossy, dark green leaves maturing to broadly ovate to heart-shaped. In mid-summer bears bell-shaped, greyish-lavender-blue flowers on scapes to 45cm (18in) long.
***H.* 'Dream Weaver'** (illus. p.273). Vigorous, clump-forming perennial. **H** 45cm (18in), **S** 90cm (36in). Has large, broadly ovate, strongly-ribbed, chartreuse-green leaves, later ivory-white in the centre, with very broad, dark blue-green margins, glaucous beneath. Produces funnel-shaped, lavender-striped, white flowers, on scapes to 70cm (28in) long, in mid- and late summer.
***H.* 'Fire and Ice'** (illus. p.273). Upright, mounding, clump-forming perennial. **H** 20cm (8in), **S** 30cm (12in). Has small, narrowly ovate to ovate, ivory to white leaves, irregularly margined dark green, with twisted, acute tips. Produces narrowly funnel-shaped, pale lavender flowers on scapes, 60cm (20in) long, in mid- and late summer.
***H.* 'Fire Island'** Clump-forming perennial. **H** 25cm (10in), **S** 45cm (18in). Bright red stems bear ovate, puckered, bright yellow leaves becoming more green as the season progress, the red stem colouring seeping into the leaf blade. In mid-summer has bell-shaped, lavender flowers on scapes 50cm (20in) long.
***H. fluctuans* 'Variegated'** see *H.* 'Sagae'.
H. fortunei*.** Group of vigorous, clump-forming, hybrid perennials. **H** 75cm–1m (2½–3ft), **S** 1m (3ft) or more. Leaves are oval to heart-shaped. ♀ **var. *albopicta (syn. *H.f.* 'Albopicta') has pale green leaves, with creamy-yellow centres, fading to dull green from mid-summer. Racemes of trumpet-shaped, pale violet flowers on scapes, 75cm (30in) long, open above foliage in early summer. ♀ **var. *aureomarginata*** (syn. *H.f.* 'Aureomarginata', *H.f.* 'Yellow Edge') has mid-green leaves with irregular, creamy-yellow edges. In mid-summer, trumpet-shaped, violet flowers on scapes, 75cm (30in) long, are carried in racemes above foliage. Mass planting looks very effective. Tolerates full sun. **'Yellow Edge'** see *H.f. f.aureomarginata.*
***H.* 'Fragrant Bouquet'** (illus. p.273). Mounded, clump-forming perennial. **H** 45cm (18in), **S** 65cm (26in). Produces heart-shaped, slightly puckered, slightly wavy, chartreuse leaves edged in cream. In late summer, large, fragrant, flared, very pale lavender flowers are borne on scapes 90cm (36in) long.
♀ ***H.* 'Francee'.** Vigorous, clump-forming perennial. **H** 55cm (22in), **S** 1m (3ft). Has oval to heart-shaped, slightly cupped and puckered, olive-green leaves with irregular, white margins. In summer, produces arching, leafy scapes, 70cm (28in) long, bearing funnel-shaped, lavender-blue flowers. Is late to emerge.
***H.* 'Ginko Craig'** (illus. p.273). Low-growing, clump-forming perennial. **H** and **S** 30cm (1ft). Has small, narrow, dark green leaves irregularly margined white. In summer produces spikes of bell-shaped, deep mauve flowers on scapes, 55cm (22in) long. Is a good edging plant.
***H.* 'Gold Edger'** (illus. p.272). Densely mounded, clump-forming perennial. **H** to 30cm (12in), **S** 30cm (12in) or more. Has heart-shaped, matt, golden-yellow leaves that fade to chartreuse with age. In late summer produces bell-shaped, lavender flowers on scapes to 30cm (12in) long.
***H.* 'Golden'.** See *H.* 'Birchwood Parky's Gold'.
***H.* 'Golden Nakaiana'.** See *H.* 'Birchwood Parky's Gold'.
***H.* 'Golden Prayers'** (illus. p.273). Upright, clump-forming perennial. **H** 15cm (6in), **S** 30cm (12in). Cupped leaves are puckered and bright golden-green. Flowers on scapes, 45cm (18in) long, are white suffused with pale lavender. Suits a rock garden.
♀ ***H.* 'Golden Tiara'** (illus. p.273). Clump-forming perennial. **H** 15cm (6in), **S** 30cm (12in). Neat, broadly heart-shaped, dark green leaves have well-defined, chartreuse-yellow margins. In summer produces long spikes of lavender-purple flowers on scapes 60cm (24in) long.
***H.* 'Gold Standard'.** Vigorous, clump-forming perennial. **H** 75cm (2½ft), S 1m (3ft). Oval to heart-shaped leaves are pale green, turning to gold from mid-summer, with narrow, regular, dark green margins. Racemes of trumpet-shaped, violet flowers on scapes, 1.1m (3½ft) long, are produced above leaves in mid-summer. Prefers partial shade.
***H. gracillima*.** Clump-forming perennial. **H** 5cm (2in), **S** 18cm (7in). Has lance-shaped, wavy-margined, glossy, deep green leaves, paler beneath. In summer–autumn, produces purple-dotted scapes, 25cm (10in) long, of widely funnel-shaped, lavender-blue flowers, purple striped within.
***H.* 'Grand Tiara'.** Vigorous perennial forming a compact mound. **H** 30cm (12in), **S** 50cm (20in). Has ovate to heart-shaped, mid-green leaves with irregular, wide, yellow margins. In summer produces bell-shaped, sometimes remontant, deep purple flowers, on scapes 80cm (32in) long, each striped lavender-blue within.
***H.* 'Great Expectations'** (illus. p.273). Clump-forming perennial. **H** 55cm (22in), **S** 85cm (34in). Green-margined, white leaf stalks bear heart-shaped, stiff, puckered, thick leaves that are glaucous, blue-green, and irregularly but widely splashed with yellow, fading to white in the centres. In early summer, bell-shaped, greyish-white flowers are borne on leafy scapes, 70cm (28in) long, .
***H.* 'Green Fountain'.** Clump-forming perennial. **H** 60cm (24in), **S** 45cm (18in). Red-dotted leaf stalks bear arching, lance-shaped, wavy-margined, glossy, mid-green leaves. Funnel-shaped, pale mauve flowers are borne in summer, on scapes 60cm (24in) long.
***H.* 'Ground Master'** (illus. p.272). Vigorous, stoloniferous, prostrate perennial. **H** 25cm (10in), **S** 55cm (22in). Has ovate to lance-shaped, matt, olive-green leaves with wavy, irregular, creamy margins, fading to white. In summer, bears straight, leafy scapes, 60cm (24in) long, of funnel-shaped, purple flowers, .
***H.* 'Guacamole'.** Vigorous, clump-forming perennial. **H** 45cm (18in), **S** 65cm (26in). Bold, heart-shaped, slightly wavy, soft gold leaves are irregularly edged in green. In mid-summer has flared, very pale lavender flowers on scapes 85cm (34in) long. Leaves colour best in good light.
***H.* 'Hadspen Blue'** (illus. p.272). Slow-growing, clump-forming perennial. **H** and **S** 30cm (12in). Smooth leaves are heart-shaped and deep glaucous blue. Produces short spikes of lavender flowers, on scapes 35cm (14in) long, in summer.
♀ ***H.* 'Halcyon'** (illus. p.272). Robust, clump-forming perennial. **H** 30cm (1ft), **S** 1m (3ft). Has heart-shaped, tapering, greyish-blue leaves that fade to muddy-green in full sun; texture may be spoiled by heavy rain. Heavy clusters of trumpet-shaped, violet-mauve flowers, on scapes 45cm (18in) long, open just above foliage in mid-summer.
♀ ***H.* 'Honeybells'.** Clump-forming perennial. **H** 1m (3ft), **S** 60cm (2ft). Light green leaves are blunt at the tips and have wavy margins. In late summer bears fragrant, pale lilac flowers on 1.1m (3½ft) long scapes.
***H.* 'Hydon Sunset'** (illus. p.273). Densely mounded, clump-forming perennial. **H** and **S** to 60cm (24in). Has heart-shaped leaves, bright gold in spring that turn mid-green by late summer. In late summer produces bell-shaped, purple flowers on scapes to 60cm (24in) long.
H. hypoleuca (White-backed hosta). Clump-forming perennial. **H** 45cm (1½ft), **S** 1m (3ft). Broadly oval leaves have widely spaced veins and are pale green above, striking white beneath. In late summer bears drooping racemes of trumpet-shaped, milky-violet flowers, on scapes 35cm (14in) long, with mauve-flecked, pale green bracts. Tolerates full sun.
***H.* 'Inniswood'.** Densely mounding, clump-forming perennial. **H** 60cm (24in), **S** 90cm (36in). Has large, broadly ovate to rounded, heart-shaped, seersuckered, rich golden-yellow leaves, with somewhat glaucous, dark green leaves that are glaucous beneath. In mid-summer produces funnel-shaped, pale lavender flowers on scapes 75cm (30in) long.
***H.* 'Invincible'** (illus. p.272). Densely mounded, clump-forming perennial. **H** and **S** to 60cm (24in). Has heart-shaped, long-tipped, leathery, glossy, olive-green leaves. In late summer produces slightly fragrant, funnel-shaped, pale lavender flowers on scapes to 60cm (24in) long.
♀ ***H.* 'June'** (illus. p.272). Dense, clump-forming perennial. **H** 38cm (15in), **S** 70cm (28in). Has heart-shaped, smooth, grey-blue leaves irregularly splashed in centres with yellow and yellowish green. Bell-shaped, lavender-grey flowers, on scapes 45cm (18in) long, are borne in late summer. Is a sport of *H.* 'Halcyon'.
***H.* 'Kabitan'.** See *H. sieboldii* f. *kabitan.*
H. kikutii*.** Clump-forming perennial. **H** 40cm (16in), **S** 60cm (2ft). Has oval to lance-shaped, deeply veined, dark green leaves. Racemes of bell-shaped, near-white flowers are borne in a tight bunch at the top of the raceme on conspicuously leaning scapes, 60cm (24in) long, in mid-summer. **var. *caput-avis is smaller, and the flower bud resembles a bird's head. **'Kifukurin'** has larger leaves, attractively margined with cream.
♀ ***H.* 'Krossa Regal'.** Vase-shaped, clump-forming perennial. **H** and **S** 1m (3ft). Arching, deeply ribbed leaves are greyish-blue. Produces long spikes of pale lilac flowers, on scapes 1.4m (4½ft) long, in summer. Tolerates sun.
♀ ***H. lancifolia*** (illus. p.273). Clump-forming perennial. **H** 45cm (18in), **S** 75cm (30in). Arching, narrowly lance-shaped, glossy, dark green leaves overlap neatly into a dense mound. Bell-shaped, lavender flowers, on scapes 65cm (26in) long, are produced in late summer.
♀ ***H.* 'Love Pat'.** Vigorous, clump-forming perennial. **H** and **S** to 60cm (2ft). Produces rounded, deeply puckered, deep glaucous blue leaves. Bears racemes of pale lilac flowers, on scapes 55cm (22in) long, during summer.
***H.* 'Minuteman'** (illus. p.272). Clump-forming perennial. **H** 75cm (30in), **S** 60cm (24in). Has oval, slightly wavy-rimmed, white-margined, dark green leaves. In mid- and late summer produces funnel-shaped, lavender flowers on scapes 75cm (30in) long.
***H. montana*.** Vigorous, clump-forming perennial. **H** 1.1m (3½ft), **S** 1m (3ft). Has oval, prominently veined, glossy, dark

green leaves. Racemes of trumpet-shaped, pale violet flowers, on scapes 90cm (36in) long, open well above foliage in mid-summer. Slower-growing **'Aureomarginata'** has leaves irregularly edged with golden-yellow. Is always the first hosta to appear in spring.

***H.* 'Moonlight'.** Clump-forming perennial. **H** 50cm (20in), **S** 70cm (28in). Has pale yellow leaves that emerge olive-green, narrowly margined white. Produces funnel-shaped, violet-budded, pinkish-lavender flowers, on scapes 70cm (28in) long, in mid-summer. Requires full shade.

***H.* 'Morning Light'.** Clump-forming perennial forming upright mounds of foliage. **H** 45cm (18in), **S** 70cm (28in). Has ovate, long-pointed, rich ivory-yellow leaves, with irregular, dark green margins. Produces narrowly funnel-shaped, lavender flowers, on scapes to 70cm (28in) long, in mid-summer.

***H.* 'Night Before Christmas'** (illus. p.272). Clump-forming perennial. **H** 60cm (2ft), **S** 1.5m (5ft). Large, oval, slightly wavy, rich dark green leaves are boldly splashed with a central, bright white flash. Has narrowly funnel-shaped, lavender flowers, on scapes 90cm (36in) long, in mid-summer.

H. nigrescens (illus. p.272). Vigorous, clump-forming perennial. **H** 70cm (28in), **S** 65cm (26in). In late summer has oval to heart-shaped, concave, puckered, glaucous grey-green leaves, and racemes of funnel-shaped, pearl-grey to white flowers, on undulating scapes 1.4m (4½ft) long.

***H.* 'Paxton's Original'.** See *H. sieboldii* 'Paxton's Original'.

***H.* 'Piedmont Gold'.** Slow-growing, clump-forming perennial. **H** 60cm (2ft), **S** 75cm (2½ft). Smooth leaves are bright yellowish-green with fluted margins. Racemes of white flowers, on scapes to 65cm (26in) long, are produced in summer. Is best in light shade.

H. plantaginea (August lily). Lax, clump-forming perennial. **H** 60cm (2ft), **S** 1.2m (4ft). Leaves are oval and glossy, pale green. Rising well above these are scapes, to 65–75cm (26–30in) long, crowned in late summer and early autumn with fragrant, trumpet-shaped, white flowers that open in the evening. Prefers sunny conditions. ♀ **var. *japonica*,** syn *H.p.* 'Grandiflora' has larger, longer-tubed flowers, to 13cm (5in) long. Prefers sun. **'Grandiflora'.** See *H.p.* var. *japonica*.

***H. rectifolia*.** Upright, clump-forming perennial. **H** 1m (3ft), **S** 75cm (2½ft). Produces oval to lance-shaped, dark green leaves and racemes of large, trumpet-shaped, violet flowers, to 60–75cm (24–30in) long, from mid- to late summer.

***H.* 'Regal Splendor'** (illus. p.272). Clump-forming perennial. **H** and **S** 1m (3ft). Arching, greyish-blue leaves are suffused white or yellow at the margins. Lilac flowers, on scapes 1.4m (4½ft) long, are produced in summer.

***H.* 'Remember Me'** (illus. p.273). Densely mounded, clump-forming perennial. **H** 40cm (16in), **S** 30cm (12in). Has narrowly oval, bright ivory-white to creamy-yellow leaves with irregular, green-margins. Tubular, lavender flowers, on 40cm (16in) long scapes, are produced in mid-summer.

***H.* 'Revolution'** (illus. p.273). Clump-forming perennial. **H** 50cm (20in), **S** 1.1m (3½ft). Ivory-white leaf stalks, finely outlined dark green, bear broadly ovate, wavy, lustrous, green-flecked, ivory-cream leaves, margined and splashed dark green and overlaid with light olive-green. In mid-summer has narrowly funnel-shaped, lavender-blue flowers on scapes 50cm (20in) long.

♀ ***H.* 'Royal Standard'.** Upright, clump-forming perennial. **H** 60cm (2ft), **S** 1.2m (4ft). Broadly oval leaves are glossy, pale green. Pure white, slightly fragrant, trumpet-shaped flowers, to 1m (3ft) long, are carried well above foliage and open in the evening. Prefers sun.

♀ ***H.* 'Sagae'**, syn. *H. fluctuans* 'Variegated' (illus. p.273). Semi-erect, clump-forming perennial. **H** 75cm (2½ft), **S** 1.5m (5ft). Very large, roughly triangular, dark green leaves have gold edges which fade to cream or white. Flared, lavender flowers are borne, on scapes 1.2m (4ft) long, in mid-summer.

***H.* 'Sea Thunder'.** Vigorous, dense-mounding, clump-forming perennial. **H** 40–50cm (16–20in), **S** 1m (3ft). Has narrowly ovate to ovate, ivory-cream leaves, irregularly margined dark olive-green, often with intrusions of olive-green towards the centre. Produces broadly funnel-shaped, purple flowers, on scapes 90cm (36in) long, in late summer.

♀ ***H.* 'Shade Fanfare'.** Vigorous, clump-forming perennial. **H** 45cm (1½ft), **S** 75cm (2½ft). Heart-shaped leaves are pale green with cream margins. In summer has an abundance of lavender flowers on scapes 60cm (24in) long.

H. sieboldiana (illus. p.272). Robust, clump-forming perennial. **H** 1m (3ft) or more, **S** 1.5m (5ft). Large, heart-shaped, deeply ribbed, puckered leaves are bluish-grey. Racemes of trumpet-shaped, very pale lilac flowers, on scapes 60cm (24in) long, open in early summer, just above foliage. Makes good ground cover. Tolerates sun, but leaves may then turn dull green. ♀ **var. *elegans*** has larger, bluer leaves and scapes 70cm (28in) long. ♀ **'Frances Williams'** has yellow-margined leaves, scapes 70cm (28in) long, is slower-growing and should not be grown in full sun.

H. sieboldii* f. *kabitan, syn. *H.* 'Kabitan'. Clump-forming perennial, spreading by short runners. **H** to 30cm (1ft), **S** 60cm (2ft). Lance-shaped, thin-textured, glossy leaves are yellow-centred and have narrow, undulating, dark green margins. In early summer produces small, trumpet-shaped, pale violet flowers on scapes 30–40cm (12–16in) long. Is suitable for a shaded rock garden. Needs establishing in a pot for first few years. ♀ **'Paxton's Original'** (syn. *H. albomarginata*, *H.* 'Paxton's Original'), **H** 45cm (1½ft), is vigorous, and has round-tipped, mid- to dark green leaves with irregular, white margins. Violet flowers appear in late summer and are followed by ovoid, glossy, dark green, then brown seed heads, which are useful for flower arrangements.

***H.* 'Snowden'.** Clump-forming perennial. **H** and **S** 1m (3ft) or more. Has large, pointed, glaucous, blue leaves that age to sage-green. Long stems produce white flowers tinged with green, on thick scapes 1m (3ft) long, during summer.

***H.* 'So Sweet'** (illus. p.273). Clump-forming perennial. **H** 35cm (14in), **S** 55cm (22in). Has ovate to lance-shaped, glossy, mid-green leaves margined creamy-white. In mid- and late summer lavender-blue buds open to fragrant, funnel-shaped, purple-striped, white flowers on scapes 60cm (24in) long.

***H.* 'Stiletto'.** Vigorous, clump-forming perennial. **H** 15cm (6in), **S** 20cm (8in). Has lance-shaped, rippled, mid-green leaves margined creamy-white. In summer produces funnel-shaped, purple-striped, lavender-blue flowers on scapes 30cm (12in) long.

***H.* 'Striptease'.** Densely mounding, clump-forming perennial. **H** 50cm (20in), **S** 1.2m (4ft). Has narrowly ovate to ovate leaves, dark green leaves, glaucous beneath, with chartreuse-green centres, sometimes white-flecked, later becoming ivory-yellow. Produces funnel-shaped, violet then lavender flowers on scapes, 70cm (28in) long, in mid-summer.

♀ ***H.* 'Sum and Substance'.** Vigorous, clump-forming perennial. **H** and **S** to 1m (3ft). Produces large, greenish-gold leaves that are thick in texture and, in mid-summer, pale lavender flowers on scapes 1m (3ft) long. Tolerates full sun.

***H.* 'Tall Boy'.** Clump-forming perennial. **H** and **S** 60cm (2ft). Has large, bright green leaves ending in long points. In summer an abundance of rich lilac flowers is produced on scapes 1.2m (4ft) long or more.

***H. tardiflora*.** Slow-growing, clump-forming perennial. **H** 30cm (1ft), **S** 75cm (2½ft). Has narrowly lance-shaped, thick-textured, dark green leaves. Dense racemes of trumpet-shaped, lilac-purple flowers, on scapes 35cm (14in) long, open just above foliage from late summer to early autumn.

***H.* 'Tattoo'** (illus. p.273). Clump-forming perennial. **H** 30cm (12in), **S** 45cm (18in). Broadly ovate, slightly puckered, pale green leaves have a maple-leaf-shaped, gold centres edged in darker green. Bears bell-shaped, lavender flowers, on scapes 45cm (18in) long, in mid-summer.

***H.* 'Thomas Hogg'.** See *H. undulata* var. *albomarginata*.

H. tokudama, syn. *H.* 'Tokudama'. Very slow-growing, clump-forming perennial. **H** 45cm (1½ft), **S** 75cm (2½ft). Produces cup-shaped, puckered, blue leaves. Racemes of trumpet-shaped, pale lilac-grey flowers, on scapes 40cm (16in) long, appear just above foliage in mid-summer. **f. *aureonebulosa*** (syn. *H.t.* 'Aureonebulosa', *H.t.* 'Variegata') illus. p.274. **f. *flavocircinalis*,** (illus. p.272), often mistaken for a juvenile *H. sieboldiana* 'Frances Williams', has heart-shaped leaves with wide, irregular, creamy-yellow margins. **'Variegata'** see *H.t.* f. *aureonebulosa*.

***H.* 'Tokudama'.** See *H. tokudama*.

***H.* 'Torchlight'.** Clump-forming perennial. **H** 35cm (14in), **S** 85cm (34in). Strongly red-streaked leaf stalks bear ovate, slightly folded, wavy, smooth, dark olive-green leaves lightly streaked chartreuse, with irregular, ivory margins. Bears funnel-shaped, rich lavender-blue flowers, on scapes 75cm (30in) long, in late summer.

♀ ***H. undulata* var. *undulata*,** syn. *H.* 'Undulata'. Clump-forming perennial. **H** to 1m (3ft), **S** 45cm (18in). Has lance-shaped to elliptic or narrowly ovate, slightly pointed, twisted, deeply channelled, mid-green leaves that are thin but leathery and strongly wavy-margined, with central, white or pale yellow-white markings. Funnel-shaped, mauve flowers, on arching leaf scapes 50–80cm (20–32in) long, are produced in early and mid-summer. **var. *albomarginata*** (syn. *H.* 'Thomas Hogg', *H.* 'Undulata Albomarginata'), **H** 55cm (22in), **S** 60cm (24in), has broadly oval, flat or slightly wavy-margined, dark green leaves, with irregular, cream or pale yellow margins. ♀ **var. *erromena*** (syn. *H.* 'Undulata Erromena'), **H** 45cm (1½ft), **S** 60cm (2ft), is robust and bears broadly oval, tapering, matt, mid-green leaves. ♀ **var. *univittata*** (syn. *H.* 'Undulata Univittata'), **H** 45cm (1½ft), **S** 70cm (28in), has oval, twisted, matt, olive-green leaves that have narrow, cream centres.

***H.* 'Undulata'.** See *H. undulata* var. *undulata*.

***H.* 'Undulata Albomarginata'.** See *H. undulata* var. *albomarginata*.

***H.* 'Undulata Erromena'.** See *H. undulata* var. *erromena*.

***H.* 'Undulata Univittata'.** See *H. undulata* var. *univittata*.

♀ ***H. ventricosa*.** Clump-forming perennial. **H** 70cm (28in), **S** 1m (3ft) or more. Has heart-shaped to oval, slightly wavy-margined, glossy, dark green leaves. Racemes of bell-shaped, deep purple flowers, on scapes 80cm–1m (32–36in) long, are produced above foliage in late summer. Usually comes true from seed. **'Variegata'** (syn. *H.v.* 'Aureomarginata') produces leaves with irregular, cream margins.

♀ ***H. venusta*.** Vigorous, mat-forming perennial. **H** 2.5cm (1in), **S** to 30cm (12in). Has oval to lance-shaped, mid- to dark green leaves. Abundant racemes of trumpet-shaped, purple flowers, on scapes 25–35cm (10–14in) long, are borne well above foliage in mid-summer. Is suitable for a rock garden. **'Suzuki Thumbnail'** produces small leaves up to 5cm (2in) long by 2.5cm (1in) across.

***H.* 'Whirlwind'** (illus. p.273). Clump-forming perennial. **H** 43cm (17in), **S** 85cm (34in). Has ovate to heart-shaped, folded, twisted and pointed, white to yellowish-green leaves, with wide dark green margins. Funnel-shaped, lavender-blue flowers, on scapes 60cm (24in) long, are produced in mid- and late summer.

♀ ***H.* 'Wide Brim'.** Vigorous, clump-forming perennial. **H** and **S** to 75cm (2½ft). Leaves are heavily puckered and dark blue-green, with wide, irregular, creamy-white margins. Produces white or very pale lavender flowers, on scapes 55cm (22in) long, in summer.

***H.* 'Yellow River'.** Clump-forming perennial. **H** 55cm (22in), **S** 1m (3ft). Has ovate to heart-shaped, pointed, thick, dark green leaves with irregular, yellow margins. Leafy scapes, 1m (3ft) long, of funnel-shaped, very pale lavender-blue flowers are produced in early summer.

***H.* 'Zounds'.** Slow-growing, clump-forming perennial. **H** and **S** to 1m (3ft).

Large, bright gold leaves are corrugated and have metallic sheen. White or pale lavender flowers, on scapes 60cm (24in) long, are produced in early summer.

HOTTONIA

PRIMULACEAE

Genus of deciduous, perennial, submerged water plants, grown for their handsome foliage and delicate, primula-like flowers. Fully hardy. Needs sun and clear, cool water, still or running. Periodically thin overcrowded growth. Propagate by stem cuttings in spring or summer.
H. palustris illus. p.435.

Houstonia serpyllifolia. See *Hedyotis michauxii.*

HOUTTUYNIA

SAURURACEAE

Genus of one species of perennial or deciduous marginal water plant, with far-spreading rhizomes. Is suitable for ground cover, although invasive. Fully hardy. Prefers position in semi-shade and moist soil or shallow water, beside streams and ponds. Propagate by runners in spring.
***H. cordata* 'Chameleon'**, syn. *H.c.* 'Variegata', illus. p.444. **'Flore Pleno'** (syn. *H.c.* 'Plena') is a spreading perennial. **H** 15–60cm (6–24in), **S** indefinite. Spikes of insignificant flowers, surrounded by 8 or more oval, white bracts, are produced above aromatic, fleshy, leathery, heart-shaped, pointed leaves, in spring. **'Plena'** see *H.c.* 'Flore Pleno'. **'Variegata'** see *H.c.* 'Chamaeleon'.

HOVENIA

RHAMNACEAE

Genus of one species of deciduous, summer-flowering tree, grown for its foliage. Fully hardy, but young, unripened growth is susceptible to frost damage. Does best in a position in full sun and requires fertile, well-drained soil. Propagate by softwood cuttings in summer or by seed in autumn.
H. dulcis illus. p.74.

HOWEA

SYN. HOWEIA, KENTIA

PALMAE/ARECACEAE

Genus of evergreen palms, grown for their ornamental appearance. Frost tender, min. 16–18°C (61–4°F). Needs partial shade and humus-rich, well-drained soil. Water containerized specimens freely in summer, minimally in winter and moderately at other times. Propagate by seed in spring at not less than 26°C (79°F). Is prone to red spider mite.
♀ ***H. forsteriana***, syn. *Kentia fosteriana* (Paradise palm, Sentry palm, Thatch-leaf palm). Evergreen, upright palm with a slender stem. **H** 10m (30ft), **S** 3–4m (10–12ft). Has spreading, feather-shaped leaves, 1.5–2.5m (5–8ft) long, made up of strap-shaped leaflets. Branching clusters of several spikes of small, greenish-brown flowers are produced in winter.

Howeia. See *Howea.*

HOYA

ASCLEPIADACEAE/APOCYNACEAE

Genus of evergreen, woody-stemmed, twining and/or root climbers and loose shrubs, grown for their flowers and foliage. Frost tender, min. 5–18°C (41–64°F). Grow in humus-rich, well-drained soil with semi-shade in summer. Water moderately when in full growth, sparingly at other times. Stems require support. Cut back and thin out crowded stems after flowering or in spring. Propagate by semi-ripe cuttings in summer.
H. australis, syn. *H. darwinii* of gardens. Moderately vigorous, evergreen, woody-stemmed, twining, root climber. **H** to 5m (15ft). Frost tender, min. 15°C (59°F). Has fleshy, rich green leaves. In summer produces trusses of 20–50 fragrant, star-shaped flowers, white with red-purple markings.
H. bella. See *H. lanceolata* subsp. *bella.*
♀ ***H. carnosa*** illus. p.460.
H. coronaria. Slow-growing, evergreen, woody-stemmed, twining and root climber. **H** 2–3m (6–10ft). Min. 16–18°C (61–4°F). Bears thick, leathery, oblong to oval leaves. In summer, bell-shaped, yellow to white flowers are borne, each spotted with red.
H. darwinii of gardens. See *H. australis.*
H. imperialis. Vigorous, evergreen, woody-stemmed, twining and root climber. **H** to 6m (20ft). Min. 16–18°C (61–4°F). Oval, leathery, leaves are covered with down and 10–23cm (4–9in) long. In summer, produces large, star-shaped, brown-purple to deep magenta flowers, each with a cream centre.
♀ ***H. lanceolata* subsp. *bella***, syn. *H. bella*, illus. p.460.
H. macgillivrayi illus. p.462.

HUERNIA

ASCLEPIADACEAE/APOCYNACEAE

Genus of clump-forming, perennial succulents with finger-like, usually 4-angled stems. Has minute, short-lived, deciduous leaves on new growth. Frost tender, min. 8–11°C (46–52°F). Needs sun or partial shade and very well-drained soil. Is one of easiest stapeliads to grow. Propagate by seed or stem cuttings in spring or summer.
H. macrocarpa, syn. *H.m.* var. *arabica*, illus p.488. **var. *arabica*** see *H. macrocarpa.*
H. pillansii. Deciduous, clump-forming, perennial succulent. **H** 5cm (2in), **S** 10cm (4in). Min. 11°C (52°F). Has a finger-like, light green stem that is densely covered with short tubercles with hair-like tips. Produces bell-shaped, creamy-red flowers, with red spots, at base of new growth, in summer through to autumn.
H. primulina. See *H. thuretii* var. *primulina.*
H. thuretii* var. *primulina, syn. *H. primulina.* Deciduous, clump-forming, perennial succulent. **H** 10cm (4in), **S** 15cm (6in). Min. 11°C (52°F). Stems are short, thick and grey-green. In summer through to autumn bell-shaped, dull yellow flowers, 2cm (¾in) across, with reflexed, blackish tips, are produced at base of new growth.
H. zebrina (Owl-eyes). Deciduous, clump-forming, perennial succulent. **H** 10cm (4in), **S** 15cm (6in). Min. 11°C (52°F). Is similar to *H. thuretii* var. *primulina*, but has pale yellow-green flowers with bands of red-brown.

Humea. See *Calomeria.*

HUMULUS

Hop

CANNABACEAE

Genus of herbaceous, twining climbers. Is useful for concealing unsightly garden sheds or tree-stumps. Male and female flowers are borne on separate plants; female flower spikes become drooping clusters known as 'hops'. Fully hardy. Grow in a position in sun or semi-shade and in any well-drained soil. Propagate by tip cuttings in spring.
H. lupulus (Common hop). ♀ **'Aureus'** illus. p.194.

HUNNEMANNIA

PAPAVERACEAE

Genus of poppy-like perennials, usually grown as annuals. Half hardy. Grow in sun and in poor to fertile, very well-drained soil. Dead-head plants regularly. Provide support, especially in windy areas. Propagate by seed sown under glass in early spring, or outdoors in mid-spring.
H. fumariifolia (Mexican tulip poppy). ♀ **'Sunlite'** is a fast-growing, upright perennial, grown as an annual. **H** 60cm (24in), **S** 20cm (8in). Has oblong, very divided, bluish-green leaves and, in summer and early autumn, poppy-like, semi-double, bright yellow flowers, to 8cm (3in) wide.

HYACINTHELLA

LILIACEAE/HYACINTHACEAE

Genus of spring-flowering bulbs with short spikes of small, bell-shaped flowers, suitable for rock gardens and cold greenhouses. Frost hardy. Requires an open, sunny situation and well-drained soil, which partially dries out while bulbs are dormant in summer. Propagate by seed in autumn.
H. leucophaea illus. p.421.

HYACINTHOIDES

SYN. ENDYMION

Bluebell

LILIACEAE/HYACINTHACEAE

Genus of spring-flowering bulbs, grown for their bluebell flowers. Is suitable for growing in borders and for naturalizing in grass beneath trees and shrubs. Fully hardy. Requires partial shade and plenty of moisture. Prefers heavy soil. Plant bulbs in autumn 10–15cm (4–6in) deep. Propagate by division in late summer or by seed in autumn. ⓘ All parts may irritate skin on contact, and may cause severe discomfort if ingested.
H. hispanica of gardens. See *H.* x *massartiana.*
♀ ***H. italica***, syn. *Scilla italica.* Spring-flowering bulb. **H** 15–20cm (6–8in), **S** 5–8cm (2–3in). Produces a basal cluster of narrowly strap-shaped, semi-erect leaves. Leafless stem produces a conical spike of many flattish, star-shaped, blue flowers, 1cm (½in) across.
H.* x *massartiana (*H. hispanica* x *H. non-scripta*), syn. *H. hispanica* of gardens, *Scilla campanulata, S. hispanica*, illus. p.403.
H. non-scripta, syn. *Scilla non-scripta, S. nutans*, illus. p.403.

HYACINTHUS

Hyacinth

LILIACEAE/HYACINTHACEAE

Genus of bulbs, grown for their dense spikes of fragrant, tubular flowers; is ideal for spring bedding displays and for pot cultivation indoors. Frost hardy. Needs an open, sunny situation or partial shade and well-drained soil. Plant in autumn. For winter flowers, force large-size, specially "treated" bulbs of *H. orientalis* cultivars by potting in early autumn, then keep cool and damp for several weeks to ensure adequate root systems develop. When shoot tips are visible, move into max. 10°C (50°F) at first, raising temperature as more shoot appears and giving as much light as possible. After forcing, keep in a cool place to finish growth, then plant out to recover. Propagate by offsets in late summer or early autumn. ⓘ All parts may cause stomach upset if ingested; contact with the bulbs may aggravate skin allergies.
H. amethystinus. See *Brimeura amethystina.*
H. azureus. See *Muscari azureum.*
***H. orientalis* 'Amsterdam'.** Winter- or spring-flowering bulb. **H** 10–20cm (4–8in), **S** 6–10cm (2½–4in). Has strap-shaped, channelled, semi-erect, glossy, basal leaves that develop fully only after flowering. Flower stem carries a dense, cylindrical spike of fragrant, tubular, bright rose-red flowers, each with 6 recurving petals.
♀ **'Blue Jacket'** illus. p.403. ♀ **'City of Haarlem'** illus. p.407. ♀ **'Delft Blue'** has violet-flushed, soft blue flowers. **'Distinction'** produces slender, open spikes of reddish-purple flowers; those of ♀ **'Jan Bos'** are crimson. **'Lady Derby'** bears rose-pink flowers. ♀ **'L' Innocence'** has ivory-white flowers. ♀ **'Ostara'** has a large spike of blue flowers, with a dark stripe along each petal centre. ♀ **'Pink Pearl'** has a dense spike of carmine-pink flowers. Flowers of **'Princess Maria Christina'** are salmon-pink; those of **'Queen of the Pinks'** are soft pink. **'Violet Pearl'** produces spikes of violet flowers. **'White Pearl'** illus. p.415.

HYDRANGEA

HYDRANGEACEAE

Genus of deciduous shrubs and deciduous or evergreen, root climbers, grown for their mainly domed or flattened flower heads. Each head usually consists of masses of small, inconspicuous, fertile flowers, surrounded by or mixed with much larger, sterile flowers bearing showy, petal-like sepals. However, in some forms, all or most of the flowers are sterile. Fully to half hardy. Prefers full sun or semi-shade and fertile, moist but well-drained soil. Needs more shade in dry areas. Propagate by softwood cuttings in

summer. ① All parts of hydrangeas may cause mild stomach upset if ingested; contact with the foliage may aggravate skin allergies. See also feature panel pp.134–135.
H. anomala* subsp. *petiolaris. See *H. petiolaris*.
♀ ***H. arborescens* 'Annabelle'** (illus. p.134). Deciduous, open shrub. **H** and **S** 2.5m (8ft). Fully hardy. Long-stalked, broadly oval leaves are glossy, dark green above, paler beneath. Very large, rounded heads of mainly sterile, white flowers are borne in summer. ♀ **'Grandiflora'** has smaller flower heads but larger sterile flowers.
♀ ***H. aspera.*** Deciduous, upright shrub with arching branches. **H** and **S** to 4m (13ft). Fully hardy. Young stems are finely haired. Has lance-shaped to ovate, dark green leaves, downy beneath. Pale blue, inner flowers, surrounded by lilac-pink to white, outer ones, are borne in summer. **'Mauvette'** (illus. p.135) has slightly deeper purple-mauve flowers. **subsp. *sargentiana*** see *H. sargentiana.* ♀ **Villosa Group** (syn. *H. villosa*) illus. p.133.
H. bretschneideri. See *H. heteromalla* 'Bretschneideri'.
H. heteromalla. Deciduous, arching shrub. **H** 5m (15ft), **S** 3m (10ft). Fully hardy. Narrowly oval, dark green leaves turn yellow in autumn. Broad, flat, open heads of white flowers, 17cm (7in) across, are borne in mid- and late summer. **'Bretschneideri'** (syn. *H. bretschneideri*) has peeling, chestnut-brown bark and large leaves, to 12cm (5in) long and half as much wide. **'Snowcap'** (illus. p.134) has large, flat, white flower heads, to 25cm (10in) across.
H. integerrima. See *H. serratifolia.*
H. involucrata. Deciduous, spreading, open shrub. **H** 1m (3ft), **S** 2m (6ft). Frost hardy. Has broadly heart-shaped, bristly, mid-green leaves. During late summer and autumn bears heads of small, blue, inner flowers surrounded by large, pale blue to white, outer ones. ♀ **'Hortensis'** is smaller and has clusters of cream, pink and green flowers.
H. longipes. Deciduous shrub with lax, spreading habit. **H** and **S** to 3m (10ft). Fully hardy. Rounded to ovate, toothed, rough, grey-green leaves are produced on long leaf stalks. Has flat, white flower heads in mid-summer.
H. macrophylla. Deciduous, bushy shrub. **H** 1.5–2m (5–6ft), **S** 2–2.5m (6–8ft). Frost hardy. Has oval, toothed, glossy, light green leaves. In mid- to late summer, blue or purple flowers are produced in acid soils with a pH of up to about 5.5. In neutral or alkaline soils above this level, flowers are pink or red. White flowers are not affected by pH. Prune older shoots back to base in spring. Trim back winter-damaged shoots to new growth and remove spent flower heads in spring. Is divided into 2 groups: Hortensias, which have domed, dense heads of mainly sterile flowers; and Lacecaps, which have flat, open heads, each with fertile flowers in the centre and larger, sterile flowers on the outside that are green in bud.
♀ **'Altona'** (Hortensia; illus. p.134), **H** 1m (3ft), **S** 1.5m (5ft), has large heads of rich pink to deep purple-blue flowers. ♀ **'Ami Pasquier'** (Hortensia; illus. p.135), **H** 60cm (2ft), **S** 1m (3ft), is compact, with deep crimson or blue- purple flowers. **'Ayesha'** (Hortensia; illus. p.135), **H** and **S** 1m (3ft), has flattened heads of pink to lilac flowers and deep green leaves.**'Blue Bonnet'** (Hortensia; illus. p.135), **H** 2m (6ft), **S** to 2.5m (8ft), produces heads of rich blue or lilac to pink flowers. **'Blue Wave'** see *H.m.* 'Mariesii Perfecta'. ♀ **'Europa'** (Hortensia; illus. p.135), **H** 1.5m (5ft), **S** 1m (3ft), produces large florets of rich pink flowers. Flower heads of ♀ **'Générale Vicomtesse de Vibraye'** (Hortensia; illus. p.134), **H** and **S** 1.5m (5ft), are rounded and pale blue or pink. Foliage is light green. ♀ **'Goliath'** (Hortensia), **H** and **S** 1m (3ft), has dark green leaves and produces very large florets of soft pink to pale blue flowers in small heads. **'Hamburg'** (Hortensia; illus. p.134), **H** 1m (3ft), **S** 1.5m (5ft), is vigorous and has large, deep pink to deep blue flowers with serrated sepals. ♀ **'Lanarth White'** (Lacecap), **H** and **S** 1.5m (5ft), has pink or blue fertile flowers edged with pure white sterile flowers. **'Libelle'** (Lacecap; illus. p.135), **H** and **S** 1.5m (5ft), produces very pale blue flowers, fading to creamy-white, over a long period. ♀ **'Lilacina'** (syn. *H.m.* 'Mariesii Lilacina'; Lacecap; illus. p.134), **H** and **S** 2m (6ft), has deep lilac central flowers and pinkish-purple outer flowers. ♀ **'Madame Emile Mouillère'** (Hortensia; illus. p.134) has white flowers, becoming pale pink, and prefers partial shade. **'Mariesii Lilacina'** see *H.m.* 'Lilacina'. ♀ **'Mariesii Perfecta'** (syn. *H.m.* 'Blue Wave'; Lacecap), **H** 2m (6ft), **S** to 2.5m (8ft), produces heads of rich blue or lilac to pink flowers. ♀ **'Möwe'** (Lacecap; illus. p.135), **H** and **S** 1m (3ft), has broad, flat flower heads ranging in colour from purple-red to deep pink. ♀ **'Nigra'** (Hortensia), **H** and **S** 1m (3ft), has almost black stems bearing pink or occasionally blue flowers. **subsp. *serrata*** see *H. serrata.* **subsp. *serrata* 'Preziosa'** see *H.* 'Preziosa'. ♀ **'Tokyo Delight'** (Lacecap), **H** and **S** 1m (3ft), produces pink or white flowers maturing to red-wine. **'Tricolor'** (Lacecap), **H** 2m (6ft), **S** 1.5m (5ft), has variegated, grey-green and yellow leaves and bears pale pink to white in late summer. ♀ **'Veitchii'** (Lacecap) has lilac-blue flowers. ♀ **'Westfallen'** (Hortensia), **H** and **S** 1m (3ft), bears bright red to purple flowers.
H. paniculata. Vigorous, deciduous, spreading to upright shrub. **H** 2–3m (6–10ft), **S** 2.5–3m (8–10ft). Fully hardy. Has ovate, pointed, toothed, mid- to dark green leaves. In summer and early autumn produces large, usually conical panicles of tiny, sometimes rose-tinted, creamy-white, fertile flowers surrounded by large, petal-like, white, sterile flowers (florets) that usually mature to varying shades of pink. Prune moderately to hard annually to promote vigorous growth and large inflorescences. ♀ **'Big Ben'** (illus. p.134), **H** and **S** 1.7m (5½ft), has an upright habit, red stems and, in mid-summer, produces masses of large, conical panicles of pale green, sterile florets that turn white and then mature to deep pink in mid-autumn. Needs moderate to hard pruning. **'Brussels Lace'** has dark green leaves and white flowers in late summer and early autumn. Needs moderate pruning. **'Dharuma'** (illus. p.135), **H** and **S** 1.2m (4ft), is a compact, relatively slow-growing cultivar with mahogany-red stems, dark green leaves and rounded panicles of white, sterile florets in mid-summer; these mature to deep pink by mid-autumn. when fully mature. Is best left unpruned or given only light pruning annually. Is good in a small garden. **'Dvppinky'** see *H.p.* PINKY-WINKY. **'Floribunda'** has dense conical heads of small, fertile, central flowers surrounded by large, white ray flowers. ♀ **'Grandiflora'** has large, oval and dark green leaves. Large, conical panicles of mostly sterile, white flowers turn pink or red from late summer. Prune back hard in spring to obtain largest panicles. **'Interhydia'** see *H.p.* PINK DIAMOND. ♀ **'Limelight'** (illus. p.135), **H** 1.7m (5½ft), **S** 2.2m (7ft), is robust and produces very dense, broadly conical panicles of lime-green, sterile florets in mid-summer gradually maturing to a mixture of lime-green and warm pink by mid-autumn. Needs moderate pruning. ♀ **'Phantom'** (illus. p.134), **H** 1.5m (5ft), **S** 2.2m (7ft), is a robust, upright cultivar producing dense, conical, rounded panicles of sterile, white florets, flushed yellow-green at tips, in mid-summer; these mature to warm, deep pink by early autumn. Needs moderate to hard pruning. Flower heads of ♀ **PINK DIAMOND ('Interhydia')** illus. p.135, turn pink with age. ♀ **PINKY-WINKY ('Dvppinky')** illus. p.134, **H** 1.4m (4½ft), **S** 1.6m (5½ft), has a compact, upright, slightly spreading habit with dark red stems, yellowish-green leaves and dense, tapered, conical panicles of lime-green, sterile florets in mid-summer; these mature to deep pink by early autumn. Responds well to moderate pruning. Is good in a small garden. **'Praecox'** flowers from mid-summer. ♀ **'Silver Dollar'** (illus. p.134), **H** 1.2m (4ft), **S** 1.7m (5½ft), is compact with strong stems supporting very dense, rounded panicles of white, sterile florets, tipped pale yellow-green, produced in mid-summer and mature to pink in mid-autumn. Responds well to hard pruning. Is very good in a small garden. **'Tardiva'** has both fertile and sterile flowers from early to mid-autumn. ♀ **'Unique'** is similar to 'Grandiflora' but more vigorous and has larger flowers.
♀ ***H. petiolaris*** (Climbing hydrangea), syn. *H. anomala* subsp. *petiolaris*, illus. p.195.
♀ ***H.* 'Preziosa'**, syn. *H. macrophylla* subsp. *serrata* 'Preziosa', *H. serrata* 'Preziosa'. Deciduous, bushy shrub. **H** 1.5–2m (5–6ft), **S** 2–2.5m (6–8ft). Frost hardy. Has oval, toothed, light green leaves. Pink flowers turn to deep crimson.
♀ ***H. quercifolia*** (Oak-leaved hydrangea). Deciduous, bushy, mound-forming shrub. **H** and **S** 2m (6ft). Frost hardy. Deeply lobed, dark green leaves turn red and purple in autumn. Has white flower heads from mid-summer to mid-autumn. **'Brido'** see *H.q.* SNOWFLAKE. **SNOWFLAKE ('Brido')** illus. p.134, produces pure white fertile flower bracts surrounded by a double rank of white sterile flower bracts.
♀ ***H. sargentiana***, syn. *H. aspera* subsp. *sargentiana* (illus. p.135). Deciduous, upright, gaunt shrub. **H** 2.5m (8ft), **S** 2m (6ft). Frost hardy. Has peeling bark, stout shoots and very large, narrowly oval, bristly, dull green leaves with grey down beneath. In late summer to mid-autumn bears broad heads of flowers, the inner ones small and blue or deep purple, the outer ones larger and white, sometimes flushed purplish-pink.
H. scandens* subsp. *chinensis. Deciduous, woody-stemmed, scandent shrub. **H** and **S** to 3m (10ft). Fully hardy. Has spreading, often pendent, branchlets and lance-shaped, slightly leathery, toothed, mid-green leaves. In summer produces numerous, flattened flower heads with central clusters of small, white, sterile flowers and several blue to white, sterile flowers along the margins. Is suitable for training along a low wall.
H. seemanii illus. p.196.
H. serrata, syn. *H. macrophylla* subsp. *serrata*. Deciduous, bushy, dense shrub. **H** and **S** 1.2m (4ft). Frost hardy. Has slender stems and light green leaves. From mid- to late summer bears flat heads of pink, lilac or white inner and pink or blue outer flowers. ♀ **'Bluebird'** (illus. p.135) has pale pink, pale purple or blue flowers. ♀ **'Diadem'** (illus. p.134) has a compact habit and bright blue – sometimes pink – flowers. ♀ **'Grayswood'** (illus. p.135), **H** and **S** 1.5m (5ft), is slow-growing and bears blue fertile flowers surrounded by white to pink, sterile flowers. **'Kiyosumi'** (illus. p.134) produces purple, young leaves and pink to white fertile flowers surrounded by red-edged, white sterile flowers. **'Preziosa'** see *H.* 'Preziosa'.
H. serratifolia, syn. *H. integerrima*, illus. p.196.
H. villosa. See *H. aspera* Villosa Group.

HYDROCHARIS

HYDROCHARITACEAE

Genus of one species of deciduous, perennial, floating water plant, grown for its foliage and flowers. Fully hardy. Requires an open, sunny position in still water. Propagate by detaching young plantlets as required.
H. morsus-ranae illus. p.434.

Hydrocleis. See *Hydrocleys.*

HYDROCLEYS

SYN. HYDROCLEIS

LIMNOCHARITACEAE

Genus of deciduous or evergreen, annual or perennial, water plants, grown for their floating foliage and attractive flowers. Frost tender, min. 1°C (34°F). Is best grown in large aquariums and tropical pools with good light. Propagate by seed when ripe or by tip cuttings year-round.
H. nymphoides (Water poppy). Deciduous, perennial, deep-water plant, evergreen in tropical conditions. **S** to 60cm (2ft). Has floating, oval, mid-green leaves and poppy-like, yellow flowers held above foliage during summer.

HYGROPHILA

ACANTHACEAE

Genus of deciduous or evergreen, perennial, submerged water plants and marsh plants, grown for their foliage. Frost tender, min. 13°C (55°F). Remove fading leaves regularly. Propagate by stem cuttings in spring or summer.

H. polysperma. Deciduous, perennial, submerged water plant. **S** indefinite. Lance-shaped, pale green leaves are borne on woody stems. In water above 16°C (61°F), is evergreen. Is suitable for a tropical aquarium.

HYLOCEREUS

CACTACEAE

Genus of fast-growing, perennial cacti with erect, slender, climbing stems that are jointed into sections, and many aerial roots. Makes successful grafting stock, except in northern Europe. Frost tender, min. 11°C (52°F). Needs sun or partial shade and very well-drained soil. Propagate by stem cuttings in spring or summer.

H. undatus (Night-blooming cereus, Queen-of-the-night). Fast-growing, climbing, perennial cactus. **H** 1m (3ft), **S** indefinite. Has freely branching, 3-angled, weakly spined, dark green stems, 7cm (3in) wide and jointed into sections. In summer bears flattish, white flowers, 30cm (12in) across, that last only one night.

HYLOMECON

PAPAVERACEAE

Genus of one species of vigorous perennial, grown for its large, cup-shaped flowers. Is good for rock gardens, borders and woodlands but may be invasive. Fully hardy. Prefers a partially shaded position and humus-rich, moist soil. Propagate by division in spring or by seed in autumn.

H. japonica illus. p.335.

Hylotelephium anacampseros. See *Sedum anacampseros.*
Hylotelephium cauticola. See *Sedum cauticola.*
Hylotelephium ewersii. See *Sedum ewersii.*
Hylotelephium populifolium. See *Sedum populifolium.*
Hylotelephium spectabile. See *Sedum spectabile.*
Hylotelephium sieboldii. See *Sedum sieboldii*
Hylotelephium tatarinowii. See *Sedum tatarinowii.*
Hymenanthera. See *Melicytus.*

HYMENOCALLIS

AMARYLLIDACEAE

Genus of bulbs, some of which are evergreen, grown for their fragrant flowers, somewhat like those of large daffodils. Half hardy to frost tender, min. 15°C (59°F). Needs a sheltered site, full sun or partial shade and well-drained soil. Plant in early summer, lifting for winter in cold districts. Alternatively, grow in a heated greenhouse; reduce water in winter, without drying out completely, then repot in spring. Propagate by offsets in spring or early summer.

H. calathina. See *Ismene narcissiflora.*
♀ ***H. x festalis.*** See *Ismene* x *deflexa.*
H. x macrostephana. See *Ismene* x *macrostephana.*
H. narcissiflora. See *Ismene narcissiflora.*
H. speciosa. Evergreen, winter-flowering bulb. **H** and **S** 30–45cm (12–18in). Frost tender. Has broadly elliptic, semi-erect, basal leaves. Produces a head of 5–10 fragrant, white or green-white flowers, each 20–30cm (8–12in) wide with a funnel-shaped cup and 6 long, narrow petals.
♀ ***H. x spofforthiae* 'Sulphur Queen'.** See *Ismene* x *spofforthiae* 'Sulphur Queen'.

HYMENOSPORUM

PITTOSPORACEAE

Genus of one species of evergreen shrub or tree, grown for its flowers and overall appearance. Frost tender, min. 5–7°C (41–45°F). Prefers full sun, though some shade is tolerated. Requires humus-rich, well-drained soil, ideally neutral to acid. Water containerized specimens freely when in full growth, less at other times. Propagate by seed when ripe, in autumn, or in spring or by semi-ripe cuttings in late summer.

H. flavum (Native Australian frangipani). Evergreen, erect shrub or tree, gradually spreading with age. **H** 10m (30ft) or more, **S** 5m (15ft) or more. Has oval to oblong, lustrous, rich green leaves. In spring–summer bears terminal panicles of very fragrant, tubular, 5-petalled, cream flowers that age to deep sulphur-yellow.

HYPERICUM

HYPERICACEAE/CLUSIACEAE

Genus of perennials and deciduous, semi-evergreen or evergreen sub-shrubs and shrubs, grown for their conspicuous yellow flowers with prominent stamens. Fully to half hardy. Large species and cultivars need sun or semi-shade and fertile, not too dry soil. Smaller types, which are good in rock gardens, do best in full sun and well-drained soil. Propagate species sub-shrubs and shrubs by softwood cuttings in summer or by seed in autumn, cultivars by softwood cuttings only in summer; perennials by seed or division in autumn or spring. Is generally trouble-free but *H.* x *inodorum* 'Elstead' is susceptible to rust, which produces orange spots on leaves, *H.* 'Hidcote' to a virus that makes leaves narrow and variegated.

H. balearicum. Evergreen, compact shrub. **H** and **S** to 60cm (2ft). Frost hardy. Small, oval, green leaves have wavy edges and rounded tips. Solitary, large, fragrant, shallowly cup-shaped, yellow flowers are produced at stem tips above foliage from early summer to autumn.

***H. beanii* 'Gold Cup'.** See *H.* x *cyathiflorum* 'Gold Cup'.

H. bellum. Semi-evergreen, arching, graceful shrub. **H** 1m (3ft), **S** 1.5m (5ft). Fully hardy. Cup-shaped, golden-yellow flowers are borne from mid-summer to early autumn. Shoots are red. Oval, wavy-edged, mid-green leaves redden in autumn.

H. calycinum illus. p.161.

H. cerastioides, syn. *H. rhodoppeum.* Vigorous, evergreen sub-shrub with upright and arching branches. **H** 15cm (6in) or more, **S** 40–50cm (16–20in). Fully hardy. Leaves are oval, hairy and soft greyish-green. In late spring and early summer produces masses of saucer-shaped, bright yellow flowers in terminal clusters. Cut back hard after flowering. Is suitable for a large rock garden.

H. coris. Evergreen, open, dome-shaped, occasionally prostrate, sub-shrub. **H** 15–30cm (6–12in), **S** 20cm (8in) or more. Frost hardy. Bears long-stemmed whorls of 3 or 4 pointed-oval leaves. Produces panicles of shallowly cup-shaped, bright yellow flowers, streaked red, in summer. Suits a sheltered rock garden.

***H. x cyathiflorum* 'Gold Cup'**, syn. *H. beanii* 'Gold Cup'. Semi-evergreen, arching shrub. **H** and **S** 1m (3ft). Frost hardy. Produces pinkish-brown shoots, oval, dark green leaves and, from mid-summer to early autumn, large, cup-shaped, golden-yellow flowers.

H. empetrifolium* subsp. *oliganthum*.** See *H.e.* var. *prostratum* of gardens. **var. *prostratum of gardens (syn. *H.e.* subsp. *oliganthum*) illus. p.373.
♀ ***H.* 'Hidcote'** illus. p.160.
***H. x inodorum* 'Elstead'** illus. p.161.
♀ ***H. kouytchense***, syn. *H. patulum* var. *grandiflorum*, illus. p.161.
♀ ***H. x moserianum.*** Deciduous, arching shrub. **H** 30cm (12in), **S** 60cm (24in). Frost hardy. Small, bowl-shaped, yellow flowers are produced above oval, dark green leaves from mid-summer to mid-autumn. **'Tricolor'** has leaves margined white and pink. Prefers a sheltered position.
♀ ***H. olympicum.*** Deciduous, upright, slightly spreading, dense sub-shrub. **H** 15–30cm (6–12in), **S** to 15cm (6in). Fully hardy. Tufts of upright stems are covered in small, oval, grey-green leaves. Produces terminal clusters of up to 5 cup-shaped, bright yellow flowers in summer.
♀ **f. *uniflorum* 'Citrinum'** (syn. *H.o.* 'Sulphureum') illus. p.343.

H. patulum. Evergreen or semi-evergreen, upright shrub. **H** and **S** 1m (3ft). Frost hardy. Large, cup-shaped, golden-yellow flowers open above oval, dark green leaves from mid-summer to mid-autumn. **var. *grandiflorum*** see *H. kouytchense.*

H. reptans. Deciduous, mat-forming shrub. **H** 5cm (2in), **S** 20cm (8in). Frost hardy. Oval, green leaves turn yellow or bright red in autumn. In summer produces flattish, golden-yellow flowers, crimson-flushed outside. Suits a rock garden.

H. rhodoppeum. See *H. cerastioides.*
♀ ***H.* 'Rowallane'** illus. p.206.

Hypocyrta radicans. See *Nematanthus gregarius.*
Hypocyrta strigillosa. See *Nematanthus strigillosus.*

HYPOESTES

ACANTHACEAE

Genus of mainly evergreen perennials, shrubs and sub-shrubs, grown for their flowers and foliage. Frost tender, min. 10°C (50°F). Needs bright light and well-drained soil. Water often in growing season, less in winter. Straggly stems should be cut back. Propagate by stem cuttings in spring or summer. *H. phyllostachya* may be grown as an annual using seed sown in spring.

H. aristata. Evergreen, bushy perennial or sub-shrub. **H** to 1m (3ft), **S** 60cm (2ft). Has oval, mid-green leaves to 8cm (3in) long. Small, tubular, deep pink to purple flowers are produced in terminal spikes in late winter.

♀ ***H. phyllostachya***, syn. *H. sanguinolenta* of gardens, illus. p.300.
H. sanguinolenta of gardens. See *H. phyllostachya.*

HYPOXIS

HYPOXIDACEAE

Genus of spring- or summer-flowering corms, grown for their flat, star-shaped flowers. Suits rock gardens. Frost to half hardy. Requires full sun and light, well-drained soil. Propagate by seed in autumn or spring.

H. angustifolia. Summer-flowering corm. **H** 10–20cm (4–8in), **S** 5–8cm (2–3in). Half hardy. Has slender, hairy, semi-erect, basal leaves. Stems each bear 3–7 star-shaped, yellow flowers, 1.5–2cm (5/8–3/4in) across.

H. capensis, syn. *H. stellata, Spiloxene capensis.* Spring-flowering corm with a basal leaf cluster. **H** 10–20cm (4–8in), **S** 5–8cm (2–3in). Half hardy. Has very slender, narrowly lance-shaped, erect leaves. Stems each produce an upward-facing flower with pointed, white or yellow petals and a purple eye.

H. stellata. See *H. capensis.*

HYPSELA

CAMPANULACEAE

Genus of vigorous, creeping perennials, grown for their flowers and heart-shaped leaves. Good as ground cover, especially in rock gardens. Frost hardy. Needs shade and moist soil. Propagate by division in spring.

H. longiflora. See *H. reniformis.*
H. reniformis, syn. *H. longiflora.* Vigorous, creeping, stemless perennial. **H** 2cm (3/4in), **S** indefinite. Has tiny, heart-shaped, fleshy leaves and, in spring–summer, small, star-shaped, pink-and-white flowers.

HYSSOPUS

LABIATAE/LAMIACEAE

Genus of perennials and semi-evergreen or deciduous shrubs, grown for their flowers, which attract bees and butterflies, and for their aromatic foliage, which has culinary and medicinal uses. May be grown as a low hedge. Fully hardy. Requires full sun and fertile, well-drained soil. Cut back hard or, if grown as a hedge, trim lightly, in spring. Propagate by softwood cuttings in summer or by seed in autumn.

H. officinalis (Hyssop) illus. p.157. **subsp. *aristatus*** is a semi-evergreen or deciduous, upright, dense shrub. **H** 60cm (2ft), **S** 1m (3ft). Aromatic, narrowly lance-shaped leaves are bright green. Densely clustered, small, 2-lipped, dark blue flowers are produced from mid-summer through to early autumn.

I

IBERIS

CRUCIFERAE/BRASSICACEAE

Genus of annuals, perennials, evergreen sub-shrubs and shrubs, grown for their flowers and excellent for rock gardens. Some species are short-lived, flowering themselves to death. Fully to half hardy. Requires sun and well-drained soil. Propagate by seed in spring, and sub-shrubs and shrubs by semi-ripe cuttings in summer.

I. amara illus. p.299. **'Giant Hyacinth-flowered'** is a group of fast-growing, upright, bushy annuals. **H** 30cm (12in), **S** 15cm (6in). Fully hardy. Has lance-shaped, mid-green leaves and, in summer, flattish heads of large, scented, 4-petalled flowers in a variety of colours.

I. commutata. See *I. sempervirens*.

I. saxatilis illus. p.360.

♀ ***I. sempervirens***, syn. *I. commutata*, illus. p.332.

♀ **'Snowflake'** (syn. *I.s.* 'Schneeflocke') is an evergreen, spreading sub-shrub. **H** 15–30cm (6–12in), **S** 45–60cm (18–24in). Fully hardy. Leaves are narrowly oblong, glossy and dark green. Dense, semi-spherical heads of 4-petalled, white flowers are produced in late spring and early summer. Trim after flowering.

I. umbellata. Fast-growing, upright, bushy annual. **H** 15–30cm (6–12in), **S** 20cm (8in). Fully hardy. Has lance-shaped, mid-green leaves. Heads of small, 4-petalled, white or pale purple flowers, sometimes bicoloured, are carried in summer and early autumn. **Fairy Series** illus. p.304.

IDESIA

FLACOURTIACEAE

Genus of one species of deciduous, summer-flowering tree, grown for its foliage and fruits. Both male and female plants are required to obtain fruits. Fully hardy. Needs sun or semi-shade and fertile, moist but well-drained soil, preferably neutral to acid. Propagate by softwood cuttings in summer or by seed in autumn.

I. polycarpa illus. p.75.

ILEX

Holly

AQUIFOLIACEAE

Genus of evergreen or deciduous trees and shrubs, grown for their foliage and fruits (berries). Mainly spherical berries, ranging in colour from red through yellow to black, are produced in autumn, following insignificant, usually white, flowers borne in spring. Almost all plants are unisexual, and to obtain fruits on a female plant, a male also needs to be grown. Fully to half hardy. All prefer well-drained soil. Grow in sun or shade, but deciduous plants and those with variegated foliage do best in sun or semi-shade. Hollies resent being transplanted, but respond well to hard pruning and pollarding, which should be done in late spring. Propagate by seed in spring or by semi-ripe cuttings from late summer to early winter. Holly leaf miner and holly aphid may cause problems. ⓘ Berries may cause mild stomach upset if ingested. See also feature panel p.94.

I. x altaclerensis. Group of vigorous, evergreen shrubs and trees. Frost hardy. Is resistant to pollution and coastal exposure. **'Balearica'** (illus. p.94) is an erect, female tree. **H** 12m (40ft), **S** 5m (15ft). Has green to olive-green young branches. Large, broadly oval leaves are spiny- or smooth-edged and glossy, dark green. Freely produces large, bright red berries. **'Belgica'** is an erect, dense, female tree. **H** 12m (40ft), **S** 5m (15ft). Young branches are green to yellowish-green. Has large, lance-shaped to oblong, spiny- or smooth-edged, glossy, mid-green leaves. Large, orange-red fruits are freely produced. ♀ **'Belgica Aurea',** syn. *I. x a.* 'Silver Sentinel', *I. perado* 'Aurea', (illus. p.94) is an upright, female tree. **H** 8m (25ft), **S** 3m (10ft). Young branches are green with yellow streaks. Has large, lance-shaped, mainly spineless, dark green leaves, mottled with grey-green and irregularly edged with yellow. Red berries are produced only rarely. ♀ **'Camelliifolia'** (illus. p.94) is a narrow, pyramidal, female tree. **H** 14m (46ft), **S** 3m (10ft). Has purple young branches and large, oblong, mainly smooth-edged, glossy, dark green leaves. Reliably produces large, scarlet fruits; is an excellent specimen tree. **'Camelliifolia Variegata'** (illus. p.94), **H** 8m (25ft), **S** 3m (10ft), is similar to *I. x a.* 'Camelliifolia', but leaves have broad, yellow margins. ♀ **'Golden King'** (illus. p.94) is a bushy, female shrub. **H** 6m (20ft), **S** 5m (15ft). Young branches are green with a purplish flush. Has large, oblong to oval, sometimes slightly spiny, dark green leaves, each splashed with grey-green in the centre and with a bright yellow margin that turns to cream on older leaves. Is not a good fruiter, bearing only a few reddish-brown berries, but is excellent as a hedge or a specimen plant. ♀ **'Hodginsii'** is a vigorous, dense, male tree. **H** 14m (46ft), **S** 10m (30ft). Shoots are purple; leaves are broadly oval, sparsely spiny and glossy, blackish-green. ♀ **'Lawsoniana'** is a bushy, female shrub. **H** 6m (20ft), **S** 5m (15ft). Is similar to *I. x a.* 'Golden King', but has leaves splashed irregularly in the centre with gold and lighter green. Foliage tends to revert to plain green. **'N.F. Barnes'** is a dense, female shrub. **H** 5.5m (18ft), **S** 4m (12ft). Has purple shoots and oval, mainly entire but spine-tipped, glossy, dark green leaves and red berries. **'Silver Sentinel'** see *I. x a.* 'Belgica Aurea'. **'Wilsonii'** is a vigorous, female tree. **H** 8m (25ft), **S** 5m (15ft). Has purplish-green young branches and large, oblong to oval, glossy, mid-green leaves with prominent veins and large spines. Freely produces large, scarlet fruits and makes a good hedging or specimen plant.

♀ ***I. aquifolium*** (Common holly; illus. p.94). Evergreen, much-branched, erect shrub or tree. **H** 20m (70ft), **S** 6m (20ft). Frost hardy. Has variably shaped, wavy, sharply spined, glossy, dark green leaves and bright red berries. ♀ **'Amber'** illus. p.92. ♀ **'Argentea Marginata'** (Silver-margined holly; illus. p.94) is a columnar, female tree. **H** 14m (46ft), **S** 5m (15ft). Young branches are green, streaked with cream. Broadly oval, spiny, dark green leaves, with wide, cream margins, are shrimp-pink when young. Bears an abundance of bright red berries. Is good for hedging. **'Argentea Marginata Pendula'** (Perry's weeping silver holly) is a slow-growing, weeping, female tree. **H** 6m (20ft), **S** 5m (15ft). Has purple young branches and broadly oval, spiny, dark green leaves, mottled with grey-green and broadly edged with cream. Bears red fruits. Is good as a specimen plant in a small garden. **'Atlas'** is an erect, male shrub. **H** 5m (15ft), **S** 3m (10ft). Has green young branches and oval, spiny, glossy, dark green leaves. Is useful for landscaping and hedging. **'Aurea Regina'** see *I.a.* 'Golden Queen'. **'Aurifodina'** is an erect, dense, female shrub. **H** 6m (20ft), **S** 3m (10ft). Young branches are purplish. Oval, spiny leaves are olive-green with golden margins that turn tawny-yellow in winter. Produces a good crop of deep scarlet fruits. **'Bacciflava'**, syn. f. *bacciflava* (illus. p.94) is a much-branched, usually erect shrub or tree. **H** 20m (70ft), **S** 6m (20ft). Has variably shaped, wavy, sharply spined, glossy, dark green leaves and yellow fruits. **'Crispa Aureopicta'** is a male tree of open habit. **H** 10m (30ft), **S** 6m (20ft). Narrowly oval, twisted, sparsely spiny, blackish-green leaves are centrally blotched with golden-yellow. Foliage tends to revert to plain green. **'Ferox'** (Hedgehog holly) is an open, male shrub. **H** 6m (20ft), **S** 4m (12ft). Has purple young branches and oval, dark green leaves with spines over the entire leaf surface. ♀ **'Ferox Argentea'** (Silver hedgehog holly; illus. p.94) is similar to *I.a.* 'Ferox', but has leaves with cream margins. **'Flavescens'** (Moonlight holly) is a columnar, female shrub. **H** 6m (20ft), **S** 5m (15ft). Young branches are purplish-red. Variably shaped leaves are dark green, with a yellowish flush when young that will last year-round when grown in good light. Produces plentiful, red berries. **'Golden Milkboy'** (illus. p.94) is a dense, male shrub. **H** 6m (20ft), **S** 4m (12ft). Has purplish-green young branches and oval, very spiny, bright green leaves with heavily blotched, bright yellow centres. Leaves tend to revert to plain green. ♀ **'Golden Queen'** (syn. *I.a.* 'Aurea Regina') is a dense tree that, despite its name, is male. **H** 10m (30ft), **S** 6m (20ft). Broadly oval, very spiny, mid-green leaves are edged with golden-yellow. **'Golden van Tol'**, a sport of *I.a.* 'J.C. van Tol', is an upright, female shrub. **H** 4m (12ft), **S** 3m (10ft). Young branches are purple. Oval, puckered, slightly spiny, dark green leaves have irregular, clear yellow margins. Produces a sparse crop of red fruits. Is good for hedging or as a specimen plant. ♀ **'Handsworth New Silver'** is a dense, columnar, female shrub. **H** 8m (25ft), **S** 5m (15ft). Branches are purple. Oblong to oval, spiny, dark green leaves have broad, cream margins. Bears a profusion of bright red fruits. Is excellent as a hedge or specimen plant and is good for a small garden. **'Hascombensis'** is a slow-growing, dense shrub of unknown sex. **H** 1.5m (5ft), **S** 1–1.2m (3–4ft). Has purplish-green young branches and small, oval, spiny, dark green leaves. Does not produce berries. Suits a rock garden. ♀ **'J.C. van Tol'** is an open, female shrub that does not require cross-fertilization to produce fruits. **H** 6m (20ft), **S** 4m (12ft). Branches are dark purple when young. Oval, puckered, slightly spiny leaves are dark green. Produces a good crop of red berries. Is useful as a hedge or for a tub. ♀ **'Madame Briot'** (illus. p.94) is a vigorous, bushy, female tree. **H** 10m (30ft), **S** 5m (15ft). Young branches are purplish-green. Leaves are large, broadly oval, spiny and dark green with bright golden borders. Bears scarlet berries. **'Ovata Aurea'** is a dense, male shrub. **H** 5m (15ft), **S** 4m (12ft). Has reddish-brown young branches and oval, regularly spiny, dark green leaves with bright golden margins. ♀ **'Pyramidalis'** is a dense, female tree that does not require cross-fertilization to produce fruits. **H** 6m (20ft), **S** 5m (15ft). Has green young branches and narrowly elliptic, slightly spiny, mid-green leaves. Produces masses of scarlet fruits. Is suitable for a small garden. **'Pyramidalis Aureomarginata'** (illus. p.94) is an upright, female shrub. **H** 6m (20ft), **S** 5m (15ft). Young branches are green. Has narrowly elliptic, mid-green leaves with prominent, golden margins and spines on upper half. Bears a large crop of red berries. ♀ **'Pyramidalis Fructu Luteo'** is a conical, female shrub that broadens with age. **H** 6m (20ft), **S** 4m (12ft). Branches are green when young. Has oval, often spineless, dark green leaves and bears yellow berries. Is excellent for a small garden. **'Scotica'** is a large, stiff, compact, female shrub. **H** 6m (20ft), **S** 4m (12ft). Oval, usually spineless, glossy, very dark green leaves are slightly twisted. Bears red fruits. **'Silver King'** see *I.a.* 'Silver Queen'. **'Silver Milkboy'** see *I.a.* 'Silver Milkmaid'. **'Silver Milkmaid'**, syn. *I.a.* 'Silver Milkboy' (illus. p.94) is a dense, female shrub. **H** 5.5m (18ft), **S** 4m (12ft). Oval, wavy-edged, very spiny leaves are bronze when young, maturing to bright green, each with a central, creamy-white blotch, but tend to revert to plain green. Produces an abundance of scarlet berries. Makes a very attractive specimen plant. ♀ **'Silver Queen'**, syn. *I.a.* 'Silver King' (illus. p.94) is a dense shrub that, despite its name, is male. **H** 5m (15ft), **S** 4m (12ft). Has purple young branches. Oval, spiny leaves, pink when young, mature to very dark green, almost black, with broad, cream edging. **'Watereriana'** (syn. *I.a.* 'Waterer's Gold') is a dense, male bush. **H** and **S** 5m (15ft). Young branches are green, streaked with yellow. Oval, spiny- or smooth-edged leaves are greyish-green, with broad, golden margins. Is best grown as a specimen plant. **'Waterer's Gold'** see *I.a.* 'Watereriana'.

I. x aquipernyi. Evergreen, upright shrub. **H** 5m (15ft), **S** 3m (10ft). Frost hardy. Has small, oval, spiny, glossy, dark green leaves with long tips. Berries are large and red.

I. chinensis of gardens. See *I. purpurea*.

I. ciliospinosa. Evergreen, upright shrub or tree. **H** 6m (20ft), **S** 4m (12ft).

Frost hardy. Has small, oval, weak-spined, dull green leaves and red berries.
I. cornuta (Horned holly). Evergreen, dense, rounded shrub. **H** 4m (12ft), **S** 5m (15ft). Frost hardy. Rectangular, dull green leaves are spiny except on older bushes. Produces large, red berries. **'Burfordii'** is female, **S** 2.5m (8ft), has glossy leaves with only a terminal spine and bears a profusion of fruits. **'Rotunda'**, **H** 2m (6ft), **S** 1.2m (4ft), is also female and produces a small crop of fruits; is useful for a tub or small garden.
I. crenata (Box-leaved holly, Japanese holly). Evergreen, spreading shrub or tree. **H** 5m (15ft), **S** 3m (10ft). Fully hardy. Has very small, oval, dark green leaves with rounded teeth. Bears glossy, black fruits. Is useful for landscaping or as hedging. **'Bullata'** see *I.c.* 'Convexa'. ♀ **'Convexa'**, syn. *I.c.* 'Bullata' (illus. p.94) is a dense, female shrub. **H** 2.5m (8ft), **S** 1.2–1.5m (4–5ft). Has purplish-green young branches and oval, puckered, glossy leaves. Bears glossy, black fruits. **'Helleri'** is a spreading, female shrub. **H** 1.2m (4ft), **S** 1–1.2m (3–4ft). Has green young branches and oval leaves with few spines. Has glossy, black fruits. Is much used for landscaping.
f. *latifolia* (syn. *I.c.* 'Latifolia') is a spreading to erect, female shrub or tree. **H** 6m (20ft), **S** 3m (10ft). Young branches are green and broadly oval leaves have tiny teeth. Produces glossy, black berries. **var. *paludosa*** is a prostrate shrub or tree. **H** 15–30cm (6–12in), **S** indefinite. Has very small, oval, dark green leaves with rounded teeth. Bears glossy, black fruits. **'Variegata'** is an open, male shrub. **H** 4m (12ft), **S** 2.5m (8ft). Oval leaves are spotted or blotched with yellow, but tend to revert to plain green.
I. dipyrena (Himalayan holly). Evergreen, dense, upright tree. **H** 12m (40ft), **S** 8m (25ft). Frost hardy. Elliptic, dull green leaves are spiny when young, later smooth-edged. Bears large, red fruits.
I. fargesii. Evergreen, broadly conical tree or shrub. **H** 6m (20ft), **S** 5m (15ft). Frost hardy. Has green or purple shoots and oval, small-toothed, mid- to dark green leaves. Produces red berries. **var. *brevifolia***, **H** 4m (12ft), is dense and rounded.
I. georgei. Evergreen, compact shrub. **H** 5m (15ft), **S** 4m (12ft). Half hardy. Has small, lance-shaped or oval, weak-spined, glossy, dark green leaves with long tips. Berries are red.
I. glabra (Inkberry). Evergreen, dense, upright shrub. **H** 2.5m (8ft), **S** 2m (6ft). Fully hardy. Small, oblong to oval, dark green leaves are smooth-edged or may have slight teeth near tips. Produces black fruits.
I. insignis. See *I. kingiana*.
I. integra. Evergreen, dense, bushy shrub or tree. **H** 6m (20ft), **S** 5m (15ft). Frost hardy. Has oval, blunt-tipped, bright green leaves with smooth edges. Bears large, deep red berries.
***I.* 'Jermyns Dwarf'.** See *I. pernyi* 'Jermyns Dwarf'.
I. kingiana, syn. *I. insignis*. Evergreen, upright tree. **H** 6m (20ft), **S** 4m (12ft). Half hardy. Very large, oblong, leathery, dark green leaves have small spines. Berries are bright red.
I. x koehneana. Evergreen, conical shrub. **H** 6m (20ft), **S** 5m (15ft). Fully hardy. Young branches are green. Has very large, oblong, spiny, mid-green leaves and red fruits. ♀**'Chestnut Leaf'** (illus. p.94) has elliptic, regularly spined, yellow-green leaves reminiscent of sweet chestnut.
I. latifolia (Tarajo holly). Evergreen, upright shrub. **H** 6m (20ft), **S** 5m (15ft). Half hardy. Has stout, olive-green young branches, very large, oblong, dark green leaves with short spines and plentiful, red fruits.
I. macrocarpa. Deciduous, upright tree. **H** 10m (30ft), **S** 6m (20ft). Frost hardy. Has large, oval, saw-toothed, mid-green leaves and very large, black berries.
I. x meserveae (Blue holly). Group of vigorous, evergreen, dense shrubs. Fully hardy, but does not thrive in a maritime climate. Has oval, glossy, greenish-blue leaves. **'Conapri'** see Blue Princess. **Blue Princess ('Conapri')** (illus. p.94), **H** 3m (10ft), **S** 1.2m (4ft), is female and has purplish-green young branches, small, oval, wavy, spiny leaves and an abundance of red fruits.
I. opaca (American holly). Evergreen, erect tree. **H** 14m (46ft), **S** 1.2m (4ft). Fully hardy, but does not thrive in a maritime climate. Oval leaves are dull green above, yellow-green beneath and spiny- or smooth-edged. Has red fruits.
I. pedunculosa. Evergreen, upright shrub or tree. **H** 10m (30ft), **S** 6m (20ft). Fully hardy. Oval, dark green leaves are smooth-edged. Bright red berries appear on very long stalks.
***I. perado* 'Aurea'**. See *I.* x *altaclerensis* 'Belgica Aurea'.
I. pernyi (illus. p.94). Slow-growing, evergreen, stiff shrub. **H** 8m (25ft), **S** 4m (12ft). Fully hardy. Has pale green young branches and small, oblong, spiny, dark green leaves. Produces red berries. **'Jermyns Dwarf'** (syn. *I.* 'Jermyns Dwarf'), **H** 60cm (2ft), **S** 1.2m (4ft), is low-growing and female, with glossy, very spiny leaves.
I. purpurea, syn. *I. chinensis* of gardens. Evergreen, upright tree. **H** 12m (40ft), **S** 6m (20ft). Half hardy. Oval, thin-textured, glossy, dark green leaves have rounded teeth. Lavender flowers are followed by egg-shaped, glossy, scarlet fruits.
I. serrata. Deciduous, bushy shrub. **H** 4m (12ft), **S** 2.5m (8ft). Fully hardy. Small, oval, finely toothed, bright green leaves are downy when young. Pink flowers are followed by small, red fruits. **f. *leucocarpa*** bears white berries.
I. verticillata (Winterberry; illus. p.94.) Deciduous, dense, suckering shrub. **H** 2m (6ft), **S** 1.2–1.5m (4–5ft). Fully hardy. Young branches are purplish-green. Produces oval or lance-shaped, saw-toothed, bright green leaves. Bears masses of long-lasting, red berries that remain on bare branches during winter.
I. yunnanensis. Evergreen, spreading to erect shrub. **H** 4m (12ft), **S** 2.5m (8ft). Frost hardy. Branches are downy. Small, oval leaves, with rounded teeth, are brownish-green when young, glossy, dark green in maturity. Produces red berries.

ILLICIUM

ILLICIACEAE/SCHISANDRACEAE

Genus of evergreen, spring- to early summer-flowering trees and shrubs, grown for their foliage and unusual flowers. Frost to half hardy. Does best in semi-shade or shade and moist, neutral to acid soil. Propagate by semi-ripe cuttings in summer.
I. anisatum (Chinese anise). Slow-growing, evergreen, conical tree or shrub. **H** and **S** 6m (20ft). Frost hardy. Produces oval, aromatic, glossy, dark green leaves. Star-shaped, greenish-yellow flowers, with numerous narrow petals, are carried in mid-spring.
I. floridanum (Purple anise). Evergreen, bushy shrub. **H** and **S** 2m (6ft). Half hardy. Lance-shaped, leathery, deep green leaves are very aromatic. Star-shaped, red or purplish-red flowers, with numerous, narrow petals, are produced in late spring and early summer.

IMPATIENS

BALSAMINACEAE

Genus of annuals and mainly evergreen perennials and sub-shrubs, often with succulent but brittle stems. In cold climates some may be herbaceous. Fully hardy to frost tender, min. 5–10°C (41–50°F). Prefers sun or semi-shade and moist but not waterlogged soil. Propagate by seed or by stem cuttings in spring or summer. Red spider mite, aphids and whitefly may cause problems under glass.
***I.* 'Balfuspeafro'.** See *I.* Fusion Series Fusion Peach Frost.
I. balsamina (illus. p.300). **'Blackberry Ice'** is a fast-growing, upright, bushy annual. **H** 70cm (28in), **S** 45cm (18in). Half hardy. Has lance-shaped, pale green leaves and, in summer and early autumn, large, double, purple flowers, splashed with white. **Tom Thumb Series** is a dwarf, sparsely branched, slightly hairy annual with toothed leaves. **H** to 30cm (12in), **S** 45cm (18in). Frost tender, min. 5°C (41°F). From summer to early autumn, produces double, pink, scarlet, violet or white flowers.
***I.* Expo Series 'Expo Pink'** illus. p.307.
***I.* Fusion Series Fusion Peach Frost ('Balfuspeafro')** illus. p.325.
***I.* New Guinea Group 'Mimas'.** Sub-shrubby hybrid perennial, grown as an annual. **H** 30cm (12in), **S** 35–40cm (14–16in). Frost tender, min. 10°C (50°F). Opposite or whorled, mid-green, toothed leaves often have central yellowish-green marks. Bears large, red open-faced flowers in spring–autumn.
I. niamniamensis. Evergreen, bushy perennial. **H** to 90cm (3ft), **S** 30cm (1ft). Frost tender, min. 15°C (59°F). Has reddish-green stems and oval, toothed leaves to 20cm (8in) long. Showy, 5-petalled, hooded, yellowish-green flowers, 2.5cm (1in) long and each with a long, orange, red, crimson or purple spur, appear in summer–autumn. **'Congo Cockatoo'** has red, green and yellow flowers.
I. oliveri. See *I. sodenii*.
♀ ***I. repens*** illus. p.476.
***I.* 'Sakimp011'.** See *I.* Sunpatiens Series Sunpatiens Compact Orange.
I. sodenii, syn. *I. oliveri*. Evergreen, strong-growing, bushy perennial. **H** 1.2m (4ft) or more, **S** 60cm (2ft). Frost tender, min 10°C (50°F). Narrowly oval, toothed leaves, in whorls of 4–10, are 15cm (6in) or more long. Almost flat, white or pale pink to mauve flowers, 5cm (2in) or more wide, are produced mainly in summer.
***I.* Sunpatiens Series Sunpatiens Compact Orange ('Sakimp011')** illus. p.325.
♀ **Super Elfin Series, H** and **S** 20cm (8in), has flattish flowers in mixed colours. **Swirl Series** are subshrubby perennials, usually grown as annuals. **H** 15–20cm (6–8in), **S** to 60cm (24in). Frost tender, min. 10°C (50°F). Have light green to red-flushed stems and leaves. In summer, bear flattened, slender-spurred, pink-and-orange flowers margined in rose-red. Flowers of ♀ **Tempo Series, H** to 23cm (9in), include shades of violet, orange, pink and red, as well as bicolours and picotees.
I. tinctoria illus. p.216.
I. walleriana (Busy lizzie). Fast-growing, evergreen, bushy perennial, usually grown as an annual. **H** and **S** to 60cm (2ft). Half hardy. Has oval, fresh green leaves. Flattish, 5-petalled, spurred, bright red, pink, purple, violet or white flowers appear from spring to autumn. **Accent Series 'Accent Pink'** is a compact, very long-flowering perennial, grown as an annual. **H** 20–25cm (8–10in), **S** 25–30cm (10–12in). Has succulent stems and rounded, flat, 5-petalled, spurred, blush-pink flowers, with dark centres, in summer and autumn. Hates drought. **Confection Series, H** and **S** 20–30cm (8–12in) have fresh green leaves and small, flat, spurred, double or semi-double flowers, in shades of red or pink, from spring to autumn. **Fiesta Series 'Fiesta Apple Blossom'** is a mound-forming, well-branched, prolific perennial, grown as an annual. **H** 25–40cm (10–16in), **S** 25– 35cm (10–14in). Half hardy. Produces rose-like, fully double, dark-centred, blush-pink flowers in summer and autumn. Is good in a hanging basket or other container or in a border. Hates drought. **Masquerade ('Tuckmas')** illus. p.307.

IMPERATA

GRAMINAE/POACEAE

See also GRASSES, BAMBOOS, RUSHES and SEDGES.
***I. cylindrica* 'Rubra'** illus. p.285.

INCARVILLEA

BIGNONIACEAE

Genus of late spring- or summer-flowering perennials, suitable for rock gardens and borders. Fully to frost hardy, but protect crowns with bracken or compost in winter. Requires sun and fertile, well-drained soil. Propagate by seed in autumn or spring.
I. delavayi illus. p.265.
I. mairei illus. p.265.

INDIGOFERA

LEGUMINOSAE/PAPILIONACEAE

Genus of perennials and deciduous shrubs, grown for their foliage and small, pea-like flowers. Fully to frost hardy; in cold areas, hard frosts may cut plants to ground, but they usually regrow from base in spring. Needs full sun and fertile, well-drained soil. Cut out dead wood in spring. Propagate by softwood cuttings in summer or by seed in autumn.

I. decora. Deciduous, bushy shrub. **H** 45cm (1½ft), **S** 1m (3ft). Frost hardy. Glossy, dark green leaves each have 7–13 oval leaflets. Long spikes of pink or white flowers appear from mid- to late summer.

I. dielsiana illus. p.152.

I. gerardiana. See *I. heterantha.*

♀ ***I. heterantha,*** syn. *I. gerardiana*, illus. p.133.

I. pseudotinctoria. Deciduous, arching shrub. **H** 1m (3ft) or more, **S** 2m (6ft). Fully hardy. Each dark green leaf has usually 7–9 oval leaflets. Long, dense racemes of small, pale pink flowers are borne in mid-summer to early autumn.

INULA

COMPOSITAE/ASTERACEAE

Genus of summer-flowering, clump-forming, sometimes rhizomatous perennials. Fully hardy. Most need sun and moist but well-drained soil. Propagate by seed or division in spring or autumn.

I. acaulis. Tuft-forming, rhizomatous perennial. **H** 5–10cm (2–4in), **S** 15cm (6in). Has lance-shaped to elliptic, hairy leaves. Solitary, almost stemless, daisy-like, golden-yellow flower heads are produced in summer. Is good for a rock garden.

I. ensifolia illus. p.277.

I. hookeri illus. p.243.

I. macrocephala of gardens. See *I. royleana.*

I. magnifica illus. p.219.

I. oculis-christi. Spreading, rhizomatous perennial. **H** 45cm (18in), **S** 60cm (24in). Stems each bear 2 or 3 daisy-like, yellow flower heads, which appear in summer. Has lance-shaped to elliptic, hairy, mid-green leaves.

I. royleana, syn. *I. macrocephala* of gardens, illus. p.277.

IOCHROMA

SOLANACEAE

Genus of evergreen, semi-evergreen and deciduous shrubs and small trees, grown for their flowers. Half hardy to frost tender, min. 7–10°C (45–50°F). Needs full light or partial shade and fertile, well-drained soil. Water potted plants freely when in full growth, moderately at other times. Tip prune young plants to stimulate a bushy habit. Cut back flowered stems by half in late winter. Propagate by greenwood or semi-ripe cuttings in summer. Whitefly and red spider mite are sometimes troublesome.

I. australe, syn. *Acnistus australis*, illus. p.138.

I. cyaneum, syn. *I. tubulosum*, illus. p.457.

I. tubulosum. See *I. cyaneum.*

IONOPSIDIUM

CRUCIFERAE/BRASSICACEAE

Genus of annuals. Only one species is usually cultivated, for rock gardens and as edging. Frost hardy. Grow in semi-shade and in fertile, well-drained soil. Propagate by seed sown outdoors in spring, early summer or early autumn.

I. acaule (Violet cress). Fast-growing, upright annual. **H** 5–8cm (2–3in), **S** 2.5cm (1in). Rounded leaves are mid-green. Tiny, 4-petalled, lilac or white flowers, flushed with deep blue, are produced in summer and early autumn.

IPHEION

LILIACEAE/ALLIACEAE

Genus of bulbs that freely produce many star-shaped, blue, white or yellow flowers in spring and make excellent pot plants in cold greenhouses. Frost hardy. Prefers a sheltered situation in dappled sunlight and well-drained soil. Plant in autumn; after flowering, dies down for summer. Propagate by offsets in late summer or early autumn.

♀ ***I. uniflorum* 'Froyle Mill'** illus. p.419. ♀ **'Wisley Blue'** is a spring-flowering bulb. **H** 10–15cm (4–6in), **S** 5–8cm (2–3in). Bears linear, semi-erect, basal, pale green leaves, which smell of onions if damaged. Leafless stems each produce an upward-facing, pale blue flower, 3–4cm (1¼–1½in) across.

IPOMOEA

SYN. MINA, PHARBITIS

CONVOLVULACEAE

Genus of mainly evergreen shrubs, perennials, annuals and soft- or woody-stemmed, twining climbers. Half hardy to frost tender, min. 7–10°C (45–50°F). Provide full light and humus-rich, well-drained soil. Water freely when in full growth, less at other times. Support is needed. Thin out or cut back congested growth in spring. Propagate by seed in spring or by softwood or semi-ripe cuttings in summer. Whitefly and red spider mite may cause problems. ① Seeds are highly toxic if ingested.

I. acuminata. See *I. indica.*

I. alba, syn. *Calonyction aculeatum, I. bona-nox* (Moon flower). Evergreen, soft-stemmed, twining climber with prickly stems that exude milky juice when cut. **H** 7m (22ft) or more. Frost tender, min. 10°C (50°F). Oval or sometimes 3-lobed leaves are 20cm (8in) long. Fragrant, tubular, white flowers, to 15cm (6in) long and expanded at the mouths to 15cm (6in) across, open at night in summer.

***I. batatus* 'Blackie'** illus. p.311. **'Margarita'** illus. p.318.

I. bona-nox. See *I. alba.*

I. coccinea, syn. *Quamoclit coccinea* (Red morning glory, Star ipomoea). Annual, twining climber. **H** to 3m (10ft). Frost tender, min. 10°C (50°F). Arrow- or heart-shaped leaves are long-pointed and often toothed. Fragrant, tubular, scarlet flowers, with yellow throats and expanded mouths, are produced in late summer and autumn.

I. hederacea illus. p.204.

♀ ***I. horsfalliae.*** Strong-growing, evergreen, woody-stemmed, twining climber. **H** 2–3m (6–10ft). Frost tender, min. 7–10°C (45–50°F). Leaves have 5–7 radiating lobes or leaflets; stalked clusters of funnel-shaped, deep rose-pink or rose-purple flowers, 6cm (2½in) long, appear from summer to winter. The flowers of **'Briggsii'** are larger and more richly coloured than those of the species.

I. imperialis. See *I. nil.*

♀ ***I. indica,*** syn. *I. acuminata, I. learii*, illus. p.462.

I. learii. See *I. indica.*

I. lobata, syn. *I. versicolor, Quamoclit lobata*, illus. p.202.

I. x multifida, syn. *I. x sloteri* (Cardinal climber, Hearts-and-honey vine). Annual, twining climber. **H** 3m (10ft). Frost tender, min. 10°C (50°F). Triangular-oval leaves are divided into 7–15 segments. Tubular, wide-mouthed, crimson flowers with white eyes appear in summer.

I. nil, syn. *I. imperialis.* **'Early Call'** is a short-lived, soft-stemmed, perennial, twining climber with hairy stems, best grown as an annual. **H** to 4m (12ft). Half hardy. Leaves are heart-shaped or 3-lobed. From summer to early autumn bears large, funnel-shaped flowers in a range of colours, with white tubes. **'Scarlett O'Hara'** has deep red flowers.

I. purpurea, syn. *Convolvulus purpureus* (Common morning glory). Short-lived, soft-stemmed, perennial, twining climber, best grown as an annual, with hairy stems. **H** to 5m (15ft). Half hardy. Leaves are heart-shaped or 3-lobed. From summer to early autumn has funnel-shaped, deep purple to bluish-purple or reddish flowers with white throats and bristly sepals.

I. quamoclit, syn. *Quamoclit pennata*, illus. p.202.

***I. rubrocaerulea* 'Heavenly Blue'.** See *I. tricolor* 'Heavenly Blue'.

I. x sloteri. See *I. x multifida.*

♀ ***I. tricolor* 'Heavenly Blue'**, syn. *I. rubrocaerulea* 'Heavenly Blue', illus. p.205.

I. tuberosa. See *Merremia tuberosa.*

I. versicolor. See *I. lobata.*

IPOMOPSIS

POLEMONIACEAE

Genus of perennials and biennials, often grown as pot plants for green-houses and conservatories. Half hardy. Grow in cool, airy conditions with bright light and in fertile, well-drained soil. Propagate by seed sown under glass in early spring or early summer.

I. aggregata. Slow-growing biennial with upright, slender, hairy stems. **H** to 1m (3ft), **S** 30cm (1ft). Mid-green leaves are divided into linear leaflets. Fragrant, trumpet-shaped flowers, borne in summer, are usually brilliant red, sometimes spotted yellow, but may be rose, yellow or white.

IRESINE

AMARANTHACEAE

Genus of perennials, grown for their colourful leaves. Frost tender, min. 10–15°C (50–59°F). Requires bright light to retain leaf colour and a good, loamy, well-drained soil. Pinch out tips in growing season to obtain bushy plants. Propagate by stem cuttings in spring.

I. herbstii (Beefsteak plant). Bushy perennial. **H** to 60cm (24in), **S** 45cm (18in). Has red stems and rounded, purplish-red leaves, notched at their tips and 10cm (4in) long, with paler or yellowish-red veins. Flowers are insignificant.

'Aureoreticulata' illus. p.319.

♀ ***I. lindenii*** (Blood leaf). Bushy perennial. **H** 60cm (24in), **S** 45cm (18in). Has lance-shaped, dark red leaves, 5–10cm (2–4in) long. Flowers are insignificant.

IRIS

IRIDACEAE

Genus of upright, rhizomatous or bulbous (occasionally fleshy-rooted) perennials, some of which are evergreen, grown for their distinctive and colourful flowers. Each flower has 3 usually large 'falls' (pendent or semi-pendent petals), which in a number of species have conspicuous beards or crests; 3 generally smaller 'standards' (erect, horizontal or, occasionally, pendent petals); and a 3-branched style. In many irises the style branches are petal-like. Unless otherwise stated below, flower stems are unbranched. Green, then brown seed pods are ellipsoid to cylindrical and often ribbed. Irises are suitable for borders, rock gardens, woodlands, watersides, bog gardens, alpine houses, cold frames and containers. Species and cultivars described are fully hardy unless otherwise stated, but some groups may thrive only in the specific growing conditions mentioned below. Propagate species by division of rhizomes or offsets in late summer or by seed in autumn, named cultivars by division only.

Botanically, irises are divided into a number of sub-genera and sections, and it is convenient, for horticultural purposes, to use some of these botanical names for groups of irises with similar characteristics and requiring comparable cultural treatment. ① All parts may cause severe discomfort if ingested; contact with the sap may irritate skin. See also feature panel pp.224–5.

Rhizomatous These irises have rhizomes as rootstocks; leaves are sword-shaped and usually in a basal fan.

Bearded irises are rhizomatous and have 'beards', consisting of numerous often coloured hairs, along the centre of each fall. In some irises, the end of the beard is enlarged into the shape of a horn. The group covers the vast majority of irises, including many named cultivars, grown in gardens; all are derived from *I. pallida* and related species. Bearded irises thrive in full sun in fairly rich, well-drained, preferably slightly alkaline soil. Some are very tolerant and will grow and flower reasonably in partial shade in poorer soil. For horticultural purposes, various groupings of hybrid bearded irises are recognized, based mainly on the height of the plants in flower. These include **Miniature Dwarf, H** to 20cm (8in); **Standard Dwarf, H** 20–40cm (8–16in); **Intermediate**, **H** 40–70cm (16–28in); and

Tall, **H** 70cm (28in) or more (this last category may be further subdivided). In general, the shorter the iris, the earlier the flowering season (from early spring to early summer). **Oncocyclus** irises are rhizomatous, with very large and often bizarrely coloured flowers, one to each stem, which have bearded falls. They require full sun, sharply drained but fairly rich soil and, after flowering, a dry period of dormancy in summer and early autumn. Difficult to cultivate successfully, they are best grown in an alpine house or covered frame in climates subject to summer rains.

Regelia irises are closely related to Oncocyclus irises, differing in having bearded standards as well as falls and in having 2 flowers to each stem. They require similar conditions of cultivation, although a few species, such as *I. hoogiana*, have proved easier to grow than Oncocyclus irises. Hybrids between the 2 groups have been raised and are known as **Regeliocyclus** irises.

Beardless irises, also rhizomatous, lack hairs on the falls; most have very similar cultural requirements to bearded irises but some prefer heavier soil. Various groupings are recognized, of which the following are the most widely known. **Pacific Coast** irises, a group of Californian species and their hybrids, prefer acid to neutral soil and grow well in sun or partial shade, appreciating some humus in the soil; they are best grown from seed as they resent being moved. **Spuria** irises (*I. spuria* and its relatives) grow in sun or semi-shade and well-drained but moist soil. A number of species and hybrids prefers moist, waterside conditions; these include the well-known Siberian irises (*I. sibirica* and its relatives) and the **Japanese** water irises, such as *I. ensata* and *I. laevigata*, which may also be grown as border plants, but succeed best in open, sunny, humus-rich, moist positions.

Crested irises, also rhizomatous, have ridges, or cockscomb-like crests, instead of beards. They include the **Evansia** irises, with often widely spreading, creeping stolons. Most have very similar cultivation requirements to bearded irises but some prefer damp, humus-rich conditions; a few are half hardy to frost tender, min. 5°C (41°F).

Bulbous irises are distinguished by having bulbs as storage organs, sometimes with thickened, fleshy roots, and leaves that are lance-shaped and channelled; 4-sided (more or less square in cross section); or almost cylindrical – unlike the flat and usually sword-shaped leaves of the rhizomatous irises. **Xiphium** irises include the commonly grown Spanish, English and Dutch irises, which are excellent both for garden decoration and as cut flowers. All are easy to cultivate in sunny, well-drained sites, preferring slightly alkaline conditions, but also growing well on acid soil. **Spanish** irises are derived from *I. xiphium*, which is variable in flower colour, from blue and violet to yellow and white, and produces its channelled leaves in autumn. **English** irises have been produced from *I. latifolia*, which varies from blue to violet (occasionally white) and produces its channelled leaves in spring. **Dutch** irises are hybrids of *I. xiphium* and the related pale to deep blue *I. latifolia*. They are extremely variable in flower colour. **Juno** irises have bulbs with thickened, fleshy roots, channelled leaves and very small standards that are sometimes only bristle-like and usually horizontally placed. Although very beautiful in flower, they are mostly difficult to grow successfully, requiring the same cultivation conditions as Oncocyclus irises to thrive. Care must be taken not to damage the fleshy roots when transplanting or dividing clumps.

Reticulata irises include the dwarf, bulbous irises valuable for flowering early in the year. Unlike other bulbous irises, they have net-like bulb tunics and leaves that are 4-sided, or occasionally cylindrical. With few exceptions (not described here), Reticulata irises grow well in open, sunny, well-drained sites.

***I.* 'About Town'.** Vigorous, rhizomatous, bearded iris (Tall). **H** 1m (39in), **S** indefinite. Very frilly flowers with soft mauve-lilac standards and deep violet falls, edged with soft mauve-lilac, appear from early to mid-summer. The beards are orange.

I. acutiloba. Rhizomatous Oncocyclus iris. **H** 8–25cm (3–10in), **S** 30–38cm (12–15in). Has narrowly sickle-shaped, mid-green leaves. In late spring produces solitary, strongly purple-violet- or brownish-purple-veined, white flowers, 5–7cm (2–3in) across, with a dark brown blaze around the beard of each fall.

***I.* 'Alida'.** Bulbous Reticulata iris. **H** 10–15cm (4–6in), **S** 4–6cm (1½–2½in). In early spring bears a solitary, fragrant, long-tubed, light blue flower, 4–6cm (1½–2½in) wide, with a yellow ridge down each fall centre.

***I.* 'Alizes'.** Vigorous, rhizomatous, bearded iris (Tall). **H** 80cm (32in), **S** indefinite. In summer, large, frilly white flowers are produced with violet-blue falls that pale to white in the centre of the petals. The flowers have yellow beards.

***I.* 'Amethyst Dancer'.** Rhizomatous, bearded iris (Tall). **H** 85cm (34in), **S** indefinite. Scented flowers with peach-buff standards, crinkled around the edges, are produced in summer. The wine-purple falls are faded around the edges, and white veins sit around orange-tipped beards.

***I.* 'Annabel Jane'.** Vigorous, rhizomatous, bearded iris (Tall). **H** 1.2m (4ft), **S** indefinite. Well-branched stem bears 8–12 flowers, 15–25cm (6–10in) across, with pale lilac falls and paler standards. Flowers in early summer.

***I.* 'Anniversary'.** Rhizomatous, beardless Siberian iris. **H** 75cm (2½ft), **S** indefinite. In mid- and late spring bears 1–4 white flowers, 5–10cm (2–4in) across, with a yellow stripe in the throat of each fall. Grows well in moist soil or a bog garden.

I. aphylla. Rhizomatous, bearded iris. **H** 15–30cm (6–12in), **S** indefinite. Branched stem produces up to 5 pale to dark purple or blue-violet flowers, 6–7cm (2½–3in) across, in late spring and sometimes again in autumn if conditions suit.

🏆 ***I. aucheri.*** Bulbous Juno iris. **H** 15–25cm (6–10in), **S** 15cm (6in). Has channelled, mid-green leaves packed closely together on stem, looking somewhat leek-like. In late spring bears up to 6 blue to white flowers, 6–7cm (2½–3in) across with yellow-ridged falls, in leaf axils.

I. aurea. See *I. crocea*.

***I.* 'Autumn Circus'** (illus. p.224). Vigorous, rhizomatous, bearded iris (Tall). **H** 80cm (32in), **S** indefinite. Well-branched stems bear scented, gently ruffled, white flowers, with violet-blue margins and violet-blue feathering and pencilling on the standards and falls, in late spring. Often blooms again in summer.

***I.* 'Autumn Leaves'.** Vigorous, rhizomatous, bearded iris (Tall). **H** 80cm (32in), **S** indefinite. In mid-spring produces branched sprays of sweetly scented, caramel-coloured flowers, a blend of brown and purple, with orange-yellow beards.

***I.* 'Badlands'.** Rhizomatous, bearded iris (Tall). **H** 95cm (38in), **S** indefinite. In early to mid-summer, branched stem produces large, ruffled, black, beautifully proportioned flowers.

I. bakeriana. Bulbous Reticulata iris. **H** 10cm (4in), **S** 5–6cm (2–2½in). In early spring bears a solitary, long-tubed, pale blue flower, 5–6cm (2–2½in) across, with each fall having a dark blue blotch at the tip and a spotted, deep blue centre. Has narrow, almost cylindrical leaves that are very short at flowering time but elongate later.

***I.* 'Ballyhoo'.** Robust, rhizomatous, bearded iris (Tall). **H** 90–100cm (36–39in), **S** indefinite. In mid- to late spring produces large blooms with ruffled, lemon-white standards and veined, rosy-purple falls with yellow-tipped, white beards.

🏆 ***I.* 'Banbury Beauty'.** Rhizomatous, beardless Pacific Coast iris. **H** 45cm (18in), **S** indefinite. In late spring and early summer, branched stem produces 2–10 light lavender flowers, 10–15cm (4–6in) across, with a purple zone on each fall.

🏆 ***I.* 'Berlin Tiger'** (illus. p.225). Rhizomatous, beardless Japanese iris. **H** 1.2m (4ft), **S** indefinite. In early summer, branched stems bear 3–5 small, dark yellow flowers, 5cm (2in) across, strongly netted with deep brownish-purple veins. Grow in rich, moist soil.

🏆 ***I.* 'Bibury'.** Rhizomatous, bearded iris (Standard Dwarf). **H** 30cm (12in), **S** indefinite. Has 2–4 cream flowers, 10cm (4in) wide, on a branched stem in late spring.

***I.* 'Blenheim Royal'.** Rhizomatous, bearded iris (Tall). **H** 1m (3ft), **S** indefinite. A vigorous plant with ruffled rich blue, lightly scented flowers in summer.

***I.* 'Blue Eyed Brunette'.** Rhizomatous, bearded iris (Tall). **H** 1m (3ft), **S** indefinite. Well-branched stem produces 7–10 brown flowers, 10–15cm (4–6in) wide, with a blue blaze and a golden beard on each fall, in early summer.

***I.* 'Blue Notes Blue'.** Rhizomatous, bearded iris (Tall). **H** 90cm (36in), **S** indefinite. Scented, ruffled mid-blue flowers, paler around the edges, appear in summer. The white beards are tipped with orange towards the back.

***I.* 'Blue Rhythm'** (illus. p.225). Vigorous, rhizomatous, bearded iris (Tall). **H** 1.1m (3½ft), **S** indefinite. In early and mid-summer produces lemon-scented, well-formed, violet-blue flowers, the veins on the standards slightly paler than those on the broad falls, with their yellow-tipped, white beards.

***I.* 'Bold Print'** (illus. p.224). Rhizomatous, bearded iris (Intermediate). **H** 55cm (22in), **S** indefinite. In late spring or early summer, branched stem bears up to 6 flowers, 13cm (5in) wide, with purple-edged, white standards and white falls that are each purple-stitched at the edge and have a bronze-tipped, white beard.

***I.* 'Bronze Queen'.** Bulbous Xiphium iris (Dutch). **H** to 80cm (32in), **S** 15cm (6in). In spring and early summer produces 1 or 2 golden-brown flowers, 8–10cm (3–4in) wide, flushed bronze and purple. Lance-shaped, channelled, mid-green leaves are scattered up flower stem.

🏆 ***I.* 'Brown Lasso'.** Rhizomatous, bearded iris (Intermediate). **H** 55cm (22in), **S** indefinite. In early summer, sturdy, well-branched stem bears 6–10 flowers, 10–13cm (4–5in) across, with deep butterscotch standards and brown-edged, light violet falls.

🏆 ***I. bucharica*** (illus. p.224). Vigorous, bulbous Juno iris. **H** 20–40cm (8–16in), **S** 12cm (5in). In late spring produces 2–6 flowers, 6cm (2½in) across, golden-yellow to white with yellow falls, from leaf axils. Has narrowly lance-shaped, channelled, glossy, mid-green leaves scattered up flower stem. Is easier to grow than most Juno irises.

🏆 ***I.* 'Bumblebee Deelite'** (illus. p.225). Rhizomatous, bearded iris (Miniature Tall). **H** 45cm (18in), **S** indefinite. In late spring and early summer has flowers with yellow standards, yellow-margined, maroon falls and orange beards.

🏆 ***I.* 'Butter and Sugar'** illus. p.227.

***I.* 'Carnaby'** (illus. p.225). Rhizomatous, bearded iris (Tall). **H** to 1m (3ft), **S** indefinite. Well-branched stem bears 6–8 flowers, 15–18cm (6–7in) wide, with pale pink standards and deep rose-pink falls with orange beards, in early summer.

I. chamaeiris. See *I. lutescens*.

***I.* 'Champagne Elegance'** (illus. p.224). Vigorous, rhizomatous, bearded iris (Tall). **H** 85cm (34in), **S** indefinite. In early to mid-spring and again in summer produces scented, strongly ruffled flowers, with pink-washed, white standards and flaring, apricot-pink falls with darker veining and pale orange beards.

***I.* 'Change of Pace'.** Vigorous, rhizomatous, bearded iris (Tall). **H** 90cm (36in), **S** indefinite. Large, scented flowers are produced from early to late spring, the ruffled, veined, delicate pink standards contrasting with the brilliant white falls, which are broadly margined and flecked deep rosy-violet.

***I.* 'Chasing Rainbows'.** Rhizomatous, bearded iris (Tall). **H** 80cm (32in), **S** indefinite. In summer, strongly scented flowers with buff-peach standards, flushed with lilac appear. The falls are pale violet, fading to buff-peach at the edges, with orange beards.

***I.* 'Chief Moses'.** Rhizomatous, bearded

iris (Tall). **H** 95cm (38in), **S** indefinite. From early to mid-summer, large ruffled brown scented flowers are produced, with falls flushed with yellow, and orange beards.
🏆 ***I. chrysographes*** (illus. p.225). Rhizomatous, beardless Siberian iris. **H** 40cm (16in), **S** indefinite. From late spring–early summer, branched stem bears 1–4 deep red-purple or purple-black flowers, 5–10cm (2–4in) across, with gold etching down falls. Prefers a moist site.
***I.* 'Clairette',** syn. *I. reticulata* 'Clairette'. Bulbous Reticulata iris. **H** 10–15cm (4–6in), **S** 4–6cm (1½–2½in). In early spring bears a solitary, fragrant, long-tubed, pale blue flower, 4–6cm (1½–2½in) wide, with white-flecked, deep violet falls. Narrow, squared leaves elongate after flowering time.
I. clarkei. Rhizomatous, beardless Siberian iris. **H** 60cm (2ft), **S** indefinite. From late spring to early summer, solid stem produces 2–3 branches each with 2 blue to red-purple flowers, 5–10cm (2–4in) across, with a violet-veined, white blaze on each fall. Prefers moist conditions.
I. colchica. See *I. graminea.*
🏆 ***I. confusa*** (illus. p.224). Evergreen or semi-evergreen, rhizomatous Crested iris. **H** 1m (3ft) or more, **S** indefinite. Frost hardy. Bamboo-like, erect stem is crowned by a fan of broad leaves. In mid-spring, widely branched flower stem produces a long succession of up to 30 short-lived, white flowers, 4–5cm (1½–2in) across, with yellow or purple spots around the yellow crests. Prefers well-drained soil and the protection of a south-facing wall.
***I.* 'Conjuration'.** Rhizomatous, bearded iris (Tall). **H** 90cm (3ft), **S** indefinite. In early summer bears 6–11 flowers with standards that are white at the margins, suffusing inwards to pale violet-blue, and white falls suffusing to deep amethyst-violet at the margins. The white horned beard is yellow tipped.
I. cretensis. See *I. unguicularis* subsp. cretensis.
🏆 ***I. cristata*** (illus. p.224). Evansia iris with much-branched rhizomes. **H** 10cm (4in), **S** indefinite. Has neat fans of lance-shaped leaves. In early summer produces 1 or 2 virtually stemless, long-tubed, lilac, blue, lavender or white flowers, 3–4cm (1¼–1½in) across, with a white patch and orange crest on each fall. Prefers semi-shade and moist soil; is ideal for peat banks.
🏆 ***I. crocea,*** syn. *I. aurea.* Rhizomatous, beardless Spuria iris. **H** 1–1.2m (3–4ft), **S** indefinite. Has long leaves. Strong, erect, sparsely branched stem produces terminal clusters of 2–10 golden-yellow flowers, 12–18cm (5–7in) across, with wavy-margined falls, in early summer. Resents being disturbed.
I. cuprea. See *I. fulva.*
***I.* 'Custom Design'.** Rhizomatous, beardless Spuria iris. **H** 1m (3ft), **S** indefinite. Strong, erect-branched stem produces 2–10 deep maroon-brown flowers, each 5–12cm (2–5in) wide, with a heavily veined, bright yellow blaze on each fall, from early to mid-summer.
I. danfordiae. Bulbous Reticulata iris. **H** 5–10cm (2–4in), **S** 5cm (2in). In early spring bears usually one yellow flower, 3–5cm (1¼–2in) across, with green spots on each fall. Standards are reduced to short bristles. Narrow, squared leaves are very short at flowering time but elongate later. Tends to produce masses of small bulblets and requires deeper planting than other Reticulata irises to maintain bulbs at flowering size.
***I.* 'Deep Black'** (illus. p.224). Rhizomatous, bearded iris (Tall). **H** 85cm (34in), **S** indefinite. In early summer, branched stem produces unruffled flowers, 7–10cm (3–4in) across, with deep purple standards and dark indigo falls, each with an orange-tipped beard.
***I.* 'Desert Song'.** Rhizomatous, bearded iris (Tall). **H** 90cm (36in), **S** indefinite. In summer, pale yellow flowers appear with slightly crinkled petals and a long white flash in front of bright yellow beards.
I. domestica. See *Belamcanda chinensis.*
🏆 ***I. douglasiana.*** Evergreen, rhizomatous, beardless Pacific Coast iris. **H** 25–70cm (10–28in), **S** indefinite. Leathery, dark green leaves are stained red-purple at base. Branched stem produces 1–3 lavender to purple, occasionally white, flowers, 7–12cm (3–5in) wide, with variable, central, yellowish zones on the falls, in late spring and early summer.
🏆 ***I.* 'Dreaming Spires'.** Rhizomatous, beardless Siberian iris. **H** 1m (3ft), **S** indefinite. From late spring to early summer, branched stem produces 1–4 flowers, 5–10cm (2–4in) wide, with lavender standards and royal-blue falls. Prefers moist soil.
🏆 ***I.* 'Dreaming Yellow'** (illus. p.224). Rhizomatous, beardless Siberian iris. **H** 1m (3ft), **S** indefinite. From late spring to early summer, branched stem produces 1–4 flowers, 5–10cm (2–4in) across. Standards are white, falls creamy-yellow fading to white with age. Prefers moist soil.
🏆 ***I.* 'Early Light'.** Rhizomatous, bearded iris (Tall). **H** 1m (3ft), **S** indefinite. In early summer, well-branched stem bears 8–10 ruffled, white flowers, 15–18cm (6–7in) wide, heavily flushed lemon-yellow on the standards; yellow-veined falls have broad margins flushed slightly deeper lemon-yellow and a yellow beard.
***I.* 'Electric Rays'.** Strong-growing, rhizomatous Japanese iris. **H** 1m (3ft), **S** indefinite. Ruffled, double, rich violet flowers, with white and intense, deep blue veining, are borne freely in early summer.
***I.* 'Elmohr'.** Rhizomatous, bearded iris. **H** 1m (3ft), **S** indefinite. In early summer, well-branched stem produces 2–5 strongly veined, red-purple flowers, 15–20cm (6–8in) across.
***I.* 'English Charm'** Rhizomatous, bearded iris (Tall). **H** 85cm (34in), **S** indefinite. Gently ruffled flowers with cream standards, heavily veined with soft apricot yellow appear in summer. The soft apricot falls are paler along the edges and the beards are reddy-orange.
***I.* 'English Cottage'** (illus. p.224). Robust, rhizomatous, bearded iris (Tall). **H** 90–100cm (36–39in), **S** indefinite. In mid- to late spring and again in summer or early autumn produces large, white flowers with the margins of both standards and falls washed pale blue-violet. Has deeper veining at the base of the falls and yellow-tipped, white beards.
🏆 ***I. ensata,*** syn. *I. kaempferi* (Japanese flag). Rhizomatous, beardless Japanese iris. **H** 60cm–1m (2–3ft), **S** indefinite. Branched stem produces 3–15 purple or red-purple flowers, 8–15cm (3–6in) across, with a yellow blaze on each fall, from early to mid-summer. May be distinguished from the related, smooth-leaved *I. laevigata* by the prominent midrib on the leaves. Has produced many hundreds of garden forms, some with double flowers, in shades of purple, pink, lavender and white, sometimes bicoloured. Prefers partial shade and thrives in a water or bog garden. 🏆 **'Caprician Butterfly'**, **H** 90cm (36in), has dark purple standards with fringed white margins; falls are white with dark purple veins and gold patches. **'Galathea'** (syn. *I.* 'Galatea'), **H** 80cm (32in), has blue-purple flowers with a yellow blaze on each fall. **'Moonlight Waves'** (illus. p.224), **H** 90cm (36in), is strong-growing and produces large, open, spreading, white flowers, with lime-green blazes at the base of each petal. 🏆 **'Rose Queen'**, syn. *I. laevigata* 'Rose Queen' (illus. p.224), **H** 90–100cm (36–39in), is strong-growing and produces large, soft pink flowers, with deeper pink veining and a yellow blaze at the base of each fall. 🏆**'Variegata'**, **H** 75cm (30in), has narrow foliage, brightly edged in white.
I. extremorientalis. See *I. sanguinea.*
🏆 ***I.* 'Eyebright'** (illus. p.225). Rhizomatous, bearded iris (Standard Dwarf). **H** 30cm (12in), **S** indefinite. In late spring produces 2–4 bright yellow flowers, 7–10cm (3–4in) wide, each with a brown zone on the falls surrounding the beard, on usually an unbranched stem.
***I.* 'Feminine Charm'.** Rhizomatous, bearded iris (Tall). **H** 90cm (36in), **S** indefinite. Scented soft pinkish-apricot flowers with a hint of yellow appear in summer. The falls are apricot and edged with white.
***I.* 'Filibuster'.** Rhizomatous, bearded iris (Tall). **H** 90cm (36in), **S** indefinite. Heavily scented, frilly flowers with rosy-purple standards are produced in summer. The pale peach falls are stained with rosy-purple, and the beards are burnt orange.
***I.* 'Flamenco'.** Rhizomatous, bearded iris (Tall). **H** 1m (3ft), **S** indefinite. In early summer, well-branched stem produces 6–9 flowers, 15cm (6in) wide, with gold standards, infused red, and white to yellow falls with red borders.
***I.* 'Flight of Butterflies'.** Elegant, rhizomatous, beardless Siberian iris. **H** 90cm (36in), **S** indefinite. From early to mid-summer produces delicate flowers with violet-blue standards and white falls veined deep violet-blue.
I. florentina. See *I. germanica* 'Florentina'.
🏆 ***I. foetidissima*** (Gladwin, Roast-beef plant, Stinking iris; illus. p.225). Evergreen, rhizomatous, beardless iris. **H** 30cm–1m (1–3ft), **S** indefinite. Branched stem bears up to 9 yellow-tinged, dull purple or occasionally pure yellow flowers, 5–10cm (2–4in) wide, from early to mid-summer. Cylindrical seed pods open to reveal rounded, bright scarlet fruits throughout winter. Thrives in a bog or water garden, although tolerates drier conditions.
🏆 ***I. forrestii.*** Rhizomatous, beardless Siberian iris. **H** 15–40cm (6–16in), **S** indefinite. From late spring to early summer, unbranched stem produces 1 or 2 fragrant, yellow flowers, 5–6cm (2–2½in) across, with black lines on each fall and occasionally brownish-flushing on standards. Has linear, glossy, mid-green leaves, grey-green below. Prefers moist, lime-free soil.
***I.* 'Fortunate Son'.** Rhizomatous, bearded iris (Tall). **H** 90cm (36in), **S** indefinite. Branches of scented, velvety, rich burgundy flowers with purple beards appear from early to mid-summer. .
I. fosteriana. Bulbous Juno iris. **H** 10–15cm (4–6in), **S** 6cm (2½in). In spring produces 1 or 2 long-tubed flowers, 4–5cm (1½–2in) wide, with downward-turned, rich purple standards, which are larger than those of most Juno irises, and creamy-yellow falls. Has narrowly lance-shaped, channelled, silver-edged, mid-green leaves scattered on flower stem. Is difficult to grow and is best in an alpine house or cold frame.
***I.* 'Frank Elder'.** Bulbous Reticulata iris. **H** 6–10cm (2½–4in), **S** 5–7cm (2–3in). Has a solitary, very pale blue flower, 6–7cm (2½–3in) wide, suffused pale yellow and veined and spotted darker blue, in early spring. Narrow, squared leaves are very short at flowering time but elongate later.
***I.* 'Frost and Flame'** (illus. p.224). Strong-growing, rhizomatous, bearded iris (Tall). **H** 90cm (36in), **S** indefinite. In early to mid-spring produces fragrant, glistening, white flowers with gently ruffled standards, rounded falls and bright orange beards.
🏆 ***I. fulva,*** syn. *I. cuprea*, illus. p.439.
🏆 ***I. x fulvala,*** syn. *I.* 'Fulvala'. Rhizomatous, beardless iris. **H** 45cm (18in), **S** indefinite. Frost hardy. In summer, zigzag stem produces 4–6 (occasionally more) velvety, deep red-purple flowers, 5–12cm (2–5in) across, with 2 flowers per leaf axil. Has a yellow blaze on each fall. Thrives in a bog or water garden.
***I.* 'Galatea'.** See *I. ensata* 'Galatea'.
***I.* 'Geisha Gown'.** Robust, rhizomatous, beardless Japanese iris. **H** 90cm (36in), **S** indefinite. In mid- and late spring produces large, delicate, double, white ruffled flowers with dark violet-blue veining and a central, deep purple-violet centre.
🏆 ***I. germanica*** (Common German flag). Rhizomatous, bearded iris. **H** to 60cm–1.2m (2–4ft), **S** indefinite. Sparsely branched stem produces up to 6 yellow-bearded, blue-purple or blue-violet flowers, 10–15cm (4–6in) wide, in late spring and early summer. 🏆 **'Florentina'**, syn. *I. florentina* (Orris root; illus. p.224) has strongly scented, white flowers.
***I.* 'Golden Harvest'.** Bulbous Xiphium iris (Dutch). **H** to 80cm (32in), **S** 15cm (6in). Bears 1 or 2 deep rich yellow flowers, 6–8cm (2½–3in) wide, in spring and early summer. Has scattered, narrowly lance-shaped, channelled, mid-green leaves.
I. gracilipes. Clump-forming, rhizomatous Evansia iris with short stolons. **H** 15–20cm (6–8in), **S** indefinite. In late spring and early summer, slender, branched stem produces a succession of 4 or 5 lilac-blue flowers, each 3–4cm (1¼–1½in) across, with a violet-veined, white zone surrounding a yellow-and-white crest. Has narrow, grass-like leaves.

Prefers semi-shade and peaty soil.
I. graeberiana. Bulbous Juno iris. **H** 15–35cm (6–14in), **S** 6–8cm (2½–3in). In late spring produces 4–6 bluish-lavender flowers, 6–8cm (2½–3in) across, with a white crest on each fall, from leaf axils. Lance-shaped, channelled leaves are white-margined, glossy, mid-green above, greyish-green below, and scattered up flower stem. Is easier to grow than most Juno irises.
♀ ***I. graminea,*** syn. *I. colchica.* Rhizomatous, beardless Spuria iris. **H** 20–40cm (8–16in), **S** indefinite. In late spring, narrowly lance-shaped leaves partially hide up to 10 plum-scented flowers, 5–12cm (2–5in) wide, with wine-purple standards and heavily veined, violet-blue falls, borne on flattened, angled stem. Resents being disturbed.
♀ ***I.* 'Green Spot'** (illus. p.224). Rhizomatous, bearded iris (Standard Dwarf). **H** 30cm (12in), **S** indefinite. In late spring, branched stems bear 2–4 ivory-white flowers, 10cm (4in) across, with an olive-green mark and a yellow throat on each fall.
***I.* 'Harmony'.** Bulbous Reticulata iris. **H** 6–10cm (2½–4in), **S** 6–7cm (2½–3in). In early spring bears a solitary, fragrant, long-tubed, clear pale blue flower, 5–6cm (2–2½in) across, with white marks and a yellow ridge down each fall centre. Narrow, squared leaves are very short at flowering time but elongate later.
I. histrioides. Bulbous Reticulata iris. **H** 6–10cm (2½–4in), **S** 6–7cm (2½–3in). In early spring produces solitary flowers, 6–7cm (2½–3in) across, which vary from light to deep violet-blue. Each fall is lightly to strongly spotted with dark blue and has white marks and a yellow ridge down centre. Narrow, squared leaves are very short at flowering time but elongate later. **'Lady Beatrix Stanley'** has light blue flowers and heavily spotted falls. **'Major'** has darker blue-violet flowers.
♀ ***I.* 'Holden Clough'** (illus. p.225). Rhizomatous, beardless iris. **H** 50–70cm (20–28in), **S** indefinite. In early summer, branched stem bears 6–12 yellow flowers, each 5cm (2in) wide, with very heavy, burnt-sienna veining. Is excellent in a bog or water garden, but also grows well in any rich, well-drained soil.
♀ ***I. hoogiana*** (illus. p.224). Regelia iris with stout rhizomes. **H** 40–60cm (16–24in), **S** indefinite. Produces 2 or 3 scented, delicately veined, lilac-blue flowers, 7–10cm (3–4in) across, in late spring and early summer. Is relatively easy to cultivate.
I. iberica. Rhizomatous Oncocyclus iris. **H** 15–20cm (6–8in), **S** indefinite. Has narrow, strongly curved, grey-green leaves. Bears solitary, bicoloured flowers, 10–12cm (4–5in) across, in late spring. Standards are white, pale yellow, or pale blue with slight brownish-purple veining; spoon-shaped falls are white or pale lilac, spotted and strongly veined brownish-purple. Grows best in a frame or alpine house.
I. innominata. Evergreen or semi-evergreen, rhizomatous, beardless Pacific Coast iris. **H** 16–25cm (6–10in), **S** indefinite. Stem bears 1 or 2 flowers, 6.5–7.5cm (2½–3in) across, from late spring to early summer. Varies greatly in colour from cream to yellow or orange and from lilac-pink to blue or purple; falls are often veined with maroon or brown.
♀ ***I. japonica*** (illus. p.224). Vigorous, rhizomatous Evansia iris with slender stolons. **H** 45–80cm (18–32in), **S** indefinite. Frost hardy. Has fans of broadly lance-shaped, glossy leaves. In late spring produces branched flower stem with a long succession of flattish, frilled or ruffled, pale lavender or white flowers, 1–8cm (½–3in) across, marked violet around an orange crest on each fall. Prefers the protection of a sheltered, sunny wall. ♀ **'Variegata'**, **H** 70cm (28in). Has mid-green leaves boldly striped with white.
***I.* 'Jesse's Song'.** Vigorous, rhizomatous, bearded iris (Tall). **H** 90cm (36in), **S** indefinite. In early to mid-spring produces scented, ruffled, white flowers, the standards heavily suffused violet, the falls irregularly margined and speckled violet and the white beard tipped pale violet.
***I.* 'Joette'.** Rhizomatous, bearded iris (Intermediate). **H** 45cm (18in), **S** indefinite. In late spring or early summer, branched stems carry uniformly lavender-blue flowers with yellow beards. Is excellent in flower arrangements.
***I.* 'Joyce'** (illus. p.225). Bulbous Reticulata iris. **H** 6–10cm (2½–4in), **S** 6–7cm (2½–3in). In early spring bears a solitary, fragrant, long-tubed, clear blue flower, 5–6cm (2–2½in) across, with white marks and a yellow ridge down each fall centre. Narrow, squared leaves are very short at flowering time but elongate later.
***I.* 'June Prom'.** Vigorous, rhizomatous, bearded iris (Intermediate). **H** 50cm (20in), **S** indefinite. In late spring or early summer, branched stem bears up to 6 pale blue flowers, 8–10cm (3–4in) wide, with a green tinge on each fall.
I. kaempferi. See *I. ensata.*
♀ ***I.* 'Katharine Hodgkin'** (illus. p.225). Bulbous Reticulata iris. **H** 6–10cm (2½–4in), **S** 5–7cm (2–3in). Is similar to *I.* 'Frank Elder', but has yellower flowers, 6–7cm (2½–3in) wide, suffused pale blue, lined and dotted with dark blue. Flowers in early spring.
***I.* 'Kent Pride'** (illus. p.225). Strong-growing, rhizomatous, bearded iris (Tall). **H** 90cm (36in), **S** indefinite. In mid-spring produces deep chestnut-brown and white flowers; the standards are faintly suffused yellow and the falls have a white central patch, yellow beards and yellow and brown veining, surrounded by chestnut-brown margins.
♀ ***I. kerneriana.*** Rhizomatous, beardless Spuria iris. **H** 25cm (10in), **S** indefinite. Has very narrow, grass-like leaves. Strong, erect-branched stem bears 2–4 soft lemon- or creamy-yellow flowers, 5–12cm (2–5in) across, from each pair of bracts, in early summer. Resents being disturbed.
I. korolkowii. Regelia iris with stout rhizomes. **H** 40–60cm (16–24in), **S** indefinite. From late spring to early summer, each spathe encloses 2 or 3 delicately blackish-maroon- or olive-green-veined, creamy-white or light purple flowers, 6–8cm (2½–3in) across. Is best grown in a bulb frame.
***I.* 'Krasnia'.** Rhizomatous, bearded iris (Tall). **H** 1m (3ft), **S** indefinite. In early summer, the well-branched stem produces 8–12 flowers, 13–18cm (5–7in) wide, with purple standards and purple-margined, white falls.
***I.* 'Lady Mohr'.** Rhizomatous, bearded Arilbred iris. **H** 75cm (30in), **S** indefinite. In early spring produces flowers with pearly-white standards and pale yellow falls veined and spotted brownish-purple around the chrome-yellow beards.
***I.* 'Lady of Quality'.** Rhizomatous, beardless Siberian iris. **H** to 1m (3ft), **S** indefinite. In mid- and late spring produces flowers with light blue-violet standards and lighter blue falls.
♀ ***I. laevigata.*** Rhizomatous, beardless Japanese iris. **H** 60–90cm (2–3ft) or more, **S** indefinite. Sparsely branched stem produces 2–4 blue, blue-purple or white flowers, 5–12cm (2–5in) across, from early to mid-summer. Is related to *I. ensata* but has smooth, not ridged leaves. Grows well in sun or semi-shade in moist conditions or in shallow water. **'Regal'** bears single, cyclamen-red flowers. **'Rose Queen'** see *I. ensata* 'Rose Queen'. **'Rowden Starlight'** illus. p.437. **'Snowdrift'** has single, white flowers marked yellow at the bases of the falls. ♀ **'Variegata'**, **H** 25cm (10in), has white-and-green-striped leaves and often flowers a second time in early autumn. **'Weymouth Midnight'** illus. p.442.
***I.* 'Langport Storm'.** Strong-growing, rhizomatous, bearded iris (Intermediate). **H** 45cm (18in), **S** indefinite. In mid-spring produces neat, smoky-chartreuse blooms, the falls overlaid with deep red-brown patches suffused and veined yellow, with cream beards.
♀ ***I. latifolia,*** syn. *I. xiphioides* (English iris). Bulbous Xiphium iris (English). **H** 80cm (32in), **S** 15cm (6in). In late spring and summer, 1 or 2 blue to deep violet flowers, 8–10cm (3–4in) wide, with a yellow stripe down centre of each very broad fall, are produced from the bracts. Lance-shaped, channelled, mid-green leaves are scattered up flower stem. **'Duchess of York'** bears purple flowers. Flowers of **'Mont Blanc'** are pure white. **'Queen of the Blues'** has blue standards and purple-blue falls.
***I.* 'Lavender Royal'.** Rhizomatous, beardless Pacific Coast iris. **H** 45cm (18in), **S** indefinite. In late spring to early summer, branched stems carry lavender flowers with darker flushes.
♀ ***I. lazica.*** Evergreen, rhizomatous, beardless iris. **H** 15–25cm (6–10in), **S** indefinite. Has arching fans of broad, bright green leaves. In early spring produces stemless, long-tubed, lavender-blue flowers. Falls are white in the lower halves, spotted and veined lavender, each with a central yellow stripe. Thrives in slight shade in moist soil.
♀ ***I. lutescens,*** syn. *I. chamaeiris.* Fast-growing, very variable, rhizomatous, bearded iris. **H** 5–30cm (2–12in), **S** indefinite. Branched stem produces 1 or 2 yellow-bearded, violet, purple, yellow, white or bicoloured flowers, 6–8cm (2½–3in) across, in early summer. **'Nancy Lindsay'** has scented, yellow flowers.
***I.* 'Magic Man'.** Rhizomatous, bearded iris (Tall). **H** 1m (3ft), **S** indefinite. In early summer, branched stems carry flowers that have light blue standards and velvety purple falls with light blue margins; beards are orange.
♀ ***I. magnifica*** (illus. p.224). Bulbous Juno iris. **H** 30–60cm (12–24in), **S** 15cm (6in). In late spring produces 3–7 very pale lilac flowers, 6–8cm (2½–3in) across, with a central, yellow area on each fall, from leaf axils. Bears scattered, lance-shaped, channelled, glossy, mid-green leaves.
***I.* 'Making Eyes'.** Rhizomatous, bearded iris (Standard Dwarf). **H** 30–35cm (12–14in), **S** indefinite. In early spring produces neat flowers with pale lemon-white standards, narrow, white-margined, dark purple-violet falls and yellowish-white beards.
***I.* 'Margot Holmes'.** Rhizomatous, beardless Siberian iris. **H** 25cm (10in), **S** indefinite. Frost hardy. In early summer produces 2 or 3 purple-red flowers, 10–15cm (4–6in) across, with yellow veining on each fall.
***I.* 'Marhaba'.** Rhizomatous, bearded iris (Miniature Dwarf). **H** 15cm (6in), **S** indefinite. Bears 1, rarely 2 deep blue flowers, 5–8cm (2–3in) wide, in mid-spring.
***I.* 'Mary Frances'.** Rhizomatous, bearded iris (Tall). **H** 1m (3ft), **S** indefinite. In early summer, well-branched stem bears 6–9, occasionally to 12 pink-lavender flowers, 15cm (6in) wide.
♀ ***I.* 'Mary McIlroy'.** Rhizomatous, bearded iris (Intermediate). **H** 40–50cm (16–20in), **S** indefinite. In early to mid-spring produces bright yellow blooms, the standards veined slightly deeper yellow, with darker veins on the falls and lemon-yellow beards.
***I.* 'Matinata'.** Rhizomatous, bearded iris (Tall). **H** 1m (3ft), **S** indefinite. In early summer, well-branched stem produces 6–9, occasionally to 12 flowers, 15cm (6in) wide, that are dark purple-blue throughout.
♀ ***I. missouriensis,*** syn. *I. tolmeiana* (Missouri flag). Very variable, rhizomatous, beardless Pacific Coast iris. **H** to 75cm (2½ft), **S** indefinite. Branched stem produces 2 or 3 pale blue, lavender, lilac, blue or white flowers, 5–8cm (2–3in) wide, in each spathe, in late spring or early summer. Falls are veined and usually have a yellow blaze.
♀ ***I.* 'Morwenna'.** Robust, rhizomatous, bearded iris (Tall). **H** 70–80cm (28–32in), **S** indefinite. In mid- to late spring bears ruffled, pale blue flowers, with both standards and falls feathered a slightly deeper blue, and with white beards.
***I.* 'Mountain Lake'** (illus. p.224). Rhizomatous, beardless Siberian iris. **H** 1m (3ft), **S** indefinite. From late spring to early summer, branched stem produces 1–4 mid-blue flowers, 5–10cm (2–4in) across, with darker veining on falls. Prefers moist soil.
***I.* 'Natascha'** illus. p.415.
I. ochroleuca. See *I. orientalis.*
***I.* 'Ola Kala'** (illus. p.225). Robust, rhizomatous, bearded iris (Tall). **H** 1m (3ft), **S** indefinite. Produces neat, scented, rich deep yellow flowers; the falls have darker yellow bases and yellow beards.
***I.* 'Oriental Eyes'** (illus. p.224). Vigorous, rhizomatous, beardless Japanese iris. **H** 1m

(3ft), **S** indefinite. In early summer produces large, ruffled, strongly veined, purple violet flowers, with bright golden-yellow flares at the base of each petal.

♀ ***I. orientalis,*** syn. *I. ochroleuca* (illus. p.224). Rhizomatous, beardless Spuria iris. **H** to 90cm (3ft), **S** indefinite. In late spring each stem, usually with one branch, bears 3–5 white flowers, 8–10cm (3–4in) wide. Falls are white with yellow centres. Leaves are often present over winter.

I. orientalis of gardens. See *I. sanguinea*.

I. pallida (Dalmatian iris). Rhizomatous, bearded iris. **H** 70–90cm (28–36in) or more, **S** indefinite. In late spring and early summer produces 2–6 scented, lilac-blue flowers, 8–12cm (3–5in) across and with yellow beards, from silvery spathes on strong, branched stems. Leaves of ♀ **'Variegata'** (syn. *I.p.* 'Aurea Variegata') are striped green and yellow.

♀ ***I.* 'Paradise Bird'.** Rhizomatous, bearded iris (Tall). **H** 85cm (34in), **S** indefinite. In early summer, well-branched stem produces 8–10 flowers, 14–15cm (5½–6in) wide, with magenta falls and paler standards.

***I.* 'Peach Frost'.** Rhizomatous, bearded iris (Tall). **H** 1m (3ft), **S** indefinite. Well-branched stem bears 6–10 flowers, 15cm (6in) wide, in early summer. Standards are peach-pink, falls white with peach-pink margins and tangerine beards.

***I.* 'Perry's Blue'** (illus. p.225). Robust, rhizomatous, beardless Siberian iris. **H** 1m (3ft), **S** indefinite. In late spring and early summer produces neat, pale purplish-blue flowers, with noticeably deeper blue veins. Slightly twisted standards and broad, rounded falls are white margined and creamy-white near the bases, and have dark yellow markings in the throats.

***I.* 'Piona'.** Rhizomatous, bearded iris (Intermediate). **H** 45cm (18in), **S** indefinite. In late spring and early summer, branched stem bears up to 6 deep violet flowers, 8–10cm (3–4in) wide, with golden beards. Mid-green leaves have purple bases.

***I.* 'Pixie'** illus. p.418.

♀ ***I.* 'Professor Blaauw'.** Bulbous Xiphium iris (Dutch). **H** 80cm (32in), **S** 15cm (6in). From spring to early summer produces 1 or 2 rich violet-blue flowers, 6–8cm (2½–3in) across. Narrowly lance-shaped, channelled, mid-green leaves are scattered up flower stem.

♀ ***I. pseudacorus*** (Yellow flag; illus. p.225). Robust, rhizomatous, beardless iris. **H** to 2m (6ft), **S** indefinite. Branched stem produces 4–12 golden-yellow flowers, 5–12cm (2–5in) wide, usually with brown or violet veining and a darker yellow patch on the falls, from early to mid-summer. Leaves are broad, ridged and greyish-green. Prefers semi-shade and thrives in a water garden. **var. *bastardii*** (syn. *I.p.* 'Sulphur Queen') illus. p.445. **'Sulphur Queen'** see *I.p.* var. *bastardii*. ♀ **'Variegata'** has yellow-and-green-striped foliage in spring, often turning green before flowering.

I. pumila (Dwarf bearded iris). Rhizomatous, bearded iris. **H** 10–15cm (4–6in), **S** indefinite. In mid-spring has a 1cm (½in) long flower stem bearing 2or 3 long-tubed flowers, 2.5–5cm (1–2in) wide, varying from violet-purple to white, yellow or blue, with yellow or blue beards on the falls. Prefers very well-drained, slightly alkaline soil.

***I.* 'Rare Treat'.** Robust, rhizomatous, bearded iris (Tall). **H** 90cm (36in), **S** indefinite. In mid- to late spring produces ruffled, snow-white flowers, with both standards and falls margined deep purple-blue, and the bases of the falls and beards similarly coloured.

***I.* 'Raspberry Candy'.** Vigorous, rhizomatous, beardless Japanese iris. **H** 80–90cm (32–36in), **S** indefinite. In late spring and early summer produces large, open, white flowers strongly veined red-violet, with bright yellow blazes at the bases of the falls.

♀ ***I. reticulata.*** Bulbous Reticulata iris. **H** 10–15cm (4–6in), **S** 4–6cm (1½–2½in). In early spring bears a solitary, fragrant, long-tubed, deep violet-purple flower, 4–6cm (1½–2½in) wide, with a yellow ridge down each fall centre. Narrow, squared leaves elongate after flowering time. **'Cantab'** (illus. p.225) has clear pale blue flowers with a deep yellow ridge on each fall. **'Clairette'** see *I.* 'Clairette'. **'Edward',** **H** 15cm (6in), **S** 2cm (¾in), has solitary, slightly fragrant, orange-striped, blue-purple flowers from late winter to early spring. Leaves are linear and mid-green. Flowers of **'J.S. Dijt'** are reddish-purple with an orange ridge on each fall. **'Violet Beauty'** see *I.* 'Violet Beauty'.

***I.* 'Ringo'** (illus. p.224). Vigorous, rhizomatous, bearded iris (Tall). **H** 90cm (36in), **S** indefinite. In late spring and early summer, lightly ruffled flowers have white standards touched purple on the midribs and dark reddish-purple falls with narrow, white margins and orange beards.

***I.* 'Rippling Rose'.** Rhizomatous, bearded iris (Tall). **H** 1m (3ft), **S** indefinite. In early summer, well-branched stem has 6–10 white flowers, 15cm (6in) wide, with purple marks and lemon-yellow beards.

♀***I.* x *robusta* 'Gerald Darby'** (illus. p.224). Rhizomatous, beardless Species Hybrid iris. **H** 80cm (32in), **S** indefinite. In late spring and early summer, unbranched purplish-green stems bear up to 4 violet-blue flowers, with deep yellow signals on the falls. Leaves are stained purple at the bases. Prefers wet conditions.

I. rosenbachiana. Bulbous Juno iris. **H** 10–15cm (4–6in), **S** 6cm (2½in). In spring produces 1 or 2 long-tubed flowers, 4–5cm (1½–2in) wide, with small, downward-turned, rich purple standards and reddish-purple falls, each with a yellow ridge in the centre. Has lance-shaped, channelled, mid-green leaves in a basal tuft. Is difficult to grow and is best in an alpine house or cold frame.

***I.* 'Ruban Bleu'.** Strong-growing, rhizomatous, bearded iris (Tall). **H** 85–90cm (32–36in), **S** indefinite. In late spring and early summer, has scented flowers with snow-white standards and slightly ruffled, dark blue-violet falls each with a large, white basal patch and orange beard.

♀ ***I.* 'Ruffled Velvet'.** Rhizomatous, beardless Siberian iris. **H** to 1m (3ft), **S** indefinite. In early summer produces 2 or 3 red-purple flowers marked with yellow.

***I.* 'Saffron Jewel'.** Rhizomatous, bearded iris (Intermediate). **H** 75cm (30in), **S** indefinite. In early summer, branched stem produces 2–5 flowers, 5–10cm (2–4in) across, with oyster falls, veined chartreuse, and paler standards. Falls each have a blue blaze and beard.

♀ ***I. sanguinea,*** syn. *I. extremorientalis, I. orientalis* of gardens. Rhizomatous, beardless Siberian iris. **H** to 1m (3ft), **S** indefinite. From late spring to early summer, branched stem produces 2 or 3 deep purple or red-purple flowers, 5–10cm (2–4in) wide, from each set of bracts. Falls are red-purple with white throats finely veined purple. **'Snow Queen'** (illus. p.224) has pure white flowers with yellow-green marks at the bases of the falls.

***I.* 'Sapphire Star'.** Rhizomatous, beardless Japanese iris. **H** 1.2m (4ft), **S** indefinite. In summer, branched stem bears 3–5 white-veined, lavender flowers, 15–30cm (6–12in) wide, pencilled with a white halo around a yellow blaze on each fall. Prefers moist soil.

***I.* 'Saturday Night Live'.** Vigorous, rhizomatous, bearded iris (Tall). **H** 90–95cm (36–38in), **S** indefinite. Has mildly scented, deep red-brown to burgundy-red flowers, with bronze-yellow beards and faint, light yellow veining near the bases of the falls, from mid-spring to early summer.

♀ ***I. setosa*** illus. p.441.

***I.* 'Shepherd's Delight'.** Rhizomatous, bearded iris (Tall). **H** 1m (3ft), **S** indefinite. In early summer, well-branched stem produces 6–10 clear pink flowers, 15–18cm (6–7in) wide, with a yellow cast.

♀ ***I. sibirica*** (Siberian flag; illus. p.441), Rhizomatous, beardless Siberian iris. **H** 50–120cm (20–48in), **S** indefinite. From late spring to early summer, branched stem bears 2 or 3 dark-veined, blue or blue-purple flowers, 5–10cm (2–4in) across, from each spathe. Prefers moist or boggy conditions. **'Papillon'** (illus. p.225), **H** 90cm (36in), produces a prolific display of soft blue flowers, veined in white on the falls. ♀**'Shirley Pope'** (illus. p.225), **H** 85cm (34in), has velvety, dark, almost blue-back flowers, with a white zone veined in purple at the base of the horizontal falls. ♀ **'Soft Blue'** (illus. p.225).

♀ ***I. sintenisii.*** Rhizomatous, beardless Spuria iris. **H** 30cm (12in), **S** indefinite. Has linear, dark green leaves. In late spring produces 2 white flowers, densely veined blue-purple.

***I.* 'Soft Blue'.** Robust, rhizomatous, beardless Siberian iris. **H** 75cm (30in), **S** indefinite. In early to mid-spring produces pale blue flowers; the long, arching falls have yellow basal markings and darker blue veins.

***I.* 'Splash Down'.** Rhizomatous, beardless Siberian iris. **H** 1m (3ft), **S** indefinite. From late spring to early summer, branched stem produces 1–4 flowers, 5–10cm (2–4in) across. Standards are pale blue and falls speckled blue on a pale ground. Prefers moist soil.

I. spuria. Very variable, rhizomatous, beardless Spuria iris. **H** 50–90cm (20–36in), **S** indefinite. Strong, erect-branched stem produces 2–5 pale blue-purple, sky-blue, violet-blue, white or yellow flowers, 5–12cm (2–5in) across, in early summer. Prefers moist soil.

♀ ***I.* 'Stepping Out'.** Rhizomatous, bearded iris (Tall). **H** 1m (3ft), **S** indefinite. Well-branched stem produces 8–11 white flowers, 14–15cm (5½–6in) wide, with deep blue-purple marks in early summer.

I. stylosa. See *I. unguicularis*.

***I.* 'Sun Miracle'.** Rhizomatous, bearded iris (Tall). **H** 1m (3ft), **S** indefinite. Well-branched stem produces 7–10 pure yellow flowers, 15–18cm (6–7in) wide, in early summer.

***I.* 'Supreme Sultan'.** Vigorous, rhizomatous, bearded iris (Tall). **H** 1m (3ft), **S** indefinite. In late spring and early summer bears large, ruffled flowers, with deep golden-yellow standards, rich dark red-brown falls that are paler at the margins, and deep yellow beards.

I. susiana (Mourning iris). Rhizomatous Oncocyclus iris. **H** 35–40cm (14–16in), **S** indefinite. In late spring produces a solitary, greyish-white flower, 8–15cm (3–6in) wide, heavily veined deep purple. Standards appear larger than incurved falls, which each carry a black blaze and a deep purple beard. Grows best in a frame or alpine house.

***I.* 'Sweet Musette'.** Vigorous, rhizomatous, bearded iris (Tall). **H** 90–95cm (36–38in), **S** indefinite. In mid-and late spring produces large, ruffled, frilly flowers, with lavender-flushed, peach-pink standards, purplish-pink falls and orange beards.

I. tectorum (Japanese roof iris, Wall flag). Evansia iris with stout rhizomes. **H** 25–35cm (10–14in), **S** indefinite. Frost hardy. Has fans of broadly lance-shaped, ribbed leaves. In early summer, sparsely branched stem produces 2–3 darker-veined, bright lilac flowers, 1–8cm (½–3in) across with a white crest on each fall, from each spathe. Prefers a sheltered, sunny site near a south- or west-facing wall.

I. tenax. Rhizomatous, beardless Pacific Coast iris. **H** 15–30cm (6–12in), **S** indefinite. From late spring to early summer produces 1 or 2 deep purple to lavender-blue flowers, 8–12cm (3–5in) across, often with yellow-and-white marking on falls. White, cream and yellow variants also occur. Narrow, dark green leaves are stained pink at base.

***I.* 'Theseus'.** Rhizomatous Regeliocyclus iris. **H** 45cm (18in), **S** indefinite. From late spring to early summer produces usually 2 flowers, 10–15cm (4–6in) across, with violet standards and violet-veined, cream falls. Is best in a frame or alpine house.

♀ ***I.* 'Thornbird'.** Rhizomatous, bearded iris (Tall). **H** 90cm (3ft), **S** indefinite. In early summer, produces up to 7 flowers, with pale greenish-white standards and greenish-brown falls overlaid with deep violet lines. Long, horned beard is violet, tipped with mustard-yellow.

***I.* 'Titan's Glory'.** Robust, rhizomatous, well-branched, bearded iris (Tall). **H** 90–100cm (36–38in), **S** indefinite. Produces very large, deep purple-blue flowers, with an almost silken texture, in mid-spring.

I. tolmeiana. See *I. missouriensis*.

***I.* 'Tropic Night'** (illus. p.225). Strong-growing, rhizomatous, beardless Siberian iris. **H** 90cm (36in), **S** indefinite. In late spring and early summer produces deep violet-blue flowers; upright standards and

rounded falls have strong, white feathering and veining near the bases and are touched yellow around the throats.
I. tuberosa. See *Hermodactylus tuberosus.*
🏆 ***I. unguicularis,*** syn. *I. stylosa* (Algerian iris, Algerian winter iris, Winter iris). Evergreen, rhizomatous, beardless iris. **H** to 20cm (8in), **S** indefinite. Has narrow, tough leaves. Almost stemless, primrose-scented, lilac flowers, 5–8cm (2–3in) across with yellow centres to the falls and with very long tubes, appear from late autumn to early spring. Buds are prone to slug attack. Is excellent for cutting. Prefers a sheltered site against a south- or west-facing wall. 🏆 **'Mary Barnard'** has deep violet-blue flowers. ***subsp. cretensis,*** syn. *I. cretensis* (illus. p.224), **H** 10cm (4in), has violet or lavender-blue standards and white or yellow falls with violet veining at the bases and clear violet tips. Flowers of **'Walter Butt'** are pale silvery-lavender.
🏆 ***I. variegata*** (Variegated iris; illus. p.225). Rhizomatous, bearded iris. **H** 30–50cm (12–20in), **S** indefinite. In early summer, branched stem produces 3–6 flowers, 5–8cm (2–3in) across, with bright yellow standards and white or pale yellow falls, heavily veined red-brown and appearing striped.
I. verna. Rhizomatous, beardless iris. **H** 5cm (2in), **S** indefinite. In mid-spring bears 1, occasionally 2, lilac-blue flowers, 2.5–5cm (1–2in) across, with a narrow, orange stripe in the centre of each fall. Prefers semi-shade and moist but well-drained soil.
🏆 ***I. versicolor*** (Blue flag, Wild iris; illus. p.442.). Prefers partial shade and thrives in moist soil or in shallow water. **'Kermesina'** (illus. p.225) is robust, rhizomatous, beardless iris. **H** 60cm (2ft), **S** indefinite. From early to mid-summer produces red-purple flowers, with dense, white feathering at the bases of the falls. **'Rowden Cadenza'** illus. p.438.
I. 'Violet Beauty', syn. *I. reticulata* 'Violet Beauty'. Bulbous Reticulata iris. **H** 10–15cm (4–6in), **S** 4–6cm (1½–2½in). In early spring bears a solitary, fragrant, long-tubed, deep violet-purple flower, 4–6cm (1½–2½in) wide, with an orange ridge down the centre of each fall. Narrow, squared leaves elongate after flowering time.
I. warleyensis. Bulbous Juno iris. **H** 20–45cm (8–18in), **S** 7–8cm (3in). In spring produces up to 5 pale lilac or violet-blue flowers, 5–7cm (2–3in) across, in leaf axils. Each fall has a darker blue apex and a yellow stain in the centre. Bears scattered, lance-shaped, channelled, mid-green leaves. Is best in an unheated greenhouse.
I. 'White Excelsior'. Bulbous Xiphium iris (Dutch). **H** to 80cm (32in), **S** 15cm (6in). From spring to early summer bears 1 or 2 white flowers, 6–8cm (2½–3in) wide, with a yellow stripe down each fall centre. Narrowly lance-shaped, channelled, mid-green leaves are scattered on flower stem.
🏆 ***I. winogradowii*** (illus. p.225) Bulbous Reticulata iris. **H** 6–10cm (2½–4in), **S** 6–7cm (2½–3in). Solitary pale primrose-yellow flower, 6–7cm (2½–3in) wide, spotted green on falls, appears in early spring. Narrow, squared leaves are very short at flowering time but elongate later.
I. 'Wisley White'. Rhizomatous, beardless Siberian iris. **H** to 1m (3ft), **S** indefinite. Each stem carries 2 or 3 white flowers, held well above the foliage, in early summer.
I. xiphioides. See *I. latifolia.*
I. xiphium. Bulbous Xiphium iris (Spanish). **H** to 80cm (32in), **S** 15cm (6in). Has 1 or 2 blue or violet, occasionally yellow or white, flowers, 6–8cm (2½–3in) across, with central orange or yellow marks on the falls, in spring and early summer. Narrowly lance-shaped, channelled, mid-green leaves are scattered on flower stem. **'Blue Angel'** bears bright mid-blue flowers with a yellow mark in the centre of each fall. Flowers of **'Lusitanica'** are pure yellow. **'Queen Wilhelmina'** produces white flowers in spring. **'Wedgwood'** has bright blue flowers.

ISATIS

CRUCIFERAE/BRASSICACEAE

Genus of summer-flowering annuals, biennials and perennials. Fully hardy. Needs sun and fertile, well-drained soil. Propagate by seed in autumn or spring.
I. tinctoria (Woad). Vigorous, upright biennial. **H** to 1.2m (4ft), **S** 45cm (1½ft). Has oblong to lance-shaped, glaucous leaves and, in summer, large, terminal panicles of 4-petalled, yellow flowers.

ISMELIA

COMPOSITAE/ASTERACEAE

Genus of one species of annuals, grown for its daisy-like flower heads. Half hardy. Needs full sun and well-drained soil. Propagate by seed in spring.
I. carinata, syn. *Chrysanthemum carinatum, C. tricolor.* **'Monarch Court Jesters'** is a fast-growing, erect, branching annual. **H** 60cm (24in), **S** 30cm (12in). Has feathery, grey-green leaves and, in summer, daisy-like, zoned flower heads, to 8cm (3in) wide, in various colour combinations. **Tricolor Series** is a group of fast-growing, upright, branching annuals. **H** 30–60cm (12–24in), **S** 30cm (12in). Has feathery, light green leaves and, in summer, daisy-like, single or double flower heads, to 8cm (3in) wide, in many colour combinations. Tall cultivars, **H** 60cm (24in), **S** 30cm (12in), and dwarf, **H** and **S** 30cm (12in), are available.

ISMENE

AMARYLLIDACEAE

A genus of 10–15 species of half-hardy to frost tender bulbs grown for their large white scented flowers. Similar to *Hymenocallis* and *Pancratium*. Requires sheltered site in sun or partial shade, in a rich, well drained soil. Plant in early summer, lifting before the first frosts in cold areas, or grow under glass with a winter min. 10–15°C (50–59°F), reduce watering in winter, repot in spring. Propagate by offsets when repotting or seed sown when ripe.
I. calathina. See *I. narcissiflora.*
🏆 ***I. x deflexa,*** syn. *Hymenocallis festalis.* Spring- or summer-flowering bulb with a basal leaf cluster. **H** to 80cm (32in), **S** 30–45cm (12–18in). Frost tender. Bears strap-shaped, semi-erect leaves. Produces a head of 2–5 scented, white flowers, each 20cm (8in) across with a deep, central cup and 6 narrow, reflexed petals.
🏆 ***I. x macrostephana,*** syn. *Hymenocallis x macrostephana.* Evergreen, spring- or summer-flowering bulb. **H** 80cm (32in), **S** 30–45cm (12–18in). Has strap-shaped, semi-erect, basal leaves and fragrant, white or cream- to greenish-yellow flowers which are 15–20cm (6–8in) wide.
I. narcissiflora, syn. *Hymenocallis calathina, H. narcissiflora, I. calanthina,* illus. p.408.
🏆 ***I. x spofforthiae*** **'Sulphur Queen',** syn. *Hymenocallis x spofforthiae* 'Sulphur Queen', illus p.412.

ISOLEPIS

CYPERACEAE

See also GRASSES, BAMBOOS, RUSHES and SEDGES.
I. setaceus, syn. *Scirpus setaceus* (Bristle club-rush). Tuft-forming, annual or short-lived, perennial rush. **H** 10–15cm (4–6in), **S** 8cm (3in). Fully hardy. Has very slender, lax, basal leaves. Very slender, unbranched stems each bear 1–3 minute, egg-shaped, green spikelets in summer.

ISOPLEXIS

SCROPHULARIACEAE

Genus of evergreen, mainly summer-flowering shrubs, grown for their flowers. Is closely related to *Digitalis*. Frost tender, min. 7°C (45°F). Tolerates full light or partial shade and prefers well-drained soil. Water potted specimens freely when in full growth, moderately at other times. Remove spent flower spikes. Propagate by seed in spring or by semi-ripe cuttings in late summer.
I. canariensis, syn. *Digitalis canariensis,* illus. p.459.

ISOPYRUM

RANUNCULACEAE

Genus of spring-flowering perennials, grown for their small flowers and delicate foliage. Is suitable for peat beds, woodlands and rock gardens. Fully hardy. Requires shade and humus-rich, moist soil. Propagate by seed when fresh or by division in autumn. Self-seeds readily.
I. thalictroides. Dainty, clump-forming perennial. **H** and **S** 25cm (10in). Central stalk bears fern-like, 3-parted leaves, each leaflet being cut into 3. Produces small, nodding, cup-shaped, white flowers in spring.

ISOTOMA

CAMPANULACEAE

A genus of 8 species of half hardy perennials, often grown as annuals, for their long tubular flowers. Frequently used in containers and summer bedding. Propagation is by division, cuttings and seed.
I. **Avant-Garde Series** illus. p.313

Isotrema griffithii. See *Aristolochia griffithii.*

ITEA

ESCALLONIACEAE/ITEACEAE

Genus of deciduous or evergreen trees and shrubs, grown for their foliage and flowers. Frost hardy, but in most areas protect by growing against a south- or west-facing wall. Needs sun or semi-shade and fertile, well-drained but not too dry soil. Propagate by softwood cuttings in summer.
🏆 ***I. ilicifolia*** illus. p.211.

IXIA

IRIDACEAE

Genus of spring- and summer-flowering corms with wiry stems and spikes of flattish flowers. Half hardy. Grow in an open, sunny situation and in well-drained soil. Plant in autumn for spring and early summer flowers; plant in spring for later summer display. Dry off after flowering. Propagate in autumn by seed or by offsets at replanting time.
I. 'Mabel'. Spring- to early summer-flowering corm. **H** 40cm (16in), **S** 2.5–5cm (1–2in). Has linear, basal, mid-green leaves and spikes of deep pink flowers.
I. maculata. Spring- to early summer-flowering corm. **H** 40cm (16in), **S** 2.5–5cm (1–2in). Leaves are linear, erect and mostly basal. Wiry stem bears a spike of flattish, orange or yellow flowers, 2.5–5cm (1–2in) across, with brown or black centres.
I. monadelpha. Spring- to early summer-flowering corm. **H** 30cm (12in), **S** 2.5–5cm (1–2in). Linear, erect leaves are mostly basal. Stem produces a dense spike of 5–10 flattish, white, pink, purple or blue flowers, 3–4cm (1¼–1½in) across, often with differently coloured eyes.
I. viridiflora illus. p.406.

IXIOLIRION

AMARYLLIDACEAE

Genus of bulbs, grown for their funnel-shaped flowers mainly in spring. Fully hardy. Needs a sheltered, sunny site and well-drained soil that becomes hot and dry in summer to ripen the bulb. Propagate, by seed or offsets, in autumn.
I. montanum. See *I. tataricum.*
I. tataricum, syn. *I. montanum,* illus. p.403.

IXORA

RUBIACEAE

Genus of evergreen, summer-flowering shrubs, grown primarily for their flowers, some also for their foliage. Frost tender, min. 13–16°C (55–61°F). Prefers full sun and humus-rich, well-drained soil. Water containerized specimens freely when in full growth, moderately at other times. Propagate by seed in spring or by semi-ripe cuttings in summer.
I. coccinea illus. p.456.

JK

JACARANDA

BIGNONIACEAE

Genus of deciduous or evergreen trees, grown for their flowers in spring–summer and their foliage. Frost tender, min. 7–10°C (45–50°F). Grow in fertile, well-drained soil and in full light. Water potted specimens freely when in full growth, sparingly at other times. Potted plants grown for their foliage only may be cut back hard in late winter. Propagate by seed in spring or by semi-ripe cuttings in summer.
J. acutifolia of gardens. See *J. mimosifolia.*
J. mimosifolia, syn. *J. acutifolia* of gardens, *J. ovalifolia*, illus. p.451.
J. ovalifolia. See *J. mimosifolia.*

Jacobinia carnea. See *Justicia carnea.*
Jacobinia coccinea. See *Pachystachys coccinea.*
Jacobinia pohliana. See *Justicia carnea.*
Jacobinia spicigera. See *Justicia spicigera.*

JACQUEMONTIA

CONVOLVULACEAE

Genus of evergreen, twining climbers, grown for their flowers. Frost tender, min. 16–18°C (61–4°F). Any well-drained soil is suitable with full light. Water freely except in cold weather. Provide support and thin out by cutting old stems to ground level in spring. Propagate by seed in spring or by semi-ripe cuttings in summer. Red spider mite and whitefly may cause problems.
J. pentantha, syn. *J. violacea.* Fast-growing, evergreen, twining climber. **H** 2–3m (6–10ft). Has heart-shaped, pointed leaves and 2.5cm (1in) wide, funnel-shaped, rich violet-blue or pure blue flowers in long-stalked clusters in summer–autumn.
J. violacea. See *J. pentantha.*

JAMESBRITTENIA

SCROPHULARIACEAE

Genus of annuals, perennials and evergreen shrubs. Frost hardy to frost tender. Needs a position in sun and in moist but well-drained soil. Propagate by seed or division in spring or by softwood cuttings in spring or summer.
J. grandiflora, syn. *Sutera grandiflora.* Much-branched, sub-shrubby perennial, used for summer bedding. **H** 1m (3ft), **S** 30–45cm (12–18in). Frost tender, min. 5°C (41°F). Has oval to oblong, round-toothed leaves. Tubular, 5-lobed, frilled, deep purple flowers are produced from mid-summer to autumn.

JAMESIA

HYDRANGEACEAE

Genus of one species of deciduous shrub, grown for its flowers. Fully hardy. Needs full sun and fertile, well-drained soil. Propagate by softwood cuttings in summer.
J. americana. Deciduous, bushy shrub. **H** 1.5m (5ft), **S** 2.5m (8ft). Rounded, grey-green leaves are grey-white beneath. Clusters of small, slightly fragrant, star-shaped, white flowers are produced during late spring.

JANCAEA,

SYN. JANKAEA

GESNERIACEAE

Genus of one species of evergreen, rosetted perennial, grown for its flowers and silver-green leaves. Makes a good alpine house plant. Frost hardy. Is difficult to grow, as needs shade from mid-day sun in high summer, a humus-rich, gritty, moist, alkaline soil and a gritty collar. Dislikes winter wet. Propagate by seed in spring or by leaf cuttings in mid-summer.
J. heldreichii illus. p.355.

Jankaea. See *Jancaea.*

JASIONE

CAMPANULACEAE

Genus of summer-flowering annuals, biennials and perennials, grown for their attractive flower heads. Fully hardy. Needs sun and sandy soil. Remove old stems in autumn. Propagate by seed in autumn or by division in spring.
J. laevis, syn. *J. perennis* (Sheep's bit). Tufted perennial. **H** 5–30cm (2–12in), **S** 10–20cm (4–8in). Has narrowly oblong, very hairy or glabrous, grey-green leaves and, in summer, spiky, spherical, blue flower heads borne on erect stems. Is good for a rock garden.
J. perennis. See *J. laevis.*

JASMINUM

Jasmine

OLEACEAE

Genus of deciduous or evergreen shrubs and woody-stemmed, scrambling or twining climbers, grown for their star-shaped, often fragrant flowers and their foliage. Fully hardy to frost tender, min. 7–18°C (45–64°F). Needs full sun and fertile, well-drained soil. *J. nudiflorum*, which needs supporting, benefits from having its old shoots thinned out after flowering, when others may be pruned. Propagate by semi-ripe cuttings in summer.
🏆 ***J. angulare***, syn. *J. capense.* Evergreen, woody-stemmed, scrambling climber. **H** 2m (6ft) or more. Frost tender, min. 7–10°C (45–50°F). Dark green leaves have 3 oval leaflets. Small clusters of fragrant, tubular, 5-lobed, white flowers are carried in late summer.
J. beesianum illus. p.193.
J. capense. See *J. angulare.*
J. grandiflorum of gardens. See *J. officinale* f. *affine.*
J. humile (Yellow jasmine) illus. p.139.
🏆 **'Revolutum'** illus. p.206.
f. *wallichianum* has semi-pendent flowers and 7–13 leaflets.
🏆 ***J. mesnyi***, syn. *J. primulinum* (Primrose jasmine), illus. p.195.
J. nobile* subsp. *rex, syn. *J. rex.* Evergreen, woody-stemmed, twining climber. **H** 3m (10ft). Frost tender, min. 18°C (64°F). Has broadly oval, leathery, deep green leaves, 10–20cm (4–8in) long. Scentless, tubular, 5-lobed, pure white flowers are pink-tinged in bud and appear intermittently all year if warm enough.
🏆 ***J. nudiflorum*** illus. p.144.
🏆 ***J. officinale*** (Common jasmine, Jessamine). Semi-evergreen or deciduous, woody-stemmed, twining climber. **H** to 12m (40ft). Leaves comprise 7 or 9 leaflets. Has clusters of fragrant, 4- or 5-lobed, white flowers in summer–autumn. **f. *affine*** (syn. *J. grandiflorum* of gardens) illus. p.196.
J. parkeri. Evergreen, domed shrub. **H** 15cm (6in), **S** 38cm (18in) or more. Frost hardy. Produces a tangled mass of fine stems and twigs bearing minute, oval leaves. Masses of tiny, tubular, 5-lobed, yellow flowers appear from leaf axils in early summer.
🏆 ***J. polyanthum*** illus. p.208.
J. primulinum. See *J. mesnyi.*
J. rex. See *J. nobile* subsp. *rex.*
J. x stephanense illus. p.201.

JEFFERSONIA

BERBERIDACEAE

Genus of spring-flowering perennials. Fully hardy. Needs shade or partial shade and humus-rich, moist soil. Extensive root systems resent disturbance. Top-dress crown in late autumn. Propagate by seed as soon as ripe.
J. diphylla illus. p.333.
J. dubia, syn. *Plagiorhegma dubia*, illus. p.355.

JOVIBARBA

CRASSULACEAE

Genus of evergreen perennials that spread by short stolons and are grown for their symmetrical rosettes of oval to strap-shaped, pointed, fleshy leaves. Makes ground-hugging mats, suitable for rock gardens, screes, walls, banks and alpine houses. Fully hardy. Needs sun and gritty soil. Takes several years to reach flowering size. Rosettes die after plants have flowered, but leave numerous offsets. Propagate by offsets in summer.
J. hirta, syn. *Sempervivum globiferum* subsp. *hirtum*, illus. p.374.
J. sobolifera, syn. *Sempervivum globiferum* subsp. *globiferum.* Vigorous, evergreen, mat-forming perennial. **H** 10cm (4in), **S** 20cm (8in). Rounded, greyish-green or olive-green rosettes are often red-tinged. Flower stems bear terminal clusters of small, cup-shaped, 6-petalled (rarely 5 or 7), pale yellow flowers in summer.

JUANULLOA

SOLANACEAE

Genus of evergreen, summer-flowering shrubs, grown for their flowers. Frost tender, min. 13–15°C (55–9°F). Low temperatures cause leaf drop. Prefers full light and fertile, freely draining soil. Water potted specimens moderately, less when not in full growth. To encourage a branching habit, tip prune young plants. Propagate by semi-ripe cuttings in summer. Whitefly, red spider mite and mealy bug may be troublesome.
J. aurantiaca. See *J. mexicana.*
J. mexicana, syn. *J. aurantiaca.* Evergreen, upright, sparingly branched shrub. **H** 2m (6ft) or more, **S** 60–100cm (24–39in). Leaves are felted beneath. Has orange flowers, each with a ribbed calyx, in short, nodding clusters in summer.

JUBAEA

PALMAE/ARECACEAE

Genus of one species of evergreen palm, grown for its overall appearance. Frost hardy. Needs full light and fertile, well-drained soil. Water potted specimens moderately, less frequently in winter. Propagate by seed in spring at not less than 25°C (77°F). Red spider mite may be a nuisance.
J. chilensis, syn. *J. spectabilis*, illus. p.80.
J. spectabilis. See *J. chilensis.*

JUGLANS

Walnut

JUGLANDACEAE

Genus of deciduous trees, with aromatic leaves, grown for their foliage, stately habit and, in some species, edible nuts (walnuts). Produces greenish-yellow catkins in spring and early summer. Fully hardy, but young plants are prone to frost damage. Requires full sun and deep, fertile, well-drained soil. Propagate by seed, when ripe, in autumn.
J. ailantifolia, syn. *J. sieboldiana* (Japanese walnut). Deciduous, spreading tree with stout shoots. **H** and **S** 15m (50ft). Very large leaves consist of 11–17 oblong, glossy, bright green leaflets. Bears edible walnuts in autumn. **var. *cordiformis*** (syn. *J. cordiformis*) illus. p.67.
J. cathayensis (Chinese walnut). Deciduous, spreading tree. **H** and **S** 20m (70ft). Has very large leaves, consisting of 11–17 oval to oblong, dark green leaflets. Bears edible walnuts in autumn.
J. cinerea (Butternut). Fast-growing, deciduous, spreading tree. **H** 25m (80ft), **S** 20m (70ft). Leaves are large and very aromatic, with 7–19 oval to oblong, pointed, bright green leaflets. Bears dense clusters of large, rounded nuts in autumn.
J. cordiformis. See *J. ailantifolia* var. *cordiformis.*
J. microcarpa, syn. *J. rupestris*, illus. p.88.
🏆 ***J. nigra*** illus. p.63.
🏆 ***J. regia*** illus. p.62.
J. rupestris. See *J. microcarpa.*
J. sieboldiana. See *J. ailanthifolia.*

JUNCUS

JUNCACEAE

See also GRASSES, BAMBOOS, RUSHES and SEDGES.
J. effusus* f. *spiralis, syn. *J. effusus* 'Spiralis' illus. p.286.

JUNIPERUS

Juniper

CUPRESSACEAE

See also CONIFERS.

J. chinensis (Chinese juniper). Conical conifer, making a tree. **H** 15m (50ft), **S** 2–3m (6–10ft), or a spreading shrub **H** 1–5m (3–15ft), **S** 3–5m (10–15ft). Fully hardy. Has peeling bark. Both scale- and needle-like, aromatic, dark green leaves, paired or in 3s, are borne on same shoot. Globose, fleshy, berry-like fruits are glaucous white. Many cultivars commonly listed under *J. chinensis* are forms of *J.* x *pfitzeriana*. See also feature panel p.105. ♀**'Aurea'**, **H** 10–15m (30–50ft), **S** 3–4m (10–12ft), is a slow-growing, oval or conical form with gold foliage and abundant yellow, male cones. ♀**'Blaauw'** (syn. *J.* x *media* 'Blaauw'), **H** and **S** 2m (6ft), is a spreading shrub with blue-green foliage. **'Expansa Variegata'** (syn. *J. davurica* 'Expansa Variegata') is a conifer with trailing or ascending branchlets. **H** 75cm (30in), **S** 1.5–2m (5–6ft). Fully hardy. Bears scale- and needle-like, aromatic, yellow-variegated, bluish-green leaves. ♀**'Kaizuka'**, **H** 5m (15ft), **S** 3–5m (10–15ft), forms a sprawling, irregular bush and has a profusion of cones. **'Keteleeri'** illus. p.100. ♀**'Obelisk'** illus. p.103. ♀**'Plumosa Aurea'** (syn. *J.* x *media* 'Plumosa Aurea') is more erect, with green-gold foliage, turning bronze in winter. ♀**'Pyramidalis'**, **H** 10m (30ft), **S** 1–2m (3–6ft), is a columnar, dense form with ascending branches bearing needle-like, blue-green leaves. **'Robusta Green'**, syn. *J. virginiana* 'Robusta Green', illus. p.103. **'Stricta'**, **H** to 5m (15ft), **S** to 1m (3ft), is conical, with soft, blue-green, young foliage.

J. communis (Common juniper). Conifer, ranging from a spreading shrub to a narrow, upright tree. **H** 30cm–8m (1–25ft), **S** 1–4m (3–12ft). Fully hardy. Has needle-like, aromatic, glossy, mid- or yellow-green leaves in 3s and bears globular to ovoid, fleshy, greenish berries that become glaucous blue, then ripen to black in their third year. ♀**'Compressa'**, **H** 75cm (30in), **S** 15cm (6in), is a dwarf, erect form. ♀**'Hibernica'**, **H** 3–5m (10–15ft), **S** 30cm (12in), is columnar. ♀**'Hornibrookii'**, **H** 50cm (20in), **S** 2m (6ft), and **'Prostrata'**, **H** 20–30cm (8–12in), **S** 1–2m (3–6ft), are carpeting plants.

J. conferta, syn. *J. rigida* subsp. *conferta* (Shore juniper). Prostrate, shrubby conifer. **H** 15cm (6in), **S** 1–2m (3–6ft). Fully hardy. Spreading branches bear dense, needle-like, aromatic, glossy, bright green leaves, glaucous beneath. Produces glaucous black berries. Tolerates salty, coastal air.

***J. davurica* 'Expansa Variegata'.** See *J. chinensis* 'Expansa Variegata'.

J. drupacea (Syrian juniper). Columnar conifer. **H** 10–15m (30–50ft), **S** 1–2m (3–6ft). Fully hardy. Has needle-like, aromatic, light green leaves, in 3s, and ovoid or almost globose, fleshy, brown berries.

J. horizontalis (Creeping juniper). Prostrate, wide-spreading, shrubby conifer, eventually forming mats up to 50cm (20in) thick. Fully hardy. Has scale- or needle-like, aromatic, blue-green or -grey leaves and pale blue-grey berries. Leaves of **'Andorra Compact'** (syn. *J.h.* 'Plumosa Compacta') turn bronze-purple in winter. **'Douglasii'** has glaucous blue foliage that turns plum-purple in winter. **'Plumosa'** is less dense than 'Andorra Compact' and has grey-green leaves, becoming purple during winter. **'Plumosa Compacta'** see *J.h.* 'Andorra Compact'. **'Prince of Wales'** has bright green foliage, tinged blue when young and turning purple-brown in winter. **'Turquoise Spreader'** has turquoise-green foliage. ♀**'Wiltonii'** has bluish-grey leaves that retain their colour over winter.

***J.* x *media*.** See *J.* x *pfitzeriana*. **'Blaauw'** see *J. chinensis* 'Blaauw'. **'Blue and Gold'** see *J.* x *pfitzeriana* 'Blue and Gold'. **'Hetzii'** see *J. virginiana* 'Hetzii'. **'Pfitzeriana'** see *J.* x *pfitzeriana* 'William Pfitzer'. **'Pfitzeriana Aurea'** see *J.* x *pfitzeriana* 'Aurea'. **'Pfitzeriana Glauca'** see *J.* x *pfitzeriana* 'Glauca'. **'Plumosa'**, **H** 1m (3ft), **S** 2–3m (6–10ft), is a spreading shrub with drooping sprays of mid-green foliage. **'Plumosa Aurea'** see *J. chinensis* 'Plumosa Aurea'.

J.* x *pfitzeriana, syn. *J.* x *media*. Group of spreading to conical conifers. **H** 15m (50ft), **S** 2–3m (6–10ft). Fully hardy. Has peeling bark. Mainly scale-like, dark green leaves exude a fetid smell when crushed. Fruits are globose to rounded, white or blue-black. Cultivars are suitable as ground cover or as specimen plants in a small garden. Some forms are commonly listed under *J. chinensis*. **'Aurea'** (syn. *J.* x *media* 'Pfitzeriana Aurea') has golden foliage. **'Blue and Gold'**, syn. *J.* x *media* 'Blue and Gold', **H** to 1m (3ft), **S** 1m (3ft), is a spreading form with leaves variegated sky-blue and gold. **'Glauca'** (syn. *J.* x *media* 'Pfitzeriana Glauca') produces grey-blue leaves. ♀**'Old Gold'** (illus. p.105), **H** 1m (3ft), **S** 2.5m (8ft), has a compact, spreading, flat-topped habit and bronze-yellow leaves. ♀**'Pfitzeriana Compacta'**, **H** and **S** 1.5m (5ft), has a dense, compact habit and a tendency to produce more juvenile leaves. **'William Pfitzer'** (syn. *J.* x *media* 'Pfitzeriana'), **H** 3m (10ft), **S** 3–5m (10–15ft), is a spreading, flat-topped shrub and produces greyish-green leaves.

J. procumbens (Bonin Isles juniper). Spreading, prostrate, shrubby conifer. **H** 75cm (30in), **S** 2m (6ft). Fully hardy. Has red-brown bark. Thick branches carry needle-like, aromatic, light green or yellow-green leaves and globose, fleshy, brown or black berries. ♀**'Nana'**, **H** 15–20cm (6–8in), **S** 75cm (30in), is less vigorous and is mat-forming.

J. recurva (Drooping juniper, Himalayan weeping juniper) illus. p.103. **var. *coxii*** illus. p.100. **'Densa'** (syn. *J. recurva* 'Nana') is a spreading conifer. **H** 30cm (1ft), **S** 1m (3ft). Fully hardy. Shaggy bark flakes in thin sheets. Sprays of long, needle-like, aromatic, dark green leaves are erect at tips. Ovoid, fleshy berries are black. **'Nana'** see *J.r.* 'Densa'.

J. rigida (Temple juniper). Sprawling, shrubby conifer. **H** and **S** 8m (25ft). Fully hardy. Grey or brown bark peels in strips. Very sharp, needle-like, aromatic, bright green leaves, in 3s, are borne in nodding sprays. Globose, fleshy fruits are purplish-black. **subsp. *conferta*** see *J. conferta*.

J. sabina (Savin). Spreading, shrubby conifer. **H** to 4m (12ft), **S** 3–5m (10–15ft). Fully hardy. Has flaking, red-brown bark. Slender shoots bear mainly scale-like, aromatic, dark green leaves that give off a fetid smell when crushed. Produces rounded, blue-black berries. **'Blaue Donau'** (syn. *J.s.* 'Blue Danube'), **H** 2m (6ft), **S** 2–4m (6–12ft), is a spreading form with branch tips curved upwards and grey-blue foliage. **'Blue Danube'** see *J.s.* 'Blaue Donau'. **'Cupressifolia'**, **H** 2m (6ft), **S** 4m (12ft), is a free-fruiting, female form with horizontal or ascending branches and blue-green leaves. **'Mas'** has ascending branches. Leaves are blue above, green below, purplish in winter. **var. *tamariscifolia***, **H** 1m (3ft), **S** 2m (6ft), produces tiered layers of mainly needle-like, bright green or blue-green leaves.

J. scopulorum (Rocky Mountain juniper). Slow-growing, round-crowned conifer. **H** 10m (30ft), **S** 4m (12ft). Fully hardy. Reddish-brown bark is furrowed into strips or squares and peels on branches. Scale-like, aromatic leaves are grey-green to dark green. Bears globose, fleshy, blue berries. **'Skyrocket'**, syn. *J. virginiana* 'Skyrocket' (illus. p.105), **H** 8m (26ft), **S** 75cm (2½ft), is very narrow in habit with glaucous blue foliage. **'Springbank'** is narrowly conical with drooping branch tips and intense silvery-blue foliage. **'Tabletop'**, **H** 2m (6ft), **S** 5m (15ft), has a flat-topped habit and silvery-blue leaves.

J. squamata (Flaky juniper). Prostrate to sprawling, shrubby conifer. **H** 30cm–4m (1–12ft), **S** 1–5m (3–15ft). Fully hardy. Bark is red-brown and flaking. Needle-like, aromatic, fresh green or bluish-green leaves spread at tips of shoots. Produces ovoid, fleshy, black berries. ♀ **'Blue Carpet'** (illus. p.105), **H** 30cm (1ft), **S** 2–3m (6–10ft), is vigorous and prostrate, with glaucous blue foliage. ♀**'Blue Star'**, **H** 50cm (20in), **S** 60cm (24in), forms a dense, rounded bush and has blue foliage. **'Chinese Silver'**, **H** and **S** 3–4m (10–12ft), has branches with nodding tips and bluish leaves with bright silver undersides. ♀**'Holger'** (illus. p.105), **H** and **S** 2m (6ft), produces sulphur-yellow young leaves that contrast with steel-blue old foliage. **'Meyeri'**, **H** and **S** 5m (15ft), has a sprawling habit and produces steel-blue foliage.

J. virginiana (Pencil cedar). Slow-growing, conical or broadly columnar conifer. **H** 15–20m (50–70ft), **S** 6–8m (20–25ft). Fully hardy. Both scale- and needle-like, aromatic, grey-green leaves are borne on same shoot. Ovoid, fleshy berries are brownish-violet and extremely glaucous. **'Burkii'**, **H** to 6m (20ft), **S** 1m (3ft), has blue-grey leaves that become purple-tinged over winter. ♀**'Grey Owl'**, **H** 3m (10ft), **S** 3–5m (10–15ft), is a low, spreading cultivar with ascending branches and silvery-grey foliage. **'Hetzii'** (syn. *J.* x *media* 'Hetzii'), **H** 3–4m (10–12ft), **S** 4m (12ft), produces tiers of grey-green foliage. **'Robusta Green'** see *J. chinensis* 'Robusta Green'. **'Skyrocket'** see *J. scopulorum* 'Skyrocket'.

JUSTICIA

ACANTHACEAE

Genus of evergreen perennials, sub-shrubs and shrubs, grown mainly for their flowers. Frost tender, min. 7–15°C (45–59°F). Requires full light or partial shade and fertile, well-drained soil. Water containerized specimens freely when in full growth, moderately at other times. Some species need regular pruning. Propagate by softwood or greenwood cuttings in spring or early summer. Whitefly may cause problems.

J. adhatoda, syn. *Adhatoda duvernoia*, *Duvernoia adhatodoides* (Snake bush). Evergreen, erect shrub. **H** 2–3m (6–10ft), **S** 1–2m (3–6ft). Frost tender, min. 7°C (45°F). Has elliptic, dark green leaves. Fragrant, tubular, white or mauve flowers, with pink, red or purple marks, appear in summer–autumn.

♀***J. brandegeeana***, syn. *Beloperone guttata*, *Drejerella guttata*, illus. p.455. **'Chartreuse'** is an evergreen, arching shrub. **H** to 1m (3ft), **S** 60–90cm (24–36in). Frost tender, min. 10–15°C (50–59°F). Has white flowers surrounded by pale yellow-green bracts mainly in summer but also intermittently during the year.

J. carnea, syn. *Jacobinia carnea*, *J. pohliana*, illus. p.455.

***J. coccinea*.** See *Pachystachys coccinea*.

***J. floribunda*.** See *J. rizzinii*.

J. ghiesbreghtiana of gardens. See *J. spicigera*.

***J. pauciflora*.** See *J. rizzinii*.

♀***J. rizzinii***, syn. *J. floribunda*, *J. pauciflora*, *Libonia floribunda*. Evergreen, rounded, freely branching shrub. **H** and **S** 30–60cm (1–2ft). Frost tender, min. 15°C (59°F) to flower well in winter. Leaves are oval and mid-green. Bears nodding clusters of tubular, yellow-tipped, scarlet flowers mainly autumn–spring; propagate every few years.

J. spicigera, syn. *J. ghiesbreghtiana* of gardens, *Jacobinia spicigera*. Evergreen, well-branched shrub. **H** to 1–1.8m (3–6ft), **S** 75–120cm (2½–4ft). Frost tender, min. 10–15°C (50–59°F). Has spikes of tubular, orange or red flowers in summer and occasionally other seasons.

KADSURA

SCHISANDRACEAE

Genus of evergreen, twining climbers, grown for their foliage and fruits. Male and female flowers are borne on separate plants, so plants of both sexes must be grown to obtain fruits. Frost hardy. Grow in semi-shade and in any soil. Propagate by stem cuttings in late summer.

***K. japonica*.** Evergreen, twining climber. **H** 3–4m (10–12ft). Has oval or lance-shaped, mid-green leaves. Solitary small, fragrant, cream flowers are produced in leaf axils in summer, followed by bright red berries. Prefers well-drained soil.

KAEMPFERIA

ZINGIBERACEAE

Genus of tufted, rhizomatous perennials, grown for their aromatic leaves and their flowers. Frost tender, min. 5–18°C

(41–64°F). Needs a moist atmosphere, partial shade and moist, humus-rich soil. Allow to dry out when plants become dormant. Propagate by division in late spring. See also feature panel p.477.
K. pulchra (illus. p.477). Tufted, rhizomatous perennial. **H** 15cm (6in), **S** 30cm (12in). Frost tender, min. 10°C (50°F). Has horizontal, aromatic, dark green leaves, variegated with paler green above. Short spikes of lilac-pink flowers appear from the centre of tufts in summer.
K. roscoeana. Rhizomatous perennial without an obvious stem. **H** 5–10cm (2–4in), **S** 20–25cm (8–10in). Frost tender, min. 18°C (64°F). Usually has only 2 almost rounded, aromatic leaves, to 10cm (4in) long, dark green with pale green marks above, reddish- green below, that are held horizontally. A short spike of pure white flowers, each with a deeply lobed lip, appears from the centre of the leaf tuft in autumn.
K. rotunda. Herbacous, rhizomatous perennial. **H** 60cm (2ft), **S** 30cm (1ft). Frost tender, min. 5°C (41°F). Has 2–4 broadly lance-shaped leaves, 20–25cm (8–10in) long, patterned silver and deep green, with red undersides. White flowers, with pink to purple lips, borne on a separate stem before the leafy stem emerges, open in succession from late spring to summer. A number of cultivars are grown for their patterned foliage.

KALANCHOE

SYN. BRYOPHYLLUM

CRASSULACEAE

Genus of perennial succulents or shrubs with very fleshy, mainly cylindrical, oval or linear leaves and bell-shaped to tubular flowers. Many species produce new plantlets from indented leaf margins. Frost tender, min. 7–15°C (45–59°F). Requires a position in full sun or partial shade and well-drained soil. Keep moist from spring to autumn. Water lightly and only occasionally in winter. Propagate by seed, offsets or stem cuttings in spring or summer.
♈ ***K. beharensis.*** Bushy, perennial succulent. **H** and **S** to 4m (12ft). Frost tender, min. 10°C (50°F). Has triangular to lance-shaped, olive-green leaves, covered with fine, brown hairs. Bell-shaped, yellow flowers appear in late winter, only on plants over 2m (6ft) high.
K. blossfeldiana (Flaming Katy; illus. p.487). Bushy, perennial succulent. **H** and **S** 30cm (12in). Min. 10°C (50°F). Has oval to oblong, glossy, dark green leaves with toothed edges and clusters of tubular, scarlet flowers, 0.5cm (¼in) across, in spring. Prefers partial shade. Many hybrids are available in a range of colours (salmon pink, illus. p.487). **'Calandiva'** illus. p.482.
K. daigremontiana illus. p.492.
K. delagoensis, syn. *K. tubiflora*, illus. p.496.
K. fedtschenkoi. Bushy, perennial succulent. **H** and **S** 1m (3ft). Min. 10°C (50°F). Produces oval, indented, blue-grey leaves with new plantlets in each notch. Bell-shaped, brownish-pink flowers, 2cm (¾in) long, appear in late winter. Prefers a sunny position. **'Variegata'** illus. p.482.
K. laetivirens. Evergreen, perennial succulent. **H** 25cm (10in), **S** 15cm (6in). Min. 10°C (50°F). Oblong to elliptic, glaucous, mid-green leaves, turning pink in strong light, produce small plantlets from notches along the margins. Bears clusters of tubular, greenish-white to purplish flowers, 1.5cm (⅝in) long, in winter.
♈ ***K. pumila.*** Creeping, perennial succulent. **H** 10cm (4in), **S** indefinite. Min. 10°C (50°F). Has oval, powdery grey-white leaves with indented margins. Tubular, pink flowers, 1cm (½in) long, are produced in spring. Suits a hanging basket in a sunny position.
♈ ***K. 'Tessa'*** illus. p.487.
♈ ***K. tomentosa*** illus. p.490.
K. tubiflora. See *K. delagoensis.*
K. uniflora, syn. *Kitchingia uniflora.* Creeping, perennial succulent. **H** 6cm (2½in), **S** indefinite. Min. 15°C (59°F). Produces rounded, mid-green leaves, 0.5–3cm (¼–1¼in) long, and bell-shaped, yellow-flushed, reddish-purple flowers, 1cm (½in) long, in late winter. Prefers partial shade.
♈ ***K. 'Wendy'*** illus. p.485.

KALMIA

ERICACEAE

Genus of evergreen, summer-flowering shrubs, grown for their clusters of distinctive, usually cup-shaped flowers. Fully hardy. Needs sun or semi-shade and moist, peaty, acid soil. Propagate species by softwood cuttings in summer or by seed in autumn, selected forms by softwood cuttings in summer. ⓘ All parts may cause severe discomfort if ingested.
♈ ***K. angustifolia*** (Sheep laurel).
♈ **f. *rubra*** (syn. *K. angustifolia* 'Rubra') illus. p.156.
♈ ***K. latifolia*** (Calico bush) illus. p.136. **'Ostbo Red'** is an evergreen, bushy, dense shrub. **H** and **S** 3m (10ft). Has oval, glossy, rich green leaves. Large, showy clusters of deep pink flowers open in early summer from distinctively crimped, deep red buds. Prefers full sun.

KALMIOPSIS

ERICACEAE

Genus of one species of evergreen, spring-flowering shrub, grown for its flowers. Fully hardy. Requires a position in semi-shade and moist, peaty, acid soil. Propagate by softwood or semi-ripe cuttings in summer. Suits a cool place in a peat garden.
***K. leachiana* 'La Piniec'**, syn. *K.l.* 'M. le Piniec'. Evergreen, bushy shrub. **H** and **S** 30cm (12in). Terminal clusters of small, widely bell-shaped, purplish-pink flowers are produced from early to late spring. Has small, oval, glossy, dark green leaves.

KALOPANAX

ARALIACEAE

Genus of one species of deciduous, autumn-flowering tree, grown for its foliage and fruits. Fully hardy, but unripened wood on young plants is susceptible to frost damage. Does best in sun or semi-shade and in fertile, moist but well-drained soil. Propagate by softwood cuttings in summer.
K. pictus. See *K. septemlobus.*
K. ricinifolius. See *K. septemlobus.*
K. septemlobus, syn. *Acanthopanax ricinifolius, K. pictus, K. ricinifolius,* illus. p.74.

KELSEYA

ROSACEAE

Genus of one species of extremely small, evergreen sub-shrub. Is difficult to grow and is best in an alpine house as foliage deeply resents both summer and winter wet. Fully hardy. Requires full sun and moist, alkaline soil. Propagate by soft-tip cuttings in late spring or by seed in autumn. Is susceptible to moulds, so remove any dead rosettes at once.
K. uniflora. Slow-growing, evergreen, rosetted sub-shrub. **H** 1cm (½in), **S** to 20cm (8in). Forms a hard mat of closely packed, small rosettes of tiny, oval, dark green leaves. In early spring carries stemless, star-shaped, occasionally pink-flushed, white flowers.

KENNEDIA

SYN. KENNEDYA

LEGUMINOSAE/PAPILIONACEAE

Genus of evergreen, woody-stemmed, trailing and twining climbers, grown for their pea-like flowers. Frost tender, min. 5–7°C (41–5°F). Provide full light and moderately fertile, sandy soil. Water regularly when in full growth, sparingly in cold weather. Requires support. Thin out congested growth after flowering or in spring. Propagate by seed in spring or by semi-ripe cuttings in summer.
K. nigricans (Black bean). Vigorous, evergreen, woody-stemmed, twining climber. **H** to 2m (6ft). Leaves are divided into 3 leaflets with notched tips. Has small trusses of pea-like, velvety, black-purple flowers, with yellow blazes, in spring–summer.
K. rubicunda illus. p.462.

Kennedya. See *Kennedia.*
Kentia fosteriana. See *Howea fosteriana.*

KERRIA

ROSACEAE

Genus of one species of deciduous shrub, grown for its showy, yellow flowers. Fully hardy. Needs sun or semi-shade and fertile, well-drained soil. Thin out old shoots after flowering. Propagate by softwood cuttings in summer or by division in autumn.
♈ ***K. japonica* 'Pleniflora'** illus. p.127. **var. *simplex*** is a deciduous, arching, graceful shrub. **H** and **S** 2m (6ft). Has bright green foliage. Single, buttercup-like, golden yellow flowers are borne from mid- to late spring.

KIGELIA

BIGNONIACEAE

Genus of one species of evergreen tree, grown for its flowers, curious, sausage-like fruits and for shade. Frost tender, min. 16°C (61°F). Requires full light and humus-rich, well-drained soil. Water potted specimens moderately, very little when temperatures low. Propagate by seed in spring at not less than 23°C (73°F).
K. africana, syn. *K. pinnata* (Sausage tree). Evergreen, spreading, fairly bushy tree. **H** and **S** 8m (25ft) or more. Leaves have 7–11 oblong to oval leaflets. Scented, bell-shaped, purplish-red flowers open at night from autumn to spring. Bears inedible, cylindrical, hard-shelled, brown fruits, 30–45cm (12–18in) long.
K. pinnata. See *K. africana.*

KIRENGESHOMA

HYDRANGEACEAE

Genus of late summer- and autumn-flowering perennials. Fully hardy. Grow in light shade and in deep, moist, lime-free soil. Propagate by seed or division in autumn or spring.
♈ ***K. palmata*** illus. p.251.

KITAIBELA

SYN. KITAIBELIA

MALVACEAE

Genus of one species of summer-flowering perennial. Fully hardy. Needs full sun and fertile, preferably dry soil. Propagate by seed in autumn or spring.
K. vitifolia. Bushy, upright perennial. **H** to 1.5m (5ft), **S** 60cm (2ft). In summer bears small clusters of open cup-shaped, white or rose-pink flowers. Has palmately lobed, coarsely toothed leaves.

Kitaibelia. See *Kitaibela*
Kitchingia uniflora. See *Kalanchoe uniflora.*
Kleinia articulata. See *Senecio articulatus.*
Kleinia rowleyana. See *Senecio rowleyanus.*

KNAUTIA

DIPSACACEAE

Genus of summer-flowering annuals and perennials. Fully hardy. Needs sun and well-drained soil. Requires staking. Propagate by basal cuttings in spring or by seed in autumn.
K. arvensis, syn. *Scabiosa arvensis* (Scabious). Erect perennial. **H** 1.2m (4ft), **S** 45cm (1½ft). Produces heads of pincushion-like, bluish-lilac flowers in summer. Stems are clothed in narrowly oval to lyre-shaped, deeply divided leaves.
K. macedonica, syn. *Scabiosa rumelica,* illus. p.235.

KNIGHTIA

PROTEACEAE

Genus of evergreen, summer-flowering trees, grown for their flowers, foliage and overall appearance. Half hardy, but is best at min. 3–5°C (37–41°F). Grows in any

reasonably fertile, well-drained soil and in sun or partial shade. Water potted specimens moderately, less in winter. Propagate by seed in spring.
K. excelsa (New Zealand honeysuckle, Rewa rewa). Evergreen, upright tree. **H** 20m (70ft) or more, **S** 2–4m (6–12ft). Has oblong to lance-shaped, coarsely serrated, leathery leaves, glossy and deep green. Dense racemes of slender, tubular, deep red flowers are produced in summer.

KNIPHOFIA

Red-hot poker, Torch lily

LILIACEAE/ASPHODELACEAE

Genus of perennials, some of which are evergreen. Fully to half hardy. Needs full sun and well-drained conditions, with constantly moist soil in summer. Propagate species by seed or division in spring, cultivars by division only in spring. See also feature panel p.254.
***K.* 'Ada'.** Semi-evergreen, clump-forming perennial. **H** 100m (36in), **S** 45cm (18in). Frost hardy. Has long, lance-shaped, mid-green, basal leaves. In summer, upright, dark green stems bear racemes of tubular, orange-yellow flowers, the buds rather darker in colour.
***K.* 'Alcazar'.** Semi-evergreen, clump-forming perennial. **H** 100cm (36in), **S** 45cm (18in). Fully hardy. Has long, lance-shaped, mid-green, basal leaves. In summer, upright, dark green stems bear racemes of reddish-orange buds opening to tubular, golden-yellow flowers.
***K.* 'Atlanta'** (illus. p.254). Evergreen, upright perennial. **H** to 1m (3ft), **S** 45cm (1½ft). Fully hardy. In summer, stout stems bear dense, terminal racemes of tubular, bright orange-yellow flowers. Has thick, grass-like, channelled leaves. Does well in a coastal area.
***K.* 'Bee's Lemon'.** Upright perennial. **H** 1m (3ft), **S** 45cm (1½ft). Fully hardy. Has dense, terminal racemes of tubular, green-tinged, citron-yellow flowers on stout stems in late summer and autumn. Grass-like, deep green leaves have serrated edges.
♡***K.* 'Bees' Sunset'** (illus. p.254). Semi-evergreen, clump-forming perennial. **H** 120cm (48in), **S** 45cm (18in). Frost hardy. Has long, grass-like, mid-green, basal leaves. In summer, upright, purplish-green stems bear slender racemes of tubular, warm orange-flushed, yellow flowers.
♡***K.* 'Brimstone'.** Semi-evergreen, clump-forming perennial. **H** 100cm (36in), **S** 45cm (18in). Frost hardy. Has long, narrowly lance-shaped, mid-green, basal leaves. In summer, upright stems bear slender racemes of tubular, soft greenish-yellow flowers.
♡***K. caulescens*** (illus. p.254). Stately, evergreen, upright perennial. **H** 1.2m (4ft), **S** 60cm (2ft). Frost hardy. Has basal tufts of narrow, blue-green leaves and smooth, stout stems bearing terminal spikes of reddish-salmon flowers in autumn.
***K.* 'C.M. Prichard'** of gardens. See *K. rooperi*.
***K.* 'Cobra'.** Semi-evergreen, clump-forming perennial. **H** 100cm (36in) or more, **S** 45cm (18in). Frost hardy. Has long, lance-shaped, mid-green, basal leaves. In summer, upright stems bear stout, broad, dense racemes of tubular, brown-tinged, orange flowers that age to yellowish-white.
***K.* 'Green Jade'** (illus. p.254). Semi-evergreen, clump-forming perennial. Frost hardy. **H** 120cm (48in), **S** 55cm (22in). Has long, lance-shaped, mid-green, basal leaves. In summer, upright stems bear elegant, rather slender racemes of tubular, pale green flowers, fading to warm ivory-white.
K. linearifolia. Semi-evergreen, clump-forming perennial. **H** 1.5m (60in), **S** 80cm (32in). Frost hardy. Has very long, rather lax, grass-like, mid-green leaves. In summer, upright stems bear dense racemes of orange-red buds opening to tubular, bright yellow flowers.
***K.* 'Little Maid'.** Semi-evergreen, clump-forming perennial. **H** 60cm (2ft), **S** 30cm (1ft). Frost hardy. Has long, grass-like, mid-green, basal leaves. In summer, upright stems bear dainty racemes of tubular, greenish yellow flowers that fade to creamy-white.
***K.* 'Maid of Orleans'.** Upright perennial. **H** 1.2m (4ft), **S** 45cm (1½ft). Frost hardy. In summer, slender stems are each crowned with a dense raceme of yellow buds that open to tubular, creamy-white flowers. Leaves are fresh green, basal and strap-shaped.
♡***K. northiae.*** Evergreen, rosette-forming perennial. **H** 1.5m (5ft), **S** 1m (3ft) or more. Frost hardy. Has rather lax, broadly strap shaped, pointed, pale green leaves. In summer produces dense racemes of tubular, greenish-yellow flowers.
***K.* 'Percy's Pride'** illus. p.251.
***K.* 'Prince Igor'** (illus. p.254). Semi-evergreen, clump-forming perennial. **H** 2m (6ft) or more, **S** 1m (3ft). Frost hardy. Has long, lance-shaped, mid-green, basal leaves. In summer, upright stems bear racemes of tubular, yellow-tinged, reddish-orange flowers.
♡***K. rooperi***, syn. *K.* 'C.M. Prichard' of gardens (illus. p.254). Robust, evergreen perennial. **H** 1.2m (4ft), **S** 60cm (2ft). Fully hardy. Has arching, linear, dark green leaves. From early to late autumn, produces broadly ellipsoid racemes of orange-red flowers, becoming orange-yellow.
♡***K.* 'Royal Standard'** (illus. p.254). Semi-evergreen, clump-forming perennial. **H** 100cm (36in) or more, **S** 55cm (22in). Frost hardy. Bears long, lance-shaped, mid-green, basal leaves. In summer, upright stems bear 2-toned racemes of bright red buds opening to tubular, yellow flowers.
♡***K.* 'Samuel's Sensation'.** Semi-evergreen, clump-forming perennial. **H** 165cm (66in) or more, **S** 80cm (32in). Frost hardy. Bears long, lance-shaped, mid-green, basal leaves. In summer, upright stems bear racemes of tubular, pinkish-red flowers ageing to orange-yellow.
K. snowdenii of gardens. See *K. thomsonii* var. *snowdenii.*
***K.* 'Star of Baden-Baden'.** Semi-evergreen, clump-forming perennial. **H** 180m (72in), **S** 80cm (32in). Frost hardy. Has long, lance-shaped, mid-green, basal leaves. In summer, upright stems bear racemes of tubular, greenish-golden-yellow flowers.
***K.* 'Strawberries and Cream'.** Largely herbaceous, rather compact, clump-forming perennial. **H** 60cm (24in), **S** 35cm (14in). Frost hardy. Has lance-shaped, mid-green, basal leaves. In summer, bears upright racemes of tubular, pinkish-ivory flowers, opening from darker buds.
***K.* 'Tetbury Torch'.** Semi-evergreen, clump-forming perennial. **H** 100cm (36in), **S** 45cm (18in). Frost hardy. Bears lance-shaped, mid-green, basal leaves. In early summer and often in later summer produces upright racemes of tubular, orange flowers that fade to warm yellow.
K. thomsonii* var. *snowdenii, syn. *K. snowdenii* of gardens (illus. p.254). Upright perennial. **H** 1m (3ft), **S** 50cm (20in). Frost hardy. Has grass-like, basal foliage and in summer bears coral-pink flowers, with yellowish interiors, spaced widely along terminal spikes.
***K.* 'Timothy'.** Semi-evergreen, clump-forming perennial. **H** 100cm (36in), **S** 45cm (18in). Frost hardy. Has long, lance-shaped, mid-green, basal leaves. In summer, upright, purplish-green stems bear racemes of tubular, warm peachy-pink flowers.
♡***K.* 'Toffee Nosed'** (illus. p.254). Semi-evergreen, clump-forming perennial. **H** 100cm (36in), **S** 45cm (18in). Frost hardy. Has long, lance-shaped, mid-green, basal leaves. In summer, upright stems bear racemes of tubular, brown-orange flowers that fade to warm cream.
K. uvaria (Red-hot poker). ♡**'Nobilis'** is an upright perennial with erect, then spreading leaves. **H** 2m (6ft), **S** 1m (3ft). Fully hardy. In late summer and autumn, stout stems each bear a dense, terminal raceme of tubular, bright red flowers. Has strap-shaped, channelled, dark green leaves.
***K.* 'Wrexham Buttercup'** (illus. p.254). Semi-evergreen, clump-forming perennial. **H** 120cm (48in), **S** 55cm (22in). Frost hardy. Has long, lance-shaped, mid-green, basal leaves. In summer, upright stems bear broad racemes of tubular, bright yellow flowers, opening from greenish buds.

Kochia. See *Bassia.*

KOELREUTERIA

SAPINDACEAE

Genus of deciduous, summer-flowering trees, grown for their foliage, flowers and fruits. Fully hardy to frost tender, min. 10°C (50°F). Requires full sun, doing best in hot summers, and fertile, well-drained soil. Propagate by seed in autumn or by root cuttings in late winter.
♡***K. paniculata*** (Golden rain tree, Pride of India) illus. p.89.

KOHLERIA

GESNERIACEAE

Genus of erect perennials with scaly rhizomes, grown for their showy, tubular flowers borne mainly in summer. Frost tender, min. 15°C (59°F). Grow in moist but well-drained soil and in full sun or semi-shade. Water sparingly in winter; over-watering will cause rhizomes to rot. Propagate in spring by division of rhizomes or by seed if available.
K. amabilis. Rhizomatous perennial. **H** 8–16cm (3–6in), **S** 60cm (2ft). Oval, hairy leaves, to 8cm (3in) long, are often marked with silver and brown above. Small, nodding, tubular, deep pink flowers, with red-marked lobes, appear in summer. Is useful for a hanging basket.
K. bogotensis. Erect, rhizomatous perennial. **H** and **S** 45cm (18in) or more. Oval, velvety, green leaves, to 8cm (3in) long, are sometimes marked with paler green above. In summer has small, tubular flowers, red with a yellow base outside, red-dotted, yellow within.
K. digitaliflora illus. p.469.
♡***K. eriantha*** illus. p.470.
♡***K. warscewiczii.*** Erect, rhizomatous perennial. **H** 1m (3ft), **S** 60cm (2ft). Oval, dark green leaves have scalloped margins. In summer and autumn, produces tubular, hairy, yellow-based, scarlet flowers with red- or brown spotted, greenish-yellow or bright yellow lobes.

KOLKWITZIA

CAPRIFOLIACEAE

Genus of one species of deciduous shrub, grown for its abundant flowers. Fully hardy. Prefers full sun and fertile, well-drained soil. Cut out old shoots after flowering. Propagate by softwood cuttings in summer.
K. amabilis (Beauty bush). Deciduous, arching shrub. **H** and **S** 3m (10ft). Has peeling bark and oval, dark green leaves. Bell-shaped, yellow-throated, white or pink flowers are borne in late spring and early summer. ♡**'Pink Cloud'** illus. p.114.

Korolkowia sewerzowii. See *Fritillaria sewerzowii.*

KUNZEA

MYRTACEAE

Genus of evergreen shrubs and trees, grown for their flowers and overall appearance. Frost tender, min. 5–7°C (41–5°F). Prefers full light and sandy, well-drained, neutral to acid soil. Water potted specimens moderately, less when not in full growth. Propagate by semi-ripe cuttings in late summer or by seed in spring.
K. baxteri. Evergreen, rounded, wiry-stemmed shrub. **H** and **S** to 2m (6ft). Has narrow, cylindrical, pointed leaves and, in early summer, deep red flowers, each with a brush of stamens, in 5cm (2in) long spikes.

L

LABLAB

LEGUMINOSAE/PAPILIONACEAE

Genus of one species of deciduous, woody-stemmed, twining climber, grown for its attractive, pea-like flowers (in tropics is grown for green manure and animal feed, and for its edible pods and seeds). Is often raised as an annual. Frost tender, min. 5–10°C (41–50°F). Grow in sun and in any well-drained soil. Propagate by seed in spring.

L. purpureus, syn. *Dolichos lablab, D. purpureus*, illus. p.203.

+ LABURNOCYTISUS

LEGUMINOSAE/PAPILIONACEAE

Deciduous tree, grown for its flowers. Is a graft hybrid between *Laburnum anagyroides* and *Cytisus purpureus*. Fully hardy. Requires full sun; grows in any but waterlogged soil. Propagate by grafting on laburnum in late summer.

***L.* 'Adamii'.** Deciduous, spreading tree. **H** 8m (25ft), **S** 6m (20ft). In late spring and early summer bears 3 types of blooms: yellow, laburnum flowers; purple, cytisus flowers; and laburnum-like, yellow and pinkish-purple flowers. Leaves, with 3 oval leaflets, are dark green.

LABURNUM

LEGUMINOSAE/PAPILIONACEAE

Genus of deciduous trees, grown for their profuse, pendent flower clusters in spring and summer. Fully hardy. Does best in full sun; grows in any but waterlogged soil. Seeds are very poisonous. Propagate species by seed in autumn, hybrids by budding in summer. ① All parts are highly toxic if ingested.

L. alpinum illus. p.89.

L. anagyroides, syn. *L. vulgare* (Common laburnum, Golden chain). Deciduous, spreading tree. **H** and **S** 7m (22ft). Leaves have 3 oval leaflets and are grey-green. Short, pendent, dense clusters of large, pea-like, yellow flowers appear in late spring and early summer.

L. vulgare. See *L. anagyroides*.

♀***L.* x *watereri* 'Vossii'** illus. p.84.

LACHENALIA

LILIACEAE/HYACINTHACEAE

Genus of winter- and spring-flowering bulbs with tubular or bell-shaped flowers; some have attractively mottled leaves. Useful as pot plants and in open borders. Half hardy. Requires light, well-drained soil and a sunny site. Plant in early autumn; dry off in summer when foliage has died down. Propagate in autumn by seed or freely produced offsets.

L. aloides, syn. *L. tricolor, L.* 'Tricolor'. Winter- and spring-flowering bulb. **H** 15–25cm (6–10in), **S** 5–8cm (2–3in). Has 2 strap-shaped, semi-erect, basal, purple-spotted, green leaves. Produces a spike of 10–20 pendent flowers, each 3cm (1¼in) long with a yellow tube shading to red at the apex and with flared, green tips. **'Nelsonii'** (syn. *L.* 'Nelsonii') illus. p.429. ♀**var. *quadricolor*** illus. p.429.

L. angustifolia. See *L. contaminata*.

♀***L. contaminata***, syn. *L. angustifolia*. Winter- and spring-flowering bulb. **H** to 20cm (8in), **S** 5–8cm (2–3in). Has narrowly strap-shaped, semi-erect leaves in a basal cluster. Bears a spike of bell-shaped, white flowers, 0.5cm (¼in) long, suffused and tipped with red and green.

L. glaucina. See *L. orchioides* var. *glaucina*.

L. mutabilis. Winter- and spring-flowering bulb. **H** to 30cm (12in), **S** 5–8cm (2–3in). Has 2 strap-shaped, semi-erect, basal leaves. Stem bears a loose spike of up to 25 tubular, 1cm (½in) long flowers that are purple or lilac in bud and open to reddish-brown-tipped petals with a green tube base.

***L.* 'Nelsonii'.** See *L. aloides* 'Nelsonii'.

♀***L. orchioides.*** Winter- and spring-flowering bulb. **H** 15–30cm (6–12in), **S** 5–8cm (2–3in). Has 2 strap-shaped, semi-erect, basal, green leaves, sometimes spotted blackish- or purple-brown. Stem produces a dense spike of fragrant, semi-erect, tubular, white flowers, 1cm (½in) long, blue-tinged and tipped with green. **var. *glaucina*** (syn. *L. glaucina*) flowers in late winter and early spring. **H** to 30cm (12in), **S** 5–8cm (2–3in). Leaves are usually spotted purple. Has a spike of fragrant, whitish-blue or pale lilac flowers.

L. rubida. Winter-flowering bulb. **H** to 25cm (10in), **S** 5–8cm (2–3in). Bears 2 strap-shaped, purple-spotted, green leaves, semi-erect and basal, and a loose spike of pendent, tubular, red flowers, 2–3cm (¾–1¼in) long, shading to yellow at tips.

L. tricolor. See *L. aloides*.

***L.* 'Tricolor'.** See *L. aloides*.

Lactuca alpina. See *Cicerbita alpina*.

Lactuca bourgaei. See *Cicerbita bourgaei*.

LAELIA

ORCHIDACEAE

See also ORCHIDS.

L. anceps (illus. p.466). Evergreen, epiphytic orchid for a cool greenhouse. **H** 25cm (10in). Lilac-pink flowers, 6cm (2½in) wide, each with a deep mauve lip, are carried in tall spikes in autumn. Has oval, rigid leaves, 10–15cm (4–6in) long. Needs semi-shade in summer.

L. cinnabarina. See *Cattleya cinnabarina*.

x ***Laeliocattleya* Rojo gx 'Mont Millais'.** See x *Cattlianthe* Rojo gx 'Mont Millais'.

LAGAROSIPHON

HYDROCHARITACEAE

Genus of semi-evergreen, perennial, spreading, submerged water plants grown for their decorative foliage. Oxygenates water. Fully hardy. Needs full sun. Thin regularly to keep under control. Propagate by stem cuttings in spring or summer.

L. major, syn. *Elodea crispa* of gardens. Semi-evergreen, perennial, spreading, submerged water plant. **S** indefinite. Forms dense, underwater swards of foliage. Ascending stems are covered in narrow, reflexed, dark green leaves. Bears insignificant flowers in summer.

LAGERSTROEMIA

LYTHRACEAE

Genus of deciduous or evergreen, summer-flowering shrubs and trees, grown for their flowers. Frost hardy to frost tender, min. 3–5°C (37–41°F). Prefers fertile, well-drained soil and full light. Water potted specimens freely when in full growth, less at other times. To maintain as shrubs, cut back hard the previous season's stems each spring. Propagate by seed in spring or by semi-ripe cuttings in summer.

♀***L. indica*** (Crepe myrtle; illus. p.86). Deciduous, rounded tree or large shrub. **H** and **S** 8m (25ft). Half hardy. Has trusses of flowers with strongly waved, pink, white or purple petals in summer and early autumn. **'Seminale'**.

L. speciosa (Pride of India, Queen's crape myrtle). Deciduous, rounded tree. **H** 15–20m (50–70ft), **S** 10–15m (30–50ft). Frost tender. Mid- to deep green leaves are narrowly oval, 8–18cm (3–7in) long. Has panicles of funnel-shaped, rose-pink to rose-purple flowers in summer–autumn, often when leafless.

LAGUNARIA

MALVACEAE

Genus of one species of evergreen tree, grown for its flowers in summer–autumn and its overall appearance. Frost tender, min. 3–5°C (37–41°F). Prefers fertile, well-drained soil and full light. Water potted plants freely when in full summer growth, moderately at other times. Pruning is tolerated if required. Propagate by seed in spring or by semi-ripe cuttings in summer. Under cover, red spider mite may be troublesome. ① Contact with the seeds may irritate skin.

L. patersonii (Norfolk Island hibiscus, Queensland pyramidal tree). Fast-growing, evergreen, upright tree, pyramidal when young. **H** 10–14m (30–46ft), **S** 5–7m (15–22ft). Oval, rough-textured leaves are matt-green above, whitish-green beneath. Bears hibiscus-like, rose-pink flowers, 5cm (2in) wide, in summer.

LAGURUS

GRAMINEAE/POACEAE

See also GRASSES, BAMBOOS, RUSHES and SEDGES.

♀***L. ovatus*** illus. p.284.

LAMARCKIA

GRAMINEAE/POACEAE

See also GRASSES, BAMBOOS, RUSHES and SEDGES.

L. aurea (Golden top). Tuft-forming, annual grass. **H** and **S** 20cm (8in). Fully hardy. Wiry stems bear scattered, pale green leaves and, in summer, erect, dense, one-sided, golden panicles. Needs sun.

LAMIUM

Deadnettle

LABIATAE/LAMIACEAE

Genus of spring- or summer-flowering perennials, most of which are semi-evergreen, including a number of weeds; some species make useful ground cover. Fully hardy. Prefers full or partial shade and moist but well-drained soil. Resents excessive winter wet. Propagate by stem-tip cuttings of non-flowering shoots in mid-summer or by division in autumn or early spring.

***L. galeobdolon* subsp. *montanum* 'Florentinum'**, syn. *L.g.* 'Variegatum'. Semi-evergreen, carpeting perennial. **H** to 30cm (12in), **S** indefinite. Oval, mid-green leaves are marked with silver. Has racemes of tubular, 2-lipped, lemon-yellow flowers in summer.

L. maculatum. Semi-evergreen, mat-forming perennial. **H** 15cm (6in), **S** 90cm (36in). Has mauve-tinged, often pink-flushed, leaves with central, silvery stripes. Clusters of hooded, mauve-pink flowers are borne in mid-spring. **'Album'** illus. p.255. **'Aureum'** (syn. *L.m.* 'Gold Leaf'), **H** 20cm (8in), **S** 60cm (24in), produces oval, yellow leaves with paler white centres. Whorls of hooded, pink flowers appear on short stems in summer. **'Beacon Silver'** bears mauve-tinged, silver leaves, sometimes with narrow, green margins, and clear pale pink flowers. **'Gold Leaf'** see *L.m.* 'Aureum'. ♀**'White Nancy'** illus. p.254.

L. orvala illus. p.260.

LAMPRANTHUS

AIZOACEAE

Genus of creeping, bushy, perennial succulents and sub-shrubs with daisy-like flowers. Becomes woody after several years, when is best replenished. Plants are good for summer bedding, particularly in arid conditions. Leaves redden in strong sun. Frost tender, min. 7°C (45°F) if dry. Requires full sun and very well-drained soil. Propagate by seed or stem cuttings in spring or autumn.

L. aurantiacus. syn. *L. glaucoides*, illus. p.496

L. deltoides. See *Oscularia deltoides*, illus. p.485.

L. glaucoides, See *L. aurantiacus*.

L. haworthii. Erect to creeping, perennial succulent. **H** 50cm (20in), **S** indefinite. Blue-grey leaves are cylindrical and 5cm (2in) long. In spring bears masses of daisy-like, cerise flowers, 7cm (3in) across, that only open in sun.

L. roseus, syn. *Mesembryanthemum multiradiatum*. Creeping, perennial succulent. **H** 15cm (6in), **S** indefinite. Produces solid, 3-angled, mid- to glaucous green leaves, 5cm (2in) long. Daisy-like, dark rose-red flowers, 4cm (1½in) across, open only in sun from spring to autumn.

L. spectabilis illus. p.484.

***Lamprocapnos spectabilis*.** See *Dicentra spectabilis*, illus. p.223.
♀***f. alba*** (syn. *D. s.* 'Alba'). p.223

LANTANA

VERBENACEAE

Genus of evergreen perennials and shrubs, grown for their flowers. Frost tender, min. 10–13°C (50–55°F). Needs full sunlight and fertile, well-drained soil. Water containerized specimens freely when in full growth, moderately at other times. Tip-prune young plants to promote a bushy habit and more flowering stems. Propagate by seed in spring or by semi-ripe cuttings in summer. Red spider mite and whitefly may be troublesome. ⓘ All parts may cause severe discomfort if ingested, and contact with foliage may irritate skin.

L. camara. Evergreen, rounded to spreading shrub. **H** and **S** 1–2m (3–6ft). Bears oval, finely wrinkled, deep green leaves. From spring to autumn, tiny, tubular, 5-lobed flowers, in dense, domed heads, open yellow, then turn red. Many colour forms have been selected. **'Baluclush'.** See *L. c.* Lucky Series LUCKY HONEY BLUSH. **Lucky Series LUCKY HONEY BLUSH ('Baluclush')** illus. p.301.

L. delicatissima. See *L. montevidensis.*

L. montevidensis, syn. *L. delicatissima*, *L. sellowiana*, illus. p.310.

L. sellowiana. See *L. montevidensis.*

***L.* 'Spreading Sunset'** illus. p.325.

LAPAGERIA

PHILESIACEAE/LILIACEAE

Genus of one species of evergreen, woody-stemmed, twining climber, grown for its large, waxy blooms. Half hardy. Requires humus-rich, well-drained soil and partial shade. Water moderately, scarcely at all when not in full growth. Provide support. Thin out congested growth in spring. Propagate in spring by seed, soaked for 2 days before sowing, or in spring or autumn by layering.

♀ ***L. rosea*** illus. p.202. **var. *albiflora*** is an evergreen, woody-stemmed, twining climber. **H** to 5m (15ft). Has oblong to oval, leathery, dark green leaves. From summer to late autumn bears pendent, fleshy, narrowly bell-shaped, white flowers.

Lapeirousia cruenta. See *Anomatheca laxa.*

Lapeirousia laxa. See *Anomatheca laxa.*

LARDIZABALA

LARDIZABALACEAE

Genus of evergreen, woody-stemmed, twining climbers, grown for their foliage. Male and female flowers are produced on the same plant in late autumn to winter. Is useful for growing on trellises or pergolas. Frost to half hardy. Grow in any well-drained soil and in sun or partial shade. Propagate by seed in spring, or by stem cuttings in late summer or autumn.

L. biternata. See *L. funaria.*

L. funaria, syn *L. biternata*. Evergreen, woody-stemmed, twining climber. **H** 3–4m (10–12ft). Half hardy. Rounded leaves have broadly oval, leathery, dark green leaflets. In winter produces brown flowers with tiny, whitish petals, the males in drooping spikes, the females solitary. In winter–spring bears many-seeded, berry-like, purple fruits, 5–8cm (2–3in) long.

LARIX

PINACEAE

See also CONIFERS.

♀ ***L. decidua***, (European larch) syn. *L. europaea*, illus. p.97.

L. europaea. See *L. decidua.*

♀ ***L. kaempferi***, syn. *L. leptolepis* (Japanese larch). Fast-growing, deciduous, columnar conifer with a conical tip. **H** 25–30m (80–100ft), **S** 5–8m (15–25ft). Fully hardy. Shoots are purplish-red and leaves are needle-like, flattened, greyish-green or bluish. Small cones have reflexed scales.

L. leptolepis. See *L. kaempferi.*

LATHRAEA

SCROPHULARIACEAE

Genus of spreading perennials that grow as parasites on the roots of trees, in the case of *L. clandestina* on willow or poplar. True leaves are not produced. Fully hardy. Grows in dappled shade cast by host tree and prefers moist conditions. Roots resent being disturbed. Propagate by seed when fresh, in late summer.

L. clandestina illus. p.260.

LATHYRUS

LEGUMINOSAE/PAPILIONACEAE

Genus of annuals and perennials, many of them tendril climbers, grown for their racemes of attractive flowers. Flowers are followed by long, thin seed pods. Fully to frost hardy. Grow in humus-rich, fertile, well-drained soil and in full light. Provide support and remove dead flowers regularly. Cut down perennials in late autumn. Propagate annuals by seed (soaked before sowing) in early spring or early autumn, perennials by seed in autumn or by division in spring. Botrytis and mildew may cause problems. ⓘ Seeds may cause mild stomach upset if ingested.

L. grandiflorus (Everlasting pea). Herbaceous, tendril climber. **H** to 1.5m (5ft). Fully hardy. Has unwinged stems, and neat racemes of pink-purple and red flowers in summer.

♀ ***L. latifolius*** (Everlasting pea) i llus. p.201.

L. magellanicus of gardens. See *L. nervosus.*

L. nervosus, syn. *L. magellanicus* of gardens (Lord Anson's blue pea). Herbaceous, tendril climber. **H** to 5m (15ft). Frost hardy. Grey-green leaves each have a pair of leaflets, a 3-branched tendril and large stipules. Fragrant, purplish-blue flowers appear in long-stalked racemes in summer.

L. odoratus (Sweet pea). Moderately fast-growing, annual, tendril climber. **H** to 3m (10ft). Fully hardy. Has oval, mid-green leaves with tendrils. Scented flowers are produced in shades of pink, blue, purple or white, from summer to early autumn. Dwarf, non-climbing cultivars are available. **'Barry Dare'** illus. p.202. **'Bijou', H** and **S** 45cm (18in), has oval, divided, mid-green leaves and large, fragrant flowers, in shades of pink, red or blue, that are carried in summer or early autumn. **'Charles Unwin'** illus. p.201. Cupid Series **'Cupid Pink'** illus. p.301. ♀ **'Jayne Amanda'** bears racemes of usually 4, rarely 5, rose-pink flowers, and may be grown as a cordon or bush. **'Knee Hi', H** and **S** 90cm (3ft), has oval, divided, mid-green leaves and large, fragrant flowers, in shades of pink, red, blue or white, that are borne in summer or early autumn. **'Lady Diana'** illus. p.201. ♀ **'Mrs Bernard Jones'** illus. p.201. ♀ ***L. rotundifolius*** (Persian everlasting pea). Herbaceous, tendril climber with winged stems. **H** to 1m (3ft). Fully hardy. Leaves each have narrow stipules, a pair of leaflets and a 3-branched tendril. Has small racemes of 3–8 pink to purplish flowers in summer.

L. sylvestris (Everlasting pea, Perennial pea). Herbaceous, tendril climber with winged stems. **H** to 2m (6ft). Fully hardy. Leaves each have narrow stipules, a pair of leaflets and a terminal, branched tendril. In summer and early autumn bears racemes of 4–10 rose-pink flowers, marked with green and purple.

♀ ***L. vernus***, syn. *Orobus vernus*, illus. p.260. ♀ **'Alboroseus'** is a clump-forming perennial. **H** and **S** 30cm (12in). Fully hardy. In spring, slender stems each bear 3–5 white-and-deep-pink flowers. Has fern-like, much-divided, soft leaves.

LAURELIA

MONIMIACEAE

Genus of evergreen trees and shrubs, grown for their aromatic foliage. Frost hardy, but needs shelter from cold winds. Requires sun or semi-shade; grows in any but very dry soil. Propagate by semi-ripe cuttings in summer.

L. sempervirens, syn. *L. serrata* of gardens (Chilean laurel). Evergreen, broadly conical tree or shrub. **H** and **S** to 15m (50ft). Oval, leathery leaves are glossy, dark green and very aromatic. In summer it bears small, inconspicuous flowers.

L. serrata of gardens. See *L. sempervirens.*

LAURUS

Bay tree, Laurel

LAURACEAE

Genus of evergreen trees, grown for their foliage. Frost hardy, but foliage may be scorched by extremely cold weather or strong, cold winds. Needs a sheltered position in sun or semi-shade and fertile, well-drained soil. In tubs may be grown well as standards, which should be trimmed during summer. Propagate by semi-ripe cuttings in summer or by seed in autumn.

♀ ***L. nobilis*** illus. p.80.

LAVANDULA

Lavender

LABIATAE/LAMIACEAE

Genus of evergreen, mainly summer-flowering shrubs, with entire or divided, often grey-green leaves, grown for their aromatic foliage and flowers. Makes an effective, low hedge. Fully to half hardy. Needs full sun and fertile, well-drained soil. Trim hedges lightly in spring to maintain a compact habit. New growth is rarely produced from old wood. Propagate by semi-ripe cuttings in summer. See also feature panel p.158.

L. angustifolia. Evergreen, bushy shrub. **H** 40–80cm (16–32in), **S** 40–60cm (16–24in). Fully hardy. Has linear to narrowly ovate, aromatic, grey-felted leaves. In mid-summer produces small, fragrant, compact, violet-blue, sometimes pink or white flower spikes, on stalks 10–30cm (4–12in) long. **'Batlad'** see *L.a.* LITTLE LADY. **'Clarmo'** see *L.a.* LITTLE LOTTIE. ♀ **'Hidcote'** syn. *L.* 'Hidcote' (illus. p.158). Evergreen, bushy shrub. **H** 60m (24in), **S** 75cm (30in). Fully hardy. Has dense spikes of fragrant, deep purple flowers from mid- to late summer and narrow, aromatic, silver-grey leaves. ♀ **'Imperial Gem'** (illus. p.158) is an evergreen, bushy, compact shrub. **H** and **S** 60cm (2ft). Fully hardy. Has narrowly oblong, aromatic, silvery-grey leaves and produces dense spikes of tiny, fragrant, tubular, deep purple flowers from mid- to late summer. **LITTLE LADY ('Batlad')** illus. p.158, **H** 65cm (26in), **S** 80cm (32in), has a compact, erect habit, grey- to sage-green leaves and bears abundant spikes of white-centred, dark violet flowers, on stalks to 30cm (12in) long, from summer to early autumn. ♀ **LITTLE LOTTIE ('Clarmo')** illus. p.158, **H** 40cm (16in), **S** 65cm (26in), is a neat, domed shrub, spreading with age, with bright grey-green leaves and, in mid-summer, dense spikes of pale mauve-pink flowers with bluish stripes down the centre of each corolla lobe. ♀ **'Lodden Blue'** (illus. p.158), **H** to 40cm (16in), bears lilac-blue flowers. **'Lodden Pink', H** to 75cm (30in), has pale pink flowers. ♀ **'Miss Katherine'** (illus. p.158) bears deep pink flowers. **'Munstead', H** and **S** 60cm (24in), has grey-green leaves and blue flowers from mid- to late summer. ♀ **'Nana Alba', H** to 30cm (12in), produces white flowers. **'Old English Lavender', H** to 50cm (20in), has purple flowers borne on long, erect stems. ♀ **'Wendy Carlile'** (illus. p.158), **H** to 30cm (12in), is similar to 'Nana Alba' but with a more erect, uniform habit.

♀ ***L.* x *chaytoriae* 'Richard Gray'.** Evergreen, bushy, compact shrub. **H** and **S** 50cm (20in). Fully hardy. Has linear, aromatic, silvery-grey leaves. Cylindrical spikes of deep purple flowers are borne in summer. ♀ **'Sawyers'** (illus. p.158), **H** to 60cm (24in), has large, more pointed, deep purple flower spikes.

L. dentata. Evergreen, bushy shrub. **H** and **S** 1m (3ft). Frost hardy. Aromatic leaves are fern-like, toothed and grey-green. Dense spikes of small, slightly fragrant, tubular, lavender-blue flowers and purple bracts are borne from mid- to late summer.

***L.* 'Fathead'** (illus. p.158). Evergreen, robust, rounded, bushy shrub. **H** 50cm (20in), **S** 60cm (24in). Frost hardy. Has linear, aromatic, mid- to dark green leaves and dark violet flower spikes, with large, petal-like, reddish-purple, terminal bracts, borne on dark green stalks to 12cm (5in) long. Flowers from late spring through summer if deadheaded regularly.

L. 'Grappenhall'. See *L.* x *intermedia* 'Pale Pretender'.
L. 'Helmsdale' (illus. p.158). Evergreen, robust, rounded shrub. **H** 70cm (28in), **S** 110cm (43in). Frost hardy. Has linear, aromatic, mid- to dark leaves. Bright green stalks, to 12cm (5in) long, bear dark violet flower spikes with reddish-purple bracts. Flowers from mid-spring through summer if deadheaded regularly.
L. 'Hidcote'. See *L angustifolia* 'Hidcote'.
L. x intermedia (*L. angustifolia* x *L. latifolia*). Evergreen, spreading shrub. **H** 80–140cm (32–56in), **S** 70–90cm (28–36in). Has narrowly elliptic to obovate, very aromatic, silver- to greenish-grey leaves, covered in fine, silvery-grey hairs. From mid-summer to early autumn, long, sometimes branched, stalks, 20–70cm (8–28in) long, bear spikes of fragrant, tubular, violet-blue to white flowers, with green to dark violet calyces. Is the main source of commercial lavender, lavandine. ♀**'Alba'** (illus. p.158) is a vigorous, erect shrub with white flowers, occasionally tinted pale purple. **'Grappenhall'** (syn. *L.* 'Grappenhall') has blue-purple flowers in mid- and late summer. ♀**'Hidcote Giant'**, **H** to 1.2m (4ft), has dense spikes of deep lavender-blue flowers. **'Pale Pretender'** (syn. *L.* 'Grappenhall', *L. x i.* 'Grappenhall'), **H** to 1.2m (4ft), **S** 1.5m (5ft), produces blue-purple flowers.
♀**L. lanata** (illus. p.158). Evergreen, bushy shrub. **H** and **S** 50cm (20in). Frost hardy. Young shoots and linear leaves are covered with whitish "wool". Produces strongly fragrant, tubular, bright violet flowers on erect spikes throughout summer.
L. pedunculata. Evergreen, erect shrub. **H** and **S** 80cm (32in). Fully hardy. Linear leaves are covered with felt-like, greenish-grey hairs. In spring and summer, compact, deep purple flower spikes, with dark purple apical terminal bracts, are borne on stalks 30cm (12in) long.
♀ **subsp. pedunculata**, syn. *L. stoechas* subsp. *pedunculata*. Evergreen, clump-forming shrub. **H** and **S** 50–80cm (20–32in). Frost hardy. Ascending branches bear linear, aromatic, grey-green leaves covered with greenish-grey hairs. Produces short, dense spikes of violet-blue aromatic flowers in summer. **'James Compton'** (illus. p.158), **H** 70cm (28in), **S** 50cm (20in), has purple-margined, green stalks, to 20cm (8in) long, bearing dark purple flower spikes with dark purplish-mauve, apical bracts. Flowers from mid-spring to summer if regularly deadheaded.
L. 'Regal Splendour' (illus. p.158). Evergreen, erect shrub. **H** 70cm (28in), **S** 50cm (20in). Frost hardy. Has linear, aromatic, bright green leaves. Dark violet-blue flower spikes, with dark purple, apical terminal bracts, are produced on stems to 12cm (5in) long. Flowers from mid-spring to summer if regularly deadheaded.
♀**L. stoechas** (French lavender; illus. p.157). Evergreen, spreading shrub. **H** and **S** 20–70cm (8–28in). Frost hardy. Has linear, grey-green leaves, with soft, white hairs. From mid-spring to autumn (if regularly deadheaded) produces dark violet-purple flower spikes, with purplish-violet apical terminal bracts, on stalks to 3cm (1¼in) long. **f. leucantha** has white flowers. **f. rosea** produces pink to rose-red flowers and reddish-purple bracts. **f. rosea 'Kew Red'** (illus. p.158), **H** and **S** 45cm (18in), is a compact, upright cultivar with mid- to grey-green leaves and pale green, purple-flushed stalks, 3–5cm (1¼–2in) long, bearing rounded, cerise-crimson flower spikes with soft pink bracts. **subsp. stoechas f. leucantha 'Snowman'** (illus. p.158) is an evergreen, compact shrub. **H** and **S** 50cm (20in). Fully hardy. Numerous short, dense spikes of small, fragrant, white flowers, topped by white bracts, are produced in summer. Mature, linear leaves are grey-green and strongly aromatic.
♀**L. 'Willow Vale'** (illus. p.158). Evergreen, compact shrub. **H** and **S** 50–70cm (20–28in). Frost hardy. Has linear, aromatic, grey-green leaves and bears long spikes of purple flowers, with wavy or crinkly flower bracts, in summer.

LAVATERA

Tree mallow

MALVACEAE

Genus of mainly summer-flowering annuals, biennials, perennials and semi-evergreen sub-shrubs and shrubs. Fully to frost hardy. Needs sun and well-drained soil. Propagate perennials, sub-shrubs and shrubs by softwood cuttings in early spring or summer, annuals and biennials by seed in spring or early autumn.
L. assurgentiflora illus. p.133.
L. cachemiriana, syn. *L. cachemirica*. Semi-evergreen, woody-based perennial or sub-shrub. **H** 1.5–2m (5–6ft), **S** 1m (3ft). Frost hardy. Has wiry stems bearing panicles of trumpet-shaped, silky, clear pink flowers in summer and ivy-shaped, downy, mid-green leaves.
L. cachemirica. See *L. cachemiriana*.
L. x clementii 'Barnsley'. Vigorous, semi-evergreen sub-shrub. **H** and **S** 2m (6ft). Fully hardy. Mid-green, palmate leaves have 3–5 lobes. Throughout summer bears profuse clusters of open funnel-shaped, red-eyed, white flowers, ageing to soft pink, with deeply notched petals.
♀**L.'Rosea'** (syn. *L. olbia* 'Rosea') illus. p.136.
L. olbia 'Rosea'. See *L.* x *clementii* 'Rosea'.
L. trimestris 'Mont Blanc' illus. p.299.
♀**'Silver Cup'** illus. p.305.

LAYIA

COMPOSITAE/ASTERACEAE

Genus of annuals, useful for hot, dry places. Fully hardy. Grow in sun and in poor to fertile, very well-drained soil. Propagate by seed sown outdoors in spring or early autumn.
L. elegans. See *L. platyglossa*.
L. platyglossa, syn. *L. elegans* (Tidy tips). Fast-growing, upright, bushy annual. **H** 45cm (18in), **S** 30cm (12in). Has lance-shaped, greyish-green leaves. Daisy-like flower heads, 5cm (2in) wide, with white-tipped, yellow ray petals and yellow centres, are produced from early summer to early autumn. Is suitable for cutting.

Lechenaultia. See *Leschenaultia*.

LEDEBOURIA

LILIACEAE/HYACINTHACEAE

Genus of bulbs, some of which are evergreen, with ornamental, narrowly lance-shaped leaves. Produces very small flowers with reflexed tips. Makes good pot plants in cool greenhouses. Half hardy. Needs full light, to allow leaf marks to develop well, and loose, open soil. Propagate by offsets in spring.
L. cooperi, syn. *Scilla adlamii, S.cooperi*. Summer-flowering bulb. **H** 5–10cm (2–4in), **S** 2.5–5cm (1–2in). Semi-erect, basal, green leaves, with brownish-purple stripes, die away in winter. Stem carries a short spike of small, bell-shaped, greenish-purple flowers.
L. socialis, syn. *Scilla socialis, S. violacea*, illus. p.421.

LEDUM

ERICACEAE

Genus of evergreen shrubs, grown for their aromatic foliage and small, white flowers. Fully hardy. Needs shade or partial shade and moist, peaty, acid soil. Benefits from dead-heading. Propagate by semi-ripe cuttings in summer or by seed in autumn.
L. groenlandicum illus. p.145.

LEIOPHYLLUM

ERICACEAE

Genus of one species of evergreen shrub with an extensive, spreading root system. Fully hardy. Prefers semi-shade and well-drained, peaty, acid soil. Top-dress regularly with peaty soil. Propagate by seed in spring or by semi-ripe cuttings in summer.
♀**L. buxifolium.** Evergreen, dome-shaped shrub. **H** 25cm (10in), **S** 45cm (18in). Stems are covered with tiny, oval, leathery, dark green leaves. In late spring, terminal clusters of deep pink buds develop into small, star-shaped, white flowers, with prominent stamens.

Lemaireocereus euphorbioides. See *Neobuxbaumia euphorbioides*.
Lemaireocereus marginatus. See *Pachycereus marginatus*.
Lemaireocereus thurberi. See *Stenocereus thurberi*.
Lemboglossum bictoniense. See *Rhynchostele bictoniensis*.
Lemboglossum cervantesii. See *Rhynchostele cervantesii*.
Lemboglossum cordatum. See *Rhynchostele cordatum*.
Lemboglossum rossii. See *Rhynchostele rossii*.
Lembotropis nigricans. See *Cytisus nigricans*.

LEONOTIS

LABIATAE/LAMIACEAE

Genus of annuals, evergreen and semi-evergreen perennials, sub-shrubs and shrubs, grown for their flowers and overall appearance. Half hardy to frost tender, min. 5–7°C (41–5°F). Needs full sun and rich, well-drained soil. Water containerized specimens freely when in full growth, much less at other times of year. Cut back perennials, sub-shrubs and shrubs to within 15cm (6in) of the ground in early spring. Propagate by seed in spring or by greenwood cuttings taken in early summer.
L. leonurus illus. p.141.

LEONTOPODIUM

Edelweiss

COMPOSITAE/ASTERACEAE

Genus of short-lived, spring-flowering, woolly perennials, grown for their distinctive flower heads. Is suitable for rock gardens, containers, and alpine troughs. Fully hardy. Requires sun, gritty, well-drained soil, and a deep collar of grit to improve surface drainage. Shelter from prevailing, rain-bearing winds, because the crowns are extremely intolerant of winter wet and may rot off. Propagate by division in spring, or by seed when fresh. Many seeds are not viable.
L. alpinum illus. p.332.
L. stracheyi. Mound-forming, spreading, woolly perennial. **H** and **S** 10cm (4in). Star-shaped, glistening, white flower heads are produced among thick, oval, silver leaves in spring. Makes a good alpine house plant.

Leopoldia comosa. See *Muscari comosum*.

LEPISMIUM

CACTACEAE

Genus of epiphytic and lithophytic (growing on rocks) perennial cacti often pendulous in habit with cylindrical, ribbed, angled or flat, usually segmented stems. Small, funnel- to disc-shaped flowers are followed by spherical, often purple or red berries. Frost tender, min. 6–10°C (43–50°F). Needs partial shade and rich, well-drained soil. Prefers 80% relative humidity – higher than for most cacti. Give only occasional, very light watering in winter. Propagate by seed or stem cuttings in spring or summer.
L. warmingianum, syn. *Rhipsalis warmingiana*. Erect, then pendent, perennial cactus. **H** 1m (3ft), **S** 50cm (20in). Frost tender, min. 11°C (52°F). Has slender, notched, cylindrical, green branches, sometimes tinged red or brown, with 2–4 angles, and green-white flowers in winter and spring, followed by violet berries.

LEPTINELLA

COMPOSITAE/ASTERACEAE

Genus of annuals and creeping perennials that are effective as low ground cover. Fully hardy. Grow in full sun and moderately fertile, sharply drained soil. Propagate by seed as soon as ripe or by division in spring.
L. atrata, syn. *Cotula atrata*. Evergreen, mat-forming perennial. **H** 2.5cm (1in), **S** to 25cm (10in). Has small, finely cut, greyish-green leaves and blackish-red flower heads in late spring and early summer. Is uncommon and not easy to grow successfully. **subsp. luteola** illus. p.349.

LEPTOSPERMUM

MYRTACEAE

Genus of evergreen trees and shrubs, grown for their foliage and small, often profuse flowers. Grows well in coastal areas if not too exposed. Frost to half hardy, but in cold areas plant against a south- or west-facing wall. Needs full sun and fertile, well-drained soil. Propagate by semi-ripe cuttings in summer.

L. flavescens. See *L. polygalifolium.*

L. humifusum. See *L. rupestre.*

L. polygalifolium, syn. *L. flavescens*, illus. p.131.

♀***L. rupestre***, syn. *L. humifusum*, illus. p.151.

L. scoparium (Manuka, New Zealand tea-tree). ♀**var. *incanum* 'Keatleyi'** is an evergreen, rounded shrub. **H** and **S** 3m (10ft). Half hardy. Narrowly lance-shaped, aromatic, grey-green leaves set off a profusion of large, star-shaped, pale pink flowers during late spring and summer. ♀**'Nicholsii'** produces bronze-purple leaves and smaller, crimson flowers. ♀**'Red Damask'** illus. p.123. **'Snow White'** illus. p.130.

LESCHENAULTIA

SYN. LECHENAULTIA

GOODENIACEAE

Genus of evergreen shrubs, grown for their flowers. Frost tender, min. 7–10°C (45–50°F). Needs full light and peaty, well-drained soil with few phosphates and nitrates. Water containerized plants moderately during growing season, sparingly at other times. Shorten over-long stems after flowering. Propagate by seed in spring or by semi-ripe cuttings in summer. Most species are not easy to grow under glass; good ventilation is essential.

L. floribunda. Evergreen, domed, wiry-stemmed shrub. **H** and **S** 30–60cm (12–24in). Has narrow, cylindrical, pointed leaves, and in spring-summer, short, tubular, pale blue flowers, with 5 angular petals, in terminal clusters.

LEUCADENDRON

PROTEACEAE

Genus of evergreen shrubs and trees, grown for their flower heads from autumn to spring and for their foliage. Frost tender, min. 5–7°C (41–5°F). Needs full light and sharply drained soil, mainly of sand and peat, ideally with very little nitrogen and phosphates. Water potted specimens moderately while in growth, sparingly at other times. Propagate by seed in spring.

L. argenteum (Silver tree) illus. p.451.

LEUCANTHEMELLA

COMPOSITAE/ASTERACEAE

Genus of hairy perennials, grown for their daisy-like flower heads in autumn. Fully hardy. Grow in full sun or partial shade and reliably moist soil. Propagate by division or basal cuttings in spring.

♀***L. serotina***, syn. *Chrysanthemum serotinum, C. uliginosum*, illus. p.220.

LEUCANTHEMOPSIS

COMPOSITAE/ASTERACEAE

Genus of dwarf, tufted, clump- or mat-forming perennials, grown for their solitary, daisy-like flower heads in summer. Fully hardy. Grow in full sun and sharply drained soil. Propagate by seed as soon as they are ripe, or by division or basal cuttings taken in spring.

L. alpina, syn. *Chrysanthemum alpinum.* Tuft-forming, short-lived perennial. **H** 10cm (4in), **S** 20cm (8in). Small tufts of deeply cut leaves are produced from short, rhizomatous stems. Has large, white flower heads, with yellow centres, in summer. Is good for rock or scree gardens, or alpine planters.

LEUCANTHEMUM

COMPOSITAE/ASTERACEAE

Genus of annuals and perennials, grown for their attractive flowers. Fully hardy. Cultivars of *L.* x *superbum* are valued for their profusion of large daisy-like summer flowers. Some species are suitable for rock gardens. Needs full sun and well-drained soil. Taller cultivars require staking. Propagate species by seed or division, cultivars by division only.

L.* x *superbum, syn. *Chrysanthemum maximum* of gardens, *C.* x *superbum* (Shasta daisy). Robust perennial. **H** 1m (3ft), **S** 60cm (2ft). Lift, divide and replant plants every 2 years to maintain vigour. ♀**'Aglaia'** illus. p.230. **'Elizabeth'** has large, daisy-like, single, pure white flower heads borne singly in summer. **'Esther Read'** illus. p.263. **'Sonnenschein'** illus. p.231. **'Wirral Pride'** illus. p.246. ♀**'Wirral Supreme'** is double with short, central florets.

LEUCHTENBERGIA

CACTACEAE

Genus of one species of perennial cactus. Looks like *Agave* in foliage, but its flowers, seed pods and seeds are similar to *Ferocactus*. Tubercles eventually form on short, rough, woody stems. Frost tender, min. 6°C (43°F). Needs full sun and very well-drained soil. Keep completely dry in winter; water sparingly from spring to autumn. Propagate by seed in spring or summer.

L. principis illus. p.490.

LEUCOCORYNE

LILIACEAE/ALLIACEAE

Genus of spring-flowering bulbs with loose heads of flattish flowers. Half hardy. Needs sun and well-drained soil. Plant in autumn, water well during their growing season, and keep almost dry when dormant in summer. Propagate by seed, or offsets in autumn.

L. ixioides (Glory-of-the-sun). Spring-flowering bulb. H 30–40cm (12–16in), **S** 8–10cm (3–4in). Has long, narrow, semi-erect, basal leaves that are withered by flowering time. Wiry, slender flower stem has a loose head of up to 10 lilac-blue flowers.

LEUCOGENES

New Zealand edelweiss

COMPOSITAE/ASTERACEAE

Genus of evergreen, woody-based perennials, grown for foliage. Is excellent for alpine houses in areas where summers are cool. Frost to half hardy. Needs sun and gritty, well-drained, peaty soil. Resents winter wet. Propagate by seed when fresh or by softwood cuttings in late spring.

L. grandiceps illus. p.356.

L. leontopodium, syn. *Raoulia leontopodium* (North Island edelweiss). Evergreen, rosetted perennial. **H** and **S** 12cm (5in). Half hardy. Has oblong to oval, overlapping, silvery-white to yellowish leaves. In early summer has up to 15 small, star-shaped, woolly, silvery-white flower heads surrounded by thick, felted, white bracts.

LEUCOJUM

SYN. ACIS

Snowflake

AMARYLLIDACEAE

Genus of bulbs, grown for their pendent, bell-shaped, white or pink flowers in autumn or spring. Fully to frost hardy. Some species prefer a moist, partially shaded site, others do best in sun and well-drained soil. Propagate by division in spring or early autumn or by seed in autumn.

L. aestivum illus. p.436.

L. autumnale. See *Acis autumnalis.*

L. roseum. See *Acis rosea.*

♀***L. vernum*** illus. p.414.

LEUCOPHYTA

Cushion bush

COMPOSITAE/ASTERACEAE

Genus of annuals, evergreen perennials and small shrubs, often used as summer bedding. Frost tender, min. 7–10°C (45–50°F). Requires well-drained soil and full light. Water containerized plants moderately when in full growth, sparingly at other times. Remove tips to promote a bushy habit. Propagate by semi-ripe cuttings in late summer. Botrytis may be troublesome if plants are kept too cool and damp in winter.

L. brownii, syn. *Calocephalus brownii*, illus. p.315.

LEUCOPOGON

EPACRIDACEAE/ERICACEAE

Genus of evergreen, heath-like shrubs, suitable for rock gardens and peat beds. Frost hardy to frost tender, min. 7°C (45°F). Needs a sheltered, shaded site and gritty, moist, peaty soil. Propagate in summer by seed or semi-ripe cuttings.

L. colensoi, syn. *Cyathodes colensoi*, illus. p.346.

LEUCOSPERMUM

PROTEACEAE

Genus of evergreen shrubs, grown for their flower heads. Frost tender, min. 7–10°C (45–50°F). Requires full light and sandy, well-drained soil with few phosphates and nitrates. Water containerized specimens moderately when in growth, sparingly at other times. Propagate by seed in spring. Is not easy to cultivate long term under glass; good ventilation is essential.

L. cordifolium, syn. *L. nutans.* Evergreen, rounded to spreading, well-branched shrub. **H** and **S** 1.2m (4ft). Elongated, heart-shaped, blue-grey leaves each have a 3-toothed tip. In summer, very slender, tubular, brick-red to orange flowers, each with a long style, are borne in tight heads that resemble single blooms.

L. nutans. See *L. cordifolium.*

L. reflexum illus. p.456.

LEUCOTHÖE

ERICACEAE

Genus of evergreen, semi-evergreen or deciduous shrubs, grown for their white flowers and their foliage. Fully to frost hardy. Needs shade or semi-shade and moist, peaty, acid soil. Propagate by semi-ripe cuttings in summer.

L. catesbaei of gardens. See *L. fontanesiana.*

♀***L. fontanesiana***, syn. *L. catesbaei* of gardens, *L. walteri.* Evergreen, arching shrub. **H** 1.5m (5ft), **S** 3m (10ft). Fully hardy. Lance-shaped, leathery, glossy, dark green leaves have long points and sharp teeth. Short racemes of small, urn-shaped, white flowers are borne beneath shoots from mid- to late spring. **'Rainbow'** illus. p.167. **SCARLETTA ('Zeblid')** has dark red-purple young foliage, which turns dark green, then bronze in winter. **'Zeblid'** see *L.f.* SCARLETTA.

L. keiskei. Evergreen shrub with erect or semi-procumbent stems. **H** 15–60cm (6–24in), **S** 30–60cm (12–24in). Frost hardy. Oval, thin-textured, glossy, dark green leaves have a red flush when young and a leathery appearance. Bears pendent, urn-shaped, white flowers from leaf axils in summer. Is good for a rock garden, peat bed or alpine house. Prefers mild, damp climates.

L. walteri. See *L. fontanesiana.*

LEWISIA

PORTULACACEAE

Genus of perennials, some of which are evergreen, with rosettes of succulent leaves and deep tap roots. Most species are good in alpine houses, troughs and rock gardens. Fully to frost hardy. Evergreen species need semi-shaded, humus-rich, moist or well-drained, neutral to acid soil and resent water in their rosettes at all times. Herbaceous species shed their leaves in summer and require sun and well-drained, neutral to acid soil; dry off after flowering. Propagate herbaceous species by seed in spring or autumn, evergreen species by seed in spring or by offsets in summer. Seed of *L.* Cotyledon Hybrids may not come true.

L. columbiana. Evergreen, basal-rosetted perennial. **H** 15cm (6in) or more, **S** 10–15cm (4–6in). Fully hardy. Bears thick, narrowly oblong, flat, glossy, green leaves and, in early summer, terminal sprays of small, cup-shaped, deeply veined, white to deep pink flowers. Prefers moist soil.

***L.* Cotyledon Hybrids** illus. p.340.

***L.* 'George Henley'** illus. p.338.
L. nevadensis. Loose, basal-rosetted perennial. **H** 4–6cm (1½–2½in), **S** 8cm (3in). Fully hardy. In summer, large, almost stemless, cup-shaped, white flowers appear above small clusters of strap-shaped, dark green leaves. ***L. rediviva*** (Bitter root) [pink form] illus. p.365; [white form] illus. p.360.
🏆***L. tweedyi,*** syn. *Cistanthe tweedyi, Lewisiopsis tweedi*, illus. p.351.

Lewisiopsis tweedi. See *Lewisia tweedyi.*

LEYCESTERIA

CAPRIFOLIACEAE

Genus of deciduous shrubs, grown for their showy flower clusters. Frost to half hardy. Needs full sun and fertile, well-drained soil. Propagate by softwood cuttings in summer or by seed or division in autumn.
🏆***L. formosa*** (Himalayan honeysuckle). Deciduous, upright shrub. **H** and **S** 2m (6ft). Frost hardy. Has blue-green shoots and slender, oval, dark green leaves. In summer and early autumn, small, funnel-shaped, white flowers are produced at tip of each pendent cluster of purplish-red bracts and are followed by spherical, reddish-purple fruits. Cut weak shoots to ground level in early spring.

LEYMUS

GRAMINEAE/POACEAE

See also GRASSES, BAMBOOS, RUSHES and SEDGES.
L. arenarius, syn. *Elymus arenarius* (Lyme grass). Vigorous, spreading, herbaceous, rhizomatous, perennial grass. **H** to 1.5m (5ft), **S** indefinite. Fully hardy. Has broad, glaucous leaves. Has stout, terminal spikes of greyish-green flowers on erect stems in late summer. Is useful for binding coastal dunes.

LIATRIS

Gay feathers

COMPOSITAE/ASTERACEAE

Genus of summer-flowering perennials with thickened, corm-like rootstocks. Fully hardy. Prefers sun and well-drained soil. Propagate by division in spring.
L. callilepis of gardens. See *L. spicata.*
L. pycnostachya (Kansas gay feather). Clump-forming perennial. **H** 1.2m (4ft), **S** 30cm (1ft). In summer bears tall spikes of clustered, feathery, mauve-pink flower heads. Grass-like, dark green leaves form basal tufts.
L. spicata, syn. *L. callilepis* of gardens, illus. p.438.

LIBERTIA

IRIDACEAE

Genus of rhizomatous perennials, grown for their foliage, decorative seed pods and flowers. Frost to half hardy. Needs a sheltered, sunny or partially shaded site and well-drained soil. Propagate new plants by division in spring, or by seed in autumn or spring.
🏆 ***L. grandiflora*** illus. p.230.
L. ixioides. Clump-forming, rhizomatous perennial. **H** and **S** 60cm (24in). Frost hardy. Produces panicles of saucer-shaped, white flowers in summer. Grass-like, dark green leaves turn orange-brown during winter. **'Goldfinger'** illus. p.277.

Libocedrus chilensis. See *Austrocedrus chilensis.*
Libocedrus decurrens. See *Calocedrus decurrens.*
Libonia floribunda. See *Justicia rizzinii.*

LIGULARIA

COMPOSITAE/ASTERACEAE

Genus of perennials, grown for their foliage and large, daisy-like flower heads. Fully to half hardy. Grow in sun or semi-shade and in moist but well-drained soil. Propagate by division in spring or by seed in autumn or spring. Is prone to damage by slugs and snails.
***L. clivorum* 'Desdemona'.** See *L. dentata* 'Desdemona'.
***L. dentata* 'Britt Marie Crawford'** illus. p.445. 🏆**'Desdemona'** (syn. *L. clivorum* 'Desdemona') is a compact, clump-forming perennial. **H** 1.2m (4ft), **S** 60cm (2ft). Fully hardy. Has heart-shaped, long-stalked, leathery, basal, dark brownish-green leaves, almost mahogany beneath, and bears terminal clusters of large, daisy-like, vivid orange flower heads on branching stems from mid- to late summer.
🏆***L.* 'Gregynog Gold'.** Clump-forming perennial. **H** 2m (6ft), **S** 60cm (2ft). Fully hardy. Leaves are large, heart-shaped and deep green. Conical panicles of daisy-like, orange-yellow flower heads are borne from mid- to late summer.
🏆***L. przewalskii***, syn. *Senecio przewalskii*, illus. p.445.
L. stenocephala. Loosely clump-forming perennial. **H** 1.2m (4ft) or more, **S** 60cm (2ft). Fully hardy. Has jagged-edged, round, mid-green leaves. Large heads of daisy-like, yellow-orange flowers open on purplish stems from mid- to late summer.
🏆 ***L.* 'The Rocket'** illus. p.219.
L. tussilaginea. See *Farfugium japonicum.*

LIGUSTRUM

Privet

OLEACEAE

Genus of deciduous, semi-evergreen or evergreen shrubs and trees, grown for their foliage and, in some species, flowers. Fully to frost hardy. Requires sun or semi-shade, the variegated forms doing best in full sun. Thrives on any well-drained soil, including chalky soil. All except *L. lucidum* occasionally need cutting back in mid-spring to restrict growth. Propagate by semi-ripe cuttings in summer. ⚠All parts may cause severe discomfort if ingested.
L. japonicum (Japanese privet). Evergreen, bushy, dense shrub. **H** 3m (10ft), **S** 2.5m (8ft). Frost hardy. Has oval, glossy, very dark green leaves and, from mid-summer to early autumn, large, conical panicles of small, tubular, white flowers with lobes. **'Coriaceum'** see *L.j.* 'Rotundifolium'. **'Rotundifolium'**, syn. *L.j.* 'Coriaceum', is slow-growing, and produces a dense mass of rounded, leathery leaves.
🏆***L. lucidum*** (Chinese privet). Evergreen, upright shrub or tree. **H** 10m (30ft), **S** 8m (25ft). Frost hardy. Bears large, oval, glossy, dark green leaves. Produces large panicles of small, tubular, white flowers, with 4 lobes, in late summer and early autumn. 🏆**'Excelsum Superbum'** has bright green leaves, marked with pale green and yellow-edged, and small, tubular, white flowers.
L. ovalifolium illus. p.119. 🏆**'Aureum'** is a vigorous, evergreen or semi-evergreen, upright, dense shrub. **H** 4m (12ft), **S** 3m (10ft). Fully hardy. Leaves are oval, glossy and mid-green, broadly edged with bright yellow. Dense panicles of small, rather unpleasantly scented, tubular, white flowers, with 4 lobes, appear in mid- summer and are succeeded by spherical, black fruits. Cut back hedges to 30cm (1ft) after planting and prune hard for first 2 years; then trim as necessary during the growing season.
L. sinense illus. p.112.
***L.* 'Vicaryi'**, syn. *L.* x *vicaryi*, illus. p.140.
L.* x *vicaryi. See *L.* 'Vicaryi'.
L. vulgare. Deciduous or semi-evergreen, bushy shrub. **H** and **S** 3m (10ft). Fully hardy. Leaves are narrowly lance-shaped and dark green. Produces panicles of small, strongly scented, tubular, white flowers, with 4 lobes, from early to mid-summer, then spherical, black fruits. Cut back hedges to 30cm (1ft) after planting and prune hard for first 2 years; then trim as necessary during the growing season. **'Aureum'**, **H** and **S** 2m (6ft), has golden-yellow foliage.

LILIUM

Lily

LILIACEAE

Genus of mainly summer-flowering bulbs, grown for their often fragrant, brightly coloured flowers. Each fleshy-scaled bulb produces one unbranched, leafy stem, in some cases with annual roots in lower part. Mostly lance-shaped or linear leaves, to 22cm (9in) long, are scattered or in whorls, sometimes with bulbils in axils. Flowers, usually several per stem, are mainly trumpet- to bowl-shaped or with the 6 petals strongly reflexed to form a turkscap shape. (Petals of *Lilium* are known botanically as perianth segments.) Three categories of flower size – small, medium and large – are used in the descriptions below. For turkscap, bowl-, cup- and star-shaped flowers: small is up to 5cm (2in) across; medium is 5–7cm (2–3in) across; large is over 7cm (3in) across. For trumpet- and funnel-shaped flowers: small is up to 7cm (3in) long; medium is 7–10cm (3–4in) long; large is over 10cm (4in) long. Each plant has a spread of up to 30cm (12in). Frost hardy, unless otherwise stated. Needs sun and well-drained soil, unless otherwise stated. Propagate by seed in autumn or spring, by bulb scales in summer or by stem bulbils (where present) in autumn. Virus, fungal diseases, and lily beetle may cause problems. Lilies are classified into 9 divisions. See feature panel pp.388–391.

Division 1 (Asiatic hybrids)
These lilies are derived from various Asiatic species, including *L. bulbiferum, L. cernuum, L. concolor, L. davidii, L. lancifolium* and *L.maculatum.* The flowers are borne in racemes or umbels, and are usually unscented. The leaves are narrowly ovate and arranged alternatively. There are 3 subdivisions: **1a**) upward-facing flowers; **1b**) outward-facing flowers; **1c**) pendent flowers.
Division 2 (Martagon hybrids)
Derived primarily from *L. hansonii* and *L. martagon*, these lilies produce racemes of turkscap, sometimes scented flowers, and have whorls of elliptic leaves.
Division 3 (Candidum hybrids)
Derived from *L. candicum* and other European species, except *L. martagon*, these lilies produce sometimes scented, mostly turkscap flowers, singly or in umbels or racemes. Leaves are elliptic, and spirally arranged or scattered.
Division 4 (American hybrids) Derived from American species, these lilies bear racemes of sometimes scented, mostly turkscap, but occasionally funnel-shaped flowers, and have whorls of lance-shaped to elliptic leaves.
Division 5 (Longiflorum hybrids)
Derived from *L. formosanum* and *L.longiflorum*, these lilies bear racemes or umbels of large, often sweetly scented, trumpet- or funnel-shaped flowers, sometimes only 2 or 3 per stem. Leaves are linear to narrowly lance-shaped, and scattered.
Division 6 (Trumpet and Aurelian hybrids)
Derived from Asiatic species, including *L. regale, L. henryi* and *L. sargentiae*, these lilies bear racemes or umbels of usually scented flowers. Leaves are elliptic to linear, and alternate or spirally arranged. There are 4 subdivisions: **6a**) trumpet-shaped flowers; **6b**) bowl-shaped flowers; **6c**) very shallowly bowl-shaped flowers, some almost flat; **6d**) distinctly recurved flowers.
Division 7 (Oriental hybrids)
Derived from E. Asian species, such as *L. auratum, L. japonicum* and *L.speciosum*, as well as their hybrids with *L. henryi*, these lilies have flowers borne in racemes or panicles, and are often scented. Leaves are lance-shaped and alternate. There are 4 subdivisions: **7a**) trumpet-shaped flowers; **7b**) bowl-shaped flowers; **7c**) flat or very shallowly bowl-shaped flowers; **7d**) turkscap or various recurved flowers.
Division 8. Other hybrids
Division 9. All true species.

🏆***L.* African Queen Group** (illus. p.391). Summer-flowering Division 6 lily. **H** 1m (3ft). Produces 3 large fragrant flowers, brownish-purple outside and apricot-orange on the inside, with recurved petals.
***L.* 'Altari'** (illus. p.388). Summer-flowering Division 5 and 7 crossbred lily. **H** 1m (3ft). Highly scented, white flowers have cranberry-red inner throats.
L. amabile. Summer-flowering Division 9 lily with stem roots. **H** 30cm–1m (1–3ft). Scattered leaves are lance-shaped. Has up to 10 unpleasant-smelling, nodding, turkscap, black-spotted, red flowers; each petal is 5–5.5cm (2–2¼in) long.

L

L. 'Amber Gold'. Summer-flowering Division 1c lily. **H** 1.2–1.5m (4–5ft). Has medium-sized, nodding, turkscap, deep yellow flowers, each with maroon spots in throat.
L. 'Angela North'. Mid-summer flowering Division 1c lily. H to 1m (3ft). Has medium-sized, slightly fragrant, dark red flowers, spotted darker red, that have strongly recurved petals.
♀**L. 'Apollo'** (illus. p.391). Summer-flowering Division 1a lily. **H** 1.2m (4ft). Has downward-facing, turkscap, pale orange flowers with strongly reflexed petals.
L. 'Arena' (illus. p.388). Vigorous, summer-flowering, Division 7b lily. **H** 1.25m (4ft). Large, outward-facing, bowl-shaped to slightly trumpet-shaped, recurving, greenish- to yellowish-white flowers have deep red central veining on the insides and yellow-green throats with deep red spots.
L. auratum (Golden-rayed lily of Japan). Summer- and autumn-flowering, Division 9 lily with stem roots. **H** 60cm–1.5m (2–5ft). Has long, scattered, lance-shaped leaves. Produces up to 10, sometimes more, fragrant, outward-facing, widely bowl-shaped, white flowers; each petal is 12–18cm (5–7in) long with a central, red or yellow band and often red or yellow spots. Requires semi-shade and neutral to acid soil. **var. *platyphyllum*** (illus. p.388) has broader leaves; petals have a central, yellow band and fewer spots.
L. 'Black Beauty'. Summer-flowering Division 7d lily. **H** 1.5–2m (5–6ft). Has medium-sized, outward-facing, flattish, green-centred, very deep red flowers with recurved, white-margined petals.
L. 'Black Dragon'. Summer-flowering Division 6a lily. **H** 1.5m (5ft). Has large, outward-facing, trumpet-shaped flowers with dark purplish-red outsides and white insides.
L. 'Black Magic' (illus. p.388). Summer-flowering Division 6a lily. **H** 1.2–2m (4–6ft). Scented, outward-facing, trumpet-shaped flowers are purplish-brown outside and white inside.
L. 'Black Out' (illus. p.389). Summer-flowering Division 1b lily. **H** 1.2m (4ft). Glossy, dark red flowers have black-red throats, with tiny, black spots.
L. 'Black Pearl'. Summer-flowering Division 1a lily. **H** 1m (3ft). Bears deep purple-red flowers.
L. 'Bonfire'. Late summer-flowering Division 7b lily. **H** 1.2–1.5m (4–5ft). Produces outward-facing, bowl-shaped flowers with broad petals, white outside flushed with pink, and dark crimson inside, spotted paler crimson.
L. 'Boogie Woogie' (illus. p.390). Summer-flowering Division 5 and 6 crossbred Orienpet lily. **H** 1m (3ft). Bears large, fragrant flowers with recurved, pink-edged, yellow petals.
L. 'Bright Star' (illus. p.390). Summer-flowering Division 6b lily. **H** 1–1.5m (3–5ft). Has large, flattish, white flowers; petals have recurved tips and a central, orange streak inside.
L. 'Brocade'. Early summer-flowering Division 2 lily. **H** 1.5m (5ft). Produces nodding, turkscap, orange-yellow flowers, suffused rosy-pink, with purple-red spots on the insides of the recurved petals.
L. 'Bronwen North'. Mid-summer-flowering Division 1c lily. H to 1m (3ft). Each stem carries 7 or more medium-sized, slightly fragrant flowers with strongly recurving, pale mauve-pink petals, paler at the tips, and pale pink throats with dark spots and lines; nectaries are reddish-black.
L. 'Brushmarks'. Early summer-flowering Division 1a lily. **H** 1.35m (4½ft). Large, upward-facing, cup-shaped, orange flowers are green-throated. Petals have deep red blotches and sometimes spots.
L. bulbiferum (Fire lily, Orange lily). Summer-flowering Division 9 lily with stem roots. **H** 40cm–1.5m (16in–5ft). Stem bears scattered, lance-shaped leaves and, usually, bulbils in leaf axils. Bears 1–5 or more upward-facing, shallowly cup-shaped, orange-red flowers. Each petal is 6–8.5cm (2½–3¼in) long and spotted black or deep red. **var. *croceum*** (illus. p.391) has orange flowers and does not normally bear bulbils.
L. 'California Gold'. Vigorous, summer-flowering, Division 6a lily. **H** 1–1.2m (3–4ft). Produces sprays of outward-facing, trumpet- to bowl-shaped, deep lemon-yellow flowers, with the reverses of the gently recurving petals bronze-green.
L. canadense (Canada lily, Meadow lily, Wild yellow lily; illus. p.390). Summer-flowering Division 9 lily with stem roots. **H** to 1.5m (5ft). Narrowly to broadly lance-shaped leaves are mainly in whorls. Bears about 10 nodding, bell-shaped, yellow or red flowers; each petal is 5–8cm (2–3in) long, with dark red or purple spots in lower part.
♀***L. candidum*** (Madonna lily). Summer-flowering Division 9 lily. **H** 1–2m (3–6ft). Flower stem bears scattered, lance-shaped leaves and 5–20 fragrant, outward-facing, broadly funnel-shaped, white flowers. Each petal is 5–8cm (2–3in) long with a yellow base and a slightly recurved tip. In autumn bears basal leaves, which remain throughout winter but die off as flowering stems mature. Prefers lime-rich soil.
L. carniolicum. See *L. pyrenaicum* subsp. *carniolicum*.
♀**L. 'Casa Blanca'** (illus. p.388). Late summer-flowering Division 7b lily. **H** 90cm (3ft). Large, waxy, white flowers, have yellowish-white midribs and violet-red nectaries.
L. cernuum (illus. p.389). Summer-flowering Division 9 lily with stem roots. **H** to 60cm (2ft). Long, linear leaves are scattered. Produces 7–15 fragrant, nodding, turkscap flowers, usually pinkish-purple with purple spots. Each petal is 3.5–5cm (1½–2in) long.
L. chalcedonicum, syn. *L. heldreichii* (Scarlet turkscap lily; illus. p.391). Summer-flowering Division 9 lily with stem roots. **H** 50cm–1.5m (20in–5ft). Leaves are scattered and mostly lance-shaped, lower ones spreading, upper ones smaller and closer to stem. Bears up to 12 slightly scented, nodding, turkscap flowers with red or reddish-orange petals, each 5–7cm (2–3in) long.
L. Citronella Group (illus. p.390). Mid-summer-flowering Division 1 lily. **H** 1m (3ft). Produces nodding heads of large, scented flowers with recurved, black-spotted, bright yellow petals.
L. 'Conca d'Or' (illus. p.390). Summer-flowering Division 5 and 6 crossbred Orienpet lily. **H** 1.2m (4ft). Produces to 3 large, spicy-scented, creamy-yellow flowers with lemon-yellow throats.
L. 'Connecticut King' (illus. p.390). Early to mid-summer-flowering Division 1a lily. **H** 1m (3ft). Flowers are medium-sized, upward-facing, cup-shaped and bright yellow.
L. 'Corsage'. Summer-flowering Division 1b lily. **H** 1.2m (4ft). Bears outward-facing, bowl-shaped flowers with recurved petals, pink-flushed outside and pink inside with white centres and maroon spots.
L. 'Côte d'Azur' (illus. p.389). Summer-flowering Division 1a lily. **H** 40cm (16in). Strong stems bear deep rose-pink flowers with darker-spotted throats.
L. 'Cover Girl'. Summer to early autumn-flowering Division 7c lily. **H** 1.5–1.9m (5–6ft). Has very large, outward- or slightly downward-facing, soft pink flowers, with white at the tips of the gently recurved petals which are centrally banded deep pink and strongly red-spotted.
L. 'Crimson Pixie' (illus. p.391). Early summer-flowering Division 1a lily. **H** 40cm (16in). Has umbels of upright, open bowl-shaped, unspotted, deep warm red-orange flowers. Is good as a pot plant.
***L.* x *dalhansonii*.** Variable, summer-flowering Division 9 lily. **H** 1.5–2m (5–6ft). Has unpleasant-smelling, turkscap flowers, chestnut brown or dark maroon with gold spots. **'Marhan'** see *L.* 'Marhan'.
L. davidii. Summer-flowering Division 9 lily with stem roots. **H** 1–1.4m (3–4½ft). Linear leaves are scattered. Produces 5–20 nodding, turkscap, red or reddish-orange flowers; each petal is 5–8cm (2–3in) long with dark purple spots. **var. *willmottiae*** differs in its slender, arching stems to 2m (6ft) and pendent flower stalks.
L. 'Destiny'. Early summer-flowering Division 1a lily. **H** 1–1.2m (3–4ft). Flowers are medium-sized, upward-facing, cup-shaped and yellow with brown spots.
L. duchartrei. Summer-flowering Division 9 lily. **H** 60cm–1m (2–3ft). Lance-shaped leaves are scattered up stems. Has up to 12 fragrant, nodding, turkscap, white flowers that are flushed purple outside and spotted deep purple inside.
L. 'Ed', syn. *L.* 'Mr Ed'. Summer to early autumn-flowering Division 7 lily. **H** 40cm (16in). Has large, outward-facing, bowl-shaped, greenish-white flowers, with the petals centrally banded pale yellow and flushed pale red, and dark red spots on one-third of each petal.
L. 'Elodie' (illus. p.389). Summer-flowering Division 1a lily. **H** 1.2m (4ft). Semi-double, pale pink flowers have dark pink-freckled centres.
L. 'Enchantment' (illus. p.391). Early summer-flowering Division 1a lily. **H** 1m (3ft). Produces medium-sized, upward-facing, cup-shaped, orange-red flowers with black-spotted throats.
L. 'Eros'. Mid-summer-flowering Division 1c lily. **H** 90cm–1.1m (3–3½ft). Has small, unscented, turkscap, buff flowers.
♀**L. 'Garden Party'.** Summer-flowering Division 7 lily. **H** 50cm (20in) Produces large, fragrant, outward-facing, red-speckled, white flowers with gold and red or pink stripes in the centre of each petal.
L. Golden Clarion Group. Late spring to early summer-flowering bulb. **H** 1–2m (3–6ft). Produces outward-facing, trumpet-shaped, pale to deep yellow flowers that may be flushed with reddish-purple on the outside.
♀**L. Golden Splendor Group** illus. p.393.
♀**L.'Grand Cru'** (illus. p.391). Early summer-flowering Division 1a lily. **H** 1.2m (4ft). Has upright, open bowl-shaped, vivid-yellow flowers, strongly red-suffused in the throats for about half the petal lengths, and with a few red spots at the base internally. Is good as a pot plant.
L. 'Gran Paradiso' (illus. p.391). Mid-summer-flowering Division 1a lily. **H** 1m (3ft). Produces medium-sized, unscented, bowl-shaped, red flowers with slightly recurved petals.
L. hansonii (illus. p.391). Summer-flowering Division 9 lily with stem roots. **H** 1–1.5m (3–5ft). Long leaves in whorls are lance-shaped to oval. Has 3–12 scented, nodding, turkscap, orange-yellow flowers. Each thick petal is 3–4cm (1¼–1½in) long with brown-purple spots towards base.
L. 'Harmony'. Summer-flowering Division 1a lily. **H** 50cm–1m (1½–3ft). Orange flowers are upward-facing, cup-shaped and spotted with maroon.
L. heldreichii. See *L. chalcedonicum.*
♀***L. henryi*** (illus. p.391). Late summer-flowering Division 9 lily with stem roots. **H** 1–3m (3–10ft). Has scattered, lance-shaped leaves. Produces 5–20, sometimes up to 70, nodding, turkscap, orange flowers; petals are 6–8cm (2½–3in) long with dark spots and prominent warts towards bases. Prefers lime-rich soil.
L. Imperial Crimson Group. Late summer-flowering Division 7c lily. **H** 1.5m (5ft). Large, fragrant, flattish, deep crimson flowers have white throats and white-margined petals.
L. Imperial Gold Group. Summer-flowering Division 7c lily. **H** 2m (6ft). Bears large, fragrant, flattish, white flowers, spotted maroon, and with a yellow stripe up each petal centre.
L. 'Journey's End' (illus. p.389). Late summer-flowering Division 7d lily. **H** 2m (6ft). Large, outward-facing, bowl-shaped, maroon-spotted, deep pink flowers have recurved petals, white at tips and edges.
L. 'Karen North' (illus. p.391). Summer-flowering Division 1c lily. **H** to 1.4m (4½ft). Turkscap flowers are medium-sized, downward-facing, with orange-pink petals sparsely spotted with deep pink.
L. 'Lady Alice' (illus. p.388). Summer-flowering Divison 8 lily. **H** 1.2m (4ft). Pendent, turkscap flowers have recurved, brown-speckled, cream petals with apricot-orange centres.
L. 'Lady Bowes Lyon' (illus. p.391). Summer-flowering Division 1c lily. **H** 1–1.2m (3–4ft). Downward-facing, black-spotted, red flowers have reflexed petals.
L. lancifolium, syn. *L. tigrinum* (Tiger lily). Summer- to early autumn-flowering, Division 9 lily with stem roots. **H** 60cm–1.5m (2–5ft). Produces long, scattered, narrowly lance-shaped leaves. Produces 5–10, sometimes up to 40, nodding, turkscap, pink- to red-orange flowers; each petal is 7–10cm (3–4in) long and spotted with purple. **var. *flaviflorum*** has yellow flowers. Vigorous.

L

♀ **L.'Splendens'** (illus. p.391) bears larger, brighter red-orange flowers.
L. lankongense (illus. p.389). Summer-flowering Division 9 lily with stem roots. **H** to 1.2m (4ft). Leaves are scattered and lance-shaped. Has up to 15 scented, nodding, turkscap, pink flowers. Petals, each 4–6.5cm (1½–2½in) long with a central, green stripe and red-purple spots mainly on edges, are often mauve-flushed. Needs partial shade in warm areas.
L. leichtlinii (illus. p.390). Summer-flowering Division 9 lily with stem roots. **H** to 1.2m (4ft). Scattered leaves are linear to narrowly lance-shaped. Produces 1–6 nodding, turkscap, yellow flowers; each petal is 6–8.5cm (2½–3¼in) long with dark reddish-purple spots. Needs semi-shade.
***L.* 'Limelight'** (illus. p.390). Moderately robust, mid-summer-flowering, Division 9 lily. **H** 1–2m (3–6ft). Large, fragrant, slightly pendent, trumpet-shaped, lime-yellow flowers are flushed with green, especially outside.
***L.* 'Lime Star'.** Vigorous, summer-flowering, Division 7a/b lily. **H** 1.2m (4ft). Has outward-facing, bowl-shaped to flat flowers, with recurving, white petals. Each petal is strongly banded bright greenish-yellow and has slightly ruffled margins.
***L.* 'Lollypop'.** See *L.* Lollypop 'Holebibi'.
***L.* Lollypop 'Holebibi',** syn. *L.* 'Lollypop'. Early summer-flowering Division 1a lily. **H** 60cm (2ft). Has upright, open bowl-shaped, white flowers, with the upper parts of the gently recurving petals strongly suffused deep red.
♀ ***L. longiflorum*** (Bermuda lily, Easter lily, White trumpet lily; illus. p.388). Summer-flowering Division 9 lily with stem roots. **H** 30cm–1m (1–3ft). Leaves are scattered and lance-shaped. Produces 1–6 fragrant, outward-facing, funnel-shaped, white flowers. Each petal is 13–20cm (5–8in) long with slightly recurved tips. **'White American'**, **H** 1m (3ft), is a Division 5 lily and produces white flowers with green tips and deep yellow anthers. Often grown for cutting. **'White Heaven'** (illus. p.388), **H** 1.2m (4ft), is a Division 5 lily with delicately scented, pure white flowers.
***L.* 'Luxor'.** Vigorous, summer-flowering, Division 1b lily. **H** 90cm–1.5m (3–5ft). Produces large, outward-facing, bowl-shaped, bright yellow flowers, slightly darker yellow and speckled with dark red spots on the lower half of each petal.
L. mackliniae (Manipur lily; illus. p.389). Late spring- to summer-flowering, Division 9 lily with stem roots. **H** to 40cm (16in). Small, narrowly lance-shaped to narrowly oval leaves are scattered or whorled near top of stem. Has 1–6 usually nodding, broadly bell-shaped, purplish-pink flowers; each petal is 4.5–5cm (1¾–2in) long. Needs semi-shade.
L. maculatum, syn. *L. thunbergianum.* Summer-flowering Division 9 lily with stem roots. **H** to 60cm (2ft). Fully hardy. Scattered leaves are lance-shaped or oval. Has 1–6 upward-facing, cup-shaped, yellow, orange or red flowers with darker spots; each petal is 8–10cm (3–4in) long.
***L.* 'Magic Pink'.** Early summer-flowering Division 7b lily. **H** 1–1.2m (3–4ft). Large flowers are pink with darker pink spots.
***L.* 'Marhan'**, syn. *L.* x *dalhansonii* 'Marhan'. Early summer-flowering Division 2 lily. **H** 1.2–2m (4–6ft). Medium-sized, nodding, turkscap, deep orange flowers are spotted red-brown.
♀ ***L. martagon*** (Martagon lily; illus. p.389). Summer-flowering Division 9 lily with stem roots. **H** 1–2m (3–6ft). Fully hardy. Has lance-shaped to oval leaves in whorls and up to 50 scented, nodding, turkscap flowers. Petals are 3–4.5cm (1¼–1¾in) long and pink or purple, often with darker spots. ♀ **var. *album*** (illus. p.388) has pure white flowers.
L. medeoloides (illus. p.390). Summer-flowering Division 9 lily. **H** to 75cm (2½ft). Has lance-shaped leaves and up to 10 turkscap, apricot to orange-red flowers, usually with darker spots.
***L.* 'Miss Lucy'** (illus. p.389). Summer-flowering Division 7 lily. **H** 1.2m (4ft). Produces highly fragrant, double, pinkish-white flowers with 18 petals.
L. monadelphum, syn. *L. szovitsianum*, (illus. p.390). Summer-flowering Division 9 lily with stem roots. **H** 50cm–2m (1½–6ft). Has scattered, lance-shaped to oval leaves. Produces usually 1–5, sometimes up to 30, scented, nodding, turkscap, yellow flowers, usually with deep red or purple spots inside. Petals 6–10cm (2½–4in) long.
***L.* 'Mona Lisa'** (illus. p.388). Summer-flowering Division 7b/c lily. **H** 45cm (18in). Has large, shallowly bowl-shaped to flat, light reddish-purple flowers, with ivory-white margins suffused red, greenish petal tips, dark red spots on the lower half of each petal and light green throats.
***L.* 'Mont Blanc'.** Summer-flowering Division 1a lily. **H** 90cm (3ft). Has large, upward-facing, creamy-white flowers, spotted with brown.
***L.* 'Montreux'.** Mid-summer-flowering Division 1a lily. **H** 1m (3ft). Bears about 8 medium-sized, pink flowers with darker pink midribs; orange-pink throats are spotted with brown.
***L.* 'Mr Ed'.** See *L.* 'Ed'.
***L.* 'Muscadet'.** Summer-flowering Division 7 lily. **H** 1m (3ft). Large, fragrant, white flowers have pink markings and maroon spots.
L. nanum, syn. *Nomocharis nana.* Late spring- or summer-flowering, Division 9 lily. **H** 6–45cm (2½–18in). Scattered leaves are linear. Bears a usually nodding, broadly bell-shaped, purplish-pink flower, with 4.5–5cm (1¾–2in) long petals. Needs partial shade. **var. *flavidum*** has pale yellow flowers.
L. nepalense. Summer-flowering Division 9 lily with stem roots. **H** 70cm–1m (28–36in). Has scattered, lance-shaped leaves. Produces often unpleasant-smelling, nodding, funnel-shaped, greenish-white or greenish-yellow flowers, each with a dark reddish-purple base inside and petals to 15cm (6in) long.
***L.* 'Netty's Pride'** (illus. p.389). Summer-flowering Division 1b lily. **H** 60cm (2ft). Bears dark maroon flowers with ivory-tipped petals.
***L.* 'New Wave'** (illus. p.389). Early to mid-summer-flowering Division 1a lily. **H** 60cm (2ft). Produces large, pure white flowers with scattered, maroon spots.
***L.* 'Nymph'** (illus. p.388). Summer-flowering Division 7 lily. **H** 1.2m (4ft). Produces large, scented, white flowers with deep pink stripes along the centre of each petal.
***L.* 'Olivia'** (illus. p.388). Late summer-flowering Division 7b lily. **H** 75cm–1m (2½–3ft). Has medium-sized, scented, slightly reflexed, bowl-shaped, white flowers.
***L.* Olympic Group.** Vigorous, summer-flowering, Division 6a lily. **H** 1.2–2m (4–6ft). Produces racemes of up to 15 l arge, sweetly scented, trumpet-shaped flowers ranging from white, greenish-white, cream and yellow to pink and purple, often yellow in the throats. Petals are flushed pink or purplish-red on the outside.
***L.* 'Orange Electric'** (illus. p.391). Summer-flowering Division 1a lily. **H** 1.2m (4ft). Bears white flowers with orange and yellow stripes and brown spots.
***L.* 'Orange Pixie'** (illus. p.391). Early summer-flowering Division 1a lily. **H** 25–30cm (10–12in). Has upright umbels of open bowl-shaped, deep golden-orange flowers. Is good as a pot plant.
♀ ***L. pardalinum*** (Leopard lily, Panther lily; illus. p.391). Summer-flowering Division 9 lily. **H** 2–3m (6–10ft). Long, narrowly elliptic leaves are mainly in whorls. Has up to 10 often scented, nodding, turkscap flowers. Each petal is 5–9cm (2–3½in) long with red upper parts. Orange lower parts have maroon spots, some of which are encircled with yellow. **subsp. *wigginsii*** (illus. p.390).
♀ ***L.* Pink Perfection Group.** Summer-flowering Division 6a lily with stout stems. **H** 1.5–2m (5–6ft). Produces large, scented, slightly nodding, trumpet-shaped flowers, which are deep purplish-red or purple-pink, with bright orange anthers.
***L.* 'Pink Tiger'.** Vigorous, late summer-flowering, Division 1b lily. **H** 1.2m (4ft). Produces medium-sized, unscented, turkscap, pink flowers.
L. pomponium (illus. p.391). Slender, stem-rooting, summer-flowering, Division 9 lily with green stems that are spotted purple on the lower halves. **H** 1m (3ft). Has scattered, linear, mid-green leaves with silver-hairy margins. Produces racemes of up to 6 (rarely up to 10) pungently scented, pendent, turkscap, sealing-wax-red flowers, generally with black spots and streaks in the throats. Alkaline soil in full sun or partial shade.
L. ponticum. See *L. pyrenaicum* subsp. *ponticum.*
♀ ***L. pumilum***, syn. *L. tenuifolium.* Summer-flowering Division 9 lily with stem roots. **H** 15cm–1m (6–36in). Small, scattered leaves are linear. Produces usually up to 7 but occasionally up to 30 slightly scented, nodding, turkscap flowers; each petal is 3–3.5cm (1¼–1½in) long and scarlet with or without basal, black spots.
L. pyrenaicum (Yellow turkscap lily; illus. p.390). Late spring to early summer-flowering, Division 9 lily, often with stem roots. **H** 30cm–1.35m (1–4½ft). Has scattered, linear to narrowly elliptic, hairless leaves. Produces up to 12 unpleasant-smelling, nodding, turkscap flowers. Each petal is 4–6.5cm (1½–2½in) long and yellow or green-yellow with prominent dark purple spots and lines. **subsp. *carniolicum*** (syn. *L. carniolicum*) has red- or orange-spotted flowers. Leaves may be hairless or downy. **subsp. *ponticum*** (syn. *L. ponticum*) bears deep yellow flowers, densely lined and spotted with red-brown or purple; leaves are downy beneath. **f. *rubrum*** (illus. p.391) has orange-red or dark red flowers.
***L.* 'Red Carpet'** (illus. p.391). Early summer-flowering Division 1a lily. **H** 30cm (1ft). Has upright umbels of open bowl-shaped, unspotted, deep red flowers. Is good as a pot plant.
♀ ***L. regale*** (Regal lily; illus. p.388). Summer-flowering Division 9 lily with stem roots. **H** 50cm–2m (20in–6ft). Linear leaves are scattered. Produces up to 25 fragrant, outward-facing, funnel-shaped flowers. Petals are each 12–15cm (5–6in) long, white inside with a yellow base and pinkish-purple outside. **'Royal Gold'** syn. *L.* 'Royal Gold' (illus. p.390). Vigorous, summer-flowering, Division 9 lily. **H** 1.2–1.5m (4–5ft). Produces clusters of large, outward-facing, trumpet-shaped flowers, mid-yellow inside and purple-brown outside.
***L.* 'Roma'** (illus. p.390). Early summer-flowering Division 1a lily. **H** 1.5m (5ft). Green buds open to cream flowers that sometimes age to pale greenish-yellow.
***L.* 'Rosemary North'** (illus. p.390). Mid- to late summer-flowering, Division 1c lily. **H** to 1m (3ft). Produces 12 or more medium-sized, slightly fragrant, rich orange flowers that sometimes have darker spots.
***L.* 'Rosita'** (illus. p.389). Early summer-flowering Division 1a lily. **H** 75cm (2½ft). Has umbels of upright, open bowl-shaped, green-centred, blush-pink flowers, with slightly recurving petals.
L. rosthornii (illus. p.390). Vigorous, stem-rooting, clump-forming, summer-flowering, Division 9 lily. **H** 40–100cm (16–39in). Has long, scattered, lance-shaped leaves on the lower part of the stem, the upper stem leaves being much shorter and oval in shape. Produces up to 9 nodding, turkscap, orange or orange-yellow flowers. Strongly recurved, channelled petals have green central bands and purple-red basal spots.
***L.* 'Royal Gold'**, syn. *L. regale* 'Royal Gold'
L. rubellum (illus. p.389). Early summer-flowering Division 9 lily with stem roots. **H** 30–80cm (12–32in). Has scattered, narrowly oval leaves and up to 9 scented, outward-facing, broadly funnel-shaped, pink flowers with dark red spots at bases; each petal is 6–8cm (2½–3in) long.
***L.* 'Shuksan'.** Summer-flowering Division 4 lily. **H** 1.2–2m (4–6ft). Medium-sized, nodding, turkscap, yellowish-orange flowers are flushed red at petal tips and sparsely spotted with black.
***L.* 'Sixth Sense'.** Summer-flowering Division 1b lily. **H** 70cm (28in). Produces white-edged, dark burgundy-red flowers with dark purple-brown spots.
L. speciosum. Late summer-flowering Division 9 lily with stem roots. **H** 1–1.7m (3–5½ft). Has long, scattered, broadly lance-shaped leaves. Produces up to 12 scented, nodding, turkscap, white or pink flowers; each petal is up to 10cm (4in) long, with pink or crimson spots.

L

Requires neutral to acid soil. **var. *album*** has white flowers and purple stems. Flowers of **var. *rubrum*** are carmine, stems are purple.
***L.* 'Starfighter'** (illus. p.389). Summer-flowering Division 7 lily. **H** 50cm (20in). Bears spicy-scented, maroon-speckled, deep pinkish-purple flowers with prominent white-edges.
***L.* 'Star Gazer'.** Late summer-flowering Division 7c lily. **H** 90cm (3ft). Large, highly fragrant, rich crimson flowers are spotted maroon, with white edges.
***L.* 'Sterling Star'** (illus. p.388). Summer-flowering Division 1a lily. **H** 1–1.2m (3–4ft). Has large, upward-facing, cup-shaped, white flowers with tiny, brown spots.
***L.* 'Sumatra'** (illus. p.389). Summer-flowering Division 7 lily. **H** 90cm (36in). Produces large, scented, dark wine-red flowers with a hint of white at the tips of the petals.
L. superbum (Swamp lily, Turkscap lily; illus. p.390). Late summer- to early autumn-flowering, Division 9 lily with stem roots. **H** 1.5–3m (5–10ft). Lance-shaped to elliptic leaves are mainly in whorls. Bears up to 40 nodding, turkscap, orange flowers. Each petal is 6–10cm (2½–4in) long, with a green base inside and usually flushed red and spotted maroon. Requires neutral to acid soil.
***L.* 'Sweet Lord'** (illus. p.389). Early to mid-summer-flowering Division 1a lily. **H** 50cm (20in). Produces purple-red flowers.
L. szovitsianum. See *L. monadelphum.*
L. tenuifolium. See *L. pumilum.*
♀***L.* x *testaceum*** (Nankeen lily). Summer-flowering Division 9 lily. **H** 1–1.5m (3–5ft). Has scattered, linear, often twisted leaves. Produces 6–12 fragrant, nodding, turkscap, light orange to brownish-yellow flowers; each petal is 8cm (3in) long, usually with reddish spots inside.
L. thunbergianum. See *L. maculatum.*
***L.* 'Tiger Woods'** (illus. p.389). Summer-flowering Division 7 lily. **H** 1m (3ft). Bears very large, scented, white flowers with a rich crimson stripe down the centre of each petal surrounded by crimson spots.
L. tigrinum. See *L. lancifolium.*
***L.* 'Tom Pouce'** (illus. p.389). Summer-flowering Division 7 lily. **H** 90cm (36in). Bears large, highly scented, pink flowers with a pale yellow stripe down the centre of each petal and pale yellow freckles.
***L.* TRIUMPHATOR ('Zanlophator')** (illus. p.388). Summer-flowering Division 6 lily. **H** 1m (3ft). Produces large, fragrant, outward-facing, white flowers with rich rose-pink centres.
L. tsingtauense (illus. p.391). Summer-flowering Division 9 lily with stem roots. **H** 1m (3ft). Lance-shaped leaves are mainly in whorls. Produces 1–5 upward-facing, cup-shaped, orange to orange-red flowers; petals are up to 5cm (2in) long and spotted with maroon.
L. wallichianum. Late summer- to autumn-flowering, Division 9 lily with stem roots. **H** to 2m (6ft). Half hardy. Long, scattered leaves are linear or lance-shaped. Bears 1–4 fragrant, outward-facing, funnel-shaped, white or cream flowers that are green or yellow towards bases. Each petal is 15–30cm (6–12in) long.
***L.* 'White Heaven'** illus. p.388.
L. wigginsii (illus. p.390). Stem-rooting, mid-summer-flowering, Division 9 lily with hairless stems. **H** 90cm–1.2m (3–4ft). Linear-lance-shaped, deep green leaves are scattered and in 2–4 whorls roughly halfway up the stems. Produces few-flowered racemes of unscented, pendent, turkscap, deep yellow flowers, with purple spots. Needs moist acid soil, and partial or dappled shade.
***L.* 'Zanlophator'.** See *L.* TRIUMPHATOR.

Limnanthemum nymphoides. See *Nymphoides peltata.*

LIMNANTHES

LIMNANTHACEAE

Genus of annuals, useful for rock gardens, containers and for edging borders. Fully hardy. Prefers a sunny situation and fertile, well-drained soil. Propagate by seed sown outdoors in spring or early autumn. Self seeds very freely, although easy to control.
♀***L. douglasii*** illus. p.321.

LIMONIUM

Sea lavender

PLUMBAGINACEAE

Genus of summer- and autumn-flowering perennials, sometimes grown as annuals, and sub-shrubs, some of which are evergreen. Fully hardy to frost tender, min. 7–10°C (45–50°F). Grows in full sun and in well-drained soil. Propagate by division in spring, by seed in autumn or early spring or by root cuttings in winter.
L. bellidifolium, syn. *L. reticulatum.* Evergreen, dome-shaped perennial with a woody base. **H** 15–20cm (6–8in), **S** 10cm (4in). Frost hardy. Has basal rosettes of rounded, dark green leaves. Much-branched flower stems produce masses of small, "everlasting", trumpet-shaped blue flowers in summer–autumn. Is excellent for a rock garden.
***L. latifolium* 'Blue Cloud'.** Clump-forming perennial. **H** 30cm (12in), **S** 45cm (18in). Fully hardy. In late summer carries diffuse clusters of bluish-mauve flowers that can be dried for indoor decoration. Has large, leathery, dark green leaves.
L. perezii. Evergreen, rounded sub-shrub. **H** and **S** 1m (3ft) or more. Frost tender, min. 7–10°C (45–50°F). Has long-stalked, oval to diamond-shaped, deep green leaves. Dense clusters, 20cm (8in) wide, of tiny, tubular, deep mauve-blue flowers are carried well above the leaves in autumn. Needs good ventilation if grown under glass.
L. reticulatum. See *L. bellidifolium.*
L. sinuatum. Fairly slow-growing, bushy, upright perennial, grown as an annual. **H** 45cm (18in), **S** 30cm (12in). Half hardy. Has lance-shaped, lobed, deep green leaves and, in summer and early autumn, tiny, blue, pink or white flowers borne in clusters on winged stems. **Fortress Series** have small, tubular flowers in a mixture of shades such as pink, yellow or blue. The leaves are often wavy-margined.
L. suworowii. See *Psylliostachys suworowii.*

LINARIA

Toadflax

SCROPHULARIACEAE

Genus of spring-, summer- or autumn-flowering annuals, biennials and perennials, useful for rock gardens and borders. Fully to frost hardy. Prefers a position in sun or light shade; thrives in any well-drained soil. Propagate by seed in autumn or spring. Self seeds freely.
L. alpina (Alpine toadflax). Tuft-forming, compact, annual, biennial or short-lived perennial with a sparse root system. **H** 15cm (6in), **S** 10–15cm (4–6in). Fully hardy. Has whorls of linear to lance-shaped, fleshy, grey-green leaves. A succession of snapdragon-like, yellow-centred, purple-violet flowers is borne in loose racemes in summer.
L. dalmatica. See *L. genistifolia* var. *dalmatica.*
L. genistifolia. Upright perennial. **H** 60cm–1.2m (2–4ft), **S** 23cm (9in). Fully hardy. From mid-summer to autumn produces racemes of small, snapdragon-like, orange-marked, yellow flowers. Lance-shaped, glossy, mid-green leaves clasp the stems. **var. *dalmatica*,** syn. ***L. dalmatica*** (Dalmatian toadflax), **H** 1–1.2m (3–4ft), **S** 60cm (2ft), bears much larger, golden-yellow flowers, from mid- to late summer, and has broader, more glaucous leaves.
***L. maroccana* 'Fairy Lights'.** Fast-growing, erect, bushy annual. **H** 20cm (8in), **S** 15cm (6in). Fully hardy. Has lance-shaped, pale green leaves. Tiny, snapdragon-like flowers, in shades of red, pink, purple, yellow or white, are borne throughout summer.
L. purpurea (Purple toadflax). Upright perennial. **H** 60cm–1m (2–3ft), **S** 60cm (2ft). Fully hardy. From mid- to late summer, racemes of snapdragon-like, purplish-blue flowers, touched with white at throats, are produced above narrowly oval, grey-green leaves. **'Canon J. Went'** illus. p.232.
L. triornithophora illus. p.239.

LINDERA

LAURACEAE

Genus of deciduous or evergreen shrubs and trees, grown for their foliage, which is often aromatic, and their autumn colour. Fruits are produced on female plants if male plants are also grown. Fully to frost hardy. Needs semi-shade and moist, acid soil. Propagate by softwood cuttings in summer or by seed in autumn.
L. benzoin illus. p.127.
♀***L. obtusiloba.*** Deciduous, bushy shrub. **H** and **S** 6m (20ft). Fully hardy. Bears 3-lobed, aromatic, glossy, dark green leaves, becoming butter-yellow in autumn. Clusters of small, star-shaped, deep yellow flowers, borne on bare shoots from early to mid-spring, are followed by small, spherical, black fruits.

LINDHEIMERA

COMPOSITAE/ASTERACEAE

Genus of late summer- and early autumn-flowering annuals. Fully hardy. Grow in sun and in fertile, well-drained soil. Propagate by seed sown under glass in early spring or outdoors in late spring.
L. texana (Star daisy). Moderately fast-growing, erect, branching annual. **H** 30–60cm (12–24in), **S** 30cm (12in). Has hairy stems and oval, serrated, hairy leaves. Daisy-like, yellow flower heads appear in late summer and early autumn.

LINNAEA

Twin flower

CAPRIFOLIACEAE

Genus of one species of evergreen, creeping, summer-flowering, sub-shrubby perennial that makes an extensive, twiggy mat. Is useful as ground cover on peat beds and rock gardens. Fully hardy. Requires partial shade and moist, peaty, acid soil. Propagate by rooted runners in spring, by softwood cuttings in summer or by seed in autumn.
L. borealis illus. p.363.

LINUM

LINACEAE

Genus of annuals, biennials, perennials, sub-shrubs and shrubs, some of which are evergreen or semi-evergreen, grown for their flowers. Is suitable for rock gardens. Fully to half hardy, but in cold areas some species need a sheltered position. Prefers sun and humus-rich, well-drained, peaty soil. Propagate sub-shrubs and shrubs by semi-ripe cuttings in summer or by seed in autumn, annuals, biennials and perennials by seed in autumn.
♀***L. arboreum*** illus. p.344.
L. flavum (Golden flax, Yellow flax). Bushy perennial with a woody rootstock. **H** 30cm (12in), **S** 15cm (6in). Fully hardy. Has narrowly oval, green leaves and, in summer, upward-facing, funnel-shaped, yellow flowers in terminal clusters. **'Compactum'** illus. p.372.
♀***L.* 'Gemmell's Hybrid'.** Semi-evergreen, domed perennial with a woody rootstock. **H** 15cm (6in), **S** 20cm (8in). Frost hardy. Leaves are oval and grey-green. In summer, short-stalked, broadly funnel-shaped, bright chrome-yellow flowers are produced in terminal clusters. Prefers alkaline soil.
***L. grandiflorum* 'Rubrum'** illus. p.308.
L. narbonense. Clump-forming, short-lived perennial, best renewed frequently from seed. **H** 30–60cm (12–24in), **S** 30cm (12in). Fully hardy. Has lance-shaped, greyish-green leaves and heads of somewhat cup-shaped, pale to deep blue flowers in spring-summer.
L. perenne illus. p.342.
L. salsoloides. See *L. suffruticosum* subsp. *salsoloides.*
***L. suffruticosum* subsp. *salsoloides*,** syn. *L. salsoloides.* Perennial with spreading, sometimes woody-based, stems. **H** 5–20cm (2–8in), **S** 8cm (3in). Frost hardy. Slender stems produce fine, heath-like, grey-green leaves and, in summer, a succession of short-lived, saucer-shaped, pearl-white flowers, flushed blue or pink, in terminal clusters.

Lippia citriodora. See *Aloysia triphylla.*

LIQUIDAMBAR

HAMAMELIDACEAE

Genus of deciduous trees, with inconspicuous flowers, grown for their maple-like foliage and autumn colour. Fully to frost hardy. Requires sun or semi-shade and fertile, moist but well-drained soil; grows poorly on shallow, chalky soil. Propagate by softwood cuttings in summer or by seed in autumn.

L. formosana, syn. *L. monticola*. Deciduous, broadly conical tree. **H** 12m (40ft), **S** 10m (30ft). Frost hardy. Has large, 3-lobed, toothed leaves, purple when young, dark green in summer and turning orange, red and purple in autumn.

L. monticola. See *L. formosana*.

L. orientalis (Oriental sweet gum). Slow-growing, deciduous, bushy tree. **H** 6m (20ft), **S** 4m (12ft). Frost hardy. Small, 5-lobed, mid-green leaves turn vivid orange in autumn.

L. styraciflua (Sweet gum) illus. p.65. ♀**'Lane Roberts'** is a deciduous, broadly conical to spreading tree. **H** 25m (80ft), **S** 12m (40ft). Fully hardy. Shoots usually have corky ridges. Glossy, green leaves, each with 5 lobes, turn deep reddish-purple in autumn.

LIRIODENDRON

MAGNOLIACEAE

Genus of deciduous trees, grown for their foliage and flowers in summer. Flowers are almost hidden by unusual leaves and are not produced on young trees. Fully hardy. Requires sun or semi-shade and deep, fertile, well-drained, preferably slightly acid, soil. Propagate species from seed in autumn, and selected forms by budding in late summer.

L. chinense (Chinese tulip tree). Fast-growing, deciduous, spreading tree. **H** 25m (80ft), **S** 12m (40ft). Bears large, deep green leaves, cut off at the tips and with a deep lobe on each side; leaves become yellow in autumn. Cup-shaped, orange-based, greenish-white flowers appear in mid-summer.

♀***L. tulipifera*** illus. p.60.

♀**'Aureomarginatum'** illus. p.65.

LIRIOPE

Lilyturf

LILIACEAE/CONVALLARIACEAE

Genus of evergreen perennials with swollen, fleshy rhizomes. Some are grown as ground cover. Fully to frost hardy. Requires sun and well-drained soil. Propagate by division in spring or by seed in autumn.

***L. graminifolia* var. *densiflora*.** See *L. muscari*.

♀***L. muscari***, syn. *L. graminifolia* var. *densiflora*, *L. platyphylla*, illus. p.280. **'Majestic'** is an evergreen, spreading, rhizomatous perennial. **H** 30cm (12in), **S** 45cm (18in). Frost hardy. In late autumn, it produces spikes of thickly clustered, rounded-bell-shaped, violet flowers among linear, glossy, green leaves.

L. platyphylla. See *L. muscari*.

L. spicata. Evergreen, spreading, rhizomatous perennial. **H** 30cm (12in), **S** 30–40cm (12–16in). Fully hardy. Grass-like, glossy, dark green leaves make good ground cover. Produces spikes of rounded-bell-shaped, pale lavender flowers in late summer.

Lisianthus russellianus. See *Eustoma grandiflorum*.

LITHOCARPUS

FAGACEAE

Genus of evergreen trees, grown for their foliage. Frost hardy. Needs sun or semi-shade. Prefers well-drained, neutral to acid soil. Shelter from strong winds. Propagate by seed, when ripe, in autumn.

L. densiflorus (Tanbark oak). Evergreen, spreading tree. **H** and **S** 10m (30ft). Has sweet chestnut-like, leathery, glossy, dark green leaves and upright, pale yellow flower spikes borne in spring and often again in autumn.

L. henryi illus. p.93.

LITHODORA

BORAGINACEAE

Genus of evergreen sub-shrubs and shrubs, grown for their flowers. Is excellent in rock gardens. Fully to frost hardy. Needs full sun and moist, well-drained soil; some species are limestone haters and require acid conditions. Resents root disturbance. Propagate by semi-ripe cuttings in mid-summer or by seed in autumn.

L. diffusa, syn. *Lithospermum diffusum*. ♀**'Grace Ward'** is an evergreen, compact, semi-prostrate shrub. **H** 15–30cm (6–12in), **S** to 30cm (12in). Frost hardy. Trailing stems bear lance-shaped, hairy, dull green leaves. In early summer bears masses of funnel-shaped, deep blue flowers in terminal clusters. Needs acid soil. Plants should be trimmed back after flowering. ♀**'Heavenly Blue'** illus. p.343.

♀***L. oleifolia***, syn. *Lithospermum oleifolium*, illus. p.342.

L. zahnii, syn. *Lithospermum zahnii*. Evergreen, much-branched, upright shrub. **H** and **S** 30cm (12in) or more. Frost hardy. Stems are covered in oval, hairy, dark green or greyish-green leaves. Funnel-shaped, azure-blue flowers, with spreading lobes, open in succession from early spring to mid-summer. Sets buds and flowers intermittently until mid-autumn. Prefers alkaline soil.

LITHOPHRAGMA

SAXIFRAGACEAE

Genus of tuberous perennials, grown for their campion-like flowers. Is dormant in summer. Fully hardy. Tolerates all but deepest shade and prefers humus-rich, moist soil. Propagate by seed or division in spring or autumn.

L. parviflorum illus. p.332.

LITHOPS

Living stones, Stone plant

AIZOACEAE

Genus of prostrate, egg-shaped, perennial succulents, with almost united pairs of swollen, erect leaves that are separated on upper surface by a fissure from which a daisy-like flower emerges. Each pair of old leaves splits and dries away to papery skin in spring to reveal a pair of new leaves growing at right angles to old ones. Slowly forms clumps after 3–5 years. Frost tender, min. 5°C (41°F). Needs full sun and extremely well-drained soil or gritty compost. Water regularly in growing season (mid-summer to early autumn), not at all in winter. Propagate by seed in spring or summer.

♀***L. aucampiae.*** Egg-shaped, perennial succulent. **H** 1cm (½in), **S** 3cm (1¼in). Pairs of brown leaves have flat, upper surfaces bearing darker marks. Produces a yellow flower in late summer or early autumn.

L. bella. See *L. karasmontana* subsp. *bella*.

♀***L. bromfieldii.*** Egg-shaped, perennial succulent. **H** 2–3cm (¾–1¼in), **S** 2cm (¾in). Slightly convex, upper surfaces of paired, brown leaves have dark green windows and red dots and lines. Produces a yellow flower in late summer or early autumn.

L. dorotheae illus. p.491.

L. fulleri. Egg-shaped, perennial succulent. **H** and **S** 2cm (¾in). Pairs of leaves are dove-grey to brown-yellow. Convex, upper surfaces have sunken, darker marks. In late summer or early autumn bears a white flower.

♀***L. hookeri.*** See *L. turbiniformis*.

L. julii. Egg-shaped, perennial succulent.**H** 2–3cm (¾–1¼in), **S** 5cm (2in). Has paired, pearl- to pink-grey leaves, each with a slightly convex, darker-marked, upper surface. In late summer or autumn produces a white flower.

♀***L. karasmontana*** illus. p.481. **subsp. *bella***, syn. *L. bella*, is an egg-shaped, perennial succulent. **H** 2–3cm (¾–1¼in), **S** 1.5cm (⅝in). Has pairs of brown to brown-yellow leaves with darker marks on convex, upper surfaces. Produces a white flower in late summer or early autumn.

♀***L. lesliei.*** Egg-shaped, perennial succulent. **H** 1cm (½in), **S** 2cm (¾in). Is similar to *L. aucampiae*, but upper leaf surfaces are convex. **var. *albinica*** illus. p.491.

L. marmorata illus. p.489.

♀***L. olivacea.*** Egg-shaped, perennial succulent. **H** and **S** 2cm (¾in). Paired, dark olive-green leaves have darker windows on convex, upper surfaces. Yellow flower appears in late summer or early autumn.

L. otzeniana. Egg-shaped, perennial succulent. **H** 3cm (1¼in), **S** 2cm (¾in). Paired, grey-violet leaves each have a convex, upper surface with a light border and large, semi-translucent windows. In late summer or early autumn bears a yellow flower.

♀***L. pseudotruncatella.*** Egg-shaped, perennial succulent. **H** 3cm (1¼in), **S** 4cm (1½in). Bears pairs of pale grey or blue to lilac leaves with darker marks on convex, upper surfaces. Fissure reaches from side to side only on mature plants. Has a yellow flower in late summer or early autumn. **subsp. *dendritica*** illus. p.495.

♀***L. schwantesii*** illus. p.495.

L. turbiniformis. Syn. *L. hookeri*. Egg-shaped, perennial succulent. **H** 4cm (1½in), **S** 2cm (¾in). Has a flattish, upper surface with, usually, sunken, dark brown marks on paired, brown leaves. Has yellow flower in late summer or early autumn.

Lithospermum diffusum. See *Lithodora diffusa*.

Lithospermum oleifolium. See *Lithodora oleifolia*.

Lithospermum zahnii. See *Lithodora zahnii*.

Litsia glauca. See *Neolitsia sericea*.

LITTONIA

LILIACEAE/COLCHICACEAE

Genus of deciduous, perennial, scandent, tuberous climbers, grown for their pendent, bell-shaped flowers in summer. Frost tender, min. 8–16°C (46–61°F). Requires full sun and rich, well-drained soil. Provide support. Dies down in winter; lift and dry off tubers and store in a frost-free place. Propagate by seed in spring; tubers sometimes will divide naturally.

L. modesta illus. p.395.

LIVISTONA

PALMAE/ARECACEAE

Genus of evergreen palms, grown for their overall appearance. Has clusters of insignificant flowers in summer. Frost tender, min. 7°C (45°F). Needs full light or partial shade and fertile, well-drained soil, ideally neutral to acid. Water potted specimens moderately, less in winter. Propagate by seed in spring at not less than 23°C (73°F). Red spider mite may be a nuisance on containerized plants.

L. australis (Australian cabbage palm, Gippsland fountain palm). Slow-growing, evergreen palm with a fairly slender trunk. **H** 15–20m (50–70ft), **S** 3–6m (10–20ft). Has fan-shaped leaves, 1.2–2.5m (4–8ft) wide, divided into narrow, slender-pointed, glossy, green leaflets. Leaf stalks are spiny.

♀***L. chinensis*** illus. p.451.

LLOYDIA

LILIACEAE

Genus of summer-flowering bulbs, grown for their small, graceful, bell-shaped flowers. Fully to half hardy. Is not easy to grow. Requires partial shade and well-drained, peaty soil; provide plenty of moisture in summer but, preferably, keep fairly dry in winter. Propagate by seed in spring.

L. graeca. See *Gagea graeca*.

L. serotina. Early summer-flowering bulb. **H** 5–15cm (2–6in), **S** 2.5–5cm (1–2in). Fully hardy. Has wiry stems bearing scattered, threadlike, semi-erect leaves near stem base. Carries 1 or 2 bell-shaped, white flowers, 1–1.5cm (½–⅝in) long, with purple or purple-red veins.

LOBELIA

CAMPANULACEAE

Genus of annuals, perennials and deciduous or evergreen shrubs, grown for their flowers. Some are suitable for wild gardens or by the waterside. Fully hardy to frost tender, min. 5°C (41°F). Prefers sun and moist but well-drained soil. Resents wet conditions in winter; in cold areas some perennials and shrubs are therefore best lifted in autumn and placed in well-drained compost in frames. Propagate annuals by seed in spring,

perennial species by seed or division in spring, perennial cultivars by division only, and shrubs by semi-ripe cuttings in summer. ⓘContact with the milky sap of some species may irritate skin.
L. angulata, syn. *Pratia angulata*. Evergreen, creeping perennial. **H** 1cm (½in), **S** indefinite. Frost hardy. Bears small, broadly oval, dark green leaves. Star-shaped, white flowers, with 5 unevenly spaced petals, are carried in leaf axils in late spring and are followed by globose, purplish-red fruits in autumn.
♀ **L. cardinalis,** syn. *L. fulgens, L. splendens* (Cardinal flower), illus. p.439. ♀**'Queen Victoria'** illus. p.248.
L. 'Cherry Ripe' illus. p.439.
L. 'Dark Crusader'. Clump-forming perennial. **H** 1m (3ft), **S** 23cm (9in). Half hardy. From mid- to late summer bears racemes of 2-lipped, dark red flowers above lance-shaped, fresh green or red-bronze leaves.
L. erinus 'Blue Cascade'. Slow-growing, pendulous, spreading annual, occasionally perennial. **H** 10–20cm (4–8in), **S** 10–15cm (4–6in). Half hardy. Oval to lance-shaped leaves are pale green. Small, 2-lipped, pale blue flowers are produced continuously in summer and early autumn. ♀**'Cambridge Blue'** is compact and has blue flowers. ♀**'Colour Cascade'** has flowers in a mixture of colours, such as blue, red, pink, mauve or white. ♀**'Crystal Palace'** illus. p.315. **'Red Cascade'** produces white-eyed, purple-red flowers. **'Sapphire'** illus. p.314. **Waterfall Series 'Waterfall Blue'** illus. p.314. **Waterfall Series 'Waterfall Light Lavender'** illus. p.311.
L. fulgens. See *L. cardinalis*.
L. x gerardii 'Vedrariensis'. See *L. x speciosa* 'Vedrariensis'.
L. pedunculata, syn. *Pratia pendunculata*. **'County Park'** is a vigorous, evergreen, creeping perennial. **H** 1cm (½in), **S** indefinite. Frost hardy. Has small, rounded to oval leaves and, in summer, a profusion of star-shaped, rich violet-blue flowers. Makes good ground cover.
L. siphilitica illus. p.441.
L. x speciosa 'Vedrariensis', syn. *L. x gerardii* 'Vedrariensis', *L.* 'Vedrariensis'. Clump-forming perennial. **H** 1m (3ft), **S** 30cm (1ft). Frost hardy. In late summer produces racemes of 2-lipped, purple flowers. Has lance-shaped, dark green leaves.
L. splendens. See *L. cardinalis*.
L. tupa. Clump-forming perennial. **H** 1.5–2m (5–6ft), **S** 1m (3ft). Half hardy. Bears large spikes of 2-lipped, vivid brick-red flowers in late summer, above narrowly oval, hairy, light green leaves. Performs best in a sheltered, sunny site with well-drained soil.
L. 'Vedrariensis'. See *L. x speciosa* 'Vedrariensis'.
L. 'Will Scarlet'. Clump-forming perennial. **H** 1m (3ft), **S** 30cm (1ft). Frost hardy. Racemes of 2-lipped, bright red flowers are borne in summer. Lance-shaped leaves are coppery-green.

Lobivia aurea. See *Echinopsis aurea*.
Lobivia backebergii.
See *Echinopsis bachebergii*.
Lobivia cinnabarina.
See *Echinopsis cinnabarina*.
Lobivia cylindrica.
See *Echinopsis aurea*.
Lobivia haageana.
See *Echinopsis marsoneri*.
Lobivia pentlandii.
See *Echinopsis pentlandii*.
Lobivia pygmaea.
See *Rebutia pygmaea*.
Lobivia shaferi. See *Echinopsis aurea*.
Lobivia silvestrii.
See *Echinopsis chamaecereus*.

LOBULARIA

CRUCIFERAE/BRASSICACEAE

Genus of summer- and early autumn-flowering annuals. Fully hardy. Grow in sun and in fertile, well-drained soil. Dead-head to encourage continuous flowering. Ideal for containers and edging. Propagate by seed sown under glass in spring, or outdoors in late spring. May self-seed.
L. maritima, syn. *Alyssum maritimum* (Sweet alyssum). Fast-growing, spreading annual. **H** 8–15cm (3–6in), **S** 20–30cm (8–12in). Has lance-shaped, greyish-green leaves. Rounded heads of tiny, scented, 4-petalled, white flowers are produced in summer and early autumn. **'Carpet of Snow',** **H** to 10cm (4in), **S** 20–30cm (8–12in), is a ground-hugging, mound-forming annual with narrow leaves and heads of tiny, 4-petalled, white flowers summer–autumn. ♀ **'Rosie O' Day'** illus. p.304. **'Snow Crystals'** illus. p.298.

LOISELEURIA

ERICACEAE

Genus of one species of evergreen, creeping, prostrate shrub, grown for its flowers. Fully hardy. Requires full light and humus-rich, well-drained, acid soil. Is difficult to grow. Propagate by seed in spring or by softwood or semi-ripe cuttings in summer.
L. procumbens (Alpine azalea, Trailing azalea) illus. p.364.

LOMATIA

PROTEACEAE

Genus of evergreen shrubs and trees, grown for their foliage and flowers, which have 4 narrow, twisted petals. Frost hardy, but in cold areas needs shelter from strong winds. Requires sun or semi-shade and moist but well-drained, acid soil. Propagate by softwood or semi-ripe cuttings in summer.
L. ferruginea. Evergreen, upright shrub or tree. **H** 10m (30ft), **S** 5m (15ft). Stout, brown-felted shoots bear oblong to oval, dark green leaves, deeply cut into 6–15 oblong lobes. Racemes of yellow-and-red flowers are borne in mid-summer. Thrives outside only in mild, moist areas.
L. silaifolia illus. p.151.

LONICERA

Honeysuckle

CAPRIFOLIACEAE

Genus of deciduous, semi-evergreen or evergreen shrubs and woody-stemmed, twining climbers, grown mainly for their flowers, which are often fragrant. Flowers are tubular, with spreading, 2-lipped petal lobes. Climbers may be trained into large shrubs. Fully hardy to frost tender, min. 5°C (41°F). Grows in any fertile, well-drained soil in sun or semi-shade. Prune out flowered wood of climbers after flowering. Prune shrubs only to remove dead shoots or restrain growth. Propagate by seed in autumn or spring, by semi-ripe cuttings in summer or by hardwood cuttings in late autumn. Aphids may be a problem. The berries may cause mild stomach upset if ingested. See also feature panel p.207.
L. x americana, syn. *L. x italica* of gardens, illus. p.206.
L. x brownii (Scarlet trumpet honeysuckle). **'Dropmore Scarlet'** is a deciduous, woody-stemmed, twining climber. **H** to 4m (12ft). Frost hardy. Has oval, blue-green leaves. Small, fragrant, red flowers with orange throats are borne throughout summer.
L. etrusca (Etruscan honeysuckle). Deciduous or semi-evergreen, woody-stemmed, twining climber. **H** to 4m (12ft). Half hardy. Oval, mid-green leaves are blue-green beneath, the upper ones united into cups. Fragrant, long-tubed, pale yellow flowers, borne in summer–autumn, turn deeper yellow and become red-flushed with age. Grow in sun. **'Michael Rosse'** (illus. p. 207) has glaucous leaves and pale yellow flowers that deepen in colour as they mature. ♀ **'Superba'** (illus. p. 207) is very vigorous and has red-flushed young shoots and bright red and white flowers that turn orange-yellow as they age.
L. fragrantissima. Deciduous or semi-evergreen, bushy, spreading shrub. **H** 2m (6ft), **S** 4m (12ft). Fully hardy. Bears oval, dark green leaves. Fragrant, short-tubed, creamy-white flowers open in winter and early spring.
L. 'Gold Flame'. See *L. x heckrottii* 'Gold Flame'.
L. x heckrottii. Deciduous or semi-evergreen, twining climber. **H** 5m (15ft). Fully hardy. Oval, dark green leaves are blue-green beneath, the upper pairs united. Bears terminal whorls of fragrant, pink flowers, orange-yellow inside, in summer, sometimes followed by red berries. **'Gold Flame'** (syn. *L.* 'Gold Flame') is deciduous and requires support. Frost hardy. Has oblong or oval leaves, bluish beneath, upper ones joined into shallow cups. Scented, orange-throated, pink flowers appear in clusters in summer.
L. henryi (illus. p.207). Evergreen or semi-evergreen, woody-stemmed, twining climber. **H** to 10m (30ft). Frost hardy. Narrowly oval, dark green leaves are paler beneath. Terminal clusters of long-tubed, red-purple flowers appear in summer–autumn, followed by black berries.
L. hildebrandiana (Giant Burmese honeysuckle). Evergreen or semi-evergreen, woody-stemmed, twining climber. **H** to 20m (70ft). Frost tender. Oval or rounded, mid-green leaves are paler beneath. Long-tubed, white or cream flowers, ageing to creamy-orange or brownish-yellow, appear in pairs in leaf axils or at shoot tips in summer. Grow in full sun.
L. x italica of gardens. See *L. x americana*.
L. japonica (Japanese honeysuckle). Vigorous, evergreen or semi-evergreen, twining climber. **H** to 10m (30ft). Fully hardy. Has soft-hairy, woody stems and ovate, sometimes lobed, dark green leaves. Throughout summer and early autumn produces fragrant, long-tubed, 2-lipped, white flowers that turn yellow as they mature. Is ideal for hiding an unsightly fence, shed or wall and also good as ground cover although requires control if space is limited. **'Aureoreticulata'** (illus. p.207) has bright green leaves with bright yellow veining. ♀ **'Halliana'** is fully hardy and has very fragrant, white flowers, ageing to pale yellow, in summer and autumn.
L. ledebourii illus. p.136.
L. maackii. Vigorous, deciduous, bushy shrub. **H** and **S** 5m (15ft). Fully hardy. Leaves are oval and dark green. Fragrant, short-tubed, white, later yellow flowers, in early summer, are followed by spherical, bright red fruits.
L. morrowii. Deciduous, spreading shrub with arching branches. **H** 2m (6ft), **S** 3m (10ft). Fully hardy. Has oval, dark green leaves and, in late spring and early summer, small, short-tubed, creamy-white flowers that age to yellow.
L. nitida. Evergreen, bushy, dense shrub. **H** 2m (6ft), **S** 3m (10ft). Fully hardy. Leaves are small, oval, glossy and dark green. Tiny, fragrant, short-tubed, creamy-white flowers appear in late spring and are followed by small, spherical, purple fruits. Is good for hedging. ♀**'Baggesen's Gold'** illus. p.167. **'Yunnan'** is more upright, has stouter shoots and larger leaves and flowers more freely.
L. periclymenum (Common honeysuckle, Woodbine). Vigorous, deciduous, twining or scrambling climber. **H** 6–7m (20–22ft). Fully hardy. Has ovate to oblong, mid-green leaves, greyish-green beneath. From early summer to early autumn produces terminal clusters of very fragrant, long-tubed, 2-lipped, purple-red and/or yellow flowers, with creamy-white to white insides. ♀**'Graham Thomas'** is a deciduous, woody-stemmed, twining climber. H to 7m (23ft). Fully hardy. Has oval or oblong leaves that are bluish beneath. Fragrant, white flowers, which age to yellow, appear in summer. ♀**'Red Gables'** (illus. p.207). ♀**'Serotina'** (Late Dutch honeysuckle); illus. p.207) has rich red-purple flowers, white inside. **'Sweet Sue'** bears very fragrant, creamy-white flowers that mature to yellow.
L. pileata illus. p.167.
L. x purpusii illus. p.163. ♀**'Winter Beauty'** has red-purple shoots and freely bears very fragrant, white flowers on bare, leaf-less stems.
♀**L. sempervirens** (Coral honeysuckle; illus. p.207). Evergreen or deciduous, woody-stemmed, twining climber. **H** to 4m (12ft). Frost hardy. Has oval leaves, upper ones united and saucer like, and salmon-red to orange flowers, yellow inside, in whorls on shoot tips in summer.
L. standishii. Evergreen, bushy shrub. **H** and **S** 2m (6ft). Fully hardy. Has peeling bark, oblong, bristly, dark green leaves and, in winter, fragrant, short-tubed, creamy-white flowers.

L. tatarica illus. p.133. **'Hack's Red'** is a deciduous, bushy shrub. **H** and **S** 2.5m (8ft). Fully hardy. Produces short-tubed, deep pink flowers in late spring and early summer, followed by spherical, red fruits. Leaves are oval and dark green.
L.* x *tellmanniana. Deciduous, woody-stemmed, twining climber. **H** to 5m (15ft). Frost hardy. Has oval leaves; the upper ones are joined and resemble saucers. The bright yellow-orange flowers are carried in clusters.
♀***L. tragophylla.*** Deciduous, woody-stemmed, twining climber. **H** 5–6m (15–20ft). Frost hardy. Oval leaves are bluish-green, the uppermost pair united into a cup. Produces clusters of up to 20 long-tubed, bright yellow flowers in early summer.
***L.* x *xylosteoides* 'Clavey's Dwarf'.** Deciduous, upright, dense shrub. **H** 2m (6ft), **S** 1m (3ft). Fully hardy. Leaves are oval and grey-green. Bears short-tubed, pink flowers in late spring, then spherical, red fruits.
L. xylosteum illus. p.131.

Lophocereus schottii. See *Pachycereus schottii.*

LOPHOMYRTUS

MYRTACEAE

Genus of evergreen shrubs or small trees, grown for their flowers, foliage and fruit. Frost to half hardy. Needs partial shade and fertile, humus-rich, moist but well-drained soil. Propagate by seed sown as soon as ripe or by semi-ripe cuttings in summer.
L. bullata, syn. *Myrtus bullata.* Evergreen, upright shrub. **H** 5m (15ft), **S** 3m (10ft). Half hardy. Rounded, puckered leaves, bronze-purple when young, mature to gloss, dark green. Produces saucer-shaped, white flowers in late spring and early summer, then egg-shaped, black-red fruits.

LOPHOPHORA

Peyote

CACTACEAE

Genus of very slow-growing, perennial cacti that resemble small, blue dumplings, with up to 10 ribs, each separated by an indented line. Has long tap roots. Flowering areoles each produce tufts of short, white hairs. Frost tender, min. 5–10°C (41–50°F). Needs sun and well-drained soil. Is very prone to rotting, so water lightly from spring to autumn. Propagate by seed in spring or summer.
L. echinata. See *L. williamsii.*
L. lutea. See *L. williamsii.*
L. williamsii, syn. *L. echinata, L. lutea,* illus. p.492.

LOPHOSPERMUM

SCROPHULARIACEAE

Genus of deciduous and evergreen, perennial climbers and shrubs. Has triangular to rounded leaves and tubular to funnel-shaped flowers. Half hardy to frost tender, min. 5°C (41°F). Needs sun and moist but well-drained soil. Propagate by seed in spring or semi-ripe cuttings in late summer.
♀***L. erubescens***, syn. *Asarina erubescens, Maurandya erubescens,* illus. p.460.

LOPHOSTEMON

MYRTACEAE

Genus of evergreen trees and shrubs, grown for their overall appearance when mature and for shade. Is related to *Tristania* and *Eucalyptus.* Half hardy to frost tender, min. 3–5°C (37–41°F). Needs sun or partial shade and fertile, well-drained soil. Other than shaping plants in winter, pruning is seldom necessary. Propagate by seed in spring or by semi-ripe cuttings in summer.
L. confertus, syn. *Tristania conferta.* (Brisbane box, Brush-box tree). Fast-growing, evergreen, round-headed tree. **H** and **S** 15–40m (50–130ft). Frost tender. Produces lance-shaped, leathery, lustrous leaves. In spring bears white flowers with prominent, feathery stamen bundles. **'Perth Gold'** has bright green leaves strongly variegated yellow.

LOROPETALUM

HAMAMELIDACEAE

Genus of evergreen shrubs, grown for their flowers. Half hardy, but needs min. 5°C (41°F) to flower well. Requires full light or semi-shade and rich, well-drained, neutral to acid soil. Water containerized plants freely when in full growth, moderately at other times. Propagate by layering or seed in spring or by semi-ripe cuttings in late summer.
L. chinense. Evergreen, rounded, well-branched shrub. **H** and **S** 1.2m (4ft). Asymmetrically oval leaves are deep green. White flowers, each with 4 strap-shaped petals, are borne in tufted, terminal clusters, mainly in winter–spring.

LOTUS

LEGUMINOSAE/PAPILIONACEAE

Genus of summer-flowering perennials, some of which are semi-evergreen, and evergreen sub-shrubs, grown for their foliage and flowers. Fully hardy to frost tender, min. 5°C (41°F). Prefers sun and well-drained soil. Propagate by softwood cuttings from early to mid-summer or by seed in autumn or spring.
♀***L. berthelotii*** illus. p.306.
♀***L. hirsutus***, syn. *Dorycnium hirsutum.* Deciduous, upright sub-shrub. **H** and **S** 60cm (24in). Bears silver-grey leaves with 3 oval leaflets. Dense clusters of pea-like, pink-tinged, white flowers in summer and early autumn are followed by oblong to ovoid, reddish-brown seed pods.

LUCULIA

RUBIACEAE

Genus of evergreen shrubs, grown for their flowers and foliage. Frost tender, min. 5–10°C (41–50°F). Needs full light or partial shade and fertile, well-drained soil. Water potted specimens freely when in full growth, moderately at other times. Cut back flowered stems hard in spring, if container-grown. Propagate by seed in spring or by semi-ripe cuttings in summer.
L. grandifolia. Evergreen, rounded to upright, robust shrub. **H** and **S** 3–6m (10–20ft). Min. 5°C (41°F). Oval, green leaves have red veins and stalks. Fragrant, tubular, white flowers, each 6cm (2½in) long, with 5 rounded petal lobes, appear in terminal clusters in summer.

LUETKEA

ROSACEAE

Genus of one species of deciduous sub-shrub, grown for its fluffy flower heads. Is suitable for banks and rock gardens. Fully hardy. Requires shade and well-drained but not too dry soil. Propagate by division or seed in spring.
L. pectinata. Deciduous, spreading, decumbent sub-shrub. **H** to 30cm (12in), **S** 20cm (8in). Stems are clothed in finely dissected, very dark green leaves. In summer has terminal racemes of small, fluffy, off-white flower heads.

LUMA

MYRTACEAE

Genus of evergreen shrubs and small trees, grown for their aromatic leaves and cup-shaped, white flowers. Frost hardy. Grow in full sun or partial shade and fertile, ideally humus-rich, well-drained soil. Propagate by seed in spring or by semi-ripe cuttings in late summer. See also feature panel p.78.
♀***L. apiculata***, syn. *Amomyrtus luma, Myrceugenia apiculata, Myrtus apiculata, M. luma* (illus. p.78). Strong-growing, evergreen shrub. **H** and **S** 10–15m (30–50ft). Has peeling, golden-brown and grey-white bark and cup-shaped flowers amid aromatic leaves in summer–autumn.
♀**'Glanleam Gold'**, **H** and **S** 10m (30ft), has stout stems, peeling, brown-and-white bark and oval, bright green leaves edged with creamy-yellow. Slightly fragrant flowers are borne from mid-summer to mid-autumn.
L. chequen, syn. *Myrtus chequen.* Strong growing upright-shrub or small tree. **H** 6m (20ft), **S** 5m (15ft). Frost hardy. Has broadly ovate, wavy-margined, aromatic, dark green leaves. In late summer and early autumn bears cup-shaped white flowers singly or in small clusters followed by black berries.

LUNARIA

Honesty

CRUCIFERAE/BRASSIACEAE

Genus of biennials and perennials, grown for their flowers and silvery seed pods. Fully hardy. Will grow in sun or shade, but prefers partial shade and well-drained soil. Propagate perennials by seed in autumn or spring, or by division in spring, biennials by seed only. Self-seeds prolifically.
L. annua, syn. *L. biennis*, illus. p.310. **'Variegata'** illus. p.306.
L. biennis. See *L. annua.*
L. rediviva. Rosette-forming perennial. **H** 60–75cm (24–30in), **S** 30cm (12in). Produces racemes of 4-petalled, lilac or white flowers in spring, followed by elliptical, silvery seed pods that are useful for indoor decoration. Has oval, coarse, often maroon-tinted, mid-green leaves.

LUPINUS

Lupin

LEGUMINOSAE/PAPILIONACEAE

Genus of annuals, perennials and semi-evergreen shrubs, grown for their large, imposing racemes of pea-like flowers. Fully to frost hardy. Prefers sun and well-drained soil. Remove seed heads of most varieties to prevent self-seeding. Propagate species by seed when fresh in autumn; selected forms by cuttings from non-flowering side-shoots in spring or early summer. ①The seeds may cause severe discomfort if ingested. Aphids can be a problem.
♀***L. arboreus*** illus. p.159.
♀***L.* Band of Nobles Series.** Clump-forming perennial. **H** to 1.5m (5ft), **S** 75cm (2½ft). Fully hardy. In early and mid-summer, racemes of flowers in white, yellow, pink, red, blue or bicolours (usually white or yellow in combination with another colour) arise above palmate, deeply divided, mid-green leaves.
***L.* 'My Castle'.** Clump-forming perennial. **H** 90cm (3ft), **S** 75cm (2½ft). Fully hardy. Bears racemes of deep rose-pink flowers above palmate, deeply divided, mid-green leaves in early and mid-summer.
***L.* 'Noble Maiden'.** Clump-forming perennial. **H** 90cm (3ft), **S** 75cm (2½ft). Fully hardy. In early and mid-summer, racemes of cream-white flowers rise above deeply divided, palmate, mid-green leaves.
***L.* 'The Chatelaine'** illus. p.232. ***L.* 'The Page'.** Clump-forming perennial. **H** 90–100cm (36–39in), **S** 75cm (30in). Fully hardy. Bears spikes of intense, deep red flowers above palmate, divided, basal mid-green leaves from early to mid-summer.

LURONIUM

ALISMATACEAE

Genus of deciduous, perennial, marginal water plants and marsh plants, grown for their foliage and flowers. Fully hardy. Requires shallow water and full sun. Thin plants when overcrowded. Propagate in spring by seed or division.
L. natans, syn. *Alisma natans* (Floating water plantain). Deciduous, perennial, marginal water plant. **H** 2.5–5cm (1–2in), **S** 30cm (12in). Produces small, elliptic to lance-shaped, mid-green leaves and, in summer, small, 3-lobed, yellow-spotted, white flowers.

LUZULA

Woodrush

JUNCACEAE

See also GRASSES, BAMBOOS, RUSHES and SEDGES.
L. maxima. See *L. sylvatica.*
L. nivea illus. p.284.
L. sylvatica, syn. *L. maxima* (Greater woodrush). **'Hohe Tatra'** illus. p.288. **'Marginata'** (syn. *L.s.* 'Aureomarginata') is a slow-growing, evergreen, spreading, rhizomatous, perennial grass. **H** to 30cm (12in), **S** indefinite. Fully hardy. Produces thick tufts of broad, hairy-edged, mid-green leaves, with white margins. Leafy stems bear terminal, open, brown flower spikes in summer. Tolerates shade; suitable for woodland gardens.

LYCASTE

ORCHIDACEAE

See also ORCHIDS.
L. cruenta (illus. p.467). Vigorous, deciduous, epiphytic orchid for a cool greenhouse. **H** 30cm (12in). Fragrant, triangular, green-and-yellow flowers, 5cm (2in) across, are produced singly in spring. Has broadly oval, ribbed, soft leaves, to 30cm (12in) long. Grow in semi-shade during summer and avoid spraying, which can mark leaves.

LYCHNIS

CARYOPHYLLACEAE

Genus of summer-flowering annuals, biennials and perennials. Fully hardy. Require a wide of soil-types, from dry to wet, also sunny to partially shaded positions. Propagate by division or seed in autumn or spring.
***L.* 'Abbotswood Rose'.** See *L.* x *walkeri* 'Abbotswood Rose'.
L. alpina, syn. *Viscaria alpina* (Alpine catchfly). Tuft-forming perennial. **H** 5–15cm (2–6in), **S** 10–15cm (4–6in). Has dense tufts of thick, linear, deep green leaves. In summer, sticky stems each bear a rounded head of pale to deep pink or, rarely, white flowers with spreading, frilled petals. Suits a rock garden.
♀***L. chalcedonica*** illus. p.235.
L. coeli-rosa. See *Silene coeli-rosa*.
♀***L. coronaria*** illus. p.268.
♀***L. flos-jovis*** illus. p.265.
L.* x *haageana, syn. *L.* x *haagena*. Short-lived, clump-forming perennial. **H** 45cm (18in), **S** 30cm (12in). Produces clusters of large, 5-petalled, white, orange or red flowers in summer. Oval leaves are mid-green. Is best raised regularly from seed.
***L.* x *haagena*.** See *L.* x *haageana*.
***L. viscaria*.** Clump-forming perennial. **H** 30cm (12in), **S** 30–45cm (12–18in). From early to mid-summer, rather sticky, star-shaped, reddish-purple flowers are borne in dense clusters above narrowly oval to oblong, dark green leaves. Is suitable for the front of a border or a rock garden.
♀**'Splendens Plena'** illus. p.265.
♀***L.* x *walkeri* 'Abbotswood Rose'**, syn. *L.* 'Abbotswood Rose'. Neat, clump-forming perennial. **H** 30–38cm (12–15in), **S** 23cm (9in). Has oval, grey leaves and grey, branching stems that, from mid- to late summer, bear sprays of rounded, 5-petalled, bright rose-pink flowers.

LYCIANTHES

SOLANACEAE

A genus of half hardy perennials and shrubs grown for their attractive flowers, and sometimes also their coloured or variegated foliage. Commonly grown in containers for summer bedding, it can also be grown in borders. Min. 5–10°C (41–50°F). Requires a sunny position with moist, but not wet, fertile soil. Propagate by semi-ripe cuttings taken in summer or from seed sown in autumn or spring.
L. rantonnetii, syn. *Solanum rantonnetii, S. rantonnei* (Blue potato bush). **'Royal Robe'** illus. p.310.

LYCIUM

SOLANACEAE

Genus of deciduous shrubs, sometimes with long, scandent branches, grown for their habit, flowers and fruits. Is useful for poor, dry soil and coastal gardens. May be grown as a hedge. Fully hardy. Prefers full sun and not too rich, well-drained soil. Remove dead wood in winter and cut back to restrict growth if necessary. Cut back hedges hard in spring. Propagate by softwood cuttings in summer, by seed in autumn or by hardwood cuttings in winter.
L. barbarum, syn. *L. halimifolium* (Chinese box thorn, Duke of Argyll's tea-tree). Deciduous, arching, often spiny shrub. **H** 2.5m (8ft), **S** 5m (15ft). Funnel-shaped, purple or pink flowers in late spring and summer are followed by spherical, orange-red berries. Leaves are lance-shaped, bright green or grey-green.
***L. halimifolium*.** See *L. barbarum*.

LYCORIS

AMARYLLIDACEAE

Genus of late summer- and early autumn-flowering bulbs with showy flower heads on leafless stems. Frost hardy; in cool areas is best grown in pots or planted in greenhouse borders. Needs sun, well-drained soil and a warm period in summer to ripen bulbs so they flower. Provide regular liquid feed while in growth. After summer dormancy, water from early autumn until following summer, when foliage dies away. Propagate by seed when ripe or in spring or summer or by off-sets in late summer.
L. aurea (Golden spider lily). Late summer- and early autumn-flowering bulb. **H** 30–40cm (12–16in), **S** 10–15cm (4–6in). Produces a head of 5 or 6 bright yellow flowers that have narrow, reflexed petals, with very wavy margins, and conspicuous stamens. Strap-shaped, semi-erect, basal leaves appear after flowering.
L. radiata illus. p.410.
***L. squamigera*.** Late summer- or early autumn-flowering bulb. **H** 45–60cm (18–24in), **S** 10–15cm (4–6in). Carries a head of 6–8 fragrant, funnel-shaped, rose-pink flowers, 10cm (4in) long, with reflexed petal tips. Strap-shaped, semi-erect, basal leaves form after flowers.

LYGODIUM

SCHIZAEACEAE

Genus of deciduous or semi-evergreen, climbing ferns, usually with 2 kinds of fronds: vegetative and fertile. Half hardy to frost tender, min. 5°C (41°F). Needs shade or semi-shade and humus-rich, moist, peaty soil. Is best grown among shrubby plants that can provide support. Plants grown under glass in pots need support. Remove faded fronds regularly. Propagate by division in spring or by fresh spores in summer.
L. japonicum (Japanese climbing fern). Deciduous, climbing fern. **H** 2m (6ft), **S** indefinite. Frost tender. Mid-green, fronds consist of delicate, finger-shaped pinnae; fertile fronds are broader and 3–5 lobed, with a longer, terminal lobe.

LYONIA

ERICACEAE

Genus of deciduous, semi-evergreen or evergreen shrubs and trees, grown for their racemes of urn-shaped flowers. Fully hardy. Needs full or semi-shade and moist, peaty, acid soil. Propagate by semi-ripe cuttings in summer.
***L. ligustrina*.** Deciduous, bushy shrub. **H** and **S** 2m (6ft). Oval, dark green leaves set off dense racemes of globular urn-shaped, white flowers from mid- to late summer.
***L. ovalifolia*.** Deciduous or semi-evergreen, bushy shrub. **H** and **S** 2m (6ft). Produces red shoots and oval, dark green leaves. Racemes of urn-shaped, white flowers appear in late spring and early summer.

LYONOTHAMNUS

ROSACEAE

Genus of one species of evergreen tree, grown for its foliage and flowers. Frost hardy. Needs sun or semi-shade, a warm, sheltered position and fertile, well-drained soil. Propagate by softwood cuttings in summer or by seed in autumn.
L. floribundus (Catalina ironwood). Evergreen tree grown only in the form **subsp. *aspleniifolius*.** This slender tree, **H** 12m (40ft), **S** 6m (20ft), has rather stringy, reddish-brown bark and much divided, fern-like, dark green leaves. Large, flattened heads of 5-petalled, star-shaped white flowers are produced in early summer.

LYSICHITON

ARACEAE

Genus of deciduous, perennial, marginal water plants and bog plants, grown for their handsome spathes and very large, glossy foliage. Fully hardy. Prefers full sun, but tolerates semi-shade. Tolerates both still and running water. Propagate by seed sown when fresh, in late summer.
***L. americanum*.** See *L. americanus*.
♀***L. americanus***, syn. *L. americanum*, illus. p.444.
♀***L. camtschatcensis*** illus. p.434.

LYSIMACHIA

Loosestrife

PRIMULACEAE

Genus of summer-flowering annuals and perennials, suitable for the border or rock garden. Fully to half hardy. Prefers a sunny or semi-shaded position and moist but well-drained soil. Propagate by division in spring or by seed in autumn.
♀***L. clethroides*** illus. p.437.
***L. congestiflora* 'Outback Sunset'** illus. p.323.
***L. ephemerum*.** Neat, clump-forming perennial. **H** 1m (3ft), **S** 30cm (1ft). Fully hardy. Erect, terminal racemes of star-shaped, greyish-white flowers are borne on slender stems in summer, followed by light green seed heads. Lance-shaped leaves are leathery and glaucous.
***L. nummularia*.** ♀**'Aurea'** illus. p.372.
L. punctata illus. p.243.

LYSIONOTUS

GESNERIACEAE

Genus of evergreen, creeping, shrubby perennials, grown for their relatively large, tubular, inflated, white to pink flowers. Half hardy. Requires humus-rich, moist but well-drained soil in partial or full shade. Propagate by cuttings in summer or by seed in spring.
***L. pauciflorus*.** Evergreen, suckering, shrubby perennial. **H** 20–30cm (8–12in), **S** 50cm (20in). Erect, woody stems have ovate, toothed, rigid, leathery, dark green leaves, 2–3cm (¾–1¼in) long, and bear tubular, purple-striped, pale lilac flowers in summer–autumn.

LYTHRUM

Purple loosestrife

LYTHRACEAE

Genus of summer-flowering perennials that thrive by the waterside and in bog gardens. Fully hardy. Grows in full sun or semi-shade and in moist or wet soil. Propagate cultivars by division in spring, species by seed or division in spring or autumn. Some species have become noxious weeds in the USA.
♀***L. salicaria* 'Feuerkerze'**, syn. *L.s.* 'Firecandle', illus. p.234. **'Firecandle'** see *L.s.* 'Feuerkerze'. **'Robert'** is a clump-forming perennial. **H** 75cm (30in), **S** 45cm (18in). Produces racemes of 4-petalled, clear pink flowers from mid- to late summer. Leaves are mid-green and lance-shaped.
***L. virgatum* 'Rose Queen'.** Clump-forming perennial. **H** 1m (3ft), **S** 60cm (2ft). Racemes of 4-petalled, star-shaped, light pink flowers are produced from mid- to late summer above lance-shaped, hairless, mid-green leaves. **'The Rocket'**, **H** 1m (3ft), **S** 45cm (1½ft), carries slender spikes of rose-red flowers above mid-green foliage during summer. Good for a waterside or bog garden.

M

MAACKIA

LEGUMINOSAE/PAPILIONACEAE

Genus of deciduous, summer-flowering trees, grown for their foliage and flowers. Fully hardy. Requires full sun and fertile, well-drained soil. Propagate by seed in autumn.

M. amurensis illus. p.85

MACADAMIA

PROTEACEAE

Genus of evergreen trees, grown for their foliage and fruits. Frost tender, min. 10–13°C (50–55°F). Prefers full light, though some shade is tolerated. Provide humus-rich, moisture-retentive but well-drained soil. Water freely while in full growth, moderately at other times. Pruning is not usually necessary, but is tolerated in autumn. Propagate by seed when ripe, in autumn, or in spring.

M. integrifolia (Macadamia nut, Queensland nut). Spreading tree. **H** and **S** 15m (50ft). Has whorls of leathery, semi-glossy leaves and edible, brown nuts in autumn. Produces panicles of small, creamy-yellow flowers in spring.

MACFADYENA

SYN. DOXANTHA

BIGNONIACEAE

Genus of evergreen, woody-stemmed, tendril climbers, grown for their foxglove-like flowers. Frost tender, min. 5°C (41°F). Any fertile, well-drained soil is suitable with full light. Water regularly, less when not in full growth. Provide support for stems. Thin out crowded shoots after flowering or in spring. Propagate by semi-ripe cuttings in summer.

M. unguis-cati, syn. *Bignonia unguis-cati, Doxantha unguis-cati* (Cat's claw). Fast-growing, evergreen, woody-stemmed, tendril climber. **H** 8–10m (25–30ft). Leaves have 2 leaflets and a tendril. Has yellow flowers, 10cm (4in) long, in late spring or early summer.

MACKAYA

ACANTHACEAE

Genus of one species of evergreen shrub, grown for its flowers and overall appearance. Frost tender, min. 7–10°C (45–50°F). Requires full light or partial shade and fertile, well-drained soil. Water potted plants freely when in full growth, moderately at other times. Pruning is tolerated in winter if necessary. Propagate by greenwood cuttings in spring or by semi-ripe cuttings in summer.

♀***M. bella***, syn. *Asystasia bella*. Evergreen, erect, then spreading, well-branched shrub. **H** to 1.5m (5ft), **S** 1.2–1.5m (4–5ft). Leaves are oval, pointed, glossy and mid- to deep green. Has spikes of tubular, dark-veined, lavender flowers, each with 5 large, flared petal lobes, from spring to autumn. In warm conditions, above 13°C (55°F), will flower into winter.

MACLEANIA

ERICACEAE

Genus of evergreen, spring- to summer-flowering shrubs and scrambling climbers, grown primarily for their flowers. Frost tender, min. 10°C (50°F). Needs partial shade and humus-rich, freely draining, neutral to acid soil. Water potted specimens moderately, less when not in full growth. Long shoots may be shortened in winter or after flowering. Propagate by seed in spring, by semi-ripe cuttings in summer or by layering in autumn.

M. insignis. Evergreen, scrambling climber with erect, sparingly branched, wand-like stems. **H** 3m (10ft), **S** 1–3m (3–10ft). Has oval, leathery, deep green leaves, red-flushed when young. Tubular, waxy, scarlet flowers, with white tips, hang in clusters in summer. Needs support.

MACLEAYA

Plume poppy

PAPAVERACEAE

Genus of summer-flowering perennials, grown for their overall appearance. Fully hardy. Requires a position in sun and in well-drained soil. May spread rapidly. Propagate by division in early spring or by root cuttings in winter.

♀***M. cordata***, syn. *Bocconia cordata*. Spreading, clump-forming perennial. **H** 1.5m (5ft) or more, **S** 60cm (2ft) or more. Large, rounded, lobed, grey-green leaves, grey-white beneath, are produced at base of plant and up lower parts of stems. Large, feathery panicles of dainty, creamy-white flowers are produced in summer.

***M. microcarpa* 'Kelway's Coral Plume'.** See *M.m.* 'Kelway's Coral Plume'.

♀**'Kelway's Coral Plume'** (syn. *M.m.* 'Kelway's Coral Plume) illus. p.216.

MACLURA

MORACEAE

Genus of one species of deciduous tree, grown for its foliage and unusual fruits. Both male and female trees need to be planted to obtain fruits. Fully hardy, but young plants are susceptible to frost damage. Requires full sun and needs hot summers to thrive in cold areas. Grows in any but waterlogged soil. Propagate by softwood cuttings in summer, by seed in autumn or by root cuttings in late winter.

M. aurantiaca. See *M. pomifera*.

M. pomifera, syn. *M. aurantiaca* (Osage orange). Deciduous, rounded, spreading tree. **H** 15m (50ft), **S** 12m (40ft). Has spiny shoots and oval, dark green leaves that turn yellow in autumn. Tiny, cup-shaped, yellow flowers in summer are followed on female trees by large, rounded, wrinkled, pale green fruits.

M. tricuspidata, syn. *Cudrania tricuspidata*. Deciduous, spreading tree. **H** 7m (22ft), **S** 6m (20ft). Bears oval, dark green leaves that are sometimes 3-lobed. Produces small, rounded clusters of tiny, green flowers in mid-summer.

Macroplectrum sesquipedale. See *Angraecum sesquipedale*.

Macrotomia echioides. See *Arnebia pulchra*.

MACROZAMIA

ZAMIACEAE

Genus of slow-growing, evergreen shrubs and small trees, with or without trunks, grown for their palm-like appearance. Mature plants may produce conical, green flower spikes. Frost tender, min. 13–16°C (55–61°F). Needs full light or partial shade and well-drained soil. Water containerized plants moderately when in full growth, less at other times. Propagate by seed in spring.

M. corallipes. See *M. spiralis*.

M. spiralis, syn. *M. corallipes*. Evergreen, palm-like shrub with a very short, mainly underground trunk. **H** and **S** 60cm–1m (2–3ft). Has a rosette of deep green leaves, each with a spirally twisted mid-rib and very narrow, leathery leaflets.

MAGNOLIA

MAGNOLIACEAE

Genus of deciduous, semi-evergreen or evergreen trees and shrubs, grown for their showy, usually fragrant flowers. Leaves are mainly oval. Fully to half hardy. Flowers and buds of early-flowering magnolias may be damaged by late frosts. Needs sun or semi-shade and shelter from strong winds. Does best in fertile, well-drained soil. *M. delavayi, M. kobus, M. sieboldii* and *M. wilsonii* grow on chalky soil. Other species prefer neutral to acid soil, but will grow in alkaline soil if deep and humus-rich. Dry, sandy soils should be generously enriched with manure and leaf mould before planting. Propagate species by semi-ripe cuttings in summer or by seed, when ripe, in autumn, selected forms by semi-ripe cuttings in summer or by grafting in winter. See also feature pp.70–71.

M. acuminata (Cucumber tree). Vigorous, deciduous tree, conical when young, later spreading. **H** 20m (70ft), **S** 10m (30ft). Fully hardy. Has fragrant, cup-shaped, bluish-green flowers from early to mid-summer amid large, oval, pale green leaves, followed by small, egg-shaped, green, later red fruits.

♀ ***M.* 'Ann'** (illus. p.70). Deciduous, erect, multi-stemmed tree. **H** and **S** to 6m (20ft). Fully hardy. Has oval, deep green leaves. In spring produces an abundance of fragrant, narrowly goblet-shaped, rich pinkish-red flowers, to 20cm (8in) long.

***M.* Black Tulip ('Jurmag1')** (illus. p.70). Deciduous, densely branched tree. **H** to 12m (40ft), **S** 6m (20ft). Fully hardy. Has large, goblet-shaped, deep wine-red flowers, 20cm (8in) across or more, borne in early spring before the large, oval, mid-green leaves unfold.

***M. x brooklynenesis* 'Yellow Bird'** (illus. p.70). Deciduous, upright, slightly pyramidal tree. **H** 12m (40ft), 6m (20ft). Fully hardy. Has oval mid-green leaves. Goblet-shaped, dark yellow flowers, 10cm (4in) or more across, sometimes tinted green, are borne in spring.

***M.* 'Butterflies'** (illus. p.70). Deciduous, upright tree. H and S 3m (10ft). Fully hardy. Has oval, mid-green leaves. Goblet- to tulip-shaped, bright deep yellow flowers, 10cm (4in) across or more, are borne in mid-spring opening widely as they mature to reveal orange-red stamens.

M. campbellii. Deciduous tree, upright when young, later spreading. **H** 15m (50ft), **S** 10m (30ft). Frost hardy. Large, slightly fragrant, pale to deep pink flowers are borne on leafless branches from late winter to mid-spring on trees 15–20 years old or more. **'Charles Raffill'** bears large, fragrant, cup-shaped, purplish-pink flowers from late winter to mid-spring on trees at least 15 years old. Leaves are large, oval and mid-green. **'Darjeeling'** has large, very deep pink flowers. **'Kew's Surprise'** produces deep purplish-pink flowers. **subsp. *mollicomata*** (illus. p.70) has lilac-pink flowers slightly earlier in the year.

***M.* 'Charles Coates'.** Deciduous, rounded, open, spreading tree. **H** 19m (70ft), **S** 8m (25ft). Fully hardy. Extremely fragrant, creamy-white flowers with conspicuous, red stamens are produced in late spring and early summer amid large, light green leaves.

M. cylindrica. Deciduous, spreading tree or large shrub. **H** and **S** 5m (15ft). Fully hardy. Fragrant, upright, creamy-white flowers are produced in mid-spring, after which the young leaves turn dark green.

M. cylindrica of gardens. See *M.* 'Pegasus'.

M. dawsoniana. Deciduous tree or shrub, with a broadly oval head. **H** 15m (50ft), **S** 10m (30ft). Frost hardy. In early spring, large, fragrant, pendent, open cup-shaped, pale lilac-pink flowers are carried profusely on older plants (20 years from seed, 10 years from grafting). Leaves are oval, leathery and deep green.

M. delavayi. Evergreen, rounded, dense shrub or tree. **H** and **S** 10m (30ft). Frost hardy. Large, slightly fragrant, bowl-shaped, parchment-white flowers are short-lived and open intermittently from mid-summer to early autumn. Large, oval leaves are deep blue-green above and bluish-white beneath.

♀***M. denudata***, syn. *M. heptapeta* (Lily tree, Yulan). Deciduous, rounded, bushy shrub or spreading tree. **H** and **S** 10m (30ft). Fully hardy. Produces masses of fragrant, cup-shaped, white flowers from mid- to late spring before oval, mid-green leaves appear.

M. doltsopa. See *Michelia doltsopa*.

***M.* 'Elizabeth'** (illus. p.70). Small to medium-sized deciduous, multi-stemmed conical tree. **H** to 8m (25ft), **S** to 6m (20ft). Fully hardy. In spring produces cupped, fragrant, primrose-yellow flowers to 20cm (8in) across, with 6–9 petals and red stamens. Obovate, dark green leaves, 12–15cm (4–6in) long, are coppery in colour when they unfold in spring.

M. figo. See *Michelia figo*.

M. fraseri. Deciduous, spreading, open tree. **H** 10m (30ft), **S** 8m (25ft). Fully hardy. Fragrant white or pale yellow flowers open in late spring and early summer amid large, pale green leaves.

***M.* 'Galaxy'** (illus. p.70). Deciduous, conical to upright tree. **H** 6m (20ft), **S** 3m (10ft). Fully hardy. Large, slightly fragrant, narrowly goblet-shaped, pinkish-purple flowers, purple-red outside, open from deep purple buds in early spring before elliptic, mid-green leaves emerge.

M. globosa. Deciduous, bushy shrub. **H** and **S** 5m (15ft). Frost hardy. In early summer, large, oval, glossy, dark green leaves set off fragrant, cup-shaped, creamy-white flowers with red anthers.

M. grandiflora (Bull bay). Evergreen, broadly conical or rounded, dense tree. **H** and **S** 10m (30ft). Frost hardy. Bears large, very fragrant, bowl-shaped, white flowers intermittently from mid-summer to early autumn. Has oblong, glossy, mid- to dark green leaves. ♀**'Exmouth'** (illus. p.70) produces creamy-white flowers and narrow, leathery leaves. **'Ferruginea'** produces dark green leaves that are rust-brown beneath.

♀***M.* 'Heaven Scent'** illus. p.72.

M. heptapeta. See *M. denudata.*

M. hypoleuca. See *M. obovata.*

M. insignis. See *Manglietia insignis.*

***M.* x *kewensis* 'Wada's Memory'.** See *M. salicifolia* 'Wada's Memory'.

M. kobus. Deciduous, broadly conical tree. **H** 10m (30ft), **S** 8m (25ft). Fully hardy. Bears a profusion of fragrant, pure white flowers in mid-spring before small, slightly aromatic, dark green leaves appear.

M. liliiflora, syn. *M. quinquepeta.* Deciduous, bushy shrub. **H** 3m (10ft), **S** 4m (12ft). Fully hardy. Has fragrant, upright, vase-shaped, purplish-pink flowers that are borne amid oval, very dark green leaves from mid-spring to mid-summer. ♀**'Nigra'** (illus. p.70) has large, deep purple flowers.

♀***M.* x *loebneri* 'Leonard Messel'** (illus. p.70). Deciduous, upright shrub or small tree. **H** 8m (25ft), **S** 6m (20ft). Fully hardy. In mid-spring, fragrant flowers with many pale lilac-pink petals appear before and after oval, deep green leaves emerge. ♀**'Merrill'** has funnel-shaped, white flowers.

M. macrophylla. Deciduous, broadly upright tree, becoming rounded with age. **H** and **S** 10m (30ft). Frost hardy. Produces stout, blue-grey shoots and very large, oval, bright green leaves. Large, fragrant, bowl-shaped, parchment-white flowers are borne in early summer.

***M.* 'Manchu Fan'.** Vigorous, deciduous shrub or tree. **H** 6m (20ft), **S** 5m (15ft). Fully hardy. In late spring has large, goblet-shaped, creamy-white flowers with usually 9 petals, the inner ones flushed purple-pink at the base. Leaves are ovate.

***M.* 'Norman Gould'.** Deciduous, spreading tree or bushy shrub. **H** and **S** 5m (15ft). Fully hardy. Silky buds open into fragrant, star-shaped, white flowers in mid-spring. Leaves are oblong and dark green.

♀***M. obovata***, syn. *M. hypoleuca* (Japanese big-leaf magnolia). Vigorous, deciduous, upright tree. **H** 15m (50ft), **S** 10m (30ft). Fully hardy. Large, fragrant, pink-flushed, white or pale cream flowers with crimson stamens appear in early summer.

***M.* 'Pegasus'**, syn. *M. cylindrica* of gardens. Deciduous shrub or multi-stemmed tree, initially vase-shaped, later spreading. **H** and **S** 6m (20ft). Fully hardy. Has elliptic, dark green leaves, pale green beneath. In spring, before and with the young leaves, produces cup-shaped, creamy-white or yellowish-white flowers, suffused purplish-pink at the bases.

***M.* 'Pinkie'** illus. p.70. Deciduous shrub. **H** and **S** to 4m (12ft). Fully hardy. In spring produces cup-shaped, pale pinkish-purple flowers, 18cm (7in) across, with white inner surfaces, followed by ovate to elliptic mid-green leaves, to 15cm (6in) long.

M. quinquepeta. See *M. liliiflora.*

***M.* 'Ricki'.** Upright, deciduous shrub. **H** and **S** 4m (12ft). Fully hardy. Goblet-shaped flowers, each with 15 twisted petals that are pink to dark purple-pink at the bases, are produced from dark purple-pink buds in mid-spring. Leaves are broadly oval and mid-green.

♀***M. salicifolia*** (Willow-leaved magnolia). Deciduous, conical tree. **H** 10m (30ft), **S** 5m (15ft). Fully hardy. Has aromatic, oval leaves, mid-green above, grey-white beneath. Fragrant, pure white flowers open in mid-spring before foliage appears. ♀**'Wada's Memory'** (syn. *M.* x *kewensis* 'Wada's Memory') has dark green foliage and a profusion of large flowers borne from mid- to late spring.

M. sargentiana. Deciduous, broadly conical tree. **H** 15m (50ft), **S** 10m (30ft). Fully hardy. Large, fragrant, narrowly bowl-shaped, many-petalled flowers, white inside, purplish-pink outside, open from mid- to late spring, before oval, dark green leaves emerge.

♀***M. sieboldii.*** Deciduous, arching shrub or wide-spreading tree. **H** 8m (25ft), **S** 12m (40ft). Frost hardy. Fragrant, cup-shaped, white flowers, with crimson anthers, are carried above oval, dark green leaves from late spring to late summer. **subsp. *sinensis*** (syn. *M. sinensis*) has slightly larger, fully pendent flowers and more rounded, oval leaves.

M. sinensis. See. *M. sieboldii* subsp. *sinensis.*

***M.* x *soulangeana* 'Alba'** see *M.* x *s* 'Alba Superba'. **'Alba Superba'** (syn. *M.* x *s.* 'Alba') is a deciduous, rounded, spreading shrub or small tree. **H** and **S** 6m (20ft). Fully hardy. Bears large, fragrant, tulip-like, white flowers, faintly flushed with pink at the bases, from mid- to early spring, the first before mid- to dark green leaves emerge. ♀**'Brozzonii'**, **H** 8m (25ft), **S** 6m (20ft), is tree-like, with large, purple-flushed, white flowers. ♀**'Etienne Soulange-Bodin'** bears purple-flushed, white blooms. Flowers of ♀**'Lennei'** are large, goblet-shaped and deep rose-purple. ♀**'Lennei Alba'** has ivory-white blooms. **'Picture'**, **H** 8m (25ft), **S** 6m (20ft), is vigorous, compact and upright, with large, erect, deep reddish-purple flowers.**'Rubra'** of gardens see *M.* x *s.* 'Rustica Rubra'. ♀**'Rustica Rubra'** (syn. *M.* x *s.* 'Rubra' of gardens; illus. p.70), has purplish-red blooms suffused pink.

M. sprengeri. Deciduous, spreading tree. **H** 15m (50ft), **S** 10m (30ft). Frost hardy. In mid-spring has fragrant, bowl-shaped, white flowers sometimes fringed with red or pale pink, before oval, dark green leaves appear. **var. *diva***, (illus. p.70) is fully hardy and bears deep purplish-pink flowers, to 20cm (8in) across. **H** 17m (56ft), **S** 12m (40ft) **'Wakehurst'** has deep purplish-pink flowers.

♀***M. stellata*** (Star magnolia). Deciduous, bushy, dense shrub. **H** 3m (10ft), **S** 4m (12ft). Fully hardy. Fragrant, star-shaped flowers with many narrow petals open from silky buds during early to mid-spring. Leaves are narrow and deep green. **'Rosea'** (illus. p.70) has warm pink buds that open pale pink. ♀**'Waterlily'** (illus. p.70) has large, white flowers with many petals.

M. tripetala. Deciduous, spreading, open tree, conical when young. **H** 10m (30ft), **S** 8m (25ft). Fully hardy. Has large, dark green leaves, clustered about shoot tips, and rather unpleasantly scented, creamy-white flowers with narrow petals in late spring and early summer.

***M.* x *veitchii* 'Peter Veitch'.** Fast-growing, deciduous, spreading tree. **H** 20m (60ft), **S** 15m (52ft). Frost hardy. Produces large, fragrant, pale pink and white flowers in mid-spring, before dark green leaves emerge. Usually flowers within 10 years of planting.

M. virginiana (Sweet bay). Deciduous or semi-evergreen, conical shrub or tree. **H** 9m (28ft), **S** 6m (20ft). Fully hardy. Has very fragrant, cup-shaped, creamy-white flowers from early summer to early autumn. Oblong, glossy, mid- to dark green leaves are bluish-white beneath.

***M.* 'Vulcan'** (illus. p.70). Deciduous, open-branched tree. **H** 6m (20ft), **S** 4m (13ft). Fully hardy. Has oval, mid-green leaves. In spring bears large, cup- to goblet-shaped, erect, deep wine-red flowers, to 20cm (8in) across, with outward curved petals. Flowers from a young age.

M.* x *watsonii. See *M.* x *wieseneri.*

M.* x *wieseneri, syn. *M.* x *watsonii* (illus. p.70). Deciduous, spreading, open tree or shrub. **H** 8m (25ft), **S** 5m (15ft). Fully hardy. Rounded, white buds open in late spring to early summer to fragrant, creamy-white flowers, flushed pink outside and with crimson stamens.

♀***M. wilsonii.*** Deciduous, spreading tree or shrub. **H** 8m (25ft), **S** 7m (22ft). Frost hardy. In late spring and early summer, fragrant, cup-shaped, white flowers with crimson stamens hang from arching branches amid narrow, dark green leaves.

x MAHOBERBERIS

BERBERIDACEAE

Hybrid genus (*Berberis* x *Mahonia*) of evergreen shrubs, grown for their foliage, flowers and botanical interest. Fully hardy. Needs sun or semi-shade and fertile, well-drained soil. Propagate by semi-ripe cuttings in summer.

M. aquisargentii. Evergreen, upright, densely leaved shrub. **H** and **S** 2m (6ft). Leaves are bright green, often with 3 leaflets, some oblong and finely toothed, others holly-shaped. Terminal clusters of berberis-like, yellow flowers are sparsely produced in late spring.

MAHONIA

BERBERIDACEAE

Genus of evergreen shrubs, grown for their foliage, their usually short racemes of often fragrant, rounded, bell-shaped, yellow flowers and, with tall species and cultivars, for their deeply fissured bark. Large mahonias make good specimen plants; low-growing ones are excellent for ground cover. Fully to half hardy. Prefers shade or semi-shade and fertile, well-drained but not too dry soil. Propagate species by leaf-bud or semi-ripe cuttings in summer, or by seed in autumn, selected forms by leaf-bud or semi-ripe cuttings only.

M. acanthifolia. See *M. napaulensis.*

M. aquifolium illus. p.148.

M. bealei. See *M. japonica* Bealei Group.

***M.* 'Heterophylla'.** Evergreen, upright shrub. **H** 1m (3ft), **S** 1.5m (5ft). Frost hardy. Has reddish-purple shoots and glossy, bright green leaves, each composed of 5 or 7 narrowly lance-shaped, wavy-edged or curled leaflets that turn reddish-purple in winter. Small clusters of yellow flowers appear in spring.

♀***M. japonica*** illus. p.144. **Bealei Group** (syn. *M. bealei*). Bears blue-green leaves divided into broad leaflets and fragrant, pale yellow flowers in shorter, upright racemes.

♀***M. lomariifolia.*** Evergreen, very upright shrub. **H** 3m (10ft), **S** 2m (6ft). Frost hardy. Large, dark green leaves each have 19–37 narrow, holly-like, spiny leaflets. Fragrant, bright yellow flowers are produced in dense, upright racemes during late autumn and winter.

M.* x *media. ♀**'Buckland'** and **'Charity'** illus. p.118.

M. napaulensis, syn. *M. acanthifolia.* Evergreen, upright, open shrub. **H** 2.5m (8ft), **S** 3m (10ft). Frost hardy. Leaves are composed of up to 15 holly-like, spiny, dark green leaflets. Produces long, slender racemes of yellow flowers in early and mid-spring.

M. repens. Evergreen, upright shrub that spreads by underground stems. **H** 30cm (1ft), **S** 2m (6ft). Fully hardy. Blue-green leaves each consist of 3–7 oval leaflets, with bristle-like teeth. Dense clusters of deep yellow flowers are borne from mid- to late spring.

***M.* x *wagneri* 'Undulata'.** Evergreen, upright shrub. **H** and **S** 2m (6ft). Fully hardy. Glossy, dark green leaves each have 5–9 holly-like, wavy-edged leaflets that become bronzed in winter. Bears dense clusters of deep yellow flowers in mid- and late spring.

MAIANTHEMUM

May lily

LILIACEAE/CONVALLARIACEAE

Genus of perennials with extensive, spreading rhizomes. Is useful as ground cover in woodlands and wild areas. Fully hardy. Prefers shade and humus-rich, moist, sandy, neutral to acid soil. Propagate by seed in autumn or by division in any season.

M. bifolium illus. p.348.

M. canadense. Vigorous, ground-cover, rhizomatous perennial. **H** 10cm (4in), **S** indefinite. Has large, upright, oval, wavy-edged, glossy leaves. Slender stems bear sprays of small, white flowers in late spring and early summer followed by red berries.

M. racemosum. See *Smilacina racemosa.*

MAIHUENIA

CACTACEAE

Genus of slow-growing, summer-flowering, alpine cacti, clump-forming with age, with cylindrical stems. Fully to frost hardy. Requires sun and well-drained soil. Protect from winter rain. Propagate by seed or stem cuttings in spring or summer.
M. poeppigii illus. p.490.

MALCOLMIA

CRUCIFERAE/BRASSICACEAE

Genus of spring- to autumn-flowering annuals. Fully hardy. Grow in sun and in fertile, well-drained soil. Propagate by seed sown outdoors in spring, summer or early autumn. Self-seeds freely.
M. maritima illus. p.304.

MALEPHORA

AIZOACEAE

Genus of erect or spreading, perennial succulents with semi-cylindrical leaves. Frost tender, min. 5°C (41°F). Needs sun and very well-drained soil. Propagate by seed or stem cuttings in spring or summer.
M. crocea illus. p.496.

MALOPE

MALVACEAE

Genus of annuals, grown for their showy flowers that are ideal for cutting. Fully hardy. Grow in sun and in fertile, well-drained soil. Propagate by seed sown outdoors in spring. Self-seeds freely.
M. trifida illus. p.305.

MALUS

Crab apple

ROSACEAE

Genus of deciduous, mainly spring-flowering trees and shrubs, grown for their shallowly cup-shaped flowers, fruits, foliage or autumn colour. Crab apples may be used to make preserves. Fully hardy. Prefers full sun, but tolerates semi-shade; grows in any but waterlogged soil. In winter, cut out dead or diseased wood and prune to maintain a balanced branch system. Propagate by budding in late summer or by grafting in mid-winter. Trees are sometimes attacked by aphids, caterpillars and red spider mite, and are susceptible to fireblight and apple scab.
***M.* 'Almey'.** Deciduous, rounded tree. **H** and **S** 8m (25ft). Oval leaves are reddish-purple when young, maturing to dark green. Single, deep pink flowers, with paler pink, almost white centres, in late spring are followed by long-lasting, rounded, orange-red crab apples, which are subject to apple scab.
M.* x *arnoldiana illus. p.82.
***M.* x *atrosanguinea*.** Deciduous, spreading tree. **H** and **S** 6m (20ft). Produces oval, glossy, dark green leaves. Red flower buds open to single, rich pink blooms in late spring. Bears small, rounded, red-flushed, yellow crab apples.
M. baccata (Siberian crab). Deciduous, spreading tree. **H** and **S** 15m (50ft). Has oval, dark green leaves, a profusion of single, white flowers from mid- to late spring followed by tiny, rounded, red or yellow crab apples in autumn. **var. *mandschurica*** illus. p.69.
***M.* 'Chilko'.** Deciduous, spreading tree. **H** and **S** 8m (25ft). Oval, dark green leaves are reddish-purple when young. Has single, rose-pink flowers in mid-spring, followed by large, rounded, bright crimson crab apples.
***M. coronaria* 'Charlottae'**. Deciduous, spreading tree. **H** and **S** 9m (28ft). Broadly oval, lobed or deeply toothed leaves are dark green, turning red in autumn. Semi-double, pale pink flowers are borne in late spring and early summer.
***M.* 'Cowichan'** illus. p.90.
***M.* 'Dorothea'.** Deciduous, spreading tree. **H** and **S** 8m (25ft). Semi-double, silvery-pink flowers, red in bud, are borne in late spring, followed by rounded, yellow crab apples. Oval leaves are mid-green. Is subject to apple scab.
***M.* 'Eleyi'**, syn. *M.* x *purpurea* 'Eleyi'. Deciduous, spreading tree. **H** and **S** 8m (25ft). Oval leaves are dark reddish-purple when young, dark green when mature. Bears single, deep purplish-red flowers from mid- to late spring and rounded, purplish-red crab apples.
♀***M. floribunda*** illus. p.84.
***M.* 'Frettingham's Victoria'.** Deciduous, upright tree. **H** 8m (25ft), **S** 4m (12ft). Single, white flowers, borne amid oval, dark green leaves in late spring, are followed by rounded, red-flushed, yellow crab apples.
♀***M.* 'Golden Hornet'**, syn. *M.* x *zumi* 'Golden Hornet', illus. p.92.
***M.* x *hartwigii* 'Katherine'.** See *M.* 'Katherine'.
***M.* 'Hopa'.** Deciduous, spreading tree. **H** and **S** 10m (30ft). Oval, dark green leaves are reddish-purple when young. Single, deep pink flowers in mid-spring are succeeded by rounded, orange-and-red crab apples.
♀***M. hupehensis*** illus. p.69.
***M.* 'John Downie'** illus. p.91.
***M.* 'Katherine'**, syn. *M.* x *hartwigii* 'Katherine'. Deciduous, round-headed tree. **H** and **S** 6m (20ft). Has oval, mid-green leaves, large, double, pale pink flowers, fading to white, from mid- to late spring and tiny, rounded, yellow-flushed, red crab apples.
***M.* 'Lemoinei'**, syn. *M.* x *purpurea* 'Lemoinei', illus. p.84.
M.* x *magdeburgensis illus. p.83.
***M.* 'Marshall Oyama'** illus. p.90.
***M.* x *moerlandsii* 'Profusion'.** See *M.* 'Profusion'.
***M.* 'Neville Copeman'**, syn. *M.* x *purpurea* 'Neville Copeman'. Deciduous, spreading tree. **H** and **S** 9m (28ft). Oval, dark green leaves are purplish-red when young. Single, dark purplish-pink flowers, are borne from mid- to late spring; these are followed by rounded, orange-red to carmine crab apples.
M. niedzwetskyana, syn. *M. pumila* var. *niedzwetskyana*. Deciduous, spreading tree. **H** 6m (20ft), **S** 8m (25ft). Oval leaves are red when young, later purple. Produces clusters of single, deep reddish-purple flowers in late spring, then very large, conical, reddish-purple crab apples.
***M. prattii*.** Deciduous tree, upright when young, later spreading. **H** and **S** 10m (30ft). Oval, red-stalked, glossy, mid-green leaves become orange and red in autumn. Single, white flowers in late spring are followed by small, rounded or egg-shaped, white-flecked, red crab apples.
***M.* 'Professor Sprenger'** illus. p.91.
***M.* 'Profusion'**, syn. *M.* x *moerlandsii* 'Profusion', illus. p.71.
M. prunifolia illus. p.90.
***M. pumila* var. *niedzwetskyana*.** See *M. niedzwetskyana*.
M.* x *purpurea (Purple crab). Deciduous, spreading tree. **H** 8m (25ft), **S** 10m (30ft). Oval, young leaves are reddish, maturing to green. Single, deep ruby-red flowers, which become paler with age, are produced in late spring and are followed by rounded, reddish-purple crab apples. **'Eleyi'** see *M.* 'Eleyi'.**'Lemoinei'** see *M.* 'Lemoinei'. **'Neville Copeman'** see *M.* 'Neville Copeman'.
***M.* x *robusta*.** Vigorous, deciduous, spreading tree. **H** 12m (40ft), **S** 10m (30ft). Bears masses of single, white or pink flowers above oval, dark green leaves in late spring. These are followed by long-lasting, rounded, yellow or red crab apples. **'Yellow Siberian'** produces white flowers, which are sometimes pink-tinged, and yellow crab apples.
***M.* 'Royalty'** illus. p.84.
***M. sargentii*,** syn. *M. sieboldii, M. toringo* subsp. *sargentii*. (illus. p.110). Deciduous, spreading shrub with arching branches. **H** 4m (12ft), **S** 5m (15ft). Dark green leaves, often lobed, turn red or yellow in autumn. Bears white or pale to deep pink flowers in mid-spring followed by small, red or yellow fruits.
***M.* x *scheidekeri* 'Red Jade'**. Deciduous, weeping tree. **H** 4m (12ft), **S** 6m (20ft). In late spring has single, white flowers, sometimes pale pink-flushed, then long-lasting, rounded to egg-shaped, red crab apples. Leaves are dark green and oval.
***M. sieboldii*.** See *M. sargentii*.
***M.* 'Snowcloud'** illus. p.81.
***M. spectabilis*.** Deciduous, round-headed tree. **H** and **S** 10m (30ft). Has oval, dark green leaves, large, single, blush-pink flowers, rose-red in bud, from mid- to late spring and large, rounded, yellow crab apples.
M. toringo. See *M. sargentii*.
***M. toringoides*.** Deciduous, spreading tree. **H** 8m (25ft), **S** 10m (30ft). Oval, deeply lobed, glossy, bright green leaves turn yellow in autumn. Bears single, white flowers in late spring and rounded or egg-shaped, red-flushed, yellow crab apples in autumn.
♀***M. transitoria*.** Deciduous, spreading, elegant tree. **H** 8m (25ft), **S** 10m (30ft). Oval, deeply lobed, mid-green leaves turn yellow in autumn. Has masses of single, white flowers in late spring, followed by small, rounded, pale yellow crab apples.
***M. trilobata*.** Deciduous, conical tree. **H** 15m (50ft), **S** 7m (22ft). Has maple-like, lobed, glossy, bright green leaves that often become brightly coloured in autumn. Bears single, white flowers in early summer, followed by small, rounded or pear-shaped, red or yellow crab apples.
♀***M. tschonoskii*** illus. p.77.
***M.* 'Van Eseltine'.** Deciduous, upright tree. **H** 6m (20ft), **S** 4m (12ft). Bears double, pink flowers in late spring and rounded, yellow crab apples in autumn. Has oval, dark green leaves.
***M.* 'Veitch's Scarlet'** illus. p.89.
M. yunnanensis* var. *veitchii illus. p.86.
M.* x *zumi* var. *calocarpa, syn. *M.* x *z.* var. *calocarpa*. Deciduous, spreading tree. **H** 9m (28ft), **S** 8m (25ft). Dark green leaves are sometimes deeply lobed. White flowers in late spring are followed by dense clusters of long-lasting, cherry-like, red crab apples in autumn. **var. *calocarpa*** see *M.* x *z.* 'Calocarpa'. **'Golden Hornet'** see *M.* 'Golden Hornet'.

MALVA

Mallow

MALVACEAE

Genus of annuals, biennials and free-flowering, short-lived perennials. Fully hardy. Requires sun and fertile, well-drained soil. Propagate species by seed in autumn, selected forms by cuttings from firm, basal shoots in late spring or summer. These shoots may be encouraged by cutting plant back after first flowers have faded.
M. moschata illus. p.232.

***Malvastrum capensis*.** See *Anisodontea capensis*.

MALVAVISCUS

MALVACEAE

Genus of evergreen shrubs and trees, grown for their flowers. Frost tender, min. 13–16°C (55–61°F). Requires a position in full light and in fertile, well-drained soil. Water containerized plants freely during growing season, moderately at other times. To maintain shape, flowered stems may be cut back hard in late winter. Propagate by seed in spring or by semi-ripe cuttings in summer. Whitefly and red spider mite may be troublesome.
M. arboreus (Sleepy mallow). Vigorous, evergreen, rounded shrub. **H** to 4m (12ft) or more, **S** 1.5–3m (5–10ft). Serrated, bright green leaves are soft-haired. Has bright red flowers with protruding stamens in summer-autumn.

MAMMILLARIA

Pincushion cactus

CACTACEAE

Genus of hemispherical, spherical or columnar cacti, grown for their rings of funnel-shaped flowers that develop near crowns. Flowers, offsets and long, slender to spherical seed pods grow between tubercles on a spiny, green stem with extended areoles. Frost tender, min. 5–10°C (41–50°F). Requires full sun and very well-drained soil. Keep completely dry in winter, otherwise plants rot easily. Propagate by seed in spring or summer.
♀***M. bocasana*** illus. p.480.
***M. candida*.** See *Mammilloydia candida*
***M. centricirrha*.** See *M. magnimamma*.
***M. conoidea*.** See *Neolloydia conoidea*.
M. crinita of gardens. See *M. zeilmanniana*.
***M. densispina*.** Slow-growing, spherical, perennial cactus. **H** 10cm (4in), **S** 20cm

(8in). Min. 5°C (41°F). Has a green stem densely covered with stout, golden spines and, in spring, yellow flowers, 1–2cm (½–¾in) wide.
M. elegans of gardens. See *M. haageana.*
♀***M. elongata*** illus. p.494.
♀***M. geminispina*** illus. p.480.
M. gracilis. See *M. vetula* subsp. *gracilis.*
M. haageana, syn. *M. elegans* of gardens. Spherical to columnar, perennial cactus. **H** 30cm (12in), **S** 20cm (8in). Min. 5°C (41°F). Bears a green stem densely covered with short, bristly spines and bright red flowers, 1cm (½ in) across, in spring. Offsets occasionally.
♀***M. hahniana*** illus. p.479.
M. magnimamma, syn. *M. centricirrha.* Clump-forming, perennial cactus. **H** 30cm (1ft), **S** 60cm (2ft). Min. 5°C (41°F). Green stem has very pronounced, angular, dark green tubercles with white spines of variable length. Bears cream, pink or red flowers, 1–2cm (½–¾in) wide, in spring and possibly again in late summer.
M. microhelia illus. p.491.
♀***M. plumosa*** illus. p.483.
♀***M. prolifera*** (Strawberry cactus). Clump-forming, perennial cactus. **H** 10cm (4in), **S** 30cm (12in). Min 5°C (41°F). Green stem bears dense, golden to white spines. Produces masses of cream or yellow flowers, 1–2cm (½–¾in) wide, in summer, followed by edible red berries that taste like strawberries.
M. rhodantha. Spherical to columnar, perennial cactus. **H** and **S** 60cm (2ft). Min. 5°C (41°F). Green stem, branching from crown with age, is densely covered with brown to yellow spines, often curved. In late summer produces bright red flowers, 1–2cm (½–¾in) across.
M. schiedeana Clump-forming, perennial cactus. **H** 10cm (4in), **S** 30cm (12in). Min. 10°C (50°F). The green stem is covered with short, feathery, yellow spines that turn white. Produces cream flowers and narrow, red seed pods in late summer.
M. sempervivi illus. p.484.
M. vetula subsp. gracilis, syn. *M. gracilis.* Clump-forming, perennial cactus. **H** 5cm (2in), **S** 20cm (8in). Min. 5°C (41°F). Produces a columnar, green stem densely covered with pure white spines. In early summer carries pale cream flowers, 1–2cm (½–¾in) across. Stem is shallow-rooted and reroots readily. **var. *fragilis***, **H** 4cm (1½in), is more fragile and has off-white spines.
M. zeilmanniana, syn. *M. crinita,* illus. p.486.

MAMMILLOYDIA

CATACEAE

Genus of a single species of clump-forming cactus grown for ornamental spines and rings of small flowers. Frost tender, min. 5–10°C (41–50°F). Grow in well-drained soil in full sun. Keep dry in winter. Propagate by seed sown in spring.
♀***M. candida***, syn. *Mammillaria candida* (Snowball pincushion). Slow-growing, clump-forming, perennial cactus. **H** and **S** 15cm (6in). Min. 5°C (41°F). Columnar, green stem is densely covered with short, stiff, white spines. Produces cream to rose flowers, 1–2cm (½–¾in) across, in spring. Water sparingly in summer.

MANDEVILLA

SYN. DIPLADENIA

APOCYNACEAE

Genus of evergreen, semi-evergreen or deciduous, woody-stemmed, twining climbers, grown for their large, trumpet-shaped flowers. Half hardy to frost tender, min. 7–10°C (45–50°F). Grow in any well-drained soil, with light shade in summer. Water freely when in full growth, sparingly at other times. Provide support and thin out and spur back congested growth in early spring. Propagate by seed in spring or by semi-ripe cuttings in summer. Whitefly and red spider mite may cause problems. ⓘContact with the sap may cause skin irritation, and all parts may cause mild stomach upset if ingested.
***M.* x *amabilis* 'Alice du Pont'.** See *M.* x *amoena* 'Alice du Pont'.
***M.* x *amoena* 'Alice du Pont'**, syn. *M.* x *amabilis* 'Alice du Pont', illus. p.461.
M. boliviensis, syn. *Dipladenia boliviensis.* Vigorous, evergreen, woody-stemmed, twining climber. Frost tender. **H** to 4m (12ft). Oblong, pointed leaves are lustrous green. Has large, trumpet-shaped, white flowers with gold eyes in small clusters in summer.
M. laxa, syn. *M. suaveolens, M. tweediana* (Chilean jasmine). Fast-growing, deciduous or semi-evergreen, woody-stemmed, twining climber. **H** 5m (15ft) or more. Half hardy. Oval leaves have heart-shaped bases. Clusters of fragrant, white flowers are borne in summer.
M. splendens, syn. *Dipladenia splendens,* illus. p.460.
M. suaveolens. See *M. laxa.*
M. tweediana. See *M. laxa.*

MANDRAGORA

Mandrake

SOLANACEAE

Genus of rosetted perennials with large, deep, fleshy roots. Fully to frost hardy. Needs sun or partial shade and deep, humus-rich, well-drained soil. Resents being transplanted. Propagate by seed in autumn. ⓘAlkaloids in the plant may be harmful if ingested.
M. officinarum illus. p.356..

MANGLIETIA

MAGNOLIACEAE

Genus of evergreen trees, grown for their foliage and flowers. Half hardy, but is best at min. 3–5°C (37–41°F). Provide humus-rich, moisture-retentive but well-drained, acid soil and full light or partial shade. Water potted plants freely when in full growth, less at other times. Pruning is tolerated if necessary. Propagate by seed in spring.
M. insignis, syn. *Magnolia insignis.* Evergreen, broadly conical tree. **H** 8–12m (25–40ft) or more, **S** 3–5m (10–15ft) or more. Half hardy, min. 3–5°C (37–41°F). Leaves are narrowly oval, lustrous, dark green above, bluish-green beneath. In early summer produces solitary, magnolia-like, pink to carmine flowers that are cream-flushed.

MANETTIA

RUBIACEAE

Genus of evergreen, soft- or semi-woody-stemmed, twining climbers, grown for their small but showy flowers. Frost tender, min. 5°C (41°F), but 7–10°C (45–50°F) is preferred. Grow in any humus-rich, well-drained soil, with partial shade in summer. Water regularly, sparingly when temperatures are low. Stems need support. Cut back if required in spring. Propagate by softwood or semi-ripe cuttings in summer. Whitefly is sometimes a problem.
M. bicolor. See *M. luteorubra.*
M. cordifolia (Firecracker vine). Fast-growing, evergreen, soft-stemmed, twining climber. **H** 2m (6ft) or more. Has narrowly heart-shaped, glossy leaves. Funnel-shaped, red flowers, sometimes yellow flushed on the lobes, appear in small clusters in summer.
M. inflata. See *M. luteorubra.*
M. luteorubra, syn. *M. bicolor, M. inflata* (Brazilian firecracker). Fast-growing, evergreen, semi-woody-stemmed, twining climber. **H** 2m (6ft). Has glossy leaves and small, funnel-shaped, red flowers, with yellow tips, in spring–summer.

Manfreda maculosa. See *Agave maculosa.*
Manglietia. See. *Magnolia.*

MARANTA

MARANTACEAE

Genus of evergreen perennials, grown for their distinctively patterned, coloured foliage. Frost tender, min. 10–15°C (50–59°F). Needs constant, high humidity and a shaded position away from draughts or wind. Grow in humus-rich, well-drained soil. Propagate by division in spring or summer or by stem cuttings in summer.
M. leuconeura (Prayer plant). **'Erythroneura'** (syn. *M.l.* 'Erythrophylla') illus. p.475. **'Erythrophylla'.** See *M.l.* 'Erythroneura'. ♀**'Kerchoveana'** illus. p.475. **'Massangeana'** is an evergreen, short-stemmed perennial, branching at the base. **H** and **S** 30cm (1ft). Each oblong, velvety, dark green leaf, 15cm (6in) long, has a wide, irregular, pale midrib, white, lateral veins and often purplish-green below, stand upright at night but lie flat during the day. Bears small, 3-petalled, white to mauve flowers in slender, upright spikes year-round.

Marginatocereus marginatus. See *Pachycereus marginatus.*

MARGYRICARPUS

ROSACEAE

Genus of evergreen shrubs, grown for their fruits. Is good for rock gardens. Frost hardy. Needs a sheltered, sunny position and well-drained soil. Propagate by softwood cuttings in early summer or by seed in autumn.
M. pinnatus, syn. *M. setosus* (Pearl berry). Evergreen, prostrate shrub. **H** 23–30cm (9–12in), **S** 1m (3ft). Has dark green leaves divided into linear, silky leaflets. Has tiny, inconspicuous, green flowers in early summer, then small, globose, glossy, white fruits.
M. setosus. See *M. pinnatus.*

Marsdenia erecta. See *Cionura erecta.*

MARTYNIA

PEDALIACEAE

Genus of annuals, grown for their flowers and horned fruits. Half hardy. Requires a sunny, sheltered site and fertile, well-drained soil. Propagate by seed sown under glass in early spring.
M. annua illus. p.300.
M. louisianica. See *Proboscidea louisianica.*

MASDEVALLIA

ORCHIDACEAE

See also ORCHIDS.
M. coccinea (illus. p.466). Evergreen, epiphytic orchid for a cool greenhouse. **H** 15cm (6in). Narrowly oval leaves are 10cm (4in) long. Bears rich cerise flowers, 8cm (3in) long, in summer. Needs shade in summer.
M. infracta. Evergreen, epiphytic orchid for a cool greenhouse. **H** 15cm (6in). Narrowly oval leaves are 10cm (4in) long. Bears rounded, red- and-white flowers, 5cm (2in) long, with tail-like, greenish sepals, in summer. Needs shade from hot summer sun.
M. tovarensis (illus. p.466). Evergreen, epiphytic orchid for a cool greenhouse. **H** 15cm (6in). Has oval leaves, 10cm (4in) long, and in autumn milky-white flowers, 4cm (1½in) long, with short-tailed sepals, singly or up to 3 to a stem. Grow in shade in summer.
M. wageneriana (illus. p.466). Evergreen, epiphytic orchid for a cool greenhouse. **H** 8cm (3in). Narrowly oval leaves are 10cm (4in) long. Bears pale yellow flowers, 4cm (1½in) long, with long, tail-like sepals, singly or in pairs in summer. Needs summer shade.

MATHIASELLA

APIACEAE/UMBELLIFERAE

A genus of a single species.
***M. bupleuroides* 'Green Dream'** illus. p.242.

MATTEUCCIA

DRYOPTERIDACEAE/WOODSIACEAE

Genus of deciduous, rhizomatous ferns. Fully hardy. Prefers semi-shade and wet soil. Remove faded fronds regularly and divide plants when crowded. Propagate by division in autumn or winter.
M. orientalis. Deciduous, rhizomatous fern. **H** and **S** to 1m (3ft). Produces a "shuttlecock" of sterile, arching, broadly ovate, divided fronds, to 80cm (32in) long, light green when young, becoming darker. Fertile, erect, blackish-green fronds appear from the centre of the plant in summer.
♀***M. struthiopteris*** illus. p.443.

MATTHIOLA
Stock
CRUCIFERAE/BRASSICACEAE

Genus of annuals, biennials, perennials and evergreen sub-shrubs. Flowers of most annual or biennial stocks are highly scented and excellent for cutting. Fully hardy to frost tender, min. 4°C (39°F). Grow in sun or semi-shade and in fertile, well-drained, ideally lime-rich soil. Tall cultivars may need support. If grown as biennials outdoors, provide cloche protection during winter. To produce flowers outdoors the same summer, sow seed of annuals under glass in early spring, or outdoors in mid-spring. Sow seed of perennials under glass in spring. Propagate sub-shrubs by semi-ripe cuttings in summer. Is prone to aphids, flea beetle, club root, downy mildew and botrytis.
***M.* Brompton Group.** Fast-growing, erect, bushy biennial, grown as an annual. **H** 45cm (18in), **S** 30cm (12in). Fully hardy. Lance-shaped leaves are greyish-green; long spikes of highly scented flowers in shades of pink, red, purple, yellow or white are borne in summer.
***M.* East Lothian Group.** Group of fast-growing, upright, bushy biennials and short-lived perennials, grown as annuals. **H** and **S** 30cm (1ft). Fully hardy. Has lance-shaped, greyish-green leaves and, in summer, spikes, 15cm (6in) or more long, of scented, 4-petalled, single or double flowers, in shades of pink, red, purple, yellow or white.
***M.* 'Giant Excelsior'** illus. p.303.
***M.* 'Giant Imperial'.** Fast-growing, erect, bushy biennial, grown as an annual. **H** to 60cm (24in), **S** 30cm (12in). Fully hardy. Has lance-shaped, greyish-green leaves and long spikes of highly scented, white to creamy-yellow flowers in summer.
M. incana (Brompton stock). Fast-growing, upright, bushy biennial or short-lived perennial, grown as an annual. **H** 30–60cm (1–2ft), **S** 30cm (1ft). Fully hardy. Has lance-shaped, greyish-green leaves and, in summer, scented, 4-petalled, light purple flowers borne in spikes, 7–15cm (3–6in) long.
***M.* 'Mammoth Column'.** Fast-growing, upright, bushy biennial or short-lived perennial, grown as an annual. **H** to 75cm (2½ft), **S** 30cm (1ft). Fully hardy. Has lance-shaped, greyish-green leaves and, in summer, 30–38cm (12–15in) long spikes, of scented, 4-petalled flowers, available in mixed or single colours. Flowers are excellent for cutting.
***M.* Park Series.** Group of fast-growing, upright, bushy biennials and short-lived perennials, grown as annuals. **H** and **S** to 30cm (1ft). Fully hardy. Lance-shaped leaves are greyish-green. In summer, spikes, at least 15cm (6in) long, of scented, 4-petalled flowers are borne in a wide range of colours.
***M.* Ten-week Group.** Group of fast-growing, upright, bushy biennials and short-lived perennials, grown as annuals. **H** and **S** to 30cm (1ft). Fully hardy. Has lance-shaped, greyish-green leaves. Has scented, 4-petalled flowers, in spikes at least 15cm (6in) long, in a wide range of colours in summer. Dwarf and "selectable" cultivars have double flowers.
***M.* 'Trysomic'.** Fast-growing, upright, bushy biennial or short-lived perennial, grown as an annual. **H** and **S** to 30cm (1ft). Fully hardy. Lance-shaped leaves are greyish-green. Spikes, at least 15cm (6in) long, of scented, mostly double flowers are produced in a wide range of colours in summer.

MATUCANA
CACTACEAE

Genus of low-growing, spherical to shortly cylindrical, solitary to clustering perennial cacti, with thick, ribbed stems, often with some spines, usually branching from the base. Solitary, narrowly funnel-shaped yellow, orange or red flowers are produced around the stem tips in summer. Frost tender, min. 10°C (50°F). Needs full sun and very well-drained, slightly alkaline soil. Propagate by seed in spring or summer.
♀ ***M. aurantiaca***, syn. *Oreocereus aurantiacus*. Spherical, perennial cactus. **H** 12cm (5in), **S** 40cm (16in). Has a 15–17-ribbed stem and elongated areoles each bear up to 30 spines. Produces orange-yellow flowers in summer.
***M. haynei*.** Slow-growing, spherical to columnar, perennial cactus. **H** 60cm (24in), **S** 10cm (4in). Has a cylindrical, much-ribbed, grass-green stem densely covered with short, white or yellow spines. Has red, orange-brown or purple-crimson flowers in summer on plants over 15cm (6in) high.

MAURANDYA
SCROPHULARIACEAE

Genus of twining, woody-based, perennial climbers, grown against a wall or to clothe a trellis. Half hardy. Needs full sun and moderately fertile, moist but well-drained soil. Propagate by seed in spring, or softwood cuttings in late spring.
M. barclayana, syn. *Asarina barclayana*. Evergreen, soft-stemmed, scandent climber, herbaceous in cold climates. **H** to 2m (6ft). Has angular, heart-shaped, hairless leaves. Trumpet-shaped, white, pink or purple flowers, each with a green or whitish throat, 6–7cm (2½–3in) long, are produced in summer-autumn.
***M. erubescens*.** See *Lophospermum erubescens*.

***Maxillaria picta*.** See *Brasiliorchis picta*.
***Maxillaria porphyrostele*.** See *Brasiliorchis porphyrostele*.
***Maxillaria tenufolia*.** See *Maxillariella tnufolia*.

MAXILLARIELLA
ORCHIDACEAE

See also ORCHIDS.
♀***M. tenuifolia*,** syn. *Maxillaria tenuifolia*. Evergreen, epiphytic orchid for a cool greenhouse. **H** 15cm (6in). Fragrant, yellow flowers, 2.5cm (1in) across, heavily overlaid with red and with white lips, are borne singly throughout summer. Has narrowly oval leaves, 15cm (6in) long. Needs good light in summer.

MAYTENUS
CELASTRACEAE

Genus of evergreen trees, grown for their neat foliage. Frost hardy, but needs shelter from strong, cold winds when young. Requires sun or semi-shade and fertile, well-drained soil. Propagate by semi-ripe cuttings in summer or by suckers in autumn or spring.
M. boaria, syn. *M. chilensis* (Maiten). Evergreen, bushy-headed, elegant tree. **H** 10m (30ft), **S** 8m (25ft). Bears narrowly oval, glossy, dark green leaves on slender shoots, and tiny, star-shaped, green flowers in late spring.
***M. chilensis*.** See *M. boaria*.

MAZUS
SCROPHULARIACEAE

Genus of creeping, spring-flowering perennials. Is useful for rock gardens and in paving. Frost hardy. Needs a sheltered, sunny site and moist soil. Propagate by division in spring or by seed in autumn.
M. reptans illus. p.351.

MECONOPSIS
PAPAVERACEAE

Genus of perennials, some long-lived, some short-lived and others monocarpic (die after flowering), grown for their flowers. Fully hardy. Needs shade and, in warm areas, a cool position. Most prefer humus-rich, moist, neutral to acid soil. *M. baileyi* and *M.* 'Crewdson Hybrid' tolerate more alkaline oil. Propagate sterile perennial hybrids and perennial species by division in late summer or early spring. Propagate fertile species and hybrids (which set viable seed) by seed in late summer or in winter. Division of perennial species and cultivars is advisable every 3 years.
♀ ***M. baileyi***, syn. *M. betonicifolia* of gardens (Blue poppy). Clump-forming perennial. **H** 1–1.2m (3–4ft), **S** 45cm (1½ft). Bears clusters of cup-shaped, blue flowers in late spring and early summer. Oblong, hairy, mid-green leaves, with heart-shaped bases, are produced in basal rosettes and in decreasing size up flowering stems. **'Alba'** (illus. p.218), **H** 1.2–1.5m (4–5ft), **S** 45–60cm (1½–2ft), has pure white flowers in early summer.
***M. betonicifolia* of gardens**. See *M. baileyi*.
M. cambrica illus. p.263.
***M.* x *cookei* 'Old Rose'** (illus. p.218). Clump forming, long-lived perennial. **H** 45cm (18in), **S** 30cm. Produces numerous pendent, cup-shaped, deep pink flowers in late spring and early summer. Has basal rosettes of oval–oblong, bristly, mid-green leaves. Does not produce viable seed.
***M.* Fertile Blue Group 'Lingholm'** (illus. p.218). Clump-forming perennial. **H** 1.2–1.5m (4–5ft), **S** 45–60cm (1½–2ft). In early summer bears clusters of shallow cup-shaped, sky-blue flowers. Has rosettes of oblong to oval–lance-shaped, slightly toothed, hairy, mid-green leaves. Divide every 3 years to maintain vigour.
♀***M. grandis*** illus. p.218.
***M.* Infertile Blue Group 'Crewdson Hybrid'** (illus. p.218). Clump forming, long-lived perennial. **H** 1–1.2m (3–4ft), **S** 45–60cm (1½–2ft). In early summer bears clusters of funnel- to cup-shaped, clear deep blue flowers. Has rosettes of oblong, hairy, mid-green leaves with a brownish tinge and scalloped edges.
♀ ***M.* Infertile Blue Group 'Slieve Donard'** (illus. p.218). Clump forming, long-lived perennial. **H** 1.2–1.5m (4–5ft), **S** 45–60cm (1½–2ft). In early summer bears clusters of shallow cup-shaped, sky-blue flowers. Has rosettes of oblong to oval, hairy, mid-green leaves with marginal teeth absent or very few and tiny. Fertile seed is not produced.
M. integrifolia (Lampshade poppy). Rosette-forming biennial or short-lived perennial. **H** 45–60cm (18–24in), **S** 60cm (24in). Produces spikes of large, cup-shaped, pale yellow flowers in late spring and early summer. Has large, oval–oblong, hairy, pale green leaves.
***M.* 'Jimmy Bayne'** (George Sherriff Group) illus. p.218. Rhizomatous, long-lived perennial. **H** 1.2–1.5m (4–5ft), **S** 45–60cm (1½–2ft). In early summer bears clusters of shallowly bowl-shaped flowers, deep blue or with a purplish tinge. Has rosettes of oval–lance-shaped, hairy, mid-green leaves edged with rounded teeth.
***M.* 'Marit'** (illus. p.218). Clump forming, long-lived perennial. **H** 1.2–1.5m (4–5ft), **S** 45–60cm (1½–2ft). In early summer bears clusters of cup-shaped, white to pale creamy-white flowers. Has rosettes of oblong to lance-shaped, hairy, mid-green leaves with regular and neatly toothed edges. Divide every 3 years to maintain vigour. Seed is not produced.
***M. napaulensis* of gardens** (illus. p.218). Clump-forming, short-lived perennial that dies after flowering. **H** 1.5m (5ft), **S** 60cm (2ft). Produces racemes of nodding, shallowly cup-shaped, yellow, pink, red, or white flowers in late spring or early summer. Bears large rosettes of oblong to lance-shaped, deeply lobed and cut, hairy, yellowish-green leaves.
♀ ***M. quintuplinervia*** (Harebell poppy). Mat-forming perennial. **H** 30–45cm (12–18in), **S** 30cm (12in). Cup-shaped, nodding, lavender-blue flowers, deepening to purple at the bases, are carried singly on hairy stems in late spring and early summer above a dense mat of large, oblong to lance-shaped, mid-green leaves. Seed is notoriously difficult to germinate.

MEDICAGO
LEGUMINOSAE/PAPILIONACEAE

Genus of annuals, perennials and evergreen shrubs, grown for their flowers. Is good in mild, coastal areas as is very wind-resistant. Frost hardy, but in cold areas plant against a south- or west-facing wall. Requires sun and well-drained soil. Cut out dead wood in spring. Propagate shrubs by semi-ripe or softwood cuttings in summer or by seed in autumn or spring, annuals and perennials by seed in autumn or spring.
M. arborea (Moon trefoil, Tree medick). Evergreen, bushy, dense shrub. **H** and

S 2m (6ft). Bears clusters of small, pea-like, yellow flowers from mid-spring to late autumn or winter, followed by curious, flattened, snail-like, green, then brown seed pods. Has dark green leaves, each composed of 3 narrowly triangular leaflets, which are silky-haired when young.

MEDINILLA

MELASTOMATACEAE

Genus of evergreen shrubs and scrambling climbers, grown for their flowers and foliage. Frost tender, min. 16–18°C (61–4°F). Needs partial shade and humus-rich, well-drained soil. Water potted plants freely when in full growth, moderately at other times. Propagate by greenwood cuttings in spring or summer.
M. magnifica illus. p.455.

MEEHANIA

LABIATAE/LAMIACEAE

Genus of perennials often with creeping stems, grown mainly as ground cover. Frost hardy. Prefers shade and well-drained but not dry, humus-rich soil. May be propagated by seed, division or stem cuttings in spring.
M. urticifolia. Trailing, hairy perennial with long, creeping, leafy stems and erect flowering stems. **H** to 30cm (1ft), **S** indefinite. Oval to triangular, toothed leaves are 10cm (4in) or more long on the creeping stems – smaller on flowering stems. Whorls of fragrant, 2-lipped, purplish-blue flowers, to 5cm (2in) long, are carried in erect spikes in late spring.

Megasea. Reclassified as *Bergenia*.

MELALEUCA

MYRTACEAE

Genus of evergreen, spring- and summer-flowering trees and shrubs, grown for their flowers and overall appearance. Half hardy to frost tender, min. 4–7°C (39–45°F). Needs full light and well-drained soil, preferably without much nitrogen. Some species tolerate waterlogged soils. Water containerized specimens moderately, less in low temperatures. Propagate by seed in spring or by semi-ripe cuttings in summer.
M. armillaris (Bracelet honey myrtle). Evergreen, rounded, wiry-stemmed shrub or tree. **H** 3–6m (10–20ft), **S** 1.2–3m (4–10ft). Frost tender. Has needle-like, deep green leaves and, in summer, dense, bottlebrush-like clusters, 3–6cm (1¼–2½in) long, each flower consisting of a small brush of white stamens.
M. elliptica illus. p.137.
M. hypericifolia. Evergreen, rounded shrub. **H** and **S** 2–5m (6–15ft). Frost tender. Leaves are oblong to elliptic and mid- to deep green above, paler beneath. Crimson flowers, each composed of a 2–2.5cm (¾–1in) long brush of stamens of the same colour, are produced in summer, mainly in bottlebrush-like spikes, 4–8cm (1½–3in) long.
M. nesophila, syn. *M. nesophylla*, illus. p.133.
M. nesophylla. See *M. nesophila*.
M. quinquenervia. See *M. viridiflora* var. *rubriflora*.
M. squarrosa (Scented paper-bark). Evergreen, erect, wiry-stemmed shrub or tree. **H** 3–6m (10–20ft), **S** 2–4m (6–12ft). Frost tender. Has tiny, oval, deep green leaves. Bears 4cm (1½in) long spikes of scented flowers, each comprising a tiny brush of cream stamens, in late spring and summer.
M. viridiflora* var. *rubriflora, syn. *M. quinquenervia* (Paper-bark tree). Strong-growing, evergreen, rounded tree. **H** 6–12m (20–40ft), **S** 3–6m (10–20ft). Frost tender. Leaves are elliptic and lustrous. Has peeling, papery, tan-coloured bark and, in spring, small, white or creamy-pink flowers in bottlebrush-like clusters. Tolerates waterlogged soil.

MELASPHAERULA

IRIDACEAE

Genus of one species of spring-flowering corm, grown mainly for botanical interest. Half hardy. Needs sun and well-drained soil. Plant in autumn and keep watered until after flowering, then dry off. Propagate by seed or offsets in autumn.
M. graminea. See *M. ramosa*.
M. ramosa, syn. *M. graminea*. Spring-flowering corm. **H** to 60cm (24in), **S** 10–15cm (4–6in). Has narrowly sword-shaped, semi-erect leaves in a basal fan. Wiry, branched stem bears loose sprays of small, pendent, funnel-shaped, yellowish-green flowers with pointed petals.

MELASTOMA

MELASTOMATACEAE

Genus of evergreen, mainly summer-flowering shrubs and trees, grown for their flowers and foliage. Frost tender, min. 10–13°C (50–55°F). Requires full light or partial shade and fertile, well-drained soil. Water containerized specimens freely when in full growth, moderately at other times. Pruning is tolerated in late winter if necessary. Propagate by softwood or greenwood cuttings in spring or summer. Red spider mite and whitefly may cause problems.
M. candidum. Evergreen, rounded, bristly-stemmed shrub. **H** and **S** 1–2m (3–6ft). Bears oval, leathery, bristly leaves. Small, terminal clusters of fragrant, 5–7-petalled, white or pink flowers are produced profusely in summer.

MELIA

MELIACEAE

Genus of deciduous, spring-flowering trees, grown for their foliage, flowers and fruits. Is useful for very dry soil and does well in coastal gardens in mild areas. Frost hardy. Requires a position in full sun; grows in any well-drained soil. Propagate by seed in autumn.
M. azedarach illus. p.71.

MELIANTHUS

MELIANTHACEAE

Genus of evergreen perennials and shrubs, grown primarily for their foliage. Half hardy to frost tender, min. 5°C (41°F). Requires sun and fertile, well-drained soil. Water potted specimens freely in summer, moderately at other times. Long stems may be shortened in early spring. May be propagated by seed in spring or by greenwood cuttings in summer. Red spider mite may be troublesome.
♀ ***M. major*** illus. p.145.

MELICA

GRAMINEAE/POACEAE

See also GRASSES, BAMBOOS, RUSHES and SEDGES.
M. altissima (Siberian melic, Tall melic). Evergreen, tuft-forming, perennial grass. **H** 60cm (24in), **S** 20cm (8in). Fully hardy. Bears slender stems and broad, mid-green leaves, rough beneath. In summer, produces pendent, tawny spikelets in narrow panicles. **'Atropurpurea'** illus. p.286.

MELICYTUS,

SYN. HYMENANTHERA

VIOLACEAE

Genus of evergreen shrubs and trees, grown for their overall appearance and ornamental fruits. Fully hardy to frost tender, min. 3–5°C (37–41°F). Requires a position in full light or partial shade and in well-drained soil. Water pot plants moderately, less in winter. Pruning is tolerated if required. Propagate by seed when ripe, in autumn, or in spring.
M. crassifolius, syn. *Hymenanthera crassifolia*. Evergreen, densely twiggy shrub of irregular outline. **H** and **S** to 1.2m (4ft). Frost hardy. Bears narrowly oval to oblong, leathery, mid-green leaves. Carries tiny, bell-shaped, 5-petalled, yellow flowers in spring-summer, followed by egg-shaped, purple fruits.
M. ramiflorus (Mahoe, Whiteywood). Evergreen, spreading shrub or tree. **H** and **S** 6–10m (20–30ft). Frost tender. Bark is grey-white. Bears lance-shaped, bluntly serrated, bright green leaves. Small, rounded, greenish flowers are produced in axillary clusters in summer, followed by tiny, violet to purple-blue berries.

MELINIS

GRAMINEAE/POACEAE

See also GRASSES, BAMBOOS, RUSHES and SEDGES.
M. repens, syn. *Rhynchelytrum repens*, *R. roseum* (Natal grass, Ruby grass). Tuft-forming, annual or short-lived, perennial grass. **H** 1.2–2m (4–6ft), **S** 60cm–1m (2–3ft). Frost tender, min. 5°C (41°F). Leaves are mid-green, flat and finely pointed. Produces loose panicles of awned, pink spikelets in summer.

MELIOSMA

MELIOSMACEAE

Genus of deciduous trees and shrubs, grown for their habit, foliage and flowers, which, however, do not appear reliably. Frost hardy. Prefers full sun and deep, fertile, well-drained soil. Propagate by seed in autumn.
M. oldhamii. See *M. pinnata* var. *oldhamii*.
M. pinnata* var. *oldhamii, syn. *M. oldhamii*. Deciduous, stout-branched tree, upright when young, spreading when mature. **H** 10m (30ft), **S** 6m (20ft). Has very large, dark green leaves divided into 5–13 oval leaflets. Bears large clusters of small, fragrant, star-shaped, white flowers in early summer.
M. veitchiorum illus. p.74.

MELITTIS

Bastard balm

LABIATAE/LAMIACEAE

Genus of one species of summer-flowering perennial. Fully hardy. Does best in light shade and requires fertile, well-drained soil. Propagate by seed in autumn or by division in spring or autumn.
M. melissophyllum illus. p.264.

MELOCACTUS

Turk's cap

CACTACEAE

Genus of spherical, ribbed, perennial cacti. On reaching flowering size, usually 15cm (6in) high, stems produce woolly crowns; then stems appear to stop growing while woolly crowns develop into columns. Has funnel-shaped flowers in summer, followed by elongated or rounded, red, pink or white seed pods. Frost tender, min. 11–15°C (52–9°F). Requires a position in full sun and extremely well-drained soil. Propagate by seed in spring or summer.
M. actinacanthus. See *M. matanzanus*.
M. bahiensis. Spherical, perennial cactus. **H** and **S** 15cm (6in). Min. 15°C (59°F). Dull green stem bears 10–15 ribs. Produces stout, slightly curved, dark brown spines that become paler with age. Crown bears brown bristles and pink flowers, 1–2cm (½–¾in) across, in summer.
M. communis. See *M. intortus*.
M. curvispinus, syn. *M. oaxacensis*. Spherical to columnar, perennial cactus. **H** 20cm (8in), **S** 15cm (6in). Min. 15°C (59°F). Green stem has 15 rounded ribs. Areoles each bear a straight central spine and curved radial spines. Flat, woolly crown bears deep pink flowers, 1cm (½in) across, in summer.
M. intortus, syn. *M. communis*, illus. p.494.
M. matanzanus, syn. *M. actinacanthus*. Spherical, perennial cactus. **H** and **S** 10cm (4in). Min. 15°C (59°F). Dark green stem has neat, short spines and develops a woolly crown about 5 years from seed. In summer produces pink flowers, 1cm (½in) across.
M. oaxacensis. See *M. curvispinus*.

MENISPERMUM

Moonseed

MENISPERMACEAE

Genus of deciduous, woody or semi-woody, twining climbers, grown for their attractive fruits that each contain a crescent-shaped seed – hence the common name. Male and female flowers are carried on separate plants; to produce fruits, plants of both sexes must be grown. Frost hardy. Grow in sun and in any well-drained soil. Propagate by seed or suckers in spring. ⓘ The fruits may cause severe discomfort if ingested.

M. canadense (Canada moonseed, Yellow parilla). Vigorous, deciduous, woody-stemmed, twining climber, producing a dense tangle of stems and spreading by underground suckers. **H** to 5m (15ft). Oval to heart-shaped, rounded leaves are usually 3–7-lobed. Has small, cup-shaped, greenish-yellow flowers in summer, then poisonous, spherical, glossy, blackish fruits.

MENTHA

Mint

LABIATAE/LAMIACEAE

Genus of perennials, some of which are semi-evergreen, grown for their aromatic foliage, which is both decorative and used as a culinary herb. Plants are invasive, however, and should be used with caution. Fully to frost hardy. Grow in a sunny or shady position and in well-drained soil. Propagate by division in spring or autumn.

M. corsica. See *M. requienii.*

M. x gentilis 'Variegata'. See *M.* x *gracilis* 'Variegata'.

M. x gracilis 'Variegata', syn. *M.* x *gentilis* 'Variegata'. Spreading perennial. **H** 45cm (18in), **S** 60cm (24in). Fully hardy. Forms a mat of oval, dark green leaves that are speckled and striped with yellow, most conspicuously in full sun. Produces stems that carry whorls of small, 2-lipped, pale mauve flowers in summer.

M. x piperita f. citrata (Eau-de-Cologne mint) is a vigorous, spreading perennial. **H** 30–60cm (12–24in), **S** 60cm (24in). Fully hardy. Reddish-green stems, bearing terminal spikes of small, 2-lipped, purple flowers in summer, arise from a carpet of oval, slightly toothed, mid-green leaves that have a scent which is similar to *eau de Cologne*.

M. requienii, syn. *M. corsica* (Corsican mint). Semi-evergreen, mat-forming, creeping perennial. **H** to 1cm (½in), **S** indefinite. Frost hardy. When they are crushed, the rounded, bright apple-green leaves exude a strong peppermint fragrance. Carries tiny, stemless, lavender-purple flowers in summer. Is suitable for a rock garden or paved path. Needs shade and moist soil.

M. rotundifolia of gardens. See *M. suaveolens.*

M. suaveolens, syn. *M. rotundifolia* of gardens (Apple mint). **'Variegata'** illus. p.274.

MENTZELIA

LOASACEAE

Genus of annuals, perennials and evergreen shrubs. Fully hardy to frost tender, min. 4°C (39°F). Requires sun and fertile, very well-drained soil; tender species are best grown in pots under glass. Propagate by seed in spring; shrubs may also be propagated by semi-ripe cuttings in summer.

M. lindleyi, syn. *Bartonia aurea.* Fairly fast-growing, bushy annual. **H** 45cm (18in), **S** 20cm (8in). Fully hardy. Has fleshy stems and lance-shaped, serrated leaves. In summer, has fragrant, cup-shaped, deep yellow flowers, with conspicuous stamens.

MENYANTHES

MENYANTHACEAE

Genus of deciduous, perennial, marginal water plants, grown for their foliage and flowers. Fully hardy. Prefers an open, sunny position. Remove fading flower heads and foliage, and divide overcrowded clumps in spring. Propagate by stem cuttings in spring.

M. trifoliata illus. p.434.

MENZIESIA

ERICACEAE

Genus of deciduous shrubs, grown for their small, urn-shaped flowers. Fully hardy. Needs semi-shade and fertile, moist, peaty, acid soil. Propagate by softwood cuttings in summer or by seed in autumn.

M. ciliicalyx var. lasiophylla. See *M.c.* var. *purpurea.* **var. purpurea** (syn. *M.c.* var. *lasiophylla*) illus. p.146.

MERENDERA

LILIACEAE/COLCHICACEAE

Genus of corms similar to *Colchicum* but with less showy flowers. Fully to frost hardy. Needs a sunny position and well-drained soil. In cool, damp areas grow in an unheated greenhouse or frame where corms can dry out in summer. Plant in autumn and keep watered through winter and spring. Propagate by seed or offsets in autumn.

M. bulbocodium. See *M. montana.*

M. montana, syn. *M. bulbocodium.* Autumn-flowering corm. **H** to 5cm (2in), **S** 5–8cm (2–3in). Fully hardy. Has narrowly strap-shaped, semi-erect, basal leaves, produced just after upright, broad-petalled, funnel-shaped, rose- or purple-lilac flowers appear.

M. robusta. Spring-flowering corm. **H** 8cm (3in), **S** 5–8cm (2–3in). Frost hardy. Narrowly lance-shaped, semi-erect, basal leaves appear at the same time as upright, funnel-shaped flowers, 5–6cm (2–2½in) wide, with narrow, pale purplish-pink or white petals.

MERREMIA

CONVOLVULACEAE

Genus of evergreen, twining climbers, grown for their flowers and fruits. Frost tender, min. 7–10°C (45–50°F). Prefers fertile, well-drained soil and full light. Water moderately, much less when not in full growth. Provide support. Thin out congested stems during spring. Propagate by seed in spring. Red spider mite may be a problem.

M. tuberosa, syn. *Ipomoea tuberosa, Operculina tuberosa* (Wood rose, Yellow morning glory). Fast-growing, evergreen, twining climber. **H** 6m (20ft) or more. Leaves have 7 radiating lobes. In summer bears funnel-shaped, yellow flowers, followed by semi-woody, globose, ivory-brown fruits.

MERTENSIA

BORAGINACEAE

Genus of perennials, grown for their funnel-shaped flowers. Fully hardy. Requires sun or shade and deep, well-drained soil. Propagate by division in spring or by seed in autumn.

M. echioides. Clump-forming perennial. **H** 15–23cm (6–9in), **S** 15cm (6in). Has basal rosettes of long, oval, hairy, blue-green leaves. Slender stems carry many open funnel-shaped, dark blue flowers in summer.

M. maritima illus. p.356.

M. pulmonarioides. See *M. virginica.*

♀ **M. virginica**, syn. *M. pulmonarioides*, illus. p.261.

MERWILLA

HYACINTHACEAE/LILIACEAE

Genus of 3 half hardy bulbs grown for their spikes of blue flowers in summer. Grows in well-drained soil in full sun or semi-shade. Propagate by division when dormant or by seed in autumn.

M. plumbea, syn. *Scilla natalensis.* Clump-forming, summer-flowering bulb. **H** 30–45cm (12–18in), **S** 15–20cm (6–8in). Has lance-shaped, semi-erect, finely hairy basal leaves with a long spike of up to 100 flattish, blue flowers, each one 1.5–2cm (⅝–¾in) across.

MERYTA

ARALIACEAE

Genus of evergreen trees, grown for their handsome foliage. Frost tender, min. 5°C (41°F). Requires full light or partial shade and humus-rich, moisture-retentive but moderately drained soil. Water freely containerized plants in full growth, less at other times. Propagate by semi-ripe cuttings in summer or by seed when ripe in late summer.

M. sinclairii illus. p.451.

Mesembryanthemum cordifolium. See *Aptenia cordifolia.*

Mesembryanthemum criniflorum. See *Dorotheanthus bellidiformis.*

Mesembryanthemum multiradiatum. See *Lampranthus roseus.*

MESPILUS

Medlar

ROSACEAE

Genus of one species of deciduous tree or shrub, grown for its habit, flowers, foliage and edible fruits. Fully hardy. Requires sun or semi-shade and fertile, well-drained soil. Propagate species by seed in autumn and named forms (for fruit) by budding during late summer.

M. germanica illus. p.80.

METASEQUOIA

TAXODIACEAE

See also CONIFERS.

♀ **M. glyptostroboides** illus. p.96.

METROSIDEROS

MYRTACEAE

Genus of evergreen, winter-flowering shrubs, trees and scrambling climbers, grown for their flowers, the trees also for their overall appearance and for shade. Frost tender, min. 5°C (41°F). Grows in fertile, well-drained soil and in full light. Water freely containerized specimens in full growth, moderately at other times. Pruning is tolerated if necessary. Propagate by seed in spring or by semi-ripe cuttings in summer.

M. excelsa, syn. *M. tomentosa*, illus. p.450.

M. robusta (Rata). Robust, evergreen, rounded tree. **H** 20–25m (70–80ft) or more, **S** 10–15m (30–50ft). Oblong to elliptic, leathery leaves are dark green and lustrous. Has large clusters of flowers, which are mostly composed of long, dark red stamens, in winter.

M. tomentosa. See *M. excelsa.*

MEUM

UMBELLIFERAE/APIACEAE

Genus of summer-flowering perennials, grown for their aromatic leaves. Is useful on banks and in wild gardens. Fully hardy. Needs sun and well-drained soil. Propagate by seed when fresh, in autumn.

M. athamanticum (Baldmoney, Spignel). Upright, clump-forming perennial. **H** 15–45cm (6–18in), **S** 10–15cm (4–6in). Mainly basal and deeply dissected leaves have narrowly linear leaflets. In summer, has flattish flower heads consisting of clusters of tiny, white or purplish-white flowers.

MICHELIA

MAGNOLIACEAE

Genus of evergreen, winter- to summer-flowering shrubs and trees, grown for their flowers and foliage. Half hardy to frost tender, min. 5°C (41°F). Provide humus-rich, well-drained, neutral to acid soil and full light or partial shade. Water potted specimens freely when in full growth, less in winter. Pruning is seldom necessary. Propagate by semi-ripe cuttings in summer or by seed when ripe, in autumn, or in spring.

M. doltsopa, syn. *Magnolia doltsopa*, illus. p.71.

M. figo, syn. *Magnolia figo.* Evergreen tree or rounded shrub. **H** 3–6m (10–20ft), **S** 1.5–3.5 (5–11ft). Frost tender, min. 5°C (41°F). Has oval, glossy, rich green leaves and banana-scented, creamy-yellow flowers, edged maroon, in spring-summer.

MICROBIOTA

CUPRESSACEAE

See also CONIFERS.

♀ **M. decussata** (illus. p.105). Spreading, shrubby conifer. **H** 50cm (20in), **S** 2–3m (6–10ft). Fully hardy. Flat sprays of scale-like, yellow-green leaves turn bronze in winter. Globose, yellow-brown cones had only one seed.

Microglossa albescens. See *Aster albescens.*

MICROLEPIA

DENNSTAEDTIACEAE

Genus of deciduous, semi-evergreen or evergreen ferns, best grown in pans and hanging baskets. Frost tender, min. 5°C (41°F). Requires shade or semi-shade and moist soil. Remove faded fronds regularly. Propagate by division in spring or by spores in summer.
M. speluncae illus. p.478.

MICROMERIA

LABIATAE/LAMIACEAE

Genus of evergreen or semi-evergreen shrubs, subshrubs and perennials, suitable for rock gardens and banks. Frost hardy. Needs sun and well-drained soil. Propagate by seed in spring or by softwood cuttings in early summer.
M. juliana. Evergreen or semi-evergreen, bushy shrub or sub-shrub. **H** and **S** 30cm (12in). Produces small, oval, aromatic, green leaves pressed close to stems. In summer, minute, tubular, bright deep pink flowers are carried in whorls on upper parts of stems.

MIKANIA

COMPOSITAE/ASTERACEAE

Genus of evergreen or herbaceous, scrambling or twining climbers, shrubs and erect perennials, grown for their foliage and flower heads. Half hardy to frost tender, min. 7°C (45°F). Any fertile, well-drained soil is suitable, with partial shade in summer. Water regularly, less when not in full growth. Stem support is needed. Thin out congested growth in spring. Propagate by semi-ripe or softwood cuttings in summer. Aphids may be a problem.

M. scandens. Herbaceous, twining climber. **H** 3–5m (10–15ft). Half hardy. Oval to triangular, mid-green leaves have 2 basal lobes. Tiny, groundsel-like, pink to purple flower heads appear in compact clusters in summer-autumn.

MILIUM

GRAMINEAE/POACEAE

See also GRASSES, BAMBOOS, RUSHES and SEDGES.
M. effusum (Wood millet). **'Aureum'** is an evergreen, tuft-forming, perennial grass. **H** 1m (3ft), **S** 30cm (1ft). Fully hardy. Has flat, golden-yellow leaves. Produces open, tiered panicles of greenish-yellow spikelets in summer. Self seeds readily in shady sites.

MILLA

LILIACEAE/ALLIACEAE

Genus of summer-flowering bulbs, grown for their fragrant flowers, each comprising a slender tube with 6 spreading, star-shaped petals at the tip. Half hardy. Needs a sheltered, sunny position and well-drained soil. Plant in spring. After flowering lift bulbs and partially dry off for winter. Propagate by seed or offsets in spring.
M. biflora. Summer-flowering bulb. **H** 30–45cm (12–18in), **S** 8–10cm (3–4in). Has long, narrow, semi-erect, basal leaves. Stem bears a loose head of 2–6 erect, white flowers, 3–6cm (1¼–2½in) across, each on a slender stalk to 20cm (8in) long.

MILTONIA

ORCHIDACEAE

See also ORCHIDS.
M. candida. Evergreen, epiphytic orchid for a cool or intermediate greenhouse. **H** 20cm (8in). Cream-lipped, green-patterned, brown flowers, 5cm (2in) across, are borne in spikes in autumn. Has narrowly oval leaves, 10–12cm (4–5in) long. Grow in semi-shade in summer.
M. clowesii. Evergreen, epiphytic orchid for an intermediate greenhouse. **H** 20cm (8in). In early summer produces large spikes of 4cm (1½in) wide, yellow flowers, barred with reddish-brown and each with a white-and-mauve lip. Has broadly oval leaves, 30cm (12in) long. Grow in semi-shade in summer.

MILTONIOPSIS

Pansy orchid

ORCHIDACEAE

See also ORCHIDS.
***M.* Anjou gx 'St Patrick'** (illus. p.467). Evergreen, epiphytic orchid for a cool greenhouse. **H** 15cm (6in). Has sprays of deep crimson flowers, 10cm (4in) across, with red and yellow patterns on each lip, mainly in summer. Narrowly oval, soft leaves are 10–12cm (4–5in) long. Needs shade in summer.
***M.* Robert Strauss gx 'Ardingly'** (illus. p.466). Evergreen, epiphytic orchid for a cool greenhouse. **H** 15cm (6in). Bears sprays of white flowers, 10cm (4in) across, marked reddish-brown and purple; flowering season varies. Narrowly oval, soft leaves are 10–12cm (4–5in) long. Requires shade in summer.

MIMOSA

LEGUMINOSAE/MIMOSACEAE

Genus of annuals, evergreen perennials, shrubs, trees and scrambling climbers, cultivated for their flowers and foliage. *M. pudica* is usually grown as an annual. Frost tender, min. 13–16°C (55–61°F). Needs partial shade and fertile, well-drained soil. Water potted specimens freely when in full growth, moderately at other times. Propagate by seed in spring, shrubs also by semi-ripe cuttings in summer. Red spider mite may be a nuisance.
M. pudica illus. p.457.

MIMULUS

Monkey musk

SCROPHULARIACEAE

Genus of annuals, perennials and evergreen shrubs. Small species suit damp pockets in rock gardens. Fully to half hardy. Most prefer full sun and wet or moist soil; some, such as *M. aurantiacus* need a dry site. Propagate perennials by division in spring, sub-shrubs by softwood cuttings in late summer; annuals and all species by seed in autumn or early spring.
***M.* 'Andean Nymph'.** See *M. naiandinus.*
♀***M. aurantiacus***, syn. *Diplacus glutinosus, M. glutinosus*, illus. p.162.
♀***M. cupreus* 'Whitecroft Scarlet'.** Short-lived, spreading perennial. **H** 20–30cm (8–12in), **S** 30cm (12in). Half hardy. Bears snapdragon-like, scarlet flowers freely from early to late summer. Has oval, toothed, mid-green leaves.
M. glutinosus. See *M. aurantiacus.*
M. guttatus, syn. *M. langsdorffii.* Spreading, mat-forming perennial. **H** and 60cm (24in). Frost hardy. Snapdragon-like, bright yellow flowers, spotted with reddish-brown on lower lobes, are borne in succession in summer and early autumn. Oval leaves are coarsely or sometimes deeply toothed and mid-green.
M.* x *hybrida illus. p.445.
M. langsdorffii. See *M. guttatus.*
♀***M. lewisii.*** Upright perennial. **H** 60cm (24in), **S** 45cm (18in). Frost hardy. Has downy, sticky, grey leaves that provide an excellent foil for snapdragon-like, deep rose-pink flowers borne singly in summer.
M. luteus (Yellow musk). Spreading perennial. **H** and **S** 30cm (12in). Frost hardy. Throughout summer, snapdragon-like, occasionally red-spotted, yellow flowers are freely produced above hairy, mid-green foliage.
***M.* Magic Series.** Early-flowering perennial. **H** 15–20cm (6–8in). Produces small flowers, ranging from bright orange, yellow, and red to more usual pastel shades and bicolours. **'Magic Yellow Blotch'** illus. p.322.
M. moschatus (Musk). Deciduous, prostrate, perennial, bog plant. **H** 10cm (4in), **S** 15cm (6in). Frost hardy. Has oval, hairy, pale green leaves. Small, pale yellow flowers, lightly speckled with brown, are borne in late summer.
♀***M. naiandinus***, syn. **'Andean Nymph'** illus. p.264.
M. ringens illus. p.441.
***M.* 'Royal Velvet'.** Compact perennial, often grown as an annual. **H** 30cm (12in), **S** 23cm (9in). Half hardy. Leaves are mid-green. Produces many large, snapdragon-like, mahogany-red flowers with mahogany-speckled, gold throats throughout the summer.

Mina. See *Ipomoea.*

MIRABILIS

Four o'clock flower, Marvel of Peru

NYCTAGINACEAE

Genus of summer-flowering annuals and tuberous perennials. Half hardy. Is best grown in a sheltered position in fertile, well-drained soil and in full sun. Lift tubers and store over winter in frost-free conditions. Propagate by seed or division of tubers in early spring.
M. jalapa illus. p.233.

MISCANTHUS

GRAMINEAE/POACEAE

See also GRASSES, BAMBOOS, RUSHES and SEDGES.
M. sacchariflorus (Amur silver grass). Vigorous, herbaceous, slow-spreading, rhizomatous, perennial grass. **H** 3m (10ft), **S** indefinite. Frost hardy. Hairless, mid-green leaves last into winter, often turning bronze. Produces open, branched panicles of hairy, purplish-brown spikelets in summer followed by attractive seedheads.
***M. sinensis* var. *condensatus* 'Cosmopolitan'** illus. p.285. **'Flamingo'** illus. p.286. **'Gracillimus'** illus. p.286. **'Yakushima Dwarf'** illus. p.285. **'Zebrinus'** illus. p.284.

MITCHELLA

RUBIACEAE

Genus of evergreen, trailing sub-shrubs, grown for their foliage and fruits. Makes excellent ground cover, especially in woodlands, although is sometimes difficult to establish. Fully hardy. Prefers shade and humus-rich, neutral to acid soil. Propagate by division of rooted runners in spring or by seed in autumn.
M. repens (Partridge berry). Evergreen, trailing, mat-forming sub-shrub. **H** 5cm (2in), **S** indefinite. Bears small, oval, white-striped, green leaves with heart-shaped bases. In early summer has pairs of tiny, fragrant, tubular, white flowers, sometimes purple-tinged, followed by spherical, bright red fruits. Suits a rock garden or peat bed.

MITELLA

SAXIFRAGACEAE

Genus of clump-forming, summer-flowering, slender-stemmed, rhizomatous perennials. Fully hardy. Requires shade and humus-rich, moist soil. Propagate by division in spring or by seed in autumn.
M. breweri illus. p.371.

MITRARIA

GESNERIACEAE

Genus of one species of evergreen, woody-stemmed, scrambling climber. Half hardy. Requires a position in semi-shade and in peaty, acid soil. Propagate by seed in spring or by stem cuttings in summer.
M. coccinea illus. p.193.

MOLINIA

GRAMINEAE/POACEAE

See also GRASSES, BAMBOOS, RUSHES and SEDGES.
M. altissima. See *M. caerulea* subsp. *arundinacea.*
M. caerulea* subsp. *arundinacea, syn. *M. altissima.* Tuft-forming, herbaceous, perennial grass. **H** 2.5m (8ft), **S** 60cm (2ft). Fully hardy. Has broad, flat, grey-green leaves and spreading panicles of purple spikelets on stiff, erect stems in summer. Needs a dry, sunny position and acid soil. **'Transparent'** (illus. p.286), ♀**'Variegata'** (Variegated purple moor grass), **H** 60cm (2ft), has yellow-striped, mid-green leaves and, in late summer, panicles of purplish spikelets.
***M. caerulea* subsp. *caerulea* 'Heidebraut'** (illus. p.233)

MOLTKIA

BORAGINACEAE

Genus of deciduous, semi-evergreen or evergreen sub-shrubs and perennials, grown for their funnel-shaped flowers in

summer. Fully to frost hardy. Prefers sun and well-drained, neutral to acid soil. Propagate by semi-ripe cuttings in summer or by seed in autumn.
♀ ***M.* x *intermedia*.** Evergreen, open, dome-shaped sub-shrub. **H** 30cm (12in), **S** 50cm (20in). Fully hardy. Stems are clothed in narrowly linear, dark green leaves. Masses of loose spikes of small, open funnel-shaped, bright blue flowers appear in summer.
***M. petraea*.** Semi-evergreen, bushy shrub. **H** 30cm (12in), **S** 60cm (24in). Fully hardy. Has long, narrow, hairy l eaves and clusters of pinkish-purple buds open into funnel-shaped, violet-blue flowers in summer.
M. suffruticosa illus. p.342.

MOLUCCELLA

LABIATAE/LAMIACEAE

Genus of annuals and perennials, grown for their flowers that may be dried successfully. Half hardy. Grow in sun and in rich, very well-drained soil. May be propagated by seed sown under glass in spring, or outdoors in late spring.
M. laevis illus. p.316.

MONARDA

Bergamot

LABIATAE/LAMIACEAE

Genus of annuals and perennials, grown for their aromatic foliage as well as their flowers. Fully hardy. Requires sun and moist soil. Propagate species and cultivars by division in spring, species only by seed in spring.
***M.* 'Adam'.** Clump-forming perennial. **H** 75cm (30in), **S** 45cm (18in). Bears dense whorls of 2-lipped, cerise flowers throughout summer. Oval, usually toothed, mid-green leaves are aromatic and hairy.
M. didyma (Bee balm, Bergamot).
♀ **'Cambridge Scarlet'** illus. p.235.
♀ **'Croftway Pink'** illus. p.233.
M. fistulosa illus. p.239.
***M.* 'Prairie Night'.** See *M.* 'Prärienacht'.
***M.* 'Prärienacht'**, syn. *M.* 'Prairie Night'. Clump-forming perennial. **H** 1.2m (4ft), **S** 45cm (1½ft). Produces dense whorls of 2-lipped, rich violet-purple flowers from mid- to late summer. Oval, toothed leaves are mid-green.

MONSTERA

ARACEAE

Genus of evergreen, woody-stemmed, root climbers, grown for their large, handsome leaves. Bears insignificant, creamy-white flowers with hooded spathes intermittently. Frost tender, min. 15–18°C (59–64°F). Provide humus-rich, well-drained soil and light shade in summer. Water moderately, less when temperatures are low. Provide support. If necessary, shorten long stems in spring. Propagate by leaf-bud or stem-tip cuttings in summer. ⓘ All parts except the fruit may cause mild stomach upset when ingested, and contact with the fruit may irritate skin.
M. acuminata (Shingle plant). Evergreen, woody-stemmed, root climber with robust stems. **H** 3m (10ft) or more. Has lopsided, oval, pointed, rich green leaves with a heart-shaped base, sometimes cleft into a few large lobes, to 25cm (10in) long.
♀ ***M. deliciosa*** illus. p.463.

MORAEA

IRIDACEAE

Genus of corms with short-lived, iris-like flowers. Divides into 2 groups: winter- and summer-growing species. Winter-growing species are half hardy, need full sun and well-drained soil; keep dry in summer during dormancy and start into growth by watering in autumn. Summer-growers are frost hardy and dormant in winter; grow in a sheltered, sunny site and well-drained soil. Propagate winter growers by seed in autumn, spring for summer growers.
M. huttonii illus. p.393.
***M. polystachya*.** Winter-growing corm. **H** to 30cm (12in), **S** 5–8cm (2–3in). Bears long, narrow, semi-erect, basal leaves. Stem has a succession of erect, flattish, blue or lilac flowers, 8cm (3in) wide, in winter-spring. Outer petals each have a central, yellow mark.
***M. ramosissima*.** Late spring- to early summer-flowering corm. **H** 50–120cm (20–48in), **S** 10cm (4in). Has numerous, semi-erect, narrowly linear, channelled, basal leaves. Bears yellow flowers, with deeper yellow marks on the inner petals, on many-branched stems.
***M. sisyrinchium*,** syn. *Gynandiris sisyrinchium*, illus. p.419.
***M. spathacea*.** See *M. spathulata*.
M. spathulata, syn. *M. spathacea*. Summer-growing corm. **H** to 1m (3ft), **S** 10–15cm (4–6in). Has one long, narrow, semi-erect, basal leaf. Tough flower stem carries a succession of up to 5 upward-facing, yellow flowers, 5–7cm (2–3in) wide, with reflexed, outer petals, in summer.

MORINA

Whorl flower

MORINACEAE

Genus of evergreen perennials, only one species of which is in general cultivation: this is grown for its thistle-like foliage and its flowers. Frost hardy, but protect from drying spring winds. Needs full sun and well-drained, idealy sandy soil. Propagate by division directly after flowering or by seed when fresh, in late summer.
M. longifolia illus. p.231.

MORISIA

CRUCIFERAE/BRASSICACEAE

Genus of one species of rosetted perennial with a long tap root. Is good for rock gardens and alpine houses. Fully hardy. Needs sun and gritty, well-drained soil. Propagate by seed in autumn or by root cuttings in winter.
***M. hypogaea*.** See *M. monanthos*.
M. monanthos, syn. *M. hypogaea*, illus. p.358.

MORUS

Mulberry

MORACEAE

Genus of deciduous trees, grown for foliage and edible fruits. Tiny flowers appear in spring. Fully hardy. Requires full sun and fertile, well-drained soil. Propagate by softwood cuttings in summer or by seed in autumn.
M. alba (White mulberry). **'Laciniata'** illus. p.88. **'Pendula'** is a deciduous, weeping tree. **H** 3m (10ft), **S** 5m (15ft). Rounded, sometimes lobed, glossy, deep green leaves turn yellow in autumn. Edible, oval, fleshy, pink, red or purple fruits ripen in summer.
♀ ***M. nigra*** (Black mulberry). Deciduous, round-headed tree. **H** 12m (40ft), **S** 15m (50ft). Heart-shaped, dark green leaves turn yellow in autumn. Bears edible, oval, succulent, dark purplish-red fruits in late summer or early autumn.

MUCUNA

LEGUMINOSAE/PAPILIONACEAE

Genus of vigorous, evergreen, twining climbers, grown for their large, pea-like flowers. Frost tender, min. 18°C (64°F). Humus-rich, moist but well-drained soil is essential, with partial shade in summer. Water freely when in full growth, less at other times. Needs plenty of space to climb; provide support. Thin out crowded stems in spring. Propagate by seed in spring or by layering in late summer. Whitefly and red spider mite may cause problems.
***M. bennettii*.** Strong- and fast-growing, evergreen, twining climber. **H** 15–25m (50–80ft). Leaves are divided into 3 oval leaflets. In summer has pendent clusters of pea-like, orange-scarlet flowers.
***M. deeringiana*.** See *M. pruriens* var. *utilis*.
M. pruriens* var. *utilis, syn. *M. deeringiana*. Vigorous, evergreen, twining climber. **H** 15m (50ft) or more. Has pea-like, both green- and red-purple flowers in long, pendent clusters in summer-autumn. Leaves, of 3 oval leaflets, are used for fodder and green manure. May be short-lived.

MUEHLENBECKIA

POLYGONACEAE

Genus of deciduous or evergreen, slender-stemmed, summer-flowering shrubs and woody-stemmed, scrambling climbers, grown for their foliage. Frost hardy. Grow in sun or shade and in well-drained soil. Propagate by semi-ripe cuttings in summer.
M. axillaris of gardens. See *M. complexa*.
M. complexa, syn. *M. axillaris* of gardens. Deciduous, mound-forming shrub or twining climber. **H** 60cm–1m (2–3ft), **S** 1m (3ft). Slender, wiry stems bear variably shaped (oval to fiddle-shaped), dark green leaves. Produces tiny, star-shaped, greenish-white flowers in mid-summer that are followed by small, spherical, waxy, white fruits.

***Mulgedium*.** See *Cicerbita*.

MURRAYA

RUTACEAE

Genus of evergreen trees and shrubs, grown for their overall appearance. Frost tender, min. 13–15°C (55–9°F). Requires a position in full light or partial shade and in humus-rich, well-drained soil. Water containerized plants freely when in full growth, moderately at other times. Pruning is tolerated in late winter if necessary. Propagate by seed in spring or by semi-ripe cuttings in summer. Whitefly may be troublesome.
***M. exotica*.** See *M. paniculata*.
M. paniculata, syn. *M. exotica* (Orange jasmine). Evergreen, rounded shrub or tree. **H** and **S** 2–4m (6–12ft). Pungently aromatic, edible, glossy, rich green leaves each have 9 or more oval leaflets. Carries fragrant, 5-petalled, white flowers in terminal clusters year-round, followed by tiny, egg-shaped, red fruits.

MUSA

Banana

MUSACEAE

Genus of evergreen, palm-like, suckering perennials, with false stems formed from overlapping leaf sheaths, grown for their foliage, flowers and fruits (bananas), not all of which are edible. Frost hardy to frost tender, min. 18°C (64°F). Grow in sun or partial shade and in humus-rich, well-drained soil. Propagate by division year-round, by offsets in summer or by suckers after flowering.
***M. arnoldiana*.** See *Ensete ventricosum*.
M. basjoo, syn. *M. japonica*, illus. p.219.
♀ ***M. coccinea***, syn. *M. uranoscopus* of gardens (Scarlet banana). Evergreen, palm-like perennial. **H** to 1m (3ft), **S** 1.5m (5ft). Frost tender. Bears oblong to oval, dark green leaves, to 1m (3ft) long, that are paler below. In summer produces erect spirals of tubular, yellow flowers, enclosed in red bracts, followed by banana-like, orange-yellow fruits, 5cm (2in) long.
***M. ensete*.** See *Ensete ventricosum*.
***M. japonica*.** See *M. basjoo*.
♀ ***M. ornata*** illus. p.470.
M. uranoscopus of gardens. See *M. coccinea*.

MUSCARI

Grape hyacinth

LILIACEAE/HYACINTHACEAE

Genus of spring-flowering bulbs, each with a cluster of narrowly strap-shaped, basal leaves, usually appearing in spring just before flowers. Leafless flower stems bear dense spikes of small flowers, most of which have constricted mouths. Fully to half hardy. Needs sun and fairly well-drained soil. Plant in autumn. Propagate by division in late summer or by seed in autumn.
♀ ***M. armeniacum*** illus. p.420. **'Blue Spike'** is a spring-flowering bulb. **H** 15–20cm (6–8in), **S** 8–10cm (3–4in). Frost hardy. Produces 3–6 long, narrow, semi-erect, basal leaves. Bears dense spikes of fragrant, bell-shaped, deep blue flowers; constricted mouths have rims of paler blue or white 'teeth'.
♀ ***M. aucheri***, syn. *M. lingulatum*, illus. p.420.
♀ ***M. azureum***, syn. *Hyacinthus azureus*, *Pseudomuscari azureum*. Spring-flowering bulb. **H** 10–15cm (4–6in), **S** 5–8cm (2–3in). Frost hardy. Bears 2 or 3 narrow, semi-erect, basal, greyish-green leaves, slightly

M

wider towards the tips. Produces a very dense spike of bell-shaped, pale clear blue flowers; mouths have small 'teeth' with central, dark blue stripes. May self-seed freely.
M. botryoides. Spring-flowering bulb. **H** 15–20cm (6–8in), **S** 5–8cm (2–3in). Frost hardy. Bears 2–4 narrow, semi-erect, basal leaves that widen slightly at the tips. Each minute, nearly spherical, bright blue flower has a constricted mouth and white-toothed rim. **'Album'** illus. p.415.
M. comosum, syn. *Leopoldia comosa* (Tassel grape hyacinth). Late spring-flowering bulb. **H** 20–30cm (8–12in), **S** 10–12cm (4–5in). Frost hardy. Has up to 5 strap-shaped, semi-erect, basal, grey-green leaves. Bears a loose spike of bell-shaped, fertile, brownish-yellow flowers with a tuft of thread-like, sterile, purplish-blue flowers at the tip.
'Monstrosum' see *M.c.* 'Plumosum'.
'Plumosum' (syn. *M.c.* 'Monstrosum') illus. p.419.
M. latifolium illus. p.403.
M. lingulatum. See *M. aucheri*.
M. macrocarpum illus. p.421.
M. neglectum, syn. *M. racemosum*, illus. p.420.
M. paradoxum of gardens. See *Bellevalia pycnantha*.
M. pycnantha. See *Bellevalia pycnantha*.
M. racemosum. See *M. neglectum*.

MUSSAENDA

RUBIACEAE

Genus of evergreen shrubs and scrambling climbers, grown for their flowers. Frost tender, min. 16–18°C (61–4°F). Requires a position in full light and fertile, well-drained soil. Water freely when in full growth, less at other times. Provide support and thin out crowded stems in spring. Propagate by seed in spring or by air-layering in summer. Whitefly and red spider mite may cause problems.
M. erythrophylla. Moderately vigorous, evergreen, scrambling climber. **H** 6–10m (20–30ft). Frost tender, min. 16–18°C (61–4°F). Has broadly oval, bright green leaves and flowers in summer-autumn. Each flower has one greatly enlarged, oval, bract-like, red sepal, a red tube and yellow petal lobes.

MUTISIA

COMPOSITAE/ASTERACEAE

Genus of evergreen, tendril climbers, grown for their long-lasting flower heads. Frost to half hardy. Plant with roots in shade and leafy parts in sun, in well-drained soil. Propagate by seed in spring, by stem cuttings in summer or by layering in autumn.
M. decurrens illus. p.208.
M. oligodon. Evergreen, tendril climber. **H** to 1.5m (5ft). Frost hardy. Oblong, glossy, green leaves with sharply toothed margins are 2.5–3.5cm (1–1½in) long. In summer-autumn produces long-stalked, daisy-like, pink flower heads with yellow centres. Grow against a low wall or through a shrub.

MYOPORUM

MYOPORACEAE

Genus of evergreen shrubs and trees, grown for their overall appearance and as hedges and windbreaks. Frost tender, min. 2–5°C (36–41°F). Prefers full light and well-drained soil; will tolerate poor soil. Water potted specimens moderately. Propagate by seed when ripe or in spring or by semi-ripe cuttings in late summer.
M. laetum. Evergreen, rounded to upright shrub or tree. **H** 3–10m (10–30ft), **S** 2–5m (6–15ft). Has fleshy, oval, lustrous, bright green leaves and axillary clusters of small, bell-shaped, white flowers, dotted with purple, in spring-summer, then tiny, narrowly oblong, pale to deep red-purple fruits.
M. parvifolium illus. p.454.

MYOSOTIDIUM

Chatham Island forget-me-not

BORAGINACEAE

Genus of one species of evergreen perennial that is suitable for mild, coastal areas. Half hardy. Prefers semi-shade and moist soil. Seaweed is often recommended as a mulch. Is not easy to cultivate, and once established should not be disturbed. Propagate by division in spring or by seed when ripe, in summer or autumn.
M. hortensia, syn. *M. nobile*, illus. p.271. Bears oval to heart-shaped, glossy leaves. **H** and **S** 60cm (24in). In early summer produces bell-shaped, pale to dark blue flowers, sometimes with white-margined lobes.
M. nobile. See *M. hortensia*.

MYOSOTIS

Forget-me-not

BORAGINACEAE

Genus of annuals, biennials and perennials, grown for their flowers. Most species are good for rock gardens and screes; *M. scorpioides* is best grown as a marginal water plant. Fully hardy. Most prefer sun or semi-shade and fertile, well-drained soil. Propagate by seed in autumn.
M. alpestris, syn. *M. rupicola*, (Alpine forget-me-not), illus. p.356.
M. australis. Short-lived, tuft-forming perennial. **H** 12cm (5in), **S** 8cm (3in). Has oval, rough-textured leaves and, in summer, tight sprays of open funnel-shaped, yellow or white flowers. Is good for a scree.
M. caespitosa. See *M. laxa* subsp. *caespitosa*.
M. laxa* subsp. *caespitosa, syn. *M. caespitosa*. Clump-forming annual or short-lived perennial. **H** 12cm (5in), **S** 15cm (6in). Lance-shaped, leathery leaves are dark green. Bears rounded, bright blue flowers in summer.
M. palustris. See *M. scorpioides*.
M. rupicola. See *M. alpestris*.
M. scorpioides, syn. *M. palustris* (Water forget-me-not). **'Mermaid'** illus. p.441.
***M. sylvatica* 'Blue Ball'** illus. p.315. **'White Ball'** is a slow-growing, short-lived, bushy, compact perennial, grown as a biennial. **H** to 20cm (8in), **S** 15cm (6in). Leaves are lance-shaped. Sprays of tiny, 5-lobed, pure white flowers are produced in early summer.
***M.* Sylva Series** illus. p.313.

Myrceugenia apiculata. See *Luma apiculata*.

MYRICA

MYRICACEAE

Genus of deciduous and evergreen, usually suckering shrubs and trees found in moist soils worldwide. They have alternate, lance- to ovate-shaped dark green leaves. Requires humus-rich, moist soil, and a position in full sun or partial shade.
M. gale (Bog myrtle) illus. p.162.

MYRIOPHYLLUM

HALORAGIDACEAE

Genus of deciduous, perennial, submerged water plants, grown for their foliage. Most species are ideal as depositories for fish spawn. Fully hardy to frost tender, min. 5°C (41°F). Requires full sun. Spreads widely; keep in check by removing excess growth as required. Propagate by stem cuttings in spring or summer.
M. aquaticum, syn. *M. proserpinacoides* (Parrot feather). Deciduous, perennial, partially or completely submerged water plant. **S** indefinite. Half hardy. Spreading, finely divided, blue-green foliage turns reddish in autumn if it surfaces.
M. hippuroides. Deciduous, perennial, spreading, submerged water plant with thin stems. **S** indefinite. Half hardy. Produces a dense mass of small, feathery, pale green leaves. Inconspicuous, greenish-cream flowers are borne from the axils of the emergent leaves in summer. Is suitable for a cold-water aquarium.
M. proserpinacoides. See *M. aquaticum*.
M. verticillatum illus. p.443.

MYRRHIS

Sweet Cicely

UMBELLIFERAE/APIACEAE

Genus of one species of summer-flowering perennial. Fully hardy. Requires a position in sun or shade and in well-drained soil. Propagate by seed in autumn or spring.
M. odorata illus. p.230.

MYRSINE

MYRSINACEAE

Genus of evergreen shrubs and trees, with inconspicuous flowers, grown mainly for their foliage. Also bears decorative fruits, to obtain which plants of both sexes must be grown. Is suitable for rock and peat gardens. Frost hardy, but in cold areas requires shelter. Requires a position in sun or shade and in any fertile, well-drained soil other than a shallow, chalky one. Propagate by semi-ripe cuttings in summer.
M. africana (Cape myrtle). Very slow-growing, evergreen, bushy, dense shrub. **H** and **S** 75cm (30in). Small, glossy, dark green leaves are aromatic and rounded. Tiny, yellowish-brown flowers in late spring are succeeded by spherical, pale blue fruits.

MYRTILLOCACTUS

CACTACEAE

Genus of branching, perennial cacti with ribbed, spiny, blue-green stems. Bears star-shaped flowers that open at night. Frost tender, min. 11–12°C (52–4°F). Needs a sunny, well-drained site. Propagate by seed or stem cuttings in spring or summer.
M. geometrizans illus. p.489.

MYRTUS

Myrtle

MYRTACEAE

Genus of evergreen shrubs, sometimes tree-like, grown for their flowers, fruits and aromatic foliage. Frost to half hardy; in cold areas plant against a south- or west-facing wall. Requires full sun and fertile, well-drained soil. May be pruned in spring. Propagate by semi-ripe cuttings in late summer.
M. apiculata. See *Luma apiculata*.
M. bullata. See *Lophomyrtus bullata*.
M. chequen. See *Luma chequen*.
♀ ***M. communis*** (Common myrtle) illus. p.122. ♀ ***subsp. tarentina*** is an evergreen, bushy shrub. **H** and **S** 2m (6ft). Frost hardy. Bears small leaves that are narrowly oval, glossy and dark green. Produces fragrant, saucer-shaped, white flowers, each with a dense cluster of stamens, from mid-spring to early summer, followed by spherical, white fruits. Is very wind-resistant and good for hedging in mild areas.
M. luma. See *Lum apiculata*. **'Glanleam Gold'** see *Luma apiculata* 'Glanleam Gold'.
M. ugni. See *Ugni molinae*.

M

N

NANDINA

BERBERIDACEAE

Genus of one species of evergreen or semi-evergreen, summer-flowering shrub, grown for its foliage and flowers. Frost hardy. Prefers a sheltered, sunny site and fertile, well-drained but not too dry soil. On established plants prune untidy, old stems to base in spring. Propagate by semi-ripe cuttings in summer.

🏆 ***N. domestica*** (Heavenly bamboo, Sacred bamboo). Evergreen or semi-evergreen, upright, elegant shrub. **H** and **S** 2m (6ft). Leaves have narrowly lance-shaped, dark green leaflets, purplish-red when young and in autumn-winter. Large panicles of small, star-shaped, white flowers, with large yellow anthers, in mid-summer are followed in warm climates by spherical, red fruits. 🏆 **'Fire Power'** illus. p.143.

NARCISSUS

Daffodil

AMARYLLIDACEAE

Genus of bulbs, grown for their ornamental flowers. Daffodils have usually linear, basal leaves and a spread of up to 20cm (8in). Each flower has a trumpet or cup (the corona) and petals (botanically known as perianth segments). Fully hardy, except where otherwise stated. Prefer sun or light shade and well-drained soil, but Div.8 cultivars (*see below*) prefer a sunny site and tolerate lighter soils. Dead-head flowers as they fade flowers and remove the spent foliage during mid-summer. Most cultivars increase naturally by offsets; dense clumps should be divided no sooner than 6 weeks after flowering every 3–5 years. Species may be propagated by fresh seed in late summer or autumn. Narcissus yellow stripe virus, basal rot, slugs, large narcissus fly and bulb and stem eelworm may cause problems. ⓘContact with the sap of daffodils may irritate skin or aggravate skin allergies. See also feature panel pp.404–405). Horticulturally, *Narcissus* is split into the following divisions.

Div.1 Trumpet – usually solitary flowers each have a trumpet that is as long as, or longer than, the petals. Early to late spring-flowering.
Div.2 Large-cupped – solitary flowers each have a cup at least one-third the length of, but shorter than, the petals. Spring-flowering.
Div.3 Small-cupped – flowers are often borne singly; each has a cup not more than one-third the length of the petals. Spring- or early summer-flowering.
Div.4 Double – most have solitary, large, fully or semi-double flowers, sometimes scented, with both cup and petals or cup alone replaced by petaloid structures. Some have smaller flowers, produced in clusters of 4 or more, which are often sweetly fragrant. Spring- or early summer-flowering.
Div.5 Triandrus – nodding flowers, with short, sometimes straight-sided cups and narrow, reflexed petals, are borne 2–6 per stem. Flowers are produced in spring.
Div.6 Cyclamineus – flowers are borne usually 1 or 2 per stem, each with a cup sometimes flanged and often longer than those of Div.5. Petals are narrow, pointed and reflexed. Early to mid-spring-flowering.
Div.7 Jonquil and Apodanthus – sweetly scented flowers are borne usually 2 or more per stem. Cup is short, sometimes flanged; petals are often flat, fairly broad and rounded. Spring-flowering.
Div.8 Tazetta – sweetly fragrant flowers of small-flowered cultivars are borne in clusters of 12 or more per stem; large-flowered cultivars have 3 or 4 flowers per stem. All have a small, often straight-sided cup and broad, mostly pointed petals. Late autumn- to mid-spring-flowering. Most are frost to half hardy. Autumn-flowering hybrids provide valuable cut flowers; "prepared" bulbs may be grown in pots for mid-winter flowering.
Div.9 Poeticus – flowers, sometimes borne 2 per stem, may be sweetly fragrant. Each has a small, coloured cup and glistening white petals. Some *N. poeticus* hybrids are categorized as Div.3 or 8. Late spring- or early summer-flowering.
Div.10 Bulbocodium – flowers usually borne singly on very short stems, showing all the hallmarks of hoop-petticoat daffodils (*N. bulbocodium* subsp. *bulbocodium*), with insignificant petals and a disproportionately large, widely flaring cup. Winter- to spring-flowering.
Div.11 Split-corona – usually solitary flowers that have cups split for more than half their length. In (**a**), Collar daffodils, the overlapping segments of the cup lie against the petals, but in (**b**), Papillon daffodils, the segments of the cup tend to be narrower, with their tips arranged at the margin of the petals. Most flowers fall into category (a). Spring-flowering.
Div.12 Miscellaneous – a miscellaneous category containing hybrids with varying, intermediate flower shapes that cannot be satisfactorily classified elsewhere. Autumn- to spring-flowering.
Div.13 Daffodils distinguished solely by botanical name – a wide variety of flowers showing the huge range of floral characteristics of wild daffodils, from the tiny *N. cyclamineus* and the sweetly scented, many-flowered *N. tazetta* to the stately trumpet species. Flower in early autumn to early summer.

***N.* 'Acropolis'**, Div.4. Mid-to late spring-flowering bulb. **H** 42cm (17in). Large, double flowers have white, outer petals and petaloids; white, inner petals are interspersed with shorter, orange-red petaloids. Is suitable for exhibition.
🏆 ***N.* 'Actaea'** (illus. p.404), Div.9. Late spring-flowering bulb. **H** 40cm (16in). Fragrant flowers have glistening white petals and shallow, flanged, rich lemon cups with narrow, orange-red rims.
***N.* 'Aircastle'** (illus. p.405), Div.3. Mid-spring-flowering bulb. **H** 40cm (16in). Flowers have white petals that age greenish; shallow, flat, lemon-yellow cups deepen in colour at the rim.
***N.* 'Albus Plenus Odoratus'.** See *N. poeticus* 'Plenus'.
***N.* 'Altruist'** (illus. p.405), Div.3. Mid-spring-flowering bulb. **H** 45cm (18in). Flowers have smooth, pale orange petals and a neat, ribbed, shallow, orange-red cup.
***N.* 'Ambergate'** (illus. p.405), Div.2. Mid-spring-flowering bulb. **H** 45cm (18in). Flowers each have a shallow, widely expanded, fiery scarlet cup and soft tangerine petals.
🏆 ***N.* 'Arctic Gold'**, Div.1. Mid-spring-flowering bulb. **H** 40cm (16in). Rich golden-yellow flowers have broad petals and well-proportioned, flanged trumpets with neatly serrated rims. Is suitable for exhibition.
N. assoanus, syn. *N. juncifolius*, *N. requienii*, Div.13. Mid-spring-flowering bulb. **H** 15cm (6in). Is similar to *N. jonquilla*, but has thin, cylindrical leaves and rounded, bright clear yellow flowers with a sweet, slightly lemony fragrance. Thrives in sunny, gritty soil.
N. asturiensis, syn. *N. minimus* of gardens, Div.13. Late winter- or early spring-flowering bulb. **H** 8cm (3in). Small, pale yellow flowers have waisted trumpets and slender petals. Prefers full sun.
***N.* 'Avalon'**, Div.2. Mid-spring-flowering bulb. **H** 35cm (14in). Fully hardy. Rounded, bright lemon-yellow flowers have wide, fluted cups that become white with age.
🏆 ***N.* 'Avalanche'** (illus. p.405), Div.8. Early spring-flowering bulb. **H** 35cm (14in). Half hardy. Produces 8 or more sweetly fragrant flowers, each with white petals and a primrose-yellow cup that scarcely fades. May be forced for mid-winter flowering.
***N.* 'Barrett Browning'**, Div.3. Early to mid-spring-flowering bulb. **H** 40cm (16in). Flowers have pure white petals and short, frilled, orange-red cups.
***N.* 'Bartley'** (illus. p.405), Div.6. Early spring-flowering bulb. **H** 35cm (14in). Long, slender, golden flowers have reflexed petals and narrow, angled trumpets. Flowers are long-lasting.
***N.* 'Belcanto'**, Div.11a. Late spring-flowering bulb. **H** 45cm (18in). Flowers, 8–12cm (3–5in) across, have rounded perianth segments, almost obscured by flattened, pale yellow cups.
***N.* x *biflorus*.** See *N.* x *medioluteus*.
***N.* 'Binkie'** (illus. p.405), Div.2. Early spring-flowering bulb. **H** 30cm (12in). Flowers open pale lemon and cups turn sulphur-white with ruffled, lemon rims.
***N.* 'Birma'**, Div.3. Mid-spring-flowering bulb. **H** 45cm (18in). Flowers have soft yellow petals and fiery orange cups with heavily ruffled rims.
🏆 ***N.* 'Bravoure'**, Div.1. Early to mid-spring-flowering bulb. **H** 38cm (15in). Large flowers have overlapping, white petals and unusually slender, only slightly flared, lemon-yellow trumpets, with entire rims.
🏆 ***N.* 'Bridal Crown'** (illus. p.404), Div.4. Late spring-flowering bulb. **H** 40cm (16in). Long-lasting, small, sweetly scented flowers are semi-double, with rounded, milk-white petals and white petaloids interspersed with shorter, saffron-orange ones towards centre.
***N.* 'Broadway Star'** (illus. p.404), Div.11b. Mid-spring-flowering bulb. **H** 40cm (16in). Has white flowers, 8cm (3in) across. The expanded segments of the split cups are flattened against the perianth segments; each has a narrow, orange mid-stripe running lengthways.
***N.* 'Brunswick'**, Div.2. Early spring-flowering bulb. **H** 40cm (16in). Long-lasting flowers have white petals and long, flared, primrose cups, which fade to lemon, with darker rims. Foliage is a bluish-green. Is suitable for cutting.
N. bulbocodium (Hoop-petticoat daffodil; illus. p.405), Div.13. Vigorous, spring-flowering bulb. **H** 8–15cm (3–6in). Flowers are golden-yellow with conical cups and narrow, pointed petals. Thrives in moist turf in full sun. **var. *citrinus***, **H** 15cm (6in), has slender, dark green leaves and clear pale lemon flowers. Hybrids of this species are in Div.10.
***N. campernelli*.** See *N.* x *odorus*.
***N.* 'Canaliculatus'** of gardens (illus. p.404), Div.8. Mid-spring-flowering bulb. **H** 23cm (9in). Frost hardy. Produces a cluster of 4 or more small, fragrant flowers per stem, each with reflexed, white petals and a shallow, straight-sided, yellow cup.
***N.* 'Canisp'**, Div.2. Mid-spring-flowering bulb. **H** 40cm (16in). A robust garden and exhibition daffodil with large, milk-white flowers, with broad, overlapping petals, lightly reflexed at the apex, and a slightly darker, flanged, trumpet-like cup, with a rolled, crenate mouth.
🏆 ***N.* 'Cantabile'**, Div.9. Late spring-flowering bulb. **H** 25cm (10in). Stiff stems bear neat, well-rounded, glistening white flowers, with tiny, red-rimmed, yellow cups and a prominent green eye.
N. cantabricus, Div.13. Spring- and sometimes winter-flowering bulb. **H** 10cm (4in). Is similar in form to *N. bulbocodium* subsp. *bulbocodium*, but is less robust. Flowers are milk- or ice-white. Thrives in an alpine house or greenhouse.
***N.* 'Cantatrice'**, Div.1. Mid-spring-flowering bulb. **H** 40cm (16in). Flowers have pure white petals and slender, milk-white trumpets.
***N.* 'Capax Plenus'.** See *N.* 'Eystettensis'.
***N.* 'Cassata'** (illus. p.405), Div.11a. Mid-spring-flowering bulb. **H** 40cm (16in). Cups are soft primrose and distinctly split into segments with ruffled margins, while petals are broad and milk-white.
🏆 ***N.* 'Charity May'** (illus. p.405), Div.6. Early to mid-spring-flowering bulb. **H** 30cm (12in). Small, pale lemon flowers each have broad, reflexed petals and slightly darker cups.
🏆 ***N.* 'Cheerfulness'** (illus. p.404), Div.4. Mid-spring-flowering bulb. **H** 40cm (16in). Long-lasting, small, sweetly scented, fully double flowers, 5.5cm (2¼in) across, are borne several to a stem, with milk-white petals and petaloids interspersed with shorter, orange-yellow ones at the centre. Is excellent for cutting.
***N.* 'Cool Crystal'**, Div.3. Mid-spring bulb. **H** 50cm (20in). Has white flowers with bowl-shaped, green-eyed cups.
N. cyclamineus, Div.13. Late winter- to early spring-flowering bulb. **H** 15cm (6in). Slender, nodding, clear gold flowers have narrow, reflexed petals and long, slender, flanged, waisted trumpets.

N

***N.* 'Daydream'**, Div.2. Mid-spring-flowering bulb. **H** 35cm (14in). Flowers have green-yellow petals and a pale trumpet that fades to white as it ages.
***N.* 'Diversity'**, Div.11a. Mid-spring-flowering bulb. **H** 40cm (16in). Flowers have pure white petals and a large, pink-tinted shallow, bowl-shaped cup. Flowers very freely and is suitable for cutting.
♀ ***N.* 'Dove Wings'** (illus. p.404), Div.6. Mid-spring-flowering bulb. **H** 30cm (12in). Has small flowers with milk-white petals and fairly long, soft primrose cups.
***N.* 'Dutch Delight',** Div.2. Early- or mid-spring-flowering bulb. **H** 45cm (18in). Has large flowers, 10cm (4in) across, with bright yellow petals and a deep, orange-red trumpet. Is a vigorous grower.
***N.* 'Dutch Delight'**, Div.1. Mid-spring-flowering bulb. **H** 30cm (12in). Golden yellow petals and trumpet. Flowers prolifically and is good for cutting.
***N.* 'Electrus'**, Div.11a. Mid-spring-flowering bulb. **H** 40cm (16in). Bears large flowers, 10cm (4in) across, with white petals, and a flattened pink-orange cup with a green eye in the centre.
♀ ***N.* 'Empress of Ireland'** (illus. p.404), Div.1. Mid-spring-flowering bulb. **H** 40cm (16in). Large, robust, milk-white flowers have broad, overlapping petals, reflexed at the apex, and a slightly darker, flanged trumpet with a rolled, crenate mouth.
***N.* 'Eystettensis'**, syn. *N.* 'Capax Plenus' (Queen Anne's double daffodil), Div.4. Mid-spring-flowering bulb. **H** 20cm (8in). Dainty, double flowers are composed of pointed, soft pale primrose petaloids neatly arranged in whorls.
♀ ***N.* 'February Gold'**, Div.6. Early spring-flowering bulb. **H** 32cm (13in). Solitary, long-lasting flowers have clear golden petals and long, flanged, slightly darker trumpets. Is useful for borders and naturalizing.
***N.* 'February Silver'** (illus. p.405), Div.6. Robust, early spring-flowering bulb. **H** 32cm (13in). Long-lasting flowers with milk-white petals and long, sturdy, nodding trumpets open rich lemon and age to creamy-yellow.
***N.* 'Fortune'**, Div.2. Early to mid-spring-flowering bulb. **H** 40cm (16in). Flowers have ribbed, dark lemon petals and bold, flared, copper-orange cups; they are very good for cutting.
***N.* 'Foxfire'**, Div.2. Mid-spring-flowering bulb. **H** 35cm (14in). Has very rounded flowers with conspicuously white petals. Small, greenish-cream cups each have a small, green eye zone and a coral-orange outer rim.
***N.* 'Fragrant Breeze'** (illus. p.404), Div.2. Early to mid-spring-flowering bulb. **H** 43cm (17in). Fragrant flowers have pure white petals and vase-shaped, apricot-yellow cups.
***N.* 'Fragrant Rose'**, Div.2. Late-spring-flowering bulb. **H** 45cm (18in). Flowers have white petals that develop a pink tint with age, and a red-pink conical-shaped cup with a green eye in the centre. Is not widely available or grown.
♀ ***N.* 'Gay Kybo'**, Div.4. Mid-spring-flowering bulb. **H** 45cm (18in). Bears large, 10cm (4in) double flowers, consisting of multiple layers of creamy white petals and shorter, orange, trumpet segments.
***N.* 'Geranium'**, Div.8. Mid- to late-spring-flowering bulb. **H** 35cm (14in).Stems bear up to 6 scented flowers, with white petals and flattened, flared, orange-red cups. Is excellent for cutting, and can be grown for indoor pots.
♀ ***N.* 'Gold Convention'**, Div.2. Mid-spring-flowering bulb. **H** 50cm (20in). Large, 11cm (4½in), flowers have rich golden petals and a deep trumpet in the same colour.
***N.* 'Golden Ducat'** (illus. p.405), Div.4. Mid-spring-flowering bulb. **H** 38cm (15in). Produces variable, sometimes poorly formed, double, rich golden flowers. Is suitable for cutting.
♀ ***N.* 'Golden Vale'**, Div.1. Mid-spring-flowering bulb. **H** 45cm (18in). Flowers have rich, golden yellow petals and a matching, flared trumpet. Is suitable for cutting.
***N.* 'Grand Primo Citronière'**, Div.8. Late autumn- to early spring-flowering bulb. **H** 32cm (13in). Half hardy. Bears 8 or more fragrant flowers, each with milk-white petals and a clear lemon cup, which fades to cream. 'Treated' bulbs may be forced for mid-winter flowering. Is good for cutting.
***N.* 'Grand Soleil d'Or'**, Div.8. Late autumn- to early spring-flowering bulb. **H** 35cm (14in). Half hardy. Flowers are sweetly scented with a dash of lemon. Each has rich golden petals and a clear tangerine cup. May be forced for mid-winter flowering, but staking is needed. Is excellent for cutting.
♀ ***N.* 'Hawera'** (illus. p.405), Div.5. Mid-spring-flowering bulb. **H** 20cm (8in). Nodding flowers are a delicate lemon-yellow. Requires a sunny position. Suitable for rockeries and alpine beds; also makes a good indoor pot plant.
♀ ***N.* 'Highfield Beauty'**, Div.8. Mid-spring-flowering bulb. **H** 50cm (20in). Stems bears up to 3 slightly scented flowers, with butter-yellow petals and slightly darker trumpets.
***N.* 'Home Fires'** (illus. p.405), Div.2. Early spring-flowering bulb. **H** 45cm (18in). Flowers each have pointed, rich lemon petals and an orange-scarlet cup with a lobed and frilled rim.
***N.* 'Honeybird'**, Div.1. Mid-spring-flowering bulb. **H** 50cm (20in). Well-proportioned flowers, 10.5cm (4½in) across, open greenish-yellow. The trumpets gradually fade almost to pure white as they age.
♀ ***N.* 'Ice Follies'** (illus. p.404), Div.2. Early spring-flowering bulb. **H** 40cm (16in). Flowers have milk-white petals and very wide, almost flat, primrose-yellow cups, fading to cream. Is excellent for cutting.
***N.* 'Irene Copeland'** (illus. p.405), Div.4. Mid-spring-flowering bulb. **H** 35cm (14in). Bears large, fully double flowers of neatly arranged, milk-white petaloids interspersed with shorter, pale creamy-yellow ones. Is excellent for cutting.
♀ ***N.* 'Jack Snipe'** (illus. p.405), Div.6. Sturdy, early to mid-spring-flowering bulb. **H** 23cm (9in). Long-lasting, milk-white flowers are similar to those of *N.* 'Dove Wings', but have narrower petals with incurved margins and medium-length cups of rich dark lemon-yellow.
♀ ***N.* 'Jenny'** (illus. p.405), Div.6. Early to mid- spring-flowering bulb. **H** 30cm (12in). Bears long-lasting flowers, each with milk-white petals and a medium-length, flanged, soft lemon trumpet that turns creamy-white.
♀ ***N.* 'Jetfire'**, Div.6. Floriferous, early spring-flowering bulb. **H** 23cm (9in). Flowers have overlapping, reflexed, clear golden-yellow petals and a cylindrical, ribbed, vibrant orange cup, slightly waisted before the crenate rim.
♀ ***N. jonquilla*** (Wild jonquil), Div.13. Mid-spring-flowering bulb. **H** 30cm (12in). Richly fragrant flowers are borne in a cluster of 6 or more; each has tapering, yellow petals and a shallow, dark gold cup. Distinctive foliage is semi-cylindrical, dark, shining and grooved. **'Flore Pleno'** (Queen Anne's jonquil) has loosely double flowers; broad, incurved, yellow petals are interspersed with short, darker ones.
♀ ***N.* 'Jumblie'**, Div.12. Early spring-flowering bulb. **H** 20cm (8in). Bears 2 or 3 long-lasting flowers, each with broad, golden petals and a sturdy, flanged, orange-yellow cup. Is ideal as a pot plant.
N. juncifolius. See *N. assoanus.*
***N.* 'Kilworth'**, Div.2. Vigorous, late spring-flowering bulb. **H** 38cm (15in). Flowers have pointed, milk-white petals and dark reddish-orange cups with green eyes. Is effective in large groups.
♀ ***N.* 'Kingscourt'**, Div.1. Sturdy, mid-spring-flowering bulb. **H** 42cm (17in). Flowers have flanged, flared, rich gold trumpets with broad, rounded, paler gold petals.
***N.* 'Liberty Bells'** (illus. p.405), Div.5. Sturdy, mid-spring-flowering bulb. **H** 32cm (13in). Paired, nodding flowers, 9cm (3½in) across, are slightly fragrant and clear lemon yellow.
♀ ***N.* 'Little Beauty'**, Div.1. **H** 14cm (14in). Early-spring-flowering bulb. Small, 3cm (1¼in) flowers have creamy white petals and a yellow trumpet. Dwarf variety, suitable for rock gardens and containers.
***N.* 'Little Witch'**, Div.6. Early to mid-spring-flowering bulb. **H** 23cm (9in). Produces golden-yellow flowers with reflexed petals and trumpet-shaped cups.
♀ ***N.* 'Manley'**, Div.4. **H** 45cm (18in). Early- to mid-spring-flowering bulb. Produces double flowers consisting of whorls of greenish-yellow petals, interspersed with bright orange trumpet segments.
N.* x *medioluteus, syn. *N.* x *biflorus* (Primrose peerless), Div.13. Mid-to late-spring-flowering bulb. **H** 40cm (16in). Produces neat, medium-sized, sweetly scented flowers of rounded outline, with overlapping, almost pure white petals and a small, shallow, solid primrose-yellow, bowl-shaped cup. Is usually twin-headed.
♀ ***N.* 'Merlin'**, Div.3. Mid-spring-flowering bulb. **H** 35cm (14in). Flowers have broad, rounded, glistening white petals and relatively large, almost flat, rich gold cups, each with a small, green eye and a broad, lightly ruffled, orange-red rim. Is excellent for exhibition.
N. minimus of gardens. See *N. asturiensis.*
♀ ***N.* 'Minnow'**, Div.8. Robust, early to mid-spring-flowering bulb. **H** 18cm (7in). Has a cluster of 4 or more fragrant flowers per stem, each with rounded, creamy-yellow petals and a lemon cup. Increases freely and will naturalize in grass. It is suitable for rockeries and can be grown indoors as a pot plant.
♀ ***N. minor***, syn. *N. nanus* of gardens, Div.13. Early spring-flowering bulb. **H** 20cm (8in). Flowers have slightly overlapping, soft yellow petals and almost straight, darker yellow trumpets with frilled rims. **subsp. *pumilus*** see *N. pumilus.*
N. minor of gardens. See *N. pumilus.*
♀ ***N.* 'Mission Bells'**, Div.5. Mid-spring-flowering bulb. **H** 25cm (10in). Stems bear 1–3 flowers with white petals, and matching trumpets with greenish centres.
♀ ***N.* 'Mount Hood'** (illus. p.404), Div.1. Vigorous, mid-spring-flowering bulb. **H** 40cm (16in). Trumpet-shaped, creamy-yellow flowers soon fade to white.
N. nanus, Div.13. Early spring-flowering bulb. **H** 12cm (5in). Flowers each have twisted, cream petals and a stout, straight, dull yellow trumpet with a frilled rim. Leaves are particularly broad. Is suitable for naturalizing.
N. nanus of gardens. See *N. minor.*
♀ ***N. obvallaris***, syn. *N. pseudonarcissus* subsp. *obvallaris* (Tenby daffodil), Div.13. Sturdy, early spring-flowering bulb. **H** 30cm (12in). Gold flowers have short petals and broad trumpets, and are borne on stiff stems.
N.* x *odorus, syn. *N. campernelli* (Campernelle jonquil), Div.13. Robust, mid-spring-flowering bulb. **H** 20–30cm (8–12in). Has usually 2 richly fragrant, dark gold flowers. ♀ **'Rugulosus'**, Div.7, **H** 28cm (11in), is more vigorous and produces up to 4 small-cupped, rich gold flowers.
***N.* 'Panache'** (illus. p.405), Div.1. Mid-spring-flowering bulb. **H** 40cm (16in). Produces very large, pure white flowers with well-balanced trumpets tinged green at the bases and broad overlapping petals.
***N.* 'Paper White Grandiflorus'**, syn. *N. papyraceus* 'Grandiflorus', *N.* 'Paper White Snowflake', Div.8. Winter- to mid-spring-flowering bulb. **H** 35cm (14in). Half hardy. Has 10 or more long-lived, heavily fragrant, star-shaped, glistening white flowers, each with long, spreading petals and a small, flanged cup containing conspicuous, saffron-yellow stamens. Produces flowers continuously through winter indoors.
***N.* 'Paper White Snowflake'.** See *N.* 'Paper White Grandiflorus'.
***N. papyraceus* 'Grandiflorus'.** See *N.* 'Paper White Grandiflorus'.
♀ ***N.* 'Passionale'** (illus. p.405), Div.2. Mid-spring-flowering bulb. **H** 40cm (16in). Each flower has milk-white petals and a long, flanged, apricot-tinged, pink cup.
***N.* 'Pencrebar'** (illus. p.405), Div.4. Mid-spring-flowering bulb. **H** 18cm (7in). Fragrant flowers are small, rounded and fully double, often in pairs. Outer petaloids and large, inner ones are pale gold and are evenly interspersed with darker ones.
♀ ***N.* 'Pipit'** (illus. p.405), Div.7. Mid-spring-flowering bulb. **H** 25cm (10in). Bears up to 3 scented flowers per stem, slightly greenish sulphur-yellow on opening. The ruffled, flared cup and the base of the overlapping petals become almost white at maturity.

N. poeticus (Poet's daffodil, Poet's narcissus), Div.13. Variable, late spring-flowering bulb. **H** 22–42cm (9–17in). Each fragrant flower comprises glistening white petals and a small, shallow, yellow or orange cup with a red rim. Is ideal for naturalizing in moist turf although slow to establish. **'Flore Pleno'** see *N.p.* 'Plenus'. **'Plenus'** (syn. *N.* 'Albus Plenus Odoratus', *N.p.* 'Flore Pleno'), **H** 40cm (16in), has loosely double, pure white flowers, with inconspicuous, greenish-yellow or orange centres, in late spring or early summer. Is good for cutting. ♀ **var. *recurvus*** (Pheasant's eye), **H** 42cm (17in), bears larger, long-lasting flowers with strongly swept-back petals and very shallow, greenish-yellow cups, with crimson rims, in early summer.

***N.* 'Portrush'**, Div.3. Late spring- to early summer-flowering bulb. **H** 35cm (14in). Produces small flowers, each with green-tinged, glistening milk-white petals and a small, shallow, flanged, creamy-white cup with a bright green eye.

***N.* 'Pride of Cornwall'**, Div.8. Mid-spring-flowering bulb. **H** 38cm (15in). Bears several large, fragrant flowers, each with milk-white petals and a rich yellow cup shading to an orange-red rim outside. Is excellent for cutting. *N.* 'Martha Washington' and *N.* 'Geranium' are similar in appearance.

♀ ***N. pseudonarcissus*** (Lent lily, Wild daffodil), Div.13. Extremely variable, early spring-flowering bulb. **H** 15–30cm (6–12in). Nodding flowers have overlapping, straw-yellow petals and large, darker yellow trumpets. Is ideal for naturalizing. **subsp. *obvallaris*** see *N. obvallaris*.

N. pumilus, syn. *N. minor* of gardens, *N. minor* subsp. *pumilus*, Div.13. Early spring-flowering bulb. **H** 15–22cm (6–9in). Bears bright gold flowers with separated, slightly paler petals and large trumpets with lobed and frilled rims. **'Plenus'** see *N.* 'Rip van Winkle'.

♀ ***N.* 'Rainbow'**, Div.2. Vigorous, mid-spring-flowering bulb. **H** 45cm (18in). White flowers have cups that are broadly banded with coppery-pink at the rim.

***N.* 'Replete'**, Div.4. Mid-spring-flowering bulb. **H** 40cm (16in). Produces double flowers with white petals, interspersed with reddish-orange trumpet fragments.

N. requienii. See *N. assoanus*.

***N.* 'Rip van Winkle'**, syn. *N. pumilus* 'Plenus', Div.4. Early spring-flowering bulb. **H** 15cm (6in). Shaggy, double flowers have densely arranged, flat, tapering, greenish-lemon petals with incurving tips.

***N.* 'Rockall'**, Div.3. Mid-spring-flowering bulb. **H** 50cm (20in). Produces neat flowers with overlapping, white petals and a shallow, ribbed, intense orange-red, bowl-shaped cup.

♀ ***N. romieuxii***, Div.13. Early spring-flowering bulb. **H** 10cm (4in). Frost hardy, but is best grown in a frame or an alpine house. Is similar to *N. bulbocodium*, but each fragrant flower has a large, almost flat, flanged cup of pale primrose.

N. rupicola, Div.13. Mid-spring-flowering bulb. **H** 8cm (3in). Is similar to *N. assoanus*, but has more angled, bluish-green foliage and solitary, less scented, lemon flowers, each with a 6-lobed cup. **subsp. *watieri***, **H** 10cm (4in), produces relatively large, fragrant, crystalline-textured, white flowers with shallow, lobed cups.

♀ ***N.* 'Saint Keverne'**, Div.11b. Sturdy, early to mid-spring-flowering bulb. **H** 42cm (17in). Solitary flowers have clear rich golden petals and slightly darker cups of almost trumpet proportions.

***N.* 'Saint Patrick's Day'**, Div.2. Early spring-flowering bulb. **H** 40cm (16in). Flowers have broad, flattish, greenish-yellow petals and large cups with dark yellow margins.

***N.* 'Salome'**, Div.2. Early to mid-spring-flowering bulb. **H** 35cm (14in). Flowers have white petals and a long pink trumpet-shaped cups, which are slightly frilled with a hint of warm gold at the edge. Is excellent for cutting.

***N.* 'Satin Pink'**, Div.2. Mid-spring-flowering bulb. **H** 42cm (17in). Each flower has broad, ribbed, milk-white petals and a long, barely flared, flanged, soft buff-pink cup of almost trumpet proportions.

***N.* 'Sempre Avanti'**, Div.2. Early to mid-spring-flowering bulb. **H** 40cm (16in). Flowers have creamy-white petals and contrasting yellow cups. Good for naturalizing in grass.

***N.* 'Scarlet Gem'**, Div.8. Mid-spring-flowering bulb. **H** 35cm (14in). Frost hardy. Produces 7–8 scented flowers with golden petals and contrasting scarlet or deep orange-red cups.

***N.* 'Segova'**, Div.3. Mid-spring-flowering bulb. **H** 40cm (16in). Flowers have pure white petals and small lemon-yellow cups.

***N.* 'Shepherds Hey'**, Div.7. Mid-spring-flowering bulb. **H** 25cm (10in). Produces two or more fragrant flowers per stem, with golden-yellow overlapping petals and small fluted cups.

***N.* 'Shining Light'**, Div.2. Mid-spring-flowering bulb. **H** 42cm (17in). Refined, well-balanced flowers have smooth, overlapping, clear, pale golden-yellow petals, and the slightly ribbed, cup-shaped cup is rich orange-red. The lightly dentate rim is slightly darker. Is excellent for exhibition.

***N.* 'Silver Chimes'** illus. p.407.

***N.* 'Sinopel'**, Div.3. Mid-spring-flowering bulb. **H** 45cm (18in). Flowers have pure white petals and green shallow-bowled cups edged with deep yellow.

♀ ***N.* 'Sir Winston Churchill'** (illus. p.405), Div.4. Mid-spring-flowering bulb. **H** 35cm (14in). Produces fragrant, double, white flowers with orange-yellow segments in the centres.

***N.* 'Slim Whitman'**, Div.2. Early to mid-spring-flowering bulb. **H** 40cm (16in). Flowers have ivory white petals and orange cups with a sulphur-yellow rim.

♀ ***N.* 'Spellbinder'** (illus. p.405), Div.1. Early spring-flowering bulb. **H** 42cm (17in). Long-lasting, bright sulphur-yellow flowers each have a slender, flanged trumpet, reversing to palest sulphur-white inside, except for the lobed, rolled-back rim, which is tinged with lemon.

***N.* 'Spring Pride'**, Div.2. Early to mid-spring-flowering bulb. **H** 40cm (16in). Flowers have ivory white petals and yellow cups edged with apricot.

***N.* 'Stint'**, Div.5. Mid-spring-flowering bulb. **H** 30cm (12in). Produces two or more pendent bright yellow flowers with pale lemon yellow cups.

♀ ***N.* 'Stratosphere'** (illus. p.405), Div.7. Mid-spring-flowering bulb. **H** 40cm (16in). Bears usually 3 fragrant flowers, each with rich golden petals and a darker gold cup. Is excellent for exhibition.

***N.* 'Sun Disc'**, Div.7. Mid-spring-flowering bulb. **H** 15cm (6in). Produces two or more rounded, sweetly scented flowers per stem, with yellow petals and small flat cups.

♀ ***N.* 'Suzy'** (illus. p.405), Div.7. Robust, mid-spring-flowering bulb. **H** 38cm (15in). Produces 3 or 4 long-lasting, large, fragrant flowers, each with clear golden petals and a large, flanged, rich tangerine cup. Suitable for cutting.

♀ ***N.* 'Sweetness'**, Div.7. Early spring-flowering bulb. **H** 38cm (15in). Sweetly fragrant flowers, occasionally borne in pairs, have intense, golden-yellow petals and a darker, waved cup of strong substance. Good for cutting.

♀ ***N.* 'Tahiti'** (illus. p.405), Div.4. Robust, mid-spring-flowering bulb. **H** 38cm (15in). Solitary, loosely double flowers have golden petals and petaloids, interspersed with short, fiery orange, inner petaloids.

N. tazetta (Bunch-flowered daffodil, Polyanthus daffodil), Div.13. Extremely variable, late autumn- to mid-spring-flowering bulb. **H** 30–40cm (12–16in). Bears usually 12 or more fragrant flowers, generally with slender, white or yellow petals and shallow, white or yellow cups.

♀ ***N.* 'Tête-à-Tête'**, Div.12. Early spring-flowering bulb. **H** 15–30cm (6–12in). Long-lasting flowers each have reflexed, rich golden petals and a square, flanged, warm yellowish-orange cup. Should be twin-flowered. Is very susceptible to viruses.

***N.* 'Thalia'** (illus. p.404), Div.5. Vigorous, mid-spring-flowering bulb. **H** 38cm (15in). Has 3 or more long-lived, charming, milk-white flowers per stem, each with irregularly formed, often propeller-shaped petals and a flanged, bold cup.

***N.* 'Tresamble'**, Div.5. Sturdy, early spring-flowering bulb. **H** 40cm (16in). Bears up to 6 flowers per stem, each with milk-white petals and a flanged, creamy-white cup that is paler at the rim.

♀ ***N.* 'Trevithian'**, Div.7. Vigorous, early to mid-spring-flowering bulb. **H** 45cm (18in). Produces 2 or 3 large, fragrant flowers, rounded and soft primrose, each with broad petals and a short cup.

♀ ***N. triandrus*** (Angel's tears), Div.13. Early spring-flowering bulb. **H** 12cm (5in). Bears nodding, milk-white flowers, each with narrow, reflexed petals and a fairly long, straight-sided cup. Suitable for rockeries and is a good pot plant.

***N.* 'Tripartite'**, Div.11. Mid-spring-flowering bulb. **H** 25cm (10in). Produces 2–3 lemon and golden-yellow flowers per stem, each with split trumpets that sit flat against the petals.

***N.* 'Trousseau'**, Div.1. Early spring-flowering bulb. **H** 42cm (17in). Flowers each have milk-white petals and a straight, flanged, soft lemon trumpet, with a flared, lobed rim turning rich creamy-buff tinged with pale pink.

***N.* 'Tudor Minstrel'**, Div.2. Mid-spring-flowering bulb. **H** 42cm (17in). Produces flowers with white, pointed petals. Chrome-yellow cups are slender and flanged outwards.

***N.* 'Verger'**, Div.3. Mid-spring flowering bulb. **H** 40cm (16in). Flowers have pure white petals and small, shallow, deep orange-red cups.

***N.* 'Waterperry'**, Div.7. Mid-spring-flowering bulb. **H** 25cm (10in). Flowers have dull creamy-white petals; lightly flanged, spreading, primrose cups turn rich buff-yellow, shading to pinkish-apricot rims.

***N.* 'White Lady'**, Div.3. Vigorous, mid- to late-spring-flowering bulb. **H** 45cm (18in). Large, scented flowers have spreading, slightly overlapping, pure white petals. The small, shallow, heavily frilled cup is strong primrose-yellow on opening, becoming more creamy-yellow with maturity.

***N.* 'White Lion'**, Div.4. Mid-spring-flowering bulb. **H** 35cm (14in). Produces double white flowers interspersed with bright yellow.

***N.* 'White Marvel'**, Div.5. Mid-spring-flowering bulb. **H** 35cm (14in). Produces two or more pendent, fragrant, double white flowers per stem.

***N.* 'Woodland Star'**, Div.3. Mid-spring-flowering bulb. **H** 50cm (20in). Large flowers have white petals and small, bowl-shaped, deep red cups.

***N.* 'W.P. Milner'**, Div.1. Early spring-flowering bulb. **H** 23cm (9in). Nodding flowers each have slender, twisted, light creamy-yellow petals and a flared, pale lemon trumpet, which fades to palest sulphur.

***N.* 'Yellow Cheerfulness'**, Div.8. Mid-spring-flowering bulb. **H** 35cm (14in). Produces multi-headed stems of fragrant pale yellow blooms.

NAUTILOCALYX

GESNERIACEAE

Genus of evergreen, erect, bushy perennials, grown for their flowers and foliage. Frost tender, min. 15°C (59°F). Requires high humidity, partial shade and well-drained soil; avoid waterlogging, especially in winter. Propagate by stem cuttings in summer or by seed, if available, in spring.

N. bullatus, syn. *N. tessellatus*. Evergreen, erect, bushy perennial. **H** and **S** 60cm (2ft). Narrowly oval, wrinkled leaves, to 23cm (9in) long, are dark green with a bronze sheen above, reddish-green beneath. Clusters of small, tubular, white-haired, pale yellow flowers are produced in the leaf axils mainly in summer.

N. lynchii illus. p.471.

N. tessellatus. See *N. bullatus*.

Neanthe bella.
See *Chamaedorea elegans*.

NECTAROSCORDUM

LILIACEAE/ALLIACEAE

Genus of summer-flowering bulbs, related to *Allium* and *Lilium*, with long, linear, erect leaves, and umbels of bell-shaped flowers. Exudes a very strong onion-like smell when bruised. Stems with erect, shuttlecock-like seed heads may be dried for winter decoration. Frost hardy. Needs dappled or partial shade. Grow in rough grass or borders, in any soil that is neither

too dry nor waterlogged. Propagate by freely produced offsets in late summer or by seed in autumn.
N. dioscoridis. See *N. siculum* subsp. *bulgaricum.*
***N. siculum* subsp. *bulgaricum*,** syn. *N. dioscoridis,* illus. p.385.

NEILLIA

ROSACEAE

Genus of deciduous shrubs, grown for their graceful habit and profuse clusters of small flowers. Fully hardy. Requires sun or semi-shade and fertile, well-drained soil. Established plants benefit from having some older shoots cut to base after flowering. Propagate by softwood cuttings in summer or by suckers in autumn.
N. longiracemosa. See *N. thibetica.*
N. sinensis. Deciduous, arching shrub. **H** and **S** 2m (6ft). Has peeling brown bark and oval, sharply toothed, mid-green leaves. Bears nodding racemes of small, tubular, pinkish-white flowers in late spring and early summer.
***N. thibetica*,** syn. *N. longiracemosa,* illus. p.133.

NELUMBO

NYMPHAEACEAE

Genus of deciduous, perennial, marginal water plants, grown for their foliage and flowers. Half hardy to frost tender, min. 1–7°C (34–45°F). Needs an open, sunny position and 60cm (24in) depth of water. Remove fading foliage; flowers may be left to develop into decorative seed pods. Divide overgrown plants in spring. Propagate species by seed in spring, selected forms by division in spring.
N. lutea (American lotus). Vigorous, deciduous, perennial, marginal water plant. **H** and **S** 1m (3ft). Half hardy. Rounded, blue-green leaves, prominently veined beneath, develop on stout, 30–60cm (1–2ft) long stems. Large, chalice-shaped, yellow flowers open in summer.
N. nucifera (Sacred lotus) illus. p.438. **'Alba Grandiflora'** is a vigorous, deciduous, perennial, marginal water plant. **H** 1.2–1.8m (4–6ft), **S** 1.2m (4ft). Frost tender, min. 1°C (34°F). Has very large, rounded, wavy-margined, dark green leaves, on sturdy stems, with large, fragrant, chalice-shaped, white flowers, 22–25cm (9–10in) across, in summer. **'Alba Striata'** bears white flowers, 15cm (6in) across, with jagged red margins. **'Rosea Plena'** produces double, soft pink flowers to 30cm (12in) across.

NEMATANTHUS

GESNERIACEAE

Genus of perennials and soft-stemmed, evergreen shrubs, grown for their flowers and foliage. Frost tender, min. 13–15°C (55–9°F). Requires partial shade and humus-rich, moist but well-drained soil. Water potted specimens moderately, allowing soil almost to dry out between applications. Tip prune young plants to stimulate branching. Propagate by softwood or greenwood cuttings in summer.
♀ ***N. gregarius*,** syn. *Hypocyrta radicans, N. radicans,* illus. p.459.
N. radicans. See *N. gregarius.*
***N. strigillosus*,** syn. *Hypocyrta strigillosa.* Evergreen, prostrate shrub. **H** 15–30cm (6–12in), **S** 60cm–1m (2–3ft). Elliptic, slightly cupped leaves are clothed in dense down. Small, tubular, orange or orange-red flowers appear in leaf axils mainly from spring to autumn.

NEMESIA

SCROPHULARIACEAE

Genus of annuals, perennials and evergreen sub-shrubs, commonly grown for summer bedding and as greenhouse plants. Half to frost hardy. Prefers sun and fertile, well-drained soil. Cut back stems after flowering to encourage new buds. Pinch out growing shoots of young plants to ensure a bushy habit. Propagate by seed sown under glass in early spring, or outdoors in late spring.
***N.* Amelie ('Fleurame')** illus. p.301.
***N.* 'Fleurame'.** See *N.* Amelie.
***N.* 'Inupyel'.** See *N.* Sunsatia Series Sunsatia Mango.
***N.* Maritana Series *Maritana Blue Lagoon* ('Pengoon').** Rather upright, twiggy perennial, grown as an annual. **H** 35cm (14in), **S** 60cm (24in). Frost hardy. Slightly fragrant, 2-lipped, blue-purple flowers, 2cm (¾in) across are borne in dense spikes in summer and autumn above lance-shaped, slightly scalloped, mid-green leaves. Prefers moist soil.
***N.* 'Pengoon'.** See *N.* Maritana Series Maritana Blue Lagoon.
N. strumosa. Fast-growing, bushy annual. **H** 20–45cm (8–18in), **S** 15cm (6in). Half hardy. Has lance-shaped, serrated, pale green leaves and, in summer, trumpet-shaped, yellow, white or purple flowers, 2.5cm (1in) across, that are suitable for cutting. **Carnival Series,** illus. p.307.
***N.* Sunsatia Series Sunsatia mango ('Inupyel')** illus. p.320.

NEMOPHILA

HYDROPHYLLACEAE

Genus of annuals, useful for rock gardens and for edging. Fully hardy. Grow in sun or semi-shade and in fertile, well-drained soil. Propagate by seed sown outdoors in spring or early autumn. Is prone to aphids.
N. insignis. See *N. menziesii.*
N. maculata illus. p.299.
***N. menziesii*,** syn. *N. insignis,* illus. p.314.

NEOBUXBAUMIA

CACTACEAE

Genus of columnar or tree-like perennial cacti with cylindrical stems and usually low-set ribs. Nocturnal flowers, produced in summer, are followed by angular fruits, which open like stars when ripe. Frost tender, min. 15°C (59°F). Requires a sunny position and poor to moderately fertile, sharply drained, gritty soil. Propagate by seed in spring.
***N. euphorbioides*,** syn. *Lemaireocereus euphorbioides, Rooksbya euphorbioides,* illus. p.494.

Neochilenia mitis of gardens. See *Eriosyce napina.*

NEOLITSEA

LAURACEAE

Genus of evergreen trees and shrubs, grown for their foliage. Frost to half hardy. In cold areas needs shelter from strong winds; does best against a south-or west-facing wall. Requires sun or semi-shade and fertile, well-drained soil. Propagate by semi-ripe cuttings in late summer.
N. glauca. See *N. sericea.*
***N. sericea*,** syn. *Litsea glauca, N. glauca.* Evergreen, broadly conical, dense tree or shrub. **H** and **S** 6m (20ft). Frost hardy. Narrowly oval, pointed leaves are glossy, mid-green above, white beneath and, when young, are densely covered with silky, brown hairs. Small, star-shaped, yellow flowers are borne in autumn.

NEOLLOYDIA

CACTACEAE

Genus of spherical to columnar, perennial cacti with dense spines and short tubercles in spirals. Most species are exceptionally difficult to cultivate unless grafted. Frost tender, min. 10°C (50°F). Needs full sun and well-drained soil. Water sparingly from spring to autumn; keep dry in winter. Propagate by seed in spring or summer.
***N. conoidea*,** syn. *Mammillaria conoidea,* illus. p.483.
N. macdowellii. See *Thelocactus macdowellii.*

NEOMARICA

IRIDACEAE

Genus of evergreen, summer-flowering, iris-like, rhizomatous perennials with clusters of short-lived flowers. Frost tender, min. 10°C (50°F). Needs partial shade and fertile, moist, preferably humus-rich soil. Water freely in summer; reduce water in winter but do not allow plants to dry out. Propagate by seed in spring or by division in spring or summer.
N. caerulea illus. p.393.

NEOPANAX

ARALIACEAE

Small genus of evergreen shrubs, grown for their foliage. Half hardy to frost hardy. Grow in sun or semi-shade in a good, well-drained soil. Propagate by semi-ripe cuttings in summer or by seed in autumn.
***N. arboreus*,** syn. *Nothopanax arboreus, Pseudopanax arboreus* (Five fingers). Evergreen, round-headed, stout-branched tree. **H** 6m (20ft), **S** 4m (12ft). Frost hardy. Large, glossy, dark green leaves are divided into 5 or 7 oblong leaflets. Produces tiny, honey-scented, green flowers in summer, followed by rounded, purplish-black fruits on female plants.
***N. laetus*,** syn. *Nothopanax laetus, Pseudopanax laetus.* Evergreen, round-headed, stout-branched tree or shrub. **H** and **S** 3m (10ft). Half hardy. Has large, long-stalked, leathery leaves composed of 5 or 7 oblong, dark green leaflets, to 30cm (12in) long. Bears tiny, greenish-purple flowers, to 20cm (8in) across, in summer, followed by rounded, purplish-black fruits on female plants in autumn.

Neoporteria. See *Eriosyce.*

NEOREGELIA

BROMELIACEAE

Genus of evergreen, rosette-forming, epiphytic perennials, grown for their overall appearance. Frost tender, min. 10°C (50°F). Requires semi-shade and a rooting medium of equal parts humus-rich soil and sphagnum moss or bark or plastic chips used for orchid culture. Using soft water, water moderately during growing season, sparingly at other times, and keep rosette centres filled with water from spring to autumn. Propagate by offsets in spring or summer.
N. carolinae*,** syn. *Aregelia carolinae, Nidularium carolinae* (Blushing bromeliad). Evergreen, spreading, basal-rosetted, epiphytic perennial. **H** 20–30cm (8–12in), **S** 40–60cm (16–24in). Strap-shaped, finely spine-toothed, lustrous, bright green leaves are produced in dense rosettes. A compact cluster of tubular, blue-purple flowers, surrounded by red bracts, is borne at the heart of each mature rosette, usually in summer. ♀ ***f. tricolor (syn. *N.c.* 'Tricolor') has leaves striped with ivory-white, that flush pink with age.
♀ **'Tricolor'** see *N.c.* f. *tricolor.*
N. concentrica (illus. p.471). Evergreen, spreading, basal-rosetted, epiphytic perennial. **H** 20–30cm (8–12in), **S** to 70cm (28in). Very broadly strap-shaped to oval, glossy, dark green leaves, with spiny, black teeth and usually with dark blotches, are borne in dense rosettes. In summer, a compact cluster of tubular, pale blue flowers, surrounded by pinkish-lilac bracts, is produced at the heart of each mature rosette. **var. *plutonis*** (syn. *N.c.* 'Plutonis') has bracts flushed with red. **'Plutonis'** see *N.c.* var. *plutonis.*

NEPENTHES

Pitcher plant

NEPENTHACEAE

Genus of evergreen, insectivorous, mostly epiphytic perennials, with leaves adapted to form pendulous, lidded, coloured pitchers that trap and digest insects. Is suitable for hanging baskets. Frost tender, min. 18°C (64°F). Requires a humid atmosphere, partial shade and moist, fertile soil with added peat and moss. Propagate by seed in spring or by stem cuttings in spring or summer.
N.* x *hookeriana illus. p.473.
N. rafflesiana. Evergreen, epiphytic, insectivorous perennial. **H** 3m (10ft), **S** 1–1.2m (3–4ft). Has lance-shaped, dark green leaves. Greenish-yellow pitchers, to 25cm (10in) long, are mottled purple and brown and have spurred lids. Inconspicuous, green flowers are borne in racemes and produced intermittently.

NEPETA

Catmint

LABIATAE/LAMIACEAE

Genus of summer-flowering perennials, useful for edging, particularly where they can tumble over paving. Fully hardy. Grows in sun or partial shade and any

well-drained soil. Propagate by division in spring or by stem-tip or softwood cuttings in spring or summer, species only by seed in autumn. Cats may be attracted to this plant, rolling on it and crushing it. Leaves can be dried and used in cat toys.
***N.* 'Blue Beauty'.** See *N.* 'Souvenir d'André Chaudon'.
♀***N.* x *faassenii*** (Catmint) illus. p.270.
***N. grandiflora*.** Neat, erect perennial. **H** 40–80cm (16–32in), **S** 45–60cm (18–24in). Has slightly hairy stems, oval, round-toothed, light green leaves, with heart-shaped bases, and, in summer, racemes of small, hooded, blue flowers.
***N. macrantha*.** See *N. sibirica.*
***N. nervosa*.** Clump-forming perennial. **H** 35cm (14in), **S** 30cm (12in). Forms a mound of narrowly oblong to lance-shaped, pointed, prominently veined, mid-green leaves. Dense racemes of small, tubular, pale blue flowers are produced from early to mid-summer.
N. sibirica, syn. *Dracocephalum sibiricum, N. macrantha*. Erect, leafy perennial. H 90cm (36in), **S** 45cm (18in). Bears long, whorled cymes of blue to lavender-blue flowers in mid- and late summer. Leaves are dark green and aromatic. **'Souvenir d'André Chaudron'** see *N.* 'Souvenir d'André Chaudron'.
***N.* 'Six Hills Giant'** illus. p.240.
***N.* 'Souvenir d'André Chaudron'**, syn. *N.* 'Blue Beauty', *N. sibirica* 'Souvenir d'André Chaudron'. Spreading, clump-forming perennial. **H** and **S** 45cm (18in). Tubular, blue flowers are borne throughout summer above oval to lance-shaped, toothed, grey leaves.

NEPHROLEPIS

NEPHROLEPIDACEAE/OLEANDRACEAE

Genus of evergreen or semi-evergreen ferns. Frost tender, min. 5°C (41°F). Needs a shady position. Prefers moist soil, but is extremely tolerant of both drought and waterlogging. Remove fading fronds and divide regularly. Propagate by division in summer or early autumn.
N. cordifolia (Ladder fern, Sword fern). Semi-evergreen fern. **H** 45cm (18in), **S** 30cm (12in). Has narrowly lance-shaped, arching, dark green fronds with rounded, finely serrated pinnae.
♀***N. exaltata*** illus. p.478.

NEPHTHYTIS

ARACEAE

Genus of evergreen, tufted perennials, with horizontal, creeping rhizomes, grown for their foliage. Frost tender, min. 18°C (64°F). Requires a humid atmosphere, moist, humus-rich soil and partial shade. Propagate by division in spring or summer.
***N. afzelii*.** Evergreen, creeping, rhizomatous perennial. **H** to 75cm (30in), **S** indefinite. Has tufts of arrow-shaped, lobed, dark green leaves, to 25cm (10in) long. Intermittently bears a hooded, greenish spathe, enclosing a green spadix, followed by spherical, orange fruits.
N. triphylla of gardens. See *Syngonium podophyllum.*

NERINE

AMARYLLIDACEAE

Genus of bulbs, some of which are semi-evergreen, grown for their spherical heads of wavy-petalled, pink to red, occasionally white, flowers. Most flower in autumn before leaves appear. Frost to half hardy. Needs full sun and light, sandy soil. Plant in early autumn. Dislikes being disturbed. Water until leaves die down, then dry off. Propagate by seed when fresh or divide offsets in autumn or when leaves have died down. ⓘ All parts may cause mild stomach upset if ingested.
***N.* 'Baghdad'.** Autumn-flowering bulb. **H** 60cm (24in), **S** 15–20cm (6–8in). Half hardy. Leaves are strap-shaped, semi-erect and basal. Has crimson flowers, paler towards centres; long, narrow petals have recurved tips and crisped margins.
***N.* 'Blanchefleur'.** Autumn-flowering bulb. **H** 30–50cm (12–20in), **S** 15–20cm (6–8in). Half hardy. Produces strap-shaped, semi-erect, basal leaves and a tight head of 5–10 pure white flowers. Upper parts of petals are twisted.
♀***N. bowdenii*** illus. p.413. **f. alba** illus. p.413. **'Rowie'**, **H** 60cm (24in), **S** 8cm (3in), is an autumn-flowering bulb. Frost hardy. Bears umbels of soft apricot-pink flowers with recurved petal tips. Strap-shaped, semi-erect, basal leaves persist throughout winter and die down in spring.
***N.* 'Brian Doe'.** Autumn-flowering bulb. **H** 30–50cm (12–20in), **S** 20–25cm (8–10in). Half hardy. Has strap-shaped, semi-erect, basal leaves. Stout, leafless stem bears a head of salmon flowers with 6 reflexed, wavy-margined petals.
***N.* 'Corusca Major'**, syn. *N. sarniensis* var. *corusca* 'Major'. Autumn-flowering bulb. **H** 60cm (24in), **S** 12–15cm (5–6in). Half hardy. Forms strap-shaped, semi-erect, basal leaves. Stout stem bears 10–15 scarlet-red flowers with narrow petals. Is useful for cutting.
***N. crispa*.** See *N. undulata.*
***N. filifolia*.** Autumn-flowering bulb. **H** to 25cm (10in), **S** 8–10cm (3–4in). Half hardy. Has thread-like, semi-erect leaves in a basal tuft. Slender stem has pale pink flowers with narrow petals.
***N. flexuosa*.** (syn. *N. undulata* Flexuosa Group.) Semi-evergreen, autumn-flowering bulb. **H** 40–50cm (16–20in), **S** 12–15cm (5–6in). Half hardy. Bears strap-shaped, semi-erect, basal leaves and 10–15 pink flowers; each petal has a deeper pink mid-vein and a recurved, wavy upper half. **'Alba'** has white flowers.
***N.* 'Fothergillii Major'.** Late summer- to early autumn-flowering bulb. **H** 45–60cm (18–24in), **S** 12–15cm (5–6in). Half hardy. Leaves are strap-shaped, semi-erect and basal. Very strong stem has about 10 bright scarlet-salmon flowers with recurved petals.
***N. masoniorum*.** Autumn-flowering bulb. **H** 15–20cm (6–8in), **S** 8–10cm (3–4in). Half hardy. Produces thread-like, semi-erect leaves in a basal tuft. Stem bears pink flowers with very crisped petal margins.
***N.* 'Nikita'.** Autumn-flowering bulb. **H** 45cm (18in), **S** 8cm (3in). Frost hardy. Has a stout stem and broadly strap-shaped, semi-erect, basal leaves. Produces loose umbels of funnel-shaped, pale pink flowers with wavy-margined, recurved petal tips.
***N.* 'Orion'** illus. p.413.
♀***N. sarniensis*** illus. p.414. **var. *corusca* 'Major'** see *N.* 'Corusca Major'.
N. undulata, syn. *N. crispa*, illus. p.413.

NERIUM

APOCYNACEAE

Genus of evergreen shrubs, grown for their flowers. Frost tender, min. 10°C (50°F). Needs full sun and well-drained soil. Water potted plants freely when in full growth, sparingly at other times. Tip prune young plants to promote branching. Propagate by seed in spring or by semi-ripe cuttings in summer. ⓘ All parts are highly toxic if ingested; contact with foliage may irritate skin.
N. oleander illus. p.455.

NERTERA

RUBIACEAE

Genus of creeping perennials, grown for their mass of spherical, bead-like fruits in autumn. Makes excellent alpine house plants. Half hardy. Requires a sheltered, semi-shaded position in gritty, moist but well-drained, sandy soil. Resents winter wet. Propagate in spring by seed, division or tip cuttings.
***N. depressa*.** See *N. granadensis.*
N. granadensis, syn. *N. depressa*, illus. p.373.

NICANDRA

Apple of Peru, Shoo-fly

SOLANACEAE

Genus of one species of annual with short-lived flowers. Fully hardy. Grow in sun and in rich, well-drained soil. Propagate by seed sown in spring.
N. physalodes (Apple of Peru, Shoo-fly). Fast-growing, upright, branching annual. **H** 1m (3ft), **S** 30cm (1ft) or more. Has oval, serrated, mid-green leaves. In summer to early autumn has bell-shaped, white-throated, light violet-blue flowers, over 2.5cm (1in) wide that last one day. Spherical, green fruits, 5cm (2in) wide, are surrounded by purple and green calyces. Is thought to repel flies, hence its name.

***Nicodemia madagascariensis*.** See *Buddleja madagascariensis.*

NICOTIANA

Tabacco plant

SOLANACEAE

Genus of annuals, perennials, that are usually grown as annuals, and semi-evergreen shrubs. Frost hardy to frost tender, min. 1°C (34°F). Needs sun or partial shade and fertile, well-drained soil. Propagate annuals and perennials by seed in early spring, shrubs by seed in spring or by semi-ripe cuttings in summer. ⓘ Contact with the foliage may irritate skin.
***N. affinis*.** See *N. alata.*
N. alata, syn. *N. affinis*, illus. p.231.
***N. glauca*.** Semi-evergreen, upright shrub. **H** and **S** 2.5–3m (8–10ft). Half hardy. Stout, blue-grey shoots bear narrowly oval, fleshy, blue-grey leaves. Showy, tubular, bright yellow flowers are produced in summer and early autumn.
♀***N. langsdorffii*** illus. p.316.
♀***N.* 'Lime Green'.** Upright annual. **H** 60cm (24in), **S** 25cm (10in). Half hardy. Mid-green leaves are spoon-shaped. In late summer and autumn produces racemes of open trumpet-shaped, greenish-yellow flowers that are fragrant at night.
***N.* x *sanderae* 'Crimson Rock'.** Fairly slow-growing, bushy annual. **H** 60cm (2ft), **S** 30cm (1ft). Half hardy. Oval leaves are mid-green. Evening-scented, trumpet-shaped, bright crimson flowers, to 8cm (3in) long, are produced throughout summer and early autumn. **Nicki Series**, **H** 38cm (15in), produces fragrant flowers in an extensive colour range that includes white, pink, red and purple. **Saratoga Series** (rose), illus. p.305; (white), illus. p.299.
♀***N. sylvestris*** (Flowering tobacco). Branching perennial, often grown as an annual. Frost hardy. Prefers sun. **H** 1.5m (5ft), **S** 75cm (2½ft). Carries panicles of fragrant, tubular, white flowers at the ends of stems in late summer. The sweet flower scent is strongest at night. Has long, rough, mid-green leaves that are sticky to the touch.

NIDULARIUM

BROMELIACEAE

Genus of evergreen, rosette-forming, epiphytic perennials, grown for their overall appearance. Frost tender, min. 10–15°C (50–59°F). Requires a position in semi-shade and a rooting medium of equal parts humus-rich soil and sphagnum moss or bark or plastic chips generally used for orchid culture. Using soft water, water moderately during the growing season, sparingly at other times, and keep centres of rosettes filled with water from spring to autumn. Propagate by offsets in spring or summer.
***N. carolinae*.** See *Neoregelia carolinae.*
N. fulgens (Blushing bromeliad). Evergreen, spreading, basal-rosetted, epiphytic perennial. **H** 20cm (8in) or more, **S** 40–50cm (16–20in). Has dense rosettes of strap-shaped, spiny-toothed, arching, glossy, rich green leaves. Tubular, white-and-purple flowers, almost hidden in a rosette of bright scarlet bracts, are mainly produced in summer.
N. innocentii (Bird's-nest bromeliad). Evergreen, spreading, basal-rosetted, epiphytic perennial. **H** 20–30cm (8–12in), **S** 60cm (24in). Has dense rosettes of strap-shaped, prickle-toothed, arching, dark green, sometimes reddish-green leaves with reddish-purple undersides. Tubular, white flowers, partially hidden in a rosette of bright red bracts, appear mainly in summer.
***N. procerum*.** Evergreen, spreading, basal-rosetted, epiphytic perennial. **H** 20–30cm (8–12in), **S** 50–75cm (20–30in). Strap-shaped, spiny-toothed, bright green leaves are produced in dense rosettes. Clusters of small, tubular, blue flowers are produced in summer.

NIEREMBERGIA

SOLANACEAE

Genus of summer-flowering perennials, sometimes grown as annuals, and deciduous or semi-evergreen sub-shrubs. Frost to half hardy. Prefers sun and moist but well-drained soil. Propagate by division in spring, by semi-ripe cuttings in summer or by seed in autumn.

N. caerulea. See *N. linariifolia*.

N. linariifolia, syn. *N. caerulea. N. hippomanica*, **'Purple Robe'** illus. p.312.

N. hippomanica. See *N. linariifolia*.

N. repens, syn. *N. rivularis*, illus. p.361.

N. rivularis. See *N. repens*.

NIGELLA

RANUNCULACEAE

Genus of annuals, grown for their attractive flowers, which are suitable for cutting, and their ornamental seed pods. Fully hardy. Grows best in sun and in fertile, well-drained soil. Dead-head plants to prolong flowering if seed heads are not required. Propagate by seed sown outdoors in spring or early autumn.

N. damascena (Love-in-a-mist). Fast-growing, upright annual. **H** 60cm (24in), **S** 20cm (8in). Has feathery, bright green leaves. Spurred, many-petalled, blue or white flowers are produced in summer, followed by inflated, rounded, green, then brown seed pods that may be cut and dried. ♀**'Miss Jekyll'** illus. p.315, **Persian Jewels Series** illus. p.314.

NOLANA

SOLANACEAE

Genus of annuals, useful for growing in hot, dry sites and rock gardens and as edging. Frost hardy. Grow in sun and in fertile, well-drained soil. Propagate by seed sown outdoors in spring.

N. atriplicifolia. See *N. paradoxa*.

N. grandiflora. See *N. paradoxa*.

N. paradoxa, syn. *N. atriplicifolia, N. grandiflora*. Moderately fast-growing, prostrate annual. **H** 8cm (3in), **S** 15cm (6in). Has oval, mid-green leaves and, in summer, funnel-shaped, purplish-blue flowers, to 5cm (2in) wide, that have white-zoned, yellow throats.

Nolina recurvata. See *Beaucarnea recurvata*.

Nolina tuberculata. See *Beaucarnea recurvata*.

NOMOCHARIS

LILIACEAE

Genus of bulbs with a lily-like habit and, in summer, loose spikes of flattish flowers, often conspicuously spotted. Fully hardy. Requires partial shade and rich, well-drained soil with a high humus content. In summer needs moist but not waterlogged soil. Remains dormant throughout winter. Propagate by seed in winter or spring.

N. mairei. See *N. pardanthina*.

N. nana. See *Lilium nanum*.

N. pardanthina, syn. *N. mairei*, illus. p.385.

N. saluenensis. Summer-flowering bulb. **H** 85cm (34in), **S** 12–15cm (5–6in). Leafy stems bear lance-shaped, scattered leaves. Has a loose spike of 2–6 saucer-shaped, white or pink flowers, with dark purple eyes and purple spots.

Nopalxochia. See *Discocactus*.

NOTHOFAGUS

Southern beech

FAGACEAE/NOTHOFAGACEAE

Genus of deciduous or evergreen trees, grown for their habit, foliage and, in the case of deciduous species, autumn colour. Has inconspicuous flowers in late spring. Fully to frost hardy. Requires sun or semi-shade and, because it is not very resistant to strong winds, should have the shelter of other trees. Prefers deep, fertile, moist but well-drained soil; is not suitable for shallow, chalky soil. Propagate by seed in autumn.

N.* x *alpina, syn. *N. procera*, illus. p.64.

N. antarctica (Antarctic beech, Nirre). Deciduous, broadly conical tree, sometimes with several main stems. **H** 15m (50ft), **S** 10m (30ft). Fully hardy. Small, oval, crinkly-edged, glossy, dark green leaves turn yellow in autumn.

N. betuloides illus. p.69.

N. dombeyi illus. p.68.

♀***N. menziesii*** illus. p.69.

N. obliqua illus. p.63.

N. procera. See *N.* x *alpina*.

NOTHOLIRION

LILIACEAE

Genus of summer-flowering bulbs, related to *Lilium*, grown for their funnel-shaped flowers. Frost hardy. Often produces early leaves, which may be damaged by spring frosts, so grow in a cool greenhouse in areas subject to alternating mild and cold periods in spring. Prefers partial shade or full sun and humus-rich, well-drained soil. Bulb dies after flowering. Propagate in spring or autumn by offsets, which take 2–3 years to reach flowering size. Alternatively propagate by seed in winter or spring.

N. campanulatum illus. p.386.

Nothopanax. See *Pseudopanax*.

Nothoscordum neriniflorum. See *Caloscordum neriniflorum*.

Notocactus apricus. See *Parodia concinna*.

Notocactus graessneri. See *Parodia haselbergii* subsp. *graessneri*.

Notocactus haselbergii. See *Parodia haselbergii* subsp. *haselbergii*, illus p.487.

Notocactus leninghausii. See *Parodia leninghausii*.

Notocactus mammulosus. See *Parodia mammulosa*.

Notocactus ottonis. See *Parodia ottonis*.

Notocactus rutilans. See *Parodia rutilans*.

Notocactus scopa. See *Parodia scopa*.

Notospartium carmichaeliae. See *Carmichaelia carmichaeliae*.

NUPHAR

NYMPHAEACEAE

Genus of deciduous, perennial, deep-water plants, grown for their floating foliage and spherical flowers. Fully to frost hardy. Grows in shade or sun and in running or still water; is often grown for a water-lily effect in conditions where true water lilies would not thrive. Remove fading foliage and flowers, and divide crowded plants. Propagate by division in spring.

N. advena (American spatterdock, Yellow pond lily). Deciduous, perennial, deep-water plant. **S** 1.2m (4ft). Fully hardy. Has broadly oval, floating, mid-green leaves; central ones are occasionally erect. Small, purple-tinged, yellow flowers in summer are followed by decorative seed heads.

N. lutea illus. p.444.

Nutallia. See *Oemleria*.

NYMANIA

AITONIACEAE/MELIACEAE

Genus of one species of evergreen, spring-flowering shrub, grown for its flowers and fruits. Frost tender, min. 7–10°C (45–50°F). Needs full light and fertile, well-drained soil. Water potted specimens moderately, less when not in full growth. Propagate by seed in spring or by semi-ripe cuttings in summer.

N. capensis illus. p.456.

NYMPHAEA

Water lily

NYMPHAEACEAE

Genus of deciduous, summer-flowering, perennial water plants, grown for their floating, usually rounded leaves and brightly coloured flowers. Fully hardy to frost tender, min. 10°C (50°F). Needs an open, sunny position and still water; they are not suitable for streams, or positions close to fountains. Remove fading foliage to prevent it polluting water. Plants have tuber-like rhizomes and require dividing and replanting in spring or early summer every 3 or 4 years. Most frost tender plants may be treated as annuals. May also be propagated by seed or by separating plantlets in spring or early summer. Water lily beetle and China mark moth eat the foliage and can be problems. See also feature panel p.440.

***N.* 'Amabilis'.** Deciduous, perennial water plant with floating leaves. **S** 1.5–2.2m (5–7ft). Fully hardy. Rounded leaves, reddish-purple when young, mature to dark green with red-margined, light green undersides. In summer, has star-shaped, pink flowers, 15–19cm (6–7in) across, with light pink tips and dark yellow stamens.

***N.* 'American Star'** (illus. p.440). Deciduous, perennial water plant with floating leaves. **S** to 1.2m (4ft). Frost hardy. Young leaves are purplish-green or bronze, maturing to bright green. Star-shaped flowers, 10cm (4in) across, are deep pink and are held above water throughout summer.

***N.* 'Attraction'** (illus. p.440). Deciduous, perennial water plant with floating leaves. **S** to 2m (6ft). Fully hardy. Has dark green leaves. In summer bears cup-shaped, garnet-red flowers, 15cm (6in) across and flecked with white.

***N.* 'Aurora'.** Deciduous, perennial water plant with floating leaves. **S** to 75cm (30in). Frost hardy. Olive-green leaves are mottled with purple. In summer has star-shaped flowers, 5cm (2in) across, cream in bud, opening to yellow, then passing through orange to blood-red. Suits a small- to medium-sized pool.

***N.* 'Black Princess'** (illus. p.440). Deciduous, perennial water plant with floating leaves. **S** 1.2m (4ft). Fully hardy. Rounded, red-bronze leaves mature to dark green. In summer produces cup-shaped, very dark blackish-purple flowers, 8cm (3in) across, with dark orange stamens.

***N.* 'Blue Beauty'** (illus. p.440). Deciduous, perennial water plant with floating leaves. **S** to 2.5m (8ft). Frost tender. Leaves are brown-freckled, dark green above, purplish-green beneath. Fragrant, rounded, deep blue flowers, to 30cm (12in) across, are produced in summer.

N. capensis (Cape blue water lily). Deciduous, perennial water plant with floating leaves. **S** to 2m (6ft). Frost tender. Large, mid-green leaves are often splashed with purple beneath. Star-shaped, bright blue flowers, 15–20cm (6–8in) across, appear in summer.

***N.* 'Emily Grant Hutchings'.** Deciduous, perennial water plant with floating leaves. **S** to 1.2m (4ft). Frost tender. Has small, green leaves overlaid with bronze-crimson. Cup-shaped, pinkish-red flowers, 15–20cm (6–8in) across, open during the night in summer.

♀***N.* 'Escarboucle'** (illus. p.440). Deciduous, perennial water plant with floating leaves. **S** to 3m (10ft). Fully hardy. Leaves are dark green. In summer has cup-shaped, deep crimson flowers, 10–15cm (4–6in) across, with bright golden centres.

***N.* 'Fabiola'.** Deciduous, perennial water plant with floating leaves. **S** to 1.5m (5ft). Fully hardy. In summer, produces fragrant, peony-shaped flowers, 15–18cm (6–7in) across, with strongly flecked pink petals, above mid-green leaves.

***N.* 'Fire Crest'** (illus. p.440). Deciduous, perennial water plant with floating leaves. **S** to 1.2m (4ft). Fully hardy. Dark green leaves are suffused with purple. In summer bears star-shaped, deep pink flowers, 15–20cm (6–8in) across, with bold, red-tipped stamens.

***N.* 'Froebelii'** (illus. p.440). Deciduous, perennial water plant with floating leaves. **S** 90cm (3ft). Fully hardy. Has rounded, pale green leaves, bronzed when young. In summer, produces cup-shaped, later star-shaped, burgundy-red flowers, 10–12cm (4–5in) across, with red stamens.

***N.* 'General Pershing'.** Deciduous, perennial water plant with floating leaves. **S** 1.5–1.8m (5–6ft). Frost tender. Leaves are rounded, wavy-margined, olive-green and marked with purple. In summer, bears day-blooming, cup-shaped, later flat, highly fragrant, lavender-pink flowers, 20–27cm (8–11in) across, with contrasting yellow stamens.

♀***N.* 'Gladstoneana'.** Deciduous, perennial water plant with floating leaves.

S to 3m (10ft). Frost hardy. Leaves are mid-green. Star-shaped, white flowers, 15–30cm (6–12in) across, open in summer.
♀ ***N.* 'Gonnère'** (illus. p.440). Deciduous, perennial water plant with floating leaves. **S** to 1.5m (5ft). Fully hardy. Has bright pea-green leaves and, in summer, rounded, white flowers, 15–20cm (6–8in) across.
***N.* 'Green Smoke'.** Deciduous, perennial water plant with floating leaves. **S** to 2m (6ft). Frost tender. Bronze-green leaves have bronze speckling. Star-shaped flowers, 10–20cm (4–8in) across, are chartreuse, shading to blue.
***N.* 'Helvola'** (syn. *N. pygmaea* 'Helvola', *N. tetragona* 'Helvola', illus. p.440), **S** to 45cm (18in), is frost hardy and has small, olive-green leaves with heavy purple or brown mottling. Produces star-shaped, yellow flowers, 2–4cm (¾–1¼in) across, in summer.
♀ ***N.* 'James Brydon'** (illus. p.440). Deciduous, perennial water plant with floating leaves. **S** to 2.5m (8ft). Frost hardy. Fragrant, peony-shaped, orange-suffused, crimson flowers, 15–20cm (6–8in) across, are borne in summer above dark green glossy leaves.
***N.* 'Laydekeri Fulgens'.** See *N.* Laydekeri Group 'Fulgens'.
***N.* Laydekeri Group 'Fulgens'**, syn. *N.* 'Laydekeri Fulgens' (illus. p.440). Deciduous, perennial water plant with floating leaves. **S** to 1m (3ft). Fully hardy. Dark green leaves have purplish-green undersides. Star-shaped, bright crimson flowers, 5–10cm (2–4in) across, appear in summer.
***N.* 'Lemon Chiffon'** (illus. p.440). Deciduous, perennial water plant with floating leaves. S 2m (6ft). Fully hardy. Rounded, mid-green leaves, red spotted underneath, are strongly splashed with bronze. Produces spherical, pale lemon flowers, 15cm (6in) across, in summer.
***N.* 'Lucida'** (illus. p.440). Deciduous, perennial water plant with floating leaves. **S** 1.5–1.8m (5–6ft). Fully hardy. Produces broadly ovate, mid-green leaves, and star-shaped flowers, 12–15cm (5–6in) across, with red inner petals, pink-veined, whitish-pink outer petals, and yellow stamens, in summer.
***N.* 'Madame Wilfon Gonnère'.** Deciduous, perennial water plant with floating leaves. **S** to 1.5m (5ft). Frost hardy. Has mid-green leaves and, in summer, cup-shaped, white flowers, 15cm (6in) across, spotted with deep rose-pink.
***N.* Marliacea Group 'Albida'** (illus. p.440). Deciduous, perennial water plant with floating leaves. **S** to 2m (6ft). Fully hardy. Deep green leaves have red or purplish-green undersides. Bears fragrant, cup-shaped, pure white flowers, 15–20cm (6–8in) across, in summer.
♀ **'Chromatella'** (illus. p.440), has olive-green leaves, heavily mottled with maroon and bronze, and cup-shaped, canary-yellow flowers, 15–20cm (6–8in) across.
***N. odorata* 'Sulphurea Grandiflora'**, syn *N.* 'Odorata Sulphurea Grandiflora'. Deciduous, perennial water plant with floating leaves. **S** to 1m (3ft). Fully hardy. Dark green leaves are heavily mottled with maroon. Bears fragrant, star-shaped, yellow flowers, 10–15cm (4–6in) across, throughout summer.
N. odorata var. minor (illus. p.440). Deciduous, perennial water plant with floating leaves. **S** 1m (3ft). Fully hardy. Small, rounded, soft green leaves have dark red undersides. Produces fragrant, star-shaped, white flowers 8cm (3in) across, in summer.
***N.* 'Odorata Sulphurea Grandiflora'.** See *N. odorata* 'Sulphurea Grandiflora'.
***N.* 'Pink Sensation'.** Deciduous, perennial water plant with floating leaves. **S** 1.2m (4ft). Fully hardy. In summer, bears cup-shaped, later star-shaped, pink flowers, 12–15cm (5–6in) across, with yellow inner stamens and pink outer stamens. Has rounded, mid-green leaves, purple-green when young.
N. pygmaea. See *N. tetragona.* **'Helvola'** see. *N.* 'Helvola'
***N.* 'Pygmaea Rubra'.** Deciduous, perennial water plant with floating leaves. **S** 60cm (2ft). Frost hardy. Small, reddish-green young leaves mature to purplish-green. Produces cup-shaped, blood-red flowers, 5cm (2in) across, in summer.
***N.* 'Ray Davies'.** Deciduous, perennial water plant with floating leaves. **S** to 1.5m (5ft). Fully hardy. In summer, produces peony-shaped, light pink flowers, 15–18cm (6–7in) across, slightly yellow in the centre, above rounded, deep green leaves.
***N.* 'Red Flare'.** Deciduous, perennial water plant with floating leaves. **S** 1.5–1.8m (5–6ft). Frost tender. Leaves are rounded, strongly toothed and reddish-green. In summer, bears night-blooming, flat, dark red flowers, 17–25cm (7–10in) across, with light pink or yellowish stamens.
***N.* 'Rose Arey'** (illus. p.440). Deciduous, perennial water plant with floating leaves. **S** to 1.5m (5ft). Frost hardy. Leaves are reddish-green, purple when young. In summer bears star-shaped, deep rose-pink flowers, 10–15cm (4–6in) across, that pale with age and have a strong aniseed fragrance.
***N.* 'Saint Louis'.** Deciduous, perennial water plant with floating leaves. **S** to 2m (6ft). Frost tender. Bright green leaves are spotted with brown when young. Produces open, star-shaped, bright yellow flowers, 15–25cm (6–10in) across, in summer.
***N.* 'Sunrise'** (illus. p.440). Deciduous, perennial water plant with floating leaves. **S** to 2m (6ft). Frost hardy. Mid-green leaves have downy stalks and undersides. Bears star-shaped, yellow flowers, 10–15cm (4–6in) across, in summer.
N. tetragona, syn. *N. pygmaea.* **'Alba'** (illus. p.440) is a deciduous, perennial water plant with floating leaves. **S** to 30cm (12in). Fully hardy. Has small, dark green leaves, purplish-green beneath, and, in summer, star-shaped, white flowers, 2–3cm (¾–1¼in) across. **'Helvola'** see. *N.* 'Helvola'
***N.* 'Virginia'.** Deciduous, perennial water plant with floating leaves. **S** to 1.5m (5ft). Fully hardy. Produces purplish-green leaves and, in summer, star-shaped, white flowers, 10–15cm (4–6in) across.
***N.* 'Wood's White Knight'.** Deciduous, perennial water plant with floating leaves. **S** to 2m (6ft). Frost tender. Leaves are mid-green, dappled with darker green beneath. In summer, produces star-shaped, creamy-white flowers, 10–20cm (4–8in) across and with prominent, gold stamens, that open at night.

NYMPHOIDES

MENYANTHACEAE

Genus of deciduous, perennial, deep-water plants, with floating foliage, grown for their flowers. Fully hardy to frost tender, min. 5°C (41°F). Requires an open, sunny position. Propagate by division in spring or summer.
N. peltata, syn. *Limnanthemum nymphoides, Villarsia nymphoides,* llus. p.444.

NYSSA

Tupelo

CORNACEAE/NYSSACEAE

Genus of deciduous trees grown for their foliage and brilliant autumn colour. Fully hardy. Needs sun or semi-shade; does best in hot summers. Requires moist, neutral to acid soil. Resents being transplanted. Propagate by softwood cuttings in summer or by seed in autumn.
♀ ***N. sinensis*** illus. p.77.
♀ ***N. sylvatica*** illus. p.66.

O

OCHNA

OCHNACEAE

Genus of mainly evergreen trees and shrubs, grown mostly for their flowers and fruits. Frost tender, min. 10°C (50°F). Prefers full light and well-drained soil. Water containerized specimens moderately, less when not in full growth. Prune, if necessary, in early spring. Propagate by seed in spring or by semi-ripe cuttings in summer.
O. multiflora. See *O. serrulata.*
O. serratifolia of gardens. See *O. serrulata.*
O. serrulata, syn. *O. multiflora, O. serratifolia* of gardens (Mickey-mouse plant). Evergreen, irregularly rounded, twiggy shrub that is semi-evergreen in low temperatures. **H** to 2m (6ft), **S** 1–2m (3–6ft) or more. Leaves are narrowly elliptic, toothed and glossy. Has 5-petalled, bright yellow flowers in spring-summer, then shuttlecock-shaped, red fruits, each with 1–5 berry-like seeds clustered on top.

x ODONTIODA

ORCHIDACEAE

See also ORCHIDS.
x *O.* (*O.* Chantos x *O.* Marzorka)
x *Odontoglossum* Buttercrisp. See *Oncidium* Julia Barbara Good gx.
x *O.* Mount Bingham gx. See *Oncidium* Mount Bingham gx.
x *O.* Pacific Gold x *Odontoglossum cordatum.* See x *Oncostele* Pacific Mystery gx.

x *Odontocidium.* See *Oncidium.*
Odontoglossum bictoniense. See *Rhynchostele bictoniense.*
Odontoglossum cervantesii. See *Rhynchostele cervantesii.*
Odontoglossum cordatum. See *Rhynchostele cordatum.*
Odontoglossum crispum. See *Oncidium alexandrae.*
***Odontoglossum* Eric Young gx.** See *Oncidium* Eric Young gx.
Odontoglossum grande. See *Rossioglossum grande.*
***Odontoglossum* Le Nez Point gx.** See *Oncidium* Le Nez Point gx.
Odontoglossum rossii. See *Rhynchostele rossii.*
***Odontoglossum* Royal Occasion gx.** See *Oncidium* Royal Occasion gx.

OEMLERIA

SYN. NUTTALLIA, OSMARONIA

ROSACEAE

Genus of one species of deciduous, early spring-flowering shrub, grown for its fragrant flowers and decorative fruits. Separate male and female plants are needed in order to obtain fruits. Fully hardy. Prefers sun or semi-shade and moist soil. To restrict growth remove suckers and cut old shoots back or down to base in late winter. Propagate by suckers in autumn.

O. cerasiformis. (Indian plum, Oso berry). Deciduous, upright, then arching shrub that forms dense thickets. **H** 2.5m (8ft), **S** 4m (12ft). Leaves are narrowly oval and dark blue-green. Has nodding clusters of small, fragrant, bell-shaped, white flowers in early spring, then small, plum-shaped, purple fruits.

OENOTHERA
Evening primrose

ONAGRACEAE

Genus of annuals, biennials and perennials, grown for their profuse but short-lived flowers in summer. Fully to frost hardy. Needs full sun and well-drained, sandy soil. Propagate by seed or division in autumn or spring or by softwood cuttings in late spring.

O. acaulis. Tuft-forming perennial. **H** 15cm (6in), **S** 20cm (8in). Fully hardy. Has oblong to oval, deeply toothed or lobed leaves. Cup-shaped, white flowers, turning pink, open at sunset in summer.

O. caespitosa. Clump-forming, stemless perennial. **H** 12cm (5in), **S** 20cm (8in). Fully hardy. Has narrowly oval, entire or toothed, mid-green leaves. Flowers, opening at sunset in summer, are fragrant, cup-shaped and white, becoming pink with age. Suits a rock garden.

O. fraseri. See *O. fruticosa* subsp. *glauca*.

O. fruticosa 'Fireworks'. See *O.f.* 'Fyrverkeri'. ♀ **'Fyrverkeri'** (syn. *O.f.* 'Fireworks') illus. p.275. ♀ **subsp. *glauca*** (syn. *O. fraseri, O. glauca, O. tetragona*) is a clump-forming perennial. **H** 45–60cm (18–24in), **S** 45cm (18in). Fully hardy. Dense spikes of fragrant, cup-shaped, bright yellow flowers appear from mid- to late summer. Leaves, borne on reddish-green stems, are narrowly oval to lance-shaped and glossy, mid-green.

O. glauca. See *O. fruticosa* subsp. *glauca*.

♀ ***O. macrocarpa***, syn. *O. missouriensis*, illus. p.372.

O. missouriensis. See *O. macrocarpa*.

O. perennis, syn. *O. pumila*. Clump-forming perennial. **H** 15–60cm (6–4in), **S** 30cm (12in). Fully hardy. In summer, loose spikes of nodding buds open to fragrant, funnel-shaped, yellow flowers above spoon-shaped, mid-green leaves.

O. pumila. See *O. perennis*.

O. speciosa (White evening primrose). Often short-lived, clump-forming perennial with running rhizomes. **H** 45cm (18in), **S** 30cm (12in) or more. Frost hardy. In summer bears spikes of fragrant, saucer-shaped, green-centred, pure white flowers that age to pink and open flat. Leaves are narrowly spoon-shaped, deeply cut and mid-green.

O. tetragona. See *O. fruticosa* subsp. *glauca*.

OLEA

OLEACEAE

Genus of evergreen trees, grown for their foliage and edible fruits. Frost to half hardy; in cold areas requires the protection of a sheltered, south- or west-facing wall. Needs full sun and deep, fertile, very well-drained soil. Propagate by semi-ripe cuttings in summer or by seed in autumn.

O. europaea (Olive). Slow-growing, evergreen, spreading tree. **H** and **S** 10m (30ft). Frost hardy. Is very long-lived. Narrowly oblong leaves are grey-green above, silvery beneath. Tiny, fragrant, white flowers, borne in short racemes in late summer, are followed by edible, oval, green, later purple fruits.

OLEARIA
Daisy bush

COMPOSITAE/ASTERACEAE

Genus of evergreen shrubs and trees, grown for their foliage and daisy-like flower heads. In mild, coastal areas provides good, very wind-resistant shelter. Frost to half hardy. Needs full sun and well-drained soil. Cut out dead wood in spring. Propagate by semi-ripe cuttings in summer.

O. albida of gardens. See *O.* 'Talbot de Malahide'.

O. avicenniifolia. Evergreen, rounded, dense shrub. **H** 3m (10ft), **S** 5m (15ft). Frost hardy. Oval to lance-shaped, dark grey-green leaves are white beneath. Bears wide heads of fragrant, white flowers in late summer and early autumn.

O. x *haastii* illus. p.130.

O. 'Henry Travers', syn. *O. semidentata* of gardens. Evergreen, rounded, compact shrub. **H** and **S** 3m (10ft). Half hardy. Has white shoots and narrowly lance-shaped, leathery, grey-green leaves. Large heads of purple-centred, lilac flowers appear from early to mid-summer.

O. ilicifolia, illus. p.130. Evergreen, bushy, dense shrub. **H** and **S** 3m (10ft). Frost hardy. Narrowly oblong, rigid leaves are sharply toothed, grey-green and musk-scented. Fragrant, white flower heads are borne in clusters in early summer.

O. lacunosa. Evergreen, upright, dense shrub. **H** and **S** 3m (10ft). Frost hardy. Narrowly oblong, pointed, rigid leaves have rust-brown hairs when young and mature to glossy, dark green with central, white veins. Produces white flowerheads only rarely.

♀ **O. macrodonta.** (illus. p.132). Vigorous, evergreen, upright shrub, often tree-like. **H** 6m (20ft), **S** 5m (15ft). Frost hardy. Has holly-shaped, sharply toothed, grey-green leaves, silvery-white beneath. Large heads of fragrant, white flowers appear in early summer.

O. x mollis. Evergreen, rounded, dense shrub. **H** 1m (3ft), **S** 1. 5m (5ft). Frost hardy. Has oval, wavy-edged, silvery-grey leaves. Large heads of small, white flowers are borne profusely in late spring.

♀ **'Zennorensis'**, **H** and **S** 2m (6ft), has narrowly oblong leaves.

O. nummulariifolia illus. p.128.

O. phlogopappa. Evergreen, upright, compact shrub. **H** and **S** 2m (6ft). Half hardy. Leaves are grey-green and oblong, with wavy edges. Massed, white flower heads are carried in late spring. **var. *subrepanda*** illus. p.149.

♀ **O. x scilloniensis.** Evergreen, upright, then rounded, dense shrub. **H** and **S** 2m (6ft). Frost hardy. Narrowly oblong, wavy-edged, grey-green leaves set off masses of white flower heads in late spring.

O. semidentata of gardens. See *O.* 'Henry Travers'.

O. 'Talbot de Malahide', syn. *O. albida* of gardens. Evergreen, bushy, dense shrub. **H** 3m (10ft), **S** 5m (15ft). Frost hardy. Oval, dark green leaves are silvery beneath. Bears broad heads of fragrant, white flowers in late summer. Excellent for exposed, coastal gardens.

O. virgata illus. p.112.

OLSYNIUM

IRIDACEAE

Genus of fibrous-rooted, clump-forming perennials, grown for their nodding, trumpet- to bell-shaped flowers in spring. Fully hardy. Requires partial shade and moist, humus-rich, moderately fertile soil. Propagate by seed in autumn. Young plants take 2 or 3 years to flower.

O. biflorum, syn. *Phaiophleps biflora, Sisyrinchium odoratissimum*. Clump-forming, spring- to summer-flowering, rhizomatous perennial. **H** 25–35cm (10–14in), **S** 5–8cm (2–3in). Has cylindrical, rush-like, erect, basal leaves. Bears a small head of pendent, white flowers that are striped and veined red.

♀ **O. douglasii**, syn. *Sisyrinchium douglasii, S. grandiflorum* (Grass widow, Spring bell). Stiff, upright, summer-deciduous perennial. **H** 25cm (10in), **S** 15cm (6in). Has grass-like leaves sheathing very short, thread like flowering stems and, in early spring, a succession of pendent, bell-shaped, violet to red-purple, or sometimes white, flowers. Suits a rock garden or alpine house.

OMPHALODES

BORAGINACEAE

Genus of annuals and perennials, some of which are evergreen or semi-evergreen. Makes good ground cover, especially in rock gardens. Fully to half hardy. Needs shade or semi-shade and moist but well-drained soil, except for *O. linifolia* and *O. luciliae*, which prefer sun. Propagate by seed or division in spring.

♀ **O. cappadocica** illus. p.334. **'Cherry Ingram'** illus. p.261.

♀ **O. linifolia** illus. p.299.

O. luciliae. Semi-evergreen, mound-forming perennial. **H** 7cm (3in), **S** 15cm (6in). Half hardy. Has oval, blue-grey leaves. In spring-summer, loose sprays of pink buds develop into flattish, sky-blue flowers. Resents winter wet, so plant in a sheltered site or alpine house. Prefers sun and very gritty soil.

O. verna illus. p.334.

OMPHALOGRAMMA

PRIMULACEAE

Genus of perennials, closely related to *Primula*, grown for their flowers. Makes good rock garden plants, but is difficult to grow, especially in hot, dry areas. Frost hardy. Needs shade and gritty, moist but well-drained, peaty soil. Propagate by seed in spring.

O. vinciflorum. Basal-rosetted perennial. **H** 15cm (6in), **S** 10cm (4in). Has oval, hairy leaves that are mid-green in colour. In spring produces nodding, funnel-shaped, violet flowers, each with a deeper violet throat and a flat, flared mouth.

ONCIDIUM

ORCHIDACEAE

See also ORCHIDS.

O. alexandrae, syn. *Odontoglossum crispum* (illus. p.466). Evergreen, epiphytic orchid for a cool greenhouse or conservatory. **H** 15cm (6in). Bears long sprays of rounded flowers, 8cm (3in) across, white or spotted or flushed with pink, each with a red-and-yellow-marked lip; flowering season varies. Has narrowly oval leaves, 10–15cm (4–6in) long. Requires shade in summer.

O. Artur Elle gx 'Colombian', syn. x *Odontocidium* Artur Elle 'Colombian' (illus. p.467). Evergreen, epiphytic orchid for a cool greenhouse. **H** 23cm (9in). Produces tall spikes of pale yellow flowers, 6cm (2½in) across and intricately patterned with brown; flowering season varies. Has narrowly oval leaves, 10–15cm (4–6in) long. Requires shade in summer.

O. Eric Young gx, syn. *Odontoglossum* Eric Young (illus. p.467). Evergreen, epiphytic orchid for a cool greenhouse. **H** 15cm (6in). Has spikes of white-lipped, pale yellow flowers, 8cm (3in) across, spotted with rich yellow; flowering season varies. Bears narrowly oval leaves, 10–15cm (4–6in) long. Grow in cool shade in summer.

O. flexuosum. See *Gomesa flexuosum*.

O. Hambühren Stern gx 'Cheam', syn. x *Wilsonara* Hambühren Stern gx 'Cheam', illus. p.467. Evergreen, epiphytic orchid for a cool greenhouse. **H** 23cm (9in). Narrowly oval leaves are 10cm (4in) long. Bears spikes of deep reddish-brown flowers, 9cm (3½in) across, each with a yellow lip; flowering season varies. Requires shade in summer.

O. Julie Barbara Good gx, syn. x *Odontioda* (*O.* Chantos x *O.* Marzorka) x *Odontoglossum Buttercrisp* (illus. p.467). Evergreen, epiphytic orchid for a cool greenhouse. **H** 23cm (9in). Produces arching spikes of intricately patterned, red, tan, orange and yellow flowers, 8cm (3in) across; flowering season varies. Has narrowly oval leaves, 10–15cm (4–6in) long. Needs shade in summer.

O. Le Nez Point, syn. *Odontoglossum* Le Nez Point. Evergreen, epiphytic orchid for a cool greenhouse. **H** 15cm (6in). Crimson flowers, 6cm (2½in) across, are borne in spikes; flowering season varies. Has narrowly oval leaves, 10–15cm (4–6in) long. Needs shade in summer.

O. Memoria Commander Wiggs gx 'Kay', syn. x *Odontocidium* Tiger Butter x *Wilsonara* Wigg's 'Kay' (illus. p.467). Evergreen, epiphytic orchid for a cool greenhouse. **H** 23cm (9in). Bears spikes of mottled, deep reddish-brown flowers, 5cm (2in) across, each with a rich golden-yellow lip; flowering season varies. Narrowly oval leaves are 10–15cm (4–6in) long. Grow in shade in summer.

O. Mount Bingham, syn. x *Odontioda* Mount Bingham. Evergreen, epiphytic orchid for a cool greenhouse. **H** 23cm (9in). Bears pink-edged, red flowers, 9cm (3½in) across, in spikes; flowering season varies. Has narrowly oval leaves, 10–15cm (4–6in) long. Needs shade in summer.

O. ornithorrhynchum. See *O. sotoanum*.

O. Petit Port, syn. x *Odontioda* Petit Port. Evergreen, epiphytic orchid for a cool greenhouse. **H** 23cm (9in). Bears spikes of rich red flowers, 8cm (3in) across, each with a pink-and-yellow-marked lip; flowering season varies. Narrowly oval leaves are 10–15cm (4–6in) long. Needs shade in summer.
O. Royal Occasion, syn. *Odontoglossum* Royal Occasion. Evergreen, epiphytic orchid for a cool greenhouse. **H** 15cm (6in). Has spikes of white flowers, 8cm (3in) across, with deep yellow markings in the centres of the lips, in autumn-winter. Leaves are narrowly oval and 10–15cm (4–6in) long. Shade in summer.
O. papilio. See *Psychopsis papilio*.
O. sotoanum. This plant has been widely grown under the alternative name of *O. ornithorrhynchum* of gardens (illus. p.466). Evergreen, epiphytic orchid for a cool greenhouse. **H** 15cm (6in). Dense, arching sprays of very fragrant, rose-lilac flowers, 0.5cm (¼in) across, with a yellow highlight, are borne freely in autumn. Has narrowly oval leaves, 10cm (4in) long. Requires semi-shade in summer.
O. Tiger Hambuhren, syn. x *Odontocidium* Tiger Hambuhren. Evergreen, epiphytic orchid for a cool greenhouse. **H** 23cm (9in). Deep yellow flowers, 8cm (3in) across and heavily patterned with chestnut-brown, are borne in tall spikes; flowering season varies. Has narrowly oval leaves, 10–15cm (4–6in) long. Needs shade in summer.
O. Tigersun gx 'Orbec', syn. x *Odontocidium* Tigersun 'Orbec' (illus. p.467). Evergreen, epiphytic orchid for a cool greenhouse. Is very similar to x *O.* Tiger Hambuhren, but the flowers are slightly smaller, with lighter patterning.
O. tigrinum (illus. p.467). Evergreen, epiphytic orchid for a cool or intermediate greenhouse. **H** 23cm (9in). Branching spikes of fragrant, yellow-marked, brown flowers, 5cm (2in) across, each with a large, yellow lip, open in autumn. Has oval leaves, 15cm (6in) long. Requires semi-shade in summer.

x ONCIDOPSIS

ORCHIDACEAE

See also ORCHIDS.
x O. Olga. Evergreen, epiphytic orchid for a cool greenhouse. **H** 15cm (6in). Pure white flowers, 10cm (4in) across, with large, reddish-brown-blotched lips, are borne in tall, arching racemes, mainly in autumn. Produces ovoid pseudobulbs and narrowly oval leaves, 12cm (5in) long. Is best grown in shade during the summer.

x ONCOSTELE

ORCHIDACEAE

See also ORCHIDS.
♀ **x O. Cambria gx 'Lensing's Favorite',** syn. x *Vuylstekeara* Cambria gx 'Lensing's Favorite', illus. p.467. Evergreen, epiphytic orchid for a cool greenhouse. **H** 23cm (9in). Has narrowly oval leaves, 10–15cm (4–6in) long. Bears long sprays of wine-red flowers, 10cm (4in) across, heavily marked with white; flowering season varies. Needs shade in summer.
x O. Pacific Mystery gx, syn. x *Odontioda* Pacific Gold x *Odontoglossum cordatum*. Evergreen, epiphytic orchid for a cool greenhouse. **H** 23cm (9in). Bears long spikes of yellow-striped and -marked, rich chocolate-brown flowers, 7cm (3in) across; flowering season varies. Leaves are narrowly oval and 10–15cm (4–6in) long. Grow in shade in summer.

ONIXOTIS

SYN. DIPIDAX

LILIACEAE/COLCHICACEAE

Genus of spring-flowering corms, cultivated mainly for botanical interest. Half hardy. Requires sun and well-drained soil. Plant corms in early autumn and keep them watered until after flowering. Dry off in summer. Propagate by seed in autumn.
O. triquetra, syn. *Dipidax triquetrum*. Spring-flowering corm. **H** 20–30cm (8–12in), **S** 5–8cm (2–3in). Long, narrow leaves are semi-erect and basal. Carries a spike of flattish, star-shaped, white flowers, each narrow petal having a basal, red mark.

ONOCLEA

WOODSIACEAE

Genus of one species of deciduous fern that rapidly colonizes wet areas via spreading under ground rhizomes. Fully hardy. Grows in sun or shade and in wet soil. Remove fronds as they fade. Propagate by division in autumn or winter.
♀ **O. sensibilis** illus. p.443.

ONONIS

LEGUMINOSAE/PAPILIONACEAE

Genus of summer-flowering annuals, perennials and deciduous or semi-evergreen shrubs and sub-shrubs, grown for their pea-like flowers. Is good for rock gardens, walls and banks. Fully hardy. Needs a sunny position in well-drained soil. Propagate by seed in autumn or spring, shrubs also by softwood cuttings in summer.
O. fruticosa illus. p.339.
O. natrix illus. p.345.
O. rotundifolia. Deciduous or semi-evergreen, glandular, upright sub-shrub. **H** 20–60cm (8–24in), **S** 20–30cm (8–12in) or more. Bears small, rounded, 3-parted, toothed, hairy, green leaves, with the terminal leaflet long-stalked. Flowers that are relatively large, red-streaked, and rose-pink appear in small clusters in summer.

Onopordon. See *Onopordum*.

ONOPORDUM

SYN. ONOPORDON

COMPOSITAE/ASTERACEAE

Genus of annuals, biennials and perennials, ranging from stemless to tall, branching plants. Fully hardy. Grow in sun or semi-shade and in rich, well-drained soil. To prevent self seeding remove dead flower heads. Propagate by seed sown outdoors in autumn or spring. Leaves are prone to slug and snail damage.
O. acanthium illus. p.304.

ONOSMA

BORAGINACEAE

Genus of summer-flowering annuals, semi-evergreen biennials, perennials and sub-shrubs, grown for their long, pendent, tubular flowers. Is suitable for rock gardens. Fully to frost hardy. Needs full sun and well-drained soil. Dislikes wet summers. Propagate by softwood cuttings in summer or by seed in autumn.
O. alborosea illus. p.338.
O. stellulata. Semi-evergreen, upright sub-shrub. **H** and **S** 15cm (6in). Fully hardy. Leaves are oblong and covered in hairs which may irritate the skin. Clusters of yellow flowers open in late spring and summer.

OOPHYTUM

AIZOACEAE

Genus of clump-forming, egg-shaped, perennial succulents with 2 united, very fleshy leaves. These are covered in dry, papery sheaths, except in spring when sheaths split open, revealing a new pair of leaves. Flowers are produced from a slight central fissure on upper surface. Is difficult to grow. Frost tender, min. 5°C (41°F). Requires sun and well-drained soil. Propagate by seed or stem cuttings in spring or summer.
O. nanus. Clump-forming, perennial succulent. **H** 2cm (¾in), **S** 1cm (½in). Has 2 united, fleshy, green leaves and daisy-like, white flowers, 1cm (½in) wide, in autumn.

Operculina tuberosa.
See *Merremia tuberosa*.

OPHIOPOGON

LILIACEAE/CONVALLARIACEAE

Genus of evergreen perennials, grown for their grass-like foliage. Fully to half hardy. Grows in sun or partial shade and in fertile, well-drained soil. Propagate by division in spring or by seed in autumn.
O. jaburan. (illus. p.283) Evergreen, clump-forming perennial. **H** 15cm (6in), **S** 30cm (12in). Frost hardy. Has dark green foliage. In early summer produces racemes of bell-shaped, white flowers, followed by deep blue berries. **'Variegatus'** see *O.j.* 'Vittatus'.
'Vittatus' (syn. *O.j.* 'Variegatus') is half hardy, has white- or yellow-striped foliage and is much less robust.
O. japonicus illus. p.283.
♀ **O. planiscapus 'Nigrescens'** illus. p.280.

OPHRYS

ORCHIDACEAE

See also ORCHIDS.
O. aranifera. See *O. sphegodes*.
O. fuciflora of gardens, syn. *O. holoserica*. Deciduous, terrestrial orchid. **H** 15–55cm (6–22in). Frost hardy. Spikes of flowers, 1cm (½in) long, from white through pink to blue and green, appear in spring-summer. Leaves are oval to oblong, 5–10cm (2–4in) long. Grow in shade outdoors. Containerized plants require semi-shade in summer.
O. fusca. Deciduous, terrestrial orchid. **H** 10–40cm (4–16in). Frost hardy. Spikes of greenish, yellow or brown flowers, 5cm (¼in) long, each with a yellow-edged, bluish, brown or purple lip, are produced in spring. Has oval or lance-shaped leaves, 8–12cm (3–5in) long. Cultivate as for *O. fuciflora* of gardens.
O. holoserica of gardens. See *O. fuciflora* of gardens.
O. lutea (illus. p.467). Deciduous, terrestrial orchid. **H** 8–30cm (3–12in). Frost hardy. In spring bears short spikes of flowers, 1cm ((½in) long, with greenish sepals, yellow petals and brown-centred, bright yellow lips. Has oval, basal leaves, 5–10cm (2–4in) long. Cultivate as for *O. fuciflora* of gardens.
O. speculum, syn. *O. vernixia*. Deciduous, terrestrial orchid. **H** 8–30cm (3–12in). Frost hardy. In spring produces dense spikes of flowers, 1cm (½in) long, with greenish or yellow sepals, purple petals and 3-centred, brown lips. Has oblong to lance-shaped leaves, 4–7cm (1½–3in) long. Cultivate as for *O. fuciflora* of gardens.
O. sphegodes, syn. *O. aranifera* (Spider orchid). Deciduous, terrestrial orchid. **H** 10–45cm (4–18in). Frost hardy. In spring-summer carries spikes of flowers, 1cm (½in) long, that vary from green to yellow and have spider-like, blackish-brown marks on lips. Leaves are oval to lance-shaped and 4–8cm (1½–3in) long. Cultivate as for *O. fuciflora* of gardens.
O. tenthredinifera (Sawfly orchid; illus. p.466). Deciduous, terrestrial orchid. **H** 15–55cm (6–22in). Frost hardy. In spring has spikes of flowers, 1cm (½in) long, in colours of white to pink, or blue and green, each with a violet or bluish lip edged with pale green. Has a basal rosette of oval to oblong leaves, 5–9cm (2–3½in) long. Cultivate as for *O. fuciflora* of gardens.
O. vernixia. See *O. speculum*.

Ophthalmophyllum.
See *Conophytum*.

OPLISMENUS

GRAMINEAE/POACEAE

See also GRASSES, BAMBOOS, RUSHES and SEDGES.
O. africanus, syn. *O. hirtellus* (Basket grass). ♀ **'Variegatus'** illus. p.469.
O. hirtellus. See *O. africanus*.

OPLOPANAX

ARALIACEAE

Genus of deciduous, summer-flowering shrubs, grown for their habit, fruits and spiny foliage. Fully hardy, but young growths may be damaged by late frosts. Does best in a cool, partially shaded position and in moist soil. Propagate by seed in autumn or by root cuttings in late winter.
O. horridus (Devil's club). Deciduous, spreading, open, sparsely branched shrub. **H** and **S** 2m (6ft). Prickly stems bear large, oval, 7–9-lobed, toothed, mid-green leaves. Bears dense umbels of small, star-shaped, greenish-white flowers from mid- to late summer, then spherical, red fruits.

OPUNTIA

Prickly pear

CACTACEAE

Genus of perennial cacti, ranging from small, alpine, ground-cover plants to large, evergreen, tropical trees, with at times insignificant glochids – short, soft, barbed spines produced on areoles. Mature plants carry masses of short-spined, pear-shaped, green, yellow, red or purple fruits (prickly pears), edible in some species. Fully hardy to frost tender, min. 5–10°C (41–50°F). Hardy species must be kept dry during winter in order to survive low temperatures. Needs sun and well-drained soil. Water containerized specimens when in full growth. Propagate by seed or stem cuttings in spring or summer. Some species can spread and become invasive. Contact with the bristles causes intense irritation to skin, and they are difficult to remove.

O. brasiliensis, syn. *Brasiliopuntia brasiliensis*. Tree-like, perennial cactus. **H** 5.5m (18ft), **S** 3m (10ft). Frost tender, min. 10°C (50°F). Has a cylindrical, green stem bearing bright green branches of flattened, oval, spiny segments. Sheds 2–3-year-old side branches. Masses of shallowly saucer-shaped, yellow flowers, 4cm (1½in) across, appear in spring summer, only on plants over 60cm (2ft) tall, and are followed by small, yellow fruits.

O. cylindrica, syn. *Austrocylindropuntia cylindrica*. Bushy, perennial cactus. **H** 4–6m (12–20ft), **S** 1m (3ft). Frost tender, min. 10°C (50°F). On cylindrical stems, 4–5cm (1½–2in) across, are borne short-lived, cylindrical, dark green leaves, to 2cm (¾in) long, on new growth. Areoles may lack spines or each produce 2 or 3 barbed ones. Shallowly saucer-shaped, pink-red flowers appear in spring-summer, only on plants over 2m (6ft) tall, and are followed by greenish-yellow fruits.

O. erinacea. See *O. polyacantha.*

O. ficus-indica (Edible prickly pear, Indian fig). Bushy to tree-like, perennial cactus. **H** and **S** 5m (15ft). Frost tender, min. 10°C (50°F). Bears flattened, oblong, blue-green stem segments, 50cm (20in) long and spineless. In spring-summer has masses of shallowly saucer-shaped, yellow flowers, 10cm (4in) across, followed by edible, purple fruits.

O. humifusa illus. p.494.

O. microdasys (Bunny ears). Bushy, perennial cactus. **H** and **S** 60cm (2ft). Frost tender, min. 10°C (50°F). Has flattened, oval, green stem segments, 8–18cm (3–7in) long, that develop brown marks in low temperatures. Bears spineless areoles, with white, yellow, brown or red glochids, closely set in diagonal rows. Masses of funnel-shaped, yellow flowers, 5cm (2in) across, appear in summer on plants over 15cm (6in) tall, and are followed by small, dark red fruits. **var. *albispina*** illus. p.483.

O. polycantha, syn. *O. erinacea*, illus. p.481.

O. robusta illus. p.488.

O. tunicata, syn. *Cylindropuntia tunicata*, illus. p.496.

O. verschaffeltii, syn. *Austrocylindropuntia verschaffeltii*, illus. p.486.

ORBEA

ASCLEPIADACEAE/APOCYNACEAE

Genus of clump-forming, perennial succulents with erect, 4-angled stems. Stem edges are often indented and may produce small leaves that drop after only a few weeks. Frost tender, min. 11°C (52°F). Needs sun or partial shade and well-drained soil. Propagate by seed or stem cuttings in spring or summer.

🏆 ***O. variegata***, syn. *Stapelia variegata*, (Star flower) illus. p.488.

ORCHIDS

ORCHIDACEAE

Family of perennials, some of which are evergreen or semi-evergreen, grown for their beautiful, unusual flowers. These consist of 3 outer sepals and 3 inner petals, the lowest of which, known as the lip, is usually enlarged and different from the others in shape, markings and colour. There are about 750 genera and 22,500 species, together with an even greater number of hybrids, bred partly for their vigour and ease of care. They are divided into epiphytic and terrestrial plants. (The spread of an orchid is indefinite.)

Epiphytic orchids

Epiphytes have more flamboyant flowers than terrestrial orchids and are more commonly grown. In the wild, they grow on tree branches or rocks (lithophytes), obtaining nourishment through clinging roots and moisture through aerial roots. Most consist of a horizontal rhizome, from which arise vertical, water-storing, often swollen stems known as pseudobulbs. Flowers and foliage are produced from the newest pseudobulbs. Other epiphytes consist of a continuously growing upright rhizome; on these, flower spikes appear in the axils of leaves growing from the rhizome. In temperate climates, epiphytes need to be grown under glass.

Cultivation of epiphytes

For cultivation purposes, epiphytes, which are all frost tender, may be divided into 3 groups: cool-greenhouse types, which require min. 10°C (50°F) and max. 24°C (75°F); intermediate-greenhouse types, needing a range of 13–27°C (55–80°F); and warm-greenhouse types, requiring 18–27°C (65–80°F). In summer, temperatures need to be controlled by shading the glass and by ventilation. Cool-greenhouse orchids may be placed outdoors in summer; this improves flowering. Other types may also be grown outdoors if the air temperature remains within these ranges.

The amount of light required in summer is given in individual plant entries. All epiphytic orchids, however, need to be kept out of direct sun in summer to avoid scorching, and require full light in winter.

Epiphytic orchids, whether grown indoors or outside, require a special soil-free compost obtained from an orchid nursery or made by mixing 2 parts fibrous material (such as bark chippings and/or peat) with 1 part porous material (such as moss and/or expanded clay pellets). Most epiphytes may be grown in pots, although some may be successfully cultivated in a hanging basket or on a slab of bark (with moss around their roots) suspended in the greenhouse.

In summer, water plants freely and spray regularly. Those suspended on bark slabs need a constantly moist atmosphere. In winter, water moderately and, if plants are in growth, spray occasionally. Some orchids rest in winter and require scarcely any water or none at all. Orchids benefit from weak foliar feeds; apply as for watering. Repot plants every other year, in spring; if they are about to flower, repot after flowering.

Terrestrial orchids

Terrestrial orchids, some of which also produce pseudobulbs, grow in soil or leaf mould, sustaining themselves in the normal way through roots or tubers. Some may be grown in borders, but many in temperate climates need to be cultivated in pots and protected under glass during winter.

Cultivation of terrestrial orchids

Terrestrial orchids are fully hardy to frost tender, min. 18°C (65°F). *Cypripedium* species may be grown outdoors in any area, preferably in neutral to acid soil, but cannot withstand severe frost, if frozen solid in pots or without snow cover, or tolerate very wet soil in winter. Other terrestrial orchids, except in very mild areas, are best grown in pots; use the same compost as for epiphytes but add 1 part grit to 2 parts compost. Place pots outdoors in a peat bed or in a glasshouse in the growing season. Keep dry when dormant. Under glass, light requirements, watering, feeding and repotting are as for epiphytes.

Orchid propagation

Orchids with pseudobulbs may be increased by removing and replanting old, leafless pseudobulbs when repotting in spring. Take care to retain at least 4 pseudobulbs on the parent plant. Some genera that may be propagated in this way are: *Ada*, x *Aliceara*, *Anguloa*, *Bletilla*, *Brassavola* (large plants only and retaining at least 6 pseudobulbs on the parent), x *Brassocattleya*, x *Brassolaeliocattleya*, *Bulbophyllum*, *Calanthe*, *Cattleya*, *Coelogyne*, *Cymbidium*, *Dendrobium*, *Dendrochilum*, *Encyclia*, *Gomesa*, *Gongora*, *Laelia*, x *Laeliocattleya*, *Lycaste*, *Maxillaria*, *Miltonia*, *Miltoniopsis*, x *Odontioda*, x *Odontocidium*, *Odontoglossum*, x *Odontonia*, *Oncidium*, *Phaius*, *Pleione*, x *Potinara*, x *Sophrolaeliocattleya*, *Stanhopea*, x *Vuylstekeara*, x *Wilsonara* and *Zygopetalum*.

Some orchids without pseudobulbs produce new growth from the base. When a plant has 6 new growths, divide it in spring into 2 and repot both portions. Propagate *Disa*, *Paphiopedilum* and *Phragmipedium* in this way. Large specimens of *Eria*, *Masdevallia* and *Pleurothallis* may be divided in spring, leaving 4–6 stems on each portion.

Propagation of *Phalaenopsis* is by stem cuttings taken soon after flowering. *Vanda* may be increased by removing the top half of the stem once it has produced aerial roots and leaves; new growths will develop from the leafless base. With both these methods achieving success is difficult and not recommended for the beginner.

Propagate terrestrial orchids with tubers by division of the tubers. Genera that may be increased in this way are: *Cypripedium* (in spring), *Dactylorhiza* (spring), *Ophrys* (autumn), *Orchis* (spring), *Serapias* (autumn) and *Spiranthes* (spring). *Calypso* is rarely propagated successfully in cultivation. *Angraecum* should not be propagated in cultivation, because the parent plant is easily endangered. Propagate *Ponerorchis* by small tubers that form around the base of the stem, when repotting tubers before growth commences in early spring. Seedlings may appear in the compost around the parent plant.

The most easily increased orchids are *Cymbidium*. Propagation of *Epidendrum* may be extremely difficult; see genus for specific details.

Orchids are illustrated on pp.466–47. See also *Ada*, x *Aliceara*, *Angraecum*, *Anguloa*, *Bletilla*, *Brassavola*, x *Brassocattleya*, *Bulbophyllum*, *Calanthe*, *Calypso*, *Cattleya*, x *Cattlianthe*, *Coelogyne*, *Cymbidium*, *Cypripedium*, *Dactylorhiza*, *Dendrobium*, *Dendrochilum*, *Encyclia*, *Epidendrum*, *Eria*, *Gomesa*, *Gongora*, *Guarianthe*, *Laelia*, x *Laeliocattleya*, *Lycaste*, *Masdevallia*, *Maxillariella*, *Miltonia*, *Miltoniopsis*, *Oncidium*, x *Oncidopsis*, *Ophrys*, *Orchis*, *Paphiopedilum*, *Phaius*, *Phalaenopsis*, *Phragmipedium*, *Pleione*, *Pleurothallis*, x *Potinara*, *Psychopsis*, x *Rhyncattleanthe*, *Rossioglossum*, *Serapias*, *Spiranthes*, *Stanhopea*, *Vanda*, x *Vuylstekeara*, x *Wilsonara* and *Zygopetalum*.

Orchis elata. See *Dactylorhiza elata.*

Orchis morio. See *Anacamptis morio.*

OREOCEREUS

CACTACEAE

Genus of mainly columnar, perennial cacti with thick, cylindrical, much-ribbed stems with spines, usually branching from the base, and, in some species, are covered in long hairs. Solitary, tubular-funnel-shaped flowers are produced near stem tips during the day in summer. Frost tender, min. 10°C (50°F). Requires full sun and very well-drained, slightly alkaline soil. Water well during the spring and summer, much less so in autumn and winter. Propagate by seed in spring or summer.

O. aurantiacus. See *Matucana aurantiaca.*

O. celsianus, syn. *Cleistocactus celsianus*, illus. p.493.

O. trollii, syn. *Cleistocactus trollii* (Old man of the Andes). Slow-growing, columnar, perennial cactus. **H** 70cm (28in), **S** 10cm (4in). Cylindrical, green stem, 7–10cm (3–4in), with thick, golden spines is almost hidden by long, wispy, hair-like, white spines. Has pink flowers, recurved at tips and 10cm (4in) long, in summer on fully mature plants.

OREOPTERIS

THELYPTERIDACEAE

Genus of deciduous ferns. Fully hardy. Tolerates sun or semi-shade. Grow in moist or very moist soil. Remove fading fronds regularly. Spreads via under ground rhizomes to form colonies. Some species can be invasive. Propagate by division in spring.

O. limbosperma, syn. *Thelypteris oreopteris* (Mountain buckler fern, Mountain fern, Mountain wood fern). Deciduous fern. **H** 60cm–1m (2–3ft), **S** 30cm (1ft). Has mainly lance-shaped, much-divided fronds, with oblong to lance-shaped, mid-green pinnae.

ORIGANUM

Marjoram, Oregano

LABIATAE/LAMIACEAE

Genus of deciduous sub-shrubs and perennials, sometimes with overwintering leaf rosettes. Some species are grown as culinary herbs, others for their clusters of tubular, usually pink flowers. Most species have arching, prostrate stems and are useful for trailing over rocks, banks and walls. Fully to frost hardy. Prefers sun and well-drained, alkaline soil. Propagate by division in spring, by cuttings of non-flowering shoots in early summer or by seed in autumn or spring.

♀ ***O. amanum.*** Deciduous, rounded, compact sub-shrub. **H** and **S** 15–20cm (6–8in). Frost hardy. Open funnel-shaped, pale pink or white flowers are borne all summer above small, heart-shaped, pale green leaves. Makes a good alpine house plant; dislikes a damp atmosphere.

O. dictamnus (Cretan dittany). Prostrate perennial. **H** 12–15cm (5–6in), **S** 40cm (16in). Frost hardy. Arching stems are clothed in rounded, aromatic, hairy, grey-white leaves. Has pendent heads of open funnel-shaped, purplish-pink flowers in summer.

O. 'Kent Beauty' illus. p.339.

♀ ***O. laevigatum*** illus. p.340.

♀ ***O. rotundifolium.*** Deciduous, prostrate sub-shrub. **H** 23–30cm (9–12in), **S** 30cm (12in). Fully hardy. Throughout summer bears whorls of pendent, funnel-shaped, pale pink flowers, surrounded by yellow-green bracts. Has small, rounded, mid-green leaves.

O. vulgare (Wild marjoram). Mat-forming, woody-based perennial. **H** and **S** 45cm (18in). Fully hardy. Has oval, aromatic, dark green leaves, above which branched, wiry stems bear clusters of tiny, tubular, 2-lipped, mauve flowers in summer. ♀ **'Aureum'** illus. p.274.

ORNITHOGALUM

Star-of-Bethlehem

LILIACEAE/HYACINTHACEAE

Genus of bulbs, grown for their mostly star-shaped, white flowers, usually backed with green. Fully hardy to frost tender, min. 7°C (45°F). Needs sun or partial shade and well-drained soil. Lift and dry tender species for winter, if grown outside in summer, and replant in spring. Propagate by seed or offsets, in autumn for spring-flowering plants, in spring for summer-flowering ones. ⓘ Handle carefuly as all parts may cause severe discomfort if ingested; the sap may irritate skin.

O. arabicum illus. p.408.

O. balansae, syn. *O. oligophyllum* of gardens, illus. p.414.

O. lanceolatum illus. p.415.

O. magnum illus. p.382.

O. montanum illus. p.415.

O. narbonense illus. p.408.

♀ ***O. nutans*** (Drooping star-of-Bethlehem) illus. p.399. Spring-flowering bulb. **H** 15–35cm (6–14in), **S** 8–10cm (3–4in). Frost hardy. Has a cluster of linear, channelled, semi-erect, basal leaves. Stem bears a spike of pendent, bell-shaped, translucent, white flowers, 2–3cm (¾–1¼in) long with pale green outsides. Prefers partial shade.

O. oligophyllum of gardens. See *O. balansae*.

O. saundersiae. Summer-flowering bulb. **H** to 1m (3ft), **S** 15–20cm (6–8in). Half hardy. Produces a basal cluster of strap- or lance-shaped, semi-erect leaves. Stem bears a flat-topped head of erect, flattish, white or cream flowers, each with a blackish-green ovary forming a dark eye.

O. thyrsoides illus. p.408.

O. umbellatum (illus. p.416.) Spring-flowering bulb. **H** 10–30cm (4–12in), **S** 10–15cm (4–6in). Frost hardy. Linear, channelled, semi-erect, green leaves each have a white line on upper surface. Bears a loose, flat-topped head of star-shaped, white flowers, backed with green.

Orobus vernus. See *Lathyrus vernus*.

ORONTIUM

Golden club

ARACEAE

Genus of one species of deciduous, perennial, deep-water plant, grown for its floating foliage and flower spikes. Fully hardy. Needs full sun. Remove faded flower spikes. Propagate by seed when fresh, in mid-summer.

O. aquaticum illus. p.444.

OROSTACHYS

CRASSULACEAE

Genus of short-lived, basal-rosetted, perennial succulents with very fleshy, sword-shaped leaves. Produces flowers 3 years from sowing seed, then dies. Frost tender, min. 8°C (46°F). Requires sun and well-drained soil. Propagate by seed or division in spring or summer.

O. chanetii. Basal-rosetted, perennial succulent. **H** 4cm (1½in), **S** 8cm (3in). Bears grey-green leaves that are shorter in rosette centre. Flower stem produces a dense, tapering spike of star-shaped, white or pink flowers, 1–2cm (½–¾in) across, in spring-summer.

OROYA

CACTACEAE

Genus of spherical, perennial cacti. Inner flower petals form a tube and outer ones open fully. Frost tender, min. 10°C (50°F). Needs a sunny, well-drained site. Propagate by seed in spring or summer.

O. neoperuviana. See *O. peruviana*.

O. peruviana, syn. *O. neoperuviana*, illus. p.486.

Orphanidesia gaultherioides. See *Epigaea gaultheriodes*.

ORTHROSANTHUS

IRIDACEAE

Genus of perennials with short, woody rhizomes, grown for their flowers. Frost tender, min. 5°C (41°F). Prefers sun and well-drained soil. Propagate by division or seed in spring.

O. chimboracensis. Tufted, rhizomatous perennial. **H** 60cm (2ft) in flower, **S** 15cm (6in). Has very narrow, grass-like, ribbed, stiff leaves, to 45cm (18in) long, with finely toothed margins. In summer, produces clusters of short-lived, long-stalked, shallowly bowl-shaped, lavender-blue flowers, each enclosed in 2 leaf-like bracts.

ORYCHOPHRAGMUS

CRUCIFERAE/BRASSICACEAE

Genus of late spring- to summer-flowering annuals. Half hardy. Grow in sun and in fertile, well-drained soil. Propagate by seed in spring.

O. violaceus. Moderately fast-growing, upright annual or biennial. **H** 30–60cm (12–24cm), **S** 30cm (12in). Has branching flower stems and pointed-oval, pale green leaves. Heads of 4-petalled, purple-blue flowers are carried in spring.

Osage orange. See *Maclura pomifera*.

OSBECKIA

MELASTOMATACEAE

Genus of evergreen, summer-flowering perennials, sub-shrubs and shrubs, grown for their flowers and foliage. Frost tender, min. 16°C (61°F). Needs full light or partial shade and humus-rich, well-drained soil. Water potted specimens freely when in full growth, moderately at other times. Cut back flowered stems by at least half in early spring to maintain vigour and to produce large flower trusses. Propagate by seed in spring or by greenwood cuttings in summer.

O. stellata. Evergreen, rounded, stiff-stemmed shrub. **H** and **S** 1–2m (3–6ft). Has narrowly oval, hairy, prominently veined leaves. Bears terminal clusters of 4-petalled, rose-purple flowers in late summer.

OSCULARIA

AIZOCEACE

Genus of spreading, sometimes erect, subshrubby perennial succulents with daisy-like, white to pink flowers, and usually angular, fleshy, greyish-green leaves. Frost tender, min 7°C (41°F), if dry. Use for summer bedding or as pot plants. Becomes woody with age. Requires full sun and very well-drained soil. Propagate by seed or stem cuttings in spring or autumn.

♀ ***O. deltoides***, syn. *Lampranthus deltoides*, illus. p.485.

OSMANTHUS

OLEACEAE

Genus of evergreen shrubs and trees, grown for their foliage and small, fragrant flowers. *O.* x *burkwoodii* and *O. heterophyllus* may be used for hedging. Fully to half hardy. Tolerates sun or shade and fertile, well-drained soil. Restrict growth by cutting back after flowering; trim hedges in mid-summer. Propagate by semi-ripe cuttings in summer.

O. armatus. Evergreen, bushy, dense shrub. **H** and **S** 4m (12ft). Frost hardy. Large, oblong, dark green leaves are rigid and sharply toothed. Has tubular, 4-lobed, white flowers in autumn, then egg-shaped, dark violet fruits.

♀ ***O. x burkwoodii***, syn. x *Osmarea burkwoodii*, illus. p.110.

O. decorus, syn. *Phillyrea decora*. Evergreen, upright, rounded, dense shrub. **H** 3m (10ft), **S** 5m (15ft). Fully hardy. Has large, oblong, glossy, dark green leaves. Bears tubular, 4-lobed, white flowers in mid-spring, then egg-shaped, blackish-purple fruits.

♀ ***O. delavayi***, syn. *Siphonosmanthus delavayi*, illus. p.110.

O. forrestii. See *O. yunnanensis*.

O. fragrans (Fragrant olive). Evergreen, upright shrub or tree. **H** and **S** 6m (20ft). Half hardy. Very fragrant, tubular, 4-lobed, white flowers are borne amid oblong, glossy, dark green leaves from early to late summer, followed by ovoid, blue-black fruits. Is suitable only for very mild areas. **f. aurantiacus** has orange flowers.

***O. heterophyllus* 'Aureomarginatus'** illus. p.119. ♀ **'Gulftide'** is an evergreen, bushy, dense shrub. **H** 2.5m (8ft), **S** 3m (10ft). Frost hardy. Holly-shaped, sharply toothed, glossy, dark green leaves set off tubular, 4-lobed, white flowers in autumn.

O. yunnanensis, syn. *O. forrestii*. Evergreen, tree-like, upright, then spreading shrub. **H** and **S** 10m (30ft). Frost hardy. Has large, oblong, glossy, bright green leaves, bronze when young. Produces tubular, 4-lobed, creamy-white flowers in clusters in late winter or early spring.

x *Osmarea burkwoodii.* See *Osmanthus* x *burkwoodii*.

Osmaronia. See *Oemleria*.

OSMUNDA

OSMUNDACEAE

Genus of deciduous ferns. Fully hardy. Requires shade, except for *O. regalis*, which also tolerates sun. *O. cinnamomea* and *O. claytoniana* need moist soil; *O. regalis* does best in very wet conditions. Remove fading fronds regularly. Propagate by division in autumn or winter or by spores as soon as ripe.

♀ ***O. cinnamomea*** (Cinnamon fern). Deciduous fern. **H** 1m (3ft), **S** 45cm (18in). Outer, lance-shaped, divided, pale green sterile fronds, with deeply cut pinnae, surround brown fertile fronds, all arising from a fibrous rootstock.

♀ ***O. claytoniana*** (Interrupted fern). Deciduous fern. **H** 60cm (2ft), **S** 30cm (1ft). Has lance-shaped, pale green fronds,

divided into oblong, blunt pinnae; outer sterile fronds are larger than fertile ones at centre of plant.
♀ ***O. regalis*** (Royal fern) illus. p.443.

OSTEOMELES

ROSACEAE

Genus of evergreen, summer-flowering shrubs, grown for their habit, foliage and flowers. Frost to half hardy. In most areas plant against a south- or west-facing wall. Requires a position in sun and fertile, well-drained soil. Propagate by semi-ripe cuttings in summer.
O. schweriniae illus. p.129.

OSTEOSPERMUM

COMPOSITAE/ASTERACEAE

Genus of evergreen, semi-woody perennials. Frost to half hardy; does best in warm areas. Requires sun and well-drained soil. Propagate by cuttings of non-flowering shoots in mid-summer.
O. barberae of gardens.
See *O. jucundum*.
O. 'Blue Streak', syn. *O. ecklonis* 'Blue Streak'. Evergreen, upright perennial. **H** and **S** 45cm (18in). Half hardy. In summer-autumn, daisy-like flower heads, with dark slate-blue centres and white ray florets, blue on the reverse, are borne above lance-shaped, grey-green leaves.
♀ ***O. 'Buttermilk'*** illus. p.319.
O. 'Cannington Roy'. Evergreen, clump-forming, prostrate perennial. **H** 30cm (12in), **S** 45cm (18in). Half hardy. Large, daisy-like, pink flower heads, with darker eyes, are borne profusely in summer-autumn. Leaves are linear and grey.
***O.* Cape Daisy Series NASINGA PURPLE ('Aksullo')** illus. p.311.
O. ecklonis. Evergreen, upright or somewhat straggling perennial. **H** and **S** 45cm (18in). Half hardy. In summer-autumn, daisy-like, white flower heads, with dark blue centres, are borne singly above lance-shaped, grey-green leaves.
'Blue Streak' see *O.* 'Blue Streak'.
♀ ***O. jucundum***, syn. *Dimorphotheca barberae* of gardens, *O. barberae* of gardens, illus. p.265.
O. 'Nairobi Purple'. Evergreen, semi-prostrate perennial. **H** 30cm (12in), **S** 30–45cm (12–18in). Half hardy. Bears daisy-like, velvety, deep purple-red flower heads, with darker streaks on outside of ray petals, in summer. Has fresh green, lance-shaped leaves. Will not flower freely in rich soils.
***O.* Sunny Series 'Sunny Marina'** illus. p.301.
♀ ***O. 'Whirlygig'*** illus. p.298.

OSTROWSKIA

CAMPANULACEAE

Genus of one species of summer-flowering perennial. Fully hardy. Prefers a warm, sunny situation and rich, moist but well-drained soil. May be difficult to grow because it requires a resting period after flowering, so cover with a frame until late autumn to keep dry. Propagate by seed in autumn or spring.
O. magnifica. Erect perennial. **H** 1.5m (5ft), **S** 45cm (1½ft). From early to mid-summer produces very large, bell-shaped blooms of delicate light blue-purple, veined with darker purple. Produces whorls of oval, blue-grey leaves.

OSTRYA

CORYLACEAE/BETULACEAE

Genus of deciduous trees, grown for their foliage, catkins and fruits. Fully hardy. Needs sun or semi-shade and fertile, well-drained soil. Propagate by seed in autumn.
O. carpinifolia (Hop hornbeam). Deciduous, rounded tree. **H** and **S** 15m (50ft). Has grey bark and oval, glossy, dark green leaves that turn yellow in autumn. Yellow catkins in mid-spring are followed by hop-like, greenish-white fruit clusters that become brown in autumn.
O. virginiana illus. p.72.

OTHONNA

SYN. OTHONNOPSIS

COMPOSITAE/ASTERACEAE

Genus of evergreen shrubs, grown for their daisy-like flower heads in summer. Half hardy. Needs sun and well-drained soil. Propagate by softwood cuttings in early summer.
O. cheirifolia illus. p.344.

Othonnopsis. See *Othonna*.

OURISIA

SCROPHULARIACEAE

Genus of evergreen perennials with creeping rootstocks. Excellent for peat beds and walls. Fully to frost hardy. Needs shade and moist, peaty soil. Propagate by division or seed in spring.
O. caespitosa illus. p.360.
O. coccinea illus. p.269.
O. 'Loch Ewe'. Vigorous, evergreen, rosetted perennial. **H** and **S** 30cm (12in). Frost hardy. Prostrate stems have heart-shaped, leathery, green leaves. Produces dense spikes of outward-facing, tubular, salmon-pink flowers in late spring and early summer.
O. macrocarpa. Vigorous, evergreen, prostrate perennial. **H** 60cm (24in), **S** 20cm (8in). Frost hardy. Has rosettes of heart-shaped, leathery, dark green leaves. Produces spikes of open cup-shaped, yellow-centred, white flowers in late spring.
O. magellanica. See *O. ruellioides*.
O. microphylla illus. p.362.
O. ruellioides, syn. *O. magellanica*. Evergreen, straggling perennial. **H** 4cm (1½in), **S** to 15cm (6in). Frost hardy. In summer produces tubular, scarlet flowers above broadly heart-shaped leaves.

OXALIS

OXALIDACEAE

Genus of tuberous, rhizomatous or fibrous-rooted perennials and semi-evergreen sub-shrubs, grown for their colourful flowers, which in bud are rolled like an umbrella, and their often attractive leaves. Leaves are mostly less than 2cm (¾in) across and are divided into 3 or more leaflets. Some species may be invasive; smaller species and cultivars suit a rock garden. Fully hardy to frost tender, min. 5°C (41°F). Needs full sun or semi-shade and well-drained soil. Propagate by division in autumn or early spring.
O. acetosella (Wood sorrel). Creeping, spring-flowering, rhizomatous perennial. **H** 5cm (2in), **S** 30–45cm (12–18in). Fully hardy. Forms mats of clover-like, 3-lobed leaves. Delicate stems bear cup-shaped, white flowers, each 1cm (½in) across with 5 purple-veined petals. Prefers semi-shade. **var. *purpurascens*** see *O.a.* var. *subpurpurascens*. **var. *subpurpurascens***, syn. *O.a.* var. *purpurascens*, illus. p.352.
♀ ***O. adenophylla*** illus. p.352.
O. bowiei, syn. *O. purpurata* var. *bowiei*. Spring- to summer-flowering, tuberous perennial. **H** to 30cm (12in), **S** 15cm (6in). Half hardy. Has long-stalked, clover-like, 3-lobed leaves. Stems each produce a loose head of 3–10 widely funnel-shaped, pinkish-purple flowers, 3–4cm (1¼–1½in) across. Needs a sheltered, sunny site.
O. chrysantha. Creeping, fibrous-rooted perennial. **H** 4–5cm (1½–2in), **S** 15–30cm (6–12in). Half hardy. Forms mats of clover-like, 3-lobed leaves. Stems each produce a funnel-shaped, bright yellow flower, 2–3cm (¾–1¼in) across, in summer. Requires a sheltered position.
O. deppei. See *O. tetraphylla*.
O. depressa, syn. *O. inops*, illus. p.364.
♀ ***O. enneaphylla*** (Scurvy grass). Tuft-forming, rhizomatous perennial. **H** 5–7cm (2–3in), **S** 8–10cm (3–4in). Frost hardy. Grey-green leaves are divided into narrowly oblong to oval leaflets. In summer, stems bear widely funnel-shaped, 3–4cm (1¼–1½in) wide, lilac-pink or white flowers.
O. hedysaroides. Semi-evergreen, bushy sub-shrub. **H** 1m (3ft), **S** 30–45cm (1–1½ft). Half hardy. Stems have clover-like, green leaves with 3 elliptical leaflets, the central leaflet on a stalk. Leaf axils bear clusters of widely funnel-shaped, yellow flowers, 2–3cm (¾–1¼in) across, in spring-summer.
O. hirta. Late summer-flowering, tuberous perennial. **H** 30cm (12in), **S** 10–15cm (4–6in). Half hardy. Stem produces scattered leaves, with 3 narrowly lance-shaped leaflets. Leaf axils each produce a widely funnel-shaped, rose-purple flower, 2–3cm (¾–1¼in) wide, with a yellow centre.
O. inops. See *O. depressa*.
♀ ***O. 'Ione Hecker'.*** Tuft-forming, rhizomatous perennial. **H** 5cm (2in), **S** 5–8cm (2–3in). Frost hardy. Grey leaves are composed of narrowly oblong, wavy leaflets. In summer bears funnel-shaped, pale purple-blue flowers, 4cm (1½in) across, with darker veins.
O. laciniata. Tuft-forming, rhizomatous perennial. **H** 5cm (2in), **S** 5–8cm (2–3in). Frost hardy. Has blue-grey leaves with narrowly oblong, crinkly-edged leaflets. In summer bears wide funnel-shaped, steel-blue flowers, 4cm (1½) across, with darker veins.
O. perdicaria illus. p.371.
***O. purpurata* var. *bowiei*.**
See *O. bowiei*.
O. spiralis* subsp. *vulcanicola, syn. *O. vulcanicola*. Evergreen sub-shrub. **H** and **S** 30cm (12in). Half hardy. Succulent red stems bear clover-like, 3-lobed leaves in shades of reddish-yellow to dark or mid-green. Widely funnel-shaped, yellow flowers, 1.5cm (⅝in) across, are borne in clusters from spring to autumn. Is often used in summer bedding or in a hanging basket.
O. tetraphylla, syn. *O. deppei*, illus. p.338.
O. vulcanicola. See *O. spiralis* subsp. *vulcanicola*.

OXYDENDRUM

ERICACEAE

Genus of one species of deciduous tree, grown for its flowers and spectacular autumn colour. Fully hardy. For good colouring plant in an open position in sun or semi-shade. Needs moist, acid soil. Propagate by softwood cuttings in summer or by seed in autumn.
O. arboreum illus. p.76.

Oxypetalum caeruleum.
See *Tweedia caerulea*.

OZOTHAMNUS

COMPOSITAE/ASTERACEAE

Genus of evergreen, summer-flowering shrubs, grown for their foliage and small, densely clustered flower heads. Fully to half hardy. Requires full sun and well-drained soil. Propagate by semi-ripe cuttings in summer.
♀ ***O. coralloides***, syn. *Helichrysum coralloides*, illus. p.347.
♀ ***O. ledifolius***, syn. *Helichrysum ledifolium*, illus. p.151.
O. rosmarinifolius, syn. *Helichrysum rosmarinifolium*.
O. selago, syn. *Helichrysum selago*, illus. p.347.

PQ

PACHYCEREUS

CACTACEAE

Genus of slow-growing, columnar, perennial cacti, branching with age. The funnel-shaped flowers are unlikely to appear in cultivation as they are produced only on plants over 3m (10ft) high. Frost tender, min. 10°C (50°F). Requires sun and well-drained soil. Propagate by seed in spring or summer.

P. marginatus, syn. *Lemaireocereus marginatus, Marginatocereus marginatus, Stenocereus marginatus*, illus. p.494.

P. pecten-aboriginum. Columnar, perennial cactus. **H** 11m (35ft), **S** 3m (10ft). Dark green stems bear 9–11 deep ribs. Each areole has 8 radial spines, 1cm (½in) long, and longer central spines. Red-based, dark brown spines fade to grey.

P. pringlei illus. p.483.

P. schottii, syn. *Lophocereus schottii*, illus. p.493. **'Monstrosus'** is a columnar, perennial cactus. **H** 7m (22ft), **S** 2m (6ft). Irregular, olive- to dark green stems have 4–15 ribs and no spines. Has funnel-shaped, pink flowers, 3cm (1¼in) wide, at night in summer.

Pachyphragma. See *Thlaspi.*

PACHYPHYTUM

CRASSULACEAE

Genus of rosetted, perennial succulents, closely related to *Echeveria*, with which it hybridizes. Frost tender, min. 5–10°C (41–50°F). Needs sun and well-drained soil. Propagate by seed, or leaf or stem cuttings in spring or summer.

P. compactum illus. p.491.

P. oviferum illus. p.490.

PACHYPODIUM

APOCYNACEAE

Genus of bushy or tree-like, perennial succulents, mostly with swollen stems, closely related to *Adenium*, except that most species have spines. Frost tender, min. 10–15°C (50–59°F). Requires full sun and very well-drained soil. May be very difficult to grow. Propagate by seed in spring or summer.

♀ ***P. lamerei*** illus. p.494.

P. succulentum. Tree-like, perennial succulent. **H** 60cm (2ft), **S** 30cm (1ft). Min. 10°C (50°F). Swollen trunk, 15cm (6in) across, has narrow, vertical, green to grey-brown stems. Has trumpet-shaped, pink-crimson flowers, 2cm (¾in) across, near stem tips in summer.

PACHYSANDRA

BUXACEAE

Genus of evergreen, creeping perennials and sub-shrubs, grown for their tufted foliage. Is useful for ground cover. Fully hardy. Tolerates dense shade and grows in any but very dry soil. Propagate by division in spring.

P. axillaris. Evergreen, mat-forming sub-shrub. **H** 20cm (8in), **S** 25cm (10in). Stems are each crowned by 3–6 oval, toothed, leathery leaves. Carries small, white flowers in erect spikes in late spring.

P. terminalis illus. p.375. ♀ **'Variegata'** is an evergreen, creeping perennial. **H** 10cm (4in), **S** 20cm (8in). Diamond-shaped, cream-variegated leaves are clustered at stem tips. In early summer, bears spikes of tiny, white flowers, sometimes flushed purple.

PACHYSTACHYS

ACANTHACEAE

Genus of evergreen perennials and shrubs, grown for their flowers. Frost tender, min. 13–18°C (55–64°F). Needs partial shade and fertile, well-drained soil. Water potted plants freely when in full growth, moderately at other times. Cut back flowered stems in late winter to maintain a bushy habit. Propagate by greenwood cuttings in early summer. Whitefly and red spider mite may cause problems.

P. cardinalis. See *P. coccinea.*

P. coccinea, syn. *Jacobinia coccinea, Justicia coccinea, P. cardinalis* (Cardinal's guard). Evergreen, erect, robust shrub. **H** 1.2–2m (4–6ft), **S** 60cm–1m (2–3ft). Min. 15–18°C (59–64°F) to flower well. Leaves are oval and deep green. Has tubular, bright red flowers in tight, green-bracted spikes, 15cm (6in) long, in winter.

♀ ***P. lutea*** illus. p.459.

Pachystima. See *Paxistima.*

x PACHYVERIA

CRASSULACEAE

Hybrid genus (*Echeveria* x *Pachyphytum*) of clump-forming, rosetted, perennial succulents, sometimes almost stemless. Frost tender, min. 5–7°C (41–45°F). Requires full sun or partial shade and very well-drained soil. Propagate by leaf or stem cuttings in spring or summer.

x *P. glauca* illus. p.490.

PAEONIA

Peony

PAEONIACEAE

Genus of late spring-flowering perennials and deciduous shrubs ("tree peonies"), valued for their bold foliage, showy blooms and, in some species, colourful seed pods. Fully hardy, unless otherwise stated, although young growth (especially on tree peonies) may be damaged by late spring frosts. Prefers sun (but tolerates light shade) and rich, well-drained soil. Tall and very large-flowered cultivars need support. Propagate all species by seed in autumn (may take up to 3 years to germinate), tuberous species by root cuttings in winter, tree peonies by semi-ripe cuttings in late summer or by grafting in winter. Perennials may also be propagated by division in autumn or early spring. Is prone to peony wilt. ⓘ All parts can cause mild stomach upset if ingested. See also feature panel pp.228–229.

Flower forms

Unless stated otherwise, peonies described below flower between late spring and early to mid-summer and have large, alternate leaves divided into oval to lance-shaped or linear leaflets. Flowers are single, semi-double, double or anemone-form.

Single – flowers are mostly cup-shaped, with 1 or 2 rows of large, often lightly ruffled, incurving petals and a conspicuous central boss of stamens.

Semi-double – flowers are similar to single ones, but have 2 or 3 rows of petals.

Double – flowers are rounded, usually composed of 1 or 2 outer rows of large, often lightly ruffled, incurving petals, the remaining petals being smaller, usually becoming more densely arranged and diminishing in size towards the centre. Stamens are few, inconspicuous, or absent.

Anemone-form (Imperial or Japanese) – flowers usually have 1 or 2 rows of broad, incurving, outer petals; the centre of the flower is often filled entirely with numerous densely arranged, sometimes deeply cut, narrow petaloids derived from stamens.

***P.* 'Alice Harding'.** Clump-forming perennial. **H** and **S** to 1m (3ft). Bears very large, fragrant, double, creamy-white flowers.

***P.* 'America'** (illus. p.229). Clump-forming perennial. **H** and **S** to 1m (3ft). Has large, single flowers with very broad, crimson petals, lightly ruffled at edges.

***P.* 'Argosy'.** Deciduous, upright shrub (tree peony). **H** and **S** to 1.5m (5ft). Magnificent, large, single flowers are lemon-yellow, each with a crimson-purple blotch at base. Is hard to propagate.

P. arietina. See *P. mascula* subsp. *arietina.*

***P.* 'Auguste Dessert'.** Clump-forming perennial. **H** and **S** to 75cm (30in). Foliage provides rich autumn colour. Has masses of fragrant, semi-double flowers; carmine petals are tinged salmon-pink and have slightly ruffled, striking silvery-white edges.

***P.* 'Avant Garde'.** Clump-forming perennial. **H** and **S** to 1m (3ft). Has luxuriant foliage. Medium-sized to large, fragrant, single flowers are pale rose-pink with darker veins and bright golden anthers that have yellow-red filaments. Flowers are borne on stiff, straight stems in mid-spring and are ideal for cutting.

***P.* 'Ballerina'.** Clump-forming perennial. **H** and **S** 1m (3ft). Foliage provides autumn colour. Fragrant, double flowers are soft blush-pink, tinged lilac at first, later fading to white. Outer rows of petals are loosely arranged, very broad and incurving; inner petals are also incurving, but more densely arranged, narrower, more uneven in size and often have slightly ruffled margins.

***P.* 'Baroness Schroeder'.** Vigorous, clump-forming perennial. **H** and **S** to 1m (3ft). Is very free-flowering with large, fragrant, globe-shaped, double flowers, tinged with pale flesh-pink on opening but fading to almost pure white. Produces several rows of nearly flat, outer petals; inner petals are incurving, ruffled and very tightly arranged. Is one of the best peonies for cutting.

***P.* 'Barrymore'.** Clump-forming perennial. **H** and **S** to 85cm (34in). Has very large, anemone-form flowers with broad, outer petals that are palest blush-pink on opening, later white. Clear pale golden-yellow petaloids are very narrow, relatively short and are neatly and densely arranged.

***P.* 'Bartzella'** (illus. p.229). Clump-forming, free-flowering hybrid between a herbaceous perennial and a tree peony. **H** and **S** 90cm (3ft). In early summer bears large, scented, double, lemon-yellow flowers, marked with red.

♀ ***P.* 'Bowl of Beauty'** (illus. p.228). Clump-forming perennial. **H** and **S** to 1m (3ft). Has very large, striking, anemone-form flowers with pale carmine-pink, outer petals and numerous narrow, densely arranged, ivory-white petaloids.

***P.* 'Buckeye Belle'** (illus. p.229) Clump-forming perennial. **H** and **S** 90cm (3ft). Has red-tinged, mid-green leaves and semi-double, dark red flowers with a mass of central, golden staminodes.

***P.* 'Callie's Memory'.** Clump-forming, free-flowering hybrid between a herbaceous perennial and a tree peony. **H** 60–80cm (24–28in), **S** 60cm (24in). Produces large, scented, double, dark-centred, cream flowers marked red-pink at the edges and base.

♀ ***P. cambessedesii*** (Majorcan peony; illus. p.228). Clump-forming perennial. **H** and **S** 45cm (18in). Half hardy. Has especially attractive foliage, dark green above with veins, stalks and under-surfaces suffused purple-red. Single, deep rose-pink flowers are borne in mid-spring.

***P.* 'Cheddar Cheese'.** Clump-forming perennial. **H** and **S** to 1m (3ft). Produces well-formed, large, double flowers in mid-summer. Neatly and densely arranged, slightly ruffled, ivory-white petals, the inner ones incurving, are interspersed with shorter, yellow petals.

♀ ***P.* 'Cheddar Gold'** (illus. p.228). Clump-forming perennial, **H** and **S** 70–80cm (28–32in). In spring produces bronze or reddish-brown stems bearing dark green leaves, divided into 9 lance-shaped leaflets. In late spring or early summer has strongly scented flowers, with rounded white petals surrounding a central boss of golden staminodes.

***P.* 'Chocolate Soldier'.** Clump-forming perennial. **H** and **S** to 1m (3ft). Has mid- to dark green leaves that are often tinged bronze-red when young. Semi-double, purple-red flowers, borne in early summer, have yellow-mottled centres.

***P.* 'Claire de Lune'** (illus. p.229). Clump-forming perennial. **H** and **S** 70–80cm (28–32in). In mid-spring, single, pale yellow flowers, each with a central boss of golden staminodes, are borne in pairs.

***P.* 'Colonel Heneage'.** Clump-forming perennial of upright habit. **H** and **S** to 85cm (34in). Has masses of anemone-form flowers with both outer petals and inner petaloids of dark rose-crimson.

***P.* 'Coral Charm'** (illus. p.228). Clump-forming perennial. **H** and **S** 70 cm (28in). Bears semi-double, peach-pink flowers opening from darker buds.

***P.* 'Coral Fay'.** Clump-forming perennial forming a rather spreading dome. **H** and **S** 80–90cm (32–36in). Semi-double, pink-tinged, rich crimson flowers are paler towards the petal bases; stamens are golden-yellow.

P. corallina. See *P. mascula* subsp. *mascula.*

***P.* 'Cora Louise'.** Clump-forming, free-flowering hybrid between a herbaceous perennial and a tree peony. **H** 60–80cm

(24–32in), **S** 60cm (24in). Bears large, scented, semi-double, white flowers; each petal has a purplish blotch at the base.
***P.* 'Cornelia Shaylor'.** Erect, clump-forming perennial. **H** and **S** to 85cm (34in). Fragrant, double flowers, flushed rose-pink on opening and fading to blush-white, are borne freely from early to mid-summer. Ruffled petals are neatly and densely arranged.
***P.* 'Dayspring'.** Clump-forming perennial. **H** and **S** to 70cm (28in). Has an abundance of fragrant, single, clear pink flowers borne in trusses.
P. decora. See *P. peregrina.*
***P.* 'Defender'.** Clump-forming, vigorous perennial. **H** and **S** to 1m (3ft). Single, satiny crimson flowers, to 15cm (6in) across, with a central boss of golden anthers, are carried on strong stems.
♀ ***P. delavayi*** illus. p.136. **var. *angustiloba*** is a deciduous, upright, open, suckering shrub or sub-shrub (tree peony). **H** to 1m (3ft), **S** to 1.2m (4ft). Leaves are divided into pointed-oval leaflets, often with reddish stalks. Produces small, bowl-shaped, red, red-purple, yellow, orange or white flowers, 5–6cm (2–2½in) across, with conspicuous, leafy bracts beneath, in late spring. **var. *angustiloba* f. *alba*** (syn. *P. potaninii* f. *alba*) has white flowers. **var. *angustiloba* f. *angustifolia*** (syn. *P. potaninii*) produces dark red, red or reddish-purple flowers. **var. *angustiloba* f. *trollioides*** (syn. *P. potaninii* var. *trollioides*, *P. trollioides*) has yellow or orange flowers. **var. *delavayi* f. *delavayi*** has dark red to purplish flowers. **var. *delavayi* f. *lutea*** (syn. *P. lutea*) has orange, yellow or greenish-yellow flowers, sometimes red at the bases or on the petal margins. **var. *ludlowii*.** See *P. ludlowii.*
***P.* 'Dresden'.** Robust, clump-forming perennial. **H** and **S** to 85cm (34in). Foliage provides autumn colour. Has single, ivory-white flowers tinged soft blush-rose-pink.
♀ ***P.* 'Duchesse de Nemours'**, syn. *P.* 'Mrs Gwyn Lewis'. Vigorous, clump-forming perennial. **H** and **S** to 70cm (28in). Produces masses of richly fragrant, double flowers with very large, incurving, outer petals, tinged palest green at first, soon fading to pure white; inner petals with irregular margins are densely arranged towards the centre and are creamy-yellow at their base.
***P.* 'Early Windflower'.** Clump-forming perennial. **H** 70cm (28in), **S** 50cm (20in). Has bronze-tinged, mid-green leaves. Produces pendent, cupped, single, pure white flowers.
P. emodi (illus. p.228). Clump-forming perennial. **H** to 1.2m (4ft), **S** to 1m (3ft). Glossy, green foliage is topped by tall stems bearing several large, fragrant, single, pure white flowers with golden-yellow anthers.
***P.* 'Evening World'.** Clump-forming perennial. **H** and **S** to 1m (3ft). Has abundant, large, anemone-form flowers with soft blush-pink, outer petals and very tightly arranged, pale flesh-pink petaloids.
♀ ***P.* 'Félix Crousse'**, syn. *P.* 'Victor Hugo' (illus. p.229). Vigorous, clump-forming perennial. **H** and **S** to 75cm (30in). Bears a profusion of fragrant, double, rich carmine-pink flowers with darker red centres. Petals are ruffled, very numerous and tightly arranged, with edges sometimes tipped silvery-white.
♀ ***P.* 'Festiva Maxima'** (illus. p.228). Clump-forming perennial. **H** and **S** to 1m (3ft). Has dense, spreading foliage and huge, fragrant, double flowers borne on strong stems. Rather loosely arranged petals are large with irregular margins; outer petals are pure white, inner ones each have a basal, crimson blotch.
***P.* 'Flamingo'.** Clump-forming perennial. **H** and **S** to 85cm (34in). Foliage provides autumn colour. Double flowers are large and clear pale salmon-pink.
***P.* 'Garden Treasure'** (illus. p.229). Clump-forming, free-flowering hybrid between a herbaceous perennial and a tree peony. **H** and **S** 70–80cm (28–32in). Has large, semi-double, bright yellow flowers.
***P.* 'Globe of Light'.** Clump-forming perennial. **H** and **S** to 1m (3ft). Has large, fragrant, anemone-form flowers. Outer petals are pure rose-pink, petaloids clear golden-yellow.
***P.* 'Heirloom'.** Compact, clump-forming perennial. **H** and **S** to 70cm (28in). Bears masses of large, fragrant, double, pale lilac-pink flowers.
***P.* 'Instituteur Doriat'.** Clump-forming perennial. **H** and **S** to 1m (3ft). Foliage provides autumn colour. Has abundant, large, anemone-form flowers with reddish-carmine, outer petals and densely arranged, relatively broad petaloids, paler and more pink than outer petals, with ruffled, silvery-white margins.
***P.* 'Jan van Leeuwen'** (illus. p.228). Clump-forming perennial, **H** 90cm (36in), **S** 70cm (28in). In spring produces bronze or reddish-brown stems bearing dark green leaves divided into leaflets. In late spring or early summer, produces scented, white, bowl-shaped flowers with large, floppy petals and yellow staminodes.
P. japonica (illus. p.228). Compact, clump-forming perennial. **H** 30–40cm (12–16in), **S** 20cm (8in). In early spring produces pink-tinged stems bearing soft green leaves with 7–9 rounded leaflets. Produces short-lived, cup-shaped, single, white flowers; after flowering, the leaves continue to develop and turn to green.
***P.* 'Kelway's Fairy Queen'** (illus. p.228). Clump-forming, compact perennial, **H** and **S** 70–80cm (28–32in). In spring produces bronze-brown stems bearing dark green leaves divided into lance-shaped leaflets. In late spring to early summer, bears bowl-shaped, semi-double, soft pink flowers, with deeper outer petals and golden staminodes.
***P.* 'Kelway's Gorgeous'** (illus. p.229). Clump-forming perennial. **H** and **S** to 85cm (34in). Single, intense clear carmine flowers, with a hint of salmon-pink, are borne very freely.
***P.* 'Kelway's Majestic'.** Clump-forming perennial. **H** and **S** to 1m (3ft). Freely borne, large, fragrant, anemone-form flowers have bright cherry rose-pink, outer petals and lilac-pink petaloids flecked with silver or pale gold.
***P.* 'Kelway's Supreme'.** Clump-forming perennial. **H** and **S** to 1m (3ft). Foliage provides autumn colour. Has large, strongly fragrant, double flowers, produced over a long period, sometimes borne in clusters on well-established plants. Petals are broad, incurving, soft blush-pink, fading to milk-white. Single or semi-double axillary flowers are often produced.
***P.* 'Knighthood'** (illus. p.229). Clump-forming perennial. **H** and **S** to 75cm (30in). Double flowers have densely arranged, rather narrow, ruffled petals of unusually rich burgundy-red.
***P.* 'Krinkled White'.** Robust, clump-forming perennial. **H** and **S** to 80cm (32in). Large, bowl-shaped, single, milk-white flowers are sometimes flushed palest pink. Petals are large with ruffled margins.
P. lactiflora. Variable, clump-forming perennial. **H** 70–120cm (28–48in), **S** 70–100cm (28–39in). In spring produces bronze or reddish-brown stems bearing dark green leaves divided into 9 lance-shaped leaflets. In late spring or early summer, 1–3 scented, bowl-shaped, white flowers are borne on each stem. Is more often represented in garden by named selections, most of which are hybrids.
♀ ***P.* 'Lady Alexandra Duff'** (illus. p.228). Clump-forming perennial, **H** and **S** 90cm (36in). In spring produces bronze or reddish-brown stems bearing dark green leaves divided into leaflets. Late spring or early summer, has large, scented, double flowers with soft pink outer petals and smaller, white inner ones. Flowers fade white in sun.
♀ ***P.* 'Laura Dessert'** (illus. p.229). Clump-forming perennial. **H** and **S** to 75cm (30in). Produces fragrant, double flowers with creamy blush-white, outer petals. Densely arranged, incurving, inner petals are flushed rich lemon-yellow, and their margins are sometimes deeply cut.
P.* x *lemoinei (*P. suffruticosa* and *P. lutea*). Variable, deciduous, upright, open shrub. **H** 2m (6ft) or more, **S** 1m (3ft). Bears bold, mid-green leaves divided into pointed leaflets. In early summer produces large, bowl-shaped, often double flowers in a range of colours, notably yellow. **'High Noon'** (illus. p.229), **H** and **S** 1.3m (4½ft), has semi-double, bright yellow flowers, often marked with crimson towards the centres.
***P.* 'L'Espérance'**, syn. *P.* x *lemoinei* 'L'Espérance' (illus. p.229). Has very large, single, primrose-yellow flowers with a carmine blotch at the base of each petal.
***P.* x *lemoinei* 'L'Espérance'.** See *P.* 'L'Espérance'.
P. lobata. See *P. peregrina.*
♀ ***P. ludlowii***, syn. *P. delavayi* var. *ludlowii*, *P. lutea* var. *ludlowii* (illus. p.229). Deciduous, upright, slightly suckering shrub. **H** to 3.5m (11ft), **S** to 1.5m (5ft). Leaves are divided into sharply pointed, bright green leaflets. Produces large, bright yellow flowers, to 12cm (5in) across, in late spring.
P. lutea. See *P. delavayi* var. *delavayi* f. *lutea*. **var. *ludlowii*** see *P. ludlowii.*
***P.* 'Madame Louis Henri'.** Deciduous, upright shrub (tree peony). **H** and **S** to 1.5m (5ft). Has loosely semi-double, whitish-yellow flowers with large, incurving, outer petals very heavily suffused with rusty-red. Smaller, often darker, inner petals each have a basal, dull red blotch.
***P.* 'Magic Orb'** (illus. p.229). Clump-forming perennial. **H** and **S** to 1m (3ft). Foliage provides autumn colour. Bears masses of large, strongly fragrant, double flowers, each with several outer whorls of fairly broad, ruffled, intense cherry-pink petals and a centre of densely arranged, smaller, incurving petals. Outermost rows of central petals are blush-white, heavily shaded with mid-rose-carmine; the innermost petals are mostly creamy-white.
P. mascula* subsp. *arietina, syn. *P. arietina*. Tuberous perennial. **H** and **S** to 75cm (30in). Foliage is hairy underneath and dark green; stems are dark red. Has single, reddish-pink flowers. Seed capsules with 2–5 boat-shaped sections split to reveal purplish-black seeds. **subsp. *mascula*** (syn. *P. corallina*) is clump-forming, **H** and **S** to 1m (3ft), with hairless leaflets. Produces purple- or carmine-red, occasionally pink or white, flowers with bosses of golden-yellow anthers borne on purple filaments.
♀ ***P. mlokosewitschii*** illus. p.227.
***P.* 'Mother of Pearl'.** Clump-forming perennial. **H** to 75cm (30in) and **S** to 60cm (24in). Has greyish-green leaves and single, dog rose-pink flowers.
***P.* 'Mrs Gwyn Lewis'.** See *P.* 'Duchesse de Nemours'.
♀ ***P. obovata* var. *alba*** (illus. p.228). Clump-forming perennial. **H** and **S** 70–90cm (28–36in). Has erect stems and large, deep green leaves, each with 9 uneven, broadly elliptic leaflets, pale grey-green and slightly hairy beneath. Bears single, cup-shaped, white flowers with purple filaments.
P. officinalis. Clump-forming, tuberous perennial. **H** and **S** to 60cm (24in). This single, red apothecaries' peony has long been in cultivation, but is seldom seen today, having been superseded by larger, often double-flowered hybrids, such as the following. **'Alba Plena'**, **H** and **S** to 75cm (30in), has double, white flowers that are sometimes tinged with pink. **'China Rose'**, **H** and **S** to 45cm (18in), has handsome, dark green foliage and single flowers with incurving, clear dark salmon-rose petals contrasting with central bosses of orange-yellow anthers. **'Crimson Globe'** **H** and **S** 70–85cm (28–34in), produces single, garnet-red flowers with golden-yellow stamens. ♀ **'Rubra Plena'** (illus. p.229), **H** and **S** to 75cm (30in), is long-lived and has distinctive foliage, divided into broadly oval leaflets, and double, vivid pinkish-crimson flowers with ruffled petals.
***P.* 'Paul M. Wild'** (illus. p.229). Clump-forming perennial, **H** and **S** 90cm (36in). In spring produces bronze-brown stems bearing dark green leaves, divided into 9 lance-shaped leaflets. In late spring or early summer, it produces large, fully double, bowl-shaped, ruby-red flowers.
P. peregrina, syn. *P. decora*, *P. lobata*. Clump-forming, tuberous perennial. **H** and **S** to 1m (3ft). Bears bowl-shaped, single, ruby-red flowers. ♀ **'Otto Froebel'** (illus. p.229), has glossy, bright green leaves and bears large, single, vermilion flowers, tinged with salmon-rose.
***P.* 'Pillow Talk'** (illus. p.228). Clump-forming perennial, **H** and **S** 70–80cm (28–32in). In spring produces bronze or reddish-stems bearing dark green leaves divided into leaflets. Between late spring or early summer bears double, soft pastel-pink flowers, slightly richer at petal tips.

P. potaninii. See *P. delavayi* var. *angustiloba* f. *angustiloba*. **f. *alba*** see *P. delavayi* var. *angustiloba* f. *alba*. **var. *trollioides*** see *P. delavayi* var. *angustiloba* f. *trollioides*.
***P.* 'Président Poincaré'.** Clump-forming perennial. **H** and **S** to 1m (3ft). Foliage provides autumn colour. Fragrant, double, clear rich ruby-crimson flowers are borne very freely.
***P.* 'Red Charm'.** Clump-forming perennial with a rather spreading dome. **H** and **S** 80cm (32in). Bears large, double, rich red flowers. Is good for cut flowers.
P. rockii, syn. *P. suffruticosa* subsp. *rockii*. Deciduous, upright shrub (tree peony). **H** and **S** to 2.2m (7ft). Produces large, spreading, semi-double, white flowers; inner petals each have a basal, dark maroon blotch. Is difficult to propagate.
🏆 ***P.* 'Sarah Bernhardt'** (illus. p.228). Vigorous, erect, clump-forming perennial. **H** and **S** to 1m (3ft). Bears masses of huge, fragrant, fully double flowers with large, ruffled, slightly dull rose-pink petals, fading to silvery blush-white at margins.
***P.* 'Shirley Temple'** (illus. p.228). Clump-forming perennial. **H** and **S** to 85cm (34in). Profuse, soft rose-pink flowers, fading to palest buff-white, are fully double, with broad petals arranged in whorls; innermost petals are smaller and more loosely packed.
***P.* 'Silver Flare'.** Clump-forming perennial. **H** and **S** to 1m (3ft). Foliage gives autumn colour. Stems are flushed dull reddish-brown. Produces masses of fragrant, single flowers with rather long, slender, rich carmine-pink petals, each feathering to a striking silvery-white edge.
***P.* 'Sir Edward Elgar'.** Clump-forming perennial. **H** and **S** to 75cm (30in). Foliage provides autumn colour. Has masses of single, chocolate-brown-tinged, rich crimson flowers with bosses of loosely arranged, clear lemon-yellow anthers.
***P.* x *smouthii*.** Clump-forming perennial. **H** and **S** to 60cm (24in). Produces masses of fragrant, single, glistening, dark crimson flowers, to 10cm (4in) across, with yellow stamens, although both flowers and foliage may vary in colour.
***P.* 'Souvenir de Maxime Cornu'.** Deciduous, upright shrub (tree peony). **H** and **S** to 1.5m (5ft). Large, richly fragrant flowers are fully double with warm golden-yellow petals densely arranged towards centres; ruffled margins are dull reddish-orange.
P. suffruticosa (Moutan). Deciduous, upright shrub (tree peony). **H** and **S** to 2.2m (7ft). Bears variable, large, cup-shaped flowers, single or semi-double, with incurving, rose-pink or white petals, each sometimes with a basal, usually chocolate-maroon blotch. Has given rise to many cultivars with semi-double and double flowers. **'Cardinal Vaughan'** (illus. p.229) has semi-double, ruby-purple flowers.**'Duchess of Marlborough'**, **H** and **S** 1.5m (5ft) or more, produces semi-double, soft, warm pink flowers with feathery petals. **'Godaishu'** ('Large Globe'), bears semi- or fully double, white flowers with yellow centres amid light green leaves that are fringed and twisted. **'Hana-daijin'** ('Magnificent Flower'), **H** and **S** 2m (6ft) or more, is a vigorous cultivar that bears masses of double, purple flowers. **'Hakuo-jisi'** (illus. p.228), **H** and **S** 1.5m (5ft) or more, is strong growing and bears large, double, white flowers in early summer; petals are finely marked with purple at the base. **'Hana-kisoi'** ('Floral Rivalry'; illus. p.228) has double, pale cerise-pink flowers. **'Kamada-nishiki'** ('Kamada Brocade'), **H** and **S** to 1.2m (4ft), produces large, double flowers, to 20cm (8in) across, that are lilac-pink striped white at the edge of each petal. **'Quing Long Wo Mo Chi'**, **H** and **S** 3m (10ft), is a Chinese tree peony with large, scented, semi-double, dark purple flowers, with petals marked green towards the base. **'Reine Elizabeth'**, **H** and **S** to 2m (6ft), has large, fully double flowers with broad, salmon-pink petals, flushed with bright copper-red and lightly ruffled at margins. **'Renkaku'** ('Flight of Cranes'), **H** and **S** to 1m (3ft), bears double flowers, each with broad, incurving, slightly ruffled, ivory-white petals, loosely arranged in 3 or more whorls, that surround a large boss of long, golden-yellow anthers. **'Rimpo'** (illus. p.229), **H** and **S** 1.5m (5ft) or more, has large, scented, semi-double, dark mauve-purple flowers with ruffled petals. **subsp. *rockii*** see *P. rockii*. **'Tama-fuyo'** ('Jewel in the Lotus') is vigorous and freely produces double, pink flowers earlier than most other cultivars.**'Wu Long Peng Sheng'**, **H** and **S** 3m (10ft), is a Chinese tree peony with scented, rounded, double, magenta-red flowers with golden staminodes. **'Yachiyo-tsubaki'** (illus. p.228), **H** and **S** 1.5m (5ft) or more, produces masses of semi-double, clear pink flowers.
***P. tenuifolia*.** Clump-forming perennial. **H** and **S** to 45cm (18in). Elegant leaves are finely divided into many linear segments. Has single, dark crimson flowers, with golden-yellow anthers.
***P.* 'Thunderbolt'** (illus. p.229). Clump-forming perennial. **H** 1.1m (3½ft), **S** 70–80cm (28–32in). In mid-spring has masses of slightly pendent, single, deep red flowers, often streaked dark purple.
P. trollioides. See *P. delavayi* var. *angustiloba* f. *trollioides*.
P. veitchii (illus. p.229). Clump-forming perennial. **H** and **S** to 75cm (30in). Shiny, bright green leaves are divided into oblong to elliptic leaflets. In early summer produces nodding, cup-shaped, single, purple-pink flowers.
***P.* 'Victor Hugo'.** See *P.* 'Félix Crousse'.
***P.* 'White Wings'** (illus. p.228). Clump-forming perennial. **H** and **S** to 85cm (34in). Glossy, dark green foliage also provides autumn colour. In mid-summer, produces masses of large, fragrant, single flowers with broad, white petals, sometimes tinged sulphur-yellow, that are each slightly ruffled at the apex.
🏆 ***P.* 'Whitleyi Major'** (illus. p.228). Clump-forming perennial. **H** to 1m (3ft), **S** to 60cm (2ft). Foliage and stems are flushed rich reddish-brown. Large, single, ivory-white flowers have a satin sheen and central bosses of clear yellow anthers.
***P. wittmanniana*.** Clump-forming perennial. **H** and **S** to 1m (3ft). Has large, single, pale primrose-yellow flowers, each with a large, central boss of yellow anthers on purple-red filaments. Leaves are divided into broadly oval leaflets, shiny dark green above, paler beneath.

PALIURUS

RHAMNACEAE

Genus of deciduous, spiny, summer-flowering shrubs and trees, grown for their foliage and flowers. *P. spinachristi* is also grown for its religious association, reputedly being the plant from which Christ's crown of thorns was made. Frost hardy. Requires full sun and well-drained soil. Propagate by softwood cuttings in summer or by seed in autumn.
P. spina-christi illus. p.116.

PAMIANTHE

AMARYLLIDACEAE

Genus of one species of evergreen, spring-flowering bulb, grown for its large, strongly fragrant, showy flowers. Frost tender, min. 12°C (54°F). Needs partial shade and rich, well-drained soil. Feed with high-potash liquid fertilizer in summer. Reduce watering in winter but do not allow to dry out. Propagate by seed in spring or by offsets in late winter.
P. peruviana illus. p.399.

PANCRATIUM

AMARYLLIDACEAE

Genus of bulbs with large, fragrant, daffodil-like flowers in summer. Frost to half hardy. Needs sun and well-drained soil that is warm and dry in summer when bulbs are dormant. Plant at least 15cm (6in) deep. Feed with a high-potash liquid fertilizer every 2 weeks from autumn to spring. Propagate by seed in autumn or by offsets detached in early autumn.
P. illyricum illus. p.408.
P. maritimum (Sea daffodil, Sea lily). Late summer-flowering bulb. **H** 45cm (18in), **S** 25–30cm (10–12in). Half hardy. Has strap-shaped, erect, basal, greyish-green leaves. Produces a head of 5–12 white flowers, each with a large, deep cup in the centre and 6 spreading petals. Is shy-flowering in cultivation.

PANDANUS

Screw pine

PANDANACEAE

Genus of evergreen trees, shrubs and scramblers, grown for their foliage and overall appearance. Flowers and fruits appear only on large, mature specimens. Frost tender, min. 13–16°C (55–61°F). Needs full light or partial shade and fertile, well-drained soil. Water containerized plants freely when in full growth, moderately at other times. Propagate by seed or suckers in spring or by cuttings of lateral shoots in summer. Red spider mite may be troublesome.
P. odoratissimus of gardens. See *P. tectorius*.
P. tectorius, syn. *P. odoratissimus* of gardens. Evergreen, rounded tree. **H** to 6m (20ft), **S** 3m (10ft) or more. Has rosettes of strap-shaped, deep green leaves, each 1–1.5m (3–5ft) long, with spiny margins and a spiny midrib beneath. Small flowers, the males in clusters, each with a lance-shaped, white bract, appear mainly in summer. Fruits are like round pineapples. 🏆 **'Veitchii'** (syn. *P. veitchii*) illus. p.454.
***P. veitchii*.** See *P. tectorius* 'Veitchii'.

PANDOREA

BIGNONIACEAE

Genus of evergreen, woody-stemmed, twining climbers, grown for their flowers and leaves. Frost tender, min. 5°C (41°F). Grow in sun and in any well-drained soil. Prune after flowering to restrain growth. Propagate by seed sown in spring or by stem cuttings or layering in summer.
P. jasminoides, syn. *Bignonia jasminoides*, illus. p.459.
***P. lindleyana*.** See *Clytostoma callistegioides*.
P. pandorana, syn. *Bignonia pandorana*, *Tecoma australis* (Wonga-wonga vine). Fast-growing, evergreen, woody-stemmed, twining climber. **H** 6m (20ft) or more. Leaves have 3–9 scalloped leaflets. Bears small, funnel-shaped, cream flowers, streaked and often spotted with red, brown or purple, in clusters in summer.
***P. ricasoliana*.** See *Podranea ricasoliana*.

PANICUM

GRAMINEAE/POACEAE

See also GRASSES, BAMBOOS, RUSHES and SEDGES.
P. capillare (Old-witch grass). Tuft-forming, annual grass. **H** 60cm–1m (2–3ft), **S** 30cm (1ft). Half hardy. Has broad leaves and hairy stems. Top half of each stem carries a dense panicle of numerous, minute, greenish-brown spikelets on delicate stalks in summer.
***P. virgatum* 'Northwind'**, illus. p.289.

PAPAVER

Poppy

PAPAVERACEAE

Genus of annuals, biennials and perennials, some of which are semi-evergreen, grown for their cup-shaped flowers. Fully hardy. Needs sun or semi-shade and prefers moist but well-drained soil. Propagate by seed in autumn or spring. *P. orientale* and its cultivars are best propagated by root cuttings in winter. Self-seeds readily.
***P. alpinum* subsp. *burseri*.** See *P. burseri*.
***P. atlanticum*.** Clump-forming, short-lived perennial. **H** and **S** 10cm (4in). Has oval, toothed, hairy leaves and, in summer, single, dull orange flowers. Is good for a rock garden.
P. burseri, syn. *P. alpinum* subsp. *burseri* (Alpine poppy). Semi-evergreen, tuft-forming, short-lived perennial, best treated as an annual or biennial. **H** 15–20cm (6–8in), **S** 10cm (4in). Has finely cut, grey leaves. Produces single, white flowers in summer. Suits a rock garden, wall or bank.
🏆 ***P. commutatum***, syn. *P.c.* 'Ladybird'. Fast-growing, erect, branching annual. **H** and **S** 45cm (18in). Has elliptic, deeply lobed, mid-green leaves and, in summer, single, red flowers, each with a black blotch in centre. **'Ladybird'** see *P. commutatum*.

P. croceum, syn. *P. nudicaule* of gardens (Iceland poppy). Tuft-forming perennial. **H** to 30cm (12in), **S** 10cm (4in). Hairy stems each produce a fragrant, single, white-and-yellow flower, sometimes marked green outside, in summer. Many colour forms have been selected. Leaves are oval, toothed and soft green. Needs partial shade. Is good for a rock garden.
P. fauriei, syn. *P. miyabeanum* of gardens, illus. p.373.
P. 'Fire Ball' (illus. p.238). Tuft-forming perennial, spreading by stolons. **H** 35cm (14in), **S** 30–60cm (12–24in). Has elliptical, lobed, toothed, hairy, mid-green leaves. In early summer, upright, rather wiry stems produce large, solitary, double, bright tangerine-orange flowers.
P. 'Medallion' (illus. p.238). Tuft-forming perennial, spreading by stolons. **H** 85cm (34in), **S** 70–100cm (28–39in). Has elliptical, lobed, toothed, hairy, mid-green leaves. In early and late summer, numerous upright, stout stems bear large, solitary pinkish-purple flowers that last for several days.
P. miyabeanum of gardens. See *P. fauriei.*
P. nudicaule of gardens. See *P. croceum.*
P. orientale (Oriental poppy). Rosetted perennial. **H** 1m (3ft), **S** 30cm–1m (1–3ft). Single, brilliant vermilion flowers, with dark blotches at bases of petals, are borne in early summer. Has broadly lance-shaped, toothed or cut, rough, mid-green leaves. Flowering stems need support. **'Allegro'** (syn. *P.o.* 'Allegro Viva'), H 60–75cm (24–30in), has bright scarlet flowers. **'Allegro Viva'** see *P.o.* 'Allegro'. **'Beauty of Livermere'** illus. p.235. 🏆**'Black and White'** (illus. p.238) is vigorous and has large, white flowers. 🏆**var. bracteatum** (illus. p.238), **H** 1.2m (4ft), is a robust, vigorous perennial with a ruff of bract-like leaves held below the large deeply cupped, blood-red flowers, which have black blotches at the base. 🏆**'Cedric Morris'**, **H** 70cm (28in), produces pastel greyish-pink flowers. **'Choir Boy'** (illus. p.238) is variable, compact and bears ruffled, white flowers marked at the base with 4 black blotches. **'Graue Witwe'** has ruffled, grey-white flowers. **'Indian Chief'** has deep mahogany-red flowers. 🏆**'Karine'** (illus. p.238) has bowl-shaped, soft pale pink flowers marked with dark red blotches. **'Kleine Tänzerin'** bears abundant, ruffled, dark pink flowers. **'Lauren's Lilac'** has soft lilac-mauve flowers. **'May Queen'** bears double, orange flowers. **'Mrs Perry'** has large, salmon-pink flowers. **'Patty's Plum'** (illus. p.238) produces rich muddy-purple flowers that fade as they age. **'Perry's White'**, **H** 80cm (32in), has satiny, white flowers with purple centres. **'Prinzessin Victoria Louise'** has large, salmon-pink flowers. **'Turkish Delight'** (illus. p.238) bears unblotched, bright salmon-pink flowers. 'Watermelon' has flowers of vivid watermelon-pink.
P. rhoeas (Corn poppy, Field poppy). **Shirley Group** (double) Fast-growing, slender, erect annual. **H** 60cm (24in), **S** 30cm (12in). Has lobed, light green leaves. In summer has rounded, often cup-shaped, double flowers, in shades of red, pink or white, including bicolours; (single) illus. p.310.
P. somniferum (Opium poppy). Fast-growing, upright annual. **H** 75cm (30in), **S** 30cm (12in). Has oblong, lobed, light greyish-green leaves. Large, single flowers, to 10cm (4in) wide, in shades of red, pink, purple or white, are produced in summer. Several double-flowered forms are available, including **Carnation-flowered Series**, with fringed flowers in mixed colours; **'Paeoniiflorum Group'** illus. p.303; **'Pink Beauty'**, which has salmon-pink flowers; and **'White Cloud'**, which produces large, white flowers.

PAPHIOPEDILUM

Slipper orchid

ORCHIDACEAE

ⓘ Contact with foliage may aggravate skin allergies. See also ORCHIDS.
P. appletonianum. Evergreen, terrestrial orchid. **H** 8cm (3in). Frost tender, min. 13°C (55°F). In spring, green flowers, 6cm (2½in) across and each with a pouched, brownish lip and pink-flushed petals, are borne singly on tall, slender stems. Has oval, mottled leaves, 10cm (4in) long. Needs shade in summer.
P. armeniacum (illus. p.467). Evergreen, terrestrial orchid. **H** 50cm (20in), **S** 25cm (10in). Frost tender, min. 10°C (50°F). In spring, pouch-lipped, bright yellow flowers, 6–11cm (2½–4½in) across, with red lines in the centres, are borne singly on a stem 20–40cm (8–16in) long. Strap-shaped leaves, 6–15cm (2½–16in) long, marbled light and dark green above, purple spotted beneath, are borne from a creeping rhizome. Needs shade in summer.
P. bellatulum (illus. p.467). Evergreen, terrestrial orchid. **H** 5cm (2in). Frost tender, min. 18°C (64°F). Bears almost stemless, rounded, pouch-lipped, white flowers, 8cm (3in) across, spotted with dark maroon, singly in spring. Oval, marbled leaves are 8cm (3in) long. Grow in shade in summer.
P. Buckhurst gx 'Mont Millais' (illus. p.467). Evergreen, terrestrial orchid. **H** 10cm (4in). Frost tender, min. 13°C (55°F). Rounded, yellow-and-white flowers, to 12cm (5in) across and lined and spotted with red, are produced singly in winter. Has oval leaves, 10cm (4in) long. Requires shade in summer.
P. callosum. Evergreen, terrestrial orchid. **H** 8cm (3in). Frost tender, min. 13°C (55°F). Purple- and green-veined, white flowers, 8cm (3in) across, are borne on tall stems in spring–summer. Has oval, mottled leaves, 10cm (4in) long. Needs shade in summer.
P. fairrieanum (illus. p.467). Evergreen, terrestrial orchid. **H** 8cm (3in). Frost tender, min. 10°C (50°F). Rich purple- and green-veined flowers, 5cm (2in) across, with curved petals and orange-brown pouches, are borne singly in autumn. Oval leaves are 8cm (3in) long. Grow in shade in summer.
P. Freckles gx (illus. p.466). Evergreen, terrestrial orchid. **H** 10cm (4in). Frost tender, min. 13°C (55°F). Rounded, reddish-brown-spotted and pouched, white flowers, 10cm (4in) across, are produced singly in winter. Has oval leaves, 10cm (4in) long. Grow in shade in summer.
P. haynaldianum. Evergreen, terrestrial orchid. **H** 12cm (5in). Frost tender, min. 13°C (55°F). In summer, long-petalled, brown-marked, green-, pink-and-white flowers, to 15cm (6in) across, are produced singly. Has oval leaves, 20–23cm (8–9in) long. Requires shade in summer.
P. Lyric gx 'Glendora' (illus. p.467). Evergreen, terrestrial orchid. **H** 10cm (4in). Frost tender, min. 13°C (55°F). Rounded, glossy, white-red-and-green flowers, 10cm (4in) across, are produced singly in winter. Has oval leaves, 15cm (6in) long. Needs shade in summer.
P. Maudiae gx (illus. p.467). Evergreen, terrestrial orchid. **H** 10cm (4in). Frost tender, min. 13°C (55°F). Clear apple-green or deep reddish-purple flowers, 10cm (4in) across, appear singly on long stems in spring or early summer. Has oval, mottled leaves, 10cm (4in) long. Requires shade in summer.
P. niveum. Evergreen, terrestrial orchid. **H** 5cm (2in). Frost tender, min. 13–18°C (55–64°F). White flowers, 4cm (1½in) across, are produced singly, mainly in spring. Oval, marbled leaves are 8cm (3in) long. Needs shade in summer.
P. rothschildianum (illus. p.467). Evergreen, clump-forming, terrestrial orchid. **H** and **S** 50cm (20in). Frost tender, min. 13°C (55°F). Spikes, 45cm (18in) long, of 2–6 pouch-lipped, creamy-yellow flowers, with maroon stripes, mahogany pouch and elongated petals, to 14cm (5½in) long, are produced in summer. Has strap-shaped, mid-green leaves, to 60cm (24in) long. Needs shade in summer.
P. sukhakulii. Evergreen, terrestrial orchid. **H** 8cm (3in). Frost tender, min. 13°C (55°F). In spring-summer, purple-pouched, black-spotted, green flowers, 8cm (3in) across, appear singly on tall stems. Has oval, mottled leaves, 10cm (4in) long. Grow in shade in summer.
P. venustum. Evergreen, terrestrial orchid. **H** 10cm (4in). Frost tender, min. 13°C (55°F). Variably coloured flowers, ranging from pink to orange with green veins and darker spots, are 6cm (2½in) across and borne singly in autumn. Has oval, mottled leaves, 10cm (4in) long. Needs shade in summer.

PARADISEA

LILIACEAE/ASPHODELACEAE

Genus of perennials, grown for their flowers and foliage. Fully hardy. Requires a sunny site and fertile, well-drained soil. Propagate by division in spring or by seed in autumn. After division may not flower for a season.
🏆 **P. liliastrum** (St Bruno's lily). Clump-forming, fleshy-rooted perennial. **H** 30–60cm (12–24in), **S** 30cm (12in). Slender stems, bearing racemes of saucer-shaped, white flowers in early summer, arise above broad, grass-like, greyish-green leaves.

PARAHEBE

SCROPHULARIACEAE

Genus of evergreen or semi-evergreen, summer-flowering perennials, sub-shrubs and shrubs, similar to *Hebe* and *Veronica.* Is suitable for rock gardens. Frost hardy. Needs sun and well-drained, peaty, sandy soil. Propagate by semi-ripe cuttings in early summer.
P. catarractae illus. p.342.
P. lyallii. Semi-evergreen, prostrate shrub. **H** 15cm (6in), **S** 20–25cm (8–10in). Has oval, toothed, leathery leaves. In early summer, erect stems bear loose sprays of flattish, pink-veined, white flowers.
🏆 **P. perfoliata**, syn. *Veronica perfoliata,* illus. p.271.

PARAQUILEGIA

RANUNCULACEAE

Genus of tufted perennials, grown for their cup-shaped flowers and fern-like foliage. Is difficult to cultivate and flower successfully. Prefers dry winters and cool climates. Is good in alpine houses and troughs. Fully hardy. Needs sun and gritty, well-drained, alkaline soil. Propagate by seed in autumn.
P. anemonoides, syn. *P. grandiflora,* illus. p.350.
P. grandiflora. See *P. anemonoides.*

PARASERIANTHES

LEGUMINOSAE/MIMOSACEAE

Genus of deciduous or semi-evergreen trees, grown for their feathery foliage and unusual flower heads, composed of numerous stamens and resembling bottlebrushes. Half hardy to frost tender, min. 4–5°C (39–41°F). In frost-prone areas, grow half hardy species against a south- or west-facing wall and tender species under glass; in cold areas, do not plant out until late spring. Needs full sun and well-drained soil. Propagate by seed in spring.
🏆 **P. lophantha**, syn. *Albizia distachya, A. lophantha,* illus. p.89.

PARIS

Herb Paris

LILIACEAE/TRILLIACEAE

Genus of summer-flowering, rhizomatous perennials. Fully hardy. Requires shade or semi-shade and humus-rich soil. Propagate by division in spring or by seed in autumn. Flowers are followed by fleshy fruits with black or red seeds. ⓘ These may cause mild stomach upset if ingested.
🏆 **P. polyphylla**, syn. *Daiswa polyphylla.* Erect, rhizomatous perennial. **H** 60cm–1m (2–3ft), **S** to 30cm (1ft). In early summer, at tips of slender stems, produces unusual flowers consisting of a ruff of green sepals, with another ruff of greenish-yellow petals, marked with crimson above, crowned by a violet-purple stigma. Leaves, borne in whorls at stem tips, are lance-shaped to oval and mid-green.

PARKINSONIA

LEGUMINOSAE/CAESALPINIACEAE

Genus of evergreen, spring-flowering shrubs and trees, grown for their flowers and overall appearance. Frost tender, min. 15°C (59°F). Needs as much sunlight as possible to thrive, a dry atmosphere and fertile, free-draining soil. Water potted specimens moderately when in full growth, sparingly at other times. Pruning is tolerated, but spoils the natural habit. Propagate by seed in spring.
P. aculeata (Jerusalem thorn, Mexican palo verde). Evergreen, feathery shrub or

tree with a spiny, green stem. **H** and **S** 3–6m (10–20ft) or more. Long, linear leaves have winged midribs bearing tiny, elliptic, short-lived leaflets. Produces fragrant, 5-petalled, yellow flowers in arching racemes in spring.

PARNASSIA

PARNASSIACEAE

Genus of rosetted, mainly summer-flowering perennials, grown for their saucer-shaped flowers. Is good for rock gardens. Fully hardy. Needs sun and wet soil. Propagate by seed in autumn.
P. palustris illus. p.336.

PAROCHETUS

LEGUMINOSAE/PAPILIONACEAE

Genus of two species of evergreen perennial. Grows best in alpine houses. Half hardy. Needs semi-shade and gritty, moist soil. Propagate by division of rooted runners in any season.
P. communis illus. p.370.

PARODIA

CACTACEAE

Genus of rounded, perennial cacti with tubercles arranged in ribs that often spiral around green stems. Crown forms woolly buds, then funnel-shaped flowers. Frost tender, min. 5–10°C (41–50°F). Requires full sun or partial shade and very well-drained soil. Water very lightly in winter; tends to lose roots during a long period of drought. Propagate by seed in spring or summer.
P. chrysacanthion illus. p.496.
🏆 ***P. concinna***, syn. *Notocactus apricus*. Flattened spherical, perennial cactus. **H** 7cm (3in), **S** 10cm (4in). Min. 10°C (50°F). Much-ribbed, pale green stem is densely covered with short, soft, golden-brown spines. In summer, crown produces flattish, glossy, bright yellow flowers, 8cm (3in) across, with purple stigmas. Prefers partial shade.
P. erinacea, syn. *Wigginsia vorwerkiana* (Colombian ball cactus). Slow-growing, flattened spherical, perennial cactus. **H** 8cm (3in), **S** 9cm (3½in). Min. 10°C (50°F). Glossy stem, with up to 20 wart-like ribs, has yellow-white spines and bears yellow flowers in summer.
P. haselbergii* subsp. *graessneri (syn. *Notocactus graessneri*) is a slow-growing, flattened spherical, perennial cactus. **H** 10cm (4in), **S** 25cm (10in). Min 10°C (50°F). Bristle-like, golden spines cover much-ribbed, green stem. Slightly sunken crown bears funnel-shaped, glossy, greenish-yellow flowers, with yellow stigmas, in early spring. Prefers partial shade. **subsp. *haselbergii***, syn. *Notocactus haselbergii*, illus. p.487.
P. leninghausii, syn. *Notocactus leninghausii* (Golden ball cactus). Clump-forming, perennial cactus. **H** 1m (3ft), **S** 30cm (1ft). Min. 10°C (50°F). Woolly crown always slopes towards sun. In summer, on plants more than 10cm (4in) tall, yellow blooms open flat.
P. mammulosa, syn. *Notocactus mammulosus*. Spherical, perennial cactus. **H** and **S** 10cm (4in). Min. 10°C (50°F). Green stem has about 20 ribs and straight, stiff, yellow-brown to white spines, to 1cm (½in) long. Woolly crown produces masses of golden flowers in summer.
P. microsperma, syn. *P. sanguiniflora*, illus. p.487.
P. mueller-melchersii, syn. *P. rutilans, Notocactus rutillans*, illus. p.486.
P. nivosa illus. p.487.
P. ottonis, syn. *Notocactus ottonis*. Variable, spherical, perennial cactus. **H** and **S** 10cm (4in). Min. 5°C (41°F). Has pale to dark green stem with 8–12 rounded ribs bearing stiff, golden radial spines and longer, soft, red central spines. In summer, crown bears flattish, glossy, golden flowers, 8cm (3in) across, with purple stigmas. Offsets freely from stolons. Prefers sun.
P. sanguiniflora. See *P. microsperma.*
P. scopa, syn. *Notocactus scopa* (Silver ball cactus). Spherical to columnar, perennial cactus. **H** 25cm (10in), **S** 15cm (6in). Min. 10°C (50°F). Stem, with 30–35 ribs, is densely covered with white radial spines and longer, red central spines, 3 or 4 per areole. Crown bears funnel-shaped, glossy, yellow flowers, 4cm (1½in) across, with purple stigmas, in summer. Prefers a sunny position.

PARONYCHIA

CARYOPHYLLACEAE/ILLECEBRACEAE

Genus of evergreen perennials making loose mats of prostrate stems. Is useful for rock gardens and walls. Fully to frost hardy. Needs sun and well-drained soil. Propagate by division in spring.
P. capitata. Vigorous, evergreen, mat-forming perennial. **H** 1cm (½in), **S** 40cm (16in). Fully hardy. Silvery leaves are small and oval. In summer, produces inconspicuous flowers surrounded by papery bracts. Makes good ground cover.
P. kapela* subsp. *serpyllifolia illus. p.375.

PARROTIA

HAMAMELIDACEAE

Genus of one species of deciduous tree, grown for its flowers and autumn colour. Fully hardy, but flower buds may be killed by hard frosts. Requires full sun and grows best in fertile, moist but well-drained soil. Is lime-tolerant, but usually colours best in acid soil. Propagate by softwood cuttings in summer or by seed in autumn.
🏆 ***P. persica*** illus. p.77.

PARROTIOPSIS

HAMAMELIDACEAE

Genus of one species of deciduous tree or shrub, grown for its ornamental, dense flower heads surrounded by conspicuous bracts. Fully hardy. Needs sun or semi-shade. Grows in any fertile, well-drained soil except very shallow soil over chalk. Propagate by softwood cuttings in summer or by seed in autumn.
P. jacquemontiana. Deciduous, shrubby or upright tree. **H** 6m (20ft), **S** 4m (12ft). Has witch-hazel-like, dark green leaves that turn yellow in autumn. From mid- to late spring and in summer, bears clusters of minute flowers, with tufts of yellow stamens, surrounded by white bracts.

PARTHENOCISSUS

VITACEAE

Genus of deciduous, woody-stemmed, tendril climbers, grown for their leaves, which often turn beautiful colours in autumn. Broad tips of tendrils have sucker-like pads that cling to supports. Has insignificant, greenish flowers in summer. Will quickly cover north-or east-facing walls or fences and may be grown up large trees. Fully to half hardy. Grow in semi-shade or shade and in well-drained soil. Propagate by softwood or greenwood cuttings in summer or by hardwood cuttings in early spring. ⓘThe berries may cause mild stomach upset if ingested.
🏆 ***P. henryana***, syn. *Vitis henryana*. Deciduous, tendril climber with 4-angled, woody stems. **H** to 10m (30ft) or more. Frost hardy. Leaves have 3–5 toothed, oval leaflets, each 4–13cm (1½–5in) long, and are velvety, deep green or bronze with white or pinkish veins. Small, dark blue berries are produced in autumn. Leaf colour is best with a north or east aspect.
🏆 ***P. quinquefolia***, syn. *Vitis quinquefolia* (Five-leaved ivy, Virginia creeper). Deciduous, woody-stemmed, tendril climber. **H** 15m (50ft) or more. Frost hardy. Leaves have 5 oval, toothed, dull green leaflets, paler beneath, that turn a beautiful crimson in autumn. Blue-black berries are produced in autumn. Is ideal for covering a high wall or building.
P. striata. See *Cissus striata*.
P. thomsonii. See *Cayratia thomsonii*.
🏆 ***P. tricuspidata***, illus. p.209. **'Lowii'** illus. p.209. **'Veitchii'** (syn. *Ampelopsis veitchii*) illus. p.210.

PASSIFLORA

Passion flower

PASSIFLORACEAE

Genus of evergreen or semi-evergreen, woody-stemmed, tendril climbers, grown for their unique flowers, each one with a central corona of filaments. Produces egg-shaped to rounded, fleshy, edible fruits that mature to orange or yellow in autumn. Half hardy to frost tender, min. 5–16°C (41–61°F). Grow in full sun or partial shade and in any fertile, well-drained soil. Water freely in full growth, less at other times. Stems need support. Thin out and spur back crowded growth in spring. Propagate by seed in spring or by semi-ripe cuttings in summer.
P. x allardii, syn. *P.* 'Allardii'. Strong-growing, evergreen, woody-stemmed, tendril climber. **H** 7–10m (22–30ft). Frost tender, min. 7°C (45°F). Has 3-lobed leaves. Flowers, 7–10cm (3–4in) wide, are white, tinted pink, with purple-banded crowns, and are carried in summer–autumn.
P. 'Allardii'. See *P. x allardii*.
🏆 ***P. antioquiensis***, syn. *Tacsonia van-volxemii* (Banana passion fruit). Fast-growing, evergreen, woody-stemmed, tendril climber. **H** 5m (15ft) or more. Frost tender, min. 7°C (45°F). Has downy leaves, with 3 deep lobes. Bears long-tubed, rose-red flowers, 10–12cm (4–5in) across, with purplish-blue centres, in summer–autumn.
🏆 ***P. caerulea*** illus. p.204. **'Constance Elliot'** is a fast-growing, evergreen or semi-evergreen, woody-stemmed, tendril climber. **H** 10m (30ft) or more. Frost hardy. Has rich green leaves. In summer–autumn produces bowl-shaped, fragrant, white flowers with pale blue or white filaments.
P. x caeruleoracemosa. See *P. x violacea*.
***P. x caponii* 'John Innes'.** Strong-growing, evergreen, woody-stemmed, tendril climber. **H** 8m (25ft). Frost tender, min. 7°C (45°F). Has 3-lobed leaves and bowl-shaped, nodding, white flowers, flushed claret-purple, with purple-banded, white crowns, in summer–autumn.
P. coccinea illus. p.462.
🏆 ***P. x exoniensis.*** Fast-growing, evergreen, woody-stemmed, tendril climber. **H** 8m (25ft) or more. Frost tender, min. 7°C (45°F). Leaves have 3 deep lobes and are softly downy. Rose-pink flowers, 8cm (3in) across, with purplish-blue crowns, are produced in summer–autumn.
P. manicata. Fast-growing, evergreen, woody-stemmed, tendril climber. **H** 3–5m (10–15ft). Frost tender, min. 7°C (45°F). Has slender, angular stems and 3-lobed leaves. Red flowers, with deep purple and white crowns, are borne in summer–autumn.
🏆 ***P. mollissima***, syn. *Tacsonia mollissima*. Fast-growing, evergreen, woody-stemmed, tendril climber. **H** 5m (15ft) or more. Frost tender, min. 7°C (45°F). Softly downy leaves have 3 deep lobes. Long-tubed, pink flowers, to 8cm (3in) wide, each with a purplish-blue crown, appear in summer–autumn.
🏆 ***P. quadrangularis*** illus. p.462.
🏆 ***P. racemosa*** (Red passion flower). Fast-growing, evergreen, tendril climber with slender, woody stems. **H** 5m (15ft). Frost tender, min. 15°C (59°F). Has wavy, leathery leaves with 3 deep lobes. In summer–autumn bears terminal racemes of pendent, crimson flowers, 8–10cm (3–4in) across, with white- and purple-banded crowns.
P. sanguinea. See *P. vitifolia*.
🏆 ***P. x violacea***, syn. *P. x caeruleoracemosa*. Vigorous, evergreen, woody-stemmed, tendril climber. **H** 10m (30ft). Frost tender, min. 7–10°C (45–50°F). Has 3-lobed leaves. Purple flowers, 8cm (3in) across, appear in summer–autumn.
P. vitifolia, syn. *P. sanguinea*. Evergreen, woody-stemmed, tendril climber; slender stems have fine, brown hairs. **H** to 5m (15ft). Frost tender, min. 16°C (61°F). Has 3-lobed, lustrous leaves. In summer–autumn, bears bright scarlet flowers, 13cm (5in) wide, each with a short crown, banded red, yellow and white.

PATERSONIA

IRIDACEAE

Genus of evergreen, clump-forming, spring- and early summer-flowering, rhizomatous perennials. Half hardy. Needs full sun and light, well-drained soil. Leave undisturbed once planted. Propagate by seed in autumn. Leave undisturbed once planted. Propagate by seed in autumn.
P. umbrosa. Evergreen, clump-forming, spring- and early summer-flowering rhizomatous perennial. **H** 30–45cm (12–18in), **S** 30–60cm (12–24in). Has erect, basal leaves and tough flower stems bearing a succession of iris-like, purple-blue flowers, 3–4cm (1¼–1½in) across.

PATRINIA

VALERIANACEAE

Genus of perennials, with neat clumps, grown for their flowers. Is suitable for rock gardens and peat beds. Fully hardy. Needs a site in partial shade with moist soil. Propagate by division in spring or by seed in autumn. Self-seeds freely.
P. triloba illus. p.275.

PAULOWNIA

SCROPHULARIACEAE

Genus of deciduous trees, grown for their large leaves and foxglove-like flowers, borne before the foliage emerges. Fully to frost hardy, but flower buds and young growth of small plants may be damaged by very hard frosts. Requires full sun and fertile, moist but well-drained soil. Propagate by seed in autumn or spring, or by root cuttings in winter.
P. fortunei. Deciduous, spreading tree. **H** and **S** 8m (25ft). Fully hardy. Has large, oval, mid-green leaves. In late spring, bears large, fragrant flowers, purple-spotted and white inside, pale purple outside.
P. imperialis. See *P. tomentosa.*
♀ ***P. tomentosa***, syn. *P. imperialis*, illus. p.72.

PAVONIA

MALVACEAE

Genus of evergreen, mainly summer-flowering perennials and shrubs, grown usually for their flowers. Frost tender, min. 16–18°C (61–4°F). Needs full light or partial shade and humus-rich, well-drained soil. Water freely when in full growth, moderately at other times. Leggy stems may be cut back hard in spring. Propagate by seed in spring or by greenwood cuttings in summer. Whitefly and red spider mite may be troublesome.
P. hastata. Evergreen, erect shrub. **H** 2–3m (6–10ft), **S** 1–2m (3–6ft). Has lance-shaped to oval, mid-green leaves, each with 2 basal lobes. Funnel-shaped, pale red to white flowers, with darker basal spotting, appear in summer.

PAXISTIMA

SYN. PACHYSTIMA

CELASTRACEAE

Genus of evergreen, spreading shrubs and sub-shrubs, grown for their foliage. Is suitable for ground cover. Fully hardy. Prefers shade and humus-rich, moist soil. Propagate by division in spring or by semi-ripe cuttings in summer.
P. canbyi. Evergreen, spreading sub-shrub. **H** 15–30cm (6–12in), **S** 20cm (8in). Leaves are linear or oblong, and short, pendent spikes of tiny, greenish-white flowers are produced in summer.

Pedilanthus. See *Euphorbia.*

PELARGONIUM

Geranium

GERANIACEAE

Genus of mainly summer-flowering perennials, most of which are evergreen, often cultivated as annuals. Is grown for its colourful flowers and is useful in pots or as bedding plants; in warm conditions flowers are borne almost continuously. Frost tender, min. 2°C (36°F), unless otherwise stated. A sunny site with 12 hours of daylight is required for good flowering. Prefers well-drained, neutral to alkaline soil. Dislikes very hot, humid conditions. Dead-head frequently and fertilize regularly if grown in containers; do not overwater. Plants may be kept through winter in the greenhouse by cutting back in autumn–winter to 12cm (5in) and repotting. Propagate by softwood cuttings from spring to autumn. ⓘContact with the foliage may occasionally aggravate skin allergies.

Pelargoniums may be divided into 6 groups; all flower in summer–autumn unless stated otherwise. See also feature panel p.309.

Angel – plants with rounded, sometimes scented, usually mid-green leaves, and clusters of small, single flowers of the regal type.
Ivy-leaved – trailing, evergreen plants, ideal for hanging baskets, with lobed, sometimes pointed, stiff, fleshy, usually mid-green leaves and flowers similar to those of zonal pelargoniums.
Regal – shrubby, evergreen plants with rounded, sometimes lobed or partially toothed, mid-green leaves and clusters of single, rarely double, broadly trumpet-shaped, exotic-coloured flowers that are prone to weather damage in the open.
Scented-leaved and species – evergreen plants with small, single, often irregularly star-shaped flowers; scented-leaved forms are grown for their fragrance.
Unique – Tall-growing, evergreen sub-shrubs with rounded or lobed, sometimes incised, mid-green leaves, often with a pungent scent when crushed. Produces clusters of single, trumpet-shaped, brightly coloured flowers of the regal type, which appear continuously through the season.
Zonal – succulent-stemmed, evergreen plants with rounded, leaves, distinctively marked with a darker 'zone', and single (5-petalled), semi-double or fully double flowers. Zonal pelargoniums can be separated into the following groups: cactus-flowered; double- and semi-double-flowered; fancy-leaved; Formosum hybrids; Rosebud; Single-flowered; and Stellar.

P. acetosum. Species pelargonium. **H** 50–60cm (20–24in), **S** 20–25cm (8–10in). Stems are succulent with fleshy, grey-green leaves that are often margined red. Bears single, salmon-pink flowers. Is good as a pot plant in a greenhouse.
***P.* 'Alberta'** (illus. p.309). Evergreen, single-flowered zonal pelargonium. **H** 45cm (18in), **S** 30cm (12in). Bears clusters of small, crimson-and-white flowers. Is best grown as a bedding plant.
♀ ***P.* AMETHYST ('Fisdel')**. Evergreen, trailing ivy-leaved pelargonium. **H** and **S** to 1.5m (5ft). Leaves are fleshy with pointed lobes. Bears fully double, light mauve-purple flowers.
***P.* Antik Series.** Vigorous, evergreen, single-flowered zonal pelargonium grown as a climber or, with pinching, as ground cover. **H** and **S** 90–120cm (36–48in). Has rounded, lobed, plain green leaves and large clusters of flowers in orange, pink, violet, salmon or scarlet. **ANTIK SALMON ('Tiksal')** (illus. p.309) bears salmon-pink flowers.
♀ ***P.* 'Apple Blossom Rosebud'.** Evergreen, rosebud zonal pelargonium. **H** 30cm (12in), **S** 23cm (9in). Fully double, pinkish-white flowers, margined with red, look like miniature rosebuds.
***P.* 'Autumn Festival'.** Evergreen, bushy regal pelargonium. **H** and **S** 30cm (12in). Salmon-pink flowers have pronounced, white throats.
♀ ***P.* 'Bird Dancer'.** Dwarf, stellar zonal pelargonium. **H** 15–20cm (6–8in), **S** 12–15cm (5–6in). Has clusters of single flowers, with pale pink lower petals and salmon-pink upper petals.
***P.* BLUE WONDER ('Pacbla')** (illus. p.309). Evergreen, semi-double-flowered zonal pelargonium. **H** 30cm (12in), **S** 40cm (16in). Has rounded, lobed, plain green leaves and large clusters of vivid rich lilac flowers (not blue).
♀ ***P.* 'Bredon'.** Strong-growing, evergreen regal pelargonium. **H** 45cm (18in), **S** to 30cm (12in). Bears large, maroon flowers.
***P.* 'Brookside Primrose'** (illus. p.309). Dwarf, fancy-leaved zonal pelargonium. **H** 10–12cm (4–5in), **S** 7–10cm (3–4in). Bears double, pale pink flowers. Leaves have a butterfly mark in the centre of each leaf. Is good as a pot plant or for bedding.
***P.* Bulls Eye Series.** Evergreen, single-flowered zonal pelargonium. **H** 33–38cm (13–15in), **S** 28–33cm (11–13in). Has rounded, lobed, chocolate-brown leaves with green edges. Produces large clusters of flowers in shades of red, pink or a mixture. Propagate by seed. **'Bulls Eye Salmon'** (illus. p.309) is salmon-pink.
***P.* 'Butterfly Lorelei'.** Fancy-leaved, zonal pelargonium. **H** 25–30cm (10–12in), **S** 15–20cm (6–8in). Has butterfly-shaped leaves and double, pale salmon-pink flowers. Is suitable as a pot plant in a greenhouse.
***P.* 'Caligula'.** Evergreen, miniature, semi-double-flowered zonal pelargonium. **H** 15–20cm (6–8in), **S** 10cm (4in). Has small, crimson flowers and tiny, dark green leaves. Suits a windowsill.
***P.* 'Capen'.** Bushy, semi-double-flowered zonal pelargonium. **H** 38–45cm (15–18in), **S** 15–20cm (6–8in). Bears coral-pink, semi-double flowers. Is good as a pot plant.
P. capitatum. Evergreen, scented-leaved pelargonium. **H** 30–60cm (12–24in), **S** 30cm (12in). Has mauve flowers and irregularly 3-lobed leaves that smell faintly of roses. Is mainly used to produce geranium oil for the perfume industry, but may be grown as a pot plant.
P. carnosum. Deciduous, shrubby pelargonium (unclassified), with thick, succulent stems and a woody, swollen, tuber-like rootstock. **H** and **S** 30cm (12in). Min. 10°C (50°F). Has long, grey-green leaves with triangular, deeply lobed leaflets. Produces branched, umbel-like flower heads with white or greenish-yellow flowers, the upper petals streaked red and shorter than the green sepals.
***P.* 'Cherry Blossom'.** Vigorous, evergreen, single-flowered zonal pelargonium. **H** and **S** to 45cm (18in). Mauve-pink flowers have white centres.
***P.* 'Chew Magna'.** Evergreen regal pelargonium. **H** 30–45cm (12–18in), **S** to 30cm (12in). Each petal of the pale pink flowers has a wine-red blaze.
***P.* 'Clorinda'** (illus. p.309). Vigorous, scented-leaved pelargonium. **H** 45–50cm (18–20in), **S** 20–25cm (8–10in). Leaves smell of cedar and are 3-lobed. Bears large, single, rose-pink flowers. Is suitable for a greenhouse or patio.
***P.* 'Coddenham'.** Miniature, double-flowered zonal pelargonium. **H** 10–12cm (4–5in), **S** 7–10cm (3–4in). Produces clusters of orange-red flowers.
♀ ***P. crispum* 'Variegatum'.** Evergreen, upright, scented-leaved pelargonium. **H** to 1m (3ft), **S** 30–45cm (1–1½ft). Has gold-variegated leaves and small, pale lilac flowers. Foliage tends to become creamy-white in winter.
***P.* 'Dale Queen'.** Evergreen, bushy, single-flowered zonal pelargonium. **H** 23–30cm (9–12in), **S** 23cm (9in). Flowers are delicate salmon-pink. Is particularly suitable for a pot.
***P.* Decora Series.** Evergreen, trailing ivy-leaved pelargonium. **H** 15–20cm (6–8in), **S** to 1.2m (4ft). Bears fresh green leaves without a dark zone, and narrow-petalled flowers in red, lilac or shades of pink. **'Decora Dark Pink'** (illus. p.309) is dark rose-pink.
♀ ***P.* 'Dolly Varden'.** Evergreen, fancy-leaved zonal pelargonium. **H** 30cm (12in), **S** 23cm (9in). Green leaves have purple-brown, white and crimson markings. Single, scarlet flowers are insignificant.
***P.* 'Emma Hössle'.** See *P.* 'Frau Emma Hössle'.
***P.* 'Evka'** (illus. p.309). Evergreen, trailing, bushy ivy-leaved pelargonium. **H** 15cm (6in), **S** 45cm (18in). Has pale green leaves edged in creamy white. Bears clusters of small, single, deep rose-red flowers.
***P.* 'Fair Ellen'.** Compact scented-leaved pelargonium. **H** and **S** 30cm (12in). Has dark green leaves and pale pink flowers marked with red.
***P.* Fireworks Series.** Bushy, compact evergreen perennial with matt, shallowly 5-lobed, aromatic, dark green leaves, the lobes suffused purplish-green. From spring to early autumn, produces upright, dense clusters of red, white, pink or bicoloured flowers, each with 5 sharply pointed lobes. **H** 20–25cm (8–10in), **S** 15–20cm (6–8in). **FIREWORKS SCARLET ('Fiwoscarl')** (illus. p.309) has bright scarlet flowers.
♀ ***P.* 'Flower of Spring'** (Silver-leaved geranium). Vigorous, evergreen, fancy-leaved zonal pelargonium. **H** 60cm (24in), **S** 30cm (12in). Has green-and-white leaves and single, red flowers.
P. x fragrans. See *P.* 'Fragrans'.
***P.* 'Fragrans'**, syn. *P. x fragrans*, *P.* Fragrans Group. Evergreen, very bushy, scented-leaved pelargonium. **H** and **S** 30cm (12in). Rounded, shallowly lobed, grey-green leaves smell strongly of pine. Bears small, white flowers.
***P.* Fragrans Group.** See *P.* 'Fragrans'.
***P.* 'Fraiche Beauté'**, syn. *P.* 'Fraicher Beauty' (illus. p.309). Evergreen, double-flowered zonal pelargonium. **H** 30cm (12in), **S** 23cm (9in). Flowers are perfectly formed with delicate colouring: white with a thin, red edge to each petal. Is excellent as a pot plant.

P. 'Fraicher Beauty'. See *P.* 'Fraiche Beauté'.

♀ **P. 'Francis Parrett'.** Evergreen, short-jointed, double-flowered zonal pelargonium. **H** 15–20cm (6–8in), **S** 10cm (4in). Bears purplish-mauve flowers and small, green leaves. Is good for a windowsill.

P. 'Frau Emma Hössle', syn. *P.* 'Emma Hössle'. Evergreen, dwarf, double-flowered zonal pelargonium. **H** 20–25cm (8–10in), **S** 15cm (6in). Bears large, mauve-pink flowers. Is useful for a window box.

P. 'Friesdorf'. Evergreen, fancy-leaved zonal pelargonium. **H** 25cm (10in), **S** 15cm (6in). Has dark green foliage and narrow-petalled, single, orange-scarlet flowers. Is good for a window box or planted in a large group.

P. 'Golden Lilac Mist'. Bushy, fancy-leaved zonal pelargonium. **H** 25–30cm (10–12in), **S** 15–20cm (6–8in). Leaves are gold marked with bronze. Bears double, lavender-pink flowers. Is a good window-box plant.

P. 'Gustav Emich'. Vigorous, evergreen, semi-double-flowered zonal pelargonium. **H** and **S** to 60cm (24in). Semi-double flowers are vivid scarlet.

♀ **P. 'Happy Thought'** illus. p.307.

P. Horizon Devas Series. Evergreen, single-flowered zonal pelargonium. **H** and **S** 30–45cm (12–18in). Has rounded, lobed, often bronze-zoned, mid-green leaves and large, domed heads of flowers with a speckled or picotee pattern, or a combination of the two. Propagate by seed. **'Horizon Deva Orange Ice'** (illus. p.309) is white with an orange picotee and veining and orange on the reverse. **'Horizon Deva Raspberry Ripple'** (illus. p.309) is white with a rich pattern of deep red speckles and occasional streaks.

♀ **P. 'Irene'.** Evergreen, semi-double-flowered zonal pelargonium. **H** 45cm (18in), **S** 23–30cm (9–12in). Bears large, light crimson blooms.

P. 'Ivalo'. Evergreen, bushy, short-jointed, semi-double-flowered zonal pelargonium. **H** 23–30cm (9–12in), **S** 23cm (9in). Large, semi-double flowers are pale pink with crimson-dotted, white centres.

P. 'Lachsball'. Vigorous, semi-double-flowered zonal pelargonium. **H** 45–50cm (18–20in), **S** 15–20cm (6–8in). Bears salmon-pink flowers each with a scarlet eye. Is good for summer bedding.

P. 'Lachskönigin' (illus. p.309). Evergreen, trailing, brittle-jointed pelargonium. **H** and **S** to 60cm (24in). Has fleshy leaves, with pointed lobes, and semi-double, deep rosy-pink flowers. Suits a hanging basket or window box.

♀ **P. 'Lady Plymouth'** (illus. p.309). Scented-leaved pelargonium. **H** 30–40cm (11–16in), **S** 15–20cm (6–8in). Has eucalyptus-scented, silver-margined leaves and lavender-pink flowers, borne in clusters.

♀ **P. 'L'Elégante'.** Evergreen, trailing ivy-leaved pelargonium. **H** and **S** to 60cm (24in). Foliage is variegated with creamy-white margins, sometimes turning pink at the edges; semi-double flowers are pale mauve. Is best grown in a hanging basket.

P. 'Lesley Judd'. Vigorous, evergreen, bushy regal pelargonium. **H** 30–45cm (12–18in), **S** to 30cm (12in). Flowers are soft salmon-pink with a central, red blotch. Pinch out growing tips before flowering to control shape.

♀ **P. 'Mabel Grey'.** Evergreen, scented-leaved pelargonium. **H** 45–60cm (18–24in), **S** 30–45cm (12–18in). Has diamond-shaped, rough-textured, toothed, strongly lemon-scented leaves, with 5–7 pointed lobes, and mauve flowers.

P. 'Madame Fournier'. Evergreen, short-jointed, single-flowered zonal pelargonium. **H** 15–20cm (6–8in), **S** 10cm (4in). Small, scarlet flowers contrast well with almost black leaves. Is useful for a pot or as a summer bedding plant.

P. 'Manx Maid'. Evergreen regal pelargonium. **H** 30–38cm (12–15in), **S** 25cm (10in). Flowers and leaves are small for regal type. Pink flowers are veined and blotched with burgundy.

P. 'Mauritania'. Evergreen, single-flowered zonal pelargonium. **H** 30cm (12in), **S** 23cm (9in). White flowers are ringed towards centres with pale salmon-pink.

P. Maverick Series. Evergreen, single-flowered zonal pelargonium. **H** and **S** 30–45cm (12–18in). Has rounded, lobed, mainly bronze-zoned, mid-green leaves. Produces large, domed heads of flowers in reds, pinks, a bicolour or white. Propagate by seed. **'Maverick Star'** (illus. p.309) is blushed white with deep rose-pink eyes.

P. 'Mini Cascade'. Evergreen, trailing, short-jointed, ivy-leaved pelargonium. **H** and **S** 30–45cm (12–18in). Bears many single, red flowers. Regular dead-heading is essential for continuous display.

P. 'Mr Everaarts'. Bushy, dwarf, double-flowered zonal pelargonium. **H** 15–20cm (6–8in), **S** 10–12cm (4–5in). Bears bright pink flowers. Is good in a window box.

♀ **P. 'Mr Henry Cox'**, syn. *P.* 'Mrs Henry Cox'. Evergreen, fancy-leaved zonal pelargonium. **H** 30cm (12in), **S** 15cm (6in). Mid-green leaves are marked with red, yellow and purple-brown. Flowers are single and pink.

P. 'Mrs Henry Cox'. See *P.* 'Mr Henry Cox'.

P. 'Mrs Pollock'. Evergreen, single-flowered zonal pelargonium. **H** 30cm (12in), **S** 15cm (6in). Each golden leaf has a grey-green butterfly mark in centre, with a bronze zone running through it. Bears small, orange-red flowers.

♀ **P. 'Mrs Quilter'.** Evergreen, fancy-leaved zonal pelargonium. **H** 30cm (12in), **S** 23cm (9in). Has yellow leaves with wide, chestnut-brown zones and single, pink flowers.

♀ **P. Multibloom Series**. Seed-raised, single-flowered zonal pelargonium. **H** 25–30cm (10–12in) and **S** 30cm (12in). Abundant flowers in shades of white, pink and red, some with white eyes, are borne in clusters. Early flowering over a long period. Is tolerant of wet conditions.

P. 'Orange Ricard'. Vigorous, robust, evergreen, semi-double-flowered zonal pelargonium. **H** 45–60cm (18–24in), **S** 30cm (12in). Has masses of large, orange blooms.

♀ **P. 'Paton's Unique'.** Vigorous unique pelargonium with pungent-smelling leaves. **H** 38–45cm (15–18in), **S** 15–20cm (6–8in). Flowers are single, red or pale pink, each with a small, white eye.

P. peltatum. Evergreen, trailing, brittle-jointed pelargonium from which ivy-leaved cultivars have been derived. **H** and **S** to 1.5m (5ft). Has fleshy leaves, with pointed lobes, and produces single, mauve or white flowers. Cultivars suit hanging baskets and window boxes.

P. 'Polka'. Vigorous unique pelargonium. **H** 45–50cm (18–20in), **S** 20–25cm (8–10in). Flowers are semi-double. Upper petals are orange-red, blotched and feathered deep purple; lower ones are salmon-orange.

P. 'Prince of Orange'. Scented-leaved pelargonium. **H** 25–30cm (10–12in), **S** 15–20cm (6–8in). Small, rounded leaves smell of orange. Bears single, mauve flowers. Is good as a pot plant indoors.

P. 'Purple Emperor'. Evergreen regal pelargonium. **H** 45cm (18in), **S** 30cm (12in). Pink-mauve flowers have a deeper, central coloration. Flowers well into autumn.

P. 'Purple Unique'. Vigorous, evergreen, upright, shrubby unique pelargonium. **H** and **S** 1m (3ft) or more. Rounded, large-lobed leaves are very aromatic. Has single, open trumpet-shaped, light purple flowers. Does well when trained against a sunny wall.

P. Regalia Series. Evergreen, bushy, single-flowered regal pelargonium. **H** and **S** 30–38cm (12–15in). Has clusters of prolific flowers in pink, deep purple, red, lilac or salmon, all with darker marks in throats. **'Regalia Chocolate'** (illus. p.309) is crimson with deep purplish-red marks.

P. 'Rica'. Bushy, single-flowered zonal pelargonium. **H** 30–38cm (12–15in), **S** 15–20cm (6–8in). Flowers are deep rose-pink, each with a large, white eye. Is good in a window box or as a greenhouse pot plant.

P. 'Robe'. Vigorous, semi-double-flowered zonal pelargonium. **H** 38–45cm (15–18in), **S** 15–20cm (6–8in). Bears cerise-crimson flowers. Is suitable as a pot plant in a greenhouse, or as a bedding plant, and is good for exhibition.

P. 'Rollisson's Unique'. Evergreen, shrubby, unique, pelargonium. **H** 60cm (24in) or more, **S** 30cm (12in). Has oval, notched, pungent leaves and small, single, open trumpet-shaped, wine-red flowers with purple veins.

P. 'Rouletta'. Vigorous, evergreen, trailing ivy-leaved pelargonium. **H** and **S** 60cm–1m (2–3ft). Bears semi-double, red-and-white flowers. To control shape, growing tips should be pinched out regularly.

♀ **P. 'Royal Oak'.** Evergreen, bushy, compact scented-leaved pelargonium. **H** 38cm (15in), **S** 30cm (12in). Oak-like, slightly sticky leaves have a spicy fragrance and are dark green with central, brown markings. Flowers are small and mauve-pink.

P. 'Schöne Helena'. Evergreen, semi-double-flowered zonal pelargonium. **H** 30–45cm (12–18in), **S** 23cm (9in). Produces masses of large, salmon-pink blooms.

P. 'Splendide'. Slow-growing, short-branching pelargonium. **H** 25–30cm (10–12in), **S** 15–20cm (6–8in). Butterfly-shaped flowers are borne singly or in clusters. Dark red upper petals each have a black spot at the base; lower petals are white, sometimes stained red.

P. Sprinter Series. Group of slow-growing, evergreen, branching, bushy, single-flowered zonal pelargoniums, grown as annuals. **H** and **S** 30–60cm (12–24in). Has rounded, lobed, light to mid-green leaves. Bears large, domed flower heads in shades of red. Is very free-flowering.

P. 'Tavira'. Evergreen, trailing, brittle-jointed pelargonium. **H** and **S** 30–40cm (12–16in). Has fleshy leaves, with pointed lobes, and single, soft cerise-red flowers. Is suitable for growing in a hanging basket or window box.

♀ **P. 'The Boar'.** Evergreen, trailing pelargonium. **H** and **S** to 60cm (24in). Has unusual, 5-lobed, notched leaves, each with a central, dark brown blotch, and long-stemmed, single, salmon-pink flowers. Is useful for a hanging basket.

P. 'Timothy Clifford'. Evergreen, short-jointed, semi-double-flowered zonal pelargonium. **H** 15–20cm (6–8in), **S** 10cm (4in). Has dark green leaves and fully double, salmon-pink flowers. Suits a windowsill.

♀ **P. 'Tip Top Duet'** (illus. p.309). Evergreen, bushy, free-branching regal pelargonium. **H** 30–38cm (12–15in), **S** 25cm (10in). Leaves and blooms are small for regal type. Bears pink-veined, white flowers; uppermost petals have dark burgundy blotches.

♀ ***P. tomentosum*** (Peppermint geranium). Evergreen, bushy scented-leaved pelargonium. **H** 30–60cm (12–24in), **S** 1m (36in). Large, rounded, shallowly lobed, velvety, grey-green leaves have a strong peppermint aroma. Bears clusters of small, white flowers. Growing tips should be pinched out to control spread. Dislikes full sun.

♀ **P. Video Series.** Group of slow-growing, evergreen, branching, bushy, single-flowered zonal pelargoniums, grown as annuals. **H** and **S** 30–60cm (12–24in). Has rounded, lobed, bronze-zoned, deep green leaves and large, domed, single flower heads in white and shades of pink or red.

♀ **P. 'Voodoo'** (illus. p.309). Unique pelargonium. **H** 50–60cm (20–24in), **S** 20–25cm (8–10in). Flowers are single and pale burgundy with a purple-black blaze on each petal. Is suitable as a greenhouse pot plant.

PELLAEA

ADIANTACEAE

Genus of deciduous, semi-evergreen or evergreen ferns. Half hardy to frost tender, min. 5°C (41°F). Grow in semi-shade and gritty, moist but well-drained soil. Remove fading fronds regularly. Propagate by spores in summer.

P. atropurpurea (Purple rock brake, Purple-stemmed cliff brake). Semi-evergreen or evergreen fern. **H** and **S** 30cm (12in). Frost tender. Small, narrowly lance-shaped, divided fronds have oblong, blunt pinnae and are dark green with a purplish tinge.

♀ ***P. rotundifolia*** (Button fern). Evergreen fern. **H** and **S** 15cm (6in). Frost tender. Small, narrowly lance-shaped, divided fronds are dark green and have rounded pinnae.

PELIOSANTHES

LILIACEAE/CONVALLARIACEAE

Genus of evergreen, rhizomatous perennials, grown for their foliage and delicate flowers. Fully to half hardy. Grow in moist but well-drained, fertile, acid soil in semi- or full shade. Propagate by divisions of the rhizome in spring or by seed in autumn.
P. arisanensis illus. p.472.

Pellionia. See *Elatostema*.

PELTANDRA

ARACEAE

A genus of 2 species of hardy, herbaceous perennials suitable for wet soils. Propagation is by division of the rhizome when dormant, or by seed sown in spring.
P. undulata. See *P. virginica*.
P. virginica, syn. *P. undulata*, illus. p.443.

Peltiphyllum. See *Darmera*.

PENNISETUM

GRAMINEAE/POACEAE

See also GRASSES, BAMBOOS, RUSHES and SEDGES.
P. alopecuroides, syn. *P. compressum* (Chinese fountain grass). Tuft-forming, herbaceous, perennial grass. **H** 1m (3ft), **S** 45cm (1½ft). Frost hardy. Has narrow, mid-green leaves; leaf sheaths each have a hairy tip. In late summer bears arching, cylindrical panicles with decorative, purple bristles that last well into winter.
P. compressum. See *P. alopecuroides*.
***P.* Fairy Tails.** Clump-forming, herebaceous, perennial grass. **H** 1.2m (4ft), **S** 60cm (24in). Frost hardy. Has long, bottlebrush-like panicles of beige spikelets, with pinkish bristles, borne in late summer above slender, mid-green leaves.
***P. glaucum* 'Purple Majesty'** illus. p.311.
P. longistylum. See *P. villosum*.
P. rueppellii. See *P. setaceum*.
🏆 ***P. setaceum***, syn. *P. rueppellii* (African fountain grass). Tuft-forming, herbaceous, perennial grass. **H** 1m (3ft), **S** 45cm (1½ft). Frost hardy. Has very rough, mid-green leaves and stems. In summer, bears dense, cylindrical panicles of copper-red spikelets, with decorative, bearded bristles, that last well into winter. **'Rubrum'** (illus. p.312).
🏆 ***P. villosum***, syn. *P. longistylum*, illus. p.286.

PENSTEMON

SCROPHULARIACEAE

Genus of annuals, perennials, sub-shrubs and shrubs, most of which are semi-evergreen or evergreen. Fully to half hardy. Prefers full sun and fertile, well-drained soil. Propagate species by seed in autumn or spring, or by softwood or semi-ripe cuttings of non-flowering shoots in mid-summer, cultivars by cuttings only. See also feature panel pp.236-237.
🏆 ***P.* 'Alice Hindley'** (illus. p.236). Large-leaved, semi-evergreen perennial. **H** 90cm (36in), **S** 45cm (18in). Frost hardy. Bears tubular to bell-shaped, pale lilac-blue flowers, white inside, tinged mauve-pink outside, from mid-summer to early or mid-autumn. Leaves are linear to lance-shaped and mid-green.
🏆 ***P.* 'Andenken an Friedrich Hahn'**, syn. *P.* 'Garnet' (illus. p.237). **H** 60–75cm (2–2½ft), **S** 60cm (2ft). Vigorous, semi-evergreen, bushy perennial. Frost hardy. Bears sprays of tubular, deep wine-red flowers from mid-summer to autumn. Has narrow, fresh green leaves.
🏆 ***P.* 'Apple Blossom'** (illus. p.236). Semi-evergreen, bushy perennial. **H** and **S** 60cm (24in). Frost hardy. Carries sprays of small, tubular, pale pink flowers from mid-summer onwards above narrow, fresh green foliage.
***P.* 'Barbara Barker'.** See *P.* 'Beech Park'.
P. barbatus, syn. *Chelone barbata* (illus. p.237). Semi-evergreen, rosette-forming perennial. **H** 1m (3ft), **S** 30cm (1ft). Frost hardy. From mid-summer to early autumn, bears racemes of slightly nodding, tubular, 2-lipped, rose-red flowers. Flower stems rise from rosettes of oblong to oval, mid-green leaves.
🏆 ***P.* 'Beech Park'**, syn. *P.* 'Barbara Barker' (illus. p.236). Semi-evergreen perennial. **H** and **S** 60cm (24in). Frost hardy. Bears bright pink and white flowers. Leaves are linear and light green.
***P.* 'Blackbird'.** Vigorous, semi-evergreen perennial. **H** 1.2m (4ft), **S** 45cm (18in). Frost hardy. Produces willowy, purplish-red stems clothed in long, lance-shaped, dark green leaves and racemes of deep red-purple flowers, the throats densely streaked deep red, from mid-summer to autumn.
***P.* 'Burford Seedling'.** See *P.* 'Burgundy'.
***P.* 'Burford White'.** See *P.* 'White Bedder'.
***P.* 'Burgundy'**, syn. *P.* 'Burford Seedling' (illus. p.237). Robust, semi-evergreen perennial. **H** 1.2m (4ft), **S** 60cm (2ft). Frost hardy. Produces purplish-red flowers with white throats streaked dark red. Leaves are linear and light green.
P. campanulatus, syn. *P. pulchellus*. Semi-evergreen, upright perennial. **H** 30–60cm (12–24in), **S** 30cm (12in). Frost hardy. Long racemes of bell-shaped, dark purple, violet or, occasionally, white flowers appear in early summer above lance-shaped, toothed, mid-green leaves.
***P.* 'Candy Pink'** See *P.* 'Old Candy Pink'.
P. cardwellii. Spreading, sometimes stem-rooting, evergreen sub-shrub. **H** and **S** 30–50cm (12–20in). Fully hardy. In early summer, produces raceme-like panicles of slender, tubular to funnel-shaped, deep purple flowers. Leaves are elliptic, finely toothed and mid-green.
***P.* 'Cherry'** of gardens See *P.* 'Cherry Ripe'.
🏆 ***P.* 'Cherry Ripe'**, syn. *P.* 'Cherry' of gardens (illus. p.237). Semi-evergreen perennial. **H** 1.1m (3½ft), **S** 45–60cm (1½–2ft). Frost hardy. Has lance-shaped, mid-green leaves. From mid-summer to autumn, produces an abundance of deep rose-red flowers, with a golden sheen and white throats, streaked deep red.
🏆 ***P.* 'Chester Scarlet'** (illus. p.237). Semi-evergreen perennial. **H** and **S** 90cm (36in). Frost hardy. Large, bright red flowers are borne above narrowly lance-shaped, light green leaves.
P. confertus. Semi-evergreen, neat, clump-forming perennial. **H** 45cm (18in), **S** 30cm (12in). Frost hardy. Bears spikes of tubular, creamy-yellow flowers above long, lance-shaped, mid-green leaves in early summer.
🏆 ***P.* 'Connie's Pink'.** Erect, much-branched, semi-evergreen perennial. **H** 1.2m (4ft), **S** 60cm (2ft). Frost hardy. Has slender, bright rose-pink flowers, with deep pink corolla lobes and red-pencilled, white throats, from early summer to autumn. Pale green leaves are lance-shaped to oval.
***P.* 'Countess of Dalkeith'.** Erect, semi-evergreen perennial. **H** 1m (3ft), **S** 60cm (2ft). Frost hardy. Produces large, deep purple flowers, each with a pure white throat. Leaves are linear and light green.
P. davidsonii. Evergreen, prostrate shrub. **H** 8cm (3in), occasionally more, **S** 15cm (6in) or more. Frost hardy. In late spring and early summer, funnel-shaped, violet to ruby-red flowers, with protruding lips, develop from leaf axils. Leaves are small, oval to rounded and leathery. Trim after flowering. 🏆 **var. *menziesii*** (syn. *P. menziesii*), **H** 5cm (2in), **S** 20cm (8in), produces lavender-blue flowers and rounded, toothed leaves.
P. diffusus. See *P. serrulatus*.
***P. digitalis* 'Husker Red'** (illus. p.236). Vigorous, semi-evergreen or deciduous, basal-rosetted perennial. **H** 50–75cm (20–30in), **S** 30cm (12in). Fully hardy. Has stems often marked reddish-purple bearing inversely lance-shaped, entire or sparsely toothed, mid-green leaves that are maroon-red when young. Produces panicles of tubular to bell-shaped, pink-tinted, white flowers, with purple lines inside, in summer.
***P.* 'Ellenbank Amethyst'.** Bushy, semi-evergreen perennial. **H** 90cm (36in), **S** 45cm (18in). Frost hardy. Has lance-shaped, mid-green leaves. In summer bears racemes of large, tubular, soft purple flowers, each with a white throat, edged with vivid rosy-purple.
🏆 ***P.* 'Evelyn'** illus. p.233.
***P.* 'Firebird'.** See *P.* 'Schoenholzeri'.
***P.* 'Flamingo'** (illus. p.236). Open, much-branched, semi-evergreen perennial. **H** 90–95cm (36–38in), **S** 60cm (24in). Frost hardy. From summer to autumn produces white-throated, deep purplish-pink flowers, the white extending onto the corolla lobes, with a few darker, reddish-pink pencillings on the lower lobes. Leaves are mid-green, lance-shaped to oval.
P. fruticosus. Evergreen, upright, woody-based sub-shrub. **H** and **S** 15–30cm (6–12in). Frost hardy. Has lance-shaped to oval, toothed leaves and, in early summer, funnel-shaped, lipped, lavender-blue flowers. Is suitable for a rock garden. Trim back after flowering. 🏆 **var. *scouleri*** (syn. *P. scouleri*) has pale to deep purple flowers. 🏆 **var. *scouleri* f. *albus*** (syn. *P. scouleri* f. *albus*; illus. p.236) has white flowers.
***P.* 'Garnet'.** See *P.* 'Andenken an Friedrich Hahn'.
***P.* 'Geoff Hamilton'.** Vigorous, semi-evergreen perennial. **H** 75cm (30in), **S** 60cm (24in). Frost hardy. Has lance-shaped to oval, mid-green leaves. Produces large, open, purple flowers, with white throats and white-flecked lobes, from early summer to autumn.
🏆 ***P.* 'George Home'.** Narrow-leaved perennial. **H** 75cm (30in), **S** 45cm (18in). Frost hardy. Produces small, tubular to bell-shaped, wine-red flowers, with white throats, the white extending over the lips, from mid-summer to early or mid-autumn.
P. glaber (illus. p.237). Evergreen, variable sub-shrub. **H** and **S** 50–75cm (20–30in). Frost hardy. In summer produces clusters of snapdragon-like, sky-blue to indigo flowers, with maroon pencillings in the white or pale blue throats. Lance-shaped to inversely oval leaves are mid-green. Requires a sunny, dry site.
🏆 ***P. hartwegii.*** Semi-evergreen, erect perennial. **H** 60cm (24in) or more, **S** 30cm (12in). Frost hardy. Bears sprays of slightly pendent, tubular to bell-shaped, scarlet flowers from mid- to late summer. Lance-shaped leaves are mid-green.
P. heterophyllus (Foothill penstemon). Evergreen sub-shrub. **H** and **S** 30–50cm (12–20in). Fully hardy (borderline). In summer produces racemes of tubular to funnel-shaped, pinkish-blue flowers, with blue or lilac lobes. Leaves are linear to lance-shaped, entire and mid-green or bluish-green. **'Heavenly Blue'** (illus. p.237). **H** 60cm (2ft), **S** 30cm (1ft), is frost hardy and produces tubular, mauve-tinged, blue flowers from mid-summer until the first frosts. **'True Blue'** has pale green leaves and pure blue flowers, borne on short side shoots. Trim back after flowering. Is suitable for a rock garden.
🏆 ***P.* 'Hidcote Pink'** (illus. p.236). Narrow-leaved perennial. **H** 60–75cm (24–30in), **S** 45cm (18in). Frost hardy. Produces small, tubular, pale pink flowers, with spreading lobes marked with crimson lines inside, from mid-summer to early or mid-autumn.
P. hirsutus Short-lived, evergreen, open sub-shrub. **H** 60cm–1m (2–3ft), **S** 30–60cm (1–2ft). Frost hardy. In summer produces hairy, tubular, lipped, purple- or blue-flushed, white flowers. Leaves are oval and dark green. Is suitable for a rock garden. **var. *pygmaeus*** illus. p.361.
***P.* 'Hopley's Variegated'** (illus. p.237). Large-leaved, semi-evergreen perennial. **H** 90cm (36in), **S** 45cm (18in). Frost hardy. Is a sport of *P.* 'Alice Hindley' with yellow-speckled leaves.
🏆 ***P. isophyllus*** illus. p.153.
***P.* 'Kilimanjaro'.** Vigorous, semi-evergreen perennial. **H** 80cm (32in), **S** 60cm (24in). Frost hardy. Has long, lance-shaped, mid-green leaves. From summer to autumn produces long racemes of purplish-pink flowers, with white throats.
***P.* 'King George V'** (illus. p.237). Narrow-leaved perennial. **H** 60cm (24in), **S** 45cm (18in). Frost hardy. Bears small, tubular to bell-shaped, bright, deep scarlet flowers, with white throats, from mid-summer to early to mid-autumn.
P. kunthii (illus. p.236). Variable, woody-based, willowy perennial. **H** 90cm–1.2m (3–4ft), **S** 60cm (2ft). Frost hardy. Has lance-shaped, toothed, mid-green leaves. From mid-summer to late autumn produces many-flowered racemes of red to

maroon-red flowers, with white streaks in the throats. Requires a sunny, dry site.
P. 'Madame Golding'. Strong-growing, semi-evergreen perennial. **H** 75cm (30in), **S** 40–45cm (16–18in). Frost hardy. Is similar to *P.* 'Old Candy Pink' but has paler pink flowers.
♀ **P. 'Margery Fish'** (illus. p.236). Almost mat-forming, woody-based perennial. **H** and **S** 50cm (20in). Frost hardy. Has narrow, shiny, mid-green leaves. Produces dense spikes of pale blue to violet-mauve flowers, with white pencilling in the throats, in summer–autumn.
♀ **P. 'Maurice Gibbs'.** Semi-evergreen perennial. **H** 90cm (3ft), **S** 60cm (2ft). Bears claret-red flowers, with white throats. Has lance-shaped, light green leaves.
P. menziesii. See *P. davidsonii* var. *menziesii*.
P. 'Modesty'. Strong-growing, erect, semi-evergreen perennial. **H** 90cm (3ft), **S** 45cm (1½ft). Frost hardy. Has lance-shaped, glossy, olive-green leaves. Produces bright red-pink flowers, with white throats sparsely pencilled purplish-red, in summer–autumn.
P. 'Mother of Pearl' (illus. p.236). Narrow-leaved perennial. **H** to 75cm (30in), **S** 45cm (18in). Frost hardy. Has small, tubular to bell-shaped, pearl-mauve flowers, tinted pink and white, with white throats and red lines, from mid-summer to early or mid-autumn. ♀ **P. newberryi** (Mountain pride). Evergreen, mat-forming shrub. **H** 15–20cm (6–8in), **S** 30cm (12in). Frost hardy. Branches are covered in small, oval, leathery, dark green leaves. Bears short sprays of tubular, lipped, deep rose-pink flowers in early summer. Trim back after flowering. Is good for a rock garden. **f. humilior** illus. p.340.
P. 'Old Candy Pink', syn. *P.* 'Candy Pink'. Strong-growing, semi-evergreen perennial. **H** 75cm (30in), **S** 40–45cm (16–18in). Frost hardy. Has lance-shaped, mid-green leaves. Produces bright crimson flowers, with darker crimson lines in the white throats and small, rounded, white patches at the bases of each lobe, from early summer to mid-autumn.
♀ **P. 'Osprey'** (illus. p.236). Vigorous, open-branched, semi-evergreen perennial. **H** 1.1m (3½ft), **S** 60cm (2ft). Frost hardy. Has lance-shaped to oval, mid-green leaves. Produces creamy-white flowers, with spreading, purplish-pink lobes and white throats, in summer–autumn. As the flowers age the pink coloration deepens and extends into the flower tubes.
P. 'Papal Purple' (illus. p.237). Mound-forming, semi-evergreen perennial. **H** 50cm (20in), **S** 35cm (14in). Frost hardy. Has narrowly lance-shaped, mid-green leaves. In summer bears small, rather rounded, white-throated, lilac-purple flowers.
P. 'Penbow'. Bushy, rather upright, semi-evergreen perennial. **H** 90cm (36in), **S** 40cm (16in). Frost hardy. Has narrowly lance-shaped, blue-green leaves. From mid-summer to autumn bears slender racemes of small, tubular, bright azure-blue flowers.
♀ **P. 'Pennington Gem'.** Vigorous, semi-evergreen perennial. **H** 1m (3ft), **S** 45cm (18in). Frost hardy. Bears sprays of tubular, pink flowers from mid-summer to autumn. Leaves are narrow and fresh green.
P. 'Pensham Just Jane' (illus. p.237). Robust, bushy, semi-evergreen perennial. **H** 90cm–1.2m (3–4ft), **S** 60cm (2ft). Frost hardy. Has lance-shaped to oval, deep green leaves. Produces rich, deep cerise-pink flowers, with faintly white-lined, magenta throats, from early summer to autumn.
P. 'Pensham Petticoat'. Bushy, semi-evergreen perennial. **H** 60cm (24in), **S** 35cm (14in). Frost hardy. Has lance-shaped, mid-green leaves. In summer produces racemes of large, tubular, rather frilly-looking, white flowers, edged with rose-pink.
P. 'Pershore Fanfare'. Vigorous, semi-evergreen perennial. **H** 90cm (36in), **S** 45cm (18in). Frost hardy. Has lance-shaped, mid-green leaves. In summer bears racemes of large, tubular, lavender-blue flowers, each with a white throat striped in darker purple.
♀ **P. pinifolius** illus. p.340. **'Mersea Yellow'** is an evergreen, bushy sub-shrub, **H** 10–20cm (4–8in), **S** 25cm (10in), with branched stems clothed in fine, dark green leaves. In summer, very narrow, tubular, bright deep yellow flowers are borne in loose, terminal spikes.
♀ **P. 'Port Wine'** (illus. p.237). Vigorous, upright, semi-evergreen perennial. **H** 1m (3ft), **S** 60cm (2ft). Frost hardy. Has lance-shaped to oval, mid- to dark green leaves. Produces deep claret to deep purple flowers, with white throats heavily pencilled deep claret, from early summer to autumn.
P. procerus. Upright, semi-evergreen perennial. **H** 50cm (20in), **S** 20cm (8in). Frost hardy. Leaves are oblong to lance-shaped. Produces slim spikes of funnel-shaped, blue-purple flowers in summer. Is suitable for a rock garden.
P. pulchellus. See *P. campanulatus*.
♀ **P. 'Raven'** (illus. p.237). Strong-growing, erect, semi-evergreen perennial. **H** 1.1m (3½ft), **S** 60cm (2ft). Frost hardy. Has lance-shaped to oval, mid- to dark green leaves. Dark purple-red flowers, with white throats pencilled faint, dark red in the tubes, coalescing into patches of blackish-purple-red at the lobe bases, are produced freely in summer–autumn.
P. 'Red Emperor'. Robust, erect, semi-evergreen perennial. **H** 90cm (3ft), **S** 45–50cm (18–20in). Frost hardy. Has lance-shaped to oval, mid-green leaves and vivid, bright scarlet flowers, with a golden sheen and white throats streaked and suffused red, in summer–autumn.
P. 'Rich Ruby'. Strong-growing, erect, semi-evergreen perennial. **H** 80–100cm (32–39in), **S** 60cm (24in). Frost hardy. Red-purple stems bear lance-shaped to oval, dark green leaves. In summer–autumn produces large, rich, dark red-purple blooms, with white throats heavily streaked and suffused dark red, coalescing into a dark brown-purple patch at the mouth of each flower tube.
P. 'Royal White'. See *P.* 'White Bedder'.
♀ **P. 'Rubicundus'** (illus. p.237). Erect, semi-evergreen perennial. **H** 1.2m (4ft), **S** 60cm (2ft). Frost hardy. Bears very large, bright red flowers, each with a white throat. Leaves are linear and light green.
♀ **P. rupicola.** Evergreen, prostrate shrub. **H** 5cm (2in), **S** 15cm (6in). Frost hardy. Has rounded to oval, fleshy, blue-grey leaves and, in summer, variable, funnel-shaped, pale to deep pink flowers. Is best grown in a rock garden.
P. 'Russian River' (illus. p.237). Vigorous, stout, erect, semi-evergreen perennial. **H** 70cm (28in), **S** 40cm (16in). Frost hardy. Purplish stems bear mid-green, lance-shaped leaves. In summer produces racemes of tubular, plum-purple flowers, each with a lavender-purple throat lined with darker markings.
♀ **P. 'Schoenholzeri'**, syn. *P.* 'Firebird' (illus. p.237). Vigorous, semi-evergreen, upright perennial. **H** 1m (3ft), **S** 30–45cm (1–1½ft). Frost hardy. Produces racemes of trumpet-shaped, brilliant scarlet flowers from mid-summer to autumn. Lance-shaped to narrowly oval leaves are mid-green.
P. scouleri. See *P. fruticosus* var. *scouleri*. **f. albus** see *P. fruticosus* var. *scouleri* f. *albus*.
P. serrulatus, syn. *P. diffusus*, illus. p.341.
P. 'Six Hills'. Evergreen, prostrate shrub. **H** 5cm (2in), **S** 15cm (6in). Frost hardy. Has rounded, fleshy, grey-green leaves. In summer carries funnel-shaped, cool lilac flowers at stem tips. Is suitable for a rock garden.
P. 'Snow Storm'. See *P.* 'White Bedder'.
♀ **P. 'Sour Grapes'** (illus. p.237). Semi-evergreen perennial. **H** 90cm (36in), **S** 60cm (24in). Light green leaves are narrowly lance-shaped. Bears deep purple-blue flowers suffused violet.
P. 'Southgate Gem'. Vigorous, semi-evergreen perennial. **H** 75cm (30in), **S** 45cm (18in). Frost hardy. Has lance-shaped, dark green leaves. Produces an abundance of bright rose-red flowers, with white throats sparsely pencilled crimson, in summer–autumn.
♀ **P. 'Stapleford Gem'** (illus. p.236). Large-leaved, semi-evergreen perennial. **H** to 60cm (24in), **S** 45cm (18in). Fully hardy. Bears large, tubular to bell-shaped, lilac-purple flowers from mid-summer to early or mid-autumn; upper lips are pale pink-lilac; lower lips and throats are white with purple lines. Leaves are linear to lance-shaped and mid-green.
P. 'Stromboli' (illus. p.236). Vigorous, semi-evergreen perennial. **H** 60–90cm (2–3ft), **S** 45–60cm (1½–2ft). Frost hardy. Produces pale creamy-white flowers, with purplish-pink lobes and faintly purple-pink-streaked, white throats, in summer–autumn. Mid-green leaves are lance-shaped to oval.
P. 'The Juggler' (illus. p.236). Erect, semi-evergreen perennial. **H** 110cm (3½ft), **S** 45–60cm (1½–2ft). Frost hardy. Produces white-throated, magenta flowers in summer–autumn.
P. 'Torquay Gem'. Semi-evergreen, woody-based perennial. **H** 60cm (2ft), **S** 30–40cm (12–16in). Frost hardy. Has long, lance-shaped, light green leaves. Produces deep rose-red flowers, with a few carmine lines in the white throats, in summer–autumn.
P. whippleanus (illus. p.237). Erect, semi-evergreen, basal-rosetted perennial. **H** 60cm (2ft), **S** 30cm (1ft). Frost hardy. Has rounded basal leaves and slender stems bearing lance-shaped, glossy, pale green leaves. In summer, pendent, tubular, dark purple flowers, with cream-marked throats, are borne in clusters around raceme.
♀ **P. 'White Bedder'**, syn. *P.* 'Burford White', *P.* 'Royal White', *P.* 'Snow Storm' (illus p.236). Semi-evergreen, free-flowering perennial. **H** 70cm (28in), **S** 60cm (24in). Frost hardy. Has white flowers with dark anthers, and linear, fresh green leaves.

PENTACHONDRA

ERICACEAE/EPACRIDACEAE

Genus of evergreen, spreading shrubs with heath-like leaves. Frost hardy. Needs full light and gritty, moist, peaty soil. Is difficult to grow, especially in hot, dry areas. Propagate by rooted offsets in spring, by semi-ripe cuttings in summer or by seed in autumn.
P. pumila. Evergreen, mat-forming, dense shrub. **H** 3–10cm (1¼–4in), **S** 20cm (8in) or more. Has oblong to narrowly oval, purplish-green leaves. Small, tubular, white flowers, with reflexed lobes, open in early summer, followed, though rarely in cultivation, by small, spherical, orange fruits.

Pentapterygium. See *Agapetes*.

PENTAS

RUBIACEAE

Genus of mainly evergreen perennials and shrubs, grown for their flowers. Frost tender, min. 10–15°C (50–59°F). Needs full light or partial shade and fertile, well-drained soil. Water freely when in full growth, moderately at other times. May be hard pruned in winter. Propagate by softwood cuttings in summer or by seed in spring. Is prone to whitefly.
P. carnea. See *P. lanceolata*.
P. lanceolata, syn. *P. carnea*, illus. p.300.

PEPEROMIA

PIPERACEAE

Genus of annuals and evergreen perennials, grown for their foliage. Frost tender, min. 10°C (50°F). Grow in full light or partial shade, ideally in a peat-based compost. Do not overwater. Propagate by division, by seed or by leaf or stem cuttings in spring or summer.
♀ **P. argyreia**, syn. *P. sandersii* (Watermelon plant). Evergreen, bushy, compact perennial. **H** and **S** 20cm (8in). Has red-stalked, oval, fleshy, dark green leaves, to 10cm (4in) or more long, striped with broad bands of silver. Flowers are insignificant.
P. caperata illus. p.465.
P. clusiifolia (Baby rubber plant). Evergreen perennial with branching, sometimes prostrate, reddish-green stems. **H** to 20cm (8in), **S** 25cm (10in). Narrowly oval, fleshy leaves, 8–15cm (3–6in) long, are dark green, edged with red. Flowers are insignificant. Leaves of **'Variegata'** have cream- and-red margins.
P. glabella illus. p.474.
♀ **P. griseoargentea**, syn. *P. hederifolia* (Ivy peperomia, Silver-leaf peperomia). Evergreen, bushy perennial. **H** to 15cm

(6in), **S** 20cm (8in). Oval, fleshy leaves, 5cm (2in) or more long, each have a heart-shaped base, a quilted green surface and a silvery sheen. Flowers are insignificant.
P. hederifolia. See *P. griseoargentea.*
P. magnoliifolia. See *P. obtusifolia.*
P. marmorata illus. p.474.
P. metallica. Evergreen perennial with erect, branching, reddish-green stems. **H** and **S** to 15cm (6in). Narrowly oval, dark green leaves, to 2.5cm (1in) long, have a metallic sheen, and wide, pale midribs above, reddish-green veins below. Flowers are insignificant.
P. nummulariifolia. See *P. rotundifolia.*
♀ ***P. obtusifolia***, syn. *P. magnoliifolia* (Pepper face) Evergreen perennial with leathery, dull green leaves. **H** and **S** 25cm (10in). Bears spikes of white flowers. **'Green and Gold'** has green leaves with golden-yellow margins. **'Variegata'** illus. p.474.
P. rotundifolia, syn. *P. nummulariifolia.* Evergreen, creeping perennial. **H** 5–8cm (2–3in), **S** 30cm (12in) or more. Very slender stems produce tiny, rounded, fleshy, bright green leaves, 1cm (½in) wide. Flowers are insignificant. Is useful for a hanging basket.
P. rubella. Evergreen perennial with erect, branching, red stems. **H** and **S** 15cm (6in). Leaves, in whorls of 4, are 1cm (½in) long, narrowly oval, fleshy and dark green above, crimson below. Flowers are insignificant.
P. sandersii. See *P. argyreia.*
♀ ***P. scandens*** (Cupid peperomia). Evergreen, climbing or trailing perennial with pinkish-green stems. **H** and **S** to 1m (3ft). Oval, pointed, fleshy leaves, to 5cm (2in) or more long, are waxy and bright green. Flowers are insignificant.

PERESKIA

CACTACEAE

Genus of deciduous cacti, some of which are climbing, with fleshy leaves and woody, green, then brown stems. Is considered the most primitive genus of the Cactaceae, producing true leaves unlike most members of the family. Frost tender, min. 5–10°C (41–50°F). Needs sun and well-drained soil. Water moderately in summer. Propagate by stem cuttings in spring or summer.
P. aculeata illus. p.479. **'Godseffiana'** (syn. *P.a.* var. *godseffiana*) is a fast-growing, deciduous, erect, then climbing cactus. **H** to 10m (30ft), **S** 5m (15ft). Min. 5°C (41°F). Broadly oval, slightly fleshy, orange-brown leaves, usually purplish beneath and 9cm (3½in) long, mature to glossy green. Short flower stems, carrying rose-like, single, orange-centred, cream flowers, 5cm (2in) across, appear in autumn only on plants over 1m (3ft) high. Cut back hard to main stems in autumn.
P. grandifolia, syn. *Rhodocactus grandifolius*, illus. p.485.

PERICALLIS

COMPOSITAE/ASTERACEAE

Genus of perennials and sub-shrubs, sometimes grown as annuals, especially for their daisy-like flower heads. Frost tender, min. 5°C (41°F). Requires sun or partial shade and fertile, well-drained soil. Propagate by seed sown from spring to mid-summer.
P. x hybrida, syn. *Cineraria cruentus* of gardens, *C.* x *hybridus, Senecio* x *hybridus* (Cineraria). **H** 45–60cm (18–24in), **S** 25–60cm (10–24in). Slow-growing, evergreen, mound- or dome-shaped perennial. Cultivars are grown as biennials. Half hardy. All have oval, serrated, mid- to deep green leaves. Large, daisy-like, single, semi-double or double flower heads, in shades of blue, red, pink or white, sometimes bicoloured, are produced in winter or spring. **'Brilliant'** has large flower heads in a mixture of white, blue, deep red, copper and rose-pink, and bicolours. **Royalty'** is late-flowering, with flower heads in sky-blue, cherry-red, lilac with a white eye, and bicolours. **'Spring Glory'** has flowers in a mixture of colours in spring. **'Star Wars'**, **H** 15cm (6in), **S** 20cm (8in), is compact, with flower heads in a mixture of white, blue, rose-pink, carmine-red and purple; ideal for small containers.
***P.* Senetti Series Senetti Blue Bi-color ('Sunseneribuba')** illus. p.314.
***P.* 'Sunseneribuba'.** See *P.* Senetti Series Senetti Blue Bi-color.

PERILLA

LABIATAE/LAMIACEAE

Genus of annuals, grown for their foliage. Half hardy. Grow in sun and in fertile, well-drained soil. Pinch out growing tips of young plants to encourage a bushy habit. Propagate by seed sown under glass in early spring.
P. frutescens. Moderately fast-growing, upright, bushy annual. **H** 60cm (24in), **S** 30cm (12in). Has oval, serrated, aromatic, reddish-purple leaves. In summer produces spikes of very small, tubular, white flowers.
***P.* 'Magilla Vanilla'** illus. p.318.

PERIPLOCA

ASCLEPIADACEAE/APOCYNACEAE

Genus of deciduous or evergreen, twining climbers, grown for their leaves. Stems exude milky juice if cut. Frost hardy. Grow in sun and in any well-drained soil. Propagate by seed in spring or by semi-ripe cuttings in summer. ⓘThe fruits and sap may cause stomach upset if ingested.
P. graeca (Silk vine). Deciduous, twining climber. **H** to 9m (28ft). Oval, glossy leaves are 2.5–5cm (1–2in) long. In summer has clusters of 8–12 greenish-yellow flowers, purplish-brown inside, each with 5 lobes. Pairs of narrowly cylindrical seed pods, 12cm (5in) long, contain winged, tufted seeds. Scent of the flowers is thought by some to be unpleasant.

PERISTROPHE

ACANTHACEAE

Genus of mainly evergreen perennials and sub-shrubs, grown usually for their flowers. Frost tender, min. 15°C (59°F). Grow in a sunny or partially shaded position and in well-drained soil; do not overwater plants in winter. Propagate by stem cuttings in spring or summer.
P. angustifolia. See *P. hyssopifolia.*
P. hyssopifolia, syn. *P. angustifolia.* Evergreen, bushy perennial. **H** to 60cm (2ft), **S** 1–1.2m (3–4ft). Broadly lance-shaped leaves, with long-pointed tips, are 8cm (3in) long. Small clusters of tubular, deep rose-pink flowers are borne in winter. **'Aureovariegata'** illus. p.476.

Pernettya mucronata. See *Gaultheria mucronata.*
Pernettya prostrata. See *Gaultheria myrsinoides.*
Pernettya pumila. See *Gaultheria pumila.*
Pernettya tasmanica. See *Gaultheria tasmanica.*

PEROVSKIA

LABIATAE/LAMIACEAE

Genus of deciduous sub-shrubs, grown for their aromatic, grey-green foliage and blue flowers. Fully hardy. Requires a position in full sun and very well-drained soil. Cut plants back hard, almost to base, in spring, as new growth starts. Propagate by softwood cuttings in late spring.
P. atriplicifolia. Deciduous, upright sub-shrub. **H** 1.2m (4ft), **S** 1m (3ft). Grey-white stems bear narrowly oval, coarsely toothed leaves. Bears 2-lipped, violet-blue flowers in long, slender spikes from late summer to mid-autumn.
♀ ***P.* 'Blue Spire'** illus. p.159.
***P.* 'Hybrida'.** Deciduous, upright sub-shrub. **H** 1m (3ft), **S** 75cm (2½ft). Has oval, deeply lobed and toothed leaves and, from late summer to mid-autumn, tall spires of 2-lipped, deep lavender-blue flowers.

PERSICARIA

Knotweed

POLYGONACEAE

Genus of annuals, sometimes invasive perennials and rarely evergreen, semi-evergreen or deciduous sub-shrubs, grown for their autumn leaf colour. Has spikes or panicles of small, usually long-lasting, white, pink or red flowers. Fully to frost hardy. Needs sun or partial shade and moist soil. Propagate by seed in spring. Divide perennials in spring or autumn. ⓘContact with all parts may irritate skin; the sap may cause mild stomach upset if ingested.
P. affinis, syn. *Polygonum affine.* Mat-forming, evergreen perennial. **H** 15–30cm (6–12in), **S** 30cm (12in) or more. Fully hardy. Stout stems bear small, lance-shaped, glossy, green leaves that turn red-bronze in winter. From midsummer to mid-autumn carries dense spikes of small, funnel-shaped, rose-red flowers, fading to pale pink. Is good on a bank or in a rock garden. ♀ **'Darjeeling Red'**, **H** 20–25cm (8–10in), has long spikes of deep red flowers. ♀ **'Donald Lowndes'** illus. p.365. **'Superba'** (illus. p.234) is vigorous and has pale pink flowers, becoming deep pinkish-red, with red calyces; leaves turn rich brown in autumn.
P. amplexicaulis, syn. *Polygonum amplexicaule.* Clump-forming, leafy perennial. **H** and **S** 1.2m (4ft). Fully hardy. Bears profuse spikes of small, rich red flowers in summer–autumn. Has oval to heart-shaped, mid-green leaves. **'Alba'**, **H** 90cm (36in), **S** 120cm (48in), has showy spikes of white flowers. **'Blotau'** see *P.a.* Taurus. ♀ **'Firetail'** (illus. p.234), **H** to 1–1.2m (3–4ft), **S** to 60cm (24in), carries slender spikes of bright red flowers above heart-shaped leaves in summer–autumn. **Taurus ('Blotau'),** **H** to 80cm (32in), **S** to 100cm (36in), bears bright crimson-red flowers; is reputed to be less spreading than many other selections.
P. bistorta, syn. *Polygonum bistorta* (Bistort). ♀ **'Superba'** (illus. p.234) is a vigorous, clump-forming perennial. **H** 60–75cm (24–40in), **S** to 60cm (24in). Fully hardy. Produces spikes of soft pink flowers above oval leaves in summer.
P. campanulata, syn. *Polygonum campanulatum* (illus. p.234). Compact, mat-forming perennial. **H** and **S** 1m (3ft). Fully hardy. Bears branching heads of bell-shaped, pink or white flowers from mid-summer to early autumn. Has oval leaves, brown-felted beneath. **'Rosenrot'** (illus. p.234), H 1.2m (4ft), **S** 1m (3ft), has reddish-pink flowers in summer.
P. capitata, syn. *Polygonum capitatum.* Compact, spreading perennial. **H** 5cm (2in), **S** 15–20cm (6–8in). Frost hardy. Small, oval leaves are green with darker marks. Small, spherical heads of pink flowers are borne in summer. Is suitable for a rock garden or bank.
P. macrophylla, syn. *P. sphaerostachya, Polygonum macrophyllum, Polygonum sphaerostachyum*, illus. p.265.
P. microcephala. Spreading, leafy, rhizomatous perennial. **H** to 60cm (2ft), **S** 1m (3ft) or more. Fully hardy. Has lance-shaped, reddish-green leaves with darker zonal markings. Branching stems bear small, rounded heads of minute, white flowers in summer.
P. milletii, syn. *Polygonum milletii.* Compact perennial. **H** and **S** 60cm (24in). Fully hardy. Produces slender spikes of rich crimson flowers from mid-summer to early autumn. Narrow, lance-shaped leaves are mid-green.
P. polymorpha (illus. p.234). Clump-forming, leafy perennial. **H** and **S** 2m (6ft) or more. Fully hardy. Stout, branching stems bear large, elliptic-lance-shaped, mid-green leaves. In mid-summer produces frothy, terminal heads of tiny, long-lasting, creamy-white flowers.
***P.* 'Red Dragon'** (illus. p.234), **H** 70cm (28in), has deep red leaves, each marked with a silvery chevron. Leaves develop greenish tints as they age.
P. sphaerostachya. See *P. macrophylla.*
♀ ***P. vacciniifolia***, syn. *Polygonum vacciniifolium*, illus. p.373.
P. virginiana. Rather variable, clump-forming perennial. **H** to 1.2m (4ft), **S** to 60cm (2ft). Fully hardy. Oval, pale green leaves have brownish-mauve blotches, brightest in spring. In late summer produces spikes of insignificant, green flowers. **'Batwings'**, **H** and **S** to 80cm (32in), has narrowly oval leaves with a dark red chevron mark. **'Lance Corporal'** (illus. p.234), **H** and **S** to 80cm (32in), has a rich brown chevron mark on each leaf. **'Painter's Palette'** (syn. *Polygonum virginianum* 'Painter's Palette', *Tovara virginiana* 'Painter's Palette'; illus. p.234) has green leaves with central,

brown zones, ivory-yellow splashes and stripes and an overall deep pink tinge. Seldom flowers in cultivation.

PETASITES

COMPOSITAE/ASTERACEAE

Genus of invasive perennials, grown for their usually large leaves and value as ground cover. Fully hardy. Tolerates sun or shade and prefers moist but well-drained soil. Propagate by division in spring or autumn.

P. fragrans (Winter heliotrope). Spreading, invasive perennial. **H** 23–30cm (9–12in), **S** 1.2m (4ft). Has rounded to heart-shaped, dark green leaves. Small, vanilla-scented, daisy-like, pinkish-white flower heads are produced in late winter before foliage.

P. japonicus. Spreading, invasive perennial. **H** 60cm (2ft), **S** 1.5m (5ft). In early spring produces dense cones of small, daisy-like, yellowish-white flowers before large, light green leaves appear.

x PETCHOA

SOLANACEAE

Hybrids obtained from Calibrachoa x Petunia. Trailing half-hardy perennials grown for colourful flowers in hanging baskets and containers. Propagate only by cuttings, does not set seed.

x *P.* Supercal® Series SUPERCAL NEON ROSE ('KAKegawa S89') illus. p.303.

x *P.* 'KAKegawa S89'. See x *P.* Supercal® Series SUPERCAL NEON ROSE.

PETREA

VERBENACEAE

Genus of evergreen shrubs and woody-stemmed, twining climbers, grown for their flowers. Frost tender, min. 13–15°C (55–9°F). Needs full light and fertile, well-drained soil. Water regularly, less when not in full growth. Provide support. Thin out and spur back crowded growth in spring. Propagate by semi-ripe cuttings in summer. Mealy bug and whitefly may cause problems.

P. volubilis illus. p.463.

PETROCOSMEA

GESNERIACEAE

Genus of evergreen, rhizomatous perennials. Frost tender, min. 2–5°C (36–41°F). Needs shade and well-drained, peaty soil. Propagate by seed in early spring or by leaf cuttings in early summer.

P. kerrii illus. p.361.

Petrophyton. See *Petrophytum.*

PETROPHYTUM

SYN. PETROPHYTON

ROSACEAE

Genus of evergreen, summer-flowering shrubs, grown for their spikes of small, fluffy flowers. Is good for growing on tufa or in alpine houses. Fully hardy. Needs sun and gritty, well-drained, alkaline soil. May be difficult to grow. Propagate by softwood or semi-ripe cuttings in summer or by seed in autumn. Aphids and red spider mite may be troublesome in hot weather.

P. caespitosum. Evergreen, mat-forming shrub. **H** 5–8cm (2–3in), **S** 10–15cm (4–6in). Has clusters of small, spoon-shaped, silky-hairy, bluish-green leaves. Flower stems, 2cm (¾in) long, each carry a conical spike of small, fluffy, white flowers, with prominent stamens, in summer.

P. hendersonii. Evergreen, mound-forming shrub. **H** 5–10cm (2–4in), **S** 10–15cm (4–6in). Has branched stems covered in hairy, rounded, blue-green leaves. Conical spikes of small, cup-shaped, fluffy, white to creamy flowers are produced on 2.5cm (1in) stems in summer.

PETRORHAGIA

CARYOPHYLLACEAE

Genus of annuals and perennials, grown for their flowers. Is suitable for rock gardens and banks. Fully hardy. Prefers sun and well-drained, sandy soil. Propagate by seed in autumn. Self-seeds readily.

♀ ***P. saxifraga***, syn. *Tunica saxifraga* (Tunic flower), illus. p.361. **'Rosette'** is a mat-forming perennial. **H** 10cm (4in), **S** 15cm (6in). Has tufts of grass-like leaves. In summer, slender stems carry a profusion of cup-shaped, double, white to pale pink flowers, sometimes veined deeper pink.

PETTERIA

LEGUMINOSAE/PAPILIONACEAE

Genus of one species of deciduous shrub, grown for its flowers. Is related to *Laburnum*, differing in its erect racemes. Fully hardy. Requires full sun and fertile, well-drained soil. Propagate by softwood cuttings in summer or by seed in autumn. ⓘ The seeds may cause stomach upset if ingested.

P. ramentacea (Dalmatian laburnum). Deciduous, upright shrub. **H** 2m (6ft), **S** 1m (3ft). Has dense, upright spikes of fragrant, laburnum-like, yellow flowers in late spring and early summer. Mid-green leaves each have 3 oval leaflets.

PETUNIA

SOLANACEAE

Genus of annuals and perennials, wholly grown as annuals, with showy, colourful flowers. Half hardy. Grow in a sunny position that is sheltered from wind and in fertile, well-drained soil. Dead-head regularly. Propagate by seed sown under glass in autumn or mid-spring. May suffer from viruses, including cucumber mosaic and tomato spotted wilt.

The many cultivars that have been produced are moderately fast-growing, branching, bushy plants, **H** 15–30cm (6–12in), **S** 30cm (12in), with oval, mid- to deep green leaves, usually 5–12cm (2–5in) long. In summer–autumn, they produce flared, trumpet-shaped, single or double flowers in a wide range of colours (available in mixtures or singly), including blue, violet, purple, red, pink and white. Some have dark veining, central white stars, halos (throats in contrasting colours), or picotee margins. The cultivars are divided into 2 groups, Grandiflora and Multiflora petunias.

Grandiflora petunias have very large flowers, 8–10cm (3–4in) wide, but they are easily damaged by rain and are best grown in sheltered hanging baskets and pots.

Multiflora petunias are bushier than the Grandiflora petunias, and produce smaller flowers, 5cm (2in) wide, in greater quantity. They tend to be more resistant to rain damage, and are excellent for summer bedding or for a mixed border.

***P.* Aladdin Series.** Grandiflora petunia. **H** to 30cm (12in), **S** 30–90cm (12–36in). Has flowers in a range of colours, including strong shades of red and salmon-pink.

***P.* Carpet Series.** Multiflora petunia. H 20–25cm (8–10in), **S** 30–90cm (12–36in). Bears flowers in a colour range that includes strong reds and oranges.

***P.* Cascade Series.** Grandiflora petunia. **H** 20–30cm (8–12in), **S** 30–90cm (12–36in). Trailing stems produce flowers in a wide range of colours.

***P.* 'Cherry Tart'.** Multiflora petunia. **H** 5–30cm (6–12in), **S** 30–60cm (12–24in). Bears double, deep pink-and-white flowers.

***P.* 'Colour Parade'.** Grandiflora petunia. **H** 20–30cm (8–12in), **S** 30–90cm (12–36in). Has a wide colour range of flowers with ruffled petals.

***P.* Daddy Series.** Grandiflora petunia. **H** 35cm (14in), **S** 30–90cm (12–36in). Bear large, heavily veined flowers in pastel to deep pink, salmon-pink, purple or lavender-blue. **'Sugar Daddy'** illus p.312.

***P.* Flash Series.** Compact, Grandiflora petunia. **H** 23–40cm (9–16in), **S** 30–90cm (12–36in). Produce flowers in a range of bright colours, including bicolours.

***P.* 'Gypsy'.** Multiflora petunia. **H** 5–30cm (6–12in), **S** 30–60cm (12–24in). Has salmon-red flowers.

***P.* Jamboree Series.** Multiflora petunia. **H** 15–30cm (6–12in), **S** 30–90cm (12–36in). Produce pendulous stems bearing flowers in a range of colours.

***P.* 'Keiyeul'.** See *Petunia* Surfinia Series SURFINIA LIME.

***P.* 'Kerpril'.** See *P.* Tumbelina Series PRISCILLA.

***P.* 'Magic Cherry'.** Compact, Grandiflora petunia. **H** 20–30cm (8–12in), **S** 30–60cm (12–24in). Has cherry-red flowers.

***P.* 'Mirage Velvet'.** Multiflora petunia, illus. p.308.

***P.* Pearl Series.** Dwarf, Multiflora petunia. **H** 15–20cm (6–8in), **S** 20–50cm (8–20in). Bear small flowers in a wide range of colours.

***P.* Picotee Ruffled Series.** Multiflora petunia. **H** 15–30cm (6–12in), **S** 30–90cm (12–36in). Bear ruffled flowers, edged with white, in a range of colours.

***P.* Picotee Series.** Grandiflora petunia. **H** 15–30cm (6–12in), **S** 30cm (12in). Has flared, somewhat trumpet-shaped, red flowers, edged with white.

***P.* Plum Crazy Series.** Multiflora petunia. **H** 15–20cm (6–8in), **S** 30–90cm (12–36in). Produce flowers that have contrasting veins and throats. Colours available include white, with yellow throat and veins, and shades of violet, pink and magenta, all with darker throats and veins.

***P.* Primetime Series.** Multiflora petunia. H to 35cm (14in), **S** 30–90cm (12–36in). Bears flowers in a very wide range of colours, including white, blue, pink or red, some with dark veins or central stars, or picotee margin.

***P.* 'Razzle Dazzle'.** Grandiflora petunia. **H** 20–30cm (8–12in), **S** 30–90cm (12–36in). Has flowers in various colours, striped with white.

***P.* Recoverer Series.** Grandiflora petunia. H 15–30cm (6–12in), **S** 30cm (12in). Has large, flared, trumpet-shaped, white flowers.

***P.* 'Red Satin'.** Multiflora petunia. **H** 5–30cm (6–12in), **S** 30–60cm (12–24in). Has brilliant scarlet flowers.

***P.* Resisto Series.** Multiflora petunia. H 15–30cm (6–12in), **S** 30cm (12in). Has intense blue and rose-pink flowers.

***P.* 'Sunsolos'.** See *P.* Surfinia Series SURFINIA BLUE VEIN.

♀ ***P.* Surfinia Series SURFINIA BLUE VEIN ('Sunsolos')** illus. p.311. **SURFINIA LIME ('Keiyeul')** illus. p.316. **'Surfinia Purple'** is a vigorous Grandiflora petunia. **H** 23–40cm (9–16in), **S** 30–90cm (12–36in). Bears masses of magenta flowers with purple veining. Has good wet-weather tolerance.

***P.* Tumbelina Series PRISCILLA ('Kerpril')** illus. p.311.

***P.* WonderWave Series 'Wave Purple'.** **H** 10–15cm (4–6in), **S** 1m (3ft). Has prolific, deep purple flowers, 5–7.5cm (2–3in) across.

PHACELIA

HYDROPHYLLACEAE

Genus of annuals, biennials and perennials. Fully hardy. Grow in sun and in fertile, well-drained soil. Tall species may need support. Propagate by seed sown outdoors in spring or early autumn. ⓘ Contact with foliage may aggravate skin allergies.

P. campanularia illus. p.314.

P. tanacetifolia. Moderately fast-growing, upright annual. **H** 60cm (24in) or more, **S** 30cm (12in). Has feathery, deep green leaves. In summer, bears spikes of bell-shaped, lavender-blue flowers.

PHAEDRANASSA

AMARYLLIDACEAE

Genus of bulbs with tubular, often pendent flowers. Half hardy. Needs full sun or partial shade and fairly rich, well-drained soil. Feed with high-potash fertilizer in summer. Reduce watering in winter. Propagate by seed or offsets in spring.

P. carmiolii illus. p.410.

Phaedranthus buccinatorius. See *Distictis buccinatoria.*

Phaiophleps biflora. See *Olsynium biflorum.*

PHAIUS

ORCHIDACEAE

See also ORCHIDS.

P. tankervilleae (illus. p.467). Semi-evergreen, terrestrial orchid. **H** 75cm (30in). Frost tender, min. 10°C (55°F). Tall spikes of flowers, 9cm (3½in) across, brown within, silvery-grey outside and each with a long, red-marked, pink lip, open in early summer. Leaves are broadly oval, ribbed and 60cm (24in) long. Provide semi-shade in summer.

PHALAENOPSIS

ORCHIDACEAE

See also ORCHIDS.

***P.* Allegria.** Evergreen, epiphytic orchid for a warm greenhouse. **H** 15cm (6in). Carries sprays of white flowers, to 12cm (5in) across; flowering season varies. Broadly oval, fleshy leaves are 15cm (6in) long. Needs shade in summer.

P. cornu-cervi. Evergreen, epiphytic orchid for a warm greenhouse. **H** 15cm (6in). Yellowish-green flowers, 5cm (2in) across, with brown marks, are borne successively, either singly or in pairs, in summer. Has broadly oval leaves, 10cm (4in) long. Needs shade in summer.

***P.* Lady Pink Lips gx** (illus. p.466). Evergreen, epiphytic orchid for a warm greenhouse. **H** 15cm (6in). Tall, pendent spikes of pink flowers, 9cm (3½in) across, appear at varying times of year. Broadly oval leaves are 10cm (4in) long. Requires shade in summer.

***P.* Lundy gx** (illus. p.467). Evergreen, epiphytic orchid for a warm greenhouse. **H** 15cm (6in). Has sprays of red-striped, yellow flowers, 8cm (3in) across; flowering season varies. Broadly oval leaves are 23cm (9in) long. Grow in shade in summer.

PHALARIS

GRAMINEAE/POACEAE

See also GRASSES, BAMBOOS, RUSHES and SEDGES.

♀ ***P. arundinacea* var. *picta***, syn. *P.a.* 'Picta' (Gardener's garters). Evergreen, spreading, perennial grass. **H** 1m (3ft), **S** indefinite. Fully hardy. Has broad, white-striped leaves and produces narrow panicles of spikelets in summer.

Phanerophlebia fortunei. See *Cyrtomium fortunei.*
Pharbitis. See *Ipomoea.*
Phaseolus caracalla. See *Vigna caracalla.*
Phedimus aizoon. See *Sedum aizoon.*
Phedimus kamtschaticus. See *Sedum kamtschaticum.*
Phedimus spurius. See *Sedum spurium.*

PHEGOPTERIS

THELYPTERIDACEAE

Genus of deciduous ferns. Fully hardy. Grow in semi-shade and in humus-rich, moist but well-drained soil. Propagate by division in spring or by spores in summer.

P. connectilis, syn. *Thelypteris phegopteris* (Beech fern). Deciduous fern. **H** 23cm (9in), **S** 30cm (12in). Broadly lance-shaped, mid-green fronds, each consisting of tiny, triangular pinnae on wiry stalks, arise from a creeping rootstock. Is useful for ground cover.

PHELLODENDRON

RUTACEAE

Genus of deciduous trees, grown for their foliage, which colours well in autumn. Male and female flowers are produced on different plants. Fully hardy, but young growth is susceptible to damage by late frosts. Needs full sun and fertile, well-drained soil. Does best in hot summers. Propagate by softwood cuttings in summer, by seed in autumn or by root cuttings in late winter.

P. amurense (Amur cork tree). Deciduous, spreading tree. **H** 12m (40ft), **S** 15m (50ft). Has corky, dark bark when old. Aromatic leaves, each with 5 to 11 oblong leaflets, are glossy, dark green, becoming yellow in autumn. Tiny, green flowers in early summer are followed by small, rounded, black fruits.

P. chinense illus. p.75.

Phemeranthus sediformis, See *Talinum okanoganense.*

PHILADELPHUS

HYDRANGEACEAE/PHILADELPHACEAE

Genus of deciduous, mainly summer-flowering shrubs, grown for their usually fragrant flowers. Fully to frost hardy. Needs sun and fertile, well-drained soil. After flowering, cut some older shoots back to young growths, leaving young shoots to flower the following year. Propagate by softwood cuttings in summer. May become infested with aphids.

♀ ***P.* 'Beauclerk'** illus. p.127.
♀ ***P.* 'Belle Etoile'** illus. p.128.
***P.* 'Boule d' Argent'** illus. p.128.

P. coronarius (Mock orange). ♀ **'Aureus'** is a deciduous, upright shrub. **H** 2.5m (8ft), **S** 1.5m (5ft). Fully hardy. Clusters of very fragrant, 4-petalled, creamy-white flowers are produced in late spring and early summer. Oval, golden-yellow, young leaves turn yellow-green in summer. Protect from full sun. ♀ **'Variegatus'** illus. p.131.

***P.* 'Dame Blanche'** illus. p.129.

P. delavayi. Deciduous, upright shrub. **H** 3m (10ft), **S** 2.5m (8ft). Frost hardy. Dense clusters of very fragrant, 4-petalled, white flowers, with sometimes purple-flushed, green sepals, open from early to mid-summer. Leaves are dark green, oval and toothed. **f. *melanocalyx*** (syn. *P. purpurascens*) illus. p.131.

P. x lemoinei. See *P.* 'Lemoinei'.

***P.* 'Lemoinei'**, syn. *P.* x *lemoinei*, illus. p.129.

P. magdalenae. Deciduous, bushy shrub. **H** and **S** 4m (12ft). Fully hardy. Bark peels on older shoots. Narrowly oval, dark green leaves set off fragrant, 4-petalled, white flowers in late spring and early summer.

♀ ***P.* 'Manteau d' Hermine'** illus. p.149.

P. purpurascens. See *P. delavayi* f. *melanocalyx.*

♀ ***P.* 'Sybille'.** Deciduous, arching shrub. **H** 1.2m (4ft), **S** 2m (6ft). Fully hardy. Bears fragrant, 4-petalled, white flowers, each with a central, pink stain, profusely in early and mid-summer. Leaves are mid-green and oval.

***P.* 'Virginal'.** Vigorous, deciduous, upright shrub. **H** 3m (10ft), **S** 2.5m (8ft). Fully hardy. Has oval, dark green leaves. Produces masses of large, very fragrant, double or semi-double, pure white flowers in loose racemes from early to mid-summer.

x PHILAGERIA

LILIACEAE/PHILESIACEAE

Hybrid genus (*Philesia* x *Lapageria*) of one evergreen, scrambling or twining shrub. Frost tender, min. 5°C (41°F). Grow in semi-shade and in well-drained, preferably acid soil. Propagate by layering in late summer or autumn.

x *P. veitchii.* Evergreen, scrambling or twining shrub. **H** 3–4m (10–12ft). Has oblong, slightly toothed leaves. Nodding, tubular, rose-pink flowers are produced in leaf axils in summer.

PHILESIA

LILIACEAE/PHILESIACEAE

Genus of one species of evergreen shrub, grown for its showy flowers. Frost hardy, but thrives only in mild, moist areas. Needs semi-shade and humus-rich, moist, acid soil. Apply an annual dressing of leaf mould. Propagate by semi-ripe cuttings in summer or by suckers in autumn.

P. magellanica. Evergreen, erect shrub. **H** 90cm (3ft), **S** 2m (6ft). Bears trumpet-shaped, waxy, crimson-pink flowers, in leaf axils, from mid-summer to late autumn. Narrowly oblong, dark green leaves are bluish white beneath.

PHILLYREA

OLEACEAE

Genus of evergreen shrubs and trees, with inconspicuous flowers, grown for their foliage. Frost hardy, but in cold areas requires shelter. Does best in full sun and in fertile, well-drained soil. To restrict growth, cut back in spring. Propagate by semi-ripe cuttings in summer.

P. angustifolia. Evergreen, bushy, dense shrub. **H** and **S** 3m (10ft). Leaves are narrowly oblong and dark green. Small, fragrant, 4-lobed, greenish-white flowers in late spring and early summer are followed by spherical, blue-black fruits.

P. decora. See *Osmanthus decorus.*

P. latifolia. Evergreen, rounded shrub or tree. **H** and **S** 8m (25ft). Has oval, glossy, dark green leaves. Bears tiny, fragrant, 4-lobed, greenish-white flowers from late spring to early summer, then spherical, blue-black fruits.

PHILODENDRON

ARACEAE

Genus of evergreen shrubs and woody-based root-climbers, grown for their handsome leaves. Intermittently bears insignificant flowers. Frost tender, min. 15–18°C (59–64°F). Needs partial shade and humus-rich, well-drained soil. Water moderately, sparingly in cold weather. Provide support. Young stem tips may be removed to promote branching. Propagate by leaf-bud or stem-tip cuttings in summer. ⓘ All parts may cause severe discomfort if ingested; contact with sap may irritate skin.

P. auritum of gardens. See *Syngonium auritum.*

♀ ***P. bipinnatifidum***, syn. *P. selloum* (Tree philodendron), illus. p.458. Tree-like shrub with a single, erect stem and very long-stalked leaves.

♀ ***P.* 'Burgundy'.** Slow-growing, evergreen, woody-based, root climber. **H** 2m (6ft) or more. Has narrowly oblong, red-flushed, deep green leaves, to 30cm (12in) long, wine-red beneath.

P. cordatum. See *P. hederaceum.*

P. domesticum, syn. *P. hastatum* of gardens (Elephant's ear, Spade leaf). Fairly slow-growing, evergreen, woody-based, root climber. **H** 2–3m (6–10ft). Lustrous, bright green leaves, 30–40cm (12–16in) long, are arrow-shaped on young plants and later have prominent, basal lobes.

♀ ***P. erubescens*** (Blushing philodendron). Evergreen, erect, woody-based, root climber. **H** to 3m (10ft). Oval to triangular leaves, 15–25cm (6–10in) long, have long, red stalks and are dark green with a lustrous, coppery flush.

P. hastatum of gardens. See *P. domesticum.*

P. hederaceum, syn. *H. cordatum* (Heart leaf). Moderately vigorous, evergreen, woody-based, root climber. **H** 3m (10ft) or more. Has heart-shaped, lustrous, rich green leaves, to 45cm (18in) long.

P. laciniatum. See *P. pedatum.*

P. melanochrysum. Robust, fairly slow-growing, evergreen, woody-based, root climber. **H** 3m (10ft) or more. Heart-shaped leaves, to 75cm (30in) long, are lustrous, deep olive-green with a coppery sheen and pale veins.

P. pedatum, syn. *P. laciniatum.* Slow-growing, evergreen, woody-based, root climber. **H** 2–3m (6–10ft). Has oval, glossy, deep green leaves, 30–80cm (12–32in) long, with 5 or 7 prominent lobes.

P. sagittatum. See *P. sagittifolium.*

P. sagittifolium, syn. *P. sagittatum.* Slow-growing, evergreen, woody-based, root climber. **H** 2–3m (6–10ft). Oval leaves with basal lobes are up to 40–60cm (16–24in) long and glossy, bright green.

♀ ***P. scandens*** illus. p.463.

P. selloum. See *P. bipinnatifidum.*

P. trifoliatum. See *Syngonium auritum.*

PHLEBODIUM

POLYPODIACEAE

Genus of evergreen or semi-evergreen ferns. Frost tender, min. 5°C (41°F). Needs full light or semi-shade and humus-rich, moist but well-drained soil. Remove fading fronds regularly. Propagate by division in spring or by spores in summer.

♀ ***P. aureum***, syn. *Polypodium aureum*, illus. p.478. **'Mandaianum'** illus. p.479.

PHLOMIS

LABIATAE/LAMIACEAE

Genus of evergreen, summer-flowering shrubs and perennials, grown for their conspicuous, hooded flowers, which are borne in dense whorls, and for their foliage. Fully to frost hardy. Prefers full sun and well-drained soil. Propagate by seed in autumn; increase shrubs from softwood cuttings in summer, perennials by division in spring.

P. cashmeriana. Evergreen, upright shrub. **H** 60cm (24in), **S** 45cm (18in). Frost hardy. Produces masses of 2-lipped, pale lilac flowers in summer. Narrowly oval, mid-green leaves have woolly, white undersides.

♀ **P. chrysophylla.** Evergreen, rounded, stiffly branched shrub. **H** and **S** 1m (3ft). Frost hardy. Bears 2-lipped, golden-yellow flowers in early summer. Oval leaves are grey-green when young, becoming golden-green.
♀ **P. fruticosa** illus. p.160.
P. italica illus. p.152.
P. longifolia var. bailanica. Evergreen, bushy shrub. **H** 1.2m (4ft), **S** 1m (3ft). Frost hardy. Leaves are oblong to heart-shaped, deeply veined and bright green. Has 2-lipped, deep yellow flowers from early to mid-summer.
♀ **P. russeliana** illus. p.243.

PHLOX

POLEMONIACEAE

Genus of mainly late spring- or summer-flowering annuals and perennials, some of which are semi-evergreen or evergreen, grown for their terminal panicles or profusion of brightly coloured flowers. Fully to half hardy. Does best in sun or semi-shade and in fertile, moist but well-drained soil; some species prefer acid soil; in light, dry soils is better grown in partial shade. Trim back rock garden species after flowering. Propagate rock garden species and hybrids by cuttings from non-flowering shoots in spring or summer; species by seed in autumn or spring; *P. maculata, P. paniculata* and their cultivars also by division in early spring or by root cuttings in winter; and annuals by seed in spring. *P. maculata, P. paniculata* and their cultivars are susceptible to eelworm. See also feature panel p.240.
♀ **P. adsurgens.** Evergreen, mat-forming, prostrate perennial. **H** 10cm (4in), **S** 30cm (12in). Fully hardy. Woody-based stems are clothed in oval, light to mid-green leaves. In summer produces terminal clusters of short-stemmed, saucer-shaped, purple, pink or white flowers with overlapping petals. Is good for a rock garden or peat bed. Prefers partial shade and gritty, peaty, acid soil. **'Wagon Wheel'** illus. p.363.
P. amoena 'Variegata'. See *P. x procumbens* 'Variegata'.
P. bifida illus. p.366.
P. caespitosa. Evergreen, mound-forming, compact perennial. **H** 8cm (3in), **S** 12cm (5in). Fully hardy. Leaves are narrow and needle-like. Solitary almost stemless, saucer-shaped, lilac or white flowers are borne in summer. Suits a rock garden or trough. Needs sun and very well-drained soil.
P. 'Camla' illus. p.365.
P. 'Chattahoochee'. See *P. divaricata* subsp. *laphamii* 'Chattahoochee'.
♀ **P. divaricata.** Semi-evergreen, creeping perennial. **H** 30cm (12in) or more, **S** 20cm (8in). Fully hardy. In early summer, upright stems carry saucer-shaped, lavender-blue flowers in loose clusters. Leaves are oval. Suits a rock garden or peat bed. Prefers semi-shade and moist but well-drained, peaty soil. **subsp. *laphamii*** illus. p.341. ♀ **subsp. *laphamii* 'Chattahoochee'** (syn. *P.* 'Chattahoochee') illus. p.341.
♀ **P. douglasii 'Boothman's Variety'** illus. p.366 .♀ **'Crackerjack'** illus. p.365. **'May Snow'** is an evergreen, mound-forming perennial. **H** 8cm (3in), **S** 20cm (8in). Fully hardy. Has lance-shaped, mid-green leaves. Masses of saucer-shaped, white flowers are borne in early summer. Is suitable for a rock garden, wall or bank. Vigorous, compact ♀ **'Red Admiral'**, **H** 5cm (6in), has crimson flowers.
P. drummondii (Annual phlox). **Beauty Series** is a group of moderately fast-growing, compact, upright annuals. **H** 5cm (6in), **S** 10cm (4in). Half hardy. Has lance-shaped, pale green leaves and, from summer to early autumn, heads of star-shaped flowers in many colours, including red, pink, blue, purple and white. ♀ **Buttons Series**, **H** and **S** 15–25cm (6–10in), has flowers in a range of colours from deep red to pink and white. **'Carnival'** has larger flowers with contrasting centres. **'Chanal'** illus. p.305. **'Petticoat'** has bicoloured flowers. **'Sternenzauber'** (syn. *P.d.* 'Twinkle'), **H** 15cm (6in), has star-shaped flowers in a bright mixture of colours, some with contrasting centres. **'Twinkle'** see *P.d.* 'Sternenzauber'.
P. 'Emerald Cushion' illus. p.367.
P. hoodii. Evergreen, compact, prostrate perennial. **H** 5cm (2in), **S** 10cm (4in). Fully hardy. Solitary, flat, white flowers open in early summer above fine, needle-like, hairy leaves. Suits a rock garden. Needs sun and very well-drained soil.
P. maculata. Erect perennial. **H** 1m (3ft), **S** 45cm (1½ft). Fully hardy. In summer produces cylindrical panicles of tubular, 5-lobed, mauve-pink flowers above oval, mid-green leaves. ♀**'Alpha'** has rose-pink flowers. ♀ **'Omega'** has white flowers, each with a lilac eye.
P. paniculata. Upright perennial, seldom grown, as is replaced in gardens by its more colourful cultivars. **H** 1.2m (4ft), **S** 60cm (2ft). Fully hardy. Tubular, 5-lobed flowers are borne in conical heads above oval, mid-green leaves in late summer. **'Aida'** is purple-red, each flower with a purple eye. Flowers of **'Amethyst'** (illus. p.240) are pale lilac with paler-edged petals.**'Balmoral'** has large, rosy-mauve flowers. ♀**'Brigadier'** (illus. p.240) has deep orange-red flowers. ♀ **'Bright Eyes'** has pale pink flowers, each with a red eye.**'Eva Cullum'** (illus. p.240) has clear pink flowers with magenta eyes. ♀**'Eventide'** produces lavender-blue flowers.♀ **'Fujiyama'.** See *P.p.* 'Mount Fuji'. ♀ **'Mount Fuji'** (syn. *P.p.* 'Fujiyama'; illus. p.230). Flowers of **'Graf Zeppelin'** are white with red centres. **'Hampton Court'** (illus. p.240) is a mauve-blue cultivar, with dark green foliage. **'Harlequin'** has reddish-purple flowers. Leaves are variegated ivory-white. **'Junior Bouquet'** has deep pink flowers with a prominent white eye. ♀ **'Le Mahdi'** has deep purple flowers. **'Mia Ruys'** (illus. p.240), **H** 45cm (18in), has large, white flowers, and is shorter than most other cultivars. ♀**'Mother of Pearl'** has white flowers tinted pink. **'Norah Leigh'** (illus. p.240) has pale lilac flowers and ivory-variegated leaves. ♀**'Prince of Orange'** illus. p.235. **'Russian Violet'** is of open habit and has pale lilac-blue flowers. Flowers of **'Sandringham'** have widely spaced petals and are pink with darker centres. **'Sir John Falstaff'** has large, deep salmon flowers, each with a cherry-red eye. ♀ **'White Admiral'** bears pure white flowers. Those of ♀ **'Windsor'** (illus. p.240) are carmine-rose with red eyes.
♀ **P. x procumbens 'Millstream'.** Evergreen, prostrate perennial. **H** to 15cm (6in), **S** 30cm (12in). Fully hardy. Has narrowly oval, glossy, green leaves. In early summer bears small, saucer-shaped, white-eyed, deep lavender-pink flowers. Is suitable for a rock garden. **'Variegata'** (syn. *P. amoena* 'Variegata'), **H** 2.5cm (1in), **S** 25cm (10in), has white-margined leaves and bright cerise-pink flowers.
P. stolonifera (Creeping phlox). Evergreen, prostrate, spreading perennial. **H** 10–15cm (4–6in), **S** 30cm (12in) or more. Fully hardy. Has small, saucer-shaped, pale blue flowers in early summer. Leaves are oblong to oval. Prefers moist, peaty, acid soil; is good for a peat bed or rock garden. **'Ariane'** illus. p.359. ♀ **'Blue Ridge'** has masses of lavender-blue flowers.
P. subulata. Evergreen, mound-forming perennial. **H** 10cm (4in), **S** 20cm (8in). Fully hardy. Bears fine, needle-like leaves. Masses of star-shaped, white, pink or mauve flowers appear in early summer. Is good for a sunny rock garden. **'Marjorie'** illus. p.365.

PHOENIX

PALMAE/ARECACEAE

Genus of evergreen palms, grown for their overall appearance and their edible fruits. Frost tender, min. 10–15°C (50–59°F). Grows in full light, though tolerates partial shade, in any fertile, well-drained soil. Water potted specimens moderately, less during winter. Propagate by seed in spring at not less than 24°C (75°F). Red spider mite may be a nuisance.
♀ **P. canariensis** (Canary Island date palm). Evergreen, upright palm with a robust trunk. **H** 18m (60ft) or more, **S** 10m (30ft) or more. Min. 10°C (50°F). Feather-shaped, arching leaves, each to 5m (15ft) long, are divided into narrowly lance-shaped, leathery, bright green leaflets. Bears large, pendent clusters of tiny, yellowish-brown flowers that on mature specimens are followed by shortly oblong, yellow to red fruits in autumn–winter.
♀ **P. roebelenii** (Miniature date palm, Pygmy date palm). Evergreen palm with a slender trunk. **H** 2–4m (6–12ft), **S** 1–2m (3–6ft). Min. 15°C (59°F). Has feather-shaped, arching, glossy, dark green leaves, 1–1.2m (3–4ft) long, and, in summer, large panicles of tiny, yellow flowers. Egg-shaped, black fruits are borne in pendent clusters, 45cm (18in) long, in autumn.

PHORMIUM

New Zealand flax

AGAVACEAE/PHORMIACEAE

Genus of evergreen perennials, grown for their bold, sword-shaped leaves. Frost hardy. Requires sun and moist but well-drained soil. Propagate by division or seed in spring.
P. 'Bronze Baby'. Evergreen, upright perennial. **H** and **S** 45–60cm (18–24in). Has tufts of bold, stiff, pointed, wine-red leaves. Panicles of reddish flowers are occasionally produced on purplish stems in summer.
P. colensoi. See *P. cookianum*.
P. cookianum, syn. *P. colensoi* (Mountain flax). Evergreen, upright perennial. **H** 1–2m (3–6ft), **S** 30cm (1ft). Has tufts of sword-shaped, dark green leaves. Panicles of tubular, pale yellowish-green flowers are borne in summer. **'Black Adder'** has burgundy-black leaves. ♀ **subsp. *hookeri* 'Tricolor'** has leaves striped vertically with red, yellow and green. **'Variegatum'** has cream-striped leaves.
P. 'Dazzler' illus. p.216.
♀ **P. tenax.** Evergreen, upright perennial. **H** 3m (10ft), **S** 1–2m (3–6ft). Has tufts of sword-shaped, stiff, dark green leaves. Panicles of tubular, dull red flowers are produced on short, slightly glaucous green stems in summer. Thrives by the sea. **'Aurora'** has leaves vertically striped with red, bronze, salmon-pink and yellow. ♀ **Purpureum Group**, **H** 2–2.5m (6–8ft), **S** 1m (3ft), has rich reddish-purple to dark copper leaves. **'Veitchianum'** (syn. *P.t.* 'Veitchii') bears broad, creamy-white-striped leaves. **'Veitchii'** see *P.t.* 'Veitchianum'.

PHOTINIA

SYN. STRANVAESIA

ROSACEAE

Genus of evergreen or deciduous shrubs and trees, with small white flowers, grown for their foliage and, in the case of deciduous species, for their autumn colour and fruits. Fully to frost hardy, but protect evergreen species from strong, cold winds. Requires sun or semi-shade and fertile, well-drained soil; some species prefer acid soil. Propagate evergreen and deciduous species by semi-ripe cuttings in summer, deciduous species also by seed in autumn.
P. arbutifolia. See *Heteromeles salicifolia*.
P. davidiana illus. p.90.
P. x fraseri. Group of evergreen, hybrid shrubs. **H** and **S** 5m (15ft). Frost hardy. Has oblong, dark green leaves. Young growths are attractive over a long period. Has good resistance to damage by late frosts. **'Birmingham'** has heads of small, white flowers in late spring. ♀ **Red Robin'** illus. p.111.
P. nussia. Evergreen, spreading tree. **H** and **S** 6m (20ft). Frost hardy. Produces oblong, leathery, glossy, dark green leaves and saucer-shaped, 5-petalled, white flowers in mid-summer, followed by rounded, orange-red fruits.
P. serratifolia, syn. *P. serrulata*, illus. p.111.
P. serrulata. See *P. serratifolia*.
♀ **P. villosa.** Deciduous, upright shrub or spreading tree. **H** and **S** 5m (15ft). Fully hardy. Oval, dark green leaves, bronze-margined when young, become brilliant orange-red in autumn. Clusters of 5-petalled flowers, produced in late spring, are followed by spherical, red fruits. Prefers acid soil.

PHRAGMIPEDIUM

ORCHIDACEAE

See also ORCHIDS.
P. besseae (illus. p.467). Evergreen, terrestrial orchid for an intermediate

greenhouse. **H** 1m (3ft), **S** 50cm (20in). Frost tender, min. 13°C (55°F). Pouch-lipped, bright scarlet red, orange-red or yellow flowers are borne in upright racemes in spring. Has strap-shaped leaves. Needs shade in summer.
P. caudatum. Evergreen, epiphytic orchid for an intermediate greenhouse. **H** 3cm (9in). In summer produces sprays of flowers with light green and tan sepals and pouches and drooping, ribbon-like, yellow and brownish-crimson petals, to 30cm (12in) long. Has narrowly oval leaves, 30cm (12in) long. Needs shade in summer.

PHUOPSIS

RUBIACEAE

Genus of one species of mat-forming, summer-flowering perennial, grown for its small, pungent, tubular flowers. Is good for ground cover, especially on banks and in rock gardens. Fully hardy. Needs sun and well-drained soil. Propagate by division in spring, by semi-ripe cuttings in summer or by seed sown in autumn.
P. stylosa, syn. *Crucianella stylosa*, illus. p.338.

PHYGELIUS

SCROPHULARIACEAE

Genus of evergreen or semi-evergreen shrubs and sub-shrubs, grown for their showy, tubular flowers. Frost hardy, but in most areas plant in a sheltered site; will attain a considerably greater height when grown against a south- or west-facing wall. Needs sun and fertile, well-drained but not too dry soil. Usually loses leaves or has shoots cut to ground by frosts. Cut back to just above ground level in spring, or, if plants have woody bases, prune to live wood. Propagate by softwood cuttings in summer.
P. aequalis illus. p.156. ♀ **'Yellow Trumpet'** illus. p.160.
♀ ***P. capensis.*** Evergreen or semi-evergreen, upright sub-shrub. **H** 1.5m (5ft), **S** 2m (6ft). Has tubular, curved, bright orange-red flowers, each with a red mouth and a yellow throat, from mid-summer to early autumn, in tall, slender spires amid triangular, dark green leaves.
P. x rectus **'Winchester Fanfare'.** Evergreen or semi-evergreen, upright sub-shrub. **H** 1.5m (5ft), **S** 2m (6ft). Has pendulous, tubular, dusky, reddish-pink flowers, each with scarlet lobes and a yellow throat, from mid-summer to early autumn, and triangular, dark green leaves.

Phyllanthus nivosus. See *Breynia disticha*.

x PHYLLIOPSIS

ERICACEAE

Hybrid genus (*Phyllodoce* x *Kalmiopsis*) of one species of evergreen shrub, grown for its flowers. Is suitable for peat beds and rock gardens. Fully hardy. Needs partial shade and peaty, acid soil. Trim back after flowering to maintain a compact habit. Propagate by semi-ripe cuttings in late summer.
x *P. hillieri* 'Pinocchio'. Evergreen, upright shrub. **H** 20cm (8in), **S** 25cm (10in). Branched stems bear thin, oval leaves. Long, open clusters of bell-shaped, very deep pink flowers appear in spring and intermittently thereafter.

Phyllitis scolopendrium. See *Asplenium scolopendrium*.
***Phyllitis scolopendrium* 'Marginatum'.** See *Asplenium scolopendrium* Marginatum Group.

PHYLLOCLADUS

PHYLLOCLADACEAE

See also CONIFERS.
P. aspleniifolius (Tasman celery pine). Slow-growing, upright conifer. **H** 5–10m (15–30ft), **S** 3–5m (10–15ft). Half hardy. Instead of true leaves has flattened, leaf-like shoots known as phylloclades; these are dull dark green and resemble celery leaves in outline. Produces inedible, white-coated nuts with fleshy, red bases.
P. trichomanoides illus. p.101.

PHYLLODOCE

ERICACEAE

Genus of evergreen shrubs, grown for their heath-like leaves and attractive flowers. Fully to frost hardy. Needs semi-shade and moist, peaty, acid soil. Propagate by semi-ripe cuttings in late summer or by seed in spring.
♀ ***P. caerulea***, syn. *P. taxifolia*, illus. p.334.
P. empetriformis illus. p.334.
***P. x intermedia* 'Drummondii'** illus. p.333. **'Fred Stoker'** is an evergreen, upright shrub. **H** and **S** 23cm (9in). Fully hardy. Has narrow, glossy, green leaves. From late spring to early summer carries terminal clusters of pitcher-shaped, bright reddish-purple flowers on slender, red stalks.
♀ ***P. nipponica.*** Evergreen, upright shrub. **H** 10–20cm (4–8in), **S** 10–15cm (4–6in). Frost hardy. Freely branched stems bear fine, linear leaves and, in late spring and summer, stalked, bell-shaped, white flowers from their tips.
P. taxifolia. See *P. caerulea*.

PHYLLOSTACHYS

GRAMINEAE/POACEAE

See also GRASSES, BAMBOOS, RUSHES and SEDGES.
♀ ***P. aurea***, illus. p.288.
P. aureosulcata (Golden-groove bamboo). Evergreen, clump-forming bamboo. **H** 6–8m (20–25ft), **S** indefinite. Frost hardy. Bears striped sheaths and yellow grooves on rough, brownish-green stems. Mid-green leaves are up to 15cm (6in) long; flowers are unimportant as they are so rarely produced.
P. bambusoides illus. p.287.
P. flexuosa (Zigzag bamboo). Evergreen, clump-forming bamboo. **H** 6–8m (20–25ft), **S** indefinite. Fully hardy. Has slender, markedly zigzag stems that turn black with age. Leaf sheaths have no bristles. Leaves stay fresh green all winter.
***P.* 'Henonis'.** See *P. nigra* f. *henonis*.
♀ ***P. nigra*** illus. p.286. ♀ **f. *henonis*** (syn. *P.* 'Henonis') illus. p.287.
P. viridiglaucescens illus. p.287.
P. vivax* f. *aureocaulis illus. p.289.

x PHYLLOTHAMNUS

ERICACEAE

Hybrid genus (*Phyllodoce* x *Rhodothamnus*) of one species of evergreen shrub, grown for its foliage and flowers. Is good for peat beds and rock gardens. Fully hardy. Needs a sheltered, semi-shaded site and moist, acid soil. Propagate by semi-ripe cuttings in late summer.
x *P. erectus.* Evergreen, upright shrub. **H** and **S** 15cm (6in). Has small, linear, glossy, deep green leaves. Clusters of slender-stalked, bell-shaped, soft rose-pink flowers are produced in late spring and early summer.

PHYSALIS

Chinese lantern

SOLANACEAE

Genus of summer-flowering perennials and annuals, grown mainly for their decorative, lantern-like calyces and fruits, produced in autumn. Fully to half hardy. Grows in sun or shade and in well-drained soil. Propagate by division or softwood cuttings in spring, annuals by seed in spring or autumn. ① All parts of *P. alkekengi*, except the fully ripe fruit, may cause mild stomach upset if ingested; contact with foliage may irritate skin.
♀ ***P. alkekengi*** (Bladder cherry, Winter cherry). Spreading perennial, grown as an annual. **H** 45cm (18in), **S** 60cm (24in). Fully hardy. Inconspicuous, nodding, star-shaped, white flowers in summer are followed, in autumn, by rounded, bright orange-red fruits, surrounded by inflated, orange calyces. Leaves are mid-green and oval.

PHYSOCARPUS

ROSACEAE

Genus of deciduous, mainly summer-flowering shrubs, grown for their foliage and flowers. Fully hardy. Requires sun and fertile, not too dry soil. Prefers acid soil and does not grow well on shallow, chalky soil. Thin established plants occasionally by cutting some older shoots back to ground level after flowering. Propagate by softwood cuttings in summer.
P. opulifolius (Ninebark). Deciduous, arching, dense shrub. **H** 3m (10ft), **S** 5m (15ft). Has peeling bark and broadly oval, toothed and lobed, mid-green leaves. Bears clusters of tiny, at times pink-tinged, white flowers in early summer. ♀ **'Dart's Gold'** illus. p.159.

PHYSOPLEXIS

CAMPANULACEAE

Genus of one species of tufted perennial, grown for its flowers. Is good grown on tufa, in rock gardens, troughs and alpine houses. Fully hardy. Needs sun and very well-drained, alkaline soil, but should face away from midday sun. Keep fairly dry in winter. Propagate by seed in autumn or by softwood cuttings in early summer. Is susceptible to slug damage.
♀ ***P. comosa***, syn. *Phyteuma comosum*, illus. p.366.

PHYSOSTEGIA

Obedient plant

LABIATAE/LAMIACEAE

Genus of summer- to early autumn-flowering perennials. Fully hardy. Needs sun and fertile, moist but well-drained soil. Propagate by division in spring.
P. virginiana. Erect perennial. **H** 1m (3ft), **S** 60cm (2ft). In late summer, produces spikes of hooded, 2-lipped, rose-purple flowers with hinged stalks that allow flowers to remain in position once moved. Has lance-shaped, toothed, mid-green leaves. **subsp. *speciosa* 'Variegata'** see *P.v.* 'Variegata'. ♀ **'Summer Snow'** has pure white flowers. **'Variegata'** (syn. *P.v.* subsp. *speciosa* 'Variegata') illus. p.233. ♀ **'Vivid'** illus. p.280.

PHYTEUMA

CAMPANULACEAE

Genus of early- to mid-summer-flowering perennials that are useful for rock gardens. Fully hardy. Needs sun and well-drained soil. Propagate by seed in autumn.
P. comosum. See *Physoplexis comosa*.
P. scheuchzeri illus. p.342.

PHYTOLACCA

PHYTOLACCACEAE

Genus of perennials and evergreen shrubs and trees, grown for their overall appearance and decorative but poisonous fruits. Fully hardy to frost tender, min. 5°C (41°F). Tolerates sun or shade and requires fertile, moist soil. Propagate by seed in autumn or spring. ① All parts may cause severe discomfort if ingested; the fruit of *P. americana* may be lethal if eaten. Contact with the sap may irritate skin.
P. americana, syn. *P. decandra* (Red-ink plant, Virginian pokeweed). Upright, spreading perennial. **H** and **S** 1.2–1.5m (4–5ft). Fully hardy. Oval to lance-shaped, mid-green leaves are tinged purple in autumn. Shallowly cup-shaped, sometimes pink-flushed, white-and-green flowers, borne in terminal racemes in summer, are followed by poisonous, rounded, fleshy, blackish-purple berries.
P. clavigera. See *P. polyandra*.
P. decandra. See *P. americana*.
P. polyandra, syn. *P. clavigera*. Stout, upright perennial. **H** and **S** 1.2m (4ft). Fully hardy. Has brilliant crimson stems, oval to lance-shaped, mid-green leaves that turn yellow in autumn. In summer bears clusters of shallowly cup-shaped, pink flowers, followed by poisonous, blackish-purple berries.

PICEA

Spruce

PINACEAE

Genus of conifers with needle-like leaves set on a pronounced peg on the shoots and arranged spirally. Cones are pendulous and ripen in their first autumn; scales are woody and flexible. See also CONIFERS.
P. abies (Common spruce, Norway

spruce) illus. p.98. **'Clanbrassiliana'**, **H** 5m (15ft), **S** 3–5m (10–15ft), is slow-growing, rounded and spreading. **'Gregoryana'**, **H** and **S** 60cm (2ft), is slow-growing, with a dense, globose form. **'Inversa'**, **H** 5–10m (15–30ft), **S** 2m (6ft), has an erect leader, but pendent side branches. ♀ **'Little Gem'**, **H** and **S** 30–50cm (12–20in), has a nest-shaped, central depression caused by spreading branches. ♀ **'Nidiformis'**, **H** 1m (3ft), **S** 1–2m (3–6ft), is larger and faster-growing. **'Ohlendorffii'** (illus. p.105), **H** and **S** 1m (3ft), is slow-growing, initially rounded, becoming conical with age. **'Reflexa'**, **H** 30cm (1ft), **S** 5m (15ft), is prostrate and ground-hugging, but may be trained up a stake, to form a mound of weeping foliage.

♀ ***P. breweriana*** illus. p.99.

P. engelmannii illus. p.99.

P. glauca (White spruce). Narrowly conical conifer. **H** 10–15m (30–50ft), **S** 4–5m (12–15ft). Fully hardy. Glaucous shoots produce blue-green leaves. Ovoid, light brown cones fall after ripening. **var. *albertiana* 'Conica'** (syn. *P.g.* 'Albertiana Conica'), **H** 2–5m (6–15ft), **S** 1–2m (3–6ft), is of neat, pyramidal habit and slow-growing, with longer leaves and smaller cones. **'Albertiana Conica'** see *P.g.* var. *albertiana* 'Conica'. **'Coerulea'** illus. p.99. ♀ **'Echiniformis'**, **H** 50cm (20in), **S** 90cm (36in), is a dwarf, flat-topped, rounded form.

P. likiangensis illus. p.100.

P. mariana (Black spruce). Conical conifer, whose lowest branches often layer naturally, forming a ring of stems around the parent plant. **H** 10–15m (30–50ft), **S** 3m (10ft). Fully hardy. Leaves are bluish-green or bluish-white. Oval cones are dark grey-brown. **'Doumetii'** illus. p.103. ♀ **'Nana'**, **H** 50cm (20in), **S** 50–80cm (20–32in), is a neat shrub with blue-grey foliage.

***P. x mariorika* 'Gnom'**, syn. *P. omorika* 'Gnom', is a shrub-like conifer with pendent branches arching at tips. **H** to 1.5m (5ft), **S** 1–2m (3–6ft). Fully hardy. Dark green leaves are white beneath.

P. morrisonicola illus. p.101.

♀ ***P. omorika*** illus. p.98. **'Gnom'** see *P. x mariorika* 'Gnom'. ♀ **'Nana'**, **H** and **S** 1m (3ft), is a slow-growing, rounded or oval cultivar.

♀ ***P. orientalis*** (Caucasian spruce, Oriental spruce). Columnar, dense conifer. **H** 20m (70ft), **S** 5m (15ft). Fully hardy. Has glossy, deep green leaves and ovoid to conical cones, 6–10cm (2½–4in) long, dark purple, ripening to brown, the males brick-red in spring. ♀ **'Aurea'** has golden, young foliage in spring, later turning green. **'Skylands'** illus. p.99.

P. pungens (Colorado spruce). Columnar conifer. **H** 15m (50ft), **S** 5m (15ft). Fully hardy. Has scaly, grey bark and very sharp, stout, greyish-green or bright blue leaves. Cylindrical, light brown cones have papery scales. ♀**'Globosa'** (illus. p.105) is a slow-growing, rounded form of dense habit and glaucous-blue leaves. ♀ **'Hoopsii'**, **H** 10–15m (30–50ft), hassilvery-blue foliage. ♀ **'Koster'** illus. p.99. **'Montgomery'**, **H** and **S** 1m (3ft), is dwarf, compact, spreading or conical, with grey-blue leaves.

P. sitchensis (Sitka spruce). Very vigorous, broadly conical conifer. **H** 30–50m (100–160ft) in damp locations, 15–20m (50–70ft) in dry situations, **S** 6–10m (20–30ft). Fully hardy. Bark scales on old trees. Has prickly, bright deep green leaves and cylindrical, papery, pale brown or whitish cones, 5–10cm (2–4in) long. Is good on an exposed or poor site.

P. smithiana (Morinda spruce, West Himalayan spruce). Slow-growing conifer, conical when young, columnar with horizontal branches and weeping shoots when mature. **H** 25–30m (80–100ft), **S** 6m (20ft). Fully hardy. Has dark green leaves and produces cylindrical, bright brown cones, 10–20cm (4–8in) long.

PICRASMA

SIMAROUBACEAE

Genus of deciduous trees, grown for their brilliant autumn colour. Produces insignificant flowers in late spring. Fully hardy. Requires sun or semi-shade and fertile, well-drained soil. Propagate by seed in autumn.

P. ailanthoides. See *P. quassioides.*

P. quassioides, syn. *P. ailanthoides*, illus. p.92.

PIERIS

ERICACEAE

Genus of evergreen shrubs, grown for their foliage and small, profuse, urn-shaped flowers. Fully to frost hardy. Needs a sheltered site in semi-shade or shade and in moist, peaty, acid soil. *P. floribunda*, however, grows well in any acid soil. Young shoots are sometimes frost-killed in spring and should be cut back as soon as possible. Dead-heading after flowering improves growth. Propagate by soft tip or semi-ripe cuttings in summer. ⓘ Leaves may cause severe discomfort if ingested.

***P.* 'Bert Chandler'.** Evergreen, bushy shrub. **H** 2m (6ft), **S** 1.5m (5ft). Frost hardy. Lance-shaped leaves are bright pink when young, becoming creamy-yellow, then white and finally dark green. Produces white flowers only very rarely. Likes an open position.

P. floribunda illus. p.120.

♀ ***P.* 'Forest Flame'.** Evergreen, upright shrub. **H** 4m (12ft), **S** 2m (6ft). Frost hardy. Narrowly oval, glossy leaves are brilliant red when young, then turn pink, cream and finally dark green. White flowers are borne with the young leaves from mid- to late spring.

P. formosa. Evergreen, bushy, dense shrub. **H** and **S** 4m (12ft). Frost hardy. Large, oblong, glossy, dark green leaves are bronze when young. Bears large clusters of white flowers from mid- to late spring. ♀ **var. *forrestii* 'Wakehurst'** illus. p.137. **'Henry Price'** has deep-veined leaves, which are bronze-red when young.

P. japonica illus. p.110. **'Daisen'** is an evergreen, rounded, dense shrub. **H** and **S** 3m (10ft). Fully hardy. Oval, bronze leaves mature to glossy, dark green. Bears drooping clusters of red-budded, deep pink flowers in spring. **'Dorothy Wyckoff'** has deep crimson buds, opening to pink blooms; foliage is bronze in winter. Young foliage of ♀ **'Mountain Fire'** is brilliant red. **'Scarlett O'Hara'** illus. p.120. The leaves of **Taiwanensis Group** (syn. *P. taiwanensis*), **S** 5m (15ft), are narrow, and bronze-red when young. Bears clusters of white flowers in early and mid-spring. Slow-growing **'Variegata'** has small leaves, edged with white.

P. nana, syn. *Arcterica nana*. Evergreen, prostrate, dwarf shrub. **H** 2.5–5cm (1–2in), **S** 10–15cm (4–6in). Fully hardy. Has tiny, oval, leathery, dark green leaves, usually in whorls of 3, on fine stems that root readily. In early spring bears small, terminal clusters of white flowers with green or red calyces. Is excellent for binding a peat wall or in a rock garden.

P. taiwanensis. See *P. japonica* Taiwanensis Group.

PILEA

URTICACEAE

Genus of bushy or trailing annuals and evergreen perennials, grown for their ornamental foliage. Frost tender, min. 10°C (50°F). Grow in any well-drained soil out of direct sunlight and draughts; do not overwater in winter. Pinch out tips in growing season to avoid straggly plants. Propagate perennials by stem cuttings in spring or summer, annuals by seed in spring or autumn. Red spider mite may be a problem.

♀ ***P. cadierei*** (Aluminium plant) illus. p.465.

P. involucrata, syn. *P. mollis* (Friendship plant). Evergreen, bushy perennial. **H** 15cm (6in), **S** 30cm (12in). Oval to rounded, corrugated, bronze leaves, to 5cm (2in) long, are reddish-green below; leaves are green when grown in shade.

P. mollis. See *P. involucrata.*

P. nummulariifolia illus. p.474.

PILEOSTEGIA

HYDRANGEACEAE

Genus of evergreen, woody-stemmed root climbers. Frost hardy. Grows in sun or shade and in any well-drained soil; is therefore useful for planting against a north wall. Prune in spring, if required. Propagate by semi-ripe cuttings in summer.

♀ ***P. viburnoides***, syn. *Schizophragma viburnoides*, illus. p.196.

PILOSOCEREUS

CACTACEAE

Genus of columnar, summer-flowering, perennial cacti with wool-like spines in flowering zones at crowns. Some species are included in *Cephalocereus*. Frost tender, min. 11°C (52°F). Needs full sun and very well-drained soil. Propagate by seed or stem cuttings in spring or summer.

P. leucocephalus, syn. *P. palmeri*, illus. p.483.

P. palmeri. See *P. leucocephalus.*

PIMELEA

THYMELAEACEAE

Genus of evergreen shrubs, grown for their flowers and overall appearance. Frost hardy to frost tender, min. 5–7°C (41–45°F). Needs full sun and well-drained, neutral to acid soil. Water potted plants moderately, less when temperatures are low. Needs good winter light and ventilation in northern temperate greenhouses. Propagate by seed in spring or by semi-ripe cuttings in late summer.

P. ferruginea illus. p.454.

PINELLIA

ARACEAE

Genus of summer-flowering, tuberous perennials that produce slender, hood-like, green spathes, each enclosing and concealing a pencil-shaped spadix. Frost hardy. Needs partial shade or sun and humus-rich soil. Water well in spring–summer. Is dormant in winter. Propagate in early spring by offsets, or in late summer by bulbils borne in leaf axils.

P. ternata. Summer-flowering, tuberous perennial. **H** 15–25cm (6–10in), **S** 10–15cm (4–6in). Has erect stems crowned by oval, flat, 3-parted leaves. Leafless stem bears a tubular, green spathe, 5–6cm (2–2½in) long, with a hood at the tip.

PINGUICULA

LENTIBULARIACEAE

Genus of summer-flowering perennials with sticky leaves that trap insects and digest them for food. Is useful in pots under glass among plants at risk from aphids. Fully hardy to frost tender, min. 7°C (45°F). Needs sun and wet soil. Propagate by division in early spring or by seed in autumn.

P. caudata. See *P. moranensis* var. *caudata*.

P. grandiflora illus. p.368.

P. moranensis* var. *caudata, syn. *P. caudata*. Basal-rosetted perennial. **H** 12–15cm (5–6in), **S** 5cm (2in). Frost tender. Leaves are narrowly oval and dull green with inrolled, purplish margins. In summer, 5-petalled, deep carmine flowers are produced on long stems.

PINUS

Pine

PINACEAE

Genus of small to large conifers with spirally arranged leaves in bundles, usually of 2, 3 or 5 needles. Cones ripen over 2 years and are small in the first year. See also CONIFERS.

P. aristata illus. p.103.

P. armandii (Armand pine, David's pine). Conical, open conifer. **H** 10–15m (30–50ft), **S** 5–8m (15–25ft). Fully hardy. Has pendent, glaucous blue leaves and conical, green cones, 8–25cm (3–10in) long, ripening to brown.

P. ayacahuite (Mexican white pine) illus. p.95.

P. banksiana illus. p.102.

P. bungeana (Lace-bark pine; illus. p.78). Slow-growing, bushy conifer. **H** 10–15m (30–50ft), **S** 5–6m (15–20ft). Fully hardy. Has grey-green bark that flakes to reveal creamy-yellow patches, darkening to red or purple. Leaves are dark green.

P. cembra illus. p.101.

P. cembroides illus. p.103.

P. chylla. See *P. wallichiana.*

P. contorta illus. p.102. **var. *latifolia*** illus. p.101. **'Spaan's Dwarf'** is a conical, open, dwarf conifer with short, stiffly erect shoots. **H** and **S** 75cm (30in). Fully hardy. Has bright green leaves in 2s.
♀ ***P. coulteri*** illus. p.96.
P. densiflora (Japanese red pine). Flat-topped conifer. **H** 15m (50ft), **S** 5–7m (15–22ft). Fully hardy. Has scaling, reddish-brown bark, bright green leaves and conical, yellow or pale brown cones. **'Alice Verkade'**, **H** and **S** 75cm (30in), is a diminutive, rounded form with fresh green leaves. **'Tagyosho'** see *P.d.* 'Umbraculifera'.**'Umbraculifera'** (syn. *P.d.* 'Tagyosho'), **H** 4m (12ft), **S** 6m (20ft), is a slow-growing, rounded or umbrella-shaped form.
P. excelsa. See *P. wallichiana.*
P. griffithii. See *P. wallichiana.*
P. halepensis illus. p.102.
♀ ***P. heldreichii***, syn. *P.h.* var. *leucodermis, P. leucodermis*, illus. p.98. **'Compact Gem'** (syn. *P.h.*var. *leucodermis* 'Compact Gem') is a broadly conical, dense, dwarf conifer. **H** and **S** 25–30cm (10–12in). Fully hardy. Has very dark green leaves in 2s. Grows only 2.5cm (1in) a year. **var. *leucodermis*** see *P. heldreichii.*
♀ **'Smidtii'** (syn *P.h.* var. *leucodermis* 'Schmidtii'; illus. p.105) is a dwarf form with an ovoid habit and sharp, dark green leaves.
P.* x *holfordiana illus. p.95.
P. insignis. See *P. radiata.*
♀ ***P. jeffreyi*** illus. p.97.
P. leucodermis. See *P. heldreichii.*
P. mugo (Dwarf pine, Mountain pine, Swiss mountain pine). Spreading, shrubby conifer. **H** 3–5m (10–15ft), **S** 5–8m (15–25ft). Fully hardy. Has bright to dark green leaves in 2s and ovoid, brown cones. **'Gnom'**, **H** and **S** to 2m (6ft), and ♀ **'Mops'** (illus. p.105), **H** 1m (3ft), **S** 2m (6ft), are rounded cultivars.
♀ ***P. muricata*** illus. p.97.
♀ ***P. nigra*** (Black pine). Upright, later spreading conifer, generally grown in one of the following forms. **'Hornibrookiana'**, **H** 1.5–2m (5–6ft), **S** 2m (6ft), is fully hardy and shrubby with stout, spreading or erect branches and dark green leaves in 2s. ♀ **subsp. *laricio*** (syn. *P.n.* var. *maritima*; Corsican pine), **H** 25–30m (80–100ft), **S** 8m (25ft), is fast-growing and narrowly conical with an open crown; bears grey-green leaves, in 2s, and ovoid to conical, yellow- or pale grey-brown cones. **var. *maritima*** see *P.n.* subsp. *laricio*. **subsp. *nigra*** illus. p.98.
P. patula (Mexican weeping pine) illus. p.97.
P. parviflora illus. p.99. ♀ **'Adcock's Dwarf'** is a slow-growing, rounded, dense, dwarf conifer. **H** 2–3m (6–10ft), **S** 1.5–2m (5–6ft). Fully hardy. Bears grey-green leaves in 5s.
P. peuce illus. p.95.
♀ ***P. pinaster*** illus. p.97.
♀ ***P. pinea*** illus. p.104.
♀ ***P. ponderosa*** illus. p.97.
P. pumila (Dwarf Siberian pine). Spreading, shrubby conifer. **H** 2–3m (6–10ft), **S** 3–5m (10–15ft). Fully hardy. Has bright blue-green leaves in 5s. Ovoid cones are violet-purple, ripening to red-brown or yellow-brown, the males bright red-purple in spring. **'Globe'**, **H** and **S** 50cm–1m (1½–3ft), is a rounded cultivar with blue foliage.
♀ ***P. radiata***, syn. *P. insignis*, illus. p.98.
P. rigida illus. p.100.
P. strobus illus. p.96. ♀ **'Radiata'** is a rounded, dwarf conifer with an open, sparse, whorled crown. **H** 1–2m (3–6ft), **S** 2–3m (6–10ft). Fully hardy. Grey bark is smooth at first, later fissured. Bears grey-green leaves in 5s.
♀ ***P. sylvestris*** (Scots pine; illus. p.78). Conifer, upright and with whorled branches when young, that develops a spreading, rounded crown with age. **H** 15–25m (50–80ft), **S** 8–10m (25–30ft). Fully hardy. Bark is flaking and red-brown on upper trunk, fissured and purple-grey at base. Has blue-green leaves in 2s and conical, green cones that ripen to pale grey- or red-brown. ♀ **'Aurea'** illus. p.104. ♀ **'Beuvronensis'**, **H** and **S** 1m (3ft), is a rounded shrub. **'Doone Valley'**, **H** and **S** 1m (3ft), is an upright, irregularly shaped shrub. **f. *fastigiata*** see *P.s.* 'Fastigiata'. **'Fastigiata'** (syn. *P.s.* f. *fastigiata*), **H** up to 8m (25ft), **S** 1–3m (3–10ft), has a narrow, obelisk habit; suffers wind damage in an exposed site. **'Gold Coin'**, **H** and **S** 2m (6ft), is a dwarf version of *P.s.* 'Aurea'. **'Nana'** of gardens see *P.s.* 'Watereri'. **'Watereri'** (syn. *P.s.* 'Nana' of gardens), **H** and **S** 50cm (20in), is a very dense cultivar with widely spaced leaves.
P. thunbergii illus. p.100.
P. virginiana (Scrub pine, Virginia pine). Conifer of untidy habit. **H** 12m (40ft), **S** 8m (25ft). Grey- to yellow-green leaves are 4–7cm (1½–3in) long. Fully hardy. Young shoots have a pinkish-white bloom. Bears oblong to conical, red-brown cones, 4–7cm (1½–3in) long.
♀ ***P. wallichiana***, syn. *P. chylla, P. excelsa, P. griffithii*, illus. p.97.

PIPTANTHUS

LEGUMINOSAE/PAPILIONACEAE

Genus of deciduous or semi-evergreen shrubs, grown for their foliage and flowers. Frost hardy. In cold areas needs the protection of a south- or west-facing wall. Requires sun and fertile, well-drained soil. In spring cut some older shoots back to ground level and prune any frost-damaged growths back to healthy wood. Propagate by seed in autumn.
P. laburnifolius. See *P. nepalensis.*
P. nepalensis, syn. *P. laburnifolius*, illus. p.206.

PISONIA

NYCTAGINACEAE

Genus of evergreen shrubs and trees, grown for their foliage and overall appearance. Frost tender, min. 10–15°C (50–59°F). Needs full light or partial shade and humus-rich, well-drained soil. Water containerized specimens freely when in full growth, moderately at other times. Pruning is tolerated if required. Propagate by seed in spring or by semi-ripe cuttings in summer.
P. brunoniana. See *P. umbellifera.*
P. umbellifera, syn. *Heimerliodendron brunonianum, P. brunoniana* (Bird-catcher tree, Para para). Evergreen, rounded large shrub or small tree. **H** and **S** 3–6m (10–20ft). Bears oval, leathery, lustrous leaves. In spring, produces clusters of tiny, green or pink flowers, followed by 5-winged, sticky, brownish fruits.

PISTACIA

ANACARDIACEAE

Genus of evergreen or deciduous trees, grown for their foliage and overall appearance. Frost tender, min. 10°C (50°F). Requires full light and free-draining, even dry soil. Water containerized plants moderately when in full growth, sparingly at other times. Pruning is tolerated if necessary. Propagate by seed in spring or by semi-ripe cuttings in summer.
P. lentiscus (Mastic tree). Evergreen, irregularly rounded shrub or tree. **H** 5m (15ft), **S** to 3m (10ft). Bears leaves that are divided into 2–5 pairs of oval, leathery, glossy leaflets. Produces auxillary clusters of insignificant flowers from spring to early summer that develop into globose, red, then black fruits in autumn.
P. terebinthus (Cyprus turpentine, Terebinth tree). Deciduous, rounded to ovoid tree. **H** 6–9m (20–28ft), **S** 3–6m (10–20ft). Leaves have 5–9 oval, usually lustrous, rich green leaflets. Axillary clusters of small flowers borne in spring and early summer develop into tiny, globular to ovoid, red, then purple-brown fruits in autumn.

PISTIA

ARACEAE

Genus of one species of deciduous, perennial, floating water plant, grown for its foliage. In water above 19–21°C (66–70°F), is evergreen. Is suitable for tropical aquariums and frost-free pools. Frost tender, min 10–15°C (50–59°F). Grows in sun or semi-shade. Remove fading foliage and thin plants out as necessary. Propagate by separating plantlets in summer.
P. stratiotes illus. p.442.

PITCAIRNIA

BROMELIACEAE

Genus of evergreen, rosette-forming perennials, grown for their overall appearance. Frost tender, min. 10°C (50°F). Needs semi-shade and well-drained soil. Water moderately during growing season, sparingly at other times. Propagate by offsets or division in spring.
P. andreana. Evergreen, clump-forming, basal-rosetted perennial. **H** 20cm (8in), **S** 30cm (12in) or more. Loose rosettes comprise narrowly lance-shaped, strongly arching, green leaves, grey-scaled beneath. Racemes of tubular, orange-and-red flowers are borne in summer.
P. heterophylla. Evergreen, basal-rosetted perennial with swollen, much-branched rhizomes. **H** 10cm (4in) or more, **S** to 30cm (12in). Forms loose rosettes; outer leaves resemble barbed spines, inner leaves are strap-shaped, low-arching and green, with downy, white undersides. Produces almost stemless spikes of tubular, bright red, or rarely white flowers in summer.

PITTOSPORUM

PITTOSPORACEAE

Genus of evergreen trees and shrubs, grown for their ornamental foliage and fragrant flowers. Frost hardy to frost tender, min. 7°C (45°F). Does best in mild areas; in cold regions, grow against a south- or west-facing wall. *P. crassifolium* and *P. ralphii* make wind-resistant hedges in mild, coastal areas; like forms with variegated or purple leaves, prefer sun. Others will grow in sun or semi-shade. All need well-drained soil. Propagate *P. dallii* by budding in summer, other species by seed in autumn or spring or by semi-ripe cuttings in summer; selected forms by semi-ripe cuttings only in summer.
P. crassifolium (Karo). Evergreen, bushy-headed, dense tree or shrub. **H** 5m (15ft), **S** 3m (10ft). Frost hardy. Has oblong, dark green leaves, grey-felted beneath. Clusters of small, fragrant, star-shaped, dark reddish-purple flowers are borne in spring.
P. dallii illus. p.119.
P. eugenioides. Evergreen, columnar tree. **H** 10m (30ft), **S** 5m (15ft). Frost hardy. Narrowly oval, wavy-edged leaves are glossy, dark green. Honey-scented, star-shaped, pale yellow flowers are produced in spring. ♀ **'Variegatum'** illus. p.93.
♀ ***P.* 'Garnettii'** illus. p.119.
P. ralphii. Evergreen, bushy-headed tree or shrub. **H** 4m (12ft), **S** 3m (10ft). Frost hardy. Large leaves are oblong, leathery and grey-green, very hairy beneath. Produces small, fragrant, star-shaped, dark red flowers in spring.
♀ ***P. tenuifolium*** illus. p.120. **'Margaret Turnbull'** is an evergreen, compact shrub. **H** 1.8m (6ft), **S** 1m (3ft). Frost hardy. Has dark green leaves, centrally splashed golden yellow. ♀ **'Tom Thumb'** illus. p.164.
♀ ***P. tobira*** (Japanese pittosporum, Mock orange). Evergreen, bushy-headed, dense tree or shrub. **H** 6m (20ft), **S** 4m (12ft). Frost hardy. Has oblong to oval, glossy, dark green leaves. Very fragrant, star-shaped, white flowers, opening in late spring, later become creamy-yellow.
P. undulatum (Victorian box). Evergreen, broadly conical tree. **H** 12m (40ft), **S** 8m (25ft). Half hardy. Has long, narrowly oval, pointed, wavy-edged, dark green leaves. Fragrant, star-shaped, white flowers are borne in late spring and early summer, followed by rounded, orange fruits.

PITYROGRAMMA

PTERIDACEAE/ADIANTACEAE

Genus of semi-evergreen or evergreen ferns, suitable for hanging baskets. Frost tender, min. 10°C (50°F). Needs semi-shade and humus-rich, moist but well-drained soil. Remove fading fronds regularly. Water carefully to avoid spoiling farina on fronds. Propagate by spores in late summer.
P. triangularis. Semi-evergreen or evergreen fern. **H** and **S** 45cm (18in). Has broadly triangular, delicately divided, mid-green fronds with orange or creamy-white farina.

Plagiorhegma dubia. See *Jeffersonia dubia.*

PLANTAGO

PLANTAGINACEAE

Genus of summer-flowering annuals, biennials and evergreen perennials and shrubs. Many species are weeds, but a few are grown for their foliage and architectural value. Fully hardy to frost tender, min. 7–10°C (45–50°F). Needs full sun and well-drained soil. Water potted plants moderately, sparingly in winter. Propagate by seed or division in spring.
P. nivalis, illus. p.376, has lance-shaped, silky-hairy, silver-green leaves and tiny, grey-brown flowers.

PLATANUS

Plane

PLATANACEAE

Genus of deciduous trees, grown for their habit, foliage and flaking bark. Flowers are inconspicuous. Spherical fruit clusters hang from shoots in autumn. Fully to half hardy. Needs full sun and deep, fertile, well-drained soil. Propagate species by seed in autumn, *P.* x *hispanica* by hardwood cuttings in early winter. All except *P. orientalis* are susceptible to the fungal disease plane anthracnose. ⓘContact with the basal tufts of hair on the fruits may irritate the skin and respiratory system.
P.* x *acerifolia. See *P.* x *hispanica.*
♀ ***P.* x *hispanica***, syn. *P.* x *acerifolia*, illus. p.63. **'Suttneri'** is a vigorous, deciduous, spreading tree. **H** 20m (70ft), **S** 15m (50ft). Fully hardy. Has flaking bark and large, palmate, 5-lobed, sharply toothed, bright green leaves that are blotched with creamy-white.
♀ ***P. orientalis*** illus. p.63.

PLATYCARYA

JUGLANDACEAE

Genus of one species of deciduous tree, grown for its foliage and catkins. Fully hardy. Requires full sun and fertile, well-drained soil. Propagate by seed in autumn.
P. strobilacea. Deciduous, spreading tree. **H** and **S** 10m (30ft). Has ash-like, bright green leaves with 5–15 leaflets. Upright, green catkins are borne from mid- to late summer; males are slender and cylindrical, often drooping at tips, females are cone-like, become brown and persist through winter.

PLATYCERIUM

Stag's-horn fern

POLYPODIACEAE

Genus of evergreen, epiphytic ferns, best grown in hanging baskets or fastened to and suspended from pieces of wood. Produces 2 kinds of fronds: permanent, broad, sterile "nest leaves" forming the main part of the plant; and strap-shaped, usually partly bifurcated, arching fertile fronds. Frost tender, min. 5°C (41°F). Thrives in warm, humid conditions in semi-shade, and needs fibrous, peaty compost with hardly any soil. Propagate by detaching buds in spring or summer and planting in compost, or by spores in summer or early autumn.
P. alcicorne of gardens. See *P. bifurcatum.*
♀ ***P. bifurcatum***, syn. *P. alcicorne* of gardens, illus. p.479.

PLATYCLADUS

CUPRESSACEAE

See also CONIFERS. ⓘContact with the foliage may aggravate skin allergies.
P. orientalis, syn. *Biota orientalis, Thuja orientalis* (Biota, Chinese arbor-vitae, Chinese thuja). Conifer with an irregularly rounded crown. **H** 10–15m (30–50ft), **S** 5m (15ft). Fully hardy. Has fibrous bark and flattened, vertical sprays of scale-like, scentless, dark green leaves. Egg-shaped cones are glaucous grey. ♀ **'Aurea Nana'** (illus. p.105), **H** and **S** 60cm (24in), is a dwarf cultivar with yellow-green foliage that turns bronze in winter. **'Semperaurea'**, **H** 3m (10ft), **S** 2m (6ft), is compact, with golden leaves.

PLATYCODON

Balloon flower

CAMPANULACEAE

Genus of one species of perennial, grown for its flowers in summer. Fully hardy. Needs sun and light, sandy soil. Propagate by basal cuttings of non-flowering shoots in summer, with a bit of root attached, or by seed in autumn.
♀ ***P. grandiflorus*** illus. p.269. ♀ **var. *mariesii*** (syn. *P.g.* 'Mariesii') is a clump-forming perennial. **H** and **S** 30–45cm (12–18in). In mid-summer, produces solitary terminal, large, balloon-like flower buds opening to bell-shaped, blue or purplish-blue flowers. Has oval, sharply toothed, bluish-green leaves. **'Mariesii'** see *P.g.* var. *mariesii.*

PLATYSTEMON

PAPAVERACEAE

Genus of one species of summer-flowering annual. Fully hardy. Grow in sun and in fertile, well-drained soil. Propagate by seed sown outdoors in spring or early autumn.
P. californicus illus. p.321.

PLECTRANTHUS

LABIATAE/LAMIACEAE

Genus of evergreen, trailing or bushy perennials, grown for their foliage. Frost tender, min. 4–10°C (39–50°F). Is easy to grow if kept moist in partial shade or bright light. Cut back stem tips in growing season if plants become too straggly. Propagate by stem cuttings or division in spring or summer.
P. australis of gardens. See *P. verticillatus.*
***P. coleoides* 'Variegatus'** of gardens. See *P. madagascariensis* 'Variegated Mintleaf'.
***P. forsteri* 'Marginatus'**, illus. p.298.
***P. fruticosus* 'James'** illus. p.454.
P. madagascariensis (Mintleaf). Creeping perennial. **H** 30cm (12in), **S** indefinite. Min. 10°C (50°F). Has rounded, scalloped, fleshy leaves. Bears 2-lipped, lavender-blue or white flowers, often dotted with red. ♀ **'Variegated Mintleaf'** (syn. *P. coleoides* 'Variegatus' of gardens) has variegated white leaves.
♀ ***P. oertendahlii*** (Prostrate coleus, Swedish ivy). Evergreen, prostrate perennial. **H** to 15cm (6in), **S** indefinite. Min. 10°C (50°F). Rounded, scalloped, dark green leaves are reddish-green below, with white veins above. Has racemes of tubular, white or pale mauve flowers at irregular intervals throughout the year.
P. scutellarioides. See *Solenostemon scutellarioides.*
P. thyrsoideus, syn. *Coleus thyrsoideus.* Fast-growing, bushy perennial, often grown as an annual. **H** to 1m (3ft), **S** 60cm (2ft). Min. 4°C (39°F). Has heart-shaped, serrated, mid-green leaves. Produces spikes of tubular, bright blue flowers at various times of year.
P. verticillatus, syn. *P. australis* of gardens (Swedish ivy). Evergreen, trailing perennial with square stems. **H** to 15cm (6in), **S** indefinite. Min.10°C (50°F). Has rounded, waxy, glossy, green leaves with scalloped edges. Racemes of tubular, white or pale mauve flowers are produced intermittently through the year.

PLEIOBLASTUS

GRAMINEAE/POACEAE

See also GRASSES, BAMBOOS, RUSHES and SEDGES.
♀ ***P. variegatus***, syn. *Arundinaria fortunei, A. variegata*, illus. p.284.
P. viridistriatus, syn. *Arundinaria auricoma*, illus. p.289.

PLEIONE

ORCHIDACEAE

See also ORCHIDS.
P. bulbocodioides (illus. p.466). Deciduous, terrestrial orchid. **H** 20cm (8in). Frost hardy. In spring, usually before solitary leaf appears, bears pink, rose or magenta flowers, 5–12cm (2–5in) across, with darker purple marks on lips. Leaf is narrowly lance-shaped, 14cm (5½in) long. Is often difficult to flower: regular feeding helps to increase pseudobulbs to flowering size.
P.* x *confusa. Deciduous, terrestrial orchid. **H** 15cm (6in). Frost hardy. Canary-yellow flowers, 5–8cm (2–3in) across, with brown or purple blotches on lips, appear singly in spring, before foliage. Has lance-shaped leaves, 10–18cm (4–7in) long. Does best in an alpine house. Needs semi-shade.
P. hookeriana. Deciduous, terrestrial orchid. **H** 8–15cm (3–6in). Frost hardy. Lilac-pink, rose or white flowers, 5–7cm (2–3in) across, each with a brown- or purplish-spotted lip, are borne singly in spring with lance-shaped leaves, 5–20cm (2–8in) long. Cultivate as for *P.* x *confusa.*
P. humilis. Deciduous, terrestrial orchid. **H** 5–8cm (2–3in). Frost hardy. In winter, before foliage appears, white flowers, 7–9cm (3–3½in) across, each with a crimson-spotted lip, are borne singly or in pairs. Lance-shaped leaves are 18–25cm (7–10in) long. Cultivate as for *P.* x *confusa.*
P. praecox. Deciduous, terrestrial orchid. **H** 8–13cm (3–5in). Frost hardy. Flowers, to 8cm (3in) across, appear in pairs in autumn, after foliage. They are white to pinkish-purple or lilac-purple, with violet marks. Leaves are oblong to lance-shaped and 15–25cm (6–10in) long. Cultivate as for *P.* x *confusa.*

PLEIOSPILOS

AIZOACEAE

Genus of clump-forming, perennial succulents with almost stemless rosettes bearing up to 4 pairs of fleshy, erect leaves, like pieces of granite, each with a flat upper surface and each pair united at the base. Flowers are daisy-like. Individual species are very similar, and many are difficult to identify. Frost tender, min. 5°C (41°F). Needs sun and well-drained soil. Propagate by seed or division in spring or summer.
♀ ***P. bolusii*** illus. p.495.
♀ ***P. compactus*** illus. p.495.

Pleurothallis grobyi. See *Specklinia grobyi.*

PLUMBAGO

PLUMBAGINACEAE

Genus of annuals, evergreen or semi-evergreen shrubs, perennials and woody-stemmed, scrambling climbers, grown for their primrose-shaped flowers. Frost hardy to frost tender, min. 7°C (45°F). Grow in full light or semi-shade and in fertile, well-drained soil. Water regularly, less when not in full growth. Tie stems to supports. Thin out or spur back all previous year's growth in early spring. Propagate by semi-ripe cuttings in summer. Whitefly may be a problem.
♀ ***P. auriculata***, syn. *P. capensis*, illus. p.205.
P. capensis. See *P. auriculata.*
♀ ***P. indica***, syn. *P. rosea.* Evergreen or semi-evergreen, spreading shrub or semi-climber. **H** 2m (6ft), **S** 1–2m (3–6ft). Frost tender. Leaves are oval to elliptic and mid-green. Has terminal racemes of primrose-shaped, red or pink flowers, 2.5cm (1in) long. These are produced in summer, if hard-pruned annually in spring, or from late winter onwards, if left unpruned and trained as a climber.
P. rosea. See *P. indica.*

PLUMERIA

Frangipani

APOCYNACEAE

Genus of mainly deciduous, fleshy-branched shrubs and trees, grown for their flowers in summer–autumn. Frost tender, min. 13°C (55°F). Requires full sun and freely draining soil. Water potted specimens moderately while in growth, keep dry in winter when leafless. Stem tips may be cut out to induce branching. Propagate by seed or leafless stem-tip cuttings in late spring. Red spider mite may be a nuisance. ⓘThe milky sap may cause mild stomach upset if ingested.
P. acuminata. See *P. rubra* f. *acutifolia.*
P. acutifolia. See *P. rubra* f. *acutifolia.*
P. alba (West Indian jasmine). Deciduous, rounded, sparingly branched tree. **H** to 6m (20ft), **S** to 4m (12ft). Leaves are lance-shaped and slender-pointed, to 30cm (12in)

long. Terminal clusters of fragrant, yellow-eyed, white flowers, each with 5 spreading petals and a tubular base, appear in summer.
🏆 ***P. rubra*** illus. p.453. **f. *acutifolia*** (syn. *P. acuminata, P. acutifolia*) is a deciduous, spreading, sparsely branched tree or shrub. **H** and **S** 4m (12ft) or more. Produces fragrant, yellow-centred, white flowers, with 5 spreading petals, in summer–autumn. Leaves are lance-shaped to oval and 20–30cm (8–12in) long.

PODALYRIA

LEGUMINOSAE/PAPILIONACEAE

Genus of evergreen, mainly summer-flowering shrubs, grown for their flowers and overall appearance. Frost tender, min. 7–10°C (45–50°F). Requires full light and fertile, well-drained soil. Water containerized plants moderately, less when not in full growth. Prune, if necessary, after flowering. Propagate by seed in spring or by semi-ripe cuttings in summer.
P. sericea. Vigorous, evergreen, rounded shrub. **H** and **S** 1.2–3m (4–10ft). Has oval, downy, mid-green leaves and sweet pea-like, pink flowers, 3–4cm (1¼–1½in) wide, in summer.

PODOCARPUS

PODOCARPACEAE

See also CONIFERS.
P. alpinus (Tasmanian podocarp). Rounded, spreading, shrubby conifer. **H** 2m (6ft), **S** 3–5m (10–15ft). Frost hardy. Has linear, dull green leaves and rounded, egg-shaped, fleshy, bright red fruits.
P. andinus. See *Prumnopitys andina*.
P. macrophyllus (Kusamaki). Erect conifer. **H** 10m (30ft), **S** 3–5m (10–15ft). Half hardy. Long, linear leaves are bright green above, glaucous beneath. May be grown as a shrub, **H** and **S** 1–2m (3–6ft), and planted in a tub in hot climates.
P. nivalis (Alpine totara; illus. p.105). Rounded, spreading, shrubby conifer. **H** 2m (6ft), **S** 3–5m (10–15ft). Frost hardy. Is very similar to *P. alpinus*, but bears longer, broader, more rigid leaves.
🏆 ***P. salignus*** illus. p.100.

PODOPHYLLUM

BERBERIDACEAE

Genus of spring-flowering, rhizomatous perennials. Fully hardy, but young leaves may be damaged by frost. Prefers semi-shade and moist, peaty soil. Propagate by division in spring or by seed in autumn. ⚠ All parts of the plants are highly toxic if ingested.
P. emodi. See *Sinopodophyllum hexandrum*.
P. hexandrum. See *Sinopodophyllum hexandrum*.
P. peltatum (May apple). Vigorous, spreading, rhizomatous perennial. **H** 30–45cm (12–18in), **S** 30cm (12in). Palmate, sometimes brown-mottled, light green leaves, with 3–5 deep lobes, push up through soil, looking like closed umbrellas, and are followed, in spring, by nodding, cup-shaped, white flowers. Produces large, fleshy, plum-like, glossy, deep rose-pink fruits in autumn.

PODRANEA

BIGNONIACEAE

Genus of evergreen, twining climbers, grown for their foxglove-like flowers. Frost tender, min. 5–10°C (41–50°F). Grow in full light and any fertile, well-drained soil. Water regularly, less in cold weather. Provide support. Thin out crowded growth in winter or early spring. Propagate by seed in spring or by semi-ripe cuttings in summer.
P. ricasoliana, syn. *Pandorea ricasoliana, Tecoma ricasoliana*. Fast-growing, evergreen, twining climber. **H** 4m (12ft) or more. Has leaves of 7 or 9 lance-shaped to oval, wavy, deep green leaflets. Bears loose clusters of fragrant, pink flowers, with darker veins, from spring to autumn.

Poinciana gilliesii. See *Caesalpinia gilliesii*.
Poinciana pulcherrima. See *Caesalpinia pulcherrima*.

POLEMONIUM

Jacob's ladder

POLEMONIACEAE

Genus of late spring- or summer-flowering annuals and perennials, some perennials tending to be short-lived. Fully hardy. Prefers sun and fertile, well-drained soil. Propagate by division in spring or by seed in autumn.
P. caeruleum illus. p.270. **Brise d'Anjou ('Blanjou')** illus. p.270.
P. carneum illus. p.269.
P. foliosissimum. Vigorous, clump-forming perennial. **H** 75cm (30in), **S** 60cm (24in). Terminal clusters of cup-shaped, lilac flowers, with yellow stamens, are borne in summer above oblong to lance-shaped, mid-green leaves, each composed of numerous, small leaflets. **var. *flavum***, **H** 40–70cm (16–28in), produces yellow flowers shaded orange-red outside
P. pulcherrimum. Vigorous, summer-flowering perennial. **H** 50cm (20in), **S** 30cm (12in). Has bright green leaves divided into leaflets and tubular, purple-blue flowers with throats of yellow or white.

POLIANTHES

AGAVACEAE

Genus of tuberous perennials, grown for their fragrant flowers in summer. Half hardy to frost tender, min. 15–20°C (59–68°F). Needs a sheltered site in full sun and well-drained soil. Water well in spring–summer; feed liquid fertilizer every 2 weeks when in growth. Dry off after leaves die down in winter. Propagate by seed or offsets in spring.
P. geminiflora, syn. *Agave duplicata, Bravoa geminiflora*, illus. p.413.
🏆 ***P. tuberosa*** syn. *Agave polianthes* (Tuberose). Summer-flowering, tuberous perennial. **H** 60–90cm (24–36in), **S** 10–15cm (4–6in). Half hardy. Has a basal cluster of strap-shaped, erect leaves; flower stem also bears leaves on lower part. Produces a spike of funnel-shaped, single, white flowers with 6 spreading petals. A double form is also available. **'The Pearl'** illus. p.385.

POLIOTHYRSIS

FLACOURTIACEAE

Genus of one species of deciduous tree, grown for its foliage and flowers. Fully hardy. Needs a position in sun or semi-shade and in fertile, well-drained soil. Propagate by softwood cuttings in summer.
🏆 ***P. sinensis.*** Deciduous, spreading tree. **H** 10m (30ft), **S** 6m (20ft). Bears long, oval, sharply toothed leaves, glossy and dark green, with wine-red stalks. Fragrant, star-shaped, white, later yellow flowers are produced in late summer and early autumn.

POLYGALA

POLYGALACEAE

Genus of annuals, evergreen perennials, shrubs and trees, grown mainly for their pea-like flowers. Fully hardy to frost tender, min. 7°C (45°F). Needs full light or partial shade and moist but sharply drained soil. Water potted specimens freely when in full growth, moderately at other times. Lanky stems may be cut back hard in late winter. Propagate by seed in spring or by semi-ripe cuttings in late summer. Is susceptible to whitefly.
P. calcarea illus. p.370. **'Bulley's Form'** is an evergreen, prostrate perennial. **H** 2.5cm (1in), **S** 8–10cm (3–4in). Fully hardy. Has rosettes of small, narrowly oval leaves. Bears loose heads of deep blue flowers in late spring and early summer. Prefers humus-rich soil. 🏆 **'Lillet'** illus. p.369.
🏆 ***P. chamaebuxus*** illus. p.371. 🏆 **var. *grandiflora*** (syn. *P.c.* var. *purpurea, P.c.* var. *rhodoptera*) illus. p.354. **var. *purpurea*** see *P.c.* var. *grandiflora*. **var. *rhodoptera*** see *P.c.* var. *grandiflora*.
🏆 ***P. x dalmaisiana***, syn. *P. myrtifolia* var. *grandiflora* of gardens, illus. p.457.
P. myrtifolia* var. *grandiflora of gardens. See *P.* x *dalmaisiana*.
P. vayredae. Evergreen, mat-forming shrub. **H** 5–10cm (2–4in), **S** 20–30cm (8–12in). Frost hardy. Slender, prostrate stems bear small, linear leaves. Pea-like, reddish-purple flowers, each with a yellow lip, are produced in late spring and early summer. Suitable for a rock garden or alpine house.

POLYGONATUM

Solomon's seal

LILIACEAE/CONVALLARIACEAE

Genus of spring- or early summer-flowering, rhizomatous perennials. Fully hardy to frost tender, min. 5°C (41°F). Requires a cool, shady situation and fertile, well-drained soil. Propagate by division in early spring or by seed in autumn. Sawfly caterpillar is a common pest. ⚠ All parts may cause mild stomach upset if ingested.
P. biflorum, syn. *P. canaliculatum, P. commutatum, P. giganteum* (Great Solomon's seal). Arching, rhizomatous perennial. **H** 1.5m (5ft) or more, **S** 60cm (2ft). Fully hardy. Bears oval to oblong, mid-green leaves. Pendent clusters of bell-shaped, white flowers are borne in leaf axils during late spring.
P. canaliculatum. See *P. biflorum*.
P. commutatum. See *P. biflorum*.
P. giganteum. See *P. biflorum*.
P. hirtum, syn. *P. latifolium*. Upright, then arching, rhizomatous perennial. **H** 1m (3ft), **S** 30cm (1ft). Fully hardy. Clusters of 2–5 drooping, tubular, green-tipped, white flowers open in late spring. Undersides of stems, leaf stalks and oval to lance-shaped, mid-green leaves are hairy.
P. hookeri illus. p.353.
🏆 ***P. x hybridum*** illus. p.223.
P. latifolium. See *P. hirtum*.
P. multiflorum. Arching, leafy perennial with fleshy rhizomes. **H** 1m (3ft), **S** 30cm (1ft). Fully hardy. Bears clusters of 2–6 pendent, tubular, green-tipped, white flowers in late spring, then spherical, black fruit. Has oval to lance-shaped, mid-green leaves. **'Flore Pleno'** has double flowers that look like ballet dancers' skirts. **'Striatum'** (syn. *P.m.* 'Variegatum'), **H** 60cm (2ft), has leaves with creamy-white stripes. **'Variegatum'** see *P.m.* 'Striatum'.
🏆 ***P. odoratum*** (Angled Solomon's seal). Arching, rhizomatous perennial. **H** 60cm (24in), **S** 30cm (12in). Fully hardy. Produces pairs of fragrant, tubular to bell-shaped, green-tipped, white flowers in late spring. Oval to lance-shaped leaves are mid-green.
P. verticillatum (Whorled Solomon's seal). Upright, rhizomatous perennial. **H** 1.2m (4ft), **S** 45cm (1½ft). Fully hardy. Bears whorls of stalkless, lance-shaped, mid-green leaves. In early summer produces narrowly bell-shaped, greenish-white flowers.

Polygonum affine. See *Persicaria affinis*.
Polygonum amplexicaule. See *Persicaria amplexicaulis*.
Polygonum aubertii. See *Fallopia aubertii*.
Polygonum baldschuanicum. See *Fallopia baldschuanica*.
Polygonum bistorta. See *Persicaria bistorta*.
Polygonum campanulatum. See *Persicaria campanulata*.
Polygonum capitatum. See *Persicaria capitata*.
Polygonum macrophyllum. See *Persicaria macrophylla*.
Polygonum milletii. See *Persicaria milletii*.
Polygonum sphaerostachyum. See *Persicaria macrophylla*.
Polygonum vacciniifolium. See *Persicaria vacciniifolia*.
***Polygonum virginianum* 'Painter's Palette'.** See *Persicaria virginiana* 'Painter's Palette'.

POLYPODIUM

POLYPODIACEAE

Genus of deciduous, semi-evergreen or evergreen ferns, grown for their sculptural fronds. Fully hardy to frost tender, min. 10°C (50°F). Grow in semi-shade and fibrous, moist but well-drained soil. Propagate by division in spring or by spores in late summer.
P. aureum. See *Phlebodium aureum*.
P. australe. See *P. cambricum*.
P. cambricum, syn. *P. australe, P. vulgare* subsp. *serratum* (Southern polypody,

Wintergreen fern). Deciduous, creeping fern. **H** 15–60cm (6–24in), **S** indefinite. Fully hardy. Has broadly lance-shaped to broadly triangular-ovate, divided, mid-green fronds, to 60cm (24in) long, with linear or oblong pinnae that often have toothed margins. New fronds appear in late summer and die back by early summer. Sori are conspicuously yellow in winter. **'Richard Kayse'** illus. p.293.
P. glycyrrhiza (Liquorice fern). Terrestrial, deciduous fern. **H** and **S** 45cm (18in). Fully hardy. Has oblong-triangular to narrowly oval, divided, mid-green fronds, with lance-shaped to oblong pinnae that arise from a liquorice-scented rootstock.
♀ ***P. interjectum* 'Cornubiense'**, syn. *P. vulgare* 'Cornubiense', illus. p.291.
P. vulgare illus. p.291. **'Cornubiense'** see *P. interjectum* 'Cornubiense'. **'Cristatum'** is an evergreen, creeping fern. **H** and **S** 25–30cm (10–12in). Fully hardy. Narrowly lance-shaped, divided, mid-green fronds, with semi-pendulous, terminal crests, grow from creeping rhizomes covered with copper-brown scales. **subsp. *serratum*** see *P. cambricum*.

POLYSCIAS

ARALIACEAE

Genus of evergreen trees and shrubs, grown for their foliage. Sometimes has insignificant flowers in summer, but only on large, mature specimens. Frost tender, 15–18°C (59–64°F). Needs partial shade and humus-rich, well-drained soil. Water containerized plants freely when in full growth, moderately at other times. Straggly stems may be cut out in spring. Propagate by seed in spring or by stem-tip or leafless stem-section cuttings in summer. Red spider mite may be troublesome.
P. filicifolia illus. p.458. **'Marginata'** is an evergreen, erect, sparsely branched shrub. **H** 2m (6ft) or more, **S** 1m (3ft) or more. Has 30cm (1ft) long leaves with many small, oval to lance-shaped, serrated, bright green leaflets with white edges.
♀ ***P. guilfoylei*** (Wild coffee). Slow-growing, evergreen, rounded tree. **H** 3–8m (10–25ft), **S** to 2m (6ft) or more. Leaves are 25–40cm (10–16in) long and divided into oval to rounded, serrated, deep green leaflets. ♀ **'Victoriae'** illus. p.458.

POLYSPORA

SYN. GORDONIA

THEACEAE

Genus of evergreen shrubs and trees, grown for their flowers and overall appearance. Half hardy, but best at min. 3°C (37°F). Prefers sun or partial shade and humus-rich, acid soil. Water potted plants moderately, less in winter. Propagate by semi-ripe cuttings in late summer or by seed when ripe, in autumn, or in spring.
P. axillaris, syn. *Gordonia axillaris*. Evergreen, bushy shrub or tree. **H** and **S** 3–5m (10–15ft), sometimes much more. Has lance-shaped, leathery, glossy leaves, each with a blunt tip, and bears, from autumn to spring, saucer-shaped, white flowers.
P. lasianthus, syn. *Gordonia lasianthus* (Loblolly bay). Evergreen, upright tree. **H** to 20m (70ft), **S** to 10m (30ft). Lance-shaped to elliptic leaves are shallowly serrated. Has fragrant, saucer- to bowl-shaped, white flowers in summer. Needs sub-tropical summer warmth to grow and flower well.

POLYSTICHUM

DRYOPTERIDACEAE

Genus of evergreen, semi-evergreen or deciduous ferns. Fully to frost hardy. Does best in semi-shade and moist but well-drained soil enriched with fibrous organic matter. Remove faded fronds regularly. Propagate species by division in spring or by spores in summer, selected forms by division in spring.
P. acrostichoides (Christmas fern). Evergreen fern. **H** 60cm (24in), **S** 45cm (18in). Fully hardy. Slender, lance-shaped, deep green fronds have small, holly-like pinnae. Is excellent for cutting.
♀ ***P. aculeatum*** (Hard shield fern, Prickly shield fern). Semi-evergreen fern. **H** 60cm (24in), **S** 75cm (30in). Fully hardy. Broadly lance-shaped, yellowish-green, then deep green fronds, with oblong to oval, spiny-edged, glossy pinnae, are produced on stems often covered in brown scales. **'Pulcherrimum'** see *P. setiferum* 'Pulcherrimum Bevis'.
P. braunii. Evergreen or semi-evergreen fern. **H** and **S** 45–75cm (18–30in). Fully hardy. Produces a rosette of spreading to arching, lance-shaped, divided, dark green fronds, to 60cm (2ft) long. Young fronds are densely covered with orange-brown scales when unfurling in spring.
♀ ***P. munitum*** illus. p.293.
♀ ***P. polyblepharum.*** Evergreen fern. **H** 60–80cm (24–32in), **S** 90cm (36in). Fully hardy. Produces 'shuttlecocks' of spreading, lance-shaped, divided, shiny, dark green fronds, 30–80cm (12–32in) long, covered with golden hairs when they unfurl. Pinnae lobes are oblong-ovate and have spiny-toothed margins.
P. rigens. Evergreen fern. **H** 40cm (16in), **S** 60cm (24in). Fully hardy. Has 'shuttlecocks' of narrowly ovate-oblong, divided, leathery, harsh-textured, dull green fronds, 30–45cm (12–18in) long. Broad, lance-shaped pinnae are divided into ovate, spiny-toothed lobes. Fronds are yellowish-green in spring.
♀ ***P. setiferum*** (Soft shield fern). **'Divisilobum'** see *P.s.* Divisilobum Group. **Divisilobum Group** (syn. *P.s.* 'Divisilobum') illus. p.291. **Plumoso-divisilobum Group** illus. p.291.
♀ **'Pulcherrimum Bevis'** (syn. *P. aculeatum* 'Pulcherrimum') illus p.290.
♀ ***P. tsussimense***, illus. p.292.

PONCIRUS

RUTACEAE

Genus of one species of very spiny, deciduous shrub or small tree, grown for its foliage, showy flowers and orange-like fruits. Is very effective as a protective hedge. Fully hardy. Needs sun and fertile, well-drained soil. Cut out dead wood in spring, and trim hedges in early summer. Propagate by semi-ripe cuttings in summer or by seed when ripe, in autumn.
P. trifoliata (Japanese bitter orange; illus. p.142). Deciduous, bushy shrub or tree. **H** and **S** 5m (15ft). Stout, spiny, green shoots bear dark green leaves each with 3 oval leaflets. Has fragrant, white flowers, with 4 or 5 large petals, in late spring and often again in autumn. Rounded fruits are 2–3cm (¾–1¼in) wide.

PONERORCHIS

ORCHIDACEAE

See also ORCHIDS.
P. graminifolia. Deciduous, terrestrial orchid for an alpine greenhouse. **H** 15cm (6in), **S** 10cm (4in). Frost tender, min. 1°C (34°F). Terminal racemes of variable 2–15 flowers, with 3-lobed lips and pronounced spurs, are borne in late spring and summer in shades of pink, purple and white. Has 2–4 narrowly linear leaves, to 15cm (6in) long.

PONTEDERIA

PONTEDERIACEAE

Genus of deciduous, perennial, marginal water plants, grown for their foliage and flower spikes. Fully to frost hardy. Needs full sun and up to 23cm (9in) depth of water. Remove fading flowers regularly. Propagate in spring by division or seed.
♀ ***P. cordata*** illus. p.441.

POPULUS

Poplar

SALICACEAE

Genus of deciduous trees, grown for their habit, foliage and very quick growth. Has catkins in late winter or spring. Female trees produce copious amounts of fluffy, white seeds. Fully hardy. Prefers full sun and needs deep, fertile, moist but well-drained soil; resents dry soil, apart from *P. alba*, which thrives in coastal gardens. Extensive root systems can undermine foundations and so make poplars unsuitable for planting close to buildings, particularly on clay soil. Propagate by hardwood cuttings in winter. Is susceptible to bacterial canker and fungal diseases.
P. alba illus. p.60. Is much confused with the commoner *P.* x *canescens*. **f. *pyramidalis*** (syn. *P.a.* 'Pyramidalis') is a vigorous, deciduous, upright tree. **H** 20m (70ft), **S** 5m (15ft). Broadly oval, wavy-margined or lobed, dark green leaves, white beneath, turn yellow in autumn. **'Pyramidalis'** see *P.a.* f. *pyramidalis*. **'Raket'** (syn. *P.a.* 'Rocket'), **S** 8m (25ft), is narrowly conical. **'Richardii'**, **H** 15m (50ft), **S** 12m (40ft), has leaves golden-yellow above. **'Rocket'** see *P.a.* 'Raket'.
P. balsamifera (Balsam poplar, Tacamahac). Fast-growing, deciduous, upright tree. **H** 30m (100ft), **S** 8m (25ft). Oval, glossy, dark green leaves, whitish beneath, have a strong fragrance of balsam when young.
P.* x *berolinensis (Berlin poplar). Deciduous, columnar tree. **H** 25m (80ft), **S** 8m (25ft). Has broadly oval, bright green leaves, white beneath.
P.* x *canadensis (Canadian poplar). **'Eugenei'** is a deciduous, columnar tree. **H** 30m (100ft), **S** 12m (40ft). Has broadly oval, bronze, young leaves, maturing to dark green, and red catkins in spring. **'Robusta'** illus. p.62. **'Serotina de Selys'** (syn. *P.* x *c.* 'Serotina Erecta') illus. p.61.
P.* x *candicans of gardens. See *P.* x *jackii*.
P.* x *canescens illus. p.60.
P. deltoides (Cottonwood, Eastern cottonwood, Necklace poplar). Very fast-growing, deciduous, spreading tree. **H** 30m (100ft), **S** 20m (70ft). Has lush growth of broadly oval, glossy, bright green leaves.
P. gileadensis. See *P.* x *jackii*.
P.* x *jackii, syn. *P.* x *candicans* of gardens, *P. gileadensis* (Balm of Gilead). Very fast-growing, deciduous, conical tree. **H** 25m (80ft), **S** 10m (30ft). Oval leaves are dark green and, when young, balsam-scented. Is very susceptible to canker. **'Aurora'**, **H** 15m (50ft) or more, **S** 6m (20ft), has leaves that are heavily but irregularly blotched with creamy-white.
♀ ***P. lasiocarpa*** (Chinese necklace poplar). Very fast-growing, deciduous, spreading tree. **H** 15m (50ft), **S** 12m (40ft). Has stout shoots and very large, heart-shaped, mid-green leaves with red veins, on long, red stalks. Bears stout, drooping, yellow catkins in spring.
P. maximowiczii illus. p.61.
P. nigra (Black poplar). Fast-growing, deciduous, spreading tree. **H** 25m (80ft), **S** 20m (70ft). Has dark bark. Diamond-shaped, bronze young leaves turn bright green, then yellow in autumn. Male trees bear red catkins in mid-spring. ♀ **'Italica'** illus. p.63.
P. szechuanica. Very fast-growing, deciduous, conical tree. **H** 25m (80ft), **S** 10m (30ft). Has flaking, pinkish-grey bark and large, heart-shaped, dark green leaves.
♀ ***P. tremula*** (Aspen). Vigorous, deciduous, spreading tree. **H** 15m (50ft), **S** 10m (30ft). Rounded leaves are bronze-red when young, grey-green when mature, and yellow in autumn. Flattened stalks make foliage tremble and rattle in wind. **'Erecta'**, **S** 5m (15ft), has an upright habit. **'Pendula'** illus. p.74.
P. tremuloides (American aspen, Quaking aspen). Very fast-growing, deciduous, spreading tree. **H** 15m (50ft) or more, **S** 10m (30ft). Has rounded, finely toothed, glossy, dark green leaves that flutter in the wind and turn yellow in autumn.
P. trichocarpa (Black cottonwood, Western balsam poplar). Very fast-growing, deciduous, conical tree. **H** 30m (100ft) or more, **S** 10m (30ft). Bears dense growth of oval, glossy, dark green leaves with green-veined, white undersides, strongly balsam-scented when young. Foliage turns yellow in autumn.

PORANA

CONVOLVULACEAE

Genus of evergreen or deciduous, twining climbers, grown for their flowers. Frost tender, min. 5–7°C (41–45°F), 10–13°C (50–55°F) for good winter blooms. Provide full light and fertile, moisture-retentive, well-drained soil. Water freely in full growth, sparingly in cold weather. Stems require support. Thin out evergreen species and cut back deciduous ones to

just above ground level in late winter or early spring. Propagate by basal, softwood cuttings in late spring or early summer or by seed in spring.
P. paniculata (Bridal bouquet, Snow creeper). Vigorous, evergreen, twining climber. **H** 6–10m (20–30ft). Large, loose panicles of small, elder-scented, trumpet-shaped, white flowers are produced from late summer to mid-winter. Leaves are heart-shaped.

PORTULACA

PORTULACACEAE

Genus of fleshy annuals and perennials with flowers that open in sun and close in shade. Half hardy. Needs full light and any well-drained soil. Propagate by seed sown under glass in early spring, or outdoors in late spring. Is prone to attack by aphids.
P. grandiflora (Sun plant). Slow-growing, partially prostrate annual. **H** 15–20cm (6–8in), **S** 15cm (6in). Has lance-shaped, succulent, bright green leaves. In summer and early autumn bears shallowly bowl-shaped flowers, 2.5cm (1in) wide and with conspicuous stamens, in shades of yellow, red, orange, pink or white. **Minilaca Hybrids** have a double-flowered cultivars. **Sundance Hybrids** are semi-trailing and have semi-double or double flowers, 5cm (2in) wide, in a broad range of colours. **Sundial Series** has double flowers in a broad colour range. Bred for longer flowering in poor conditions and cooler climates. **Sundial Series 'Mango'** illus. p.324.

PORTULACARIA

PORTULACACEAE

Genus of one species of evergreen or semi-evergreen, succulent-leaved shrub, grown for its foliage. Frost tender, min. 7–10°C (45–50°F). Needs full sun and well-drained soil. Water potted plants moderately when in full growth, sparingly at other times. Propagate by semi-ripe cuttings in summer.
P. afra illus. p.457. **'Foliisvariegatus'** (syn. *P.a.* 'Variegatus') is an evergreen or semi-evergreen, erect shrub with more or less horizontal branches. **H** and **S** 2–3m (6–10ft). Has oval to rounded, fleshy, cream-edged, bright green leaves. From late spring to summer, bears tiny, star-shaped, pale pink flowers in small clusters. **'Variegatus'** see *P.a.* 'Foliisvariegatus'.

POTAMOGETON

POTAMOGETONACEAE

Genus of deciduous, perennial, submerged water plants, grown for their foliage. Is suitable for cold-water pools and aquariums. Fully hardy. Prefers sun. Remove fading foliage and thin plants as necessary. Propagate by stem cuttings in spring or summer.
P. crispus illus. p.442.
P. pectinatus (Fennel-leaved pondweed). Deciduous, perennial, submerged water plant. **S** 3m (10ft). Has very narrow, linear, green to brownish-green leaves, and produces inconspicuous flowers in summer. Is suitable for a medium to large pool.

POTENTILLA

ROSACEAE

Genus of perennials and deciduous shrubs, grown for their clusters of small, flattish to saucer-shaped flowers and for their foliage. Tall species – particularly the shrubs – are useful in borders. Dwarf potentillas are good for rock gardens. Fully hardy. Does best in full sun, but flower colour is better on orange-, red- and pink-flowered cultivars if they are shaded from hottest sun. Needs well-drained soil. Propagate perennial species by seed in autumn or by division in spring or autumn; selected forms by division only in spring or autumn. Shrubby species may be raised by seed in autumn or by softwood or greenwood cuttings in summer, selected forms by softwood or greenwood cuttings during summer.
***P.* 'Abbotswood'.** See *P. fruticosa* 'Abbotswood'.
P. alba illus. p.359.
P. arbuscula. See *P. fruticosa* var. *arbuscula*.
***P.* 'Arc-en-ciel'** illus. p.268.
P. argyrophylla. See *P. atrosanguinea* var. *argyrophylla*.
P. atrosanguinea illus. p.269. **var. *argyrophylla*** (syn. *P. argyrophylla*) is a clump-forming perennial. **H** 45cm (18in), **S** 60cm (24in). Saucer-shaped, yellow or yellow-orange flowers are produced in profusion from early to late summer above strawberry-like, silvery leaves.
P. aurea illus. p.372.
***P.* 'Beesii'.** See *P. fruticosa* 'Beesii'.
P. crantzii (Alpine cinquefoil). Upright perennial with a thick, woody rootstock. **H** and **S** 10–20cm (4–8in). Produces wedge-shaped, 5-lobed leaves and, in spring, flattish, yellow flowers with orange centres. Is good in a rock garden.
P. davurica* var. *mandschurica of gardens. See *P. fruticosa* 'Manchu'.
***P.* 'Daydawn'.** See *P. fruticosa* 'Daydawn'.
***P.* 'Elizabeth'.** See *P. fruticosa* 'Elizabeth'.
P. eriocarpa illus. p.372.
***P.* 'Etna'.** Clump-forming perennial. **H** 75cm (30in), **S** 45cm (18in). In mid-summer produces saucer-shaped, maroon flowers above strawberry-like, dark green leaves.
P. fruticosa. Deciduous, bushy, dense shrub. **H** 1m (3ft), **S** 1.5m (5ft). From late spring to late summer produces saucer-shaped, bright yellow flowers. Dark green leaves have 5 narrowly oblong leaflets. ♀ **'Abbotswood'** (syn. *P.* 'Abbotswood') illus. p.149. **var. *arbuscula*** (syn. *P. arbuscula*), **S** 1.2m (4ft), bears golden-yellow flowers amid grey-green to silver-grey leaves. **'Beesii'** (syn. *P.* 'Beesii', *P.* 'Nana Argentea'), **H** 75cm (30in), **S** 1m (3ft), is slow-growing and compact. Has golden-yellow flowers and silver leaves. **'Daydawn'** (syn. *P.* 'Daydawn') illus. p.162. **'Elizabeth'** (syn. *P.* 'Elizabeth') illus. p.160. **'Farrer's White'** illus. p.149. **'Friedrichsenii'** illus. p.160. **'Gold Drop'** (syn. *P. parvifolia* 'Gold Drop'), **H** and **S** 1.2m (4ft), bears a mass of golden-yellow flowers amid bright green leaves. ♀ **'Goldfinger'** (syn. *P.* 'Goldfinger') bears large, rich yellow flowers in profusion. ♀ **'Jackman's Variety'** (syn. *P.* 'Jackman's Variety'), **H** 1.2m (4ft), has large, bright yellow flowers. **'Maanelys'** (syn. *P.* 'Maanelys', *P.* 'Manelys', *P.* 'Moonlight'), **H** 1.2m (4ft), **S** 2m (6ft), has soft yellow flowers and grey-green foliage. **'Manchu'** (syn. *P. davurica* var. *mandschurica* of gardens, *P.* 'Manchu') has pure white flowers and silvery-grey leaves. **'Red Ace'** (syn. *P.* 'Red Ace') illus. p.156. **'Royal Flush'** (syn. *P.* 'Royal Flush'), **H** 45cm (18in), **S** 75cm (30in), produces mid-green leaves and sometimes semi-double, yellow-stamened, rich pink flowers, fading to white in full sun. **'Sunset'** (syn. *P.* 'Sunset') illus. p.162. **'Tangerine'** (syn. *P.* 'Tangerine'), **H** 1.2m (4ft), bears yellow flowers, flushed with pale orange-red, amid mid-green leaves. **'Vilmoriniana'** (syn. *P.* 'Vilmoriniana') illus. p.159.
♀ ***P.* 'Gibson's Scarlet'.** Clump-forming perennial. **H** and **S** 45cm (18in). Bears saucer-shaped, brilliant scarlet flowers from mid- to late summer. Dark green leaves are strawberry-like.
***P.* 'Gloire de Nancy'**, syn. *P.* 'Glory of Nancy'. Clump-forming perennial. **H** and **S** 45cm (18in). Very large, saucer-shaped, semi-double, orange and coppery-red flowers appear throughout summer. Has strawberry-like, dark green leaves.
***P.* 'Glory of Nancy'.** See *P.* 'Gloire de Nancy'.
***P.* 'Goldfinger'.** See *P. fruticosa* 'Goldfinger'.
***P.* 'Jackman's Variety'.** See *P. fruticosa* 'Jackman 's Variety'.
***P.* 'Maanelys'.** See *P. fruticosa* 'Maanelys'.
***P.* 'Manchu'.** See *P. fruticosa* 'Manchu'.
***P.* 'Manelys'.** See *P. fruticosa* 'Maanelys'.
♀ ***P. megalantha*** illus. p.276.
***P.* 'Monsieur Rouillard'.** Clump-forming perennial. **H** and **S** 45cm (18in). Bears saucer-shaped, double, blood-red flowers in summer above strawberry-like, dark green leaves.
***P.* 'Moonlight'.** See *P. fruticosa* 'Maanelys'.
***P.* 'Nana Argentea'.** See *P. fruticosa* 'Beesii'.
♀ ***P. nepalensis* 'Miss Willmott'** illus. p.265.
P. nitida. Dense, mat-forming perennial. **H** 2.5–5cm (1–2in), **S** 20cm (8in). Has rounded, 3-lobed, silver leaves. Flower stems each carry 1–2 rose-pink flowers with dark centres in early summer. Is often shy-flowering. Suits a rock garden or trough.
***P. parvifolia* 'Gold Drop'.** See *P. fruticosa* 'Gold Drop'.
P. recta. Clump-forming, hairy perennial. **H** 60cm (24in), **S** 45cm (18in). From early to late summer, bears pale yellow flowers. **'Macrantha'** see *P.r.* 'Warrenii'. **'Warrenii'** (syn. *P.r.* 'Macrantha') has rich, golden-yellow flowers throughout summer..
***P.* 'Red Ace'.** See *P. fruticosa* 'Red Ace'.
***P.* 'Royal Flush'.** See *P. fruticosa* 'Royal Flush'.
***P.* 'Sunset'.** See *P. fruticosa* 'Sunset'.
***P.* 'Tangerine'.** See *P. fruticosa* 'Tangerine'.
♀ ***P.* x *tonguei*.** Mat-forming perennial. **H** 5cm (2in), **S** 25cm (10in). Has rounded, 3–5 lobed, dark green leaves. Prostrate branches bear flattish, orange-yellow flowers with red centres during summer. Is good for a rock garden.
***P.* 'Vilmoriniana'.** See *P. fruticosa* 'Vilmoriniana'.
♀ ***P.* 'William Rollison'.** Clump-forming perennial. **H** and **S** 45cm (18in). From mid- to late summer bears saucer-shaped, semi-double, scarlet-suffused, deep orange flowers with yellow centres. Has dark green leaves.
***P.* 'Yellow Queen'.** Clump-forming perennial. **H** to 60cm (24in) or more, **S** 45cm (18in). Has strawberry-like, dark green leaves. Produces bright yellow flowers in mid-summer.

Pothos. See *Epipremnum*.
x *Potinara* Cherub 'Spring Daffodil'. See x *Rhyncattleanthe* Cherub 'Spring Daffodil'.
Pratia. See *Lobelia*.

PRIMULA

Primrose

PRIMULACEAE

Genus of mainly herbaceous perennials, some woody-based and evergreen. All have leaves in basal rosettes and tubular, bell- or primrose-shaped (flat) flowers. In some primulas, the flower stems, leaves, sepals and, occasionally, sections of the petals are covered with a waxy powder known as farina. There are primulas suitable for almost every type of site: the border, scree garden, rock garden, peat garden, bog garden, pool margin, greenhouse and alpine house. Some may be difficult to grow as they dislike winter damp or summer heat. Fully hardy to frost tender, min. 7–10°C (45–50°F). Repot pot grown plants annually. Tidy up fading foliage and dead-head as flowering ceases. Propagate species by seed when fresh or in spring; increase selected forms when dormant, either by division in autumn–spring, or by root cuttings in winter. Propagate auricula primulas by offsets in early spring or early autumn. Border cultivars may be prone to slug damage in damp places and to attack by root aphids when grown in very dry conditions or in pots. Primulas are divided into many different horticultural groups, of which the following are in common use. See also feature panel pp.258–259.

Auricula primulas
These are evergreen primulas, derived from hybrids between *P. auricula* and *P. hirsuta*, producing flat, smooth flowers carried in an umbel on a stem above the foliage. There are 3 main sub-groups: alpine, show and border.

Alpine Auricula Group. In these, the colour of the flower centre is strikingly different from that of the petals. They may be either light-centred (white or pale in the centre) or gold-centred (yellow or gold in the centre). There is no meal or "farina" on either leaves or flowers. Grow in an alpine house or rock garden.

Show Auricula Group has flowers with a distinct circle of white meal or "paste" in the centre. Some are self-coloured, with one colour, which may be red, yellow, blue or violet, from the central paste to the petal margins; edged cultivars have a black ring surrounding the central paste, feathering out to an often green, grey or white margin; in fancy cultivars, the paste is surrounded by a colour other than black, with a green, grey or white margin. Show Auriculas have white farina on their foliage (except those with green-edged flowers), on their flower eyes and, sometimes, on their petal margins. Grow under glass to protect flowers from rain.

Border Auricula Group has generally robust, garden Auricula primulas, which are often very fragrant. Some have farina on flower stems and leaves. Grow in a mixed or herbaceous border.

Candelabra primulas

These are robust, herbaceous perennials with tubular, flat-faced flowers borne in tiered whorls up tall, sturdy stems. Some are deciduous, dying back to basal buds; others are semi-evergreen, dying back to reduced rosettes. Grow in moist shade or woodland, especially by streams.

Primrose-Polyanthus primulas

A diverse group of evergreen, semi-evergreen or deciduous perennial hybrids, derived from *P. vulgaris*, crossed with *P. veris*, *P. juliae* and other species. They are divided into two main groups.

Primrose Group Most produce solitary flowers among the leaves. Are mainly grown as herbaceous perennials, flowering in spring, or as biennial greenhouse container plants flowering in winter-spring.

Polyanthus Group Produce flowers in long-stalked umbels. Usually grown as biennials for bedding, sown in summer to flower in winter and the following spring, or under glass as winter- and spring-flowering container plants.

Cultivation

Primulas have varying cultivation requirements. For ease of reference, these have been grouped as follows:

1 – Full sun or partial shade, in moist, but well-drained, humus-rich soil.

2 – Partial shade, in deep, humus-rich, moist, neutral to acid soil.

3 – Deep or partial shade, in peaty, gritty, moist but sharply drained, acid soil. Protect from excessive winter wet.

4 – Under glass in an alpine house or frame. Avoid wetting foliage of mealy species and hybrids.

5 – Full sun with some midday shade, or partial shade, in moist but sharply drained, gritty, humus-rich, slightly alkaline soil.

6 – In a cool or temperate greenhouse, or as a houseplant, in bright, filtered light.

***P.* 'Adrian'.** Alpine Auricula primula. **H** and **S** 10cm (4in). Fully hardy. Produces flat, light to dark blue flowers, with light centres and paler margins, in mid- to late spring. Leaves are oval to rounded and mid-green. Is useful for exhibition. Cultivation group 1 or 4.

🏆 ***P. allionii*** (illus. p.257). Rosette-forming, evergreen perennial. **H** 7–10cm (3–4in), **S** 20cm (8in). Fully hardy, but better grown in an alpine house. Tubular, rose, mauve or white flowers cover a tight cushion of oval, mid-green leaves in spring. Cultivation group 4.

🏆 ***P. alpicola*** (illus. p.259). Compact, rosette-forming perennial. **H** 50cm (20in), **S** 30cm (12in). Fully hardy. Produces terminal clusters of pendent, bell-shaped, yellow to white or purple flowers on slender stems in early summer. Mid-green leaves are oval to lance-shaped. Cultivation group 2. **var. *alpicola*** (syn. *P.a.* var. *luna*) has soft sulphur-yellow flowers. **var. *luna*** see *P.a.* var. *alpicola*.

P. aurantiaca. Small, rosette-forming Candelabra primula. **H** 30cm (12in), **S** 40cm (16in). Fully hardy. Tubular, reddish-orange flowers are borne in early summer. Has long, broadly oval to lance-shaped, coarse, mid-green leaves. Cultivation group 2.

P. aureata (illus. p.259). Rosette-forming, evergreen perennial. **H** 15cm (6in), **S** 20cm (8in). Frost hardy. Bears small umbels of flat, cream to yellow flowers in spring. In summer, oval, toothed, mid-green leaves have purple-red midribs; in winter, leaves form tight buds covered with whitish farina. Cultivation group 3 or 4.

🏆 ***P. auricula.*** Rosette-forming, evergreen, sometimes white-mealy perennial. **H** 20cm (8in), **S** 25cm (10in). Fully hardy. Bears fragrant, flat, yellow flowers in large umbels in spring. Oval, soft, pale green to grey-green leaves are densely covered with white farina. Cultivation group 1, 4 or 5.

🏆 ***P.* Barnhaven Blues Group** (illus. p.258). Vigorous, rosette-forming, evergreen or semi-evergreen, Primrose Group primula. **H** and **S** 15–20cm (6–8in). Fully hardy. Flat flowers in a range of mainly dark blue shades, all with small, yellow eyes, are borne singly on reddish stems in spring. Has long, oval, slightly purple-tinted, green leaves. Cultivation group 1 or 2.

P. beesiana, syn. *P. bulleyana* subsp. *beesiana* (illus. p.258). Rosette-forming, deciduous or semi-evergreen Candelabra primula. **H** and **S** 60cm (2ft). Fully hardy. In summer, stout, white-mealy stems bear whorls of tubular, yellow-eyed, reddish-pink flowers. Has inversely lance-shaped to oval, toothed, mid-green leaves, with red midribs. Cultivation group 2.

***P.* Belarina Series.** Vigorous, rosette-forming, evergreen or semi-evergreen, Primrose Group primula. **H** 15cm (6in), **S** 23cm (9in). Fully to frost hardy. Has oval to lance-shaped, dark green leaves. In late winter and spring produces flat, fully double flowers with slightly ruffled petals. Cultivation group 1 or 2. **'Belarina Cobalt Blue'** (illus. p.258) has very dark green leaves and vivid deep blue flowers. **'Belarina Pink Ice'**, illus. p.303.

***P. bhutanica* 'Sherriff's Variety'**, syn. *P. whitei* 'Sherriff's Variety'. Rosette-forming perennial. **H** 15cm (6in), **S** 20cm (8in). Fully hardy, but often short-lived. In spring produces neat umbels of tubular, pale ice-blue to sky-blue flowers, with strongly-toothed petals and a greenish-yellow eye surrounded by a broad white zone, close to oval to lance-shaped, crinkled, mid-green leaves. Cultivation group 3.

***P.* 'Blairside Yellow'** (illus. p.259). Compact, border Auricula primula. **H** 10cm (4in), **S** 20cm (8in). Fully hardy. In early spring, bell-shaped, golden-yellow flowers nestle in a rosette of tiny, rounded to oval, pale green leaves. Cultivation group 2 or 5.

***P.* 'Blossom'.** Vigorous, alpine Auricula primula. **H** and **S** 10cm (4in). Fully hardy. Flat, deep crimson to bright red flowers with golden centres are borne profusely in spring. Has oval, dark green leaves. Is suitable for exhibition. Cultivation group 1 or 4.

🏆 ***P. bulleyana*** (illus. p.259). Rosette-forming, semi-evergreen, Candelabra primula. **H** and **S** 60cm (24in). Fully hardy. Tubular, deep orange flowers appear in early summer. Leaves are oval to lance-shaped, toothed and dark green. Cultivation group 2. **subsp. *beesiana*** see *P. beesiana*.

🏆 ***P.* Charisma Series.** Rosette-forming, semi-evergreen or evergreen, Primrose Group primula. **H** and **S** 20cm (8in). Frost hardy. Has inversely oval, wrinkled, dark green leaves. In spring produces tubular flowers in a variety of different colours or self-coloured. Usually grown as a biennial. Cultivation group 1, 2 or 6. **'Charisma Blue'** (illus. p.258) has yellow-eyed, blue to purple-blue flowers. **'Charisma Red'** (illus. p.257) has pink to red flowers, with yellow centres.

P. chionantha* subsp. *melanops, syn. *P. melanops*. Rosette-forming perennial. **H** 35cm (14in), **S** 50cm (20in). Fully hardy. In summer has umbels of pendent, narrowly funnel-shaped, deep violet-purple flowers, with black eyes, above long, strap-shaped, mid-green leaves. Cultivation group 2 or 4.

***P.* 'Chloë'.** Green-edged, show Auricula primula. **H** and **S** 10cm (4in). Fully hardy. In late spring produces flat, dark-green-edged flowers with a black body colour and brilliant white paste centres. Oval leaves are dark green and have no farina. Is good for exhibition. Cultivation group 4.

P. chungensis (illus. p.259). Vigorous, rosette-forming Candelabra primula. **H** 80cm (32in), **S** 60cm (24in). Fully hardy. In summer bears tiered whorls of tubular, orange flowers among oval to lance-shaped, mid-green leaves. Cultivation group 2.

P. clarkei. Small, rosette-forming perennial. **H** 7cm (3in), **S** 15cm (6in). Fully hardy. In spring has flat, rose-pink flowers, with yellow eyes, just above a clump of rounded to oval, pale green leaves. Cultivation group 2 or 4. Divide in late winter.

P. clusiana. Small, rosette-forming, evergreen perennial. **H** 8cm (3in), **S** 15cm (6in). Fully hardy. In spring bears umbels of tubular, rose-pink flowers with white eyes. Leaves are oval, glossy and mid-green. Cultivation group 4 or 5.

***P.* 'Craddock White'.** Rosette-forming, deciduous or semi-evergreen, Primrose Group primula. **H** to 12cm (5in), **S** 25cm (10in). Fully hardy. Fragrant, upward-facing, flat, white flowers, with yellow eyes, are borne in spring just above long, oval, red-veined, dark green leaves. Cultivation group 1 or 2.

***P.* Crescendo Series** (illus. p.258). Rosette-forming, evergreen or semi-evergreen, Polyanthus Group primula. **H** and **S** 20cm (8in). Fully hardy. Has inversely oval, wrinkled, dark green leaves. In spring produces umbels of flat, yellow-centred flowers. Is usually grown as a biennial. Cultivation group 1 or 2. 🏆**'Crescendo Bright Red'** (illus. p.258) has bright scarlet flowers. 🏆**'Crescendo Pink and Rose Shades'** (illus. p.257) produces flowers in shades of rich purplish-pink.

***P.* 'David Green'.** Rosette-forming, Primrose Group primula. **H** 10cm (4in), **S** 15–20cm (6–8in). Fully hardy. In spring, produces flat, bright crimson-purple flowers amid oval, coarse, mid-green leaves. Cultivation group 1 or 2.

***P.* 'Dawn Ansell'** (illus. p.257). Vigorous, evergreen or semi-evergreen, Primrose Group primula. **H** 20cm (8in), **S** 30cm (12in). Fully hardy. Has oval to lance-shaped, slightly toothed, fresh green leaves. In spring produces double, white flowers set in an enlarged, leafy green calyx. Cultivation group 2.

🏆 ***P. denticulata*** (Drumstick primula). Robust, rosette-forming perennial. **H** and **S** 45cm (18in). Fully hardy. From early to mid-spring, dense, rounded heads of flat, lilac, purple or pink flowers are borne on tops of stout stems. Mid-green leaves are broadly lance-shaped and toothed. Cultivation group 1 or 2. **var. *alba*** (illus. p.257) has white flowers.

***P.* 'Don Keefe'** (illus. p.258). Vigorous, rosette-forming, evergreen or semi-evergreen, Polyanthus Group primula. **H** and **S** 20cm (8in). Fully hardy. Reddish stems bear umbels of flat, slightly wavy flowers in soft orange-red, with tiny yellow eyes, in spring. Has long, oval, dark green leaves. Cultivation group 2.

***P.* 'Dreamer'.** Rosette-forming, Primrose Group primula. **H** 8–10cm (3–4in), **S** 15–20cm (6–8in). Half hardy. Has oval leaves and, in spring, bears flat flowers in cream, apricot, pink or rose-pink; all bicolours have darker eyes and yellow centres. Cultivation group 2.

P. edgeworthii. See *P. nana*.

🏆 ***P. elatior*** (Oxlip; illus. p.259). Variable, rosette-forming, evergreen or semi-evergreen perennial. **H** 30cm (12in), **S** 25cm (10in). Fully hardy. Has umbels of small, fragrant, tubular, yellow flowers in spring, above neat, oval to lance-shaped, toothed, mid-green leaves. Cultivation group 1 or 2.

***P.* 'Elizabeth Killelay'** (illus. p.258). Vigorous, rosette-forming, evergreen or semi-evergreen, Polyanthus Group primula. **H** and **S** 20cm (8in). Fully hardy. Small, fragrant, double, maroon flowers, with a creamy edge to each petal and a yellow eye, are borne in umbels on reddish stems in spring. Has long, oval, dark green leaves. Cultivation group 2.

***P.* 'E.R. Janes'.** Vigorous, rosette-forming, semi-evergreen, Primrose Group primula. **H** 10–15cm (4–6in), **S** 30–40cm (12–16in). Fully hardy. Flat, pale rose-pink flowers, flushed with orange, are borne in spring amid broadly oval, toothed, mid-green leaves. Cultivation group 1 or 2.

P. farinosa (Bird's-eye primrose). Rosette-forming perennial. **H** and **S** 25cm (10in). Fully hardy. In spring, umbels of tubular, lilac-pink, occasionally white, flowers are borne on short, stout stems. Oval, toothed, mid-green leaves are densely covered with white farina. Cultivation group 2 or 4.

P. flaccida, syn. *P. nutans* of gardens. Lax, rosette-forming, short-lived perennial. **H** 50cm (20in), **S** 30cm (12in). Fully hardy. In early summer, each stout stem produces a conical head of pendent, bell-shaped, lavender or violet flowers above narrowly oval, pale to mid-green leaves. Cultivation group 3 or 4.
♈ ***P. florindae*** illus. p.445.
P. forrestii (illus. p.259). Rosette-forming, evergreen perennial. **H** 60cm (24in), **S** 45cm (18in). Frost hardy. Dense umbels of flat, yellow flowers with orange eyes are borne in late spring or early summer. Has oval, toothed, dark green leaves. Cultivation group 4 or 5.
***P.* 'Francisca'** (illus. p.259). Vigorous, rosette-forming, evergreen or semi-evergreen, Polyanthus Group primula. **H** and **S** 20cm (8in) Fully hardy. In spring has umbels of large, flat, slightly ruffled, pale green flowers, each with a large, star-shaped, yellow eye marked with 5 slender, orange streaks. Cultivation group 2.
♈ ***P. frondosa*** (illus. p.257). Compact, rosette-forming perennial. **H** 15cm (6in), **S** 25cm (10in). Fully hardy. In spring bears umbels of flat, yellow-eyed, lilac-rose to reddish-purple flowers on short stems above neat, oval, mid-green leaves, densely covered with white farina. Cultivation group 2 or 4.
***P.* 'Garryarde Guinevere'.** See *P.* 'Guinevere'.
***P.* Gold-laced Group** (illus. p.259). Erect, semi-evergreen or evergreen, Polyanthus Group primulas. **H** 25cm (10in), **S** 30cm (12in). Fully hardy. Produces flat flowers, in a variety of colours, with gold-laced margins, from mid- to late spring. Leaves are oval and mid-green, sometimes tinged red. Raise annually by seed. Cultivation group 2 or 4.
P. gracilipes. Rosette-forming, evergreen or semi-evergreen perennial. **H** 1cm (4in), **S** 20cm (8in). Fully hardy. Tubular, purplish-pink flowers with greenish-yellow eyes are borne singly in spring or early summer among oval, wavy, toothed, mid-green leaves. Cultivation group 3 or 4.
***P.* Grand Burgundy Series.** Rosette-forming, semi-evergreen or evergreen, Polyanthus Group primula. **H** and **S** 15–20cm (6–8in). Frost hardy. Has inversely oval, wrinkled, mid- to dark green leaves. In spring produces umbels of tubular, yellow-eyed flowers in a variety of colours. Cultivation group 1, 2 or 6.
♈ ***P.* 'Guinevere'**, syn. *P.* 'Garryarde Guinevere' (illus. p.257). Vigorous, rosette-forming, evergreen Polyanthus Group primula. **H** 12cm (5in), **S** 25cm (10in). Fully hardy. Flat, purplish-pink flowers with yellow eyes are produced in spring among oval, toothed, bronze-green leaves. Cultivation group 2.
***P.* 'Harlow Carr'.** Rosette-forming, Alpine Auricula primula. **H** 10–15cm (4–6in), **S** 15–20cm (6–8in). Fully hardy. In spring produces flat, white flowers on short stems above oval, soft, mid-green leaves. Cultivation group 1 or 4.
P. helodoxa. See *P. prolifera.*
P. hirsuta, syn. *P. rubra*. Rosette-forming, evergreen perennial. **H** 10cm (4in), **S** 25cm (10in). Fully hardy. Produces small umbels of flat, rose or lilac flowers in spring. Has small, rounded to oval, sticky, mid-green leaves. Cultivation group 1, 2 or 4.
***P.* Husky Mixed.** Rosette-forming, evergreen or semi-evergreen, Primrose Group primula. **H** and **S** 20cm (8in). Fully hardy. Has inversely oval, wrinkled, dark green leaves. In late winter and spring produces flat, brightly yellow-eyed flowers in 8 colours. Is usually grown as a biennial. Cultivation group 1 or 2.
***P.* Husky Series [white]** (illus. p.257).
♈ ***P.* 'Inverewe'** (illus. p.258). Vigorous, rosette-forming, semi-evergreen, Candelabra primula. **H** 75cm (30in), **S** 60cm (24in). Fully hardy. Tubular, bright orange-red flowers are produced in summer on stems coated with white farina. Has oval to lance-shaped, toothed, coarse, mid-green leaves. Cultivation group 2.
P. ioessa. Rosette-forming perennial. Clustered heads of funnel-shaped, pink or pinkish-mauve, or sometimes white, flowers are borne in spring or early summer above oval to lance-shaped, toothed, mid-green leaves. Cultivation group 2, 3 or 4.
***P.* 'Janet'.** Vigorous, rosette-forming, alpine Auricula. **H** 15–20cm (6–8in), **S** 15cm (6in). Fully hardy. In spring, clusters of outward-facing, flat, purplish-pink flowers are produced above a rosette of oval to rounded, soft, mid-green leaves. Cultivation group 1 or 4. Propagate by offsets after flowering.
***P.* 'Janie Hill'.** Rosette-forming, alpine Auricula. **H** 10cm (4in), **S** 15cm (6in). Fully hardy. Flat, dark to golden-brown flowers, with golden centres, open in mid- to late spring. Has oval, mid-green leaves. Is useful for exhibition. Cultivation group 4 or 5.
P. japonica. Robust, rosette-forming, Candelabra primula. **H** and **S** 45cm (18in). Fully hardy. In early summer produces tubular, deep red flowers on stout stems above oval to lance-shaped, toothed, coarse, pale green leaves. Cultivation group 2. ♈ **'Miller's Crimson'** (illus. p.257) has intense crimson flowers. ♈ **'Postford White'** (illus. p.257) bears white flowers.
***P.* Joker Series**. Compact, rosette-forming, evergreen or semi-evergreen perennial. **H** 8–10cm (3–4in), **S** 25cm (10in). Half hardy. Has short-stemmed, inversely lance-shaped to oval, mid-green leaves. In spring, produces tubular flowers, in a range of colours, including bicolours, with yellow or creamy-yellow eyes. Is also available in selected colour variants. **'Cherry'** has mid-pink petals with crimson bases. **'Red and Gold'** has golden-yellow flowers with wide, red margins.
***P.* 'Kerbelpice'.** See *P.* Belarina Series Belarina Pink Ice.
♈ ***P. kewensis*** (illus. p.259). Rosette-forming, evergreen perennial. **H** 45cm (18in), **S** 20cm (8in). Half hardy. Produces whorls of fragrant, tubular, bright yellow flowers in early spring. Oval to spoon-shaped, toothed, mid-green leaves are sparsely covered with white farina. Cultivation group 6.
♈ ***P.* 'Lady Greer'** (illus. p.257). Semi-creeping, rosette-forming, semi-evergreen, Polyanthus Group primula. **H** and **S** 10–15cm (4–6in). Has umbels of fragrant, funnel-shaped, creamy-yellow flowers in spring. Small, bright green leaves are produced close to the ground. Cultivation group 2.
***P.* 'Linda Pope'**, syn. *P. marginata* 'Linda Pope'. Vigorous, rosette-forming, evergreen or semi-evergreen perennial derived from *P. marginata*. **H** 15cm (6in), **S** 30cm (12in). Fully hardy. In spring bears flat, mauve-blue flowers on short stems above oval, toothed, mid-green leaves covered with white farina. Cultivation group 4 or 5.
P. malacoides. Erect, rosette-forming, evergreen perennial, usually grown as an annual. **H** 30–45cm (12–18in), **S** 20cm (8in). Half hardy. In winter–spring, small, flat, single or double, pale lilac-purple, reddish-pink and white flowers are borne in whorls of decreasing size up slender, softly hairy stems. Leaves are dainty, oval, slightly frilly-margined, softly downy and pale green. Cultivation group 6.
***P.* 'Margaret Martin'** (illus. p.259). Rosette-forming, show Auricula primula. **H** 10cm (4in), **S** 15cm (6in). Fully hardy. Bears flat, grey-edged flowers, with a black body colour and white centres, in mid- to late spring. Has spoon-shaped, grey-green leaves covered with white farina. Is excellent for exhibition. Cultivation group 4.
♈ ***P. marginata.*** Rosette-forming, evergreen or semi-evergreen perennial. **H** 15cm (6in), **S** 30cm (12in). Fully hardy. In spring, clusters of funnel-shaped, blue-lilac flowers appear above oval, toothed, mid-green leaves densely covered with white farina. Cultivation group 4 or 5. **'Linda Pope'** see *P.* 'Linda Pope'.
♈ **'Prichard's Variety'** has lilac-purple flowers with white eyes.
***P.* 'Mark'** (illus. p.258). Vigorous, alpine Auricula primula. **H** and **S** 10cm (4in). Fully hardy. Produces flat, pink flowers, with light yellow centres, in spring. Has oval, vibrant green leaves. Is good for exhibition. Cultivation group 4.
***P.* 'Matthew Yates'** (illus. p.258). Vigorous, double auricula. **H** and **S** 12cm (5in). Fully hardy. Produces fully double, very dark blackish-red flowers in tight trusses in spring. Leaves are inversely oval and mid-green with some farina. Is good for exhibition. Cultivation group 1 or 4.
P. melanops. See *P. chionantha* subsp. *melanops*.
***P.* 'Miss Indigo'**, syn. *P. vulgaris* 'Miss Indigo' (illus. p.258). Vigorous, rosette-forming, evergreen or semi-evergreen perennial. **H** 20cm (8in), **S** 35cm (14in). Fully hardy. Has oval to lance-shaped, toothed, bright green leaves. In spring produces flat, double, deep rich purple flowers, with creamy-white tips. Cultivation group 2.
P. modesta. Rosette-forming perennial. **H** and **S** 20cm (8in). Fully hardy. Dense heads of small, tubular, pinkish-purple flowers appear on short stems in spring. Rounded to oval, mid-green leaves are covered with yellow farina. Cultivation group 1 or 4. **var. *fauriae***, **H** and **S** 5cm (2in), produces yellow-eyed, pinkish-purple flowers and leaves covered with white farina.
***P.* 'Moonstone'.** Rosette-forming, border Auricula primula. **H** 12cm (5in), **S** 15cm (6in). Fully hardy. Rounded, double, whitish- or greenish-yellow flowers are produced in profusion in spring. Leaves are oval and mid-green. Preferably, grow under glass. Cultivation group 4 or 5.
***P.* 'Mrs J.H. Wilson'**, syn. *P.* x *pubescens* 'Mrs J.H. Wilson'. Rosette-forming, alpine Auricula primula. **H** and **S** 10–15cm (4–6in). Fully hardy. Bears small umbels of flat, white-centred, purple flowers in spring. Oval leaves are greyish-green. Cultivation group 1 or 4.
P. nana, syn. *P. edgeworthii*. Rosette-forming perennial. **H** 10cm (4in), **S** 15cm (6in). Fully hardy. Flat, pale mauve flowers with white eyes appear singly among oval, toothed, pale green leaves in spring. Cultivation group 3 or 4.
P. nutans of gardens. See *P. flaccida*.
P. obconica. Erect, rosette-forming, evergreen perennial, usually grown as an annual. **H** 23–40cm (9–16in), **S** 25cm (10in). Frost tender to frost hardy. Flat, purple, lilac or white flowers, with yellow eyes, are borne in dense umbels during winter–spring. Leaves are oval, toothed, hairy and pale green. Cultivation group 6.
***P.* 'Orb'.** Neat, show Auricula primula. **H** and **S** 10cm (4in). Fully hardy. Flat, dark-green-edged flowers, each with a black body colour and a central zone of white paste, are produced from mid- to late spring. Has spoon-shaped, dark green leaves without farina. Is good for exhibition. Cultivation group 4.
***P.* Pacific Series.** Polyanthus Group primula. **H** and **S** 20–22cm (8–9in); dwarf: **H** 10–15cm (4–6in). Fully hardy. Rosette-forming perennial, normally grown as a biennial, with lance-shaped leaves. Has heads of large, fragrant, flat flowers in shades of blue, yellow, red, pink or white in spring. Cultivation group 1, 2, 4 or 6.
P. palinuri (illus. p.259). Rosette-forming, evergreen perennial. **H** and **S** 30cm (12in). Fully to frost hardy. One-sided clusters of semi-pendent, narrowly funnel-shaped, yellow flowers appear on thick stems in early summer. Has rounded to oval, lightly toothed, thick-textured, powdered, green leaves. Cultivation group 1 or 4; requires full sun.
P. petiolaris. Rosette-forming, evergreen perennial. **H** 10cm (4in), **S** 20cm (8in). Fully hardy. Tubular, purplish-pink flowers, with toothed petals, are borne singly in spring. Has small, oval, toothed, mid-green leaves. Cultivation group 3 or 4.
P. poissonii. Rosette-forming, evergreen perennial. **H** 45–50cm (18–20in), **S** 20–25cm (8–10in). Fully hardy. Has long, inversely lance-shaped, dark green leaves. Produces 4–5 whorls of tubular, plum-purple flowers, with golden (rarely white) eyes, in early and mid-summer. Cultivation Group 3.
P. polyneura (illus. p.258). Rosette-forming perennial. **H** and **S** 45cm (18in). Fully to frost hardy. Dense heads of tubular, pale rose, rich rose or purple-rose flowers are produced in late spring or early summer. Rounded to oval, shallowly lobed, downy, soft leaves are mid-green. Cultivation group 2.
♈ ***P. prolifera***, syn. *P. helodoxa*, illus. p.445.
***P.* x *pubescens* 'Mrs J.H. Wilson'.** See *P.* 'Mrs J.H. Wilson'.
♈ ***P. pulverulenta*** (illus. p.258). Rosette-

P
Q

forming, Candelabra primula. **H** 90cm (36in), **S** 60cm (24in). Fully hardy. In early summer bears tubular, deep red flowers with purple-red eyes on stems covered with white farina. Has broadly lance-shaped, toothed, coarse, mid-green leaves. Cultivation group 2. ♀ **'Bartley'** has pink flowers.
P. reidii. Robust, rosette-forming perennial. **H** 5–15cm (2–6in), **S** 10–15cm (4–6in). Fully to frost hardy. Produces dense clusters of bell-shaped, pure white flowers on slender stems in early summer. Has oval, hairy, pale green leaves. Cultivation group 3 or 4. **var. *williamsii*** is more robust and has purplish-blue to pale blue flowers.
♀ ***P. rosea.*** Rosette-forming perennial. **H** and **S** 20cm (8in). Fully hardy. In early spring bears small clusters of flat, glowing rose-pink flowers on short stems, among oval to lance-shaped, mid-green leaves, often bronze-flushed when young. Cultivation group 2.
***P.* 'Royal Velvet'.** Vigorous, rosette-forming, border Auricula primula. **H** and **S** 15–20cm (6–8in). Fully hardy. Flat, velvety, blue-tinged, maroon flowers, with frilled petals and large, creamy-yellow centres, are produced in spring. Has large, spoon-shaped, pale green leaves. Cultivation group 2 or 5.
P. rubra. See *P. hirsuta*.
P. x scapeosa. Vigorous, rosette-forming perennial. **H** 10cm (4in), **S** 25cm (10in). Fully hardy. Clusters of outward-facing, flat, mauve-pink flowers, in early spring, are initially hidden by broadly oval, sharply toothed, mid-green leaves covered at first with slight farina; later, flower stem elongates above leaves. Cultivation group 3 or 4.
P. secundiflora. Rosette-forming, evergreen or semi-evergreen perennial. **H** 60–90cm (24–36in), **S** 60cm (24in). Fully hardy. Has clusters of pendent, funnel-shaped, reddish-purple flowers in summer above lance-shaped, toothed leaves. Cultivation group 2.
♀ ***P. sieboldii*** (illus. p.258). Rosette-forming perennial. **H** 30cm (12in), **S** 45cm (18in). Fully hardy. Umbels of flat, white, pink or purple flowers, with white eyes, open above oval, round-toothed, downy, soft, pale green leaves in early summer. Cultivation group 2. **'Geisha Girl'** (illus. p.257) bears large, pink flowers with deeply cut petals. **'Sumina'** bears large, wisteria-blue flowers. **'Wine Lady'** has white flowers, strongly suffused with purplish-red.
♀ ***P. sikkimensis*** (illus. p.259). Rosette-forming perennial. **H** 60–90cm (24–36in), **S** 60cm (24in). Fully hardy. Pendent clusters of funnel-shaped, yellow flowers are borne in summer. Has rounded to oval, toothed, pale green leaves. Cultivation group 2.
P. sinensis. Erect, rosette-forming, evergreen perennial. **H** and **S** 15–20cm (6–8in). Frost tender. Flat, purple, purple-rose, pink or white flowers, with yellow eyes, are produced in neat whorls in winter–spring. Leaves are oval, toothed, hairy and mid-green. Cultivation group 6.
P. sonchifolia. Rosette-forming, deciduous perennial. **H** 5cm (2in), **S** 30cm (12in). Fully hardy. Produces dense umbels of tubular, blue-purple flowers with white eyes and yellow margins in spring. Leaves are oval to lance-shaped, toothed and mid-green. Cultivation group 3 or 4.
***P.* Super Giants Series.** Rosette-forming Polyanthus Group primulas, usually grown as biennials. **H** and **S** 15–20cm (6–8in). Fully hardy. Produce large, fragrant, flat flowers in a wide range of colours in spring. Cultivation group 1 or 2.
***P.* 'Tawny Port'.** Very dwarf, rosette-forming, evergreen or semi-evergreen, Polyanthus Group primula. **H** 10–15cm (4–6in), **S** 15–20cm (6–8in). Fully hardy. Bears flat, port-wine-coloured flowers on short stems in spring. Rounded to oval, toothed leaves are reddish-green. Cultivation group 1, 2 or 4.
***P.* 'Trouble'** (illus. p.259). Vigorous, double auricula. **H** and **S** 12cm (5in). Fully hardy. Leaves are broad, inversely oval, mid-green and irregularly toothed. Produces fully double flowers, a blend of yellow and pink, resulting in pale coffee-coloured blooms borne in tight trusses in spring. Cultivation group 1 or 4.
♀ ***P. veris*** illus. p.263. **'Katy McSparron'** (illus. p.259) bears fully double flowers with an enlarged, greyish calyx.
P. verticillata (illus. p.259). Rosette-forming perennial. **H** 20–25cm (8–10in), **S** 15–20cm (6–8in). Half hardy. Fragrant, bell-shaped, yellow flowers are borne in whorls in spring. Has oval, toothed, mid-green leaves. Cultivation group 4 or 6.
♀ ***P. vialii*** (illus. p.257). Rosette-forming, often short-lived perennial. **H** 30–60cm (12–24in), **S** 30cm (12in). Fully to frost hardy. Dense, conical spikes of tubular, bluish-purple and red flowers are produced in late spring. Has lance-shaped, toothed, soft, mid-green leaves. Cultivation group 1 or 2.
♀ ***P. vulgaris*** (Primrose; illus. p.259). Rosette-forming, evergreen or semi-evergreen perennial. **H** 20cm (8in), **S** 35cm (14in). Fully hardy. Flat, soft yellow flowers, with darker eyes, are borne singly among oval to lance-shaped, toothed, bright green leaves in spring. Cultivation group 2. **'Alba Plena'** (illus. p.257) has double, white flowers. **'Gigha White'** is very floriferous and has yellow-eyed, white flowers. **'Lilacina Plena'** is vigorous and free-flowering, with fully double, lilac-purple flowers. **'Miss Indigo'** see *P.* 'Miss Indigo'. ♀ **subsp. *sibthorpii*** (illus. p.258) has pink or purplish-pink flowers.
***P.* Wanda Supreme Series.** Evergreen or semi-evergreen perennial. **H** 8–10cm (3–4in), **S** 15cm (6in). Frost hardy. Has inversely lance-shaped to oval, bronze to dark green foliage. From winter to mid-spring, has flowers in different shades of blue, yellow, purple, burgundy, red, rose and pink bicolours. Cultivation group 1 or 2.
P. warshenewskiana. Rosette-forming perennial. **H** 7cm (3in), **S** 15cm (6in). Fully hardy. Tiny, flat, white-eyed, bright pink flowers sit just above spoon-shaped, dark green leaves in early spring. Cultivation group 2 or 4. Divide clumps regularly in late winter before flowering.
***P. whitei* 'Sherriff's Variety'.** See *P. bhutanica* 'Sherriff's Variety'.
***P.* 'Woodland Walk'** (illus. p.257) Rosette-forming, evergreen or semi-evergreen, Primrose Group primula. **H** and **S** 20cm (8in). Fully hardy. Has inversely oval, wrinkled, dark green leaves tinted with bronze. In late winter and spring, flat flowers, with heart-shaped petals, are borne on single stems and range in colour from faintly pink-tinted white to vivid pink, each petal edged in darker pink. Cultivation group 2.
***P.* 'Yellow Dream'.** Rosette-forming, Polyanthus Group primula. **H** and **S** 15–23cm (6–9in). Fully hardy. Has ovate, toothed leaves. Produces large, fragrant bright yellow flower heads, with slightly darker yellow centres, in late winter and spring.

PRINSEPIA

ROSACEAE

Genus of deciduous, usually spiny, spring- and early summer-flowering shrubs, grown for their habit, flowers and fruits. Fully hardy. Needs sun and any not too dry soil. Does well against a south- or west-facing wall. Propagate by softwood cuttings in summer or by seed in autumn.
P. uniflora illus. p.129.

PROBOSCIDEA

MARTYNIACEAE/PEDALIACEAE

Genus of annuals and perennials. Half hardy. Grow in a sunny, sheltered position and in fertile, well-drained soil. Propagate by seed sown under glass in early spring.
P. fragrans. Moderately fast-growing, upright annual. **H** 60cm (24in), **S** 30cm (12in). Has rounded, serrated or lobed leaves. Fragrant, bell-shaped, crimson-purple flowers, to 5cm (2in) long, appear in summer–autumn, followed by rounded, horned, brown fruits, 8–10cm (3–4in) long, which, if gathered young, may be pickled and eaten.
P. jussieui. See *P. louisianica*.
P. louisianica, syn. *Martynia louisianica*, *P. jussieui*, *P. proboscidea* (Common devil's claw, Common unicorn plant, Ram's horn). Erect to spreading annual. Has rounded to ovate, unlobed leaves. In summer, bears funnel-shaped, fragrant, reddish-purple to purple flowers, followed by narrow, crested fruit, to 6cm (2½in) long, with beak-like projections.
P. proboscidea. See *P. louisianica*.

Prometheum sempervivoides. See *Sedum sempervivoides*.

PROSTANTHERA

Mint bush

LABIATAE/LAMIACEAE

Genus of evergreen shrubs, grown for their flowers and mint-scented foliage. Frost hardy to frost tender, min. 5°C. Requires full light or partial shade and fertile, well-drained soil. Water containerized specimens freely when in full growth, moderately at other times. Leggy stems may be cut back after flowering. Propagate by seed in spring or by semi-ripe cuttings in late summer.
♀ ***P. cuneata*** illus. p.197.
P. lasianthos. Evergreen, erect shrub. **H** and **S** to 2m (6ft). Half hardy. Has lance-shaped, aromatic, mid-green leaves. In spring produces branched, terminal panicles of 2-lipped, purple-tinted, white or cream flowers in profusion.
P. melissifolia. Evergreen, erect shrub. **H** and **S** 2m (6ft). Frost tender, min. 5°C (41°F). Has ovate-elliptic, very aromatic, mid-green leaves. In summer produces terminal racemes of 2-lipped, bright lilac, purple or pink flowers.
♀ ***P. ovalifolia*** illus. p.457.
♀ ***P. rotundifolia*** illus. p.138. ♀ **'Rosea'** (syn. 'Chelsea Pink') illus. p.192.

PROTEA

PROTEACEAE

Genus of evergreen shrubs and trees, grown mainly for their colourfully bracted flower heads. Is difficult to grow. Frost tender, min. 5–7°C (41–45°F). Requires full light and well-drained, neutral to acid soil, low in phosphates and nitrates. Water containerized specimens moderately, less when not in full growth. Plants under glass must have plenty of ventilation throughout the year. Prune, if necessary, in early spring. Propagate by seed in spring or by semi-ripe cuttings in summer.
P. barbigera. See *P. magnifica*.
P. cynaroides illus. p.454.
P. magnifica, syn. *P. barbigera*. Evergreen, rounded to spreading shrub. **H** and **S** 1m (3ft). Has oblong to elliptic, leathery, mid- to greyish-green leaves. Spherical flower heads, 15–20cm (6–8in) wide, with petal-like, pink, red, yellow or white bracts, appear in spring–summer.
P. mellifera. See *P. repens*.
P. neriifolia illus. p.454.
P. repens, syn. *P. mellifera* (Sugar bush). Evergreen, ovoid to rounded shrub. **H** and **S** 2–3m (6–10ft). Mid-green leaves are narrowly oblong to elliptic and tinted blue-grey. In spring–summer produces cup-shaped, 13cm (5in) long flower heads, with petal-like, pink, red or white bracts.

PRUMNOPITYS

PODOCARPACEAE

See also CONIFERS.
P. andina, syn. *Podocarpus andinus* (Plum yew, Plum-fruited yew). Conifer with a domed crown on several stems. **H** 15m (50ft), **S** 8m (25ft). Frost hardy. Has smooth, grey-brown bark, needle-like, flattened, bluish-green leaves and edible, yellowish-white fruits like small plums.

PRUNELLA

Self-heal

LABIATAE/LAMIACEAE

Genus of semi-evergreen perennials with spreading mats of leaves from which arise short, stubby flower spikes in mid-summer. Suits rock gardens. Fully hardy. Grows well in a position in sun or shade and in moist but well-drained soil. Propagate by division in spring.
P. grandiflora, syn. *P. x webbiana*, illus. p.368. ♀ **'Loveliness'** , basal-rosetted, ground-cover perennial. **H** 10–15cm (4–6in), **S** 30cm (12in). Bears whorls of pale purple flowers in terminal spikes on leafy stems in summer. May be invasive; cut old flower stems before they seed. **'Pink Loveliness'** bears soft pink flowers in

terminal spikes in summer. Makes good ground cover, but may be invasive. Cut off old flower stems before they produce seed. **'White Loveliness'** has white flowers.
***P.* x *webbiana*.** See *P. grandiflora*.

PRUNUS

Cherry

ROSACEAE

Genus of deciduous or evergreen shrubs and trees. The trees are grown mainly for their single (5-petalled) to double flowers and autumn colour; the shrubs for their autumn colour, bark, flowers or fruits. All have oval to oblong leaves. Plants described here are fully hardy, unless otherwise stated. Evergreen species tolerate sun or shade; deciduous species prefer full sun. All may be grown in any but waterlogged soil. Trim deciduous hedges after flowering, evergreen ones in early or mid-spring. Propagate deciduous species by seed in autumn, deciduous hybrids and selected forms by softwood cuttings in summer. Increase evergreens by semi-ripe cuttings in summer. Bullfinches may eat flower buds and foliage may be attacked by aphids, caterpillars and the fungal disease silver leaf. Flowering cherries are prone to a fungus that causes "witches" brooms' (abnormal, crowded shoots). Certain *Prunus* species and cultivars, notably cultivars of the almond (*P. dulcis*) and the peach (*P. persica*), are grown for their edible fruits. ⓘ Leaves and fruits of most other species may cause severe discomfort if ingested.

PQ

♀ ***P.* 'Accolade'** illus. p.83.
♀ ***P.* 'Amanogawa'.** Deciduous, upright tree. **H** 10m (30ft), **S** 4m (12ft). Bears fragrant, semi-double, pale pink flowers in late spring. Oblong to oval, taper-pointed, dark green leaves turn orange and red in autumn.
***P.* x *amygdalopersica* 'Pollardii'.** See *P.* x *persicoides*.
♀ ***P. avium*** illus. p.67. ♀ **'Plena'** illus. p.71.
♀ ***P.* x *blireana*.** Deciduous, spreading shrub or small tree. **H** and **S** 4m (12ft). Bears double, pink flowers in mid-spring and has oval, purple leaves.
P. campanulata (Bell-flowered cherry, Taiwan cherry). Deciduous, spreading tree. **H** and **S** 8m (25ft). Frost hardy. Shallowly bell-shaped, deep rose-red flowers are produced from early to mid-spring, before or with oval, taper-pointed, dark green leaves. Fruits are small, rounded and reddish.
P. cerasifera (Cherry plum, Myrobalan). ♀ **'Nigra'** illus. p.86. **'Pissardii'** is a deciduous, round-headed tree. **H** and **S** 10m (30ft). Small, 5-petalled, pale pink flowers open from early to mid-spring and are often followed by edible, plum-like, red fruits. Has oval, red, young leaves turning deeper red, then purple. May be used for hedging.
***P.* 'Cheal's Weeping'.** See *P.* 'Kiku-shidare-zakura'.
♀ ***P.* x *cistena*** illus. p.146.
P. davidiana (David's peach). Deciduous, spreading tree. **H** and **S** 8m (25ft). Saucer-shaped, 5-petalled, white or pale pink flowers are carried on slender shoots in late winter and early spring, but are susceptible to late frosts. Leaves are narrowly oval and dark green. Fruits are rounded and reddish.
P. dulcis (Almond). **'Roseoplena'** is a deciduous, spreading tree. **H** and **S** 8m (25ft). Bears double, pink flowers in late winter and early spring, before oblong, pointed, toothed, dark green leaves.
***P. glandulosa* 'Alba Plena'** illus. p.145. **'Rosea Plena'** see *P.g.* 'Sinensis'.
♀ **'Sinensis'** (syn. *P.g.* 'Rosea Plena') is a deciduous, rounded, open shrub. **H** and **S** 1.5m (5ft). Produces double, bright rose-pink flowers in late spring and oval, mid-green leaves. Flowers best when grown against a south- or west-facing wall. Cut back young shoots to within a few buds of old wood after flowering.
***P.* 'Hally Jolivette'.** Deciduous, rounded, compact tree. **H** and **S** 5m (15ft). Double, white flowers open from pink buds in late spring. Leaves are oval and dark green.
***P.* x *hillieri* 'Spire'.** See *P.* 'Spire'.
***P.* 'Hokusai'**, syn. *P.* 'Uzuzakura', illus. p.82.
P. incisa (Fuji cherry) illus. p.81. **'February Pink'** is a deciduous, spreading tree. **H** and **S** 8m (25ft). Oval, sharply toothed, dark green leaves are reddish when young, orange-red in autumn. During mild, winter periods bears 5-petalled, pale pink flowers. Has tiny, rounded, reddish fruits.
P. jamasakura, syn. *P. serrulata* var. *spontanea*, illus. p.71.
♀ ***P.* 'Kanzan'** illus. p.72.
♀ ***P.* 'Kiku-shidare-zakura'**, syn. *P.* 'Cheal's Weeping', illus. p.83.
♀ ***P.* 'Kursar'.** Deciduous, spreading tree. **H** and **S** 8m (25ft). Bears masses of small, 5-petalled, deep pink flowers in early spring. Oval, dark green leaves turn brilliant orange in autumn.
♀ ***P. laurocerasus*** (Cherry laurel, Laurel). Evergreen, dense, bushy shrub becoming spreading and open. **H** 6m (20ft), **S** 10m (30ft). Frost hardy. Has long spikes of small, single, white flowers from mid- to late spring, large, oblong, glossy, bright green leaves and cherry-shaped, red, then black fruits. Restrict growth by cutting back hard in spring. ♀ **'Otto Luyken'** illus. p.145. **'Schipkaensis'**, **H** 2m (6ft), **S** 3m (10ft), is fully hardy and of elegant, spreading habit, with narrow leaves and freely borne flowers in upright spikes. **'Zabeliana'** illus. p.145.
♀ ***P. lusitanica*** (Laurel, Portugal laurel). Evergreen, bushy, dense shrub or spreading tree. **H** and **S** 6–10m (20–30ft). Frost hardy. Reddish-purple shoots bear oval, glossy, dark green leaves. Slender spikes of small, fragrant, 5-petalled, white flowers appear in early summer, followed by egg-shaped, fleshy, deep purple fruits. Restrict growth by pruning hard in spring. **subsp. *azorica*** illus. p.119. **'Variegata'** illus. p.119.
***P. maackii*.** Deciduous, spreading tree. **H** 10m (30ft), **S** 8m (25ft). Has peeling, yellowish-brown bark. Produces spikes of small, white flowers in mid-spring. Pointed, dark green leaves turn yellow in autumn..
P. mahaleb illus. p.71.
***P.* 'Mount Fuji'.** See *P.* 'Shirotae'.
***P. mume* 'Beni-chidori'** syn. *P.m.* 'Beni-shidon', illus. p.123. **'Omoi-no-mama'** (syn. *P.m.* 'Omoi-no-wac') is a deciduous, spreading shrub. **H** and **S** 2.5m (8ft). Has fragrant, semi-double, occasionally single, pink-flushed, white flowers wreathing young growths in early spring, before broadly oval, toothed leaves appear. Sometimes produces edible, apricot-like, yellow fruits.**'Pendula'**, **H** and **S** 6m (20ft), has weeping branches and pink flowers
♀ ***P.* 'Okame'.** Deciduous, bushy-headed tree. **H** 10m (30ft), **S** 8m (25ft). Bears masses of 5-petalled, carmine-pink flowers in early spring. Oval, sharply toothed, dark green leaves turn orange-red in autumn.
P. padus (Bird cherry). Deciduous, spreading tree, conical when young. **H** 15m (50ft), **S** 10m (30ft). Bears fragrant, white flowers in pendent spikes in late spring, followed by small, black fruits. Dark green leaves turn yellow in autumn.
♀ **'Colorata'** illus. p.72. **'Grandiflora'** see *P.p.* 'Watereri'. **'Plena'** has double, pink flowers and oval, reddish-purple young leaves that mature to dark green and then turn to red or yellow in autumn.
♀ **'Watereri'**, illus. p.71. (syn. *P.p.* 'Grandiflora') bears long racemes of flowers from mid- to late spring.
♀ ***P.* 'Pandora'** illus. p.82.
♀ ***P. pendula* 'Pendula Rubra'.** See *P.* x *subhirtella* 'Pendula Rubra'. **'Stellata'** (syn. *P.* 'Pink Star', *P.* x *subhirtella* 'Stellata') illus. p.83.
P. pensylvanica (Pin cherry). Deciduous, spreading tree. **H** 15m (50ft), **S** 10m (30ft). Has peeling, red-banded bark and oval, taper-pointed, bright green leaves. Produces clusters of small, star-shaped, 5-petalled, white flowers from mid- to late spring, then small, pea-shaped, red fruits.
P. persica (Peach). **'Clara Meyer'** is a deciduous, spreading tree. **H** 5m (15ft), **S** 6m (20ft). Bears double, bright pink flowers in mid-spring. Has slender, lance-shaped, bright green leaves. Is susceptible to the fungal disease peach leaf curl. **'Prince Charming'** illus. p.83.
P.* x *persicoides, syn. *P. amygdalopersica* **'Pollardii'**. Deciduous, spreading tree. **H** and **S** 7m (22ft). Large, 5-petalled, bright pink flowers open from early to mid-spring, before oval, glossy, mid-green leaves emerge. Green, then brown fruits are like almonds in shape and taste.
♀ ***P.* 'Pink Perfection'** illus. p.83.
***P.* 'Pink Shell'** illus. p.84.
***P.* 'Pink Star'.** See *P. pendula* 'Stellata'.
♀ ***P. sargentii*** illus. p.77.
P. serotina illus. p.66.
♀ ***P. serrula*** (illus. p.78). Deciduous, round-headed tree. **H** and **S** 10m (30ft). Has gleaming, coppery-red bark that peels. In late spring bears small, 5-petalled, white flowers amid oval, tapering, toothed, dark green leaves that turn yellow in autumn. Fruits are tiny, rounded and reddish-brown.
***P. serrulata* var. *spontanea*.** See *P. jamasakura*.
***P.* 'Shimidsu'.** See *P.* 'Shogetsu'
♀ ***P.* 'Shirofugen'** illus. p.83.
♀ ***P.* 'Shirotae'**, syn. *P.* 'Mount Fuji', illus. p.82.
♀ ***P.* 'Shogetsu'**, syn. *P.* 'Shimidsu', illus. p.81.
P. spinosa (Blackthorn, Sloe). **'Purpurea'** illus. p.115.
♀ ***P.* 'Spire'**, syn. *P.* x *hillieri* 'Spire', illus. p.82.
P.* x *subhirtella (Higan cherry, Rosebud cherry). Deciduous, spreading tree. **H** and **S** 8m (25ft). From early to mid-spring, a profusion of small, 5-petalled, pale pink flowers appear before oval, taper-pointed, dark green leaves, which turn yellow in autumn. Has small, rounded, reddish-brown fruits. ♀ **'Autumnalis'** semi-double,white flowers, pink in bud, in mild periods in winter. ♀ **'Pendula Rubra'** (syn. *P. pendula* 'Pendula Rubra') illus. p.83. **'Stellata'** see *P. pendula* 'Stellata'.
♀ ***P.* 'Taihaku'** illus. p.82.
P. tenella illus. p.146. ♀ **'Fire Hill'** is a deciduous, bushy shrub with upright, then spreading branches. **H** and **S** 2m (6ft). Narrowly oval, glossy, dark green leaves are a foil for small, almond-like, single, very deep pink flowers borne profusely from mid- to late spring, followed by small, almond-like fruits.
P. tomentosa (Downy cherry). Deciduous, bushy, dense shrub. **H** 1.5m (5ft), **S** 2m (6ft). Has small, 5-petalled, pale pink flowers from early to mid-spring before oval, downy, dark green leaves appear. Fruits are spherical and bright red. Thrives in hot summers.
***P.* 'Trailblazer'.** Deciduous, spreading tree. **H** and **S** 5m (15ft). Bears 5-petalled, white flowers from early to mid-spring, sometimes followed by edible, plum-like, red fruits. Oval, light green, young leaves mature to deep red-purple.
***P. triloba* 'Multiplex'.** Deciduous, bushy, spreading tree or shrub. **H** and **S** 4m (12ft). Double, pink flowers are borne in mid-spring. Has oval, dark green leaves, often 3-lobed, that turn yellow in autumn. Does best against a sunny wall. Cut back young shoots to within a few buds of old wood after flowering.
♀ ***P.* 'Ukon'** illus. p.82.
***P.* 'Uzuzakura'.** See *P.* 'Hokusai'.
P. virginiana (Virginian bird cherry). **'Schubert'** is a deciduous, conical tree. **H** 10m (30ft), **S** 8m (25ft). Produces dense spikes of small, star-shaped, white flowers from mid- to late spring, followed by dark purple-red fruits. Has oval, pale green, young leaves, turning deep reddish-purple in summer.
***P.* 'Yae-murasaki'** illus. p.82.
P.* x *yedoensis illus. p.82.

PSEUDERANTHEMUM

ACANTHACEAE

Genus of evergreen perennials and shrubs, grown mainly for their foliage. Frost tender, min. 16°C (61°F). Requires partial shade and fertile, well-drained soil. Water potted plants freely when in full growth, moderately at other times. Tip prune young plants to promote a bushy habit. Cut leggy plants back hard in spring. Propagate annually or biennially as a pot plant by greenwood cuttings in spring or summer. Whitefly may sometimes be troublesome.
P. atropurpureum, syn. *Eranthemum atropurpureum*. Evergreen, erect shrub. **H** 1–1.2m (3–4ft), **S** 30–6 0cm (1–2ft). Has oval, strongly purple-flushed leaves and, mainly in summer, short spikes of tubular, purple-marked, white flowers.

PSEUDOCYDONIA

ROSACEAE

Genus of one species of deciduous or semi-evergreen, spring-flowering tree, grown for its bark, flowers and fruits. Frost hardy, but in cool areas grow against a south- or west-facing wall. Requires full sun and does well only in hot summers. Needs well-drained soil. Propagate by seed in autumn.

P. sinensis, syn. *Cydonia sinensis*. Deciduous or semi-evergreen, spreading tree. **H** and **S** 6m (20ft). Has decorative, flaking bark. Shallowly cup-shaped, pink flowers, borne from mid- to late spring, are followed after hot summers by large, egg-shaped, yellow fruits. Oval, finely toothed leaves are dark green.

Pseudofumaria lutea. See *Corydalis lutea.*

Pseudofumaria ochroleuca. See *Corydalis ochroleuca.*

PSEUDOGYNOXYS

ASTERACEAE/COMPOSITAE

Genus of about 15 species of half hardy shrubs and climbers grown for their large yellow and orange daisy-like flowers. Propagate by semi-ripe cuttings and layering in summer or seed in autumn.

P. chenopodioides, syn. *Senecio confusus* (Mexican flame vine). Evergreen, woody-stemmed, twining climber. **H** to 3m (10ft) or more. Min. 7–10°C (45–50°F). Bears clusters of daisy-like, orange-yellow flower heads, ageing to orange-red, mainly in summer.

Pseudogynoxys chenopodioides. See *Senecio confusus.*

PSEUDOLARIX

PINACEAE

See also CONIFERS.

♀ ***P. amabilis***, syn. *P. kaempferi*, illus. p.102.

P. kaempferi. See *P. amabilis.*

Pseudolobivia aurea. See *Echinopsis aurea.*

Pseudomuscari azureum. See *Muscari azureum.*

PSEUDOPANAX

SYN. NOTHOPANAX

ARALIACEAE

Genus of evergreen trees and shrubs, grown for their unusual foliage and fruits. Is excellent for landscaping and may also be grown in large containers. Insignificant flowers are produced in summer. Frost to half hardy. Grows in sun or semi-shade and in fertile, well-drained soil. Propagate by semi-ripe cuttings in summer or by seed in autumn or spring.

P. arboreus. See *Neopanax arboreus.*

P. crassifolius (Lancewood). Evergreen tree, unbranched for many years, then becoming round-headed. **H** 6m (20ft), **S** 2m (6ft). Frost hardy. Dark green leaves are very variable in shape on young trees, but eventually become long, narrow, rigid and downward-pointing on older specimens. Female plants bear small, rounded, black fruits.

P. ferox illus. p.88.

P. laetus. See *Neopanax laetus.*

PSEUDOSASA

GRAMINEAE/POACEAE

See also GRASSES, BAMBOOS, RUSHES and SEDGES.

♀ ***P. japonica***, syn. *Arundinaria japonica*, illus. p.287.

PSEUDOTSUGA

PINACEAE

See also CONIFERS.

P. douglasii. See *P. menziesii.*

♀ ***P. menziesii***, syn. *P. douglasii*, *P. taxifolia* (Douglas fir). Fast-growing, conical conifer. **H** 25m (80ft), **S** 8–12m (25–40ft). Fully hardy. Has thick, corky, fissured, grey-brown bark. Spirally arranged, aromatic, needle-like, slightly flattened leaves, which develop from sharply pointed buds, are dark green with white bands beneath. Elliptic cones, 8–10cm (3–4in) long, with projecting bracts, are dull brown. **'Fletcheri'**, **H** 3m (10ft), **S** 2–3m (6–10ft), makes a flat-topped shrub. **'Fretsii'**, **H** 6m (20ft) or more, **S** 3–4m (10–12ft), is slow-growing, with very short, dull green leaves. **var. *glauca*** illus. p.96. **'Oudemansii'** is very slow-growing, with ascending branches and short, glossy leaves, dark green all over.

P. taxifolia. See *P. menziesii.*

PSEUDOWINTERA

WINTERACEAE

Genus of evergreen shrubs and trees, grown for their foliage. Frost to half hardy. Needs full light or partial shade and humus-rich, well-drained but moisture-retentive soil, ideally neutral to acid. Water containerized plants freely when in full growth, only moderately at other times. Pruning is tolerated if needed. Propagate by semi-ripe cuttings taken in summer or by seed when ripe, in autumn, or in spring.

P. axillaris, syn. *Drimys axillaris* (Heropito, Pepper-tree). Evergreen, rounded shrub or tree. **H** and **S** 3–8m (10–25ft). Half hardy. Has oval, lustrous, mid-green leaves, blue-grey beneath. Tiny, star-shaped, greenish-yellow flowers appear in spring–summer, followed by bright red fruits.

P. colorata, syn. *Drimys colorata*. Evergreen, bushy, spreading shrub. **H** 1m (3ft), **S** 1.5m (5ft). Half hardy. Has oval, leathery, pale yellow-green leaves, to 8cm (3in) long, blotched with pink and narrowly edged with deep red-purple; undersides are bluish-white. Clusters of 2–5 small, star-shaped, greenish-yellow flowers appear in mid-spring. Provide shelter in all but the mildest areas.

PSYCHOPSIS

ORCHIDACEAE

See also ORCHIDS.

P. papilio, syn. *Oncidium papilio* (Butterfly orchid; illus. p.467). Evergreen, epiphytic orchid for a warm greenhouse. **H** 15cm (6in). In summer, rich yellow-marked, orange-brown flowers, 8cm (3in) long, are borne singly and in succession on tops of stems. Has oval, semi-rigid, mottled leaves, 10–15cm (4–6in) long. Grow in good light in summer.

PSYLLIOSTACHYS

Statice

PLUMBAGINACEAE

Genus of annuals, perennials and evergreen sub-shrubs, grown for cut flowers and for drying. Is suitable for coastal areas. Fully to half hardy. Grow in sun and fertile, well-drained soil. If required for drying, cut flowers before they are fully open. Cut down dead stems of perennials in autumn. Propagate by seed sown under glass in early spring; perennials and sub-shrubs may also be increased by softwood cuttings in spring. Botrytis and powdery mildew may be troublesome.

P. suworowii, syn. *Limonium suworowii*, *Statice suworowii*. Fairly slow-growing, erect, branching annual. **H** 45cm (18in), **S** 30cm (12in). Half hardy. Has lance-shaped leaves. Bears branching spikes of small, tubular, pink to purple flowers in summer and early autumn.

PTELEA

RUTACEAE

Genus of deciduous trees and shrubs, grown for their foliage and fruits. Fully hardy. Needs sun and fertile soil. Propagate species by softwood cuttings in summer or by seed in autumn, selected forms by softwood cuttings only in summer.

P. trifoliata (Hop tree). Deciduous, bushy, spreading tree or shrub. **H** and **S** 7m (22ft). Produces aromatic, dark green leaves with 3 narrowly oval leaflets. Clusters of small, star-shaped, green flowers from early to mid-summer are succeeded by clusters of winged, pale green fruits. ♀ **'Aurea'** illus. p.138.

PTERIS

PTERIDACEAE/ADIANTACEAE

Genus of deciduous, semi-evergreen or evergreen ferns. Frost tender, min. 5°C (41°F). Tolerates sun or shade. Grow in moist, peaty soil. Remove faded fronds regularly. Propagate by division in spring or by spores in summer.

♀ ***P. cretica*** (Cretan brake). Evergreen or semi-evergreen fern. **H** 45cm (18in), **S** 30cm (12in). Frost tender, min. 5°C (41°F). Produces triangular to broadly oval, divided, pale green fronds that have finger-like pinnae. **var. *albolineata*** see *P.c.* 'Albolineata'.

♀ **'Albolineata'** (syn. *P.c.* var. *albolineata*) has pale green fronds centrally variegated with creamy-white. Variegated **'Mayi'**, **H** 30cm (12in), has crested frond tips. **'Wimsettii'**, illus. p.478, is compact, with the margins of the pinnae deeply and irregularly lobed.

P. ensiformis (Snow brake). Deciduous or semi-evergreen fern. **H** 30cm (12in), **S** 23cm (9in). Dark green fronds, often greyish-white around the midribs, are coarsely divided into finger-shaped pinnae. **'Arguta'**, **H** 45cm (18in), has deeper green fronds with central, silver-white marks.

PTEROCARYA

Wing nut

JUGLANDACEAE

Genus of deciduous trees, grown for their foliage and catkins. Fully hardy. Needs full sun and any deep, moist but well-drained soil. Suckers should be removed regularly. Propagate by softwood cuttings in summer or by suckers or seed, when ripe, in autumn.

♀ ***P. fraxinifolia*** (Caucasian wing nut). Deciduous, spreading tree. **H** 25m (80ft), **S** 20m (70ft). Large, ash-like glossy, dark green leaves turn yellow in autumn. Long green catkins are borne in summer, the females developing winged, green, then brown fruits.

P. x rehderiana illus. p.65.

P. stenoptera (Chinese wing nut). Deciduous, spreading tree. **H** 20m (70ft), **S** 15m (50ft). Ash-like, bright green leaves, each with a winged stalk, turn yellow in autumn. Produces long green catkins in summer; the females develop winged, pink-tinged, green fruits.

PTEROCELTIS

ULMACEAE

Genus of one species of deciduous tree, with inconspicuous flowers in summer, grown for its foliage and fruits. Fully hardy. Needs full sun and does best in hot summers. Requires well-drained soil. Propagate by seed in autumn.

P. tatarinowii. Deciduous, spreading tree with arching branches. **H** 12m (40ft), **S** 10m (30ft). Has peeling, grey bark, and oval, dark green leaves, to 10cm (4in) long, with toothed margins. In autumn, bears small, spherical, green fruits, each with a broad, circular wing.

PTEROCEPHALUS

DIPSACACEAE

Genus of compact, summer-flowering annuals, perennials and semi-evergreen sub-shrubs, grown for their scabious-like flower heads and feathery seed heads. Is useful for rock gardens. Fully hardy. Requires sun and well-drained soil. Propagate by softwood or semi-ripe cuttings in summer or by seed in autumn. Self-seeds moderately.

P. parnassi. See *P. perennis.*

P. perennis, syn. *P. parnassi*, illus. p.364.

PTEROSTYRAX

STYRACACEAE

Genus of deciduous trees and shrubs, grown for their foliage and fragrant flowers. Fully hardy. Requires sun or semi-shade and deep, well-drained, neutral to acid soil. Propagate by softwood or semi-ripe cuttings in summer or by seed in autumn.

♀ ***P. hispida*** illus. p.73.

Ptilotrichum spinosum. See *Alyssum spinosum.*

PUERARIA

LEGUMINOSAE/PAPILIONACEAE

Genus of deciduous, woody-stemmed or herbaceous, twining climbers. Half hardy. Grow in full sun and in any well-drained soil. Propagate by seed in spring.

P. hirsuta. See *P. lobata.*

P. lobata, syn. *P. hirsuta, P. montana* var. *lobata, P. thunbergiana* (Kudzu vine). Deciduous, woody-stemmed, twining climber with hairy stems. **H** to 5m (15ft) or to 30m (100ft) in the wild. Leaves have 3 broadly oval leaflets. In summer produces racemes, to 30cm (12in) long, of small, scented, sweet pea-like, reddish-purple flowers, followed by long, slender, hairy pods, 6–8cm (2½–3in) long. In cold areas is best grown as an annual.

P. montana* var. *lobata. See *P. lobata.*

P. thunbergiana. See *P. lobata.*

PULMONARIA

Lungwort

BORAGINACEAE

Genus of mainly spring-flowering perennials, some of which are semi-evergreen with small, overwintering rosettes of leaves. Fully hardy. Prefers shade; grows in any moist but well-drained soil. Propagate by division in spring or autumn.

♀ ***P. angustifolia.*** Clump-forming, usually deciduous perennial. **H** 23cm (9in), **S** 20–30cm (8–12in) or more. Has lance-shaped, unspotted, mid-green leaves, 40cm (16in) long. In early spring produces heads of tubular, 5-lobed, borage-like, sometimes pink-tinged, deep blue flowers. **'Azurea'**, **H** and **S** 30cm (12in), has dark green leaves and produces pinkish buds that open to rich gentian-blue flowers.

***P.* 'Beth's Pink'.** Semi-evergreen, clump-forming perennial. **H** 25cm (10in), **S** 50cm (20in). Has oval-lance-shaped, hairy, dark green leaves spotted with silvery-white. In early and mid-spring bears heads of tubular, 5-lobed, borage-like, purplish-pink flowers.

***P.* 'Blue Ensign'.** Semi-evergreen, clump-forming perennial. **H** 25cm (10in), **S** 50cm (20in). Has broadly oval, hairy, dark green leaves. In early and mid-spring produces heads of tubular, 5-lobed, borage-like, rich blue flowers.

***P.* 'Cotton Cool'.** Semi-evergreen, clump-forming perennial. **H** 30cm (12in), **S** 50cm (20in). Has narrowly elliptic, hairy, dark green leaves marked almost entirely with silver. In early and mid-spring bears heads of tubular, 5-lobed, borage-like, pink and blue flowers.

***P.* 'Excalibur'** (illus. p.261). Vigorous, semi-evergreen, clump-forming perennial. **H** 30cm (12in), **S** 50cm (20in). Has narrowly lance-shaped hairy, silver leaves with a narrow, green edge. In early and mid-spring, heads of tubular, 5-lobed, borage-like, light blue flowers open from pink buds.

***P.* 'Glacier'.** Semi-evergreen, clump-forming perennial. **H** 20–30cm (8–12in), **S** 50cm (20in). Has broadly oval, hairy, mid-green leaves spotted with silver. In early and mid-spring produces heads of tubular, 5-lobed, borage-like, pale blue and pale pink flowers.

***P.* 'Ice Ballet'.** Vigorous, semi-evergreen, clump-forming perennial. **H** 30cm (12in), **S** 50cm (20in). Has broadly oval, hairy, mildew-resistant, mid-green leaves well spotted with silver. In early and mid-spring bears heads of large, tubular, 5-lobed, borage-like, pure white flowers.

♀ ***P.* 'Lewis Palmer'** (illus. p.261). Vigorous, semi-evergreen, clump-forming perennial. **H** 35cm (14in), **S** 50cm (20in). Has oval, hairy, silver-spotted, mid-green leaves. In early and mid-spring, heads of tubular, 5-lobed, borage-like, clear blue flowers open from pinkish buds.

P. longifolia. Clump-forming, deciduous perennial. **H** 30cm (12in), **S** 45cm (18in). Bears very narrowly lance-shaped, dark green leaves, to 45cm (18in), spotted with silvery white. Heads of tubular, 5-lobed, borage-like, vivid blue flowers appear in late spring. **'Bertram Anderson'** has long leaves especially well spotted with silver and bears brighter blue flowers.

♀ ***P.* 'Margery Fish'** (illus. p.261). Semi-evergreen, clump-forming perennial. **H** 30cm (12in), **S** 50cm (20in). Has narrowly lance-shaped, hairy, mid-green leaves marked heavily with silver. In early spring, heads of tubular, 5-lobed, borage-like, pink flowers gradually turn to blue as they age.

***P.* 'Mary Mottram'** (illus. p.261). Vigorous, semi-evergreen, clump-forming perennial. **H** 35cm (14in), **S** 50cm (20in). Has oval, hairy leaves marked heavily with silver with a narrow green margin. In early spring bears heads of large, tubular, 5-lobed, borage-like, pink and violet flowers.

***P.* 'Mawson's Blue'** (illus. p.261). Semi-evergreen, clump-forming perennial. **H** 20–30cm (8–12in), **S** 50cm (20in). Has oval, hairy, mid-green leaves, bronze tinged when young. In early spring, heads of tubular, 5-lobed, borage-like, azure-blue flowers are often produced before the leaves fully develop.

***P.* 'Ocupol'.** See *P.* Opal.

♀ ***P. officinalis* 'Sissinghurst White'**, syn. *P. saccharata* 'Sissinghurst White', illus. p.254.

***P.* Opal ('Ocupol')** illus. p.261. Semi-evergreen, clump-forming perennial. **H** 25cm (10in), **S** 50cm (20in). Has oval, hairy, silver-spotted, mid-green leaves. In spring, heads of tubular, 5-lobed, borage-like, glowing, pale blue flowers open from pink buds.

♀ ***P. rubra*** (illus. p.261). Semi-evergreen, clump-forming perennial. **H** 30cm (12in), **S** 60cm (24in). Has oval, velvety, mid-green leaves. Heads of tubular, 5-lobed, borage-like, brick-red flowers open from late winter to early spring. **'David Ward'** (illus. p.261) has narrow, white-edged, soft green leaves and pale red flowers. Needs a sheltered spot.

P. saccharata. Semi-evergreen, clump-forming perennial. **H** 30cm (12in), **S** 60cm (24in). Long, elliptic leaves are variably spotted with creamy-white. In spring, bears funnel-shaped flowers, opening pink and turning to blue. **'Leopard'** has silver-spotted, dark green leaves and reddish-pink flowers that fade to lilac. **'Mrs Moon'** bears leaves spotted liberally with silver and heads of pinkish-mauve flowers. **'Sissinghurst White'** see *P. officinalis* 'Sissinghurst White'.

***P.* 'Weetwood Blue'.** Usually semi-evergreen, clump-forming perennial. **H** 20cm (8in), **S** 50cm (20in). Has lance-shaped, hairy, green leaves occasionally spotted with white. In spring bears heads of tubular, 5-lobed, borage-like, clear blue flowers that darken as they age.

PULSATILLA

RANUNCULACEAE

Genus of perennials, some of which are evergreen, grown for their large, feathery leaves, upright or pendent, bell- or cup-shaped flowers, covered in fine hairs, and feathery seed heads. Has fibrous, woody rootstocks. Leaves increase in size after flowering time. Is suitable for large rock gardens. Fully hardy. Needs full sun and humus-rich, well-drained soil. Resents disturbance to roots. Propagate by root cuttings in winter or by seed when fresh. ⓘ All parts of the plant may cause mild stomach upset if ingested, and, in rare instances, contact with the sap may irritate skin.

P. alpina (Alpine anemone) illus. p.332. ♀ **subsp. *apiifolia*** (syn. *P.a.* subsp. *sulphurea*) is a clump-forming perennial. **H** 15–30cm (6–12in), **S** to 10cm (4in). Has feathery, soft green leaves. Bears upright, bell-shaped, soft pale yellow flowers in spring, followed by feathery, silvery seed heads. **subsp. *sulphurea*** see *P.a.* subsp. *apiifolia.*

♀ ***P. halleri*** illus. p.334. **subsp. *grandis*** (syn. *P. vulgaris* subsp. *grandis*) is a clump-forming perennial. **H** and **S** 15–23cm (6–9in). In spring, before feathery, light green leaves appear, bears large, upright, shallowly bell-shaped, lavender-blue flowers, 5cm (2in) wide, with bright yellow centres. Flower stems rapidly elongate as the feathery, silvery seed heads mature.

P. occidentalis. Clump-forming perennial. **H** 20cm (8in), **S** 15cm (6in). In late spring to early summer, solitary nodding buds develop into erect, goblet-shaped, white flowers, stained blue-violet at base outside and sometimes flushed pink, followed by feathery, silvery seed heads. Bears feathery leaves. Is extremely difficult to grow and flower well at low altitudes.

♀ ***P. vernalis*** illus. p.349.

♀ ***P. vulgaris*** illus. p.334. **subsp. *grandis*** see *P. halleri* subsp. *grandis.*

PUNICA

Pomegranate

LYTHRACEAE/PUNICACEAE

Genus of deciduous, summer-flowering shrubs and trees, grown for their bright red flowers and yellow to orange-red fruits, which ripen and become edible only in warm climates. Frost to half hardy. Needs a sheltered, sunny position and well-drained soil. Propagate by seed in spring or by semi-ripe cuttings in summer.

P. granatum. Deciduous, rounded shrub or tree. **H** and **S** 2–8m (6–25ft). Half hardy. Has narrowly oblong leaves and, in summer, funnel-shaped, bright red flowers, with crumpled petals. Fruits are spherical and deep yellow to orange. May be grown in a southern or eastern aspect, either free-standing or, in frost-prone climates, against a wall. ♀ **var. *nana*** illus. p.340.

PUSCHKINIA

LILIACEAE/HYACINTHACEAE

Genus of dwarf, *Scilla*-like bulbs, grown for their early spring flowers. Fully hardy. Needs sun or partial shade and humus-rich soil that has grit or sand added to ensure good drainage. Plant in autumn. Dies down in summer. Propagate by offsets in late summer or by seed in autumn.

P. libanotica. See *P. scilloides* var. *libanotica.*

P. scilloides* var. *libanotica, syn. *P. libanotica*, illus. p.421. **'Alba'** illus. p.415.

PUYA

BROMELIACEAE

Genus of evergreen, rosette-forming perennials and shrubs, grown for their overall appearance. Half hardy to frost tender, min. 5–7°C (41–5°F). Requires full light and well-drained soil. Water moderately during the growing season, sparingly at other times. Propagate by seed or offsets in spring.

P. alpestris. Evergreen perennial with stout, branched, prostrate stems. **H** to 2m (6ft), **S** 3m (10ft). Half hardy. Linear, tapering, arching, bright green leaves are fleshy, with hooked, spiny teeth along the edges and dense, white scales beneath. Tubular, deep metallic-blue flowers, ageing to purple-red, are borne in stiff, erect panicles in early summer.

P. chilensis (illus. p.471). Evergreen, upright perennial with a short, woody stem. **H** and **S** to 2m (6ft). Half hardy. Stem is crowned by a dense rosette of linear, tapering, arching, fleshy, grey-green leaves with margins of hooked, spiny teeth. Bears tubular, metallic- or greenish-yellow flowers in erect, branched panicles in summer.

PYCNOSTACHYS

LABIATAE/LAMIACEAE

Genus of bushy perennials, grown for their whorled clusters of flowers. Frost tender, min. 15°C (59°F). Grow in bright light and in fertile, well-drained soil. Propagate by stem cuttings in early summer.

P. dawei illus. p.473.

P. urticifolia. Strong-growing, erect perennial with square stems. **H** 1–2m (3–6ft), **S** 20–60cm (8–24in). Has oval, toothed, hairy, mid-green leaves. Bears whorls of small, tubular, bright blue flowers in racemes in winter.

PYRACANTHA

Firethorn

ROSACEAE

Genus of evergreen, spiny, summer-flowering shrubs, grown for their foliage, flowers and fruits. Fully to frost hardy. Requires a sheltered site in sun or semi-shade and fertile soil. To produce a compact habit on a plant grown against a wall, train and cut back long shoots after flowering. Propagate by semi-ripe cuttings in summer. Is susceptible to scab and fireblight. ⓘThe seeds may cause mild stomach upset if ingested.

P. angustifolia. Evergreen, bushy, dense shrub. **H** and **S** 3m (10ft). Frost hardy. Has narrowly oblong leaves, dark green above, grey beneath. Bears clusters of small, 5-petalled, white flowers in early summer, followed by spherical, orange-yellow fruits, 8mm (5⁄16in) across, in autumn.

P. atalantioides. Vigorous, evergreen shrub, part upright, part arching. **H** 5m (15ft), **S** 4m (12ft). Frost hardy. Oblong leaves are glossy and dark green. Large clusters of small, 5-petalled, white flowers in early summer are followed by spherical, red fruits in early autumn. **'Aurea'** illus. p.118.

P. coccinea. Evergreen, dense, bushy shrub. **H** and **S** 4m (12ft). Fully hardy. Dense clusters of small, 5-petalled, white flowers open amid oval, dark green leaves in early summer and are succeeded by spherical, bright red fruits. **'Lalandei'** has larger leaves and larger, orange-red fruits.

🏆 ***P.* 'Golden Charmer'** illus. p.141.

***P.* 'Golden Dome'** illus. p.144.

***P.* 'Mohave'**, illus. p.209.

🏆 ***P.* 'Orange Glow'.** Evergreen, upright, dense shrub. **H** 5m (15ft), **S** 3m (10ft). Frost hardy. Has oblong, glossy, dark green leaves. Clusters of small, 5-petalled, white flowers, in early summer, are followed by spherical, orange fruits.

🏆 ***P. rogersiana.*** Evergreen, upright, then arching shrub. **H** and **S** 3m (10ft). Frost hardy. Leaves are narrowly oblong, glossy and bright green. Produces clusters of small, 5-petalled, white flowers in early summer, followed by round, orange-red or yellow fruits.

P. x watereri, syn. *P.* 'Waterer's Orange', illus. p.128.

***P.* 'Waterer's Orange'.** See *P. x watereri.*

Pyrethropsis hosmariense. See *Rhodanthemum hosmariense.*

Pyrethrum. See *Tanacetum coccineum.*

***Pyrethrum* 'Brenda'.** See *Tanacetum coccineum* 'Brenda'.

Pyrethrum coccineum. See *Tanacetum coccineum.*

Pyrethrum parthenium. See *Tanacetum parthenium.*

Pyrethrum roseum. See *Tanacetum coccineum.*

PYROLA

Wintergreen

PYROLACEAE/ERICACEAE

Genus of evergreen, spreading, spring- and summer-flowering perennials. Fully hardy. Needs partial shade, cool conditions and well-drained, peaty, acid soil; is best suited to light woodland. Resents disturbance. Propagate by seed in autumn or spring or by division in spring.

P. asarifolia. Evergreen, rosette-forming perennial. **H** 15–25cm (6–10in), **S** 15cm (6in) or more. Has kidney-shaped, leathery, glossy, light green leaves. Bears tubular, pale to deep pink flowers in spring.

P. rotundifolia (Round-leaved wintergreen, Wild lily-of-the-valley). Creeping, evergreen, rosette-forming perennial. **H** 23cm (9in), **S** 30cm (12in). Produces rounded, leathery, glossy, mid-green leaves and, in late spring and early summer, sprays of fragrant, white flowers that resemble lily-of-the-valley.

PYROSTEGIA

BIGNONIACEAE

Genus of evergreen, woody-stemmed, tendril climbers, grown for their flowers. Frost tender, min. 13–15°C (55–59°F). Needs full light and fertile, well-drained soil. Water regularly, less in winter. Provide support. Thin stems after flowering. Propagate by semi-ripe cuttings or layering in summer.

P. ignea. See *P. venusta.*

P. venusta, syn. *P. ignea*, illus. p.464.

PYRUS

Pear

ROSACEAE

Genus of deciduous, spring-flowering trees, grown for their habit, foliage, flowers and edible fruits (pears). Fully hardy. Does best in full sun and needs well-drained soil. Propagate species by seed in autumn, cultivars by budding in summer or by grafting in winter. Many species are susceptible to fireblight and scab and, in North America, pear decline.

P. amygdaliformis. Deciduous, spreading tree. **H** 10m (30ft), **S** 8m (25ft). Lance-shaped leaves are grey when young, maturing to glossy, dark green. Clusters of 5-petalled, white flowers are produced in mid-spring, and are followed by small, brownish fruits.

P. calleryana (Callery pear). Deciduous, broadly conical tree. **H** and **S** to 15m (50ft). Oval, glossy, dark green leaves often turn red in autumn. Bears 5-petalled, white flowers from mid- to late spring and small, brownish fruits. **'Bradford'**, **S** 10m (30ft), is resistant to fireblight. 🏆 **'Chanticleer'** illus. p.71.

P. communis (Common pear). **'Beech Hill'** is a deciduous, narrowly conical tree. **H** 10m (30ft), **S** 7m (22ft). Oval, glossy, dark green leaves often turn orange and red in autumn. From mid- to late spring bears 5-petalled, white flowers as leaves emerge, followed by small, brownish fruits.

P. elaeagrifolia. Deciduous, spreading, thorny tree. **H** and **S** 8m (25ft). Has lance-shaped, grey-green leaves. Produces loose clusters of 5-petalled, creamy white flowers in mid-spring, followed by small, pear-shaped, brownish fruits.

P. salicifolia. Deciduous, mound-shaped tree with slightly drooping branches. **H** 5–8m (15–25ft), **S** 4m (12ft). White flowers, with 5 petals, open as lance-shaped, grey leaves emerge in mid-spring. Fruits are small and brownish.

🏆 **'Pendula'** illus. p.88.

Quamoclit coccinea. See *Ipomoea coccinea.*

Quamoclit lobata. See *Ipomoea lobata.*

Quamoclit pennata. See *Ipomoea quamoclit.*

QUERCUS

Oak

FAGACEAE

Genus of deciduous or evergreen trees and shrubs, grown for their habit, foliage and, in some deciduous species, autumn colour. Produces insignificant flowers from late spring to early summer, followed by egg-shaped to rounded, brownish fruits (acorns). Fully to frost hardy. Does best in sun or semi-shade and in deep, well-drained soil. Except where stated otherwise, will tolerate limestone. Propagate species by seed in autumn, selected forms and hybrids by grafting in late winter. May be affected, though not usually seriously, by mildew and various galls, and in North America, by oak wilt.

Q. acutissima (Sawtooth oak). Deciduous, round-headed tree. **H** and **S** 15m (50ft). Fully hardy. Has sweet-chestnut-like, glossy, dark green leaves, edged with bristle-tipped teeth, that last until late in the year.

Q. aegilops. See *Q. ithaburensis* subsp. *macrolepis.*

Q. agrifolia illus. p.80.

Q. alba (American white oak) illus. p.66.

Q. aliena (Oriental white oak). Deciduous, spreading tree. **H** 15m (50ft), **S** 12m (40ft). Fully hardy. Has large, oblong, prominently toothed, glossy, dark green leaves.

Q. alnifolia (Golden oak of Cyprus). Evergreen, spreading tree. **H** 6m (20ft), **S** 5m (15ft). Frost hardy. Rounded, leathery leaves are glossy, dark green above, with mustard-yellow or greenish-yellow felt beneath.

🏆 ***Q. canariensis*** illus. p.62.

Q. castaneifolia illus. p.64.

Q. cerris (Turkey oak). Fast-growing, deciduous, spreading tree of stately habit. **H** 30m (100ft), **S** 25m (80ft). Fully hardy. Oblong, glossy, dark green leaves are deeply lobed. Thrives on shallow, chalky soil. **'Argenteovariegata'** illus. p.73.

Q. coccifera (Kermes oak). Evergreen, bushy, compact tree or shrub. **H** and **S** 5m (15ft). Frost hardy. Holly-like leaves are glossy, dark green and rigid with spiny margins.

Q. coccinea illus. p.65. 🏆 **'Splendens'** is a deciduous, round-headed tree. **H** 20m (70ft), **S** 15m (50ft). Fully hardy. Oblong, glossy, mid-green leaves, with deep, tooth-like lobes, turn deep scarlet in autumn. Prefers acid soil.

Q. dentata (Daimio oak). Deciduous, spreading, stout-branched tree of rugged habit. **H** 15m (50ft), **S** 10m (30ft). Fully hardy. Has oval, lobed, dark green leaves, 30cm (12in) or more long. Prefers acid soil.

Q. ellipsoidalis illus. p.65.

Q. frainetto illus. p.64.

Q. garryana illus. p.74.

Q. x heterophylla illus. p.77.

🏆 ***Q. x hispanica* 'Lucombeana'**, syn. *Q. x lucombeana* 'William Lucombe', illus. p.68.

🏆 ***Q. ilex*** (Holm oak). Evergreen, round-headed tree. **H** 25m (80ft), **S** 20m (70ft). Frost hardy. Glossy, dark green leaves are silvery-grey when young and very variably shaped, but are most often oval. Thrives on shallow chalk and is excellent for an exposed, coastal position.

Q. imbricaria (Shingle oak). Deciduous, spreading tree. **H** 20m (70ft), **S** 15m (50ft). Fully hardy. Produces long, narrow leaves that are yellowish when young, dark green in summer and yellowish-brown in autumn.

Q. ithaburensis* subsp. *macrolepis, syn. *Q. aegilops, Q. macrolepis*, illus. p.75.

Q. laurifolia illus. p.64.

***Q. x lucombeana* 'William Lucombe'.** See *Q. x hispanica* 'Lucombeana'.

Q. macranthera illus. p.61.

Q. macrocarpa illus. p.75.

Q. macrolepis. See *Q. ithaburensis* subsp. *macrolepis.*

Q. marilandica illus. p.75.

Q. mongolica* subsp. *crispula* var. *grosseserrata. Deciduous, spreading tree. **H** 20m (70ft), **S** 15m (50ft). Fully hardy. Has large, oblong, lobed, dark green leaves with prominent, triangular teeth.

Q. muehlenbergii illus. p.62.

Q. myrsinifolia illus. p.80.

Q. nigra illus. p.63.

🏆 ***Q. palustris*** illus. p.66.

🏆 ***Q. petraea*** (Durmast oak, Sessile oak). Deciduous, spreading tree. **H** 30m (100ft), **S** 25m (80ft). Fully hardy. Has oblong, lobed, leathery, dark green leaves with yellow stalks. **'Columna'** illus. p.63.

Q. phellos illus. p.67.

Q. pontica (Armenian oak, Pontine oak). Deciduous, sometimes shrubby tree with upright, stout branches and broadly oval head. **H** 6m (20ft), **S** 5m (15ft). Fully hardy. Large, oval, toothed, glossy, bright green leaves turn yellow in autumn.

🏆 ***Q. robur*** (Common oak, Pedunculate oak). Deciduous, spreading, rugged tree. **H** and **S** 25m (80ft). Fully hardy. Bears oblong, wavy, lobed, dark green leaves. **'Concordia'**, **H** 10m (30ft), is slow-growing and has golden-yellow, young foliage that becomes yellowish-green in mid-summer. ***f. fastigiata*** illus. p.62.

🏆 ***Q. rubra*** illus. p.65. **'Aurea'** illus. p.72.

Q. suber (Cork oak; illus. p.78). Evergreen, round-headed tree. **H** and **S** 20m (70ft). Frost hardy. Has thick, corky bark. Oval, leathery leaves are glossy, dark green above and greyish beneath.

Q. x turneri illus. p.68.

Q. velutina (Black oak). Fast-growing, deciduous, spreading tree. **H** 30m (100ft), **S** 25m (80ft). Fully hardy. Large, oblong, lobed, glossy, dark green leaves turn reddish-brown in autumn.

QUISQUALIS

COMBRETACEAE

Genus of evergreen or deciduous, scandent shrubs and twining climbers, grown for their flowers. Frost tender, min. 10–18°C (50–64°F). Provide humus-rich, moist but well-drained soil and full light or semi-shade. Water freely when in full growth, less in cold weather. Stems need support. Thin out crowded growth in spring. Propagate by seed in spring or by semi-ripe cuttings in summer.

Q. indica, syn. *Combretum indicum*, illus. p.462.

R

RAMONDA

GESNERIACEAE

Genus of evergreen perennials, grown for their rosettes of rounded, crinkled, hairy leaves and for their flowers. Is useful for rock gardens and peat walls. Fully hardy. Prefers shade and moist soil. Water plants well if they curl in a dry spell. Propagate by rooting offsets in early summer or by leaf cuttings or seed in early autumn.

♀ ***R. myconi***, syn. *R. pyrenaica*, illus. p.369.

♀ ***R. nathaliae.*** Evergreen, basal-rosetted perennial. **H** and **S** 10cm (4in). Has small, pale green leaves and, in late spring and early summer, bears umbels of small, outward-facing, flattish, white or lavender flowers, with yellow anthers.

R. pyrenaica. See *R. myconi.*

R. serbica. Evergreen, basal-rosetted perennial. **H** and **S** 10cm (4in). Is similar to *R. nathaliae*, but has cup-shaped, lilac-blue flowers and dark violet-blue anthers. May be difficult to grow.

RANUNCULUS

Buttercup

RANUNCULACEAE

Genus of annuals, aquatics and perennials, some of which are evergreen or semi-evergreen, grown mainly for their flowers. Many species grow from a thickened rootstock or a cluster of tubers. Some are invasive. Aquatic species are seldom cultivated. Fully to half hardy. Grows in a sunny or shaded position and in moist but well-drained soil. Propagate by seed when fresh or by division in spring or autumn.

ⓣ Contact with the sap may irritate skin.

R. aconitifolius, illus p.223, and ♀ **'Flore Pleno'** illus. p.230.

R. acris (Meadow buttercup). **'Flore Pleno'** illus. p.276.

R. alpestris (Alpine buttercup) illus. p.349.

R. amplexicaulis. Upright perennial. **H** 25cm (10in), **S** 10cm (4in). Fully hardy. Has narrowly oval, blue-grey leaves. In early summer produces clusters of shallowly cup-shaped, white flowers with yellow anthers. Needs humus-rich soil.

R. aquatilis (Water crowfoot). Aquatic annual or usually evergreen perennial. **H** 1cm (½in), **S** indefinite. Fully hardy. Submerged, branched, slender stems bear dark green leaves with many thread-like segments; floating leaves are kidney-shaped to rounded, deeply divided into 3–7 lobes. In mid-summer produces solitary, bowl- or saucer-shaped, white-based, yellow flowers, on the surface.

R. asiaticus (Persian buttercup) illus. p.410. **var. *flavus*** illus. p.412.

***R. bulbosus* 'Speciosus Plenus'** of gardens. See *R. constantinopolitanus* 'Plenus'.

R. bullatus. Clump-forming perennial with thick, fibrous roots. **H** 5–8cm (2–3in), **S** 8–10cm (3–4in). Half hardy. Has fragrant, shallowly cup-shaped, bright yellow flowers in autumn. Oblong to oval, puckered, dark green leaves have sharply toothed tips. Suits an alpine house or rock garden.

♀ ***R. calandrinioides*** illus. p.346.

***R. constantinopolitanus* 'Plenus'**, syn. *R. bulbosus* 'Speciosus Plenus' of gardens, *R. gouanii* 'Plenus', *R. speciosus* 'Plenus', illus. p.275.

R. crenatus. Semi-evergreen, rosetted perennial with thick, fibrous roots. **H** and **S** 10cm (4in). Fully hardy. Produces rounded, toothed, green leaves and, in summer, short stems bearing 1 or 2 shallowly cup-shaped, white flowers just above foliage. May also be propagated by removing a flower stem at its first joint in summer; rosettes will form and may then be rooted. Rarely sets seed in cultivation. Suits an alpine house or rock garden.

R. ficaria, syn. *Ficaria verna* (Lesser celandine). **var. *albus*** (syn. *R.f.* 'Albus') illus. p.349. **var. *aurantiacus*** (syn. *R.f.* 'Aurantiacus') illus. p.359.

'Brazen Hussy' is a mat-forming, tuberous perennial. **H** 5cm (2in), **S** to 20cm (8in). Fully hardy. Is grown for its heart-shaped, purple-bronze leaves produced in spring. Shallowly cup-shaped, glossy, sulphur-yellow flowers, with bronze reverses, appear in early spring. All *R. ficaria* forms die down in late spring. May spread rapidly; is good for a wild garden.

Flore Pleno Group (syn. *R.f.* 'Flore Pleno', *R.f.* var. *flore-pleno*) illus. p.357.

R. glacialis. Hummock-forming perennial with fibrous roots. **H** 5–25cm (2–10in), **S** 5cm (2in) or more. Fully hardy. Bears rounded, deeply lobed, glossy, dark green leaves and, in late spring and early summer, clusters of shallowly cup-shaped, white or pink flowers. Is very difficult to grow at low altitudes. Suits a scree or alpine house. Prefers humus-rich, moist, acid soil that is drier in winter. Slugs may be troublesome.

***R. gouanii* 'Plenus'.** See *R. constantinopolitanus* 'Plenus'.

♀ ***R. gramineus*** illus. p.345.

R. lingua illus. p.444. **'Grandiflorus'** is a deciduous, perennial, marginal water plant. **H** 1m (3ft), **S** 30cm (1ft). Fully hardy. Has stout, pinkish-green stems, lance-shaped, glaucous leaves and, in late spring, racemes of large, saucer-shaped, yellow flowers.

R. lyallii (Giant buttercup). Evergreen, stout, upright, tufted perennial. **H** and **S** 30cm (12in) or more. Frost hardy. Has rounded, leathery, dark green leaves, each 15cm (6in) or more across, and, in summer, bears panicles of large, shallowly cup-shaped, white flowers. Is very difficult to flower in hot, dry climates. Is suitable for an alpine house. Rarely sets seed in cultivation.

♀ ***R. montanus* 'Molten Gold'.** Clump-forming, compact perennial. **H** 15cm (6in), **S** 10cm (4in). Fully hardy. Leaves are rounded and 3-lobed. Flower stems each produce a shallowly cup-shaped, shiny, bright golden-yellow flower in early summer. Is useful for a sunny rock garden.

***R. speciosus* 'Plenus'.** See *R. constantinopolitanus* 'Plenus'.

RANZANIA

BERBERIDACEAE

Genus of one species of perennial, grown for its unusual appearance as well as its flowers. Is ideal for woodland gardens. Fully hardy. Prefers shade or semi-shade and humus-rich, moist soil. Propagate by division in spring or by seed in autumn.

R. japonica. Upright perennial. **H** 45cm (18in), **S** 30cm (12in). Produces 3-parted, fresh green leaves and, in early summer, small clusters of nodding, shallowly cup-shaped, pale mauve flowers.

RAOULIA

COMPOSITAE/ASTERACEAE

Genus of evergreen, mat-forming perennials, grown for their foliage. Some species are suitable for alpine houses, others for rock gardens. Fully to frost hardy. Needs sun or semi-shade and gritty, moist but well-drained, peaty soil. Propagate by seed when fresh or by division in spring.

R. australis illus. p.376.

R. eximia. Evergreen, cushion-forming perennial. **H** 2.5cm (1in), **S** 5cm (2in). Fully hardy. Has oblong to oval, overlapping, woolly, grey leaves. In late spring-summer bears small, rounded heads of yellowish-white flowers. Suits an alpine house. Prefers some shade.

R. haastii illus. p.376.

R. hookeri* var. *albosericea illus. p.374.

R. leontopodium. See *Leucogenes leontopodium.*

RAVENALA

STRELITZIACEAE

Genus of one species of evergreen, palm-like tree, grown for its foliage and overall appearance. Is related to *Strelitzia*. Frost tender, min. 16°C (61°F). Requires full light and humus-rich, well-drained soil. Water potted specimens freely in summer, less in winter or when temperatures are low. Propagate by seed in spring. Red spider mite may be troublesome.

R. madagascariensis (Traveller's tree). Evergreen, upright, fan-shaped tree. **H** and to 10m (30ft). Has banana- like, long-stalked leaves, each 3–6m (10–20ft) long, with expanded stalk bases. Groups of boat-shaped spathes with 6-parted, white flowers emerge from leaf axils in summer.

REBUTIA

CACTACEAE

Genus of mostly clump-forming, spherical to columnar, perennial cacti. Produces flowers in profusion from plant bases, usually 2–3 years after raising from seed. Much-ribbed, tuberculate, green stems have short spines. A few species are sometimes included in *Aylostera*. Frost tender, min. 5–10°C (41–50°F). Requires a position in sun or partial shade and well-drained soil. Is easy to grow. Propagate by seed in spring or summer.

R. arenacea, syn. *Sulcorebutia arenacea*, illus. p.496.

♀ ***R. aureiflora.*** See *R. einsteinii* subsp. *aureiflora.*

***R.* 'Carnival'** illus. p.483.

R. deminuta, syn. *R. spegazziniana*, illus. p.486.

♀ ***R. einsteinii* subsp. *aureiflora***, syn. *R. aureiflora*. Clump-forming, perennial cactus. **H** 10cm (4in), **S** 20cm (8in). Min. 5°C (41°F). Dark green stem, often tinged violet-red, has stiff, radial spines and longer, soft, central spines. Bears masses of yellow, violet or red flowers in late spring.

♀ ***R. fiebrigii***, syn. *R. muscula*, illus. p.496.

***R.* 'Jenny'** illus. p.484.

R. krainziana. See *R. minuscula.*

R. marsoneri. See *R. minuscula.*

♀ ***R. minuscula***, syn. *R. krainziana, R. marsoneri, R. senilis, R. violaciflora.* (illus. p.486) Clump-forming, perennial cactus. **H** 5cm (2in), **S** 15cm (6in). Min. 5°C (41°F). Has a tuberculate, dark green stem. Areoles each produce 15–20 brown spines, to 0.5cm (¼in) long. Has trumpet-shaped, deep pink to violet flowers, to 2cm (¾in) across, in spring.

R. muscula. See *R. fiebrigii.*

♀ ***R. neocumingii***, syn. *Weingartia neocumingii.* Spherical, perennial cactus. **H** and **S** 10cm (4in). Stem is tuberculate and green. Areoles bear dense clusters of yellow spines, 1.5cm (⅝in) long, some thicker than others, and cup-shaped, dark yellow flowers, 3cm (1¼in) long, in spring.

R. pygmaea, syn. *Lobivia pygmaea.* Clump-forming, columnar, perennial cactus. **H** 5cm (2in), **S** 10cm (4in). Very short, comb-like spines are pressed against grey- to purple-green stem. Trumpet-shaped, pink to salmon or rose-purple flowers, to 2cm (¾in) across, appear in spring. Prefers a sunny position.

R. rauschii. See *R. steinmannii.*

R. senilis. See *R. minuscula.*

R. spegazziniana. See *R. deminuta.*

R. steinmannii, syn. *R. rauschii, Sulcorebutia rauschii.* Flattened spherical, perennial cactus. **H** 5cm (2in), **S** 10cm (4in). Grey-green stem bears very short, comb-like, golden or black spines. Bears flattish, 3cm (1¼) wide, deep purple flowers in spring. Grows better when grafted.

R. steinbachii* subsp. *tiraquensis, syn. *R. tiraquensis, Sulcorebutia tiraquensis*, illus. p.487.

R. tiraquensis. See *R. steinbachii* subsp. *tiraquensis.*

R. violaciflora. See *R. minuscula.*

REHDERODENDRON

STYRACACEAE

Genus of deciduous, spring-flowering trees, grown for their flowers and fruits. Frost hardy. Needs sun or semi-shade, some shelter and fertile, moist, but well-drained, acid soil. Propagate by semi-ripe cuttings in summer or by seed in autumn.

R. macrocarpum. Deciduous, spreading tree. **H** 10m (30ft), **S** 7m (22ft). Young shoots are red. Pendent clusters of lemon-scented, cup-shaped, pink-tinged, white flowers are borne amid oblong, taper-pointed, red-stalked, glossy, dark green leaves in late spring. Bears cylindrical, woody, red, then brown fruits in autumn.

REHMANNIA

SCROPHULARIACEAE

Genus of spring- and summer-flowering perennials. Half hardy to frost tender, min. 1–5°C (34–41°F). Needs a sunny site and light soil. Propagate by seed in autumn or spring or by root cuttings in winter.

R. angulata of gardens. See *R. elata.*

♀ ***R. elata***, syn. *R. angulata* of gardens, illus. p.234.

R

♀ ***R. glutinosa.*** Rosette-forming perennial. **H** 30cm (12in), **S** 25cm (10in). Frost tender, min. 1°C (34°F). Bears tubular, purple-veined, pink, red-brown or yellow flowers, on leafy shoots in late spring and early summer. Has lance-shaped to oval, toothed, hairy, light green leaves.

REINWARDTIA

LINACEAE

Genus of evergreen sub-shrubs, grown for their flowers. Frost tender, min. 7–10°C (45–50°F). Needs full light or semi-shade and fertile, well-drained soil. Water freely when growing, moderately at other times. Tip prune young plants to promote branching; cut back hard after flowering. Raise softwood cuttings annually in late spring. Red spider mite may cause problems.

R. indica, syn. *R. trigyna*, illus. p.459.

R. trigyna. See *R. indica*.

RESEDA

Mignonette

RESEDACEAE

Genus of annuals and biennials with flowers that attract bees and that are also suitable for cutting. Fully hardy. Grow in a sunny position and in any fertile, well-drained soil. Dead-heading regularly ensures a prolonged flowering period. Propagate by sowing seed outdoors in spring or early autumn.

R. odorata illus. p.300.

RETAMA

LEGUMINOSAE/PAPILIONACEAE

Genus of deciduous shrubs grown for their willowy, dark green or silky grey stems and pea-like, white or yellow flowers. Half hardy. Needs full sun, sharply drained soil and a sheltered site against a south- or west-facing wall. Propagate from seed in a cold frame or under glass or by semi-ripe cuttings in summer.

R. monosperma, syn. *Genista monosperma*. Deciduous, almost leafless, graceful, arching shrub. **H** to 4m (12ft), **S** 1.5m (5ft). Half hardy. Slender, silky-grey shoots bear clusters of small, very fragrant, white flowers in early spring. Has a few linear leaves, which soon fall. Grow against a south- or west-facing wall.

Reynoutria. See *Fallopia*.

RHAMNUS

Buckthorn

RHAMNACEAE

Genus of deciduous or evergreen shrubs and trees, with inconspicuous flowers, grown mainly for their foliage and fruits. Fully to frost hardy. Requires sun or semi-shade and fertile soil. Propagate deciduous species by seed in autumn, evergreen species by semi-ripe cuttings in summer. ⓘAll parts may cause severe discomfort if ingested.

R. alaternus (Italian buckthorn).

♀ **'Argenteovariegata'** is an evergreen, bushy shrub. **H** and **S** 3m (10ft). Frost hardy. Has oval, leathery, glossy, grey-green leaves margined creamy-white. Tiny, yellowish-green flowers are produced from early to mid-summer and followed by spherical red, then black fruits.

R. imeretina. Deciduous, spreading, open shrub. **H** 3m (10ft), **S** 5m (15ft). Fully hardy. Stout shoots bear large, broadly oblong, prominently veined, dark green leaves that turn bronze-purple in autumn. Small, green flowers are borne in summer.

RHAPHIOLEPIS

ROSACEAE

Genus of evergreen shrubs, grown for their flowers and foliage. Frost to half hardy. In most areas does best against a sheltered wall; *R. umbellata* is the most hardy. Needs sun and fertile, well-drained soil. Propagate by semi-ripe cuttings in late summer.

***R. x delacourii* 'Coates' Crimson'.** Evergreen, rounded shrub. **H** 2m (6ft), **S** 2.5m (8ft). Frost hardy. Clusters of fragrant, star-shaped, deep pink flowers, produced in spring or summer, are set off by the oval, leathery, dark green leaves.

R. indica (Indian hawthorn). Evergreen, bushy shrub. **H** 1.5m (5ft), **S** 2m (6ft). Half hardy. Clusters of fragrant, star-shaped, white flowers, flushed with pink, are borne in spring or early summer amid narrowly lance-shaped, glossy, dark green leaves.

R. japonica. See *R. umbellata*.

R. ovata. See *R. umbellata*.

♀ ***R. umbellata***, syn. *R. japonica, R. ovata*, illus. p.150.

RHAPIS

PALMAE/ARECACEAE

Genus of evergreen fan palms, grown for their foliage and overall appearance. May have tiny, yellow flowers in summer. Frost tender, min.15°C (59°F). Needs partial shade and humus-rich, well-drained soil. Water containerized specimens freely when growing, moderately at other times. Propagate by seed, suckers or division in spring. Is susceptible to red spider mite.

♀ ***R. excelsa*** (Bamboo palm, Slender lady palm), syn. *R. flabelliformis*, illus. p.458.

R. flabelliformis. See *R. excelsa*.

Rhazya orientalis. See *Amsonia orientalis*.

RHEUM

Rhubarb

POLYGONACEAE

Genus of perennials, grown for their foliage and overall appearance. Includes the edible rhubarb and various ornamental plants. Some species are extremely large and require plenty of space. Fully hardy. Prefers sun or semi-shade and deep, rich, well-drained soil. Propagate by division in spring or by seed in autumn. ⓘLeaves may cause severe discomfort if ingested.

R. nobile. Clump-forming perennial. **H** 15m (5ft), **S** 1m (3ft). Leaves are oblong to oval, leathery, basal, mid-green, 60cm (2ft) long. In late summer produces long stems and conical spikes of large, overlapping, pale cream bracts that hide insignificant flowers.

R. palmatum. Clump-forming perennial. **H** and **S** 2m (6ft). Has 60–75cm (2–2½ft) long, rounded, 5-lobed, mid-green leaves. In early summer has broad panicles of small, creamy-white flowers.

♀ **'Atrosanguineum'** illus. p.439.

Rhipsalidopsis gaertneri. See *Hatiora gaertneri*.

Rhipsalidopsis rosea. See *Hatiora rosea*.

RHIPSALIS

Mistletoe cactus

CACTACEAE

Genus of epiphytic, perennial cacti with usually pendent, variously formed stems. Flowers are followed by spherical, translucent berries. Frost tender, min. 10–11°C (50–52°F). Needs partial shade and rich, well-drained soil. Prefers 80% relative humidity – higher than for most cacti. Give only occasional, very light watering in winter. Propagate by seed or stem cuttings in spring or summer.

R. capilliformis. See *R. teres*.

R. cereuscula (Coral cactus) illus. p.483.

R. clavata. See *R. gaertneri*.

R. crispata. Bushy, then pendent, perennial cactus. **H** 1m (3ft), **S** indefinite. Min. 11°C (52°F). Has leaf-like, elliptic to oblong, pale green stem segments, to 12cm (5in) long, with undulating edges that produce short, funnel-shaped, cream or pale yellow flowers, to 1cm (½in) across, with recurved tips, in winter-spring, then white berries.

R. floccosa illus. p.493.

R. gaertneri, syn. *R. clavata, Hatiora clavata*. Pendent, perennial, epiphytic cactus. **H** 60cm (2ft), **S** 1m (3ft).min. 11°C (52°F). Multi-branched, cylindrical, dark green stems that widen towards tips. Masses of terminal, bell-shaped, white flowers, 1.5cm (5/8in) wide, are produced in late winter and early spring on plants over 30cm (1ft) high.

R. paradoxa (Chain cactus). Bushy, then pendent, perennial cactus. **H** 1m (3ft), **S** indefinite. Min. 11°C (52°F). Triangular, green stems have segments alternately set at different angles. Short, funnel-shaped, white flowers, 2cm (¾in) across, with recurved tips, in winter–spring are followed by red berries.

R. salicornioides. See *Hatiora salicornioides*.

R. teres, syn. *R. capilliformis*. Pendent, perennial cactus. **H** 1m (3ft), **S** 50cm (20in). Min. 10°C (50°F). Has freely branching, cylindrical, green stems and, in winter-spring, short, funnel-shaped, white flowers, to 1cm (½in) wide, with recurved tips, then white berries.

R. warmingiana. See *Lepismium warmingianum*.

RHODANTHE

SYN. ACROCLINIUM

Strawflower

COMPOSITAE/ASTERACEAE

Genus of drought-tolerant annuals, perennials and sub-shrubs, grown for their daisy-like, papery flower heads, which are excellent for cutting and drying. Half hardy. Grow in sun and in poor, very well-drained soil. Propagate by seed sown outdoors in mid-spring. Aphids may cause problems.

R. chlorocephala* subsp. *rosea, syn. *Acroclinium roseum, Helipterum roseum*, illus. p.303.

R. manglesii, syn. *Helipterum manglesii*. Moderately fast-growing, erect annual. **H** 30cm (12in), **S** 15cm (6in). Has pointed-oval, greyish-green leaves and daisy-like, papery, red, pink or white flower heads, in summer and early autumn.

RHODANTHEMUM

COMPOSITAE/ASTERACEAE

Genus of mat-forming, often rhizomatous perennials and sub-shrubs, grown for their solitary, large, daisy-like, white flower heads, surrounded by prominent, usually green bracts. Fully to frost hardy. Needs full sun and moderately fertile, very well-drained soil. Propagate by seed in spring or by softwood cuttings in summer.

♀ ***R. hosmariense***, syn. *Chrysanthemum hosmariense, Pyrethropsis hosmariense*, illus. p.332.

RHODIOLA

CRASSULACEAE

Genus of perennials, some dioecious, with thick, fleshy rhizomes producing scaly, brown basal leaves and stiffly erect stems that bear triangular-oval to lance-shaped, fleshy, grey-green leaves. Star-shaped flowers have prominent stamens, and may be unisexual or bisexual. Fully hardy. Grow in full sun and moderately fertile soil. Propagate by seed in spring or autumn, divide rhizomes in spring or early summer or take leaf cuttings in summer.

R. heterodonta, syn. *Sedum heterodontum, S. rosea* var. *heterodontum*, illus. p.268.

R. rosea, syn. *Sedum rosea* (Roseroot). Clump-forming perennial. **H** and **S** 30cm (12in). Stems are clothed with oval to inversely lance-shaped, toothed, fleshy, glaucous leaves. In late spring or early summer, pink buds on dense, terminal heads open to small, star-shaped, greenish-, yellowish- or purplish-white flowers.

Rhodocactus grandifolius. See *Pereskia grandifolia*.

RHODOCHITON

SCROPHULARIACEAE

Genus of one species of evergreen, leaf-stalk climber, grown for its unusual flowers. Does best when grown as an annual. May be planted against fences and trellises or used as ground cover. Frost tender, min. 5°C (41°F). Grow in sun and in any well-drained soil. Propagate by seed in early spring.

♀ ***R. atrosanguineus***, syn. *R. volubilis*, illus. p.203.

R. volubilis. See *R. atrosanguineus*.

RHODODENDRON

Azalea, rhododendron

ERICACEAE

Genus of evergreen, semi-evergreen or deciduous shrubs, ranging from a dwarf habit to a tree-like stature, grown mainly for beauty of flower. Fully hardy to frost tender, min. 4–7°C (39–45°F). Most prefer dappled shade, but a considerable number tolerates full sun, especially in cool climates. Needs neutral to acid soil – ideally, humus-rich and well-drained. Shallow planting is essential, as plants are surface-rooting. Dead-head spent flowers, wherever practical, to encourage energy into growth rather than seed production. Propagate by layering or semi-ripe cuttings in late summer. Yellowing leaves are usually caused by poor drainage, excessively deep planting or lime in soil. Weevils and powdery mildew may also cause problems. ①The nectar of some rhododendron flowers may cause severe discomfort if ingested. See also feature panel pp.124–25.

Rhododendrons and azaleas

The genus *Rhododendron* includes not only evergreen, large-leaved and frequently large-flowered species and hybrids, but also dwarf, smaller-leaved shrubs, both evergreen and deciduous, with few-flowered clusters of usually small blooms. "Azalea" is the common name given to the deciduous species and hybrids, as well as to a group of compact, evergreen shrubs derived mainly from Japanese species. They are valued for their mass of small colourful blooms produced in late spring. Many of the evergreen azaleas (sometimes known as Belgian azaleas) may also be grown as house plants. Botanically, however, all are classified as *Rhododendron*. The flowers are usually single, but may be semi-double or double, including hose-in-hose (one flower tube inside the other). Unless otherwise stated below, flowers are single and leaves mid- to dark green and oval.

R

R. aberconwayi. Evergreen, distinctly erect rhododendron. **H** to 2.5m (8ft), **S** 1.2m (4ft). Frost hardy. Has small, broadly lance-shaped, rigid, deep green leaves. Bears saucer-shaped, white flowers in late spring.
R. albrechtii. Deciduous, upright, bushy azalea. **H** to 3m (10ft), **S** 2m (6ft). Fully hardy. Has spoon-shaped leaves, clustered at branch tips, and, in spring, loose clusters of 3–5 bell-shaped, green-spotted, purple or pink flowers.
***R.* 'Alison Johnstone'.** Evergreen, bushy, compact rhododendron. **H** and **S** 2m (6ft). Frost hardy. Produces an abundance of exquisite, bell-shaped, peach-pink flowers in spring and bears waxy, grey-green leaves.
***R.* 'Angelo'.** Evergreen, bushy rhododendron. **H** and **S** to 4m (12ft). Frost hardy. Has bold foliage and large, fragrant, bell-shaped, white flowers in mid-summer. Is good in light woodland.
R. arboreum (illus. p.125). Evergreen, tree-like rhododendron. **H** to 12m (40ft), **S** 3m (10ft). Frost hardy. Undersides of broadly lance-shaped leaves are silver, fawn or cinnamon. In spring has dense clusters of bell-shaped flowers in colours ranging from red (most tender form) through pink to white.
R. argyrophyllum. Evergreen, spreading rhododendron. **H** and **S** to 5m (15ft). Fully hardy. Oblong leaves are silvery-white on undersides. Loose bunches of bell-shaped, rich pink flowers, sometimes with deeper coloured spots, are borne in spring. Is ideal for a light woodland.
R. arizelum. See *R. rex* subsp. *arizelum*.
***R.* 'Ascot Brilliant'.** Evergreen, bushy rhododendron. **H** and **S** 3m (10ft). Frost hardy. Leaves are broadly oval. In spring produces loose bunches of funnel-shaped, waxy, rose-red blooms with darker edges.
R. augustinii (illus. p.125). Evergreen, bushy rhododendron. **H** and **S** to 4m (12ft). Fully hardy. Has lance-shaped to oblong, light green leaves and, in spring, bears an abundance of multi-stemmed, widely funnel-shaped, pale to deep blue or lavender flowers.
R. auriculatum. Evergreen, bushy, widely branching rhododendron. **H** and **S** to 6m (20ft). Fully hardy. Has large, oblong, hairy leaves with distinct, ear-like lobes at their base. In late summer bears loose bunches of 7–15 large, heavily scented, tubular to funnel-shaped, white flowers. Is best in light woodland.
***R.* 'Azor'.** Evergreen, upright rhododendron. **H** and **S** to 4m (12ft). Frost hardy. Leaves are broadly oval. Especially valuable as it produces large, fragrant, funnel-shaped, salmon-pink flowers in mid-summer.
***R.* 'Azuma-kagami'.** Evergreen, compact azalea. **H** and **S** 1.2m (4ft). Frost hardy. Bears many small, hose-in-hose, deep pink flowers in mid-spring. Is best in semi-shade.
R. barbatum. Evergreen, upright rhododendron. **H** and **S** to 10m (30ft). Fully hardy. Bears lance-shaped, dark green leaves covered with bristles, on stems; bark is plum-coloured and peeling. Bears tight bunches of tubular to bell-shaped, bright scarlet flowers in early spring.
***R.* 'Beauty of Littleworth'.** Evergreen, open, shrubby rhododendron. **H** and **S** 4m (12ft). Frost hardy. In late spring bears huge, conical bunches of scented, funnel-shaped, crimson-spotted, white flowers.
***R.* 'Beefeater'.** Evergreen, bushy rhododendron. **H** and **S** to 2.5m (8ft). Frost hardy. Leaves are broadly lance-shaped. Produces striking, flat-topped bunches of bell-shaped, scarlet flowers in late spring and early summer.
🏆 ***R.* 'Blaauw's Pink'** (illus. p.125). Evergreen, compact azalea. **H** and **S** 1.5m (5ft). Fully hardy. Bears masses of funnel-shaped, salmon-pink flowers, with paler blush, in late spring.
🏆 ***R.* 'Blue Danube'** (illus. p.125). Evergreen, upright azalea. **H** 2m (6ft), **S** 1.5m (5ft). Fully hardy. Produces bell-shaped, vivid violet-blue flowers in spring.
***R.* 'Blue Diamond'.** Evergreen, upright rhododendron. **H** and **S** to 1.5m (5ft). Fully hardy. Small, neat leaves contrast with funnel-shaped, bright blue flowers borne in mid- to late spring. Likes full sun.
🏆 ***R.* 'Blue Peter'.** Evergreen, bushy rhododendron. **H** and **S** to 4m (12ft). Fully hardy. In early summer produces bold, open funnel-shaped, 2-tone lavender-purple flowers, with frilled petal margins.
R. calendulaceum (Flame azalea). Deciduous, bushy azalea. **H** and **S** 2–3m (6–10ft). Fully hardy. In early summer bears funnel-shaped, scarlet or orange flowers in bunches of 5–7.
🏆 ***R. calophytum*** (illus. p.124). Evergreen, widely-branched rhododendron. **H** and **S** to 6m (20ft). Frost hardy. Produces large, lance-shaped leaves and, in early spring, huge bunches of bell-shaped, white or pale pink flowers, with crimson spots.
R. calostrotum. Evergreen, compact rhododendron. **H** and to 1m (3ft). Fully hardy. Has blue-green leaves and, in late spring, saucer-shaped, purple or scarlet flowers in clusters of 2–5.
***R.* 'Catawbiense Album'.** Evergreen, rounded rhododendron. **H** and **S** to 3m (10ft). Fully hardy. Bears glossy leaves and, in early summer, dense, rounded bunches of bell-shaped, white flowers.
***R.* 'Catawbiense Boursault'.** Evergreen, rounded rhododendron. **H** and **S** to 3m (10ft). Fully hardy. Has glossy leaves. Dense, rounded bunches of bell-shaped, lilac-purple blooms are borne in early summer.
🏆 ***R.* 'Cilpinense'**, syn. *R.* x *cilpinense*. Semi-evergreen, compact rhododendron. **H** and **S** to 1.5m (5ft). Frost hardy. Leaves are dark green and glossy. Bears masses of large, bell-shaped, blush-pink flowers, flushed deeper in bud, in early spring. Flowers are vulnerable to frost damage.
R. cinnabarinum (illus. p.125). Evergreen, upright rhododendron. **H** and 1.5–4m (5–12ft). Frost hardy. Has blue-green leaves with small scales. Narrowly tubular, waxy, orange to red flowers are borne in loose, drooping bunches in late spring. **subsp. *xanthocodon*** (syn. *R. xanthocodon*) is of open, upright habit and has aromatic, mid-green leaves, which are blue-green when young. Bears bell-shaped, yellow flowers in late spring.
🏆 ***R.* 'Coccineum Speciosum'.** Deciduous, bushy azalea. **H** and **S** 1.5–2.5m (5–8ft). Fully hardy. Produces open funnel-shaped, brilliant rich orange-red blooms in early summer. Broadly lance-shaped leaves provide good autumn colour.
🏆 ***R.* 'Corneille'.** Deciduous, bushy azalea. **H** and **S** 1.5–2.5m (5–8ft). Fully hardy. In early summer produces fragrant, honeysuckle-like, cream flowers, flushed pink outside. Has colourful autumn foliage.
🏆 ***R.* 'Crest'**, syn. *R.* 'Hawk Crest'. Evergreen rhododendron of open habit. **H** and **S** 1.5–4m (5–12ft). Frost hardy. Has broadly lance-shaped leaves. Bell-shaped flowers are borne in loose, flat-topped bunches, and are apricot in bud, opening to clear sulphur-yellow in late spring.
R. cubittii. Evergreen rhododendron now included in *R. veitchianum*. **H** 1.5m (5ft), **S** to1m (3ft). Half hardy. Has purple-brown young shoots and oblong to elliptic, leathery, sparsely scaly, mid- to dark green leaves. In mid- and late spring bears funnel-shaped, white to pale pink flowers, with brownish or yellow-orange markings.
***R.* 'Cunningham's White'.** Evergreen, compact rhododendron. **H** 2.5 (8ft), **S** 2m (6ft). Fully hardy. In spring produces open trusses of funnel-shaped, pale lilac flowers, which fade to white, speckled with purple and yellow.

🏆 ***R.* 'Curlew'** (illus. p.125). Evergreen rhododendron of compact, spreading habit. **H** and **S** 30cm (1ft). Fully hardy. Produces dull green leaves and, in late spring, relatively large, open funnel-shaped, yellow flowers.
🏆 ***R.* 'Cynthia'.** Vigorous, evergreen, dome-shaped rhododendron. **H** and **S** to 6m (20ft). Fully hardy. Bears conical bunches of bell-shaped, magenta-purple flowers, marked blackish-red within, in late spring. Is excellent for sun or shade.
R. dauricum. Evergreen, upright rhododendron. **H** and **S** to 1.5m (5ft). Fully hardy. Produces funnel-shaped, vivid purple flowers in loose clusters throughout winter. Green leaves turn purple-brown in frosty conditions.
🏆 ***R. davidsonianum.*** Deciduous, upright rhododendron. **H** 1.5–4m (5–12ft). Fully hardy. Aromatic leaves are lance-shaped to oblong. In late spring has clusters of funnel-shaped flowers, ranging from pale pink to mid-lilac-mauve.
🏆 ***R.* 'Daviesii'** (illus. p.125). Deciduous, upright azalea. **H** and **S** 2m (6ft). Fully hardy. Fragrant, funnel-shaped, white flowers, each with a yellow flare, are borne in spring.
🏆 ***R. decorum*** (illus. p.124). Evergreen, bushy rhododendron. **H** and **S** 4m (12ft). Frost hardy. Oblong to lance-shaped leaves are mid-green above, paler beneath. Large, fragrant, funnel-shaped, white or shell-pink flowers, green- or pink-spotted within, are produced in early summer.
***R. degronianum* var. *heptamerum*,** syn. *R. metternichii*. Evergreen, upright rhododendron. **H** and **S** 1.5–4m (5–12ft). Fully hardy. Has oblong leaves, glossy and green above, reddish-brown-felted beneath. Bell-shaped, rose-red flowers, borne in spring, are in rounded bunches of 10–15, often subtly spotted within.
R. discolor. See *R. fortunei* subsp. *discolor*.
***R.* 'Doncaster'.** Evergreen, compact rhododendron. **H** and **S** 2–2.5m (6–8ft). Frost hardy. Has leathery, glossy leaves and, in late spring, funnel-shaped, dark red flowers in dense bunches.
🏆 ***R.* 'Dopey'.** Evergreen, compact rhododendron. **H** and **S** 1.5m (5ft). Fully hardy. In spring has bell-shaped, flame-orange flowers in rounded trusses.
🏆 ***R.* 'Dora Amateis'.** Evergreen, compact rhododendron. **H** and **S** 60cm (2ft). Fully hardy. Leaves are slender, glossy and pointed. Masses of broadly funnel-shaped, white flowers, tinged with pink and marked with green, appear in late spring. Is sun tolerant.
***R.* 'Elizabeth'.** Evergreen, dome-shaped rhododendron. **H** and **S** to 1.5m (5ft). Frost hardy. Leaves are oblong. Has large, trumpet-shaped, brilliant red flowers in late spring. Is good in sun or partial shade.
***R.* 'Elizabeth Lockhart'.** Evergreen, dome-shaped rhododendron. **H** and **S** 60cm (2ft). Frost hardy. Produces shiny, purple-green leaves that become darker in winter. Bell-shaped, deep pink flowers are carried in spring.
***R.* 'English Roseum'.** Evergreen, vigorous, bushy rhododendron. **H** and **S** to 2.5m (8ft). Fully hardy. Dark green leaves are paler beneath. Bears compact bunches of funnel-shaped, lilac-rose flowers in late spring.

🏆 ***R.* 'Fabia'.** Evergreen, dome-shaped rhododendron. **H** and **S** 2m (6ft). Frost hardy. Leaves are lance-shaped. Loose, flat trusses of funnel-shaped, orange-tinted, scarlet flowers are borne in early summer.
R. falconeri (illus. p.124). Multi-stemmed, evergreen rhododendron. **H** to 12m (40ft), **S** 5m (15ft). Fully hardy. Has flaking, red-brown bark and broadly elliptic to oval, dark green leaves, brown-felted beneath.

In mid-spring produces widely bell-shaped, fleshy, creamy-white or yellow flowers, sometimes pink-tinged, often with purple marks inside.

🏆 **R. 'Fastuosum Flore Pleno'** (illus. p.125). Evergreen, dome-shaped rhododendron. **H** and **S** 1.5–4m (5–12ft). Fully hardy. In early summer bears loose bunches of funnel-shaped, double, rich mauve flowers, with red-brown marks and wavy margins.

R. fictolacteum. See *R. rex* subsp. *fictolacteum.*

🏆 **R. 'Fireball'.** Evergreen, compact rhododendron. **H** and **S** 2m (6ft). Fully hardy. Has rounded trusses of bell-shaped, vivid scarlet flowers in early spring.

R. 'Firefly'. See *R.* 'Hexe'.

🏆 ***R. fortunei* subsp. *discolor***, syn. *R. discolor.* Evergreen, tree-like rhododendron. **H** and **S** to 8m (25ft). Frost hardy. Leaves are oblong to oval. Bears fragrant, funnel-shaped, pink flowers in mid-summer. Is ideal in a light woodland.

🏆 **R. 'Fragrantissimum'** (illus. p.124). Lax, evergreen rhododendron. **H** and **S** 2m (6ft). Half hardy. Nutmeg-scented, broadly funnel-shaped, sometimes pink-flushed, white flowers, with yellow throats, are borne in mid-spring. Leaves are hairy.

R. 'Freya'. Deciduous azalea of compact, shrubby habit. **H** and **S** 1.5m (5ft). Fully hardy. Fragrant, funnel-shaped, pink-flushed, orange-salmon flowers appear from late spring to early summer.

R. 'Frome'. Deciduous azalea of shrubby habit. **H** and **S** to 1.5m (5ft). Fully hardy. In spring bears trumpet-shaped, saffron-yellow flowers, overlaid red in throats; petals are frilled and wavy-margined.

🏆 ***R. fulvum*** (illus. p.125). Evergreen, bushy rhododendron. **H** and **S** 1.5–4m (5–12ft). Frost hardy. Oblong to oval, polished, deep green leaves are brown-felted beneath. In early spring has loose bunches of bell-shaped, red-blotched, pink flowers, which fade to white.

R. 'George Reynolds'. Deciduous, bushy azalea. **H** and **S** to 2m (6ft). Fully hardy. Large, funnel-shaped, yellow flowers, flushed pink in bud, are borne with or before the leaves in spring.

🏆 **R. 'Gibralter'** (illus. p.125). Deciduous, bushy azalea. **H** 1.5m (5ft), **S** 1m (3ft). Fully hardy. In spring produces tubular, flame-red flowers, which are deep orange in bud.

R. 'Gloria Mundi'. Deciduous, twiggy azalea. **H** and **S** to 2m (6ft). Fully hardy. Produces fragrant, honeysuckle-like, yellow-flared, orange flowers, with frilled margins, in early summer.

R. 'Glory of Littleworth'. Evergreen or semi-evergreen, bushy hybrid between a rhododendron and an azalea. **H** and **S** 1.5m (5ft). Frost hardy. Compact bunches of fragrant, bell-shaped, orange-marked, creamy-white flowers are borne abundantly in late spring and early summer. Is not easy to cultivate.

R. 'Gold Crown'. See *R.* 'Goldkrone'.

🏆 **R. 'Golden Torch'** (illus. p.124). Evergreen, compact rhododendron. **H** and **S** 1m (3ft). Fully hardy. In spring has bell-shaped, pink-budded, pale yellow flowers.

🏆 **R. 'Goldkrone'**, syn. *R.* 'Gold Crown' (illus. p.125). Compact, evergreen shrub. **H** and **S** 1.5m (5ft). Fully hardy. Funnel- to bell-shaped, bright golden-yellow flowers, delicately spotted ruby-red inside, are borne in succession in mid-spring.

🏆 **R. 'Gomer Waterer'** (illus. p.124). Evergreen, compact rhododendron. **H** and **S** 1.5–4m (5–12ft). Fully hardy. Leaves are curved back at margins. Bell-shaped flowers, borne in dense bunches in early summer, are white, flushed mauve, each with a basal, mustard blotch. Likes sun or partial shade.

R. 'Grace Seabrook' (illus. p.125). Evergreen, upright rhododendron. **H** and **S** 2m (6ft). Fully hardy. Leaves are pointed. In spring bears funnel-shaped, deep red flowers, which are paler towards edges.

R. griffithianum. Evergreen, upright rhododendron with peeling, red bark. **H** to 6m (20ft), **S** 3m (10ft). Frost hardy. Bears loose trusses of fragrant, bell-shaped, white flowers in spring. Has large, elliptic, glabrous leaves.

R. 'Hatsugiri'. Evergreen, compact azalea. **H** and **S** 60cm (2ft). Frost hardy. Has small, but very numerous, funnel-shaped, bright crimson-purple flowers in spring. Flowers very reliably.

R. 'Hawk Crest'. See *R.* 'Crest'.

R. 'Hexe', syn. *R.* 'Firefly'. Evergreen azalea of neat habit. **H** and **S** 60cm (2ft). Frost hardy. Has numerous relatively large, hose-in-hose, glowing, crimson flowers in spring.

R. 'Hinode-giri'. Evergreen, compact azalea. **H** and **S** 1.5m (5ft). Frost hardy. Funnel-shaped, bright crimson flowers are small, but produced in abundance in late spring. Likes sun or light shade.

🏆 **R. 'Hinomayo'.** Evergreen, compact azalea. **H** and **S** 1.5m (5ft). Frost hardy. Small, funnel-shaped, clear pink flowers are produced in great abundance in spring. Likes sun or light shade.

R. hippophaeoides. Evergreen, erect rhododendron. **H** and **S** 1.5m (5ft). Fully hardy. Narrowly lance-shaped, aromatic leaves are grey-green. Has small, funnel-shaped, lavender or lilac flowers in spring. Tolerates wet, but not stagnant, soil.

🏆 **R. 'Homebush'.** Deciduous, compact azalea. **H** and **S** 1.5m (5ft). Frost hardy. In late spring bears tight, rounded heads of trumpet-shaped, semi-double, rose-purple flowers with paler shading.

🏆 **R. 'Hotei'** (illus. p.125). Evergreen, rhododendron of neat, compact habit. **H** and **S** 1.5–2.5m (5–8ft). Fully hardy. Large, funnel-shaped, deep yellow flowers are freely produced in late spring.

R. 'Humming Bird'. Evergreen, dome-shaped rhododendron of neat, compact habit. **H** and **S** to 1.5m (5ft). Fully hardy. From mid- to late spring has bell-shaped, rose-pink flowers in loose, nodding bunches, above rounded, glossy leaves.

🏆 **R. 'Hydon Hunter'.** Evergreen rhododendron of neat habit. **H** and **S** to 1.5m (5ft). Fully hardy. In late spring or early summer has masses of large, narrowly bell-shaped, red-rimmed flowers, paler towards the centre and orange-spotted within.

R. impeditum. Slow-growing, evergreen rhododendron. **H** and **S** to 60cm (2ft). Fully hardy. Aromatic leaves are grey-green. Funnel-shaped, purplish-blue flowers appear in spring. Is ideal in a rock garden.

🏆 **R. 'Irohayama'.** Evergreen, compact azalea. **H** and **S** to 1.5m (5ft). Frost hardy. Has abundant, small, funnel-shaped, white flowers, with pale lavender margins and faint brown eyes, in spring. Does well in light shade.

R. 'Jalisco'. Deciduous, open, bushy rhododendron. **H** and **S** 1.5–4m (5–12ft). Frost hardy. Bears bunches of narrowly bell-shaped, straw-coloured flowers, tinted orange-rose at tips, in early summer.

R. 'Jeanette'. Semi-evergreen, upright azalea. **H** and **S** 1.5–2m (5–6ft). Frost hardy. Has funnel-shaped, vivid phlox-pink, dark blotched flowers, in spring. Is good in light shade or full sun.

R. 'John Cairns'. Evergreen, upright, compact azalea. **H** and 1.5–2m (5–6ft). Fully hardy. Bears abundant funnel-shaped, orange-red flowers in spring. Grows reliably in sun or semi-shade.

R. kaempferi. Semi-evergreen, erect, loosely branched azalea. **H** and **S** 1.5–2.5m (5–8ft). Fully hardy. Leaves are lance-shaped. Has an abundance of funnel-shaped flowers in orange or red in late spring and early summer.

R. 'Kilimanjaro'. Evergreen, bushy rhododendron. **H** and **S** 1.5–4m (5–12ft). Frost hardy. Bears broadly lance-shaped leaves. Produces large, rounded bunches of funnel- to bell-shaped, wavy-edged, maroon-red flowers, spotted chocolate within, in late spring and early summer.

R. 'Kirin'. Evergreen, compact azalea. **H** and **S** to 1.5m (5ft). Frost hardy. In spring has numerous hose-in-hose flowers that are deep rose, shaded a delicate silvery-rose. Looks best in light shade.

🏆 ***R. kiusianum.*** Semi-evergreen azalea of compact habit. **H** and **S** to 60cm (2ft). Fully hardy. Leaves are narrowly oval. Produces clusters of 2–5 funnel-shaped flowers, usually lilac-rose or mauve-purple, in late spring. Prefers full sun.

🏆 **R. 'Lady Alice Fitzwilliam'.** Evergreen, bushy rhododendron. **H** and **S** 1.5–4m (5–12ft). Half hardy. Leaves are glossy, dark green. Loose bunches of heavily scented, broadly funnel-shaped, white flowers, flushed pale pink, are produced in mid- to late spring. Grow against a south-or west-facing wall.

🏆 **R. 'Lady Clementine Mitford'.** Evergreen, rounded, dense rhododendron. **H** and **S** 4m (12ft). Fully hardy. Has broadly oval, glossy, dark green leaves that are silvery when young and, in late spring and early summer, bold bunches of tubular- to bell-shaped flowers, peach-pink fading to white in the centre, with V-shaped, pink, green and brown marks within.

R. 'Lady Rosebery'. Evergreen, stiffly branched rhododendron. **H** and **S** 1.5–4m (5–12ft). Frost hardy. Bears clusters of drooping, narrowly bell-shaped, waxy, deep pink flowers, which are paler towards petal margins, in late spring. Is ideal for a woodland margin.

R. laetum. Erect, evergreen rhododendron. **H** and **S** 1.5m (5ft). Min. 5°C (41°F). Elliptic to broadly elliptic, glossy, dark green leaves have tiny, white scales beneath. In spring, red flower stalks bear funnel-shaped, golden-yellow flowers, later suffused orange-red.

🏆 **R. 'Lem's Cameo'.** Evergreen, rounded, bushy rhododendron. **H** and **S** 1.5–2.5m (5–8ft). Frost hardy. Leaves are rounded. In spring has large-domed bunches of open funnel-shaped, pale peach flowers, deep pink in bud, shaded to pink at margins, with basal, deep rose-coloured blotches.

R. leucaspis. Densely branched, evergreen rhododendron. **H** 1m (3ft), **S** 1.5m (5ft). Frost hardy. Has broadly elliptic, dark green leaves, bristly above, scaly and yellowish-green beneath. In early spring bears saucer-shaped, white flowers, with chocolate-brown anthers.

🏆 **R. 'Loderi King George'** (illus. p.124). Large, evergreen rhododendron of open habit. **H** and 4m (12ft). Fully hardy. Has large leaves. In late spring and early summer, pale pink buds open to huge trusses of fragrant, funnel-shaped, pure white flowers, with subtle green marks in the throats.

R. lutescens. Semi-evergreen, upright rhododendron. **H** and 1.5–3m (5–10ft). Fully hardy. Has oval to lance-shaped leaves that are bronze-red when young. In early spring bears funnel-shaped, primrose-yellow flowers. Is effective in a light woodland.

🏆 ***R. luteum*** (illus. p.125). Open deciduous azalea. **H** and **S** 1.5–2.5m (5–8ft). Fully hardy. Leaves are oblong to lance-shaped. Has very fragrant, funnel-shaped, bold yellow blooms in spring. Autumn foliage is rich and colourful.

🏆 ***R. maccabeanum.*** Evergreen, tree-like rhododendron. **H** and up to 13.5m (45ft). Frost hardy. Has bold, broadly oval leaves, dark green above, grey-felted beneath, and, in early spring, large bunches of bell-shaped, yellow flowers, blotched purple within.

R. mallotum. Evergreen, upright, open rhododendron, occasionally tree-like. **H** and to 4m (12ft). Frost hardy. Oblong to oval leaves are deep green above, red-brown-felted beneath. Showy, tubular, crimson flowers in loose bunches are borne in early spring.

🏆 **R. 'May Day'.** Evergreen, spreading rhododendron. **H** and to 1.5m (5ft). Frost hardy. Leaves are fresh green above, whitish-felted beneath. Has masses of loose bunches of long-lasting, funnel-shaped, scarlet flowers in late spring; petal-like calyces match the flower colour.

R. 'Medway'. Deciduous, bushy, open azalea. **H** and **S** 1.5–2.5m (5–8ft). Fully hardy. In late spring has large, trumpet-shaped, pale pink flowers with darker margins and orange-flashed throats; petal margins are frilled.

R. metternichii. See *R. degronianum* var. *heptamerum.*

R. 'Moonshine Crescent'. Evergreen, rounded to upright rhododendron. **H** 2–2.5m (6–8ft), **S** 2m (6ft). Frost hardy. In late spring produces compact trusses of bell-shaped, yellow flowers. Leaves are oblong to oval and dark green.

🏆 **R. 'Mother's Day'** (illus. p.125). Evergreen, compact azalea. **H** and **S** 1m (3ft). Fully hardy. Has funnel-shaped, bright red flowers in spring.

R. moupinense. Evergreen, rounded, compact rhododendron. **H** and **S** to 1.5m (5ft). Frost hardy. Produces funnel-shaped, pink blooms in loose bunches in late winter and early spring. Leaves are glossy, dark green above, paler beneath. Is best grown in a sheltered situation to reduce risk of frosted flowers.

***R.* 'Mrs G.W. Leak'.** Evergreen, upright, compact rhododendron. **H** and **S** 4m (12ft). Fully hardy. In late spring bears compact, conical bunches of funnel-shaped, pink flowers, with black-brown and crimson marks within,.

R. nakaharae. Evergreen, mound-forming azalea. **H** and **S** 60cm (2ft). Frost hardy. Shoots and oblong to oval leaves are densely hairy. Funnel-shaped, dark brick-red flowers are borne in small clusters. Is valuable for mid-summer flowering and is ideal for a rock garden.

🏆 ***R.* 'Nancy Waterer'.** Deciduous, twiggy azalea. **H** and **S** 1.5–2.5m (5–8ft). Fully hardy. Has large, long-tubed and honeysuckle-like, brilliant golden-yellow flowers in early summer. Is ideal in a light woodland or full sun.

🏆 ***R.* 'Narcissiflorum'.** Vigorous, deciduous, compact azalea. **H** and **S** 1.5–2.5m (5–8ft). Fully hardy. Sweetly scented, hose-in-hose, pale yellow flowers, darker outside and in centre, are borne in late spring or early summer. Autumn foliage is bronze.

🏆 ***R. niveum*** (illus. p.125). Evergreen, shrubby rhododendron. **H** 5m (16ft), **S** 3m (10ft). Fully hardy. Narrowly oval to lance-shaped, dark green leaves are white felted when young and brown felted beneath when mature. Bell-shaped, plum-purple flowers in compact, rounded heads are borne in spring.

***R.* Nobleanum Group.** Evergreen, upright shrub or tree-like rhododendron. **H** and **S** to 5m (15ft). Frost hardy. Bears large, compact bunches of broadly funnel-shaped, rose-red, pink or white flowers in winter or early spring. Will flower for long periods in mild weather; is best in a sheltered position.

🏆 ***R.* 'Norma'.** Vigorous, deciduous, compact azalea. **H** and **S** to 1.5m (5ft). Fully hardy. Bears masses of hose-in-hose, rose-red flowers, with a salmon glow, in spring. Grows well in sun or light shade.

***R.* 'Nova Zembla'.** Vigorous, evergreen, upright rhododendron. **H** and 1.5–4m (5–12ft). Fully hardy. Has funnel-shaped, dark red flowers in closely set bunches from late spring to early summer.

🏆 ***R. occidentale.*** Bushy, deciduous, azalea. **H** and **S** 1.5–2.5m (5–8ft). Fully hardy. Glossy leaves turn yellow or orange in autumn. Bears fragrant, funnel-shaped, white or pale pink flowers, each with a basal, yellow-orange blotch, in early to mid-summer.

***R.* 'Olive'.** Upright, evergreen rhododendron. **H** 1.2m (4ft), **S** 1m (3ft). Fully hardy. Small, oval to elliptic, mid-green leaves are paler green beneath. Has funnel-shaped, mauve-pink flowers, with darker spots inside, in early spring.

🏆 ***R. orbiculare*** (illus. p.124). Evergreen rhododendron of compact habit. **H** and **S** to 3m (10ft). Fully hardy. Has rounded, bright green leaves and bell-shaped, rose-pink flowers in loose bunches in late spring.

R. oreotrephes. Deciduous, upright shrub or tree-like rhododendron. **H** and **S** to 5m (15ft). Fully hardy. Has attractive, scaly, grey-green foliage. In spring bears loose bunches of 3–10 broadly funnel-shaped flowers, usually mauve or purple, but variable, often with crimson spots.

🏆 ***R. pachysanthum*** (illus. p.124). Evergreen, compact, rounded rhododendron. **H** and **S** 2m (6ft). Fully hardy. New shoots and oblong leaves,with pointed tips, are covered in fawn felt. Trusses of open bell-shaped, white to pale pink flowers, sometimes with purple flecks, are borne in mid- and late spring.

🏆 ***R.* 'Palestrina'.** Evergreen or semi-evergreen, compact, free-flowering azalea. **H** and **S** to 1.2m (4ft). Frost hardy. Has large, open funnel-shaped, white flowers, with faint, green marks, in late spring. Grows well in light shade.

🏆 ***R.* 'Patty Bee'** (illus. p.125). Evergreen, compact rhododendron. **H** and **S** 1m (3ft). Fully hardy. Produces trusses of funnel-shaped, lemon-coloured flowers in spring.

🏆 ***R.* 'Percy Wiseman'** illus. p.122.

🏆 ***R.* 'Peter John Mezitt'**, syn. *R.* 'P.J. Mezitt'. Evergreen, compact rhododendron. **H** and **S** up to 1.5m (5ft). Fully hardy. Aromatic leaves are small, dark green in summer, bronze-purple in winter. Bears frost-resistant, funnel-shaped, lavender-pink flowers in early spring. Is good in full sun.

***R.* 'Pink Pearl'** (illus. p.125). Vigorous, evergreen, upright, open rhododendron. **H** and **S** 4m (12ft) or more. Frost hardy. Bears tall bunches of open funnel-shaped, pink flowers in late spring.

***R.* 'P.J. Mezitt'.** See *R.* 'Peter John Mezitt'.

🏆 ***R.* 'Polar Bear'** (illus. p.124). Vigorous, multi-stemmed, evergreen rhododendron. **H** 5m (15ft), **S** 4m (12ft). Fully hardy. In late summer bears strongly scented, tubular to funnel-shaped, white flowers, with light brown-flecked, pale green throats.

🏆 ***R. praecox*** (illus. p.125). Partially deciduous, compact rhododendron. **H** 1.5m (5ft), **S** 1m (3ft). Fully hardy. Funnel-shaped, rose-purple flowers, in 2s and 3s, are borne at the ends of the shoots in late winter and early spring. Elliptic leaves are aromatic when bruised.

🏆 ***R.* 'Ptarmigan'.** Evergreen, spreading rhododendron that forms a compact mound. **H** to 30cm (1ft), **S** 75cm (2½ft) or more. Fully hardy. Funnel-shaped, pure white flowers are borne in early spring. Prefers full sun.

🏆 ***R.* 'Purple Splendour'** (illus. p.125). Evergreen, bushy rhododendron. **H** and **S** to 3m (10ft). Fully hardy. Has bunches of open funnel-shaped, rich royal-purple flowers, with black marks in throats, in late spring or early summer.

🏆 ***R.* 'Queen Elizabeth II'.** Evergreen, bushy rhododendron. **H** and **S** 1.5–4m (5–12ft). Frost hardy. Bears funnel-shaped, greenish-yellow flowers in loose bunches in late spring. Leaves are narrowly oval or lance-shaped, glossy and mid-green above, paler beneath.

***R.* 'Queen of Hearts'.** Evergreen, open rhododendron. **H** and **S** 1.5–4m (5–12ft). Frost hardy. Has masses of domed bunches of funnel-shaped, deep crimson flowers, black-speckled within, in mid-spring.

R. quinquefolium (illus. p.124). Deciduous, bushy shrub. **H** 3-4m (10–13ft), **S** 3m. Fully hardy. Has obovate to diamond-shaped, mid-green leaves in whorls of 4 or 5 at shoot ends. Leaves have reddish edges when young and colour well in autumn. In mid- and late spring bears small clusters of pendent, saucer-shaped, green-spotted, white flowers.

R. racemosum. Evergreen, upright, stiffly branched rhododendron. **H** and **S** to 2.5m (8ft). Fully hardy. Has clusters of widely funnel-shaped, bright pink flowers carried along the stems in spring. Small, aromatic, broadly oval leaves are dull green above, grey-green below.

R. rex. Vigorous, evergreen, upright shrub or tree-like rhododendron. **H** and **S** 4m (12ft) or more. Frost hardy. Leaves are pale buff-felted beneath. Pink or white flowers each have a crimson blotch and a spotted throat. **subsp. *arizelum*** (syn. *R. arizelum*), **H** and **S** 8m (25ft), has inversely oval leaves and usually yellow, sometimes pink, rarely white flowers, with crimson marks in the throats. 🏆 **subsp. *fictolacteum*** (syn. *R. fictolacteum*); (illus. p.124), **H** to 13.5m (45ft), has large leaves, green above, brown-felted beneath. Bears bunches of bell-shaped, white flowers in spring, each with a maroon blotch and often a spotted throat.

***R.* 'Romany Chai'.** Vigorous, evergreen rhododendron, open when young, becoming denser with age. **H** and **S** 1.5–4m (5–12ft). Frost hardy. Has dark green, bronze-tinged foliage. In early summer, produces large, compact bunches of broadly funnel-shaped, rich brown-red flowers, each with a basal, maroon blotch. Suits a light woodland.

***R.* 'Roseum Elegans'.** Vigorous, evergreen, rounded rhododendron. **H** and **S** 2.5m (8ft) or more. Fully hardy. Foliage is bold and glossy, deep green. In early summer bears rounded bunches of broadly funnel-shaped, reddish-purple flowers, each marked with yellow-brown.

***R.* 'Roza Stevenson'.** Vigorous, evergreen, upright rhododendron of open habit. **H** and **S** 1.5–4m (5–12ft). Frost hardy. Produces masses of fine, loose bunches of saucer-shaped, lemon flowers in mid- to late spring. Is excellent in light shade.

R. rubiginosum. Vigorous, evergreen, upright, well-branched rhododendron. **H** 6m (20ft), **S** 2.5m (8ft). Frost hardy. Aromatic leaves are lance-shaped, dull green above, reddish-brown beneath. Has funnel-shaped, lilac-purple flowers in loose bunches in mid-spring.

R. schlippenbachii. Deciduous, rounded, open azalea. **H** and 2.5m (8ft). Fully hardy. Spoon-shaped leaves are in whorls at branch ends. Bears loose bunches of 3–6 saucer-shaped, pink flowers in mid-spring. Suits a light woodland.

***R.* 'Seta'** (illus. p.124). Evergreen, erect rhododendron. **H** 1.5m (5ft), **S** 1–1.5m (3–5ft). Frost hardy. In early spring bears loose bunches of tubular, vivid pink-and-white-striped flowers, fading to white at bases.

***R.* 'Seven Stars'.** Vigorous, evergreen, upright, dense rhododendron. **H** and **S** 2–3m (6–10ft). Fully hardy. Has yellowish-green foliage and, in spring, masses of bunches of large, bell-shaped, wavy-margined, white flowers, flushed with apple-blossom pink, pink in bud.

🏆 ***R. sinogrande*** (illus. p.124). Evergreen, bushy rhododendron. **H** and **S** 10m (30ft). Fully hardy. Has very large, oblong to lance-shaped, glossy, dark green leaves, silver- to buff-felted beneath. In mid- and late spring bears widely bell-shaped, pale yellow to creamy-white flowers, marked crimson inside.

***R.* 'Snowdrift'.** Deciduous, bushy azalea. **H** and **S** to 2.5m (8ft). Fully hardy. Bears bunches of large, slender-tubed flowers in spring before leaves appear. White flowers have yellow marks that deepen to orange.

R. souliei. Evergreen, open rhododendron. **H** and **S** 1.5–4m (5–12ft). Fully hardy. Has rounded leaves and, in late spring, saucer-shaped, soft pink flowers. Grows best in areas of low rainfall.

🏆 ***R.* 'Spek's Orange'.** Deciduous, bushy azalea. **H** and **S** to 2.5m (8ft). Fully hardy. In late spring bears bold bunches of large, slender-tubed, bright reddish-orange flowers, with greenish marks within.

🏆 ***R.* 'Strawberry Ice'.** Deciduous, bushy azalea. **H** and **S** 1.5–2.5m (5–8ft). Fully hardy. In late spring, deep pink buds open into trumpet-shaped, flesh-pink flowers, with deep yellow-marked throats and mottled deeper pink petal margins

***R.* 'Surprise'.** Evergreen, dense azalea. **H** and **S** to 1.5m (5ft). Frost hardy. Has abundant, small, funnel-shaped, light orange-red flowers in mid-spring. Looks effective when mass planted and is ideal in light shade or full sun.

🏆 ***R.* 'Susan'.** Close-growing, evergreen rhododendron. **H** and **S** 1.5–4m (5–12ft). Fully hardy. Foliage is glossy, dark green. In spring bears large bunches of open funnel-shaped flowers in 2 shades of blue-mauve, spotted purple within.

R. sutchuenense. Evergreen, spreading shrub or tree-like rhododendron. **H** and **S** to 5m (16ft). Frost hardy. Has large leaves and, in early spring, large bunches of broadly funnel-shaped, pink flowers, spotted deeper within. Is suitable for a light woodland.

***R.* 'Temple Belle'.** Evergreen rhododendron of neat, compact habit. **H** and **S** 1.5–2.5m (5–8ft). Fully hardy. Loose bunches of bell-shaped, clear pink flowers are produced in spring. Rounded leaves are dark green above, grey-green beneath.

R. thomsonii. Evergreen, rounded rhododendron of open habit. **H** and **S** to 5.5m (18ft). Frost hardy. Leaves are waxy, dark green above, whiter beneath. Peeling, fawn-coloured bark contrasts well with bell-shaped, waxy, red flowers in spring.

🏆 ***R.* 'Vuyk's Scarlet'.** Evergreen, compact azalea. **H** and **S** to 60cm (2ft). Frost hardy. In spring bears an abundance of relatively large, open funnel-shaped, brilliant red flowers, with wavy petals, which completely cover the glossy foliage.

R. wardii. Evergreen, compact rhododendron. **H** and **S** 1.5–4m (5–12ft). Fully hardy. Leaves are rounded. In late spring bears loose bunches of saucer-shaped, clear yellow flowers, with crimson basal blotches.

🏆 ***R. williamsianum*** (illus. p.124). Evergreen rhododendron of compact, spreading habit. **H** and **S** 1.5m (5ft). Fully hardy. Young leaves are bronze, maturing to mid-green. Has loosely clustered, bell-shaped, pink flowers in spring. Is ideal for a small garden.

***R.* 'Woodcock'.** Evergreen, compact, spreading rhododendron. **H** and **S** 1.5–2.5m (5–8ft). Fully hardy. Has semi-glossy, dark green leaves and, in spring, masses of loose bunches of funnel-shaped, rose-red flowers.

R. xanthocodon. See *R. cinnabarinum* subsp. *xanthocodon*.
R. yakushimanum (illus. p.124). Evergreen, dome-shaped rhododendron of neat, compact habit. **H** 1m (3ft), **S** 1.5m (5ft). Fully hardy. Leaves are broadly oval, silvery at first, maturing to deepest green, and brown-felted beneath. In late spring has open funnel-shaped, pink flowers, green flecked within, that fade to near white.
♀ ***R. 'Yellow Hammer'*** illus. p.126.
R. yunnanense. Semi-evergreen, open rhododendron. **H** and **S** 1.5–4m (5–12ft). Fully hardy. Has aromatic, grey-green leaves and masses of butterfly-like, pale pink or white flowers, with blotched throats, in spring.

RHODOHYPOXIS

HYPOXIDACEAE

Genus of dwarf, spring- to summer-flowering, tuberous perennials, grown for their pink, red or white flowers, each comprising 6 petals that meet at the centre, so the flower has no eye. Frost hardy, if kept fairly dry while dormant. Needs full sun, sandy, peaty soil and plenty of moisture in summer. Propagate in spring by seed or offsets.
R. 'Albrighton' illus. p.365.
♀ ***R. baurii.*** Spring- and early summer-flowering, tuberous perennial. **H** 5–10cm (2–4in), **S** 2.5–5cm (1–2in). Has an erect, basal tuft of narrowly lance-shaped, hairy leaves. Bears a succession of erect, flattish, white, pale pink or red flowers, 2cm (¾in) across, on slender stems. **var. *platypetala*** has 2.5cm (1in) wide, white or very pale pink flowers.
R. 'Douglas'. Spring- and early summer-flowering, tuberous perennial. **H** 5–10cm (2–4in), **S** 2.5–5cm (1–2in). Has an erect, basal tuft of narrowly lance-shaped, hairy leaves. Bears a succession of upright, flattish, rich deep red flowers singly on slender stems.
R. 'Margaret Rose' illus. p.362.

RHODOLEIA

HAMAMELIDACEAE

Genus of evergreen, mainly spring-flowering trees, grown for their foliage and flowers. Frost tender, min. 7–10°C (45–50°F). Needs full light or partial shade and humus-rich, well-drained, neutral to acid soil. Water potted specimens freely; sparingly when not in full growth. Tolerates pruning if necessary. Propagate by semi-ripe cuttings in summer or by seed when ripe, in autumn or in spring.
R. championii. Evergreen, bushy tree. **H** and **S** 4–8m (12–25ft). Elliptic to oval, bright green leaves, each to 9cm (3½in) long, are borne near the shoot tips. Clusters of tiny flowers, surrounded by petal-like, pink bracts, appear in spring.

RHODOPHIALA

AMARYLLIDACEAE

Genus of bulbs, grown for their large, funnel-shaped flowers. Frost hardy to frost tender, min. 13–15°C (55–9°F). Needs full sun or partial shade and well-drained soil. Keep dormant bulbs dry in winter. Propagate by seed in spring or by offsets in spring (summer-flowering species).
R. advena, syn. *Hippeastrum advenum*, illus. p.410.

RHODOTHAMNUS

ERICACEAE

Genus of one species of evergreen, semi-prostrate, open shrub, grown for its flowers. Is suitable for rock gardens and peat beds. Fully hardy. Needs sun and humus-rich, well-drained, acid soil. Propagate by seed in spring or by semi-ripe cuttings in summer.
R. chamaecistus illus. p.338.

RHODOTYPOS

ROSACEAE

Genus of one species of deciduous shrub, grown for its flowers. Fully hardy. Needs sun or semi-shade and moist but well-drained, fertile soil. After flowering, on established plants, cut back some older shoots. Propagate by softwood cuttings in summer or by seed in autumn.
R. kerrioides. See *R. scandens*.
R. scandens, syn. *R. kerrioides*, illus. p.149.

Rhoeo discolor. See *Tradescantia spathacea*.
Rhoeo spathacea. See *Tradescantia spathacea*.

RHOICISSUS

VITACEAE

Genus of evergreen, tendril climbers, grown for their handsome foliage. Bears inconspicuous flowers intermittently. Frost tender, min. 7–10°C (45–50°F). Grow in fertile, well-drained soil with light shade in summer. Water regularly, less in cold weather. Provide support. Remove crowded stems when necessary or in early spring. Propagate by seed in spring or by semi-ripe cuttings in summer.
♀ ***R. capensis*** (Cape grape). Vigorous, evergreen, tendril climber. **H** and **S** to 5m (15ft). Rounded, toothed, lustrous, mid- to deep green leaves, to 20cm (8in) wide, have deeply rounded, heart-shaped bases.
R. rhombifolia. See *Cissus rhombifolia*.
R. rhomboidea. See *Cissus rhombifolia*.

RHOMBOPHYLLUM

AIZOACEAE

Genus of mat-forming, perennial succulents with dense, basal rosettes of linear or semi-cylindrical leaves, each expanded towards middle or tip; leaf tip is reflexed or incurved. Frost tender, min. 5°C (41°F). Needs sun and very well-drained soil. Propagate by seed or stem cuttings in spring or summer.
♀ ***R. rhomboideum*** illus. p.494.

RHUS

Sumach

ANACARDIACEAE

Genus of deciduous trees, shrubs and scrambling climbers, grown for their divided, ash-like foliage, autumn colour and, in some species, showy fruit clusters. Fully to frost hardy. Requires sun and well-drained soil. Propagate by semi-ripe cuttings in summer, by seed in autumn or by root cuttings in winter. May be attacked by coral spot fungus. ⓘ All parts of *R. verniciflua* are highly toxic if ingested; contact with its foliage, and that of a number of related species, including *R. succedanea*, may aggravate skin allergies.
R. aromatica. Deciduous, bushy shrub. **H** 1m (3ft), **S** 1.5m (5ft). Fully hardy. Deep green leaves, each composed of 3 oval leaflets, turn orange or reddish-purple in autumn. Tiny, yellow flowers are borne in mid-spring, before foliage, followed by spherical, red fruits.
R. copallina (Dwarf sumach). Deciduous, upright shrub. **H** and **S** 1–1.5m (3–5ft, or more). Fully hardy. Has glossy, dark green leaves, with numerous lance-shaped leaflets, that turn red-purple in autumn. Minute, greenish-yellow flowers, borne in dense clusters from mid- to late summer, develop into narrowly egg-shaped, bright red fruits.
R. cotinoides. See *Cotinus obovatus*.
R. cotinus. See *Cotinus coggygria*.
R. glabra (Smooth sumach) illus. p.140.
R. hirta. See *R. typhina*. **'Laciniata'** see *R. typhina* 'Dissecta'.
R. potaninii. Deciduous, round-headed tree. **H** 12m (40ft), **S** 8m (25ft). Fully hardy. Has large, dark green leaves, with usually 7–11 oval leaflets that turn red in autumn. In summer produces dense clusters of tiny, yellow-green flowers. Female flower clusters develop into tiny, spherical, black or brownish fruits.
R. succedanea, syn. *Toxicodendron succedaneum* (Wax tree). Deciduous, spreading tree. **H** and **S** 10m (30ft). Frost hardy. Large, glossy, dark green leaves, each made up of 9–15 oval leaflets, turn red in autumn. Has dense clusters of tiny, yellow-green flowers in summer. Female flowers develop into tiny, spherical, black or brownish fruits.
R. trichocarpa illus. p.90.
♀ ***R. typhina***, syn. *R. hirta* (Stag's horn sumach). Deciduous, spreading, suckering, open shrub or tree. **H** 5m (15ft), **S** 6m (20ft). Fully hardy. Velvety shoots are clothed in dark green leaves with oblong leaflets. Produces minute, greenish-white flowers from mid- to late summer. Leaves become brilliant orange-red in autumn, accompanying clusters of spherical, deep red fruits on female plants. ♀ **'Dissecta'** (syn. *R. hirta* 'Laciniata', *R.t.* 'Laciniata' of gardens), illus. p.117. **'Laciniata'** of gardens see *R.t.* 'Dissecta'.
R. verniciflua, syn. *Toxicodendron vernicifluum* (Varnish tree). Deciduous, spreading tree. **H** 15m (50ft), **S** 10m (30ft). Fully hardy. Large, glossy, bright green leaves, with 7–13 oval leaflets, redden in autumn. Bears dense clusters of tiny, yellow-green flowers in summer, followed by berry-like, brownish-yellow fruits. ⓘ Contact with the sap may severely irritate the skin.

x RHYNCATTLEANTHE

ORCHIDACEAE

See also ORCHIDS.
x *R.* Cherub gx 'Spring Daffodil', syn. x *Potinara* Cherub gx 'Spring Daffodil'. Evergreen, epiphytic orchid for an intermediate greenhouse. **H** 15cm (6in). Sprays of yellow flowers, 5cm (2in) across, open in spring. Broadly oval, rigid leaves are 10cm (4in) long. Provide good light in summer.

Rhynchelytrum repens. See *Melinis repens*.
Rhynchelytrum roseum. See *Melinis repens*.

x RHYNCHOLAELIO-CATTLEYA

ORCHIDACEAE

See also ORCHIDS.
x *R.* Hetherington Horace gx 'Coronation', syn. x *Brassolaeliocattleya* Hetherington Horace gx 'Coronation'. Evergreen, epiphytic orchid for an intermediate greenhouse. **H** 45cm (18in). Bears stiff, oval leaves, 10–15cm (4–6in) long, and fragrant, light pink flowers, 10cm (4in) across, each with a deep pink-yellow lip, up to 4 to a stem, mainly in spring. Provide good light in summer.
x *R.* Mount Adams gx, syn. x *Brassocattleya* Mount Adams gx (illus. p.466). Evergreen, epiphytic orchid for an intermediate greenhouse. **H** 45cm (18in). Intermittently produces lavender-pink flowers, to 15cm (6in) across, each with a darker lip marked yellow and red, up to 4 per stem. Has oval, stiff leaves, 10–15cm (4–6in) long. Needs good light in summer.
x *R.* St Helier gx, syn. x *Brassolaeliocattleya* St Helier gx. Evergreen, epiphytic orchid for an intermediate greenhouse. **H** 45cm (18in). Produces oval, stiff leaves, 10–15cm (4–6in) long. Pinkish-purple flowers, to 10cm (4in) across, each with a yellow-marked, rich red lip, are borne 1–4 to a stem, mainly in spring. Grow in good light in summer.

RHYNCHOSPORA

CYPERACEAE

See also GRASSES, BAMBOOS, RUSHES and SEDGES.
R. colorata, syn. *Dichromena colorata*, illus. p.437.

RHYNOCHOSTELE

ORCHIDACEAE

See also ORCHIDS.
♀ ***R. bictoniensis***, syn. *Lemboglossum bictoniense, Odontoglossum bictoniense*. Evergreen, epiphytic orchid for a cool greenhouse. **H** 23cm (9in). Olive-green flowers, 4cm (1½in) across, barred with dark brown and each with a sometimes pink-flushed, white lip, are produced in spikes in late summer. Leaves are narrowly oval and 10–15cm (4–6in) long. Requires shade in summer.
R. cervantesii, syn. *Lemboglossum cervantesii, Odontoglossum cervantesii*. Evergreen, epiphytic orchid for a cool greenhouse. **H** 8cm (3in). In winter produces sprays of papery, white flowers, 2.5cm (1in) across, with cobweb-like, light brown marks. Has narrowly oval leaves, 10–15cm (4–6in) long. Grow in shade in summer.
R. cordatum, syn. *Lemboglossum cordatum, Odontoglossum cordatum*. Evergreen, epiphytic orchid for a cool

greenhouse. **H** 12cm (5in). Sprays of brown-marked, corn-yellow flowers, 2.5cm (1in) across, open in spring. Leaves are narrowly oval and 10–15cm (4–6in) long. Provide shade in summer and keep very dry in winter.
R. rossii, syn. *Lemboglossum rossii, Odontoglossum rossii* (illus. p.466). Evergreen, epiphytic orchid for a cool greenhouse. **H** 8cm (3in). In autumn–winter, white to mushroom-pink flowers, 2.5cm (1in) across, speckled beige-brown, are borne in spikes. Narrowly oval leaves are 10–15cm (4–6in) long. Needs shade in summer.

RIBES

Currant

GROSSULARIACEAE

Genus of deciduous or evergreen, mainly spring-flowering shrubs, grown for their edible fruits (currants and gooseberries) or their flowers. Fully to frost hardy. Needs full sun and well-drained, fertile soil, but *R. laurifolium* tolerates shade. After flowering, cut out some older shoots and, in winter or early spring, prune straggly, old plants hard. Propagate deciduous species by hardwood cuttings in winter, evergreens by semi-ripe cuttings in summer. Aphids attack young foliage.
R. aureum of gardens. See *R. odoratum*.
R. laurifolium illus. p.165.
R. odoratum, syn. *R. aureum* of gardens (Buffalo currant). Deciduous, upright shrub. **H** and **S** 2m (6ft). Fully hardy. Clusters of fragrant, tubular, golden-yellow flowers are borne from mid- to late spring, followed by rounded, purple fruits. Rounded, 3-lobed, bright green leaves turn red and purple in autumn.
R. sanguineum (Flowering currant). **'Brocklebankii'** is a deciduous, spreading shrub. **H** and **S** 1.2m (4ft). Fully hardy. Has aromatic, pale yellow leaves. Pendent clusters of small, pale pink flowers, in spring, are followed by white-bloomed, black fruits. **'King Edward VII'** illus. p.146. ♀ **'Pulborough Scarlet'** illus. p.123. **'Tydeman's White'**, **H** and **S** 2.5m (8ft), has pure white flowers.
♀ ***R. speciosum*** (Fuchsia-flowered currant) illus. p.193.

RICHEA

ERICACEAE/EPACRIDACEAE

Genus of evergreen, summer-flowering shrubs, grown for their foliage and densely clustered flowers. Frost to half hardy. Needs sun or semi-shade and moist, peaty, neutral to acid soil. Propagate by semi-ripe cuttings in summer or by seed in autumn.
R. scoparia. Evergreen, upright shrub. **H** and **S** 2m (6ft). Frost hardy. Shoots are covered with narrowly lance-shaped, sharp-pointed, dark green leaves. Bears dense, upright spikes of small, egg-shaped, pink, white, orange or maroon flowers in early summer.

RICINUS

EUPHORBIACEAE

Genus of one species of fast-growing, evergreen, tree-like shrub, grown for its foliage. In cool climates is grown as an annual. Half hardy. Needs sun and fertile to rich, well-drained soil. May require support in exposed areas. Propagate by seed sown under glass in early spring.
① All parts of *R. communis*, particularly the seeds, are highly toxic if ingested; contact with the foliage may aggravate skin allergies.
R. communis (Castor-oil plant) illus. p.318. **'Impala'** illus. p.308.

ROBINIA

LEGUMINOSAE/PAPILIONACEAE

Genus of deciduous, mainly summer-flowering trees and shrubs, grown for their foliage and clusters of pea-like flowers. Is useful for poor, dry soil. Fully hardy. Needs a sunny position. Grows in any but waterlogged soil. Branches are brittle and may be damaged by strong winds. Propagate by seed or suckers in autumn or by root cuttings in winter.
① All parts may cause severe discomfort if ingested.
***R. x ambigua* 'Decaisneana'.** Deciduous, spreading tree. **H** 15m (50ft), **S** 10m (30ft). Dark green leaves have numerous oval leaflets. Long, hanging clusters of pea-like, pink flowers are borne in early summer.
R. hispida (Rose acacia) illus. p.133. **var. *kelseyi*** (syn. *R. kelseyi*) is a deciduous, spreading, open shrub. **H** 2.5m (8ft), **S** 4m (12ft). Clusters of pea-like, rose-pink flowers open in late spring or early summer, followed by pendent, red seed pods. Dark green leaves consist of 9 or 11 oval leaflets.
R. kelseyi. See *R. hispida* var. *kelseyi*.
R. pseudoacacia (False acacia, Locust). Fast-growing, deciduous, spreading tree. **H** 25m (80ft), **S** 15m (50ft). Dark green leaves consist of 11–23 oval leaflets. Has dense, drooping clusters of fragrant, pea-like, white flowers in late spring and early summer. ♀ **'Frisia'** illus. p.76. **'Umbraculifera'** (Mop-head acacia), **H** and **S** 6m (20ft), rarely produces a rounded, dense flower head.
♀ ***R. x slavinii* 'Hillieri'** illus. p.86.

Rochea coccinea. See *Crassula coccinea*.

RODGERSIA

SAXIFRAGACEAE

Genus of summer-flowering, rhizomatous perennials. Is ideal for pond sides. Fully to frost hardy. Grows in sun or semi-shade and in soil that is moist; requires shelter from strong winds, which may damage foliage. Propagate by division in spring or by seed in autumn.
♀ ***R. aesculifolia*** illus. p.437.
♀ ***R. pinnata* 'Fireworks'.** Clump-forming, rhizomatous perennial. **H** 1m (3ft), **S** 60cm (2ft). Fully hardy. Has a large creeping root and large, pinnate, red-tinged, mid green leaves with narrowly oval leaflets. In summer produces much-branched, loose panicles of small, star-shaped, pink-red flowers. **'Superba'**, **H** 1–1.2m (3–4ft), **S** 75cm (2½ft), frost hardy, has bronze-tinged, emerald-green leaves and bright pink flowers.
♀ ***R. podophylla*** illus. p.436.
R. sambucifolia illus. p.437.
R. tabularis. See *Astilboides tabularis*.

ROMNEYA

Tree poppy

PAPAVERACEAE

Genus of summer-flowering, woody-based perennials and deciduous sub-shrubs. Frost hardy. Requires a warm, sunny position and deep, well-drained soil. Is difficult to establish, resents being moved and, in very cold areas, roots may need protection in winter. Once established, may spread rapidly. Propagate by softwood cuttings of basal shoots in early spring, by seed in autumn (transplanting seedlings without disturbing rootballs) or by root cuttings in winter.
♀ ***R. coulteri*** illus. p.216.
♀ ***R.* 'White Cloud'.** Vigorous, bushy, woody-based perennial. **H** and **S** 1m (3ft). Throughout summer produces large, slightly fragrant, shallowly cup-shaped, white flowers with prominent golden stamens. Leaves are oval, deeply lobed and grey.

ROMULEA

IRIDACEAE

Genus of crocus-like corms, grown for their funnel-shaped flowers. Frost to half hardy. Needs full light and well-drained, sandy soil. Water freely during the growing period. Most species die down in summer and then need warmth and dryness. *R. macowanii*, however, is dormant in winter. Propagate by seed in autumn, or in spring for *R. macowanii*.
R. bulbocodioides of gardens. See *R. flava*.
R. bulbocodium illus. p.419.
R. flava, syn. *R. bulbocodioides* of gardens. Early spring-flowering corm. **H** to 10cm (4in), **S** 2.5–5cm (1–2in). Half hardy. Has a thread-like, erect, basal leaf and 1–5 upright, widely funnel-shaped, usually yellow flowers, 2–4cm (¾–1½in) across, with deeper yellow centres.
R. longituba. See *R. macowanii* var. *alticola*.
R. macowanii* var. *alticola, syn. *R. longituba*. Summer-flowering corm. **H** and **S** 1–2cm (½–¾in). Half hardy. Leaves are thread-like, erect and basal. Produces 1–3 upright, yellow flowers, each 3cm (1¼in) across with a long tube expanding to become a wide funnel shape.
R. sabulosa. Early spring-flowering corm. **H** 5–15cm (2–6in), **S** 2.5–5cm (1–2in). Half hardy. Forms thread-like, erect, basal leaves. Stems bear 1–4 upward-facing, funnel-shaped, black-centred, bright red flowers that open flattish, to 4–5cm (1½–2in) across, in the sun.

RONDELETIA

RUBIACEAE

Genus of evergreen, mainly summer-flowering trees and shrubs, grown primarily for their flowers. Frost tender, min. 13–16°C (55–61°F). Requires full light or partial shade and fertile, well-drained soil. Water containerized specimens freely when in full growth, moderately at other times. Stems may be shortened in early spring if necessary. Propagate by seed in spring or by semi-ripe cuttings in summer.
R. amoena. Evergreen, rounded shrub. **H** and **S** 2–4m (6–12ft). Oval, dark green leaves are brown hairy beneath. Produces dense clusters of tubular, 4-or 5-lobed, pink flowers in summer.

Rooksbya euphorbioides. See *Neobuxbaumia euphorbioides*.

ROSA

Rose

ROSACEAE

Genus of deciduous or semi-evergreen, open shrubs and scrambling climbers, grown for their profusion of flowers, often fragrant, and sometimes for their fruits (rose hips). Leaves are divided into usually 5 or 7 oval leaflets, with rounded or pointed tips, that are sometimes toothed. Stems usually bear thorns, or prickles. Fully hardy, unless otherwise stated below. Prefers an open, sunny site and requires fertile, moist but well-drained soil. Avoid planting in an area where roses have been grown in recent years, as problems due to harmful organisms may occur: either exchange the soil, which may be used satisfactorily elsewhere, or choose another site for the new rose. To obtain blooms of high quality, feed in late winter or early spring with a balanced fertilizer and apply a mulch. In spring and summer feed regularly at 3-weekly intervals. Remove spent flower heads from plants that are "remontant" ("rising up again"; other terms used are repeat- or perpetual-flowering). May be trimmed for tidiness in early winter. To improve health, flower quality and shape of bush, prune in the dormant season or, preferably, in early spring, before young shoots develop from dormant growth buds: remove dead, damaged and dying wood; lightly trim Old Garden and Ground-cover roses (see below); remove two-thirds of previous summer's growth of Modern bush, including miniature, roses. Correct treatment of Modern shrub and climbing roses, ramblers and Species roses depends on the individual cultivar, but in general they should be pruned only lightly. Propagate by budding in summer or by hardwood cuttings in autumn. All roses are prone to attack by various pests and diseases, including aphids, blackspot, powdery mildew, rust and sawfly.

Rose species and cultivars are often regarded as 2 separate groups. Cultivars are further divided into Old Garden and Modern roses. Each group comprises different types, based, it is claimed, on the functional qualities of each plant, such as whether it is repeat-flowering, rather than on any historical, botanical or genetical relationships. Flowers occur in a variety of forms (illustrated and described on p.172) and are single (4–7 petals), semi-double (8–20 petals), double (20–30 petals) or fully double (over 30 petals).

Many modern rose cultivars are sold under names other than the registered Plant Breeder's Rights (PBR) names; where this is the case, the plant is listed under its trade name, with the PBR name in brackets afterwards. Roses are illustrated on pp.172–87.

Species roses
Species, or wild, roses (including those interspecific hybrids that share most of the characteristics of their parent species) are either shrubs or climbers, mostly bearing single, 5-petalled, often fragrant flowers in summer, usually in one flush on short shoots from second-year wood: the flowers are followed by red or black hips in autumn.
Old Garden roses
This category is so large that it is divided into two groups. Roses in Group A are mostly of European origin, while those in Group B are hybrids between Oriental and European roses.

Group A
Alba – large, freely branching shrubs with only a few prickles on the stems. They bear clusters of 5–7 semi- to fully double, scented flowers in mid-summer, on shoots from second-year wood. Have abundant, greyish-green leaves. Are very hardy. Most are good for borders and as hedges or as specimen plants.
Centifolia (or **Provence**) – lax, thorny shrubs that produce often scented, double to fully double flowers, borne singly or in 3s, in summer, on shoots from second-year wood. Leaves are matt, dark green. Are suitable for borders.
Damask – open shrubs with prickly stems and downy leaves. They produce often very fragrant, semi- to fully double flowers, borne singly or in loose clusters of 5–7 mainly in summer, on shoots from second-year wood; a few also flower on new wood in autumn. Are suitable for borders or training against a support.
Gallica – shrubs of fairly dense, free-branching habit, with usually thorny stems, and mostly dull, dark green leaves. Produce mostly scented, single to fully double, richly coloured flowers, often in clusters of 3, in summer on shoots from second-year wood. Are suitable for borders and as hedging.
Moss – often lax shrubs with a furry, moss-like growth on stems and calyces. Leaves are usually dark green. Usually fragrant, semi- to fully double flowers, often in clusters of 3 or more, are borne on very thorny shoots from second-year wood in summer. Are suitable for beds and borders.
Scots (or **Scotch**) – Suckering shrubs, selections or hybrids of *R. spinosissima*, of low, spreading, rarely upright habit, with prickly stems and dark green leaves. Occasionally scented, single to double flowers are solitary or borne in clusters of 3 or more, on short stems from second-year wood, usually in early summer. Are suitable for beds and borders.
Sweet Briar – Vigorous, free-branching shrubs with usually thorny stems and sweetly scented, dark green leaves. In summer, they bear usually scented, single to double flowers, singly or in clusters of up to 7, on short shoots from second-year wood. Use as hedges, as specimen plants and in large borders.

Group B
Bourbon – large, open, repeat-flowering shrubs and climbing roses, often with long, smooth or prickly stems, which may be trained to climb. They have often glossy leaves and numerous scented, double or fully double flowers, borne commonly in 3s, in flushes in summer and usually autumn. Flowers are borne on short shoots from second-year wood and on new wood. Are suitable for borders and for training over fences, walls and pillars.
Boursault – climbing roses with long, arching, usually smooth stems and dark green leaves. They bear slightly scented, semi-double or double flowers, singly or in clusters of 3, in early summer, on short shoots from second-year wood. Grow against a sheltered wall or fence.
China – spindly, repeat-flowering shrubs with mostly smooth stems, bearing only a few reddish-brown prickles, and glossy leaves. They produce sometimes scented, single to fully double flowers, singly or in clusters of 3–13, in flushes in summer–autumn. Flowers appear on short shoots from second-year wood and on new wood. Need a sheltered site. Are suitable for borders and walls.
Hybrid Musk – Vigorous, repeat-flowering shrubs with prickly stems and abundant foliage. They produce mainly double blooms, often very fragrant, either singly or in clusters of 2–7 or more, in flushes from mid-summer to autumn. Are good for shrub borders, and can be trained on walls.
Hybrid Perpetual – free-branching, repeat-flowering shrubs with upright, prickly growth and dark green leaves. They bear often scented, fully double flowers, held singly or in 3s, in flushes in summer–autumn on shoots from second-year wood and on new wood. Are suitable for beds and borders.
Noisette – repeat-flowering climbing roses that bear clusters of 3–15 usually double to fully double flowers, with a slight spicy fragrance, in flushes in summer–autumn. Flowers are borne on shoots from second-year wood, occasionally on new wood. Have generally smooth stems and glossy leaves. Are suitable for sheltered, south- or west-facing walls.
Portland (or **Damask Portland**) – upright, compact, repeat-flowering shrubs with thorny stems and usually dark green leaves. They produce usually scented, semi- to fully double flowers, held singly or in 3s, in flushes in summer–autumn, mainly on shoots from second-year wood. Are suitable for beds and borders.
Sempervirens – vigorous, semi-evergreen climbing or rambler roses with shiny, light green leaves. Arching, thorny stems bear clusters of 3–15 unscented, semi- to fully double flowers in summer, on short stems from second-year wood. Are ideal for naturalizing or for growing on fences and pergolas.
Tea – repeat-flowering shrubs and climbing roses with smooth to thorny stems, sometimes bearing a few large, red prickles, and glossy, light or sometimes dark green leaves. They produce spicy-scented, slender-stemmed, semi- to fully double flowers, borne singly or in 3s, in flushes in summer–autumn, on shoots from second-year wood and on new wood. Need a sheltered site. Are suitable for beds and borders and trained against walls.

Modern roses
Climber – often vigorous climbing roses with thorny, arching, stiff stems and usually dense, glossy, mid- to dark green foliage. They bear generally scented flowers in a variety of forms, singly or in clusters of 3–7 or more. Some bloom in summer only, on short shoots from second-year wood; many are repeat-flowering and also flower on new wood. Train against walls, fences or use to cover garden structures.
Climbing Miniature – Repeat-flowering, climbing roses with restrained, sparsely thorny growth. Clusters of 3–9 tiny, rarely scented, single to fully double flowers are borne in flushes in summer–autumn, on shoots from second-year wood and on new wood. Grow against low walls, fences and pillars.
Floribunda (or **Cluster-flowered bush**) – repeat-flowering, free-branching shrubs of upright or bushy habit, usually with prickly stems and glossy, dark green leaves. Sometimes scented, single to double flowers are usually in clusters of 3–25, rarely solitary, and are borne continuously in summer–autumn on shoots from second-year wood and on new wood. Are excellent for borders and as hedges.
Ground-cover – trailing and spreading roses, mostly with prickly stems, producing often glossy leaves. They bear clusters of numerous, sometimes scented, single to fully double flowers; some flower in summer only, on short shoots from second-year wood; others are repeat-flowering, and also flower on new wood. Many bear flowers all along the stems. Are ideal for beds, banks and containers, and for trailing over walls.
Hybrid Tea (or **Large-flowered bush**) – repeat-flowering, free-branching shrubs of upright or bushy habit, with usually thorny stems and glossy or matt, mid- to dark green leaves. Large, often scented, usually double flowers are borne singly or in 3s in flushes in summer–autumn on shoots from second-year wood and on new wood. Use in formal borders, as hedges and for cut flowers.
Miniature – repeat-flowering shrubs with very compact, rarely spreading, sparsely thorny, short growth. Sprays of 3–11 tiny, rarely scented, single to fully double flowers are borne in flushes in summer–autumn on very short shoots from second-year wood and on new wood. Have tiny leaves. Are suitable for edging paths and driveways, and for rock gardens, raised beds and container growing.
Patio (or **Dwarf cluster-flowered bush**) – repeat-flowering shrubs with compact growth, sometimes prickly stems, and usually glossy leaves. They bear clusters of 3–11 usually unscented, single to double flowers in flushes in summer–autumn, on shoots from second-year wood and on new wood. Are ideal for beds, borders and as hedges and for growing in containers.
Polyantha – compact, repeat-flowering shrubs with sparsely thorny stems and glossy leaves. Sprays of many small, rarely scented, single to double flowers are borne in summer–autumn, on shoots from second-year wood and on new wood. Are suitable for beds and borders, as hedges and for containers.
Rambler – a diverse group of vigorous roses with long, arching, thorny stems and dense, usually glossy foliage. They have clusters of 3–21 sometimes scented, single to fully double flowers, mainly in summer, on short shoots from second-year wood and on new wood. Train over walls, fences, pergolas and into trees.
Rugosa – Hardy shrubs with tough, wrinkled, usually bright green leaves and prickly stems. Most bear scented, single or semi-double flowers, in clusters of 3–11, in summer–autumn, on short shoots from second-year wood. They are often followed by tomato-like, usually red hips. Use as hedges, for beds and borders and as specimen plants.
Shrub – Roses in this diverse group are usually larger than bush roses (a general term used to describe Floribundas, Hybrid Teas, Miniatures, Patio roses and occasionally Ground-cover roses). They often have thorny stems and bear usually scented, semi-double to double flowers in few- to many-flowered clusters, sometimes singly, in summer–autumn. Some bloom in summer only from second-year wood; most are repeat-flowerers and also flower on new wood. Use as hedges, in beds and borders and as specimen plants.

***R.* ABSOLUTELY FABULOUS (‘Wekvossutono’)** illus. p.182.
***R.* ‘Aimée Vibert’**, syn. *R.* ‘Bouquet de la Mariée’. Noisette rose with smooth stems. **H** 5m (15ft), **S** 3m (10ft). Bears lightly scented, cupped, fully double, blush-pink to white flowers, 8cm (3in) across, in summer–autumn. Leaves are glossy, dark green. May be grown as a shrub.
***R.* ALAN TITCHMARSH (‘Ausjive’)**. Bushy shrub rose with good disease resistance and matt foliage. **H** 1.6m (5½ft), **S** 1.2m (4ft). Produces sweetly scented, rosette, double, deep pink flowers, 12cm (5in) across, with lighter pink outer petals, in summer and again in autumn.
♀ ***R.* ‘Alba Semiplena’**, syn. *R.* x *alba* ‘Semiplena’. Vigorous, bushy Alba rose. **H** 2m (6ft), **S** 1.5m (5ft). Bears sweetly scented, flat, semi-double, white flowers, 8cm (3in) across, in mid-summer. Leaves are greyish-green. Is suitable for a hedge.
♀ ***R.* ‘Albéric Barbier’** illus. p.184.
♀ ***R.* ‘Albertine’** illus. p.185.
***R.* Alec’s Red (‘Cored’)** illus. p.181.
♀ ***R.* ALEXANDER (‘Harlex’)**, syn. *R.* ‘Alexandra’, illus. p.180.
***R.* ‘Alfred de Dalmas’** of gardens. See *R.* ‘Mousseline’.
***R.* ALIBABA (‘Chewalibaba’)** illus. p.187.
***R.* ALISSAR PRINCESS OF PHONECIA (‘Harisdon’)** illus. p.174.
♀ ***R.* ‘Alister Stella Gray’**, syn. *R.* ‘Golden Rambler’. Noisette rose with long, vigorous, upright stems. **H** 5m (15ft), **S** 3m (10ft). Bears clusters of musk-scented, quartered, fully double, yolk-yellow flowers, 6cm (2½in) across, in summer–autumn. Has glossy, mid-green leaves.
♀ ***R.* ‘Aloha’** illus. p.185.
***R.* ‘Alpine Sunset’.** Compact Hybrid Tea rose with moderate disease resistance. **H** and **S** 60cm (2ft). Fragrant, rounded, fully double, peach-yellow flowers, 20cm (8in) across, are produced on short stems

R

in summer and again in autumn. Has large, semi-glossy leaves. May die back in hard winters.
🏆 ***R.* Amber Queen ('Harroony')**. Spreading, cluster-flowered bush rose with good disease resistance and repeat-flowering in summer–autumn. **H** and **S** 50cm (20in). Amber flowers are fragrant, rounded and fully double, 8cm (3in) across. Has abundant, reddish foliage.
***R.* 'American Pillar'.** Vigorous Rambler of lax growth. **H** to 5m (15ft), **S** 4m (12ft). Large clusters of cupped, single, carmine-red flowers, with white eyes, are borne freely in mid-summer. Leathery foliage is glossy, mid-green.
***R.* 'Amruda'.** See *R.* Red Ace.
***R.* 'Andeli'.** See *R.* Double Delight.
***R.* Angela Rippon ('Ocaru')**. Miniature rose with good disease resistance. **H** 45cm (18in), **S** 30cm (12in). Produces slightly scented, urn-shaped, fully double, salmon-pink flowers, 4cm (1½in) across, in summer and again in autumn. Has many small, dark green leaves.
***R.* 'Angelita'.** See *R.* 'Snowball'.
🏆 ***R.* Anisley Dickson ('Dickimono')**, syn. *R.* 'Dicky'. Vigorous Floribunda rose with good disease resistance. **H** 1m (3ft), **S** 75cm (2½ft). Produces large clusters of slightly scented, pointed, double, salmon-pink flowers 8cm (3in) across, in summer and again in autumn.
🏆 ***R.* Anna Ford ('Harpiccolo')** illus. p.180.
***R.* 'Anne Harkness' ('Harkaramel')**. Upright Floribunda rose with good disease resistance. **H** 1.2m (4ft), **S** 60cm (2ft). Slightly scented, urn-shaped, amber flowers, 8cm (3in) across, are borne in sprays of many blooms in summer and again in autumn.
***R.* Aphrodite ('Tanetidor')** illus. p.178.
***R.* 'Apothecary's Rose'.** See *R. gallica* var. *officinalis*.
🏆 ***R.* 'Arthur Bell'** illus. p.182.
***R.* 'Assemblage des Beautés'**, syn. *R.* 'Rouge Eblouissante'. Upright, dense Gallica rose. **H** 1.2m (4ft), **S** 1m (3ft). In summer bears faintly scented, rounded, fully double, green-eyed, cerise to crimson-purple flowers, 8cm (3in) across. Has rich green leaves.
***R.* 'Ausmary'.** See *R.* Mary Rose.
***R.* 'Ausmas'.** See *R.* Graham Thomas.
***R.* 'Austance'.** See *R.* Constance Spry.
***R.* 'Baby Carnival'.** See *R.* Baby Masquerade.
***R.* Baby Masquerade ('Tanba')**, syn. 'Baby Carnival'. Dense Miniature rose with good disease resistance. **H** and **S** 40cm (16in), more if not pruned. Bears clusters of rosette, double, yellow-pink flowers, 2.5cm (1in) across, in summer and again in autumn. Has plentiful, leathery leaves.
R. banksiae, syn. *R.b.* var. *normalis* (Banksian rose). Climbing Species rose with good disease resistance. **H** and **S** 10m (30ft). Frost hardy. Dense clusters of fragrant, flat, single, white flowers, 2.5cm (1in) across, are borne on thornless, light green stems in a single flush in summer. Leaves are small and pale green. Is uncommon in cultivation. 🏆 **'Lutea'** (syn. *R.b.* var. *lutea*) has scentless, rosette, fully double, yellow flowers, 2cm (¾in) across. Needs a sunny, sheltered wall and pruning of spent wood only.

***R.* 'Beauty of Glazenwood'.** See *R.* x *odorata* 'Pseudindica'.
***R.* 'Belle Courtisanne'.** See *R.* 'Königin von Dänemark'.
🏆 ***R.* 'Belle de Crécy'.** Gallica rose of rather lax growth, few thorns and moderate disease resistance. **H** 1.2m (4ft), **S** 1m (3ft). In a single flush in summer produces rosette, fully double, pink flowers, 8cm (3in) across, with green eyes and a spicy fragrance.
***R.* 'Belle de Londres'.** See *R.* 'Compassion'.
***R.* Belmonte ('Harpearl')** illus. p.179.
***R.* Benjamin Britten ('Ausencart')** illus. p.175.
***R.* 'Bizarre Triomphant'.** See *R.* 'Charles de Mills'.
***R.* 'Blanche Moreau'.** Moss rose of rather lax growth. **H** 1.5m (5ft), **S** 1.2m (4ft). Fragrant, cupped, fully double, white flowers, 10cm (4in) across, with brownish "mossing", appear in summer. Has dull green leaves.
🏆 ***R.* 'Blessings'.** Upright Hybrid Tea rose with moderate disease resistance. **H** 1m (3ft), **S** 75cm (2½ft). Slightly scented, urn-shaped, fully double, salmon-pink flowers are borne singly or in clusters in summer and again in autumn. Has large, dark leaves.
***R.* Blue Moon ('Tannacht')**, syn. *R.* 'Mainzer Fastnacht', *R.* 'Sissi'. Hybrid Tea rose of open habit. **H** 1m (3ft), **S** 60cm (2ft). Sweetly scented, pointed, fully double, lilac flowers, 10cm (4in) across, are borne in summer–autumn. Leaves are large and dark green.
***R.* Blue Peter ('Ruiblun')**, syn. *R.* 'Bluenette'. Miniature rose of neat habit. **H** 35cm (14in), **S** 30cm (12in). Slightly scented, cupped, double, purple flowers, 5cm (2in) across, are produced in summer–autumn. Leaves are small and plentiful.
***R.* 'Blue Rambler'.** See *R.* 'Veilchenblau'.
***R.* 'Bluenette'.** See *R.* Blue Peter.
***R.* 'Blush Noisette'.** See *R.* 'Noisette Carnée'.
***R.* 'Blush Rambler'.** Vigorous Rambler. **H** 3m (10ft), **S** 4m (12ft). Clusters of delicately fragrant, cupped, semi-double, light pink flowers, 4cm (1½in) across, are borne in summer. Has an abundance of glossy leaves. Is a particularly good scrambler for an arch, pergola or tree.
🏆 ***R.* 'Bobbie James'.** Rampant Rambler. **H** to 10m (30ft), **S** 6m (20ft). Large clusters of cupped, semi-double, scented, creamy-white flowers, 5cm (2in) across, are produced in summer. Glossy leaves are reddish-green when young, mid-green when mature.
🏆 ***R.* Bonica ('Meidomonac')**, syn. *R.* 'Bonica '82'. Vigorous, spreading shrub rose with very good disease resistance and repeat-flowering in summer–autumn. **H** 1m (3ft), **S** 1.1m (3½ft). Bears large sprays of slightly fragrant, cupped, fully double, rose-pink flowers, 7cm (3in) across. Foliage is glossy and plentiful.
***R.* 'Boule de Neige'.** Upright Bourbon rose with arching stems and very good disease resistance. **H** 1.5m (5ft), **S** 1.2m (4ft). Very fragrant, cupped to rosette, fully double, white flowers, 8cm (3in) across, sometimes tinged pink, are produced in summer–autumn. Leaves are glossy and dark green.

***R.* 'Bouquet de la Mariée'.** See *R.* 'Aimée Vibert'.
***R.* 'Brass Ring'.** See *R. Peek-a-Boo*.
***R.* Breath of Life ('Harquanne')**. Stiff, upright Climber with moderate disease resistance. **H** 2.8m (9ft), **S** 2.2m (7ft). Slightly scented, rounded, fully double, pinkish-apricot flowers, 10cm (4in) across, are borne in summer and again in autumn. Leaves are semi-glossy.
***R.* Bridge of Sighs ('Harglow')** illus. p.187.
***R.* Bright Smile ('Dicdance')**. Bushy Floribunda rose with good disease resistance and repeat-flowering in summer–autumn. **H** and **S** 45cm (18in). Bears clusters of slightly scented, flat, semi-double, yellow flowers, 8cm (3in) across. Has glossy, bright green leaves.
🏆 ***R.* 'Buff Beauty' illus. p.177.**
***R.* Burgundy Ice ('Prose')** illus. p.181.
***R. californica*.** Shrubby Species rose. **H** 2.2m (7ft), **S** 2m (6ft). Fragrant, flat, single, lilac-pink flowers, 4cm (1½in) across, are borne freely in mid-summer, sparsely in autumn. Has small dull green leaves. **'Plena'** see *R. nutkana* 'Plena'.
***R.* 'Canary Bird'.** See *R. xanthina* 'Canary Bird'.
***R.* 'Candide'.** See *R.* Goldstar.
🏆 ***R.* 'Capitaine John Ingram'.** Vigorous, bushy Moss rose. **H** and **S** 1.2m (4ft). In summer bears fragrant, cupped, fully double, rich maroon-crimson flowers, 8cm (3in) across; petals are paler on reverses. Foliage is dark green.
🏆 ***R.* 'Cardinal de Richelieu'** illus. p.175.
***R.* Cardinal Hume ('Harregale')** illus. p.175.
***R.* Carris ('Harmanna')** illus. p.180.
***R.* Casino ('Macca')**, syn. *R.* 'Gerbe d'Or'. Upright, free-branching Climber with moderate disease resistance. **H** 3m (10ft), **S** 2.2m (7ft). Slightly scented, rounded, double, yellow flowers, 9cm (3½in) across, are borne in summer and again in autumn. Sparse, dark green leaves are produced on stiffly arching stems.
🏆 ***R.* 'Cécile Brünner'** illus. p.186.
🏆 ***R.* 'Céleste'**, syn. *R.* 'Celestial', illus. p.173.
***R.* 'Celestial'.** See *R.* 'Céleste'.
🏆 ***R.* x *centifolia* 'Cristata'**, syn. *R.* 'Chapeau de Napoléon', *R.* 'Cristata' (Crested moss). Bushy, lanky Centifolia rose. **H** 1.5m (5ft), **S** 1.2m (4ft). In summer, very fragrant, cupped, fully double, pink flowers, 9cm (3½in) across and with tufted sepals, are borne on nodding stems amid dull green foliage. May be grown on a support. 🏆 **'Muscosa'** (Common moss, Old pink moss) is a vigorous, lax Moss rose. **H** 1.5m (5ft), **S** 1.2m (4ft). Bears fragrant, rounded to cupped, fully double, mossed, pink flowers, 8cm (3in) across, in summer. Leaves are matt, dull green.
🏆 ***R.* 'Cerise Bouquet'.** Very vigorous Shrub rose of arching habit. **H** and **S** to 3.5m (11ft). Produces a spectacular display of flat, semi-double, cherry-red flowers, 6cm (2½in) across, in summer. Leaves are small and greyish-green.
🏆 ***R.* Champagne Cocktail ('Horflash')**. Upright Floribunda rose with very good disease resistance. **H** 1m (3ft), **S** 60cm (2ft). Fragrant, cupped, double, yellow-pink flowers, 9cm (3½in) across, opening wide are borne in summer and again in autumn.

***R.* Champagne Moments ('Korvanaber')** illus. p.177.
***R.* Chandos Beauty ('Harmisty')** illus. p.178.
***R.* 'Chapeau de Napoléon'.** See *R.* x *centifolia* 'Cristata'.
***R.* 'Chaplin's Pink Companion'** illus. p.185.
***R.* Charles Darwin ('Auspeet')**. Bushy shrub rose with very good disease resistance and glossy, light green foliage. **H** 1.8m (6ft), **S** 1.2m (4ft). Quartered-rosette, fully double, golden-yellow flowers, 10cm (4in) across, with occasional pink flush on the outer petals, are borne in summer and again in autumn.
🏆 ***R.* 'Charles de Mills'**, syn. *R.* 'Bizarre Triomphant'. Upright, arching Gallica rose with fairly smooth stems. **H** 1.2m (4ft), **S** 1m (3ft). Very fragrant, quartered-rosette, fully double, crimson-purple flowers, 10cm (4in) across, appear in summer. Leaves are plentiful and mid-green. May be grown on a support.
***R.* 'Chewarvel'.** See *R.* Laura Ford.
***R. chinensis* var. *minima*.** See *R.* 'Rouletii'. **'Mutabilis'** see *R.* x *odorata* 'Mutabilis'.
***R.* Chris Beardshaw ('Wekmeredoc')** illus. p.179
***R.* City of London ('Harukfore')**. Rounded Floribunda rose. **H** 1m (3ft), **S** 75cm (2½ft). In summer–autumn, bears dainty sprays of sweet-smelling, urn-shaped, double, blush-pink flowers, 8cm (3in) across, amid bright green foliage.
🏆 ***R.* 'Climbing Lady Hillingdon'.** Stiff climbing Tea rose. **H** 4m (12ft), **S** 2m (6ft). Has dark green leaves on reddish-green stems. Bears spice-scented, pointed, double, apricot-yellow flowers, 10cm (4in) across, in summer–autumn. Is best in a sheltered site.
🏆 ***R.* 'Climbing Mrs Sam McGredy'.** Vigorous, stiff, branching Climber. **H** and **S** 3m (10ft). Leaves are glossy, rich reddish-green. Bears faintly fragrant, large, urn-shaped, fully double, coppery salmon-pink flowers, 11cm (4½in) across, in summer and again, sparsely, in autumn.
***R.* 'Cocabest'.** See *R.* Wee Jock.
***R.* 'Cocdestin'.** See *R.* Remember Me.
***R.* Colibre '79 ('Meidanover')**. Upright, rather open Miniature rose with good disease resistance. **H** 38cm (15in), **S** 25cm (10in). Urn-shaped, double, red-veined, orange flowers, 4cm (1½in) across, are borne in summer and again in autumn.
***R.* 'Commandant Beaurepaire'**, syn. *R.* 'Panachée d' Angers'. Vigorous, spreading Bourbon rose. **H** and **S** 1.2m (4ft). Fragrant, cupped, double flowers, 10cm (4in) across, are borne in summer–autumn. They are blush-pink, splashed with mauve, purple, crimson and scarlet. Light green leaflets have wavy margins.
🏆 ***R.* 'Compassion'**, syn. *R.* 'Belle de Londres', illus. p.185.
🏆 ***R.* 'Complicata'** illus. p.174.
***R.* 'Comte de Chambord'** of gardens. See *R.* 'Madame Knorr'.
***R.* Congratulations ('Korlift')**, syn. *R.* 'Sylvia'. Upright, vigorous Hybrid Tea rose. **H** 1.2m (4ft), **S** 1m (3ft). Produces neat, urn-shaped, fully double, deep rose-pink flowers, 11cm (4½in) across, on long stems in summer–autumn. Leaves are large and dark green. Makes a tall hedge.

***R.* 'Conrad Ferdinand Meyer'.** Vigorous, arching shrub rose with good disease resistance. **H** 2.5m (8ft), **S** 1.2m (4ft). Cupped, fully double, pink flowers, 7cm (3in) across, are richly fragrant and borne freely in a single flush in summer. Foliage is leathery and prone to rust.
♀ ***R.* Constance Spry ('Austance')** illus. p.174.
***R.* 'Cored'.** See *R.* Alec's Red.
***R.* Crazy For You ('Wekroalt')** illus. p.179.
***R.* 'Cristata'.** See *R.* x *centifolia* 'Cristata'.
***R.* 'Cuisse de Nymphe'.** See *R.* 'Great Maiden's Blush'.
***R.* 'Danse du Feu'**, syn. *R.* 'Spectacular'. Vigorous, stiffly branched Climber with moderate disease resistance. **H** and **S** 2.5m (8ft). Slightly scented, rounded, double, scarlet flowers, 8cm (3in) across, are borne in summer and again in autumn. Has abundant, glossy foliage.
***R.* Dancing Queen ('Fryfestoon')** illus. p.186.
***R.* Darcey Bussell ('Ausdecorum').** Compact shrub rose with good disease resistance and matt, mid-green leaves. **H** 1.2m (4ft), **S** 1m (3ft). Fragrant, quartered-rosette, fully double, crimson flowers, 10cm (4in) across, ageing to purple shades, are produced in summer and again in autumn.
***R.* Darling Flame ('Meilucca').** Well-branched Miniature rose. **H** 40cm (16in), **S** 30cm (12in). Leaves are glossy and dark green. Urn-shaped, double, orange-red flowers, 4cm (1½in) across, are borne freely in summer–autumn.
***R.* 'Dicdance'.** See *R.* Bright Smile.
***R.* 'Dicdivine'.** See *R.* Pot o' Gold.
***R.* 'Dicgrow'.** See *R.* Peek-a-boo.
***R.* 'Dicjana'.** See *R.* Elina.
***R.* 'Dicjem'.** See *R.* Freedom.
***R.* 'Dicjubell'.** See *R.* Lovely Lady.
***R.* 'Dickimono'.** See *R.* Anisley Dickson.
***R.* 'Dicky'.** See *R.* Anisley Dickson.
***R.* 'Diclulu'.** See *R.* Gentle Touch.
***R.* 'Dicmagic'.** See *R.* Sweet Magic.
***R.* 'Doris Tysterman'.** Vigorous, upright Hybrid Tea rose with moderate disease resistance. **H** 1.2m (4ft), **S** 75cm (2½ft). Slightly scented, pointed, fully double, orange-red flowers, 10cm (4in) across, are borne in summer and again in autumn. Leaves are large, glossy and dark green.
♀ ***R.* 'Dortmund'** illus. p.186.
***R.* Double Delight ('Andeli')** illus. p.180.
***R.* 'Double Velvet'.** See *R.* 'Tuscany Superb'.
***R.* 'Doux Parfum'.** See *R.* L'Aimant.
***R.*Drummer Boy ('Harvacity').** Dwarf Floribunda rose of bushy, spreading habit. **H** and **S** 50cm (20in). in summer–autumn bears faintly scented, cupped, double, bright crimson flowers, 5cm (2in) across, in dense sprays. Has abundant, small, dark green leaves. Makes a good, low hedge.
♀ ***R.* Dublin Bay ('Macdub')** illus. p.186.
***R.* 'Duchesse d'Istrie'.** See *R.* 'William Lobb'.
***R.* 'Duftzauber '84'.** See *R.* Royal William.
***R.* 'Du Maître d'Ecole'.** Bushy, spreading Gallica rose. **H** 1.2m (4ft), **S** 1m (3ft). Bears fragrant, quartered-rosette, fully double, carmine to light pink flowers, 10cm (4in) across, in summer. Foliage is dull green.
***R.* 'Dupontii'**, syn. *R. moschata* var. *nivea*, illus. p.173.
♀ ***R.* 'Easlea's Golden Rambler'.** Vigorous, arching Rambler. **H** 5m (15ft), **S** 3m (10ft). Pleasantly scented, cupped, fully double, yellow flowers, 10cm (4in) across and flecked with red, appear, usually in clusters, during summer. Has plentiful, leathery foliage.
***R.* 'Easter Morning'**, syn. *R.* 'Easter Morn'. Upright Miniature rose. **H** 40cm (16in), **S** 25cm (10in). In summer–autumn, faintly fragrant, urn-shaped, fully double, ivory-white flowers, 3cm (1¼in) across, are borne freely amid glossy, dark green leaves.
***R.* Easy Does It ('Harpagent')** illus. p.183.
***R.* Easy Going ('Harglow')** illus. p.182.
R. ecae. Erect, wiry Species rose with very good disease resistance. **H** 1.5m (5ft), **S** 1.2m (4ft). Cupped, single, bright yellow flowers, 2cm (¾in) across, with a light musky scent, are borne close to reddish stems in a single flush in summer. Foliage is fern-like. Needs shelter.
R. eglanteria. See *R. rubiginosa*.
♀ ***R.* Elina ('Dicjana')**, syn. *R.* 'Peaudouce'. Vigorous, shrubby Hybrid Tea rose. **H** 1.1m (3½ft), **S** 75cm (2½ft). Lightly scented, rounded, fully double, ivory-white flowers, 15cm (6in) across, with lemon-yellow centres, are borne freely in summer–autumn. Has abundant, reddish foliage.
***R.* 'Elizabeth Harkness'.** Neat, upright Hybrid Tea rose with moderate disease resistance. **H** 80cm (32in), **S** 60cm (24in). Fragrant, pointed, fully double, buff-tinted, pale creamy-pink flowers, 12cm (5in) across, are borne in summer and again in autumn. Has abundant, dark green foliage.
***R.* 'Emily Gray'** illus. p.187.
***R.* 'Empereur du Maroc'.** Compact, shrubby Hybrid Perpetual rose with good disease resistance. **H** 1.2m (4ft), **S** 1m (3ft). Fragrant, quartered-rosette, fully double, rich purplish-crimson flowers, 8cm (3in) across, are borne freely in a single flush in summer.
♀ ***R.* Escapade ('Harpade').** Dense Floribunda rose with good disease resistance. **H** 75cm (30in), **S** 60cm (24in). Fragrant, cupped, semi-double, rose-violet flowers, 8cm (3in) across, with white eyes, are borne in sprays in summer and again in autumn. Foliage is light green and glossy.
***R.* Evelyn ('Aussaucer')** illus. p.177.
♀ ***R.* 'Fantin-Latour'** illus. p.173.
♀ ***R.* Fascination ('Poulmax')**, syn. *R.* 'Fredensborg'. Vigorous Floribunda rose. **H** 1m (3ft), **S** 60cm (2ft). In summer–autumn bears fragrant, rounded, double, shrimp-pink blooms amid dark green, glossy foliage. Is good for beds and hedges.
♀ ***R.* 'Felicia'** illus. p.173.
♀ ***R.* 'Félicité Parmentier'.** Vigorous, compact, upright Alba rose. **H** 1.2m (4ft), **S** 1m (3ft). Fragrant, cupped to flat, fully double, pale flesh-pink flowers, 6cm (2½in) across, are borne in mid-summer. Has abundant, greyish-green leaves. Makes a good hedge.
♀ ***R.* 'Félicité Perpétue'** illus. p.184.
***R.* Felicity Kendal ('Lanken').** Sturdy, well-branched Hybrid Tea rose. **H** 1.1m (3½ft), **S** 75cm (2½ft). Lightly fragrant, rounded, fully double, bright red flowers, 11cm (4½in) across, appear among a mass of dark green foliage in summer–autumn.
***R.* 'Fellemberg'**, syn. *R.* 'Fellenberg'. Vigorous, shrubby Noisette rose. **H** 2.5m (8ft), **S** 1.2m (4ft). Leaves are purplish-green. Clusters of faintly scented, rounded to cupped, fully double flowers, 5cm (2in) across, in shades of light crimson, appear in summer–autumn. Prune to grow as a bedding rose or support as a climber.
***R.* Fellowship ('Harwelcome')** illus. p.183.
♀ ***R. filipes* 'Kiftsgate'** illus. p.184
***R.* 'Fire Princess'.** Upright Miniature rose with good disease rsistance. **H** 45cm (18in), **S** 30cm (12in). Bears sprays of rosette, fully double, scarlet flowers, 4cm (1½in) across, in summer and again in autumn. Has small, glossy leaves.
***R.* Flower Carpet ('Noatraum')** illus. p.179.
***R. foetida* 'Persiana'**, syn. *R.* 'Persian Yellow'. Upright, arching Species rose with moderate disease resistance. **H** and **S** 1.5m (5ft). Cupped, double, yellow flowers, 2.5cm (1in) across, are produced in a single flush in summer. Glossy leaves are prone to blackspot. Prune spent branches only. Shelter from cold winds.
***R.* 'Fortune's Double Yellow'.** See *R.* x *odorata* 'Pseudindica'.
***R.* Fragrant Cloud ('Tanellis').** Bushy, dense Hybrid Tea rose. **H** 75cm (30in), **S** 60cm (24in). Very fragrant, rounded, double, dusky-scarlet flowers, 12cm (5in) across, are borne freely in summer–autumn. Has plentiful, dark green foliage.
♀ ***R.* 'Fragrant Delight'.** Bushy Floribunda rose of uneven habit. **H** 1m (3ft), **S** 75cm (2½ft). Bears an abundance of reddish-green foliage, amid which clusters of fragrant, urn-shaped, double, salmon-pink flowers, 8cm (3in) across, are borne freely in summer–autumn.
♀ ***R.* 'François Juranville'.** Vigorous, arching Rambler. **H** 6m (20ft), **S** 5m (15ft). Bears clusters of apple-scented, rosette, fully double, rosy-salmon-pink flowers, 8cm (3in) across, in summer. Produces a mass of glossy leaves. Is prone to mildew in a dry site.
***R.* 'Fredensborg'.** See *R.* Fascination.
♀ ***R.* Freedom ('Dicjem')** illus. p.182.
***R.* 'Friesia'.** See *R.* 'Korresia'.
***R.* 'Frühlingsmorgen'**, syn. *R.* 'Spring Morning'. Open, free-branching Shrub rose. **H** 2m (6ft), **S** 1.5m (5ft). Foliage is greyish-green. In late spring, hay-scented, cupped, single, pink flowers, 12cm (5in) across, with a primrose centre and reddish stamens, are produced.
***R.* 'Fryminicot'.** See *R.* Sweet Dream.
♀ ***R. gallica* var. *officinalis***, syn. *R.* 'Apothecary's Rose', *R. officinalis* (Red rose of Lancaster). Bushy Species rose of neat habit. **H** to 80cm (32in), **S** 1m (36in). In summer, bears flat, semi-double, pinkish-red flowers, 8cm (3in) across, with a moderate scent. ♀ **'Versicolor'** illus. p.174.
***R.* Gardeners Glory ('Chewability')** illus. p.187.
***R.* 'Gaumo'.** See *R.* Rose Gaujard.
***R.* Gentle Touch ('Diclulu').** Upright, dwarf Floribunda rose. **H** 50cm (20in), **S** 30cm (12in). Bears sprays of faintly scented, urn-shaped, semi-double, pale salmon-pink flowers, 5cm (2in) across, in summer–autumn. Leaves are small and dark green. Is good as a low hedge.
***R.* Geoff Hamilton ('Ausham').** Bushy shrub rose with good disease resistanceand most flowers produced near the top of the bush. **H** 1.6m (5½ft), **S** 1m (3ft). Rounded buds open to sweetly scented, quartered-rosette, double, light rose-pink flowers, 10cm (4in) across, intensifying to rose-pink in centres, in summer and again in autumn.
***R.* George Best ('Dichimanher')** illus. p.181.
***R.* 'Geranium'.** See *R. moyesii* 'Geranium'.
***R.* 'Gerbe d'Or'.** See *R.* 'Casino'.
***R.* Gertrude Jekyll ('Ausbord')** illus. p.175.
***R.* 'Gioia'.** See *R.* 'Peace'.
***R.* 'Gipsy Boy'.** See *R.* 'Zigeunerknabe'.
***R.* Glamis Castle ('Auslevel').** Compact shrub rose with good disease resistance and glossy, mid-green leaves. **H** 1.5m (5ft), **S** 1.2m (4ft). Produces fragrant, quartered-rosette, fully double, cream-centred, white flowers, 10cm (4in) across, in summer and again in autumn.
♀ ***R. glauca***, syn. *R. rubrifolia* (illus. p.176). Vigorous, arching Species rose with very good disease resistance. **H** 2m (6ft), **S** 1.5m (5ft). Flat, single, pale-centred, cerise-pink flowers, 4cm (1½in) across, with gold stamens, in a single flush in summer, are followed by red hips in autumn. Has greyish-purple leaves and red stems.
***R.* 'Glenfiddich'.** Upright Floribunda rose with moderate disease resistance. **H** 75cm (30in), **S** 60cm (24in). Fragrant, urn-shaped, double, amber-yellow flowers, 10cm (4in) across, are borne singly or in clusters in summer and again in autumn.
***R.* 'Gloire de Dijon'** illus. p.184.
***R.* 'Gloire des Mousseux'.** Vigorous, bushy Moss rose. **H** 1.2m (4ft), **S** 1m (3ft). Has plentiful, light green foliage. In summer bears fragrant, cupped, fully double flowers, 15cm (6in) across. These are bright pink, paling to blush-pink, with light green "mossing".
***R.* 'Gloria Dei'.** See *R.* 'Peace'.
***R.* 'Gold of Ophir'.** See *R.* x *odorata* 'Pseudindica'.
***R.* Golden Beauty ('Korberbeni')** illus. p.182.
♀ ***R.* Golden Celebration ('Ausgold').** Bushy shrub rose with good disease resistance and glossy, mid-green leaves. **H** 1.5m (5ft), **S** 1.2m (4ft). In summer and again in autumn, abundant, plump, rounded buds open to slighty scented, rosette, fully double, golden-yellow flowers, 12cm (5in) across, taking on pink hues as they age.
***R.* Golden Memories ('Korholesea')** illus. p.182.
***R.* Golden Penny ('Rugul')**, syn. *R.* 'Guletta', *R.* 'Tapis Jaune'. Compact, dense Patio rose with moderate disease resistance. **H** 30cm (12in), **S** 40cm (16in). Cupped to flat, double, yellow flowers, 5cm (2in) across, are borne in summer and again in autumn. Has rich green leaves.
***R.* 'Golden Rambler'.** See *R.* 'Alister Stella Gray'.
♀ ***R.* 'Golden Showers'.** Stiff, upright Climber with moderate disease resistance.

H 2m (6ft), S 2.2m (7ft) or more. In summer and again in autumn produces many slightly scented, pointed, double, yellow flowers, 10cm (4in) across, that open flat. May be pruned to grow as a shrub.
R. 'Golden Sunblaze'. See *R.* 'Rise 'n' Shine'.
♀ **R. 'Golden Wings'.** Bushy, spreading Shrub rose. **H** 1.1m (3½ft), **S** 1.35m (4½ft). Bears fragrant, cupped, single, pale yellow flowers, 12cm (5in) across, amid light green foliage, in summer–autumn. Is good for a hedge.
R. 'Goldfinch'. Vigorous, arching Rambler. **H** 2.7m (9ft), **S** 2m (6ft). In summer produces lightly scented, rosette, double, yolk-yellow flowers, 4cm (1½in) across, that fade to white. Has plentiful, bright light green leaves.
R. 'Goldsmith'. See *R.* SIMBA.
R. GOLDSTAR ('Candide'). Neat, upright Hybrid Tea rose. **H** 1m (3ft), **S** 60cm (2ft). Amid glossy, dark green leaves, lightly scented, urn-shaped, fully double, yellow flowers, 8cm (3in) across, are borne in summer–autumn.
R. GORDON'S COLLEGE ('Cocjabby') illus. p.179.
♀ **R. GRAHAM THOMAS ('Ausmas')** illus. p.176.
R. 'Grandpa Dickson', syn. *R.* 'Irish Gold'. Neat, upright Hybrid Tea rose with moderate disease resistance. **H** 80cm (32in), **S** 60cm (24in). Bears many pointed, fully double, light yellow flowers, 18cm (7in) across, in summer and again in autumn. Has sparse, glossy, pale green leaves.
R. 'Great Maiden's Blush', syn. *R.* 'Cuisse de Nymphe', *R.* 'La Séduisante', illus. p.173.
♀ **R. GROUSE ('Korimro')**. Trailing ground-cover rose with good disease resistance. **H** 45cm (1½ft), **S** 3m (10ft). Slightly fragrant, flat, single, blush-pink flowers, 4cm (1½in) across, are borne close to stems in a single flush in summer. Has abundant, glossy foliage.
R. 'Guinée' illus. p.186.
R. 'Guletta'. See *R.* Golden Penny.
R. GUY SAVOY ('Delstrimen') illus. p.181.
R. GUY'S GOLD ('Harmatch') illus. p.182.
♀ **R. HANDEL ('Macha')**. Stiff, upright Climber with moderate disease resistance. **H** 3m (10ft), **S** 2.2m (7ft). Slightly scented, urn-shaped, double, cream flowers, 8cm (3in) across, edged with pinkish-red, are borne in clusters in summer and again in autumn. Has glossy, dark green leaves.
R. HANNAH GORDON ('Korweiso'). Bushy, open Floribunda rose. **H** 75cm (30in), **S** 60cm (2ft). Sprays of slightly fragrant, cupped, double, blush-pink flowers, 8cm (3in) across, margined with reddish-pink, appear in summer–autumn. Leaves are dark green.
R. 'Harbabble'. See *R.* SUNSET BOULEVARD.
R. 'Hardinkum'. See *R.* PRINCESS OF WALES.
R. 'Hardwell'. See *R.* PENNY LANE.
R. 'Harkaramel'. See *R.* ANNE HARKNESS.
R. 'Harkuly'. See *R.* MARGARET MERRIL.
R. 'Harlex'. See *R.* ALEXANDER.
R. 'Harmantelle'. See *R.* MOUNTBATTEN.
R. 'Harpade'. See *R.* ESCAPADE.
R. 'Harpiccolo'. See *R.* ANNA FORD.
R. 'Harquanne'. See *R.* BREATH OF LIFE.
R. 'Harqueterwife'. See *R.* PAUL SHIRVILLE.
R. 'Harregale'. See *R.* CARDINAL HUME.
R. 'Harroony'. See *R.* AMBER QUEEN.
R. 'Harrowbond'. See *R.* ROSEMARY HARKNESS.
R. 'Harsherry'. See *R.* SHEILA'S PERFUME.
R. 'Harukfore'. See *R.* CITY OF LONDON.
R. 'Harvacity'. See *R.* DRUMMER BOY.
R. 'Harwanna'. See *R.* JACQUELINE DU PRÉ.
R. 'Harwanted'. See *R.* MANY HAPPY RETURNS.
R. 'Haryup'. See *R.* HIGH HOPES.
R. 'Harzola'. See *R.* L'AIMANT.
R. 'Heartthrob'. See *R.* 'Paul Shirville'.
R. 'Heideröslein'. See *R.* 'Nozomi'.
R. 'Henri Martin', syn. *R.* 'Red Moss', illus. p.175.
♀ **R. HERTFORDSHIRE ('Kortenay')**. Free-flowering Ground-cover rose of compact, uneven, spiky habit. **H** 45cm (18in), **S** 1m (3ft). Has dense, bright green leaves and flat, single, carmine-pink flowers, 4.5cm (1¾in) across, with paler pink centres, in large clusters on short stems, from summer to autumn.
♀ **R. HIGH HOPES ('Haryup')** illus. p.185.
R. 'Honorine de Brabant'. Vigorous, bushy, sprawling Bourbon rose. **H** and **S** 2m (6ft). Fragrant, quartered, double flowers, 10cm (4in) across, lilac-pink, marked with light purple and crimson, are produced in summer–autumn. Has plentiful, light green foliage.
R. 'Horflash'. See *R.* CHAMPAGNE COCKTAIL.
R. HOT CHOCOLATE ('Wekpaltlez'). Upright Floribunda rose with good disease resistance and repeat-flowering in summer–autumn. **H** 1m (3ft), **S** 80cm (32in). Produces semi-glossy, dark green leaves and cupped, double flowers, 7cm (3in) across, in burnt-orange, tending towards brown, lighter in the centres with a hint of tangerine.
R. 'Hula Girl'. iWide, bushy Miniature rose with moderate disease resistance. **H** 45cm (18in), **S** 40cm (16in). Urn-shaped, fully double, salmon-orange flowers, 2.5cm (1in) across, are produced freely in summer and again in autumn. Has glossy, dark green leaves.
♀ **R. ICEBERG ('Korbin')**, syn. *R.* 'Schneewittchen', illus. p.177.
R. 'Iced Ginger'. Upright Floribunda rose with moderate disease resistance. **H** 90cm (36in), **S** 70cm (28in). Pointed, fully double, buff to copper-pink flowers, 11cm (4½in) across, are borne singly or in clusters in summer and again in autumn. Has sparse, reddish-green foliage.
♀ **R. INGRID BERGMAN ('Poulman')**. Upright, branching Hybrid Tea rose. **H** 75cm (30in), **S** 60cm (24in). Bears slightly scented, urn-shaped, double, dark red flowers, 11cm (4½in) across, in summer–autumn. Has leathery, semi-glossy, dark green foliage.
R. 'Interall'. See *R.* ROSY CUSHION.
R. INVINCIBLE ('Runatru'). Upright Floribunda rose. **H** 1m (3ft), **S** 60cm (2ft). Faintly scented, cupped, fully double, bright crimson flowers, 9cm (3½in) across, appear in open clusters in summer–autumn. Leaves are semi-glossy.
R. 'Irish Gold'. See *R.* 'Grandpa Dickson'.
R. ISN'T SHE LOVELY ('Diciluvit') illus. p.177.
♀ **R. 'Ispahan'**, syn. *R.* 'Pompon des Princes', *R.* 'Rose d'Isfahan'. Vigorous, bushy, dense Damask rose. **H** 1.5m (5ft), **S** 1.2m (4ft). Produces fragrant, cupped, double, clear pink flowers, 8cm (3in) across, amid greyish-green foliage in summer–autumn.
♀ **R. JACQUELINE DU PRÉ ('Harwanna')** illus. p.172.
R. JOIE DE VIVRE ('Korfloci 01') illus. p.179.
R. 'Julia's Rose'. Spindly, branching Hybrid Tea rose. **H** 75cm (30in), **S** 45cm (18in). In summer–autumn produces faintly scented, urn-shaped, double, brownish-pink to buff flowers, 10cm (4in) across. Foliage is reddish-green. Is good for flower arrangements.
♀ **R. 'Just Joey'** illus. p.183.
R. 'Kathleen Harrop'. Arching, lax Bourbon rose. **H** 2.5m (8ft), **S** 2m (6ft). Fragrant, double, cupped, pale pink flowers, 8cm (3in) across, are borne in summer–autumn. Plentiful, dark green foliage is susceptible to mildew. May be grown as a climber or hedge.
R. KEEPSAKE ('Kormalda'). Neat, bushy Hybrid Tea rose with good disease resistance. **H** 75cm (30in), **S** 60cm (24in). Scented, rounded, fully double, pink flowers, 12cm (5in) across, are freely produced in summer and again in autumn. Foliage is plentiful and glossy.
♀ **R. KENT ('Poulcov')** illus. p. 177.
♀ **R. 'Königin von Dänemark'**, syn. *R.* 'Belle Courtisanne'. Vigorous, rather open Alba rose with good disease resistance. **H** 1.5m (5ft), **S** 1.2m (4ft). Scented, quartered-rosette, fully double, warm-pink flowers, 8cm (3in) across and with green button eyes, are produced in a single flush in summer.
R. 'Korbelma'. See *R.* SIMBA.
R. 'Korbin'. See *R.* ICEBERG.
R. 'Korblue'. See *R.* SHOCKING BLUE.
R. 'Korgund'. See *R.* LOVING MEMORY.
R. 'Korimro'. See *R.* GROUSE.
R. 'Korlift'. See *R.* CONGRATULATIONS.
R. 'Kormalda'. See *R.* KEEPSAKE.
R. 'Korpeahn'. See *R.* THE TIMES ROSE.
R. 'Korresia', syn. *R.* 'Friesia'. Bushy, upright Floribunda rose with moderate disease resistance. **H** 75cm (30in), **S** 60cm (24in). Bears open sprays of strongly scented, urn-shaped, double flowers, 8cm (3in) across, with wavy, yellow petals, in summer and again in autumn.
R. 'Kortenay'. See *R.* HERTFORDSHIRE.
R. 'Korweiso'. See *R.* HANNAH GORDON.
R. 'Korzaun'. See *R.* ROYAL WILLIAM.
♀ **R. L'AIMANT ('Harzola')**, syn. *R.* 'Doux Parfum'. Vigorous Floribunda rose. **H** 1m (3ft), **S** 75cm (2½ft). Strongly fragrant, cupped, fully double, pink blooms, 9cm (3½in) across, appear in summer–autumn on dark-foliaged plants. Is good for bedding and cutting.
R. 'La Séduisante'. See *R.* 'Great Maiden's Blush'.
R. LA SÉVILLANA ('Meigekanu'). Dense, bushy Ground cover rose. **H** 75cm (2½ft), **S** 1m (3ft). Clusters of faintly scented, cupped, double, bright red flowers, 8cm (3in) across, are borne freely in summer–autumn. Produces an abundance of dark green leaves. Is suitable for growing as a hedge or ground cover.
R. 'Lady Waterlow'. Stiff Climbing Hybrid Tea rose. **H** 4m (12ft), **S** 2m (6ft). Bears pleasantly scented, pointed to cupped, double, light pink shaded, salmon flowers, 12cm (5in) across, mainly in summer, but some may also appear in autumn. Leaves are mid-green.
R. LANCASHIRE ('Korstesgli') illus. p.181.
R. 'Lanken'. See *R.* FELICITY KENDAL.
♀ **R. LAURA FORD ('Chewarvel')** illus. p.187.
♀ **R. L.D. BRAITHWAITE ('Auscrim')**. Lax, open shrub rose with moderate disease resistance and dull, mid-green leaves. **H** 1.8m (6ft), **S** 1.2m (4ft). Scented, quartered-rosette, fully double, deep crimson flowers, 12cm (5in) across, fading to lighter crimson, are produced sparingly in summer and again in autumn.
R. 'Leggab'. See *R.* PEARL DRIFT.
R. 'Legnews'. See *R.* NEWS.
R. 'Lenip'. See *R.* PASCALI.
R. LIGHT FANTASTIC ('Dicgottago'). Compact, bushy Floribunda rose with good disease resistance and repeat-flowering in summer–autumn. **H** and **S** 80cm (2½ft). Produces clusters of up to 9 rosette, double, lemon-yellow flowers, 5cm (2in) across. Has glossy, light green leaves.
♀ **R. LITTLE RAMBLER ('Chewramb')**. Climber with very good disease resistance and repeat-flowering in summer-autumn. **H** 1.5m (5ft), **S** 1.2m (4ft). Produces small, glossy, light green leaves and tight clusters of moderately-scented, cupped, semi-double, rose-pink flowers, 5cm (2in) across, fading to pale pink with a lilac hue.
R. 'Louise Odier', syn. *R.* 'Madame de Stella'. Elegant, upright Bourbon rose. **H** 2m (6ft), **S** 1.2m (4ft). Has light greyish-green foliage and fragrant, cupped, fully double, warm rose-pink flowers, 12cm (5in) across, borne in summer–autumn.
♀ **R. LOVELY LADY ('Dicjubell')**. Dense, rounded Hybrid Tea rose with moderate disease resistance. **H** 80cm (32in), **S** 70cm (28in). Slightly scented, pointed, fully double, rose-pink flowers, 10cm (4in) across, are produced freely in summer and again in autumn.
R. LOVING MEMORY ('Korgund') illus. p.181.
R. LUCKY! ('Frylucy'). Upright Floribunda rose with very good disease resistance and repeat-flowering in summer–autumn. **H** 1m (3ft), **S** 80cm (2½ft). Cupped, double flowers, 7cm (3in) across, deep rose-pink in bud, open lighter. Has matt dark green leaves.
R. 'Macangeli'. See *R.* SNOWBALL.
R. 'Macar'. See *R.* PICCADILLY.
R. 'Macca'. See *R.* CASINO.
R. 'Maccarpe'. See *R.* SNOW CARPET.
R. 'Macdub'. See *R.* DUBLIN BAY.
R. 'Macha'. See *R.* HANDEL.
R. 'Macmi'. See *R.* MISCHIEF.
R. 'Macrexy'. See *R.* SEXY REXY.
R. *macrophylla*. Vigorous Species rose. **H** 4m (12ft), **S** 3m (10ft). Bears moderately fragrant, flat, single, red flowers, 5cm (2in) across, in summer, followed by flask-shaped, red hips. Has red stems and large, mid-green leaves.
R. 'Mactru'. See *R.* TRUMPETER.
♀ **R. 'Madame Alfred Carrière'** illus. p.184.
R. 'Madame A. Meilland'. See *R.* PEACE.
R. 'Madame de Stella'. See *R.* 'Louise Odier'.

R

***R.* 'Madame Ernest Calvat'.** Vigorous, arching Bourbon rose. **H** 2–3m (6–10ft), **S** 2m (6ft). Fragrant, cupped to quartered-rosette, fully double, rose-pink flowers, 15cm (6in) across, are borne freely in summer–autumn. Has plentiful, large leaves.

♀ ***R.* 'Madame Grégoire Staechelin'**, syn. *R.* 'Spanish Beauty', illus. p.185.

♀ ***R.* 'Madame Hardy'** illus. p.172.

***R.* 'Madame Hébert'.** See *R.* 'Président de Sèze'.

♀ ***R.* 'Madame Isaac Pereire'** illus. p.174.

♀ ***R.* 'Madame Knorr'**, syn. *R.* 'Comte de Chambord' of gardens. Vigorous, erect Portland rose. **H** 1.2m (4ft), **S** 1m (3ft). In summer–autumn, fragrant, quartered-rosette, fully double, lilac-tinted, pink flowers, 10cm (4in) across, appear amid plentiful, light green foliage. Is suitable for a hedge.

***R.* 'Madame Pierre Oger'.** Lax Bourbon rose. **H** 2m (6ft), **S** 1.2m (4ft). In summer–autumn, slender stems carry sweetly scented, cupped or bowl-shaped, double, pink flowers, 8cm (3in) across, with rose-lilac tints. Has light green leaves. Grows well on a pillar.

***R.* Maid of Honour ('Jacwhink')** illus. p.178.

♀ ***R.* 'Maigold'** illus. p.187.

***R.* 'Mainzer Fastnacht'.** See *R.* Blue Moon.

♀ ***R.* Many Happy Returns ('Harwanted')** illus. p.178.

***R.* 'Maréchal Davoust'.** Vigorous, bushy Moss rose. **H** 1.5m (5ft), **S** 1.2m (4ft). In summer bears moderately fragrant, cupped, fully double, deep reddish-pink to purple flowers, 10cm (4in) across, with a green eye and brownish "mossing". Leaves are dull green and lance-shaped.

***R.* 'Maréchal Niel'.** Vigorous, spreading Noisette or climbing Hybrid Tea rose. **H** 3m (10ft), **S** 2m (6ft). Drooping stems carry rich green foliage and moderately scented, pointed, fully double, clear yellow flowers, 10cm (4in) across, in summer–autumn.

♀ ***R.* Margaret Merril ('Harkuly')** illus. p.177.

♀ ***R.* 'Marguerite Hilling'**, syn. *R.* 'Pink Nevada', illus. p.173.

♀ ***R.* Mary Rose ('Ausmary')**. Bushy, spreading Shrub rose. **H** and **S** 1.2m (4ft). Produces moderately fragrant, cupped, fully double, rose-pink flowers, 9cm (3½in) across, in summer–autumn. Has plentiful leaves.

***R.* 'Meidanover'.** See *R.* Colibre '79.

***R.* 'Meidomonac'.** See *R.* Bonica.

***R.* 'Meigekanu'.** See *R.* La Sévillana.

***R.* 'Meijikitar'.** See *R.* Orange Sunblaze.

***R.* 'Meilucca'.** See *R.* Darling Flame.

♀ ***R.* 'Mermaid'** illus. p.187.

***R.* 'Mignon'.** See *R.* 'Cécile Brünner'.

***R.* Mischief ('Macmi')**. Upright Hybrid Tea rose. **H** 1m (3ft), **S** 60cm (2ft). Moderately fragrant, urn-shaped, double, salmon-pink flowers, 10cm (4in) across, are borne freely in summer–autumn. Leaves are plentiful but prone to rust.

♀ ***R.* Molineux ('Ausmol')**. Compact shrub rose with very good disease resistance and shiny, mid-green foliage. **H** 1.5m (5ft), **S** 1.2m (4ft). Slightly scented, rosette, canary-yellow flowers, 10cm (4in) across, with slightly paler outer petalsare produced in summer and again in autumn.

♀ ***R.* 'Morning Jewel'.** Free-branching Climber. **H** 2.5m (8ft), **S** 2.2m (7ft). Has plentiful, glossy foliage and cupped, double, bright pink flowers, 9cm (3½in) across, freely borne, usually in clusters, in summer–autumn. May be pruned to a shrub.

***R.* 'Morsherry'.** See *R.* Sheri Anne.

***R. moschata* var. *nivea*.** See *R.* 'Dupontii'.

♀ ***R.* Mountbatten ('Harmantelle')** illus. p.182.

***R.* 'Mousseline'**, syn. *R.* 'Alfred de Dalmas' of gardens. Bushy Moss rose with twiggy growth. **H** and **S** 1m (3ft). Mainly in summer bears scented, cupped, fully double, blush-pink flowers, 8cm (3in) across, with little "mossing". Has matt green leaves.

***R. moyesii*.** Vigorous, arching Species rose. **H** 4m (12ft), **S** 3m (10ft). In summer, faintly scented, flat, single, dusky-scarlet flowers, 5cm (2in) across, with yellow stamens, are borne close to branches. Produces long, red hips in autumn. Sparse, small, dark green leaves are composed of 7–13 leaflets. ♀ **'Geranium'** (syn. *R.* 'Geranium'; illus. p.176), **H** 3m (10ft), **S** 2.5m (8ft), has large, red hips.

***R.* 'Mrs John Laing'** illus. p.174.

R. multibracteata (illus. p.176). Rounded, bushy Species rose with good disease resistance. **H** 2m (6ft), **S** 1.5m (5ft). Thin stems have abundant, small, grey-green leaves. Slightly scented, flat, single, pink flowers, 5cm (2in) across, with a hint of lilac, and many bracts on the stem behind each flower, are borne in a single flush in summer and are followed by small, rounded hips in autumn–winter.

***R.* 'National Trust'.** Compact Hy brid Tea rose. **H** 75cm (30in), **S** 60cm (24in). Slightly scented, urn-shaped, fully double, scarlet-crimson flowers, 10cm (4in) across, are borne freely in summer–autumn. Produces plentiful, dark green foliage. Makes a good, low hedge.

♀ ***R.* 'Nevada'** illus. p.173.

♀ ***R.* 'New Dawn'** illus. p.185.

***R.* News ('Legnews')**. Upright Floribunda rose. **H** 60cm (24in), **S** 50cm (20in). Has dark green leaves and, in summer–autumn, clusters of slightly fragrant, cupped, wide-opening, double, bright reddish-purple flowers, each 8cm (3in) across.

***R.* 'Niphetos'.** Branching, climbing Hybrid Tea rose. **H** 3m (10ft), **S** 2m (6ft). Long, pointed buds on nodding stems open to rounded, double, white flowers, 12cm (5in) across, mainly in summer, a few later. Pale green leaves are pointed.

***R.* 'Noisette Carnée'**, syn. *R.* 'Blush Noisette'. Noisette rose of branching habit and lax growth. **H** 2–4m (6–12ft), **S** 2–2.5m (6–8ft). In summer–autumn, smooth stems bear clusters of spice-scented, cupped, double, blush-pink flowers, 4cm (1½in) across. Has matt foliage. May be grown as a shrub.

***R.* Nostalgia ('Taneiglat')** illus. p.179.

♀ ***R.* 'Nozomi'**, syn. *R.* 'Heideröslein'. Creeping, ground-cover rose with good disease resistance. **H** 45cm (1½ft), **S** 1.2m (4ft). Bears slightly scented, flat, single, blush-pink and white flowers, 2.5cm (1in) across, close to stems in a single flush in summer. Has small, dark green leaves. May be used for a container.

♀ ***R.* 'Nuits de Young'**, syn. *R.* 'Old Black'. Erect Moss rose with wiry stems. **H** 1.2m (4ft), **S** 1m (3ft). In summer has slightly scented, double, flat, dark maroon-purple flowers, 5cm (2in) across, with brownish "mossing". Leaves are small and dark green.

♀ ***R. nutkana* 'Plena'** , syn. *R. californica* 'Plena'. Robust Species rose. **H** to 3m (10ft), **S** 2m (6ft). Fragrant, cupped, semi-double, pink flowers, 4cm (1½in) across, are borne singly in summer. Has toothed, mid-green leaves.

***R.* 'Ocaru'.** See *R.* Angela Rippon.

♀ ***R. x odorata* 'Mutabilis'**, syn. *R. chinensis* 'Mutabilis', illus. p.174. **'Pallida'** (Old blush china) illus. p.174. **'Pseudindica'** (syn. *R.* 'Beauty of Glazenwood', *R.* 'Fortune's Double Yellow', *R.* 'Gold of Ophir', *R.* 'San Rafael Rose') is a lax Climber of restrained growth. **H** 2.5m (8ft), **S** 1.5m (5ft). Frost hardy. In summer bears small clusters of scented, pointed to cupped, semi-double, copper-suffused, yellow flowers, 5cm (2in) across. Leaves are glossy, light green. Prune very lightly.

***R. officinalis*.** See *R. gallica* var. *officinalis*.

***R.* 'Old Black'.** See *R.* 'Nuits de Young'.

***R.* 'Omar Khayyám'.** Dense, prickly Damask rose. **H** and **S** 1m (3ft). Fragrant, quartered-rosette, fully double, light pink flowers, 8cm (3in) across, are borne amid downy, greyish foliage in summer.

***R. omeiensis* f. *pteracantha*.** See *R. sericea* subsp. *omeiensis* f. *pteracantha*.

***R.* 'Opa Potschke'.** See *R.* 'Precious Platinum'.

***R.* 'Ophelia'.** Upright, open Hybrid Tea rose. **H** 1m (3ft), **S** 60cm (2ft). In summer–autumn, produces sweetly fragrant, urn-shaped, double, creamy-blush-pink flowers, 10cm (4in) across, singly or in clusters. Dark green foliage is sparse.

***R.* Orange Sunblaze ('Meijikitar')**, syn. *R.* 'Sunblaze'. Compact Miniature rose with moderate disease resistance. **H** and **S** 30cm (12in). Rosette, fully double, bright orange-red flowers, 4cm (1½in) across, are freely produced in summer and again in autumn. Has plentiful, dark green leaves.

***R.* 'Panachée d'Angers'.** See *R.* 'Commandant Beaurepaire'.

***R.* Pascali ('Lenip')**. Upright Hybrid Tea rose. **H** 1m (3ft), **S** 60cm (2ft). Bears faintly scented, neat, urn-shaped, fully double, white flowers, 9cm (3½in) across, in summer–autumn. Has deep green leaves.

♀ ***R.* Pat Austin ('Ausmum')**. Bushy shrub rose with very good disease resistance and matt, mid-green leaves. **H** 1.2m (4ft), **S** 1m (3ft). In summer and again in autumn, cupped, fully double, rich orange flowers, with some red veining on petals, fade to peach.

♀ ***R.* Paul Shirville ('Harqueterwife')**, syn. *R.* 'Heartthrob', illus. p.178.

♀ ***R.* 'Paul Transon'.** Vigorous, rather lax Rambler. **H** 4m (12ft), **S** 1.5m (5ft). In summer has slightly fragrant, flat, double, faintly coppery, salmon-pink flowers, 8cm (3in) across, with pleated petals. Plentiful foliage is glossy, dark green.

♀ ***R.* 'Paul's Himalayan Musk'**, syn. *R.* 'Paul's Himalayan Musk Rambler'. Very vigorous Rambler. **H** and **S** 10m (30ft). Large clusters of slightly fragrant, rosette, double, blush-pink flowers, 4cm (1½in) across, are freely borne in late summer. Has thorny, trailing shoots and drooping leaves. Is suitable for growing up a tree or in a wild garden.

***R.* 'Paul's Himalayan Musk Rambler'.** See *R.* 'Paul's Himalayan Musk'.

***R.* 'Paul's Lemon Pillar'** illus. p.184.

***R.* Paul Shirville ('Harqueterwife')** illus. p.178.

♀ ***R.* Peace ('Madame A. Meilland')**, syn. *R.* 'Gioia', *R.* 'Gloria Dei', illus. p.182.

***R.* Pearl Drift ('Leggab')**. Bushy, spreading shrub roses with good disease resistance. **H** 1m (3ft), **S** 1.2m (4ft). Produces clusters of lightly scented, cupped, double, blush-pink flowers, 10cm (4in) across, in summer and again in autumn. Leaves are plentiful and glossy.

***R.* 'Peaudouce'.** See *R.* Elina.

***R.* Peek-a-boo ('Dicgrow')**, syn. *R.* 'Brass Ring'. Dense, cushion-forming Patio rose with moderate disease resistance. **H** and **S** 45cm (18in). Produces sprays of urn-shaped, double, apricot-pink flowers, 4cm (1½in) across, in summer and again in autumn. Leaves are narrow and dark green.

♀ ***R.* 'Penelope'** illus. p.172.

♀ ***R.* Penny Lane ('Hardwell')** illus. p.186.

♀ ***R.* 'Perle d'Or'.** China rose that forms a twiggy, leafy, small shrub. **H** 75cm (2½ft), **S** 60cm (2ft). Small, slightly scented, urn-shaped, fully double, honey-pink flowers, 4cm (1½in) across, are borne in summer–autumn. Leaves have pointed, glossy leaflets.

***R.* 'Persian Yellow'.** See *R. foetida* 'Persiana'.

***R.* Piccadilly ('Macar')**. Vigorous, bushy Hybrid Tea rose with moderate disease resistance. **H** 1m (3ft), **S** 60cm (2ft). Pointed, double, red and yellow flowers, 12cm (5in) across, are produced singly or in clusters in summer and again in autumn. Abundant foliage is reddish-green and glossy.

***R. pimpinellifolia*.** See *R. spinosissima*.

***R.* Pink Bells ('Poulbells')**. Very dense, spreading ground-cover rose with good disease resistance. **H** 75cm (2½ft), **S** 1.2m (4ft). Produces clusters of many pompon, fully double, pink flowers, 2.5cm (1in) across, iin summer and again in autumn. Has abundant, small, dark green leaves.

♀ ***R.* 'Pink Grootendorst'.** Upright, bushy shrub rose with very good disease resistance. **H** 2m (6ft), **S** 1.5m (5ft). Sprays of rosette, double flowers, 5cm (2in) across, with serrated, clear pink petals, are borne in summer and again in autumn.

***R.* 'Pink Nevada'.** See *R.* 'Marguerite Hilling'.

***R.* 'Pink Parfait'.** Bushy Floribunda rose. **H** 75cm (2½ft), **S** 60cm (2ft). In summer–autumn, slightly fragrant, urn-shaped, double flowers, 9cm (3½in) across, in shades of light pink, are produced freely. Has plentiful foliage.

***R.* Pink Perfection ('Korpauvio')** illus. p.180.

***R.* 'Pink Perpétué'.** Stiffly branched Climber with moderate disease resistance. **H** 2.8m (9ft), **S** 2.5m (8ft). Produces clusters of slightly scented, cupped to rosette, double, deep pink flowers, 8cm (3in)

across, in summer and again in autumn. Leathery foliage is plentiful. May be pruned to grow as a shrub.
R. 'Pompon de Paris'. See *R.* 'Rouletii'.
R. 'Pompon des Princes'. See *R.* 'Ispahan'.
R. Pot o' Gold ('Dicdivine'). Hybrid Tea rose with neat, even growth and moderate disease resistance. **H** 75cm (30in), **S** 60cm (24in). Fragrant, rounded, fully double, golden-yellow flowers, 9cm (3½in) across, are produced singly or in wide sprays in summer and again in autumn.
R. 'Poulbells'. See *R.* Pink Bells.
R. 'Poulcov'. See *R.* Kent.
R. 'Poulman'. See *R.* Ingrid Bergman.
R. 'Poulmax'. See *R.* Fascination.
R. 'Poumidor'. See *R.* Troika.
R. 'Precious Platinum', syn. *R.* 'Opa Potschke'. Vigorous Hybrid Tea rose with moderate disease resistance. **H** 1m (3ft), **S** 60cm (2ft). Bears slightly scented, rounded, fully double, deep crimson-scarlet flowers, 10cm (4in) across, in summer and again in autumn. Foliage is abundant and glossy.
🏆 **R. 'Président de Sèze'**, syn. *R.* 'Madame Hébert'. Vigorous, rather open Gallica rose. **H** and **S** 1.2m (4ft). Bears fragrant, quartered-rosette, fully double, magenta-pink to pale lilac-pink flowers, 10cm (4in) across, in summer.
R. 'Prima'. See *R.* 'Many Happy Returns'.
🏆 ***R. primula*** (Incense rose). Lax, arching Species rose with very good disease resistance. **H** and **S** 2m (6ft). Produces scented, cupped, primrose-yellow flowers, 4cm (1½in) across, in a single flush in summer. Foliage is plentiful, aromatic and fern-like. May die back in hard winters.
🏆 **R. Princess of Wales ('Hardinkum')**. Vigorous, compact Floribunda rose. **H** 80cm (30in), **S** 60cm (24in). Tight clusters of scented, rounded, fully double, paper-white blooms, 9cm (3½in) across, nestle among crisp dark leaves in summer–autumn. Is good for beds and hedges.
R. 'Queen Elizabeth', syn. *R.* 'The Queen Elizabeth', illus. p.178.
R. 'Queen of the Violets'. See *R.* 'Reine des Violettes'.
R. Rachel ('Tangust') illus. p.183.
🏆 **R. 'Rambling Rector'** illus. p.184.
R. 'Ramona', syn. *R.* 'Red Cherokee'. Rather stiff, open Climber. **H** 2.7m (9ft), **S** 3m (10ft). Fragrant, flat, single, carmine-red flowers, 10cm (4in) across, with a greyish-red reverse and gold stamens, appear mainly in summer. Has sparse foliage. Does best against a warm wall.
R. Red Ace ('Amruda'). Compact Miniature rose with good disease resistance. **H** 35cm (14in), **S** 30cm (12in). Slightly scented, rosette, double, dark red flowers, 4cm (1½in) across, are borne in summer and again in autumn.
R. 'Red Cherokee'. See *R.* 'Ramona'.
R. Red Finesse ('Korvillade') illus. p.181.
R. 'Red Moss'. See *R.* 'Henri Martin'.
R. 'Reine des Violettes', syn. *R.* 'Queen of the Violets'. Spreading, vigorous Hybrid Perpetual rose. **H** and **S** 2m (6ft). Has greyish-toned leaves and fragrant, quartered-rosette, fully double, violet to purple flowers, 8cm (3in) across, in summer–autumn. May be grown on a support.
R. 'Reine Victoria' illus. p.173.
🏆 **R. Remember Me ('Cocdestin')** illus. p.183.
R. Remembrance ('Harxampton') illus. p.181.
R. 'Rise 'n' Shine', syn. *R.* 'Golden Sunblaze'. Bushy, upright Miniature rose with moderate disease resistance. **H** 40cm (16in), **S** 25cm (10in). Bears rosette, fully double, yellow flowers, 2.5cm (1in) across, in summer and again in autumn. Foliage is dark green.
R. Rhapsody in Blue ('Frantasia') illus. p.175.
R. 'Rose d'Isfahan'. See *R.* 'Ispahan'.
R. Rose Gaujard ('Gaumo'). Upright, strong Hybrid Tea rose. **H** 1.1m (3½ft), **S** 75cm (2½ft). Has plentiful glossy foliage. Bears slightly scented, urn-shaped, double, cherry-red and blush-pink flowers, 10cm (4in) across, freely in summer–autumn.
R. Rosemary Harkness ('Harrowbond'). Vigorous Hybrid tea rose with moderate disease resistance. **H** 1m (3ft), **S** 75cm (2½ft). Bears strongly scented, pointed, double flowers, 10cm (4in) across, in salmon-pink and orange, singly or in clusters in summer and again in autumn. Has abundant, glossy leaves.
🏆 **R. 'Roseraie de l'Haÿ'** illus. p.175.
🏆 **R. Rosy Cushion ('Interall')**. Dense, spreading shrub rose with very good disease resistance and repeat-flowering in summer–autumn. **H** 1m (3ft), **S** 1.2m (4ft). Clusters of slightly scented, cupped, semi-double flowers, 6cm (2½in) across, are pink with ivory centres. Has plentiful, glossy, dark green leaves.
R. 'Rosy Mantle'. Stiff, open-branched Climber with good disease resistance. **H** 2.5m (8ft), **S** 2m (6ft). Very fragrant, pointed, fully double, rose-pink flowers, 10cm (4in) across, are borne in summer and again in autumn. Dark green foliage is rather sparse.
R. 'Rouge Eblouissante'. See *R.* 'Assemblage des Beautés'.
R. 'Rouletii', syn. *R. chinensis* var. *minima*, *R.* 'Pompon de Paris'. Compact Miniature rose with thin stems. **H** and **S** 20cm (8in). Has mid-green leaves comprising many lance-shaped leaflets, and freely produces cupped, double, deep pink flowers, 2cm (¾in) across, in summer–autumn.
R. roxburghii (Burr rose, Chestnut rose, Chinquapin rose; illus. p.176). Compact, bushy Species rose with good disease resistance. **H** and **S** 1.2m (4ft). Has flaky bark and light to mid-green leaves, often with up to 15 leaflets that look as if they are almost arranged on the plant. In a single flush in summer produces flat, double, pink flowers, 5cm (2in) across, followed by spiked hips, which remain green and fall in late summer.
R. 'Royal Dane'. See *R.* Troika.
🏆 **R. Royal William ('Korzaun')**, syn. *R.* 'Duftzauber '84', illus. p.180.
R. rubiginosa, syn. *R. eglanteria* (Eglantine, Sweet briar; illus. p.176). Vigorous, arching, thorny Species rose with very good disease resistance. **H** and **S** 2.4m (8ft). Has apple-scented foliage. Bears cupped, single, pink flowers, 2.5cm (1in) across, in a single flush in summer and red hips in autumn.
***R. rubrifolia*.** See *R. glauca*.
R. Ruby Anniversary ('Harbonny'). Bushy Patio rose with good disease resistance and repeat-flowering in summer–autumn. **H** 70cm (28in), **S** 50cm (20in). Produces highly glossy, dark green leaves and large, wide clusters of cupped, double, ruby-red flowers, 5cm (2in) across.
R. rugosa (illus. p.176). Vigorous, dense Species rose with very good disease resistance. **H** and **S** 1–2m (3–6ft). Has wrinkled leaves and large, red hips. Bears cupped, single, white or purplish-red flowers, 9cm (3½in) across, in a single flush in summer. 🏆 **var. *alba*** has white flowers opening from pale pink buds.
R. 'Rugul'. See *R.* Golden Penny.
R. 'Ruiblun'. See *R.* Blue Peter.
R. 'Runatru'. See *R.* Invincible.
R. 'Saint Nicholas'. Vigorous, erect Damask rose. **H** and **S** 1.2m (4ft). In summer bears lightly scented, cupped, semi-double, rose-pink flowers, 12cm (5in) across, with golden stamens, followed by red hips in autumn. Has plentiful, dark green foliage.
R. 'Sally Holmes' illus. p.173.
R. 'San Rafael Rose'. See *R.* x *odorata* 'Pseudindica'.
🏆 **R. 'Sander's White Rambler'.** Vigorous Rambler of lax growth. **H** 3m (10ft), **S** 2.5m (8ft). Fragrant, rosette, fully double, white flowers, 5cm (2in) across, appear in clusters in late summer. Small, glossy leaves are plentiful.
R. Savoy Hotel ('Harvintage') illus. p.178.
🏆 **R. Scepter'd Isle ('Ausland')**. Bushy shrub rose with good disease resistance and dark green foliage. **H** 1.5m (5ft), **S** 1m (3ft). In summer and again in autumn produces scented, cupped, fully double, rose-pink flowers, 10cm (4in) across, eventually opening to show yellow stamens.
R. 'Schneewittchen'. See *R.* Iceberg.
R. 'Schoolgirl'. Stiff, rather lanky, large-flowered Climber. **H** 2.7m (9ft), **S** 2.2m (7ft). Large, deep green leaves set off moderately fragrant, rounded, fully double, apricot-orange flowers, 10cm (4in) across, borne in summer–autumn.
R. sericea* subsp. *omeiensis* f. *pteracantha, syn. *R. omeiensis* f. *pteracantha* (Winged thorn rose; illus. p.176). Stiff, upright, vigorous Species rose. **H** 2.5m (8ft), **S** 2.2m (7ft). Has small, fern-like, light green leaves and large, red prickles on young stems. In summer, solitary, flat, white flowers, 2.5–6cm (1–2½in) across, are borne briefly along the stems.
🏆 **R. Sexy Rexy ('Macrexy')**. Compact, bushy Floribunda rose with moderate disease resistance. **H** and **S** 60cm (2ft). Bears clusters of slightly scented, cupped, camellia-like, fully double, pink flowers, 8cm (3in) across, in summer and again in autumn. Leaves are dark green.
R. Sheila's Perfume ('Harsherry'). Upright Floribunda rose. **H** 75cm (2½ft), **S** 60cm (2ft). Has glossy, reddish foliage. Fragrant, urn-shaped, double, red-and-yellow flowers, 9cm (3½in) across, are produced singly or in clusters in summer–autumn.
R. Sheri Anne ('Morsherry'). Upright Miniature rose with moderate disease resistance. **H** 45cm (18in), **S** 30cm (12in). Produces slightly scented, rosette, double, light red flowers, 2.5cm (1in) across, in summer and again in autumn. Has leathery, glossy leaves.
R. Shocking Blue ('Korblue'). Bushy Floribunda rose. **H** 75cm (2½ft), **S** 60cm (2ft). In summer–autumn bears fragrant, pointed, well-formed, fully double, purple flowers, 10cm (4in) across, singly or in clusters. Foliage is dark green.
R. Silver Anniversary ('Poulari') illus. p.177.
🏆 **R. 'Silver Jubilee'.** Dense, upright Hybrid Tea rose with good disease resistance. **H** 1.1m (3½ft), **S** 75cm (2½ft). Bears slightly scented, pointed, fully double, soft salmon-pink flowers, 12cm (5in) across, very freely in summer and again in autumn. Foliage is abundant and glossy.
R. Simba ('Korbelma'), syn. *R.* 'Goldsmith'. Upright Hybrid Tea rose with moderate disease resistance. **H** 75cm (30in), **S** 60cm (24in). Slightly scented, urn-shaped, fully double, yellow flowers, 9cm (3½in) across, are borne freely in summer and again in autumn. Leaves are large and dark green.
R. Simply Sally ('Harpaint') illus. p.180.
R. Simply the Best ('Macamster') illus. p.183.
R. 'Sissi'. See *R.* Blue Moon.
R. Snow Carpet ('Maccarpe'). Prostrate, creeping Miniature rose. **H** 15cm (6in), **S** 50cm (20in). Has many small glossy leaves and pompon, fully double, white flowers, 3cm (1½in) across, in summer, a few in autumn. Makes good, compact ground cover.
R. Snowball ('Macangeli'), syn. *R.* 'Angelita'. Compact, creeping Miniature rose with moderate disease resistance. **H** 20cm (8in), **S** 30cm (12in). Pompon, fully double, white flowers, 2.5cm (1in) across, are borne in summer and again in autumn. Leaves are small, glossy and plentiful.
🏆 **R. 'Southampton'**, syn. *R.* 'Susan Ann', illus. p.183.
R. 'Souvenir d'Alphonse Lavallée'. Vigorous, sprawling Hybrid Perpetual rose. **H** 2.2m (7ft), **S** 2m (6ft). Fragrant, cupped, double, burgundy-red to maroon-purple flowers, 10cm (4in) across, are borne in summer–autumn. Leaves are small and mid-green. Is best grown on a light support.
R. 'Souvenir de la Malmaison'. Dense, spreading Bourbon rose. **H** and **S** 1.5m (5ft). Bears spice-scented, quartered-rosette, fully double, blush-pink to white flowers, 12cm (5in) across, in summer–autumn. Rain spoils flowers. Has large, dark green leaves.
R. 'Spanish Beauty'. See *R.* 'Madame Grégoire Staechelin'.
'Spectacular'. See *R.* 'Danse du Feu'.
R. spinosissima, syn. *R. pimpinellifolia* (Burnet rose, Scotch rose). **'Plena'** is a dense, spreading, prickly Species rose with good disease resistance. **H** 1m (3ft), **S** 1.2m (4ft). Bears cupped, double, creamy-white flowers, 4cm (1½in) across, in a single flush in summer. Has small, fern-like, dark green leaves and blackish hips.

R

***R.* 'Spring Morning'.** See *R.* 'Frühlingsmorgen'.
***R.* 'Stacey Sue'.** Spreading Miniature rose with good disease resistance. **H** and **S** 38cm (15in). Slightly scented, rosette, fully double, pink flowers, 2.5cm (1in) across, are produced freely in summer and again in autumn. Has plentiful, dark green leaves.
***R.* Strawberry Hill ('Ausrimini')** illus. p.174.
***R.* Summer Song ('Austango')** illus. p.177.
***R.* Summer Wine ('Korizont')** illus. p.187.
***R.* 'Sunblaze'.** See *R.* Orange Sunblaze.
🏆 ***R.* Sunset Boulevard ('Harbabble')**. Upright Floribunda rose. **H** 1m (3ft), **S** 60cm (2ft). Bears open sprays of lightly scented, pointed to cupped, double, salmon-pink flowers, 9cm (3½in) across, in summer–autumn on glossy-foliaged plants. Is excellent for beds and cutting.
***R.* Super Trooper ('Fryleyeca')** illus. p.183.
***R.* 'Susan Ann'.** See *R.* 'Southampton'.
***R.* Susan Daniel ('Harlibra')** illus. p.178.
🏆 ***R.* Sweet Dream ('Fryminicot')** illus. p.179.
🏆 ***R.* Sweet Magic ('Dicmagic')** illus. p.183.
***R.* 'Sylvia'.** See *R.* Congratulations.
***R.* 'Sympathie'** illus. p.186.
***R.* 'Tanba'.** See *R.* Baby Masquerade.
***R.* 'Tanellis'.** See *R.* Fragrant Cloud.
***R.* 'Tanky'.** See *R.* Whisky Mac.
***R.* 'Tannacht'.** See *R.* Blue Moon.
***R.* 'Tapis d'Orient'.** See *R.* 'Yesterday'.
***R.* 'Tapis Jaune'.** See *R.* Golden Penny.
***R.* Teasing Georgia ('Ausbaker')** illus. p.176.
***R.* Tess of the D'Urbervilles ('Ausmove')**. Slightly lax, arching shrub rose with good disease resistance and repeat-flowering in summer–autumn. **H** 1.8m (6ft), **S** 1.5m (5ft). Scented, quartered-rosette, red flowers, 12cm (5in) across, fade with sun and age to pink-red. Foliage is mid-green.
🏆 ***R.* 'The Fairy'** illus. p.178.
***R.* The Pilgrim ('Auswalker')** illus. p.176.
***R.* The Prince's Trust ('Harholding')** illus. p.186.
***R.* 'The Queen Elizabeth'.** See *R.* 'Queen Elizabeth'.
🏆 ***R.* The Times Rose ('Korpeahn')** illus. p.180.
***R.* 'Tour de Malakoff'.** Provence rose of open habit and good disease resistance. **H** 2m (6ft), **S** 1.5m (5ft). In a single flush in summer produces scented, rosette, double, violet-veined, magenta flowers, 12cm (5in) across, fading to greyish-purple.
***R.* 'Tricolore de Flandre'.** Vigorous, upright Gallica rose. **H** and **S** 1m (3ft). Fragrant, pompon, fully double, blush-pink flowers, 6cm (2½in) across, striped with pink and purple, open in summer. Has dull green leaves.
🏆 ***R.* Troika ('Poumidor')**, syn. *R.* 'Royal Dane'. Vigorous, dense Hybrid Tea rose with moderate disease resistance. **H** 1m (3ft), **S** 75cm (2½ft). Fragrant, pointed, double, pink-tinged, orange-red flowers, 15cm (6in) across, are produced in summer and again in autumn. Has semi-glossy leaves.
🏆 ***R.* Trumpeter ('Mactru')**. Neat, bushy Floribunda rose with moderate disease resistance. **H** 60cm (24in), **S** 50cm (20in). Produces many cupped, fully double, bright red flowers, 6cm (2½in) across, in summer and again in autumn. Leaves are deep green and semi-glossy.
🏆 ***R.* 'Tuscany Superb'**, syn. *R.* 'Double Velvet'. Vigorous, upright Gallica rose. **H** 1.1m (3½ft), **S** 1m (3ft). In summer produces, slightly scented, cupped to flat, double flowers, 5cm (2in) across, deep crimson-maroon, ageing to purple, with gold stamens. Leaves are dark green.
***R.* 'Variegata di Bologna'.** Upright, arching Bourbon rose. **H** 2m (6ft), **S** 1.4m (4½ft). Has small leaves and, in summer–autumn, fragrant, quartered-rosette, fully double flowers, 8cm (3in) across, blush-pink, striped with rose-purple. Needs fertile soil and is prone to blackspot.
🏆 ***R.* 'Veilchenblau'**, syn. *R.* 'Blue Rambler', illus. p.185.
🏆 ***R.* Warm Wishes ('Fryxotic')** illus. p.179.
***R.* 'Wedding Day'.** Rampant Rambler. **H** 8m (25ft), **S** 4m (12ft). Produces large clusters of fruity-scented, flat, single, creamy-white flowers, 2.5cm (1in) across, that mature to blush-pink, in late summer. Is suitable for growing up a tree or in a wild garden.
***R.* Wee Jock ('Cocabest')**. Dense, bushy Patio rose with good disease resistance. **H** and **S** 45cm (18in). Bears rosette, fully double, crimson flowers, 4cm (1½in) across, in summer and again in autumn. Plentiful leaves are small and dark green.
***R.* Whisky Mac ('Tanky')**. Neat, upright Hybrid Tea rose. **H** 75cm (2½ft), **S** 60cm (2ft). Fragrant, rounded, fully double, amber flowers, 9cm (3½in) across, appear freely in summer–autumn. Reddish foliage is prone to mildew. May die back during a hard winter.
***R.* 'White Cockade'.** Slow-growing, bushy, upright Climber. **H** 2–3m (6–10ft), **S** 1.5m (5ft). Bears slightly fragrant, rounded, well-formed, fully double, white flowers, 9cm (3½in) across, in summer–autumn. May be pruned and grown as a shrub.
***R.* White Gold ('Cocquiriam')**. Vigorous Floribunda rose with very good disease resistance. **H** 1.2m (4ft), **S** 1m (3ft). Has semi-glossy, dark green leaves. Dense clusters of strongly scented, rounded, fully double, off-white flowers, 7cm (3in) across, with creamy-white centres, are produced in summer and again in autumn.
***R.* White Star ('Harquill')** illus. p.184.
***R.* Wild Rover ('Dichirap')**. Upright Floribunda rose with good disease resistance and repeat-flowering in summer–autumn. **H** 1m (3ft), **S** 80cm (2½ft). Produces clusters of 5 or more lightly scented, flat, semi-double, rich purple flowers, 7cm (3in) across, with yellow stamens. Has matt, mid-green leaves.
🏆 ***R.* 'William Lobb'**, syn. *R.* 'Duchesse d'Istrie', illus. p.175.
***R.* William Shakespeare 2000 ('Ausromeo')**. Bushy shrub rose with good disease resistance and dark mat green leaves. **H** 1.5m (5ft), **S** 1.0m (3ft). Strongly scented, quartered-rosette, fully double, crimson flowers, 10cm (4in) across, with slightly pink outer petals, are produced in summer and again in autumn.
***R.* Winchester Cathedral ('Auscat')**. Bushy shrub rose with good disease resistance and dark green leaves. **H** 1.2m (4ft), **S** 1m (3ft). Myrrh-scented, rosette, double, white flowers, 10cm (4 in) across, with light pink blushes when young, are produced in summer and again in autumn.
***R.* Wisley 2008 ('Ausbreeze')**. Bushy shrub rose with very good disease resistance and dull, mid-green leaves. **H** 1.2m (4ft), **S** 1.0m (3ft). Sweetly scented, quartered-rosette, fully double, light rose-pink flowers open from plump, rounded buds in summer and again in autumn.
🏆 ***R. xanthina* 'Canary Bird'**, syn. *R.* 'Canary Bird'. Vigorous, dense, arching Species hybrid with very good disease resistance. **H** and **S** 2.1m (7ft). Cupped, single, yellow flowers, 5cm (2in) across, with musky scent, are produced in a single flush in summer. Has small, fern-like leaves. May die back in hard winters.
🏆 ***R.* 'Yesterday'**, syn. *R.* 'Tapis d'Orient'. Bushy, arching Polyantha rose. **H** and **S** 75cm (30in), or more if lightly pruned. Fragrant, rosette, semi-double, lilac-pink flowers, 2.5cm (1in) across, are borne, mainly in clusters, from summer through to early winter. Produces small, dark green leaves. Makes a good hedge.
🏆 ***R.* 'Yvonne Rabier'.** Dense, bushy Polyantha rose. **H** 45cm (18in), **S** 40cm (16in). Plentiful leaves are bright green. Bears moderately scented, rounded, double, creamy-white flowers, 5cm (2in) across, in summer–autumn.
***R.* 'Zéphirine Drouhin'** illus. p.185.
***R.* 'Zigeunerknabe'**, syn. *R.* 'Gipsy Boy'. Vigorous, thorny Bourbon rose of lanky habit. **H** and **S** 2m (6ft). Faintly scented, cupped to flat, double, purplish-crimson flowers, 8cm (3in) across, are borne in summer. Leaves are dark green.
***R.* 'Zonta Rose'.** See *R.* Princess Alice.

Rosa mundi. See *Rosa gallica* 'Versicolor', illus. p.174.

ROSCOEA

ZINGIBERACEAE

Genus of late summer- and early autumn-flowering, tuberous perennials, related to ginger, grown for their orchid-like flowers. All species have a hooded, upper petal, a wide-lobed, lower lip and 2 narrower petals. Suits open borders, rock gardens and woodland gardens. Fully to frost hardy. Grows in sun or partial shade and in cool, well-drained humus-rich soil that must be kept moist in summer. Dies down in winter, when a top dressing of leaf mould or well-rotted compost is beneficial. Propagate by division in spring or by seed, exposed to frost for best germination, in autumn or winter.

R. alpina. Herbaceous, creeping, tuberous perennial. **H** and **S** 20cm (8in). Fully hardy. At the top of the leafy shoot has 1–5 deep purple, pink or white flowers borne in succession in summer. Produces 1–2 rather short, lance-shaped, mid-green leaves at flowering time, increasing to 5–6 leaves, to 25cm (10in) long. Requires a shady site.
R. auriculata illus. p.411.
R. australis. Summer-flowering, tuberous perennial. **H** 25–40cm (10–16in), **S** 25cm (10in). Frost hardy. Has 2–7 broadly lance-shaped, glossy, dark green leaves, arranged in opposite pairs, forming a pseudostem bearing 1–2 purple or white flowers, with shallowly lobed lips to 2.5cm (1in) across. Is intolerant of winter wet so is better in a cold frame. Is sometimes confused with *R. tibetica.*
🏆 ***R. cautleyoides*** illus. p.424.
🏆 ***R. humeana*** illus. p.423.
R. procera. See *R. purpurea.*
R. purpurea, syn. *R. procera*. Summer-flowering, tuberous perennial. **H** 20–30cm (8–12in), **S** 15–20cm (6–8in). Lance-shaped, erect leaves are long-pointed and wrap around each other at base to form a false stem. Produces long-tubed, purple flowers.
R. scillifolia (illus. p.477). Upright, tuberous perennial. **H** 5–30cm (2–12in), **S** 10–25cm (4–10in). Fully hardy. Small, purple-black or light pink flowers are produced in summer-autumn above narrowly lance-shaped to linear, mid-green leaves.
R. tibetica. Rosette-forming, tuberous perennial. **H** 5–20cm (2–8in), **S** 10–30cm (4–12in). Fully hardy. Broadly lance-shaped, pleated, mid-green leaves. In summer produces purple, pink or white flowers, with deeply lobed lips to 1.5–2cm (⅝–¾in) wide, at the top of the stem.

ROSMARINUS

LABIATAE/LAMIACEAE

Genus of evergreen shrubs, grown for their flowers and aromatic foliage, which can be used as a culinary herb. Frost hardy, but in cold areas grow against a south- or west-facing wall. Requires sun and well-drained soil. Cut back frost-damaged plants to healthy wood in spring; straggly, old plants may be cut back hard at same time. Trim hedges after flowering. Propagate by semi-ripe cuttings in summer.

R. lavandulaceus of gardens. See *R. officinalis* 'Prostratus'.
R. officinalis (Rosemary) illus. p.157. 🏆 **'Miss Jessopp's Upright'** is an evergreen, compact, upright shrub. **H** and **S** 2m (6ft). From mid- to late spring and sometimes again in autumn bears small, 2-lipped, blue flowers amid narrowly oblong, aromatic, dark green leaves. Is good when grown for hedging. **'Prostratus'** (syn. *R. lavandulaceus* of gardens), **H** 15cm (6in), is prostrate and the least hardy form. 🏆 **'Severn Sea'**, **H** 1m (3ft), has an arching habit, and produces bright blue flowers.

ROSSIOGLOSSUM

SYN. LEMBOGLOSSUM

ORCHIDACEAE

See also ORCHIDS.

R. grande, syn. *Odontoglossum grande* (illus. p.467). Evergreen, epiphytic orchid for a cool greenhouse. **H** 15cm (6in). Spikes of rich yellow flowers, to 15cm (6in) across and heavily marked chestnut-brown, are produced in autumn. Has broadly oval, stiff leaves, 15cm (6in) long. Provide shade in summer and keep very dry in winter.

ROTHMANNIA

RUBIACEAE

Genus of evergreen, summer-flowering shrubs and trees, grown for their flowers. Is related to *Gardenia*. Frost tender, min. 16°C (61°F). Needs a position in full light or partial shade and humus-rich, well-drained, neutral to acid soil. Water potted plants freely when in full growth, moderately at other times. Propagate by seed in spring or by semi-ripe cuttings in summer.

R. capensis, syn. *Gardenia capensis, G. rothmannia*. Evergreen, ovoid shrub or tree. **H** 6m (20ft) or more, **S** 3m (10ft) or more. Leaves are oval, lustrous and rich green. Has fragrant, tubular flowers, each with 5 arching, white to creamy-yellow petal lobes and a purple-dotted throat, in summer.

ROYSTONEA

Royal palm

PALMAE/ARECACEAE

Genus of evergreen palms, grown for their majestic appearance. Produces racemes of insignificant flowers in summer. Frost tender, min. 16–18°C (61–64°F). Needs full light or partial shade and fertile, well-drained but moisture-retentive soil. Water potted plants freely when in full growth, less at other times, especially when temperatures are low. Propagate by seed in spring at not less than 27°C (81°F). Red spider mite may be a problem.

R. regia (Cuban royal palm). Evergreen palm with an upright stem, sometimes thickened about the middle. **H** 20m (70ft) or more, **S** to 6m (20ft). Leaves are feather-shaped, 3m (10ft) long, upright at first, then becoming arching and pendent, and are divided into narrowly oblong, leathery, bright green leaflets.

RUBUS

Blackberry, Bramble

ROSACEAE

Genus of deciduous, semi-evergreen or evergreen shrubs and woody-stemmed, scrambling climbers. Some species are cultivated solely for their edible fruits, which include raspberries and blackberries. Those described here are grown mainly for their foliage, flowers or ornamental, often prickly stems, though some may also bear edible fruits. Fully to frost hardy. Deciduous species grown for their winter stems prefer full sun; other deciduous species need sun or semi-shade; evergreens and semi-evergreens tolerate sun or shade. All *Rubus* require fertile, well-drained soil. Cut old stems of *R. biflorus, R. cockburnianus* and *R. thibetanus* to ground after fruiting. Propagate by seed or cuttings (semi-ripe for evergreens, softwood or hardwood for deciduous species) in summer or winter. Or *R. odoratus* may be increased by division, and *R.* 'Benenden' and *R. ulmifolius* 'Bellidiflorus' by layering in spring.

🏆 ***R.* 'Benenden'**, syn. *R.* 'Tridel', illus. p.128.

🏆 ***R. biflorus*** illus. p.143.

R. cockburnianus. Deciduous, arching shrub. **H** and **S** 2.5m (8ft). Fully hardy. Prickly shoots are brilliant blue-white in winter. Dark green leaves, white beneath, each have usually 9 oval leaflets. Bears panicles of 5-petalled, purple flowers in early summer, followed by unpalatable, spherical, black fruits.

R. henryi* var. *bambusarum. Fast-growing, vigorous, evergreen, woody-stemmed, scrambling climber, grown mainly for its attractive foliage. **H** to 6m (20ft). Fully hardy. Leaves have 3 broadly oval leaflets, white-felted beneath. Tiny, pink flowers are borne in small clusters in summer.

R. odoratus (Flowering raspberry, Thimbleberry). Vigorous, deciduous, upright, thicket-forming shrub. **H** and **S** 2.5m (8ft). Fully hardy. Thornless, peeling shoots bear large, velvety, dark green leaves, each with 5 broadly triangular lobes. Large, fragrant, 5-petalled, rose-pink flowers appear from early summer to early autumn, and are sometimes followed by unpalatable, flattened, red fruits.

🏆 ***R. thibetanus*** illus. p.143.

R. tricolor. Evergreen shrub with both prostrate and arching shoots covered in red bristles. **H** 60cm (2ft), **S** 2m (6ft). Fully hardy. Oval, toothed, glossy, dark green leaves set off cup-shaped, 5-petalled, white flowers borne in mid-summer. Has edible, raspberry-like, red fruits. Makes good ground cover.

***R.* 'Tridel'.** See *R.* 'Benenden'.

***R. ulmifolius* 'Bellidiflorus'.** Vigorous, deciduous or semi-evergreen, arching shrub. **H** 2.5m (8ft), **S** 4m (12ft). Fully hardy. Prickly stems bear dark green leaves, with 3 or 5 oval leaflets, and, in mid- to late summer, large panicles of daisy-like, double, pink flowers.

RUDBECKIA

Coneflower

COMPOSITAE/ASTERACEAE

Genus of annuals, biennials and perennials grown for their flowers. Fully hardy. Thrives in sun or shade and well-drained or moist soil. Propagate by division in spring or by seed in autumn or spring.

R. fulgida (Black-eyed Susan). 🏆 **var. *deamii*** (illus. p.251) is an erect perennial. **H** 1m (3ft), **S** 60cm (2ft) or more. In late summer and autumn has daisy-like, yellow flower heads with central, black cones. Has narrowly lance-shaped, mid-green leaves. Prefers moist soil. 🏆 **var. *speciosa*** (illus. p.251) has elliptic to lance-shaped, almost sickle-shaped basal leaves and coarsely toothed stem leaves.

🏆 **var. *sullivantii* 'Goldsturm'** (illus. p.251), **H** 75cm (30in), **S** 30cm (12in) or more, has golden flower heads.

***R.* 'Goldquelle'.** See *R. laciniata* 'Goldquelle'.

***R.* 'Herbstsonne'** illus. p.251.

R. hirta. Moderately fast-growing, upright, branching, short-lived perennial, grown as an annual. **H** 30cm–1m (1–3ft), **S** 30–45cm (1–1½ft). Has lance-shaped, mid-green leaves and, in summer–autumn, large, daisy-like, deep yellow flower heads, with conical, purple centres. Needs sun and well-drained soil. **Becky Mixed**, **H** to 25cm (10in), has yellow, dark red or reddish brown flowers. **'Goldilocks'** illus. p.325. **'Irish Eyes'**, **H** to 75cm (2½ft), has yellow flower heads with olive-green centres. **'Marmalade'** illus. p.323. **'Rustic Dwarfs'**, **H** to 60cm (24in), bears yellow, mahogany, or bronze flower heads. **'Toto Gold'** illus. p.320.

***R. laciniata* 'Golden Glow'.** Erect perennial. **H** 2–2.2m (6–7ft), **S** 60cm–1m (2–3ft). Bears daisy-like, double, golden-yellow flower heads, with green centres, in late summer and autumn. Mid-green leaves are divided into lance-shaped leaflets, themselves further cut. Prefers well-drained soil. 🏆 **'Goldquelle'** (syn. *R.* 'Goldquelle') illus. p.222. 🏆 **'Herbstsonne'** (illus. p.251) has single, bright yellow flower heads.

R. maxima (illus. p.251). Clump-forming perennial. **H** 2m (6ft) or more, **S** 60cm (2ft). Has broadly spoon-shaped, waxy, blue-green, basal leaves. In summer, stout stems bear solitary, dairy-like, flower heads with slender, reflexed, yellow ray florets and large, central, black cones.

R. occidentalis. Clump-forming perennial. **H** 60–180cm (24–72in), **S** 45cm (18in) or more. Has oval, mid-green, basal leaves. In summer, erect, leafy, occasionally branched stems bear daisy-like flower heads with a large, central, brownish-black cone surrounded by short, pointed, green bracts; they have no true ray florets ("petals"). **'Green Wizard'** (illus. p.251), **H** 1.5m (60in), has a more even height range.

R. purpurea. See *Echinacea purpurea*.

🏆 ***R. triloba*** (illus. p.251). Short-lived, upright, clump-forming perennial. **H** 80cm (32in), **S** 40cm (16in). Has 3-lobed, hairy, mid- to pale green, basal leaves. From late summer until autumn frosts, leafy stems bear masses of daisy-like, bright yellow flower heads with central, blackish-brown cones. Self-seeds freely.

RUELLIA

ACANTHACEAE

Genus of perennials and evergreen sub-shrubs and shrubs with showy flowers. Frost tender, min. 15°C (59°F). Grow in a humid atmosphere, partial shade and in moist but well-drained soil. Propagate by stem cuttings or seed, if available, in spring.

R. amoena. See *R. graecizans*.

R. devosiana illus. p.465.

R. graecizans, syn. *R. amoena*. Evergreen, bushy sub-shrub with wide-spreading stems. **H** and **S** 60cm (24in) or more. Has oval, pointed leaves. Intermittently bears clusters of small, tubular, scarlet flowers

🏆 ***R. makoyana*** (Trailing velvet plant). Hairy, spreading perennial. **H** to 60cm (2ft), **S** 45cm (1½ft). Has oval, silver-veined purple leaves, dark purple beneath. In summer, bears funnel-shaped, carmine-pink flowers singly from the leaf axils.

RUSCHIA

AIZOACEAE

Genus of mostly small, tufted, perennial succulents and evergreen shrubs with leaves united up to one-third of their lengths around stems or with very short sheaths. Frost tender, min. 5°C (41°F). Needs a sunny position and well-drained soil. Propagate by seed or stem cuttings in spring or summer.

R. acuminata. Evergreen, erect, succulent shrub. **H** 20cm (8in), **S** 50cm (20in). Has woody stems as well as non-woody, bluish-green stems with darker dots. Produces solid, 3-angled, 3cm (1¼in) long leaves, each with a blunt keel and a short sheath. Daisy-like, white to pale pink flowers, 3cm (1¼in) across, appear in summer.

R. crassa. Evergreen, erect, succulent shrub. **H** and **S** 50cm (20in). Bears solid, 3-angled, bluish-green leaves, 2cm (¾in) long, with short, white hairs; the undersides are keeled, each with a single tooth. Has 2.5cm (1in) wide, daisy-like, white flowers in summer.

R. macowanii. Erect, then spreading, perennial succulent. **H** 15cm (6in), **S** 1m (3ft). Has solid, slightly keeled, 3-angled, bluish-green leaves, to 3cm (1¼in) long. In summer carries masses of daisy-like, bright pink flowers, 3cm (1¼in) across, with darker stripes.

RUSCUS

LILIACEAE/RUSCACEAE

Genus of evergreen, clump-forming, spring-flowering shrubs, grown for their foliage and fruits. The apparent leaves are actually flattened shoots, on which flowers and fruits are borne. Usually, separate male and female plants are required for fruiting. Is particularly useful for dry, shady sites. Fully to frost hardy. Tolerates sun or shade and any soil other than waterlogged. Cut back dead shoots to base in spring. Propagate by division in spring. ⓘThe berries of *R. aculeatus* may cause mild stomach upset if ingested.

R. aculeatus (Butcher's broom) illus. p.167.

R. hypoglossum illus. p.167.

RUSSELIA

SCROPHULARIACEAE

Genus of evergreen shrubs and sub-shrubs with showy flowers. Frost tender, min. 10–15°C (50–59°F). Needs sun or partial shade. Requires humus-rich, light, well-drained soil. Propagate by stem cuttings or division in spring.

🏆 ***R. equisetiformis*** (Coral plant), syn. *R. juncea*, illus. p.470.

R. juncea. See *R. equisetiformis*.

RUTA

Rue

RUTACEAE

Genus of evergreen, summer-flowering sub-shrubs, with deeply divided, aromatic leaves, grown for their foliage and flowers and used as a medicinal herb. Fully hardy. Requires a sunny position and well-drained soil. Cut back to old wood in spring to keep compact. Propagate by semi-ripe cuttings in summer. ⓘAll parts may cause severe discomfort if eaten; the foliage may cause photodermatitis on contact.

R. graveolens (Common rue). **'Jackman's Blue'** illus. p.159.

S

SABAL

PALMAE/ARECACEAE

Genus of evergreen fan palms, grown for their foliage and overall appearance. Half hardy to frost tender, min. 5–7°C (41–45°F). Prefers full sun and fertile, well-drained soil. Water moderately, less when not in full growth. Propagate by seed in spring. Red spider mite may be troublesome.
S. minor illus. p.457.

SAGINA

CARYOPHYLLACEAE

Genus of mat-forming annuals and evergreen perennials, grown for their foliage. Is suitable for banks and in paving. Some species may be very invasive. Fully hardy. Prefers sun and gritty, moist soil; dislikes hot, dry conditions. Propagate by division in spring, by seed in autumn or, for *S. boydii*, by tip cuttings in summer. Aphids and red spider mite may cause problems.
S. boydii, syn. *S. procumbens* 'Boydii' illus. p.376.

SAGITTARIA

Arrowhead

ALISMATACEAE

Genus of deciduous, perennial, submerged and marginal water plants, grown for their foliage and flowers. Fully hardy to frost tender, min. 5°C (41°F). Some species are suitable for pools, others for aquariums. All require full sun. Remove fading foliage as necessary. Propagate by division in spring or summer or by breaking off turions (scaly, young shoots) in spring.
***S. graminea* 'Crushed Ice'.** Deciduous, perennial, marginal water plant or bog plant. **H** 23cm (9in), **S** 15cm (6in). Half hardy. Has linear, pointed leaves marbled cream and green. Bears 3-petalled, white flowers from early to mid-summer.
S. japonica. See *S. sagittifolia* 'Flore Pleno'.
S. latifolia (American arrowhead) illus. p.434.
S. sagittifolia (Common arrowhead). Deciduous, perennial, marginal water plant. **H** 45cm (18in), **S** 30cm (12in). Fully hardy. Upright, mid-green leaves are acutely arrow-shaped. In summer produces 3-petalled, white flowers with dark purple centres. May be grown in up to 23cm (9in) depth of water. **'Flore Pleno'** (syn. *S. japonica*; Japanese arrowhead) has double flowers.

SAINTPAULIA

African violet

GESNERIACEAE

Genus of evergreen, rosette-forming perennials, grown for their showy flowers. Frost tender, min. 15°C (59°F). Needs a constant temperature, a humid atmosphere, partial shade and fertile soil. Propagate by leaf cuttings in summer. Whitefly and mealy bug may cause problems with indoor plants.

African violet cultivars
There are over 2,000 cultivars, mainly derived from *S. ionantha*, with star- or bell-shaped, white, pink, red, blue, violet, bi- or multi-coloured flowers, borne throughout the year. They may be single, semi-double or fully double. Petal edges may be ruffled, rounded, frilled or fringed. The broadly ovate to oval leaves are usually mid- or dark green, and may be feathered, flecked or variegated white, pink or cream. See also feature panel p.472.
Cultivars are divided into 5 groups, according to rosette size. The measurement given below is the diameter of the rosette; the spread of each cultivar is the same as this: Micro-miniature – less than 8cm (3in); Miniature – 8–16cm (3–6in); Semi-miniature – 16–21cm (6–8in); Standard – 21–40cm (8–16in); Large – over 40cm (16in).
***S.* 'Bright Eyes'** (illus. p.472). Standard Group. **H** to 15cm (6in). Has dark green leaves and single, deep violet-blue flowers with yellow centres.
***S.* 'Chantabent'.** Semi-miniature Group. **H** 10–15cm (4–6in). Has dark green leaves with deep red undersides, and bears large, single, violet-blue flowers.
***S.* 'Colorado'** illus. p.469.
***S.* 'Delft'.** Standard Group. **H** to 15cm (6in). Leaves are dark green, and flowers are semi-double and violet-blue.
***S.* 'Dorothy'.** Standard Group. **H** to 15cm (6in). Has long-stalked, light green leaves, and bears large, single, rich pink flowers with frilled, white margins.
***S.* 'Falling Raindrops'** (illus. p.472). Standard Group with trailing habit. **H** 10–15cm (4–6in). Has mid-green leaves and single, violet-blue flowers.
***S.* 'Garden News'** (illus. p.472). Standard Group. **H** to 15cm (6in). Has bright green leaves and double, pure white flowers.
***S.* 'Ice Maiden'** (illus. p.472). Standard Group. **H** to 15cm (6in). Bears single, white flowers with purple-blue markings.
S. ionantha. Evergreen, stemless, rosette-forming perennial, often forming clumps. **H** to 10cm (4in), **S** 25cm (10in). Almost rounded, scalloped, long-stalked, fleshy, usually hairy leaves, to 8cm (3in) long, are mid-green above and often reddish-green below. Loose clusters of 2–8 tubular, 5-lobed, violet-blue flowers, to 2.5cm (1in) across, are produced on stems held above leaves and appear year-round.
***S.* 'Pip Squeek'** (illus. p.472). Micro-miniature Group. **H** to 8cm (3in). Produces oval, unscalloped, deep green leaves, 1–2cm (½–¾in) long, and bell-shaped, pale pink flowers, 1cm (½in) wide.
***S.* 'Porcelain'** (illus. p.472). Standard Group. **H** to 15cm (6in). Bears semi-double, white flowers with purple-blue edges.
***S.* 'Powder Keg'** (illus. p.472). Large Group. **H** 10–15cm (4–6in). Bears deep green leaves and semi-double, deep red flowers, with white margins to the petals.
***S.* 'Rainbow's Limelight'.** Standard Group. **H** 10–15cm (4–6in). Has mid-green leaves and single, lime-green and yellow flowers.
***S.* 'Rococo Anna'**, syn. *S.* 'Rococo Pink'. Standard Group. **H** to 15cm (6in). Bears double, iridescent pink flowers.
***S.* 'Starry Trail'** (illus. p.472). Standard Group. **H** to 15cm (6in). Has dark green leaves and narrow-petalled, semi-double to double, white flowers, sometimes flushed pale pink.
***S.* 'Zoja'** (illus. p.472). Standard Group. **H** to 15cm (6in). Produces large, single to semi-double, purple-blue flowers with a bold white line at the margin of each petal.

SALIX

Willow

SALICACEAE

Genus of deciduous trees and shrubs, grown for their habit, foliage, catkins and, in some cases, colourful winter shoots. Male catkins are more striking than female; each plant usually bears catkins of only one sex. Fully to frost hardy. Most prefer full sun. Most species grow well in any but very dry soil; *S. caprea, S. purpurea* and their variants also thrive in dry soil. Plants grown for their colourful winter shoots should be cut back hard in early spring, every 1–3 years. Propagate by semi-ripe cuttings in summer or by hardwood cuttings in winter. Fungal diseases may cause canker, particularly in *S. babylonica* and *S.* x *sepulcralis* var. *chrysocoma*. Willows may become infested with such pests as caterpillars, aphids and gall mites.
S. aegyptiaca (Musk willow). Vigorous, deciduous, bushy shrub or tree. **H** 4m (12ft), **S** 5m (15ft). Fully hardy. Grey catkins that mature to yellow are produced on bare, stout shoots in late winter or early spring, before large, narrowly oval, deep green leaves.
S. alba (White willow). **f. *argentea*** see *S.a.* var. *sericea*. **'Britzensis'** see *S.a.* var. *vitellina* 'Britzensis'. **var. *caerulea*** (Cricket-bat willow) is a very fast-growing, deciduous, conical tree with upright branches. **H** 25m (80ft), **S** 10m (30ft). Fully hardy. Has long, narrowly lance-shaped, deep bluish-green leaves and, in early spring, small, pendent, yellowish-green catkins. **'Chermesina'** see *S.a.* var. *vitellina* 'Chermesina'. ♀ **var. *sericea*** (syn. *S.a.* f. *argentea*, *S.a.* 'Sericea'; Silver willow), **H** 15m (50ft), **S** 8m (25ft), is a spreading tree that is conical when young and has bright silver-grey leaves. **'Sericea'** see *S.a.* var. *sericea*. **'Tristis'** (syn. *S. vitellina* 'Pendula') has a more weeping habit and only produces female catkins. **'Tristis'** of gardens see *S.* x *sepulcralis* var. *chrysocoma*. ♀ **var. *vitellina*** illus. p.69. ♀ **var. *vitellina* 'Britzensis'** (syn. *S.a.* 'Britzensis'), which has green leaves and bright orange-red, young shoots, is usually cut back to near ground level to provide winter colour. **var. *vitellina* 'Chermesina'** (syn. *S.a.* 'Chermesina') has carmine-red, young winter shoots.
S. apoda illus. p.356.
S. arbuscula (Mountain willow). Deciduous, spreading shrub. **H** and **S** 60cm (2ft) or more. Fully hardy. In spring, dark brown stems produce narrowly oval, toothed leaves and white-haired, sometimes red-tinged, yellow catkins. Suits a rock garden.
S. babylonica (Weeping willow). Deciduous, weeping tree with slender, pendent shoots that reach almost to the ground. **H** and **S** 12m (40ft). Fully hardy. Bears narrowly lance-shaped, long-pointed leaves. Has yellowish-green catkins in early spring. Is susceptible to canker and has been largely replaced in cultivation by *S.* x *sepulcralis* var. *chrysocoma*. ♀ **var. *pekinensis* 'Tortuosa'** (syn. *S. matsudana* 'Tortuosa') illus. p.80.
S. bockii. Deciduous, bushy shrub. **H** and **S** 2.5m (8ft). Fully hardy. Has slender, upright, grey-hairy shoots and oblong, glossy, bright green leaves, with silky-hairy undersides. Usually female in cultivation; bears green catkins in early and mid-autumn.
♀ ***S.* x *boydii*,** syn. 'Boydii', illus. p.347.
S. caprea (Goat willow, Pussy willow). Deciduous, bushy shrub or tree. **H** 10m (30ft), **S** 8m (25ft). Fully hardy. Oval leaves are dark green above, grey beneath. Catkins are borne in spring before foliage emerges: females are silky and grey, males are grey with yellow anthers. **'Kilmarnock'** (Kilmarnock willow), **H** 1.5–2m (5–6ft), **S** 2m (6ft), is dense-headed and weeping. From early to mid-spring produces grey catkins that later become yellow.
***S.* 'Chrysocoma'.** See *S.* x *sepulcralis* var. *chrysocoma*.
S. daphnoides illus. p.69.
S. elaeagnos (Hoary willow). Deciduous, upright, dense shrub. **H** 3m (10ft), **S** 5m (15ft). Fully hardy. In spring, long shoots bear slender, yellow catkins as leaves appear. These are narrowly oblong and dark green, with white undersides, and turn yellow in autumn.
S. exigua illus. p.112.
S. fargesii, syn. *S. moupinensis* of gardens. Deciduous, upright, open shrub. **H** and **S** 3m (10ft). Fully hardy. Has purplish-red winter shoots and buds. Slender, erect, green catkins are carried in spring, at same time as bold, oblong, glossy, dark green leaves.
S. fragilis (Crack willow). Deciduous tree with a broad, bushy head. **H** 15m (50ft), **S** 12–15m (40–45ft). Fully hardy. Has long, narrow, pointed, glossy, bright green leaves. Catkins, borne in early spring, are yellow on male plants, green on females.
S. gracilistyla. Deciduous, bushy shrub. **H** 3m (10ft), **S** 4m (12ft). Fully hardy. Large, silky, grey catkins with red, then bright yellow anthers are produced from early to mid-spring, and are followed by lance-shaped, silky, grey, young leaves that mature to bright, glossy green.
♀ **'Melanostachys'** (syn. *S.* 'Melanostachys'; Black willow) bears almost black catkins, with red anthers, in early spring, before bright green leaves emerge.
♀ ***S. hastata* 'Wehrhahnii'** illus. p.145.
♀ ***S. helvetica*** illus. p.335.
S. herbacea (Dwarf willow, Least willow). Deciduous, creeping shrub. **H** 2.5cm (1in), **S** 20cm (8in) or more. Fully hardy. Has small, rounded to oval leaves and, in spring, small, yellow or yellowish-green catkins are produced. Is good for a rock garden. Needs moist soil.
S. irrorata. Deciduous, upright shrub. **H** 3m (10ft), **S** 5m (15ft). Fully hardy. Purple, young shoots are white-bloomed in winter. Catkins with red, then yellow anthers appear from early to mid-spring

before narrowly oblong, glossy, bright green leaves emerge.

♀ ***S. lanata*** illus. p.147. **'Stuartii'** see *S.* 'Stuartii'.

S. lindleyana. Deciduous, creeping, mat-forming shrub with long, creeping stems. **H** 2–3cm (¾–1¼in), **S** 40cm (16in) or more. Frost hardy. Small, narrowly oval to linear, pale green leaves are densely set on short branchlets that produce brownish-pink catkins, 1cm (½in) long, in spring. Suits a rock garden or bank. Needs partial shade and damp soil. Is often confused with the very similar *S. furcata* (syn. *S. fruticulosa, S. hylematica*), which is more lax, with spreading, sometimes erect stems.

♀ ***S. magnifica.*** Deciduous, upright shrub. **H** 5m (15ft), **S** 3m (10ft). Fully hardy. Produces very long, slender, green catkins on stout, red shoots in spring, as large, magnolia-like, blue-green leaves emerge.

***S. matsudana* 'Tortuosa'.** See *S. babylonica* var. *pekinensis* 'Tortuosa'.

***S.* 'Melanostachys'.** See *S. gracilistyla* 'Melanostachys'.

S. moupinensis of gardens. See *S. fargesii.*

S. pentandra (Bay willow). Deciduous, large shrub, then small tree with broad, bushy head. **H** and **S** 10m (30ft). Fully hardy. Oval, glossy, green leaves are blue-white beneath. Catkins – males bright yellow, females grey-green – open in early summer when the tree is in full leaf.

S. purpurea (Purple osier). Deciduous, bushy, spreading shrub. **H** and **S** 5m (15ft). Fully hardy. Grey, male catkins, with yellow anthers, and insignificant, female catkins are both borne on slender, often purple shoots in spring, before narrowly oblong, deep green leaves emerge. **'Nana'** (syn. *S.p.* f. *gracilis, S.p.* 'Gracilis'), **H** and **S** 1.5m (5ft), is dense, with silver-grey leaves; is good as a hedge.

S. repens illus. p.147.

♀ ***S. reticulata*** illus. p.357.

***S. x rubens* 'Basfordiana'.** Deciduous, spreading tree. **H** 15m (50ft), **S** 10m (30ft). Fully hardy. Has bright orange-yellow, young shoots in winter and long, narrow leaves, grey-green when young, becoming glossy, bright green in summer. Yellowish-green catkins appear in early spring.

***S. sachalinensis* 'Sekka'.** See *S. udensis* 'Sekka'.

***S. x sepulcralis* var. *chrysocoma*,** syn. *S. alba* 'Tristis' of gardens, *S.* 'Chrysocoma', illus. p.69.

***S.* 'Stuartii'**, syn. *S. lanata* 'Stuartii'. Slow-growing, deciduous, spreading shrub. **H** 1m (3ft), **S** 2m (6ft). Fully hardy. Has yellow winter shoots. Stout, grey-green catkins open from orange buds in spring, as oval, woolly, grey leaves emerge.

***S. udensis* 'Sekka'**, syn. *S. sachalinensis* 'Sekka'. Deciduous, spreading shrub. **H** 5m (15ft), **S** 10m (30ft). Fully hardy. Has flattened shoots that are red in winter and lance-shaped, glossy, bright green leaves. Silver catkins are produced in early spring.

***S. vitellina* 'Pendula'.** See *S. alba* 'Tristis'.

SALPIGLOSSIS

SOLANACEAE

Genus of annuals and biennials. Usually only annuals are cultivated, either for colour in borders or as greenhouse plants. Half hardy. Grow in sun and in rich, well-drained soil. Stems need support. Dead-head regularly. Propagate by seed sown under glass in early spring, or in early autumn for winter flowering indoors. Aphids may be troublesome.

***S. sinuata* Bolero Hybrids.** Group of moderately fast-growing, branching, upright annuals. **H** 60cm (2ft), **S** 30cm (1ft). Has lance-shaped, pale green leaves. Outward-facing, widely flared, trumpet-shaped, conspicuously veined flowers, 5cm (2in) across, appear in summer and early autumn. Is available in a mixture of rich colours. **Casino Series** is available in red, blue, purple, yellow or orange flowers. **'Friendship'** has upward-facing flowers in a range of colours.

SALVIA

Sage

LABIATAE/LAMIACEAE

Genus of annuals, biennials, perennials and evergreen or semi-evergreen shrubs and subshrubs, grown for their tubular, 2-lipped, often brightly coloured flowers and aromatic foliage. Leaves of some species may be used for flavouring foods. Fully hardy to frost tender, min. 5°C (41°F). Needs sun and fertile, well-drained soil. Propagate perennials by division in spring, perennials, shrubs and subshrubs by softwood cuttings in mid-summer. Sow seed of half-hardy annuals under glass in early spring and of fully-hardy species outdoors in mid-spring.

♀ ***S. argentea*** (illus. p.250). Rosette-forming, short-lived perennial. **H** 90cm (36in), **S** 60cm (24in). Fully hardy. Has ovate to elliptic, toothed, silvery-woolly leaves. From mid- to late summer bears many-branched, terminal panicles of white flowers, sometimes pink-flushed.

S. blepharophylla. Spreading, rhizomatous perennial. **H** and **S** 45cm (18in). Frost tender. Has oval, glossy, dark green leaves and slender racemes of bright red flowers, with maroon calyces, in summer-autumn.

S. bulleyana. Rosette-forming perennial. **H** and **S** 60cm (24in). Fully hardy. Racemes of nettle-like, yellow flowers, with maroon lips, are borne in summer above a basal mass of broadly oval, coarse, prominently veined, dark green leaves.

♀ ***S. discolor*** (Andean silver-leaf sage). Semi-evergreen, compact subshrub. **H** and **S** to 1m (3ft). Half hardy. Ovate, silver leaves and stems are covered in woolly, white hairs. Has terminal racemes of purple flowers, sometimes almost black, from late summer to early autumn.

***S. elegans* 'Scarlet Pineapple'** (Pineapple sage). Clump-forming, woody-based perennial. **H** and **S** 1m (3ft). Frost hardy. Hairy stems bear heart-shaped, downy, glaucous leaves, which are pineapple scented when bruised. Bears loose panicles of large, crimson-pink flowers from winter to spring.

***S. farinacea* f. *alba*.** Moderately fast-growing, upright perennial, grown as an annual. **H** 1m (3ft), **S** 30cm (1ft). Half hardy. Has lance-shaped, mid-green leaves. Spikes of white flowers appear in summer. **'Strata'** illus. p.314. ♀ **'Victoria'** illus. p.312. Dwarf forms are also available.

S. forsskaolii. Basal clump-forming perennial. **H** and **S** 50cm (20in). Frost hardy. Ovate, toothed, hairy, grass-green leaves mature to dark green by summer. In summer produces sparse whorls of violet-blue flowers, with white and yellow markings on the lower lips.

S. fulgens illus. p.156.

S. glutinosa (illus. p.250). Clump-forming, sticky-hairy perennial. **H** and **S** 90cm (36in). Fully hardy. Branched or unbranched stems bear heart-shaped, toothed, mid-green leaves. From mid-summer to mid-autumn produces loose, terminal racemes of softly hairy, maroon-spotted, pale yellow flowers, with red-brown marks on lower lips.

S. grahamii. See *S. microphylla* var. *microphylla.*

S. greggii. Evergreen, erect subshrub. **H** to 1m (3ft), **S** to 60cm (2ft). Frost tender. Leaves are narrowly oblong and matt, deep green. Has terminal racemes of bright red-purple flowers in autumn. **'Devon Cream'** see *S.g.* 'Sungold'. **'Icing Sugar'** (illus. p.155) has deep purplish-pink flowers, with frosted pink lower lips. **'Sungold'** (syn. *S.g.* 'Devon Cream') has warm yellow flowers.

S. guaranitica. Deciduous, upright sub-shrub. **H** 2.5m (8ft), **S** 90cm (3ft). Frost hardy. Branched, dark green stems bear ovate, hairy, wrinkled, mid-green leaves. Deep blue flowers, with purple calyces, are produced in terminal and axillary spikes from late summer to autumn. **'Black and Blue'** (illus. p.250) has rich blue flowers, with dark purple-blue calyces. ♀ **'Blue Enigma'.** Clump-forming perennial. **H** and **S** 1m (3ft). Half hardy. Has long racemes of small, slightly fragrant, pale blue flowers, with green calyces, in summer–autumn.

S. haematodes. See *S. pratensis* Haematodes Group.

S. horminum. See *S. viridis.*

♀ ***S. involucrata.*** Bushy, woody-based perennial. **H** 60–75cm (2–2½ft) or more, **S** 1m (3ft). Half hardy. Has oval, mid-green leaves and, in late summer and autumn, racemes of large, rose-crimson flowers. ♀ **'Bethellii'** illus. p.221.

S. x jamensis (*S. microphylla* x *S. greggii*). Very variable, evergreen, bushy shrub. **H** 1m (3ft), **S** 60–75cm (2–2½ft). Frost hardy. Has ovate to elliptic, toothed, mid-green leaves. In summer–autumn produces terminal racemes of 2-lipped flowers, varying in colour from red to rose-pink, salmon-pink and orange to creamy-yellow. **'Hot Lips'** (illus. p.155) has white upper flower lips and vivid red lower lips but may also produce pure white or pure red flowers. **'James Compton'** bears deep crimson flowers. **'La Luna'** (illus. p.155) has creamy-yellow flowers with reddish-brown hairs on upper lips. **'Maraschino'** (illus. p.155) has cherry-red flowers. **'Pat Vlasto'** bears pink-suffused, orange flowers. ♀ **'Raspberry Royale'** produces bright raspberry-red flowers. **'Red Velvet'** (illus. p.155) has velvety, red flowers, with dark calyces. **'Sierra San Antonio'** (illus. p.155) bears peach-rose flowers, with yellow lower lips.

S. jurisicii. Rosette-forming perennial. **H** 45cm (18in), **S** 30cm (12in). Fully hardy. Stems are clothed with mid-green leaves, divided into 4–6 pairs of linear leaflets. In early summer produces racemes of inverted, violet-blue flowers.

S. lavandulifolia (Spanish sage). Prostrate, woody-based perennial. **H** and **S** 30cm (12in). Frost hardy. Has narrowly oblong, downy, aromatic, grey-green leaves. Spike-like racemes of violet to lavender-blue flowers are borne from late spring to early summer.

♀ ***S. leucantha*** (Mexican bush sage). Evergreen, erect, well-branched shrub. **H** and **S** to 60cm (2ft) or more. Frost tender. Narrowly lance-shaped, finely wrinkled leaves are deep green above, white-downy beneath. In summer-autumn produces terminal spikes of hairy, white flowers, each from a woolly, violet calyx.

***S. microphylla* var. *microphylla*,** syn. *S. grahamii, S. neurepia*, illus. p.156. **'Cerro Potosi'** (illus. p.155) is an evergreen, erect, well-branched shrub. **H** and **S** 1–1.2m (3–4ft). Half hardy, but best at 5°C (41°F). Has oval to elliptic, mid- to deep green leaves. Racemes of magenta flowers, ageing to purple and with purple-tinted calyces, appear in late summer and autumn. ♀ **'Kew Red'** (illus. p.155) has large, almost glabrous leaves and large, vivid red flowers. **'La Foux'** (illus. p.155) is similar to 'Kew Red' but is more intense in colour and has purplish-black calyces. ♀ **Newby Hall'** (illus. p.155) has pale to mid-green leaves and bright red flowers. ♀ **Pink Blush'** (illus. p.155) bears reddish-pink flowers.

S. nemorosa, syn. *S. virgata* var. *nemorosa*. Neat, clump-forming perennial. **H** 90cm (36in), **S** 45cm (18in). Fully hardy. Has narrowly oval, rough, mid-green leaves and, in summer, branching racemes densely set with violet-blue flowers. ♀ **'Amethyst'** (illus. p.250) has violet flowers, with purple calyces and bracts. **'Caradonna'** (illus. p.250), **H** 30cm (12in), has blackish-purple stems and bracts and bright purple flowers. **'East Friesland'** see *S.n.* 'Ostfriesland'. ♀ **'Lubecca'** (illus. p.250), **H** 45cm (18in), has pinkish-purple bracts and deep blue flowers. ♀ **'Ostfriesland'** (syn. *S.n.* 'East Friesland; illus. p.250), **H** 75cm (2½ft), is smaller.

S. neurepia. See *S. microphylla* var. *microphylla.*

S. officinalis (Common sage; illus. p.155). **H** and **S** 30cm (20in). Frost hardy. Lance-shaped, downy, aromatic, grey-green leaves are used as a culinary and medicinal herb. Lax racemes of purple-blue flowers are produced in summer. **'Alba'** see *S.o.* 'Albiflora'. **'Albiflora'** (syn. *S.o.* 'Alba') is an evergreen or semi-evergreen, bushy shrub. **H** 60cm (2ft), **S** 1m (3ft). Oblong, grey-green leaves are used as a culinary herb. Racemes of white flowers are produced in summer. **'Berggarten'** (illus. p.155), **H** 40cm (16in), has a spreading habit and round-tipped, silvery-grey leaves. ♀ **'Icterina'** (illus. p.155) has aromatic, grey-green leaves variegated with pale green and yellow. Occasionally bears small spikes of tubular, 2-lipped, purplish flowers. ♀ **'Purpurascens'** (illus. p.155), **H** 60cm (2ft), **S** 1m (3ft), has blue-purple flowers and purple-flushed leaves when young. **'Tricolor'** (illus. p.155) has very aromatic, cream-margined, grey-green leaves; young leaves are flushed pinkish-purple.

♀ **S. patens** (illus. p.250). Erect, tuberous perennial often grown as an annual. **H** 45–60cm (18–24in), **S** 45cm (18in). Frost hardy. Branching stems bear ovate to triangular, mid-green leaves, spear-shaped at base. From mid-summer to mid-autumn produces terminal racemes of widely 2-lipped, deep to pale blue or white flowers. ♀ **'Cambridge Blue'** has pale blue flowers.

S. pratensis. Clump-forming, woody-based perennial. **H** 90cm (3ft), **S** 30cm (1ft). Fully hardy. Has ovate, wrinkled, toothed, mid-green, basal leaves. Erect, usually branched, terminal spikes of violet, blue, pink or white flowers are borne in summer. ♀ **Haematodes Group** (syn. *S. haematodes*), **S** 45cm (18in), has wavy-edged, rough, dark green leaves and lavender-blue flowers. ♀ **'Indigo'** (illus. p.250) bears dark blue flowers. **'Pink Delight'** (illus. p.250) produces mid- to deep pink flowers. **'Swan Lake'** (illus. p.250) has pure white flowers.

S. sclarea var. turkestanica illus. p.313.

S. splendens. Slow-growing, bushy perennial or evergreen subshrub, grown as an annual. **H** to 30cm (12in), **S** 20–30cm (8–12in). Half hardy. Has oval, serrated, fresh green leaves, and dense racemes of scarlet flowers in summer and early autumn. **'Blaze of Fire'** has brilliant scarlet flowers. **Cleopatra Series** are available in mixed or single colours including salmon-pink and deep violet-purple flowers. **'Rambo'**, **H** to 60cm (24in), is very tall, vigorous, and bushy, with dark green leaves and scarlet flowers. **'Red Riches'** (syn. *S.s.* 'Ryco'), **S** 30–40cm (12–16in) has dark green leaves and scarlet flowers. **'Ryco'** see *S.s.* 'Red Riches'. **'Scarlet King'** has bright scarlet flowers in dense, terminal spikes in early summer. **Sizzler Series 'Sizzler Salmon Bicolour'** has dense racemes of salmon-tinted, white flowers, each with a rich salmon calyx. **Vista Series** (red), illus p.308.

♀ **S. x superba.** Clump-forming, erect, branched perennial. **H** 60–90cm (24–36in), **S** 45–60cm (18–24in). Fully hardy. Leaves are lance-shaped to oblong, scalloped and mid-green, slightly hairy beneath. Slender, terminal racemes of bright violet or purple flowers, to 1.5cm (½in) long, are produced from mid-summer to early autumn.

S. x sylvestris. Clump-forming, erect, branched perennial. **H** 80cm (32in), **S** 30cm (12in). Fully hardy. Leaves are lance-shaped to oblong, scalloped and mid-green, softly hairy. Dense, terminal racemes of pinkish violet flowers, to 1cm (½in) long, are produced in early to mid-summer. ♀ **'Blauhügel'** (illus. p.250), **H** 45cm (18in), has mid-blue flowers and purple bracts. ♀ **'Mainacht'** (syn. *S. x s.* May Night; illus. p.250), **H** 90cm (36in), **S** 45cm (18in), has violet-blue flowers in late spring and summer.

♀ **S. uliginosa** (Bog sage; illus. p.250). Graceful, upright, branching perennial. **H** 2m (6ft), **S** 45cm (18in). Half hardy. Has oblong to lance-shaped, saw-edged, mid-green leaves and, in autumn, long racemes with whorls of bright blue flowers. Prefers moist soil.

S. verticillata. Erect perennial. **H** 90cm (36in), **S** 45cm (45in). Fully hardy. Has ovate to elliptic, deeply cut, dark green leaves, with large terminal lobes. Produces branched racemes with whorls of lilac to violet-blue, occasionally white, flowers in summer. **'Purple Rain'** (illus. p.250) produces dark green leaves and red-purple stems and flowers.

S. virgata var. nemorosa. See *S. nemorosa*.

S. viridis, syn. *S. horminum*. Moderately fast-growing, upright, branching annual. **H** 45cm (18in), **S** 20cm (8in). Fully hardy. Has oval leaves. Tubular, lipped flowers, enclosed by purple, pink, or white bracts, are borne in spikes at tops of stems in summer and early autumn. **'Bouquet'** (syn. *S.v.* 'Monarch Bouquet') has blue, rose-pink, white, deep carmine-pink or purple bracts; also available as single colours. Bracts of **Claryssa Series** are in a wide range of brilliant colours, including white, pink, purple and blue. **'Monarch Bouquet'** see *S.v.* 'Bouquet'. **'Oxford Blue'**, **H** 30cm (12in), has violet-blue bracts.

SALVINIA

SALVINIACEAE

Genus of deciduous, perennial, floating water ferns, evergreen in tropical conditions and aquariums. Frost tender, min. 10–15°C (50–59°F). Does best in warm water, with plenty of light. Remove fading foliage, and thin plants when crowded. Propagate by dividing young plants in summer.

S. auriculata. Deciduous, spreading, perennial, floating water plant, evergreen in tropical conditions. **S** indefinite. Has rounded, pale to mid-green leaves, sometimes suffused purplish-brown, in pairs on branching stems.

S. natans. Deciduous, perennial, floating water plant. **S** indefinite. Oval, elongated, mid-green leaves are borne on branching stems. Tolerates colder conditions than other species and is often used in a cold-water aquarium.

SAMBUCUS

Elder

CAPRIFOLIACEAE

Genus of perennials, deciduous shrubs and trees, grown for their foliage, flowers and fruits. Fully hardy. Needs sun and fertile, moist soil. For best foliage effect, either cut all shoots to ground in winter or prune out old shoots and reduce length of young shoots by half. Propagate species by softwood cuttings in summer, by seed in autumn or by hardwood cuttings in winter, some forms by cuttings only.

ⓘ All parts may cause severe discomfort if ingested, although fruits are safe when cooked; contact with the leaves may irritate skin.

S. canadensis, syn. *S. nigra* subsp. *canadensis* (American elder). **'Aurea'** is a deciduous, upright shrub. **H** and **S** 4m (12ft). Has large, golden-yellow leaves, each with usually 7 oblong leaflets. In mid-summer bears large, domed heads of small, star-shaped, creamy-white flowers, then spherical, red fruits.

S. nigra (Common elder). ♀ **'Aurea'** (Golden elder) is a deciduous, bushy shrub. **H** and **S** 6m (20ft). Has stout, corky shoots and golden-yellow leaves of usually 5 oval leaflets. Flattened heads of fragrant, star-shaped, creamy-white flowers in early summer are followed by spherical, black fruits. Dark green foliage of **f. porphyrophylla 'Guincho Purple'** matures to deep blackish-purple. Bears purple-stalked flowers, pink in bud and opening to white within, pink outside. **subsp. canadensis** see *S. canadensis*.

S. racemosa (Red-berried elder). Deciduous, bushy shrub. **H** and **S** 3m (10ft). Mid-green leaves each have usually 5 oval leaflets. Star-shaped, creamy-yellow flowers, borne in dense, conical clusters in mid-spring, are succeeded by spherical, red fruits. **'Plumosa'** has leaves with finely cut leaflets. **'Plumosa Aurea'** illus. p.139.

SANCHEZIA

ACANTHACEAE

Genus of evergreen, mainly summer-flowering perennials, shrubs and scrambling climbers, grown for their flowers and foliage. Frost tender, min. 15–18°C (59–64°F). Requires full light or partial shade and fertile, well-drained soil. Water potted plants freely when in full growth, less at other times. Tip prune young plants to promote branching. Propagate by greenwood cuttings in spring or summer. Is prone to whitefly and soft scale.

S. nobilis of gardens. See *S. speciosa*.

S. speciosa, syn. *S. nobilis* of gardens. Evergreen, erect, soft-stemmed shrub. **H** 1.2–2.2m (4–7ft), **S** 90–150cm (3–5ft). Glossy leaves have yellow- or white-banded main veins. Tubular, yellow flowers are produced in axils of red bracts, in summer.

SANDERSONIA

LILIACEAE/COLCHICACEAE

Genus of one species of deciduous, tuberous climber with urn-shaped flowers in summer. Half hardy. Needs a sheltered, sunny site and well-drained soil. Support with sticks or canes. Lift tubers for winter. Propagate in spring by seed or by naturally divided tubers.

S. aurantiaca illus. p.413.

SANGUINARIA

PAPAVERACEAE

Genus of one species of spring-flowering, rhizomatous perennial. Fully hardy. Grow in sun or semi-shade and in humus-rich, moist but well-drained soil. Propagate by division of rhizomes in summer or by seed in autumn.

S. canadensis illus. p.348. ♀ **f. multiplex 'Plena'** (syn. *S.c.* 'Flore Pleno') is a clump-forming, rhizomatous perennial with fleshy, underground stems that exude red sap when cut. **H** 15cm (6in), **S** 30–45cm (12–18in). Has short-lived, rounded, fully double, white flowers in spring, followed by large, rounded to heart-shaped, scalloped, grey-green leaves with glaucous undersides.

SANGUISORBA

Burnet

ROSACEAE

Genus of perennials, grown for their bottlebrush-like flower spikes. Fully hardy. Requires sun and moist soil. Propagate by division in spring or by seed in autumn.

S. canadensis illus. p.437.

S. obtusa. Clump-forming perennial. **H** 1–1.2m (3–4ft), **S** 60cm (2ft). Arching stems bear spikes of rose-crimson flowers in mid-summer. Pairs of oval leaflets are pale green above, blue-green beneath.

S. officinalis (Great burnet). **'Rubra'** is a clump-forming perennial. **H** 1.2m (4ft), **S** 60cm (2ft). Produces small spikes of red-brown flowers in late summer. Mid-green leaves are divided into oval leaflets.

S. tenuifolia 'Alba' illus. p.216.

SANSEVIERIA

AGAVACEAE/DRACAENACEAE

Genus of evergreen, rhizomatous perennials, grown for their rosettes of stiff, fleshy leaves. Frost tender, min. 10–15°C (50–59°F). Tolerates sun and shade and is easy to grow in most soil conditions if not overwatered. Propagate by leaf cuttings or division in summer.

S. cylindrica. Evergreen, stemless, rhizomatous perennial. **H** 45cm–1.2m (1½–4ft), **S** 10cm (4in). Has a rosette of 3–4 cylindrical, stiff, fleshy, erect leaves, to 1.2m (4ft) long, in dark green with paler horizontal bands. Racemes of small, tubular, 6-lobed, pink or white flowers are occasionally produced.

S. trifasciata (Mother-in-law's tongue). Evergreen, stemless, rhizomatous perennial. **H** 45cm–1.2m (1½–4ft), **S** 10cm (4in). Has a rosette of about 5 lance-shaped, pointed, stiff, fleshy, erect leaves, to 1.2m (4ft) long, banded horizontally with pale green and yellow. Occasionally carries racemes of tubular, 6-lobed, green flowers. ♀ **'Golden Hahnii'** illus. p.476. ♀ **'Hahnii'** illus. p.475. ♀ **'Laurentii'** illus. p.476.

SANTOLINA

COMPOSITAE/ASTERACEAE

Genus of evergreen, summer-flowering shrubs, grown for their aromatic foliage and their button-like flower heads. Frost hardy. Needs sun and not too rich, well-drained soil. Cut off old flower heads and reduce long shoots in autumn. Cut straggly plants back hard each spring. Propagate by semi-ripe cuttings in summer.

S. chamaecyparissus, syn. *S. incana* (Cotton lavender, Lavender cotton). Evergreen, rounded, dense shrub. **H** 75cm (2½ft), **S** 1m (3ft). Shoots are covered with woolly, white growth, and narrowly oblong, finely toothed leaves are also white. Bright yellow flower heads are borne in mid- and late summer.

S. incana. See *S. chamaecyparissus*.

S. neapolitana. See *S. pinnata* subsp. *neapolitana*.

S. pinnata. Evergreen shrub, mainly grown as ♀ **subsp. neapolitana** (syn. *S. neapolitana*), which is of rounded and bushy habit. **H** 75cm (2½ft), **S** 1m (3ft).

Slender flower stems bear a head of lemon-yellow flowers in mid-summer, among feathery, deeply cut, grey-green foliage. **subsp. *neapolitana* 'Sulphurea'** illus. p.159.
S. rosmarinifolia, syn. *S. virens* (Holy flax). Evergreen, bushy, dense shrub. **H** 60cm (2ft), **S** 1m (3ft). Has finely cut, bright green leaves. Each slender stem produces a head of bright yellow flowers in mid-summer. 🏆 **'Primrose Gem'** has pale yellow flower heads.
S. virens. See *S. rosmarinifolia*.

SANVITALIA

COMPOSITAE/ASTERACEAE

Genus of perennials and annuals. Fully hardy. Needs sun and fertile, well-drained soil. Propagate by seed sown outdoors in spring or early autumn.
S. procumbens illus. p.320. **'Mandarin Orange'** illus. p.324.

SAPIUM

EUPHORBIACEAE

Genus of evergreen trees, grown for their ornamental appearance. Has poisonous, milky sap. Frost tender, min. 5°C (41°F). Prefers fertile, well-drained soil and full light. Water containerized plants freely when in full growth, less at other times. Pruning is tolerated if necessary. Propagate by seed in spring or by semi-ripe cuttings in summer.
S. sebiferum (Chinese tallow tree). Fast-growing, evergreen, erect to spreading tree. **H** to 8m (25ft), **S** 4m (12ft) or more. Rhombic to oval, mid-green leaves turn red with age. Clusters of tiny, greenish-yellow flowers develop into rounded, black fruits covered by a layer of white wax.

SAPONARIA

Soapwort

CARYOPHYLLACEAE

Genus of summer-flowering annuals and perennials, grown for their flowers. Is good for rock gardens, screes and banks. Fully hardy. Needs sun and well-drained soil. Propagate by seed in spring or autumn or by softwood cuttings in early summer.
🏆 ***S.* 'Bressingham'**, syn. *S.* 'Bressingham Hybrid'. Loose, mat-forming perennial. **H** 8cm (3in), **S** 10cm (4in). Has small, narrowly oval leaves. Flattish, deep vibrant pink flowers are borne in clustered heads in summer. Is good for a trough.
***S.* 'Bressingham Hybrid'.** See *S.* 'Bressingham'.
S. caespitosa illus. p.364.
🏆 ***S. ocymoides*** illus. p.364.
***S. officinalis* 'Rubra Plena'** (Double soapwort). Upright perennial. **H** to 1m (3ft), **S** 30cm (1ft). Has oval, rough, mid-green leaves on erect stems. Clusters of ragged, double, red flowers are produced on upper part of flower stems in summer.
🏆 ***S.* x *olivana*** illus. p.362.

SARCOCAPNOS

PAPAVERACEAE/FUMARIACEAE

Genus of spring-flowering perennials. Is useful for rock gardens. Frost hardy. Prefers sun and well-drained, alkaline soil. Propagate by seed in spring.
S. enneaphylla. Loose, upright perennial. **H** and **S** 15cm (6in). Slender, much-branched stems bear small, divided, glaucous green leaves with oval to rounded segments. In spring, small, spurred, yellowish-white flowers, tipped with purple, are produced in short racemes. Protect from winter wet.

SARCOCOCCA

Christmas box, Sweet box

BUXACEAE

Genus of evergreen shrubs, grown for their foliage, fragrant, winter flowers and spherical fruits. Flowers are tiny – the only conspicuous part being the anthers. Is useful for cutting in winter. Fully to frost hardy. Grow in sun or shade and fertile, not too dry soil. Propagate by semi-ripe cuttings in summer or by seed in autumn.
🏆 ***S. confusa*** (illus. p.142). Evergreen, bushy, dense shrub. **H** and **S** 1m (3ft). Fully hardy. Leaves are small, oval, taper-pointed, glossy and dark green. Has tiny, white flowers in winter, then black fruits.
🏆 ***S. hookeriana.*** Evergreen, upright, dense, suckering shrub. **H** 1.5m (5ft), **S** 2m (6ft). Fully hardy. Forms clumps of narrowly oblong, pointed, dark green leaves and has tiny, white flowers in the leaf axils during winter. Fruits are black.
🏆 **var. *digyna*** illus. p.164. **var. *digyna* 'Purple Stem'** has young shoots flushed dark purple-pink, and pink-tinged flowers.
var. *humilis* see *S. humilis*.
S. humilis, syn. *S. hookeriana* var. *humilis*, illus. p.164.
S. ruscifolia. Evergreen, upright, arching shrub. **H** and **S** 1m (3ft). Frost hardy. Has oval, glossy, dark green leaves and, in winter, creamy-white flowers, then red fruits. 🏆 **var. *chinensis*** has narrower leaves.

SARMIENTA

GESNERIACEAE

Genus of one species of evergreen, woody-stemmed, scrambling or trailing perennial. Suits hanging baskets. Half hardy. Likes semi-shade and humus-rich soil that does not dry out. Propagate by seed in spring or by stem cuttings in summer or autumn.
🏆 ***S. repens***, syn. *S. scandens*. Evergreen, slender-stemmed, scrambling perennial. **H** and **S** 60cm (2ft) or more. Tips of oval leaves each have 3–5 teeth. In summer produces small, tubular, coral-pink flowers, each narrowed at the base and towards the mouth, which has 5 deeper pink lobes.
S. scandens. See *S. repens*.

SARRACENIA

Pitcher plant

SARRACENIACEAE

Genus of insectivorous perennials, some of which are evergreen, with pitchers formed from modified leaves with hooded tops. Frost tender, min. 5°C (41°F). Grow in sun or partial shade and in peat and moss. Keep very wet, except in winter, when drier conditions are needed. Propagate by seed in spring.
🏆 ***S. flava*** illus. p.445.
S. purpurea illus. p.439.

SASA

GRAMINEAE/POACEAE

See also GRASSES, BAMBOOS, RUSHES and SEDGES.
S. albomarginata. See *S. veitchii*.
S. palmata. Evergreen, spreading bamboo. **H** 2m (6ft), **S** indefinite. Frost hardy. A fine foliage plant, it produces very broad, rich green leaves, to 40cm (16in) long. Hollow, purple-streaked stems have one branch at each node. Flower spikes are unimportant.
S. veitchii, syn. *S. albomarginata*, illus. p.284.

SASSAFRAS

LAURACEAE

Genus of deciduous trees, with inconspicuous flowers, grown for their aromatic foliage. Fully hardy. Needs sun or light shade and deep, fertile, well-drained, preferably acid soil. Propagate by seed or suckers in autumn or by root cuttings in winter.
S. albidum illus. p.64.

SATUREJA

LABIATAE/LAMIACEAE

Genus of summer-flowering annuals, semi-evergreen perennials and subshrubs, grown for their highly aromatic leaves and attractive flowers. Is useful for rock gardens and dry banks. Fully hardy. Needs sun and well-drained soil. Propagate by seed in winter or spring or by softwood cuttings in summer.
S. montana (Winter savory). Semi-evergreen, upright perennial or subshrub. **H** 30cm (12in), **S** 20cm (8in) or more. Leaves are linear to oval, aromatic and green or greyish-green. Produces loose whorls of tubular, 2-lipped, lavender flowers in summer. **'Prostrate White'**, **H** 7–15cm (3–6in), has a prostrate habit and bears white flowers.

SAUROMATUM

ARACEAE

Genus of spring-flowering, tuberous perennials with tubular spathes that expand into waved, twisted blades. Tubers will flower without soil or moisture, and before leaves appear. Frost tender, min. 5–7°C (41–5°F). Needs a sheltered, semi-shaded position and humus-rich, well-drained soil. Water well in summer. Dry off or lift when dormant in winter. Propagate by offsets in spring.
S. guttatum. See *S. venosum*.
S. venosum, syn. *S. guttatum*, illus. p.403.

SAURURUS

SAURURACEAE

Genus of deciduous, perennial, bog and marginal water plants, grown for their foliage. Fully hardy. Prefers full sun, but tolerates some shade. Remove faded leaves and divide plants as required to maintain vigour. Propagate by division in spring.
S. cernuus illus. p.435.

SAXEGOTHAEA

PODOCARPACEAE

See also CONIFERS.
S. conspicua (Prince Albert's yew). Conifer that is conical in mild areas, more bushy in cold districts. **H** 5–15m (15–50ft), **S** 4–5m (12–15ft). Fully hardy. Needle-like, flattened, dark green leaves are produced in whorls at ends of shoots. Bears globose, fleshy, glaucous green cones.

SAXIFRAGA

Saxifrage

SAXIFRAGACEAE

Genus of often rosetted perennials, most of which are evergreen or semi-evergreen, grown for their flowers and attractive foliage. Is excellent in rock gardens, raised beds and alpine houses. Fully to half hardy. Propagate by seed in autumn or by rooted offsets in winter. For cultivation, saxifrages may be grouped as follows:
1 – Needs moist soil and protection from midday sun.
2 – Needs semi-shaded, well-drained soil. Is good among rocks and screes.
3 – Thrives in well-drained rock pockets, troughs, alpine-house pans etc, shaded from midday sun. Must never be dry at roots. Most form tight cushions and flower in early spring, flower stems being barely visible above leaves.
4 – Needs full sun and well-drained, alkaline soil. Suits rock pockets. Most have hard leaves encrusted in lime.
S. aizoides. Evergreen perennial forming a loose mat. **H** 15cm (6in), **S** 30cm (12in) or more. Fully hardy. Has small, narrowly oval, fleshy, shiny, green leaves and, in spring-summer, terminal racemes of star-shaped, bright yellow or orange flowers, often spotted red, on 8cm (3in) stems. Cultivation group 1.
S. aizoon. See *S. paniculata*.
***S.* x *anglica* 'Cranbourne'**, syn. *S.* 'Cranbourne'. Evergreen, cushion-forming perennial. **H** and **S** 12cm (5in). Fully hardy. In early spring produces solitary, cup-shaped, bright purplish-lilac flowers on short stems just above tight rosettes of linear, green leaves. Flower stems are longer if plant is grown in an alpine house. Cultivation group 3.
🏆 ***S.* x *apiculata* 'Gregor Mendel'**, syn. *S.* 'Gregor Mendel', illus. p.357; cultivation group 2.
***S.* 'Arco'.** See. *S.* x *arco-valleyi* 'Arco'.
***S.* x *arco-valleyi* 'Arco'**, syn. *S.* 'Arco'. Evergreen perennial forming a tight cushion. **H** and **S** 10cm (4in). Fully hardy. In early spring produces upturned, cup-shaped to flattish, pale lilac flowers almost resting on tight rosettes of oblong to linear leaves. Cultivation group 3.
***S.* 'Bob Hawkins'.** Evergreen perennial with a loose rosette of leaves. **H** 2.5–5cm (1–2in), **S** 15cm (6in). Fully hardy. Carries small, upturned, rounded, greenish-white flowers in summer on 5cm (2in) stems. Oval, green leaves are white-splashed. Cultivation group 1.
***S.* x *boydii* 'Hindhead Seedling'** illus. p.356; cultivation group 2.
***S.* 'Brookside'.** See *S. burseriana* 'Brookside'.

S. brunoniana. See *S. brunonis*.
S. brunonis, syn. *S. brunoniana*. Semi-evergreen, rosetted perennial. **H** 10cm (4in), **S** 20cm (8in). Frost hardy. Small, soft green rosettes of lance-shaped, rigid leaves produce masses of long, thread-like, red runners. Many of the rosettes die down to large terminal buds in winter. Short racemes of 5-petalled, spreading, pale yellow flowers are produced in late spring and summer on 5–8cm (2–3in) stems. Is difficult to grow; cultivation group 1.
S. burseriana illus. p.348. **'Brookside'** (syn. *S.* 'Brookside') is a slow-growing, evergreen perennial forming a hard cushion. **H** 2.5–5cm (1–2in), **S** to 10cm (4in). Fully hardy. Has broadly linear, spiky, grey-green leaves. In early spring bears upturned, rounded, shallowly cup-shaped, bright yellow flowers on short, red stems. Flowers of **'Crenata'** (syn. *S.* 'Crenata') have fringed, white petals and red sepals. ♀ **'Gloria'** (syn. *S.* 'Gloria') has dark reddish-brown stems, each bearing 1 or 2 flowers, with red sepals and white petals, in late spring. Cultivation group 3.
♀ **S. callosa,** syn. *S. linguata*, illus. p.337.
S. cochlearis. Evergreen, rosetted perennial. **H** 20cm (8in), **S** 25cm (10in). Fully hardy. Has spoon-shaped, green leaves with white-encrusted edges. Produces loose panicles of rounded, white flowers, often with red-spotted petals, in early summer. ♀ **'Minor'**, **H** and **S** 12cm (5in), has smaller leaf rosettes and loose panicles of red-spotted, white flowers on red stems. Is ideal for a trough. Cultivation group 4.
S. cortusifolia var. fortunei. See *S. fortunei*.
S. cotyledon. Evergreen perennial. **H** and **S** to 30cm (12in). Fully hardy. Has large, pale green rosettes of leaves, which die after flowering. In late spring and early summer produces arching, conical panicles of cup-shaped, white flowers sometimes strongly marked red internally. Cultivation group 2.
S. 'Cranbourne'. See *S.* x *anglica* 'Cranbourne'.
S. 'Crenata'. See *S. burseriana* 'Crenata'.
S. cuneifolia illus. p.337; cultivation group 1.
S. x elisabethae, syn. *S.* 'Elisabethae', illus. p.357; cultivation group 2.
S. exarata subsp. moschata, syn. *S. moschata*. Evergreen perennial forming a loose to tight hummock. **H** and **S** 10cm (4in). Fully hardy. Rosettes comprise small, lance-shaped, sometimes 3-toothed, green leaves. Bears 2–5 star-shaped, creamy-white or dull yellow flowers on slender stems in summer. **'Cloth of Gold'** illus. p.377. Cultivation group 1.
♀ **S. federici-augustii subsp. grisebachii 'Wisley Variety'**, syn. *S. grisebachii* 'Wisley Variety', illus. p.353; cultivation group 4.
♀ **S. ferdinandi-coburgi.** Evergreen, cushion-forming perennial. **H** and **S** 15cm (6in). Fully hardy. Forms rosettes of linear, spiny, glaucous green leaves and, in early spring, bears racemes of open cup-shaped, rich yellow flowers on stems 3–10cm (1–4in) long. Cultivation group 3.
♀ **S. fortunei**, syn. *S. cortusifolia* var. *fortunei*. Semi-evergreen or herbaceous, clump-forming perennial. **H** and **S** 30cm (12in). Frost hardy. Has rounded, 5- or 7-lobed, fleshy, green or brownish-green leaves, red beneath. In autumn produces panicles of tiny, moth-like, white flowers, with 4 equal-sized petals and one elongated petal, on upright stems. Propagate by division in spring. **'Rubrifolia'** has dark red flower stems and dark reddish-green leaves, beetroot-red beneath. Cultivation group 1.

S. x geum. Evergreen, mat-forming perennial. **H** 15–20cm (6–8in), **S** 30cm (12in). Fully hardy. Has shallow-rooted rosettes of spoon-shaped, hairy leaves. In summer, star-shaped, pink-spotted, white flowers, deep pink in bud, are borne on loose panicles on slender stems. Cultivation group 1.
S. 'Gloria'. See *S. burseriana* 'Gloria'.
S. granulata (Fair maids of France, Meadow saxifrage) illus. p.332. **'Plena'** is a clump-forming perennial. **H** 23–38cm (9–15in), **S** to 15cm (6in) or more. Fully hardy. Loses its kidney-shaped, glossy, pale to mid-green leaves soon after flowering. Has a loose panicle of large, rounded, double, white flowers in late spring or early summer. Bulbils or resting buds form at base of foliage. Cultivation group 1.
S. 'Gregor Mendel'. See *S.* x *apiculata* 'Gregor Mendel'.
S. grisebachii 'Wisley Variety'. See *S. federici-augustii* subsp. *grisebachii* 'Wisley Variety'.
S. hirsuta. Evergreen, mound-forming perennial. **H** 15–20cm (6–8in), **S** 20cm (8in). Fully hardy. Has rosettes of round, hairy leaves. Bears loose panicles of tiny, star-shaped, white flowers, often yellow-spotted at the base of petals, in late spring and early summer. Cultivation group 1.
S. 'Irvingii'. See *S.* x *irvingii* 'Walter Irving'.
♀ **S. x irvingii 'Jenkinsiae'**, syn. *S.* 'Jenkinsiae', illus. p.350; cultivation group 2. **'Walter Irving'** (syn. *S.* 'Irvingii') is a very slow-growing, evergreen, hard-domed perennial. **H** 2cm (¾in), **S** 8cm (3in). Fully hardy. Bears minute leaves in rosettes. Stemless, cup-shaped, lilac-pink flowers open in early spring. Cultivation group 3.
S. 'Jenkinsiae'. See *S.* x *irvingii* 'Jenkinsiae'.
S. lingulata. See *S. callosa*.
S. longifolia. Rosetted perennial. **H** 60cm (24in), **S** 20–25cm (8–10in). Fully hardy. Has long, narrow, lime-encrusted leaves forming attractive rosettes that, after 3–4 years, develop long, arching, conical to cylindrical panicles bearing numerous rounded, 5-petalled, white flowers in late spring and summer. Rosettes die after flowering, and no daughter rosettes are formed, so propagate by seed in spring or autumn. In cultivation, hybridizes readily with other related species. Cultivation group 4.
S. moschata. See *S. exarata* subsp. *moschata*.
S. oppositifolia illus. p.353. **'Ruth Draper'** is an evergreen, loose mat-forming perennial. **H** 2.5–5cm (1–2in), **S** 15cm (6in). Fully hardy. Has small, opposite, oblong to oval, white-flecked, dark green leaves closely set along prostrate stems. Large, cup-shaped, deep purple-pink flowers appear in early spring just above foliage. Prefers peaty soil. Cultivation group 1.
S. paniculata, syn. *S. aizoon*. Evergreen, tightly rosetted perennial. **H** 15–30cm (6–12in), **S** 20cm (8in). Fully hardy. In summer produces loose panicles of rounded, usually white flowers, with or without purplish-red spots, on upright stems above rosettes of oblong to oval, lime-encrusted leaves. Is very variable in size. Pale yellow or pale pink forms also occur. Cultivation group 4.
S. x primulaize, syn. *S.* 'Primulaize'. Evergreen, loosely rosetted perennial. **H** and **S** 15cm (6in). Fully hardy. In summer, branched flower stems, 5–8cm (2–3in) long, produce star-shaped, salmon-pink flowers. Leaves are tiny, narrowly oval, slightly indented and fleshy. Cultivation group 1.
S. sancta illus. p.358; cultivation group 2.
S. sarmentosa. See *S. stolonifera*.
S. scardica illus. p.348; cultivation group 3.
S. sempervivum illus. p.353; cultivation group 3.
♀ **S. 'Southside Seedling'** illus. p.338; cultivation group 4.
S. stolonifera, syn. *S. sarmentosa* (Mother of thousands). Evergreen, prostrate perennial with runners. **H** 15cm (6in) or more, **S** 30cm (12in) or more. Frost hardy. Has large, rounded, shallowly lobed, hairy, silver-veined, olive-green leaves that are reddish-purple beneath. Loose panicles of tiny, moth-like, white flowers, each with 4 equal-sized petals and one elongated petal, appear in summer on slender, upright stems. Makes good ground cover. ♀ **'Tricolor'** (syn. *S.* 'Tricolor'; Strawberry geranium) has green-and-red leaves with silver marks and is half hardy. Cultivation group 1.
S. stribrnyi illus. p.354; cultivation group 3.
S. 'Tricolor'. See *S. stolonifera* 'Tricolor'.
♀ **S. 'Tumbling Waters'** illus. p.333; cultivation group 4.
♀ **S. x urbium** (London pride). Evergreen, rosetted, spreading perennial. **H** 30cm (12in), **S** indefinite. Fully hardy. Has spoon-shaped, toothed, leathery, green leaves. Flower stems bear tiny, star-shaped, at times pink-flushed, white flowers, with red spots, in summer. Is useful as ground cover. Cultivation group 1.
S. 'Valerie Finnis'. Evergreen, hard cushion-forming perennial. **H** and **S** 10cm (4in). Fully hardy. Short, red stems carry upturned, cup-shaped, sulphur-yellow flowers above tight rosettes of oval, green leaves in spring. Cultivation group 3.

SCABIOSA

Scabious

DIPSACACEAE

Genus of annuals and perennials, some of which are evergreen, with flower heads that are good for cutting. Fully to frost hardy. Prefers sun and fertile, well-drained, alkaline soil. Propagate annuals by seed in spring and perennials by cuttings of young, basal growths in summer, by seed in autumn or by division in early spring.

S. arvensis. See *Knautia arvensis*.
S. atropurpurea (Sweet scabious). Moderately fast-growing, upright, bushy annual. **H** to 1m (3ft), **S** 20–30cm (8–12in). Fully hardy. Has lance-shaped, lobed, mid-green leaves. Domed heads of scented, pincushion-like, deep crimson flower heads, 5cm (2in) wide, are produced on wiry stems in summer and early autumn. Tall forms, **H** 1m (3ft), and dwarf, **H** 45cm (18in), are available with flower heads in shades of blue, purple, red, pink or white.
♀ **S. caucasica. 'Clive Greaves'** illus. p.270. **'Floral Queen'** is a clump-forming perennial. **H** and **S** 60cm (24in). Fully hardy. Large, frilled, violet-blue flower heads, with pincushion-like centres, are produced throughout summer. Light green leaves are lance-shaped at base of plant and segmented on stems. ♀ **'Miss Willmott'** has creamy-white flowers.
S. columbaria var. ochroleuca. See *S. ochroleuca*.
S. graminifolia. Evergreen, clump-forming perennial, often with a woody base. **H** and **S** 15–25cm (6–10 in). Frost hardy. Has tufts of narrow, grass-like, pointed, silver-haired leaves. In summer produces stiff stems with spherical, bluish-violet to lilac flower heads like pincushions. Resents disturbance. Suits a rock garden.
S. lucida illus. p.341.
S. ochroleuca, syn. *S. columbaria* var. *ochroleuca*. Clump-forming perennial. **H** and **S** 1m (3ft). Fully hardy. In late summer, branching stems carry many heads of frilled, sulphur-yellow flower heads with pincushion-like centres. Has narrowly oval, toothed, grey-green leaves.
S. rumelica. See *Knautia macedonica*.

SCADOXUS

AMARYLLIDACEAE

Genus of bulbs with dense, mainly spherical, umbels of red flowers. Frost tender, min. 10–15°C (50–59°F). Requires a position in partial shade and humus-rich, well-drained soil. Reduce watering in winter, when not in active growth. Propagate by seed or offsets in spring.
S. multiflorus, syn. *Haemanthus multiflorus*. Summer-flowering bulb. **H** to 70cm (28in), **S** 30–45cm (12–18in). Has broadly lance-shaped, semi-erect, basal leaves. Produces a spherical umbel, 10–15cm (4–6in) wide, of up to 200 narrow-petalled flowers. ♀ **subsp. katherinae** (syn. *Haemanthus katherinae*) illus. p.386.
S. puniceus, syn. *Haemanthus magnificus*, *H. natalensis*, *H. puniceus* (Royal paintbrush). Spring- and summer-flowering bulb. **H** 30–40cm (12–16in), **S** 30–45cm (12–18in). Has elliptic, semi-erect leaves in a basal cluster. Leaf bases are joined, forming a false stem. Flower stem bears up to 100 tubular, orange-red flowers in a conical umbel surrounded by a whorl of red bracts.

SCAEVOLA

GOODENIACEAE

Genus of short-lived, mainly evergreen perennials but also scrambling climbers, shrubs and small trees, grown for summer display, usually in containers. Half hardy to

frost tender, min. -2°C (28°F). Grow in moist but well-drained, fertile compost in sun or partial shade. Propagate by softwood cuttings in late spring or summer.
***S. aemula* 'Little Wonder'.** Evergreen, trailing, bushy perennial, grown as an annual. **H** 30cm (12in), **S** 40cm (16in). Half hardy. Has spoon-shaped, rich green leaves. In summer produces 5-lobed, blue flowers each with a yellow ring round the white throat.

SCHEFFLERA

SYN. BRASSAIA, HEPTAPLEURUM

ARALIACEAE

Genus of evergreen shrubs and trees, grown mainly for their handsome foliage. Half hardy to frost tender, min. 3–16°C (37–61°F). Grows in any fertile, well-drained but moisture-retentive soil and in full light or partial shade. Water potted specimens freely when in full growth, moderately at other times. Pruning is tolerated if needed. Propagate by air-layering in spring, by semi-ripe cuttings in summer or by seed as soon as ripe, in late summer.
🏆 ***S. actinophylla*** illus. p.452.
🏆 ***S. arboricola.*** Evergreen, erect, well-branched shrub or tree. **H** 2–5m (6–15ft), **S** 1–3m (3–10ft). Frost tender, min. 15°C (59°F). Leaves each have 7–16 oval, stalked, glossy, deep green leaflets. Mature plants carry small, spherical heads of tiny, green flowers in spring–summer.
S. digitata. Evergreen, rounded to ovoid shrub or bushy tree. **H** and **S** 3–8m (10–25ft). Frost tender, min. 5°C (41°F). Leaves are hand-shaped, with 5–10 oval, glossy, rich green leaflets. Has tiny, greenish flowers in large, terminal panicles in spring and tiny, globular, dark violet fruits in autumn.
🏆 ***S. elegantissima***, syn. *Aralia elegantissima, Dizygotheca elegantissima*, illus. p.457.

SCHIMA

THEACEAE

Genus of one species of very variable, evergreen tree or shrub, grown for its foliage and flowers. Is related to *Camellia*. Frost tender, min. 3–5°C (37–41°F). Prefers humus-rich, well-drained, neutral to acid soil and a sunny or partially shaded position. Water potted plants freely in full growth, moderately at other times. Pruning is tolerated if necessary. Propagate by seed as soon as ripe or by semi-ripe cuttings in summer.
S. wallichii. Robust, evergreen, ovoid tree or shrub. **H** 25–30m (80–100ft), **S** 12m (40ft) or more. Elliptic to oblong, red-veined, dark green leaves are 10–18cm (4–7in) long, red-flushed beneath. In late summer has solitary fragrant, cup-shaped, white flowers, 4cm (1½in) wide, red-flushed in bud.

SCHINUS

ANACARDIACEAE

Genus of evergreen shrubs and trees, grown mainly for their foliage and for shade. Frost tender, min. 5°C (41°F). Grows in any freely draining soil and in full light. Water potted specimens moderately, hardly at all in winter. Propagate by seed in spring or by semi-ripe cuttings in summer.
S. molle (Californian pepper-tree, Peruvian mastic tree, Peruvian pepper-tree). Fast-growing, evergreen, weeping tree. **H** and **S** to 8m (25ft). Fern-like leaves are divided into many narrowly lance-shaped, glossy, rich green leaflets. Has open clusters of tiny, yellow flowers from late winter to summer, followed by pea-sized, pink-red fruits.
S. terebinthifolius. Evergreen shrub or tree, usually of bushy, spreading habit. **H** 3m (10ft) or more, **S** 2–3m (6–10ft) or more. Leaves have 3–13 oval, mid- to deep green leaflets. Tiny, white flowers borne in clusters in summer-autumn, are followed by pea-sized, red fruits, but only if plants of both sexes are grown close together.

SCHISANDRA

SCHISANDRACEAE

Genus of deciduous, woody-stemmed, twining climbers. Male and female flowers are borne on separate plants, so grow plants of both sexes if fruits are required. Is useful for growing against shady walls and training up pillars and fences. Frost hardy. Grow in sun or partial shade and rich, well-drained soil. Propagate by greenwood or semi-ripe cuttings in summer.
S. grandiflora* var. *rubriflora of gardens. See *S. rubriflora.*
S. henryi. Deciduous, woody-stemmed, twining climber, with stems that are angled and winged when young. **H** 3–4m (10–12ft). Glossy, green leaves are oval or heart-shaped. Small, cup-shaped, white flowers appear in spring. Pendent spikes, 5–7cm (2–3in) long, of spherical, fleshy, red fruits are borne in late summer on female plants.
S. rubriflora, syn. *S. grandiflora* var. *rubriflora* of gardens, illus. p.202.

SCHIZANTHUS

Butterfly flower, Poor man's orchid

SOLANACEAE

Genus of annuals, grown for their showy flowers. Makes excellent pot plants. Half hardy to frost tender, min. 5°C (41°F). Grow in a sunny, sheltered position and in fertile, well-drained soil. Pinch out growing tips of young plants to ensure a bushy habit. Propagate by seed sown under glass in early spring for summer-autumn flowers and in late summer for plants to flower in pots in late winter or spring. Is prone to damage by aphids.
***S.* 'Dwarf Bouquet'** illus. p.304.
S. pinnatus. Moderately fast-growing, upright, bushy annual. **H** 30cm–1.2m (1–4ft), **S** 30cm (1ft). Has feathery, light green leaves. In summer–autumn bears rounded, lobed, multicoloured flowers in shades of pink, purple, white or yellow.
***S.* 'Star Parade'.** Compact annual with a distinctive pyramidal habit. **H** 20–25cm (8–10in), **S** 23–30cm (9–12in). Frost tender, min. 5°C (41°F). Has almost fern-like, light green leaves. From spring to autumn, bears tubular, then flared, 2-lipped, white, yellow, pink, purple, or red flowers.

Schizocentron elegans. See *Heterocentron elegans.*

SCHIZOPETALON

CRUCIFERAE/BRASSICACEAE

Genus of annuals. Half hardy. Grow in sun and in well-drained, fertile soil. Propagate by seed sown under glass in spring.
S. walkeri. Moderately fast-growing, upright, slightly branching annual. **H** 45cm (18in), **S** 20cm (8in). Has deeply divided, mid-green leaves and, in summer, almond-scented, white flowers with deeply cut and fringed petals.

SCHIZOPHRAGMA

HYDRANGEACEAE

Genus of deciduous, woody-stemmed, root climbers, useful for training up large trees. Frost hardy. Flowers best in sun, but will grow against a north-facing wall. Needs well-drained soil. Tie young plants to supports. Propagate by seed in spring or by greenwood or semi-ripe cuttings in summer.
S. hydrangeoides illus p.197. **'Roseum'** is a deciduous, woody-stemmed, root climber. **H** to 12m (40ft). Broadly oval leaves are 10–15cm (4–6in) long. Small, white or creamy-white flowers, in flat heads 20–25cm (8–10in) across, are produced on pendent side-branches in summer; these are surrounded by marginal, sterile flowers, which each have bract-like, pink-flushed, pale yellow sepals.
🏆 ***S. integrifolium*** illus. p.197.
S. viburnoides. See *Pileostegia viburnoides.*

SCHIZOSTYLIS

Kaffir lily

IRIDACEAE

Genus of rhizomatous perennials with flowers that are excellent for cutting. Frost hardy. Requires sun and fertile, moist soil. Divide in spring every few years to avoid congestion.
🏆 ***Schizostylis coccinea*** *syn. Hesperantha coccinea.* 🏆 **'Major'**, syn. *S.c.* 'Grandiflora', illus. p.279. **'Mrs Hegarty'** is a vigorous, clump-forming, rhizomatous perennial. **H** 60cm (24in), **S** 23–30cm (9–12in). In mid-autumn produces spikes of shallowly cup-shaped, pale pink flowers above tufts of grass-like, mid-green leaves. 🏆 **'Sunrise'** illus. p.278. **'Viscountess Byng'** has pink flowers that last until late autumn.

SCHLUMBERGERA

CACTACEAE

Genus of bushy, perennial cacti with erect, then pendent stems and flattened, oblong stem segments with indented notches at margins – like teeth in some species. Stem tips produce flowers with prominent stigmas and stamens and with petals of different lengths set in 2 rows. In the wild, frequently grows over mossy rocks, rooting at ends of stem segments. Frost tender, min. 10°C (50°F). Requires a partially shaded position and rich, well-drained soil. Propagate by stem cuttings in spring or early summer.
***S.* 'Bristol Beauty'** illus. p.488.
🏆 ***S. x buckleyi*** (Christmas cactus). Erect, then pendent, perennial cactus. **H** 15cm (6in), **S** 1m (3ft). Has glossy, green stem segments and produces red-violet flowers in mid-winter.
***S.* 'Gold Charm'** illus. p.486.
S. truncata, syn. *Zygocactus truncatus* (Lobster cactus), illus. p.487.
***S.* 'Wintermärchen'.** Erect, then pendent, perennial cactus. **H** 15cm (6in), **S** 30cm (12in). Has glossy, green stem segments. In early autumn bears white flowers that become pink-and-white in winter.
***S.* 'Zara'.** Erect, then pendent, perennial cactus. **H** 15cm (6in), **S** 30cm (12in). Has glossy, green stem segments. Deep orange-red flowers are produced in early autumn and winter.

SCHOENOPLECTUS

CYPERACEAE

See also GRASSES, BAMBOOS, RUSHES and SEDGES.
***S. lacustris* subsp. *tabernaemontani* 'Zebrinus'**, syn. *Scirpus lacustris* var. *tabernaemontani* 'Zebrinus', *Scirpus tabernaemontani* 'Zebrinus', illus. p.436.

SCHWANTESIA

AIZOACEAE

Genus of cushion-forming, perennial succulents with stemless rosettes of unequal-sized pairs of keeled leaves and daisy-like, yellow flowers. Frost tender, min. 5°C (41°F). Needs full sun and well-drained soil. Propagate by seed or stem cuttings in spring or summer.
S. ruedebuschii illus. p.491.

SCIADOPITYS

SCIADOPITYACEAE

See also CONIFERS.
🏆 ***S. verticillata*** illus. p.101.

SCILLA

LILIACEAE/HYACINTHACEAE

Genus of mainly spring- and summer-flowering bulbs with leaves in basal clusters and spikes of small, often blue flowers. Fully to half hardy. Needs an open site, sun or partial shade and well-drained soil. Propagate by division in late summer or by seed in autumn.
S. adlamii. See *Ledebouria cooperi.*
🏆 ***S. bifolia.*** Early spring-flowering bulb. **H** 5–15cm (2–6in), **S** 2.5–5cm (1–2in). Fully hardy. Has 2 narrowly strap-shaped, semi-erect, basal leaves that widen towards tips. Stem bears one-sided spike of up to 20 star-shaped, purple-blue, pink or white flowers.
S. campanulata. See *Hyacinthoides hispanica.*
S. chinensis. See *S. scilloides.*
S. cooperi. See *Ledebouria cooperi.*
S. hispanica. See *Hyacinthoides x massartiana.*
S. italica. See *Hyacinthoides italica.*
S. japonica. See *S. scilloides.*
S. litardierei, syn. *S. pratensis.* Clump-forming, early summer-flowering bulb. **H** 10–25cm (4–10in), **S** 5–8cm (2–3in). Fully hardy. Bears up to 5 narrowly strap-

shaped, semi-erect, basal leaves. Stem has a dense spike of flat, star-shaped, violet flowers, 1–1.5cm (½–⅝in) across.
🏆 ***S. mischtschenkoana***, syn. *S. tubergeniana, S.* 'Tubergeniana', illus. p.420.
S. natalensis. See *Merwilla plumbea.*
S. non-scripta. See *Hyacinthoides non-scripta.*
S. nutans. See *Hyacinthoides non-scripta.*
S. peruviana illus. p.423.
S. pratensis. See *S. litardierei.*
S. scilloides, syn. *S. chinensis, S. japonica*, illus. p.413.
S. siberica (Siberian squill). **'Alba'** illus. p.416. **'Atrocoerulea'** illus. p.420.
S. socialis. See *Ledebouria socialis.*
S. tubergeniana. See *S. mischtschenkoana.*
***S.* 'Tubergeniana'.** See *S. mischtschenkoana.*
S. violacea. See *Ledebouria socialis.*

SCINDAPSUS

ARACEAE

Genus of about 40 species of evergreen climbers, closley related to Epipremnum, which are grown for their attractive leaves with pointed tips. Frost tender, min. 15°C (59°F). In frost-prone regions grow under glass or as house plants and provide a moss pole for support. In warmer areas, grow against a wall, over a pergola, or through a tree. Outdoors requires fertile, moist, but well-drained soil and partial shade. Indoors, or under glass, needs bright, filtered light and plenty of water in the growing season; water sparingly during winter. Prune in early spring and propagate by stem-tip cuttings in summer with bottom heat, or by layering in spring and summer.
***S. aureus* 'Marble Queen'**. See *Epipremnum aureum* 'Marble Queen'.
🏆 ***S. pictus* 'Argyraeus'**, syn. *Epipremnum pictum* 'Argyraeum' (Silver vine). Slow-growing, evergreen, woody-stemmed, root climber. **H** 2–3m (6–10ft) or more. Heart-shaped leaves are dark green with silver markings.

SCIRPOIDES

CYPERACEAE

See also GRASSES, BAMBOOS, RUSHES and SEDGES.
S. holoschoenus, syn. *Scirpus holoschoenus* (Round-headed club-rush). **'Variegatus'** is an evergreen, tuft-forming, perennial rush. **H** 1m (3ft), **S** 45cm (1½ft). Fully hardy. Rounded, leafless, green stems are striped horizontally with cream and bear long-stalked, dense, spherical heads of egg-shaped, awned, brown spikelets, produced from mid-summer to early autumn.

Scirpus holoschoenus. See *Scirpoides holoschoenus.*
***Scirpus lacustris* 'Spiralis'.** See *Juncus effusus* 'Spiralis'.
***Scirpus lacustris* subsp. *tabernaemontani* 'Zebrinus'.** See *Schoenoplectus lacustris* subsp. *tabernaemontani* 'Zebrinus'.
Scirpus setaceus. See *Isolepsis setaceus.*
***Scirpus tabernaemontani* 'Zebrinus'.** See *Schoenoplectus lacustris* subsp. *tabernaemontani* 'Zebrinus'.

SCLEROCACTUS

CACTACEAE

Genus of perennial cacti, grown for their depressed-spherical to club-shaped or columnar stems, each with a long, fleshy tap root and deeply notched or warty ribs. Frost tender, min. 7–10°C (45–50°F) if completely dry. Needs full sun with some midday shade and very well-drained soil. Propagate by seed in spring.
S. scheeri, syn. *Ancistrocactus megarhizus, A. scheeri, Echinocactus scheeri*, illus. p.495.
S. uncinatus, syn. *Ancistrocactus uncinatus, Echinocactus uncinatus, Glandulicactus uncinatus, Hamatocactus uncinatus.* Globose to columnar, perennial cactus. **H** 20cm (8in), **S** 10cm (4in). Stem is blue-green. Areoles each produce 1–4 very long, hooked, reddish spines and 15–18 straight ones. Has cup-shaped, brown-green or reddish flowers, 2cm (¾in) across, in spring.

SCOLIOPUS

LILIACEAE/TRILLIACEAE

Genus of two species of spring-flowering perennial. Usually grown in alpine houses, where the neat habit and curious flowers, which arise directly from buds on the rootstock early in the season, may be better appreciated. Also suitable for rock gardens and peat beds. Frost hardy. Requires sun or partial shade and moist but well-drained soil. Propagate by seed when fresh, in summer or autumn.
S. bigelowii, syn. *S. bigelovii*, illus. p.349.

Scolopendrium vulgare. See *Asplenium scolopendrium.*

SCOPOLIA

SOLANACEAE

Genus of spring-flowering perennials. Fully hardy. Prefers shade and fertile, very well-drained soil. Propagate by division in spring or by seed in autumn. ⚠ All parts are highly toxic if ingested.
S. carniolica illus. p.260.

SCROPHULARIA

Figwort

SCROPHULARIACEAE

Genus of perennials and subshrubs, some of which are semi-evergreen or evergreen. Most species are weeds, but some are grown for their variegated foliage. Fully hardy. Does best in semi-shade and moist soil. Propagate by division in spring or by softwood cuttings in summer.
***S. aquatica* 'Variegata'.** See *S. auriculata* 'Variegata'.
***S. auriculata* 'Variegata'**, syn. *S. aquatica* 'Variegata' (Water figwort). Evergreen, clump-forming perennial. **H** 60cm (24in), **S** 30cm (12in) or more. Has attractive, oval, toothed, dark green leaves with cream marks. Remove spikes of insignificant summer flowers.

SCUTELLARIA

Skullcap

LABIATAE/LAMIACEAE

Genus of rhizomatous perennials, grown for their summer flowers. Fully hardy to frost tender, min. 7–10°C (45–50°F). Needs sun and well-drained soil. Propagate by softwood cuttings in summer or by seed in autumn.
S. indica. Upright, rhizomatous perennial. **H** 15–30cm (6–12in), **S** 10cm (4in) or more. Frost hardy. Leaves are oval, toothed and hairy. Has dense racemes of long-tubed, 2-lipped, slate-blue, occasionally white flowers in summer. Suits a rock garden.
S. orientalis illus. p.372.
S. scordiifolia. Mat-forming, rhizomatous perennial. **H** and **S** 15cm (6in) or more. Fully hardy. Bears narrowly oval, wrinkled leaves. In summer-autumn has racemes of tubular, hooded, purple flowers, each with a white-streaked lip. Propagate by division in spring.

SEDUM

Stonecrop

CRASSULACEAE

Genus of often fleshy or succulent annuals, evergreen biennials, mostly evergreen or semi-evergreen perennials and evergreen shrubs and subshrubs, suitable for rock gardens and borders. Fully hardy to frost tender, min. 5°C (41°F). Needs sun. Does best in fertile, well-drained soil. Propagate perennials, subshrubs and shrubs by division or by softwood cuttings of non-flowering shoots from spring to mid-summer or by seed in autumn or spring. Propagate annuals and biennials by seed, sown under glass in early spring or outdoors in mid-spring. ⚠ All parts may cause mild stomach upset if ingested; contact with the sap may irritate skin.
S. acre illus. p.371. **'Aureum'** illus. p.371.
S. aizoon syn. *Phedimus aizoon.* Evergreen, erect perennial. **H** and **S** 45cm (18in). Fully hardy. Mid-green leaves are oblong to lance-shaped, fleshy and toothed. In summer bears flat heads of star-shaped, yellow flowers. **'Aurantiacum'** (illus. p.279) has rounded heads of dark yellow flowers followed by red seed capsules.
S. anacampseros, syn. *Hylotelephium anacampseros.* Semi-evergreen, trailing perennial with overwintering foliage rosettes. **H** 10cm (4in), **S** 25cm (10in) or more. Frost hardy. Prostrate, loosely rosetted, brown stems bear oblong to oval, fleshy, glaucous green leaves. Has dense, sub-globose, terminal heads of small, cup-shaped, purplish-pink flowers in summer.
🏆 ***S.* 'Bertram Anderson'.** Clump-forming perennial. **H** 20cm (8in), **S** 30cm (12in). Fully hardy. Has prostrate stems bearing rounded, toothed, fleshy, dusky-purple leaves. In late summer bears rounded, flattened, terminal heads of star-shaped, dark pink flowers.
S. caeruleum illus. p.315.
🏆 ***S. cauticola***, syn. *Hylotelephium cauticola.* Trailing, shallow-rooted perennial with stolons. **H** 5cm (2in), **S** 20cm (8in). Fully hardy. Has oval to oblong, stalked, fleshy, blue-green leaves on procumbent, purplish-red stems. Bears leafy, branched, flattish heads of star-shaped, pale purplish-pink flowers in early autumn. Cut back old stems in winter.
S. erythrostictum. Clump-forming perennial. **H** 40–60cm (16–24in), **S** 40cm (16in). Fully hardy. Has unbranched stems bearing oval, toothed, fleshy, grey-green leaves. In late summer produces domed, terminal heads of star-shaped, pink and white flowers with leafy bracts. **'Frosty Morn'** has variegated, narrowly spoon-shaped leaves, edged with white. Flower heads in late summer also display variegation. **'Mediovariegatum'** (illus. p.279) bears yellow-green leaves each with a central, creamy-white mark.
S. ewersii, syn. *Hylotelephium ewersii.* Trailing perennial. **H** 5cm (2in), **S** 15cm (6in). Fully hardy. Is similar to *S. cauticola*, but has more rounded, stem-clasping leaves, often tinted red, and dense, rounded flower heads.
🏆 ***S.* 'Herbstfreude'.** Clump-forming perennial. **H** 60cm (24in), **S** 50cm (20in). Fully hardy. Has oval, toothed, fleshy, grey-green leaves on stout, erect stems. In late summer and autumn bears broad, flattened, terminal heads of small, star-shaped, brick-red flowers that fade to brown.
S. heterodontum. See *Rhodiola heterodonta.*
🏆 ***S. kamtschaticum***, syn. *Phedimus kamtschaticus.* Semi-evergreen, prostrate perennial with overwintering foliage rosettes. **H** 5–8cm (2–3in), **S** 20cm (8in). Fully hardy. Bears narrowly oval, toothed, fleshy, mid-green leaves. Spreading, terminal clusters of star-shaped, orange-flushed, yellow flowers appear in summer-autumn. 🏆 **'Variegatum'** illus. p.377.
S. lydium illus. p.374.
🏆 ***S.* 'Matrona'** (illus. p.279). Clump-forming perennial. **H** 60cm (24in), **S** 50cm (20in). Fully hardy. Has oval, toothed, fleshy, purple-flushed, brown-green leaves on erect, dark purple stems. In late summer bears flattened, terminal heads of small, star-shaped, pink flowers.
🏆 ***S. morganianum*** (Burro's tail, Donkey-tail). Evergreen, prostrate, succulent perennial. **H** 30cm (12in) or more, **S** indefinite. Frost tender. Stems are clothed in oblong to lance-shaped, almost cylindrical, fleshy, waxy, white leaves. Has terminal clusters of star-shaped, rose-pink flowers in summer.
S. obtusatum illus. p.374.
S. palmeri. Evergreen, clump-forming perennial. **H** 20cm (8in), **S** 30cm (12in). Half hardy. Bears sprays of star-shaped, yellow or orange flowers in early summer above oblong-oval to spoon-shaped, fleshy, grey-green leaves.
S. populifolium, syn. *Hylotelephium populifolium.* Semi-evergreen, bushy perennial. **H** 30–45cm (12–18in), **S** 30cm (12in). Fully hardy. Terminal clusters of hawthorn-scented, star-shaped, pale pink or white flowers are borne in late summer. Has broadly oval, irregularly toothed, fleshy, mid-green leaves.
🏆 ***S.* 'Red Cauli'** (illus. p.279). Clump-forming, compact perennial. **H** 30–40cm (12–16in), **S** 30cm (12in). Fully hardy. Has oval, toothed, fleshy, grey-purple leaves on erect stems. In summer bears cauliflower-

like, domed, terminal heads of star-shaped, rich red flowers.
S. reflexum. See *S. rupestre*.
S. rosea. See *Rhodiola rosea*. **var. *heterodontum*** see *Rhodiola heterodonta*.
♀ ***S. 'Ruby Glow'*** (illus. p.279). Clump-forming, deciduous perennial with prostrate stems. **H** 20cm, **S** 40cm, Fully hardy. Has elliptic, toothed, fleshy, grey-purple leaves. In late summer bears loose terminal heads of star-shaped, pink and ruby-red flowers.
S. rupestre, syn. *S. reflexum*, illus. p.345.
S. sempervivoides, syn. *Prometheum sempervivoides*. Evergreen, basal-rosetted biennial. **H** 8–10cm (3–4in), **S** 5cm (2in). Half hardy. Has oval to strap-shaped, leathery, glaucous green leaves marked red-purple. Bears domed heads of star-shaped, scarlet flowers in summer. Dislikes winter wet. Is good in an alpine house.
S. sieboldii syn. *Hylotelephium sieboldii* **'Mediovariegatum'** (syn. *S.s.* 'Variegatum') is an evergreen, spreading, tuberous perennial with long, tapering tap roots. **H** 10cm (4in), **S** 20cm (8in) or more. Frost tender. Rounded, fleshy, blue-green leaves, splashed cream and occasionally red-edged, are in whorls of 3. Bears open, terminal heads of star-shaped, pink flowers in late summer. Is good in an alpine house.
S. spathulifolium illus. p.374. ♀ **'Cape Blanco'** (syn. *S.s.* 'Cappa Blanca') illus. p.375.
♀ ***S. spectabile***, syn. *Hylotelephium spectabile* (Ice-plant). Clump-forming perennial. **H** and **S** 45cm (18in). Fully hardy. Has oval, indented, fleshy, grey-green leaves, above which flat heads of small, star-shaped, pink flowers that attract butterflies are borne in late summer. ♀ **'Brilliant'** illus. p.278. **'Iceberg'** (illus. p.279) has pale green leaves and heads of greenish-white flowers that develop pink tinges with age. **'Stardust'** produces flower heads that may be white or pink on the same plant.
S. spurium, syn. *Phedimus spurius*. Semi-evergreen, mat-forming, creeping perennial. **H** 10cm (4in) or more, **S** indefinite. Frost hardy. Oblong to oval, toothed leaves are borne along hairy stems. Large, slightly rounded heads of small, star-shaped flowers are borne in summer. Flower colour varies from deep purple to white.
***S* 'Stewed Rhubarb Mountain'.** Clump-forming, compact perennial. **H** and **S** 30cm (12in). Fully hardy. Has oval, toothed, fleshy, pinkish-green leaves on erect stems. In late summer bears rounded, terminal heads of star-shaped, pale green, pale pink and darker pink flowers.
S. tatarinowii, syn. *Hylotelephium tatarinowii*. Arching, spreading, tuberous perennial. **H** 10cm (4in), **S** 20cm (8in). Fully hardy. Rounded, terminal heads of star-shaped, pink-flushed, white flowers appear in late summer above small, oval, toothed, green leaves borne along purplish stems. Suits an alpine house.
S. telephium. Rather variable, clump-forming perennial, sometimes with a rather open, lax habit. **H** 60–70cm (24–28in), **S** 50cm (20in). Fully hardy. Erect stems bear oval, fleshy, blue-green leaves that are often toothed. In late summer–autumn bears domed, branched terminal heads of star-shaped, reddish- or purplish-pink flowers. ♀ **Atropurpureum Group** has red stems bearing dark red leaves with pink flowers. **'Gooseberry Fool'** (illus. p.279), **H** 50cm (20in), **S** 30cm (12in), bears red-flushed, greenish-grey leaves and domed heads of green and white flowers. ♀ **'Purple Emperor'** (illus. p.279), **H** 50cm (20in), **S** 30cm (12in), is neat and compact, with dark purple leaves and pinkish-red flowers. **'Strawberries and Cream'** (illus. p.279), **H** and **S** 50–60cm (20–24in), has purple stems, toothed, green-purple leaves and pinkish-green flowers opening from dark pink buds.

SELAGINELLA

SELAGINELLACEAE

Genus of evergreen, moss-like perennials, grown for their foliage. Frost tender, min. 5°C (41°F). Prefers semi-shade and needs moist but well-drained, peaty soil. Remove faded foliage regularly. Propagate from pieces with roots attached that have been broken off plant in any season.
♀ ***S. kraussiana*** illus. p.478. **'Aurea'** is an evergreen, moss-like perennial. **H** 1cm (½in), **S** indefinite. Spreading, filigreed, bright yellowish-green fronds are much-branched, denser towards the growing tips and easily root on soil surface.
♀ **'Variegata'** has foliage splashed with creamy-yellow.
S. lepidophylla (Resurrection plant, Rose of Jericho). Evergreen, moss-like perennial. **H** and **S** 10cm (4in). Bluntly rounded, emerald-green fronds, ageing red-brown or grey-green, are produced in dense tufts. On drying, fronds curl inwards into a tight ball; they unfold when placed in water.
♀ ***S. martensii*** illus. p.478.

SELENICEREUS

CACTACEAE

Genus of summer-flowering, perennial cacti with climbing, 4–10-ribbed, green stems, to 2cm (¾in) across. Nocturnal, funnel-shaped flowers eventually open flat. Frost tender, min. 5°C (41°F). Needs sun or partial shade and rich, well-drained soil. Propagate by seed or stem cuttings in spring or summer.
S. grandiflorus illus. p.479.

SELINUM

UMBELLIFERAE/APIACEAE

Genus of summer-flowering perennials, ideal for informal gardens and backs of borders. Fully hardy. Prefers sun, but will grow in semi-shade, and any well-drained soil. Once established, roots resent disturbance. Propagate by seed when fresh, in summer or autumn.
S. tenuifolium. See *S. wallichianum*.
S. wallichianum illus p.230.

SEMELE

LILIACEAE/RUSCACEAE

Genus of one species of evergreen, twining climber. Male and female flowers are produced on the same plant. Frost tender, min. 5°C (41°F). Needs partial shade and prefers rich, well-drained soil. Propagate by division or seed in spring.
S. androgyna (Climbing butcher's broom). Evergreen climber, twining in upper part, branched and bearing oval cladodes, 5–10cm (2–4in) long. **H** to 7m (22ft). Star-shaped, cream flowers appear in early summer, in notches on cladode margins, followed by orange-red berries.

SEMIAQUILEGIA

RANUNCULACEAE

Genus of perennials, grown for their flowers. These differ from those of *Aquilegia*, with which it is sometimes included, by having no spurs. Is good for rock gardens. Fully hardy. Requires a sunny position and moist but well-drained soil. Propagate by seed in autumn.
S. ecalcarata illus. p.341.

SEMIARUNDINARIA

GRAMINEAE/POACEAE

See also GRASSES, BAMBOOS, RUSHES and SEDGES.
♀ ***S. fastuosa***, syn. *Arundinaria fastuosa*, illus. p.287.

SEMPERVIVUM

Houseleek

CRASSULACEAE

Genus of evergreen perennials that spread by short stolons and are grown for their symmetrical rosettes of oval to strap-shaped, pointed, fleshy leaves. Makes ground-hugging mats, suitable for rock gardens, screes, walls, banks and alpine houses. Flowers are star-shaped with 8–16 spreading petals. Fully hardy. Needs sun and gritty soil. Takes several years to reach flowering size. Rosettes die after flowering but leave numerous offsets. Propagate by offsets in summer.
♀ ***S. arachnoideum*** (Cobweb houseleek; illus. p.377). Evergreen, mat-forming perennial. **H** 5–12cm (2–5in), **S** 10cm (4in) or more. Rosettes of oval, fleshy leaves with red tips are covered in a web of white hairs. Bears loose clusters of star-shaped, rose-red flowers in summer.
S. 'Blood Tip' (illus. p.377). Evergreen, basal-rosetted, mat-forming succulent. **H** to 10cm (4in), **S** to 30cm (12in). Has thick, green leaves strongly suffused purple-red with deeper red, bristle-like tips.
S. calcareum (illus. p.377). Variable, evergreen, mat-forming, basal-rosetted perennial. **H** 5–7cm (2–3in), **S** 20–25cm (8–10in). Has bluish-green leaves with dark reddish-brown tips. Erect stems bear terminal clusters of star-shaped, red-based, creamy-white flowers in summer. Is excellent in a trough or on a dry wall.
♀ **'Extra'** (illus. p.377) has intense, dark leaf tips.
♀ ***S. ciliosum*** illus. p.375.
♀ ***S. 'Commander Hay'.*** Evergreen, basal-rosetted perennial. **H** 15cm (6in), **S** to 30cm (12in). Is mainly grown for its very large, dark red rosettes to 10cm (4in) across. Terminal clusters of dull greenish-red flowers are produced in summer.
♀ ***S. 'Gallivarda'*** (illus. p.377). Evergreen, mat-forming, basal-rosetted perennial. **H** 5–8cm (2–3in), **S** 20–25cm (8–10in). Red leaves turn to orange-red in summer, then to purplish-red.
♀ ***S. giuseppii*** (illus. p.377). Vigorous, evergreen, prostrate perennial. **H** in flower 8–10cm (3–4in), **S** 10cm (4in). Leaves are hairy, especially in spring, and have dark spots at tips. Produces terminal clusters of star-shaped, deep pink or red flowers in summer.
***S. globiferum* subsp. *globiferum*.** See *Jovibarba sobolifera*. **subsp. *hirtum*.** See *Jovibarba hirta*.
S. grandiflorum. Evergreen, basal-rosetted perennial. **H** 10cm (4in), **S** to 20cm (8in). Variable, densely haired, red-tinted, dark green rosettes exude a goat-like smell when crushed. Produces loose, terminal clusters of yellow-green flowers, stained purple in centres, on long flower stems in summer. Prefers humus-rich, acid soil.
S. 'Gulle Dame' (illus. p.377). Evergreen, mat-forming, basal-rosetted perennial. **H** 5–8cm (2–3in), **S** 20–25cm (8–10in). Has dark red leaves with long, white hairs, in spring and summer, gradually changing to green in winter.
S. 'Kappa' (illus. p.377). Evergreen, mat-forming, basal-rosetted perennial. **H** 5–8cm (2–3in), **S** 15–20–25cm (6–8in). Deep purple-red leaves are covered in cobwebs of white hairs.
S. montanum (illus. p.377). Evergreen, mat-forming perennial. **H** 10–15cm (3–6in), **S** 10cm (4in). Has dark green rosettes of fleshy, hairy leaves. Star-shaped, wine-red flowers are borne in terminal clusters in summer. Is a variable plant that hybridizes freely.
S. 'Rosie' (illus. p.377). Evergreen, mat-forming, open-rosetted perennial. **H** 5–8cm (2–3in), **S** 20–25cm (8–10in). Green-flushed, purple-red leaves have short, marginal hairs.
♀ ***S. tectorum*** (Common houseleek; illus. p.377). Vigorous, evergreen perennial. **H** 10–15cm (4–6in), **S** to 20cm (8in). Has purple-tipped leaves, sometimes suffused deep red. In summer produces clusters of star-shaped, reddish-purple flowers on stems 30cm (12in) tall.

SENECIO

COMPOSITAE/ASTERACEAE

Genus of annuals, succulent and non-succulent perennials and evergreen shrubs, subshrubs and twining climbers, grown for their foliage and usually daisy-like flower heads. Some shrubby species are now referred to the genus *Brachyglottis*. Shrubs are excellent for coastal gardens. Fully hardy to frost tender, min. 5–10°C (41–50°F). Most prefer full sun and well-drained soil (although *S. articulatus* and *S. rowleyanus* tolerate partial shade and need very well-drained soil). Propagate shrubs and climbers by semi-ripe cuttings in summer, annuals by seed in spring, perennials by division in spring (*S. articulatus* and *S. rowleyanus* by seed or stem cuttings in spring or summer). ⓘ All parts may cause severe discomfort if ingested.
S. articulatus, syn. *Kleinia articulata* (Candle plant). Deciduous, spreading, perennial succulent. **H** 60cm (2ft), **S** indefinite. Frost tender, min. 10°C (50°F). Branching, grey-marked, blue stems have weak joints. Bears rounded to oval, 3–5-lobed, grey leaves and flattish heads of

S

small, cup-shaped, yellow flowers from spring to autumn. Offsets freely from stolons. **'Variegatus'** illus. p.486.
S. cineraria, syn. *S. maritimus.* Moderately fast-growing, evergreen, bushy subshrub, often grown as an annual. **H** and **S** 30cm (1ft). Half hardy. Has long, oval, very deeply lobed, hairy, silver-grey leaves. Rounded, yellow flower heads appear in summer, but are best removed. **'Cirrus'** has elliptic, finely toothed or lobed, silvery-green to white leaves. ♡ **'Silver Dust'** illus. p.315.
***S. clivorum* 'Desdemona'.** See *Ligularia dentata* 'Desdemona'.
S. compactus. See *Brachyglottis compacta.*
S. confusus. See *Pseudogynoxys chenopodioides.*
***S.* Dunedin Hybrids.** See *Brachyglottis* Dunedin Hybrids.
S. elegans. Moderately fast-growing, upright annual. **H** 45cm (18in), **S** 15cm (6in). Half hardy. Has oval, deeply lobed, deep green leaves. Daisy-like, purple flower heads appear in summer.
S. grandifolius, syn. *Telanthophora grandiflora.* Evergreen, erect, robust-stemmed shrub. **H** 3–5m (10–15ft), **S** 2–3m (6–10ft). Frost tender, min. 10°C (50°F) to flower well. Has oval, toothed, boldly veined leaves, 20–45cm (8–18in) long, glossy, rich green above, red-brown-haired beneath. Carries terminal clusters, 30cm (12in) wide, of small, daisy-like, yellow flower heads in winter-spring.
S. greyi of gardens. See *Brachyglottis* Dunedin Hybrids.
S. x hybridus. See *Pericallis x hybrida.*
S. laxifolius. See *Brachyglottis laxifolia.*
S. laxifolius of gardens. See *Brachyglottis* Dunedin Hybrids.
S. macroglossus (Natal ivy, Wax vine). Evergreen, woody-stemmed, twining climber. **H** 3m (10ft). Frost tender, min. 7°C (45°F), best at 10°C (50°F). Leaves are sharply triangular, fleshy-textured and glossy. Loose clusters of daisy-like flower heads, each with a few white ray petals and a central, yellow disc, are borne mainly in winter. ♡ **'Variegatus'** illus. p.464.
S. maritimus. See *S. cineraria.*
S. mikanioides, syn. *Delairea odorata* (German ivy). Evergreen, semi-woody, twining climber. **H** 2–3m (6–10ft). Frost tender, min. 5°C (41°F), best at 7–10°C (45–50°F). Has fleshy leaves with 5–7 broad, pointed, radiating lobes. Mature plants carry large clusters of small, yellow flower heads in autumn-winter.
S. monroi. See *Brachyglottis monroi.*
S. przewalskii. See *Ligularia przewalskii.*
S. pulcher illus. p.278.
S. reinholdii. See *Brachyglottis rotundifolia.*
S. rotundifolius. See *Brachyglottis rotundifolia.*
S. rowleyanus, syn. *Kleinia rowleyana*, illus. p.481.
S. smithii. Bushy perennial. **H** 1–1.2m (3–4ft), **S** 75cm–1m (2½–3ft). Fully hardy. Woolly stems are clothed with long, oval, toothed, leathery, dark green leaves. Daisy-like, white flower heads, with yellow centres, are borne in terminal clusters, up to 15cm (6in) across, in early summer. Likes boggy conditions.
***S.* 'Spring Glory'.** See *Pericallis x hybrida* 'Spring Glory'.
***S.* 'Sunshine'.** See *Brachyglottis* Dunedin Hybrids 'Sunshine'.
S. tamoides. Evergreen, woody-stemmed, twining climber. **H** 5m (15ft) or more. Frost tender, min. 5–10°C (41–50°F). Has ivy-shaped, light green leaves. In autumn-winter bears daisy-like, yellow flower heads with only a few ray petals.

SENNA

LEGUMINOSAE/CAESALPINIACEAE

Genus of evergreen trees, shrubs and perennials, grown for their pea-like flowers. Frost tender, min. 7–18°C (45–64°F). Requires full sun and moist but well-drained soil. Propagate by seed sown in spring, or by semi-ripe cuttings in summer. Divide perennials in spring.
♡ ***S. artemisioides***, syn. *Cassia artemisioides* (Silver cassia, Wormwood cassia). Evergreen, erect to spreading, wiry shrub. **H** and **S** 1–2m (3–6ft). Frost tender, min. 10–13°C (50–55°F). Leaves each have 6–8 linear leaflets covered with silky, white down. Axillary spikes of cup-shaped, yellow flowers appear from winter to early summer.
S. corymbosa, syn. *Cassia corymbosa*, illus. p.459.
S. didymobotrya, syn. *Cassia didymobotrya*, illus. p.459.
♡ ***S. x floribunda***, syn. *Cassia corymbosa* var. *plurijuga* of gardens, *C. x floribunda.* Vigorous, evergreen or deciduous, rounded shrub with robust stems. **H** and **S** 1.5–2m (5–6ft). Frost tender, min. 7°C (45°F). Bright green leaves consist of 4–6 oval leaflets. Has very large clusters of bowl-shaped, rich yellow flowers in late summer.
S. siamea, syn. *Cassia siamea.* Fast-growing, evergreen, rounded tree. **H** and **S** 8–10m (25–30ft) or more. Frost tender, min. 16–18°C (61–4°F). Leaves, 15–30cm (6–12in) long, have 7–12 pairs of elliptic leaflets. Large terminal panicles of small, cup-shaped, bright yellow flowers are borne in spring, followed by flat, dark brown pods, to 23cm (9in) long.

SEQUOIA

TAXODIACEAE

See also CONIFERS.
♡ ***S. sempervirens*** illus. p.97.

SEQUOIADENDRON

TAXODIACEAE

See also CONIFERS.
♡ ***S. giganteum*** illus. p.98. **'Pendulum'** is a weeping conifer. **H** 10m (30ft), **S** 2m (6ft) or more. Fully hardy. Bark is thick, soft, fibrous and red-brown. Has spiralled, needle-like, incurved, grey-green leaves that darken and become glossy.

SERAPIAS

ORCHIDACEAE

See also ORCHIDS.
S. cordigera. Deciduous, terrestrial orchid. **H** 40cm (16in). Half hardy. Spikes of reddish or dark purple flowers, 4cm (1½in) long, are borne in spring. Has lance-shaped, red-spotted leaves, 15cm (6in) long. Grow in semi-shade.

SERENOA

PALMAE/ARECACEAE

Genus of one species of evergreen fan palm, grown for its foliage. Frost tender, min. 10–13°C (50–55°F). Requires full light or partial shade and well-drained soil. Water potted plants moderately during growing season, less at other times. Propagate by seed or suckers in spring. Red spider mite may be troublesome.
S. repens (Saw palmetto, Scrub palmetto). Evergreen, rhizomatous fan palm, usually stemless. **H** 60cm–1m (2–3ft), **S** 2m (6ft) or more. Palmate leaves, 45–75cm (18–30in) wide, are grey to blue-green, and each divided into 6–20 strap-shaped lobes. Clusters of tiny, fragrant, cream flowers are hidden among leaves in summer, followed by egg-shaped, purple-black fruits.

SERISSA

RUBIACEAE

Genus of one species of evergreen shrub, grown for its overall appearance. Frost tender, min. 7–10°C (45–50°F). Needs sun or partial shade and fertile, well-drained soil. Water containerized specimens moderately, less when not in growth. May be trimmed after flowering. Propagate by semi-ripe cuttings in summer.
S. foetida. See *S. japonica.*
S. japonica, syn. *S. foetida.* Evergreen, spreading to rounded, freely branching shrub. **H** to 60cm (2ft), **S** 60cm–1m (2–3ft). Has tiny, oval, lustrous, deep green leaves. Small, funnel-shaped, 4- or 5-lobed, white flowers are borne from spring to autumn.

SERRATULA

COMPOSITAE/ASTERACEAE

Genus of perennials, grown for their thistle-like flower heads. Fully hardy. Requires sun and well-drained soil. Propagate by seed or by division in spring.
S. seoanei, syn. *S. shawii.* Upright, compact perennial. **H** 23cm (9in), **S** 12–15cm (5–6in). Stems bear feathery, finely cut leaves and, in autumn, terminal panicles of small, thistle-like, purple flower heads. Is useful in a rock garden.
S. shawii. See *S. seoanei.*

SESLERIA

GRAMINEAE/POACEAE

See also GRASSES, BAMBOOS, RUSHES and SEDGES.
S. heufleriana (Balkan blue grass). Evergreen, tuft-forming, perennial grass. **H** 50cm (20in), **S** 30–45cm (12–18in). Fully hardy. Bears rich green leaves, glaucous beneath, and, in spring, compact panicles of purple spikelets.

SETARIA

GRAMINEAE/POACEAE

See also GRASSES, BAMBOOS, RUSHES and SEDGES.
S. italica (Foxtail millet, Italian millet). Moderately fast-growing, annual grass with stout stems. **H** 1.5m (5ft), **S** to 1m (3ft). Half hardy. Has lance-shaped, mid-green leaves, to 45cm (1½ft) long, and loose panicles of white, cream, yellow, red, brown or black flowers from summer to autumn.
♡ ***S. macrostachya*** illus. p.318.

Setcreasea purpurea. See *Tradescantia pallida* 'Purpurea'.

SHEPHERDIA

ELAEAGNACEAE

Genus of deciduous or evergreen shrubs, grown for their foliage and fruits. Separate male and female plants are needed in order to obtain fruits. Fully hardy. Requires sun and well-drained soil. Propagate by softwood cuttings in summer or by seed in autumn.
S. argentea (Buffalo berry). Deciduous, bushy, often tree-like shrub. **H** and **S** 4m (12ft). Bears tiny, inconspicuous, yellow flowers amid oblong, silvery leaves in spring, followed by small, egg-shaped, bright red fruits.

SHIBATAEA

GRAMINEAE/POACEAE

See also GRASSES, BAMBOOS, RUSHES and SEDGES.
S. kumasasa illus. p.287.

SHORTIA

DIAPENSIACEAE

Genus of evergreen, spring-flowering perennials with leaves that often turn red in autumn-winter. Fully hardy, but buds may be frosted in areas without snow cover. Is difficult to grow in hot, dry climates. Needs shade or semi-shade and well-drained, peaty, sandy, acid soil. Propagate by runners in summer or by seed when available.
S. galacifolia illus. p.349.
S. soldanelloides illus. p.352. **var. *ilicifolia*** is an evergreen, mat-forming perennial. **H** 5–10cm (2–4in), **S** 10–15cm (4–6in). Has rounded, toothed leaves. In late spring each flower stem carries 4–6 small, pendent, bell-shaped flowers with fringed edges and rose-pink centres shading to white. Flowers of **var. *magna*** are rose-pink throughout.
***S. uniflora* 'Grandiflora'.** Vigorous, evergreen, mat-forming perennial with a few rooted runners. **H** 8cm (3in), **S** 20cm (8in). Leaves are rounded, toothed, leathery and glossy. Flower stems bear cup-shaped, 5cm (2in) wide, white-pink flowers, with serrated petals, in spring.

SIBIRAEA

ROSACEAE

Genus of deciduous shrubs, grown for their foliage and flowers. Fully hardy. Needs sunny, well-drained soil. Prune out old or weak shoots to base after flowering. Propagate by softwood cuttings in summer.
S. altaiensis. See. *S. laevigata.*
S. laevigata. syn *S. altaiensis.* Deciduous, spreading, open shrub. **H** 1m (3ft), **S** 1.5m (5ft). Has narrowly oblong, blue-green leaves and, in late spring and early summer, dense, terminal clusters of tiny, star-shaped, white flowers.

SIDALCEA

MALVACEAE

Genus of summer-flowering perennials, grown for their hollyhock-like flowers. Fully hardy. Needs sun and well-drained soil. Propagate by division in spring.

S. 'Loveliness'. Upright perennial. **H** 1m (3ft), **S** 45cm (1½ft). Has buttercup-like, divided leaves with narrowly oblong segments. In summer bears racemes of shallowly cup-shaped, shell-pink flowers.

S. 'Oberon' illus. p.233.

S. 'Puck'. Upright perennial. **H** 60cm (2ft), **S** 45cm (1½ft). Has buttercup-like, divided leaves with narrowly oblong segments. In summer bears racemes of shallowly cup-shaped, deep pink flowers.

S. 'Sussex Beauty'. Upright perennial. **H** 1.2m (4ft), **S** 45cm (1½ft). Has buttercup-like, divided leaves, with narrowly oblong segments, and, in summer, shallowly cup-shaped, deep rose-pink flowers.

SIDERITIS

LABIATAE/LAMIACEAE

Genus of evergreen perennials, subshrubs and shrubs, grown mainly for their foliage. Half hardy to frost tender, min. 7–10°C (45–50°F). Needs full light and well-drained soil. Water containerized plants moderately, less when temperatures are low. Remove spent flower spikes after flowering. Propagate by seed in spring or by semi-ripe cuttings in summer.

S. candicans. Evergreen, erect, well-branched shrub. **H** to 75cm (2½ft), **S** to 60cm (2ft). Frost tender. Lance-shaped to narrowly oval or triangular leaves bear dense, white wool. Produces leafy, terminal spikes of tubular, pale yellow-and-light-brown or orange-red flowers in summer.

SILENE

Campion, Catchfly

CARYOPHYLLACEAE

Genus of annuals and perennials, some of which are evergreen, grown for their mass of 5-petalled flowers. Fully to half hardy. Needs sun and fertile, well-drained soil. Propagate by softwood cuttings in spring or by seed in spring or early autumn.

S. acaulis illus. p.352.

S. alpestris, syn. *Heliosperma alpestre*, illus. p.359.

S. armeria 'Electra'. Moderately fast-growing, erect annual. **H** 30cm (12in), **S** 15cm (6in). Fully hardy. Has oval, greyish-green leaves. Heads of 5-petalled, bright rose-pink flowers are produced in summer and early autumn.

S. coeli-rosa, syn. *Agrostemma coeli-rosa, Lychnis coeli-rosa, Viscaria elegans*, illus. p.303.

S. elisabethae. Basal-rosetted perennial. **H** 10cm (4in), **S** 20cm (8in). Fully hardy. Has rosettes of strap-shaped, mid-green leaves. In summer, stems bear large, often solitary, deep rose-red flowers with green centres and long-clawed petals. Is suitable for a rock garden.

S. hookeri. Short-lived, trailing, prostrate, late summer-deciduous perennial with a long, slender tap root. **H** 5cm (2in), **S** 20cm (8in). Fully hardy. Slender stems bear oval, grey leaves and, in late summer, soft pink, salmon or orange flowers, deeply cleft to base.

S. maritima 'Flore Pleno'. See *S. uniflora* 'Robin Whitebreast'.

S. pendula (Nodding catchfly). Moderately fast-growing, bushy annual. **H** and **S** 15–20cm (6–8in). Half hardy. Has oval, hairy, mid-green leaves and, in summer and early autumn, clusters of light pink flowers.

🏆 **S. schafta** illus. p.346.

S. uniflora 'Robin Whitebreast', syn. *S. maritima* 'Flore Pleno', *S.u.* 'Flore Pleno', *S. vulgaris* subsp. *maritima* 'Flore Pleno' (Double sea campion). Lax perennial with deep, wandering roots. **H** and **S** 20cm (8in). Fully hardy. Has lance-shaped, grey-green leaves. Bears pompon-like, double, white flowers on branched stems in summer.

S. vulgaris subsp. maritima 'Flore Pleno'. See *S. uniflora* 'Robin Whitebreast'.

SILPHIUM

COMPOSITAE/ASTERACEAE

Genus of fairly coarse, summer-flowering perennials. Fully hardy. Does best in sun or semi-shade and in moist but well-drained soil. Propagate by division in spring or by seed when fresh, in autumn.

S. laciniatum (Compass plant). Clump-forming perennial. **H** 2m (6ft), **S** 60cm (2ft). Mid-green leaves, composed of opposite pairs of oblong to lance-shaped leaflets, face north and south wherever the plant is grown, hence the common name. Large clusters of slightly pendent, daisy-like, yellow flower heads are borne in late summer.

SILYBUM

COMPOSITAE/ASTERACEAE

Genus of thistle-like biennials, grown for their spectacular foliage. Fully hardy. Grow in sun and in any well-drained soil. Propagate by seed in late spring or early summer. Is prone to slug and snail damage.

S. marianum illus. p.304.

Sinarundinaria jaunsarensis. See *Yushania anceps*.

Sinarundinaria murieliae. See *Fargesia murieliae*.

Sinarundinaria nitida. See *Fargesia nitida*.

SINNINGIA

GESNERIACEAE

Genus of usually summer-flowering, tuberous perennials and deciduous subshrubs with showy flowers. Frost tender, min. 15°C (59°F). Grow in bright light but not direct sun. Prefers a humid atmosphere and moist but not waterlogged, peaty soil. When leaves die down after flowering, allow tubers to dry out; then store in a frost-free area. Propagate in spring by seed or in late spring or summer by stem cuttings or by dividing tubers into sections, each with a young shoot.

S. barbata. Bushy, tuberous perennial with square, red stems. **H** and **S** 60cm (2ft) or more. Broadly lance-shaped, glossy, mid-green leaves, to 15cm (6in) long, are reddish-green beneath. In summer has 5-lobed, pouched, white flowers, 4cm (1½in) long.

S. concinna. Rosetted perennial with very small tubers. **H** and **S** to 15cm (6in). Oval to almost round, scalloped, velvety, red-veined, mid-green leaves, 2cm (¾in) long, are red below. Trumpet-shaped, bicoloured, purple and white or yellowish-white flowers, to 2cm (¾in) long, appear in summer.

S. 'Etoile du Feu'. Short-stemmed, rosetted, tuberous perennial. **H** 30cm (12in), **S** 40cm (16in) or more. Has oval, velvety leaves, 20–24cm (8–9½in) long. Upright, trumpet-shaped, carmine-red flowers appear in summer.

S. 'Mont Blanc'. Short-stemmed, rosetted, tuberous perennial. **H** 30cm (12in), **S** 40cm (16in) or more. Oval, velvety, mid-green leaves are 20–24cm (8–9½in) long. In summer has upright, trumpet-shaped, pure white flowers.

S. 'Red Flicker'. Short-stemmed, tuberous perennial. **H** to 30cm (12in), **S** 45cm (18in). Has rosettes of oval, velvety leaves, to 20cm (8in) long. Fleshy, nodding, funnel-shaped, pinkish-red flowers, pouched on lower sides, are borne in summer.

S. speciosa, syn. *Gloxinia speciosa* (Gloxinia). Short-stemmed, rosetted, tuberous perennial. **H** and **S** to 30cm (1ft). Oval, velvety, green leaves are 20cm (8in) long. Nodding, funnel-shaped, fleshy, violet, red or white flowers, to 5cm (2in) long and pouched on lower sides, are produced in summer. Is a parent of many named hybrids, of which a selection is included above and below.

S. 'Switzerland' illus. p.470.

S. 'Waterloo'. Short-stemmed, rosetted, tuberous perennial. **H** 30cm (12in), **S** 40cm (16in) or more. Has oval, velvety leaves, 20–24cm (8–9½in) long. Upright, trumpet-shaped, bright scarlet flowers open in summer.

SINOFRANCHETIA

LARDIZABALACEAE

Genus of one species of deciduous, twining climber, grown mainly for its handsome leaves. Is suitable for covering buildings and growing up large trees. Male and female flowers are produced on separate plants. Frost hardy. Grow in semi-shade and in any well-drained soil. Propagate by semi-ripe cuttings in summer.

S. chinensis. Deciduous, twining climber. **H** to 15m (50ft). Mid- to dark green leaves have 3 oblong to oval leaflets, each 5–15cm (2–6in) long. In late spring has small, dull white flowers in pendent racemes, to 10cm (4in) long. Pale purple berries, containing many seeds, follow in summer.

SINOJACKIA

STYRACACEAE

Genus of deciduous shrubs and trees, grown for their flowers. Fully hardy. Requires a sheltered position in sun or partial shade and fertile, humus-rich, moist, acid soil. Propagate by softwood cuttings in summer.

S. rehderiana. Deciduous, bushy shrub or spreading tree. **H** and **S** 6m (20ft). Nodding, saucer-shaped, white flowers, each with a central cluster of yellow anthers, are produced in late spring and early summer. Oval leaves are dark green and glossy.

SINOPODOPHYLLUM

BERBERIDACEAE

Genus of a single spring flowering rhizomatous perennial species, grown for its flowers, often marbled foliage and large red fruit. Fully hardy. Requires semi-shade, moist, humus-rich soil. Propagate by division of the rhizome or seed sown in autumn. All parts toxic if eaten.

S. hexandrum, syn. *Podophyllum hexandrum, P. emodii*, illus. p.255.

SINOWILSONIA

HAMAMELIDACEAE

Genus of one species of deciduous tree, grown for its foliage and catkins. Fully hardy. Requires sun or semi-shade and fertile, moist but well-drained soil. Propagate by seed in autumn.

S. henryi. Deciduous, spreading, sometimes shrubby tree. **H** and **S** 8m (25ft). Has oval, toothed, glossy, bright green leaves, and long, pendent, green catkins in late spring.

Siphonosmanthus delavayi. See *Osmanthus delavayi*.

SISYRINCHIUM

IRIDACEAE

Genus of annuals and perennials, some of which are semi-evergreen. Fully to half hardy. Prefers sun, but tolerates partial shade, and well-drained or moist soil. Propagate by division in early spring or by seed in spring or autumn.

S. angustifolium. See *S. graminoides*.

S. bellum of gardens. See *S. idahoense*.

S. bermudiana. See *S. graminoides*.

S. brachypus. See *S. californicum*.

S. californicum (Golden-eyed grass). Semi-evergreen, upright perennial. **H** 30–60cm (12–24in), **S** 30cm (12in). Frost hardy. Has grass-like tufts of basal, light green leaves. For a long period in spring-summer produces flattish, bright yellow flowers, with slightly darker veins, on winged stems. Outer leaves may die off and turn black in autumn. Dwarf forms are known as *S. brachypus*. Prefers moist soil.

S. douglasii. See *Olsynium douglasii*.

S. graminoides, syn. *S. angustifolium*.

S. 'E.K. Balls' illus. p.342.

S. graminoides. Semi-evergreen, erect perennial. **H** to 30cm (12in), **S** 8cm (3in). Fully hardy. Has tufts of grass-like leaves. Small, iris-like, pale to dark purplish-blue flowers with yellow bases are borne in terminal clusters in late spring and early summer.

S. grandiflorum. See *Olsynium douglasii*.

S. idahoense, syn. *S. bellum* of gardens, illus. p.369.

S. odoratissimum. See *Olsynium biflorum*.

S. palmifolium. Semi-evergreen, upright perennial. **H** 45cm (18in), **S** 30cm (12in). Half hardy. Produces a fan of narrowly sword-shaped, mid-green leaves. In

S

summer bears dense spikes of widely funnel-shaped, golden-yellow flowers.
S. striatum illus. p.274. **'Aunt May'** (syn. *S.s.* 'Variegatum') is a semi-evergreen, upright perennial. **H** 45–60cm (18–24in), **S** 30cm (12in). Fully hardy. Produces tufts of long, narrow, cream-striped, greyish-green leaves. Slender spikes of trumpet-shaped, purple-striped, straw-yellow flowers are borne in summer.

SKIMMIA

RUTACEAE

Genus of evergreen shrubs and trees, grown for their spring flowers, aromatic foliage and their fruits. Except with *S. japonica* subsp. *reevesiana*, separate male and female plants are needed in order to obtain fruits. Fully to frost hardy. Requires shade or semi-shade and fertile, moist soil. Poor soil or too much sun may cause chlorosis. Propagate by semi-ripe cuttings in late summer or by seed in autumn.
⚠ The fruits may cause mild stomach upset if ingested.
S. anquetilia. Evergreen, bushy, open shrub. **H** 1.2m (4ft), **S** 2m (6ft). Fully hardy. Produces small clusters of tiny, yellow flowers from mid- to late spring, then spherical, scarlet fruits. Leaves are oblong to oval, pointed, strongly aromatic and dark green.
S. x foremanii of gardens. See *S. japonica* 'Veitchii'.
S. japonica illus. p.164. **'Fructo Albo'** (female) illus. p.163. 🏆 **subsp. *reevesiana* 'Robert Fortune'** (syn. *S. reevesiana; hermaphrodite*), illus. p.164. 🏆 **'Rubella'** (male) illus. p.164. **'Veitchii'** (syn. *S. x foremanii* of gardens) is a vigorous, evergreen, upright, dense, female shrub. **H** and **S** 1.5m (5ft). Fully hardy. Broadly oval leaves are rich green. In mid- and late spring bears dense clusters of small, star-shaped, white flowers, followed by large, spherical, bright red fruits.
S. reevesiana. See *S. japonica* subsp. *reevesiana* 'Robert Fortune'.

SMILACINA

LILIACEAE/CONVALLARIACEAE

Genus of perennials, grown for their graceful appearance. Fully hardy. Prefers semi-shade and humus-rich, moist, neutral to acid soil. Propagate by division in spring or by seed in autumn.
S. racemosa, syn. *Maianthemum racemosum*, illus. p.223.

SMILAX

LILIACEAE/SMILACACEAE

Genus of deciduous or evergreen, woody-stemmed or herbaceous, scrambling climbers with tubers or rhizomes. Male and female flowers are borne on separate plants. Frost hardy to frost tender, min. 5°C (41°F). Grow in any well-drained soil and in sun or semi-shade. Propagate by division or seed in spring or by semi-ripe cuttings in summer.
S. china. Deciduous, woody-based, scrambling climber with straggling, sometimes spiny stems. **H** to 5m (15ft). Frost hardy. Leaves are broadly oval to rounded. Umbels of yellow-green flowers are produced in spring; tiny, red berries appear in autumn.

SMITHIANTHA

Temple bells

GESNERIACEAE

Genus of bushy, erect perennials with tuber-like rhizomes, grown for their flowers and foliage. Frost tender, min. 15°C (59°F). Grow in humus-rich, well-drained soil and in bright light but out of direct sun. Reduce watering after flowering and water sparingly in winter. Propagate by division of rhizomes in early spring.
S. cinnabarina (Temple bells). Robust, erect, rhizomatous perennial. **H** and **S** to 60cm (2ft). Broadly oval to almost rounded, toothed leaves, to 15cm (6in) long, are dark green with dark red hairs. Bell-shaped, orange-red flowers, lined with pale yellow, are produced in summer-autumn.
***S.* 'Orange King'** illus. p.471.
S. zebrina. Bushy, rhizomatous perennial with velvety-haired stems. **H** and **S** to 1m (3ft). Oval, toothed, hairy leaves, to 18cm (7in) long, are deep green marked with reddish-brown. In summer produces tubular flowers, scarlet above, yellow below, spotted red inside and with orange-yellow lobes.

SMYRNIUM

UMBELLIFERAE/APIACEAE

Genus of biennials, grown for their flowers. Fully hardy. Grow in sun and in fertile, well-drained soil. Propagate by seed sown outdoors in autumn or spring.
S. perfoliatum illus. p.321.

SOLANDRA

SOLANACEAE

Genus of evergreen, woody-stemmed, scrambling climbers, grown for their large, trumpet-shaped flowers. Frost tender, min. 10°C (50°F), but prefers 13–16°C (55–61°F). Needs full light and fertile, well-drained soil. Water freely when in full growth, sparingly in cold weather. Tie to supports. Thin out crowded stems after flowering. Propagate by semi-ripe cuttings in summer.
S. maxima, syn. *S. grandiflora* of gardens, illus. p.464.

SOLANUM

SOLANACEAE

Genus of annuals, perennials (some of which are evergreen) and evergreen, semi-evergreen or deciduous subshrubs, shrubs (occasionally scandent) and woody-stemmed, scrambling or leaf-stalk climbers, grown for their flowers and ornamental fruits. Frost hardy to frost tender, min. 5–10°C (41–50°F). Requires full sun and fertile, well-drained soil. Water regularly but sparingly in winter. Support scrambling climbers. Thin out and spur back crowded growth of climbers in spring. Propagate by seed in spring or by semi-ripe cuttings in summer. Red spider mite, whitefly and aphids may cause problems. ⚠ All parts of most species, especially the fruits of *S. capsicastrum* and *S. pseudocapsicum*, can cause severe discomfort if ingested.
S. betaceum, syn. *Cyphomandra betacea, C. crassicaulis* (Tree tomato), illus. p.456.
S. capsicastrum (Winter cherry). Fairly slow-growing, evergreen, bushy subshrub, grown as an annual. **H** and **S** 30–45cm (1–1½ft). Half hardy. Has lance-shaped, deep green leaves. In summer bears small, star-shaped, white flowers, followed by egg-shaped, pointed, orange-red or scarlet fruits, at least 1cm (½in) in diameter, which are at their best in winter.
🏆 ***S. crispum* 'Glasnevin'** illus. p.204.
S. jasminoides. See *S. laxum*.
S. laxum, syn. *S. jasminoides* (Potato vine). Semi-evergreen, woody-stemmed, scrambling climber. **H** to 6m (20ft). Half hardy. Oval to lance-shaped leaves may be lobed or have leaflets at base. Small, 5-petalled, pale grey-blue flowers are produced in summer-autumn; tiny, purple berries appear in autumn. 🏆 **'Album'** illus. p.195.
S. pseudocapsicum (Jerusalem cherry). Fairly slow-growing, evergreen, bushy shrub, usually grown as an annual. **H** and **S** to 1.2m (4ft). Half hardy. Has oval or lance-shaped, bright green leaves. Small, star-shaped, white flowers appear in summer and are followed by spherical, scarlet fruits. Has several smaller selections: **'Balloon'** illus. p.327; **'Fancy'**, **H** 30cm (1ft), with scarlet fruits; **'Joker'** has yellow fruit turning orange and red; **'Red Giant'** illus. p.327; and **'Snowfire'**, **H** 30cm (1ft), with white fruits that later turn red.
S. rantonnei. See *Lycianthes rantonnetii.*
S. rantonnetii. See *Lycianthes rantonnetii.*
S. seaforthianum illus. p.463.
S. wendlandii illus. p.463.

SOLDANELLA

Snowbell

PRIMULACEAE

Genus of evergreen perennials, grown for their early spring flowers. Is good for rock gardens, troughs and alpine houses. Fully hardy, but flower buds are set in autumn and may be destroyed by frost if there is no snow cover. Requires partial shade and humus-rich, well-drained, peaty soil. Propagate by seed in spring or by division in late summer. Slugs may attack flower buds.
S. alpina (Alpine snowbell) illus. p.354.
S. minima (Least snowbell). Evergreen, prostrate perennial. **H** 2.5cm (1in), **S** 10cm (4in). Forms a mat of minute, rounded leaves on soil surface. In early spring produces solitary almost stemless, bell-shaped, pale lavender-blue or white flowers with fringed mouths.
S. montana (Mountain tassel). Evergreen, mound-forming perennial. **H** 10cm (4in), **S** 15cm (6in). In early spring produces tall flower stems bearing long, pendent, bell-shaped, lavender-blue flowers with fringed mouths. Leaves are rounded and leathery.
S. villosa illus. p.354.

SOLEIROLIA

Baby's tears, Mind-your-own-business, Mother of thousands

URTICACEAE

Genus of one species of usually evergreen, prostrate perennial that forms a dense carpet of foliage. Frost hardy, although leaves are killed by winter frost. Recovers to grow vigorously again in spring. Tolerates sun or shade, and prefers moist soil. Propagate by division from spring to mid-summer.
S. soleirolii, syn. *Helxine soleirolii*, illus. p.283.

SOLENOSTEMON

Flame nettle, Painted nettle

LABIATAE/LAMIACEAE

Genus of evergreen, bushy, subshrubby perennials, grown for their colourful leaves amd flowers. Makes excellent pot plants. Frost tender, min. 4–10°C (39–50°F). Grow in sun or partial shade and in fertile, well-drained soil, choosing a sheltered position. Water freely in summer, much less at other times. Pinch out growing shoots of young plants to encourage a bushy habit. Propagate by seed sown under glass in spring or by softwood cuttings in spring or summer. Mealy bugs and whitefly may cause problems.
***S.* 'Chocolate Mint'** illus. p.311.
S. scutellarioides, syn. *Coleus blumei* var. *verschaffeltii, Plectranthus scutellarioides.* Fast-growing, bushy perennial, grown as an annual. **H** to 45cm (18in), **S** 30cm (12in) or more. Leaves are a mixture of colours, including pink, red, green or yellow. Flower spikes should be removed. **'Brightness'** Has rust-red leaves, edged with green. **'Fashion Parade'** has multicoloured, serrated leaves of various shapes, from oval and unlobed to deeply lobed. **'Inky Fingers'** illus. p.311. **Kong Series 'Kong Scarlet'** illus. p.310. **'Scarlet Poncho'**, with a pendulous habit and oval, serrated, bright red leaves, and **Wizard Series**, also with oval, serrated leaves, but in a very wide range of leaf colours, are both dwarf forms, **H** 30cm (12in).

SOLIDAGO

Golden rod

COMPOSITAE/ASTERACEAE

Genus of summer- and autumn-flowering perennials, some species of which are vigorous, coarse plants that tend to crowd out others in borders. Fully hardy. Most tolerate sun or shade and any well-drained soil. Propagate by division in spring. Occasionally self-seeds.
***S.* 'Golden Wings'.** Upright perennial. **H** 1.5m (5ft), **S** 1m (3ft). Bears large, feathery panicles of small, bright yellow flower heads in early autumn. Has lance-shaped, toothed, hairy, mid-green leaves.
🏆 ***S.* 'Goldenmosa'** illus. p.251.
***S.* 'Laurin'.** Compact perennial. **H** 60–75cm (24–30in), **S** 45cm (18in). Has mid-green leaves. Bears spikes of deep yellow flowers in late summer.
S. x luteus, syn. x *Solidaster hybridus*, x *S. luteus*, illus. p.275.

S. virgaurea* subsp. *minuta, syn. *S.v.* subsp. *alpestris*. Mound-forming perennial. **H** and **S** 10cm (4in). Has small, lance-shaped, green leaves and, in autumn, neat spikes of small, yellow flower heads. Is suitable for a rock garden, trough or alpine house. Needs shade and moist soil.

x *Solidaster hybridus*. See *Solidago* x *hybridus*.
x *Solidaster luteus*. See *Solidago* x *luteus*.

SOLLYA
Bluebell creeper
PITTOSPORACEAE

Genus of evergreen, woody-based, twining climbers, grown for their attractive flowers. Half hardy. Grow in sun and well-drained soil. Propagate by seed in spring or by softwood or greenwood cuttings in summer.
♀ ***S. heterophylla*** illus. p.194.

SONERILA
MELASTOMATACEAE

Genus of evergreen, bushy perennials and shrubs, grown for their foliage and flowers. Frost tender, min. 15°C (59°F). Prefers a humid atmosphere in semi-shade and peaty soil. Propagate by tip cuttings in spring.
♀ ***S. margaritacea*.** Evergreen, bushy, semi-prostrate perennial. **H** and **S** 20–25cm (8–10in). Red stems produce oval, dark green leaves, 5–8cm (2–3in) long, reddish below, silver-patterned above. Has racemes of 3-petalled, rose-pink flowers in summer. **'Argentea'** has more silvery leaves with green veins; **'Hendersonii'** is more compact with white-spotted leaves.

SOPHORA
Kowhai
LEGUMINOSAE/PAPILIONACEAE

Genus of deciduous or semi-evergreen trees and shrubs, grown for their habit, foliage and flowers. Fully to frost hardy. Requires full sun (*S. microphylla* and *S. tetraptera* usually need to be grown against a south- or west-facing wall) and fertile, well-drained soil. Propagate by seed in autumn; semi-evergreens may also be raised from cuttings in summer.
S. davidii, syn. *S. viciifolia*, illus. p.138.
♀ ***S. japonica*** (Pagoda tree). Deciduous, spreading tree. **H** and **S** 20m (70ft). Fully hardy. Dark green leaves consist of 9–15 oval leaflets. On mature trees, long clusters of pea-like, creamy-white flowers appear in late summer and early autumn. Does best in hot summers. **'Pendula'**, **H** and **S** 3m (10ft), has long, hanging shoots clothed with dark green foliage. **'Violacea'** illus. p.67.
S. microphylla, syn. *Edwardsia microphylla*. Semi-evergreen, spreading tree. **H** and **S** 8m (25ft). Frost hardy. Dark green leaves are composed of numerous tiny, oblong leaflets. Produces clusters of pea-like, deep yellow flowers in late spring.
♀ ***S. tetraptera*** illus. p.84.
***S. viciifolia*.** See *S. davidii*.

x *Sophrolaeliocattleya* Hazel Boyd 'Apricot Glow'. See x *Cattlianthe* Hazel Boyd gx 'Apricot Glow'.
x *Sophrolaeliocattleya* Trizac gx 'Purple Emperor'. See *Cattleya Trizac* gx 'Purple Emperor'.

x SOPHROLAELIOCATTLEYA
ORCHIDACEAE

See also ORCHIDS.
x *S.* Trizac gx 'Purple Emperor', syn. x *Sophrolaeliocattleya* Trizac gx 'Purple Emperor'. Evergreen, epiphytic orchid for an intermediate greenhouse. **H** 10cm (4in). In spring, has crimson-lipped, pinkish-purple flowers, 6cm (2½in) across, in small heads. Has oval, rigid leaves, 10cm (4in) long. Provide good light in summer.

SORBARIA
ROSACEAE

Genus of deciduous, summer flowering shrubs, grown for their foliage and large panicles of small, white flowers. Fully hardy. Prefers sun and deep, fertile, moist soil. In winter, cut out some older stems on mature plants and prune back remaining shoots to growing points. Remove suckers at base to prevent *Sorbaria* spreading too widely. Propagate by softwood cuttings in summer, by division in autumn or by root cuttings in late winter.
***S. aitchisonii*.** See *S. tomentosa* var. *angustifolia*.
***S. arborea*.** See *S. kirilowii*.
S. kirilowii, syn. *S. arborea*, *Spiraea arborea*. Vigorous, deciduous, arching shrub. **H** and **S** 6m (20ft). Leaves are composed of 13–17 lance-shaped, taper-pointed, deep green leaflets. Nodding panicles of star-shaped, white flowers are produced in mid- and late summer.
S. sorbifolia, syn. *Spiraea sorbifolia*, illus. p.128.
♀ ***S. tomentosa* var. *angustifolia***, syn. *S. aitchisonii*, *Spiraea aitchisonii*. Deciduous, arching shrub. **H** and **S** 3m (10ft). Shoots are red when young. Leaves have 11–23 narrowly lance-shaped, taper-pointed, dark green leaflets. Upright panicles of star-shaped, white flowers are produced from mid- to late summer.

SORBUS
ROSACEAE

Genus of deciduous trees and shrubs, grown for their foliage, small, 5-petalled flowers, attractive fruits and, in some species, autumn colour. Leaves may be whole or divided into leaflets. Fully to frost hardy. Needs sun or semi-shade and fertile, well-drained but moist soil. Species with leaves composed of leaflets do not grow well in very dry soil. Propagate by softwood cuttings or budding in summer, by seed in autumn or by grafting in winter. Is susceptible to fireblight. ⓘ Raw fruit may cause mild stomach upset if ingested.
S. alnifolia (Korean mountain ash). Deciduous, conical, then spreading tree. **H** 15m (50ft), **S** 8m (25ft). Fully hardy. Oval, toothed, bright green leaves turn orange and red in autumn. Produces small, white flowers in late spring, then egg-shaped, orange-red fruits.
S. americana (American mountain ash). Deciduous, round-headed tree. **H** 10m (30ft), **S** 7m (22ft). Fully hardy. Light green leaves, divided into 11–17 narrowly oval leaflets, usually colour well in autumn. Bears small, white flowers in early summer, then rounded, bright red fruits, ripening in early autumn.
S. aria (Whitebeam). Deciduous, spreading tree. **H** 15m (50ft), **S** 10m (30ft). Fully hardy. Oval, toothed leaves are silver-grey when young, maturing to dark green above, white-felted beneath. Clusters of small, white flowers in late spring are followed by rounded, brown-speckled, deep red fruits. **'Chrysophylla'**, **H** 10m (30ft), **S** 7m (22ft), bears golden-yellow, young leaves. **'Decaisneana'** see *S.a.* 'Majestica'. ♀ **'Lutescens'** (illus. p.91) has orange-red fruits. ♀ **'Majestica'** (syn. *S.a.* 'Decaisneana') has larger leaves, white-haired when young, and larger fruits.
S. aucuparia (Mountain ash, Rowan; illus. p.91). Deciduous, spreading tree. **H** 15m (50ft), **S** 7m (22ft). Fully hardy. Leaves have mid-green leaflets that turn red or yellow in autumn. Bears white flowers in spring and red fruits in autumn. **'Fastigiata'** (syn. *S. scopulina* of gardens), **H** 8m (25ft), **S** 5m (15ft), is a conical tree with upright branches and dark green leaves. ♀ **'Fructu Luteo'** a spreading tree, **H** 15m (50ft), **S** 8m (25ft). Leaves consist of 13–15 narrowly oval, mid-green leaflets that turn yellow or red in autumn. Bears orange-yellow fruits. Fruits of **'Rossica Major'** (syn. *S.a.* 'Rossica') are large and deep red. ♀ **'Sheerwater Seedling'**, **S** 4m (12ft), has a narrow, upright habit.
♀ ***S. cashmiriana*** (illus. p.91). Deciduous, spreading tree. **H** 8m (25ft), **S** 7m (22ft). Has leaves consisting of 6–9 pairs of rich green leaflets. Pink-flushed, white flowers in early summer are followed by large, white fruits in autumn.
S. commixta, syn. *S. discolor* of gardens (illus. p.91). Vigorous, deciduous, spreading tree. **H** 10m (30ft), **S** 7m (22ft). Fully hardy. Leaves have 6–8 pairs of glossy, deep green leaflets that turn orange and red in autumn. White flowers in spring are followed by bright red fruits. ♀ **'Embley'**, **H** 12m (40ft), **S** 9m (28ft), has steeply ascending branches, bright red leaves, each with 13–17 leaflets, in late autumn, and fruits profusely.
***S. cuspidata*.** See *S. vestita*.
***S. decora*.** Deciduous, spreading, sometimes shrubby tree. **H** 10m (30ft), **S** 8m (25ft). Fully hardy. Leaves are composed of oblong, blue-green leaflets. Small, white flowers in late spring are succeeded by rounded, orange-red fruits.
S. discolor of gardens. See *S. commixta*.
S. esserteauana (illus. p.91). Deciduous, spreading tree. **H** and **S** 10m (30ft). Fully hardy. Dark green leaves, with broadly oblong leaflets, redden in autumn. Has small, white flowers in late spring, followed by large clusters of rounded, bright red, sometimes orange-yellow fruits.
S. forrestii (illus. p.91). Deciduous, spreading tree. **H** 6m (20ft), **S** 4m (13ft). Fully hardy. Bluish-green leaves, to 20cm (8in) long, have 15–19 oval to elliptic, toothed leaflets. Corymbs of creamy-white flowers, in spring, are followed by small, spherical, fleshy, white fruits, tinted crimson at the bases.
S. hupehensis (Hupeh rowan). Deciduous, spreading tree. **H** 12m (40ft), **S** 8m (25ft). Fully hardy. Leaves have 9–17 oblong, blue-green leaflets that turn orange-red in late autumn. Small, white flowers in late spring are followed by clusters of rounded, pink-tinged, white fruits. ♀ **var. *obtusa*** has heavy trusses of rose-pink fruits. **'Rosea'** See *S. pseudohupehensis*.
♀ ***S. hybrida* 'Gibbsii'.** Deciduous, compact tree. **H** to 7m (22ft), **S** 4m (13ft). Fully hardy. Broadly ovate, mid-green leaves, with grey undersides, are more deeply lobed towards the base. Produces large clusters of cream flowers in spring, followed by bright red fruits.
***S. insignis*.** Deciduous, spreading tree. **H** 8m (25ft), **S** 6m (20ft). Frost hardy. Leaves consist of usually 9–21 large, oblong, glossy, dark green leaflets. Large clusters of small, creamy-white flowers in late spring are followed by rounded, pink fruits that become white in winter.
S. intermedia (Swedish whitebeam; illus. p.91). Deciduous, broad-headed, dense tree. **H** and **S** 12m (40ft). Fully hardy. Has broadly oval, deeply lobed, dark green leaves. Carries clusters of small, white flowers in late spring, succeeded by rounded, red fruits.
***S.* 'Joseph Rock'.** Deciduous, upright tree. **H** 10m (30ft), **S** 7m (22ft). Bright green leaves composed of many leaflets turn orange, red and purple in autumn. White flowers in late spring are followed by large clusters of small, yellow berries in late summer and autumn.
S.* x *kewensis (illus. p.91), syn. *S. pohuashanensis* of gardens. Deciduous, spreading tree. **H** 10m (30ft), **S** 8m (25ft). Fully hardy. Dark green leaves are divided into 11–15 oblong leaflets. Has small, white flowers in late spring, followed by dense clusters of rounded, red fruits.
S. latifolia (Service tree of Fontainebleau). Deciduous, spreading tree. **H** 12m (40ft), **S** 10m (30ft). Fully hardy. Has peeling bark and broadly oval, sharply lobed, glossy, dark green leaves. Small, white flowers in late spring are succeeded by rounded, brownish-red fruits.
S. megalocarpa (illus. p.91). Deciduous, spreading tree with stout branches. **H** to 7m (22ft), **S** 4m (13ft). Fully hardy. Has oval, coarsely toothed, dark green leaves. Corymbs of pungent, creamy-white flowers in spring] are followed by speckled-brown fruits.
***S.* 'Mitchellii'.** See *S. thibetica* 'John Mitchell'.
S. pohuashanensis of gardens. See *S.* x *kewensis*.
***S. prattii*.** Deciduous, spreading tree. **H** and **S** 6m (20ft). Fully hardy. Dark green leaves are divided into 21–9 oblong, sharply toothed leaflets. Produces small, white flowers in late spring, followed by rounded, white fruits
♀ ***S. pseudohupehensis*** (syn. *S. hupehensis* 'Rosea') illus. p.73.
♀ ***S. reducta*** illus. p.346.
♀ ***S. sargentiana*** (Sargent's rowan; illus. p.91). Deciduous, sparsely branched, spreading tree. **H** and **S** 6m (20ft). Fully hardy. Has stout shoots and large, mid-

S

green leaves, consisting of 7–11 oblong leaflets, that turn brilliant red in autumn. Small, white flowers in late spring are succeeded by rounded, red fruits.
S. scalaris (illus. p.91). Deciduous, spreading, graceful tree. **H** and **S** 10m (30ft). Fully hardy. Produces leaves with 21–33 narrowly oblong, glossy, deep green leaflets that become deep red and purple in autumn. Produces small, white flowers in late spring, followed by rounded, red fruits in large, dense clusters.
S. scopulina of gardens. See *S. aucuparia* 'Fastigiata'.
S. thibetica. Deciduous, conical tree. **H** 20m (70ft), **S** 15m (50ft). Fully hardy. Large, broadly oval, dark green leaves are silvery-white when young and remain so on undersides. Heads of small, white flowers in late spring are followed by rounded, brown fruits. 🏆 **'John Mitchell'** (syn. *S.* 'Mitchellii'; illus. p.91) has white flowers in spring and brown fruits in late summer.
S. x thuringiaca. Deciduous, broadly conical, compact tree. **H** 12m (40ft), **S** 8m (25ft). Fully hardy. Oval, dark green leaves are deeply lobed and have 3 pairs of basal leaflets. Small, white flowers appear in late spring, followed by rounded, bright red fruits. **'Fastigiata'** has upright branches and a broad, oval, dense crown. **'Scarlet King'** produces bright scarlet-red fruits in larger trusses and has large leaves bearing up to 6 pairs of leaflets.
S. vestita. syn. *S. cuspidata*. Deciduous, broadly conical tree. **H** to 25m (80ft), **S** 10m (30ft). Has very large, veined, grey-green leaves, white-haired when young. Heads of pink-stamened, white flowers in late spring or early summer are followed by russet or yellowish-red fruits.
🏆 **S. vilmorinii** (illus. p.91). Deciduous, spreading, arching, elegant tree. **H** and **S** 5m (15ft). Leaves of 9–14 pairs of dark green leaflets turn to orange- or bronze-red in autumn. Has white blooms in late spring and small, deep pink fruits in autumn.
S. 'Wilfred Fox'. Deciduous tree, upright when young, later with a dense, oval head. **H** 15m (50ft), **S** 10m (30ft). Fully hardy. Has broadly oval, glossy, dark green leaves and small, white flowers in late spring, followed by rounded, orange-brown fruits.

SPARAXIS

Harlequin flower

IRIDACEAE

Genus of spring- and early summer-flowering corms, grown for their very gaudy flowers. Half hardy. Needs a sunny, well-drained site. Plant in autumn. Dry off corms after flowering. Propagate by offsets in late summer or by seed in autumn.
S. elegans, syn. *Streptanthera cuprea, S. elegans*. Spring-flowering corm. **H** 10–25cm (4–10in), **S** 8–12cm (3–5in). Has lance-shaped leaves in an erect, basal fan. Stem produces a loose spike of 1–5 flattish, orange or white blooms, each 3–4cm (1¼–1½in) wide and with a yellow centre surrounded by a purple-black band.
S. fragrans subsp. grandiflora, syn. *S. grandiflora*. Spring-flowering corm. **H** 15–40cm (6–16in), **S** 8–12cm (3–5in). Has sword-shaped leaves in an erect, basal fan. Stem bears a loose spike of up to 5 flattish, yellow-tubed, deep purple flowers, each 4–5cm (1½–2in) across.
S. grandiflora. See *S. fragrans* subsp. *grandiflora*.
S. tricolor illus. p.418.

SPARGANIUM

Bur reed

SPARGANIACEAE/TYPHACEAE

Genus of deciduous or semi-evergreen, perennial, marginal water plants, grown for their foliage. Fully hardy. Tolerates deep shade and cold water. Remove faded foliage and cut plants back regularly to control growth. Propagate by seed or division in spring.
S. erectum, syn. *S. ramosum*, illus. p.442.
S. minimum. See *S. natans*.
S. natans, syn. *S. minimum* (Least bur reed). Vigorous, deciduous or semi-evergreen, perennial, marginal water plant. **H** 30cm–1m (1–3ft), **S** 30cm (1ft). Mid-green leaves are grass-like, some erect, some floating. In summer has insignificant, brownish-green flowers, in the form of burs.
S. ramosum. See *S. erectum*.

SPARRMANNIA

SYN. SPARMANNIA

African hemp

TILIACEAE/SPARRMANNIACEAE

Genus of evergreen trees and shrubs, grown for their flowers and foliage. Frost tender, min. 7°C (45°F). Prefers a position in full light and fertile, well-drained soil. Water freely when in full growth, moderately at other times. Flowered stems may be cut back after flowering to promote a more compact habit. Propagate by greenwood cuttings in late spring.
🏆 **S. africana** illus. p.453.

SPARTINA

GRAMINEAE/POACEAE

See also GRASSES, BAMBOOS, RUSHES and SEDGES.
S. pectinata 'Aureomarginata', syn. *S.p.* 'Aureovariegata', illus. p.289.

SPARTIUM

LEGUMINOSAE/PAPILIONACEAE

Genus of one species of deciduous, almost leafless shrub, grown for its green shoots and showy flowers. Frost hardy. Needs sun and not too rich, well-drained soil. To maintain a compact habit, trim in early spring. Propagate by seed in autumn.
🏆 **S. junceum** illus. p.140.

SPATHIPHYLLUM

ARACEAE

Genus of evergreen perennials, with rhizomes, grown for their foliage and flowers. Frost tender, min. 15°C (59°F). Prefers a humid atmosphere, humus-rich, moist soil and partial shade. Propagate by division in spring or summer. ⓘ All parts of the plants may cause mild stomach upset if ingested, and contact with the sap may irritate skin.
S. 'Clevelandii'. See *S. wallisii* 'Clevelandii'.
S. floribundum. Evergreen, tufted, short-stemmed perennial. **H** and **S** to 30cm (1ft). Has clusters of lance-shaped, long-pointed, long-stalked, glossy, dark green leaves, to 15cm (6in) long. Intermittently, bears narrowly oval, white spathes, to 8cm (3in) long, each enclosing a green-and-white spadix.
🏆 **S. 'Mauna Loa'** illus. p.468.
S. wallisii illus. p.468. **'Clevelandii'** (syn. *S.* 'Clevelandii') is an evergreen, tufted perennial. **H** and **S** to 60cm (2ft). Has broadly lance-shaped, semi-erect, glossy, mid-green leaves, 30cm (1ft) or more long. Intermittently bears oval, white spathes, each 15cm (6in) long with a central, green line, that surround fragrant, white spadices.

SPATHODEA

BIGNONIACEAE

Genus of evergreen trees, grown for their flowers, mainly from autumn to spring, and for their overall appearance. Frost tender, min. 16–18°C (61–4°F). Needs full light and fertile, well-drained but moisture-retentive soil. Container-grown and immature plants seldom bear flowers. Propagate by seed in spring or by semi-ripe cuttings in summer.
S. campanulata (African tulip tree) illus. p.453.

SPECKLINIA

BIGNONIACEAE

See also ORCHIDS.
S. grobyi. Evergreen, epiphytic orchid for a cool greenhouse. **H** 2.5cm (1in). In summer produces sprays of minute, white flowers, 0.25cm (⅛in) long. Leaves are oval, fleshy and 0.5cm (¼in) long. Provide shade in summer.

SPHAERALCEA

MALVACEAE

Genus of perennials and deciduous subshrubs, evergreen in warm climates. Half hardy. Requires a warm, sunny situation and fertile, well-drained soil. Propagate by seed or division in spring, softwood cuttings in mid-summer.
S. ambigua illus. p.246.
S. munroana. Branching, woody- based perennial. **H** and **S** 45cm (18in). Broadly funnel-shaped, brilliant coral-pink flowers are borne singly in leaf axils from summer until first frosts. Has oval, round-toothed, hairy, mid-green leaves.

Sphaeropteris. See *Cyathea*.

SPIRAEA

ROSACEAE

Genus of deciduous or semi-evergreen shrubs, grown for their mass of small flowers and, in some species, their foliage. Fully hardy. Requires sun and fertile, well-drained but not over-dry soil. On species and cultivars that flower on the current year's growth – *S. x billiardii, S. douglasii* and *S. japonica* and its cultivars – cut back young stems and remove very old ones in early spring. On species that flower on old wood, cut out older shoots in early spring, leaving young shoots to flower that year. Propagate *S. douglasii* by division between late autumn and early spring, other species and cultivars by softwood cuttings in summer.
S. aitchisonii. See *Sorbaria tomentosa* var. *angustifolia*.
S. arborea. See *Sorbaria kirilowii*.
S. 'Arguta' (Bridal wreath, Foam of May). Deciduous, arching, dense shrub. **H** and **S** 2.5m (8ft). Produces clusters of 5-petalled, white flowers from mid- to late spring. Leaves are narrowly oblong and bright green.
S. aruncus. See *Aruncus dioicus*.
S. x billiardii. Deciduous, upright, dense shrub. **H** and **S** 2.5m (8ft). Has oval, finely toothed, dark green leaves and dense panicles of 5-petalled, pink flowers in summer. **'Triumphans'** has large, broadly conical panicles of bright purplish-pink flowers.
S. canescens illus. p.128.
S. douglasii. Vigorous, deciduous, upright shrub. **H** and **S** 2m (6ft). Dense, narrow panicles of 5-petalled, purplish-pink flowers are borne from early to mid-summer among oblong, mid-green leaves with grey-white undersides. Leaves of **subsp. menziesii**, **H** 1m (3ft), are green on both sides.
S. japonica 'Anthony Waterer' illus. p.154, **'Goldflame'** illus. p.156, and **'Little Princess'** illus. p.153.
S. nipponica. Deciduous, arching shrub. **H** and **S** 2.5m (8ft). Bears dense clusters of 5-petalled, white flowers in early summer. Stout, red shoots carry small, rounded, dark green leaves. **'Halward's Silver'**, **H** and **S** 1m (3ft), is slow-growing, very dense and flowers profusely.
🏆 **'Snowmound'** (syn. *S.n.* var. *tosaensis* of gardens) illus. p.131.
S. prunifolia. Deciduous, arching, graceful shrub. **H** and **S** 2m (6ft). In mid- and late spring has clusters of rosette-like, double, white flowers amid rounded to oblong, bright green leaves, colouring to bronze-yellow in autumn.
S. 'Snow White', syn. *S. trichocarpa* 'Snow White'. Deciduous, arching shrub. **H** and **S** 2m (6ft). Leaves are oblong and mid-green. Dense clusters of 5-petalled, white flowers are borne in late spring and early summer.
S. sorbifolia. See *Sorbaria sorbifolia*.
🏆 **S. thunbergii.** Deciduous or semi-evergreen, arching, dense shrub. **H** 1.5m (5ft), **S** 2m (6ft). Small clusters of 5-petalled, white flowers are borne from early to mid-spring. Has narrowly oblong, pale green leaves.
S. trichocarpa 'Snow White'. See *S.* 'Snow White'.
S. trilobata. Deciduous, arching, graceful shrub. **H** 1m (3ft), **S** 1.5m (5ft). In early summer bears 5-petalled, white flowers in clusters along slender shoots. Has rounded, shallowly lobed, toothed, blue-green leaves.
S. ulmaria. See *Filipendula ulmaria*.
S. x vanhouttei illus. p.145.
S. veitchii. Vigorous, deciduous, upright shrub. **H** and **S** 3m (10ft). Has arching, red branches and oblong, dark green leaves. Produces heads of 5-petalled, white flowers from early to mid-summer.

S

SPIRANTHES

ORCHIDACEAE

See also ORCHIDS.

S. cernua (illus. p.466). Deciduous, terrestrial orchid. **H** 50cm (20in). Frost hardy. Spikes of delicate, white flowers, 1cm (½in) long, with pale yellow centres, appear in autumn. Has narrowly lance-shaped leaves, 5–12cm (2–5in) long. Requires semi-shade in summer.

SPREKELIA

AMARYLLIDACEAE

Genus of one species of bulb, grown for its showy, red flowers in spring. Half hardy. Needs an open, sunny site and well-drained soil. Keep dry in winter; start into growth by watering in spring. Propagate by offsets in early autumn.

S. formosissima illus. p.402.

STACHYS

LABIATAE/LAMIACEAE

Genus of late spring- or summer-flowering perennials, shrubs and subshrubs, some of which are evergreen. Fully hardy to frost tender, min. 5°C (41°F). Grows in any well-drained soil, tolerating even poor soil. Species mentioned below prefer an open, sunny position; others are woodland plants and grow better in semi-shade. Propagate by division in spring.

S. byzantina, syn. *S. lanata, S. olympica*, illus. p.274. **'Primrose Heron'** illus. p.275. **'Silver Carpet'** is an evergreen, mat-forming perennial. **H** 15cm (6in), **S** 60cm (24in). Fully hardy. Has oval, woolly, grey leaves. Rarely produces flowers. Makes an excellent front-of-border or ground-cover plant.

S. coccinea. Clump-forming perennial. **H** 60cm (24in), **S** 45cm (18in). Frost tender. Has oval, mid-green leaves with a pronounced network of veins. From early to late summer, spikes of small, hooded, bright scarlet flowers, protruding from purple calyces, arise from leaf axils.

S. lanata. See *S. byzantina.*

S. macrantha. Clump-forming perennial. **H** and **S** 30cm (12in). Fully hardy. Has heart-shaped, crinkled, round-toothed, soft green leaves. Whorls of large, hooded, rose-purple flowers are produced in summer. **'Superba'** illus. p.270.

S. officinalis, syn. *Betonica officinalis* (Betony). Mat-forming perennial. **H** 45–60cm (18–24in), **S** 30–45cm (12–18in). Fully hardy. Produces whorls of hooded, tubular, purple, pink or white flowers on sturdy stems, arising, in summer, from mats of oval to oblong, round-toothed, mid-green leaves. **'Hummelo'** illus. p268. **'Rosea'** has flowers of clearer pink.

S. olympica. See *S. byzantina.*

STACHYURUS

STACHYURACEAE

Genus of deciduous shrubs, grown for their flowers, which are borne before the leaves. Fully to half hardy; flower spikes, formed in autumn, are usually unharmed by hard frosts. Requires a position in sun or semi-shade, and fertile, moist but well-drained, not too heavy soil, preferably peaty and acid. Does well when trained against a south- or west-facing wall. Propagate by softwood cuttings in summer.

S. chinensis. Deciduous, spreading, open shrub. **H** 2m (6ft), **S** 4m (12ft). Fully hardy. Pendent spikes of small, bell-shaped, pale yellow flowers open in late winter and early spring. Leaves are oval and deep green.

♀ ***S. praecox*** illus. p.144. **'Magpie'** is a deciduous, spreading, open shrub, less vigorous than the species. **H** 1.5m (5ft), **S** 2m (6ft). Has arching, red-purple shoots and oval, tapered, grey-green leaves, edged with creamy-white. Bell-shaped, pale yellow flowers are borne in late winter and early spring.

STANHOPEA

ORCHIDACEAE

See also ORCHIDS.

S. tigrina. Evergreen, epiphytic orchid for a cool greenhouse. **H** 23cm (9in). Pendent spikes of fragrant, waxy, rich yellow and maroon flowers, 15cm (6in) across, with red-spotted, white lips, are produced in summer. Has broadly oval, ribbed leaves, 30cm (12in) long. Is best grown in a hanging, slatted basket. Provide semi-shade in summer.

STAPELIA

ASCLEPIADACEAE/APOCYNACEAE

Genus of clump-forming, perennial succulents with erect, 4-angled stems. Stem edges are often indented and may bear small leaves that drop after only a few weeks. Flowers are often foul-smelling. Frost tender, min. 11°C (52°F). Requires a position in sun or partial shade, and moderately fertile, gritty, well-drained soil. Propagate by seed or stem cuttings in spring or summer.

S. europaea. See *Caralluma europaea.*

S. flavirostris. See *S. grandiflora.*

♀ ***S. gigantea*** illus. p.496.

S. grandiflora, syn. *S. flavirostris*, illus. p.488.

S. variegata. See *Orbea variegata.*

STAPHYLEA

Bladder nut

STAPHYLEACEAE

Genus of deciduous, spring-flowering shrubs and trees, grown for their flowers and bladder-like fruits. Fully hardy. Requires sun or semi-shade and fertile, moist soil. Propagate species by softwood or greenwood cuttings in summer or by seed in autumn, selected forms by softwood or greenwood cuttings in summer.

S. colchica. Deciduous, upright shrub. **H** and **S** 3.5m (11ft). Erect panicles of bell-shaped, white flowers are borne in late spring and are followed by inflated, greenish-white fruits. Bright green leaves each consist of 3–5 oval leaflets.

***S. holocarpa* 'Rosea'** illus. p.111.

S. pinnata illus. p.110.

Statice. See *Limonium* except for: ***S. suworowii*** for which see *Psylliostachys suworowii.*

STAUNTONIA

LARDIZABALACEAE

Genus of evergreen, woody-stemmed, twining climbers. Male and female flowers are produced on separate plants. Frost hardy. Grow in any well-drained soil and in sun or semi-shade. Prune in early spring. Propagate by seed in spring or by stem cuttings in summer or autumn.

S. hexaphylla illus. p.192.

STENANTHIUM

LILIACEAE/MELANTHIACEAE

Genus of summer-flowering bulbs, attractive but seldom cultivated. Frost hardy. Needs an open, sunny position in any well-drained soil. In cool areas, plant in a warm, sheltered site in light soil that does not dry out excessively. Propagate by seed in autumn or by division in spring.

S. gramineum. Summer-flowering bulb. **H** to 1.5m (5ft), **S** 45–60cm (1½–2ft). Has long, narrowly strap-shaped, semi-erect, basal leaves. Stem produces a dense, branched, often arching spike of fragrant, star-shaped, white or green flowers, each 1–1.5cm (½–⅝in) across.

STENOCACTUS

SYN. ECHINOFOSSULOCACTUS

CACTACEAE

Genus of spherical, perennial cacti with spiny, green stems that have very narrow, wavy ribs. Frost tender, min. 7°C (45°F). Needs sun and well-drained soil. Water well during the growing season, much less when dormant in winter as it may rot off. Propagate by seed in spring or summer.

S. coptonogonus illus. p.487.

S. crispatus syn. *Echinofossulatus lamellosus.* Spherical, perennial cactus. **H** and **S** 8cm (3in). Green stem has 30–35 ribs. Funnel-shaped, flesh-coloured or red flowers, 1–3cm (½–1¼in) across, are produced from crown in spring. Has flattened upper radial spines, shorter, more rounded lower ones and longer, rounded central spines with darker tips.

S. lamellosus. See *S. obvallatus.*

S. obvallatus, syn. *Echinofossulatus pentacanthus, E. violaciflorus, Stenocactus lamellosus*, illus. p.484.

STENOCARPUS

PROTEACEAE

Genus of evergreen, summer- and autumn-flowering trees, grown for their flowers and foliage. Frost tender, min. 5–7°C (41–5°F). Needs full light and fertile, well-drained soil. Water containerized plants moderately, less in winter. Pruning is rarely necessary. Propagate by seed in spring or by semi-ripe cuttings in summer.

S. sinuatus (Australian firewheel tree). Slow-growing, evergreen, upright tree. **H** 12m (40ft) or more, **S** 5m (15ft). Has lustrous, deep green leaves, each 12–25cm (5–10in) long, lance-shaped and entire or with pairs of oblong lobes. Bottle-shaped, bright scarlet flowers, clustered like the spokes of a wheel, are produced from late summer to autumn.

STENOCEREUS

CACTACEAE

Genus of tree-like or shrubby, perennial cacti with prominently ribbed stems often densely spined. Frost tender, min. 13°C (55°F), otherwise plants may become badly marked. Needs full sun and very well-drained soil. Propagate by seed in spring or stem cuttings in summer.

S. marginatus. See *Pachycereus marginatus.*

S. thurberi, syn. *Lemaireocereus thurberi.* Columnar, perennial cactus, branching from low down. **H** to 7m (22ft), **S** 1m (3ft). Has 5–6-ribbed, glossy, dark green stems with very short-spined areoles set in close rows down each rib. Produces funnel-shaped, purple or pink flowers with red sepals in summer.

Stenolobium stans. See *Tecoma stans.*

STENOMESSON

AMARYLLIDACEAE

Genus of about 13 species of bulbs, grown for their long, often pendent, tubular flowers. Frost tender, min. 5–10°C (41–50°F). Needs an open, sunny situation and well-drained soil. Propagate by offsets in autumn.

S. miniatum, syn. *Urceolina peruviana*, illus. p.407.

S. variegatum illus. p.407.

STENOTAPHRUM

GRAMINEAE/POACEAE

See also GRASSES, BAMBOOS, RUSHES and SEDGES.

S. secundatum (St Augustine grass) ♀ **'Variegatum'** is an evergreen, spreading, rhizomatous, perennial grass. **H** 15cm (6in), **S** indefinite. Frost tender, min. 5°C (41°F). Cream-striped, mid-green leaves last well into winter. In summer has erect racemes of brownish-green spikelets. In warm climates is used for a lawn.

STEPHANANDRA

ROSACEAE

Genus of deciduous, summer-flowering shrubs, grown for their habit, foliage, autumn colour and winter shoots. Fully hardy. Needs sun or semi-shade and fertile, not too dry soil. On established plants, cut out some older shoots after flowering. Propagate by softwood cuttings in summer or by division in autumn.

S. incisa. Deciduous, arching shrub. **H** 1.5m (5ft), **S** 3m (10ft). Oval, deeply lobed and toothed, bright green leaves turn orange-yellow in autumn and stems become rich brown in winter. Produces crowded panicles of tiny, star-shaped, greenish-white flowers in early summer. **'Crispa'**, **H** 60cm (2ft), has wavy-edged and more deeply lobed leaves.

S. tanakae illus. p.132.

STEPHANOTIS

ASCLEPIADACEAE/APOCYNACEAE

Genus of evergreen, woody-stemmed, twining climbers, grown for their scented, waxy flowers. Frost tender, min. 13–16°C (55–61°F). Provide a humus-rich, well-drained soil and partial shade in summer. Water moderately, less in cold weather. Provide stems with support. Shorten over-long or crowded stems in spring. Propagate by seed in spring or by semi-ripe cuttings in summer.

♀ ***S. floribunda*** illus. p.460.

Sterculia acerifolia. See *Brachychiton acerifolius.*
Sterculia diversifolia. See *Brachychiton populneus.*
Sterculia platanifolia. See *Firmiana simplex.*

STERNBERGIA

AMARYLLIDACEAE

Genus of spring- or autumn-flowering bulbs, grown for their large, crocus-like flowers. Frost hardy, but in cool areas grow against a sunny wall. Needs full sun and any well-drained, heavy or light soil that dries out in summer, when bulbs die down and need warmth and dryness. Leave undisturbed to form clumps. Propagate by division in spring or autumn.
S. candida illus. p.415.
S. clusiana. Autumn-flowering bulb. **H** to 2cm (¾in), **S** 8–10cm (3–4in). Strap-shaped, semi-erect, basal, greyish-green leaves, often twisted lengthways, appear after flowering. Stems carry erect, goblet-shaped, yellow or greenish-yellow flowers, 4–8cm (1½–3in) long.
S. lutea. Autumn-flowering bulb. **H** 2.5–15cm (1–6in), **S** 8–10cm (3–4in). Has strap-shaped, semi-erect, basal, deep green leaves appearing together with a funnel-shaped, bright yellow flower, 2.5–6cm (1–2½in) long, on a leafless stem.
S. sicula. Autumn-flowering bulb. **H** 2.5–7cm (1–3in), **S** 5–8cm (2–3in). Narrowly strap-shaped, semi-erect, basal, deep green leaves, each with a central, paler green stripe, appear with flowers. Each stem bears a funnel-shaped, bright yellow flower, 2–4cm (¾–1½in) long.

STETSONIA

CACTACEAE

Genus of one species of tree-like, perennial cactus with a stout trunk. Nocturnal, funnel-shaped flowers are 15cm (6in) long. Frost tender, min. 10°C (50°F). Needs a sunny, well-drained position. Propagate by seed in spring or summer.
S. coryne. Tree-like, perennial cactus. **H** 8m (25ft), **S** 4m (12ft). Has a short, swollen trunk bearing 8- or 9-ribbed, blue-green stems. Black spines fade with age to white with black tips. Funnel-shaped, white flowers appear at night in summer.

STEWARTIA

SYN. STUARTIA

THEACEAE

Genus of deciduous trees and shrubs, grown for their flowers, autumn colour and usually peeling bark. Fully to frost hardy. Needs a sunny position, but preferably with roots in shade, and shelter from strong winds. Requires fertile, moist but well-drained, neutral to acid soil. Resents being transplanted. Propagate by softwood cuttings in summer or by seed in autumn.
S. malacodendron. Deciduous, spreading tree or shrub. **H** 4m (12ft), **S** 3m (10ft). Frost hardy. Rose-like, purple-stamened, white flowers, some-times purple-streaked, are borne in mid-summer amid oval, dark green leaves.
S. monadelpha illus. p.76.
♀ ***S. pseudocamellia*** (illus. p.78). Deciduous, spreading tree. **H** 20m (70ft), **S** 8m (25ft). Fully hardy. Has ornamental, peeling bark and bears white flowers in mid-summer. Foliage is mid-green, turning orange and red in autumn.
♀ ***S. sinensis.*** Deciduous, spreading tree. **H** 12m (40ft), **S** 7m (22ft). Fully hardy. Has peeling bark and oval, bright green leaves that turn brilliant red in autumn. Fragrant, rose-like, white flowers are produced in mid-summer.

STIGMAPHYLLON

MALPIGHIACEAE

Genus of evergreen, woody-stemmed, twining climbers, grown for their flowers. Frost tender, min. 15–18°C (59–64°F). Fertile, well-drained soil is needed with partial shade in summer. Water freely when in full growth, less in low temperatures. Provide stems with support. Thin out crowded stems in spring. Propagate by semi-ripe cuttings in summer.
S. ciliatum illus. p.464.

STIPA

GRAMINEAE/POACEAE

See also GRASSES, BAMBOOS, RUSHES and SEDGES.
S. arundinacea. See *Anemanthele lessoniana.*
S. calamagrostis illus. p.286.
♀ ***S. gigantea*** illus. p.287.
♀ ***S. lessoniana*** illus. p.289.
S. tenuissima illus. p.288.

STOKESIA

COMPOSITAE/ASTERACEAE

Genus of one species of evergreen, summer-flowering perennial. Fully hardy. Requires sun or semi-shade and fertile, well-drained soil. Propagate by division in spring or by seed in autumn.
S. laevis illus. p.269. **'Blue Star'** is an evergreen, basal-rosetted perennial. **H** and **S** 30–45cm (12–18in). Bears cornflower-like, deep blue flower heads singly at stem tips in summer. Has rosettes of narrowly lance-shaped, dark green leaves.

STOMATIUM

AIZOACEAE

Genus of mat-forming, perennial succulents with short stems, each bearing 4–6 pairs of solid, 3-angled or semi-cylindrical leaves, often with toothed edges and incurved tips. Frost tender, min. 5°C (41°F). Needs sun and well-drained soil. Propagate by seed or stem cuttings in spring or summer.
S. agninum. Mat-forming, perennial succulent. **H** 5cm (2in), **S** 1m (3ft) or more. Has solid, 3-angled or semi-cylindrical, soft grey-green leaves, 4–5cm (1½–2in) long, often without teeth. In summer, fragrant, daisy-like, yellow flowers, 2–5cm (¾–2in) across, open in evening.
S. patulum. Mat-forming, perennial succulent. **H** 3cm (1¼in), **S** 1m (3ft). Has semi-cylindrical, grey-green leaves, each 2cm (¾in) long, with rough dots and 2–9 teeth-like tubercles on upper surface. Bears 2cm (¾in) wide, fragrant, daisy-like, pale yellow flowers in evening in summer.

Strangweja spicata. See *Bellevalia hyacinthoides.*

STRATIOTES

HYDROCHARITACEAE

Genus of semi-evergreen, perennial, submerged, free-floating water plants, grown for their foliage. Fully hardy. Requires sun. Grows in any depth of cool water. Thin plants as required. Propagate by separating young plants from runners in summer.
S. aloides illus. p.435.

STRELITZIA

Bird-of-paradise flower

MUSACEAE/STRELITZIACEAE

Genus of large, evergreen, tufted, clump-forming, palm-like perennials, grown for their showy flowers. Frost tender, min. 5–10°C (41–50°F). Grow in fertile, well-drained soil and in bright light shaded from direct sun in summer. Reduce watering in low temperatures. Propagate by seed or division of suckers in spring.
S. nicolai. Evergreen, palm-like perennial with a stout trunk. **H** 8m (25ft), **S** 5m (15ft). Has leaves, 1.5m (5ft) or more long, on very long stalks and intermittently bears beak-like, white and pale blue flowers in boat-shaped, dark purple bracts..
♀ ***S. reginae*** illus. p.476.

Streptanthera cuprea. See *Sparaxis elegans.*
Streptanthera elegans. See *Sparaxis elegans.*

STREPTOCARPUS

GESNERIACEAE

Genus of perennials, some of which are evergreen, with showy flowers. Frost tender, min. 10–15°C (50–59°F). Grow in a humid atmosphere in humus-rich, moist soil and in bright light away from direct sunlight. Avoid wetting leaves when watering; water less during cold periods. Propagate by seed in spring, by division after flowering or by tip cuttings from bushy species or leaf cuttings from stemless species in spring or summer.
♀ ***S.*** **'Amanda'** illus. p.473.
S. caulescens. Erect perennial. **H** and **S** 45cm (18in) or more. Has small, narrow to oval, fleshy, dark green leaves. Stalked clusters of small, tubular, violet-striped, violet or white flowers are carried in leaf axils intermittently.
S. **'Constant Nymph'.** Evergreen, stemless perennial. **H** 25cm (10in), **S** 50cm (20in). Has a rosette of strap-shaped, wrinkled leaves. Funnel-shaped, purplish-blue flowers, darker veined and yellow-throated, are intermittently produced in small clusters.
♀ ***S.*** **'Crystal Ice'** illus. p.465.
S. kentaniensis. Herbaceous, stemless perennial. **H** 25cm (10in), **S** 20cm (8in). Has loose whorls of narrowly lance-shaped, wrinkled, hairy, dark green leaves, with a prominent mid-vein, held semi-erect. Clusters of 2–5 small, white flowers, with a radiating, violet vein pattern, are borne mainly in winter but can appear all year long under ideal conditions.
S. **'Nicola'** illus. p.469.
S. rexii (Cape primrose). Stemless perennial. **H** to 25cm (10in), **S** to 50cm (20in). Has a rosette of strap-shaped, wrinkled, green leaves. Stems, 15cm (6in) or more long, bear loose clusters of funnel-shaped, pale blue or mauve flowers, 5cm (2in) long and with darker lines, intermittently at any time of year.
♀ ***S. saxorum*** illus. p.310.

STREPTOSOLEN

SOLANACEAE

Genus of one species of evergreen or semi-evergreen, loosely scrambling shrub, grown for its flowers. Frost tender, min. 7–10°C (45–50°F). Requires full sun and humus-rich, well-drained soil. Water freely when in full growth, less at other times. After flowering or in spring, remove flowered shoots and tie in new growths. Propagate by softwood or semi-ripe cuttings in summer.
♀ ***S. jamesonii*** illus. p.464.

STROBILANTHES

ACANTHACEAE

Genus of perennials and evergreen subshrubs, grown for their flowers. Frost hardy to frost tender, min. 15°C (59°F). Grow in semi-shade in fertile, well-drained soil. Propagate by seed, basal stem cuttings or division in spring.
S. atropurpurea illus. p.250.
♀ ***S. dyerinanus*** illus. p.311.
S. **Purple Shield.** See *Strobilanthes dyerinanus.*

STROMANTHE

MARANTACEAE

Genus of evergreen, creeping perennials, grown mainly for their foliage. Frost tender, min. 15°C (59°F). Prefers high humidity and partial shade. Grow in open soil or compost, use soft water if possible and do not allow to dry out completely. Propagate by division in spring.
S. sanguinea. Strong-growing, evergreen, creeping perennial. **H** and **S** to 1.5m (5ft). Lance-shaped leaves, to 45cm (18in) long, are glossy, green above with paler midribs, reddish below. Bears panicles of small, 3 petalled, white flowers in axils of showy, bright red bracts, usually in spring but also in summer-autumn.

STROMBOCACTUS

CACTACEAE

Genus of extremely slow-growing, hemispherical to cylindrical, perennial cacti. Takes 5 years from seed to reach 1cm (½in) high. Funnel-shaped flowers are 4cm

(1½in) across. Frost tender, min. 5°C (41°F). Needs sun and very well-drained soil. Susceptible to overwatering. Propagate by seed in spring or summer.
S. disciformis illus. p.481.

STRONGYLODON

LEGUMINOSAE/PAPILIONACEAE

Genus of evergreen, woody-stemmed, twining climbers, grown for their large, claw-like flowers. Frost tender, min. 18°C (64°F). Needs humus-rich, moist but well-drained soil and partial shade in summer. Water freely when in full growth, less at other times. Provide support. If necessary, thin crowded stems in spring. Propagate by seed or stem cuttings in summer or by layering in spring.
S. macrobotrys (Jade vine). Fast-growing, evergreen, woody-stemmed, twining climber. **H** to 20m (70ft). Leaves have 3 oval, glossy leaflets. Has claw-like, luminous, blue-green flowers in long, pendent spikes in winter–spring.

STYLIDIUM

STYLIDIACEAE

Genus of perennials with grass-like leaves, grown for their unusual flowers that have fused, "triggered" stamens adapted for pollination by insects. Frost tender, min. 10°C (50°F). Grow in fertile soil and in bright light. Propagate by seed in spring.
S. graminifolium (Trigger plant). Rosetted perennial. **H** and **S** to 15cm (6in) or more. Grass-like, stiff, dark green leaves, with toothed margins, rise from ground level. Bears tiny, pale pinkish-mauve flowers in narrow spikes, 30cm (12in) or more long, in summer.

STYLOPHORUM

PAPAVERACEAE

Genus of spring-flowering perennials with large, deeply lobed leaves, nearly all as basal rosettes. Fully hardy. Needs semi-shade and humus-rich, moist, peaty soil. Propagate by division in spring or by seed in autumn.
S. diphyllum. Perennial with basal rosettes of large, lobed, hairy leaves. **H** and **S** to 30cm (12in) or more. Bears open cup-shaped, golden-yellow flowers in spring on upright, branched stems. Prefers rich, woodland conditions.

STYRAX

STYRACACEAE

Genus of deciduous, summer-flowering trees and shrubs, grown for their foliage and flowers. Fully hardy to frost tender, min. 7–10°C (45–50°F). Prefers a sheltered position in sun or semi-shade and moist, neutral to acid soil. Propagate by softwood cuttings in summer or by seed in autumn.
♀ ***S. japonicus*** illus. p.72.
♀ ***S. obassia*** (Fragrant snowbell). Deciduous, spreading tree. **H** 12m (40ft), **S** 7m (22ft). Fully hardy. Bears long, spreading clusters of fragrant, bell- to funnel-shaped, white flowers in early summer. Has rounded green leaves.
S. officinalis illus. p.112.
S. wilsonii illus. p.129.

Sulcorebutia arenacea. See *Rebutia arenacea.*
Sulcorebutia rauschii. See *Rebutia steinmannii.*
Sulcorebutia tiraquensis. See *Rebutia steinmannii* subsp. *tiraquensis.*
Sutera grandiflora. See *Jamesbrittenia grandiflora.*

SUTERA

SCROPHULARIACEAE

A genus of some 60 species of creeping perennial half hardy perennials, often found in wet places. Grown for showy, but small, flowers in hanging baskets and containers. Propagate cultivars by cuttings, or seed. Grow in full sun and moist soil.
***S. cordata* Snowstorm Series Giant Snowflake ('Danova906')** illus. p.298.
***S.* 'Danova906'**. See *S. cordata* Snowstorm Series Giant Snowflake.
♀ ***B.* 'Snowflake' H** 10cm, **S** 20 cm or more. Trailing perennial, freely branching, half hardy perennial, with small heart shaped, hairy leaves 1–2 cm wide. Flowers white, 5-lobed, 2 cm wide, with yellow stamens, borne towards shoot tips.

SUTHERLANDIA

LEGUMINOSAE/PAPILIONACEAE

Genus of evergreen shrubs, grown for their flowers and fruits. Frost tender, min. 7–10°C (45–50°F). Requires full light and fertile, well-drained soil. Water containerized specimens freely when in full growth, moderately at other times. Remove old, twiggy stems at ground level in late winter. Propagate by seed in spring. Red spider mite may be troublesome.
S. frutescens illus. p.456.

SWAINSONA

LEGUMINOSAE/PAPILIONACEAE

Genus of annuals, evergreen perennials, subshrubs and shrubs, grown for their flowers. Frost tender, min. 5–7°C (41–5°F). Needs full light or partial shade and humus-rich, well-drained soil. Water freely when in active growth, moderately at other times. Propagate by seed in spring or by semi-ripe cuttings in summer.
S. galegifolia (Darling pea). Evergreen, sprawling subshrub. **H** 60cm–1.2m (2–4ft), **S** 30–60cm (1–2ft). Leaves have 11–25 narrowly oval, mid- to deep green leaflets. Bears pea-like, red, pink, purple, blue or yellow flowers in late spring and summer. Remove old, flowered shoots in late winter.

SYAGRUS

Queen palm

PALMAE/ARECACEAE

Genus of one species of evergreen palm, grown for its majestic appearance. Frost tender, min. 18°C (64°F). Requires full light or partial shade and humus-rich, well-drained soil. Water containerized specimens moderately, less when temperatures are low. Propagate by seed in spring at not less than 24°C (75°F). Red spider mite may be a nuisance.
S. romanzoffiana (Queen palm). Sturdy, evergreen palm. **H** to 20m (70ft), **S** 6–10m (20–30ft). Has feather-shaped leaves with lustrous, green leaflets. Mature trees bear clusters of yellow flowers in summer.

SYCOPSIS

HAMAMELIDACEAE

Genus of evergreen trees and shrubs, grown for their foliage and flowers. Frost hardy. Needs a sheltered position in sun or semi-shade and fertile, not too dry, peaty soil. Propagate by semi-ripe cuttings in summer.
S. sinensis. Evergreen, upright shrub. **H** 5m (15ft), **S** 4m (12ft). Leaves are oval, glossy and dark green. Flowers lack petals but have showy, dense clusters of red-tinged, yellow anthers in late winter or early spring.

SYMPHORICARPOS

CAPRIFOLIACEAE

Genus of deciduous shrubs, with inconspicuous, bell-shaped flowers, grown mainly for their clusters of showy, long-persistent fruits. Fully hardy. Requires sun or semi-shade and fertile soil. Propagate by softwood cuttings in summer or by division in autumn. ⓘ Fruits may cause mild stomach upset if ingested; contact with them may irritate skin.
S. albus (Snowberry). **var. *laevigatus*** (illus. p.142) is a vigorous, deciduous, dense shrub, part upright, part arching. **H** and **S** 2m (6ft). Large, marble-like, white fruits follow pink flowers borne in summer. Rounded leaves are dark green.
***S. x chenaultii* 'Hancock'.** Deciduous, procumbent, dense shrub. **H** 1m (3ft), **S** 3m (10ft). Has oval, bronze leaves maturing to bright green. White flowers appear from early to mid-summer. Small, spherical, deep lilac-pink fruits are sparsely borne. Makes excellent ground cover.
S. orbiculatus (Coralberry, Indian currant). Deciduous, bushy, dense shrub. **H** and **S** 2m (6ft). Has white or pink flowers in late summer and early autumn, then spherical, deep purplish-red fruits. Oval leaves are dark green. Does best after a hot summer. **'Foliis Variegatis'** (syn. *S.o.* 'Variegatus') illus. p.160.

Symphandra armena. See *Campanula armena.*
Symphandra pendula. See. *Campanula pendula.*
Symphandra wanneri. See *Campanula wanneri.*

SYMPHYTUM

Comfrey

BORAGINACEAE

Genus of vigorous, coarse perennials, best suited to wild gardens. Fully hardy. Prefers sun or semi-shade and moist soil. Propagate by division in spring or by seed in autumn; usually self-seeds. Propagate named cultivars by division only. ⓘ Roots and leaves may cause severe discomfort if ingested; contact with foliage may irritate skin.
♀ ***S. caucasicum*** illus. p.227.
***S.* 'Goldsmith'**, syn. *S. ibericum* 'Jubilee', *S. ibericum* 'Variegatum', *S.* 'Jubilee'. Clump-forming perennial. **H** and **S** 30cm (12in). Has ovate, hairy, dark green leaves with gold and cream markings. Bears pale blue flowers, tinged cream or pink, in spring.
S. grandiflorum of gardens. See *S. ibericum.*
***S.* 'Hidcote Blue'.** Clump-forming perennial. **H** 50cm (20in), **S** 60cm (24in). Is similar to *S. ibericum*, but has pale blue flowers.
S. ibericum, syn. *S. grandiflorum* of gardens. Clump-forming perennial. **H** 25cm (10in), **S** 60cm (24in). Has lance-shaped, hairy, rich green leaves. Bears one-sided racemes of tubular, creamy flowers in spring. Makes good ground cover. **'Jubilee'** see *S.* 'Goldsmith'. **'Variegatum'** see *S.* 'Goldsmith'.
***S.* 'Jubilee'.** See *S.* 'Goldsmith'.
S. x uplandicum (Russian comfrey). ♀ **'Variegatum'** illus. p.227.

SYMPLOCOS

SYMPLOCACEAE

Genus of evergreen or deciduous trees and shrubs, of which only the species described is in general cultivation. This is grown for its flowers and fruits. Fruits are most prolific when several plants are grown together. Fully hardy. Needs full sun and fertile, moist but well-drained soil. Propagate by seed in autumn.
S. paniculata (Sapphire berry; illus. p.142). Deciduous, bushy shrub or small tree. **H** and **S** 5m (15ft). Has dark green leaves. Panicles of small, fragrant, white flowers in late spring and early summer are followed by small, metallic blue fruits.

***Synadenium compactum* var. *rubrum*.** See *Euphorbia bicompacta* var. *rubra.*
***Synadenium grantii* of gardens 'Rubrum'.** See *Euphorbia bicompacta* var. *rubra.*

SYNGONIUM

ARACEAE

Genus of evergreen, woody-stemmed, root climbers, grown for their ornamental foliage. Flowers are seldom produced in cultivation. Frost tender, min. 16–18°C (61–4°F). Needs partial shade and humus-rich, well-drained soil. Water moderately, less in low temperatures. Provide support, ideally with moss poles. Remove young stem tips to promote branching. Propagate by leaf-bud or stem-tip cuttings in summer. ⓘ All parts may cause mild stomach upset if ingested; contact with the sap may irritate skin.
S. auritum, syn. *Philodendron auritum* of gardens *P. trifoliatum*, (Five fingers). Fairly slow-growing, evergreen, woody-stemmed, root climber. **H** 1–2m (3–6ft). Has glossy, rich green leaves divided into 3, sometimes 5, oval leaflets, the central one the largest.
S. erythrophyllum. Slow-growing, evergreen, root climber with slender, woody stems. **H** 1m (3ft) or more. Young plants have arrowhead-shaped leaves, flushed purple beneath. Leaves on mature plants have 3 lobes or leaflets and thicker, longer stems.

S

S. hoffmannii. Moderately vigorous, evergreen, woody-stemmed, root climber. **H** 2–3m (6–10ft). Young plants have arrowhead-shaped leaves; mature ones have leaves divided into 3 grey-green leaflets with silvery-white veins.
♀ ***S. podophyllum***, syn. *Nephthytis triphylla* of gardens, illus. p.463. **'Trileaf Wonder'** illus. p.460.

SYNNOTIA

IRIDACEAE

Genus of spring-flowering corms, with fans of lance-shaped leaves, grown for their loose spikes of flowers, each with 6 unequal petals, hooded like a small gladiolus. Half hardy. Needs sun and well-drained soil. Plant in autumn. Dry off after flowering. Propagate by seed or offsets in autumn.
S. variegata. Spring-flowering corm. **H** 10–35cm (4–14in), **S** 8–10cm (3–4in). Produces erect leaves in a basal fan. Flowers are long-tubed with upright, purple, upper petals and narrower, pale yellowish-purple, lower ones curving downwards. **var. *metelerkampiae*** produces smaller flowers.

SYNTHYRIS

SCROPHULARIACEAE

Genus of evergreen or deciduous, spring-flowering perennials with gently spreading, rhizomatous rootstocks. Is useful for rock gardens and peat beds. Fully hardy. Prefers partial shade and moist soil. Propagate in late spring by seed or division.
***S. missurica* var. *stellata*.** See *S. stellata*.
S. reniformis. Evergreen, clump-forming perennial. **H** 8–10cm (3–4in), **S** 15cm (6in). Has kidney-shaped to rounded, toothed, dark green leaves and, in spring, short, dense racemes of small, bell-shaped, blue flowers.
S. stellata, syn. *S. missurica* var. *stellata*, illus. p.355.

SYRINGA

Lilac

OLEACEAE

Genus of deciduous shrubs and trees, grown for their dense panicles of small, tubular flowers, usually extremely fragrant. Fully hardy. Needs sun and deep, fertile, well-drained, preferably alkaline soil. Obtain plants on their own roots, since grafted plants usually sucker freely. Remove flower heads from newly planted lilacs, and dead-head for first few years. Cut out weak shoots in winter and, to maintain shape, prune after flowering. Straggly, old plants may be cut back hard in winter, but the next season's flowers will then be lost. Propagate by softwood cuttings in summer. Leaf miners, leaf spot and lilac blight may be troublesome. See also feature panel p.115.
***S.* 'Belle de Nancy'.** See *S. vulgaris* 'Belle de Nancy'.
***S.* 'Bellicent'.** See *S.* x *josiflexa* 'Bellicent'.
***S.* 'Blue Hyacinth'.** See *S.* x *hyacinthiflora* 'Blue Hyacinth'.
***S.* 'Charles Joly'.** See *S. vulgaris* 'Charles Joly'.
S.* x *chinensis (Rouen lilac). Deciduous, arching shrub. **H** and **S** 4m (12ft). Bears large, arching panicles of fragrant, tubular, single, lilac-purple flowers in late spring. Oval leaves are dark green. **'Alba'** has white flowers.
***S.* 'Clarke's Giant'.** See *S.* x *hyacinthiflora* 'Clarke's Giant'.
***S.* 'Congo'.** See *S. vulgaris* 'Congo'.
***S.* 'Cora Brandt'.** See *S.* x *hyacinthiflora* 'Cora Brandt'.
***S.* 'Decaisne'.** See *S. vulgaris* 'Decaisne'.
S. emodi (Himalayan lilac). Vigorous, deciduous, upright shrub. **H** 5m (15ft), **S** 4m (12ft). Bears unpleasantly scented, tubular, single, very pale lilac flowers in large, upright panicles in early summer. Has large, oval, dark green leaves.
***S.* 'Esther Staley'.** See *S.* x *hyacinthiflora* 'Esther Staley'.
***S.* 'Fountain'.** Vigorous, deciduous, arching, open shrub. **H** 4m (12ft), **S** 5m (15ft). Large, nodding panicles of fragrant, tubular, single, deep pink flowers open above large, oval, dark green leaves in early summer.
***S.* x *hyacinthiflora* 'Blue Hyacinth'**, syn. *S.* 'Blue Hyacinth'. Deciduous, bushy shrub, upright when young, later spreading. **H** and **S** 3m (10ft). Bears large, loose panicles of fragrant, single, pale lilac-blue flowers from mid-spring to early summer and has broadly heart-shaped, mid-green leaves. Vigorous **'Clarke's Giant'** (syn. *S.* 'Clarke's Giant'), **H** and **S** 5m (15ft), has lavender flowers, mauve-pink within, opening from mauve-pink buds from mid- to late spring. Has dark green leaves. **'Cora Brandt'** (syn. *S.* 'Cora Brandt') produces double, white flowers in large open panicles. ♀ **'Esther Staley'** (syn. *S.* 'Esther Staley') is vigorous, with broadly conical panicles of red buds opening to lilac-pink flowers.
***S.* 'Isabella'.** See *S.* x *prestoniae* 'Isabella'.
***S.* 'Jan van Tol'.** See *S. vulgaris* 'Jan van Tol'.
♀ ***S.* x *josiflexa* 'Bellicent'**, syn. *S.* 'Bellicent'. Deciduous, upright, then arching shrub. **H** 4m (12ft), **S** 5m (15ft). Large panicles of fragrant, tubular, single, clear pink flowers are borne above oval, dark green leaves in late spring and early summer.
***S.* 'Katherine Havemeyer'.** See *S. vulgaris* 'Katherine Havemeyer'.
S. komarowii* subsp. *reflexa (illus. p.115). Vigorous, upright shrub. **H** and **S** 4m (13ft). Stout stems bear elliptic–oblong, dark green leaves. Rich purple-pink flowers are borne in slender, nodding panicles in late spring and early summer.
***S.* 'Madame Antoine Buchner'.** See *S. vulgaris* 'Madame Antoine Buchner'.
***S.* 'Madame F. Morel'.** See *S. vulgaris* 'Madame F. Morel'.
***S.* 'Madame Florent Stepman'.** See *S. vulgaris* 'Madame Florent Stepman'.
***S.* 'Madame Lemoine'.** See *S. vulgaris* 'Madame Lemoine'.
***S.* 'Maréchal Foch'.** See *S. vulgaris* 'Maréchal Foch'.
***S.* 'Masséna'.** See *S. vulgaris* 'Masséna'.
***S.* 'Maud Notcutt'.** See *S. vulgaris* 'Maud Notcutt'.
♀ ***S. meyeri* 'Palibin'**, syn. *S. palibianina* of gardens, *S. velutina* of gardens (illus. p.115). Slow-growing, deciduous, bushy, dense shrub. **H** 1.5–2m (5–6ft), **S** 1.5m (5ft). Has small, oval, deep green leaves. Produces dense panicles of fragrant, tubular, single, lilac-pink flowers in late spring and early summer.
***S.* 'Michel Buchner'.** See *S. vulgaris* 'Michel Buchner'.
S. microphylla. See *S. pubescens* subsp. *microphylla*.
***S.* 'Monge'.** See *S. vulgaris* 'Monge'.
***S.* 'Mrs Edward Harding'.** See *S. vulgaris* 'Mrs Edward Harding'.
S. palibiniana of gardens. See *S. meyeri* 'Palibin'.
***S.* 'Paul Thirion'.** See *S. vulgaris* 'Paul Thirion'.
♀ ***S.* x *persica*** (Persian lilac; illus. p.115). Deciduous, bushy, dense shrub. **H** and **S** 2m (6ft). Produces small, dense panicles of fragrant, purple flowers in late spring. Leaves are narrow, pointed and dark green. ♀**'Alba'** (illus. p.115) has white flowers.
***S.* 'Président Grévy'.** See *S. vulgaris* 'Président Grévy'.
***S.* x *prestoniae* 'Isabella'**, syn. *S.* 'Isabella'. Vigorous, deciduous, upright shrub. **H** and **S** 4m (12ft). Has large, nodding panicles of fragrant, tubular, single, lilac-purple flowers, almost white within, in early summer, and large, oval, dark green leaves.
***S.* 'Primrose'.** See *S. vulgaris* 'Primrose'.
S. pubescens* subsp. *microphylla, syn. *S. microphylla*. Deciduous, bushy shrub. **H** and **S** 2m (6ft). Small panicles of very fragrant, tubular, single, pink flowers appear in early summer, and often again in autumn, amid oval, mid-green leaves.
♀**subsp. *patula* 'Miss Kim'** (illus. p.115) bears purple flowers maturing to bluish-white. ♀ **'Superba'** (illus. p.115).
S. reticulata. Deciduous, broadly conical tree or shrub. **H** 10m (30ft), **S** 6m (20ft). Large panicles of fragrant, tubular, single, creamy-white flowers open above oval, taper-pointed, bright green leaves from early to mid-summer.
***S.* 'Souvenir de Louis Spaeth'.** See *S. vulgaris* 'Andenken an Ludwig Spaeth'.
S. velutina of gardens. See *S. meyeri* 'Palibin'.
S. vulgaris. ♀ **'Andenken an Ludwig Späth'** (syn. *S.* 'Souvenir de Louis Späth'; illus. p.115) is a deciduous, upright, then spreading shrub. **H** and **S** 5m (15ft). Long, slender panicles of fragrant, tubular, single, deep purplish-red flowers are borne profusely above heart-shaped, dark green leaves in late spring. **'Belle de Nancy'** (syn. *S.* 'Belle de Nancy') has large, dense panicles of double, mauve-pink flowers opening from purple-red buds.
♀ **'Charles Joly'** (syn. *S.* 'Charles Joly'), **H** and **S** 3m (10ft), carries deep purple-red flowers from mid-spring to early summer. **'Congo'** (syn. *S.* 'Congo'), bears large panicles of single, deep lilac-purple flowers, purplish-red in bud, in spring. **'Decaisne'** (syn. *S.* 'Decaisne'), is compact, with masses of single, dark blue flowers that are shaded purple, and mid-green leaves. ♀**'Firmament'** (illus. p.115) bears masses of lilac-blue flowers in mid-spring. **'Jan van Tol'** (syn. *S.* 'Jan van Tol'), bears long, semi-pendent panicles of single, narrow-petalled, pure white flowers. ♀ **'Katherine Havemeyer'** (syn. *S.* 'Katherine Havemeyer'; illus. p.115) has double, lavender-purple, then lavender-pink flowers in dense, conical panicles. **'Madame Antoine Buchner'** (syn. *S.* 'Madame Antoine Buchner'), carries long, narrow panicles of deep purple-red buds, which open to double, pinkish-mauve flowers, fading with age. **'Madame F. Morel'** (syn. *S.* 'Madame F. Morel'), produces large panicles of single, light violet-purple flowers that are purple in bud. **'Madame Florent Stepman'** (syn. *S.* 'Madame Florent Stepman') illus p.113. ♀ **'Madame Lemoine'** (syn. *S.* 'Madame Lemoine'; illus. p.115.) bears compact panicles of large, double, white flowers. **'Maréchal Foch'** (syn. *S.* 'Maréchal Foch'), has broad, open panicles of very large, single, carmine-pink flowers. **'Masséna'** (syn. *S.* 'Masséna'), bears loose panicles of large, deep red-purple flowers. **'Maud Notcutt'** (syn. *S.* 'Maud Notcutt') produces large panicles of single, pure white flowers. **'Michel Buchner'** (syn. *S.* 'Michel Buchner'), has large panicles of double, pink-lilac flowers, each with a white eye. **'Monge'** (syn. *S.* 'Monge'), produces masses of very large, single, deep purple-red flowers. ♀ **'Mrs Edward Harding'** (syn. *S.* 'Mrs Edward Harding'), has large panicles of double or semi-double, purple-red flowers that fade to pink. **'Paul Thirion'** (syn. *S.* 'Paul Thirion'), carries double lilac-pink flowers that open from deep purple-red buds. **'Président Grévy'** (syn. *S.* 'Président Grévy'), bears very large panicles of double, lilac-blue flowers that open from red-violet buds. **'Primrose'** (syn. *S.* 'Primrose'), has small, dense panicles of pale yellow flowers.
S. yunnanensis. Deciduous, upright shrub. **H** 3m (10ft), **S** to 3m (10ft). In early summer, large, oval, pointed, dark green leaves set off slender panicles of 4-petalled, pale pink or white flowers.

SYZYGIUM

MYRTACEAE

Genus of evergreen shrubs and trees, grown for their overall appearance. Frost tender, min. 10–13°C (50–56°F). Prefers full light (but tolerates some shade) and fertile, well-drained soil. Water potted plants freely when in full growth, moderately at other times. Is very tolerant of pruning, but is best grown naturally. Propagate by seed in spring or semi-ripe cuttings in summer.
S. paniculatum, syn. *Eugenia australis* of gardens, *E. paniculata*, illus. p.450.

T

TABEBUIA

BIGNONIACEAE

Genus of deciduous or evergreen, mainly spring-flowering trees, grown for their flowers and for shade. Frost tender, min. 16–18°C (61–4°F). Requires full light and fertile, well-drained but not dry soil. Pot-grown plants are unlikely to flower. Pruning, other than shaping while young in autumn, is not needed. Propagate by seed or air-layering in spring or by semi-ripe cuttings in summer.
T. chrysotricha (Golden trumpet tree) illus. p.452.
T. donnell-smithii. See *Cybistax donnell-smithii.*
T. pentaphylla of gardens. See *T. rosea.*
T. rosea, syn. *T. pentaphylla* of gardens (Pink trumpet tree). Fast-growing, evergreen, rounded tree, deciduous in cool climates. **H** and **S** 15m (50ft) or more. Leaves have 5 oval leaflets. Produces trumpet-shaped rose- to lavender-pink or white flowers, with yellow throats, in terminal clusters in spring.

TACCA

TACCACEAE/DIOSCOREACEAE

Genus of perennials with rhizomes, grown for their curious flowers. Frost tender, min. 18°C (64°F). Needs a fairly humid atmosphere, partial shade and peaty soil. Water sparingly during resting period in winter. Propagate by division or seed, if available, in spring.
T. chantrieri (Bat flower, Cat's whiskers). Clump-forming, rhizomatous perennial. **H** and **S** 30cm (1ft). Narrowly oblong, stalked, arching leaves are 45cm (1½ft) or more long. In summer produces flower umbels with green or purplish bracts on stems up to 60cm (2ft) long. Individual flowers are nodding, bell-shaped, 6-petalled and green, turning purple with long, pendent, maroon to purple threads.
T. leontopetaloides (East Indian arrowroot, South Sea arrowroot). Clump-forming, rhizomatous perennial. **H** and **S** 45cm (1½ft). Green leaves, to 1m (3ft) long, are deeply 3-lobed, each lobe also divided, on stalks to over 1m (3ft). In summer, on stems up to 1m (3ft) long, flower umbels are produced with 4–12 purple or brown bracts and 20–40 small, 6-petalled, yellow or purplish-green flowers, with long, purple to brown threads. Rhizomes yield edible starch.

Tacitus bellus.
See *Graptopetalum bellum.*
Tacsonia mollissima.
See *Passiflora mollissima.*
Tacsonia van-volxemii.
See *Passiflora antioquiensis.*

TAGETES

COMPOSITAE/ASTERACEAE

Genus of annuals that flower continuously throughout summer and until the autumn frosts. Is useful as bedding plants and for edging. Half hardy. Grow in sun and in fertile, well-drained soil. Dead-head to ensure a long flowering period. Propagate by seed sown under glass in mid-spring. Is prone to slugs, snails and botrytis. The African marigolds are excellent for formal bedding, whereas the French, Afro-French, and Signet marigolds are more suitable for the edge of a mixed border. All are good in containers and provide long-lasting cut flowers. ⚠ Contact with the foliage may aggravate skin allergies. Four main hybrid groups are grown.
African marigolds (African Group)
Compact annuals, derived from *T. erecta*, with angular, hairless stems and pinnate, sparsely glandular leaves, 5–10cm (2–4in) long, each with 11–17 narrowly lance-shaped, pointed, sharply toothed leaflets, to 5cm (2in) long. Large, densely double, pompon-like, terminal flower heads, usually to 12cm (5in) across, each with 5–8 or more ray-florets and numerous orange to yellow disc-florets, are produced from late spring to autumn. **S** to 45cm (18in).
French marigolds (French Group)
Compact annuals, derived from *T. patula*, with hairless, purple-tinged stems and pinnate leaves, to 10cm (4in) long, with lance-shaped to narrowly lance-shaped, toothed leaflets, to 3cm (1¼in) long. Solitary, usually double flower heads, typically to 5cm (2in) across, with few to many red-brown, yellow, orange, or parti-coloured ray-florets and usually several disc-florets, are borne singly or in cyme-like inflorescences from late spring to autumn. **S** to 30cm (12in).
Afro-French marigolds (Afro-French Group)
Bushy annuals, derived from crosses of *T. erecta* and *T. patula*, with angular to rounded stems, branched and sometimes stained purple, and pinnate leaves, 5–13cm (2–5in) long, with lance-shaped leaflets, to 5cm (2in) long. Numerous small, single or double, yellow or orange flower heads, usually 2.5–6cm (1–2½in) across, often marked red-brown, are borne singly or in cyme-like inflorescences from late spring to autumn. **S** 30–40cm (12–16in).
Signet marigolds (Signet Group)
Upright annuals, derived from *T. tenuifolia*, with cylindrical, simple or many-branched stems and pinnate leaves, 5–13cm (2–5in) long, with narrowly lance-shaped, toothed leaflets, to 2cm (¾ in) long. Many single flower heads, usually to 2.5cm (1in) across, with yellow or orange florets (few ray-florets and several disc-florets), are borne in cyme-like inflorescences from late spring to autumn. **S** to 40cm (16in).

***T.* Antigua Series**. Compact African marigolds. **H** to 30cm (12in). Bear orange, lemon-yellow, golden-yellow, or primrose-yellow flower heads from late spring to early autumn.
***T.* Beaux Series.** Afro-French marigolds. **H** 35cm (14in). Bear double flower heads of rich golden-yellow, orange with a red splash, or copper-red, from late spring to early autumn.
🏆 ***T.* Bonanza Series.** French marigolds. **H** 30cm (12in). In summer, they have double flowers in deep orange-mahogany with gold margins, golden orange-mahogany, or orange-yellow-mahogany.
***T.* Boy Series** Compact French marigolds. **H** 20–30cm (8–12in). Have divided, mid-green leaves. Produce double, crested flower heads in shades of orange, yellow, gold, mahogany red, and yellow with mahogany brown centres from late spring to summer. [Orange], illus. p.324.
***T.* 'Cinnabar'** illus. p.308.
***T.* Disco Series.** French marigolds. **H** 20–25cm (8–10in). Single, weather-resistant flower heads in a range of colours, including yellow, golden-yellow with mahogany markings, golden-red and red-orange, are borne from late spring to early autumn.
T. erecta (African marigold, Aztec marigold). Fast-growing, upright, bushy annual. **H** 30cm–1m (1–3ft), **S** 30–45cm (1–1½ft). Has very deeply divided, aromatic, glossy, deep green leaves. Daisy-like, double flower heads, 5cm (2in) wide, are carried in summer and early autumn.
***T.* Gem Series.** Signet marigolds. **H** to 23cm (9in). Produce flower heads in lemon-yellow, deep orange, or bright orange with darker markings. **'Lemon Gem'** has lemon-yellow flower heads. **'Tangerine Gem'** illus. p.326.
🏆 ***T.* Gold Coins Series** illus. p.320.
🏆 ***T.* 'Honeycomb'.** French marigold. **H** 25cm (10in). Produces crested, double, yellow- and reddish-orange flower heads.
***T.* Lady Series.** African marigolds. **H** 40–45cm (16–18in). Produce orange, primrose-yellow, yellow, or golden-yellow flower heads from late spring to early autumn.
***T.* Marvel Series.** Compact African marigolds. **H** 45cm (18in). Produce densely double flower heads in gold, orange, yellow, lemon-yellow, or in a formula mixture of colours, from late spring to early autumn.
***T.* Mischief Series.** French marigolds. **H** to 30cm (12in) or more. Have single flower heads in mahogany-red, yellow, or golden-yellow, with some bicolours, from late spring to early autumn.
***T.* 'Naughty Marietta'** illus. p.322.
T. patula (French marigold). Fast-growing, bushy annual. **H** and **S** to 30cm (1ft). Has deeply divided, aromatic, deep green leaves. Single or carnation-like, double flower heads, in shades of yellow, orange, red or mahogany, are borne in summer and early autumn.
🏆 ***T.* Safari Series 'Safari Tangerine'.** French marigolds. **H** 20–25cm (8–10in). Has double, broad-petalled, rich tangerine-orange flower heads from late spring to early autumn.
***T.* 'Vanilla'.** African marigold. **H** to 35cm (14in). Has creamy-white flower heads from late spring to early autumn.
***T.* Voyager Series.** Compact African marigolds. **H** 30–35cm (12–14in). Large, yellow or orange flower heads, to 10cm (4in) across, are borne from late spring to early autumn.
***T.* Zenith Series.** Afro-French marigolds. **H** 30cm (12in). Have flower heads in yellow, golden-yellow, lemon-yellow, red, or orange, from late spring to early autumn.

Talbotia elegans. See *Vellozia elegans.*

TALINUM

PORTULACACEAE

Genus of summer-flowering perennials, some of which are evergreen, grown for their flowers and succulent foliage. Is useful for rock gardens, troughs and alpine houses and as pot plants. Fully hardy to frost tender, min. 7°C (45°F). Needs sun and gritty, not too dry, well-drained soil. Propagate by seed in autumn.
T. okanoganense. syn. *T. sediforme, Phemeranthus sediformis.* Cushion-or mat-forming, prostrate perennial. H to 4cm (1½in), S to 10cm (4in). Fully hardy. Succulent stems produce tufts of cylindrical, succulent, greyish-green leaves. Tiny, cup-shaped, white flowers are borne in summer. Is excellent for cultivating in a trough or alpine house.

TAMARINDUS

LEGUMINOSAE/CAESALPINIACEAE

Genus of one species of evergreen tree, grown for its edible fruits and overall appearance as well as for shade. Frost tender, min. 15–18°C (59–64°F). Needs full light and well-drained soil. Propagate by seed or air-layering in spring.
T. indica (Tamarind). Slow-growing, evergreen, rounded tree. **H** and **S** to 25m (80ft). Leaves have 10–15 pairs of oblong to elliptic, bright green leaflets. Produces profuse racemes of asymmetric, 5-petalled, pale yellow flowers, veined red, in summer, then long, brownish pods containing edible but acidic pulp.

TAMARIX

Tamarisk

TAMARICACEAE

Genus of deciduous or evergreen shrubs and trees, grown for their foliage, habit and abundant racemes of small flowers. In mild areas is very wind-resistant and thrives in exposed, coastal positions, making excellent hedges. Fully to frost hardy. Requires sun and fertile, well-drained soil. Restrict growth by cutting back in spring; trim hedges at the same time. Propagate by semi-ripe cuttings in summer or by hardwood cuttings taken in winter.
T. gallica. Deciduous, spreading shrub or tree. **H** 4m (12ft), **S** 6m (20ft). Frost hardy. Purple, young shoots are clothed with tiny, scale-like, blue-grey leaves. Star-shaped, pink flowers are borne in slender racemes in summer.
T. pentandra. See *T. ramosissima.*
T. ramosissima, syn. *T. pentandra*, illus. p.114.

TANACETUM

COMPOSITAE/ASTERACEAE

Genus of perennials, some of which are evergreen, often with aromatic foliage, grown for their daisy-like flower heads. Fully to frost hardy. Grow in sun and in fertile, well-drained soil. Propagate by division in spring. ⚠ Contact with the foliage may aggravate skin allergies. *T. parthenium* will self-seed freely.
T. argenteum, syn. *Achillea argentea*, illus. p.346.

T. coccineum, syn. *Chrysanthemum coccineum, Pyrethrum coccineum, Pyrethrum roseum* (Pyrethrum). **'Brenda'** (syn. *Pyrethrum* 'Brenda') is an erect perennial, **H** 60cm (24in), **S** 45cm (18in) or more. Fully hardy. Has somewhat aromatic, feathery leaves. Single, magenta-pink flower heads are borne in late spring and early summer.
♀ **'Eileen May Robinson'** illus. p.232.
♀ **'James Kelway'** has deep crimson flower heads ageing to pink.
T. densum* subsp. *amani, syn. *Chrysanthemum densum*, illus. p.347.
T. haradjanii, syn. *Chrysanthemum haradjanii*. Evergreen, mat-forming, woody-based perennial with a tap root. **H** and **S** 23–38cm (9–15in). Frost hardy. Has broadly lance-shaped, much-divided, silvery-grey leaves and, in summer, terminal clusters of bright yellow flower heads. Is useful for a rock garden or an alpine house.
T. parthenium (Feverfew), syn. *Chrysanthemum parthenium, Pyrethrum parthenium*, illus. p.300. **'Aureum'** is a short-lived, bushy perennial, grown as an annual. **H** and **S** 20–45cm (8–18in). Half hardy. Has oval, lobed, aromatic, green-gold leaves and, in summer and early autumn, daisy-like, white flower heads.

TANAKAEA

SAXIFRAGACEAE

Genus of one species of evergreen, spreading perennial, grown for its foliage and flowers. Is suitable for rock gardens and peat beds. Fully hardy. Needs partial shade and well-drained, peaty, sandy soil. Propagate by runners in spring.
T. radicans. Evergreen, dense, basal-rosetted perennial. **H** 6–8cm (2½–3in), **S** 20cm (8in). Leaves are narrowly oval to heart-shaped, leathery and mid- to dark green. Bears small panicles of tiny, outward-facing, star-shaped, white flowers in late spring.

TAPEINOCHILOS

COSTACEAE/ZINGIBERACEAE

Genus of mostly evergreen perennials, grown for their colourful, leaf-like bracts. Frost tender, min. 18°C (64°F). Needs high humidity, partial shade and humus-rich soil. Is not easy to grow successfully in pots. Propagate by division in spring. Red spider mite may be a problem with pot-grown plants.
T. ananassae. Evergreen, tufted perennial. **H** to 2m (6ft), **S** 75cm (2½ft). Non-flowering stems are erect and unbranched, with narrowly oval, long-pointed leaves, to 15cm (6in) long. Flowering stems are leafless, to over 1m (3ft) long, and, in summer, bear ovoid, dense spikes, 15cm (6in) or more long, of small, tubular, yellow flowers. Showy, recurved, hard, scarlet bracts enclose and almost hide flowers.

TAXODIUM

TAXODIACEAE

See also CONIFERS.
♀ ***T. distichum*** (Bald cypress, Swamp cypress) illus. p.99.

TAXUS

TAXACEAE

① All parts (but not the seed coating) are highly toxic if ingested. See also CONIFERS.
♀ ***T. baccata*** (Yew). Slow-growing conifer with a broadly conical, later dome-shaped crown. **H** 10–15m (30–50ft), **S** 5–10m (15–30ft). Fully hardy. Needle-like, flattened leaves are dark green. Female plants bear cup-shaped, fleshy, bright red fruits; only the red part, not the seed, is edible. Will regrow if cut back. The following forms are **H** 6–10m (20–30ft), **S** 5–8m (15–25ft) unless otherwise stated. **'Adpressa'** is a shrubby, female form with short, broad leaves. **Aurea Group** (syn. *T.b.* 'Aurea') has golden-yellow foliage. ♀ **'Dovastoniana'** is spreading, with weeping branchlets. ♀ **'Dovastonii Aurea'** (illus. p.105) is similar to *T.b.* 'Dovastoniana', but has golden shoots and yellow-margined leaves. ♀ **'Fastigiata'** illus. p.101. **'Fastigiata Aurea'** is similar to *T.b.* 'Fastigiata', but has gold-variegated leaves. **'Lutea'**(Yellow-berried yew) illus. p.102. ♀ **'Repandens'**, **H** 60cm (2ft), **S** 5m (15ft), is a spreading form.
♀ **'Semperaurea'**, **H** 3m (10ft), **S** 5m (15ft), has ascending branches with dense, golden foliage.
T. cuspidata (Japanese yew) illus. p.104. **'Aurescens'** is a spreading, bushy, dwarf conifer. **H** 30cm (1ft), **S** 1m (3ft). Fully hardy. Is hardier than *T. baccata* forms. Needle-like, flattened leaves are deep golden-yellow in their first year and mature to dark green. **'Capitata'**, **H** 10m (30ft), **S** 2m (6ft), is upright in habit. **'Densa'**, **H** 1.2m (4ft), **S** 6m (20ft), is a female form with short, erect shoots.
T. x media. Dense conifer that is very variably shaped. **H** and **S** 3–6m (10–20ft). Fully hardy. Has needle-like, flattened leaves, spreading either side of olive-green shoots. Leaves are stiff, broad and widen abruptly at the base. Fruits are similar to those of *T. baccata*. **'Brownii'**, **H** 2.5m (8ft), **S** 3.5m (11ft), is a dense, globose form with dark green foliage. **'Densiformis'**, **H** 2–3m (6–10ft), is dense and rounded, with masses of shoots that have bright green leaves. ♀ **'Hicksii'**, **H** to 6m (20ft), is columnar and has ascending branches. Male and female forms exist. **'Hillii'**, **H** and **S** 3m (10ft), is a broadly conical to rounded, dense bush with glossy, green leaves. **'Wardii'**, **H** 2m (6ft), **S** 6m (20ft), is a flat, globose, female form.

TECOMA,

SYN. TECOMARIA

BIGNONIACEAE

Genus of mainly evergreen shrubs and trees, grown for their flowers from spring to autumn. Frost tender, min. 5–13°C (41–55°F). Prefers moist but well-drained soil and full light. Water potted specimens moderately, hardly at all in winter. May be pruned annually after flowering to maintain as a shrub. Propagate by seed in spring or by semi-ripe cuttings in summer. Red spider mite may be troublesome.
T. australis. See *Pandorea pandorana*.
♀ ***T. capensis***, syn. *Bignonia capensis, Tecomaria capensis* (Cape honeysuckle). Evergreen, scrambling climber, shrub-like when young. **H** 2–3m (6–10ft). Leaves have 5–9 rounded, serrated, glossy, dark green leaflets. Tubular, orange-red flowers are carried in short spikes mainly in spring–summer. **'Aurea'** (syn. *Tecomaria capensis* 'Aurea') illus. p.464.
T. grandiflora. See *Campsis grandiflora*.
T. radicans. See *Campsis radicans*.
T. ricasoliana. See *Podranea ricasoliana*.
T. stans (Yellow bells), syn. *Bignonia stans, Stenolobium stans*, illus. p.452.

TECOMANTHE

BIGNONIACEAE

Genus of evergreen, twining climbers, grown for their flowers. Frost tender, min. 16–18°C (61–64°F). Provide humus-rich, well-drained soil and light shade in summer. Water freely when in full growth, less at other times. Provide stems with support. If necessary, thin out crowded stems in spring. Propagate by seed in spring or by semi-ripe cuttings in summer.
T. speciosa. Strong-growing, evergreen, twining climber. **H** to 10m (30ft) or more. Has leaves of 3 or 5 oval leaflets. Bears dense clusters of foxglove-like, fleshy-textured, cream flowers, tinged with green, in autumn.

TECOPHILAEA

LILIACEAE/TECOPHILAEACEAE

Genus of spring-flowering corms, rare in cultivation and extinct in the wild, grown for their beautiful flowers. Fully hardy, but because of rarity usually grown in a cold greenhouse or cold frame. Requires sun and well-drained soil. Water in winter and spring. Keep corms dry, but not sunbaked, from early summer to autumn, then replant. Propagate in autumn by seed or by taking offsets.
♀ ***T. cyanocrocus*** (Chilean blue crocus) illus. p.420. ♀ **var. *leichtlinii*** (syn. *T.c.* 'Leichtlinii') illus. p.420.

TELEKIA

COMPOSITAE/ASTERACEAE

Genus of summer-flowering perennials, grown for their bold foliage and large flower heads. Fully hardy. Grows in sun or shade and in moist soil. Propagate by division in spring or by seed in autumn.
T. speciosa, syn. *Buphthalmum speciosum*. Upright, spreading perennial. **H** 1.2–1.5m (4–5ft), **S** 1–1.2m (3–4ft). Mid-green leaves are heart-shaped at base of plant, oval on stems. In late summer, branched stems bear large, daisy-like, rich gold flower heads. Is ideal for a pool side or woodland.

Telesonix jamesii.
See *Boykinia jamesii*.

TELLIMA

SAXIFRAGACEAE

Genus of one species of semi-evergreen, late spring-flowering perennial. Makes good ground cover and is ideal for cool, semi-shaded woodland gardens and beneath shrubs in sunny borders. Fully hardy. Grows in any well-drained soil. Propagate by division in spring or by seed in autumn.
T. grandiflora (Fringecups). Semi-evergreen, clump-forming perennial. **H** and **S** 60cm (24in). Has heart-shaped, toothed, hairy, purple-tinted, bright green leaves. Bears racemes of small, bell-shaped, fringed, cream flowers, well above foliage, in late spring. **Rubra Group** (syn. *T.g.* 'Purpurea', *T.g.* 'Rubra Group') illus. p.279.

TELOPEA

PROTEACEAE

Genus of evergreen trees and shrubs, grown mainly for their flower heads. Half hardy to frost tender, min. 5°C (41°F). Requires full sun or semi-shade and humus-rich, moist but well-drained, neutral to acid soil. Water containerized plants freely when in full growth, moderately at other times. Propagate by seed in spring or by layering in winter.
T. speciosissima (Waratah) illus. p.137.
T. truncata (Tasmanian waratah) illus. p.123.

TEMPLETONIA

LEGUMINOSAE/PAPILIONACEAE

Genus of evergreen shrubs, grown for their flowers. Frost tender, min. 7°C (45°F). Prefers full light and freely draining, alkaline soil. Water potted specimens moderately, less in winter. Propagate by seed in spring or by semi-ripe cuttings taken in summer.
T. retusa (Coral bush). Evergreen, erect, irregularly branched shrub. **H** 2m (6ft), **S** 1–1.5m (3–5ft). Has oval to elliptic, leathery, bluish-green leaves. Pea-like, red flowers, sometimes pink or cream, are produced in spring–summer.

TERMINALIA

COMBRETACEAE

Genus of evergreen trees and shrubs, grown for their overall appearance, edible seeds (nuts) and for shade. Frost tender, min. 16–18°C (61–4°F). Requires full light and well-drained soil. Water potted specimens moderately, scarcely at all when temperatures are low. Pruning is seldom necessary. Propagate by seed in spring.
T. catappa (Indian almond, Tropical almond). Evergreen, rounded tree. **H** and **S** 15m (50ft) or more. Has broadly oval, lustrous, green leaves at stem tips. Small, greenish-white flowers appear in spring, followed by flattened ovoid, keeled, green to red fruits, each with an edible seed.

TERNSTROEMIA

THEACEAE

Genus of evergreen trees and shrubs, grown for their overall appearance. Half hardy. Requires full sun or semi-shade and humus-rich, well-drained, neutral to acid soil. Water containerized specimens copiously when in full growth, moderately at other times. Prune in spring. Propagate by seed when ripe or in spring or by semi-ripe cuttings in late summer.

T. gymnanthera, syn. *T. japonica.* Evergreen, rounded, dense shrub. **H** and **S** 2m (6ft). Oval leaves are lustrous, mid- to deep green. In summer, pendent, 5-petalled, white flowers are borne singly from leaf axils. Pea-sized, berry-like, bright red fruits appear in autumn. Leaves of **'Variegata'** are white-bordered with a pink tinge.
T. japonica. See *T. gymnanthera.*

Testudinaria elephantipes.
See *Dioscorea elephantipes.*

TETRACENTRON

TETRACENTRACEAE

Genus of one species of deciduous tree, grown for its foliage and catkins. Fully hardy. Needs sun or partial shade and fertile, well-drained soil. Propagate by seed in autumn.
T. sinense. Deciduous, spreading tree of graceful habit. **H** and **S** 10m (30ft) or more. Bears oval, finely toothed, dark green leaves and long, slender, yellow catkins in early summer.

TETRADIUM,

SYN. EUODIA, EVODIA

RUTACEAE

Genus of deciduous trees, grown for their foliage, late flowers, and fruits. Fully hardy. Needs full sun and fertile, well-drained soil. Propagate by softwood cuttings in summer, by seed in autumn, or by root cuttings in late winter.
T. daniellii, syn. *Euodia hupehensis.* Deciduous, spreading tree. **H** and **S** 15m (50ft). Ash-like, dark green leaves, with 5–11 oval to oblong leaflets, turn yellow in autumn. Has small, fragrant, 5-petalled, white flower clusters in early autumn, then beaked, red fruits.

TETRANEMA

SCROPHULARIACEAE

Genus of shrubby, evergreen perennials, grown for their trumpet-shaped flowers in summer. Frost tender, min. 13°C (55°F). Grow in a light position, shaded from direct sunlight, and in well-drained soil; avoid waterlogging and a humid atmosphere. Propagate by division, or seed if available, in spring.
T. mexicanum. See *T. roseum.*
🏆 ***T. roseum*** (Mexican foxglove, Mexican violet) , syn. *T. mexicanum*, illus. p.472.

TETRAPANAX

ARALIACEAE

Genus of one species of evergreen, summer- to autumn-flowering shrub, grown for its foliage. Half hardy. Requires full sun or partial shade and humus-rich, moist but well-drained soil. Water containerized specimens freely, less in winter. Leggy stems may be cut back to near ground level in winter. Propagate by suckers or seed in early spring. Severe frosts can cause stems to die back but will re-grow in spring
🏆 ***T. papyrifer*** (Rice-paper plant), syn. *Fatsia papyrifera*, illus. p.120.

TETRASTIGMA

VITACEAE

Genus of evergreen, woody-stemmed, tendril climbers, grown for their handsome leaves. Frost tender, min. 15–18°C (59–64°F). Grow in any fertile, well-drained soil, with shade in summer. Water freely while in active growth, less in low temperatures. Provide stems with support; cut out crowded stems in spring. Propagate by layering in spring or by semi-ripe cuttings in summer.
🏆 ***T. voinierianum*** (Chestnut vine), syn. *Cissus voinieriana*, illus. p.463.

TEUCRIUM

LABIATAE/LAMIACEAE

Genus of evergreen or deciduous shrubs, sub-shrubs and perennials, grown for their flowers, foliage (sometimes aromatic) or habit. Fully to half hardy. Needs full sun and well-drained soil. Propagate shrubs and sub-shrubs by softwood or semi-ripe cuttings in summer, perennials by seed or division in spring.
T. aroanium. Evergreen, procumbent, much-branched sub-shrub. **H** 2.5cm (1in), **S** 10–15cm (4–6in). Frost hardy. Has white-haired twigs and oblong to oval, slightly hairy leaves, which are densely hairy below, and, in summer, whorls of small, tubular, 2-lipped, purple flowers. Is good for a trough.
T. fruticans (Shrubby germander, Tree germander). 🏆 **'Azureum'** is an evergreen, arching shrub. **H** 2m (6ft), **S** 4m (12ft). Half hardy. Has oval, aromatic, grey-green leaves, white beneath. Bears tubular, 2-lipped, deep blue flowers with prominent stamens in summer. Cut out dead wood in spring.
T. polium illus. p.366.

THALIA

MARANTACEAE

Genus of deciduous, perennial, marginal water plants, grown for their foliage and flowers. Frost tender, min. 7°C (45°F). Needs an open, sunny position in up to 45cm (18in) depth of water. Some species tolerate cool water. Remove fading foliage regularly. Propagate in spring by division or seed.
T. dealbata. Deciduous, perennial, marginal water plant. **H** 1.5m (5ft), **S** 60cm (2ft). Oval, long-stalked, blue-green leaves have a mealy, white covering. Spikes of narrowly tubular, violet flowers in summer are followed by decorative seed heads. Tolerates cool water.
T. geniculata. Deciduous, perennial, marginal water plant. **H** 2m (6ft), **S** 60cm (2ft). Has oval, long-stalked, blue-green leaves and, in summer, spikes of narrowly tubular, violet flowers. Needs a warm pool.

THALICTRUM

Meadow rue

RANUNCULACEAE

Genus of perennials, grown for their divided foliage and fluffy flower heads. Flowers lack petals, but each has prominent tufts of stamens and 4 or 5 sepals, which rapidly fall. Does well at edges of woodland gardens. Tall species and cultivars make excellent foils in borders for perennials with bolder leaves and flowers. Fully hardy. Requires sun or light shade. Grows in any well-drained soil, although some species prefer cool, moist conditions. Propagate by seed when fresh, in autumn, or by division in spring.
T. aquilegiifolium illus. p.239. **'White Cloud'**, **H** 1–1.2m (3–4ft), **S** 30cm (1ft), has divided, greyish-green leaves. In summer produces terminal sprays of fluffy, white flowers. 🏆 **'Thundercloud'** illus. p.233.
T. chelidonii. Clump-forming perennial. **H** 1–1.5m (3–5ft), **S** 60cm (2ft). Has finely divided, mid-green leaves and, in summer, produces panicles of fluffy, 4- or 5-sepalled, mauve flowers. Prefers cool soil that does not dry out.
🏆 ***T. delavayi***, syn. *T. dipterocarpum* of gardens. Elegant, clump-forming perennial. **H** 1.5–2m (5–6ft), **S** 60cm (2ft). Has divided, mid-green leaves, and bears large panicles of nodding, lilac flowers, with 4 or 5 sepals and prominent, yellow stamens, from mid- to late summer.
🏆 **'Hewitt's Double'** illus. p.220.
T. diffusiflorum. Clump-forming perennial. **H** 1m (3ft), **S** 30–60cm (1–2ft). Has much-divided, basal, mid-green leaves. Slender stems produce large sprays of delicate, drooping, mauve flowers in summer. Prefers cool, moist soil.
T. dipterocarpum of gardens. See *T. delavayi.*
***T.* 'Elin'** illus. p.218.
T. flavum. Clump-forming perennial. **H** 1.2m–1.5m (4–5ft), **S** 60cm (2ft). Has much-divided, glaucous blue-green leaves and, from mid- to late summer, clusters of fluffy, pale yellow flowers on slender stems. **'Illuminator'** is a pale yellow cultivar with bright green foliage.
T. kiusianum. Mat-forming perennial with short runners. **H** 8cm (3in), **S** 15cm (6in). Has small, fern-like, 3-lobed leaves and, throughout summer, loose clusters of tiny, purple flowers. Is excellent in a peat bed, rock garden, trough or alpine house. Is difficult to grow in hot, dry areas. Prefers shade and moist, sandy, peaty soil.
T. lucidum, *syn. T. angustifolium.* Perennial. H 1–1.2m (3–4ft), **S** 50cm (20in). Has glossy leaves composed of numerous leaflets. Stout stems bear loose panicles of fluffy, greenish-yellow flowers in summer.
T. orientale. Spreading perennial with short runners. **H** 15cm (6in), **S** 20cm (8in). Leaves are fern-like with oval to rounded, lobed leaflets. Bears small, saucer-shaped, blue-mauve to violet flowers, with yellow stamens and large sepals, in late spring.

Thamnocalamus falconeri.
See *Himalayacalamus falconeri.*
Thamnocalamus murieliae.
See *Fargesia murieliae.*
***Thamnocalamus spathaceus* of gardens.** See *Fargesia murieliae.*

THAMNOCALAMUS

GRAMINEAE/POACEAE

See also GRASSES, BAMBOOS, RUSHES and SEDGES.
***Thamnocalamus crassinodus* 'Kew Beauty'** illus. p.286.

THELOCACTUS

CACTACEAE

Genus of spherical to columnar, perennial cacti with ribbed or tuberculate stems. Elongated areoles in crowns produce funnel-shaped flowers. Frost tender, min. 7°C (45°F). Requires sun and well-drained soil. Propagate by seed spring or summer.
🏆 ***T. bicolor*** illus. p.484.
T. leucacanthus. Clump-forming, perennial cactus. **H** 10cm (4in), **S** 30cm (12in). Spherical to columnar, green stem has 8–13 tuberculate ribs. Areoles bear up to 20 short, golden spines and yellow flowers, 5cm (2in) across, in summer.
T. macdowellii, syn. *Echinomastus macdowellii.* Also sometimes included in *Neolloydia.* Spherical, perennial cactus. **H** and **S** 15cm (6in). Has a tuberculate, dark green stem densely covered with white spines, to 3cm (1¼in) long. Violet-red flowers, 4cm (1½in) across, appear in spring–summer.
🏆 ***T. setispinus***, syn. *Ferocactus setispinus*, illus. p.495.

THELYPTERIS

THELYPTERIDACEAE

Genus of deciduous ferns. Fully hardy. Tolerates sun or semi-shade. Grow in moist or very moist soil. Remove fading fronds regularly. Propagate by division in spring.
T. oreopteris. See *Oreopteris limbosperma.*
T. palustris (Marsh buckler fern, Marsh fern) illus. p.291.
T. phegopteris. See *Phegopteris connectilis.*

THERMOPSIS

LEGUMINOSAE/PAPILIONACEAE

Genus of summer-flowering perennials. Fully hardy. Prefers sun and rich, light soil. Propagate by division in spring or by seed in autumn.
T. caroliniana. See *T. villosa.*
T. montana. See *T. rhombifolia.*
T. rhombifolia, syn. *T. montana*, illus. p.243.
T. villosa, syn. *T. caroliniana.* Straggling perennial. **H** 1m (3ft) or more, **S** 60cm (2ft). Bears racemes of pea-like, yellow flowers in late summer. Glaucous leaves are divided into 3 oval leaflets.

THESPESIA

MALVACEAE

Genus of evergreen perennials, shrubs and trees, grown for their flowers. Frost tender, min. 16–18° C (61–4°F). Requires a position in full light and well-drained soil. Water containerized plants freely when in full growth, less at other times. Prune in early spring to maintain as a shrub. Propagate by seed in spring or by semi-ripe cuttings in summer. Whitefly and red spider mite may be a nuisance.
T. populnea (Mahoe, Portia oil nut). Evergreen tree, bushy when young, thinning with age. **H** 12m (40ft) or more, **S** 3–6m (10–20ft). Leaves are heart-shaped. Intermittently, or all year round if warm enough, produces cup-shaped, yellow

flowers, each with a maroon eye, that age to purple. Grows well by the sea.

THEVETIA

APOCYNACEAE

Genus of evergreen shrubs and trees, grown for their flowers from winter to summer. Is related to *Frangipani*. Has poisonous, milky sap. Frost tender, min. 16–18°C (61–4°F). Needs full light and well-drained soil. Water containerized specimens moderately, less in winter. Young stems may be tip pruned in winter to promote branching. Propagate by seed in spring or by semi-ripe cuttings in summer. ⓘ The seeds are highly toxic if ingested.

T. neriifolia. See *T. peruviana*.

T. peruviana, syn. *T. neriifolia* (Yellow oleander). Evergreen, erect tree. **H** 2–8m (6–25ft), **S** 1–3m (3–10ft). Has narrow, lance-shaped, rich green leaves and funnel-shaped, yellow or orange-yellow flowers from winter to summer.

THLADIANTHA

CUCURBITACEAE

Genus of herbaceous or deciduous, tendril climbers, grown for their bell-shaped, yellow flowers and oval to heart-shaped, mid-green leaves. Frost hardy to frost tender, min. 4°C (39°F). Requires a sheltered position in full sun and fertile, well-drained soil. Propagate by seed sown in spring or by division in early spring.

T. dubia illus. p.206.

THLASPI

CRUCIFERAE/BRASSICACEAE

Genus of annuals and perennials, some of which are evergreen, grown for their flowers. Small plants may flower themselves to death, so remove buds for 2 years, to encourage a large plant. Is difficult to grow at low altitudes and may require frequent renewal from seed. Is good for screes and troughs. Fully hardy. Needs sun and moist but well-drained soil. Propagate by seed in autumn.

T. alpestre of gardens. See *T. alpinum*.

T. alpinum, syn. *T. alpestre* of gardens (Alpine penny-cress). Evergreen, mat-forming perennial. **H** 5cm (2in), **S** 10cm (4in). Has small, oval, mid-green leaves. Produces racemes of small, 4-petalled, white flowers in spring.

T. bulbosum. Clump-forming, tuberous perennial. **H** 8cm (3in), **S** 15–20cm (6–8in). Bears broadly oval, glaucous leaves and, in summer, racemes of 4-petalled, dark violet flowers. Suits a rock garden.

T. cepaeifolium* subsp. *rotundifolium, syn. *T. rotundifolium* , illus. p.352.

T. macrophyllum, syn. *Pachyphragma macrophyllum*, illus. p.255.

T. rotundifolium. See *T. cepaeifolium* subsp. *rotundifolium*.

THUJA

CUPRESSACEAE

ⓘ Contact with the foliage may aggravate skin allergies. See also CONIFERS.

T. koraiensis (Korean thuja). Upright conifer, sometimes sprawling and shrubby. **H** 3–10m (10–30ft), **S** 3–5m (10–15ft). Fully hardy. Scale-like foliage is bright green or yellow-green above, glaucous silver beneath, and smells of almonds when crushed. ⓘ Contact with the foliage may aggravate skin allergies.

T. occidentalis (American arbor-vitae, Eastern white cedar, White cedar). Slow-growing conifer with a narrow crown. **H** 15m (50ft), **S** 3–5m (10–15ft). Fully hardy. Has orange-brown bark and flat sprays of scale-like, yellowish-green leaves, pale or greyish-green beneath, smelling of apples when crushed. Ovoid cones are yellow-green, ripening to brown. **'Caespitosa'**, **H** 30cm (12in), **S** 40cm (16in), is a cushion-shaped, dwarf cultivar. **'Fastigiata'**, **H** to 15m (50ft), **S** to 5m (15ft), is broadly columnar, with erect, spreading branches and light green leaves. **'Filiformis'**, **H** 1.5m (5ft), **S** 1.5–2m (5–6ft), forms a mound with pendent, whip-like shoots. **'Hetz Midget'**, **H** and **S** 50cm (20in), growing only 2.5cm (1in) each year, is a globose, dwarf form with blue-green foliage. ♀ **'Holmstrup'**, **H** 3–4m (10–12ft), **S** 1m (3ft), is slow-growing, dense and conical, with rich green foliage. **'Little Champion'**, **H** and **S** 50cm (20in) or more, is a globose, dwarf form, conical when young, with foliage turning brown in winter. ♀ **'Lutea Nana'**, **H** 2m (6ft), **S** 1–2m (3–6ft), is a dwarf form with golden-yellow foliage. ♀ **'Rheingold'**, **H** 3–4m (10–12ft), **S** 2–4m (6–12ft), is slow-growing, with golden-yellow foliage that becomes bronze in winter. ♀ **'Smaragd'**, **H** 2–2.5m (6–8ft), **S** 60–75cm (2–2½ft), is slow-growing and conical, with erect sprays of bright green leaves. **'Spiralis'**, **H** 10–15m (30–50ft), **S** 2–3m (6–10ft), has foliage in twisted, fern-like sprays. **'Woodwardii'**, **H** 2.5m (8ft), **S** to 5m (15ft), is very slow-growing and globose, with mid-green foliage.

T. orientalis. See *Platycladus orientalis*.

T. plicata (Western red cedar). Fast-growing, conical conifer that has great, curving branches low down. **H** 20–30m (70–100ft), **S** 5–8m (15–25ft), greater if lower branches self-layer. Fully hardy. Has red-brown bark, scale-like, glossy, dark green leaves, which have a pineapple aroma when crushed, and erect, ovoid, green cones, ripening to brown. ♀ **'Atrovirens'** has darker green foliage. ♀ **'Aurea'** has golden-yellow foliage. **'Collyer's Gold'**, **H** to 2m (6ft), **S** 1m (3ft), is a dwarf form with yellow, young foliage turning light green. **'Cuprea'**, **H** 1m (3ft), **S** 75cm–1m (2½–3ft), is a conical shrub with copper- to bronze-yellow leaves. **'Hillieri'**, **H** and **S** to 1m (3ft), is a slow-growing, dense, rounded, dwarf shrub with moss-like, rich green foliage. ♀ **'Stoneham Gold'** (illus. p.105), **H** 1–2m (3–6ft), **S** 1m (3ft), is a conical, dwarf form with bright gold foliage. **'Zebrina'**, **H** 15m (50ft), has leaves banded with yellowish-white.

THUJOPSIS

CUPRESSACEAE

See also CONIFERS.

♀ ***T. dolabrata*** (Hiba). Conical or bushy conifer with a mass of stems. **H** 10–20m (30–70ft), **S** 8–10m (25–30ft). Fully hardy. Produces heavy, flat sprays of scale-like leaves, glossy, bright green above, silvery-white beneath. Small, rounded cones are blue-grey. **'Variegata'** illus. p.104.

THUNBERGIA

ACANTHACEAE

Genus of annual or mainly evergreen, perennial, twining climbers, perennials and shrubs, grown for their flowers. Half hardy to frost tender, min. 10–15°C (50–59°F). Any fertile, well-drained soil is suitable, with full sun or light shade in summer. Water freely when in full growth, less at other times. Requires support. Thin out crowded stems in early spring. Propagate by seed in spring or from softwood or semi-ripe cuttings in summer.

T. alata (Black-eyed Susan) illus. p.207.

T. coccinea. Evergreen, woody-stemmed, perennial, twining climber with narrowly oval leaves. **H** 6m (20ft) or more. Frost tender, min. 15°C (59°F). Pendent racemes of tubular, scarlet flowers are produced in winter-spring.

T. gibsonii. See *T. gregorii*.

♀ ***T. grandiflora*** (Blue trumpet vine). Evergreen, woody-stemmed, perennial, twining climber. **H** 6–10m (20–30ft). Frost tender, min. 10°C (50°F). Oval leaves, 10–20cm (4–8in) long, have a few tooth-like lobes. In summer has trumpet-shaped, pale to deep violet-blue flowers.

♀ ***T. gregorii***, syn. *T. gibsonii*. Evergreen, woody-stemmed, twining climber, usually grown as an annual. **H** to 3m (10ft). Frost tender, min. 10°C (50°F). Triangular-oval leaves have winged stalks. Glowing orange flowers are carried in summer.

♀ ***T. mysorensis*** illus. p.464.

THYMUS

Thyme

LABIATAE/LAMIACEAE

Genus of evergreen, mat-forming and dome-shaped shrubs, sub-shrubs and woody-based perennials with aromatic leaves. Is useful for growing on banks and in rock gardens, troughs and paving. Commonly grown as a culinary herb, it is also suitable for containers. Fully to half hardy. Requires sun and moist but well-drained soil. Propagate by seed in spring, or softwood or semi-ripe cuttings taken in summer.

T. azoricus. See *T. caespititius*.

***T.* 'Bressingham'** illus. p.365

T. caespititius, syn. *T. azoricus, T. cilicicus*, illus. p.366.

T. carnosus. Evergreen, spreading shrub. **H** and **S** 20cm (8in). Frost hardy. Has tiny, narrowly oval, aromatic leaves. Erect flowering stems bear whorls of small, 2-lipped, white flowers in summer. Needs a sheltered position.

♀ ***T.* x *citriodorus* 'Silver Queen'.** Evergreen, rounded shrub. **H** to 30cm (12in), **S** to 25cm (10in). Has narrow, oval-diamond-shaped to lance-shaped, more or less hairless, aromatic, silvery-green leaves, with creamy-white markings. In summer, produces 2-lipped, pale lavender-pink flowers in terminal clusters.

T. herba-barona (Caraway thyme). Evergreen sub-shrub. **H** in flower 5–10cm (2–4in), **S** to 20cm (8in). Forms a loose mat of tiny, caraway-scented, dark green leaves. In summer, small, lilac flowers are borne in terminal clusters.

T. micans. See *T. caespititius*.

***T.* 'Peter Davis'** syn. *T. leucotrichus* of gardens, illus. p.367

***T.* 'Porlock'.** Evergreen, dome-shaped perennial. **H** 8cm (3in), **S** 20cm (8in). Fully hardy. Thin stems are covered in small, rounded to oval, very aromatic, glossy, green leaves. In summer, produces clusters of small, 2-lipped, pink flowers.

T. pseudolanuginosus. Evergreen, prostrate shrub. **H** 2.5–5cm (1–2in), **S** 20cm (8in) or more. Fully hardy. Has dense mats of very hairy stems bearing tiny, aromatic, grey leaves. Produces 2-lipped, pinkish-lilac flowers in leaf axils in summer.

♀ ***T. pulegioides* 'Aureus'.** Evergreen, spreading shrub. **H** 10cm (4in), **S** 10–25cm (4–10in). Frost hardy. Tiny, rounded to oval, golden-yellow leaves are very fragrant when crushed. Produces terminal clusters of small, 2-lipped, lilac flowers in summer. Cut back in spring.

T. serpyllum. Evergreen, mat-forming sub-shrub. **H** 25cm (10in), **S** 45cm (18in). Fully hardy. Finely hairy, trailing stems bear linear to elliptic to oval, mid-green leaves. Whorls of two-lipped, purple flowers are borne in summer. **'Annie Hall'**, **H** 5cm (2in), **S** 20cm (8in), has pale purple-pink flowers and light green leaves. **'Elfin'**, **H** 5cm (2in), **S** 10cm (4in), produces emerald-green leaves in dense hummocks; occasionally bears purple flowers.

TIARELLA

Foamflower

SAXIFRAGACEAE

Genus of perennials, some of which are evergreen, that spread by runners. Is excellent as ground cover. Fully hardy. Tolerates deep shade and prefers moist, well-drained soil. Suitable for woodland gardens. Propagate by division in spring.

♀ ***T. cordifolia*** (Foamflower) illus. p.333. **var. *collina*** see *T. wherryi*.

♀ ***T. wherryi***, syn. *T. cordifolia* var. *collina*. Slow-growing, clump-forming perennial. **H** 10cm (4in), **S** 15cm (6in). Triangular, lobed, hairy, basal, green leaves are stained dark red, with heart-shaped bases. Bears racemes of tiny, star-shaped, soft pink or white flowers from late spring to early summer.

TIBOUCHINA

MELASTOMATACEAE

Genus of evergreen perennials, sub-shrubs, shrubs and scandent climbers, grown for their flowers and leaves. Frost tender, min. 5–7°C (41–5°F). Prefers full sun and fertile, well-drained, neutral to acid soil. Water potted specimens freely when in full growth, moderately at other times. Cut back flowered stems, to 2 pairs of buds each, in spring. Tip prune young plants to promote branching. Propagate by greenwood or semi-ripe cuttings in late spring or summer.

T. semidecandra of gardens. See *T. urvilleana*.

♀ ***T. urvilleana*** (Glory bush), syn. *T. semidecandra* of gardens, illus. p.457.

TIGRIDIA

IRIDACEAE

Genus of summer-flowering bulbs, grown for their highly colourful but short-lived flowers, rather iris-like in shape, with 3 large, outer petals. Half hardy. Needs sun and well-drained soil, with ample water in summer. Plant in spring. Lift in autumn; then partially dry bulbs and store in peat or sand at 8–12°C (46–54°F). Propagate by seed in spring.

T. pavonia (Peacock flower) illus. p.413.

TILIA

Lime, Linden

TILIACEAE

Genus of deciduous trees, grown for their small, fragrant, cup-shaped flowers and stately habit. Flowers attract bees, but are toxic to them in some cases. Fully hardy. Requires sun or semi-shade and fertile, well-drained soil. Propagate species by seed in autumn, selected forms and hybrids by grafting in late summer. Except for *T.* x *euchlora*, trees are usually attacked by aphids, which cover growth and ground beneath with sticky honeydew. ⓘThe nectar of *T.* 'Petiolaris' and *T. tomentosa* may be toxic, especially to bumblebees.

T. americana (American lime, Basswood). Deciduous, spreading tree. **H** 25m (80ft), **S** 12m (40ft). Has large, rounded, sharply toothed, glossy, dark green leaves. Small, yellowish-white flowers appear in summer.

🏆 ***T. cordata*** (Small-leaved lime). Deciduous, spreading tree. **H** 30m (100ft), **S** 12m (40ft). In mid-summer has small, glossy, dark green leaves and small, yellowish-white flowers.

🏆 **'Greenspire'**, **S** 8m (25ft), is very vigorous and pyramidal in habit, even when young. **'Rancho'** illus. p.75.

🏆 ***T. x euchlora*** (Caucasian lime, Crimean lime). Deciduous, spreading tree with lower branches that droop with age. **H** 20m (70ft), **S** 10m (30ft). Rounded, very glossy, deep green leaves turn yellow in autumn. Bears small, yellowish-white flowers, toxic to bees, in summer. Is relatively pest-free.

T. x europaea, syn. *T.* x *vulgaris*. (Common lime). Vigorous, deciduous, spreading tree. **H** 35m (120ft), **S** 15m (50ft). Trunk develops many burs. Has rounded, dark green leaves. Small, yellowish-white flowers that are toxic to bees appear in summer. Periodically remove shoots from burrs at base.

T. henryana. Deciduous, spreading tree. **H** and **S** 10m (30ft). Broadly heart-shaped, glossy, bright green leaves, fringed with long teeth, are often tinged red when young. Has masses of small, creamy-white flowers in autumn.

T. mongolica (Mongolian lime). Deciduous, spreading, graceful tree. **H** 15m (50ft), **S** 12m (40ft). Young shoots are red. Heart-shaped, coarsely toothed, glossy, dark green leaves turn yellow in autumn. Small, yellowish-white flowers appear in summer.

T. oliveri illus. p.63.

T. petiolaris. See *T.* 'Petiolaris'.

🏆 ***T.* 'Petiolaris'** (Pendent silver lime), syn. *T. petiolaris*, illus. p.64.

T. platyphyllos (Broad-leaved lime, Large-leaved lime). Deciduous, spreading tree. **H** 30m (100ft), **S** 20m (70ft). Has rounded, dark green leaves and small, dull yellowish-white flowers in mid-summer. **'Prince's Street'** is upright, with bright red shoots in winter. 🏆 **'Rubra'** (Red-twigged lime) illus. p.63.

T. tomentosa (European white lime, Silver lime). Deciduous, spreading tree. **H** 25m (80ft), **S** 20m (70ft). Leaves are large, rounded, sharply toothed, dark green above and white beneath. Very fragrant, small, dull white flowers, toxic to bees, are borne in late summer.

T. x vulgaris. See *T.* x *europaea*.

TILLANDSIA

BROMELIACEAE

Genus of evergreen, epiphytic perennials, often rosette-forming, some with branching stems and spirally arranged leaves, all grown for their flowers or overall appearance. Frost tender, min. 7–10°C (45–50°F). Requires semi-shade. Provide a rooting medium of equal parts humus-rich soil and either sphagnum moss or bark or plastic chips used for orchid culture. May also be grown on slabs of bark or sections of trees. Using soft water, water moderately in summer, sparingly at other times; spray plants grown on bark or tree sections with water several times a week from mid-spring to mid-autumn. Propagate by offsets or division during spring. See also feature panel p.471.

🏆 ***T. argentea*** (illus. p.471). Evergreen, basal-rosetted, epiphytic perennial. **H** and **S** 10–15cm (4–6in). Very narrow, almost thread-like leaves, covered with white scales, are produced in dense, near-spherical rosettes, each with a fleshy, bulb-like base. In summer, small, loose racemes of tubular, red flowers are produced.

T. caput-medusae. Evergreen, basal-rosetted, epiphytic perennial. **H** and **S** 15cm (6in) or more. Linear, channelled, twisted and rolled, incurved leaves, covered in grey scales, develop in loose rosettes that have hollow, bulb-like bases. In summer, spikes of tubular, violet-blue flowers appear above foliage.

🏆 ***T. cyanea.*** Evergreen, basal-rosetted, epiphytic perennial. **H** and **S** 25cm (10in). Forms dense rosettes of linear, pointed, channelled, arching, usually deep green leaves. In summer, broadly oval, blade-like spikes of pansy-shaped, deep purple-blue flowers, emerging from pink or red bracts, are produced among foliage.

T. fasciculata. Evergreen, basal-rosetted, epiphytic perennial. **H** and **S** 30cm (12in) or more. Has dense rosettes of narrowly triangular, tapering, arching, mid-green leaves. In summer, flat spikes of tubular, purple-blue flowers emerge from red or reddish-yellow bracts, just above leaf tips. Bracts require strong light to develop reddish tones.

T. ionantha (Sky plant). Evergreen, clump-forming, basal-rosetted, epiphytic perennial. **H** and **S** 12cm (5in). Linear, incurved, arching leaves, covered in grey scales, are produced in dense rosettes; the inner leaves turn red at flowering time. Spikes of tubular, violet-blue flowers, emerging in summer from narrow, white bracts, are borne just above foliage.

🏆 ***T. lindenii*** (Blue-flowered torch; illus. p.471). Evergreen, basal-rosetted, epiphytic perennial. **H** and **S** 40cm (16in). Linear, pointed, channelled, arching, mid-green leaves, with red-brown lines, form dense rosettes. In summer, produces blade-like spikes of widely pansy-shaped, deep blue flowers, emerging from sometimes pink-tinted, green bracts, which are borne just above leaves.

T. recurvata. Evergreen, basal-rosetted, epiphytic perennial. **H** and **S** 10–20cm (4–8in). Has long, loose, stem-like rosettes of linear, arching to recurved leaves, densely covered in silvery-grey scales. In summer produces short, dense spikes of small, tubular, pale blue or pale green flowers, which appear above the leaves.

T. stricta (illus. p.471). Evergreen, clump-forming, basal-rosetted, epiphytic perennial. **H** and **S** 20–30cm (8–12in). Narrowly triangular, tapering, arching, mid-green leaves, usually with grey scales, are produced in dense rosettes. Large, tubular, blue flowers emerge from drooping, cone-like spikes of bright red bracts, usually in summer.

T. usneoides (Spanish moss). Evergreen, pendent, epiphytic perennial. **H** 1m (3ft) or more, **S** 10–20cm (4–8in). Slender, branched, drooping stems bear linear, incurved leaves, densely covered in silvery- white scales. Inconspicuous, tubular, greenish-yellow or pale blue flowers, hidden among foliage, are produced in summer.

TIPUANA

LEGUMINOSAE/PAPILIONACEAE

Genus of one species of evergreen, spring-flowering tree, grown for its flowers and overall appearance when mature and for shade. In certain conditions, may be deciduous. Frost tender, min. 10–13°C (50–55°F). Requires full light and fertile, well-drained soil. Container-grown plants will not produce flowers. Young specimens may be pruned in winter. Propagate by seed in spring.

T. speciosa. See *T. tipu*.

T. tipu, syn. *T. speciosa* (Pride of Bolivia, Tipa tree, Tipu tree). Fast-growing, mainly evergreen, bushy tree. **H** 10m (30ft), **S** 8–10m (25–30ft). Bears leaves, 25cm (10in) long, with 11–25 oval leaflets. Produces pea-like, orange-yellow flowers, 3cm (1¼in) wide, in spring, followed by short, woody, winged, brownish pods in autumn–winter.

TITANOPSIS

AIZOACEAE

Genus of basal-rosetted, perennial succulents eventually forming small, dense clumps. Produces 6–8 opposite pairs of fleshy, triangular leaves, 2–3cm (¾–1¼in) long, narrow at stems and expanding to straight tips. Frost tender, min. 8°C (46°F). Requires a position in sun and well-drained soil. Propagate by seed in spring or summer.

🏆 ***T. calcarea*** illus. p.496.

T. schwantesii. Clump-forming, perennial succulent. **H** 3cm (1¼in), **S** 10cm (4in). Has a basal rosette of triangular, grey-blue leaves, covered with small, wart-like, yellow-brown tubercles. Carries daisy-like, light yellow flowers, 2cm (¾in) wide, in summer–autumn.

TITHONIA

COMPOSITAE/ASTERACEAE

Genus of annuals. Half hardy. Grow in sun and in fertile, well-drained soil. Provide support and dead-head regularly. Propagate by seed sown under glass in late winter or early spring.

T. rotundifolia (Mexican sunflower). **'Torch'** illus. p.324.

TOLMIEA

SAXIFRAGACEAE

Genus of one species of perennial that is sometimes semi-evergreen and is grown as ground cover. Is suitable for cool woodland gardens. Fully hardy. Prefers a position in shade and requires well-drained, neutral to acid soil. Propagate by division in spring or by seed in autumn.

T. menziesii (Pick-a-back-plant, Youth-on-age). Mat-forming perennial, sometimes semi-evergreen. **H** 45–60cm (18–24in), **S** 30cm (12in) or more. Young plantlets develop where ivy-shaped, mid-green leaves join stem. Produces spikes of tiny, nodding, tubular to bell-shaped, green and chocolate-brown flowers, which appear in spring.

TOLPIS

COMPOSITAE/ASTERACEAE

Genus of summer-flowering annuals and perennials. Fully hardy. Grow in sun and in fertile, well-drained soil. Propagate by seed sown outdoors in spring.

T. barbata. Moderately fast-growing, upright, branching annual. **H** 45–60cm (1½–2ft), **S** 30cm (1ft). Has lance-shaped, serrated, mid-green leaves. Daisy-like, bright yellow flower heads, 2.5cm (1in) or more wide, with maroon centres, are produced in summer.

TOONA

MELIACEAE

Genus of deciduous trees, grown for their foliage, autumn colour and flowers. Fully hardy. Prefers full sun; requires fertile, well-drained soil. Propagate by seed in autumn, root cuttings in winter.

T. sinensis, syn. *Cedrela sinensis*, illus. p.73.

TORENIA

SCROPHULARIACEAE

Genus of annuals and perennials. Half hardy to frost tender, min. 5°C (41°F). Often grown as summer bedding. Grow in semi-shade and in a sheltered position in fertile, well-drained soil. Pinch out growing shoots of young plants to encourage a busy habit. Propagate by seed sown under glass in early spring.

***T.* 'Dantmoon'.** See *T.* Moon Series Blue Moon.

T. fournieri (Wishbone flower). Moderately fast-growing, erect, branching annual. **H** 30cm (12in), **S** 20cm (8in). Frost tender, min. 5°C (41°F). Has serrated, light green leaves. Dark blue-purple flowers, paler and yellow within, are carried in summer and early autumn.
***T.* Moon Series Blue Moon ('Dantmoon')**. Dense, trailing perennial, grown as an annual. **H** 15– 20cm (6–8in), **S** 45cm (18in). Half hardy. Has oval, toothed, dark green leaves. In summer-autumn bears tubular, flared, 2-tone blue flowers with dark throats.

TORREYA

TAXACEAE

See also CONIFERS.
T. californica illus. p.101.

***Tovara virginiana* 'Painter's Palette'.** See *Persicaria virginiana* 'Painter's Palette'.

TOWNSENDIA

COMPOSITAE/ASTERACEAE

Genus of evergreen, short-lived perennials and biennials, grown for their daisy-like flower. Suits alpine houses as dislikes winter wet. Fully hardy. Needs sun and moist soil. Propagate by seed in autumn.
T. grandiflora illus. p.369.
T. parryi. Evergreen, basal-rosetted, short-lived perennial. **H** 7–15cm (3–6in), **S** 5cm (2in). In late spring produces daisy-like, lavender or violet-blue flower heads, with bright yellow centres, above spoon-shaped leaves.

Toxicodendron succedaneum. See *Rhus succedanea.*
Toxicodendron vernicifluum. See *Rhus verniciflua.*

TRACHELIUM, syn. DIOSPHAERA

CAMPANULACEAE

Genus of small perennials, useful for rock gardens and mixed borders. Some are good in alpine houses. Flowers of half-hardy species are ideal for cutting. Fully to half hardy, but protect fully hardy species under glass in winter as they resent damp conditions. Grow in a sunny, sheltered position and in fertile, very well-drained soil (*T. asperuloides* prefers lime-rich soil). Propagate by seed in early or mid-spring or by softwood cuttings in spring.
T. asperuloides, syn. *Diosphaera asperuloides*, illus. p.369.
♀ ***T. caeruleum*** (Throatwort) illus. p.313.

TRACHELOSPERMUM

APOCYNACEAE

Genus of evergreen, woody-stemmed, twining climbers with stems that exude milky sap when cut. Frost hardy. Grow in any well-drained soil and in sun or semi-shade. Propagate by seed in spring, by layering in summer or by semi-ripe cuttings in late summer or autumn.
♀ ***T. asiaticum*** illus. p.195.
♀ ***T. jasminoides*** (Confederate jasmine, Star jasmine) illus. p.195.

TRACHYCARPUS

PALMAE/ARECACEAE

Genus of evergreen, summer-flowering palms, grown for their habit, foliage and flowers. Frost hardy. Requires full sun and does best in a position sheltered from strong, cold winds, especially when young. Needs fertile, well-drained soil. Propagate by seed in autumn or spring.
♀ ***T. fortunei*** (Chusan palm) illus. p.80.

TRACHYMENE

UMBELLIFERAE/APIACEAE

Genus of summer-flowering annuals. Half hardy. Grow in a sunny, sheltered position and in fertile, well-drained soil. Support with sticks. Propagate by seed sown under glass in early spring.
T. coerulea, syn. *Didiscus coeruleus* (Blue lace flower). Moderately fast-growing, upright, branching annual. **H** 45cm (18in), **S** 20cm (8in). Has deeply divided, pale green leaves. Spherical heads, to 5cm (2in) wide, of tiny, blue flowers are produced in summer. Flowers are excellent for cutting.

TRADESCANTIA

Spiderwort

COMMELINACEAE

Genus of perennials, some of which are evergreen, grown for their flowers or ornamental foliage. Fully hardy to frost tender, min. 10–15°C (50–59°F). Grow in fertile, moist to dry soil and in sun or partial shade. Cut back or repropagate trailing species when they become straggly. Propagate hardy species by division or seed, and frost-tender species by tip cuttings in spring, summer or autumn. Hardy species are useful in shady gardens. ① Contact with the foliage may cause skin irritation.
T. albiflora. See *T. fluminensis.*
♀ ***T.* Andersoniana Group 'J.C. Weguelin'**, syn. *T.* 'J.C. Weguelin'. Clump-forming perennial. **H** to 60cm (2ft), **S** 45cm (1½ft). Fully hardy. Has narrowly lance-shaped, fleshy, green leaves, 15–30cm (6–12in) long. In summer producess clusters of 3-petalled, lavender-blue flowers, 2.5cm (1in) or more wide, surrounded by 2 leaf-like bracts.
♀ **'Osprey'** (syn. *T.* 'Osprey') illus. p.263. **'Purple Dome'** (syn. *T.* 'Purple Dome') illus. p.269.
T. blossfeldiana. See *T. cerinthoides.*
T. cerinthoides, syn. *T. blossfeldiana.* Evergreen, creeping perennial. **H** 5cm (2in), **S** indefinite. Frost tender. Narrowly oval, fleshy, stem-clasping leaves, to 10cm (4in) long, are glossy, dark green above, purple with long, white hairs below. Intermittently produces clusters of tiny, pink flowers, with white centres, surrounded by 2 leaf-like bracts. Leaves of ♀ **'Variegata'** have longitudinal, cream stripes.
T. fluminensis, syn. *T. albiflora* (Wandering Jew). Evergreen perennial with trailing, rooting stems. **H** 5cm (2in), **S** to 60cm (24in) or more. Frost tender. Oval, fleshy leaves, 4cm (1½in) long, that clasp the stem, are glossy and green above, sometimes tinged purple below. Intermittently has clusters of tiny, white flowers enclosed in 2 leaf-like bracts. **'Albovittata'** illus. p.468. **'Variegata'**, **H** 30cm (12in), **S** indefinite, has irregularly striped creamy-white leaves. Intermittently has clusters of white flowers.
***T.* 'J.C. Weguelin'.** See *T.* Andersoniana Group 'J.C. Weguelin'.
T. navicularis. See *Callisia navicularis.*
***T.* 'Osprey'.** See *T.* Andersoniana Group 'Osprey'.
♀ ***T. pallida* 'Purpurea'**, syn. *T.p.* 'Purple Heart', *Setcreasea purpurea*, illus. p.310.
T. pexata. See *T. sillamontana.*
***T.* 'Purple Dome'.** See *T.* Andersoniana Group 'Purple Dome'.
T. purpusii. See *T. zebrina* 'Purpusii'.
♀ ***T. sillamontana***, syn. *T. pexata*, *T. velutina*, illus. p.469.
T. spathacea, syn. *Rhoeo discolor*, *R. spathacea* (Boat lily, Moses-in-the-cradle). Evergreen, clump-forming perennial. **H** 50cm (20in), **S** 25cm (10in). Frost tender. Rosette of lance-shaped, fleshy leaves, to 30cm (12in) long, is green above, purple below. Bears tiny, white flowers, enclosed in boat-shaped, leaf-like bracts, year-round. ♀ **'Vittata'** has leaves striped longitudinally with pale yellow.
T. velutina. See *T. sillamontana.*
♀ ***T. zebrina*** (Silver inch plant), syn. *Zebrina pendula*, illus. p.469. ♀ **'Purpusii'** (syn. *T. purpusii*) is a strong-growing, evergreen, trailing or mat-forming perennial. **H** 10cm (4in), **S** indefinite. Frost tender. Has elliptic, purple- tinged, bluish-green leaves and tiny, shallowly cup-shaped, pink flowers.
♀ **'Quadricolor'** has leaves striped green, pink, red and white.

TRAPA

Water chestnut

TRAPACEAE/LYTHRACEAE

Genus of deciduous, perennial and annual, floating water plants, grown for their foliage and flowers. Frost hardy to frost tender, min. 5°C (41°F). Requires sun. Propagate in spring from seed gathered in autumn and stored frost-free, in water or damp moss.
T. natans (Water chestnut) illus. p.442.

Trichocereus bridgesii. See *Echinopsis lageniformis.*
Trichocereus candicans. See *Echinopsis candicans.*
Trichocereus spachianus. See *Echinopsis spachiana.*

TRICHODIADEMA

AIZOACEAE

Genus of bushy, perennial succulents with woody or tuberous roots and cylindrical to semi-cylindrical leaves. Frost tender, min. 5°C (41°F). Needs a sunny position and well-drained soil. Propagate by seed or stem cuttings in spring or summer.
♀ ***T. densum.*** Tufted, perennial succulent. **H** 10cm (4in), **S** 20cm (8in). Cylindrical, pale green leaves are each 1–2cm (½–¾in) long and tipped with clusters of white bristles. Roots and prostrate, green stem are both fleshy and form caudex. The stem tip bears daisy-like, cerise-pink flower heads, 3cm (1¼in) across, in summer.
T. mirabile illus. p.481.

TRICHOSANTHES

CUCURBITACEAE

Genus of annual and evergreen, perennial, tendril climbers, grown for their fruits and overall appearance. Frost tender, min. 15–18°C (59–64°F). Needs full sun or partial shade and humus-rich soil. Water freely in growing season, less in cool weather. Provide support. Propagate by seed in spring at not less than 21°C (70°F).
T. anguina. See *T. cucumerina* var. *anguina.*
T. cucumerina* var. *anguina, syn. *T. anguina* (Snake gourd). Erect to spreading, annual, tendril climber. **H** 3–5m (10–15ft). Has broadly oval to almost triangular, sometimes shallowly 3- to 5-lobed, mid- to pale green leaves, to 20cm (8in) long. In summer produces 5-petalled, white flowers, 2.5–5cm (1–2in) across, with heavily fringed petals; females are solitary, the males in racemes. Cylindrical fruits, 60cm (2ft) or rarely to 2m (6ft) long, often twisted or coiled, are green-and-white striped and ripen to dull orange.

Trichosma suavis. See *Eria coronaria.*
Tricuspidaria lanceolata. See *Crinodendron hookerianum.*

TRICYRTIS

Toad lily

LILIACEAE/CONVALLARIACEAE

Genus of late summer- and autumn-flowering, rhizomatous perennials. Fully hardy. Grows in sun or, in warm areas, in partial shade. Needs humus-rich, moist soil. Propagate by division in spring or by seed in autumn.
♀ ***T. formosana***, syn. *T. stolonifera*, illus. p.247.
T. hirta. Upright, rhizomatous perennial. **H** 30cm–1m (1–3ft), **S** 45cm (1½ft). In late summer and early autumn, clusters of large, open bell-shaped, white-spotted, purple flowers appear from axils of uppermost leaves. Leaves are narrowly oval, hairy and dark green and clasp stems. **var. *alba*** illus. p.277.
T. macrantha. Upright, rhizomatous perennial. **H** and **S** 60cm (24in). In early autumn has loose sheaves of open bell-shaped, deep primrose-yellow flowers, spotted light chocolate, at tips of arching stems; small, oval leaves are dark green.
T. stolonifera. See *T. formosana.*

TRIFOLIUM

Clover

LEGUMINOSAE/PAPILIONACEAE

Genus of annuals, biennials and perennials, some of which are semi-evergreen, with round, usually 3-lobed leaves and heads of pea-like flowers. Some species are useful in rock gardens or on banks, others in agriculture. Many are invasive. Fully to frost hardy. Needs sun and well-drained soil. Propagate by division in spring or by seed in autumn. Self-seeds readily.
***T. repens* 'Purpurascens'** illus. p.375.

TRILLIUM

Trinity flower, Wood lily

LILIACEAE/TRILLIACEAE

Genus of rhizomatous perennials with petals, sepals and leaves that are all borne in whorls of 3. Is excellent for woodland gardens, and also shaded borders and rockeries. Fully hardy. Enjoys partial shade and fertile, moist but well-drained, neutral to acid soil. Propagate by division after foliage has died down in summer or by seed in autumn.

T. cernuum. Clump-forming perennial. **H** 30–45cm (12–18in), **S** 30cm (12in). Has nodding, maroon-centred, white flowers borne in spring beneath luxuriant, 3-parted, mid-green leaves.

T. chloropetalum illus. p.255.

♀ ***T. erectum*** (Birthroot) illus. p.260.

♀ ***T. grandiflorum*** (Wake-robin) illus. p.255. **'Flore Pleno'** is a clump-forming perennial. **H** 38cm (15in), **S** 30cm (12in). Large, double, pure white flowers, are borne singly in spring, turning pink with age. Has large broadly oval, dark green leaves.

T. nivale (Dwarf white wood lily, Snow trillium). Early spring-flowering, rhizomatous perennial. **H** 7cm (3in), **S** 10cm (4in). Whorls of 3 oval leaves emerge at same time as outward-facing, slightly nodding, white flowers, each with 3 narrowly oval petals. Thrives in a trough or alpine house. Is difficult to grow.

T. ovatum illus. p.255.

♀ ***T. rivale*** illus. p.350.

T. sessile (Toadshade) illus. p.260.

T. undulatum (Painted trillium, Painted wood lily). Clump-forming perennial. **H** 10–20cm (4–8in), **S** 15–20cm (6–8in). Open funnel-shaped flowers with red-bordered, green sepals and 3 white or pink petals, each with a basal carmine stripe, are borne singly in spring, above broadly oval, basal, blue-green leaves.

TRIPETALEIA

ERICACEAE

Genus of one species of deciduous shrub, grown for its flowers; is now often included in *Elliottia*. Fully hardy. Needs semi-shade and moist, peaty, neutral to acid soil. Propagate by softwood cuttings in summer or by seed in autumn.

T. paniculata, syn. *Elliottia paniculata*. Deciduous, upright shrub. **H** and **S** 1.5m (5ft). Bears upright panicles of pink-tinged, white flowers, each with 3 (or 4 or 5) narrow petals, from mid-summer to early autumn. Lance-shaped, dark green leaves persist well into autumn.

TRIPTERYGIUM

CELASTRACEAE

Genus of deciduous, twining or scrambling climbers, grown for their foliage and fruits. Frost hardy. Grow in any fertile, well-drained soil and in full sun or light shade. Water freely while in full growth, less in low temperatures. Provide stems with support. Thin out crowded stems in winter or early spring. Propagate by seed when ripe or in spring, or by semi-ripe cuttings taken in summer.

T. regelii. Deciduous, thin-stemmed, twining or scrambling climber. **H** 10m (30ft). Leaves are oval and usually rich green. In late summer produces clusters, 20–25cm (8–10in) long, of small, off-white flowers, followed by winged, green fruits.

Tristania conferta. See *Lophostemon confertus.*

TRITELEIA

LILIACEAE/ALLIACEAE

Genus of late spring- and early summer-flowering corms with wiry stems carrying *Allium*-like umbels of funnel-shaped flowers. Long, narrow leaves usually die away by flowering time. Frost hardy. Needs an open but sheltered, sunny situation and well-drained soil that dries out to some extent in summer. Dies down in mid- to late summer until spring; plant during dormancy in early autumn. Propagate by seed or offsets in autumn.

T. hyacinthina, syn. *Brodiaea hyacinthina*, *B. lactea*, illus. p.408.

T. ixioides, syn. *Brodiaea ixioides*, *B. lutea*. Early summer-flowering corm. **H** to 50cm (20in), **S** 8–10cm (3–4in). Bears semi-erect, basal leaves. Stem has a loose umbel, to 12cm (5in) across, of yellow flowers; petals each have a purple-stripe. **'Starlight'** illus. p.407.

T. laxa, syn. *Brodiaea laxa*, illus. p.411. **'Koningin Fabiola'**, syn. *Brodiaea laxa* 'Queen Fabiola', illus. p.411.

T. peduncularis, syn. *Brodiaea peduncularis*. Early summer-flowering corm. **H** 10–40cm (4–16in), **S** 10–15cm (4–6in). Bears semi-erect, basal leaves. Stem has a loose umbel, to 35cm (14in) across, of white flowers, each 1.5–3cm (⅝–1¼in) long, faintly tinged blue.

TRITONIA

IRIDACEAE

Genus of corms, with sword-shaped, erect leaves, grown for their spikes of colourful flowers. Frost to half hardy. Needs a sunny, sheltered site and well-drained soil. Plant corms in autumn (*T. disticha* subsp. *rubrolucens* in spring). Dry off once leaves die back in summer (winter for *T. disticha* subsp. *rubrolucens*). Propagate by seed in autumn or by offsets at replanting time.

♀ ***T. crocata***, syn. *T. hyalina*. Spring-flowering corm. **H** 15–35cm (6–14in), **S** 5–8cm (2–3in). Half hardy. Has erect, basal leaves. Each wiry stem has a loose spike of up to 10 widely cup-shaped, orange or pink flowers, 4–5cm (1½–2in) across, with transparent margins.

T. disticha* subsp. *rubrolucens, syn. *T. rosea*, *T. rubrolucens*, illus. p.409.

T. hyalina. See *T. crocata*.

T. rosea. See *T. disticha* subsp. *rubrolucens*.

T. rubrolucens. See *T. disticha* subsp. *rubrolucens*.

TROCHOCARPA

ERICACEAE/EPACRIDACEAE

Genus of evergreen shrubs, grown for their nodding flower spikes. Frost hardy to frost tender, min. 7°C (45°F). Requires sun and moist but well-drained, peaty, sandy soil. Propagate by semi-ripe cuttings in summer.

T. thymifolia. Slow-growing, evergreen, erect shrub. **H** 30cm (12in), **S** to 20cm (8in). Frost hardy. Stems are covered in minute, thyme-like leaves. Carries 4cm (1½in) long spikes of tiny, bell-shaped, pink flowers in summer–autumn. Suits an alpine house.

TROCHODENDRON

TROCHODENDRACEAE

Genus of one species of evergreen tree, grown for its foliage and flowers. Frost hardy, but needs shelter from strong, cold winds. Tolerates a sunny or shady position and requires moist but well-drained soil; dislikes very dry or very shallow, chalky soil. Propagate by semi-ripe cuttings in summer or by seed in autumn.

T. aralioides illus. p.79.

TROLLIUS

Globeflower

RANUNCULACEAE

Genus of spring- or summer-flowering perennials that thrive beside pools and streams. Fully hardy. Tolerates sun or shade. Does best in moist soil. Propagate by division in early autumn or by seed in summer or autumn.

***T. x cultorum* 'Alabaster'** illus. p.436. **'Earliest of All'** is a clump-forming perennial. **H** 60cm (24in), **S** 45cm (18in). Globular, butter-yellow flowers are borne singly in spring, above rounded, deeply divided, mid-green leaves.

♀ **'Goldquelle'** has large, rich orange flowers. ♀ **'Orange Princess'**, **H** 75cm (30in), **S** 45cm (18in), bears orange-gold flowers.

T. europaeus illus. p.445. **'Canary Bird'** is a clump-forming perennial. **H** 60cm (24in), **S** 45cm (18in). In spring bears globular, canary-yellow flowers above rounded, deeply divided, mid-green leaves.

T. pumilus illus. p.358.

T. yunnanensis. Clump-forming perennial. **H** 60cm (2ft), **S** 30cm (1ft). Has broadly oval leaves with 3–5 deep lobes. Buttercup-like, bright yellow flowers are produced in late spring or summer.

TROPAEOLUM

Nasturtium

TROPAEOLACEAE

Genus of annuals, perennials and herbaceous, twining climbers, grown for their brightly coloured flowers. Fully hardy to frost tender, min. 5°C (41°F). Most species prefer sun and well-drained soil. Propagate by seed, tubers or basal stem cuttings in spring. Aphids and caterpillars of cabbage white butterfly and its relatives may cause problems.

♀ ***T.* Alaska Series.** See *T. majus* Alaska Series.

T. azureum. Herbaceous, leaf-stalk climber with small tubers. **H** to 1.2m (4ft). Frost tender. Leaves, to 5cm (2in) across, have 5 narrow lobes. Small, purple-blue flowers, with notched petals, open in late summer.

T. canariense. See *T. peregrinum*.

***T.* 'Empress of India'.** Fast-growing, bushy annual. **H** 23cm (12in), **S** 45cm (18in). Fully hardy. Has rounded, purple-green leaves. Trumpet-shaped, spurred, semi-double, rich scarlet flowers, 5cm (2in) wide, are borne from early summer to early autumn.

***T.* Gleam Series.** Fast-growing, semi-trailing annual. **H** 40cm (16in), **S** 60cm (24in). Fully hardy. Have rounded, mid-green leaves. From early summer to early autumn, bears trumpet-shaped, spurred, semi-double flowers, 5cm (2in) wide, in single colours or in a mixture that includes scarlet, yellow and orange and pastel shades.

***T.* Jewel Series** illus. p.327.

T. majus. Fast-growing, bushy annual. **H** 1–3m (3–10ft), **S** 1.5–5m (5–15ft). Frost tender. Has rounded to kidney-shaped, wavy-margined, pale green leaves. From summer to autumn, bears long-spurred, red, orange or yellow flowers, 5–6cm (2–2½in) wide. Many cultivars often attributed to *T. majus*, and with similar characteristics to the species, are of hybrid origin, and are described in this book under their cultivar names. ♀ **Alaska Series** illus. p. 323. ♀ **'Hermine Grashoff'** illus. p.307.

***T.* 'Peach Melba'.** Fast-growing, bushy annual. **H** to 45cm (18in), **S** 30cm (12in). Fully hardy. Bears rounded, mid-green leaves. Trumpet-shaped, spurred, pale yellow, flowers, 5cm (2in) wide, and blotched with scarlet are produced from early summer to early autumn.

T. peregrinum, syn. *T. canariense* (Canary creeper). Herbaceous, leaf-stalk climber. **H** to 2m (6ft). Frost tender. Grey-green leaves have 5 broad lobes. Small, bright yellow flowers, the 2 upper petals much larger and fringed, are borne from summer until first frosts. In cool areas, is best grown as an annual.

T. polyphyllum illus. p.276.

♀ ***T. speciosum*** (Flame creeper, Flame nasturtium) illus. p.202.

T. tricolor. See *T. tricolorum*.

♀ ***T. tricolorum***, syn. *T. tricolor*, illus. p.461.

T. tuberosum. Herbaceous, tuberous-rooted, leaf-stalk climber. **H** 2–3m (6–10ft). Half hardy. Greyish-green leaves have 3–5 lobes; from mid-summer to late autumn has cup-shaped flowers with orange-yellow petals, orange-red sepals and a long spur. ♀ **var. *lineamaculatum* 'Ken Aslet'** illus. p.207.

♀ ***T.* Whirlybird Series'.** Fast-growing, bushy annual. **H** 25cm (10in), **S** 35cm (14in). Fully hardy. Have rounded, mid-green leaves. Trumpet-shaped, spurred, single to semi-double flowers, 5cm (2in) wide, are borne in a mixture or in single colours from early summer to early autumn.

TSUGA

PINACEAE

See also CONIFERS.

T. canadensis (Canada Hemlock, Eastern hemlock) illus. p.102. **'Aurea'** is a broadly conical-shaped conifer, often with several stems. **H** 5m (15ft) or more, **S** 2–3m (6–10ft). Fully hardy. Shoots are pake grey with spirally-arranged, needle-like, flattened leaves, golden-yellow when young, ageing to green in their second year, those along the top are inverted to show silver bands. Has ovoid, light brown cones. **'Bennett'**, **H** 1–2m (3–6ft), **S** 2m (6ft), is a compact, dwarf form with arching

branches and a nest-shaped, central depression. ♀ **'Pendula'** (syn. *T.c.* f. *pendula*) has weeping branches that may be trained to create a dome. **H** and **S** 3–5m (10–15ft); if left to spread at ground level, **H** 50cm (20in), **S** 2–5m (6–15ft).
T. caroliniana (Carolina hemlock). Conifer with a conical or ovoid crown. **H** 10–15m (30–50ft), **S** 5–8m (15–25ft). Fully hardy. Red-brown shoots produce spirally set, needle-like, flattened, glossy, dark green leaves. Bears ovoid, green cones, ripening to brown.
T. diversifolia (Japanese hemlock, Northern Japanese hemlock). Conifer with a broad, dense crown. **H** 10–15m (30–50ft), **S** 8–12m (25–40ft). Fully hardy. Has orange shoots and needle-like, flattened, glossy, deep green leaves, banded with white beneath, that are spirally set. Ovoid cones are dark brown.
♀ ***T. heterophylla*** (Western hemlock). Vigorous, conical conifer with drooping branchlets. **H** 20–30m (70–100ft), **S** 8–10m (25–30ft). Fully hardy. Grey shoots bear spirally set, needle-like, flattened, dark green leaves with silvery bands beneath. Green cones ripen dark brown.
T. mertensiana (Mountain hemlock). Narrowly conical conifer with short, horizontal branches. **H** 8–15m (25–50ft), **S** 3–6m (10–20ft). Fully hardy. Red-brown shoots bear needle-like, flattened, glaucous blue-green or grey-green leaves, spirally arranged. Cones are cylindrical and yellow-green to purple, ripening to dark brown. **'Glauca'** illus. p.99.
T. sieboldii (Japanese hemlock, Southern Japanese hemlock). Broadly conical conifer. **H** 15m (50ft), **S** 8–10m (25–30ft). Fully hardy. Has glossy, buff shoots that bear needle-like, flattened, lustrous, dark green leaves, set spirally. Cones are ovoid and dark brown.

TSUSIOPHYLLUM

ERICACEAE

Genus of one species of semi-evergreen shrub, grown for its flowers. Is similar to *Rhododendron* and is suitable for rock gardens and peat beds. Frost hardy. Requires shade and well-drained, peaty, sandy soil. Propagate by softwood cuttings in spring or early summer or by seed in autumn or spring.
T. tanakae. Semi-evergreen, spreading shrub. **H** 15cm (6in) or more, **S** 25cm (10in). Twiggy, branched stems bear tiny, narrowly oval, hairy leaves. In early summer produces small, tubular, white or pinkish-white flowers at stem tips.

TUBERARIA

CISTACEAE

Genus of annuals, grown for their flowers. Fully hardy. Requires sun and in very well-drained soil. Propagate by seed in spring.
T. guttata, syn. *Helianthemum guttatum*. Moderately fast-growing, upright, branching annual. **H** and **S** 10–30cm (4–12in). Has lance-shaped, hairy, mid-green leaves and, in summer, yellow flowers, sometimes red-spotted at base of petals, that look like small, single roses.

TULBAGHIA

LILIACEAE/ALLIACEAE

Genus of clump-forming, mainly deciduous, sometimes semi-evergreen, rhizomatous or bulbous perennials. Frost to half hardy. Needs full sun and well-drained soil. Propagate by division or seed in spring.
T. fragrans. See *T. simmleri*.
T. natalensis. Semi-evergreen, clump-forming perennial. **H** 12cm (5in), **S** 10cm (4in). Frost hardy. In mid-summer, umbels of delicately fragrant, tubular, yellow-centred, white flowers, with spreading petal lobes, open above fine, grass-like, mid-green foliage.
T. pulchella. See *T. simmleri*.
T. simmleri, syn. *T. fragrans*, *T. pulchella*, *T. simmieri*, illus. p.411.
T. violacea illus. p.280.

TULIPA

Tulip

LILIACEAE

Genus of mainly spring-flowering bulbs, grown for their bright, upward-facing flowers. Each bulb produces a few linear to lance-shaped, green or grey-green leaves on the stem. Flowers bear 6 usually pointed petals (botanically known as perianth segments) and 6 stamens, singly, unless otherwise stated below. Each plant has a spread of up to 20cm (8in). All are fully hardy unless otherwise stated. Requires a sunny position with well-drained soil and appreciates a summer baking; in cool, wet areas, bulbs may be lifted, when the leaves have died down, and stored in a dry place for replanting in autumn. Propagate by division of bulbs in autumn or, for species, by seed in spring or autumn. ⓘ If ingested, all parts may cause mild stomach upset, and contact with any part may aggravate skin allergies. See also feature panel pp.400–401. Horticulturally, tulips are grouped into the following divisions.

Single Early Group (Div.1) – has cup-shaped, single, white to dark purple flowers, to 7cm (3in) across, often margined, "flamed" or flecked with a contrasting colour, from early to mid-spring. **H** 15–45cm (6–18in).
Double Early Group (Div.2) – has bowl-shaped, fully double, dark red to yellow or white flowers, to 8cm (3in) across, often margined or flecked with another colour, borne in mid-spring. **H** 30–40cm (12–16in).
Triumph Group (Div.3) – sturdy stems bear cup-shaped, single flowers, to 6cm (2½in) across, in a range of colour and often margined or flecked with a contrasting colour, in mid- and late spring. **H** 35–60cm (14–24in).
Darwin Hybrid Group (Div.4) – has egg-shaped, single flowers, to 7cm (3in) across, in a range of colours and usually flushed, "flamed" or margined with a different colour and often with contrasting bases, from mid- to late spring. **H** 50–70cm (20–28in).
Single Late Group including Cottage and Darwin Hybrids (Div.5) – has cup- or goblet-shaped, single flowers, sometimes several to a stem, in white to yellow, pink, red or almost black, often with contrasting margins, in late spring. **H** 45–75cm (18–30in).
Lily-flowered Group (Div.6) – strong stems bear goblet-shaped, single flowers, to 8cm (3in) across, with reflexed, pointed petal tips and sometimes margined, "flamed" or flushed with a contrasting colour, in late spring. **H** 45–65cm (18–26in).
Fringed Group (Div.7) – flowers are similar to those in Div.6, but have fringed petals. **H** 35–65cm (14–26in).
Viridiflora Group (Div.8) – has cup- or almost closed bowl-shaped, single flowers, to 8cm (3in) across, sometimes entirely green, margined with another colour, or white to yellow, red or purple, "flamed" or striped green, with contrasting centres, borne in late spring. **H** 40–55cm (16–22in).
Rembrandt Group (Div.9) – comprises mostly very old cultivars, similar to Div.6, but has colours "broken" into striped or feathered patterns owing to virus. Flowers in late spring. **H** 45–65cm (18–26in).
Parrot Group (Div.10) – has cup-shaped, single, white to pink or violet-blue flowers, to 10cm (4in) across, often unevenly striped with different colours, including green, borne in late spring. Petals are finely and irregularly cut. **H** 35–65cm (14–26in).
Double Late Group (peony-flowered) (Div.11) – has bowl-shaped, fully double flowers, to 12cm (5in) across, in white to purple, sometimes margined or "flamed" in a different colour, borne in late spring. **H** 35–60cm (14–24in).
Kaufmanniana Group (Div.12) – comprises *T. kauffmanniana* and hybrids and has bowl-shaped, single flowers, 8–10cm (3–4in) across, frequently multicoloured and usually with distinctively coloured bases, in early or mid-spring. Leaves are sometimes marked bronze, red or purple. **H** 15–30cm (6–12in).
Fosteriana Group (Div.13) – comprises *T. fosteriana* and hybrids and has bowl-shaped, single flowers, to 12cm (5in) across, in white to yellow or dark red, often margined or "flamed" in another colour and with contrasting bases, borne in mid-spring. Leaves are sometimes marked red-purple. **H** 20–65cm (8–26in).
Greigii Group (Div.14) – comprises *T. greigii* and hybrids and has bowl-shaped, single, yellow to red flowers, to 10cm (4in) across, sometimes "flamed" or margined in a different colour and with contrasting bases, borne in early or mid-spring. Blue-green leaves are generally wavy-margined and always marked dark bluish-maroon. **H** 15–30cm (6–12in).
Miscellaneous Group (Div.15) – comprises all species and hybrids not included in other divisions. Flowers are produced from late winter to late spring.

***T.* 'Abu Hassan'** (illus. p.401), Div.3. Mid- to late-flowering spring bulb. **H** 50cm (20in). Produces cardinal-red flowers with pinkish-red stripes and yellow edges.
T. acuminata (Horned tulip; illus. p.401), Div.15. Mid-spring-flowering bulb. **H** 30–45cm (12–18in). Flowers are 7–13cm (3–5in) long, with long-pointed, tapered, pale red or yellow petals, often tinged with red or green outside.
***T.* 'Ad Rem'**, Div.4. Mid- to late spring-flowering bulb. **H** 60cm (24in). Flowers are scarlet with black bases and yellow margins. Anthers are yellow.
T. aitchisonii. See *T. clusiana*.
***T.* 'Albert Heyn'**, Div.13. (illus. p.400). Early spring-flowering bulb. **H** 35cm (14in). Bears deep rose-pink flowers with a purple sheen and paler pink edges.
♀ ***T.* 'Ancilla'**, Div.12. Early spring-flowering bulb. **H** 15cm (6in). Flowers are pink and reddish outside, white inside, each with a central, red ring.
♀ ***T.* 'Angélique'**, Div.11. Late spring-flowering bulb. **H** 40cm (16in). Delicately scented, double, pale pink flowers deepen with age. Each petal has paler streaks and a lighter margin. Is good for bedding.
♀ ***T.* 'Apeldoorn's Elite'** (illus. p.401), Div.4. Mid- to late spring-flowering bulb. **H** 60cm (24in). Has buttercup-yellow flowers feathered with cherry-red and with yellowish-green bases.
♀ ***T.* 'Apricot Beauty'**, Div.1. Early spring-flowering bulb. **H** 40cm (16in). Flowers salmon-pink faintly tinged red.
♀ ***T.* 'Artist'** (illus. p.401), Div.8. Late spring-flowering bulb. **H** 45cm (18in). Flowers are salmon-pink and purple outside, sometimes marked with green, and deep salmon-pink and green inside.
***T.* 'Attila'**, Div.3. Mid-spring-flowering bulb. **H** 40cm (16in). Strong stems carry long-lasting, pink flowers.
♀ ***T. aucheriana***, Div.15. Early spring-flowering bulb. **H** to 20cm (8in). Has grey-green leaves. Bears yellow-centred, pink flowers, 2–5cm (¾–2in) long, each tapered at the base, and with oval petals.
T. australis. See *T. sylvestris*.
T. bakeri. See *T. saxatilis*.
***T.* 'Balalaika'**, Div.5. Late spring-flowering bulb. **H** 50cm (20in). Bright red flowers each have a yellow base and black stamens.
♀ ***T.* 'Ballade'** (illus. p.400), Div.6. Late spring-flowering bulb. **H** 50cm (20in). Reddish-magenta flowers with a white-margined, yellow base have long petals that are margined white.
♀ ***T.* 'Ballerina'** (illus. p.401), Div.6. Late-flowering spring bulb. **H** 60cm (24in). Produces lemon-yellow flowers with blood-red, flame-like markings, orange-yellow veins near the margins, and star-shaped yellow bases. Inner surfaces are bright red, feathered marigold-orange, with pale golden-yellow anthers.
♀ ***T. batalinii***, Div.15. Early spring-flowering bulb. **H** 10–30cm (4–12in). Is often included under *T. linifolia*. Leaves are grey-green. Flowers, 2–6cm (¾–2½in) long, have broadly oval petals and are bowl-shaped at the base. Pale yellow petals are darker yellow or brown at bases inside. Several cultivars are hybrids between *T. batalinii* and *T. linifolia*. These include **'Apricot Jewel'** with flowers that are orange-red outside, yellow inside. ♀ **'Bright Gem'**, which has yellow flowers flushed with orange; and **'Bronze Charm'**, which bears yellow flowers with bronze feathering.
***T.* 'Bellona'** (illus. p.401), Div.1. Early spring-flowering bulb. **H** 30cm (12in). Fragrant flowers are deep golden-yellow. Is good for bedding and forcing.
T. biflora, syn. *T. polychroma*, Div.15. Early spring-flowering bulb. **H** 5–10cm

T

(2–4in). Has grey-green leaves. Stem bears 1–5 fragrant, yellow-centred, white flowers, 1.5–3.5cm (⅝–1½in) long and tapered at the bases. Narrowly oval petals are flushed outside with greenish-grey or greenish-pink. Suits a rock garden.

***T.* 'Bing Crosby'**, Div.3. Mid- to late spring-flowering bulb. **H** 50cm (20in). Has scarlet flowers.

***T.* 'Bird of Paradise'** (illus. p.400), Div.10. Late spring-flowering bulb. **H** 45cm (18in). Produces orange-margined, cardinal-red flowers with bright yellow bases. Anthers are purple.

***T.* 'Black Hero'** (illus. p.401), Div.11. Late spring-flowering bulb. **H** 60cm (24in). Flowers have maroon outer petals and darker, almost black edges and dark purple-black inner petals.

***T.* 'Black Jewel'**, Div.7. Late spring-flowering bulb. **H** 50cm (20in). Produces deep maroon-purple, almost black flowers with a crystalline fringe very lightly marked with golden-yellow.

***T.* 'Blue Parrot'** (illus. p.401), Div.10. Late spring-flowering bulb. **H** 60cm (24in). Very large, bright violet flowers, sometimes bronze outside, are borne on strong stems.

***T.* 'Burgundy Lace'**, Div.7. Late spring-flowering bulb. **H** 60cm (24in). Flowers are wine-red with fringed margins.

🏆 ***T.* 'Candela'** (illus. p.401), Div.13. Early to mid-spring-flowering bulb. **H** 30cm (12in). Large flowers are yellow, with black anthers, and long-lasting.

***T.* 'Cape Cod'**, Div.14. Mid- to late spring-flowering bulb. **H** 45cm (18in). Grey-green leaves have reddish stripes. Yellowish-bronze flowers each have a black-and-red base; petals are margined yellow outside.

🏆 ***T.* 'Carnaval de Nice'** (illus. p.400), Div.11. Late spring-flowering bulb. **H** 40cm (16in). Double flowers are white feathered with deep red.

🏆 ***T.* 'China Pink'** (illus. p.400), Div.6. Late spring-flowering bulb. **H** 55cm (22in). Flowers are pink, each with a white base, and have slightly reflexed petals.

***T.* 'Chopin'**, Div.12. Early spring-flowering bulb. **H** 20cm (8in). Has brown-mottled, grey-green leaves. Lemon-yellow flowers have black bases.

T. chrysantha. See *T. clusiana* var. *chrysantha*.

***T.* 'Clara Butt'**, Div.5. Late spring-flowering bulb. **H** 60cm (24in). Flowers are salmon-pink. Good for bedding.

T. clusiana, syn. *T. aitchisonii* (Lady tulip), Div.15. Mid-spring-flowering bulb. **H** to 30cm (12in). Has grey-green leaves. Each stem bears 1 or 2 flowers, 2–6.5cm (¾–2½in) long, that are bowl-shaped at the base. Narrowly oval, white petals are purple or crimson at base inside, striped deep pink outside. Stamens are purple. Flowers of 🏆 **var. *chrysantha*,** syn. *T. chrysantha* (illus. p.401) are yellow, flushed red or brown outside, with yellow stamens, **var. *stellata*** has white flowers with yellow bases and yellow stamens.

***T.* 'Couleur Cardinal'**, Div.3. Mid-spring-flowering bulb. **H** 35cm (14in). Plum-purple flowers are dark crimson-scarlet inside.

T. dasystemon of gardens. See *T. tarda*.

***T.* 'Dawnglow'**, Div.4. Mid- to late-spring-flowering bulb. **H** 60cm (24in). Pale apricot flowers are flushed with deep pink outside and are deep yellow inside.

***T.* 'Diana'**, Div.1. Early spring-flowering bulb. **H** 28cm (11in). Large, pure white flowers are carried on strong stems.

***T.* 'Dillenburg'**, Div.5. Late spring-flowering bulb. **H** 65cm (26in). Flowers are brick-orange and are good for bedding.

🏆 ***T.* 'Don Quichotte'**, Div.3. Mid-spring-flowering bulb. **H** 40cm (16in). Purple-pink flowers are long-lasting.

***T.* 'Dreamboat'**, Div.14. Mid- to late spring-flowering bulb. **H** 25cm (10in). Produces grey-green leaves with brown stripes. Urn-shaped, red-tinged, amber-yellow flowers have greenish-bronze bases with red blotches.

***T.* 'Dreaming Maid'** (illus. p.401), Div.3. Mid- to late spring-flowering bulb. **H** 55cm (22in). Flowers have white-margined, violet petals.

🏆 ***T.* 'Dreamland'** (illus. p.400), Div.5. Late spring-flowering bulb. **H** 60cm (24in). Flowers are red with white bases and yellow anthers.

T. eichleri. See *T. undulatifolia*.

🏆 ***T.* 'Esperanto'** (illus. p.400), Div.8. Late spring-flowering bulb. **H** 30cm (12in). Produces flowers with rose-pink petals that fade to pale pink towards the bottom, with green feathered bases. Has cream-edged, grey-green leaves.

***T.* 'Estella Rijnveld'** (illus. p.400), Div.10. Late spring-flowering bulb. **H** 60cm (24in). Large flowers are red, streaked with white and green.

🏆 ***T.* 'Fancy Frills'**, Div.10. Late spring-flowering bulb. **H** 50cm (20in). Fringed, ivory-white petals are striped and margined pink outside; inside, base is rose-pink. Anthers are pale yellow.

***T.* 'Flaming Parrot'**, Div.10. Late-spring flowering bulb. **H** 55cm (22in). Deep yellow flowers, "flamed" dark red, have primrose-yellow bases. Insides are primrose-yellow with glowing, blood-red 'flames'. Anthers are purple-black.

T. fosteriana, Div.15. Early spring-flowering bulb. **H** 20–45cm (8–18in). Has a downy stem and grey-green leaves, downy above. Flowers 4.5–10cm (1¾–4in) long, are bowl-shaped at the base with narrowly oval, bright red petals, and each has a purplish-black centre inside, ringed with yellow.

🏆 ***T.* 'Fringed Beauty'**, Div.7. Early to mid-spring-flowering bulb. **H** 32cm (13in). Fringed petals are bright red with yellow margins. Is excellent for forcing.

🏆 ***T.* 'Fringed Elegance'**, Div.7. Late spring-flowering bulb. **H** 50cm (20in). Produces pale yellow flowers dotted with pink outside; inside, bases have bronze-green blotches. Each petal has a yellow fringe. Anthers are purple.

***T.* 'Gala Beauty'**, Div.9. Late spring-flowering bulb. **H** 60cm (24in). Yellow flowers are streaked with crimson.

🏆 ***T.* 'Garden Party'**, Div.3. Mid- to late spring-flowering bulb. **H** 40–45cm (16–18in). Produces white flowers; petals are margined deep pink outside, and inside are streaked with deep pink.

***T.* 'Giuseppe Verdi'** illus. p.407.

🏆 ***T.* 'Glück'** (illus. p.401), Div.12. Early spring-flowering bulb. **H** 15cm (6in). Has reddish-brown-mottled, grey-green leaves. Petals are red outside, margined bright yellow, and yellow inside, each with a darker base.

***T.* 'Golden Apeldoorn'** (illus. p.401), Div.4. Mid- to late spring-flowering bulb. **H** 50–60cm (20–24in). Golden-yellow flowers have a black base and stamens.

***T.* 'Golden Artist'**, Div.8. Late spring-flowering bulb. **H** 45cm (18in). Flowers are bright golden-yellow.

***T.* 'Gordon Cooper'**, Div.4. Mid- to late spring-flowering bulb. **H** 60cm (24in). Petals are deep pink outside, margined red; inside they are red with blue-and-yellow bases. Has black anthers.

***T.* 'Greenland'.** See *T.* 'Groenland'.

T. greigii, Div.15. Early spring-flowering bulb. **H** 20–45cm (8–18in). Has downy stems. Leaves are streaked or mottled with red or purple. Cup-shaped flowers, 3–10cm (1¼–4in) long, with broadly oval, red or yellow petals, have yellow-ringed, black centres.

***T.* 'Greuze'**, Div.5. Late spring-flowering bulb. **H** 65cm (26in). Flowers are dark violet-purple and are good for bedding.

***T.* 'Groenland'**, syn. *T.* 'Greenland' (illus. p.400), Div.8. Late spring-flowering bulb. **H** 50cm (20in). Bears flowers with green petals that are margined rose-pink. Is a good bedding tulip.

T. hageri, Div.15. Mid-spring-flowering bulb. **H** 10–30cm (4–12in). Frost hardy. Stem has 1–4 flowers, 3–6cm (1½–2½in) long, tapered at the base and with oval, dull red petals tinged with green outside.

***T.* 'Heart's Delight'**, Div.12. Early spring-flowering bulb. **H** 20–25cm (8–10in). Has green leaves striped red-brown. Deep pinkish-red flowers, margined pale pink, have pale pink inside with red-blotched, yellow bases.

***T.* 'Hollywood'**, Div.8. Late spring-flowering bulb. **H** 30cm (12in). Red flowers, tinged and streaked with green, have yellow bases. Is good for bedding.

T. humilis, Div.15. Early spring-flowering bulb. A variable species, often considered to include *T. aucheriana*, *T. pulchella* and *T. violacea*. **H** to 20cm (8in). Has grey-green leaves. Stem bears usually 1, sometimes 2 or 3, pinkish-magenta flowers, 2–5cm (¾–2in) long, tapered at the base and with a yellow centre inside. Petals are oval. Suitable for a rock garden.

***T.* 'Jack Laan'**, Div.9. Late spring-flowering bulb. **H** 60cm (24in). Purple flowers are shaded with brown and feathered with white and yellow.

🏆 ***T.* 'Juan'**, Div.13. Early to mid-spring-flowering bulb. **H** 35cm (14in). Flowers are deep orange overlaid with scarlet. Leaves are marked with reddish-brown.

T. kaufmanniana (Water lily tulip; illus. p.401), Div.15. Early spring-flowering bulb. **H** 10–35cm (4–14in). Leaves are grey-green. Stem has 1–5 often scented flowers, 3–10cm (1½–4in) long and bowl-shaped at the base. Narrowly oval petals are usually either cream or yellow, flushed with pink or grey-green outside; centres are often a different colour. Pink, orange or red forms occasionally occur.

🏆 ***T.* 'Keizerskroon'**, Div.1. Early spring-flowering bulb. **H** 35cm (14in). Flowers have crimson-scarlet petals, with broad, bright yellow margins. Is a good, reliable bedding tulip.

🏆 ***T.* 'Kingsblood'**, Div.5. Late spring-flowering bulb. **H** 60cm (24in). Cherry-red flowers are margined scarlet.

🏆 ***T. linifolia***, Div.15. Early spring-flowering bulb. **H** 10–30cm (4–12in). A variable species, often considered to include *T. batalinii* and *T. maximowiczii*. Has grey-green leaves. Red flowers, 2–6cm (¾–2in) long, are bowl-shaped at the base and, inside, have blackish-purple centres that are usually ringed with cream or yellow. Petals are broadly oval.

***T.* 'Lustige Witwe'**, syn. *T.* 'Merry Widow', Div.3. Mid- to late spring-flowering bulb. Flowers have deep glowing red petals margined white.

***T.* 'Madame Lefeber'**, syn. *T.* 'Red Emperor' (illus. p.401), Div.13. Early to mid-spring-flowering bulb. **H** 35–40cm (14–16in). Produces very large, brilliant red flowers.

***T.* 'Maja'** (illus. p.401), Div.7. Late spring-flowering bulb. **H** 50cm (20in). Has egg-shaped, pale yellow flowers, with fringed petals, that are bronze-yellow at the base. Anthers are yellow.

***T.* 'Margot Fonteyn'**, Div.3. Mid- to late spring flowering bulb. **H** 40 45cm (16 18in). Flowers have yellow-margined, bright red petals, each with a yellow base inside. Anthers are black.

T. marjolletii, Div.15. Mid-spring-flowering bulb. **H** 40–50cm (16–20in). Produces flowers, 4–6cm (1½–2½in) long and bowl-shaped at the base, with broadly oval, creamy-white petals, margined and marked deep pink.

🏆 ***T.* 'Maureen'**, Div.5. Late spring-flowering bulb. **H** 70cm (28in). Bears marble-white flowers.

T. maximowiczii, Div.15. Early spring-flowering bulb. **H** 10–30cm (4–12in). Has grey-green leaves. Bright red flowers, 2–6cm (¾–2½in) long, with broadly oval petals, have white-bordered, black centres and are bowl-shaped at the base.

🏆 ***T.* 'Menton'** (illus. p.401), Div.5. Late spring-flowering bulb. **H** 60cm (24in). Flowers have light orange-margined, rose-pink petals with bright yellow and white bases. Anthers are yellow.

***T.* 'Merry Widow'.** See *T.* 'Lustige Witwe'.

🏆 ***T.* 'Monte Carlo'**, Div.2. Early spring-flowering bulb. **H** 40cm (16in). Has double, bright yellow flowers decorated with sparse, red streaks.

***T.* 'Negrita'** (illus. p.401), Div.3. Mid- to late spring-flowering bulb. H 45cm (18in). Produces deep purple flowers with red-purple streaks.

***T.* 'New Design'**, Div.3. Mid-spring-flowering bulb. **H** 40cm (16in). Flowers have yellow petals that fade to pinkish-white and are margined red outside and marked apricot inside. Leaves have pinkish-white margins.

🏆 ***T.* 'Orange Emperor'**, Div.13. Early to mid-spring-flowering bulb. **H** 40cm (16in). Flowers are bright orange, each with a yellow base inside and have black anthers.

***T.* 'Orange Triumph'**, Div.11. Late spring-flowering bulb. **H** 50cm (20in). Has double, soft orange-red flowers flushed with brown, and yellow margins.

🏆 ***T.* 'Oranje Nassau'**, Div.2. Early spring-flowering bulb. **H** 25–30cm (10–12in). Has double, blood-red flowers flushed fiery orange-red.

🏆 ***T.* 'Oratorio'**, Div.14. Mid- to late spring-flowering bulb. **H** 20cm (8in). Has

brown-mottled, grey-green leaves. Broadly urn-shaped flowers are rose-pink outside, apricot-pink inside with black bases.
T. orphanidea (illus. p.401), Div.15. Mid-spring-flowering bulb. **H** 10–30cm (4–12in). Frost hardy. Green leaves often have reddish margins. Stem has 1–4 flowers, 3–6cm (1¼–2½in) long and tapered at the base. Oval petals are orange-brown, tinged outside green and often purple.
***T.* 'Page Polka'**, Div.3. Mid-spring-flowering bulb. Large, deep red flowers have white bases and are striped with white. Anthers are yellow.
***T.* 'Palestrina'**, Div.5. Late spring-flowering bulb. **H** 45cm (18in). Petals of large, salmon-pink flowers are green outside.
***T.* 'Peach Blossom'**, Div.2. Early spring-flowering bulb. **H** 25–30cm (10–12in). Produces double, silvery-pink flowers flushed with deep pink.
***T.* 'Peer Gynt'**, Div.3. Mid- to late spring-flowering bulb. **H** 50cm (20in). Purple-margined, fuchsia-red flowers have white bases spotted with yellow. Anthers are purplish-grey.
🏆 ***T.* 'Plaisir'**, Div.14. Mid- to late spring-flowering bulb. **H** 15–20cm (6–8in). Has grey-green leaves mottled with red-brown. Bears broadly urn-shaped, pale yellow-margined, deep pinkish-red flowers, with black-and-yellow bases.
T. polychroma. See *T. biflora*.
🏆 ***T. praestans* 'Fusilier'**, Div.15. Early spring-flowering bulb. **H** 10–45cm (4–18in). Has a minutely downy stem and downy, grey-green leaves. Stem bears 3–5 flowers that are 5.5–6.5cm (2¼–2½in) long and bowl-shaped at the base. Oval petals are orange-scarlet. **'Unicum'** (illus. p.401) has leaves that are margined pale yellow. Flowers have bright red petals with yellow bases and blue-black anthers. **'Van Tubergen's Variety'** produces 2–5 flowers per stem that are often yellow at the base; it increases very freely.
🏆 ***T.* 'Prinses Irene'** (illus. p.401), Div.1. Early spring-flowering bulb. **H** 30–35cm (12–14in). Produces orange flowers streaked with purple.
T. pulchella, Div.15. Early spring-flowering bulb. **H** to 20cm (8in). Has grey-green leaves. Flowers, 2–5cm (¾–2in) long and tapered at the base, have oval, purple petals and yellow or bluish-black centres inside. Is useful for a rock garden.
🏆 ***T.* 'Purissima'**, syn. *T.* 'White Emperor' (illus. p.400), Div.13. Early to mid-spring-flowering bulb. **H** 35–40cm (14–16in). Flowers are pure white.
***T.* 'Queen of Night'** (illus. p.401), Div.5. Late spring-flowering bulb. **H** 60cm (24in). The darkest of all tulips, has long-lasting, very dark maroon-black flowers on sturdy stems. Is useful for bedding.
🏆 ***T.* 'Queen of Sheba'**, Div.6. Late-spring-flowering bulb. **H** 60cm (24in). Bears orange-margined, glowing, brownish-red flowers.
***T.* 'Red Emperor'.** See *T.* 'Madame Lefeber'.
***T.* 'Red Parrot'**, Div.10. Late spring-flowering bulb. **H** 60cm (24in). Large, raspberry-red flowers are carried on strong stems.
🏆 ***T.* 'Red Riding Hood'** (illus. p.401), Div.14. Late spring-flowering bulb. **H** 20cm (8in). Has vivid, black-based, scarlet flowers amid spreading, dark green leaves mottled brownish-purple.
T. saxatilis, syn. *T. bakeri* (illus. p.400), Div.15. Early spring-flowering bulb. **H** 15–45cm (6–18in). Frost hardy. Has shiny, green leaves. Stem produces 1–4 scented flowers, 4–5.5cm (1½–2¼in) long and tapered at the base. Oval, pink to lilac petals are yellow at the base inside.
***T.* 'Shakespeare'**, Div.12. Early spring-flowering bulb. **H** 12–15cm (5–6in). Petals are deep red outside, margined salmon, and salmon inside, flushed red with a yellow base.
***T.* 'Shirley'** (illus. p.400), Div.3. Mid- to late spring-flowering bulb. **H** 50cm (20in). Bears ivory-white flowers with pinkish-purple petal edges and flecks.
🏆 ***T. sprengeri*** (illus. p.401), Div.15. Late spring- and early summer-flowering bulb. **H** 30–45cm (12–18in). Flowers are 4.5–6.5cm (1¼–2½in) long and tapered at the base. Bears narrowly oval, orange-red petals, the outer 3 with buff-yellow backs. Latest-flowering tulip; increases rapidly.
🏆 ***T.* 'Spring Green'** (illus. p.400), Div.8. Late spring-flowering bulb. **H** 35–38cm (14–15in). Has white flowers feathered with green. Anthers are pale green.
T. sylvestris, syn. *T. australis* (illus. p.401), Div.15. Early spring-flowering bulb. **H** 10–45cm (4–18in). Yellow flowers, usually borne singly, are 3.5–6.5cm (1–2½in) long and tapered at the base. Narrowly oval petals are often tinged with green outside.
🏆 ***T. tarda***, syn. *T. dasystemon* of gardens, Div.15. Early spring-flowering bulb. **H** to 15cm (6in). Has glossy, green leaves. Flowers, 4–6 per stem, are 3–4cm (1¼–1½in) long and tapered at the base. Oval, white petals have yellow lower halves inside and are tinged with green and sometimes red outside. Suits a rock garden or raised bed.
🏆 ***T.* 'Toronto'**, Div.14. Mid- to late spring-flowering bulb. **H** 30cm (12in). Has mottled leaves and 2 or 3 long-lasting flowers per stem. Open, broadly cup-shaped flowers have pointed, bright red petals each with a brownish-green-yellow base inside. Anthers are bronze.
🏆 ***T. turkestanica*** (illus. p.400), Div.15. Early spring-flowering bulb. **H** 10–30cm (4–12in). Has a hairy stem and grey-green leaves. Unpleasant-smelling flowers, up to 12 per stem, are 1.5–3.5cm (⅝–1½in) long and tapered at the base. Oval, white petals are flushed green or pink outside; flowers have yellow or orange centres inside.
***T.* 'Uncle Tom'** (illus. p.401), Div.11. Late spring-flowering bulb. **H** 50cm (20in). Double flowers are maroon-red.
T. undulatifolia, syn. *T. eichleri*. Div.15. Early to mid-spring-flowering bulb. **H** 15–50cm (6–20in). Has a downy stem and grey-green leaves. Flowers, 3–8cm (1¼–3in) long, are bowl-shaped at the base. Narrowly oval, red or orange-red petals each have a pale red or buff back and a yellow-bordered, dark green or black blotch at the base inside.
🏆 ***T.* 'Union Jack'**, Div.5. Late spring-flowering bulb. **H** 60cm (24in). Ivory-white petals, marked with deep pinkish-red 'flames', have blue-margined, white bases.
🏆 ***T. urumiensis***, Div.15. Early spring-flowering bulb. **H** 10–20cm (4–8in). Stem is mostly below soil level. Leaves are green or greyish-green. Bears 1 or 2 flowers, each 4cm (1½in) long and tapered at the base. Narrowly oval, yellow petals are flushed mauve or red-brown outside. Is useful for a rock garden.
T. violacea Div.15. Early spring-flowering bulb. **H** to 20cm (8in). Has grey-green leaves. Violet-pink flowers, 2–5cm (¾–2in) long, are tapered at the base and have yellow or bluish-black centres inside. Petals are oval. Suits a rock garden or raised bed.
🏆 ***T.* 'West Point'**, Div.6. Late spring-flowering bulb. **H** 50cm (20in). Primrose-yellow flowers have long-pointed, recurved petals.
***T.* 'White Dream'** (illus. p.400), Div.3. Mid- to late spring-flowering bulb. **H** 40–45cm (16–18in). Flowers are white with yellow anthers.
***T.* 'White Emperor'.** See *T.* 'Purissima'.
***T.* 'White Parrot'**, Div.10. Late spring-flowering bulb. **H** 55cm (22in). Large flowers have ruffled, white petals, flecked green near the base. Is good for cutting.
🏆 ***T.* 'White Triumphator'** (illus. p.400), Div.6. Late spring-flowering bulb. **H** 65–70cm (26–28in). White flowers have elegantly reflexed petals.
T. whittallii, Div.15. Mid-spring-flowering bulb. **H** 30–35cm (12–14in). Frost hardy. Stem produces 1–4 flowers, 3–6cm (1¼–2½in) long, and tapered at the base. Oval petals are bright brownish-orange.
***T.* 'Yokohama'**, Div.1. Early to mid-spring-flowering bulb. **H** 35cm (14in). Pointed flowers are deep yellow.

Tunica saxifraga. See *Petrorhagia saxifraga*.

TURRAEA

MELIACEAE

Genus of evergreen trees and shrubs, grown for their flowers and foliage. Frost tender, min. 12–15°C (54–9°F). Prefers full sun. Needs fertile, well-drained soil. Water freely in full growth, less at other times. Young plants may need growing point removed to promote branching. Prune after flowering if necessary. Propagate by seed in spring or by semi-ripe cuttings in summer.
T. obtusifolia. Evergreen, rounded, bushy, arching shrub. Frost tender, min. 13°C (55°F). Has oval to lance-shaped leaves. Bears fragrant, white flowers from autumn to spring, followed by orange-yellow fruits like tiny, peeled tangerines.

TWEEDIA

ASCLEPIADACEAE/APOCYNACEAE

Genus of herbaceous, twining climbers; only one species is in general cultivation. Frost tender, min. 5°C (41°F). In cool climates, may be grown as an annual. Requires a position in sun and in well-drained soil. Pinch out tips of shoots to encourage branching. Propagate by seed in spring.
🏆 ***T. caerulea***, syn. *Oxypetalum caeruleum*. Herbaceous, twining climber with white-haired stems. **H** to 1m (3ft). Pink-flushed buds open to reveal small, fleshy, pale blue flowers, maturing purple, appear in summer and early autumn. Has green fruits to 15cm (6in) long.

TYLECODON

CRASSULACEAE

Genus of deciduous, bushy, winter-growing, succulent shrubs with very swollen stems. Frost tender, min. 7°C (45°F). Requires a sunny position and very well-drained soil. Propagate by seed or stem cuttings in summer. ⚠The leaves of *T. wallichii* are highly toxic if ingested.
T. paniculatus, syn. *Cotyledon paniculata* (Butter tree). Deciduous, bushy, succulent shrub. **H** and **S** 2m (6ft). Swollen stem and branches have papery, yellow coverings. Leaves are oblong to oval, fleshy and bright green. In summer, clusters of tubular, green-striped, red flowers are produced at the stem tips.
***T. papillaris* subsp. *wallichii*.** See *T. wallichii*.
T. reticulatus, syn. *Cotyledon reticulata* (Barbed-wire plant). Deciduous, bushy, succulent shrub. **H** and **S** 30cm (1ft). Swollen branches bear cylindrical leaves in winter. Has tubular, green-yellow flowers on a woody stem in autumn.
T. wallichii, syn. *Cotyledon wallichii*, *T. papillaris* subsp. *wallichii*. Deciduous, bushy, succulent shrub. **H** and **S** 30cm (1ft). Has 3cm (1¼in) thick stems with cylindrical, grooved-topped, green leaves at tips. After leaf fall, stems are neatly covered in raised leaf bases. Bears tubular, yellow-green flowers, 2cm (¾in) long, in autumn.

TYPHA

TYPHACEAE

Genus of deciduous, perennial, marginal water plants, grown for their decorative, cylindrical seed heads. Fully hardy. Requires a position in sun or shade. Propagate in spring by seed or division.
T. latifolia (Bulrush) illus. p.442. **'Variegata'** is a deciduous, perennial marginal water plant. **H** 90cm–1.2m (3–4ft), **S** indefinite. Strap-shaped, mid-green leaves have longitudinal, cream stripes. Produces spikes of beige flowers in late summer; these are followed by decorative, cylindrical, dark brown seed heads.
T. minima illus. p.443.

UVW

UGNI

MYRTACEAE

Genus of densely leafy, evergreen shrubs or trees. *U. molinae*, the only species usually cultivated, is valued for its foliage, flowers and fruit. Frost hardy. Needs full sun or partial shade and moist but well-drained soil. Propagate by semi-ripe cuttings in late summer.

U. molinae, syn. *Eugenia ugni, Myrtus ugni.* Evergreen, upright, densely branched shrub. **H** 1.5m (5ft), **S** 1m (3ft). Glossy, dark green leaves are oval. Has fragrant, slightly nodding, cup-shaped, white-pink-tinted flowers in late spring, then aromatic, edible, spherical, dark red fruits. Is good for hedging in mild areas.

ULEX

LEGUMINOSAE/PAPILIONACEAE

Genus of leafless, or almost leafless, shrubs that appear evergreen as a result of their year-round, green shoots and spines. Is grown for its flowers in spring. Fully hardy. Needs full sun, and prefers poor, well-drained, acid soil. Trim each year after flowering to maintain compact habit. Straggly, old plants may be cut back hard in spring. Propagate by seed in autumn.

(!) The seeds may cause mild stomach upset if ingested.

U. europaeus (Gorse) illus. p.148.

🏆 **'Flore Pleno'** is a leafless, or almost leafless, bushy shrub. **H** 1m (3ft), **S** 1.2m (4ft). In spring, bears masses of fragrant, pea-like, double, yellow flowers on leafless, dark green shoots.

ULMUS

Elm

ULMACEAE

Genus of deciduous or, rarely, semi-evergreen trees and shrubs, often large and stately, grown for their foliage and habit. Inconspicuous flowers appear in spring. Fully hardy. Requires full sun and fertile, well-drained soil. Propagate by softwood cuttings in summer or by seed or suckers in autumn. Is susceptible to Dutch elm disease, which is quickly fatal, although *U. parvifolia* and *U. pumila* appear more resistant than other species and hybrids.

U. americana (American white elm, White elm). Deciduous, spreading tree. **H** and **S** 30m (100ft). Has grey bark and drooping branchlets. Large, oval, dark green leaves are sharply toothed and rough-textured.

U. angustifolia. See *U. minor* subsp. *angustifolia*. **var. *cornubiensis*** see *U. minor* 'Cornubiensis'.

***U.* 'Camperdownii'.** See *U. glabra* 'Camperdownii'.

U. carpinifolia. See *U. minor*.

***U.* 'Dicksonii'.** See *U. minor* 'Dicksonii'.

U. glabra (Wych elm). Deciduous, spreading tree. **H** 30m (100ft), **S** 25m (80ft). Has broadly oval, toothed, very rough, dark green leaves, often slightly lobed at tips. From mid- to late spring bears clusters of winged, green fruits on bare branches. **'Camperdownii'** (syn. *U.* 'Camperdownii') illus. p.88. **'Exoniensis'** (Exeter elm), **H** 15m (50ft), **S** 5m (15ft), is narrow with upright branches when young, later becoming more spreading.

U. x hollandica (Dutch elm). Vigorous, deciduous tree with a short trunk and spreading to arching branches. **H** 30m (100ft), **S** 25m (80ft). Has oval, toothed, glossy, dark green leaves. Is very susceptible to Dutch elm disease. **'Jacqueline Hillier'**, **H** and **S** 2m (6ft), is slow-growing and suitable for hedging. Small leaves, rough-textured and sharply toothed, form 2 rows on each shoot; they persist into early winter. **'Vegeta'** (Huntingdon elm) **H** 35m (120ft), has upright, central branches and pendent, outer shoots. Broadly oval leaves turn yellow in autumn.

U. minor, syn. *U. carpinifolia* (Smooth-leaved elm). Deciduous, spreading tree with arching branches and pendent shoots. **H** 30m (100ft), **S** 20m (70ft). Small, oval, toothed, glossy, bright green leaves turn yellow in autumn. **subsp. *angustifolia*** (syn. *U. angustifolia;* Goodyer's elm) has a rounded canopy and elliptic to oval, double-toothed, mid- to dark green leaves, paler beneath. **'Cornubiensis'** (syn. *U. angustifolia* var. *cornubiensis;* Cornish elm), **S** 15m (50ft), is conical when young and with a vase-shaped head when mature. **'Dicksonii'** (syn. *U.m.* 'Sarniensis Aurea', *U.* 'Dicksonii', *U.* 'Wheatleyi Aurea'; Cornish golden elm, Dickson's golden elm) illus. p.76. **'Sarniensis'** (Jersey elm, Wheatley elm), **S** 10m (30ft), is a conical, dense tree with upright branches. Small, broadly oval leaves are mid-green.

'Sarniensis Aurea' see *U.m.* 'Dicksonii'.

U. parvifolia (Chinese elm). Deciduous or semi-evergreen, rounded tree. **H** and **S** 15m (50ft). Small, oval, glossy, dark green leaves last well into winter or, in mild areas, may persist until fresh growth appears.

U. procera (English elm). Vigorous, deciduous, spreading tree with a bushy, dense, dome-shaped head. **H** 35m (120ft), **S** 15m (50ft). Broadly oval, toothed, rough, dark green leaves turn yellow in autumn.

U. pumila (Siberian elm). Deciduous, spreading, sometimes shrubby tree. **H** 15m (50ft), **S** 12m (40ft). Has oval, toothed, dark green leaves. Has some resistance to Dutch elm disease, but seedlings may be susceptible in hot summers.

***U.* 'Wheatleyi Aurea'.** See *U. minor* 'Dicksonii'.

UMBELLULARIA

Headache tree

LAURACEAE

Genus of evergreen, spring-flowering trees, grown for their aromatic foliage, although the scent of the crushed leaves may induce headaches and nausea in some people. Frost hardy, but requires shelter from strong, cold winds when young. Needs sun and fertile, moist but well-drained soil. Propagate by seed in autumn.

U. californica (Californian laurel) illus. p.69.

Urceolina peruviana. See *Stenomesson miniatum.*

Urginea maritima. See *Drimia maritima.*

URSINIA

COMPOSITAE/ASTERACEAE

Genus of annuals, evergreen perennials and sub-shrubs, grown mainly for their flower heads usually in summer, a few species for their foliage. Half hardy to frost tender, min. 5–7°C (41–45°F). Needs full light and well-drained soil. Water potted plants moderately, less when not in full growth. Requires good ventilation if grown under glass. Propagate by seed or greenwood cuttings in spring. Aphids are sometimes troublesome.

U. anthemoides illus. p.322.

U. chrysanthemoides. Evergreen, bushy perennial. **H** and **S** 60cm (2ft) or more. Frost tender. Narrowly oval, feathery, strongly scented, green leaves are 5cm (2in) long. Has small, long-stalked, daisy-like, yellow flower heads, sometimes coppery below, in summer.

U. sericea. Evergreen, bushy sub-shrub. **H** and **S** 25–45cm (10–18in). Frost tender. Leaves are cut into an elegant filigree of very slender, silver-haired segments. Daisy-like, yellow flower heads, 4cm (½in) across, in summer. Mainly grown for its foliage.

UTRICULARIA

LENTIBULARIACEAE

Genus of deciduous or evergreen, perennial, carnivorous water plants with bladder-like, modified leaves that trap and digest insects. Most species in cultivation are free-floating. Frost hardy to frost tender, min. 7°C (45°F). Some species are suitable only for tropical aquariums; those grown in outdoor pools require full sun. Thin out plants that are overcrowded or become laden with algae. Propagate by division of floating foliage in spring or summer.

U. exoleta. See *U. gibba.*

U. gibba, syn. *U. exoleta.* Deciduous, perennial, free-floating water plant. **S** 15cm (6in). Frost tender. Slender stems carry finely divided, mid-green leaves on which small bladders develop. Pouched, bright yellow flowers are borne in summer. Is evergreen in very warm water; suitable only for a tropical aquarium.

U. vulgaris. Deciduous, perennial, free-floating water plant. **S** 30cm (12in). Frost hardy. Much-divided, bronze-green leaves, studded with small bladders, are produced on slender stems. Bears pouched, bright yellow flowers in summer. May be grown in a pool or cold-water aquarium.

UVULARIA

LILIACEAE/CONVALLARIACEAE

Genus of spring-flowering perennials that thrive in moist woodlands. Fully hardy. Requires semi-shade and prefers moist but well-drained, peaty soil. Propagate in early spring, before flowering, by division.

🏆 ***U. grandiflora*** (Bellwort, Merry-bells) illus. p.262.

U. perfoliata. Clump-forming perennial. **H** 45cm (18in), **S** 30cm (12in). In spring, clusters of pendent, bell-shaped, pale yellow flowers with twisted petals appear on numerous slender stems above stem-clasping, narrowly oval, mid-green leaves.

VACCINIUM

ERICACEAE

Genus of deciduous or evergreen sub-shrubs, shrubs and trees, grown for their foliage, autumn colour (on deciduous species), flowers and fruits, which are often edible. Fully to frost hardy. Needs sun or semi-shade and moist but well-drained, peaty or sandy, acid soil. Propagate by semi-ripe cuttings in summer or by seed in autumn.

V. angustifolium* var. *laevifolium (Low-bush blueberry) illus. p.163.

V. arctostaphylos (Caucasian whortleberry). Deciduous, upright shrub. **H** 3m (10ft), **S** 2m (6ft). Fully hardy. Has red-brown young shoots and oval, dark green leaves that mature to red and purple in autumn. Bell-shaped, white flowers, tinged with red, are produced in spreading racemes in early summer, followed by spherical, purplish-black fruits.

🏆 ***V. corymbosum*** (Highbush blueberry) illus. p.150. **'Pioneer'** illus. p.163.

🏆 ***V. glaucoalbum*** illus. p.165.

V. myrtillus (Bilberry, Whortleberry). Deciduous, usually prostrate shrub. **H** 15cm (6in) or more, **S** 30cm (12in) or more. Fully hardy. Bears small, heart-shaped, leathery, bright green leaves. Pendent, bell-shaped, pale pink flowers in early summer are followed by edible, round, blue-black fruits.

V. nummularia. Evergreen, prostrate shrub. **H** 10cm (4in), **S** 20cm (8in). Frost hardy. Slender stems, covered in red-brown bristles, bear oval, wrinkled, bright green leaves with red-brown bristles at their margins. Small racemes of bell-shaped, white to deep pink flowers at stem tips in early summer are followed by small, round, black fruits. Is suitable for a rock garden or peat bed. Needs semi-shade. May also be propagated by division in spring.

V. parvifolium illus. p.163.

V. vitis-idaea. Vigorous, evergreen, prostrate shrub, spreading by underground runners. **H** 2–25cm (¾–10in), **S** indefinite. Fully hardy. Forms hummocks of oval, hard, leathery leaves. Bell-shaped, white to pink flowers are borne in nodding racemes from early summer to autumn, followed by bright red fruits in autumn–winter. May also be propagated by division in spring. **subsp. *minus*** (syn. *V.v-i.* 'Minus') illus. p.351.

VALERIANA

Valerian

VALERIANACEAE

Genus of summer-flowering perennials that are suitable for growing in borders and rock gardens. Fully hardy. Requires a position in sun and well-drained soil. Propagate by division in autumn, but *V. officinalis* is best propagated by seed in spring.

V. officinalis (Cat's valerian, Common valerian) illus. p.231.

***V. phu* 'Aurea'** illus. p.262.

VALLEA

ELAEOCARPACEAE

Genus of one species of evergreen shrub, grown for its overall appearance. Half hardy, but best at 3–5°C (37–41°F) to prevent foliage being damaged by cold. Prefers a position in full sun and humus-rich, well-drained soil. Containerized plants should be watered freely during the growing season, moderately at other times. Untidy growth may be cut out in early spring. Propagate by seed in spring or by semi-ripe cuttings in summer. Red spider mite may be a nuisance.

V. stipularis. Evergreen, erect, then loose and spreading shrub. **H** and **S** 2–5m (6–15ft). Leaves are lance-shaped to rounded and lobed, deep green above, grey beneath. Small, cup-shaped flowers, each with 5 deep pink petals that have 3 lobes, are borne in small, terminal and lateral clusters in spring–summer.

VALLISNERIA

HYDROCHARITACEAE

Genus of evergreen, perennial, submerged water plants, grown for their foliage. Is suitable for pools and aquariums. Frost tender, min. 5°C (41°F). Requires sun or semi-shade and deep, clear water. Remove fading foliage, and thin overcrowded plants as required. Propagate by division in spring or summer.

V. americana, syn. *V. gigantea.* Vigorous, evergreen, perennial, submerged water plant. **S** indefinite. Quickly grows to form colonies of long, strap-shaped, mid-green leaves. Produces insignificant, greenish flowers all year-round.

V. gigantea. See *V. americana.*

V. spiralis (Eel grass, Tape grass). Vigorous, evergreen, perennial, submerged water plant. **S** indefinite. Forms a mass of long, strap-shaped, mid-green leaves, but on a smaller scale than *V. americana.* Insignificant, greenish flowers are borne year-round.

Vallota speciosa. See *Cyrtanthus elatus.*

VANCOUVERIA

BERBERIDACEAE

Genus of perennials, some of which are evergreen, suitable for ground cover. Fully hardy. Prefers cool, partially shaded positions and moist, peaty soil. Propagate by division in spring.

V. chrysantha. Evergreen, sprawling perennial. **H** 30cm (12in), **S** indefinite. Oval, dark green leaves borne on flower stems are divided into rounded diamond-shaped leaflets with thickened, undulating margins. Loose sprays of small, bell-shaped, yellow flowers are borne in spring.

V. hexandra. Vigorous, spreading perennial. **H** 20cm (8in), **S** indefinite. Leathery leaves are divided into almost hexagonal leaflets. Bears open sprays of many tiny, white flowers in late spring and early summer. Makes good woodland ground cover.

VANDA

ORCHIDACEAE

See also ORCHIDS.

♀ ***V. Rothschildiana gx*** (illus. p.466). Evergreen, epiphytic orchid for a cool or intermediate greenhouse. **H** 60cm (24in). Sprays of dark-veined, violet-blue flowers, 10cm (4in) across, are borne twice a year in varying seasons. Has narrowly oval, rigid leaves, 10–12cm (4–5in) long. Grow in a hanging basket and provide good light in summer.

VELLOZIA

VELLOZIACEAE

Genus of evergreen perennials and shrubs, grown for their showy flowers. Frost tender, min. 10°C (50°F). Grow in full sun and moderately fertile, sharply drained soil. Propagate by seed or division in spring.

V. elegans, syn. *Barbacenia elegans, Talbotia elegans.* Evergreen, mat-forming perennial with slightly woody stems. **H** to 15cm (6in), **S** 15–30cm (6–12in). Lance-shaped, leathery, dark green leaves, to 20cm (8in) long, each has a V-shaped keel. In late spring bears solitary small, star-shaped, white flowers on slender stems above leaves.

VELTHEIMIA

LILIACEAE/HYACINTHACEAE

Genus of winter-flowering bulbs with dense spikes of pendent, tubular flowers and rosettes of basal leaves. Frost tender, min. 10°C (50°F). Needs good light, to keep foliage compact and to develop flower colours fully, and well-drained soil. Plant in autumn with tips above soil surface. Reduce watering in summer. Propagate by seed or offsets in autumn.

♀ ***V. bracteata,*** syn. *V. capensis* of gardens, *V. undulata, V. viridifolia,* illus. p.414.

♀ ***V. capensis,*** syn. *V. glauca, V. viridifolia* of gardens. Winter- flowering bulb. **H** 30–45cm (12–18in), **S** 20–30cm (8–12in). Has a basal rosette of lance-shaped leaves, usually with very wavy edges. Stem produces a dense spike of pink or red flowers, each 2–3cm (¾–1½in) long.

V. capensis of gardens. See *V. bracteata.*

V. glauca. See *V. capensis.*

V. undulata. See *V. bracteata.*

V. viridifolia. See *V. bracteata.*

V. viridifolia of gardens. See *V. capensis.*

x *Venidioarctotis.* See *Arctotis; Arctotis* Harlequin Hybrids.

VERATRUM

LILIACEAE/MELANTHIACEAE

Genus of perennials, with poisonous black rhizomes, ideal for woodland gardens. Fully hardy. Requires semi-shade and fertile, moist soil. Propagate by division or seed in autumn. ⓘ All parts are highly toxic if ingested. Contact with the foliage may irritate the skin.

♀ ***V. album*** (White false hellebore). Clump-forming perennial. **H** 2m (6ft), **S** 60cm (2ft). Basal leaves are pleated, oval and dark green. Stems bear dense, terminal panicles of saucer-shaped, yellowish-white flowers in summer.

♀ ***V. nigrum*** (Black false hellebore) illus. p.216.

VERBASCUM

Mullein

SCROPHULARIACEAE

Genus of mainly summer-flowering perennials, some of which are semi-evergreen or evergreen, and evergreen biennials and shrubs. Fully to frost hardy. Tolerates shade, but prefers an open, sunny site and well-drained soil. Propagate species by seed in spring or late summer or by root cuttings in winter, selected forms by root cuttings only. Some species self seed freely.

V. bombyciferum. Evergreen, erect biennial. **H** 1.2–2m (4–6ft), **S** 60cm (2ft). Fully hardy. Oval leaves and stems are covered with silver hairs. Produces upright racemes densely set with 5-lobed, yellow flowers in summer.

V. chaixii. Erect perennial, covered with silvery hairs. **H** 1m (3ft), **S** 60cm (2ft). Fully hardy. Has oval, toothed, rough, nettle-like leaves. Produces slender spires of 5-lobed, yellow, sometimes white flowers, with purple stamens, in summer.

***V.* 'Cotswold Beauty'** illus. p.246.

***V.* 'Cotswold Queen'.** Short-lived, rosette-forming perennial. **H** 1–1.2m (3–4ft), **S** 30–60cm (1–2ft). Fully hardy. Throughout summer, branched racemes of 5-lobed, apricot-buff flowers are borne on stems that arise from oval, mid-green leaves.

V. densiflorum, syn. *V. thapsiforme.* Fairly slow-growing, semi-evergreen, upright perennial. **H** 1.2–1.5m (4–5ft), **S** 60cm (2ft). Fully hardy. Has a rosette of large, oval, crinkled, hairy, mid-green leaves. Hairy stems each produce a bold spike of flattish, 5-lobed, yellow flowers in summer.

♀ ***V. dumulosum*** illus. p.345.

♀ ***V.* 'Gainsborough'** illus. p.243.

♀ ***V.* 'Letitia'** illus. p.343.

V. lychnitis (White mullein). Slow-growing, evergreen, upright, branching biennial. **H** 60cm–1m (2–3ft), **S** 60cm (2ft). Fully hardy. Has lance-shaped, dark grey-green leaves. Flattish, 5 lobed, white flowers are borne on branching stems in summer.

V. nigrum. Semi-evergreen, clump-forming perennial. **H** 60cm–1m (2–3ft), **S** 60cm (2ft). Fully hardy. Bears narrow spikes of small, 5-lobed, purple-centred, yellow flowers during summer and autumn. Oblong, mid-green leaves are downy beneath.

V. olympicum illus. p.219.

♀ ***V.* 'Pink Domino'.** Short-lived, rosette-forming perennial. **H** 1.2m (4ft), **S** 30–60cm (1–2ft). Fully hardy. Produces branched racemes of 5-lobed, rose-pink flowers throughout summer above oval, mid-green leaves.

V. thapsiforme. See *V. densiflorum.*

VERBENA

VERBENACEAE

Genus of summer- and autumn-flowering biennials and perennials, some of which are semi-evergreen. Frost hardy to frost tender, min. 1°C (34°F). Prefers sun and well-drained soil. Propagate by stem cuttings in late summer or autumn or by seed in autumn or spring.

V. alpina of gardens. See *Glandularia x maonettii.*

♀ ***V. bonariensis,*** syn. *V. patagonica,* illus. p.221.

V. chamaedrifolia. See *Glandularia peruviana.*

V. chamaedrioides. See *Glandularia peruviana.*

V.* x *hybrida. See *Glandularia x hybrida.*

V. patagonica. See *V. bonariensis.*

♀ ***V. rigida,*** syn. *V. venosa,* illus. p.269.

***V.* 'Sissinghurst'.** See *Glandularia* 'Sissinghurst'.

V. tenera* var. *maonettii. See *Glandularia. x maonettii.*

V. venosa. See *V. rigida.*

VERONICA

SCROPHULARIACEAE

Genus of perennials and sub-shrubs, some of which are semi-evergreen or evergreen, grown for their usually blue flowers. Fully to frost hardy. Some need sun and well-drained soil, others prefer a moist site in sun or partial shade. Propagate by division in spring or autumn, by softwood or semi-ripe cuttings in summer or by seed in autumn.

V. austriaca. Mat-forming or upright perennial. **H** and **S** 25–50cm (10–20in). Fully hardy. Leaves are very variable: from broadly oval to narrowly oblong, and from entire to deeply cut and fern-like. Short, dense or lax racemes of small, saucer-shaped, bright blue flowers appear in early summer. Suits a rock garden or bank. **subsp. *teucrium*** (syn. *V. teucrium*) illus. p.343. **subsp. *teucrium* 'Kapitan',** syn. *V. prostrata* 'Kapitan', illus. p.343. ♀ **subsp. *teucrium* 'Royal Blue'** has deep royal-blue flowers. Propagate by division in spring or by softwood cuttings in summer.

V. beccabunga (Brooklime) illus. p.442.

♀ ***V. cinerea.*** Spreading, much-branched, woody-based perennial. **H** 15cm (6in), **S** 30cm (12in). Fully hardy. Has small, linear, occasionally oval, hairy, silvery-white leaves. Trailing flower stems bear saucer-shaped, deep blue to purple flowers, with white eyes, in early summer. Is suitable for a sunny rock garden.

V. exaltata. See *V. longifolia.*

V. fruticans (Rock speedwell). Deciduous, upright to procumbent sub-shrub. **H** 15cm (6in), **S** 30cm (12in). Fully hardy. Leaves are oval and green. Spikes of saucer-shaped, bright blue flowers, each with a red eye, are borne in summer. Is suitable for a rock garden.

♀ ***V. gentianoides*** illus. p.271.

V. incana. See *V. spicata* subsp. *incana.*

V. longifolia, syn. *V. exaltata.* Variable, upright perennial. **H** 1–1.2m (3–4ft), **S** 30cm (1ft) or more. Fully hardy. In late summer and early autumn, long, terminal racemes of star-shaped, lilac-blue flowers are borne on stems with whorls of narrowly oval to lance-shaped, toothed, mid-green leaves.

V. pectinata. Dense, mat-forming perennial that is sometimes semi-erect. **H** and **S** 20cm (8in). Fully hardy. Has small, narrowly oval, hairy leaves and bears

loose sprays of saucer-shaped, soft blue to blue-violet flowers in summer. Is good for a rock garden or bank. **'Rosea'**, **H** 8cm (3in), has rose-lilac flowers.
V. peduncularis illus. p.271.
V. perfoliata. See *Parahebe perfoliata*.
♀ ***V. prostrata*** (Prostrate speedwell), syn. *V. rupestris*, illus. p.343. **'Kapitan'** see *V.a.* subsp. *teucrium* 'Kapitan'. **'Trehane'** illus. p.343. ♀ **'Spode Blue'** is a dense, mat-forming perennial. **H** to 30cm (12in), **S** indefinite. Fully hardy. Upright spikes of small, saucer-shaped, china-blue flowers appear in early summer. Leaves are narrowly oval and toothed.
V. rupestris. See *V. prostrata*.
V. spicata (Spiked speedwell). Clump-forming perennial. **H** 30–60cm (12–24in), **S** 45cm (18in). Fully hardy. Spikes of small, star-shaped, bright blue flowers are borne in summer above narrowly oval, toothed, mid-green leaves. ♀ **subsp. *incana*** (syn. *V. incana*) illus. p.271. **'Romiley Purple'** illus. p.239.
V. teucrium. See *V. austriaca* subsp. *teucrium*.
V. virginica. See *Veronicastrum virginicum*. **f. *alba*** see *Veronicastrum virginicum* f. *album*.

VERONICASTRUM

SCROPHULARIACEAE

Genus of evergreen perennials, grown for their elegant, pale blue flowers. Fully hardy. Requires a position in sun and moist soil. Propagate by division in spring or autumn, by softwood or semi-ripe cuttings in summer or by seed in autumn.
V. virginicum, syn. *Veronica virginica*. Upright perennial. **H** 1.2m (4ft), **S** 45cm (1½ft). Fully hardy. In late summer, racemes of small, star-shaped, purple-blue or pink flowers crown stems clothed with whorls of narrowly lance-shaped, dark green leaves. **'Fascination'** illus. p.220. **f. album** (syn. *Veronica virginica* f. *alba*) has spires of small, white flowers in late summer, with pink-flushed bases and pink anthers, on stems clothed with whorls of narrow, dark green leaves.

VESTIA

SOLANACEAE

Genus of one species of evergreen shrub, grown for its flowers and foliage. Frost hardy, but in cold areas is best cut to ground level and grown against a south-facing wall. Requires sun and well-drained soil. Propagate by semi-ripe cuttings in summer or by seed in autumn or spring.
♀ ***V. foetida,*** syn. *V. lycioides*, illus. p.194.
V. lycioides. See *V. foetida*.

VIBURNUM

CAPRIFOLIACEAE

Genus of deciduous, semi-evergreen or evergreen shrubs and trees, grown for their foliage, autumn colour (in many deciduous species), flowers and, often, fruits. Fruiting is generally most prolific when several plants of different clones are planted together. Fully to frost hardy. Grow in sun or semi-shade and in deep, fertile, not too dry soil. To thin out overgrown plants cut out some older shoots after flowering. Propagate by cuttings (softwood for deciduous species, semi-ripe for evergreens) in summer or by seed in autumn. ⓘ The fruits of viburnums may cause mild stomach upset if ingested. See also feature panel p.142.
V. acerifolium illus. p.151.
V. betulifolium (illus. p.142). Deciduous, upright, arching shrub. **H** and **S** 3m (10ft). Fully hardy. Bright green leaves are slightly glossy beneath. Heads of small, white flowers in early summer succeeded by profuse nodding clusters of decorative, bright red fruits in autumn–winter.
V. bitchiuense illus. p.122.
♀ ***V.* x *bodnantense* 'Dawn'** illus. p.143. ♀ **'Deben'** is a deciduous, upright shrub. **H** 3m (10ft), **S** 2m (6ft). Fully hardy. Oval, toothed, dark green leaves are bronze when young. Clusters of fragrant, tubular, white flowers, tinted with pale pink, open during mild periods from late autumn through to early spring.
V.* x *burkwoodii. Semi-evergreen, bushy, open shrub. **H** and **S** 2.5m (8ft). Fully hardy. Rounded heads of fragrant, tubular, pink, then white flowers are borne amid oval, glossy, dark green leaves from mid- to late spring. ♀ **'Anne Russell'**, **H** and **S** 1.5m (5ft), is deciduous and has very fragrant, white flowers. ♀ **'Park Farm Hybrid'** bears very fragrant, white flowers that are slightly pink in bud, and older leaves turn bright red in autumn.
♀ ***V.* x *carlcephalum*** illus. p.111.
V. carlesii illus. p.146. **'Diana'** is a deciduous, bushy, dense shrub. **H** and **S** 2m (6ft). Fully hardy. Broadly oval leaves are bronze when young and turn purple-red in autumn. From mid- to late spring bears rounded heads of red buds that open to very fragrant, tubular, pink flowers fading to white.
♀ ***V. cinnamomifolium.*** Evergreen, bushy or tree-like shrub. **H** and **S** 5m (15ft). Frost hardy. Large, oval leaves, each has 3 prominent veins. Bears broad clusters of small, star-shaped, white flowers in early summer, then egg-shaped, blue fruits.
♀ ***V. davidii*** illus. p.165.
V. dilatatum. Deciduous, upright shrub. **H** 3m (10ft), **S** 2m (6ft). Fully hardy. Oval, sharply toothed, dark green leaves sometimes redden in autumn. Flat heads of small, star-shaped, white flowers in late spring and early summer are succeeded by showy, egg-shaped, bright red fruits. **'Catskill'** illus. p.130.
♀ ***V. farreri,*** syn. *V. fragrans*, illus. p.143. **'Candidissimum'** is a deciduous, upright shrub. **H** 3m (10ft), **S** 2m (6ft). Fully hardy. Oval, toothed, dark green leaves are pale green when young. Produces clusters of fragrant, tubular, pure white flowers in late autumn and during mild periods in winter and early spring.
V. foetens, syn. *V. grandiflorum* f. *foetens*, illus. p.143.
V. fragrans. See *V. farreri*.
V. grandiflorum. Deciduous, upright, open shrub. **H** and **S** 2m (6ft). Fully hardy. Stiff branches bear oblong, dark green leaves that become deep purple in autumn. Dense clusters of fragrant, tubular, white-and-pink flowers open from deep pink buds from mid-winter to early spring. **f. *foetens*** see *V. foetens*.
♀ ***V.* x *juddii*** illus. p.146.
V. lantana (Wayfaring tree). Vigorous, deciduous, upright shrub. **H** 5m (15ft), **S** 4m (12ft). Fully hardy. Has broadly oval, grey-green leaves that redden in autumn, flattened heads of small, 5-lobed, white flowers in late spring and early summer, then egg-shaped, red fruits that ripen to black.
V. lentago (Sheepberry). Vigorous, deciduous, upright shrub. **H** 4m (12ft), **S** 3m (10ft). Fully hardy. Oval, glossy, dark green leaves turn red and purple in autumn. Bears flattened heads of small, fragrant, star-shaped, white flowers in late spring and early summer, then egg-shaped, blue-black fruits.
V. odoratissimum (Sweet viburnum). Evergreen, bushy shrub. **H** and **S** 5m (15ft). Frost hardy. Clusters of small, fragrant, star-shaped, white flowers, borne amid oval, leathery, glossy, dark green leaves in late spring, are followed by egg-shaped, red fruits that ripen to black.
V. opulus (Guelder rose). Vigorous, deciduous, bushy shrub. **H** and **S** 4m (12ft). Fully hardy. Bears broadly oval, lobed, deep green leaves that redden in autumn and, in late spring and early summer, flattened, lace-cap-like heads of white flowers. Produces large bunches of spherical, bright red fruits.
♀ **'Compactum'** illus. p.162.
♀ **'Xanthocarpum'** has yellow fruits and mid-green leaves that become yellow in autumn.
V. plicatum (Japanese snowball tree). Deciduous, bushy, spreading shrub. **H** 3m (10ft), **S** 4m (12ft). Fully hardy. Leaves are oval, toothed, deeply veined and dark green, turning reddish-purple in autumn. Dense, rounded heads of large, sterile, flattish, white flowers are borne along branches in late spring and early summer. ♀ **f. *tomentosum* 'Mariesii'**, syn. *V.p.* 'Mariesii', illus. p.110. **'Nanum Semperflorens'** (syn. *V.p.* 'Watanabe', *V.p.* 'Watanabei', *V. watanabei*), **H** 2m (6ft), **S** 1.5m (5ft), is slow-growing, conical and dense, and produces small flower heads from late spring until early autumn.
♀ **'Pink Beauty'** (illus. p.142) is a deciduous, bushy shrub. Dark green leaves become reddish-purple in autumn. In late spring and early summer bears white, later pink, blooms, followed by red, then black, fruits. **f. *tomentosum*** has tiered branches, flattish, lacecap-like flower heads and red fruits, ripening to black. **'Watanabe'** see *V.p.* 'Nanum Semperflorens'. **'Watanabei** see *V.p.* 'Nanum Semperflorens'.
V.* x *pragense. See *V.* 'Pragense'.
♀ ***V.* 'Pragense',** syn. *V.* x *pragense*, illus. p.131.
V. rhytidophyllum illus. p.112.
V. sargentii. Deciduous, bushy shrub. **H** and **S** 3m (10ft). Fully hardy. Maple-like, mid-green foliage often changes to yellow or red in autumn. Broad, flattish, lace-cap-like heads of white flowers in late spring are followed by spherical, bright red fruits. ♀ **'Onondaga'**, **S** 2m (6ft), has bronze-red, young leaves, becoming deep green, then bronze-red again in autumn. Flower buds are pink.
V. sieboldii. Deciduous, rounded, dense shrub. **H** 4m (12ft), **S** 6m (20ft). Fully hardy. Has large, oblong to oval, glossy, bright green leaves. Rounded heads of tubular, creamy-white flowers are borne in late spring, followed by egg-shaped, red-stalked, red fruits that ripen to black.
V. tinus (Laurustinus). Evergreen, bushy, compact shrub. **H** and **S** 3m (10ft). Frost hardy. Has oval, dark green leaves. Freely produced flat heads of small, white blooms open from pink buds during late winter and spring. ♀ **'Eve Price'** illus. p.143. ♀ **'Gwenllian'** has flattened heads of small, star-shaped, pale pink flowers freely borne from deep pink buds amid oval, dark green leaves in winter–spring and followed by abundant, ovoid, blue fruits.
V. watanabei. See *V. plicatum* 'Nanum Semperflorens'.

VIGNA

LEGUMINOSAE/PAPILIONACEAE

Genus of evergreen, annual and perennial, erect or scrambling and twining climbers, grown mainly as crop plants for their leaves, pods and seeds. Frost tender, min. 13–15°C (55–59°F). Provide full light and humus-rich, well-drained soil. Water freely when in full growth, sparingly at other times. Stems require support. Thin crowded stems or cut back hard in spring. Propagate by seed in autumn or spring.
V. caracalla, syn. *Phaseolus caracalla* (Snail flower). Evergreen, perennial, fast-growing, twining climber. **H** 3–5m (10–15ft). Leaves comprise 3 oval leaflets. From summer to early autumn carries pea-like, purple-marked, cream flowers that turn orange-yellow.

Villarsia nymphoides. See *Nymphoides peltata*.

VINCA

Periwinkle

APOCYNACEAE

Genus of evergreen, trailing sub-shrubs and perennials, grown for their foliage and flowers. Flowers are tubular with 5 spreading lobes. Fully to frost hardy. Is useful for ground cover in shade, but flowers more freely given some sun. Grows in any soil that is not too dry. Propagate by semi-ripe cuttings in summer or by division from autumn to spring. ⓘ All parts may cause mild stomach upset if ingested.
♀ ***V. difformis.*** Evergreen, prostrate sub-shrub. **H** 30cm (12in), **S** indefinite. Frost hardy. Slender, trailing stems bear oval, glossy, dark green leaves. Erect flower stems produce pale blue flowers in late autumn and early winter.
V. major (Greater periwinkle, Quater). Evergreen, prostrate, arching sub-shrub. **H** 45cm (18in), **S** indefinite. Fully hardy. Leaves are broadly oval, glossy and dark green. Large, bright blue flowers are produced from late spring to early autumn. **subsp. *hirsuta*** see *V.m.* var. *oxyloba*. **var. *oxyloba*** (syn. *V.m.* subsp. *hirsuta*) has leaves, leaf stalks and calyces edged with long hairs. ♀ **'Variegata'** (Greater periwinkle) illus. p.164.
V. minor (Lesser periwinkle) illus. p.165. **'Alba Variegata'** is an evergreen, prostrate sub-shrub. **H** 15cm (6in), **S** indefinite. Fully hardy. Forms extensive

U V W

mats of small, oval, glossy, dark green leaves, edged with pale yellow, above which white flowers are carried from mid-spring to early summer, then intermittently into autumn. **'Bowles' Blue'** see *V.m.* 'La Grave'. **'Bowles' White'** bears large, white flowers that are pinkish-white in bud. ♀ **'Gertrude Jekyll'** is of dense growth and produces a profusion of small, white flowers. Flowers of ♀ **'La Grave'** (syn. *V.m.* 'Bowles' Blue') are large and lavender-blue.
V. rosea. See *Catharanthus roseus.*

VIOLA
Violet

VIOLACEAE

Genus of annuals, perennials, some of which are semi-evergreen, and deciduous sub-shrubs, grown for their distinctive flowers. Annuals are suitable as summer bedding, perennials and sub-shrubs are good in rock gardens, screes and alpine houses. Fully to half hardy. Grow in sun or shade and well-drained but moisture-retentive soil unless otherwise stated; a few species prefer acid soil. Propagate annuals by seed sown according to flowering season, perennials and sub-shrubs by softwood cuttings in spring unless otherwise stated. Species may also be propagated by seed in spring or autumn.
V. aetolica illus. p.359.
V. biflora (Twin-flowered violet). Creeping, rhizomatous perennial. **H** 5–15cm (2–6in), **S** 15cm (6in). Fully hardy. Flat-faced, deep lemon-yellow flowers, veined dark brown, are borne singly or in pairs on upright stems in summer. Leaves are kidney-shaped and mid-green. Needs shade. May be propagated by division.
***V.* 'Bowles' Black',** syn. *V. tricolor* 'Bowles' Black', illus. p.355.
V. calcarata illus. p.354.
V. cazorlensis. Tufted, woody-based perennial. **H** to 5cm (2in), **S** to 8cm (3in). Frost hardy. Has small, linear to lance-shaped leaves and in late spring carries small, flat-faced, long-spurred, deep pink flowers, singly on short stems. Suits an alpine house. Is difficult to grow.
V. cenisia. Spreading perennial with runners. **H** 7cm (3in), **S** 10cm (4in). Fully hardy. Small, flat-faced, bright violet flowers, each with a deep purple line radiating from the centre, are produced on very short stems in summer. Has a deep tap root and tiny, heart-shaped or oblong, dark green leaves. Suits a scree. Propagate by division in spring.
♀ ***V. cornuta*** (Horned violet). Rhizomatous perennial. **H** 12–20cm (8in), **S** to 20cm (8in) or more. Fully hardy. Has oval, toothed leaves and flat-faced, angular, spurred, pale to deep purplish-blue, occasionally white flowers in spring and much of summer. ♀**'Minor'** illus. p.356.
V. cucullata. See *V. obliqua.*
V. elatior. Upright, little-branched perennial. **H** 20–30cm (8–12in), **S** 15cm (6in). Fully hardy. Leaves are broadly lance-shaped and toothed. Produces flat-faced, pale blue flowers, with white centres, in early summer. Prefers semi-shade and moist soil. Propagate in spring by division.
V. glabella. Clump-forming perennial with a scaly, horizontal rootstock. **H** 10cm (4in), **S** 20cm (8in). Fully hardy. Produces flat-faced, bright yellow flowers, with purplish-veined lower petals, in late spring above toothed, heart-shaped, bright green leaves. Needs shade. Propagate by division in spring.
V. gracilis. Mat-forming perennial. **H** 12cm (5in), **S** 15cm (6in) or more. Fully hardy. Flat-faced, yellow-centred, violet-blue or sometimes yellow flowers are produced in summer. Has small, dissected leaves with linear or oblong segments. Needs sun.
***V.* 'Green Goddess',** syn. *V. tricolor* 'Green Goddess', illus. p.318.
V. 'Haslemere'. See *V.* 'Nellie Britton'.
V. hederacea, syn. *Erpetion reniforme, V. reniforme* (Australian violet, Ivy-leaved violet). Evergreen, creeping, mat-forming perennial. **H** 2.5–5cm (1–2in), **S** indefinite. Half hardy. Has tiny, rounded leaves and bears purple or white flowers, with a squashed appearance, on short stems in summer. Is suitable for growing in an alpine house. Prefers semi-shade. Propagate by division in spring.
♀ ***V.* 'Huntercombe Purple'** illus. p.368.
***V.* 'Irish Molly'.** Evergreen, clump-forming, short-lived perennial. **H** 10cm (4in), **S** 15–20cm (6–8in). Fully hardy. Has broadly oval, dissected leaves and, in summer, a succession of flat-faced, old-gold flowers with brown centres. Flowers itself to death. Needs sun.
♀ ***V.* 'Jackanapes'** illus. p.359.
***V.* Joker Series** (summer-flowering) illus. p.312.
***V. labradorica* 'Purpurea'.** See *V. riviniana* 'Purpurea'.
V. lutea (Mountain pansy). Mat-forming, rhizomatous perennial. **H** 10cm (4in), **S** 15cm (6in). Fully hardy. Has small, oval to lance-shaped leaves. Flat-faced, yellow, violet or bicoloured flowers are produced in spring and summer.
♀ ***V.* 'Nellie Britton',** syn. *V.* 'Haslemere', illus. p.367.
♀ ***V. obliqua***, syn. *V. cucullata.* Variable, spreading perennial with fleshy rhizomes. **H** 5cm (2in), **S** 10–15cm (4–6in). Fully hardy. Has kidney-shaped, toothed, mid-green leaves. In late spring produces flat-faced, blue-violet, sometimes white or pale blue flowers. Propagate in spring.
V. odorata (Sweet violet). Semi-evergreen, spreading, rhizomatous perennial. **H** 7cm (3in), **S** 15cm (6in) or more. Fully hardy. Leaves are heart-shaped and toothed. Long stems each carry a fragrant, flat-faced, violet or white flower from late winter to early spring. Is useful in a wild garden. Self seeds prolifically. May also be propagated by division.
V. palmata. Spreading perennial. **H** 10cm (4in), **S** 15cm (6in). Fully hardy. Has short-stemmed, flat-faced, pale violet flowers in late spring and deeply dissected leaves. Prefers dry, well-drained soil. Self seeds readily.
V. pedata (Bird's-foot violet) illus. p.355. **var. *bicolor*** is a clump-forming perennial with a thick rootstock. **H** 5cm (2in), **S** 8cm (3in). Fully hardy. Flat-faced, velvety-purple or white flowers are borne singly on slender stems in late spring and early summer. Leaves are finely divided into 5–7 or more, narrow, toothed segments. Suits an alpine house. May be difficult to grow; needs peaty, sandy soil.
V. reniforme. See *V. hederacea.*
***V. riviniana* Purpurea Group,** syn. *V. labradorica* 'Purpurea', *V. riviniana* 'Purpurea', illus. p.355.
***V.* 'Sunvioki'.** See *V.* x *wittrockiana* Friolina Gold.
V. tricolor (Heartsease, Wild pansy) illus. p.355.
V.* x *wittrockiana (Pansy). Group of slow- to moderately fast-growing, mainly bushy perennials, usually grown as annuals or biennials. **H** 15–20cm (6–8in), **S** 20cm (8in). Fully hardy. Has oval, often serrated, mid-green leaves. Flattish, 5-petalled flowers, 2.5–10cm (1–4in) across, in a very wide colour range, appear throughout summer or in winter–spring. The following are among those available: **Angel Series 'Tiger Eye'** illus. p.323. **'Baby Lucia'** (summer-flowering) has small, deep blue flowers. **Clear Crystals Series** (summer-flowering) is in a wide range of clear colours. **'Clear Sky Primrose'** (winter- to spring-flowering) produces primrose-yellow flowers brushed in canary yellow. **Crystal Bowl Series** (summer-flowering) are in a range of colours, including yellow. **Floral Dance Series** (winter-flowering) have a wide range of colours, including white (mixed, illus. p.308). **Forerunner Series** (winter- to spring-flowering) bear medium-sized flowers in a range of bright, single colours and bicolours. **Friolina Gold ('Sunvioki')** has yellow flowers, with faintly streaked orange centres. Frost hardy. Is ideal in a basket. **Imperial Series 'Imperial Frosty Rose'** (summer-flowering) illus. p.312. **Imperial Series 'Orange Prince'** (summer-flowering) has orange flowers with black blotches. **Imperial Series 'Sky Blue'** (summer-flowering) has sky-blue flowers, each with a deeper-coloured blotch. ♀ **Joker Series**, see *V.* Joker Series. **'Majestic Giants'** (summer-flowering) has large flowers in a wide colour range. **Panola Series** (yellow) produce a long display of large, 5-petalled, bright yellow, black-centred flowers in summer. ♀ **Princess Series** (spring- to summer-flowering) are neat in habit, and produce small flowers in blue, cream, bicoloured purple and white, dark purple or yellow. **'Silver Princess'** (summer-flowering) has white flowers, each with a deep pink blotch. **Sorbet Series** (winter- to spring-flowering) has small flowers, with or without whiskers, in more than 20 colour combinations. **Sorbet Series 'Sorbet Black Delight'** (winter- to spring-flowering) illus. p.312. **'Super Chalon Giants'** (summer- to autumn-flowering) have ruffled and waved, bicoloured flowers. **'True Blue'** (winter- to summer-flowering) bears large, clear sky-blue flowers each with a small, yellow eye. **Ultima Radiance Series** (winter- to spring-flowering) has large, neatly rounded flowers in up to 30 colour combinations (deep blue, illus. p.313). **Ultima Series** (winter- to spring-flowering) have medium-sized flowers in a very broad range of colours, including bicolours. ♀ **Universal Series** (winter- to spring-flowering) produce flowers in an extensive range of separate colours as well as in a mixture of colours.

VIRGILIA

LEGUMINOSAE/PAPILIONACEAE

Genus of short-lived, evergreen shrubs and trees, grown for their flowers which are borne in spring and summer. Frost tender, min. 5°C (41°F). Prefers a position in full light and well-drained soil. Water pot-grown plants freely when in full growth, less at other times. Pruning is usually not required. Propagate in spring by seed, ideally soaked in warm water for 24 hours before sowing.
V. capensis. See *V. oroboides.*
V. oroboides, syn. *V. capensis.* Fast-growing, evergreen, rounded shrub or tree. **H** and **S** 6–10m (20–30ft). Has leaves of 11–21 oblong leaflets. Racemes of fragrant, pea-like, bright mauve-pink flowers, sometimes pink, crimson or white, are produced in late spring and summer, usually in great profusion.

Viscaria alpina. See *Lychnis alpina.*
Viscaria elegans. See *Silene coeli-rosa.*

VITALIANA

PRIMULACEAE

Genus of one species of evergreen, spring-flowering perennial, grown for its flowers. Is often included in *Douglasia* and is useful for rock gardens, screes and alpine houses. Fully hardy. Requires sun and moist but well-drained soil. Propagate by softwood cuttings in summer or by seed in autumn.
V. primuliflora, syn. *Douglasia vitaliana,* illus. p.358.

VITEX

VERBENACEAE/LAMIACEAE

Genus of evergreen or deciduous trees and shrubs, grown for their flowers. Cultivated species are frost hardy, but in cold areas grow against a south- or west-facing wall. Needs full sun and well-drained soil. Propagate by semi-ripe cuttings in summer or by seed in autumn or spring.
V. agnus-castus (Chaste tree). Deciduous, spreading, open, aromatic shrub. **H** and **S** 2.5m (8ft). Upright panicles of fragrant, tubular, violet-blue flowers appear in early and mid-autumn. Dark green leaves are each divided into 5 or 7 long, narrowly lance-shaped leaflets.
V. negundo. Deciduous, bushy shrub. **H** and **S** 3m (10ft). Mid-green leaves are each composed of 3–7 narrowly oval, sharply toothed leaflets. Has loose panicles of small, tubular, violet-blue flowers from late summer through to early autumn.

VITIS
Vine

VITACEAE

Genus of deciduous, woody-stemmed, tendril climbers, grown for their foliage and fruits (grapes), which are produced in bunches. Fully to half hardy. Prefers fertile, well-drained, chalky soil and sun or semi-shade. Produces the best fruits and autumn leaf-colour when planted in a warm situation. Propagate by hardwood cuttings in late autumn.

V. aconitifolia. See *Ampelopsis aconitifolia.*

V. amurensis (Amur grape). Vigorous, deciduous, woody-stemmed, tendril climber. **H** 6m (20ft). Fully hardy. Bears dark green, 3- or 5-lobed leaves, 12–30cm (5–12in) long, that mature to red and purple in autumn. Has inconspicuous flowers through the summer, followed in late summer and autumn, by tiny, black fruits.

♀ ***V. 'Brant'*** (illus. p.208). Deciduous, woody-stemmed, tendril climber. **H** to 7m (22ft) or more. Fully hardy. Bears leaves that are lobed, toothed, 10–22cm (4–9in) long and bright green. In autumn they mature to brown-red, except for the veins. Has inconspicuous flowers in summer, followed by green or purple fruits.

♀ ***V. coignetiae*** (Crimson glory vine) illus. p.209.

V. davidii. Deciduous, woody-stemmed, tendril climber; young stems are densely covered with short prickles. **H** to 8m (25ft) or more. Half hardy. Heart-shaped leaves, 10–25cm (4–10in) long, are blue- or grey-green beneath, turning scarlet in autumn. Insignificant, greenish flowers in summer are followed by small, black fruits.

V. henryana. See *Parthenocissus henryana.*

V. heterophylla. See *Ampelopsis brevipedunculata* var. *maximowiczii.*

V. quinquefolia. See *Parthenocissus quinquefolia.*

V. striata. See *Cissus striata.*

V thomsonii. See *Cayratia thomsonii.*

V. vinifera (Grape vine). ♀ **'Purpurea'** illus. p.210.

VRIESEA

BROMELIACEAE

Genus of evergreen, rosette-forming, epiphytic perennials, grown for their flowers and overall appearance. Frost tender, min. 15°C (59°F). Needs a position in semi-shade and a rooting medium of equal parts humus-rich soil and either sphagnum moss or bark or plastic chips used for orchid culture. Using soft water, water moderately when in growth, sparingly at other times, and from mid-spring to mid-autumn keep rosette centres filled with water. Propagate plants by offsets or seed in spring. See also feature panel p.471.

V. fenestralis. Evergreen, epiphytic perennial with dense, funnel-shaped rosettes. **H** and **S** 30–40cm (12–16in). Pale green leaves, with dark lines and cross-bands, are very broadly strap-shaped and arching or rolled under at tips. In summer, flat racemes of tubular, yellowish-green flowers, with green bracts, are carried above the foliage.

♀ ***V. fosteriana***. Evergreen, epiphytic perennial with dense, funnel-shaped rosettes. **H** and **S** 60cm (24in) or more. Has broadly strap-shaped, arching, yellowish- to deep green leaves, cross-banded with reddish-brown, particularly beneath. In summer–autumn, flat spikes of tubular, pale yellow or greenish-yellow flowers, with brownish-red tips, are produced well above the foliage.

V. hieroglyphica (King of the bromeliads). Evergreen perennial with dense, funnel-shaped rosettes. **H** and **S** 60cm–1m (2–3ft). Produces broadly strap-shaped, arching, yellowish-green leaves, cross-banded and chequered with dark brownish-green. In summer bears panicles of tubular, yellow flowers well above the leaves.

V. platynema. Evergreen, basal-rosetted, epiphytic perennial. **H** and **S** 60cm (24in). Broadly strap-shaped, mid- to light green leaves, with purple tips, form dense rosettes. In summer flat racemes of tubular, green-and-yellow flowers, with red or yellow bracts, are produced.

♀ ***V. psittacina.*** Evergreen, spreading, basal-rosetted, epiphytic perennial. **H** and **S** 40–60cm (16–24in). Has dense rosettes of strap-shaped, arching, pale green leaves. Flat spikes of tubular, yellow flowers with green tips, emerging from red-and-yellow or red-and-green bracts, are borne above foliage in summer–autumn.

♀ ***V. splendens*** (Flaming sword; illus. p.471). Evergreen, basal-rosetted, epiphytic perennial. **H** and **S** 30cm (12in). Has dense rosettes of strap-shaped, arching, olive-green leaves, with purple to reddish-brown cross-bands. Bears flat, sword-shaped racemes of tubular, yellow flowers, between bright red bracts, in summer and autumn.

x *Vuylstekeara* Cambria gx 'Lensing's Favorite'. See x *Oncidopsis* Cambria gx 'Lensing's Favorite'.

WACHENDORFIA

HAEMODORACEAE

Genus of summer-flowering perennials with deep roots, to guard against frost. Half hardy. Requires a position in full sun and in moist soil. Propagate by division in spring or by seed in autumn or spring.

W. thyrsiflora. Clump-forming perennial. **H** 1.5–2m (5–6ft), **S** 45cm (1½ft). Shallowly cup-shaped, yellow to orange flowers are produced in dense panicles in early summer. Mid-green leaves are narrowly sword-shaped, pleated and rather coarse.

WAHLENBERGIA

CAMPANULACEAE

Genus of summer-flowering annuals, biennials and short-lived perennials, grown for their bell-shaped flowers. Is useful for alpine houses. Frost hardy. Needs a sheltered site, partial shade and well-drained, peaty, sandy soil. Propagate by seed in autumn.

W. albomarginata (New Zealand bluebell). Basal-rosetted, rhizomatous perennial. **H** and **S** 15cm (6in) or more. Slender stems each carry a bell-shaped, clear blue flower that opens flat in summer. Has narrowly elliptic to oval, mid-green leaves in tufts. Is good in a rock garden.

W. congesta, syn. *W. saxicola* var. *congesta*. Mat-forming, creeping, rhizomatous perennial. **H** 7cm (3in), **S** 10cm (4in). Has small, rounded or spoon-shaped, mid-green leaves and, in summer, bell-shaped, lavender-blue or white flowers held singly on wiry stems.

W. saxicola var. congesta. See *W. congesta.*

W. serpyllifolia. See *Edraianthus serpyllifolius.*

WALDSTEINIA

ROSACEAE

Genus of semi-evergreen, creeping perennials with runners. Makes good ground cover. Fully hardy. Needs sun and well-drained soil. Propagate by division in early spring.

W. ternata, syn. *W. trifolia*, illus. p.372.

W. trifolia. See *W. ternata.*

WASHINGTONIA

ARECACEAE/PALMAE

Genus of evergreen palms, grown for their stately appearance. Frost tender, min. 10°C (50°F). Grows in fertile, well-drained soil and in full sun. Water containerized specimens freely in summer, moderately at other times. Remove skirt of persistent, dead leaves regularly as they are a fire risk. Propagate by seed in spring at not less than 24°C (75°F). Red spider mite may be a nuisance.

♀ ***W. filifera*** (Desert fan palm). Fast-growing, evergreen palm. **H** and **S** to 25m (80ft). Has fan-shaped, long-stalked, grey-green leaves, each lobe with a filamentous tip. Long-stalked clusters of tiny, creamy-white flowers are borne in summer and berry-like, black fruits in winter.

W. robusta (Thread palm) illus. p.451.

WATSONIA

IRIDACEAE

Genus of clump-forming corms, *Gladiolus*-like in overall appearance, although flowers are more tubular. Half hardy. Requires an open, sunny position and light, well-drained soil. Plant in autumn, 10–15cm (4–6in) deep; protect with bracken, loose peat or similar during first winter, if frost is expected. Feed with slow-acting fertilizer, such as bonemeal, in summer. Corms are best left undisturbed to form clumps. Propagate by seed in autumn.

W. beatricis. See *W. pillansii.*

W. borbonica, syn. *W. pyramidata*, illus. p.386.

W. fourcadei. Clump-forming, summer-flowering corm. **H** to 1.5m (5ft), **S** 30–45cm (1–1½ft). Sword-shaped, erect leaves are mostly basal. Has a dense spike of tubular, salmon-red flowers, each 8–9cm (3–3½in) long and with 6 lobes.

W. meriania illus. p.385.

W. pillansii, syn. *W. beatricis*, illus. p.386.

W. pyramidata. See *W. borbonica.*

Wattakaka sinensis. See *Dregea sinensis.*

WEIGELA

CAPRIFOLIACEAE

Genus of deciduous shrubs, grown for their showy, funnel-shaped flowers. Fully hardy. Prefers sunny, fertile soil. To maintain vigour, prune out a few older branches to ground level, after flowering each year. Straggly, old plants may be pruned hard in spring (although this will lose one season's flowers). Propagate by softwood cuttings in summer.

W. 'Bristol Ruby'. Vigorous, deciduous, upright shrub. **H** 2.5m (8ft), **S** 2m (6ft). Deep red flowers open from darker buds amid oval, toothed, mid-green leaves in late spring and early summer.

W. 'Candida'. Deciduous, bushy shrub. **H** and **S** 2.5m (8ft). Pure white flowers appear in late spring and early summer. Leaves are oval, toothed and bright green.

W. 'Eva Rathke'. Deciduous, upright, dense shrub. **H** and **S** 1.5m (5ft). Has oval, toothed, dark green leaves. Broad-mouthed, crimson flowers open from darker buds from late spring to early summer.

W. florida. Deciduous, arching shrub. **H** and **S** 2.5m (8ft). Bears deep pink flowers, pale pink to white inside, in late spring and early summer. Oval, toothed leaves are mid-green. ♀ **'Foliis Purpureis'** illus. p.153. ♀ **'Variegata'** illus. p.152.

W. 'Looymansii Aurea'. Weak-growing, deciduous, upright shrub. **H** 1.5m (5ft), **S** 1m (3ft). From late spring through to early summer, produces pale pink flowers amid oval, toothed, golden-yellow leaves with narrow red rims. Needs protection from hot sun.

W. middendorffiana illus. p.159.

W. praecox. Deciduous, upright shrub. **H** 2.5m (8ft), **S** 2m (6ft). Fragrant, pink flowers, marked inside with yellow, are produced in late spring. Leaves are bright green, oval and toothed. ♀ **'Variegata'** has leaves with broad, creamy-white margins.

Weingartia neocumingii. See *Rebutia neocumingii.*

WEINMANNIA

CUNONIACEAE

Genus of evergreen trees and shrubs, grown for their foliage, flowers and overall appearance. Frost tender, min. 5–7°C (41–5°F). Requires a position in partial shade or full light and humus-rich, well-drained but not dry soil, ideally neutral to acid. Water containerized plants freely when in full growth, moderately at other times. Pruning is tolerated if needed. Propagate by seed in spring or by semi-ripe cuttings in summer.

W. trichosperma. Evergreen, ovoid to round-headed tree. **H** 12m (40ft) or more, **S** 8–10m (25–30ft). Glossy, rich green leaves have 9–19 oval, boldly toothed leaflets that are borne on a winged midrib. Spikes of tiny, fragrant, white flowers, with pink stamens, are produced in early summer.

WELDENIA

COMMELINACEAE

Genus of one species of summer-flowering, tuberous perennial, grown for its flowers. Half hardy. Needs sun and gritty, well-drained soil. Keep dry from autumn until growth restarts in late winter. Is suitable for alpine houses. Propagate by

root cuttings in winter or by division in early spring.
W. candida illus. p.348.

WELWITSCHIA

WELWITSCHIACEAE

Genus of one species of evergreen, desert-growing perennial with a deep tap root. Has only 2 leaves, which lie on the ground and grow continuously from the base for up to 100 years. Frost tender, min. 10°C (50°F). Requires sun and sharply drained soil. Requires desert conditions: may succeed in a mixture of stone chippings and leaf mould, in a length of drainpipe to take its long tap root. Propagate by seed when ripe.
W. bainesii. See *W. mirabilis*.
W. mirabilis, syn. *W. bainesii*. Evergreen perennial with a short, woody trunk. **H** to 30cm (12in), **S** indefinite. Has 2 strap-shaped leaves, to 2.5m (8ft) long, with tips splitting to form many tendril-like strips. Bears small, reddish-brown cones.

WESTRINGIA

LABIATAE/LAMIACEAE

Genus of evergreen shrubs, grown for their flowers and overall appearance. Frost tender, min. 5–7°C (41–45°F). Requires full light and well-drained soil. Water containerized specimens moderately, less when not in full growth. Propagate by seed in spring or by semi-ripe cuttings in late summer.
♀ ***W. fruticosa*** (Australian rosemary), syn. *W. rosmariniformis*, illus. p.453.
W. rosmariniformis. See *W. fruticosa*.

WIGANDIA

HYDROPHYLLACEAE

Genus of evergreen perennials and shrubs, grown for their flowers and foliage. Frost tender, min. 7–10°C (45–50°F). Needs full light and moist but well-drained soil. Water potted plants freely when in full growth, moderately at other times. Cut down flowered stems in spring to prevent plants becoming straggly. Propagate by seed or softwood cuttings in spring. Whitefly is sometimes troublesome. ⓘContact with foliage may aggravate skin allergies.
W. caracasana. Evergreen, erect, sparsely branched shrub. **H** 2–3m (6–10ft), **S** 1–2m (3–6ft). Produces oval, wavy-edged, toothed, deep green leaves, 45cm (18in) long and covered with white hairs beneath. Carries 5-petalled, violet-purple flowers in large, terminal clusters from spring through to autumn. Is often grown annually from seed for its leaves.

Wigginsia vorwerkiana. See *Parodia erinacea*.
Wilcoxia albiflora. See *Echinocereus leucanthus*.
Wilcoxia schmollii. See *Echinocereus schmollii*.
x *Wilsonara* Hambühren Stern gx 'Cheam'. See Oncidium Hambühren Stern gx 'Cheam'.
Wintera aromatica. See *Drimys winteri*.

WISTERIA

LEGUMINOSAE/PAPILIONACEAE

Genus of deciduous, woody-stemmed, twining climbers, grown for their spectacular flowers and suitable for walls and pergolas and for growing against buildings and trees. Fully to frost hardy. Needs a position in sun and in fertile, well-drained soil. Prune after flowering and again in late winter. Propagate by bench grafting in winter or by seed in autumn or spring. Plants grown from seed may not flower for some years and often have poor flowers. ⓘAll parts may cause severe discomfort if ingested. See also feature panel p.205.
W. brachybotrys (Silky wisteria). Deciduous, woody-stemmed, twining climber. **H** to 9m (28ft) or more. Fully hardy. Leaves are 20–35cm (8–14in) long, each with 9–13 oval leaflets. Has 10–15cm (4–6in) long racemes of scented, pea-like, violet to white flowers, each with a yellow blotch at base of upper petal, in early summer. It sometimes flowers again sparsely in autumn. **f. *alba*** see 'Shiro-kapitan'. **'Alba'** see 'Shiro-kapitan'. **'Alba Plena'** see 'Shiro-kapitan'. **'Murasaki-kapitan'** (syn. *W. venusta* f. *violacea*, *W.v.* 'Violacea') has deep blue-violet flowers with prominent white, slightly yellow-tinged markings on the standards. **f. *plena*** see *W.b.* 'Shiro-kapitan'. **'Shiro-kapitan'**, syn. *W.b.* f. *alba*, *W.b.* 'Alba', *W.b.* 'Alba Plena', *W.b.* f. *plena*, *W. venusta*, *W.v.* f. *alba*, *W.v.* 'Alba', *W.v.* 'Alba Plena' (illus. p.205) has white flowers with a yellow stain at the base of each standard. Occasionally bears double flowers. **'White Silk'** (illus. p.205) is similar to 'Shiro-kapitan' but produces much longer racemes.
W. chinensis. See *W. sinensis*.
W. floribunda (Japanese wisteria). Vigorous twining climber. **H** 9m (28ft) or more. Fully hardy. Has pinnate leaves, each composed of 11–19 ovate to lance-shaped leaflets. In early summer, pea-like, fragrant, blue to violet, pink, or white flowers, the standards marked with white and yellow, are produced in pendent racemes, to 30cm (12in) or more long, the flowers opening gradually from the bases to the tips; they are often followed by bean-like, velvety green seed pods, to 15cm (6in) long. ♀ **'Alba'** (syn. *W.f.* 'Shiro Noda') bears white flowers in racemes 60cm (24in) long, illus. p.196. **'Black Dragon'**, see. *W.f.* 'Yae-kokuryu' (illus. p.205) has racemes 30–50cm (12–20in) long with violet-purple flowers. **'Domino'** (illus. p.205) has blue-violet flowers with light purple-blue standards, marked yellow at base, and darker purple-blue wing and keel petals, borne in spring and sometimes again in autumn. **'Hon-Beni'** see *W.f.* 'Rosea' (illus. p.205). **'Lawrence'** (illus. p.205) has densely packed racemes of pale violet-blue flowers, with greenish-yellow bases on standards and darker blue-violet on keel and wing petals, borne in spring. **'Macrobotrys'** see *W.f.* 'Multijuga'. ♀ **'Multijuga'** (syn. *W.f.* 'Macrobotrys') has lilac-blue flowers in racemes that are 90–120cm (3–4ft) long. ♀ **'Rosea'** (syn. *W.f.* 'Hon-beni'; illus. p.205) has racemes that are 30–40cm (12–16in) long and have dark purplish-pink flowers with a yellow mark on standard bases. **'Shiro Noda'** see *W.f.* 'Alba'. **'Violacea Plena'** is similar to 'Yae Kokuryu' but has double, lavender-purple flowers and no dark purple-indigo central petals. **'Yae-kokuryu'** (syn. *W.f.* 'Black Dragon', *W.* x *formosa* 'Black Dragon', *W.* x *f.* 'Double Black Dragon'; illus. p.205) has racemes, 35cm (14in) long, of slightly ragged, fully double, lilac-purple flowers with dark purple-indigo centres.
W.* x *formosa (*W. floribunda* x *W. sinensis*). Vigorous twining climber with pinnate leaves, each composed of 9–15, broadly ovate to elliptic leaflets. **H** 9m (28ft) or more. Fully hardy. Pea-like, fragrant, violet-blue flowers, with white and yellow markings, are borne in pendent racemes, to 25cm (10in) long, in late spring and early summer, often followed by bean-like velvety green seed pods to 15cm (6in) long. **'Black Dragon'** see *W. floribunda* 'Yae Kokuryu'. **'Double Black Dragon'** see *W. floribunda* 'Yae Kokuryu'.
♀ ***W. sinensis***, syn. *W. chinensis* (Chinese wisteria). Vigorous, deciduous, woody-stemmed, twining climber. **H** to 30m (100ft). Fully hardy. Has leaves of 11 leaflets and fragrant, lilac or pale violet flowers, in racemes 20–30cm (8–12in) long, in early summer, followed by velvety pods. ♀ **'Alba'** has strongly scented, pea-like, white flowers in racemes, 25–30cm (8–12in) long, in early summer. **'Prolific'** (illus. p.205), **H** to 30m (100ft), is vigorous, with masses of single, lilac-blue to pale violet-blue flowers in longer racemes.
W. venusta. See *W. brachybotrys* 'Shiro-kapitan'. **f. *alba*** see *W. brachybotrys* 'Shiro-kapitan'. **'Alba'** see *W. brachybotrys* 'Shiro-kapitan'. **'Alba Plena'** see *W. brachybotrys* 'Shiro-kapitan'. **f. *violacea*** see *W. brachybotrys* 'Murasaki-kapitan'. **'Violacea'** see *W. brachybotrys* 'Murasaki-kapitan'.

WOLFFIA

Duckweed

LEMNACEAE/ARACEAE

Genus of semi-evergreen, perennial, floating water plants, grown for their curiosity value as the smallest-known flowering plants. Is ideal for cold-water aquariums. Half hardy. Needs a sunny position. Remove excess plantlets as required. Propagate by redistribution of plantlets as required.
W. arrhiza (Least duckweed). Semi-evergreen, perennial, floating water plant. **S** indefinite. Leaves are rounded and mid-green. Insignificant, greenish flowers appear year-round.

WOLLEMIA

Wollemi pine

ARAUCARIACEAE

Genus of conifers with narrowly oblong, pointed, needle-like, dark green leaves set opposite each other along shoot. See also CONIFERS.
W. nobilis (Wollemi pine) illus. p.96.

WOODSIA

DRYOPTERIDACEAE

Genus of deciduous ferns, suitable for rock gardens and alpine houses. Fully hardy. Tolerates sun or semi-shade. May be difficult to cultivate: soil must provide constant moisture and also be quick-draining, and crowns of plants must sit above soil to avoid rotting. Propagate by division in early spring.
♀ ***W. polystichoides*** (Holly-fern woodsia). Deciduous, tufted fern. **H** 10–30cm (4–12in), **S** 20–40cm (8–16in). In early spring, has lance-shaped, divided, pale green fronds, to 35cm (14in) long, softly hairy on both surfaces and scaly beneath; each is composed of 15–30 pairs of narrowly sickle-shaped or oblong pinnae, with slightly toothed margins. May be damaged by late frosts.

WOODWARDIA

BLECHNACEAE

Genus of evergreen or deciduous ferns. Fully to frost hardy. Prefers semi-shade and fibrous, moist, peaty soil. Remove faded fronds regularly. Propagate by division in spring.
♀ ***W. radicans*** (Chain fern). Vigorous, evergreen, spreading fern. Fully hardy. **H** 1.2m (4ft), **S** 60cm (2ft). Large, broadly lance-shaped, coarsely divided, mid-green arching fronds, with narrowly oval pinnae.
W. unigemmata (Asian chain fern). Evergreen fern very similar to *W. radicans*. **H** 1m (3ft), **S** 3m (10ft). Frost hardy. New foliage emerges brilliant red and fades to brown and then green.

WORSLEYA

Blue amaryllis

AMARYLLIDACEAE

Genus of one species of evergreen, winter-flowering bulb, with a neck up to 75cm (2½ft) high crowned by a tuft of leaves and a 20–30cm (8–12in) leafless flower stem. Frost tender, min. 15°C (59°F). Needs full sun and well-drained soil, or compost mixed with osmunda fibre, perlite or bark chips and some leaf mould. Soil should never dry out. Propagate by seed in spring.
W. procera. See *W. rayneri*.
W. rayneri, syn. *Hippeastrum procerum*, *W. procera*. Evergreen, winter-flowering bulb. **H** 1–1.2m (3–4ft), **S** 45–60cm (1½–2ft). Bears long, strap-shaped, strongly curved leaves and up to 14 funnel-shaped, lilac-blue flowers, 15cm (6in) long, with wavy-edged petals.

WULFENIA

SCROPHULARIACEAE

Genus of evergreen, basal-rosetted perennials, suitable for an alpine house. Fully hardy. Needs full sun and well-drained soil. Propagate by division in spring or by seed in autumn.
W. amherstiana illus. p.341.
W. carinthiaca. Evergreen perennial. **H** and **S** 25cm (10in). Has oblong to oval, toothed, dark green leaves, hairy beneath. Has a dense spike of small, tubular, violet-blue flowers in summer.

XYZ

XANTHOCERAS

SAPINDACEAE

Genus of one species of deciduous, spring- to summer-flowering shrub or tree, grown for its foliage and flowers. Fully hardy. Requires a sunny position and fertile, well-drained soil. Does best in areas with hot summers. Propagate by seed sown in autumn or by root cuttings or suckers in late winter. Is susceptible to coral spot fungus.
♀ ***X. sorbifolium*** illus. p.112.

XANTHOPHTHALMUM

COMPOSITAE/ASTERACEAE

Genus of annuals, grown for their daisy-like flower heads. Fully hardy. Prefers full sun and well-drained soil. Propagate by seed in spring.
X. coronarium, syn. *Chrysanthemum coronarium.* Fast-growing, upright, branching annual. **H** 30cm–90cm (1–3ft), **S** 38cm (15in). Has feathery, divided, light green leaves. In summer bears single or semi-double, daisy-like, yellow or yellow-and-white flower heads, to 5cm (2in) across.
X. segetum, syn. *Chrysanthemum segetum,* illus. p.322.

XANTHORHIZA

RANUNCULACEAE

Genus of one species of deciduous, spring-flowering shrub, grown for its leaves, clustered at the shoot tips, and star-shaped flowers. Fully hardy. Prefers a position in shade or semi-shade and in moist soil. Propagate by division in autumn.
X. apiifolia. See *X. simplicissima.*
X. simplicissima, syn. *X. apiifolia* (Yellow-root). Deciduous, upright shrub that spreads by underground stems. **H** 60cm (2ft), **S** 1.5m (5ft) Bright green leaves, each consisting of usually 5 oval to lance-shaped, sharply toothed leaflets, turn bronze or purple in autumn. Bears nodding panicles of tiny, star-shaped, purple flowers from early to mid-spring as foliage emerges.

XANTHORRHOEA

Blackboy, Grass tree

XANTHORRHOEACEAE

Genus of evergreen, long-lived perennials, grown mainly as foliage plants. Frost tender, min. 10°C (50°F). Needs full sun, well-drained soil and a fairly dry atmosphere. Propagate by basal offsets or seed in spring.
X. australis. Evergreen perennial with a stout, dark trunk. **H** 60cm–1.2m (2–4ft), **S** 1.2–1.5m (4–5ft). Very narrow, arching, flattened, silvery-green leaves, 60cm (2ft) or more long, 2mm (1/10in) wide, spread from top of the trunk. In summer may produce small, fragrant, 6-petalled, white flowers, in dense, candle-like spikes, 60cm (2ft) or more long, on stems of similar length.

XANTHOSOMA

ARACEAE

Genus of perennials, with underground tubers or thick stems above ground, grown mainly for their attractive foliage. Many species are cultivated in the tropics for their edible tubers. Frost tender, min. 15°C (59°F). Requires a position in partial shade and rich, moist soil. The atmosphere should be kept moist at all times. Propagate by division; alternatively take stem cuttings in spring or summer.
X. nigrum, syn. *X. violaceum.* Stemless perennial with large, underground tubers and leaves rising from ground level. **H** and **S** 1.2m (4ft). Purplish leaf stalks, to over 60cm (2ft) long, carry arrow-shaped leaf blades, 70cm (28in) long, dark green with purple midribs and veins. Intermittently bears greenish-purple spathes, yellower within, surrounding a brownish spadix.
X. sagittifolium illus. p.474.
X. violaceum. See *X. nigrum.*

XERANTHEMUM

Immortelle

COMPOSITAE/ASTERACEAE

Genus of summer-flowering annuals. Half hardy. Grow in sun and in fertile, very well-drained soil. Propagate by seed sown outdoors in spring.
X. annuum [double] illus. p.305.

XEROCHRYSUM

SYN. BRACHTEANTHA

COMPOSITAE/ASTERACEAE

Genus of herbaceous perennials and annuals, grown for their daisy-like flower heads with papery bracts. Stalkless, hairy leaves are borne on erect, branching stems. Frost to half hardy. Needs full sun and moderately fertile, moist but well-drained soil. Propagate by seed sown in spring. *X. bracteatum* is often grown for cutting and drying.
X. bracteatum (Everlasting flower, Immortelle, Strawflower). Moderately fast-growing, upright, branching annual. Half hardy. ♀ **'Bright Bikini', H** and **S** 30cm (12in), has lance-shaped, mid-green leaves. From summer to early autumn produces papery, daisy-like flower heads in many colours. **Monstrosum Series, H** 90cm (3ft), has double flower heads in summer and early autumn. Flowers dry well. **Sundaze Series SUNDAZE GOLD ('Redbragol')** illus. p.320.
***X.* 'Redbragol'.** See *X. bracteatum* Sundaze Series SUNDAZE GOLD.

XERONEMA

AGAVACEAE/PHORMIACEAE

Genus of evergreen, robust, tufted perennials, with short, creeping rootstocks, grown for their flowers. Frost tender, min. 10°C (50°F). Grow in sun or partial shade and in humus-rich, well-drained soil. Propagate by seed or division in spring.
X. callistemon. Evergreen, iris-like, clump-forming perennial. **H** 60cm–1m (2–3ft), **S** indefinite. Erect, folded leaves, 60cm–1m (2–3ft) long, are very narrow and hard-textured. In summer, short-stalked, 6-petalled, red flowers, to 3cm (1¼in) wide, are borne on one-sided racemes, 15–30cm (6–12in) long.

XEROPHYLLUM

LILIACEAE/MELANTHIACEAE

Genus of elegant, summer-flowering, rhizomatous perennials. Frost hardy. Prefers full sun and moist, peaty soil. May be difficult to cultivate. Propagate by seed in autumn.
X. tenax. Clump-forming perennial. **H** 1–1.2m (3–4ft), **S** 30–60cm (1–2ft). Star-shaped, white flowers, with violet anthers, borne in dense, terminal racemes in summer. Basal leaves are mid-green.

YUCCA

SYN. HESPEROYUCCA

AGAVACEAE

Genus of evergreen shrubs and trees, grown for the architectural value of their bold, sword-shaped, clustered leaves and showy panicles of usually white flowers. Makes fine container-grown plants. Fully hardy to frost tender, min. 7°C (45°F). Requires full sun and well-drained soil. Water container specimens moderately and reduce when they are not in full growth. Regularly remove spent flowering stems. Propagate in spring: frost-tender species by seed or suckers, hardier species by root cuttings or division.
Y. aloifolia (Spanish bayonet). Slow-growing, evergreen shrub or small tree with few branches. **H** 8m (25ft), **S** 4–5m (12–15ft). Frost tender. Has sword-shaped, deep green leaves, 50–75cm (20–30in) long, and large panicles of purple-tinted, white flowers in summer–autumn.
***Y. elephantipes* 'Variegata'.** Evergreen, large, upright shrub or small tree. **H** to 10m (30ft), **S** 5–8m (15–25ft), min. 10°C (50°F). Several to many sparsely branched trunks arise near ground level. Leaves are narrowly lance-shaped, leathery, light to mid-green and creamy-white at the margins. On mature plants, hemispherical, white to cream flowers are borne in dense, erect panicles from summer to autumn.
♀ ***Y. filamentosa*** (Adam's needle). Clump-forming, evergreen, basal-rosetted shrub. **H** 2m (6ft), **S** 1.5m (5ft) Fully hardy. From mid-through to late summer produces tall panicles of pendulous, tulip-shaped, white flowers, which rise up through low-growing tufts of sword-shaped, deep green leaves, edged with white threads.
Y. filifera* 'Ivory'.** See ***Y. flaccida 'Ivory'.
♀ ***Y. flaccida* 'Ivory',** syn. *Y. filifera* 'Ivory', illus. p.151.
♀ ***Y. gloriosa*** (Spanish dagger) illus. p.132. **'Nobilis'** is an evergreen shrub. **H** and **S** 2m (6ft) Frost hardy. Stem is stout and usually unbranched, and crowned with a large tuft of long, sword-shaped, sharply pointed, blue-green leaves, the outer ones semi-pendent. Pendulous, tulip-shaped, red-backed, white flowers are borne in long, erect panicles from mid-summer to early autumn.
Y. parviflora. See *Hesperaloe parviflora.*
Y. whipplei illus. p.151.

YUSHANIA

GRAMINEAE/POACEAE

See also GRASSES, BAMBOOS, RUSHES and SEDGES.
Y. anceps, syn. *Arundinaria anceps, A. jaunsarensis, Sinarundinaria jaunsarensis* (Anceps bamboo). Evergreen, spreading bamboo. **H** 2–3m (6–10ft), **S** indefinite. Fully hardy. Erect, later arching, stems bearing several branches at each node. **'Pitt White'** illus. p.288.

ZALUZIANSKYA

SCROPHULARIACEAE

Genus of sticky, low-growing annuals and evergreen perennials and sub-shrubs, with spikes of fragrant, tubular flowers with spreading petals. Frost hardy. Needs full sun and moist, sharply drained, humus-rich soil. Propagate by stem-tip cuttings in summer. Plants are short-lived.
Z. ovata. Clump-forming, evergreen perennial. **H** to 25cm (10in), **S** to 60cm (24in) Branching, brittle stems bear ovate, toothed, sticky, grey-green leaves. Crimson-backed, white flowers are produced over a long period in summer.

ZANTEDESCHIA

ARACEAE

Genus of summer-flowering, tuberous perennials, usually remaining evergreen in a warm climate, grown for their erect, funnel-shaped spathes and club-shaped spadix. Frost hardy to frost tender, min. 10°C (50°F). Requires full sun or partial shade and well-drained soil. *Z. aethiopica* will also grow in 15–30cm (6–12in) of water and therefore is suitable as a marginal water plant. Propagate by offsets in winter.
ⓘ All parts of the plant may cause mild stomach upset if ingested, and contact with the sap may irritate the skin.
♀ ***Z. aethiopica*** (Arum lily).
♀ **'Crowborough'** illus. p.437.
♀ **'Green Goddess'** illus. p.408.
Z. albomaculata, syn. *Z. melanoleuca.* Summer-flowering, tuberous perennial. **H** 30–40cm (12–16in), **S** 30cm (12in). Frost tender. Bears arrow-shaped, semi-erect, basal leaves with transparent spots. Has a yellow spadix inside a white spathe, 12–20cm (5–8in) long, shading to green at the base and a purple blotch inside.
***Z.* 'Black-eyed Beauty'.** Summer-flowering, tuberous perennial. **H** 30–40cm (12–16in), **S** 15cm (6in). Frost tender. Broadly heart-shaped, semi-erect, mid- to dark green, basal leaves are heavily white spotted. Each flower stem has a yellow spadix and cream spathe, 15cm (6in) long, with a central black mark in the throat.
Z. 'Black Magic'. Summer-flowering, tuberous perennial. **H** 75cm (30in), **S** 20cm (8in.) Frost tender. Broadly heart-shaped, semi-erect, mid- to dark green, basal leaves are heavily mottled with white. Each flower stem produces a golden-yellow spadix, surrounded by a black-throated, yellow spathe, 15cm (6in) long.
***Z.* 'Cameo'** illus. p.395.
♀ ***Z. elliottiana*** (Golden arum lily) illus. p.393.
Z. melanoleuca. See *Z. albomaculata.*

♡ ***Z. rehmannii*** (Pink arum). Summer-flowering, tuberous perennial. **H** 40cm (16in), **S** 30cm (12in). Frost tender. Green basal leaves are arrow-shaped and semi-erect. Each flower stem has a yellow spadix, surrounded by a reddish-pink spathe, 7–8cm (3in) long.

ZANTHOXYLUM

RUTACEAE

Genus of deciduous or evergreen, spiny shrubs and trees, grown for their aromatic foliage, fruits and habit. Fully to frost hardy. Requires sun or semi-shade and in fertile soil. Propagate by seed in autumn or by root cuttings in late winter.

Z. piperitum (Japan pepper). Deciduous, bushy, spiny shrub or small tree. **H** and **S** 2.5m (8ft). Fully hardy. Has aromatic, glossy, dark green leaves composed of many leaflets. Small, red fruits follow tiny, greenish-yellow, spring flowers.

Z. simulans illus. p.141.

ZAUSCHNERIA

ONAGRACEAE

Genus of sub-shrubby, evergreen or deciduous perennials, grown for their mass of flowers. Fully to frost hardy. Requires sun and well-drained soil. Propagate by seed or division in spring or by taking side-shoot cuttings in summer.

Z. californica, syn. *Epilobium californicum*. Clump-forming, woody-based, evergreen or semi-evergreen perennial. **H** and **S** 45cm (18in). Frost hardy. Terminal clusters of tubular, bright scarlet flowers, borne on slender stems, are produced in late summer and early autumn. Bears lance-shaped, rich green leaves. ♡ **'Dublin'** (syn. *Z.c.* 'Glasnevin', *Z.c.* subsp. *cana* 'Dublin') illus. p.340. **'Glasnevin'** see *Z.c.* subsp. *cana* 'Dublin'. **subsp. *cana*** (syn. *Epilobium canum*, *Z. cana*), **H** 30cm (12in) is deciduous and produces linear, grey leaves and fuchsia-like, brilliant scarlet flowers. **subsp. *cana* 'Dublin'** see *Z.c* 'Dublin'.

Z. cana. See *Z. californica* subsp. *cana*.

Z. septentrionalis, syn. *Epilobium septentrionale*. Mat-forming, non-woody, deciduous perennial. **H** 10–20cm (4–8in), **S** to 20cm (8in) Fully hardy. Terminal clusters of numerous, short-stalked, tubular, scarlet flowers are produced in late summer. Has oval to lance-shaped, grey to grey-green leaves.

ZEA

Indian corn, Maize

GRAMINEAE/POACEAE

See also GRASSES, BAMBOOS, RUSHES and SEDGES.

Z. mays (Ornamental maize, Sweet corn). Fairly fast-growing, upright annual with lance-shaped leaves. **H** to 4m (12ft), **S** 60cm (2ft). Half hardy. **'Gracillima Variegata'**, **H** 90cm (3ft), **S** 30–45cm (1–1½ft), has leaves striped green and creamy. Tassel-like, silvery flower heads are followed by large, bright yellow seed heads (cobs). **'Harlequin'**, **H** 1–2m (3–6ft), **S** 60cm (2ft), has leaves 60cm (2ft) long and striped with green, red and white. Feathery, silky flower heads, 15cm (6in) long, borne on long stems, are produced in mid-summer, followed by large, cylindrical, green-sheathed, yellow seed heads (cobs), with deep red grains. **'Strawberry Corn'**, **H** 1.2m (4ft), produces seed heads with small, yellow to burgundy-red grains within yellow-green spathe-bracts.

Zebrina pendula. See *Tradescantia zebrina*.

ZELKOVA

ULMACEAE

Genus of deciduous trees, grown mainly for foliage and habit and are best when planted as single specimens. Has insignificant flowers in spring. Fully hardy, but prefers some shelter. Does best in full sun and requires deep, fertile, moist but well-drained soil. Propagate by seed in autumn.

Z. abelicea, syn. *Z. cretica*. Deciduous, bushy-headed, spreading tree. **H** 5m (15ft), **S** 7m (22ft) Produces small, oval, dark green leaves that are prominently toothed.

Z. carpinifolia (Caucasian elm) illus. p.64.

Z. cretica. See *Z. abelicea*.

♡ ***Z. serrata*** illus. p.67.

ZENOBIA

ERICACEAE

Genus of one species of deciduous or semi-evergreen, summer-flowering shrub, grown for its flowers. Fully hardy. Requires semi-shade and moist, peaty, acid soil. Prune out older, weaker shoots after flowering to maintain vigour. Propagate by semi-ripe cuttings in summer.

Z. pulverulenta illus. p.130.

ZEPHYRANTHES

Rain lily, Windflower

AMARYLLIDACEAE

Genus of clump-forming bulbs with an erect, crocus-like flower on each stem. Frost to half hardy. Needs a sheltered, sunny site and open, well-drained but moist soil. Container-grown bulbs need a dryish, warm period after foliage dies down in summer, followed by copious amounts of water to stimulate flowering. Propagate by seed in autumn or in spring.

Z. atamasco (Atamasco lily) Clump-forming, early summer-flowering bulb. **H** 15–25cm (6–10in), **S** 8–10cm (3–4in) Half hardy. Basal leaves are very narrow, grass-like and semi-erect. Each stem produces a widely funnel-shaped, purple-tinged, white flower, opening to 10cm (4in) wide, in spring or summer.

Z. candida illus. p.424.

Z. carinata, syn. *Z. grandiflora* of gardens, illus. p.413.

Z. citrina. Clump-forming, autumn-flowering bulb. **H** 10–15cm (4–6in), **S** 5–8cm (2–3in) Half hardy. Has rush-like, erect, basal, green leaves. Stems produce funnel-shaped, bright yellow flowers, opening to 4–5cm (1½–2in) wide, in autumn.

Z. grandiflora of gardens. See *Z. carinata*.

Z. robusta. See *Habranthus robustus*.

Z. rosea. Autumn-flowering bulb. **H** 20cm (8in), **S** 5cm (2in). Half hardy. Short-tubed, funnel-shaped, sugar-pink flowers among narrowly linear, semi-erect, green, basal leaves.

ZIGADENUS

LILIACEAE/MELANTHIACEAE

Genus of summer-flowering bulbs with spikes of star-shaped, 6-petalled flowers. Frost hardy. It requires sun or partial shade and well-drained soil. Water copiously in spring and summer, when in growth; less at other times. Remains dormant in winter. Propagate by division in early spring or by seed sown in autumn or spring. ⓘ All parts are highly toxic if ingested.

Z. elegans. Clump-forming, summer-flowering bulb. **H** 30–50cm (12–20in), **S** 10–15cm (4–6in). Bears long, narrow, semi-erect, basal leaves. Every stem has a spike of greenish-white flowers, 1cm (½in) wide and with yellowish-green nectaries.

Z. fremontii. Clump-forming, early summer-flowering bulb. **H** 30–50cm (12–20in), **S** 10–15cm (4–6in). Has long, strap-shaped, semi-erect, basal leaves. Stem produces a spike of star-shaped, pale creamy-green flowers with darker green nectaries on petal bases.

Z. nuttallii. Clump-forming, summer-flowering bulb. **H** 30–60cm (12–24in), **S** 8cm (3in) Narrowly strap-shaped, semi-erect, basal leaves are mid- to dark green. Produces dense spikes of tiny, creamy-yellow flowers, 6–8mm (¼–⅜in) across.

ZINGIBER

Ginger

ZINGIBERACEAE

Genus of herbaceous or evergreen perennials, grown for their spicy rhizomes and flowers arranged in a pine-cone-shaped head, borne on separate stems to the leaves. Frost hardy to frost tender, min. 10°C (50°F). Needs humus-rich, moist but well-drained soil in partial shade. Propagate by division in spring.

Z. mioga. Herbaceous, clump-forming perennial. **H** 80cm (32in), **S** 50cm (20in). Frost hardy. Short-stemmed spikes, 5–15cm (2–6in) long, of pale cream to yellow flowers, 5cm (2in) across, with reddish-purple bracts, are borne in late summer. Has tall, leafy pseudostems of narrowly lance-shaped, pale green leaves.

ZINNIA

COMPOSITAE/ASTERACEAE

Genus of annuals with large, dahlia-like flower heads that are excellent for cutting. Half hardy. Requires a position in sun and in fertile, well-drained soil. Dead flower heads should be removed regularly to promote flowering. Propagate by seed sown under glass in early spring.

***Z. angustifolia* 'Orange Star'.** See *Z. haageana 'Orange Star'*. **'Persian Carpet'** see *Z. haageana* 'Persian Carpet'.

Z. elegans. Moderately fast-growing, upright, sturdy annual. **H** 60–75cm (2–2½ft), **S** 30cm (1ft) Bears oval to lance-shaped leaves that are pale or mid-green. Purple flower heads, over 5cm (2in) wide, are produced in summer and early autumn. Hybrids of *Z. elegans* are available in various shades. **Cactus-flowered Group**, **H** 60–90cm (24–36in), have large, semi-double flower heads, similar to those of cactus dahlias, with long, narrow, quilled petals, in a broad range of colours. **Dreamland Series [Yellow]**. **H** and **S** 30cm (12in). In summer and autumn has large, daisy-like, semi-double flower heads. **[Scarlet]** illus. p.306. **'Envy'** illus. p.316. **Hobgoblin Series, H** to 45cm (18in), produce sturdy plants, with small, single flower heads in a broad range of colours. **Peter Pan Series, H** 20cm (8in), are dwarf, with double flower heads in a wide range of colours. **'Red Sun', H** and **S** 30–40cm (12–16in), has semi- to fully double, daisy-like, deep bright red flower heads. **Short Stuff Series, H** 25cm (10in), are dwarf, with double flower heads in a broad range of colours. **Small World Series, H** to 45cm (18in), are dwarf and have double flower heads in a wide range of colours. **'State Fair', H** to 75cm (30in), is vigorous, and produces large, double flower heads in many colours.

***Z. haageana* 'Classic'.** See *Z.h.* 'Orange Star'. **'Orange Star'** (syn. *Z.angustifolia* 'Orange Star', *Z. haageana* 'Classic') illus p.325. **'Persian Carpet'** (syn. *Z. angustifolia* 'Persian Carpet') is a moderately fast-growing, upright, dwarf annual. **H** 38cm (15in), **S** 30cm (12in). Pale-green leaves are lance-shaped and hairy. Small, weather-resistant, dahlia-like, double flower heads, opening to over 2.5cm (1in) wide, are produced through the summer, in a range of colours.

***Z. x marylandica* Profusion Series 'Profusion Cherry'** illus. p.307 . **Zahara Series 'Zahara Starlight Rose'** illus. p.298.

ZIZANIA

GRAMINEAE/POACEAE

See also GRASSES, BAMBOOS, RUSHES and SEDGES.

Z. aquatica (Canada wild rice). Annual, grass-like, marginal water plant. **H** 3m (10ft), **S** 45cm (18in). Half hardy. Has grass-like, mid-green leaves and, in summer, grass-like, pale green flowers, followed by rice-like seeds that attract waterfowl. Needs sun; suitable for up to 23cm (9in) deep water. Propagate from seed stored damp and sown in spring.

Zygocactus truncatus. See *Schlumbergera truncata*.

ZYGOPETALUM

ORCHIDACEAE

See also ORCHIDS.

Z. mackaii. See *Z. mackayi*.

Z. mackayi, syn. *Z. mackaii*. Evergreen, epiphytic orchid for growing in a cool or intermediate greenhouse. **H** 30cm (12in). In autumn produces long sprays of fragrant, brown-blotched, green flowers, 8cm (3in) across, with reddish-indigo veins, and white lips. Ribbed leaves are narrowly oval, and 30cm (12in) long. Requires semi-shade in summer.

***Z. Perrenoudii* gx** (illus. p.466). Evergreen, epiphytic orchid for a cool or intermediate greenhouse. **H** 30cm (12in) Spikes of fragrant, violet-purple-lipped, dark brown flowers, 8cm (3in) across, appear in winter. Has narrowly oval, ribbed leaves, 30cm (12in) long. Requires a position in semi-shade in summer.

INDEX OF COMMON NAMES

A

B

C

Caucasian elm. See *Zelkova carpinifolia.*
Caucasian fir. See *Abies nordmanniana.*
Caucasian lime. See *Tilia* x *euchlora.*
Caucasian oak. See *Quercus macranthera.*
Caucasian spruce. See *Picea orientalis.*
Caucasian whortleberry. See *Vaccinium arctostaphylos.*
Caucasian wing nut. See *Pterocarya fraxinifolia.*

D

E

F

G

D

H

I

J

K

L

M

N

O

M

PQ

R

U

VW

XYZ

GLOSSARY OF TERMS

Terms printed in italics refer to other glossary entries.

Acid [of soil]. With a *pH* value of less than 7; see also *alkaline* and neutral.

Adventitious [of roots]. Arising directly from a stem or leaf.

Aerial root. See *root.*

Air-layering. A method of propagation by which a portion of stem is induced to root by enclosing it in a suitable medium, such as damp moss, and securing it with plastic sheeting; roots will form if the moss is kept moist.

Alkaline [of soil]. With a *pH* value of more than 7; some plants will not tolerate alkaline soils and must be grown in *neutral* or *acid* soil.

Alpine house. An unheated greenhouse, used for the cultivation of mainly alpine and bulbous plants, that provides greater ventilation and usually more light than a conventional greenhouse.

Alternate [of leaves]. Borne singly at each *node*, on either side of a stem.

Annual. A plant that completes its life cycle, from germination through to flowering and seeding and then death, in one growing season.

Anther. The part of a stamen that produces pollen; it is usually borne on a filament.

Apex. The tip or growing point of an organ such as a leaf or shoot.

Areole. A modified, cushion-like *tubercle*, peculiar to the family Cactaceae, that bears hairs, spines, leaves, side-branches or flowers.

Asclepiad. A member of the family Asclepiadaceae, e.g. *Asclepias, Hoya, Stephanotis.*

Auricle. An ear-like lobe such as is sometimes found at the base of a leaf.

Awn. A stiff, bristle-like projection commonly found on grass seeds and *spikelets.*

Axil. The angle between a leaf and stem where an axillary bud develops.

Bedding plant. A plant that is mass-planted to provide a temporary display.

Biennial. A plant that flowers, seeds and dies in the second season after germination, producing only stems, roots and leaves in the first season.

Blade. The flattened and often broad part of a leaf.

Bloom. 1. A flower or blossom. 2. A fine, waxy, whitish or bluish-white coating on stems, leaves or fruits.

Bog garden. An area where the soil is kept permanently damp but not waterlogged.

Bole. The trunk of a *tree* from ground level to the first major branch.

Bolt. To produce flowers and seed prematurely, particularly in the case of vegetables such as lettuce and beetroot.

Bonsai. A method of producing dwarf trees or shrubs by special techniques that include pruning roots, pinching out shoots, removing growth buds and training branches and stems.

Bract. A modified leaf at the base of a flower or flower cluster. Bracts may resemble normal leaves or be reduced and scale-like in appearance; they are often large and brightly coloured.

Bud. A rudimentary or condensed shoot containing embryonic leaves or flowers.

Bulb. A storage organ consisting mainly of fleshy scales and swollen, modified leaf-bases on a much reduced stem. Bulbs usually, but not always, grow underground.

Bulbil. A small, *bulb*-like organ, often borne in a leaf *axil*, occasionally in a *flower head;* it may be used for propagation.

Bulblet. A small *bulb* produced at the base of a mature one.

Bur. 1. A prickly or spiny *fruit*, or aggregate of fruits. 2. A woody outgrowth on the stems of certain trees.

Cactus (pl. cacti). A member of the family Cactaceae, often *succulent* and spiny.

Calyx (pl. calyces). The outer part of a flower, usually small and green but sometimes showy and brightly coloured, that encloses the petals in bud and is formed from the *sepals.*

Capsule. A dry *fruit* that splits open when ripe to release its seeds.

Carpel. The female portion of a flower, or part of it, consisting of an *ovary, stigma* and *style.*

Catkin. A flower cluster, normally pendulous. Flowers lack petals, are often stalkless, surrounded by scale-like *bracts*, and are usually unisexual.

Caudex (pl. caudices). The stem base of a woody plant such as a *palm* or tree fern.

Cladode. A stem, often flattened, with the function and appearance of a leaf.

Claw. The narrow, basal portion of petals in some genera, e.g. *Dianthus.*

Climber. A plant that climbs using other plants or objects as a support: a **leaf-stalk** climber by coiling its leaf stalks around supports; a **root** climber by producing aerial, supporting roots; a **self-clinging** climber by means of suckering pads; a **tendril** climber by coiling its tendrils; a **twining** climber by coiling stems. **Scandent, scrambling** and **trailing climbers** produce long stems that grow over plants or other supports; they attach themselves only loosely, if at all.

Clone. A group of genetically identical plants, propagated vegetatively.

Compound. Made up of several or many parts, e.g. a leaf divided into 2 or more *leaflets.*

Cone. The clustered flowers or woody, seed-bearing structures of a conifer.

Coppice. To cut back to near ground level each year in order to produce vigorous, ornamental shoots, as is usual with some *Cornus* and *Eucalyptus.*

Cordon. A trained plant restricted in growth to one main stem, occasionally 2–4 stems.

Corm. A bulb-like, underground storage organ consisting mainly of a swollen stem base and often surrounded by a papery tunic.

Cormlet. A small *corm* arising at the base of a mature one.

Corolla. The part of a flower formed by the petals.

Corona (crown). A petal-like outgrowth sometimes borne on the *corolla*, e.g. the trumpet or cup of a *Narcissus.*

Corymb. A racemose flower cluster in which the inner flower stalks are shorter than the outer, resulting in a rounded or flat-topped head.

Cotyledon. See *seed leaf.*

Creeper. A plant that grows close to the ground, usually rooting as it spreads.

Crisped. Minutely wavy-edged.

Crown. 1. The part of the plant at or just below the soil surface from which new shoots are produced and to which they die back in autumn. 2. The upper, branched part of a tree above the *bole*. 3. A *corona.*

Culm. The usually hollow stem of a grass or bamboo.

Cutting. A section of a plant that is removed and used for propagation. The various types of cutting are: **basal** – taken from the base of a plant (usually herbaceous) as it begins to produce growth in spring; **greenwood** – made from the tip of young growth; **hardwood** – mature wood taken at the end of the growing season; **leaf** – a detached leaf or part of a leaf; **root** – part of a semi-mature or mature root; **semi-ripe** – half-ripened wood taken during the growing season; softwood – young growth taken at the beginning of the growing season; **stem** – a greenwood, hardwood, semi-ripe or softwood cutting; **tip** – a greenwood cutting.

Cyme. A flower cluster in which each growing point terminates in a flower.

Dead-head. To remove spent flower heads so as to promote further growth or flowering, prevent seeding or improve appearance.

Deciduous. Losing its leaves annually at the end of the growing season; **semi-deciduous** plants lose only some leaves.

Decumbent. Growing close to the ground but ascending at the tips.

Dentate. With toothed margins.

Die-back. Death of the tips of shoots due to frost or disease.

Dioecious. Bearing male and female flowers on separate plants.

Disbud. To remove surplus buds to promote larger flowers or fruits.

Disc floret, disc flower. A small and often inconspicuous, usually tubular flower, one of many that comprise the central portion of a composite flower head such as a daisy.

Division. A method of propagation by which a clump is divided into several parts during dormancy.

Elliptic [of leaves]. Broadening in the centre and narrowing towards each end.

Entire [of leaves]. With untoothed margins.

Epiphyte. A plant that grows on the surface of another without being parasitic.

Evergreen. Retaining its leaves at the end of the growing season although losing some older leaves regularly throughout the year; **semi-evergreen** plants retain only some leaves or lose older leaves only when the new growth is produced.

F1 hybrid. The first generation derived from crossing 2 distinct plants, usually when the parents are pure-bred lines and the offspring are vigorous. Seed from F1 hybrids does not come *true* to type.

Fall. An outer *perianth segment* of an iris, which projects outwards or downwards from the inner segments.

Fan palm. A *palm* with *palmate* rather than *pinnate* leaves.

Farina. A powdery, white, sometimes yellowish deposit naturally occurring on some leaves and flowers.

Fibrous root. A fine, young root, usually one of many.

Filament. The stalk of an *anther.*

Floret. A single flower in a head of many flowers.

Flower. The basic flower forms are: single, with one row of usually 4–6 petals; **semi-double,** with more petals, usually in 2 rows; **double,** with many petals in several rows and few or no stamens; **fully double,** usually rounded in shape, with densely packed petals and the stamens absent or obscured.

Flower head. A mass of small *flowers* or *florets* that together appear as one flower, e.g. a daisy.

Force. To induce artificially the early production of growth, flowers or *fruits.*

Frond. The leaf-like organ of a fern. Some ferns produce both barren and fertile fronds, the fertile fronds bearing *spores.*

Fruit. The structure in plants that bears one or more ripe seeds, e.g. a berry or nut.

Glabrous. Not hairy.

Glaucous. Bluish-white, bluish-green or bluish-grey.

Globose. Spherical.

Glochid. One of the barbed bristles or hairs, usually small, borne on a cactus *areole.*

Grafting. A method of propagation by which an artificial union is made between different parts of individual plants; usually the *shoot* (scion) of one is grafted onto the *rootstock* (stock) of another.

Heel. The small portion of old wood that is retained at the base of a cutting when it is removed from the stem.

Herbaceous. Dying down at the end of the growing season.

Hose-in-hose [of flowers]. With one *corolla* borne inside another, forming a double or semi-double *flower.*

Inflorescence. A cluster of flowers with a distinct arrangement, e.g. *corymb, cyme, panicle, raceme, spike, umbel.*

Insectivorous plant. A plant that traps and digests insects and other small animals to supplement its nutrient intake.

Key. A winged seed like those produced by the sycamore (*Acer pseudoplatanus*).

Lateral. A side growth that arises from the side of a shoot or root.

Layering. A method of propagation by which a stem is induced to root by being pegged down into the soil while it is still attached to the parent plant. See also *air-layering.*

Leaflet. The subdivision of a compound leaf.

Lenticel. A small, usually corky area on a stem or other part of a plant, which acts as a breathing pore.

Lime. Compounds of calcium; the amount of lime in soil determines whether it is *alkaline, neutral* or *acid.*

Linear [of leaves]. Very narrow with parallel sides.

Lip. A lobe comprising 2 or more flat or sometimes pouched *perianth segments*.

Loam. Well-structured, fertile soil that is moisture-retentive but free-draining.

Marginal water plant. A plant that grows partially submerged in shallow water or in moist soil at the edge of a pond.

Midrib. The main, central vein of a leaf or the central stalk to which the *leaflets* of a *pinnate* leaf are attached.

Monocarpic. Flowering and fruiting only once before dying; such plants may take several years to reach flowering size.

Mulch. A layer of organic matter applied to the soil over or around a plant to conserve moisture, protect the roots from frost, reduce the growth of weeds and enrich the soil.

Naturalize. To establish and grow as if in the wild.

Nectar. A sweet, sugary liquid secreted by the **nectary** – glandular tissue usually found in the flower but sometimes found on the leaves or stems.

Neutral [of soil]. With a *pH* value of 7, the point at which soil is neither *acid* nor *alkaline*.

Node. The point on a stem from which a leaf or leaves arise.

Offset. A small plant that arises by natural vegetative reproduction, usually at the base of the mother plant.

Opposite [of leaves]. Borne 2 to each *node*, one opposite the other.

Ovary. The part of the female portion of the flower, containing embryonic seeds, that will eventually form the *fruit*.

Palm. An evergreen *tree* or *shrub*-like plant, normally single-stemmed, with *palmate* or *pinnate* leaves usually in terminal rosettes; strictly a member of the family Palmae.

Palmate. Lobed in the fashion of a hand, with 5 lobes arising from the same point.

Pan. A shallow, free-draining pot in which alpine plants or bulbs are grown.

Panicle. A branched *raceme*.

Papilla (pl. papillae). A minute protuberance or gland-like structure.

Pea-like [of flowers]. Of the same structure as a pea flower.

Peat bed. A specially constructed area, edged with peat blocks and containing moisture-retentive, acidic, peaty soil.

Pedicel. The stalk of an individual flower.

Peduncle. The stalk of a flower cluster.

Peltate [of leaves]. Shield-shaped, with the stalk inserted towards or at the centre of the blade and not at the margin.

Perennial. Living for at least 3 seasons. In this book the term when used as a noun, and unless qualified, denotes an *herbaceous* perennial. A woody-based perennial dies down only partially, leaving a woody stem at the base.

Perianth. The outer parts of the flower comprising the *calyx* and the *corolla*. The term is often used when the calyx and the corolla are very similar in form.

Perianth segment. One portion of the *perianth*, resembling a *petal* and sometimes known as a tepal.

Petal. One portion of the often showy and coloured part of the *corolla*. In some families, e.g. Liliaceae, the *perianth segments* are petal-like and referred to horticulturally as petals.

Petaloid. Like a petal.

Petiole. The stalk of a *leaf*.

pH. The scale by which the acidity or alkalinity of soil is measured. See also *acid, alkaline, neutral*.

Phyllode. A flattened leaf stalk, which functions as and resembles a leaf.

Pinch out. To remove the growing tips of a plant to induce the production of side-shoots.

Pinna (pl. pinnae). The primary division of a *pinnate* leaf. The fertile pinnae of ferns produce spores, vegetative pinnae do not.

Pinnate [of leaves]. Compound, with *leaflets* arranged on opposite sides of a central stalk.

Pistil. The female part of a flower comprising the *ovary, stigma* and *style*.

Pollard [of a tree]. To cut back to its main branches in order to restrict growth.

Pollination. The transfer of pollen from the *anthers* to the *stigma* of the same or different flowers, resulting in fertilization of the embryonic seeds in the *ovary*.

Procumbent. Prostrate, creeping along the ground.

Raceme. An unbranched flower cluster with several or many stalked flowers borne singly along a main axis, the youngest at the apex.

Ray floret, ray flower. One of the flowers, usually with strap-shaped petals, that together form the outer ring of flowers in a composite *flower head* such as a daisy.

Ray petal. The petal or fused petals, often showy, of a ray *floret*.

Recurved. Curved backwards.

Reflexed. Bent sharply backwards.

Revert. To return to its original state, as when a plain green leaf is produced on a variegated plant.

Rhizome. An underground, creeping stem that acts as a storage organ and bears leafy shoots.

Root. The part of a plant, normally underground, that functions as anchorage and through which water and nutrients are absorbed. An **aerial root** emerges from the stem at some distance above the soil level.

Rootball. The roots and accompanying soil or compost visible when a plant is lifted.

Rootstock. A well-rooted plant onto which a scion is grafted; see *grafting*.

Rosette. A group of leaves radiating from approximately the same point, often borne at ground level at the base of a very short stem.

Runner. A horizontally spreading, usually slender stem that forms roots at each node; often confused with *stolon*.

Scale. 1. A reduced or modified leaf. 2. Part of a conifer cone.

Scandent. See *climber*.

Scarify. To scar the coat of a seed by abrasion in order to speed water intake and hence germination.

Scion. See *grafting*.

Scree. An area composed of a deep layer of stone chippings mixed with a small amount of loam. It provides extremely sharp drainage for plants that resent moisture at their base.

Seed head. Any usually dry *fruit* that contains ripe seeds.

Seed leaf (cotyledon). The first leaf, pair of leaves or occasionally group of leaves produced by a seed as it germinates. In some plants they remain below ground.

Self-seed. To produce seedlings around the parent plant.

Sepal. Part of a *calyx*, usually insignificant but sometimes showy.

Series. The name applied to a group of similar but not identical plants, usually annuals, linked by one or more common features.

Sessile. Without a stalk.

Sheath. A cylindrical structure that surrounds or encircles, partially or fully, another plant organ such as a stem.

Shoot. The aerial part of a plant which bears leaves. A **side-shoot** arises from the side of a main shoot.

Shrub. A plant with *woody stems*, usually well-branched from or near the base.

Shy-flowering. Reluctant to flower; producing few flowers.

Simple [of leaves]. Not divided into leaflets.

Soft-stemmed. The opposite of *woody-stemmed*.

Spadix (*pl. spadices*). A *spike*-like flower cluster that is usually fleshy and bears numerous small flowers. Spadices are characteristic of the family Araceae, e.g. *Arum*.

Spathe. A large *bract*, or sometimes 2, frequently coloured and showy, that surrounds a *spadix* (as in *Arum*) or an individual flower bud (as in *Narcissus*).

Sphagnum. Mosses common to bogs; their moisture-retentive character makes them ideal components of some growing media. They are used particularly for orchid cultivation.

Spike. A racemose flower cluster with several or many unstalked flowers borne along a common axis.

Spikelet. 1. The flowering unit of grasses comprising one or several flowers with basal *bracts*. 2. A small *spike*, part of a branched flower cluster.

Spore. The minute reproductive structure of flowerless plants, e.g. ferns, fungi and mosses.

Sporangium (*pl. sporangia*). A body that produces *spores*.

Sport. A mutation, caused by an accidental or induced change in the genetic make-up of a plant, which gives rise to a shoot with different characteristics to those of the parent plant.

Spur. 1. A hollow projection from a petal, often producing *nectar*. 2. A short stem bearing a group of flower buds such as is found on fruit trees.

Spur back. To cut back side-shoots to within 2 or 3 buds of the main shoot.

Stamen. The *anther* and *filament*.

Standard. 1. A *tree* or *shrub* with a clear length of bare stem below the first branches. Certain shrubs, e.g. roses and fuchsias, may be trained to form standards. 2. One of the 3 inner and often erect *perianth segments* of the iris flower. 3. The larger, usually upright back petal of a flower in the family Leguminosae, e.g. *Lathyrus*.

Stapeliad. A member of the genus *Stapelia* and closely related genera of the family Asclepiadaceae.

Stem segment. A portion of a jointed stem between 2 *nodes*, most frequently occurring in cacti.

Sterile. Infertile, not bearing *spores*, pollen, seeds etc.

Stigma. The part of the female portion of the flower, borne at the tip of the *style*, that receives pollen.

Stipule. A small scale, or leaf-like appendage, usually one of a pair, mostly borne at a *node* or below a leaf stalk.

Stock. See *rootstock*.

Stolon. A horizontally spreading or arching stem, usually above ground, which roots at its tip to produce a new plant.

Stop. To remove certain growing points of a plant so as to control growth or the size and number of flowers.

Stratify. To break the dormancy of some seeds by exposing them to a period of cold.

Style. The part of the flower on which the *stigma* is borne.

Sub-globose. Almost spherical.

Sub-shrub. A plant that is woody at the base although the terminal shoots die back in winter.

Succulent. A plant with thick, fleshy leaves and/or stems; in this book, it is evergreen unless otherwise stated.

Sucker. A shoot that arises from below ground level, directly from the *root* or *rootstock*.

Summer-deciduous. Losing its leaves naturally in summer.

Taproot. The main, downward-growing root of a plant; it is also applied generally to any strong, downward-growing root.

Tendril. A thread-like structure, used to provide support; see also *climber*.

Tooth. A small, marginal, often pointed lobe on a leaf, *calyx* or *corolla*.

Tepal. See *perianth segment*.

Tree. A woody plant usually having a well-defined trunk or stem with a head of branches above.

Trifoliate. With 3 leaves; loosely, with 3 leaflets; **trifoliolate,** with 3 leaflets.

True [of seedlings]. Retaining the distinctive characteristics of the parent when raised from seed.

Truss. A compact cluster of flowers, often large and showy, e.g. those of pelargoniums and rhododendrons.

Tuber. A thickened, usually underground, storage organ derived from a stem or root.

Tubercle. A small, rounded protuberance; see also *areole*.

Turion. 1. A bud on a *rhizome*. 2. A fleshy, overwintering bud found on certain water plants.

Umbel. A usually flat-topped or rounded flower cluster in which the individual flower stalks arise from a central point. In a compound umbel each primary stalk ends in an umbel.

Upright [of habit]. With vertical or semi-vertical main branches.

Water bud. See *turion*.

Whorl. The arrangement of 3 or more organs arising from the same point.

Winged [of seeds or fruits]. Having a marginal flange or membrane.

Woody-stemmed. With a stem composed of woody fibres and therefore persistent, as opposed to soft-stemmed and *herbaceous*. A **semi-woody stem** contains some softer tissue and may be only partially persistent.

x The sign used to denote a hybrid plant derived from the crossing of 2 or more botanically distinct plants.

+ The sign used to denote a graft hybrid; see *grafting*.

ACKNOWLEDGMENTS

Special thanks to **John R.L. Carter** for pictures of water plants; **Tony Russell** for his tree and shrub photography; **Dr Evelyn Stevens** for her help with *Meconopsis* entries and images, and also to **Julian Shaw** for additional help and support throughout the preparation of the 5th edition.

The publisher would like to thank the following for their kind permission to reproduce their photographs. Illustrations elsewhere in the book use the key: a=above; b=below/bottom; c=centre; l=left; r=right; t=top.

Every effort has been made to trace the copyright holders. Dorling Kindersley apologizes for any unintentional ommissions, and would be pleased, if any such case should arise, to add an appropriate acknowledgement in future editions.

2 Corbis: Eric Crichton. **3 Getty Images:** Gyro Photography/amanaimages RF. **4 Getty Images:** Evan Sklar. **6 Corbis:** Radius Images. **12-13 GAP Photos:** Richard Bloom/Design: Adrian Bloom. **13 GAP Photos:** Jerry Harpur/Design: Andy Sturgeon, RHS Chelsea Flower Show 2006 (tl). **Clive Nichols:** Pettifers Garden, Oxfordshire (ftr). **14 Marianne Majerus Garden Images:** Marianne Majerus. **15 Clive Nichols:** Lady Farm, Somerset: Designer, Judy Pearce (t). **Photolibrary:** Friedrich Strauss (b). **16 GAP Photos:** Marcus Harpur (t). **Getty Images:** John Glover (bc). **Clive Nichols:** Designer: Dominic Skinner (bl); Marianne Majerus/RHS Hyde Hall Garden (br). **17 Marianne Majerus Garden Images:** Marianne Majerus/Susanne Blair (t). **18 Clive Nichols:** Design: Ivan Tucker (b). **Photolibrary:** Ellen Rooney (t). **19 Photolibrary:** Allan Mandell (tl). **20 Marianne Majerus Garden Images:** Marianne Majerus/Hermannshof, Weinheim, Germany / Cassian Schmidt (b). **Clive Nichols:** Wollerton Old Hall, Shropshire (t). **21 GAP Photos:** Elke Borkowski (cra); Martin Hughes-Jones (br). **Marianne Majerus Garden Images:** Andrew Lawson/Piet Oudolf/Bury Court, Hants. (bl). **22 GAP Photos:** Designer: Marcus Barnett and Philip Nixon (bl); Location: The Summer Garden, Bressingham Gardens, Norfolk, UK (br). **Clive Nichols:** Pettifers Garden, Oxfordshire (cr); Winkworth Arboretum, Surrey (tr). **23 Clive Nichols:** (tr) (br) (cr) (crb). **24 GAP Photos:** Matt Anker (tl); Jonathan Buckley, Design:Carol and Malcolm Skinner (br). **Marianne Majerus Garden Images:** Marianne Majerus (clb). **Clive Nichols:** (cl) (bl). **25 GAP Photos:** (br); Friedrich Strauss (bc). **Marianne Majerus Garden Images:** Bennet Smith (bl). **56-57 Clive Nichols. 57 Clive Nichols:** (ftl) (ftr) (tl) (tr). **58 Garden World Images:** MAP/Arnaud Descat. **59 Alamy Images:** K-Pix. **GAP Photos:** Elke Borkowski (tr). **59 Garden World Images:** Gilles Delacroix. **60 Garden World Images:** MAP/Arnaud Descat: *Fraxinus excelsior* 'Jaspidea'. **Photolibrary:** Paroli Galperti: *Davidia involucrata* **61 Alamy:** K-Pix: *Fagus sylvatica* 'Riversii'. **Garden World Images:** Gilles Delacroix: *Fagus sylvatica* 'Rohanii' **62 Alamy:** blickwinkel: *Celtis australis*. **Getty:** DEA/D. Dagli Orti: *Juglans regia*. **Marianne Majerus Garden Images:** Marianne Majerus: *Quercus robur f. fastigiata* **63 Alamy:** CuboImages srl: *Platanus x hispanica*. **GAP Photos:** Martin Hughes-Jones: *Tilia platyphyllos* 'Rubra'. **Garden World Images:** W E Procter: *Platanus orientalis* **64 Alamy:** blickwinkel: *Fagus sylvatica* 'Aspleniifolia'. **Getty:** DEA/C. Sappa: *Zelkova carpinifolia*. **Photoshot:** Michael Warren: *Tilia* 'Petiolaris'. **Science Photo Library (SPL):** Vaughan Fleming: *Quercus frainetto* **65 Garden World Images:** *Pterocarya x rehderiana*. **Science Photo Library (SPL):** Bob Gibbons: *Quercus coccinea* **66 Alamy:** Holmes Garden Photos: *Acer rubrum*. **GAP Photos:** Heather Edwards: *Cercidiphyllum japonicum*; Martin Hughes-Jones: *Fraxinus angustifolia* 'Raywood'. **Garden World Images:** MAP/Frédéric Didillon: *Quercus palustris* **67 Alamy:** Bob Gibbons: *Prunus avium*; Steffen Hauser/botanikfoto: *Juglans ailantifolia var. cordiformis* **68 Alamy:** John Glover: *Quercus x turneri*. **Garden World Images:** Gilles Delacroix: *Eucalyptus johnstonii* **69 Alamy:** John Glover: *Salix daphnoides*; Martin Hughes-Jones: *Malus hupehensis*. **Frank Lane Picture Agency (FLPA):** Keith Rushforth: *Nothofagus menziesii*. **Science Photo Library (SPL):** John Stiles: *Nothofagus betuloides* **70 Alamy:** CuboImages srl: *Magnolia* 'Ann'; fotoFlora: *Magnolia campbellii subsp. mollicomata*; Andrea Jones: *Magnolia sprengeri var. diva*, *Magnolia x brooklynensis* 'Yellow Bird'; The Garden Picture Library: *Magnolia grandiflora* 'Exmouth'. **Corbis:** Mark Bolton: *Magnolia liliiflora* 'Nigra'; Clive Nichols: *Magnolia* 'Galaxy'. **Garden World Images:** Adrian James: *Magnolia* 'Butterflies'; J Lilly: *Magnolia wilsonii*; John Martin: *Magnolia* 'Pinkie'. **Getty:** Richard Bloom: *Magnolia* 'Black Tulip'. **Photolibrary:** Howard Rice: *Magnolia* 'Vulcan'; J S Sira: *Magnolia x loebneri* 'Leonard Messel', *Magnolia x soulangeana* 'Rustica Rubra' **71 Marianne Majerus Garden Images:** Marianne Majerus: *Halesia monticola* **72 Garden World Images:** Paul Lane: *Paulownia tomentosa*; John Martin: *Quercus rubra* 'Aurea'. **The Garden Collection:** Derek Harris: *Aesculus x neglecta* 'Erythroblastos' **73 A-Z Botanical Collection:** *Drimys winteri*. **Alamy:** CuboImages srl: *Quercus cerris* 'Argenteovariegata'. **Frank Lane Picture Agency (FLPA):** Keith Rushforth: *Toona sinensis*. **GAP Photos:** Dianna Jazwinski: *Eucryphia cordifolia*. **Photolibrary:** J S Sira: *Catalpa fargesii f. duclouxii*. **Science Photo Library (SPL):** Jim D Saul: *Acer pseudoplatanus* 'Simon Louis Frères' **74 Alamy:** blickwinkel: *Acer negundo* 'Variegatum'. **GardenPhotos.com:** judywhite: *Kalopanax septemlobus* **75 Frank Lane Picture Agency (FLPA):** Keith Rushforth: *Phellodendron chinense*, *Quercus marilandica*. **GardenPhotos.com:** judywhite: *Quercus ithaburensis subsp. macrolepis*. **Science Photo Library (SPL):** John Stiles: *Emmenopterys henryi* **76 Frank Lane Picture Agency (FLPA):** David Hosking: *Oxydendrum arboreum*. **Garden World Images:** John Swithinbank: *Acer henryi* **77 Alamy:** Andrea Jones: *Acer capillipes*. **Garden World Images:** *Nyssa sinensis*. **Marianne Majerus Garden Images:** Fiona Edmond: *Parrotia persica* **78 Alamy:** Mark Boulton: *Quercus suber*; John Glover: *Acer pensylvanicum* 'Erythrocladum', *Betula ermanii*; Brian Hoffman: *Acer griseum*; MBP-One: *Betula utilis var. jacquemontii* 'Grayswood Ghost'; Wildscape: *Acer grosseri*. **GAP Photos:** Fiona Lea: *Betula utilis var. jacquemontii* 'Jermyns'. **Garden World Images:** T Sims: *Acer palmatum* 'Sango-kaku'. **Getty:** Clive Nichols: *Pinus sylvestris*. **Photolibrary:** Richard Bloom: *Pinus bungeana*; Mark Bolton: *Stewartia pseudocamellia*; John Glover: *Prunus serrula*; Francois de Heel: *Acer davidii* **79 Frank Lane Picture Agency (FLPA):** Martin B Withers: *Fraxinus excelsior* 'Pendula'. **The Garden Collection:** Andrew Lawson: *Acer pensylvanicum* **80 Garden World Images:** John Swithinbank: *Trachycarpus fortunei* **81 Garden World Images:** *Aesculus californica* **83 Garden World Images:** Gilles Delacroix: *Prunus persica* 'Prince Charming' **84 Garden World Images:** *Laburnum x watereri* 'Vossii'. **Getty:** Geoff Kidd: *Malus floribunda* **85 Alamy:** fotoFlora: *Eucryphia glutinosa*; Martin Hughes-Jones: *Hoheria lyallii*. **GAP Photos:** Martin Hughes-Jones: *Hoheria angustifolia*. **Getty:** Scientifica: *Cornus kousa*. **Science Photo Library (SPL):** Adrian Thomas: *Eucryphia lucida* **87 Alamy:** Holmes Garden Photos: *Cornus mas*; Martin Hughes-Jones: *Cornus capitata*, *Cornus kousa* 'National'; John Martin: *Cornus kousa* 'Miss Satomi'; Organica: *Cornus kousa var. chinensis*. **GAP Photos:** Dave Bevan: *Cornus kousa var. chinensis* 'China Girl'; Dave Zubraski: *Cornus nuttallii* 'Monarch'. **Garden World Images:** G. Delacroix: *Cornus alternifolia*; Paul Lane: *Cornus florida* 'Cherokee Chief'; MAP/Arnaud Descat: *Cornus florida* 'Cherokee Princess'; MAP/Nicole et Patrick Mioulane: *Cornus mas* 'Aureoelegantissima'; L Thomas: *Cornus florida* 'Rainbow' **88 Frank Lane Picture Agency (FLPA):** Keith Rushforth: *Ehretia dicksonii*. **Garden World Images:** *Ulmus glabra* 'Camperdownii' **89 Frank Lane Picture Agency (FLPA):** Ron Boardman, Life Science Image: *Koelreuteria paniculata*. **Garden World Images:** *Paraserianthes lophantha* **90 Alamy:** imagebroker: *Acer palmatum* 'Osakazuki' **91 Alamy:** Richard Becker: *Sorbus aucuparia*; blickwinkel: *Sorbus intermedia*. **GAP Photos:** Dave Bevan: *Sorbus x kewensis*; Sarah Cuttle: *Sorbus esserteauana*: Howard Rice: *Sorbus thibetica* 'John Mitchell'. **Photoshot:** Photos Horticultural: *Sorbus megalocarpa*. **Science Photo Library (SPL):** Malcolm Richards: *Sorbus forrestii* **92 Corbis:** Eric Crichton: *Malus* 'Golden Hornet'. **Garden World Images:** MAP/Arnaud Descat: *Acer laxiflorum* **93 GAP Photos:** Martin Hughes-Jones: *Pittosporum eugenioides* 'Variegatum'. **Garden World Images:** *Arbutus unedo* **94 Alamy:** Holmes Garden Photos: *Ilex aquifolium* 'Ferox Argentea'; Martin Hughes-Jones: *Ilex aquifolium* 'Madame Briot', *Ilex x altaclerensis* 'Belgica Aurea'; Plantography: *Ilex x altaclerensis* 'Camelliifolia'; The Garden Picture Library: *Ilex aquifolium* 'Bacciflava', *Ilex x altaclerensis* 'Golden King'. **Garden World Images:** Floramedia: *Ilex aquifolium* 'Silver Queen'; M Hughes-Jones: *Ilex aquifolium*; MAP/Arnaud Descat: *Ilex pernyi*. **Photolibrary:** Carole Drake: *Ilex crenata* 'Convexa' **95 Alamy:** Arco Images GmbH: *Abies procera* **96 Alamy:** WILDLIFE GmbH: *Wollemia nobilis*. **Garden World Images:** *Chamaecyparis lawsoniana* 'Intertexta'. **Photolibrary:** Leonie Lambert: *Cedrus deodara* **97 Garden World Images:** *Cedrus libani* **98 Alamy:** F Davis: *Araucaria araucana*. **Getty:** Tim Gainey: *Araucaria araucana* **99 GAP Photos:** Adrian Bloom, location: David Wards Garden, Leeds, Yorkshire: *Picea engelmannii*. **Garden World Images:** *Taxodium distichum*. **Photoshot:** *Tsuga mertensiana* 'Glauca'. **Savill Gardens:** *Picea glauca* 'Coerulea' **100 Alamy:** kpzfoto: *Juniperus chinensis* 'Keteleeri'. **GAP Photos:** FhF Greenmedia: *Picea likiangensis* **102 Photolibrary:** *Pinus contorta*, *Pseudolarix amabilis*, *Pseudolarix amabilis*, *Taxus baccata* 'Lutea'; Leonie Lambert: *Pseudolarix amabilis*; Fritz Polking: *Pinus contorta*; Howard Rice: *Taxus baccata* 'Lutea' **103 Garden World Images:** *Juniperus chinensis* 'Obelisk'. **Science Photo Library (SPL):** Chris Hellier: *Juniperus chinensis* 'Robust Green' **104 Alamy:** Martin Hughes-Jones: *Pinus sylvestris* 'Aurea'. **Frank Lane Picture Agency (FLPA):** R P Lawrence: *Taxus cuspidata*. **Garden World Images:** *Pinus pinea*. **Photolibrary:** Ron Evans: *Chamaecyparis obtusa* 'Crippsii' **105 Alamy:** CuboImages srl: *Podocarpus nivalis*; Martin Hughes-Jones: *Juniperus squamata* 'Blue Carpet'. **Corbis:** Patrick Johns: *Abies cephalonica* 'Meyer's Dwarf'. **GAP Photos:** Adrian Bloom: *Abies concolor* 'Compacta', *Pinus heldreichii* 'Smidtii', *Taxus baccata* 'Dovastonii Aurea'; J S Sira/Design: Collin Elliott: *Juniperus x pfitzeriana* 'Old Gold'. **Garden World Images:** *Chamaecyparis obtusa* 'Nana Gracilis', *Juniperus squamata* 'Holger', *Microbiota decussata*, *Platycladus orientalis* 'Aurea Nana', *Thuja plicata* 'Stoneham Gold'; R Coates: *Juniperus squamata* 'Holger'; G. Delacroix: *Microbiota decussata*; MAP/Nathalie Pasquel: *Chamaecyparis obtusa* 'Nana Gracilis', *Platycladus orientalis* 'Aurea Nana'. **GardenPhotos.com:** judywhite: *Chamaecyparis pisifera* 'Filifera Aurea', *Juniperus scopulorum* 'Skyrocket'. **Photolibrary:** Jerry Pavia: *Picea pungens* 'Globosa' **106-107 GAP Photos:** Richard Bloom. **107 GAP Photos:** Sharon Pearson (ftl). **Clive Nichols:** (tl) (ftr) (tr). **110 Garden World Images:** *Amelanchier lamarckii* **111 Garden World Images:** *Dipelta floribunda*. **Photolibrary:** Howard Rice: *Berberis valdiviana* **112 Alamy:** Holmes Garden Photos: *Salix exigua* **113 Garden World Images:** Martin Hughes-Jones: *Crinodendron patagua*, *Elaeagnus umbellata* **114 GAP Photos:** Christina Bollen: *Buddleja davidii* 'White Profusion'; FhF Greenmedia: *Buddleja salviifolia*; Lynn Keddie: *Buddleja x weyeriana* 'Moonlight'; Rob Whitworth: *Abutilon vitifolium* 'Veronica Tennant'. **Garden World Images:** D Brown: *Buddleja colvilei* 'Kewensis'; M Hughes-Jones: *Buddleja* 'Lochinch', *Buddleja davidii* 'Pink Delight', *Buddleja x weyeriana* 'Sungold'. **The Garden Collection:** Jonathan Buckley: *Buddleja* 'Lochinch', *Buddleja davidii* 'Black Knight'; Nicola Stocken Tomkins: *Buddleja davidii* 'Dartmoor' **115 Alamy:** Holmes Garden Photos: *Syringa vulgaris* 'Andenken an Ludwig Späth'. **Garden World Images:** G. Delacroix: *Syringa pubescens subsp. patula* 'Miss Kim'; M Hughes-Jones: *Syringa x persica*; MAP/Arnaud Descat: *Syringa komarowii subsp. reflexa*, *Syringa vulgaris* 'Firmament', *Syringa vulgaris* 'Katherine Havemeyer'. **Marianne Majerus Garden Images:** Marianne Majerus: *Syringa x persica* 'Alba' **116 Garden World Images:** Derek Gould: *Genista tenera* 'Golden Shower' **117 Garden World Images:** *Cotoneaster* 'Cornubia'. **John Glover:** *Cotinus* 'Flame' **118 Alamy:** John Glover: *Hamamelis x intermedia* 'Arnold Promise', *Hamamelis x intermedia* 'Barmstedt Gold', *Hamamelis x intermedia* 'Jelena'; MBP-Plants: *Hamamelis x intermedia* 'Pallida'. **GAP Photos:** Richard Bloom: *Hamamelis x intermedia* 'Jelena'. **Garden World Images:** Jacqui Dracup: *Hamamelis x intermedia* 'Robert'. **Marianne Majerus Garden Images:** Marianne Majerus: *Azara microphylla*. **Photolibrary:** Richard Bloom: *Hamamelis x intermedia* 'Primavera' **119 GAP Photos:** Geoff Kidd: *Pittosporum dallii*. **Garden World Images:** G Kidd: *Prunus lusitanica subsp. variegata*; Geoff Kidd: *Prunus lusitanica subsp. variegata* **120 Alamy:** Martin Hughes-Jones: *Camellia* 'Cornish Snow'. **GAP Photos:** Fiona Lea: *Camellia japonica* 'Hagoromo'. **Garden World Images:** *Camellia japonica* 'Alba Plena', *Camellia japonica* 'Nobilissima', *Tetrapanax papyrifer*, *Tetrapanax papyrifer*; MAP/A Descat/Collection Pepineiere Stervinou: *Camellia japonica* 'Nobilissima'; John Martin: *Camellia japonica* 'Alba Plena' **121 Alamy:** blickwinkel/Jagel: *Camellia* 'Spring Festival'; John Glover: *Camellia japonica* 'Lavinia Maggi'. **GAP Photos:** Richard Bloom: *Camellia* 'Inspiration'; Lynn Keddie: *Camellia x williamsii* 'J.C. Williams'; Geoff Kidd: *Camellia japonica* 'Brushfield's Yellow'; Howard Rice: *Camellia japonica* 'Tricolor'; S & O: *Camellia x williamsii* 'Jury's Yellow'; J S Sira: *Camellia japonica* 'Bob's Tinsie'. **Garden World Images:** G. Delacroix: *Camellia reticulata* 'Captain Rawes'; MAP/A Descat/Collection Pepineiere Stervinou: *Camellia* 'Black Lace', *Camellia* 'Freedom Bell'; T Sims: *Camellia japonica* 'Adolphe Audusson'. **Photolibrary:** Clive Nichols /GPL: *Camellia x williamsii* 'Debbie' **122 GAP Photos:** J S Sira: *Viburnum bitchiuense*. **Garden World Images:** *Choisya* 'Aztec Pearl', *Rhododendron* 'Percy Wiseman'; MAP/Nicole et Patrick Mioulane: *Choisya* 'Aztec Pearl' **123 Alamy:** Auscape International Pty Ltd: *Telopea truncata*; John Glover: *Prunus mume* 'Beni-chidori'. **GAP Photos:** S & O: *Ribes sanguineum* 'Pulborough Scarlet'. **Garden World Images:** *Leptospermum scoparium* 'Red Damask' **124 GAP Photos:** Dave Bevan: *Rhododendron sinogrande*. **Garden World Images:** M Hughes-Jones: *Rhododendron* 'Gomer Waterer', *Rhododendron quinquefolium*; MAP/Nathalie Pasquel: *Rhododendron* 'Golden Torch'; J Need: *Rhododendron calophytum*. **Photolibrary:** Georgianna Lane: *Rhododendron decorum*; Brigitte Thomas: *Rhododendron williamsianum*. **Photoshot:** Michael Warren: *Rhododendron decorum*. **Royal Horticultural Society (RHS):** Carol Sheppard: *Rhododendron pachysanthum* **125 Alamy:** Brian Hoffman: *Rhododendron arboreum*; Holmes Garden Photos: *Rhododendron praecox*. **GAP Photos:** Richard Bloom: *Rhododendron* 'Fastuosum Flore Pleno'; Christina Bollen: *Rhododendron niveum*; FhF Greenmedia: *Rhododendron cinnabarinum*; Neil Holmes: *Rhododendron* 'Blue Danube'. **Garden World Images:** G Delacroix: *Rhododendron* 'Blaauw's Pink', *Rhododendron* 'Purple Splendour'; M Hughes-Jones: *Rhododendron* 'Daviesii', *Rhododendron fulvum*; Christopher Lavis-Jones: *Rhododendron* 'Patty Bee'. **Photolibrary:** Georgianna Lane: *Rhododendron* 'Hotei'. **Royal Horticultural Society (RHS):** Rebecca Ross: *Rhododendron* 'Gibraltar' **126 Alamy:** Holmes Garden Photos: *Cornus sericea* 'Flaviramea'; J Need: *Cornus sericea* 'White Gold'; Plantography: *Cornus alba* 'Elegantissima'. **GAP Photos:** J S Sira: *Corylopsis pauciflora*; Jo Whitworth: *Cornus sericea* 'Kelseyi'. **Garden World Images:** Jacqui Dracup: *Edgeworthia chrysantha*; T Sims: *Cornus alba* 'Aurea', *Cornus sanguinea* 'Midwinter Fire' **127 GAP Photos:** Neil Holmes: *Forsythia x intermedia* 'Beatrix Farrand'. **Garden World Images:** *Deutzia scabra*, *Kerria japonica* 'Pleniflora', *Lindera benzoin*; Liz Cole: *Deutzia scabra*. **Photolibrary:** Mel Watson: *Philadelphus* 'Beauclerk' **129 Garden World Images:** Martin Hughes-Jones: *Clethra barbinervis* **130 Garden World Images:** Gilles Delacroix: *Leptospermum scoparium* 'Snow White'; Trevor Sims: *Colletia hystrix*. **P-Pod:** Tim Argles: *Olearia ilicifolia*. **Photoshot:** Photos Horticultural: *Zenobia pulverulenta*. **Science Photo Library (SPL):** Nick Wiseman: *Escallonia virgata* **132 Alamy:** Holmes Garden Photos: *Olearia macrodonta*. **GAP Photos:** Martin Hughes-Jones: *Hibiscus syriacus* 'Red Heart'; Mel Watson: *Aloysia triphylla* **133 Garden World Images:** *Robinia hispida* **134 Alamy:** Martin Hughes-Jones: *Hydrangea paniculata* 'Silver Dollar'; Andrea Jones: *Hydrangea paniculata* PINKY WINKY. **GAP Photos:** Martin Hughes-Jones: *Hydrangea serrata* 'Diadem'; Rob Whitworth: *Hydrangea macrophylla* 'Madame Emile Mouillère'. **Garden World Images:** G. Delacroix: *Hydrangea arborescens* 'Annabelle', *Hydrangea quercifolia* 'Snowflake'. **Marianne Majerus Garden Images:** Marianne Majerus: *Hydrangea serrata* 'Kiyosumi'; Marianne Majerus/RHS Wisley Garden: *Hydrangea paniculata* 'Big Ben'. **Photolibrary:** Sunniva Harte: *Hydrangea heteromalla* 'Snowcap'; Marga Werner: *Hydrangea paniculata* 'Phantom'. **Science Photo

Library (SPL): A-Z Botanical Collection: *Hydrangea macrophylla* 'Générale Vicomtesse de Vibraye' **135 Alamy:** John glover: *Hydrangea paniculata PINK DIAMOND* Hydrangea paniculata PINK DIAMOND; Holmes Garden Photos: *Hydrangea macrophylla* 'Ami Pasquier'; Andrea Jones: *Hydrangea paniculata* 'Dharuma'. **GAP Photos:** Martin Hughes-Jones: *Hydrangea paniculata* 'Limelight'. **Garden World Images:** R Coates: *Hydrangea macrophylla* 'Europa', *Hydrangea serrata* 'Grayswood'; Rita Coates: *Hydrangea aspera* 'Mauvette'; G. Delacroix: *Hydrangea macrophylla* 'Libelle', *Hydrangea macrophylla* 'Möwe'; Steffen Hauser: *Hydrangea aspera subsp. sargentiana;* K Howchin: *Hydrangea macrophylla* 'Ayesha' **136 Alamy:** The Garden Picture Library: *Paeonia delavayi.* **Garden World Images:** MAP/Nathalie Pasquel: *Erythrina x bidwillii* **137 Alamy:** Milestone Media: *Abutilon* 'Ashford Red'. **Garden World Images:** *Camellia japonica* 'Mathotiana' **138 Garden World Images:** *Ceanothus impressus.* **Photolibrary:** Sunniva Harte: *Iochroma australe* **140 Garden World Images:** *Euonymus europaeus* 'Red Cascade'. **The Garden Collection:** Andrew Lawson: *Rhus glabra* **141 GAP Photos:** David Dixon: *Berberis x carminea* 'Barbarossa'. **Garden World Images:** *Leonotis leonurus.* **Getty:** Rob Whitworth: *Disanthus cercidifolius* **142 Alamy:** CuboImages srl: *Cotoneaster conspicuus, Cotoneaster x watereri* 'John Waterer'; Steffen Hauser/ botanikfoto: *Cotoneaster salicifolius;* Colin Underhill: *Euonymus hamiltonianus subsp. sieboldianus.* **Garden World Images:** S Hauser: *Daphne mezereum;* D Murphy: *Cotoneaster frigidus.* **Janet Johnson:** *Hippophae rhamnoides.* **Photolibrary:** Richard Bloom: *Cornus alba* 'Sibirica Variegata' **143 Alamy:** Steffen Hauser/ botanikfoto: *Viburnum farreri.* **Garden World Images:** *Nandina domestica* 'Fire Power', *Viburnum tinus* 'Eve Price'; Christopher Lavis-Jones: *Viburnum tinus* 'Eve Price'. **The Garden Collection:** Jonathan Buckley: *Viburnum foetens* **144 GAP Photos:** John Glover: *Fatsia japonica* 'Variegata'. **Getty:** Hemant Jariwala: *Mahonia japonica* **145 Alamy:** blickwinkel: *Buxus balearica.* **Garden World Images:** *Gaultheria x wisleyensis* 'Wisley Pearl', *Prunus laurocerasus* 'Zabeliana'; Trevor Sims: *Prunus laurocerasus* 'Zabeliana' **146 Alamy:** Holmes Garden Photos: *Ribes sanguineum* 'Edward VII'; Martin Hughes-Jones: *Chaenomeles speciosa* 'Snow' **148 Alamy:** Chris Howes/Wild Places Photography: *Ulex europaeus.* **The Garden Collection:** Derek Harris: *Choisya ternata* SUNDANCE **149 Garden World Images:** *Convolvulus cneorum, x Halimiocistus sahucii* **150 Garden World Images:** *Rhaphiolepis umbellata* **151 GAP Photos:** J S Sira: *Hebe recurva.* **Garden World Images:** Martin Hughes-Jones: *Ozothamnus ledifolius;* M Hughes-Jones: *Ozothamnus ledifolius.* **Science Photo Library (SPL):** Anthony Cooper: *Lomatia silaifolia* **152 GAP Photos:** Dianna Jazwinski: *Deutzia* 'Mont Rose' **154 Alamy:** Arco Images GmbH: *Fuchsia* 'Riccartonii'; John Glover: *Fuchsia magellanica;* Martin Hughes-Jones: *Escallonia* 'Donard Beauty'. **GAP Photos:** Dave Zubraski: *Fuchsia* 'Howlett's Hardy'. **Garden World Images:** T Sims: *Fuchsia* 'Corallina'. **Getty:** Dave Zubraski: *Fuchsia* 'Mrs Popple', *Fuchsia magellanica* 'Thompsonii'. **Marianne Majerus Garden Images:** Marianne Majerus: *Fuchsia magellanica var. gracilis.* **Science Photo Library (SPL):** Mike Danson: *Fuchsia* 'Madame Cornélissen' **155 Alamy:** Martin Hughes-Jones: *Salvia x jamensis* 'La Luna'; Plantography: *Salvia microphylla* 'La Foux', *Salvia x jamensis* 'Maraschino'. **GAP Photos:** Heather Edwards: *Salvia microphylla* 'Cerro Potosi'; FhF Greenmedia: *Salvia x jamensis* 'Red Velvet'; Marcus Harpur: *Salvia microphylla* 'Kew Red'. **Garden World Images:** N R Colborn: *Salvia x jamensis* 'Hot Lips'; G Delacroix: *Salvia x jamensis* 'Sierra San Antonio'; G. Delacroix: *Salvia officinalis* 'Berggarten'; L Thomas: *Salvia greggii* 'Icing Sugar'. **Getty:** *Salvia officinalis, Salvia officinalis* 'Purpurascens', *Salvia officinalis* 'Tricolor'; De Agostini: *Salvia officinalis;* Linda Lewis: *Salvia officinalis* 'Tricolor'. **Photolibrary:** Geoff Kidd: *Salvia microphylla* 'Newby Hall'; Juliette Wade: *Salvia microphylla* 'Pink Blush' **158 Alamy:** John Glover: *Lavandula x chaytorae* 'Sawyers'; Holmes Garden Photos: *Lavandula* 'Fathead', *Lavandula angustifolia* 'Miss Katherine'. **GAP Photos:** Elke Borkowski: *Lavandula pedunculata subsp. pedunculata* 'James Compton'; Suzie Gibbons: *Lavandula angustifolia* 'Wendy Carlile'; Dianna Jazwinski: *Lavandula angustifolia* 'Imperial Gem'; J S Sira: *Lavandula* 'Helmsdale', *Lavandula angustifolia* 'Loddon Blue', *Lavandula stoechas f. rosea* 'Kew Red'. **Garden World Images:** G. Delacroix: *Lavandula lanata;* C Fairweather: Lavandula angustifolia LITTLE LOTTIE, *Lavandula stoechas* 'Snowman'; MAP/N Pasquel: *Lavandula angustifolia* 'Little Lady'; T Sims: *Lavandula angustifolia* 'Hidcote'; L Thomas: *Lavandula* 'Regal Splendour', *Lavandula* 'Willow Vale'. **Photolibrary:** Chris L Jones: *Lavandula x intermedia* 'Alba' **159 Alamy:** Martin Hughes-Jones: *Ceanothus thyrsiflorus var. repens.* **Garden World Images:** *Ceratostigma willmottianum* **160 Garden World Images:** Gilles Delacroix: *Symphoricarpos orbiculatus* 'Foliis Variegatis' **161 GAP Photos:** Martin Hughes-Jones: *Hypericum x inodorum* 'Elstead'; J S Sira: *Halimium lasianthum subsp. formosum.* **Garden World Images:** *Coriaria terminalis var. xanthocarpa, Hypericum kouytchense* **162 Garden World Images:** *Berberis* 'Rubrostilla', *Cytisus scoparius f. andreanus.* **Photolibrary:** Mark Bolton: *Cuphea cyanea;* Mark Turner/GPL: *Myrica gale* **163 GAP Photos:** Adrian Bloom: *Fothergilla gardenii.* **The Garden Collection:** Jonathan Buckley: *Lonicera x purpusii* **164 Alamy:** Plantography: *Pittosporum tenuifolium* 'Tom Thumb' **165 GAP Photos:** Friedrich Strauss: *Artemisia abrotanum* Artemisia abrotanum. **Garden World Images:** *Hebe cupressoides* **166 Alamy:** J S Sira/ GPL: *Erica carnea* 'Challenger'; Arco Images GmbH: *Erica vagans* 'St Keverne'; John Glover: *Calluna vulgaris* 'Annemarie', *Calluna vulgaris* 'Peter Sparkes', *Calluna vulgaris* 'Wickwar Flame'; Martin Hughes-Jones: *Erica carnea* 'Ann Sparkes'; Piotr & Irena Kolasa: *Calluna vulgaris* 'Dark Star'. **GAP Photos:** Mark Bolton: *Erica x darleyensis* 'Arthur Johnson'; Geoff Kidd: *Erica x darleyensis* 'Furzey'. **Garden World Images:** I Anderson: *Erica erigena* 'Irish Dusk'; G. Delacroix: *Erica erigena f. alba* 'Brian Proudley'; T Jennings: *Erica vagans* 'Birch Glow'; M Hughes-Jones: *Erica carnea* 'Golden Starlet'; MAP/N Pasquel: *Erica vagans* 'Mrs D. F. Maxwell'. **GardenPhotos.com:** Judy White: *Calluna vulgaris* 'Beoley Gold' **167 GAP Photos:** Geoff Kidd: *Ruscus aculeatus* Ruscus aculeatus. **Garden World Images:** Trevor Sims: *Leucothöe fontanesiana* 'Rainbow' **168 GAP Photos:** Geoff Kidd. **168 Garden World Images:** Trevor Sims. **169 GAP Photos:** Mark Anker (ftr); FhF Greenmedia (ftl); Leigh Clapp (tr). **176 Alamy:** John Glover: *R. moyesii* 'Geranium'; Holmes Garden Photos: *R. sericia subsp. omeiensis f. ptenracantha.* **GAP Photos:** Jonathan Need: *R. roxburghii.* **Garden World Images:** MAP/Jean-Yves Grospas: *R. rubiginosa;* Trevor Sims: *R. multibracteata.* **Getty:** Rob Whitworth: *R. rugosa.* **Marianne Majerus Garden Images:** Marianne Majerus: *R. glauca* **177 Alamy:** Martin Hughes-Jones: *R.* 'Buff Beauty'. **GAP Photos:** Michael Howes: *R.* EVELYN; Rob Whitworth: *R.* KENT. **Photoshot:** Photos Horticultural: *R.* SILVER ANNIVERSARY. **Roses UK:** *R.* ISN'T SHE LOVELY **178 Alamy:** Natural Garden Images: *R.* . MANY HAPPY RETURNS. **GAP Photos:** FhF Greenmedia: *R.* SUSAN DANIEL. **Photolibrary:** Leonie Lambert: *R.* SAVOY HOTEL **179 Alamy:** Roger Cope: *R.* NOSTALGIA. **C & K Jones:** *R.* CHRIS BEARDSHAW. **David Austin Roses:** *R.* BRAVEHEART. **Garden World Images:** Gilles Delacroix: *R.* FLOWER CARPET **181 Garden World Images:** MAP/Nicole et Patrick Mioulane: *R.* GUY SAVOY. **Photoshot:** Michael Warren: *R.* LANCASHIRE **182 Garden World Images:** G Delacroix: *R.* ABSOLUTELY FABULOUS; Christopher Lavis-Jones: *R.* 'Arthur Bell'; Jenny Lilly: *R.* GOLDEN BEAUTY. **The Garden Collection:** Derek Harris: *R.* GUY'S GOLD **183 GAP Photos:** Howard Rice: *R.* SIMPLY THE BEST. **Harkness Roses, roses.co.uk:** *R.* EASY DOES IT. **Roses UK:** *R.* SUPER TROOPER **184 Botanical Garden Collection:** *R. filipes* 'Kiftsgate'. **Garden World Images:** *R.* 'Félicité Perpétue' **185 Garden World Images:** *R.* 'Veilchenblau' **186 GAP Photos:** Howard Rice: *R.* 'Cécile Brünner'. **Garden World Images:** *R.* 'Guinée' **187 Chris Warner:** *R.* GARDENERS GLORY. **GAP Photos:** Maxine Adcock: *R.* SUMMER WINE; Visions Premium: *R.* BRIDGE OF SIGHS. **Garden World Images:** *R.* 'Mermaid'. **Roses UK:** *R.* ALIBABA **189 GAP Photos:** Andrea Jones (tl); Jerry Harpur (ftl); Marcus Harpur (ftr). **190 GAP Photos:** John Glover (bl). **191 GAP Photos:** Maddie Thornhill (tr). **192 Alamy:** Holmes Garden Photos: *Prostanthera rotundifolia* 'Rosea'; Martin Hughes-Jones: *Acradenia frankliniae;* JTB Photo Communications, Inc.: *Stauntonia hexaphylla.* **Garden Picture Library:** *Ercilla volubilis.* **Garden World Images:** Trevor Sims: *Holboellia latifolia.* **Photos Horticultural:** *Decumaria sinensis* **193 Alamy:** John Glover: *Jasminum beesianum.* **Garden World Images:** *Campsis radicans* 'Indian Summer', *Clianthus puniceus, Mitraria coccinea, Ribes speciosum;* MAP/Arnaud Descat: *Mitraria coccinea;* Trevor Sims: *Campsis radicans* 'Indian Summer', *Ribes speciosum* **194 GAP Photos:** Martin Hughes-Jones: *Sollya heterophylla.* **Garden World Images:** Lee Thomas: *Humulus lupulus* 'Aureus'. **Photolibrary:** Mark Bolton: *Ceanothus arboreus* 'Trewithen Blue'; Philippe Bonduel: *Eriobotrya japonica* **195 GAP Photos:** John Glover: *Ampelopsis brevipedunculata var. maximowiczii* 'Elegans'. **Garden World Images:** *Araujia sericifera, Hydrangea petiolaris, Jasminum mesnyi;* Geoff Kidd: *Araujia sericifera;* Trevor Sims: *Hydrangea petiolaris* **196 Garden World Images:** Trevor Sims: *Hydrangea seemannii;* Lee Thomas: *Jasminum officinale f. affine.* **Science Photo Library (SPL):** Bob Gibbons: *Hydrangea serratifolia.* **The Garden Collection:** Andrew Lawson: *Trachelospermum asiaticum* **197 Alamy:** Holmes Garden Photos: *Prostanthera cuneata.* **GAP Photos:** Geoff Kidd: *Drimys lanceolata.* **Garden World Images:** *Anredera cordifolia, Schizophragma hydrangeoides;* Gilles Delacroix: *Schizophragma hydrangeoides.* **Photolibrary:** Howard Rice: *Dregea sinensis* **198 GAP Photos:** Fiona Lea: *Clematis* 'Avalanche'; J S Sira: *Clematis cartmannii* 'Joe'. **Garden World Images:** MAP/A Descat: *Clematis fasciculiflora;* T Sims: *Clematis* 'Andromeda'; Trevor Sims: *Clematis* 'Andromeda'; Lee Thomas: *Clematis* 'Avalanche', *Clematis* 'Early Sensation', *Clematis* ARCTIC QUEEN, *Clematis cartmannii* 'Joe'. **Photolibrary:** Ron Evans: *Clematis montana;* Abbe Green-Armytage: *Clematis* 'Guernsey Cream'. **Photoshot:** Photos Horticultural: *Clematis* 'Bella' **199 Alamy:** Roger Cope: *Clematis* PINK CHAMPAGNE. **GAP Photos:** Martin Hughes-Jones: *Clematis* 'Barbara Jackman'. **Garden World Images:** R Coates: *Clematis* 'Jacqueline du Pré'; A Graham: *Clematis* 'Barbara Jackman'; C Lavis-Jones: *Clematis* 'Barbara Dibley', *Clematis* 'Barbara Dibley'; B Stojanovic: *Clematis* 'Corona'. **Marianne Majerus Garden Images:** Marianne Majerus, RHS Wisley Garden: *Clematis cirrhosa.* **Photolibrary:** Howard Rice: *Clematis* 'Jan Lindmark', *Clematis montana var. rubens.* **Raymond Evison:** *Clematis* BLUE MOON, *Clematis* CHANTILLY, *Clematis florida* PISTACHIO, *Clematis* VIENNETTA **200 Alamy:** CuboImages srl: *Clematis* 'Perle d'Azur'; John Glover: *Clematis* 'Abundance'. **GAP Photos:** Mark Bolton: *Clematis* 'Silver Moon'. **Garden World Images:** Floramedia: *Clematis* 'Columella', *Clematis* 'Frankie'; Martin Hughes-Jones: *Clematis* 'Frances Rivis'; C Lavis-Jones: *Clematis* 'Westerplatte'; MAP/A Descat: *Clematis* 'Black Prince'; MAP/N Pasquel: *Clematis* 'Abundance', *Clematis* 'Betty Corning'. **Raymond Evison:** *Clematis* AVANT-GARDE, *Clematis* BOURBON, *Clematis* ROSEMOOR, *Clematis* VINO. **The Garden Collection:** Torie Chugg: *Clematis* 'Betty Corning' **201 Alamy:** Niall McDiarmid: *Bomarea edulis.* **Garden World Images:** *Lathyrus odoratus* 'Lady Diana'. **Photolibrary:** Anne Green-Armytage: *Jasminum x stephanense.* **Photos Horticultural:** *Lathyrus odoratus* 'Charles Unwin', *Lathyrus odoratus* 'Mrs Bernard Jones' **202 Garden World Images:** *Ipomoea lobata.* **Getty:** Ron Evans: *Lapageria rosea;* Leroy Simon: *Ipomoea quamoclit.* **Paul Beard Photo Agency:** *Lathyrus odoratus* 'Barry Dare' **203 Alamy:** Holmes Garden Photos: *Callistemon subulatus;* Martin Hughes-Jones: *Desfontainia spinosa.* **GAP Photos:** Martin Hughes-Jones: *Grevillea rosmarinifolia.* **Garden World Images:** *Callistemon citrinus* 'Splendens', *Cestrum* 'Newellii'; Trevor Sims: *Cestrum* 'Newellii'. **Getty:** *Abutilon megapotamicum.* **Photolibrary:** J S Sira: *Campsis grandiflora* **204 GAP Photos:** Geoff Kidd: *Aconitum hemsleyanum;* J S Sira: *Ipomoea hederacea.* **Garden World Images:** *Akebia trifoliata, Cobaea scandens;* Trevor Sims: *Akebia trifoliata.* **Marianne Majerus Garden Images:** Andrew Lawson: *Passiflora caerulea* **205 Frank Lane Picture Agency (FLPA):** Brian Davis: *Wisteria brachybotrys* 'White Silk'. **GAP Photos:** Richard Bloom: *Ceanothus* 'Puget Blue'; Neil Holmes: *Plumbago auriculata.* **Garden World Images:** MAP/Arnaud Descat: *Wisteria floribunda* 'Yae Kokoryu'; John Martin: *Wisteria floribunda* 'Domino', *Wisteria sinensis* 'Prolific'; Ellen McKnight: *Wisteria floribunda* 'Lawrence'. **Photolibrary:** Mark Turner: *Wisteria floribunda* 'Hon-Beni'. **Royal Horticultural Society (RHS):** Graham Titchmarsh: *Ceanothus* 'Burkwoodii' **206 GAP Photos:** John Glover: *Fremontodendron* 'California Glory'; Martin Hughes-Jones: *Campsis radicans f. flava;* Geoff Kidd: *Hypericum* 'Rowallane'; Howard Rice: *Jasminum humile* 'Revolutum'. **Garden World Images:** *Piptanthus nepalensis* **207 Alamy:** Martin Hughes-Jones: *Lonicera periclymenum* 'Red Gables'. **GAP Photos:** Howard Rice: *Lonicera etrusca* 'Michael Rosse'. **Garden World Images:** MAP/Arnaud Descat: *Lonicera henryi.* **Photolibrary:** Kate Boykin: *Lonicera sempervirens;* Howard Rice: *Lonicera etrusca* 'Superba' **208 Alamy:** Charles Stirling: *Cotoneaster horizontalis.* **Garden World Images:** *Jasminum polyanthum, Vitis* 'Brant'; Lee Thomas: *Vitis* 'Brant'. **Marianne Majerus Garden Images:** Marianne Majerus: *Campsis x tagliabuana* 'Madame Galen'. **Photolibrary:** Howard Rice: *Campsis radicans* 'Flamenco' **209 Photolibrary:** Gert Tabak: *Celastrus orbiculatus* 'Diana' **210 Alamy:** Andrea Jones: *Ampelopsis megalophylla* **211 Alamy:** John Glover: *Acacia dealbata.* **Garden World Images:** Martin Hughes-Jones: *Garrya elliptica* 'James Roof' **212-213 GAP Photos:** Elke Borkowski. **213 GAP Photos:** Lynn Keddie (tl); Clive Nichols (tr); Howard Rice (ftl); Visions (ftr). **214 GAP Photos:** Richard Bloom (crb); Howard Rice (bl). **215 GAP Photos:** John Glover (bc/metal spirals). **216 GAP Photos:** Geoff Kidd: *Impatiens tinctoria;* Rob Whitworth: *Sanguisorba tenuifolia* 'Alba'. **Garden World Images:** Derek Gould: *Artemisia lactiflora* **217 GAP Photos:** Mark Bolton: *Delphinium* 'Red Caroline'. **Photolibrary:** Paroli Galperti: *Delphinium* 'Cliveden Beauty'; J S Sira/GPL: *Delphinium* 'Elizabeth Cook' **218 Alamy:** John Glover: *Meconopsis paniculata.* **Dr Evelyn Stevens:** *Meconopsis grandis, Meconopsis* 'Jimmy Bayne', *Meconopsis* 'Marit', *Meconopsis baileyi* 'Alba', *Meconopsis x cookei* 'Old Rose'; Plant Heritage National Plant Collection: *Meconopsis* 'Marit', *Meconopsis baileyi* 'Alba', *Meconopsis x cookei* 'Old Rose'. **GAP Photos:** Leigh Clapp: *Meconopsis* 'Lingholm'; Fiona Lea: *Galega x hartlandii* 'Lady Wilson'; Howard Rice: *Meconopsis* 'Slieve Donard'. **Garden World Images:** Martin Hughes-Jones: *Thalictrum* 'Elin'. **Photolibrary:** Howard Rice: *Meconopsis* 'Crewdson Hybrid' **219 Alamy:** Florapix: *Ligularia* 'The Rocket'; John Glover: *Musa basjoo, Musa basjoo.* **Photoshot:** Photos Horticultural: *Acanthus mollis* 'Hollard's Gold' **220 Alamy:** Jim Allan: *Thalictrum delavayi* 'Hewitt's Double'. **Eric Crichton Photos:** *Anemone x hybrida* 'Honorine Jobert'. **GAP Photos:** Victoria Firmston: *Veronicastrum virginicum* 'Fascination'. **Marianne Majerus Garden Images:** Marianne Majerus: *Hedychium x moorei* 'Tara'. **Photoshot:** Photos Horticultural: *Eremurus x isabellinus* 'Cleopatra' **221 Alamy:** WILDLIFE GmbH: *Echinacea paradoxa.* **GAP Photos:** Visions: *Eupatorium maculatum* 'Riesenschirm'. **Garden World Images:** *Echinacea* 'Harvest Moon', *Echinacea purpurea* 'Coconut Lime', *Echinacea purpurea* 'Doubledecker', *Echinacea purpurea* 'Fragrant Angel', *Echinacea purpurea* 'Sundown', *Salvia involucrata* 'Bethellii'; G Delacroix: *Echinacea* 'Harvest Moon'; G. Delacroix: *Echinacea purpurea* 'Coconut Lime', *Echinacea purpurea* 'Fragrant Angel', *Echinacea purpurea* 'Sundown'; J Spears: *Echinacea purpurea* 'Doubledecker'. **Photolibrary:** Cubo Images: *Echinacea purpurea* 'Magnus'; Antonio Molero: *Echinacea angustifolia;* J S Sira: *Echinacea purpurea* 'Razzmatazz' **222 Alamy:** Steffen Hauser/ botanikfoto: *Helianthus salicifolius.* **GAP Photos:** J S Sira: *Anemone hupehensis* 'Bowles's Pink'. **Garden World Images:** L Thomas: *Anemone hupehensis* 'Praecox', *Anemone x hybrida* 'Robustissima'. **Photolibrary:** Paroli Galperti: *Anemone x hybrida* 'Whirlwind'; J S Sira: *Anemone hupehensis var. japonica* 'Pamina'; Richard Surman: *Anemone x hybrida* 'Konigin Charlotte'; Mark Turner: *Anemone x hybrida* 'September Charm'. **Royal Horticultural Society (RHS):** *Anemone hupehensis var. japonica* 'Bressingham Glow'. **The Garden Collection:** Andrew Lawson: *Helianthus* 'Lemon Queen' **223 Alamy:** Zena Elea: *Diascia personata.* **Garden World Images:** *Aquilegia vulgaris var. stellata* 'Black Barlow' **224 Alamy:** John Glover: *Iris* 'Deep Black'. **British Iris Society:** *Iris japonica.* **GAP Photos:** Mark Bolton: *Iris x robusta* 'Gerald Darby'; Jonathan Buckley: *Iris* 'Green Spot'. **Garden World Images:** *Iris hoogiana.* **Picturesmiths Ltd.:** *Iris* 'English Cottage', *Iris* 'Frost and Flame', *Iris ensata* 'Moonlight Waves', *Iris germanica* 'Florentina', *Iris orientalis, Iris sanguinea* 'Snow Queen' **225 Alamy:** John Glover: *Iris sibirica* 'Shirley Pope'; Holmes Garden Photos: *Iris* 'Berlin Tiger'. **GAP Photos:** Richard Bloom: *Iris foetidissima;* S & O: *Iris* 'Holden Clough'. **Garden World Images:** *Iris winogradowii.* **Photolibrary:** Chris Burrows/GPL: *Iris sibirica* 'Papillon'. **Picturesmiths Ltd.:** *Iris* 'Kent Pride', *Iris* 'Perry's Blue', *Iris* 'Tropic Night', *Iris sibirica* 'Soft Blue' **226 Andrew Lawson Digital:** *Aquilegia viridiflora.* **Andrew Lawson Photography:** *Aquilegia longissima.* **Anne Green-Armytage:** *Aquilegia vulgaris* 'William Guiness'. **Garden World Images:** *Aquilegia* 'Dragonfly', *Aquilegia* 'Hensol Harebell', *Aquilegia coerulea, Aquilegia flabellata var. pumila, Aquilegia Songbird Series* 'Bunting', *Aquilegia triternata;* Brian Gadsby: *Aquilegia triternata;* S Hauser: *Aquilegia coerulea;* MAP/A Descat: *Aquilegia Songbird Series* 'Bunting'; T Schilling: *Aquilegia* 'Hensol

Harebell'; Darren Warner: *Aquilegia* 'Dragonfly'. **John Glover:** *Aquilegia canadensis.* **Photolibrary:** Tracey Rich: *Aquilegia* 'Nora Barlow'. **Thompson & Morgan:** *Aquilegia chrysantha* **227 Garden World Images:** *Doronicum columnae* 'Miss Mason' **228 GAP Photos:** S & O: *Paeonia suffruticosa* 'Hakuo-jisi'; Rob Whitworth: *Paeonia* 'Coral Charm', *Paeonia* 'Kelway's Fairy Queen'. **Garden World Images:** *Paeonia* 'Cheddar Gold', *Paeonia* 'Festiva Maxima', *Paeonia* 'Jan van Leeuwen', *Paeonia obovata var. alba;* S Chesterman: *Paeonia* 'Cheddar Gold'; C Harris: *Paeonia* 'Jan van Leeuwen'; T Jennings: *Paeonia* 'Festiva Maxima'. **Marianne Majerus Garden Images:** Marianne Majerus: *Paeonia suffruticosa* 'Yachiyo-tsubaki'; Marianne Majerus/The Manor, Hemingford Grey: *Paeonia* 'Lady Alexandra Duff'. **Photolibrary:** Martin Page: *Paeonia* 'Pillow Talk' **229 Alamy:** Ros Drinkwater: *Paeonia x lemoinei* 'High Noon'. **Collection & Photo Riviere (France, 26 Drôme):** *Paeonia x lemoinei* 'L'Espérance'. **GAP Photos:** Visions: *Paeonia* 'Félix Crousse'; Rob Whitworth: *Paeonia suffruticosa* 'Rimpo'. **Garden World Images:** G Delacroix: *Paeonia* 'Thunderbolt'; L Thomas: *Paeonia* 'Paul M. Wild'. **Getty:** Martin Page: *Paeonia* 'Bartzella', *Paeonia* 'Garden Treasure'. **Marianne Majerus Garden Images:** Marianne Majerus: *Paeonia* 'Claire de Lune'. **Photolibrary:** Martin Page: *Paeonia* 'Buckeye Belle' **230 GAP Photos:** Suzie Gibbons: *Selinum wallichianum.* **Garden World Images:** Gilles Delacroix: *Leucanthemum x superbum* 'Aglaia' **231 GAP Photos:** Jo Whitworth: *Anaphalis triplinervis* 'Sommerschnee'; Rob Whitworth: *Gaura lindheimeri.* **Garden World Images:** Lee Thomas: *Leucanthemum x superbum* 'Sonnenschein' **232 Alamy:** CuboImages srl: *Astilbe* 'Europa'; John Glover: *Astilbe* 'Amethyst'; Steffen Hauser/botanikfoto: *Astilbe* 'Granat'; Martin Hughes-Jones: *Astilbe* 'Europa'. **Garden World Images:** G Delacroix: *Astilbe* 'Deutschland'; M Thornhill: *Astilbe x crispa* 'Perkeo' **233 Marianne Majerus Garden Images:** Marianne Majerus: *Thalictrum aquilegiifolium* 'Thundercloud' **234 GAP Photos:** Richard Bloom: *Persicaria campanulata* 'Rosenrot'. **Garden World Images:** *Persicaria* 'Red Dragon', *Persicaria virginiana* 'Lance Corporal', *Persicaria virginiana* 'Painter's Palette', *Rehmannia elata;* M Hughes-Jones: *Persicaria* 'Red Dragon'; T Sims: *Persicaria virginiana* 'Lance Corporal', *Persicaria virginiana* 'Painter's Palette'. **Getty:** Dave Zubraski: *Persicaria affinis* 'Superba'. **Photolibrary:** Carole Drake/GPL: *Persicaria polymorpha* **235 GAP Photos:** J S Sira: *Hemerocallis* 'Red Precious'. **Garden World Images:** *Lychnis chalcedonica, Lychnis chalcedonica, Phlox paniculata* 'Prince of Orange'; Rodger Tamblyn: *Lychnis chalcedonica, Lychnis chalcedonica* **236 Photolibrary:** J S Sira: *Penstemon* 'The Juggler' **237 bloompictures:** *Penstemon* 'Chester Scarlet', *Penstemon* 'King George V'. **Garden World Images:** *Penstemon* 'Cherry Ripe', *Penstemon* 'Papal Purple', *Penstemon* 'Russian River'; G. Delacroix: *Penstemon* 'Cherry Ripe'; Derek Gould: *Penstemon* 'Russian River'. **Marianne Majerus Garden Images:** Marianne Majerus/Little Llanavon, Herefordshire: *Penstemon heterophyllus* 'Heavenly Blue'. **Photolibrary:** Chris Burrows: *Penstemon whippleanus* **238 Alamy:** Holmes Garden Photos: *Astrantia major* 'Ruby Wedding'; Martin Hughes-Jones: *Papaver* 'Fireball'; Wildscape: *Papaver orientale* 'Black and White'. **GAP Photos:** J S Sira: *Filipendula purpurea.* **Garden World Images:** M Hughes-Jones: *Papaver orientale* 'Karine'; MAP/A Descat: *Papaver* 'Patty's Plum'; L Thomas: *Papaver* 'Medallion'. **Marianne Majerus Garden Images:** Marianne Majerus, Bankton Cottage, Sussex: *Geranium palmatum.* **Photolibrary:** Chris Burrows/GPL: *Papaver orientale* 'Choir Boy'; John Glover: *Papaver orientale* 'Turkish Delight'; Hermant Jariwala/GPL: *Papaver orientale var. bracteatum* **239 Alamy:** blickwinkel: *Linaria triornithophora, Linaria triornithophora;* WILDLIFE GmbH: *Monarda fistulosa, Monarda fistulosa* **240 Alamy:** Shorelark Nigel Downer: *Eryngium alpinum.* **GAP Photos:** Mark Bolton: *Nepeta* 'Six Hills Giant'. **Garden World Images:** *Agapanthus inapertus subsp. pendulus* 'Graskop', *Phlox paniculata* 'Windsor'; Martin Hughes-Jones: *Agapanthus inapertus subsp. pendulus* 'Graskop'. **John Glover:** *Phlox paniculata* 'Hampton Court'. **Science Photo Library (SPL):** A-Z Botanical Collection: *Phlox paniculata* 'Amethyst' **241 Alamy:** Holmes Garden Photos: *Campanula persicifolia* 'Chettle Charm'; imagebroker: *Echinops bannaticus* 'Taplow Blue'. **GAP Photos:** Jonathan Buckley: *Agapanthus* 'Purple Cloud'; Clive Nichols: *Agapanthus* 'Northern Star'. **Garden World Images:** G Delacroix: *Campanula takesimana;* M Hughes-Jones: *Campanula lactiflora* 'Prichard's Variety'; P Smith: *Campanula punctata* 'Cherry Bells'; L Thomas: *Campanula trachelium* 'Bernice'; Lee Thomas: *Aconitum* 'Stainless Steel' **242 Alamy:** Holmes Garden Photos: *Astelia chathamica.* **GAP Photos:** Jonathan Buckley: *Astelia chathamica.* **Garden World Images:** Gilles Delacroix: *Artemisia* 'Powis Castle'. **Marianne Majerus Garden Images:** Marianne Majerus, The Old Vicarage, East Ruston: *Mathiasella bupleuroides* 'Green Dream' **243 GAP Photos:** Flora Press: *Gentiana lutea;* Martin Hughes-Jones: *Berkheya macrocephala.* **GardenPhotos.com:** Judy White: *Phlomis russeliana* **244 bloompictures:** *Hemerocallis* 'Cherry Cheeks'. **GAP Photos:** Clive Nichols: *Hemerocallis* 'Pardon Me'. **Garden Picture Library:** J S Sira: *Hemerocallis* 'Neyron Rose'. **Garden World Images:** *Hemerocallis* 'Canadian Border Patrol', *Hemerocallis* 'Luxury Lace', *Hemerocallis* 'Prairie Blue Eyes'; G Delacroix: *Hemerocallis* 'Luxury Lace'; L Thomas: *Hemerocallis* 'Canadian Border Patrol'. **The Garden Collection:** Derek Harris: *Hemerocallis* 'Stoke Poges' **245 bloompictures:** *Hemerocallis* 'Cream Drop'. **GAP Photos:** Adrian Bloom: *Hemerocallis* 'Whichford'; Martin Hughes-Jones: *Hemerocallis* 'Cathy's Sunset'. **Garden Picture Library:** M Bolton: *Hemerocallis dumortieri;* C Burrows: *Hemerocallis* 'Little Wine Cup'. **Garden World Images:** G Delacroix: *Hemerocallis* 'Green Flutter'; G Harper: *Hemerocallis* 'Lemon Bells'; T Jennings: *Hemerocallis* 'Chicago Sunrise'. **Peter Stiles Photography:** *Hemerocallis* 'Cartwheels'. **The Garden Collection:** Andrew Lawson: *Hemerocallis* 'Bonanza'; Nicola Stocken Tomkins: *Hemerocallis* 'Black Magic' **246 Alamy:** Holmes Garden Photos: *Euphorbia griffithii* 'Fireglow'. **Garden World Images:** Martin Hughes-Jones: *Verbascum* 'Cotswold Beauty' **247 Alamy:** Holmes Garden Photos: *Achillea ptarmica* 'The Pearl'. **GAP Photos:** Lynn Keddie: *Achillea* 'Belle Epoque'; J S Sira: *Achillea* 'Christine's Pink'. **Garden World Images:** A Biddle: *Achillea* 'Lachsschönheit'; N R Colborn: *Achillea* 'Heidi'; G. Delacroix: *Achillea millefolium* 'Red Velvet'; D Rose: *Achillea millefolium* 'Kelwayi'; L Thomas: *Achillea* 'Terracotta'. **Getty:** Martin Page: *Achillea filipendulina* 'Parker's Variety' **248 Alamy:** Steffen Hauser/botanikfoto: *Helenium* 'Feuersiegel'; Martin Hughes-Jones: *Helenium* 'Potter's Wheel'; Leonie Lambert: *Lobelia cardinalis* 'Queen Victoria', *Lobelia cardinalis* 'Queen Victoria'. **Garden World Images:** G. Delacroix: *Helenium* 'Waltraut'; G Harper: *Helenium* 'Indianersommer'; M Hughes-Jones: *Helenium* 'Double Trouble', *Helenium* 'Red Army', *Helenium* 'Rubinzwerg'. **Photolibrary:** Neil Holmes: *Helenium* 'Butterpat' **249 Alamy:** John Martin: *Aster* 'Photograph'. **Garden World Images:** G. Delacroix: *Aster x frikartii* 'Wunder von Stäfa'; MAP/A Descat: *Aster novae-angliae* 'Rosa Sieger'; T Sims: *Aster novi-belgii* 'Carnival'. **GardenPhotos.com:** Graham Rice: *Aster* 'Sunhelene'. **Getty:** Rob Whitworth: *Aster novi-belgii* 'Chequers'. **Photolibrary:** Mark Bolton: *Aster* 'Little Carlow', *Aster novae-angliae* 'Violetta'; Sunniva Harte: *Aster* 'Coombe Fishacre'; Stephen Henderson: *Aster divaricatus* **250 Alamy:** Carole Drake: *Salvia glutinosa.* **GAP Photos:** Richard Bloom: *Salvia nemorosa* 'Ostfriesland'; Jonathan Buckley: *Salvia guaranitica* 'Black and Blue'; Heather Edwards: *Salvia patens;* John Glover: *Salvia verticillata* 'Purple Rain'; Marcus Harpur: *Salvia nemorosa* 'Lubecca'; Neil Holmes: *Salvia x sylvestris* 'Blauhügel'. **Garden World Images:** Gilles Delacroix: *Salvia argentea, Salvia nemorosa* 'Caradonna', *Salvia pratensis* 'Indigo', *Salvia pratensis* 'Swan Lake'; Martin Hughes-Jones: *Salvia pratensis* 'Pink Delight'. **Marianne Majerus Garden Images:** Marianne Majerus: *Salvia nemorosa* 'Amethyst'. **Photolibrary:** Ron Evans: *Salvia x sylvestris* 'Mainacht' **251 Alamy:** blickwinkel: *Rudbeckia fulgida var. speciosa;* Organica: *Rudbeckia triloba;* The Garden Picture Library: *Rudbeckia occidentalis* 'Green Wizard'. **GAP Photos:** Richard Bloom: *Rudbeckia maxima;* Marcus Harpur: *Kirengeshoma palmata, Kirengeshoma palmata.* **Garden World Images:** *Rudbeckia fulgida var. deamii, Rudbeckia laciniata* 'Herbstsonne'; John Martin: *Rudbeckia fulgida var. deamii.* **Photolibrary:** Brian Carter: *Solidago* 'Goldenmosa' **252 Garden World Images:** M Hughes-Jones: *Chrysanthemum* 'Innocence'; J Need: *Chrysanthemum* 'Chesapeake'. **GardenPhotos.com:** Graham Rice: *Chrysanthemum* 'Emperor of China', *Chrysanthemum* 'Nell Gwynn', *Chrysanthemum* 'Purleigh White'. **Royal Horticultural Society (RHS):** Ali Cundy: *Chrysanthemum* 'Aunt Millicent', *Chrysanthemum* 'Spartan Seagull' **253 Alamy:** Martin Hughes-Jones: *Chrysanthemum* 'Duchess of Edinburgh'. **GAP Photos:** Richard Bloom: *Chrysanthemum* 'Cottage Apricot'; Howard Rice: *Chrysanthemum* 'Mary Stoker'. **Garden World Images:** *Chrysanthemum* 'Apollo', *Chrysanthemum* 'Doctor Tom Parr', *Chrysanthemum* 'Nantyderry Sunshine', *Chrysanthemum* 'Ruby Mound', *Chrysanthemum* 'Tapestry Rose'; R Coates: *Chrysanthemum* 'Ruby Mound'; R Ditchfield: *Chrysanthemum* 'Doctor Tom Parr'; G Harper: *Chrysanthemum* 'Nantyderry Sunshine'; MAP/A Kubacsi: *Chrysanthemum* 'Apollo'. **GardenPhotos.com:** Graham Rice: *Chrysanthemum* 'Bronze Elegance', *Chrysanthemum* 'Grandchild', *Chrysanthemum* 'Perry's Peach', *Chrysanthemum* 'Sea Urchin'. **John McCormack:** *Chrysanthemum* 'Chelsea Physic Garden'. **Marianne Majerus Garden Images:** Marianne Majerus/NCCPG National Plant Collection: *Chrysanthemum* 'Mrs Jessie Cooper', *Chrysanthemum* 'Paul Boissier', *Chrysanthemum* 'Rumpelstilzchen'. **Photoshot:** Photos Horticultural: *Chrysanthemum* 'Anastasia'. **Royal Horticultural Society (RHS):** Ali Cundy: *Chrysanthemum* 'Carmine Blush' **254 GAP Photos:** FhF Greenmedia: *Kniphofia* 'Atlanta'. **Garden World Images:** *Kniphofia* 'Green Jade', *Kniphofia* 'Prince Igor', *Kniphofia* 'Royal Standard', *Kniphofia* 'Toffee Nosed', *Kniphofia* 'Wrexham Buttercup', *Kniphofia caulescens, Kniphofia thomsonii* var. *snowdenii;* G Delacroix: *Kniphofia* 'Royal Standard'; D Gould: *Kniphofia* 'Prince Igor'; M Hughes-Jones: *Kniphofia* 'Wrexham Buttercup'; MAP/N Pasquel: *Kniphofia* 'Green Jade'; T Sandell: *Kniphofia* 'Toffee Nosed'. **Getty:** Martin Page: *Kniphofia* 'Wrexham Buttercup'. **Photolibrary:** Chris Burrows/GPL: *Kniphofia* 'Bees' Sunset'; Howard Rice/GPL: *Kniphofia rooperi* **255 Alamy:** Steffen Hauser/botanikfoto: *Convallaria majalis.* **Garden World Images:** *Sinopodophyllum hexandrum.* **Marianne Majerus Garden Images:** Marianne Majerus: *Helleborus x ericsmithii* 'Bob's Best' **256 Alamy:** GardenPhotos.com: *Cypripedium* Ulla Silkens gx; Martin Hughes-Jones: *Geranium macrorrhizum* 'Ingwersen's Variety'. **GAP Photos:** FhF Greenmedia: *Helleborus x ericsmithii* IVORY PRINCE; Andrea Jones: *Chrysosplenium macrophyllum;* Gerald Majumdar: *Geranium macrorrhizum* 'Ingwersen's Variety'. **Marianne Majerus Garden Images:** Marianne Majerus/Emile Becker: *Helleborus thibetanus.* **Photolibrary:** Clive Nichols: *Bergenia* 'Beethoven' **257 Alamy:** John Glover: *Primula* 'Guinevere', *Primula* 'Woodland Walk'; June Green: *Primula Husky Series [white].* **GAP Photos:** J S Sira: *Primula sieboldii* 'Geisha Girl'. **Garden World Images:** *Primula* 'Dawn Ansell', *Primula* 'Lady Greer', *Primula vialii;* T Sims: *Primula* 'Lady Greer'; D Wildridge: *Primula* 'Dawn Ansell'. **Science Photo Library (SPL):** Bjanka Kadic: *Primula Crescendo Series* 'Crescendo Pink and Rose Shades' **258 Alamy:** John Glover: *Primula* 'Elizabeth Killelay'. **GAP Photos:** Visions: *Primula* 'Don Keefe'. **Garden World Images:** *Primula* 'Belarina Cobalt Blue', *Primula* 'Mark'; L Thomas: *Primula* 'Belarina Cobalt Blue'. **Photolibrary:** Sunniva Harte: *Primula Crescendo Series* 'Crescendo Bright Red' **259 Garden World Images:** M Hughes-Jones: *Primula* 'Fransisca'. **Photolibrary:** Sunniva Harte: *Primula veris* 'Katy McSparron'. **Picturesmiths Ltd.:** R. Smith: *Primula* 'Trouble' **260 Alamy:** Karen Appleyard: *Helleborus purpurascens;* Florapix: *Lathyrus vernus, Lathyrus vernus.* **Garden World Images:** *Glaucidium palmatum, Lathraea clandestina, Lathraea clandestina;* Dr Alan Beaumont: *Lathraea clandestina, Lathraea clandestina.* **The Garden Collection:** Nicola Stocken Tomkins: *Epimedium epsteinii* **261 Alamy:** Martin Hughes-Jones: *Brunnera macrophylla* 'Jack Frost'. **GAP Photos:** Carole Drake, courtesy The Sir Harold Hillier Gardens/Hampshire County Council: *Pulmonaria* 'Lewis Palmer'; Heather Edwards: *Pulmonaria* 'Mawson's Blue'. **Garden World Images:** G Delacroix: *Pulmonaria* 'Margery Fish'; G. Delacroix: *Pulmonaria* 'Excalibur'; MAP/A Descat: *Pulmonaria* 'Mary Mottram'; L Thomas: *Pulmonaria OPAL* Pulmonaria OPAL. **Getty:** Martin Page: *Mertensia virginica, Mertensia virginica.* **Photolibrary:** John Glover /GPL: *Pulmonaria rubra* 'David Ward'; Howard Rice/GPL: *Pulmonaria rubra* **262 GAP Photos:** Richard Bloom: *Helleborus argutifolius* 'Silver Lace'; Martin Hughes-Jones: *Euphorbia amygdaloides var. robbiae.* **Garden World Images:** F Davis: *Helleborus argutifolius* 'Pacific Frost'. **Photolibrary:** Howard Rice: *Valeriana phu* 'Aurea' **263 Alamy:** The Garden Picture Library: *Doronicum orientale* 'Magnificum'. **Garden World Images:** *Epimedium* 'Amber Queen', *Leucanthemum x superbum* 'Esther Read'; N R Colborn: *Epimedium* 'Amber Queen' **264 Photolibrary:** Joshua McCullough: *Deinanthe bifida.* **Photos Horticultural:** *Diplarrhena moraea* **265 Eric Crichton Photos:** *Osteospermum jucundum.* **Photolibrary:** Rex Butcher: *Dactylorhiza foliosa.* **Science Photo Library (SPL):** A-Z Botanical Collection: *Lychnis viscaria* 'Splendens Plena' **266 Alamy:** The Garden Picture Library: *Dianthus* 'Inchmery'. **Garden World Images:** T Sims: *Dianthus* 'Cranmere Pool'; L Thomas: *Dianthus* 'Devon Dove', *Dianthus* CANDY FLOSS, *Dianthus* LADY MADONNA. **GardenPhotos.com:** Graham Rice: *Dianthus* 'Brilliant Star', *Dianthus* 'Evening Star'. **Royal Horticultural Society (RHS):** Sue Drew: *Dianthus* 'Coquette', *Dianthus* 'Milky Way' **267 Alamy:** Christopher Burrows: *Dianthus superbus* 'Crimsonia'; Glenn Harper: *Dianthus* 'Neon Star'. **Allwoods Nursery:** *Dianthus* 'Tayside Red'. **Garden World Images:** *Dianthus* 'Devon Wizard', *Dianthus* 'Fusilier', *Dianthus* 'Lily the Pink', *Dianthus* 'Monica Wyatt', *Dianthus* 'Moulin Rouge', *Dianthus* 'Passion', *Dianthus* 'Pixie Star', *Dianthus* 'Rose de Mai', *Dianthus* 'Tickled Pink', *Dianthus* 'Valda Wyatt', *Dianthus* FEUREHEXE, *Dianthus* STARLIGHT; R Coates: *Dianthus* 'Monica Wyatt'; G Delacroix: G Harper: *Dianthus* 'Moulin Rouge'; T Sims: *Dianthus* 'Rose de Mai'; L Thomas: *Dianthus* 'Fusilier', *Dianthus* 'Lily the Pink', *Dianthus* 'Passion', *Dianthus* 'Pixie Star', *Dianthus* 'Tickled Pink', *Dianthus* 'Valda Wyatt', **GardenPhotos.com:** Graham Rice: *Dianthus* 'India Star'. **Marianne Majerus Garden Images:** Marianne Majerus: *Dianthus* 'Queen of Sheba'. **Royal Horticultural Society (RHS):** Sue Drew: *Dianthus* 'Prado Mint' **268 Alamy:** Christopher Burrows: *Potentilla* 'Arc-en-ciel'; CuboImages srl: *Stachys officinalis* 'Hummelo'. **Bleddyn Wynn Jones:** *Crusea coccinea.* **Photolibrary:** Richard Bloom: *Geum* 'Bell Bank'. **Photoshot:** Photos Horticultural: *Coreopsis* 'Limerock Ruby' **269 GAP Photos:** Jonathan Buckley: *Berkheya purpurea.* **Garden World Images:** Tony Schilling: *Ourisia coccinea* **270 Alamy:** Hillhead: *Geranium* 'Johnson's Blue' **271 Alamy:** CuboImages srl: *Geranium* ROZANNE; Martin Hughes-Jones: *Amsonia orientalis.* **Garden World Images:** *Myosotidium hortensia* **272 Alamy:** Ros Drinkwater: *Hosta* 'Invincible'; Holmes Garden Photos: *Hosta* 'June'. **GAP Photos:** Dave Bevan: *Hosta* 'Gold Edger'; Clive Nichols: *Hosta* 'Night Before Christmas'. **Garden World Images:** L Thomas: *Hosta* 'Minuteman'. **GardenPhotos.com:** judywhite: *Hosta* 'Cherry Berry' **273 GAP Photos:** Howard Rice: *Hosta* 'Brim Cup'; Jo Whitworth: *Hosta lancifolia.* **Garden World Images:** G Delacroix: *Hosta* 'Fragrant Bouquet '; Ellen McKnight: *Hosta* 'Sagae'. **Photoshot:** Photos Horticultural: *Hosta* 'Hydon Sunset', *Hosta* 'Remember Me', *Hosta* 'Revolution'. **The Garden Collection:** Torie Chugg: *Hosta* 'Tattoo' **274 Alamy:** John Glover: *Mentha suaveolens* 'Variegata', *Mentha suaveolens* 'Variegata'. **GAP Photos:** Neil Holmes: *Artemisia ludoviciana* 'Valerie Finnis'. **Garden World Images:** *Hosta tokudama f. aureonebulosa* **275 Alamy:** blickwinkel: *Alchemilla conjuncta.* **Photolibrary:** Howard Rice: *Stachys byzantina* 'Primrose Heron', *Stachys byzantina* 'Primrose Heron'. **Rosemary Kautzky:** photographersdirect.com: *Calanthe striata* **276 Alamy:** Holmes Garden Photos: *Tropaeolum polyphyllum* **277 Alamy:** Holmes Garden Photos: *Hieracium lanatum.* **GAP Photos:** Visions: *Gaillardia* 'Oranges and Lemons'. **Garden World Images:** Richard Shiell: *Libertia ixioides* 'Goldfinger' **278 Alamy:** The Garden Picture Library: *Astrantia maxima.* **GAP Photos:** J S Sira: *Astrantia major* 'Roma'. **John Fielding:** *Begonia taliensis.* **Marianne Majerus Garden Images:** Marianne Majerus: *Begonia grandis subsp. evansiana* **279 GAP Photos:** Paul Debois: *Sedum telephium* 'Strawberries and Cream'. **Garden World Images:** N Appleby: *Sedum* 'Matrona'; L Every: *Sedum telephium* 'Purple Emperor'; D Gould: *Sedum spectabile* 'Iceberg'; G Harper: *Sedum telephium* 'Gooseberry Fool'; L Thomas: *Sedum erythrostictum* 'Mediovariegatum'. **Marianne Majerus Garden Images:** Marianne Majerus: *Sedum* 'Red Cauli'. **Photolibrary:** Mark Bolton: *Sedum* 'Ruby Glow' **280 Alamy:** John Glover: *Heuchera* 'Plum Pudding', *Heuchera* 'Plum Pudding'. **GAP Photos:** Martin Hughes-Jones: *Agastache* 'Black Adder', *Geranium* 'Orion'. **Garden World Images:** *Bergenia purpurascens, Tulbaghia violacea;* Gilles Delacroix: *Bergenia purpurascens* **281 GAP Photos:** FhF Greenmedia: *Helleborus niger* 'HGC Joseph Lemper'; John Glover: *Helleborus x hybridus Harvington hybrids* [single, white]; Marcus Harpur: *Helleborus x hybridus Bradfield hybrids* [double, apricot with spots]; Howard Rice: *Helleborus x hybridus* [single, apricot]. **Garden World Images:** L Thomas: *Helleborus niger* 'Potter's Wheel', *Helleborus x nigercors.* **GardenPhotos.com:** Graham Rice: *Helleborus x hybridus* [single, white with spots]. **Getty:** Richard Bloom: *Helleborus x hybridus* [double, slate]; Jonathan Buckley: *Helleborus x* *hybridus Ashwood Garden hybrids* [double, black]; Dave Zubraski: *Helleborus x hybridus* [single, yellow with spots]. **Marianne Majerus Garden Images:** Marianne Majerus/The Old Rectory, Sudborough: *Helleborus x hybridus* [single, yellow]. **Peter Stiles Photography:** *Helleborus x hybridus* [single, red]. **Photolibrary:** Clive Nichols /GPL: *Helleborus x hybridus Harvington hybrids* [double, apricot]; Garden Pix Ltd/GPL: *Helleborus x hybridus Ashwood Garden hybrids* [double, pink]; Anne Green-Armytage/GPL: *Helleborus x hybridus* [double, white]; Howard Rice: *Helleborus x hybridus* [single, green]; Howard Rice/GPL: *Helleborus x hybridus* [double, plum]. **The Garden Collection:** Nicola Stocken Tomkins: *Helleborus x hybridus* [double, white with spots] **282 GAP Photos:** BBC Magazines Ltd: *Heuchera* 'Black Beauty'; Jonathan Buckley: *Heuchera* 'Silver Scrolls'; Lynn Keddie: *Heuchera* 'Peppermint Spice'; Visions Premium: *Heuchera* 'Ginger Ale'; Rob Whitworth: *Heuchera* 'Ebony and Ivory', *Heuchera* 'Southern Comfort'. **Garden World Images:** Rita Coates: *Heuchera* 'Midnight Rose'; G Delacroix: *Heuchera* 'Purple Petticoats', *Heuchera sanguinea var. pulchra* 'Snow Storm', *Heucherella tiarelloides* 'Stoplight'; G. Delacroix: *Heuchera* 'Lime Rickey'; Richard Shiell: *Heuchera* 'Amber Waves'; L Thomas: *Heuchera* 'Beauty Colour', *Heuchera* 'Blackbird', *Heuchera* 'Can-can', *Heuchera* 'Georgia Peach', *Heuchera* 'Green Spice', *Heuchera* 'Peach Flambé', *Heuchera* 'Tiramisu', *Heuchera* CRÈME BRÛLÉE, *Heucherella tiarelloides* 'Kimono'; D Wildridge: *Heuchera* 'Pewter Moon'. **GardenPhotos.com:** Graham Rice: *Heuchera* 'Cinnabar Silver'. **Getty:** Jo Whitworth: *Heuchera* 'Chocolate Ruffles' **283 Alamy:** John Glover: *Helleborus foetidus Wester Flisk Group.* **GAP Photos:** Geoff Kidd: *Ophiopogon japonicus;* Howard Rice: *Helleborus odorus;* J S Sira: *Helleborus cyclophyllus.* **Garden World Images:** Gilles Delacroix: *Dianella caerulea* CASSA BLUE. **Marianne Majerus Garden Images:** Marianne Majerus/Harveys Garden Plants: *Helleborus x sternii* 'Boughton Beauty' **284 GAP Photos:** Mark Bolton: *Cortaderia richardii.* **Garden World Images:** Gilles Delacroix: *Calamagrostis brachytricha* **285 Alamy:** The Garden Picture Library: *Miscanthus sinensis* 'Yakushima Dwarf'. **GAP Photos:** Adrian Bloom: *Miscanthus sinensis var. condensatus* 'Cosmopolitan'; Ron Evans: *Chionochloa rubra;* Jo Whitworth, location: Knoll Gardens: *Eragrostis curvula* 'Totnes Burgandy'. **Garden World Images:** Martin Hughes-Jones: *Molinia caerulea subsp. caerulea* 'Heidebraut'. **Photolibrary:** Jerry Pavia: *Elegia capensis* **286 GAP Photos:** Carole Drake, courtesy The Sir Harold Hillier Gardens/Hampshire County Council: *Thamnocalamus crassinodus* 'Kew Beauty'. **GardenPhotos.com:** judywhite: *Miscanthus sinensis* 'Gracillimus'. **Getty:** Richard Bloom: *Miscanthus sinensis* 'Flamingo'; Rob Whitworth: *Stipa calamagrostis.* **Photolibrary:** Stephen Henderson: *Molinia caerulea subsp. arundinacea* 'Transparent' **287 Alamy:** Holmes Garden Photos: *Chimonobambusa timidissinoda.* **GAP Photos:** Howard Rice: *Ampelodesmos mauritanica* **288 Alamy:** Holmes Garden Photos: *Yushania anceps* 'Pitt White'. **GAP Photos:** BBC Magazines Ltd: *Phyllostachys aurea.* **Photoshot:** Photos Horticultural: *Luzula sylvatica* 'Hohe Tatra' **289 Photolibrary:** Adrian Bloom: *Panicum virgatum* 'Northwind'. **The Garden Collection:** Andrew Lawson: *Phyllostachys vivax f. aureocaulis* **290 Alamy:** Debbie Monique Jolliff: *Athyrium niponicum var. pictum* 'Burgandy Lace'. **Garden World Images:** Lee Thomas: *Athyrium* 'Ghost' **292 Eric Crichton Photos:** *Adiantum venustum.* **Garden World Images:** Lee Thomas: *Polystichum tsussimense.* **The Garden Collection:** Andrew Lawson: *Blechnum chilense* **293 Alamy:** Dave Gowan: *Polystichum munitum;* John Swithinbank: *Dryopteris erythrosora.* **The Garden Collection:** Torie Chugg: *Polypodium cambricum* 'Richard Kayse' **294-295 GAP Photos:** Elke Borkowski. **295 GAP Photos:** Lee Avison (ftr); John Glover (ftl); Sharon Pearson (tl); Dave Zubraski (tr). **296 GAP Photos:** Charles Hawes (t); Martin Hughes-Jones (b). **298 Garden World Images:** Anthony Baggett: *Dahlia Gallery Series* 'Gallery Art Fair'; Dr Alan Beaumont: *Dahlia Gallery Series* 'Gallery Art Fair'; G Delacroix: *Euphorbia hypericifolia* DIAMOND FROST, *Lobularia maritima* 'Snow Crystals', *Sutera cordata* Snowstorm Series GIANT SNOWFLAKE; Gilles Delacroix: *Euphorbia hypericifolia* DIAMOND FROST, *Lobularia maritima* 'Snow Crystals', *Sutera cordata* Snowstorm Series GIANT SNOWFLAKE; R Shiell: *Zinnia x marylandica Zahara Series* 'Zahara Starlight Rose'; Richard Shiell: *Zinnia x marylandica Zahara Series* 'Zahara Starlight Rose' **299 Garden World Images:** *Euphorbia marginata, Eustoma grandiflorum, Nicotiana x sanderae* 'Saratoga Series' [white] **300 Alamy:** Martin Hughes-Jones: *Argyranthemum* 'Summer Melody'. **Garden World Images:** *Catharanthus roseus* Boa Series 'Boa Peach', *Martynia annua;* R Shiell: *Calibrachoa* Caberet Series LIGHT PINK, *Catharanthus roseus Boa Series* 'Boa Peach'; Richard Shiell: *Calibrachoa* Calibrachoa Caberet Series LIGHT PINK, *Catharanthus roseus Boa Series* 'Boa Peach'. **Photolibrary:** Chris Burrows: *Brachyscome* 'Strawberry Mousse'; Chris Burrows/GPL: *Brachyscome* 'Strawberry Mousse' **301 Garden World Images:** N R Colborn: *Diascia* LITTLE DANCER; G Delacroix: *Lantana camara* Lucky Series LUCKY HONEY BLUSH; Trevor Sims: *Lathyrus odoratus* Cupid Series 'Cupid Pink'; L Thomas: *Nemesia* AMELIE, *Osteospermum* Sunny Series 'Sunny Marina'. **The Garden Collection:** Liz Eddison: *Gaura lindheimeri* 'Rosyjane' **302 Garden World Images:** *Fuchsia* 'Dollar Prinzessin', *Fuchsia* 'Nellie Nuttall', *Fuchsia* 'Sunray', *Fuchsia triphylla* 'Firecracker', *Fuchsia Windchimes Series* 'Windchimes Pink and White'; G. Delacroix: *Fuchsia Windchimes Series* 'Windchimes Pink and White'; MAP/N Pasquel: *Fuchsia triphylla* 'Firecracker'; P Smith: *Fuchsia* 'Sunray'. **Marianne Majerus Garden Images:** Simon Meaker: *Fuchsia California Dreamers Series* 'Snowburner'. **Young Plants Limited:** *Fuchsia* 'Joanna Lumley', *Fuchsia Mojo* 'Beebop', *Fuchsia Shadowdancer* PEGGY; Proven Winners: Chris Wright Photography: *Fuchsia* 'Joanna Lumley' **303 GAP Photos:** Geoff Kidd: *Primula* Belarina Series BELARINA PINK ICE. **Garden World Images:** MAP/N Pasquel: *Antirrhinum* Luminaire Series LUMINAIRE HOT PINK; MAP/Nathalie Pasquel: *Antirrhinum* Luminaire Series LUMINAIRE HOT PINK; R Shiell: *Petchoa* Supercal Series SUPERCAL NEON ROSE; Lee Thomas: *Glandularia x hybrida* Aztec Magic Series AZTEC DARK PINK MAGIC. **Unwins Seeds Ltd:** *Gomphrena globosa* **304 Garden World Images:** *Lobularia maritima* 'Rosie O'Day', *Schizanthus* 'Dwarf Bouquet' [mixed]. **Unwins Seeds Ltd:** *Iberis umbellata* Fairy Series **305 Andrew Lawson Photography:** *Clarkia amoena* 'Sybil Sherwood'. **Garden World Images:** *Nicotiana x sanderae* Saratoga Series [deep rose] **306 Andrew Lawson Photography:** T Chugg: *Zinnia elegans* Dreamland Series [scarlet]. **GAP Photos:** Rob Whitworth: *Antirrhinum majus* 'Black Prince'. **Garden World Images:** G Delacroix: *Calibrachoa* Million Bells Series MILLION BELLS CHERRY PINK; Simon Keeble: *Brassica Northern Lights Series;* Richard Shiell: *Catharanthus roseus* Cobra Series 'Cobra Burgundy'; L Thomas: *Cuphea x purpurea* 'Firecracker', *Dahlia* HAPPY SINGLE ROMEO; **Thompson & Morgan:** *Cosmos atrosanguineus* CHOCAMOCHA **307 Garden World Images:** Eric Crichton: *Nemesia strumosa Carnival Series;* Dan Sams: *Impatiens Expo Series* 'Expo Pink'; Richard Shiell: *Glandularia x hybrida* Corsage Series 'Corsage Red'; Trevor Sims: *Tropaeolum majus* 'Hermine Grashoff'. **Photolibrary:** J S Sira: *Zinnia x marylandica* Profusion Series 'Profusion Cherry'. **Thompson & Morgan:** *Impatiens walleriana* MASQUERADE **308 Garden World Images:** *Salvia splendens Vista Series [red], Tagetes* 'Cinnabar'. **Photoshot:** *Alonsoa warscewiczii.* **Unwins Seeds Ltd:** *Petunia* 'Mirage Velvet' **309 Chris Burrows:** *Pelargonium Horizon Deva Series* 'Horizon Deva Raspberry Ripple'. **GAP Photos:** Friedrich Strauss: *Pelargonium* Antik Series ANTIK SALMON; Graham Strong: *Pelargonium* Maverick Series 'Maverick Star'. **Garden World Images:** R Coates: *Pelargonium* Regalia Series 'Regalia Chocolate'; J Spears: *Pelargonium* BLUE WONDER; L Thomas: *Pelargonium Bulls Eye Series* 'Bulls Eye Salmon', *Pelargonium* Fireworks Series FIREWORKS SCARLET. **Photolibrary:** Chris Burrows/GPL: *Pelargonium* Decora Series 'Decora Dark Pink', *Pelargonium* Horizon Deva Series 'Horizon Deva Orange Ice'; Andrew Lord/GPL: *Pelargonium* 'Evka' **310 Alamy:** WILDLIFE GmbH: *Heliotropium arborescens.* **Garden World Images:** MAP/N Pasquel: *Solenostemon scutellarioides Kong Series* 'Kong Scarlet'; **311 GAP Photos:** Christina Bollen: *Lobelia erinus* Waterfall Series 'Waterfall Light Lavender'; J S Sira: *Petunia* Petunia Surfinia Series SURFINIA BLUE VEIN, *Solenostemon scutellarioides* 'Inky Fingers'. **Garden World Images:** G Delacroix: *Ipomoea batatas* 'Blackie', *Osteospermum* Cape Daisy Series NASINGA PURPLE, *Solenostemon* 'Chocolate Mint'; Steffen Hauser: *Pennisetum glaucum* 'Purple Majesty'; T Sims: *Dahlia* HAPPY SINGLE WINK; L Thomas: *Angelonia angustifolia AngelMist Series* 'AngelMist Lavender Stripe', *Petunia* Tumbelina Series PRISCILLA. **Photolibrary:** Photos Lamontagne/GPL: *Alternanthera dentata* 'Purple Knight'. **The Garden Collection:** Liz Eddison: *Strobilanthes dyerinanus* **312 GAP Photos:** Friedrich Strauss: *Viola x wittrockiana* Sorbet Series 'Sorbet Black Delight'. **Garden Picture Library:** *Cerinthe major* 'Purpurascens'. **Garden World Images:** *Nierembergia linariifolia* 'Purple Robe', Gilles Delacroix: *Glandularia x hybrida* Aztec Magic Series AZTEC SILVER MAGIC, *Pennisetum setaceum* 'Rubrum'. **Suttons Seeds:** *Viola x wittrockiana Imperial Series* 'Imperial Frosty Rose' **313 GAP Photos:** Marcus Harpur: *Myosotis Sylva Series.* **Garden World Images:** *Campanula medium* 'Bells of Holland', *Salvia sclarea var. turkestanica , Trachelium caeruleum,* Gilles Delacroix: *Viola x wittrockiana* Ultima Radiance Series [deep blue]; Trevor Sims: *Salvia sclarea var. turkestanica .* **Thompson & Morgan:** *Isotoma Avant-Garde Series* **314 Alamy:** Anna Yu: *Salvia farinacea* 'Strata'. **Garden World Images:** Lee Thomas: *Lobelia erinus Waterfall Series* 'Waterfall Blue', *Pericallis* Senetti Series SENETTI BLUE BICOLOR **315 Alpine Garden Society:** *Cynoglossum amabile* 'Firmament'. **Garden World Images:** *Commelina coelestis, Myosotis sylvatica* 'Blue Ball' **316 Alamy:** Christopher Burrows: *Petunia* Surfinia Series SURFINIA LIME. **Garden World Images:** Gilles Delacroix: *Zinnia elegans* 'Envy' **317 Alamy:** WILDLIFE GmbH: *Begonia x tuberhybrida Mocha Series* [Scarlet]. **Garden World Images:** G. Delacroix: *Begonia* 'Dragon Wing Red', *Begonia* 'Ikon White Blush'; R Shiell: *Begonia Illumination Series* 'Illumination Salmon Pink', *Begonia x tuberhybrida Non Stop Series [White].* **The Garden Collection:** Liz Eddison: *Begonia boliviensis* 'Bonfire' **318 Garden World Images:** MAP/Nathalie Pasquel: *Perilla* 'Magilla Vanilla'; MAP/Nicole et Patrick Mioulane: *Ipomoea batatus* 'Margarita'. **Photolibrary:** Chris Burrows: *Viola* 'Green Goddess'; Stephen Henderson: *Setaria macrostachya* **319 Eric Crichton Photos:** *Argyranthemum* 'Jamaica Primrose'. **Garden World Images:** *Brugmansia x candida* 'Grand Marnier', Gilles Delacroix: *Antirrhinum majus Liberty Classic Series* 'Liberty Yellow'; Lee Thomas: *Duranta erecta* 'Gold Edge'. **Photolibrary:** Photos Lamontagne/GPL: *Argyranthemum* BUTTERFLY, *Bidens* 'Gold Star' **320 GAP Photos:** Friedrich Strauss: *Nemesia Sunsatia Series SUNSATIA MANGO.* **Garden World Images:** *Antirrhinum majus* Chimes Series [yellow]. **Photolibrary:** Photos Lamontagne/GPL: *Xerochrysum bracteatum* Sundaze Series SUNDAZE GOLD. **Thompson & Morgan:** *Rudbeckia hirta* 'Toto Gold' **321 Photos Horticultural:** *Calendula officinalis* 'Daisy May'. **Thompson & Morgan:** *Platystemon californicus* **322 GAP Photos:** Paul Debois: *Mimulus Magic Series* 'Magic Yellow Blotch' **323 Alamy:** CuboImages srl: *Gazania Daybreak Series* 'Daybreak Bright Yellow'. **Garden World Images:** Trevor Sims: *Carthamus tinctorius.* **Photolibrary:** Michael Davis: *Viola x wittrockiana Angel Series* 'Tiger Eye'; J S Sira: *Lysimachia congestiflora* 'Outback Sunset' **324 Alamy:** Kevin Wheal Commercial: *Gazania Kiss Series* 'Kiss Orange Flame'. **Garden World Images:** *Erysimum x allionii* 'Orange Bedder', Gilles Delacroix: *Portulaca* Sundial Series 'Mango' **325 GAP Photos:** Friedrich Strauss: *Impatiens* Sunpatiens Series SUNPATIENS COMPACT ORANGE. **Garden World Images:** *Calendula officinalis Fiesta Gitana Group,* Richard Shiell: *Impatiens* Fusion Series FUSION PEACH FROST **326 Garden World Images:** *Calendula officinalis* 'Geisha Girl', *Coreopsis* 'Rum Punch'; Lee Thomas: *Coreopsis* 'Rum Punch' **327 Eric Crichton Photos:** *Gaillardia pulchella* 'Lollipops'. **Garden World Images:** *Solanum pseudocapsicum* 'Red Giant'. **Photolibrary:** Photos Lamontagne/GPL: *Dahlia Dahlietta Surprise Kelly.* **Plant Pictures World Wide:** *Eschscholzia californica Thai Silk Series* **328-329 GAP Photos:** Christina Bollen. **329 GAP Photos:** Lee Avison (tl). **330 GAP Photos:** Elke Borkowski (r). **332 Alamy:** WILDLIFE GmbH: *Pulsatilla alpina.* **GAP Photos:** John Glover: *Cassiope tetragona* **333 Garden World Images:** *Saxifraga* 'Tumbling Waters'. **Photolibrary:** Mark Turner: *Dodecatheon hendersonii.* **The Garden Collection:** Andrew Lawson: *Dodecatheon meadia f. album, Jeffersonia diphylla* **334 Alpine Garden Society:** *Aquilegia alpina, Daphne x hendersonii* 'Blackthorn Rose', *Phyllodoce empetriformis.* **Garden World Images:** *Omphalodes verna.* **Photolibrary:** Harald Lange: *Pulsatilla halleri* **335 Eric Crichton Photos:** *Aurinia saxatilis* 'Variegata'. **Garden World Images:** *Chiastophyllum oppositifolium.* **Photolibrary:** Howard Rice: *Corydalis cheilanthifolia* **336 Alamy:** AP: *Armeria pseudarmeria* **337 Clive Nichols:** *Saxifraga callosa.* **Garden World Images:** *Hebe vernicosa;* Derek Gould: *Diascia* ICE CRACKER **338 Garden World Images:** *Rhodothamnus chamaecistus.* **The Garden Collection:** Torie Chugg: *Oxalis tetraphylla* **339 Alpine Garden Society:** *Dianthus carthusianorum.* **Garden World Images:** Martin Hughes-Jones: *Crassula sarcocaulis* **340 The Garden Collection:** Andrew Lawson: *Origanum laevigatum* **342 Alamy:** Martin Hughes-Jones: *Phyteuma scheuchzeri.* **Alpine Garden Society:** *Lithodora oleifolia.* **Garden World Images:** *Convolvulus sabatius* **343 Eric Crichton Photos:** *Hypericum olympicum f. uniflorum* 'Citrinum', *Lithodora diffusa* 'Heavenly Blue' **345 Alamy:** National Geographic Image Collection: *Ononis natrix.* **Eric Crichton Photos:** *Helianthemum* 'Ben More' **346 Alamy:** Steffen Hauser/botanikfoto: *Ceratostigma plumbaginoides.* **Garden World Images:** *Gaultheria cuneata, Ranunculus calandrinioides.* **Photolibrary:** DEA: *Sorbus reducta* **347 Alpine Garden Society:** *Androsace vandellii.* **Garden World Images:** *Hebe cupressoides* 'Boughton Dome' **348 Photolibrary:** Rex Butcher: *Weldenia candida* **349 Garden World Images:** Gilles Delacroix: *Leptinella atrata subsp. luteola* **350 Alpine Garden Society:** *Paraquilegia anemonoides* **351 Garden World Images:** *Daphne arbuscula, Epigaea gaultherioides* **352 Garden World Images:** *Arabis alpina subsp. caucasica* 'Douler Angevine', *Silene acaulis;* Dave Bevan: *Arabis alpina subsp. caucasica* 'Douler Angevine' **354 Garden World Images:** Lee Thomas: *Aubrieta* 'Greencourt Purple'. **Photos Horticultural:** *Soldanella villosa* **355 Alpine Garden Society:** *Jancaea heldreichii.* **Spectrum Photofile:** *Aubrieta* 'Purple Charm' **356 Alamy:** blickwinkel: *Mertensia maritima.* **Garden World Images:** Martin Hughes-Jones: *Viola cornuta* 'Minor' **357 GAP Photos:** Juliette Wade: *Ranunculus ficaria Flore Pleno Group.* **Garden World Images:** *Draba longisiliqua, Draba rigida, Saxifraga x elizabethae* **358 Garden World Images:** *Erysimum helveticum* **359 Garden World Images:** *Viola aetolica* **360 Alpine Garden Society:** *Lewisia rediviva* [white form] **361 Eric Crichton Photos:** *Carlina acaulis.* **Garden World Images:** *Alstroemeria hookeri* **362 Alpine Garden Society:** *Convolvulus althaeoides* **363 Garden World Images:** *Dianthus pavonius* **364 Alamy:** Bob Gibbons: *Pterocephalus perennis.* **Alpine Garden Society:** *Dianthus alpinus.* **Eric Crichton Photos:** *Dianthus* 'Annabelle' **365 Alpine Garden Society:** *Lewisia rediviva [pink form]* **367 Garden World Images:** *Viola* 'Nellie Britton' **368 Alamy:** Brian & Sophia Fuller: *Pinguicula grandiflora.* **Alpine Garden Society:** *Aquilegia jonesii.* **Eric Crichton Photos:** *Edraianthus pumilio* **369 Eric Crichton Photos:** *Globularia cordifolia.* **GAP Photos:** Neil Holmes: *Polygala calcarea* 'Lillet'. **Garden World Images:** *Cyananthus microphyllus, Townsendia grandiflora* **370 GAP Photos:** Michael Howes: *Gentiana* 'Inverleith', *Gentiana* 'Shot Silk'. **Garden World Images:** *Gentiana sino-ornata;* Jenny Lilly: *Gentiana* 'Soutra'; Lee Thomas: *Gentiana* 'Blue Silk'. **Marianne Majerus Garden Images:** Marianne Majerus: *Gentiana* 'Ettrick', *Gentiana* 'Eugen's Allerbester'. **Muriel Hodgeman:** *Eritrichium nanum.* **Photolibrary:** Sunniva Harte: *Parochetus communis.* **The Garden Collection:** Jonathan Buckley: *Gentiana* 'Strathmore' **371 Garden World Images:** Dave Bevan: *Gunnera magellanica* **373 Eric Crichton Photos:** *Gaultheria procumbens.* **Garden World Images:** *Hippocrepis comosa, Nertera granadensis* **375 Alamy:** Steffen Hauser/ botanikfoto: *Paronychia kapela* subsp. *serpyllifolia;* Organica: *Arabis procurrens* 'Variegata'. **Garden World Images:** *Arctostaphylos uva-ursi* 'Point Reyes' **376 Alpine Garden Society:** *Arctostaphylos uva-ursi* **377 Fernwood Nursery:** *Sempervivum* 'Blood Tip', *Sempervivum* 'Gallivarda', *Sempervivum* 'Gulle Dame', *Sempervivum* 'Kappa', *Sempervivum* 'Rosie', *Sempervivum calcareum* 'Extra'. **Photolibrary:** Frederic Didillon: *Sempervivum calcareum* **378-379 GAP Photos:** Richard Bloom. **379 GAP Photos:** Carole Drake (ftl); Dianna Jazwinski (tl); Clive Nichols (ftr). **380 Corbis:** Clive Nichols (bl). **GAP Photos:** (fcla); FhF Greenmedia (fcl); Virginia Grey (cl); Geoff Kidd (cla). **Getty Images:** Wally Eberhart (bl/tuber). **Marianne Majerus Garden Images:** Marianne Majerus, Goodnestone Park Gardens (br). **382 Alamy:** MBP-Plants: *Fritillaria imperialis* 'Lutea'. **Eric Crichton Photos:** *Fritillaria persica.* **GAP Photos:** Sabina Ruber: *Fritillaria persica* 'Ivory Bells'. **Getty:** Ron Evans: *Allium aflatunense.* **Photolibrary:** Chris Burrows: *Ornithogalum magnum* **383 Alamy:** Michel Foret: *Fritillaria recurva;* Jacky Parker: *Gladiolus murielae* **384 Alamy:** CuboImages srl: *Gladiolus* 'Wine and Roses'. **GAP Photos:** John Glover: *Gladiolus* 'White Prosperity'; Martin Hughes-Jones: *Gladiolus* 'Impressive'; Visions:

Gladiolus 'Blue Frost', *Gladiolus* 'Columbine', *Gladiolus* 'Her Majesty', *Gladiolus* 'Morning Gold', *Gladiolus* 'Nova Lux', *Gladiolus* 'Nymph', *Gladiolus* 'Oscar', *Gladiolus* 'Purple Flora', *Gladiolus* 'Velvet Eyes'. **Garden World Images:** *Gladiolus* 'Green Woodpecker'. **Getty:** Gerald Majumdar: *Gladiolus* 'Stella'. **Photoshot:** Photos Horticultural: *Gladiolus* 'Sancerre' **385 Alamy:** The National Trust Photolibrary: *Cardiocrinum giganteum*. **GAP Photos:** Carole Drake: *Allium* 'Mount Everest'. **Garden World Images:** *Watsonia meriana;* John Martin: *Allium* 'Mount Everest'. **Marianne Majerus Garden Images:** Marianne Majerus, Rita Streitz: *Polianthes tuberosa* 'The Pearl' **386 Garden World Images:** *Notholirion campanulatum, Watsonia borbonica* **387 Alamy:** Holmes Garden Photos: *Alstroemeria* 'Blushing Bride'. **GAP Photos:** Howard Rice: *Alstroemeria* 'Apollo', *Alstroemeria* 'Moulin Rouge', *Alstroemeria* 'Serenade'; Visions: *Alstroemeria* 'Inca Ice', *Alstroemeria* 'Inca Tropic', *Alstroemeria* 'Tara'. **Garden World Images:** G Harper: *Alstroemeria* 'Friendship'; J Lloyd: *Alstroemeria psittacina;* MAP/A Descat: *Alstroemeria aurea* 'Orange King'; L Thomas: *Alstroemeria* PRINCESS ARIANE, *Alstroemeria* PRINCESS JULIETA. **Science Photo Library (SPL):** Neil Joy: *Alstroemeria* 'Red Beauty'. **Viv Marsh:** *Alstroemeria* 'Elvira' **388 Alamy:** Gig Binder: *Lilium* 'White Heaven'. **Andrew Lawson Photography:** *Lilium* 'Arena', *Lilium* 'Sterling Star'. **Garden World Images:** *Lilium* 'Altari', *Lilium* 'Black Magic', *Lilium* 'Olivia'; G Delacroix: *Lilium* 'Altari'. **Photolibrary:** James Guilliam/GPL: *Lilium TRIUMPHATOR* Lilium TRIUMPHATOR. **Science Photo Library (SPL):** Ian Gowland: *Lilium* 'Lady Alice'. **The Garden Collection:** Derek Harris: *Lilium* 'Nymph' **389 Alamy:** Chris Burrows/GPL: *Lilium cernuum;* Brian Hoffman: *Lilium* 'Elodie'; The Garden Picture Library: *Lilium cernuum*. **Andrew Lawson Photography:** *Lilium lankongense*. **GAP Photos:** Paul Debois: *Lilium* 'Tiger Woods'; Clive Nichols: *Lilium* 'Miss Lucy'; Visions: *Lilium* 'Star Fighter', *Lilium* 'Sweet Lord'. **Garden World Images:** G. Delacroix: *Lilium* 'Tom Pouce'; N Johnson: *Lilium* 'Netty's Pride'. **GardenPhotos.com:** Graham Rice: *Lilium* 'Sumatra'. **Jerry Harpur:** Cherry Williams: *Lilium* 'Rosita'. **Photolibrary:** Sarah Cuttle/GPL: *Lilium* 'Black Out' **390 Andrew Lawson Photography:** *Lilium regale* 'Royal Gold', *Lilium rosthornii*. **Garden Library:** *Lilium* 'Roma'. **Garden World Images:** *Lilium* 'Bright Star', G Delacroix: *Lilium* 'Conca d'Or'; Floramedia: *Lilium* 'Boogie Woogie'; John Swithinbank: *Lilium leichtlinii*. **Jerry Harpur:** *Lilium* 'Limelight'. **Photolibrary:** Richard Bloom/GPL: *Lilium Citronella Group* **391 Alamy:** Martin Hughes-Jones: *Lilium* African Queen Group. **Andrew Lawson Photography:** *Lilium* 'Crimson Pixie', *Lilium* 'Karen North', *Lilium pomponium*. **GAP Photos:** Graham Strong: *Lilium* 'Orange Electric'. **Garden Library:** *Lilium* 'Gran Paradiso', *Lilium* 'Red Carpet'. **Picturesmiths Ltd.:** *Lilium* 'Grand Cru' **392 GAP Photos:** Clive Nichols: *Allium atropurpureum;* Clive Nichols, Design: Angel Collins: *Allium* 'Gladiator'. **Photolibrary:** Suzie Gibbons: *Allium* 'Globemaster' **393 Garden World Images:** *Lilium Golden Splendor Group* **394 Alamy:** John Henwood: *Canna* 'Brillant'. **GAP Photos:** Richard Bloom: *Canna* 'Lucifer', *Canna* 'Lucifer'; Sarah Cuttle: *Canna* 'Richard Wallace'; Neil Holmes: *Canna* 'Picasso'. **Garden World Images:** Anthony Baggett: *Canna* 'Louis Cottin', *Canna x ehemanii*; Eric Crichton: *Canna* 'Striata'; G. Delacroix: *Canna* 'Ambassadour'. **Marianne Majerus Garden Images:** Marianne Majerus: *Canna* 'Stuttgart'. **Photolibrary:** Mark Bolton: *Canna* 'Durban'; Mark Bolton/GPL: *Canna* 'Durban'; David Cavagnaro: *Canna* 'Konigin Charlotte', *Canna* 'Konigin Charlotte'. **Reedy Meadow Nursery:** *Canna* 'Wyoming', *Canna* 'Wyoming' **395 Garden World Images:** *Amaryllis belladonna* 'Hathor', *Canna iridiflora, Gladiolus papilio, Zantedeschia* 'Cameo'; Liz Cole: *Zantedeschia* 'Cameo' **396 Alamy:** Holmes Garden Photos: *Dahlia* 'White Moonlight'. **Aylett Nurseries:** *Dahlia* 'White Ballet'. **GAP Photos:** Lucy Griffiths: *Dahlia* 'Eveline'. **Garden World Images:** T Sandell: *Dahlia* 'Café au Lait'. **Peter Stiles Photography:** *Dahlia* 'B. J. Beauty' **397 Alamy:** John Maud: *Dahlia* 'Tiptoe'. **GAP Photos:** Jonathan Buckley: *Dahlia* 'Bishop of Auckland'; Clive Nichols: *Dahlia* 'Carolina Moon'; J S Sira: *Dahlia* 'Gerrie Hoek'; Visions: *Dahlia* 'Karma Choc', *Dahlia* 'Natal', *Dahlia* 'Sorbet'; Visions/Elburg Botanic Media: *Dahlia* 'New Dimension'. **GardenPhotos.com:** Graham Rice: *Dahlia* 'Gallery Art Nouveau'. **Photolibrary:** Ron Evans: *Dahlia* 'Franz Kafka'; Michael Howes: *Dahlia* 'Cornel'; Ellen Rooney: *Dahlia* 'Ruskin Charlotte' **398 Alamy:** RDE Flora: *Dahlia* 'Ellen Huston'. **Eric Crichton Photos:** *Dahlia* 'Comet'. **GAP Photos:** Graham Rice: *Dahlia* 'Happy Single First Love'. **Garden World Images:** T Jennings: *Dahlia* 'Bishop of York'. **P-Pod:** *Dahlia* 'Moonglow'. **Photolibrary:** Richard Surman: *Dahlia* 'Alva's Supreme' **399 Garden World Images:** *Pamianthe peruviana*. **Getty:** Clive Nichols: *Ornithogalum nutans*. **Trecanna Nursery:** *Bellevalia romana* **400 Alamy:** John Glover: *Tulipa* 'Shirley'. **Eric Crichton Photos:** *Tulipa* 'Purissima'. **GAP Photos:** Visions: *Tulipa* 'Esperanto'. **Garden World Images:** Nathalie Pasquel: *Tulipa* 'Albert Heijn' **401 Alamy:** West Country Images: *Tulipa* 'Ballerina'. **GAP Photos:** Clive Nichols: *Tulipa* 'Abu Hassan'; Visions: *Tulipa* 'Black Hero', *Tulipa* 'Negrita' **403 Alamy:** Organica: *Ixiolirion tataricum*. **GAP Photos:** Clive Nichols: *Anemone coronaria De Caen Group* 'Mister Fokker'; Visions: *Hyacinthus orientalis* 'Blue Jacket' **404 GAP Photos:** Richard Bloom: *Narcissus* 'Fragrant Breeze'. **Photoshot:** Photos Horticultural: *Narcissus* 'Mount Hood' **405 GAP Photos:** Rob Whitworth: *Narcissus* 'Sir Winston Churchill'. **Garden World Images:** Martin Hughes-Jones: *Narcissus* 'Jenny' **407 Alamy:** CuboImages srl: *Ferraria crispa*. **GAP Photos:** J S Sira: *Triteleia ixioides* 'Starlight' **408 Alamy:** Hideo Kurihara: *Habenaria radiata*. **Eric Crichton Photos:** *Ornithogalum thyrsoides*. **Garden World Images:** *Ornithogalum arabicum* **409 Alamy:** Christopher Burrows: *Calochortus superbus;* Plantography: *Eucomis pallidiflora;* The Garden Picture Library: *Tritonia disticha subsp. rubrolucens*. **GAP Photos:** Jonathan Buckley: *Allium schubertii*. **The Garden Collection:** Jonathan Buckley: *Allium neapolitanum Cowanii Group* **410 GAP Photos:** Martin Hughes-Jones: *Crocosmia* 'Severn Sunrise'; Visions Premium: *Crocosmia* 'Honey Angels'. **Marianne Majerus Garden Images:** Andrew Lawson: *Crocosmia* 'Star of the East'; Marianne Majerus: *Crocosmia* 'George Davison'. **Photolibrary:** Mark Bolton: *Crocosmia* 'Solfatare' **411 GAP Photos:** Richard Bloom: *Camassia quamash;* J S Sira: *Roscoea auriculata, Triteleia laxa* 'Koningin Fabiola'. **Photolibrary:** Michele Lamontagne: *Tulbaghia simmleri* **412 GAP Photos:** J S Sira: *Ismene x spofforthiae* 'Sulphur Queen'. **Garden World Images:** *Arisaema griffithii, Eucomis bicolor, Ranunculus asiaticus var. flavus* **413 Alamy:** Emmanuel Lattes: *Tigridia pavonia*. **Photos Horticultural:** *Nerine* 'Orion' **414 Garden World Images:** *Eucharis amazonica, Ornithogalum balansae* **415 Alamy:** Jacquie Green: *Hyacinthus orientalis* 'White Pearl'. **International Flower Bulb Centre:** *Iris* 'Natascha'. **Photolibrary:** Howard Rice: *Muscari botryoides* 'Album' **416 Alamy:** Elizabeth Whiting & Associates: *Allium acuminatum;* WoodyStock: *Ornithogalum umbellatum*. **GAP Photos:** John Glover: *Scilla siberica* 'Alba'. **Garden World Images:** *Anemone tschaernjaewii* **417 Alamy:** idp crocus collection: *Crocus chrysanthus* 'Zwanenberg Bronze'. **Garden World Images:** *Crocus* 'Blue Bird', *Crocus* 'Cream Beauty', *Crocus* 'Eyecatcher', *Crocus speciosus* 'Conqueror'. **Pat Brindley:** *Crocus vernus* 'Remembrance'. **Photolibrary:** Howard Rice: *Crocus goulimyi;* Francesca York: *Crocus vernus* 'Queen of the Blues' **418 Alamy:** Bob Gibbons: *Babiana rubrocyanea;* J Marshall - Tribaleye Images: *Sparaxis tricolor*. **GAP Photos:** Visions: *Iris* 'Pixie' **420 Garden World Images:** *Tecophilaea cyanocrocus var. leichtlinii* **421 Alamy:** Holmes Garden Photos: *Puschkinia scilloides var. libanotica*. **Garden World Images:** *Crocus* 'Blue Pearl', *Hyacinthella leucophaea* **422 Garden World Images:** *Allium narcissiflorum, Cyclamen purpurascens, Dipcadi serotinum* **423 Garden World Images:** *Scilla peruviana*. **Photolibrary:** Chris Burrows: *Anomatheca laxa* **424 Alamy:** Neil Overy: *Acis autumnalis*. **Garden World Images:** *Chlidanthus fragrans* **425 Garden World Images:** *Cyclamen graecum* **426 Garden World Images:** *Colchicum autumnale, Cyclamen rohlfsianum* **427 GAP Photos:** Mark Bolton: *Galanthus* 'Hill Poë' **428 GAP Photos:** Richard Bloom: *Cyclamen coum Pewter Group* 'Maurice Dryden'. **Garden World Images:** *Galanthus nivalis* 'Sandersii'. **Getty:** Garden Picture/Photolibrary: *Galanthus woronowii* **429 Garden World Images:** *Lachenalia aloides* 'Nelsonii', *Lachenalia aloides var. quadricolor* **430-431 GAP Photos:** Fiona Lea. **431 GAP Photos:** Pernilla Bergdahl (tl); Jo Whitworth (tr); Mark Bolton (ftr); S&O (fl). **432 GAP Photos:** (cra). **435 Garden World Images:** *Caltha leptosepala, Hottonia palustris*. **Science Photo Library (SPL):** *Aponogeton distachyos, Stratiotes aloides* **436 GardenPhotos.com:** judywhite: *Filipendula ulmaria* **437 GAP Photos:** Frederic Didillon: *Rodgersia sambucifolia* **438 Corbis:** Markus Botzek: *Nelumbo nucifera*. **Garden World Images:** G. Delacroix: *Filipendula rubra;* M Hughes-Jones: *Cardamine pratensis* Cardamine pratensis. **Photoshot:** Dave Watts: *Cardamine raphanifolia* **439 GardenPhotos.com:** judywhite: *Geum coccineum, Lobelia cardinalis*. **Getty:** John & Barbara Gerlach: *Sarracenia purpurea* Sarracenia purpurea. **Photolibrary:** Claire Takacs: *Iris fulva* **440 Eric Crichton Photos:** *Nymphaea* 'James Brydon' **441 Corbis:** Fred Hirschmann/Science Faction: *Iris setosa*. **Frank Lane Picture Agency (FLPA):** Winfried Wisniewski: *Iris sibirica*. **Garden World Images:** M Hughes-Jones: *Iris ensata*. **GardenPhotos.com:** judywhite: *Myosotis scorpioides* 'Mermaid'. **Photoshot:** Michael Warren: *Lobelia siphilitica*. **Science Photo Library (SPL):** *Pontederia cordata*. **The Garden Collection:** Liz Eddison: *Mimulus ringens* **442 Biophoto Associates:** *Potamogeton crispus*. **Garden World Images:** *Sparganium erectum*. **Photolibrary:** Ulrich Niehoff: *Iris versicolor* **443 Photolibrary:** Fredrik Ehrenstrom: *Myriophyllum verticillatum*. **Photoshot:** Michael Warren: *Peltandra virginica* **444 Alamy:** Arco Images GmbH: *Nymphoides peltata* **445 Frank Lane Picture Agency (FLPA):** Michael Durham: *Mimulus x hybrida*. **GAP Photos:** Richard Bloom: *Ligularia* 'Britt Marie Crawford' **446-447 GAP Photos:** Martin Hughes-Jones. **447 GAP Photos:** Lee Avison (tl); Frederic Didillon (ftr); John Glover (ftl); Jo Whitworth (tr). **448 Alamy Images:** Douglas Peebles Photography (bl). **GAP Photos:** Jerry Harpur (r); Visions (cl). **450 Garden World Images:** *Bauhinia variegata, Chorisia speciosa*. **Photolibrary:** Gerry Whitmont: *Brachychiton acerifolius* **451 GAP Photos:** Trevor Nicholson Christie: *Jacaranda mimosifolia* **452 Garden World Images:** *Ficus benghalensis* **453 Garden World Images:** *Sparrmannia africana, Spathodea campanulata*. **Photolibrary:** Ed Reschke: *Calliandra eriophylla* **454 P-Pod:** *Plectranthus fructicosus* 'James' **455 Garden World Images:** *Epacris impressa, Medinilla magnifica;* Sam Tran: *Medinilla magnifica* **456 Garden World Images:** Gilles Delacroix: *Ixora coccinea* **457 Garden World Images:** *Polygala x dalmaisiana, Tibouchina urvilleana* **459 Garden World Images:** *Senna corymbosa, Senna didymobotrya* **460 Garden World Images:** *Lophospermum erubescens* **461 Alamy:** The Garden Picture Library: *Mandevilla x amabilis* 'Alice du Pont'. **GAP Photos:** Jerry Harpur: *Clytostoma callistegioides*. **Photos Horticultural:** *Agapetes variegata var. macrantha* **462 Eric Crichton Photos:** *Passiflora quadrangularis*. **Garden Picture Library:** *Hardenbergia violacea* 'Happy Wanderer'. **Garden World Images:** *Aristolochia littoralis* **464 Garden World Images:** *Streptosolen jamesonii* **465 Alamy:** blickwinkel: *Episcia dianthiflora*. **Photolibrary:** Chris Burrows: *Streptocarpus* 'Crystal Ice' **467 Alamy:** CuboImages srl: *Paphiopedilum armeniacum*. **Garden World Images:** MAP/Arnaud Descat: *Phragmipedium besseae*. **Photolibrary:** Paroli Galperti: *Paphiopedilum rothschildianum* **469 GAP Photos:** J S Sira: *Tradescantia zebrina*. **Garden World Images:** *Achimenes* 'Little Beauty' **470 Garden World Images:** *Russelia equisetiformis, Sinningia* 'Switzerland'; Gilles Delacroix: *Russelia equisetiformis* **471 Alamy:** CuboImages srl: *Episcia cupreata* **472 Bleddyn Wynn Jones:** *Peliosanthes arisanensis*. **Dibleys Nurseries:** *Saintpaulia* 'Falling Raindrops', *Saintpaulia* 'Powder Keg'. **Garden World Images:** *Browallia speciosa* **473 Alamy:** Steffen Hauser/botanikfoto: *Hemigraphis repanda*. **GAP Photos:** Lynn Keddie: *Streptocarpus* 'Amanda' **474 Photolibrary:** Georgianna Lane: *Asparagus densiflorus* **476 Garden World Images:** *Impatiens repens* **477 Alamy:** Christopher Burrows: *Roscoea scillifolia;* Tim Gainey: *Costus speciosus;* Inga Spence: *Curcuma petiola*. **Bleddyn Wynn Jones:** *Hedychium stenopetalum*. **Dave Skinner:** *Alpinia hainanensis, Cornukaempferia aurantiflora* 'Jungle Gold', *Curcuma zedoaria, Hedychium thyrsiforme*. **GAP Photos:** Martin Hughes-Jones: *Hedychium yunnanense*. **Marianne Majerus Garden Images:** Marianne Majerus: *Hedychium maximum* **478 Garden World Images:** *Aeschynanthus speciosus* **482 Alamy:** John Glover: *Agave americana* 'Marginata'. **Roy Mottram:** *Agave macroacantha, Agave parrasana, Agave polianthiflora, Agave potatorum* **483 Garden World Images:** J Lilly: *Rebutia* 'Carnival' **484 Roy Mottram:** *Rebutia* 'Jenny' **485 Alamy:** GFC Collection: *Frithia pulchra* **486 Photolibrary:** Harald Lange: *Adenium obesum* **488 Garden World Images:** *Schlumbergera* 'Bristol Beauty' **490 Garden World Images:** *Kalanchoe tomentosa* **493 Roy Mottram:** *Aloe hemmingii* **494 Alamy:** shapencolour: *Mammillaria elongata* **496 Alamy:** John Glover: *Kalanchoe delagoensis*.

The publishers would like to thank all those who generously assisted the photographers and provided plants for photography, in particular the curators, directors and staff of the following organizations and those private individuals listed below. Special thanks are due to those at the Royal Botanic Gardens, Kew, and the Royal Horticultural Society's Garden, Wisley, for their invaluable assistance and support.

African Violet Centre, Terrington St Clement, Norfolk; Ken Akers, Great Saling, Essex; Jacques Amand Ltd, Clamphill, Middx; Anmore Exotics, Havant, Hants; David Austin Roses, Albrighton, Shrops; Avon Bulbs, Bradford-on-Avon, Wilts; Ayletts Nurseries, St Albans, Herts; Steven Bailey Ltd, Sway, Hants; Bill Baker, Tidmarsh, Berks; Batsford Arboretum, Moreton-in-Marsh, Glos; Booker Seeds, Sleaford, Lincs; Rupert Bowlby, Reigate, Surrey; Bressingham Gardens, Diss, Norfolk; Roy Brooks, Newent, Glos; British Orchid Growers' Association; Broadleigh Gardens, Somerset; Burford House Gardens, Tenbury Wells, Shrops; Cambridge Bulbs, Newton, Cambs; Nola Carr, Sydney, Australia; Beth Chatto Gardens, Colchester, Essex; Chelsea Physic Garden, London; Colegrave Seeds, Banbury, Oxon; County Park Nurseries, Hornchurch, Essex; Jill Cowley, Chelmsford, Essex; Mrs Anne Dexter, Oxford; Edrom Nurseries, Coldingham, Berwicks; Dr Jack Elliott, Ashford, Kent; Joe Elliott, Broadwell, Glos; Erdigg (National Trust), Clwyd, Wales; Fibrex Nurseries, Pebworth, Warwicks; Fisk's Clematis Nursery, Westleton, Suffolk; Mr & Mrs Thomas Gibson, Westwell, Oxon; Glasgow Botanic Garden, Glasgow; 'Glazenwood', Braintree, Essex. R. Harkness & Co. Ltd, Hitchin, Herts; Harry Hay, Lower Kingswood, Surrey; Hazeldene Nurseries, East Farleigh, Kent; Hidcote Manor (National Trust), Chipping Camden, Glos; Hillier Gardens and Arboretum, Romsey, Hants; Hillier Nurseries (Winchester) Ltd, Romsey, Hants; Holly Gate Cactus Nursery, Ashington, Sussex; Hopleys Plants, Much Hadham, Herts; Huntingdon Botanical Gardens, San Marino, California; W.E.Th. Ingwersen Ltd, East Grinstead, Sussex; the late Clive Innes; Kelways Nurseries, Langport, Somerset; Kiftsgate Court Gardens, Chipping Camden, Glos; Lechlade Fuchsia Centre, Lechlade, Glos; The Living Desert, Palm Desert, California; Robin Loder, Leonardslee, Sussex; Los Angeles State and County Arboreta and Botanical Gardens, Los Angeles, California; Lotusland Foundation, Santa Barbara, California; McBeans Orchids, Lewes, Sussex; Merrist Wood Agricultural College, Worplesdon, Surrey; Mrs J.F. Phillips, Westwell, Oxon; Mr & Mrs Richard Purdon, Ramsden, Oxon; Ramparts Nurseries, Colchester, Essex; Ratcliffe Orchids, Didcot, Oxon; Mrs Joyce Robinson, Denmans, Fontwell, Sussex; Peter Q. Rose, Castle Cary, Somerset; Royal Botanic Garden, Edinburgh; Royal Botanic Gardens, Kew, Surrey; Royal Botanic Gardens, Sydney, Australia; Royal National Rose Society, St Albans, Herts; Royal Horticultural Society's Garden, Wisley, Surrey. Santa Barbara Botanic Garden, Santa Barbara, California; Savill Garden, Windsor, Berks; Mr & Mrs K. Schoenenberger, Shipton-under-Wychwood, Oxon; Mrs Martin Simmons, Burghclere, Berks; Dr James Smart, Barnstaple, Devon; Arthur Smith, Wigston, Leics; P.J. Smith, Ashington, Sussex; Springfields Gardens, Spalding, Lincs; Staite & Sons, Evesham, Worcs; Stapeley Water Gardens, Nantwich, Cheshire; Strybing Arboreta Society of Golden Gate Park, San Francisco, California; David Stuart, Dunbar, East Lothian; Suffolk Herbs, Sudbury, Suffolk; University Botanic Garden, Cambridge; University of British Columbia Botanical Garden, Vancouver; University of California Arboretum, Davis, California; University of California Arboretum, Santa Cruz, California; University of California Botanical Garden, Berkeley, California; University of California Botanical Gardens, Los Angeles, California; University of Reading Botanic Garden, Reading, Berks; Unwins Seeds Ltd, Histon, Cambridge; Jack Vass, Haywards Heath, Sussex; Rosemary Verey, Barnsley, Glos; Vesutor Air Plants, Ashington, Sussex; Wakehurst Place (Royal Botanic Gardens, Kew), Ardingly, Sussex; Primrose Warburg, Oxford; Waterperry Gardens, Wheatley, Oxon; Westonbirt Arboretum, Westonbirt, Glos; Woolman's Nurseries, Dorridge, West Midlands; Wyld Court Orchids, Newbury, Berks; Eric Young Orchid Foundation, Jersey, Channel Islands.